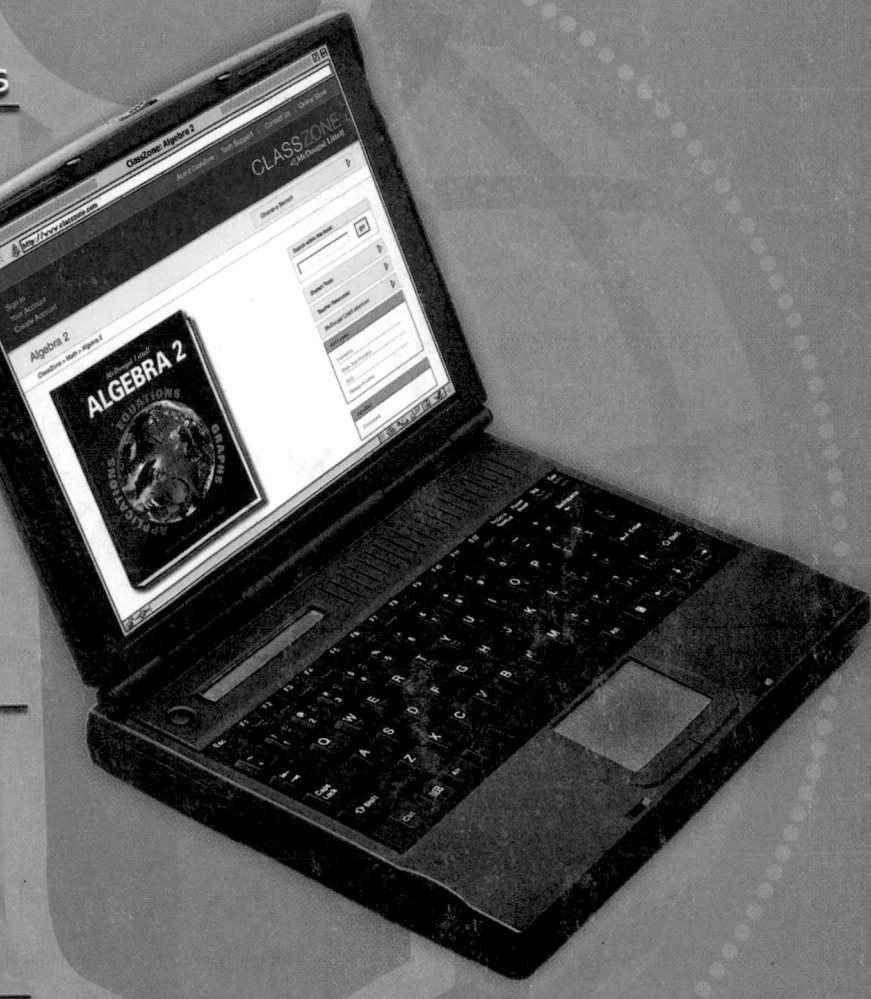

ALGEBRA 2

Ron Larson

Laurie Boswell

Timothy D. Kanold

Lee Stiff

EQUATIONS

APPLICATIONS

GRAPHS

McDougal Littell

A HOUGHTON MIFFLIN COMPANY

Evanston, Illinois • Boston • Dallas

About the Cover

Algebra 2 brings math to life with many real-life applications. The cover illustrates some of the applications used in this book. Examples of mathematics in architecture, bicycling, amusement parks, and animal motion are shown on pages 46, 342, 809, 811, and 818. Circling the globe are three key aspects of Algebra 2—the *equations*, *graphs*, and *applications* that you will use in this course. They will help you understand how mathematics relates to the world. As you explore the applications presented in the book, try to make your own connections between mathematics and the world around you!

ISBN-13: 978-0-618-25020-2   ISBN-10: 0-618-25020-4   10 11 12 13 14–DWO–07 06

Internet Web Site: http://www.classzone.com

About the Authors

▶ **Ron Larson** is a professor of mathematics at Penn State University at Erie. He is the author of a broad range of mathematics textbooks for middle school, high school, and college students. He is one of the pioneers in the use of multimedia and the Internet to enhance the learning of mathematics. Dr. Larson is a member of the National Council of Teachers of Mathematics and is a frequent speaker at NCTM and other national and regional mathematics meetings.

▶ **Laurie Boswell** is a mathematics teacher at Profile Junior-Senior High School in Bethlehem, New Hampshire. She is active in NCTM and local mathematics organizations. A recipient of the 1986 Presidential Award for Excellence in Mathematics Teaching, she is also the 1992 Tandy Technology Scholar and the 1991 recipient of the Richard Balomenos Mathematics Education Service Award presented by the New Hampshire Association of Teachers of Mathematics.

▶ **Timothy D. Kanold** is Director of Mathematics and a teacher at Adlai E. Stevenson High School in Lincolnshire, IL. In 1995 he received the Award of Excellence from the Illinois State Board of Education for outstanding contributions to education. He served on NCTM's Professional Standards for Teaching Mathematics Commission. A 1986 recipient of the Presidential Award for Excellence in Mathematics Teaching, he served as president of the Council of Presidential Awardees of Mathematics.

▶ **Lee Stiff** is a professor of mathematics education in the College of Education and Psychology of North Carolina State University at Raleigh and has taught mathematics at the high school and middle school levels. He served on the NCTM Board of Directors and was elected President of NCTM for the years 2000–2002. He is the 1992 recipient of the W. W. Rankin Award for Excellence in Mathematics Education presented by the North Carolina Council of Teachers of Mathematics.

REVIEWERS

Jimmy Bostock
Mathematics Department Chair
Hepzibah High School
Hepzibah, GA

Phyllis Carter
Mathematics Department Head
Parkway North High School
Creve Coeur, MO

Theresa Cepaitis
Instructional Specialist, Secondary
    Mathematics
Anne Arundel County Public Schools
Annapolis, MD

Linda M. Fulmore
Assistant Principal, Instruction
Camelback High School
Phoenix, AZ

David Sanchez
Mathematics Teacher
Orosi High School
Orosi, CA

CALIFORNIA TEACHER PANEL

Courteney Dawe
Mathematics Teacher
Placerita Junior High School
Valencia, CA

Dave Dempster
Mathematics Teacher
Temecula Valley High School
Temecula, CA

Pauline Embree
Mathematics Department Chair
Rancho San Joaquin Middle School
Irvine, CA

Tom Griffith
Mathematics Teacher
Scripps Ranch High School
San Diego, CA

Diego Gutierrez
Mathematics Teacher
Crawford High School
San Diego, CA

Roger Hitchcock
Mathematics Teacher
Buchanan High School
Clovis, CA

Joseph Jacobs
Mathematics Teacher
Luther Burbank High School
Sacramento, CA

Louise McComas
Mathematics Teacher
Fremont High School
Sunnyvale, CA

Viola Okoro
Mathematics Teacher
Laguna Creek High School
Elk Grove, CA

Jon Simon
Mathematics Department Chair
Casa Grande High School
Petaluma, CA

CLEVELAND TEACHER PANEL

Laura Anfang
University Supervisor, Teacher of
    Secondary Math Methods
John Carroll University
University Heights, OH

Patricia Benedict
Mathematics Department Liaison
Cleveland Heights High School
Cleveland Heights, OH

Carol Caroff
Mathematics Department
    Chair/Teacher
Solon High School
Solon, OH

Fred Dillon
Mathematics Teacher
Strongsville High School
Strongsville, OH

Bill Hunt
Past President, Ohio Council
    of Teachers of Mathematics
Strongsville, OH

Dr. Margie Raub Hunt
Executive Director, Ohio Council
    of Teachers of Mathematics
Strongsville, OH

Robert Jones
Mathematics Supervisor (K–12)
Cleveland City School District
Cleveland, OH

Andrea Kopco
Mathematics Teacher
Midpark High School
Cleveland, OH

Sandy Sikorski
Mathematics Teacher
Berea High School
Berea, OH

Gil Stevens
Mathematics Teacher
Brunswick High School
Brunswick, OH

▶ KANSAS TEACHER PANEL

Rosemary Arb
Mathematics Department Chair
North Kansas City High School
Kansas City, MO

Jerry Belshe
Mathematics Teacher
Indian Woods Middle School
Overland Park, KS

Carol Edwards
Mathematics Teacher
Belton High School
Belton, MO

Robert Franks
Mathematics Teacher
Park Hill High School
Kansas City, MO

Cynthia Hardy
Mathematics Teacher
Oxford Middle School
Overland Park, KS

Julie Knittle
Secondary Mathematics Resource Specialist
Shawnee Mission District Office
Shawnee Mission, KS

Glenda Morrison
Mathematics Teacher
Central High School
Kansas City, MO

Mitch Shea
Mathematics Teacher
Leavenworth High School
Leavenworth, KS

Ginny Taylor
Mathematics Department Chair
Santa Fe Trail Junior High School
Olathe, KS

▶ STUDENT REVIEW PANEL

Jacquelyn J. Arnold
Dunbar High School
Ohio

Michael Aznavour
William S. Hart High School
California

Kristopher Cadena
Las Cruces High School
New Mexico

Jonathan Ellenberger
Plymouth North High School
Massachusetts

Kari Frick
Standley Lake High School
Colorado

Nour Ghazi
Watertown High School
Massachusetts

Rebekah Good
Broadneck Sr. High School
Maryland

Lauren Henderson
Harriton High School
Pennsylvania

Amanda L. Hood
Robert S. Alexander High School
Georgia

Amanda Jakuszanek
Stevenson High School
Michigan

Jennifer Kelley
Lakota West High School
Ohio

David Lai
Holmdel High School
New Jersey

Melissa Machit
Polytechnic High School
California

Tracy A. Marynowski
Mother McAuley High School
Illinois

Ben McLain
Clarke Central High School
Georgia

Shoshana Muhammad
Skyline High School
California

Dayle Pivetta
Churchill High School
Michigan

Khandicia Nichelle Randolph
Whitney Young Magnet High School
Illinois

Tomekia Yoshida Mattice Reed
Murrah High School
Mississippi

Marianne Roller
Cedar Cliff High School
Pennsylvania

Brice Roncace
Meridian High School
Idaho

Joshua D. Rosenfeld
South High School
California

Nancy Ruiz
Santa Ana High School
California

Mahdi Salehi
El Camino Real High School
California

Paul Jared Schmidt
California

Tara Schoop
Glenbard East High School
Illinois

Sammy Shreibati
Westmoor High School
California

Michele D. Unruh
Truman High School
Missouri

Kristal M. Watrous
Mead High School
Washington

Equations and Inequalities

CHAPTER

2

Linear Equations and Functions

CHAPTER
3

Systems of Linear Equations and Inequalities

Matrices and Determinants

CHAPTER
5

Quadratic Functions

Polynomials and Polynomial Functions

Powers, Roots, and Radicals

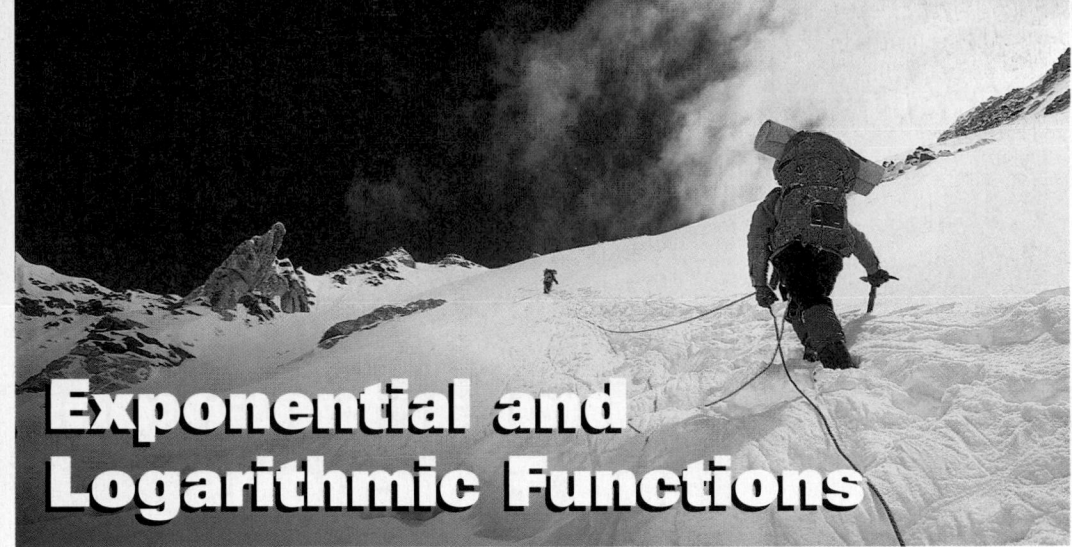

CHAPTER
8

Exponential and Logarithmic Functions

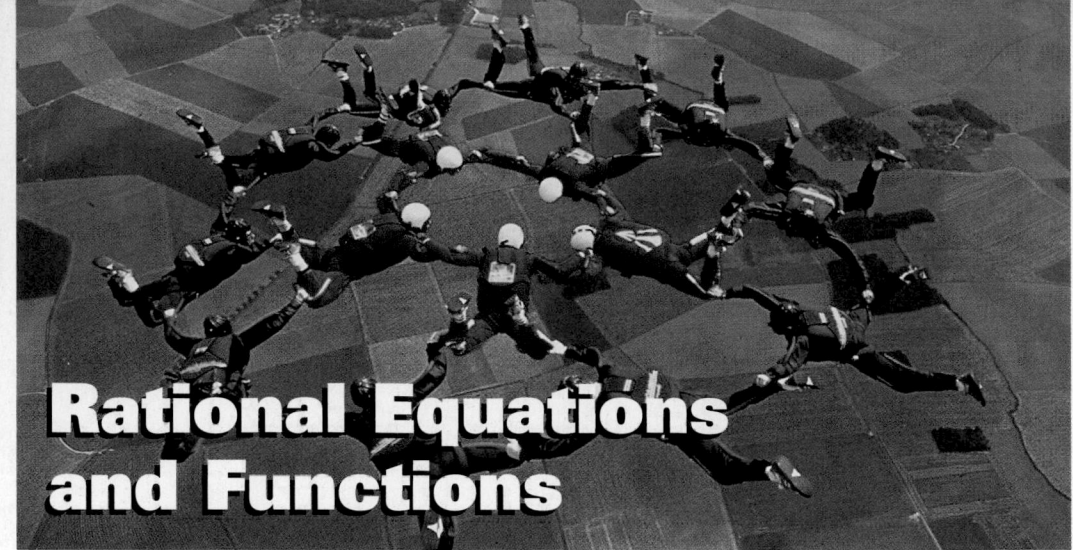

Rational Equations and Functions

Quadratic Relations and Conic Sections

Sequences and Series

Probability and Statistics

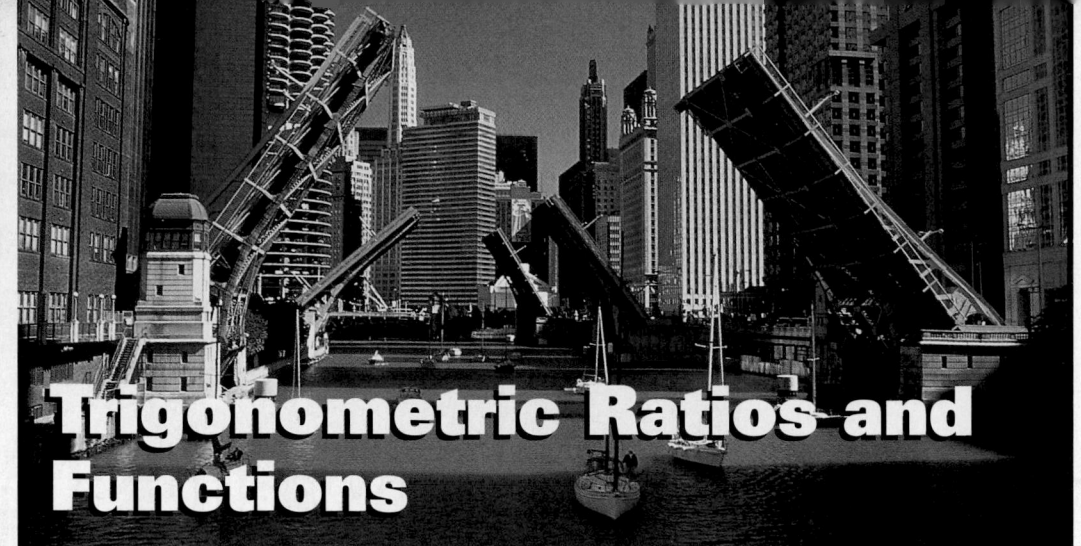

CHAPTER
13

Trigonometric Ratios and Functions

CHAPTER 14

Trigonometric Graphs, Identities, and Equations

▶ Student Resources

▶ Who Uses Mathematics in Real Life?

Here are some careers that use the mathematics in Algebra 2.

REAL LIFE

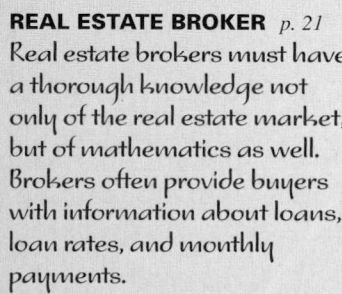

WEB DEVELOPER *p. 296*
Web developers use hypertext markup language (HTML) to create electronic pages for the World Wide Web. A Web browser translates HTML into pages that can be viewed on a computer screen.

CIVIL ENGINEER *p. 252*
Civil engineers design bridges, roads, buildings, and other structures. In 1996 civil engineers held about 196,000 jobs in the United States.

PALEONTOLOGIST *p. 419*
A paleontologist is a scientist who studies fossils of dinosaurs and other prehistoric life forms. Most paleontologists work as college professors.

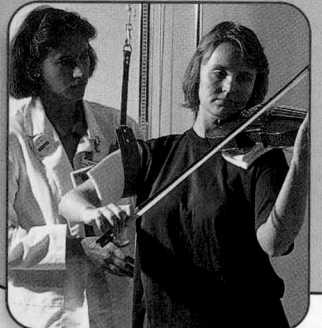

PHYSICAL THERAPIST *p. 16*
Physical therapists help restore function, improve mobility, and relieve pain in patients with injuries or disease.

REAL ESTATE BROKER *p. 21*
Real estate brokers must have a thorough knowledge not only of the real estate market, but of mathematics as well. Brokers often provide buyers with information about loans, loan rates, and monthly payments.

▶ *Your textbook contains* many special elements to help you learn. It provides several study helps that may be new to you. For example, every chapter begins with a Study Guide.

Chapter Preview The Study Guide starts with a short description of what you will be learning.

Key Vocabulary This list highlights important new terms that will be introduced in the chapter and reviews terms that you already know.

Skill Review These exercises review key skills that you'll apply in the chapter. They will help you identify any topics that you need to review.

Study Strategy The study strategies suggest ideas to help you better understand the math you are learning as well as help you prepare for tests.

CHAPTER 2

Study Guide

PREVIEW

What's the chapter about?

Chapter 2 is about **linear equations and functions**. In Chapter 2 you'll learn

- how to graph ordered pairs, relations, functions, linear equations and inequalities in two variables, piecewise functions, and absolute value functions.
- how to write equations of lines.
- how to solve real-life problems using graphs and equations.

KEY VOCABULARY

▶ Review
- graph, p. 3
- linear equation, p. 19
- solution, p. 19
- linear inequality in one variable, p. 41
- absolute value, p. 50

▶ New
- relation, p. 67
- function, p. 67
- ordered pair, p. 67
- coordinate plane, p. 67
- linear function, p. 69
- slope, p. 75

- slope-intercept form, p. 82
- standard form, p. 84
- direct variation, p. 94
- scatter plot, p. 100
- linear inequality in two variables, p. 108
- piecewise function, p. 114

PREPARE

Are you ready for the chapter?

SKILL REVIEW Do these exercises to review key skills that you'll apply in this chapter. See the given **reference page** if there is something you don't understand.

STUDENT HELP

▶ **Study Tip**
"Student Help" boxes throughout the chapter give you study tips and tell you where to look for extra help in this book and on the Internet.

Evaluate the expression for the given values of x and y. (Review Example 3, p. 12)

1. $\frac{y-7}{x-3}$; $x = 2, y = 5$ **2.** $\frac{5-y}{6-x}$; $x = 4, y = 1$ **3.** $\frac{8-y}{3-x}$; $x = -1, y = -4$

Solve the equation for y. (Review Example 1, p. 26)

4. $3x + y = 4$ **5.** $x - 2y = 10$ **6.** $5x + 6y = -60$

Solve the inequality. (Review Examples 1 and 2, p. 42)

7. $2x + 9 < 18$ **8.** $6 - 0.5y \leq 19$ **9.** $2x + 3 > 6x - 7$

STUDY STRATEGY

Here's a study strategy!

Skills File

In a notebook, make a file of the skills you learn throughout this course. On the left side of the paper, write an important skill and the lesson that it comes from. On the right side of the paper, give an example of the skill in use. Go back now and make a skills file for Chapter 1. Then continue with Chapter 2.

66 Chapter 2

Also, in every lesson you will find a variety of Student Help notes.

STUDENT HELP

 In the Book

Study Tip The study tips will help you avoid common errors.

Skills Review Here you can find where to review skills you've studied in earlier math classes.

Look Back Here are references to material in earlier lessons that may help you understand the lesson.

Extra Practice Your book contains more exercises to practice the skills you are learning.

Homework Help Here you can find suggestions about which Examples may help you solve Exercises.

 On the Internet

Homework Help: *Extra Examples* These are places where you can find additional examples on the Web site.

Homework Help: *Problem Solving Help* Here you can find additional suggestions for solving an exercise.

Keystroke Help These provide the exact keystroke sequences for many different kinds of calculators.

STUDENT HELP
➤ **Study Tip**
For an expression like $2x - 3$, think of the expression as $2x + (-3)$, so the terms are $2x$ and -3.

STUDENT HELP
➤ **Skills Review**
For help with opposites, see p. 936.

GOAL 2 SIMPLIFYING ALGEBRAIC EXPRESSIONS

For an expression such as $2x + 3$, the parts that are added together, $2x$ and 3, are called **terms**. When a term is the product of a number and a power of a variable, such as $2x$ or $4x^3$, the number is the **coefficient** of the power.

Terms such as $3x^2$ and $-5x^2$ are **like terms** because they have the same variable part. **Constant terms** such as -4 and 2 are also like terms. The distributive property lets you *combine like terms* that have variables by adding the coefficients.

EXAMPLE 5 *Simplifying by Combining Like Terms*

a. $7x + 4x = (7 + 4)x$ **Distributive property**
      $= 11x$ **Add coefficients.**

b. $3n^2 + n - n^2 = (3n^2 - n^2) + n$ **Group like terms.**
      $= 2n^2 + n$ **Combine like terms.**

c. $2(x + 1) - 3(x - 4) = 2x + 2 - 3x + 12$ **Distributive property**
      $= (2x - 3x) + (2 + 12)$ **Group like terms.**
      $= -x + 14$ **Combine like terms.**

· · · · · · · · · ·

Two algebraic expressions are **equivalent** if they have the same value for all values of their variable(s). For instance, the expressions $7x + 4x$ and $11x$ are equivalent, as are the expressions $5x - (6x + y)$ and $-x - y$. A statement such as $7x + 4x = 11x$

GUIDED PRACTICE

Vocabulary Check ✓
1. Explain the difference between a simple linear inequality and a compound linear inequality.

Concept Check ✓
2. Tell whether this statement is *true* or *false*: Multiplying both sides of an inequality by the same number always produces an equivalent inequality. Explain.

3. Explain the difference between solving $2x < 7$ and solving $-2x < 7$.

Skill Check ✓ **Solve the inequality. Then graph your solution.**

4. $x - 5 < 8$ 5. $3x \geq 15$ 6. $-x + 4 > 3$

7. $\frac{1}{2}x \leq 6$ 8. $x + 8 > -2$ 9. $-x - 3 < -5$

Graph the inequality.

10. $-2 \leq x < 5$ 11. $x \geq 3$ or $x < -3$

12. 🚗 **WINTER DRIVING** You are moving to Montana and need to lower the freezing point of the cooling system in the car from Example 6 to $-50°C$. This will also raise the boiling point to $140°C$. Write a compound inequality that models this situation. Then write the inequality in degrees Fahrenheit.

PRACTICE AND APPLICATIONS

STUDENT HELP
➤ **Extra Practice**
to help you master skills is on p. 941.

MATCHING INEQUALITIES Match the inequality with its graph.

13. $x \geq 4$ 14. $x < 4$ 15. $-4 < x \leq 4$

16. $x \geq 4$ or $x < -4$ 17. $-4 \leq x \leq 4$ 18. $x > 4$ or $x \leq -4$

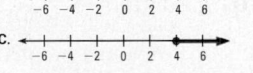 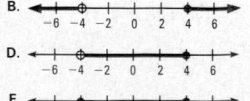

CHECKING SOLUTIONS Decide whether the given number is a solution of the inequality.

19. $2x + 9 < 16; 4$ 20. $10 - x \geq 3; 7$ 21. $7x - 12 < 8; 3$

22. $-\frac{1}{3}x - 2 \leq -4; 9$ 23. $-3 < 2x \leq 6; 3$ 24. $-8 < x - 11 < -6; 5$

SIMPLE INEQUALITIES Solve the inequality. Then graph your solution.

25. $4x + 5 > 25$ 26. $7 - n \leq 19$ 27. $5 - 2x \geq 27$

28. $\frac{1}{2}x - 4 > -6$ 29. $\frac{3}{2}x - 7 < 2$ 30. $5 + \frac{1}{3}n \leq 6$

31. $4x - 1 > 14 - x$ 32. $-n + 6 < 7n + 4$ 33. $4.7 - 2.1x > -7.9$

34. $2(n - 4) \leq 6$ 35. $2(4 - x) > 8$ 36. $5 - 5x > 4(3 - x)$

STUDENT HELP
➤ **HOMEWORK HELP**
Examples 1, 2: Exs. 13, 14, 19–22, 25–36
Example 3: Exs. 49–51
Examples 4, 5: Exs. 15–18, 23, 24, 37–48
Example 6: Exs. 52–54
Example 7: Exs. 55, 56

1.6 Solving Linear Inequalities **45**

EQUATIONS AND INEQUALITIES

▶ *How fast can trains travel?*

APPLICATION: High-Speed Trains

Many countries now have high-speed trains. Some of these trains can travel 150 mi/h or faster. The diagram below shows the average speeds for a number of the world's fastest trains.

Fastest Trains in Each Country

Spain	209.1 km/h
U.S.A.	97.7 mi/h
Japan	261.8 km/h
Italy	164.9 km/h
France	254.3 km/h
England	111.8 mi/h

To find the fastest train, you need to convert all the speeds to the same units of measure. The formula to convert kilometers per hour to miles per hour is:

$$\text{speed in mi/h} = 0.621(\text{speed in km/h})$$

Think & Discuss

1. Use the given formula to convert all the train speeds to miles per hour.

2. How would you convert miles per hour to kilometers per hour? Write a formula to do this.

3. Convert all the train speeds to kilometers per hour.

Learn More About It

You will calculate the average speed of another Japanese high-speed train in Example 1 on p. 33.

 APPLICATION LINK Visit www.mcdougallittell.com for more information on high-speed trains.

Study Guide

PREVIEW

What's the chapter about?

Chapter 1 is about **expressions, equations, and inequalities**. In Chapter 1 you'll learn

- how to evaluate and simplify numerical and algebraic expressions.
- how to solve linear and absolute value equations and inequalities.
- how to use algebra to model and solve real-life problems.

KEY VOCABULARY

- graph of a real number, p. 3
- numerical expression, p. 11
- order of operations, p. 11
- variable, p. 12
- algebraic expression, p. 12

- mathematical model, p. 12
- terms of an expression, p. 13
- linear equation in one variable, p. 19
- verbal model, p. 33

- algebraic model, p. 33
- linear inequality in one variable, p. 41
- compound inequality, p. 43
- absolute value, p. 50

PREPARE

Are you ready for the chapter?

SKILL REVIEW Do these exercises to review key skills that you'll apply in this chapter. See the given **reference page** if there is something you don't understand.

STUDENT HELP

▶ **Study Tip**
"Student Help" boxes throughout the chapter give you study tips and tell you where to look for extra help in this book and on the Internet.

Perform the operation. **(Skills Review, p. 905)**

1. $-3 + 14$ **2.** $7(-10)$ **3.** $-1 - (-9)$ **4.** $-45 \div (-5)$

5. $(-12)(-2)$ **6.** $8 - 15$ **7.** $30 \div (-3)$ **8.** $-6 + (-2)$

Find the area of the figure. **(Skills Review, p. 914)**

9. triangle   **10.** square   **11.** rectangle   **12.** circle

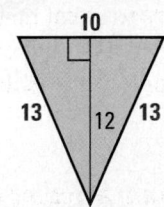
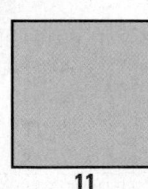
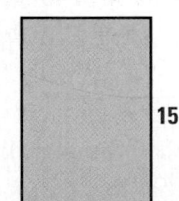
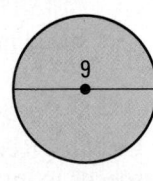

STUDY STRATEGY

Here's a study strategy!

Vocabulary File

Make a flashcard file of vocabulary words.

On the front of an index card, write an important vocabulary word or phrase. On the back of the card write the definition given in the book, along with your own definition if that helps you. Also include symbols, diagrams, examples, and your own notes.

1.1

Real Numbers and Number Operations

What you should learn

GOAL 1 Use a number line to graph and order real numbers.

GOAL 2 Identify properties of and use operations with real numbers, as applied in **Exs. 64 and 65**.

Why you should learn it

▼ To solve **real-life** problems, such as how to exchange money in **Example 7**.

GOAL 1 USING THE REAL NUMBER LINE

The numbers used most often in algebra are the *real numbers*. Some important subsets of the real numbers are listed below.

SUBSETS OF THE REAL NUMBERS

WHOLE NUMBERS   0, 1, 2, 3, . . .

INTEGERS   . . . , −3, −2, −1, 0, 1, 2, 3, . . .

RATIONAL NUMBERS   Numbers such as $\frac{3}{4}$, $\frac{1}{3}$, and $\frac{-4}{1}$ (or −4) that can be written as the ratio of two integers. When written as decimals, rational numbers terminate or repeat. For example, $\frac{3}{4} = 0.75$ and $\frac{1}{3} = 0.333. . . .$

IRRATIONAL NUMBERS   Real numbers that are not rational, such as $\sqrt{2}$ and π. When written as decimals, irrational numbers neither terminate nor repeat.

The three dots in the lists of the whole numbers and the integers above indicate that the lists continue without end.

Real numbers can be pictured as points on a line called a *real number line*. The numbers increase from left to right, and the point labeled 0 is the **origin**.

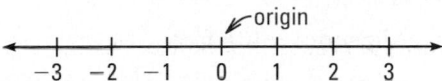

The point on a number line that corresponds to a real number is the **graph** of the number. Drawing the point is called *graphing* the number or *plotting* the point. The number that corresponds to a point on a number line is the **coordinate** of the point.

EXAMPLE 1   *Graphing Numbers on a Number Line*

Graph the real numbers $-\frac{4}{3}$, $\sqrt{2}$, and 2.7.

SOLUTION

First, recall that $-\frac{4}{3}$ is $-1\frac{1}{3}$, so $-\frac{4}{3}$ is between −2 and −1. Then, approximate $\sqrt{2}$ as a decimal to the nearest tenth: $\sqrt{2} \approx 1.4$. (The symbol $\approx$ means *is approximately equal to*.) Finally, graph the numbers.

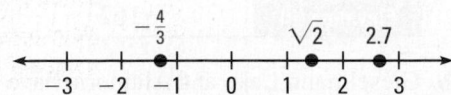

A number line can be used to order real numbers. The *inequality symbols* $<$, $\leq$, $>$, and $\geq$ can be used to show the order of two numbers.

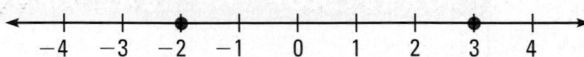

EXAMPLE 2 *Ordering Real Numbers*

Use a number line to order the real numbers.

    a. -2 and 3 **b.** -1 and -3

SOLUTION

  a. Begin by graphing both numbers.

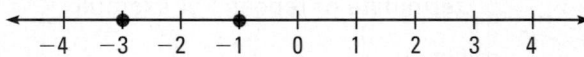

Because -2 is to the left of 3, it follows that -2 *is less than* 3, which can be written as $-2 < 3$. This relationship can also be written as $3 > -2$, which is read as "3 *is greater than* -2."

  b. Begin by graphing both numbers.

Because -3 is to the left of -1, it follows that -3 *is less than* -1, which can be written as $-3 < -1$. (You can also write $-1 > -3$.)

EXAMPLE 3 *Ordering Elevations*

Geography

Here are the elevations of five locations in Imperial Valley, California.

    Alamorio: -135 feet

    Curlew: -93 feet

    Gieselmann Lake: -162 feet

    Moss: -100 feet

    Orita: -92 feet

  a. Order the elevations from lowest to highest.

  b. Which locations have elevations below -100 feet?

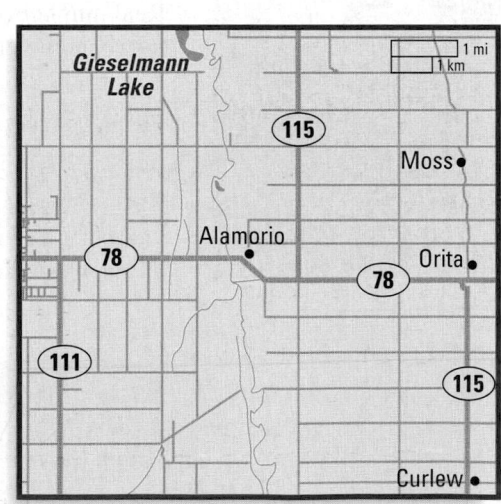

SOLUTION

  a. From lowest to highest, the elevations are as follows.

Location	Gieselmann Lake	Alamorio	Moss	Curlew	Orita
Elevation (ft)	-162	-135	-100	-93	-92

  b. Gieselmann Lake and Alamorio have elevations below -100 feet.

GOAL 2 USING PROPERTIES OF REAL NUMBERS

When you add or multiply real numbers, there are several properties to remember.

CONCEPT SUMMARY	PROPERTIES OF ADDITION AND MULTIPLICATION	

Let a, b, and c be real numbers.

Property	Addition	Multiplication
CLOSURE	$a + b$ is a real number.	ab is a real number.
COMMUTATIVE	$a + b = b + a$	$ab = ba$
ASSOCIATIVE	$(a + b) + c = a + (b + c)$	$(ab)c = a(bc)$
IDENTITY	$a + 0 = a, 0 + a = a$	$a \cdot 1 = a, 1 \cdot a = a$
INVERSE	$a + (-a) = 0$	$a \cdot \dfrac{1}{a} = 1, a \neq 0$

The following property involves both addition and multiplication.

DISTRIBUTIVE	$a(b + c) = ab + ac$

EXAMPLE 4 *Identifying Properties of Real Numbers*

Identify the property shown.

  a. $(3 + 9) + 8 = 3 + (9 + 8)$ **b.** $14 \cdot 1 = 14$

SOLUTION

  a. Associative property of addition   **b.** Identity property of multiplication

· · · · · · · · · ·

The **opposite,** or *additive inverse*, of any number a is $-a$. The **reciprocal,** or *multiplicative inverse*, of any nonzero number a is $\dfrac{1}{a}$. Subtraction is defined as *adding the opposite*, and division is defined as *multiplying by the reciprocal.*

$a - b = a + (-b)$	**Definition of subtraction**
$\dfrac{a}{b} = a \cdot \dfrac{1}{b}, b \neq 0$	**Definition of division**

STUDENT HELP

➤ **Study Tip**
- If a is positive, then its opposite, $-a$, is negative.
- The opposite of 0 is 0.
- If a is negative, then its opposite, $-a$, is positive.

EXAMPLE 5 *Operations with Real Numbers*

  a. The difference of 7 and -10 is:

$$7 - (-10) = 7 + 10 \qquad \text{Add 10, the opposite of } -10.$$
$$= 17 \qquad \text{Simplify.}$$

  b. The quotient of -24 and $\dfrac{1}{3}$ is:

$$\dfrac{-24}{\frac{1}{3}} = -24 \cdot 3 \qquad \text{Multiply by 3, the reciprocal of } \tfrac{1}{3}.$$
$$= -72 \qquad \text{Simplify.}$$

When you use the operations of addition, subtraction, multiplication, and division in real life, you should use *unit analysis* to check that your units make sense.

EXAMPLE 6   *Using Unit Analysis*

Perform the given operation. Give the answer with the appropriate unit of measure.

a. 345 miles $-$ 187 miles $=$ 158 miles

b. $(1.5 \text{ hours})\left(\dfrac{50 \text{ miles}}{1 \text{ hour}}\right) = 75 \text{ miles}$

c. $\dfrac{24 \text{ dollars}}{3 \text{ hours}} = 8 \text{ dollars per hour}$

d. $\left(\dfrac{88 \text{ feet}}{1 \text{ second}}\right)\left(\dfrac{3600 \text{ seconds}}{1 \text{ hour}}\right)\left(\dfrac{1 \text{ mile}}{5280 \text{ feet}}\right) = 60 \text{ miles per hour}$

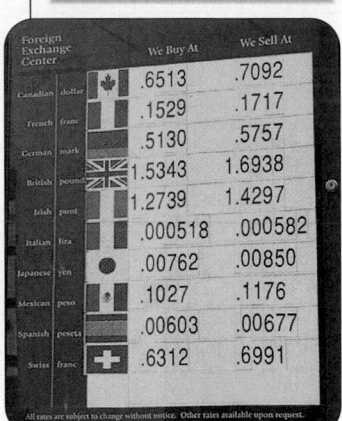
EXAMPLE 7   *Operations with Real Numbers in Real Life*

MONEY EXCHANGE You are exchanging $400 for Mexican pesos. The exchange rate is 8.5 pesos per dollar, and the bank charges a 1% fee to make the exchange.

a. How much money should you take to the bank if you do not want to use part of the $400 to pay the exchange fee?

b. How much will you receive in pesos?

c. When you return from Mexico you have 425 pesos left. How much can you get in dollars? Assume that you use other money to pay the exchange fee.

SOLUTION

a. To find 1% of $400, multiply to get:

$1\% \times \$400 = 0.01 \times \$400$ **Rewrite 1% as 0.01.**

$= \$4$ **Simplify.**

▶ You need to take $400 + $4 = $404 to the bank.

b. To find the amount you will receive in pesos, multiply $400 by the exchange rate.

$(400 \text{ dollars})\left(\dfrac{8.5 \text{ pesos}}{1 \text{ dollar}}\right) = (400 \times 8.5) \text{ pesos}$

$= 3400 \text{ pesos}$

▶ You receive 3400 pesos for $400.

c. To find the amount in dollars, divide 425 pesos by the exchange rate.

$\dfrac{425 \text{ pesos}}{8.5 \text{ pesos per dollar}} = (425 \text{ pesos})\left(\dfrac{1 \text{ dollar}}{8.5 \text{ pesos}}\right)$

$= \dfrac{425}{8.5} \text{ dollars}$

$= \$50$

▶ You receive $50 for 425 pesos.

GUIDED PRACTICE

Vocabulary Check ✓ 1. What is a rational number? What is an irrational number?

Concept Check ✓ 2. Give an example of each of the following: a whole number, an integer, a rational number, and an irrational number.

3. Which of the following is false? Explain.

   A. No integer is an irrational number.

   B. Every integer is a rational number.

   C. Every integer is a whole number.

Skill Check ✓ **Graph the numbers on a number line. Then decide which number is the greatest.**

4. $-3, 4, 0, -8, -10$

5. $\frac{3}{2}, -1, -\frac{5}{2}, 3, -5$

6. $1, -2.5, 4.5, -0.5, 6$

7. $3.2, -0.7, \frac{3}{4}, -\frac{3}{2}, 0$

Identify the property shown.

8. $5 + 2 = 2 + 5$

9. $6 + (-6) = 0$

10. $24 \cdot 1 = 24$

11. $8 \cdot 10 = 10 \cdot 8$

12. $13 + 0 = 13$

13. $7\left(\frac{1}{7}\right) = 1$

14. Find the product. Give the answer with the appropriate unit of measure. Explain your reasoning.

$$\left(\frac{90 \text{ miles}}{1 \text{ hour}}\right)\left(\frac{5280 \text{ feet}}{1 \text{ mile}}\right)\left(\frac{1 \text{ hour}}{60 \text{ minutes}}\right)\left(\frac{1 \text{ minute}}{60 \text{ seconds}}\right)$$

PRACTICE AND APPLICATIONS

STUDENT HELP

▶ **Extra Practice**
to help you master skills is on p. 940.

USING A NUMBER LINE **Graph the numbers on a number line. Then decide which number is greater and use the symbol < or > to show the relationship.**

15. $\frac{1}{2}, -5$

16. $4, \frac{3}{4}$

17. $2.3, -0.6$

18. $0.3, -2.1$

19. $-\frac{5}{3}, \sqrt{3}$

20. $0, -\sqrt{10}$

21. $-\frac{9}{4}, -3$

22. $-\frac{3}{2}, -\frac{11}{3}$

23. $\sqrt{5}, 2$

24. $-2, \sqrt{2}$

25. $\sqrt{8}, 2.5$

26. $-4.5, -\sqrt{24}$

STUDENT HELP

▶ **HOMEWORK HELP**
Examples 1, 2: Exs. 15–32
Example 3: Exs. 55, 56
Example 4: Exs. 33–42
Example 5: Exs. 43–50
Example 6: Exs. 51–54
Example 7: Exs. 57–65

ORDERING NUMBERS **Graph the numbers on a number line. Then write the numbers in increasing order.**

27. $-\frac{1}{2}, 2, \frac{13}{4}, -3, -6$

28. $\sqrt{15}, -4, -\frac{2}{9}, -1, 6$

29. $-\sqrt{5}, -\frac{5}{2}, 0, 3, -\frac{1}{3}$

30. $\frac{1}{6}, 2.7, -1.5, -8, -\sqrt{7}$

31. $0, -\frac{12}{5}, -\sqrt{12}, 0.3, -1.5$

32. $0.8, \sqrt{10}, -2.4, -\sqrt{6}, \frac{9}{2}$

IDENTIFYING PROPERTIES Identify the property shown.

33. $-8 + 8 = 0$

34. $(3 \cdot 5) \cdot 10 = 3 \cdot (5 \cdot 10)$

35. $7 \cdot 9 = 9 \cdot 7$

36. $(9 + 2) + 4 = 9 + (2 + 4)$

37. $12(1) = 12$

38. $2(5 + 11) = 2 \cdot 5 + 2 \cdot 11$

LOGICAL REASONING Tell whether the statement is true for all real numbers *a*, *b*, and *c*. Explain your answers.

39. $(a + b) + c = a + (b + c)$

40. $(a - b) - c = a - (b - c)$

41. $(a \cdot b) \cdot c = a \cdot (b \cdot c)$

42. $(a \div b) \div c = a \div (b \div c)$

OPERATIONS Select and perform an operation to answer the question.

43. What is the sum of 32 and -7?

44. What is the sum of -9 and -6?

45. What is the difference of -5 and 8?

46. What is the difference of -1 and -10?

47. What is the product of 9 and -4?

48. What is the product of -7 and -3?

49. What is the quotient of -5 and $-\frac{1}{2}$?

50. What is the quotient of -14 and $\frac{7}{4}$?

UNIT ANALYSIS Give the answer with the appropriate unit of measure.

51. $8\frac{1}{6}$ feet $+ 4\frac{5}{6}$ feet

52. $27\frac{1}{2}$ liters $- 18\frac{5}{8}$ liters

53. $(8.75 \text{ yards})\left(\dfrac{\$70}{1 \text{ yard}}\right)$

54. $\left(\dfrac{50 \text{ feet}}{1 \text{ second}}\right)\left(\dfrac{1 \text{ mile}}{5280 \text{ feet}}\right)\left(\dfrac{3600 \text{ seconds}}{1 \text{ hour}}\right)$

55. STATISTICS CONNECTION The lowest temperatures ever recorded in various cities are shown. List the cities in decreasing order based on their lowest temperatures. How many of these cities have a record low temperature below $-25°F$? ▶ Source: National Climatic Data Center

City	Low temp.	City	Low temp.
Albany, NY	$-28°F$	Jackson, MS	$2°F$
Atlanta, GA	$-8°F$	Milwaukee, WI	$-26°F$
Detroit, MI	$-21°F$	New Orleans, LA	$11°F$
Helena, MT	$-42°F$	Norfolk, VA	$-3°F$
Honolulu, HI	$53°F$	Seattle-Tacoma, WA	$0°F$

56. MASTERS GOLF The table shows the final scores of 10 competitors in the 1998 Masters Golf Tournament. List the players in increasing order based on their golf scores. ▶ Source: Sports Illustrated

Player	Score	Player	Score
Paul Azinger	-6	Lee Janzen	$+6$
Tiger Woods	-3	Jeff Maggert	$+1$
Jay Haas	-2	Mark O'Meara	-9
Jim Furyk	-7	Corey Pavin	$+9$
Vijay Singh	$+12$	Jumbo Ozaki	$+8$

0   25215 04658   2

↑ first digit   ↑ check digit

BAR CODES Using the operations on this bar code produces
$(0 + 5 + 1 + 0 + 6 + 8)(3)$
$+ (2 + 2 + 5 + 4 + 5) = 78$.
The next highest multiple of 10 is 80, and $80 - 78 = 2$, which is the check digit.

STUDENT HELP

Skills Review
For help with significant digits, see p. 911.

🌐 **BAR CODES** In Exercises 57 and 58, use the following information.

All packaged products sold in the United States have a Universal Product Code (UPC), or bar code, such as the one shown at the left. The following operations are performed on the first eleven digits, and the result should equal the twelfth digit, called the *check digit*.

• Add the digits in the odd-numbered positions. Multiply by 3.

• Add the digits in the even-numbered positions.

• Add the results of the first two steps.

• Subtract the result of the previous step from the next highest multiple of 10.

57. Does a UPC of 0 76737 20012 9 check? Explain.

58. Does a UPC of 0 41800 48700 3 check? Explain.

59. **SOCIAL STUDIES** **CONNECTION** Two of the tallest buildings in the world are the Sky Central Plaza in Guangzhou, China, which reaches a height of 1056 feet, and the Petronas Tower I in Kuala Lumpur, Malaysia, which reaches a height of 1483 feet. Find the heights of both buildings in yards, in inches, and in miles. Give your answers to four significant digits.

▶ Source: Council on Tall Buildings and Urban Habitat

Petronas Tower I

60. 🌐 **ELEVATOR SPEED** The elevator in the Washington Monument takes 75 seconds to travel 500 feet to the top floor. What is the speed of the elevator in miles per hour? Give your answer to two significant digits.

▶ Source: National Park Service

🌐 **TRAVEL** In Exercises 61–63, use the following information.

You are taking a trip to Switzerland. You are at the bank exchanging $600 for Swiss francs. The exchange rate is 1.5 francs per dollar, and the bank charges a 1.5% fee to make the exchange.

61. You brought $10 extra with you to pay the exchange fee. Do you have enough to pay the fee?

62. How much will you receive in Swiss francs for your $600?

63. After your trip, you have 321 Swiss francs left. How much is this amount in dollars? Assume that you use other money to pay the exchange fee.

HISTORY **CONNECTION** In Exercises 64 and 65, use the following information.

In 1862, James Glaisher and Henry Coxwell went up too high in a hot-air balloon. At 25,000 feet, Glaisher passed out. To get the balloon to descend, Coxwell grasped a valve, but his hands were too numb to pull the cord. He was able to pull the cord with his teeth. The balloon descended, and both men made it safely back. The temperature of air drops about 3°F for each 1000 foot increase in altitude.

64. How much had the temperature dropped from the sea level temperature when Glaisher and Coxwell reached an altitude of 25,000 feet?

65. If the temperature at sea level was 60°F, what was the temperature at 25,000 feet?

Test Preparation

66. MULTI-STEP PROBLEM You are taking a trip through the provinces of Alberta and British Columbia in Canada. You are at Quesnel Lake when you decide to visit some of the national parks. You visit the following places in order: Kamloops, Revelstoke, Lethbridge, and Red Deer. After you visit Red Deer, you return to Quesnel Lake.

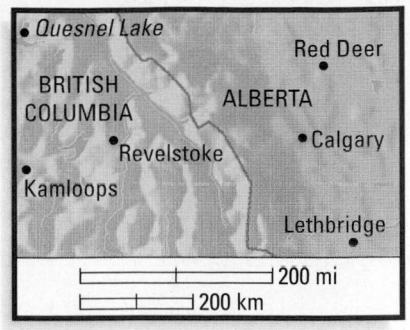

a. Using the scale on the map, estimate the distance traveled (in kilometers) for the entire trip. Approximately where was the "halfway point" of your trip?

b. Your car gets 12 kilometers per liter of gasoline. If your gas tank holds 60 liters and the cost of gasoline is $.29 per liter, about how much will you spend on gasoline for the entire trip? How many times will you have to stop for gasoline if you begin the trip with a full tank?

c. If you drive at an average speed of 88 kilometers per hour, how many hours will you spend driving on your trip?

★ **Challenge**

67. LOGICAL REASONING Show that $a + (a + 2) = 2(a + 1)$ for all values of a by justifying the steps using the properties of addition and multiplication.

$$a + (a + 2) = (a + a) + 2 \qquad \textbf{a.} \underline{\ ?\ }$$
$$= (1 \cdot a + 1 \cdot a) + 2 \qquad \textbf{b.} \underline{\ ?\ }$$
$$= (1 + 1)a + 2 \qquad \textbf{c.} \underline{\ ?\ }$$
$$= 2a + 2 \cdot 1 \qquad \textbf{d.} \underline{\ ?\ }$$
$$= 2(a + 1) \qquad \textbf{e.} \underline{\ ?\ }$$

MIXED REVIEW

OPERATIONS WITH SIGNED NUMBERS Perform the operation.
(Skills Review, p. 905)

68. $4 - 12$ **69.** $(-7)(-9)$ **70.** $-20 \div 5$ **71.** $6(-5)$

72. $-14 + 9$ **73.** $6 - (-13)$ **74.** $56 \div (-7)$ **75.** $-16 + (-18)$

ALGEBRAIC EXPRESSIONS Write the given phrase as an algebraic expression.
(Skills Review, p. 929 for 1.2)

76. 7 more than a number   **77.** 3 less than a number

78. 6 times a number   **79.** $\frac{1}{4}$ of a number

GEOMETRY ▶ **CONNECTION** Find the area of the figure. (Skills Review, p. 914)

80. Triangle with base 6 inches and height 4 inches

81. Triangle with base 7 inches and height 3 inches

82. Rectangle with sides 5 inches and 7 inches

83. Rectangle with sides 25 inches and 30 inches

Algebraic Expressions and Models

What you should learn

GOAL 1 Evaluate algebraic expressions.

GOAL 2 Simplify algebraic expressions by combining like terms, as applied in **Example 6**.

Why you should learn it

▼ To solve **real-life** problems, such as finding the population of Hawaii in **Ex. 57**.

GOAL 1 EVALUATING ALGEBRAIC EXPRESSIONS

A **numerical expression** consists of numbers, operations, and grouping symbols. In Lesson 1.1 you worked with addition, subtraction, multiplication, and division. In this lesson you will work with *exponentiation*, or raising to a power.

Exponents are used to represent repeated factors in multiplication. For instance, the expression 2^5 represents the number that you obtain when 2 is used as a factor 5 times.

$$2^5 = \underbrace{2 \cdot 2 \cdot 2 \cdot 2 \cdot 2}_{\textbf{5 factors of 2}} \qquad \textbf{2 to the fifth power}$$

The number 2 is the **base**, the number 5 is the **exponent**, and the expression 2^5 is a **power**. The exponent in a power represents the number of times the base is used as a factor. For a number raised to the first power, you do not usually write the exponent 1. For instance, you usually write 2^1 simply as 2.

EXAMPLE 1   *Evaluating Powers*

a. $(-3)^4 = (-3) \cdot (-3) \cdot (-3) \cdot (-3) = 81$

b. $-3^4 = -(3 \cdot 3 \cdot 3 \cdot 3) = -81$

. . . .

In Example 1, notice how parentheses are used in part (a) to indicate that the base is -3. In the expression -3^4, however, the base is 3, not -3. An **order of operations** helps avoid confusion when evaluating expressions.

ORDER OF OPERATIONS

1. First, do operations that occur within grouping symbols.
2. Next, evaluate powers.
3. Then, do multiplications and divisions from left to right.
4. Finally, do additions and subtractions from left to right.

EXAMPLE 2   *Using Order of Operations*

$$-4 + 2(-2 + 5)^2 = -4 + 2(3)^2 \qquad \textbf{Add within parentheses.}$$
$$= -4 + 2(9) \qquad \textbf{Evaluate power.}$$
$$= -4 + 18 \qquad \textbf{Multiply.}$$
$$= 14 \qquad \textbf{Add.}$$

A **variable** is a letter that is used to represent one or more numbers. Any number used to replace a variable is a **value of the variable**. An expression involving variables is called an **algebraic expression**.

When the variables in an algebraic expression are replaced by numbers, you are *evaluating* the expression, and the result is called the **value of the expression**. To evaluate an algebraic expression, use the following flow chart.

| Write algebraic expression. | → | Substitute values of variables. | → | Simplify. |

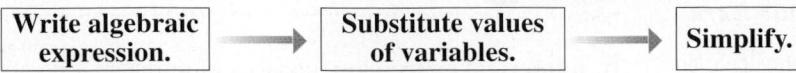 **EXAMPLE 3** *Evaluating an Algebraic Expression*

Evaluate $-3x^2 - 5x + 7$ when $x = -2$.

$$-3x^2 - 5x + 7 = -3(-2)^2 - 5(-2) + 7$$ **Substitute −2 for x.**

$$= -3(4) - 5(-2) + 7$$ **Evaluate power.**

$$= -12 + 10 + 7$$ **Multiply.**

$$= 5$$ **Add.**

· · · · · · · · · ·

An expression that represents a real-life situation is a **mathematical model**. When you create the expression, you are *modeling* the real-life situation.

EXAMPLE 4 *Writing and Evaluating a Real-Life Model*

Movies

You have $50 and are buying some movies on videocassettes that cost $15 each. Write an expression that shows how much money you have left after buying n movies. Evaluate the expression when $n = 2$ and $n = 3$.

SOLUTION

PROBLEM SOLVING STRATEGY

VERBAL MODEL

| Original amount | − | Price per movie | · | Number of movies bought |

LABELS

Original amount = **50**   (dollars)

Price per movie = **15**   (dollars per movie)

Number of movies bought = n (movies)

ALGEBRAIC MODEL

$$50 - 15n$$

When you buy **2** movies, you have $50 - 15(2) = \$20$ left.

When you buy **3** movies, you have $50 - 15(3) = \$5$ left.

UNIT ANALYSIS You can use unit analysis to check your verbal model.

$$\text{dollars} - \left(\frac{\text{dollars}}{\text{movie}}\right)(\text{movies}) = \text{dollars} - \text{dollars} = \text{dollars}$$

For an expression such as $2x + 3$, the parts that are added together, $2x$ and 3, are called **terms**. When a term is the product of a number and a power of a variable, such as $2x$ or $4x^3$, the number is the **coefficient** of the power.

Terms such as $3x^2$ and $-5x^2$ are **like terms** because they have the same variable part. **Constant terms** such as -4 and 2 are also like terms. The distributive property lets you *combine like terms* that have variables by adding the coefficients.

STUDENT HELP

↳ **Study Tip**
For an expression like $2x - 3$, think of the expression as $2x + (-3)$, so the terms are $2x$ and -3.

EXAMPLE 5 *Simplifying by Combining Like Terms*

STUDENT HELP

↳ **Skills Review**
For help with opposites, see p. 936.

a. $7x + 4x = (7 + 4)x$ **Distributive property**
$\qquad\qquad\quad = 11x$ **Add coefficients.**

b. $3n^2 + n - n^2 = (3n^2 - n^2) + n$ **Group like terms.**
$\qquad\qquad\qquad = 2n^2 + n$ **Combine like terms.**

c. $2(x + 1) - 3(x - 4) = 2x + 2 - 3x + 12$ **Distributive property**
$\qquad\qquad\qquad\qquad = (2x - 3x) + (2 + 12)$ **Group like terms.**
$\qquad\qquad\qquad\qquad = -x + 14$ **Combine like terms.**

· · · · · · · · · ·

Two algebraic expressions are **equivalent** if they have the same value for all values of their variable(s). For instance, the expressions $7x + 4x$ and $11x$ are equivalent, as are the expressions $5x - (6x + y)$ and $-x - y$. A statement such as $7x + 4x = 11x$ that equates two equivalent expressions is called an **identity**.

EXAMPLE 6 *Using a Real-Life Model*

MUSIC You want to buy either a CD or a cassette as a gift for each of 10 people. CDs cost $13 each and cassettes cost $8 each. Write an expression for the total amount you must spend. Then evaluate the expression when 4 of the people get CDs.

SOLUTION

VERBAL MODEL	Price per CD	·	Number of CDs	+	Price per cassette	·	Number of cassettes

LABELS		
	CD price = **13**	(dollars per CD)
	Number of CDs = n	(CDs)
	Cassette price = **8**	(dollars per cassette)
	Number of cassettes = **10 − n**	(cassettes)

ALGEBRAIC MODEL

$13\,n + 8\,(10 - n) = 13n + 80 - 8n$
$\qquad\qquad\qquad = 5n + 80$

▶ When $n = 4$, the total cost is $5(4) + 80 = 20 + 80 = \$100$.

FOCUS ON PEOPLE

HEITARO NAKAJIMA could be called the inventor of the compact disc (CD). He was head of the research division of the company that developed the first CDs in 1982. A CD usually has a diameter of 12 centimeters, just the right size to hold Beethoven's Ninth Symphony.

GUIDED PRACTICE

Vocabulary Check ✔

Concept Check ✔

1. Copy 8^4 and label the base and the exponent. What does each number represent?

2. Identify the terms of $6x^3 - 17x + 5$.

3. Explain how the order of operations is used to evaluate $3 - 8^2 \div 4 + 1$.

ERROR ANALYSIS Find the error. Then write the correct steps.

4.
$$5 + 2(16 \div 2)^2 = 5 + 2(16 \div 4)$$
$$= 5 + 2(4)$$
$$= 5 + 8$$
$$= 13$$

5.
$$4x - (3y + 7x) = 4x - 3y + 7x$$
$$= (4x + 7x) - 3y$$
$$= (4 + 7)x - 3y$$
$$= 11x - 3y$$

Skill Check ✔

Evaluate the expression for the given value of x.

6. $x - 8$ when $x = 2$

7. $3x + 14$ when $x = -3$

8. $x(x + 4)$ when $x = 5$

9. $x^2 - 9$ when $x = 6$

Simplify the expression.

10. $9y - 14y$

11. $11x + 6y - 2x + 3y$

12. $3(x + 4) - (6 + 2x)$

13. $3x^2 - 5x + 5x^2 - 3x$

14. 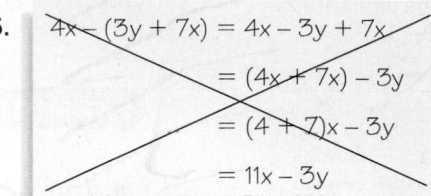 **RETAIL BUYING** When you arrive at the music store to buy the CDs and cassettes for the 10 people mentioned in Example 6, you find that the store is having a sale. CDs now cost $11 each and cassettes now cost $7 each. Write an expression for the new total amount you will spend. Then evaluate the expression when 6 of the people get CDs.

PRACTICE AND APPLICATIONS

STUDENT HELP

→ **Extra Practice**
to help you master
skills is on p. 940.

WRITING WITH EXPONENTS Write the expression using exponents.

15. eight to the third power

16. x to the fifth power

17. 5 to the nth power

18. $x \cdot x \cdot x \cdot x \cdot x \cdot x \cdot x$

EVALUATING POWERS Evaluate the power.

19. 4^4

20. $(-4)^4$

21. -2^5

22. $(-2)^5$

23. 5^3

24. 3^5

25. 2^8

26. 8^2

STUDENT HELP

→ **HOMEWORK HELP**
Example 1: Exs. 15–26
Example 2: Exs. 27–32
Example 3: Exs. 33–46
Example 4: Exs. 56–61
Example 5: Exs. 47–52
Example 6: Exs. 56–61

USING ORDER OF OPERATIONS Evaluate the expression.

27. $13 + 20 - 9$

28. $14 \cdot 3 - 2$

29. $6 \cdot 2 + 35 \div 5$

30. $-6 + 3(-3 + 7)^2$

31. $24 - 8 \cdot 12 \div 4$

32. $16 \div (2 + 6) \cdot 10$

EVALUATING EXPRESSIONS Evaluate the expression for the given value of x.

33. $x - 12$ when $x = 7$

34. $6x + 9$ when $x = 4$

35. $25x(x - 4)$ when $x = -1$

36. $x^2 + 5 - x$ when $x = 5$

EVALUATING EXPRESSIONS Evaluate the expression for the given values of x and y.

37. $x^4 + 3y$ when $x = 2$ and $y = -8$

38. $(3x)^2 - 7y^2$ when $x = 3$ and $y = 2$

39. $9x + 8y$ when $x = 4$ and $y = 5$

40. $5\left(\dfrac{x}{y}\right) - x$ when $x = 6$ and $y = \dfrac{2}{3}$

41. $\dfrac{x^2}{2y + 1}$ when $x = -3$ and $y = 2$

42. $\dfrac{(x + 3)^2}{3y - 2}$ when $x = 2$ and $y = 4$

43. $\dfrac{x + y}{x - y}$ when $x = -4$ and $y = 9$

44. $\dfrac{2x + y}{3y + x}$ when $x = 10$ and $y = 6$

45. $\dfrac{4(x - 2y)}{x + y}$ when $x = 4$ and $y = -2$

46. $\dfrac{4y - x}{3(2x + y)}$ when $x = -3$ and $y = 3$

SIMPLIFYING EXPRESSIONS Simplify the expression.

47. $7x^2 + 12x - x^2 - 40x$

48. $4x^2 + x - 3x - 6x^2$

49. $12(n - 3) + 4(n - 13)$

50. $5(n^2 + n) - 3(n^2 - 2n)$

51. $4x - 2y + y - 9x$

52. $8(y - x) - 2(x - y)$

STUDENT HELP

▶ **Skills Review**
For help with area,
see p. 914.

HOMEWORK HELP
Visit our Web site
www.mcdougallittell.com
for help with problem
solving in Ex. 56.

GEOMETRY CONNECTION Write an expression for the area of the figure. Then evaluate the expression for the given value(s) of the variable(s).

53. $n = 40$

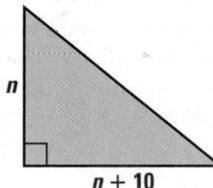

n

$n + 10$

54. $a = 8, b = 3$

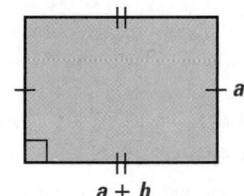

a

$a + b$

55. $x = 12, y = 5$

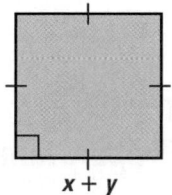

$x + y$

56. 🌐 **AVERAGE SALARIES** In 1980, a public high school principal's salary was approximately \$30,000. From 1980 through 1996, the average salary of principals at public high schools increased by an average of \$2500 per year. Use the verbal model and labels below to write an algebraic model that gives a public high school principal's average salary t years after 1980. Evaluate the expression when $t = 5$, 10, and 15.

▶ Source: Educational Research Service

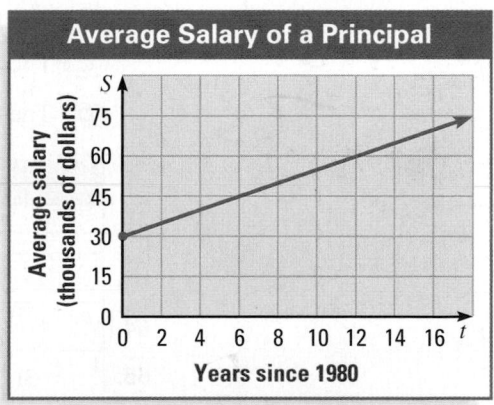

Average Salary of a Principal

VERBAL MODEL

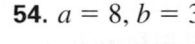 $+$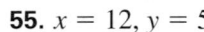

| Salary in 1980 | $+$ | Average increase per year | $\cdot$ | Years since 1980 |

LABELS

Salary in 1980 = **30** (thousands of dollars)

Average increase per year = **2.5** (thousands of dollars per year)

Years since 1980 = t (years)

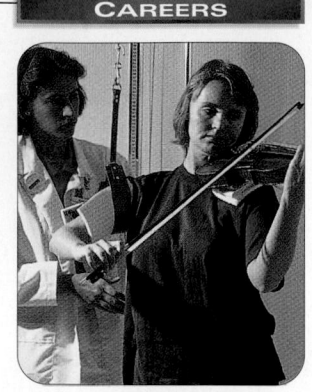

57. **SOCIAL STUDIES** **CONNECTION** For 1980 through 1998, the population (in thousands) of Hawaii can be modeled by $13.2t + 965$ where t is the number of years since 1980. What was the population of Hawaii in 1998? What was the population increase from 1980 to 1998? ▶ Source: U.S. Bureau of the Census

58. **PHYSICAL THERAPY** In 1996 there were approximately 115,000 physical therapy jobs in the United States. The number of jobs is expected to increase by 8100 each year. Write an expression that gives the total number of physical therapy jobs each year since 1996. Evaluate the expression for the year 2010.

DATA UPDATE of U.S. Bureau of Labor Statistics data at www.mcdougallittell.com

59. **MOVIE RENTALS** You buy a VCR for $149 and plan to rent movies each month. Each rental costs $3.85. Write an expression that gives the total amount you spend during the first twelve months that you own the VCR, including the price of the VCR. Evaluate the expression if you rent 6 movies each month.

60. **USED CARS** You buy a used car with 37,148 miles on the odometer. Based on your regular driving habits, you plan to drive the car 15,000 miles each year that you own it. Write an expression for the number of miles that appears on the odometer at the end of each year. Evaluate the expression to find the number of miles that will appear on the odometer after you have owned the car for 4 years.

61. **WALK-A-THON** You are taking part in a charity walk-a-thon where you can either walk or run. You walk at 4 kilometers per hour and run at 8 kilometers per hour. The walk-a-thon lasts 3 hours. Money is raised based on the total distance you travel in the 3 hours. Your sponsors donate $15 for each kilometer you travel. Write an expression that gives the total amount of money you raise. Evaluate the expression if you walk for 2 hours and run for 1 hour.

**Test
Preparation**

QUANTITATIVE COMPARISON In Exercises 62–67, choose the statement that is true about the given quantities.

(A) The quantity in column A is greater.

(B) The quantity in column B is greater.

(C) The two quantities are equal.

(D) The relationship cannot be determined from the given information.

	Column A	Column B
62.	2^6	$(-2)^6$
63.	-4^4	$(-4)^4$
64.	x^4	x^5
65.	$3(x - 2)$ when $x = 4$	$3x - 6$ when $x = 4$
66.	$x + 10(x^2 - 3)$ when $x = 3$	x^6 when $x = 2$
67.	$2(x^2 - 1)$	$2x^2 - 1$

★ **Challenge**

68. MATH CLUB SHIRTS The math club is ordering shirts for its 8 members. The club members have a choice of either a $15 T-shirt or a $25 sweatshirt. Make a table showing the total amount of money needed for each possible combination of T-shirts and sweatshirts that the math club can order. Describe any patterns you see. Write an expression that gives the total cost of the shirts. Explain what each term in the expression represents.

MIXED REVIEW

LEAST COMMON DENOMINATOR Find the least common denominator.
(Skills Review, p. 908)

69. $\frac{1}{2}, \frac{3}{4}, \frac{4}{5}$ **70.** $\frac{1}{2}, \frac{3}{4}, \frac{5}{6}$ **71.** $\frac{1}{3}, \frac{2}{5}, -\frac{14}{15}$

72. $\frac{1}{4}, -\frac{3}{8}, \frac{7}{12}$ **73.** $\frac{1}{3}, \frac{4}{5}, \frac{6}{7}$ **74.** $\frac{1}{2}, \frac{3}{4}, -\frac{1}{16}$

USING A NUMBER LINE Graph the numbers on a number line. Then decide which number is greater and use the symbol $<$ or $>$ to show the relationship. (Review 1.1)

75. $-\sqrt{3}, -3$ **76.** $-\frac{1}{2}, -\frac{11}{2}$ **77.** $2.75, \frac{7}{2}$

IDENTIFYING PROPERTIES Identify the property shown. (Review 1.1)

78. $(7 \cdot 9)8 = 7(9 \cdot 8)$ **79.** $-13 + 13 = 0$

80. $27 + 6 = 6 + 27$ **81.** $19 \cdot 1 = 19$

FINDING RECIPROCALS Give the reciprocal of the number. (Review 1.1 for 1.3)

82. -22 **83.** $\frac{7}{8}$ **84.** 12 **85.** $-\frac{5}{4}$

86. $\frac{11}{16}$ **87.** $-\frac{1}{9}$ **88.** 37 **89.** -14

QUIZ 1
Self-Test for Lessons 1.1 and 1.2

Graph the numbers on a number line. Then write the numbers in increasing order. (Lesson 1.1)

1. $\frac{9}{2}, -2.5, 0, -\frac{3}{4}, 1$ **2.** $\frac{10}{3}, 0.8, \frac{15}{8}, -1.5, -0.25$

Identify the property shown. (Lesson 1.1)

3. $5(3 - 7) = 5 \cdot 3 - 5 \cdot 7$ **4.** $(8 + 6) + 4 = 8 + (6 + 4)$

Evaluate the expression for the given value(s) of the variable(s). (Lesson 1.2)

5. $12x - 21$ when $x = 3$ **6.** $7x - (9x + 5)$ when $x = \frac{1}{3}$

7. $x^2 + 5x - 8$ when $x = -3$ **8.** $x^3 + 4(x - 1)$ when $x = 4$

9. $x^2 - 11x + 40y - 14$ when $x = 5$ and $y = -2$

Simplify the expression. (Lesson 1.2)

10. $3x - 2y - 9y + 4 + 5x$ **11.** $3(x - 2) - (4 + x)$

12. $5x^2 - 3x + 8x - 6 - 7x^2$ **13.** $4(x + 2x) - 2(x^2 - x)$

14. 🌐 **COMPUTER DISKS** You are buying a total of 15 regular floppy disks and high capacity storage disks for your computer. Regular floppy disks cost $.35 each and high capacity disks cost $13.95 each. Write an expression for the total amount you spend on computer disks. (Lesson 1.2)

Evaluating Expressions

You can use a scientific calculator or a graphing calculator to evaluate expressions. Keystrokes for evaluating several expressions are shown below. Because the keystrokes shown may not agree precisely with the keystrokes for *your* calculator, you should make sure you know how to evaluate the expressions using your own calculator.

▶ **EXAMPLE**

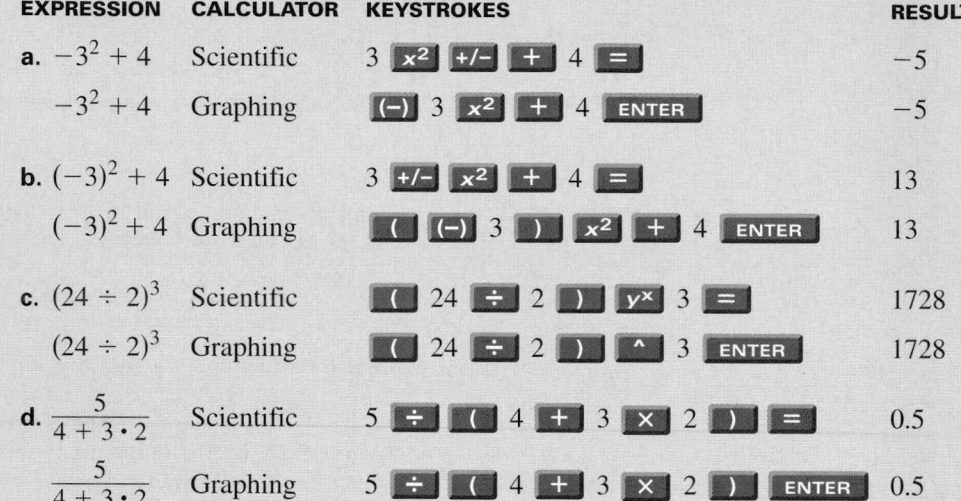

EXPRESSION	CALCULATOR	KEYSTROKES	RESULT
a. $-3^2 + 4$	Scientific	3 [x²] [+/–] [+] 4 [=]	-5
$-3^2 + 4$	Graphing	[(–)] 3 [x²] [+] 4 [ENTER]	-5
b. $(-3)^2 + 4$	Scientific	3 [+/–] [x²] [+] 4 [=]	13
$(-3)^2 + 4$	Graphing	[(] [(–)] 3 [)] [x²] [+] 4 [ENTER]	13
c. $(24 \div 2)^3$	Scientific	[(] 24 [÷] 2 [)] [yˣ] 3 [=]	1728
$(24 \div 2)^3$	Graphing	[(] 24 [÷] 2 [)] [^] 3 [ENTER]	1728
d. $\dfrac{5}{4 + 3 \cdot 2}$	Scientific	5 [÷] [(] 4 [+] 3 [×] 2 [)] [=]	0.5
$\dfrac{5}{4 + 3 \cdot 2}$	Graphing	5 [÷] [(] 4 [+] 3 [×] 2 [)] [ENTER]	0.5

On a scientific calculator, notice the difference between the change sign key, [+/–], and the subtraction key, [–]. Likewise, on a graphing calculator, the negation key, [(–)], and the subtraction key, [–], do not perform the same operation.

▶ **EXERCISES**

Write an expression that corresponds to the calculator keystrokes. Then evaluate the expression.

1. Scientific: 4 [+/–] [x²] [–] 5 [=]

2. Scientific: 7 [÷] [(] 3 [+/–] [–] 5 [)] [=]

3. Graphing: [(] 1 [+] 4 [)] [^] 6 [ENTER]

4. Graphing: 3 [×] [(] 5 [–] 2 [)] [ENTER]

Use a calculator to evaluate the expression. Round the result to three decimal places.

5. $3(5.3 - 4.1)^2$ 6. $(-2.6 - 12.5)^4$ 7. $(0.21 + 5.23)^3$

8. $\frac{4}{3}\pi(5.5)^3$ 9. $\dfrac{9.2 - 4.5}{0.6}$ 10. $\dfrac{7.3}{-6.2 - 3.6}$

11. $1024(1 + 0.42)^5$ 12. $\dfrac{1 + 3 \cdot 4^2}{7.25}$ 13. $\left(\dfrac{2^3 + 1}{2 \cdot 5}\right)^2$

1.3

Solving Linear Equations

What you should learn

GOAL 1 Solve linear equations.

GOAL 2 Use linear equations to solve **real-life** problems, such as finding how much a broker must sell in **Example 5**.

Why you should learn it

▼ To solve **real-life** problems, such as finding the temperature at which dry ice changes to a gas in **Ex. 43**.

An **equation** is a statement in which two expressions are equal. A **linear equation** in one variable is an equation that can be written in the form $ax = b$ where a and b are constants and $a \neq 0$. A number is a **solution** of an equation if the statement is true when the number is substituted for the variable.

Two equations are **equivalent** if they have the same solutions. For instance, the equations $x - 4 = 1$ and $x = 5$ are equivalent because both have the number 5 as their only solution. The following *transformations*, or changes, produce equivalent equations and can be used to solve an equation.

TRANSFORMATIONS THAT PRODUCE EQUIVALENT EQUATIONS

ADDITION PROPERTY OF EQUALITY	*Add* the same number to both sides: If $a = b$, then $a + c = b + c$.
SUBTRACTION PROPERTY OF EQUALITY	*Subtract* the same number from both sides: If $a = b$, then $a - c = b - c$.
MULTIPLICATION PROPERTY OF EQUALITY	*Multiply* both sides by the same nonzero number: If $a = b$ and $c \neq 0$, then $ac = bc$.
DIVISION PROPERTY OF EQUALITY	*Divide* both sides by the same nonzero number: If $a = b$ and $c \neq 0$, then $a \div c = b \div c$.

EXAMPLE 1 *Solving an Equation with a Variable on One Side*

Solve $\frac{3}{7}x + 9 = 15$.

SOLUTION

Your goal is to isolate the variable on one side of the equation.

$$\frac{3}{7}x + 9 = 15 \qquad \text{Write original equation.}$$

$$\frac{3}{7}x = 6 \qquad \text{Subtract 9 from each side.}$$

$$x = \frac{7}{3}(6) \qquad \text{Multiply each side by } \tfrac{7}{3}, \text{ the reciprocal of } \tfrac{3}{7}.$$

$$x = 14 \qquad \text{Simplify.}$$

▶ The solution is 14.

✓ **CHECK** Check $x = 14$ in the original equation.

$$\frac{3}{7}(14) + 9 \stackrel{?}{=} 15 \qquad \text{Substitute 14 for } x.$$

$$15 = 15 \checkmark \qquad \text{Solution checks.}$$

EXAMPLE 2 *Solving an Equation with a Variable on Both Sides*

Solve $5n + 11 = 7n - 9$.

SOLUTION

$5n + 11 = 7n - 9$	Write original equation.
$11 = 2n - 9$	Subtract $5n$ from each side.
$20 = 2n$	Add 9 to each side.
$10 = n$	Divide each side by 2.

▶ The solution is 10. Check this in the original equation.

EXAMPLE 3 *Using the Distributive Property*

Solve $4(3x - 5) = -2(-x + 8) - 6x$.

SOLUTION

$4(3x - 5) = -2(-x + 8) - 6x$	Write original equation.
$12x - 20 = 2x - 16 - 6x$	Distributive property
$12x - 20 = -4x - 16$	Combine like terms.
$16x - 20 = -16$	Add $4x$ to each side.
$16x = 4$	Add 20 to each side.
$x = \dfrac{1}{4}$	Divide each side by 16.

▶ The solution is $\dfrac{1}{4}$. Check this in the original equation.

EXAMPLE 4 *Solving an Equation with Fractions*

Solve $\dfrac{1}{3}x + \dfrac{1}{4} = x - \dfrac{1}{6}$.

SOLUTION

$\dfrac{1}{3}x + \dfrac{1}{4} = x - \dfrac{1}{6}$	Write original equation.
$12\left(\dfrac{1}{3}x + \dfrac{1}{4}\right) = 12\left(x - \dfrac{1}{6}\right)$	Multiply each side by the LCD, 12.
$4x + 3 = 12x - 2$	Distributive property
$3 = 8x - 2$	Subtract $4x$ from each side.
$5 = 8x$	Add 2 to each side.
$\dfrac{5}{8} = x$	Divide each side by 8.

▶ The solution is $\dfrac{5}{8}$. Check this in the original equation.

GOAL 2 **USING LINEAR EQUATIONS IN REAL LIFE**

EXAMPLE 5 *Writing and Using a Linear Equation*

REAL ESTATE A real estate broker's base salary is $18,000. She earns a 4% commission on total sales. How much must she sell to earn $55,000 total?

SOLUTION

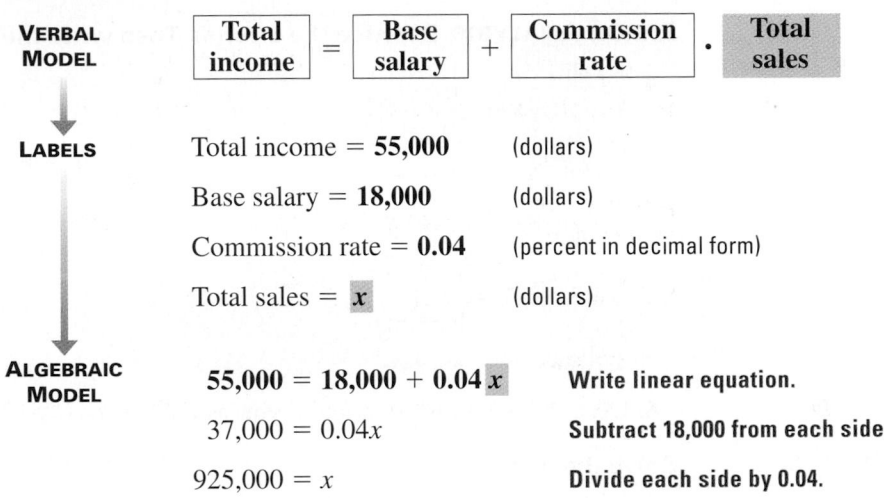

VERBAL MODEL

| Total income | = | Base salary | + | Commission rate | · | Total sales |

LABELS

Total income = **55,000**   (dollars)

Base salary = **18,000**   (dollars)

Commission rate = **0.04**   (percent in decimal form)

Total sales = **x**   (dollars)

ALGEBRAIC MODEL

$55,000 = 18,000 + 0.04x$ Write linear equation.

$37,000 = 0.04x$ Subtract 18,000 from each side.

$925,000 = x$ Divide each side by 0.04.

▶ The broker must sell real estate worth a total of $925,000 to earn $55,000.

Photo Framing

EXAMPLE 6 *Writing and Using a Geometric Formula*

You have a 3 inch by 5 inch photo that you want to enlarge, mat, and frame. You want the width of the mat to be 2 inches on all sides. You want the perimeter of the framed photo to be 44 inches. By what percent should you enlarge the photo?

SOLUTION

Let x be the percent (in decimal form) of enlargement relative to the original photo. So, the dimensions of the enlarged photo (in inches) are $3x$ by $5x$. Draw a diagram.

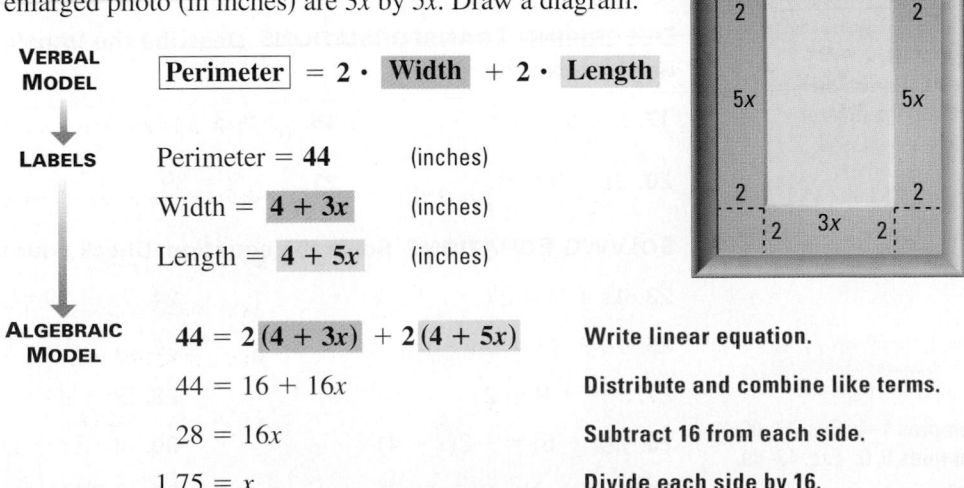

PROBLEM SOLVING STRATEGY

VERBAL MODEL

| **Perimeter** | = | 2 · | **Width** | + | 2 · | **Length** |

LABELS

Perimeter = **44**   (inches)

Width = **4 + 3x**   (inches)

Length = **4 + 5x**   (inches)

ALGEBRAIC MODEL

$44 = 2(4 + 3x) + 2(4 + 5x)$ Write linear equation.

$44 = 16 + 16x$ Distribute and combine like terms.

$28 = 16x$ Subtract 16 from each side.

$1.75 = x$ Divide each side by 16.

▶ You should enlarge the photo to 175% of its original size.

REAL ESTATE BROKER
Real estate brokers must have a thorough knowledge not only of the real estate market, but of mathematics as well. Brokers often provide buyers with information about loans, loan rates, and monthly payments.

CAREER LINK
www.mcdougallittell.com

GUIDED PRACTICE

Vocabulary Check ✔

1. What is an equation?

Concept Check ✔

2. What does it mean for two equations to be equivalent? Give an example of two equivalent equations.

3. How does an equation such as $2(x + 3) = 10$ differ from an identity such as $2(x + 3) = 2x + 6$?

ERROR ANALYSIS Describe the error(s). Then write the correct steps.

4.

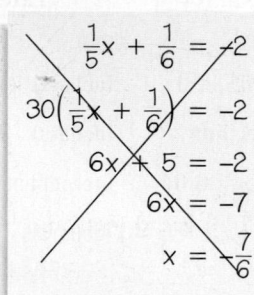

$$\frac{1}{5}x + \frac{1}{6} = -2$$
$$30\left(\frac{1}{5}x + \frac{1}{6}\right) = -2$$
$$6x + 5 = -2$$
$$6x = -7$$
$$x = -\frac{7}{6}$$

5.

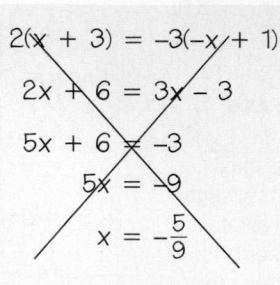

$$2(x + 3) = -3(-x + 1)$$
$$2x + 6 = 3x - 3$$
$$5x + 6 = -3$$
$$5x = -9$$
$$x = -\frac{5}{9}$$

6. Describe the transformation(s) you would use to solve $2x - 8 = 14$.

Skill Check ✔

Solve the equation.

7. $x + 4 = 9$

8. $4x = 24$

9. $2x - 3 = 7$

10. $0.2x - 8 = 0.6$

11. $\frac{1}{3}x + \frac{1}{2} = \frac{11}{12}$

12. $\frac{3}{4}x - \frac{2}{3} = \frac{5}{6}$

13. $1.5x + 9 = 4.5$

14. $6x - 4 = 2x + 10$

15. $2(x + 2) = 3(x - 8)$

16. 🌎 **REAL ESTATE SALES** The real estate broker's base salary from Example 5 has been raised to $21,000 and the commission rate has been increased to 5%. How much real estate does the broker have to sell now to earn $70,000?

PRACTICE AND APPLICATIONS

STUDENT HELP

▶ **Extra Practice**
to help you master skills is on p. 940.

DESCRIBING TRANSFORMATIONS Describe the transformation(s) you would use to solve the equation.

17. $x + 5 = -7$

18. $\frac{1}{6}x = 3$

19. $-\frac{4}{7}x = 6$

20. $2x - 9 = 0$

21. $\frac{x}{3} + 2 = 89$

22. $3 = -x - 5$

SOLVING EQUATIONS Solve the equation. Check your solution.

23. $4x + 7 = 27$

24. $7s - 29 = -15$

25. $3a + 13 = 9a - 8$

26. $m - 30 = 6 - 2m$

STUDENT HELP

▶ **HOMEWORK HELP**
Examples 1–4: Exs. 17–40
Examples 5, 6: Exs. 43–49

27. $15n + 9 = 21$

28. $2b + 11 = 15 - 6b$

29. $2(x + 6) = -2(x - 4)$

30. $4(-3x + 1) = -10(x - 4) - 14x$

31. $-(x + 2) - 2x = -2(x + 1)$

32. $-4(3 + x) + 5 = 4(x + 3)$

SOLVING EQUATIONS Solve the equation. Check your solution.

33. $\frac{7}{2}x - 1 = 2x + 5$

34. $\frac{1}{2}x - \frac{5}{3} = -\frac{1}{2}x + \frac{19}{4}$

35. $\frac{3}{4}\left(\frac{4}{5}x - 2\right) = \frac{11}{4}$

36. $-\frac{2}{3}\left(\frac{6}{5}x - \frac{7}{10}\right) = \frac{17}{20}$

37. $2.7n + 4.3 = 12.94$

38. $-4.2n - 6.5 = -14.06$

39. $3.1(x + 2) - 1.5x = 5.2(x - 4)$

40. $2.5(x - 3) + 1.7x = 10.8(x + 1.5)$

GEOMETRY ▸ CONNECTION Find the dimensions of the figure.

41. Area = 504

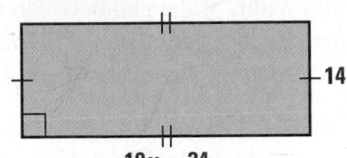
14
10x − 24

42. Perimeter = 23

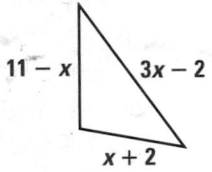
11 − x   3x − 2
x + 2

In Exercises 43 and 44, use the following formula.

$$\text{degrees Fahrenheit} = \frac{9}{5}(\text{degrees Celsius}) + 32$$

43. 🌐 **DRY ICE** Dry ice is solid carbon dioxide. Dry ice does not melt — it changes directly from a solid to a gas. Dry ice changes to a gas at −109.3°F. What is this temperature in degrees Celsius?

44. 🌐 **VETERINARY MEDICINE** The normal body temperature of a dog is 38.6°C. Your dog's temperature is 101.1°F. Does your dog have a fever? Explain.

45. 🌐 **CAR REPAIR** The bill for the repair of your car was $390. The cost for parts was $215. The cost for labor was $35 per hour. How many hours did the repair work take?

46. 🌐 **SUMMER JOBS** You have two summer jobs. In the first job, you work 28 hours per week and earn $7.25 per hour. In the second job, you earn $6.50 per hour and can work as many hours as you want. If you want to earn $255 per week, how many hours must you work at your second job?

47. 🌐 **STOCKBROKER** A stockbroker earns a base salary of $40,000 plus 5% of the total value of the stocks, mutual funds, and other investments that the stockbroker sells. Last year, the stockbroker earned $71,750. What was the total value of the investments the stockbroker sold?

48. 🌐 **WORD PROCESSING** You are writing a term paper. You want to include a table that has 5 columns and is 360 points wide. $\left(\text{A point is } \frac{1}{72} \text{ of an inch.}\right)$ You want the first column to be 200 points wide and the remaining columns to be equal in width. How wide should each of the remaining columns be?

49. 🌐 **WALKWAY CONSTRUCTION** You are building a walkway of uniform width around a 100 foot by 60 foot swimming pool. After completing the walkway, you want to put a fence along the outer edge of the walkway. You have 450 feet of fencing to enclose the walkway. What is the maximum width of the walkway?

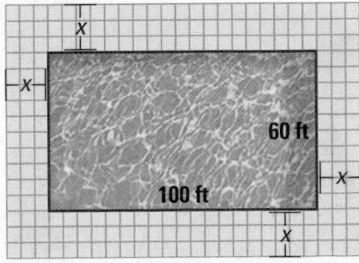
x
x
60 ft
100 ft
x

FOCUS ON CAREERS

REAL LIFE **STOCKBROKER**
Stockbrokers buy and sell stocks, bonds, and other securities for clients as discussed in Ex. 47. Stockbrokers typically study economics in college.

INTERNET **CAREER LINK**
www.mcdougallittell.com

50. MULTI-STEP PROBLEM You are in charge of constructing a fence around the running track at a high school. The fence is to be built around the track so that there is a uniform gap between the outside edge of the track and the fence.

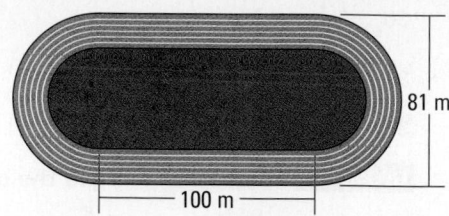

81 m

100 m

a. What is the maximum width of the gap between the track and the fence if no more than 630 meters of fencing is used? (*Hint:* Use the equation for the circumference of a circle, $C = 2\pi r$, to help you.)

b. You are charging the school $10.50 for each meter of fencing. The school has $5250 in its budget to spend on the fence. How many meters of fencing can you use with this budget?

c. **CRITICAL THINKING** Explain whether or not it is geometrically reasonable to put up the new fence with the given budget.

★ **Challenge**

SOLVING EQUATIONS Solve the equation. If there is no solution, write *no solution*. If the equation is an identity, write *all real numbers*.

51. $5(x - 4) = 5x + 12$ **52.** $3(x + 5) = 3x + 15$

53. $7x + 14 - 3x = 4x + 14$ **54.** $11x - 3 + 2x = 6(x + 4) + 7x$

EXTRA CHALLENGE
www.mcdougallittell.com

55. $-2(4 - 3x) + 7 = -2x + 6 + 8x$ **56.** $5(2 - x) = 3 - 2x + 7 - 3x$

MIXED REVIEW

GEOMETRY **CONNECTION** Find the area of the figure. (Skills Review, p. 914)

57. Circle with radius 5 inches   **58.** Square with side 4 inches

59. Circle with radius 7 inches   **60.** Square with side 9 inches

EVALUATING EXPRESSIONS Evaluate the expression. (Review 1.2 for 1.4)

61. $24 - (9 + 7)$ **62.** $-16 + 3(8 - 4)$

63. $-3 + 6(1 - 3)^2$ **64.** $2(3 - 5)^3 + 4(-4 + 7)$

65. $2x + 3$ when $x = 4$ **66.** $8(x - 2) + 3x$ when $x = 6$

67. $5x - 7 + 2x$ when $x = -3$ **68.** $6x - 3(2x + 4)$ when $x = 5$

SIMPLIFYING EXPRESSIONS Simplify the expression. (Review 1.2)

69. $3(7 + x) - 8x$ **70.** $2(8 + x) + 2x - x$

71. $4x - (6 - 3x)$ **72.** $2x - 3(4x + 7)$

73. $3(x + 9) + 2(4 - x)$ **74.** $-4(x - 3) - 2(x + 7)$

75. $2(x^2 + 2) - x + x^2 + 7$ **76.** $2(x^2 - 81) - 3x^2$

77. $x^2 - 5x + 3(x^2 + 7x)$ **78.** $4x^2 - 2(x^2 - 3x) + 6x + 8$

▶ ACTIVITY 1.3

Using Technology

Using Tables to Solve Equations

You can use the *Table* feature of a graphing calculator to solve linear equations.

▶ **EXAMPLE**

Use the *Table* feature of a graphing calculator to solve the equation $7x - 2 = 4x + 13$.

▶ **SOLUTION**

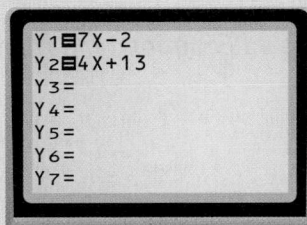

	Y₁ = 7X − 2
	Y₂ = 4X + 13
	Y₃ =
	Y₄ =
	Y₅ =
	Y₆ =
	Y₇ =

X	Y₁	Y₂
0	-2	13
1	5	17
2	12	21
3	19	25
4	26	29
5	33	33

1 To use the *Table* feature to solve the equation, let y_1 equal the left side of the equation, and let y_2 equal the right side as shown above.

2 Then set the starting x-value of the table to 0 and the step value (the value by which the x-values increase) to 1. The table should look similar to the one shown above.

3 Scroll through the table until you find an x-value for which both sides of the equation have the same y-value or until the difference in the y-values changes sign. If both of the y-values are the same, that x-value is the solution of the equation. For the given equation, the solution is $x = 5$.

X	Y₁	Y₂
0	-2	13
1	5	17
2	12	21
3	19	25
4	26	29
5	33	33

▶ **EXERCISES**

Use the table shown to decide whether the statement is *true* or *false*. Explain your reasoning.

1. The solution of $4 - 5x = 16 + x$ is 2.

2. The solution of $3x + 4 = x + 10$ is 3.

X	Y₁	Y₂
-3	19	13
-2	14	14
-1	9	15
0	4	16
1	-1	17
2	-6	18

X	Y₁	Y₂
-2	-2	8
-1	1	9
0	4	10
1	7	11
2	10	12
3	13	13

Use the *Table* feature of a graphing calculator to solve the equation.

3. $2x + 4 = -3x - 6$

4. $-4x + 4 = -x - 5$

5. $-2x - 5 = 3 - 10x$

6. $-4x + 10 = 4 - 10x$

7. $15x - 3 = 15 - 3x$

8. $2x - 18 = -5x - 4$

Rewriting Equations and Formulas

What you should learn

GOAL 1 Rewrite equations with more than one variable.

GOAL 2 Rewrite common formulas, as applied in **Example 5**.

Why you should learn it

▼ To solve **real-life** problems, such as finding how much you should charge for tickets to a benefit concert in **Example 4**.

FARM AID

FARM AID

GOAL 1 EQUATIONS WITH MORE THAN ONE VARIABLE

In Lesson 1.3 you solved equations with one variable. Many equations involve more than one variable. You can solve such an equation for one of its variables.

EXAMPLE 1 *Rewriting an Equation with More Than One Variable*

Solve $7x - 3y = 8$ for y.

SOLUTION

$7x - 3y = 8$	Write original equation.
$-3y = -7x + 8$	Subtract $7x$ from each side.
$y = \dfrac{7}{3}x - \dfrac{8}{3}$	Divide each side by -3.

▶ **ACTIVITY**

Developing Concepts

Equations with More Than One Variable

Given the equation $2x + 5y = 4$, use each method below to find y when $x = -3, -1, 2,$ and 6. Tell which method is more efficient.

Method 1 Substitute $x = -3$ into $2x + 5y = 4$ and solve for y. Repeat this process for the other values of x.

Method 2 Solve $2x + 5y = 4$ for y. Then evaluate the resulting expression for y using each of the given values of x.

EXAMPLE 2 *Calculating the Value of a Variable*

Given the equation $x + xy = 1$, find the value of y when $x = -1$ and $x = 3$.

SOLUTION

Solve the equation for y.

$x + xy = 1$	Write original equation.
$xy = 1 - x$	Subtract x from each side.
$y = \dfrac{1 - x}{x}$	Divide each side by x.

Then calculate the value of y for each value of x.

When $x = -1$: $y = \dfrac{1 - (-1)}{-1} = -2$ When $x = 3$: $y = \dfrac{1 - 3}{3} = -\dfrac{2}{3}$

Benefit Concert

EXAMPLE 3 *Writing an Equation with More Than One Variable*

You are organizing a benefit concert. You plan on having only two types of tickets: adult and child. Write an equation with more than one variable that represents the revenue from the concert. How many variables are in your equation?

SOLUTION

PROBLEM SOLVING STRATEGY

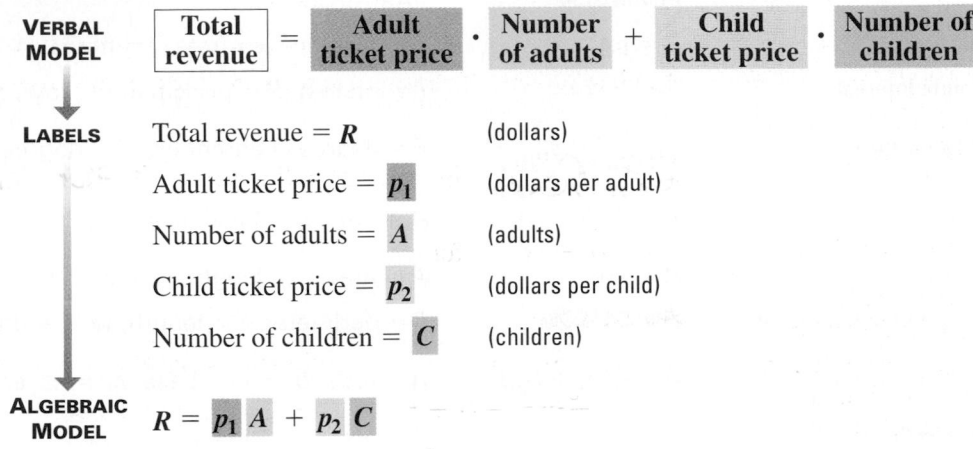

VERBAL MODEL

| Total revenue | = | Adult ticket price | · | Number of adults | + | Child ticket price | · | Number of children |

LABELS

Total revenue = R (dollars)

Adult ticket price = p_1 (dollars per adult)

Number of adults = A (adults)

Child ticket price = p_2 (dollars per child)

Number of children = C (children)

ALGEBRAIC MODEL

$R = p_1 A + p_2 C$

This equation has five variables. The variables p_1 and p_2 are read as "p sub one" and "p sub two." The small lowered numbers 1 and 2 are subscripts used to indicate the two different price variables.

EXAMPLE 4 *Using an Equation with More Than One Variable*

BENEFIT CONCERT For the concert in Example 3, your goal is to sell $25,000 in tickets. You plan to charge $25.25 per adult and expect to sell 800 adult tickets. You need to determine what to charge for child tickets. How much should you charge per child if you expect to sell 200 child tickets? 300 child tickets? 400 child tickets?

FOCUS ON APPLICATIONS

SOLUTION

First solve the equation $R = p_1 A + p_2 C$ from Example 3 for p_2.

$R = p_1 A + p_2 C$ **Write original equation.**

$R - p_1 A = p_2 C$ **Subtract $p_1 A$ from each side.**

$\dfrac{R - p_1 A}{C} = p_2$ **Divide each side by C.**

Now substitute the known values of the variables into the equation.

BENEFIT CONCERT
Farm Aid, a type of benefit concert, began in 1985. Since that time Farm Aid has distributed more than $13,000,000 to family farms throughout the United States.

If $C = 200$, the child ticket price is $p_2 = \dfrac{25,000 - 25.25(800)}{200} = \$24$.

If $C = 300$, the child ticket price is $p_2 = \dfrac{25,000 - 25.25(800)}{300} = \$16$.

If $C = 400$, the child ticket price is $p_2 = \dfrac{25,000 - 25.25(800)}{400} = \$12$.

GOAL 2 REWRITING COMMON FORMULAS

Throughout this course you will be using many formulas. Several are listed below.

COMMON FORMULAS

	FORMULA	VARIABLES
Distance	$d = rt$	d = distance, r = rate, t = time
Simple Interest	$I = Prt$	I = interest, P = principal, r = rate, t = time
Temperature	$F = \frac{9}{5}C + 32$	F = degrees Fahrenheit, C = degrees Celsius
Area of Triangle	$A = \frac{1}{2}bh$	A = area, b = base, h = height
Area of Rectangle	$A = \ell w$	A = area, ℓ = length, w = width
Perimeter of Rectangle	$P = 2\ell + 2w$	P = perimeter, ℓ = length, w = width
Area of Trapezoid	$A = \frac{1}{2}(b_1 + b_2)h$	A = area, b_1 = one base, b_2 = other base, h = height
Area of Circle	$A = \pi r^2$	A = area, r = radius
Circumference of Circle	$C = 2\pi r$	C = circumference, r = radius

---

EXAMPLE 5 *Rewriting a Common Formula*

STUDENT HELP

→ **Skills Review**
For help with perimeter,
see p. 914.

The formula for the perimeter of a rectangle is $P = 2\ell + 2w$. Solve for w.

SOLUTION

$P = 2\ell + 2w$	**Write perimeter formula.**
$P - 2\ell = 2w$	**Subtract 2ℓ from each side.**
$\dfrac{P - 2\ell}{2} = w$	**Divide each side by 2.**

EXAMPLE 6 *Applying a Common Formula*

Gardening

You have 40 feet of fencing with which to enclose a rectangular garden. Express the garden's area in terms of its length only.

SOLUTION

Use the formula for the area of a rectangle, $A = \ell w$, and the result of Example 5.

$A = \ell w$	**Write area formula.**
$A = \ell\left(\dfrac{P - 2\ell}{2}\right)$	**Substitute $\dfrac{P - 2\ell}{2}$ for w.**
$A = \ell\left(\dfrac{40 - 2\ell}{2}\right)$	**Substitute 40 for P.**
$A = \ell(20 - \ell)$	**Simplify.**

GUIDED PRACTICE

1. Complete this statement: $A = \ell w$ is an example of a(n) _?_.

2. Which of the following are equations with more than one variable?

    A. $2x + 5 = 9 - 5x$ **B.** $4x + 10y = 62$ **C.** $x - 8 = 3y + 7$

3. Use the equation from Example 3. Describe how you would solve for A.

Solve the equation for y.

4. $4x + 8y = 17$ 5. $5x - 3y = 9$ 6. $5y - 3x = 15$

7. $\frac{3}{4}x + 5y = 20$ 8. $xy + 2x = 8$ 9. $\frac{2}{3}x - \frac{1}{2}y = 12$

In Exercises 10 and 11, use the following information.
The area A of an ellipse is given by the formula $A = \pi ab$ where a and b are half the lengths of the major and minor axes. (The longer chord is the major axis.)

10. Solve the formula for a.

11. Use the result from Exercise 10 to find the length of the major axis of an ellipse whose area is 157 square inches and whose minor axis is 10 inches long. (Use 3.14 for π.)

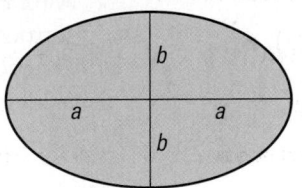

PRACTICE AND APPLICATIONS

EXPLORING METHODS Find the value of y for the given value of x using two methods. First, substitute the value of x into the equation and then solve for y. Second, solve for y and then substitute the value of x into the equation.

12. $4x + 9y = 30; x = 3$ 13. $5x - 7y = 12; x = 1$

14. $xy + 3x = 25; x = 5$ 15. $9y - 4x = -16; x = 8$

16. $-y - 2x = -11; x = -4$ 17. $-x = 3y - 55; x = 20$

18. $x = 24 + xy; x = -12$ 19. $-xy + 3x = 30; x = 15$

20. $-4x + 7y + 7 = 0; x = 7$ 21. $6x - 5y - 44 = 0; x = 4$

22. $\frac{1}{2}x - \frac{4}{5}y = 19; x = 6$ 23. $\frac{3}{4}x = -\frac{9}{11}y + 12; x = 10$

REWRITING FORMULAS Solve the formula for the indicated variable.

24. Circumference of a Circle

    Solve for r: $C = 2\pi r$

25. Volume of a Cone

    Solve for h: $V = \frac{1}{3}\pi r^2 h$

26. Area of a Triangle

    Solve for b: $A = \frac{1}{2}bh$

27. Investment at Simple Interest

    Solve for P: $I = Prt$

28. Celsius to Fahrenheit

    Solve for C: $F = \frac{9}{5}C + 32$

29. Area of a Trapezoid

    Solve for b_2: $A = \frac{1}{2}(b_1 + b_2)h$

GEOMETRY CONNECTION In Exercises 30–32, solve the formula for the indicated variable. Then evaluate the rewritten formula for the given values. (Include units of measure in your answer.)

30. Area of a circular ring: $A = 4\pi pw$ Solve for p. Find p when $A = 22$ cm² and $w = 2$ cm.

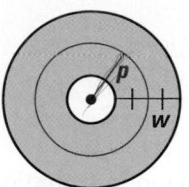

31. Surface area of a cylinder: $S = 2\pi rh + 2\pi r^2$ Solve for h. Find h when $S = 105$ in.² and $r = 3$ in.

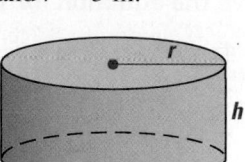

32. Perimeter of a track: $P = 2\pi r + 2x$ Solve for r. Find r when $P = 440$ yd and $x = 110$ yd.

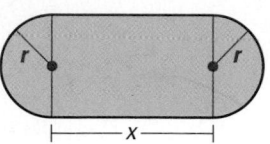

🌐 **HONEYBEES** In Exercises 33 and 34, use the following information.

A forager honeybee spends about three weeks becoming accustomed to the immediate surroundings of its hive and spends the rest of its life collecting pollen and nectar. The total number of miles T a forager honeybee flies in its lifetime L (in days) can be modeled by $T = m(L - 21)$ where m is the number of miles it flies each day.

33. Solve the equation $T = m(L - 21)$ for L.

34. A forager honeybee's flight muscles last only about 500 miles; after that the bee dies. Some forager honeybees fly about 55 miles per day. Approximately how many days do these bees live?

🌐 **BASEBALL** In Exercises 35 and 36, use the following information.

The Pythagorean Theorem of Baseball is a formula for approximating a team's ratio of wins to games played. Let R be the number of runs the team scores during the season, A be the number of runs allowed to opponents, W be the number of wins, and T be the total number of games played. Then the formula

$$\frac{W}{T} \approx \frac{R^2}{R^2 + A^2}$$

approximates the team's ratio of wins to games played. ▶ Source: *Inside Sports*

35. Solve the formula for W.

36. The 1998 New York Yankees scored 965 runs and allowed 656. How many of its 162 games would you estimate the team won?

🌐 **FUNDRAISER** In Exercises 37–39, use the following information.

Your tennis team is having a fundraiser. You are going to help raise money by selling sun visors and baseball caps.

37. Write an equation that represents the total amount of money you raise.

38. How many variables are in the equation? What does each represent?

39. Your team raises a total of $4480. Give three possible combinations of sun visors and baseball caps that could have been sold if the price of a sun visor is $3.00 and the price of a baseball cap is $7.00.

40. **GEOMETRY CONNECTION** The formula for the area of a circle is $A = \pi r^2$. The formula for the circumference of a circle is $C = 2\pi r$. Write a formula for the area of a circle in terms of its circumference.

41. **GEOMETRY** ▶ **CONNECTION** The formula for the height h of an equilateral triangle is $h = \frac{\sqrt{3}}{2}b$ where b is the length of a side. Write a formula for the area of an equilateral triangle in terms of the following.

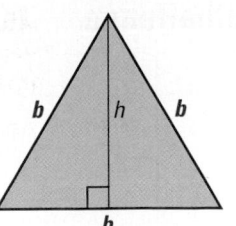

a. the length of a side only

b. the height only

42. **GEOMETRY** ▶ **CONNECTION** The surface area S of a cylinder is given by the formula $S = 2\pi rh + 2\pi r^2$. The height h of the cylinder shown at the right is 5 more than 3 times its radius r.

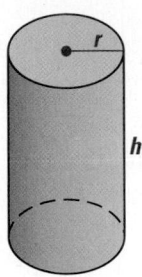

a. Write a formula for the surface area of the cylinder in terms of its radius.

b. Find the surface area of the cylinder for $r = 3, 4,$ and 6.

Test Preparation

QUANTITATIVE COMPARISON In Exercises 43 and 44, choose the statement that is true about the given quantities.

  (A) The quantity in column A is greater.

  (B) The quantity in column B is greater.

  (C) The two quantities are equal.

  (D) The relationship cannot be determined from the given information.

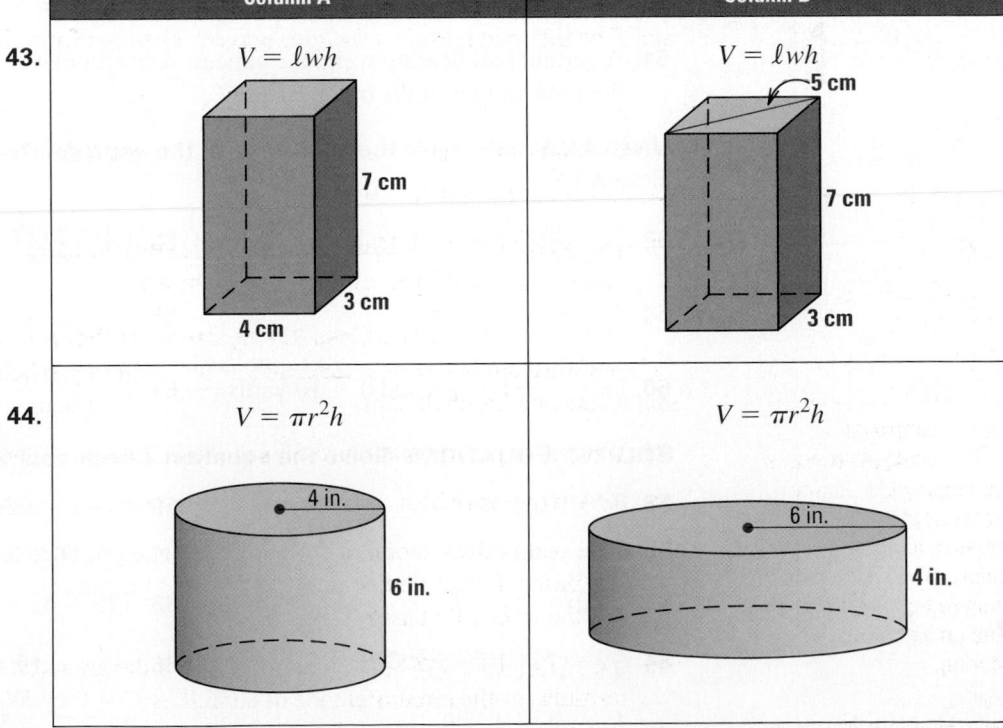

	Column A	Column B
43.	$V = \ell wh$	$V = \ell wh$
44.	$V = \pi r^2 h$	$V = \pi r^2 h$

★ **Challenge**

45. 🌐 **FUEL EFFICIENCY** The more aerodynamic a vehicle is, the less fuel the vehicle's engine must use to overcome air resistance. To design vehicles that are as fuel efficient as possible, automotive engineers use the formula

$$R = 0.00256 \times D_C \times F_A \times s^2$$

where R is the air resistance (in pounds), D_C is the drag coefficient, F_A is the frontal area of the vehicle (in square feet), and s is the speed of the vehicle (in miles per hour). The formula assumes that there is no wind.

a. Rewrite the formula to find the drag coefficient in terms of the other variables.

b. Find the drag coefficient of a car when the air resistance is 50 pounds, the frontal area is 25 square feet, and the speed of the car is 45 miles per hour.

EXTRA CHALLENGE
➜ www.mcdougallittell.com

MIXED REVIEW

WRITING EXPRESSIONS Write an expression to answer the question. (Skills Review, p. 929)

46. You buy x birthday cards for $1.85 each. How much do you spend?

47. You have $30 and spend x dollars. How much money do you have left?

48. You drive 55 miles per hour for x hours. How many miles do you drive?

49. You have $250 in your bank account and you deposit x dollars. How much money do you now have in your account?

50. You spend $42 on x music cassettes. How much does each cassette cost?

51. A certain ball bearing weighs 2 ounces. A box contains x ball bearings. What is the total weight of the ball bearings?

UNIT ANALYSIS Give the answer with the appropriate unit of measure. (Review 1.1)

52. $\left(\dfrac{7 \text{ meters}}{1 \text{ minute}}\right)(60 \text{ minutes})$

53. $\left(\dfrac{168 \text{ hours}}{1 \text{ week}}\right)(52 \text{ weeks})$

54. $4\frac{1}{4}$ feet $+ 7\frac{3}{4}$ feet

55. $13\frac{1}{4}$ liters $- 8\frac{7}{8}$ liters

56. $\left(\dfrac{3 \text{ yards}}{1 \text{ second}}\right)(12 \text{ seconds}) - 10 \text{ yards}$

57. $\left(\dfrac{15 \text{ dollars}}{1 \text{ hour}}\right)(8 \text{ hours}) + 45 \text{ dollars}$

SOLVING EQUATIONS Solve the equation. Check your solution. (Review 1.3)

58. $3d + 16 = d - 4$

59. $5 - x = 23 + 2x$

60. $10(y - 1) = y + 4$

61. $p - 16 + 4 = 4(2 - p)$

62. $-10x = 5x + 5$

63. $12z = 4z - 56$

64. $\frac{2}{3}x - 7 = 1$

65. $-\frac{3}{4}x + 19 = -11$

66. $\frac{1}{4}x + \frac{3}{8} = \frac{1}{5} - \frac{1}{5}x$

67. $\frac{5}{4}x - \frac{3}{4} = \frac{5}{6}x + \frac{1}{2}$

Problem Solving Using Algebraic Models

GOAL 1 USING A PROBLEM SOLVING PLAN

One of your major goals in this course is to learn how to use algebra to solve real-life problems. You have solved simple problems in previous lessons, and this lesson will provide you with more experience in problem solving.

As you have seen, it is helpful when solving real-life problems to first write an equation in words *before* you write it in mathematical symbols. This word equation is called a **verbal model**. The verbal model is then used to write a mathematical statement, which is called an **algebraic model**. The key steps in this problem solving plan are shown below.

Write a verbal model. ⇒ Assign labels. ⇒ Write an algebraic model. ⇒ Solve the algebraic model. ⇒ Answer the question.

EXAMPLE 1 *Writing and Using a Formula*

The Bullet Train runs between the Japanese cities of Osaka and Fukuoka, a distance of 550 kilometers. When it makes no stops, it takes 2 hours and 15 minutes to make the trip. What is the average speed of the Bullet Train?

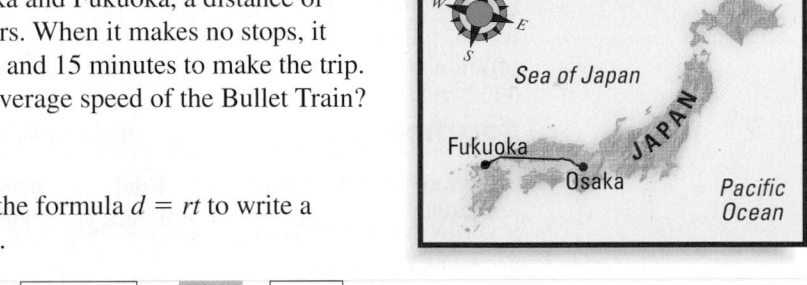

SOLUTION

You can use the formula $d = rt$ to write a verbal model.

VERBAL MODEL | Distance | = | Rate | · | Time |

LABELS   Distance = **550**   (kilometers)

Rate = **r**   (kilometers per hour)

Time = **2.25**   (hours)

ALGEBRAIC MODEL $550 = r\,(2.25)$ **Write algebraic model.**

$\dfrac{550}{2.25} = r$ **Divide each side by 2.25.**

$244 \approx r$ **Use a calculator.**

▶ The Bullet Train's average speed is about 244 kilometers per hour.

UNIT ANALYSIS You can use unit analysis to check your verbal model.

$$550 \text{ kilometers} \approx \frac{244 \text{ kilometers}}{\text{hour}} \cdot 2.25 \text{ hours}$$

Water Conservation

EXAMPLE 2 *Writing and Using a Simple Model*

A water-saving faucet has a flow rate of at most 9.6 cubic inches per second. To test whether your faucet meets this standard, you time how long it takes the faucet to fill a 470 cubic inch pot, obtaining a time of 35 seconds. Find your faucet's flow rate. Does it meet the standard for water conservation?

SOLUTION

VERBAL MODEL

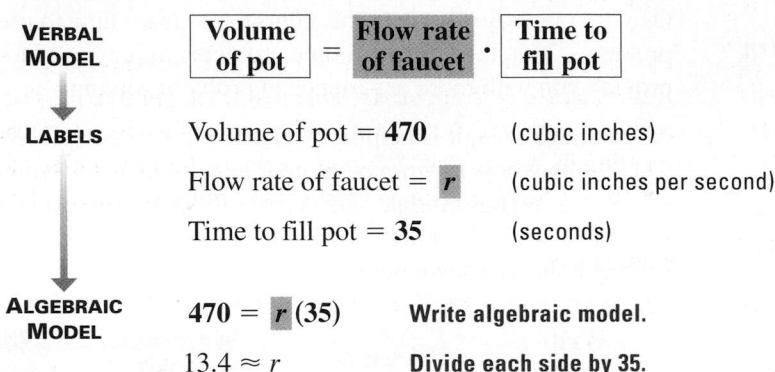

LABELS

Volume of pot = **470**   (cubic inches)

Flow rate of faucet = **r**   (cubic inches per second)

Time to fill pot = **35**   (seconds)

ALGEBRAIC MODEL

$470 = r\,(35)$ **Write algebraic model.**

$13.4 \approx r$ **Divide each side by 35.**

▶ The flow rate is about 13.4 in.^{3}/sec, which does not meet the standard.

Gasoline Cost

EXAMPLE 3 *Writing and Using a Model*

You own a lawn care business. You want to know how much money you spend on gasoline to travel to out-of-town clients. In a typical week you drive 600 miles and use 40 gallons of gasoline. Gasoline costs $1.25 per gallon, and your truck's fuel efficiency is 21 miles per gallon on the highway and 13 miles per gallon in town.

SOLUTION

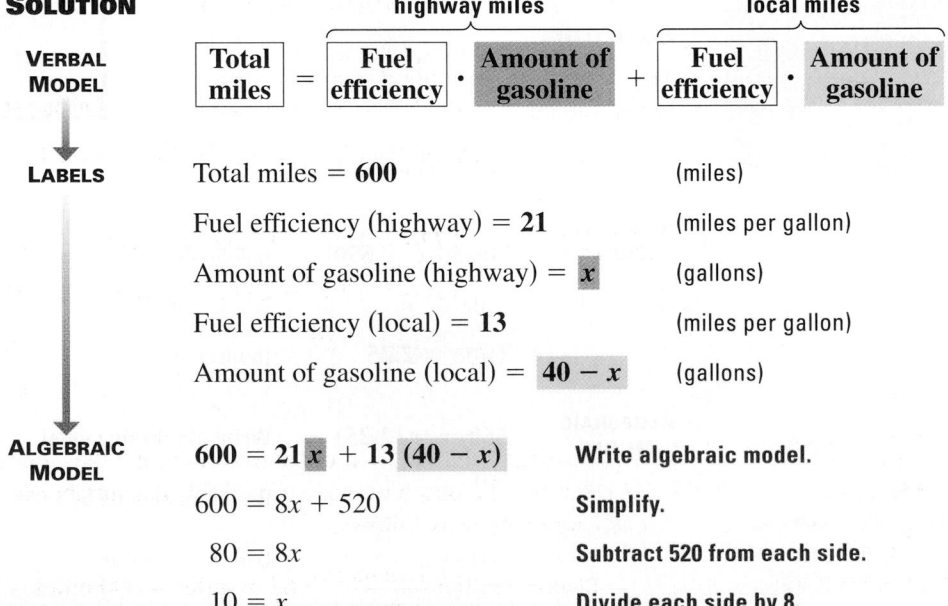

LABELS

Total miles = **600**   (miles)

Fuel efficiency (highway) = **21**   (miles per gallon)

Amount of gasoline (highway) = **x**   (gallons)

Fuel efficiency (local) = **13**   (miles per gallon)

Amount of gasoline (local) = **$40 - x$**   (gallons)

ALGEBRAIC MODEL

$600 = 21x + 13\,(40 - x)$ **Write algebraic model.**

$600 = 8x + 520$ **Simplify.**

$80 = 8x$ **Subtract 520 from each side.**

$10 = x$ **Divide each side by 8.**

▶ In a typical week you use 10 gallons of gasoline to travel to out-of-town clients. The cost of the gasoline is (10 gallons)($1.25 per gallon) = $12.50.

STUDENT HELP

▶ **Study Tip**

The solutions of the equations in Examples 2 and 3 are 13.4 and 10, respectively. However, these are not the answers to the questions asked. In Example 2 you must compare 13.4 to 9.6, and in Example 3 you must multiply 10 by $1.25. Be certain to answer the question asked.

When you are writing a verbal model to represent a real-life problem, remember that you can use other problem solving strategies, such as *draw a diagram, look for a pattern*, or *guess, check, and revise*, to help create the verbal model.

EXAMPLE 4 *Drawing a Diagram*

RAILROADS Use the information under the photo at the left. The Central Pacific Railroad averaged about 10.3 miles of track per month. The Union Pacific Railroad averaged about 23.6 miles of track per month. The photo shows the two companies meeting in Promontory Summit, Utah, as the 1776 miles of track were completed. When was the photo taken? How many miles of track did each company build?

SOLUTION

Begin by drawing and labeling a diagram, as shown below.

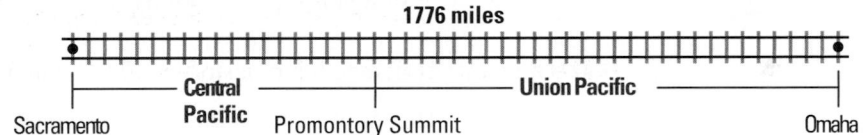

RAILROADS In 1862, two companies were given the rights to build a railroad from Omaha, Nebraska to Sacramento, California. The Central Pacific Railroad began from Sacramento in 1863. Twenty-one months later, the Union Pacific Railroad began from Omaha.

APPLICATION LINK
www.mcdougallittell.com

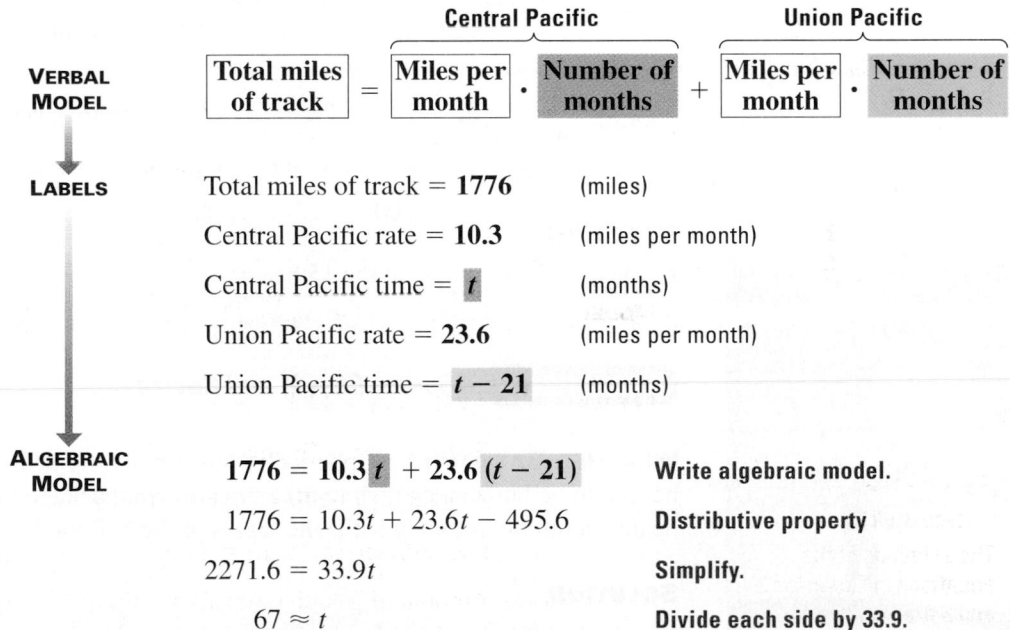

VERBAL MODEL

		Central Pacific			**Union Pacific**	
Total miles of track	=	Miles per month	·	Number of months	+ Miles per month	· Number of months

LABELS

Total miles of track = **1776**   (miles)

Central Pacific rate = **10.3**   (miles per month)

Central Pacific time = **t**   (months)

Union Pacific rate = **23.6**   (miles per month)

Union Pacific time = **t − 21**   (months)

ALGEBRAIC MODEL

$1776 = 10.3\,t + 23.6\,(t - 21)$ **Write algebraic model.**

$1776 = 10.3t + 23.6t - 495.6$ **Distributive property**

$2271.6 = 33.9t$ **Simplify.**

$67 \approx t$ **Divide each side by 33.9.**

▶ The construction took 67 months from the time the Central Pacific Railroad began in 1863. So, the photo was taken in 1869. The number of miles of track built by each company is as follows.

Central Pacific: $\dfrac{10.3 \text{ miles}}{\text{month}} \cdot 67 \text{ months} \approx 690$ miles

Union Pacific: $\dfrac{23.6 \text{ miles}}{\text{month}} \cdot (67 - 21) \text{ months} \approx 1086$ miles

STUDENT HELP

Skills Review
For help with additional problem solving strategies, see p. 930.

Heights

EXAMPLE 5 *Looking for a Pattern*

The table gives the heights to the top of the first few stories of a tall building. Determine the height to the top of the 15th story.

Story	Lobby	1	2	3	4
Height to top of story (feet)	20	32	44	56	68

SOLUTION

Look at the differences in the heights given in the table. After the lobby, the height increases by 12 feet per story.

Heights: 20   32   44   56   68
            +12   +12   +12   +12

You can use the observed pattern to write a model for the height.

PROBLEM SOLVING STRATEGY

VERBAL MODEL

Height to top of a story	=	Height of lobby	+	Height per story	·	Story number

LABELS

Height to top of a story = h (feet)

Height of lobby = **20**   (feet)

Height per story = **12**   (feet per story)

Story number = n (stories)

ALGEBRAIC MODEL

$h = 20 + 12n$ Write algebraic model.

$= 20 + 12(15)$ Substitute 15 for n.

$= 200$ Simplify.

▶ The height to the top of the 15th story is 200 feet.

EXAMPLE 6 *Guess, Check, and Revise*

WEATHER BALLOONS A spherical weather balloon needs to hold 175 cubic feet of helium to be buoyant enough to lift an instrument package to a desired height. To the nearest tenth of an foot, what is the radius of the balloon?

SOLUTION

Use the formula for the volume of a sphere, $V = \frac{4}{3}\pi r^3$.

$175 = \frac{4}{3}\pi r^3$ Substitute 175 for V.

$42 \approx r^3$ Divide each side by $\frac{4}{3}\pi$.

You need to find a number whose cube is 42. As a first guess, try $r = 4$. This gives $4^3 = 64$. Because $64 > 42$, your guess of 4 is too high. As a second guess, try $r = 3.5$. This gives $(3.5)^3 = 42.875$, and $42.875 \approx 42$. So, the balloon's radius is about 3.5 feet.

GUIDED PRACTICE

Vocabulary Check ✓
Concept Check ✓
Skill Check ✓

1. What is a verbal model? What is it used for?

2. Describe the steps of the problem solving plan.

3. How does this diagram help you set up the algebraic model in Example 3?

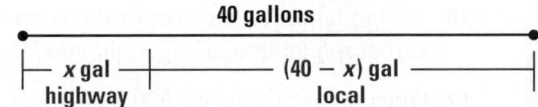

SCIENCE CONNECTION **In Exercises 4–7, use the following information.**
To study life in Arctic waters, scientists worked in an underwater building called a *Sub-Igloo* in Resolute Bay, Canada. The water pressure at the floor of the Sub-Igloo was 2184 pounds per square foot. Water pressure is zero at the water's surface and increases by 62.4 pounds per square foot for each foot of depth.

4. Write a verbal model for the water pressure.

5. Assign labels to the parts of the verbal model. Indicate the units of measure.

6. Use the labels to translate the verbal model into an algebraic model.

7. Solve the algebraic model to find the depth of the Sub-Igloo's floor.

PRACTICE AND APPLICATIONS

STUDENT HELP

▶ **Extra Practice**
to help you master skills is on p. 940.

🌐 **BOAT TRIP** **In Exercises 8–11, use the following information.**
You are on a boat on the Seine River in France. The boat's speed is 32 kilometers per hour. The Seine has a length of 764 kilometers, but only 547 kilometers can be navigated by boats. How long will your boat ride take if you travel the entire navigable portion of the Seine? Use the following verbal model.

$$\boxed{\text{Distance}} = \boxed{\text{Rate}} \cdot \boxed{\text{Time}}$$

8. Assign labels to the parts of the verbal model.

9. Use the labels to translate the verbal model into an algebraic model.

10. Solve the algebraic model.

11. Answer the question.

🌐 **MUSIC** **In Exercises 12–14, use the following information.**
A *metronome* is a device similar to a clock and is used to maintain the tempo of a musical piece. Suppose one particular piece has 180 measures with 3 beats per measure and a metronome marking of 80 beats per minute. Determine the length (in minutes) of the musical piece by using the following verbal model.

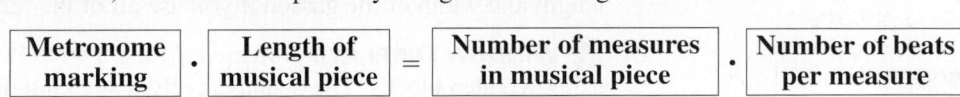

STUDENT HELP

▶ **HOMEWORK HELP**
Examples 1–3: Exs. 8–17
Examples 4–6: Exs. 18–27

12. Assign labels to the parts of the verbal model.

13. Use the labels to translate the verbal model into an algebraic model.

14. Answer the question. Use unit analysis to check your answer.

CALORIE INTAKE In Exercises 15–17, use the following information.
To determine the total number of calories of a food, you must add the number of calories provided by the grams of fat, the grams of protein, and the grams of carbohydrates. There are 9 Calories per gram of fat. A gram of protein and a gram of carbohydrates each have about 4 Calories. ▶ Source: U.S. Department of Agriculture

15. Write a verbal model that gives the total number of calories of a certain food.

16. Assign labels to the parts of the verbal model. Use the labels to translate the verbal model into an algebraic model.

17. One cup of raisins has 529.9 Calories and contains 0.3 gram of fat and 127.7 grams of carbohydrates. Solve the algebraic model to find the number of grams of protein in the raisins. Use unit analysis to check your answer.

18. **BORROWING MONEY** You have borrowed $529 from your parents to buy a mountain bike. Your parents are not charging you interest, but they want to be repaid as soon as possible. You can afford to repay them $20 per week. How long will it take you to repay your parents?

19. **THE CHUNNEL** The Chunnel connects the United Kingdom and France by a railway tunnel under the English Channel. The British started tunneling 2.5 months before the French and averaged 0.63 kilometer per month. The French averaged 0.47 kilometer per month. When the two sides met, they had tunneled 37.9 kilometers. How many kilometers of tunnel did each country build? If the French started tunneling on February 28, 1988, approximately when did the two sides meet?

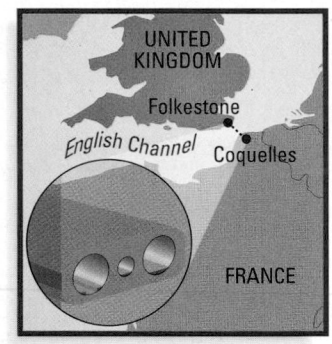

20. **FLYING LESSONS** You are taking flying lessons to get a private pilot's license. The cost of the introductory lesson is $\frac{5}{8}$ the cost of each additional lesson, which is $80. You have a total of $375 to spend on the flying lessons. How many lessons can you afford? How much money will you have left?

21. **TYPING PAPERS** Some of your classmates ask you to type their history papers throughout a 7 week summer course. How much should you charge per page if you want to earn enough to pay for the flying lessons in Exercise 20 and have $75 left over for spending money? You estimate that you can type 40 pages per week. Assume that you have to take 9 flying lessons plus the introductory lesson and that you already have $375 to spend on the lessons.

22. **WOODSHOP** You are working on a project in woodshop. You have a wooden rod that is 72 inches long. You need to cut the rod so that one piece is 6 inches longer than the other piece. How long should each piece be?

23. **GARDENING** You have 480 feet of fencing to enclose a rectangular garden. You want the length of the garden to be 30 feet greater than the width. Find the length and width of the garden if you use all of the fencing.

24. **WINDOW DISPLAYS** You are creating a window display at a toy store using wooden blocks. The display involves stacking blocks in triangular forms. You begin the display with 1 block, which is your first "triangle," and then stack 3 blocks, two on the bottom and one on the top, to get the next triangle. You create the next three triangles by stacking 6 blocks, then 10 blocks, and then 15 blocks. How many blocks will you need for the ninth triangle?

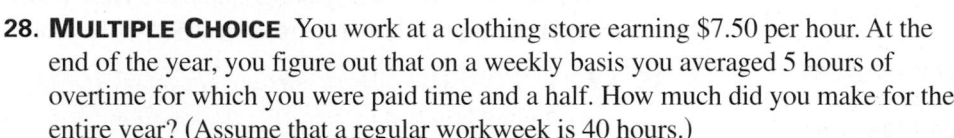

SCIENCE ▶ CONNECTION In Exercises 25–27, use the following information.
As part of a science experiment, you drop a ball from various heights and measure how high it bounces on the first bounce. The results of six drops are given below.

Drop height (m)	0.5	1.5	2	2.5	4	5
First bounce height (m)	0.38	1.15	1.44	1.90	2.88	3.85

25. How high will the ball bounce if you drop it from a height of 6 meters?

26. To continue the experiment, you must find the number of bounces the ball will make before it bounces less than a given number of meters. Your experiment shows the ball's bounce height is always the same percent of the height from which it fell before the bounce. Find the average percent that the ball bounces each time.

27. Find the number of times the ball bounces before it bounces less than 1 meter if it is dropped from a height of 3 meters.

Test Preparation

28. MULTIPLE CHOICE You work at a clothing store earning $7.50 per hour. At the end of the year, you figure out that on a weekly basis you averaged 5 hours of overtime for which you were paid time and a half. How much did you make for the entire year? (Assume that a regular workweek is 40 hours.)

    Ⓐ $15,600   **Ⓑ** $17,550   **Ⓒ** $18,000   **Ⓓ** $18,525   **Ⓔ** $19,500

29. MULTIPLE CHOICE You are taking piano lessons. The cost of the first lesson is one and one half times the cost of each additional lesson. You spend $260 for six lessons. How much did the first lesson cost?

    Ⓐ $52   **Ⓑ** $40   **Ⓒ** $43.33   **Ⓓ** $60   **Ⓔ** $34.67

★ Challenge

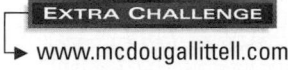

EXTRA CHALLENGE
www.mcdougallittell.com

30. 🌐 OWNING A BUSINESS You have started a business making papier-mâché sculptures. The cost to make a sculpture is $.75. Your sculptures sell for $14.50 each at a craft store. You receive 50% of the selling price. Each sculpture takes about 2 hours to complete. If you spend 14 hours per week making sculptures, about how many weeks will you work to earn a profit of $360?

MIXED REVIEW

LOGICAL REASONING Tell whether the compound statement is *true* or *false*. (Skills Review, p. 924)

31. $-3 < 5$ and $-3 > -5$ **32.** $1 > -2$ or $1 < -2$

33. $-4 > -5$ and $1 < -2$ **34.** $-2.7 > -2.5$ or $156 > 165$

ORDERING NUMBERS Write the numbers in increasing order. (Review 1.1)

35. $-1, -5, 4, -10, -55$ **36.** $-\dfrac{2}{3}, \dfrac{5}{8}, \dfrac{1}{100}, -2, 1$

37. $-1.2, 2, -2.9, 2.09, -2.1$ **38.** $-\sqrt{3}, 1, \sqrt{10}, \sqrt{2}, \dfrac{8}{5}$

SOLVING EQUATIONS Solve the equation. Check your solution. (Review 1.3 for 1.6)

39. $6x + 5 = 17$ **40.** $5x - 4 = 7x + 12$

41. $2(3x - 1) = 5 - (x + 3)$ **42.** $\dfrac{2}{3}x + \dfrac{1}{4} = 2x - \dfrac{5}{6}$

Solve the equation. Check your solution. (Lesson 1.3)

1. $5x - 9 = 11$

2. $6y + 8 = 3y - 16$

3. $\frac{1}{4}z + \frac{2}{3} = \frac{1}{2}z - \frac{3}{4}$

4. $0.4(x - 50) = 0.2x + 12$

Solve the equation for y. Then find the value of y when $x = 2$. (Lesson 1.4)

5. $3x + 5y = 9$

6. $4x - 3y = 14$

7. The formula for the area of a rhombus is $A = \frac{1}{2}d_1d_2$ where d_1 and d_2 are the lengths of the diagonals. Solve the formula for d_1. **(Lesson 1.4)**

8. 🌐 **GIRL SCOUT COOKIES** Your sister is selling Girl Scout cookies that cost $2.80 per box. Your family bought 6 boxes. How many more boxes of cookies must your sister sell in order to collect $154? **(Lesson 1.5)**

MATH & History ▶ **Problem Solving**

APPLICATION LINK
www.mcdougallittell.com

THEN ▶ **MANY CULTURES,** such as the Egyptians, Greeks, Hindus, and Arabs, solved problems by using the *rule of false position*. This technique was similar to the problem solving strategy of guess, check, and revise. As an example of how to use the rule of false position, consider this problem taken from the Ahmes papyrus:

> *You want to divide 700 loaves of bread among four people in the ratio $\frac{2}{3}:\frac{1}{2}:\frac{1}{3}:\frac{1}{4}$. Choose a number divisible by the denominators 2, 3, and 4, such as 48. Then evaluate $\frac{2}{3}(48) + \frac{1}{2}(48) + \frac{1}{3}(48) + \frac{1}{4}(48)$, which has a value of 84.*

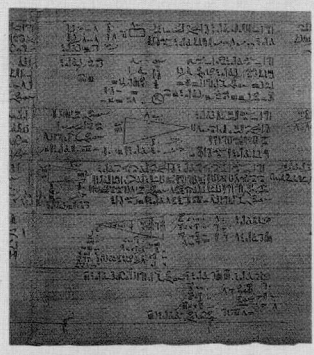

Ahmes papyrus

1. The next step is to multiply 48 by a number so that when the resulting product is substituted for 48 in the expression above, you get a new expression whose value is 700. By what number should you multiply 48? How did you use the original expression's value of 84 to get your answer?

2. Use your result from Exercise 1 to find the number of loaves for each person.

NOW ▶ **TODAY,** we would model this problem using $\frac{2}{3}x + \frac{1}{2}x + \frac{1}{3}x + \frac{1}{4}x = 700$. Equations like this can now be solved with symbolic manipulation software.

Brahmagupta solves linear equations in India.

Francois Viéte introduces symbolic algebra.

432 B.C.

Greeks solve quadratic equations geometrically.

A.D. 628

1591

1988

Symbolic and graphical manipulation software is introduced.

1.6

Solving Linear Inequalities

What you should learn

GOAL 1 Solve simple inequalities.

GOAL 2 Solve compound inequalities, as applied in **Example 6**.

Why you should learn it

▼ To model **real-life** situations, such as amusement park fees in **Ex. 50**.

GOAL 1 SOLVING SIMPLE INEQUALITIES

Inequalities have properties that are similar to those of equations, but the properties differ in some important ways.

> **ACTIVITY**
> Developing Concepts
> ## Investigating Properties of Inequalities
>
> **1** Write two true inequalities involving integers, one using $<$ and one using $>$.
>
> **2** Add, subtract, multiply, and divide each side of your inequalities by 2 and -2. In each case, decide whether the new inequality is true or false.
>
> **3** Write a general conclusion about the operations you can perform on a true inequality to produce another true inequality.

Inequalities such as $x \leq 1$ and $2n - 3 > 9$ are examples of **linear inequalities** in one variable. A **solution** of an inequality in one variable is a value of the variable that makes the inequality true. For instance, -2, 0, 0.872, and 1 are some of the many solutions of $x \leq 1$.

In the activity you may have discovered some of the following properties of inequalities. You can use these properties to solve an inequality because each transformation produces a new inequality having the same solutions as the original.

TRANSFORMATIONS THAT PRODUCE EQUIVALENT INEQUALITIES

- *Add* the same number to both sides.
- *Subtract* the same number from both sides.
- *Multiply* both sides by the same *positive* number.
- *Divide* both sides by the same *positive* number.
- *Multiply* both sides by the same *negative* number and *reverse* the inequality.
- *Divide* both sides by the same *negative* number and *reverse* the inequality.

The **graph** of an inequality in one variable consists of all points on a real number line that correspond to solutions of the inequality. To graph an inequality in one variable, use an open dot for $<$ or $>$ and a solid dot for $\leq$ or $\geq$. For example, the graphs of $x < 3$ and $x \geq -2$ are shown below.

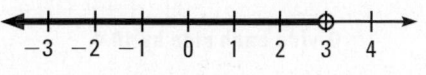

Graph of $x < 3$

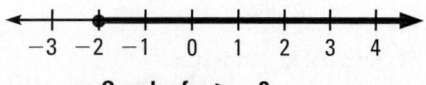

Graph of $x \geq -2$

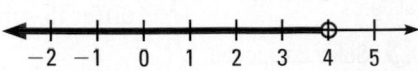

EXAMPLE 1 **Solving an Inequality with a Variable on One Side**

Solve $5y - 8 < 12$.

SOLUTION

$5y - 8 < 12$	**Write original inequality.**
$5y < 20$	**Add 8 to each side.**
$y < 4$	**Divide each side by 5.**

▶ The solutions are all real numbers less than 4, as shown in the graph at the right.

(number line graph with open circle at 4, marked −2 −1 0 1 2 3 4 5)

✓ **CHECK** As a check, try several numbers that are less than 4 in the original inequality. Also, try checking some numbers that are greater than or equal to 4 to see that they are *not* solutions of the original inequality.

EXAMPLE 2 **Solving an Inequality with a Variable on Both Sides**

Solve $2x + 1 \le 6x - 1$.

SOLUTION

$2x + 1 \le 6x - 1$	**Write original inequality.**
$-4x + 1 \le -1$	**Subtract 6x from each side.**
$-4x \le -2$	**Subtract 1 from each side.**
$x \ge \dfrac{1}{2}$	**Divide each side by −4 and reverse the inequality.**

▶ The solutions are all real numbers greater than or equal to $\dfrac{1}{2}$. Check several numbers greater than or equal to $\dfrac{1}{2}$ in the original inequality.

EXAMPLE 3 **Using a Simple Inequality**

(REAL LIFE) *Fish*

The weight w (in pounds) of an Icelandic saithe is given by

$$w = 10.4t - 2.2$$

where t is the age of the fish in years. Describe the ages of a group of Icelandic saithe that weigh up to 29 pounds. ▶ Source: Marine Research Institute

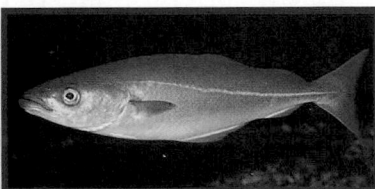

Icelandic saithe

SOLUTION

$w \le 29$	**Weights are at most 29 pounds.**
$10.4t - 2.2 \le 29$	**Substitute for w.**
$10.4t \le 31.2$	**Add 2.2 to each side.**
$t \le 3$	**Divide each side by 10.4.**

▶ The ages are less than or equal to 3 years.

GOAL 2 SOLVING COMPOUND INEQUALITIES

A **compound inequality** is two simple inequalities joined by "and" or "or." Here are two examples.

$$-2 \leq x < 1$$

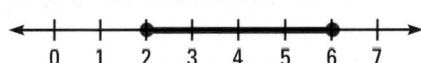

All real numbers that are greater than or equal to -2 *and* less than 1.

$$x < -1 \text{ or } x \geq 2$$

All real numbers that are less than -1 *or* greater than or equal to 2.

> **STUDENT HELP**
>
> **Study Tip**
> The inequality $a < x < b$ is read as "*x* is between *a* and *b*." The inequality $a \leq x \leq b$ is read as "*x* is between *a* and *b*, inclusive."

EXAMPLE 4 *Solving an "And" Compound Inequality*

Solve $-2 \leq 3t - 8 \leq 10$.

SOLUTION

To solve, you must isolate the variable between the two inequality signs.

$-2 \leq 3t - 8 \leq 10$	**Write original inequality.**
$6 \leq 3t \leq 18$	**Add 8 to each expression.**
$2 \leq t \leq 6$	**Divide each expression by 3.**

▶ Because t is between 2 and 6, inclusive, the solutions are all real numbers greater than or equal to 2 *and* less than or equal to 6. Check several of these numbers in the original inequality. The graph is shown below.

EXAMPLE 5 *Solving an "Or" Compound Inequality*

Solve $2x + 3 < 5$ or $4x - 7 > 9$.

> **STUDENT HELP**
>
> **HOMEWORK HELP**
> Visit our Web site
> www.mcdougallittell.com
> for extra examples.

SOLUTION

A solution of this compound inequality is a solution of *either* of its simple parts, so you should solve each part separately.

SOLUTION OF FIRST INEQUALITY		**SOLUTION OF SECOND INEQUALITY**	
$2x + 3 < 5$	**Write first inequality.**	$4x - 7 > 9$	**Write second inequality.**
$2x < 2$	**Subtract 3 from each side.**	$4x > 16$	**Add 7 to each side.**
$x < 1$	**Divide each side by 2.**	$x > 4$	**Divide each side by 4.**

▶ The solutions are all real numbers less than 1 *or* greater than 4. Check several of these numbers to see that they satisfy one of the simple parts of the original inequality. The graph is shown below.

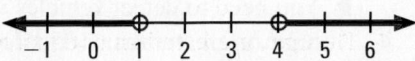

1.6 *Solving Linear Inequalities*   **43**

EXAMPLE 6 *Using an "And" Compound Inequality*

You have added enough antifreeze to your car's cooling system to lower the freezing point to $-35°C$ and raise the boiling point to $125°C$. The coolant will remain a liquid as long as the temperature C (in degrees Celsius) satisfies the inequality $-35 < C < 125$. Write the inequality in degrees Fahrenheit.

SOLUTION

Let F represent the temperature in degrees Fahrenheit, and use the formula $C = \frac{5}{9}(F - 32)$.

$-35 < C < 125$	Write original inequality.
$-35 < \frac{5}{9}(F - 32) < 125$	Substitute $\frac{5}{9}(F - 32)$ for *C*.
$-63 < F - 32 < 225$	Multiply each expression by $\frac{9}{5}$, the reciprocal of $\frac{5}{9}$.
$-31 < F < 257$	Add 32 to each expression.

▶ The coolant will remain a liquid as long as the temperature stays between $-31°F$ and $257°F$.

EXAMPLE 7 *Using an "Or" Compound Inequality*

TRAFFIC ENFORCEMENT You are a state patrol officer who is assigned to work traffic enforcement on a highway. The posted minimum speed on the highway is 45 miles per hour and the posted maximum speed is 65 miles per hour. You need to detect vehicles that are traveling outside the posted speed limits.

a. Write these conditions as a compound inequality.

b. Rewrite the conditions in kilometers per hour.

SOLUTION

a. Let m represent the vehicle speeds in miles per hour. The speeds that you need to detect are given by:

$$m < 45 \text{ or } m > 65$$

b. Let k be the vehicle speeds in kilometers per hour. The relationship between miles per hour and kilometers per hour is given by the formula $m \approx 0.621k$. You can rewrite the conditions in kilometers per hour by substituting $0.621k$ for m in each inequality and then solving for k.

$m < 45$	or	$m > 65$
$0.621k < 45$	or	$0.621k > 65$
$k < 72.5$	or	$k > 105$

▶ You need to detect vehicles whose speeds are less than 72.5 kilometers per hour or greater than 105 kilometers per hour.

POLICE RADAR Police radar guns emit a continuous radio wave of known frequency. The radar gun compares the frequency of the wave reflected from a vehicle to the frequency of the transmitted wave and then displays the vehicle's speed.

GUIDED PRACTICE

Vocabulary Check ✔ **1.** Explain the difference between a simple linear inequality and a compound linear inequality.

Concept Check ✔ **2.** Tell whether this statement is *true* or *false:* Multiplying both sides of an inequality by the same number always produces an equivalent inequality. Explain.

3. Explain the difference between solving $2x < 7$ and solving $-2x < 7$.

Skill Check ✔ **Solve the inequality. Then graph your solution.**

4. $x - 5 < 8$ **5.** $3x \geq 15$ **6.** $-x + 4 > 3$

7. $\frac{1}{2}x \leq 6$ **8.** $x + 8 > -2$ **9.** $-x - 3 < -5$

Graph the inequality.

10. $-2 \leq x < 5$ **11.** $x \geq 3$ or $x < -3$

12. 🌎 **WINTER DRIVING** You are moving to Montana and need to lower the freezing point of the cooling system in the car from Example 6 to $-50°C$. This will also raise the boiling point to $140°C$. Write a compound inequality that models this situation. Then write the inequality in degrees Fahrenheit.

PRACTICE AND APPLICATIONS

STUDENT HELP

▸ **Extra Practice**
to help you master
skills is on p. 941.

MATCHING INEQUALITIES Match the inequality with its graph.

13. $x \geq 4$ -C   **14.** $x < 4$ -A   **15.** $-4 < x \leq 4$ D

16. $x \geq 4$ or $x < -4$ -E   **17.** $-4 \leq x \leq 4$ -F   **18.** $x > 4$ or $x \leq -4$ -B

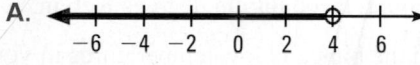

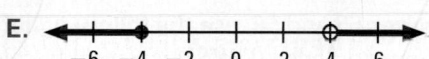

CHECKING SOLUTIONS Decide whether the given number is a solution of the inequality.

19. $2x + 9 < 16$; 4   **20.** $10 - x \geq 3$; 7   **21.** $7x - 12 < 8$; 3

22. $-\frac{1}{3}x - 2 \leq -4$; 9   **23.** $-3 < 2x \leq 6$; 3   **24.** $-8 < x - 11 < -6$; 5

STUDENT HELP

▸ **HOMEWORK HELP**
Examples 1, 2: Exs. 13,
14, 19–22, 25–36
Example 3: Exs. 49–51
Examples 4, 5: Exs. 15–18,
23, 24, 37–48
Example 6: Exs. 52–54
Example 7: Exs. 55, 56

SIMPLE INEQUALITIES Solve the inequality. Then graph your solution.

25. $4x + 5 > 25$ **26.** $7 - n \leq 19$ **27.** $5 - 2x \geq 27$

28. $\frac{1}{2}x - 4 > -6$ **29.** $\frac{3}{2}x - 7 < 2$ **30.** $5 + \frac{1}{3}n \leq 6$

31. $4x - 1 > 14 - x$ **32.** $-n + 6 < 7n + 4$ **33.** $4.7 - 2.1x > -7.9$

34. $2(n - 4) \leq 6$ **35.** $2(4 - x) > 8$ **36.** $5 - 5x > 4(3 - x)$

COMPOUND INEQUALITIES Solve the inequality. Then graph your solution.

37. $-2 \leq x - 7 \leq 11$ **38.** $-16 \leq 3x - 4 \leq 2$ **39.** $-5 \leq -n - 6 \leq 0$

40. $-2 < -2n + 1 \leq 7$ **41.** $-7 < 6x - 1 < 5$ **42.** $-8 < \frac{2}{3}x - 4 < 10$

43. $x + 2 \leq 5$ or $x - 4 \geq 2$ **44.** $3x + 2 < -10$ or $2x - 4 > -4$

45. $-5x - 4 < -1.4$ or $-2x + 1 > 11$ **46.** $x - 1 \leq 5$ or $x + 3 \geq 10$

47. $-0.1 \leq 3.4x - 1.8 < 6.7$ **48.** $0.4x + 0.6 < 2.2$ or $0.6x > 3.6$

49.  **COMMISSION** Your salary is $1250 per week and you receive a 5% commission on your sales each week. What are the possible amounts (in dollars) that you can sell each week to earn at least $1500 per week?

50. **PARK FEES** You have $50 and are going to an amusement park. You spend $25 for the entrance fee and $15 for food. You want to play a game that costs $.75. Write and solve an inequality to find the possible numbers of times you can play the game. If you play the game the maximum number of times, will you have spent the entire $50? Explain.

51. **GRADES** A professor announces that course grades will be computed by taking 40% of a student's project score (0–100 points) and adding 60% of the student's final exam score (0–100 points). If a student gets an 86 on the project, what scores can she get on the final exam to get a course grade of at least 90?

SCIENCE CONNECTION In Exercises 52–54, use the following information.
The international standard for scientific temperature measurement is the Kelvin scale. A Kelvin temperature can be obtained by adding 273.15 to a Celsius temperature. The daytime temperature on Mars ranges from $-89.15°C$ to $-31.15°C$. ▶ Source: NASA

52. Write the daytime temperature range on Mars as a compound inequality in degrees Celsius.

53. Rewrite the compound inequality in degrees Kelvin.

54. **RESEARCH** Find the high and low temperatures in your area for any particular day. Write three compound inequalities representing the temperature range in degrees Fahrenheit, in degrees Celsius, and in degrees Kelvin.

WINTER In Exercises 55 and 56, use the following information.
The Ontario Winter Severity Index (OWSI) is a weekly calculation used to determine the severity of winter conditions. The OWSI for deer is given by

$$I = \frac{p}{30} + \frac{d}{30} + c$$

where p represents the average Snow Penetration Gauge reading (in centimeters), d represents the average snow depth (in centimeters), and c represents the *chillometer reading*, which is a measure of the cold (in kilowatt-hours) based on temperature and wind chill. An extremely mild winter occurs when $I < 5$ on average, and an extremely severe winter occurs when $I > 6.5$ on average. A deer can tolerate a maximum snow penetration of 50 centimeters. Assume the average snow depth is 60 centimeters. ▶ Source: Snow Network for Ontario Wildlife

55. What weekly chillometer readings will produce extremely severe winter readings?

56. What weekly chillometer readings will produce extremely mild winter readings?

57. *Writing* The first transformation listed in the box on page 41 can be written symbolically as follows: If a, b, and c are real numbers and $a > b$, then $a + c > b + c$. Write similar statements for the other transformations.

58. MULTI-STEP PROBLEM You are vacationing at Lake Tahoe, California. You decide to spend a day sightseeing in other places. You want to go from Lake Tahoe to Sacramento, from Sacramento to Sonora, and then from Sonora back to Lake Tahoe. You know that it is about 85 miles from Lake Tahoe to Sacramento and about 75 miles from Sacramento to Sonora.

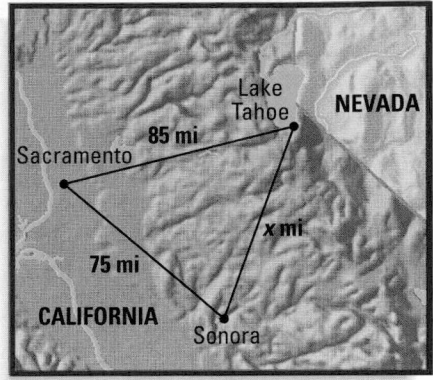

a. The triangle inequality theorem states that the sum of the lengths of any two sides of a triangle is greater than the length of the third side. Write a compound inequality that represents the distance from Sonora to Lake Tahoe.

b. CRITICAL THINKING You are reading a brochure which states that the distance between Sonora and Lake Tahoe is 170 miles. You know that the distance is a misprint. How can you be so sure? Explain.

c. You keep a journal of the distances you have traveled. Many of your distances represent triangular circuits. Your friend is reading your journal and states that you must have recorded a wrong distance for one of these circuits. To which one of the following is your friend referring? Explain.

    A. 35 miles, 65 miles, 45 miles   **B.** 15 miles, 50 miles, 64 miles

    C. 49 miles, 78 miles, 28 miles   **D.** 55 miles, 72 miles, 41 miles

★ Challenge

59. Write an inequality that has no solution. Show why it has no solution.

60. Write an inequality whose solutions are all real numbers. Show why the solutions are all real numbers.

MIXED REVIEW

IDENTIFYING PROPERTIES Identify the property shown. **(Review 1.1)**

61. $(7 \cdot 3) \cdot 11 = 7 \cdot (3 \cdot 11)$ **62.** $34 + (-34) = 0$

63. $37 + 29 = 29 + 37$ **64.** $3(9 + 4) = 3(9) + 3(4)$

SOLVING EQUATIONS Solve the equation. Check your solution. **(Review 1.3 for 1.7)**

65. $5x + 4 = -2(x + 3)$ **66.** $2(3 - x) = 16(x + 1)$

67. $-(x - 1) + 10 = -3(x - 3)$ **68.** $\frac{1}{8}x + \frac{3}{2} = \frac{3}{4}x - 1$

69. **CONCERT TRIP** You are going to a concert in another town 48 miles away. You can average 40 miles per hour on the road you plan to take to the concert. What is the minimum number of hours before the concert starts that you should leave to get to the concert on time? **(Review 1.5)**

● ACTIVITY 1.6

Using Technology

Solving an Inequality

Most graphing calculators are able to evaluate whether a statement is true or false. If a statement is true, the calculator returns a 1; if a statement is false, it returns a 0. You can use this *Test* feature of a graphing calculator to solve a linear inequality.

▶ EXAMPLE

Use the *Test* feature of a graphing calculator to solve the inequality $3x + 2 > -4$.

▶ SOLUTION

① To solve the inequality, you must find the values of x for which the inequality is true. Enter the inequality as the *truth function* $y = (3x + 2 > -4)$, as shown in the calculator screen below.

② In the graph below you can see that the y-values are 1 for all x-values greater than -2. So, the solutions are given by $x > -2$. Check several solutions in the original inequality.

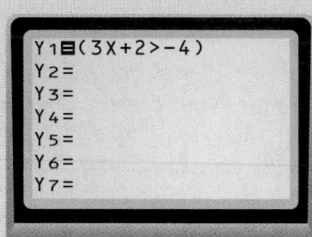

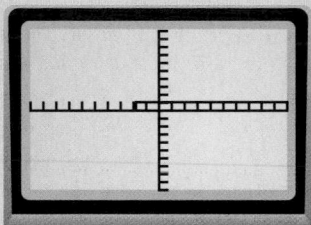

▶ EXERCISES

In Exercises 1 and 2, the *Test* feature of a graphing calculator was used to create the graph. Use the graph to solve the inequality. Check several solutions in the original inequality.

1. $y = (4x - 5 \le 11)$

2. $y = (5x + 6 \ge -14)$

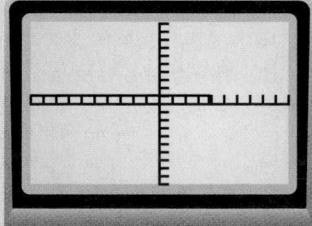

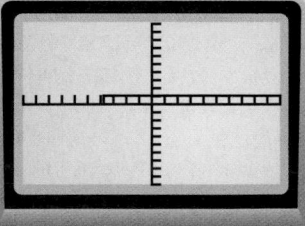

Use the *Test* feature of a graphing calculator to solve the inequality. Check several solutions in the original inequality.

3. $2x - 7 > -1$ **4.** $4x + 2 < 18$ **5.** $0.5x + 2 \le -1$

6. $-x + 5 \ge -3$ **7.** $-6x + 3 > -9$ **8.** $-0.5x - 1.5 \le 3$

9. $5x < 4x + 6$ **10.** $4 - x \ge 2 - \frac{1}{2}x$ **11.** $3x - 4 \le 2x + 5$

12. $2x - 1 < \frac{7}{3} + \frac{4}{3}x$ **13.** $5 - 5x > 12 - 4x$ **14.** $8 - 4x \le 5 - x$

○ ACTIVITY 1.7

Developing Concepts

Absolute Value
Equations and Inequalities

SET UP
Work with a partner.

MATERIALS
11 index cards numbered
from −5 to 5

▶ **QUESTION** **What does the solution of an absolute value equation or inequality look like on a number line?**

The *absolute value* of a number x, written $|x|$, is the distance on a number line that the number is from 0. Because both 2 and −2 are 2 units from 0, $|2| = 2$ and $|-2| = 2$. Notice that the absolute value of a number is always positive or 0.

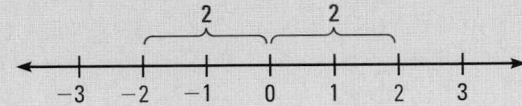

▶ **EXPLORING THE CONCEPT**

1 You should work with a partner. Each pair of partners should have a set of index cards numbered from −5 to 5. The cards should be placed face up in numerical order to form a number line.

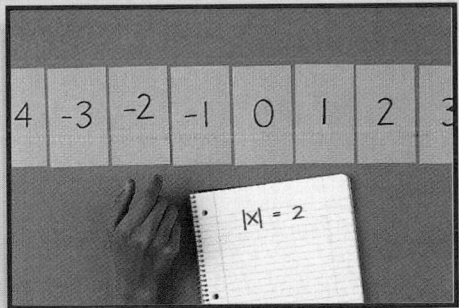 

2 For each absolute value equation or inequality below, one partner should turn over the cards whose numbers are solutions. The other partner should then agree or disagree as to whether the solutions are correct. Once in agreement, both of you should graph the solutions on a number line. You should take turns turning over the cards and checking the solutions.

a. $|x| = 4$ 　　 b. $|x| \le 4$ 　　 c. $|x| \ge 4$

d. $|3x| = 9$ 　　 e. $|3x| \le 9$ 　　 f. $|3x| \ge 9$

g. $|x - 1| = 2$ 　　 h. $|x - 1| \le 2$ 　　 i. $|x - 1| \ge 2$

▶ **DRAWING CONCLUSIONS**

1. Describe the nature of the solutions of the absolute value equations in parts (a), (d), and (g). Do you think that all absolute value equations will have solutions of this nature? Will all absolute value equations have the same number of solutions?

2. Describe the nature of the solutions of the absolute value inequalities in parts (b), (e), and (h), all of which involve the $\le$ sign. What difference, if any, would there be if the inequalities involved the $<$ sign?

3. Describe the nature of the solutions of the absolute value inequalities in parts (c), (f), and (i), all of which involve the $\ge$ sign. What difference, if any, would there be if the inequalities involved the $>$ sign?

Solving Absolute Value Equations and Inequalities

GOAL 1 SOLVING EQUATIONS AND INEQUALITIES

The **absolute value** of a number x, written $|x|$, is the distance the number is from 0 on a number line. Notice that the absolute value of a number is always nonnegative.

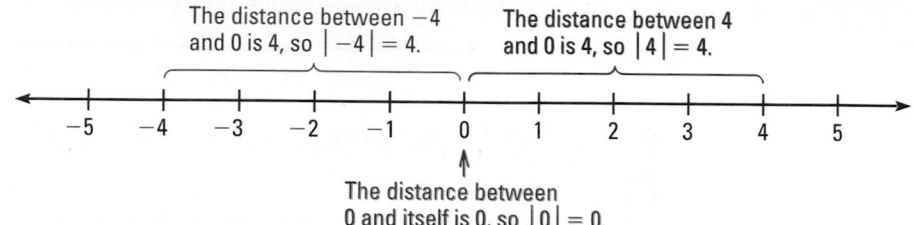

The distance between -4 and 0 is 4, so $|-4| = 4$.

The distance between 4 and 0 is 4, so $|4| = 4$.

The distance between 0 and itself is 0, so $|0| = 0$.

The absolute value of x can be defined algebraically as follows.

$$|x| = \begin{cases} x, & \text{if } x \text{ is positive} \\ 0, & \text{if } x = 0 \\ -x, & \text{if } x \text{ is negative} \end{cases}$$

To solve an absolute value equation of the form $|x| = c$ where $c > 0$, use the fact that x can have two possible values: a positive value c or a negative value $-c$. For instance, if $|x| = 5$, then $x = 5$ or $x = -5$.

SOLVING AN ABSOLUTE VALUE EQUATION

The absolute value equation $|ax + b| = c$, where $c > 0$, is equivalent to the compound statement $ax + b = c$ or $ax + b = -c$.

EXAMPLE 1 *Solving an Absolute Value Equation*

Solve $|2x - 5| = 9$.

SOLUTION

Rewrite the absolute value equation as two linear equations and then solve each linear equation.

$\|2x - 5\| = 9$		**Write original equation.**
$2x - 5 = 9$ or $2x - 5 = -9$		**Expression can be 9 or −9.**
$2x = 14$ or $2x = -4$		**Add 5 to each side.**
$x = 7$ or $x = -2$		**Divide each side by 2.**

▶ The solutions are 7 and -2. Check these by substituting each solution into the original equation.

An absolute value inequality such as $|x - 2| < 4$ can be solved by rewriting it as a compound inequality, in this case as $-4 < x - 2 < 4$.

TRANSFORMATIONS OF ABSOLUTE VALUE INEQUALITIES

- The inequality $|ax + b| < c$, where $c > 0$, means that $ax + b$ is *between* $-c$ and c. This is equivalent to $-c < ax + b < c$.

- The inequality $|ax + b| > c$, where $c > 0$, means that $ax + b$ is *beyond* $-c$ and c. This is equivalent to $ax + b < -c$ or $ax + b > c$.

In the first transformation, $<$ can be replaced by $\leq$. In the second transformation, $>$ can be replaced by $\geq$.

STUDENT HELP

HOMEWORK HELP
Visit our Web site
www.mcdougallittell.com
for extra examples.

EXAMPLE 2   *Solving an Inequality of the Form $|ax + b| < c$*

Solve $|2x + 7| < 11$.

SOLUTION

$\|2x + 7\| < 11$	**Write original inequality.**
$-11 < 2x + 7 < 11$	**Write equivalent compound inequality.**
$-18 < 2x < 4$	**Subtract 7 from each expression.**
$-9 < x < 2$	**Divide each expression by 2.**

▶ The solutions are all real numbers greater than -9 and less than 2. Check several solutions in the original inequality. The graph is shown below.

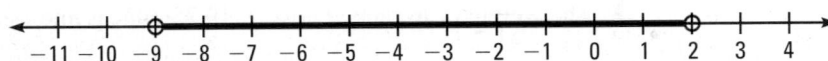

EXAMPLE 3   *Solving an Inequality of the Form $|ax + b| \geq c$*

Solve $|3x - 2| \geq 8$.

SOLUTION

This absolute value inequality is equivalent to $3x - 2 \leq -8$ or $3x - 2 \geq 8$.

SOLVE FIRST INEQUALITY		**SOLVE SECOND INEQUALITY**
$3x - 2 \leq -8$	**Write inequality.**	$3x - 2 \geq 8$
$3x \leq -6$	**Add 2 to each side.**	$3x \geq 10$
$x \leq -2$	**Divide each side by 3.**	$x \geq \dfrac{10}{3}$

▶ The solutions are all real numbers less than or equal to -2 or greater than or equal to $\dfrac{10}{3}$. Check several solutions in the original inequality. The graph is shown below.

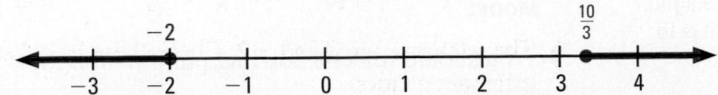

GOAL 2 USING ABSOLUTE VALUE IN REAL LIFE

In manufacturing applications, the maximum acceptable deviation of a product from some ideal or average measurement is called the *tolerance*.

Manufacturing

EXAMPLE 4 *Writing a Model for Tolerance*

A cereal manufacturer has a tolerance of 0.75 ounce for a box of cereal that is supposed to weigh 20 ounces. Write and solve an absolute value inequality that describes the acceptable weights for "20 ounce" boxes.

SOLUTION

PROBLEM SOLVING STRATEGY

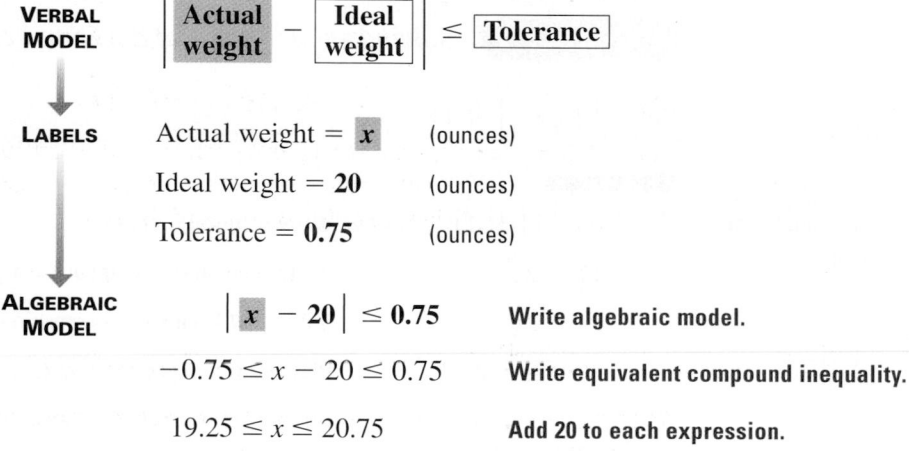

VERBAL MODEL

$$\left| \boxed{\text{Actual weight}} - \boxed{\text{Ideal weight}} \right| \le \boxed{\text{Tolerance}}$$

LABELS

Actual weight $= x$ (ounces)

Ideal weight $= 20$ (ounces)

Tolerance $= 0.75$ (ounces)

ALGEBRAIC MODEL

$$|x - 20| \le 0.75$$ **Write algebraic model.**

$$-0.75 \le x - 20 \le 0.75$$ **Write equivalent compound inequality.**

$$19.25 \le x \le 20.75$$ **Add 20 to each expression.**

▶ The weights can range between 19.25 ounces and 20.75 ounces, inclusive.

EXAMPLE 5 *Writing an Absolute Value Model*

FOCUS ON APPLICATIONS

QUALITY CONTROL You are a quality control inspector at a bowling pin company. A regulation pin must weigh between 50 ounces and 58 ounces, inclusive. Write an absolute value inequality describing the weights you should reject.

SOLUTION

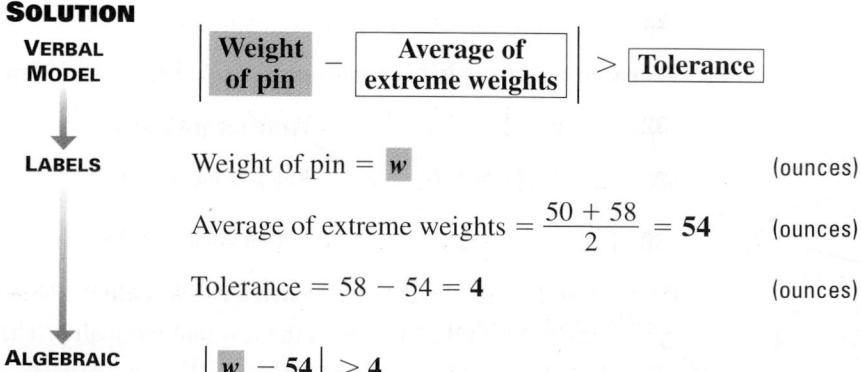

VERBAL MODEL

$$\left| \boxed{\text{Weight of pin}} - \boxed{\text{Average of extreme weights}} \right| > \boxed{\text{Tolerance}}$$

LABELS

Weight of pin $= w$ (ounces)

Average of extreme weights $= \dfrac{50 + 58}{2} = 54$ (ounces)

Tolerance $= 58 - 54 = 4$ (ounces)

ALGEBRAIC MODEL

$$|w - 54| > 4$$

▶ You should reject a bowling pin if its weight w satisfies $|w - 54| > 4$.

BOWLING Bowling pins are made from maple wood, either solid or laminated. They are given a tough plastic coating to resist cracking. The lighter the pin, the easier it is to knock down.

GUIDED PRACTICE

Vocabulary Check ✓

1. What is the absolute value of a number?

Concept Check ✓

2. The absolute value of a number cannot be negative. How, then, can the absolute value of a be $-a$?

3. Give an example of the absolute value of a number. How many other numbers have this absolute value? State the number or numbers.

Skill Check ✓ **Decide whether the given number is a solution of the equation.**

4. $|3x + 8| = 20; -4$ **5.** $|11 - 4x| = 7; 1$ **6.** $|2x - 9| = 11; -1$

7. $|-x + 9| = 4; -5$ **8.** $|6 + 3x| = 0; -2$ **9.** $|-5x - 3| = 8; -1$

Rewrite the absolute value inequality as a compound inequality.

10. $|x + 8| < 5$ **11.** $|11 - 2x| \geq 13$ **12.** $|9 - x| > 21$

13. $|x + 5| \leq 9$ **14.** $|10 - 3x| \geq 17$ **15.** $\left|\frac{1}{4}x + 10\right| < 18$

16. 🌐 **TOLERANCE** Suppose the tolerance for the "20 ounce" cereal boxes in Example 4 is now 0.45 ounce. Write and solve an absolute value inequality that describes the new acceptable weights of the boxes.

PRACTICE AND APPLICATIONS

STUDENT HELP

▸ **Extra Practice**
to help you master skills is on p. 941.

REWRITING EQUATIONS Rewrite the absolute value equation as two linear equations.

17. $|x - 8| = 11$ **18.** $|5 - 2x| = 13$ **19.** $|6n + 1| = \frac{1}{2}$

20. $|5n - 4| = 16$ **21.** $|2x + 1| = 5$ **22.** $|2 - x| = 3$

23. $|15 - 2x| = 8$ **24.** $\left|\frac{1}{2}x + 4\right| = 6$ **25.** $\left|\frac{2}{3}x - 9\right| = 18$

CHECKING A SOLUTION Decide whether the given number is a solution of the equation.

26. $|4x + 1| = 11; 3$ **27.** $|8 - 2n| = 2; -5$ **28.** $\left|6 + \frac{1}{2}x\right| = 14; -40$

29. $\left|\frac{1}{5}x - 2\right| = 4; 10$ **30.** $|4n + 7| = 1; 2$ **31.** $|-3x + 5| = 7; 4$

SOLVING EQUATIONS Solve the equation.

32. $|11 + 2x| = 5$ **33.** $|10 - 4x| = 2$ **34.** $|22 - 3n| = 5$

35. $|2n - 5| = 7$ **36.** $|8x + 1| = 23$ **37.** $|30 - 7x| = 4$

STUDENT HELP

▸ **HOMEWORK HELP**
Example 1: Exs. 17–40
Examples 2, 3:
     Exs. 41–58
Examples 4, 5:
     Exs. 65–76

38. $\left|\frac{1}{4}x - 5\right| = 8$ **39.** $\left|\frac{2}{3}x + 2\right| = 10$ **40.** $\left|\frac{1}{2}x - 3\right| = 2$

REWRITING INEQUALITIES Rewrite the absolute value inequality as a compound inequality.

41. $|3 + 4x| \leq 15$ **42.** $|4n - 12| > 16$ **43.** $|3x + 2| < 7$

44. $|2x - 1| \geq 12$ **45.** $|8 - 3n| \leq 18$ **46.** $|11 + 4x| < 23$

SOLVING AND GRAPHING Solve the inequality. Then graph your solution.

47. $|x + 1| < 8$

48. $|12 - x| \leq 19$

49. $|16 - x| \geq 10$

50. $|x + 5| > 12$

51. $|x - 8| \leq 5$

52. $|x - 16| > 24$

53. $|14 - 3x| > 18$

54. $|4x + 10| < 20$

55. $|8x + 28| \geq 32$

56. $\left|20 + \frac{1}{2}x\right| > 6$

57. $|7x + 5| < 23$

58. $|11 + 6x| \leq 47$

STUDENT HELP

KEYSTROKE HELP
Visit our Web site
www.mcdougallittell.com
to see keystrokes for
several models of
calculators.

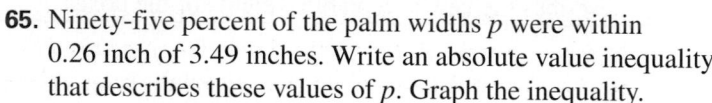 **SOLVING INEQUALITIES** Use the *Test* feature of a graphing calculator to solve the inequality. Most calculators use *abs* for absolute value. For example, you enter $|x + 1|$ as abs($x + 1$).

59. $|x + 1| < 3$

60. $\left|\frac{2}{3}x - \frac{1}{3}\right| \leq \frac{1}{3}$

61. $|2x - 4| > 10$

62. $\left|\frac{1}{2}x - 1\right| \leq 3$

63. $|4x - 10| > 6$

64. $|1 - 2x| \geq 13$

🌎 **PALM WIDTHS** In Exercises 65 and 66, use the following information.
In a sampling conducted by the United States Air Force,
the right-hand dimensions of 4000 Air Force men were
measured. The gathering of such information is useful when
designing control panels, keyboards, gloves, and so on.

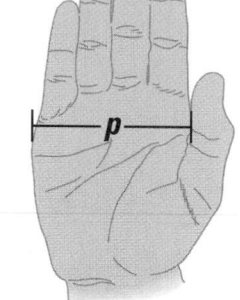

65. Ninety-five percent of the palm widths p were within
0.26 inch of 3.49 inches. Write an absolute value inequality
that describes these values of p. Graph the inequality.

66. Ninety-nine percent of the palm widths p were within
0.37 inch of 3.49 inches. Write an absolute value inequality
that describes these values of p. Graph the inequality.

67. 🌎 **ACCURACY OF MEASUREMENTS** Your woodshop instructor requires that
you cut several pieces of wood within $\frac{3}{16}$ inch of his specifications. Let p
represent the specification and let x represent the length of a cut piece of wood.
Write an absolute value inequality that describes the acceptable values of x. One
piece of wood is specified to be $p = 9\frac{1}{8}$ inches. Describe the acceptable lengths
for the piece of wood.

68. 🌎 **BASKETBALL** The length of a standard basketball court can vary from
84 feet to 94 feet, inclusive. Write an absolute value inequality that describes the
possible lengths of a standard basketball court.

69. 🌎 **BODY TEMPERATURE** Physicians consider an adult's normal body
temperature to be within 1°F of 98.6°F, inclusive. Write an absolute value
inequality that describes the range of normal body temperatures.

🌎 **WEIGHING FLOUR** In Exercises 70 and 71, use the following information.
A 16 ounce bag of flour probably does not weigh exactly 16 ounces. Suppose the
actual weight can be between 15.6 ounces and 16.4 ounces, inclusive.

70. Write an absolute value inequality that describes the acceptable weights for a
"16 ounce" bag of flour.

71. A case of flour contains 24 of these "16 ounce" bags. What is the greatest
possible weight of the flour in a case? What is the least possible weight? Write
an absolute value inequality that describes the acceptable weights of a case.

FOCUS ON APPLICATIONS

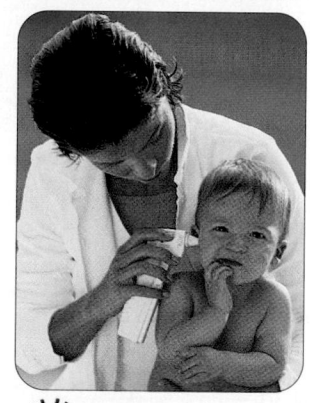

🌎 **BODY TEMPERATURE**
Doctors routinely use ear
thermometers to measure
body temperature. The first
ear thermometers were used
in 1990. The thermometers
use an infrared sensor and
microprocessors.

SPORTS EQUIPMENT In Exercises 72 and 73, use the table giving the recommended weight ranges for the balls from five different sports.

Sport	Weight range of ball used
Volleyball	260–280 grams
Basketball	600–650 grams
Water polo	400–450 grams
Lacrosse	142–149 grams
Football	14–15 ounces

72. Write an absolute value inequality for the weight range of each ball.

73. For each ball, write an absolute value inequality describing the weights of balls that are *outside* the recommended range.

74. **SCIENCE CONNECTION** Green plants can live in the ocean only at depths of 0 feet to 100 feet. Write an absolute value inequality describing the range of possible depths for green plants in an ocean.

75. **BOTTLING** A juice bottler has a tolerance of 9 milliliters in a two liter bottle, of 5 milliliters in a one liter bottle, and of 2 milliliters in a 500 milliliter bottle. For each size of bottle, write an absolute value inequality describing the capacities that are outside the acceptable range.

76. **SCIENCE CONNECTION** To determine height from skeletal remains, scientists use the equation $H = 2.26f + 66.4$ where H is the person's height (in centimeters) and f is the skeleton's femur length (in centimeters). The equation has a margin of error of ± 3.42 centimeters. Suppose a skeleton's femur length is 51.6 centimeters. Write an absolute value inequality that describes the person's height. Then solve the inequality to find the range of possible heights.

Test Preparation

77. **MULTIPLE CHOICE** Which of the following are solutions of $|3x - 7| = 14$?

(A) $x = \frac{7}{3}$ or $x = 7$

(B) $x = -\frac{7}{3}$ or $x = 7$

(C) $x = \frac{7}{3}$ or $x = -7$

(D) $x = -\frac{7}{3}$ or $x = -7$

78. **MULTIPLE CHOICE** Which of the following is equivalent to $|2x - 9| < 3$?

(A) $-3 \le x \le 6$

(B) $3 < x < 6$

(C) $3 \le x \le 6$

(D) $-3 < x < -6$

79. **MULTIPLE CHOICE** Which of the following is equivalent to $|3x + 5| \ge 19$?

(A) $x \le -\frac{14}{3}$ or $x \ge 8$

(B) $x < -8$ or $x > \frac{14}{3}$

(C) $x \le -8$ or $x \ge \frac{14}{3}$

(D) $x < -\frac{14}{3}$ or $x > 8$

★ Challenge

SOLVING INEQUALITIES Solve the inequality. If there is no solution, write *no solution*.

80. $|2x + 3| \ge -13$

81. $|5x + 2| \le -2$

82. $|3x - 8| < -10$

83. $|4x - 2| > -6$

84. $|6 - 2x| > -8$

85. $|7 - 3x| \le -14$

SOLVING INEQUALITIES Solve for *x*. Assume *a* and *b* are positive numbers.

86. $|x + a| < b$

87. $|x - a| > b$

88. $|x + a| \ge a$

89. $|x - a| \le a$

MIXED REVIEW

LOGICAL REASONING Tell whether the statement is *true* or *false*. If the statement is false, explain why. (Skills Review, p. 926)

90. A triangle is a right triangle if and only if it has a right angle.

91. $2x = 14$ if and only if $x = -7$.

92. All rectangles are squares.

EVALUATING EXPRESSIONS Evaluate the expression for the given value(s) of the variable(s). (Review 1.2 for 2.1)

93. $5x - 9$ when $x = 6$

94. $-2y + 4$ when $y = 14$

95. $11c + 6$ when $c = -3$

96. $-8a - 3$ when $a = -4$

97. $a - 11b + 2$ when $a = 61$ and $b = 7$

98. $15x + 8y$ when $x = \frac{1}{2}$ and $y = \frac{1}{3}$

99. $\frac{1}{5}\left(8g + \frac{1}{3}h\right)$ when $g = 6$ and $h = 6$

100. $\frac{1}{5}(p + q) - 7$ when $p = 5$ and $q = 3$

SOLVING INEQUALITIES Solve the inequality. (Review 1.6)

101. $6x + 9 > 11$

102. $15 - 2x \geq 45$

103. $-3x - 5 \leq 10$

104. $13 + 4x < 9$

105. $-18 < 2x + 10 < 6$

106. $x + 2 \leq -1$ or $4x \geq 8$

QUIZ 3

Self-Test for Lessons 1.6 and 1.7

Solve the inequality. Then graph your solution. (Lesson 1.6)

1. $4x - 3 \leq 17$

2. $2y - 9 > 5y + 12$

3. $-8 < 3x + 4 < 22$

4. $3x - 5 \leq -11$ or $2x - 3 > 3$

Solve the equation. (Lesson 1.7)

5. $|x + 5| = 4$

6. $|x - 3| = 2$

7. $|6 - x| = 9$

8. $|4x - 7| = 13$

9. $|3x + 4| = 20$

10. $|15 - 3x| = 12$

Solve the inequality. Then graph your solution. (Lesson 1.7)

11. $|y + 2| \geq 3$

12. $|x + 6| < 4$

13. $|x - 3| > 7$

14. $|2y - 5| \leq 3$

15. $|2x - 3| > 1$

16. $|4x + 5| \geq 13$

17. **FUEL EFFICIENCY** Your car gets between 20 miles per gallon and 28 miles per gallon of gasoline and has a 16 gallon gasoline tank. Write a compound inequality that represents your fuel efficiency. How many miles can you travel on one tank of gasoline? (Lesson 1.6)

18. **MANUFACTURING TOLERANCE** The ideal diameter of a certain type of ball bearing is 30 millimeters. The manufacturer has a tolerance of 0.045 millimeter. Write an absolute value inequality that describes the acceptable diameters for these ball bearings. Then solve the inequality to find the range of acceptable diameters. (Lesson 1.7)

Chapter Summary

WHAT did you learn?

Graph and order real numbers. **(1.1)**

Identify properties of and perform operations with real numbers. **(1.1)**

Evaluate and simplify algebraic expressions. **(1.2)**

Solve equations.
- linear equations **(1.3)**

- absolute value equations **(1.7)**

Rewrite equations and common formulas with more than one variable. **(1.4)**

Use a problem solving plan and strategies to solve real-life problems. **(1.5)**

Solve and graph inequalities in one variable.
- linear inequalities **(1.6)**

- absolute value inequalities **(1.7)**

Write and use algebraic models to solve real-life problems. **(1.2–1.7)**

WHY did you learn it?

Analyze record low temperatures. **(p. 8)**

Learn how to exchange money. **(p. 6)**

Find the population of Hawaii. **(p. 16)**

Find the temperature in degrees Celsius at which dry ice changes from a solid to a gas. **(p. 23)**
Solve problems that involve tolerance. **(p. 52)**

Find how much you should charge for tickets to a benefit concert. **(p. 27)**

Find the average speed of the Bullet Train. **(p. 33)**

Decide how to spend your money at an amusement park. **(p. 46)**

Describe recommended weight ranges for balls used in various sports. **(p. 55)**

Use femur length to find a range of possible heights for a person. **(p. 55)**

How does Chapter 1 fit into the BIGGER PICTURE of algebra?

Chapter 1 provides a review of skills and strategies you learned in Algebra 1 and a foundation for continuing your study of algebra and its applications. The primary use of algebra is to model and solve real-life problems. You will use algebra in this way throughout the course, in future courses, and perhaps in a future career.

STUDY STRATEGY

How did you make and use a vocabulary file?

Here is an example of one flashcard for your vocabulary file, following the **Study Strategy** on page 2.

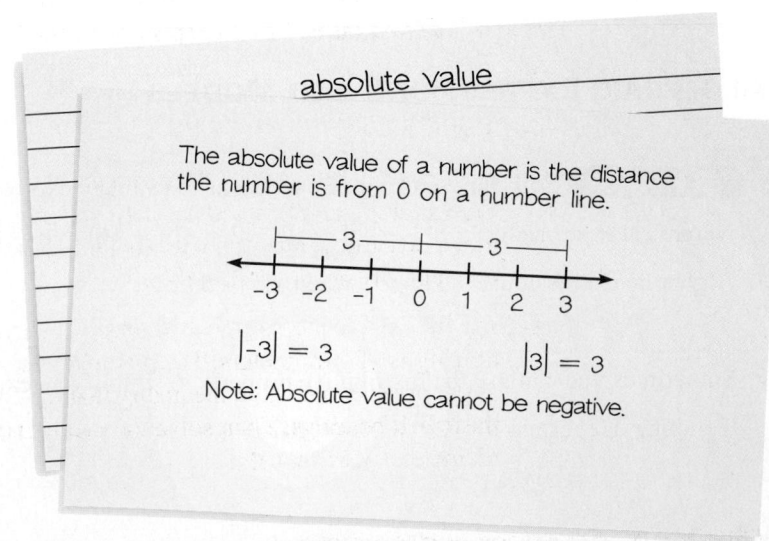

absolute value

The absolute value of a number is the distance the number is from 0 on a number line.

$|-3| = 3 \qquad |3| = 3$

Note: Absolute value cannot be negative.

VOCABULARY

- whole numbers, p. 3
- integers, p. 3
- rational numbers, p. 3
- irrational numbers, p. 3
- origin, p. 3
- graph of a real number, p. 3
- coordinate, p. 3
- opposite, p. 5
- reciprocal, p. 5
- numerical expression, p. 11

- base, p. 11
- exponent, p. 11
- power, p. 11
- order of operations, p. 11
- variable, p. 12
- value of a variable, p. 12
- algebraic expression, p. 12
- value of an expression, p. 12
- mathematical model, p. 12
- terms of an expression, p. 13

- coefficient, p. 13
- like terms, p. 13
- constant terms, p. 13
- equivalent expressions, p. 13
- identity, p. 13
- equation, p. 19
- linear equation, p. 19
- solution of an equation, p. 19
- equivalent equations, p. 19

- verbal model, p. 33
- algebraic model, p. 33
- linear inequality in one variable, p. 41
- solution of a linear inequality in one variable, p. 41
- graph of a linear inequality in one variable, p. 41
- compound inequality, p. 43
- absolute value, p. 50

1.1 REAL NUMBERS AND NUMBER OPERATIONS

Examples on pp. 3–6

> **EXAMPLE** You can use a number line to graph and order real numbers.
>
>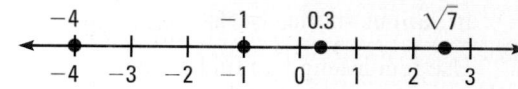
>
> Increasing order (left to right):
> $-4, -1, 0.3, \sqrt{7}$
>
> Properties of real numbers include the closure, commutative, associative, identity, inverse, and distributive properties.

Graph the numbers on a number line. Then write the numbers in increasing order.

1. $-2, 0.2, -\pi, -\sqrt{6}, \dfrac{6}{5}$

2. $\dfrac{3}{4}, \sqrt{3}, -1.75, -3, -\dfrac{4}{3}$

Identify the property shown.

3. $4(5 + 1) = 4 \cdot 5 + 4 \cdot 1$

4. $8 + (-8) = 0$

1.2 ALGEBRAIC EXPRESSIONS AND MODELS

Examples on pp. 11–13

> **EXAMPLES** You can use order of operations to evaluate expressions.
>
> Numerical expression: $8(3 + 4^2) - 12 \div 2 = 8(3 + 16) - 6 = 8(19) - 6 = 152 - 6 = 146$
>
> Algebraic expression: $3x^2 - 1$ when $x = -5$
>
> $3(-5)^2 - 1 = 3(25) - 1 = 75 - 1 = 74$
>
> Sometimes you can use the distributive property to simplify an expression.
>
> Combine like terms: $2x^2 - 4x + 10x - 1 = 2x^2 + (-4 + 10)x - 1 = 2x^2 + 6x - 1$

Evaluate the expression.

5. $-3 - 6 \div 2 - 12$

6. $-5 \div 1 + 2(7 - 10)^2$

7. $7x - 3x - 8x^3$ when $x = -1$

8. $3ab^2 + 5a^2b - 1$ when $a = 2$ and $b = -2$

Simplify the expression.

9. $7y - 2x + 5x - 3y + 2x$

10. $4(3 - x) + 5(x - 6)$

11. $6x^2 - 3x + 5x^2 + 2x$

12. $2(x^2 + x) - 3(x^2 - 4x)$

Examples on pp. 19–21

1.3	SOLVING LINEAR EQUATIONS

> **EXAMPLE** You can use properties of real numbers and transformations that produce equivalent equations to solve linear equations.
>
> Solve: $-2(x - 4) = 12$
>
> $\qquad -2x + 8 = 12$ $\qquad$ Then check: $-2(-2 - 4) \overset{?}{=} 12$
>
> $\qquad\qquad -2x = 4$ $\qquad\qquad\qquad\qquad\qquad -2(-6) \overset{?}{=} 12$
>
> $\qquad\qquad\quad x = -2$ $\qquad\qquad\qquad\qquad\qquad\qquad 12 = 12$ ✓

Solve the equation. Check your solution.

13. $-5x + 3 = 18$

14. $\frac{2}{3}n - 5 = 1$

15. $\frac{1}{2}y = -\frac{3}{4}y - 40$

16. $2 - 3a = 4 + a$

17. $8(z - 6) = -16$

18. $-4x - 4 = 3(2 - x)$

Examples on pp. 26–28

1.4	REWRITING EQUATIONS AND FORMULAS

> **EXAMPLES** You can solve an equation that has more than one variable, such as a formula, for one of its variables.
>
> Solve the equation for y. $\qquad\qquad$ Solve the formula for the area of a trapezoid for h.
>
> $\qquad 2x - 3y = 6$ $\qquad\qquad\qquad\qquad\qquad A = \frac{1}{2}(b_1 + b_2)h$
>
> $\qquad\quad -3y = -2x + 6$ $\qquad\qquad\qquad\qquad 2A = (b_1 + b_2)h$
>
> $\qquad\qquad y = \frac{2}{3}x - 2$ $\qquad\qquad\qquad\qquad \frac{2A}{b_1 + b_2} = h$

Solve the equation for y.

19. $5x - y = 10$

20. $x + 4y = -8$

21. $0.1x + 0.5y = 3.5$

22. $2x = 3y + 9$

23. $5x - 6y + 12 = 0$

24. $x - 2xy = 1$

Solve the formula for the indicated variable.

25. Perimeter of a Rectangle

Solve for ℓ: $P = 2\ell + 2w$

26. Celsius to Fahrenheit

Solve for C: $F = \frac{9}{5}C + 32$

1.5 PROBLEM SOLVING USING ALGEBRAIC MODELS

Examples on
pp. 33–36

EXAMPLE You can use a problem solving plan in which you write a verbal model, assign labels, write and solve an algebraic model, and then answer the question.

How far can you drive at 55 miles per hour for 4 hours?

VERBAL MODEL

$$\boxed{\text{Distance}} = \boxed{\text{Rate}} \cdot \boxed{\text{Time}}$$

LABELS Distance = d (miles), Rate = **55** (miles per hour), Time = **4** (hours)

ALGEBRAIC MODEL $d = 55 \cdot 4 = 220$

▶ You can drive 220 miles.

27. How long will it take to drive 325 miles at 55 miles per hour?

28. While on vacation, you take a taxi from the airport to your hotel for $21.85. The taxi costs $2.95 plus $1.35 per mile. How far is it from the airport to the hotel?

1.6 SOLVING LINEAR INEQUALITIES

Examples on
pp. 41–44

EXAMPLES You can use transformations to solve inequalities. Reverse the inequality when you multiply or divide both sides by a negative number.

$4x + 1 < 7x - 5$
$-3x < -6$
$x > 2$

$0 \le 6 - 2n \le 10$
$-6 \le -2n \le 4$
$3 \ge n \ge -2$

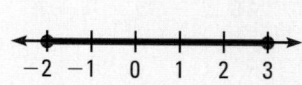

Solve the inequality. Then graph your solution.

29. $2x - 10 > 6$ **30.** $12 - 5x \ge -13$ **31.** $-3x + 4 \ge 2x + 19$

32. $0 < x - 7 \le 5$ **33.** $-3 \le 2y + 1 \le 5$ **34.** $3a + 1 < -2$ or $3a + 1 > 7$

1.7 SOLVING ABSOLUTE VALUE EQUATIONS AND INEQUALITIES

Examples on
pp. 50–52

EXAMPLES To solve an absolute value equation, rewrite it as two linear equations. To solve an absolute value inequality, rewrite it as a compound inequality.

$|x + 3| = 5$
$x + 3 = 5$ or $x + 3 = -5$
$x = 2$ or $x = -8$

$|x - 7| \ge 2$
$x - 7 \ge 2$ or $x - 7 \le -2$
$x \ge 9$ or $x \le 5$

Solve the equation or inequality.

35. $|x + 1| = 4$ **36.** $|2x - 1| = 15$ **37.** $|10 - 6x| = 26$

38. $|x + 8| > 0$ **39.** $|2x - 5| < 9$ **40.** $|3x + 4| \ge 2$

Graph the numbers on a number line. Then write the numbers in increasing order.

1. $-0.98, -0.9, -1, -1.95$

2. $\frac{2}{3}, -\frac{3}{2}, -\frac{2}{3}, 0, \frac{3}{2}$

3. $\sqrt{4}, 4, 2\frac{3}{4}, \sqrt{10}, \frac{7}{2}$

Identify the property shown.

4. $7(11 + 9) = 7 \cdot 11 + 7 \cdot 9$

5. $8xy = 8yx$

6. $50 + 0 = 50$

Select and perform an operation to answer the question.

7. What is the product of -5 and -3?

8. What is the difference of 29 and -20?

Evaluate the expression.

9. $18 - 7 \cdot 15 \div 3$

10. $36 - 5^2 \cdot 2 + 7$

11. $12 - 3(1 - 17) \div 4$

12. $-4x^2 + 6xy$ when $x = -2$ and $y = 5$

13. $\frac{3}{5}x - \frac{7}{2}y$ when $x = 3$ and $y = 4$

Simplify the expression.

14. $-2x + 4y - 10 + x$

15. $4y + 6x - 3(x - 2y)$

16. $5(x^2 - 9x) - 2(3x + 4) + 7$

Solve the equation.

17. $7x + 12 = -16$

18. $1.2x = 2.3x - 2.2$

19. $4x + 21 = 7(x + 9)$

20. $|x - 4| = 15$

21. $|5x + 11| = 9$

22. $|13 + 2x| = 5$

Solve the equation for y.

23. $5x + y = 7$

24. $6x - 3y = 1$

25. $2xy + x = 12$

Solve the inequality. Then graph your solution.

26. $4x - 5 \le 15$

27. $3 < 2x + 11 < 17$

28. $8x < 1$ or $x - 9 > -5$

29. $|3x - 1| > 7$

30. $|x + 3| \ge 4$

31. $|1 - 2x| \le 3$

32. **GEOMETRY CONNECTION** The formula for the volume of a cylinder is $V = \pi r^2 h$. Solve the formula for h. How tall is a cylindrical can with radius 3 centimeters and volume 200 cubic centimeters?

33. **PHONE CALLS** A company charges $.09 per minute for any long distance call, along with a $5 monthly fee. Your monthly bill shows that you owe $27.23. For how many minutes of long distance calls were you charged?

34. **SAVING MONEY** You plan to save $15 per week from your allowance to buy a snowboard for $400. How many *months* will it take?

35. **HOT WATER LAKE** Boiling Lake is a small lake on the island of Dominica. The water temperature of the lake is between 180°F and 197°F. Write a compound inequality for this temperature range. Graph the inequality.

36. **BASKETBALL BOUNCE** If manufactured correctly, a basketball should bounce from 48 inches to 56 inches when dropped from a height of 6 feet. Determine the tolerance for the bounce height of a basketball and write an absolute value inequality for acceptable bounce heights.

Chapter Standardized Test

● **TEST-TAKING STRATEGY** Draw an arrow on your test booklet next to questions that you do not answer. This will enable you to find the questions quickly when you go back.

1. MULTIPLE CHOICE Which list of numbers is written in increasing order?

(A) $-\sqrt{7}, -3, -\frac{5}{2}, 0, \frac{3}{4}$

(B) $-6, -4.5, -4.8, 1, 1.9$

(C) $-\sqrt{3}, -\frac{8}{5}, -\frac{1}{2}, 0, \frac{1}{8}$

(D) $-\frac{11}{2}, -\sqrt{2}, -\frac{1}{7}, -\frac{1}{4}, \frac{5}{2}$

(E) $-0.5, -\sqrt{2}, -\frac{7}{2}, -\sqrt{13}, -13$

2. MULTIPLE CHOICE Which property is illustrated by the statement $6(8 + 4) = 6(4 + 8)$?

(A) Distributive property

(B) Associative property of addition

(C) Associative property of multiplication

(D) Commutative property of addition

(E) Commutative property of multiplication

3. MULTIPLE CHOICE Which expression *cannot* be simplified?

(A) $8x - 8$ (B) $8x - x$

(C) $8x + 5x$ (D) $(8 + 5)x$

(E) $-(x + x)$

4. MULTIPLE CHOICE Which number does $(7 + 1)^2 - 16 \div 2 + 6 \div 3$ equal?

(A) $\frac{62}{3}$ (B) $\frac{23}{3}$ (C) 10

(D) 2 (E) 58

5. MULTIPLE CHOICE Which number does $4x^2 - 5x + 3$ equal when $x = -3$?

(A) -48 (B) 24 (C) 54

(D) -54 (E) -18

6. MULTIPLE CHOICE Which number is the solution of the equation $-4x + 8 = x - 7$?

(A) -3 (B) -5 (C) 3

(D) 5 (E) $-\frac{1}{5}$

7. MULTIPLE CHOICE A real estate broker earns a salary of $21,000 plus 2.5% of the value of any real estate sold. Last year the broker earned $52,000. What was the total value of all real estate sold by the broker?

(A) $12,400   (B) $31,000

(C) $124,000   (D) $1,240,000

(E) $12,400,000

8. MULTIPLE CHOICE Which gives the equation $C = 2\pi r$ solved for r?

(A) $r = 2\pi C$ (B) $r = \frac{C}{2\pi}$

(C) $r = \frac{2\pi}{C}$ (D) $r = \frac{2C}{\pi}$

(E) $r = 2\frac{\pi}{2C}$

9. MULTIPLE CHOICE Which inequality is the solution of $6x - 3 \geq 7 + 4x$?

(A) $x \geq -5$ (B) $x > 5$ (C) $x \leq 5$

(D) $x \leq -5$ (E) $x \geq 5$

10. MULTIPLE CHOICE Which number is *not* a solution of the inequality $-3 \leq -6x + 3 \leq 9$?

(A) -1 (B) 0 (C) 0.5

(D) 1 (E) 2

11. MULTIPLE CHOICE Which number is a solution of the equation $|5x - 2| = 8$?

(A) $\frac{6}{5}$ (B) $-\frac{6}{5}$ (C) $\frac{1}{2}$

(D) -2 (E) -1

12. MULTIPLE CHOICE Which graph represents $|2x - 11| > 3$?

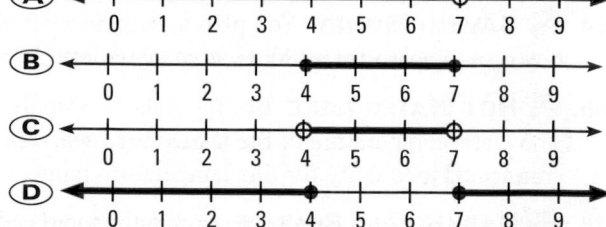
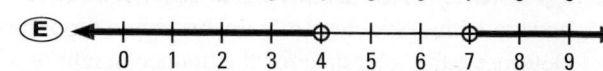

QUANTITATIVE COMPARISON In Exercises 13–15, choose the statement that is true about the given quantities.

    (A) The quantity in column A is greater.

    (B) The quantity in column B is greater.

    (C) The two quantities are equal.

    (D) The relationship cannot be determined from the given information.

	Column A	Column B
13.	$x^2 + (2x - 15) - 9x + 52 \div 2$ when $x = 1$	$x^2 + (2x - 15) - 9x + 52 \div 2$ when $x = -1$
14.	a if $6a + 7 = -5$	b if $b - 5 = 2b - 7$
15.	t if $I = Prt$, $I = \$100$, $P = \$1000$, and $r = 4\%$	t if $I = Prt$, $I = \$200$, $P = \$2000$, and $r = 4\%$

16. **MULTI-STEP PROBLEM** You buy a new car with a fuel efficiency of 31 miles per gallon on the highway and 26 miles per gallon in town. The gas tank holds 12.9 gallons. How far can you travel on the highway in your new car with a full tank of gas?

    a. Write a verbal model for this problem.

    b. Assign labels to each part of the verbal model.

    c. Use the labels to translate the verbal model into an algebraic model.

    d. Solve the algebraic model.

    e. Answer the question.

    f. How far can you travel *in town* in your new car with a full tank of gas?

17. **MULTI-STEP PROBLEM** The table below gives the average weight range for different types of dogs.

Dog	Average weight range (pounds)
Beagle	18–30
Bloodhound	80–100
Bulldog	40–50
Great Dane	120–150
Mastiff	165–185

▶ Source: American Kennel Club

    a. For each type of dog, write the average weight range as a compound inequality.

    b. For each type of dog, write the average weight range as an absolute value inequality.

    c. *Writing* Choose one type of dog from the table. Explain how the two inequalities you wrote for the average weight range for this type of dog are related.

LINEAR EQUATIONS AND FUNCTIONS

▶ *How can you predict membership enrollments for an organization?*

APPLICATION: Youth Service

City Year is a national youth service program that began with 57 members in Boston in 1989. The organization has expanded since then and currently has sites in cities across the country.

Think & Discuss

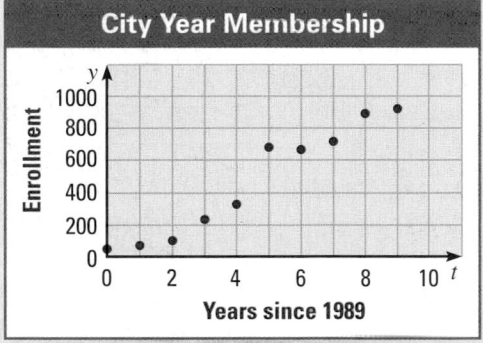

City Year Membership

Years since 1989

1. What trend do you see in the membership enrollment for City Year?

2. Based on the graph, how can you predict future membership enrollments?

Learn More About It

You will predict the number of members in City Year in 2010 in Exercises 24 and 25 on p. 105.

APPLICATION LINK Visit www.mcdougallittell.com for more information about youth service.

Study Guide

What's the chapter about?

Chapter 2 is about **linear equations and functions**. In Chapter 2 you'll learn

- how to graph ordered pairs, relations, functions, linear equations and inequalities in two variables, piecewise functions, and absolute value functions.

- how to write equations of lines.

- how to solve real-life problems using graphs and equations.

KEY VOCABULARY

▶ **Review**
- graph, p. 3
- linear equation, p. 19
- solution, p. 19
- linear inequality in one variable, p. 41
- absolute value, p. 50

▶ **New**
- relation, p. 67
- function, p. 67
- ordered pair, p. 67
- coordinate plane, p. 67
- linear function, p. 69
- slope, p. 75

- slope-intercept form, p. 82
- standard form, p. 84
- direct variation, p. 94
- scatter plot, p. 100
- linear inequality in two variables, p. 108
- piecewise function, p. 114

Are you ready for the chapter?

SKILL REVIEW Do these exercises to review key skills that you'll apply in this chapter. See the given **reference page** if there is something you don't understand.

Evaluate the expression for the given values of x and y. (Review Example 3, p. 12)

1. $\dfrac{y-7}{x-3}$; $x = 2$, $y = 5$

2. $\dfrac{5-y}{6-x}$; $x = 4$, $y = 1$

3. $\dfrac{8-y}{3-x}$; $x = -1$, $y = -4$

Solve the equation for y. (Review Example 1, p. 26)

4. $3x + y = 4$

5. $x - 2y = 10$

6. $5x + 6y = -60$

Solve the inequality. (Review Examples 1 and 2, p. 42)

7. $2x + 9 < 18$

8. $6 - 0.5y \le 19$

9. $2x + 3 > 6x - 7$

▶ **Study Tip**
"Student Help" boxes throughout the chapter give you study tips and tell you where to look for extra help in this book and on the Internet.

Here's a study strategy!

Skills File

In a notebook, make a file of the skills you learn throughout this course. On the left side of the paper, write an important skill and the lesson that it comes from. On the right side of the paper, give an example of the skill in use. Go back now and make a skills file for Chapter 1. Then continue with Chapter 2.

2.1

Functions and Their Graphs

What you should learn

GOAL 1 Represent relations and functions.

GOAL 2 Graph and evaluate linear functions, as applied in **Exs. 55 and 56**.

Why you should learn it

▼ To model **real-life** quantities, such as the distance a hot air balloon travels in **Example 6**.

GOAL 1 REPRESENTING RELATIONS AND FUNCTIONS

A **relation** is a *mapping*, or pairing, of input values with output values. The set of input values is the **domain**, and the set of output values is the **range**. A relation is a **function** provided there is exactly one output for each input. It is not a function if at least one input has more than one output.

Relations (and functions) between two quantities can be represented in many ways, including mapping diagrams, tables, graphs, equations, and verbal descriptions.

EXAMPLE 1   *Identifying Functions*

Identify the domain and range. Then tell whether the relation is a function.

a.   Input   Output
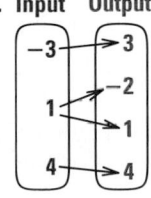

b.   Input   Output
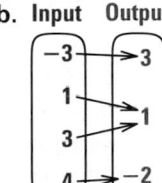

SOLUTION

a. The domain consists of −3, 1, and 4, and the range consists of −2, 1, 3, and 4. The relation is not a function because the input 1 is mapped onto both −2 and 1.

b. The domain consists of −3, 1, 3, and 4, and the range consists of −2, 1, and 3. The relation is a function because each input in the domain is mapped onto exactly one output in the range.

· · · · · · · · · ·

A relation can be represented by a set of **ordered pairs** of the form (x, y). In an ordered pair the first number is the **x-coordinate** and the second number is the **y-coordinate**. To graph a relation, plot each of its ordered pairs in a **coordinate plane**, such as the one shown. A coordinate plane is divided into four **quadrants** by the **x-axis** and the **y-axis**. The axes intersect at a point called the **origin**.

┌─ **STUDENT HELP**

▶ **Study Tip**
Although the origin O is not usually labeled, it is understood to be the point $(0, 0)$.

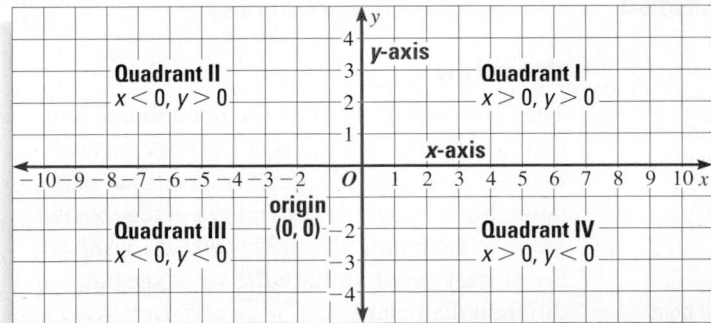

EXAMPLE 2 *Graphing Relations*

Graph the relations given in Example 1.

STUDENT HELP

▶ **Skills Review**
For help with plotting points in a coordinate plane, see p. 933.

SOLUTION

a. Write the relation as a set of ordered pairs: $(-3, 3)$, $(1, -2)$, $(1, 1)$, $(4, 4)$. Then plot the points in a coordinate plane.

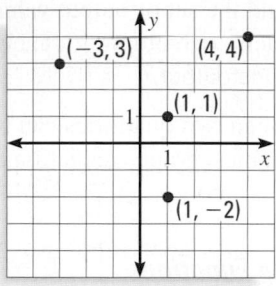

b. Write the relation as a set of ordered pairs: $(-3, 3)$, $(1, 1)$, $(3, 1)$, $(4, -2)$. Then plot the points in a coordinate plane.

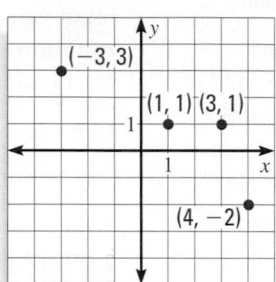

· · · · · · · · · ·

In Example 2 notice that the graph of the relation that is not a function (the graph on the left) has two points that lie on the same vertical line. You can use this property as a graphical test for functions.

VERTICAL LINE TEST FOR FUNCTIONS

A relation is a function if and only if no vertical line intersects the graph of the relation at more than one point.

FOCUS ON CAREERS

Variables other than x and y are often used when working with relations in real-life situations, as shown in the next example.

EXAMPLE 3 *Using the Vertical Line Test in Real Life*

FORESTRY The graph shows the ages a and diameters d of several pine trees at Lundbreck Falls in Canada. Are the diameters of the trees a function of their ages? Explain.

▶ Source: National Geographical Data Center

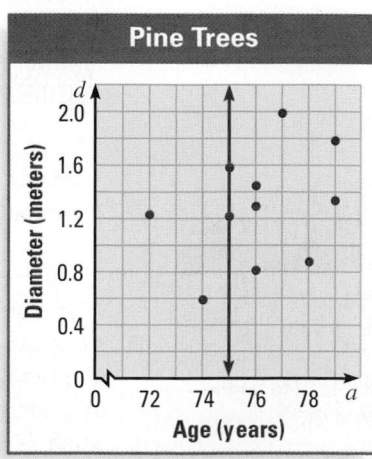

SOLUTION

The diameters of the trees are not a function of their ages because there is at least one vertical line that intersects the graph at more than one point. For example, a vertical line intersects the graph at the points $(75, 1.22)$ and $(75, 1.58)$. So, at least two trees have the same age but different diameters.

FORESTER
A forester manages, develops, and protects natural resources. To measure the diameter of trees, a forester uses a special tool called diameter tape.

CAREER LINK
www.mcdougallittell.com

GOAL 2 GRAPHING AND EVALUATING FUNCTIONS

Many functions can be represented by an **equation** in two variables, such as $y = 2x - 7$. An ordered pair (x, y) is a **solution** of such an equation if the equation is true when the values of x and y are substituted into the equation. For instance, $(2, -3)$ is a solution of $y = 2x - 7$ because $-3 = 2(2) - 7$ is a true statement.

In an equation, the input variable is called the **independent variable**. The output variable is called the **dependent variable** and depends on the value of the input variable. For the equation $y = 2x - 7$, the independent variable is x and the dependent variable is y.

The **graph** of an equation in two variables is the collection of all points (x, y) whose coordinates are solutions of the equation.

GRAPHING EQUATIONS IN TWO VARIABLES

To graph an equation in two variables, follow these steps:

STEP ❶ Construct a table of values.

STEP ❷ Graph enough solutions to recognize a pattern.

STEP ❸ Connect the points with a line or a curve.

EXAMPLE 4 *Graphing a Function*

Graph the function $y = x + 1$.

SOLUTION

❶ Begin by constructing a table of values.

Choose x.	-2	-1	0	1	2
Evaluate y.	-1	0	1	2	3

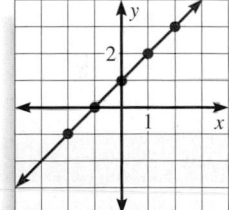

❷ Plot the points. Notice the five points lie on a line.

❸ Draw a line through the points.

. . . .

The function in Example 4 is a **linear function** because it is of the form

$$y = mx + b \qquad \text{**Linear function**}$$

where m and b are constants. The graph of a linear function is a line. By naming a function "f" you can write the function using **function notation.**

$$f(x) = mx + b \qquad \text{**Function notation**}$$

The symbol $f(x)$ is read as "the value of f at x," or simply as "f of x." Note that $f(x)$ is another name for y. The domain of a function consists of the values of x for which the function is defined. The range consists of the values of $f(x)$ where x is in the domain of f. Functions do not have to be represented by the letter f. Other letters such as g or h can also be used.

EXAMPLE 5 Evaluating Functions

Decide whether the function is linear. Then evaluate the function when $x = -2$.

a. $f(x) = -x^2 - 3x + 5$ **b.** $g(x) = 2x + 6$

STUDENT HELP

↳ INTERNET
HOMEWORK HELP
Visit our Web site
www.mcdougallittell.com
for extra examples.

SOLUTION

a. $f(x)$ is not a linear function because it has an x^2-term.

$f(x) = -x^2 - 3x + 5$	**Write function.**
$f(-2) = -(-2)^2 - 3(-2) + 5$	**Substitute −2 for x.**
$= 7$	**Simplify.**

b. $g(x)$ is a linear function because it has the form $g(x) = mx + b$.

$g(x) = 2x + 6$	**Write function.**
$g(-2) = 2(-2) + 6$	**Substitute −2 for x.**
$= 2$	**Simplify.**

· · · · · · · · · ·

In Example 5 the domain of each function is all real numbers. In real-life problems the domain is restricted to the numbers that make sense in the real-life context.

EXAMPLE 6 Using a Function in Real Life

BALLOONING In March of 1999, Bertrand Piccard and Brian Jones attempted to become the first people to fly around the world in a balloon. Based on an average speed of 97.8 kilometers per hour, the distance d (in kilometers) that they traveled can be modeled by $d = 97.8t$ where t is the time (in hours). They traveled a total of about 478 hours. The rules governing the record state that the minimum distance covered must be at least 26,700 kilometers. ▶ Source: Breitling

a. Identify the domain and range and determine whether Piccard and Jones set the record.

b. Graph the function. Then use the graph to approximate how long it took them to travel 20,000 kilometers.

FOCUS ON
PEOPLE

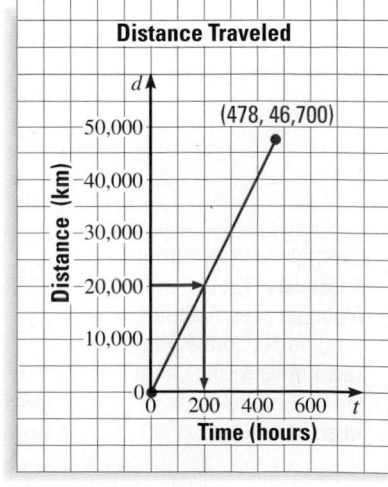

PICCARD AND JONES are the first pilots to fly around the world in a balloon. Piccard is a medical doctor in Switzerland specializing in psychiatry, and Jones is a member of the Royal Air Force in the United Kingdom.

SOLUTION

a. Because their trip lasted 478 hours, the domain is $0 \le t \le 478$. The distance they traveled was $d = 97.8(478) \approx 46,700$ kilometers, so the range is $0 \le d \le 46,700$. Since $46,700 > 26,700$, they did set the record.

b. The graph of the function is shown. Note that the graph ends at (478, 46,700). To find how long it took them to travel 20,000 kilometers, start at 20,000 on the d-axis and move right until you reach the graph. Then move down to the t-axis. It took them about 200 hours to travel 20,000 kilometers.

GUIDED PRACTICE

Vocabulary Check ✔   1. What are the domain and range of a relation?

Concept Check ✔   2. Explain why a vertical line, rather than a horizontal line, is used to determine if a graph represents a function.

3. Explain the process for graphing an equation.

Skill Check ✔   4. Identify the domain and range of the relation shown. Then tell whether the relation is a function.

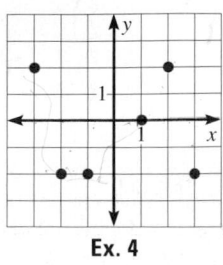
Ex. 4

Graph the function.

5. $y = x - 1$ 6. $y = 4x$ 7. $y = 2x + 5$

8. $y = x$ 9. $y = -2x$ 10. $y = -x + 9$

Evaluate the function when $x = 3$.

11. $f(x) = x$ 12. $f(x) = 6x$ 13. $f(x) = x^2$

14. $g(x) = 2x + 7$ 15. $h(x) = -x^2 + 10$ 16. $j(x) = x^3 - 7x$

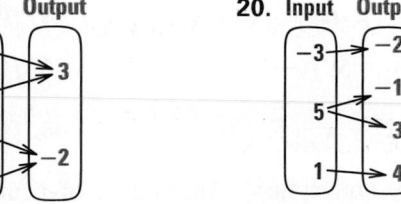 **HIGHWAY DRIVING** In Exercises 17 and 18, use the following information. A car has a 16 gallon gas tank. On a long highway trip, gas is used at a rate of about 2 gallons per hour. The gallons of gas g in the car's tank can be modeled by the equation $g = 16 - 2t$ where t is the time (in hours).

17. Identify the domain and range of the function. Then graph the function.

18. At the end of the trip there are 2 gallons of gas left. How long was the trip?

PRACTICE AND APPLICATIONS

STUDENT HELP

➤ **Extra Practice**
to help you master
skills is on p. 941.

DOMAIN AND RANGE Identify the domain and range.

19. Input Output

```
2
         3
5
-1
         -2
6
```

20. Input Output

```
-3 ---- -2
        -1
5
        3
1 ----- 4
```

21. Input Output

```
4 ---- 1
3 ---- 2
2 ---- 3
1 ---- 4
```

GRAPHS Graph the relation. Then tell whether the relation is a function.

22.

x	0	0	2	2	4	4
y	−4	4	−3	3	−1	1

STUDENT HELP

➤ **HOMEWORK HELP**
Example 1: Exs. 19–27
Example 2: Exs. 22–27
Example 3: Exs. 30–32, 51–54
Example 4: Exs. 34–42
Example 5: Exs. 43–50
Example 6: Exs. 55–58

23.

x	−5	−4	−3	0	3	4	5
y	−6	−4	−2	−1	−2	−4	−6

24.

x	−2	−2	0	2	2
y	1.5	−3.5	0	1.5	−3.5

MAPPING DIAGRAMS Use a mapping diagram to represent the relation. Then tell whether the relation is a function.

25.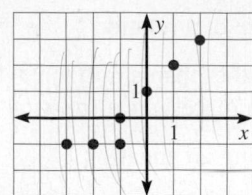

26.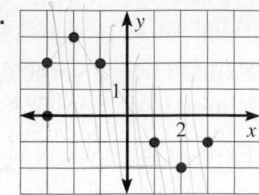

27.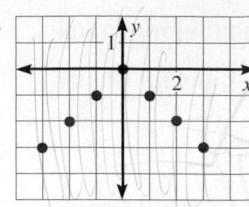

28. *Writing* Is a function always a relation? Is a relation always a function? Explain your reasoning.

<u>**STUDENT HELP**</u>

▶ **Skills Review**
For help with if-then statements, see p. 926.

29. **LOGICAL REASONING** Rewrite the vertical line test as two if-then statements.

VERTICAL LINE TEST Use the vertical line test to determine whether the relation is a function.

30.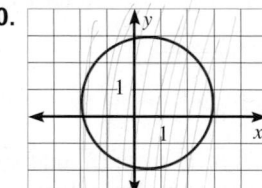

31.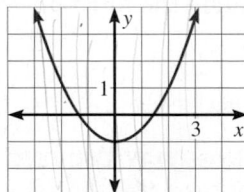

32.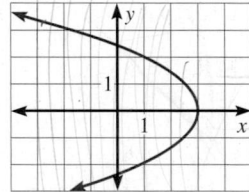

33. **CRITICAL THINKING** Why does $y = 3$ represent a function, but $x = 3$ does not?

GRAPHING FUNCTIONS Graph the function.

34. $y = x - 3$

35. $y = -x + 6$

36. $y = 2x + 7$

37. $y = -5x + 1$

38. $y = 3x - 4$

39. $y = -2x - 3$

40. $y = 10x$

41. $y = 5$

42. $y = -\frac{2}{3}x + 4$

EVALUATING FUNCTIONS Decide whether the function is linear. Then evaluate the function for the given value of *x*.

43. $f(x) = x - 11$; $f(4)$

44. $f(x) = 2$; $f(-4)$

45. $f(x) = |x| - 5$; $f(-6)$

46. $f(x) = 9x^3 - x^2 + 2$; $f(2)$

47. $f(x) = -\frac{2}{3}x^2 - x + 5$; $f(6)$

48. $f(x) = -3 + 4x$; $f\left(-\frac{1}{2}\right)$

49. **GEOMETRY ▶ CONNECTION** The volume of a cube with side length *s* is given by the function $V(s) = s^3$. Find $V(5)$. Explain what $V(5)$ represents.

50. **GEOMETRY ▶ CONNECTION** The volume of a sphere with radius *r* is given by the function $V(r) = \frac{4}{3}\pi r^3$. Find $V(2)$. Explain what $V(2)$ represents.

51. 🌐 **BOSTON MARATHON** The graph shows the ages and finishing places of the top three competitors in each of the four categories of the 100th Boston Marathon. Is the finishing place of a competitor a function of his or her age? Explain your reasoning.

▶ Source: Boston Athletic Association

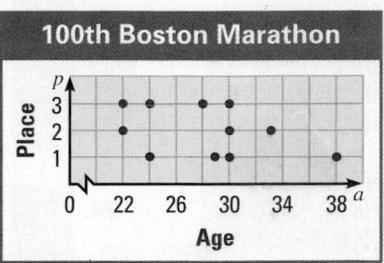

52. 🌐 **HOUSE OF REPRESENTATIVES**
The graph shows the number of
Independent representatives for the
100th–105th Congresses. Is the
number of Independent representatives
a function of the Congress number?
Explain your reasoning.

▶ Source: The Office of the Clerk, United States
House of Representatives

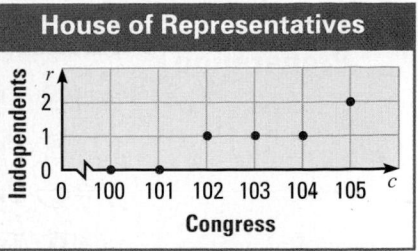

House of Representatives

53. Identify the domain and range of the relation. Then graph the relation.

STATISTICS ▷ CONNECTION In Exercises 53 and 54, use the table which shows the number of shots attempted and the number of shots made by 9 members of the Utah Jazz basketball team in Game 1 of the 1998 NBA Finals. ▶ Source: NBA

Player	Shots attempted, x	Shots made, y
Bryon Russell	12	6
Karl Malone	25	9
Greg Foster	5	1
Jeff Hornacek	10	2
John Stockton	12	9
Howard Eisley	6	4
Chris Morris	6	3
Greg Ostertag	1	1
Shandon Anderson	5	3

53. Identify the domain and range of the relation. Then graph the relation.

54. Is the relation a function? Explain.

🌐 **WATER PRESSURE** In Exercises 55 and 56, use the information below and in the caption to the photo.
Water pressure can be measured in atmospheres, where 1 atmosphere equals 14.7 pounds per square inch. At sea level the water pressure is 1 atmosphere, and it increases by 1 atmosphere for every 33 feet in depth. Therefore, the water pressure p can be modeled as a function of the depth d by this equation:

$$p = \frac{1}{33}d + 1, \quad 0 \le d \le 130$$

55. Identify the domain and range of the function. Then graph the function.

56. What is the water pressure at a depth of 100 feet?

🌐 **CAP SIZES** In Exercises 57 and 58, use the following information.
Your cap size is based on your head circumference (in inches). For head circumferences from $20\frac{7}{8}$ inches to 25 inches, cap size s can be modeled as a function of head circumference c by this equation:

$$s = \frac{c - 1}{3}$$

57. Identify the domain and range of the function. Then graph the function.

58. If you wear a size 7 cap, what is your head circumference?

Test Preparation

QUANTITATIVE COMPARISON In Exercises 59–62, choose the statement that is true about the given quantities.

   Ⓐ The quantity in column A is greater.

   Ⓑ The quantity in column B is greater.

   Ⓒ The two quantities are equal.

   Ⓓ The relationship cannot be determined from the given information.

	Column A	Column B
59.	$f(x) = 3x + 10$ when $x = 0$	$f(x) = 2x - 4$ when $x = 7$
60.	$f(x) = x^2 - 4x - 11$ when $x = 6$	$f(x) = x^2 - 3x + 5$ when $x = 4$
61.	$f(x) = x^3 - 7x + 1$ when $x = -3$	$f(x) = -x^3 - 4$ when $x = 2$
62.	$f(x) = 2x + 8$ when $x = \frac{3}{2}$	$f(x) = -8x + 9$ when $x = -\frac{1}{4}$

★ Challenge

EXTRA CHALLENGE

www.mcdougallittell.com

63. 🌐 **TELEPHONE KEYPADS** For the numbers 2 through 9 on a telephone keypad, draw two mapping diagrams: one mapping numbers onto letters, and the other mapping letters onto numbers. Are both relations functions? Explain.

MIXED REVIEW

EVALUATING EXPRESSIONS Evaluate the expression for the given values of *x* and *y*. (Review 1.2 for 2.2)

64. $\dfrac{y - 6}{x - 9}$ when $x = -3$ and $y = -2$

65. $\dfrac{y - 11}{x - 2}$ when $x = -4$ and $y = 5$

66. $\dfrac{y - (-5)}{x - 3}$ when $x = 2$ and $y = 5$

67. $\dfrac{y - (-1)}{x - (-4)}$ when $x = 6$ and $y = 4$

68. $\dfrac{4 - y}{1 - x}$ when $x = 2$ and $y = 3$

69. $\dfrac{10 - y}{14 - x}$ when $x = 6$ and $y = 8$

SOLVING EQUATIONS Solve the equation. Check your solution. (Review 1.3)

70. $2x + 13 = 31$

71. $-2.4x + 11.8 = 29.8$

72. $x + 17 = 10 - 3x$

73. $\dfrac{5}{2} - 7x = 40 + x$

74. $-\dfrac{1}{3}(x - 15) = -48$

75. $6x + 5 = 0.5(x + 6) - 4$

CHECKING SOLUTIONS Decide whether the given number is a solution of the inequality. (Review 1.6)

76. $3x - 4 < 10$; 5

77. $\dfrac{1}{2}x - 8 \le 0$; 16

78. $10 - x \ge 6$; 2

79. $3 + 2x > -5$; -2

80. $-5 \le x + 8 < 15$; $\dfrac{3}{2}$

81. $x - 2.7 < -1$ or $3x > 6.9$; 2.5

2.2

Slope and Rate of Change

What you should learn

GOAL 1 Find slopes of lines and classify parallel and perpendicular lines.

GOAL 2 Use slope to solve **real-life** problems, such as how to safely adjust a ladder in **Example 5**.

Why you should learn it

▼ To model **real-life** quantities, such as the average rate of change in the temperature of the Grand Canyon in **Ex. 52**.

GOAL 1 FINDING SLOPES OF LINES

The **slope** of a nonvertical line is the ratio of vertical change (the *rise*) to horizontal change (the *run*).

The slope of a line is represented by the letter m. Just as two points determine a line, two points are all that are needed to determine a line's slope. The slope of a line is the same regardless of which two points are used.

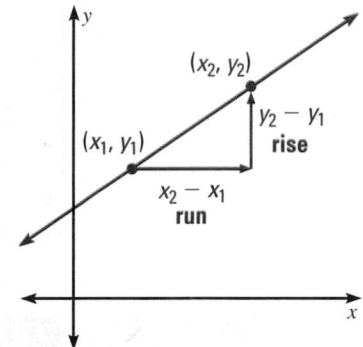

THE SLOPE OF A LINE

The slope of the nonvertical line passing through the points (x_1, y_1) and (x_2, y_2) is:

$$m = \frac{y_2 - y_1}{x_2 - x_1} = \frac{\text{rise}}{\text{run}}$$

When calculating the slope of a line, be careful to subtract the coordinates in the correct order.

EXAMPLE 1 *Finding the Slope of a Line*

Find the slope of the line passing through $(-3, 5)$ and $(2, 1)$.

SOLUTION Let $(x_1, y_1) = (-3, 5)$ and $(x_2, y_2) = (2, 1)$.

$$m = \frac{y_2 - y_1}{x_2 - x_1} \quad \longleftarrow \text{ Rise: Difference of } y\text{-values}$$
$$\longleftarrow \text{ Run: Difference of } x\text{-values}$$

$$= \frac{1 - 5}{2 - (-3)} \quad \text{Substitute values.}$$

$$= \frac{-4}{2 + 3} \quad \text{Simplify.}$$

$$= -\frac{4}{5} \quad \text{Simplify.}$$

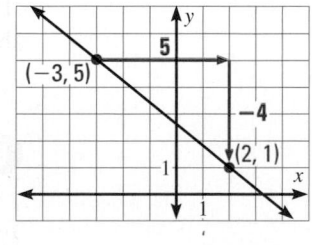

STUDENT HELP

▶ **Look Back**
For help with evaluating expressions, see p. 12.

In Example 1 notice that the line *falls* from left to right and that the slope of the line is *negative*. This suggests one of the important uses of slope—to decide whether y decreases, increases, or is constant as x increases.

- A line with a *positive* slope *rises* from left to right. ($m > 0$)
- A line with a *negative* slope *falls* from left to right. ($m < 0$)
- A line with a slope of *zero* is *horizontal*. ($m = 0$)
- A line with an *undefined* slope is *vertical*. (m is undefined.)

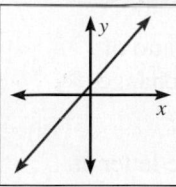 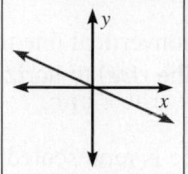 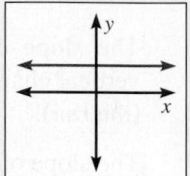 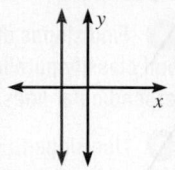

Positive slope   **Negative slope**   **Zero slope**   **Undefined slope**

EXAMPLE 2   *Classifying Lines Using Slope*

Without graphing tell whether the line through the given points *rises*, *falls*, *is horizontal*, or *is vertical*.

   a. $(3, -4), (1, -6)$ **b.** $(2, -1), (2, 5)$

SOLUTION

  a. $m = \dfrac{-6 - (-4)}{1 - 3} = \dfrac{-2}{-2} = 1$ Because $m > 0$, the line rises.

  b. $m = \dfrac{5 - (-1)}{2 - 2} = \dfrac{6}{0}$ Because m is undefined, the line is vertical.

· · · · · · · · · ·

The slope of a line tells you more than whether the line rises, falls, is horizontal, or is vertical. It also tells you the steepness of the line. For two lines with **positive slopes**, the line with the greater slope is steeper. For two lines with **negative slopes**, the line with the slope of greater absolute value is steeper.

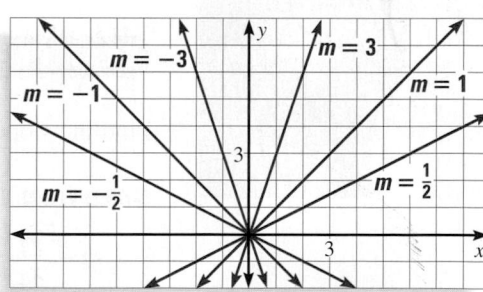

EXAMPLE 3   *Comparing Steepness of Lines*

Tell which line is steeper.

Line 1: through $(2, 3)$ and $(4, 7)$ Line 2: through $(-1, 2)$ and $(4, 5)$

SOLUTION

The slope of line 1 is $m_1 = \dfrac{7 - 3}{4 - 2} = 2$ and the slope of line 2 is $m_2 = \dfrac{5 - 2}{4 - (-1)} = \dfrac{3}{5}$.

▶ Because the lines have positive slopes and $m_1 > m_2$, line 1 is steeper than line 2.

Two lines in a plane are **parallel** if they do not intersect. Two lines in a plane are **perpendicular** if they intersect to form a right angle. Slope can be used to determine whether two different (nonvertical) lines are parallel or perpendicular.

SLOPES OF PARALLEL AND PERPENDICULAR LINES

Consider two different nonvertical lines ℓ_1 and ℓ_2 with slopes m_1 and m_2.

PARALLEL LINES The lines are parallel if and only if they have the same slope.

$$m_1 = m_2$$

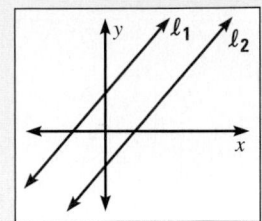

PERPENDICULAR LINES The lines are perpendicular if and only if their slopes are negative reciprocals of each other.

$$m_1 = -\frac{1}{m_2} \text{ or } m_1 m_2 = -1$$

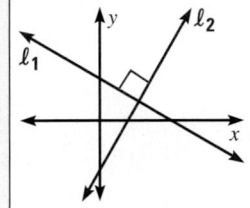

EXAMPLE 4 *Classifying Parallel and Perpendicular Lines*

Tell whether the lines are *parallel*, *perpendicular*, or *neither*.

a. Line 1: through $(-3, 3)$ and $(3, -1)$
   Line 2: through $(-2, -3)$ and $(2, 3)$

b. Line 1: through $(-3, 1)$ and $(3, 4)$
   Line 2: through $(-4, -3)$ and $(4, 1)$

SOLUTION

a. The slopes of the two lines are:

$$m_1 = \frac{-1 - 3}{3 - (-3)} = \frac{-4}{6} = -\frac{2}{3}$$

$$m_2 = \frac{3 - (-3)}{2 - (-2)} = \frac{6}{4} = \frac{3}{2}$$

Because $m_1 m_2 = -\frac{2}{3} \cdot \frac{3}{2} = -1$, m_1 and m_2 are negative reciprocals of each other. Therefore, you can conclude that the lines are perpendicular.

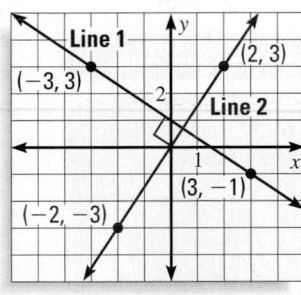

b. The slopes of the two lines are:

$$m_1 = \frac{4 - 1}{3 - (-3)} = \frac{3}{6} = \frac{1}{2}$$

$$m_2 = \frac{1 - (-3)}{4 - (-4)} = \frac{4}{8} = \frac{1}{2}$$

Because $m_1 = m_2$ (and the lines are different), you can conclude that the lines are parallel.

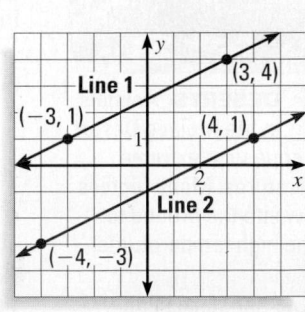

EXAMPLE 5 *Geometrical Use of Slope*

Ladder Safety

In a home repair manual the following ladder safety guideline is given.

Adjust the ladder until the distance from the base of the ladder to the wall is at least one quarter of the height where the top of the ladder hits the wall. For example, a ladder that hits the wall at a height of 12 feet should have its base at least 3 feet from the wall.

a. Find the maximum recommended slope for a ladder.

b. Find the minimum distance a ladder's base should be from a wall if you need the ladder to reach a height of 20 feet.

SOLUTION

a. A ladder that hits the wall at a height of 12 feet with its base about 3 feet from the wall has slope $m = \dfrac{\text{rise}}{\text{run}} = \dfrac{12}{3} = 4$. The maximum recommended slope is 4.

STUDENT HELP

▸ **Skills Review**
For help with solving proportions, see p. 910.

b. Let x represent the minimum distance that the ladder's base should be from the wall for the ladder to safely reach a height of 20 feet.

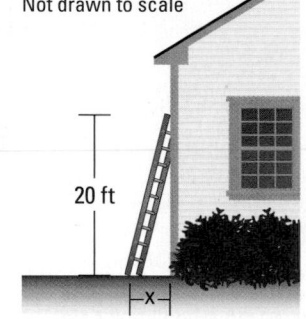

Not drawn to scale

20 ft

$\dfrac{\text{rise}}{\text{run}} = \dfrac{4}{1}$ **Write a proportion.**

$\dfrac{20}{x} = \dfrac{4}{1}$ **The rise is 20 and the run is *x*.**

$20 = 4x$ **Cross multiply.**

$5 = x$ **Solve for *x*.**

▸ The ladder's base should be at least 5 feet from the wall.

· · · · · · · · · ·

In real-life problems slope is often used to describe an *average rate of change*. These rates involve units of measure, such as miles per hour or dollars per year.

EXAMPLE 6 *Slope as a Rate of Change*

FOCUS ON APPLICATIONS

DESERTS In the Mojave Desert in California, temperatures can drop quickly from day to night. Suppose the temperature drops from 100°F at 2 P.M. to 68°F at 5 A.M. Find the average rate of change and use it to determine the temperature at 10 P.M.

SOLUTION

$$\text{Average rate of change} = \frac{\text{Change in temperature}}{\text{Change in time}}$$

$$= \frac{68°F - 100°F}{5\ \text{A.M.} - 2\ \text{P.M.}} = \frac{-32°F}{15\ \text{hours}} \approx -2°F \text{ per hour}$$

Because 10 P.M. is 8 hours after 2 P.M., the temperature changed $8(-2°F) = -16°F$. That means the temperature at 10 P.M. was about $100°F - 16°F = 84°F$.

DESERTS Animals in the Mojave Desert must cope with extreme temperatures. Many reptiles burrow into the ground to escape high temperatures.

APPLICATION LINK
www.mcdougallittell.com

GUIDED PRACTICE

Vocabulary Check ✓

1. Describe what is meant by the slope of a nonvertical line. Explain how your description relates to the definition of slope.

Concept Check ✓

2. What type of line has a slope of zero? What type of line has a slope that is undefined?

3. How can you decide, using slope, whether two nonvertical lines are parallel? whether two nonvertical lines are perpendicular?

Skill Check ✓

Find the slope of the line passing through the given points. Then tell whether the line *rises, falls, is horizontal*, or *is vertical*.

4. $(4, 2), (14, 3)$

5. $(8, 4), (8, 1)$

6. $(-3, 4), (3, -5)$

7. $(-2, 4), (-6, 8)$

8. $(-7, 3), (4, 3)$

9. $(6, 9), (-2, -7)$

Tell which line is steeper.

10. Line 1: through $(-5, 0)$ and $(3, 4)$
    Line 2: through $(0, 4)$ and $(1, 6)$

11. Line 1: through $(2, 4)$ and $(1, 7)$
    Line 2: through $(5, 2)$ and $(3, 12)$

Tell whether the lines are *parallel, perpendicular*, or *neither*.

12. Line 1: through $(1, 5)$ and $(-4, -2)$
    Line 2: through $(3, 0)$ and $(-2, -7)$

13. Line 1: through $(2, -2)$ and $(-2, 7)$
    Line 2: through $(4, -5)$ and $(5, 1)$

14. Line 1: through $(3, 6)$ and $(2, -1)$
    Line 2: through $(-1, 2)$ and $(6, 1)$

15. Line 1: through $(9, 0)$ and $(3, 4)$
    Line 2: through $(-5, 6)$ and $(4, 0)$

16. 🌐 **AVERAGE SPEED** You are driving through Europe. At 9:00 A.M. you are 420 kilometers from Rome. At 3:00 P.M. you are 108 kilometers from Rome. Find your average speed.

PRACTICE AND APPLICATIONS

STUDENT HELP

▶ **Extra Practice**
to help you master
skills is on p. 941.

ESTIMATING SLOPE Estimate the slope of the line.

17.
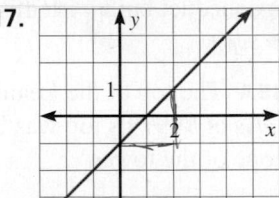

18.
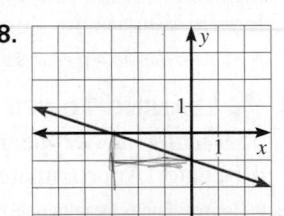

19.
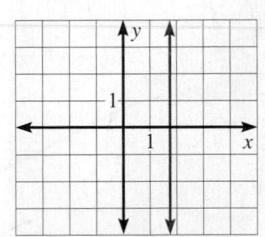

STUDENT HELP

▶ **HOMEWORK HELP**
Example 1: Exs. 17–31
Example 2: Exs. 20–31
Example 3: Exs. 32–35,
           37–40
Example 4: Exs. 41–44
Example 5: Exs. 48–50
Example 6: Exs. 45–47,
           51, 52

FINDING SLOPE Find the slope of the line passing through the given points. Then tell whether the line *rises, falls, is horizontal*, or *is vertical*.

20. $(3, 2), (-4, 3)$

21. $(1, -4), (2, 6)$

22. $(14, -3), (4, 11)$

23. $(-10, -12), (2, -6)$

24. $(-7, 3), (-2, 3)$

25. $(6, -6), (-6, 6)$

26. $(4, 2), (-18, 1)$

27. $(-9, 8), (-9, 2)$

28. $(3, 4), \left(2, -\frac{5}{4}\right)$

29. $\left(0, \frac{7}{2}\right), \left(2, \frac{5}{2}\right)$

30. $\left(\frac{1}{5}, -1\right), \left(\frac{3}{5}, -2\right)$

31. $\left(\frac{4}{3}, -\frac{9}{5}\right), \left(\frac{4}{3}, -\frac{8}{5}\right)$

MATCHING SLOPES AND LINES Match the given slopes with the given lines.

32. $-\dfrac{5}{4}$ 33. 5

34. 2 35. $-\dfrac{2}{3}$

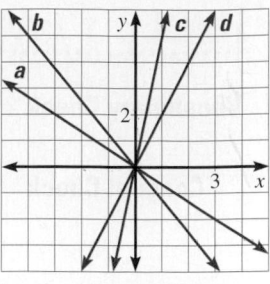

36. **LOGICAL REASONING** Use the formula for slope to verify that a horizontal line has a slope of zero and that a vertical line has an undefined slope.

DETERMINING STEEPNESS Tell which line is steeper.

37. Line 1: through $(-2, 6)$ and $(2, 8)$
    Line 2: through $(0, -4)$ and $(5, -3)$

38. Line 1: through $(4, 1)$ and $(-8, 6)$
    Line 2: through $(-2, 4)$ and $(-1, -8)$

39. Line 1: through $(3, -10)$ and $(2, -10)$
    Line 2: through $(-6, 8)$ and $(2, 12)$

40. Line 1: through $(-5, 6)$ and $(-2, -9)$
    Line 2: through $\left(1, \dfrac{1}{2}\right)$ and $\left(\dfrac{5}{4}, 1\right)$

TYPES OF LINES Tell whether the lines are *parallel*, *perpendicular*, or *neither*.

41. Line 1: through $(-1, 9)$ and $(-6, -6)$
    Line 2: through $(-7, -23)$ and $(0, -2)$

42. Line 1: through $(4, -3)$ and $(-8, 1)$
    Line 2: through $(5, 11)$ and $(8, 20)$

43. Line 1: through $(0, 3)$ and $(0, -7)$
    Line 2: through $(-6, -4)$ and $(12, -4)$

44. Line 1: through $(1, 10)$ and $(5, 15)$
    Line 2: through $\left(\dfrac{3}{2}, \dfrac{3}{2}\right)$ and $(4, 2)$

AVERAGE RATE OF CHANGE Find the average rate of change in *y* for the given *xy*-pairs. State the unit of measure for the average rate of change.

45. $(4, 3)$ and $(8, 27)$ *x* is measured in hours and *y* is measured in dollars

46. $(0, 5)$ and $(3, 17)$ *x* is measured in seconds and *y* is measured in meters

47. $(2, 10)$ and $(4, 16)$ *x* is measured in years and *y* is measured in inches

48. **HISTORY** **CONNECTION** Aqueducts were once used to carry water from rivers using gravity. Water flowing too quickly might damage an aqueduct, but water flowing too slowly might not keep the aqueduct clear. One of the best and most common designs for an aqueduct was to raise it 3 meters for every kilometer in length. What is the slope of an aqueduct built with this design?
▶ Source: *Roman Aqueducts and Water Supply*

49. **LEANING TOWER OF PISA** The top of the Leaning Tower of Pisa is about 55.9 meters above the ground. As of 1997 its top was leaning about 5.2 meters off-center. Approximate the slope of the tower.
▶ Source: Endex Engineering

50. **PITCH OF A ROOF** Building codes require the minimum slope, or pitch, of a roof with asphalt shingles to be such that it rises at least 4 feet for every 12 feet of horizontal distance. A 72 foot wide apartment building has a 12 foot high roof. Does it meet the building code? Explain.

51. **OCEANOGRAPHY** Loihi is the name of an underwater volcano that has formed twenty miles off the coast of Hawaii. The peak of the volcano is currently 3100 feet below sea level. Oceanographers estimate that it will take about 50,000 years before the peak breaks the water. If this holds true, what will be the rate of change in the volcano's height? Explain.
▶ Source: United States Geological Survey

52.  **GRAND CANYON** You are camping at the Grand Canyon. When you pitch your tent at 1:00 P.M. the temperature is 81°F. When you wake up at 6:00 A.M. the temperature is 47°F. What is the average rate of change in the temperature? Estimate the temperature when you went to sleep at 9:00 P.M.

53. CRITICAL THINKING Does it make a difference what two points on a line you choose when finding slope? Does it make a difference which point is (x_1, y_1) and which point is (x_2, y_2) in the formula for slope? Draw a line and calculate its slope using several pairs of points to support your answer.

Test Preparation

54. MULTI-STEP PROBLEM You are in charge of building a wheelchair ramp for a doctor's office. Federal regulations require that the ramp must extend 12 inches for every 1 inch of rise. The ramp needs to rise to a height of 18 inches.

▶ Source: *Uniform Federal Accessibility Standards*

18 in.

STUDENT HELP

▶ **Skills Review**
For help with the Pythagorean theorem, see p. 917.

  a. How far should the end of the ramp be from the base of the building?

  b. Use the Pythagorean theorem to determine the length of the ramp.

  c. Some northern states require that outdoor ramps extend 20 inches for every 1 inch of rise because of the added problems of winter weather. Under this regulation, what should be the length of the ramp?

  d. *Writing* How does changing the slope of the ramp affect the required length of the ramp?

★ Challenge

MISSING COORDINATES Find the value of *k* so that the line through the given points has the given slope. Check your solution.

55. $(5, k)$ and $(k, 7)$, $m = 1$ **56.** $(-3, 2k)$ and $(k, 6)$, $m = 4$

57. $(-2, k)$ and $(k, 4)$, $m = 3$ **58.** $(9, -k)$ and $(3k, -1)$, $m = -\dfrac{1}{3}$

MIXED REVIEW

IDENTIFYING PROPERTIES Identify the property shown. (Review 1.1)

59. $12 + (-12) = 0$ **60.** $(16 + 5) + 10 = 16 + (5 + 10)$

61. $8(2 + 13) = 8 \cdot 2 + 8 \cdot 13$ **62.** $22 \cdot \dfrac{1}{22} = 1$

REWRITING EQUATIONS Solve the equation for *y*. (Review 1.4 for 2.3)

63. $8x + y = 15$ **64.** $-2x - y = 11$

65. $\dfrac{8}{3}x + 2y = 16$ **66.** $-6y + \dfrac{4}{5}x = 10$

SOLVING EQUATIONS Solve the equation. (Review 1.7)

67. $|9 + 2x| = 7$ **68.** $|4 - 6x| = 2$

69. $|-3x + 1| = 4$ **70.** $|0.25x - 9| = 6$

71.  **MIXED NUTS** A 16 ounce can of mixed nuts costs $5.82, but peanuts cost only $.25 per ounce. The can contains 7 ounces of peanuts and 9 ounces of other nuts. What is the cost per ounce of the other nuts? **(Review 1.5 for 2.3)**

Quick Graphs of Linear Equations

GOAL 1 SLOPE-INTERCEPT FORM

In Lesson 2.1 you graphed a linear equation by creating a table of values, plotting the corresponding points, and drawing a line through the points. In this lesson you will study two quicker ways to graph a linear equation.

If the graph of an equation intersects the y-axis at the point $(0, b)$, then the number b is the **y-intercept** of the graph. To find the y-intercept of a line, let $x = 0$ in an equation for the line and solve for y.

> ◐ **ACTIVITY**
> Developing Concepts

Investigating Slope and *y*-intercept

Equation	Points on graph of equation	Slope	y-intercept
$y = 2x + 3$	$(0, ?), (1, ?)$	?	?
$y = -x + 2$	$(0, ?), (1, ?)$	?	?
$y = \frac{1}{2}x - 4$	$(0, ?), (1, ?)$	?	?
$y = -2x$	$(0, ?), (1, ?)$	?	?
$y = 7$	$(0, ?), (1, ?)$	?	?

1 Copy and complete the table.

2 What do you notice about each equation and the slope of the line?

3 What do you notice about each equation and the y-intercept of the line?

The **slope-intercept form** of a linear equation is $y = mx + b$. As you saw in the activity, a line with equation $y = mx + b$ has slope m and y-intercept b.

GRAPHING EQUATIONS IN SLOPE-INTERCEPT FORM

The slope-intercept form of an equation gives you a quick way to graph the equation.

STEP 1 Write the equation in slope-intercept form by solving for y.

STEP 2 Find the y-intercept and use it to plot the point where the line crosses the y-axis.

STEP 3 Find the slope and use it to plot a second point on the line.

STEP 4 Draw a line through the two points.

EXAMPLE 1 **Graphing with the Slope-Intercept Form**

Graph $y = \frac{3}{4}x - 2$.

SOLUTION

1 The equation is already in slope-intercept form.

2 The y-intercept is -2, so plot the point $(0, -2)$ where the line crosses the y-axis.

3 The slope is $\frac{3}{4}$, so plot a second point on the line by moving 4 units to the right and 3 units up. This point is $(4, 1)$.

4 Draw a line through the two points.

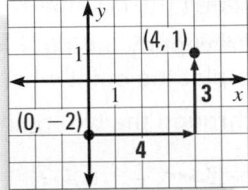 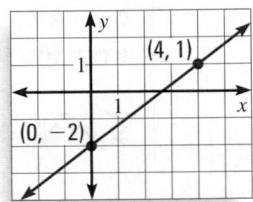

· · · · · · · · · ·

In a real-life context the y-intercept often represents an initial amount and, as you saw in Lesson 2.2, the slope often represents a rate of change.

Buying a Computer

EXAMPLE 2 **Using the Slope-Intercept Form**

You are buying an $1100 computer on layaway. You make a $250 deposit and then make weekly payments according to the equation $a = 850 - 50t$ where a is the amount you owe and t is the number of weeks.

a. What is the original amount you owe on layaway?

b. What is your weekly payment?

c. Graph the model.

SOLUTION

a. First rewrite the equation as $a = -50t + 850$ so that it is in slope-intercept form. Then you can see that the a-intercept is 850. So, the original amount you owe on layaway (the amount when $t = 0$) is $850.

b. From the slope-intercept form you can also see that the slope is $m = -50$. This means that the amount you owe is changing at a rate of $-$50 per week. In other words, your weekly payment is $50.

c. The graph of the model is shown. Notice that the line stops when it reaches the t-axis (at $t = 17$) so the computer is completely paid for at that point.

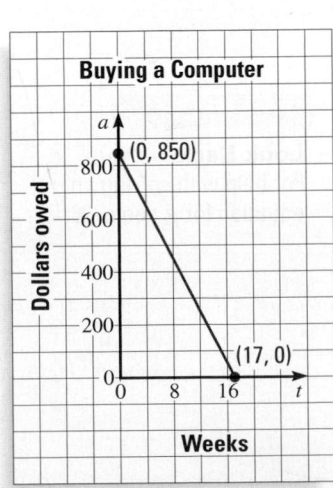

GOAL 2 STANDARD FORM

The **standard form** of a linear equation is $Ax + By = C$ where A and B are not both zero. A quick way to graph an equation in standard form is to plot its intercepts (when they exist). You found the y-intercept of a line in Goal 1. The **x-intercept** of a line is the x-coordinate of the point where the line intersects the x-axis.

GRAPHING EQUATIONS IN STANDARD FORM

The standard form of an equation gives you a quick way to graph the equation:

STEP ❶ Write the equation in standard form.

STEP ❷ Find the x-intercept by letting $y = 0$ and solving for x. Use the x-intercept to plot the point where the line crosses the x-axis.

STEP ❸ Find the y-intercept by letting $x = 0$ and solving for y. Use the y-intercept to plot the point where the line crosses the y-axis.

STEP ❹ Draw a line through the two points.

EXAMPLE 3 *Drawing Quick Graphs*

Graph $2x + 3y = 12$.

SOLUTION

Method 1 USE STANDARD FORM

❶ The equation is already written in standard form.

❷ $2x + 3(\mathbf{0}) = 12$ **Let $y = 0$.**

$x = 6$ **Solve for x.**

The x-intercept is 6, so plot the point $(6, 0)$.

❸ $2(\mathbf{0}) + 3y = 12$ **Let $x = 0$.**

$y = 4$ **Solve for y.**

The y-intercept is 4, so plot the point $(0, 4)$.

❹ Draw a line through the two points.

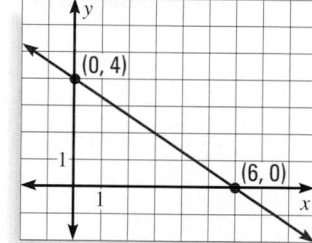

STUDENT HELP

▶ **Look Back**
For help with solving an equation for y, see p. 26.

Method 2 USE SLOPE-INTERCEPT FORM

❶ $2x + 3y = 12$

$3y = -2x + 12$

$y = -\frac{2}{3}x + 4$ **Slope-intercept form**

❷ The y-intercept is 4, so plot the point $(0, 4)$.

❸ The slope is $-\frac{2}{3}$, so plot a second point by moving 3 units to the right and 2 units down. This point is $(3, 2)$.

❹ Draw a line through the two points.

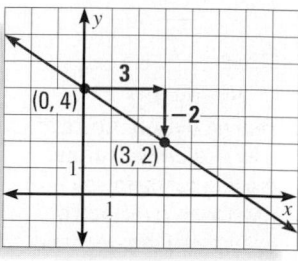

The equation of a vertical line cannot be written in slope-intercept form because the slope of a vertical line is not defined. Every linear equation, however, can be written in standard form—even the equation of a vertical line.

HORIZONTAL AND VERTICAL LINES

HORIZONTAL LINES   The graph of $y = c$ is a horizontal line through $(0, c)$.

VERTICAL LINES   The graph of $x = c$ is a vertical line through $(c, 0)$.

EXAMPLE 4   *Graphing Horizontal and Vertical Lines*

Graph (**a**) $y = 3$ and (**b**) $x = -2$.

SOLUTION

a. The graph of $y = 3$ is a horizontal line that passes through the point $(0, 3)$. Notice that every point on the line has a y-coordinate of 3.

b. The graph of $x = -2$ is a vertical line that passes through the point $(-2, 0)$. Notice that every point on the line has an x-coordinate of -2.

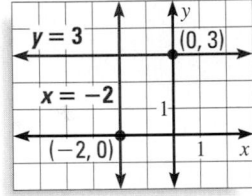

EXAMPLE 5   *Using the Standard Form*

Fundraising

The school band is selling sweatshirts and T-shirts to raise money. The goal is to raise \$1200. Sweatshirts sell for a profit of \$2.50 each and T-shirts for \$1.50 each. Describe numbers of sweatshirts and T-shirts the band can sell to reach the goal.

SOLUTION

First write a model for the problem.

PROBLEM SOLVING STRATEGY

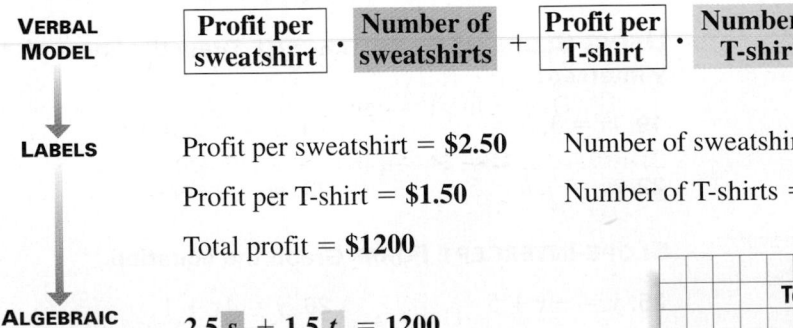

| **VERBAL MODEL** | $\boxed{\text{Profit per sweatshirt}} \cdot \boxed{\text{Number of sweatshirts}} + \boxed{\text{Profit per T-shirt}} \cdot \boxed{\text{Number of T-shirts}} = \boxed{\text{Total Profit}}$ |

LABELS   Profit per sweatshirt = **\$2.50**   Number of sweatshirts = **s**

Profit per T-shirt = **\$1.50**   Number of T-shirts = **t**

Total profit = **\$1200**

ALGEBRAIC MODEL   **2.5 s** + **1.5 t** = **1200**

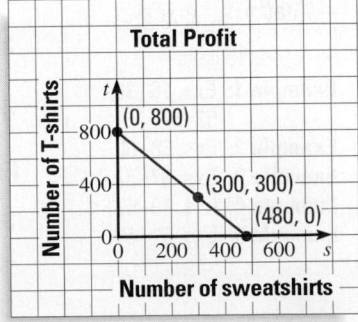

STUDENT HELP

➤ **Study Tip**
Finding the intercepts of a line before you draw the line can help you determine reasonable scales for the x-axis and the y-axis.

The graph of $2.5s + 1.5t = 1200$ is a line that intersects the s-axis at $(480, 0)$ and intersects the t-axis at $(0, 800)$. Points with integer coordinates on the line segment joining $(480, 0)$ and $(0, 800)$ represent ways to reach the goal. For instance, the band can sell 300 sweatshirts and 300 T-shirts.

GUIDED PRACTICE

Vocabulary Check ✓

1. What are the slope-intercept and standard forms of a linear equation?

Concept Check ✓

2. Which of the two quick-graph techniques discussed in the lesson would you use to graph $y = -2x + 4$? Explain.

3. Which of the two quick-graph techniques discussed in the lesson would you use to graph $3x + 4y = 24$? Explain.

Skill Check ✓

Find the slope and *y*-intercept of the line.

4. $y = x + 10$

5. $y = -2x - 7$

6. $2x - 3y = 18$

Find the intercepts of the line.

7. $x - y = 11$

8. $5x - 2y = 20$

9. $y = 5x - 15$

Graph the equation.

10. $y = 2x + 1$

11. $y = \frac{1}{3}x - 4$

12. $y = 7$

13. $x = -5$

14. $2x - 6y = 6$

15. $5x + 3y = -15$

PRACTICE AND APPLICATIONS

STUDENT HELP

→ **Extra Practice**
to help you master
skills is on p. 941.

MATCHING GRAPHS Match the equation with its graph.

16. $y = -5x + 10$

17. $y = -\frac{1}{2}x - 5$

18. $y = 4x - 12$

A.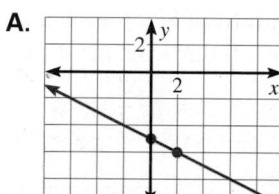

B.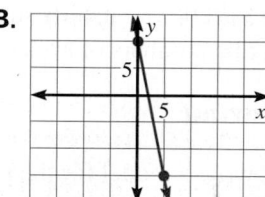

C.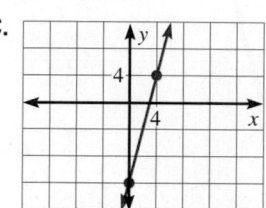

USING SLOPE AND *y*-INTERCEPT Draw the line with the given slope and *y*-intercept.

19. $m = 3, b = -2$

20. $m = -2, b = 0$

21. $m = 1, b = 1$

22. $m = \frac{1}{2}, b = 5$

23. $m = 0, b = -7$

24. $m = -\frac{3}{7}, b = 14$

SLOPE-INTERCEPT FORM Graph the equation.

25. $y = -x + 5$

26. $y = 4x + 1$

27. $y = \frac{4}{5}x - 1$

28. $y = 2x - 3$

29. $y = -\frac{5}{2}x - 3$

30. $y = 5x - \frac{5}{2}$

STUDENT HELP

→ **HOMEWORK HELP**
Example 1: Exs. 16–36,
  52–57
Example 2: Exs. 58–60
Example 3: Exs. 37–57
Example 4: Exs. 49–57
Example 5: Exs. 61–63

FINDING SLOPE AND *y*-INTERCEPT Find the slope and *y*-intercept of the line.

31. $y = 6x + 10$

32. $y = -9x$

33. $y = 100$

34. $2x + y = 14$

35. $8x - 2y = 14$

36. $x + 10y = 7$

MATCHING GRAPHS Match the equation with its graph.

37. $x - 4y = -8$ **38.** $3x + 6y = -9$ **39.** $2x - 3y = -12$

A. 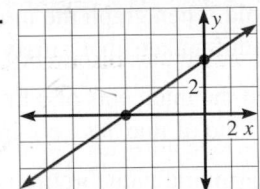 **B.** 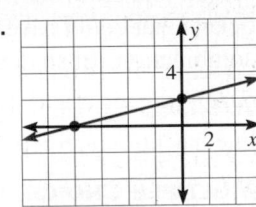 **C.**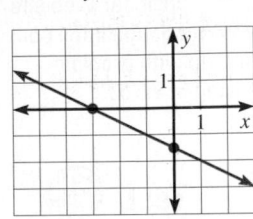

USING INTERCEPTS Draw the line with the given intercepts.

40. x-intercept: 3
y-intercept: 5

41. x-intercept: 2
y-intercept: -6

42. x-intercept: -4
y-intercept: $-\frac{1}{2}$

STANDARD FORM Graph the equation. Label any intercepts.

43. $2x + y = 8$ **44.** $x + 2y = 8$ **45.** $3x + 4y = -10$

46. $3x - y = 3$ **47.** $5x - 6y = -2$ **48.** $3x + 0.2y = 2$

49. $y = 6$ **50.** $x = -5$ **51.** $y = -\frac{1}{2}$

CHOOSE A METHOD Graph the equation using any method.

52. $y = 3x + 7$ **53.** $x = -10$ **54.** $2x - 7y = 14$

55. $y = \frac{3}{4}$ **56.** $5x + 10y = 30$ **57.** $y = \frac{5}{2}x - 2$

58. ⊕ **IRS** The amount a (in billions of dollars) of annual taxes collected by the Internal Revenue Service can be modeled by $a = 57.1t + 488$ where t represents the number of years since 1980. Graph the equation.

▶ Source: *Statistical Abstract of the United States*

59. ⊕ **PLACING AN AD** The cost C (in dollars) of placing a color advertisement in a newspaper can be modeled by $C = 7n + 20$ where n is the number of lines in the ad. Graph the equation. What do the slope and C-intercept represent?

60. ⊕ **RAINFORESTS** The area A (in millions of hectares) of land covered by rainforests can be modeled by $A = 718.3 - 4.6t$ where t represents the number of years since 1990. Graph the equation. What are three predicted future areas of land covered by rainforests? ▶ Source: Food and Agriculture Organization

61. ⊕ **CAR WASH** A car wash charges $8 per wash and $12 per wash-and-wax. After a busy day sales totaled $3464. Use the verbal model to write an equation that shows the different numbers of washes and wash-and-waxes that could have been done. Then graph the equation.

Price per wash	·	Number of washes	+	Price per wash-and-wax	·	Number of wash-and-waxes	=	Total sales

62. ⊕ **SAILING** The owner of a sailboat takes passengers to an island 5 miles away to go snorkeling. A sailboat averages about 9 miles per hour when using its sails and about 14 miles per hour when using its motor. Write an equation that shows the numbers of *minutes* the sailboat can use its sails and its motor to get to the island. Then graph the equation.

HOMEWORK HELP
Visit our Web site
www.mcdougallittell.com
for help with problem
solving in Ex. 63.

63.  **TICKET PRICES** Student tickets at a high school basketball game cost $2.50 each. Adult tickets cost $6.00 each. The ticket sales at the first game of the season totaled $7000. Write a model that shows the numbers of student and adult tickets that could have been sold. Then graph the model and determine three combinations of student and adult tickets that satisfy the model.

64. *Writing* Explain how to find the intercepts of a line if they exist. What kind of line has no x-intercept? What kind of line has no y-intercept?

Test Preparation

65. **MULTIPLE CHOICE** You have an individual retirement account (IRA). The amount a you have deposited into your account after t years can be modeled by $a = 4500 + 2000t$. How much money do you put into your IRA every year?

Ⓐ $1000   Ⓑ $2000   Ⓒ $2500   Ⓓ $4500   Ⓔ $6500

66. **MULTIPLE CHOICE** What is the slope-intercept form of $4x - 6y = 18$?

Ⓐ $x = \frac{3}{2}y + \frac{9}{2}$ Ⓑ $y = \frac{2}{3}x - 3$ Ⓒ $-y = \frac{4}{6}x + 3$

Ⓓ $6y = -4x + 18$ Ⓔ $4x = 6y + 18$

★ **Challenge**

67. **CALCULATING SLOPE** For the line $y = 7x + 6$, show that the slope is 7 regardless of the points (x_1, y_1) and (x_2, y_2) you use to calculate the slope. (*Hint:* Substitute x_1 and x_2 into the equation to obtain expressions for y_1 and y_2.)

MIXED REVIEW

SOLVING INEQUALITIES Solve the inequality. Then graph your solution. (Review 1.6)

68. $9 + x \leq 21$

69. $-\frac{2}{3}x + 3 < 11$

70. $2x - 11 > 34 - x$

71. $64 - 3x \geq 19 - 2x$

72. $-5 < 2x - 0.5 \leq 23$

73. $x + 12 \leq 5$ or $3x - 21 \geq 0$

EVALUATING FUNCTIONS Evaluate the function for the given value of x. (Review 2.1)

74. $f(x) = \frac{1}{2}x - 13; f(8)$

75. $f(x) = x^2 - 3x + 2; f(5)$

76. $f(x) = -x^3 + 8x^2 + 3; f(-7)$

77. $f(x) = 10 - 2x; f(1)$

78. $f(x) = |x + 17|; f(-5)$

79. $f(x) = 12x^2 - 19; f\left(\frac{1}{2}\right)$

FINDING SLOPE Find the slope of the line passing through the given points. (Review 2.2 for 2.4)

80. $(3, 2), (7, 2)$

81. $(16, -3), (2, 9)$

82. $(-12, -9), (1, -8)$

83. $(-1, -1), (-1, -5)$

84. $(5, -2), (-3, 2)$

85. $(-4, 7), (2, -5)$

86. **READING SPEED** You can read a novel at a rate of 2 pages per minute. Write a model that shows the number of pages you can read in h *hours*. Then find how long it will take you to read a 1048 page novel. (**Review 1.5 for 2.4**)

Identify the domain and range. Then tell whether the relation is a function. (Lesson 2.1)

1.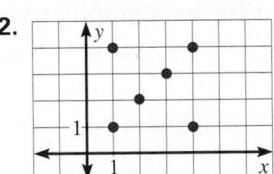

2.

3.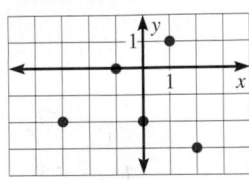

Evaluate the function for the given value of *x*. (Lesson 2.1)

4. $f(x) = -2x - 13; f(4)$

5. $f(x) = 5x^2 - x + 9; f(-5)$

Tell whether the lines are *parallel, perpendicular,* or *neither*. (Lesson 2.2)

6. Line 1: through $(2, 10)$ and $(1, 5)$
Line 2: through $(3, -7)$ and $(8, -8)$

7. Line 1: through $(4, 5)$ and $(9, -2)$
Line 2: through $(6, -6)$ and $(-2, -1)$

Graph the equation. (Lesson 2.3)

8. $y = 3x + 5$

9. $2x - 3y = 10$

10. $y = -11$

11. 🌐 **BICYCLING** There is an annual seven day bicycle ride across Iowa that covers about 468 miles. If a participant rides each day from 8:00 A.M. to 5:00 P.M., stopping only 1 hour for lunch, what is the rider's average speed in miles per hour? (Lesson 2.2)

MATH & History

Transatlantic Voyages

🌐 **APPLICATION LINK**
www.mcdougallittell.com

THEN

AT 2:00 P.M. ON APRIL 11, 1912, the *Titanic* left Cobh, Ireland, on her maiden voyage to New York City. At 11:40 P.M. on April 14, the *Titanic* struck an iceberg and sank, having covered only about 2100 miles of the approximately 3400 mile trip.

1. What was the total length of the *Titanic*'s maiden voyage in hours?

2. What was the *Titanic*'s average speed in miles per hour?

3. Write an equation relating the *Titanic*'s distance from New York City and the number of hours traveled. Identify the domain and range.

4. Graph the equation from Exercise 3.

NOW

TODAY, ocean liners still cross the Atlantic Ocean. The *Queen Elizabeth 2*, or *QE2*, is one of the fastest with a top speed of 32.5 knots (about 37 miles per hour).

Titanic's maiden voyage

1912

1927
Charles Lindbergh makes the first solo transatlantic flight.

QE2's maiden voyage

1969

Benoit Lecomte swims across the Atlantic.

1998

● ACTIVITY 2.3

Using Technology

Graphing Equations

You can use a graphing calculator to graph equations of the form $y = f(x)$.

▶ **EXAMPLE**

Use a graphing calculator to graph the equation $x + 6y = 30$.

▶ **SOLUTION**

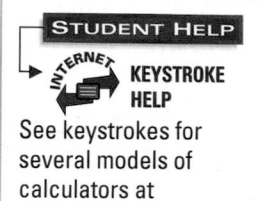
① First solve the equation for y so that it can be entered into the calculator.

$$x + 6y = 30$$
$$6y = -x + 30$$
$$y = -\frac{1}{6}x + 5$$

② When you have fractional coefficients, you must use parentheses. So, enter the equation as $y = -(1/6)x + 5$.

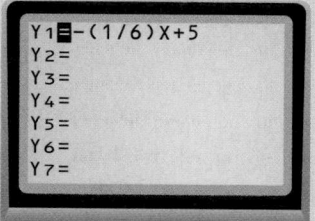

③ Finally, set a viewing window for the graph by entering the least and greatest x- and y-values and the x- and y-scales. The *standard viewing window* is $-10 \le x \le 10$ and $-10 \le y \le 10$, both with a scale of 1. The viewing window you choose should show all of the important features of the graph, such as the intercepts. The settings for the viewing window and the corresponding graph of the equation $y = -\frac{1}{6}x + 5$ are shown.

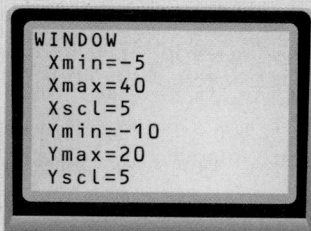

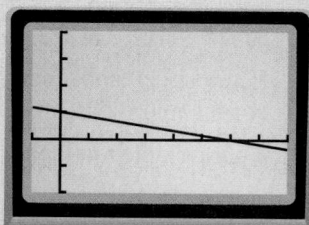

▶ **EXERCISES**

Use a graphing calculator to graph the equation in the standard viewing window.

1. $y + 11 = 16 - 3x$ **2.** $2x - y = 6$ **3.** $x - 3y = -2$

Use a graphing calculator to graph the equation in the indicated viewing window.

4. $17 - 2x = -y$ $\text{Xmin} = -2, \text{Xmax} = 12, \text{Xscl} = 2,$
                   $\text{Ymin} = -20, \text{Ymax} = 2, \text{Yscl} = 5$

5. $y + 4 = 2x + 1$ $\text{Xmin} = -2, \text{Xmax} = 5, \text{Xscl} = 1,$
                    $\text{Ymin} = -4, \text{Ymax} = 1, \text{Yscl} = 1$

Use a graphing calculator to graph the equation. Choose a viewing window that shows the x- and y-intercepts.

6. $7x = 3y + 20$ **7.** $1.54x + 2.1y = 63.4$ **8.** $\frac{7}{10}x = 5y - 104$

2.4 Writing Equations of Lines

What you should learn

GOAL 1 Write linear equations.

GOAL 2 Write direct variation equations, as applied in **Example 7**.

Why you should learn it

▼ To model **real-life** quantities, such as the number of calories you burn while dancing in **Ex. 64.**

GOAL 1 WRITING LINEAR EQUATIONS

In Lesson 2.3 you learned to find the slope and *y*-intercept of a line whose equation is given. In this lesson you will study the reverse process. That is, you will learn to write an equation of a line using one of the following: the slope and *y*-intercept of the line, the slope and a point on the line, or two points on the line.

CONCEPT SUMMARY **WRITING AN EQUATION OF A LINE**

SLOPE-INTERCEPT FORM Given the slope *m* and the *y*-intercept *b*, use this equation:

$$y = mx + b$$

POINT-SLOPE FORM Given the slope *m* and a point (x_1, y_1), use this equation:

$$y - y_1 = m(x - x_1)$$

TWO POINTS Given two points (x_1, y_1) and (x_2, y_2), use the formula

$$m = \frac{y_2 - y_1}{x_2 - x_1}$$

to find the slope *m*. Then use the point-slope form with this slope and either of the given points to write an equation of the line.

Every nonvertical line has only one slope and one *y*-intercept, so the slope-intercept form is unique. The point-slope form, however, depends on the point that is used. Therefore, in this book equations of lines will be simplified to slope-intercept form so a unique solution may be given.

EXAMPLE 1 *Writing an Equation Given the Slope and the y-intercept*

Write an equation of the line shown.

SOLUTION

From the graph you can see that the slope is $m = \frac{3}{2}$. You can also see that the line intersects the *y*-axis at the point $(0, -1)$, so the *y*-intercept is $b = -1$.

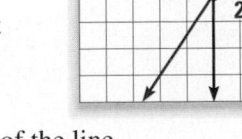

Because you know the slope and the *y*-intercept, you should use the slope-intercept form to write an equation of the line.

$y = mx + b$ **Use slope-intercept form.**

$y = \frac{3}{2}x - 1$ **Substitute $\frac{3}{2}$ for *m* and -1 for *b*.**

▶ An equation of the line is $y = \frac{3}{2}x - 1$.

EXAMPLE 2 **Writing an Equation Given the Slope and a Point**

Write an equation of the line that passes through $(2, 3)$ and has a slope of $-\frac{1}{2}$.

SOLUTION

Because you know the slope and a point on the line, you should use the point-slope form to write an equation of the line. Let $(x_1, y_1) = (2, 3)$ and $m = -\frac{1}{2}$.

$$y - y_1 = m(x - x_1) \qquad \text{Use point-slope form.}$$

$$y - 3 = -\frac{1}{2}(x - 2) \qquad \text{Substitute for } m, x_1, \text{ and } y_1.$$

Once you have used the point-slope form to find an equation, you can simplify the result to the slope-intercept form.

$$y - 3 = -\frac{1}{2}(x - 2) \qquad \text{Write point-slope form.}$$

$$y - 3 = -\frac{1}{2}x + 1 \qquad \text{Distributive property}$$

$$y = -\frac{1}{2}x + 4 \qquad \text{Write in slope-intercept form.}$$

✓ **CHECK** You can check the result graphically. Draw the line that passes through the point $(2, 3)$ with a slope of $-\frac{1}{2}$. Notice that the line has a y-intercept of 4, which agrees with the slope-intercept form found above.

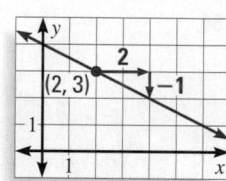

EXAMPLE 3 **Writing Equations of Perpendicular and Parallel Lines**

Write an equation of the line that passes through $(3, 2)$ and is **(a)** perpendicular and **(b)** parallel to the line $y = -3x + 2$.

SOLUTION

a. The given line has a slope of $m_1 = -3$. So, a line that is perpendicular to this line must have a slope of $m_2 = -\frac{1}{m_1} = \frac{1}{3}$. Because you know the slope and a point on the line, use the point-slope form with $(x_1, y_1) = (3, 2)$ to find an equation of the line.

$$y - y_1 = m_2(x - x_1) \qquad \text{Use point-slope form.}$$

$$y - 2 = \frac{1}{3}(x - 3) \qquad \text{Substitute for } m_2, x_1, \text{ and } y_1.$$

$$y - 2 = \frac{1}{3}x - 1 \qquad \text{Distributive property}$$

$$y = \frac{1}{3}x + 1 \qquad \text{Write in slope-intercept form.}$$

b. For a parallel line use $m_2 = m_1 = -3$ and $(x_1, y_1) = (3, 2)$.

$$y - y_1 = m_2(x - x_1) \qquad \text{Use point-slope form.}$$

$$y - 2 = -3(x - 3) \qquad \text{Substitute for } m_2, x_1, \text{ and } y_1.$$

$$y - 2 = -3x + 9 \qquad \text{Distributive property}$$

$$y = -3x + 11 \qquad \text{Write in slope-intercept form.}$$

EXAMPLE 4 *Writing an Equation Given Two Points*

Write an equation of the line that passes through $(-2, -1)$ and $(3, 4)$.

SOLUTION

The line passes through $(x_1, y_1) = (-2, -1)$ and $(x_2, y_2) = (3, 4)$, so its slope is:

$$m = \frac{y_2 - y_1}{x_2 - x_1} = \frac{4 - (-1)}{3 - (-2)} = \frac{5}{5} = 1$$

Because you know the slope and a point on the line, use the point-slope form to find an equation of the line.

$y - y_1 = m(x - x_1)$	Use point-slope form.
$y - (-1) = 1[x - (-2)]$	Substitute for m, x_1, and y_1.
$y + 1 = x + 2$	Simplify.
$y = x + 1$	Write in slope-intercept form.

EXAMPLE 5 *Writing and Using a Linear Model*

POLITICS In 1970 there were 160 African-American women in elected public office in the United States. By 1993 the number had increased to 2332. Write a linear model for the number of African-American women who held elected public office at any given time between 1970 and 1993. Then use the model to predict the number of African-American women who will hold elected public office in 2010.

 DATA UPDATE of Joint Center for Political and Economic Studies data at www.mcdougallittell.com

SOLUTION

The average rate of change in officeholders is $m = \dfrac{2332 - 160}{1993 - 1970} \approx 94.4$.

You can use the average rate of change as the slope in your linear model.

PROBLEM SOLVING STRATEGY

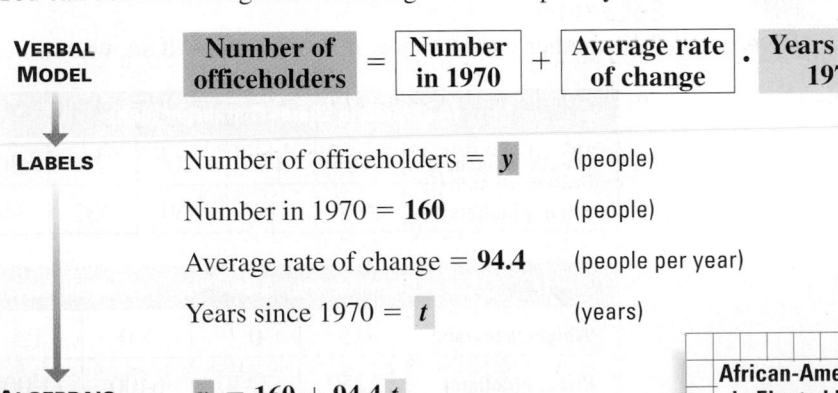

| VERBAL MODEL | Number of officeholders | = | Number in 1970 | + | Average rate of change | · | Years since 1970 |

LABELS

Number of officeholders = y	(people)	
Number in 1970 = **160**	(people)	
Average rate of change = **94.4**	(people per year)	
Years since 1970 = t	(years)	

ALGEBRAIC MODEL

$$y = 160 + 94.4\,t$$

In 2010, which is 40 years since 1970, you can predict that there will be

$$y = 160 + 94.4(\mathbf{40}) \approx 3936$$

African-American women in elected public office. You can graph the model to check your prediction visually.

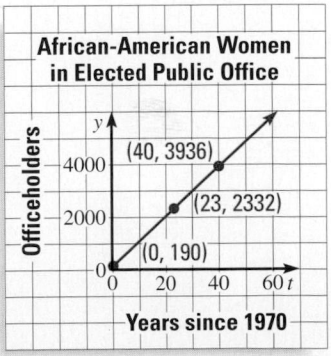

African-American Women in Elected Public Office

(40, 3936)
(23, 2332)
(0, 190)

Officeholders

Years since 1970

GOAL 2 WRITING DIRECT VARIATION EQUATIONS

Two variables x and y show **direct variation** provided $y = kx$ and $k \neq 0$. The nonzero constant k is called the **constant of variation**, and y is said to *vary directly* with x. The graph of $y = kx$ is a line through the origin.

EXAMPLE 6 *Writing and Using a Direct Variation Equation*

The variables x and y vary directly, and $y = 12$ when $x = 4$.

a. Write and graph an equation relating x and y.　　**b.** Find y when $x = 5$.

SOLUTION

a. Use the given values of x and y to find the constant of variation.

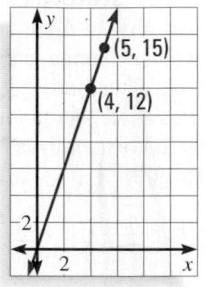

$y = kx$	**Write direct variation equation.**
$12 = k(4)$	**Substitute 12 for *y* and 4 for *x*.**
$3 = k$	**Solve for *k*.**

The direct variation equation is $y = 3x$. The graph of $y = 3x$ is shown.

b. When $x = 5$, the value of y is $y = 3(5) = 15$.

· · · · · · · · · ·

The equation for direct variation can be rewritten as $\dfrac{y}{x} = k$. This tells you that a set of data pairs (x, y) shows direct variation if the quotient of y and x is constant.

REAL LIFE

Jewelry

EXAMPLE 7 *Identifying Direct Variation*

Tell whether the data show direct variation. If so, write an equation relating x and y.

a.

14-karat Gold Chains (1 gram per inch)					
Length, *x* (inches)	16	18	20	24	30
Price, *y* (dollars)	288	324	360	432	540

b.

Loose Diamonds (round, colorless, very small flaws)					
Weight, *x* (carats)	0.5	0.7	1.0	1.5	2.0
Price, *y* (dollars)	2250	3430	6400	11,000	20,400

SOLUTION For each data set, check whether the quotient of y and x is constant.

a. For the 14-karat gold chains, $\dfrac{288}{16} = \dfrac{324}{18} = \dfrac{360}{20} = \dfrac{432}{24} = \dfrac{540}{30} = 18$. The data do show direct variation, and the direct variation equation is $y = 18x$.

b. For the loose diamonds, $\dfrac{2250}{0.5} = 4500$, but $\dfrac{3430}{0.7} = 4900$. The data do not show direct variation.

GUIDED PRACTICE

Vocabulary Check ✓

1. Define the constant of variation for two variables x and y that vary directly.

Concept Check ✓

2. How can you find an equation of a line given the slope and the y-intercept of the line? given the slope and a point on the line? given two points on the line?

3. Give a real-life example of two quantities that vary directly.

Skill Check ✓

Write an equation of the line that has the given properties.

4. slope: $\frac{2}{5}$, y-intercept: 2

5. slope: 2, passes through $(0, -4)$

6. slope: -3, passes through $(5, 2)$

7. slope: $-\frac{3}{4}$, passes through $(-7, 0)$

8. passes through $(4, 8)$ and $(1, 2)$

9. passes through $(0, 2)$ and $(-5, 0)$

10. Write an equation of the line that passes through $(1, -6)$ and is perpendicular to the line $y = 3x + 7$.

11. Write an equation of the line that passes through $(3, 9)$ and is parallel to the line $y = 5x - 15$.

12. 🌍 **LAW OF SUPPLY** The *law of supply* states that the quantity supplied of an item varies directly with the price of that item. Suppose that for $4 per tape 5 million cassette tapes will be supplied. Write an equation that relates the number c (in millions) of cassette tapes supplied to the price p (in dollars) of the tapes. Then determine how many cassette tapes will be supplied for $5 per tape.

PRACTICE AND APPLICATIONS

STUDENT HELP

➤ **Extra Practice**
to help you master
skills is on p. 942.

SLOPE-INTERCEPT FORM Write an equation of the line that has the given slope and y-intercept.

13. $m = 5, b = -3$

14. $m = -3, b = -4$

15. $m = -4, b = 0$

16. $m = 0, b = 4$

17. $m = \frac{3}{5}, b = 6$

18. $m = -\frac{3}{4}, b = \frac{7}{3}$

POINT-SLOPE FORM Write an equation of the line that passes through the given point and has the given slope.

19. $(0, 4), m = 2$

20. $(1, 0), m = 3$

21. $(-6, 5), m = 0$

22. $(9, 3), m = -\frac{2}{3}$

23. $(3, -2), m = -\frac{4}{3}$

24. $(7, -4), m = \frac{2}{5}$

STUDENT HELP

➤ **HOMEWORK HELP**
Example 1: Exs. 13–18
Example 2: Exs. 19–24
Example 3: Exs. 25–28
Example 4: Exs. 29–40
Example 5: Exs. 59–62
Example 6: Exs. 43–54
Example 7: Exs. 55–58,
 63–68

25. Write an equation of the line that passes through $(1, -1)$ and is perpendicular to the line $y = -\frac{1}{2}x + 6$.

26. Write an equation of the line that passes through $(6, -10)$ and is perpendicular to the line that passes through $(4, -6)$ and $(3, -4)$.

27. Write an equation of the line that passes through $(2, -7)$ and is parallel to the line $x = 5$.

28. Write an equation of the line that passes through $(4, 6)$ and is parallel to the line that passes through $(6, -6)$ and $(10, -4)$.

VISUAL THINKING Write an equation of the line.

29.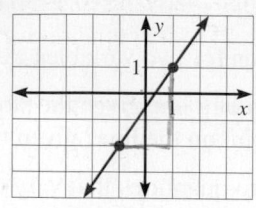

30.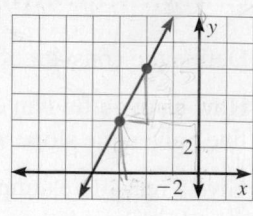

31.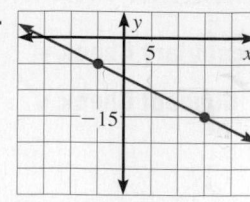

32.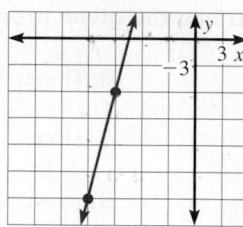

33.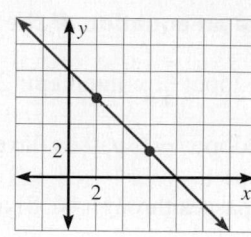

34.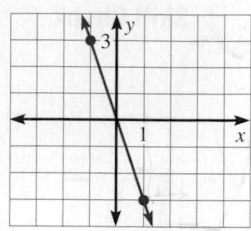

WRITING EQUATIONS Write an equation of the line that passes through the given points.

35. $(8, 5), (11, 14)$ **36.** $(-5, 9), (-4, 7)$ **37.** $(-8, 8), (0, 1)$

38. $(2, 0), (4, -6)$ **39.** $(-20, -10), (5, 15)$ **40.** $(-2, 0), (0, 6)$

41. LOGICAL REASONING Redo Example 2 by substituting the given point and slope into $y = mx + b$. Then solve for b to write an equation of the line. Explain why using this method does not change the equation of the line.

42. LOGICAL REASONING Redo Example 4 by substituting $(3, 4)$ for (x_1, y_1) into $y - y_1 = m(x - x_1)$. Then rewrite the equation in slope-intercept form. Explain why using the point $(3, 4)$ does not change the equation of the line.

RELATING VARIABLES The variables x and y vary directly. Write an equation that relates the variables. Then find y when $x = 8$.

43. $x = 2, y = 7$ **44.** $x = -6, y = 15$ **45.** $x = -3, y = 9$

46. $x = 24, y = 4$ **47.** $x = 1, y = \frac{1}{2}$ **48.** $x = 0.8, y = 1.6$

RELATING VARIABLES The variables x and y vary directly. Write an equation that relates the variables. Then find x when $y = -5$.

49. $x = 6, y = 3$ **50.** $x = 9, y = 15$ **51.** $x = -5, y = -1$

52. $x = 100, y = 2$ **53.** $x = \frac{5}{2}, y = \frac{5}{4}$ **54.** $x = -0.3, y = 2.2$

IDENTIFYING DIRECT VARIATION Tell whether the data show direct variation. If so, write an equation relating x and y.

55.

x	2	4	6	8	10
y	1	2	3	4	5

56.

x	1	2	3	4	5
y	5	4	3	2	1

57.

x	3	6	9	12	15
y	-3	-6	-9	-12	-15

58.

x	-5	-4	-3	-2	-1
y	10	8	6	4	2

59. 🌎 **POPULATION OF OREGON** From 1990 to 1996 the population of Oregon increased by about 60,300 people per year. In 1996 the population was about 3,204,000. Write a linear model for the population P of Oregon from 1990 to 1996. Let t represent the number of years since 1990. Then estimate the population of Oregon in 2014. ▶ Source: *Statistical Abstract of the United States*

60. 🌎 **AIRFARE** In 1998 an airline offered a special airfare of $201 to fly from Cincinnati to Washington, D.C., a distance of 386 miles. Special airfares offered for longer flights increased by about $.138 per mile. Write a linear model for the special airfares a based on the total number of miles t of the flight. Estimate the airfare offered for a flight from Boston to Sacramento, a distance of 2629 miles.

61. 🌎 **BOOKSTORE SALES** In 1990 retail sales at bookstores were about $7.4 billion. In 1997 retail sales at bookstores were about $11.8 billion. Write a linear model for retail sales s (in billions of dollars) at bookstores from 1990 through 1997. Let t represent the number of years since 1990. Then estimate the retail sales at bookstores in 2012. ▶ Source: American Booksellers Association

62. **SCIENCE ▸ CONNECTION** The velocity of sound in dry air increases as the temperature increases. At 40°C sound travels at a rate of about 355 meters per second. At 49°C it travels at a rate of about 360 meters per second. Write a linear model for the velocity v (in meters per second) of sound based on the temperature T (in degrees Celsius). Then estimate the velocity of sound at 60°C.
▶ Source: *CRC Handbook of Chemistry and Physics*

63. 🌎 **BREAKING WAVES** The height h (in feet) at which a wave breaks varies directly with the wave length l (in feet), which is the distance from the crest of one wave to the crest of the next. A wave that breaks at a height of 4 feet has a wave length of 28 feet. Write a linear model that gives h as a function of l. Then estimate the wave length of a wave that breaks at a height of 5.5 feet.
▶ Source: Rhode Island Sea Grant

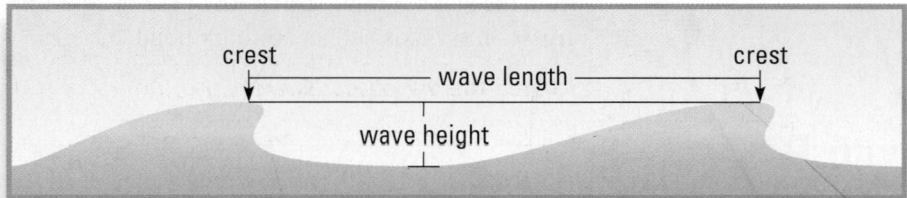

64. 🌎 **DANCING** The number C of calories a person burns performing an activity varies directly with the time t (in minutes) the person spends performing the activity. A 160 pound person can burn 73 Calories by dancing for 20 minutes. Write a linear model that gives C as a function of t. Then estimate how long a 160 pound person should dance to burn 438 Calories. ▶ Source: *Health Journal*

65. 🌎 **HAILSTONES** Hailstones are formed when frozen raindrops are caught in updrafts and carried into high clouds containing water droplets. As a rule of thumb, the radius r (in inches) of a hailstone varies directly with the time t (in seconds) that the hailstone is in a high cloud. After a hailstone has been in a high cloud for 60 seconds, its radius is 0.25 inch. Write a linear model that gives r as a function of t. Then estimate how long a hailstone was in a high cloud if its radius measures 2.75 inches. ▶ Source: National Oceanic and Atmospheric Administration

66. **GEOMETRY ▸ CONNECTION** When the length of a rectangle is fixed, the area A (in square inches) of the rectangle varies directly with its width w (in inches). When the width of a particular rectangle is 12 inches, its area is 36 square inches. Write an equation that gives A as a function of w. Then find A when w is 7.5 inches.

FOCUS ON APPLICATIONS

HAILSTONES The largest hailstone ever recorded fell at Coffeyville, Kansas. It weighed 1.67 pounds and had a radius of about 2.75 inches.

STATISTICS ▶ **CONNECTION** Tell whether the data show direct variation. If so, write an equation relating *x* and *y*.

67.

Applesauce					
Ounces, *x*	8	16	24	36	48
Price, *y*	$.89	$1.25	$1.39	$2.09	$2.49

68.

Fresh Apples					
Pounds, *x*	1	1.5	2	2.5	3
Price, *y*	$.89	$1.34	$1.78	$2.23	$2.49

Test Preparation

69. MULTI-STEP PROBLEM Besides slope-intercept and point-slope forms, another form that can be used to write equations of lines is *intercept form*: $\frac{x}{a} + \frac{y}{b} = 1$

a. Graph $\frac{x}{5} + \frac{y}{3} = 1$.   **b.** Graph $\frac{x}{-2} + \frac{y}{9} = 1$.

c. *Writing* Geometrically, what do *a* and *b* represent in the intercept form of a linear equation?

d. Write an equation of the line shown using intercept form.

e. Write an equation of the line with *x*-intercept −5 and *y*-intercept −8 using intercept form.

f. Write an equation of the line that passes through (0, −3) and (2, 0) using intercept form.

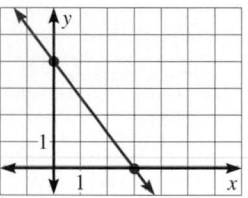

★ Challenge

70. SLOPE-INTERCEPT FORM Derive the slope-intercept form of a linear equation from the slope formula using (0, *b*) as the coordinates of the point where the line crosses the *y*-axis and an arbitrary point (*x*, *y*).

MIXED REVIEW

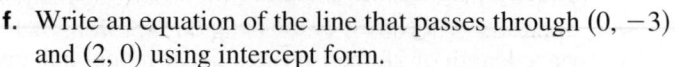

SOLVING EQUATIONS Solve the equation. **(Review 1.7)**

71. $|x - 10| = 17$ **72.** $|7 - 2x| = 5$ **73.** $|-x - 9| = 1$

74. $|4x + 1| = 0.5$ **75.** $|22x + 6| = 9.2$ **76.** $|5.2x + 7| = 3.8$

FINDING SLOPE Find the slope of the line passing through the given points. **(Review 2.2 for 2.5)**

77. (1, −7), (2, 7)   **78.** (−1, −1), (−5, −4)   **79.** (2, 4), (5, 10)

80. (5, −2), (−3, −1)   **81.** (−2, 4), (2, 4)   **82.** (−4, −1), (5, −4)

83. (0, −8), (−9, 10)   **84.** (6, 11), (6, −5)   **85.** (−11, 4), (−4, 11)

GRAPHING EQUATIONS Graph the equation. **(Review 2.3 for 2.5)**

86. $y = \frac{3}{4}x - 5$ **87.** $y = -\frac{1}{5}x + 2$ **88.** $y = -\frac{3}{7}x + 2$

89. $3x + 7y = 42$ **90.** $2x - 8y = -15$ **91.** $-5x + 3y = 10$

92. $x = 0$ **93.** $y = -3$ **94.** $y = x$

98   **Chapter 2** *Linear Equations and Functions*

● ACTIVITY 2.5

Developing Concepts

Fitting a Line to a Set of Data

GROUP ACTIVITY
Work in a small group.

MATERIALS
• overhead projector
• overhead transparency
• metric ruler
• meter stick
• graph paper

▶ **QUESTION** How can you approximate the *best-fitting line* for a set of data?

▶ **EXPLORING THE CONCEPT**

❶ Draw a line segment 15 centimeters long on an overhead transparency. Place the transparency on an overhead projector. First measure the distance (in centimeters) from the overhead projector to the screen, and then measure the length (in centimeters) of the line segment as it appears on the screen. Record the data in a table like the one shown.

❷ Repeat **Step 1** using nine other locations of the overhead projector.

❸ Graph the data pairs (x, y). Describe the pattern of the data.

Distance from projector to screen (cm), x	Length of line segment on screen (cm), y
200	?
210	?
220	?
230	?
240	?
250	?
260	?
270	?
280	?
290	?

❹ Use a ruler to draw a line that lies as close as possible to all of the points on the graph. The line does not have to pass through any of the points. Your line is an approximation of the best-fitting line for the data.

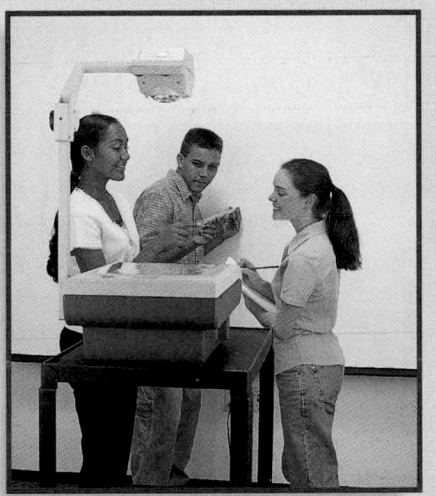
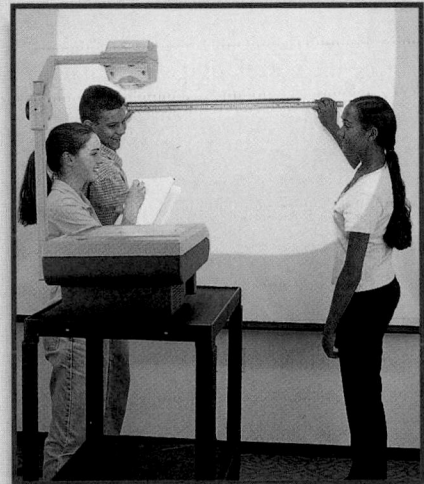
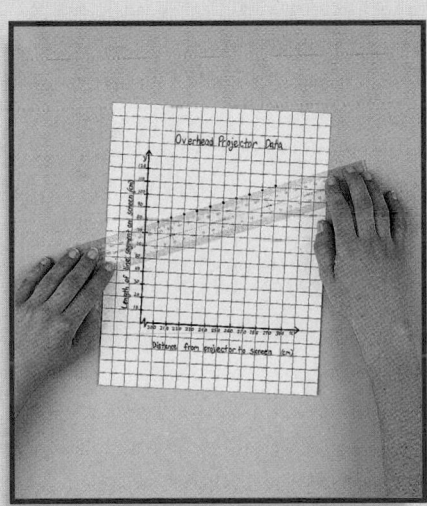

▶ **DRAWING CONCLUSIONS**

1. Find the slope of your line. What does the slope represent?

2. Find the y-intercept of your line. What does the y-intercept represent?

3. Use the slope and y-intercept to write an equation of your line.

4. Use your equation from Exercise 3 to estimate the length of the line segment as it appears on the screen if the distance from the overhead projector to the screen is 300 centimeters.

5. Test your prediction from Exercise 4. How accurate was your prediction?

6. Did every group in your class have the same line? Did every group have the same prediction?

Correlation and Best-Fitting Lines

GOAL 1 SCATTER PLOTS AND CORRELATION

A **scatter plot** is a graph used to determine whether there is a relationship between paired data. In many real-life situations, scatter plots follow patterns that are approximately linear. If y tends to increase as x increases, then the paired data are said to have a **positive correlation**. If y tends to decrease as x increases, then the paired data are said to have a **negative correlation**. If the points show no linear pattern, then the paired data are said to have **relatively no correlation**.

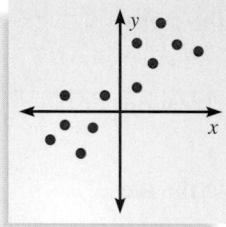

| **Positive correlation** | **Negative correlation** | **Relatively no correlation** |

EXAMPLE 1 *Determining Correlation*

MUSIC Describe the correlation shown by each scatter plot.

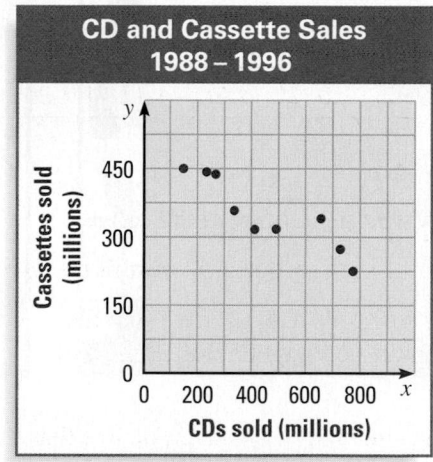

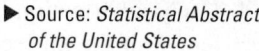

▶ Source: *Statistical Abstract of the United States*

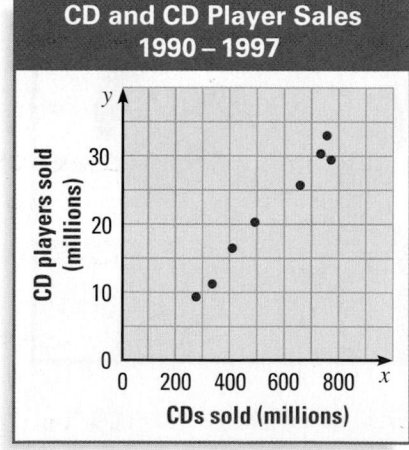

▶ Sources: *Electronic Market Data Book, Recording Industry Association of America*

SOLUTION

The first scatter plot shows a negative correlation, which means that as CD sales increased, the sales of cassettes tended to decrease.

The second scatter plot shows a positive correlation, which means that as CD sales increased, the sales of CD players tended to increase.

GOAL 2 APPROXIMATING BEST-FITTING LINES

When data show a positive or negative correlation, you can approximate the data with a line. Finding the line that *best* fits the data is tedious to do by hand. (See page 107 for a description of how to use technology to find the best-fitting line.) You can, however, approximate the best-fitting line using the following graphical approach.

APPROXIMATING A BEST-FITTING LINE: GRAPHICAL APPROACH

STEP 1 Carefully *draw a scatter plot* of the data.

STEP 2 *Sketch the line* that appears to follow most closely the pattern given by the points. There should be as many points above the line as below it.

STEP 3 *Choose two points* on the line, and estimate the coordinates of each point. These two points do not have to be original data points.

STEP 4 *Find an equation of the line* that passes through the two points from Step 3. This equation models the data.

EXAMPLE 2 *Fitting a Line to Data*

Walking Speeds   Researchers have found that as you increase your walking speed (in meters per second), you also increase the length of your step (in meters). The table gives the average walking speeds and step lengths for several people. Approximate the best-fitting line for the data.

▶ Source: *Biomechanics and Energetics of Muscular Exercise*

Speed	0.8	0.85	0.9	1.3	1.4	1.6	1.75	1.9
Step	0.5	0.6	0.6	0.7	0.7	0.8	0.8	0.9
Speed	2.15	2.5	2.8	3.0	3.1	3.3	3.35	3.4
Step	0.9	1.0	1.05	1.15	1.25	1.15	1.2	1.2

SOLUTION

1 Begin by drawing a scatter plot of the data.

2 Next, sketch the line that appears to best fit the data.

3 Then, choose two points on the line. From the scatter plot shown, you might choose (0.9, 0.6) and (2.5, 1).

4 Finally, find an equation of the line. The line that passes through the two points has a slope of:

$$m = \frac{1 - 0.6}{2.5 - 0.9} = \frac{0.4}{1.6} = 0.25$$

Use the point-slope form to write the equation.

$$y - y_1 = m(x - x_1)$$ **Use point-slope form.**

$$y - 0.6 = 0.25(x - 0.9)$$ **Substitute for** *m*, x_1, **and** y_1.

$$y = 0.25x + 0.375$$ **Simplify.**

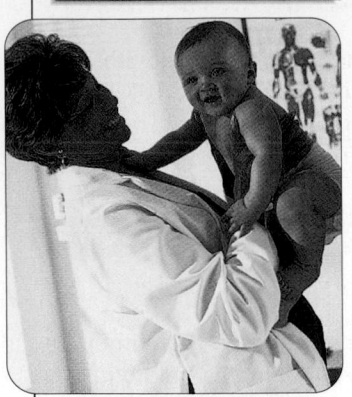
EXAMPLE 3 *Using a Fitted Line*

SLEEP REQUIREMENTS The table shows the age *t* (in years) and the number *h* of hours slept per day by 24 infants who were less than one year old.

Infant Sleep Requirements								
Age, *t*	0.03	0.05	0.05	0.08	0.11	0.19	0.21	0.26
Sleep, *h*	15.0	15.8	16.4	16.2	14.8	14.7	14.5	15.4
Age, *t*	0.34	0.35	0.35	0.44	0.52	0.69	0.70	0.75
Sleep, *h*	15.2	15.3	14.4	13.9	14.4	13.2	14.1	14.2
Age, *t*	0.80	0.82	0.86	0.91	0.94	0.97	0.98	0.98
Sleep, *h*	13.4	13.2	13.9	13.1	13.7	12.7	13.7	13.6

a. Approximate the best-fitting line for the data.

b. Use the fitted line to estimate the number of hours that a 6 month old infant sleeps per day.

SOLUTION

a. *Draw* a scatter plot of the data.

Sketch the line that appears to best fit the data.

Choose two points on the line. From the scatter plot shown, you might choose:

$(0, 15.5)$ and $(0.52, 14.4)$

Find an equation of the line. The line that passes through the two points has a slope of:

$$m = \frac{14.4 - 15.5}{0.52 - 0} = \frac{-1.1}{0.52} \approx -2.12$$

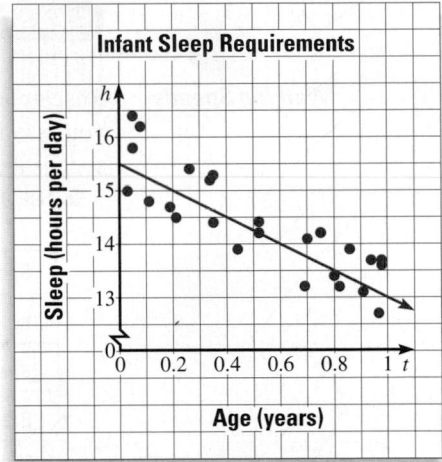

Because the *h*-intercept was chosen as one of the two points for determining the line, you can use the slope-intercept form to approximate the best-fitting line as follows:

$h = mt + b$ **Use slope-intercept form.**

$h = -2.12t + 15.5$ **Substitute for *m* and *b*.**

▶ An equation of the line is $h = -2.12t + 15.5$. Notice that a newborn infant sleeps about 15.5 hours per day and tends to sleep less as he or she gets older.

b. To estimate the number of hours that a 6 month old infant sleeps, use the model from part (a) and the fact that 6 months = 0.5 years.

$h = -2.12t + 15.5$ **Write linear model.**

$h = -2.12(0.5) + 15.5$ **Substitute 0.5 for *t*.**

$h \approx 14.4$ **Simplify.**

▶ A 6 month old infant sleeps about 14.4 hours per day.

GUIDED PRACTICE

Vocabulary Check ✓

Concept Check ✓

Skill Check ✓

1. Explain the meaning of the terms *positive correlation*, *negative correlation*, and *relatively no correlation*.

2. Suppose you were given the shoe sizes *s* and the heights *h* of one hundred 25 year old men. Do you think that *s* and *h* would have a *positive correlation*, a *negative correlation*, or *relatively no correlation*? Explain.

3. **ERROR ANALYSIS** Explain why the line shown at the right is not a good fit for the data.

4. Does the scatter plot at the right show a *positive correlation*, a *negative correlation*, or *relatively no correlation*? Explain.

5. Look back at Example 2. Estimate the step length of a person who walks at a speed of 4 meters per second.

🌐 **FM RADIO STATIONS** In Exercises 6 and 7, use the table below which gives the number of FM radio stations from 1989 to 1995. ▶ Source: *Statistical Abstract of the United States*

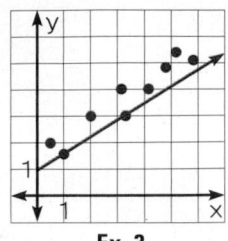
Ex. 3

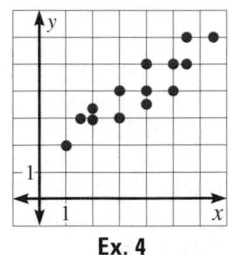
Ex. 4

Years since 1989	0	1	2	3	4	5	6
FM radio stations	4269	4392	4570	4785	4971	5109	5730

6. Approximate the best-fitting line for the data.

7. If the pattern continues, how many FM radio stations will there be in 2010?

PRACTICE AND APPLICATIONS

STUDENT HELP

→ **Extra Practice**
to help you master
skills is on p. 942.

DETERMINING CORRELATION Tell whether *x* and *y* have a *positive correlation*, a *negative correlation*, or *relatively no correlation*.

8.
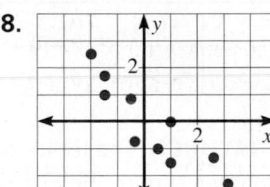

9.
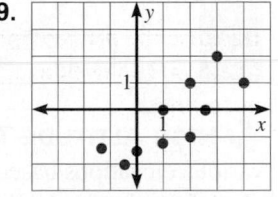

10.
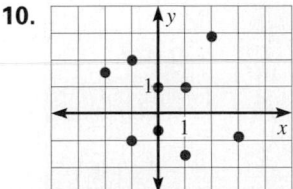

DRAWING SCATTER PLOTS Draw a scatter plot of the data. Then tell whether the data have a *positive correlation*, a *negative correlation*, or *relatively no correlation*.

STUDENT HELP

→ **HOMEWORK HELP**
Example 1: Exs. 8–14,
22, 23
Example 2: Exs. 16–21
Example 3: Exs. 24–27

11.

x	1	2	3	3	5	5	6	7	8	9
y	1	3	3	4	4	5	7	6	8	7

12.

x	1	1	3	4	4	5	7	7	8	8
y	8	2	5	8	3	5	3	5	1	8

DRAWING SCATTER PLOTS Draw a scatter plot of the data. Then tell whether the data have a *positive correlation*, a *negative correlation*, or *relatively no correlation*.

13.

x	1.5	2	3	3.5	4.5	5	6	6.5	8	8
y	7	8	6	7.5	5	6.5	3.5	5	5	4

14.

x	2	3	3.5	4	4.5	5.5	5.5	7	8	8.5
y	9	7.5	7.5	5.5	6.5	5	4	3.5	2	1.5

15. **LOGICAL REASONING** Explain how you can determine the type of correlation for data by examining the data in a table as opposed to drawing a scatter plot.

APPROXIMATING BEST-FITTING LINES Copy the scatter plot. Then approximate the best-fitting line for the data.

16. 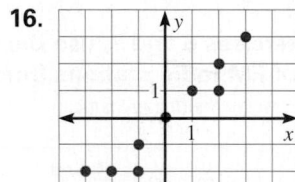 17. 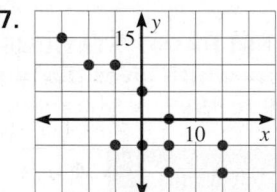 18.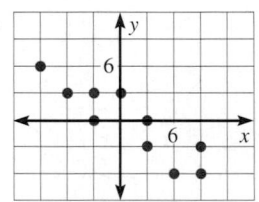

FITTING A LINE TO DATA Draw a scatter plot of the data. Then approximate the best-fitting line for the data.

19.

x	−2	−1	0	0.5	1	2	2.5	3.5	4	5
y	4	3	2.5	2.5	2	0.5	−1	−3	−2.5	−2.5

20.

x	−4	−3	−2	−1.5	0	0.5	2	2.5	3	4
y	−2	−1	−1.5	0	0.5	0.5	2.5	2	3	3

21.

x	−4	−3	−2	−1.5	−0.5	0	1	2	2.5	3
y	6	4	4.5	3	2	3	1.5	2	0.5	0

22. 🌐 **HIGH ALTITUDE TEMPERATURES** The table shows the temperature for various elevations based on a temperature of 59°F at sea level. Draw a scatter plot of the data and describe the correlation shown.

Elevation (ft)	1000	5000	10,000	15,000	20,000	30,000
Temperature (°F)	56	41	23	5	−15	−47

23. 🌐 **OLD FAITHFUL** Old Faithful is a geyser in Yellowstone National Park. The table shows the duration of eruptions and the time interval between eruptions for a typical day. Draw a scatter plot of the data and describe the correlation shown.

Duration (min)	4.4	3.9	4	4	3.5	4.1	2.3	4.7	1.7	4.9	1.7	4.6	3.4
Interval (min)	78	74	68	76	80	84	50	93	55	76	58	74	75

STUDENT HELP

HOMEWORK HELP

Visit our Web site
www.mcdougallittell.com
for help with problem
solving in Exs. 24–27.

🌐 **CITY YEAR** In Exercises 24 and 25, use the table below which gives the enrollment for the City Year national youth service program from 1989 to 1998.

Years since 1989	0	1	2	3	4	5	6	7	8	9
Enrollment	57	76	107	234	371	688	678	716	894	918

24. Approximate the best-fitting line for the data.

25. If the pattern continues, how many people will enroll in City Year in 2010?

BIOLOGY ▶ **CONNECTION** In Exercises 26 and 27, use the table below which gives the average life expectancy (in years) of a person based on various years of birth. ▶ Source: National Center for Health Statistics

Year of birth	1900	1910	1920	1930	1940
Life expectancy	47.3	50	54.1	59.7	62.9
Year of birth	1950	1960	1970	1980	1990
Life expectancy	68.2	69.7	70.8	73.7	75.4

26. Approximate the best-fitting line for the data.

27. Predict the life expectancy for someone born in 2010.

Test Preparation

28. **MULTI-STEP PROBLEM** The table below gives the numbers (in thousands) of black-and-white and color televisions sold in the United States for various years from 1955–1995. ▶ Source: Electronic Industries Association

Year	Black-and-white TVs sold (thousands)	Color TVs sold (thousands)
1955	7,738	20
1960	5,709	120
1965	8,753	2,694
1970	4,704	5,320
1975	4,955	6,486
1980	6,684	10,897
1985	3,684	16,995
1990	1,411	20,384
1995	480	25,600

a. Draw a scatter plot of the data pairs (*year, black-and-white TVs sold*). Then describe the correlation shown by the scatter plot.

b. Draw a scatter plot of the data pairs (*year, color TVs sold*). Then describe the correlation shown by the scatter plot.

c. **CRITICAL THINKING** Based on your answers to parts (a) and (b), are black-and-white television sales and color television sales *positively correlated*, *negatively correlated*, or *neither*? Explain.

★ **Challenge**

29. **BEST-FITTING LINES** Describe a set of real-life data where the best-fitting line could *not* be used to make a prediction. Explain.

MIXED REVIEW

SOLVING INEQUALITIES Solve the inequality. Then graph your solution.
(Review 1.6 for 2.6)

30. $2x - 9 \geq 14$

31. $3(x + 7) < -x + 10$

32. $17 \leq 2x - 7 \leq 29$

33. $x - 4 < 0$ or $x - 6 \geq 4$

DETERMINING STEEPNESS Tell which line is steeper. (Review 2.2)

34. Line 1: through $(-3, 4)$ and $(1, 6)$
Line 2: through $(1, -5)$ and $(6, 2)$

35. Line 1: through $(6, 1)$ and $(-4, 4)$
Line 2: through $(-2, 3)$ and $(1, -6)$

36. Line 1: through $(2, 4)$ and $(1, 7)$
Line 2: through $(-5, 8)$ and $(3, 8)$

37. Line 1: through $(4, 3)$ and $(1, -9)$
Line 2: through $(-2, -4)$ and $(3, -7)$

GRAPHING EQUATIONS Graph the equation. (Review 2.3 for 2.6)

38. $y = \frac{1}{3}x + 5$

39. $y = -10x + 9$

40. $y = \frac{7}{3}$

41. $-x + 2y = -8$

42. $4x + 2y = 1$

43. $x = 12$

QUIZ 2

Self-Test for Lessons 2.4 and 2.5

Write an equation of the line that passes through the given point and has the given slope. (Lesson 2.4)

1. $(0, 6)$, $m = \frac{2}{3}$

2. $(-4, -3)$, $m = 2$

3. $(2, -7)$, $m = -\frac{1}{5}$

4. Write an equation of the line that passes through $(1, -2)$ and is perpendicular to the line that passes through $(4, 2)$ and $(0, 4)$. (Lesson 2.4)

Tell whether *x* and *y* have a *positive correlation*, a *negative correlation*, or *relatively no correlation*. (Lesson 2.5)

5.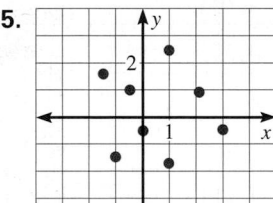

6.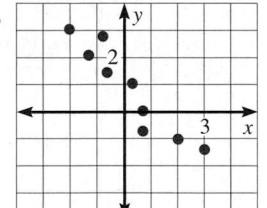

7.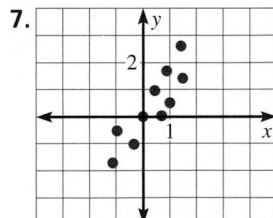

8. 🌎 **WAVES** The water depth *d* (in feet) at which a wave breaks varies directly with the height *h* (in feet) of the wave. A 6.5 foot wave breaks at a water depth of 8.45 feet. Write a linear model that gives *d* as a function of *h*. If a wave breaks at a depth of 5.2 feet, what is its height? (Lesson 2.4)

9. 🌎 **HEIGHTS OF CHILDREN** The table gives the average heights of children for ages 1–10. Draw a scatter plot of the data and approximate the best-fitting line for the data. (Lesson 2.5)

Age (years)	1	2	3	4	5	6	7	8	9	10
Height (cm)	73	85	93	100	107	113	120	124	130	135

● ACTIVITY 2.5

Using Technology

Using Linear Regression

Many graphing calculators have a *linear regression* feature that can be used to find the best-fitting line for a set of data.

▶ EXAMPLE

The table gives the price p (in cents) of a first-class stamp over time where t is the number of years since 1970. Use the linear regression feature of a graphing calculator to find an equation of the best-fitting line for the data.

t	1	4	5	8	11	11	15	18	21	25	29
p	8	10	13	15	18	20	22	25	29	32	33

▶ SOLUTION

1 Use the *Stat Edit* feature to enter the data into two *lists* such as L_1 and L_2. Enter the years since 1970 in L_1 and the prices in L_2.

2 Find an equation of the best-fitting line by using the *Stat Calc* feature. The linear regression equation can be rounded to $p = 0.947t + 7.71$.

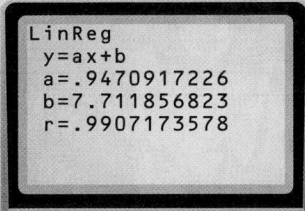

3 To see that the data have a positive correlation, graph the data pairs. To do this, make a scatter plot using the *Stat Plot* feature.

4 Graph the regression equation in an appropriate viewing window. The graph shows that the line fits the data well.

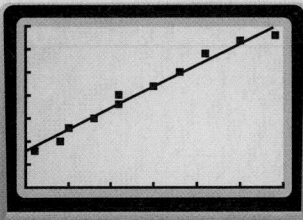

▶ EXERCISES

Use a graphing calculator to find and graph an equation of the best-fitting line.

1.

x	50	75	80	100	150	175	210	250	260	320
y	0.3	0.5	0.6	0.7	0.75	0.85	1.05	0.9	1.1	1.15

2.

x	4	7	8.5	10	11	14	15	16	18	19
y	150	450	600	600	900	1100	1250	1400	1400	1650

2.6
Linear Inequalities in Two Variables

What you should learn

GOAL 1 Graph linear inequalities in two variables.

GOAL 2 Use linear inequalities to solve **real-life** problems, such as finding the number of minutes you can call relatives using a calling card in **Example 4**.

Why you should learn it

▼ To model **real-life** data, such as blood pressures in your arm and ankle in **Ex. 45**.

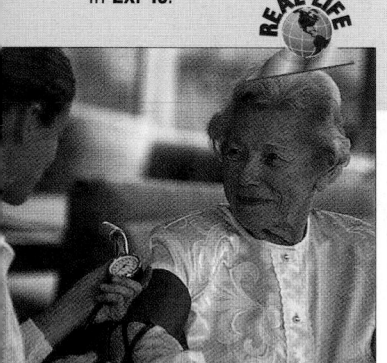

GOAL 1 GRAPHING LINEAR INEQUALITIES

A **linear inequality** in two variables is an inequality that can be written in one of the following forms:

$$Ax + By < C, \quad Ax + By \leq C, \quad Ax + By > C, \quad Ax + By \geq C$$

An ordered pair (x, y) is a **solution** of a linear inequality if the inequality is true when the values of x and y are substituted into the inequality. For instance, $(-6, 2)$ is a solution of $y \geq 3x - 9$ because $2 \geq 3(-6) - 9$ is a true statement.

EXAMPLE 1 *Checking Solutions of Inequalities*

Check whether the given ordered pair is a solution of $2x + 3y \geq 5$.

   a. $(0, 1)$ **b.** $(4, -1)$ **c.** $(2, 1)$

SOLUTION

ORDERED PAIR	SUBSTITUTE	CONCLUSION
a. $(0, 1)$	$2(0) + 3(1) = 3 \ngeq 5$	$(0, 1)$ is not a solution.
b. $(4, -1)$	$2(4) + 3(-1) = 5 \geq 5$	$(4, -1)$ is a solution.
c. $(2, 1)$	$2(2) + 3(1) = 7 \geq 5$	$(2, 1)$ is a solution.

▶ ACTIVITY
Developing Concepts
Investigating the Graph of an Inequality

1 Copy the scatter plot.

2 Test each circled point to see whether it is a solution of $x + y \geq 1$. If it is a solution, color it blue. If it is not a solution, color it red.

3 Graph the line $x + y = 1$. What relationship do you see between the colored points and the line?

4 Describe a general strategy for graphing an inequality in two variables.

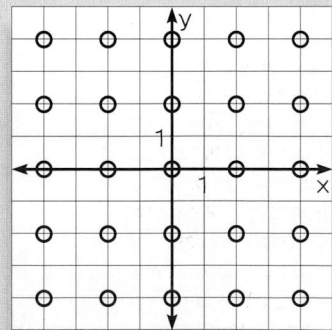

The **graph** of a linear inequality in two variables is the graph of all solutions of the inequality. The boundary line of the inequality divides the coordinate plane into two **half-planes**: a shaded region which contains the points that are solutions of the inequality, and an unshaded region which contains the points that are not.

GRAPHING A LINEAR INEQUALITY

The graph of a linear inequality in two variables is a half-plane. To graph a linear inequality, follow these steps:

STEP ❶ Graph the boundary line of the inequality. Use a dashed line for < or > and a solid line for ≤ or ≥.

STEP ❷ To decide which side of the boundary line to shade, test a point *not* on the boundary line to see whether it is a solution of the inequality. Then shade the appropriate half-plane.

EXAMPLE 2 *Graphing Linear Inequalities in One Variable*

STUDENT HELP

▸ **Look Back**
For help with inequalities in one variable, see p. 42.

Graph (**a**) $y < -2$ and (**b**) $x \le 1$ in a coordinate plane.

SOLUTION

a. *Graph* the boundary line $y = -2$. Use a dashed line because $y < -2$.

Test the point $(0, 0)$. Because $(0, 0)$ is *not* a solution of the inequality, shade the half-plane below the line.

b. *Graph* the boundary line $x = 1$. Use a solid line because $x \le 1$.

Test the point $(0, 0)$. Because $(0, 0)$ *is* a solution of the inequality, shade the half-plane to the left of the line.

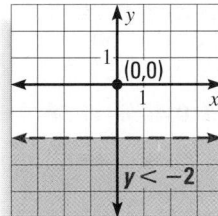

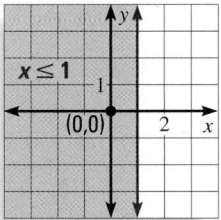

EXAMPLE 3 *Graphing Linear Inequalities in Two Variables*

STUDENT HELP

▸ **Study Tip**
Because your test point must *not* be on the boundary line, you may not always be able to use (0, 0) as a convenient test point. In such cases test a different point, such as (1, 1) or (1, 0).

Graph (**a**) $y < 2x$ and (**b**) $2x - 5y \ge 10$.

SOLUTION

a. *Graph* the boundary line $y = 2x$. Use a dashed line because $y < 2x$.

Test the point $(1, 1)$. Because $(1, 1)$ *is* a solution of the inequality, shade the half-plane below the line.

b. *Graph* the boundary line $2x - 5y = 10$. Use a solid line because $2x - 5y \ge 10$.

Test the point $(0, 0)$. Because $(0, 0)$ is *not* a solution of the inequality, shade the half-plane below the line.

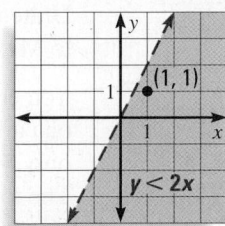

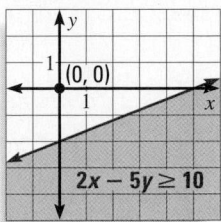

GOAL 2 USING LINEAR INEQUALITIES IN REAL LIFE

EXAMPLE 4 *Writing and Using a Linear Inequality*

Communication

You have relatives living in both the United States and Mexico. You are given a prepaid phone card worth $50. Calls within the continental United States cost $.16 per minute and calls to Mexico cost $.44 per minute.

a. Write a linear inequality in two variables to represent the number of minutes you can use for calls within the United States and for calls to Mexico.

b. Graph the inequality and discuss three possible solutions in the context of the real-life situation.

SOLUTION

PROBLEM SOLVING STRATEGY

a.

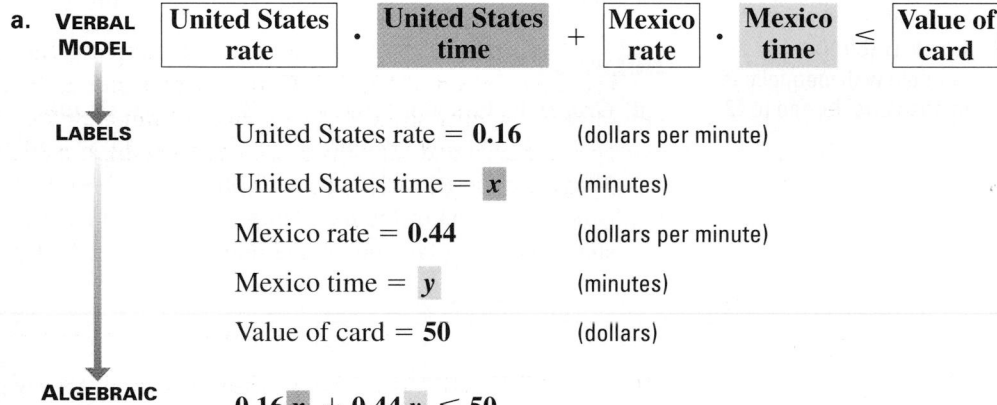

VERBAL MODEL

| United States rate | · | United States time | + | Mexico rate | · | Mexico time | ≤ | Value of card |

LABELS

United States rate = **0.16**   (dollars per minute)

United States time = x (minutes)

Mexico rate = **0.44**   (dollars per minute)

Mexico time = y (minutes)

Value of card = **50**   (dollars)

ALGEBRAIC MODEL

$$0.16\,x + 0.44\,y \le 50$$

STUDENT HELP

HOMEWORK HELP
Visit our Web site
www.mcdougallittell.com
for extra examples.

b. **Graph** the boundary line $0.16x + 0.44y = 50$. Use a solid line because $0.16x + 0.44y \le 50$.

Test the point $(0, 0)$. Because $(0, 0)$ *is* a solution of the inequality, shade the half-plane below the line. Finally, because x and y cannot be negative, restrict the graph to points in the first quadrant.

Possible solutions are points within the shaded region shown.

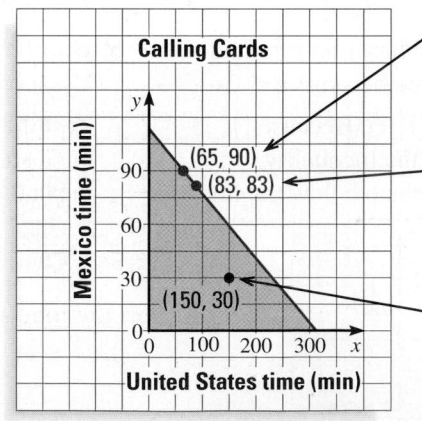

Calling Cards

Mexico time (min)

(65, 90)
(83, 83)
(150, 30)

United States time (min)

One solution is to spend 65 minutes on calls within the United States and 90 minutes on calls to Mexico. The total cost will be $50.

To split the time evenly, you could spend 83 minutes on calls within the United States and 83 minutes on calls to Mexico. The total cost will be $49.80.

You could instead spend 150 minutes on calls within the United States and only 30 minutes on calls to Mexico. The total cost will be $37.20.

GUIDED PRACTICE

Vocabulary Check ✔

1. Compare the graph of a linear inequality with the graph of a linear equation.

Concept Check ✔

2. Would you use a dashed line or a solid line for the graph of $Ax + By < C$? for the graph of $Ax + By \leq C$? Explain.

Tell whether the statement is *true* or *false*. Explain.

3. The point $\left(\frac{4}{3}, 0\right)$ is a solution of $3x - y > 4$.

4. The graph of $y < 3x + 5$ is the half-plane below the line $y = 3x + 5$.

Skill Check ✔

GRAPHING INEQUALITIES Graph the inequality in a coordinate plane.

5. $x > 5$ 6. $y < -4$ 7. $3x \leq 1$ 8. $-y \geq \frac{4}{3}$

9. $y \geq -x + 7$ 10. $y > \frac{2}{3}x - 1$ 11. $2x - 3y < 6$ 12. $x + 5y \leq -10$

13. 🌐 **CALLING CARDS** Look back at Example 4. Suppose you have relatives living in China instead of Mexico. Calls to China cost \$.75 per minute. Write and graph a linear inequality showing the number of minutes you can use for calls within the United States and for calls to China. Then discuss three possible solutions in the context of the real-life situation.

PRACTICE AND APPLICATIONS

STUDENT HELP

▸ **Extra Practice**
to help you master
skills is on p. 942.

CHECKING SOLUTIONS Check whether the given ordered pairs are solutions of the inequality.

14. $x \leq -5$; $(0, 2)$, $(-5, 1)$ 15. $2y \geq 7$; $(1, -6)$, $(0, 4)$

16. $y < -9x + 7$; $(-2, 2)$, $(3, -8)$ 17. $19x + y \geq -0.5$; $(2, 3)$, $(-1, 0)$

INEQUALITIES IN ONE VARIABLE Graph the inequality in a coordinate plane.

18. $x \leq 6$ 19. $-x \geq 20$ 20. $10x \geq \frac{10}{3}$

21. $-3y < 21$ 22. $8y > -4$ 23. $y < 0.75$

MATCHING GRAPHS Match the inequality with its graph.

24. $2x - y \geq 4$ 25. $-2x - y < 4$ 26. $2x + y \leq 4$

A. 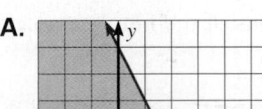   B. 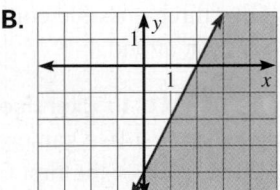   C.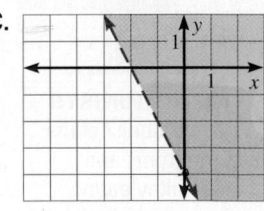

STUDENT HELP

▸ **HOMEWORK HELP**
Example 1: Exs. 14–17
Example 2: Exs. 18–23,
        33–44
Example 3: Exs. 24–44
Example 4: Exs. 45–51

INEQUALITIES IN TWO VARIABLES Graph the inequality.

27. $y \leq 3x + 11$ 28. $y > -4 - x$ 29. $y < 0.75x - 5$

30. $3x + 12y > 4$ 31. $9x - 9y > -36$ 32. $\frac{3}{2}x + \frac{2}{3}y > 1$

MATCHING GRAPHS Match the inequality with its graph.

33. $x + y > 2$ **34.** $x \geq 2$ **35.** $y \leq -x + 2$

A. 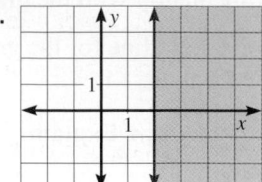   B. 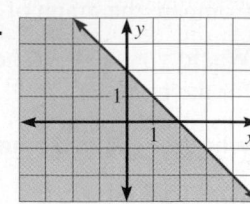   C.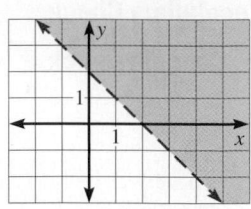

GRAPHING INEQUALITIES Graph the inequality in a coordinate plane.

36. $9x - 2y \leq -18$ **37.** $y < 3x - \dfrac{3}{4}$ **38.** $5x > -20$

39. $y \geq \dfrac{1}{5}x + 10$ **40.** $4y \leq -6$ **41.** $2x + 3y > 4$

42. $6x \geq -\dfrac{1}{3}y$ **43.** $0.25x + 3y > 19$ **44.** $x + y < 0$

45. **HEALTH RISKS** By comparing the blood pressure in your ankle with the blood pressure in your arm, a physician can determine whether your arteries are becoming clogged with plaque. If the blood pressure in your ankle is less than 90% of the blood pressure in your arm, you may be at risk for heart disease. Write and graph an inequality that relates the unacceptable blood pressure in your ankle to the blood pressure in your arm.

NUTRITION In Exercises 46 and 47, use the following information.
Teenagers should consume at least 1200 milligrams of calcium per day. Suppose you get calcium from two different sources, skim milk and cheddar cheese. One cup of skim milk supplies 296 milligrams of calcium, and one slice of cheddar cheese supplies 338 milligrams of calcium. ▶ *Source: Nutrition in Exercise and Sport*

46. Write and graph an inequality that represents the amounts of skim milk and cheddar cheese you need to consume to meet your daily requirement of calcium.

47. Determine how many cups of skim milk you should drink if you have eaten two slices of cheddar cheese.

MOVIES In Exercises 48 and 49, use the following information.
You receive a gift certificate for $25 to your local movie theater. Matinees are $4.50 each and evening shows are $7.50 each.

48. Write and graph an inequality that represents the numbers of matinees and evening shows you can attend.

49. Give three possible combinations of the numbers of matinees and evening shows you can attend.

FOOTBALL In Exercises 50 and 51, use the following information.
In one of its first five games of a season, a football team scored a school record of 63 points. In all of the first five games, points came from touchdowns worth 7 points and field goals worth 3 points.

50. Write and graph an inequality that represents the numbers of touchdowns and field goals the team could have scored in any of the first five games.

51. Give five possible numbers of points scored, including the number of touchdowns and the number of field goals, for the first five games.

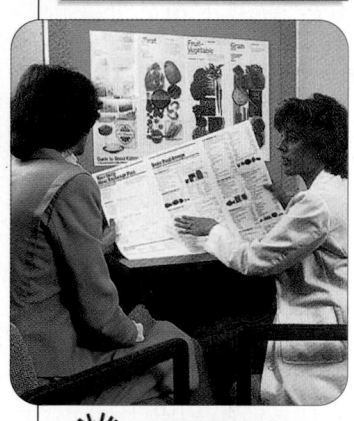

Test Preparation

52. **MULTI-STEP PROBLEM** You want to open your own truck rental company. You do some research and find that the majority of truck rental companies in your area charge a flat fee of $29.99, plus $.29 for every mile driven. You want to charge less so that you can advertise your lower rate and get more business.

   a. Write and graph an equation for the cost of renting a truck from other truck rental companies.

   b. Shade the region of the coordinate plane where the amount you will charge must fall.

   c. To charge less than your competitors, will you offer a lower flat fee, a lower rate per mile, or both? Explain your choice.

   d. Write and graph an equation for the cost of renting a truck from your company in the same coordinate plane used in part (a).

   e. **CRITICAL THINKING** Why can't you offer a lower rate per mile but a higher flat fee and still always charge less?

★ **Challenge**

VISUAL THINKING In Exercises 53–55, use the graph shown.

53. Write the inequality whose graph is shown.

54. Explain how you came up with the inequality.

EXTRA CHALLENGE
www.mcdougallittell.com

55. What real-life situation could the first–quadrant portion of the graph represent?

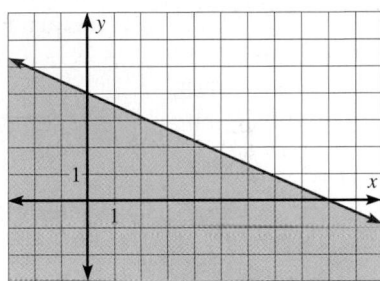

MIXED REVIEW

SCIENTIFIC NOTATION Write the number in scientific notation. (Skills Review, p. 913)

56. 10,000,000
57. 1,650,000,000
58. 203,000

59. 0.00067
60. 0.0000009
61. 0.0808

GRAPHING EQUATIONS Graph the equation. (Review 2.3 for 2.7)

62. $y = \frac{5}{2}x - 5$
63. $y = -5x - 1$
64. $y = -\frac{1}{2}x + 6$

65. $x - y = 4$
66. $2x + y = 6$
67. $-4x + y = 4$

WRITING EQUATIONS Write an equation of the line that passes through the given points. (Review 2.4 for 2.7)

68. $(2, 2), (5, 5)$
69. $(0, 7), (5, 1)$
70. $(-1, 6), (8, -2)$

71. $(3, 2), (3, -4)$
72. $(1, 9), (-10, -6)$
73. $(4, -8), (-7, -8)$

74. **GARDENING** The horizontal middle of the United States is at about 40°N latitude. As a rule of thumb, plants will bloom earlier south of 40°N latitude and later north of 40°N latitude. The function $w = \frac{3}{5}(l - 40)$ gives the number of weeks w (earlier or later) that plants at latitude l°N will bloom compared with those at 40°N. The equation is valid from 35°N to 45°N latitude. Identify the domain and range of the function and then graph the function. **(Review 2.1)**

2.7

Piecewise Functions

What you should learn

GOAL 1 Represent piecewise functions.

GOAL 2 Use piecewise functions to model **real-life** quantities, such as the amount you earn at a summer job in **Example 6**.

Why you should learn it

▼ To solve **real-life** problems, such as determining the cost of ordering silk-screen T-shirts in **Exs. 54 and 55**.

GOAL 1 REPRESENTING PIECEWISE FUNCTIONS

Up to now in this chapter a function has been represented by a single equation. In many real-life problems, however, functions are represented by a combination of equations, each corresponding to a part of the domain. Such functions are called **piecewise functions**. For example, the piecewise function given by

$$f(x) = \begin{cases} 2x - 1, & \text{if } x \le 1 \\ 3x + 1, & \text{if } x > 1 \end{cases}$$

is defined by two equations. One equation gives the values of $f(x)$ when x is less than or equal to 1, and the other equation gives the values of $f(x)$ when x is greater than 1.

EXAMPLE 1 *Evaluating a Piecewise Function*

Evaluate $f(x)$ when (**a**) $x = 0$, (**b**) $x = 2$, and (**c**) $x = 4$.

$$f(x) = \begin{cases} x + 2, & \text{if } x < 2 \\ 2x + 1, & \text{if } x \ge 2 \end{cases}$$

SOLUTION

  a. $f(x) = x + 2$ **Because 0 < 2, use first equation.**

       $f(0) = 0 + 2 = 2$ **Substitute 0 for x.**

  b. $f(x) = 2x + 1$ **Because 2 ≥ 2, use second equation.**

       $f(2) = 2(2) + 1 = 5$ **Substitute 2 for x.**

  c. $f(x) = 2x + 1$ **Because 4 ≥ 2, use second equation.**

       $f(4) = 2(4) + 1 = 9$ **Substitute 4 for x.**

EXAMPLE 2 *Graphing a Piecewise Function*

Graph this function: $f(x) = \begin{cases} \frac{1}{2}x + \frac{3}{2}, & \text{if } x < 1 \\ -x + 3, & \text{if } x \ge 1 \end{cases}$

SOLUTION

To the left of $x = 1$, the graph is given by $y = \frac{1}{2}x + \frac{3}{2}$.

To the right of and including $x = 1$, the graph is given by $y = -x + 3$.

The graph is composed of two rays with common initial point (1, 2).

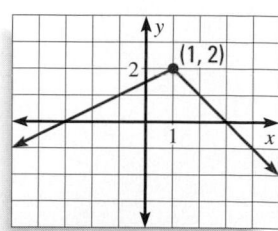

EXAMPLE 3 *Graphing a Step Function*

Graph this function: $f(x) = \begin{cases} 1, & \text{if } 0 \le x < 1 \\ 2, & \text{if } 1 \le x < 2 \\ 3, & \text{if } 2 \le x < 3 \\ 4, & \text{if } 3 \le x < 4 \end{cases}$

SOLUTION

The graph of the function is composed of four line segments. For instance, the first line segment is given by the equation $y = 1$ and represents the graph when x is greater than or equal to 0 and less than 1.

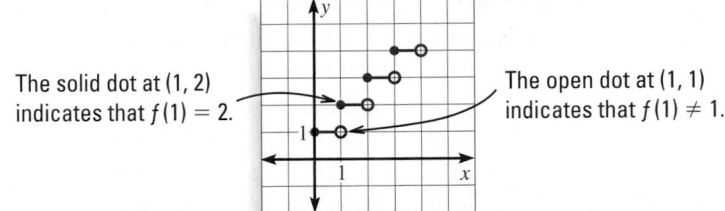

The solid dot at (1, 2) indicates that $f(1) = 2$.

The open dot at (1, 1) indicates that $f(1) \ne 1$.

· · · · · · · · · ·

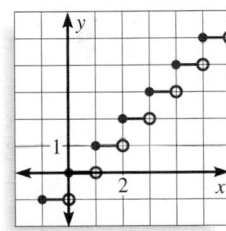

The function in Example 3 is called a **step function** because its graph resembles a set of stair steps. Another example of a step function is the *greatest integer function*. This function is denoted by $g(x) = [\![x]\!]$. For every real number x, $g(x)$ is the greatest integer less than or equal to x. The graph of $g(x)$ is shown at the right. Note that in Example 3 the function f could have been written as $f(x) = [\![x]\!] + 1, 0 \le x < 4$.

EXAMPLE 4 *Writing a Piecewise Function*

Write equations for the piecewise function whose graph is shown.

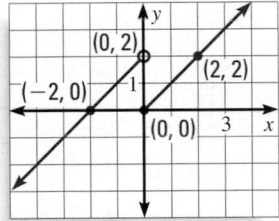

SOLUTION

To the left of $x = 0$, the graph is part of the line passing through $(-2, 0)$ and $(0, 2)$. An equation of this line is given by:

$$y = x + 2$$

To the right of and including $x = 0$, the graph is part of the line passing through $(0, 0)$ and $(2, 2)$. An equation of this line is given by:

$$y = x$$

▶ The equations for the piecewise function are:

$$f(x) = \begin{cases} x + 2, & \text{if } x < 0 \\ x, & \text{if } x \ge 0 \end{cases}$$

Note that $f(x) = x + 2$ does *not* correspond to $x = 0$ because there is an *open* dot at $(0, 2)$, but $f(x) = x$ *does* correspond to $x = 0$ because there is a *solid* dot at $(0, 0)$.

GOAL 2 USING PIECEWISE FUNCTIONS IN REAL LIFE

Urban Parking

EXAMPLE 5 *Using a Step Function*

a. Write and graph a piecewise function for the parking charges shown on the sign.

b. What are the domain and range of the function?

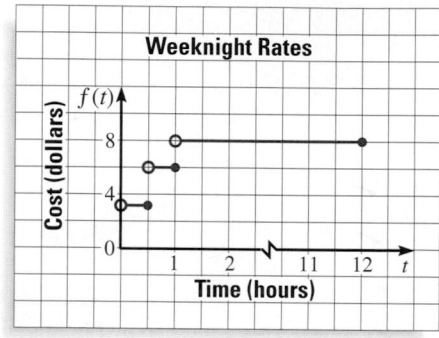

Garage Rates (Weekends)
$3 per half hour
$8 maximum for 12 hours

SOLUTION

a. For times up to one half hour, the charge is $3. For each additional half hour (or portion of a half hour), the charge is an additional $3 until you reach $8. Let t represent the number of hours you park. The piecewise function and graph are:

$$f(t) = \begin{cases} 3, & \text{if } 0 < t \le 0.5 \\ 6, & \text{if } 0.5 < t \le 1 \\ 8, & \text{if } 1 < t \le 12 \end{cases}$$

b. The domain is $0 < t \le 12$, and the range consists of 3, 6, 8

Wages

EXAMPLE 6 *Using a Piecewise Function*

You have a summer job that pays time and a half for overtime. That is, if you work more than 40 hours per week, your hourly wage for the extra hours is 1.5 times your normal hourly wage of $7.

a. Write and graph a piecewise function that gives your weekly pay P in terms of the number h of hours you work.

b. How much will you get paid if you work 45 hours?

SOLUTION

a. For up to 40 hours your pay is given by $7h$. For over 40 hours your pay is given by:

$$7(40) + 1.5(7)(h - 40) = 10.5h - 140$$

▶ The piecewise function is:

$$P(h) = \begin{cases} 7h, & \text{if } 0 \le h \le 40 \\ 10.5h - 140, & \text{if } h > 40 \end{cases}$$

The graph of the function is shown. Note that for up to 40 hours the rate of change is $7 per hour, but for over 40 hours the rate of change is $10.50 per hour.

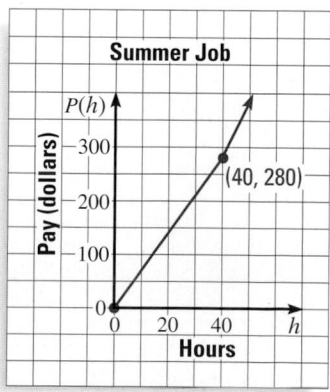

b. To find how much you will get paid for working 45 hours, use the equation $P(h) = 10.5h - 140$.

$$P(\mathbf{45}) = 10.5(\mathbf{45}) - 140 = 332.5$$

▶ You will earn $332.50.

GUIDED PRACTICE

Vocabulary Check ✓

1. Define piecewise function and step function. Give an example of each.

Concept Check ✓

2. Look back at Example 3. What does a solid dot on the graph of a step function indicate? What does an open dot indicate?

Tell whether the statement is *True* or *False*. Explain.

3. In the graph of a piecewise function, the separate pieces are always connected.

4. $f(x) = \begin{cases} 2, & \text{if } 1 \le x < 2 \\ 4, & \text{if } 2 \le x < 3 \\ 6, & \text{if } 3 \le x < 4 \end{cases}$ can be rewritten as $f(x) = 2[\![x]\!]$, $1 \le x < 4$.

Skill Check ✓

Evaluate $f(x) = \begin{cases} 3x - 1, & \text{if } x \le 4 \\ 2x + 7, & \text{if } x > 4 \end{cases}$ for the given value of *x*.

5. $x = 10$ 6. $x = -\dfrac{1}{3}$ 7. $x = 4$ 8. $x = -2$

Graph the function.

9. $f(x) = \begin{cases} 2x + 1, & \text{if } x < 1 \\ -x + 4, & \text{if } x \ge 1 \end{cases}$ 10. $f(x) = \begin{cases} 4, & \text{if } 0 \le x < 2 \\ 5, & \text{if } 2 \le x < 4 \\ 6, & \text{if } 4 \le x < 6 \end{cases}$

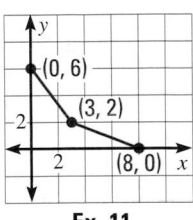

Ex. 11

11. Write equations for the piecewise function whose graph is shown.

12. 🌎 **PARKING RATES** The weekday parking rates for a garage are shown. Write and graph a piecewise function for the weekday parking charges at that garage.

> **Garage Rates** (Weekdays)
> **$3** per half hour
> **$18** maximum for 12 hours

PRACTICE AND APPLICATIONS

EVALUATING FUNCTIONS Evaluate the function for the given value of *x*.

$f(x) = \begin{cases} 5x - 1, & \text{if } x < -2 \\ x - 9, & \text{if } x \ge -2 \end{cases}$

13. $f(-4)$ 14. $f(-2)$
15. $f(0)$ 16. $f(5)$

$h(x) = \begin{cases} \dfrac{1}{2}x - 10, & \text{if } x \le 6 \\ -x - 1, & \text{if } x > 6 \end{cases}$

17. $h(1)$ 18. $h(-10)$
19. $h(6)$ 20. $h(0)$

GRAPHING FUNCTIONS Graph the function.

21. $f(x) = \begin{cases} 2x, & \text{if } x \ge 1 \\ -x + 3, & \text{if } x < 1 \end{cases}$ 22. $f(x) = \begin{cases} x + 6, & \text{if } x \le -3 \\ -\dfrac{2}{3}x - 3, & \text{if } x > -3 \end{cases}$

23. $f(x) = \begin{cases} 2x + 13, & \text{if } x \ge -5 \\ x + \dfrac{1}{2}, & \text{if } x < -5 \end{cases}$ 24. $f(x) = \begin{cases} -x, & \text{if } x > 2 \\ x - 4, & \text{if } x \le 2 \end{cases}$

25. $f(x) = \begin{cases} 3x - 14, & \text{if } x \le 4 \\ -2x + 6, & \text{if } x > 4 \end{cases}$ 26. $f(x) = \begin{cases} x - 8, & \text{if } x < 9 \\ \dfrac{1}{3}x - 2, & \text{if } x \ge 9 \end{cases}$

GRAPHING STEP FUNCTIONS Graph the step function.

27. $f(x) = \begin{cases} 3, & \text{if } -1 \le x < 2 \\ 5, & \text{if } 2 \le x < 4 \\ 8, & \text{if } 4 \le x < 9 \\ 10, & \text{if } 9 \le x < 12 \end{cases}$

28. $f(x) = \begin{cases} 6.5, & \text{if } -4 \le x < -2 \\ 4.1, & \text{if } -2 \le x < 1 \\ 0.9, & \text{if } 1 \le x < 3 \\ -2.1, & \text{if } 3 \le x < 6 \end{cases}$

29. $f(x) = \begin{cases} -1, & \text{if } 0 \le x < 1 \\ -3, & \text{if } 1 \le x < 2 \\ -5, & \text{if } 2 \le x < 3 \\ -7, & \text{if } 3 \le x < 4 \\ -9, & \text{if } 4 \le x < 5 \end{cases}$

30. $f(x) = \begin{cases} 4, & \text{if } -10 < x \le -8 \\ 6, & \text{if } -8 < x \le -6 \\ 8, & \text{if } -6 < x \le -4 \\ 9.1, & \text{if } -4 < x \le -2 \\ 10, & \text{if } -2 < x \le 0 \end{cases}$

SPECIAL STEP FUNCTIONS Graph the special step function. Then explain how you think the function got its name.

31. CEILING FUNCTION

$f(x) = \lceil x \rceil = \begin{cases} \dots \\ 1, & \text{if } 0 < x \le 1 \\ 2, & \text{if } 1 < x \le 2 \\ 3, & \text{if } 2 < x \le 3 \\ \dots \end{cases}$

32. ROUNDING FUNCTION

$f(x) = \text{ROUND}(x) = \begin{cases} \dots \\ 1, & \text{if } 0.5 \le x < 1.5 \\ 2, & \text{if } 1.5 \le x < 2.5 \\ 3, & \text{if } 2.5 \le x < 3.5 \\ \dots \end{cases}$

33. **CRITICAL THINKING** Look back at Example 2. How would the graph of the function change if $<$ was replaced with $\le$ and $\ge$ was replaced with $>$? Explain your answer.

34. **CRITICAL THINKING** Look back at Example 3. How would the graph of the function change if each $\le$ was replaced with $<$ and each $<$ was replaced with $\le$? Explain your answer.

WRITING PIECEWISE FUNCTIONS Write equations for the piecewise function whose graph is shown.

35.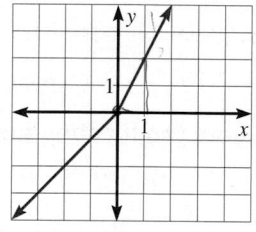

36.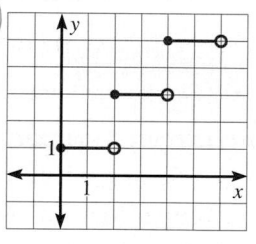

37.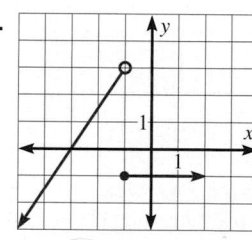

38.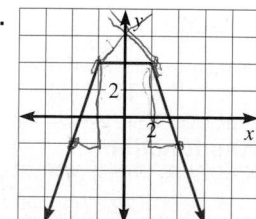

39.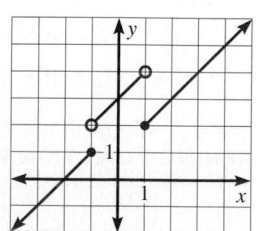

40.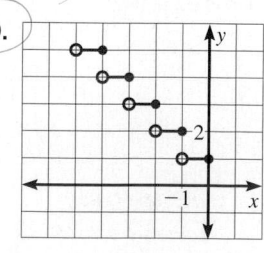

GREATEST INTEGER FUNCTION On many graphing calculators $\llbracket x \rrbracket$ is denoted by int(x). Use a graphing calculator to graph the function.

41. $g(x) = \llbracket x \rrbracket$

42. $g(x) = \llbracket 2x \rrbracket$

43. $g(x) = \llbracket x \rrbracket - 1$

44. $g(x) = \llbracket x + 3 \rrbracket$

45. $g(x) = 6\llbracket x \rrbracket$

46. $g(x) = \llbracket 3x \rrbracket + 4$

47. $g(x) = 4\llbracket x + 7 \rrbracket$

48. $g(x) = -\llbracket x \rrbracket$

49. $g(x) = 3\llbracket x - 2 \rrbracket + 5$

POSTAL RATES In Exercises 50 and 51, use the following information.

As of January 10, 1999, the cost C (in dollars) of sending next-day mail using the United States Postal Service, depending on the weight x (in ounces) of a package up to five pounds, is given by the function below.

 DATA UPDATE of United States Postal Service data at www.mcdougallittell.com

$$C(x) = \begin{cases} 11.75, & \text{if } 0 < x \le 8 \\ 15.75, & \text{if } 8 < x \le 32 \\ 18.50, & \text{if } 32 < x \le 48 \\ 21.25, & \text{if } 48 < x \le 64 \\ 24.00, & \text{if } 64 < x \le 80 \end{cases}$$

50. Graph the function.

51. Identify the domain and range of the function.

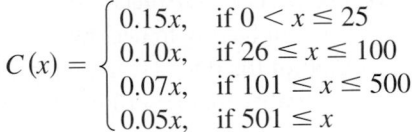 **PHOTOCOPY RATES** In Exercises 52 and 53, use the function given for the cost C (in dollars) of making x photocopies at a copy shop.

$$C(x) = \begin{cases} 0.15x, & \text{if } 0 < x \le 25 \\ 0.10x, & \text{if } 26 \le x \le 100 \\ 0.07x, & \text{if } 101 \le x \le 500 \\ 0.05x, & \text{if } 501 \le x \end{cases}$$

52. Graph the function.

53. VISUAL THINKING Use your graph to explain why it would not be cost-effective to make 450 photocopies.

SILK-SCREEN T-SHIRTS In Exercises 54 and 55, use the following silk-screen shop charges.

- An initial charge of $20 to create the silk screen

- $17.00 per shirt for orders of 50 or fewer shirts

- $15.80 per shirt for orders of more than 50 shirts

54. Write a piecewise function that gives the cost C for an order of x shirts.

55. Graph the function.

SOCIAL SECURITY In Exercises 56 and 57, use the following information.

The amount of Social Security tax you pay, part of your Federal Insurance Contributions Act (FICA) deductions, depends on your annual income. As of 1999 you pay 6.2% of your income if it is less than $72,600. If your income is at least $72,600, you pay a fixed amount of $4501.20.

DATA UPDATE of Social Security Administration data at www.mcdougallittell.com

56. Write and graph a piecewise function that gives the Social Security tax.

57. How much Social Security tax do you pay if you make $30,000 per year?

SNOWSTORM In Exercises 58 and 59, use the following information.

During a nine hour snowstorm it snows at a rate of 1 inch per hour for the first two hours, at a of rate of 2 inches per hour for the next six hours, and at a rate of 1 inch per hour for the final hour.

58. Write and graph a piecewise function that gives the depth of the snow during the snowstorm.

59. How many inches of snow accumulated from the storm?

STUDENT HELP

 **HOMEWORK HELP**
Visit our Web site www.mcdougallittell.com for help with problem solving in Exs. 52 and 53.

FOCUS ON APPLICATIONS

 **SNOWSTORM**
By weighing snow at the end of a snowstorm you can determine the water content of the snow. This information is one of the factors used to determine avalanche warnings.

APPLICATION LINK www.mcdougallittell.com

Test Preparation

QUANTITATIVE COMPARISON In Exercises 60 and 61, choose the statement that is true about the given quantities.

Ⓐ The quantity in column A is greater.

Ⓑ The quantity in column B is greater.

Ⓒ The two quantities are equal.

Ⓓ The relationship cannot be determined from the given information.

Column A	Column B
60. $f(3)$ where $f(x) = \begin{cases} 2x - 7, & \text{if } x \le 1 \\ -x + 9, & \text{if } x > 1 \end{cases}$	$f(2)$ where $f(x) = \begin{cases} x + 2, & \text{if } x < 8 \\ 3x - 3, & \text{if } x \ge 8 \end{cases}$
61. $f(0)$ where $f(x) = \begin{cases} 5x + 1, & \text{if } x < 9 \\ 6x - 4, & \text{if } x \ge 9 \end{cases}$	$f(-4)$ where $f(x) = \begin{cases} 9, & \text{if } x \le -4 \\ 11, & \text{if } x > -4 \end{cases}$

★ **Challenge**

62. 🤿 **SCUBA DIVING** The time t (in minutes) that a person may safely scuba dive without having to decompress while surfacing is determined by the depth d (in feet) of the dive. Using the information below, write and graph a piecewise inequality that describes the time limits for scuba divers at various depths.

- For depths from 40 feet (the minimum depth requiring decompression) to $53\frac{1}{3}$ feet, the time must not exceed 600 minutes minus ten times the depth.

- For depths greater than $53\frac{1}{3}$ feet to less than 90 feet, the time must not exceed 120 minutes minus the depth.

- For depths from 90 feet to 130 feet (the maximum safe depth for a recreational diver), the time must not exceed 75 minutes minus one half the depth.

EXTRA CHALLENGE
www.mcdougallittell.com

MIXED REVIEW

SOLVING EQUATIONS Solve the equation. **(Review 1.7 for 2.8)**

63. $|9 + 4x| = 15$

64. $|7x + 3| = 11$

65. $|21 - 2x| = 9$

66. $|2x + 8| = 1$

67. $\left|\frac{1}{2}x - 5\right| = 11$

68. $\left|1 - \frac{3}{4}x\right| = 6$

SCATTER PLOTS Draw a scatter plot of the data. Then tell whether the data have a *positive*, a *negative*, or *relatively no correlation*. **(Review 2.5)**

69.

x	−8	−8	−7	−6	−5	−4	−4	−2	−2	−1
y	−2	−8	−5	−7	−1	−4	−8	−1	−3	−7

70.

x	1	1.5	1.5	2.5	3	3.5	5	5.5	7	8
y	9	8	6	5	6	4	2	3	1	2

71. 🛏️ **SLEEPING BAGS** To be comfortable, sleeping bags rated for −40°F have 3.5 inches of insulation, and those rated for 40°F have 1.5 inches. Write a linear model for the amount a of insulation needed to be comfortable at temperature T. How much insulation would you need to be comfortable at 0°F? **(Review 2.4)**

▶ ACTIVITY 2.7

Using Technology

Graphing Piecewise Functions

You can use a graphing calculator to graph a piecewise function.

STUDENT HELP

INTERNET **KEYSTROKE HELP**

See keystrokes for several models of calculators at www.mcdougallittell.com

▶ EXAMPLE

Use a graphing calculator to graph the function f given below. Use the *Trace* feature to evaluate $f(x)$ when $x = 4$ and when $x = 10$.

$$f(x) = \begin{cases} 3x - 1, & \text{if } x < 2 \\ 7, & \text{if } 2 \le x \le 5 \\ 2x - 3, & \text{if } x > 5 \end{cases}$$

▶ SOLUTION

1 Put the calculator in dot mode so that the calculator does not connect separate pieces of the graph.

STUDENT HELP

▶ **Look Back**
For help with truth functions, see p. 48.

2 Enter the piecewise function by entering each piece of the function multiplied by a truth function specifying the values of x for which the piece applies. Add the products together. For any particular x-value, all of the products will evaluate to 0 except for the product whose truth function is satisfied.

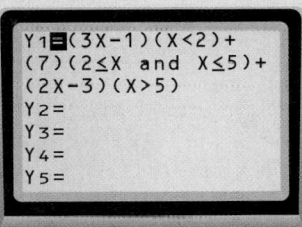

3 Choose an appropriate viewing window and graph the function. Note that the calculator does not distinguish between open and solid dots. Using the *Trace* feature, you can find that $f(4) \approx 7$ and that $f(10) \approx 17$, which you can check by substituting $x = 4$ and $x = 10$ into the function by hand.

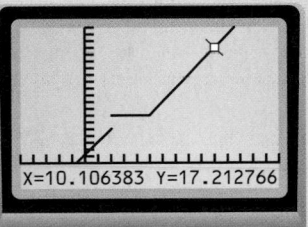

▶ EXERCISES

Use a graphing calculator to graph the piecewise function. Then use the *Trace* feature to evaluate the function when $x = 2$.

1. $f(x) = \begin{cases} 2x + 1, & \text{if } x < 0 \\ 2x + 2, & \text{if } x \ge 0 \end{cases}$

2. $f(x) = \begin{cases} 2x + 3, & \text{if } x \le 3 \\ 3 - x, & \text{if } x > 3 \end{cases}$

3. $f(x) = \begin{cases} \frac{1}{2}x + 1, & \text{if } x \le 2 \\ x - 2, & \text{if } x > 2 \end{cases}$

4. $f(x) = \begin{cases} 3, & \text{if } x < 2 \\ 2x - 1, & \text{if } x \ge 2 \end{cases}$

5. $f(x) = \begin{cases} x + 3, & \text{if } x \le 1 \\ 2(x + 1), & \text{if } 1 < x \le 3 \\ 11 - x, & \text{if } x > 3 \end{cases}$

6. $f(x) = \begin{cases} 5 - x, & \text{if } x \le 4 \\ 0.25x, & \text{if } 4 < x \le 8 \\ 10 - x, & \text{if } x > 8 \end{cases}$

2.8

Absolute Value Functions

What you should learn

GOAL 1 Represent absolute value functions.

GOAL 2 Use absolute value functions to model **real-life** situations, such as playing pool in **Example 4**.

Why you should learn it

▼ To solve **real-life** problems, such as when an orchestra should reach a desired sound level in **Exs. 44 and 45**.

GOAL 1 REPRESENTING ABSOLUTE VALUE FUNCTIONS

In Lesson 1.7 you learned that the absolute value of x is defined by:

$$|x| = \begin{cases} x, & \text{if } x > 0 \\ 0, & \text{if } x = 0 \\ -x, & \text{if } x < 0 \end{cases}$$

The graph of this piecewise function consists of two rays, is V-shaped, and opens up. The corner point of the graph, called the **vertex**, occurs at the origin.

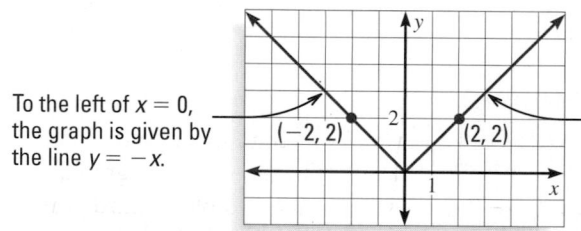

To the left of $x = 0$, the graph is given by the line $y = -x$.

$(-2, 2)$ $(2, 2)$

To the right of $x = 0$, the graph is given by the line $y = x$.

Notice that the graph of $y = |x|$ is symmetric in the y-axis because for every point (x, y) on the graph, the point $(-x, y)$ is also on the graph.

▶ ACTIVITY

Developing Concepts

Graphs of Absolute Value Functions

1 In the same coordinate plane, graph $y = a|x|$ for $a = -2, -\frac{1}{2}, \frac{1}{2},$ and 2. What effect does a have on the graph of $y = a|x|$? What is the vertex of the graph of $y = a|x|$?

2 In the same coordinate plane, graph $y = |x - h|$ for $h = -2, 0,$ and 2. What effect does h have on the graph of $y = |x - h|$? What is the vertex of the graph of $y = |x - h|$?

3 In the same coordinate plane, graph $y = |x| + k$ for $k = -2, 0,$ and 2. What effect does k have on the graph of $y = |x| + k$? What is the vertex of the graph of $y = |x| + k$?

Although in the activity you investigated the effects of a, h, and k on the graph of $y = a|x - h| + k$ separately, these effects can be combined. For example, the graph of $y = 2|x - 4| + 3$ is shown in red along with the graph of $y = |x|$ in blue. Notice that the vertex of the red graph is (4, 3) and that the red graph is narrower than the blue graph.

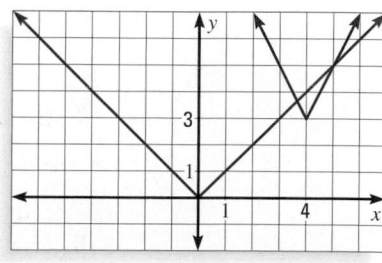

GRAPHING ABSOLUTE VALUE FUNCTIONS

The graph of $y = a|x - h| + k$ has the following characteristics.

- The graph has vertex (h, k) and is symmetric in the line $x = h$.
- The graph is V-shaped. It opens up if $a > 0$ and down if $a < 0$.
- The graph is wider than the graph of $y = |x|$ if $|a| < 1$.
  The graph is narrower than the graph of $y = |x|$ if $|a| > 1$.

STUDENT HELP

↪ **Skills Review**
For help with
symmetry, see p. 919.

To graph an absolute value function you may find it helpful to plot the vertex and one other point. Use symmetry to plot a third point and then complete the graph.

EXAMPLE 1 *Graphing an Absolute Value Function*

Graph $y = -|x + 2| + 3$.

SOLUTION

To graph $y = -|x + 2| + 3$, plot the vertex at $(-2, 3)$. Then plot another point on the graph, such as $(-3, 2)$. Use symmetry to plot a third point, $(-1, 2)$. Connect these three points with a V-shaped graph. Note that $a = -1 < 0$ and $|a| = 1$, so the graph opens down and is the same width as the graph of $y = |x|$.

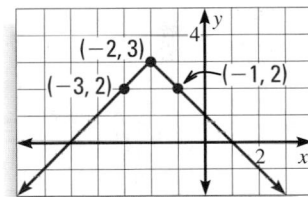

EXAMPLE 2 *Writing an Absolute Value Function*

Write an equation of the graph shown.

SOLUTION

The vertex of the graph is $(0, -3)$, so the equation has the form:

$$y = a|x - 0| + (-3) \quad \text{or} \quad y = a|x| - 3$$

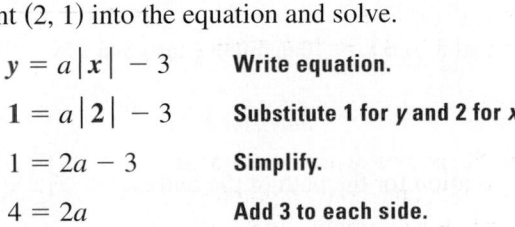

To find the value of a, substitute the coordinates of the point $(2, 1)$ into the equation and solve.

$y = a|x| - 3$	**Write equation.**
$1 = a|2| - 3$	**Substitute 1 for y and 2 for x.**
$1 = 2a - 3$	**Simplify.**
$4 = 2a$	**Add 3 to each side.**
$2 = a$	**Divide each side by 2.**

▶ An equation of the graph is $y = 2|x| - 3$.

✓ **CHECK** Notice the graph opens up and is narrower than the graph of $y = |x|$, so 2 is a reasonable value for a.

GOAL 2 USING ABSOLUTE VALUE FUNCTIONS IN REAL LIFE

EXAMPLE 3   *Interpreting an Absolute Value Function*

Camping   The front of a camping tent can be modeled by the function

$$y = -1.4\,|x - 2.5| + 3.5$$

where x and y are measured in feet and the x-axis represents the ground.

   a. Graph the function.

   b. Interpret the domain and range of the function in the given context.

SOLUTION

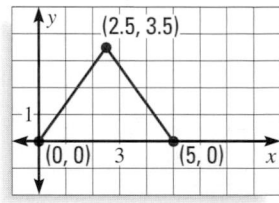

   a. The graph of the function is shown. The vertex is (2.5, 3.5) and the graph opens down. It is narrower than the graph of $y = |x|$.

   b. The domain is $0 \le x \le 5$, so the tent is 5 feet wide. The range is $0 \le y \le 3.5$, so the tent is 3.5 feet tall.

EXAMPLE 4   *Interpreting an Absolute Value Graph*

Billiards   While playing pool, you try to shoot the eight ball into the corner pocket as shown. Imagine that a coordinate plane is placed over the pool table. The eight ball is at $\left(5, \dfrac{5}{4}\right)$ and the pocket you are aiming for is at (10, 5). You are going to bank the ball off the side at (6, 0).

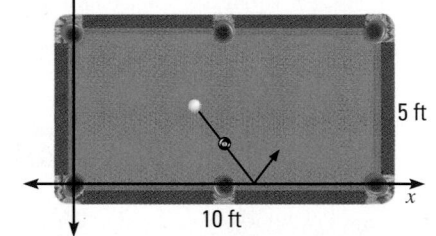

   a. Write an equation for the path of the ball.

   b. Do you make your shot?

SOLUTION

   a. The vertex of the path of the ball is (6, 0), so the equation has the form $y = a\,|x - 6|$. Substitute the coordinates of the point $\left(5, \dfrac{5}{4}\right)$ into the equation and solve for a.

$$\frac{5}{4} = a\,|5 - 6| \qquad \text{Substitute } \tfrac{5}{4} \text{ for } y \text{ and 5 for } x.$$

$$\frac{5}{4} = a \qquad \text{Solve for } a.$$

   ▶ An equation for the path of the ball is $y = \dfrac{5}{4}\,|x - 6|$.

   b. You will make your shot if the point (10, 5) lies on the path of the ball.

$$5 \overset{?}{=} \frac{5}{4}\,|10 - 6| \qquad \text{Substitute 5 for } y \text{ and 10 for } x.$$

$$5 = 5 \checkmark \qquad \text{Simplify.}$$

   ▶ The point (10, 5) satisfies the equation, so you do make your shot.

GUIDED PRACTICE

Vocabulary Check ✓

1. What do the coordinates (h, k) represent on the graph of $y = a|x - h| + k$?

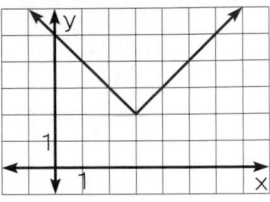

Concept Check ✓

2. How do you know if the graph of $y = a|x - h| + k$ opens up or down? How do you know if it is wider, narrower, or the same width as the graph of $y = |x|$?

3. **ERROR ANALYSIS** Explain why the graph shown is not the graph of $y = |x + 3| + 2$.

Ex. 3

Skill Check ✓

Graph the function. Then identify the vertex, tell whether the graph opens up or down, and tell whether the graph is wider, narrower, or the same width as the graph of $y = |x|$.

4. $y = \frac{1}{2}|x|$

5. $y = |x + 5|$

6. $y = |x| - 10$

7. $y = |x| + 5$

8. $y = 2|x + 6| - 10$

9. $y = -\left|x - \frac{1}{2}\right| - 14$

10. Write an equation for the function whose graph is shown.

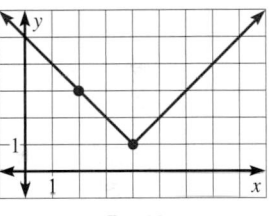

11. **CAMPING** Suppose that the tent in Example 3 is 7 feet wide and 5 feet tall. Write a function that models the front of the tent. Let the x-axis represent the ground. Then graph the function and identify the domain and range of the function.

Ex. 10

PRACTICE AND APPLICATIONS

STUDENT HELP

↳ **Extra Practice**
to help you master skills is on p. 942.

EXAMINING THE EFFECT OF *a* Match the function with its graph.

12. $f(x) = 3|x|$

13. $f(x) = -3|x|$

14. $f(x) = \frac{1}{3}|x|$

A.
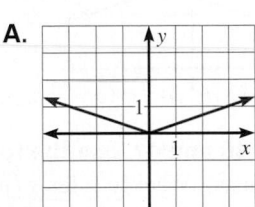

B.
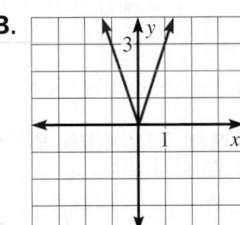

C.
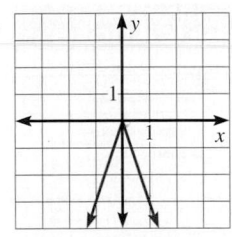

EXAMINING THE EFFECTS OF *h* AND *k* Match the function with its graph.

15. $y = |x - 2|$

16. $y = |x| - 2$

17. $y = |x + 2|$

STUDENT HELP

↳ **HOMEWORK HELP**
Example 1: Exs. 12–25
Example 2: Exs. 34–39
Example 3: Exs. 40–45
Example 4: Exs. 46–48

A.
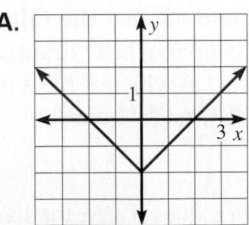

B.
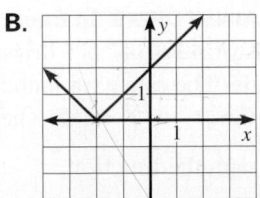

C.
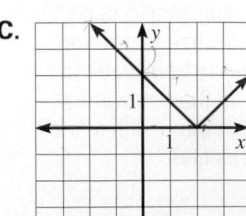

GRAPHING ABSOLUTE VALUE FUNCTIONS Graph the function. Then identify the vertex, tell whether the graph opens up or down, and tell whether the graph is wider, narrower, or the same width as the graph of $y = |x|$.

18. $y = 6|x - 7|$

19. $y = |x| + 9$

20. $y = -|x - 8| + 1$

21. $y = -|x + 2| + 11$

22. $y = \frac{1}{3}|x - 3| + 4$

23. $y = -2|x + 9| + 3$

24. $y = |x| - \frac{5}{2}$

25. $y = -\frac{1}{2}|x + 6|$

ABSOLUTE VALUE On many graphing calculators $|x|$ is denoted by ABS(x). Use a graphing calculator to graph the absolute value function. Then use the *Trace* feature to find the corresponding x-value(s) for the given y-value.

26. $y = |x| + 4; y = 10$

27. $y = |x + 14|; y = 9$

28. $y = 15|x|; y = \frac{3}{2}$

29. $y = |x + \frac{4}{7}| - 5; y = 0$

30. $y = -|x - 2| + 5; y = 0.5$

31. $y = -3.2|x| + 7; y = -2$

32. $y = -3.75|x + 1.5| - 5; y = -5$

33. $y = 1.5|x - 3| + 6; y = 8.25$

WRITING EQUATIONS Write an equation of the graph shown.

34.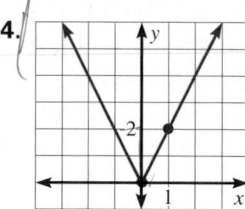

35.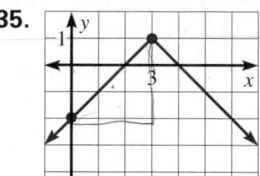

36.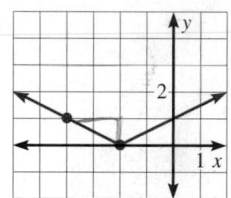

37.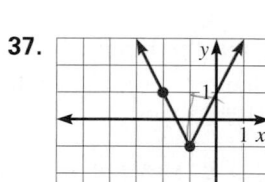

38.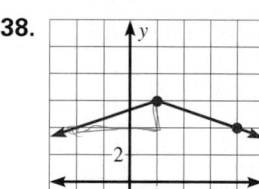

39.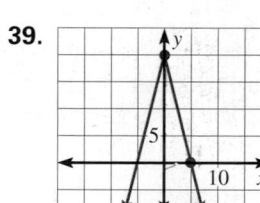

MUSIC SINGLES In Exercises 40 and 41, use the following information.
A musical group's new single is released. Weekly sales s (in thousands) increase steadily for a while and then decrease as given by the function $s = -2|t - 20| + 40$ where t is the time (in weeks).

40. Graph the function.

41. What was the maximum number of singles sold in one week?

RAINSTORMS In Exercises 42 and 43, use the following information.
A rainstorm begins as a drizzle, builds up to a heavy rain, and then drops back to a drizzle. The rate r (in inches per hour) at which it rains is given by the function $r = -0.5|t - 1| + 0.5$ where t is the time (in hours).

42. Graph the function.

43. For how long does it rain and when does it rain the hardest?

🌐 **SOUND LEVELS** In Exercises 44 and 45, use the following information.

Suppose a musical piece calls for an orchestra to start at *fortissimo* (about 90 decibels), decrease in loudness to *pianissimo* (about 50 decibels) in four measures, and then increase back to *fortissimo* in another four measures. The sound level *s* (in decibels) of the musical piece can be modeled by the function $s = 10|m - 4| + 50$ where *m* is the number of measures.

44. Graph the function for $0 \le m \le 8$.

45. After how many measures should the orchestra be at the loudness of *mezzo forte* (about 70 decibels)?

46. 🌐 **MINIATURE GOLF** You are trying to make a hole-in-one on the miniature golf green shown. Imagine that a coordinate plane is placed over the golf green. The golf ball is at (2.5, 2) and the hole is at (9.5, 2). You are going to bank the ball off the side wall of the green at (6, 8). Write an equation for the path of the ball and determine if you make your shot.

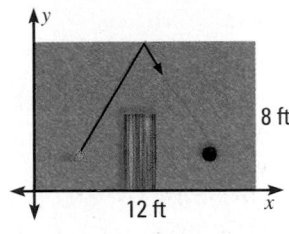
8 ft
12 ft

47. 🌐 **REFLECTING SUNLIGHT** You are sitting in a boat on a lake. You can get a sunburn from sunlight that hits you directly and from sunlight that reflects off the water. Sunlight reflects off the water at the point (2, 0) and hits you at the point (3.5, 3). Write and graph the function that shows the path of the sunlight.

STUDENT HELP

🌐 **HOMEWORK HELP**
Visit our Web site
www.mcdougallittell.com
for help with problem
solving in Ex. 48.

48. 🌐 **TRANSAMERICA PYRAMID** The Transamerica Pyramid, shown at the right, is an office building in San Francisco. It stands 853 feet tall and is 145 feet wide at its base. Imagine that a coordinate plane is placed over a side of the building. In the coordinate plane, each unit represents one foot, and the origin is at the center of the building's base. Write an absolute value function whose graph is the V-shaped outline of the sides of the building, ignoring the "shoulders" of the building.

Test Preparation

49. MULTIPLE CHOICE Which statement is true about the graph of the function $y = -|x + 2| + 3$?

A Its vertex is at (2, 3).   **B** Its vertex is at (−2, −3).

C It opens down.   **D** It is wider than the graph of $y = |x|$.

50. MULTIPLE CHOICE Which function is represented by the graph shown?

A $y = -|x - 10| + 2$
B $y = -|x + 10| - 2$
C $y = -|x - 2| - 10$
D $y = -|x + 2| + 10$

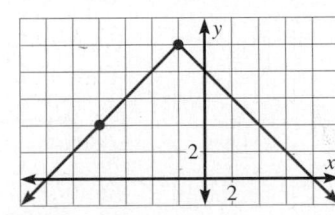

★ **Challenge**

GRAPHING Graph the functions.

51. $y = |2x|$ and $y = 2|x|$ **52.** $y = |-5x|$ and $y = 5|x|$

53. $y = |x + 6|$ and $y = |x| + 6$ **54.** $y = |x + (-3)|$ and $y = |x| + 3$

55. Based on your answers to Exercises 51–54, do you think $|ab| = |a| \cdot |b|$ and $|a + b| = |a| + |b|$ are true statements? Explain.

EXTRA CHALLENGE
www.mcdougallittell.com

MIXED REVIEW

REWRITING EQUATIONS Solve the equation for *y*. **(Review 1.4)**

56. $3x - 5y = 8$ 　　　**57.** $6x + 2y = -9$ 　　　**58.** $-\frac{1}{5}x - \frac{3}{2}y = 1$

GRAPHING EQUATIONS Graph the equation. **(Review 2.3 for 3.1)**

59. $y = x - 5$ 　　　**60.** $y = 6x + 7$ 　　　**61.** $y = -\frac{1}{2}x + 10$

62. $x + y = 8$ 　　　**63.** $4x + y = 2$ 　　　**64.** $3x - y = -1$

FITTING A LINE TO DATA Draw a scatter plot of the data. Then approximate the best-fitting line for the data. **(Review 2.5)**

65.

x	−2	−1.5	−1	−0.5	0.5	1	1	1.5	2	2
y	−5	−3	−1	−2	1	−1	2	4	3	3

66.

x	−2	−1	0	0.5	1	2	2.5	3.5	4	4.5
y	5	3	3.5	1.5	2	0	−2	−3.5	−2	−3.5

QUIZ 3

Graph the inequality in a coordinate plane. **(Lesson 2.6)**

1. $y \le -8$ 　　　**2.** $2x \ge -5$ 　　　**3.** $y > 3x - 4$ 　　　**4.** $2x + 5y < 15$

Evaluate the function for the given value of *x*. **(Lesson 2.7)**

5. $f(5)$ where $f(x) = \begin{cases} 3x + 9, & \text{if } x \le 3 \\ 2x - 3, & \text{if } x > 3 \end{cases}$ 　　**6.** $f(0)$ where $f(x) = \begin{cases} 10, & \text{if } -1 \le x < 0 \\ 5, & \text{if } 0 \le x < 1 \\ 0, & \text{if } 1 \le x < 2 \end{cases}$

Graph the function. **(Lesson 2.8)**

7. $y = 3|x - 2|$ 　　　**8.** $y = -|x| + 6$ 　　　**9.** $y = -5|x + 3| - 8$

Write an equation of the graph shown. **(Lesson 2.8)**

10. 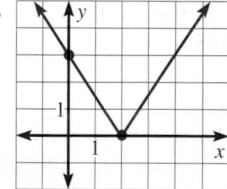 　　　**11.** 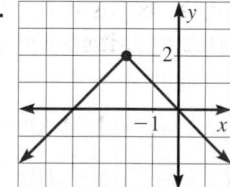 　　　**12.**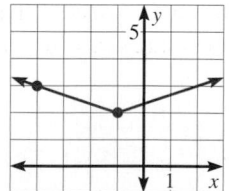

13. 🌎 **BEACH SNACKS** You and four friends have $15 to spend on snacks at the beach. A medium box of popcorn costs $2.50 and a medium soft drink costs $1.25. Write and graph an inequality that represents the numbers of medium boxes of popcorn and medium soft drinks you can buy. **(Lesson 2.6)**

14. 🌎 **RENTING A CAR** A local car rental company charges a weekly rate of $200 with 1000 free miles. Each additional mile is $.20. Write and graph a piecewise function that shows the car rental charge. If you drive 1200 miles in one week, how much will the rental car cost? **(Lesson 2.7)**

Chapter Summary

WHAT did you learn?

Represent relations and functions. **(2.1)**

Graph and evaluate linear functions. **(2.1)**

Find and use the slope of a line. **(2.2)**

Write linear equations. **(2.4)**

Write direct variation equations. **(2.4)**

Use a scatter plot to identify the correlation shown by a set of data. **(2.5)**

Approximate the best-fitting line for a set of data. **(2.5)**

Graph linear equations, inequalities, and functions.
  • linear equations **(2.3)**

  • linear inequalities in two variables **(2.6)**
  • piecewise functions **(2.7)**
  • absolute value functions **(2.8)**

Use linear equations, inequalities, and functions to solve real-life problems. **(2.3–2.8)**

WHY did you learn it?

Determine if the diameters of trees are a function of their ages. **(p. 68)**

Model the distance a hot-air balloon travels. **(p. 70)**

Find the average rate of change in temperature. **(p. 81)**

Predict the number of African-American women who will hold elected public office in 2010. **(p. 93)**

Model calories burned while dancing. **(p. 97)**

Identify the relationship between when and for how long Old Faithful will erupt. **(p. 104)**

Predict how many people will enroll in City Year in 2010. **(p. 105)**

Identify relationships between sales of student and adult basketball tickets. **(p. 88)**

Model blood pressures in your arm and ankle. **(p. 112)**
Determine the cost of ordering T-shirts. **(p. 119)**
Model the sound level of an orchestra. **(p. 127)**

Determine how much your summer job will pay. **(p. 116)**

How does Chapter 2 fit into the BIGGER PICTURE of algebra?

Your study of functions began in Chapter 2 and will continue throughout Algebra 2 and in future mathematics courses. To represent different kinds of functions with graphs and equations is a very important part of algebra. A relationship between two variables or two sets of data is often linear, but as you will see later in this course, it can also be quadratic, cubic, exponential, logarithmic, or trigonometric.

STUDY STRATEGY

How did you make and use a skills file?

Here is an example of a skill from Lesson 2.4 for your skills file, following the **Study Strategy** on page 66.

Write an equation of a line that passes through the given points. (Lesson 2.4)

Skills File

Points: $(-1, 6), (3, -2)$
Find slope:

$$m = \frac{-2 - 6}{3 - (-1)} = \frac{-8}{4} = -2$$

Use point-slope form:
$$y - 6 = -2[x - (-1)]$$
$$y - 6 = -2x - 2$$
$$y = -2x + 4$$

Chapter Review

- relation, p. 67
- domain, p. 67
- range, p. 67
- function, p. 67
- ordered pair, p. 67
- coordinate plane, p. 67
- equation in two variables, p. 69
- solution of an equation in two variables, p. 69
- independent variable, p. 69

- dependent variable, p. 69
- graph of an equation in two variables, p. 69
- linear function, p. 69
- function notation, p. 69
- slope, p. 75
- parallel lines, p. 77
- perpendicular lines, p. 77
- y-intercept, p. 82
- slope-intercept form of a linear equation, p. 82

- standard form of a linear equation, p. 84
- x-intercept, p. 84
- direct variation, p. 94
- constant of variation, p. 94
- scatter plot, p. 100
- positive correlation, p. 100
- negative correlation, p. 100
- relatively no correlation, p. 100

- linear inequality in two variables, p. 108
- solution of a linear inequality in two variables, p. 108
- graph of a linear inequality in two variables, p. 108
- half-plane, p. 108
- piecewise function, p. 114
- step function, p. 115
- vertex of an absolute value graph, p. 122

2.1 FUNCTIONS AND THEIR GRAPHS

Examples on pp. 67–70

EXAMPLE You can represent a relation with a table of values or a graph of ordered pairs.

x	0	1	−2	3	1
y	1	−1	0	0	2

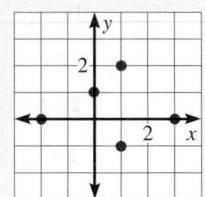

This relation is not a function because $x = 1$ is paired with both $y = -1$ and $y = 2$.

Graph the relation. Then tell whether the relation is a function.

1.

x	−1	0	1	2	3
y	10	7	4	1	−2

2.

x	6	1	0	4	3	5
y	2	4	2	1	5	0

2.2 SLOPE AND RATE OF CHANGE

Examples on pp. 75–78

EXAMPLE You can find the slope of a line passing through two given points.

Points: $(5, 0)$ and $(-3, 4)$ **Slope:** $m = \dfrac{y_2 - y_1}{x_2 - x_1} = \dfrac{4 - 0}{-3 - 5} = \dfrac{4}{-8} = -\dfrac{1}{2}$

Find the slope of the line passing through the given points.

3. $(3, 6), (-6, 0)$ **4.** $(2, 4), (-2, 4)$ **5.** $(-7, 2), (-1, -4)$ **6.** $(5, 1), (5, 4)$

QUICK GRAPHS OF LINEAR EQUATIONS

Examples on pp. 82–85

EXAMPLES You can graph a linear equation in slope-intercept or in standard form.

$y = -3x + 1$

slope $= -3$

y-intercept $= 1$

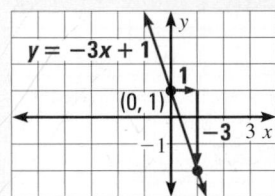

$4x - 3y = 12$

x-intercept $= 3$

y-intercept $= -4$

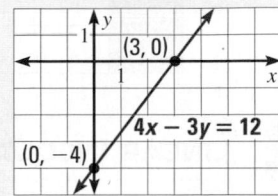

Graph the equation.

7. $y = -x + 3$ **8.** $y = \frac{1}{2}x - 7$ **9.** $4x + y = 2$ **10.** $-4x + 8y = -16$

WRITING EQUATIONS OF LINES

Examples on pp. 91–94

EXAMPLES You can write an equation of a line using (**a**) the slope and y-intercept, (**b**) the slope and a point on the line, or (**c**) two points on the line.

    a. Slope-intercept form, $m = 2$ and $b = -3$: $y = 2x - 3$

    b. Point-slope form, $m = 2$ and $(x_1, y_1) = (2, 1)$: $y - 1 = 2(x - 2)$
                                            $y = 2x - 3$

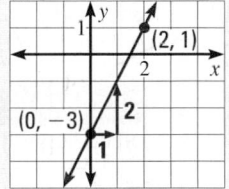

    c. Points $(0, -3)$ and $(2, 1)$:   slope $= \dfrac{1 - (-3)}{2 - 0} = 2$

        Use either slope-intercept form or point-slope form: $y = 2x - 3$

Write an equation of the line that has the given properties.

11. slope: -1, y-intercept: 2   **12.** slope: 3, point: $(-4, 1)$ **13.** points: $(3, -8)$, $(8, 2)$

CORRELATION AND BEST-FITTING LINES

Examples on pp. 100–102

EXAMPLE You can graph paired data to see what relationship, if any, exists. The table shows the price p (in dollars per pound) of bread where t is the number of years since 1990.

t	0	1	2	3	4	5	6
p	0.70	0.72	0.74	0.76	0.75	0.84	0.87

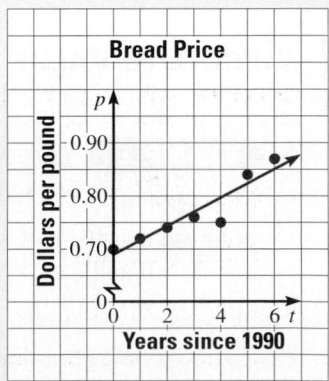

Bread Price

Approximate the best-fitting line using $(4, 0.80)$ and $(6, 0.85)$,

$m = \dfrac{0.85 - 0.80}{6 - 4} = 0.025$ $y - 0.80 = 0.025(x - 4)$

                                    $y = 0.025x + 0.70$

Approximate the best-fitting line for the data.

14.

x	14	11	21	3	4	19	10	1	17	6
y	4	6	1	10	9	0	5	10	2	7

2.6 LINEAR INEQUALITIES IN TWO VARIABLES

Examples on pp. 108–110

EXAMPLE You can graph a linear inequality in two variables in a coordinate plane.

To graph $y < x + 2$, first graph the boundary line $y = x + 2$. Use a dashed line since the symbol is $<$, not $\leq$. Test the point $(0, 0)$. Since $(0, 0)$ *is* a solution of the inequality, shade the half-plane that contains it.

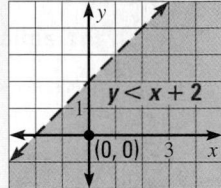

Graph the inequality in a coordinate plane.

15. $2x < 6$ **16.** $y \leq 7$ **17.** $y \geq -x + 4$ **18.** $x + 8y > 8$

2.7 PIECEWISE FUNCTIONS

Examples on pp. 114–116

EXAMPLE You can graph a piecewise function by graphing each piece separately.

$$y = \begin{cases} x - 1, & \text{if } x < 0 \\ -x + 2, & \text{if } x \geq 0 \end{cases}$$

Graph $y = x - 1$ to the left of $x = 0$.
Graph $y = -x + 2$ to the right of and including $x = 0$.

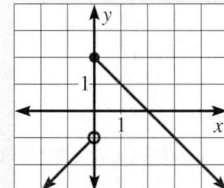

Graph the function.

19. $y = \begin{cases} 2x, & \text{if } x < -1 \\ 2x + 1, & \text{if } x \geq -1 \end{cases}$ **20.** $y = \begin{cases} -x, & \text{if } x \leq 0 \\ 3x, & \text{if } x > 0 \end{cases}$ **21.** $y = \begin{cases} -2, & \text{if } x \leq 2 \\ 2, & \text{if } x > 2 \end{cases}$

2.8 ABSOLUTE VALUE FUNCTIONS

Examples on pp. 122–124

EXAMPLE You can graph an absolute value function using symmetry.

The graph of $y = 3|x + 1| - 2$ has vertex $(-1, -2)$. Plot a second point such as $(0, 1)$. Use symmetry to plot a third point, $(-2, 1)$. Note that $a = 3 > 0$ and $|a| > 1$, so the graph opens up and is narrower than the graph of $y = |x|$.

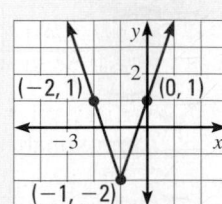

Graph the function.

22. $y = -|x| + 1$ **23.** $y = |x - 4| + 3$ **24.** $y = 2|x| - 5$ **25.** $y = 3|x + 6| - 2$

Graph the relation. Then tell whether the relation is a function.

1.

x	−4	−2	0	2	4
y	−1	0	1	2	3

2.

x	2	−3	4	0	−3	1
y	2	−2	0	2	3	−1

Evaluate the function for the given value of x.

3. $f(x) = 80 - 3x; f(5)$

4. $f(x) = x^2 + 4x - 7; f(-1)$

5. $f(x) = 3|x - 4| + 2; f(2)$

Graph the equation.

6. $y = -\frac{2}{3}x + 2$

7. $y = -3$

8. $5x - 2y = 10$

9. $x = 4$

Write an equation of the line with the given characteristics.

10. slope: $\frac{3}{4}$, y-intercept: -5

11. slope: -1, point: $(2, -4)$

12. points: $(-2, 5), (-6, 8)$

13. Write an equation of the line that passes through $(-3, 2)$ and is parallel to the line $x - y = 7$.

14. Write an equation of the line that passes through $(1, 4)$ and is perpendicular to the line $y = -3x + 1$.

Graph the inequality in a coordinate plane.

15. $x + 4y \le 0$

16. $y > 3x - 1$

17. $x - y > 3$

18. $-x \ge 2$

Graph the function.

19. $f(x) = \begin{cases} -2x + 3, & \text{if } x \le 1 \\ x, & \text{if } x > 1 \end{cases}$

20. $f(x) = \begin{cases} 2, & \text{if } -4 < x \le -2 \\ 5, & \text{if } -2 < x \le 0 \\ 7, & \text{if } 0 < x \le 2 \\ 10, & \text{if } 2 < x \le 4 \end{cases}$

21. $f(x) = \begin{cases} x - 2, & \text{if } x \le 0 \\ x + 2, & \text{if } x > 0 \end{cases}$

22. $y = -|x + 3|$

23. $y = 2|x| - 1$

24. $y = -\frac{1}{3}|x - 2| + 2$

25. **ROLLER COASTERS** One of the world's faster roller coasters is located in a theme park in Valencia, California. Riders go from 0 to 100 miles per hour in 7 seconds. Find the acceleration of the roller coaster during this time interval in miles per second squared.

26. **MIRROR LENGTH** To be able to see your complete reflection in a mirror that is hanging on a wall, the mirror must have a minimum length of m inches. The value of m varies directly with your height h (in inches). A person 71 inches tall requires a 35.5 inch mirror. Write a linear model that gives m as a function of h. Then find the minimum mirror length required for a person who is 66 inches tall.

27. **PATENTS** The table shows the number p (in thousands) of patents issued to United States residents where t is the number of years since 1985. Draw a scatter plot of the data and describe the correlation shown. Then approximate the best-fitting line for the data.
▶ Source: Statistical Abstract of the United States

t	0	1	2	3	4	5	6	7	8	9	10
p	43.3	42.0	47.7	44.6	54.6	52.8	57.7	58.7	61.1	64.2	64.4

Chapter Standardized Test

▶ **TEST-TAKING STRATEGY** Read the test questions carefully. Also try to find short cuts that will help you move through the questions quicker.

1. MULTIPLE CHOICE Which of the following relations is *not* a function?

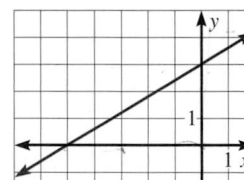

(A)
x	1	2	3
y	1	2	3

(B)
x	0	1	3
y	2	2	2

(C)
x	1	1	1
y	0	2	3

(D)
x	1	2	3
y	2	1	3

(E)
x	0	3	1
y	1	2	3

2. MULTIPLE CHOICE If $f(x) = -x^2 - 7x - 22$, what is $f(-5)$?

(A) -82 (B) -32 (C) -12

(D) 12 (E) 38

3. MULTIPLE CHOICE What is the slope of the line that passes through $(-4, -9)$ and $(0, 5)$?

(A) $-\dfrac{7}{2}$ (B) $-\dfrac{2}{7}$ (C) $\dfrac{2}{7}$

(D) 1 (E) $\dfrac{7}{2}$

4. MULTIPLE CHOICE Which function is represented by the graph shown?

(A) $3x - 5y = 15$

(B) $3x - 5y = 0$

(C) $3x - 5y = -15$

(D) $3x + 5y = 15$

(E) $3x + 5y = -15$

5. MULTIPLE CHOICE What is the y-intercept of the line $y = 4x - 3$?

(A) 1 (B) 3 (C) 4

(D) -3 (E) -4

6. MULTIPLE CHOICE The variables x and y vary directly, and $y = 20$ when $x = 5$. Which equation relates the variables?

(A) $y = \dfrac{1}{5}x$ (B) $y = \dfrac{1}{4}x$ (C) $y = 5x$

(D) $y = 20x$ (E) $y = 4x$

7. MULTIPLE CHOICE What is the equation of the line that passes through $(-4, -1)$ and $(0, 7)$?

(A) $y = 2x + 9$ (B) $y = \dfrac{1}{2}x + 7$

(C) $y = 2x + 7$ (D) $y = -\dfrac{1}{2}x + 7$

(E) $y = -2x + 7$

8. MULTIPLE CHOICE What is the equation of the line that contains $(3, 3)$ and is perpendicular to the line $y = -2x + 3$?

(A) $y = \dfrac{1}{2}x + \dfrac{3}{2}$ (B) $y = -2x + 9$

(C) $y = -\dfrac{1}{2}x + \dfrac{3}{2}$ (D) $y = 2x + 9$

(E) $y = \dfrac{1}{2}x$

9. MULTIPLE CHOICE Which inequality is represented by the graph shown?

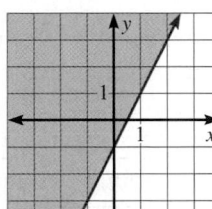

(A) $y < 2x - 1$

(B) $y > 2x - 1$

(C) $y \le 2x - 1$

(D) $y \ne 2x - 1$

(E) $y \ge 2x - 1$

10. MULTIPLE CHOICE If $f(x) = \begin{cases} 2x - 3, & \text{if } x < 4 \\ -x + 6, & \text{if } x \ge 4 \end{cases}$, what is $f(4)$?

(A) 2 (B) 4

(C) 5 (D) 10

(E) 11

11. MULTIPLE CHOICE Which function is represented by the graph shown?

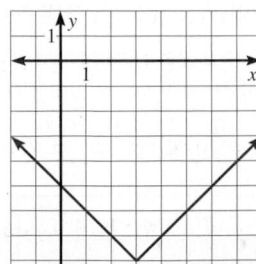

(A) $y = |x - 3| + 8$

(B) $y = |x + 3| - 8$

(C) $y = |x + 3| + 8$

(D) $y = |x - 3| - 8$

(E) $y = -|x - 3| - 8$

QUANTITATIVE COMPARISON In Exercises 12 and 13, choose the statement that is true about the given quantities.

(A) The quantity in column A is greater.

(B) The quantity in column B is greater.

(C) The two quantities are equal.

(D) The relationship cannot be determined from the given information.

Column A	Column B
12. slope of the line that passes through $(-6, 1)$ and $(2, 8)$	slope of the line that passes through $(0, 5)$ and $(-4, -9)$
13. $f(-3)$ where $f(x) = x^2 - 7x - 24$	$f(-3)$ where $f(x) = \begin{cases} 2x, & \text{if } x \le 0 \\ -2x, & \text{if } x > 0 \end{cases}$

14. **MULTI-STEP PROBLEM** You are planting an herb garden. The garden has 120 inches of row space, the amount of space needed *between* rows of plants. Parsley seeds need 15 inches of row space and garlic cloves need 12 inches of row space.

   a. If you plant only parsley seeds, at most how many rows can you plant?

   b. If you plant only garlic cloves, at most how many rows can you plant?

   c. Write a model that shows the maximum number of rows you can plant if you plant both herbs and leave 12 inches of row space between the parsley and the garlic.

   d. If you plant five rows of parsley seeds, how many rows of garlic cloves can you plant?

15. **MULTI-STEP PROBLEM** The table gives the number n of nurses per 100,000 people in the United States where t is the number of years since 1990.

t	0	1	2	3	4	5	6
n	713	730	748	767	785	805	815

   a. Draw a scatter plot of the data.

   b. Describe the correlation shown by the scatter plot.

   c. Approximate the best-fitting line for the data.

   d. Use your equation from part (c) to predict the number of nurses per 100,000 people in the United States in 2010.

16. **MULTI-STEP PROBLEM** While playing pool, you try to shoot the eight ball into the upper right corner pocket. Imagine that a coordinate plane is placed over the pool table. The eight ball is at $(4, 3)$ and the pocket you are aiming for is at $(10, 5)$. You are trying to decide at which point to bank the ball off the side.

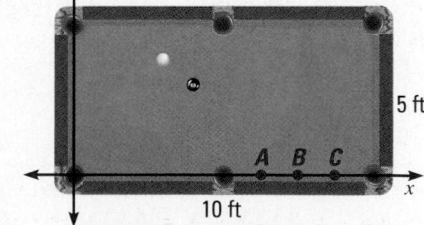

5 ft

10 ft

   a. Write an equation for the path of the ball if you aim for the point $(6.25, 0)$.

   b. Write an equation for the path of the ball if you aim for the point $(7.5, 0)$.

   c. Write an equation for the path of the ball if you aim for the point $(8.75, 0)$.

   d. Which point should you aim for to make your shot?

SYSTEMS OF LINEAR EQUATIONS AND INEQUALITIES

How can you combine swimming and inline skating to burn 300 Calories?

APPLICATION: Cross-Training

Cross-training involves doing a combination of two or more types of exercise. Since different exercises use different muscle groups, cross-training is a good way to get a well-rounded workout.

Think & Discuss

You burn about 12 Calories per minute swimming and about 8 Calories per minute inline skating. You want to do a combination of both activities for a total of 30 minutes and 300 Calories burned.

Minutes swimming, s	Minutes inline skating, i	$12s + 8i$
0	?	?
5	?	?
10	?	?
15	?	?
20	?	?
25	?	?
30	?	?

1. Copy the table above. Complete the second column so that $s + i = 30$.

2. What does the expression $12s + 8i$ represent? Complete this column in your table.

3. How long should you spend doing each activity?

Learn More About It

You will find another cross-training combination in Ex. 57 on p. 154.

APPLICATION LINK Visit www.mcdougallittell.com for more information about cross-training.

Study Guide

What's the chapter about?

Chapter 3 is about **systems of linear equations and inequalities**. In Chapter 3 you'll learn

- how to solve linear systems in two or three variables by graphing and by using algebraic methods.

- how to write and use linear systems to solve real-life problems.

PREVIEW

KEY VOCABULARY

▶ **Review**
- solution of an equation in two variables, p. 69
- solution of a linear inequality in two variables, p. 108

▶ **New**
- system of two linear equations in two variables, p. 139

- substitution method, p. 148
- linear combination method, p. 149
- system of linear inequalities, p. 156
- linear programming, p. 163
- three-dimensional coordinate system, p. 170

- ordered triple, p. 170
- linear equation in three variables, p. 171
- function of two variables, p. 171
- system of three linear equations in three variables, p. 177

PREPARE

Are you ready for the chapter?

SKILL REVIEW Do these exercises to review key skills that you'll apply in this chapter. See the given **reference page** if there is something you don't understand.

Check whether the ordered pair is a solution of the given equation or inequality. (Review p. 69; Example 1, p. 108)

1. $y = \frac{2}{3}x - 4, (0, 4)$ **2.** $x = -3, (-3, 1)$ **3.** $5x + y = 10, (1, 5)$

4. $y \geq 0, (-4, 5)$ **5.** $2x - 3y > 6, (6, 2)$ **6.** $x + y \leq 3, (-7, 9)$

Graph in a coordinate plane. (Review Examples 1–5, pp. 83–85; Examples 2 and 3, p. 109)

7. $y = \frac{1}{2}x + 1$ **8.** $2x + 5y = 20$ **9.** $y = 3$

10. $x \geq -2$ **11.** $y < -x$ **12.** $x - 3y \geq 9$

STUDY STRATEGY

Here's a study strategy!

Building on Previous Skills

Many of the ideas and skills you will learn in Chapter 3 directly build upon those in Chapter 2. As you study Chapter 3, make a list of important ideas and skills. To help you understand the new material, review the related ideas and skills from Chapter 2. Write these in a second column.

3.1

Solving Linear Systems by Graphing

What you should learn

GOAL 1 Graph and solve systems of linear equations in two variables.

GOAL 2 Use linear systems to solve **real-life** problems, such as choosing the least expensive long-distance telephone service in **Ex. 64**.

Why you should learn it

▼ To solve **real-life** problems, such as how to stay within a budget on a vacation in Florida in **Example 4**.

GOAL 1 GRAPHING AND SOLVING A SYSTEM

A **system of two linear equations** in two variables x and y consists of two equations of the following form.

$$Ax + By = C \qquad \text{Equation 1}$$
$$Dx + Ey = F \qquad \text{Equation 2}$$

A **solution** of a system of linear equations in two variables is an ordered pair (x, y) that satisfies each equation.

EXAMPLE 1   Checking Solutions of a Linear System

Check whether (**a**) $(2, 2)$ and (**b**) $(0, -1)$ are solutions of the following system.

$$3x - 2y = 2 \qquad \text{Equation 1}$$
$$x + 2y = 6 \qquad \text{Equation 2}$$

SOLUTION

a. $3(2) - 2(2) = 2 \checkmark$ **Equation 1 checks.**

   $2 + 2(2) = 6 \checkmark$ **Equation 2 checks.**

▶ Since $(2, 2)$ is a solution of each equation, it is a solution of the system.

b. $3(0) - 2(-1) = 2 \checkmark$ **Equation 1 checks.**

   $0 + 2(-1) = -2 \neq 6$ **Equation 2 does not check.**

▶ Since $(0, -1)$ is not a solution of Equation 2, it is not a solution of the system.

EXAMPLE 2   Solving a System Graphically

Solve the system.

$$2x - 3y = 1 \qquad \text{Equation 1}$$
$$x + y = 3 \qquad \text{Equation 2}$$

SOLUTION

Begin by graphing both equations as shown at the right. From the graph, the lines appear to intersect at $(2, 1)$. You can check this algebraically as follows.

   $2(2) - 3(1) = 1 \checkmark$ **Equation 1 checks.**

   $2 + 1 = 3 \checkmark$ **Equation 2 checks.**

▶ The solution is $(2, 1)$.

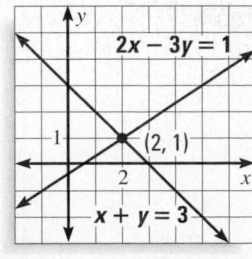

The system in Example 2 has exactly one solution. It is also possible for a system of linear equations to have infinitely many solutions or no solution.

STUDENT HELP

HOMEWORK HELP
Visit our Web site
www.mcdougallittell.com
for extra examples.

EXAMPLE 3 *Systems with Many or No Solutions*

Tell how many solutions the linear system has.

a. $3x - 2y = 6$
$\quad 6x - 4y = 12$

b. $3x - 2y = 6$
$\quad 3x - 2y = 2$

SOLUTION

a. The graph of the equations is the same line. So, each point on the line is a solution and the system has infinitely many solutions.

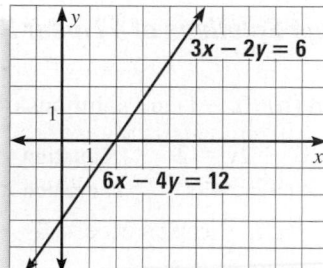

b. The graphs of the equations are two parallel lines. Because the two lines have no point of intersection, the system has no solution.

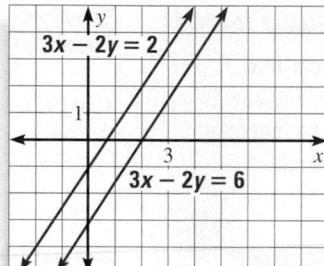

CONCEPT SUMMARY   **NUMBER OF SOLUTIONS OF A LINEAR SYSTEM**

The relationship between the graph of a linear system and the system's number of solutions is described below.

GRAPHICAL INTERPRETATION	**ALGEBRAIC INTERPRETATION**
The graph of the system is a pair of lines that intersect in one point.	The system has exactly one solution.
The graph of the system is a single line.	The system has infinitely many solutions.
The graph of the system is a pair of parallel lines so that there is no point of intersection.	The system has no solution.

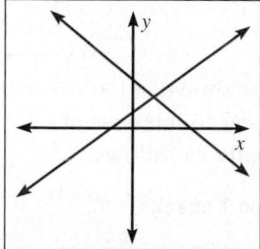

Exactly one solution

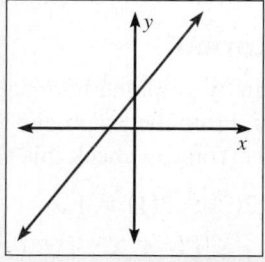

Infinitely many solutions

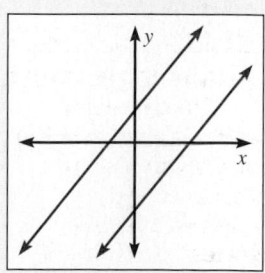

No solution

EXAMPLE 4 *Writing and Using a Linear System*

VACATION COSTS Your family is planning a 7 day trip to Florida. You estimate that it will cost $275 per day in Tampa and $400 per day in Orlando. Your total budget for the 7 days is $2300. How many days should you spend in each location?

SOLUTION

You can use a verbal model to write a system of two linear equations in two variables.

PROBLEM
SOLVING
STRATEGY

VERBAL MODEL

| Time spent in Tampa | + | Time spent in Orlando | = | Total vacation time |

| Daily rate in Tampa | · | Time spent in Tampa | + | Daily rate in Orlando | · | Time spent in Orlando | = | Total 7 day budget |

LABELS

Equation 1
Time spent in Tampa = x (days)
Time spent in Orlando = y (days)
Total vacation time = **7**   (days)

Equation 2
Daily rate in Tampa = **275**   (dollars per day)
Time spent in Tampa = x (days)
Daily rate in Orlando = **400**   (dollars per day)
Time spent in Orlando = y (days)
Total 7 day budget = **2300**   (dollars)

ALGEBRAIC MODEL

Equation 1 $x + y = 7$ **Total vacation time**

Equation 2 $275x + 400y = 2300$ **Total 7 day budget**

To solve the system, graph each equation as shown at the right.

Notice that you need to graph the equations only in the first quadrant because only positive values of x and y make sense in this situation.

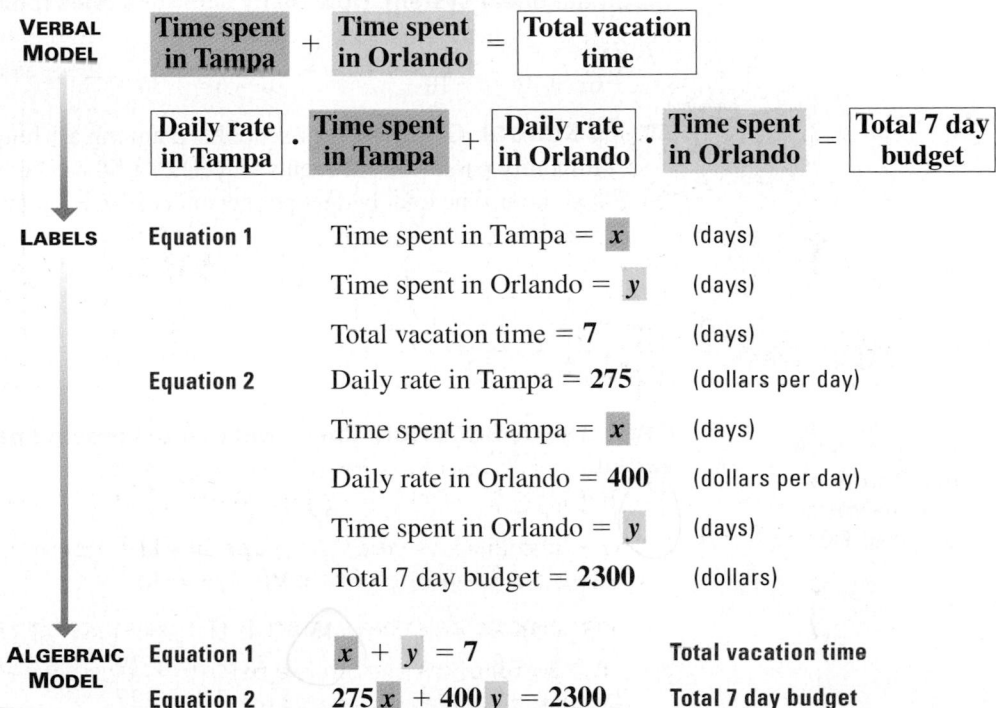
$x + y = 7$
$(4, 3)$
$275x + 400y = 2300$

The lines appear to intersect at the point $(4, 3)$. You can check this algebraically as follows.

$4 + 3 = 7$ ✓   **Equation 1 checks.**

$275(4) + 400(3) = 2300$ ✓   **Equation 2 checks.**

▶ The solution is $(4, 3)$, which means that you should plan to spend 4 days in Tampa and 3 days in Orlando.

GUIDED PRACTICE

Vocabulary Check ✓

1. Complete this statement: A(n) _?_ of a system of linear equations in two variables is an ordered pair (x, y) that satisfies each equation.

Concept Check ✓

2. How can you use the graph of a linear system to decide how many solutions the system has?

3. Explain why a linear system in two variables cannot have exactly two solutions.

Skill Check ✓

Check whether the ordered pair (5, 6) is a solution of the system.

4. $-2x + 4y = -14$
   $3x + y = 21$

5. $7x - 2y = 23$
   $-x + 3y = 13$

6. $x + y = 11$
   $-x - y = -11$

Graph the linear system. How many solutions does it have?

7. $2x - y = 4$
   $-6x + 3y = -18$

8. $14x + 3y = 16$
   $7x - 5y = 34$

9. $21x - 7y = 7$
   $-3x + y = -1$

10. 🌐 **SCHOOL OUTING** Your school is planning a 5 hour outing at the community park. The park rents bicycles for $8 per hour and inline skates for $6 per hour. The total budget per person is $34. How many hours should students spend doing each activity?

PRACTICE AND APPLICATIONS

STUDENT HELP

▶ **Extra Practice**
to help you master
skills is on p. 943.

CHECKING A SOLUTION Check whether the ordered pair is a solution of the system.

11. $(6, -1)$
    $4x - y = 25$
    $-3x - 2y = -16$

12. $(3, 0)$
    $-x + 2y = 3$
    $10x + y = 30$

13. $(-2, -8)$
    $2x - y = 52$
    $9x - y = -10$

14. $(-3, -5)$
    $-x - y = 8$
    $2x + 5y = -31$

15. $(-4, 1)$
    $-4x + 3y = 19$
    $5x - 7y = -27$

16. $(10, 8)$
    $-3x - y = -38$
    $-8x + 8y = -16$

17. $(1, -1)$
    $-3x + y = -4$
    $7x + 2y = -5$

18. $(-2, -7)$
    $5x - y = -3$
    $x + 3y = -23$

19. $(0, 2)$
    $17x + 8y = 16$
    $-x - 4y = 8$

GRAPH AND CHECK Graph the linear system and estimate the solution. Then check the solution algebraically.

20. $2x + y = 13$
    $5x - 2y = 1$

21. $x + 2y = 9$
    $-x + 6y = -1$

22. $-2x + y = 5$
    $x + y = 2$

23. $3x + 4y = -10$
    $-7x - y = -10$

24. $2x + y = -11$
    $-6x - 3y = 33$

25. $y = 5x$
    $y = x + 4$

26. $-x + 3y = 3$
    $2x - 6y = -6$

27. $2x + y = -2$
    $x - 2y = 19$

28. $3x - y = 12$
    $-x + 8y = -4$

29. $3x - y = 8$
    $\frac{1}{3}x - \frac{1}{6}y = 1$

30. $y = \frac{1}{6}x - 2$
    $y = -\frac{1}{6}x + 2$

31. $-x + 4y = 10$
    $4x - y = -10$

STUDENT HELP

▶ **HOMEWORK HELP**
Example 1: Exs. 11–19
Example 2: Exs. 20–31
Example 3: Exs. 32–52
Example 4: Exs. 54–59

INTERPRETING A GRAPH The graph of a system of two linear equations is shown. Tell whether the linear system has *infinitely many solutions, one solution,* or *no solution.* Explain your reasoning.

32.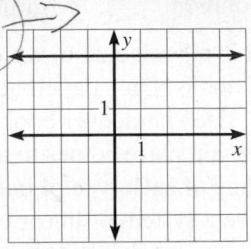

33.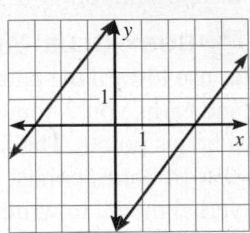

34.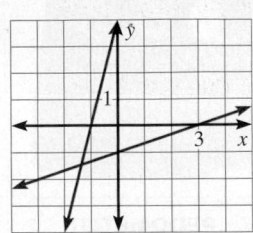

MATCHING GRAPHS Match the linear system with its graph. Tell how many solutions the system has.

35. $2x - y = -5$
$x + 2y = 0$

36. $-2x + 3y = 12$
$2x - 3y = 6$

37. $2x - y = 5$
$-4x + 2y = -10$

38. $x + 5y = -12$
$x - 5y = 8$

39. $-x + 5y = 8$
$2x - 10y = 7$

40. $4x - 7y = 27$
$-6x - 9y = -21$

A.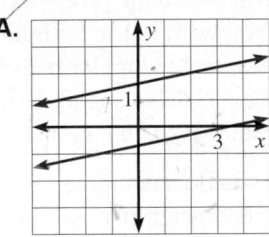

B.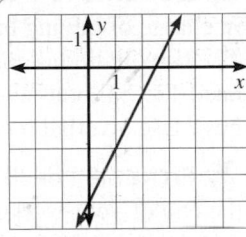

C.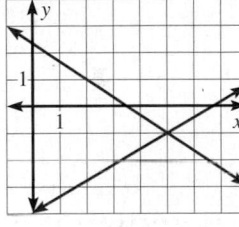

D.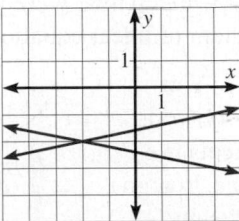

E.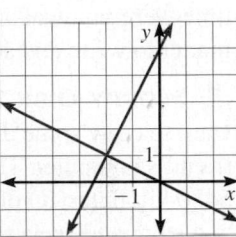

F.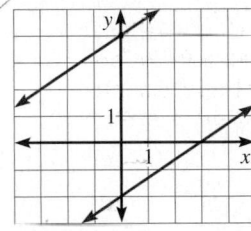

STUDENT HELP

► **Skills Review**
For help with
graphing, see p. 933.

NUMBER OF SOLUTIONS Graph the linear system and tell how many solutions it has. If there is exactly one solution, estimate the solution and check it algebraically.

41. $x = 5$
$x + y = 1$

42. $7x + y = 10$
$3x - 2y = -3$

43. $y = \frac{1}{2}x - 5$
$y = \frac{1}{2}x + 3$

44. $y = -5 - x$
$x + 3y = -15$

45. $\frac{1}{3}x + 7y = 2$
$\frac{2}{3}x + 14y = 4$

46. $-4y = 24x + 4$
$y = -6x - 1$

47. $2x - y = 7$
$y = 2x + 8$

48. $y = \frac{3}{4}x + 3$
$y = 3x - 6$

49. $6x - 2y = -2$
$-3x - 7y = 17$

50. $\frac{1}{2}x + 3y = 6$
$\frac{1}{3}x - 5y = -3$

51. $-6x + 2y = 8$
$y = 3x + 4$

52. $\frac{3}{4}x + y = 5$
$3x + 4y = 2$

53. CRITICAL THINKING Write a system of two linear equations that has the given number of solutions.

    a. one solution   **b.** no solution   **c.** infinitely many solutions

54. 🌐 **BOOK CLUB** You enroll in a book club in which you can earn bonus points to use toward the purchase of books. Each paperback book you order costs $6.95 and earns you 2 bonus points. Each hardcover book costs $19.95 and earns you 4 bonus points. The first order you place comes to a total of $60.75 and earns you 14 bonus points. How many of each type of book did you order? Use the verbal model to write and solve a system of linear equations.

Price of paperback book	·	Number of paperback books	+	Price of hardcover book	·	Number of hardcover books	=	Total cost of order

Bonus points for paperback book	·	Number of paperback books	+	Bonus points for hardcover book	·	Number of hardcover books	=	Total number of bonus points

55. 🌐 **DECORATION COSTS** You are on the prom decorating committee and are in charge of buying balloons. You want to use both latex and mylar balloons. The latex balloons cost $.10 each and the mylar balloons cost $.50 each. You need 125 balloons and you have $32.50 to spend. How many of each can you buy? Use a verbal model to write and solve a system of linear equations.

56. 🌐 **FITNESS** For 30 minutes you do a combination of walking and jogging. At the end of your workout your pedometer displays a total of 2.5 miles. You know that you walk 0.05 mile per minute and jog 0.1 mile per minute. For how much time were you walking? For how much time were you jogging? Use a verbal model to write and solve a system of linear equations.

57. 🌐 **FLOPPY DISK STORAGE** You want to copy some documents on your friend's computer. The documents use 6480 kilobytes(K) of disk space. You go to a store and see a sign advertising double-density disks and high-density disks. If you have $6 to spend, how many of each type of disk can you buy to get the disk space you need? Use a verbal model to write and solve a system of linear equations.

Floppy Disks

DOUBLE DENSITY 720K

HIGH DENSITY 1440K

$1.00 each $1.25 each

58. 🌐 **BATTERY POWER** Your portable stereo requires 10 size D batteries. You have $25 to spend on 5 packages of 2 batteries each and would like to maximize your battery power. Each regular package of batteries costs $4.25 and each alkaline package of batteries costs $5.50 (because alkaline batteries last longer). How many packages of each type of battery should you buy? Use a verbal model to write and solve a system of linear equations.

59. 🌐 **AIRPORT SHUTTLE** A bus station 15 miles from the airport runs a shuttle service to and from the airport. The 9:00 A.M. bus leaves for the airport traveling 30 miles per hour. The 9:05 A.M. bus leaves for the airport traveling 40 miles per hour. Write a system of linear equations to represent distance as a function of time for each bus. Graph and solve the system. How far from the airport will the 9:05 A.M. bus catch up to the 9:00 A.M. bus?

TYPES OF SYSTEMS In Exercises 60–62, use the following definitions to tell whether the system is *consistent and independent*, *consistent and dependent*, or *inconsistent*.

A system that has at least one solution is *consistent*. A consistent system that has exactly one solution is *independent*, and a consistent system that has infinitely many solutions is *dependent*. If a system has no solution, the system is *inconsistent*.

60. $-5x + 2y = 12$
$10x - 4y = -24$

61. $-3x - 3y = -6$
$7x + 4y = 20$

62. $2x - y = -12$
$-6x + 3y = 8$

63. **GEOMETRY CONNECTION** Graph the equations $x + y = 2$, $-5x + y = 20$, and $-\frac{5}{7}x + y = -\frac{10}{7}$. What geometric figure do the graphs of the equations form? What are the coordinates of the vertices of the figure? Explain the steps you used to find the coordinates.

Test Preparation

64. MULTI-STEP PROBLEM You are choosing between two long-distance telephone companies. Company A charges $.09 per minute plus a $4 monthly fee. Company B charges $.11 per minute with no monthly fee.

a. Let x be the number of minutes you call long distance in one month, and let y be the total cost of long-distance phone service. Write and graph two equations representing the cost of each company's service for one month.

b. Estimate the coordinates of the point where the two graphs intersect. Check your estimate algebraically.

c. *Writing* What does the point of intersection you found in part (b) represent? How can it help you decide which long-distance company to use?

★ Challenge

65. **BUYING A DIGITAL CAMERA** The school yearbook staff is purchasing a digital camera. Recently the staff received two ads in the mail. The ad for Store 1 states that all digital cameras are 15% off. The ad for Store 2 gives a $300 coupon to use when purchasing any digital camera. Assume that the lowest priced digital camera is $700. Write and graph two equations that describe the prices at both stores. When does Store 1 have a better deal than Store 2?

EXTRA CHALLENGE
www.mcdougallittell.com

MIXED REVIEW

SOLVING EQUATIONS Solve the equation. Check your solution. (Review 1.3 for 3.2)

66. $4x + 11 = 39$

67. $\frac{1}{2}x - 10 = 8$

68. $6x - 8 = 3x + 16$

69. $-9x - 2 = x + 1$

70. $2(3x - 5) = 7(x + 2)$

71. $10(x + 1) = \frac{1}{2}(x - 18)$

CHECKING SOLUTIONS Check whether the ordered pairs are solutions of the inequality. (Review 2.6)

72. $12x + 4y \geq 3$; $(1, -3)$, $(0, 2)$

73. $-x - y \leq -10$; $(-3, -7)$, $(5, 4)$

74. $15 > 2x - 2y$; $(10, 3)$, $(-5, 7)$

75. $6x + \frac{1}{2}y \leq -5$; $(2, -6)$, $(-1, 7)$

GRAPHING ABSOLUTE VALUE FUNCTIONS Graph the function. (Review 2.8)

76. $y = |x| - 5$

77. $y = |x - 9|$

78. $y = -|x - 8| + 3$

79. $y = |7 - x| + 4$

Graphing Systems of Equations

In Lesson 3.1 you learned how to *estimate* the solution of a linear system by graphing. With a graphing calculator, you can get an answer that is very close to, and sometimes *exactly* equal to, the actual solution.

▶ EXAMPLE

Solve the linear system using a graphing calculator.

$$5x + 3y = -15$$
$$4x - 2y = 45$$

▶ SOLUTION

1 Solve each equation for y.

$$5x + 3y = -15$$
$$3y = -5x - 15$$
$$y = -\frac{5}{3}x - 5$$
$$4x - 2y = 45$$
$$-2y = -4x + 45$$
$$y = 2x - \frac{45}{2}$$

2 Enter the equations. It's a good idea to use parentheses to enter fractions.

```
Y1❚(-5/3)X-5
Y2❚2X-(45/2)
Y3=
Y4=
Y5=
Y6=
Y7=
```

3 Using a standard viewing window, graph the equations.

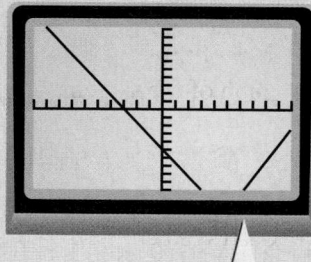

If the graphs do not intersect on the screen, set a different viewing window.

4 Use the *Intersect* feature to find the point where the graphs intersect.

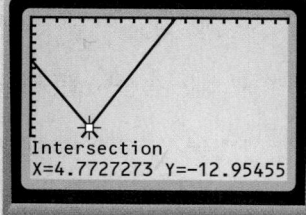

```
Intersection
X=4.7727273  Y=-12.95455
```

▶ The solution is about $(4.77, -12.95)$.

▶ EXERCISES

Solve the linear system using a graphing calculator.

1. $y = x + 4$
   $y = 2x + 5$

2. $y = -2x + 13$
   $y = 6x - 5$

3. $3x - y = 16$
   $-5x + 8y = 13$

4. $5x + 2y = 6$
   $x - 3y = -5$

5. $6x + 9y = -13$
   $-x + 2y = 10$

6. $2x + 8y = -53$
   $3x + 4y = 26$

○ ACTIVITY 3.2

Developing Concepts

GROUP ACTIVITY
Work with a partner.

MATERIALS
• graph paper
• ruler

Combining Equations in a Linear System

▶ QUESTION

For a system of two linear equations with exactly one solution, how is the graph of the *sum* of the equations related to the graph of the system?

▶ EXPLORING THE CONCEPT

1 Graph the system and label the point of intersection.

$$3x - y = -5$$
$$3x + y = -1$$

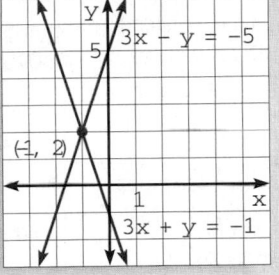

2 Add the two equations in the system. Graph the resulting equation in the same coordinate plane you used to graph the system.

$$\begin{array}{r} 3x - y = -5 \\ 3x + y = -1 \\ \hline 6x = -6 \\ x = -1 \end{array}$$

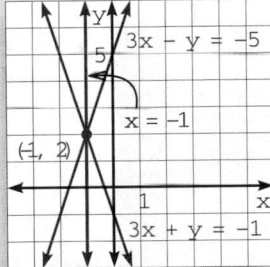

3 Note how the graph of the sum of the equations is related to the graph of the system.

▶ DRAWING CONCLUSIONS

1. Repeat the steps above for each system.

   a. $10x + 4y = 24$
   $-6x - 4y = 8$

   b. $x - 2y = 2$
   $-x + 4y = -20$

   c. $6x - 3y = 27$
   $2x + y = -9$

   d. $x - y = -3$
   $-2x + 5y = 6$

   e. $7x + 20y = 0$
   $-3x + 6y = 4$

   f. $2x - y = -3$
   $x + 2y = 6$

2. What seems to be true about the graph of the sum of two equations in a system if the system has exactly one solution?

3. Consider the following general system that has a single solution (p, q).

$$Ax + By = C$$
$$Dx + Ey = F$$

Use this system to justify your conclusion from Exercise 2 algebraically.

3.2

Solving Linear Systems Algebraically

What you should learn

GOAL 1 Use algebraic methods to solve linear systems.

GOAL 2 Use linear systems to model **real-life** situations, such as catering an event in **Example 5**.

Why you should learn it

▼ To solve **real-life** problems, such as how to plan a 40 minute workout in **Ex. 57**.

GOAL 1 USING ALGEBRAIC METHODS TO SOLVE SYSTEMS

In this lesson you will study two algebraic methods for solving linear systems. The first method is called *substitution*.

THE SUBSTITUTION METHOD

STEP 1 Solve one of the equations for one of its variables.

STEP 2 Substitute the expression from Step 1 into the other equation and solve for the other variable.

STEP 3 Substitute the value from Step 2 into the revised equation from Step 1 and solve.

EXAMPLE 1 *The Substitution Method*

Solve the linear system using the substitution method.

$$3x + 4y = -4 \quad \text{Equation 1}$$
$$x + 2y = 2 \quad \text{Equation 2}$$

SOLUTION

1 Solve Equation 2 for x.

$$x + 2y = 2 \quad \text{Write Equation 2.}$$
$$x = -2y + 2 \quad \text{Revised Equation 2}$$

2 Substitute the expression for x into Equation 1 and solve for y.

$$3x + 4y = -4 \quad \text{Write Equation 1.}$$
$$3(-2y + 2) + 4y = -4 \quad \text{Substitute } -2y + 2 \text{ for } x.$$
$$y = 5 \quad \text{Solve for } y.$$

3 Substitute the value of y into revised Equation 2 and solve for x.

$$x = -2y + 2 \quad \text{Write revised Equation 2.}$$
$$x = -2(5) + 2 \quad \text{Substitute 5 for } y.$$
$$x = -8 \quad \text{Simplify.}$$

▶ The solution is $(-8, 5)$.

✓**CHECK** Check the solution by substituting back into the original equations.

$$3x + 4y = -4 \quad \text{Write original equations.} \quad x + 2y = 2$$
$$3(-8) + 4(5) \stackrel{?}{=} -4 \quad \text{Substitute for } x \text{ and } y. \quad -8 + 2(5) \stackrel{?}{=} 2$$
$$-4 = -4 ✓ \quad \text{Solution checks.} \quad 2 = 2 ✓$$

CHOOSING A METHOD In Step 1 of Example 1, you could have solved for either x or y in either Equation 1 or Equation 2. It was easiest to solve for x in Equation 2 because the x-coefficient is 1. In general you should solve for a variable whose coefficient is 1 or -1.

$$x - 5y = 11 \longleftarrow \textbf{Solve for } \textit{x}. \qquad 4x - 2y = -1$$
$$2x + 7y = -3 \qquad\qquad\qquad 3x - y = 8 \longleftarrow \textbf{Solve for } \textit{y}.$$

If neither variable has a coefficient of 1 or -1, you can still use substitution. In such cases, however, the *linear combination* method may be better. The goal of this method is to add the equations to obtain an equation in one variable.

THE LINEAR COMBINATION METHOD

STEP ❶ Multiply one or both of the equations by a constant to obtain coefficients that differ only in sign for one of the variables.

STEP ❷ Add the revised equations from Step 1. Combining like terms will eliminate one of the variables. Solve for the remaining variable.

STEP ❸ Substitute the value obtained in Step 2 into either of the original equations and solve for the other variable.

EXAMPLE 2 *The Linear Combination Method: Multiplying One Equation*

Solve the linear system using the linear combination method.

$$2x - 4y = 13 \qquad \textbf{Equation 1}$$
$$4x - 5y = 8 \qquad \textbf{Equation 2}$$

SOLUTION

❶ Multiply the first equation by -2 so that the x-coefficients differ only in sign.

$$2x - 4y = 13 \quad \times \ -2 \quad \longrightarrow \quad -4x + 8y = -26$$
$$4x - 5y = 8 \quad \longrightarrow \qquad\qquad \underline{4x - 5y = 8}$$

❷ Add the revised equations and solve for y.
$$3y = -18$$
$$y = -6$$

❸ Substitute the value of y into one of the original equations. Solve for x.

$$2x - 4y = 13 \qquad \textbf{Write Equation 1.}$$
$$2x - 4(-6) = 13 \qquad \textbf{Substitute }-6 \textbf{ for } \textit{y}.$$
$$2x + 24 = 13 \qquad \textbf{Simplify.}$$
$$x = -\frac{11}{2} \qquad \textbf{Solve for } \textit{x}.$$

▶ The solution is $\left(-\dfrac{11}{2}, -6\right)$.

✓ **CHECK** You can check the solution algebraically using the method shown in Example 1. You can also use a graphing calculator to check the solution.

Intersection
X=-5.5   Y=-6

EXAMPLE 3 **The Linear Combination Method: Multiplying Both Equations**

Solve the linear system using the
linear combination method.

$$7x - 12y = -22 \qquad \text{Equation 1}$$
$$-5x + 8y = 14 \qquad \text{Equation 2}$$

SOLUTION

Multiply the first equation by **2** and the second equation by **3** so that the coefficients of *y* differ only in sign.

$$7x - 12y = -22 \quad \boxed{\times\,2} \rightarrow \quad 14x - 24y = -44$$
$$-5x + 8y = 14 \quad \boxed{\times\,3} \rightarrow \quad -15x + 24y = 42$$

Add the revised equations
and solve for *x*.

$$-x = -2$$
$$x = 2$$

Substitute the value of *x* into one of the original equations. Solve for *y*.

$$-5x + 8y = 14 \qquad \text{Write Equation 2.}$$
$$-5(\mathbf{2}) + 8y = 14 \qquad \text{Substitute 2 for } x.$$
$$y = 3 \qquad \text{Solve for } y.$$

▶ The solution is (2, 3). Check the solution algebraically or graphically.

EXAMPLE 4 **Linear Systems with Many or No Solutions**

Solve the linear system.

a. $x - 2y = 3$
   $2x - 4y = 7$

b. $6x - 10y = 12$
   $-15x + 25y = -30$

SOLUTION

a. Since the coefficient of *x* in the first equation is 1, use substitution.

Solve the first equation for *x*.

$$x - 2y = 3$$
$$x = 2y + 3$$

Substitute the expression for *x* into the second equation.

$$2x - 4y = 7 \qquad \text{Write second equation.}$$
$$2(\mathbf{2y + 3}) - 4y = 7 \qquad \text{Substitute } 2y + 3 \text{ for } x.$$
$$6 = 7 \qquad \text{Simplify.}$$

▶ Because the statement 6 = 7 is never true, there is *no solution.*

b. Since no coefficient is 1 or −1, use the linear combination method.

Multiply the first equation by **5** and the second equation by **2**.

$$6x - 10y = 12 \quad \boxed{\times\,5} \rightarrow \quad 30x - 50y = 60$$
$$-15x + 25y = -30 \quad \boxed{\times\,2} \rightarrow \quad -30x + 50y = -60$$

Add the revised equations. $\qquad\qquad\qquad 0 = 0$

▶ Because the equation 0 = 0 is always true, there are *infinitely many solutions.*

EXAMPLE 5 *Using a Linear System as a Model*

CATERING A caterer is planning a party for 64 people. The customer has $150 to spend. A $39 pan of pasta feeds 14 people and a $12 sandwich tray feeds 6 people. How many pans of pasta and how many sandwich trays should the caterer make?

SOLUTION

PROBLEM SOLVING STRATEGY

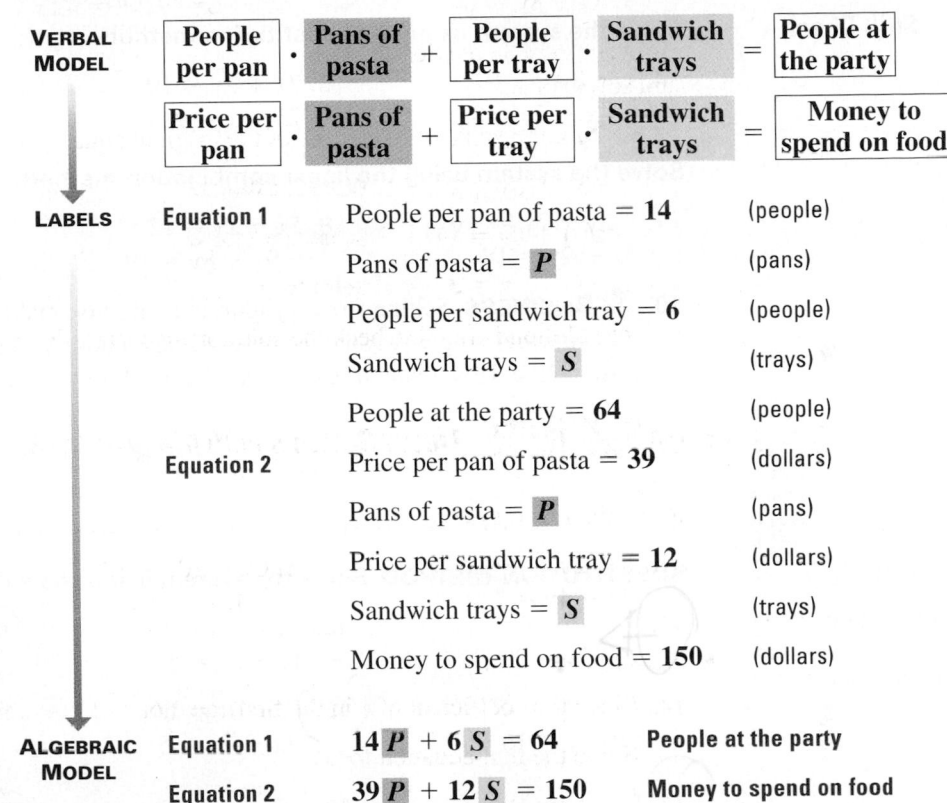

VERBAL MODEL

| People per pan | · | Pans of pasta | + | People per tray | · | Sandwich trays | = | People at the party |

| Price per pan | · | Pans of pasta | + | Price per tray | · | Sandwich trays | = | Money to spend on food |

LABELS

Equation 1

People per pan of pasta = **14**	(people)
Pans of pasta = **P**	(pans)
People per sandwich tray = **6**	(people)
Sandwich trays = **S**	(trays)
People at the party = **64**	(people)

Equation 2

Price per pan of pasta = **39**	(dollars)
Pans of pasta = **P**	(pans)
Price per sandwich tray = **12**	(dollars)
Sandwich trays = **S**	(trays)
Money to spend on food = **150**	(dollars)

ALGEBRAIC MODEL

Equation 1 $14P + 6S = 64$ **People at the party**

Equation 2 $39P + 12S = 150$ **Money to spend on food**

Use the linear combination method to solve the system.

Multiply Equation 1 by **−2** so that the coefficients of S differ only in sign.

$$14P + 6S = 64 \quad \times -2 \quad \longrightarrow \quad -28P - 12S = -128$$
$$39P + 12S = 150 \quad \longrightarrow \quad \underline{39P + 12S = 150}$$

Add the revised equations and solve for P.
$$11P = 22$$
$$P = 2$$

Substitute the value of P into one of the original equations and solve for S.

$14P + 6S = 64$	**Write Equation 1.**
$14(2) + 6S = 64$	**Substitute 2 for P.**
$28 + 6S = 64$	**Multiply.**
$S = 6$	**Solve for S.**

▶ The caterer should make 2 pans of pasta and 6 sandwich trays for the party.

FOCUS ON CAREERS

CATERER
A caterer prepares food for special events. When planning a meal, a caterer needs to consider both the cost of the food and the number of guests.

CAREER LINK
www.mcdougallittell.com

GUIDED PRACTICE

Vocabulary Check ✔

1. Complete this statement: To solve a linear system where one of the coefficients is 1 or −1, it is usually easiest to use the ? method.

Concept Check ✔

2. Read Step 3 in the box on page 148. Why do you think it recommends substituting into the revised equation from Step 1 instead of one of the original equations?

3. When solving a linear system algebraically, how do you know when there is no solution? How do you know when there are infinitely many solutions?

Skill Check ✔

Solve the system using the substitution method.

4. $x + 3y = -2$
   $-4x - 5y = 8$

5. $3x + 2y = 10$
   $2x - y = 9$

6. $-3x + y = -7$
   $5x - 2y = 12$

Solve the system using the linear combination method.

7. $-3x + 2y = -6$
   $5x - 2y = 18$

8. $5x - 2y = 12$
   $-9x - 8y = 19$

9. $4x - 3y = 0$
   $-10x + 7y = -2$

10. 🌐 **BUSINESS** Selling frozen yogurt at a fair, you make $565 and use 250 cones. A single-scoop cone costs $2 and a double-scoop cone costs $2.50. How many of each type of cone did you sell?

PRACTICE AND APPLICATIONS

STUDENT HELP

▶ **Extra Practice**
to help you master
skills is on p. 943.

SUBSTITUTION METHOD Solve the system using the substitution method.

11. $2x + 3y = 5$
    $x - 5y = 9$

12. $-2x + y = 6$
    $4x - 2y = 5$

13. $-x + 2y = 3$
    $4x - 5y = -3$

14. $5x + 3y = 4$
    $5x + y = 16$

15. $4x + 6y = 15$
    $-x + 2y = 5$

16. $3x - y = 4$
    $5x + 3y = 9$

17. $\frac{1}{2}x + y = 9$
    $7x + 4y = 24$

18. $-3x + y = 2$
    $8x - 15y = 7$

19. $5x + 6y = -45$
    $x - \frac{1}{2}y = 8$

20. $-x - 4y = -3$
    $2x + y = 15$

21. $x + 2y = 2$
    $7x - 3y = -20$

22. $3x - y = 4$
    $-9x + 3y = -12$

LINEAR COMBINATION METHOD Solve the system using the linear combination method.

23. $3x + 5y = -16$
    $3x - 2y = -9$

24. $3x + 2y = 6$
    $-6x - 3y = -6$

25. $-6x + 5y = 4$
    $7x - 10y = -8$

STUDENT HELP

▶ **HOMEWORK HELP**
Example 1: Exs. 11–22,
    35–49
Examples 2, 3: Exs. 23–49
Example 4: Exs. 11–49
Example 5: Exs. 54–62

26. $7x - 4y = -3$
    $2x + 5y = -7$

27. $-9x + 6y = 0$
    $-12x + 8y = 0$

28. $5x + 6y = -16$
    $2x + 10y = 5$

29. $21x - 8y = -1$
    $9x + 5y = 8$

30. $-15x - 2y = -31$
    $4x + 6y = 11$

31. $\frac{1}{4}x + 5y = 37$
    $-4x + 2y = 13$

32. $7x + 2y = -3$
    $-14x - 4y = 6$

33. $6x - y = -2$
    $-18x + 3y = 4$

34. $-5x + 2y = -10$
    $3x - 6y = -18$

CHOOSING A METHOD Solve the system using any algebraic method.

35. $-5x + 7y = 11$
$-5x + 3y = 19$

36. $x - y = 3$
$-2x + 2y = -6$

37. $2x - 5y = 10$
$-3x + 4y = -15$

38. $-3x + y = 11$
$5x - 2y = -16$

39. $-4x - 6y = 11$
$6x + 9y = -3$

40. $x - 4y = -2$
$-3x + 8y = -1$

41. $2x + 5y = 17$
$-5x - 7y = -10$

42. $-3x + 7y = 6$
$5x - y = 10$

43. $-2x + 3y = 20$
$4x + 4y = -15$

44. $3x - 7y = 20$
$-11x + 10y = 5$

45. $x - y = 17$
$\frac{1}{2}x - 3y = 1$

46. $4x + 9y = -10$
$-8x - 12y = 8$

47. $12x + 3y = 16$
$-36x - 9y = 32$

48. $-x + 5y = 17$
$2x - 10y = -34$

49. $\frac{1}{3}x + y = 9$
$-2x + 2y = -6$

50. *Writing* Explain how you can tell whether the system has infinitely many solutions or no solution without trying to solve the system.

a. $5x - 2y = 6$
$-10x + 4y = -12$

b. $-2x + y = 8$
$-6x + 3y = 12$

GEOMETRY CONNECTION Find the coordinates of the point where the diagonals of the quadrilateral intersect.

51.

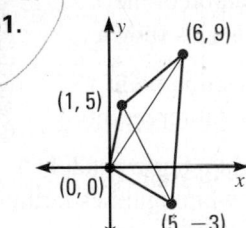

52.

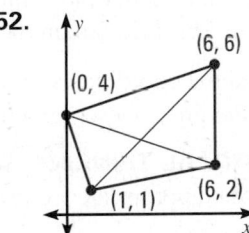

53.

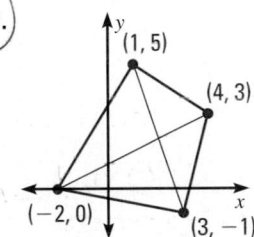

54. **BREAKING EVEN** You are starting a business selling boxes of hand-painted greeting cards. To get started, you spend $36 on paint and paintbrushes that you need. You buy boxes of plain cards for $3.50 per box, paint the cards, and then sell them for $5 per box. How many boxes must you sell for your revenue to equal your expenses? What will your revenue and expenses equal when you break even?

55. **HOME ELECTRONICS** To connect a VCR to a television set, you need a cable with special connectors at both ends. Suppose you buy a 6 foot cable for $15.50 and a 3 foot cable for $10.25. Assuming that the cost of a cable is the sum of the cost of the two connectors and the cost of the cable itself, what would you expect to pay for a 4 foot cable? Explain how you got your answer.

56. **SCIENCE CONNECTION** Weights of atoms and molecules are measured in *atomic mass units* (u). A molecule of C_2H_6 (ethane) is made up of 2 carbon atoms and 6 hydrogen atoms and weighs 30.07 u. A molecule of C_3H_8 (propane) is made up of 3 carbon atoms and 8 hydrogen atoms and weighs 44.097 u. Find the weights of a carbon atom and a hydrogen atom.

Ethane molecule

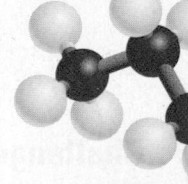

Propane molecule

REAL LIFE **SWIMMING**
One way swimmers
improve their racing times is
by training at high altitudes.
Many elite swimmers train at
the Olympic Training Center
in Colorado Springs,
Colorado, at an altitude of
6035 feet above sea level.

57. CROSS-TRAINING You want to burn 380 Calories during 40 minutes of exercise. You burn about 8 Calories per minute inline skating and 12 Calories per minute swimming. How long should you spend doing each activity?

58. RENTING AN APARTMENT Two friends rent an apartment for $975 per month. Since one bedroom is 60 square feet larger than the other bedroom, each person's rent contribution is based on bedroom size. Each person agrees to pay $3.25 per square foot of bedroom area. Let x be the area (in square feet) of the larger bedroom, and let y be the area (in square feet) of the smaller bedroom. Write and solve a system of linear equations to find the area of each bedroom.

 SWIMMING In Exercises 59–62, use the table below of winning times in the Olympic 100 meter freestyle swimming event for the period 1968–1996.

Years since 1968, x	0	4	8	12	16	20	24	28
Men's time (sec), m	52.2	51.2	50.0	50.4	49.8	48.6	49.0	48.7
Women's time (sec), w	60.0	58.6	55.7	54.8	55.9	54.9	54.6	54.5

INTERNET **DATA UPDATE** of USA Swimming data at www.mcdougallittell.com

59. Use a graphing calculator to make scatter plots of the data pairs (x, m) and (x, w).

60. For each scatter plot, find an equation of the line of best fit. Graph the equations, as shown.

61. Find the coordinates of the intersection point of the lines. Describe what this point represents.

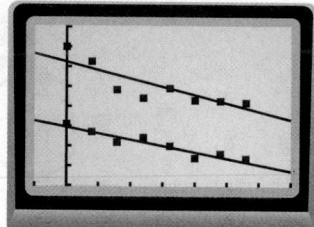

62. CRITICAL THINKING Why might a linear model not be appropriate for projecting winning times far into the future?

Test Preparation

QUANTITATIVE COMPARISON In Exercises 63 and 64, choose the statement that is true about the given quantities.

ⓐ The quantity in column A is greater.

ⓑ The quantity in column B is greater.

ⓒ The two quantities are equal.

ⓓ The relationship cannot be determined from the given information.

	Column A	Column B
63.	The x-coordinate of the solution of: $$7x - y = 19$$ $$10x + 2y = 34$$	3
64.	-5	The y-coordinate of the solution of: $$-2x + 6y = -26$$ $$x + 3y = 11$$

 **Challenge**

65. CRITICAL THINKING Find values of r, s, and t that produce the solution(s).

$$-3x - 5y = 9$$
$$rx + sy = t$$

a. no solution   **b.** infinitely many solutions   **c.** a solution of $(2, -3)$

MIXED REVIEW

ABSOLUTE VALUE EQUATIONS Solve the equation. (Review 1.7)

66. $|6x| = 12$ **67.** $|x + 5| = 3$ **68.** $|2x - 1| = 7$

69. $|4x + 1| = 5$ **70.** $|3x - 2| = 8$ **71.** $|-x + 10| = 14$

WRITING EQUATIONS Write an equation of the line. (Review 2.4)

72. 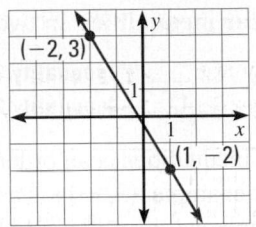   **73.** 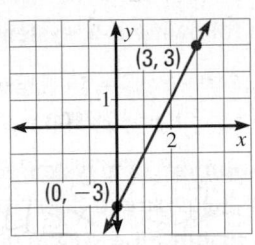   **74.**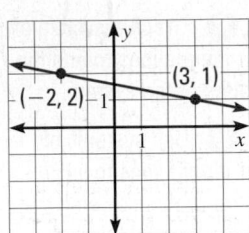

GRAPHING INEQUALITIES Graph the inequality in a coordinate plane. (Review 2.6 for 3.3)

75. $y < 4$ **76.** $x \geq -2$ **77.** $3x - y \geq 0$

78. $y < -x + 4$ **79.** $4x - y < 5$ **80.** $y \geq -2x - 1$

81. **CONSUMER ECONOMICS** You plan to buy a pair of jeans for $25 and some T-shirts for $12 each. You have only $60 to spend. Write and solve an inequality for the number of T-shirts you can buy. **(Review 1.6 for 3.3)**

QUIZ 1

Self-Test for Lessons 3.1 and 3.2

Use a graph to solve the system. (Lesson 3.1)

1. $y = 2x + 5$ **2.** $y = -4x + 1$ **3.** $-3x + 2y = 4$
    $y = -2x - 3$ $y = x - 4$ $6x - 4y = 14$

4. $-2x - y = -2$ **5.** $y = -x + 5$ **6.** $4x + 5y = -9$
    $3x - 3y = 15$ $3x - y = -1$ $x + 3y = -4$

Tell how many solutions the linear system has. (Lessons 3.1 and 3.2)

7. $6x + 6y = 3$ **8.** $-2x + y = 13$ **9.** $-5x + 7y = 10$
    $4x + 4y = 2$ $x - 4y = -31$ $15x - 21y = 22$

10. $3x - 3y = 3$ **11.** $x - 6y = 6$ **12.** $-4x + 8y = 24$
    $-4x + y = -21$ $-3x + 2y = -2$ $-x + 2y = 6$

Solve the system using any algebraic method. (Lesson 3.2)

13. $-2x + 2y = -5$ **14.** $-3x + 2y = -6$ **15.** $-4x - y = -1$
    $x + y = -5$ $5x - 2y = 18$ $12x + 3y = 3$

16. $-3x - 4y = -2$ **17.** $3x - 8y = 11$ **18.** $3x - 8y = -7$
    $x + 2y = 3$ $-6x + 16y = -5$ $-5x - 6y = 3$

19. 🌎 **THEATER** Tickets for your school's play are $3 for students and $5 for non-students. On opening night 937 tickets are sold and $3943 is collected. How many tickets were sold to students? to non-students? **(Lesson 3.2)**

3.3 Graphing and Solving Systems of Linear Inequalities

What you should learn

GOAL 1 Graph a system of linear inequalities to find the solutions of the system.

GOAL 2 Use systems of linear inequalities to solve **real-life** problems, such as finding a person's target heart rate zone in **Example 3**.

Why you should learn it

▼ To solve **real-life** problems, such as finding out how a moose can satisfy its nutritional requirements in **Ex. 58**.

GOAL 1 GRAPHING A SYSTEM OF INEQUALITIES

The following is a **system of linear inequalities** in two variables.

$$x + y \leq 6 \qquad \textbf{Inequality 1}$$
$$2x - y > 4 \qquad \textbf{Inequality 2}$$

A **solution** of a system of linear inequalities is an ordered pair that is a solution of each inequality in the system. For example, $(3, -1)$ is a solution of the system above. The **graph** of a system of linear inequalities is the graph of all solutions of the system.

▶ ACTIVITY
Developing Concepts

Investigating Graphs of Systems of Inequalities

The coordinate plane shows the four regions determined by the lines $3x - y = 2$ and $2x + y = 1$. Use the labeled points to help you match each region with one of the systems of inequalities.

a. $3x - y \leq 2$
  $2x + y \leq 1$

b. $3x - y \geq 2$
  $2x + y \geq 1$

c. $3x - y \geq 2$
  $2x + y \leq 1$

d. $3x - y \leq 2$
  $2x + y \geq 1$

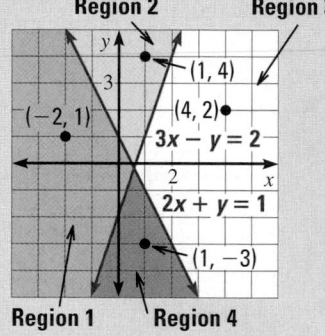

As you saw in the activity, a system of linear inequalities defines a region in a plane. Here is a method for graphing the region.

GRAPHING A SYSTEM OF LINEAR INEQUALITIES

To graph a system of linear inequalities, do the following for each inequality in the system:

- Graph the line that corresponds to the inequality. Use a dashed line for an inequality with $<$ or $>$ and a solid line for an inequality with $\leq$ or $\geq$.

- Lightly shade the half-plane that is the graph of the inequality. Colored pencils may help you distinguish the different half-planes.

The graph of the system is the region common to all of the half-planes. If you used colored pencils, it is the region that has been shaded with *every* color.

EXAMPLE 1 *Graphing a System of Two Inequalities*

STUDENT HELP

▸ **Look Back**
For help with graphing a linear inequality, see p. 109.

Graph the system.

$$y \geq -3x - 1 \qquad \text{Inequality 1}$$
$$y < x + 2 \qquad \text{Inequality 2}$$

SOLUTION

Begin by graphing each linear inequality. Use a different color for each half-plane. For instance, you can use red for Inequality 1 and blue for Inequality 2. The graph of the system is the region that is shaded purple.

Shade the half-plane on and to the right of $y = -3x - 1$ red.

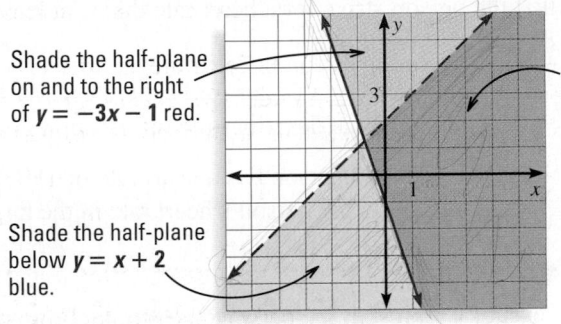

The graph of the system is the intersection of the red and blue regions.

Shade the half-plane below $y = x + 2$ blue.

· · · · · · · · · ·

You can also graph a system of three or more linear inequalities.

EXAMPLE 2 *Graphing a System of Three Inequalities*

Graph the system.

$$x \geq 0 \qquad \text{Inequality 1}$$
$$y \geq 0 \qquad \text{Inequality 2}$$
$$4x + 3y \leq 24 \qquad \text{Inequality 3}$$

SOLUTION

Inequality 1 and Inequality 2 restrict the solutions to the first quadrant. Inequality 3 is the half-plane that lies on and below the line $4x + 3y = 24$. The graph of the system of inequalities is the triangular region shown below.

STUDENT HELP

▸ **Study Tip**
From this point on, only the solution region will be shaded on graphs of systems of linear inequalities.

The inequality $x \geq 0$ implies that the region is on and to the right of the y-axis.

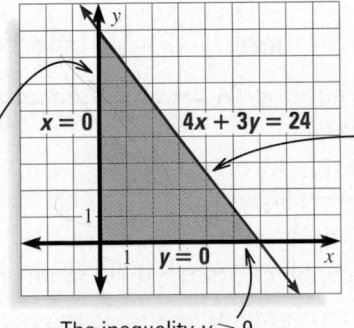

The inequality $4x + 3y \leq 24$ implies that the region is on and below the line $4x + 3y = 24$.

The inequality $y \geq 0$ implies that the region is on and above the x-axis.

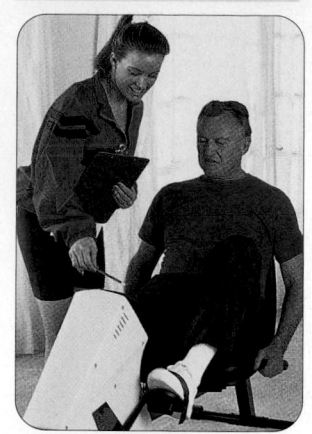

GOAL 2 **USING SYSTEMS OF INEQUALITIES IN REAL LIFE**

You can use a system of linear inequalities to describe a real-life situation, as shown
in the following example.

EXAMPLE 3 *Writing and Using a System of Inequalities*

HEART RATE A person's theoretical maximum heart rate is $220 - x$ where x is the
person's age in years ($20 \le x \le 65$). When a person exercises, it is recommended
that the person strive for a heart rate that is at least 70% of the maximum and at most
85% of the maximum.

  a. You are making a poster for health class. Write and graph a system of linear
  inequalities that describes the information given above.

  b. A 40-year-old person has a heart rate of 150 (heartbeats per minute) when
  exercising. Is the person's heart rate in the target zone?

SOLUTION

  a. Let y represent the person's heart rate. From the given information, you can write
  the following four inequalities.

$x \ge 20$	**Person's age must be at least 20.**
$x \le 65$	**Person's age can be at most 65.**
$y \ge 0.7(220 - x)$	**Target rate is at least 70% of maximum rate.**
$y \le 0.85(220 - x)$	**Target rate is at most 85% of maximum rate.**

  The graph of the system is shown below.

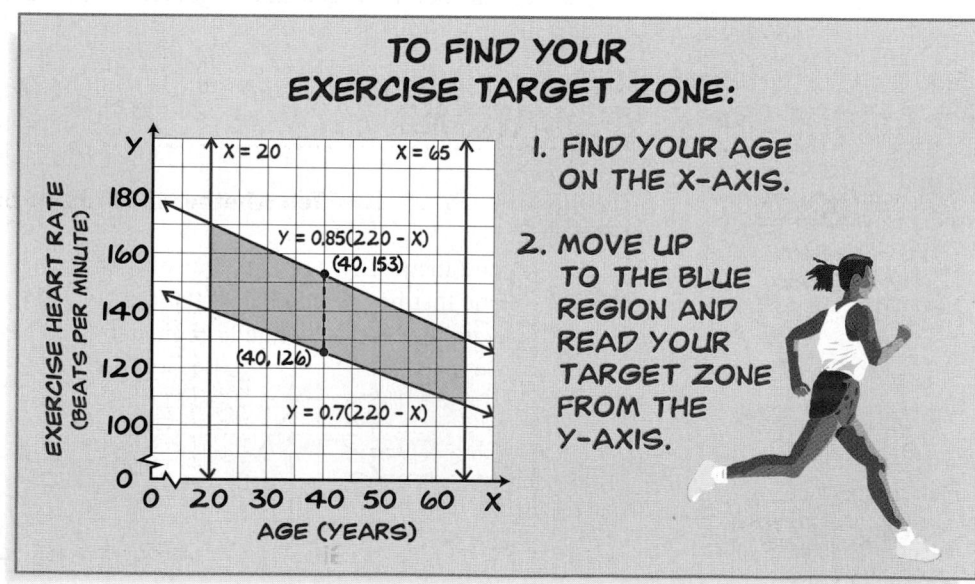

  b. From the graph you can see that the target zone for a 40-year-old person is
  between 126 and 153, inclusive. That is,

$$126 \le y \le 153.$$

  ▶ A 40-year-old person who has a heart rate of 150 is within the target zone.

GUIDED PRACTICE

Vocabulary Check ✓

1. What must be true in order for an ordered pair to be a solution of a system of linear inequalities?

Concept Check ✓

2. Look back at Example 1 on page 157. Explain why the ordered pair $(-1, -5)$ is *not* a solution of the system.

3. **ERROR ANALYSIS** Explain what is wrong with the graph of the following system of inequalities.

$$y \le 3$$
$$x + y \ge 5$$

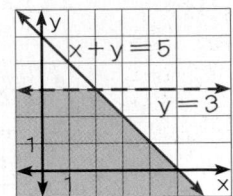

Skill Check ✓

Tell whether the ordered pair is a solution of the following system.

$$x \ge -1$$
$$y > 2x + 2$$

4. $(-1, 2)$ **5.** $(0, 0)$ **6.** $(1, 4)$ **7.** $(2, 7)$

Graph the system of linear inequalities.

8. $x \ge -1$
    $y > 2x + 2$

9. $x + y \le 3$
    $y > 1$

10. $x > 0$
     $y \le x - 5$

11. 🌐 **FLIGHT ATTENDANTS** To be a flight attendant, you must be at least 18 years old and at most 55 years old, and you must be between 60 and 74 inches tall, inclusive. Let x represent a person's age (in years) and let y represent a person's height (in inches). Write and graph a system of linear inequalities showing the possible ages and heights for flight attendants.

PRACTICE AND APPLICATIONS

STUDENT HELP

→ **Extra Practice**
to help you master skills is on p. 943.

CHECKING A SOLUTION Tell whether the ordered pair is a solution of the system.

12. $(25, -5)$

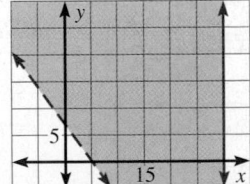

13. $(2, 3)$

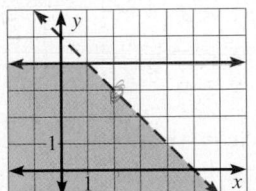

14. $(2, 6)$

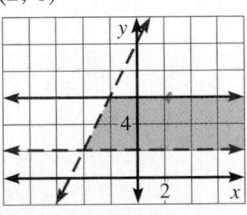

STUDENT HELP

→ **HOMEWORK HELP**
Example 1: Exs. 12, 13, 15–17, 21, 22, 27–38
Example 2: Exs. 14, 18–20, 23–26, 39–50
Example 3: Exs. 51–58

FINDING A SOLUTION Give an ordered pair that is a solution of the system.

15. $x - y \ge 3$
     $y < 15$

16. $x + y < 6$
     $x \ge -2$

17. $4x > y$
     $x \le 12$

18. $x \ge -7$
     $y < 10$
     $x < y$

19. $y > -5$
     $x > 3$
     $2x + y < 13$

20. $y \ge -x$
     $y \ge 0$
     $x < 0$

MATCHING SYSTEMS AND GRAPHS Match the system of linear inequalities
with its graph.

21. $y \le 4$
$x > -2$

22. $y > -4$
$x > -2$

23. $y > x$
$x > -3$
$y \ge 0$

24. $y > x$
$y > -3$
$x \le 0$

25. $x \le 3$
$y > 1$
$y \ge -x + 1$

26. $y > -1$
$x \ge -1$
$y \ge -x + 1$

A.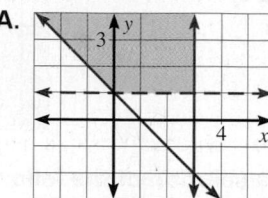

B.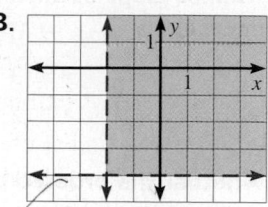

C.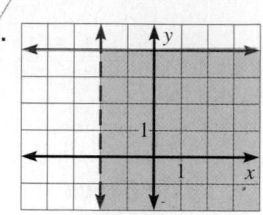

D.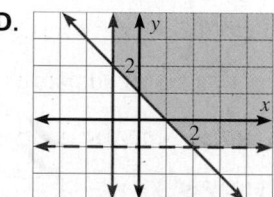

E.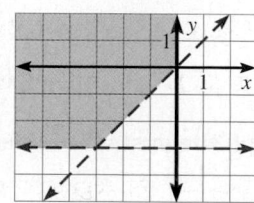

F.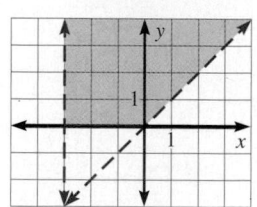

SYSTEMS OF TWO INEQUALITIES Graph the system of linear inequalities.

27. $x < 5$
$x > -4$

28. $y > -2$
$y \le 1$

29. $x \ge 0$
$x + y < 11$

30. $x + y \ge -2$
$-5x + y < -3$

31. $y \ge -4$
$y < -2x + 10$

32. $y > 2x - 7$
$4x + 4y < -12$

33. $y < x + 4$
$y \ge -2x + 1$

34. $x + y > -8$
$x + y \le 6$

35. $y > -3x$
$x \le 5y$

36. $x - y > 7$
$2x + y < 8$

37. $7x + y > 0$
$3x - 2y \le 5$

38. $-x < y$
$x + 3y > 8$

SYSTEMS OF THREE OR MORE INEQUALITIES Graph the system of linear
inequalities.

39. $y < 4$
$x > -3$
$y > x$

40. $y \ge 1$
$x \le 6$
$y < 2x - 5$

41. $2x - 3y > -6$
$5x - 3y < 3$
$x + 3y > -3$

42. $x - 4y > 0$
$x + y \le 1$
$x + 3y > -1$

43. $2x + 1 \ge y$
$x < 5$
$y < x + 2$

44. $5x - 3y \le 4$
$x + y < 8$
$y > 3$

45. $x \ge y - 2$
$x + y > 1$
$x < 10$

46. $y \ge 0$
$x - 4y < 2$
$y < x$

47. $x - y \ge 0$
$y < 2x$
$5x + 6y \ge 1$

48. $y \ge 0$
$x \le 9$
$x + y < 15$
$y < x$

49. $x + y \le 4$
$x + y \ge -1$
$x - y \ge -2$
$x - y \le 2$

50. $y < 5$
$y > -6$
$2x + y \ge -1$
$y \le x + 3$

51.  **POOL CHEMICALS** You are a lifeguard at a community pool, and you are in charge of maintaining the proper pH (amount of acidity) and chlorine levels. The water test-kit says that the pH level should be between 7.4 and 7.6 pH units and the chlorine level should be between 1.0 and 1.5 PPM (parts per million). Let p be the pH level and let c be the chlorine level (in PPM). Write and graph a system of inequalities for the pH and chlorine levels the water should have.

HEALTH **In Exercises 52–54, use the following information.**
For a healthy person who is 4 feet 10 inches tall, the recommended lower weight limit is about 91 pounds and increases by about 3.7 pounds for each additional inch of height. The recommended upper weight limit is about 119 pounds and increases by about 4.9 pounds for each additional inch of height.
▶ Source: Dietary Guidelines Advisory Committee

52. Let x be the number of inches by which a person's height exceeds 4 feet 10 inches and let y be the person's weight in pounds. Write a system of inequalities describing the possible values of x and y for a healthy person.

53. Use a graphing calculator to graph the system of inequalities from Exercise 52.

54. What is the recommended weight range for someone 6 feet tall?

SHOE SALE **In Exercises 55 and 56, use the shoe store ad shown below.**

55. Let x be the regular footwear price and y be the discount price. Write a system of inequalities for the regular footwear prices and possible sale prices.

56. Graph the system you wrote in Exercise 55. Use your graph to estimate the range of possible sale prices for shoes that are regularly priced at $65.

HUGE ONE-DAY SALE!
Save **10%–25%** on all athletic footwear.
(Regular price: $20–$80)

57.  **WEIGHTLIFTING RECORDS** The men's world weightlifting records for the 105-kg-and-over weight category are shown in the table. The combined lift is the sum of the snatch lift and the clean and jerk lift. Let s be the weight lifted in the snatch and let j be the weight lifted in the clean and jerk. Write and graph a system of inequalities to describe the weights you could lift to break the records for both the snatch and combined lifts, but *not* the clean and jerk lift.

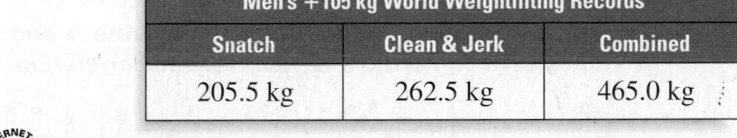

Men's +105 kg World Weightlifting Records		
Snatch	**Clean & Jerk**	**Combined**
205.5 kg	262.5 kg	465.0 kg

DATA UPDATE of International Weightlifting Federation data at www.mcdougallittell.com

58. **BIOLOGY** **CONNECTION** Each day, an average adult moose can process about 32 kilograms of terrestrial vegetation (twigs and leaves) and aquatic vegetation. From this food, it needs to obtain about 1.9 grams of sodium and 11,000 Calories of energy. Aquatic vegetation has about 0.15 gram of sodium per kilogram and about 193 Calories of energy per kilogram, while terrestrial vegetation has minimal sodium and about four times more energy than aquatic vegetation. Write and graph a system of inequalities describing the amounts t and a of terrestrial and aquatic vegetation, respectively, for the daily diet of an average adult moose.
▶ Source: *Biology by Numbers*

59. CRITICAL THINKING Write a system of three linear inequalities that has no solution. Graph the system to show that it has no solution.

60. MULTIPLE CHOICE Which system of inequalities is graphed at the right?

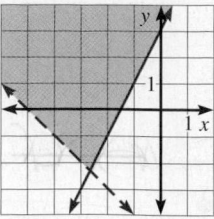

Ⓐ $x + y > -5$
   $-2x + y \geq 3$

Ⓑ $x + y > -5$
   $-2x + y < 3$

Ⓒ $x + y > -5$
   $-2x + y \leq 3$

Ⓓ $x + y > -5$
   $-2x + y > 3$

61. MULTIPLE CHOICE Which ordered pair is *not* a solution of the following system of inequalities?

$$3x + 2y \geq -2$$
$$x - y < 3$$

Ⓐ $(0, 0)$ Ⓑ $(-1, 2)$ Ⓒ $(4, 1)$ Ⓓ $(2, 2)$

★ **Challenge**

WRITING A SYSTEM Write a system of linear inequalities for the region.

62.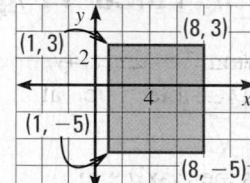

63.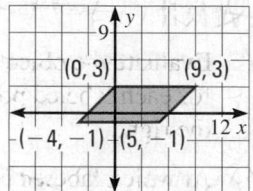

64.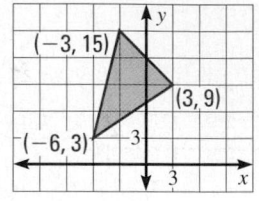

EXTRA CHALLENGE
www.mcdougallittell.com

65. VISUAL THINKING Write a system of linear inequalities whose graph is a pentagon and its interior.

MIXED REVIEW

EVALUATING EXPRESSIONS Evaluate the expression for the given values of *x* and *y*. (Review 1.2 for 3.4)

66. $2x + 7y$ when $x = 5$ and $y = -3$ **67.** $-4x - 3y$ when $x = -6$ and $y = -1$

68. $10x - 3y$ when $x = -4$ and $y = 2$ **69.** $-y + 8x$ when $y = -3$ and $x = -2$

DETERMINING CORRELATION Tell whether *x* and *y* have a *positive correlation*, a *negative correlation*, or *relatively no correlation*. (Review 2.5)

70.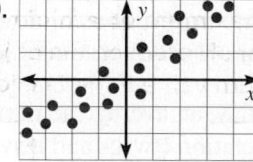

71.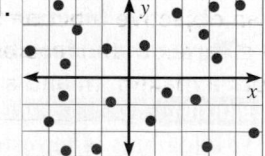

72.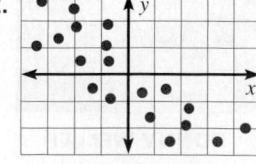

CHOOSING A METHOD Solve the system using any algebraic method. (Review 3.2)

73. $13x + 5y = 2$
   $x - 4y = 10$

74. $-2x + 7y = 10$
   $x - 3y = -3$

75. $5x + 6y = -12$
   $10x + 12y = 24$

76. $-7x + 5y = 0$
   $14x - 8y = 2$

77. $-4x - 10y = 12$
   $x + 5y = 2$

78. $6x - 8y = -18$
   $-3x + 4y = 9$

3.4

Linear Programming

Many real-life problems involve a process called **optimization,** which means finding the maximum or minimum value of some quantity. In this lesson you will study one type of optimization process called *linear programming*.

Linear programming is the process of optimizing a linear **objective function** subject to a system of linear inequalities called **constraints**. The graph of the system of constraints is called the **feasible region**.

▶ **ACTIVITY**
Developing Concepts

Investigating Linear Programming

❶ Evaluate the objective function $C = 2x + 4y$ for each labeled point in the feasible region at the right.

❷ At which labeled point does the maximum value of C occur? At which labeled point does the minimum value of C occur?

❸ What are the maximum and minimum values of C on the entire feasible region? Try other points in the region to see if you can find values of C that are greater or lesser than those you found in **Step 2**.

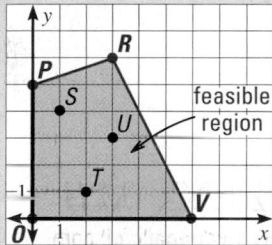

Constraints:
$x \geq 0$
$y \geq 0$
$-x + 3y \leq 15$
$2x + y \leq 12$

In the activity you may have discovered that the optimal values of the objective function occurred at vertices of the feasible region.

OPTIMAL SOLUTION OF A LINEAR PROGRAMMING PROBLEM

If an objective function has a maximum or a minimum value, then it must occur at a vertex of the feasible region. Moreover, the objective function will have both a maximum and a minimum value if the feasible region is bounded.

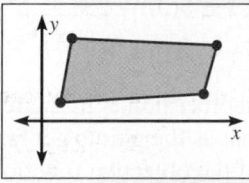

Bounded region

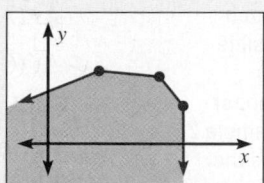

Unbounded region

EXAMPLE 1 **Solving a Linear Programming Problem**

Find the minimum value and the maximum value of

$$C = 3x + 4y \qquad \text{Objective function}$$

subject to the following constraints.

$$
\begin{aligned}
x &\geq 0 \\
y &\geq 0 \qquad\qquad \text{Constraints}\\
x + y &\leq 8
\end{aligned}
$$

SOLUTION

The feasible region determined by the constraints is shown. The three vertices are $(0, 0)$, $(8, 0)$, and $(0, 8)$. To find the minimum and maximum values of C, evaluate $C = 3x + 4y$ at each of the three vertices.

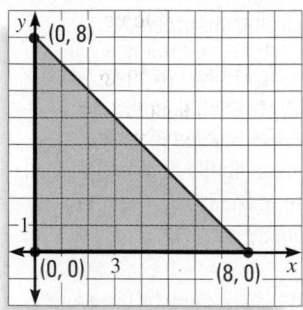

At $(0, 0)$: $C = 3(0) + 4(0) = 0$ ⟵ **Minimum**

At $(8, 0)$: $C = 3(8) + 4(0) = 24$

At $(0, 8)$: $C = 3(0) + 4(8) = 32$ ⟵ **Maximum**

The minimum value of C is 0. It occurs when $x = 0$ and $y = 0$. The maximum value of C is 32. It occurs when $x = 0$ and $y = 8$.

EXAMPLE 2 **A Region that is Unbounded**

Find the minimum value and the maximum value of

$$C = 5x + 6y \qquad \text{Objective function}$$

subject to the following constraints.

$$
\begin{aligned}
x &\geq 0 \\
y &\geq 0 \qquad\qquad \text{Constraints}\\
x + y &\geq 5 \\
3x + 4y &\geq 18
\end{aligned}
$$

SOLUTION

The feasible region determined by the constraints is shown. The three vertices are $(0, 5)$, $(2, 3)$, and $(6, 0)$. First evaluate $C = 5x + 6y$ at each of the vertices.

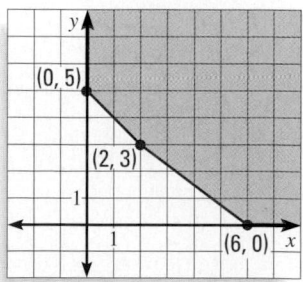

At $(0, 5)$: $C = 5(0) + 6(5) = 30$

At $(2, 3)$: $C = 5(2) + 6(3) = 28$

At $(6, 0)$: $C = 5(6) + 6(0) = 30$

If you evaluate several other points in the feasible region, you will see that as the points get farther from the origin, the value of the objective function increases without bound. Therefore, the objective function has no maximum value. Since the value of the objective function is always at least 28, the minimum value is 28.

STUDENT HELP

▶ **Study Tip**
You can find the coordinates of each vertex in the feasible region by solving systems of two linear equations. In Example 2 the vertex $(2, 3)$ is the solution of this system:
$$
\begin{aligned}
x + y &= 5 \\
3x + 4y &= 18
\end{aligned}
$$

BICYCLES In China bicycles are a popular means of transportation. In 1999 China had an estimated 700–800 million bicycles.

GOAL 2 **LINEAR PROGRAMMING IN REAL LIFE**

EXAMPLE 3 *Using Linear Programming to Find the Maximum Profit*

BICYCLE MANUFACTURING Two manufacturing plants make the same kind of bicycle. The table gives the hours of general labor, machine time, and technical labor required to make one bicycle in each plant. For the two plants combined, the manufacturer can afford to use up to 4000 hours of general labor, up to 1500 hours of machine time, and up to 2300 hours of technical labor per week. Plant A earns a profit of $60 per bicycle and Plant B earns a profit of $50 per bicycle. How many bicycles per week should the manufacturer make in each plant to maximize profit?

Resource	Hours per bicycle in Plant A	Hours per bicycle in Plant B
General labor	10	1
Machine time	1	3
Technical labor	5	2

SOLUTION

Write an objective function. Let a and b represent the number of bicycles made in Plant A and Plant B, respectively. Because the manufacturer wants to maximize the profit P, the objective function is:

$$P = 60a + 50b$$

Write the constraints in terms of a and b. The constraints are given below and the feasible region determined by the constraints is shown at the right.

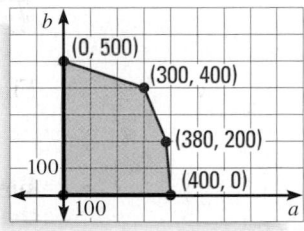

$10a + b \leq 4000$ **General labor: up to 4000 hours**

$a + 3b \leq 1500$ **Machine time: up to 1500 hours**

$5a + 2b \leq 2300$ **Technical labor: up to 2300 hours**

$a \geq 0$ **Cannot produce a negative amount**

$b \geq 0$ **Cannot produce a negative amount**

Calculate the profit at each vertex of the feasible region.

At (0, 500): $\quad P = 60(0) + 50(500) = 25{,}000$

At (300, 400): $\quad P = 60(\mathbf{300}) + 50(\mathbf{400}) = 38{,}000 \longleftarrow$ **Maximum**

At (380, 200): $\quad P = 60(380) + 50(200) = 32{,}800$

At (400, 0): $\quad P = 60(400) + 50(0) = 24{,}000$

At (0, 0): $\quad P = 60(0) + 50(0) = 0$

▶ The maximum profit is obtained by making 300 bicycles in Plant A and 400 bicycles in Plant B.

GUIDED PRACTICE

Vocabulary Check ✔

1. Define linear programming.

Concept Check ✔

2. How is the objective function used in a linear programming problem? How is the system of constraints used?

3. In a linear programming problem, which ordered pairs should be tested to find a minimum or maximum value?

Skill Check ✔

In Exercises 4 and 5, use the feasible region at the right.

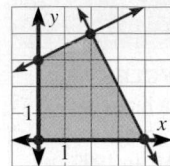

4. What are the vertices of the feasible region?

5. What are the minimum and maximum values of the objective function $C = 5x + 7y$?

Find the minimum and maximum values of the objective function subject to the given constraints.

6. **Objective function:** $C = x + y$; **Constraints:** $y \le 5,\ y \ge 0,\ y - 2x \ge 0$

7. **Objective function:** $C = 2x - y$; **Constraints:** $x \ge 0,\ x + y \le 20,\ y \ge 3$

8. 🌐 **PLANNING A FUNDRAISER** Your club plans to raise money by selling two sizes of fruit baskets. The plan is to buy small baskets for $10 and sell them for $16 and to buy large baskets for $15 and sell them for $25. The club president estimates that you will not sell more than 100 baskets. Your club can afford to spend up to $1200 to buy the baskets. Find the number of small and large fruit baskets you should buy in order to maximize profit.

PRACTICE AND APPLICATIONS

STUDENT HELP

▶ **Extra Practice**
to help you master
skills is on p. 943.

CHECKING VERTICES Find the minimum and maximum values of the objective function for the given feasible region.

9. $C = x - y$

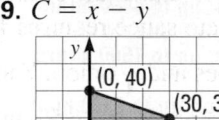

10. $C = 2x + 5y$

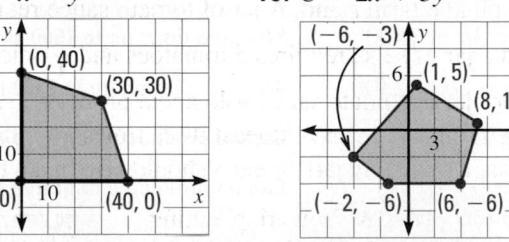

11. $C = 4x + 2y$

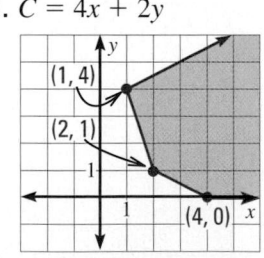

FINDING VALUES In Exercises 12–20, find the minimum and maximum values of the objective function subject to the given constraints.

12. **Objective function:**
$C = 2x + 3y$

Constraints:
$x \ge 0$
$y \ge 0$
$x + y \le 9$

13. **Objective function:**
$C = x + 4y$

Constraints:
$x \ge 2$
$x \le 5$
$y \ge 1$
$y \le 6$

14. **Objective function:**
$C = 2x + y$

Constraints:
$x \ge -5$
$x \le 0$
$y \ge -2$
$y \le 2$

STUDENT HELP

▶ **HOMEWORK HELP**
Examples 1, 2: Exs. 9–20
Example 3: Exs. 21–24

15. Objective function:
$$C = 10x + 7y$$

Constraints:
$$0 \le x \le 60$$
$$0 \le y \le 45$$
$$5x + 6y \le 420$$

16. Objective function:
$$C = -2x + y$$

Constraints:
$$x \ge 0$$
$$y \ge 0$$
$$x + y \ge 7$$
$$5x + 2y \ge 20$$

17. Objective function:
$$C = 4x + 6y$$

Constraints:
$$-x + y \le 11$$
$$x + y \le 27$$
$$2x + 5y \le 90$$

18. Objective function:
$$C = 5x + 4y$$

Constraints:
$$x \ge 0$$
$$y \ge 0$$
$$y \le 8$$
$$x + y \le 14$$
$$5x + y \le 50$$

19. Objective function:
$$C = 4x + 3y$$

Constraints:
$$x \ge 0$$
$$2x + 3y \ge 6$$
$$3x - 2y \le 9$$
$$x + 5y \le 20$$

20. Objective function:
$$C = 10x + 3y$$

Constraints:
$$x \ge 0$$
$$y \ge 0$$
$$-x + y \ge 0$$
$$2x + y \ge 4$$
$$2x + y \le 13$$

21. 🌐 **JUICE BLENDS** A juice company makes two kinds of juice: Orangeade and Berry-fruity. One gallon of Orangeade is made by mixing 2.5 quarts of orange juice and 1.5 quarts of raspberry juice, while one gallon of Berry-fruity is made by mixing 3 quarts of raspberry juice and 1 quart of orange juice. A profit of $.50 is made on every gallon of Orangeade sold, and a profit of $.40 is made on every gallon of Berry-fruity sold. If the company has 150 gallons of raspberry juice and 125 gallons of orange juice on hand, how many gallons of each type of juice should be made to maximize profit?

22. 🌐 **FILE CABINETS** An office manager is purchasing file cabinets and wants to maximize storage space. The office has 60 square feet of floor space for the cabinets and $600 in the budget to purchase them. Cabinet A requires 3 square feet of floor space, has a storage capacity of 12 cubic feet, and costs $75. Cabinet B requires 6 square feet of floor space, has a storage capacity of 18 cubic feet, and costs $50. How many of each cabinet should the office manager buy?

23. 🌐 **HOME CANNING** You have 180 tomatoes and 15 onions left over from your garden. You want to use these to make jars of tomato sauce and jars of salsa to sell at a farm stand. A jar of tomato sauce requires 10 tomatoes and 1 onion, and a jar of salsa requires 5 tomatoes and $\frac{1}{4}$ onion. You'll make a profit of $2 on every jar of tomato sauce sold and a profit of $1.50 on every jar of salsa sold. The farm stand wants at least three times as many jars of tomato sauce as jars of salsa. How many jars of each should you make to maximize profit?

24. 🌐 **NUTRITION** You are planning a dinner of pinto beans and brown rice. You want to consume at least 2100 Calories and 44 grams of protein per day, but no more than 2400 milligrams of sodium and 73 grams of fat. So far today, you have consumed 1600 Calories, 24 grams of protein, 2370 milligrams of sodium, and 65 grams of fat. Pinto beans cost $.57 per cup and brown rice costs $.78 per cup. How many cups of pinto beans and brown rice should you make to minimize cost while satisfying your nutritional requirements?

Contents	1 cup pinto beans	1 cup brown rice (with salt)
Calories	265	230
Protein (g)	15	5
Sodium (mg)	3	10
Fat (g)	1	1

Test Preparation

25. **MULTIPLE CHOICE** Given the feasible region shown, what is the maximum value of the objective function $C = 2x + 6y$?

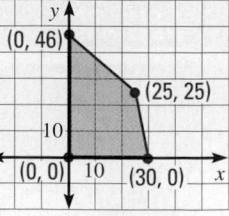

(0, 46)
(25, 25)
10
(0, 0) 10 (30, 0) x

   Ⓐ 0   Ⓑ 60   Ⓒ 200

   Ⓓ 276   Ⓔ 326

26. **MULTIPLE CHOICE** Given the constraints $y \geq 0$, $y \leq x + 8$, and $y \geq 2x + 8$, what is the minimum value of the objective function $C = -2x - y$?

   Ⓐ -8 Ⓑ 16   Ⓒ -16 Ⓓ 8

★ Challenge

27. **CONSECUTIVE VERTICES** Find the value of the objective function at each vertex of the feasible region and at two points on each line segment connecting two vertices. What can you conclude?

  a. Objective function:
    $C = 2x + 2y$

    Constraints:
    $y \leq 4$
    $x \leq 5$
    $x + y \leq 6$

  b. Objective function:
    $C = 5x - y$

    Constraints:
    $y \geq -1$
    $x \leq 3$
    $-5x + y \leq 4$

EXTRA CHALLENGE
www.mcdougallittell.com

MIXED REVIEW

GRAPHING EQUATIONS Graph the equation. Label any intercepts. (Review 2.3 for 3.5)

28. $x - y = 10$ **29.** $3x + 4y = -12$ **30.** $y = -3x + 2$

31. $5x - 15y = 15$ **32.** $y = -\frac{3}{4}x + 2$ **33.** $y = -\frac{1}{2}x + 7$

EVALUATING FUNCTIONS Evaluate the function for the given value of *x*. (Review 2.7)

$$f(x) = \begin{cases} 3x - 1, & \text{if } x < -2 \\ x - 5, & \text{if } x \geq -2 \end{cases} \qquad g(x) = \begin{cases} -7x, & \text{if } x \leq 0 \\ 2x + 1, & \text{if } x > 0 \end{cases}$$

34. $f(0)$ **35.** $f(-2)$ **36.** $f(-10)$ **37.** $f(-1)$

38. $g(1)$ **39.** $g(-5)$ **40.** $g(-1)$ **41.** $g(7)$

GRAPHING SYSTEMS OF INEQUALITIES Graph the system of linear inequalities. (Review 3.3)

42. $x > 2$ **43.** $x + y \leq 5$ **44.** $x < -1$
    $y < 6$ $y > 0$ $x - y \geq 4$

45. $y < 5$ **46.** $-x + y > 2$ **47.** $x + y \leq 6$
    $x \geq -1$ $y > 0$ $-\frac{1}{2}x + y \leq 3$
    $y \geq 1$ $2x + y \leq 3$ $y \leq 3$

48. 🌐 **AMUSEMENT CENTER** You have 30 tokens for playing video games and pinball. It costs 3 tokens to play a video game and 2 tokens to play pinball. You want to play an equal number of video games and pinball games. Use an algebraic model to find how many games of each you can play. (Review 1.5)

Graph the system of linear inequalities. (Lesson 3.3)

1. $y > -2$
$x \geq -4$
$y \leq -x + 1$

2. $y > -5$
$x \leq 2$
$y \leq x + 2$

3. $x \leq 3$
$y < 2$
$y > -x + 1$

Find the minimum and maximum values of the objective function $C = 5x + 2y$ subject to the given constraints. (Lesson 3.4)

4. Constraints:
$x \leq -2$
$x \geq -4$
$y \geq 1$
$y \leq 6$

5. Constraints:
$x \geq 0$
$y \geq 2$
$2x + y \leq 10$
$x - 3y \geq -3$

6. Constraints:
$x \geq 0$
$y \geq 0$
$y \leq 8$
$x + y \leq 14$

7. 🌐 **MAXIMUM INCOME** You are stenciling wooden boxes to sell at a fair. It takes you 2 hours to stencil a small box and 3 hours to stencil a large box. You make a profit of $10 for a small box and $20 for a large box. If you have no more than 30 hours available to stencil and want at least 12 boxes to sell, how many of each size box should you stencil to maximize your profit? **(Lesson 3.4)**

MATH & History   **Linear Programming in World War II**    **APPLICATION LINK** www.mcdougallittell.com

THEN

DURING WORLD WAR II, the need for efficient transportation of supplies inspired mathematician George Dantzig to develop linear programming.

The LST was a ship used during World War II that carried 3 ton trucks and 25 ton tanks. The upper deck could carry 27 trucks, but no tanks. The tank deck could carry 500 tons, but no more than 33 trucks.

1. What is the maximum number of tanks that an LST could hold?

2. What is the maximum number of trucks that an LST could hold?

3. Suppose an LST was to be loaded with as many tanks and trucks as possible, and at least three times as many trucks as tanks. What is the maximum number of tanks and trucks that could be loaded?

U.S. Marines loading military supplies on an LST (Landing Ship, Tank)

NOW

IN 1984 mathematician Narendra Karmarkar developed a new time-saving linear programming method. Today his method is used by industries that deal with allocation of resources, such as telephone companies, airlines, and manufacturers.

L.V. Kantorovich and T.C. Koopmans receive Nobel Prize for their linear programming work.

A Soviet Discovery Rocks World of Mathematics

1947

George Dantzig develops simplex method.

1975

1979

L.G. Khachyan develops ellipsoid method.

1984

N. Karmarkar devises a polynomial-time algorithm.

Graphing Linear Equations in Three Variables

What you should learn

GOAL 1 Graph linear equations in three variables and evaluate linear functions of two variables.

GOAL 2 Use functions of two variables to model **real-life** situations, such as finding the cost of planting a lawn in **Example 4**.

Why you should learn it

▼ To solve **real-life** problems, such as finding how many times to air a radio commercial in **Ex. 53**.

GOAL 1 GRAPHING IN THREE DIMENSIONS

Solutions of equations in three variables can be pictured with a **three-dimensional coordinate system**. To construct such a system, begin with the *xy*-coordinate plane in a horizontal position. Then draw the **z-axis** as a vertical line through the origin.

In much the same way that points in a two-dimensional coordinate system are represented by ordered pairs, each point in space can be represented by an **ordered triple** (*x, y, z*).

Drawing the point represented by an ordered triple is called *plotting* the point.

The three axes, taken two at a time, determine three coordinate planes that divide space into eight **octants**. The first octant is the one for which all three coordinates are positive.

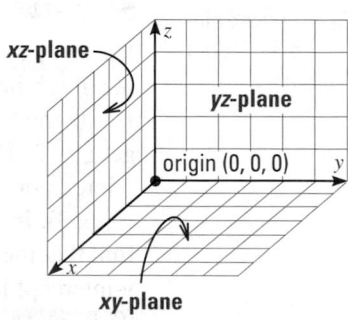

EXAMPLE 1 *Plotting Points in Three Dimensions*

Plot the ordered triple in a three-dimensional coordinate system.

a. $(-5, 3, 4)$ **b.** $(3, -4, -2)$

SOLUTION

a. To plot $(-5, 3, 4)$, it helps to first find the point $(-5, 3)$ in the *xy*-plane. The point $(-5, 3, 4)$ lies four units above.

b. To plot $(3, -4, -2)$, find the point $(3, -4)$ in the *xy*-plane. The point $(3, -4, -2)$ lies two units below.

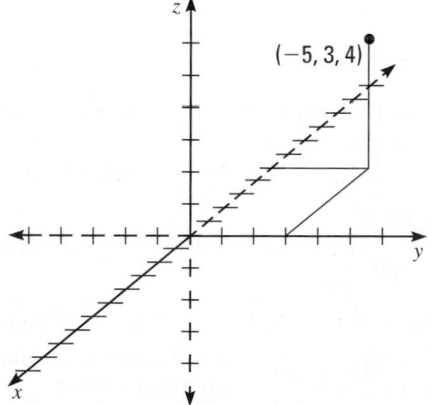

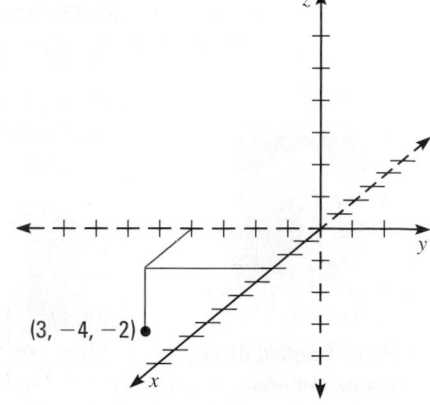

A **linear equation in three variables** x, y, and z is an equation of the form

$$ax + by + cz = d$$

where a, b, and c are not all zero. An ordered triple (x, y, z) is a *solution* of this equation if the equation is true when the values of x, y, and z are substituted into the equation. The *graph* of an equation in three variables is the graph of all its solutions. The graph of a linear equation in three variables is a plane.

EXAMPLE 2 *Graphing a Linear Equation in Three Variables*

Sketch the graph of $3x + 2y + 4z = 12$.

SOLUTION

Begin by finding the points at which the graph intersects the axes. Let $x = 0$ and $y = 0$, and solve for z to get $z = 3$. This tells you that the z-intercept is 3, so plot the point $(0, 0, 3)$. In a similar way, you can find that the x-intercept is 4 and the y-intercept is 6. After plotting $(0, 0, 3)$, $(4, 0, 0)$, and $(0, 6, 0)$, you can connect these points with lines to form the triangular region of the plane that lies in the first octant.

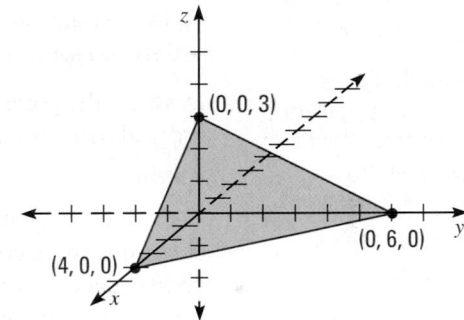

· · · · · · · · · ·

A linear equation in x, y, and z can be written as a **function of two variables**. To do this, solve the equation for z. Then replace z with $f(x, y)$.

EXAMPLE 3 *Evaluating a Function of Two Variables*

a. Write the linear equation $3x + 2y + 4z = 12$ as a function of x and y.

b. Evaluate the function when $x = 1$ and $y = 3$. Interpret the result geometrically.

SOLUTION

a.

$3x + 2y + 4z = 12$	**Write original equation.**
$4z = 12 - 3x - 2y$	**Isolate z-term.**
$z = \frac{1}{4}(12 - 3x - 2y)$	**Solve for z.**
$f(x, y) = \frac{1}{4}(12 - 3x - 2y)$	**Replace z with f(x, y).**

b. $f(\mathbf{1}, \mathbf{3}) = \frac{1}{4}(12 - 3(\mathbf{1}) - 2(\mathbf{3})) = \frac{3}{4}$. This tells you that the graph of f contains the point $\left(1, 3, \frac{3}{4}\right)$.

GOAL 2 **USING FUNCTIONS OF TWO VARIABLES IN REAL LIFE**

EXAMPLE 4 *Modeling a Real-Life Situation*

LANDSCAPING You are planting a lawn and decide to use a mixture of two types of grass seed: bluegrass and rye. The bluegrass costs $2 per pound and the rye costs $1.50 per pound. To spread the seed you buy a spreader that costs $35.

a. Write a model for the total amount you will spend as a function of the number of pounds of bluegrass and rye.

b. Evaluate the model for several different amounts of bluegrass and rye, and organize your results in a table.

SOLUTION

a. Your total cost involves two variable costs (for the two types of seed) and one fixed cost (for the spreader).

VERBAL MODEL

| Total cost | = | Blue-grass cost | · | Blue-grass amount | + | Rye cost | · | Rye amount | + | Spreader cost |

LABELS

Total cost = C (dollars)

Bluegrass cost = 2   (dollars per pound)

Bluegrass amount = x (pounds)

Rye cost = 1.5   (dollars per pound)

Rye amount = y (pounds)

Spreader cost = 35   (dollars)

ALGEBRAIC MODEL

$$C = 2x + 1.5y + 35$$

b. To evaluate the function of two variables, substitute values of x and y into the function. For instance, when $x = 10$ and $y = 20$, the total cost is:

$$C = 2x + 1.5y + 35 \qquad \text{Write original function.}$$
$$= 2(10) + 1.5(20) + 35 \qquad \text{Substitute for } x \text{ and } y.$$
$$= 85 \qquad \text{Simplify.}$$

The table shows the total cost for several different values of x and y.

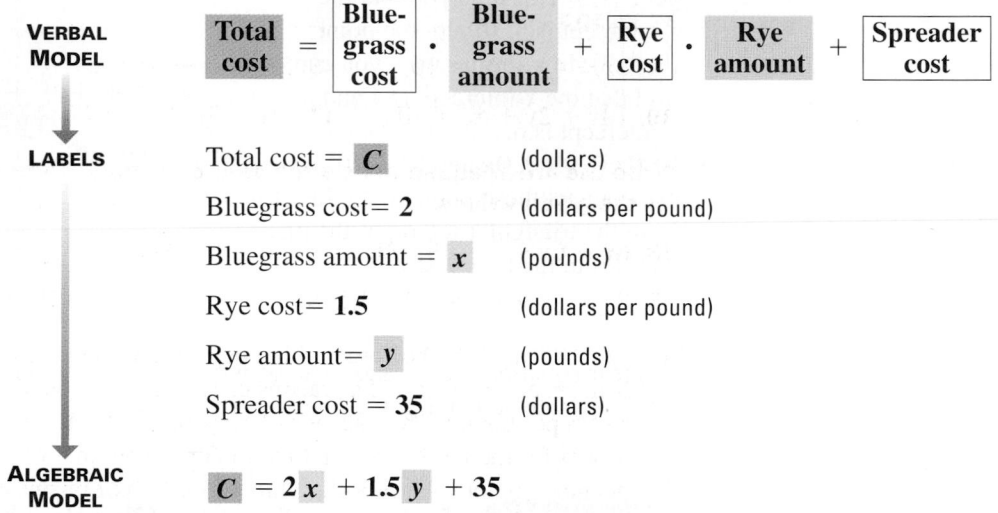

	Rye (lb)				
	0	**10**	**20**	**30**	**40**
10	$70	**$85**	$100	$115	
20	$90	$105	$120	$135	
30	$110	$125	$140	$155	
40	$130	$145	$160	$175	

(left axis label: Bluegrass (lb))

GUIDED PRACTICE

Vocabulary Check ✓

1. Write the general form of a linear equation in three variables. How is the solution of such an equation represented?

Concept Check ✓

2. **LOGICAL REASONING** Tell whether this statement is *true* or *false*: The graph of a linear equation in three variables consists of three different lines.

3. How are octants and quadrants similar?

4. Describe how you would graph a linear equation in three variables.

Skill Check ✓

5. Draw a three-dimensional coordinate system and plot the ordered triple $(2, -4, -6)$.

6. Write the coordinates of the vertices A, B, C, and D of the rectangular prism shown, given that one vertex is the point $(2, 3, 4)$.

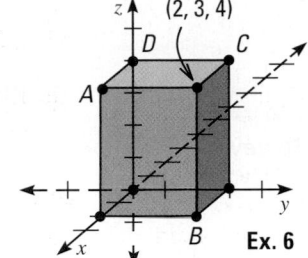

Ex. 6

Sketch the graph of the equation. Label the points where the graph crosses the *x*-, *y*-, and *z*-axes.

7. $8x + 4y + 2z = 16$
8. $2x + 4y + 5z = 20$
9. $3x + 3y + 7z = 21$

10. $10x + 2y + 5z = 10$
11. $9x + 3y + 3z = 27$
12. $4x + y + 2z = 8$

Write the linear equation as a function of *x* and *y*. Then evaluate the function for the given values.

13. $6x + 6y + 3z = 9$, $f(1, 2)$
14. $-2x - y + z = 7$, $f(-3, 2)$

15. $8x + 2y + 4z = -16$, $f(5, 6)$
16. $5x - 10y - 5z = 15$, $f(2, 2)$

17. 🌐 **TRAIL MIX** You are making bags of a trail mix called GORP (Good Old Raisins and Peanuts). The raisins cost $2.25 per pound and the peanuts cost $2.95 per pound. The package of bags for the trail mix costs $2.65. Write a model for the total cost as a function of the number of pounds of raisins and peanuts you buy. Evaluate the model for 5 lb of raisins and 8 lb of peanuts.

PRACTICE AND APPLICATIONS

STUDENT HELP

→ **Extra Practice**
to help you master
skills is on p. 943.

PLOTTING POINTS Plot the ordered triple in a three-dimensional coordinate system.

18. $(2, 4, 0)$
19. $(4, -1, -6)$
20. $(5, -2, -2)$
21. $(0, 6, -3)$

22. $(3, 4, -2)$
23. $(-2, 1, 1)$
24. $(5, -1, 5)$
25. $(-3, 2, -7)$

SKETCHING GRAPHS Sketch the graph of the equation. Label the points where the graph crosses the *x*-, *y*-, and *z*-axes.

STUDENT HELP

→ **HOMEWORK HELP**
Example 1: Exs. 18–25
Example 2: Exs. 26–37

continued on p. 174

26. $x + y + z = 7$
27. $5x + 4y + 2z = 20$
28. $x + 6y + 4z = 12$

29. $12x + 3y + 8z = 24$
30. $2x + 18y + 3z = 36$
31. $7x + 9y + 21z = 63$

32. $7x + 7y + 2z = 14$
33. $6x + 4y + 3z = 10$
34. $3x + 5y + 3z = 15$

35. $\frac{1}{2}x + 4y - 3z = 8$
36. $5x + y + 2z = -4$
37. $-2x + 9y + 3z = 18$

STUDENT HELP

→ **HOMEWORK HELP**
continued from p. 173
Example 3: Exs. 38–45
Example 4: Exs. 48–52

EVALUATING FUNCTIONS Write the linear equation as a function of x and y. Then evaluate the function for the given values.

38. $6x + 2y + 3z = 18$, $f(2, 1)$

39. $-2x - 5y + 5z = 15$, $f\left(\frac{3}{2}, -2\right)$

40. $x + 6y + z = 10$, $f(-4, -1)$

41. $3x - \frac{3}{4}y + \frac{5}{2}z = 9$, $f(-3, 16)$

42. $-x - 2y - 7z = 14$, $f(-5, -10)$

43. $10x + 15y + 60z = 12$, $f\left(-3, \frac{4}{5}\right)$

44. $x - 5y - z = 14$, $f(3, 6)$

45. $-x + 6y - 9z = 12$, $f\left(-\frac{1}{2}, 12\right)$

STUDENT HELP

→ **Skills Review**
For help with volume, see p. 914.

46. GEOMETRY CONNECTION Use the given point $(4, 7, 2)$ to find the volume of the rectangular prism.

47. GEOMETRY CONNECTION Use the given point $(5, 6, -2)$ to find the volume of the rectangular prism.

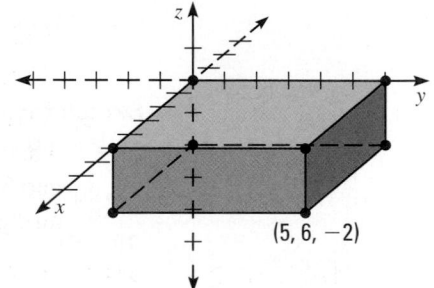

48. 🌐 **HOME AQUARIUM** You want to buy an aquarium and stock it with goldfish and angelfish. The pet store sells goldfish for $.40 each and angelfish for $4 each. The aquarium starter kit costs $65. Write a model for the amount you will spend as a function of the number of goldfish and angelfish you buy. Make a table that shows the total cost for several different numbers of goldfish and angelfish.

49. 🌐 **POTTERY** A craft store has paint-your-own pottery sessions available. You pick out a piece of pottery that ranges in price from $8 to $50 and pick out paint colors for $1.50 per color. The craft store charges a base fee of $16 for sitting time, brushes, glaze, and kiln time. Write a model for the total cost of making a piece of pottery as a function of the price of the pottery and the number of paint colors you use. Make a table that shows the total cost for several different pieces of pottery and numbers of paint colors.

FOCUS ON APPLICATIONS

→ **TRANSPORTATION**
The Massachusetts Bay Transit Authority (MBTA) is the nation's oldest subway system. On an average weekday, the MBTA serves about 1.2 million passengers on its bus, ferry, and train lines.

🌐 **APPLICATION LINK**
www.mcdougallittell.com

50. 🌐 **FLOWER ARRANGEMENT** You are buying tulips, carnations, and a glass vase to make a flower arrangement. The flower shop sells tulips for $.70 each and carnations for $.30 each. The glass vase costs $12. Write a model for the total cost of the flower arrangement as a function of the number of tulips and carnations you use. Make a table that shows the total cost for several different numbers of tulips and carnations.

51. 🌐 **TRANSPORTATION** Every month you buy a local bus pass for $20 that is worth $.60 toward the fare for the local bus, the express bus, or the subway. The local bus costs $.60, the express bus costs $1.50, and the subway costs $.85. Write a model for the total cost of transportation in a month as a function of the number of times you take the express bus and the number of times you take the subway. Evaluate the model for 8 express bus rides and 10 subway rides. Make a table that shows the total cost for several different numbers of rides.

52. 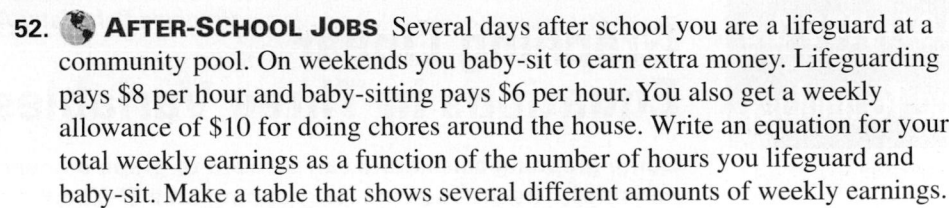 **AFTER-SCHOOL JOBS** Several days after school you are a lifeguard at a community pool. On weekends you baby-sit to earn extra money. Lifeguarding pays $8 per hour and baby-sitting pays $6 per hour. You also get a weekly allowance of $10 for doing chores around the house. Write an equation for your total weekly earnings as a function of the number of hours you lifeguard and baby-sit. Make a table that shows several different amounts of weekly earnings.

Test Preparation

53. MULTI-STEP PROBLEM You are deciding how many times to air a 60 second commercial on a radio station. The station charges $100 for a 60 second spot during off-peak listening hours and $350 for a 60 second spot during peak listening hours. The company you have hired to make your commercial charges $500.

a. Write a model for the total amount that will be spent making and airing the commercial as a function of the number of times it is aired during off-peak and peak listening hours.

b. Evaluate the model for several different numbers of off-peak airings and peak airings. Organize your results in a table.

c. *Writing* Suppose your advertising budget is $4000. Using the table you made in part (b), can you air the commercial 8 times during off-peak hours and 8 times during peak hours? What combination of off-peak and peak airings would you recommend? Explain.

★ **Challenge**

WRITING EQUATIONS Write an equation of the plane having the given *x*-, *y*-, and *z*-intercepts. Explain the method you used.

→ www.mcdougallittell.com

54. *x*-intercept: 4
y-intercept: -2
z-intercept: 4

55. *x*-intercept: $\frac{3}{2}$
y-intercept: 12
z-intercept: 6

56. *x*-intercept: 4
y-intercept: -6
z-intercept: -9

MIXED REVIEW

SOLVING INEQUALITIES Solve the inequality. Then graph the solution. (Review 1.6)

57. $3 + x \le 17$

58. $2x + 5 \ge 21$

59. $-x + 3 < 3x + 11$

60. $-13 < 6x - 1 < 11$

61. $24 \le 2x - 12 \le 30$

62. $-3 < 2x - 3 \le 17$

TYPES OF LINES Tell whether the lines are *parallel*, *perpendicular*, or *neither*. (Review 2.2)

63. Line 1: through $(1, 7)$ and $(-3, -5)$
Line 2: through $(-6, 20)$ and $(0, 2)$

64. Line 1: through $(4, -4)$ and $(-16, 1)$
Line 2: through $(1, 5)$ and $(5, 21)$

65. Line 1: through $(-2, 1)$ and $(0, 3)$
Line 2: through $(2, 1)$ and $(0, -1)$

66. Line 1: through $(0, 6)$ and $(5, -2)$
Line 2: through $(-1, -1)$ and $(7, 4)$

67. 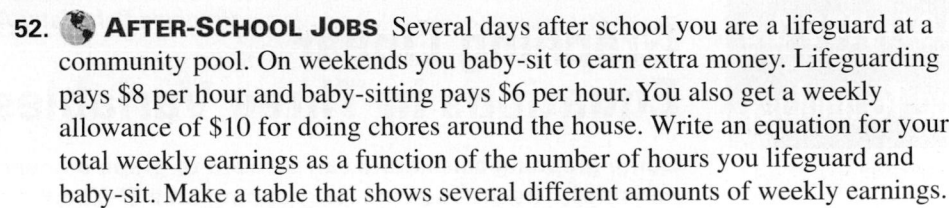 **HOME CARPENTRY** You have budgeted $48.50 to purchase red oak and poplar boards to make a bookcase. Each red oak board costs $3.95 and each poplar board costs $3.10. You need a total of 14 boards for the bookcase. Write and solve a system of equations to find the number of red oak boards and the number of poplar boards you should buy. **(Review 3.1, 3.2 for 3.6)**

ACTIVITY 3.5

Using Technology

Graphing Linear Equations in Three Variables

Some graphing calculators can be used to graph a linear equation in three variables. The instructions for graphing on a TI-92 are given below.

MATERIALS

TI-92 graphing calculator or computer with 3-D graphing software

▶ **EXAMPLE**

Use a graphing calculator (or a computer) to graph the equation $3x + 5y + 6z = 30$.

▶ **SOLUTION**

1 Solve the equation for z.

$$3x + 5y + 6z = 30 \qquad \text{Write equation.}$$

$$6z = 30 - 3x - 5y \qquad \text{Isolate the } z\text{-term.}$$

$$z = 5 - \frac{1}{2}x - \frac{5}{6}y \qquad \text{Solve for } z.$$

2 Enter the equation in the [Z=] editor.

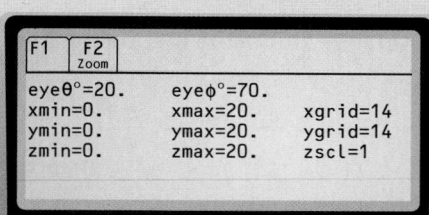

3 Display the axes in box format and turn the labels on.

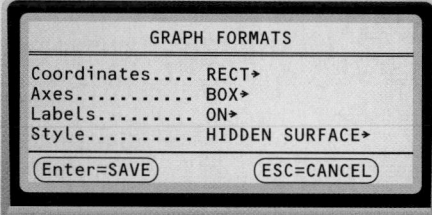

4 Set the window values as shown.

5 Graph the equation. You can use the *Evaluate* feature to evaluate z for values of x and y.

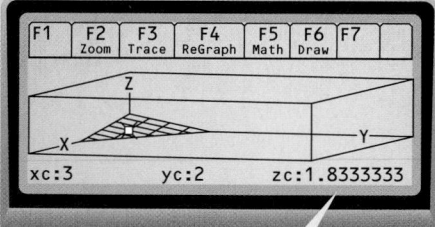

When $x = 3$ and $y = 2$, $z \approx 1.83$.

▶ **EXERCISES**

Use a graphing calculator (or a computer) to graph the equation. Then evaluate z for the given values of x and y.

1. $4x + 18y + 3z = 54$; $x = 6$, $y = 4$ **2.** $3x + y + z = 24$; $x = 1.5$, $y = 19$

3. $x + 3y + 10z = 45$; $x = 20$, $y = 7$ **4.** $7x + 6y + 2z = 61$; $x = 4$, $y = 4$

5. $4x + 13y - 5z = 26$; $x = 14$, $y = 6$ **6.** $3x - 25y + 20z = 35$; $x = 5$, $y = 0$

3.6
Solving Systems of Linear Equations in Three Variables

What you should learn

GOAL 1 Solve systems of linear equations in three variables.

GOAL 2 Use linear systems in three variables to model **real-life** situations, such as a high school swimming meet in **Example 4**.

Why you should learn it

▼ To solve **real-life** problems, such as finding the number of athletes who placed first, second, and third in a track meet in **Ex. 35**.

GOAL 1 SOLVING A SYSTEM IN THREE VARIABLES

In Lessons 3.1 and 3.2 you learned how to solve a system of two linear equations in two variables. In this lesson you will learn how to solve a **system of three linear equations** in three variables. Here is an example.

$$x + 2y - 3z = -3 \qquad \text{Equation 1}$$
$$2x - 5y + 4z = 13 \qquad \text{Equation 2}$$
$$5x + 4y - z = 5 \qquad \text{Equation 3}$$

A **solution** of such a system is an ordered triple (x, y, z) that is a solution of all three equations. For instance, $(2, -1, 1)$ is a solution of the system above.

$$2 + 2(-1) - 3(1) = 2 - 2 - 3 = -3 \checkmark$$
$$2(2) - 5(-1) + 4(1) = 4 + 5 + 4 = 13 \checkmark$$
$$5(2) + 4(-1) - 1 = 10 - 4 - 1 = 5 \checkmark$$

From Lesson 3.5 you know that the graph of a linear equation in three variables is a plane. Three planes in space can intersect in different ways.

If the planes intersect in a single point, as shown below, the system has exactly one solution.

If the planes intersect in a line, as shown below, the system has infinitely many solutions.

If the planes have no point of intersection, the system has no solution. In the example on the left, the planes intersect pairwise, but all three have no points in common. In the example on the right, the planes are parallel.

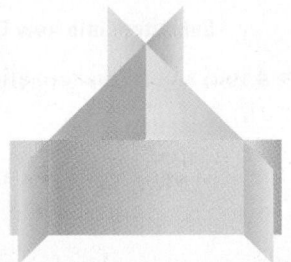

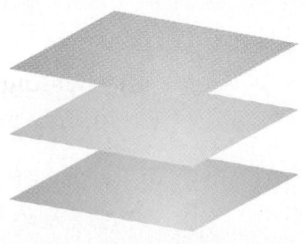

The linear combination method you learned in Lesson 3.2 can be extended to solve a system of linear equations in three variables.

THE LINEAR COMBINATION METHOD (3-VARIABLE SYSTEMS)

STEP ❶ Use the linear combination method to rewrite the linear system in three variables as a linear system in *two* variables.

STEP ❷ Solve the new linear system for both of its variables.

STEP ❸ Substitute the values found in Step 2 into one of the original equations and solve for the remaining variable.

Note: If you obtain a false equation, such as $0 = 1$, in any of the steps, then the system has no solution. If you do not obtain a false solution, but obtain an identity, such as $0 = 0$, then the system has infinitely many solutions.

EXAMPLE 1 *Using the Linear Combination Method*

STUDENT HELP

HOMEWORK HELP
Visit our Web site
www.mcdougallittell.com
for extra examples.

Solve the system.

$3x + 2y + 4z = 11$	**Equation 1**
$2x - y + 3z = 4$	**Equation 2**
$5x - 3y + 5z = -1$	**Equation 3**

SOLUTION

❶ Eliminate one of the variables in two of the original equations.

$$3x + 2y + 4z = 11$$
$$\underline{4x - 2y + 6z = 8}$$

Add 2 times the second equation to the first.

$$7x + 10z = 19 \qquad \text{New Equation 1}$$

$$5x - 3y + 5z = -1$$
$$\underline{-6x + 3y - 9z = -12}$$

Add -3 times the second equation to the third.

$$-x - 4z = -13 \qquad \text{New Equation 2}$$

❷ Solve the new system of linear equations in two variables.

$$7x + 10z = 19 \qquad \text{New Equation 1}$$
$$\underline{-7x - 28z = -91} \qquad \text{Add 7 times new Equation 2.}$$
$$-18z = -72$$

$$z = 4 \qquad \text{Solve for } z.$$

$$x = -3 \qquad \text{Substitute into new Equation 1 or 2 to find } x.$$

❸ Substitute $x = -3$ and $z = 4$ into an original equation and solve for y.

$$2x - y + 3z = 4 \qquad \text{Equation 2}$$
$$2(-3) - y + 3(4) = 4 \qquad \text{Substitute } -3 \text{ for } x \text{ and 4 for } z.$$
$$y = 2 \qquad \text{Solve for } y.$$

▶ The solution is $x = -3$, $y = 2$, and $z = 4$, or the ordered triple $(-3, 2, 4)$. Check this solution in each of the original equations.

STUDENT HELP

Look Back
For help with solving linear systems with many or no solutions, see p. 150.

EXAMPLE 2 *Solving a System with No Solution*

Solve the system.

$$x + y + z = 2 \qquad \text{Equation 1}$$
$$3x + 3y + 3z = 14 \qquad \text{Equation 2}$$
$$x - 2y + z = 4 \qquad \text{Equation 3}$$

SOLUTION

When you multiply the first equation by -3 and add the result to the second equation, you obtain a false equation.

$$\begin{array}{rl} -3x - 3y - 3z = -6 & \quad\text{Add } -3 \text{ times the first} \\ \underline{3x + 3y + 3z = 14} & \quad\text{equation to the second.} \\ 0 = 8 & \quad\text{New Equation 1} \end{array}$$

▶ Because you obtained a false equation, you can conclude that the original system of equations has no solution.

EXAMPLE 3 *Solving a System with Many Solutions*

Solve the system.

$$x + y + z = 2 \qquad \text{Equation 1}$$
$$x + y - z = 2 \qquad \text{Equation 2}$$
$$2x + 2y + z = 4 \qquad \text{Equation 3}$$

SOLUTION

Rewrite the linear system in three variables as a linear system in two variables.

$$\begin{array}{rl} x + y + z = 2 & \quad\text{Add the first equation} \\ \underline{x + y - z = 2} & \quad\text{to the second.} \\ 2x + 2y = 4 & \quad\text{New Equation 1} \end{array}$$

$$\begin{array}{rl} x + y - z = 2 & \quad\text{Add the second equation} \\ \underline{2x + 2y + z = 4} & \quad\text{to the third.} \\ 3x + 3y = 6 & \quad\text{New Equation 2} \end{array}$$

The result is a system of linear equations in two variables.

$$2x + 2y = 4 \qquad \text{New Equation 1}$$
$$3x + 3y = 6 \qquad \text{New Equation 2}$$

Solve the new system by adding -3 times the first equation to 2 times the second equation. This produces the identity $0 = 0$. So, the system has infinitely many solutions.

Describe the solution. One way to do this is to divide new Equation 1 by 2 to get $x + y = 2$, or $y = -x + 2$. Substituting this into original Equation 1 produces $z = 0$. So, any ordered triple of the form

$$(x, -x + 2, 0)$$

is a solution of the system. For instance, $(0, 2, 0)$, $(1, 1, 0)$, and $(2, 0, 0)$ are all solutions.

EXAMPLE 4 *Writing and Solving a Linear System*

SPORTS Use a system of equations to model the information in the newspaper article. Then solve the system to find how many swimmers finished in each place.

In yesterday's swim meet, **Roosevelt High** dominated in the individual events, with 24 individual-event placers scoring a total of 56 points. A first-place finish scores 5 points, a second-place finish scores 3 points, and a third-place finish scores 1 point. Having as many third-place finishers as first- and second-place finishers combined really shows the team's depth.

SOLUTION

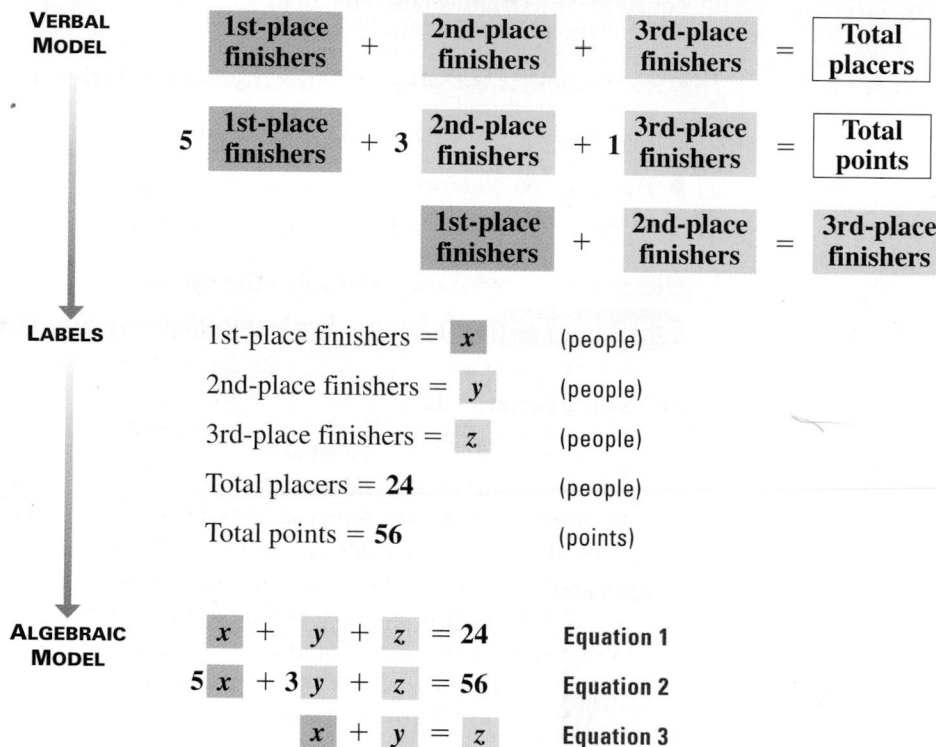

VERBAL MODEL

$\boxed{\text{1st-place finishers}} + \boxed{\text{2nd-place finishers}} + \boxed{\text{3rd-place finishers}} = \boxed{\text{Total placers}}$

$5\,\boxed{\text{1st-place finishers}} + 3\,\boxed{\text{2nd-place finishers}} + 1\,\boxed{\text{3rd-place finishers}} = \boxed{\text{Total points}}$

$\boxed{\text{1st-place finishers}} + \boxed{\text{2nd-place finishers}} = \boxed{\text{3rd-place finishers}}$

LABELS

1st-place finishers = x (people)

2nd-place finishers = y (people)

3rd-place finishers = z (people)

Total placers = **24**   (people)

Total points = **56**   (points)

ALGEBRAIC MODEL

$x + y + z = 24$ **Equation 1**

$5x + 3y + z = 56$ **Equation 2**

$x + y = z$ **Equation 3**

Substitute the expression for *z* from Equation 3 into Equation 1.

$x + y + z = 24$ **Write Equation 1.**

$x + y + (x + y) = 24$ **Substitute $x + y$ for z.**

$2x + 2y = 24$ **New Equation 1**

Substitute the expression for *z* from Equation 3 into Equation 2.

$5x + 3y + z = 56$ **Write Equation 2.**

$5x + 3y + (x + y) = 56$ **Substitute $x + y$ for z.**

$6x + 4y = 56$ **New Equation 2**

You now have a system of two equations in two variables.

$2x + 2y = 24$ **New Equation 1**
$6x + 4y = 56$ **New Equation 2**

▶ When you solve this system you get $x = 4$ and $y = 8$. Substituting these values into original Equation 3 gives you $z = 12$. There were 4 first-place finishers, 8 second-place finishers, and 12 third-place finishers.

GUIDED PRACTICE

Vocabulary Check ✔

Concept Check ✔

1. Give an example of a system of three linear equations in three variables.

2. ERROR ANALYSIS A student correctly solves a system of equations in three variables and obtains the equation $0 = 3$. The student concludes that the system has infinitely many solutions. Explain the error in the student's reasoning.

3. Look back at the intersecting planes on page 177. How else can three planes intersect so that the system has infinitely many solutions?

4. Explain how to use the substitution method to solve a system of three linear equations in three variables.

Skill Check ✔ **Decide whether the given ordered triple is a solution of the system.**

5. $(1, 4, 2)$
$$-2x - y + 5z = 12$$
$$3x + 2y - z = -7$$
$$-5x + 4y + 2z = -17$$

6. $(7, -1, 0)$
$$-4x + 6y - z = -34$$
$$-2x - 5y + 8z = -9$$
$$5x + 2y - 4z = 33$$

7. $(-2, 3, 3)$
$$5x - 2y + z = -13$$
$$x + 4y + 3z = 19$$
$$-3x + y + 6z = 15$$

Use the indicated method to solve the system.

8. linear combination
$$x + 5y - z = 16$$
$$3x - 3y + 2z = 12$$
$$2x + 4y + z = 20$$

9. substitution
$$-2x + y + 3z = -8$$
$$3x + 4y - 2z = 9$$
$$x + 2y + z = 4$$

10. any method
$$9x + 5y - z = -11$$
$$6x + 4y + 2z = 2$$
$$2x - 2y + 4z = 4$$

11. 🌎 INVESTMENTS Your aunt receives an inheritance of $20,000. She wants to put some of the money into a savings account that earns 2% interest annually and invest the rest in certificates of deposit (CDs) and bonds. A broker tells her that CDs pay 5% interest annually and bonds pay 6% interest annually. She wants to earn $1000 interest per year, and she wants to put twice as much money in CDs as in bonds. How much should she put in each type of investment?

PRACTICE AND APPLICATIONS

STUDENT HELP

▶ **Extra Practice**
to help you master
skills is on p. 944.

LINEAR COMBINATION METHOD Solve the system using the linear combination method.

12. $3x + 2y - z = 8$
$$-3x + 4y + 5z = -14$$
$$x - 3y + 4z = -14$$

13. $x + 2y + 5z = -1$
$$2x - y + z = 2$$
$$3x + 4y - 4z = 14$$

14. $3x + 2y - 3z = -2$
$$7x - 2y + 5z = -14$$
$$2x + 4y + z = 6$$

15. $5x - 4y + 4z = 18$
$$-x + 3y - 2z = 0$$
$$4x - 2y + 7z = 3$$

16. $x + y - 2z = 5$
$$x + 2y + z = 8$$
$$2x + 3y - z = 13$$

17. $-5x + 3y + z = -15$
$$10x + 2y + 8z = 18$$
$$15x + 5y + 7z = 9$$

STUDENT HELP

▶ **HOMEWORK HELP**
Example 1: Exs. 12–17,
24–33
Examples 2, 3: Exs. 12–33
Example 4: Exs. 18–23,
34–39

SUBSTITUTION METHOD Solve the system using the substitution method.

18. $-2x + y + 6z = 1$
$$3x + 2y + 5z = 16$$
$$7x + 3y - 4z = 11$$

19. $x - 6y - 2z = -8$
$$-x + 5y + 3z = 2$$
$$3x - 2y - 4z = 18$$

20. $x + y + z = 4$
$$5x + 5y + 5z = 12$$
$$x - 4y + z = 9$$

21. $x - 3y + 6z = 21$
$$3x + 2y - 5z = -30$$
$$2x - 5y + 2z = -6$$

22. $x + y - 2z = 5$
$$x + 2y + z = 8$$
$$2x + 3y - z = 1$$

23. $2x - 3y + z = 10$
$$y + 2z = 13$$
$$z = 5$$

CHOOSING A METHOD Solve the system using any algebraic method.

24. $2x - 2y + z = 3$
$5y - z = -31$
$x + 3y + 2z = -21$

25. $17x - y + 2z = -9$
$x + y - 4z = 8$
$3x - 2y - 12z = 24$

26. $-2x + y + z = -2$
$5x + 3y + 3z = 71$
$4x - 2y - 3z = 1$

27. $x - 9y + 4z = 1$
$-4x + 18y - 8z = -6$
$2x + y - 4z = -3$

28. $2x + y + 2z = 7$
$2x - y + 2z = 1$
$5x + y + 5z = 13$

29. $7x - 3y + 4z = -14$
$8x + 2y - 24z = 18$
$6x - 10y + 8z = -24$

30. $12x + 6y + 7z = -35$
$7x - 5y - 6z = 200$
$x + y = -10$

31. $7x - 10y + 8z = -50$
$-2x - 5y + 12z = -90$
$3x + 4y + 4z = 26$

32. $-2x - 3y - 6z = -26$
$5x + 5y + 4z = 24$
$3x + 4y - 5z = -40$

33. $3x + 3y + z = 30$
$10x - 3y - 7z = 17$
$-6x + 7y + 3z = -49$

34. 🌐 **FIELD TRIP** You and two friends buy snacks for a field trip. Using the information given in the table, determine the price per pound for mixed nuts, granola, and dried fruit.

Shopper	Mixed nuts	Granola	Dried fruit	Total price
You	1 lb	$\frac{1}{2}$ lb	$\frac{1}{2}$ lb	$5.97
Kenny	$1\frac{1}{3}$ lb	$\frac{1}{4}$ lb	$\frac{3}{2}$ lb	$9.22
Vanessa	$\frac{1}{3}$ lb	$1\frac{1}{2}$ lb	2 lb	$10.96

35. 🌐 **TRACK MEET** Use a system of linear equations to model the data in the following newspaper article. Solve the system to find how many athletes finished in each place.

> **Lawrence High** prevailed in Saturday's track meet with the help of 20 individual-event placers earning a combined 68 points. A first-place finish earns 5 points, a second-place finish earns 3 points, and a third-place finish earns 1 point. Lawrence had a strong second-place showing, with as many second-place finishers as first- and third-place finishers combined.

36. 🌐 **CHINESE RESTAURANT** Jeanette, Raj, and Henry go to a Chinese restaurant for lunch and order three different luncheon combination platters. Jeanette orders 2 portions of fried rice and 1 portion of chicken chow mein. Raj orders 1 portion of fried rice, 1 portion of chicken chow mein, and 1 portion of sautéed broccoli. Henry orders 1 portion of sautéed broccoli and 2 portions of chicken chow mein. Jeanette's platter costs $5, Raj's costs $5.25, and Henry's costs $5.75. How much does 1 portion of chicken chow mein cost?

FURNITURE SALE In Exercises 37 and 38, use the furniture store ad shown at the right.

$1300
Sofa and love seat
$1400
Sofa and two chairs
$1600
Sofa, love seat, and one chair

Sam's Furniture Store

37. Write a system of equations for the three combinations of furniture.

38. What is the price of each piece of furniture?

39. **SOCIAL STUDIES** **CONNECTION** For several political parties, the table shows the approximate percent of votes for the party's presidential candidate that were cast in 1996 by voters in two regions of the United States. Write and solve a system of equations to find the *total* number of votes for each party (Democrat, Republican, and Other). Use the fact that a total of about 100 million people voted in 1996. ▶ Source: *Statistical Abstract of the United States*

Region	Democrat (%)	Republican (%)	Other parties (%)	Total voters (millions)
Northeast	20	15	20	18
South	30	35	25	31.5

40. GOING IN REVERSE Which values should be given to a, b, and c so that the linear system shown has $(-1, 2, -3)$ as its only solution?

$$x + 2y - 3z = a$$
$$-x - y + z = b$$
$$2x + 3y - 2z = c$$

41. CRITICAL THINKING Write a system of three linear equations in three variables that has the given number of solutions.

    a. one solution   **b.** no solution   **c.** infinitely many solutions

Test Preparation

42. MULTI-STEP PROBLEM You have $25 to spend on picking 21 pounds of three different types of apples in an orchard. The Empire apples cost $1.40 per pound, the Red Delicious apples cost $1.10 per pound, and the Golden Delicious apples cost $1.30 per pound. You want twice as many Red Delicious apples as the other two kinds combined.

    a. Write a system of equations to represent the given information.

    b. How many pounds of each type of apple should you buy?

    c. *Writing* Create your own situation in which you are buying three different types of fruit. State the total amount of fruit you need, the price of each type of fruit, the amount of money you have to spend, and the desired ratio of one type of fruit to the other two types. Write a system of equations representing your situation. Then solve your system to find the number of pounds of each type of fruit you should buy.

★ **Challenge**

SYSTEMS OF FOUR EQUATIONS Solve the system of equations. Describe what you are doing at each step in your solution process.

43. $w + x + y + z = 6$
$3w - x + y - z = -3$
$2w + 2x - 2y + z = 4$
$2w - x - y + z = -4$

44. $2w - x + 5y + z = -3$
$3w + 2x + 2y - 6z = -32$
$w + 3x + 3y - z = -47$
$5w - 2x - 3y + 3z = 49$

MIXED REVIEW

PERFORMING AN OPERATION Perform the indicated operation.
(Review 1.1 for 4.1)

45. $-10 + 21$

46. $15 - (-1)$

47. $12 \cdot 7$

48. $-2 - (-20)$

49. $-9 + (-7)$

50. $-8(-6)$

51. $-\dfrac{1}{2} + \dfrac{4}{5}$

52. $-\dfrac{1}{3}\left(-\dfrac{2}{7}\right)$

53. $\dfrac{3}{4} - 3$

SOLVING AND GRAPHING Solve the inequality. Then graph your solution.
(Review 1.7)

54. $\left|11 - x\right| < 20$

55. $\left|2x + 3\right| \geq 26$

56. $\left|18 + \dfrac{1}{2}x\right| \geq 10$

57. $\left|7 + 8x\right| > 5$

58. $\left|5 - x\right| < 10$

59. $\left|3x - 1\right| \leq 30$

60. $\left|-3x + 6\right| \geq 12$

61. $\left|6x + 4\right| < 40$

62. $\left|15 - 3x\right| > 3$

PLOTTING POINTS Plot the ordered triple in a three-dimensional coordinate
system. (Review 3.5)

63. $(3, 6, 0)$

64. $(-3, -6, -4)$

65. $(-5, 9, 2)$

66. $(-9, 4, -7)$

67. $(6, -2, -6)$

68. $(-8, 5, -6)$

69. $(0, -3, -3)$

70. $(2, 2, -2)$

71. $(-4, -7, -3)$

QUIZ 3

Self-Test for Lessons 3.5 and 3.6

Sketch the graph of the equation. Label the points where the graph crosses the
x-, *y*-, and *z*-axes. (Lesson 3.5)

1. $2x + 5y + 3z = 15$

2. $x + 4y + 16z = 8$

3. $3x + y + z = 10$

4. $3x + 12y + 6z = 9$

5. $5x - 2y + z = 15$

6. $-x + 9y - 3z = 18$

Write the linear equation as a function of *x* and *y*. Then evaluate the function
for the given values. (Lesson 3.5)

7. $-x + \dfrac{1}{2}y + 3z = 18,\ f(2, 0)$

8. $4x + 8y - 8z = -16,\ f(-4, 4)$

9. $20x - 3y - z = 15,\ f(3, -7)$

10. $-2x + y + 6z = 24,\ f(12, 7)$

Solve the system using any algebraic method. (Lesson 3.6)

11. $2x + 4y + 3z = 10$
$3x - y + 6z = 15$
$5x + 2y - z = 25$

12. $3x - 2y + 3z = 11$
$5x + 2y - 2z = 4$
$-x + y + z = -7$

13. $x - 2y + 3z = -9$
$2x + 5y + z = 10$
$3x - 6y + 9z = 12$

14. 🌐 **STATE ORCHESTRA** Fifteen band members from your school were
selected to play in the state orchestra. Twice as many students who play a wind
instrument were selected as students who play a string or percussion instrument.
Of the students selected, one fifth play a string instrument. How many students
playing each type of instrument were selected to play in the state orchestra?
(Lesson 3.6)

CHAPTER 3

Chapter Summary

WHAT did you learn?

Solve systems of linear equations in two variables.
- by graphing **(3.1)**
- using algebraic methods **(3.2)**

Graph and solve systems of linear inequalities. **(3.3)**

Solve linear programming problems. **(3.4)**

Graph linear equations in three variables. **(3.5)**

Model real-life problems with functions of two variables. **(3.5)**

Solve systems of linear equations in three variables. **(3.6)**

Identify the number of solutions of a linear system. **(3.1, 3.2, 3.6)**

Solve real-life problems.
- using a system of linear equations **(3.1, 3.2, 3.6)**
- using a system of linear inequalities **(3.3, 3.4)**

WHY did you learn it?

Plan a vacation within a budget. **(p. 141)**
Find the weights of atoms in a molecule. **(p. 153)**

Describe conditions that will satisfy nutritional requirements of wildlife. **(p. 161)**

Plan a meal that minimizes cost while satisfying nutritional requirements. **(p. 167)**

Find the volume of a geometric figure graphed in a three-dimensional coordinate system. **(p. 174)**

Evaluate advertising costs of a commercial. **(p. 175)**

Use regional data to find the number of voters for different political parties in the United States. **(p. 183)**

See if a bus catches up to another one before arriving at a common destination. **(p. 144)**

Find the break-even point of a business. **(p. 153)**
Display possible sale prices for shoes. **(p. 161)**

How does Chapter 3 fit into the BIGGER PICTURE of algebra?

Linear algebra is an important branch of mathematics that begins with solving linear systems. It has widespread applications to other areas of mathematics and to real-life problems, especially in business and the sciences. You will continue your study of linear algebra in the next chapter with matrices.

STUDY STRATEGY

Did you recognize when new skills related to previously learned skills?

The two-column list you made, following the **Study Strategy** on page 138, may resemble this one.

Building on Previous Skills

Chapter 3
Graph a system of linear equations or inequalities.
Check a solution of a system.
Tell the number of solutions a system has.
Plot an ordered triple.
Graph $ax + by + cz = d$.
Function notation: $f(x, y)$

Chapter 2
Graph a linear equation or inequality.
Check a solution of an equation or inequality.
Decide if lines are parallel.
Plot an ordered pair.
Graph $Ax + By = C$.
Function notation: $f(x)$

185

- system of two linear equations in two variables, p. 139
- solution of a system of linear equations, p. 139
- substitution method, p. 148
- linear combination method, p. 149

- System of linear inequalities in two variables, p. 156
- solution of a system of linear inequalities, p. 156
- graph of a system of linear inequalities, p. 156
- optimization, p. 163
- linear programming, p. 163

- objective function, p. 163
- constraints, p. 163
- feasible region, p. 163
- three-dimensional coordinate system, p. 170
- z-axis, p. 170
- ordered triple, p. 170
- octants, p. 170

- linear equation in three variables, p. 171
- function of two variables, p. 171
- system of three linear equations in three variables, p. 177
- solution of a system of three linear equations, p. 177

3.1 SOLVING LINEAR SYSTEMS BY GRAPHING

Examples on pp. 139–141

EXAMPLE You can solve a system of two linear equations in two variables by graphing.

$$x + 2y = -4 \quad \textbf{Equation 1}$$
$$3x + 2y = 0 \quad \textbf{Equation 2}$$

From the graph, the lines appear to intersect at $(2, -3)$. You can check this algebraically as follows.

$$2 + 2(-3) = -4 \checkmark \quad \textbf{Equation 1 checks.}$$
$$3(2) + 2(-3) = 0 \checkmark \quad \textbf{Equation 2 checks.}$$

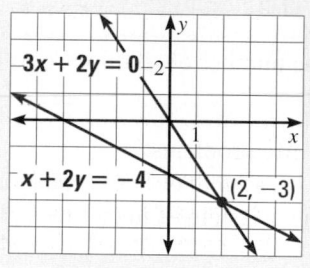

Graph the linear system and tell how many solutions it has. If there is exactly one solution, estimate the solution and check it algebraically.

1. $x + y = 2$
   $-3x + 4y = 36$

2. $x - 5y = 10$
   $-2x + 10y = -20$

3. $2x - y = 5$
   $2x + 3y = 9$

4. $y = \dfrac{1}{3}x$
   $y = \dfrac{1}{3}x - 2$

3.2 SOLVING LINEAR SYSTEMS ALGEBRAICALLY

Examples on pp. 148–151

EXAMPLE 1 You can use the substitution method to solve a system algebraically.

① Solve the first equation for x.

② Substitute the value of x into the second equation and solve for y.

$$x - 4y = -25 \longrightarrow x = 4y - 25 \longrightarrow 2(4y - 25) + 12y = 10$$
$$2x + 12y = 10 \qquad\qquad\qquad\qquad\qquad\qquad y = 3$$

When you substitute $y = 3$ into one of the original equations, you get $x = -13$.

EXAMPLE 2 You can also use the linear combination method to solve a system of equations algebraically.

1 Multiply the first equation by 3 and add to the second equation. Solve for x.

$x - 4y = -25 \longrightarrow 3x - 12y = -75$
$2x + 12y = 10 \longrightarrow \underline{2x + 12y = 10}$
$\;\; 5x = -65$
$\;\;\; x = -13$

2 Substitute $x = -13$ into the original first equation and solve for y.

$-13 - 4y = -25$
$-4y = -12$
$y = 3$

Solve the system using any algebraic method.

5. $9x - 5y = -30$
$x + 2y = 12$

6. $x + 3y = -2$
$x + y = 2$

7. $2x + 3y = -7$
$-4x - 5y = 13$

8. $3x + 3y = 0$
$-2x + 6y = -24$

3.3 **GRAPHING AND SOLVING SYSTEMS OF LINEAR INEQUALITIES**

Examples on pp. 156–158

EXAMPLE You can use a graph to show all the solutions of a system of linear inequalities.

$$x \geq 0$$
$$y \geq 0$$
$$x + 2y < 10$$

Graph each inequality. The graph of the system is the region common to *all* of the shaded half-planes and includes any solid boundary line.

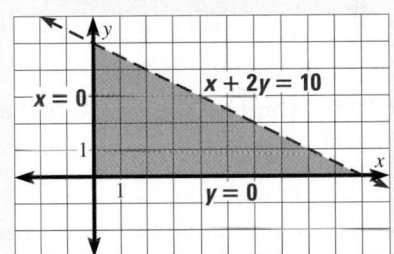

Graph the system of linear inequalities.

9. $y < -3x + 3$
$y > x - 1$

10. $x \geq 0$
$y \geq 0$
$-x + 2y < 8$

11. $x \geq -2$
$x \leq 5$
$y \geq -1$
$y \leq 3$

12. $x + y \leq 8$
$2x - y > 0$
$y \leq 4$

3.4 **LINEAR PROGRAMMING**

Examples on pp. 163–165

EXAMPLE You can find the minimum and maximum values of the objective function $C = 6x + 5y$ subject to the constraints graphed below. They must occur at vertices of the feasible region.

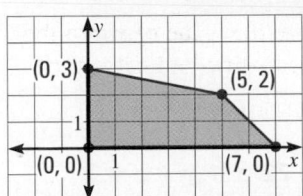

At $(0, 0)$: $C = 6(0) + 5(0) = 0 \longleftarrow$ **Minimum**

At $(0, 3)$: $C = 6(0) + 5(3) = 15$

At $(5, 2)$: $C = 6(5) + 5(2) = 40$

At $(7, 0)$: $C = 6(7) + 5(0) = 42 \longleftarrow$ **Maximum**

Find the minimum and maximum values of the objective function
$C = 5x + 2y$ subject to the given constraints.

13. $x \geq 0$
$y \geq 0$
$x + y \leq 10$

14. $x \geq 0$
$y \geq 0$
$4x + 5y \leq 20$

15. $x \geq 1; x \leq 4$
$y \geq 0; y \leq 9$

16. $y \leq 6; x + y \leq 10$
$x \geq 0; x - y \leq 0$

3.5 GRAPHING LINEAR EQUATIONS IN THREE VARIABLES

Examples on pp. 170–172

EXAMPLE You can sketch the graph of an equation in
three variables in a three-dimensional coordinate system.

To graph $3x + 4y - 3z = 12$, find x-, y-, and z-intercepts.

If $y = 0$ and $z = 0$, then $x = 4$. Plot $(4, 0, 0)$.

If $x = 0$ and $z = 0$, then $y = 3$. Plot $(0, 3, 0)$.

If $x = 0$ and $y = 0$, then $z = -4$. Plot $(0, 0, -4)$.

Draw the plane that contains $(4, 0, 0)$, $(0, 3, 0)$, and $(0, 0, -4)$.

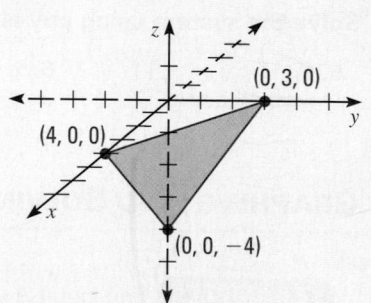

Sketch the graph of the equation. Label the points where the graph crosses the
x-, y-, and z-axes.

17. $x + y + z = 5$

18. $5x + 3y + 6z = 30$

19. $3x + 6y - 4z = -12$

3.6 SOLVING SYSTEMS OF LINEAR EQUATIONS IN THREE VARIABLES

Examples on pp. 177–180

EXAMPLE You can use algebraic methods to solve a system of linear equations in
three variables. First rewrite it as a system in two variables.

1 Add the first and second equations.

$$x - 3y + z = 22 \qquad\qquad x - 3y + z = 22$$
$$2x - 2y - z = -9 \qquad\qquad \underline{2x - 2y - z = -9}$$
$$x + y + 3z = 24 \qquad\qquad 3x - 5y = 13$$

2 Multiply the second equation by 3
and add to the third equation.

$$6x - 6y - 3z = -27$$
$$\underline{x + y + 3z = 24}$$
$$7x - 5y = -3$$

3 Solve the new system.

$$3x - 5y = 13$$
$$\underline{-7x + 5y = 3}$$
$$-4x = 16$$
$$x = -4 \text{ and } y = -5$$

When you substitute $x = -4$ and $y = -5$ into one of the original
equations, you get the value of the last variable: $z = 11$.

Solve the system using any algebraic method.

20. $x + 2y - z = 3$
$-x + y + 3z = -5$
$3x + y + 2z = 4$

21. $2x - 4y + 3z = 1$
$6x + 2y + 10z = 19$
$-2x + 5y - 2z = 2$

22. $x + y + z = 3$
$x + y - z = 3$
$2x + 2y + z = 6$

Chapter Test

Graph the linear system and tell how many solutions it has. If there is exactly one solution, estimate the solution and check it algebraically.

1. $x + y = 1$
$2x - 3y = 12$

2. $y = -\frac{1}{3}x + 4$
$y = 6$

3. $y = 2x + 2$
$y = 2x - 3$

4. $\frac{1}{2}x + 5y = 2$
$-x - 10y = -4$

Solve the system using any algebraic method.

5. $3x + 6y = -9$
$x + 2y = -3$

6. $x - y = -5$
$x + y = 11$

7. $7x + y = -17$
$3x - 10y = 24$

8. $8x + 3y = -2$
$-5x + y = -3$

Graph the system of linear inequalities.

9. $2x + y \geq 1$
$x \leq 3$

10. $x \geq 0$
$y < x$
$y > -x$

11. $x + 2y \geq -6$
$x + 2y \leq 2$
$y \geq -1$

12. $x + y < 7$
$2x - y \geq 5$
$x \geq -2$

Find the minimum and maximum values of the objective function subject to the given constraints.

13. Objective function: $C = 7x + 4y$

Constraints: $x \geq 0$
$y \geq 0$
$4x + 3y \leq 24$

14. Objective function: $C = 3x + 4y$

Constraints: $x + y \leq 10$
$-x + y \leq 5$
$2x + 4y \leq 32$

Plot the ordered triple in a three-dimensional coordinate system.

15. $(-1, 3, 2)$

16. $(0, 4, -2)$

17. $(-5, -1, 2)$

18. $(6, -2, 1)$

Sketch the graph of the equation. Label the points where the graph crosses the x-, y-, and z-axes.

19. $2x + 3y + 5z = 30$

20. $4x + y + 2z = 8$

21. $3x + 12y - 6z = 24$

22. Write the linear equation $2x - 5y + z = 9$ as a function of x and y. Then evaluate the function when $x = 10$ and $y = 3$.

Solve the system using any algebraic method.

23. $x + 2y - 6z = 23$
$x + 3y + z = 4$
$2x + 5y - 4z = 24$

24. $x + y + 2z = 1$
$x - y + z = 0$
$3x + 3y + 6z = 4$

25. $x + 3y - z = 1$
$-4x - 2y + 5z = 16$
$7x + 10y + 6z = -15$

26. 🌐 **CRAFT SUPPLIES** You are buying beads and string to make a necklace. The string costs $1.50, a package of 10 decorative beads costs $.50, and a package of 25 plain beads costs $.75. You can spend only $7.00 and you need 150 beads. How many packages of each type of bead should you buy?

27. 🌐 **BUSINESS** An appliance store manager is ordering chest and upright freezers. One chest freezer costs $250 and delivers a $40 profit. One upright freezer costs $400 and delivers a $60 profit. Based on previous sales, the manager expects to sell at least 100 freezers. Total profit must be at least $4800. Find the least number of each type of freezer the manager should order to minimize costs.

Chapter Standardized Test

● **TEST-TAKING STRATEGY** If you find yourself spending too much time on one test question and getting frustrated, move on to the next question. You can revisit a difficult problem later with a fresh perspective.

1. **MULTIPLE CHOICE** Which ordered pair is a solution of the following system of linear equations?

$$2x - 5y = -12$$
$$-x + 4y = 9$$

Ⓐ $(-6, 0)$ Ⓑ $(3, 3)$ Ⓒ $(-1, 2)$

Ⓓ $(-9, 0)$ Ⓔ $(2, 2)$

2. **MULTIPLE CHOICE** How many solutions does the following system have?

$$8x - 4y = 20$$
$$2x - y = 5$$

Ⓐ 0   Ⓑ 1   Ⓒ 2

Ⓓ 4   Ⓔ infinitely many

3. **MULTIPLE CHOICE** A total of $6500 is invested in two funds. One fund pays 4% interest annually and the other fund pays 6% interest annually. The combined annual interest earned is $350. How much of the $6500 is invested in one of the funds?

Ⓐ $2000   Ⓑ $2500   Ⓒ $3250

Ⓓ $4000   Ⓔ $5500

4. **MULTIPLE CHOICE** Which ordered pair is *not* a solution of the following system of linear inequalities?

$$x \geq -2$$
$$y \geq -3$$
$$y < 3x + 3$$

Ⓐ $(4, -3)$ Ⓑ $(0, 0)$ Ⓒ $(1, 6)$

Ⓓ $(5, 17)$ Ⓔ $(-1, -1)$

5. **MULTIPLE CHOICE** What is the minimum value of the objective function $C = 4x + 3y$ subject to the following constraints?

$$x \geq 0$$
$$y \geq 0$$
$$2x + 3y \leq 18$$
$$3x + y \geq 6$$

Ⓐ 0   Ⓑ 2   Ⓒ 8

Ⓓ 18   Ⓔ 36

6. **MULTIPLE CHOICE** Which linear equation is graphed below?

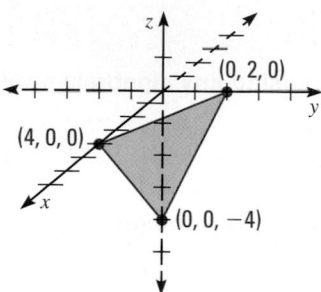

Ⓐ $x - 2y - z = 4$ Ⓑ $x - 2y + z = -4$

Ⓒ $x + 2y - z = -4$ Ⓓ $x + 2y - z = 4$

Ⓔ $-x + 2y + z = 4$

7. **MULTIPLE CHOICE** At which point does the graph of $15x - 6y - 3z = 30$ cross the y-axis?

Ⓐ $(0, -6, 0)$ Ⓑ $(2, 0, 0)$

Ⓒ $(0, -3, 0)$ Ⓓ $(0, 0, -10)$

Ⓔ $(0, -5, 0)$

8. **MULTIPLE CHOICE** Which ordered triple is a solution of the following linear system?

$$2x + 5y + 3z = 10$$
$$3x - y + 4z = 8$$
$$5x - 2y + 7z = 12$$

Ⓐ $(7, 1, -3)$ Ⓑ $(7, -1, -3)$

Ⓒ $(7, 1, 3)$ Ⓓ $(7, -1, 3)$

Ⓔ $(-7, 1, -3)$

9. **MULTIPLE CHOICE** A cashier at a restaurant made the chart below for popular lunch combinations. What is the individual price of soup?

Lunch Combinations
Soup + Salad = $4.25
Soup + Sandwich = $4.75
Salad + Sandwich = $5.50

Ⓐ $1.50   Ⓑ $1.75   Ⓒ $2.25

Ⓓ $2.50   Ⓔ $3.00

QUANTITATIVE COMPARISON In Exercises 10 and 11, choose the statement that is true about the given quantities.

(A) The quantity in column A is greater.

(B) The quantity in column B is greater.

(C) The two quantities are equal.

(D) The relationship cannot be determined from the given information.

Column A	Column B
10. $f(x, y) = \frac{1}{5}(20 - 2x + y)$, $f(4, 8)$	$f(x, y) = \frac{1}{5}(20 - 2x + y)$, $f(-1, 3)$
11. $f(x, y) = \frac{1}{2}(10 + 4x - 3y)$, $f(-2, -1)$	$f(x, y) = \frac{1}{2}(10 + 4x - 3y)$, $f(2, 1)$

12. MULTI-STEP PROBLEM Use the following system of linear equations.

$$x - 2y = 2 \qquad \textbf{Equation 1}$$
$$5x - 4y = -8 \qquad \textbf{Equation 2}$$

a. Solve the system by graphing.

b. Solve the system using the substitution method. Show your work.

c. Solve the system using the linear combination method. Show your work.

d. *Writing* Which method do you prefer for solving this system? Explain.

13. MULTI-STEP PROBLEM Write an equation which, when paired with $-2x + 3y = 12$ to form a system, has the given number of solutions.

a. exactly one solution

b. no solution

c. infinitely many solutions

d. *Writing* Explain how you wrote each of the equations in parts (a)–(c).

14. MULTI-STEP PROBLEM The cholesterol in your blood is necessary, but too much cholesterol can lead to health problems. A blood cholesterol test gives three readings: LDL "bad" cholesterol, HDL "good" cholesterol, and total cholesterol (LDL + HDL). It is recommended that your LDL cholesterol be less than 130 milligrams per deciliter, HDL cholesterol be at least 35 milligrams per deciliter, and total cholesterol be no more than 200 milligrams per deciliter.

a. Write a system of three linear inequalities for the recommended cholesterol readings. Let x represent HDL cholesterol and y represent LDL cholesterol.

b. Graph the system. Label any vertices of the solution region.

c. Are the cholesterol readings at the right within recommendations?

d. Give an example of blood cholesterol test results in which the LDL cholesterol is too high, but HDL and total cholesterol readings are fine. Write a system of linear inequalities to describe all the examples of this type.

LDL: 120 mg/dL

HDL: 90 mg/dL

Total: 210 mg/dL

e. Another recommendation is that the ratio of total cholesterol to HDL cholesterol be less than 4. Find a point in your solution region from part (b) that meets this recommendation and show that it does.

Plot the numbers on a number line. Write the numbers in increasing order. (1.1)

1. $0, \pi, 2\frac{3}{4}, -\frac{3}{2}, 4$

2. $\frac{5}{2}, -\frac{1}{10}, -2, \sqrt{5}, 1.9$

3. $-4.25, -\frac{16}{3}, -\sqrt{9}, -0.4, -1$

Identify the property shown. (1.1)

4. $8 \cdot \frac{1}{8} = 1$

5. $-1(9 + 7) = (-1)9 + (-1)7$

6. $-6 \cdot (-3 \cdot 4) = (-6 \cdot (-3)) \cdot 4$

Evaluate the expression. (1.2)

7. $12 \div 2 - 4 \cdot 7$

8. $-8 + 3(1 - 5)^2$

9. $17 - 2^4 \div 8 + 1$

10. $-2(16 + 7) \div -10$

Simplify the expression. (1.2)

11. $18a + 7a - 9a + 11$

12. $10x - (4y - x) + y$

13. $6(n^2 - n) - 5n^2 + 8n$

Solve the equation. (1.3, 1.7)

14. $\frac{5}{8}x - 9 = 21$

15. $-75 = 9x - 3$

16. $4(2x - 1) = -20$

17. $3 - x = 5x + 27$

18. $|x| = 9$

19. $|4x + 1| = 39$

20. $|7 - 2x| = 15$

21. $|x - 10| = 0$

Solve the formula for the indicated variable. (1.4)

22. Distance
Solve for r: $d = rt$

23. Volume of a Cylinder
Solve for h: $V = \pi r^2 h$

24. Area of a Trapezoid
Solve for h: $A = \frac{1}{2}(b_1 + b_2)h$

Solve the inequality. Then graph the solution. (1.6, 1.7)

25. $14 - 5x > -6$

26. $1 \le x - 13 \le 20$

27. $3x - 2 \le 0$ or $x + 6 > 8$

28. $|x - 7| \le 1$

29. $|7x - 9| \ge 12$

30. $\left|\frac{1}{4}x + 3\right| > 5$

31. $|-5x| < 10$

Graph the relation. Then tell whether the relation is a function. (2.1)

32.

x	2	−4	2	−1	0
y	1	0	5	−1	3

33.

x	−3	−1	1	3	5
y	1	0	−1	−2	−3

Graph in a coordinate plane. (2.1, 2.3, 2.6–2.8)

34. $y = -2x + 5$

35. $x - 3y = 6$

36. $y = 2$

37. $x = -4$

38. $y > \frac{2}{5}x - 2$

39. $y \le -1$

40. $4x + 3y \le 24$

41. $y > -x$

42. $f(x) = 4|x|$

43. $f(x) = |x| - 3$

44. $f(x) = 2|x + 2|$

45. $f(x) = -|x - 5| + 1$

46. $f(x) = \begin{cases} 2x, & \text{if } x \le 0 \\ -2x, & \text{if } x > 0 \end{cases}$

47. $f(x) = \begin{cases} \frac{1}{2}x + 1, & \text{if } x \le -2 \\ x + 1, & \text{if } x > -2 \end{cases}$

48. $f(x) = \begin{cases} 4, & \text{if } -5 \le x < 0 \\ -4, & \text{if } 0 \le x \le 5 \end{cases}$

Graph the system. Describe the solution(s). (3.1, 3.3)

49. $4x - 2y = 8$
$4x + y = 2$

50. $y = x$
$y = x - 3$
$y = x + 5$

51. $2x - y > 1$
$x < 3$

52. $x \ge 0$
$y \ge 0$
$x + y \le 8$

Tell whether the lines are *perpendicular, parallel,* or *neither*. (2.2)

53. Line 1: through $(0, 7)$ and $(3, 6)$
Line 2: through $(-2, -9)$ and $(0, -3)$

54. Line 1: through $(-6, -3)$ and $(0, 1)$
Line 2: through $(0, -5)$ and $(4, -2)$

Write an equation of the line with the given characteristics. (2.4)

55. slope: -3, y-intercept: 7

56. vertical line through $(2, 5)$

57. x-intercept: -2, y-intercept: 1

Evaluate the function for the given value(s). (2.1, 2.7, 2.8, 3.5)

58. $f(x) = 5x - 17$, $f(-3)$

59. $f(x) = x^2 - 2x + 11$, $f(2)$

60. $f(x) = \begin{cases} x - 4, & \text{if } x \le 0 \\ x + 2, & \text{if } x > 0 \end{cases}$, $f(-2)$

61. $f(x) = -|12 - 8x|$, $f(1)$

62. $f(x, y) = 8x - 5y$, $f(3, -2)$

63. $f(x, y) = 2(-x + y)$, $f(-1, 0)$

Solve the system using any algebraic method. (3.2, 3.6)

64. $-x + 5y = 8$
$-3x + 15y = 24$

65. $x - 3y = 7$
$2x + y = 7$

66. $x + y - z = 7$
$-x + 2y + 2z = 3$
$3x - y - z = 1$

67. $2x + y + z = 4$
$x - y - 2z = -9$
$2x - y + z = 6$

Graph in a three-dimensional coordinate system. (3.5)

68. $(1, -4, 2)$

69. $(-2, 3, -5)$

70. $x + 2y + 3z = 6$

71. $10x + 4y + 5z = 20$

72. 🌏 **SWEATER SALE** You pay $38.50 for a sweater that is marked 30% off the regular price. What is the regular price of the sweater? How much did you save by buying it on sale? **(1.5)**

73. 🌏 **BODY TEMPERATURE** Although the average body temperature of a healthy baby is 98.6°F, the temperature can vary from 97°F to 100°F. Write an inequality to describe the range of healthy temperatures. On a number line, graph the inequality and mark the average body temperature of a healthy baby. **(1.6)**

74. 🌏 **HIGHWAY TRAVEL** If you drive at a constant speed then the distance you travel d varies directly with the time t. Suppose you use cruise control and drive 180 miles in 3 hours. Write an equation to show the relationship between d and t. What is the constant of variation and what does it represent? **(2.4)**

75. 🌏 **SOLID WASTE** The table gives the amount of material recovered from solid waste (in millions of tons) in the United States from 1988 to 1996. Make a scatter plot of the data and approximate a best-fitting line. Predict the amount of material recovered in the United States in 2002. **(2.5)**

Years since 1988, t	0	1	2	3	4	5	6	7	8
Material, m	23.5	29.9	33.6	37.0	40.6	43.8	50.9	55.1	57.3

▶ Source: *Statistical Abstract of the United States*

76. 🌏 **AUTO RENTAL** An automobile rental agency charges $60 per day with unlimited mileage. A second agency charges $45 per day plus $.25 per mile after the first 100 miles. For a one-day rental, after how many miles will the first agency be less expensive? **(3.1, 3.2)**

77. 🌏 **STIR-FRY RECIPE** A restaurant serves a stir-fry dish containing vegetables and beef. The recipe calls for no more than twice as many pounds of vegetables as beef. The owner buys vegetables at $1.39 per pound and beef at $1.79 per pound and will order a total of 150 pounds. To minimize the cost yet satisfy the recipe, how much of each food should the owner order? What will be the total cost? **(3.4)**

Drawing with Linear Perspective

OBJECTIVE Use linear equations to represent a drawing made with linear perspective.

Materials: graph paper, ruler

During the Renaissance, artists turned to mathematics to develop *perspective*, a method for realistically depicting a three-dimensional object on a two-dimensional surface. A drawing with linear perspective has all slanted lines converging toward a point or points on the horizon. These points are called *vanishing points*. The painting below and on the left has all slanted lines converging toward a single vanishing point at the far end of the road. The painting on the right has all slanted lines converging toward one of two vanishing points, one on either side of the building.

The Avenue at Middelharnis, painted in 1689 by Meindert Hobbema

Corner of George and Hunter Streets, Sydney, painted in 1849 by A. Torning

HOW TO DRAW AN OBJECT IN TWO-POINT PERSPECTIVE

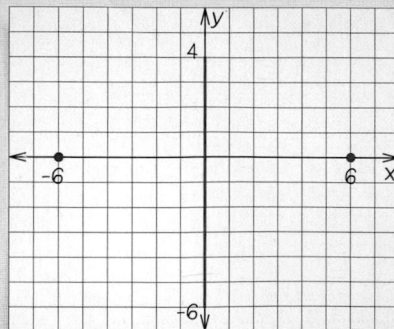

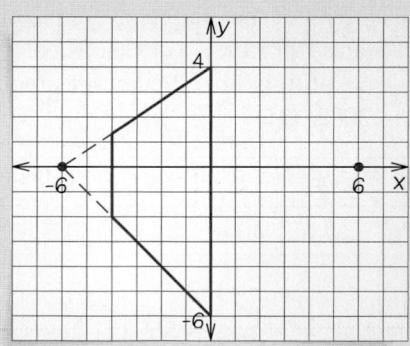

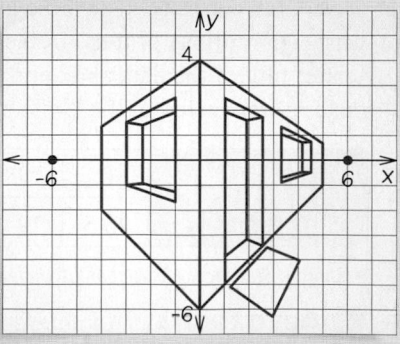

1 Use the *x*-axis as the horizon. Select two points equidistant from the origin and on the *x*-axis as the vanishing points. Draw a vertical segment to represent the front edge of the object—in this case, the front edge of a building.

2 To draw the left wall of the building, draw segments from the endpoints of the front edge toward the vanishing point on the left. Connect the segments with a vertical line to represent the end of the wall.

3 Continue drawing slanted lines that are to the left of the front edge toward the vanishing point on the left, and lines that are to the right of the front edge toward the vanishing point on the right.

INVESTIGATION

1. Choose an object that has many parallel edges, such as a building, courtyard, or computer. Use the method given on the previous page to draw the object in two-point perspective.

2. Experiment with using a lower or higher horizon line, as well as vanishing points that are farther apart or closer together, until your drawing has the look you want. How does the placement of the horizon line and the vanishing points affect the way your drawing looks?

3. Write an equation for each line in your drawing. Include the domain to indicate the length of the line. For example, the upper left edge of the building on the previous page is defined by $y = \frac{2}{3}x + 4$ for $-4 \leq x \leq 0$.

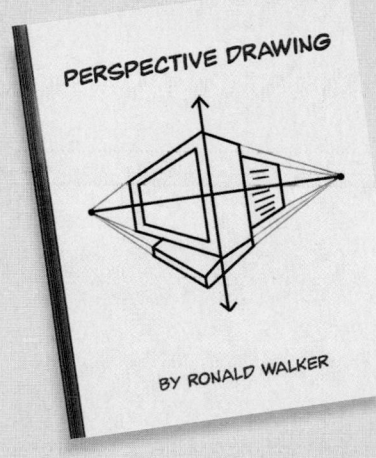

PERSPECTIVE DRAWING

BY RONALD WALKER

PRESENT YOUR RESULTS

Write a report to present your results.

- Include your drawing and any preliminary sketches you did.

- Include your answers to Exercises 1–3 above.

- Write a set of instructions for how to draw the object just as you have drawn it. Include the equations you wrote.

- Tell how this project has helped you mathematically.

Test your results.

- Trade drawing instructions with a partner (do not trade actual drawings). Follow the instructions to create your partner's drawing.

- Compare your drawing with the original.

EXTENSION

Another way to suggest a three-dimensional object on a two-dimensional surface is to add shadowing. Select a point for a light source and decide where the shadows cast by your object would fall. Write a system of linear inequalities to indicate each shaded region. Add these to your report.

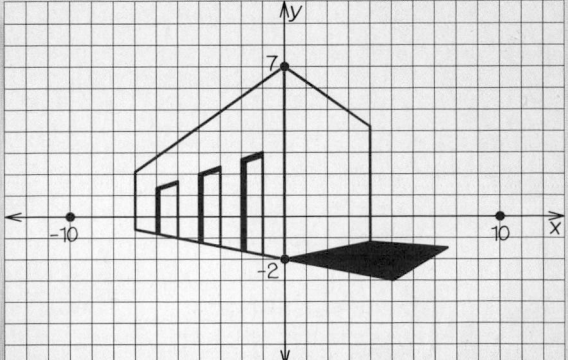

System of inequalities for the building's shadow:

$$y \leq \frac{1}{5}x - 2$$

$$y \geq -\frac{1}{5}x - 2$$

$$y \geq \frac{3}{5}x - 6$$

$$y \leq -\frac{3}{35}x - \frac{6}{7}$$

MATRICES AND DETERMINANTS

▶ *How can you organize data about music sales?*

APPLICATION: Music Sales

When you shop for music, your purchases matter. Music sales by people age 15 to 19 years accounted for about 16% of the $13.7 billion total music purchases in 1998. The tables below give the dollar value of the music sold by age category in 1997 and 1998.

1997 Music Sales	
Age (years)	Sales (billions)
10–14	108.58
15–19	204.96
20–24	168.36
25–29	142.74
30–34	134.2
35–39	141.52
40–44	107.36
45+	201.3

1998 Music Sales	
Age (years)	Sales (billions)
10–14	124.67
15–19	216.46
20–24	167.14
25–29	156.18
30–34	156.18
35–39	172.52
40–44	113.71
45+	247.97

Think & Discuss

1. From 1997 to 1998, how much did sales in the 15–19 age category increase? How much did sales in the 20–24 age category decrease?

2. Make a new table that gives the change in the sales in each age category from 1997 to 1998. (Use negative numbers to indicate decreases.)

Learn More About It

You will find the total Hispanic music sales for 1996 and 1997 in Exercise 40 on p. 204.

 APPLICATION LINK Visit www.mcdougallittell.com for more information about music sales.

Study Guide

PREVIEW

What's the chapter about?

Chapter 4 is about **matrices and determinants**. You can use matrices to organize numerical data. In Chapter 4 you'll learn

• how to add, subtract, and multiply matrices, and how to evaluate determinants.

• how to solve linear systems using Cramer's rule and inverse matrices.

KEY VOCABULARY

▶ **Review**
• multiplicative inverse, p. 5
• coefficient, p. 13
• constant, p. 13
• solution of a system of linear equations, p. 139

▶ **New**
• matrix, p. 199
• equal matrices, p. 199
• scalar, p. 200
• scalar multiplication, p. 200

• determinant, p. 214
• Cramer's rule, p. 216
• identity matrix, p. 223
• inverse matrix, p. 223

PREPARE

Are you ready for the chapter?

SKILL REVIEW Do these exercises to review key skills that you'll apply in this chapter. See the given **reference page** if there is something you don't understand.

STUDENT HELP

▶ **Study Tip**
"Student Help" boxes throughout the chapter give you study tips and tell you where to look for extra help in this book and on the Internet.

Perform the operation(s). (Skills Review, p. 905)

1. $4 + (-5)$ **2.** $-10 - 3$ **3.** $(-1)6 - 4(2)$ **4.** $12(5) + 2(-10)$

Identify the property shown. (Review Example 4, p. 5)

5. $3(-9) = -9(3)$ **6.** $7 + y = y + 7$ **7.** $4(x - 2) = 4x - 4(2)$

Solve the system of linear equations using any algebraic method. (Review p. 149)

8. $2x = 30$
$x + 4y = 27$

9. $x - y = 7$
$3x - 7y = 61$

10. $x - 2y = 24$
$x + 3y = 20$

11. $3x + y = -8$
$8x - 3y = -10$

STUDY STRATEGY

Here's a study strategy!

Writing Out the Steps

In this chapter you will perform calculations with numbers in matrices. When you work with matrices, point your fingers at the numbers you will add, subtract, or multiply. Before calculating, write the numbers and the operation symbols in the correct location of the solution matrix. By doing this step, you are less likely to make a mistake. If you do make a mistake, you can easily trace backwards to find it.

EXPLORING DATA
AND STATISTICS

4.1

What you should learn

GOAL 1 Add and subtract
matrices, multiply a matrix by
a scalar, and solve matrix
equations.

GOAL 2 Use matrices in
real-life situations, such as
organizing data about health
care plans in **Example 5**.

Why you should learn it

▼ To organize **real-life**
data, such as the data for
Hispanic CD, cassette,
and music video sales
in **Exs. 39–41**.

Matrix Operations

GOAL 1 USING MATRIX OPERATIONS

A **matrix** is a rectangular arrangement of numbers in rows and columns. For
instance, matrix A below has two rows and three columns. The **dimensions** of
this matrix are 2×3 (read "2 by 3"). The numbers in a matrix are its **entries**.
In matrix A, the entry in the second row and third column is **5**.

$$A = \begin{bmatrix} 6 & 2 & -1 \\ -2 & 0 & 5 \end{bmatrix} \Big\} \text{2 rows}$$

$$\underbrace{}_{\text{3 columns}}$$

Some *matrices* (the plural of *matrix*) have special names because of their dimensions
or entries.

NAME	DESCRIPTION	EXAMPLE
Row matrix	A matrix with only 1 row	$\begin{bmatrix} 3 & -2 & 0 & 4 \end{bmatrix}$
Column matrix	A matrix with only 1 column	$\begin{bmatrix} 1 \\ 3 \end{bmatrix}$
Square matrix	A matrix with the same number of rows and columns	$\begin{bmatrix} 4 & -1 & 5 \\ 2 & 0 & 1 \\ 1 & -3 & 6 \end{bmatrix}$
Zero matrix	A matrix whose entries are all zeros	$\begin{bmatrix} 0 & 0 \\ 0 & 0 \\ 0 & 0 \end{bmatrix}$

Two matrices are **equal** if their dimensions are the same and the entries in
corresponding positions are equal.

EXAMPLE 1 *Comparing Matrices*

a. The following matrices are equal because corresponding entries are equal.

$$\begin{bmatrix} 5 & 0 \\ -\frac{4}{4} & \frac{3}{4} \end{bmatrix} = \begin{bmatrix} 5 & 0 \\ -1 & 0.75 \end{bmatrix}$$

b. The following matrices are not equal because corresponding entries in the second
row are not equal.

$$\begin{bmatrix} -2 & 6 \\ 0 & -3 \end{bmatrix} \neq \begin{bmatrix} -2 & 6 \\ 3 & 0 \end{bmatrix}$$

· · · · · · · · · ·

To add or subtract matrices, you simply add or subtract corresponding entries.
You can add or subtract matrices only if they have the same dimensions.

4.1 *Matrix Operations* **199**

EXAMPLE 2 **Adding and Subtracting Matrices**

Perform the indicated operation, if possible.

a. $\begin{bmatrix} 3 \\ -4 \\ 7 \end{bmatrix} + \begin{bmatrix} 1 \\ 0 \\ 3 \end{bmatrix}$
b. $\begin{bmatrix} 8 & 3 \\ 4 & 0 \end{bmatrix} - \begin{bmatrix} 2 & -7 \\ 6 & -1 \end{bmatrix}$
c. $\begin{bmatrix} 2 & 0 \\ 3 & 4 \end{bmatrix} + \begin{bmatrix} 1 \\ 5 \end{bmatrix}$

SOLUTION

a. Since the matrices have the same dimensions, you can add them.

$$\begin{bmatrix} 3 \\ -4 \\ 7 \end{bmatrix} + \begin{bmatrix} 1 \\ 0 \\ 3 \end{bmatrix} = \begin{bmatrix} 3+1 \\ -4+0 \\ 7+3 \end{bmatrix} = \begin{bmatrix} 4 \\ -4 \\ 10 \end{bmatrix}$$

b. Since the matrices have the same dimensions, you can subtract them.

$$\begin{bmatrix} 8 & 3 \\ 4 & 0 \end{bmatrix} - \begin{bmatrix} 2 & -7 \\ 6 & -1 \end{bmatrix} = \begin{bmatrix} 8-2 & 3-(-7) \\ 4-6 & 0-(-1) \end{bmatrix} = \begin{bmatrix} 6 & 10 \\ -2 & 1 \end{bmatrix}$$

c. Since the dimensions of $\begin{bmatrix} 2 & 0 \\ 3 & 4 \end{bmatrix}$ are 2 × 2 and the dimensions of $\begin{bmatrix} 1 \\ 5 \end{bmatrix}$ are 2 × 1, you cannot add the matrices.

. . . .

In matrix algebra, a real number is often called a **scalar**. To multiply a matrix by a scalar, you multiply each entry in the matrix by the scalar. This process is called **scalar multiplication**.

EXAMPLE 3 **Multiplying a Matrix by a Scalar**

Perform the indicated operation(s), if possible.

a. $3\begin{bmatrix} -2 & 0 \\ 4 & -7 \end{bmatrix}$
b. $-2\begin{bmatrix} 1 & -2 \\ 0 & 3 \\ -4 & 5 \end{bmatrix} + \begin{bmatrix} -4 & 5 \\ 6 & -8 \\ -2 & 6 \end{bmatrix}$

> **STUDENT HELP**
>
> ► **Study Tip**
> The order of operations for matrix expressions is similar to that for real numbers. In particular, you perform scalar multiplication before matrix addition and subtraction, as shown in part (b) of Example 3.

SOLUTION

a. $3\begin{bmatrix} -2 & 0 \\ 4 & -7 \end{bmatrix} = \begin{bmatrix} 3(-2) & 3(0) \\ 3(4) & 3(-7) \end{bmatrix} = \begin{bmatrix} -6 & 0 \\ 12 & -21 \end{bmatrix}$

b. $-2\begin{bmatrix} 1 & -2 \\ 0 & 3 \\ -4 & 5 \end{bmatrix} + \begin{bmatrix} -4 & 5 \\ 6 & -8 \\ -2 & 6 \end{bmatrix} = \begin{bmatrix} -2(1) & -2(-2) \\ -2(0) & -2(3) \\ -2(-4) & -2(5) \end{bmatrix} + \begin{bmatrix} -4 & 5 \\ 6 & -8 \\ -2 & 6 \end{bmatrix}$

$$= \begin{bmatrix} -2 & 4 \\ 0 & -6 \\ 8 & -10 \end{bmatrix} + \begin{bmatrix} -4 & 5 \\ 6 & -8 \\ -2 & 6 \end{bmatrix}$$

$$= \begin{bmatrix} -6 & 9 \\ 6 & -14 \\ 6 & -4 \end{bmatrix}$$

You can use what you know about matrix operations and matrix equality to solve a matrix equation.

EXAMPLE 4 *Solving a Matrix Equation*

Solve the matrix equation for x and y: $2\left(\begin{bmatrix} 3x & -1 \\ 8 & 5 \end{bmatrix} + \begin{bmatrix} 4 & 1 \\ -2 & -y \end{bmatrix} \right) = \begin{bmatrix} 26 & 0 \\ 12 & 8 \end{bmatrix}$

SOLUTION

Simplify the left side of the equation.

$$2\left(\begin{bmatrix} 3x & -1 \\ 8 & 5 \end{bmatrix} + \begin{bmatrix} 4 & 1 \\ -2 & -y \end{bmatrix} \right) = \begin{bmatrix} 26 & 0 \\ 12 & 8 \end{bmatrix}$$

$$2\begin{bmatrix} 3x + 4 & 0 \\ 6 & 5 - y \end{bmatrix} = \begin{bmatrix} 26 & 0 \\ 12 & 8 \end{bmatrix}$$

$$\begin{bmatrix} 6x + 8 & 0 \\ 12 & 10 - 2y \end{bmatrix} = \begin{bmatrix} 26 & 0 \\ 12 & 8 \end{bmatrix}$$

Equate corresponding entries and solve the two resulting equations.

$$6x + 8 = 26 \qquad\qquad 10 - 2y = 8$$
$$x = 3 \qquad\qquad\qquad y = 1$$

· · · · · · · · · ·

STUDENT HELP

▶ **Look Back**
For help with properties of real numbers, see p. 5.

In Example 4, you could have distributed the scalar 2 to each matrix inside the parentheses before adding the matrices.

$$2\left(\begin{bmatrix} 3x & -1 \\ 8 & 5 \end{bmatrix} + \begin{bmatrix} 4 & 1 \\ -2 & -y \end{bmatrix} \right) = 2\begin{bmatrix} 3x & -1 \\ 8 & 5 \end{bmatrix} + 2\begin{bmatrix} 4 & 1 \\ -2 & -y \end{bmatrix}$$

$$= \begin{bmatrix} 6x & -2 \\ 16 & 10 \end{bmatrix} + \begin{bmatrix} 8 & 2 \\ -4 & -2y \end{bmatrix}$$

$$= \begin{bmatrix} 6x + 8 & 0 \\ 12 & 10 - 2y \end{bmatrix}$$

This illustrates one of several properties of matrix operations stated below.

CONCEPT SUMMARY   **PROPERTIES OF MATRIX OPERATIONS**

Let A, B, and C be matrices with the same dimensions and let c be a scalar.

When adding matrices, you can regroup them and change their order without affecting the result.

ASSOCIATIVE PROPERTY OF ADDITION	$(A + B) + C = A + (B + C)$
COMMUTATIVE PROPERTY OF ADDITION	$A + B = B + A$

Multiplication of a sum or difference of matrices by a scalar obeys the distributive property.

DISTRIBUTIVE PROPERTY OF ADDITION	$c(A + B) = cA + cB$
DISTRIBUTIVE PROPERTY OF SUBTRACTION	$c(A - B) = cA - cB$

GOAL 2 **USING MATRICES IN REAL LIFE**

Health Care

EXAMPLE 5 *Using Matrices to Organize Data*

Use matrices to organize the following information about health care plans.

This Year *For individuals, Comprehensive, HMO Standard, and HMO Plus cost $694.32, $451.80, and $489.48, respectively. For families, the Comprehensive, HMO Standard, and HMO Plus plans cost $1725.36, $1187.76, and $1248.12.*

Next Year *For individuals, Comprehensive, HMO Standard, and HMO Plus will cost $683.91, $463.10, and $499.27, respectively. For families, the Comprehensive, HMO Standard, and HMO Plus plans will cost $1699.48, $1217.45, and $1273.08.*

SOLUTION

One way to organize the data is to use 3×2 matrices, as shown.

	THIS YEAR (*A*)		**NEXT YEAR (*B*)**	
	Individual	Family	Individual	Family
Comprehensive	$694.32	$1725.36	$683.91	$1699.48
HMO Standard	$451.80	$1187.76	$463.10	$1217.45
HMO Plus	$489.48	$1248.12	$499.27	$1273.08

You can also organize the data using 2×3 matrices where the row labels are levels of coverage (individual and family) and the column labels are the types of plans (Comprehensive, HMO Standard, and HMO Plus).

EXAMPLE 6 *Using Matrix Operations*

FOCUS ON CAREERS

HEALTH CARE A company offers the health care plans in Example 5 to its employees. The employees receive monthly paychecks from which health care payments are deducted. Use the matrices in Example 5 to write a matrix that shows the monthly changes in health care payments from this year to next year.

SOLUTION

Begin by subtracting matrix *A* from matrix *B* to determine the yearly changes in health care payments. Then multiply the result by $\frac{1}{12}$ and round answers to the nearest cent to find the monthly changes.

$$\frac{1}{12}(B - A) = \frac{1}{12}\left(\begin{bmatrix} 683.91 & 1699.48 \\ 463.10 & 1217.45 \\ 499.27 & 1273.08 \end{bmatrix} - \begin{bmatrix} 694.32 & 1725.36 \\ 451.80 & 1187.76 \\ 489.48 & 1248.12 \end{bmatrix}\right)$$

$$= \frac{1}{12}\begin{bmatrix} -10.41 & -25.88 \\ 11.30 & 29.69 \\ 9.79 & 24.96 \end{bmatrix}$$

$$\approx \begin{bmatrix} -\$.87 & -\$2.16 \\ \$.94 & \$2.47 \\ \$.82 & \$2.08 \end{bmatrix}$$

HEALTH SERVICES MANAGER
Health services managers in health maintenance organizations (HMOs) plan and organize the delivery of health care.

CAREER LINK
www.mcdougallittell.com

▶ The monthly deductions for the Comprehensive plan will decrease, but the monthly deductions for the other two plans will increase.

GUIDED PRACTICE

1. What is a matrix? Describe and give an example of a row matrix, a column matrix, and a square matrix.

2. Are the two matrices equal? Explain.
$$\begin{bmatrix} -6 & \frac{1}{2} \\ 4 & -5 \\ 3 & 5 \end{bmatrix} \stackrel{?}{=} \begin{bmatrix} -6 & 0.5 \\ 4 & -5 \\ 3 & 5 \end{bmatrix}$$

3. To add or subtract two matrices, what must be true?

4. Use the matrices at the right to find $-2(A + B)$. Is your answer the same as that for part (b) of Example 3? Explain.
$$A = \begin{bmatrix} 1 & -2 \\ 0 & 3 \\ -4 & 5 \end{bmatrix} \quad B = \begin{bmatrix} -4 & 5 \\ 6 & -8 \\ -2 & 6 \end{bmatrix}$$

5. Rework Example 5 by organizing the data using 2×3 matrices.

Perform the indicated operation(s), if possible.

6. $\begin{bmatrix} 20 \\ -22 \\ 9 \end{bmatrix} - \begin{bmatrix} -11 \\ -10 \\ -6 \end{bmatrix}$

7. $\begin{bmatrix} -6 & -7 & 4 \\ -4 & 0 & -1 \end{bmatrix} + \begin{bmatrix} -1 & -5 & 8 \\ 9 & 12 & -9 \end{bmatrix}$

8. $-4\begin{bmatrix} 2 & 0 \\ -4 & -5 \end{bmatrix}$

9. $6\begin{bmatrix} -5 & -1 \\ 2 & 0 \end{bmatrix} - 5\begin{bmatrix} -1 & 0 \\ 4 & -3 \end{bmatrix}$

10. 🌐 **HEALTH CARE** In Example 5, suppose the annual health care costs given in matrix B increase by 4% the following year. Write a matrix that shows the new *monthly* payment.

PRACTICE AND APPLICATIONS

COMPARING MATRICES Tell whether the matrices are *equal* or *not equal*.

11. $\begin{bmatrix} 5 & -1 & 7 \end{bmatrix}, \begin{bmatrix} 5 \\ -1 \\ 7 \end{bmatrix}$

12. $\begin{bmatrix} 1 & 0 & -8 \\ 8 & 0 & 1 \end{bmatrix}, \begin{bmatrix} 1 & 0 & -8 \\ 8 & 0 & 1 \end{bmatrix}$

13. $\begin{bmatrix} 4 & 0 \\ 2 & -4 \end{bmatrix}, \begin{bmatrix} 4 & 0 \\ -2 & -4 \end{bmatrix}$

14. $\begin{bmatrix} 2 & 1.5 & 4.25 \\ 0.5 & -0.5 & 0 \end{bmatrix}, \begin{bmatrix} 2 & \frac{3}{2} & \frac{17}{4} \\ \frac{1}{2} & -\frac{1}{2} & 0 \end{bmatrix}$

ADDING AND SUBTRACTING MATRICES Perform the indicated operation, if possible. If not possible, state the reason.

15. $\begin{bmatrix} 1 & -4 \\ -7 & 2 \end{bmatrix} + \begin{bmatrix} 3 & 5 \\ -5 & 2 \end{bmatrix}$

16. $\begin{bmatrix} 4 & -2 \\ 0 & -6 \end{bmatrix} + \begin{bmatrix} 4 \\ -1 \end{bmatrix}$

17. $\begin{bmatrix} -8 & -2 \\ 6 & -6 \end{bmatrix} - \begin{bmatrix} -4 & 5 \\ 1 & -1 \end{bmatrix}$

18. $\begin{bmatrix} -3 & 5 \\ 0 & -1 \end{bmatrix} + \begin{bmatrix} 2 & -7 \\ -4 & 9 \end{bmatrix}$

19. $\begin{bmatrix} 1.2 & 3.5 \\ 0.2 & 5.1 \end{bmatrix} + \begin{bmatrix} 4.1 & 8.7 \\ 2.6 & 5.3 \end{bmatrix}$

20. $\begin{bmatrix} 7 & -1 & 4 \\ 11 & -9 & 2 \end{bmatrix} + \begin{bmatrix} -3 & 6 & 3 \\ 10 & 1 & -5 \end{bmatrix}$

21. $\begin{bmatrix} 1 & 6 \\ -1 & -6 \\ 2 & 8 \end{bmatrix} - \begin{bmatrix} 7 & -3 & 9 \\ -2 & -7 & 9 \\ 11 & -1 & 2 \end{bmatrix}$

22. $\begin{bmatrix} \frac{1}{2} & \frac{1}{4} \\ \frac{2}{3} & \frac{3}{8} \end{bmatrix} - \begin{bmatrix} 2 & \frac{3}{4} \\ \frac{1}{2} & 5 \end{bmatrix}$

MULTIPLYING BY A SCALAR Perform the indicated operation.

23. $-4\begin{bmatrix} -1 & -3 & 7 \\ -4 & 0 & 6 \end{bmatrix}$

24. $5\begin{bmatrix} -2 & -6 \\ 3 & 1 \end{bmatrix}$

25. $4\begin{bmatrix} 1 & 3 & 9 \\ -5 & 5 & 15 \\ -3 & -5 & -11 \end{bmatrix}$

26. $-9\begin{bmatrix} 0 & 0 \\ -2 & -2 \\ \frac{1}{3} & \frac{4}{9} \end{bmatrix}$

27. $\frac{1}{2}\begin{bmatrix} -2 & -2 & 4 \\ \frac{1}{4} & \frac{6}{11} & -10 \end{bmatrix}$

28. $2.5\begin{bmatrix} -8.6 & 3.4 \\ 1.2 & -5.1 \\ -4.8 & 4.4 \\ 10 & -8 \end{bmatrix}$

COMBINING MATRIX OPERATIONS Perform the indicated operations.

29. $\begin{bmatrix} 12 & -8 \\ 0 & 5 \\ 0 & 3 \end{bmatrix} + 4\begin{bmatrix} -1 & 0 \\ 3 & -2 \\ -4 & 5 \end{bmatrix}$

30. $2\begin{bmatrix} -6 & -10 & 2 \\ 4 & -7 & -4 \end{bmatrix} - \begin{bmatrix} -1 & 5 & 13 \\ -3 & -6 & 19 \end{bmatrix}$

31. $2\begin{bmatrix} 7 & -7 \\ -1 & 3 \end{bmatrix} + 4\begin{bmatrix} 2 & -4 \\ -5 & -6 \end{bmatrix}$

32. $3\begin{bmatrix} -7 & 1 & 0 \\ 8 & -6 & -2 \end{bmatrix} - 2\begin{bmatrix} 4 & -1 & -7 \\ -3 & -5 & 5 \end{bmatrix}$

STUDENT HELP

HOMEWORK HELP
Visit our Web site
www.mcdougallittell.com
for help with Exs. 33–36.

SOLVING MATRIX EQUATIONS Solve the matrix equation for *x* and *y*.

33. $\begin{bmatrix} -2x & -8 \\ -10 & -9 \end{bmatrix} = \begin{bmatrix} 6 & y \\ -10 & -9 \end{bmatrix}$

34. $\begin{bmatrix} 3x & -2 \\ -1 & 8 \end{bmatrix} + \begin{bmatrix} -4 & 0 \\ -7 & -8 \end{bmatrix} = \begin{bmatrix} -16 & -2 \\ y & 0 \end{bmatrix}$

35. $2x\begin{bmatrix} -3 & 4 \\ -11 & 5 \end{bmatrix} = \begin{bmatrix} 12 & -16 \\ y & -20 \end{bmatrix}$

36. $\begin{bmatrix} 4 & -3 \\ 8 & -7 \\ 1 & 2 \end{bmatrix} + \begin{bmatrix} -5 & x \\ -7 & 7 \\ 4 & -9 \end{bmatrix} = \begin{bmatrix} -1 & -8 \\ y & 0 \\ 5 & -7 \end{bmatrix}$

🌎 **BASEBALL STATISTICS** In Exercises 37 and 38, use the following information about three Major League Baseball teams' wins and losses in 1998 before and after the All-Star Game. ▶ Source: CNN/SI

Before The Atlanta Braves had 59 wins and 29 losses, the Seattle Mariners had 37 wins and 51 losses, and the Chicago Cubs had 48 wins and 39 losses.

After The Atlanta Braves had 47 wins and 27 losses, the Seattle Mariners had 39 wins and 34 losses, and the Chicago Cubs had 42 wins and 34 losses.

37. Use matrices to organize the information.

38. Using your matrices from Exercise 37, write a matrix that shows the total numbers of wins and losses for the three teams in 1998.

🌎 **HISPANIC MUSIC** In Exercises 39–41, use the following information.
The figures below give the number (in millions) of Hispanic CD, cassette, and music video units shipped to all market channels and the dollar value (in millions) of those shipments (at suggested list prices). ▶ Source: Recording Industry Association of America

1996 Number of units—CDs: 20,779; cassettes: 15,299; and music videos: 45.
    Dollar value—CDs: 268,441; cassettes: 122,329; and music videos: 916.

1997 Number of units—CDs: 26,277; cassettes: 17,799; and music videos: 70.
    Dollar value—CDs: 344,697; cassettes: 144,645; and music videos: 1,260.

39. Use matrices to organize the information.

40. Write a matrix that gives the total numbers of units shipped and total values for both years.

41. Write a matrix that gives the change in units shipped and dollar value from 1996 to 1997.

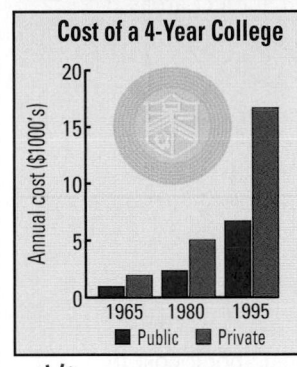

COLLEGE COSTS
Since 1980, college costs have risen substantially. After adjusting for inflation, costs rose by 48% at public 4-year colleges and 71% at private 4-year colleges between 1980 and 1995.

42. COLLEGE COSTS The matrices below show the average yearly cost (in dollars) of tuition and room and board at colleges in the United States from 1995 through 1997. Use matrix addition to write a matrix showing the totals of these costs. ▶ Source: U.S. Department of Education

	TUITION			ROOM AND BOARD		
	1995	**1996**	**1997**	**1995**	**1996**	**1997**
Public 2-year college	1,192	1,239	1,283	2,944	2,978	3,128
Public 4-year college	2,681	2,848	2,986	3,990	4,166	4,345
Private 2-year college	6,914	7,094	7,190	4,256	4,469	4,699
Private 4-year college	11,481	12,243	12,920	5,121	5,368	5,555

PSAT SCORES In Exercises 43 and 44, use the following information.
Eligibility for a National Merit Scholarship is based on a student's PSAT score. Through 1996, this total score was found by doubling a student's verbal score and adding this value to the student's mathematics score. Let V represent the average verbal scores and let M represent the average mathematics scores earned by sophomores and juniors at Central High for tests taken in 1993 through 1996.

VERBAL SCORES (V)			MATHEMATICS SCORES (M)	
	Sophomores	**Juniors**	**Sophomores**	**Juniors**
1993	48.9	49.0	49.0	50.4
1994	48.9	48.9	48.3	50.0
1995	48.7	48.8	49.4	50.8
1996	48.2	48.6	49.8	50.9

43. Write an expression in terms of V and M that you could use to determine the average total PSAT scores for sophomores and juniors at Central High from 1993 through 1996. Then evaluate the expression.

44. Use the matrix from Exercise 43 to determine the average total PSAT score for juniors at Central High in 1996.

U.S. POPULATION In Exercises 45–47, use the following information.
The matrices show the number of people (in thousands) who lived in each region of the United States in 1991 and the number of people (in thousands) projected to live in each region in 2010. The regional populations are separated into three age categories.

DATA UPDATE of U.S. Bureau of the Census data at www.mcdougallittell.com

	1991			2010		
	0–17	**18–65**	**Over 65**	**0–17**	**18–65**	**Over 65**
Northeast	12,142	31,791	7,043	12,493	33,822	7,377
Midwest	15,814	36,554	7,857	15,840	41,095	8,980
South	22,504	53,471	10,942	25,428	67,337	14,832
Mountain	3,993	8,461	1,580	5,094	12,420	2,707
Pacific	10,693	25,001	4,331	13,655	31,125	5,511

45. The total population in 1991 was 252,177,000 and the projected total population in 2010 is 297,716,000. Rewrite the matrices to give the information as percents of the total population. (*Hint:* Multiply each matrix by the reciprocal of the total population (in thousands), and then multiply by 100.)

46. Write a matrix that gives the projected change in the percent of the population in each region and age group from 1991 to 2010.

47. Based on the result of Exercise 46, which region(s) and age group(s) are projected to show relative growth from 1991 to 2010?

48. MULTI-STEP PROBLEM The matrices show the number of hardcover volumes sold and the average price per volume (in dollars) for different subject areas.

▶ Source: *The Bowker Annual*

	1995 (A)		**1996 (B)**	
	Volumes sold	Average price per volume	Volumes sold	Average price per volume
Art	1,116,000	41.23	1,070,000	53.40
Law	716,000	73.09	827,000	88.51
Music	251,000	43.27	253,000	39.21
Travel	199,000	38.30	179,000	33.92

a. Calculate $B - A$. How many more (or fewer) law volumes were sold in 1996 than in 1995? How much more (or less) did the average music book cost in 1996 than in 1995?

b. Calculate $B + A$. Does the "volumes sold" column in $B + A$ give you meaningful information? Does the "average price per volume" column in $B + A$ give you meaningful information? Explain.

c. *Writing* What conclusions can you make about the number of volumes sold and the average price per volume of these books from 1995 to 1996?

★ **Challenge**

49. GEOMETRY CONNECTION A triangle has vertices (2, 2), (8, 2), and (5, 6). Assign a letter to each vertex and organize the triangle's vertices in a matrix. When you multiply the matrix by 4, what does the "new" triangle look like? How are the two triangles related? Use a graph to help you.

MIXED REVIEW

TRANSFORMING FIGURES Draw the figure produced by each transformation of the figure shown. (Skills Review, p. 921)

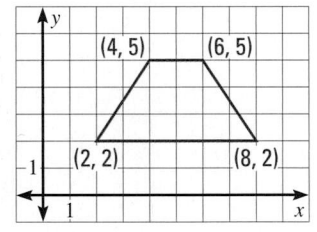

50. a 270° counterclockwise rotation about the origin

51. a translation by 2 units right and 4 units down

52. a reflection over the *y*-axis

MULTIPLYING REAL NUMBERS Find the product. (Skills Review, p. 905)

53. $-4(-5)$

54. $8(-2)$

55. $-7(-1)$

56. $\frac{1}{2}(-7)$

57. $\frac{5}{6} \cdot \frac{3}{7}$

58. $3.2(2.4 + 8.1)$

CHECKING SOLUTIONS Check whether the ordered pairs are solutions of the inequality. (Review 2.6)

59. $x + 2y \le -3$; (0, 3), (−5, 1)

60. $5x - y > 2$; (−5, 0), (5, 23)

61. $-8x - 3y < 5$; (−1, 1), (3, −9)

62. $21x - 10y > 4$; (2, 3), (−1, 0)

FINDING A SOLUTION Give an ordered pair that is a solution of the system. (Lesson 3.3)

63. $x + y < 10$
$y > 1$

64. $x - y \ge 3$
$y < 12$

65. $3x > y$
$x \le 15$

ACTIVITY 4.1

Using Technology

Using Matrix Operations

You can use a graphing calculator to perform matrix operations.

▶ **EXAMPLE**

The matrices show music sales (in thousands) for a chain of stores during a two-month period. The music formats are CDs and cassette tapes. The categories of music are Rock (R), Country (C), Jazz (J), and Easy Listening (E).

	MAY				**JUNE**			
	R	C	J	E	R	C	J	E
CDs	32	16	3	8	24	15	3	7
Tapes	28	12	5	15	25	10	4	15

a. Find the total sales for each format and category for May and June.

b. Estimate the sales for July if they are expected to decrease 3% from the June sales.

▶ **SOLUTION**

a. To find the total sales in each format and category for May and June, let matrix *A* represent May sales and let matrix *B* represent June sales. Use a graphing calculator to enter each matrix. Then find the sum of matrix *A* and matrix *B*.

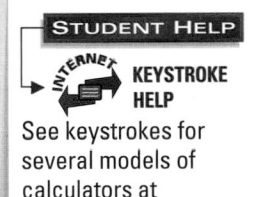
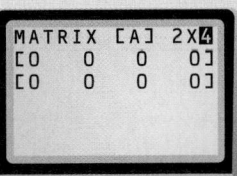

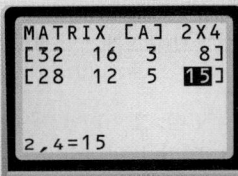

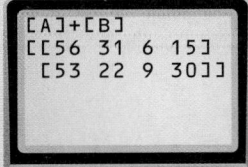

For each matrix, enter the dimensions of the matrix.

Then enter the data row by row until all 8 entries have been filled for each matrix.

To find the sum, select each matrix from the matrix menu and add.

b. To estimate the sales for July, multiply matrix *B* by the scalar 0.97. The calculator shows, for instance, that July sales for rock CDs are expected to be 23,280.

▶ **EXERCISES**

Use a graphing calculator to perform the indicated operation(s).

1. $\begin{bmatrix} -4.9 & 3.1 \\ 9.3 & -2.5 \end{bmatrix} + \begin{bmatrix} 11.5 & -9.2 \\ 6.03 & 4.22 \end{bmatrix}$

2. $\begin{bmatrix} 418 & 418 \\ 452 & 452 \\ 146 & 146 \end{bmatrix} - \begin{bmatrix} 512 & 359 \\ 428 & 184 \\ 735 & 299 \end{bmatrix}$

3. $1.043 \begin{bmatrix} 6.2 & 1.6 \\ 22.1 & 7 \end{bmatrix}$

4. $5.08 \begin{bmatrix} 0.06 & 1.25 \\ 3.32 & 0.01 \end{bmatrix} - 0.07 \begin{bmatrix} 1.009 & 0.052 \\ 11.2 & 34.15 \end{bmatrix}$

5. 🌎 **MUSIC** Write a matrix that gives the change in sales from May to June for the chain of stores discussed in the example. For which categories of CDs and cassettes did sales increase from May to June? For which did sales decrease?

Multiplying Matrices

What you should learn

GOAL 1 Multiply two matrices.

GOAL 2 Use matrix multiplication in **real-life** situations, such as finding the number of calories burned in **Ex. 40**.

Why you should learn it

▼ To solve **real-life** problems, such as calculating the cost of softball equipment in **Example 5**.

GOAL 1 MULTIPLYING TWO MATRICES

The product of two matrices A and B is defined provided the number of columns in A is equal to the number of rows in B.

If A is an $m \times n$ matrix and B is an $n \times p$ matrix, then the product AB is an $m \times p$ matrix.

$$
\begin{array}{ccccc}
A & \cdot & B & = & AB \\
m \times n & & n \times p & & m \times p
\end{array}
$$

↑   ↑ ↑   ↑
    equal
dimensions of AB

EXAMPLE 1 *Describing Matrix Products*

State whether the product AB is defined. If so, give the dimensions of AB.

  a. A: 2×3, B: 3×4 **b.** A: 3×2, B: 3×4

SOLUTION

  a. Because A is a **2 × 3** matrix and B is a **3 × 4** matrix, the product AB is defined and is a **2 × 4** matrix.

  b. Because the number of columns in A (two) does not equal the number of rows in B (three), the product AB is not defined.

EXAMPLE 2 *Finding the Product of Two Matrices*

Find AB if $A = \begin{bmatrix} -2 & 3 \\ 1 & -4 \\ 6 & 0 \end{bmatrix}$ and $B = \begin{bmatrix} -1 & 3 \\ -2 & 4 \end{bmatrix}$.

SOLUTION

Because A is a 3×2 matrix and B is a 2×2 matrix, the product AB is defined and is a 3×2 matrix. To write the entry in the first row and first column of AB, multiply corresponding entries in the first row of A and the first column of B. Then add. Use a similar procedure to write the other entries of the product.

$$
AB = \begin{bmatrix} -2 & 3 \\ 1 & -4 \\ 6 & 0 \end{bmatrix} \begin{bmatrix} -1 & 3 \\ -2 & 4 \end{bmatrix}
$$

$$
= \begin{bmatrix} (-2)(-1) + (3)(-2) & (-2)(3) + (3)(4) \\ (1)(-1) + (-4)(-2) & (1)(3) + (-4)(4) \\ (6)(-1) + (0)(-2) & (6)(3) + (0)(4) \end{bmatrix}
$$

$$
= \begin{bmatrix} -4 & 6 \\ 7 & -13 \\ -6 & 18 \end{bmatrix}
$$

EXAMPLE 3 *Finding the Product of Two Matrices*

STUDENT HELP

INTERNET

HOMEWORK HELP
Visit our Web site
www.mcdougallittell.com
for extra examples.

If $A = \begin{bmatrix} 3 & 2 \\ -1 & 0 \end{bmatrix}$ and $B = \begin{bmatrix} 1 & -4 \\ 2 & 1 \end{bmatrix}$, find each product.

a. AB **b.** BA

SOLUTION

a. $AB = \begin{bmatrix} 3 & 2 \\ -1 & 0 \end{bmatrix} \begin{bmatrix} 1 & -4 \\ 2 & 1 \end{bmatrix} = \begin{bmatrix} 7 & -10 \\ -1 & 4 \end{bmatrix}$

b. $BA = \begin{bmatrix} 1 & -4 \\ 2 & 1 \end{bmatrix} \begin{bmatrix} 3 & 2 \\ -1 & 0 \end{bmatrix} = \begin{bmatrix} 7 & 2 \\ 5 & 4 \end{bmatrix}$

· · · · · · · · ·

Notice in Example 3 that $AB \neq BA$. Matrix multiplication is not, in general, commutative.

EXAMPLE 4 *Using Matrix Operations*

If $A = \begin{bmatrix} 2 & 1 \\ -1 & 3 \end{bmatrix}$, $B = \begin{bmatrix} -2 & 0 \\ 4 & 2 \end{bmatrix}$, and $C = \begin{bmatrix} 1 & 1 \\ 3 & 2 \end{bmatrix}$, simplify each expression.

a. $A(B + C)$ **b.** $AB + AC$

SOLUTION

a. $A(B + C) = \begin{bmatrix} 2 & 1 \\ -1 & 3 \end{bmatrix} \left(\begin{bmatrix} -2 & 0 \\ 4 & 2 \end{bmatrix} + \begin{bmatrix} 1 & 1 \\ 3 & 2 \end{bmatrix} \right)$

$= \begin{bmatrix} 2 & 1 \\ -1 & 3 \end{bmatrix} \begin{bmatrix} -1 & 1 \\ 7 & 4 \end{bmatrix} = \begin{bmatrix} 5 & 6 \\ 22 & 11 \end{bmatrix}$

b. $AB + AC = \begin{bmatrix} 2 & 1 \\ -1 & 3 \end{bmatrix} \begin{bmatrix} -2 & 0 \\ 4 & 2 \end{bmatrix} + \begin{bmatrix} 2 & 1 \\ -1 & 3 \end{bmatrix} \begin{bmatrix} 1 & 1 \\ 3 & 2 \end{bmatrix}$

$= \begin{bmatrix} 0 & 2 \\ 14 & 6 \end{bmatrix} + \begin{bmatrix} 5 & 4 \\ 8 & 5 \end{bmatrix} = \begin{bmatrix} 5 & 6 \\ 22 & 11 \end{bmatrix}$

· · · · · · · · ·

Notice in Example 4 that $A(B + C) = AB + AC$, which is true in general. This and other properties of matrix multiplication are summarized below.

CONCEPT SUMMARY **PROPERTIES OF MATRIX MULTIPLICATION**

Let A, B, and C be matrices and let c be a scalar.

ASSOCIATIVE PROPERTY OF MATRIX MULTIPLICATION	$A(BC) = (AB)C$
LEFT DISTRIBUTIVE PROPERTY	$A(B + C) = AB + AC$
RIGHT DISTRIBUTIVE PROPERTY	$(A + B)C = AC + BC$
ASSOCIATIVE PROPERTY OF SCALAR MULTIPLICATION	$c(AB) = (cA)B = A(cB)$

GOAL 2 USING MATRIX MULTIPLICATION IN REAL LIFE

Matrix multiplication is useful in business applications because an *inventory* matrix, when multiplied by a *cost per item* matrix, results in a *total cost* matrix.

$$\begin{bmatrix} \text{Inventory} \\ \text{matrix} \end{bmatrix} \cdot \begin{bmatrix} \text{Cost per item} \\ \text{matrix} \end{bmatrix} = \begin{bmatrix} \text{Total cost} \\ \text{matrix} \end{bmatrix}$$
$$\quad m \times n \qquad\qquad n \times p \qquad\qquad m \times p$$

For the total cost matrix to be meaningful, the column labels for the inventory matrix must match the row labels for the cost per item matrix.

EXAMPLE 5 *Using Matrices to Calculate the Total Cost*

SPORTS Two softball teams submit equipment lists for the season.

Women's team	Men's team
12 bats	15 bats
45 balls	38 balls
15 uniforms	17 uniforms

Each bat costs $21, each ball costs $4, and each uniform costs $30. Use matrix multiplication to find the total cost of equipment for each team.

SOLUTION

To begin, write the equipment lists and the costs per item in matrix form. Because you want to use matrix multiplication to find the total cost, set up the matrices so that the columns of the equipment matrix match the rows of the cost matrix.

EQUIPMENT

	Bats	Balls	Uniforms
Women's team	12	45	15
Men's team	15	38	17

COST

	Dollars
Bats	21
Balls	4
Uniforms	30

The total cost of equipment for each team can now be obtained by multiplying the equipment matrix by the cost per item matrix. The equipment matrix is 2×3 and the cost per item matrix is 3×1, so their product is a 2×1 matrix.

$$\begin{bmatrix} 12 & 45 & 15 \\ 15 & 38 & 17 \end{bmatrix} \begin{bmatrix} 21 \\ 4 \\ 30 \end{bmatrix} = \begin{bmatrix} 12(21) + 45(4) + 15(30) \\ 15(21) + 38(4) + 17(30) \end{bmatrix} = \begin{bmatrix} 882 \\ 977 \end{bmatrix}$$

The labels for the product matrix are as follows.

TOTAL COST

	Dollars
Women's team	882
Men's team	977

▶ The total cost of equipment for the women's team is $882, and the total cost of equipment for the men's team is $977.

GUIDED PRACTICE

Vocabulary Check ✔

1. Complete this statement: The product of matrices A and B is defined provided the number of _?_ in A is equal to the number of _?_ in B.

Concept Check ✔

2. Matrix A is 6×1. Matrix B is 1×2. Which of the products is defined, AB or BA? Explain.

3. Tell whether the matrix equation is *true* or *false*. Explain.

$$\begin{bmatrix} 5 & 3 \\ -3 & 5 \end{bmatrix} \begin{bmatrix} 2 & 0 \\ 0 & 1 \end{bmatrix} = \begin{bmatrix} 2 & 0 \\ 0 & 1 \end{bmatrix} \begin{bmatrix} 5 & 3 \\ -3 & 5 \end{bmatrix}$$

Skill Check ✔

State whether the product AB is defined. If so, give the dimensions of AB.

4. A: 3×2, B: 2×3
5. A: 3×3, B: 3×3
6. A: 3×2, B: 3×2

Find the product.

7. $\begin{bmatrix} 1 & 0 \\ -2 & -1 \end{bmatrix} \begin{bmatrix} 2 & 0 \\ 1 & 3 \end{bmatrix}$

8. $\begin{bmatrix} 4 & 4 \end{bmatrix} \begin{bmatrix} -2 \\ -3 \end{bmatrix}$

9. $\begin{bmatrix} -3 & 3 \\ 3 & -2 \\ 0 & -1 \end{bmatrix} \begin{bmatrix} 1 & 0 \\ -2 & -1 \end{bmatrix}$

10. 🌐 **SOFTBALL EQUIPMENT** Use matrix multiplication to find the total cost of equipment in Example 5 if the women's team needs 16 bats, 42 balls, and 16 uniforms and the men's team needs 14 bats, 43 balls, and 15 uniforms.

PRACTICE AND APPLICATIONS

STUDENT HELP

▶ **Extra Practice**
to help you master
skills is on p. 944.

MATRIX PRODUCTS State whether the product AB is defined. If so, give the dimensions of AB.

11. A: 1×3, B: 3×2
12. A: 2×4, B: 4×3
13. A: 4×2, B: 3×5

14. A: 5×5, B: 5×4
15. A: 3×4, B: 4×1
16. A: 3×3, B: 2×4

FINDING MATRIX PRODUCTS Find the product. If it is not defined, state the reason.

17. $\begin{bmatrix} -\dfrac{1}{6} & \dfrac{1}{2} & -\dfrac{1}{3} \end{bmatrix} \begin{bmatrix} 12 \\ 0 \\ -12 \end{bmatrix}$

18. $\begin{bmatrix} 7.3 & 1.5 \\ 1.8 & 0 \\ 2.9 & 3.2 \end{bmatrix} \begin{bmatrix} -4.2 & 2.6 & -8.7 \end{bmatrix}$

19. $\begin{bmatrix} 1 & -4 \\ 3 & -2 \end{bmatrix} \begin{bmatrix} 4 & -1 \\ 0 & -3 \end{bmatrix}$

20. $\begin{bmatrix} -6 & -2 \\ 0 & 3 \end{bmatrix} \begin{bmatrix} -1 & 4 \\ -5 & 3 \end{bmatrix}$

21. $\begin{bmatrix} 2 & -8 & 1 \\ 0 & -5 & 2 \end{bmatrix} \begin{bmatrix} 0 & 1 & -2 \\ 8 & -2 & -5 \end{bmatrix}$

22. $\begin{bmatrix} 6.0 & 0 \\ -0.2 & 0.2 \\ 2.9 & 0.3 \end{bmatrix} \begin{bmatrix} 1 & 0 \\ 1.5 & -0.5 \end{bmatrix}$

STUDENT HELP

▶ **HOMEWORK HELP**
Example 1: Exs. 11–16
Examples 2, 3: Exs. 17–26
Example 4: Exs. 27–32
Example 5: Exs. 35–40

23. $\begin{bmatrix} -1 & -0.5 & 1.25 \\ 1 & -1.5 & -0.25 \end{bmatrix} \begin{bmatrix} 1.2 \\ 0.2 \\ 0 \end{bmatrix}$

24. $\begin{bmatrix} -6 & 1 & 1 \\ -2 & 3 & 8 \\ 0.1 & 7 & 1 \end{bmatrix} \begin{bmatrix} 0 & -1 & 3 \\ -7 & -2 & 4 \\ -1 & 3 & 4 \end{bmatrix}$

25. $\begin{bmatrix} 6 & -2 \\ 1 & 4 \\ 0 & 5 \end{bmatrix} \begin{bmatrix} -4 & -2 & 5 \\ 4 & -6 & -1 \end{bmatrix}$

26. $\begin{bmatrix} 0 & 1 & 0 \\ 6 & -3 & -1 \\ -2 & 5 & 3 \end{bmatrix} \begin{bmatrix} 5 & -7 & 4 \\ 3 & 12 & 6 \\ -4 & -5 & -12 \end{bmatrix}$

SIMPLIFYING EXPRESSIONS Using the given matrices, simplify the expression.

$$A = \begin{bmatrix} 4 & -2 \\ 6 & -1 \end{bmatrix}, B = \begin{bmatrix} 1 & 0 \\ -2 & 4 \end{bmatrix}, C = \begin{bmatrix} -1 & 3 \\ -2 & 1 \end{bmatrix}, D = \begin{bmatrix} 3 & -2 & 1 \\ -1 & 2 & 4 \\ -2 & -3 & 3 \end{bmatrix}, E = \begin{bmatrix} -2 & 5 & 6 \\ -1 & 4 & 2 \\ 3 & 1 & -4 \end{bmatrix}$$

27. $2AB$

28. $AB + AC$

29. $D(D + E)$

30. $(E + D)E$

31. $-3(AC)$

32. $0.5(AB) + 2AC$

SOLVING MATRIX EQUATIONS Solve for x and y.

33. $\begin{bmatrix} -2 & 1 & 2 \\ 3 & 2 & 4 \\ 0 & -2 & 4 \end{bmatrix} \begin{bmatrix} 1 \\ x \\ 3 \end{bmatrix} = \begin{bmatrix} 6 \\ 19 \\ y \end{bmatrix}$

34. $\begin{bmatrix} 4 & 1 & 3 \\ -2 & x & 1 \end{bmatrix} \begin{bmatrix} 9 & -2 \\ 2 & 1 \\ -1 & 4 \end{bmatrix} = \begin{bmatrix} y & 5 \\ -13 & 11 \end{bmatrix}$

STUDENT HELP

DATA UPDATE
Visit our Web site
www.mcdougallittell.com

🌐 **AGRICULTURE** In Exercises 35 and 36, use the following information.

The percents of the total 1997 world production of wheat, rice, and maize are shown in the matrix for the four countries that grow the most grain: China, India, the Commonwealth of Independent States (formerly the Soviet Union), and the United States. The total 1997 world production (in thousands of metric tons) of wheat, rice, and maize is 608,846, 570,906, and 586,923, respectively.

▶ Source: Food and Agriculture Organization of the United Nations

GRAIN PRODUCTION

	Wheat	Rice	Maize
China	20.1%	34.8%	18%
India	22%	21.5%	1.7%
C.I.S.	7.3%	0.1%	0.5%
U.S.	11.3%	1.4%	40.5%

35. Rewrite the matrix to give the percents as decimals.

36. Show how matrix multiplication can be used to determine how many metric tons of all three grains were produced in each of the four countries.

🌐 **CLASS DEBATE** In Exercises 37–39, use the following information.

Three teams participated in a debating competition. The final score for each team is based on how many students ranked first, second, and third in a debate. The results of 12 debates are shown in matrix A.

MATRIX A

	1st	2nd	3rd
Team 1	3	5	4
Team 2	5	2	5
Team 3	4	6	2

37. Teams earn 6 points for each first place, 5 points for each second place, and 4 points for each third place. Organize this information into a matrix B.

38. Find the product AB.

39. **LOGICAL REASONING** Which team won the competition? How many points did the winning team score?

FOCUS ON APPLICATIONS

REAL LIFE EXERCISE
A 120 pound person walking at a moderate pace of 3 mi/h would burn about 64 Cal in 20 min. At a brisk pace of 4.5 mi/h, the person would burn about 82 Cal in 20 min.

40. 🌐 **EXERCISE** The numbers of calories burned by people of different weights doing different activities for 20 minutes are shown in the matrix. Show how matrix multiplication can be used to write the total number of calories burned by a 120 pound person and a 150 pound person who each bicycled for 40 minutes, jogged for 10 minutes, and then walked for 60 minutes.

▶ Source: *Medicine and Science in Sports and Exercise*

CALORIES BURNED

	120 lb person	150 lb person
Bicycling	109	136
Jogging	127	159
Walking	64	79

Test Preparation

41. *Writing* Describe the process you use when multiplying any two matrices.

42. **MULTIPLE CHOICE** What is the product of $\begin{bmatrix} 0 & -1 \\ -4 & -2 \end{bmatrix}$ and $\begin{bmatrix} 7 & -2 \\ -1 & 0 \end{bmatrix}$?

Ⓐ $\begin{bmatrix} 2 & 0 \\ -26 & -24 \end{bmatrix}$　Ⓑ $\begin{bmatrix} 8 & 0 \\ -30 & 6 \end{bmatrix}$　Ⓒ $\begin{bmatrix} 1 & 0 \\ -26 & 8 \end{bmatrix}$　Ⓓ $\begin{bmatrix} 1 & 0 \\ -30 & 8 \end{bmatrix}$

43. **MULTIPLE CHOICE** If A is a 2×3 matrix and B is a 3×2 matrix, what are the dimensions of BA?

Ⓐ 2×2　　Ⓑ 3×3　　Ⓒ 3×2　　Ⓓ 2×3　　Ⓔ BA not defined

★ **Challenge**

44. **ROTATIONAL MATRIX** Matrix A is a 90° rotational matrix. Matrix B contains the coordinates of the triangle's vertices shown in the graph.

$$A = \begin{bmatrix} 0 & -1 \\ 1 & 0 \end{bmatrix} \qquad B = \begin{bmatrix} -7 & -4 & -4 \\ 4 & 8 & 2 \end{bmatrix}$$

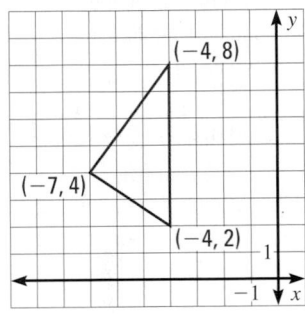

a. Calculate AB. Graph the coordinates of the vertices given by AB. What rotation does AB represent in the graph?

b. Find the 180° and 270° rotations of the original triangle by using repeated multiplication of the 90° rotational matrix. What are the coordinates of the vertices of the rotated triangles?

EXTRA CHALLENGE
→ www.mcdougallittell.com

MIXED REVIEW

CALCULATING AREA Find the area of the figure. **(Skills Review, p. 914)**

45.
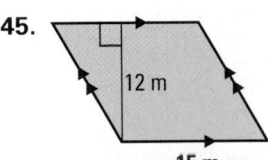

46.
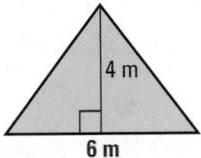

47.
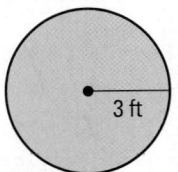

WRITING EQUATIONS Write an equation of the line with the given properties. **(Review 2.4)**

48. slope: $\frac{1}{2}$, passes through $(1, 8)$　　49. slope: $-\frac{1}{4}$, passes through $(0, 4)$

50. passes through $(3, -6)$ and $(2, 10)$　　51. passes through $(1, 5)$ and $(4, 14)$

52. x-intercept: -7, y-intercept: -5　　53. x-intercept: 4, y-intercept: -6

SOLVING SYSTEMS Solve the system of linear equations using any algebraic method. **(Review 3.2 for 4.3)**

54. $4x + y = 6$
$-3x - 2y = 8$

55. $2x + y = -9$
$3x + 5y = 4$

56. $-9x + 5y = 1$
$3x - 2y = 2$

57. $2x - 2y = 8$
$x - y = 1$

58. $-3x + 4y = -1$
$6x + 2y = 7$

59. $5x + 2y = -10$
$-3x - 8y = 40$

60. $7x + 3y = 11$
$-2x + 5y = 32$

61. $5x - 4y = -1$
$2x - 9y = 10$

62. $-x + 7y = -49$
$12x + y = -24$

4.3
Determinants and Cramer's Rule

What you should learn

GOAL 1 Evaluate determinants of 2 × 2 and 3 × 3 matrices.

GOAL 2 Use Cramer's rule to solve systems of linear equations, as applied in **Example 5**.

Why you should learn it

▼ To solve **real-life** problems, such as finding the area of the Golden Triangle of India in **Ex. 58**.

GOAL 1 EVALUATING DETERMINANTS

Associated with each square matrix is a real number called its **determinant**. The determinant of a matrix A is denoted by det A or by $|A|$.

THE DETERMINANT OF A MATRIX

DETERMINANT OF A 2 × 2 MATRIX

$$\det \begin{bmatrix} a & b \\ c & d \end{bmatrix} = \begin{vmatrix} a & b \\ c & d \end{vmatrix} = ad - cb$$

The determinant of a 2 × 2 matrix is the difference of the products of the entries on the diagonals.

DETERMINANT OF A 3 × 3 MATRIX

❶ Repeat the first two columns to the right of the determinant.

❷ Subtract the sum of the products in red from the sum of the products in blue.

$$\det \begin{bmatrix} a & b & c \\ d & e & f \\ g & h & i \end{bmatrix} = \begin{vmatrix} a & b & c \\ d & e & f \\ g & h & i \end{vmatrix} \begin{matrix} a & b \\ d & e \\ g & h \end{matrix} = (aei + bfg + cdh) - (gec + hfa + idb)$$

EXAMPLE 1 *Evaluating Determinants*

Evaluate the determinant of the matrix.

a. $\begin{bmatrix} 1 & 3 \\ 2 & 5 \end{bmatrix}$

b. $\begin{bmatrix} 2 & -1 & 3 \\ -2 & 0 & 1 \\ 1 & 2 & 4 \end{bmatrix}$

SOLUTION

a. $\begin{vmatrix} 1 & 3 \\ 2 & 5 \end{vmatrix} = 1(5) - 2(3) = 5 - 6 = -1$

b. $\begin{vmatrix} 2 & -1 & 3 \\ -2 & 0 & 1 \\ 1 & 2 & 4 \end{vmatrix} \begin{matrix} 2 & -1 \\ -2 & 0 \\ 1 & 2 \end{matrix} = [0 + (-1) + (-12)] - (0 + 4 + 8) = -13 - 12$

$$= -25$$

You can use a determinant to find the area of a triangle whose vertices are points in a coordinate plane.

AREA OF A TRIANGLE

The area of a triangle with vertices (x_1, y_1), (x_2, y_2), and (x_3, y_3) is given by

$$\text{Area} = \pm\frac{1}{2}\begin{vmatrix} x_1 & y_1 & 1 \\ x_2 & y_2 & 1 \\ x_3 & y_3 & 1 \end{vmatrix}$$

where the symbol $\pm$ indicates that the appropriate sign should be chosen to yield a positive value.

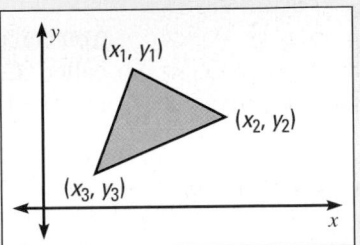

EXAMPLE 2   *The Area of a Triangle*

The area of the triangle shown is:

$$\text{Area} = \pm\frac{1}{2}\begin{vmatrix} 1 & 2 & 1 \\ 4 & 0 & 1 \\ 6 & 2 & 1 \end{vmatrix}$$

$$= \pm\frac{1}{2}[(0 + 12 + 8) - (0 + 2 + 8)] = 5$$

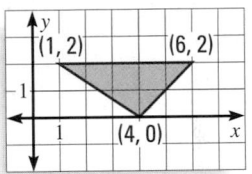

EXAMPLE 3   *The Area of a Triangular Region*

BERMUDA TRIANGLE The Bermuda Triangle is a large triangular region in the Atlantic Ocean. Many ships and airplanes have been lost in this region. The triangle is formed by imaginary lines connecting Bermuda, Puerto Rico, and Miami, Florida. Use a determinant to estimate the area of the Bermuda Triangle.

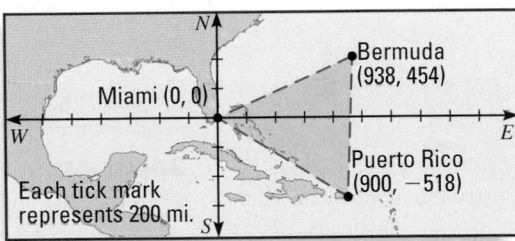

SOLUTION

The approximate coordinates of the Bermuda Triangle's three vertices are $(938, 454)$, $(900, -518)$, and $(0, 0)$. So, the area of the region is as follows:

$$\text{Area} = \pm\frac{1}{2}\begin{vmatrix} 938 & 454 & 1 \\ 900 & -518 & 1 \\ 0 & 0 & 1 \end{vmatrix}$$

$$= \pm\frac{1}{2}[(-485{,}884 + 0 + 0) - (0 + 0 + 408{,}600)]$$

$$= 447{,}242$$

▶ The area of the Bermuda Triangle is about 447,000 square miles.

You can use determinants to solve a system of linear equations. The method, called **Cramer's rule** and named after the Swiss mathematician Gabriel Cramer (1704−1752), uses the **coefficient matrix** of the linear system.

LINEAR SYSTEM

$$ax + by = e$$
$$cx + dy = f$$

COEFFICIENT MATRIX

$$\begin{bmatrix} a & b \\ c & d \end{bmatrix}$$

CRAMER'S RULE FOR A 2 X 2 SYSTEM

Let A be the coefficient matrix of this linear system:

$$ax + by = e$$
$$cx + dy = f$$

If det $A \neq 0$, then the system has exactly one solution. The solution is:

$$x = \frac{\begin{vmatrix} e & b \\ f & d \end{vmatrix}}{\det A} \quad \text{and} \quad y = \frac{\begin{vmatrix} a & e \\ c & f \end{vmatrix}}{\det A}$$

In Cramer's rule, notice that the denominator for x and y is the determinant of the coefficient matrix of the system. The numerators for x and y are the determinants of the matrices formed by using the column of constants as replacements for the coefficients of x and y, respectively.

EXAMPLE 4 *Using Cramer's Rule for a 2 × 2 System*

Use Cramer's rule to solve this system: $\begin{array}{l} 8x + 5y = 2 \\ 2x - 4y = -10 \end{array}$

SOLUTION

Evaluate the determinant of the coefficient matrix.

$$\begin{vmatrix} 8 & 5 \\ 2 & -4 \end{vmatrix} = -32 - 10 = -42$$

Apply Cramer's rule since the determinant is not 0.

$$x = \frac{\begin{vmatrix} 2 & 5 \\ -10 & -4 \end{vmatrix}}{-42} = \frac{-8 - (-50)}{-42} = \frac{42}{-42} = -1$$

$$y = \frac{\begin{vmatrix} 8 & 2 \\ 2 & -10 \end{vmatrix}}{-42} = \frac{-80 - 4}{-42} = \frac{-84}{-42} = 2$$

▶ The solution is $(-1, 2)$.

✓ **CHECK** Check this solution in the original equations.

$$8(-1) + 5(2) \stackrel{?}{=} 2 \qquad 2(-1) - 4(2) \stackrel{?}{=} -10$$
$$2 = 2 \checkmark \qquad\qquad -10 = -10 \checkmark$$

CRAMER'S RULE FOR A 3 X 3 SYSTEM

Let A be the coefficient matrix of this linear system:

$$ax + by + cz = j$$
$$dx + ey + fz = k$$
$$gx + hy + iz = l$$

If det $A \neq 0$, then the system has exactly one solution. The solution is:

$$x = \frac{\begin{vmatrix} j & b & c \\ k & e & f \\ l & h & i \end{vmatrix}}{\det A}, \quad y = \frac{\begin{vmatrix} a & j & c \\ d & k & f \\ g & l & i \end{vmatrix}}{\det A}, \quad \text{and} \quad z = \frac{\begin{vmatrix} a & b & j \\ d & e & k \\ g & h & l \end{vmatrix}}{\det A}$$

EXAMPLE 5 *Using Cramer's Rule for a 3 × 3 System*

SCIENCE CONNECTION The atomic weights of three compounds are shown. Use a linear system and Cramer's rule to find the atomic weights of carbon (C), hydrogen (H), and oxygen (O).

Compound	Formula	Atomic weight
Methane	CH_4	16
Glycerol	$C_3H_8O_3$	92
Water	H_2O	18

SOLUTION

Write a linear system using the formula for each compound. Let C, H, and O represent the atomic weights of carbon, hydrogen, and oxygen.

$$C + 4H \quad\quad = 16$$
$$3C + 8H + 3O = 92$$
$$\quad\quad 2H + O = 18$$

Evaluate the determinant of the coefficient matrix.

$$\begin{vmatrix} 1 & 4 & 0 \\ 3 & 8 & 3 \\ 0 & 2 & 1 \end{vmatrix} = (8 + 0 + 0) - (0 + 6 + 12) = -10$$

Apply Cramer's rule since the determinant is not 0.

$$C = \frac{\begin{vmatrix} 16 & 4 & 0 \\ 92 & 8 & 3 \\ 18 & 2 & 1 \end{vmatrix}}{-10} = \frac{-120}{-10} = 12 \quad \textbf{Atomic weight of carbon}$$

$$H = \frac{\begin{vmatrix} 1 & 16 & 0 \\ 3 & 92 & 3 \\ 0 & 18 & 1 \end{vmatrix}}{-10} = \frac{-10}{-10} = 1 \quad \textbf{Atomic weight of hydrogen}$$

$$O = \frac{\begin{vmatrix} 1 & 4 & 16 \\ 3 & 8 & 92 \\ 0 & 2 & 18 \end{vmatrix}}{-10} = \frac{-160}{-10} = 16 \quad \textbf{Atomic weight of oxygen}$$

▶ The weights of carbon, hydrogen, and oxygen are 12, 1, and 16, respectively.

GUIDED PRACTICE

Vocabulary Check ✓   1. Explain Cramer's rule and how it is used.

Concept Check ✓   2. Can two different matrices have the same determinant? If so, give an example.

3. **ERROR ANALYSIS** Find the error in each calculation.

a.
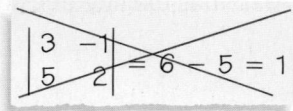
$$\begin{vmatrix} 3 & -1 \\ 5 & 2 \end{vmatrix} = 6 - 5 = 1$$

b.
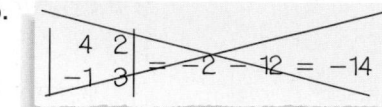
$$\begin{vmatrix} 4 & 2 \\ -1 & 3 \end{vmatrix} = -2 - 12 = -14$$

4. To use Cramer's rule to solve a linear system, what must be true of the determinant of the coefficient matrix?

Skill Check ✓   Evaluate the determinant of the matrix.

5. $\begin{bmatrix} 0 & 1 \\ 6 & 2 \end{bmatrix}$ 6. $\begin{bmatrix} -1 & 4 \\ 5 & -1 \end{bmatrix}$ 7. $\begin{bmatrix} 8 & -2 \\ -2 & 4 \end{bmatrix}$

Use Cramer's rule to solve the linear system.

8. $6x - 8y = 4$ 9. $2x + 7y = -3$ 10. $12x - 2y = 2$
   $4x - 5y = -4$ $3x - 8y = -23$ $-14x + 11y = 51$

11. 🌐 **SCHOOL SPIRIT** You are making a large pennant for your school football team. A diagram of the pennant is shown at the right. The coordinates given are measured in inches. How many square inches of material will you need to make the pennant?

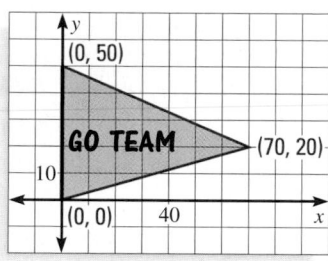

PRACTICE AND APPLICATIONS

STUDENT HELP

▶ **Extra Practice**
to help you master
skills is on p. 945.

2 × 2 DETERMINANTS Evaluate the determinant of the matrix.

12. $\begin{bmatrix} -4 & 2 \\ 5 & -2 \end{bmatrix}$ 13. $\begin{bmatrix} 8 & 0 \\ -1 & 3 \end{bmatrix}$ 14. $\begin{bmatrix} 9 & 3 \\ -2 & 1 \end{bmatrix}$

15. $\begin{bmatrix} -7 & 11 \\ -7 & 2 \end{bmatrix}$ 16. $\begin{bmatrix} 4 & 0 \\ -3 & 4 \end{bmatrix}$ 17. $\begin{bmatrix} 1 & 8 \\ 5 & 9 \end{bmatrix}$

18. $\begin{bmatrix} -6 & 5 \\ -3 & 9 \end{bmatrix}$ 19. $\begin{bmatrix} 0 & -3 \\ 8 & 10 \end{bmatrix}$ 20. $\begin{bmatrix} 12 & 2 \\ -5 & 8 \end{bmatrix}$

3 × 3 DETERMINANTS Evaluate the determinant of the matrix.

STUDENT HELP

▶ **HOMEWORK HELP**
Example 1: Exs. 12–29
Example 2: Exs. 30–35
Example 3: Exs. 54–58
Example 4: Exs. 36–44,
59
Example 5: Exs. 45–53,
60

21. $\begin{bmatrix} 12 & 4 & -1 \\ -2 & 3 & 2 \\ 5 & 8 & 1 \end{bmatrix}$ 22. $\begin{bmatrix} 5 & -9 & 4 \\ 4 & 2 & 1 \\ 0 & 1 & 1 \end{bmatrix}$ 23. $\begin{bmatrix} 0 & 5 & 2 \\ 10 & 13 & -4 \\ -5 & 4 & -1 \end{bmatrix}$

24. $\begin{bmatrix} 1 & 16 & -2 \\ 20 & 4 & 2 \\ 7 & 1 & -4 \end{bmatrix}$ 25. $\begin{bmatrix} -4 & 0 & -1 \\ 0 & 8 & 9 \\ 0 & 5 & 2 \end{bmatrix}$ 26. $\begin{bmatrix} 8 & 2 & 9 \\ 12 & 3 & 9 \\ 3 & 13 & 4 \end{bmatrix}$

27. $\begin{bmatrix} 3 & 12 & -1 \\ 10 & 9 & 0 \\ -5 & 6 & -2 \end{bmatrix}$ 28. $\begin{bmatrix} -3 & 2 & 20 \\ -10 & 9 & 18 \\ 11 & 15 & 12 \end{bmatrix}$ 29. $\begin{bmatrix} 15 & 4 & -10 \\ -10 & 0 & 6 \\ -8 & 2 & -14 \end{bmatrix}$

AREA OF A TRIANGLE Find the area of the triangle with the given vertices.

30. $A(0, 1)$, $B(2, 7)$, $C(5, 5)$ **31.** $A(3, 6)$, $B(3, 0)$, $C(1, 3)$

32. $A(6, -1)$, $B(2, 2)$, $C(4, 8)$ **33.** $A(-4, 2)$, $B(3, -1)$, $C(-2, -2)$

34. $A(2, -6)$, $B(-1, -4)$, $C(0, 2)$ **35.** $A(1, 3)$, $B(-2, 6)$, $C(-1, 1)$

USING CRAMER'S RULE Use Cramer's rule to solve the linear system.

36. $2x + y = 3$
$5x + 6y = 4$

37. $7x - 5y = 11$
$3x + 10y = -56$

38. $9x + 2y = 7$
$4x - 3y = 42$

39. $x + 7y = -3$
$3x - 5y = 17$

40. $-x - 12y = 44$
$12x - 15y = -51$

41. $4x - 3y = 18$
$8x - 7y = 34$

42. $4x - 5y = 13$
$2x - 7y = 24$

43. $8x - 9y = 32$
$-5x + 7y = 40$

44. $3x + 10y = 50$
$12x + 15y = 64$

SOLVING SYSTEMS Use Cramer's rule to solve the linear system.

45. $x + 2y - 3z = -2$
$x - y + z = -1$
$3x + 4y - 4z = 4$

46. $x + 3y - z = 1$
$-2x - 6y + z = -3$
$3x + 5y - 2z = 4$

47. $3x + 2y - 5z = -10$
$6x - z = 8$
$-y + 3z = -2$

48. $x + 2y + z = 9$
$x + y + z = 3$
$5x - 2z = -1$

49. $4x + y + 6z = 7$
$3x + 3y + 2z = 17$
$-x - y + z = -9$

50. $x + 4y - z = -7$
$2x - y + 2z = 15$
$-3x + y - 3z = -22$

51. $2x + y + z = 5$
$x + 4y - 2z = 9$
$6x + 5y = 16$

52. $-x + 2y + 7z = 13$
$2x - y - 2z = -2$
$3x + 5y + 2z = -14$

53. $-3x + y + 2z = -14$
$9x - y + 2z = -8$
$8x + 5y - 4z = 6$

54. 🌐 **BIRDS** Black-necked stilts are birds that live throughout Florida and surrounding areas but breed mostly in the triangular region shown on the map. Estimate the area of this region. The coordinates given are measured in miles.

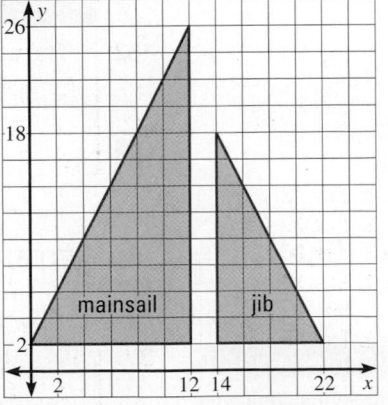

Each tick mark represents 50 miles.

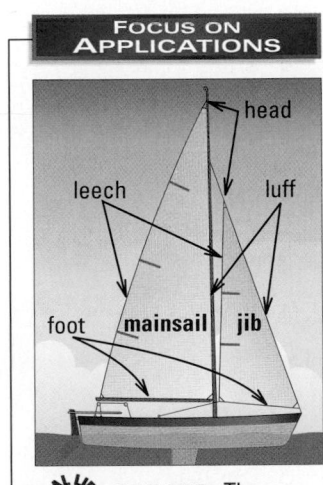

head

leech   luff

foot   **mainsail**   **jib**

SAILING The edges of a sail are called the luff, leech, and foot. The luff length of the jib is usually 80% to 90% of the distance from the deck to the head of the jib.

🌐 **SAILING** In Exercises 55–57, use the following information.

On a Marconi-rigged sloop, there are two triangular sails, a mainsail and a jib. These sails are shown in a coordinate plane at the right. The coordinates in the plane are measured in feet.

55. Find the area of the mainsail shown.

56. Find the area of the jib shown.

57. Suppose you are making a scale model of the sailboat with the sails shown using a scale of 1 in. = 6 ft. What is the area of the model's mainsail?

58. **SOCIAL STUDIES** **CONNECTION**   The Golden Triangle refers to a large triangular region in India. The Taj Mahal is one of the many wonders that lie within the boundaries of this triangle. The triangle is formed by imaginary lines that connect the cities of New Delhi, Jaipur, and Agra. Use the coordinates on the map and a determinant to estimate the area of the Golden Triangle. The coordinates given are measured in miles.

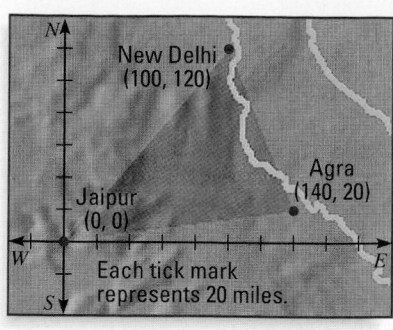

59. 🌐 **BUYING GASOLINE** You fill up your car with 10 gallons of premium gasoline and fill a small gas can with 2 gallons of regular gasoline for your lawn mower. You pay the cashier $13.56. The price of premium gasoline is 12 cents more per gallon than the price of regular gasoline. Use a linear system and Cramer's rule to find the price per gallon for regular and premium gasoline.

60. **SCIENCE** **CONNECTION**   The atomic weights of three compounds are shown.

Compound	Formula	Atomic weight
Tetrasulphur tetranitride	S_4N_4	184
Sulphur hexaflouride	SF_6	146
Dinitrogen tetraflouride	N_2F_4	104

Use a linear system and Cramer's rule to find the atomic weights of sulphur (S), nitrogen (N), and flourine (F).

61. **LOGICAL REASONING** Explain what happens to the determinant of a matrix when you switch two rows or two columns.

Test Preparation

QUANTITATIVE COMPARISON In Exercises 62 and 63, choose the statement that is true about the given quantities.

Ⓐ The quantity in column A is greater.

Ⓑ The quantity in column B is greater.

Ⓒ The two quantities are equal.

Ⓓ The relationship cannot be determined from the given information.

	Column A	Column B
62.	The area of a triangle with vertices $(-3, 4)$, $(4, 2)$, and $(1, -2)$	The area of a triangle with vertices $(4, 2)$, $(1, -2)$, and $(3, -4)$
63.	$\det \begin{bmatrix} -5 & 6 \\ -2 & 10 \end{bmatrix}$	$\det \begin{bmatrix} -7 & 1 \\ 3 & 5 \end{bmatrix}$

★ **Challenge**

64. **DETERMINANT RELATIONSHIPS** Let $A = \begin{bmatrix} 2 & -1 \\ 3 & 2 \end{bmatrix}$ and $B = \begin{bmatrix} 3 & 5 \\ -2 & -4 \end{bmatrix}$.

a. How is det AB related to det A and det B?

EXTRA CHALLENGE

www.mcdougallittell.com

b. How is det kA related to det A if k is a constant? Check your answer using matrix B and several other 2×2 matrices.

MIXED REVIEW

EVALUATING FUNCTIONS Find the indicated value of $f(x)$. (Review 2.1)

65. $f(x) = x - 10, f(7)$

66. $f(x) = 3x + 7, f(-2)$

67. $f(x) = -x^2 + 5, f(-1)$

68. $f(x) = x^2 - 2x - 4, f(7)$

69. $f(x) = x^2 + 4x - 1, f\left(\frac{1}{2}\right)$

70. $f(x) = x^5 - 2x - 10, f(3)$

GRAPHING SYSTEMS Graph the system of linear inequalities. (Review 3.3)

71. $x < 3$
$x > -2$

72. $y \geq 2x - 3$
$y > -5x - 8$

73. $y > -x - 5$
$y > 3x + 1$

74. $x + y > 3$
$4x + y < 4$

75. $2x - y \geq 2$
$5x - y \geq 2$

76. $4x - 3y > 1$
$-x + y \geq 4$

MULTIPLYING MATRICES Find the product. (Review 4.2 for 4.4)

77. $\begin{bmatrix} -2 & -4 \\ 5 & 1 \end{bmatrix} \begin{bmatrix} 6 & -1 \\ 3 & -3 \end{bmatrix}$

78. $\begin{bmatrix} 7 & -1 \\ 4 & -10 \end{bmatrix} \begin{bmatrix} 0 & -3 \\ 4 & 8 \end{bmatrix}$

79. $\begin{bmatrix} 11 & -2 \\ 0 & 4 \end{bmatrix} \begin{bmatrix} -8 & 3 \\ 8 & -1 \end{bmatrix}$

80. $\begin{bmatrix} 3 & -5 \\ -7 & 2 \end{bmatrix} \begin{bmatrix} 10 & 9 \\ 12 & 16 \end{bmatrix}$

81. $\begin{bmatrix} 0.5 & 3 \\ 0.2 & 1 \end{bmatrix} \begin{bmatrix} 0 & 0.6 \\ 4 & 0.8 \end{bmatrix}$

82. $\begin{bmatrix} -2 & 1.3 \\ 1.5 & -3 \end{bmatrix} \begin{bmatrix} 1.6 & 6 \\ -4 & 1.9 \end{bmatrix}$

QUIZ 1

Self-Test for Lessons 4.1–4.3

Perform the indicated operation(s). (Lessons 4.1, 4.2)

1. $\begin{bmatrix} -2 & 5 & 10 \\ 4 & -6 & 8 \end{bmatrix} + \begin{bmatrix} -3 & -1 & 5 \\ -2 & -8 & -7 \end{bmatrix}$

2. $\begin{bmatrix} -8 & 0 \\ 5 & -2 \end{bmatrix} - \begin{bmatrix} -3 & 7 \\ 5 & -1 \end{bmatrix}$

3. $-2 \begin{bmatrix} 7 & -2 \\ 4 & 9 \end{bmatrix} + 2 \begin{bmatrix} 6 & -3 \\ -5 & 3 \end{bmatrix}$

4. $\begin{bmatrix} 4 & -6 & 10 \\ 3 & 6 & 0 \\ 9 & -4 & 5 \end{bmatrix} - 4 \begin{bmatrix} 2 & -1 & -3 \\ 0 & 6 & -5 \\ -2 & 0 & 1 \end{bmatrix}$

5. $\begin{bmatrix} 8 & -1 \\ 6 & -2 \end{bmatrix} \begin{bmatrix} 3 & 7 \\ -2 & 0 \end{bmatrix}$

6. $\begin{bmatrix} 2 & -1 & 3 \\ 2 & 4 & 0 \end{bmatrix} \begin{bmatrix} 1 & 0 \\ 9 & -3 \\ 4 & -6 \end{bmatrix}$

Evaluate the determinant of the matrix. (Lesson 4.3)

7. $\begin{bmatrix} -4 & 3 \\ -6 & 2 \end{bmatrix}$

8. $\begin{bmatrix} 9 & -3 \\ 6 & -2 \end{bmatrix}$

9. $\begin{bmatrix} -1 & 2 & 3 \\ 5 & 0 & -2 \\ 6 & 8 & 1 \end{bmatrix}$

10. $\begin{bmatrix} 12 & 5 & -6 \\ 2 & 2 & 3 \\ 1 & 0 & -3 \end{bmatrix}$

Use Cramer's rule to solve the linear system. (Lesson 4.3)

11. $-8x + y = -6$
$-5x + 4y = 3$

12. $3x - 2y = 10$
$-6x + y = -7$

13. $5x + 4y = 12$
$3x - 6y = 3$

14. $4x + y + 6z = 2$
$2x + 2y + 4z = 1$
$-x - y + z = -5$

15. $x + y + 4z = 7$
$2x - 3y - z = -24$
$-4x + 2y + 2z = 8$

16. $3x + 3y - 2z = -18$
$-5x - 2y - 3z = -1$
$7x + y + 6z = 14$

17. 🌍 **GARDENING** You are planning to turn a triangular region of your yard into a garden. The vertices of the triangle are (0, 0), (5, 2), and (3, 6) where the coordinates are measured in feet. Find the area of the triangular region. (**Lesson 4.3**)

Investigating Identity and Inverse Matrices

▶ **QUESTION** What are some properties of identity and inverse matrices?

▶ **EXPLORING THE CONCEPT**

1 Let $A = \begin{bmatrix} 1 & 3 \\ 2 & 5 \end{bmatrix}$, $B = \begin{bmatrix} -4 & 0 \\ -7 & 6 \end{bmatrix}$, and $C = \begin{bmatrix} 0.1 & 0.8 \\ 0.6 & 0.3 \end{bmatrix}$. Consider the 2 × 2 *identity matrix* $I = \begin{bmatrix} 1 & 0 \\ 0 & 1 \end{bmatrix}$. Find AI, BI, and CI. What do you notice?

2 Find IA, IB, and IC using the matrices from **Step 1**. Is multiplication by the identity matrix commutative?

3 Let $D = \begin{bmatrix} 7 & 5 \\ 4 & 3 \end{bmatrix}$. The *inverse* of D is $E = \begin{bmatrix} 3 & -5 \\ -4 & 7 \end{bmatrix}$. Find DE and ED. What do you notice?

4 Use matrix multiplication to decide which of the following is the inverse of the matrix A in **Step 1**: $\begin{bmatrix} 5 & -3 \\ -2 & 1 \end{bmatrix}$, $\begin{bmatrix} -5 & 3 \\ 2 & -1 \end{bmatrix}$, or $\begin{bmatrix} -1 & 2 \\ 3 & -5 \end{bmatrix}$.

▶ **DRAWING CONCLUSIONS**

1. For any 2 × 2 matrix A, what is true of the products AI and IA where I is the 2 × 2 identity matrix? Justify your answer mathematically.

(*Hint:* Let $A = \begin{bmatrix} a & b \\ c & d \end{bmatrix}$, and compute AI and IA.)

2. How is the relationship between $I = \begin{bmatrix} 1 & 0 \\ 0 & 1 \end{bmatrix}$ and other 2 × 2 matrices similar to the relationship between 1 and other real numbers?

3. What do you think is the identity matrix for the set of 3 × 3 matrices? Check your answer by multiplying your proposed identity matrix by several 3 × 3 matrices.

4. What is the relationship between a matrix, its inverse, and the identity matrix? How is this relationship like the one that exists between a nonzero real number, its reciprocal, and 1?

5. Does every nonzero matrix have an inverse? Explain. (*Hint:* Consider a 2 × 2 matrix whose first row contains all nonzero entries and whose second row contains all zero entries.)

6. Find the inverse of $F = \begin{bmatrix} 2 & 7 \\ 1 & 4 \end{bmatrix}$ by finding values of a, b, c, and d such that

$$\begin{bmatrix} 2 & 7 \\ 1 & 4 \end{bmatrix} \begin{bmatrix} a & b \\ c & d \end{bmatrix} = \begin{bmatrix} 1 & 0 \\ 0 & 1 \end{bmatrix}.$$

4.4

Identity and Inverse Matrices

What you should learn

GOAL 1 Find and use inverse matrices.

GOAL 2 Use inverse matrices in **real-life** situations, such as encoding a message in **Example 5**.

Why you should learn it

▼ To solve **real-life** problems, such as decoding names of landmarks in **Exs. 44–48**.

The artist Jim Sanborn uses cryptograms in his work, such as *Kryptos* above.

GOAL 1 USING INVERSE MATRICES

The number 1 is the multiplicative identity for real numbers because $1 \cdot a = a$ and $a \cdot 1 = a$. For matrices, the $n \times n$ **identity matrix** is the matrix that has 1's on the main diagonal and 0's elsewhere.

2 × 2 IDENTITY MATRIX

$$I = \begin{bmatrix} 1 & 0 \\ 0 & 1 \end{bmatrix}$$

3 × 3 IDENTITY MATRIX

$$I = \begin{bmatrix} 1 & 0 & 0 \\ 0 & 1 & 0 \\ 0 & 0 & 1 \end{bmatrix}$$

If A is any $n \times n$ matrix and I is the $n \times n$ identity matrix, then $IA = A$ and $AI = A$.

Two $n \times n$ matrices are **inverses** of each other if their product (in *both* orders) is the $n \times n$ identity matrix. For example, matrices A and B below are inverses of each other.

$$AB = \begin{bmatrix} 3 & -1 \\ -5 & 2 \end{bmatrix} \begin{bmatrix} 2 & 1 \\ 5 & 3 \end{bmatrix} = \begin{bmatrix} 1 & 0 \\ 0 & 1 \end{bmatrix} = I \quad BA = \begin{bmatrix} 2 & 1 \\ 5 & 3 \end{bmatrix} \begin{bmatrix} 3 & -1 \\ -5 & 2 \end{bmatrix} = \begin{bmatrix} 1 & 0 \\ 0 & 1 \end{bmatrix} = I$$

The symbol used for the inverse of A is A^{-1}.

THE INVERSE OF A 2 X 2 MATRIX

The inverse of the matrix $A = \begin{bmatrix} a & b \\ c & d \end{bmatrix}$ is

$$A^{-1} = \frac{1}{|A|} \begin{bmatrix} d & -b \\ -c & a \end{bmatrix} = \frac{1}{ad - cb} \begin{bmatrix} d & -b \\ -c & a \end{bmatrix} \text{ provided } ad - cb \neq 0.$$

EXAMPLE 1 *Finding the Inverse of a 2 × 2 Matrix*

Find the inverse of $A = \begin{bmatrix} 3 & 1 \\ 4 & 2 \end{bmatrix}$.

SOLUTION

$$A^{-1} = \frac{1}{6 - 4} \begin{bmatrix} 2 & -1 \\ -4 & 3 \end{bmatrix} = \frac{1}{2} \begin{bmatrix} 2 & -1 \\ -4 & 3 \end{bmatrix} = \begin{bmatrix} 1 & -\frac{1}{2} \\ -2 & \frac{3}{2} \end{bmatrix}$$

✓ **CHECK** You can check the inverse by showing that $AA^{-1} = I = A^{-1}A$.

$$\begin{bmatrix} 3 & 1 \\ 4 & 2 \end{bmatrix} \begin{bmatrix} 1 & -\frac{1}{2} \\ -2 & \frac{3}{2} \end{bmatrix} = \begin{bmatrix} 1 & 0 \\ 0 & 1 \end{bmatrix} \text{ and } \begin{bmatrix} 1 & -\frac{1}{2} \\ -2 & \frac{3}{2} \end{bmatrix} \begin{bmatrix} 3 & 1 \\ 4 & 2 \end{bmatrix} = \begin{bmatrix} 1 & 0 \\ 0 & 1 \end{bmatrix}$$

STUDENT HELP

► **Look Back**
For help with multiplicative inverses of real numbers, see p. 5.

EXAMPLE 2 *Solving a Matrix Equation*

Solve the matrix equation $AX = B$ for the 2×2 matrix X.

$$\overbrace{\begin{bmatrix} 4 & -1 \\ -3 & 1 \end{bmatrix}}^{A} X = \overbrace{\begin{bmatrix} 8 & -5 \\ -6 & 3 \end{bmatrix}}^{B}$$

SOLUTION

Begin by finding the inverse of A.

$$A^{-1} = \frac{1}{4-3} \begin{bmatrix} 1 & 1 \\ 3 & 4 \end{bmatrix} = \begin{bmatrix} 1 & 1 \\ 3 & 4 \end{bmatrix}$$

To solve the equation for X, multiply both sides of the equation by A^{-1} *on the left.*

$$\begin{bmatrix} 1 & 1 \\ 3 & 4 \end{bmatrix}\begin{bmatrix} 4 & -1 \\ -3 & 1 \end{bmatrix} X = \begin{bmatrix} 1 & 1 \\ 3 & 4 \end{bmatrix}\begin{bmatrix} 8 & -5 \\ -6 & 3 \end{bmatrix} \qquad \textbf{\textit{A}}^{-1}\textbf{\textit{AX}} = \textbf{\textit{A}}^{-1}\textbf{\textit{B}}$$

$$\begin{bmatrix} 1 & 0 \\ 0 & 1 \end{bmatrix} X = \begin{bmatrix} 2 & -2 \\ 0 & -3 \end{bmatrix} \qquad \textbf{\textit{IX}} = \textbf{\textit{A}}^{-1}\textbf{\textit{B}}$$

$$X = \begin{bmatrix} 2 & -2 \\ 0 & -3 \end{bmatrix} \qquad \textbf{\textit{X}} = \textbf{\textit{A}}^{-1}\textbf{\textit{B}}$$

✓**CHECK** You can check the solution by multiplying A and X to see if you get B.

· · · · · · · · · ·

Some matrices do not have an inverse. You can tell whether a matrix has an inverse by evaluating its determinant. If det $A = 0$, then A does not have an inverse. If det $A \neq 0$, then A has an inverse.

The inverse of a 3×3 matrix is difficult to compute by hand. A calculator that will compute inverse matrices is useful in this case.

EXAMPLE 3 *Finding the Inverse of a 3 × 3 Matrix*

Use a graphing calculator to find the inverse of A. Then use the calculator to verify your result.

$$A = \begin{bmatrix} 1 & -1 & 0 \\ 1 & 0 & -1 \\ 6 & -2 & -3 \end{bmatrix}$$

SOLUTION

Enter the matrix A into the graphing calculator and calculate A^{-1}. Then compute AA^{-1} and $A^{-1}A$ to verify that you obtain the 3×3 identity matrix.

```
[A]-1
  [[-2 -3 1]
   [-3 -3 1]
   [-2 -4 1]]
```

```
[A][A]-1
  [[1 0 0]
   [0 1 0]
   [0 0 1]]
```

```
[A]-1[A]
  [[1 0 0]
   [0 1 0]
   [0 0 1]]
```

GOAL 2 USING INVERSE MATRICES IN REAL LIFE

A *cryptogram* is a message written according to a secret code. (The Greek word *kruptos* means *hidden* and the Greek word *gramma* means *letter*.) The following technique uses matrices to encode and decode messages.

First assign a number to each letter in the alphabet with 0 assigned to a blank space.

__ = 0	E = 5	J = 10	O = 15	T = 20	Y = 25
A = 1	F = 6	K = 11	P = 16	U = 21	Z = 26
B = 2	G = 7	L = 12	Q = 17	V = 22	
C = 3	H = 8	M = 13	R = 18	W = 23	
D = 4	I = 9	N = 14	S = 19	X = 24	

Then convert the message to numbers partitioned into 1×2 *uncoded row matrices*.

To *encode* a message, choose a 2×2 matrix A that has an inverse and multiply the uncoded row matrices by A *on the right* to obtain *coded row matrices*.

Cryptography

EXAMPLE 4 *Converting a Message*

Use the list above to convert the message GET HELP to row matrices.

SOLUTION

$$\begin{matrix} \text{G} & \text{E} & \text{T} & \_\_ & \text{H} & \text{E} & \text{L} & \text{P} \\ \begin{bmatrix} 7 & 5 \end{bmatrix} & & \begin{bmatrix} 20 & 0 \end{bmatrix} & & \begin{bmatrix} 8 & 5 \end{bmatrix} & & \begin{bmatrix} 12 & 16 \end{bmatrix} \end{matrix}$$

NAVAJO CODE During World War II, a Marine Corps code based on the complex Navajo language was used to send messages.

APPLICATION LINK
www.mcdougallittell.com

EXAMPLE 5 *Encoding a Message*

CRYPTOGRAPHY Use $A = \begin{bmatrix} 2 & 3 \\ -1 & -2 \end{bmatrix}$ to encode the message GET HELP.

SOLUTION

The coded row matrices are obtained by multiplying each of the uncoded row matrices from Example 4 by the matrix A *on the right*.

UNCODED ROW MATRIX	ENCODING MATRIX A	CODED ROW MATRIX

$$\begin{bmatrix} 7 & 5 \end{bmatrix} \begin{bmatrix} 2 & 3 \\ -1 & -2 \end{bmatrix} = \begin{bmatrix} 9 & 11 \end{bmatrix}$$

$$\begin{bmatrix} 20 & 0 \end{bmatrix} \begin{bmatrix} 2 & 3 \\ -1 & -2 \end{bmatrix} = \begin{bmatrix} 40 & 60 \end{bmatrix}$$

$$\begin{bmatrix} 8 & 5 \end{bmatrix} \begin{bmatrix} 2 & 3 \\ -1 & -2 \end{bmatrix} = \begin{bmatrix} 11 & 14 \end{bmatrix}$$

$$\begin{bmatrix} 12 & 16 \end{bmatrix} \begin{bmatrix} 2 & 3 \\ -1 & -2 \end{bmatrix} = \begin{bmatrix} 8 & 4 \end{bmatrix}$$

▶ The coded message is 9, 11, 40, 60, 11, 14, 8, 4.

DECODING USING MATRICES Decoding the cryptogram created in Example 5 would be difficult for people who do not know the matrix A. When larger coding matrices are used, decoding is even more difficult. But for an authorized receiver who knows the matrix A, decoding is simple. The receiver only needs to multiply the coded row matrices by A^{-1} *on the right* to retrieve the uncoded row matrices.

EXAMPLE 6 *Decoding a Message*

CRYPTOGRAPHY Use the inverse of $A = \begin{bmatrix} 3 & -1 \\ -2 & 1 \end{bmatrix}$ to decode this message:

$$-4, 3, -23, 12, -26, 13, 15, -5, 31, -5,$$
$$-38, 19, -21, 12, 20, 0, 75, -25$$

SOLUTION

First find A^{-1}: $\quad A^{-1} = \dfrac{1}{3-2} \begin{bmatrix} 1 & 1 \\ 2 & 3 \end{bmatrix} = \begin{bmatrix} 1 & 1 \\ 2 & 3 \end{bmatrix}$

To decode the message, partition it into groups of two numbers to form coded row matrices. Then multiply each coded row matrix by A^{-1} *on the right* to obtain the uncoded row matrices.

CODED ROW MATRIX	DECODING MATRIX A^{-1}		UNCODED ROW MATRIX
$\begin{bmatrix} -4 & 3 \end{bmatrix}$	$\begin{bmatrix} 1 & 1 \\ 2 & 3 \end{bmatrix}$	$=$	$\begin{bmatrix} 2 & 5 \end{bmatrix}$
$\begin{bmatrix} -23 & 12 \end{bmatrix}$	$\begin{bmatrix} 1 & 1 \\ 2 & 3 \end{bmatrix}$	$=$	$\begin{bmatrix} 1 & 13 \end{bmatrix}$
$\begin{bmatrix} -26 & 13 \end{bmatrix}$	$\begin{bmatrix} 1 & 1 \\ 2 & 3 \end{bmatrix}$	$=$	$\begin{bmatrix} 0 & 13 \end{bmatrix}$
$\begin{bmatrix} 15 & -5 \end{bmatrix}$	$\begin{bmatrix} 1 & 1 \\ 2 & 3 \end{bmatrix}$	$=$	$\begin{bmatrix} 5 & 0 \end{bmatrix}$
$\begin{bmatrix} 31 & -5 \end{bmatrix}$	$\begin{bmatrix} 1 & 1 \\ 2 & 3 \end{bmatrix}$	$=$	$\begin{bmatrix} 21 & 16 \end{bmatrix}$
$\begin{bmatrix} -38 & 19 \end{bmatrix}$	$\begin{bmatrix} 1 & 1 \\ 2 & 3 \end{bmatrix}$	$=$	$\begin{bmatrix} 0 & 19 \end{bmatrix}$
$\begin{bmatrix} -21 & 12 \end{bmatrix}$	$\begin{bmatrix} 1 & 1 \\ 2 & 3 \end{bmatrix}$	$=$	$\begin{bmatrix} 3 & 15 \end{bmatrix}$
$\begin{bmatrix} 20 & 0 \end{bmatrix}$	$\begin{bmatrix} 1 & 1 \\ 2 & 3 \end{bmatrix}$	$=$	$\begin{bmatrix} 20 & 20 \end{bmatrix}$
$\begin{bmatrix} 75 & -25 \end{bmatrix}$	$\begin{bmatrix} 1 & 1 \\ 2 & 3 \end{bmatrix}$	$=$	$\begin{bmatrix} 25 & 0 \end{bmatrix}$

From the uncoded row matrices you can read the message as follows.

$$\begin{bmatrix} 2 & 5 \end{bmatrix}\begin{bmatrix} 1 & 13 \end{bmatrix}\begin{bmatrix} 0 & 13 \end{bmatrix}\begin{bmatrix} 5 & 0 \end{bmatrix}\begin{bmatrix} 21 & 16 \end{bmatrix}\begin{bmatrix} 0 & 19 \end{bmatrix}\begin{bmatrix} 3 & 15 \end{bmatrix}\begin{bmatrix} 20 & 20 \end{bmatrix}\begin{bmatrix} 25 & 0 \end{bmatrix}$$
$$\text{B E A M \_ M E \_ U P \_ S C O T T Y \_}$$

GUIDED PRACTICE

Vocabulary Check ✔

Concept Check ✔

1. What is the identity matrix for 2×2 matrices? for 3×3 matrices?

2. For two 2×2 matrices A and B to be inverses of each other, what must be true of AB and BA?

3. Explain how to find the inverse of a 2×2 matrix.

4. How do you know that the matrix X in Example 2 must be 2×2?

5. If $B = \begin{bmatrix} 8 & -4 \\ -2 & 1 \end{bmatrix}$, does B have an inverse? Explain.

Skill Check ✔ **Find the inverse of the matrix.**

6. $\begin{bmatrix} -4 & 3 \\ -3 & 2 \end{bmatrix}$
7. $\begin{bmatrix} -3 & 2 \\ 0 & -1 \end{bmatrix}$
8. $\begin{bmatrix} -1 & 0 \\ 6 & 4 \end{bmatrix}$

9. $\begin{bmatrix} \frac{1}{2} & 4 \\ -2 & \frac{1}{4} \end{bmatrix}$
10. $\begin{bmatrix} 0.5 & 3 \\ 2.5 & 4 \end{bmatrix}$
11. $\begin{bmatrix} 1.6 & 2 \\ 3.2 & 0.2 \end{bmatrix}$

12. 🌐 **DECODING A MESSAGE** Use the coding information on pages 225 and 226 and the inverse of the matrix D to decode the following message.

$$D = \begin{bmatrix} -5 & 3 \\ -2 & 1 \end{bmatrix} \qquad -71, 39, -35, 20, -118, 69, -84, 49, -95, 57$$

PRACTICE AND APPLICATIONS

STUDENT HELP

▶ **Extra Practice**
to help you master
skills is on p. 945.

FINDING INVERSES **Find the inverse of the matrix.**

13. $\begin{bmatrix} 4 & -5 \\ -3 & 4 \end{bmatrix}$
14. $\begin{bmatrix} 6 & 2 \\ 8 & 3 \end{bmatrix}$
15. $\begin{bmatrix} 1 & 8 \\ 1 & 7 \end{bmatrix}$

16. $\begin{bmatrix} -6 & 17 \\ 1 & -3 \end{bmatrix}$
17. $\begin{bmatrix} 7 & 2 \\ 3 & 1 \end{bmatrix}$
18. $\begin{bmatrix} -7 & -2 \\ -4 & 1 \end{bmatrix}$

19. $\begin{bmatrix} -6 & -7 \\ 2 & 2 \end{bmatrix}$
20. $\begin{bmatrix} 5 & -4 \\ -4 & 4 \end{bmatrix}$
21. $\begin{bmatrix} 11 & -3 \\ -9 & 3 \end{bmatrix}$

22. $\begin{bmatrix} \frac{3}{2} & \frac{1}{2} \\ -2 & 1 \end{bmatrix}$
23. $\begin{bmatrix} 2.2 & 2.5 \\ 8 & 10 \end{bmatrix}$
24. $\begin{bmatrix} \frac{4}{5} & \frac{3}{4} \\ -1 & \frac{5}{2} \end{bmatrix}$

SOLVING EQUATIONS **Solve the matrix equation.**

25. $\begin{bmatrix} -5 & -13 \\ 0 & 5 \end{bmatrix} X = \begin{bmatrix} 3 & 1 \\ -4 & 0 \end{bmatrix}$
26. $\begin{bmatrix} 5 & -1 \\ 8 & 2 \end{bmatrix} X = \begin{bmatrix} 17 & 20 \\ 26 & 20 \end{bmatrix}$

STUDENT HELP

▶ **HOMEWORK HELP**
Example 1: Exs. 13–24, 33
Example 2: Exs. 25–32
Example 3: Exs. 34–39
Examples 4, 5: Exs. 40–43
Example 6: Exs. 44–48

27. $\begin{bmatrix} 2 & 4 \\ 0 & 1 \end{bmatrix} X = \begin{bmatrix} 4 & 0 & 6 \\ 3 & -1 & 5 \end{bmatrix}$
28. $\begin{bmatrix} -5 & -3 \\ 4 & 1 \end{bmatrix} X = \begin{bmatrix} -12 & -5 & 18 \\ 4 & -3 & -13 \end{bmatrix}$

29. $\begin{bmatrix} 3 & 7 \\ 1 & 4 \end{bmatrix} X + \begin{bmatrix} 8 & 5 \\ 1 & 15 \end{bmatrix} = \begin{bmatrix} 7 & -3 \\ -2 & -9 \end{bmatrix}$
30. $\begin{bmatrix} -7 & -9 \\ 4 & 5 \end{bmatrix} X + \begin{bmatrix} 3 & 4 \\ 4 & -3 \end{bmatrix} = \begin{bmatrix} 1 & 9 \\ 6 & -6 \end{bmatrix}$

31. $\begin{bmatrix} -1 & 2 \\ -4 & 6 \end{bmatrix} X - \begin{bmatrix} 2 & 1 \\ 3 & 0 \end{bmatrix} = \begin{bmatrix} 3 & -2 \\ 1 & -1 \end{bmatrix}$
32. $\begin{bmatrix} 4 & -3 \\ 6 & -2 \end{bmatrix} X - \begin{bmatrix} -1 & 1 \\ 5 & 7 \end{bmatrix} = \begin{bmatrix} 4 & 6 \\ 8 & 2 \end{bmatrix}$

IDENTIFYING INVERSES Tell whether the matrices are inverses of each other.

33. $\begin{bmatrix} 10 & -3 \\ 3 & -1 \end{bmatrix}$ and $\begin{bmatrix} 1 & 3 \\ 3 & -10 \end{bmatrix}$

34. $\begin{bmatrix} 0 & 2 & -1 \\ 5 & 2 & 3 \\ 7 & 3 & 4 \end{bmatrix}$ and $\begin{bmatrix} -2 & -10 & 8 \\ 11 & 7 & -5 \\ 1 & 12 & -10 \end{bmatrix}$

35. $\begin{bmatrix} 11 & 2 & -8 \\ 4 & 1 & -3 \\ -8 & -1 & 6 \end{bmatrix}$ and $\begin{bmatrix} 3 & -4 & 2 \\ 0 & 2 & 1 \\ 4 & -5 & 3 \end{bmatrix}$

36. $\begin{bmatrix} 10 & 2 & -25 \\ 4 & 1 & -10 \\ -9 & -2 & 23 \end{bmatrix}$ and $\begin{bmatrix} 3 & 4 & 5 \\ -2 & 5 & 0 \\ 1 & 2 & 2 \end{bmatrix}$

FINDING INVERSES Use a graphing calculator to find the inverse of the matrix *A*. Check the result by showing that $AA^{-1} = I$ and $A^{-1}A = I$.

37. $A = \begin{bmatrix} -3 & 4 & 5 \\ 1 & 5 & 0 \\ 5 & 2 & 2 \end{bmatrix}$

38. $A = \begin{bmatrix} -7 & 0 & -6 \\ -4 & 1 & 3 \\ 11 & -3 & -9 \end{bmatrix}$

39. $A = \begin{bmatrix} 2 & 1 & -2 \\ 5 & 3 & 0 \\ 4 & 3 & 8 \end{bmatrix}$

ENCODING Use the code on page 225 and the matrix to encode the message.

40. JOB WELL DONE

$A = \begin{bmatrix} 1 & -2 \\ -2 & 5 \end{bmatrix}$

41. STAY THERE

$A = \begin{bmatrix} 1 & 2 \\ 1 & 3 \end{bmatrix}$

42. COME TO DINNER

$A = \begin{bmatrix} 4 & -1 \\ -3 & 1 \end{bmatrix}$

43. HAPPY BIRTHDAY

$A = \begin{bmatrix} 5 & -2 \\ -4 & 2 \end{bmatrix}$

🌎 **TRAVEL** In Exercises 44–48, use the following information.

Your friend is traveling abroad and is sending you postcards with encoded messages. You must decipher what landmarks your friend has visited. Use the inverse of matrix *D* to decode each message. Each message represents a landmark in the country where your friend is traveling. Use the coding information on pages 225 and 226 to help you.

$$D = \begin{bmatrix} 2 & -3 \\ -1 & 2 \end{bmatrix}$$

44. $-1, 4, 30, -41, 39, -58, 22, -33, 31, -46, 23, -34, 1, 1$

45. $21, -31, 22, -26, -9, 19, -20, 40, -3, 11, 20, -24, 10, -15$

46. $39, -58, -2, 12, 0, 9, -19, 38, 13, -9, -16, 33, 10, -15$

47. $32, -44, 10, -15, -4, 15, 9, -13, 40, -60, 22, -25, 7, -6, 4, 6$

48. Using the decoded messages, tell what country your friend is visiting.

STUDENT HELP

▶ **Skills Review**
For help with transformations, see p. 921.

49. **GEOMETRY ▸ CONNECTION** Use the matrices shown. The columns of matrix *T* give the coordinates of the vertices of a triangle. Matrix *A* is a transformation matrix.

$$A = \begin{bmatrix} 0 & -1 \\ 1 & 0 \end{bmatrix} \qquad T = \begin{bmatrix} 1 & 2 & 3 \\ 1 & 4 & 2 \end{bmatrix}$$

a. Find *AT* and *AAT*. Then draw the original triangle and the two transformed triangles. What transformation does *A* represent?

b. Suppose you start with the triangle determined by *AAT* and want to reverse the transformation process to produce the triangle determined by *AT* and then the triangle determined by *T*. Describe how you can do this.

50. *Writing* Describe the process used to solve a matrix equation.

51. MULTIPLE CHOICE What is the inverse of $\begin{bmatrix} -2 & -2 \\ 7 & 6 \end{bmatrix}$?

(A) $\begin{bmatrix} \dfrac{3}{13} & -\dfrac{1}{13} \\ \dfrac{7}{26} & -\dfrac{1}{13} \end{bmatrix}$
(B) $\begin{bmatrix} -3 & 1 \\ -\dfrac{7}{2} & 1 \end{bmatrix}$
(C) $\begin{bmatrix} \dfrac{3}{13} & -\dfrac{1}{13} \\ -\dfrac{7}{26} & \dfrac{1}{13} \end{bmatrix}$
(D) $\begin{bmatrix} 3 & 1 \\ -\dfrac{7}{2} & -1 \end{bmatrix}$

52. MULTIPLE CHOICE What is the solution of $\begin{bmatrix} 5 & 2 \\ 3 & 1 \end{bmatrix} X = \begin{bmatrix} 4 & 43 \\ 2 & 25 \end{bmatrix}$?

(A) $\begin{bmatrix} 0 & 7 \\ 2 & 4 \end{bmatrix}$
(B) $\begin{bmatrix} 0 & 7 \\ -2 & 4 \end{bmatrix}$
(C) $\begin{bmatrix} 0 & 2 \\ 7 & 4 \end{bmatrix}$
(D) $\begin{bmatrix} 0 & 4 \\ 2 & 7 \end{bmatrix}$
(E) $\begin{bmatrix} 0 & 7 \\ 4 & 2 \end{bmatrix}$

★ **Challenge**

53. 🌐 **CODE BREAKER** You are a code breaker and intercept the encoded message
$45, -35, 38, -30, 18, -18, 35, -30, 81, -60, 42, -28, 75, -55, 2, -2, 22,$
$-21, 15, -10$ that you know is being sent to someone named John. You can
conclude that $\begin{bmatrix} 45 & -35 \end{bmatrix} A^{-1} = \begin{bmatrix} 10 & 15 \end{bmatrix}$ and $\begin{bmatrix} 38 & -30 \end{bmatrix} A^{-1} = \begin{bmatrix} 8 & 14 \end{bmatrix}$
where A^{-1} is the inverse of the encoding matrix A, 10 represents J, 15 represents
O, 8 represents H, and 14 represents N.

Let $A^{-1} = \begin{bmatrix} w & x \\ y & z \end{bmatrix}$.

a. Write and solve two systems of equations to find w, x, y, and z.

b. Find A^{-1}, and decode the rest of the message.

EXTRA CHALLENGE
www.mcdougallittell.com

MIXED REVIEW

SOLVING SYSTEMS Solve the system of linear equations using any algebraic method. (Review 3.2, 3.6 for 4.5)

54. $3x + 5y = 12$
$x + 4y = 11$

55. $4x - 12y = 2$
$-2x + 6y = -1$

56. $-5x + 7y = 33$
$4x - 9y = -40$

57. $7x + y + 3z = 22$
$2x - 2y + 9z = -10$
$-3x - 5y - 10z = 8$

58. $x + 3z = 6$
$-2x + 3y + z = -11$
$3x - y + 2z = 13$

59. $2x + y - 4z = 4$
$4x - 3y + 8z = -8$
$-2x + 7y - 12z = 24$

MATRIX OPERATIONS Perform the indicated operation, if possible. If not possible, state the reason. (Review 4.1)

60. $\begin{bmatrix} -4 & 2 \\ -5 & -1 \end{bmatrix} + \begin{bmatrix} 4 & -3 \\ -2 & 0 \end{bmatrix}$

61. $\begin{bmatrix} 8 & -6 \\ -2 & 5 \end{bmatrix} - \begin{bmatrix} -2 & -3 & -5 \\ 2 & -1 & 3 \end{bmatrix}$

62. $-8 \begin{bmatrix} -1 & 3 & 4 \\ -6 & 8 & 0 \end{bmatrix}$

63. $\begin{bmatrix} 7 & -5 & 8 \\ -9 & 13 & 16 \end{bmatrix} - \begin{bmatrix} -10 & -2 & 9 \\ -9 & -12 & -15 \end{bmatrix}$

64. $\begin{bmatrix} 6 & -2 & -1 \\ -3 & 5 & 4 \end{bmatrix} + \begin{bmatrix} 3 & 4 & -1 \\ -2 & 8 & -9 \end{bmatrix}$

65. $\dfrac{1}{2} \begin{bmatrix} 4 & 10 & 2 \\ 6 & 8 & 16 \end{bmatrix}$

66. 🌐 **CATERING** You are in charge of catering for a school function. To limit the cost, you will serve only two entrees. One is a vegetarian dish that costs $6 and the other is a chicken dish that costs $8. If there will be 150 people at the function and your budget for the food is $1000, how many of each type of entree will be served? (Review 3.1, 3.2)

4.4 *Identity and Inverse Matrices* **229**

4.5 Solving Systems Using Inverse Matrices

What you should learn

GOAL 1 Solve systems of linear equations using inverse matrices.

GOAL 2 Use systems of linear equations to solve **real-life** problems, such as determining how much money to invest in **Example 4**.

Why you should learn it

▼ To solve **real-life** problems, such as planning a stained glass project in **Ex. 42**.

GOAL 1 SOLVING SYSTEMS USING MATRICES

In Lesson 4.3 you learned how to solve a system of linear equations using Cramer's rule. Here you will learn to solve a system using inverse matrices.

> **⊙ ACTIVITY**
> **Developing Concepts**
> **Investigating Matrix Equations**
>
> **1** Write the left side of the matrix equation as a single matrix. Then equate corresponding entries of the matrices. What do you obtain?
>
> $$\begin{bmatrix} 5 & -4 \\ 1 & 2 \end{bmatrix}\begin{bmatrix} x \\ y \end{bmatrix} = \begin{bmatrix} 8 \\ 6 \end{bmatrix}$$ **Matrix equation**
>
> **2** Use what you learned in **Step 1** to write the following linear system as a matrix equation.
>
> $2x - y = -4$ **Equation 1**
> $-4x + 9y = 1$ **Equation 2**

In the activity you learned that a linear system can be written as a matrix equation $AX = B$. The matrix A is the coefficient matrix of the system, X is the **matrix of variables**, and B is the **matrix of constants**.

EXAMPLE 1 *Writing a Matrix Equation*

Write the system of linear equations as a matrix equation.

$$-3x + 4y = 5 \qquad \text{Equation 1}$$
$$2x - y = -10 \qquad \text{Equation 2}$$

SOLUTION

$$\overset{A}{\begin{bmatrix} -3 & 4 \\ 2 & -1 \end{bmatrix}} \overset{X}{\begin{bmatrix} x \\ y \end{bmatrix}} = \overset{B}{\begin{bmatrix} 5 \\ -10 \end{bmatrix}}$$

Once you have written a linear system as $AX = B$, you can solve for X by multiplying each side of the matrix by A^{-1} *on the left.*

$$AX = B \qquad \text{Write original matrix equation.}$$
$$A^{-1}AX = A^{-1}B \qquad \text{Multiply each side by } \boldsymbol{A^{-1}}.$$
$$IX = A^{-1}B \qquad \boldsymbol{A^{-1}A = I}$$
$$X = A^{-1}B \qquad \boldsymbol{IX = X}$$

SOLUTION OF A LINEAR SYSTEM Let $AX = B$ represent a system of linear equations. If the determinant of A is nonzero, then the linear system has exactly one solution, which is $X = A^{-1}B$.

STUDENT HELP

➤ **Look Back**
For help with systems of linear equations, see p. 150.

EXAMPLE 2 *Solving a Linear System*

Use matrices to solve the linear system in Example 1.

$$-3x + 4y = 5 \qquad \textbf{Equation 1}$$
$$2x - y = -10 \qquad \textbf{Equation 2}$$

SOLUTION

Begin by writing the linear system in matrix form, as in Example 1. Then find the inverse of matrix A.

$$A^{-1} = \frac{1}{3-8}\begin{bmatrix} -1 & -4 \\ -2 & -3 \end{bmatrix} = \begin{bmatrix} \frac{1}{5} & \frac{4}{5} \\ \frac{2}{5} & \frac{3}{5} \end{bmatrix}$$

Finally, multiply the matrix of constants by A^{-1}.

$$X = A^{-1}B = \begin{bmatrix} \frac{1}{5} & \frac{4}{5} \\ \frac{2}{5} & \frac{3}{5} \end{bmatrix}\begin{bmatrix} 5 \\ -10 \end{bmatrix} = \begin{bmatrix} -7 \\ -4 \end{bmatrix} = \begin{bmatrix} x \\ y \end{bmatrix}$$

▶ The solution of the system is $(-7, -4)$. Check this solution in the original equations.

EXAMPLE 3 *Using a Graphing Calculator*

 Use a matrix equation and a graphing calculator to solve the linear system.

$$2x + 3y + z = -1 \qquad \textbf{Equation 1}$$
$$3x + 3y + z = 1 \qquad \textbf{Equation 2}$$
$$2x + 4y + z = -2 \qquad \textbf{Equation 3}$$

STUDENT HELP

➤ **Study Tip**
Remember that you can use the method shown in Examples 2 and 3 provided A has an inverse. If A does not have an inverse, then the system has either no solution or infinitely many solutions, and you should use a different technique.

SOLUTION

The matrix equation that represents the system is $\begin{bmatrix} 2 & 3 & 1 \\ 3 & 3 & 1 \\ 2 & 4 & 1 \end{bmatrix}\begin{bmatrix} x \\ y \\ z \end{bmatrix} = \begin{bmatrix} -1 \\ 1 \\ -2 \end{bmatrix}.$

Using a graphing calculator, you can solve the system as shown.

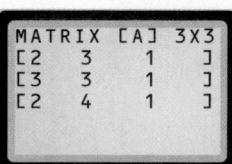

```
MATRIX [A] 3X3
[2    3    1   ]
[3    3    1   ]
[2    4    1   ]
```

```
MATRIX [B] 3X1
[-1         ]
[1          ]
[-2         ]
```

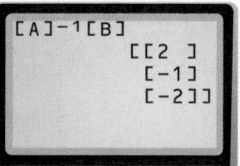

```
[A]-1[B]
            [[2 ]
             [-1]
             [-2]]
```

Enter matrix **A**.   Enter matrix **B**.   Multiply **B** by A^{-1}.

▶ The solution is $(2, -1, -2)$. Check this solution in the original equations.

GOAL 2 **USING LINEAR SYSTEMS IN REAL LIFE**

EXAMPLE 4   *Writing and Using a Linear System*

INVESTING You have $10,000 to invest. You want to invest the money in a stock mutual fund, a bond mutual fund, and a money market fund. The expected annual returns for these funds are given in the table.

You want your investment to obtain an overall annual return of 8%. A financial planner recommends that you invest the same amount in stocks as in bonds and the money market combined. How much should you invest in each fund?

Investment	Expected return
Stock mutual fund	10%
Bond mutual fund	7%
Money market (MM) fund	5%

SOLUTION

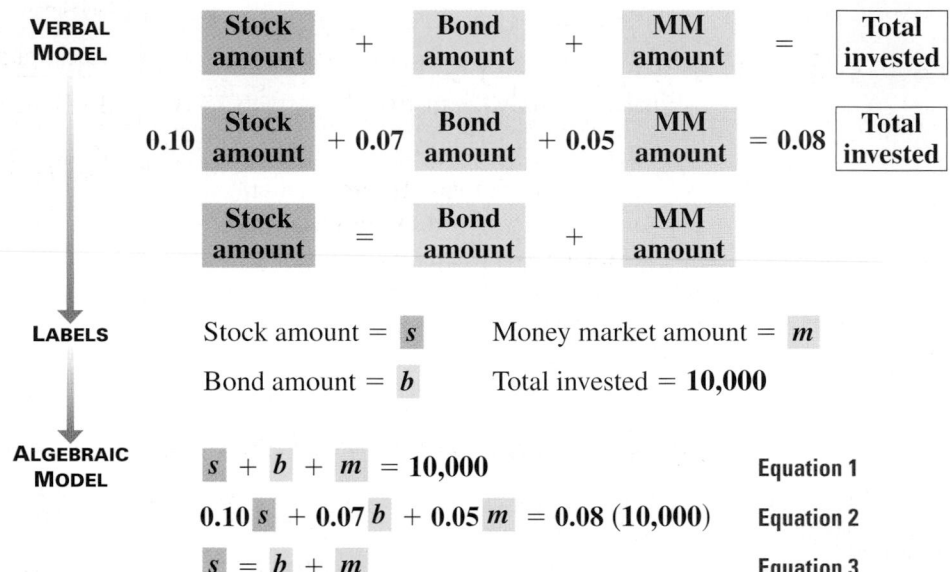

VERBAL MODEL

Stock amount	+	Bond amount	+	MM amount	=	Total invested

$$0.10 \text{ Stock amount} + 0.07 \text{ Bond amount} + 0.05 \text{ MM amount} = 0.08 \text{ Total invested}$$

Stock amount	=	Bond amount	+	MM amount

LABELS

Stock amount = s Money market amount = m

Bond amount = b Total invested = **10,000**

ALGEBRAIC MODEL

$s + b + m = 10,000$ **Equation 1**

$0.10\,s + 0.07\,b + 0.05\,m = 0.08\,(10,000)$ **Equation 2**

$s = b + m$ **Equation 3**

First rewrite the equations above in standard form and then in matrix form.

$$\begin{aligned} s + b + m &= 10,000 \\ 0.10s + 0.07b + 0.05m &= 800 \\ s - b - m &= 0 \end{aligned}$$

$$\begin{bmatrix} 1 & 1 & 1 \\ 0.1 & 0.07 & 0.05 \\ 1 & -1 & -1 \end{bmatrix} \begin{bmatrix} s \\ b \\ m \end{bmatrix} = \begin{bmatrix} 10,000 \\ 800 \\ 0 \end{bmatrix}$$

Enter the coefficient matrix A and the matrix of constants B into a graphing calculator. Then find the solution $X = A^{-1}B$.

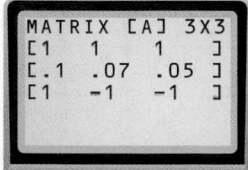

```
MATRIX [A] 3X3
[1    1    1    ]
[.1   .07  .05  ]
[1    -1   -1   ]
```

```
MATRIX [B] 3X1
[10000        ]
[800          ]
[0            ]
```

```
[A]⁻¹[B]
         [[5000]
          [2500]
          [2500]]
```

▶ You should invest $5000 in the stock mutual fund, $2500 in the bond mutual fund, and $2500 in the money market fund.

GUIDED PRACTICE

Vocabulary Check ✔

1. What are a matrix of variables and a matrix of constants, and how are they used to solve a system of linear equations?

Concept Check ✔

2. If $|A| \neq 0$, what is the solution of $AX = B$ in terms of A and B?

3. Explain why the solution of $AX = B$ is *not* $X = BA^{-1}$.

Skill Check ✔

Write the linear system as a matrix equation.

4. $x + y = 8$
$2x - y = 6$

5. $x + 3y = 9$
$4x - 2y = 7$

6. $x + y + z = 10$
$5x - y = 1$
$3x + 4y + z = 8$

Use an inverse matrix to solve the linear system.

7. $x + y = 2$
$7x + 8y = 21$

8. $-x - 2y = 3$
$2x + 8y = 1$

9. $4x + 3y = 6$
$6x - 2y = 10$

10. 🌐 **INVESTING** Look back at Example 4 on page 232. Suppose you have $60,000 to invest and you want an overall annual return of 9%. Use the expected annual returns shown to determine how much you should invest in each fund. Assume you are investing as much in stocks as in bonds and the money market combined.

Investment	Expected return
Stock mutual fund	12%
Bond mutual fund	8%
Money market fund	5%

PRACTICE AND APPLICATIONS

STUDENT HELP

→ **Extra Practice**
to help you master
skills is on p. 945.

WRITING MATRIX EQUATIONS Write the linear system as a matrix equation.

11. $x + y = 5$
$3x - 4y = 8$

12. $x + 2y = 6$
$4x - y = 5$

13. $5x - 3y = 9$
$-4x + 2y = 10$

14. $2x - 5y = -11$
$-3x + 7y = 15$

15. $x + 8y = 4$
$4x - 5y = -11$

16. $2x - 5y = 4$
$x - 3y = 1$

17. $x - 4y + 5z = -4$
$2x + y - 7z = -23$
$-4x + 5y + 2z = 38$

18. $3x - y + 4z = 16$
$2x + 4y - z = 10$
$x - y + 3z = 31$

19. $0.5x + 3.1y - 0.2z = 5.9$
$1.2x - 2.5y + 0.7z = 2.2$
$0.3x + 4.8y - 4.3z = 4.8$

20. $x + z = 9$
$-x - y + 2z = 6$
$2x + 7y - z = -4$

21. $8y - 10z = -23$
$6y - 12z = 14$
$-9x + 5z = 0$

22. $x + y - z = 0$
$2x - z = 1$
$y + z = 2$

SOLVING SYSTEMS Use an inverse matrix to solve the linear system.

STUDENT HELP

→ HOMEWORK HELP
Example 1: Exs. 11–22
Example 2: Exs. 23–31
Example 3: Exs. 32–39
Example 4: Exs. 40–44

23. $3x + y = 8$
$5x + 2y = 11$

24. $x + y = -1$
$11x + 12y = 8$

25. $2x + 7y = -53$
$x + 3y = -22$

26. $7x + 5y = 8$
$4x + 3y = 4$

27. $5x - 7y = 54$
$2x - 4y = 30$

28. $-5x - 7y = -9$
$2x + 3y = 3$

29. $x + 2y = -9$
$-2x - 3y = 14$

30. $2x + 4y = -26$
$2x + 5y = -31$

31. $9x - 5y = 43$
$-2x + 2y = -22$

STUDENT HELP

HOMEWORK HELP
Visit our Web site
www.mcdougallittell.com
for help with Exs. 32 and 33.

SOLVING SYSTEMS Use the given inverse of the coefficient matrix to solve the linear system.

32. $2y - z = -2$
$5x + 2y + 3z = 4$
$7x + 3y + 4z = -5$

$$A^{-1} = \begin{bmatrix} -1 & -11 & 8 \\ 1 & 7 & -5 \\ 1 & 14 & -10 \end{bmatrix}$$

33. $x - y - 3z = 9$
$5x + 2y + z = -30$
$-3x - y = 4$

$$A^{-1} = \begin{bmatrix} 1 & 3 & 5 \\ -3 & -9 & -16 \\ 1 & 4 & 7 \end{bmatrix}$$

SOLVING SYSTEMS Use an inverse matrix and a graphing calculator to solve the linear system.

34. $3x + 2y = 13$
$3x + 2y + z = 13$
$2x + y + 3z = 9$

35. $-x + y - 3z = -4$
$3x - 2y + 8z = 14$
$2x - 2y + 5z = 7$

36. $3x + 5y - 5z = 21$
$-4x + 8y - 5z = 1$
$2x - 5y + 6z = -16$

37. $2x + z = 2$
$5x - y + z = 5$
$-x + 2y + 2z = 0$

38. $4x + 3y + z = 14$
$6x + y = 9$
$3x + 5y + 3z = 21$

39. $x + y - 3z = -17$
$2x + z = 12$
$-7x - 2y + z = -11$

40. **SKATING PARTY** You are planning a birthday party for your younger brother at a skating rink. The cost of admission is $3.50 per adult and $2.25 per child, and there is a limit of 20 people. You have $50 to spend. Use an inverse matrix to determine how many adults and how many children you can invite.

41. **DENTAL FILLINGS** Dentists use various amalgams for silver fillings. The matrix shows the percents (expressed as decimals) of powdered alloys used in preparing three different amalgams. Suppose a dentist has 5483 grams of silver, 2009 grams of tin, and 129 grams of copper. How much of each amalgam can be made?

PERCENT ALLOY BY WEIGHT
Amalgam

	A	B	C
Silver	0.70	0.72	0.73
Tin	0.26	0.25	0.27
Copper	0.04	0.03	0.00

42. **STAINED GLASS** You are making mosaic tiles from three types of stained glass. You need 6 square feet of glass for the project and you want there to be as much iridescent glass as red and blue glass combined. The cost of a sheet of glass having an area of 0.75 square foot is $6.50 for iridescent, $4.50 for red, and $5.50 for blue. How many sheets of each type should you purchase if you plan to spend $45 on the project?

43. **WALKWAY LIGHTING** A walkway lighting package includes a transformer, a certain length of wire, and a certain number of lights on the wire. The price of each lighting package depends on the length of wire and the number of lights on the wire.

- A package that contains a transformer, 25 feet of wire, and 5 lights costs $20.
- A package that contains a transformer, 50 feet of wire, and 15 lights costs $35.
- A package that contains a transformer, 100 feet of wire, and 20 lights costs $50.

Write and solve a system of equations to find the cost of a transformer, the cost per foot of wire, and the cost of a light. Assume the cost of each item is the same in each lighting package.

FOCUS ON CAREERS

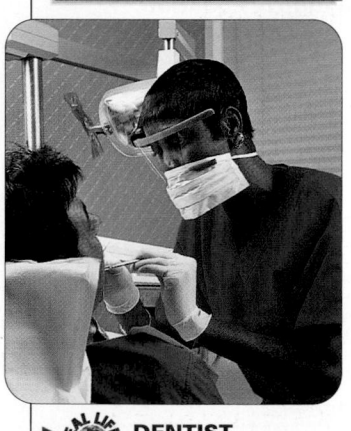

DENTIST
Dentists diagnose, prevent, and treat problems of the teeth and mouth. Dental amalgams have been used for more than 150 years to restore the teeth of over 100 million Americans.

CAREER LINK
www.mcdougallittell.com

44. 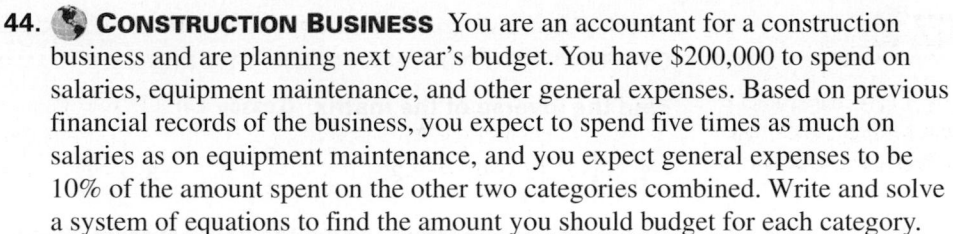 **CONSTRUCTION BUSINESS** You are an accountant for a construction business and are planning next year's budget. You have $200,000 to spend on salaries, equipment maintenance, and other general expenses. Based on previous financial records of the business, you expect to spend five times as much on salaries as on equipment maintenance, and you expect general expenses to be 10% of the amount spent on the other two categories combined. Write and solve a system of equations to find the amount you should budget for each category.

Test  Preparation

45. MULTI-STEP PROBLEM A company sells different sizes of gift baskets with a varying assortment of meat and cheese. A basic basket with 2 cheeses and 3 meats costs $15, a big basket with 3 cheeses and 5 meats costs $24, and a super basket with 7 cheeses and 10 meats costs $50.

    a. Write and solve a system of equations using the information about the basic and big baskets.

    b. Write and solve a system of equations using the information about the big and super baskets.

    c. *Writing* Compare the results from parts (a) and (b) and make a conjecture about why there is a discrepancy.

★ **Challenge**

46. SOLVING SYSTEMS OF FOUR EQUATIONS Solve the linear system using the given inverse of the coefficient matrix.

$$
\begin{aligned}
w + 6x + 3y - 3z &= 2 \\
2w + 7x + y + 2z &= 5 \\
w + 5x + 3y - 3z &= 3 \\
-6x - 2y + 3z &= 6
\end{aligned}
\qquad
A^{-1} =
\begin{bmatrix}
40 & -3 & -33 & 9 \\
1 & 0 & -1 & 0 \\
-39 & 3 & 33 & -8 \\
-24 & 2 & 20 & -5
\end{bmatrix}
$$

EXTRA CHALLENGE
www.mcdougallittell.com

MIXED REVIEW

EVALUATING FUNCTIONS Evaluate $f(x)$ or $g(x)$ for the given value of x.
(Review 2.7)

$$
f(x) = \begin{cases} \frac{3}{4}x - 8, & \text{if } x \le 8 \\ -x + 6, & \text{if } x > 8 \end{cases}
\qquad
g(x) = \begin{cases} \frac{1}{8}x + 8, & \text{if } x < -1 \\ 2x - 1, & \text{if } x \ge -1 \end{cases}
$$

47. $f(8)$ **48.** $f(11)$ **49.** $f(-2)$ **50.** $f(0)$

51. $g(3)$ **52.** $g(0)$ **53.** $g(-1)$ **54.** $g(-3)$

GRAPHING FUNCTIONS Graph the function and label the vertex.
(Review 2.8 for 5.1)

55. $y = |x - 5|$ **56.** $y = |x| + 8$ **57.** $y = -|x - 8| - 9$

58. $y = |x - 5| + 4$ **59.** $y = -|x + 3| + 4$ **60.** $y = -|x + 6| - 2$

FINDING INVERSES Find the inverse of the matrix. **(Review 4.4)**

61. $\begin{bmatrix} 7 & -4 \\ -5 & 3 \end{bmatrix}$ **62.** $\begin{bmatrix} 5 & 2 \\ 2 & 1 \end{bmatrix}$ **63.** $\begin{bmatrix} 8 & 17 \\ -1 & -2 \end{bmatrix}$

64. $\begin{bmatrix} 11 & -5 \\ 3 & -1 \end{bmatrix}$ **65.** $\begin{bmatrix} 7 & 4 \\ 3 & 2 \end{bmatrix}$ **66.** $\begin{bmatrix} 6 & -2 \\ 7 & -2 \end{bmatrix}$

Find the inverse of the matrix. (Lesson 4.4)

1. $\begin{bmatrix} 4 & 1 \\ 7 & 2 \end{bmatrix}$
2. $\begin{bmatrix} -7 & 5 \\ 4 & -3 \end{bmatrix}$
3. $\begin{bmatrix} -6 & 1 \\ 9 & -3 \end{bmatrix}$
4. $\begin{bmatrix} 6 & 5 \\ 8 & 7 \end{bmatrix}$

Use an inverse matrix to solve the linear system. (Lesson 4.5)

5. $4x + 7y = 24$
$x + 2y = 7$

6. $-9x + 13y = 3$
$2x - 3y = -1$

7. $8x + 7y = 3$
$-2x - 2y = 0$

8.  **BUYING FLATWARE** The price of flatware varies depending on the number of place settings you buy as well as other items included in the set. Suppose a set with 4 place settings costs $142 and a set with 8 place settings and a serving set costs $351. Find the cost of a place setting and a serving set. Assume that the cost of each item is the same for each flatware set. **(Lesson 4.5)**

MATH & History

Systems of Equations

THEN

OVER 2000 YEARS AGO, a method for solving systems of equations using rectangular arrays of counting rods was presented in *Nine Chapters on the Mathematical Art*, an early Chinese mathematics text. A problem from this book is given below.

Three bundles of top-grade ears of rice, two bundles of medium-grade ears of rice, and one bundle of low-grade ears of rice make 39 dou (of rice by volume); two bundles of top-grade ears of rice, three bundles of medium-grade ears of rice, and one bundle of low-grade ears of rice make 34 dou; one bundle of top-grade ears of rice, two bundles of medium-grade ears of rice, and three bundles of low-grade ears of rice make 26 dou. How many dou are there in a bundle of each grade of rice?

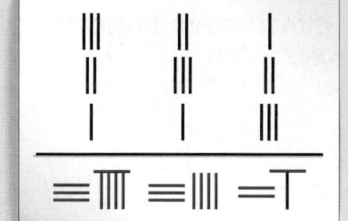

Top-grade ears of rice

Medium-grade ears of rice

Low-grade ears of rice

Total produce

1. Use matrices to organize the given information and solve the problem.

2. How is the arrangement of counting rods similar to your matrices? How is it different?

NOW

TODAY, computers use matrices representing systems with many variables to solve complicated problems like predicting weather and designing aircraft.

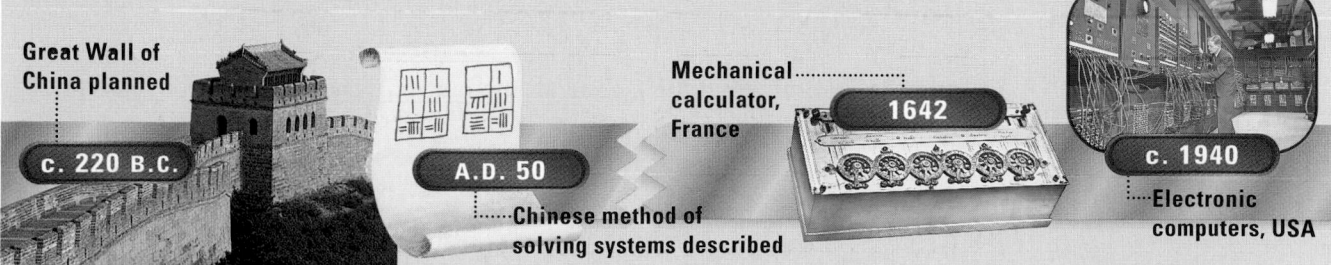

Great Wall of China planned

c. 220 B.C.

A.D. 50

Chinese method of solving systems described

Mechanical calculator, France

1642

c. 1940

Electronic computers, USA

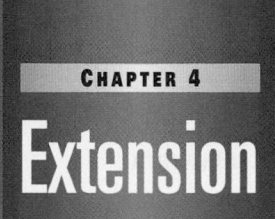
Solving Systems Using Augmented Matrices

GOAL **USING ELEMENTARY ROW OPERATIONS**

A matrix containing the coefficient matrix and the matrix of constants for a system of linear equations is called the **augmented matrix** of the system.

LINEAR SYSTEM

$$x - 2y = 7$$
$$-3x + 5y = -4$$

AUGMENTED MATRIX

$$\begin{bmatrix} 1 & -2 & \vdots & 7 \\ -3 & 5 & \vdots & -4 \end{bmatrix}$$

Recall from Chapter 3 that equations in a system can be multiplied by a constant, or a multiple of one equation can be added to another equation. Similar operations can be performed on the rows of an augmented matrix to solve the corresponding system.

ELEMENTARY ROW OPERATIONS

Two augmented matrices are *row-equivalent* if their corresponding systems have the same solution(s). Any of these row operations performed on an augmented matrix will produce a matrix that is row-equivalent to the original:

- Interchange two rows.
- Multiply a row by a nonzero constant.
- Add a multiple of one row to another row.

To solve a system, use elementary row operations to transform the original augmented matrix into a matrix having 1's along the main diagonal and 0's below the main diagonal. A matrix of this form is said to be in *triangular form*.

EXAMPLE 1 *Using Row Operations to Solve a Two-Variable System*

LINEAR SYSTEM

$$x - 2y = 7$$
$$-3x + 5y = -4$$

AUGMENTED MATRIX

$$\begin{bmatrix} 1 & -2 & \vdots & 7 \\ -3 & 5 & \vdots & -4 \end{bmatrix}$$

Add 3 times the first equation to the second equation. You get this system:

$$x - 2y = 7$$
$$-y = 17$$

Add 3 times the first row, R_1, to the second row, R_2.

$$3R_1 + R_2 \rightarrow \begin{bmatrix} 1 & -2 & \vdots & 7 \\ 0 & -1 & \vdots & 17 \end{bmatrix}$$

Multiply the second equation by -1.

$$x - 2y = 7$$
$$y = -17$$

Multiply the second row by -1.

$$(-1)R_2 \rightarrow \begin{bmatrix} 1 & -2 & \vdots & 7 \\ 0 & 1 & \vdots & -17 \end{bmatrix}$$

The second row of the matrix tells you that $y = -17$. Substitute -17 for y in the equation for the first row: $x - 2(-17) = 7$, or $x = -27$. The solution is $(-27, -17)$.

EXAMPLE 2 *Using Row Operations to Solve a Three-Variable System*

LINEAR SYSTEM	AUGMENTED MATRIX

$$2x + 4y + 5z = 5$$
$$x + 3y + 3z = 2$$
$$2x + 4y + 6z = 2$$

$$\begin{bmatrix} 2 & 4 & 5 & \vdots & 5 \\ 1 & 3 & 3 & \vdots & 2 \\ 2 & 4 & 6 & \vdots & 2 \end{bmatrix}$$

Add -1 times the first equation to the third equation. You get this system:

Add -1 times the first row to the third row.

$$2x + 4y + 5z = 5$$
$$x + 3y + 3z = 2$$
$$z = -3$$

$$(-1)R_1 + R_3 \rightarrow \begin{bmatrix} 2 & 4 & 5 & \vdots & 5 \\ 1 & 3 & 3 & \vdots & 2 \\ 0 & 0 & 1 & \vdots & -3 \end{bmatrix}$$

Add -0.5 times the first equation to the second equation.

Add -0.5 times the first row to the second row.

$$2x + 4y + 5z = 5$$
$$y + 0.5z = -0.5$$
$$z = -3$$

$$-0.5R_1 + R_2 \rightarrow \begin{bmatrix} 2 & 4 & 5 & \vdots & 5 \\ 0 & 1 & 0.5 & \vdots & -0.5 \\ 0 & 0 & 1 & \vdots & -3 \end{bmatrix}$$

Multiply the first equation by 0.5.

Multiply the first row by 0.5.

$$x + 2y + 2.5z = 2.5$$
$$y + 0.5z = -0.5$$
$$z = -3$$

$$0.5R_1 \rightarrow \begin{bmatrix} 1 & 2 & 2.5 & \vdots & 2.5 \\ 0 & 1 & 0.5 & \vdots & -0.5 \\ 0 & 0 & 1 & \vdots & -3 \end{bmatrix}$$

The third row of the matrix tells you that $z = -3$. Substitute -3 for z in the equation for the second row, $y + 0.5z = -0.5$, to obtain $y + 0.5(-3) = -0.5$, or $y = 1$. Then substitute -3 for z and 1 for y in the equation for the first row, $x + 2y + 2.5z = 2.5$, to obtain $x + 2(1) + 2.5(-3) = 2.5$, or $x = 8$. The solution is $(8, 1, -3)$.

EXERCISES

SOLVING SYSTEMS Use an augmented matrix to solve the linear system.

1. $6x + 4y = 8$
$3x + 3y = 9$

2. $x + y = 2$
$7x + 8y = 21$

3. $x + 2y = -9$
$-2x - 3y = 14$

4. $x - 3y = 5$
$-2x - 4y = 20$

5. $3x + 2y = 2$
$5x - 6y = 50$

6. $x + y = -1$
$7x + 9y = -19$

7. $-2x - y = -5$
$6x + 5y = 17$

8. $9x - 4y = 2$
$-6x - 16y = -6$

9. $-12x + 15y = 3$
$-7x - 20y = -4$

10. $2x + 6y + 3z = 2$
$x + 3y + z = 1$
$x + 5y + 2z = -1$

11. $2x + 6y + 3z = 8$
$x + 5y + 5z = 1$
$x + 3y + z = 3$

12. $2x + 10y = 28$
$x + 3y + 4z = 22$
$x + 5y - z = 10$

13. $x + 4y - 2z = 3$
$x + 3y + 7z = 1$
$2x + 9y + z = 8$

14. $x - y + 3z = 6$
$x - 2y = 5$
$2x - 2y + 5z = 9$

15. $x + 2z = 4$
$x + y + z = 6$
$3x + 3y + 4z = 28$

16. CRITICAL THINKING Try using an augmented matrix to solve the given system. What happens? What can you say about the system's solution(s)?

$$x - 2y + 7z = 6$$
$$5x - 10y + 35z = 30$$
$$3x - 6y + 21z = 18$$

WHAT did you learn?

Use matrices and determinants in real-life situations. **(4.1–4.5)**

Perform matrix operations.
- add and subtract matrices **(4.1)**

- multiply a matrix by a scalar **(4.1)**

- multiply two matrices **(4.2)**

Evaluate the determinant of a matrix. **(4.3)**

Find the inverse of a matrix. **(4.4)**

Solve matrix equations. **(4.1, 4.4, 4.5)**

Solve systems of linear equations.
- using Cramer's rule **(4.3)**
- using inverse matrices **(4.5)**

Use systems of linear equations to solve real-life problems. **(4.3, 4.5)**

WHY did you learn it?

Organize data, such as the number and dollar value of Hispanic music products shipped. **(p. 204)**

Find the total cost of college tuition plus room and board. **(p. 205)**

Write U.S. population data as percents of total population. **(p. 205)**

Calculate the cost of softball equipment. **(p. 210)**

Find the area of the Golden Triangle. **(p. 220)**

Encode or decode a cryptogram. **(pp. 225, 226)**

Extend the process of equation solving to equations whose solutions are matrices. **(pp. 201, 224)**

Find the cost of gasoline. **(p. 220)**
Calculate a budget. **(p. 235)**

Decide how much money to invest in each of three types of mutual funds. **(p. 232)**

How does Chapter 4 fit into the BIGGER PICTURE of algebra?

Your study of linear algebra has continued with Chapter 4. Matrices are used throughout linear algebra, especially for solving linear systems. This introduction to matrices, their uses, and properties of matrix operations also connects to your past. For example, instead of multiplying real numbers, or variables that represent real numbers, you multiplied matrices. You also saw properties, such as the commutative property of multiplication, that apply to real numbers but not to matrices.

STUDY STRATEGY

Did you write out the steps?

Here is an example of several steps you can write when multiplying two matrices, following the **Study Strategy** on page 198.

Writing Out the Steps

$$\begin{bmatrix} 1 & -6 \\ -3 & 2 \end{bmatrix}\begin{bmatrix} -9 & 0 \\ -2 & 7 \end{bmatrix}$$

$$= \begin{bmatrix} 1(-9)+(-6)(-2) & 1(0)+(-6)7 \\ -3(-9)+2(-2) & -3(0)+2(7) \end{bmatrix}$$

$$= \begin{bmatrix} -9+12 & 0-42 \\ 27-4 & 0+14 \end{bmatrix}$$

$$= \begin{bmatrix} 3 & -42 \\ 23 & 14 \end{bmatrix}$$

VOCABULARY

- matrix, p. 199
- dimensions of a matrix, p. 199
- entries of a matrix, p. 199
- row matrix, p. 199
- column matrix, p. 199
- square matrix, p. 199
- zero matrix, p. 199
- equal matrices, p. 199
- scalar, p. 200
- determinant, p. 214
- Cramer's rule, p. 216
- coefficient matrix, p. 216
- identity matrix, p. 223
- inverse matrix, p. 223
- matrix of variables, p. 230
- matrix of constants, p. 230

4.1 MATRIX OPERATIONS

*Examples on
pp. 199–202*

EXAMPLES You can add or subtract matrices that have the same dimensions by adding or subtracting corresponding entries.

$$\begin{bmatrix} 5 & -2 \\ 0 & 6 \end{bmatrix} + \begin{bmatrix} 9 & 1 \\ -4 & 4 \end{bmatrix} = \begin{bmatrix} 5+9 & -2+1 \\ 0+(-4) & 6+4 \end{bmatrix} = \begin{bmatrix} 14 & -1 \\ -4 & 10 \end{bmatrix}$$

You cannot subtract these matrices because they have different dimensions.

$$\begin{bmatrix} -2 & 1 \\ 0 & -3 \end{bmatrix} - \begin{bmatrix} 1 & -5 & -4 \\ 2 & 7 & 1 \end{bmatrix}$$

To do scalar multiplication, multiply each entry in the matrix by the scalar.

$$-3\begin{bmatrix} -12 & -6 \\ 3 & 1 \\ 2 & 8 \end{bmatrix} = \begin{bmatrix} (-3)(-12) & (-3)(-6) \\ (-3)(3) & (-3)(1) \\ (-3)(2) & (-3)(8) \end{bmatrix} = \begin{bmatrix} 36 & 18 \\ -9 & -3 \\ -6 & -24 \end{bmatrix}$$

To solve this matrix equation, equate corresponding entries and solve for x and y.

$$\begin{bmatrix} x+2 & 2 \\ -1 & 9 \end{bmatrix} = \begin{bmatrix} -6 & 2 \\ -1 & 3y \end{bmatrix} \qquad \begin{array}{ll} x+2=-6 & 3y=9 \\ x=-8 & y=3 \end{array}$$

Perform the indicated operation if possible. If not possible, state the reason.

1. $\begin{bmatrix} 15 & 4 \\ 3 & 12 \end{bmatrix} - \begin{bmatrix} 0 & 9 \\ 2 & 7 \end{bmatrix}$

2. $\begin{bmatrix} 3 & -2 \\ -4 & 1 \end{bmatrix} - \begin{bmatrix} 5 \\ -3 \end{bmatrix}$

3. $\begin{bmatrix} 6 & 10 \\ 9 & 6 \\ 4 & -1 \end{bmatrix} + \begin{bmatrix} 2 & 1 \\ 0 & 7 \\ 4 & 7 \end{bmatrix}$

4. $\begin{bmatrix} 0 & 1 & 5 \\ -2 & 3 & 1 \\ 1 & 2 & -4 \end{bmatrix} + \begin{bmatrix} 1 & -2 \\ 4 & 1 \\ 2 & -3 \end{bmatrix}$

5. $2\begin{bmatrix} 4 & 6 & -1 \\ 10 & -5 & 2 \\ 0 & 11 & 1 \end{bmatrix}$

6. $\frac{1}{2}\begin{bmatrix} -2 & 0 \\ 4 & 8 \\ -6 & -2 \end{bmatrix}$

Solve the matrix equation for *x* and *y*.

7. $\begin{bmatrix} 1 & 14 \\ -5x & 10 \end{bmatrix} = \begin{bmatrix} y-9 & 14 \\ 5 & 10 \end{bmatrix}$

8. $\begin{bmatrix} 3 & 4y \\ -1 & 13 \end{bmatrix} + \begin{bmatrix} -6 & 5 \\ 8 & 0 \end{bmatrix} = \begin{bmatrix} -3 & -7 \\ x & 13 \end{bmatrix}$

9. $\begin{bmatrix} 2 & 3y \\ 4 & -1 \end{bmatrix} + \begin{bmatrix} 0 & -4 \\ x & -2 \end{bmatrix} = \begin{bmatrix} 2 & 11 \\ 3 & -3 \end{bmatrix}$

10. $\begin{bmatrix} 7y & -2 \\ -3 & 5 \end{bmatrix} - \begin{bmatrix} 1 & 5 \\ x & -3 \end{bmatrix} = \begin{bmatrix} 6 & -7 \\ -2 & 8 \end{bmatrix}$

4.2 MULTIPLYING MATRICES

EXAMPLE You can multiply a matrix with n columns by a matrix with n rows.

$$\begin{bmatrix} -6 & 1 \\ 5 & -2 \end{bmatrix}\begin{bmatrix} 6 & 3 \\ 0 & 1 \end{bmatrix} = \begin{bmatrix} (-6)(6) + (1)(0) & (-6)(3) + (1)(1) \\ (5)(6) + (-2)(0) & (5)(3) + (-2)(1) \end{bmatrix} = \begin{bmatrix} -36 & -17 \\ 30 & 13 \end{bmatrix}$$

Write the product. If it is not defined, state the reason.

11. $\begin{bmatrix} 12 \\ -4 \end{bmatrix}\begin{bmatrix} -10 & -7 \end{bmatrix}$

12. $\begin{bmatrix} 2 & 15 \\ -3 & 10 \end{bmatrix}\begin{bmatrix} -5 & 12 \\ 1 & 0 \end{bmatrix}$

13. $\begin{bmatrix} 1 & 7 \\ 0 & 9 \end{bmatrix}\begin{bmatrix} 3 & -1 & 8 \\ 2 & -4 & 8 \end{bmatrix}$

4.3 DETERMINANTS AND CRAMER'S RULE

EXAMPLES You can evaluate the determinant of a 2 × 2 or a 3 × 3 matrix. Find products of the entries on the diagonals and subtract.

$$\det \begin{bmatrix} -2 & -6 \\ 1 & 4 \end{bmatrix} = \begin{vmatrix} -2 & -6 \\ 1 & 4 \end{vmatrix} = -2(4) - 1(-6) = -8 + 6 = -2$$

$$\det \begin{bmatrix} 2 & 1 & 5 \\ -1 & 6 & 3 \\ 2 & -4 & 2 \end{bmatrix} = \begin{vmatrix} 2 & 1 & 5 \\ -1 & 6 & 3 \\ 2 & -4 & 2 \end{vmatrix} \begin{matrix} 2 & 1 \\ -1 & 6 \\ 2 & -4 \end{matrix} = (24 + 6 + 20) - [60 + (-24) + (-2)] = 16$$

You can find the area of a triangle with vertices (x_1, y_1), (x_2, y_2), and (x_3, y_3) using

$$\text{Area} = \pm \frac{1}{2} \begin{vmatrix} x_1 & y_1 & 1 \\ x_2 & y_2 & 1 \\ x_3 & y_3 & 1 \end{vmatrix}$$

where $\pm$ indicates you should choose the sign that yields a positive value.

You can use Cramer's rule to solve a system of linear equations. First find the determinant of the coefficient matrix and then use Cramer's rule to solve for x and y.

$$\begin{matrix} 3x - 4y = 12 \\ x + 2y = 14 \end{matrix} \qquad \det \begin{bmatrix} 3 & -4 \\ 1 & 2 \end{bmatrix} = \begin{vmatrix} 3 & -4 \\ 1 & 2 \end{vmatrix} = 3(2) - 1(-4) = 6 + 4 = 10$$

$$x = \frac{\begin{vmatrix} 12 & -4 \\ 14 & 2 \end{vmatrix}}{10} = \frac{12(2) - 14(-4)}{10} = \frac{80}{10} = 8 \qquad y = \frac{\begin{vmatrix} 3 & 12 \\ 1 & 14 \end{vmatrix}}{10} = \frac{3(14) - 1(12)}{10} = \frac{30}{10} = 3$$

Evaluate the determinant of the matrix.

14. $\begin{bmatrix} -9 & 1 \\ 3 & 2 \end{bmatrix}$

15. $\begin{bmatrix} 6 & -3 \\ 2 & 1 \end{bmatrix}$

16. $\begin{bmatrix} 3 & 1 & 0 \\ 2 & 1 & 1 \\ 0 & 3 & 4 \end{bmatrix}$

17. $\begin{bmatrix} 2 & -3 & 4 \\ 0 & 1 & -2 \\ 1 & 2 & -3 \end{bmatrix}$

18. Find the area of a triangle with vertices $A(0, 1)$, $B(2, 4)$, and $C(1, 8)$.

Use Cramer's rule to solve the linear system.

19. $7x - 4y = -3$
$2x + 5y = -7$

20. $2x + y = -2$
$x - 2y = 19$

21. $5x - 4y + 4z = 18$
$-x + 3y - 2z = 0$
$4x - 2y + 7z = 3$

IDENTITY AND INVERSE MATRICES

Examples on
pp. 222–226

EXAMPLES You can find the inverse of an $n \times n$ matrix provided its determinant does not equal zero.

The inverse of $A = \begin{bmatrix} a & b \\ c & d \end{bmatrix}$ is $A^{-1} = \dfrac{1}{|A|}\begin{bmatrix} d & -b \\ -c & a \end{bmatrix}$.

If $A = \begin{bmatrix} 7 & 3 \\ 5 & 2 \end{bmatrix}$, then $A^{-1} = \dfrac{1}{7(2) - 5(3)}\begin{bmatrix} 2 & -3 \\ -5 & 7 \end{bmatrix} = -1\begin{bmatrix} 2 & -3 \\ -5 & 7 \end{bmatrix} = \begin{bmatrix} -2 & 3 \\ 5 & -7 \end{bmatrix}$.

You can use the inverse of a matrix A to solve a matrix equation $AX = B$: $X = A^{-1}B$.

$$\begin{bmatrix} 1 & 3 \\ 2 & 7 \end{bmatrix}X = \begin{bmatrix} 3 & 0 \\ 5 & 2 \end{bmatrix}$$

$$A^{-1} = \dfrac{1}{7 - 6}\begin{bmatrix} 7 & -3 \\ -2 & 1 \end{bmatrix} = \begin{bmatrix} 7 & -3 \\ -2 & 1 \end{bmatrix}$$

$$X = \begin{bmatrix} 7 & -3 \\ -2 & 1 \end{bmatrix}\begin{bmatrix} 3 & 0 \\ 5 & 2 \end{bmatrix} = \begin{bmatrix} 6 & -6 \\ -1 & 2 \end{bmatrix}$$

Find the inverse of the matrix.

22. $\begin{bmatrix} 2 & 3 \\ 7 & 11 \end{bmatrix}$ **23.** $\begin{bmatrix} 2 & 2 \\ 1 & 3 \end{bmatrix}$ **24.** $\begin{bmatrix} -3 & 6 \\ 2 & -4 \end{bmatrix}$ **25.** $\begin{bmatrix} 6 & -1 \\ -5 & 1 \end{bmatrix}$

Solve the matrix equation.

26. $\begin{bmatrix} 5 & 3 \\ 3 & 2 \end{bmatrix}X = \begin{bmatrix} 0 & 9 \\ -1 & 4 \end{bmatrix}$ **27.** $\begin{bmatrix} -7 & -5 \\ 4 & 3 \end{bmatrix}X + \begin{bmatrix} 8 & -2 \\ 6 & 1 \end{bmatrix} = \begin{bmatrix} 9 & -3 \\ 6 & 2 \end{bmatrix}$

SOLVING SYSTEMS USING INVERSE MATRICES

Examples on
pp. 230–232

EXAMPLE You can use inverse matrices to solve a system of linear equations.

$\begin{matrix} x + 3y = 10 \\ 2x + 5y = -2 \end{matrix}$ **Write in matrix form.** ➡ $\underset{A}{\begin{bmatrix} 1 & 3 \\ 2 & 5 \end{bmatrix}} \underset{X}{\begin{bmatrix} x \\ y \end{bmatrix}} = \underset{B}{\begin{bmatrix} 10 \\ -2 \end{bmatrix}}$

Then $X = A^{-1}B = \dfrac{1}{1(5) - 2(3)}\begin{bmatrix} 5 & -3 \\ -2 & 1 \end{bmatrix}\begin{bmatrix} 10 \\ -2 \end{bmatrix} = -1\begin{bmatrix} 56 \\ -22 \end{bmatrix} = \begin{bmatrix} -56 \\ 22 \end{bmatrix}$.

The solution is $(-56, 22)$.

Use an inverse matrix to solve the linear system.

28. $\begin{aligned} 9x + 8y &= -6 \\ -x - y &= 1 \end{aligned}$ **29.** $\begin{aligned} x - 3y &= -2 \\ 5x + 3y &= 17 \end{aligned}$ **30.** $\begin{aligned} 4x - 14y &= -15 \\ 18x - 12y &= 9 \end{aligned}$

Use an inverse matrix and a graphing calculator to solve the linear system.

31. $\begin{aligned} x - y - 4z &= 3 \\ -x + 3y - z &= -1 \\ x - y + 5z &= 3 \end{aligned}$ **32.** $\begin{aligned} 4x + 10y - z &= -3 \\ 11x + 28y - 4z &= 1 \\ -6x - 15y + 2z &= -1 \end{aligned}$ **33.** $\begin{aligned} 5x - 3y + 5z &= -1 \\ 3x + 2y + 4z &= 11 \\ 2x - y + 3z &= 4 \end{aligned}$

<CHAPTER 4>

Chapter Test

CHAPTER 4

Perform the indicated operation(s).

1. $\begin{bmatrix} 2 & 5 & -4 \\ 3 & 0 & -2 \end{bmatrix} + \begin{bmatrix} 3 & 2 & 7 \\ -2 & -5 & 7 \end{bmatrix}$

2. $0.25 \begin{bmatrix} 8 & 20 & -12 \\ -8 & -4 & 36 \end{bmatrix}$

3. $-4 \left(\begin{bmatrix} 1 & 10 \\ -4 & -6 \end{bmatrix} - \begin{bmatrix} 4 & 8 \\ -3 & -8 \end{bmatrix} \right)$

4. $\begin{bmatrix} 4 & 1 & 4 \\ -1 & 8 & -3 \\ 4 & 3 & 0 \end{bmatrix} \begin{bmatrix} -2 \\ 2 \\ 6 \end{bmatrix}$

5. $\begin{bmatrix} -6 & 1 \\ 9 & 2 \end{bmatrix} \begin{bmatrix} 3 & 0 \\ -5 & 4 \end{bmatrix}$

6. $\begin{bmatrix} 0 & 1 & 0 \\ 2 & -1 & 1 \\ 0 & 2 & -1 \end{bmatrix} \begin{bmatrix} -1 & 2 & 0 \\ 4 & 6 & 0 \\ 1 & 0 & 1 \end{bmatrix}$

Solve the matrix equation for x and y.

7. $\begin{bmatrix} -1 & y+6 \\ x-4 & 3 \end{bmatrix} = \begin{bmatrix} -1 & 8 \\ -9 & 3 \end{bmatrix}$

8. $\begin{bmatrix} -22 & 9 \\ 1 & -y \end{bmatrix} = \begin{bmatrix} 2x & 9 \\ 1 & 4 \end{bmatrix}$

9. $3 \begin{bmatrix} x & 1 \\ 8 & -4 \end{bmatrix} = \begin{bmatrix} -15 & 3 \\ y & -12 \end{bmatrix}$

Evaluate the determinant of the matrix.

10. $\begin{bmatrix} 7 & -9 \\ -3 & 4 \end{bmatrix}$

11. $\begin{bmatrix} -2 & -1 \\ 1 & -1 \end{bmatrix}$

12. $\begin{bmatrix} 4 & 0 & 1 \\ 1 & 5 & 3 \\ 2 & 2 & 0 \end{bmatrix}$

13. $\begin{bmatrix} -1 & 3 & 4 \\ 6 & 0 & -2 \\ 0 & -5 & 1 \end{bmatrix}$

Find the area of the triangle with the given vertices.

14. $A(2, 1), B(5, 3), C(7, 1)$

15. $A(-1, 0), B(-3, 3), C(0, 4)$

16. $A(-3, 2), B(-1, 4), C(-4, 3)$

Use Cramer's rule to solve the linear system.

17. $2x + y = 12$
$5x + 3y = 27$

18. $-4x + 5y = -10$
$5x - 6y = 13$

19. $x + y = 2$
$2y - z = 0$
$-x - y + z = -1$

20. $5x - 2y + 7z = 12$
$2x + 5y + 3z = 10$
$3x - y + 4z = 8$

Find the inverse of the matrix.

21. $\begin{bmatrix} 4 & 5 \\ 3 & 9 \end{bmatrix}$

22. $\begin{bmatrix} -1 & -2 \\ 1 & 1 \end{bmatrix}$

23. $\begin{bmatrix} -6 & 4 \\ 6 & -5 \end{bmatrix}$

24. $\begin{bmatrix} 1 & 0 \\ 0 & -5 \end{bmatrix}$

Solve the matrix equation.

25. $\begin{bmatrix} 8 & 7 \\ 1 & 1 \end{bmatrix} X = \begin{bmatrix} 3 & -6 \\ -2 & 9 \end{bmatrix}$

26. $\begin{bmatrix} 2 & 5 \\ 2 & 6 \end{bmatrix} X = \begin{bmatrix} 1 & 0 \\ 0 & 1 \end{bmatrix}$

27. $\begin{bmatrix} 1 & 0 \\ -6 & 2 \end{bmatrix} X = \begin{bmatrix} 10 & 6 & 8 \\ 4 & 12 & 2 \end{bmatrix}$

Use an inverse matrix to solve the linear system.

28. $x - y = 5$
$-2x + 3y = -9$

29. $3x + 2y = -8$
$-2x + 5y = 18$

30. $2x - 7y = 6$
$-3x + 11y = -10$

31. 🟢 **STAINED GLASS** You are making a stained glass panel using different colors as shown. The coordinates given are measured in inches. Find the area of the red triangle.

32. 🟢 **DECODING** Use the inverse of $A = \begin{bmatrix} 2 & -1 \\ 3 & -1 \end{bmatrix}$ and the coding information on pages 225 and 226 to decode the message below.

44, −15, 3, −1, 80, −32, 39, −17, 3, −1, 12, −4, 77, −26

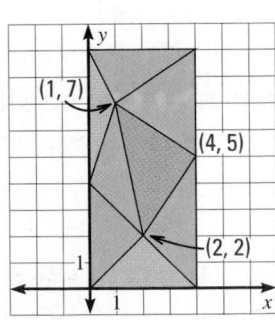

33. 🟢 **BUDGETING MEALS** You have $18 to spend for lunch during a 5 day work week. It costs you about $1.50 to make a lunch at home and about $5 to buy a lunch. How many times each work week should you make a lunch at home?

Chapter Test 243

Chapter Standardized Test

● **TEST-TAKING STRATEGY** During a test it is important to stay mentally focused, but also physically relaxed. If you start to get tense, put your pencil down and take some deep breaths. This may help you regain control.

1. MULTIPLE CHOICE Which matrix equals

$$2\left(\begin{bmatrix} 2 & -7 \\ -4 & 3 \end{bmatrix} + \begin{bmatrix} 0 & -5 \\ -3 & 6 \end{bmatrix}\right)?$$

Ⓐ $\begin{bmatrix} 4 & -4 \\ -2 & 18 \end{bmatrix}$ Ⓑ $\begin{bmatrix} 4 & -24 \\ -14 & 18 \end{bmatrix}$

Ⓒ $\begin{bmatrix} 6 & -22 \\ -12 & 20 \end{bmatrix}$ Ⓓ $\begin{bmatrix} -24 & 60 \\ -6 & 30 \end{bmatrix}$

Ⓔ $\begin{bmatrix} 42 & -104 \\ -18 & 76 \end{bmatrix}$

2. MULTIPLE CHOICE What are the values of x and y in the matrix equation?

$$2x\begin{bmatrix} -2 & -1 \\ -10 & 5 \end{bmatrix} = \begin{bmatrix} -16 & -8 \\ y & 40 \end{bmatrix}$$

Ⓐ $x = 8, y = -80$ Ⓑ $x = -4, y = -80$

Ⓒ $x = 4, y = 80$ Ⓓ $x = 4, y = -80$

Ⓔ $x = 2, y = -40$

3. MULTIPLE CHOICE What is the product of

$$\begin{bmatrix} -1 & 0 & 4 \\ -2 & 1 & 3 \\ 3 & 2 & -1 \end{bmatrix} \text{ and } \begin{bmatrix} 1 & -2 \\ 0 & 1 \\ 5 & -1 \end{bmatrix}?$$

Ⓐ $\begin{bmatrix} 19 & -2 \\ 13 & 2 \\ -2 & -3 \end{bmatrix}$ Ⓑ $\begin{bmatrix} 19 & -2 \\ 13 & -6 \\ -2 & -3 \end{bmatrix}$

Ⓒ $\begin{bmatrix} 19 & -2 \\ 13 & 2 \\ -2 & -7 \end{bmatrix}$ Ⓓ $\begin{bmatrix} 19 & -2 \\ 13 & 2 \\ 2 & -3 \end{bmatrix}$

Ⓔ $\begin{bmatrix} 21 & -2 \\ 13 & 8 \\ -2 & -3 \end{bmatrix}$

4. MULTIPLE CHOICE What is the determinant of

$$\begin{bmatrix} 2 & 1 & 5 \\ -3 & -1 & 2 \\ 0 & 4 & -2 \end{bmatrix}?$$

Ⓐ -78 Ⓑ -34 Ⓒ -16

Ⓓ 34 Ⓔ 78

5. MULTIPLE CHOICE What is the inverse of

$$\begin{bmatrix} 9 & -5 \\ 7 & -4 \end{bmatrix}?$$

Ⓐ $\begin{bmatrix} 4 & -5 \\ -7 & -9 \end{bmatrix}$ Ⓑ $\begin{bmatrix} -4 & 5 \\ 7 & 9 \end{bmatrix}$

Ⓒ $\begin{bmatrix} -4 & -5 \\ -7 & -9 \end{bmatrix}$ Ⓓ $\begin{bmatrix} 4 & -5 \\ 7 & -9 \end{bmatrix}$

Ⓔ $\begin{bmatrix} -4 & 5 \\ -7 & 9 \end{bmatrix}$

6. MULTIPLE CHOICE Which matrix has no inverse?

Ⓐ $\begin{bmatrix} 6 & 0 \\ 0 & 5 \end{bmatrix}$ Ⓑ $\begin{bmatrix} 4 & 6 \\ -6 & -9 \end{bmatrix}$

Ⓒ $\begin{bmatrix} -2 & 4 \\ 3 & 6 \end{bmatrix}$ Ⓓ $\begin{bmatrix} 1 & 1 \\ 0 & 1 \end{bmatrix}$

Ⓔ $\begin{bmatrix} -4 & 4 \\ 2 & 1 \end{bmatrix}$

7. MULTIPLE CHOICE What is the area of the triangle in square units?

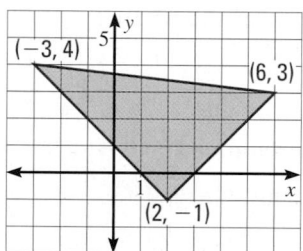

Ⓐ 40   Ⓑ 30   Ⓒ 26

Ⓓ 20   Ⓔ 13

8. MULTIPLE CHOICE What is the solution of the linear system?

$$7x + 5y = 6$$
$$4x + 3y = 3$$

Ⓐ $x = 3, y = 3$ Ⓑ $x = -3, y = -3$

Ⓒ $x = 3, y = -3$ Ⓓ $x = -3, y = 3$

Ⓔ $x = 8, y = -10$

9. **QUANTITATIVE COMPARISON** Choose the statement that is true about the given quantities.

    Ⓐ The quantity in column A is greater.

    Ⓑ The quantity in column B is greater.

    Ⓒ The two quantities are equal.

    Ⓓ The relationship cannot be determined from the given information.

Column A	Column B
$\det \begin{bmatrix} 0 & 1 \\ -8 & 2 \end{bmatrix}$	$\det \begin{bmatrix} -2 & -1 \\ 3 & 5 \end{bmatrix}$

10. **MULTI-STEP PROBLEM** The School Spirit club ordered shirts to sell at basketball games. The number of each size and type of shirt they ordered is shown in the matrix at the right.

FUNDRAISING

$$\begin{array}{c} \\ S \\ M \\ L \\ XL \end{array} \begin{array}{cc} \text{T-shirt} & \text{Sweatshirt} \\ \begin{bmatrix} 25 & 20 \\ 25 & 20 \\ 100 & 40 \\ 50 & 20 \end{bmatrix} \end{array}$$

    a. At the first basketball game the club sold 17 T-shirts (4 small, 5 medium, 6 large, and 2 extra large) and 12 sweatshirts (3 medium, 5 large, and 4 extra large). Write a matrix that gives the number of each size and type of shirt sold at the game. Then write a matrix that shows the number of shirts left.

    b. The wholesale price of a T-shirt is $8, and the club sells them for $10 each. The wholesale price of a sweatshirt is $20, and the club sells them for $25 each. Write a row matrix for the number of each type of shirt (T-shirt or sweatshirt) sold at the game from part (a). Write a column matrix for the profit on each type of shirt. Multiply the row matrix by the column matrix and interpret the result.

11. **MULTI-STEP PROBLEM** You and a friend are planning a secret meeting. You agree that $A = \begin{bmatrix} 1 & 1 \\ 1 & 2 \end{bmatrix}$ will be your coding matrix. Use the coding information on pages 225 and 226.

    a. Use matrix A to encode the message SATURDAY.

    b. Use the inverse of A to decode your answer to part (a).

    c. Your friend replied with the message below. Use the inverse of A to decode it.

        34, 49, 6, 9, 23, 41, 6, 12, 14, 19, 16, 20

    d. Use matrix A to encode your answer to part (c).

12. **MULTI-STEP PROBLEM** Use the following linear system.

$$\begin{aligned} x - 2y &= 1 \\ 3x - 5y &= 4 \end{aligned}$$

    a. Use Cramer's rule to solve the system.

    b. Use inverse matrices to solve the system.

    c. Use the substitution or linear combination method to solve the system.

    d. Solve the system by graphing. Label the solution on your graph.

    e. *Writing* Which method do you prefer for solving this linear system?

QUADRATIC FUNCTIONS

▶ *How can you model the height of lava from an erupting volcano?*

CHAPTER
5

APPLICATION: Volcanoes

Volcanic eruptions can eject lava hundreds of feet into the air, creating spectacular but dangerous "lava fountains." As the lava cools and hardens, it may accumulate to form the cone shape of a volcano.

Think & Discuss

The highest recorded lava fountain occurred during a 1959 eruption at Kilauea Iki Crater in Hawaii. The graph models the height of a typical lava fragment in the fountain while the fragment was in the air.

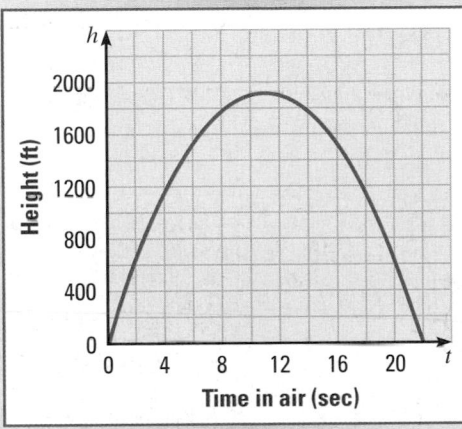

1. Estimate the lava fragment's maximum height above the ground.

2. For how long was the lava fragment in the air? How did you use the graph to get your answer?

Learn More About It

You will work with an equation modeling the height of lava in Exercise 80 on p. 297.

 APPLICATION LINK Visit www.mcdougallittell.com for more information about volcanoes.

Study Guide

PREVIEW

What's the chapter about?

Chapter 5 is about **quadratic functions, equations, and inequalities**. Many real-life situations can be modeled by quadratic functions. In Chapter 5 you'll learn

- four ways to solve quadratic equations.
- how to graph quadratic functions and inequalities.

KEY VOCABULARY

▶ **Review**
- linear equation, p. 19
- linear inequality, pp. 41, 108
- absolute value, p. 50
- linear function, p. 69
- x-intercept, p. 84
- best-fitting line, p. 101
- vertex, p. 122

▶ **New**
- quadratic function, p. 249
- parabola, p. 249
- factoring, p. 256
- quadratic equation, p. 257
- zero of a function, p. 259
- square root, p. 264
- complex number, p. 272

- completing the square, p. 282
- quadratic formula, p. 291
- discriminant, p. 293
- quadratic inequality, pp. 299, 301
- best-fitting quadratic model, p. 308

PREPARE

Are you ready for the chapter?

SKILL REVIEW Do these exercises to review key skills that you'll apply in this chapter. See the given **reference page** if there is something you don't understand.

STUDENT HELP

▶ **Study Tip**
"Student Help" boxes throughout the chapter give you study tips and tell you where to look for extra help in this book and on the Internet.

Solve the equation. (Review Examples 1–3, pp. 19 and 20)

1. $3x - 5 = 0$ **2.** $4(x + 6) = 12$ **3.** $2x + 1 = -x + 7$

Graph the inequality. (Review Example 3, p. 109)

4. $x + y > 5$ **5.** $3x - 2y \le 12$ **6.** $y \ge -2x$

Graph the function and label the vertex. (Review Example 1, p. 123)

7. $y = |x| + 2$ **8.** $y = |x - 3|$ **9.** $y = -2|x + 1| - 4$

STUDY
STRATEGY

Here's a study strategy!

Troubleshoot

After you complete each lesson, look back and identify your trouble spots, such as concepts you didn't understand or homework problems you had difficulty solving. Review the material given in the lesson and try to solve any difficult problems again. If you're still having trouble, seek the help of another student or your teacher.

5.1

Graphing Quadratic Functions

What you should learn

GOAL 1 Graph quadratic functions.

GOAL 2 Use quadratic functions to solve **real-life** problems, such as finding comfortable temperatures in **Example 5**.

Why you should learn it

▼ To model **real-life** objects, such as the cables of the Golden Gate Bridge in **Example 6**.

GOAL 1 GRAPHING A QUADRATIC FUNCTION

A **quadratic function** has the form $y = ax^2 + bx + c$ where $a \neq 0$. The graph of a quadratic function is U-shaped and is called a **parabola**.

For instance, the graphs of $y = x^2$ and $y = -x^2$ are shown at the right. The origin is the lowest point on the graph of $y = x^2$ and the highest point on the graph of $y = -x^2$. The lowest or highest point on the graph of a quadratic function is called the **vertex**.

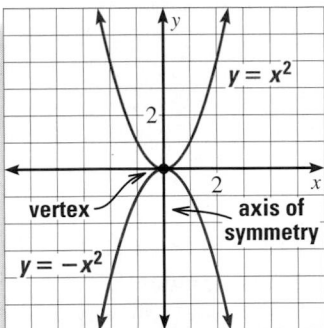

The graphs of $y = x^2$ and $y = -x^2$ are symmetric about the y-axis, called the *axis of symmetry*. In general, the **axis of symmetry** for the graph of a quadratic function is the vertical line through the vertex.

> **● ACTIVITY**
>
> **Developing Concepts**
>
> ## Investigating Parabolas
>
> **❶** Use a graphing calculator to graph each of these functions in the same viewing window: $y = \frac{1}{2}x^2$, $y = x^2$, $y = 2x^2$, and $y = 3x^2$.
>
> **❷** Repeat **Step 1** for these functions: $y = -\frac{1}{2}x^2$, $y = -x^2$, $y = -2x^2$, and $y = -3x^2$.
>
> **❸** What are the vertex and axis of symmetry of the graph of $y = ax^2$?
>
> **❹** Describe the effect of a on the graph of $y = ax^2$.

In the activity you examined the graph of the simple quadratic function $y = ax^2$. The graph of the more general function $y = ax^2 + bx + c$ is described below.

> **CONCEPT SUMMARY**   **THE GRAPH OF A QUADRATIC FUNCTION**
>
> The graph of $y = ax^2 + bx + c$ is a parabola with these characteristics:
>
> • The parabola opens up if $a > 0$ and opens down if $a < 0$. The parabola is wider than the graph of $y = x^2$ if $|a| < 1$ and narrower than the graph of $y = x^2$ if $|a| > 1$.
>
> • The x-coordinate of the vertex is $-\dfrac{b}{2a}$.
>
> • The axis of symmetry is the vertical line $x = -\dfrac{b}{2a}$.

EXAMPLE 1 *Graphing a Quadratic Function*

Graph $y = 2x^2 - 8x + 6$.

SOLUTION

Note that the coefficients for this function are $a = 2$, $b = -8$, and $c = 6$. Since $a > 0$, the parabola opens up.

Find and plot the vertex. The *x*-coordinate is:

$$x = -\frac{b}{2a} = -\frac{-8}{2(2)} = \mathbf{2}$$

The *y*-coordinate is:

$$y = 2(\mathbf{2})^2 - 8(\mathbf{2}) + 6 = -2$$

So, the vertex is $(2, -2)$.

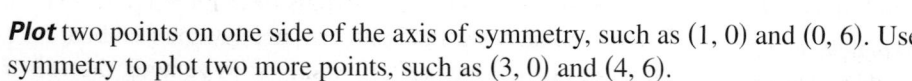

STUDENT HELP

→ **Skills Review**
For help with symmetry, see p. 919.

Draw the axis of symmetry $x = 2$.

Plot two points on one side of the axis of symmetry, such as $(1, 0)$ and $(0, 6)$. Use symmetry to plot two more points, such as $(3, 0)$ and $(4, 6)$.

Draw a parabola through the plotted points.

· · · · · · · · · ·

The quadratic function $y = ax^2 + bx + c$ is written in **standard form**. Two other useful forms for quadratic functions are given below.

VERTEX AND INTERCEPT FORMS OF A QUADRATIC FUNCTION

FORM OF QUADRATIC FUNCTION	CHARACTERISTICS OF GRAPH
Vertex form: $y = a(x - h)^2 + k$	The vertex is (h, k).
	The axis of symmetry is $x = h$.
Intercept form: $y = a(x - p)(x - q)$	The *x*-intercepts are *p* and *q*.
	The axis of symmetry is halfway between $(p, 0)$ and $(q, 0)$.

For both forms, the graph opens up if $a > 0$ and opens down if $a < 0$.

EXAMPLE 2 *Graphing a Quadratic Function in Vertex Form*

STUDENT HELP

→ **Look Back**
For help with graphing functions, see p. 123.

Graph $y = -\frac{1}{2}(x + 3)^2 + 4$.

SOLUTION

The function is in vertex form $y = a(x - h)^2 + k$ where $a = -\frac{1}{2}$, $h = -3$, and $k = 4$. Since $a < 0$, the parabola opens down. To graph the function, first plot the vertex $(h, k) = (-3, 4)$. Draw the axis of symmetry $x = -3$ and plot two points on one side of it, such as $(-1, 2)$ and $(1, -4)$. Use symmetry to complete the graph.

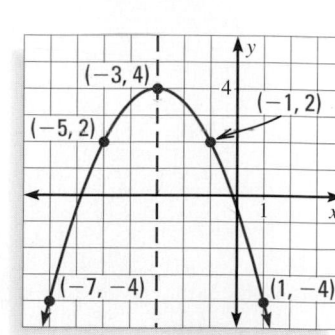

EXAMPLE 3 *Graphing a Quadratic Function in Intercept Form*

Graph $y = -(x + 2)(x - 4)$.

SOLUTION

The quadratic function is in intercept form $y = a(x - p)(x - q)$ where $a = -1$, $p = -2$, and $q = 4$. The x-intercepts occur at $(-2, 0)$ and $(4, 0)$. The axis of symmetry lies halfway between these points, at $x = 1$. So, the x-coordinate of the vertex is $x = 1$ and the y-coordinate of the vertex is:

$$y = -(1 + 2)(1 - 4) = 9$$

The graph of the function is shown.

. . . .

STUDENT HELP

▸ **Skills Review**
For help with multiplying algebraic expressions, see p. 937.

You can change quadratic functions from intercept form or vertex form to standard form by multiplying algebraic expressions. One method for multiplying expressions containing two terms is *FOIL*. Using this method, you add the products of the *F*irst terms, the *O*uter terms, the *I*nner terms, and the *L*ast terms. Here is an example:

$$\text{F} \quad \text{O} \quad \text{I} \quad \text{L}$$
$$(x + 3)(x + 5) = x^2 + 5x + 3x + 15 = x^2 + 8x + 15$$

Methods for changing from standard form to intercept form or vertex form will be discussed in Lessons 5.2 and 5.5.

EXAMPLE 4 *Writing Quadratic Functions in Standard Form*

Write the quadratic function in standard form.

a. $y = -(x + 4)(x - 9)$ **b.** $y = 3(x - 1)^2 + 8$

SOLUTION

a. $y = -(x + 4)(x - 9)$ Write original function.

$ = -(x^2 - 9x + 4x - 36)$ Multiply using FOIL.

$ = -(x^2 - 5x - 36)$ Combine like terms.

$ = -x^2 + 5x + 36$ Use distributive property.

b. $y = 3(x - 1)^2 + 8$ Write original function.

$ = 3(x - 1)(x - 1) + 8$ Rewrite $(x - 1)^2$.

$ = 3(x^2 - x - x + 1) + 8$ Multiply using FOIL.

$ = 3(x^2 - 2x + 1) + 8$ Combine like terms.

$ = 3x^2 - 6x + 3 + 8$ Use distributive property.

$ = 3x^2 - 6x + 11$ Combine like terms.

GOAL 2 **USING QUADRATIC FUNCTIONS IN REAL LIFE**

Temperature

EXAMPLE 5 *Using a Quadratic Model in Standard Form*

Researchers conducted an experiment to determine temperatures at which people feel comfortable. The percent y of test subjects who felt comfortable at temperature x (in degrees Fahrenheit) can be modeled by:

$$y = -3.678x^2 + 527.3x - 18,807$$

What temperature made the greatest percent of test subjects comfortable? At that temperature, what percent felt comfortable? ▶ Source: *Design with Climate*

SOLUTION

Since $a = -3.678$ is negative, the graph of the quadratic function opens down and the function has a maximum value. The maximum value occurs at:

$$x = -\frac{b}{2a} = -\frac{527.3}{2(-3.678)} \approx \mathbf{72}$$

The corresponding value of y is:

$$y = -3.678(\mathbf{72})^2 + 527.3(\mathbf{72}) - 18,807 \approx 92$$

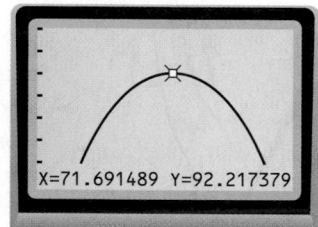

X=71.691489 Y=92.217379

▶ The temperature that made the greatest percent of test subjects comfortable was about 72°F. At that temperature about 92% of the subjects felt comfortable.

EXAMPLE 6 *Using a Quadratic Model in Vertex Form*

CIVIL ENGINEER
Civil engineers design bridges, roads, buildings, and other structures. In 1996 civil engineers held about 196,000 jobs in the United States.

CAREER LINK
www.mcdougallittell.com

CIVIL ENGINEERING The Golden Gate Bridge in San Francisco has two towers that rise 500 feet above the road and are connected by suspension cables as shown. Each cable forms a parabola with equation

$$y = \frac{1}{8960}(x - 2100)^2 + 8$$

where x and y are measured in feet.
▶ Source: Golden Gate Bridge, Highway and Transportation District

a. What is the distance d between the two towers?

b. What is the height ℓ above the road of a cable at its lowest point?

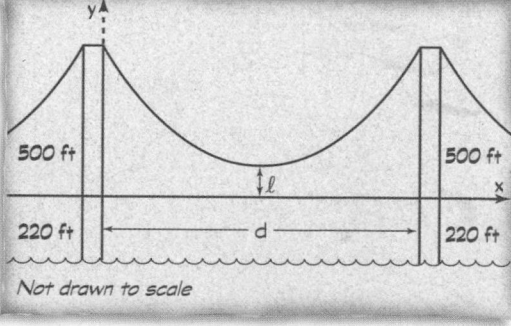

500 ft   500 ft
ℓ
220 ft d 220 ft
Not drawn to scale

SOLUTION

a. The vertex of the parabola is (2100, 8), so a cable's lowest point is 2100 feet from the left tower shown above. Since the heights of the two towers are the same, the symmetry of the parabola implies that the vertex is also 2100 feet from the right tower. Therefore, the towers are $d = 2(2100) = 4200$ feet apart.

b. The height ℓ above the road of a cable at its lowest point is the y-coordinate of the vertex. Since the vertex is (2100, 8), this height is $\ell = 8$ feet.

GUIDED PRACTICE

Vocabulary Check ✔   **1.** Complete this statement: The graph of a quadratic function is called a(n) _?_.

Concept Check ✔   **2.** Does the graph of $y = 3x^2 - x - 2$ open up or down? Explain.

3. Is $y = -2(x - 5)(x - 8)$ in standard form, vertex form, or intercept form?

Skill Check ✔   **Graph the quadratic function. Label the vertex and axis of symmetry.**

4. $y = x^2 - 4x + 7$ **5.** $y = 2(x + 1)^2 - 4$ **6.** $y = -(x + 2)(x - 1)$

7. $y = -\frac{1}{3}x^2 - 2x - 3$ **8.** $y = -\frac{3}{5}(x - 4)^2 + 6$ **9.** $y = \frac{5}{2}x(x - 3)$

Write the quadratic function in standard form.

10. $y = (x + 1)(x + 2)$ **11.** $y = -2(x + 4)(x - 3)$ **12.** $y = 4(x - 1)^2 + 5$

13. $y = -(x + 2)^2 - 7$ **14.** $y = -\frac{1}{2}(x - 6)(x - 8)$ **15.** $y = \frac{2}{3}(x - 9)^2 - 4$

16. [SCIENCE] CONNECTION   The equation given in Example 5 is based on temperature preferences of both male and female test subjects. Researchers also analyzed data for males and females separately and obtained the equations below.

Males: $y = -4.290x^2 + 612.6x - 21,773$

Females: $y = -6.224x^2 + 908.9x - 33,092$

What was the most comfortable temperature for the males? for the females?

PRACTICE AND APPLICATIONS

STUDENT HELP

▶**Extra Practice**
to help you master
skills is on p. 945.

MATCHING GRAPHS Match the quadratic function with its graph.

17. $y = (x + 2)(x - 3)$ **18.** $y = -(x - 3)^2 + 2$ **19.** $y = x^2 - 6x + 11$

A. 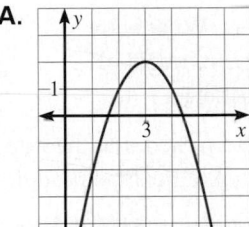   **B.** 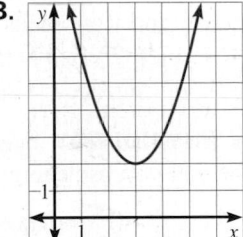   **C.**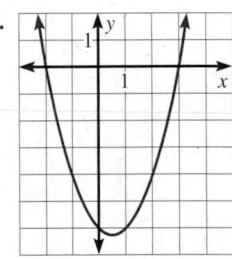

GRAPHING WITH STANDARD FORM Graph the quadratic function. Label the vertex and axis of symmetry.

20. $y = x^2 - 2x - 1$ **21.** $y = 2x^2 - 12x + 19$ **22.** $y = -x^2 + 4x - 2$

23. $y = -3x^2 + 5$ **24.** $y = \frac{1}{2}x^2 + 4x + 5$ **25.** $y = -\frac{1}{6}x^2 - x - 3$

GRAPHING WITH VERTEX FORM Graph the quadratic function. Label the vertex and axis of symmetry.

26. $y = (x - 1)^2 + 2$ **27.** $y = -(x - 2)^2 - 1$ **28.** $y = -2(x + 3)^2 - 4$

29. $y = 3(x + 4)^2 + 5$ **30.** $y = -\frac{1}{3}(x + 1)^2 + 3$ **31.** $y = \frac{5}{4}(x - 3)^2$

STUDENT HELP

▶ **HOMEWORK HELP**
Example 1: Exs. 17–25
Example 2: Exs. 17–19,
   26–31
Example 3: Exs. 17–19,
   32–37
Example 4: Exs. 38–49
Examples 5, 6: Exs. 51–54

GRAPHING WITH INTERCEPT FORM Graph the quadratic function. Label the vertex, axis of symmetry, and x-intercepts.

32. $y = (x - 2)(x - 6)$

33. $y = 4(x + 1)(x - 1)$

34. $y = -(x + 3)(x + 5)$

35. $y = \frac{1}{3}(x + 4)(x + 1)$

36. $y = -\frac{1}{2}(x - 3)(x + 2)$

37. $y = -3x(x - 2)$

WRITING IN STANDARD FORM Write the quadratic function in standard form.

38. $y = (x + 5)(x + 2)$

39. $y = -(x + 3)(x - 4)$

40. $y = 2(x - 1)(x - 6)$

41. $y = -3(x - 7)(x + 4)$

42. $y = (5x + 8)(4x + 1)$

43. $y = (x + 3)^2 + 2$

44. $y = -(x - 5)^2 + 11$

45. $y = -6(x - 2)^2 - 9$

46. $y = 8(x + 7)^2 - 20$

47. $y = -(9x + 2)^2 + 4x$

48. $y = -\frac{7}{3}(x + 6)(x + 3)$

49. $y = \frac{1}{2}(8x - 1)^2 - \frac{3}{2}$

50. **VISUAL THINKING** In parts (a) and (b), use a graphing calculator to examine how b and c affect the graph of $y = ax^2 + bx + c$.

a. Graph $y = x^2 + c$ for $c = -2, -1, 0, 1,$ and 2. Use the same viewing window for all the graphs. How do the graphs change as c increases?

b. Graph $y = x^2 + bx$ for $b = -2, -1, 0, 1,$ and 2. Use the same viewing window for all the graphs. How do the graphs change as b increases?

51. **AUTOMOBILES** The engine torque y (in foot-pounds) of one model of car is given by

$$y = -3.75x^2 + 23.2x + 38.8$$

where x is the speed of the engine (in thousands of revolutions per minute). Find the engine speed that maximizes torque. What is the maximum torque?

52. **SPORTS** Although a football field appears to be flat, its surface is actually shaped like a parabola so that rain runs off to either side. The cross section of a field with synthetic turf can be modeled by

$$y = -0.000234(x - 80)^2 + 1.5$$

where x and y are measured in feet. What is the field's width? What is the maximum height of the field's surface? ▶ Source: Boston College

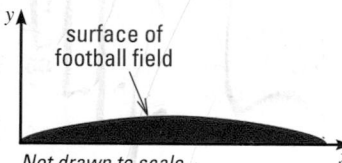

surface of football field

Not drawn to scale

53. **PHYSIOLOGY** Scientists determined that the rate y (in calories per minute) at which you use energy while walking can be modeled by

$$y = 0.00849(x - 90.2)^2 + 51.3, \quad 50 \le x \le 150$$

where x is your walking speed (in meters per minute). Graph the function on the given domain. Describe how energy use changes as walking speed increases. What speed minimizes energy use? ▶ Source: *Bioenergetics and Growth*

54. **BIOLOGY** **CONNECTION** The woodland jumping mouse can hop surprisingly long distances given its small size. A relatively long hop can be modeled by

$$y = -\frac{2}{9}x(x - 6)$$

where x and y are measured in feet. How far can a woodland jumping mouse hop? How high can it hop?
▶ Source: University of Michigan Museum of Zoology

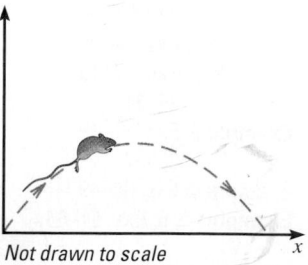

Not drawn to scale

55. MULTI-STEP PROBLEM A kernel of popcorn contains water that expands when the kernel is heated, causing it to pop. The equations below give the "popping volume" y (in cubic centimeters per gram) of popcorn with moisture content x (as a percent of the popcorn's weight). ▶ Source: *Cereal Chemistry*

Hot-air popping: $y = -0.761x^2 + 21.4x - 94.8$

Hot-oil popping: $y = -0.652x^2 + 17.7x - 76.0$

a. For hot-air popping, what moisture content maximizes popping volume? What is the maximum volume?

b. For hot-oil popping, what moisture content maximizes popping volume? What is the maximum volume?

c. The moisture content of popcorn typically ranges from 8% to 18%. Graph the equations for hot-air and hot-oil popping on the interval $8 \le x \le 18$.

d. *Writing* Based on the graphs from part (c), what general statement can you make about the volume of popcorn produced from hot-air popping versus hot-oil popping for any moisture content in the interval $8 \le x \le 18$?

★ **Challenge**

56. LOGICAL REASONING Write $y = a(x - h)^2 + k$ and $y = a(x - p)(x - q)$ in standard form. Knowing that the vertex of the graph of $y = ax^2 + bx + c$ occurs at $x = -\dfrac{b}{2a}$, show that the vertex for $y = a(x - h)^2 + k$ occurs at $x = h$ and that the vertex for $y = a(x - p)(x - q)$ occurs at $x = \dfrac{p + q}{2}$.

EXTRA CHALLENGE
www.mcdougallittell.com

MIXED REVIEW

SOLVING LINEAR EQUATIONS Solve the equation. **(Review 1.3 for 5.2)**

57. $x - 2 = 0$ **58.** $2x + 5 = 0$ **59.** $-4x - 7 = 21$

60. $3x + 9 = -x + 1$ **61.** $6(x + 8) = 18$ **62.** $5(4x - 1) = 2(x + 3)$

63. $0.6x = 0.2x + 2.8$ **64.** $\dfrac{7x}{8} - \dfrac{3x}{5} = \dfrac{11}{2}$ **65.** $\dfrac{5x}{12} + \dfrac{1}{4} = \dfrac{x}{6} - \dfrac{1}{2}$

GRAPHING IN THREE DIMENSIONS Sketch the graph of the equation. Label the points where the graph crosses the x-, y-, and z-axes. **(Review 3.5)**

66. $x + y + z = 4$ **67.** $x + y + 2z = 6$ **68.** $3x + 4y + z = 12$

69. $5x + 5y + 2z = 10$ **70.** $2x + 7y + 3z = 42$ **71.** $x + 3y - 3z = 9$

USING CRAMER'S RULE Use Cramer's rule to solve the linear system. **(Review 4.3)**

72. $x + y = 1$
$-5x + y = 19$

73. $2x + y = 5$
$3x - 4y = 2$

74. $7x - 10y = -15$
$x + 2y = -9$

75. $5x + 2y + 2z = 4$
$3x + y - 6z = -4$
$-x - y - z = 1$

76. $x + 3y + z = 5$
$-x + y + z = 7$
$2x - 7y + 5z = 28$

77. $2x - 3y - 9z = 11$
$6x + y - z = 45$
$9x - 2y + 4z = 56$

78. 🌎 **WEATHER** In January, 1996, rain and melting snow caused the depth of the Susquehanna River in Pennsylvania to rise from 7 feet to 22 feet in 14 hours. Find the average rate of change in the depth during that time. **(Review 2.2)**

Solving Quadratic Equations by Factoring

What you should learn

GOAL 1 Factor quadratic expressions and solve quadratic equations by factoring.

GOAL 2 Find zeros of quadratic functions, as applied in **Example 8**.

Why you should learn it

▼ To solve **real-life** problems, such as finding appropriate dimensions for a mural in **Ex. 97**.

GOAL 1 FACTORING QUADRATIC EXPRESSIONS

You know how to write $(x + 3)(x + 5)$ as $x^2 + 8x + 15$. The expressions $x + 3$ and $x + 5$ are **binomials** because they have two terms. The expression $x^2 + 8x + 15$ is a **trinomial** because it has three terms. You can use **factoring** to write a trinomial as a product of binomials. To factor $x^2 + bx + c$, find integers m and n such that:

$$x^2 + bx + c = (x + m)(x + n)$$
$$= x^2 + (m + n)x + mn$$

So, the *sum* of m and n must equal b and the *product* of m and n must equal c.

EXAMPLE 1 *Factoring a Trinomial of the Form $x^2 + bx + c$*

Factor $x^2 - 12x - 28$.

SOLUTION

You want $x^2 - 12x - 28 = (x + m)(x + n)$ where $mn = -28$ and $m + n = -12$.

Factors of -28 (m, n)	$-1, 28$	$1, -28$	$-2, 14$	$2, -14$	$-4, 7$	$4, -7$
Sum of factors $(m + n)$	27	-27	12	-12	3	-3

▶ The table shows that $m = 2$ and $n = -14$. So, $x^2 - 12x - 28 = (x + 2)(x - 14)$.

. . . .

To factor $ax^2 + bx + c$ when $a \neq 1$, find integers $k, l, m,$ and n such that:

$$ax^2 + bx + c = (kx + m)(lx + n)$$
$$= klx^2 + (kn + lm)x + mn$$

Therefore, k and l must be factors of a, and m and n must be factors of c.

EXAMPLE 2 *Factoring a Trinomial of the Form $ax^2 + bx + c$*

Factor $3x^2 - 17x + 10$.

SOLUTION

You want $3x^2 - 17x + 10 = (kx + m)(lx + n)$ where k and l are factors of 3 and m and n are (negative) factors of 10. Check possible factorizations by multiplying.

$(3x - 10)(x - 1) = 3x^2 - 13x + 10$ $(3x - 1)(x - 10) = 3x^2 - 31x + 10$

$(3x - 5)(x - 2) = 3x^2 - 11x + 10$ $(3x - 2)(x - 5) = 3x^2 - 17x + 10$ ✓

▶ The correct factorization is $3x^2 - 17x + 10 = (3x - 2)(x - 5)$.

STUDENT HELP

▶ **Skills Review**
For help with factoring, see p. 938.

As in Example 2, factoring quadratic expressions often involves trial and error. However, some expressions are easy to factor because they follow special patterns.

SPECIAL FACTORING PATTERNS		
PATTERN NAME	**PATTERN**	**EXAMPLE**
Difference of Two Squares	$a^2 - b^2 = (a + b)(a - b)$	$x^2 - 9 = (x + 3)(x - 3)$
Perfect Square Trinomial	$a^2 + 2ab + b^2 = (a + b)^2$	$x^2 + 12x + 36 = (x + 6)^2$
	$a^2 - 2ab + b^2 = (a - b)^2$	$x^2 - 8x + 16 = (x - 4)^2$

EXAMPLE 3 *Factoring with Special Patterns*

Factor the quadratic expression.

a. $4x^2 - 25 = (2x)^2 - 5^2$ **Difference of two squares**

$\qquad\qquad = (2x + 5)(2x - 5)$

b. $9y^2 + 24y + 16 = (3y)^2 + 2(3y)(4) + 4^2$ **Perfect square trinomial**

$\qquad\qquad\qquad = (3y + 4)^2$

c. $49r^2 - 14r + 1 = (7r)^2 - 2(7r)(1) + 1^2$ **Perfect square trinomial**

$\qquad\qquad\qquad = (7r - 1)^2$

· · · · · · · · · ·

A **monomial** is an expression that has only one term. As a first step to factoring, you should check to see whether the terms have a common monomial factor.

EXAMPLE 4 *Factoring Monomials First*

STUDENT HELP

▶ **Study Tip**
It is not always possible to factor a trinomial into a product of two binomials with integer coefficients. For instance, the trinomial $x^2 + x - 1$ in part (d) of Example 4 cannot be factored. Such trinomials are called *irreducible*.

Factor the quadratic expression.

a. $5x^2 - 20 = 5(x^2 - 4)$ **b.** $6p^2 + 15p + 9 = 3(2p^2 + 5p + 3)$

$\qquad\qquad = 5(x + 2)(x - 2)$ $= 3(2p + 3)(p + 1)$

c. $2u^2 + 8u = 2u(u + 4)$ **d.** $4x^2 + 4x - 4 = 4(x^2 + x - 1)$

· · · · · · · · · ·

You can use factoring to solve certain *quadratic equations*. A **quadratic equation** in one variable can be written in the form $ax^2 + bx + c = 0$ where $a \neq 0$. This is called the **standard form** of the equation. If the left side of $ax^2 + bx + c = 0$ can be factored, then the equation can be solved using the *zero product property*.

ZERO PRODUCT PROPERTY
Let *A* and *B* be real numbers or algebraic expressions. If $AB = 0$, then $A = 0$ or $B = 0$.

EXAMPLE 5 Solving Quadratic Equations

STUDENT HELP

Look Back
For help with
solving equations,
see p. 19.

Solve (a) $x^2 + 3x - 18 = 0$ and (b) $2t^2 - 17t + 45 = 3t - 5$.

SOLUTION

a. $x^2 + 3x - 18 = 0$ **Write original equation.**

$(x + 6)(x - 3) = 0$ **Factor.**

$x + 6 = 0$ or $x - 3 = 0$ **Use zero product property.**

$x = -6$ or $x = 3$ **Solve for x.**

▶ The solutions are -6 and 3. Check the solutions in the original equation.

b. $2t^2 - 17t + 45 = 3t - 5$ **Write original equation.**

$2t^2 - 20t + 50 = 0$ **Write in standard form.**

$t^2 - 10t + 25 = 0$ **Divide each side by 2.**

$(t - 5)^2 = 0$ **Factor.**

$t - 5 = 0$ **Use zero product property.**

$t = 5$ **Solve for t.**

▶ The solution is 5. Check the solution in the original equation.

EXAMPLE 6 Using a Quadratic Equation as a Model

Crafts

You have made a rectangular stained glass window that is
2 feet by 4 feet. You have 7 square feet of clear glass to create
a border of uniform width around the window. What should
the width of the border be?

SOLUTION

**PROBLEM
SOLVING
STRATEGY**

**VERBAL
MODEL**

$$\boxed{\text{Area of border}} = \boxed{\text{Area of border and window}} - \boxed{\text{Area of window}}$$

LABELS

Width of border $= x$ (feet)

Area of border $= 7$ (square feet)

Area of border and window $= (2 + 2x)(4 + 2x)$ (square feet)

Area of window $= 2 \cdot 4 = 8$ (square feet)

**ALGEBRAIC
MODEL**

$7 = (2 + 2x)(4 + 2x) - 8$ **Write algebraic model.**

$0 = 4x^2 + 12x - 7$ **Write in standard form.**

$0 = (2x + 7)(2x - 1)$ **Factor.**

$2x + 7 = 0$ or $2x - 1 = 0$ **Use zero product property.**

$x = -3.5$ or $x = 0.5$ **Solve for x.**

▶ Reject the negative value, -3.5. The border's width should be 0.5 ft, or 6 in.

GOAL 2 FINDING ZEROS OF QUADRATIC FUNCTIONS

In Lesson 5.1 you learned that the x-intercepts of the graph of $y = a(x - p)(x - q)$ are p and q. The numbers p and q are also called **zeros** of the function because the function's value is zero when $x = p$ and when $x = q$. If a quadratic function is given in standard form $y = ax^2 + bx + c$, you may be able to find its zeros by using factoring to rewrite the function in intercept form.

EXAMPLE 7   *Finding the Zeros of a Quadratic Function*

Find the zeros of $y = x^2 - x - 6$.

SOLUTION

Use factoring to write the function in intercept form.

$$y = x^2 - x - 6$$
$$= (x + 2)(x - 3)$$

▶ The zeros of the function are -2 and 3.

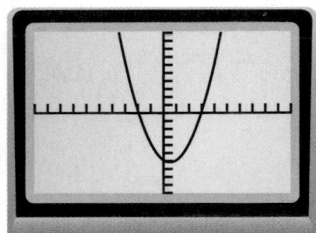

✓ **CHECK** Graph $y = x^2 - x - 6$. The graph passes through $(-2, 0)$ and $(3, 0)$, so the zeros are -2 and 3.

· · · · · · · · · ·

From Lesson 5.1 you know that the vertex of the graph of $y = a(x - p)(x - q)$ lies on the vertical line halfway between $(p, 0)$ and $(q, 0)$. In terms of zeros, the function has its maximum or minimum value when x equals the *average* of the zeros.

EXAMPLE 8   *Using the Zeros of a Quadratic Model*

BUSINESS You maintain a music-oriented Web site that allows subscribing customers to download audio and video clips of their favorite bands. When the subscription price is $16 per year, you get 30,000 subscribers. For each $1 increase in price, you expect to lose 1000 subscribers. How much should you charge to maximize your annual revenue? What is your maximum revenue?

SOLUTION

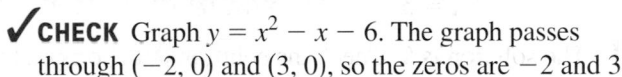

Let R be your annual revenue and let x be the number of $1 price increases.

$$R = (30,000 - 1000x)(16 + x)$$
$$= (-1000x + 30,000)(x + 16)$$
$$= -1000(x - 30)(x + 16)$$

The zeros of the revenue function are 30 and -16. The value of x that maximizes R is the average of the zeros, or $x = \dfrac{30 + (-16)}{2} = 7$.

▶ To maximize revenue, charge $16 + $7 = $23 per year for a subscription. Your maximum revenue is $R = -1000(7 - 30)(7 + 16) = \$529,000$.

GUIDED PRACTICE

Vocabulary Check ✓

1. What is a zero of a function $y = f(x)$?

Concept Check ✓

2. In Example 2, how do you know that m and n must be *negative* factors of 10?

3. ERROR ANALYSIS A student solved $x^2 + 4x + 3 = 8$ as shown. Explain the student's mistake. Then solve the equation correctly.

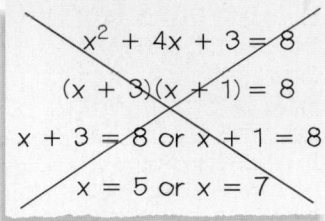

$$x^2 + 4x + 3 = 8$$
$$(x + 3)(x + 1) = 8$$
$$x + 3 = 8 \text{ or } x + 1 = 8$$
$$x = 5 \text{ or } x = 7$$

Skill Check ✓ **Factor the expression.**

4. $x^2 - x - 2$ **5.** $2x^2 + x - 3$ **6.** $x^2 - 16$

7. $y^2 + 2y + 1$ **8.** $p^2 - 4p + 4$ **9.** $q^2 + q$

Solve the equation.

10. $(x + 3)(x - 1) = 0$ **11.** $x^2 - 2x - 8 = 0$ **12.** $3x^2 + 10x + 3 = 0$

13. $4u^2 - 1 = 0$ **14.** $v^2 - 14v = -49$ **15.** $5w^2 = 30w$

Write the quadratic function in intercept form and give the function's zeros.

16. $y = x^2 - 6x + 5$ **17.** $y = x^2 + 6x + 8$ **18.** $y = x^2 - 1$

19. $y = x^2 + 10x + 25$ **20.** $y = 2x^2 - 2x - 24$ **21.** $y = 3x^2 - 8x + 4$

22. 🌐 **URBAN PLANNING** You have just planted a rectangular flower bed of red roses in a park near your home. You want to plant a border of yellow roses around the flower bed as shown. Since you bought the same number of red and yellow roses, the areas of the border and inner flower bed will be equal. What should the width x of the border be?

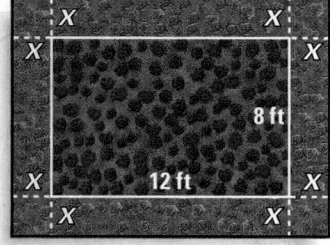

PRACTICE AND APPLICATIONS

STUDENT HELP

► **Extra Practice**
to help you master skills is on p. 945.

FACTORING $x^2 + bx + c$ **Factor the trinomial. If the trinomial cannot be factored, say so.**

23. $x^2 + 5x + 4$ **24.** $x^2 + 9x + 14$ **25.** $x^2 + 13x + 40$

26. $x^2 - 4x + 3$ **27.** $x^2 - 8x + 12$ **28.** $x^2 - 16x + 51$

29. $a^2 + 3a - 10$ **30.** $b^2 + 6b - 27$ **31.** $c^2 + 2c - 80$

32. $p^2 - 5p - 6$ **33.** $q^2 - 7q - 10$ **34.** $r^2 - 14r - 72$

FACTORING $ax^2 + bx + c$ **Factor the trinomial. If the trinomial cannot be factored, say so.**

35. $2x^2 + 7x + 3$ **36.** $3x^2 + 17x + 10$ **37.** $8x^2 + 18x + 9$

38. $5x^2 - 7x + 2$ **39.** $6x^2 - 9x + 5$ **40.** $10x^2 - 19x + 6$

41. $3k^2 + 32k - 11$ **42.** $11m^2 + 14m - 16$ **43.** $18n^2 + 9n - 14$

44. $7u^2 - 4u - 3$ **45.** $12v^2 - 25v - 7$ **46.** $4w^2 - 13w - 27$

FACTORING WITH SPECIAL PATTERNS Factor the expression.

47. $x^2 - 25$ **48.** $x^2 + 4x + 4$ **49.** $x^2 - 6x + 9$

50. $4r^2 - 4r + 1$ **51.** $9s^2 + 12s + 4$ **52.** $16t^2 - 9$

53. $49 - 100a^2$ **54.** $25b^2 - 60b + 36$ **55.** $81c^2 + 198c + 121$

FACTORING MONOMIALS FIRST Factor the expression.

56. $5x^2 + 5x - 10$ **57.** $18x^2 - 2$ **58.** $3x^2 + 54x + 243$

59. $8y^2 - 28y - 60$ **60.** $112a^2 - 168a + 63$ **61.** $u^2 + 7u$

62. $6t^2 - 36t$ **63.** $-v^2 + 2v - 1$ **64.** $2d^2 + 12d - 16$

EQUATIONS IN STANDARD FORM Solve the equation.

65. $x^2 - 3x - 4 = 0$ **66.** $x^2 + 19x + 88 = 0$ **67.** $5x^2 - 13x + 6 = 0$

68. $8x^2 - 6x - 5 = 0$ **69.** $k^2 + 24k + 144 = 0$ **70.** $9m^2 - 30m + 25 = 0$

71. $81n^2 - 16 = 0$ **72.** $40a^2 + 4a = 0$ **73.** $-3b^2 + 3b + 90 = 0$

EQUATIONS NOT IN STANDARD FORM Solve the equation.

74. $x^2 + 9x = -20$ **75.** $16x^2 = 8x - 1$

76. $5p^2 - 25 = 4p^2 + 24$ **77.** $2y^2 - 4y - 8 = -y^2 + y$

78. $2q^2 + 4q - 1 = 7q^2 - 7q + 1$ **79.** $(w + 6)^2 = 3(w + 12) - w^2$

FINDING ZEROS Write the quadratic function in intercept form and give the function's zeros.

80. $y = x^2 - 3x + 2$ **81.** $y = x^2 + 7x + 12$ **82.** $y = x^2 + 2x - 35$

83. $y = x^2 - 4$ **84.** $y = x^2 + 20x + 100$ **85.** $y = x^2 - 3x$

86. $y = 3x^2 - 12x - 15$ **87.** $y = -x^2 + 16x - 64$ **88.** $y = 2x^2 - 9x + 4$

89. LOGICAL REASONING Is there a formula for factoring the *sum* of two squares? You will investigate this question in parts (a) and (b).

    a. Consider the sum of squares $x^2 + 9$. If this sum can be factored, then there are integers m and n such that $x^2 + 9 = (x + m)(x + n)$. Write two equations relating the sum and the product of m and n to the coefficients in $x^2 + 9$.

    b. Show that there are no integers m and n that satisfy both equations you wrote in part (a). What can you conclude?

90. QUILTING You have made a quilt that is 4 feet by 5 feet. You want to use the remaining 10 square feet of fabric to add a decorative border of uniform width. What should the width of the border be?

91. CONSTRUCTION A high school wants to double the size of its parking lot by expanding the existing lot as shown. By what distance x should the lot be expanded?

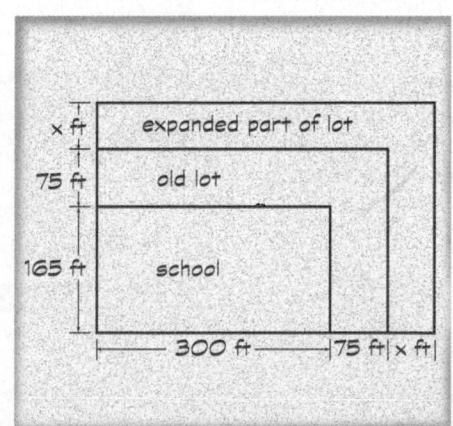

STUDENT HELP

▶ **HOMEWORK HELP**
Example 1: Exs. 23–34
Example 2: Exs. 35–46
Example 3: Exs. 47–55
Example 4: Exs. 56–64
Example 5: Exs. 65–79
Example 6: Exs. 90, 91, 97, 98
Example 7: Exs. 80–88
Example 8: Exs. 99–101

STUDENT HELP

► **Skills Review**
For help with areas of
geometric figures,
see p. 914.

GEOMETRY CONNECTION Find the value of x.

92. Area of rectangle = 40

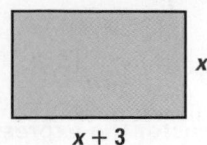

x

$x + 3$

93. Area of rectangle = 105

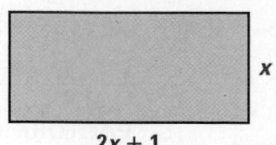

x

$2x + 1$

94. Area of triangle = 22

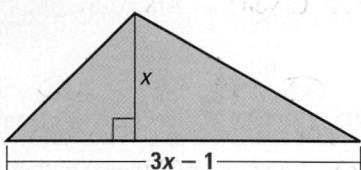

x

$3x - 1$

95. Area of trapezoid = 114

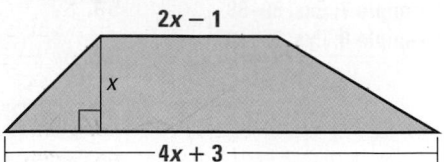

$2x - 1$

x

$4x + 3$

96. VISUAL THINKING Use the diagram shown at the right.

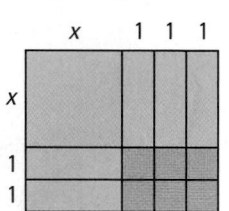

x 1 1 1

a. Explain how the diagram models the factorization
$x^2 + 5x + 6 = (x + 2)(x + 3)$.

b. Draw a diagram that models the factorization
$x^2 + 7x + 12 = (x + 3)(x + 4)$.

97. ART CONNECTION As part of Black History Month in February, an artist is creating a mural on the side of a building. A painting of Dr. Martin Luther King, Jr., will occupy the center of the mural and will be surrounded by a border of uniform width showing other prominent African-Americans. The side of the building is 50 feet wide by 30 feet high, and the artist wants to devote 25% of the available space to the border. What should the width of the border be?

FOCUS ON APPLICATIONS

► **ENVIRONMENT**
Ecology gardens
are often used to conduct
research with different plant
species under a variety of
growing conditions.

98. ENVIRONMENT A student environmental group wants to build an ecology garden as shown. The area of the garden should be 800 square feet to accommodate all the species of plants the group wants to grow. A construction company has donated 120 feet of iron fencing to enclose the garden. What should the dimensions of the garden be?

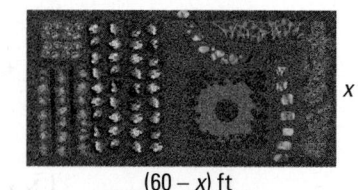

x ft

$(60 - x)$ ft

99. ATHLETIC WEAR A shoe store sells about 200 pairs of a new basketball shoe each month when it charges $60 per pair. For each $1 increase in price, about 2 fewer pairs per month are sold. How much per pair should the store charge to maximize monthly revenue? What is the maximum revenue?

100. HOME ELECTRONICS The manager of a home electronics store is considering repricing a new model of digital camera. At the current price of $680, the store sells about 70 cameras each month. Sales data from other stores indicate that for each $20 decrease in price, about 5 more cameras per month would be sold. How much should the manager charge for a camera to maximize monthly revenue? What is the maximum revenue?

101. HISTORY CONNECTION Big Bertha, a cannon used in World War I, could fire shells incredibly long distances. The path of a shell could be modeled by $y = -0.0196x^2 + 1.37x$ where x was the horizontal distance traveled (in miles) and y was the height (in miles). How far could Big Bertha fire a shell? What was the shell's maximum height? ► Source: World War I: Trenches on the Web

102. MULTIPLE CHOICE Suppose $x^2 + 4x + c = (x + m)(x + n)$ where c, m, and n are integers. Which of the following are *not* possible values of m and n?

(A) $m = 2, n = 2$ (B) $m = -1, n = 5$

(C) $m = -2, n = -2$ (D) $m = 1, n = 3$

103. MULTIPLE CHOICE What are all solutions of $2x^2 - 11x + 16 = x^2 - 3x$?

(A) 2, 6   (B) -4   (C) -4, 4   (D) 4

104. MULTIPLE CHOICE Given that 4 is a zero of $y = 3x^2 + bx - 8$, what is the value of b?

(A) -40   (B) -10   (C) -8   (D) 2

★ **Challenge**

105. MULTICULTURAL MATHEMATICS The following problem is from the *Chiu chang suan shu*, an ancient Chinese mathematics text. Solve the problem. (*Hint:* Use the Pythagorean theorem.)

> *A rod of unknown length is used to measure the dimensions of a rectangular door. The rod is 4* ch'ih *longer than the width of the door, 2* ch'ih *longer than the height of the door, and the same length as the door's diagonal. What are the dimensions of the door?* (*Note:* 1 ch'ih *is slightly greater than 1 foot.*)

EXTRA CHALLENGE
→ www.mcdougallittell.com

MIXED REVIEW

ABSOLUTE VALUE Solve the equation or inequality. (Review 1.7)

106. $|x| = 3$

107. $|x - 2| = 6$

108. $|4x - 9| = 2$

109. $|-5x + 4| = 14$

110. $|7 - 3x| = -8$

111. $|x + 1| < 3$

112. $|2x - 5| \le 1$

113. $|x - 4| > 7$

114. $\left|\frac{1}{3}x + 1\right| \ge 2$

GRAPHING LINEAR EQUATIONS Graph the equation. (Review 2.3)

115. $y = x + 1$

116. $y = -2x + 3$

117. $y = 3x - 5$

118. $y = -\frac{5}{2}x + 7$

119. $x + y = 4$

120. $2x - y = 6$

121. $3x + 4y = -12$

122. $-5x + 3y = 15$

123. $y = 2$

124. $y = -3$

125. $x = -1$

126. $x = 4$

GRAPHING QUADRATIC FUNCTIONS Graph the function. (Review 5.1 for 5.3)

127. $y = x^2 - 2$

128. $y = 2x^2 - 5$

129. $y = -x^2 + 3$

130. $y = (x + 1)^2 - 4$

131. $y = -(x - 2)^2 + 1$

132. $y = -3(x + 3)^2 + 7$

133. $y = \frac{1}{4}x^2 - 1$

134. $y = \frac{1}{2}(x - 4)^2 - 6$

135. $y = -\frac{2}{3}(x + 1)(x - 3)$

136. 🌎 **COMMUTING** You can take either the subway or the bus to your after-school job. A round trip from your home to where you work costs $2 on the subway and $3 on the bus. You prefer to take the bus as often as possible but can afford to spend only $50 per month on transportation. If you work 22 days each month, how many of these days can you take the bus? **(Review 1.5)**

5.3
Solving Quadratic Equations by Finding Square Roots

What you should learn

GOAL 1 Solve quadratic equations by finding square roots.

GOAL 2 Use quadratic equations to solve **real-life** problems, such as finding how long a falling stunt man is in the air in **Example 4**.

Why you should learn it

▼ To model **real-life** quantities, such as the height of a rock dropped off the Leaning Tower of Pisa in **Ex. 69**.

GOAL 1 SOLVING QUADRATIC EQUATIONS

A number r is a **square root** of a number s if $r^2 = s$. A positive number s has two square roots denoted by $\sqrt{s}$ and $-\sqrt{s}$. The symbol $\sqrt{}$ is a **radical sign**, the number s beneath the radical sign is the **radicand**, and the expression $\sqrt{s}$ is a **radical**.

For example, since $3^2 = 9$ and $(-3)^2 = 9$, the two square roots of 9 are $\sqrt{9} = 3$ and $-\sqrt{9} = -3$. You can use a calculator to approximate $\sqrt{s}$ when s is not a perfect square. For instance, $\sqrt{2} \approx 1.414$.

▶ ACTIVITY
Developing Concepts
Investigating Properties of Square Roots

① Evaluate the two expressions. What do you notice about the square root of a product of two numbers?

a. $\sqrt{36}$, $\sqrt{4} \cdot \sqrt{9}$ **b.** $\sqrt{8}$, $\sqrt{4} \cdot \sqrt{2}$ **c.** $\sqrt{30}$, $\sqrt{3} \cdot \sqrt{10}$

② Evaluate the two expressions. What do you notice about the square root of a quotient of two numbers?

a. $\sqrt{\dfrac{4}{9}}$, $\dfrac{\sqrt{4}}{\sqrt{9}}$ **b.** $\sqrt{\dfrac{25}{2}}$, $\dfrac{\sqrt{25}}{\sqrt{2}}$ **c.** $\sqrt{\dfrac{19}{7}}$, $\dfrac{\sqrt{19}}{\sqrt{7}}$

In the activity you may have discovered the following properties of square roots. You can use these properties to simplify expressions containing square roots.

PROPERTIES OF SQUARE ROOTS ($a > 0$, $b > 0$)
Product Property: $\sqrt{ab} = \sqrt{a} \cdot \sqrt{b}$ **Quotient Property:** $\sqrt{\dfrac{a}{b}} = \dfrac{\sqrt{a}}{\sqrt{b}}$

A square-root expression is considered simplified if (1) no radicand has a perfect-square factor other than 1, and (2) there is no radical in a denominator.

EXAMPLE 1 *Using Properties of Square Roots*

Simplify the expression.

a. $\sqrt{24} = \sqrt{4} \cdot \sqrt{6} = 2\sqrt{6}$ **b.** $\sqrt{6} \cdot \sqrt{15} = \sqrt{90} = \sqrt{9} \cdot \sqrt{10} = 3\sqrt{10}$

c. $\sqrt{\dfrac{7}{16}} = \dfrac{\sqrt{7}}{\sqrt{16}} = \dfrac{\sqrt{7}}{4}$ **d.** $\sqrt{\dfrac{7}{2}} = \dfrac{\sqrt{7}}{\sqrt{2}} \cdot \dfrac{\sqrt{2}}{\sqrt{2}} = \dfrac{\sqrt{14}}{2}$

In part (d) of Example 1, the square root in the denominator of $\frac{\sqrt{7}}{\sqrt{2}}$ was eliminated by multiplying both the numerator and the denominator by $\sqrt{2}$. This process is called **rationalizing the denominator**.

You can use square roots to solve some types of quadratic equations. For instance, if $s > 0$, then the quadratic equation $x^2 = s$ has two real-number solutions: $x = \sqrt{s}$ and $x = -\sqrt{s}$. These solutions are often written in condensed form as $x = \pm\sqrt{s}$. The symbol $\pm\sqrt{s}$ is read as "plus or minus the square root of s."

EXAMPLE 2 *Solving a Quadratic Equation*

Solve $2x^2 + 1 = 17$.

SOLUTION

Begin by writing the equation in the form $x^2 = s$.

$2x^2 + 1 = 17$	**Write original equation.**
$2x^2 = 16$	**Subtract 1 from each side.**
$x^2 = 8$	**Divide each side by 2.**
$x = \pm\sqrt{8}$	**Take square roots of each side.**
$x = \pm2\sqrt{2}$	**Simplify.**

▶ The solutions are $2\sqrt{2}$ and $-2\sqrt{2}$.

✔ **CHECK** You can check the solutions algebraically by substituting them into the original equation. Since this equation is equivalent to $2x^2 - 16 = 0$, you can also check the solutions by graphing $y = 2x^2 - 16$ and observing that the graph's x-intercepts appear to be about $2.8 \approx 2\sqrt{2}$ and $-2.8 \approx -2\sqrt{2}$.

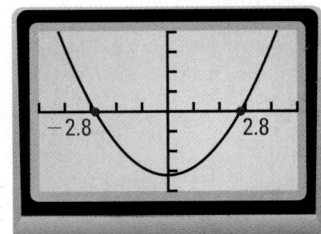

EXAMPLE 3 *Solving a Quadratic Equation*

STUDENT HELP

HOMEWORK HELP
Visit our Web site
www.mcdougallittell.com
for extra examples.

Solve $\frac{1}{3}(x + 5)^2 = 7$.

SOLUTION

$\frac{1}{3}(x + 5)^2 = 7$	**Write original equation.**
$(x + 5)^2 = 21$	**Multiply each side by 3.**
$x + 5 = \pm\sqrt{21}$	**Take square roots of each side.**
$x = -5 \pm \sqrt{21}$	**Subtract 5 from each side.**

▶ The solutions are $-5 + \sqrt{21}$ and $-5 - \sqrt{21}$.

✔ **CHECK** Check the solutions either by substituting them into the original equation or by graphing $y = \frac{1}{3}(x + 5)^2 - 7$ and observing the x-intercepts.

GOAL 2 USING QUADRATIC MODELS IN REAL LIFE

When an object is dropped, its speed continually increases, and therefore its height above the ground decreases at a faster and faster rate. The height h (in feet) of the object t seconds after it is dropped can be modeled by the function

$$h = -16t^2 + h_0$$

where h_0 is the object's initial height. This model assumes that the force of air resistance on the object is negligible. Also, the model works only on Earth. For planets with stronger or weaker gravity, different models are used (see Exercise 71).

REAL LIFE

Movies

EXAMPLE 4 *Modeling a Falling Object's Height with a Quadratic Function*

A stunt man working on the set of a movie is to fall out of a window 100 feet above the ground. For the stunt man's safety, an air cushion 26 feet wide by 30 feet long by 9 feet high is positioned on the ground below the window.

   a. For how many seconds will the stunt man fall before he reaches the cushion?

   b. A movie camera operating at a speed of 24 frames per second records the stunt man's fall. How many frames of film show the stunt man falling?

SOLUTION

a. The stunt man's initial height is $h_0 = 100$ feet, so his height as a function of time is given by $h = -16t^2 + 100$. Since the top of the cushion is 9 feet above the ground, you can determine how long it takes the stunt man to reach the cushion by finding the value of t for which $h = 9$. Here are two methods:

Method 1: Make a table of values.

t	0	1	2	3
h	100	84	36	-44

▶ From the table you can see that $h = 9$ at a value of t between $t = 2$ and $t = 3$. It takes between 2 sec and 3 sec for the stunt man to reach the cushion.

Method 2: Solve a quadratic equation.

$h = -16t^2 + 100$	**Write height function.**
$9 = -16t^2 + 100$	**Substitute 9 for h.**
$-91 = -16t^2$	**Subtract 100 from each side.**
$\dfrac{91}{16} = t^2$	**Divide each side by –16.**
$\sqrt{\dfrac{91}{16}} = t$	**Take positive square root.**
$2.4 \approx t$	**Use a calculator.**

▶ It takes about 2.4 seconds for the stunt man to reach the cushion.

b. The number of frames of film that show the stunt man falling is given by the product (2.4 sec)(24 frames/sec), or about 57 frames.

GUIDED PRACTICE

Vocabulary Check ✓

1. Explain what it means to "rationalize the denominator" of a quotient containing square roots.

Concept Check ✓

2. State the product and quotient properties of square roots in words.

3. How many real-number solutions does the equation $x^2 = s$ have when $s > 0$? when $s = 0$? when $s < 0$?

Skill Check ✓

Simplify the expression.

4. $\sqrt{49}$
5. $\sqrt{12}$
6. $\sqrt{45}$
7. $\sqrt{3} \cdot \sqrt{27}$

8. $\sqrt{\dfrac{16}{25}}$
9. $\sqrt{\dfrac{7}{9}}$
10. $\dfrac{1}{\sqrt{3}}$
11. $\sqrt{\dfrac{5}{2}}$

Solve the equation.

12. $x^2 = 64$
13. $x^2 - 9 = 16$
14. $4x^2 + 7 = 23$

15. $\dfrac{x^2}{6} - 2 = 0$
16. $5(x-1)^2 = 50$
17. $\dfrac{1}{2}(x+8)^2 = 14$

18. 🌐 **ENGINEERING** At an engineering school, students are challenged to design a container that prevents an egg from breaking when dropped from a height of 50 feet. Write an equation giving a container's height h (in feet) above the ground after t seconds. How long does the container take to hit the ground?

PRACTICE AND APPLICATIONS

STUDENT HELP

▶ **Extra Practice**
to help you master
skills is on p. 946.

USING THE PRODUCT PROPERTY **Simplify the expression.**

19. $\sqrt{18}$
20. $\sqrt{48}$
21. $\sqrt{27}$
22. $\sqrt{52}$

23. $\sqrt{72}$
24. $\sqrt{175}$
25. $\sqrt{98}$
26. $\sqrt{605}$

27. $2\sqrt{7} \cdot \sqrt{7}$
28. $\sqrt{8} \cdot \sqrt{2}$
29. $\sqrt{3} \cdot \sqrt{12}$
30. $3\sqrt{20} \cdot 6\sqrt{5}$

31. $\sqrt{12} \cdot \sqrt{2}$
32. $\sqrt{6} \cdot \sqrt{10}$
33. $4\sqrt{3} \cdot \sqrt{21}$
34. $\sqrt{8} \cdot \sqrt{6} \cdot \sqrt{3}$

USING THE QUOTIENT PROPERTY **Simplify the expression.**

35. $\sqrt{\dfrac{1}{9}}$
36. $\sqrt{\dfrac{4}{49}}$
37. $\sqrt{\dfrac{36}{25}}$
38. $\sqrt{\dfrac{100}{81}}$

39. $\sqrt{\dfrac{3}{16}}$
40. $\sqrt{\dfrac{11}{64}}$
41. $\sqrt{\dfrac{75}{36}}$
42. $\sqrt{\dfrac{40}{169}}$

43. $\dfrac{2}{\sqrt{3}}$
44. $\dfrac{5}{\sqrt{17}}$
45. $\sqrt{\dfrac{6}{5}}$
46. $\sqrt{\dfrac{144}{11}}$

47. $\sqrt{\dfrac{7}{8}}$
48. $\sqrt{\dfrac{18}{13}}$
49. $\sqrt{\dfrac{45}{32}}$
50. $\sqrt{\dfrac{15}{7}} \cdot \sqrt{\dfrac{4}{3}}$

STUDENT HELP

▶ **HOMEWORK HELP**
Example 1: Exs. 19–50
Example 2: Exs. 51–59
Example 3: Exs. 60–68
Example 4: Exs. 69–73

SOLVING QUADRATIC EQUATIONS **Solve the equation.**

51. $x^2 = 121$
52. $x^2 = 90$
53. $3x^2 = 108$

54. $2x^2 + 5 = 41$
55. $-x^2 - 12 = -87$
56. $7 - 10u^2 = 1$

57. $\dfrac{v^2}{25} - 1 = 11$
58. $6 - \dfrac{p^2}{8} = -4$
59. $\dfrac{5q^2}{6} - \dfrac{q^2}{3} = 72$

SOLVING QUADRATIC EQUATIONS Solve the equation.

60. $2(x - 3)^2 = 8$ **61.** $4(x + 1)^2 = 100$ **62.** $-3(x + 2)^2 = -18$

63. $5(x - 7)^2 = 135$ **64.** $8(x + 4)^2 = 9$ **65.** $2(a - 6)^2 - 45 = 53$

66. $\frac{1}{4}(b - 8)^2 = 7$ **67.** $(2r - 5)^2 = 81$ **68.** $\frac{(s + 1)^2}{10} - \frac{12}{5} = \frac{15}{2}$

69. **HISTORY** **CONNECTION** According to legend, in 1589 the Italian scientist Galileo Galilei dropped two rocks of different weights from the top of the Leaning Tower of Pisa. He wanted to show that the rocks would hit the ground at the same time. Given that the tower's height is about 177 feet, how long would it have taken for the rocks to hit the ground?

70. **ORNITHOLOGY** Many birds drop shellfish onto rocks to break the shell and get to the food inside. Crows along the west coast of Canada use this technique to eat whelks (a type of sea snail). Suppose a crow drops a whelk from a height of 20 feet, as shown.

▶ Source: *Cambridge Encyclopedia of Ornithology*

a. Write an equation giving the whelk's height h (in feet) after t seconds.

b. Use the *Table* feature of a graphing calculator to find h when $t = 0, 0.1, 0.2, 0.3, \ldots, 1.4, 1.5$. (You'll need to scroll down the table to see all the values.) To the nearest tenth of a second, how long does it take for the whelk to hit the ground? Check your answer by solving a quadratic equation.

20 ft

ASTRONOMY The acceleration due to gravity on the moon is about 5.3 ft/sec². This means that the moon's gravity is only about one sixth as strong as Earth's.

APPLICATION LINK www.mcdougallittell.com

71. **ASTRONOMY** On *any* planet, the height h (in feet) of a falling object t seconds after it is dropped can be modeled by

$$h = -\frac{g}{2}t^2 + h_0$$

where h_0 is the object's initial height and g is the acceleration (in feet per second squared) due to the planet's gravity. For each planet in the table, find the time it takes for a rock dropped from a height of 200 feet to hit the ground.

Planet	Earth	Mars	Jupiter	Neptune	Pluto
g (ft/sec²)	32	12	81	36	2.1

▶ Source: STARLab, Stanford University

72. **OCEANOGRAPHY** The equation $h = 0.019s^2$ gives the height h (in feet) of the largest ocean waves when the wind speed is s knots. How fast is the wind blowing if the largest waves are 15 feet high? ▶ Source: *Encyclopaedia Britannica*

STUDENT HELP

▶ **Skills Review**
For help with the Pythagorean theorem, see p. 917.

73. **TELEVISION** The *aspect ratio* of a TV screen is the ratio of the screen's width to its height. For most TVs, the aspect ratio is 4:3. What are the width and height of the screen for a 27 inch TV? (*Hint:* Use the Pythagorean theorem and the fact that TV sizes such as 27 inches refer to the length of the screen's diagonal.)

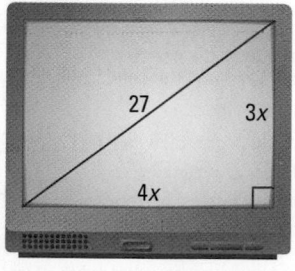

27
3x
4x

74. MULTI-STEP PROBLEM Building codes often require that buildings be able to withstand a certain amount of wind pressure. The pressure P (in pounds per square foot) from wind blowing at s miles per hour is given by $P = 0.00256s^2$.

▶ Source: *The Complete How to Figure It*

a. You are designing a two-story library. Buildings this tall are often required to withstand wind pressure of 20 lb/ft^2. Under this requirement, how fast can the wind be blowing before it produces excessive stress on a building?

b. To be safe, you design your library so that it can withstand wind pressure of 40 lb/ft^2. Does this mean that the library can survive wind blowing at twice the speed you found in part (a)? Justify your answer mathematically.

c. *Writing* Use the pressure formula to explain why even a relatively small increase in wind speed could have potentially serious effects on a building.

★ Challenge

75. SCIENCE CONNECTION For a bathtub with a rectangular base, *Torricelli's law* implies that the height h of water in the tub t seconds after it begins draining is given by

$$h = \left(\sqrt{h_0} - \frac{2\pi d^2\sqrt{3}}{lw}t \right)^2$$

where l and w are the tub's length and width, d is the diameter of the drain, and h_0 is the water's initial height. (All measurements are in inches.) Suppose you completely fill a tub with water. The tub is 60 inches long by 30 inches wide by 25 inches high and has a drain with a 2 inch diameter.

a. Find the time it takes for the tub to go from being full to half-full.

b. Find the time it takes for the tub to go from being half-full to empty.

c. **CRITICAL THINKING** Based on your results, what general statement can you make about the speed at which water drains?

EXTRA CHALLENGE
→ www.mcdougallittell.com

MIXED REVIEW

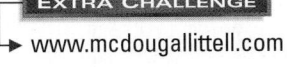

SOLVING SYSTEMS Solve the linear system by graphing. (Review 3.1)

76. $x + y = 5$
$-x + 2y = 4$

77. $x - y = -1$
$3x + y = 5$

78. $-3x + y = 7$
$2x + y = 2$

79. $2x - 3y = 9$
$4x - 3y = 3$

80. $x + 4y = 4$
$3x - 2y = 12$

81. $2x + 3y = 6$
$x - 6y = 18$

MATRIX OPERATIONS Perform the indicated operation(s). (Review 4.1)

82. $\begin{bmatrix} 6 & -1 \\ 8 & 2 \end{bmatrix} + \begin{bmatrix} -5 & -4 \\ 10 & -2 \end{bmatrix}$

83. $\begin{bmatrix} 7 & 3 \\ -2 & 0 \end{bmatrix} - \begin{bmatrix} -6 & 4 \\ 9 & -1 \end{bmatrix}$

84. $-4\begin{bmatrix} -3 & 5 & -1 \\ 4 & -4 & 8 \end{bmatrix}$

85. $-2\begin{bmatrix} 12 & 10 \\ 20 & -9 \end{bmatrix} + 7\begin{bmatrix} 15 & 11 \\ 0 & -7 \end{bmatrix}$

WRITING IN STANDARD FORM Write the quadratic function in standard form. (Review 5.1 for 5.4)

86. $y = (x + 5)(x - 2)$

87. $y = (x - 1)(x - 8)$

88. $y = (2x + 7)(x + 4)$

89. $y = (4x + 9)(4x - 9)$

90. $y = (x - 3)^2 + 1$

91. $y = 5(x + 6)^2 - 12$

Graph the function. (Lesson 5.1)

1. $y = x^2 - 2x - 3$ **2.** $y = 2(x + 2)^2 + 1$ **3.** $y = -\frac{1}{3}(x + 5)(x - 1)$

Solve the equation. (Lesson 5.2)

4. $x^2 - 6x - 27 = 0$ **5.** $4x^2 + 21x + 20 = 0$ **6.** $7t^2 - 4t = 3t^2 - 1$

Simplify the expression. (Lesson 5.3)

7. $\sqrt{54}$ **8.** $7\sqrt{2} \cdot \sqrt{10}$ **9.** $\sqrt{\dfrac{36}{5}}$ **10.** $\dfrac{4}{\sqrt{12}}$

11. 🌐 **SWIMMING** The drag force F (in pounds) of water on a swimmer can be modeled by $F = 1.35s^2$ where s is the swimmer's speed (in miles per hour). How fast must you swim to generate a drag force of 10 pounds? (Lesson 5.3)

MATH & History

Telescopes

APPLICATION LINK
www.mcdougallittell.com

THEN THE FIRST TELESCOPE is thought to have been made in 1608 by Hans Lippershey, a Dutch optician. Lippershey's telescope, called a *refracting telescope*, used lenses to magnify objects. Another type of telescope is a *reflecting telescope*. Reflecting telescopes magnify objects with parabolic mirrors, traditionally made from glass.

NOW RECENTLY "liquid mirrors" for telescopes have been made by spinning reflective liquids, such as mercury. A cross section of the surface of a spinning liquid is a parabola with equation

$$y = \frac{\pi^2 f^2}{16}x^2 - \frac{\pi^2 f^2 R^2}{32}$$

where f is the spinning frequency (in revolutions per second) and R is the radius (in feet) of the container.

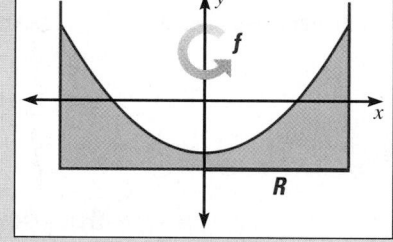

1. Write an equation for the surface of a liquid before it is spun. What does the equation tell you about the location of the x-axis relative to the liquid?

2. Suppose mercury is spun with a frequency of 0.5 revolution/sec in a container with radius 2 feet. Write and graph an equation for the mercury's surface.

3. Find the x-intercepts of the graph of $y = \dfrac{\pi^2 f^2}{16}x^2 - \dfrac{\pi^2 f^2 R^2}{32}$. Does changing the spinning frequency affect the x-intercepts? Explain.

Galileo first uses a refracting telescope for astronomical purposes.

1609

1668
Isaac Newton builds first reflecting telescope.

Maria Mitchell is first to use a telescope to discover a comet.

1847

1987
Liquid mirrors are first used to do astronomical research.

▶ ACTIVITY 5.3
Using Technology

Solving Quadratic Equations

You can use a graphing calculator to solve quadratic equations having real-number solutions.

▶ EXAMPLE

Solve $2(x - 3)^2 = 5$.

▶ SOLUTION

❶ Write the equation in the form $f(x) = 0$.

$$2(x - 3)^2 = 5$$

$$2(x - 3)^2 - 5 = 0$$

Therefore, the solutions of the original equation are the zeros of the function $y = 2(x - 3)^2 - 5$, or equivalently, the x-intercepts of this function's graph.

❷ Enter $y = 2(x - 3)^2 - 5$ into your graphing calculator.

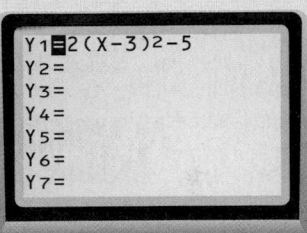

```
Y1◼2(X-3)2-5
Y2=
Y3=
Y4=
Y5=
Y6=
Y7=
```

❸ Graph the function you entered in **Step 2**. Use your calculator's *Zero* or *Root* feature to find the x-intercepts of the graph. (*Root* is another word for a solution of an equation, in this case $2(x - 3)^2 - 5 = 0$.)

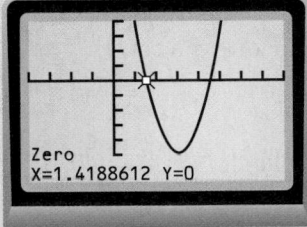

```
Zero
X=1.4188612  Y=0
```

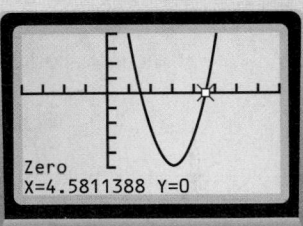

```
Zero
X=4.5811388  Y=0
```

▶ The solutions are about 1.42 and about 4.58.

▶ EXERCISES

Use a graphing calculator to solve the equation.

1. $3x^2 - 7 = 0$

2. $-2x^2 + 9 = 3$

3. $5x^2 + 2 = 6x^2 - 4$

4. $1.2x^2 - 5.6 = 0.8x^2 - 2.3$

5. $(x + 1)^2 - 3 = 0$

6. $-\frac{1}{3}(x - 4)^2 = -8$

7. $x^2 + 2x - 6 = 0$

8. $2x^2 + 8x + 3 = 4x^2 + 5x - 1$

9. 🌐 **MANUFACTURING** A company sells ground coffee in cans having a radius of 2 inches and a height of 6 inches. The company wants to manufacture a larger can that has the same height but holds twice as much coffee. Write an equation you can use to find the larger can's radius. (*Hint:* Use the formula $V = \pi r^2 h$ for the volume of a cylinder.) Solve the equation with a graphing calculator.

5.4

Complex Numbers

What you should learn

GOAL 1 Solve quadratic equations with complex solutions and perform operations with complex numbers.

GOAL 2 Apply complex numbers to fractal geometry.

Why you should learn it

▼ To solve problems, such as determining whether a complex number belongs to the Mandelbrot set in **Example 7**.

GOAL 1 OPERATIONS WITH COMPLEX NUMBERS

Not all quadratic equations have real-number solutions. For instance, $x^2 = -1$ has no real-number solutions because the square of any real number x is never negative. To overcome this problem, mathematicians created an expanded system of numbers using the **imaginary unit** i, defined as $i = \sqrt{-1}$. Note that $i^2 = -1$. The imaginary unit i can be used to write the square root of *any* negative number.

THE SQUARE ROOT OF A NEGATIVE NUMBER

PROPERTY	EXAMPLE
1. If r is a positive real number, then $\sqrt{-r} = i\sqrt{r}$.	$\sqrt{-5} = i\sqrt{5}$
2. By Property (1), it follows that $(i\sqrt{r})^2 = -r$.	$(i\sqrt{5})^2 = i^2 \cdot 5 = -5$

EXAMPLE 1 Solving a Quadratic Equation

Solve $3x^2 + 10 = -26$.

SOLUTION

$3x^2 + 10 = -26$	**Write original equation.**
$3x^2 = -36$	**Subtract 10 from each side.**
$x^2 = -12$	**Divide each side by 3.**
$x = \pm\sqrt{-12}$	**Take square roots of each side.**
$x = \pm i\sqrt{12}$	**Write in terms of i.**
$x = \pm 2i\sqrt{3}$	**Simplify the radical.**

▶ The solutions are $2i\sqrt{3}$ and $-2i\sqrt{3}$.

· · · · · · · · · ·

A **complex number** written in **standard form** is a number $a + bi$ where a and b are real numbers. The number a is the *real part* of the complex number, and the number bi is the *imaginary part*. If $b \neq 0$, then $a + bi$ is an **imaginary number**. If $a = 0$ and $b \neq 0$, then $a + bi$ is a **pure imaginary number**. The diagram shows how different types of complex numbers are related.

Complex Numbers ($a + bi$)

Real Numbers ($a + 0i$)	Imaginary Numbers ($a + bi, b \neq 0$)
-1 $\frac{5}{2}$	$2 + 3i$ $5 - 5i$
3	**Pure Imaginary Numbers** ($0 + bi, b \neq 0$)
π $\sqrt{2}$	$-4i$ $6i$

Just as every real number corresponds to a point on the real number line, every complex number corresponds to a point in the **complex plane**. As shown in the next example, the complex plane has a horizontal axis called the *real axis* and a vertical axis called the *imaginary axis*.

EXAMPLE 2 *Plotting Complex Numbers*

Plot the complex numbers in the complex plane.

  a. $2 - 3i$ **b.** $-3 + 2i$ **c.** $4i$

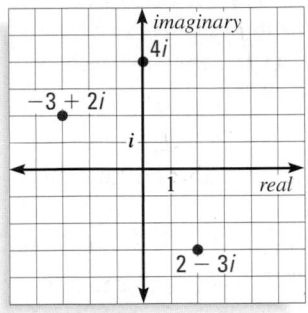

SOLUTION

  a. To plot $2 - 3i$, start at the origin, move 2 units to the right, and then move 3 units down.

  b. To plot $-3 + 2i$, start at the origin, move 3 units to the left, and then move 2 units up.

  c. To plot $4i$, start at the origin and move 4 units up.

· · · · · · · · · ·

Two complex numbers $a + bi$ and $c + di$ are equal if and only if $a = c$ and $b = d$. For instance, if $x + yi = 8 - i$, then $x = 8$ and $y = -1$.

To add (or subtract) two complex numbers, add (or subtract) their real parts and their imaginary parts separately.

  Sum of complex numbers: $(a + bi) + (c + di) = (a + c) + (b + d)i$

  Difference of complex numbers: $(a + bi) - (c + di) = (a - c) + (b - d)i$

EXAMPLE 3 *Adding and Subtracting Complex Numbers*

Write the expression as a complex number in standard form.

  a. $(4 - i) + (3 + 2i)$ **b.** $(7 - 5i) - (1 - 5i)$ **c.** $6 - (-2 + 9i) + (-8 + 4i)$

SOLUTION

  a. $(4 - i) + (3 + 2i) = (4 + 3) + (-1 + 2)i$ Definition of complex addition

          $= 7 + i$ Standard form

  b. $(7 - 5i) - (1 - 5i) = (7 - 1) + (-5 + 5)i$ Definition of complex subtraction

          $= 6 + 0i$ Simplify.

          $= 6$ Standard form

  c. $6 - (-2 + 9i) + (-8 + 4i) = [(6 + 2) - 9i] + (-8 + 4i)$ Subtract.

             $= (8 - 9i) + (-8 + 4i)$ Simplify.

             $= (8 - 8) + (-9 + 4)i$ Add.

             $= 0 - 5i$ Simplify.

             $= -5i$ Standard form

To multiply two complex numbers, use the distributive property or the FOIL method just as you do when multiplying real numbers or algebraic expressions. Other properties of real numbers that also apply to complex numbers include the associative and commutative properties of addition and multiplication.

EXAMPLE 4 *Multiplying Complex Numbers*

Write the expression as a complex number in standard form.

   a. $5i(-2 + i)$ **b.** $(7 - 4i)(-1 + 2i)$ **c.** $(6 + 3i)(6 - 3i)$

SOLUTION

   a. $5i(-2 + i) = -10i + 5i^2$ **Distributive property**

               $= -10i + 5(-1)$ **Use $i^2 = -1$.**

               $= -5 - 10i$ **Standard form**

   b. $(7 - 4i)(-1 + 2i) = -7 + 14i + 4i - 8i^2$ **Use FOIL.**

                   $= -7 + 18i - 8(-1)$ **Simplify and use $i^2 = -1$.**

                   $= 1 + 18i$ **Standard form**

   c. $(6 + 3i)(6 - 3i) = 36 - 18i + 18i - 9i^2$ **Use FOIL.**

                 $= 36 - 9(-1)$ **Simplify and use $i^2 = -1$.**

                 $= 45$ **Standard form**

· · · · · · · · · ·

In part (c) of Example 4, notice that the two factors $6 + 3i$ and $6 - 3i$ have the form $a + bi$ and $a - bi$. Such numbers are called **complex conjugates**. The product of complex conjugates is always a real number. You can use complex conjugates to write the quotient of two complex numbers in standard form.

EXAMPLE 5 *Dividing Complex Numbers*

Write the quotient $\dfrac{5 + 3i}{1 - 2i}$ in standard form.

SOLUTION

The key step here is to multiply the numerator and the denominator by the complex conjugate of the denominator.

$$\frac{5 + 3i}{1 - 2i} = \frac{5 + 3i}{1 - 2i} \cdot \frac{1 + 2i}{1 + 2i} \qquad \textbf{Multiply by } 1 + 2i, \textbf{ the conjugate of } 1 - 2i.$$

$$= \frac{5 + 10i + 3i + 6i^2}{1 + 2i - 2i - 4i^2} \qquad \textbf{Use FOIL.}$$

$$= \frac{-1 + 13i}{5} \qquad \textbf{Simplify.}$$

$$= -\frac{1}{5} + \frac{13}{5}i \qquad \textbf{Standard form}$$

REAL LIFE **BENOIT MANDELBROT**
was born in Poland in 1924, came to the United States in 1958, and is now a professor at Yale University. He pioneered the study of fractal geometry in the 1970s.

GOAL 2 **USING COMPLEX NUMBERS IN FRACTAL GEOMETRY**

In the hands of a person who understands *fractal geometry*, the complex plane can become an easel on which stunning pictures called *fractals* are drawn. One very famous fractal is the *Mandelbrot set*, named after mathematician Benoit Mandelbrot. The Mandelbrot set is the black region in the complex plane below. (The points in the colored regions are *not* part of the Mandelbrot set.)

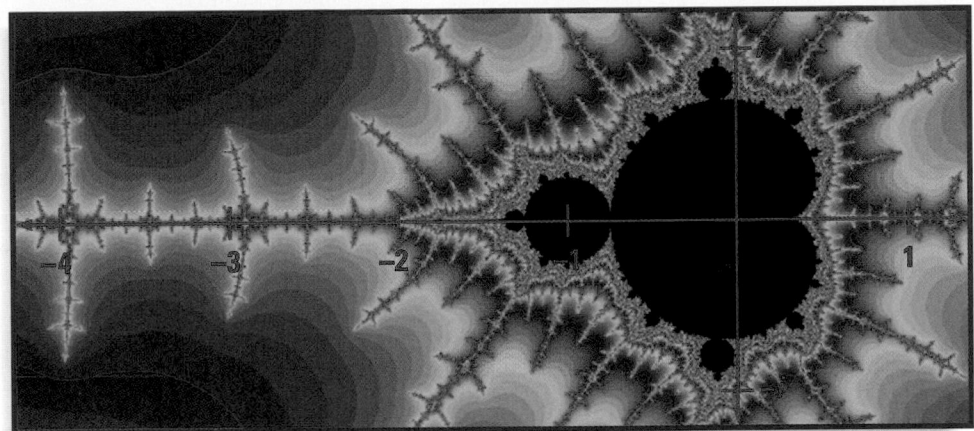

To understand how the Mandelbrot set is constructed, you need to know how the *absolute value* of a complex number is defined.

ABSOLUTE VALUE OF A COMPLEX NUMBER

The **absolute value** of a complex number $z = a + bi$, denoted $|z|$, is a nonnegative *real* number defined as follows:

$$|z| = \sqrt{a^2 + b^2}$$

Geometrically, the absolute value of a complex number is the number's distance from the origin in the complex plane.

EXAMPLE 6 *Finding Absolute Values of Complex Numbers*

Find the absolute value of each complex number. Which number is farthest from the origin in the complex plane?

   a. $3 + 4i$ **b.** $-2i$ **c.** $-1 + 5i$

SOLUTION

  a. $|3 + 4i| = \sqrt{3^2 + 4^2} = \sqrt{25} = 5$

  b. $|-2i| = |0 + (-2i)| = \sqrt{0^2 + (-2)^2} = 2$

  c. $|-1 + 5i| = \sqrt{(-1)^2 + 5^2} = \sqrt{26} \approx 5.10$

Since $-1 + 5i$ has the greatest absolute value, it is farthest from the origin in the complex plane.

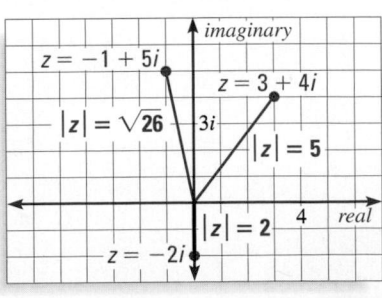

The following result shows how absolute value can be used to tell whether a given complex number belongs to the Mandelbrot set.

COMPLEX NUMBERS IN THE MANDELBROT SET

To determine whether a complex number c belongs to the Mandelbrot set, consider the function $f(z) = z^2 + c$ and this infinite list of complex numbers:

$$z_0 = 0, \ z_1 = f(z_0), \ z_2 = f(z_1), \ z_3 = f(z_2), \ \ldots$$

- If the absolute values $|z_0|, |z_1|, |z_2|, |z_3|, \ldots$ are all less than some fixed number N, then c belongs to the Mandelbrot set.

- If the absolute values $|z_0|, |z_1|, |z_2|, |z_3|, \ldots$ become infinitely large, then c does not belong to the Mandelbrot set.

EXAMPLE 7 *Determining if a Complex Number Is in the Mandelbrot Set*

Tell whether the complex number c belongs to the Mandelbrot set.

a. $c = i$ **b.** $c = 1 + i$ **c.** $c = -2$

SOLUTION

a. Let $f(z) = z^2 + i$.

$z_0 = 0$ $|z_0| = 0$

$z_1 = f(0) = 0^2 + i = i$ $|z_1| = 1$

$z_2 = f(i) = i^2 + i = -1 + i$ $|z_2| = \sqrt{2} \approx 1.41$

$z_3 = f(-1 + i) = (-1 + i)^2 + i = -i$ $|z_3| = 1$

$z_4 = f(-i) = (-i)^2 + i = -1 + i$ $|z_4| = \sqrt{2} \approx 1.41$

At this point the absolute values alternate between 1 and $\sqrt{2}$, and so all the absolute values are less than $N = 2$. Therefore, $c = i$ belongs to the Mandelbrot set.

b. Let $f(z) = z^2 + (1 + i)$.

$z_0 = 0$ $|z_0| = 0$

$z_1 = f(0) = 0^2 + (1 + i) = 1 + i$ $|z_1| \approx 1.41$

$z_2 = f(1 + i) = (1 + i)^2 + (1 + i) = 1 + 3i$ $|z_2| \approx 3.16$

$z_3 = f(1 + 3i) = (1 + 3i)^2 + (1 + i) = -7 + 7i$ $|z_3| \approx 9.90$

$z_4 = f(-7 + 7i) = (-7 + 7i)^2 + (1 + i) = 1 - 97i$ $|z_4| \approx 97.0$

The next few absolute values in the list are (approximately) 9409, 8.85×10^7, and 7.84×10^{15}. Since the absolute values are becoming infinitely large, $c = 1 + i$ does not belong to the Mandelbrot set.

c. Let $f(z) = z^2 + (-2)$, or $f(z) = z^2 - 2$. You can show that $z_0 = 0$, $z_1 = -2$, and $z_n = 2$ for $n > 1$. Therefore, the absolute values of $z_0, z_1, z_2, z_3, \ldots$ are all less than $N = 3$, and so $c = -2$ belongs to the Mandelbrot set.

GUIDED PRACTICE

Vocabulary Check ✓

1. Complete this statement: For the complex number $3 - 7i$, the real part is ? and the imaginary part is ? .

Concept Check ✓

2. **ERROR ANALYSIS** A student thinks that the complex conjugate of $-5 + 2i$ is $5 - 2i$. Explain the student's mistake, and give the correct complex conjugate of $-5 + 2i$.

3. Geometrically, what does the absolute value of a complex number represent?

Skill Check ✓

Solve the equation.

4. $x^2 = -9$ **5.** $2x^2 + 3 = -13$ **6.** $(x - 1)^2 = -7$

Write the expression as a complex number in standard form.

7. $(1 + 5i) + (6 - 2i)$ **8.** $(4 + 3i) - (-2 + 4i)$

9. $(1 - i)(7 + 2i)$ **10.** $\dfrac{3 - 4i}{1 + i}$

Find the absolute value of the complex number.

11. $1 + i$ **12.** $3i$ **13.** $-2 + 3i$ **14.** $5 - 5i$

15. Plot the numbers in Exercises 11–14 in the same complex plane.

16. **FRACTAL GEOMETRY** Tell whether $c = 1 - i$ belongs to the Mandelbrot set. Use absolute value to justify your answer.

PRACTICE AND APPLICATIONS

STUDENT HELP

▸ **Extra Practice**
to help you master
skills is on p. 946.

SOLVING QUADRATIC EQUATIONS Solve the equation.

17. $x^2 = -4$ **18.** $x^2 = -11$ **19.** $3x^2 = -81$

20. $2x^2 + 9 = -41$ **21.** $5x^2 + 18 = 3$ **22.** $-x^2 - 4 = 14$

23. $8r^2 + 7 = 5r^2 + 4$ **24.** $3s^2 - 1 = 7s^2$ **25.** $(t - 2)^2 = -16$

26. $-6(u + 5)^2 = 120$ **27.** $-\frac{1}{8}(v + 3)^2 = 7$ **28.** $9(w - 4)^2 + 1 = 0$

PLOTTING COMPLEX NUMBERS Plot the numbers in the same complex plane.

29. $4 + 2i$ **30.** $-1 + i$ **31.** $-4i$ **32.** 3

33. $-2 - i$ **34.** $1 + 5i$ **35.** $6 - 3i$ **36.** $-5 + 4i$

STUDENT HELP

▸ **HOMEWORK HELP**
Example 1: Exs. 17–28
Example 2: Exs. 29–36
Example 3: Exs. 37–46
Example 4: Exs. 47–55
Example 5: Exs. 56–63
Example 6: Exs. 64–71
Example 7: Exs. 72–79

ADDING AND SUBTRACTING Write the expression as a complex number in standard form.

37. $(2 + 3i) + (7 + i)$ **38.** $(6 + 2i) + (5 - i)$

39. $(-4 + 7i) + (-4 - 7i)$ **40.** $(-1 - i) + (9 - 3i)$

41. $(8 + 5i) - (1 + 2i)$ **42.** $(2 - 6i) - (-10 + 4i)$

43. $(-0.4 + 0.9i) - (-0.6 + i)$ **44.** $(25 + 15i) - (25 - 6i)$

45. $-i + (8 - 2i) - (5 - 9i)$ **46.** $(30 - i) - (18 + 6i) + 30i$

MULTIPLYING Write the expression as a complex number in standard form.

47. $i(3 + i)$

48. $4i(6 - i)$

49. $-10i(4 + 7i)$

50. $(5 + i)(8 + i)$

51. $(-1 + 2i)(11 - i)$

52. $(2 - 9i)(9 - 6i)$

53. $(7 + 5i)(7 - 5i)$

54. $(3 + 10i)^2$

55. $(15 - 8i)^2$

DIVIDING Write the expression as a complex number in standard form.

56. $\dfrac{8}{1 + i}$

57. $\dfrac{2i}{1 - i}$

58. $\dfrac{-5 - 3i}{4i}$

59. $\dfrac{3 + i}{3 - i}$

60. $\dfrac{2 + 5i}{5 + 2i}$

61. $\dfrac{-7 + 6i}{9 - 4i}$

62. $\dfrac{\sqrt{10}}{\sqrt{10} - i}$

63. $\dfrac{6 - i\sqrt{2}}{6 + i\sqrt{2}}$

ABSOLUTE VALUE Find the absolute value of the complex number.

64. $3 - 4i$

65. $5 + 12i$

66. $-2 - i$

67. $-7 + i$

68. $2 + 5i$

69. $4 - 8i$

70. $-9 + 6i$

71. $\sqrt{11} + i\sqrt{5}$

MANDELBROT SET Tell whether the complex number c belongs to the Mandelbrot set. Use absolute value to justify your answer.

72. $c = 1$

73. $c = -1$

74. $c = -i$

75. $c = -1 - i$

76. $c = 2$

77. $c = -1 + i$

78. $c = -0.5$

79. $c = 0.5i$

STUDENT HELP

▶ **Skills Review**
For help with
disproving statements
by counterexample,
see p. 927.

LOGICAL REASONING In Exercises 80–85, tell whether the statement is *true* or *false*. If the statement is false, give a counterexample.

80. Every complex number is an imaginary number.

81. Every irrational number is a complex number.

82. All real numbers lie on a single line in the complex plane.

83. The sum of two imaginary numbers is always an imaginary number.

84. Every real number equals its complex conjugate.

85. The absolute values of a complex number and its complex conjugate are always equal.

86. **VISUAL THINKING** The graph shows how you can geometrically add two complex numbers (in this case, $3 + 2i$ and $1 + 4i$) to find their sum (in this case, $4 + 6i$). Find each of the following sums by drawing a graph.

    a. $(2 + i) + (3 + 5i)$

    b. $(-1 + 6i) + (7 - 4i)$

COMPARING REAL AND COMPLEX NUMBERS Tell whether the property is true for (a) the set of real numbers and (b) the set of complex numbers.

87. If r, s, and t are numbers in the set, then $(r + s) + t = r + (s + t)$.

88. If r is a number in the set and $|r| = k$, then $r = k$ or $r = -k$.

89. If r and s are numbers in the set, then $r - s = s - r$.

90. If r, s, and t are numbers in the set, then $r(s + t) = rs + rt$.

91. If r and s are numbers in the set, then $|r + s| = |r| + |s|$.

92. CRITICAL THINKING Evaluate $\sqrt{-4} \cdot \sqrt{-9}$ and $\sqrt{36}$. Does the rule $\sqrt{a} \cdot \sqrt{b} = \sqrt{ab}$ on page 264 hold when a and b are negative numbers?

93. Writing Give both an algebraic argument and a geometric argument explaining why the definitions of absolute value on pages 50 and 275 are consistent when applied to real numbers.

94. EXTENSION: ADDITIVE AND MULTIPLICATIVE INVERSES The *additive inverse* of a complex number z is a complex number z_a such that $z + z_a = 0$. The *multiplicative inverse* of z is a complex number z_m such that $z \cdot z_m = 1$. Find the additive and multiplicative inverses of each complex number.

a. $z = 1 + i$ **b.** $z = 3 - i$ **c.** $z = -2 + 8i$

ELECTRICITY In Exercises 95 and 96, use the following information.

Electrical circuits may contain several types of components such as resistors, inductors, and capacitors. The resistance of each component to the flow of electrical current is the component's *impedance*, denoted by Z. The value of Z is a real number R for a resistor of R ohms (Ω), a pure imaginary number Li for an inductor of L ohms, and a pure imaginary number $-Ci$ for a capacitor of C ohms. Examples are given in the table.

Component	Symbol	Z
Resistor	—⋀⋀⋁— 3Ω	3
Inductor	-0000- 5Ω	5i
Capacitor	—╫— 6Ω	-6i

95. SERIES CIRCUITS A *series circuit* is a type of circuit found in switches, fuses, and circuit breakers. In a series circuit, there is only one pathway through which current can flow. To find the total impedance of a series circuit, add the impedances of the components in the circuit. What is the impedance of each series circuit shown below? (*Note:* The symbol ⊙ denotes an alternating current source and does not affect the calculation of impedance.)

a.

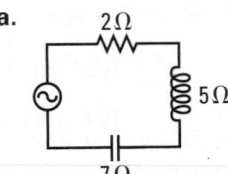

2Ω, 5Ω, 7Ω

b.

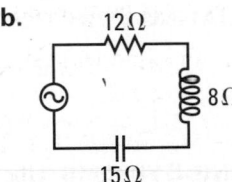

12Ω, 8Ω, 15Ω

c.

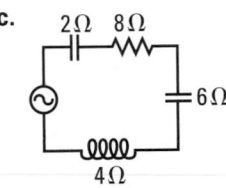

2Ω 8Ω, 6Ω, 4Ω

96. PARALLEL CIRCUITS *Parallel circuits* are used in household lighting and appliances. In a parallel circuit, there is more than one pathway through which current can flow. To find the impedance Z of a parallel circuit with two pathways, first calculate the impedances Z_1 and Z_2 of the pathways separately by treating each pathway as a series circuit. Then apply this formula:

$$Z = \frac{Z_1 Z_2}{Z_1 + Z_2}$$

What is the impedance of each parallel circuit shown below?

a.

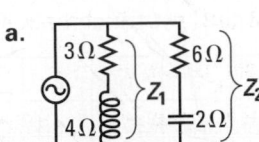

3Ω, 6Ω, 4Ω, 2Ω, Z_1, Z_2

b.

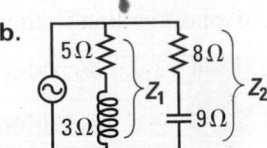

5Ω, 8Ω, 3Ω, 9Ω, Z_1, Z_2

c.

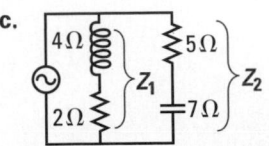

4Ω, 5Ω, 2Ω, 7Ω, Z_1, Z_2

QUANTITATIVE COMPARISON In Exercises 97–99, choose the statement that is true about the given quantities.

   Ⓐ The quantity in column A is greater.

   Ⓑ The quantity in column B is greater.

   Ⓒ The two quantities are equal.

   Ⓓ The relationship cannot be determined from the given information.

	Column A	Column B
97.	$\lvert 5 + 4i \rvert$	$\lvert 3 - 6i \rvert$
98.	$\lvert -6 + 8i \rvert$	$\lvert -10i \rvert$
99.	$\lvert 2 + bi \rvert$ where $b < -1$	$\lvert \sqrt{3} + ci \rvert$ where $0 < c < 1$

★ **Challenge**

100. POWERS OF i In this exercise you will investigate a pattern that appears when the imaginary unit i is raised to successively higher powers.

a. Copy and complete the table.

Power of i	i^1	i^2	i^3	i^4	i^5	i^6	i^7	i^8
Simplified form	i	-1	$-i$	?	?	?	?	?

EXTRA CHALLENGE
www.mcdougallittell.com

b. *Writing* Describe the pattern you observe in the table. Verify that the pattern continues by evaluating the next four powers of i.

c. Use the pattern you described in part (b) to evaluate i^{26} and i^{83}.

MIXED REVIEW

EVALUATING FUNCTIONS Evaluate $f(x)$ for the given value of x. **(Review 2.1)**

101. $f(x) = 4x - 1$ when $x = 3$ **102.** $f(x) = x^2 - 5x + 8$ when $x = -4$

103. $f(x) = \lvert -x + 6 \rvert$ when $x = 9$ **104.** $f(x) = 2$ when $x = -30$

SOLVING SYSTEMS Use an inverse matrix to solve the system. **(Review 4.5)**

105. $3x + y = 5$ **106.** $x + y = 2$ **107.** $x - 2y = 10$
       $5x + 2y = 9$ $7x + 8y = 21$ $3x + 4y = 0$

SOLVING QUADRATIC EQUATIONS Solve the equation. **(Review 5.3 for 5.5)**

108. $(x + 4)^2 = 1$ **109.** $(x + 2)^2 = 36$ **110.** $(x - 11)^2 = 25$

111. $-(x - 5)^2 = -10$ **112.** $2(x + 7)^2 = 24$ **113.** $3(x - 6)^2 - 8 = 13$

114. **STATISTICS** **CONNECTION** The table shows the cumulative number N (in thousands) of DVD players sold in the United States from the end of February, 1997, to time t (in months). Make a scatter plot of the data. Approximate the equation of the best-fitting line. **(Review 2.5)**

t	1	2	3	4	5	6	7	8	9	10	11	12
N	34	69	96	125	144	178	213	269	307	347	383	416

 DATA UPDATE of *DVD Insider* data at www.mcdougallittell.com

▶ ACTIVITY 5.5

Developing Concepts

GROUP ACTIVITY
Work with a partner.

MATERIALS
algebra tiles

Using Algebra Tiles to Complete the Square

▶ **QUESTION** Given *b*, what is the value of *c* that makes $x^2 + bx + c$ a perfect square trinomial?

▶ **EXPLORING THE CONCEPT**

① Use algebra tiles to model the expression $x^2 + 6x$.

> You will need one x^2-tile and six *x*-tiles.

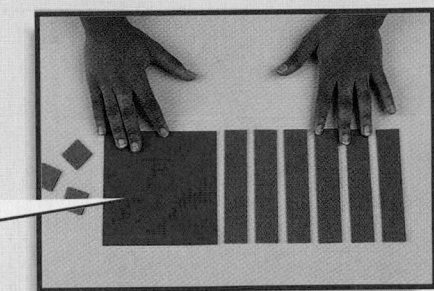

② Arrange the tiles in a square. Your arrangement will be incomplete in one corner.

> You want the length and width of your "square" to be equal.

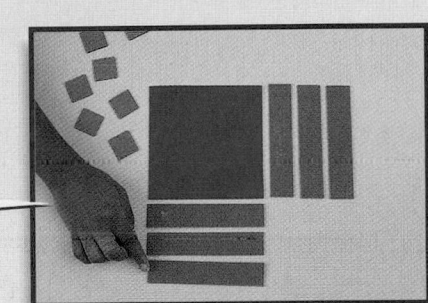

③ Determine the number of 1-tiles needed to complete the square.

> By adding nine 1-tiles, you can see that $x^2 + 6x + 9 = (x + 3)^2$.

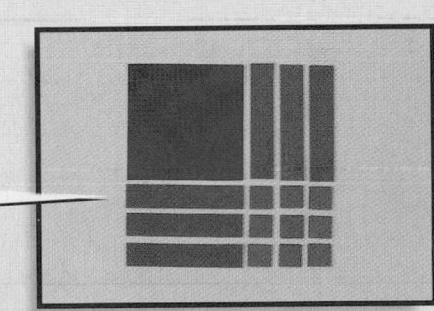

Completing the Square

Expression	Number of 1-tiles needed to complete the square	Expression written as a square
$x^2 + 2x + \underline{?}$	?	?
$x^2 + 4x + \underline{?}$	? ·	?
$x^2 + 6x + \underline{?}$	9	$x^2 + 6x + 9 = (x + 3)^2$
$x^2 + 8x + \underline{?}$	?	?
$x^2 + 10x + \underline{?}$	?	?

▶ **DRAWING CONCLUSIONS**

1. Copy and complete the table at the left by following the steps above.

2. Look for patterns in the last column of your table. Consider the general statement $x^2 + bx + c = (x + d)^2$.

   a. How is *d* related to *b* in each case?

   b. How is *c* related to *d* in each case?

   c. How can you obtain the numbers in the second column of the table directly from the coefficients of *x* in the expressions from the first column?

5.5

Completing the Square

What you should learn

GOAL 1 Solve quadratic equations by completing the square.

GOAL 2 Use completing the square to write quadratic functions in vertex form, as applied in **Example 7**.

Why you should learn it

▼ To solve **real-life** problems, such as finding where to position a fire hose in **Ex. 91**.

GOAL 1 SOLVING QUADRATIC EQUATIONS BY COMPLETING THE SQUARE

Completing the square is a process that allows you to write an expression of the form $x^2 + bx$ as the square of a binomial. This process can be illustrated using an area model, as shown below.

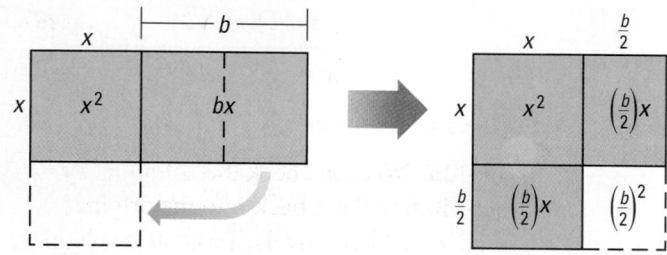

You can see that to complete the square for $x^2 + bx$, you need to add $\left(\frac{b}{2}\right)^2$, the area of the incomplete corner of the square in the second diagram. This diagram models the following rule:

$$x^2 + bx + \left(\frac{b}{2}\right)^2 = \left(x + \frac{b}{2}\right)^2$$

EXAMPLE 1 *Completing the Square*

Find the value of c that makes $x^2 - 7x + c$ a perfect square trinomial. Then write the expression as the square of a binomial.

SOLUTION

In the expression $x^2 - 7x + c$, note that $b = -7$. Therefore:

$$c = \left(\frac{b}{2}\right)^2 = \left(\frac{-7}{2}\right)^2 = \frac{49}{4}$$

Use this value of c to write $x^2 - 7x + c$ as a perfect square trinomial, and then as the square of a binomial.

$$x^2 - 7x + c = x^2 - 7x + \frac{49}{4} \qquad \text{Perfect square trinomial}$$

$$= \left(x - \frac{7}{2}\right)^2 \qquad \text{Square of a binomial: } \left(x + \frac{b}{2}\right)^2$$

. . . .

In Lesson 5.2 you learned how to solve quadratic equations by factoring. However, many quadratic equations, such as $x^2 + 10x - 3 = 0$, contain expressions that cannot be factored. Completing the square is a method that lets you solve *any* quadratic equation, as the next example illustrates.

EXAMPLE 2   *Solving a Quadratic Equation if the Coefficient of x^2 Is 1*

Solve $x^2 + 10x - 3 = 0$ by completing the square.

SOLUTION

$x^2 + 10x - 3 = 0$	**Write original equation.**
$x^2 + 10x = 3$	**Write the left side in the form $x^2 + bx$.**
$x^2 + 10x + 5^2 = 3 + 25$	**Add $\left(\frac{10}{2}\right)^2 = 5^2 = 25$ to each side.**
$(x + 5)^2 = 28$	**Write the left side as a binomial squared.**
$x + 5 = \pm\sqrt{28}$	**Take square roots of each side.**
$x = -5 \pm \sqrt{28}$	**Solve for x.**
$x = -5 \pm 2\sqrt{7}$	**Simplify.**

▶ The solutions are $-5 + 2\sqrt{7}$ and $-5 - 2\sqrt{7}$.

✓**CHECK** You can check the solutions by
substituting them back into the original
equation. Alternatively, you can graph
$y = x^2 + 10x - 3$ and observe that the
x-intercepts are about $0.29 \approx -5 + 2\sqrt{7}$
and $-10.29 \approx -5 - 2\sqrt{7}$.

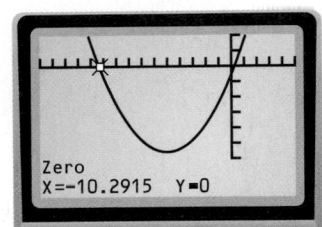

· · · · · · · · · ·

If the coefficient of x^2 in a quadratic equation is not 1, you should divide each side of
the equation by this coefficient before completing the square.

EXAMPLE 3   *Solving a Quadratic Equation if the Coefficient of x^2 Is Not 1*

Solve $3x^2 - 6x + 12 = 0$ by completing the square.

SOLUTION

$3x^2 - 6x + 12 = 0$	**Write original equation.**
$x^2 - 2x + 4 = 0$	**Divide each side by the coefficient of x^2.**
$x^2 - 2x = -4$	**Write the left side in the form $x^2 + bx$.**
$x^2 - 2x + (-1)^2 = -4 + 1$	**Add $\left(\frac{-2}{2}\right)^2 = (-1)^2 = 1$ to each side.**
$(x - 1)^2 = -3$	**Write the left side as a binomial squared.**
$x - 1 = \pm\sqrt{-3}$	**Take square roots of each side.**
$x = 1 \pm \sqrt{-3}$	**Solve for x.**
$x = 1 \pm i\sqrt{3}$	**Write in terms of the imaginary unit i.**

▶ The solutions are $1 + i\sqrt{3}$ and $1 - i\sqrt{3}$.

✓**CHECK** Because the solutions are imaginary, you cannot check them graphically.
However, you can check the solutions algebraically by substituting them back into
the original equation.

STUDENT HELP

▶ **Study Tip**
In Example 2 note that
you must add 25 to *both*
sides of the equation
$x^2 + 10x = 3$ when
completing the square.

EXAMPLE 4 *Using a Quadratic Equation to Model Distance*

Traffic Engineering

On dry asphalt the distance d (in feet) needed for a car to stop is given by

$$d = 0.05s^2 + 1.1s$$

where s is the car's speed (in miles per hour). What speed limit should be posted on a road where drivers round a corner and have 80 feet to come to a stop?

SOLUTION

$d = 0.05s^2 + 1.1s$	Write original equation.
$\mathbf{80} = 0.05s^2 + 1.1s$	Substitute 80 for d.
$1600 = s^2 + 22s$	Divide each side by the coefficient of s^2.
$1600 + \mathbf{121} = s^2 + 22s + \mathbf{11^2}$	Add $\left(\dfrac{22}{2}\right)^2 = 11^2 = 121$ to each side.
$1721 = (s + 11)^2$	Write the right side as a binomial squared.
$\pm\sqrt{1721} = s + 11$	Take square roots of each side.
$-11 \pm \sqrt{1721} = s$	Solve for s.
$s \approx 30 \text{ or } s \approx -52$	Use a calculator.

▶ Reject the solution -52 because a car's speed cannot be negative. The posted speed limit should be at most 30 miles per hour.

EXAMPLE 5 *Using a Quadratic Equation to Model Area*

Landscape Design

You want to plant a rectangular garden along part of a 40 foot side of your house. To keep out animals, you will enclose the garden with wire mesh along its three open sides. You will also cover the garden with mulch. If you have 50 feet of mesh and enough mulch to cover 100 square feet, what should the garden's dimensions be?

SOLUTION

Draw a diagram. Let x be the length of the sides of the garden perpendicular to the house. Then $50 - 2x$ is the length of the third fenced side of the garden.

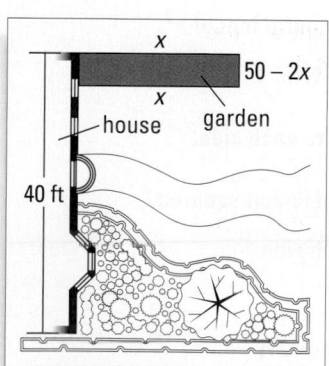

$x(50 - 2x) = 100$	Length × Width = Area
$50x - 2x^2 = 100$	Distributive property
$-2x^2 + 50x = 100$	Write the x^2-term first.
$x^2 - 25x = -50$	Divide each side by -2.
$x^2 - 25x + (\mathbf{-12.5})^2 = -50 + \mathbf{156.25}$	Complete the square.
$(x - 12.5)^2 = 106.25$	Write as a binomial squared.
$x - 12.5 = \pm\sqrt{106.25}$	Take square roots of each side.
$x = 12.5 \pm \sqrt{106.25}$	Solve for x.
$x \approx 22.8 \text{ or } x \approx 2.2$	Use a calculator.

▶ Reject $x = 2.2$ since $50 - 2x = 45.6$ is greater than the house's length. If $x = 22.8$, then $50 - 2x = 4.4$. The garden should be about 22.8 feet by 4.4 feet.

284 **Chapter 5** *Quadratic Functions*

GOAL 2 WRITING QUADRATIC FUNCTIONS IN VERTEX FORM

Given a quadratic function in standard form, $y = ax^2 + bx + c$, you can use completing the square to write the function in vertex form, $y = a(x - h)^2 + k$.

STUDENT HELP

HOMEWORK HELP
Visit our Web site
www.mcdougallittell.com
for extra examples.

EXAMPLE 6 *Writing a Quadratic Function in Vertex Form*

Write the quadratic function $y = x^2 - 8x + 11$ in vertex form. What is the vertex of the function's graph?

SOLUTION

$$y = x^2 - 8x + 11$$ **Write original function.**

$$y + \underline{\ ?\ } = (x^2 - 8x + \underline{\ ?\ }) + 11$$ **Prepare to complete the square for $x^2 - 8x$.**

$$y + 16 = (x^2 - 8x + 16) + 11$$ **Add $\left(\dfrac{-8}{2}\right)^2 = (-4)^2 = 16$ to each side.**

$$y + 16 = (x - 4)^2 + 11$$ **Write $x^2 - 8x + 16$ as a binomial squared.**

$$y = (x - 4)^2 - 5$$ **Solve for y.**

▶ The vertex form of the function is $y = (x - 4)^2 - 5$. The vertex is $(4, -5)$.

EXAMPLE 7 *Finding the Maximum Value of a Quadratic Function*

REAL LIFE

Agriculture

The amount s (in pounds per acre) of sugar produced from sugarbeets can be modeled by the function

$$s = -0.0655n^2 + 7.855n + 5562$$

where n is the amount (in pounds per acre) of nitrogen fertilizer used. How much fertilizer should you use to maximize sugar production? What is the maximum amount of sugar you can produce?

▶ Source: Sugarbeet Research and Education Board of Minnesota and North Dakota

SOLUTION

The optimal amount of fertilizer and the maximum amount of sugar are the coordinates of the vertex of the function's graph. One way to find the vertex is to write the function in vertex form.

$$s = -0.0655n^2 + 7.855n + 5562$$

$$s = -0.0655(n^2 - 120n) + 5562$$

$$s - 0.0655(\underline{\ ?\ }) = -0.0655(n^2 - 120n + \underline{\ ?\ }) + 5562$$

$$s - 0.0655(3600) = -0.0655(n^2 - 120n + 3600) + 5562$$

$$s - 236 = -0.0655(n - 60)^2 + 5562$$

$$s = -0.0655(n - 60)^2 + 5798$$

▶ The vertex is approximately $(60, 5798)$. To maximize sugar production, you should use about 60 pounds per acre of nitrogen fertilizer. The maximum amount of sugar you can produce is about 5800 pounds per acre.

GUIDED PRACTICE

Vocabulary Check ✓

1. Describe what it means to "complete the square" for an expression of the form $x^2 + bx$.

Concept Check ✓

2. Which method for solving quadratic equations—factoring or completing the square—is more general? Explain.

3. **ERROR ANALYSIS** A student tried to write $y = -x^2 - 6x + 4$ in vertex form as shown. Explain the student's mistake. Then write the correct vertex form of the function.

$$y = -x^2 - 6x + 4$$
$$y = -(x^2 + 6x) + 4$$
$$y + 9 = -(x^2 + 6x + 9) + 4$$
$$y + 9 = -(x + 3)^2 + 4$$
$$y = -(x + 3)^2 - 5$$

Skill Check ✓

Find the value of *c* that makes the expression a perfect square trinomial. Then write the expression as the square of a binomial.

4. $x^2 + 2x + c$

5. $x^2 + 14x + c$

6. $x^2 - 6x + c$

7. $x^2 - 10x + c$

8. $x^2 + 5x + c$

9. $x^2 - 13x + c$

Solve the equation by completing the square.

10. $x^2 + 4x = -1$

11. $x^2 - 2x = 4$

12. $x^2 - 16x + 76 = 0$

13. $x^2 + 8x + 9 = 0$

14. $2x^2 + 12x = 4$

15. $3x^2 - 12x + 93 = 0$

Write the quadratic function in vertex form and identify the vertex.

16. $y = x^2 + 12x$

17. $y = x^2 - 4x + 7$

18. $y = x^2 - 8x + 31$

19. $y = x^2 + 10x + 17$

20. $y = -x^2 + 14x - 45$

21. $y = 2x^2 + 4x - 4$

22. **LANDSCAPE DESIGN** Suppose the homeowner in Example 5 has 60 feet of wire mesh to put around the garden and enough mulch to cover an area of 140 square feet. What should the dimensions of the garden be?

PRACTICE AND APPLICATIONS

STUDENT HELP

► **Extra Practice**
to help you master
skills is on p. 946.

REWRITING EXPRESSIONS Write the expression as the square of a binomial.

23. $x^2 + 16x + 64$

24. $x^2 + 20x + 100$

25. $x^2 - 24x + 144$

26. $x^2 - 38x + 361$

27. $x^2 + x + 0.25$

28. $x^2 - 1.4x + 0.49$

29. $x^2 - 3x + \dfrac{9}{4}$

30. $x^2 + \dfrac{1}{6}x + \dfrac{1}{144}$

31. $x^2 - \dfrac{4}{9}x + \dfrac{4}{81}$

COMPLETING THE SQUARE Find the value of *c* that makes the expression a perfect square trinomial. Then write the expression as the square of a binomial.

32. $x^2 - 12x + c$

33. $x^2 + 18x + c$

34. $x^2 + 26x + c$

35. $x^2 - 44x + c$

36. $x^2 + 9x + c$

37. $x^2 - 11x + c$

38. $x^2 - 23x + c$

39. $x^2 + 15x + c$

40. $x^2 - 0.2x + c$

41. $x^2 - 5.8x + c$

42. $x^2 + 1.6x + c$

43. $x^2 + 9.4x + c$

44. $x^2 - \dfrac{2}{7}x + c$

45. $x^2 + \dfrac{10}{3}x + c$

46. $x^2 + \dfrac{17}{8}x + c$

STUDENT HELP

↳ **HOMEWORK HELP**
Example 1: Exs. 23–46
Example 2: Exs. 47–54,
    63–64
Example 3: Exs. 55–72
Example 4: Exs. 89–91
Example 5: Exs. 92, 93
Example 6: Exs. 73–84
Example 7: Exs. 94, 95

COEFFICIENT OF x^2 IS 1 Solve the equation by completing the square.

47. $x^2 + 2x = 9$

48. $x^2 - 12x = -28$

49. $x^2 + 20x + 104 = 0$

50. $x^2 + 3x - 1 = 0$

51. $u^2 - 4u = 2u + 35$

52. $v^2 - 17v + 200 = 13v - 43$

53. $m^2 + 1.8m - 1.5 = 0$

54. $n^2 - \frac{4}{3}n - \frac{14}{9} = 0$

COEFFICIENT OF x^2 IS NOT 1 Solve the equation by completing the square.

55. $2x^2 - 12x = -14$

56. $-3x^2 + 24x = 27$

57. $6x^2 + 84x + 300 = 0$

58. $4x^2 + 40x + 280 = 0$

59. $-4r^2 + 21r = r + 13$

60. $3s^2 - 26s + 2 = 5s^2 + 1$

61. $0.4t^2 + 0.7t = 0.3t - 0.2$

62. $\frac{w^2}{24} - \frac{w}{2} + \frac{13}{6} = 0$

SOLVING BY ANY METHOD Solve the equation by factoring, by finding square roots, or by completing the square.

63. $x^2 + 4x - 12 = 0$

64. $x^2 - 6x - 15 = 0$

65. $9x^2 - 23 = 0$

66. $2x^2 + 9x + 7 = 0$

67. $3x^2 + x = 2x - 6$

68. $4(x + 8)^2 = 144$

69. $7k^2 + 10k - 100 = 2k^2 + 55$

70. $14b^2 - 19b + 4 = -11b^2 + 11b - 5$

71. $0.01p^2 - 0.22p + 2.9 = 0$

72. $\frac{q^2}{4} - \frac{9q^2}{20} = 18$

WRITING IN VERTEX FORM Write the quadratic function in vertex form and identify the vertex.

73. $y = x^2 - 6x + 11$

74. $y = x^2 - 2x - 9$

75. $y = x^2 + 16x + 14$

76. $y = x^2 + 26x + 68$

77. $y = x^2 - 3x - 2$

78. $y = x^2 + 7x - 1$

79. $y = -x^2 + 20x - 80$

80. $y = -x^2 - 14x - 47$

81. $y = 3x^2 - 12x + 1$

82. $y = -2x^2 - 2x - 7$

83. $y = 1.4x^2 + 5.6x + 3$

84. $y = \frac{2}{3}x^2 - \frac{4}{5}x$

STUDENT HELP

↳ **Skills Review**
For help with areas of geometric figures, see p. 914.

GEOMETRY CONNECTION Find the value of x.

85. Area of rectangle = 100

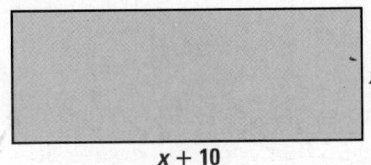

86. Area of triangle = 40

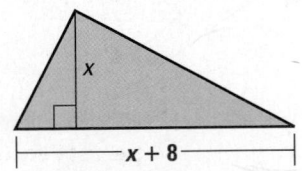

87. Area of trapezoid = 70

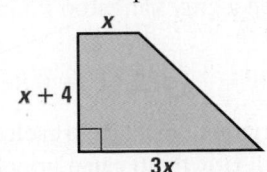

88. Area of parallelogram = 54

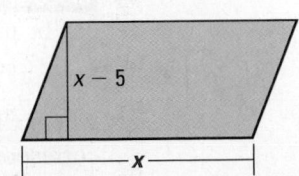

89. 🌎 **TRAFFIC ENGINEERING** For a road covered with dry, packed snow, the formula for a car's stopping distance given in Example 4 becomes:

$$d = 0.08s^2 + 1.1s$$

Show that, in snowy conditions, a driver cannot safely round the corner in Example 4 when traveling at the calculated speed limit of 30 miles per hour. What is a safe speed limit if the road is covered with snow?

90. 🌎 **SPORTS** Jackie Joyner-Kersee won the women's heptathlon during the 1992 Olympics in Barcelona, Spain. Her throw in the shot put, one of the seven events in the heptathlon, can be modeled by

$$y = -0.0241x^2 + x + 5.5$$

where x is the shot put's horizontal distance traveled (in feet) and y is its corresponding height (in feet). How long was Joyner-Kersee's throw?

91. 🌎 **FIREFIGHTING** In firefighting, a good water stream can be modeled by

$$y = -0.003x^2 + 0.62x + 3$$

where x is the water's horizontal distance traveled (in feet) and y is its corresponding height (in feet). If a firefighter is aiming a good water stream at a building's window 25 feet above the ground, at what two distances can the firefighter stand from the building?

92. 🌎 **CORRALS** You have 240 feet of wooden fencing to form two adjacent rectangular corrals as shown. You want each corral to have an area of 1000 square feet.

Not drawn to scale

a. Show that $w = 80 - \frac{4}{3}\ell$.

b. Use your answer from part (a) to find the possible dimensions of each corral.

93. 🌎 **POTTERY** You are taking a pottery class. As an assignment, you are given a lump of clay whose volume is 200 cubic centimeters and asked to make a cylindrical pencil holder. The pencil holder should be 9 centimeters high and have an inner radius of 3 centimeters. What thickness x should your pencil holder have if you want to use all the clay? (*Hint:* The volume of clay equals the difference of the volumes of two cylinders.)

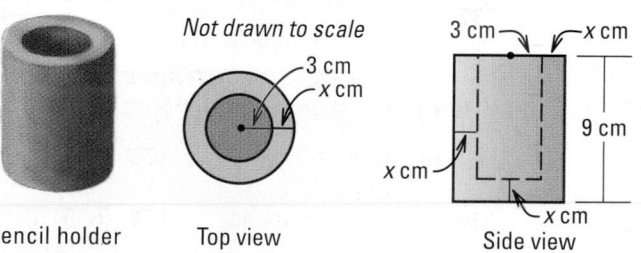

Pencil holder   Top view   Side view

94. **BIOLOGY** **CONNECTION** When a gray kangaroo jumps, its path through the air can be modeled by

$$y = -0.0267x^2 + 0.8x$$

where x is the kangaroo's horizontal distance traveled (in feet) and y is its corresponding height (in feet). How high can a gray kangaroo jump? How far can it jump?

95. SCIENCE ▷ CONNECTION In a fireplace, the heat loss q (in Btu/ft^3) resulting from hot gases escaping through the chimney can be modeled by

$$q = -0.00002T^2 + 0.0203T - 1.24$$

where T is the temperature (in degrees Fahrenheit) of the gases. (This model assumes an indoor temperature of 65°F.) For what gas temperature is heat loss maximized? What is the maximum heat loss? ▶ Source: *Workshop Math*

Test Preparation

96. MULTIPLE CHOICE If $x^2 - 28x + c$ is a perfect square trinomial, what is the value of c?

   Ⓐ -14 Ⓑ 28 Ⓒ 196 Ⓓ 784

97. MULTIPLE CHOICE What are the solutions of $x^2 + 12x + 61 = 0$?

   Ⓐ $-1, -11$ Ⓑ $-6 \pm 5i$ Ⓒ $-6 \pm \sqrt{97}$ Ⓓ $-6 \pm i\sqrt{61}$

98. MULTIPLE CHOICE What is the vertex form of $y = 2x^2 - 8x + 3$?

   Ⓐ $y = 2(x - 2)^2 - 5$ Ⓑ $y = 2(x - 2)^2 + 3$

   Ⓒ $y = 2(x - 4)^2 - 29$ Ⓓ $y = 2(x - 4)^2 + 3$

★ **Challenge**

CRITICAL THINKING Exercises 99 and 100 should be done together.

99. Graph the two functions in the same coordinate plane.

   a. $y = x^2 + 2x$ **b.** $y = x^2 + 4x$ **c.** $y = x^2 - 6x$

        $y = (x + 1)^2$ $y = (x + 2)^2$ $y = (x - 3)^2$

EXTRA CHALLENGE
→ www.mcdougallittell.com

100. Compare the graphs of $y = x^2 + bx$ and $y = \left(x + \dfrac{b}{2}\right)^2$. What happens to the graph of $y = x^2 + bx$ when you complete the square for $x^2 + bx$?

MIXED REVIEW

EVALUATING EXPRESSIONS Evaluate $b^2 - 4ac$ for the given values of a, b, and c. (Review 1.2 for 5.6)

101. $a = 1, b = 5, c = 2$ **102.** $a = 3, b = -8, c = 7$

103. $a = -5, b = 0, c = 2.6$ **104.** $a = 11, b = 4, c = -1$

105. $a = 16, b = -24, c = 9$ **106.** $a = -1.4, b = 2, c = -0.5$

EQUATIONS OF LINES Write an equation in slope-intercept form of the line through the given point and having the given slope. (Review 2.4)

107. $(3, 1), m = 2$ **108.** $(2, -4), m = 1$ **109.** $(-7, 10), m = -5$

110. $(-8, -8), m = -3$ **111.** $(6, 9), m = \dfrac{1}{3}$ **112.** $(11, -2), m = -\dfrac{5}{4}$

SYSTEMS OF LINEAR INEQUALITIES Graph the system of inequalities. (Review 3.3)

113. $x \geq 2$ **114.** $y > -1$ **115.** $x \geq 0$
      $y \leq 3$ $y < 2$ $x + y < 4$

116. $y < x - 2$ **117.** $3x - 2y < 8$ **118.** $y \leq 2x + 3$
      $x - 3y \leq 6$ $2x + y > 0$ $y \geq 2x - 3$

● **ACTIVITY 5.5**

Using Technology

Finding Maximums and Minimums

You can use a graphing calculator to find maximum or minimum values of quadratic functions.

▶ **EXAMPLE**

Find the maximum value of $y = -x^2 - 7x - 6$ and the value of x where it occurs.

STUDENT HELP

🌐 **KEYSTROKE HELP**

See keystrokes for several models of calculators at www.mcdougallittell.com

▶ **SOLUTION**

❶ Graph the given function and select the *Maximum* feature.

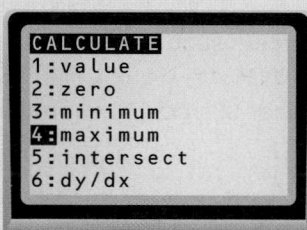

❷ Move the cursor to the left of the maximum point. Press `ENTER`.

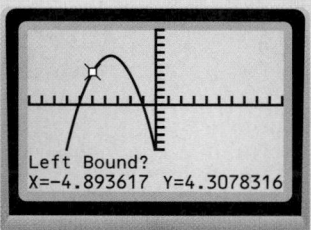

❸ Move the cursor to the right of the maximum point. Press `ENTER`.

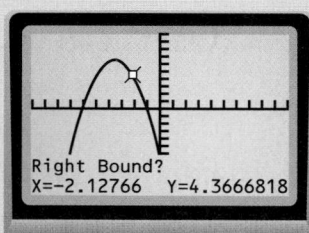

❹ Put the cursor approximately on the maximum point. Press `ENTER`.

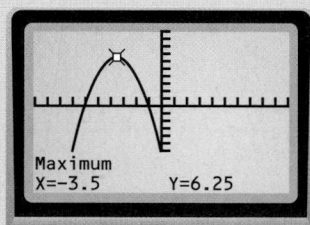

▶ The maximum value of the function is $y = 6.25$ and occurs at $x = -3.5$.

▶ **EXERCISES**

STUDENT HELP

↳ **Study Tip**
To find the minimum value of a function, select the *Minimum* feature instead of the *Maximum* feature from the menu in **Step 1**.

Tell whether the function has a maximum value or a minimum value. Then find the maximum or minimum value and the value of *x* where it occurs.

1. $y = x^2 - 5x + 2$
2. $y = -x^2 + 8x - 11$
3. $y = x^2 + 6x + 13$

4. $y = 3x^2 + 24x + 43$
5. $y = -2x^2 - 3x + 7$
6. $y = -1.2x^2 - 9x - 19$

7. $y = 0.4x^2 - 3x + 8$
8. $y = \frac{1}{2}x^2 + x - \frac{7}{2}$
9. $y = -\frac{8}{5}x^2 + \frac{22}{3}x + \frac{1}{4}$

10. 🌐 **TRAFFIC FLOW** On a typical single-lane highway, the traffic flow F (in cars per hour) can be modeled by $F = -0.313C^2 + 50C$ where C is the traffic concentration (in cars per mile). For what traffic concentration is traffic flow maximized? What is the maximum traffic flow?

▶ Source: *Towing Icebergs, Falling Dominoes, and Other Adventures in Applied Mathematics*

5.6

The Quadratic Formula and the Discriminant

What you should learn

GOAL 1 Solve quadratic equations using the quadratic formula.

GOAL 2 Use the quadratic formula in **real-life** situations, such as baton twirling in **Example 5**.

Why you should learn it

▼ To solve **real-life** problems, such as finding the speed and duration of a thrill ride in **Ex. 84**.

GOAL 1 SOLVING EQUATIONS WITH THE QUADRATIC FORMULA

In Lesson 5.5 you solved quadratic equations by completing the square for *each equation separately*. By completing the square *once* for the general equation $ax^2 + bx + c = 0$, you can develop a formula that gives the solutions of *any* quadratic equation. The formula for the solutions is called the **quadratic formula**. A derivation of the quadratic formula appears on page 895.

THE QUADRATIC FORMULA

Let a, b, and c be real numbers such that $a \neq 0$. The solutions of the quadratic equation $ax^2 + bx + c = 0$ are:

$$x = \frac{-b \pm \sqrt{b^2 - 4ac}}{2a}$$

Remember that *before* you apply the quadratic formula to a quadratic equation, you must write the equation in standard form, $ax^2 + bx + c = 0$.

EXAMPLE 1 *Solving a Quadratic Equation with Two Real Solutions*

Solve $2x^2 + x = 5$.

SOLUTION

$2x^2 + x = 5$	**Write original equation.**
$2x^2 + x - 5 = 0$	**Write in standard form.**
$x = \dfrac{-b \pm \sqrt{b^2 - 4ac}}{2a}$	**Quadratic formula**
$x = \dfrac{-1 \pm \sqrt{1^2 - 4(2)(-5)}}{2(2)}$	$a = 2, b = 1, c = -5$
$x = \dfrac{-1 \pm \sqrt{41}}{4}$	**Simplify.**

▶ The solutions are

$$x = \frac{-1 + \sqrt{41}}{4} \approx 1.35$$

and

$$x = \frac{-1 - \sqrt{41}}{4} \approx -1.85.$$

✓**CHECK** Graph $y = 2x^2 + x - 5$ and note that the x-intercepts are about 1.35 and about -1.85.

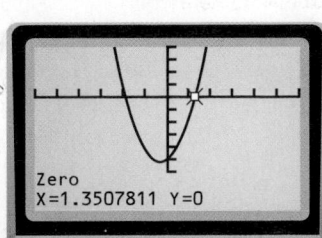

Zero
X=1.3507811 Y=0

EXAMPLE 2 **Solving a Quadratic Equation with One Real Solution**

Solve $x^2 - x = 5x - 9$.

SOLUTION

$$x^2 - x = 5x - 9$$ Write original equation.

$$x^2 - 6x + 9 = 0$$ $a = 1, b = -6, c = 9$

$$x = \frac{6 \pm \sqrt{(-6)^2 - 4(1)(9)}}{2(1)}$$ Quadratic formula

$$x = \frac{6 \pm \sqrt{0}}{2}$$ Simplify.

$$x = 3$$ Simplify.

▶ The solution is 3.

✓ **CHECK** Graph $y = x^2 - 6x + 9$ and note that the only *x*-intercept is 3. Alternatively, substitute 3 for *x* in the original equation.

$$3^2 - 3 \overset{?}{=} 5(3) - 9$$

$$9 - 3 \overset{?}{=} 15 - 9$$

$$6 = 6 \checkmark$$

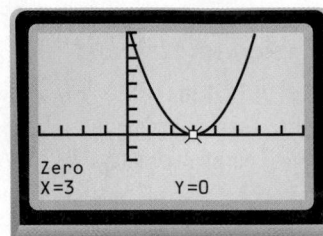

Zero
X=3   Y=0

EXAMPLE 3 **Solving a Quadratic Equation with Two Imaginary Solutions**

Solve $-x^2 + 2x = 2$.

SOLUTION

$$-x^2 + 2x = 2$$ Write original equation.

$$-x^2 + 2x - 2 = 0$$ $a = -1, b = 2, c = -2$

$$x = \frac{-2 \pm \sqrt{2^2 - 4(-1)(-2)}}{2(-1)}$$ Quadratic formula

$$x = \frac{-2 \pm \sqrt{-4}}{-2}$$ Simplify.

$$x = \frac{-2 \pm 2i}{-2}$$ Write using the imaginary unit *i*.

$$x = 1 \pm i$$ Simplify.

▶ The solutions are $1 + i$ and $1 - i$.

✓ **CHECK** Graph $y = -x^2 + 2x - 2$ and note that there are no *x*-intercepts. So, the original equation has no real solutions. To check the imaginary solutions $1 + i$ and $1 - i$, substitute them into the original equation. The check for $1 + i$ is shown.

$$-(1 + i)^2 + 2(1 + i) \overset{?}{=} 2$$

$$-2i + 2 + 2i \overset{?}{=} 2$$

$$2 = 2 \checkmark$$

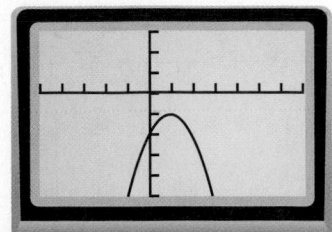

In the quadratic formula, the expression $b^2 - 4ac$ under the radical sign is called the **discriminant** of the associated equation $ax^2 + bx + c = 0$.

$$x = \frac{-b \pm \sqrt{b^2 - 4ac}}{2a} \longleftarrow \text{discriminant}$$

You can use the discriminant of a quadratic equation to determine the equation's number and type of solutions.

NUMBER AND TYPE OF SOLUTIONS OF A QUADRATIC EQUATION

Consider the quadratic equation $ax^2 + bx + c = 0$.

- If $b^2 - 4ac > 0$, then the equation has two real solutions.
- If $b^2 - 4ac = 0$, then the equation has one real solution.
- If $b^2 - 4ac < 0$, then the equation has two imaginary solutions.

EXAMPLE 4 *Using the Discriminant*

Find the discriminant of the quadratic equation and give the number and type of solutions of the equation.

a. $x^2 - 6x + 10 = 0$ **b.** $x^2 - 6x + 9 = 0$ **c.** $x^2 - 6x + 8 = 0$

SOLUTION

EQUATION $ax^2 + bx + c = 0$	DISCRIMINANT $b^2 - 4ac$	SOLUTION(S) $x = \dfrac{-b \pm \sqrt{b^2 - 4ac}}{2a}$
a. $x^2 - 6x + 10 = 0$	$(-6)^2 - 4(1)(10) = -4$	Two imaginary: $3 \pm i$
b. $x^2 - 6x + 9 = 0$	$(-6)^2 - 4(1)(9) = 0$	One real: 3
c. $x^2 - 6x + 8 = 0$	$(-6)^2 - 4(1)(8) = 4$	Two real: 2, 4

· · · · · · · · · ·

In Example 4 notice that the number of real solutions of $x^2 - 6x + c = 0$ can be changed just by changing the value of c. A graph can help you see why this occurs. By changing c, you can move the graph of

$$y = x^2 - 6x + c$$

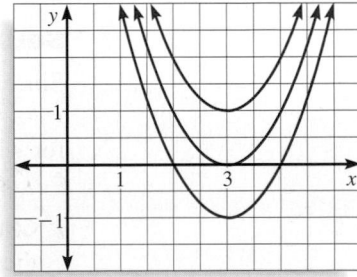

up or down in the coordinate plane. If the graph is moved too high, it won't have an x-intercept and the equation $x^2 - 6x + c = 0$ won't have a real-number solution.

$y = x^2 - 6x + 10$	Graph is above x-axis (no x-intercept).
$y = x^2 - 6x + 9$	Graph touches x-axis (one x-intercept).
$y = x^2 - 6x + 8$	Graph crosses x-axis (two x-intercepts).

In Lesson 5.3 you studied the model $h = -16t^2 + h_0$ for the height of an object that is *dropped*. For an object that is *launched or thrown*, an extra term v_0t must be added to the model to account for the object's initial vertical velocity v_0.

Models	$h = -16t^2 + h_0$	**Object is dropped.**
	$h = -16t^2 + v_0t + h_0$	**Object is launched or thrown.**
Labels	h = height	(feet)
	t = time in motion	(seconds)
	h_0 = initial height	(feet)
	v_0 = initial vertical velocity	(feet per second)

The initial vertical velocity of a launched object can be positive, negative, or zero. If the object is launched upward, its initial vertical velocity is positive ($v_0 > 0$). If the object is launched downward, its initial vertical velocity is negative ($v_0 < 0$). If the object is launched parallel to the ground, its initial vertical velocity is zero ($v_0 = 0$).

Entertainment

EXAMPLE 5 *Solving a Vertical Motion Problem*

A baton twirler tosses a baton into the air. The baton leaves the twirler's hand 6 feet above the ground and has an initial vertical velocity of 45 feet per second. The twirler catches the baton when it falls back to a height of 5 feet. For how long is the baton in the air?

SOLUTION

Since the baton is thrown (not dropped), use the model $h = -16t^2 + v_0t + h_0$ with $v_0 = 45$ and $h_0 = 6$. To determine how long the baton is in the air, find the value of t for which $h = 5$.

$h = -16t^2 + v_0t + h_0$	**Write height model.**
$5 = -16t^2 + 45t + 6$	**$h = 5$, $v_0 = 45$, $h_0 = 6$**
$0 = -16t^2 + 45t + 1$	**$a = -16$, $b = 45$, $c = 1$**
$t = \dfrac{-45 \pm \sqrt{2089}}{-32}$	**Quadratic formula**
$t \approx -0.022$ or $t \approx 2.8$	**Use a calculator.**

▶ Reject the solution -0.022 since the baton's time in the air cannot be negative. The baton is in the air for about 2.8 seconds.

GUIDED PRACTICE

Vocabulary Check ✓

1. In the quadratic formula, what is the expression $b^2 - 4ac$ called?

Concept Check ✓

2. How many solutions does a quadratic equation have if its discriminant is positive? if its discriminant is zero? if its discriminant is negative?

3. Describe a real-life situation in which you can use the model $h = -16t^2 + v_0 t + h_0$ but not the model $h = -16t^2 + h_0$.

Skill Check ✓

Use the quadratic formula to solve the equation.

4. $x^2 - 4x + 3 = 0$

5. $x^2 + x - 1 = 0$

6. $2x^2 + 3x + 5 = 0$

7. $9x^2 + 6x - 1 = 0$

8. $-x^2 + 8x = 1$

9. $5x^2 - 2x + 37 = x^2 + 2x$

Find the discriminant of the quadratic equation and give the number and type of solutions of the equation.

10. $x^2 + 5x + 2 = 0$

11. $x^2 + 2x + 5 = 0$

12. $4x^2 - 4x + 1 = 0$

13. $-2x^2 + 3x - 7 = 0$

14. $9x^2 + 12x + 4 = 0$

15. $5x^2 - x - 13 = 0$

16. 🌐 **BASKETBALL** A basketball player passes the ball to a teammate who catches it 11 ft above the court, just above the rim of the basket, and slam-dunks it through the hoop. (This play is called an "alley-oop.") The first player releases the ball 5 ft above the court with an initial vertical velocity of 21 ft/sec. How long is the ball in the air before being caught, assuming it is caught as it rises?

PRACTICE AND APPLICATIONS

STUDENT HELP

▶ **Extra Practice**
to help you master
skills is on p. 946.

EQUATIONS IN STANDARD FORM Use the quadratic formula to solve the equation.

17. $x^2 - 5x - 14 = 0$

18. $x^2 + 3x - 2 = 0$

19. $x^2 - 2x - 4 = 0$

20. $x^2 + 10x + 22 = 0$

21. $x^2 + 6x + 58 = 0$

22. $-x^2 + 7x - 19 = 0$

23. $5x^2 + 3x - 1 = 0$

24. $3x^2 - 11x - 4 = 0$

25. $2x^2 + x + 1 = 0$

26. $6p^2 - 8p + 3 = 0$

27. $-7q^2 + 2q + 9 = 0$

28. $8r^2 + 4r + 5 = 0$

29. $-4t^2 - 9t - 3 = 0$

30. $9u^2 - 12u + 85 = 0$

31. $10v^2 + 8v - 1 = 0$

EQUATIONS NOT IN STANDARD FORM Use the quadratic formula to solve the equation.

32. $x^2 + 4x = -20$

33. $x^2 - 2x = 99$

34. $x^2 + 14 = 10x$

35. $x^2 = 8x - 35$

36. $-x^2 - 3x = -7$

37. $-x^2 = 16x + 46$

38. $3x^2 + 6x = -2$

39. $8x^2 - 8x = 1$

40. $5x^2 + 9x = -x^2 + 5x + 1$

41. $40x - 7x^2 = 101 - 3x^2$

42. $-16k^2 = 20k^2 + 24k + 5$

43. $13n^2 + 11n - 9 = 4n^2 - n - 4$

44. $3(d - 1)^2 = 4d + 2$

45. $3.5y^2 + 2.6y - 8.2 = -0.4y^2 - 6.9y$

STUDENT HELP

▶ **HOMEWORK HELP**
Examples 1–3: Exs. 17–55
Example 4: Exs. 56–64
Example 5: Exs. 74–80

SOLVING BY ANY METHOD Solve the equation by factoring, by finding square roots, or by using the quadratic formula.

plug-in

46. $6x^2 - 12 = 0$

47. $x^2 - 3x - 15 = 0$

48. $x^2 + 4x + 29 = 0$

49. $x^2 - 18x + 32 = 0$

50. $4x^2 + 28x = -49$

51. $3(x + 4)^2 = -27$

52. $-2u^2 + 5 = 3u^2 - 10u$

53. $11m^2 - 1 = 7m^2 + 2$

54. $-9v^2 + 35v - 30 = 1 - v$

55. $20p^2 + 6p = 6p^2 - 13p + 3$

USING THE DISCRIMINANT Find the discriminant of the quadratic equation and give the number and type of solutions of the equation.

56. $x^2 - 4x + 10 = 0$

57. $x^2 + 3x - 6 = 0$

58. $x^2 + 14x + 49 = 0$

59. $3x^2 - 10x - 5 = 0$

60. $64x^2 - 16x + 1 = 0$

61. $-2x^2 - 5x - 4 = 0$

62. $7r^2 - 3 = 0$

63. $s^2\sqrt{5} + s + \sqrt{5} = 0$

64. $-4t^2 + 20t - 25 = 0$

VISUAL THINKING In Exercises 65–67, the graph of a quadratic function $y = ax^2 + bx + c$ is shown. Tell whether the discriminant of $ax^2 + bx + c = 0$ is *positive*, *negative*, or *zero*.

65.
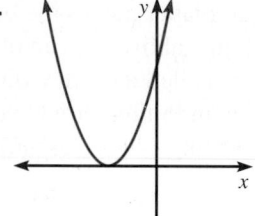

66.
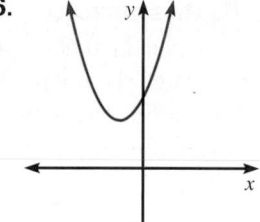

67.
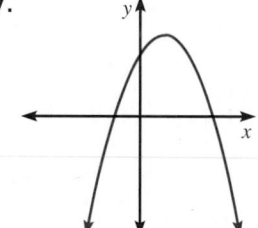

THE CONSTANT TERM Find all values of *c* for which the equation has (a) two real solutions, (b) one real solution, and (c) two imaginary solutions.

68. $x^2 - 2x + c = 0$

69. $x^2 + 4x + c = 0$

70. $x^2 + 10x + c = 0$

71. $x^2 - 8x + c = 0$

72. $x^2 + 6x + c = 0$

73. $x^2 - 12x + c = 0$

74. **CRITICAL THINKING** Explain why the height model $h = -16t^2 + v_0 t + h_0$ applies not only to launched or thrown objects, but to dropped objects as well. (*Hint:* What is the initial vertical velocity of a dropped object?)

75. **DIVING** In July of 1997, the first Cliff Diving World Championships were held in Brontallo, Switzerland. Participants performed acrobatic dives from heights of up to 92 feet. Suppose a cliff diver jumps from this height with an initial upward velocity of 5 feet per second. How much time does the diver have to perform acrobatic maneuvers before hitting the water?
▶ Source: World High Diving Federation

76. **WORLD WIDE WEB** A Web developer is creating a Web site devoted to mountain climbing. Each page on the Web site will have frames along its top and left sides showing the name of the site and links to different parts of the site. These frames will take up one third of the computer screen. What will the width *x* of the frames be on the screen shown?

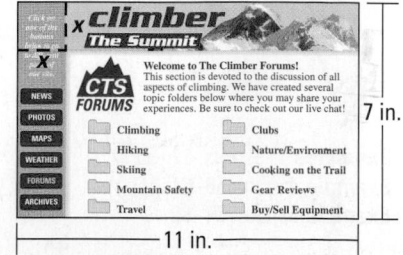

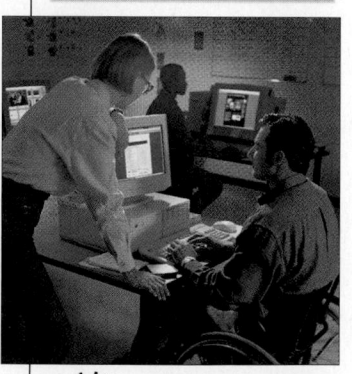

77.  **VOLLEYBALL** In a volleyball game, a player on one team spikes the ball over the net when the ball is 10 feet above the court. The spike drives the ball downward with an initial vertical velocity of -55 feet per second. Players on the opposing team must hit the ball back over the net before the ball touches the court. How much time do the opposing players have to hit the spiked ball?

78.  **AVIATION** The length l (in feet) of runway needed for a small airplane to land is given by $l = 0.1s^2 - 3s + 22$ where s is the airplane's speed (in feet per second). If a pilot is landing a small airplane on a runway 2000 feet long, what is the maximum speed at which the pilot can land?

79.  **TELECOMMUNICATIONS** For the years 1989–1996, the amount A (in billions of dollars) spent on long distance telephone calls in the United States can be modeled by $A = 0.560t^2 + 0.488t + 51$ where t is the number of years since 1989. In what year did the amount spent reach $60 billion?

 **DATA UPDATE** of *Statistical Abstract of the United States* data at www.mcdougallittell.com

80.  **EARTH SCIENCE** The volcanic cinder cone Puu Puai in Hawaii was formed in 1959 when a massive "lava fountain" erupted at Kilauea Iki Crater, shooting lava hundreds of feet into the air. When the eruption was most intense, the height h (in feet) of the lava t seconds after being ejected from the ground could be modeled by $h = -16t^2 + 350t$. ▶ Source: Volcano World

a. What was the initial vertical velocity of the lava? What was the lava's maximum height above the ground?

b. **CHOOSING A METHOD** For how long was the lava in the air? Solve the problem either by factoring or by using the quadratic formula.

Test Preparation

QUANTITATIVE COMPARISON In Exercises 81–83, choose the statement that is true about the given quantities.

Ⓐ The quantity in column A is greater.

Ⓑ The quantity in column B is greater.

Ⓒ The two quantities are equal.

Ⓓ The relationship cannot be determined from the given information.

	Column A	Column B
81.	Discriminant of $x^2 - 6x - 1 = 0$	Discriminant of $x^2 + 5x - 4 = 0$
82.	Discriminant of $x^2 + 2kx + 1 = 0$	Discriminant of $kx^2 + 3x - k = 0$
83.	Least zero of $f(x) = x^2 - 10x + 23$	Greatest zero of $f(x) = x^2 - 2x - 2$

★ Challenge

84.  **THRILL RIDES** The Stratosphere Tower in Las Vegas is 921 feet tall and has a "needle" at its top that extends even higher into the air. A thrill ride called the Big Shot catapults riders 160 feet up the needle and then lets them fall back to the launching pad. ▶ Source: Stratosphere Tower

a. The height h (in feet) of a rider on the Big Shot can be modeled by $h = -16t^2 + v_0 t + 921$ where t is the elapsed time (in seconds) after launch and v_0 is the initial vertical velocity (in feet per second). Find v_0 using the fact that the maximum value of h is $921 + 160 = 1081$ feet.

b. A brochure for the Big Shot states that the ride up the needle takes 2 seconds. Compare this time with the time given by the model $h = -16t^2 + v_0 t + 921$ where v_0 is the value you found in part (a). Discuss the model's accuracy.

EXTRA CHALLENGE
www.mcdougallittell.com

MIXED REVIEW

SOLVING LINEAR INEQUALITIES Solve the inequality. Then graph your solution. **(Review 1.6 for 5.7)**

85. $3x + 6 > 12$

86. $16 - 7x \geq -5$

87. $-2(x + 9) \leq 8$

88. $10x + 3 < 6x - 1$

89. $4 \leq 5x - 11 \leq 29$

90. $\frac{3}{2}x + 20 \leq 14$ or $1 > 8 - x$

GRAPHING LINEAR INEQUALITIES Graph the inequality. **(Review 2.6 for 5.7)**

91. $y > x$

92. $y \leq -2x$

93. $y < 3x - 2$

94. $x + y > 5$

95. $2x - 3y \geq 12$

96. $7x + 4y \leq -28$

ABSOLUTE VALUE FUNCTIONS Graph the function. **(Review 2.8)**

97. $y = |x - 3|$

98. $y = |x| + 2$

99. $y = -2|x| - 1$

100. $y = 3|x + 4|$

101. $y = |x + 2| + 3$

102. $y = \frac{1}{2}|x - 5| - 4$

QUIZ 2

Self-Test for Lessons 5.4–5.6

Write the expression as a complex number in standard form. **(Lesson 5.4)**

1. $(7 + 5i) + (-2 + 11i)$

2. $(-1 + 8i) - (3 - 2i)$

3. $(4 - i)(6 + 7i)$

4. $\frac{1 - 3i}{5 + i}$

Plot the numbers in the same complex plane and find their absolute values. **(Lesson 5.4)**

5. $2 + 4i$

6. $-5i$

7. $-3 + i$

8. $4 + 3i$

9. -4

10. $-\frac{3}{2} - \frac{7}{2}i$

Solve the quadratic equation by completing the square. **(Lesson 5.5)**

11. $x^2 + 8x = -14$

12. $x^2 - 2x + 17 = 0$

13. $4p^2 - 40p - 8 = 0$

14. $3q^2 + 20q = -2q^2 - 19$

Write the quadratic function in vertex form. **(Lesson 5.5)**

15. $y = x^2 + 6x + 1$

16. $y = x^2 - 18x + 50$

17. $y = -2x^2 + 8x - 7$

Use the quadratic formula to solve the equation. **(Lesson 5.6)**

18. $x^2 + 2x - 10 = 0$

19. $x^2 - 16x + 73 = 0$

20. $3w^2 + 3w = 4w^2 + 4$

21. $14 + 2y - 25y^2 = 42y + 6$

22. 🌐 **ENTERTAINMENT** A juggler throws a ball into the air, releasing it 5 feet above the ground with an initial vertical velocity of 15 ft/sec. She catches the ball with her other hand when the ball is 4 feet above the ground. Using the model $h = -16t^2 + v_0 t + h_0$, find how long the ball is in the air. **(Lesson 5.6)**

5.7 Graphing and Solving Quadratic Inequalities

GOAL 1 QUADRATIC INEQUALITIES IN TWO VARIABLES

In this lesson you will study four types of **quadratic inequalities in two variables**.

$$y < ax^2 + bx + c \qquad\qquad y \leq ax^2 + bx + c$$
$$y > ax^2 + bx + c \qquad\qquad y \geq ax^2 + bx + c$$

The graph of any such inequality consists of all solutions (x, y) of the inequality. The steps used to graph a quadratic inequality are very much like those used to graph a linear inequality. (See Lesson 2.6.)

GRAPHING A QUADRATIC INEQUALITY IN TWO VARIABLES

To graph one of the four types of quadratic inequalities shown above, follow these steps:

STEP 1 Draw the parabola with equation $y = ax^2 + bx + c$. Make the parabola *dashed* for inequalities with $<$ or $>$ and *solid* for inequalities with $\leq$ or $\geq$.

STEP 2 Choose a point (x, y) inside the parabola and check whether the point is a solution of the inequality.

STEP 3 If the point from Step 2 is a solution, shade the region inside the parabola. If it is not a solution, shade the region outside the parabola.

EXAMPLE 1 *Graphing a Quadratic Inequality*

Graph $y > x^2 - 2x - 3$.

SOLUTION

Follow Steps 1–3 listed above.

1 Graph $y = x^2 - 2x - 3$. Since the inequality symbol is $>$, make the parabola dashed.

2 Test a point inside the parabola, such as $(1, 0)$.

$$y > x^2 - 2x - 3$$
$$0 \overset{?}{>} 1^2 - 2(1) - 3$$
$$0 > -4 \checkmark$$

So, $(1, 0)$ is a solution of the inequality.

3 Shade the region inside the parabola.

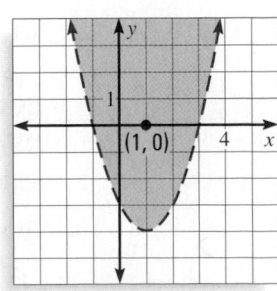

EXAMPLE 2 *Using a Quadratic Inequality as a Model*

You are building a wooden bookcase. You want to choose a thickness d (in inches) for the shelves so that each is strong enough to support 60 pounds of books without breaking. A shelf can safely support a weight of W (in pounds) provided that:

$$W \le 300d^2$$

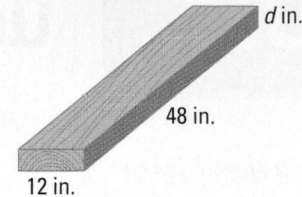

a. Graph the given inequality.

b. If you make each shelf 0.75 inch thick, can it support a weight of 60 pounds?

SOLUTION

a. Graph $W = 300d^2$ for nonnegative values of d. Since the inequality symbol is $\le$, make the parabola solid. Test a point inside the parabola, such as (0.5, 240).

$$W \le 300d^2$$

$$240 \overset{?}{\le} 300(0.5)^2$$

$$240 \not\le 75$$

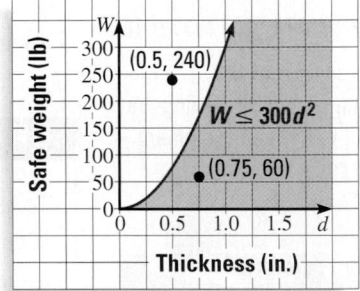

Since the chosen point is not a solution, shade the region outside (below) the parabola.

b. The point (0.75, 60) lies in the shaded region of the graph from part (a), so (0.75, 60) is a solution of the given inequality. Therefore, a shelf that is 0.75 inch thick *can* support a weight of 60 pounds.

· · · · · · · · · ·

Graphing a *system* of quadratic inequalities is similar to graphing a system of linear inequalities. First graph each inequality in the system. Then identify the region in the coordinate plane common to all the graphs. This region is called the *graph of the system.*

EXAMPLE 3 *Graphing a System of Quadratic Inequalities*

Graph the system of quadratic inequalities.

$$y \ge x^2 - 4 \qquad \text{Inequality 1}$$
$$y < -x^2 - x + 2 \qquad \text{Inequality 2}$$

SOLUTION

Graph the inequality $y \ge x^2 - 4$. The graph is the red region inside and including the parabola $y = x^2 - 4$.

Graph the inequality $y < -x^2 - x + 2$. The graph is the blue region inside (but not including) the parabola $y = -x^2 - x + 2$.

Identify the **purple region** where the two graphs overlap. This region is the graph of the system.

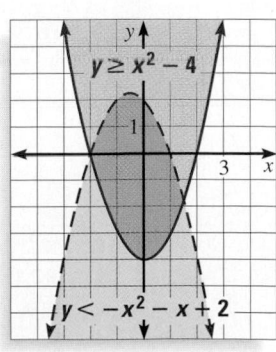

One way to solve a **quadratic inequality in one variable** is to use a graph.

- To solve $ax^2 + bx + c < 0$ (or $ax^2 + bx + c \le 0$), graph $y = ax^2 + bx + c$ and identify the x-values for which the graph lies *below* (or *on and below*) the x-axis.

- To solve $ax^2 + bx + c > 0$ (or $ax^2 + bx + c \ge 0$), graph $y = ax^2 + bx + c$ and identify the x-values for which the graph lies *above* (or *on and above*) the x-axis.

EXAMPLE 4 *Solving a Quadratic Inequality by Graphing*

STUDENT HELP

Look Back
For help with solving inequalities in one variable, see p. 41.

Solve $x^2 - 6x + 5 < 0$.

SOLUTION

The solution consists of the x-values for which the graph of $y = x^2 - 6x + 5$ lies below the x-axis. Find the graph's x-intercepts by letting $y = 0$ and using factoring to solve for x.

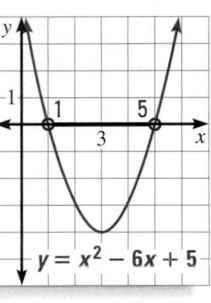

$$0 = x^2 - 6x + 5$$

$$0 = (x - 1)(x - 5)$$

$$x = 1 \text{ or } x = 5$$

Sketch a parabola that opens up and has 1 and 5 as x-intercepts. The graph lies below the x-axis between $x = 1$ and $x = 5$.

▶ The solution of the given inequality is $1 < x < 5$.

EXAMPLE 5 *Solving a Quadratic Inequality by Graphing*

Solve $2x^2 + 3x - 3 \ge 0$.

SOLUTION

The solution consists of the x-values for which the graph of $y = 2x^2 + 3x - 3$ lies on and above the x-axis. Find the graph's x-intercepts by letting $y = 0$ and using the quadratic formula to solve for x.

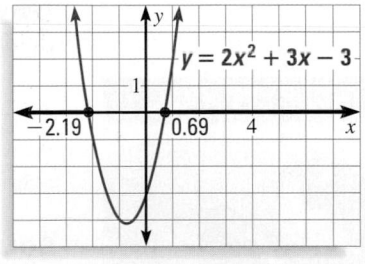

$$0 = 2x^2 + 3x - 3$$

$$x = \frac{-3 \pm \sqrt{3^2 - 4(2)(-3)}}{2(2)}$$

$$x = \frac{-3 \pm \sqrt{33}}{4}$$

$$x \approx 0.69 \text{ or } x \approx -2.19$$

Sketch a parabola that opens up and has 0.69 and -2.19 as x-intercepts. The graph lies on and above the x-axis to the left of (and including) $x = -2.19$ and to the right of (and including) $x = 0.69$.

▶ The solution of the given inequality is approximately $x \le -2.19$ or $x \ge 0.69$.

You can also use an algebraic approach to solve a quadratic inequality in one variable, as demonstrated in Example 6.

EXAMPLE 6 *Solving a Quadratic Inequality Algebraically*

Solve $x^2 + 2x \leq 8$.

SOLUTION

First write and solve the equation obtained by replacing the inequality symbol with an equals sign.

$$x^2 + 2x \leq 8 \qquad \text{Write original inequality.}$$
$$x^2 + 2x = 8 \qquad \text{Write corresponding equation.}$$
$$x^2 + 2x - 8 = 0 \qquad \text{Write in standard form.}$$
$$(x + 4)(x - 2) = 0 \qquad \text{Factor.}$$
$$x = -4 \text{ or } x = 2 \qquad \text{Zero product property}$$

The numbers -4 and 2 are called the *critical x-values* of the inequality $x^2 + 2x \leq 8$. Plot -4 and 2 on a number line, using solid dots because the values satisfy the inequality. The critical x-values partition the number line into three intervals. Test an x-value in each interval to see if it satisfies the inequality.

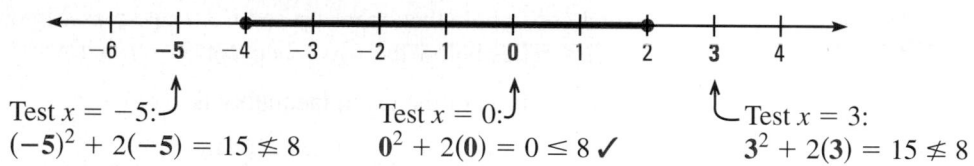

Test $x = -5$:
$(-5)^2 + 2(-5) = 15 \not\leq 8$

Test $x = 0$:
$0^2 + 2(0) = 0 \leq 8$ ✓

Test $x = 3$:
$3^2 + 2(3) = 15 \not\leq 8$

▶ The solution is $-4 \leq x \leq 2$.

EXAMPLE 7 *Using a Quadratic Inequality as a Model*

DRIVING For a driver aged x years, a study found that the driver's reaction time $V(x)$ (in milliseconds) to a visual stimulus such as a traffic light can be modeled by:

$$V(x) = 0.005x^2 - 0.23x + 22, \quad 16 \leq x \leq 70$$

At what ages does a driver's reaction time tend to be greater than 25 milliseconds?
▶ Source: *Science Probe!*

SOLUTION

You want to find the values of x for which:

$$V(x) > 25$$
$$0.005x^2 - 0.23x + 22 > 25$$
$$0.005x^2 - 0.23x - 3 > 0$$

Zero
X=56.600595 Y=0

Graph $y = 0.005x^2 - 0.23x - 3$ on the domain $16 \leq x \leq 70$. The graph's x-intercept is about 57, and the graph lies above the x-axis when $57 < x \leq 70$.

▶ Drivers over 57 years old tend to have reaction times greater than 25 milliseconds.

GUIDED PRACTICE

Vocabulary Check ✓

1. Give one example each of a quadratic inequality in one variable and a quadratic inequality in two variables.

Concept Check ✓

2. How does the graph of $y > x^2$ differ from the graph of $y \geq x^2$?

3. Explain how to solve $x^2 - 3x - 4 > 0$ graphically and algebraically.

Skill Check ✓

Graph the inequality.

4. $y \geq x^2 + 2$

5. $y \leq -2x^2$

6. $y < x^2 - 5x + 4$

Graph the system of inequalities.

7. $y \leq -x^2 + 3$
   $y \geq x^2 + 2x - 4$

8. $y \geq -x^2 + 3$
   $y \geq x^2 + 2x - 4$

9. $y \geq -x^2 + 3$
   $y \leq x^2 + 2x - 4$

Solve the inequality.

10. $x^2 - 4 < 0$

11. $x^2 - 4 \geq 0$

12. $x^2 - 4 > 3x$

13. 🌐 **ARCHITECTURE** The arch of the Sydney Harbor Bridge in Sydney, Australia, can be modeled by $y = -0.00211x^2 + 1.06x$ where x is the distance (in meters) from the left pylons and y is the height (in meters) of the arch above the water. For what distances x is the arch above the road?

PRACTICE AND APPLICATIONS

STUDENT HELP

↳ **Extra Practice**
to help you master
skills is on p. 947.

MATCHING GRAPHS Match the inequality with its graph.

14. $y \geq x^2 - 4x + 1$

15. $y < x^2 - 4x + 1$

16. $y \leq -x^2 - 4x + 1$

A.
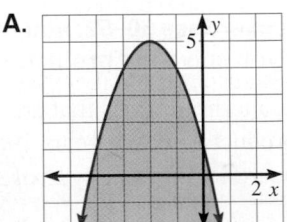

B.
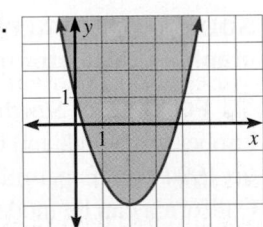

C.
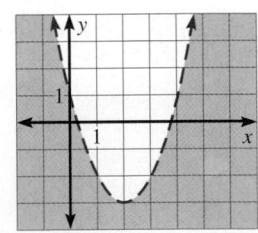

STUDENT HELP

↳ **HOMEWORK HELP**
Example 1: Exs. 14–28
Example 2: Exs. 47–49
Example 3: Exs. 29–34,
      49
Examples 4, 5: Exs. 35–40
Example 6: Exs. 41–46
Example 7: Exs. 50, 51

GRAPHING QUADRATIC INEQUALITIES Graph the inequality.

17. $y \geq 3x^2$

18. $y \leq -x^2$

19. $y > -x^2 + 5$

20. $y < x^2 - 3x$

21. $y \leq x^2 + 8x + 16$

22. $y \leq -x^2 + x + 6$

23. $y \geq 2x^2 - 2x - 5$

24. $y \geq -2x^2 - x + 3$

25. $y > -3x^2 + 5x - 4$

26. $y < -\frac{1}{2}x^2 - 2x + 4$

27. $y > \frac{4}{3}x^2 - 12x + 29$

28. $y < 0.6x^2 + 3x + 2.4$

5.7 *Graphing and Solving Quadratic Inequalities* **303**

GRAPHING SYSTEMS Graph the system of inequalities.

29. $y \geq x^2$
$\quad y \leq x^2 + 3$

30. $y < -3x^2$
$\quad y \geq -\frac{1}{2}x^2 - 5$

31. $y > x^2 - 6x + 9$
$\quad y < -x^2 + 6x - 3$

32. $y \geq x^2 + 2x + 1$
$\quad y \geq x^2 - 4x + 4$

33. $y < 3x^2 + 2x - 5$
$\quad y \geq -2x^2 + 1$

34. $y \leq 2x^2 - 9x + 8$
$\quad y > -x^2 - 6x - 4$

SOLVING BY GRAPHING Solve the inequality by graphing.

35. $x^2 + x - 2 < 0$

36. $2x^2 - 7x + 3 \geq 0$

37. $-x^2 - 2x + 8 \leq 0$

38. $-x^2 + x + 5 > 0$

39. $3x^2 + 24x \geq -41$

40. $-\frac{3}{4}x^2 + 4x - 8 < 0$

SOLVING ALGEBRAICALLY Solve the inequality algebraically.

41. $x^2 + 3x - 18 \geq 0$

42. $3x^2 - 16x + 5 \leq 0$

43. $4x^2 < 25$

44. $-x^2 - 12x < 32$

45. $2x^2 - 4x - 5 > 0$

46. $\frac{1}{2}x^2 + 3x \leq -6$

THEATER In Exercises 47 and 48, use the following information.
You are a member of a theater production crew. You use manila rope and wire rope
to support lighting, scaffolding, and other equipment. The weight W (in pounds) that
can be safely supported by a rope with diameter d (in inches) is given below for both
types of rope. ▶ Source: *Workshop Math*

> **Manila rope:** $W \leq 1480d^2$ **Wire rope:** $W \leq 8000d^2$

47. Graph the inequalities in separate coordinate planes for $0 \leq d \leq 1\frac{1}{2}$.

48. Based on your graphs, can 1000 pounds of theater equipment be supported by
a $\frac{1}{2}$ inch manila rope? by a $\frac{1}{2}$ inch wire rope?

49. **HEALTH** For a person of height h (in inches), a healthy weight W
(in pounds) is one that satisfies this system of inequalities:

$$W \geq \frac{19h^2}{703} \quad \text{and} \quad W \leq \frac{25h^2}{703}$$

Graph the system for $0 \leq h \leq 80$. What is the range of healthy weights for a
person 67 inches tall? ▶ Source: *Parade Magazine*

SOLVING INEQUALITIES In Exercises 50–52, you may want to use a
graphing calculator to help you solve the problems.

50. **FORESTRY** *Sawtimber* is a term for trees that are suitable for sawing into
lumber, plywood, and other products. For the years 1983–1995, the unit value y
(in 1994 dollars per million board feet) of one type of sawtimber harvested in
California can be modeled by

$$y = 0.125x^2 - 569x + 848{,}000, \quad 400 \leq x \leq 2200$$

where x is the volume of timber harvested (in millions of board feet).
▶ Source: *California Department of Forestry and Fire Protection*

a. For what harvested timber volumes is the value of the timber at least $400,000
per million board feet?

b. **LOGICAL REASONING** What happens to the unit value of the timber as the
volume harvested increases? Why would you expect this to happen?

51. 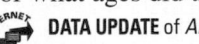 **MEDICINE** In 1992 the average income I (in dollars) for a doctor aged x years could be modeled by:

$$I = -425x^2 + 42{,}500x - 761{,}000$$

For what ages did the average income for a doctor exceed $250,000?

▶ **DATA UPDATE** of *American Almanac of Jobs and Salaries* data at www.mcdougallittell.com

Test Preparation

52. MULTI-STEP PROBLEM A study of driver reaction times to audio stimuli found that the reaction time $A(x)$ (in milliseconds) of a driver can be modeled by

$$A(x) = 0.0051x^2 - 0.319x + 15, \quad 16 \le x \le 70$$

where x is the driver's age (in years). ▶ Source: *Science Probe!*

a. Graph $y = A(x)$ on the given domain. Also graph $y = V(x)$, the reaction-time model for visual stimuli from Example 7, in the same coordinate plane.

b. For what values of x in the interval $16 \le x \le 70$ is $A(x) < V(x)$?

c. *Writing* Based on your results from part (b), do you think a driver would react more quickly to a traffic light changing from green to yellow or to the siren of an approaching ambulance? Explain.

★ **Challenge**

53. GEOMETRY CONNECTION The area A of the region bounded by a parabola and a horizontal line is given by $A = \frac{2}{3}bh$ where b and h are as defined in the diagram. Find the area of the region determined by each pair of inequalities.

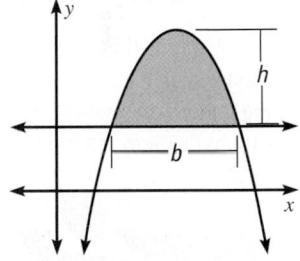

EXTRA CHALLENGE

www.mcdougallittell.com

a. $y \le -x^2 + 4x$
    $y \ge 0$

b. $y \ge x^2 - 4x - 5$
    $y \le 3$

MIXED REVIEW

SOLVING FOR A VARIABLE Solve the equation for y. (Review 1.4)

54. $3x + y = 1$ **55.** $8x - 2y = 10$ **56.** $-2x + 5y = 9$

57. $\frac{1}{6}x + \frac{1}{3}y = -\frac{11}{12}$ **58.** $xy - x = 2$ **59.** $\frac{x - 3y}{4} = 7x$

SOLVING SYSTEMS Solve the system of linear equations. (Review 3.6 for 5.8)

60. $5x - 3y - 2z = -17$
$\quad -x + 7y - 3z = 6$
$\quad 3x + 2y + 4z = 13$

61. $x - 4y + z = -14$
$\quad 2x + 3y + 7z = -15$
$\quad -3x + 5y - 5z = 29$

COMPLEX NUMBERS Write the expression as a complex number in standard form. (Review 5.4)

62. $(3 + 4i) + (10 - i)$ **63.** $(-11 - 2i) + (5 + 2i)$

64. $(9 + i) - (4 - i)$ **65.** $(5 - 3i) - (-1 + 2i)$

66. $6i(8 + i)$ **67.** $(7 + 3i)(2 - 5i)$

68. $\frac{1}{3 - i}$ **69.** $\frac{4 - 3i}{9 + 2i}$

5.8

Modeling with Quadratic Functions

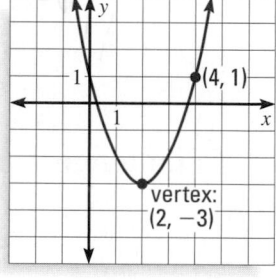

GOAL 1 **WRITING QUADRATIC FUNCTIONS**

In Lesson 5.1 you learned how to graph a given quadratic function. In this lesson you will write quadratic functions when given information about their graphs.

EXAMPLE 1 *Writing a Quadratic Function in Vertex Form*

Write a quadratic function for the parabola shown.

SOLUTION

Because you are given the vertex $(h, k) = (2, -3)$, use the vertex form of the quadratic function.

$$y = a(x - h)^2 + k$$

$$y = a(x - 2)^2 - 3$$

Use the other given point, (**4, 1**), to find a.

$\quad 1 = a(\mathbf{4} - 2)^2 - 3$ **Substitute 4 for *x* and 1 for *y*.**

$\quad 1 = 4a - 3$ **Simplify coefficient of *a*.**

$\quad 4 = 4a$ **Add 3 to each side.**

$\quad 1 = a$ **Divide each side by 4.**

▶ A quadratic function for the parabola is $y = (x - 2)^2 - 3$.

EXAMPLE 2 *Writing a Quadratic Function in Intercept Form*

Write a quadratic function for the parabola shown.

SOLUTION

Because you are given the x-intercepts $p = -2$ and $q = 3$, use the intercept form of the quadratic function.

$$y = a(x - p)(x - q)$$

$$y = a(x + 2)(x - 3)$$

Use the other given point, $(-1, 2)$, to find a.

$\quad \mathbf{2} = a(\mathbf{-1} + 2)(\mathbf{-1} - 3)$ **Substitute −1 for *x* and 2 for *y*.**

$\quad 2 = -4a$ **Simplify coefficient of *a*.**

$\quad -\dfrac{1}{2} = a$ **Divide each side by −4.**

▶ A quadratic function for the parabola is $y = -\dfrac{1}{2}(x + 2)(x - 3)$.

● ACTIVITY
Developing Concepts

Writing a Quadratic in Standard Form

In this activity you will write a quadratic function in standard form, $y = ax^2 + bx + c$, for the parabola in Example 2.

❶ The parabola passes through $(-2, 0)$, $(-1, 2)$, and $(3, 0)$. Substitute the coordinates of each point into $y = ax^2 + bx + c$ to obtain three equations in a, b, and c. For instance, the equation for $(-2, 0)$ is:

$$0 = a(-2)^2 + b(-2) + c, \text{ or}$$

$$0 = 4a - 2b + c$$

❷ Solve the system from **Step 1** to find a, b, and c. Use these values to write a quadratic function in standard form for the parabola.

❸ As a check of your work, use multiplication to write the function

$y = -\frac{1}{2}(x + 2)(x - 3)$ from Example 2 in standard form. Your answer

should match the function you wrote in **Step 2**.

REAL LIFE

Fuel Economy

EXAMPLE 3 *Finding a Quadratic Model for a Data Set*

A study compared the speed x (in miles per hour) and the average fuel economy y (in miles per gallon) for cars. The results are shown in the table. Find a quadratic model in standard form for the data. ▶ Source: *Transportation Energy Data Book*

Speed, x	15	20	25	30	35	40
Fuel economy, y	22.3	25.5	27.5	29.0	28.8	30.0
Speed, x	45	50	55	60	65	70
Fuel economy, y	29.9	30.2	30.4	28.8	27.4	25.3

SOLUTION

Plot the data pairs (x, y) in a coordinate plane.

Draw the parabola you think best fits the data.

Estimate the coordinates of three points on the parabola, such as $(20, 25)$, $(40, 30)$, and $(60, 28)$.

Substitute the coordinates of the points into the model $y = ax^2 + bx + c$ to obtain a system of three linear equations.

$$400a + 20b + c = 25$$

$$1600a + 40b + c = 30$$

$$3600a + 60b + c = 28$$

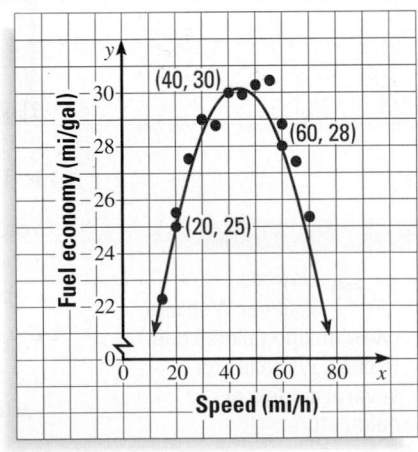

STUDENT HELP

↳ Look Back
For help with solving systems of three linear equations, see pp. 177, 217, and 231.

Solve the linear system. The solution is $a = -0.00875$, $b = 0.775$, and $c = 13$.

▶ A quadratic model for the data is $y = -0.00875x^2 + 0.775x + 13$.

GOAL 2 **USING TECHNOLOGY TO FIND QUADRATIC MODELS**

In Chapter 2 you used a graphing calculator to perform linear regression on a data set in order to find a linear model for the data. A graphing calculator can also be used to perform *quadratic regression*. Quadratic regression produces a more accurate quadratic model than the procedure in Example 3 because it uses *all* the data points. The model given by quadratic regression is called the **best-fitting quadratic model**.

EXAMPLE 4 *Using Quadratic Regression to Find a Model*

FUEL ECONOMY Use the fuel economy data given in Example 3 to complete parts (a) and (b).

a. Use a graphing calculator to find the best-fitting quadratic model for the data.

b. Find the speed that maximizes a car's fuel economy.

SOLUTION

a. Enter the data into two lists of a graphing calculator.

Make a scatter plot of the data. Note that the points show a parabolic trend.

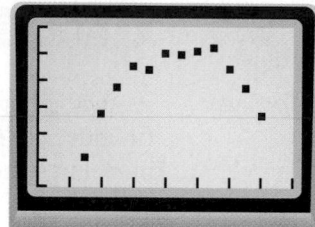

Use the quadratic regression feature to find the best-fitting quadratic model for the data.

Check how well the model fits the data by graphing the model and the data in the same viewing window.

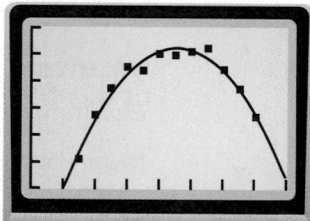

▶ The best-fitting quadratic model is $y = -0.00820x^2 + 0.746x + 13.5$.

b. You can find the speed that maximizes fuel economy by using the *Maximum* feature of a graphing calculator, as shown at the right.

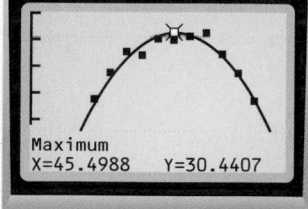

You can also find the speed algebraically using the formula for the *x*-coordinate of a parabola's vertex from Lesson 5.1:

$$x = -\frac{b}{2a} = -\frac{0.746}{2(-0.00820)} \approx 45$$

▶ The speed that maximizes a car's fuel economy is about 45 miles per hour.

GUIDED PRACTICE

Vocabulary Check ✔

1. Complete this statement: When you perform quadratic regression on a set of data, the quadratic model you obtain is called the _?_ .

Concept Check ✔

2. How many points are needed to determine a parabola if one of the points is the vertex? if none of the points is the vertex?

Skill Check ✔

Write a quadratic function in the specified form for the parabola shown.

3. vertex form

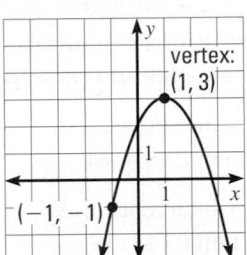

4. intercept form

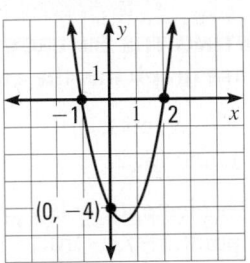

5. standard form

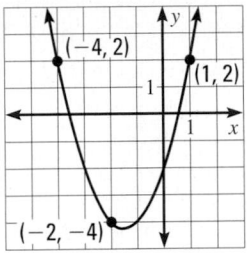

6. **REAL ESTATE** The table shows the average sale price *p* of a house in Suffolk County, Massachusetts, for various years *t* since 1988. Use a system of equations to write a quadratic model for the data. Check your model by performing quadratic regression on a graphing calculator.

Years since 1988, *t*	0	2	4	6	8	10
Average sale price (thousands of dollars), *p*	165	154.5	124.5	115	128	165

DATA UPDATE of *Boston Globe* data at www.mcdougallittell.com

PRACTICE AND APPLICATIONS

STUDENT HELP

▶ **Extra Practice**
to help you master
skills is on p. 947.

WRITING THE VERTEX FORM Write a quadratic function in vertex form for the parabola shown.

7.

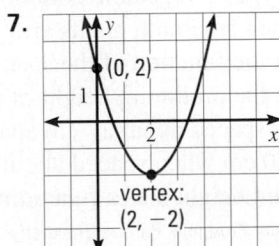

8.

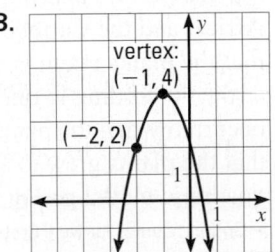

9.

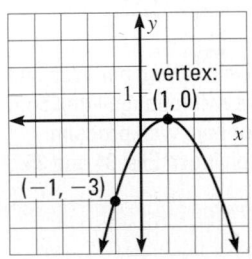

STUDENT HELP

▶ **HOMEWORK HELP**
Example 1: Exs. 7–15, 34
Example 2: Exs. 16–24, 35
Example 3: Exs. 25–33, 36–38
Example 4: Exs. 37, 38

WRITING THE VERTEX FORM Write a quadratic function in vertex form whose graph has the given vertex and passes through the given point.

10. vertex: $(2, -1)$
point: $(4, 3)$

11. vertex: $(-4, 6)$
point: $(-1, 9)$

12. vertex: $(4, 5)$
point: $(8, -3)$

13. vertex: $(0, 0)$
point: $(-2, -12)$

14. vertex: $(1, -10)$
point: $(-3, 54)$

15. vertex: $(-6, -7)$
point: $(0, -61)$

WRITING THE INTERCEPT FORM Write a quadratic function in intercept form for the parabola shown.

16.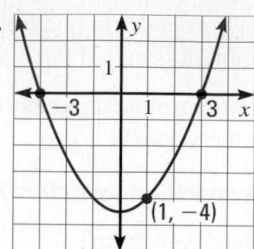

17.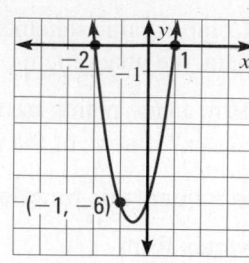

18.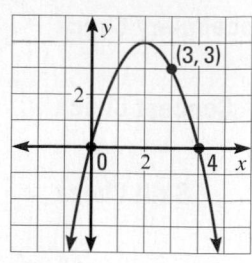

WRITING THE INTERCEPT FORM Write a quadratic function in intercept form whose graph has the given *x*-intercepts and passes through the given point.

19. *x*-intercepts: 1, 4
point: (3, 2)

20. *x*-intercepts: -2, 2
point: (-4, 8)

21. *x*-intercepts: -1, 6
point: (1, -20)

22. *x*-intercepts: -10, -8
point: (-7, -15)

23. *x*-intercepts: 3, 9
point: (14, 77)

24. *x*-intercepts: -5, 0
point: (-3, 18)

WRITING THE STANDARD FORM Write a quadratic function in standard form for the parabola shown.

25.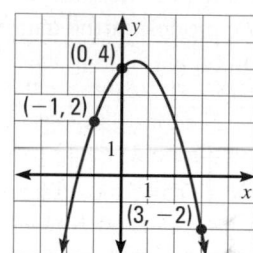

26.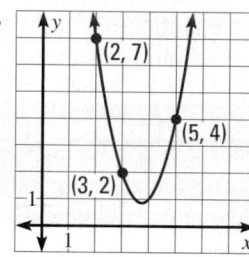

27.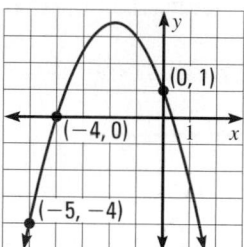

WRITING THE STANDARD FORM Write a quadratic function in standard form whose graph passes through the given points.

28. (-1, 5), (0, 3), (3, 9)

29. (1, 2), (3, 4), (6, -8)

30. (-2, -1), (1, 11), (2, 27)

31. (-4, -7), (-3, 3), (3, -21)

32. (-3, -4), (-1, 0), (9, -10)

33. (-6, 46), (2, 14), (4, 56)

STUDENT HELP

HOMEWORK HELP
Visit our Web site
www.mcdougallittell.com
for help with problem
solving in Exs. 34 and 35.

34. **BOTANY** *Amaranth* is a type of vegetable commonly grown in Asia, West Africa, and the Caribbean. When amaranth plants are grown in rows, the height that the plants attain is a quadratic function of the spacing between plants within a row. According to one study, the minimum height of the plants, about 16 cm, occurred when the plants were spaced about 27 cm apart. The study also found that the plants grew to about 20 cm when spaced about 40 cm apart. Write a quadratic model giving the plant height *h* as a function of the spacing *s*.

▶ Source: Center for New Crops and Plant Products, Perdue University

35. **TRANSPORTATION** The surfaces of some roads are shaped like parabolas to allow rain to run off to either side. (This is also true of football fields; see Exercise 52 on page 254.) Write a quadratic model for the surface of the road shown.

▶ Source: Massachusetts Highway Department

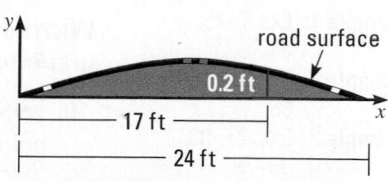

Not drawn to scale

FOCUS ON PEOPLE

MARK MCGWIRE
hit 70 home runs during the 1998 Major League Baseball season, breaking Roger Maris's record of 61. McGwire's longest home run traveled 545 ft (166 m).

APPLICATION LINK
www.mcdougallittell.com

36. **RUNNING** The table shows how wind affects a runner's performance in the 200 meter dash. Positive wind speeds correspond to tailwinds, and negative wind speeds correspond to headwinds. Positive changes in finishing time mean worsened performance, and negative changes mean improved performance. Use a system of equations to write a quadratic model for the change t in finishing time as a function of the wind speed s. ▶ Source: *The Physics of Sports*

Wind speed (m/sec), s	−6	−4	−2	0	2	4	6
Change in finishing time (sec), t	2.28	1.42	0.67	0	−0.57	−1.05	−1.42

37. **AGRICULTURE** Researchers compared protein intake to average shoulder and kidney weight for a group of pigs. The results are shown in the table. Use systems of equations to write quadratic models for the shoulder weight s and kidney weight k as a function of the protein intake p. Check your models using the quadratic regression feature of a graphing calculator.

▶ Source: *Livestock Research for Rural Development*

Protein intake (g/day), p	195	238	297	341	401	427
Shoulder weight (g), s	8130	8740	9680	9690	9810	8990
Kidney weight (g), k	239	287	288	334	379	373

38. **BASEBALL** The table shows the distance (in meters) traveled by a baseball hit at various angles and with different types of spin. (In each case the initial speed of the ball off the bat is assumed to be 40 m/sec.) Use systems of equations to write three quadratic models—one for each type of spin—that give the distance d as a function of the angle A. Check your models using the quadratic regression feature of a graphing calculator. ▶ Source: *The Physics of Sports*

Angle	10°	15°	30°	36°	42°	45°	48°	54°	60°
Distance (backspin)	61.2	83.0	130.4	139.4	143.2	142.7	140.7	132.8	119.7
Distance (no spin)	58.3	79.7	126.9	136.6	140.6	140.9	139.3	132.5	120.5
Distance (topspin)	56.1	76.3	122.8	133.2	138.3	139.0	137.8	132.1	120.9

Test
Preparation

39. MULTI-STEP PROBLEM The table shows the time t it takes to boil a potato whose smallest diameter (that is, whose shortest distance through the center) is d. ▶ Source: Dr. Peter Barham, University of Bristol

Diameter (mm), d	20	25	30	35	40	45	50
Boiling time (min), t	27	42	61	83	109	138	170

   a. Find the ratios $\frac{t}{d}$. Does boiling time vary directly with diameter? Explain.

   b. Find the ratios $\frac{t}{d^2}$. What do you notice?

   c. Use the result of part (b) to write a quadratic model for t as a function of d. Find the time needed to boil a potato whose smallest diameter is 55 mm.

40. **GEOMETRY** **CONNECTION** Let R be the maximum number of regions into which a circle can be divided using n chords. For example, the diagram shows that $R = 4$ when $n = 2$. Copy and complete the table. Then write a quadratic model giving R as a function of n.

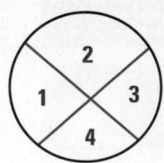

n	0	1	2	3	4	5	6
R	?	?	4	?	?	?	?

MIXED REVIEW

EVALUATING EXPRESSIONS Evaluate the expression for the given value of the variable. **(Review 1.2 for 6.1)**

41. $x^2 - 4$ when $x = 3$ **42.** x^5 when $x = 2$

43. $3u^3 + 10$ when $u = -4$ **44.** $-v^4 + 2v + 7$ when $v = -1$

SOLVING SYSTEMS Solve the system using either the substitution method or the linear combination method. **(Review 3.2)**

45. $x - y = 4$
$x + y = 2$

46. $2x - y = 0$
$5x + 3y = 11$

47. $3x + 2y = -2$
$4x + 7y = 19$

48. 🌐 **HEALTH** You belong to a health maintenance organization (HMO). Each year, you pay the HMO an insurance premium of \$1800. In addition, you pay \$15 for each visit to your doctor's office and \$10 for each prescription. Write an equation for the annual cost C of your health plan as a function of your number v of office visits and number p of prescriptions. **(Review 3.5)**

QUIZ 3

Self-Test for Lessons 5.7 and 5.8

Graph the inequality. **(Lesson 5.7)**

1. $y > x^2 + 2$ **2.** $y \geq -x^2 - x + 3$ **3.** $y \leq 2x^2 - 12x + 15$

Graph the system of inequalities. **(Lesson 5.7)**

4. $y \geq x^2$
$y \leq 2x^2 - 1$

5. $y > x^2 - 2x - 3$
$y < -x^2 + 2x + 3$

6. $y > -x^2 - 4x$
$y \leq x^2 + 7x + 10$

Write a quadratic function in the specified form whose graph has the given characteristics. **(Lesson 5.8)**

7. vertex form
vertex: $(5, -2)$
point on graph: $(4, 0)$

8. intercept form
x-intercepts: $-3, 1$
point on graph: $(2, -5)$

9. standard form
points on graph:
$(-4, 8), (-2, 1), (2, 5)$

10. 🌐 **COMPUTERS** Using an algorithm called *insertion sort*, a common minicomputer can sort N numbers from least to greatest in t milliseconds where $t = 0.00339N^2 + 0.00143N - 5.95$. How many numbers can the minicomputer sort in less than 1 second (1000 milliseconds)? Write your answer as an inequality. **(Lesson 5.7)**

Chapter Summary

WHAT did you learn?

Graph quadratic functions. **(5.1)**

Write quadratic functions in standard, intercept, and vertex forms. **(5.1, 5.2, 5.5)**

Find zeros of quadratic functions. **(5.2)**

Solve quadratic equations.
- by factoring **(5.2)**
- by finding square roots **(5.3)**
- by completing the square **(5.5)**
- by using the quadratic formula **(5.6)**

Perform operations with complex numbers. **(5.4)**

Find the discriminant of a quadratic equation. **(5.6)**

Graph quadratic inequalities in two variables. **(5.7)**

Solve quadratic inequalities in one variable. **(5.7)**

Find quadratic models for data. **(5.8)**

WHY did you learn it?

Model the suspension cables on the Golden Gate Bridge. **(p. 252)**

Find the amount of fertilizer that maximizes the sugar yield from sugarbeets. **(p. 285)**

Determine what subscription price to charge for a Web site in order to maximize revenue. **(p. 259)**

Calculate dimensions for a mural. **(p. 262)**
Find a falling rock's time in the air. **(p. 268)**
Tell how a firefighter should position a hose. **(p. 288)**
Find the speed and duration of a thrill ride. **(p. 297)**

Determine whether a complex number belongs to the Mandelbrot set. **(p. 276)**

Identify the number and type of solutions of a quadratic equation. **(p. 293)**

Calculate the weight that a rope can support. **(p. 304)**

Relate a driver's age and reaction time. **(p. 302)**

Determine the effect of wind on a runner's performance. **(p. 311)**

How does Chapter 5 fit into the BIGGER PICTURE of algebra?

In Chapter 5 you saw the relationship between the *solutions* of the quadratic equation $ax^2 + bx + c = 0$, the *zeros* of the quadratic function $y = ax^2 + bx + c$, and the *x-intercepts* of this function's graph. You'll continue to see this relationship with other types of functions. Also, the graph of a quadratic function—a parabola—is one of the four conic sections. You'll study all the conic sections in Chapter 10.

STUDY STRATEGY

How did you troubleshoot?

Here is an example of a trouble spot identified and eliminated, following the **Study Strategy** on page 248.

Troubleshoot

Trouble spot: Changing a quadratic function from standard form to vertex form by completing the square.

How to eliminate: Remember to add the same constant to *both* sides of the equation for the function.

Example:
$$y = x^2 + 10x - 3$$
$$y + 25 = (x^2 + 10x + 25) - 3$$
$$y + 25 = (x + 5)^2 - 3$$
$$y = (x + 5)^2 - 28$$

VOCABULARY

- quadratic function, p. 249
- parabola, p. 249
- vertex of a parabola, p. 249
- axis of symmetry, p. 249
- standard form of a quadratic function, p. 250
- vertex form of a quadratic function, p. 250
- intercept form of a quadratic function, p. 250
- binomial, p. 256

- trinomial, p. 256
- factoring, p. 256
- monomial, p. 257
- quadratic equation, p. 257
- standard form of a quadratic equation, p. 257
- zero product property, p. 257
- zero of a function, p. 259
- square root, p. 264
- radical sign, p. 264

- radicand, p. 264
- radical, p. 264
- rationalizing the denominator, p. 265
- imaginary unit i, p. 272
- complex number, p. 272
- standard form of a complex number, p. 272
- imaginary number, p. 272
- pure imaginary number, p. 272

- complex plane, p. 273
- complex conjugates, p. 274
- absolute value of a complex number, p. 275
- completing the square, p. 282
- quadratic formula, p. 291
- discriminant, p. 293
- quadratic inequality, pp. 299, 301
- best-fitting quadratic model, p. 308

5.1 GRAPHING QUADRATIC FUNCTIONS

Examples on pp. 249–252

EXAMPLE You can graph a quadratic function given in standard form, vertex form, or intercept form. For instance, the same function is given below in each of these forms, and its graph is shown.

Standard form: $y = x^2 + 2x - 3$;

$\qquad$ axis of symmetry: $x = -\dfrac{b}{2a} = -\dfrac{2}{2(1)} = -1$

Vertex form: $y = (x + 1)^2 - 4$; vertex: $(-1, -4)$

Intercept form: $y = (x + 3)(x - 1)$; x-intercepts: $-3, 1$

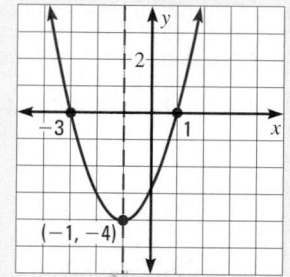

Graph the quadratic function.

1. $y = x^2 + 4x + 7$
2. $y = -3(x - 2)^2 + 5$
3. $y = \dfrac{1}{2}(x + 1)(x - 5)$

5.2–5.3 SOLVING BY FACTORING AND BY FINDING SQUARE ROOTS

Examples on pp. 256–259, 264–266

EXAMPLES You can use factoring or square roots to solve quadratic equations.

Solving by factoring:

$x^2 - 4x - 21 = 0$

$(x + 3)(x - 7) = 0$

$x + 3 = 0 \quad$ or $\quad x - 7 = 0$

$\qquad x = -3 \quad$ or $\qquad x = 7$

Solving by finding square roots:

$4x^2 - 7 = 65$

$\qquad 4x^2 = 72$

$\qquad x^2 = 18$

$\qquad x = \pm\sqrt{18} = \pm 3\sqrt{2}$

Solve the quadratic equation.

4. $x^2 + 11x + 24 = 0$ **5.** $x^2 - 8x + 16 = 0$ **6.** $2x^2 + 3x + 1 = 0$

7. $3u^2 = -4u + 15$ **8.** $25v^2 - 30v = -9$ **9.** $2x^2 = 200$

10. $5x^2 - 2 = 13$ **11.** $4(t + 6)^2 = 160$ **12.** $-(k - 1)^2 + 7 = -43$

5.4   COMPLEX NUMBERS

Examples on pp. 272–276

EXAMPLES You can add, subtract, multiply, and divide complex numbers.
You can also find the absolute value of a complex number.

Addition: $(1 + 8i) + (2 - 3i) = (1 + 2) + (8 - 3)i = 3 + 5i$

Subtraction: $(1 + 8i) - (2 - 3i) = (1 - 2) + (8 + 3)i = -1 + 11i$

Multiplication: $(1 + 8i)(2 - 3i) = 2 - 3i + 16i - 24i^2 = 2 + 13i - 24(-1) = 26 + 13i$

Division: $\dfrac{1 + 8i}{2 - 3i} = \dfrac{1 + 8i}{2 - 3i} \cdot \dfrac{2 + 3i}{2 + 3i} = \dfrac{-22 + 19i}{13} = -\dfrac{22}{13} + \dfrac{19}{13}i$

Absolute value: $|1 + 8i| = \sqrt{1^2 + 8^2} = \sqrt{65}$

In Exercises 13–16, write the expression as a complex number in standard form.

13. $(7 - 4i) + (-2 + 5i)$ **14.** $(2 + 11i) - (6 - i)$

15. $(3 + 10i)(4 - 9i)$ **16.** $\dfrac{8 + i}{1 - 2i}$

17. Find the absolute value of $6 + 9i$.

5.5   COMPLETING THE SQUARE

Examples on pp. 282–285

EXAMPLES You can use completing the square to solve quadratic equations
and change quadratic functions from standard form to vertex form.

Solving an equation:

$x^2 + 6x + 13 = 0$

$x^2 + 6x = -13$

$x^2 + 6x + \mathbf{9} = -13 + \mathbf{9}$

$(x + 3)^2 = -4$

$x + 3 = \pm\sqrt{-4}$

$x = -3 \pm 2i$

Writing a function in vertex form:

$y = x^2 + 6x + 13$

$y + \underline{\ ?\ } = (x^2 + 6x + \underline{\ ?\ }) + 13$

$y + \mathbf{9} = (x^2 + 6x + \mathbf{9}) + 13$

$y + 9 = (x + 3)^2 + 13$

$y = (x + 3)^2 + 4$

Note that the vertex is $(-3, 4)$.

Solve the quadratic equation by completing the square.

18. $x^2 + 4x = 3$ **19.** $x^2 - 10x + 26 = 0$ **20.** $2w^2 + w - 7 = 0$

Write the quadratic function in vertex form and identify the vertex.

21. $y = x^2 - 8x + 17$ **22.** $y = -x^2 - 2x - 6$ **23.** $y = 4x^2 + 16x + 23$

THE QUADRATIC FORMULA AND THE DISCRIMINANT

Examples on pp. 291–294

EXAMPLE You can use the quadratic formula to solve any quadratic equation.

$$3x^2 - 5x = -1$$
$$3x^2 - 5x + 1 = 0$$

$$x = \frac{-b \pm \sqrt{b^2 - 4ac}}{2a} = \frac{5 \pm \sqrt{(-5)^2 - 4(3)(1)}}{2(3)} = \frac{5 \pm \sqrt{13}}{6}$$

Use the quadratic formula to solve the equation.

24. $x^2 - 8x + 5 = 0$

25. $9x^2 = 1 - 7x$

26. $5v^2 + 6v + 7 = v^2 - 4v$

GRAPHING AND SOLVING QUADRATIC INEQUALITIES

Examples on pp. 299–302

EXAMPLES You can graph a quadratic inequality in two variables and solve a quadratic inequality in one variable.

Graphing an inequality in two variables: To graph $y < -x^2 + 4$, draw the dashed parabola $y = -x^2 + 4$. Test a point inside the parabola, such as $(0, 0)$. Since $(0, 0)$ is a solution of the inequality, shade the region inside the parabola.

Solving an inequality in one variable: To solve $-x^2 + 4 < 0$, graph $y = -x^2 + 4$ and identify the x-values where the graph lies below the x-axis. Or, solve $-x^2 + 4 = 0$ to find the critical x-values -2 and 2, then test an x-value in each interval determined by -2 and 2 to find the solution. The solution is $x < -2$ or $x > 2$.

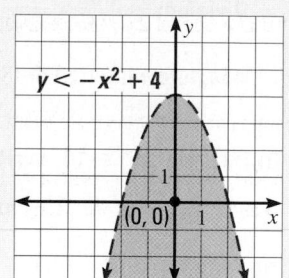

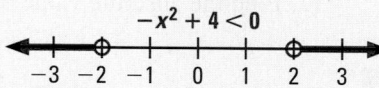

Graph the quadratic inequality.

27. $y \geq x^2 - 4x + 4$

28. $y < x^2 + 6x + 5$

29. $y > -2x^2 + 3$

Solve the quadratic inequality.

30. $x^2 - 3x - 4 \leq 0$

31. $2x^2 + 7x + 2 \geq 0$

32. $9x^2 > 49$

MODELING WITH QUADRATIC FUNCTIONS

Examples on pp. 306–308

EXAMPLE You can write a quadratic function given characteristics of its graph.

To find a function for the parabola with vertex $(1, -3)$ and passing through $(0, -1)$, use the vertex form $y = a(x - h)^2 + k$ with $(h, k) = (1, -3)$ to write $y = a(x - 1)^2 - 3$. Use the point $(0, -1)$ to find a: $-1 = a(0 - 1)^2 - 3$, so $-1 = a - 3$, and therefore $a = 2$. The function is $y = 2(x - 1)^2 - 3$.

Write a quadratic function whose graph has the given characteristics.

33. vertex: $(6, 1)$
point on graph: $(4, 5)$

34. x-intercepts: $-4, 3$
point on graph: $(1, 20)$

35. points on graph:
$(-5, 1), (-4, -2), (3, 5)$

Chapter Test

Graph the quadratic function.

1. $y = -2x^2 + 8x - 5$

2. $y = (x + 3)^2 + 1$

3. $y = -\frac{1}{3}(x + 1)(x - 5)$

4. Write $y = 4(x - 3)^2 - 7$ in standard form.

Factor the expression.

5. $x^2 - x - 20$

6. $9x^2 + 6x + 1$

7. $3u^2 - 108$

8. Write $y = x^2 - 10x + 16$ in intercept form and give the function's zeros.

9. Simplify the radical expressions $\sqrt{500}$ and $\sqrt{\frac{8}{3}}$.

10. Plot these numbers in the same complex plane: $4 + 2i$, $-5 + i$, and $-3i$.

Write the expression as a complex number in standard form.

11. $(3 + i) + (1 - 5i)$

12. $(-4 + 2i) - (7 - 3i)$

13. $(8 + i)(6 + 2i)$

14. $\frac{9 + 2i}{1 - 4i}$

15. Is $c = -0.5i$ in the Mandelbrot set? Use absolute value to justify your answer.

Find the value of c that makes the expression a perfect square trinomial. Then write the expression as the square of a binomial.

16. $x^2 - 4x + c$

17. $x^2 + 11x + c$

18. $x^2 - 0.6x + c$

19. Write $y = x^2 + 18x - 4$ in vertex form and identify the vertex.

Solve the quadratic equation using any appropriate method.

20. $7x^2 - 3 = 11$

21. $5x^2 - 60x + 180 = 0$

22. $4x^2 + 28x - 15 = 0$

23. $m^2 + 8m = -3$

24. $3(p - 9)^2 = 81$

25. $6t^2 - 2t + 2 = 4t^2 + t$

26. Find the discriminant of $7x^2 - x + 10 = 0$. What does the discriminant tell you about the number and type of solutions of the equation?

Graph the quadratic inequality.

27. $y \geq x^2 + 1$

28. $y \leq -x^2 + 4x + 2$

29. $y < 2x^2 + 12x + 15$

Solve the quadratic inequality.

30. $-x^2 + x + 6 \geq 0$

31. $2x^2 - 9 > 23$

32. $x^2 - 7x < -4$

Write a quadratic function whose graph has the given characteristics.

33. vertex: $(-3, 2)$
point on graph: $(-1, -18)$

34. x-intercepts: 1, 8
point on graph: $(2, -2)$

35. points on graph:
$(1, 7), (4, -2), (5, -1)$

36. 🌊 **WATERFALLS** Niagara Falls in New York is 167 feet high. How long does it take for water to fall from the top to the bottom of Niagara Falls?

37. 🌐 **INSURANCE** An insurance company charges a 35-year-old nonsmoker an annual premium of $118 for a $100,000 term life insurance policy. The premiums for 45-year-old and 55-year-old nonsmokers are $218 and $563, respectively. Write a quadratic model for the premium p as a function of age a.

Chapter Standardized Test

TEST-TAKING STRATEGY When checking your answer to a question, try using a method different from the one you used to get the answer. If you use the same method to find *and* check an answer, you may make the same mistake twice.

1. MULTIPLE CHOICE What is the vertex of the graph of $y = 2(x - 3)^2 - 7$?

 A $(3, 7)$ **B** $(3, -7)$ **C** $(-3, -7)$

 D $(-3, 7)$ **E** $(2, 3)$

2. MULTIPLE CHOICE What is a correct factorization of $4x^2 + 4x - 35$?

 A $(4x + 5)(x - 7)$ **B** $(4x - 5)(x + 7)$

 C $(2x + 5)(2x - 7)$ **D** $(2x + 35)(2x - 1)$

 E $(2x - 5)(2x + 7)$

3. MULTIPLE CHOICE What are the zeros of $y = x^2 - 13x + 40$?

 A $-5, -8$ **B** $5, -8$ **C** $4, 10$

 D $5, 8$ **E** $-4, -10$

4. MULTIPLE CHOICE What are all solutions of $4(x - 1)^2 - 3 = 25$?

 A 3 **B** 8 **C** $1 \pm \sqrt{7}$

 D $0.5, 3$ **E** $1 \pm 2\sqrt{7}$

5. MULTIPLE CHOICE What does the product $(-12 + 8i)(10 - i)$ equal?

 A $-128 + 68i$ **B** $-128 + 92i$

 C $-112 + 68i$ **D** $-112 + 92i$

 E $-120 - 8i^2$

6. MULTIPLE CHOICE If $x^2 + 8x + c$ is a perfect square trinomial, what is the value of c?

 A 4 **B** 8 **C** 16

 D 32 **E** 64

7. MULTIPLE CHOICE How many real and imaginary solutions does the equation $3x^2 + 2x - 7 = 0$ have?

 A 2 real solutions, no imaginary solutions

 B 1 real solution, no imaginary solutions

 C 1 real solution, 1 imaginary solution

 D no real solutions, 2 imaginary solutions

 E no real solutions, 1 imaginary solution

8. MULTIPLE CHOICE What is the solution of $x^2 + 7x - 8 > 0$?

 A $x = -8$ or $x = 1$ **B** $x < -8$ or $x > 1$

 C $-8 < x < 1$ **D** $x < -1$ or $x > 8$

 E $-1 < x < 8$

9. MULTIPLE CHOICE Which quadratic inequality is graphed?

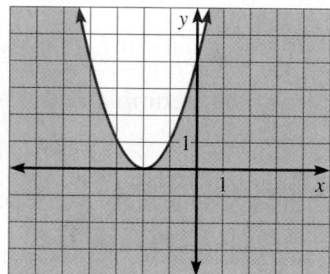

 A $y \geq x^2 + 2$ **B** $y \leq x^2 + 2$

 C $y \geq x^2 - 2$ **D** $y \leq (x + 2)^2$

 E $y \leq (x - 2)^2$

10. MULTIPLE CHOICE Which quadratic function *cannot* be represented by the graph shown?

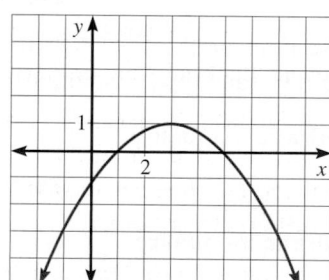

 A $y = -\frac{1}{4}(x - 1)(x - 5)$

 B $y = -\frac{1}{4}(x - 3)^2 + 1$

 C $y = -\frac{1}{4}x^2 + \frac{3}{2}x - \frac{5}{4}$

 D $y = -\frac{1}{4}(x^2 - 6x + 5)$

 E $y = -\frac{1}{4}(x + 1)(x + 5)$

QUANTITATIVE COMPARISON In Exercises 11 and 12, choose the statement that is true about the given quantities.

(A) The quantity in column A is greater.

(B) The quantity in column B is greater.

(C) The two quantities are equal.

(D) The relationship cannot be determined from the given information.

Column A	Column B
11. $\left|-3 + 2i\right|$	$\left|1 - 4i\right|$
12. Discriminant of $x^2 - 7x - 24 = 0$	Discriminant of $5x^2 - 14x + 10 = 0$

13. MULTI-STEP PROBLEM An engineer designing a curved road must make the curve's radius large enough so that car passengers are not pulled to one side as they round the curve at the posted speed limit. The minimum radius r (in feet) that should be used is given by $r = 0.334s^2$ where s is the expected speed of traffic (in miles per hour).

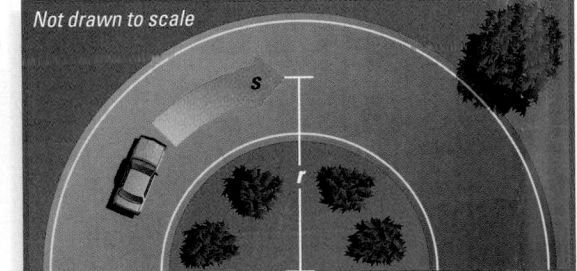

Not drawn to scale

a. If the expected speed of traffic around a curve is 30 miles per hour, what should the minimum radius of the curve be?

b. How fast can a car comfortably round a curve with a radius of 400 feet?

c. Consider a semicircular curve, as shown in the diagram. The radius of the curve is measured from the center of the semicircles formed by the road's inner and outer edges to a point on the road halfway between these edges. Write an equation giving the area A of the pavement needed for the road as a function of the radius r. Assume the road is 24 feet wide.

d. Use your answer from part (c) to write an equation giving the area A of pavement needed as a function of the expected speed s of traffic.

e. CRITICAL THINKING What type of function is the function from part (c)? What type of function is the function from part (d)?

14. MULTI-STEP PROBLEM You and your friend are playing tennis. Your friend lobs the ball high into the air, hitting it 3 feet above the court with an initial vertical velocity of 40 feet per second. You back up and prepare to hit an overhead smash to win the point.

a. Use the model $h = -16t^2 + v_0t + h_0$ to write an equation giving the height of the lobbed tennis ball as a function of time.

b. At what time t does the ball reach its maximum height above the court? What is the maximum height?

c. If you plan to hit the smash when the ball falls to a height of 8 feet above the court, how long do you have to prepare for the shot?

d. If you plan to hit the smash when the ball is between 6 feet and 9 feet above the court (inclusive), what are your possible preparation times?

e. Suppose you hit the smash when the ball is 8 feet above the court. It takes 0.1 second for the ball you smashed to hit the court on your friend's side of the net. What was the ball's initial vertical velocity coming off your racket?

POLYNOMIALS AND POLYNOMIAL FUNCTIONS

▶ *What type of function models the speed of a space shuttle?*

APPLICATION: Space Exploration

The space shuttle's engines produce immense power, equivalent to the output of 23 Hoover Dams. All this power is needed to accelerate the shuttle to more than 17,000 miles per hour in about eight minutes after launch. This speed allows the shuttle to achieve and maintain an orbit 240 miles above Earth's surface.

Think & Discuss

The table below gives the time (in seconds) after launch and the corresponding average speed (in feet per second) of the shuttle.

Time (sec)	Speed (ft/sec)
20	463.4
40	979.3
60	1421.3
80	2283.5

1. Make a scatter plot of the data. Estimate how long it takes the shuttle to reach a speed of 1000 feet per second.

2. Would either a linear function or a quadratic function be a good model for the data? Explain.

Learn More About It

You will model the speed of the space shuttle in Exercise 49 on p. 385.

 APPLICATION LINK Visit www.mcdougallittell.com for more information on space exploration.

What's the chapter about?

Chapter 6 is about **polynomials, polynomial equations, and polynomial functions**. In Chapter 6 you'll learn

- how to perform operations on polynomials and solve polynomial equations.

- how to evaluate, graph, and find zeros of polynomial functions.

KEY VOCABULARY

▶ **Review**
- power, p. 11
- *x*-intercept, p. 84
- zeros of a function, p. 259

▶ **New**
- polynomial function, p. 329

- end behavior, p. 331
- polynomial long division, p. 352
- synthetic division, p. 353
- rational zero theorem, p. 359

- fundamental theorem of algebra, p. 366
- local maximum, p. 374
- local minimum, p. 374
- finite differences, p. 380

Are you ready for the chapter?

SKILL REVIEW Do these exercises to review key skills that you'll apply in this chapter. See the given **reference page** if there is something you don't understand.

Simplify the expression. (Review Example 5, p. 13)

1. $4x^2 - 2x + x - x^2$ **2.** $2(8x + 5) - 19x$ **3.** $-x^3 - 5x^4 - 3x^3 + 7x^2$

Graph the quadratic function. (Review Examples 1–3, pp. 250 and 251)

4. $y = -3(x - 2)^2$ **5.** $y = (x + 1)(x - 5)$ **6.** $y = 2(x + 6)(x + 4)$

Write the quadratic function in standard form. (Review Example 4, p. 251)

7. $y = (x - 1)^2 - 7$ **8.** $y = 2(x + 4)^2$ **9.** $y = -(x - 2)(x + 8)$

Solve the equation. (Review Example 5, p. 258)

10. $x^2 + 6x - 27 = 0$ **11.** $x^2 + 20x + 100 = 0$ **12.** $2x^2 + 5x - 12 = 0$

Here's a study strategy!

Making a Flow Chart

A flow chart is a diagram that shows the possible paths and steps you can follow to solve a problem.

After you complete the chapter, make a flow chart that shows how to find all the zeros of a polynomial function. Include techniques and theorems you learned in Chapter 6 which you can use with various types of polynomial functions.

6.1
Using Properties of Exponents

What you should learn

GOAL 1 Use properties of exponents to evaluate and simplify expressions involving powers.

GOAL 2 Use exponents and scientific notation to solve **real-life** problems, such as finding the per capita GDP of Denmark in **Example 4**.

Why you should learn it

▼ To simplify **real-life** expressions, such as the ratio of a state's park space to total area in **Ex. 57**.

Lake Clark National Park, Alaska

GOAL 1 **PROPERTIES OF EXPONENTS**

Recall that the expression a^n, where n is a positive integer, represents the product that you obtain when a is used as a factor n times. In the activity you will investigate two properties of exponents.

> **ACTIVITY**
> **Developing Concepts**
>
> ## Products and Quotients of Powers
>
> **1** How many factors of 2 are there in the product $2^3 \cdot 2^4$? Use your answer to write the product as a single power of 2.
>
> **2** Write each product as a single power of 2 by counting the factors of 2. Use a calculator to check your answers.
>
> **a.** $2^2 \cdot 2^5$ **b.** $2^1 \cdot 2^6$ **c.** $2^3 \cdot 2^6$ **d.** $2^4 \cdot 2^4$
>
> **3** Complete this equation: $2^m \cdot 2^n = 2^?$
>
> **4** Write each quotient as a single power of 2 by first writing the numerator and denominator in "expanded form" (for example, $2^3 = 2 \cdot 2 \cdot 2$) and then canceling common factors. Use a calculator to check your answers.
>
> **a.** $\dfrac{2^3}{2^1}$ **b.** $\dfrac{2^5}{2^2}$ **c.** $\dfrac{2^7}{2^3}$ **d.** $\dfrac{2^6}{2^2}$
>
> **5** Complete this equation: $\dfrac{2^m}{2^n} = 2^?$

In the activity you may have discovered two of the following properties of exponents.

CONCEPT SUMMARY	PROPERTIES OF EXPONENTS

Let a and b be real numbers and let m and n be integers.

PRODUCT OF POWERS PROPERTY	$a^m \cdot a^n = a^{m+n}$
POWER OF A POWER PROPERTY	$(a^m)^n = a^{mn}$
POWER OF A PRODUCT PROPERTY	$(ab)^m = a^m b^m$
NEGATIVE EXPONENT PROPERTY	$a^{-m} = \dfrac{1}{a^m}, a \neq 0$
ZERO EXPONENT PROPERTY	$a^0 = 1, a \neq 0$
QUOTIENT OF POWERS PROPERTY	$\dfrac{a^m}{a^n} = a^{m-n}, a \neq 0$
POWER OF A QUOTIENT PROPERTY	$\left(\dfrac{a}{b}\right)^m = \dfrac{a^m}{b^m}, b \neq 0$

The properties of exponents can be used to evaluate numerical expressions and to simplify algebraic expressions. In this book we assume that any base with a zero or negative exponent is nonzero. A simplified algebraic expression contains only positive exponents.

EXAMPLE 1
Evaluating Numerical Expressions

a. $\left(2^3\right)^4 = 2^{3 \cdot 4}$ Power of a power property

$\qquad\quad = 2^{12}$ Simplify exponent.

$\qquad\quad = 4096$ Evaluate power.

b. $\left(\dfrac{3}{4}\right)^2 = \dfrac{3^2}{4^2}$ Power of a quotient property

$\qquad\quad = \dfrac{9}{16}$ Evaluate powers.

c. $(-5)^{-6}(-5)^4 = (-5)^{-6+4}$ Product of powers property

$\qquad\qquad\quad = (-5)^{-2}$ Simplify exponent.

$\qquad\qquad\quad = \dfrac{1}{(-5)^2}$ Negative exponent property

$\qquad\qquad\quad = \dfrac{1}{25}$ Evaluate power.

STUDENT HELP
▶ **Study Tip**

When you multiply powers, do not multiply the bases. For example, $2^3 \cdot 2^5 \ne 4^8$.

EXAMPLE 2
Simplifying Algebraic Expressions

a. $\left(\dfrac{r}{s^{-5}}\right)^2 = \dfrac{r^2}{(s^{-5})^2}$ Power of a quotient property

$\qquad\qquad = \dfrac{r^2}{s^{-10}}$ Power of a power property

$\qquad\qquad = r^2 s^{10}$ Negative exponent property

b. $\left(7b^{-3}\right)^2 b^5 b = 7^2 \left(b^{-3}\right)^2 b^5 b$ Power of a product property

$\qquad\qquad\qquad = 49 b^{-6} b^5 b$ Power of a power property

$\qquad\qquad\qquad = 49 b^{-6+5+1}$ Product of powers property

$\qquad\qquad\qquad = 49 b^0$ Simplify exponent.

$\qquad\qquad\qquad = 49$ Zero exponent property

c. $\dfrac{(xy^2)^2}{x^3 y^{-1}} = \dfrac{x^2(y^2)^2}{x^3 y^{-1}}$ Power of a product property

$\qquad\quad = \dfrac{x^2 y^4}{x^3 y^{-1}}$ Power of a power property

$\qquad\quad = x^{2-3} y^{4-(-1)}$ Quotient of powers property

$\qquad\quad = x^{-1} y^5$ Simplify exponents.

$\qquad\quad = \dfrac{y^5}{x}$ Negative exponent property

STUDENT HELP

HOMEWORK HELP
Visit our Web site
www.mcdougallittell.com
for extra examples.

Earth

Jupiter

Sun

ASTRONOMY
Jupiter is the largest planet in the solar system. It has a radius of 71,400 km— over 11 times as great as Earth's, but only about one tenth as great as the sun's.

APPLICATION LINK
www.mcdougallittell.com

STUDENT HELP

▶ **Skills Review**
For help with scientific notation, see p. 913.

GOAL 2 **USING PROPERTIES OF EXPONENTS IN REAL LIFE**

EXAMPLE 3 *Comparing Real-Life Volumes*

ASTRONOMY The radius of the sun is about 109 times as great as Earth's radius. How many times as great as Earth's volume is the sun's volume?

SOLUTION

Let r represent Earth's radius.

$$\frac{\text{Sun's volume}}{\text{Earth's volume}} = \frac{\frac{4}{3}\pi(109r)^3}{\frac{4}{3}\pi r^3}$$ The volume of a sphere is $\frac{4}{3}\pi r^3$.

$$= \frac{\frac{4}{3}\pi \cdot 109^3 r^3}{\frac{4}{3}\pi r^3}$$ Power of a product property

$$= 109^3 r^0$$ Quotient of powers property

$$= 109^3$$ Zero exponent property

$$= 1{,}295{,}029$$ Evaluate power.

▶ The sun's volume is about 1.3 million times as great as Earth's volume.

· · · · · · · · · ·

A number is expressed in **scientific notation** if it is in the form $c \times 10^n$ where $1 \le c < 10$ and n is an integer. For instance, the width of a molecule of water is about 2.5×10^{-8} meter, or 0.000000025 meter. When working with numbers in scientific notation, the properties of exponents listed on page 323 can help make calculations easier.

EXAMPLE 4 *Using Scientific Notation in Real Life*

In 1997 Denmark had a population of 5,284,000 and a gross domestic product (GDP) of $131,400,000,000. Estimate the per capita GDP of Denmark.

DATA UPDATE of UN/ECE Statistical Division data at www.mcdougallittell.com

SOLUTION

"Per capita" means per person, so divide the GDP by the population.

$$\frac{\text{GDP}}{\text{Population}} = \frac{131{,}400{,}000{,}000}{5{,}284{,}000}$$ Divide GDP by population.

$$= \frac{1.314 \times 10^{11}}{5.284 \times 10^6}$$ Write in scientific notation.

$$= \frac{1.314}{5.284} \times 10^5$$ Quotient of powers property

$$\approx 0.249 \times 10^5$$ Use a calculator.

$$= 24{,}900$$ Write in standard notation.

▶ The per capita GDP of Denmark in 1997 was about $25,000 per person.

GUIDED PRACTICE

Vocabulary Check ✓

1. State the name of the property illustrated.

   a. $a^m \cdot a^n = a^{m+n}$ **b.** $(a^m)^n = a^{mn}$ **c.** $(ab)^m = a^m b^m$

Concept Check ✓

2. **ERROR ANALYSIS** Describe the mistake made in simplifying the expression.

   a. $(-2)^2(-2)^3 = 4^5$ **b.** $\dfrac{x^8}{x^2} = x^4$ **c.** $x^4 \cdot x^3 = x^{12}$

Skill Check ✓

Evaluate the expression. Tell which properties of exponents you used.

3. $6 \cdot 6^2$ 4. $(9^6)(9^2)^{-3}$ 5. $(2^3)^2$

6. $\left(\dfrac{3}{2^{-2}}\right)\left(\dfrac{1}{2}\right)^2$ 7. $\left(\dfrac{3}{5}\right)^{-2}$ 8. $\dfrac{7^{-5}}{7^{-3}}$

Simplify the expression. Tell which properties of exponents you used.

9. $z^{-2} \cdot z^{-4} \cdot z^6$ 10. $yz^{-2}(x^2 y)^3 z$ 11. $(4x^3)^{-2}$

12. $\left(\dfrac{2}{x^{-3}}\right)^6$ 13. $\dfrac{3y^6}{y^3}$ 14. $\dfrac{(xy)^4}{xy^{-1}}$

15. 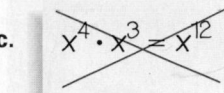 **ASTRONOMY** Earth has a radius of about 6.38×10^3 kilometers. The sun has a radius of about 6.96×10^5 kilometers. Use the formula for the volume of a sphere given on page 325 to calculate the volume of the sun and the volume of Earth. Divide the volumes. Do you get the same result as in Example 3?

PRACTICE AND APPLICATIONS

STUDENT HELP

▶ **Extra Practice**
to help you master
skills is on p. 947.

EVALUATING NUMERICAL EXPRESSIONS Evaluate the expression. Tell which properties of exponents you used.

16. $4^2 \cdot 4^4$ 17. $(5^{-2})^3$ 18. $(-9)(-9)^3$ 19. $(8^2)^3$

20. $\dfrac{5^2}{5^5}$ 21. $\left(\dfrac{3}{7}\right)^3$ 22. $\left(\dfrac{5}{9}\right)^{-3}$ 23. $11^{-2} \cdot 11^0$

24. $\dfrac{4^{-2}}{4^{-3}}$ 25. $\left(\dfrac{1}{8}\right)^{-4}$ 26. $(2^{-4})^{-2}$ 27. $\dfrac{2^2}{2^{-9}}$

28. $\dfrac{6^2}{(6^{-2} \cdot 5^1)^{-2}}$ 29. $6^0 \cdot 6^3 \cdot 6^{-4}$ 30. $\left(\dfrac{1}{10}\right)^3\left(\dfrac{1}{10}\right)^{-3}$ 31. $\left(\left(\dfrac{2}{5}\right)^{-3}\right)^2$

SIMPLIFYING ALGEBRAIC EXPRESSIONS Simplify the expression. Tell which properties of exponents you used.

32. $x^8 \cdot \dfrac{1}{x^3}$ 33. $(2^3 x^2)^5$ 34. $(x^2 y^2)^{-1}$ 35. $\dfrac{x^5}{x^{-2}}$

STUDENT HELP

▶ **HOMEWORK HELP**
Example 1: Exs. 16–31
Example 2: Exs. 32–51
Examples 3, 4: Exs. 52–56

36. $\dfrac{x^5 y^2}{x^4 y^0}$ 37. $(x^4 y^7)^{-3}$ 38. $\dfrac{x^{11} y^{10}}{x^{-3} y^{-1}}$ 39. $-3x^{-4} y^0$

40. $(10x^3 y^5)^{-3}$ 41. $\dfrac{x^{-1} y}{xy^{-2}}$ 42. $(4x^2 y^5)^{-2}$ 43. $\dfrac{2x^2 y}{6xy^{-1}}$

44. $\dfrac{5x^3 y^9}{20x^2 y^{-2}}$ 45. $\dfrac{xy^9}{3y^{-2}} \cdot \dfrac{-7y}{21x^5}$ 46. $\dfrac{y^{10}}{2x^3} \cdot \dfrac{20x^{14}}{xy^6}$ 47. $\dfrac{12xy}{7x^4} \cdot \dfrac{7x^5 y^2}{4y}$

GEOMETRY CONNECTION Write an expression for the area or volume of the figure in terms of *x*.

48. $A = \frac{\sqrt{3}}{4}s^2$

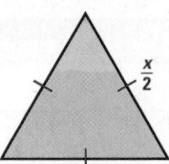

49. $A = \pi r^2$

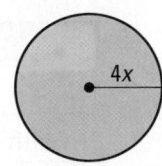

4x

50. $V = \pi r^2 h$

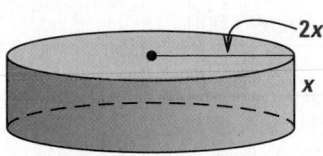

2x

x

51. $V = \frac{4}{3}\pi r^3$

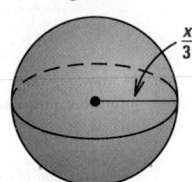

$\frac{x}{3}$

SCIENTIFIC NOTATION In Exercises 52–56, use scientific notation.

52. 🌐 **NATIONAL DEBT** On June 8, 1999, the national debt of the United States was about $5,608,000,000,000. The population of the United States at that time was about 273,000,000. Suppose the national debt was divided evenly among everyone in the United States. How much would each person owe?

🔗 **DATA UPDATE** of Bureau of the Public Debt and U.S. Census Bureau data at www.mcdougallittell.com

53. **SOCIAL STUDIES CONNECTION** The table shows the population and gross domestic product (GDP) in 1997 for each of six different countries. Calculate the per capita GDP for each country.

🔗 **DATA UPDATE** of UN/ECE Statistical Division data at www.mcdougallittell.com

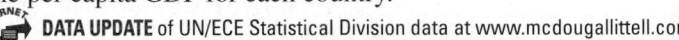

Country	Population	GDP (U.S. dollars)
France	58,607,000	1,249,600,000,000
Germany	82,061,000	1,839,300,000,000
Ireland	3,661,000	71,300,000,000
Luxembourg	420,000	13,600,000,000
The Netherlands	15,600,000	333,400,000,000
Sweden	8,849,000	177,300,000,000

54. **BIOLOGY CONNECTION** A red blood cell has a diameter of approximately 0.00075 centimeter. Suppose one of the arteries in your body has a diameter of 0.0456 centimeter. How many red blood cells could fit across the artery?

55. 🌐 **SPACE EXPLORATION** On February 17, 1998, *Voyager 1* became the most distant manmade object in space, at a distance of 10,400,000,000 kilometers from Earth. How long did it take *Voyager 1* to travel this distance given that it traveled an average of 1,390,000 kilometers per day? ▶ Source: NASA

56. 🌐 **ORNITHOLOGY** Some scientists estimate that there are about 8600 species of birds in the world. The mean number of birds per species is approximately 12,000,000. About how many birds are there in the world?

57. MULTI-STEP PROBLEM Suppose you live in a state that has a total area of 5.38×10^7 acres and 4.19×10^5 acres of park space. You think that the state should set aside more land for parks. The table shows the total area and the amount of park space for several states.

State	Total area (acres)	Amount of park space (acres)
Alaska	393,747,200	3,250,000
California	101,676,000	1,345,000
Connecticut	3,548,000	176,000
Kansas	52,660,000	29,000
Ohio	28,690,000	204,000
Pennsylvania	29,477,000	283,000

▶ Source: *Statistical Abstract of the United States*

a. Write the total area and the amount of park space for each state in scientific notation.

b. For each state, divide the amount of park space by the total area.

c. *Writing* You want to ask the state legislature to increase the amount of park space in your state. Use your results from parts (a) and (b) to write a letter that explains why your state needs more park space.

★ **Challenge**

LOGICAL REASONING In Exercises 58 and 59, refer to the properties of exponents on page 323.

58. Show how the negative exponent property can be derived from the quotient of powers property and the zero exponent property.

59. Show how the quotient of powers property can be derived from the product of powers property and the negative exponent property.

MIXED REVIEW

GRAPHING Graph the equation. **(Review 2.3, 5.1 for 6.2)**

60. $y = -4$

61. $y = -x - 3$

62. $y = 3x + 1$

63. $y = -2x + 5$

64. $y = 3x^2 + 2$

65. $y = -2x(x + 6)$

66. $y = x^2 - 2x - 6$

67. $y = 2x^2 - 4x + 10$

68. $y = -2(x - 3)^2 + 8$

SOLVING QUADRATIC EQUATIONS Solve the equation. **(Review 5.3)**

69. $2x^2 = 32$

70. $-3x^2 = -24$

71. $25x^2 = 16$

72. $3x^2 - 8 = 100$

73. $13 - 5x^2 = 8$

74. $4x^2 - 5 = 9$

75. $-x^2 + 9 = 2x^2 - 6$

76. $12 + 2x^2 = 5x^2 - 8$

77. $-2x^2 + 7 = x^2 - 2$

OPERATIONS WITH COMPLEX NUMBERS Write the expression as a complex number in standard form. **(Review 5.4)**

78. $(9 + 4i) + (9 - i)$

79. $(-5 + 3i) - (-2 - i)$

80. $(10 - i) - (4 + 7i)$

81. $-i(7 + 2i)$

82. $-11i(5 + i)$

83. $(3 + i)(9 + i)$

6.2

Evaluating and Graphing Polynomial Functions

What you should learn

GOAL 1 Evaluate a polynomial function.

GOAL 2 Graph a polynomial function, as applied in **Example 5**.

Why you should learn it

▼ To find values of **real-life** functions, such as the amount of prize money awarded at the U.S. Open Tennis Tournament in **Ex. 86**.

GOAL 1 EVALUATING POLYNOMIAL FUNCTIONS

A **polynomial function** is a function of the form

$$f(x) = a_n x^n + a_{n-1}x^{n-1} + \cdots + a_1 x + a_0$$

where $a_n \neq 0$, the exponents are all whole numbers, and the coefficients are all real numbers. For this polynomial function, a_n is the **leading coefficient**, a_0 is the **constant term**, and n is the **degree**. A polynomial function is in **standard form** if its terms are written in descending order of exponents from left to right.

You are already familiar with some types of polynomial functions. For instance, the linear function $f(x) = 3x + 2$ is a polynomial function of degree 1. The quadratic function $f(x) = x^2 + 3x + 2$ is a polynomial function of degree 2. Here is a summary of common types of polynomial functions.

Degree	Type	Standard form
0	Constant	$f(x) = a_0$
1	Linear	$f(x) = a_1 x + a_0$
2	Quadratic	$f(x) = a_2 x^2 + a_1 x + a_0$
3	Cubic	$f(x) = a_3 x^3 + a_2 x^2 + a_1 x + a_0$
4	Quartic	$f(x) = a_4 x^4 + a_3 x^3 + a_2 x^2 + a_1 x + a_0$

EXAMPLE 1 *Identifying Polynomial Functions*

Decide whether the function is a polynomial function. If it is, write the function in standard form and state its degree, type, and leading coefficient.

a. $f(x) = \frac{1}{2}x^2 - 3x^4 - 7$

b. $f(x) = x^3 + 3^x$

c. $f(x) = 6x^2 + 2x^{-1} + x$

d. $f(x) = -0.5x + \pi x^2 - \sqrt{2}$

SOLUTION

a. The function is a polynomial function. Its standard form is $f(x) = -3x^4 + \frac{1}{2}x^2 - 7$. It has degree 4, so it is a quartic function. The leading coefficient is -3.

b. The function is not a polynomial function because the term 3^x does not have a variable base and an exponent that is a whole number.

c. The function is not a polynomial function because the term $2x^{-1}$ has an exponent that is not a whole number.

d. The function is a polynomial function. Its standard form is $f(x) = \pi x^2 - 0.5x - \sqrt{2}$. It has degree 2, so it is a quadratic function. The leading coefficient is π.

One way to evaluate a polynomial function is to use direct substitution. For instance, $f(x) = 2x^4 - 8x^2 + 5x - 7$ can be evaluated when $x = 3$ as follows.

$$f(3) = 2(3)^4 - 8(3)^2 + 5(3) - 7$$
$$= 162 - 72 + 15 - 7$$
$$= 98$$

Another way to evaluate a polynomial function is to use **synthetic substitution**.

EXAMPLE 2   *Using Synthetic Substitution*

Use synthetic substitution to evaluate $f(x) = 2x^4 - 8x^2 + 5x - 7$ when $x = 3$.

STUDENT HELP

▶ **Study Tip**
In Example 2, note that the row of coefficients for $f(x)$ must include a coefficient of 0 for the "missing" x^3-term.

SOLUTION

Write the value of x and the coefficients of $f(x)$ as shown. Bring down the leading coefficient. **Multiply by 3** and write the result in the next column. **Add** the numbers in that column and write the sum below the line. Continue to multiply and add, as shown.

$$2x^4 + 0x^3 + (-8x^2) + 5x + (-7) \longleftarrow \text{ Polynomial in standard form}$$

x-value ⟶ 3 │ 2   0   −8   5   −7 ⟵ **Coefficients**
                    6   18   30   105
              2   6   10   35   98 ⟵ The value of $f(3)$ is the last number you write, in the bottom right-hand corner.

▶ $f(3) = 98$

. . . .

Using synthetic substitution is equivalent to evaluating the polynomial in *nested form*.

$$f(x) = 2x^4 + 0x^3 - 8x^2 + 5x - 7 \qquad \textbf{Write original function.}$$
$$= (2x^3 + 0x^2 - 8x + 5)x - 7 \qquad \textbf{Factor } x \textbf{ out of first 4 terms.}$$
$$= ((2x^2 + 0x - 8)x + 5)x - 7 \qquad \textbf{Factor } x \textbf{ out of first 3 terms.}$$
$$= (((2x + 0)x - 8)x + 5)x - 7 \qquad \textbf{Factor } x \textbf{ out of first 2 terms.}$$

EXAMPLE 3   *Evaluating a Polynomial Function in Real Life*

FOCUS ON CAREERS

▶ **PHOTOGRAPHER**
Some photographers work in advertising, some work for newspapers, and some are self-employed. Others specialize in aerial, police, medical, or scientific photography.

CAREER LINK
www.mcdougallittell.com

PHOTOGRAPHY The time t (in seconds) it takes a camera battery to recharge after flashing n times can be modeled by $t = 0.000015n^3 - 0.0034n^2 + 0.25n + 5.3$. Find the recharge time after 100 flashes. ▶ Source: *Popular Photography*

SOLUTION

100 │ 0.000015   −0.0034   0.25   5.3
                   0.0015   −0.19   6
       0.000015   −0.0019   0.06   11.3

▶ The recharge time is about 11 seconds.

STUDENT HELP

Look Back
For help with graphing functions, see pp. 69 and 250.

The **end behavior** of a polynomial function's graph is the behavior of the graph as x approaches positive infinity $(+\infty)$ or negative infinity $(-\infty)$. The expression $x \to +\infty$ is read as "x approaches positive infinity."

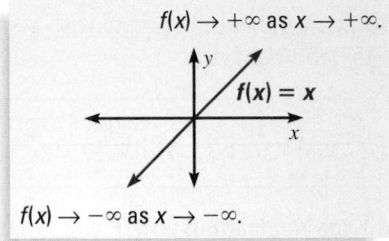

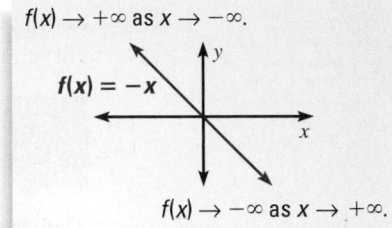

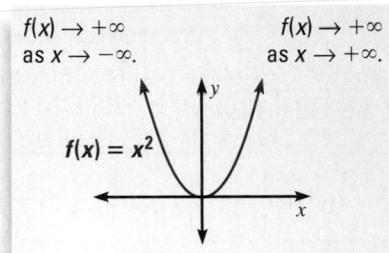

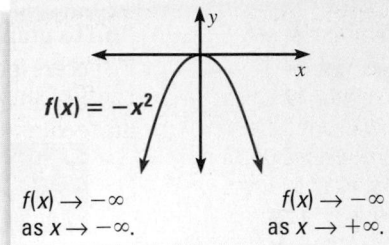

ACTIVITY

Developing Concepts

Investigating End Behavior

1 Use a graphing calculator to graph each function. Then complete these statements: $f(x) \to \underline{\ ?\ }$ as $x \to -\infty$ and $f(x) \to \underline{\ ?\ }$ as $x \to +\infty$.

   a. $f(x) = x^3$ **b.** $f(x) = x^4$ **c.** $f(x) = x^5$ **d.** $f(x) = x^6$

   e. $f(x) = -x^3$ **f.** $f(x) = -x^4$ **g.** $f(x) = -x^5$ **h.** $f(x) = -x^6$

2 How does the sign of the leading coefficient affect the behavior of a polynomial function's graph as $x \to +\infty$?

3 How is the behavior of a polynomial function's graph as $x \to +\infty$ related to its behavior as $x \to -\infty$ when the function's degree is odd? when it is even?

In the activity you may have discovered that the end behavior of a polynomial function's graph is determined by the function's degree and leading coefficient.

CONCEPT SUMMARY   **END BEHAVIOR FOR POLYNOMIAL FUNCTIONS**

The graph of $f(x) = a_n x^n + a_{n-1} x^{n-1} + \cdots + a_1 x + a_0$ has this end behavior:

- For $a_n > 0$ and n even, $f(x) \to +\infty$ as $x \to -\infty$ and $f(x) \to +\infty$ as $x \to +\infty$.
- For $a_n > 0$ and n odd, $f(x) \to -\infty$ as $x \to -\infty$ and $f(x) \to +\infty$ as $x \to +\infty$.
- For $a_n < 0$ and n even, $f(x) \to -\infty$ as $x \to -\infty$ and $f(x) \to -\infty$ as $x \to +\infty$.
- For $a_n < 0$ and n odd, $f(x) \to +\infty$ as $x \to -\infty$ and $f(x) \to -\infty$ as $x \to +\infty$.

EXAMPLE 4   *Graphing Polynomial Functions*

Graph (**a**) $f(x) = x^3 + x^2 - 4x - 1$ and (**b**) $f(x) = -x^4 - 2x^3 + 2x^2 + 4x$.

SOLUTION

a. To graph the function, make a table of values and plot the corresponding points. Connect the points with a smooth curve and check the end behavior.

x	−3	−2	−1	0	1	2	3
f(x)	−7	3	3	−1	−3	3	23

The degree is odd and the leading coefficient is positive, so $f(x) \to -\infty$ as $x \to -\infty$ and $f(x) \to +\infty$ as $x \to +\infty$.

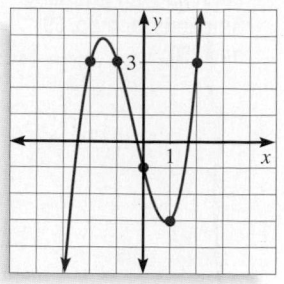

b. To graph the function, make a table of values and plot the corresponding points. Connect the points with a smooth curve and check the end behavior.

x	−3	−2	−1	0	1	2	3
f(x)	−21	0	−1	0	3	−16	−105

The degree is even and the leading coefficient is negative, so $f(x) \to -\infty$ as $x \to -\infty$ and $f(x) \to -\infty$ as $x \to +\infty$.

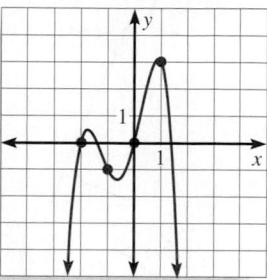

REAL LIFE

Biology

EXAMPLE 5   *Graphing a Polynomial Model*

A rainbow trout can grow up to 40 inches in length. The weight y (in pounds) of a rainbow trout is related to its length x (in inches) according to the model $y = 0.0005x^3$. Graph the model. Use your graph to estimate the length of a 10 pound rainbow trout.

SOLUTION

Make a table of values. The model makes sense only for positive values of x.

x	0	5	10	15	20	25	30	35	40
y	0	0.0625	0.5	1.69	4	7.81	13.5	21.4	32

Plot the points and connect them with a smooth curve, as shown at the right. Notice that the leading coefficient of the model is positive and the degree is odd, so the graph rises to the right.

Read the graph backwards to see that $x \approx 27$ when $y = 10$.

▶ A 10 pound trout is approximately 27 inches long.

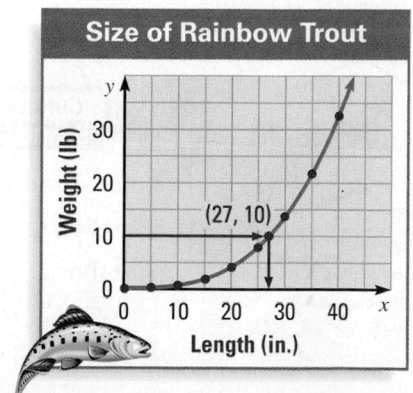

Size of Rainbow Trout

(27, 10)

Weight (lb)

Length (in.)

GUIDED PRACTICE

Vocabulary Check ✓

1. Identify the degree, type, leading coefficient, and constant term of the polynomial function $f(x) = 5x - 2x^3$.

Concept Check ✓

2. Complete the synthetic substitution shown at the right. Describe each step of the process.

$$\begin{array}{r|rrrr} -2 & 3 & 1 & -9 & 2 \\ & & ? & ? & ? \\ \hline & 3 & ? & ? & 0 \end{array}$$

3. Describe the graph of a constant function.

Skill Check ✓

Decide whether each function is a polynomial function. If it is, use synthetic substitution to evaluate the function when $x = -1$.

4. $f(x) = x^4\sqrt{5} - x$

5. $f(x) = x^3 + x^2 - x^{-3} + 3$

6. $f(x) = 6^{2x} - 12x$

7. $f(x) = 14 - 21x^2 + 5x^4$

Describe the end behavior of the graph of the polynomial function by completing the statements $f(x) \rightarrow \underline{\ ?\ }$ as $x \rightarrow -\infty$ and $f(x) \rightarrow \underline{\ ?\ }$ as $x \rightarrow +\infty$.

8. $f(x) = x^3 - 5x$

9. $f(x) = -x^5 - 3x^3 + 2$

10. $f(x) = x^4 - 4x^2 + x$

11. $f(x) = x + 12$

12. $f(x) = -x^2 + 3x + 1$

13. $f(x) = -x^8 + 9x^5 - 2x^4$

14. **VIDEO RENTALS** The total revenue (actual and projected) from home video rentals in the United States from 1985 to 2005 can be modeled by

$$R = 1.8t^3 - 76t^2 + 1099t + 2600$$

where R is the revenue (in millions of dollars) and t is the number of years since 1985. Graph the function. ▶ Source: *The Wall Street Journal Almanac*

PRACTICE AND APPLICATIONS

STUDENT HELP

▶ **Extra Practice**
to help you master
skills is on p. 947.

CLASSIFYING POLYNOMIALS Decide whether the function is a polynomial function. If it is, write the function in standard form and state the degree, type, and leading coefficient.

15. $f(x) = 12 - 5x$

16. $f(x) = 2x + \frac{3}{5}x^4 + 9$

17. $f(x) = x + \pi$

18. $f(x) = x^2\sqrt{2} + x - 5$

19. $f(x) = x - 3x^{-2} - 2x^3$

20. $f(x) = -2$

21. $f(x) = x^2 - x + 1$

22. $f(x) = 22 - 19x + 2^x$

23. $f(x) = 36x^2 - x^3 + x^4$

24. $f(x) = 3x^2 - 2x^{-x}$

25. $f(x) = 3x^3$

26. $f(x) = -6x^2 + x - \frac{3}{x}$

DIRECT SUBSTITUTION Use direct substitution to evaluate the polynomial function for the given value of x.

STUDENT HELP

▶ **HOMEWORK HELP**
Example 1: Exs. 15–26
Example 2: Exs. 37–46
Example 3: Exs. 81, 82
Example 4: Exs. 47–79
Example 5: Exs. 83–86

27. $f(x) = 2x^3 + 5x^2 + 4x + 8, x = -2$

28. $f(x) = 2x^3 - x^4 + 5x^2 - x, x = 3$

29. $f(x) = x + \frac{1}{2}x^3, x = 4$

30. $f(x) = x^2 - x^5 + 1, x = -1$

31. $f(x) = 5x^4 - 8x^3 + 7x^2, x = 1$

32. $f(x) = x^3 + 3x^2 - 2x + 5, x = -3$

33. $f(x) = 11x^3 - 6x^2 + 2, x = 0$

34. $f(x) = x^4 - 2x + 7, x = 2$

35. $f(x) = 7x^3 + 9x^2 + 3x, x = 10$

36. $f(x) = -x^5 - 4x^3 + 6x^2 - x, x = -2$

SYNTHETIC SUBSTITUTION Use synthetic substitution to evaluate the polynomial function for the given value of *x*.

37. $f(x) = 5x^3 + 4x^2 + 8x + 1, x = 2$

38. $f(x) = -3x^3 + 7x^2 - 4x + 8, x = 3$

39. $f(x) = x^3 + 3x^2 + 6x - 11, x = -5$

40. $f(x) = x^3 - x^2 + 12x + 15, x = -1$

41. $f(x) = -4x^3 + 3x - 5, x = 2$

42. $f(x) = -x^4 + x^3 - x + 1, x = -3$

43. $f(x) = 2x^4 + x^3 - 3x^2 + 5x, x = -1$

44. $f(x) = 3x^5 - 2x^2 + x, x = 2$

45. $f(x) = 2x^3 - x^2 + 6x, x = 5$

46. $f(x) = -x^4 + 8x^3 + 13x - 4, x = -2$

END BEHAVIOR PATTERNS Graph each polynomial function in the table. Then copy and complete the table to describe the end behavior of the graph of each function.

47.

Function	As $x \to -\infty$	As $x \to +\infty$
$f(x) = -5x^3$	?	?
$f(x) = -x^3 + 1$	?	?
$f(x) = 2x - 3x^3$	?	?
$f(x) = 2x^2 - x^3$	?	?

48.

Function	As $x \to -\infty$	As $x \to +\infty$
$f(x) = x^4 + 3x^3$	?	?
$f(x) = x^4 + 2$	?	?
$f(x) = x^4 - 2x - 1$	?	?
$f(x) = 3x^4 - 5x^2$	?	?

MATCHING Use what you know about end behavior to match the polynomial function with its graph.

49. $f(x) = 4x^6 - 3x^2 + 5x - 2$

50. $f(x) = -2x^3 + 5x^2$

51. $f(x) = -x^4 + 1$

52. $f(x) = 6x^3 + 1$

A.

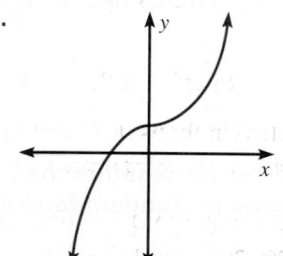

B.

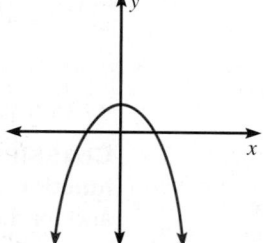

C.

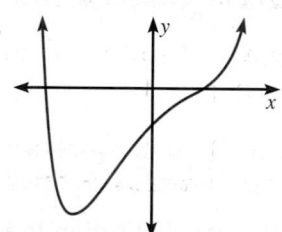

D.

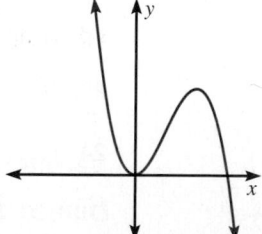

DESCRIBING END BEHAVIOR Describe the end behavior of the graph of the polynomial function by completing these statements: $f(x) \to \underline{?}$ as $x \to -\infty$ and $f(x) \to \underline{?}$ as $x \to +\infty$.

53. $f(x) = -5x^4$

54. $f(x) = -x^2 + 1$

55. $f(x) = 2x$

56. $f(x) = -10x^3$

57. $f(x) = -x^6 + 2x^3 - x$

58. $f(x) = x^5 + 2x^2$

59. $f(x) = -3x^5 - 4x^2 + 3$

60. $f(x) = x^7 - 3x^3 + 2x$

61. $f(x) = 3x^6 - x - 4$

62. $f(x) = 3x^8 - 4x^3$

63. $f(x) = -6x^3 + 10x$

64. $f(x) = x^4 - 5x^3 + x - 1$

GRAPHING POLYNOMIALS Graph the polynomial function.

65. $f(x) = -x^3$

66. $f(x) = -x^4$

67. $f(x) = x^5 + 2$

68. $f(x) = x^4 - 4$

69. $f(x) = x^4 + 6x^2 - 5$

70. $f(x) = 2 - x^3$

71. $f(x) = x^5 - 2$

72. $f(x) = -x^4 + 3$

73. $f(x) = -x^3 + 3x$

74. $f(x) = -x^3 + 2x^2 - 4$

75. $f(x) = -x^5 + x^2 + 1$

76. $f(x) = x^3 - 3x - 1$

77. $f(x) = x^5 + 3x^3 - x$

78. $f(x) = x^4 - 2x - 3$

79. $f(x) = -x^4 + 2x - 1$

80. **CRITICAL THINKING** Give an example of a polynomial function f such that $f(x) \to -\infty$ as $x \to -\infty$ and $f(x) \to +\infty$ as $x \to +\infty$.

81. **SHOPPING** The retail space in shopping centers in the United States from 1972 to 1996 can be modeled by

$$S = -0.0068t^3 - 0.27t^2 + 150t + 1700$$

where S is the amount of retail space (in millions of square feet) and t is the number of years since 1972. How much retail space was there in 1990?

82. **CABLE TELEVISION** The average monthly cable TV rate from 1980 to 1997 can be modeled by

$$R = -0.0036t^3 + 0.13t^2 - 0.073t + 7.7$$

where R is the monthly rate (in dollars) and t is the number of years since 1980. What was the monthly rate in 1983?

NURSING In Exercises 83 and 84, use the following information.
From 1985 to 1995, the number of graduates from nursing schools in the United States can be modeled by

$$y = -0.036t^4 + 0.605t^3 - 1.87t^2 - 4.67t + 82.5$$

where y is the number of graduates (in thousands) and t is the number of years since 1985. ▶ Source: *Statistical Abstract of the United States*

83. Describe the end behavior of the graph of the function. From the end behavior, would you expect the number of nursing graduates in the year 2010 to be more than or less than the number of nursing graduates in 1995? Explain.

84. Graph the function for $0 \le t \le 10$. Use the graph to find the first year in which there were over 82,500 nursing graduates.

TENNIS In Exercises 85 and 86, use the following information.
The amount of prize money for the women's U.S. Open Tennis Tournament from 1970 to 1997 can be modeled by

$$P = 1.141t^2 - 5.837t + 14.31$$

where P is the prize money (in thousands of dollars) and t is the number of years since 1970. ▶ Source: U.S. Open

85. Describe the end behavior of the graph of the function. From the end behavior, would you expect the amount of prize money in the year 2005 to be more than or less than the amount in 1995? Explain.

86. Graph the function for $0 \le t \le 40$. Use the graph to estimate the amount of prize money in the year 2005.

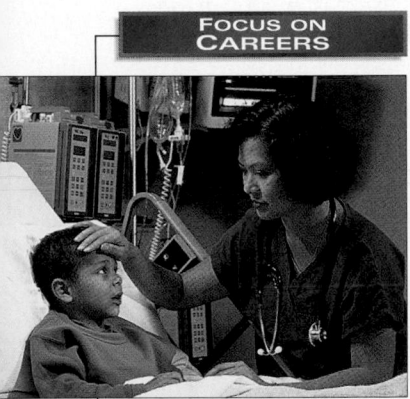

87. MULTI-STEP PROBLEM To determine whether a Holstein heifer's height is normal, a veterinarian can use the cubic functions

$$L = 0.0007t^3 - 0.061t^2 + 2.02t + 30$$

$$H = 0.001t^3 - 0.08t^2 + 2.3t + 31$$

where L is the minimum normal height (in inches), H is the maximum normal height (in inches), and t is the age (in months).

▶ Source: Journal of Dairy Science

A heifer is a young cow that has not yet had calves.

a. What is the normal height range for an 18-month-old Holstein heifer?

b. Describe the end behavior of each function's graph.

c. Graph the two height functions.

d. *Writing* Suppose a veterinarian examines a Holstein heifer that is 43 inches tall. About how old do you think the cow is? How did you get your answer?

★ Challenge

EXAMINING END BEHAVIOR Use a spreadsheet or a graphing calculator to evaluate the polynomial functions $f(x) = x^3$ and $g(x) = x^3 - 2x^2 + 4x + 5$ for the given values of x.

88. Copy and complete the table.

89. Use the results of Exercise 88 to complete this statement:

As $x \to +\infty, \dfrac{f(x)}{g(x)} \to \underline{\ ?\ }$.

Explain how this statement shows that the functions f and g have the same end behavior as $x \to +\infty$.

x	$f(x)$	$g(x)$	$\dfrac{f(x)}{g(x)}$
50	?	?	?
100	?	?	?
500	?	?	?
1000	?	?	?
5000	?	?	?

MIXED REVIEW

SIMPLIFYING EXPRESSIONS Simplify the expression. (Review 1.2 for 6.3)

90. $x + 3 - 2x - x + 2$ 91. $-2x^2 + 3x + 4x + 2x^2$ 92. $-3x^2 + 1 - (x^2 + 2)$

93. $x^2 + x + 1 + 3(x - 4)$ 94. $4x - 2x^2 + 3 - x^2 - 4$ 95. $x^2 - 1 - (2x^2 + x - 3)$

STANDARD FORM Write the quadratic function in standard form. (Review 5.1 for 6.3)

96. $y = -4(x - 2)^2 + 5$ 97. $y = -2(x + 6)(x - 5)$ 98. $y = 2(x - 7)(x + 4)$

99. $y = 4(x - 3)^2 - 24$ 100. $y = -(x + 5)^2 + 12$ 101. $y = -3(x - 5)^2 + 3$

SOLVING QUADRATIC EQUATIONS Solve the equation. (Review 5.4)

102. $x^2 = -9$

103. $x^2 = -5$

104. $-3x^2 + 1 = 7$

105. $4x^2 + 15 = 3$

106. $6x^2 + 5 = 2x^2 + 1$

107. $x^2 = 7x^2 + 1$

108. $x^2 - 4 = -3x^2 - 24$

109. $3x^2 + 5 = 5x^2 + 10$

110. $5x^2 + 2 = -2x^2 + 1$

▶ ACTIVITY 6.2
Using Technology

Setting a Good Viewing Window

When you graph a polynomial function with a graphing calculator, you must choose a viewing window that displays the important characteristics of the graph. Use what you know about end behavior to find such a viewing window.

▶ EXAMPLE

Graph $f(x) = 0.2x^3 - 5x^2 + 38x - 97$.

▶ SOLUTION

1 Graph the function using the standard viewing window.

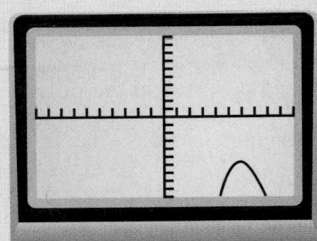

$-10 \le x \le 10, -10 \le y \le 10$

2 Adjust the horizontal scale and the vertical scale until you see the graph's end behavior and any points where it turns. A good viewing window for this graph is $-10 \le x \le 20$ and $-20 \le y \le 10$.

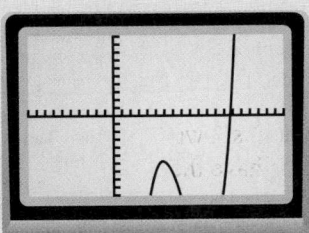

$-10 \le x \le 20, -10 \le y \le 10$

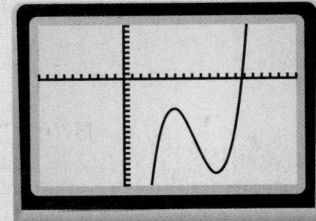

$-10 \le x \le 20, -20 \le y \le 10$

▶ EXERCISES

Find intervals for *x* and *y* that describe a good viewing window for the graph of the polynomial function.

1. $f(x) = x^3 + 6x^2 - 11x + 3$

2. $f(x) = -x^3 + 25x^2 + 4$

3. $f(x) = x^4 - 5x^2 + 6$

4. $f(x) = -x^4 - 3x^3 + x^2 - x + 5$

5. $f(x) = -x^5 + 5x^3 - 4x + 10$

6. $f(x) = x^5 - 10x^4 + 35x^3 - 50x^2 + 24x$

7. 🖌 **EDUCATION** For 1983 to 1996, the amount *P* (in millions of dollars) spent by public elementary and secondary schools and the amount *R* (in millions of dollars) spent by private elementary and secondary schools can be modeled by

$$P = 11.7x^4 - 340x^3 + 2931x^2 + 1560x + 182,000$$

$$R = 0.422x^4 - 9.84x^3 + 44.9x^2 + 779x + 15,900$$

where *x* is the number of years since 1983. Find intervals for the horizontal and vertical axes that describe a good viewing window for the graphs of both functions. ▶ Source: U.S. National Center for Education Statistics

6.3
Adding, Subtracting, and Multiplying Polynomials

What you should learn

GOAL 1 Add, subtract, and multiply polynomials.

GOAL 2 Use polynomial operations in **real-life** problems, such as finding net farm income in **Example 7**.

Why you should learn it

▼ To combine **real-life** polynomial models into a new model, such as the model for the power needed to keep a bicycle moving at a certain speed in **Ex. 66**.

GOAL 1 ADDING, SUBTRACTING, AND MULTIPLYING

To add or subtract polynomials, add or subtract the coefficients of like terms. You can use a vertical or horizontal format.

EXAMPLE 1 *Adding Polynomials Vertically and Horizontally*

Add the polynomials.

a.
$$\begin{array}{r} 3x^3 + 2x^2 - x - 7 \\ + \ x^3 - 10x^2 \quad\ + 8 \\ \hline 4x^3 - 8x^2 - x + 1 \end{array}$$

b. $(9x^3 - 2x + 1) + (5x^2 + 12x - 4) = 9x^3 + 5x^2 - 2x + 12x + 1 - 4$
$$= 9x^3 + 5x^2 + 10x - 3$$

EXAMPLE 2 *Subtracting Polynomials Vertically and Horizontally*

Subtract the polynomials.

a.
$$\begin{array}{r} 8x^3 - 3x^2 - 2x + 9 \\ - \ (2x^3 + 6x^2 - \ x + 1) \\ \hline \end{array}$$
⟶
$$\begin{array}{r} 8x^3 - 3x^2 - 2x + 9 \\ -2x^3 - 6x^2 + \ x - 1 \\ \hline 6x^3 - 9x^2 - \ x + 8 \end{array}$$
Add the opposite.

b. $(2x^2 + 3x) - (3x^2 + x - 4) = 2x^2 + 3x - 3x^2 - x + 4$ **Add the opposite.**
$$= -x^2 + 2x + 4$$

. . . .

To multiply two polynomials, each term of the first polynomial must be multiplied by each term of the second polynomial.

EXAMPLE 3 *Multiplying Polynomials Vertically*

Multiply the polynomials.

$$\begin{array}{r} -x^2 + 2x + \ 4 \\ \times \qquad\qquad x - \ 3 \\ \hline 3x^2 - 6x - 12 \\ -x^3 + 2x^2 + 4x \qquad\quad \\ \hline -x^3 + 5x^2 - 2x - 12 \end{array}$$

    Multiply $-x^2 + 2x + 4$ **by** -3.

    Multiply $-x^2 + 2x + 4$ **by** x.

    Combine like terms.

STUDENT HELP

▶ **Look Back**
For help with simplifying expressions, see p. 251.

EXAMPLE 4 *Multiplying Polynomials Horizontally*

Multiply the polynomials.

$$(x - 3)(3x^2 - 2x - 4) = (x - 3)3x^2 - (x - 3)2x - (x - 3)4$$
$$= 3x^3 - 9x^2 - 2x^2 + 6x - 4x + 12$$
$$= 3x^3 - 11x^2 + 2x + 12$$

EXAMPLE 5 *Multiplying Three Binomials*

STUDENT HELP

▶ **Look Back**
For help with multiplying binomials, see p. 251.

Multiply the polynomials.

$$(x - 1)(x + 4)(x + 3) = (x^2 + 3x - 4)(x + 3)$$
$$= (x^2 + 3x - 4)x + (x^2 + 3x - 4)3$$
$$= x^3 + 3x^2 - 4x + 3x^2 + 9x - 12$$
$$= x^3 + 6x^2 + 5x - 12$$

. . . .

Some binomial products occur so frequently that it is worth memorizing their *special product patterns*. You can verify these products by multiplying.

SPECIAL PRODUCT PATTERNS

SUM AND DIFFERENCE   **Example**

$(a + b)(a - b) = a^2 - b^2$ $(x + 3)(x - 3) = x^2 - 9$

SQUARE OF A BINOMIAL

$(a + b)^2 = a^2 + 2ab + b^2$ $(y + 4)^2 = y^2 + 8y + 16$

$(a - b)^2 = a^2 - 2ab + b^2$ $(3t^2 - 2)^2 = 9t^4 - 12t^2 + 4$

CUBE OF A BINOMIAL

$(a + b)^3 = a^3 + 3a^2b + 3ab^2 + b^3$ $(x + 1)^3 = x^3 + 3x^2 + 3x + 1$

$(a - b)^3 = a^3 - 3a^2b + 3ab^2 - b^3$ $(p - 2)^3 = p^3 - 6p^2 + 12p - 8$

EXAMPLE 6 *Using Special Product Patterns*

Multiply the polynomials.

a. $(4n - 5)(4n + 5) = (4n)^2 - 5^2$ **Sum and difference**

$$= 16n^2 - 25$$

b. $(9y - x^2)^2 = (9y)^2 - 2(9y)(x^2) + (x^2)^2$ **Square of a binomial**

$$= 81y^2 - 18x^2y + x^4$$

c. $(ab + 2)^3 = (ab)^3 + 3(ab)^2(2) + 3(ab)(2)^2 + 2^3$ **Cube of a binomial**

$$= a^3b^3 + 6a^2b^2 + 12ab + 8$$

GOAL 2 **USING POLYNOMIAL OPERATIONS IN REAL LIFE**

EXAMPLE 7 *Subtracting Polynomial Models*

FARMING From 1985 through 1995, the gross farm income G and farm expenses E (in billions of dollars) in the United States can be modeled by

$$G = -0.246t^2 + 7.88t + 159 \quad \text{and} \quad E = 0.174t^2 + 2.54t + 131$$

where t is the number of years since 1985. Write a model for the *net* farm income N for these years. ▶ Source: U.S. Department of Agriculture

SOLUTION

To find a model for the net farm income, subtract the expenses model from the gross income model.

$$
\begin{array}{r}
-0.246t^2 + 7.88t + 159 \\
-\ (0.174t^2 + 2.54t + 131) \\
\hline
-0.420t^2 + 5.34t + 28
\end{array}
$$

▶ The net farm income can be modeled by $N = -0.42t^2 + 5.34t + 28$.

The graphs of the models are shown. Although G and E both increase, the net income N eventually decreases because E increases faster than G.

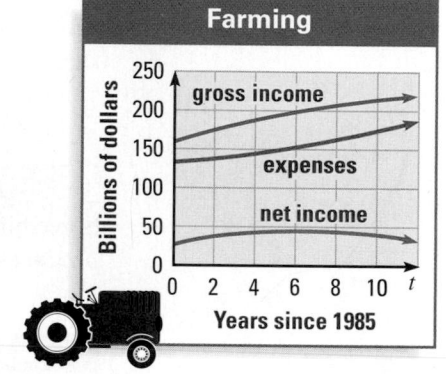

EXAMPLE 8 *Multiplying Polynomial Models*

From 1982 through 1995, the number of softbound books N (in millions) sold in the United States and the average price per book P (in dollars) can be modeled by

$$N = 1.36t^2 + 2.53t + 1076 \quad \text{and} \quad P = 0.314t + 3.42$$

where t is the number of years since 1982. Write a model for the total revenue R received from the sales of softbound books. What was the total revenue from softbound books in 1990? ▶ Source: Book Industry Study Group, Inc.

SOLUTION

To find a model for R, multiply the models for N and P.

$$
\begin{array}{r}
1.36t^2 + 2.53t + 1076 \\
\times 0.314t + 3.42 \\
\hline
4.6512t^2 + 8.6526t + 3679.92 \\
0.42704t^3 + 0.79442t^2 + 337.864t \\
\hline
0.42704t^3 + 5.44562t^2 + 346.5166t + 3679.92
\end{array}
$$

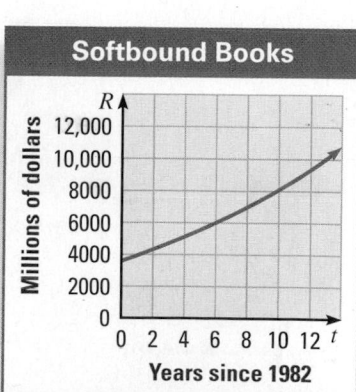

▶ The total revenue can be modeled by $R = 0.427t^3 + 5.45t^2 + 347t + 3680$. The graph of the revenue model is shown at the right. By substituting $t = 8$ into the model for R, you can calculate that the revenue was about $7020 million, or $7.02 billion, in 1990.

GUIDED PRACTICE

Vocabulary Check ✓

1. When you add or subtract polynomials, you add or subtract the coefficients of ? .

Concept Check ✓

2. **ERROR ANALYSIS** Describe the error in the subtraction shown below.

$$\overline{(x^2 - 3x + 4)} \ \cancel{- (x^2 + 7x - 2)} = x^2 - 3x + 4 - x^2 + 7x - 2$$
$$= 4x + 2$$

3. When you multiply a polynomial of degree 2 by a polynomial of degree 4, what is the degree of the product?

Skill Check ✓   **Perform the indicated operation.**

4. $(4x^2 + 3) + (3x^2 + 8)$

5. $(2x^3 - 4x^2 + 5) + (-x^2 - 3x + 1)$

6. $(x^2 + 7x - 5) - (3x^2 + 1)$

7. $(x^2 + 1) - (3x^2 - 4x + 3)$

8. $(x + 2)(2x^2 + 3)$

9. $(x^2 + 3x + 10)(4x^2 - 2x - 7)$

10. $(x - 1)(2x + 1)(x + 5)$

11. $(-3x + 1)^3$

12. **GEOMETRY CONNECTION** Write a polynomial model in standard form for the volume of the rectangular prism shown at the right.

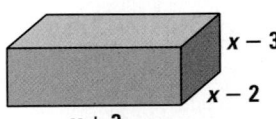

$x - 3$
$x - 2$
$x + 3$

PRACTICE AND APPLICATIONS

STUDENT HELP

▶ **Extra Practice**
to help you master
skills is on p. 948.

ADDING AND SUBTRACTING POLYNOMIALS Find the sum or difference.

13. $(8x^2 + 1) + (3x^2 - 2)$

14. $(3x^3 + 10x + 5) - (x^3 - 4x + 6)$

15. $(x^2 - 6x + 5) - (x^2 + x - 2)$

16. $(16 - 13x) + (10x - 11)$

17. $(7x^3 - 1) - (15x^3 + 4x^2 - x + 3)$

18. $8x + (14x + 3 - 41x^2 + x^3)$

19. $(4x^2 - 11x + 10) + (5x - 31)$

20. $(9x^3 - 4 + x^2 + 8x) - (7x^3 - 3x + 7)$

21. $(-3x^3 + x - 11) - (4x^3 + x^2 - x)$

22. $(6x^2 - 19x + 5) - (19x^2 - 4x + 9)$

23. $(10x^3 - 4x^2 + 3x) - (x^3 - x^2 + 1)$

24. $(50x - 3) + (8x^3 + 7x^2 + x + 4)$

25. $(10x - 3 + 7x^2) + (x^3 - 2x + 17)$

26. $(3x^3 - 5x^4 - 10x + 1) + (17x^4 - x^3)$

MULTIPLYING POLYNOMIALS Find the product of the polynomials.

27. $x(x^2 + 6x - 7)$

28. $10x^2(x - 5)$

29. $-4x(x^2 - 8x + 3)$

30. $5x(3x^2 - x + 3)$

31. $(x - 4)(x - 7)$

32. $(x + 9)(x - 2)$

STUDENT HELP

▶ **HOMEWORK HELP**
Examples 1, 2: Exs. 13–26
Examples 3, 4: Exs. 27–44
Example 5: Exs. 45–52
Example 6: Exs. 53–61
Example 7: Exs. 64, 65, 69
Example 8: Exs. 66–68

33. $(x + 3)(x^2 - 4x + 9)$

34. $(x + 8)(x^2 - 7x - 3)$

35. $(2x + 5)(3x^3 - x^2 + x)$

36. $(6x + 2)(2x^2 - 6x + 1)$

37. $(x + 11)(x^2 - 5x + 9)$

38. $(4x^2 - 1)(x^2 - 6x + 9)$

39. $(x - 1)(x^3 + 2x^2 + 2)$

40. $(x + 1)(5x^3 - x^2 + x - 4)$

41. $(3x^2 - 2)(x^2 + 4x + 3)$

42. $(-x^3 - 2)(x^2 + 3x - 3)$

43. $(x^2 + x + 4)(2x^2 - x + 1)$

44. $(x^2 - x - 3)(x^2 + 4x + 2)$

MULTIPLYING THREE BINOMIALS Find the product of the binomials.

45. $(x + 9)(x - 2)(x - 7)$ **46.** $(x + 3)(x - 4)(x - 5)$

47. $(x + 5)(x + 7)(-x + 1)$ **48.** $(2x - 3)(x + 7)(x + 6)$

49. $(x - 9)(x - 2)(3x + 2)$ **50.** $(x - 1)(-2x - 5)(x - 8)$

51. $(2x + 1)(3x + 1)(x + 4)$ **52.** $(4x - 1)(2x - 1)(3x - 2)$

SPECIAL PRODUCTS Find the product.

53. $(x + 7)(x - 7)$ **54.** $(x + 4)^2$ **55.** $(4x - 3)^3$

56. $(10x + 3)(10x - 3)$ **57.** $(6 - x^2)^2$ **58.** $(2y + 5x)^2$

59. $(3x + 7)^3$ **60.** $(7y - x)^2$ **61.** $(2x + 3y)^3$

GEOMETRY CONNECTION Write the volume of the figure as a polynomial in standard form.

62. $V = \pi r^2 h$

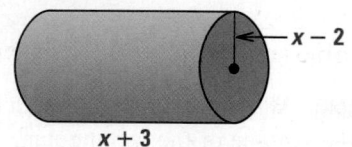

63. $V = lwh$

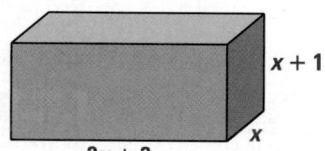

64. 🌎 **MOTOR VEHICLE SALES** For 1983 through 1996, the number of cars C (in thousands) and the number of trucks and buses T (in thousands) sold that were manufactured in the United States can be modeled by

$$C = -1.63t^4 + 49.5t^3 - 476t^2 + 1370t + 6705$$

$$T = -1.052t^4 + 31.6t^3 - 296t^2 + 1097t + 2290$$

where t is the number of years since 1983. Find a model that represents the total number of vehicles sold that were manufactured in the United States. How many vehicles were sold in 1990?

65. **SOCIAL STUDIES CONNECTION** For 1980 through 1996, the population P (in thousands) of the United States and the number of people S (in thousands) age 85 and over can be modeled by

$$P = -0.804t^4 + 26.9t^3 - 262t^2 + 3010t + 227,000$$

$$S = 0.0206t^4 - 0.670t^3 + 6.42t^2 + 213t + 7740$$

where t is the number of years since 1980. Find a model that represents the number of people in the United States under the age of 85. How many people were under the age of 85 in 1995?

DATA UPDATE of U.S. Bureau of the Census data at www.mcdougallittell.com

66. 🌐 **BICYCLING** The equation $P = 0.00267sF$ gives the power P (in horsepower) needed to keep a certain bicycle moving at speed s (in miles per hour), where F is the force of road and air resistance (in pounds). On level ground this force is given by $F = 0.0116s^2 + 0.789$. Write a polynomial function (in terms of s only) for the power needed to keep the bicycle moving at speed s on level ground. How much power does a cyclist need to exert to keep the bicycle moving at 10 miles per hour?

67. 🌐 **EDUCATION** For 1980 through 1995, the number of degrees D (in thousands) earned by people in the United States and the percent of degrees P earned by women can be modeled by

$$D = -0.096t^4 + 3t^3 - 27t^2 + 91t + 1700$$
$$P = 0.43t + 49$$

where t is the number of years since 1980. Find a model that represents the number of degrees W (in thousands) earned by women from 1980 to 1995. How many degrees were earned by women in 1991? ▶ Source: U.S. Bureau of the Census

68. 🌐 **PUBLISHING** From 1985 through 1993, the number of hardback books N (in millions) sold in the United States and the average price per book P (in dollars) can be modeled by

$$N = -0.27t^3 + 3.9t^2 + 7.9t + 650$$
$$P = 0.67t + 9.4$$

where t is the number of years since 1985. Write a model that represents the total revenue R (in millions of dollars) received from the sales of hardback books. What was the revenue in 1991?

STUDENT HELP

🌐 **HOMEWORK HELP**
Visit our Web site
www.mcdougallittell.com
for help with problem
solving in Ex. 69.

69. 🌐 **PERSONAL FINANCE** Suppose two brothers each make three deposits in accounts earning the same annual interest rate r (expressed as a decimal).

🦅 EagleBank		
Porter, Mark J.		#05-8922-4310
Date	**Transaction**	**Amount**
1/1/97	Deposit	$6000.00
1/1/98	Deposit	$8000.00
1/1/99	Deposit	$9000.00

🌐 WⓍrldBank		
Porter, Tom R.		#12-4600-2541
Date	**Transaction**	**Amount**
1/1/97	Deposit	$4000.00
1/1/98	Deposit	$5000.00
1/1/99	Deposit	$7000.00

Mark's account is worth $6000(1 + r)^3 + 8000(1 + r)^2 + 9000(1 + r)$ on January 1, 2000. Find the value of Tom's account on January 1, 2000. Then find the total value of the two accounts on January 1, 2000. Write the total value as a polynomial in standard form.

Test Preparation

70. MULTIPLE CHOICE What is the sum of $2x^4 + 5x^3 - 8x^2 - x + 10$ and $8x^4 - 4x^3 + x^2 - x + 2$?

ⓐ $10x^4 + x^3 - 9x^2 + 12$ ⓑ $10x^4 + x^3 - 9x^2 - 2x + 12$

ⓒ $10x^4 + x^3 - 7x^2 - 2x + 12$ ⓓ $10x^4 + 9x^3 - 7x^2 - 2x + 12$

71. MULTIPLE CHOICE $(3x - 8)^3 = \underline{\ ?\ }$

ⓐ $27x^3 - 216x^2 + 576x - 512$ ⓑ $27x^3 - 216x^2 + 576x + 512$

ⓒ $27x^3 - 72x^2 + 576x - 512$ ⓓ $27x^3 - 216x^2 + 72x - 512$

★ Challenge

72. FINDING A PATTERN Look at the following polynomials and their factorizations.

$$x^2 - 1 = (x - 1)(x + 1)$$
$$x^3 - 1 = (x - 1)(x^2 + x + 1)$$
$$x^4 - 1 = (x - 1)(x^3 + x^2 + x + 1)$$

a. Factor $x^5 - 1$ and $x^6 - 1$. Check your answers by multiplying.

EXTRA CHALLENGE
→ www.mcdougallittell.com

b. In general, how can $x^n - 1$ be factored? Show that this factorization works by multiplying the factors.

MIXED REVIEW

SOLVING QUADRATIC EQUATIONS Solve the equation. (Review 5.2 for 6.4)

73. $4x^2 - 36 = 0$ **74.** $x^2 + 3x - 40 = 0$ **75.** $x^2 + 16x + 64 = 0$

76. $x^2 - x - 56 = 0$ **77.** $2x^2 - 7x - 15 = 0$ **78.** $6x^2 + 10x - 4 = 0$

WRITING QUADRATIC FUNCTIONS Write a quadratic function in standard form whose graph passes through the given points. (Review 5.8)

79. $(-4, 0), (2, 0), (1, 6)$ **80.** $(10, 0), (1, 0), (4, 3)$

81. $(-6, 0), (6, 0), (-3, -9)$ **82.** $(-3, 0), (5, 0), (-2, 7)$

SIMPLIFYING ALGEBRAIC EXPRESSIONS Simplify the expression. Tell which properties of exponents you used. (Review 6.1)

83. $x^5 \cdot \dfrac{1}{x^2}$ **84.** $\dfrac{x^4 y^5}{xy^3}$ **85.** $-5^{-2}y^0$

86. $(4x^{-3})^4 \cdot \left(\dfrac{x^6}{2}\right)^2$ **87.** $\dfrac{3x^5 y^8}{6xy^{-3}}$ **88.** $\dfrac{6x^4 y^2}{30x^2 y^{-1}}$

QUIZ 1

Evaluate the expression. (Lesson 6.1)

1. $7^0 \cdot 5^{-3}$ **2.** $\left(\dfrac{4}{9}\right)^{-2}$ **3.** $\left(\dfrac{5}{3^2}\right)^2$

4. $3^2 \cdot (3^2 \cdot 2^4)^{-1}$ **5.** $(8^2 \cdot 8^{-3})^2 \cdot 8^2$ **6.** $\dfrac{(2^5 \cdot 3^2)^{-1}}{2^{-2} \cdot 3^2}$

Simplify the expression. (Lesson 6.1)

7. $(-5)^{-2}y^0$ **8.** $(3x^3 y^6)^{-2}$ **9.** $(x^3 y^{-5})(x^2 y)^2$

10. $(x^2 y^{-3})(xy^2)$ **11.** $\left(\dfrac{2x}{y^2}\right)^{-3}$ **12.** $\dfrac{x^6 y^{-2}}{x^{-1} y^5}$

Graph the polynomial function. (Lesson 6.2)

13. $f(x) = x^4 - 2$ **14.** $f(x) = -2x^5 + 3$ **15.** $f(x) = 3x^3 + 5x - 2$

16. $f(x) = -x^3 + x^2 - 2$ **17.** $f(x) = x^3 - 2x$ **18.** $f(x) = -x^4 - 3x + 6$

Perform the indicated operation. (Lesson 6.3)

19. $(7x^3 + 8x - 11) + (3x^2 - x + 8)$ **20.** $(-2x^2 + 4x) + (5x^2 - x - 11)$

21. $(-5x^2 + 12x - 9) - (-7x^2 - 6x - 7)$ **22.** $(3x^2 + 4x - 1) - (-x^3 + 2x + 5)$

23. $(x + 5)(4x^2 - x - 1)$ **24.** $(x - 3)(x + 2)(2x + 5)$

25. $(x - 6)^3$ **26.** $(2x^2 + 3)^2$

27. 🌍 **ASTRONOMY** Suppose NASA launches a spacecraft that can travel at a speed of 25,000 miles per hour in space. How long would it take the spacecraft to reach Jupiter if Jupiter is about 495,000,000 miles away? Use scientific notation to get your answer. (Lesson 6.1)

6.4 Factoring and Solving Polynomial Equations

What you should learn

GOAL 1 Factor polynomial expressions.

GOAL 2 Use factoring to solve polynomial equations, as applied in **Ex. 87**.

Why you should learn it

▼ To solve **real-life** problems, such as finding the dimensions of a block discovered at an underwater archeological site in **Example 5**.

GOAL 1 FACTORING POLYNOMIAL EXPRESSIONS

In Chapter 5 you learned how to factor the following types of quadratic expressions.

TYPE	EXAMPLE
General trinomial	$2x^2 - 5x - 12 = (2x + 3)(x - 4)$
Perfect square trinomial	$x^2 + 10x + 25 = (x + 5)^2$
Difference of two squares	$4x^2 - 9 = (2x + 3)(2x - 3)$
Common monomial factor	$6x^2 + 15x = 3x(2x + 5)$

In this lesson you will learn how to factor other types of polynomials.

> ▶ **ACTIVITY**
> Developing Concepts
>
> ### The Difference of Two Cubes
>
> Use the diagram to answer the questions.
>
> **1** Explain why $a^3 - b^3 = \boxed{\text{Volume of solid I}} + \boxed{\text{Volume of solid II}} + \boxed{\text{Volume of solid III}}$.
>
> **2** For each of solid I, solid II, and solid III, write an algebraic expression for the solid's volume. Leave your expressions in factored form.
>
> **3** Substitute your expressions from **Step 2** into the equation from **Step 1**. Use the resulting equation to factor $a^3 - b^3$ completely.

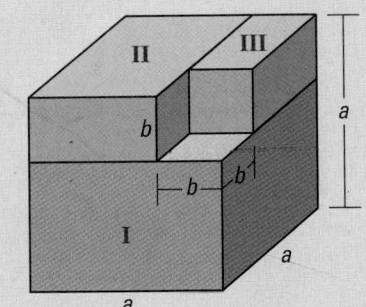

In the activity you may have discovered how to factor the difference of two cubes. This factorization and the factorization of the sum of two cubes are given below.

SPECIAL FACTORING PATTERNS

SUM OF TWO CUBES   **Example**

$a^3 + b^3 = (a + b)(a^2 - ab + b^2)$ $x^3 + 8 = (x + 2)(x^2 - 2x + 4)$

DIFFERENCE OF TWO CUBES

$a^3 - b^3 = (a - b)(a^2 + ab + b^2)$ $8x^3 - 1 = (2x - 1)(4x^2 + 2x + 1)$

EXAMPLE 1 *Factoring the Sum or Difference of Cubes*

Factor each polynomial.

a. $x^3 + 27$

b. $16u^5 - 250u^2$

SOLUTION

a. $x^3 + 27 = x^3 + 3^3$ **Sum of two cubes**

$$= (x + 3)(x^2 - 3x + 9)$$

b. $16u^5 - 250u^2 = 2u^2(8u^3 - 125)$ **Factor common monomial.**

$$= 2u^2\left[(2u)^3 - 5^3\right]$$ **Difference of two cubes**

$$= 2u^2(2u - 5)(4u^2 + 10u + 25)$$

· · · · · · · · ·

For some polynomials, you can **factor by grouping** pairs of terms that have a common monomial factor. The pattern for this is as follows.

$$ra + rb + sa + sb = r(a + b) + s(a + b)$$

$$= (r + s)(a + b)$$

EXAMPLE 2 *Factoring by Grouping*

Factor the polynomial $x^3 - 2x^2 - 9x + 18$.

SOLUTION

$$x^3 - 2x^2 - 9x + 18 = x^2(x - 2) - 9(x - 2)$$ **Factor by grouping.**

$$= (x^2 - 9)(x - 2)$$

$$= (x + 3)(x - 3)(x - 2)$$ **Difference of squares**

· · · · · · · · ·

An expression of the form $au^2 + bu + c$ where u is any expression in x is said to be in **quadratic form**. The factoring techniques you studied in Chapter 5 can sometimes be used to factor such expressions.

EXAMPLE 3 *Factoring Polynomials in Quadratic Form*

Factor each polynomial.

a. $81x^4 - 16$

b. $4x^6 - 20x^4 + 24x^2$

SOLUTION

a. $81x^4 - 16 = \left(9x^2\right)^2 - 4^2$ **b.** $4x^6 - 20x^4 + 24x^2 = 4x^2(x^4 - 5x^2 + 6)$

$$= (9x^2 + 4)(9x^2 - 4)$$ $$= 4x^2(x^2 - 2)(x^2 - 3)$$

$$= (9x^2 + 4)(3x + 2)(3x - 2)$$

GOAL 2 SOLVING POLYNOMIAL EQUATIONS BY FACTORING

In Chapter 5 you learned how to use the zero product property to solve factorable quadratic equations. You can extend this technique to solve some higher-degree polynomial equations.

EXAMPLE 4 *Solving a Polynomial Equation*

Solve $2x^5 + 24x = 14x^3$.

SOLUTION

$2x^5 + 24x = 14x^3$	**Write original equation.**
$2x^5 - 14x^3 + 24x = 0$	**Rewrite in standard form.**
$2x(x^4 - 7x^2 + 12) = 0$	**Factor common monomial.**
$2x(x^2 - 3)(x^2 - 4) = 0$	**Factor trinomial.**
$2x(x^2 - 3)(x + 2)(x - 2) = 0$	**Factor difference of squares.**
$x = 0, x = \sqrt{3}, x = -\sqrt{3}, x = -2, \text{ or } x = 2$	**Zero product property**

▶ The solutions are 0, $\sqrt{3}$, $-\sqrt{3}$, -2, and 2. Check these in the original equation.

EXAMPLE 5 *Solving a Polynomial Equation in Real Life*

ARCHEOLOGY In 1980 archeologists at the ruins of Caesara discovered a huge hydraulic concrete block with a volume of 330 cubic yards. The block's dimensions are x yards high by $13x - 11$ yards long by $13x - 15$ yards wide. What is the height?

SOLUTION

VERBAL MODEL $\boxed{\textbf{Volume}} = \boxed{\textbf{Height}} \cdot \boxed{\textbf{Length}} \cdot \boxed{\textbf{Width}}$

LABELS
Volume = **330**   (cubic yards)
Height = x (yards)
Length = $13x - 11$ (yards)
Width = $13x - 15$ (yards)

ALGEBRAIC MODEL

$330 = x\,(13x - 11)\,(13x - 15)$

$0 = 169x^3 - 338x^2 + 165x - 330$	**Write in standard form.**
$0 = 169x^2(x - 2) + 165(x - 2)$	**Factor by grouping.**
$0 = (169x^2 + 165)(x - 2)$	

▶ The only real solution is $x = 2$, so $13x - 11 = 15$ and $13x - 15 = 11$. The block is 2 yards high. The dimensions are 2 yards by 15 yards by 11 yards.

GUIDED PRACTICE

Vocabulary Check ✔   **1.** Give an example of a polynomial in quadratic form that contains an x^3-term.

Concept Check ✔   **2.** State which factoring method you would use to factor each of the following.

     a. $6x^3 - 2x^2 + 9x - 3$ **b.** $8x^3 - 125$ **c.** $16x^4 - 9$

3. ERROR ANALYSIS What is wrong with the solution at the right?

4. a. Factor the polynomial $x^3 + 1$ into the product of a linear binomial and a quadratic trinomial.

     b. Show that you can't factor the quadratic trinomial from part (a).

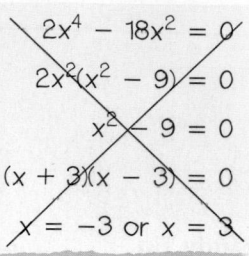

$$2x^4 - 18x^2 = 0$$
$$2x^2(x^2 - 9) = 0$$
$$x^2 - 9 = 0$$
$$(x + 3)(x - 3) = 0$$
$$x = -3 \text{ or } x = 3$$

Ex. 3

Skill Check ✔   **Factor the polynomial using any method.**

5. $x^6 + 125$ **6.** $4x^3 + 16x^2 + x + 4$ **7.** $x^4 - 1$

8. $2x^3 - 3x^2 - 10x + 15$ **9.** $5x^3 - 320$ **10.** $x^4 + 7x^2 + 10$

Find the real-number solutions of the equation.

11. $x^3 - 27 = 0$ **12.** $3x^3 + 7x^2 - 12x = 28$ **13.** $x^3 + 2x^2 - 9x = 18$

14. $54x^3 = -2$ **15.** $9x^4 - 12x^2 + 4 = 0$ **16.** $16x^8 = 81$

17. 🌐 BUSINESS The revenue R (in thousands of dollars) for a small business can be modeled by

$$R = t^3 - 8t^2 + t + 82$$

where t is the number of years since 1990. In what year did the revenue reach $90,000?

PRACTICE AND APPLICATIONS

STUDENT HELP

▶ **Extra Practice**
to help you master
skills is on p. 948.

MONOMIAL FACTORS Find the greatest common factor of the terms in the polynomial.

18. $14x^2 + 8x + 72$ **19.** $3x^4 - 12x^3$ **20.** $7x + 28x^2 - 35x^3$

21. $24x^4 - 6x$ **22.** $39x^5 + 13x^3 - 78x^2$ **23.** $145x^9 - 17$

24. $6x^6 - 3x^4 - 9x^2$ **25.** $72x^9 + 15x^6 + 9x^3$ **26.** $6x^4 - 18x^3 + 15x^2$

MATCHING Match the polynomial with its factorization.

27. $3x^2 + 11x + 6$ **A.** $2x^3(x + 2)(x - 2)(x^2 + 4)$

28. $x^3 - 4x^2 + 4x - 16$ **B.** $2x(x + 4)(x - 4)$

29. $125x^3 - 216$ **C.** $(3x + 2)(x + 3)$

30. $2x^7 - 32x^3$ **D.** $(x^2 + 4)(x - 4)$

31. $2x^5 + 4x^4 - 4x^3 - 8x^2$ **E.** $2x^2(x^2 - 2)(x + 2)$

32. $2x^3 - 32x$ **F.** $(5x - 6)(25x^2 + 30x + 36)$

STUDENT HELP

→ HOMEWORK HELP
Example 1: Exs. 18–40,
          59–67
Example 2: Exs. 18–32,
          41–49, 59–67
Example 3: Exs. 18–32,
          50–67
Example 4: Exs. 68–85
Example 5: Exs. 87–92

SUM OR DIFFERENCE OF CUBES Factor the polynomial.

33. $x^3 - 8$ **34.** $x^3 + 64$ **35.** $216x^3 + 1$ **36.** $125x^3 - 8$

37. $1000x^3 + 27$ **38.** $27x^3 + 216$ **39.** $32x^3 - 4$ **40.** $2x^3 + 54$

GROUPING Factor the polynomial by grouping.

41. $x^3 + x^2 + x + 1$ **42.** $10x^3 + 20x^2 + x + 2$ **43.** $x^3 + 3x^2 + 10x + 30$

44. $x^3 - 2x^2 + 4x - 8$ **45.** $2x^3 - 5x^2 + 18x - 45$ **46.** $-2x^3 - 4x^2 - 3x - 6$

47. $3x^3 - 6x^2 + x - 2$ **48.** $2x^3 - x^2 + 2x - 1$ **49.** $3x^3 - 2x^2 - 9x + 6$

QUADRATIC FORM Factor the polynomial.

50. $16x^4 - 1$ **51.** $x^4 + 3x^2 + 2$ **52.** $x^4 - 81$

53. $81x^4 - 256$ **54.** $4x^4 - 5x^2 - 9$ **55.** $x^4 + 10x^2 + 16$

56. $81 - 16x^4$ **57.** $32x^6 - 2x^2$ **58.** $6x^5 - 51x^3 - 27x$

CHOOSING A METHOD Factor using any method.

59. $18x^3 - 2x^2 + 27x - 3$ **60.** $6x^3 + 21x^2 + 15x$ **61.** $4x^4 + 39x^2 - 10$

62. $8x^3 - 12x^2 - 2x + 3$ **63.** $8x^3 - 64$ **64.** $3x^4 - 300x^2$

65. $3x^4 - 24x$ **66.** $5x^4 + 31x^2 + 6$ **67.** $3x^4 + 9x^3 + x^2 + 3x$

SOLVING EQUATIONS Find the real-number solutions of the equation.

68. $x^3 - 3x^2 = 0$ **69.** $2x^3 - 6x^2 = 0$ **70.** $3x^4 + 15x^2 - 72 = 0$

71. $x^3 + 27 = 0$ **72.** $x^3 + 2x^2 - x = 2$ **73.** $x^4 + 7x^3 - 8x - 56 = 0$

74. $2x^4 - 26x^2 + 72 = 0$ **75.** $3x^7 - 243x^3 = 0$ **76.** $x^3 + 3x^2 - 2x - 6 = 0$

77. $8x^3 - 1 = 0$ **78.** $x^3 + 8x^2 = -16x$ **79.** $x^3 - 5x^2 + 5x - 25 = 0$

80. $3x^4 + 3x^3 = 6x^2 + 6x$ **81.** $x^4 + x^3 - x = 1$ **82.** $4x^4 + 20x^2 = -25$

83. $-2x^6 = 16$ **84.** $3x^7 = 81x^4$ **85.** $2x^5 - 12x^3 = -16x$

86. *Writing* You have now factored several different types of polynomials.
Explain which factoring techniques or patterns are useful for factoring binomials,
trinomials, and polynomials with more than three terms.

87. 🌐 **PACKAGING** A candy factory needs a box that has a volume of 30 cubic
inches. The width should be 2 inches less than the height and the length should
be 5 inches greater than the height. What should the dimensions of the box be?

STUDENT HELP

INTERNET HOMEWORK HELP
Visit our Web site
www.mcdougallittell.com
for help with problem
solving in Ex. 88.

88. 🌐 **MANUFACTURING** A manufacturer wants to
build a rectangular stainless steel tank with a holding
capacity of 500 gallons, or about 66.85 cubic feet. If
steel that is one half inch thick is used for the walls of
the tank, then about 5.15 cubic feet of steel is needed.
The manufacturer wants the outside dimensions of
the tank to be related as follows:

• The width should be one foot less than the length.

• The height should be nine feet more than
  the length.

What should the outside dimensions of the tank be?

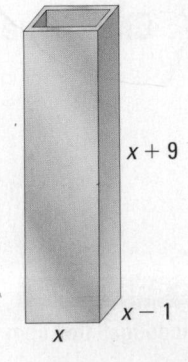

$x + 9$

$x - 1$

x

89. 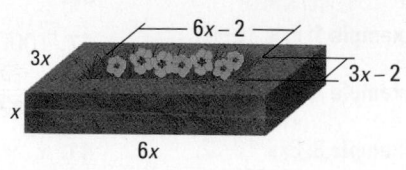 **CITY PARK** For the city park commission, you are designing a marble planter in which to plant flowers. You want the length of the planter to be six times the height and the width to be three times the height. The sides should be one foot thick. Since the planter will be on the sidewalk, it does not need a bottom. What should the outer dimensions of the planter be if it is to hold 4 cubic feet of dirt?

"Charred Sphere, Cube, and Pyramid"
by David Nash

SCULPTURE In Exercises 90 and 91, refer to the sculpture shown in the picture.

90. The "cube" portion of the sculpture is actually a rectangular prism with dimensions x feet by $5x - 10$ feet by $2x - 1$ feet. The volume of the prism is 25 cubic feet. What are the dimensions of the prism?

91. Suppose a pyramid like the one in the sculpture is $3x$ feet high and has a square base measuring $x - 5$ feet on each side. If the volume is 250 cubic feet, what are the dimensions of the pyramid? (Use the formula $V = \frac{1}{3}Bh$.)

92. 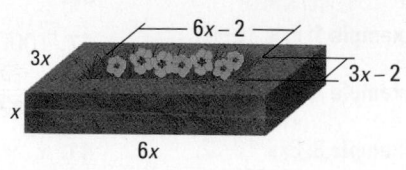 **CRAFTS** Suppose you have 250 cubic inches of clay with which to make a rectangular prism for a sculpture. If you want the height and width each to be 5 inches less than the length, what should the dimensions of the prism be?

Test Preparation

93. MULTIPLE CHOICE The expression $(3x - 4)(9x^2 + 12x + 16)$ is the factorization of which of the following?

   (A) $27x^3 - 8$ (B) $27x^3 + 36x^2$ (C) $27x^3 - 64$ (D) $27x^3 + 64$

94. MULTIPLE CHOICE Which of the following is the factorization of $x^3 - 8$?

   (A) $(x - 2)(x^2 + 4x + 4)$ (B) $(x + 2)(x^2 - 2x + 4)$
   (C) $(x + 2)(x^2 - 4x + 4)$ (D) $(x - 2)(x^2 + 2x + 4)$

95. MULTIPLE CHOICE What are the real solutions of the equation $x^5 = 81x$?

   (A) $x = \pm3, \pm3i$ (B) $x = 0, \pm9$
   (C) $x = 0, \pm3, \pm3i$ (D) $x = 0, \pm3$

★ **Challenge**

96. GEOMETRY CONNECTION Explain how the figure shown at the right can be used as a geometric factoring model for the sum of two cubes.

$$a^3 + b^3 = (a + b)(a^2 - ab + b^2)$$

Factor the polynomial.

EXTRA CHALLENGE
www.mcdougallittell.com

97. $30x^2y + 36x^2 - 20xy - 24x$

98. $2x^7 - 127x$

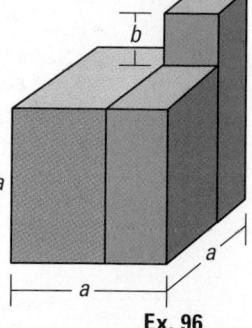
Ex. 96

Chapter 6 *Polynomials and Polynomial Functions*

MIXED REVIEW

SIMPLIFYING EXPRESSIONS Simplify the expression. **(Review 6.1 for 6.5)**

99. $\dfrac{6x^3y^9}{36x^3y^{-2}}$

100. $\dfrac{5^{-2}x^2y^{-1}}{5^2xy^3}$

101. $\dfrac{7^2x^{-3}y^2}{49x^{-3}y^{-2}}$

SYNTHETIC SUBSTITUTION Use synthetic substitution to evaluate the polynomial function for the given value of *x*. **(Review 6.2 for 6.5)**

102. $f(x) = 3x^4 + 2x^3 - x^2 - 12x + 1, \ x = 3$

103. $f(x) = 2x^5 - x^3 + 7x + 1, \ x = 3$

104. 🌐 **SEWING** At the fabric store you are buying solid fabric at $4 per yard, print fabric at $6 per yard, and a pattern for $8. Write an equation for the amount you spend as a function of the amount of solid and print fabric you buy. **(Review 3.5)**

MATH & History

Solving Polynomial Equations

APPLICATION LINK
www.mcdougallittell.com

THEN

IN 2000 B.C. the Babylonians solved polynomial equations by referring to tables of values. One such table gave the values of $y^3 + y^2$. To be able to use this table, the Babylonians sometimes had to manipulate the equation, as shown below.

$$ax^3 + bx^2 = c \qquad \text{Write original equation.}$$

$$\frac{a^3x^3}{b^3} + \frac{a^2x^2}{b^2} = \frac{a^2c}{b^3} \qquad \text{Multiply by } \frac{a^2}{b^3}.$$

$$\left(\frac{ax}{b}\right)^3 + \left(\frac{ax}{b}\right)^2 = \frac{a^2c}{b^3} \qquad \text{Re-express cubes and squares.}$$

Then they would find $\dfrac{a^2c}{b^3}$ in the $y^3 + y^2$ column of the table.

Because they knew that the corresponding *y*-value was equal to $\dfrac{ax}{b}$, they could conclude that $x = \dfrac{by}{a}$.

1. Calculate $y^3 + y^2$ for $y = 1, 2, 3, \ldots, 10$. Record the values in a table.

Use your table and the method discussed above to solve the equation.

2. $x^3 + x^2 = 252$

3. $x^3 + 2x^2 = 288$

4. $3x^3 + x^2 = 90$

5. $2x^3 + 5x^2 = 2500$

6. $7x^3 + 6x^2 = 1728$

7. $10x^3 + 3x^2 = 297$

NOW

TODAY computers use polynomial equations to accomplish many things, such as making robots move.

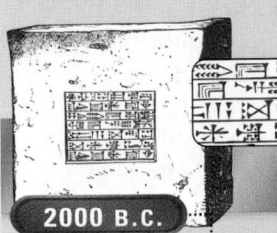

2000 B.C.
Babylonians use tables.

A.D. 1100
Chinese solve cubic equations.

1545
Cardano solves cubic equations.

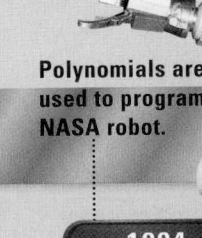

Polynomials are used to program NASA robot.

1994

The Remainder and Factor Theorems

What you should learn

GOAL 1 Divide polynomials and relate the result to the remainder theorem and the factor theorem.

GOAL 2 Use polynomial division in **real-life** problems, such as finding a production level that yields a certain profit in **Example 5**.

Why you should learn it

▼ To combine two **real-life** models into one new model, such as a model for money spent at the movies each year in **Ex. 62**.

GOAL 1 DIVIDING POLYNOMIALS

When you divide a polynomial $f(x)$ by a divisor $d(x)$, you get a quotient polynomial $q(x)$ and a remainder polynomial $r(x)$. We write this as $\frac{f(x)}{d(x)} = q(x) + \frac{r(x)}{d(x)}$. The degree of the remainder must be less than the degree of the divisor.

Example 1 shows how to divide polynomials using a method called **polynomial long division**.

EXAMPLE 1   *Using Polynomial Long Division*

Divide $2x^4 + 3x^3 + 5x - 1$ by $x^2 - 2x + 2$.

SOLUTION

Write division in the same format you would use when dividing numbers. Include a "0" as the coefficient of x^2.

$$\frac{2x^4}{x^2} \qquad \frac{7x^3}{x^2} \qquad \frac{10x^2}{x^2}$$

> At each stage, divide the term with the highest power in what's left of the dividend by the first term of the divisor. This gives the next term of the quotient.

$$
\begin{array}{r}
2x^2 + 7x + 10 \\
x^2 - 2x + 2 \overline{\smash{\big)}\, 2x^4 + 3x^3 + 0x^2 + 5x - 1} \\
\underline{2x^4 - 4x^3 + 4x^2} \qquad\qquad\qquad \\
7x^3 - 4x^2 + 5x \qquad\qquad \\
\underline{7x^3 - 14x^2 + 14x} \qquad\qquad \\
10x^2 - 9x - 1 \\
\underline{10x^2 - 20x + 20} \\
11x - 21
\end{array}
$$

Subtract $2x^2(x^2 - 2x + 2)$.

Subtract $7x(x^2 - 2x + 2)$.

Subtract $10(x^2 - 2x + 2)$.

◄ remainder

Write the result as follows.

▶ $$\frac{2x^4 + 3x^3 + 5x - 1}{x^2 - 2x + 2} = 2x^2 + 7x + 10 + \frac{11x - 21}{x^2 - 2x + 2}$$

✔ **CHECK** You can check the result of a division problem by multiplying the divisor by the quotient and adding the remainder. The result should be the dividend.

$$(2x^2 + 7x + 10)(x^2 - 2x + 2) + 11x - 21$$

$$= 2x^2(x^2 - 2x + 2) + 7x(x^2 - 2x + 2) + 10(x^2 - 2x + 2) + 11x - 21$$

$$= 2x^4 - 4x^3 + 4x^2 + 7x^3 - 14x^2 + 14x + 10x^2 - 20x + 20 + 11x - 21$$

$$= 2x^4 + 3x^3 + 5x - 1 \checkmark$$

ACTIVITY Developing Concepts

Investigating Polynomial Division

Let $f(x) = 3x^3 - 2x^2 + 2x - 5$.

1. Use long division to divide $f(x)$ by $x - 2$. What is the quotient? What is the remainder?

2. Use synthetic substitution to evaluate $f(2)$. How is $f(2)$ related to the remainder? What do you notice about the other constants in the last row of the synthetic substitution?

In the activity you may have discovered that $f(2)$ gives you the remainder when $f(x)$ is divided by $x - 2$. This result is generalized in the *remainder theorem.*

REMAINDER THEOREM

If a polynomial $f(x)$ is divided by $x - k$, then the remainder is $r = f(k)$.

STUDENT HELP

Study Tip
Notice that synthetic division could *not* have been used to divide the polynomials in Example 1 because the divisor, $x^2 - 2x + 2$, is not of the form $x - k$.

You may also have discovered in the activity that synthetic substitution gives the coefficients of the quotient. For this reason, synthetic substitution is sometimes called **synthetic division.** It can be used to divide a polynomial by an expression of the form $x - k$.

EXAMPLE 2 *Using Synthetic Division*

Divide $x^3 + 2x^2 - 6x - 9$ by **(a)** $x - 2$ and **(b)** $x + 3$.

SOLUTION

a. Use synthetic division for $k = 2$.

$$\begin{array}{r|rrrr} 2 & 1 & 2 & -6 & -9 \\ & & 2 & 8 & 4 \\ \hline & 1 & 4 & 2 & -5 \end{array}$$

▶ $\dfrac{x^3 + 2x^2 - 6x - 9}{x - 2} = x^2 + 4x + 2 + \dfrac{-5}{x - 2}$

b. To find the value of k, rewrite the divisor in the form $x - k$.
Because $x + 3 = x - (-3)$, $k = -3$.

$$\begin{array}{r|rrrr} -3 & 1 & 2 & -6 & -9 \\ & & -3 & 3 & 9 \\ \hline & 1 & -1 & -3 & 0 \end{array}$$

▶ $\dfrac{x^3 + 2x^2 - 6x - 9}{x + 3} = x^2 - x - 3$

In part (b) of Example 2, the remainder is 0. Therefore, you can rewrite the result as:

$$x^3 + 2x^2 - 6x - 9 = (x^2 - x - 3)(x + 3)$$

This shows that $x + 3$ is a factor of the original dividend.

FACTOR THEOREM

A polynomial $f(x)$ has a factor $x - k$ if and only if $f(k) = 0$.

Recall from Chapter 5 that the number k is called a *zero* of the function f because $f(k) = 0$.

EXAMPLE 3 *Factoring a Polynomial*

Factor $f(x) = 2x^3 + 11x^2 + 18x + 9$ given that $f(-3) = 0$.

SOLUTION

Because $f(-3) = 0$, you know that $x - (-3)$ or $x + 3$ is a factor of $f(x)$. Use synthetic division to find the other factors.

$$
\begin{array}{r|rrrr}
-3 & 2 & 11 & 18 & 9 \\
   &   & -6 & -15 & -9 \\
\hline
   & 2 & 5 & 3 & 0
\end{array}
$$

The result gives the coefficients of the quotient.

$$2x^3 + 11x^2 + 18x + 9 = (x + 3)(2x^2 + 5x + 3)$$
$$= (x + 3)(2x + 3)(x + 1)$$

EXAMPLE 4 *Finding Zeros of a Polynomial Function*

One zero of $f(x) = x^3 - 2x^2 - 9x + 18$ is $x = 2$. Find the other zeros of the function.

SOLUTION

To find the zeros of the function, factor $f(x)$ completely. Because $f(2) = 0$, you know that $x - 2$ is a factor of $f(x)$. Use synthetic division to find the other factors.

$$
\begin{array}{r|rrrr}
2 & 1 & -2 & -9 & 18 \\
  &   & 2 & 0 & -18 \\
\hline
  & 1 & 0 & -9 & 0
\end{array}
$$

The result gives the coefficients of the quotient.

$f(x) = (x - 2)(x^2 - 9)$ **Write $f(x)$ as a product of two factors.**

$= (x - 2)(x + 3)(x - 3)$ **Factor difference of squares.**

▶ By the factor theorem, the zeros of f are 2, -3, and 3.

GOAL 2 USING POLYNOMIAL DIVISION IN REAL LIFE

In business and economics, a function that gives the price per unit p of an item in terms of the number x of units sold is called a *demand function*.

EXAMPLE 5 *Using Polynomial Models*

ACCOUNTING You are an accountant for a manufacturer of radios. The demand function for the radios is $p = 40 - 4x^2$ where x is the number of radios produced in millions. It costs the company \$15 to make a radio.

a. Write an equation giving profit as a function of the number of radios produced.

b. The company currently produces 1.5 million radios and makes a profit of \$24,000,000, but you would like to scale back production. What lesser number of radios could the company produce to yield the same profit?

SOLUTION

PROBLEM SOLVING STRATEGY

a. VERBAL MODEL

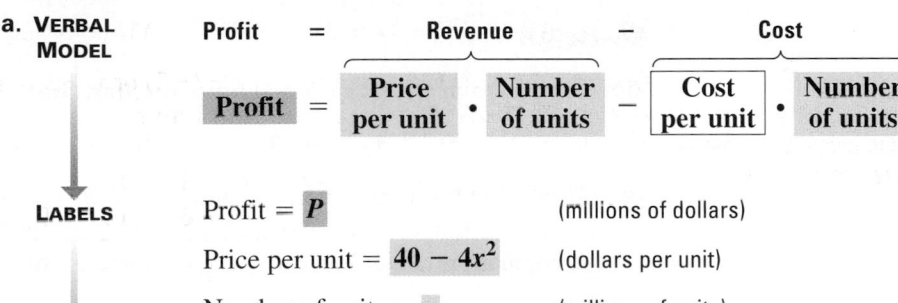

Profit = Revenue − Cost

$$\text{Profit} = \boxed{\frac{\text{Price}}{\text{per unit}}} \cdot \boxed{\frac{\text{Number}}{\text{of units}}} - \boxed{\frac{\text{Cost}}{\text{per unit}}} \cdot \boxed{\frac{\text{Number}}{\text{of units}}}$$

LABELS

Profit = P (millions of dollars)

Price per unit = $40 - 4x^2$ (dollars per unit)

Number of units = x (millions of units)

Cost per unit = 15 (dollars per unit)

ALGEBRAIC MODEL

$$P = (40 - 4x^2)\,x - 15x$$
$$P = -4x^3 + 25x$$

b. Substitute **24** for P in the function you wrote in part (a).

$$24 = -4x^3 + 25x$$
$$0 = -4x^3 + 25x - 24$$

You know that $x = 1.5$ is one solution of the equation. This implies that $x - 1.5$ is a factor. So divide to obtain the following:

$$-2(x - 1.5)(2x^2 + 3x - 8) = 0$$

Use the quadratic formula to find that $x \approx 1.39$ is the other positive solution.

▶ The company can make the same profit by selling 1,390,000 units.

✓ **CHECK** Graph the profit function to confirm that there are two production levels that produce a profit of \$24,000,000.

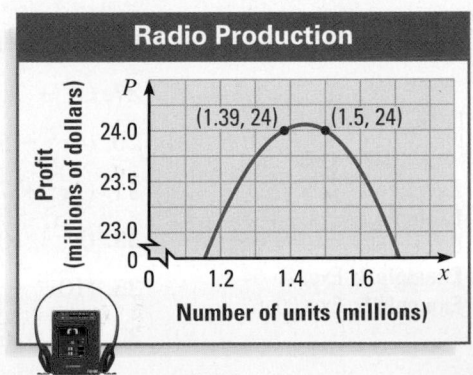

Radio Production

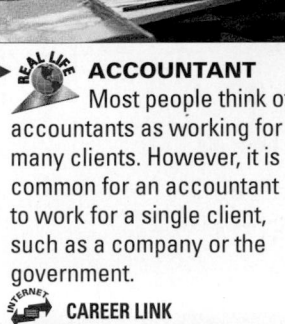

GUIDED PRACTICE

1. State the remainder theorem.

2. Write a polynomial division problem that you would use long division to solve. Then write a polynomial division problem that you would use synthetic division to solve.

3. Write the polynomial divisor, dividend, and quotient represented by the synthetic division shown at the right.

$$
\begin{array}{r|rrrr}
-3 & 1 & -2 & -9 & 18 \\
   &   & -3 & 15 & -18 \\
\hline
   & 1 & -5 & 6 & 0
\end{array}
$$

Divide using polynomial long division.

4. $(2x^3 - 7x^2 - 17x - 3) \div (2x + 3)$ **5.** $(x^3 + 5x^2 - 2) \div (x + 4)$

6. $(-3x^3 + 4x - 1) \div (x - 1)$ **7.** $(-x^3 + 2x^2 - 2x + 3) \div (x^2 - 1)$

Divide using synthetic division.

8. $(x^3 - 8x + 3) \div (x + 3)$ **9.** $(x^4 - 16x^2 + x + 4) \div (x + 4)$

10. $(x^2 + 2x + 15) \div (x - 3)$ **11.** $(x^2 + 7x - 2) \div (x - 2)$

Given one zero of the polynomial function, find the other zeros.

12. $f(x) = x^3 - 8x^2 + 4x + 48;\ 4$ **13.** $f(x) = 2x^3 - 14x^2 - 56x - 40;\ 10$

14. 🌐 **BUSINESS** Look back at Example 5. If the company produces 1 million radios, it will make a profit of $21,000,000. Find another number of radios that the company could produce to make the same profit.

PRACTICE AND APPLICATIONS

STUDENT HELP

▶ **Extra Practice**
to help you master
skills is on p. 948.

USING LONG DIVISION Divide using polynomial long division.

15. $(x^2 + 7x - 5) \div (x - 2)$ **16.** $(3x^2 + 11x + 1) \div (x - 3)$

17. $(2x^2 + 3x - 1) \div (x + 4)$ **18.** $(x^2 - 6x + 4) \div (x + 1)$

19. $(x^2 + 5x - 3) \div (x - 10)$ **20.** $(x^3 - 3x^2 + x - 8) \div (x - 1)$

21. $(2x^4 + 7) \div (x^2 - 1)$ **22.** $(x^3 + 8x^2 - 3x + 16) \div (x^2 + 5)$

23. $(6x^2 + x - 7) \div (2x + 3)$ **24.** $(10x^3 + 27x^2 + 14x + 5) \div (x^2 + 2x)$

25. $(5x^4 + 14x^3 + 9x) \div (x^2 + 3x)$ **26.** $(2x^4 + 2x^3 - 10x - 9) \div (x^3 + x^2 - 5)$

USING SYNTHETIC DIVISION Divide using synthetic division.

STUDENT HELP

▶ **HOMEWORK HELP**
Example 1: Exs. 15–26
Example 2: Exs. 27–38
Example 3: Exs. 39–46
Example 4: Exs. 47–54
Example 5: Exs. 60–62

27. $(x^3 - 7x - 6) \div (x - 2)$ **28.** $(x^3 - 14x + 8) \div (x + 4)$

29. $(4x^2 + 5x - 4) \div (x + 1)$ **30.** $(x^2 - 4x + 3) \div (x - 2)$

31. $(2x^2 + 7x + 8) \div (x - 2)$ **32.** $(3x^2 - 10x) \div (x - 6)$

33. $(x^2 + 10) \div (x + 4)$ **34.** $(x^2 + 3) \div (x + 3)$

35. $(10x^4 + 5x^3 + 4x^2 - 9) \div (x + 1)$ **36.** $(x^4 - 6x^3 - 40x + 33) \div (x - 7)$

37. $(2x^4 - 6x^3 + x^2 - 3x - 3) \div (x - 3)$ **38.** $(4x^4 + 5x^3 + 2x^2 - 1) \div (x + 1)$

FACTORING Factor the polynomial given that $f(k) = 0$.

39. $f(x) = x^3 - 5x^2 - 2x + 24$; $k = -2$
40. $f(x) = x^3 - 3x^2 - 16x - 12$; $k = 6$

41. $f(x) = x^3 - 12x^2 + 12x + 80$; $k = 10$
42. $f(x) = x^3 - 18x^2 + 95x - 126$; $k = 9$

43. $f(x) = x^3 - x^2 - 21x + 45$; $k = -5$
44. $f(x) = x^3 - 11x^2 + 14x + 80$; $k = 8$

45. $f(x) = 4x^3 - 4x^2 - 9x + 9$; $k = 1$
46. $f(x) = 2x^3 + 7x^2 - 33x - 18$; $k = -6$

FINDING ZEROS Given one zero of the polynomial function, find the other zeros.

47. $f(x) = 9x^3 + 10x^2 - 17x - 2$; -2
48. $f(x) = x^3 + 11x^2 - 150x - 1512$; -14

49. $f(x) = 2x^3 + 3x^2 - 39x - 20$; 4
50. $f(x) = 15x^3 - 119x^2 - 10x + 16$; 8

51. $f(x) = x^3 - 14x^2 + 47x - 18$; 9
52. $f(x) = 4x^3 + 9x^2 - 52x + 15$; -5

53. $f(x) = x^3 + x^2 + 2x + 24$; -3
54. $f(x) = 5x^3 - 27x^2 - 17x - 6$; 6

GEOMETRY **CONNECTION** You are given an expression for the volume of the rectangular prism. Find an expression for the missing dimension.

55. $V = 3x^3 + 8x^2 - 45x - 50$

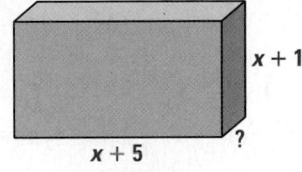

56. $V = 2x^3 + 17x^2 + 40x + 25$

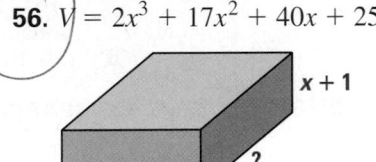

POINTS OF INTERSECTION Find all points of intersection of the two graphs given that one intersection occurs at $x = 1$.

57.

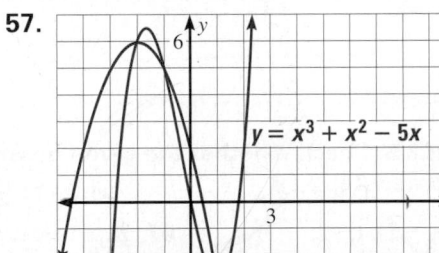

$y = x^3 + x^2 - 5x$
$y = -x^2 - 4x + 2$

58.

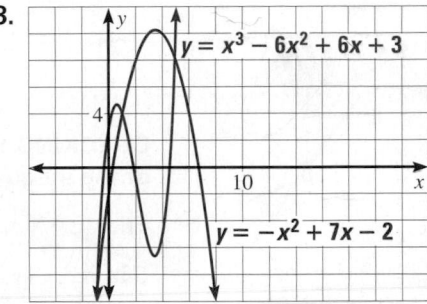

$y = x^3 - 6x^2 + 6x + 3$
$y = -x^2 + 7x - 2$

59. LOGICAL REASONING You divide two polynomials and obtain the result $5x^2 - 13x + 47 - \dfrac{102}{x + 2}$. What is the dividend? How did you find it?

60. COMPANY PROFIT The demand function for a type of camera is given by the model $p = 100 - 8x^2$ where p is measured in dollars per camera and x is measured in millions of cameras. The production cost is $25 per camera. The production of 2.5 million cameras yielded a profit of $62.5 million. What other number of cameras could the company sell to make the same profit?

61. FUEL CONSUMPTION From 1980 to 1991, the total fuel consumption T (in billions of gallons) by cars in the United States and the average fuel consumption A (in gallons per car) can be modeled by

$$T = -0.026x^3 + 0.47x^2 - 2.2x + 72 \qquad \text{and} \qquad A = -8.4x + 580$$

where x is the number of years since 1980. Find a function for the number of cars from 1980 to 1991. About how many cars were there in 1990?

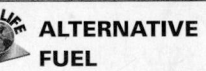

62. 🌐 **MOVIES** The amount M (in millions of dollars) spent at movie theaters from 1989 to 1996 can be modeled by

$$M = -3.05x^3 + 70.2x^2 - 225x + 5070$$

where x is the number of years since 1989. The United States population P (in millions) from 1989 to 1996 can be modeled by the following function:

$$P = 2.61x + 247$$

Find a function for the average annual amount spent per person at movie theaters from 1989 to 1996. On average, about how much did each person spend at movie theaters in 1989? ▶ Source: *Statistical Abstract of the United States*

Test Preparation

63. **MULTIPLE CHOICE** What is the result of dividing $x^3 - 9x + 5$ by $x - 3$?

Ⓐ $x^2 + 3x + 5$ Ⓑ $x^2 + 3x$ Ⓒ $x^2 + 3x + \dfrac{5}{x - 3}$

Ⓓ $x^2 + 3x - \dfrac{5}{x - 3}$ Ⓔ $x^2 + 3x - 18 + \dfrac{59}{x - 3}$

64. **MULTIPLE CHOICE** Which of the following is a factor of the polynomial $2x^3 - 19x^2 - 20x + 100$?

Ⓐ $x + 10$ Ⓑ $x + 2$ Ⓒ $2x - 5$ Ⓓ $x - 5$ Ⓔ $2x + 5$

★ **Challenge**

65. **COMPARING METHODS** Divide the polynomial $12x^3 - 8x^2 + 5x + 2$ by $2x + 1$, $3x + 1$, and $4x + 1$ using long division. Then divide the same polynomial by $x + \dfrac{1}{2}$, $x + \dfrac{1}{3}$, and $x + \dfrac{1}{4}$ using synthetic division. What do you notice about the remainders and the coefficients of the quotients from the two types of division?

EXTRA CHALLENGE
www.mcdougallittell.com

MIXED REVIEW

CHECKING SOLUTIONS Check whether the given ordered pairs are solutions of the inequality. (Review 2.6)

66. $x + 7y \le -8$; $(6, -2)$, $(-2, -3)$ 67. $2x + 5y \ge 1$; $(-2, 4)$, $(8, -3)$

68. $9x - 4y > 7$; $(-1, -4)$, $(2, 2)$ 69. $-3x - 2y < -6$; $(2, 0)$, $(1, 4)$

QUADRATIC FORMULA Use the quadratic formula to solve the equation. (Review 5.6 for 6.6)

70. $x^2 - 5x + 3 = 0$ 71. $x^2 - 8x + 3 = 0$ 72. $x^2 - 10x + 15 = 0$

73. $4x^2 - 7x + 1 = 0$ 74. $-6x^2 - 9x + 2 = 0$ 75. $5x^2 + x - 2 = 0$

76. $2x^2 + 3x + 5 = 0$ 77. $-5x^2 - x - 8 = 0$ 78. $3x^2 + 3x + 1 = 0$

POLYNOMIAL OPERATIONS Perform the indicated operation. (Review 6.3)

79. $(x^2 - 3x + 8) - (x^2 + x - 1)$ 80. $(14x^2 - 15x + 3) + (11x - 7)$

81. $(8x^3 - 1) - (22x^3 + 2x^2 - x - 5)$ 82. $(x + 5)(x^2 - x + 5)$

83. 🌐 **CATERING** You are helping your sister plan her wedding reception. The guests have chosen whether they would like the chicken dish or the vegetarian dish. The caterer charges $24 per chicken dish and $21 per vegetarian dish. After ordering the dinners for the 120 guests, the caterer's bill comes to $2766. How many guests requested chicken? (**Lesson 3.2**)

6.6 Finding Rational Zeros

What you should learn

GOAL 1 Find the rational zeros of a polynomial function.

GOAL 2 Use polynomial equations to solve **real-life** problems, such as finding the dimensions of a monument in **Ex. 60**.

Why you should learn it

▼ To model **real-life** quantities, such as the volume of a representation of the Louvre pyramid in **Example 3**.

GOAL 1 USING THE RATIONAL ZERO THEOREM

The polynomial function

$$f(x) = 64x^3 + 120x^2 - 34x - 105$$

has $-\dfrac{3}{2}$, $-\dfrac{5}{4}$, and $\dfrac{7}{8}$ as its zeros. Notice that the numerators of these zeros (-3, -5, and 7) are factors of the constant term, -105. Also notice that the denominators (2, 4, and 8) are factors of the leading coefficient, 64. These observations are generalized by the *rational zero theorem*.

THE RATIONAL ZERO THEOREM

If $f(x) = a_n x^n + \cdots + a_1 x + a_0$ has *integer* coefficients, then every rational zero of f has the following form:

$$\frac{p}{q} = \frac{\text{factor of constant term } a_0}{\text{factor of leading coefficient } a_n}$$

EXAMPLE 1 *Using the Rational Zero Theorem*

Find the rational zeros of $f(x) = x^3 + 2x^2 - 11x - 12$.

SOLUTION

List the possible rational zeros. The leading coefficient is 1 and the constant term is -12. So, the possible rational zeros are:

$$x = \pm\frac{1}{1}, \pm\frac{2}{1}, \pm\frac{3}{1}, \pm\frac{4}{1}, \pm\frac{6}{1}, \pm\frac{12}{1}$$

Test these zeros using synthetic division.

Test $x = 1$:

1	1	2	-11	-12
		1	3	-8
	1	3	-8	-20

Test $x = -1$:

-1	1	2	-11	-12
		-1	-1	12
	1	1	-12	0

Since -1 is a zero of f, you can write the following:

$$f(x) = (x + 1)(x^2 + x - 12)$$

Factor the trinomial and use the factor theorem.

$$f(x) = (x + 1)(x^2 + x - 12) = (x + 1)(x - 3)(x + 4)$$

▶ The zeros of f are -1, 3, and -4.

In Example 1, the leading coefficient is 1. When the leading coefficient is not 1, the list of possible rational zeros can increase dramatically. In such cases the search can be shortened by sketching the function's graph—either by hand or by using a graphing calculator.

EXAMPLE 2   *Using the Rational Zero Theorem*

Find all real zeros of $f(x) = 10x^4 - 3x^3 - 29x^2 + 5x + 12$.

SOLUTION

List the possible rational zeros of f: $\pm\frac{1}{1}, \pm\frac{2}{1}, \pm\frac{3}{1}, \pm\frac{4}{1}, \pm\frac{6}{1},$
$\pm\frac{12}{1}, \pm\frac{3}{2}, \pm\frac{1}{5}, \pm\frac{2}{5}, \pm\frac{3}{5}, \pm\frac{6}{5}, \pm\frac{12}{5}, \pm\frac{1}{10}, \pm\frac{3}{10}, \pm\frac{12}{10}.$

Choose values to check.

With so many possibilities, it is worth your time to sketch the graph of the function. From the graph, it appears that some reasonable choices are $x = -\frac{3}{2}, x = -\frac{3}{5}, x = \frac{4}{5},$ and $x = \frac{3}{2}.$

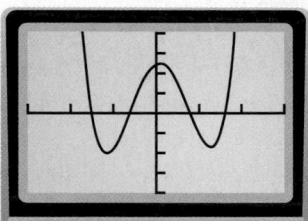

Check the chosen values using synthetic division.

$$
\begin{array}{r|rrrrr}
-\frac{3}{2} & 10 & -3 & -29 & 5 & 12 \\
  &   & -15 & 27 & 3 & -12 \\
\hline
  & 10 & -18 & -2 & 8 & 0
\end{array}
$$
$\longleftarrow -\frac{3}{2}$ is a zero.

Factor out a binomial using the result of the synthetic division.

$$f(x) = \left(x + \frac{3}{2}\right)(10x^3 - 18x^2 - 2x + 8)$$ **Rewrite as a product of two factors.**

$$= \left(x + \frac{3}{2}\right)(2)(5x^3 - 9x^2 - x + 4)$$ **Factor 2 out of the second factor.**

$$= (2x + 3)(5x^3 - 9x^2 - x + 4)$$ **Multiply the first factor by 2.**

Repeat the steps above for $g(x) = 5x^3 - 9x^2 - x + 4$.

Any zero of g will also be a zero of f. The possible *rational* zeros of g are $x = \pm1, \pm2, \pm4, \pm\frac{1}{5}, \pm\frac{2}{5},$ and $\pm\frac{4}{5}$. The graph of f shows that $\frac{4}{5}$ may be a zero.

$$
\begin{array}{r|rrrr}
\frac{4}{5} & 5 & -9 & -1 & 4 \\
  &   & 4 & -4 & -4 \\
\hline
  & 5 & -5 & -5 & 0
\end{array}
$$
$\longleftarrow \frac{4}{5}$ is a zero.

So $f(x) = (2x + 3)\left(x - \frac{4}{5}\right)(5x^2 - 5x - 5) = (2x + 3)(5x - 4)(x^2 - x - 1).$

Find the remaining zeros of f by using the quadratic formula to solve $x^2 - x - 1 = 0$.

▶ The real zeros of f are $-\frac{3}{2}, \frac{4}{5}, \frac{1 + \sqrt{5}}{2},$ and $\frac{1 - \sqrt{5}}{2}.$

GOAL 2 **SOLVING POLYNOMIAL EQUATIONS IN REAL LIFE**

Crafts

EXAMPLE 3 *Writing and Using a Polynomial Model*

You are designing a candle-making kit. Each kit will contain 25 cubic inches of candle wax and a mold for making a model of the pyramid-shaped building at the Louvre Museum in Paris, France. You want the height of the candle to be 2 inches less than the length of each side of the candle's square base. What should the dimensions of your candle mold be?

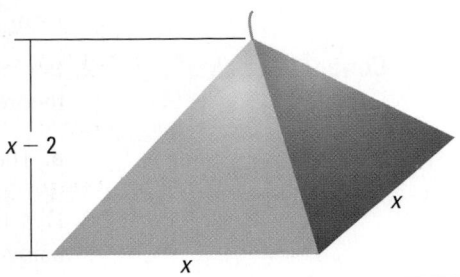

SOLUTION

The volume is $V = \frac{1}{3}Bh$ where B is the area of the base and h is the height.

PROBLEM SOLVING STRATEGY

VERBAL MODEL

$$\boxed{\text{Volume}} = \frac{1}{3} \cdot \boxed{\begin{array}{c}\text{Area of}\\\text{base}\end{array}} \cdot \boxed{\text{Height}}$$

LABELS

Volume = **25**   (cubic inches)

Side of square base = ***x***   (inches)

Area of base = ***x²***   (square inches)

Height = ***x − 2***   (inches)

ALGEBRAIC MODEL

$25 = \frac{1}{3}x^2 (x - 2)$ **Write algebraic model.**

$75 = x^3 - 2x^2$ **Multiply each side by 3 and simplify.**

$0 = x^3 - 2x^2 - 75$ **Subtract 75 from each side.**

FOCUS ON PEOPLE

 **I.M. PEI** designed the pyramid at the Louvre. His geometric architecture can be seen in Boston, New York, Dallas, Los Angeles, Taiwan, Beijing, and Singapore.

The possible rational solutions are $x = \pm\frac{1}{1}, \pm\frac{3}{1}, \pm\frac{5}{1}, \pm\frac{15}{1}, \pm\frac{25}{1}, \pm\frac{75}{1}$.

Use the possible solutions. Note that in this case, it makes sense to test only positive x-values.

```
1 | 1   -2    0   -75          3 | 1   -2    0   -75
  |      1   -1    -1            |      3    3    9
  ----------------------        ----------------------
    1   -1   -1   -76             1    1    3   -66
```

```
5 | 1   -2    0   -75
  |      5   15    75
  ----------------------
    1    3   15    0     ←── 5 is a solution.
```

So $x = 5$ is a solution. The other two solutions, which satisfy $x^2 + 3x + 15 = 0$, are $x = \frac{-3 \pm i\sqrt{51}}{2}$ and can be discarded because they are imaginary.

▶ The base of the candle mold should be 5 inches by 5 inches. The height of the mold should be $5 - 2 = 3$ inches.

GUIDED PRACTICE

Vocabulary Check ✓

1. Complete this statement of the rational zero theorem: If a polynomial function has integer coefficients, then every rational zero of the function has the form $\frac{p}{q}$, where p is a factor of the ? and q is a factor of the ? .

Concept Check ✓

2. For each polynomial function, decide whether you can use the rational zero theorem to find its zeros. Explain why or why not.

a. $f(x) = 6x^2 - 8x + 4$ b. $f(x) = 0.3x^2 + 2x + 4.5$ c. $f(x) = \frac{1}{4}x^2 - x + \frac{7}{8}$

3. Describe a method you can use to shorten the list of possible rational zeros when using the rational zero theorem.

Skill Check ✓

List the possible rational zeros of f using the rational zero theorem.

4. $f(x) = x^3 + 14x^2 + 41x - 56$

5. $f(x) = x^3 - 17x^2 + 54x + 72$

6. $f(x) = 2x^3 + 7x^2 - 7x + 30$

7. $f(x) = 5x^4 + 12x^3 - 16x^2 + 10$

Find all the real zeros of the function.

8. $f(x) = x^3 - 3x^2 - 6x + 8$

9. $f(x) = x^3 + 4x^2 - x - 4$

10. $f(x) = 2x^3 - 5x^2 - 2x + 5$

11. $f(x) = 2x^3 - x^2 - 15x + 18$

12. $f(x) = x^3 + 4x^2 + x - 6$

13. $f(x) = x^3 + 5x^2 - x - 5$

14. 🌐 **CRAFTS** Suppose you have 18 cubic inches of wax and you want to make a candle in the shape of a pyramid with a square base. If you want the height of the candle to be 3 inches greater than the length of each side of the base, what should the dimensions of the candle be?

PRACTICE AND APPLICATIONS

STUDENT HELP

▶ **Extra Practice**
to help you master skills is on p. 948.

LISTING RATIONAL ZEROS List the possible rational zeros of f using the rational zero theorem.

15. $f(x) = x^4 + 2x^2 - 24$

16. $f(x) = 2x^3 + 5x^2 - 6x - 1$

17. $f(x) = 2x^5 + x^2 + 16$

18. $f(x) = 2x^3 + 9x^2 - 53x - 60$

19. $f(x) = 6x^4 - 3x^3 + x + 10$

20. $f(x) = 4x^3 + 5x^2 - 3$

21. $f(x) = 8x^2 - 12x - 3$

22. $f(x) = 3x^4 + 2x^3 - x + 15$

USING SYNTHETIC DIVISION Use synthetic division to decide which of the following are zeros of the function: 1, −1, 2, −2.

23. $f(x) = x^3 + 7x^2 - 4x - 28$

24. $f(x) = x^3 + 5x^2 + 2x - 8$

25. $f(x) = x^4 + 3x^3 - 7x^2 - 27x - 18$

26. $f(x) = 2x^4 - 9x^3 + 8x^2 + 9x - 10$

STUDENT HELP

▶ **HOMEWORK HELP**
Example 1: Exs. 15–32
Example 2: Exs. 33–58
Example 3: Exs. 59–64

27. $f(x) = x^4 + 3x^3 + 3x^2 - 3x - 4$

28. $f(x) = 3x^4 + 3x^3 + 2x^2 + 5x - 10$

29. $f(x) = x^3 - 3x^2 + 4x - 12$

30. $f(x) = x^3 + x^2 - 11x + 10$

31. $f(x) = x^6 - 2x^4 - 11x^2 + 12$

32. $f(x) = x^5 - x^4 - 2x^3 - x^2 + x + 2$

FINDING REAL ZEROS Find all the real zeros of the function.

33. $f(x) = x^3 - 8x^2 - 23x + 30$

34. $f(x) = x^3 + 2x^2 - 11x - 12$

35. $f(x) = x^3 - 7x^2 + 2x + 40$

36. $f(x) = x^3 + x^2 - 2x - 2$

37. $f(x) = x^3 + 72 - 5x^2 - 18x$

38. $f(x) = x^3 + 9x^2 - 4x - 36$

39. $f(x) = x^4 - 5x^3 + 7x^2 + 3x - 10$

40. $f(x) = x^4 + x^3 + x^2 - 9x - 10$

41. $f(x) = x^4 + x^3 - 11x^2 - 9x + 18$

42. $f(x) = x^4 - 3x^3 + 6x^2 - 2x - 12$

43. $f(x) = x^5 + x^4 - 9x^3 - 5x^2 - 36$

44. $f(x) = x^5 - x^4 - 7x^3 + 11x^2 - 8x + 12$

ELIMINATING POSSIBLE ZEROS Use the graph to shorten the list of possible rational zeros. Then find all the real zeros of the function.

45. $f(x) = 4x^3 - 12x^2 - x + 15$

46. $f(x) = -3x^3 + 20x^2 - 36x + 16$

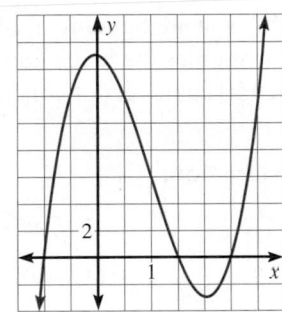

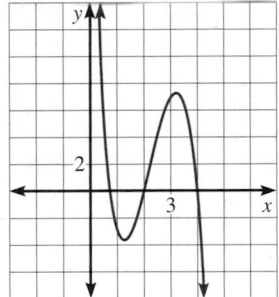

FINDING REAL ZEROS Find all the real zeros of the function.

47. $f(x) = 2x^3 + 4x^2 - 2x - 4$

48. $f(x) = 2x^3 - 5x^2 - 14x + 8$

49. $f(x) = 2x^3 - 5x^2 - x + 6$

50. $f(x) = 2x^3 + x^2 - 50x - 25$

51. $f(x) = 2x^3 - x^2 - 32x + 16$

52. $f(x) = 3x^3 + 12x^2 + 3x - 18$

53. $f(x) = 2x^4 + 3x^3 - 3x^2 + 3x - 5$

54. $f(x) = 3x^4 + 8x^3 + 14x^2 - 25$

55. $f(x) = 2x^4 + x^3 - x^2 - x - 1$

56. $f(x) = 3x^4 + 11x^3 + 11x^2 + x - 2$

57. $f(x) = 2x^5 + x^4 - 32x - 16$

58. $f(x) = 3x^5 + x^4 - 243x - 81$

59. 🌐 **HEALTH PRODUCT SALES** From 1990 to 1994, the mail order sales of health products in the United States can be modeled by

$$S = 10t^3 + 115t^2 + 25t + 2505$$

where S is the sales (in millions of dollars) and t is the number of years since 1990. In what year were about $3885 million of health products sold? (*Hint:* First substitute 3885 for S, then divide both sides by 5.)

60. 🌐 **MONUMENTS** You are designing a monument and a base as shown at the right. You will use 90 cubic feet of concrete for both pieces. Find the value of x.

61. 🌐 **MOLTEN GLASS** At a factory, molten glass is poured into molds to make paperweights. Each mold is a rectangular prism whose height is 3 inches greater than the length of each side of the square base. A machine pours 20 cubic inches of liquid glass into each mold. What are the dimensions of the mold?

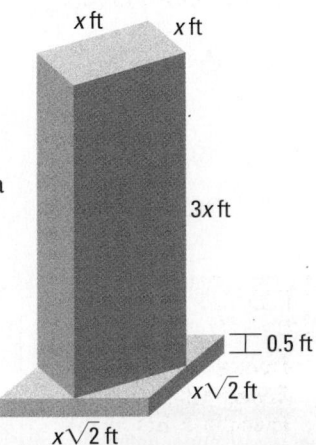

Ex. 60

62. 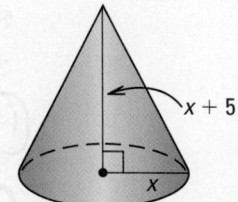 **SAND CASTLES** You are designing a kit for making sand castles. You want one of the molds to be a cone that will hold 48π cubic inches of sand. What should the dimensions of the cone be if you want the height to be 5 inches more than the radius of the base?

63. 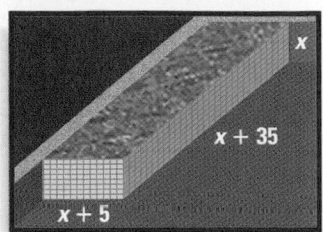 **SWIMMING POOLS** You are designing an in-ground lap swimming pool with a volume of 2000 cubic feet. The width of the pool should be 5 feet more than the depth, and the length should be 35 feet more than the depth. What should the dimensions of the pool be?

SAND SCULPTURE The tallest sand sculptures built were over 20 feet tall and each consisted of hundreds of tons of sand.

64.  **WHEELCHAIR RAMPS** You are building a solid concrete wheelchair ramp. The width of the ramp is three times the height, and the length is 5 feet more than 10 times the height. If 150 cubic feet of concrete is used, what are the dimensions of the ramp?

Test Preparation

QUANTITATIVE COMPARISON In Exercises 65 and 66, choose the statement that is true about the given quantities.

   Ⓐ The quantity in column A is greater.

   Ⓑ The quantity in column B is greater.

   Ⓒ The two quantities are equal.

   Ⓓ The relationship cannot be determined from the given information.

	Column A	Column B
65.	The number of possible rational zeros of $f(x) = x^4 - 3x^2 + 5x + 12$	The number of possible rational zeros of $f(x) = x^2 - 13x + 20$
66.	The greatest real zero of $f(x) = x^3 + 2x^2 - 5x - 6$	The greatest real zero of $f(x) = x^4 + 3x^3 - 2x^2 - 6x + 4$

★ **Challenge**

Find the real zeros of the function. Then match each function with its graph.

67. $f(x) = x^3 + 2x^2 - x - 2$ **68.** $g(x) = x^3 - 3x + 2$ **69.** $h(x) = x^3 - x^2 + 2$

A.

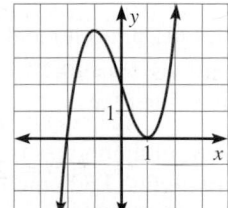

B.

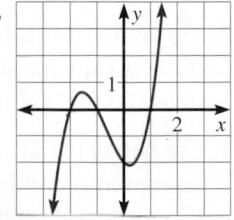

C.

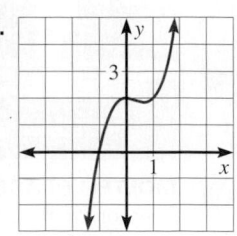

70. **CRITICAL THINKING** Is it possible for a cubic function to have more than three real zeros? Is it possible for a cubic function to have no real zeros? Explain.

MIXED REVIEW

SOLVING QUADRATIC EQUATIONS Solve the equation. (Review 5.2 for 6.7)

71. $x^2 - 6x + 9 = 0$

72. $x^2 + 12 = 10x - 13$

73. $x - 1 = x^2 - x$

74. $x^2 + 18 = 12x - x^2$

75. $2x^2 - 20x = x^2 - 100$

76. $x^2 - 12x + 49 = 6x - 32$

WRITING QUADRATIC FUNCTIONS Write a quadratic function in intercept form whose graph has the given x-intercepts and passes through the given point. (Review 5.8 for 6.7)

77. x-intercepts: $-3, 3$
point: $(0, 5)$

78. x-intercepts: $-5, 1$
point: $(-2, -6)$

79. x-intercepts: $-1, 5$
point: $(0, 10)$

80. x-intercepts: $12, 7$
point: $(-11, 7)$

81. x-intercepts: $-12, -6$
point: $(9, -5)$

82. x-intercepts: $2, 8$
point: $(3, -4)$

83. x-intercepts: $4, 10$
point: $(7, 3)$

84. x-intercepts: $-6, 0$
point: $(2, 16)$

85. x-intercepts: $-9, -1$
point: $(1, 20)$

86. 🌐 **PICTURE FRAMES** You have a picture that you want to frame, but first you have to put a mat around it. The picture is 12 inches by 16 inches. The area of the mat is 204 square inches. If the mat extends beyond the picture the same amount in each direction, what will the final dimensions of the picture and mat be? (Review 5.2)

QUIZ 2

Self-Test for Lessons 6.4–6.6

Factor the polynomial. (Lesson 6.4)

1. $5x^3 + 135$

2. $6x^3 + 12x^2 + 12x + 24$

3. $4x^5 - 16x$

4. $3x^3 - x^2 - 15x + 5$

Find the real-number solutions of the equation. (Lesson 6.4)

5. $7x^4 = 252x^2$

6. $16x^6 = 54x^3$

7. $6x^5 - 18x^4 + 12x^3 = 36x^2$

8. $2x^3 + 5x^2 = 8x + 20$

Divide. Use synthetic division when possible. (Lesson 6.5)

9. $(x^2 + 7x - 44) \div (x - 4)$

10. $(3x^2 - 8x + 20) \div (3x + 2)$

11. $(4x^3 - 7x^2 - x + 10) \div (x^2 - 3)$

12. $(12x^4 + 5x^3 + 3x^2 - 5) \div (x + 1)$

13. $(x^4 + 2x^2 + 3x + 6) \div (x^3 - 3)$

14. $(5x^4 + 2x^3 - x - 5) \div (x + 5)$

Find all the real zeros of the function. (Lesson 6.6)

15. $f(x) = x^3 - 4x^2 - 7x + 28$

16. $f(x) = x^3 - 6x^2 + 21x - 26$

17. $f(x) = 2x^3 + 15x^2 + 22x - 15$

18. $f(x) = 2x^3 + 7x^2 - 28x + 12$

19. 🌐 **DESIGNING A PATIO** You are a landscape artist designing a patio. The square patio floor is to be made from 128 cubic feet of concrete. The thickness of the floor is 15.5 feet less than each side length of the patio. What are the dimensions of the patio floor? (Lesson 6.6)

Using the Fundamental Theorem of Algebra

What you should learn

GOAL 1 Use the fundamental theorem of algebra to determine the number of zeros of a polynomial function.

GOAL 2 Use technology to approximate the real zeros of a polynomial function, as applied in **Example 5**.

Why you should learn it

▼ To solve **real-life** problems, such as finding the American Indian, Aleut, and Eskimo population in **Ex. 59**.

GOAL 1 THE FUNDAMENTAL THEOREM OF ALGEBRA

The following important theorem, called the fundamental theorem of algebra, was first proved by the famous German mathematician Carl Friedrich Gauss (1777–1855).

THE FUNDAMENTAL THEOREM OF ALGEBRA

If $f(x)$ is a polynomial of degree n where $n > 0$, then the equation $f(x) = 0$ has at least one root in the set of complex numbers.

In the following activity you will investigate how the number of solutions of $f(x) = 0$ is related to the degree of the polynomial $f(x)$.

▶ ACTIVITY
Developing Concepts
Investigating the Number of Solutions

1 Solve each polynomial equation. State how many solutions the equation has, and classify each as rational, irrational, or imaginary.

a. $2x - 1 = 0$ **b.** $x^2 - 2 = 0$ **c.** $x^3 - 1 = 0$

Make a conjecture about the relationship between the degree of a polynomial $f(x)$ and the number of solutions of $f(x) = 0$.

2 Solve the equation $x^3 + x^2 - x - 1 = 0$. How many different solutions are there? How can you reconcile this number with your conjecture?

The equation $x^3 - 6x^2 - 15x + 100 = 0$, which can be written as $(x + 4)(x - 5)^2 = 0$, has only two distinct solutions: -4 and 5. Because the factor $x - 5$ appears twice, however, you can count the solution 5 twice. So, with 5 counted as a **repeated solution,** this *third*-degree equation can be said to have *three* solutions: -4, 5, and 5.

In general, when all real and imaginary solutions are counted (with all repeated solutions counted individually), an nth-degree polynomial equation has *exactly n* solutions. Similarly, any nth-degree polynomial function has exactly n zeros.

EXAMPLE 1 *Finding the Number of Solutions or Zeros*

a. The equation $x^3 + 3x^2 + 16x + 48 = 0$ has three solutions: -3, $4i$, and $-4i$.

b. The function $f(x) = x^4 + 6x^3 + 12x^2 + 8x$ has four zeros: -2, -2, -2, and 0.

EXAMPLE 2   *Finding the Zeros of a Polynomial Function*

Find all the zeros of $f(x) = x^5 - 2x^4 + 8x^2 - 13x + 6$.

SOLUTION

The possible rational zeros are ± 1, ± 2, ± 3, and ± 6. Using synthetic division, you can determine that 1 is a repeated zero and that -2 is also a zero. You can write the function in factored form as follows:

$$f(x) = (x - 1)(x - 1)(x + 2)(x^2 - 2x + 3)$$

Complete the factorization, using the quadratic formula to factor the trinomial.

$$f(x) = (x - 1)(x - 1)(x + 2)[x - (1 + i\sqrt{2})][x - (1 - i\sqrt{2})]$$

▶ This factorization gives the following five zeros:

$$1, 1, -2, 1 + i\sqrt{2}, \text{ and } 1 - i\sqrt{2}$$

The graph of f is shown at the right. Note that only the *real* zeros appear as x-intercepts. Also note that the graph only *touches* the x-axis at the repeated zero $x = 1$, but *crosses* the x-axis at the zero $x = -2$.

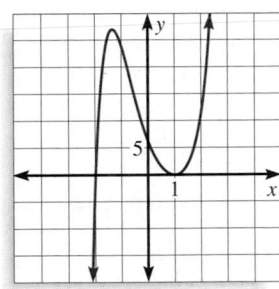

· · · · · · · · · ·

The graph in Example 2 illustrates the behavior of the graph of a polynomial function near its zeros. When a factor $x - k$ is raised to an odd power, the graph crosses the x-axis at $x = k$. When a factor $x - k$ is raised to an even power, the graph is tangent to the x-axis at $x = k$.

In Example 2 the zeros $\mathbf{1 + i\sqrt{2}}$ and $\mathbf{1 - i\sqrt{2}}$ are complex conjugates. The complex zeros of a polynomial function with *real* coefficients always occur in complex conjugate pairs. That is, if $a + bi$ is a zero, then $a - bi$ must also be a zero.

EXAMPLE 3   *Using Zeros to Write Polynomial Functions*

Write a polynomial function f of least degree that has real coefficients, a leading coefficient of 1, and 2 and $1 + i$ as zeros.

SOLUTION

Because the coefficients are real and $1 + i$ is a zero, $1 - i$ must also be a zero. Use the three zeros and the factor theorem to write $f(x)$ as a product of three factors.

$f(x) = (x - 2)[x - (1 + i)][x - (1 - i)]$	**Write $f(x)$ in factored form.**
$= (x - 2)[(x - 1) - i][(x - 1) + i]$	**Regroup terms.**
$= (x - 2)\big[(x - 1)^2 - i^2\big]$	**Multiply.**
$= (x - 2)[x^2 - 2x + 1 - (-1)]$	**Expand power and use $i^2 = -1$.**
$= (x - 2)(x^2 - 2x + 2)$	**Simplify.**
$= x^3 - 2x^2 + 2x - 2x^2 + 4x - 4$	**Multiply.**
$= x^3 - 4x^2 + 6x - 4$	**Combine like terms.**

✔**CHECK**   You can check this result by evaluating $f(x)$ at each of its three zeros.

The rational zero theorem gives you a way to find the rational zeros of a polynomial function with integer coefficients. To find the *real* zeros of *any* polynomial function, you may need to use technology.

EXAMPLE 4 *Approximating Real Zeros*

Approximate the real zeros of $f(x) = x^4 - 2x^3 - x^2 - 2x - 2$.

SOLUTION

There are several ways to use a graphing calculator to approximate the real zeros of a function. One way is to use the *Zero* (or *Root*) feature as shown below.

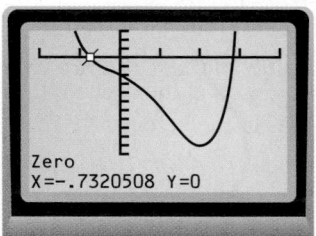
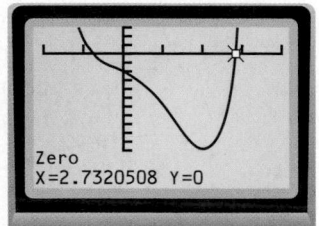

▶ From these screens, you can see that the real zeros are about −0.73 and 2.73.

Because the polynomial function has degree 4, you know that there must be two other zeros. These may be repeats of the real zeros, or they may be imaginary zeros. In this particular case, the two other zeros are imaginary: $x = \pm i$.

FOCUS ON APPLICATIONS

HARVARD STEP TEST When taking the Harvard Step Test, a person steps up and down a 20 inch platform for 5 minutes. The person's score is determined by his or her heart rate in the first few minutes after stopping.

EXAMPLE 5 *Approximating Real Zeros of a Real-Life Function*

PHYSIOLOGY For one group of people it was found that a person's score S on the Harvard Step Test was related to his or her amount of hemoglobin x (in grams per 100 milliliters of blood) by the following model:

$$S = -0.015x^3 + 0.6x^2 - 2.4x + 19$$

The normal range of hemoglobin is 12–18 grams per 100 milliliters of blood. Approximate the amount of hemoglobin for a person who scored 75.

SOLUTION

You can solve the equation

$$75 = -0.015x^3 + 0.6x^2 - 2.4x + 19$$

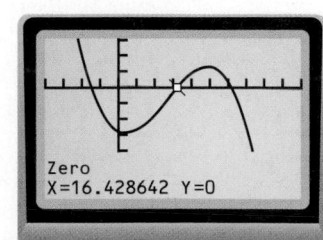

by rewriting it as $0 = -0.015x^3 + 0.6x^2 - 2.4x - 56$ and then using a graphing calculator to approximate the real zeros of $f(x) = -0.015x^3 + 0.6x^2 - 2.4x - 56$. From the graph you can see that there are three real zeros: $x \approx -7.3$, $x \approx 16.4$, and $x \approx 30.9$.

▶ The person's hemoglobin is probably about 16.4 grams per 100 milliliters of blood, since this is the only zero within the normal range.

GUIDED PRACTICE

Vocabulary Check ✓
Concept Check ✓

1. State the fundamental theorem of algebra.

2. Two zeros of $f(x) = x^3 - 6x^2 - 16x + 96$ are 4 and -4. Explain why the third zero must also be a real number.

3. The graph of $f(x) = x^3 - x^2 - 8x + 12$ is shown at the right. How many real zeros does the function have? How many imaginary zeros does the function have? Explain your reasoning.

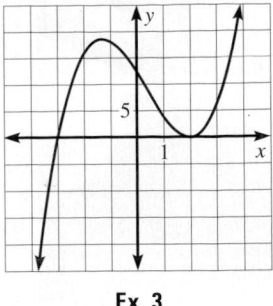

Ex. 3

Skill Check ✓

Find all the zeros of the polynomial function.

4. $f(x) = x^3 - x^2 - 2x$

5. $f(x) = x^4 + x^2 - 12$

6. $f(x) = x^3 + 5x^2 - 9x - 45$

7. $f(x) = x^4 - x^3 + 2x^2 - 4x - 8$

Write a polynomial function of least degree that has real coefficients, the given zeros, and a leading coefficient of 1.

8. $3, 0, -2$

9. $1, 1, i, -i$

10. $5, 2 + 3i$

11. $1, -1, 2, -2, 3$

12. $3, -2, -1 + i$

13. $4i, 4i$

14. 🌐 **GROCERY STORE REVENUE** For the 25 years that a grocery store has been open, its annual revenue R (in millions of dollars) can be modeled by

$$R = \frac{1}{10,000}(-t^4 + 12t^3 - 77t^2 + 600t + 13,650)$$

where t is the number of years the store has been open. In what year(s) was the revenue $1.5 million?

PRACTICE AND APPLICATIONS

STUDENT HELP

▶ **Extra Practice**
to help you master
skills is on p. 948.

CHECKING ZEROS Decide whether the given x-value is a zero of the function.

15. $f(x) = x^3 - x^2 + 4x - 4, x = 1$

16. $f(x) = x^3 + 3x^2 - 5x + 8, x = 4$

17. $f(x) = x^4 - x^2 - 3x + 3, x = 0$

18. $f(x) = x^3 + 5x^2 + x + 5, x = -5$

19. $f(x) = x^3 - 4x^2 + 16x - 64, x = 4i$

20. $f(x) = x^3 - 3x^2 + x - 3, x = -i$

FINDING ZEROS Find all the zeros of the polynomial function.

STUDENT HELP

▶ **HOMEWORK HELP**
Example 1: Exs. 21–54
Example 2: Exs. 21–34
Example 3: Exs. 35–46
Example 4: Exs. 47–54
Example 5: Exs. 55–59

21. $f(x) = x^4 + 5x^3 + 5x^2 - 5x - 6$

22. $f(x) = x^4 + 4x^3 - 6x^2 - 36x - 27$

23. $f(x) = x^3 - 4x^2 + 3x$

24. $f(x) = x^3 + 5x^2 - 4x - 20$

25. $f(x) = x^4 + 7x^3 - x^2 - 67x - 60$

26. $f(x) = x^4 - 5x^2 - 36$

27. $f(x) = x^3 - x^2 + 49x - 49$

28. $f(x) = x^3 - x^2 + 25x - 25$

29. $f(x) = x^4 + 6x^3 + 14x^2 + 54x + 45$

30. $f(x) = x^3 + 3x^2 + 25x + 75$

31. $f(x) = x^4 - x^3 - 5x^2 - x - 6$

32. $f(x) = x^4 + x^3 + 2x^2 + 4x - 8$

33. $f(x) = 2x^4 - 7x^3 - 27x^2 + 63x + 81$

34. $f(x) = 2x^4 - x^3 - 42x^2 + 16x + 160$

UNITED STATES
EXPORTS The
United States exports more
than any other country in
the world. It also imports
more than any other
country.

WRITING POLYNOMIAL FUNCTIONS Write a polynomial function of least degree that has real coefficients, the given zeros, and a leading coefficient of 1.

35. 2, 1, 4

36. 1, −4, 5

37. −6, 3, 5

38. −5, 2, −2

39. −2, −4, −7

40. 8, −i, i

41. 3i, −3i, 5

42. 2, −2, −6i

43. i, −3i, 3i

44. 3 − i, 5i

45. 4, 4, 2 + i

46. −2, −2, 3, −4i

FINDING ZEROS Use a graphing calculator to graph the polynomial function. Then use the *Zero* (or *Root*) feature of the calculator to find the real zeros of the function.

47. $f(x) = x^3 - x^2 - 5x + 3$

48. $f(x) = 2x^3 - x^2 - 3x - 1$

49. $f(x) = x^3 - 2x^2 + x + 1$

50. $f(x) = x^4 - 2x - 1$

51. $f(x) = x^4 - x^3 - 4x^2 - 3x - 2$

52. $f(x) = x^4 - x^3 - 3x^2 - x + 1$

53. $f(x) = x^4 + 3x^2 - 2$

54. $f(x) = x^4 - x^3 - 20x^2 + 10x + 27$

GRAPHING MODELS In Exercises 55–59, you may find it helpful to graph the model on a graphing calculator.

55. UNITED STATES EXPORTS For 1980 through 1996, the total exports E (in billions of dollars) of the United States can be modeled by

$$E = -0.131t^3 + 5.033t^2 - 23.2t + 233$$

where t is the number of years since 1980. In what year were the total exports about $312.76 billion? ▶ Source: U.S. Bureau of the Census

56. EDUCATION DONATIONS For 1983 through 1995, the amount of private donations D (in millions of dollars) allocated to education can be modeled by

$$D = 1.78t^3 - 6.02t^2 + 752t + 6701$$

where t is the number of years since 1983. In what year was $14.3 billion of private donations allocated to education? ▶ Source: AAFRC Trust for Philanthropy

57. SPORTS EQUIPMENT For 1987 through 1996, the sales S (in millions of dollars) of gym shoes and sneakers can be modeled by

$$S = -0.982t^5 + 24.6t^4 - 211t^3 + 661t^2 - 318t + 1520$$

where t is the number of years since 1987. Were there any years in which sales were about $2 billion? Explain. ▶ Source: National Sporting Goods Association

58. TELEVISION For 1990 through 2000, the actual and projected amount spent on television per person per year in the United States can be modeled by

$$S = -0.213t^3 + 3.96t^2 + 10.2t + 366$$

where S is the amount spent (in dollars) and t is the number of years since 1990. During which year was $455 spent per person on television?
▶ Source: Veronis, Suhler & Associates, Inc.

59. POPULATION For 1890 through 1990, the American Indian, Eskimo, and Aleut population P (in thousands) can be modeled by the function

$$P = 0.00496t^3 - 0.432t^2 + 11.3t + 212$$

where t is the number of years since 1890. In what year did the population reach 722,000? **DATA UPDATE** of *Statistical Abstract of the United States* data at www.mcdougallittell.com

60. MULTI-STEP PROBLEM Mary plans to save $1000 each summer to buy a used car at the end of the fourth summer. At the end of each summer, she will deposit the $1000 she earned from her summer job into her bank account. The table shows the value of her deposits over the four year period. In the table, g is the growth factor $1 + r$ where r is the annual interest rate expressed as a decimal.

	End of 1st summer	End of 2nd summer	End of 3rd summer	End of 4th summer
Value of 1st deposit	1000	$1000g$	$1000g^2$	$1000g^3$
Value of 2nd deposit	—	1000	?	?
Value of 3rd deposit	—	—	1000	?
Value of 4th deposit	—	—	—	1000

a. Copy and complete the table.

b. Write a polynomial function of g that represents the value of Mary's account at the end of the fourth summer.

c. *Writing* Suppose Mary wants to buy a car that costs about $4300. What growth factor does she need to obtain this amount? What annual interest rate does she need? Explain how you found your answers.

★ **Challenge**

61. a. Copy and complete the table.

Function	Zeros	Sum of zeros	Product of zeros
$f(x) = x^2 - 5x + 6$	?	?	?
$f(x) = x^3 - 7x + 6$	?	?	?
$f(x) = x^4 + 2x^3 + x^2 + 8x - 12$	?	?	?
$f(x) = x^5 - 3x^4 - 9x^3 + 25x^2 - 6x$	?	?	?

b. Use your completed table to make a conjecture relating the sum of the zeros of a polynomial function with the coefficients of the polynomial function.

c. Use your completed table to make a conjecture relating the product of the zeros of a polynomial function with the coefficients of the polynomial function.

EXTRA CHALLENGE
www.mcdougallittell.com

62. Show that the sum of a pair of complex conjugates is a real number.

63. Show that the product of a pair of complex conjugates is a real number.

MIXED REVIEW

GRAPHING WITH INTERCEPT FORM Graph the quadratic function. Label the vertex, axis of symmetry, and *x*-intercepts. (Review 5.1 for 6.8)

64. $y = -3(x - 2)(x + 2)$

65. $y = 2(x - 1)(x - 5)$

66. $y = 2(x + 4)(x - 3)$

67. $y = -(x + 1)(x - 5)$

GRAPHING POLYNOMIALS Graph the polynomial function. (Review 6.2 for 6.8)

68. $f(x) = -2x^4$

69. $f(x) = -x^3 - 4$

70. $f(x) = x^3 + 4x - 3$

71. $f(x) = x^4 - 3x^3 + x + 2$

▶ ACTIVITY 6.7
Using Technology

Solving Polynomial Equations

In Lesson 6.4 you learned to solve polynomial equations by factoring. When factoring is not possible, you can use a graphing calculator instead.

▶ EXAMPLE

Use a graphing calculator to find the real solutions of $x^3 + 4x^2 - 2x + 5 = 19$.

▶ SOLUTION

❶ To solve the equation graphically, graph each side of the equation as follows.

```
Y1◼X^3+4X2-2X+5
Y2◼19
Y3=
Y4=
Y5=
Y6=
Y7=
```

❷ When the equations are graphed in the standard viewing window, you see most of the graph of y_1, but none of the graph of y_2.

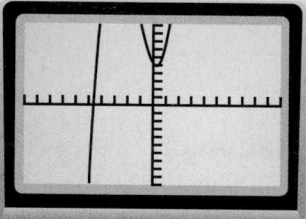

❸ You know that $y_2 = 19$ is a horizontal line. Change the viewing window so that $-10 \le x \le 10$ and $-2 \le y \le 22$.

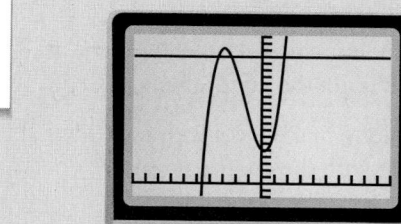

❹ The graphs of y_1 and y_2 intersect at three points. Use the *Intersect* feature to find the x-coordinates of these points.

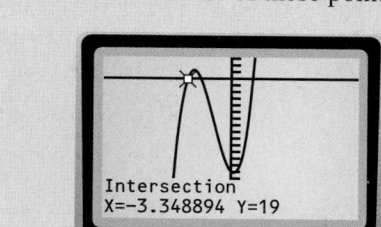

```
Intersection
X=-3.348894 Y=19
```

▶ The solutions are $x \approx -3.35$, $x \approx -2.40$, and $x \approx 1.74$.

▶ EXERCISES

Use a graphing calculator to find the real solutions of the equation.

1. $\frac{1}{2}x^3 - 3x^2 + x + 6 = 4$

2. $2x^3 - 8x^2 + 5x + 14 = 7$

3. $x^3 - 5x^2 + x + 3 = 8$

4. $0.3x^3 - 5x^2 + 8x + 15 = 13$

5. $x^4 - 6x^2 + 5 = 2$

6. $0.2x^4 - 3x^3 - 12x^2 + 8x + 22 = 13$

7. $17x^5 - 24x^3 + x^2 + 2x = 4$

8. $-1.25x^5 + 3.75x^2 + 0.4x - 6 = -4$

9. Look back at Example 5 on page 368. Use the method described above to solve the problem. Does your answer agree with the answer given in Example 5?

6.8 Analyzing Graphs of Polynomial Functions

What you should learn

GOAL 1 Analyze the graph of a polynomial function.

GOAL 2 Use the graph of a polynomial function to answer questions about **real-life** situations, such as maximizing the volume of a box in **Example 3**.

Why you should learn it

▼ To find the maximum and minimum values of **real-life** functions, such as the function modeling orange consumption in the United States in **Ex. 36**.

GOAL 1 ANALYZING POLYNOMIAL GRAPHS

In this chapter you have learned that zeros, factors, solutions, and x-intercepts are closely related concepts. The relationships are summarized below.

CONCEPT SUMMARY   **ZEROS, FACTORS, SOLUTIONS, AND INTERCEPTS**

Let $f(x) = a_n x^n + a_{n-1} x^{n-1} + \cdots + a_1 x + a_0$ be a polynomial function. The following statements are equivalent.

   ZERO: k is a zero of the polynomial function f.

   FACTOR: $x - k$ is a factor of the polynomial $f(x)$.

   SOLUTION: k is a solution of the polynomial equation $f(x) = 0$.

If k is a real number, then the following is also equivalent.

   X-INTERCEPT: k is an x-intercept of the graph of the polynomial function f.

EXAMPLE 1   *Using x-Intercepts to Graph a Polynomial Function*

Graph the function $f(x) = \frac{1}{4}(x + 2)(x - 1)^2$.

SOLUTION

Plot x-intercepts. Since $x + 2$ and $x - 1$ are factors of $f(x)$, -2 and 1 are the x-intercepts of the graph of f. Plot the points $(-2, 0)$ and $(1, 0)$.

Plot points between and beyond the x-intercepts.

x	-4	-3	-1	0	2	3
y	$-12\frac{1}{2}$	-4	1	$\frac{1}{2}$	1	5

Determine the end behavior of the graph. Because $f(x)$ has three linear factors of the form $x - k$ and a constant factor of $\frac{1}{4}$, it is a cubic function with a positive leading coefficient. Therefore, $f(x) \to -\infty$ as $x \to -\infty$ and $f(x) \to +\infty$ as $x \to +\infty$.

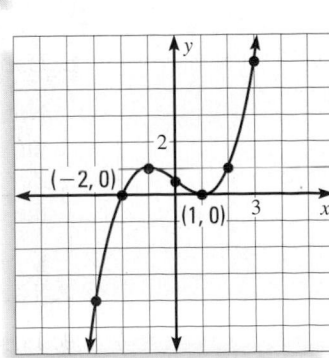

Draw the graph so that it passes through the points you plotted and has the appropriate end behavior.

TURNING POINTS Another important characteristic of graphs of polynomial functions is that they have *turning points* corresponding to local maximum and minimum values. The y-coordinate of a turning point is a **local maximum** of the function if the point is higher than all nearby points. The y-coordinate of a turning point is a **local minimum** if the point is lower than all nearby points.

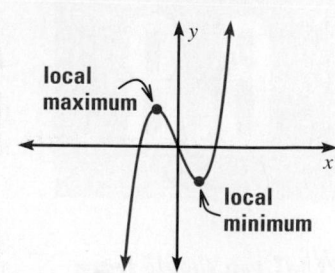

TURNING POINTS OF POLYNOMIAL FUNCTIONS

The graph of every polynomial function of degree n has *at most* $n - 1$ turning points. Moreover, if a polynomial function has n distinct real zeros, then its graph has *exactly* $n - 1$ turning points.

Recall that in Chapter 5 you used technology to find the maximums and minimums of quadratic functions. In Example 2 you will use technology to find turning points of higher-degree polynomial functions. If you take calculus, you will learn symbolic techniques for finding maximums and minimums.

EXAMPLE 2 *Finding Turning Points*

 Graph each function. Identify the x-intercepts and the points where the local maximums and local minimums occur.

a. $f(x) = x^3 - 3x^2 + 2$

b. $f(x) = x^4 - 4x^3 - x^2 + 12x - 2$

SOLUTION

a. Use a graphing calculator to graph the function.

Notice that the graph has three x-intercepts and two turning points. You can use the graphing calculator's *Zero, Maximum,* and *Minimum* features to approximate the coordinates of the points.

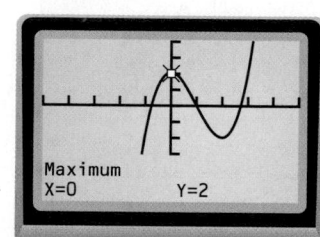

▶ The x-intercepts of the graph are $x \approx -0.73$, $x = 1$, and $x \approx 2.73$. The function has a local maximum at $(0, 2)$ and a local minimum at $(2, -2)$.

b. Use a graphing calculator to graph the function.

Notice that the graph has four x-intercepts and three turning points. You can use the graphing calculator's *Zero, Maximum,* and *Minimum* features to approximate the coordinates of the points.

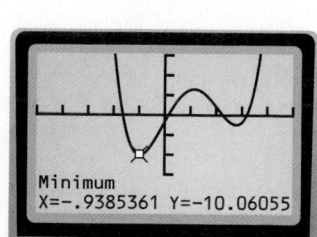

▶ The x-intercepts of the graph are $x \approx -1.63$, $x \approx 0.17$, $x \approx 2.25$, and $x \approx 3.20$. The function has local minimums at $(-0.94, -10.06)$ and $(2.79, -2.58)$, and it has a local maximum at $(1.14, 6.14)$.

In the following example, technology is used to maximize a polynomial function that models a real-life situation.

EXAMPLE 3 *Maximizing a Polynomial Model*

Manufacturing

You are designing an open box to be made of a piece of cardboard that is 10 inches by 15 inches. The box will be formed by making the square cuts shown in the diagram and folding up the sides. You want the box to have the greatest volume possible. How long should you make the cuts? What is the maximum volume? What will the dimensions of the finished box be?

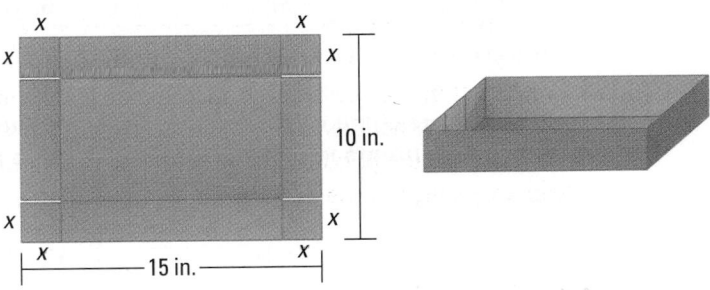

SOLUTION

PROBLEM SOLVING STRATEGY

VERBAL MODEL

| Volume | = | Width | · | Length | · | Height |

LABELS

Volume = V (cubic inches)

Width = $10 - 2x$ (inches)

Length = $15 - 2x$ (inches)

Height = x (inches)

ALGEBRAIC MODEL

$$V = (10 - 2x)(15 - 2x)x$$
$$= (4x^2 - 50x + 150)x$$
$$= 4x^3 - 50x^2 + 150x$$

To find the maximum volume, graph the volume function on a graphing calculator as shown at the right. When you use the *Maximum* feature, you consider only the interval $0 < x < 5$ because this describes the physical restrictions on the size of the flaps. From the graph, you can see that the maximum volume is about 132 and occurs when $x \approx 1.96$.

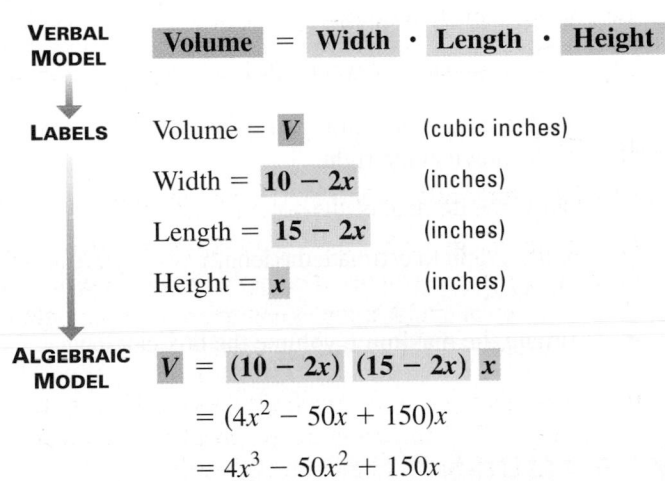

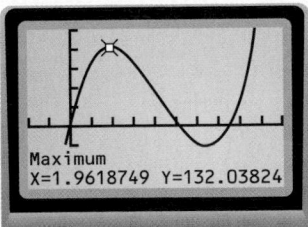

Maximum
X=1.9618749 Y=132.03824

▶ You should make the cuts approximately 2 inches long. The maximum volume is about 132 cubic inches. The dimensions of the box with this volume will be $x = 2$ inches by $10 - 2x = 6$ inches by $15 - 2x = 11$ inches.

Vocabulary Check ✓   **1.** Explain what a local maximum of a function is.

Concept Check ✓   **2.** Let f be a fourth-degree polynomial function with these zeros: $6, -2, 2i,$ and $-2i$.

     a. How many distinct linear factors does $f(x)$ have?

     b. How many distinct solutions does $f(x) = 0$ have?

     c. What are the x-intercepts of the graph of f?

   3. Let f be a fifth-degree polynomial function with five distinct real zeros. How many turning points does the graph of f have?

Skill Check ✓   **Graph the function.**

     4. $f(x) = (x - 1)(x + 3)^2$ **5.** $f(x) = (x - 1)(x + 1)(x - 3)$

     6. $f(x) = \frac{1}{8}(x + 1)(x - 1)(x - 3)$ **7.** $f(x) = \frac{1}{5}(x - 3)^2(x + 1)^2$

   Use a graphing calculator to graph the function. Identify the x-intercepts and the points where the local maximums and local minimums occur.

     8. $f(x) = 3x^4 - 5x^2 + 2x + 1$ **9.** $f(x) = x^3 - 3x^2 + x + 1$

     10. $f(x) = -2x^3 + x^2 + 4x$ **11.** $f(x) = x^5 + x^4 - 4x^3 - 3x^2 + 5x$

   12. 🌐 **MANUFACTURING** In Example 3, suppose you used a piece of cardboard that is 18 inches by 18 inches. Then the volume of the box would be given by this function:

$$V = 4x^3 - 72x^2 + 324x$$

Using a graphing calculator, you would obtain the graph shown at the right.

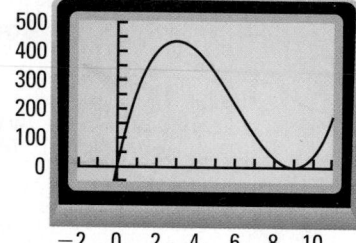

     a. What is the domain of the volume function? Explain.

     b. Use the graph to estimate the length of the cut that will maximize the volume of the box.

     c. Estimate the maximum volume the box can have.

PRACTICE AND APPLICATIONS

STUDENT HELP

▶**Extra Practice**
to help you master
skills is on p. 948.

GRAPHING POLYNOMIAL FUNCTIONS Graph the function.

   13. $f(x) = (x - 1)^3(x + 1)$ **14.** $f(x) = \frac{1}{10}(x + 3)(x - 1)(x - 4)$

   15. $f(x) = \frac{1}{8}(x + 4)(x + 2)(x - 3)$ **16.** $f(x) = 2(x + 2)^2(x + 4)^2$

   17. $f(x) = 5(x - 1)(x - 2)(x - 3)$ **18.** $f(x) = \frac{1}{12}(x + 4)(x - 3)(x + 1)^2$

   19. $f(x) = (x + 1)(x^2 - 3x + 3)$ **20.** $f(x) = (x + 2)(2x^2 - 2x + 1)$

   21. $f(x) = (x - 2)(x^2 + x + 1)$ **22.** $f(x) = (x - 3)(x^2 - x + 1)$

ANALYZING GRAPHS Estimate the coordinates of each turning point and state whether each corresponds to a local maximum or a local minimum. Then list all the real zeros and determine the least degree that the function can have.

23.
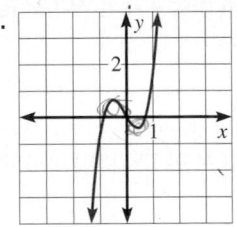

24.
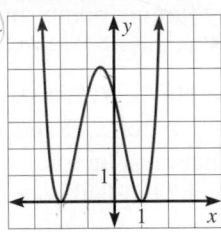

25.
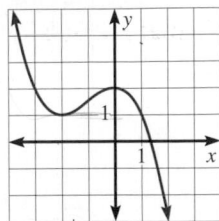

26.
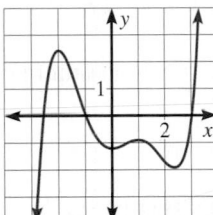

27.
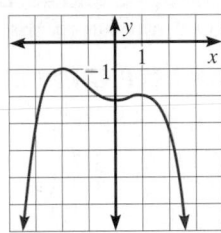

28.
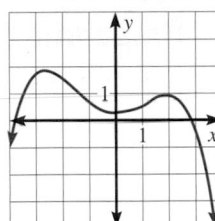

USING GRAPHS Use a graphing calculator to graph the polynomial function. Identify the *x*-intercepts and the points where the local maximums and local minimums occur.

29. $f(x) = 3x^3 - 9x + 1$

30. $f(x) = -\frac{1}{3}x^3 + x - \frac{2}{3}$

31. $f(x) = -\frac{1}{4}x^4 + 2x^2$

32. $f(x) = x^5 - 6x^3 + 9x$

33. $f(x) = x^5 - 5x^3 + 4x$

34. $f(x) = x^4 - 2x^3 - 3x^2 + 5x + 2$

35. 🌐 **SWIMMING** The polynomial function

$$S = -241t^7 + 1062t^6 - 1871t^5 + 1647t^4 - 737t^3 + 144t^2 - 2.432t$$

models the speed S (in meters per second) of a swimmer doing the breast stroke during one complete stroke, where t is the number of seconds since the start of the stroke. Graph the function. At what time is the swimmer going the fastest?

36. 🌐 **FOOD** The average amount of oranges (in pounds) eaten per person each year in the United States from 1991 to 1996 can be modeled by

$$f(x) = 0.298x^3 - 2.73x^2 + 7.05x + 8.45$$

where x is the number of years since 1991. Graph the function and identify any turning points on the interval $0 \le x \le 5$. What real-life meaning do these points have?

🌐 **QUONSET HUTS** In Exercises 37–39, use the following information.
A quonset hut is a dwelling shaped like half a cylinder. Suppose you have 600 square feet of material with which to build a quonset hut.

37. The formula for surface area is $S = \pi r^2 + \pi rl$ where r is the radius of the semicircle and l is the length of the hut. Substitute 600 for S and solve for l.

38. The formula for the volume of the hut is $V = \frac{1}{2}\pi r^2 l$. Write an equation for the volume V of the quonset hut as a polynomial function of r by substituting the expression for l from Exercise 37 into the volume formula.

39. Use the function you wrote in Exercise 38 to find the maximum volume of a quonset hut with a surface area of 600 square feet. What are the hut's dimensions?

FOCUS ON
APPLICATIONS

► **QUONSET HUTS** were invented during World War II. They were temporary structures that could be assembled quickly and easily. After the war they were sold as homes for about $1000 each.

🌐 **APPLICATION LINK**
www.mcdougallittell.com

40.  **CONSUMER ECONOMICS** The producer price index of butter from 1991 to 1997 can be modeled by $P = -0.233x^4 + 2.64x^3 - 6.59x^2 - 3.93x + 69.1$ where x is the number of years since 1991. Graph the function and identify any turning points on the interval $0 \le x \le 6$. What real-life meaning do these points have?

41. **CRITICAL THINKING** Sketch the graph of a polynomial function that has three turning points. Label each turning point as a local maximum or local minimum. What must be true about the degree of the polynomial function that has such a graph? Explain your reasoning.

In Exercises 42 and 43, use the graph of the polynomial function f shown at the right.

42. **MULTIPLE CHOICE** What is the local maximum of f on the interval $-2 \le x \le -1$?

   A $f(x) \approx 3.7$ **B** $f(x) \approx 1.4$

   C $f(x) \approx -1.4$ **D** $f(x) \approx -3.7$

43. **MULTIPLE CHOICE** What is the local maximum of f on the interval $-1 \le x \le 1$?

   A $f(x) \approx 3.7$ **B** $f(x) \approx 1.4$ **C** $f(x) \approx -1.4$ **D** $f(x) \approx -3.7$

★ Challenge

44. **GRAPHING OPPOSITES** Sketch the graph of $y = f(x)$ for this function:

$$f(x) = x^3 + 4x^2$$

Then sketch the graph of $y = -f(x)$. Explain how the graphs, the x-intercepts, the local maximums, and the local minimums are related. Finally, sketch the graph of $y = f(-x)$. Compare it with the others.

MIXED REVIEW

RELATING VARIABLES The variables x and y vary directly. Write an equation that relates the variables. **(Review 2.4)**

45. $x = 1, y = 7$ **46.** $x = -4, y = 6$ **47.** $x = 12, y = 3$

48. $x = 2, y = -5$ **49.** $x = -5, y = 3$ **50.** $x = -6, y = -15$

MATRIX PRODUCTS Let A and B be matrices with the given dimensions. State whether the product AB is defined. If so, give the dimensions of AB. **(Review 4.2)**

51. $A: 4 \times 3, B: 3 \times 1$ **52.** $A: 2 \times 4, B: 4 \times 5$

53. $A: 4 \times 3, B: 2 \times 4$ **54.** $A: 6 \times 6, B: 6 \times 5$

WRITING QUADRATIC FUNCTIONS Write a quadratic function whose graph passes through the given points. **(Review 5.8 for 6.9)**

55. vertex: $(1, 4)$; point: $(4, -5)$ **56.** vertex: $(-2, 6)$; point: $(0, 2)$

57. points: $(-5, 0), (5, 0), (7, 5)$ **58.** points: $(-2, 0), (4, 0), (1, -4)$

59.  **PLANT GROWTH** You have a kudzu vine in your back yard. On Monday, the vine is 30 inches long. The following Thursday, the vine is 60 inches long. What is the average rate of change in the length of the vine? **(Lesson 2.2)**

▶ ACTIVITY 6.9

Developing Concepts

Exploring Finite Differences

▶ **QUESTION** How are the finite differences for a polynomial function related to the function's degree?

GROUP ACTIVITY
Work with a partner.

MATERIALS
• Paper
• Pencil

▶ **EXPLORING THE CONCEPT**

The number of paths that lead, through a sequence of upward and rightward movements only, from the bottom left corner of a grid to the top right corner depends on the grid's dimensions.

For an $n \times 1$ grid, the number of paths is given by $f(n) = n + 1$.

For an $n \times 2$ grid, the number of paths is given by $g(n) = \frac{1}{2}(n + 1)(n + 2)$.

For an $n \times 3$ grid, the number of paths is given by $h(n) = \frac{1}{6}(n + 1)(n + 2)(n + 3)$.

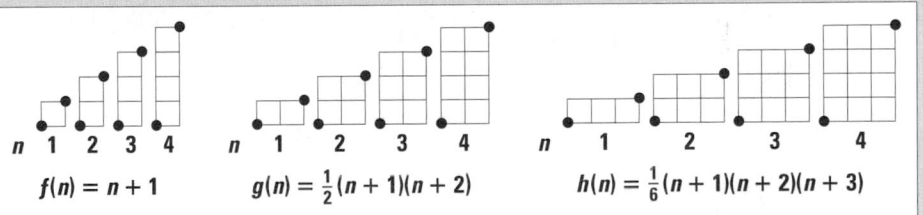

For each function given above, follow **Steps 1–4**. The steps for the first function f have been done for you.

❶ Evaluate the function when $n = 1, 2, 3, 4, 5,$ and 6.

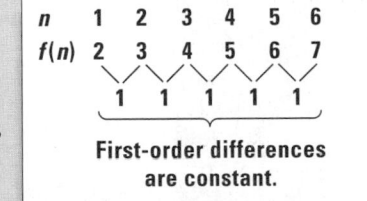

❷ For each pair of consecutive function values, find the difference of the values. These numbers are called *first-order differences*.

❸ Are the first-order differences constant? If so, stop here. Otherwise, find the differences in each pair of consecutive first-order differences. These numbers are called *second-order differences*.

❹ Are the second-order differences constant? If so, stop here. Otherwise, find the differences in each pair of consecutive second-order differences. These numbers are called *third-order differences*.

▶ **DRAWING CONCLUSIONS**

1. Repeat **Steps 1–4** for each function.

   a. $f(n) = 3n + 1$ **b.** $f(n) = n^2 + 2n - 3$ **c.** $f(n) = 2n^3 - n + 4$

2. For each function giving the number of paths through a grid and for each function in Exercise 1, state the degree of the function and the number of times differences were calculated before a row of constant, nonzero differences was obtained. What do you notice?

3. Which order differences do you think will be constant for the function $f(n) = n^4 + n$? Explain. Then find the differences to see if you are correct.

Modeling with Polynomial Functions

GOAL 1 USING FINITE DIFFERENCES

You know that two points determine a line and that three points determine a parabola. In Example 1 you will see that four points determine the graph of a cubic function.

EXAMPLE 1 *Writing a Cubic Function*

Write the cubic function whose graph is shown at the right.

SOLUTION

Use the three given x-intercepts to write the following:

$$f(x) = a(x + 3)(x - 2)(x - 5)$$

To find a, substitute the coordinates of the fourth point.

$$-15 = a(0 + 3)(0 - 2)(0 - 5), \text{ so } a = -\frac{1}{2}$$

▶ $f(x) = -\frac{1}{2}(x + 3)(x - 2)(x - 5)$

✓ **CHECK** Check the graph's end behavior. The degree of f is odd and $a < 0$, so $f(x) \to +\infty$ as $x \to -\infty$ and $f(x) \to -\infty$ as $x \to +\infty$.

. . . .

To decide whether y-values for equally-spaced x-values can be modeled by a polynomial function, you can use **finite differences**.

EXAMPLE 2 *Finding Finite Differences*

The first three triangular numbers are shown at the right.

A formula for the nth triangular number is $f(n) = \frac{1}{2}(n^2 + n)$.

Show that this function has constant second-order differences.

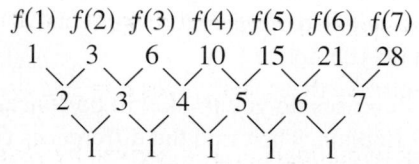

Triangular Numbers

• $f(1) = 1$

••
 • $f(2) = 3$

•
••
••• $f(3) = 6$

SOLUTION

Write the first several triangular numbers. Find the first-order differences by subtracting consecutive triangular numbers. Then find the second-order differences by subtracting consecutive first-order differences.

$$
\begin{array}{ccccccc}
f(1) & f(2) & f(3) & f(4) & f(5) & f(6) & f(7) \\
1 & 3 & 6 & 10 & 15 & 21 & 28 \\
& 2 & 3 & 4 & 5 & 6 & 7 \\
& & 1 & 1 & 1 & 1 & 1
\end{array}
$$

Function values for equally-spaced *n*-values

First-order differences

Second-order differences

In Example 2 notice that the function has degree *two* and that the *second*-order differences are constant. This illustrates the first property of finite differences.

PROPERTIES OF FINITE DIFFERENCES

1. If a polynomial function $f(x)$ has degree n, then the nth-order differences of function values for equally spaced x-values are nonzero and constant.

2. Conversely, if the nth-order differences of equally-spaced data are nonzero and constant, then the data can be represented by a polynomial function of degree n.

The following example illustrates the second property of finite differences.

EXAMPLE 3 *Modeling with Finite Differences*

STUDENT HELP

INTERNET
HOMEWORK HELP
Visit our Web site
www.mcdougallittell.com
for extra examples.

The first six triangular pyramidal numbers are shown below. Find a polynomial function that gives the nth triangular pyramidal number.

     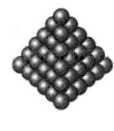 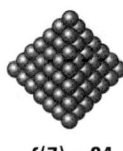

$f(1) = 1$ $f(2) = 4$ $f(3) = 10$ $f(4) = 20$ $f(5) = 35$ $f(6) = 56$ $f(7) = 84$

SOLUTION

Begin by finding the finite differences.

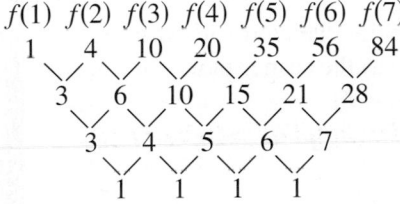

$f(1)$ $f(2)$ $f(3)$ $f(4)$ $f(5)$ $f(6)$ $f(7)$ $\quad$ 1 $\quad$ 4 $\quad$ 10 $\quad$ 20 $\quad$ 35 $\quad$ 56 $\quad$ 84	**Function values for equally-spaced n-values**
$\quad\quad$ 3 $\quad$ 6 $\quad$ 10 $\quad$ 15 $\quad$ 21 $\quad$ 28	**First-order differences**
$\quad\quad\quad$ 3 $\quad$ 4 $\quad$ 5 $\quad$ 6 $\quad$ 7	**Second-order differences**
$\quad\quad\quad\quad$ 1 $\quad$ 1 $\quad$ 1 $\quad$ 1	**Third-order differences**

Because the third-order differences are constant, you know that the numbers can be represented by a cubic function which has the form $f(n) = an^3 + bn^2 + cn + d$.

By substituting the first four triangular pyramidal numbers into the function, you can obtain a system of four linear equations in four variables.

$$a(1)^3 + b(1)^2 + c(1) + d = 1 \longrightarrow \quad a + \quad b + \quad c + d = 1$$

$$a(2)^3 + b(2)^2 + c(2) + d = 4 \longrightarrow \quad 8a + \quad 4b + 2c + d = 4$$

$$a(3)^3 + b(3)^2 + c(3) + d = 10 \longrightarrow 27a + \quad 9b + 3c + d = 10$$

$$a(4)^3 + b(4)^2 + c(4) + d = 20 \longrightarrow 64a + 16b + 4c + d = 20$$

Using a calculator to solve the system gives $a = \frac{1}{6}$, $b = \frac{1}{2}$, $c = \frac{1}{3}$, and $d = 0$.

▶ The nth triangular pyramidal number is given by $f(n) = \frac{1}{6}n^3 + \frac{1}{2}n^2 + \frac{1}{3}n$.

GOAL 2 **POLYNOMIAL MODELING WITH TECHNOLOGY**

In Examples 1 and 3 you found a cubic model that *exactly* fits a set of data points.
In many real-life situations, you cannot find a simple model to fit data points exactly.
Instead you can use the regression feature on a graphing calculator to find an *n*th-
degree polynomial model that best fits the data.

EXAMPLE 4 *Modeling with Cubic Regression*

BOATING The data in the table give the average speed y (in knots) of the *Trident*
motor yacht for several different engine speeds x (in hundreds of revolutions per
minute, or RPMs).

a. Find a polynomial model for the data.

b. Estimate the average speed of the *Trident* for an engine speed of 2400 RPMs.

c. What engine speed produces a boat speed of 14 knots?

Engine speed, x	9	11	13	15	17	19	21.5
Boat speed, y	6.43	7.61	8.82	9.86	10.88	12.36	15.24

SOLUTION

a. *Enter* the data in a graphing calculator and
make a scatter plot. From the scatter plot, it
appears that a cubic function will fit the data
better than a linear or quadratic function.

Use cubic regression to obtain a model.

▶ $y = 0.00475x^3 - 0.194x^2 + 3.13x - 9.53$

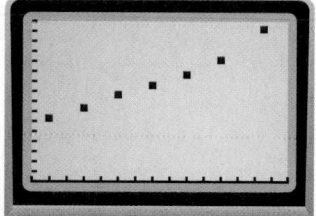

✓ **CHECK** By graphing the model in the same
viewing window as the scatter plot, you can
see that it is a good fit.

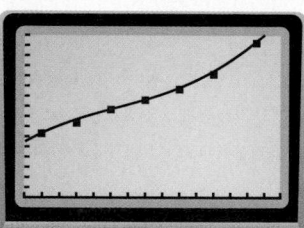

b. Substitute $x = 24$ into the model from part (a).

$$y = 0.00475(24)^3 - 0.194(24)^2 + 3.13(24) - 9.53$$

$$= 19.51$$

▶ The *Trident*'s speed for an engine speed
of 2400 RPMs is about 19.5 knots.

c. Graph the model and the equation $y = 14$ on
the same screen. Use the *Intersect* feature to
find the point where the graphs intersect.

▶ An engine speed of about 2050 RPMs
produces a boat speed of 14 knots.

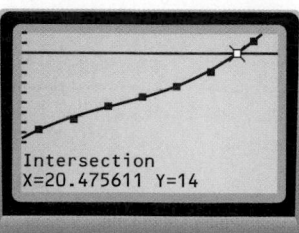

Intersection
X=20.475611 Y=14

GUIDED PRACTICE

Vocabulary Check ✓
Concept Check ✓

1. Describe what first-order differences and second-order differences are.

2. How many points do you need to determine a quartic function?

3. Why can't you use finite differences to find a model for the data in Example 4?

Skill Check ✓

4. Write the cubic function whose graph passes through $(3, 0)$, $(-1, 0)$, $(-2, 0)$, and $(1, 2)$.

Show that the nth-order finite differences for the given function of degree n are nonzero and constant.

5. $f(x) = 5x^2 - 2x + 1$

6. $f(x) = x^3 + x^2 - 1$

7. $f(x) = x^4 + 2x$

8. $f(x) = 2x^3 - 12x^2 - 5x + 3$

Use finite differences to determine the degree of the polynomial function that will fit the data.

9.

x	1	2	3	4	5	6
f(x)	−1	3	3	5	15	39

10.

x	1	2	3	4	5	6
f(x)	0	8	12	12	8	0

Find a polynomial function that fits the data.

11.

x	1	2	3	4	5	6
f(x)	6	15	22	21	6	−29

12.

x	1	2	3	4	5	6
f(x)	−1	−4	−3	8	35	84

13. **GEOMETRY** **CONNECTION** Find a polynomial function that gives the number of diagonals of a polygon with n sides.

Number of sides, n	3	4	5	6	7	8
Number of diagonals, d	0	2	5	9	14	20

PRACTICE AND APPLICATIONS

STUDENT HELP

► **Extra Practice**
to help you master
skills is on p. 949.

WRITING CUBIC FUNCTIONS Write the cubic function whose graph is shown.

14.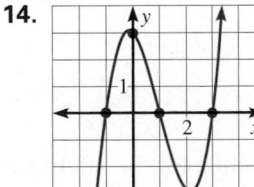

15.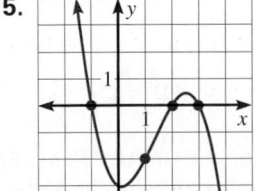

16.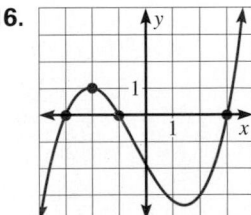

FINDING A CUBIC MODEL Write a cubic function whose graph passes through the given points.

17. $(-1, 0)$, $(-2, 0)$, $(0, 0)$, $(1, -3)$

18. $(3, 0)$, $(2, 0)$, $(-3, 0)$, $(1, -1)$

19. $(1, 0)$, $(3, 0)$, $(-2, 0)$, $(2, 1)$

20. $(-1, 0)$, $(-4, 0)$, $(4, 0)$, $(0, 3)$

21. $(3, 0)$, $(2, 0)$, $(-1, 0)$, $(1, 4)$

22. $(0, 0)$, $(-3, 0)$, $(5, 0)$, $(-2, 3)$

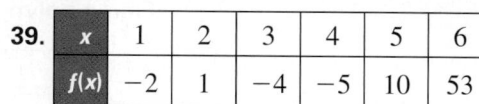
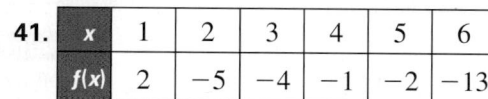

FINDING FINITE DIFFERENCES Show that the nth-order differences for the given function of degree n are nonzero and constant.

23. $f(x) = x^2 - 3x + 7$ 24. $f(x) = 2x^3 - 5x^2 - x$ 25. $f(x) = -x^3 + 3x^2 - 2x - 3$

26. $f(x) = x^4 - 3x^3$ 27. $f(x) = 2x^4 - 20x$ 28. $f(x) = -4x^2 + x + 6$

29. $f(x) = -x^4 + 5x^2$ 30. $f(x) = 3x^3 - 5x^2 - 2$ 31. $f(x) = -3x^2 + 4x + 2$

FINDING A MODEL Use finite differences and a system of equations to find a polynomial function that fits the data. You may want to use a calculator.

32.

x	1	2	3	4	5	6
$f(x)$	−4	0	10	26	48	76

33.

x	1	2	3	4	5	6
$f(x)$	17	28	33	32	25	12

34.

x	1	2	3	4	5	6
$f(x)$	−4	−6	−2	14	48	106

35.

x	1	2	3	4	5	6
$f(x)$	−2	−6	−6	4	30	78

36.

x	1	2	3	4	5	6
$f(x)$	−3	−8	−15	−21	−23	−18

37.

x	1	2	3	4	5	6
$f(x)$	2	20	58	122	218	352

38.

x	1	2	3	4	5	6
$f(x)$	−5	0	9	16	15	0

39.

x	1	2	3	4	5	6
$f(x)$	−2	1	−4	−5	10	53

40.

x	1	2	3	4	5	6
$f(x)$	20	−2	−4	2	4	−10

41.

x	1	2	3	4	5	6
$f(x)$	2	−5	−4	−1	−2	−13

42.

x	1	2	3	4	5	6
$f(x)$	26	−4	−2	2	2	16

43.

x	1	2	3	4	5	6
$f(x)$	0	6	2	6	12	−10

44. **PENTAGONAL NUMBERS** The dot patterns show pentagonal numbers. A formula for the nth pentagonal number is $f(n) = \frac{1}{2}n(3n - 1)$. Show that this function has constant second-order differences.

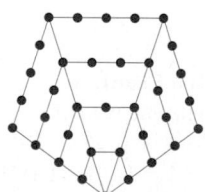

45. **HEXAGONAL NUMBERS** A formula for the nth hexagonal number is $f(n) = n(2n - 1)$. Show that this function has constant second-order differences.

46. **SQUARE PYRAMIDAL NUMBERS** The first six square pyramidal numbers are shown. Find a polynomial function that gives the nth square pyramidal number.

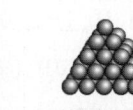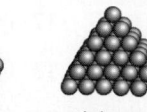

$f(1) = 1$ $f(2) = 5$ $f(3) = 14$ $f(4) = 30$ $f(5) = 55$ $f(6) = 91$ $f(7) = 140$

REAL LIFE **EILEEN COLLINS** was selected by NASA for the astronaut program in 1990. Since then she has become the first woman to pilot a spacecraft and the first woman to command a space shuttle.

FINDING MODELS In Exercises 47–49, use a graphing calculator to find a polynomial model for the data.

47. 🌐 **GIRL SCOUTS** The table shows the number of Girl Scouts (in thousands) from 1989 to 1996. Find a polynomial model for the data. Then estimate the number of Girl Scouts in 2000.

t	1989	1990	1991	1992	1993	1994	1995	1996
y	231	253.3	273.8	284.1	294.1	303.6	368.6	383.7

48. 🌐 **REAL ESTATE** The table shows the average price (in thousands of dollars) of a house in the Northeastern United States for 1987 to 1995. Find a polynomial model for the data. Then predict the average price of a house in the Northeast in 2000. 🔄 DATA UPDATE of *Statistical Abstract of the United States* data at www.mcdougallittell.com

x	1987	1988	1989	1990	1991	1992	1993	1994	1995
f(x)	140	149	159.6	159	155.9	169	162.9	169	180

49. 🌐 **SPACE EXPLORATION** The table shows the average speed y (in feet per second) of a space shuttle for different times t (in seconds) after launch. Find a polynomial model for the data. When the space shuttle reaches a speed of approximately 4400 feet per second, its booster rockets fall off. Use the model to determine how long after launch this happens.

t	10	20	30	40	50	60	70	80
y	202.4	463.4	748.2	979.3	1186.3	1421.3	1795.4	2283.5

Test Preparation

50. **MULTI-STEP PROBLEM** Your friend has a dog-walking service and your cousin has a lawn-care service. You want to start a small business of your own. You are trying to decide which of the two services you should choose. The profits for the first 6 months of the year are shown in the table.

Dog-walking service	Month, t	1	2	3	4	5	6
	Profit, P	3	5	22	54	101	163
Lawn-care service	Month, t	1	2	3	4	5	6
	Profit, P	3	21	41	68	107	163

a. Use finite differences to find a polynomial model for each business.

b. *Writing* You want to choose the business that will make the greater profit in December (when $t = 12$). Explain which business you should choose and why.

★ Challenge

51. a. Substitute the expressions x, $x + 1$, $x + 2$, ..., $x + 5$ for x in the function $f(x) = ax^3 + bx^2 + cx + d$ and show that third-order differences are constant.

b. The data below can be modeled by a cubic function. Set the variable expressions you found in part (a) equal to the first-, second-, and third-order differences for these values. Solve the equations to find the coefficients of the function that models the data. Check your work by substituting the original data values into the function.

x	1	2	3	4	5	6
f(x)	−1	1	−3	−7	−5	9

EXTRA CHALLENGE
➜ www.mcdougallittell.com

MIXED REVIEW

SOLVING QUADRATIC EQUATIONS Solve the equation. (Review 5.3 for 7.1)

52. $3x^2 = 6$ **53.** $16x^2 = 4$ **54.** $4x^2 - 5 = 9$

55. $6x^2 + 3 = 16$ **56.** $-x^2 + 9 = 2x^2 - 6$ **57.** $-x^2 + 2 = x^2 + 1$

SOLVING EQUATIONS Solve the equation by completing the square. (Review 5.5)

58. $x^2 + 12x + 27 = 0$ **59.** $x^2 + 6x - 24 = 0$ **60.** $x^2 - 3x - 18 = 0$

61. $2x^2 + 8x + 11 = 0$ **62.** $-x^2 + 14x + 15 = 0$ **63.** $3x^2 - 18x + 32 = 0$

SUM OR DIFFERENCE OF CUBES Factor the polynomial. (Review 6.4)

64. $8x^3 - 1$ **65.** $27x^3 + 8$ **66.** $216x^3 + 64$ **67.** $8x^3 - 125$

68. $3x^3 - 24$ **69.** $8x^3 + 216$ **70.** $27x^3 + 1000$ **71.** $3x^3 + 81$

QUIZ 3

Self-Test for Lessons 6.7–6.9

Find all the zeros of the polynomial function. (Lesson 6.7)

1. $f(x) = 2x^3 - x^2 - 22x - 15$ **2.** $f(x) = x^3 + 3x^2 + 3x + 2$

3. $f(x) = x^4 - 3x^3 - 2x^2 - 6x - 8$ **4.** $f(x) = 2x^4 - x^3 - 8x^2 + x + 6$

Write a polynomial of least degree that has real coefficients, the given zeros, and a leading coefficient of 1. (Lesson 6.7)

5. $-2, -2, 2$ **6.** $0, 1, -3$ **7.** $4, 2 + i, 2 - i$

8. $2, 5, -i$ **9.** $4, 2 - 3i$ **10.** $1 - i, 2 + 2i$

Graph the function. Estimate the local maximums and minimums. (Lesson 6.8)

11. $f(x) = -(x - 2)(x + 3)(x + 1)$ **12.** $f(x) = x(x - 1)(x + 1)(x + 2)$

13. $f(x) = 2(x - 2)(x - 3)(x - 4)$ **14.** $f(x) = (x + 1)(x + 3)^2$

Write a cubic function whose graph passes through the points. (Lesson 6.9)

15. $(-2, 0), (2, 0), (-4, 0), (-1, 3)$ **16.** $(-1, 0), (4, 0), (2, 0), (-3, 1)$

17. $(3, 0), (0, 0), (5, 0), (2, 6)$ **18.** $(1, 0), (-3, 0), (-5, 0), (-4, 10)$

Find a polynomial function that models the data. (Lesson 6.9)

19.

x	1	2	3	4	5	6
f(x)	−5	−6	−1	16	51	110

20.

x	1	2	3	4	5	6
f(x)	−1	−4	−3	8	35	84

21.  **SOCIAL SECURITY** The table gives the number of children (in thousands) receiving Social Security for each year from 1988 to 1995. Use a graphing calculator to find a polynomial model for the data. **(Lesson 6.9)**

Year	1988	1989	1990	1991	1992	1993	1994	1995
Number of children	3204	3165	3187	3268	3391	3527	3654	3734

Chapter Summary

WHAT did you learn?

Use properties of exponents to evaluate and simplify expressions. **(6.1)**

Evaluate polynomial functions using direct or synthetic substitution. **(6.2)**

Sketch and analyze graphs of polynomial functions. **(6.2, 6.8)**

Add, subtract, and multiply polynomials. **(6.3)**

Factor polynomial expressions. **(6.4)**

Solve polynomial equations. **(6.4)**

Divide polynomials using long division or synthetic division. **(6.5)**

Find zeros of polynomial functions. **(6.6, 6.7)**

Use finite differences and cubic regression to find polynomial models for data. **(6.9)**

Use polynomials to solve real-life problems. **(6.1–6.9)**

WHY did you learn it?

Use scientific notation to find the ratio of a state's park space to its total area. **(p. 328)**

Estimate the amount of prize money awarded at a tennis tournament. **(p. 335)**

Find maximum or minimum values of a function such as oranges consumed in the U.S. **(p. 377)**

Write a polynomial model for the power needed to move a bicycle at a certain speed. **(p. 342)**

Find the dimensions of a block discovered by archeologists. **(p. 347)**

Find the dimensions of a sculpture. **(p. 350)**

Write a function for the average annual amount of money spent per person at the movies. **(p. 358)**

Find dimensions for a candle-wax model of the Louvre pyramid. **(p. 361)**

Write and use a polynomial model for the speed of a space shuttle. **(p. 385)**

Find the maximum volume and dimensions of a box made from a piece of cardboard. **(p. 375)**

How does Chapter 6 fit into the BIGGER PICTURE of algebra?

Chapter 6 contains the fundamental theorem of algebra. Finding the solutions of a polynomial equation is the most classic problem in all of algebra. It is equivalent to finding the zeros of a polynomial function. Real-life situations have been modeled by polynomial functions for hundreds of years.

STUDY STRATEGY

How did you make and use a flow chart?

Here is a flow chart for finding all the zeros of a polynomial function, following the **Study Strategy** on page 322.

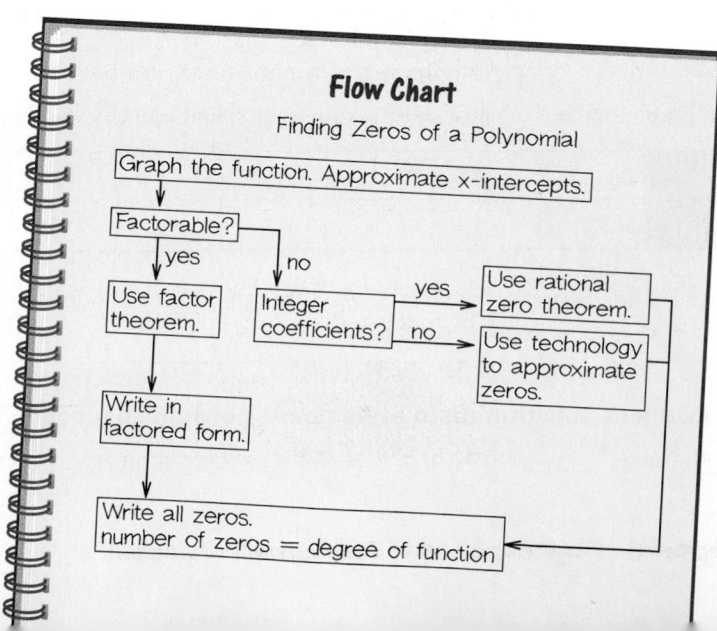

VOCABULARY

- scientific notation, p. 325
- polynomial function, p. 329
- leading coefficient, p. 329
- constant term, p. 329
- degree of a polynomial function, p. 329
- standard form of a polynomial function, p. 329

- synthetic substitution, p. 330
- end behavior, p. 331
- factor by grouping, p. 346
- quadratic form, p. 346
- polynomial long division, p. 352
- remainder theorem, p. 353
- synthetic division, p. 353

- factor theorem, p. 354
- rational zero theorem, p. 359
- fundamental theorem of algebra, p. 366
- repeated solution, p. 366
- local maximum, p. 374
- local minimum, p. 374
- finite differences, p. 380

6.1 USING PROPERTIES OF EXPONENTS

Examples on pp. 323–325

EXAMPLE You can use properties of exponents to evaluate numerical expressions and to simplify algebraic expressions.

$$\frac{(3x^2y)^5}{9x^{10}y^6} = \frac{3^5x^{2\cdot5}y^5}{9x^{10}y^6} = \frac{243}{9}x^{10-10}y^{5-6} = 27x^0y^{-1} = \frac{27}{y} \qquad \textbf{all positive exponents}$$

Simplify the expression. Tell which properties of exponents you used.

1. $\left(\frac{2}{3}\right)^2 \cdot \left(6xy^{-1}\right)^3$
2. $x^4\left(x^{-5}x^3\right)^2$
3. $\dfrac{-63xy^9}{18x^{-2}y^3}$
4. $\dfrac{5x^2}{y^{-2}} \cdot \dfrac{1}{25x^2y}$

6.2 EVALUATING AND GRAPHING POLYNOMIAL FUNCTIONS

Examples on pp. 329–332

EXAMPLES Use direct or synthetic substitution to evaluate a polynomial function.

Evaluate $f(x) = x^3 - 2x - 1$ when $x = 3$ (synthetic substitution):

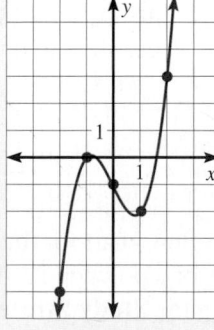

```
3 |  1   0   -2   -1
   |      3    9   21
     1   3    7   20  ← f(3) = 20
```

To graph, make a table of values, plot points, and identify end behavior.

x	−3	−2	−1	0	1	2	3
f(x)	−22	−5	0	−1	−2	3	20

The leading coefficient is positive and the degree is odd, so
$f(x) \to -\infty$ as $x \to -\infty$ and $f(x) \to +\infty$ as $x \to +\infty$.

Use synthetic substitution to evaluate the polynomial function for the given value of x.

5. $f(x) = x^3 + 3x^2 - 12x + 7, \ x = 3$

6. $f(x) = x^4 - 5x^3 - 3x^2 + x - 5, \ x = -1$

Graph the polynomial function.

7. $f(x) = -x^3 + 2$ **8.** $f(x) = x^4 - 3$ **9.** $f(x) = x^3 - 4x + 1$

6.3 ADDING, SUBTRACTING, AND MULTIPLYING POLYNOMIALS

Examples on pp. 338–340

EXAMPLES You can add, subtract, or multiply polynomials.

$$
\begin{array}{l}
4x^3 + 2x^2 + 1 \\
\underline{- (x^2 + x - 5)} \\
4x^3 + x^2 - x + 6
\end{array}
$$

$$
\begin{aligned}
(x - 3)(x^2 + 5x - 1) &= (x - 3)(x^2) + (x - 3)(5x) + (x - 3)(-1) \\
&= x^3 - 3x^2 + 5x^2 - 15x - x + 3 \\
&= x^3 + 2x^2 - 16x + 3
\end{aligned}
$$

Perform the indicated operation.

10. $(3x^3 + x^2 + 1) - (x^3 + 3)$ **11.** $(x - 3)(x^2 + x - 7)$ **12.** $(x + 3)(x - 5)(2x + 1)$

6.4 FACTORING AND SOLVING POLYNOMIAL EQUATIONS

Examples on pp. 345–347

EXAMPLES You can solve some polynomial equations by factoring.

Factor $8x^3 - 125$.

$$
\begin{aligned}
8x^3 - 125 &= (2x)^3 - 5^3 \\
&= (2x - 5)\big((2x)^2 + (2x \cdot 5) + 5^2\big) \\
&= (2x - 5)(4x^2 + 10x + 25)
\end{aligned}
$$

Solve $x^3 - 3x^2 - 5x + 15 = 0$.

$$
\begin{aligned}
x^2(x - 3) - 5(x - 3) &= 0 \\
(x - 3)(x^2 - 5) &= 0 \\
x = 3 \text{ or } x &= \pm\sqrt{5}
\end{aligned}
$$

Find the real-number solutions of the equation.

13. $x^3 + 64 = 0$ **14.** $x^4 - 6x^2 = 27$ **15.** $x^3 + 3x^2 - x - 3 = 0$

6.5 THE REMAINDER AND FACTOR THEOREMS

Examples on pp. 352–355

EXAMPLES You can use polynomial long division, and in some cases synthetic division, to divide polynomials.

$$
\begin{array}{r}
x^2 - 7x + 6 \\
x + 9\overline{\smash{\big)}\,x^3 + 2x^2 - 57x + 54} \\
\underline{x^3 + 9x^2} \\
-7x^2 - 57x \\
\underline{-7x^2 - 63x} \\
6x + 54 \\
\underline{6x + 54} \\
0
\end{array}
$$

Divide $3x^3 + 2x^2 - x + 4$ by $x + 5$.

$$
\begin{array}{c|rrrr}
-5 & 3 & 2 & -1 & 4 \\
 & & -15 & 65 & -320 \\
\hline
 & 3 & -13 & 64 & -316
\end{array}
$$

$$
\frac{x^3 + 2x^2 - 57x + 54}{x + 9} = x^2 - 7x + 6
$$

$$
\frac{3x^3 + 2x^2 - x + 4}{x + 5} = 3x^2 - 13x + 64 + \frac{-316}{x + 5}
$$

Divide. Use synthetic division if possible.

16. $(x^4 + 5x^3 - x^2 - 3x - 1) \div (x - 1)$ **17.** $(2x^3 - 5x^2 + 5x + 4) \div (2x - 5)$

> **EXAMPLE** You can use the rational zero theorem and the fundamental theorem of algebra to find all the zeros of a polynomial function.
>
> $f(x) = x^4 + 3x^3 - 5x^2 - 21x + 22$ Possible rational zeros: $\dfrac{\pm 1, \pm 2, \pm 11, \pm 22}{1}$
>
> Using synthetic division, you can find that the rational zeros are 1 and 2.
> The degree of f is 4, so f has 4 zeros. To find the other two zeros, write in factored form: $f(x) = (x - 1)(x - 2)(x^2 + 6x + 11)$. Solve $x^2 + 6x + 11 = 0$: $x = -3 \pm \sqrt{2}\,i$.
> So the zeros of $f(x) = x^4 + 3x^3 - 5x^2 - 21x + 22$ are $1, 2, -3 + \sqrt{2}\,i, -3 - \sqrt{2}\,i$.

Find all the real zeros of the function.

18. $f(x) = x^3 + 12x^2 + 21x + 10$ **19.** $f(x) = x^4 + x^3 - x^2 + x - 2$

6.8 **ANALYZING GRAPHS OF POLYNOMIAL FUNCTIONS**

> **EXAMPLE** You can identify x-intercepts and turning points when you analyze the graph of a polynomial function.
>
> The graph of $f(x) = 3x^3 - 9x + 6$ has
>
> - two x-intercepts, -2 and 1.
> - a local maximum at $(-1, 12)$.
> - a local minimum at $(1, 0)$.

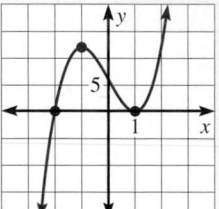

Graph the polynomial function. Identify the x-intercepts and the points where the local maximums and local minimums occur.

20. $f(x) = (x - 2)^2(x + 2)$ **21.** $f(x) = x^3 - 3x^2$ **22.** $f(x) = 3x^4 + 4x^3$

6.9 **MODELING WITH POLYNOMIALS**

> **EXAMPLE** Sometimes you can use finite differences or cubic regression to find a polynomial model for a set of data.

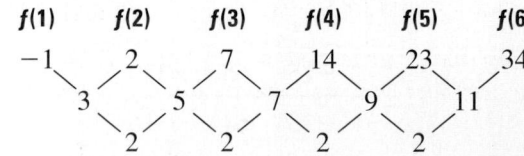

$f(1)$	$f(2)$	$f(3)$	$f(4)$	$f(5)$	$f(6)$

function values
first-order differences
second-order differences

> Since second-order differences are nonzero and constant, the data set can be modeled by a polynomial function of degree 2. The function is $f(x) = x^2 - 2$.

23. Show that the third-order differences for the function $f(n) = n^3 + 1$ are nonzero and constant.

24. Write a cubic function whose graph passes through points $(1, 0)$, $(-1, 0)$, $(4, 0)$, and $(2, -12)$. Use cubic regression on a graphing calculator to verify your answer.

CHAPTER 6

Chapter Test

Simplify the expression. Tell which properties of exponents you used.

1. $x^7 \cdot \dfrac{1}{x^2}$

2. $(3^2 x^6)^3$

3. $\dfrac{x^9}{x^{-2}}$

4. $(8x^3 y^2)^{-3}$

5. $\dfrac{15x^2 y}{6x^4 y^5} \cdot \dfrac{6x^3 y^2}{5xy}$

Describe the end behavior of the graph of the polynomial function. Then evaluate the function for $x = -4, -3, -2, \ldots, 4$. Then graph the function.

6. $y = x^4 - 2x^2 - x - 1$

7. $y = -3x^3 - 6x^2$

8. $y = (x - 3)(x + 1)(x + 2)$

Perform the indicated operation.

9. $(3x^2 - 5x + 7) - (2x^2 + 9x - 1)$

10. $(2x - 3)(5x^2 - x + 6)$

11. $(x - 4)(x + 1)(x + 3)$

Factor the polynomial.

12. $64x^3 + 343$

13. $400x^2 - 25$

14. $x^4 + 8x^2 - 9$

15. $2x^3 - 3x^2 + 4x - 6$

Solve the equation.

16. $3x^4 - 11x^2 - 20 = 0$

17. $81x^4 = 16$

18. $4x^3 - 8x^2 - x + 2 = 0$

Divide. Use synthetic division if possible.

19. $(8x^4 + 5x^3 + 4x^2 - x + 7) \div (x + 1)$

20. $(12x^3 + 31x^2 - 17x - 6) \div (x + 3)$

List all the possible rational zeros of f using the rational zero theorem. Then find all the zeros of the function.

21. $f(x) = x^3 - 5x^2 - 14x$

22. $f(x) = x^3 + 4x^2 + 9x + 36$

23. $f(x) = x^4 + x^3 - 2x^2 + 4x - 24$

Write a polynomial function of least degree that has real coefficients, the given zeros, and a leading coefficient of 1.

24. $1, -3, 4$

25. $2, 2, -1, 0$

26. $5, 2i, -2i$

27. $3, -3, 2 - i$

28. Use technology to approximate the real zeros of $f(x) = 0.25x^3 - 7x^2 + 15$.

29. Identify the x-intercepts, local maximum, and local minimum of the graph of $f(x) = \frac{1}{9}(x - 3)^2(x + 3)^2$. Then describe the end behavior of the graph.

30. Show that $f(x) = x^4 - 2x + 8$ has nonzero constant fourth-order differences.

31. The table gives the number of triangles that point upward that you can find in a large triangle that is n units on a side and divided into triangles that are each one unit on a side. Find a polynomial model for $f(n)$.

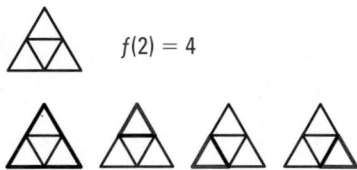

$f(2) = 4$

n	1	2	3	4	5	6	7
$f(n)$	1	4	10	20	35	56	84

32. **CELLS** An adult human body contains about 75,000,000,000,000 cells. Each is about 0.001 inch wide. If the cells were laid end to end to form a chain, about how long would the chain be in miles? Give your answer in scientific notation.

● **TEST-TAKING STRATEGY** The mathematical portion of the SAT is based on concepts and skills taught in high school mathematics courses. The best way to prepare for the SAT is to keep up with your day-to-day studies.

1. **MULTIPLE CHOICE** What is the value of -4^0?

   (A) 4　　　　(B) 1　　　　(C) 0

   (D) -1　　　(E) -4

2. **MULTIPLE CHOICE** What is the value of $f(x) = 7x^4 - 3x^3 + 8x^2 + x - 9$ when $x = -1$?

   (A) 8　　　　(B) 4　　　　(C) 2

   (D) -8　　　(E) -14

3. **MULTIPLE CHOICE** Which statement about the end behavior of the graph of $f(x) = x^4 + 1$ is true?

   (A) $f(x) \to +\infty$ as $x \to -\infty$.

   (B) $f(x) \to +\infty$ as $x \to 0$.

   (C) $f(x) \to -\infty$ as $x \to -\infty$.

   (D) $f(x) \to -\infty$ as $x \to 0$.

   (E) $f(x) \to -\infty$ as $x \to +\infty$.

4. **MULTIPLE CHOICE** For 1992 through 1995, the number of grocery stores in the United States can be modeled by $G = 0.03t^2 - 1.5t + 171$, where G is the number of stores in thousands and t is the number of years since 1990. The average sales per grocery store can be modeled by $S = 4.7t^2 + 49.1t + 2009$, where S is sales in thousands of dollars. What were the approximate total sales in millions of dollars for grocery stores in the United States in 1994?

   (A) 3.8×10^{-1}　　　(B) 3.8×10^1

   (C) 3.8×10^5　　　　(D) 3.8×10^8

   (E) 3.8×10^{11}

5. **MULTIPLE CHOICE** Which polynomial has the factorization $(2x + 1)(4x^2 - 2x + 1)$?

   (A) $2x^3 - 1$　　　　(B) $8x^3 - 1$

   (C) $2x^3 + 1$　　　　(D) $4x^3 + 1$

   (E) $8x^3 + 1$

6. **MULTIPLE CHOICE** What are all the *real* solutions of the equation $x^5 = 256x$?

   (A) $0, \pm 4$　　(B) $4, -4$　　(C) $\pm 4, \pm 4i$

   (D) $0, \pm 4i$　　(E) $0, \pm 4, \pm 4i$

7. **MULTIPLE CHOICE** What is the quotient of $(4x^3 - 11x^2 - 9x - 5) \div (x - 4)$?

   (A) $4x^3 + 5x^2 + 11x + 39$

   (B) $4x^2 + 5x + 11 + \dfrac{39}{x - 4}$

   (C) $4x^2 + 5x + 11 + \dfrac{39}{4x^3 - 11x^2 - 9x - 5}$

   (D) $4x^2 - 27x + 99 - \dfrac{401}{x - 4}$

   (E) $4x^2 - 27x + 99 - \dfrac{401}{x + 4}$

8. **MULTIPLE CHOICE** What are all the rational zeros of $f(x) = x^3 - 8x^2 + x + 42$?

   (A) $-2, -3, -7$　　　　(B) $2, 3, 7$

   (C) $2, -3, -7$　　　　(D) $0, 6, 7$

   (E) $-2, 3, 7$

9. **MULTIPLE CHOICE** How many zeros does the function $f(x) = -3x^4 + x + 2$ have?

   (A) 0　　　　(B) 1　　　　(C) 2

   (D) 3　　　　(E) 4

10. **MULTIPLE CHOICE** Which function is graphed?

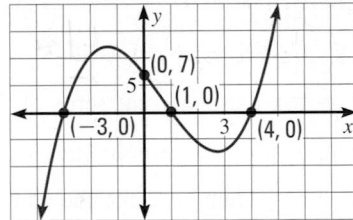

   (A) $f(x) = (x + 3)(x - 1)(x - 4)$

   (B) $f(x) = 7(x + 3)(x - 1)(x - 4)$

   (C) $f(x) = \dfrac{7}{12}(x - 3)(x + 1)(x + 4)$

   (D) $f(x) = \dfrac{7}{12}(x + 3)(x - 1)(x - 4)$

   (E) $f(x) = -\dfrac{7}{12}(x + 3)(x - 1)(x - 4)$

QUANTITATIVE COMPARISON In Exercises 11 and 12, choose the statement that is true about the given quantities.

(A) The quantity in column A is greater.

(B) The quantity in column B is greater.

(C) The two quantities are equal.

(D) The relationship cannot be determined from the given information.

Column A	Column B
11. x^{-2}	x^2
12. Degree of $f(x) = x^4 - 7x + 13$	Degree of $f(x) = 4x^3 + 2x^2 - x + 1$

13. **MULTI-STEP PROBLEM** You are designing a monument for the city park. The monument is to be a rectangular prism with dimensions $x + 1$ feet, $x - 5$ feet, and $x - 6$ feet.

   a. Write a function $f(x)$ for the volume of the monument.

   b. Use a graphing calculator to graph $f(x)$ for $-10 \le x \le 20$.

   c. *Writing* Look back at your graph from part (b). Identify the local maximums and local minimums. Do these values represent maximum and minimum possible volumes of the monument? Explain.

   d. If the volume of the monument is to be 220 cubic feet, what will the dimensions be?

14. **MULTI-STEP PROBLEM** The numbers in the table give the volumes of the first six prisms in a sequence.

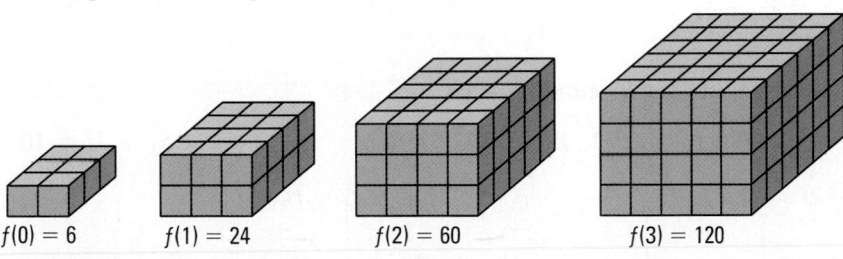

$f(0) = 6$ $f(1) = 24$ $f(2) = 60$ $f(3) = 120$

Prism (n)	0	1	2	3	4	5
Volume, $f(n)$	6	24	60	120	210	336

   a. Use finite differences to determine the degree of f.

   b. Use a system of equations to find a polynomial model for $f(n)$ in standard form.

   c. *Writing* Factor the polynomial. Explain how the factors are related to the dimensions of the prism.

   d. Use your model to find the volume of the 50th prism in the sequence.

   e. Sketch a graph of your model and label the points that represent the first six prisms. What is the domain of the function?

Solve the equation. (1.3, 1.7)

1. $5x + 4 = -21$ **2.** $3(2x + 5) = 69$ **3.** $|x - 2| = 6$ **4.** $|7 - 3x| = 23$

Solve the inequality. Then graph your solution. (1.6, 1.7)

5. $10 - 4x > -2$ **6.** $0 \le 2x - 8 \le 14$ **7.** $|x - 3| < 5$ **8.** $|5x + 2| \ge 17$

Find the slope of the line passing through the given points. (2.2)

9. $(4, 1), (-2, 1)$ **10.** $(-3, 0), (0, 2)$ **11.** $(-1, -5), (2, 7)$ **12.** $(-4, 4), (1, -3)$

Graph the equation or inequality. (2.3, 2.6–2.8)

13. $y = -2x - 1$ **14.** $3x - 7y = 21$ **15.** $x = -4$

16. $y > \frac{3}{2}x + 2$ **17.** $2x + 6y \le 12$ **18.** $y = |x| + 3$

19. $y = -2|x + 4| - 1$ **20.** $f(x) = \begin{cases} -2, & \text{if } x \le 0 \\ 3, & \text{if } x > 0 \end{cases}$ **21.** $f(x) = \begin{cases} -x, & \text{if } x < 1 \\ x - 2, & \text{if } x \ge 1 \end{cases}$

Write an equation of the line with the given characteristics. (2.4)

22. slope: 3, y-intercept: -2 **23.** points on line: $(-1, 9), (1, 1)$ **24.** vertical line through $(-8, 6)$

Solve the system of linear equations using any method. (3.1, 3.2, 3.6, 4.3, 4.5)

25. $x + y = 8$
$2x - y = 1$

26. $3x - 4y = 5$
$2x + 2y = 1$

27. $x + y + z = 4$
$x - 4y + 3z = 10$
$-4x + y + z = -1$

28. $x - y + z = 1$
$-x + y + 2z = 2$
$x + y + z = -3$

Graph the ordered triple or equation in a three-dimensional coordinate system. (3.5)

29. $(-1, -3, 0)$ **30.** $(2, 4, -2)$ **31.** $4x + 2y + z = 4$ **32.** $5x + 5y + 2z = 10$

Perform the indicated operation. (4.1, 4.2)

33. $\begin{bmatrix} -3 & 7 \\ 4 & -2 \end{bmatrix} + \begin{bmatrix} -8 & 1 \\ -3 & 0 \end{bmatrix}$ **34.** $-6 \begin{bmatrix} 2 & 3 \\ -4 & -2 \\ -5 & -1 \end{bmatrix}$ **35.** $\begin{bmatrix} 1 & -5 \\ 6 & 3 \end{bmatrix} \begin{bmatrix} 2 & -2 & 8 \\ -3 & 1 & 7 \end{bmatrix}$

Evaluate the determinant of the matrix. (4.3)

36. $\begin{bmatrix} -5 & 2 \\ 4 & -2 \end{bmatrix}$ **37.** $\begin{bmatrix} 0 & 1 \\ -3 & 6 \end{bmatrix}$ **38.** $\begin{bmatrix} 3 & 9 & 1 \\ -5 & 1 & 2 \\ -2 & 4 & 8 \end{bmatrix}$ **39.** $\begin{bmatrix} -1 & 0 & 1 \\ 3 & 7 & -2 \\ 8 & 1 & 0 \end{bmatrix}$

Find the inverse of the matrix. (4.4)

40. $\begin{bmatrix} -5 & 2 \\ -7 & 3 \end{bmatrix}$ **41.** $\begin{bmatrix} -1 & -2 \\ 4 & 7 \end{bmatrix}$ **42.** $\begin{bmatrix} 4 & 9 \\ 2 & 4 \end{bmatrix}$ **43.** $\begin{bmatrix} 4 & -2 \\ -2 & 1 \end{bmatrix}$

Graph the equation or inequality. (5.1, 5.7, 6.2, 6.8)

44. $y = x^2 + 8x + 16$ **45.** $y = -(x - 1)^2 + 3$ **46.** $y = 2(x + 1)(x - 3)$

47. $y \le \frac{1}{4}x^2 - 3$ **48.** $y < -2x^2 + 4x + 5$ **49.** $y = x^3 - 4x^2 + x + 7$

50. $y = -3x^4 + 9x^2 - 2$ **51.** $y = -(x + 2)(x - 1)(x - 2)$ **52.** $y = 2x^2(x - 3)^2$

Solve the equation or inequality. (5.2–5.7, 6.4)

53. $3x^2 - 7 = 2(x^2 + 3)$ **54.** $4x^2 + 12x + 9 = 0$ **55.** $x^2 + 64 = 0$

56. $x^2 + 4x = 4$ **57.** $100 - x^2 \geq 0$ **58.** $x^2 - 6 > -5x$

59. $x^4 - 5x^2 + 4 = 0$ **60.** $3x^4 - 15x^3 = 0$ **61.** $2x^3 + 4x^2 - 3x - 6 = 0$

Write the expression as a complex number in standard form. (5.4)

62. $\dfrac{7 + 3i}{4 - i}$ **63.** $4i(5 - 8i)$ **64.** $(9 + 5i)(9 - 5i)$ **65.** $(6 - 2i) - (-3 - 4i)$

Write a quadratic function in the specified form whose graph has the given characteristics. (5.8)

66. vertex form
vertex: $(5, 3)$
point on graph: $(7, 11)$

67. intercept form
x-intercepts: $-3, -2$
point on graph: $(0, -6)$

68. standard form
points on graph:
$(1, 4), (3, -4), (6, -61)$

Simplify the expression. (6.1)

69. $\left(6xy^3\right)^2$ **70.** $7x^{-10}y^4$ **71.** $\left(\dfrac{5}{4}\right)^{-2}$ **72.** $\dfrac{3x^2y^{-1}}{2x} \cdot \dfrac{10x^2y}{3y^{-3}}$

Perform the indicated operation. (6.3, 6.5)

73. $(x - 3)(x^3 - 2x^2 + 5x - 12)$ **74.** $(7x^3 - 9x + 2) + (5x^3 + 9x)$ **75.** $(x^4 - 3x^3 + 8x^2 - 2) \div (x + 2)$

Find all the zeros of the function. (6.6, 6.7)

76. $f(x) = 2x^3 - 5x^2 - 4x + 3$ **77.** $f(x) = x^4 - 25$ **78.** $f(x) = x^3 + 11x^2 + x + 11$

Write a cubic function whose graph passes through the given points. (6.9)

79. $(-4, 0), (-1, 0), (1, 0), (-2, 6)$ **80.** $(-6, 0), (0, 0), (3, 0), (6, -144)$

81. **SIMPLE INTEREST** The formula for simple interest is $I = Prt$. Solve the formula for r. Then find the annual interest rate if a \$1000 deposit earns \$165 of simple interest in 3 years. (1.4)

82. **COST OF BREAD** The table gives the number of one-pound loaves of bread you could buy for \$1.00 in the United States for various years since 1900. Make a scatter plot of the data and describe the correlation shown. (2.5)

Years since 1900, t	13	30	50	70	90	97
Loaves of bread, b	17.8	11.6	6.9	4.1	1.4	1.1

 DATA UPDATE of Bureau of Labor Statistics data at www.mcdougallittell.com

83. **PHONE RATES** A long distance carrier charges a flat rate of \$.09 per minute for telephone calls. A second carrier charges \$.30 for the first minute and \$.06 for each additional minute. After how many minutes will the second carrier be less expensive than the first carrier? (3.2)

84. **CRYPTOGRAMS** Use the matrix $A = \begin{bmatrix} -2 & 5 \\ 1 & 8 \end{bmatrix}$ and the coding information on page 225 to encode the message EXIT NOW. (4.4)

85. **SCIENCE > CONNECTION** Pluto is about 3,660,000,000 mi from the sun. Light travels through space at a speed of about 671,000,000 mi/h. Use scientific notation to find how long it takes light from the sun to reach Pluto. (6.1)

Magic Squares

OBJECTIVE Explore the mathematics behind magic squares.

Materials: paper, pencil

A *magic square* is a square array of consecutive integers, usually (but not always) beginning with 1, for which the sum of the entries in each row, column, and diagonal is the same. This common sum is called the *magic constant.*

For example, a 4 × 4 magic square with a magic constant of 34 is shown. This square appears in the engraving *Melancholia*, which was created in 1514 by the German artist and mathematician Albrecht Dürer.

Magic squares were discovered in China around 2200 B.C. and later spread to India, Japan, and eventually to Europe. The challenge of creating magic squares has fascinated mathematicians and puzzle lovers for many centuries.

HOW TO MAKE A 3 × 3 MAGIC SQUARE

	5	

4	9	2
3	5	7
8	1	6

❶ Draw a 3 × 3 square. You want to use the integers 1 through 9 to fill in the square. Start by writing the middle value, 5, in the center.

❷ Continue filling in numbers until you have an arrangement where the entries in each row, column, and diagonal add up to 15.

INVESTIGATION

1. Think of a magic square as a matrix. Suppose a 3 × 3 matrix containing all 2's is added to the magic square in **Step 2**. Is the resulting matrix also a magic square? If so, what is the magic constant?

2. Generalize your work from Exercise 1 by adding a 3 × 3 matrix containing all a's, where a represents *any* integer, to the magic square in **Step 2**. Is the result always a magic square? If so, what is the magic constant in terms of a?

3. Use the integers 1 through 9 to make another 3 × 3 magic square. Add your square to the one in **Step 2**. Is the result a magic square? Explain. (Remember that the square's rows, columns, and diagonals must have the same sum *and* the numbers in the square must be consecutive integers.)

4. Use scalar multiplication to multiply the magic square in **Step 2** by the scalar 2. Is the result a magic square? Explain.

5. The *transpose* of a matrix A is a matrix A^T obtained by interchanging the rows and columns of A—the first row of A becomes the first column of A^T, the second row of A becomes the second column of A^T, and so on. Find the transpose of the magic square in **Step 2**. Is the transpose also a magic square?

6. Copy and complete the 4×4 magic square shown. What reasoning did you use to place the remaining numbers?

7			14
	13	8	
	3	10	
9			4

7. The sum S of the first k positive integers is given by the quadratic function $S = \frac{1}{2}k^2 + \frac{1}{2}k$. Use this function to find the sum of the entries in the 3×3 and 4×4 magic squares from **Step 2** and Exercise 6. Check your answers by computing the sums directly.

8. Consider an $n \times n$ magic square that contains the integers 1 through n^2. Use the function from Exercise 7 to write a formula for the sum S of the entries in the square in terms of n. What type of function is this formula?

9. For an $n \times n$ magic square that contains the integers 1 through n^2, write a formula for the square's magic constant M in terms of n. (*Hint:* Note that the magic constant is the sum of all the entries in the square divided by the number of rows or columns.) What type of function is this formula?

PRESENT YOUR RESULTS

Write a report to present your results.

- Include the 3×3 and 4×4 magic squares you made.

- Tell whether a magic square is produced by performing each of the following operations on an $n \times n$ magic square A: adding the same integer to each entry of A, multiplying each entry of A by the same integer, adding another $n \times n$ magic square to A, and taking the transpose of A.

- Include the formulas you found for the sum of the entries and for the magic constant of an $n \times n$ magic square containing the integers 1 through n^2.

- Describe how you used your knowledge of matrices, quadratic functions, and higher-degree polynomial functions in this project.

EXTENSION

Consider an $n \times n$ magic square containing the integers a through $a + n^2 - 1$. Such a magic square is shown at the right for $n = 3$ and $a = 5$. For this type of magic square, write formulas for the sum S of the entries and for the magic constant M in terms of n and a. Verify that your formulas work for the magic square shown.

8	13	6
7	9	11
12	5	10

POWERS, ROOTS, AND RADICALS

▶ *How can you estimate the weight of a dinosaur?*

APPLICATION: Dinosaurs

Scientists have determined relationships between the bone measurements and the heights and weights of living animals. By applying the relationships to dinosaur bones, scientists can estimate heights and weights of these prehistoric animals.

Think & Discuss

The table below gives the femur circumference (in millimeters) and estimated weight (in kilograms) for four different dinosaurs that walk on two feet.

Femur circumference	Estimated weight
103	50
201	310
348	1400
504	3800

1. Graph the ordered pairs (*femur circumference, estimated weight*) from the table. Why can't you model the data with a linear function?

2. The femur circumference of a *Hypacrosaurus altispinus* is about 400 millimeters. Estimate a reasonable weight for this dinosaur. How did you derive your estimate?

Learn More About It

You will apply the relationship between femur circumference and weight to a *Tyrannosaurus rex* in Exercise 64 on p. 442.

APPLICATION LINK Visit www.mcdougallittell.com for more information about dinosaurs.

Study Guide

What's the chapter about?

Chapter 7 is about **powers, roots, and radicals**. In Chapter 7 you'll learn

- how to use rational exponents and *n*th roots of numbers.

- how to perform operations with and find inverses of functions.

- how to graph radical functions and solve radical equations.

KEY VOCABULARY

▶ **Review**
- exponent, p. 11
- relation, p. 67
- function, p. 67
- square root, p. 264

▶ **New**
- *n*th root of *a*, p. 401
- power function, p. 415
- composition, p. 416
- inverse function, p. 422
- radical function, p. 431

- measure of central tendency, p. 445
- measure of dispersion, p. 446
- box-and-whisker plot, p. 447
- histogram, p. 448
- frequency distribution, p. 448

Are you ready for the chapter?

SKILL REVIEW Do these exercises to review key skills that you'll apply in this chapter. See the given **reference page** if there is something you don't understand.

STUDENT HELP

▶ **Study Tip**
"Student Help" boxes throughout the chapter give you study tips and tell you where to look for extra help in this book and on the Internet.

Solve the equation for *y*. (Review Example 1, p. 26)

1. $3x - 2y = 12$

2. $x + \frac{1}{2}y = 5$

3. $x = 4y - 1$

Factor the trinomial. (Review Examples 1 and 2, p. 256)

4. $x^2 + 10x + 21$

5. $x^2 + 5x - 36$

6. $2x^2 - 16x + 30$

Simplify the expression. (Review Example 2, p. 324)

7. $(abc^2)^4$

8. $x^5 \cdot x^{-3}$

9. $\left(\dfrac{x^2}{y}\right)^2$

10. $\dfrac{3x}{y} \cdot \dfrac{3x^2y^{-2}}{12y^3}$

Perform the indicated operation. (Review Examples 1–6, pp. 338 and 339)

11. $5x^2(x - 8)$

12. $(3y - 2)^2$

13. $(7x^2 + x) - (6x - 4)$

Here's a study strategy!

Quiz Yourself

After you complete a homework assignment, copy a few representative problems from the assignment on a separate piece of paper. Record the lesson number for the problems and leave space for the answers. You can use these problems to quiz yourself later, such as before a class quiz is given.

7.1

*n*th Roots and Rational Exponents

What you should learn

GOAL 1 Evaluate *n*th roots of real numbers using both radical notation and rational exponent notation.

GOAL 2 Use *n*th roots to solve **real-life** problems, such as finding the total mass of a spacecraft that can be sent to Mars in **Example 5**.

Why you should learn it

▼ To solve **real-life** problems, such as finding the number of reptile and amphibian species that Puerto Rico can support in **Ex. 67**.

You can extend the concept of a square root to other types of roots. For instance, 2 is a cube root of 8 because $2^3 = 8$, and 3 is a fourth root of 81 because $3^4 = 81$. In general, for an integer *n* greater than 1, if $b^n = a$, then *b* is an **nth root of *a***. An *n*th root of *a* is written as $\sqrt[n]{a}$, where *n* is the **index** of the radical.

You can also write an *n*th root of *a* as a power of *a*. For the particular case of a square root, suppose that $\sqrt{a} = a^k$. Then you can determine a value for *k* as follows:

$$\sqrt{a} \cdot \sqrt{a} = a \qquad \textbf{Definition of square root}$$

$$a^k \cdot a^k = a \qquad \textbf{Substitute } a^k \textbf{ for } \sqrt{a}.$$

$$a^{2k} = a^1 \qquad \textbf{Product of powers property}$$

$$2k = 1 \qquad \textbf{Set exponents equal when bases are equal.}$$

$$k = \frac{1}{2} \qquad \textbf{Solve for } k.$$

Therefore, you can see that $\sqrt{a} = a^{1/2}$. In a similar way you can show that $\sqrt[3]{a} = a^{1/3}$ and $\sqrt[4]{a} = a^{1/4}$. In general, $\sqrt[n]{a} = a^{1/n}$ for any integer *n* greater than 1.

REAL *N*TH ROOTS

Let *n* be an integer greater than 1 and let *a* be a real number.

- If *n* is odd, then *a* has one real *n*th root: $\sqrt[n]{a} = a^{1/n}$
- If *n* is even and $a > 0$, then *a* has two real *n*th roots: $\pm\sqrt[n]{a} = \pm a^{1/n}$
- If *n* is even and $a = 0$, then *a* has one *n*th root: $\sqrt[n]{0} = 0^{1/n} = 0$
- If *n* is even and $a < 0$, then *a* has no real *n*th roots.

EXAMPLE 1 *Finding nth Roots*

Find the indicated real *n*th root(s) of *a*.

a. $n = 3, a = -125$ **b.** $n = 4, a = 16$

SOLUTION

a. Because $n = 3$ is odd, $a = -125$ has one real cube root. Because $(-5)^3 = -125$, you can write:

$$\sqrt[3]{-125} = -5 \qquad \text{or} \qquad (-125)^{1/3} = -5$$

b. Because $n = 4$ is even and $a = 16 > 0$, 16 has two real fourth roots. Because $2^4 = 16$ and $(-2)^4 = 16$, you can write:

$$\pm\sqrt[4]{16} = \pm 2 \qquad \text{or} \qquad \pm 16^{1/4} = \pm 2$$

A rational exponent does not have to be of the form $\frac{1}{n}$ where n is an integer greater than 1. Other rational numbers such as $\frac{3}{2}$ and $-\frac{1}{2}$ can also be used as exponents.

RATIONAL EXPONENTS

Let $a^{1/n}$ be an nth root of a, and let m be a positive integer.

- $a^{m/n} = (a^{1/n})^m = (\sqrt[n]{a})^m$
- $a^{-m/n} = \dfrac{1}{a^{m/n}} = \dfrac{1}{(a^{1/n})^m} = \dfrac{1}{(\sqrt[n]{a})^m}$, $a \neq 0$

EXAMPLE 2 *Evaluating Expressions with Rational Exponents*

a. $9^{3/2} = (\sqrt{9})^3 = 3^3 = 27$ **Using radical notation**

$9^{3/2} = (9^{1/2})^3 = 3^3 = 27$ **Using rational exponent notation**

b. $32^{-2/5} = \dfrac{1}{32^{2/5}} = \dfrac{1}{(\sqrt[5]{32})^2} = \dfrac{1}{2^2} = \dfrac{1}{4}$ **Using radical notation**

$32^{-2/5} = \dfrac{1}{32^{2/5}} = \dfrac{1}{(32^{1/5})^2} = \dfrac{1}{2^2} = \dfrac{1}{4}$ **Using rational exponent notation**

· · · · · · · · · ·

When using a graphing calculator to approximate an nth root, you may have to rewrite the nth root using a rational exponent. Then use the calculator's power key.

EXAMPLE 3 *Approximating a Root with a Calculator*

Use a graphing calculator to approximate $(\sqrt[4]{5})^3$.

SOLUTION First rewrite $(\sqrt[4]{5})^3$ as $5^{3/4}$. Then enter the following:

Keystrokes: 5 `^` `(` 3 `÷` 4 `)` `ENTER`   **Display:** $\boxed{3.343701525}$

▶ $(\sqrt[4]{5})^3 \approx 3.34$

· · · · · · · · · ·

To solve simple equations involving x^n, isolate the power and then take the nth root of *each* side.

STUDENT HELP

↳ **Study Tip**
To use a scientific calculator in Example 3, replace `^` with `yˣ` and replace `ENTER` with `=`.

EXAMPLE 4 *Solving Equations Using nth Roots*

a. $2x^4 = 162$

$x^4 = 81$

$x = \pm\sqrt[4]{81}$

$x = \pm 3$

b. $(x - 2)^3 = 10$

$x - 2 = \sqrt[3]{10}$

$x = \sqrt[3]{10} + 2$

$x \approx 4.15$

GOAL 2 USING *N*TH ROOTS IN REAL LIFE

Space Science

EXAMPLE 5 *Evaluating a Model with nth Roots*

The total mass *M* (in kilograms) of a spacecraft that can be propelled by a magnetic sail is, in theory, given by

$$M = \frac{0.015m^2}{fd^{4/3}}$$

where *m* is the mass (in kilograms) of the magnetic sail, *f* is the drag force (in newtons) of the spacecraft, and *d* is the distance (in astronomical units) to the sun. Find the total mass of a spacecraft that can be sent to Mars using *m* = 5000 kg, *f* = 4.52 N, and *d* = 1.52 AU. ▶ Source: *Journal of Spacecraft and Rockets*

Artist's rendition of a magnetic sail

SOLUTION

$$M = \frac{0.015\boldsymbol{m}^2}{f d^{4/3}}$$ **Write model for total mass.**

$$= \frac{0.015(\boldsymbol{5000})^2}{\boldsymbol{4.52}(\boldsymbol{1.52})^{4/3}}$$ **Substitute for *m*, *f*, and *d*.**

$$\approx 47{,}500$$ **Use a calculator.**

▶ The spacecraft can have a total mass of about 47,500 kilograms. (For comparison, the liftoff weight for a space shuttle is usually about 2,040,000 kilograms.)

EXAMPLE 6 *Solving an Equation Using an nth Root*

NAUTICAL SCIENCE The *Olympias* is a reconstruction of a trireme, a type of Greek galley ship used over 2000 years ago. The power *P* (in kilowatts) needed to propel the *Olympias* at a desired speed *s* (in knots) can be modeled by this equation:

$$P = 0.0289s^3$$

A volunteer crew of the *Olympias* was able to generate a maximum power of about 10.5 kilowatts. What was their greatest speed? ▶ Source: *Scientific American*

FOCUS ON APPLICATIONS

NAUTICAL SCIENCE The *Olympias* was completed and first launched in 1987. A crew of 170 rowers is needed to run the ship.

APPLICATION LINK
www.mcdougallittell.com

SOLUTION

$$P = 0.0289s^3$$ **Write model for power.**

$$\boldsymbol{10.5} = 0.0289s^3$$ **Substitute 10.5 for *P*.**

$$363 \approx s^3$$ **Divide each side by 0.0289.**

$$\sqrt[3]{363} \approx s$$ **Take cube root of each side.**

$$7 \approx s$$ **Use a calculator.**

▶ The greatest speed attained by the *Olympias* was approximately 7 knots (about 8 miles per hour).

7.1 *nth Roots and Rational Exponents*   **403**

GUIDED PRACTICE

Vocabulary Check ✓

1. What is the index of a radical?

Concept Check ✓

2. **LOGICAL REASONING** Let n be an integer greater than 1. Tell whether the given statement is *always true*, *sometimes true*, or *never true*. Explain.

   a. If $x^n = a$, then $x = \sqrt[n]{a}$.

   b. $a^{1/n} = \dfrac{1}{a^n}$

3. Try to evaluate the expressions $-\sqrt[4]{625}$ and $\sqrt[4]{-625}$. Explain the difference in your results.

Skill Check ✓

Evaluate the expression.

4. $\sqrt[4]{81}$ 5. $-\left(49^{1/2}\right)$ 6. $\left(\sqrt[3]{-8}\right)^5$ 7. $3125^{2/5}$

Solve the equation.

8. $x^3 = 125$ 9. $3x^5 = -3$ 10. $(x + 4)^2 = 0$ 11. $x^4 - 7 = 9993$

12. 🌐 **SHOT PUT** The shot (a metal sphere) used in men's shot put has a volume of about 905 cubic centimeters. Find the radius of the shot. (*Hint:* Use the formula $V = \dfrac{4}{3}\pi r^3$ for the volume of a sphere.)

PRACTICE AND APPLICATIONS

STUDENT HELP

→ **Extra Practice**
to help you master
skills is on p. 949.

USING RATIONAL EXPONENT NOTATION Rewrite the expression using rational exponent notation.

13. $\sqrt[4]{14}$ 14. $\sqrt[3]{11}$ 15. $\left(\sqrt[7]{5}\right)^2$ 16. $\left(\sqrt[9]{16}\right)^5$ 17. $\left(\sqrt[8]{2}\right)^{11}$

USING RADICAL NOTATION Rewrite the expression using radical notation.

18. $6^{1/3}$ 19. $7^{1/4}$ 20. $10^{3/7}$ 21. $5^{2/5}$ 22. $8^{7/4}$

FINDING NTH ROOTS Find the indicated real nth root(s) of a.

23. $n = 2, a = 100$ 24. $n = 4, a = 0$ 25. $n = 3, a = -8$

26. $n = 7, a = 128$ 27. $n = 6, a = -1$ 28. $n = 5, a = 0$

EVALUATING EXPRESSIONS Evaluate the expression without using a calculator.

29. $\sqrt[3]{64}$ 30. $\sqrt[3]{-1000}$ 31. $-\sqrt[6]{64}$

32. $4^{-1/2}$ 33. $1^{1/3}$ 34. $-\left(256^{1/4}\right)$

35. $\left(\sqrt[4]{16}\right)^2$ 36. $\left(\sqrt[3]{-27}\right)^{-4}$ 37. $\left(\sqrt[6]{0}\right)^3$

38. $-\left(25^{-3/2}\right)$ 39. $32^{4/5}$ 40. $(-125)^{-2/3}$

STUDENT HELP

→ **HOMEWORK HELP**
Example 1: Exs. 13–28
Example 2: Exs. 29–40
Example 3: Exs. 41–52
Example 4: Exs. 53–61
Example 5: Exs. 62–64
Example 6: Exs. 65–67

📟 **APPROXIMATING ROOTS** Evaluate the expression using a calculator. Round the result to two decimal places when appropriate.

41. $\sqrt[5]{-16,807}$ 42. $\sqrt[9]{1124}$ 43. $\sqrt[8]{65,536}$

44. $4^{1/10}$ 45. $10^{-1/4}$ 46. $-\left(1331^{1/3}\right)$

47. $\left(\sqrt[3]{112}\right)^{-4}$ 48. $\left(\sqrt[7]{-280}\right)^3$ 49. $\left(\sqrt[6]{6}\right)^2$

50. $(-190)^{-4/5}$ 51. $26^{-3/4}$ 52. $522^{2/7}$

SOLVING EQUATIONS Solve the equation. Round your answer to two decimal places when appropriate.

53. $x^5 = 243$ **54.** $6x^3 = -1296$ **55.** $x^6 + 10 = 10$

56. $(x - 4)^4 = 81$ **57.** $-x^7 = 40$ **58.** $-12x^4 = -48$

59. $(x + 12)^3 = 21$ **60.** $x^3 - 14 = 22$ **61.** $x^8 - 25 = -10$

62. **BIOLOGY** **CONNECTION** For mammals, the lung volume V (in milliliters) can be modeled by $V = 170m^{4/5}$ where m is the body mass (in kilograms). Find the lung volume of each mammal in the table shown.

▶ Source: *Respiration Physiology*

Mammal	Body mass (kg)
Banded mongoose	1.14
Camel	229
Horse	510
Swiss cow	700

63. **SPILLWAY OF A DAM** A dam's spillway capacity is an indication of how the dam will perform under certain flood conditions. The spillway capacity q (in cubic feet per second) of a dam can be calculated using the formula $q = c\ell h^{3/2}$ where c is the discharge coefficient, ℓ is the length (in feet) of the spillway, and h is the height (in feet) of the water on the spillway. A dam with a spillway 40 feet long, 5 feet deep, and 5 feet wide has a discharge coefficient of 2.79. What is the dam's maximum spillway capacity?

▶ Source: *Standard Handbook for Civil Engineers*

STUDENT HELP

HOMEWORK HELP
Visit our Web site
www.mcdougallittell.com
for help with problem
solving in Ex. 64.

64. **INFLATION** If the price of an item increases from p_1 to p_2 over a period of n years, the annual rate of inflation i (expressed as a decimal) can be modeled by $i = \left(\dfrac{p_2}{p_1}\right)^{1/n} - 1$. In 1940 the average value of a home was $2900. In 1990 the average value was $79,100. What was the rate of inflation for a home?

▶ Source: *Bureau of the Census*

65. **GEOMETRY** **CONNECTION** The formula for the volume V of a regular dodecahedron (a solid with 12 regular pentagons as faces) is $V \approx 7.66a^3$ where a is the length of an edge of the dodecahedron. Find the length of an edge of a regular dodecahedron that has a volume of 30 cubic feet. Round your answer to two decimal places.

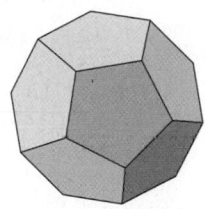

66. **GEOMETRY** **CONNECTION** The formula for the volume V of a regular icosahedron (a solid with 20 congruent equilateral triangles as faces) is $V \approx 2.18a^3$ where a is the length of an edge of the icosahedron. Find the length of an edge of a regular icosahedron that has a volume of 21 cubic centimeters. Round your answer to two decimal places.

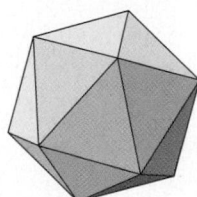

67. **ISLAND SPECIES** Philip Darlington discovered a rule of thumb that relates an island's land area A (in square miles) to the number s of reptile and amphibian species the island can support by the model $A = 0.0779s^3$. The area of Puerto Rico is roughly 4000 square miles. About how many reptile and amphibian species can it support?

▶ Source: *The Song of the Dodo: Island Biogeography in an Age of Extinctions*

68. MULTI-STEP PROBLEM A board foot is a unit for measuring wood. One board foot has a volume of 144 cubic inches. The Doyle log rule, given by $b = l\left(\dfrac{r-2}{2}\right)^2$, is a formula for approximating the number b of board feet in a log with length l (in feet) and radius r (in inches). The total volume V (in cubic inches) of wood in the main trunk of a Douglas fir can be modeled by $V = 250r^3$ where r is the radius of the trunk at the base of the tree. Suppose you need 5000 board feet from a 20 foot Douglas fir log.

Log-sawing patterns for maximum board feet

a. What volume of wood do you need?

b. What is the radius of a log that will meet your needs?

c. What is the total volume of wood in the main trunk of a Douglas fir tree that will meet your needs?

d. If you find a suitable tree, what fraction of the tree would you actually use?

e. *Writing* How does your answer to part (d) change if you instead need only 2500 board feet?

★ Challenge

69. VISUAL THINKING Copy the table. Give the number of nth roots of a for each category.

	$a < 0$	$a = 0$	$a > 0$
n is even	?	?	?
n is odd	?	?	?

70. The graph of $y = x^n$ where n is even is shown in red. Explain how the graph justifies the table for n even.

$y = a$
$a > 0$

$y = 0$ x

$y = a$
$a < 0$

Ex. 70

EXTRA CHALLENGE
www.mcdougallittell.com

71. Draw a similar graph to justify the table for n odd.

MIXED REVIEW

SOLVING SYSTEMS Use Cramer's rule to solve the linear system. **(Review 4.3)**

72. $x + 4y = 12$
$2x + 5y = 18$

73. $x - 2y = 11$
$2x + 5y = -14$

74. $2x - 4y = 7$
$-x + y = 1$

75. $-3x + 2y = -9$
$x - 4y = 2$

76. $-x - 8y = 10$
$10x + y = 1$

77. $-x - y = 0$
$5x - 6y = 13$

SIMPLIFYING EXPRESSIONS Simplify the expression. Tell which properties of exponents you used. **(Review 6.1 for 7.2)**

78. $x^4 \cdot x^{-2}$

79. $(x^{-3})^5$

80. $(2xy^3)^{-2}$

81. $5x^{-2}y^0$

82. $\dfrac{x^3}{x^{-4}}$

83. $\left(\dfrac{x^{-2}}{y}\right)^2$

84. $\dfrac{7x^3y^8}{14xy^{-2}}$

85. $\dfrac{16xy}{9x^5} \cdot \dfrac{9x^6y}{4y}$

FINDING ZEROS Find all the zeros of the polynomial function. **(Review 6.7)**

86. $f(x) = x^4 + 9x^3 - 5x^2 - 153x - 140$

87. $f(x) = x^4 + x^3 - 19x^2 + 11x + 30$

88. $f(x) = x^3 - 5x^2 + 16x - 80$

89. $f(x) = x^3 - x^2 + 9x - 9$

Properties of Rational Exponents

What you should learn

GOAL 1 Use properties of rational exponents to evaluate and simplify expressions.

GOAL 2 Use properties of rational exponents to solve **real-life** problems, such as finding the surface area of a mammal in **Example 8**.

Why you should learn it

▼ To model **real-life** quantities, such as the frequencies in the musical range of a trumpet for **Ex. 94**.

GOAL 1 PROPERTIES OF RATIONAL EXPONENTS AND RADICALS

The properties of integer exponents presented in Lesson 6.1 can also be applied to rational exponents.

CONCEPT SUMMARY — PROPERTIES OF RATIONAL EXPONENTS

Let a and b be real numbers and let m and n be rational numbers. The following properties have the same names as those listed on page 323, but now apply to rational exponents as illustrated.

	PROPERTY	EXAMPLE
1.	$a^m \cdot a^n = a^{m+n}$	$3^{1/2} \cdot 3^{3/2} = 3^{(1/2 + 3/2)} = 3^2 = 9$
2.	$(a^m)^n = a^{mn}$	$(4^{3/2})^2 = 4^{(3/2 \cdot 2)} = 4^3 = 64$
3.	$(ab)^m = a^m b^m$	$(9 \cdot 4)^{1/2} = 9^{1/2} \cdot 4^{1/2} = 3 \cdot 2 = 6$
4.	$a^{-m} = \dfrac{1}{a^m}, a \neq 0$	$25^{-1/2} = \dfrac{1}{25^{1/2}} = \dfrac{1}{5}$
5.	$\dfrac{a^m}{a^n} = a^{m-n}, a \neq 0$	$\dfrac{6^{5/2}}{6^{1/2}} = 6^{(5/2 - 1/2)} = 6^2 = 36$
6.	$\left(\dfrac{a}{b}\right)^m = \dfrac{a^m}{b^m}, b \neq 0$	$\left(\dfrac{8}{27}\right)^{1/3} = \dfrac{8^{1/3}}{27^{1/3}} = \dfrac{2}{3}$

If $m = \dfrac{1}{n}$ for some integer n greater than 1, the third and sixth properties can be written using radical notation as follows:

$$\sqrt[n]{a \cdot b} = \sqrt[n]{a} \cdot \sqrt[n]{b} \qquad \textbf{Product property}$$

$$\sqrt[n]{\frac{a}{b}} = \frac{\sqrt[n]{a}}{\sqrt[n]{b}} \qquad \textbf{Quotient property}$$

EXAMPLE 1 Using Properties of Rational Exponents

STUDENT HELP

▶ **Look Back**
For help with properties of exponents, see p. 324.

Use the properties of rational exponents to simplify the expression.

a. $5^{1/2} \cdot 5^{1/4} = 5^{(1/2 + 1/4)} = 5^{3/4}$

b. $\left(8^{1/2} \cdot 5^{1/3}\right)^2 = \left(8^{1/2}\right)^2 \cdot \left(5^{1/3}\right)^2 = 8^{(1/2 \cdot 2)} \cdot 5^{(1/3 \cdot 2)} = 8^1 \cdot 5^{2/3} = 8 \cdot 5^{2/3}$

c. $\left(2^4 \cdot 3^4\right)^{-1/4} = \left[(2 \cdot 3)^4\right]^{-1/4} = \left(6^4\right)^{-1/4} = 6^{[4 \cdot (-1/4)]} = 6^{-1} = \dfrac{1}{6}$

d. $\dfrac{7}{7^{1/3}} = \dfrac{7^1}{7^{1/3}} = 7^{(1 - 1/3)} = 7^{2/3}$

e. $\left(\dfrac{12^{1/3}}{4^{1/3}}\right)^2 = \left[\left(\dfrac{12}{4}\right)^{1/3}\right]^2 = (3^{1/3})^2 = 3^{(1/3 \cdot 2)} = 3^{2/3}$

EXAMPLE 2 *Using Properties of Radicals*

Use the properties of radicals to simplify the expression.

a. $\sqrt[3]{4} \cdot \sqrt[3]{16} = \sqrt[3]{4 \cdot 16} = \sqrt[3]{64} = 4$ **Use the product property.**

b. $\dfrac{\sqrt[4]{162}}{\sqrt[4]{2}} = \sqrt[4]{\dfrac{162}{2}} = \sqrt[4]{81} = 3$ **Use the quotient property.**

· · · · · · · · ·

For a radical to be in **simplest form**, you must not only apply the properties of radicals, but also remove any perfect nth powers (other than 1) and rationalize any denominators.

EXAMPLE 3 *Writing Radicals in Simplest Form*

STUDENT HELP

HOMEWORK HELP
Visit our Web site
www.mcdougallittell.com
for extra examples.

Write the expression in simplest form.

a. $\sqrt[3]{54} = \sqrt[3]{27 \cdot 2}$ **Factor out perfect cube.**

$\quad\quad = \sqrt[3]{27} \cdot \sqrt[3]{2}$ **Product property**

$\quad\quad = 3\sqrt[3]{2}$ **Simplify.**

b. $\sqrt[5]{\dfrac{3}{4}} = \sqrt[5]{\dfrac{3 \cdot 8}{4 \cdot 8}}$ **Make the denominator a perfect fifth power.**

$\quad\quad = \sqrt[5]{\dfrac{24}{32}}$ **Simplify.**

$\quad\quad = \dfrac{\sqrt[5]{24}}{\sqrt[5]{32}}$ **Quotient property**

$\quad\quad = \dfrac{\sqrt[5]{24}}{2}$ **Simplify.**

· · · · · · · · ·

Two radical expressions are **like radicals** if they have the same index and the same radicand. For instance, $\sqrt[3]{2}$ and $4\sqrt[3]{2}$ are like radicals. To add or subtract like radicals, use the distributive property.

EXAMPLE 4 *Adding and Subtracting Roots and Radicals*

Perform the indicated operation.

a. $7\left(6^{1/5}\right) + 2\left(6^{1/5}\right) = (7 + 2)\left(6^{1/5}\right) = 9\left(6^{1/5}\right)$

b. $\sqrt[3]{16} - \sqrt[3]{2} = \sqrt[3]{8 \cdot 2} - \sqrt[3]{2}$

$\quad\quad\quad\quad\quad = \sqrt[3]{8} \cdot \sqrt[3]{2} - \sqrt[3]{2}$

$\quad\quad\quad\quad\quad = 2\sqrt[3]{2} - \sqrt[3]{2}$

$\quad\quad\quad\quad\quad = (2 - 1)\sqrt[3]{2}$

$\quad\quad\quad\quad\quad = \sqrt[3]{2}$

The properties of rational exponents and radicals can also be applied to expressions involving variables. Because a variable can be positive, negative or zero, sometimes absolute value is needed when simplifying a variable expression.

$$\sqrt[n]{x^n} = x \text{ when } n \text{ is odd} \qquad\qquad \sqrt[7]{2^7} = 2 \text{ and } \sqrt[7]{(-2)^7} = -2$$

$$\sqrt[n]{x^n} = |x| \text{ when } n \text{ is even} \qquad\qquad \sqrt[4]{5^4} = 5 \text{ and } \sqrt[4]{(-5)^4} = 5$$

Absolute value is not needed when all variables are assumed to be positive.

EXAMPLE 5 *Simplifying Expressions Involving Variables*

Simplify the expression. Assume all variables are positive.

a. $\sqrt[3]{125y^6} = \sqrt[3]{5^3(y^2)^3} = 5y^2$

b. $\left(9u^2v^{10}\right)^{1/2} = 9^{1/2}\left(u^2\right)^{1/2}\left(v^{10}\right)^{1/2} = 3u^{(2 \cdot 1/2)}v^{(10 \cdot 1/2)} = 3uv^5$

c. $\sqrt[4]{\dfrac{x^4}{y^8}} = \dfrac{\sqrt[4]{x^4}}{\sqrt[4]{y^8}} = \dfrac{\sqrt[4]{x^4}}{\sqrt[4]{(y^2)^4}} = \dfrac{x}{y^2}$

d. $\dfrac{6xy^{1/2}}{2x^{1/3}z^{-5}} = 3x^{(1-1/3)}y^{1/2}z^{-(-5)} = 3x^{2/3}y^{1/2}z^5$

EXAMPLE 6 *Writing Variable Expressions in Simplest Form*

Write the expression in simplest form. Assume all variables are positive.

a. $\sqrt[5]{5a^5b^9c^{13}} = \sqrt[5]{5a^5b^5b^4c^{10}c^3}$ **Factor out perfect fifth powers.**

$\qquad\qquad = \sqrt[5]{a^5b^5c^{10}} \cdot \sqrt[5]{5b^4c^3}$ **Product property**

$\qquad\qquad = abc^2\sqrt[5]{5b^4c^3}$ **Simplify.**

b. $\sqrt[3]{\dfrac{x}{y^7}} = \sqrt[3]{\dfrac{xy^2}{y^7y^2}}$ **Make the denominator a perfect cube.**

$\qquad = \sqrt[3]{\dfrac{xy^2}{y^9}}$ **Simplify.**

$\qquad = \dfrac{\sqrt[3]{xy^2}}{\sqrt[3]{y^9}}$ **Quotient property**

$\qquad = \dfrac{\sqrt[3]{xy^2}}{y^3}$ **Simplify.**

EXAMPLE 7 *Adding and Subtracting Expressions Involving Variables*

Perform the indicated operation. Assume all variables are positive.

a. $5\sqrt{y} + 6\sqrt{y} = (5+6)\sqrt{y} = 11\sqrt{y}$

b. $2xy^{1/3} - 7xy^{1/3} = (2-7)xy^{1/3} = -5xy^{1/3}$

c. $3\sqrt[3]{5x^5} - x\sqrt[3]{40x^2} = 3x\sqrt[3]{5x^2} - 2x\sqrt[3]{5x^2} = (3x-2x)\sqrt[3]{5x^2} = x\sqrt[3]{5x^2}$

Biology

EXAMPLE 8 *Evaluating a Model Using Properties of Rational Exponents*

Biologists study characteristics of various living things. One way of comparing different animals is to compare their sizes. For example, a mammal's surface area S (in square centimeters) can be approximated by the model $S = km^{2/3}$ where m is the mass (in grams) of the mammal and k is a constant. The values of k for several mammals are given in the table.

Mammal	Mouse	Cat	Large dog	Cow	Rabbit	Human
k	9.0	10.0	11.2	9.0	9.75	11.0

Approximate the surface area of a cat that has a mass of 5 kilograms (5×10^3 grams). ▶ Source: *Scaling: Why Is Animal Size So Important?*

SOLUTION

$S = km^{2/3}$	**Write model.**
$= 10.0(5 \times 10^3)^{2/3}$	**Substitute for k and m.**
$= 10.0(5)^{2/3}(10^3)^{2/3}$	**Power of a product property**
$\approx 10.0(2.92)(10^2)$	**Power of a power property**
$= 2920$	**Simplify.**

▶ The cat's surface area is approximately 3000 square centimeters.

EXAMPLE 9 *Using Properties of Rational Exponents with Variables*

BIOLOGY CONNECTION You are studying a Canadian lynx whose mass is twice the mass of an average house cat. Is its surface area also twice that of an average house cat?

REAL LIFE BIOLOGY The average mass of a Canadian lynx is about 9.1 kilograms. The average mass of a house cat is about 4.8 kilograms.

SOLUTION

Let m be the mass of an average house cat. Then the mass of the Canadian lynx is $2m$. The surface areas of the house cat and the Canadian lynx can be approximated by:

$$S_{cat} = 10.0m^{2/3} \qquad S_{lynx} = 10.0(2m)^{2/3}$$

To compare the surface areas look at their ratio.

$\dfrac{S_{lynx}}{S_{cat}} = \dfrac{10.0(2m)^{2/3}}{10.0m^{2/3}}$	**Write ratio of surface areas.**
$= \dfrac{10.0(2^{2/3})(m^{2/3})}{10.0m^{2/3}}$	**Power of a product property**
$= 2^{2/3}$	**Simplify.**
≈ 1.59	**Evaluate.**

▶ The surface area of the Canadian lynx is about one and a half times that of an average house cat, not twice as much.

GUIDED PRACTICE

Vocabulary Check ✔
1. List three pairs of like radicals.

Concept Check ✔
2. If you know that $46,656,000 = 2^9 \cdot 3^6 \cdot 5^3$, what is the cube root of $46,656,000$? Explain your reasoning.

ERROR ANALYSIS Explain the error made in simplifying the expression.

3. $3\sqrt[4]{5} + 2\sqrt[4]{5} = 5\sqrt[4]{10}$

4. $\left(\dfrac{x}{y^8}\right)^{1/3} = \dfrac{x^{1/3}}{(y^8)^{1/3}} = \dfrac{x^{1/3}}{y^2}$

Skill Check ✔ **Simplify the expression.**

5. $3^{1/4} \cdot 3^{3/4}$ **6.** $(5^{1/3})^6$ **7.** $\sqrt[3]{16} \cdot \sqrt[3]{4}$ **8.** $4^{-1/2}$

9. $\sqrt[4]{\dfrac{16}{81}}$ **10.** $\sqrt[3]{\dfrac{1}{4}}$ **11.** $8^{1/7} + 2(8^{1/7})$ **12.** $\sqrt{200} - 3\sqrt{2}$

Simplify the expression. Assume all variables are positive.

13. $x^{2/3} \cdot x^{4/3}$ **14.** $(y^{1/6})^3$ **15.** $\sqrt{4a^6}$ **16.** $b^{-1/3}$

17. $\sqrt[5]{\dfrac{x^{10}}{y^5}}$ **18.** $\sqrt[3]{\dfrac{x^2}{z}}$ **19.** $2a^{1/5} - 6a^{1/5}$ **20.** $x\sqrt[3]{y^6} + y^2\sqrt[3]{x^3}$

21. 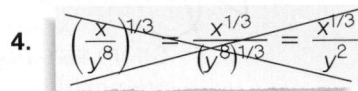 The average mass of a rabbit is 1.6 kilograms. Use the information given in Example 8 to approximate the surface area of a rabbit.

PRACTICE AND APPLICATIONS

STUDENT HELP

► **Extra Practice**
to help you master
skills is on p. 949.

PROPERTIES OF RATIONAL EXPONENTS Simplify the expression.

22. $3^{5/3} \cdot 3^{1/3}$ **23.** $(5^{2/3})^{1/2}$ **24.** $4^{1/4} \cdot 64^{1/4}$ **25.** $\dfrac{1}{36^{-1/2}}$

26. $\dfrac{7^{1/5}}{7^{3/5}}$ **27.** $\dfrac{70^{1/3}}{14^{1/3}}$ **28.** $(2^{1/4} \cdot 2^{1/3})^6$ **29.** $\left(\dfrac{5^2}{8^2}\right)^{-1/2}$

30. $\dfrac{6^{2/3} \cdot 4^{2/3}}{3^{2/3}}$ **31.** $\dfrac{125^{2/9} \cdot 125^{1/9}}{5^{1/4}}$ **32.** $\dfrac{12^{10/8}}{12^{-3/8}}$ **33.** $(10^{3/4} \cdot 4^{3/4})^{-4}$

PROPERTIES OF RADICALS Simplify the expression.

34. $\sqrt{64} \cdot \sqrt[3]{64}$ **35.** $\sqrt[4]{8} \cdot \sqrt[4]{2}$ **36.** $\sqrt[4]{5} \cdot \sqrt[4]{5}$ **37.** $(\sqrt[3]{6} \cdot \sqrt[4]{6})^{12}$

38. $\dfrac{\sqrt{7}}{\sqrt[5]{7}}$ **39.** $\dfrac{\sqrt[3]{4}}{\sqrt[3]{32}}$ **40.** $\dfrac{\sqrt[6]{8} \cdot \sqrt[6]{16}}{\sqrt[6]{2}}$ **41.** $\dfrac{\sqrt[3]{9} \cdot \sqrt[3]{6}}{\sqrt[6]{2} \cdot \sqrt[6]{2}}$

STUDENT HELP

► **HOMEWORK HELP**
Example 1: Exs. 22–33
Example 2: Exs. 34–41
Example 3: Exs. 42–49
Example 4: Exs. 50–55
Example 5: Exs. 56–67
Example 6: Exs. 68–75
Example 7: Exs. 76–81
Example 8: Exs. 90–93
Example 9: Exs. 94–97

SIMPLEST FORM Write the expression in simplest form.

42. $\sqrt{50}$ **43.** $\sqrt[5]{1215}$ **44.** $\sqrt[3]{18} \cdot \sqrt[3]{15}$ **45.** $3\sqrt[4]{24} \cdot 5\sqrt[4]{2}$

46. $\sqrt[3]{\dfrac{1}{7}}$ **47.** $\dfrac{2}{\sqrt[6]{81}}$ **48.** $\sqrt[4]{\dfrac{80}{9}}$ **49.** $\dfrac{\sqrt[3]{4}}{\sqrt[5]{8}}$

COMBINING ROOTS AND RADICALS Perform the indicated operation.

50. $\sqrt[5]{6} + 5\sqrt[5]{6}$ **51.** $5(5)^{1/7} - 7(5)^{1/7}$ **52.** $-\sqrt[8]{4} + 5\sqrt[8]{4}$

53. $160^{1/2} - 10^{1/2}$ **54.** $\sqrt[3]{375} + \sqrt[3]{81}$ **55.** $2\sqrt[4]{176} + 5\sqrt[4]{11}$

VARIABLE EXPRESSIONS Simplify the expression. Assume all variables are positive.

56. $x^{1/3} \cdot x^{1/5}$

57. $\left(y^3\right)^{1/6}$

58. $\sqrt[5]{32x^5}$

59. $\dfrac{1}{x^{-5/4}}$

60. $\dfrac{x^{3/7}}{x^{1/3}}$

61. $\sqrt[4]{\dfrac{x^{12}}{y^4}}$

62. $\dfrac{x^{5/3}y}{xy^{-1/2}}$

63. $\left(y \cdot y^{1/4}\right)^{4/3}$

64. $\left(\sqrt[4]{x^3} \cdot \sqrt[4]{x^5}\right)^{-2}$

65. $\dfrac{x^{3/4}yz^{-1/3}}{x^{1/4}z^{2/3}}$

66. $\dfrac{2\sqrt{x} \cdot \sqrt{x^3}}{\sqrt{9x^{10}}}$

67. $\dfrac{\sqrt[3]{y^6}}{\sqrt[3]{27y} \cdot \sqrt[3]{y^{11}}}$

SIMPLEST FORM Write the expression in simplest form. Assume all variables are positive.

68. $\sqrt{36x^3}$

69. $\sqrt[4]{10x^5y^8z^{10}}$

70. $\sqrt[5]{8xy^7} \cdot \sqrt[5]{6x^6}$

71. $\sqrt{xyz} \cdot \sqrt{2y^3z^4}$

72. $\dfrac{4}{\sqrt[3]{x}}$

73. $\sqrt[3]{\dfrac{x^3}{y^2}}$

74. $\sqrt{\dfrac{9x^2y}{32z^3}}$

75. $\dfrac{\sqrt[5]{x^3}}{\sqrt[5]{x^4}}$

COMBINING VARIABLE EXPRESSIONS Perform the indicated operation. Assume all variables are positive.

76. $2\sqrt[5]{y} + 7\sqrt[5]{y}$

77. $9x^{1/5} - 2x^{1/5}$

78. $-\sqrt[4]{x} + 2\sqrt[4]{x}$

79. $\left(x^9y\right)^{1/3} + \left(xy^{1/9}\right)^3$

80. $\sqrt{4x^5} - x\sqrt{x^3}$

81. $y\sqrt[3]{24x^5} + \sqrt[3]{-3x^2y^3}$

EXTENSION: IRRATIONAL EXPONENTS The properties you studied in this lesson can also be applied to irrational exponents. Simplify the expression. Assume all variables are positive.

82. $x^2 \cdot x^{\sqrt{3}}$

83. $\left(y^{\sqrt{2}}\right)^{\sqrt{2}}$

84. $(xy)^{\pi}$

85. $4^{\sqrt{7}}$

86. $\dfrac{x^{2\sqrt{5}}}{x^{\sqrt{5}}}$

87. $\left(\dfrac{x^{1/\pi}}{y^{2/\pi}}\right)^{\pi}$

88. $3x^{\sqrt{2}} + x^{\sqrt{2}}$

89. $xy^{\sqrt{11}} - 3xy^{\sqrt{11}}$

STUDENT HELP

▶ **Skills Review**
For help with perimeter and area, see p. 914.

90. **GEOMETRY CONNECTION** Find a radical expression for the perimeter of the triangle. Simplify the expression.

91. **GEOMETRY CONNECTION** The areas of two circles are 15 square centimeters and 20 square centimeters. Find the exact ratio of the radius of the smaller circle to the radius of the larger circle.

Ex. 90

92. **BIOLOGY CONNECTION** Look back at Example 8. Approximate the surface area of a human that has a mass of 68 kilograms.

93. **PINHOLE CAMERA** A pinhole camera is made out of a light-tight box with a piece of film attached to one side and a pinhole on the opposite side. The optimum diameter d (in millimeters) of the pinhole can be modeled by $d = 1.9\left[(5.5 \times 10^{-4})\ell\right]^{1/2}$, where ℓ is the length of the camera box (in millimeters). What is the optimum diameter for a pinhole camera if the camera box has a length of 10 *centimeters*?

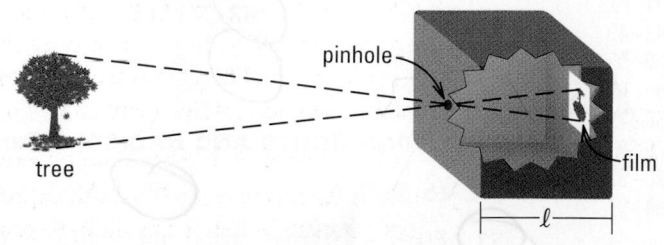

tree   pinhole   film ℓ

MUSIC In Exercises 94 and 95, use the following information.
The musical note A-440 (the A above middle C) has a frequency of 440 vibrations per second. The frequency f of any note can be found using $f = 440 \cdot 2^{n/12}$ where n represents the number of black and white keys the given note is above or below A-440. For notes above A-440, $n > 0$, and for notes below A-440, $n < 0$.

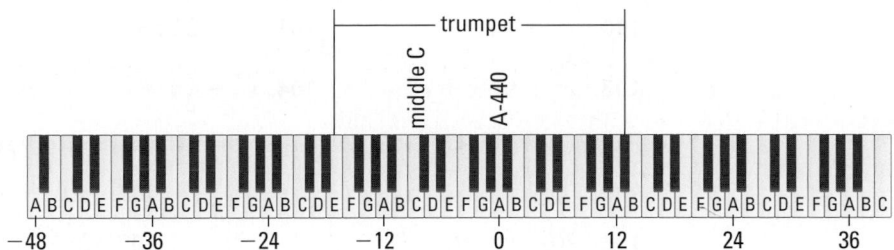

94. Find the highest and lowest frequencies in the musical range of a trumpet. What is the exact ratio of these two frequencies?

95. LOGICAL REASONING Describe the pattern of the frequencies of successive notes with the same letter.

96. **DISTANCE OF AN OBJECT** The maximum horizontal distance d that an object can travel when launched at an optimum angle of projection from an initial height h_0 can be modeled by $d = \dfrac{v_0\sqrt{(v_0)^2 + 2gh_0}}{g}$ where v_0 is the initial speed and g is the acceleration due to gravity. Simplify the model when $h_0 = 0$.

97. **BALLOONS** You have filled two round balloons with air. One balloon has twice as much air as the other balloon. The formula for the surface area S of a sphere in terms of its volume V is $S = (4\pi)^{1/3}(3V)^{2/3}$. By what factor is the surface area of the larger balloon greater than that of the smaller balloon?

98. MULTI-STEP PROBLEM A common ant absorbs oxygen at a rate of about 6.2 milliliters per second per square centimeter of exoskeleton. It needs about 24 milliliters of oxygen per second per cubic centimeter of its body. An ant is basically cylindrical in shape, so its surface area S and volume V can be approximated by the formulas for the surface area and volume of a cylinder:

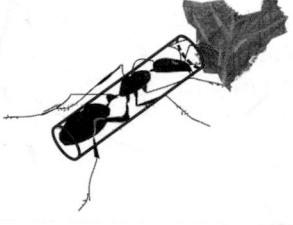

$$S = 2\pi rh + 2\pi r^2 \qquad V = \pi r^2 h$$

a. Approximate the surface area and volume of an ant that is 8 millimeters long and has a radius of 1.5 millimeters. Would this ant have a surface area large enough to meet its oxygen needs?

b. Consider a "giant" ant that is 8 meters long and has a radius of 1.5 meters. Would this ant have a surface area large enough to meet its oxygen needs?

c. *Writing* Substitute $1000r$ for r and $1000h$ for h into the formulas for surface area and volume. How does increasing the radius and height by a factor of 1000 affect surface area? How does it affect volume? Use the results to explain why "giant" ants do not exist.

★ Challenge

99. CRITICAL THINKING Substitute different combinations of odd and even positive integers for m and n in the expression $\sqrt[n]{x^m}$. Do *not* assume that x is always positive. When is absolute value needed in simplifying the expression?

MIXED REVIEW

COMPLETING THE SQUARE Find the value of *c* that makes the expression a perfect square trinomial. Then write the expression as the square of a binomial. (Review 5.5)

100. $x^2 + 14x + c$ **101.** $x^2 - 21x + c$ **102.** $x^2 - 7.6x + c$

103. $x^2 + 9.9x + c$ **104.** $x^2 + \frac{2}{3}x + c$ **105.** $x^2 - \frac{1}{4}x + c$

POLYNOMIAL OPERATIONS Perform the indicated operation. (Review 6.3 for 7.3)

106. $(-3x^3 + 6x) - (8x^3 + x^2 - 4x)$ **107.** $(50x - 3) + (8x^3 + 9x^2 + 2x + 4)$

108. $20x^2(x - 9)$ **109.** $(2x + 7)^2$

LONG DIVISION Divide using long division. (Review 6.5 for 7.3)

110. $(x^3 - 28x - 48) \div (x + 4)$ **111.** $(4x^2 + 3x - 3) \div (x + 1)$

112. $(4x^2 - 6x) \div (x - 2)$ **113.** $(x^4 - 2x^3 - 70x + 20) \div (x - 5)$

QUIZ 1

Self-Test for Lessons 7.1 and 7.2

Evaluate the expression without using a calculator. (Lesson 7.1)

1. $8^{2/3}$ **2.** $32^{-3/5}$ **3.** $-(81^{1/4})$ **4.** $(-64)^{2/3}$

Solve the equation. Round your answer to two decimal places. (Lesson 7.1)

5. $x^5 = 10$ **6.** $-9x^6 = -18$ **7.** $x^4 - 4 = 9$ **8.** $(x + 2)^3 = -15$

Write the expression in simplest form. (Lesson 7.2)

9. $\dfrac{1}{4^{-1/4}}$ **10.** $\sqrt[4]{\dfrac{16}{3}}$ **11.** $\dfrac{512^{1/3}}{8^{1/3}}$

12. $\sqrt{45}$ **13.** $\sqrt[3]{7} \cdot \sqrt[3]{49}$ **14.** $8^{1/5} + 2(8^{1/5})$

Write the expression in simplest form. Assume all variables are positive. (Lesson 7.2)

15. $\sqrt[3]{x^2} \cdot \sqrt[4]{x}$ **16.** $(x^{1/5})^{5/2}$ **17.** $\dfrac{xy^{1/2}}{x^{3/4}y^{-2}}$

18. $\sqrt[3]{5x^3y^5}$ **19.** $\sqrt{\dfrac{36x}{y^3}}$ **20.** $x(9y)^{1/2} - (x^2y)^{1/2}$

21. 🌐 **GENERATING POWER** As a rule of thumb, the power *P* (in horsepower) that a ship needs can be modeled by $P = \dfrac{d^{2/3} \cdot s^3}{c}$ where *d* is the ship's displacement (in tons), *s* is the normal speed (in knots), and *c* is the Admiralty coefficient. If a ship displaces 30,090 tons, has a normal speed of 22.5 knots, and has an Admiralty coefficient of 370, how much power does it need? (Lesson 7.1)

22. **BIOLOGY** ▸ **CONNECTION** The surface area *S* (in square centimeters) of a large dog can be approximated by the model $S = 11.2m^{2/3}$ where *m* is the mass (in grams) of the dog. A Labrador retriever's mass is about three times the mass of a Scottish terrier. Is its surface area also three times that of a Scottish terrier? (Lesson 7.2)

7.3 Power Functions and Function Operations

What you should learn

GOAL 1 Perform operations with functions including power functions.

GOAL 2 Use power functions and function operations to solve **real-life** problems, such as finding the proportion of water loss in a bird's egg in **Example 4**.

Why you should learn it

▼ To solve **real-life** problems, such as finding the height of a dinosaur in **Ex. 56**.

GOAL 1 PERFORMING FUNCTION OPERATIONS

In Chapter 6 you learned how to add, subtract, multiply, and divide polynomial functions. These operations can be defined for any functions.

CONCEPT SUMMARY — **OPERATIONS ON FUNCTIONS**

Let f and g be any two functions. A new function h can be defined by performing any of the four basic operations (addition, subtraction, multiplication, and division) on f and g.

Operation	Definition	Example: $f(x) = 2x$, $g(x) = x + 1$
ADDITION	$h(x) = f(x) + g(x)$	$h(x) = 2x + (x + 1) = 3x + 1$
SUBTRACTION	$h(x) = f(x) - g(x)$	$h(x) = 2x - (x + 1) = x - 1$
MULTIPLICATION	$h(x) = f(x) \cdot g(x)$	$h(x) = (2x)(x + 1) = 2x^2 + 2x$
DIVISION	$h(x) = \dfrac{f(x)}{g(x)}$	$h(x) = \dfrac{2x}{x + 1}$

The domain of h consists of the x-values that are in the domains of both f and g. Additionally, the domain of a quotient does not include x-values for which $g(x) = 0$.

So far you have studied various types of functions, including linear functions, quadratic functions, and polynomial functions of higher degree. Another common type of function is a **power function,** which has the form $y = ax^b$ where a is a real number and b is a rational number.

Note that when b is a positive integer, a power function is simply a type of polynomial function. For example, $y = ax^b$ is a linear function when $b = 1$, a quadratic function when $b = 2$, and a cubic function when $b = 3$.

EXAMPLE 1 *Adding and Subtracting Functions*

Let $f(x) = 2x^{1/2}$ and $g(x) = -6x^{1/2}$. Find (**a**) the sum of the functions, (**b**) the difference of the functions, and (**c**) the domains of the sum and difference.

SOLUTION

a. $f(x) + g(x) = 2x^{1/2} + \left(-6x^{1/2}\right) = (2 - 6)x^{1/2} = -4x^{1/2}$

b. $f(x) - g(x) = 2x^{1/2} - \left(-6x^{1/2}\right) = [2 - (-6)]x^{1/2} = 8x^{1/2}$

c. The functions f and g each have the same domain—all nonnegative real numbers. So, the domains of $f + g$ and $f - g$ also consist of all nonnegative real numbers.

EXAMPLE 2 **Multiplying and Dividing Functions**

STUDENT HELP

▸ **Look Back**
For help with function operations, see p. 338.

Let $f(x) = 3x$ and $g(x) = x^{1/4}$. Find (**a**) the product of the functions, (**b**) the quotient of the functions, and (**c**) the domains of the product and quotient.

SOLUTION

a. $f(x) \cdot g(x) = (3x)(x^{1/4}) = 3x^{(1 + 1/4)} = 3x^{5/4}$

b. $\dfrac{f(x)}{g(x)} = \dfrac{3x}{x^{1/4}} = 3x^{(1 - 1/4)} = 3x^{3/4}$

c. The domain of f consists of all real numbers and the domain of g consists of all nonnegative real numbers. So, the domain of $f \cdot g$ consists of all nonnegative real numbers. Because $g(0) = 0$, the domain of $\dfrac{f}{g}$ is restricted to all *positive* real numbers.

· · · · · · · · · ·

A fifth operation that can be performed with two functions is *composition*.

COMPOSITION OF TWO FUNCTIONS

The **composition** of the function f with the function g is:

$$h(x) = f(g(x))$$

The domain of h is the set of all x-values such that x is in the domain of g and $g(x)$ is in the domain of f.

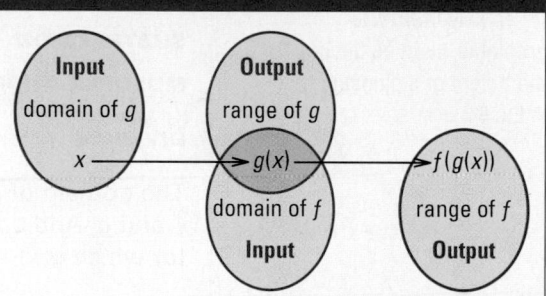

As with subtraction and division of functions, you need to pay attention to the order of functions when they are composed. In general, $f(g(x))$ is not equal to $g(f(x))$.

EXAMPLE 3 **Finding the Composition of Functions**

Let $f(x) = 3x^{-1}$ and $g(x) = 2x - 1$. Find the following.

a. $f(g(x))$ **b.** $g(f(x))$ **c.** $f(f(x))$ **d.** the domain of each composition

SOLUTION

STUDENT HELP

▸ **Study Tip**
When you are writing the composition of f with g, you may want to first rewrite $f(x) = 3x^{-1}$ as
$$f(\blacksquare) = 3(\blacksquare)^{-1}$$
and then substitute $g(x) = 2x - 1$ everywhere there is a box.

a. $f(g(x)) = f(2x - 1) = 3(2x - 1)^{-1} = \dfrac{3}{2x - 1}$

b. $g(f(x)) = g(3x^{-1}) = 2(3x^{-1}) - 1 = 6x^{-1} - 1 = \dfrac{6}{x} - 1$

c. $f(f(x)) = f(3x^{-1}) = 3(3x^{-1})^{-1} = 3(3^{-1}x) = 3^0 x = x$

d. The domain of $f(g(x))$ consists of all real numbers except $x = \dfrac{1}{2}$ because $g\left(\dfrac{1}{2}\right) = 0$ is not in the domain of f. The domains of $g(f(x))$ and $f(f(x))$ consist of all real numbers except $x = 0$, because 0 is not in the domain of f. Note that $f(f(x))$ simplifies to x, but that result is not what determines the domain.

GOAL 2 USING FUNCTION OPERATIONS IN REAL LIFE

EXAMPLE 4 *Using Function Operations*

BIOLOGY CONNECTION You are doing a science project and have found research indicating that the incubation time I (in days) of a bird's egg can be modeled by $I(m) = 12m^{0.217}$ where m is the egg's mass (in grams). You have also found that during incubation the egg's rate of water loss R (in grams per day) can be modeled by $R(m) = 0.015m^{0.742}$.

You conjecture that the proportion of water loss during incubation is about the same for any size egg. Show how you can use the two power function models to verify your conjecture. ▶ Source: *Biology by Numbers*

SOLUTION

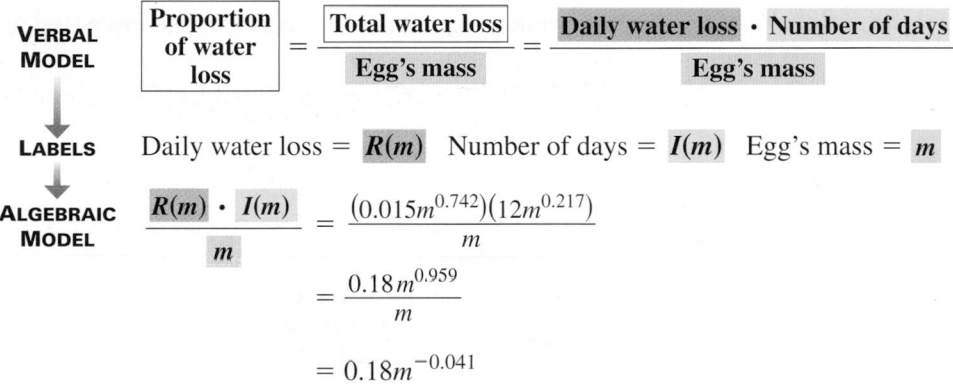

VERBAL MODEL

$$\boxed{\text{Proportion of water loss}} = \frac{\boxed{\text{Total water loss}}}{\boxed{\text{Egg's mass}}} = \frac{\boxed{\text{Daily water loss}} \cdot \boxed{\text{Number of days}}}{\boxed{\text{Egg's mass}}}$$

LABELS   Daily water loss = $R(m)$ Number of days = $I(m)$ Egg's mass = m

ALGEBRAIC MODEL

$$\frac{R(m) \cdot I(m)}{m} = \frac{(0.015m^{0.742})(12m^{0.217})}{m}$$

$$= \frac{0.18m^{0.959}}{m}$$

$$= 0.18m^{-0.041}$$

Because $m^{-0.041}$ is approximately m^0, the proportion of water loss can be treated as $0.18m^0 = (0.18)(1) = 0.18$. So, the proportion of water loss is about 18% for any size bird's egg, and your conjecture is correct.

Business

EXAMPLE 5 *Using Composition of Functions*

A clothing store advertises that it is having a 25% off sale. For one day only, the store advertises an additional savings of 10%.

a. Use composition of functions to find the total percent discount.

b. What would be the sale price of a $40 sweater?

SOLUTION

STUDENT HELP

▶ **Skills Review**
For help with calculating percents, see p. 907.

a. Let x represent the price. The sale price for a 25% discount can be represented by the function $f(x) = x - 0.25x = 0.75x$. The reduced sale price for an additional 10% discount can be represented by the function $g(x) = x - 0.10x = 0.90x$.

$$g(f(x)) = g(0.75x) = 0.90(0.75x) = 0.675x$$

▶ The total percent discount is $100\% - 67.5\% = 32.5\%$.

b. Let $x = 40$. Then $g(f(x)) = g(f(\mathbf{40})) = 0.675(\mathbf{40}) = 27$.

▶ The sale price of the sweater is $27.

GUIDED PRACTICE

Vocabulary Check ✔

1. Complete this statement: The function $y = ax^b$ is a(n) _?_ function where a is a(n) _?_ number and b is a(n) _?_ number.

Concept Check ✔

2. **LOGICAL REASONING** Tell whether the sum of two power functions is *sometimes*, *always*, or *never* a power function.

ERROR ANALYSIS Let $f(x) = x^2 + 2$ and $g(x) = 3x$. What is wrong with the composition shown? Explain.

3.
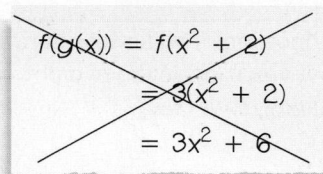

$$f(g(x)) = f(x^2 + 2)$$
$$= 3(x^2 + 2)$$
$$= 3x^2 + 6$$

4.
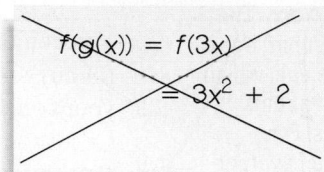

$$f(g(x)) = f(3x)$$
$$= 3x^2 + 2$$

Skill Check ✔

Let $f(x) = 4x$ and $g(x) = x - 1$. Perform the indicated operation and state the domain.

5. $f(x) + g(x)$ 6. $f(x) - g(x)$ 7. $f(x) \cdot g(x)$

8. $\dfrac{f(x)}{g(x)}$ 9. $f(g(x))$ 10. $g(f(x))$

11. 🌐 **SALES BONUS** You are a sales representative for a clothing manufacturer. You are paid an annual salary plus a bonus of 2% of your sales over $200,000. Consider two functions: $f(x) = x - 200,000$ and $g(x) = 0.02x$. If $x > \$200,000$, which composition, $f(g(x))$ or $g(f(x))$, represents your bonus? Explain.

PRACTICE AND APPLICATIONS

STUDENT HELP

▶ **Extra Practice**
to help you master
skills is on p. 949.

ADDING AND SUBTRACTING FUNCTIONS Let $f(x) = x^2 - 5x + 8$ and $g(x) = x^2 - 4$. Perform the indicated operation and state the domain.

12. $f(x) + g(x)$ 13. $g(x) + f(x)$ 14. $f(x) + f(x)$ 15. $g(x) + g(x)$

16. $f(x) - g(x)$ 17. $g(x) - f(x)$ 18. $f(x) - f(x)$ 19. $g(x) - g(x)$

MULTIPLYING AND DIVIDING FUNCTIONS Let $f(x) = 2x^{2/3}$ and $g(x) = 3x^{1/2}$. Perform the indicated operation and state the domain.

20. $f(x) \cdot g(x)$ 21. $g(x) \cdot f(x)$ 22. $f(x) \cdot f(x)$ 23. $g(x) \cdot g(x)$

24. $\dfrac{f(x)}{g(x)}$ 25. $\dfrac{g(x)}{f(x)}$ 26. $\dfrac{f(x)}{f(x)}$ 27. $\dfrac{g(x)}{g(x)}$

STUDENT HELP

▶ **HOMEWORK HELP**
Example 1: Exs. 12–19,
32–51
Example 2: Exs. 20–27,
32–51
Example 3: Exs. 28–51
Example 4: Exs. 52, 53
Example 5: Exs. 54–56

COMPOSITION OF FUNCTIONS Let $f(x) = 4x^{-5}$ and $g(x) = x^{3/4}$. Perform the indicated operation and state the domain.

28. $f(g(x))$ 29. $g(f(x))$ 30. $f(f(x))$ 31. $g(g(x))$

FUNCTION OPERATIONS Let $f(x) = 10x$ and $g(x) = x + 4$. Perform the indicated operation and state the domain.

32. $f(x) + g(x)$ 33. $f(x) - g(x)$ 34. $f(x) \cdot g(x)$ 35. $\dfrac{f(x)}{g(x)}$

36. $f(g(x))$ 37. $g(f(x))$ 38. $f(f(x))$ 39. $g(g(x))$

FUNCTION OPERATIONS Perform the indicated operation and state the domain.

40. $f + g$; $f(x) = x + 3$, $g(x) = 5x$

41. $f + g$; $f(x) = 3x^{1/2}$, $g(x) = -2x^{1/2}$

42. $f - g$; $f(x) = -x^{2/3}$, $g(x) = x^{2/3}$

43. $f - g$; $f(x) = x^2 - 3$, $g(x) = x + 5$

44. $f \cdot g$; $f(x) = 7x^{2/5}$, $g(x) = -2x^3$

45. $f \cdot g$; $f(x) = x - 4$, $g(x) = 4x^2$

46. $\dfrac{f}{g}$; $f(x) = 9x^{-1}$, $g(x) = x^{1/4}$

47. $\dfrac{f}{g}$; $f(x) = x^2 - 5x$, $g(x) = x$

48. $f(g(x))$; $f(x) = 6x^{-1}$, $g(x) = 5x - 2$

49. $g(f(x))$; $f(x) = x^2 - 3$, $g(x) = x^2 + 1$

50. $f(f(x))$; $f(x) = 2x^{1/5}$

51. $g(g(x))$; $g(x) = 9x - 2$

52.  **HEART RATE** For a mammal, the heart rate r (in beats per minute) and the life span s (in minutes) are related to body mass m (in kilograms) by these formulas:

$$r(m) = 241m^{-0.25} \qquad s(m) = (6 \times 10^6)m^{0.2}$$

Find the relationship between body mass and average number of heartbeats in a lifetime by calculating $r(m) \cdot s(m)$. Explain the results.

▶ Source: *Physiology by Numbers*

53.  **BREATHING RATE** For a mammal, the volume b (in milliliters) of air breathed in and the volume d (in milliliters) of the dead space (the portion of the lungs not filled with air) are related to body weight w (in grams) by these formulas:

$$b(w) = 0.007w \qquad d(w) = 0.002w$$

The relationship between breathing rate r (in breaths per minute) and body weight is:

$$r(w) = \frac{1.1w^{0.734}}{b(w) - d(w)}$$

Simplify $r(w)$ and calculate the breathing rate for body weights of 6.5 grams, 12,300 grams, and 70,000 grams. ▶ Source: *Respiration*

🌐 **COAT SALE** In Exercises 54 and 55, use the following information.
A clothing store is having a sale in which you can take $50 off the cost of any coat in the store. The store also offers 10% off your entire purchase if you open a charge account. You decide to open a charge account and buy a coat.

54. Use composition of functions to find the sale price of a $175 coat when $50 is subtracted before the 10% discount is applied.

55. CRITICAL THINKING Why doesn't the store apply the 10% discount before subtracting $50?

56. 🌐 **PALEONTOLOGY** The height at the hip h (in centimeters) of an ornithomimid, a type of dinosaur, can be modeled by

$$h(l) = 3.49l^{1.02}$$

where l is the length (in centimeters) of the dinosaur's instep. The length of the instep can be modeled by

$$l(f) = 1.5f$$

where f is the footprint length (in centimeters). Use composition of functions to find the relationship between height and footprint length. Then find the height of an ornithomimid with a footprint length of 30 centimeters. ▶ Source: *Dinosaur Tracks*

57. *Writing* Explain how to perform the function operations $f(x) + g(x)$, $f(x) - g(x)$, $f(x) \cdot g(x)$, $\dfrac{f(x)}{g(x)}$, and $f(g(x))$ for any two functions f and g.

Test Preparation

QUANTITATIVE COMPARISON In Exercise 58–61, choose the statement that is true about the given quantities.

   Ⓐ The quantity in column A is greater.

   Ⓑ The quantity in column B is greater.

   Ⓒ The two quantities are equal.

   Ⓓ The relationship cannot be determined from the given information.

	Column A	Column B
58.	$f(g(4)); f(x) = 6x, g(x) = 3x^2$	$f(g(2)); f(x) = x^{2/3}, g(x) = -2x$
59.	$g(f(-1)); f(x) = 5x^{-2}, g(x) = x$	$g(f(0)); f(x) = 2x + 5, g(x) = x^2$
60.	$f(f(3)); f(x) = 3x - 7$	$f(f(-2)); f(x) = 10x^3$
61.	$g(g(5)); g(x) = 16x^{-1/4}$	$g(g(7)); g(x) = x^2 + 8$

★ **Challenge**

FUNCTION COMPOSITION Find functions f and g such that $f(g(x)) = h(x)$.

62. $h(x) = (6x - 5)^3$ **63.** $h(x) = \sqrt[3]{x + 2}$

64. $h(x) = \dfrac{\sqrt[4]{x}}{2}$ **65.** $h(x) = 3x^2 + 7$

EXTRA CHALLENGE
www.mcdougallittell.com

66. $h(x) = |2x + 9|$ **67.** $h(x) = 21x$

MIXED REVIEW

REWRITING EQUATIONS Solve the equation for y. (Review 1.4 for 7.4)

68. $y - 3x = 10$ **69.** $2x + 3y = -8$ **70.** $x = -2y + 6$

71. $xy + 2 = 7$ **72.** $\dfrac{1}{2}x - \dfrac{2}{3}y = 1$ **73.** $ax + by = c$

GRAPHING FUNCTIONS Graph the function. (Review 2.1 for 7.4)

74. $y = x - 2$ **75.** $y = 4x - 3$ **76.** $y = 5x - \dfrac{2}{3}$

77. $y = -2x - 4$ **78.** $y = -\dfrac{1}{2}x + 7$ **79.** $y = -8$

SOLVING EQUATIONS Find the real-number solutions of the equation. (Review 6.4)

80. $3x^3 - 2x^2 = 0$ **81.** $2x^3 - 6x^2 + x = 3$

82. $5x^4 + 19x^2 - 4 = 0$ **83.** $x^4 + 6x^3 + 8x + 48 = 0$

84. 🌐 **CRYPTOGRAPHY** Use the inverse of $A = \begin{bmatrix} 5 & 2 \\ 2 & 1 \end{bmatrix}$ and the code on page 225 to decode the message. (Review 4.4)

45, 21, 84, 35, 92, 37, 142, 61
62, 25, 118, 49, 103, 44, 95, 38

▶ **ACTIVITY 7.4**

Developing Concepts

Exploring Inverse Functions

SET UP
Work in a group of three.

MATERIALS
• graph paper
• straightedge

▶ **QUESTION** How are a function and its *inverse* related?

▶ **EXPLORING THE CONCEPT**

Use the following steps to find the inverse of $f(x) = \dfrac{x-3}{2}$.

1 Choose values of x and find the corresponding values of $y = f(x)$. Plot the points and draw the line that passes through them.

2 Interchange the x- and y-coordinates of the ordered pairs found in **Step 1**. Plot the new points and draw the line that passes through them.

3 Write an equation of the line from **Step 2**. Call this function g.

4 Fold your graph paper so that the graphs of f and g coincide. How are the graphs geometrically related?

5 In words, f is the function that subtracts 3 from x and then divides the result by 2. Describe the function g in words.

6 Predict what the compositions $f(g(x))$ and $g(f(x))$ will be. Confirm your predictions by finding $f(g(x))$ and $g(f(x))$.

The functions f and g are inverses of each other.

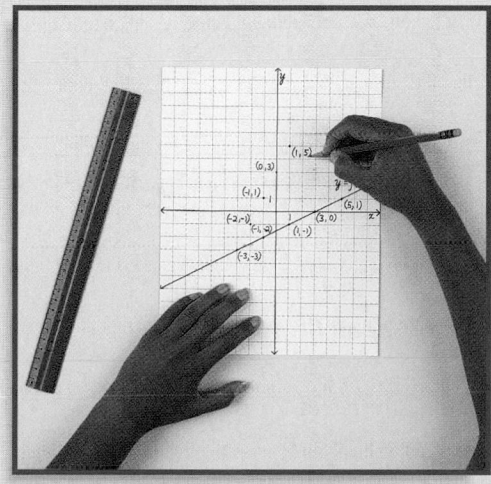 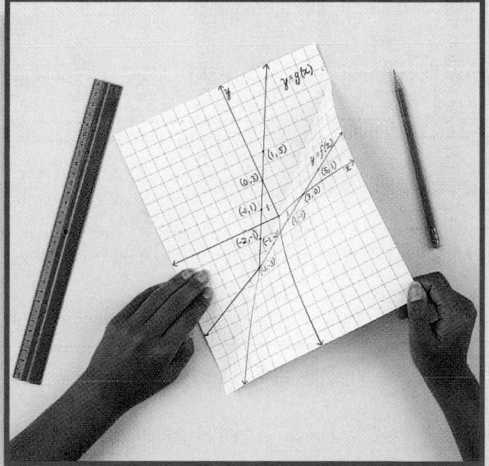

▶ **DRAWING CONCLUSIONS**

Each member in your group should choose a different function from the list below.

$$f(x) = 2x + 5 \qquad f(x) = \frac{x-2}{4} \qquad f(x) = 5 - \frac{5}{2}x$$

1. Complete **Steps 1–3** above to find the inverse of your function.

2. Complete **Step 4**. How can you graph the inverse of a function without first finding ordered pairs (x, y)?

3. Complete **Steps 5 and 6**. How can you test to see if the function you found in Exercise 1 is indeed the inverse of the original function?

Inverse Functions

What you should learn

GOAL 1 Find inverses of linear functions.

GOAL 2 Find inverses of nonlinear functions, as applied in **Example 6**.

Why you should learn it

▼ To solve **real-life** problems, such as finding your bowling average in **Ex. 59**.

GOAL 1 FINDING INVERSES OF LINEAR FUNCTIONS

In Lesson 2.1 you learned that a *relation* is a mapping of input values onto output values. An **inverse relation** maps the output values back to their original input values. This means that the domain of the inverse relation is the range of the original relation and that the range of the inverse relation is the domain of the original relation.

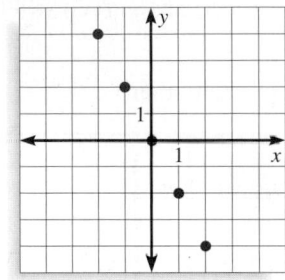

Original relation

x	-2	-1	0	1	2
y	4	2	0	-2	-4

Inverse relation

x	4	2	0	-2	-4
y	-2	-1	0	1	2

The graph of an inverse relation is the *reflection* of the graph of the original relation. The line of reflection is $y = x$.

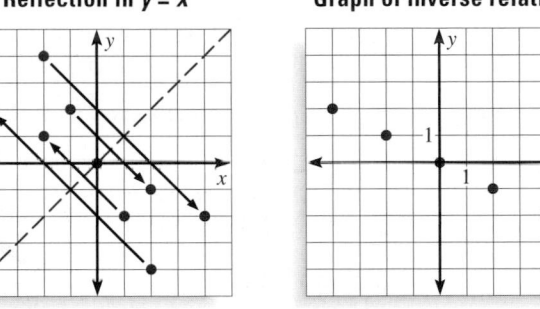

Graph of original relation   **Reflection in $y = x$**   **Graph of inverse relation**

To find the inverse of a relation that is given by an equation in x and y, switch the roles of x and y and solve for y (if possible).

EXAMPLE 1 *Finding an Inverse Relation*

Find an equation for the inverse of the relation $y = 2x - 4$.

STUDENT HELP

Look Back
For help with solving equations for y, see p. 26.

SOLUTION

$y = 2x - 4$	**Write original relation.**
$x = 2y - 4$	**Switch x and y.**
$x + 4 = 2y$	**Add 4 to each side.**
$\frac{1}{2}x + 2 = y$	**Divide each side by 2.**

▶ The inverse relation is $y = \frac{1}{2}x + 2$.

In Example 1 both the original relation and the inverse relation happen to be functions. In such cases the two functions are called **inverse functions**.

Functions f and g are inverses of each other provided:

$$f(g(x)) = x \quad \text{and} \quad g(f(x)) = x$$

The function g is denoted by f^{-1}, read as "f inverse."

Given any function, you can always find its inverse relation by switching x and y. For a linear function $f(x) = mx + b$ where $m \neq 0$, the inverse is itself a linear function.

EXAMPLE 2 *Verifying Inverse Functions*

Verify that $f(x) = 2x - 4$ and $f^{-1}(x) = \dfrac{1}{2}x + 2$ are inverses.

SOLUTION Show that $f(f^{-1}(x)) = x$ and $f^{-1}(f(x)) = x$.

$$f(f^{-1}(x)) = f\left(\frac{1}{2}x + 2\right) \qquad\qquad f^{-1}(f(x)) = f^{-1}(2x - 4)$$

$$= 2\left(\frac{1}{2}x + 2\right) - 4 \qquad\qquad\qquad = \frac{1}{2}(2x - 4) + 2$$

$$= x + 4 - 4 \qquad\qquad\qquad\qquad = x - 2 + 2$$

$$= x\ \checkmark \qquad\qquad\qquad\qquad\qquad = x\ \checkmark$$

EXAMPLE 3 *Writing an Inverse Model*

When calibrating a spring scale, you need to know how far the spring stretches based on given weights. Hooke's law states that the length a spring stretches is proportional to the weight attached to the spring. A model for one scale is $\ell = 0.5w + 3$ where ℓ is the total length (in inches) of the spring and w is the weight (in pounds) of the object.

a. Find the inverse model for the scale.

b. If you place a melon on the scale and the spring stretches to a total length of 5.5 inches, how much does the melon weigh?

spring with
weight
attached

unweighted
spring

3

0.5w

ℓ

Not drawn to scale

SOLUTION

a.

$\ell = 0.5w + 3$	**Write original model.**
$\ell - 3 = 0.5w$	**Subtract 3 from each side.**
$\dfrac{\ell - 3}{0.5} = w$	**Divide each side by 0.5.**
$2\ell - 6 = w$	**Simplify.**

b. To find the weight of the melon, substitute 5.5 for ℓ.

$$w = 2\ell - 6 = 2(5.5) - 6 = 11 - 6 = 5$$

▸ The melon weighs 5 pounds.

GOAL 2 FINDING INVERSES OF NONLINEAR FUNCTIONS

The graphs of the power functions $f(x) = x^2$ and $g(x) = x^3$ are shown below along with their reflections in the line $y = x$. Notice that the inverse of $g(x) = x^3$ is a function, but that the inverse of $f(x) = x^2$ is *not* a function.

STUDENT HELP

▶ **Look Back**
For help with recognizing when a relationship is a function, see p. 70.

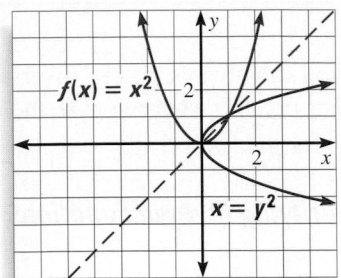
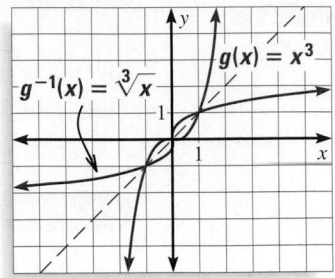

If the domain of $f(x) = x^2$ is *restricted*, say to only nonnegative real numbers, then the inverse of f *is* a function.

EXAMPLE 4   *Finding an Inverse Power Function*

Find the inverse of the function $f(x) = x^2$, $x \geq 0$.

SOLUTION

$f(x) = x^2$	**Write original function.**
$y = x^2$	**Replace $f(x)$ with y.**
$x = y^2$	**Switch x and y.**
$\pm\sqrt{x} = y$	**Take square roots of each side.**

Because the domain of f is restricted to nonnegative values, the inverse function is $f^{-1}(x) = \sqrt{x}$. (You would choose $f^{-1}(x) = -\sqrt{x}$ if the domain had been restricted to $x \leq 0$.)

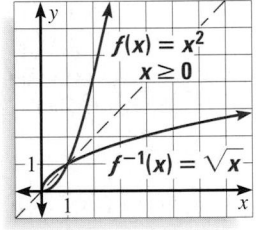

✓ **CHECK** To check your work, graph f and f^{-1} as shown. Note that the graph of $f^{-1}(x) = \sqrt{x}$ is the reflection of the graph of $f(x) = x^2$, $x \geq 0$ in the line $y = x$.

· · · · · · · · · ·

In the graphs at the top of the page, notice that the graph of $f(x) = x^2$ can be intersected twice with a horizontal line and that its inverse is *not* a function. On the other hand, the graph of $g(x) = x^3$ cannot be intersected twice with a horizontal line and its inverse *is* a function. This observation suggests the *horizontal line test*.

HORIZONTAL LINE TEST

If no horizontal line intersects the graph of a function f more than once, then the inverse of f is itself a function.

EXAMPLE 5 *Finding an Inverse Function*

Consider the function $f(x) = \frac{1}{2}x^3 - 2$. Determine whether the inverse of f is a function. Then find the inverse.

SOLUTION

Begin by graphing the function and noticing that no horizontal line intersects the graph more than once. This tells you that the inverse of f is itself a function. To find an equation for f^{-1}, complete the following steps.

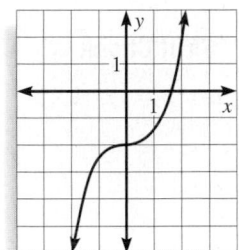

$f(x) = \frac{1}{2}x^3 - 2$	**Write original function.**
$y = \frac{1}{2}x^3 - 2$	**Replace $f(x)$ with y.**
$x = \frac{1}{2}y^3 - 2$	**Switch x and y.**
$x + 2 = \frac{1}{2}y^3$	**Add 2 to each side.**
$2x + 4 = y^3$	**Multiply each side by 2.**
$\sqrt[3]{2x + 4} = y$	**Take cube root of each side.**

▶ The inverse function is $f^{-1}(x) = \sqrt[3]{2x + 4}$.

EXAMPLE 6 *Writing an Inverse Model*

ASTRONOMY Near the end of a star's life the star will eject gas, forming a planetary nebula. The Ring Nebula is an example of a planetary nebula. The volume V (in cubic kilometers) of this nebula can be modeled by $V = (9.01 \times 10^{26})t^3$ where t is the age (in years) of the nebula. Write the inverse model that gives the age of the nebula as a function of its volume. Then determine the approximate age of the Ring Nebula given that its volume is about 1.5×10^{38} cubic kilometers.

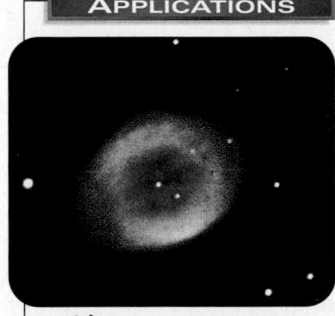

ASTRONOMY
   The Ring Nebula is part of the constellation Lyra. The radius of the nebula is expanding at an average rate of about 5.99×10^8 kilometers per year.

APPLICATION LINK
www.mcdougallittell.com

SOLUTION

$V = (9.01 \times 10^{26})t^3$	**Write original model.**
$\dfrac{V}{9.01 \times 10^{26}} = t^3$	**Isolate power.**
$\sqrt[3]{\dfrac{V}{9.01 \times 10^{26}}} = t$	**Take cube root of each side.**
$(1.04 \times 10^{-9})\sqrt[3]{V} = t$	**Simplify.**

To find the age of the nebula, substitute 1.5×10^{38} for V.

$t = (1.04 \times 10^{-9})\sqrt[3]{V}$	**Write inverse model.**
$= (1.04 \times 10^{-9})\sqrt[3]{1.5 \times 10^{38}}$	**Substitute for V.**
≈ 5500	**Use a calculator.**

▶ The Ring Nebula is about 5500 years old.

GUIDED PRACTICE

Vocabulary Check ✓

1. Explain how to use the horizontal line test to determine if an inverse relation is an inverse function.

Concept Check ✓

2. Describe how the graph of a relation and the graph of its inverse are related.

3. Explain the steps in finding an equation for an inverse function.

Skill Check ✓

Find the inverse relation.

4.

x	1	2	3	4	5
y	−1	−2	−3	−4	−5

5.

x	−4	−2	0	2	4
y	2	1	0	1	2

Find an equation for the inverse relation.

6. $y = 5x$

7. $y = 2x - 1$

8. $y = -\dfrac{2}{3}x + 6$

Verify that f and g are inverse functions.

9. $f(x) = 8x^3$, $g(x) = \dfrac{x^{1/3}}{2}$

10. $f(x) = 6x + 3$, $g(x) = \dfrac{1}{6}x - \dfrac{1}{2}$

Find the inverse function.

11. $f(x) = 3x^4$, $x \geq 0$

12. $f(x) = 2x^3 + 1$

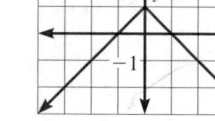

13. The graph of $f(x) = -|x| + 1$ is shown. Is the inverse of f a function? Explain.

Ex. 13

PRACTICE AND APPLICATIONS

STUDENT HELP

▶ **Extra Practice**
to help you master
skills is on p. 949.

INVERSE RELATIONS Find the inverse relation.

14.

x	1	4	1	0	1
y	3	−1	6	−3	9

15.

x	1	−2	4	2	−2
y	0	3	−2	2	−1

FINDING INVERSES Find an equation for the inverse relation.

16. $y = -2x + 5$

17. $y = 3x - 3$

18. $y = \dfrac{1}{2}x + 6$

19. $y = -\dfrac{4}{5}x + 11$

20. $y = 11x - 5$

21. $y = -12x + 7$

22. $y = 3x - \dfrac{1}{4}$

23. $y = 8x - 13$

24. $y = -\dfrac{3}{7}x + \dfrac{5}{7}$

VERIFYING INVERSES Verify that f and g are inverse functions.

STUDENT HELP

▶ **HOMEWORK HELP**
Example 1: Exs. 14–24
Example 2: Exs. 25–32
Example 3: Exs. 57–59
Example 4: Exs. 33–41
Example 5: Exs. 42–56
Example 6: Exs. 60–62

25. $f(x) = x + 7$, $g(x) = x - 7$

26. $f(x) = 3x - 1$, $g(x) = \dfrac{1}{3}x + \dfrac{1}{3}$

27. $f(x) = \dfrac{1}{2}x + 1$, $g(x) = 2x - 2$

28. $f(x) = -2x + 4$, $g(x) = -\dfrac{1}{2}x + 2$

29. $f(x) = 3x^3 + 1$, $g(x) = \left(\dfrac{x-1}{3}\right)^{1/3}$

30. $f(x) = \dfrac{1}{3}x^2$, $x \geq 0$; $g(x) = (3x)^{1/2}$

31. $f(x) = \dfrac{x^5 + 2}{7}$, $g(x) = \sqrt[5]{7x - 2}$

32. $f(x) = 256x^4$, $x \geq 0$; $g(x) = \dfrac{\sqrt[4]{x}}{4}$

VISUAL THINKING Match the graph with the graph of its inverse.

33.
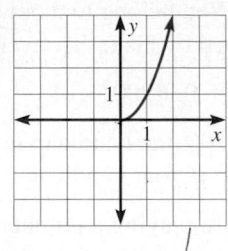

34.
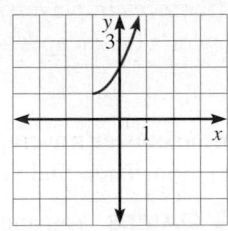

35.
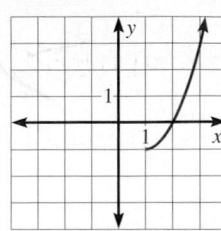

A.
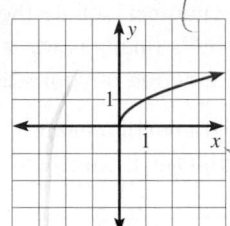

B.
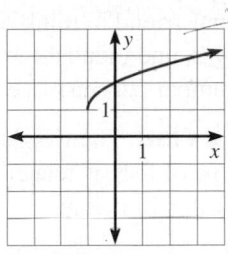

C.
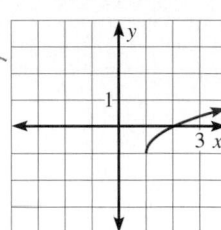

INVERSES OF POWER FUNCTIONS Find the inverse power function.

36. $f(x) = x^7$

37. $f(x) = -x^6, x \geq 0$

38. $f(x) = 3x^4, x \leq 0$

39. $f(x) = \frac{1}{32}x^5$

40. $f(x) = 10x^3$

41. $f(x) = -\frac{9}{4}x^2, x \leq 0$

INVERSES OF NONLINEAR FUNCTIONS Find the inverse function.

42. $f(x) = x^3 + 2$

43. $f(x) = -2x^5 + \frac{1}{3}$

44. $f(x) = 2 - 2x^2, x \leq 0$

45. $f(x) = \frac{3}{5}x^3 - 9$

46. $f(x) = x^4 - \frac{1}{2}, x \geq 0$

47. $f(x) = \frac{1}{6}x^5 + \frac{2}{3}$

HORIZONTAL LINE TEST Graph the function f. Then use the graph to determine whether the inverse of f is a function.

48. $f(x) = -2x + 3$

49. $f(x) = x + 3$

50. $f(x) = x^2 + 1$

51. $f(x) = -3x^2$

52. $f(x) = x^3 + 3$

53. $f(x) = 2x^3$

54. $f(x) = |x| + 2$

55. $f(x) = (x + 1)(x - 3)$

56. $f(x) = 6x^4 - 9x + 1$

57. 🌐 **EXCHANGE RATE** The Federal Reserve Bank of New York reports international exchange rates at 12:00 noon each day. On January 20, 1999, the exchange rate for Canada was 1.5226. Therefore, the formula that gives Canadian dollars in terms of United States dollars on that day is

$$D_C = 1.5226D_{US}$$

where D_C represents Canadian dollars and D_{US} represents United States dollars. Find the inverse of the function to determine the value of a United States dollar in terms of Canadian dollars on January 20, 1999.

DATA UPDATE of Federal Reserve Bank of New York data at www.mcdougallittell.com

58. 🌐 **TEMPERATURE CONVERSION** The formula to convert temperatures from degrees Fahrenheit to degrees Celsius is:

$$C = \frac{5}{9}(F - 32)$$

Write the inverse of the function, which converts temperatures from degrees Celsius to degrees Fahrenheit. Then find the Fahrenheit temperatures that are equal to 29°C, 10°C, and 0°C.

FOCUS ON CAREERS

INVESTMENT BANKER
Investment bankers have a wide variety of job descriptions. Some buy and sell international currencies at reported exchange rates, discussed in Ex. 57.

CAREER LINK
www.mcdougallittell.com

59.  **BOWLING** In bowling a *handicap* is a change in score to adjust for differences in players' abilities. You belong to a bowling league in which each bowler's handicap h is determined by his or her average a using this formula:

$$h = 0.9(200 - a)$$

(If the bowler's average is over 200, the handicap is 0.) Find the inverse of the function. Then find your average if your handicap is 27.

60. **GAMES** You and a friend are playing a number-guessing game. You ask your friend to think of a positive number, square the number, multiply the result by 2, and then add 3. If your friend's final answer is 53, what was the original number chosen? Use an inverse function in your solution.

61. **FISH** The weight w (in kilograms) of a hake, a type of fish, is related to its length l (in centimeters) by this function:

$$w = \left(9.37 \times 10^{-6}\right)l^3$$

Find the inverse of the function. Then determine the approximate length of a hake that weighs 0.679 kilogram. ▶ Source: *Fishbyte*

Hake

STUDENT HELP

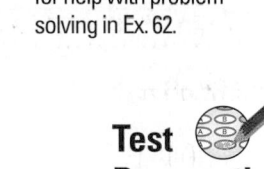

HOMEWORK HELP
Visit our Web site
www.mcdougallittell.com
for help with problem
solving in Ex. 62.

62. **SHELVES** The weight w (in pounds) that can be supported by a shelf made from half-inch Douglas fir plywood can be modeled by

$$w = \left(\frac{82.9}{d}\right)^3$$

where d is the distance (in inches) between the supports for the shelf. Find the inverse of the function. Then find the distance between the supports of a shelf that can hold a set of encyclopedias weighing 66 pounds.

Test Preparation

QUANTITATIVE COMPARISON In Exercises 63 and 64, choose the statement that is true about the given quantities.

Ⓐ The quantity in column A is greater.

Ⓑ The quantity in column B is greater.

Ⓒ The two quantities are equal.

Ⓓ The relationship cannot be determined from the given information.

	Column A	Column B
63.	$f^{-1}(3)$ where $f(x) = 6x + 1$	$f^{-1}(-4)$ where $f(x) = -2x + 9$
64.	$f^{-1}(2)$ where $f(x) = -5x^3$	$f^{-1}(0)$ where $f(x) = x^3 + 14$

★ **Challenge**

INVERSE FUNCTIONS Complete Exercises 65–68 to explore functions that are their own inverses.

65. **VISUAL THINKING** The functions $f(x) = x$ and $g(x) = -x$ are their own inverses. Graph each function and explain why this is true.

66. Graph other linear functions that are their own inverses.

67. Write equations of the lines you graphed in Exercise 66.

EXTRA CHALLENGE
www.mcdougallittell.com

68. Use your equations from Exercise 67 to find a general formula for a family of linear equations that are their own inverses.

MIXED REVIEW

ABSOLUTE VALUE FUNCTIONS Graph the absolute value function. (Review 2.8 for 7.5)

69. $f(x) = |x| - 1$

70. $f(x) = 2|x| + 7$

71. $f(x) = |x - 4| + 5$

72. $f(x) = -3|x + 2| - 7$

QUADRATIC FUNCTIONS Graph the quadratic function. (Review 5.1 for 7.5)

73. $f(x) = x^2 + 2$

74. $f(x) = (x + 3)^2 - 7$

75. $f(x) = 2(x + 2)^2 - 5$

76. $f(x) = -3(x - 4)^2 + 1$

SIMPLIFYING EXPRESSIONS Simplify the expression. Assume all variables are positive. (Review 7.2)

77. $\sqrt[4]{20} \cdot \sqrt[4]{\dfrac{4}{5}}$

78. $\left(\dfrac{1}{9}\right)^{1/6} \left(\dfrac{1}{9}\right)^{1/3}$

79. $\dfrac{(5y)^{1/5}}{(5y)^{6/5}}$

80. $\sqrt[6]{2x^6}$

81. $3\sqrt[7]{5} + 2\sqrt[7]{5}$

82. $\sqrt[3]{270} + 2\sqrt[3]{10}$

83. 🌐 **SNACK FOODS** Delia, Ruth, and Amy go to the store to buy snacks. Delia buys 3 bagels and 3 apples. Ruth buys 1 pretzel, 2 bagels, and 3 apples. Amy buys 2 pretzels and 4 bagels. Delia's bill comes to $3.72, Ruth's to $5.06, and Amy's to $6.58. How much does one bagel cost? (**Review 3.6**)

QUIZ 2

Self-Test for Lessons 7.3 and 7.4

Let $f(x) = 6x^2 - x^{1/2}$ and $g(x) = 2x^{1/2}$. Perform the indicated operation and state the domain. (Lesson 7.3)

1. $f(x) + g(x)$

2. $f(x) - g(x)$

3. $f(x) \cdot g(x)$

4. $\dfrac{f(x)}{g(x)}$

Let $f(x) = 3x^{-1}$ and $g(x) = x - 8$. Perform the indicated operation and state the domain. (Lesson 7.3)

5. $f(g(x))$

6. $g(f(x))$

7. $f(f(x))$

8. $g(g(x))$

Verify that f and g are inverse functions. (Lesson 7.4)

9. $f(x) = 2x - 3$, $g(x) = \dfrac{1}{2}x + \dfrac{3}{2}$

10. $f(x) = (x + 1)^{1/3}$, $g(x) = x^3 - 1$

Find the inverse function. (Lesson 7.4)

11. $f(x) = x + 8$

12. $f(x) = 2x^4$, $x \le 0$

13. $f(x) = -x^5 + 6$

Graph the function f. Then use the graph to determine whether the inverse of f is a function. (Lesson 7.4)

14. $f(x) = 3x^6 + 2$

15. $f(x) = -2x^5 + 3x - 1$

16. $f(x) = 6\sqrt[3]{x} + 4$

17. 🌐 **RIPPLES IN A POND** You drop a pebble into a calm pond causing ripples of concentric circles. The radius r (in feet) of the outer ripple is given by $r(t) = 0.6t$ where t is the time (in seconds) after the pebble hits the water. The area A (in square feet) of the outer ripple is given by $A(r) = \pi r^2$. Use composition of functions to find the relationship between area and time. Then find the area of the outer ripple after 2 seconds. (**Lesson 7.3**)

▶ ACTIVITY 7.4

Using Technology

Graphing Inverse Functions

You can use a graphing calculator to graph inverse functions.

▶ **EXAMPLE**

Use a graphing calculator to graph the inverse of $y = 2x - 5$.

▶ **SOLUTION**

1 Graph the original function. Use a viewing window such as $-15 \le x \le 15$ and $-10 \le y \le 10$.

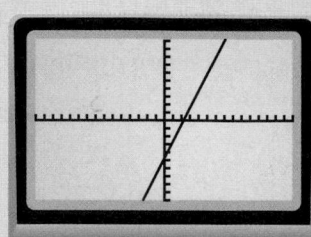

2 Use the *Draw Inverse* feature to graph the inverse.

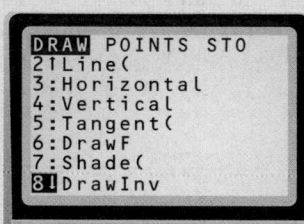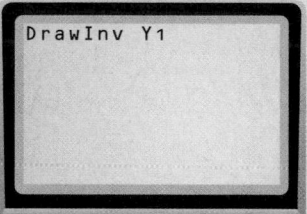

3 Display the graphs of the original function and its inverse.

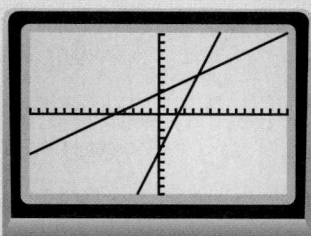

The graph of the function $y = 2x - 5$ passes the horizontal line test, so you know that the inverse of $y = 2x - 5$ is also a function. You can further verify this fact by observing that the inverse passes the vertical line test you learned in Lesson 2.1.

▶ **EXERCISES**

Graph the function on a graphing calculator. Then use the *Draw Inverse* feature to graph the function's inverse in the same viewing window. Is the inverse a function? Explain.

1. $y = 6x + 4$ **2.** $y = 0.6x - 2$ **3.** $y = 0.4x + 5$

4. $y = 0.2x^2 + 1$ **5.** $y = x^2 - 4x + 3$ **6.** $y = x^2 - 3x$

7. $y = x^3 - 4$ **8.** $y = x^3 + x$ **9.** $y = 2.1x^3 - 0.4x^2 + 1$

10. $y = |x + 4|$ **11.** $y = -|x| + 5.7$ **12.** $y = 2|x + 1| - 8$

7.5

Graphing Square Root and Cube Root Functions

GOAL 1 GRAPHING RADICAL FUNCTIONS

In Lesson 7.4 you saw the graphs of $y = \sqrt{x}$ and $y = \sqrt[3]{x}$. These are examples of **radical functions**.

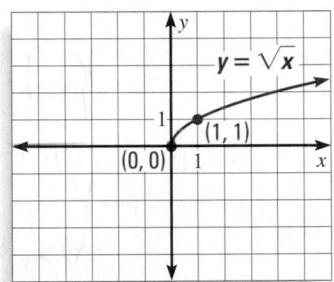

Domain: $x \geq 0$, Range: $y \geq 0$

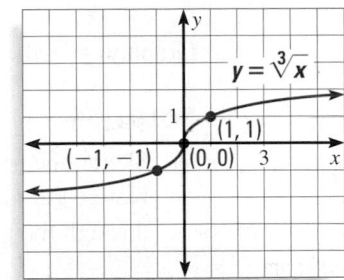

Domain and range: all real numbers

In this lesson you will learn to graph functions of the form $y = a\sqrt{x - h} + k$ and $y = a\sqrt[3]{x - h} + k$.

▶ **ACTIVITY**

Developing Concepts

Investigating Graphs of Radical Functions

❶ Graph $y = a\sqrt{x}$ for $a = 2, \frac{1}{2}, -3,$ and -1. Use the graph of $y = \sqrt{x}$ shown above and the labeled points on the graph as a reference. Describe how a affects the graph.

❷ Graph $y = a\sqrt[3]{x}$ for $a = 2, \frac{1}{2}, -3,$ and -1. Use the graph of $y = \sqrt[3]{x}$ shown above and the labeled points on the graph as a reference. Describe how a affects the graph.

In the activity you may have discovered that the graph of $y = a\sqrt{x}$ starts at the origin and passes through the point $(1, a)$. Similarly, the graph of $y = a\sqrt[3]{x}$ passes through the origin and the points $(-1, -a)$ and $(1, a)$. The following describes how to graph more general radical functions.

GRAPHS OF RADICAL FUNCTIONS

To graph $y = a\sqrt{x - h} + k$ or $y = a\sqrt[3]{x - h} + k$, follow these steps.

STEP ❶ Sketch the graph of $y = a\sqrt{x}$ or $y = a\sqrt[3]{x}$.

STEP ❷ Shift the graph h units horizontally and k units vertically.

EXAMPLE 1 *Comparing Two Graphs*

Describe how to obtain the graph of $y = \sqrt{x + 1} - 3$ from the graph of $y = \sqrt{x}$.

SOLUTION

Note that $y = \sqrt{x + 1} - 3 = \sqrt{x - (-1)} + (-3)$, so $h = -1$ and $k = -3$. To obtain the graph of $y = \sqrt{x + 1} - 3$, shift the graph of $y = \sqrt{x}$ left 1 unit and down 3 units.

EXAMPLE 2 *Graphing a Square Root Function*

Graph $y = -3\sqrt{x - 2} + 1$.

STUDENT HELP

► **Skills Review**
For help with transformations, see p. 921.

SOLUTION

❶ Sketch the graph of $y = -3\sqrt{x}$ (shown dashed). Notice that it begins at the origin and passes through the point $(1, -3)$.

❷ Note that for $y = -3\sqrt{x - 2} + 1$, $h = 2$ and $k = 1$. So, shift the graph right 2 units and up 1 unit. The result is a graph that starts at $(2, 1)$ and passes through the point $(3, -2)$.

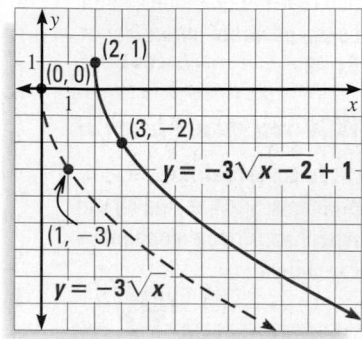

EXAMPLE 3 *Graphing a Cube Root Function*

Graph $y = 3\sqrt[3]{x + 2} - 1$.

SOLUTION

❶ Sketch the graph of $y = 3\sqrt[3]{x}$ (shown dashed). Notice that it passes through the origin and the points $(-1, -3)$ and $(1, 3)$.

❷ Note that for $y = 3\sqrt[3]{x + 2} - 1$, $h = -2$ and $k = -1$. So, shift the graph left 2 units and down 1 unit. The result is a graph that passes through the points $(-3, -4)$, $(-2, -1)$, and $(-1, 2)$.

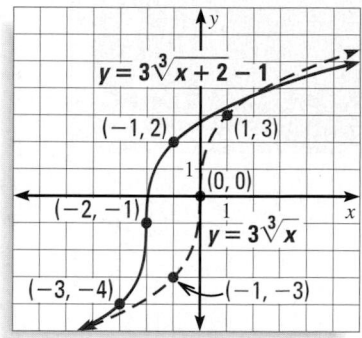

EXAMPLE 4 *Finding Domain and Range*

State the domain and range of the function in (**a**) Example 2 and (**b**) Example 3.

SOLUTION

a. From the graph of $y = -3\sqrt{x - 2} + 1$ in Example 2, you can see that the domain of the function is $x \geq 2$ and the range of the function is $y \leq 1$.

b. From the graph of $y = 3\sqrt[3]{x + 2} - 1$ in Example 3, you can see that the domain and range of the function are both all real numbers.

GOAL 2 **USING RADICAL FUNCTIONS IN REAL LIFE**

When you use radical functions in real life, the domain is understood to be restricted to the values that make sense in the real-life situation.

EXAMPLE 5 *Modeling with a Square Root Function*

AMUSEMENT PARKS At an amusement park a ride called the *rotor* is a cylindrical room that spins around. The riders stand against the circular wall. When the rotor reaches the necessary speed, the floor drops out and the centrifugal force keeps the riders pinned to the wall.

The model that gives the speed *s* (in meters per second) necessary to keep a person pinned to the wall is

$$s = 4.95\sqrt{r}$$

where *r* is the radius (in meters) of the rotor. Use a graphing calculator to graph the model. Then use the graph to estimate the radius of a rotor that spins at a speed of 8 meters per second.

SOLUTION

Graph $y = 4.95\sqrt{x}$ and $y = 8$. Choose a viewing window that shows the point where the graphs intersect. Then use the *Intersect* feature to find the *x*-coordinate of that point. You get $x \approx 2.61$.

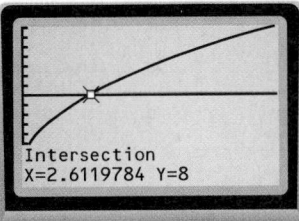

Intersection
X=2.6119784 Y=8

▶ The radius is about 2.61 meters.

EXAMPLE 6 *Modeling with a Cube Root Function*

Biologists have discovered that the shoulder height *h* (in centimeters) of a male African elephant can be modeled by

$$h = 62.5\sqrt[3]{t} + 75.8$$

where *t* is the age (in years) of the elephant. Use a graphing calculator to graph the model. Then use the graph to estimate the age of an elephant whose shoulder height is 200 centimeters. ▶ Source: *Elephants*

SOLUTION

Graph $y = 62.5\sqrt[3]{x} + 75.8$ and $y = 200$. Choose a viewing window that shows the point where the graphs intersect. Then use the *Intersect* feature to find the *x*-coordinate of that point. You get $x \approx 7.85$.

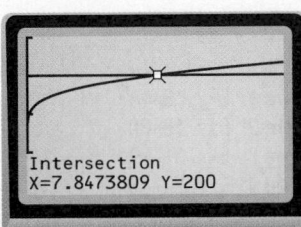

Intersection
X=7.8473809 Y=200

▶ The elephant is about 8 years old.

GUIDED PRACTICE

Vocabulary Check ✓

1. Complete this statement: Square root functions and cube root functions are examples of _?_ functions.

Concept Check ✓

2. ERROR ANALYSIS Explain why the graph shown at the near right is not the graph of $y = \sqrt{x - 1} + 2$.

3. ERROR ANALYSIS Explain why the graph shown at the far right is not the graph of $y = \sqrt[3]{x + 2} - 3$.

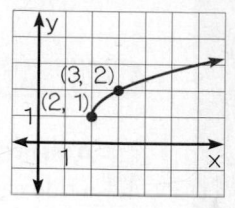

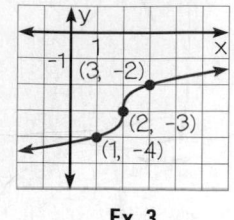

Ex. 2   Ex. 3

Skill Check ✓

Describe how to obtain the graph of _g_ from the graph of _f_.

4. $g(x) = \sqrt{x + 5}$, $f(x) = \sqrt{x}$ **5.** $g(x) = \sqrt[3]{x} - 10$, $f(x) = \sqrt[3]{x}$

Graph the function. Then state the domain and range.

6. $y = -\sqrt{x}$ **7.** $y = \sqrt{x} + 1$ **8.** $y = \sqrt{x} - 2$ **9.** $y = 2\sqrt{x + 3} - 1$

10. $y = \frac{2}{3}\sqrt[3]{x}$ **11.** $y = \sqrt[3]{x} - 6$ **12.** $y = \sqrt[3]{x + 5}$ **13.** $y = -3\sqrt[3]{x - 7} - 4$

14. ▨ **ELEPHANTS** Look back at Example 6. Use a graphing calculator to graph the model. Then use the graph to estimate the age of an elephant whose shoulder height is 250 centimeters.

PRACTICE AND APPLICATIONS

STUDENT HELP

▶ **Extra Practice**
to help you master
skills is on p. 950.

COMPARING GRAPHS Describe how to obtain the graph of _g_ from the graph of _f_.

15. $g(x) = \sqrt{x + 14}$, $f(x) = \sqrt{x}$ **16.** $g(x) = 5\sqrt{x - 10} - 3$, $f(x) = 5\sqrt{x}$

17. $g(x) = -\sqrt[3]{x} - 10$, $f(x) = -\sqrt[3]{x}$ **18.** $g(x) = \sqrt[3]{x + 6} - 5$, $f(x) = \sqrt[3]{x}$

MATCHING GRAPHS Match the function with its graph.

19. $y = \sqrt{x} - 1$ **20.** $y = \sqrt{x + 1}$ **21.** $y = \sqrt{x + 1} - 1$

A. 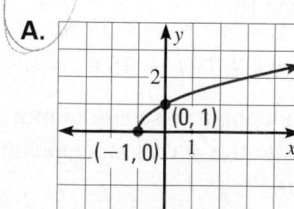   **B.** 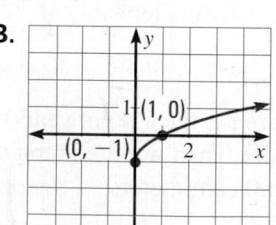   **C.**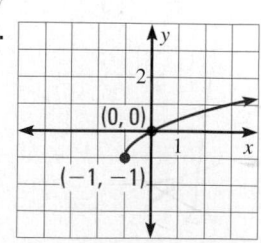

STUDENT HELP

▶ **HOMEWORK HELP**
Example 1: Exs. 15–18
Example 2: Exs. 19–30
Example 3: Exs. 31–39
Example 4: Exs. 22–45
Example 5: Exs. 46, 47
Example 6: Exs. 48, 49

SQUARE ROOT FUNCTIONS Graph the function. Then state the domain and range.

22. $y = -5\sqrt{x}$ **23.** $y = \frac{1}{3}\sqrt{x}$ **24.** $y = x^{1/2} + \frac{1}{4}$

25. $y = x^{1/2} - 2$ **26.** $y = \sqrt{x + 6}$ **27.** $y = (x - 7)^{1/2}$

28. $y = (x - 1)^{1/2} + 7$ **29.** $y = 2\sqrt{x + 5} - 1$ **30.** $y = -\frac{2}{5}\sqrt{x - 3} - 2$

CUBE ROOT FUNCTIONS Graph the function. Then state the domain and range.

31. $y = \frac{1}{2}\sqrt[3]{x}$

32. $y = -2x^{1/3}$

33. $y = \sqrt[3]{x} - 7$

34. $y = \sqrt[3]{x} + \frac{3}{4}$

35. $y = \sqrt[3]{x - 5}$

36. $y = \left(x + \frac{2}{3}\right)^{1/3}$

37. $y = \frac{1}{5}x^{1/3} - 2$

38. $y = -3\sqrt[3]{x + 4}$

39. $y = 2\sqrt[3]{x - 4} + 3$

CRITICAL THINKING Find the domain and range of the function without graphing. Explain how you found your solution.

40. $y = \sqrt{x - 13}$

41. $y = 2\sqrt{x} - 2$

42. $y = -\sqrt{x - 3} - 7$

43. $y = \sqrt[3]{x + 8}$

44. $y = -\frac{2}{3}\sqrt[3]{x} - 5$

45. $y = 4\sqrt[3]{x + 4} + 7$

GRAPHING MODELS In Exercises 46–49, use a graphing calculator to graph the models. Then use the *Intersect* feature to solve the problems.

46. 🌐 **OCEAN DISTANCES** When you look at the ocean, the distance d (in miles) you can see to the horizon can be modeled by $d = 1.22\sqrt{a}$ where a is your altitude (in feet above sea level). Graph the model. Then determine at what altitude you can see 10 miles. ▶ Source: *Mathematics in Everyday Things*

47. **GEOMETRY** **CONNECTION** In a right circular cone with a slant height of 1 unit, the radius r of the cone is given by $r = \frac{1}{\sqrt{\pi}}\sqrt{S + \frac{\pi}{4}} - \frac{1}{2}$ where S is the surface area of the cone. Graph the model. Then find the surface area of a right circular cone with a slant height of 1 unit and a radius of $\frac{1}{2}$ unit.

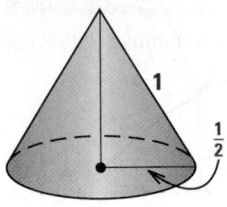

48. 🌐 **RACING** Drag racing is an acceleration contest over a distance of a quarter mile. For a given total weight, the speed of a car at the end of the race is a function of the car's power. For a total weight of 3500 pounds, the speed s (in miles per hour) can be modeled by $s = 14.8\sqrt[3]{p}$ where p is the power (in horsepower). Graph the model. Then determine the power of a car that reaches a speed of 100 miles per hour. ▶ Source: *The Physics of Sports*

49. 🌐 **STORMS AT SEA** The fetch f (in nautical miles) of the wind at sea is the distance over which the wind is blowing. The minimum fetch required to create a fully developed storm can be modeled by $s = 3.1\sqrt[3]{f + 10} + 11.1$ where s is the speed (in knots) of the wind. Graph the model. Then determine the minimum fetch required to create a fully developed storm if the wind speed is 25 knots.

▶ Source: *Oceanography*

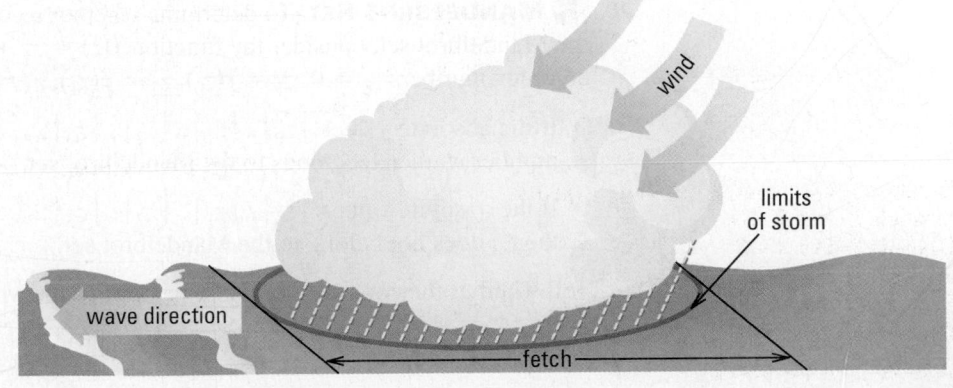

wind

limits
of storm

wave direction

fetch

50. MULTI-STEP PROBLEM Follow the steps below to graph radical functions of the form $y = f(-x)$.

   a. Graph $f_1(x) = \sqrt{x}$ and $f_2(x) = \sqrt{-x}$. How are the graphs related?

   b. Graph $g_1(x) = \sqrt[3]{x}$ and $g_2(x) = \sqrt[3]{-x}$. How are the graphs related?

   c. Graph $f_3(x) = \sqrt{-(x-2)} - 4$ and $g_3(x) = 2\sqrt[3]{-(x+1)} + 5$ using what you learned from parts (a) and (b) and what you know about the effects of a, h, and k on the graphs of $y = a\sqrt{x - h} + k$ and $y = a\sqrt[3]{x - h} + k$.

   d. *Writing* Describe the steps for graphing a function of the form $f(x) = a\sqrt{-(x - h)} + k$ or $g(x) = a\sqrt[3]{-(x - h)} + k$.

★ **Challenge**

ANALYZING GRAPHS Write an equation for the function whose graph is shown.

51. 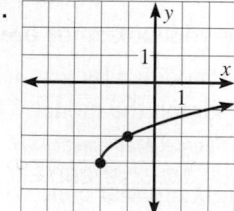 **52.** 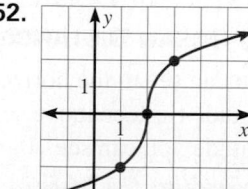 **53.**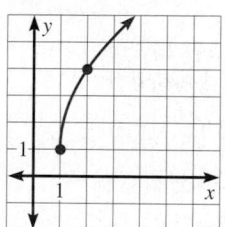

MIXED REVIEW

SOLVING EQUATIONS Solve the equation. (Review 5.3 for 7.6)

54. $2x^2 = 32$ **55.** $(x + 7)^2 = 10$ **56.** $9x^2 + 3 = 5$

57. $\frac{1}{2}x^2 - 5 = 13$ **58.** $\frac{1}{4}(x + 6)^2 = 22$ **59.** $2(x - 0.25)^2 = 16.5$

SPECIAL PRODUCTS Find the product. (Review 6.3 for 7.6)

60. $(x + 4)^2$ **61.** $(x - 9y)^2$ **62.** $(2x^3 + 7)^2$

63. $\left(-3x + 4y^4\right)^2$ **64.** $(6 - 5x)^2$ **65.** $\left(-1 - 2x^2\right)^2$

COMPOSITION OF FUNCTIONS Find $f(g(x))$ and $g(f(x))$. (Review 7.3)

66. $f(x) = x + 7$, $g(x) = 2x$ **67.** $f(x) = 2x + 1$, $g(x) = x - 3$

68. $f(x) = x^2 - 1$, $g(x) = x + 2$ **69.** $f(x) = x^2 + 7$, $g(x) = 3x - 3$

70. 🌐 **MANDELBROT SET** To determine whether a complex number c belongs to the Mandelbrot set, consider the function $f(z) = z^2 + c$ and the infinite list of complex numbers $z_0 = 0$, $z_1 = f(z_0)$, $z_2 = f(z_1)$, $z_3 = f(z_2)$, ...

   • If the absolute values $|z_0|$, $|z_1|$, $|z_2|$, $|z_3|$, ... are all less than some fixed number N, then c belongs to the Mandelbrot set.

   • If the absolute values $|z_0|$, $|z_1|$, $|z_2|$, $|z_3|$, ... become infinitely large, then c does not belong to the Mandelbrot set.

   Tell whether the complex number c belongs to the Mandelbrot set. (**Review 5.4**)

   a. $c = 3i$ **b.** $c = 2 + 2i$ **c.** $c = 6$

7.6

Solving Radical Equations

What you should learn

GOAL 1 Solve equations that contain radicals or rational exponents.

GOAL 2 Use radical equations to solve **real-life** problems, such as determining wind speeds that correspond to the Beaufort wind scale in **Example 6**.

Why you should learn it

▼ To solve **real-life** problems, such as determining which boats satisfy the rule for competing in the America's Cup sailboat race in **Ex. 68**.

GOAL 1 SOLVING A RADICAL EQUATION

To solve a *radical equation*—an equation that contains radicals or rational exponents—you need to eliminate the radicals or rational exponents and obtain a polynomial equation. The key step is to *raise each side of the equation to the same power*.

$$\text{If } a = b, \text{ then } a^n = b^n. \qquad \textbf{Powers property of equality}$$

Then solve the new equation using standard procedures. Before raising each side of an equation to the same power, you should isolate the radical expression on one side of the equation.

EXAMPLE 1 *Solving a Simple Radical Equation*

Solve $\sqrt[3]{x} - 4 = 0$.

SOLUTION

$\sqrt[3]{x} - 4 = 0$	**Write original equation.**
$\sqrt[3]{x} = 4$	**Isolate radical.**
$\left(\sqrt[3]{x}\right)^3 = 4^3$	**Cube each side.**
$x = 64$	**Simplify.**

▶ The solution is 64. Check this in the original equation.

EXAMPLE 2 *Solving an Equation with Rational Exponents*

Solve $2x^{3/2} = 250$.

SOLUTION

Because x is raised to the $\frac{3}{2}$ power, you should isolate the power and then raise each side of the equation to the $\frac{2}{3}$ power $\left(\frac{2}{3} \text{ is the reciprocal of } \frac{3}{2}\right)$.

$2x^{3/2} = 250$	**Write original equation.**
$x^{3/2} = 125$	**Isolate power.**
$\left(x^{3/2}\right)^{2/3} = 125^{2/3}$	**Raise each side to $\frac{2}{3}$ power.**
$x = \left(125^{1/3}\right)^2$	**Apply properties of roots.**
$x = 5^2 = 25$	**Simplify.**

▶ The solution is 25. Check this in the original equation.

STUDENT HELP

▶ **Study Tip**
To solve an equation of the form $x^{m/n} = k$ where k is a constant, raise both sides of the equation to the $\frac{n}{m}$ power, because $\left(x^{m/n}\right)^{n/m} = x^1 = x$.

EXAMPLE 3 | *Solving an Equation with One Radical*

Solve $\sqrt{4x - 7} + 2 = 5$.

SOLUTION

$\sqrt{4x - 7} + 2 = 5$	**Write original equation.**
$\sqrt{4x - 7} = 3$	**Isolate radical.**
$(\sqrt{4x - 7})^2 = 3^2$	**Square each side.**
$4x - 7 = 9$	**Simplify.**
$4x = 16$	**Add 7 to each side.**
$x = 4$	**Divide each side by 4.**

✓ **CHECK** Check $x = 4$ in the original equation.

$\sqrt{4x - 7} + 2 = 5$	**Write original equation.**
$\sqrt{4(4) - 7} \stackrel{?}{=} 3$	**Substitute 4 for x.**
$\sqrt{9} \stackrel{?}{=} 3$	**Simplify.**
$3 = 3$ ✓	**Solution checks.**

▶ The solution is 4.

· · · · · · · · · ·

Some equations have two radical expressions. Before raising both sides to the same power, you should rewrite the equation so that each side of the equation has only one radical expression.

EXAMPLE 4 | *Solving an Equation with Two Radicals*

Solve $\sqrt{3x + 2} - 2\sqrt{x} = 0$.

STUDENT HELP

HOMEWORK HELP
Visit our Web site
www.mcdougallittell.com
for extra examples.

SOLUTION

$\sqrt{3x + 2} - 2\sqrt{x} = 0$	**Write original equation.**
$\sqrt{3x + 2} = 2\sqrt{x}$	**Add $2\sqrt{x}$ to each side.**
$(\sqrt{3x + 2})^2 = (2\sqrt{x})^2$	**Square each side.**
$3x + 2 = 4x$	**Simplify.**
$2 = x$	**Solve for x.**

✓ **CHECK** Check $x = 2$ in the original equation.

$\sqrt{3x + 2} - 2\sqrt{x} = 0$	**Write original equation.**
$\sqrt{3(2) + 2} - 2\sqrt{2} \stackrel{?}{=} 0$	**Substitute 2 for x.**
$2\sqrt{2} - 2\sqrt{2} \stackrel{?}{=} 0$	**Simplify.**
$0 = 0$ ✓	**Solution checks.**

▶ The solution is 2.

If you try to solve $\sqrt{x} = -1$ by squaring both sides, you get $x = 1$. But $x = 1$ is not a valid solution of the original equation. This is an example of an **extraneous** (or false) **solution**. Raising both sides of an equation to the same power may introduce extraneous solutions. So, when you use this procedure it is critical that you check each solution in the *original* equation.

EXAMPLE 5 *An Equation with an Extraneous Solution*

Solve $x - 4 = \sqrt{2x}$.

STUDENT HELP

▶ **Look Back**
For help with factoring, see p. 256.

SOLUTION

$x - 4 = \sqrt{2x}$	**Write original equation.**
$(x - 4)^2 = \left(\sqrt{2x}\right)^2$	**Square each side.**
$x^2 - 8x + 16 = 2x$	**Expand left side; simplify right side.**
$x^2 - 10x + 16 = 0$	**Write in standard form.**
$(x - 2)(x - 8) = 0$	**Factor.**
$x - 2 = 0$ or $x - 8 = 0$	**Zero product property**
$x = 2$ or $x = 8$	**Simplify.**

✓ **CHECK** Check $x = 2$ in the original equation.

$x - 4 = \sqrt{2x}$	**Write original equation.**
$2 - 4 \overset{?}{=} \sqrt{2(2)}$	**Substitute 2 for x.**
$-2 \overset{?}{=} \sqrt{4}$	**Simplify.**
$-2 \neq 2$	**Solution does not check.**

✓ **CHECK** Check $x = 8$ in the original equation.

$x - 4 = \sqrt{2x}$	**Write original equation.**
$8 - 4 \overset{?}{=} \sqrt{2(8)}$	**Substitute 8 for x.**
$4 \overset{?}{=} \sqrt{16}$	**Simplify.**
$4 = 4$ ✓	**Solution checks.**

▶ The only solution is 8.

• • • • • • • • • •

If you graph each side of the equation in Example 5, as shown, you can see that the graphs of $y = x - 4$ and $y = \sqrt{2x}$ intersect only at $x = 8$. This confirms that $x = 8$ is a solution of the equation, but that $x = 2$ is not.

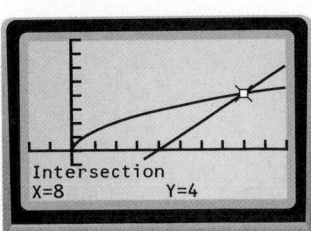

In general, all, some, or none of the apparent solutions of a radical equation can be extraneous. When all of the apparent solutions of a radical equation are extraneous, the equation has *no solution*.

EXAMPLE 6 *Using a Radical Model*

BEAUFORT WIND SCALE The Beaufort wind scale was devised to measure wind speed. The Beaufort numbers B, which range from 0 to 12, can be modeled by $B = 1.69\sqrt{s + 4.45} - 3.49$ where s is the speed (in miles per hour) of the wind. Find the wind speed that corresponds to the Beaufort number $B = 11$.

REAL LIFE

BEAUFORT WIND SCALE

The Beaufort wind scale was developed by Rear-Admiral Sir Francis Beaufort in 1805 so that sailors could detect approaching storms. Today the scale is used mainly by meteorologists.

APPLICATION LINK
www.mcdougallittell.com

Beaufort Wind Scale		
Beaufort number	Force of wind	Effects of wind
0	Calm	Smoke rises vertically.
1	Light air	Direction shown by smoke.
2	Light breeze	Leaves rustle; wind felt on face.
3	Gentle breeze	Leaves move; flags extend.
4	Moderate breeze	Small branches sway; paper blown about.
5	Fresh breeze	Small trees sway.
6	Strong breeze	Large branches sway; umbrellas difficult to use.
7	Moderate gale	Large trees sway; walking difficult.
8	Fresh gale	Twigs break; walking hindered.
9	Strong gale	Branches scattered about; slight damage to buildings.
10	Whole gale	Trees uprooted; severe damage to buildings.
11	Storm	Widespread damage.
12	Hurricane	Devastation.

SOLUTION

$B = 1.69\sqrt{s + 4.45} - 3.49$	**Write model.**
$11 = 1.69\sqrt{s + 4.45} - 3.49$	**Substitute 11 for B.**
$14.49 = 1.69\sqrt{s + 4.45}$	**Add 3.49 to each side.**
$8.57 \approx \sqrt{s + 4.45}$	**Divide each side by 1.69.**
$73.4 \approx s + 4.45$	**Square each side.**
$69.0 \approx s$	**Subtract 4.45 from each side.**

▶ The wind speed is about 69 miles per hour.

✔ **ALGEBRAIC CHECK** Substitute 69 for s into the model and evaluate.

$$1.69\sqrt{69 + 4.45} - 3.49 \approx 1.69(8.57) - 3.49$$
$$\approx 11 ✓$$

✔ **GRAPHIC CHECK** You can use a graphing calculator to graph the model, and then use the *Intersect* feature to check that $x \approx 69$ when $y = 11$.

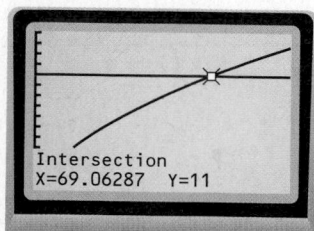

Intersection
X=69.06287   Y=11

GUIDED PRACTICE

Vocabulary Check ✔   1. What is an extraneous solution?

Concept Check ✔   2. Marcy began solving $x^{2/3} = 5$ by cubing each side. What will she have to do next? What could she have done to solve the equation in just one step?

3. Zach was asked to solve $\sqrt{5x - 2} - \sqrt{7x - 4} = 0$. His first step was to square each side. While trying to isolate x, he gave up in frustration. What could Zach have done to avoid this situation?

Skill Check ✔   **Solve the rational exponent equation. Check for extraneous solutions.**

4. $3x^{1/4} = 4$
5. $(2x + 7)^{3/2} = 27$
6. $x^{4/3} + 9 = 25$

7. $4x^{2/3} - 6 = 10$
8. $5(x - 8)^{3/4} = 40$
9. $(x + 9)^{5/2} - 1 = 31$

Solve the radical equation. Check for extraneous solutions.

10. $\sqrt[4]{x} = 3$
11. $\sqrt[3]{3x} + 6 = 10$
12. $\sqrt[5]{2x + 1} + 5 = 9$

13. $\sqrt{x - 2} = x - 2$
14. $\sqrt[3]{x + 4} = \sqrt[3]{2x - 5}$
15. $6\sqrt{x} - \sqrt{x - 1} = 0$

16. 🌐 **BEAUFORT WIND SCALE** Use the information in Example 6 to determine the wind speed that corresponds to the Beaufort number $B = 2$.

PRACTICE AND APPLICATIONS

STUDENT HELP

▶ Extra Practice
to help you master
skills is on p. 950.

CHECKING SOLUTIONS Check whether the given x-value is a solution of the equation.

17. $\sqrt{x} - 3 = 6$; $x = 81$
18. $4(x - 5)^{1/2} = 28$; $x = 12$

19. $(x + 7)^{3/2} - 20 = 7$; $x = 2$
20. $\sqrt[3]{4x} + 11 = 5$; $x = -54$

21. $2\sqrt{5x + 4} + 10 = 10$; $x = 0$
22. $\sqrt{4x - 3} - \sqrt{3x} = 0$; $x = 3$

SOLVING RATIONAL EXPONENT EQUATIONS Solve the equation. Check for extraneous solutions.

23. $x^{5/2} = 32$
24. $x^{1/3} - \frac{2}{5} = 0$
25. $x^{2/3} + 15 = 24$

26. $-\frac{1}{2}x^{1/5} = 10$
27. $4x^{3/4} = 108$
28. $(x - 4)^{3/2} = -6$

29. $(2x + 5)^{1/2} = 4$
30. $3(x + 1)^{4/3} = 48$
31. $-(x - 5)^{1/4} + \frac{7}{3} = 2$

STUDENT HELP

▶ HOMEWORK HELP
Example 1: Exs. 17–22,
        32–46
Example 2: Exs. 17–22,
        23–31
Example 3: Exs. 17–22,
        32–46
Example 4: Exs. 17–22,
        47–54
Example 5: Exs. 23–54
Example 6: Exs. 63–69

SOLVING RADICAL EQUATIONS Solve the equation. Check for extraneous solutions.

32. $\sqrt{x} = \frac{1}{9}$
33. $\sqrt[3]{x} + 10 = 16$
34. $\sqrt[4]{2x} - 13 = -9$

35. $\sqrt{x + 56} = 16$
36. $\sqrt[3]{x + 40} = -5$
37. $\sqrt{6x - 5} + 10 = 3$

38. $\frac{2}{5}\sqrt{10x + 6} = 12$
39. $2\sqrt{7x + 4} - 1 = 7$
40. $-2\sqrt[5]{2x - 1} + 4 = 0$

41. $x - 12 = \sqrt{16x}$
42. $\sqrt[4]{x^4 + 1} = 3x$
43. $\sqrt{x^2 + 5} = x + 3$

44. $\sqrt[3]{x} = x - 6$
45. $\sqrt{8x + 1} = x + 2$
46. $\sqrt{2x + \frac{1}{6}} = x + \frac{5}{6}$

SOLVING EQUATIONS WITH TWO RADICALS Solve the equation. Check for extraneous solutions.

47. $\sqrt{2x - 1} = \sqrt{x + 4}$

48. $\sqrt[4]{6x - 5} = \sqrt[4]{x + 10}$

49. $-\sqrt{8x + \frac{4}{3}} = \sqrt{2x + \frac{1}{3}}$

50. $2\sqrt[3]{10 - 3x} = \sqrt[3]{2 - x}$

51. $\sqrt[4]{2x} + \sqrt[4]{x + 3} = 0$

52. $\sqrt{x - 6} - \sqrt{\frac{1}{3}x} = 0$

53. $\sqrt{2x + 10} - 2\sqrt{x} = 0$

54. $\sqrt[3]{2x + 15} - \frac{3}{2}\sqrt[3]{x} = 0$

SOLVING EQUATIONS Use the *Intersect* feature on a graphing calculator to solve the equation.

55. $\frac{3}{4}x^{1/3} = -2$

56. $2(x + 19)^{2/5} - 1 = 17$

57. $(3.5x + 1)^{2/7} = (6.4x + 0.7)^{2/7}$

58. $\left(\frac{1}{5}x\right)^{3/4} = x - \frac{3}{8}$

59. $\sqrt{6.7x + 14} = 9.4$

60. $\sqrt[3]{70 - 2x} - 10 = -6$

61. $\sqrt[4]{x - \frac{1}{6}} = 2\sqrt[4]{3x}$

62. $\sqrt{1.1x + 2.4} = 19x - 4.2$

63. 🌐 **NAILS** The length l (in inches) of a standard nail can be modeled by

$$l = 54d^{3/2}$$

where d is the diameter (in inches) of the nail. What is the diameter of a standard nail that is 3 inches long?

64. SCIENCE ▶ CONNECTION   Scientists have found that the body mass m (in kilograms) of a dinosaur that walked on two feet can be modeled by

$$m = (1.6 \times 10^{-4})C^{273/100}$$

where C is the circumference (in millimeters) of the dinosaur's femur. Scientists have estimated that the mass of a *Tyrannosaurus rex* might have been 4500 kilograms. What size femur would have led them to this conclusion?

▶ Source: The Zoological Society of London

65. 🌐 **WOMEN IN MEDICINE** For 1970 through 1995, the percent p of Doctor of Medicine (MD) degrees earned each year by women can be modeled by

$$p = (0.867t^2 + 39.2t + 57.1)^{1/2}$$

where t is the number of years since 1970. In what year were about 36% of the degrees earned by women? ▶ Source: *Statistical Abstract of the United States*

66. 🌐 **PLUMB BOBS** You work for a company that manufactures plumb bobs. The same mold is used to cast plumb bobs of different sizes. The equation

$$h = 1.5\sqrt[3]{t}, \ 0 \le h \le 3$$

models the relationship between the height h (in inches) of the plumb bob and the time t (in seconds) that metal alloy is poured into the mold. How long should you pour the alloy into the mold to cast a plumb bob with a height of 2 inches?

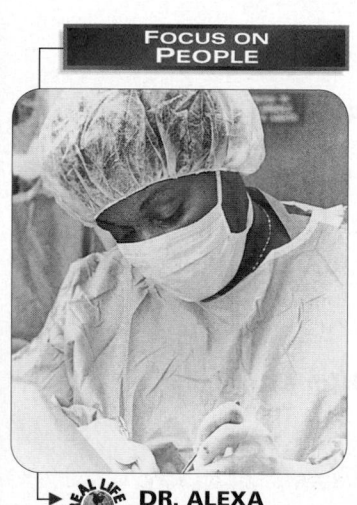

67. 🌐 **BEAUFORT WIND SCALE** Recall from Example 6 that the Beaufort number B from the Beaufort wind scale can be modeled by

$$B = 1.69\sqrt{s + 4.45} - 3.49$$

where s is the speed (in miles per hour) of the wind. Find the wind speed that corresponds to the Beaufort number $B = 7$.

68. 🌐 **AMERICA'S CUP** In order to compete in the America's Cup sailboat race, a boat must satisfy the rule

$$\frac{l + 1.25\sqrt{s} - 9.8\sqrt[3]{d}}{0.679} \leq 24$$

where l is the length (in meters) of the boat, s is the area (in square meters) of the sails, and d is the volume (in cubic meters) of water displaced by the boat. If a boat has a length of 20 meters and a sail area of 300 square meters, what is the minimum allowable value for d? ▶ Source: America's Cup

69. GEOMETRY ▶ CONNECTION   You are trying to determine the height of a truncated pyramid that cannot be measured directly. The height h and slant height l of a truncated pyramid are related by the formula

$$l = \sqrt{h^2 + \frac{1}{4}(b_2 - b_1)^2}$$

where b_1 and b_2 are the lengths of the upper and lower bases of the pyramid, respectively. If $l = 5$, $b_1 = 2$, and $b_2 = 4$, what is the height of the pyramid?

70. **CRITICAL THINKING** Look back at Example 5. Solve $x - 4 = -\sqrt{2x}$ instead of $x - 4 = \sqrt{2x}$. How does changing $\sqrt{2x}$ to $-\sqrt{2x}$ change the solution(s) of the equation?

Test Preparation

71. **MULTIPLE CHOICE** What is the solution of $\sqrt{6x - 4} = 3$?

A $-\frac{1}{6}$ **B** $\frac{5}{6}$ **C** $\frac{7}{6}$ **D** $\frac{5}{3}$ **E** $\frac{13}{6}$

72. **MULTIPLE CHOICE** What is (are) the solution(s) of $\sqrt{2x - 3} = \frac{1}{2}x$?

A 2   **B** 2, 6   **C** $\frac{18}{7}$ **D** $\frac{21}{4}$ **E** none

73. **MULTIPLE CHOICE** What is the solution of $\sqrt[3]{x - 7} = \sqrt[3]{\frac{3}{4}x + 1}$?

A -6 **B** $-\frac{24}{7}$ **C** -4 **D** 2   **E** 32

★ **Challenge**

SOLVING EQUATIONS WITH TWO RADICALS Solve the equation. Check for extraneous solutions. (*Hint:* To solve these equations you will need to square each side of the equation two separate times.)

74. $\sqrt{x + 5} = 5 - \sqrt{x}$ **75.** $\sqrt{2x + 3} = 3 - \sqrt{2x}$

76. $\sqrt{x + 3} - \sqrt{x - 1} = 1$ **77.** $\sqrt{2x + 4} + \sqrt{3x - 5} = 4$

EXTRA CHALLENGE
▶ www.mcdougallittell.com

78. $\sqrt{3x - 2} = 1 + \sqrt{2x - 3}$ **79.** $\frac{1}{2}\sqrt{2x - 5} - \frac{1}{2}\sqrt{3x + 4} = 1$

MIXED REVIEW

USING ORDER OF OPERATIONS Evaluate the expression. **(Review 1.2 for 7.7)**

80. $6 + 24 \div 3$ **81.** $3 \cdot 5 + 10 \div 2$ **82.** $27 - 4 \cdot 16 \div 8$

83. $2 - (10 \cdot 2)^2 \div 5$ **84.** $8 + (3 \cdot 10) \div 6 - 1$ **85.** $11 - 8 \div 2 + 48 \div 4$

USING GRAPHS Graph the polynomial function. Identify the *x*-intercepts, local maximums, and local minimums. **(Review 6.8)**

86. $f(x) = x^3 - 4x^2 + 3$ **87.** $f(x) = 3x^3 - 2.5x^2 + 1.25x + 6$

88. $f(x) = \frac{1}{2}x^4 - \frac{1}{2}$ **89.** $f(x) = x^5 + x^3 - 6x$

90. 🌐 **PRINTING RATES** The cost C (in dollars) of printing x announcements (in hundreds) is given by the function shown. Graph the function. **(Review 2.7)**

$$C = \begin{cases} 62 + 22(x - 1), & \text{if } 1 \le x \le 5 \\ 150 + 14(x - 5), & \text{if } x > 5 \end{cases}$$

MATH & History — Tsunamis

APPLICATION LINK
www.mcdougallittell.com

THEN

IN AUGUST OF 1883, a volcano erupted on the island of Krakatau, Indonesia. The eruption caused a *tsunami* (a type of wave) to form and travel into the Indian Ocean and into the Java Sea. The speed s (in kilometers per hour) that a tsunami travels can be modeled by $s = 356\sqrt{d}$ where d is the depth (in kilometers) of the water.

1. A tsunami from Krakatau hit Jakarta traveling about 60 kilometers per hour. What is the average depth of the water between Krakatau and Jakarta?

2. After 15 hours and 12 minutes a tsunami from Krakatau hit Port Elizabeth, South Africa, 7546 kilometers away. Find the average speed of the tsunami.

3. Based on your answer to Exercise 2, what is the average depth of the Indian Ocean between Krakatau and Port Elizabeth?

NOW

AFTER A TRAGIC TSUNAMI hit the Aleutian Islands in 1946, scientists began work on a tsunami warning system. Today that system is operated 24 hours a day at the Honolulu Observatory and effectively warns people when a tsunami might arrive.

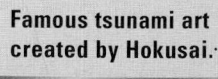

Famous tsunami art created by Hokusai.

c. 1800

1883

Krakatau erupts.

Alaskan earthquake causes Pacific-wide tsunami.

1957

1995

Prototype of tsunami real-time reporting system developed.

Statistics and Statistical Graphs

GOAL 1 MEASURES OF CENTRAL TENDENCY AND DISPERSION

What you should learn

GOAL 1 Use measures of central tendency and measures of dispersion to describe data sets.

GOAL 2 Use box-and-whisker plots and histograms to represent data graphically, as applied in **Exs. 40–42**.

Why you should learn it

▼ To use statistics and statistical graphs to analyze **real-life** data sets, such as the free-throw percentages for the players in the WNBA in **Examples 1–6**.

In this lesson you will use the following two data sets. They show the free-throw percentages for the players in the Women's National Basketball Association (WNBA) for 1998. **DATA UPDATE** of WNBA data at www.mcdougallittell.com

Women's National Basketball Association Free-Throw Percentages	
Eastern Conference	**Western Conference**
46, 47, 48, 50, 50, 50, 52, 53, 55, 57, 57, 58, 60, 61, 61, 62, 63, 63, 63, 63, 63, 63, 63, 64, 64, 67, 67, 67, 69, 71, 72, 72, 72, 72, 73, 75, 75, 75, 75, 75, 76, 77, 78, 79, 79, 80, 81, 81, 82, 82, 83, 83, 85, 89, 91, 92, 100	36, 50, 50, 56, 56, 57, 57, 58, 61, 61, 62, 62, 63, 63, 64, 64, 65, 66, 66, 66, 66, 67, 69, 69, 70, 70, 70, 70, 71, 71, 71, 71, 72, 72, 73, 73, 74, 74, 74, 74, 75, 76, 76, 76, 77, 77, 78, 80, 81, 83, 83, 83, 85, 85, 87, 100, 100, 100

Statistics are numerical values used to summarize and compare sets of data. The following **measures of central tendency** are three commonly used statistics.

1. The **mean**, or *average*, of n numbers is the sum of the numbers divided by n. The mean is denoted by $\overline{x}$, which is read as "*x*-bar." For the data $x_1, x_2, \ldots, x_n$, the mean is $\overline{x} = \dfrac{x_1 + x_2 + \cdots + x_n}{n}$.

2. The **median** of n numbers is the middle number when the numbers are written in order. (If n is even, the median is the mean of the two middle numbers.)

3. The **mode** of n numbers is the number or numbers that occur most frequently. There may be one mode, no mode, or more than one mode.

EXAMPLE 1 *Finding Measures of Central Tendency*

Find the mean, median, and mode of the two data sets listed above.

SOLUTION

EASTERN CONFERENCE: Mean: $\overline{x} = \dfrac{46 + 47 + \cdots + 100}{57} = \dfrac{3931}{57} \approx 69.0$

  Median: 69   Mode: 63

WESTERN CONFERENCE: Mean: $\overline{x} = \dfrac{36 + 50 + \cdots + 100}{58} = \dfrac{4106}{58} \approx 70.8$

  Median: 71   Modes: 66, 70, 71, 74

All three measures of central tendency for the Western Conference are greater than those for the Eastern Conference. So, the Western Conference has better free-throw percentages overall.

Measures of central tendency tell you what the *center* of the data is. Other commonly used statistics are called **measures of dispersion.** They tell you how *spread out* the data are. One simple measure of dispersion is the **range,** which is the difference between the greatest and least data values.

EXAMPLE 2 *Finding Ranges of Data Sets*

The ranges of the free-throw percentages in the two data sets on the previous page are:

EASTERN CONFERENCE: Range = $100 - 46 = 54$

WESTERN CONFERENCE: Range = $100 - 36 = 64$

Because the Western Conference's range of free-throw percentages is greater, its free-throw percentages are more spread out.

. . . .

Another measure of dispersion is **standard deviation,** which describes the typical difference (or *deviation*) between the mean and a data value.

STANDARD DEVIATION OF A SET OF DATA

The standard deviation σ (read as "sigma") of $x_1, x_2, \ldots, x_n$ is:

$$\sigma = \sqrt{\frac{(x_1 - \overline{x})^2 + (x_2 - \overline{x})^2 + \cdots + (x_n - \overline{x})^2}{n}}$$

EXAMPLE 3 *Finding Standard Deviations of Data Sets*

STUDENT HELP

HOMEWORK HELP
Visit our Web site
www.mcdougallittell.com
for extra examples.

The standard deviations of the free-throw percentages in the two data sets on the previous page are:

EASTERN CONFERENCE: $\sigma \approx \sqrt{\dfrac{(46 - 69.0)^2 + (47 - 69.0)^2 + \cdots + (100 - 69.0)^2}{57}}$

$\approx \sqrt{\dfrac{8660}{57}}$

$\approx \sqrt{152}$

≈ 12.3

WESTERN CONFERENCE: $\sigma \approx \sqrt{\dfrac{(36 - 70.8)^2 + (50 - 70.8)^2 + \cdots + (100 - 70.8)^2}{58}}$

$\approx \sqrt{\dfrac{7910}{58}}$

$\approx \sqrt{136}$

≈ 11.7

Because the Eastern Conference's standard deviation is greater, its free-throw percentages are more spread out *about the mean.*

Although statistics are useful in describing a data set, sometimes a graph of the data can be more informative. One type of statistical graph is a **box-and-whisker plot**. The "box" encloses the middle half of the data set and the "whiskers" extend to the minimum and maximum data values.

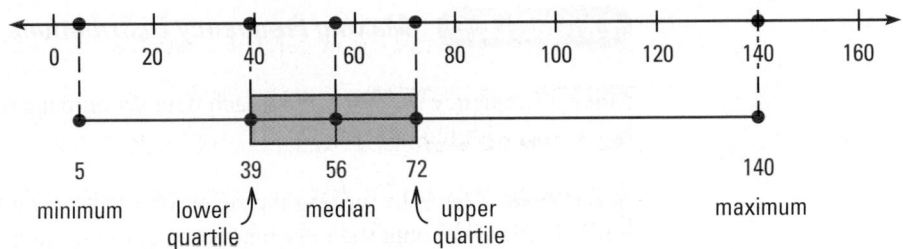

The median divides the data set into two halves. The **lower quartile** is the median of the lower half, and the **upper quartile** is the median of the upper half. You can use the following steps to draw a box-and-whisker plot.

1. Order the data from least to greatest.

2. Find the minimum and maximum values.

3. Find the median.

4. Find the lower and upper quartiles.

5. Plot these five numbers below a number line.

6. Draw the box, the whiskers, and a line segment through the median.

EXAMPLE 4 *Drawing Box-and-Whisker Plots*

Draw a box-and-whisker plot of each data set on page 445.

**SANDY BRONDELLO** was ranked first in the WNBA in 1998 for free-throw percentage (among players who attempted at least 10 free throws). As a player for the Detroit Shock, she made 96 out of 104 free throws for a free-throw percentage of 92.

SOLUTION

EASTERN CONFERENCE

The minimum is 46 and the maximum is 100. The median is 69. The lower quartile is 61 and the upper quartile is 78.5.

WESTERN CONFERENCE

The minimum is 36 and the maximum is 100. The median is 71. The lower quartile is 64 and the upper quartile is 76.

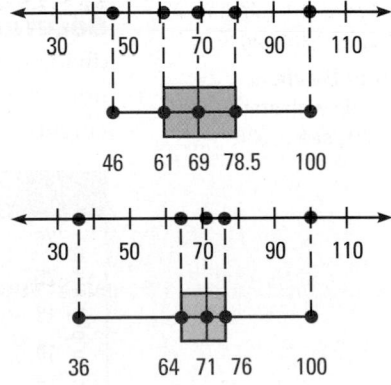

Like the computations in Examples 2 and 3, the box-and-whisker plots show you that the Western Conference's free-throw percentages are more spread out overall (comparing the entire plots) and that the Eastern Conference's free-throw percentages are more spread out about the mean (comparing the boxes).

Another way to display numerical data is with a special type of bar graph called a **histogram**. In a histogram data are grouped into intervals of *equal* width. The number of data values in each interval is the **frequency** of the interval. To draw a histogram, begin by making a **frequency distribution**, which shows the frequency of each interval.

EXAMPLE 5 *Making Frequency Distributions*

Make a frequency distribution of each data set on page 445. Use seven intervals beginning with the interval 31–40.

SOLUTION Begin by writing the seven intervals. Then tally the data values by interval. Finally, count the tally marks to get the frequencies.

Eastern Conference			Western Conference		
Interval	Tally	Frequency	Interval	Tally	Frequency
31–40		0	31–40	I	1
41–50	ⅢⅠ I	6	41–50	II	2
51–60	ⅢⅠ II	7	51–60	ⅢⅠ	5
61–70	ⅢⅠ ⅢⅠ ⅢⅠ I	16	61–70	ⅢⅠ ⅢⅠ ⅢⅠ ⅢⅠ	20
71–80	ⅢⅠ ⅢⅠ ⅢⅠ II	17	71–80	ⅢⅠ ⅢⅠ ⅢⅠ ⅢⅠ	20
81–90	ⅢⅠ III	8	81–90	ⅢⅠ II	7
91–100	III	3	91–100	III	3

EXAMPLE 6 *Drawing Histograms*

Draw a histogram of each data set on page 445.

STUDENT HELP

▶ **Skills Review**
For help with statistical graphs, see p. 934.

SOLUTION Use the frequency distributions in Example 5. Draw a horizontal axis, divide it into seven equal sections, and label the sections with the intervals. Then draw a vertical axis for measuring the frequencies. Finally, draw bars of appropriate heights to represent the frequencies of the intervals.

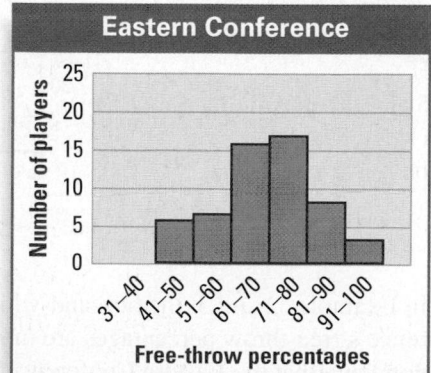

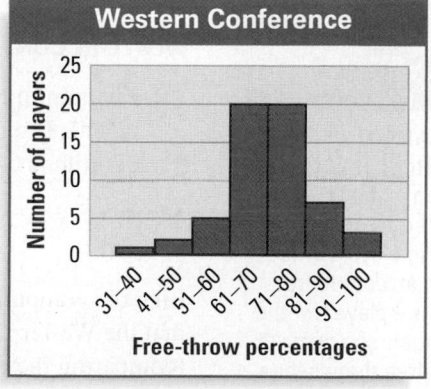

GUIDED PRACTICE

Vocabulary Check ✓

1. Define mean, median, mode, and range of a set of n numbers.

Concept Check ✓

2. Give an example of two sets of four numbers, each with a mean of 5. Choose the numbers so that one set has a range of 3 and the other set has a range of 7. Which has the greater standard deviation?

3. The following box-and-whisker plots represent two sets of data. Which data set has the greater range? Explain.

A. 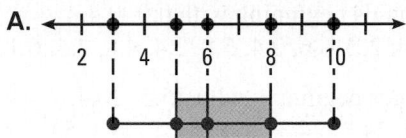 B.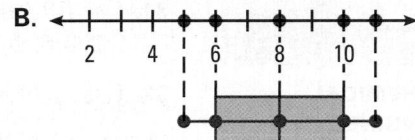

Skill Check ✓

 **HISTORY SCORES** In Exercises 4–9, use the following data set of scores received by students on a history exam.

$$68, 72, 76, 81, 84, 86, 86, 86, 89, 91, 95, 99$$

4. Find the mean, median, and mode of the data.

5. Find the range of the data.

6. Find the standard deviation of the data.

7. Draw a box-and-whisker plot of the data.

8. Make a frequency distribution of the data. Use five intervals beginning with 61–68.

9. Draw a histogram of the data.

PRACTICE AND APPLICATIONS

STUDENT HELP

▶ **Extra Practice**
to help you master
skills is on p. 950.

MEASURES OF CENTRAL TENDENCY Find the mean, median, and mode of the data set.

10. 6, 7, 9, 9, 9, 10

11. 43, 46, 47, 47, 51, 54, 59

12. 88, 83, 91, 82, 78, 81, 91, 91

13. 220, 250, 210, 290, 310, 230, 230

14. 2.9, 2.1, 2.6, 2.9, 3.0, 2.5, 3.4

15. 0, 0, 0.1, 0.2, 0.3, 0.5, 0.5, 0.6, 1.0

MEASURES OF DISPERSION Find the range and standard deviation of the data set.

STUDENT HELP

▶ **HOMEWORK HELP**
Example 1: Exs. 10–15,
33, 36, 39
Examples 2, 3: Exs. 16–21,
34, 37
Example 4: Exs. 22–27,
40, 43
Examples 5, 6: Exs. 28–32,
41, 44

16. 10, 20, 30, 40, 50, 60

17. 1, 1, 3, 4, 5, 9

18. 10, 12, 7, 11, 20, 7, 6, 8, 9

19. 1202, 1229, 1012, 1014, 1120, 1429

20. 3.1, 2.7, 6.0, 5.6, 2.3, 2.0, 1.3

21. 19.4, 16.3, 12.7, 24.8, 19.2, 15.4

BOX-AND-WHISKER PLOTS Draw a box-and-whisker plot of the data set.

22. 1, 2, 2, 4, 5, 7

23. 19, 19, 19, 89, 93, 95

24. 47, 88, 89, 61, 70, 71, 79

25. 40, 100, 20, 40, 100, 70, 90

26. 1.7, 8.5, 1.2, 3.8, 8.5, 5.2, 6.9

27. 61.2, 23.0, 72.7, 74.3, 19.1, 6.6, 28.4

HISTOGRAMS Use the given intervals to make a frequency distribution of the data set. Then draw a histogram of the data set.

28. Use five intervals beginning with 1–2.
1, 1, 1, 2, 2, 2, 3, 3, 4, 4, 4, 4, 5, 6, 6, 7, 7, 7, 7, 8, 8, 8, 8, 9, 9

29. Use five intervals beginning with 10–19.
10, 12, 14, 15, 15, 23, 26, 26, 27, 28, 37, 37, 37, 37, 38, 39, 39, 40, 48, 58

30. Use ten intervals beginning with 0–9.
66, 9, 43, 28, 5, 7, 90, 9, 78, 6, 69, 43, 28, 55, 13, 64, 45, 10, 54, 96

31. Use fifteen intervals beginning with 0.0–0.4.
2.2, 5.6, 2.2, 4.4, 2.2, 6.6, 2.4, 5.8, 2.4, 4.8, 2.4, 6.1, 5.4, 5.4

32. Use eight intervals beginning with 15.5–20.4.
22.2, 22.2, 22.6, 24.3, 24.3, 24.8, 54.5, 54.4, 54.1, 52.3, 52.3, 52.9

🌐 **SCRATCH PROTECTION** In Exercises 33–35, use the following information.
Computer chips have a silicon dioxide coating that gives them scratch protection. Phosphorus is contained in this coating and is a key to its effectiveness. A company that produces silicon dioxide has two machines that vary from run to run on the phosphorus content. The phosphorus contents for four runs on each machine are shown below.

Machine 1		Machine 2	
Run number	Percent of coating that is phosphorous (by weight)	Run number	Percent of coating that is phosphorous (by weight)
1	2.63	1	1.09
2	2.72	2	3.06
3	2.47	3	4.10
4	2.55	4	2.12

33. Find the mean, median, and mode of each data set.

34. Find the range and standard deviation of each data set.

35. CRITICAL THINKING Based on the data, which machine is more consistent? Explain your reasoning.

🌐 **REAL ESTATE** In Exercises 36–38, suppose a real estate agent has sold seven homes priced at $104,900, $119,900, $134,900, $142,000, $179,900, $199,900, and $750,000.

36. Find the mean, median, and mode of the selling prices.

37. Find the range and standard deviation of the selling prices.

38. CRITICAL THINKING How does the selling price $750,000 affect the mean? How does this explain why the most commonly used measure of central tendency for housing prices is the median rather than the mean or the mode?

39. 🌐 **POLITICAL SURVEY** A random survey of 1000 people asked their opinions on a controversial issue. The opinions are categorized as 0 = a negative opinion, 1 = a positive opinion, and 2 = a neutral opinion. The results of the survey are 212 category 0 responses, 627 category 1 responses, and 161 category 2 responses. Which measure of central tendency is most appropriate to represent the data? Explain.

HISTORY **CONNECTION** In Exercises 40–42, use the tables below which give the ages of the Presidents and Vice Presidents of the United States.

Ages of the first 42 Presidents of the United States when they first took office
42, 43, 46, 46, 47, 48, 49, 49, 50, 51, 51, 51, 51, 51, 52, 52, 54, 54, 54, 54, 55, 55, 55, 55, 56, 56, 56, 57, 57, 57, 57, 58, 60, 61, 61, 61, 62, 64, 64, 65, 68, 69

Ages of the first 47 Vice Presidents of the United States when they first took office
36, 40, 41, 42, 42, 42, 44, 45, 45, 46, 48, 49, 49, 50, 50, 51, 51, 51, 52, 52, 52, 52, 52, 53, 53, 53, 53, 56, 56, 56, 57, 57, 58, 59, 60, 60, 61, 64, 64, 65, 65, 66, 66, 68, 69, 69, 71

▶ Source: *Facts About the Presidents*

40. Draw a box-and-whisker plot of each data set.

41. Make a frequency distribution of each data set using five intervals beginning with 30–39. Then draw a histogram of each data set.

42. VISUAL THINKING What is one conclusion you can draw about the ages of the presidents and vice presidents based on your graphs?

STATISTICS **CONNECTION** In Exercises 43–45, use the tables below which give the margins of victory for each championship game in the AFC and in the NFC for the 1966–1998 seasons.

AFC Championship margins of victory
24, 33, 4, 10, 10, 21, 4, 17, 11, 6, 17, 3, 29, 14, 7, 20, 14, 16, 17, 17, 3, 5, 11, 16, 48, 3, 19, 17, 4, 4, 14, 3, 13

NFC Championship margins of victory
7, 4, 34, 20, 7, 11, 23, 17, 4, 30, 11, 17, 28, 9, 13, 1, 14, 3, 23, 24, 17, 7, 25, 27, 2, 31, 10, 17, 10, 11, 17, 13, 3

43. Draw a box-and-whisker plot of each data set.

44. Make a frequency distribution of each data set using five intervals beginning with 1–10. Then draw a histogram of each data set.

45. VISUAL THINKING What is one conclusion you *cannot* draw about the margins of victory in the AFC and NFC championship games based on your graphs?

46. RESEARCH Research two sets of data that you can compare. Find the measures of central tendency and measures of dispersion of each data set. Then draw a box-and-whisker plot and a histogram of each data set. What do you observe?

Test
Preparation

47. MULTIPLE CHOICE What is the mean of 2, 2, 6, 7, 9, 10?

(A) 2   (B) 6   (C) 6.5   (D) 7   (E) 7.2

48. MULTIPLE CHOICE What is the median of 0.5, 0.6, 0.7, 1.2, 1.5, 1.5?

(A) 0.7   (B) 0.95   (C) 1   (D) 1.2   (E) 1.5

49. MULTIPLE CHOICE What is (are) the mode(s) of 12, 13, 13, 15, 16, 16?

(A) 13   (B) 14   (C) 13, 16   (D) 17   (E) none

★ Challenge

50. ALTERNATE FORMULA The formula for standard deviation can also be written as follows:

$$\sigma = \sqrt{\frac{x_1^2 + x_2^2 + \cdots + x_n^2}{n} - \overline{x}^2}$$

For $n = 3$, show that this formula is equivalent to the formula given on page 446. (*Hint:* You will need to show that $x_1 + x_2 + x_3 = 3\overline{x}$.)

MIXED REVIEW

EVALUATING EXPRESSIONS Evaluate the expression for the given value of *x*.
(Review 1.2 for 8.1)

51. $x^5 - 8$ when $x = 2$

52. $3x^3 + 7$ when $x = \dfrac{3}{7}$

53. $(7x)^3 + 17$ when $x = -1$

54. $\dfrac{4x}{x^4 - 1}$ when $x = 0.5$

PROPERTIES OF EXPONENTS Evaluate the expression. Tell which properties of exponents you used. (Review 6.1 for 8.1)

55. $3^3 \cdot 3^4$

56. $\left(4^{-3}\right)^2$

57. $(-2)(-2)^{-3}$

58. $\left(5^{-2}\right)^{-2}$

59. $10^{-2} \cdot 10^0$

60. $7^0 \cdot 7^2 \cdot 7^{-2}$

GRAPHING POLYNOMIALS Graph the polynomial function. (Review 6.2)

61. $f(x) = 3x^5$

62. $f(x) = x^3 - 4$

63. $f(x) = -x^4 + 3x^2 - 5$

64. $f(x) = -x^3 + 2x$

65. $f(x) = x^4 - 6x^2 - 9$

66. $f(x) = x^5 - 2x + 4$

QUIZ 3

Self Test for Lessons 7.5–7.7

Graph the function. Then state the domain and range. (Lesson 7.5)

1. $y = \sqrt{x + 8}$

2. $y = (x + 7)^{1/2} - 2$

3. $y = 3\sqrt[3]{x} - 6$

Solve the equation. Check for extraneous solutions. (Lesson 7.6)

4. $\sqrt[4]{2x} = 5$

5. $\sqrt{3x + 7} = x - 1$

6. $\sqrt[3]{2x} - 2\sqrt[3]{x} = 0$

Find the mean, median, mode, range, and standard deviation of the data set.
(Lesson 7.7)

7. 0, 1, 2, 2, 5, 6, 6, 6, 7, 9

8. 15, 32, 18, 21, 26, 12, 43

9. **GEOMETRY** **CONNECTION** The radius *r* of a sphere is related to the volume *V* of the sphere by the formula $r = 0.620\sqrt[3]{V}$. Graph the formula. Then estimate the volume of a sphere with a radius of 10 units. (Lesson 7.5)

10. **ASTRONOMY** Kepler's third law of planetary motion states that a planet's orbital period *P* (in days) is related to its orbit's semi-major axis *a* (in millions of kilometers) by the formula $P = 0.199a^{3/2}$. The orbital period of Mars is about 1.88 *years*. What is its semi-major axis? (Lesson 7.6)

HISTORY **CONNECTION** In Exercises 11 and 12, use the following data set of years when each state was admitted to statehood. (Lesson 7.7)

1819, 1959, 1912, 1836, 1850, 1876, 1788, 1787, 1845, 1788,
1959, 1890, 1818, 1816, 1846, 1861, 1792, 1812, 1820, 1788,
1788, 1837, 1858, 1817, 1821, 1889, 1867, 1864, 1788, 1787,
1912, 1788, 1789, 1889, 1803, 1907, 1859, 1787, 1790, 1788,
1889, 1796, 1845, 1896, 1791, 1788, 1889, 1863, 1848, 1890

11. Draw a box-and-whisker plot of the data set.

12. Make a frequency distribution of the data set using five intervals beginning with 1750–1799. Then draw a histogram of the data set.

▶ ACTIVITY 7.7

Using Technology

Statistics and Statistical Graphs

You can use a graphing calculator to find statistics and draw statistical graphs.

▶ EXAMPLE

The fat content and number of calories in several different sandwiches available at a restaurant are shown in the tables below. Use a graphing calculator to (**a**) find the mean, median, range, and standard deviation of the fat content in the sandwiches, (**b**) draw a box-and-whisker plot of the fat content in the sandwiches, and (**c**) draw a histogram of the number of calories in the sandwiches.

Sandwich	Fat (g)	Calories
Hamburger	9	260
Cheeseburger	13	320
Quarter-pound hamburger	21	420
Quarter-pound cheeseburger	30	530
Double cheeseburger	´31	560

Sandwich	Fat (g)	Calories
Bacon cheeseburger	34	590
Fried chicken	25	500
Grilled chicken	20	440
Breaded fish on deluxe roll	28	560
Breaded fish on plain bun	25	450

▶ SOLUTION

a. Use the *Stat Edit* feature to enter the data in a list. Then use the *Stat Calc* menu to choose 1-variable statistics.

The mean is $\bar{x}$ and the standard deviation is σx. By scrolling you can find the median (Med). The range is the difference of maxX and minX.

```
EDIT CALC
1:1-Var Stats
2:2-Var Stats
3:Med-Med
4:LinReg(ax+b)
5:QuadReg
6↓CubicReg
```

```
1-Var Stats
 x̄=23.6
 Σx=236
 Σx²=6142
 Sx=7.974960815
 σx=7.565712128
↓n=10
```

b. Use the *Stat Plot* menu to choose the type of plot (box-and-whisker), the list of data, and the frequency for the data. Then set an appropriate viewing window.

Draw the box-and-whisker plot. Use the *Trace* feature to view the minimum (9), the lower quartile (20), the median (25), the upper quartile (30), and the maximum (34).

```
Plot1 Plot2 Plot3
On Off
Type: 
XList:L₁
Freq:1
```

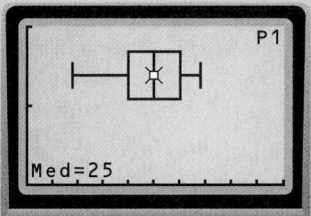

```
Med=25
```

c. Use the *Stat Edit* feature to enter the data, and use the *Stat Plot* menu to choose the type of plot (histogram), the list of data, and the frequency for the data. Then set an appropriate viewing window.

Draw the histogram. Use the *Trace* feature to view the minimum of each interval, the maximum of each interval, and the frequency of each interval.

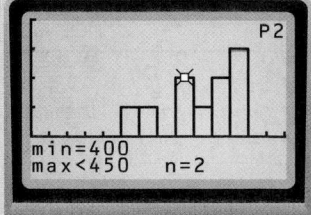

▶ EXERCISES

In Exercises 1–5, use the tables below which give the fat content and the number of calories in several different sandwiches available at a competing restaurant.

Sandwich	Fat (g)	Calories
Plain hamburger	16	360
Hamburger with everything	20	420
Bacon cheeseburger	30	580
Small hamburger	10	270
Small cheeseburger	17	360

Sandwich	Fat (g)	Calories
Small bacon cheeseburger	19	380
Grilled chicken	8	310
Breaded chicken	18	440
Chicken club	20	470
Spicy chicken	15	410

1. Use a graphing calculator to find the mean, median, range, and standard deviation of the fat content in the sandwiches.

2. How does the mean fat content in the sandwiches from the restaurant above compare with the mean fat content in the sandwiches from the restaurant in the example? Which restaurant's sandwiches have a higher median fat content? Which restaurant's sandwiches have a lower standard deviation of fat content? Based on these statistics, write a sentence that compares the fat content in the sandwiches of the two restaurants.

3. Use a graphing calculator to draw a box-and-whisker plot of the fat content in the sandwiches.

4. Use a graphing calculator to draw a box-and-whisker plot of the fat content in the sandwiches from the restaurant in the example in the same viewing window as the plot from Exercise 3. Which restaurant's sandwiches have a lower fat content? Write a sentence explaining how the box-and-whisker plots help you analyze the data.

5. Use a graphing calculator to draw a histogram of the number of calories in the sandwiches. Use an interval width of 50 for each. Write a sentence comparing the number of calories in the sandwiches from the restaurant above with the number of calories in the sandwiches from the restaurant in the example on page 453.

WHAT did you learn?

Evaluate *n*th roots of real numbers. **(7.1)**

Use properties of rational exponents to evaluate and simplify expressions. **(7.2)**

Perform function operations. **(7.3)**

Find inverses of linear and nonlinear functions. **(7.4)**

Graph square root and cube root functions. **(7.5)**

Solve equations that contain radicals or rational exponents. **(7.6)**

Use roots and rational exponents in real-life problems. **(7.1–7.6)**

Use power functions, inverse functions, and radical functions to solve real-life problems. **(7.3–7.6)**

Use measures of central tendency and measures of dispersion to describe data sets. **(7.7)**

Represent data graphically with box-and-whisker plots and histograms. **(7.7)**

WHY did you learn it?

Find the number of reptile and amphibian species that Puerto Rico can support. **(p. 405)**

Model frequencies in the musical range of a trumpet. **(p. 413)**

Find the height of a dinosaur. **(p. 419)**

Find your bowling average. **(p. 428)**

Find the age of an African elephant. **(p. 433)**

Determine which boats satisfy the rule for competing in the America's Cup. **(p. 443)**

Find surface areas of mammals. **(p. 410)**

Find wind speeds that correspond to Beaufort wind scale numbers. **(p. 440)**

Analyze data sets such as the free-throw percentages for the players in the WNBA. **(pp. 445 and 446)**

Graph data sets such as the ages of the Presidents and Vice Presidents of the United States. **(p. 451)**

How does Chapter 7 fit into the BIGGER PICTURE of algebra?

In Chapter 7 you saw the familiar ideas of squares and square roots extended. This was a significant step in your study of powers and roots as you used exponents that were *not* whole numbers in expressions, functions, and many real-life problems. You will continue to build on these ideas as long as you study mathematics.

STUDY STRATEGY

How did you quiz yourself?

Here is an example of a quiz that was written for Lesson 7.3 and used before a class quiz was given, following the **Study Strategy** on page 400.

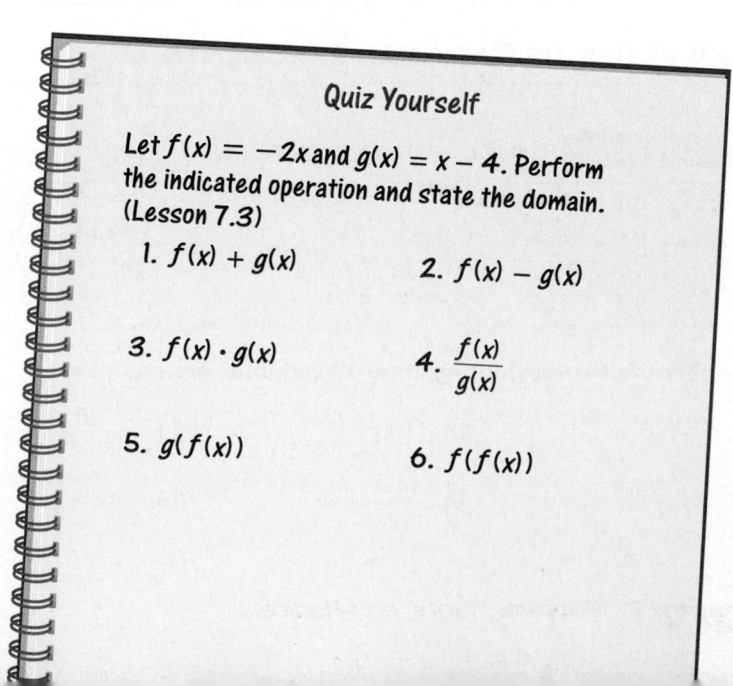

Quiz Yourself

Let $f(x) = -2x$ and $g(x) = x - 4$. Perform the indicated operation and state the domain. (Lesson 7.3)

1. $f(x) + g(x)$

2. $f(x) - g(x)$

3. $f(x) \cdot g(x)$

4. $\dfrac{f(x)}{g(x)}$

5. $g(f(x))$

6. $f(f(x))$

Chapter Review

- *n*th root of *a*, p. 401
- index, p. 401
- simplest form, p. 408
- like radicals, p. 408
- power function, p. 415
- composition, p. 416
- inverse relation, p. 422

- inverse function, p. 422
- radical function, p. 431
- extraneous solution, p. 439
- statistics, p. 445
- measure of central tendency, p. 445
- mean, p. 445

- median, p. 445
- mode, p. 445
- measure of dispersion, p. 446
- range, p. 446
- standard deviation, p. 446
- box-and-whisker plot, p. 447

- lower quartile, p. 447
- upper quartile, p. 447
- histogram, p. 448
- frequency, p. 448
- frequency distribution, p. 448

7.1 *N*TH ROOTS AND RATIONAL EXPONENTS

Examples on pp. 401–403

EXAMPLES You can evaluate *n*th roots using radicals or rational exponents.

Radical notation: $27^{-2/3} = \dfrac{1}{27^{2/3}} = \dfrac{1}{(\sqrt[3]{27})^2} = \dfrac{1}{3^2} = \dfrac{1}{9}$

Rational exponent notation: $27^{-2/3} = \dfrac{1}{27^{2/3}} = \dfrac{1}{(27^{1/3})^2} = \dfrac{1}{3^2} = \dfrac{1}{9}$

Evaluate the expression without using a calculator.

1. $\sqrt[4]{16}$ **2.** $(\sqrt[3]{64})^2$ **3.** $9^{-5/2}$ **4.** $216^{1/3}$ **5.** $\sqrt[5]{-32}$

6. Find the real *n*th root(s) of *a* if $n = 4$ and $a = 81$.

7. Find the real *n*th root(s) of *a* if $n = 5$ and $a = -1$.

8. Find the real *n*th root(s) of *a* if $n = 7$ and $a = 0$.

7.2 PROPERTIES OF RATIONAL EXPONENTS

Examples on pp. 407–410

EXAMPLES You can use properties of rational exponents to simplify expressions.

$\sqrt[3]{12} \cdot \sqrt[3]{4} = \sqrt[3]{12 \cdot 4} = \sqrt[3]{48} = \sqrt[3]{8 \cdot 6} = \sqrt[3]{8} \cdot \sqrt[3]{6} = 2\sqrt[3]{6}$

$\dfrac{(x^{1/2}y)^2}{x^{1/2}y^{3/4}} = \dfrac{x^{(1/2 \cdot 2)}y^2}{x^{1/2}y^{3/4}} = \dfrac{xy^2}{x^{1/2}y^{3/4}} = x^{(1-1/2)}y^{(2-3/4)} = x^{1/2}y^{5/4}$

Simplify the expression. Assume all variables are positive.

9. $5^{1/4} \cdot 5^{-9/4}$ **10.** $(100^{1/3})^{3/4}$ **11.** $\sqrt[3]{\dfrac{16}{1000}}$ **12.** $5\sqrt[3]{17} - 4\sqrt[3]{17}$

13. $(81x)^{1/4}$ **14.** $\dfrac{(4x)^2}{(4x)^{1/2}}$ **15.** $\sqrt[6]{6x^6y^7z^{10}}$ **16.** $\sqrt[3]{4a^6} + a\sqrt[3]{108a^3}$

POWER FUNCTIONS AND FUNCTION OPERATIONS

Examples on pp. 415–417

EXAMPLES You can add, subtract, multiply, or divide any two functions f and g. You can also find the composition of any two functions.

Let $f(x) = 2x^{1/2}$ and $g(x) = x^4$

Addition: $f(x) + g(x) = 2x^{1/2} + x^4$

Multiplication: $f(x) \cdot g(x) = 2x^{1/2} \cdot x^4 = 2x^{9/2}$

Composition: $f(g(x)) = f(x^4) = 2(x^4)^{1/2} = 2x^2$

Let $f(x) = 2x - 4$ and $g(x) = x - 2$. Perform the indicated operation.

17. $f(x) + g(x)$ **18.** $f(x) - g(x)$ **19.** $f(x) \cdot g(x)$ **20.** $\dfrac{f(x)}{g(x)}$ **21.** $f(g(x))$

INVERSE FUNCTIONS

Examples on pp. 422–425

EXAMPLES You can find the inverse relation of any function. To verify that two functions are inverses of each other, show that $f(f^{-1}(x)) = f^{-1}(f(x)) = x$.

$f(x) = y = 2x - 5$

$\quad x = 2y - 5$

$\quad x + 5 = 2y$

$\tfrac{1}{2}x + \tfrac{5}{2} = y = f^{-1}(x)$

$f(f^{-1}(x)) = 2\left(\tfrac{1}{2}x + \tfrac{5}{2}\right) - 5 = x + 5 - 5 = x$

$f^{-1}(f(x)) = \tfrac{1}{2}(2x - 5) + \tfrac{5}{2} = x - \tfrac{5}{2} + \tfrac{5}{2} = x$

Find the inverse function.

22. $f(x) = -2x + 1$ **23.** $f(x) = -x^4, x \geq 0$ **24.** $f(x) = 5x^3 + 7$

25. Verify that $f(x) = -2x^5$ and $g(x) = \sqrt[5]{-\dfrac{x}{2}}$ are inverse functions.

GRAPHING SQUARE ROOT AND CUBE ROOT FUNCTIONS

Examples on pp. 431–433

EXAMPLE You can graph a square root function by starting with the graph of $y = \sqrt{x}$. You can graph a cube root function by starting with the graph of $y = \sqrt[3]{x}$.

To graph $y = \sqrt[3]{x - 5} - 2$, first sketch $y = \sqrt[3]{x}$ (shown in red). Then shift the graph right 5 units and down 2 units. From the graph of $y = \sqrt[3]{x - 5} - 2$, you can see that the domain and range of the function are both all real numbers.

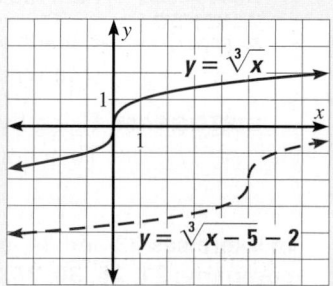

Graph the function. Then state the domain and range.

26. $y = (x - 7)^{1/3}$ **27.** $y = \sqrt{x} + 6$ **28.** $y = -2(x - 3)^{1/2}$ **29.** $y = 3\sqrt[3]{x + 4} - 9$

7.6 SOLVING RADICAL EQUATIONS

Examples on pp. 437–440

EXAMPLES You can solve equations that contain radicals or rational exponents by raising each side of the equation to the same power.

$$\sqrt{x-4} = 6 \qquad\qquad\qquad 4x^{2/3} = 100$$

$$\left(\sqrt{x-4}\right)^2 = 6^2 \quad \textbf{Square each side.} \qquad x^{2/3} = 25$$

$$x - 4 = 36 \qquad\qquad \left(x^{2/3}\right)^{3/2} = 25^{3/2} \quad \textbf{Raise each side to } \tfrac{3}{2} \textbf{ power.}$$

$$x = 40 \qquad\qquad\qquad\qquad x = 125$$

Solve the equation. Check for extraneous solutions.

30. $3(x+1)^{1/5} + 5 = 11$ **31.** $\sqrt[3]{5x+3} - \sqrt[3]{4x} = 0$ **32.** $\sqrt{4x} = x - 8$

7.7 STATISTICS AND STATISTICAL GRAPHS

Examples on pp. 445–448

EXAMPLES The table shows the normal daily high temperatures (in degrees Fahrenheit) for Phoenix, Arizona, from 1961 to 1990.

Jan.	Feb.	Mar.	Apr.	May	June	July	Aug.	Sept.	Oct.	Nov.	Dec.
65.9	70.7	75.5	84.5	93.6	103.5	105.9	103.7	98.3	88.1	74.9	66.2

MEAN Find the average of the numbers: $\dfrac{65.9 + 70.7 + \cdots + 66.2}{12} = \dfrac{1030.8}{12} = 85.9$

MEDIAN Write the numbers in increasing order and locate the middle number(s):
65.9, 66.2, 70.7, 74.9, 75.5, **84.5**, **88.1**, 93.6, 98.3, 103.5, 103.7, 105.9

There are two middle numbers, so find their mean: $\dfrac{84.5 + 88.1}{2} = 86.3$

MODE Find the number(s) that occur most frequently: none

RANGE Find the difference between the greatest and least numbers: $105.9 - 65.9 = 40$

STANDARD DEVIATION Use the formula: $\sqrt{\dfrac{(65.9 - 85.9)^2 + (70.7 - 85.9)^2 + \cdots + (66.2 - 85.9)^2}{12}} \approx 14.4$

BOX-AND-WHISKER PLOT Find the quartiles: $\dfrac{70.7 + 74.9}{2} = 72.8$ and $\dfrac{98.3 + 103.5}{2} = 100.9$

Plot the minimum, maximum, median, and quartiles. Then draw the box and the whiskers (not shown).

HISTOGRAM Using five intervals beginning with 60–69, tally the data values for each interval. Then draw a histogram of the data set (not shown).

In Exercises 33 and 34, use the following data set of employees' ages at a small company: 21, 25, 30, 36, 39, 40, 44, 45, 46, 51, 51, 63.

33. Find the mean, median, mode, range, and standard deviation of the data set.

34. Draw a box-and-whisker plot and a histogram of the data set. For the histogram, use five intervals beginning with 20–29.

Evaluate the expression without using a calculator.

1. $\sqrt[3]{-1000}$

2. $4^{5/2}$

3. $(-64)^{2/3}$

4. $243^{-1/5}$

5. $\sqrt[4]{16}$

Simplify the expression. Assume all variables are positive.

6. $(2^{1/3} \cdot 5^{1/2})^4$

7. $\sqrt[3]{27x^3y^6z^9}$

8. $\dfrac{3xy^{-1}}{12x^{1/2}y}$

9. $\left(\dfrac{81x^2}{y}\right)^{3/4}$

10. $\sqrt{18} + \sqrt{200}$

Perform the indicated operation and state the domain.

11. $f + g$; $f(x) = x - 8$, $g(x) = 3x$

12. $f - g$; $f(x) = 2x^{1/4}$, $g(x) = 5x^{1/4}$

13. $f \cdot g$; $f(x) = 5x + 7$, $g(x) = x - 9$

14. $\dfrac{f}{g}$; $f(x) = x^{-1/5}$, $g(x) = x^{3/5}$

15. $f(g(x))$; $f(x) = 4x^2 - 5$, $g(x) = -x$

16. $g(f(x))$; $f(x) = x^2 + 3x$, $g(x) = 2x + 1$

Find the inverse function.

17. $f(x) = \frac{1}{3}x - 4$

18. $f(x) = -5x + 5$

19. $f(x) = \frac{3}{4}x^2, x \geq 0$

20. $f(x) = x^5 - 2$

Graph the function. Then state the domain and range.

21. $f(x) = \sqrt{x - 6}$

22. $f(x) = \sqrt[3]{x} + 3$

23. $f(x) = 3(x + 4)^{1/3} - 2$

24. $f(x) = -2x^{1/2} + 4$

Solve the equation. Check for extraneous solutions.

25. $x^{5/2} - 10 = 22$

26. $(x + 8)^{1/4} + 1 = 0$

27. $\sqrt[3]{7x - 9} + 11 = 14$

28. $\sqrt{4x + 15} - 3\sqrt{x} = 0$

29. **BIOLOGY CONNECTION** Some biologists study the structure of animals. By studying a series of antelopes, biologists have found that the length l (in millimeters) of an antelope's bone can be modeled by
$$l = 24.1d^{2/3}$$
where d is the midshaft diameter of the bone (in millimeters). If the bone of an antelope has a midshaft diameter of 20 millimeters, what is the length of the bone? ▶ Source: *On Size and Life*

ACADEMY AWARDS In Exercises 30–33, use the tables below which give the ages of the Academy Award winners for best actress and for best actor from 1980 to 1998.

Best actress	Best actor
21, 25, 26, 29, 31, 33, 33, 34, 34, 38, 39, 41, 42, 45, 49, 49, 61, 72, 80	30, 32, 35, 37, 37, 38, 39, 42, 43, 45, 45, 46, 51, 52, 52, 54, 60, 61, 76

30. Find the mean, median, mode, range, and standard deviation of each data set.

31. Draw a box-and-whisker plot of each data set.

32. Make a frequency distribution of each data set using six intervals beginning with 21–30. Then draw a histogram of each data set.

33. *Writing* Compare the ages of the best actresses with the ages of the best actors. Use statistics and statistical graphs to support your statements.

CHAPTER 7

Chapter Standardized Test

⬤ **TEST-TAKING STRATEGY** Some college entrance exams allow the optional use of calculators. If you do use a calculator, make sure it is one you are familiar with and have used before.

1. MULTIPLE CHOICE If $x^4 = 625$, what does x equal?

- (A) 5
- (B) -5
- (C) ± 5
- (D) 25
- (E) ± 25

2. MULTIPLE CHOICE What is the simplified form of the expression $\sqrt{18} + \sqrt{200} + \sqrt{2} - \sqrt{8}$?

- (A) $12\sqrt{2}$
- (B) $14\sqrt{2}$
- (C) $18\sqrt{2}$
- (D) $14\sqrt{2} - \sqrt{8}$
- (E) $4\sqrt{2} - 4\sqrt{8}$

3. MULTIPLE CHOICE What is the simplified form of the expression $\sqrt[3]{54x^3y^6z^{10}}$? (Assume all variables are positive.)

- (A) $xy^2\sqrt[3]{54z^{10}}$
- (B) $xy^2z^3\sqrt[3]{54z}$
- (C) $3y^3z^7\sqrt[3]{5}$
- (D) $3xy^2z^3\sqrt[3]{2z}$
- (E) $18xy^3z^7$

4. MULTIPLE CHOICE Which of the following is true if $f(x) = 3x^{-1/2}$, $g(x) = 6x^{3/4}$, and $h(x) = 18x^{1/4}$?

- (A) $h(x) = f(x) + g(x)$
- (B) $h(x) = f(x) - g(x)$
- (C) $h(x) = f(x) \cdot g(x)$
- (D) $h(x) = \dfrac{f(x)}{g(x)}$
- (E) $h(x) = f(g(x))$

5. MULTIPLE CHOICE If $f(x) = x^2 - 3x + 7$ and $g(x) = x^2 + 2$, what is $f(g(x))$?

- (A) $x^4 + x^2 + 17$
- (B) $x^4 + x^2 + 5$
- (C) $x^4 + x^2 - 9$
- (D) $x^4 + x^2 - 3$
- (E) $x^4 + 7x^2 + 5$

6. MULTIPLE CHOICE Which function is the inverse of $f(x) = \frac{1}{2}x - 5$?

- (A) $f^{-1}(x) = 2x - 10$
- (B) $f^{-1}(x) = 2x + 5$
- (C) $f^{-1}(x) = 2x + 10$
- (D) $f^{-1}(x) = \frac{1}{2}x + 5$
- (E) $f^{-1}(x) = \frac{1}{2}x + \frac{5}{2}$

7. MULTIPLE CHOICE Which function is graphed?

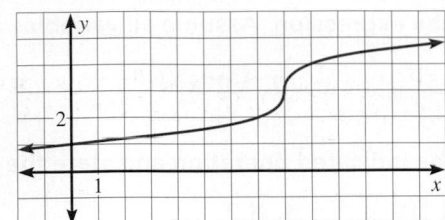

- (A) $y = \sqrt[3]{x - 3} + 8$
- (B) $y = \sqrt[3]{x + 3} + 8$
- (C) $y = \sqrt[3]{x - 8} + 3$
- (D) $y = \sqrt[3]{x + 8} - 3$
- (E) $y = \sqrt[3]{x + 8} + 3$

8. MULTIPLE CHOICE What is the solution of the equation $(3x + 5)^{1/2} - 3 = 4$?

- (A) $-\dfrac{4}{3}$
- (B) $\dfrac{8}{3}$
- (C) $\dfrac{11}{3}$
- (D) $\dfrac{14}{3}$
- (E) $\dfrac{44}{3}$

9. MULTIPLE CHOICE What is the solution of the equation $4\sqrt[3]{x - 5} = 20$?

- (A) 120
- (B) 130
- (C) 220
- (D) 2005
- (E) 4101

10. MULTIPLE CHOICE What is the median of 6, 4, 4, 10, 5, 12, 1?

- (A) 4
- (B) 5
- (C) 6
- (D) 7
- (E) 10

11. MULTIPLE CHOICE Which data set matches the box-and-whisker plot shown?

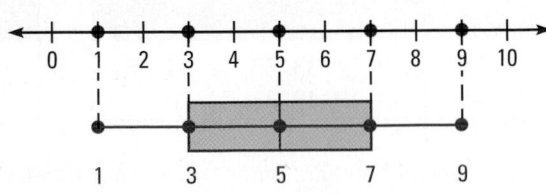

- (A) 1, 1, 3, 5, 6, 7, 9
- (B) 1, 2, 3, 5, 7, 8, 9
- (C) 1, 2, 4, 5, 6, 8, 9
- (D) 1, 3, 4, 5, 6, 7, 9
- (E) 1, 3, 5, 5, 7, 8, 9

    A The quantity in column A is greater.

    B The quantity in column B is greater.

    C The two quantities are equal.

    D The relationship cannot be determined from the given information.

	Column A	Column B
12.	$f(8)$ where $f(x) = x^{-2/3}$	$f(2)$ where $f(x) = x^{-2}$
13.	$f(f(0))$ where $f(x) = 5x - 2$	$f(f(0))$ where $f(x) = x^3 + 1$

14. **MULTI-STEP PROBLEM** The metabolic rate r (in kilocalories per day) of a mammal can be modeled by $r = km^{3/4}$ where k is a constant and m is the mass (in kilograms) of the mammal. The specific metabolic rate s (the rate per unit mass) can be modeled by $s = \dfrac{km^{3/4}}{m}$. ▶ Source: *Scaling: Why is Animal Size so Important?*

    a. A 922 kilogram cow has a metabolic rate of about 11,700 kilocalories per day. What is the value of k in the model for metabolic rate?

    b. Using the k-value from part (a), simplify the model given for specific metabolic rate.

    c. What is the specific metabolic rate of a 922 kilogram cow?

    d. What is the specific metabolic rate of a 16 *gram* mouse?

    e. *Writing* How does the specific metabolic rate change with decreasing body mass?

15. **MULTI-STEP PROBLEM** Follow the steps below to find the relationship between the number of pedal revolutions of a bicycle and the distance traveled.

    a. The rear wheel of a bicycle has a diameter of 70 centimeters. Write the function that describes the distance d traveled by the bicycle in terms of the number w of rear-wheel revolutions. (*Hint:* When $w = 1$, the distance traveled by the bicycle is equal to the circumference of the rear wheel.)

    b. The gear ratio of a bicycle is calculated by dividing the number of teeth in the chainwheel by the number of teeth in the freewheel. The number w of rear-wheel revolutions is equal to the product of the gear ratio and the number p of pedal revolutions. A bicycle in first gear has 24 teeth in the chainwheel and 32 teeth in the freewheel. Write the function that describes w in terms of p.

    c. Use composition of functions to find the relationship between d and p.

    d. Shifting gears on a bicycle changes the gear ratio. Use the table below to find how the distance traveled per pedal revolution changes as you shift gears.

Gear	Number of teeth in chainwheel	Number of teeth in freewheel
5th	24	19
10th	40	22
15th	50	19

EXPONENTIAL AND LOGARITHMIC FUNCTIONS

▶ *How does altitude affect the air?*

CHAPTER
8

APPLICATION: Mountain Climbing

A surprising fact that you may not know is that air has weight! The weight of the air above you produces what scientists call *atmospheric pressure*.

Mountain climbers need to be aware of changes in atmospheric pressure because as the pressure decreases, so does the amount of oxygen they have to breathe.

Think & Discuss

The graph below shows the relationship between atmospheric pressure and altitude.

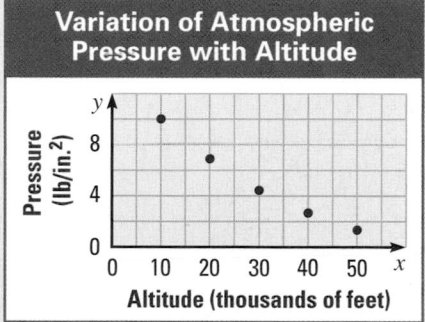

Variation of Atmospheric Pressure with Altitude

1. Describe what happens to the atmospheric pressure as the altitude increases.

2. Mount McKinley in Alaska is 20,320 feet high. Estimate the atmospheric pressure at its peak.

Learn More About It

You will find the atmospheric pressure at the peak of Mount Everest in Exercise 79 on p. 484.

APPLICATION LINK Visit www.mcdougallittell.com for more information about atmospheric pressure.

Study Guide

PREVIEW

What's the chapter about?

Chapter 8 is about **exponential and logarithmic functions**. These functions are inverses of each other. In Chapter 8 you'll learn

- how to graph and use exponential, logarithmic, and logistic growth functions.
- how to use the number e and the definition and properties of logarithms.
- how to solve exponential and logarithmic equations.

KEY VOCABULARY

▶ **Review**
- base, p. 11
- inverse function, p. 422

▶ **New**
- exponential function, p. 465

- asymptote, p. 465
- exponential growth function, p. 466
- exponential decay function, p. 474
- natural base e, p. 480

- logarithm of y with base b, p. 486
- common logarithm, p. 487
- natural logarithm, p. 487
- logistic growth function, p. 517

PREPARE

Are you ready for the chapter?

SKILL REVIEW Do these exercises to review key skills that you'll apply in this chapter. See the given **reference page** if there is something you don't understand.

STUDENT HELP

▶ Study Tip
"Student Help" boxes throughout the chapter give you study tips and tell you where to look for extra help in this book and on the Internet.

Evaluate the expression. (Review Example 1, p. 11; Example 1, p. 324)

1. 4^{-3} **2.** $\left(\dfrac{1}{3}\right)^2$ **3.** $\left(\dfrac{3}{4}\right)^0$ **4.** -5^2 **5.** $\left(\dfrac{5}{2}\right)^{-1}$

Describe the end behavior of the graph of the function by completing the statements $f(x) \to \underline{\ ?\ }$ **as** $x \to -\infty$ **and** $f(x) \to \underline{\ ?\ }$ **as** $x \to +\infty$. (Review Example 4, p. 332)

6. $f(x) = 2x^3$ **7.** $f(x) = -x^2$ **8.** $f(x) = 4x^4$ **9.** $f(x) = -5x^3$

Draw a scatter plot of the data. Then approximate an equation of the best-fitting line. (Review Example 2, p. 101)

10.

x	1	2	3	4	5	6	7	8	9	10
y	2.2	2.9	3.0	4.1	4.2	4.3	4.8	5.0	5.9	5.9

STUDY STRATEGY

Here's a study strategy!

Study Group

Form a study group. Have each group member take lessons from the chapter and summarize the important concepts and skills in those lessons. Then have each member lead a discussion on how to solve the types of problems in his or her lessons.

8.1

Exponential Growth

What you should learn

GOAL 1 Graph exponential growth functions.

GOAL 2 Use exponential growth functions to model **real-life** situations, such as Internet growth in **Example 3**.

Why you should learn it

▼ To solve **real-life** problems, such as finding the amount of energy generated from wind turbines in **Exs. 49–51**.

REAL LIFE

GOAL 1 GRAPHING EXPONENTIAL GROWTH FUNCTIONS

An **exponential function** involves the expression b^x where the **base** b is a positive number other than 1. In this lesson you will study exponential functions for which $b > 1$. To see the basic shape of the graph of an exponential function such as $f(x) = 2^x$, you can make a table of values and plot points, as shown below.

x	$f(x) = 2^x$
−3	$2^{-3} = \dfrac{1}{8}$
−2	$2^{-2} = \dfrac{1}{4}$
−1	$2^{-1} = \dfrac{1}{2}$
0	$2^0 = 1$
1	$2^1 = 2$
2	$2^2 = 4$
3	$2^3 = 8$

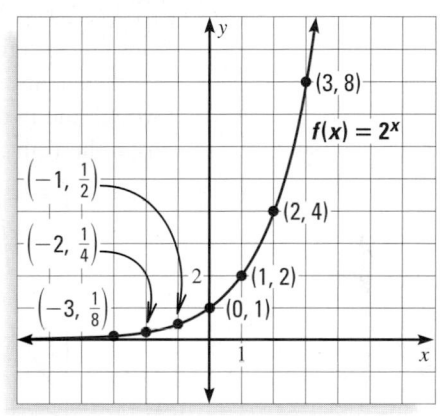

Notice the end behavior of the graph. As $x \to +\infty$, $f(x) \to +\infty$, which means that the graph moves up to the right. As $x \to -\infty$, $f(x) \to 0$, which means that the graph has the line $y = 0$ as an *asymptote*. An **asymptote** is a line that a graph approaches as you move away from the origin.

▶ ACTIVITY

Developing Concepts

Investigating Graphs of Exponential Functions

❶ Graph $y = \dfrac{1}{3} \cdot 2^x$ and $y = 3 \cdot 2^x$. Compare the graphs with the graph of $y = 2^x$.

❷ Graph $y = -\dfrac{1}{5} \cdot 2^x$ and $y = -5 \cdot 2^x$. Compare the graphs with the graph of $y = 2^x$.

❸ Describe the effect of a on the graph of $y = a \cdot 2^x$ when a is positive and when a is negative.

In the activity you may have observed the following about the graph of $y = a \cdot 2^x$:

- The graph passes through the point $(0, a)$. That is, the y-intercept is a.
- The x-axis is an asymptote of the graph.
- The domain is all real numbers.
- The range is $y > 0$ if $a > 0$ and $y < 0$ if $a < 0$.

The characteristics of the graph of $y = a \cdot 2^x$ listed on the previous page are true of the graph of $y = ab^x$. If $a > 0$ and $b > 1$, the function $y = ab^x$ is an **exponential growth function**.

EXAMPLE 1   *Graphing Exponential Functions of the Form y = abˣ*

STUDENT HELP

▶ **Look Back**
For help with end behavior of graphs, see p. 331.

Graph the function.

a. $y = \frac{1}{2} \cdot 3^x$

b. $y = -\left(\frac{3}{2}\right)^x$

SOLUTION

a. Plot $\left(0, \frac{1}{2}\right)$ and $\left(1, \frac{3}{2}\right)$. Then, from left to right, draw a curve that begins just above the *x*-axis, passes through the two points, and moves up to the right.

b. Plot $(0, -1)$ and $\left(1, -\frac{3}{2}\right)$. Then, from left to right, draw a curve that begins just below the *x*-axis, passes through the two points, and moves down to the right.

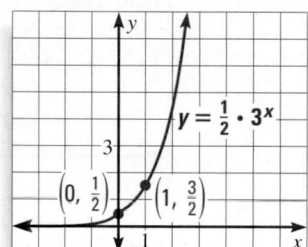

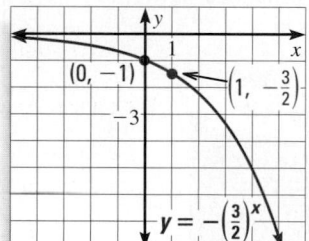

· · · · · · · · · ·

To graph a general exponential function,

$$y = ab^{x-h} + k,$$

begin by sketching the graph of $y = ab^x$. Then translate the graph horizontally by *h* units and vertically by *k* units.

EXAMPLE 2   *Graphing a General Exponential Function*

Graph $y = 3 \cdot 2^{x-1} - 4$. State the domain and range.

SOLUTION

Begin by lightly sketching the graph of $y = 3 \cdot 2^x$, which passes through $(0, 3)$ and $(1, 6)$. Then translate the graph 1 unit to the right and 4 units down. Notice that the graph passes through $(1, -1)$ and $(2, 2)$. The graph's asymptote is the line $y = -4$. The domain is all real numbers, and the range is $y > -4$.

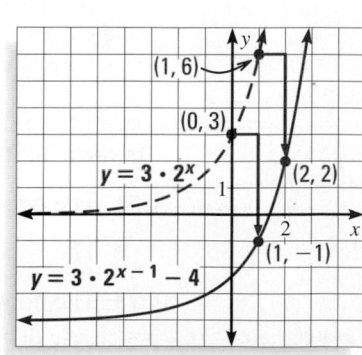

When a real-life quantity increases by a fixed percent each year (or other time period), the amount y of the quantity after t years can be modeled by this equation:

$$y = a(1 + r)^t$$

In this model, a is the initial amount and r is the percent increase expressed as a decimal. The quantity $1 + r$ is called the **growth factor**.

EXAMPLE 3 *Modeling Exponential Growth*

INTERNET HOSTS In January, 1993, there were about 1,313,000 Internet hosts. During the next five years, the number of hosts increased by about 100% per year.
▶ Source: Network Wizards

a. Write a model giving the number h (in millions) of hosts t years after 1993. About how many hosts were there in 1996?

b. Graph the model.

c. Use the graph to estimate the year when there were 30 million hosts.

SOLUTION

a. The initial amount is $a = 1.313$ and the percent increase is $r = 1$. So, the exponential growth model is:

$h = a(1 + r)^t$ **Write exponential growth model.**

$\quad = \mathbf{1.313}(1 + \mathbf{1})^t$ **Substitute for *a* and *r*.**

$\quad = 1.313 \cdot 2^t$ **Simplify.**

Using this model, you can estimate the number of hosts in 1996 ($t = 3$) to be $h = 1.313 \cdot 2^3 \approx 10.5$ million.

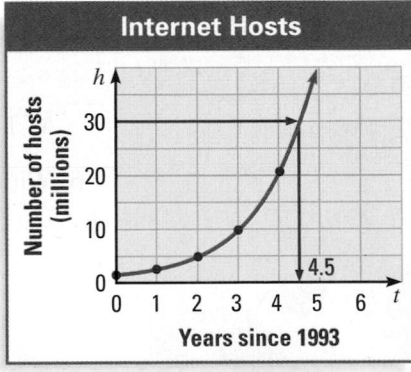

Internet Hosts

Number of hosts (millions)

Years since 1993

b. The graph passes through the points (0, 1.313) and (1, 2.626). It has the t-axis as an asymptote. To make an accurate graph, plot a few other points. Then draw a smooth curve through the points.

c. Using the graph, you can estimate that the number of hosts was 30 million sometime during 1997 ($t \approx 4.5$).

· · · · · · · · · ·

In Example 3 notice that the annual percent increase was 100%. This translated into a growth factor of 2, which means that the number of Internet hosts doubled each year.

People often confuse percent increase and growth factor, especially when a percent increase is 100% or more. For example, a percent increase of 200% means that a quantity *tripled*, because the growth factor is $1 + 2 = 3$. When you hear or read reports of how a quantity has changed, be sure to pay attention to whether a percent increase or a growth factor is being discussed.

COMPOUND INTEREST Exponential growth functions are used in real-life situations involving *compound interest*. Compound interest is interest paid on the initial investment, called the *principal,* and on previously earned interest. (Interest paid only on the principal is called *simple interest.*)

Although interest earned is expressed as an *annual* percent, the interest is usually compounded more frequently than once per year. Therefore, the formula $y = a(1 + r)^t$ must be modified for compound interest problems.

COMPOUND INTEREST

Consider an initial principal P deposited in an account that pays interest at an annual rate r (expressed as a decimal), compounded n times per year. The amount A in the account after t years can be modeled by this equation:

$$A = P\left(1 + \frac{r}{n}\right)^{nt}$$

EXAMPLE 4 *Finding the Balance in an Account*

FINANCE You deposit $1000 in an account that pays 8% annual interest. Find the balance after 1 year if the interest is compounded with the given frequency.

    a. annually   **b.** quarterly   **c.** daily

SOLUTION

    a. With interest compounded annually, the balance at the end of 1 year is:

$$A = 1000\left(1 + \frac{0.08}{1}\right)^{1 \cdot 1} \qquad \textbf{P = 1000, r = 0.08, n = 1, t = 1}$$

$$= 1000(1.08)^1 \qquad \textbf{Simplify.}$$

$$= 1080 \qquad \textbf{Use a calculator.}$$

    ▶ The balance at the end of 1 year is $1080.

    b. With interest compounded quarterly, the balance at the end of 1 year is:

$$A = 1000\left(1 + \frac{0.08}{4}\right)^{4 \cdot 1} \qquad \textbf{P = 1000, r = 0.08, n = 4, t = 1}$$

$$= 1000(1.02)^4 \qquad \textbf{Simplify.}$$

$$\approx 1082.43 \qquad \textbf{Use a calculator.}$$

    ▶ The balance at the end of 1 year is $1082.43.

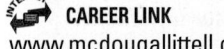
    c. With interest compounded daily, the balance at the end of 1 year is:

$$A = 1000\left(1 + \frac{0.08}{365}\right)^{365 \cdot 1} \qquad \textbf{P = 1000, r = 0.08, n = 365, t = 1}$$

$$\approx 1000(1.000219)^{365} \qquad \textbf{Simplify.}$$

$$\approx 1083.28 \qquad \textbf{Use a calculator.}$$

    ▶ The balance at the end of 1 year is $1083.28.

GUIDED PRACTICE

Vocabulary Check ✓ **1.** What is an asymptote?

Concept Check ✓ **2.** Given the general exponential function $f(x) = ab^{x-h} + k$, describe the effects of a, h, and k on the graph of the function.

3. For what values of b does $y = b^x$ represent exponential growth?

Skill Check ✓ **Graph the function. State the domain and range.**

4. $y = 4^x$ **5.** $y = 3^{x-1}$ **6.** $y = 2^{x+2}$

7. $y = 5^x - 3$ **8.** $y = 5^{x+1} + 2$ **9.** $y = 2^{x-3} + 1$

10. What is the asymptote of the graph of $y = 3 \cdot 4^{x-1} + 2$? What is the value of y when $x = 2$?

11. 🌎 **POPULATION** The population of Winnemucca, Nevada, can be modeled by $P = 6191(1.04)^t$ where t is the number of years since 1990. What was the population in 1990? By what percent did the population increase each year?

12. 🌎 **ACCOUNT BALANCE** You deposit $500 in an account that pays 3% annual interest. Find the balance after 2 years if the interest is compounded with the given frequency.

    a. annually   **b.** quarterly   **c.** daily

PRACTICE AND APPLICATIONS

STUDENT HELP

↳ **Extra Practice**
to help you master
skills is on p. 950.

INVESTIGATING GRAPHS Identify the *y*-intercept and the asymptote of the graph of the function.

13. $y = 5^x$ **14.** $y = -2 \cdot 4^x$ **15.** $y = 4 \cdot 2^x$

16. $y = 2^x - 1$ **17.** $y = 3 \cdot 2^{x-1}$ **18.** $y = 2 \cdot 3^{x-4}$

MATCHING GRAPHS Match the function with its graph.

19. $y = 2 \cdot 5^x$ **20.** $y = 3 \cdot 4^x$ **21.** $y = -2 \cdot 5^x$

22. $y = \frac{1}{3} \cdot 4^x$ **23.** $y = 3^{x-2}$ **24.** $y = 3^x - 2$

STUDENT HELP

↳ **HOMEWORK HELP**
Example 1: Exs. 13–15,
    19–22, 25–33
Example 2: Exs. 16–18,
    23, 24, 34–42
Example 3: Exs. 43–54,
    56, 58, 66
Example 4: Exs. 55, 57,
    59–65, 67

A.

B.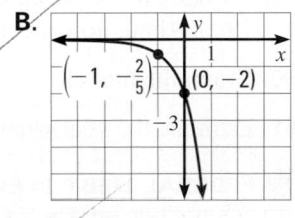

C.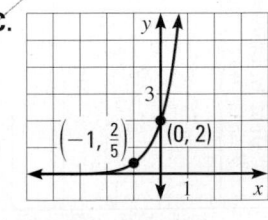

D.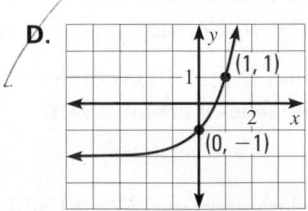

E.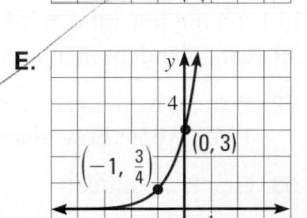

F.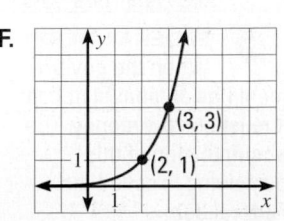

GRAPHING FUNCTIONS Graph the function.

25. $y = 5^x$ **26.** $y = -2^x$ **27.** $y = 8 \cdot 2^x$

28. $y = -3 \cdot 2^x$ **29.** $y = -2 \cdot 5^x$ **30.** $y = -(2.5)^x$

31. $y = 6\left(\dfrac{5}{4}\right)^x$ **32.** $y = -\dfrac{2}{3} \cdot 3^x$ **33.** $y = -\dfrac{1}{5}(1.5)^x$

GRAPHING FUNCTIONS Graph the function. State the domain and range.

34. $y = -2 \cdot 3^{x+2}$ **35.** $y = 4 \cdot 5^{x-1}$ **36.** $y = 7 \cdot 3^{x-2}$

37. $y = 3 \cdot 4^{x-1}$ **38.** $y = 3^{x+1} + 1$ **39.** $y = 2^{x-3} + 3$

40. $y = -3 \cdot 6^{x+2} - 2$ **41.** $y = 4 \cdot 2^{x-3} + 1$ **42.** $y = 8 \cdot 2^{x-3} - 3$

🌐 **NATURAL GAS** In Exercises 43–45, use the following information.

The amount g (in trillions of cubic feet) of natural gas consumed in the United States from 1940 to 1970 can be modeled by

$$g = 2.91(1.07)^t$$

where t is the number of years since 1940. ▶ Source: *Wind Energy Comes of Age*

43. Identify the initial amount, the growth factor, and the annual percent increase.

44. Graph the function.

45. Estimate the natural gas consumption in 1955.

🌐 **COMPUTER CHIPS** In Exercises 46–48, use the following information.

From 1971 to 1995, the average number n of transistors on a computer chip can be modeled by

$$n = 2300(1.59)^t$$

where t is the number of years since 1971.

46. Identify the initial amount, the growth factor, and the annual percent increase.

47. Graph the function.

48. Estimate the number of transistors on a computer chip in 1998.

🌐 **WIND ENERGY** In Exercises 49–51, use the following information.

In 1980 wind turbines in Europe generated about 5 gigawatt-hours of energy. Over the next 15 years, the amount of energy increased by about 59% per year.

49. Write a model giving the amount E (in gigawatt-hours) of energy t years after 1980. About how much wind energy was generated in 1984?

50. Graph the model.

51. Estimate the year when 80 gigawatt-hours of energy were generated.

🌐 **FEDERAL DEBT** In Exercises 52–54, use the following information.

In 1965 the federal debt of the United States was $322.3 billion. During the next 30 years, the debt increased by about 10.2% each year. ▶ Source: U.S. Bureau of the Census

52. Write a model giving the amount D (in billions of dollars) of debt t years after 1965. About how much was the federal debt in 1980?

53. Graph the model.

54. Estimate the year when the federal debt was $2,120 billion.

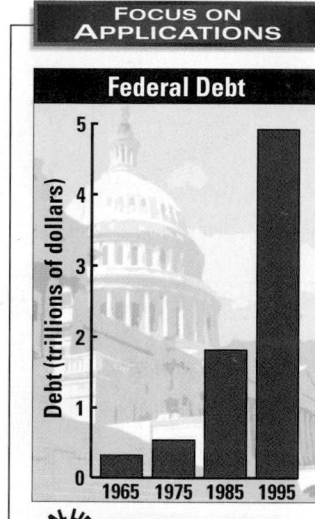

55. **EARNING INTEREST** You deposit $2500 in a bank that pays 4% interest compounded annually. Use the process below and a graphing calculator to determine the balance of your account each year.

   a. Enter the initial deposit, 2500, into the calculator. Then enter the formula ANS + ANS × 0.04 to find the balance after one year.

   b. What is the balance after five years? (*Hint:* The balance after each year will be displayed each time you press the ENTER key.)

   c. How would you enter the formula in part (a) if the interest is compounded quarterly? What do you have to do to find the balance after one year?

   d. Find the balance after 5 years if the interest is compounded quarterly. Compare this result with your answer to part (b).

WRITING MODELS In Exercises 56–58, write an exponential growth model that describes the situation.

56. **COIN COLLECTING** You buy a commemorative coin for $110. Each year t, the value V of the coin increases by 4%.

57. **SAVINGS ACCOUNT** You deposit $400 in an account that pays 2% annual interest compounded quarterly.

58. **ANTIQUES** You purchase an antique table for $525. Each year t, the value V of the table increases by 5%.

ACCOUNT BALANCE In Exercises 59–61, use the following information. You deposit $1600 in a bank account. Find the balance after 3 years for each of the following situations.

59. The account pays 2.5% annual interest compounded monthly.

60. The account pays 1.75% annual interest compounded quarterly.

61. The account pays 4% annual interest compounded yearly.

DEPOSITING FUNDS In Exercises 62–64, use the following information. You want to have $2500 after 2 years. Find the amount you should deposit for each of the situations described below.

62. The account pays 2.25% annual interest compounded monthly.

63. The account pays 2% annual interest compounded quarterly.

64. The account pays 5% annual interest compounded yearly.

65. **CRITICAL THINKING** Juan and Michelle each have $800. Juan plans to invest $200 for each of the next four years, while Michelle plans to invest all $800 now. Both accounts pay 3% annual interest compounded monthly. Will they have the same amount of money after four years? If not, explain why.

66. **LAND VALUE** You have inherited land that was purchased for $30,000 in 1960. The value V of the land increased by approximately 5% per year.

   a. Write a model for the value of the land t years after 1960.

   b. What is the approximate value of the land in the year 2010?

67. **LOGICAL REASONING** Is investing $4000 at 5% annual interest and $4000 at 7% annual interest equivalent to investing $8000 (the total of the two principals) at 6% annual interest (the average of the two interest rates)? Explain.

68. MULTIPLE CHOICE The student enrollment E of a high school was 1240 in 1990 and increased by 15% per year until 1996. Which exponential growth model shows the school's student enrollment in terms of t, the number of years since 1990?

Ⓐ $E = 15(1240)^t$ Ⓑ $E = 1240(1.15)^t$ Ⓒ $E = 1240(15)^t$

Ⓓ $E = 0.15(1240)^t$ Ⓔ $E = 1.15(1240)^t$

69. MULTIPLE CHOICE Which function is graphed below?

Ⓐ $f(x) = -3^{x+1} + 6$

Ⓑ $f(x) = -2 \cdot 3^{x+1} + 6$

Ⓒ $f(x) = 2 \cdot 3^{x+1} + 6$

Ⓓ $f(x) = 2 \cdot 3^{x-1} + 6$

Ⓔ $f(x) = 3^{x+1} + 6$

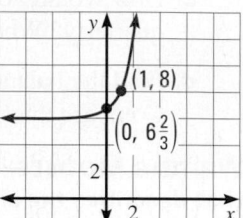

★ Challenge

70. 🖩 **IRRATIONAL EXPONENTS** Use a calculator to evaluate the following powers. Round the results to five decimal places.

$$3^{14/10}, \ 3^{141/100}, \ 3^{1,414/1,000}, \ 3^{14,142/10,000}, \ 3^{141,421/100,000}, \ 3^{1,414,213/1,000,000}$$

EXTRA CHALLENGE
➡ www.mcdougallittell.com

Each of these powers has a rational exponent. Explain how you can use these powers to define $3^{\sqrt{2}}$, which has an irrational exponent.

MIXED REVIEW

EVALUATING POWERS Evaluate the expression. **(Review 1.2 for 8.2)**

71. $\left(\frac{1}{2}\right)^3$ **72.** $\left(\frac{3}{7}\right)^3$ **73.** $\left(\frac{1}{2}\right)^5$ **74.** $\left(\frac{5}{8}\right)^4$

75. $\left(\frac{7}{12}\right)^3$ **76.** $\left(\frac{2}{3}\right)^4$ **77.** $\left(\frac{4}{5}\right)^2$ **78.** $\left(\frac{3}{10}\right)^5$

🖩 **EVALUATING EXPRESSIONS** Evaluate the expression using a calculator. Round the result to two decimal places when appropriate. **(Review 7.1)**

79. $8^{3/8}$ **80.** $15,625^{1/6}$ **81.** $-243^{1/5}$ **82.** $1024^{1/5}$

83. $10^{1/2}$ **84.** $106^{1/3}$ **85.** $\sqrt[4]{81}$ **86.** $\sqrt[7]{100}$

87. $\sqrt[3]{28}$ **88.** $\sqrt[4]{120}$ **89.** $\sqrt[4]{9}$ **90.** $\sqrt[6]{180}$

OPERATIONS WITH FUNCTIONS Let $f(x) = 6x - 11$ and $g(x) = 4x^2$. Perform the indicated operation and state the domain. **(Review 7.3)**

91. $f(x) + g(x)$ **92.** $f(x) - g(x)$ **93.** $f(x) \cdot g(x)$

94. $g(x) - f(x)$ **95.** $f(g(x))$ **96.** $g(f(x))$

97. $\dfrac{f(x)}{g(x)}$ **98.** $\dfrac{g(x)}{f(x)}$ **99.** $f(f(x))$

100. 🌐 **FENCING** You want to build a rectangular pen for your dog using 40 feet of fencing. The area of the pen should be 90 square feet. What should the dimensions of the pen be? **(Review 5.2)**

► ACTIVITY 8.2

Developing Concepts

Exponential Growth and Decay

► **QUESTION** What relationships exist between exponential growth and exponential decay when a piece of paper is folded repeatedly?

SET UP

Work with a partner.

MATERIALS
• paper
• pencil
• graph paper

► **EXPLORING THE CONCEPT**

1 Fold a rectangular piece of paper in half. The fold divides the paper into two regions, each of which has half the area of the paper.

2 Fold the paper in half again. Into how many regions has the original piece of paper been folded? What fraction of the paper's area does each region have?

3 Continue to fold the paper until it is no longer possible to make another fold. After each fold, record in a table like the one shown the fold number, the number of regions into which the paper has been folded, and the fraction of the paper's area that each region has.

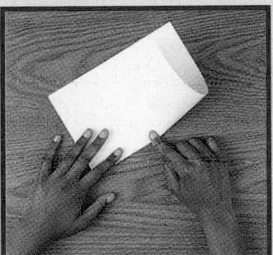  

Fold number	0	1	2	3	4	5
Number of regions	1	2	?	?	?	?
Fractional area of each region	1	$\frac{1}{2}$	?	?	?	?

4 Make two scatter plots of the data in the table. The first scatter plot will have ordered pairs of the form (*fold number*, *number of regions*) and the second will have ordered pairs of the form (*fold number*, *fractional area of each region*).

► **DRAWING CONCLUSIONS**

1. The first scatter plot is an example of exponential growth. Write an equation for the graph.

2. Use the equation from Exercise 1 to determine the number of regions there would be after 8 folds.

3. The second scatter plot is an example of exponential decay. Write an equation for the graph.

4. Use the equation from Exercise 3 to determine the fractional area of each region after 8 folds.

5. Multiply the exponential expressions from Exercise 2 and Exercise 4. Explain why the product should be 1.

8.2

Exponential Decay

What you should learn

GOAL 1 Graph exponential decay functions.

GOAL 2 Use exponential decay functions to model **real-life** situations, such as the decline of record sales in **Exs. 47–49**.

Why you should learn it

▼ To solve **real-life** problems, such as finding the depreciated value of a car in **Example 4**.

GOAL 1 GRAPHING EXPONENTIAL DECAY FUNCTIONS

In Lesson 8.1 you studied exponential growth functions. In this lesson you will study **exponential decay functions**, which have the form $f(x) = ab^x$ where $a > 0$ and $0 < b < 1$.

EXAMPLE 1 *Recognizing Exponential Growth and Decay*

State whether $f(x)$ is an exponential growth or exponential decay function.

a. $f(x) = 5\left(\dfrac{2}{3}\right)^x$ **b.** $f(x) = 8\left(\dfrac{3}{2}\right)^x$ **c.** $f(x) = 10(3)^{-x}$

SOLUTION

a. Because $0 < b < 1$, f is an exponential decay function.

b. Because $b > 1$, f is an exponential growth function.

c. Rewrite the function as $f(x) = 10\left(\dfrac{1}{3}\right)^x$. Because $0 < b < 1$, f is an exponential decay function.

· · · · · · · · · ·

To see the basic shape of the graph of an exponential decay function, you can make a table of values and plot points, as shown below.

x	$f(x) = \left(\dfrac{1}{2}\right)^x$
-3	$\left(\dfrac{1}{2}\right)^{-3} = 8$
-2	$\left(\dfrac{1}{2}\right)^{-2} = 4$
-1	$\left(\dfrac{1}{2}\right)^{-1} = 2$
0	$\left(\dfrac{1}{2}\right)^{0} = 1$
1	$\left(\dfrac{1}{2}\right)^{1} = \dfrac{1}{2}$
2	$\left(\dfrac{1}{2}\right)^{2} = \dfrac{1}{4}$
3	$\left(\dfrac{1}{2}\right)^{3} = \dfrac{1}{8}$

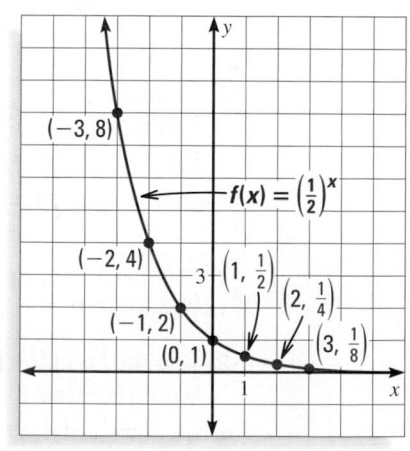

Notice the end behavior of the graph. As $x \to -\infty$, $f(x) \to +\infty$, which means that the graph moves up to the left. As $x \to +\infty$, $f(x) \to 0$, which means that the graph has the line $y = 0$ as an asymptote.

Recall that in general the graph of an exponential function $y = ab^x$ passes through the point $(0, a)$ and has the x-axis as an asymptote. The domain is all real numbers, and the range is $y > 0$ if $a > 0$ and $y < 0$ if $a < 0$.

EXAMPLE 2 *Graphing Exponential Functions of the Form $y = ab^x$*

Graph the function.

a. $y = 3\left(\dfrac{1}{4}\right)^x$

b. $y = -5\left(\dfrac{2}{3}\right)^x$

SOLUTION

a. Plot $(0, 3)$ and $\left(1, \dfrac{3}{4}\right)$.

Then, from *right* to *left*, draw a curve that begins just above the x-axis, passes through the two points, and moves up to the left.

b. Plot $(0, -5)$ and $\left(1, -\dfrac{10}{3}\right)$.

Then, from *right* to *left*, draw a curve that begins just below the x-axis, passes through the two points, and moves down to the left.

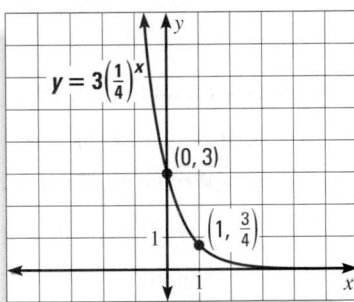

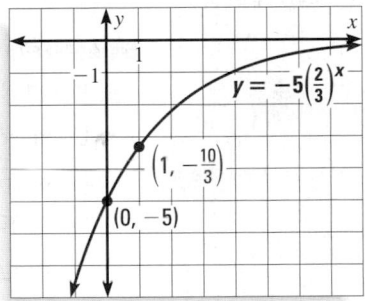

· · · · · · · · · ·

Remember that to graph a general exponential function, $y = ab^{x-h} + k$, begin by sketching the graph of $y = ab^x$. Then translate the graph horizontally by h units and vertically by k units.

EXAMPLE 3 *Graphing a General Exponential Function*

Graph $y = -3\left(\dfrac{1}{2}\right)^{x+2} + 1$. State the domain and range.

SOLUTION

Begin by lightly sketching the graph

of $y = -3\left(\dfrac{1}{2}\right)^x$, which passes through $(0, -3)$

and $\left(1, -\dfrac{3}{2}\right)$. Then translate the graph 2 units

to the left and 1 unit up. Notice that the graph

passes through $(-2, -2)$ and $\left(-1, -\dfrac{1}{2}\right)$. The

graph's asymptote is the line $y = 1$. The domain is all real numbers, and the range is $y < 1$.

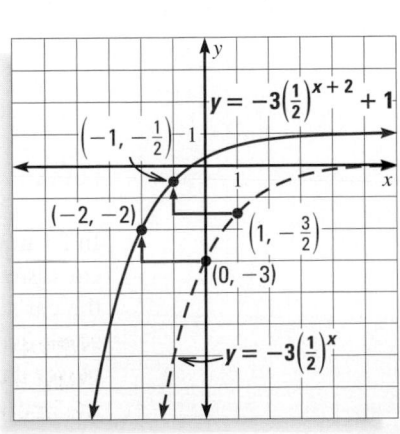

GOAL 2 USING EXPONENTIAL DECAY MODELS

When a real-life quantity decreases by a fixed percent each year (or other time period), the amount y of the quantity after t years can be modeled by the equation

$$y = a(1 - r)^t$$

where a is the initial amount and r is the percent decrease expressed as a decimal. The quantity $1 - r$ is called the **decay factor**.

Automobiles

EXAMPLE 4 *Modeling Exponential Decay*

You buy a new car for $24,000. The value y of the car decreases by 16% each year.

a. Write an exponential decay model for the value of the car. Use the model to estimate the value after 2 years.

b. Graph the model.

c. Use the graph to estimate when the car will have a value of $12,000.

SOLUTION

STUDENT HELP

HOMEWORK HELP
Visit our Web site
www.mcdougallittell.com
for extra examples.

a. Let t be the number of years since you bought the car. The exponential decay model is:

$y = a(1 - r)^t$ **Write exponential decay model.**

$= \mathbf{24{,}000}(1 - \mathbf{0.16})^t$ **Substitute for *a* and *r*.**

$= 24{,}000(0.84)^t$ **Simplify.**

When $t = 2$, the value is
$y = 24{,}000(0.84)^2 \approx \$16{,}934.$

b. The graph of the model is shown at the right. Notice that it passes through the points $(0, 24{,}000)$ and $(1, 20{,}160)$. The asymptote of the graph is the line $y = 0$.

c. Using the graph, you can see that the value of the car will drop to $12,000 after about 4 years.

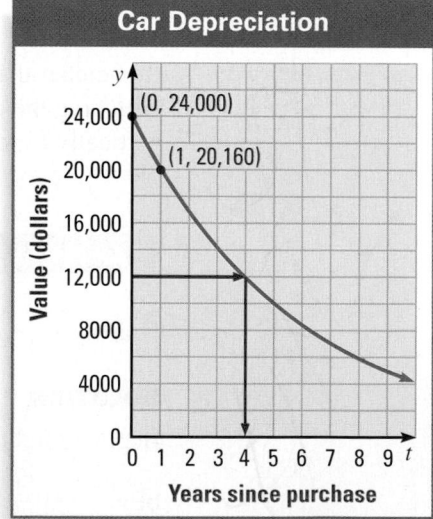

Car Depreciation

In Example 4 notice that the percent decrease, 16%, tells you how much value the car *loses* from one year to the next. The decay factor, 0.84, tells you what fraction of the car's value *remains* from one year to the next. The closer the percent decrease for some quantity is to 0%, the more the quantity is conserved or retained over time. The closer the percent decrease is to 100%, the more the quantity is used or lost over time.

GUIDED PRACTICE

Vocabulary Check ✔ 1. In the exponential decay model $y = 1500(0.65)^t$, identify the initial amount, the decay factor, and the percent decrease.

Concept Check ✔ 2. What is the asymptote of the graph of the function $y = 2\left(\frac{1}{5}\right)^{x-2} + 3$?

3. For what values of b does $y = b^x$ represent exponential decay?

Skill Check ✔ **Graph the function. State the domain and range.**

4. $y = -(0.5)^x$

5. $y = 2\left(\frac{1}{3}\right)^x$

6. $y = 4\left(\frac{2}{3}\right)^x$

7. $y = -5\left(\frac{2}{3}\right)^{x-2}$

8. $y = -4(0.25)^{x+1}$

9. $y = 5\left(\frac{1}{2}\right)^x + 2$

10. 🌐 **RADIOACTIVE DECAY** The amount y (in grams) of a sample of iodine-131 after t days is given by $y = 50(0.92)^t$.

   a. Identify the initial amount of the substance.

   b. What percent of the substance decays each day?

PRACTICE AND APPLICATIONS

STUDENT HELP

→ **Extra Practice**
to help you master
skills is on p. 950.

IDENTIFYING FUNCTIONS Tell whether the function represents *exponential growth* or *exponential decay*.

11. $f(x) = 4\left(\frac{3}{8}\right)^x$

12. $f(x) = 10 \cdot 3^x$

13. $f(x) = 8 \cdot 7^{-x}$

14. $f(x) = 8 \cdot 7^x$

15. $f(x) = 5\left(\frac{1}{8}\right)^{-x}$

16. $f(x) = 3\left(\frac{4}{3}\right)^x$

17. $f(x) = 8\left(\frac{2}{3}\right)^x$

18. $f(x) = 5(0.25)^{-x}$

MATCHING GRAPHS Match the function with its graph.

19. $y = (0.25)^x$

20. $y = -3^{x-1} + 3$

21. $y = -\left(\frac{1}{3}\right)^{x-1} + 3$

22. $y = \left(\frac{1}{2}\right)^{x-1}$

23. $y = -(0.25)^x$

24. $y = (0.5)^x - 1$

STUDENT HELP

→ **HOMEWORK HELP**
Example 1: Exs. 11–18
Example 2: Exs. 19, 23,
   25–33
Example 3: Exs. 20–22,
   24, 34–42
Example 4: Exs. 43–56

A.

B.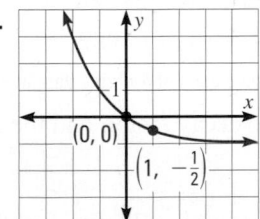

C.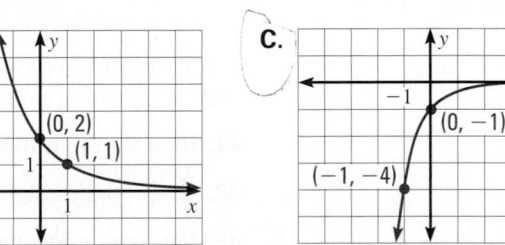

D.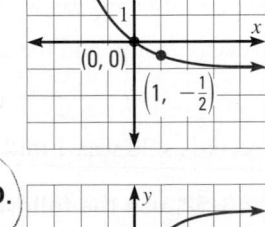

E.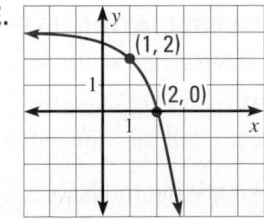

F.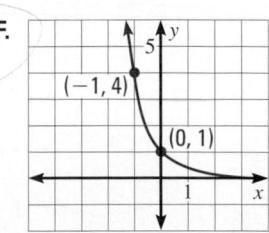

GRAPHING FUNCTIONS Graph the function.

25. $y = 3\left(\dfrac{1}{2}\right)^x$

26. $y = 2\left(\dfrac{1}{5}\right)^x$

27. $y = -2\left(\dfrac{1}{4}\right)^x$

28. $y = -5\left(\dfrac{1}{2}\right)^x$

29. $y = 4\left(\dfrac{1}{3}\right)^x$

30. $y = 5\left(\dfrac{1}{4}\right)^x$

31. $y = -3\left(\dfrac{2}{3}\right)^x$

32. $y = -5(0.75)^x$

33. $y = 3\left(\dfrac{3}{8}\right)^x$

GRAPHING FUNCTIONS Graph the function. State the domain and range.

34. $y = -\left(\dfrac{1}{2}\right)^x + 1$

35. $y = \left(\dfrac{2}{3}\right)^{x-1}$

36. $y = 4\left(\dfrac{1}{2}\right)^{x+1}$

37. $y = \left(\dfrac{1}{3}\right)^{x-2}$

38. $y = 2\left(\dfrac{1}{3}\right)^{x-1}$

39. $y = (0.25)^x + 3$

40. $y = -3\left(\dfrac{1}{3}\right)^{x-1}$

41. $y = \left(\dfrac{1}{3}\right)^x - 2$

42. $y = \left(\dfrac{2}{3}\right)^x - 1$

WRITING MODELS In Exercises 43–45, write an exponential decay model that describes the situation.

43. 🌐 **STEREO SYSTEM** You buy a stereo system for $780. Each year t, the value V of the stereo system decreases by 5%.

44. 🌐 **BEVERAGES** You drink a beverage with 120 milligrams of caffeine. Each hour h, the amount c of caffeine in your system decreases by about 12%.

45. 🌐 **MEDICINE** An adult takes 400 milligrams of ibuprofen. Each hour h, the amount i of ibuprofen in the person's system decreases by about 29%.

46. 🌐 **RADIOACTIVE DECAY** One hundred grams of plutonium is stored in a container. The amount P (in grams) of plutonium present after t years can be modeled by this equation:

$$P = 100(0.99997)^t$$

How much plutonium is present after 20,000 years?

🌐 **RECORD ALBUMS** In Exercises 47–49, use the following information.
The number A (in millions) of record albums sold each year in the United States from 1982 to 1993 can be modeled by

$$A = 265(0.39)^t$$

where t represents the number of years since 1982.

📁 **DATA UPDATE** of Recording Industry Association of America data at www.mcdougallittell.com

47. Identify the initial amount, the decay factor, and the annual percent decrease.

48. Graph the model.

49. Estimate when the number of records sold was 1 million.

🌐 **DEPRECIATION** In Exercises 50–52, use the following information.
You buy a new car for $22,000. The value of the car decreases by 12.5% each year.

50. Write an exponential decay model for the value of the car. Use the model to estimate the value after 3 years.

51. Graph the model.

52. Estimate when the car will have a value of $8000.

COMPUTERS In Exercises 53–55, use the following information.
You buy a new computer for $2100. The value of the computer decreases by about 50% annually.

53. Write an exponential decay model for the value of the computer. Use the model to estimate the value after 2 years.

54. Graph the model.

55. Estimate when the computer will have a value of $600.

56. **SCIENCE** ▶ **CONNECTION** During normal breathing, about 12% of the air in the lungs is replaced after one breath. Write an exponential decay model for the amount of the original air left in the lungs if the initial amount of air in the lungs is 500 milliliters. How much of the original air is present after 240 breaths?

Test Preparation

57. **MULTI-STEP PROBLEM** A new automobile worth $18,354 depreciates by about 17% each year. The payoff amount on a loan after making n monthly payments is given by the model

$$A(n) = \left(A_0 - \frac{P}{r}\right)(1 + r)^n + \frac{P}{r}$$

where A_0 is the original amount of the loan, P is the monthly payment, and r is the monthly interest rate expressed as a decimal.

a. Write an exponential decay model for the value V of the automobile t years after it is purchased.

b. Write a model for the payoff amount on a loan of $18,354 with a monthly payment of $280 and an *annual* interest rate of 8.5%. (*Hint:* The model for the payoff amount uses the monthly interest rate, not the annual interest rate.)

c. *Writing* Make a table showing the value of the car and the payoff amount on the loan for 5 years. When would it make sense to sell the car? Explain.

★ Challenge

58. **CRITICAL THINKING** Is the product of two exponential decay functions always another exponential decay function? Is the quotient of two exponential decay functions always another exponential decay function? Justify your answers.

MIXED REVIEW

GRAPHING FUNCTIONS Graph the function. (Review 7.5)

59. $y = (x + 1)^{1/3}$ 60. $y = \sqrt[3]{x} + 1$ 61. $y = -3x^{1/3}$

62. $y = \sqrt{x} + 4$ 63. $y = -\sqrt{x + 5}$ 64. $y = \sqrt[3]{x} + \frac{1}{4}$

USING A DATA SET Find the mean, the median, the mode, and the range for the set of data. (Review 7.7)

65. 11, 18, 13, 15, 17, 15, 23, 20, 12   66. 25, 30, 32, 42, 31, 33, 36, 22

67. **FINANCE** You deposit $2000 in a bank account. Find the balance after 4 years for each of the following situations. (Review 8.1 for 8.3)

a. The account pays 7% annual interest compounded quarterly.

b. The account pays 5% annual interest compounded monthly.

8.3

The Number *e*

What you should learn

GOAL 1 Use the number *e* as the base of exponential functions.

GOAL 2 Use the natural base *e* in **real-life** situations, such as finding the air pressure on Mount Everest in **Ex. 79**.

Why you should learn it

▼ To solve **real-life** problems, such as finding the number of listed endangered species in **Example 5**.

The grizzly bear was first listed as threatened in 1975 and remains an endangered species today.

GOAL 1 USING THE NATURAL BASE *e*

The history of mathematics is marked by the discovery of special numbers such as counting numbers, zero, negative numbers, π, and imaginary numbers. In this lesson you will study one of the most famous numbers of modern times. Like π and i, the number *e* is denoted by a letter. The number is called the **natural base *e*,** or the **Euler number,** after its discoverer, Leonhard Euler (1707–1783).

▶ ACTIVITY
Developing Concepts

Investigating the Natural Base *e*

1 Copy the table and use a calculator to complete the table.

n	10^1	10^2	10^3	10^4	10^5	10^6
$\left(1+\frac{1}{n}\right)^n$	2.594	?	?	?	?	?

2 Do the values in the table appear to be approaching a fixed decimal number? If so, what is the number rounded to three decimal places?

In the activity you may have discovered that as *n* gets larger and larger, the expression $\left(1+\frac{1}{n}\right)^n$ gets closer and closer to 2.71828 . . . , which is the value of *e*.

THE NATURAL BASE *e*

The natural base *e* is irrational. It is defined as follows:

$$\text{As } n \text{ approaches } +\infty, \left(1+\frac{1}{n}\right)^n \text{ approaches } e \approx 2.718281828459.$$

EXAMPLE 1 *Simplifying Natural Base Expressions*

Simplify the expression.

a. $e^3 \cdot e^4$ **b.** $\dfrac{10e^3}{5e^2}$ **c.** $\left(3e^{-4x}\right)^2$

SOLUTION

a. $e^3 \cdot e^4 = e^{3+4}$
           $= e^7$

b. $\dfrac{10e^3}{5e^2} = 2e^{3-2}$
           $= 2e$

c. $\left(3e^{-4x}\right)^2 = 3^2 e^{(-4x)(2)}$
           $= 9e^{-8x} = \dfrac{9}{e^{8x}}$

480   **Chapter 8** *Exponential and Logarithmic Functions*

LEONHARD EULER continued his mathematical research despite losing sight in one eye in 1735. He published more than 500 books and papers during his lifetime. Euler's use of *e* appeared in his book *Mechanica*, published in 1736.

EXAMPLE 2 *Evaluating Natural Base Expressions*

Use a calculator to evaluate the expression: **a.** e^2 **b.** $e^{-0.06}$

SOLUTION

EXPRESSION	KEYSTROKES	DISPLAY
a. e^2	2nd [e^x] 2 ENTER	7.389056
b. $e^{-0.06}$	2nd [e^x] (−) .06 ENTER	0.941765

· · · · · · · · · ·

A function of the form $f(x) = ae^{rx}$ is called a *natural base exponential function*. If $a > 0$ and $r > 0$, the function is an exponential growth function, and if $a > 0$ and $r < 0$, the function is an exponential decay function. The graphs of the basic functions $y = e^x$ and $y = e^{-x}$ are shown below.

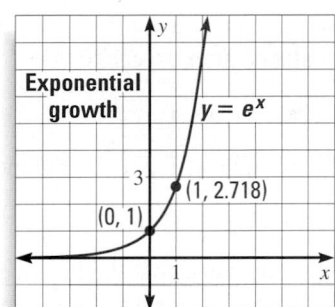

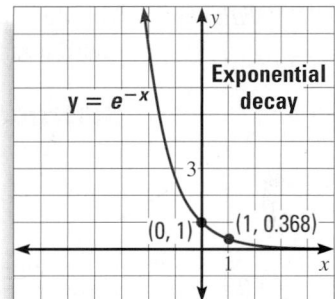

EXAMPLE 3 *Graphing Natural Base Functions*

Graph the function. State the domain and range.

a. $y = 2e^{0.75x}$

b. $y = e^{-0.5(x - 2)} + 1$

SOLUTION

a. Because $a = 2$ is positive and $r = 0.75$ is positive, the function is an exponential growth function. Plot the points $(0, 2)$ and $(1, 4.23)$ and draw the curve.

b. Because $a = 1$ is positive and $r = -0.5$ is negative, the function is an exponential decay function. Translate the graph of $y = e^{-0.5x}$ to the right 2 units and up 1 unit.

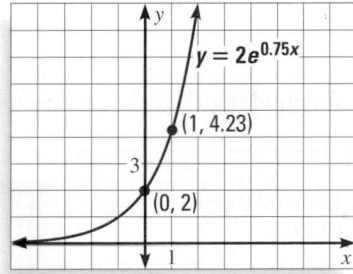

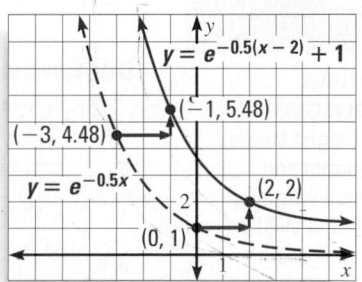

The domain is all real numbers, and the range is all positive real numbers.

The domain is all real numbers, and the range is $y > 1$.

GOAL 2 USING *e* IN REAL LIFE

In Lesson 8.1 you learned that the amount *A* in an account earning interest compounded *n* times per year for *t* years is given by

$$A = P\left(1 + \frac{r}{n}\right)^{nt}$$

where *P* is the principal and *r* is the annual interest rate expressed as a decimal. As *n* approaches positive infinity, the compound interest formula approximates the following formula for *continuously compounded interest:*

$$A = Pe^{rt}$$

Finance

EXAMPLE 4 *Finding the Balance in an Account*

You deposit $1000 in an account that pays 8% annual interest compounded continuously. What is the balance after 1 year?

SOLUTION

Note that $P = 1000$, $r = 0.08$, and $t = 1$. So, the balance at the end of 1 year is:

$$A = Pe^{rt} = 1000e^{0.08(1)} \approx \$1083.29$$

In Example 4 of Lesson 8.1, you found that the balance from daily compounding is $1083.28. So, continuous compounding earned only an additional $.01.

EXAMPLE 5 *Using an Exponential Model*

ENDANGERED SPECIES Since 1972 the U.S. Fish and Wildlife Service has kept a list of endangered species in the United States. For the years 1972–1998, the number *s* of species on the list can be modeled by

$$s = 119.6e^{0.0917t}$$

where *t* is the number of years since 1972.

a. What was the number of endangered species in 1972?

b. Graph the model.

c. Use the graph to estimate when the number of endangered species reached 1000.

SOLUTION

a. In 1972, when $t = 0$, the model gives:

$$s = 119.6e^0 = 119.6$$

So, there were about 120 endangered species on the list in 1972.

b. The graph of the model is shown.

c. Use the *Intersect* feature to determine that *s* reaches 1000 when $t \approx 23$, which is about 1995.

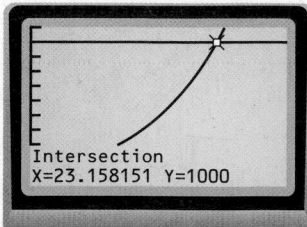

Intersection
X=23.158151 Y=1000

GUIDED PRACTICE

Vocabulary Check ✓

1. What is the Euler number? Give an approximation of the Euler number rounded to three decimal places.

Concept Check ✓

2. Tell whether the function $f(x) = \frac{1}{4}e^{2x}$ is an example of *exponential growth* or *exponential decay*. Explain.

3. Is it possible to express e as a ratio of two integers? Explain.

Skill Check ✓

Simplify the expression.

4. $e^2 \cdot e^6$
5. $e^{-2} \cdot 3e^7$
6. $(2e^{5x})^2$
7. $(4e^{-2})^3$

8. $\left(\frac{1}{2}e^{-2}\right)^4$
9. $\sqrt{36e^{4x}}$
10. $\dfrac{e^x}{e^{2x}}$
11. $\dfrac{12e^4}{36e^{-2}}$

12. What is the horizontal asymptote of the graph of $f(x) = 2e^x - 2$?

Graph the function.

13. $y = e^{-2x}$
14. $y = \frac{1}{2}e^x$
15. $y = \frac{1}{8}e^{2x}$

16. 🌐 **ENDANGERED SPECIES** Use the model in Example 5 to estimate the number of endangered species in 1998.

PRACTICE AND APPLICATIONS

STUDENT HELP

▶ **Extra Practice**
to help you master
skills is on p. 950.

SIMPLIFYING EXPRESSIONS Simplify the expression.

17. $e^2 \cdot e^4$
18. $e^{-3} \cdot e^5$
19. $(3e^{-3x})^{-1}$
20. $(3e^{4x})^2$

21. $3e^{-2} \cdot e^6$
22. $\left(\frac{1}{4}e^{-2}\right)^3$
23. $e^x \cdot e^{-3x} \cdot e^5$
24. $\sqrt{4e^{2x}}$

25. $(100e^{0.5x})^{-2}$
26. $e^x \cdot 4e^{2x+1}$
27. $\dfrac{e^x}{2e}$
28. $\dfrac{5e^x}{e^{5x}}$

29. $\sqrt[3]{27e^{6x}}$
30. $(32e^{-4x})^3$
31. $\dfrac{6e^{3x}}{4e}$
32. $\sqrt[3]{64e^{9x}}$

🖩 **EVALUATING EXPRESSIONS** Use a calculator to evaluate the expression. Round the result to three decimal places.

33. e^3
34. $e^{-2/3}$
35. $e^{1.7}$
36. $e^{1/2}$

37. $e^{-1/4}$
38. $e^{3.2}$
39. e^8
40. e^{-3}

41. e^{-4}
42. $2e^{1/2}$
43. $-4e^{-3}$
44. $0.5e^{3.2}$

45. $-1.2e^5$
46. $0.02e^{-0.3}$
47. $225e^{-50}$
48. $-8.95e^{1/5}$

STUDENT HELP

▶ **HOMEWORK HELP**
Example 1: Exs. 17–32
Example 2: Exs. 33–48
Example 3: Exs. 49–75
Example 4: Exs. 76–78
Example 5: Exs. 79, 80

GROWTH OR DECAY? Tell whether the function is an example of *exponential growth* or *exponential decay*.

49. $f(x) = 5e^{-3x}$
50. $f(x) = \frac{1}{8}e^{5x}$
51. $f(x) = e^{-4x}$
52. $f(x) = \frac{1}{6}e^{2x}$

53. $f(x) = \frac{1}{4}e^{2x}$
54. $f(x) = e^{-8x}$
55. $f(x) = e^{3x}$
56. $f(x) = \frac{1}{4}e^{-x}$

57. $f(x) = e^{-6x}$
58. $f(x) = \frac{3}{8}e^{7x}$
59. $f(x) = e^{-9x}$
60. $f(x) = e^{8x}$

MATCHING GRAPHS Match the function with its graph.

61. $y = 3e^{0.5x}$ **62.** $y = \frac{1}{3}e^{0.5x}$ **63.** $y = \frac{1}{2}e^{-(x-1)}$

64. $y = e^{-x} + 1$ **65.** $y = 3e^{-x} - 2$ **66.** $y = 3e^x - 2$

A. 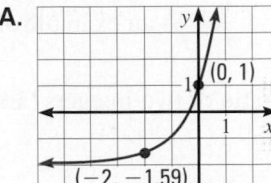   **B.** 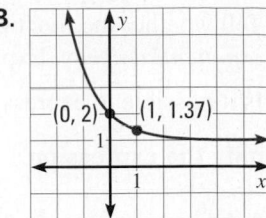   **C.**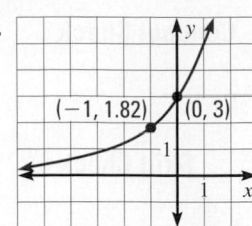

D. 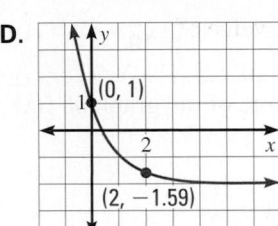   **E.** 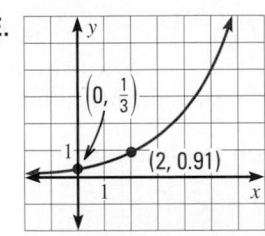   **F.**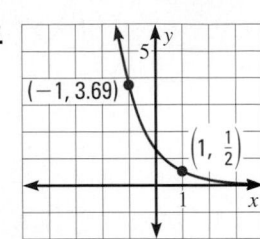

GRAPHING FUNCTIONS Graph the function. State the domain and range.

67. $y = e^{-x}$ **68.** $y = 4e^x$ **69.** $y = \frac{1}{3}e^x$

70. $y = 3e^{2x} + 2$ **71.** $y = 1.5e^{-0.5x}$ **72.** $y = 0.1e^{2x} - 4$

73. $y = \frac{1}{3}e^{x-2} - 1$ **74.** $y = \frac{4}{3}e^{x-3} + 1$ **75.** $y = 0.5e^{-2(x-1)} - 2$

76. 🌐 **CONTINUOUS COMPOUNDING** You deposit $975 in an account that pays 5.5% annual interest compounded continuously. What is the balance after 6 years?

77. 🌐 **COMPARING FORMULAS** You deposit $2500 in an account that pays 6% annual interest. Use the formulas at the top of page 482 to calculate the account balance after one year when the interest is compounded annually, semiannually, quarterly, monthly, and continuously. What do you notice? Explain.

78. *Writing* Compare the effects of compounding interest continuously and compounding interest daily using the formulas $A = Pe^{rt}$ and

$$A = P\left(1 + \frac{r}{365}\right)^{365t}.$$

79. 🌐 **MOUNT EVEREST** The air pressure P at sea level is about 14.7 pounds per square inch. As the altitude h (in feet above sea level) increases, the air pressure decreases. The relationship between air pressure and altitude can be modeled by:

$$P = 14.7e^{-0.00004h}$$

Mount Everest in Tibet and Nepal rises to a height of 29,028 feet above sea level. What is the air pressure at the peak of Mount Everest?

80. 🌐 **RATE OF HEALING** The area of a wound decreases exponentially with time. The area A of a wound after t days can be modeled by

$$A = A_0 e^{-0.05t}$$

where A_0 is the initial wound area. If the initial wound area is 4 square centimeters, how much of the wound area is present after 14 days?

Test Preparation

81. MULTIPLE CHOICE What is the simplified form of $\sqrt[3]{\dfrac{8(81e^{11}x)}{3e^5x^{-2}}}$?

Ⓐ $6e^2\sqrt[3]{x}$ Ⓑ $6x\sqrt[3]{e^6}$ Ⓒ $6\sqrt[3]{e^{16}x}$ Ⓓ $\dfrac{6e^2}{x}$ Ⓔ $6e^2x$

82. MULTIPLE CHOICE Which function is graphed at the right?

Ⓐ $f(x) = 3e^{x-2}$ Ⓑ $f(x) = 3e^x - 2$

Ⓒ $f(x) = 3e^{-x} - 2$ Ⓓ $f(x) = 3e^{-(x+2)}$

Ⓔ $f(x) = 3e^{x+2}$

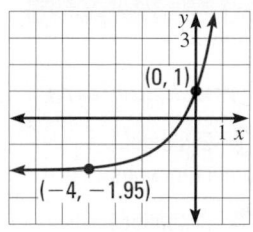

★ **Challenge**

83. CRITICAL THINKING Find a value of n for which $\left(1 + \dfrac{1}{n}\right)^n$ gives the value of e correct to 9 decimal places. Explain the process you used to find your answer.

MIXED REVIEW

FINDING INVERSE FUNCTIONS Find an equation for the inverse of the function. (Review 7.4 for 8.4)

84. $f(x) = -3x$ **85.** $f(x) = 6x + 7$ **86.** $f(x) = -5x - 24$

87. $f(x) = \frac{1}{2}x - 10$ **88.** $f(x) = -14x + 7$ **89.** $f(x) = -\frac{1}{5}x - 13$

SOLVING EQUATIONS Solve the equation. (Review 7.6)

90. $\sqrt{x} = 20$ **91.** $\sqrt[3]{5x - 4} + 7 = 10$ **92.** $2(x + 4)^{2/3} = 8$

93. $\sqrt{x^2 - 4} = x - 2$ **94.** $\sqrt{x + 3} = \sqrt{2x - 1}$ **95.** $\sqrt{3x - 5} - 3\sqrt{x} = 0$

QUIZ 1

Self-Test for Lessons 8.1–8.3

Graph the function. State the domain and range. (Lessons 8.1, 8.2)

1. $y = 4^x - 1$ **2.** $y = 3^{x+1} + 2$ **3.** $y = \frac{1}{2} \cdot 5^{x-1}$

4. $y = -2\left(\frac{1}{6}\right)^x$ **5.** $y = \left(\frac{5}{8}\right)^x + 2$ **6.** $y = -2 \cdot 6^{x-3} + 3$

Simplify the expression. (Lesson 8.3)

7. $2e^3 \cdot e^4$ **8.** $4e^{-5} \cdot e^7$ **9.** $(-3e^{2x})^2$ **10.** $(5e^{-3})^{-4x}$

11. $\dfrac{3e^x}{4e}$ **12.** $\dfrac{6e^x}{e^{5x}}$ **13.** $\sqrt{16e^2x}$ **14.** $\sqrt[3]{125e^{6x}}$

15. Graph the function $f(x) = -4e^{2x}$. (Lesson 8.3)

16. 🌎 **RADIOACTIVE DECAY** One hundred grams of radium is stored in a container. The amount R (in grams) of radium present after t years can be modeled by $R = 100e^{-0.00043t}$. Graph the model. How much of the radium is present after 10,000 years? (Lesson 8.3)

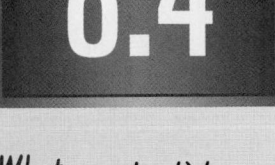

8.4

Logarithmic Functions

What you should learn

GOAL 1 Evaluate logarithmic functions.

GOAL 2 Graph logarithmic functions, as applied in **Example 8**.

Why you should learn it

▼ To model **real-life** situations, such as the slope of a beach in **Example 4**.

GOAL 1 EVALUATING LOGARITHMIC FUNCTIONS

You know that $2^2 = 4$ and $2^3 = 8$. However, for what value of x does $2^x = 6$? Because $2^2 < 6 < 2^3$, you would expect x to be between 2 and 3. To find the exact x-value, mathematicians defined *logarithms*. In terms of a logarithm, $x = \log_2 6 \approx 2.585$. (In the next lesson you will see how this x-value is obtained.)

DEFINITION OF LOGARITHM WITH BASE b

Let b and y be positive numbers, $b \neq 1$. The **logarithm of y with base b** is denoted by $\log_b y$ and is defined as follows:

$$\log_b y = x \text{ if and only if } b^x = y$$

The expression $\log_b y$ is read as "log base b of y."

This definition tells you that the equations $\log_b y = x$ and $b^x = y$ are equivalent. The first is in *logarithmic form* and the second is in *exponential form*. Given an equation in one of these forms, you can always rewrite it in the other form.

EXAMPLE 1   *Rewriting Logarithmic Equations*

LOGARITHMIC FORM	EXPONENTIAL FORM
a. $\log_2 32 = 5$	$2^5 = 32$
b. $\log_5 1 = 0$	$5^0 = 1$
c. $\log_{10} 10 = 1$	$10^1 = 10$
d. $\log_{10} 0.1 = -1$	$10^{-1} = 0.1$
e. $\log_{1/2} 2 = -1$	$\left(\frac{1}{2}\right)^{-1} = 2$

· · · · · · · · · ·

Parts (b) and (c) of Example 1 illustrate two special logarithm values that you should learn to recognize.

SPECIAL LOGARITHM VALUES

Let b be a positive real number such that $b \neq 1$.

LOGARITHM OF 1 $\log_b 1 = 0$ because $b^0 = 1$.

LOGARITHM OF BASE b $\log_b b = 1$ because $b^1 = b$.

EXAMPLE 2   *Evaluating Logarithmic Expressions*

Evaluate the expression.

a. $\log_3 81$ **b.** $\log_5 0.04$ **c.** $\log_{1/2} 8$ **d.** $\log_9 3$

SOLUTION

To help you find the value of $\log_b y$, ask yourself what power of b gives you y.

a. 3 to what power gives 81?

$3^4 = 81$, so $\log_3 81 = \textbf{4}$.

b. 5 to what power gives 0.04?

$5^{-2} = 0.04$, so $\log_5 0.04 = \textbf{-2}$.

c. $\frac{1}{2}$ to what power gives 8?

$\left(\frac{1}{2}\right)^{-3} = 8$, so $\log_{1/2} 8 = \textbf{-3}$.

d. 9 to what power gives 3?

$9^{1/2} = 3$, so $\log_9 3 = \frac{1}{2}$.

• • • • • • • • • •

The logarithm with base 10 is called the **common logarithm**. It is denoted by $\log_{10}$ or simply by log. The logarithm with base e is called the **natural logarithm**. It can be denoted by $\log_e$, but it is more often denoted by ln.

COMMON LOGARITHM

$\log_{10} x = \log x$

NATURAL LOGARITHM

$\log_e x = \ln x$

Most calculators have keys for evaluating common and natural logarithms.

EXAMPLE 3   *Evaluating Common and Natural Logarithms*

EXPRESSION	KEYSTROKES	DISPLAY
a. log 5	LOG 5 ENTER	0.698970
b. ln 0.1	LN .1 ENTER	-2.302585

EXAMPLE 4   *Evaluating a Logarithmic Function*

Sand particle	Diameter (mm)
Pebble	4
Granule	2
Very coarse sand	1
Coarse sand	0.5
Medium sand	0.25
Fine sand	0.125
Very fine sand	0.0625

SAND The table gives the diameters of different types of sand. Notice that the diameter of a pebble is about 64 times larger than the diameter of very fine sand.

SCIENCE CONNECTION The slope s of a beach is related to the average diameter d (in millimeters) of the sand particles on the beach by this equation:

$$s = 0.159 + 0.118 \log d$$

Find the slope of a beach if the average diameter of the sand particles is 0.25 millimeter.

SOLUTION

If $d = 0.25$, then the slope of the beach is:

$s = 0.159 + 0.118 \log \textbf{0.25}$ **Substitute 0.25 for d.**

$\approx 0.159 + 0.118(-0.602)$ **Use a calculator.**

≈ 0.09 **Simplify.**

▶ The slope of the beach is about 0.09. This is a gentle slope that indicates a rise of only 9 meters for a run of 100 meters.

GOAL 2 GRAPHING LOGARITHMIC FUNCTIONS

By the definition of a logarithm, it follows that the logarithmic function $g(x) = \log_b x$ is the inverse of the exponential function $f(x) = b^x$. This means that:

$$g(f(x)) = \log_b b^x = x \qquad \text{and} \qquad f(g(x)) = b^{\log_b x} = x$$

In other words, exponential functions and logarithmic functions "undo" each other.

EXAMPLE 5 *Using Inverse Properties*

STUDENT HELP

▶ **Look Back**
For help with inverses,
see p. 422.

Simplify the expression.

a. $10^{\log 2}$
b. $\log_3 9^x$

SOLUTION

a. $10^{\log 2} = 2$
b. $\log_3 9^x = \log_3 (3^2)^x = \log_3 3^{2x} = 2x$

EXAMPLE 6 *Finding Inverses*

Find the inverse of the function.

a. $y = \log_3 x$
b. $y = \ln (x + 1)$

SOLUTION

a. From the definition of logarithm, the inverse of $y = \log_3 x$ is $y = 3^x$.

b.
$y = \ln (x + 1)$	**Write original function.**
$x = \ln (y + 1)$	**Switch x and y.**
$e^x = y + 1$	**Write in exponential form.**
$e^x - 1 = y$	**Solve for y.**

▶ The inverse of $y = \ln (x + 1)$ is $y = e^x - 1$.

. . . .

The inverse relationship between exponential and logarithmic functions is also useful for graphing logarithmic functions. Recall from Lesson 7.4 that the graph of f^{-1} is the reflection of the graph of f in the line $y = x$.

Graphs of f and f^{-1} for $b > 1$

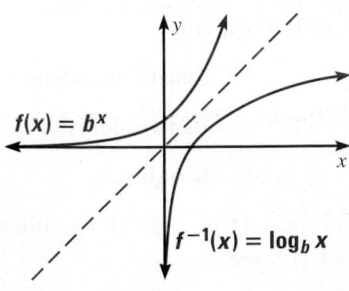

Graphs of f and f^{-1} for $0 < b < 1$

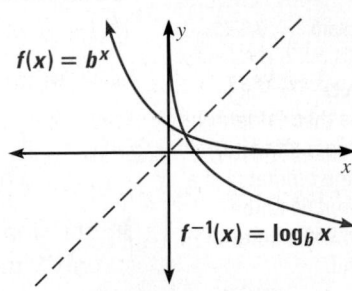

GRAPHS OF LOGARITHMIC FUNCTIONS

The graph of $y = \log_b(x - h) + k$ has the following characteristics:

- The line $x = h$ is a vertical asymptote.
- The domain is $x > h$, and the range is all real numbers.
- If $b > 1$, the graph moves up to the right. If $0 < b < 1$, the graph moves down to the right.

EXAMPLE 7 *Graphing Logarithmic Functions*

Graph the function. State the domain and range.

a. $y = \log_{1/3} x - 1$

b. $y = \log_5(x + 2)$

SOLUTION

a. Plot several convenient points, such as $\left(\frac{1}{3}, 0\right)$ and $(3, -2)$. The vertical line $x = 0$ is an asymptote. From left to right, draw a curve that starts just to the right of the y-axis and moves down.

b. Plot several convenient points, such as $(-1, 0)$ and $(3, 1)$. The vertical line $x = -2$ is an asymptote. From left to right, draw a curve that starts just to the right of the line $x = -2$ and moves up.

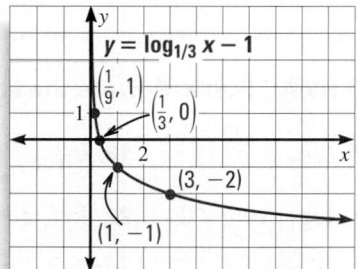

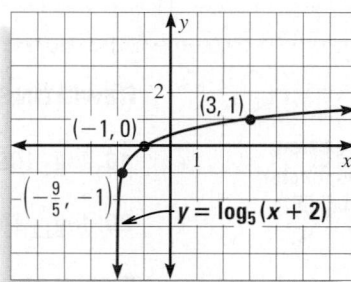

The domain is $x > 0$, and the range is all real numbers.

The domain is $x > -2$, and the range is all real numbers.

SAND A beach with very fine sand makes an angle of about 1° with the horizontal while a beach with pebbles makes an angle of about 17°.

EXAMPLE 8 *Using the Graph of a Logarithmic Function*

SCIENCE CONNECTION Graph the model from Example 4, $s = 0.159 + 0.118 \log d$. Then use the graph to estimate the average diameter of the sand particles for a beach whose slope is 0.2.

SOLUTION

You can use a graphing calculator to graph the model. Then, using the *Intersect* feature, you can determine that $s = 0.2$ when $d \approx 2.23$, as shown at the right. So, the average diameter of the sand particles is about 2.23 millimeters.

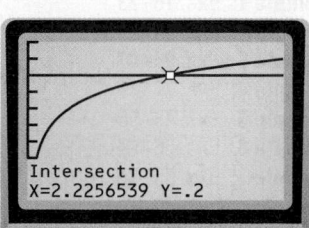

Intersection
X=2.2256539 Y=.2

8.4 *Logarithmic Functions* **489**

GUIDED PRACTICE

Vocabulary Check ✓

1. Complete this statement: The logarithm with base 10 is called the ? .

Concept Check ✓

2. Explain why the expressions $\log_3(-1)$ and $\log_1 1$ are not defined.

3. Explain the meaning of $\log_b y$.

4. **ERROR ANALYSIS** To simplify $\log_2 25$, a student reasoned as shown. Describe the error that the student made.

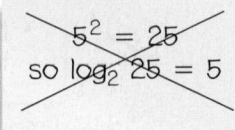
$5^2 = 25$
so $\log_2 25 = 5$

Skill Check ✓

Rewrite the equation in exponential form.

5. $\log_3 9 = 2$ 6. $\log_5 5 = 1$ 7. $\log_{1/2} 4 = -2$ 8. $\log_{19} 1 = 0$

Evaluate the expression.

9. $\log_2 64$ 10. $\log_{25} 5$ 11. $\log_6 1$ 12. $10^{\log 4}$

Graph the function. State the domain and range.

13. $y = \log_2(x + 1) - 3$ 14. $y = \log_{1/2}(x - 2) + 1$

15. ▦ **SLOPE OF A BEACH** Using the model from Example 4 and a graphing calculator, find the average diameter of the sand particles for a beach whose slope is 0.1.

PRACTICE AND APPLICATIONS

STUDENT HELP

▶ **Extra Practice**
to help you master skills is on p. 951.

REWRITING IN EXPONENTIAL FORM Rewrite the equation in exponential form.

16. $\log_4 1024 = 5$ 17. $\log_5 \frac{1}{5} = -1$ 18. $\log_{36} \frac{1}{6} = -\frac{1}{2}$ 19. $\log_8 512 = 3$

20. $\log_{12} 144 = 2$ 21. $\log_{14} 196 = 2$ 22. $\log_8 4096 = 4$ 23. $\log_{105} 11{,}025 = 2$

EVALUATING EXPRESSIONS Evaluate the expression without using a calculator.

24. $\log_5 125$ 25. $\log_7 343$ 26. $\log_8 1$ 27. $\log_{12} 12$

28. $\log_6 36$ 29. $\log_4 16$ 30. $\log_9 729$ 31. $\log_7 2401$

32. $\log_{1/4} \frac{1}{4}$ 33. $\log_4 4^{-0.38}$ 34. $\log_4 \frac{1}{2}$ 35. $\log_{1/5} 25$

STUDENT HELP

▶ **HOMEWORK HELP**
Example 1: Exs. 16–23
Example 2: Exs. 24–35
Example 3: Exs. 36–47
Example 4: Exs. 77–79
Example 5: Exs. 48–55
Example 6: Exs. 56–64
Example 7: Exs. 65–76
Example 8: Exs. 80, 81

▦ **EVALUATING LOGARITHMS** Use a calculator to evaluate the expression. Round the result to three decimal places.

36. $\log 8$ 37. $\ln 10$ 38. $\log \sqrt{2}$ 39. $\log 3.724$

40. $\log 2.54$ 41. $\log 0.3$ 42. $\log 4.05$ 43. $\log 3.5$

44. $\ln 4.6$ 45. $\ln 150$ 46. $\ln 6.9$ 47. $\ln 22.5$

USING INVERSES Simplify the expression.

48. $5^{\log_5 x}$ 49. $\log_2 2^x$ 50. $9^{\log_9 x}$ 51. $35^{\log_{35} x}$

52. $\log_4 16^x$ 53. $7^{\log_7 x}$ 54. $\log 100^x$ 55. $\log_{20} 8000^x$

FINDING INVERSES Find the inverse of the function.

56. $y = \log_9 x$

57. $y = \log_{1/4} x$

58. $y = \log_5 x$

59. $y = \log_{1/2} x$

60. $y = \log_7 49^x$

61. $y = \ln 6x$

62. $y = \ln(x - 1)$

63. $y = \ln(x + 2)$

64. $y = \ln(x - 2)$

GRAPHING FUNCTIONS Graph the function. State the domain and range.

65. $y = \log_5 x$

66. $y = \ln x + 3$

67. $y = \log_2 x + 1$

68. $y = \ln x - 1$

69. $y = \log_8 x - 2$

70. $y = \ln(x + 1)$

71. $y = \log(x - 2)$

72. $y = \ln(x - 2)$

73. $y = \log_5(x + 4)$

74. $y = \log_{1/2} x - 1$

75. $y = \log_{1/4} x - 3$

76. $y = \ln x + 5$

77. SCIENCE ▸ CONNECTION   The pH of a solution is given by the formula

$$pH = -\log [H^+]$$

where $[H^+]$ is the solution's hydrogen ion concentration (in moles per liter). Find the pH of the solution.

a. lemon juice: $[H^+] = 1 \times 10^{-2.4}$ moles per liter

b. vinegar: $[H^+] = 1 \times 10^{-3}$ moles per liter

c. orange juice: $[H^+] = 1 \times 10^{-3.5}$ moles per liter

78. GEOMETRY ▸ CONNECTION   Part of the three-dimensional mathematical figure called the horn of Gabriel is shown. The area of the cross section (in the coordinate plane) of the horn is given by:

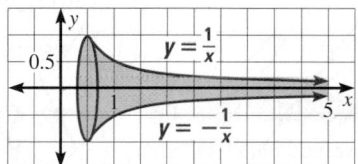

$$A = \frac{2}{\log e}$$

Approximate this area to three decimal places.

SEISMOLOGY In Exercises 79 and 80, use the following information.
The Richter scale is used for measuring the magnitude of an earthquake. The Richter magnitude R is given by the model

$$R = 0.67 \log (0.37E) + 1.46$$

where E is the energy (in kilowatt-hours) released by the earthquake.

79. Suppose an earthquake releases 15,500,000,000 kilowatt-hours of energy. What is the earthquake's magnitude? (Use a calculator.)

80. How many kilowatt-hours of energy would the earthquake in Exercise 79 have to release in order to increase its magnitude by one-half of a unit on the Richter scale? Use a graph to solve the problem.

81. 🌐 **TORNADOES** Most tornadoes last less than an hour and travel less than 20 miles. The wind speed s (in miles per hour) near the center of a tornado is related to the distance d (in miles) the tornado travels by this model:

$$s = 93 \log d + 65$$

On March 18, 1925, a tornado whose wind speed was about 280 miles per hour struck the Midwest. Use a graph to estimate how far the tornado traveled.

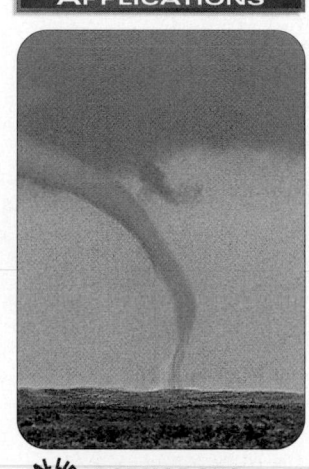

QUANTITATIVE COMPARISON In Exercises 82–87 choose the statement that is true about the given quantities.

(A) The quantity in column A is greater.

(B) The quantity in column B is greater.

(C) The two quantities are equal.

(D) The relationship cannot be determined from the given information.

	Column A	Column B
82.	$\log_9 9^{2/3}$	$\log 100$
83.	$\log_{16} 1$	0
84.	$\log_4 16$	$\log_8 64$
85.	$f(8)$ if $f(x) = \log_2 x$	4
86.	$f(-1)$ if $f(x) = \log_5 5^x$	-1
87.	$f\left(\dfrac{1}{2}\right)$ if $f(x) = \log_3 9^x$	$\log_3 81$

★ **Challenge**

EVALUATING EXPRESSIONS Evaluate the expression. (*Hint:* Each expression has the form $\log_b x$. Rewrite the base b and the x-value as powers of the same number.)

88. $\log_{16} 8$ **89.** $\log_{16} 64$ **90.** $\log_9 27$ **91.** $\log_4 512$

EXTRA CHALLENGE

→ www.mcdougallittell.com

92. CRITICAL THINKING What pattern do you recognize in your answers to Exercises 88–91?

MIXED REVIEW

EVALUATING NUMERICAL EXPRESSIONS Evaluate the numerical expression. (Review 6.1 for 8.5)

93. $5^2 \cdot 5^3$ **94.** $\left(3^{-4}\right)^2$ **95.** $7^0 \cdot 7^3 \cdot 7^{-2}$ **96.** $\left(\dfrac{3}{7}\right)^{-2}$

97. $\dfrac{6^3}{6^4}$ **98.** $\left(\dfrac{3}{8}\right)^{-3}$ **99.** $\left(-2^3\right)^2$ **100.** $\left(\dfrac{4}{5}\right)^3$

101. $\left(\dfrac{1}{2}\right)^{-4}$ **102.** $\left(-3^2\right)^{-1}$ **103.** $\dfrac{2^5}{2^9}$ **104.** $\left(\dfrac{7}{9}\right)^{-2}$

USING LONG DIVISION Divide using long division. (Review 6.5)

105. $(2x^2 + x - 1) \div (x + 4)$ **106.** $(x^2 - 5x + 4) \div (x - 1)$

107. $(4x^3 + 3x^2 + 2x - 3) \div (x^2 + 2)$ **108.** $(6x^3 - 8x^2 + 7) \div (x - 3)$

FINDING A CUBIC MODEL Write a cubic function whose graph passes through the given points. (Review 6.9)

109. $(2, 0), (-3, 0), (0, 0), (3, -3)$ **110.** $(3, 0), (2, 0), (-3, 0), (0, -1)$

111. $(4, 0), (6, 0), (-4, 0), (1, 1)$ **112.** $(-2, 0), (-3, 0), (3, 0), (0, 2)$

8.5

Properties of Logarithms

What you should learn

GOAL 1 Use properties of logarithms.

GOAL 2 Use properties of logarithms to solve **real-life** problems, such as finding the energy needed for molecular transport in **Exs. 77–79**.

Why you should learn it

▼ To model **real-life** quantities, such as the loudness of different sounds in **Example 5**.

Airport workers wear hearing protection because of the loudness of jet engines.

GOAL 1 USING PROPERTIES OF LOGARITHMS

Because of the relationship between logarithms and exponents, you might expect logarithms to have properties similar to the properties of exponents you studied in Lesson 6.1.

> **ACTIVITY**
> Developing Concepts
> ### Investigating a Property of Logarithms
>
> **1** Copy and complete the table one row at a time.
>
> | $\log_b u$ | $\log_b v$ | $\log_b uv$ |
> |---|---|---|
> | $\log 10 = ?$ | $\log 100 = ?$ | $\log 1000 = ?$ |
> | $\log 0.1 = ?$ | $\log 0.01 = ?$ | $\log 0.001 = ?$ |
> | $\log_2 4 = ?$ | $\log_2 8 = ?$ | $\log_2 32 = ?$ |
>
> **2** Use the completed table to write a conjecture about the relationship among $\log_b u$, $\log_b v$, and $\log_b uv$.

In the activity you may have discovered one of the properties of logarithms listed below.

PROPERTIES OF LOGARITHMS

Let *b, u,* and *v* be positive numbers such that $b \neq 1$.

PRODUCT PROPERTY $\qquad\qquad \log_b uv = \log_b u + \log_b v$

QUOTIENT PROPERTY $\qquad\quad \log_b \dfrac{u}{v} = \log_b u - \log_b v$

POWER PROPERTY $\qquad\qquad \log_b u^n = n \log_b u$

EXAMPLE 1 *Using Properties of Logarithms*

Use $\log_5 3 \approx 0.683$ and $\log_5 7 \approx 1.209$ to approximate the following.

a. $\log_5 \dfrac{3}{7}$ **b.** $\log_5 21$ **c.** $\log_5 49$

SOLUTION

a. $\log_5 \dfrac{3}{7} = \log_5 3 - \log_5 7 \approx 0.683 - 1.209 = -0.526$

b. $\log_5 21 = \log_5 (3 \cdot 7) = \log_5 3 + \log_5 7 \approx 0.683 + 1.209 = 1.892$

c. $\log_5 49 = \log_5 7^2 = 2 \log_5 7 \approx 2(1.209) = 2.418$

8.5 *Properties of Logarithms* **493**

You can use the properties of logarithms to expand and condense logarithmic expressions.

EXAMPLE 2

EXAMPLE 2 *Expanding a Logarithmic Expression*

Expand $\log_2 \dfrac{7x^3}{y}$. Assume x and y are positive.

SOLUTION

$$\log_2 \frac{7x^3}{y} = \log_2 7x^3 - \log_2 y \qquad \textbf{Quotient property}$$

$$= \log_2 7 + \log_2 x^3 - \log_2 y \qquad \textbf{Product property}$$

$$= \log_2 7 + 3 \log_2 x - \log_2 y \qquad \textbf{Power property}$$

STUDENT HELP

→ **Study Tip**
When you are expanding or condensing an expression involving logarithms, you may assume the variables are positive.

EXAMPLE 3 *Condensing a Logarithmic Expression*

Condense $\log 6 + 2 \log 2 - \log 3$.

SOLUTION

$$\log 6 + 2 \log 2 - \log 3 = \log 6 + \log 2^2 - \log 3 \qquad \textbf{Power property}$$

$$= \log \left(6 \cdot 2^2 \right) - \log 3 \qquad \textbf{Product property}$$

$$= \log \frac{6 \cdot 2^2}{3} \qquad \textbf{Quotient property}$$

$$= \log 8 \qquad \textbf{Simplify.}$$

· · · · · · · · ·

Logarithms with any base other than 10 or e can be written in terms of common or natural logarithms using the *change-of-base formula*.

CHANGE-OF-BASE FORMULA

Let u, b, and c be positive numbers with $b \neq 1$ and $c \neq 1$. Then:

$$\log_c u = \frac{\log_b u}{\log_b c}$$

In particular, $\log_c u = \dfrac{\log u}{\log c}$ and $\log_c u = \dfrac{\ln u}{\ln c}$.

EXAMPLE 4 *Using the Change-of-Base Formula*

Evaluate the expression $\log_3 7$ using common and natural logarithms.

SOLUTION

Using common logarithms: $\log_3 7 = \dfrac{\log 7}{\log 3} \approx \dfrac{0.8451}{0.4771} \approx 1.771$

Using natural logarithms: $\log_3 7 = \dfrac{\ln 7}{\ln 3} \approx \dfrac{1.946}{1.099} \approx 1.771$

GOAL 2 USING LOGARITHMIC PROPERTIES IN REAL LIFE

Acoustics

EXAMPLE 5 *Using Properties of Logarithms*

The loudness L of a sound (in decibels) is related to the intensity I of the sound (in watts per square meter) by the equation

$$L = 10 \log \frac{I}{I_0}$$

where I_0 is an intensity of 10^{-12} watt per square meter, corresponding roughly to the faintest sound that can be heard by humans.

a. Two roommates each play their stereos at an intensity of 10^{-5} watt per square meter. How much louder is the music when both stereos are playing, compared with when just one stereo is playing?

b. Generalize the result from part (a) by using I for the intensity of each stereo.

Decibel level	Example
130	Jet airplane takeoff
120	Riveting machine
110	Rock concert
100	Boiler shop
90	Subway train
80	Average factory
70	City traffic
60	Conversational speech
50	Average home
40	Quiet library
30	Soft whisper
20	Quiet room
10	Rustling leaf
0	Threshold of hearing

SOLUTION

Let L_1 be the loudness when one stereo is playing and let L_2 be the loudness when both stereos are playing.

a. Increase in loudness $= L_2 - L_1$

$\qquad = 10 \log \dfrac{2 \cdot 10^{-5}}{10^{-12}} - 10 \log \dfrac{10^{-5}}{10^{-12}}$ **Substitute for L_2 and L_1.**

$\qquad = 10 \log \left(2 \cdot 10^7\right) - 10 \log 10^7$ **Simplify.**

$\qquad = 10\left(\log 2 + \log 10^7 - \log 10^7\right)$ **Product property**

$\qquad = 10 \log 2$ **Simplify.**

$\qquad \approx 3$ **Use a calculator.**

▶ The sound is about 3 decibels louder.

b. Increase in loudness $= L_2 - L_1$

$\qquad = 10 \log \dfrac{2I}{10^{-12}} - 10 \log \dfrac{I}{10^{-12}}$

$\qquad = 10\left(\log \dfrac{2I}{10^{-12}} - \log \dfrac{I}{10^{-12}}\right)$

$\qquad = 10\left(\log 2 + \log \dfrac{I}{10^{-12}} - \log \dfrac{I}{10^{-12}}\right)$

$\qquad = 10 \log 2$

$\qquad \approx 3$

▶ Again, the sound is about 3 decibels louder. This result tells you that the loudness increases by 3 decibels when both stereos are played regardless of the intensity of each stereo individually.

FOCUS ON CAREERS

SOUND TECHNICIAN

Sound technicians operate technical equipment to amplify, enhance, record, mix, or reproduce sound. They may work in radio or television recording studios or at live performances.

 CAREER LINK
www.mcdougallittell.com

GUIDED PRACTICE

Vocabulary Check ✓ 1. Give an example of the property of logarithms.

        a. product property   **b.** quotient property   **c.** power property

Concept Check ✓ 2. Which is equivalent to $\log \left(\frac{7}{9} \right)^2$? Explain.

      A. $2(\log 7 - \log 9)$ **B.** $\frac{2 \log 7}{\log 9}$ **C.** Neither A nor B

3. Which is equivalent to $\log_8 (5x^2 + 3)$? Explain.

      A. $\log_8 5x^2 + \log_8 3$ **B.** $\log_8 5x^2 \cdot \log_8 3$ **C.** Neither A nor B

4. Describe two ways to find the value of $\log_6 11$ using a calculator.

Skill Check ✓ **Use a property of logarithms to evaluate the expression.**

    5. $\log_3 (3 \cdot 9)$ **6.** $\log_2 4^5$ **7.** $\log_3 \frac{1}{3}$ **8.** $\log_5 \left(\frac{1}{5} \right)^3$

Use $\log_2 7 \approx 2.81$ and $\log_2 21 \approx 4.39$ to approximate the value of the expression.

    9. $\log_2 3$ **10.** $\log_2 49$ **11.** $\log_2 147$ **12.** $\log_2 441$

13. 🌐 **SOUND INTENSITY** Use the loudness of sound equation in Example 5 to find the difference in the loudness of an average office with an intensity of 1.26×10^{-7} watt per square meter and a broadcast studio with an intensity of 3.16×10^{-10} watt per square meter.

PRACTICE AND APPLICATIONS

STUDENT HELP

▶ **Extra Practice**
to help you master
skills is on p. 951.

EVALUATING EXPRESSIONS Use a property of logarithms to evaluate the expression.

    14. $\log_2 (4 \cdot 16)$ **15.** $\ln e^{-2}$ **16.** $\log_2 4^3$ **17.** $\log_5 125$

    18. $\log_3 9^4$ **19.** $\log \frac{1}{10}$ **20.** $\ln \frac{1}{e^3}$ **21.** $\log (0.01)^3$

APPROXIMATING EXPRESSIONS Use $\log 5 \approx 0.699$ and $\log 15 \approx 1.176$ to approximate the value of the expression.

    22. $\log 3$ **23.** $\log 25$ **24.** $\log 75$ **25.** $\log 125$

    26. $\log \frac{1}{5}$ **27.** $\log 225$ **28.** $\log \frac{1}{15}$ **29.** $\log \frac{1}{3}$

STUDENT HELP

▶ **HOMEWORK HELP**
Example 1: Exs. 14–29
Example 2: Exs. 30–45
Example 3: Exs. 46–57
Example 4: Exs. 58–73
Example 5: Exs. 74–85

EXPANDING EXPRESSIONS Expand the expression.

    30. $\log_2 9x$ **31.** $\ln 22x$ **32.** $\log 4x^5$ **33.** $\log_6 x^6$

    34. $\log_4 \frac{4}{3}$ **35.** $\log_3 25$ **36.** $\log_6 \frac{10}{3}$ **37.** $\ln 3xy^3$

    38. $\log 6x^3 yz$ **39.** $\log_8 64x^2$ **40.** $\ln x^{1/2} y^3$ **41.** $\log_3 12^{5/6} x^9$

    42. $\log \sqrt{x}$ **43.** $\ln \frac{3y^4}{x^3}$ **44.** $\log \sqrt[4]{x^3}$ **45.** $\log_2 \sqrt{4x}$

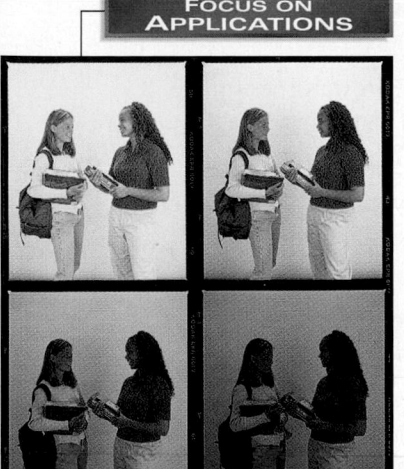

PHOTOGRAPHY
Photographers use f-stops to achieve the desired amount of light in a photo. The smaller the f-stop number, the more light the lens transmits.

APPLICATION LINK
www.mcdougallittell.com

CONDENSING EXPRESSIONS Condense the expression.

46. $\log_5 8 - \log_5 12$

47. $\ln 16 - \ln 4$

48. $2 \log x + \log 5$

49. $4 \log_{16} 12 - 4 \log_{16} 2$

50. $3 \ln x + 5 \ln y$

51. $7 \log_4 2 + 5 \log_4 x + 3 \log_4 y$

52. $\ln 20 + 2 \ln \frac{1}{2} + \ln x$

53. $\log_3 2 + \frac{1}{2} \log_3 y$

54. $10 \log x + 2 \log 10$

55. $3(\ln 3 - \ln x) + (\ln x - \ln 9)$

56. $2(\log_6 15 - \log_6 5) + \frac{1}{2} \log_6 \frac{1}{25}$

57. $\frac{1}{4} \log_5 81 - \left(2 \log_5 6 - \frac{1}{2} \log_5 4\right)$

CHANGE-OF-BASE FORMULA Use the change-of-base formula to evaluate the expression.

58. $\log_5 7$

59. $\log_7 12$

60. $\log_3 16$

61. $\log_9 25$

62. $\log_2 5$

63. $\log_6 9$

64. $\log_3 17$

65. $\log_5 32$

66. $\log_2 125$

67. $\log_6 24$

68. $\log_4 19$

69. $\log_{16} 81$

70. $\log_8 \frac{22}{7}$

71. $\log_9 \frac{5}{16}$

72. $\log_2 \frac{4}{15}$

73. $\log_5 \frac{32}{3}$

PHOTOGRAPHY In Exercises 74–76, use the following information.
The f-stops on a 35 millimeter camera control the amount of light that enters the camera. Let s be a measure of the amount of light that strikes the film and let f be the f-stop. Then s and f are related by this equation:

$$s = \log_2 f^2$$

74. Expand the expression for s.

75. The table shows the first eight f-stops on a 35 millimeter camera. Copy and complete the table. Then describe the pattern.

f	1.414	2.000	2.828	4.000	5.657	8.000	11.314	16.000
s	?	?	?	?	?	?	?	?

76. Many 35 millimeter cameras have nine f-stops. What do you think the ninth f-stop is? Explain your reasoning.

SCIENCE CONNECTION In Exercises 77–79, use the following information.
The energy E (in kilocalories per gram-molecule) required to transport a substance from the outside to the inside of a living cell is given by

$$E = 1.4(\log C_2 - \log C_1)$$

where C_2 is the concentration of the substance inside the cell and C_1 is the concentration outside the cell.

77. Condense the expression for E.

78. The concentration of a particular substance inside a cell is twice the concentration outside the cell. How much energy is required to transport the substance from outside to inside the cell?

79. The concentration of a particular substance inside a cell is six times the concentration outside the cell. How much energy is required to transport the substance from outside to inside the cell?

STUDENT HELP

HOMEWORK HELP
Visit our Web site
www.mcdougallittell.com
for help with Exs. 77–79.

RALPH E. ALLISON
developed the first single zero-point audiometer in 1937, making the equipment usable for doctors who had previously used tuning forks to test hearing.

🌐 **ACOUSTICS** In Exercises 80–85, use the table and the loudness of sound equation from Example 5.

80. The intensity of the sound made by a propeller aircraft is 0.316 watts per square meter. Find the decibel level of a propeller aircraft. To what sound in the table from Example 5 is a propeller aircraft's sound most similar?

81. The intensity of the sound made by Niagara Falls is 0.003 watts per square meter. Find the decibel level of Niagara Falls. To what sound in the table from Example 5 is the sound of Niagara Falls most similar?

82. Three groups of people are in a room, and each group is having a conversation at an intensity of 1.4×10^{-7} watt per square meter. What is the decibel level of the combined conversations in the room?

83. Five cars are in a parking garage, and the sound made by each running car is at an intensity of 3.16×10^{-4} watt per square meter. What is the decibel level of the sound produced by all five cars in the parking garage?

84. A certain sound has an intensity of I watts per square meter. By how many decibels does the sound increase when the intensity is tripled?

85. A certain sound has an intensity of I watts per square meter. By how many decibels does the sound decrease when the intensity is halved?

86. **CRITICAL THINKING** Tell whether this statement is *true* or *false*: $\log (u + v) = \log u + \log v$. If true, prove it. If false, give a counterexample.

87. *Writing* Let n be an integer from 1 to 20. Use only the fact that $\log 2 \approx 0.3010$ and $\log 3 \approx 0.4771$ to find as many values of $\log n$ as you possibly can. Show how you obtained each value. What can you conclude about the values of n for which you *cannot* find $\log n$?

Test Preparation

88. **MULTIPLE CHOICE** Which of the following is *not* correct?

   Ⓐ $\log_2 24 = \log_2 6 + \log_2 4$ Ⓑ $\log_2 24 = \log_2 72 - \log_2 3$

   Ⓒ $\log_2 24 = \log_2 8 + \log_2 16$ Ⓓ $\log_2 24 = 2 \log_2 2 + \log_2 6$

89. **MULTIPLE CHOICE** Which of the following is equivalent to $\log_5 8$?

   Ⓐ $\dfrac{\log 5}{\log 8}$ Ⓑ $\dfrac{\log 8}{\log 5}$ Ⓒ $\dfrac{\ln 8}{\ln 5}$ Ⓓ $\dfrac{\ln 13}{\ln 5}$ Ⓔ Both B and C

90. **MULTIPLE CHOICE** Which of the following is equivalent to $4 \log_3 5$?

   Ⓐ $\log_3 20$ Ⓑ $\log_3 625$ Ⓒ $\log_3 60$ Ⓓ $\log_3 243$ Ⓔ Both B and C

★ **Challenge**

91. **LOGICAL REASONING** Use the given hint and properties of exponents to prove each property of logarithms.

   a. Product property (*Hint:* Let $x = \log_b u$ and let $y = \log_b v$. Then $u = b^x$ and $v = b^y$ so that $\log_b uv = \log_b (b^x \cdot b^y)$.)

   b. Quotient property (*Hint:* Let $x = \log_b u$ and let $y = \log_b v$. Then $u = b^x$ and $v = b^y$ so that $\log_b \dfrac{u}{v} = \log_b \dfrac{b^x}{b^y}$.)

   c. Power property (*Hint:* Let $x = \log_b u$. Then $u = b^x$ and $u^n = b^{nx}$ so that $\log_b u^n = \log_b (b^{nx})$.)

   d. Change-of-base formula (*Hint:* Let $x = \log_b u$, $y = \log_b c$, and $z = \log_c u$. Then $u = b^x$, $c = b^y$, and $u = c^z$ so that $b^x = c^z$.)

EXTRA CHALLENGE
www.mcdougallittell.com

MIXED REVIEW

SIMPLIFYING EXPRESSIONS Simplify the expression. (Review 6.1)

92. $3y^2 \cdot y^2$ **93.** $(y^4)^3$ **94.** $(x^3 y)^4$ **95.** $(-3x^2)^2$

96. $4x^{-1}y$ **97.** $xy^{-2}x$ **98.** $\dfrac{x^3}{x^{-1}}$ **99.** $\dfrac{4x^2 y^7}{8xy^{-1}}$

SOLVING RADICAL EQUATIONS Solve the equation. Check for extraneous solutions. (Review 7.6 for 8.6)

100. $\sqrt[4]{x + 2} + 9 = 14$ **101.** $\sqrt[3]{3x - 4} = \sqrt[3]{x + 10}$

102. $\sqrt{3x + 7} = x + 3$ **103.** $(5x)^{1/2} - 18 = 32$

EVALUATING EXPRESSIONS Use a calculator to evaluate the expression. Round the result to three decimal places. (Review 8.3, 8.4 for 8.6)

104. e^9 **105.** e^{-12} **106.** $e^{1.7}$ **107.** $e^{-5.632}$

108. $\log 15$ **109.** $\log 1.729$ **110.** $\ln 16$ **111.** $\ln 5.89$

MATH & History   Logarithms

APPLICATION LINK
www.mcdougallittell.com

THEN

IN 1614, John Napier published his discovery of logarithms. This discovery allowed calculations with exponents to be performed more easily. In 1632 William Oughtred set two logarithmic scales side by side to form the first slide rule. Because the slide rule could be used to multiply, divide, raise to powers, and take roots, it eliminated the need for many tedious paper-and-pencil calculations.

1. To approximate the logarithm of a number, look at the number on the D row and the corresponding value on the L row of the slide rule shown above. For example, $\log 4 \approx 0.6$. Approximate $\log 3$ and $\log 5$.

2. Use the product property of logarithms to find $\log 15$.

NOW

TODAY, calculators have replaced the use of slide rules but not the use of logarithms. Logarithms are still used for scaling purposes, such as the decibel scale and the Richter scale, because the numbers involved span many orders of magnitude.

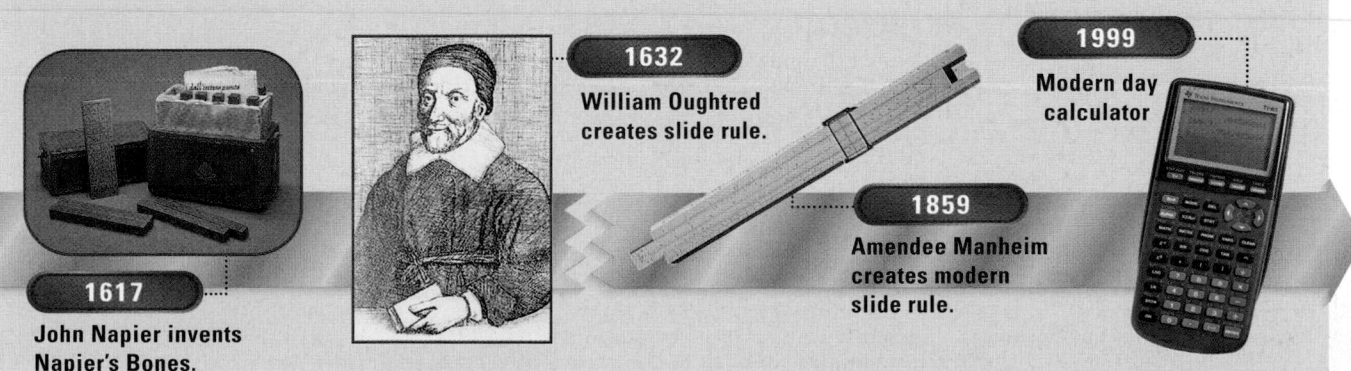

1632
William Oughtred creates slide rule.

1999
Modern day calculator

1617
John Napier invents Napier's Bones.

1859
Amendee Manheim creates modern slide rule.

▶ ACTIVITY 8.5
Using Technology

Graphing Logarithmic Functions

You can use a graphing calculator to graph logarithmic functions simply by using the [LOG] or [LN] key. To graph a logarithmic function having a base other than 10 or *e*, you need to use the change-of-base formula to rewrite the function in terms of common or natural logarithms.

▶ EXAMPLE

Use a graphing calculator to graph $y = \log_2 x$ and $y = \log_2 (x - 3) + 1$.

▶ SOLUTION

STUDENT HELP

~~INTERNET~~ **KEYSTROKE HELP**

See keystrokes for several models of calculators at www.mcdougallittell.com

❶ Rewrite each function in terms of common logarithms.

$$y = \log_2 x \qquad\qquad y = \log_2 (x - 3) + 1$$

$$= \frac{\log x}{\log 2} \qquad\qquad = \frac{\log (x - 3)}{\log 2} + 1$$

❷ Enter each function into a graphing calculator.

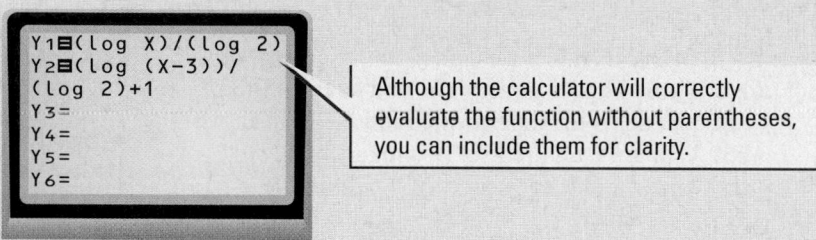

```
Y1B(log X)/(log 2)
Y2B(log (X-3))/
(log 2)+1
Y3=
Y4=
Y5=
Y6=
```

Although the calculator will correctly evaluate the function without parentheses, you can include them for clarity.

❸ Graph the functions.

The graph of $y = \log_2 x$ passes through (1, 0), and the line $x = 0$ is a vertical asymptote.

The graph of $y = \log_2 (x - 3) + 1$ passes through (4, 1), and the line $x = 3$ is a vertical asymptote.

▶ EXERCISES

Use a graphing calculator to graph the function. Give the coordinates of a point through which the graph passes, and state the vertical asymptote of the graph.

1. $y = \log_3 x$
2. $y = \log_9 x$
3. $y = \log_4 x$

4. $y = \log_7 x$
5. $y = \log_5 x$
6. $y = \log_{11} x$

7. $y = \log_5 (x - 2)$
8. $y = \log_4 (x + 1)$
9. $y = \log_2 (x - 5) - 3$

10. $y = \log_4 (x - 7) + 9$
11. $y = \log_5 (x + 2) + 6$
12. $y = \log_7 (x - 4) + 4$

13. Compare the domains of the graphs of $y = \log x$ and $y = \log |x|$.

8.6

Solving Exponential and Logarithmic Equations

What you should learn

GOAL 1 Solve exponential equations.

GOAL 2 Solve logarithmic equations, as applied in **Example 8**.

Why you should learn it

▼ To solve **real-life** problems, such as finding the diameter of a telescope's objective lens or mirror in **Ex. 69**.

GOAL 1 SOLVING EXPONENTIAL EQUATIONS

One way to solve exponential equations is to use the property that if two powers with the *same base* are equal, then their exponents must be equal.

$$\text{For } b > 0 \text{ and } b \neq 1, \text{ if } b^x = b^y, \text{ then } x = y.$$

EXAMPLE 1   Solving by Equating Exponents

Solve $4^{3x} = 8^{x+1}$.

SOLUTION

$4^{3x} = 8^{x+1}$	**Write original equation.**
$\left(2^2\right)^{3x} = \left(2^3\right)^{x+1}$	**Rewrite each power with base 2.**
$2^{6x} = 2^{3x+3}$	**Power of a power property**
$6x = 3x + 3$	**Equate exponents.**
$x = 1$	**Solve for x.**

▶ The solution is 1.

✓**CHECK** Check the solution by substituting it into the original equation.

$4^{3 \cdot 1} \stackrel{?}{=} 8^{1+1}$	**Substitute 1 for x.**
$64 = 64$ ✓	**Solution checks.**

· · · · · · · · · ·

When it is not convenient to write each side of an exponential equation using the same base, you can solve the equation by taking a logarithm of each side.

EXAMPLE 2   Taking a Logarithm of Each Side

Solve $2^x = 7$.

SOLUTION

$2^x = 7$	**Write original equation.**
$\log_2 2^x = \log_2 7$	**Take $\log_2$ of each side.**
$x = \log_2 7$	$\log_b b^x = x$
$x = \dfrac{\log 7}{\log 2} \approx 2.807$	**Use change-of-base formula and a calculator.**

▶ The solution is about 2.807. Check this in the original equation.

EXAMPLE 3 *Taking a Logarithm of Each Side*

Solve $10^{2x-3} + 4 = 21$.

SOLUTION

$10^{2x-3} + 4 = 21$	Write original equation.
$10^{2x-3} = 17$	Subtract 4 from each side.
$\log 10^{2x-3} = \log 17$	Take common log of each side.
$2x - 3 = \log 17$	$\log 10^x = x$
$2x = 3 + \log 17$	Add 3 to each side.
$x = \frac{1}{2}(3 + \log 17)$	Multiply each side by $\frac{1}{2}$.
$x \approx 2.115$	Use a calculator.

▶ The solution is about 2.115.

✓ **CHECK** Check the solution algebraically by substituting into the original equation. Or, check it graphically by graphing both sides of the equation and observing that the two graphs intersect at $x \approx 2.115$.

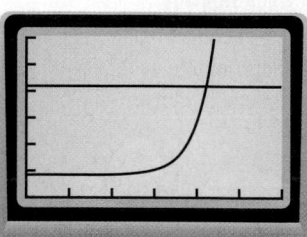

. . . .

Newton's law of cooling states that the temperature T of a cooling substance at time t (in minutes) can be modeled by the equation

$$T = (T_0 - T_R)e^{-rt} + T_R$$

where T_0 is the initial temperature of the substance, T_R is the room temperature, and r is a constant that represents the cooling rate of the substance.

REAL LIFE

Cooking

EXAMPLE 4 *Using an Exponential Model*

You are cooking *aleecha*, an Ethiopian stew. When you take it off the stove, its temperature is 212°F. The room temperature is 70°F and the cooling rate of the stew is $r = 0.046$. How long will it take to cool the stew to a serving temperature of 100°F?

SOLUTION

You can use Newton's law of cooling with $T = 100$, $T_0 = 212$, $T_R = 70$, and $r = 0.046$.

$T = (T_0 - T_R)e^{-rt} + T_R$	Newton's law of cooling
$100 = (212 - 70)e^{-0.046t} + 70$	Substitute for *T*, *T₀*, *T_R*, and *r*.
$30 = 142e^{-0.046t}$	Subtract 70 from each side.
$0.211 \approx e^{-0.046t}$	Divide each side by 142.
$\ln 0.211 \approx \ln e^{-0.046t}$	Take natural log of each side.
$-1.556 \approx -0.046t$	$\ln e^x = \log_e e^x = x$
$33.8 \approx t$	Divide each side by -0.046.

▶ You should wait about 34 minutes before serving the stew.

STUDENT HELP

INTERNET

HOMEWORK HELP
Visit our Web site
www.mcdougallittell.com
for extra examples.

GOAL 2 SOLVING LOGARITHMIC EQUATIONS

To solve a logarithmic equation, use this property for logarithms with the *same base:*

For positive numbers b, x, and y where $b \neq 1$, $\log_b x = \log_b y$ if and only if $x = y$.

EXAMPLE 5 *Solving a Logarithmic Equation*

Solve $\log_3 (5x - 1) = \log_3 (x + 7)$.

SOLUTION

$\log_3 (5x - 1) = \log_3 (x + 7)$	**Write original equation.**
$5x - 1 = x + 7$	**Use property stated above.**
$5x = x + 8$	**Add 1 to each side.**
$x = 2$	**Solve for x.**

▶ The solution is 2.

✓ **CHECK** Check the solution by substituting it into the original equation.

$\log_3 (5x - 1) = \log_3 (x + 7)$	**Write original equation.**
$\log_3 (5 \cdot 2 - 1) \stackrel{?}{=} \log_3 (2 + 7)$	**Substitute 2 for x.**
$\log_3 9 = \log_3 9$ ✓	**Solution checks.**

· · · · · · · · · ·

When it is not convenient to write both sides of an equation as logarithmic expressions with the same base, you can *exponentiate* each side of the equation.

For $b > 0$ and $b \neq 1$, if $x = y$, then $b^x = b^y$.

EXAMPLE 6 *Exponentiating Each Side*

Solve $\log_5 (3x + 1) = 2$.

SOLUTION

$\log_5 (3x + 1) = 2$	**Write original equation.**
$5^{\log_5 (3x + 1)} = 5^2$	**Exponentiate each side using base 5.**
$3x + 1 = 25$	$b^{\log_b x} = x$
$x = 8$	**Solve for x.**

▶ The solution is 8.

✓ **CHECK** Check the solution by substituting it into the original equation.

$\log_5 (3x + 1) = 2$	**Write original equation.**
$\log_5 (3 \cdot 8 + 1) \stackrel{?}{=} 2$	**Substitute 8 for x.**
$\log_5 25 \stackrel{?}{=} 2$	**Simplify.**
$2 = 2$ ✓	**Solution checks.**

Because the domain of a logarithmic function generally does not include all real numbers, you should be sure to check for extraneous solutions of logarithmic equations. You can do this algebraically or graphically.

EXAMPLE 7 *Checking for Extraneous Solutions*

STUDENT HELP

Look Back
For help with the zero product property, see p. 257.

Solve $\log 5x + \log (x - 1) = 2$. Check for extraneous solutions.

SOLUTION

$\log 5x + \log (x - 1) = 2$	**Write original equation.**
$\log [5x(x - 1)] = 2$	**Product property of logarithms**
$10^{\log (5x^2 - 5x)} = 10^2$	**Exponentiate each side using base 10.**
$5x^2 - 5x = 100$	$10^{\log x} = x$
$x^2 - x - 20 = 0$	**Write in standard form.**
$(x - 5)(x + 4) = 0$	**Factor.**
$x = 5 \quad \text{or} \quad x = -4$	**Zero product property**

The solutions appear to be 5 and -4. However, when you check these in the original equation or use a graphic check as shown at the right, you can see that $x = 5$ is the only solution.

▶ The solution is 5.

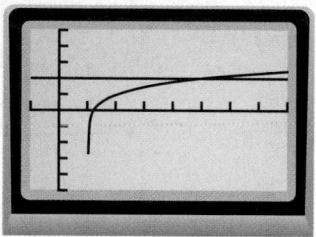

EXAMPLE 8 *Using a Logarithmic Model*

FOCUS ON PEOPLE

CHARLES RICHTER
developed the Richter scale in 1935 as a mathematical means of comparing the sizes of earthquakes. For large earthquakes, seismologists use a different measure called moment magnitude.

SEISMOLOGY The moment magnitude M of an earthquake that releases energy E (in ergs) can be modeled by this equation:

$$M = 0.291 \ln E + 1.17$$

On May 22, 1960, a powerful earthquake took place in Chile. It had a moment magnitude of 9.5. How much energy did this earthquake release?

▶ Source: U.S. Geological Survey National Earthquake Information Center

SOLUTION

$M = 0.291 \ln E + 1.17$	**Write model for moment magnitude.**
$9.5 = 0.291 \ln E + 1.17$	**Substitute 9.5 for M.**
$8.33 = 0.291 \ln E$	**Subtract 1.17 from each side.**
$28.625 \approx \ln E$	**Divide each side by 0.291.**
$e^{28.625} \approx e^{\ln E}$	**Exponentiate each side using base e.**
$2.702 \times 10^{12} \approx E$	$e^{\ln x} = e^{\log_e x} = x$

▶ The earthquake released about 2.7 trillion ergs of energy.

GUIDED PRACTICE

Vocabulary Check ✔

1. Give an example of an exponential equation and a logarithmic equation.

Concept Check ✔

2. How is solving a logarithmic equation similar to solving an exponential equation? How is it different?

3. Why do logarithmic equations sometimes have extraneous solutions?

Skill Check ✔ **Solve the equation.**

4. $3^x = 14$

5. $5^x = 8$

6. $9^{2x} = 3^{x-6}$

7. $10^{3x-4} = 0.1$

8. $2^{3x} = 4^{x-1}$

9. $10^{3x-1} + 4 = 32$

Solve the equation.

10. $\log x = 2.4$

11. $\log x = 3$

12. $\log_3 (2x - 1) = 3$

13. $12 \ln x = 44$

14. $\log_2 (x + 2) = \log_2 x^2$

15. $\log 3x + \log (x + 2) = 1$

ERROR ANALYSIS In Exercises 16 and 17, describe the error.

16.

$$4^{x+1} = 8^x$$
$$\log_4 4^{x+1} = \log_4 8^x$$
$$x + 1 = x \log_4 8$$
$$x + 1 = 2x$$
$$1 = x$$

17.

$$\log_2 5x = 8$$
$$e^{\log_2 5x} = e^8$$
$$5x = e^8$$
$$x = \frac{1}{5}e^8$$

18. 🌐 **EARTHQUAKES** An earthquake that took place in Alaska on March 28, 1964, had a moment magnitude of 9.2. Use the equation given in Example 8 to determine how much energy this earthquake released.

PRACTICE AND APPLICATIONS

STUDENT HELP

▶ **Extra Practice**
to help you master
skills is on p. 951.

CHECKING SOLUTIONS Tell whether the *x*-value is a solution of the equation.

19. $\ln x = 27, x = e^{27}$

20. $5 - \log_4 2x = 3, x = 8$

21. $\ln 5x = 4, x = \frac{1}{4}e^5$

22. $\log_5 \frac{1}{2}x = 17, x = 2e^{17}$

23. $5e^x = 15, x = \ln 3$

24. $e^x + 2 = 18, x = \log_2 16$

SOLVING EXPONENTIAL EQUATIONS Solve the equation.

STUDENT HELP

▶ **HOMEWORK HELP**
Examples 1–3:
  Exs. 23–42
Example 4: Exs. 62–68
Examples 5–7:
  Exs. 19–22, 43–60
Example 8: Exs. 69, 70

25. $10^{x-3} = 100^{4x-5}$

26. $25^{x-1} = 125^{4x}$

27. $3^{x-7} = 27^{2x}$

28. $36^{x-9} = 6^{2x}$

29. $8^{5x} = 16^{3x+4}$

30. $e^{-x} = 6$

31. $2^x = 15$

32. $1.2e^{-5x} + 2.6 = 3$

33. $4^x - 5 = 3$

34. $-5e^{-x} + 9 = 6$

35. $10^{2x} + 3 = 8$

36. $0.25^x - 0.5 = 2$

37. $\frac{1}{4}(4)^{2x} + 1 = 5$

38. $\frac{2}{3}e^{4x} + \frac{1}{3} = 4$

39. $10^{-12x} + 6 = 100$

40. $4 - 2e^x = -23$

41. $3^{0.1x} - 4 = 5$

42. $-16 + 0.2(10)^x = 35$

SOLVING LOGARITHMIC EQUATIONS Solve the equation. Check for extraneous solutions.

43. $\ln(4x + 1) = \ln(2x + 5)$

44. $\log_2 x = -1$

45. $4 \log_3 x = 28$

46. $16 \ln x = 30$

47. $\frac{1}{2} \log_6 16x = 3$

48. $1 - 2 \ln x = -4$

49. $2 \ln(-x) + 7 = 14$

50. $\log_5(2x + 15) = \log_5 3x$

51. $\ln x + \ln(x - 2) = 1$

52. $\ln x + \ln(x + 3) = 1$

53. $\log_8(11 - 6x) = \log_8(1 - x)$

54. $15 + 2 \log_2 x = 31$

55. $-5 + 2 \ln 3x = 5$

56. $\log(5 - 3x) = \log(4x - 9)$

57. $6.5 \log_5 3x = 20$

58. $\ln(x + 5) = \ln(x - 1) - \ln(x + 1)$

59. $\ln(5.6 - x) = \ln(18.4 - 2.6x)$

60. $10 \ln 100x - 3 = 117$

61. *Writing* Solve the equation $4^{3x} = 8^{x + 1}$ in Example 1 by taking the common logarithm of each side of the equation. Do you prefer this method to the method shown in Example 1? Why or why not?

62. 🌐 **COOKING** You are cooking chili. When you take it off the stove, it has a temperature of 205°F. The room temperature is 68°F and the cooling rate of the chili is $r = 0.03$. How long will it take to cool to a serving temperature of 95°F?

63. 🌐 **FINANCE** You deposit $2000 in an account that pays 2% annual interest compounded quarterly. How long will it take for the balance to reach $2400?

64. 🌐 **RADIOACTIVE DECAY** You have 20 grams of phosphorus-32 that decays 5% per day. How long will it take for half of the original amount to decay?

65. 🌐 **DOUBLING TIME** You deposit $500 in an account that pays 2.5% annual interest compounded continuously. How long will it take for the balance to double?

66. HISTORY ▶ CONNECTION   The first permanent English colony in America was established in Jamestown, Virginia, in 1607. From 1620 through 1780, the population P of colonial America can be modeled by the equation

$$P = 8863(1.04)^t$$

where t is the number of years since 1620. When was the population of colonial America about 345,000?

67. 🌐 **OCEANOGRAPHY** Oceanographers use the density d (in grams per cubic centimeter) of seawater to obtain information about the circulation of water masses and the rates at which waters of different densities mix. For water with a salinity of 30%, the density is related to the water temperature T (in degrees Celsius) by this equation:

$$d = 1.0245 - e^{0.1266T - 7.828}$$

Use the equation to find the temperature of each layer of water whose density is given in the diagram.

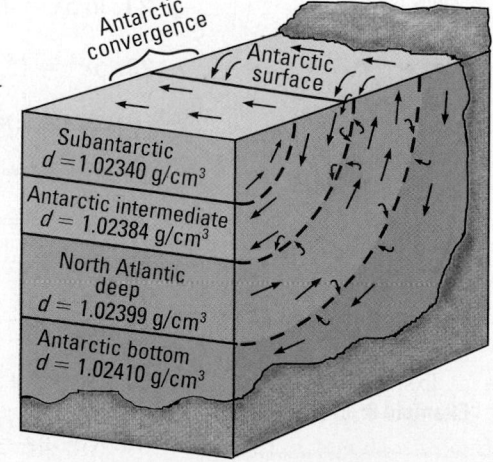

68. 🌐 **MUON DECAY** A muon is an elementary particle that is similar to an
electron, but much heavier. Muons are unstable—they very quickly decay to
form electrons and other particles. In an experiment conducted in 1943, the
number m of muon decays (of an original 5000 muons) was related to the time t
(in microseconds) by this model:

$$m = e^{6.331 - 0.403t}$$

After how many microseconds were 204 decays recorded?

69. 🌐 **ASTRONOMY** The relationship between a telescope's limiting magnitude
(the apparent magnitude of the dimmest star that can be seen with the telescope)
and the diameter of the telescope's objective lens or mirror can be modeled by

$$M = 5 \log D + 2$$

where M is the limiting magnitude and D is the diameter (in millimeters) of the
lens or mirror. If a telescope can reveal stars with a magnitude of 12, what is the
diameter of its objective lens or mirror? ▶ Source: *Practical Astronomy*

70. 🌐 **ALTIMETER** An altimeter is an instrument that finds the height above sea
level by measuring the air pressure. The height and the air pressure are related
by the model

$$h = -8005 \ln \frac{P}{101{,}300}$$

where h is the height (in meters) above sea level and P is the air pressure (in
pascals). What is the air pressure when the height is 4000 meters above sea level?

**Test
Preparation**

71. **MULTI-STEP PROBLEM** A simple
technique that biologists use to estimate the
age of an African elephant is to measure the
length of the elephant's footprint and then
calculate its age using the equation

$$l = 45 - 25.7e^{-0.09a}$$

where l is the length of the footprint (in
centimeters) and a is the age (in years).
▶ Source: *Journal of Wildlife Management*

  a. Use the equation to find the ages of the
elephants whose footprints are shown.

  b. Solve the equation for a, and use this
equation to find the ages of the elephants
whose footprints are shown.

  c. *Writing* Compare the methods you
used in parts (a) and (b). Which method
do you prefer? Explain.

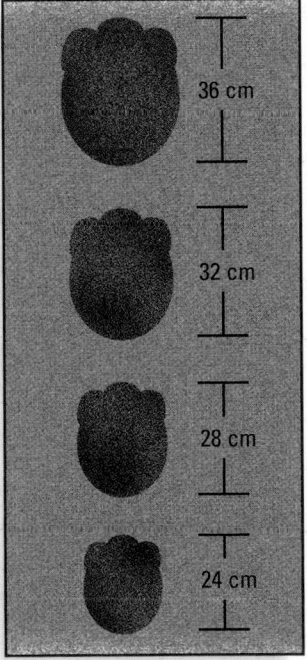

★ **Challenge**

SOLVING EQUATIONS Solve the equation.

72. $2^{x + 3} = 5^{3x - 1}$

73. $10^{5x + 2} = 5^{4 - x}$

74. $\log_3 (x - 6) = \log_9 2x$

75. $\log_4 x = \log_8 4x$

76. *Writing* In Exercises 72–75 you solved exponential and logarithmic equations
with different bases. Describe general methods for solving such equations.

MIXED REVIEW

MAKING SCATTER PLOTS Draw a scatter plot of the data. Then approximate an equation of the best-fitting line. (Review 2.5 for 8.7)

77.

x	−2	−1	−0.5	0	0.5	1	2	3	3.5	4
y	1.25	1.5	1.5	2	1.75	2	2.5	2.5	2.75	3.25

78.

x	−4	−3	−2.5	−2	−1.5	−1	0	1	1.5	2
y	1.5	1.75	1.75	2.25	2	2.25	2.75	2.75	3	3.5

THE SUBSTITUTION METHOD Solve the linear system using the substitution method. (Review 3.2 for 8.7)

79. $2x - y = 3$
$3x - 2y = 2$

80. $2x + y = 4$
$x + y = 3$

81. $x + 4y = -24$
$x - 4y = 24$

82. $x - 3y = -3$
$2x + y = 8$

83. $2x + y = -1$
$-4x - 2y = -5$

84. $-x + 6y = -32$
$7x - 2y = 24$

FACTORING Factor the polynomial by grouping. (Review 6.4)

85. $3x^3 - 6x^2 + 4x - 8$

86. $2x^3 - 5x^2 + 16x - 40$

87. $7x^3 + 4x^2 + 35x + 20$

88. $4x^3 - 3x^2 + 8x - 6$

QUIZ 2

Self-Test for Lessons 8.4–8.6

Evaluate the expression without using a calculator. (Lesson 8.4)

1. $\log_2 8$

2. $\log_5 625$

3. $\log_8 512$

4. Find the inverse of the function $y = \ln (x + 3)$. (Lesson 8.4)

Graph the function. State the domain and range. (Lesson 8.4)

5. $y = 1 + \log_4 x$

6. $y = \log_4 (x + 3)$

7. $y = 2 + \log_6 (x - 2)$

Use a property of logarithms to evaluate the expression. (Lesson 8.5)

8. $\log_3 (3 \cdot 27)$

9. $\log_2 \frac{1}{2}$

10. $\ln e^2$

11. Expand the expression $\log_4 x^{1/2}y^4$. (Lesson 8.5)

12. Condense the expression $2 \log_6 14 + 3 \log_6 x - \log_6 7$. (Lesson 8.5)

13. Use the change-of-base formula to evaluate the expression $\log_4 22$. (Lesson 8.5)

Solve the equation. (Lesson 8.6)

14. $3e^x - 1 = 14$

15. $3 \log_2 x = 28$

16. $\ln (2x + 7) = \ln (x - 4)$

17. 🌎 **EARTHQUAKES** An earthquake that took place in Indonesia on February 1, 1938, had a moment magnitude of 8.5. Use the model $M = 0.291 \ln E + 1.17$, where M is the moment magnitude and E is the energy (in ergs) of an earthquake, to determine how much energy the Indonesian earthquake released. (Lesson 8.6)

Modeling with Exponential and Power Functions

GOAL 1 MODELING WITH EXPONENTIAL FUNCTIONS

What you should learn

GOAL 1 Model data with exponential functions.

GOAL 2 Model data with power functions, as applied in **Example 5**.

Why you should learn it

▼ To solve **real-life** problems, such as finding the number of U.S. stamps issued in **Ex. 56**.

Just as two points determine a line, two points also determine an exponential curve.

EXAMPLE 1 *Writing an Exponential Function*

Write an exponential function $y = ab^x$ whose graph passes through (1, 6) and (3, 24).

SOLUTION

Substitute the coordinates of the two given points into $y = ab^x$ to obtain two equations in a and b.

$6 = ab^1$ **Substitute 6 for y and 1 for x.**

$24 = ab^3$ **Substitute 24 for y and 3 for x.**

To solve the system, solve for a in the first equation to get $a = \dfrac{6}{b}$, then substitute into the second equation.

$24 = \left(\dfrac{6}{b}\right)b^3$ **Substitute $\dfrac{6}{b}$ for a.**

$24 = 6b^2$ **Simplify.**

$4 = b^2$ **Divide each side by 6.**

$2 = b$ **Take the positive square root.**

Using $b = 2$, you then have $a = \dfrac{6}{b} = \dfrac{6}{2} = 3$. So, $y = 3 \cdot 2^x$.

· · · · · · · · · ·

When you are given more than two points, you can decide whether an exponential model fits the points by plotting the natural logarithms of the y-values against the x-values. If the new points $(x, \ln y)$ fit a linear pattern, then the original points (x, y) fit an exponential pattern.

Graph of points (x, y)

y

2

$y = 2^x$
(1, 2)

$\left(-2, \frac{1}{4}\right)$ $\left(-1, \frac{1}{2}\right)$ (0, 1)

1   x

The graph is an exponential curve.

Graph of points $(x, \ln y)$

ln y

$\ln y = x(\ln 2)$

1

(0, 0)   (1, 0.69)

(−1, −0.69)   1   x

(−2, −1.39)

The graph is a line.

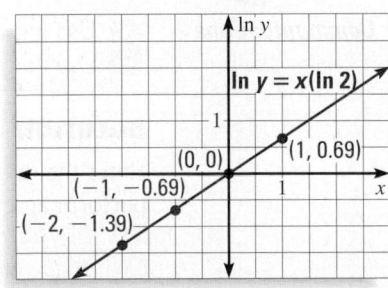

Communications

STUDENT HELP

→ **Look Back**
For help with scatter plots and best-fitting lines, see pp. 100–101.

EXAMPLE 2 *Finding an Exponential Model*

The table gives the number y (in millions) of cell-phone subscribers from 1988 to 1997 where t is the number of years since 1987.

t	1	2	3	4	5	6	7	8	9	10
y	1.6	2.7	4.4	6.4	8.9	13.1	19.3	28.2	38.2	48.7

▶ Source: Cellular Telecommunications Industry Association

a. Draw a scatter plot of ln y versus x. Is an exponential model a good fit for the original data?

b. Find an exponential model for the original data.

SOLUTION

a. Use a calculator to create a new table of values.

t	1	2	3	4	5	6	7	8	9	10
ln y	0.47	0.99	1.48	1.86	2.19	2.57	2.96	3.34	3.64	3.89

Then plot the new points as shown. The points lie close to a line, so an exponential model should be a good fit for the original data.

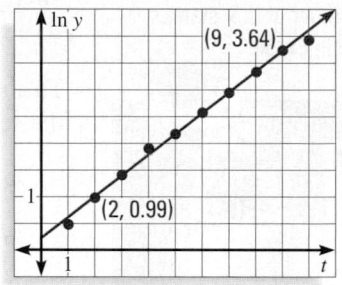

b. To find an exponential model $y = ab^t$, choose two points on the line, such as (2, 0.99) and (9, 3.64). Use these points to find an equation of the line. Then solve for y.

$\ln y = 0.379t + 0.233$	**Equation of line**
$y = e^{0.379t + 0.233}$	**Exponentiate each side using base** e.
$y = e^{0.233}\left(e^{0.379}\right)^t$	**Use properties of exponents.**
$y = 1.30(1.46)^t$	**Exponential model**

· · · · · · · · · ·

A graphing calculator that performs exponential regression does essentially what is done in Example 2, but uses all of the original data.

Communications

EXAMPLE 3 *Using Exponential Regression*

 Use a graphing calculator to find an exponential model for the data in Example 2. Use the model to estimate the number of cell-phone subscribers in 1998.

SOLUTION

Enter the original data into a graphing calculator and perform an exponential regression. The model is:

$$y = 1.30(1.46)^t$$

Substituting $t = 11$ (for 1998) into the model gives $y = 1.30(1.46)^{11} \approx 84$ million cell-phone subscribers.

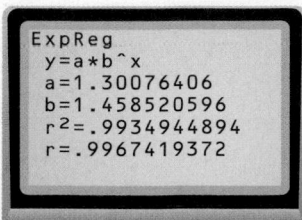

```
ExpReg
 y=a*b^x
 a=1.30076406
 b=1.458520596
 r²=.9934944894
 r=.9967419372
```

GOAL 2 MODELING WITH POWER FUNCTIONS

Recall from Lesson 7.3 that a power function has the form $y = ax^b$. Because there are only two constants (a and b), only two points are needed to determine a power curve through the points.

EXAMPLE 4 *Writing a Power Function*

Write a power function $y = ax^b$ whose graph passes through $(2, 5)$ and $(6, 9)$.

SOLUTION

Substitute the coordinates of the two given points into $y = ax^b$ to obtain two equations in a and b.

$5 = a \cdot 2^b$ **Substitute 5 for *y* and 2 for *x*.**

$9 = a \cdot 6^b$ **Substitute 9 for *y* and 6 for *x*.**

To solve the system, solve for a in the first equation to get $a = \dfrac{5}{2^b}$, then substitute into the second equation.

$9 = \left(\dfrac{5}{2^b}\right)6^b$ **Substitute $\dfrac{5}{2^b}$ for *a*.**

$9 = 5 \cdot 3^b$ **Simplify.**

$1.8 = 3^b$ **Divide each side by 5.**

$\log_3 1.8 = b$ **Take $\log_3$ of each side.**

$\dfrac{\log 1.8}{\log 3} = b$ **Use the change-of-base formula.**

$0.535 \approx b$ **Use a calculator.**

Using $b = 0.535$, you then have $a = \dfrac{5}{2^b} = \dfrac{5}{2^{0.535}} \approx 3.45$. So, $y = 3.45x^{0.535}$.

. . . .

When you are given more than two points, you can decide whether a power model fits the points by plotting the natural logarithms of the *y*-values against the natural logarithms of the *x*-values. If the new points ($\ln x$, $\ln y$) fit a linear pattern, then the original points (x, y) fit a power pattern.

Graph of points (*x, y*)

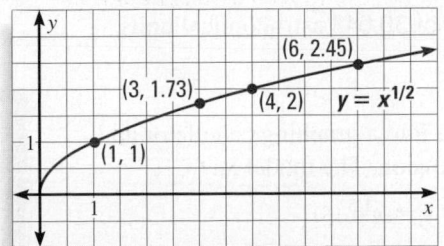

The graph is a power curve.

Graph of points (ln *x*, ln *y*)

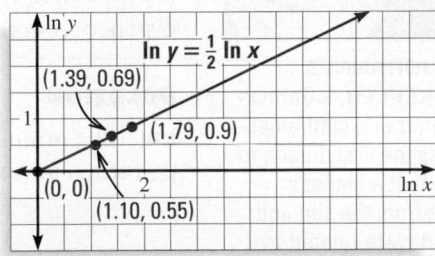

The graph is a line.

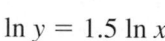

EXAMPLE 5 Finding a Power Model

Astronomy

The table gives the mean distance x from the sun (in astronomical units) and the period y (in Earth years) of the six planets closest to the sun.

Planet	Mercury	Venus	Earth	Mars	Jupiter	Saturn
x	0.387	0.723	1.000	1.524	5.203	9.539
y	0.241	0.615	1.000	1.881	11.862	29.458

a. Draw a scatter plot of $\ln y$ versus $\ln x$. Is a power model a good fit for the original data?

b. Find a power model for the original data.

SOLUTION

a. Use a calculator to create a new table of values.

$\ln x$	-0.949	-0.324	0.000	0.421	1.649	2.255
$\ln y$	-1.423	-0.486	0.000	0.632	2.473	3.383

Then plot the new points, as shown at the right. The points lie close to a line, so a power model should be a good fit for the original data.

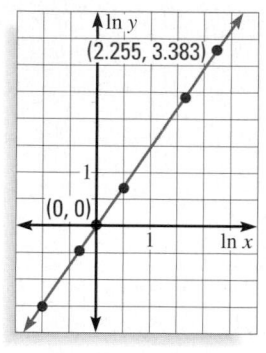

b. To find a power model $y = ax^b$, choose two points on the line, such as $(0, 0)$ and $(2.255, 3.383)$. Use these points to find an equation of the line. Then solve for y.

$\ln y = 1.5 \ln x$ **Equation of line**

$\ln y = \ln x^{1.5}$ **Power property of logarithms**

$y = x^{1.5}$ $\log_b x = \log_b y$ **if and only if** $x = y$.

· · · · · · · · · ·

A graphing calculator that performs power regression does essentially what is done in Example 5, but uses all of the original data.

EXAMPLE 6 Using Power Regression

ASTRONOMY Use a graphing calculator to find a power model for the data in Example 5. Use the model to estimate the period of Neptune, which has a mean distance from the sun of 30.043 astronomical units.

**JOHANNES
KEPLER,** a German astronomer and mathematician, was the first person to observe that a planet's distance from the sun and its period were related by the power function in Examples 5 and 6.

SOLUTION

Enter the original data into a graphing calculator and perform a power regression. The model is:

$$y = x^{1.5}$$

Substituting 30.043 for x in the model gives
$y = (30.043)^{1.5} \approx 165$ years for the period of Neptune.

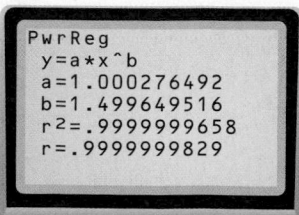

GUIDED PRACTICE

Vocabulary Check ✓

1. Complete this statement: When you are given more than two points, you can decide whether you can fit a(n) _?_ model to the points by plotting the natural logarithms of the y-values against the x-values.

Concept Check ✓

2. How many points determine an exponential function $y = ab^x$? How many points determine a power function $y = ax^b$?

3. Can you use the procedure in Example 5 to find a power model for a data set where one of the points has an x-coordinate of 0? Explain why or why not.

Skill Check ✓

Write an exponential function of the form $y = ab^x$ whose graph passes through the given points.

4. (1, 3), (2, 36)   **5.** (2, 2), (4, 18)   **6.** (1, 4), (3, 16)

7. (2, 3.5), (1, 5.2)   **8.** (5, 8), (3, 32)   **9.** $\left(1, \frac{1}{2}\right), \left(3, \frac{3}{8}\right)$

Write a power function of the form $y = ax^b$ whose graph passes through the given points.

10. (3, 27), (9, 243)   **11.** (1, 2), (4, 32)   **12.** (4, 48), (2, 6)

13. (1, 4), (3, 8)   **14.** (4.5, 9.2), (1, 6.4)   **15.** $\left(2, \frac{1}{2}\right), \left(4, \frac{3}{5}\right)$

16. 🌐 **CELL-PHONE USERS** Use the model in Example 3 to estimate the number of cell-phone users in 2005. What does your answer tell you about the model?

PRACTICE AND APPLICATIONS

STUDENT HELP

▶ **Extra Practice**
to help you master
skills is on p. 951.

WRITING EXPONENTIAL FUNCTIONS Write an exponential function of the form $y = ab^x$ whose graph passes through the given points.

17. (1, 4), (2, 12)   **18.** (2, 18), (3, 108)   **19.** (6, 8), (7, 32)

20. (1, 7), (3, 63)   **21.** (3, 8), (6, 64)   **22.** (−3, 3), (4, 6561)

23. $\left(4, \frac{112}{81}\right), \left(-1, \frac{21}{2}\right)$ **24.** (3, 13.5), (5, 30.375)   **25.** $\left(2, \frac{25}{4}\right), \left(4, \frac{625}{4}\right)$

FINDING EXPONENTIAL MODELS Use the table of values to draw a scatter plot of ln y versus x. Then find an exponential model for the data.

STUDENT HELP

▶ **HOMEWORK HELP**
Example 1: Exs. 17–25
Example 2: Exs. 26–28
Example 3: Exs. 54–56
Example 4: Exs. 29–37
Example 5: Exs. 38–40
Example 6: Exs. 57, 58

26.

x	1	2	3	4	5	6	7	8
y	14	28	56	112	224	448	896	1792

27.

x	1	2	3	4	5	6	7	8
y	10.2	30.5	43.4	61.2	89.7	120.6	210.4	302.5

28.

x	2	4	6	8	10	12	14	16
y	12.8	20.48	32.77	52.43	83.89	134.22	214.75	343.6

WRITING POWER FUNCTIONS Write a power function of the form $y = ax^b$ whose graph passes through the given points.

29. (2, 1), (6, 5)
30. (6, 8), (12, 36)
31. (5, 12), (7, 25)

32. (3, 4), (6, 18)
33. (2, 10), (8, 25)
34. (6, 11), (24, 72)

35. (2.2, 10.4), (8.8, 20.3)
36. (2.9, 9.4), (7.3, 12.8)
37. (2.71, 6.42), (13.55, 29.79)

FINDING POWER MODELS Use the table of values to draw a scatter plot of ln y versus ln x. Then find a power model for the data.

38.

x	1	2	3	4	5	6	7
y	0.78	7.37	27.41	69.63	143.47	259.00	426.79

39.

x	1	2	3	4	5	6	7
y	1.2	5.4	9.8	14.3	25.6	41.2	65.8

40.

x	2	4	6	8	10	12	14
y	1.89	1.44	1.22	1.09	1.00	0.93	0.87

WRITING EQUATIONS Write y as a function of x.

41. $\log y = 0.24x + 4.5$
42. $\log y = 0.2 \log x + 0.8$

43. $\ln y = x + 4$
44. $\log y = -0.12 + 0.88x$

45. $\log y = -0.48 \log x - 0.548$
46. $\ln y = 2.3 \ln x + 4.7$

47. $\ln y = -2.38x + 0.98$
48. $\log y = -1.48 + 3.751 \log x$

49. $\ln y = -1.5x + 2.5$
50. $1.2 \log y = 3.4 \log x$

51. $\frac{1}{2} \log y = \frac{5}{6} \log x$
52. $2\frac{1}{8} \ln y = 4\frac{1}{4} \ln x + \frac{3}{8}$

53. VISUAL THINKING Find equations of the line, the exponential curve, and the power curve that each pass through the points (1, 3) and (2, 12). Graph the equations in the same coordinate plane and then describe what happens when the equations are used as models to predict y-values for x-values greater than 2.

🖩 **MODELING DATA** In Exercises 54–58, you may wish to use a graphing calculator to perform exponential regression or power regression.

54. 🌐 **NEW WEB SITE** You have just created your own Web site. You are keeping track of the number of hits (the number of visits to the site). The table shows the number y of hits in each of the first 10 months where x is the month number.

x	1	2	3	4	5	6	7	8	9	10
y	22	39	70	126	227	408	735	1322	2380	4285

a. Find an exponential model for the data.

b. According to your model, how many hits do you expect in the twelfth month?

c. According to your model, how many hits would there be in the thirty-fourth month? What is wrong with this number?

REAL LIFE
CRANES
The red-crowned
crane (*Grus japonensis*) is
the second-rarest crane
species, with a total
population in the wild of
about 1700–2000 birds.

55. **CRANES** The table shows the number C of cranes in Izumi, Japan, from 1950 to 1990 where t represents the number of years since 1950.

▶ Source: Yamashina Institute of Ornithology

t	0	5	10	15	20	25	30	35	40
C	293	299	438	1573	2336	3649	5602	7610	9959

a. Draw a scatter plot of ln C versus t. Is an exponential model a good fit for the original data?

b. Find an exponential model for the original data. Estimate the number of cranes in Izumi, Japan, in the year 2000.

56. **UNITED STATES STAMPS** The table shows the cumulative number s of different stamps in the United States from 1889 to 1989 where t represents the number of years since 1889.

t	0	10	20	30	40	50	60	70	80	90	100
s	218	293	374	541	681	858	986	1138	1138	1794	2438

a. Draw a scatter plot of ln s versus t. Is an exponential model a good fit for the original data?

b. Find an exponential model for the original data. Estimate the cumulative number of stamps in the United States in the year 2000.

57. **CITIES OF ARGENTINA**
The table shows the population y (in millions) and the population rank x for nine cities in Argentina in 1991.

a. Draw a scatter plot of ln y versus ln x. Is a power model a good fit for the original data?

b. Find a power model for the original data. Estimate the population of the city Vicente López, which has a population rank of 20.

City	Rank, x	Population (millions), y
Cordoba	2	1.21
Rosario	3	1.12
La Matanza	4	1.11
Mendoza	5	0.77
La Plata	6	0.64
Moron	7	0.64
San Miguel de Tucuman	8	0.62
Lomas de Zamoras	9	0.57
Mar de Plata	10	0.51

STUDENT HELP

INTERNET
HOMEWORK HELP
Visit our Web site
www.mcdougallittell.com
for help with Ex. 57.

58. SCIENCE ▶ CONNECTION The table shows the atomic number x and the melting point y (in degrees Celsius) for the alkali metals.

Alkali metal	Lithium	Sodium	Potassium	Rubidium	Cesium
Atomic number, x	3	11	19	37	55
Melting point, y	180.5	97.8	63.7	38.9	28.5

a. Draw a scatter plot of ln y versus ln x. Is a power model a good fit for the original data?

b. Find a power model for the original data.

c. One of the alkali metals, francium, is not shown in the table. It has an atomic number of 87. Using your model, predict the melting point of francium.

59. MULTI-STEP PROBLEM The femur is a large bone found in the leg or hind limb of an animal. Scientists use the circumference of an animal's femur to estimate the animal's weight. The table at the right shows the femur circumference C (in millimeters) and the weight W (in kilograms) of several animals.

Animal	C (mm)	W (kg)
Meadow mouse	5.5	0.047
Guinea pig	15	0.385
Otter	28	9.68
Cheetah	68.7	38
Warthog	72	90.5
Nyala	97	134.5
Grizzly bear	106.5	256
Kudu	135	301
Giraffe	173	710

▶ Source: Zoological Society of London

a. Draw two scatter plots, one of ln W versus C and another of ln W versus ln C.

b. *Writing* Looking at your scatter plots, tell which type of model you think is a better fit for the original data. Explain your reasoning.

c. Using your answer from part (b), find a model for the original data.

d. The table at the right shows the femur circumference C (in millimeters) of four animals. Use the model you found in part (c) to estimate the weight of each animal.

Animal	C (mm)
Raccoon	28
Cougar	60.25
Bison	167.5
Hippopotamus	208

★ **Challenge**

60. DERIVING FORMULAS Using $y = ab^x$ and $y = ax^b$, take the natural logarithm of both sides of each equation. What is the slope and y-intercept of the line relating x and ln y for $y = ab^x$? of the line relating ln x and ln y for $y = ax^b$?

MIXED REVIEW

DESCRIBING END BEHAVIOR Describe the end behavior of the graph of the polynomial function by completing the statements $f(x) \to \underline{\ ?\ }$ as $x \to -\infty$ and $f(x) \to \underline{\ ?\ }$ as $x \to +\infty$. (Review 6.2 for 8.8)

61. $f(x) = -x^3 + x^2 - x + 4$

62. $f(x) = x^4 - 7x^2 + 2$

63. $f(x) = -x^4 + 3x - 3$

64. $f(x) = 3x^5 - x^4 - x^2 + 1$

65. $f(x) = x^6 - 2x - 1$

66. $f(x) = -2x^5 + 3x^4 - 2x^3 + x^2 + 5$

GRAPHING FUNCTIONS Graph the function. (Review 8.3 for 8.8)

67. $y = 4e^{-0.75x}$

68. $y = 10e^{-0.4x}$

69. $y = 2e^{x-3}$

70. $y = e^{0.5x} + 2$

71. $y = e^{-0.25x} - 4$

72. $y = 3e^{-1.5x} - 1$

73. $y = 2e^{0.25x} + 1$

74. $y = e^{x+1} - 5$

75. $y = 2.5e^{-0.6x} + 2$

CONDENSING EXPRESSIONS Condense the expression. (Review 8.5)

76. $5 \log 2 - \log 8$

77. $2 \log 9 - \log 3$

78. $\ln x + 5 \ln 3$

79. $2 \ln x - \ln 4$

80. $\log_2 8 + 3 \log_2 3 - \log_2 6$

81. $\log_7 12 + 3 \log_7 4 + \log_7 5$

Logistic Growth Functions

GOAL 1 USING LOGISTIC GROWTH FUNCTIONS

What you should learn

GOAL 1 Evaluate and graph logistic growth functions.

GOAL 2 Use logistic growth functions to model **real-life** quantities, such as a yeast population in **Exs. 50 and 51**.

Why you should learn it

▼ To solve **real-life** problems, such as modeling the height of a sunflower in **Example 5**.

In this lesson you will study a family of functions of the form

$$y = \frac{c}{1 + ae^{-rx}}$$

where a, c, and r are all positive constants. Functions of this form are called **logistic growth functions**.

EXAMPLE 1 *Evaluating a Logistic Growth Function*

Evaluate $f(x) = \dfrac{100}{1 + 9e^{-2x}}$ for each value of x.

  a. $f(-3)$ **b.** $f(0)$ **c.** $f(2)$ **d.** $f(4)$

SOLUTION

a. $f(-3) = \dfrac{100}{1 + 9e^{-2(-3)}} \approx 0.0275$ **b.** $f(0) = \dfrac{100}{1 + 9e^{-2(0)}} = \dfrac{100}{10} = 10$

c. $f(2) = \dfrac{100}{1 + 9e^{-2(2)}} \approx 85.8$ **d.** $f(4) = \dfrac{100}{1 + 9e^{-2(4)}} \approx 99.7$

▶ **ACTIVITY**

Developing Concepts

Graphs of Logistic Growth Functions

① Use a graphing calculator to graph the logistic growth function from Example 1. Trace along the graph to determine the function's end behavior.

② Use a graphing calculator to graph each of the following. Then describe the basic shape of the graph of a logistic growth function.

  a. $y = \dfrac{1}{1 + e^{-x}}$ **b.** $y = \dfrac{10}{1 + 5e^{-2x}}$ **c.** $y = \dfrac{5}{1 + 10e^{-2x}}$

In this chapter you learned that an exponential growth function $f(x)$ increases without bound as x increases. On the other hand, the logistic growth function $y = \dfrac{c}{1 + ae^{-rx}}$ has $y = c$ as an upper bound.

Logistic growth functions are used to model real-life quantities whose growth levels off because the rate of growth changes—from an increasing growth rate to a decreasing growth rate.

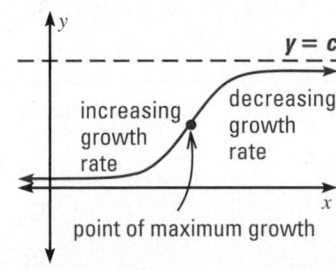

GRAPHS OF LOGISTIC GROWTH FUNCTIONS

The graph of $y = \dfrac{c}{1 + ae^{-rx}}$ has the following characteristics:

- The horizontal lines $y = 0$ and $y = c$ are asymptotes.
- The y-intercept is $\dfrac{c}{1 + a}$.
- The domain is all real numbers, and the range is $0 < y < c$.
- The graph is increasing from left to right. To the left of its point of maximum growth, $\left(\dfrac{\ln a}{r}, \dfrac{c}{2}\right)$, the rate of increase is increasing. To the right of its point of maximum growth, the rate of increase is decreasing.

EXAMPLE 2 *Graphing a Logistic Growth Function*

Graph $y = \dfrac{6}{1 + 2e^{-0.5x}}$.

SOLUTION

Begin by sketching the upper horizontal asymptote, $y = 6$. Then plot the y-intercept at $(0, 2)$ and the point of maximum growth $\left(\dfrac{\ln 2}{0.5}, \dfrac{6}{2}\right) \approx (1.4, 3)$. Finally, from left to right, draw a curve that starts just above the x-axis, curves up to the point of maximum growth, and then levels off as it approaches the upper horizontal asymptote.

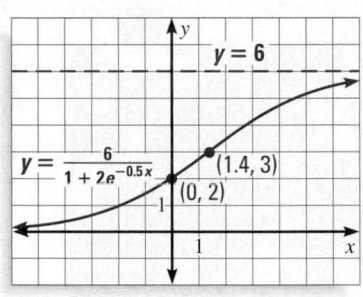

EXAMPLE 3 *Solving a Logistic Growth Equation*

Solve $\dfrac{50}{1 + 10e^{-3x}} = 40$.

SOLUTION

$$\dfrac{50}{1 + 10e^{-3x}} = 40 \qquad \textbf{Write original equation.}$$

$$50 = \left(1 + 10e^{-3x}\right)(40) \qquad \textbf{Multiply each side by } \mathbf{1 + 10e^{-3x}.}$$

$$50 = 40 + 400e^{-3x} \qquad \textbf{Use distributive property.}$$

$$10 = 400e^{-3x} \qquad \textbf{Subtract 40 from each side.}$$

$$0.025 = e^{-3x} \qquad \textbf{Divide each side by 400.}$$

$$\ln 0.025 = -3x \qquad \textbf{Take natural log of each side.}$$

$$-\dfrac{1}{3} \ln 0.025 = x \qquad \textbf{Divide each side by } \mathbf{-3.}$$

$$1.23 \approx x \qquad \textbf{Use a calculator.}$$

▶ The solution is about 1.23. Check this in the original equation.

Logistic growth functions are often more useful as models than exponential growth functions because they account for constraints placed on the growth. An example is a bacteria culture allowed to grow under initially ideal conditions, followed by less favorable conditions that inhibit growth.

EXAMPLE 4 *Using a Logistic Growth Model*

Biology

A colony of the bacteria *B. dendroides* is growing in a petri dish. The colony's area *A* (in square centimeters) can be modeled by

$$A = \frac{49.9}{1 + 134e^{-1.96t}}$$

where *t* is the elapsed time in days. Graph the function and describe what it tells you about the growth of the bacteria colony.

SOLUTION

The graph of the model is shown. The initial area is

$$A = \frac{49.9}{1 + 134e^{-1.96(0)}} \approx 0.37 \text{ cm}^2.$$

The colony grows more and more rapidly until

$$t = \frac{\ln 134}{1.96} \approx 2.5 \text{ days}.$$

Then the rate of growth decreases. The colony's area is limited to $A = 49.9 \text{ cm}^2$, which might possibly be the area of the petri dish.

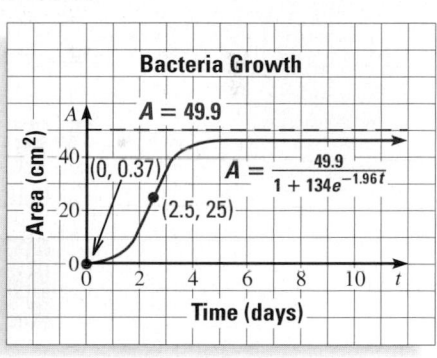

EXAMPLE 5 *Writing a Logistic Growth Model*

Botany

You planted a sunflower seedling and kept track of its height *h* (in centimeters) over time *t* (in weeks). Find a model that gives *h* as a function of *t*.

t	0	1	2	3	4	5	6	7	8	9	10
h	18	33	56	90	130	170	203	225	239	247	251

SOLUTION

A scatter plot shows that the data can be modeled by a logistic growth function.

The logistic regression feature of a graphing calculator returns the values shown at the right.

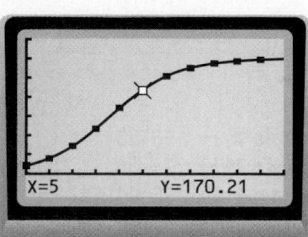

▶ The model is:

$$h = \frac{256}{1 + 13e^{-0.65t}}$$

STUDENT HELP

INTERNET
KEYSTROKE HELP
Visit our Web site
www.mcdougallittell.com
to see keystrokes for
several models of
calculators.

GUIDED PRACTICE

Vocabulary Check ✓

1. What is the name of a function having the form $y = \dfrac{c}{1 + ae^{-rx}}$ where c, a, and r are positive constants?

Concept Check ✓

2. What is a significant difference between using exponential growth functions and using logistic growth functions as models for real-life quantities?

3. What is the significance of the point $(\ln 3, 4)$ on the graph of $f(x) = \dfrac{8}{1 + 3e^{-x}}$?

Skill Check ✓

Evaluate the function $f(x) = \dfrac{12}{1 + 5e^{-2x}}$ for the given value of x.

4. $f(0)$ **5.** $f(-2)$ **6.** $f(5)$ **7.** $f\left(-\dfrac{1}{2}\right)$ **8.** $f(10)$

Graph the function. Identify the asymptotes, y-intercept, and point of maximum growth.

9. $f(x) = \dfrac{5}{1 + 4e^{-2.5x}}$ **10.** $f(x) = \dfrac{8}{1 + 3e^{-0.4x}}$ **11.** $f(x) = \dfrac{2}{1 + 4e^{-0.25x}}$

Solve the equation.

12. $\dfrac{18}{1 + 2e^{-2x}} = 10$ **13.** $\dfrac{30}{1 + 4e^{-x}} = 10$ **14.** $\dfrac{12.5}{1 + 7e^{-0.2x}} = 9$

15.  **PLANTING SEEDS** You planted a seedling and kept track of its height h (in centimeters) over time t (in weeks). Use the data in the table to find a model that gives h as a function of t.

t	0	1	2	3	4	5	6	7	8
h	5	12	26	39	51	88	94	103	112

PRACTICE AND APPLICATIONS

STUDENT HELP

→ **Extra Practice**
to help you master skills is on p. 952.

EVALUATING FUNCTIONS Evaluate the function $f(x) = \dfrac{7}{1 + 3e^{-x}}$ for the given value of x.

16. $f(1)$ **17.** $f(3)$ **18.** $f(-1)$ **19.** $f(-6)$

20. $f(0)$ **21.** $f\left(\dfrac{3}{4}\right)$ **22.** $f(2.2)$ **23.** $f(-0.9)$

MATCHING GRAPHS Match the function with its graph.

24. $f(x) = \dfrac{4}{1 + 2e^{-3x}}$ **25.** $f(x) = \dfrac{3}{1 + 2e^{-4x}}$ **26.** $f(x) = \dfrac{2}{1 + 3e^{-4x}}$

STUDENT HELP

→ **HOMEWORK HELP**
Example 1: Exs. 16–23
Example 2: Exs. 24–35
Example 3: Exs. 36–44
Example 4: Exs. 45–49
Example 5: Exs. 50, 51

A. 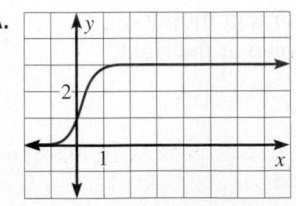   **B.** 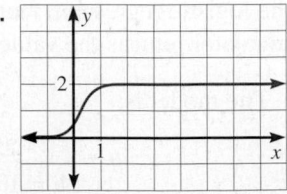   **C.**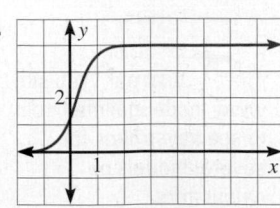

GRAPHING FUNCTIONS Graph the function. Identify the asymptotes, y-intercept, and point of maximum growth.

27. $y = \dfrac{1}{1 + 6e^{-x}}$

28. $y = \dfrac{2}{1 + 0.4e^{-0.3x}}$

29. $y = \dfrac{5}{1 + e^{-10x}}$

30. $y = \dfrac{4}{1 + 0.08e^{-2.1x}}$

31. $y = \dfrac{4}{1 + 3e^{-3x}}$

32. $y = \dfrac{3}{1 + 3e^{-8x}}$

33. $y = \dfrac{8}{1 + e^{-1.02x}}$

34. $y = \dfrac{10}{1 + 6e^{-0.5x}}$

35. $y = \dfrac{6}{1 + 0.8e^{-2x}}$

SOLVING EQUATIONS Solve the equation.

36. $\dfrac{8}{1 + 3e^{-x}} = 5$

37. $\dfrac{10}{1 + 2e^{-4x}} = 9$

38. $\dfrac{3}{1 + 18e^{-x}} = 1$

39. $\dfrac{28}{1 + 13e^{-2x}} = 20$

40. $\dfrac{82}{1 + 50e^{-x}} = 68$

41. $\dfrac{36}{1 + 7e^{-10x}} = 30$

42. $\dfrac{41}{1 + 14.9e^{-6x}} = 7$

43. $\dfrac{9}{1 + 5e^{-0.2x}} = \dfrac{3}{4}$

44. $\dfrac{40}{1 + 2.5e^{-0.4x}} = 6.4$

 **OWNING A VCR** In Exercises 45–47, use the following information.
The number of households in the United States that own VCRs has shown logistic growth from 1980 through 1999. The number H (in millions) of households can be modeled by the equation

$$H = \dfrac{91.86}{1 + 22.96e^{-0.4t}}$$

where t is the number of years since 1980. ▶ Source: Veronis, Suhler & Associates

45. In what year were there approximately 86 million households with VCRs?

46. Graph the model. In what year did the growth rate for the number of households stop increasing and start decreasing?

47. What is the long-term trend in VCR ownership?

 **ECONOMICS** In Exercises 48 and 49, use the following information.
The gross domestic product (GDP) of the United States has shown logistic growth from 1970 through 1992. The gross domestic product G (in billions of dollars) can be modeled by the equation

$$G = \dfrac{9200}{1 + 8.03e^{-0.121t}}$$

where t is the number of years since 1970. ▶ Source: U.S. Bureau of the Census

48. In what year was the GDP approximately $5000 billion?

49. Graph the model. When did the GDP reach its point of maximum growth?

YEAST POPULATION In Exercises 50 and 51, use the following information.
In biology class, you observed the biomass of a yeast population over a period of time. The table gives the yeast mass y (in grams) after t hours.

t	0	1	2	3	4	5	6	7	8	9
y	9.6	18.3	29.0	47.2	71.1	119.1	174.6	257.3	350.7	441.0

50. Draw a scatter plot of the data.

51. Find a model that gives y as a function of t using the logistic regression feature of a graphing calculator.

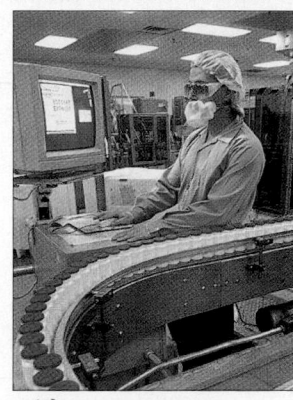

52. 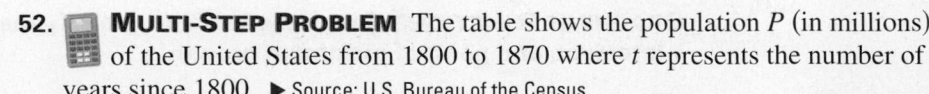 **MULTI-STEP PROBLEM** The table shows the population P (in millions) of the United States from 1800 to 1870 where t represents the number of years since 1800. ▶ Source: U.S. Bureau of the Census

a. Use a graphing calculator to find an exponential growth model and a logistic growth model for the data. Then graph both models.

b. Use the models from part (a) to find the year when the population was about 92 million. Which of the models gives a year that is closer to 1910, the correct answer? Explain why you think that model is more accurate.

c. Use each model to predict the population in 2010. Which model gives a population closer to 297.7 million, the predicted population from the U.S. Bureau of the Census?

t	P
0	5.3
10	7.2
20	9.6
30	12.9
40	17.0
50	23.2
60	31.4
70	39.8

★ **Challenge**

53. ANALYZING MODELS The graph of a logistic growth function

$$y = \frac{c}{1 + ae^{-rx}}$$ reaches its point of maximum growth where $y = \frac{c}{2}$.

Show that the x-coordinate of this point is $x = \frac{\ln a}{r}$.

MIXED REVIEW

WRITING EQUATIONS The variables x and y vary directly. Write an equation that relates the variables. (Review 2.4 for 9.1)

54. $x = 4, y = 36$ **55.** $x = -5, y = 10$ **56.** $x = 2, y = 13$

57. $x = 40, y = 5$ **58.** $x = 0.1, y = 0.9$ **59.** $x = 1, y = 0.2$

WRITING EQUATIONS Write y as a function of x. (Review 8.7)

60. $\log y = 0.9 \log x + 2.11$ **61.** $\ln y = 0.94 - 2.44x$

62. $\log y = -1.82 + 0.4x$ **63.** $\log y = -0.75 \log x - 1.76$

QUIZ 3

Self-Test for Lessons 8.7 and 8.8

Write an exponential function of the form $y = ab^x$ whose graph passes through the given points. (Lesson 8.7)

1. (2, 3), (5, 12)   **2.** (1, 16), (3, 45)   **3.** (5, 9), (8, 35)

Write a power function of the form $y = ax^b$ whose graph passes through the given points. (Lesson 8.7)

4. (2, 28), (8, 192)   **5.** (1, 0.5), (6, 48)   **6.** (5, 40), (2, 6)

7. 🌐 **FLU VIRUS** The spread of a virus through a student population can be modeled by $S = \dfrac{5000}{1 + 4999e^{-0.8t}}$ where S is the total number of students infected after t days. Graph the model and tell when the point of maximum growth in infections is reached. (Lesson 8.8)

Chapter Summary

What did you learn?

Graph exponential functions.
- exponential growth functions **(8.1)**
- exponential decay functions **(8.2)**
- natural base functions **(8.3)**

Evaluate and simplify expressions.
- exponential expressions with base e **(8.3)**
- logarithmic expressions **(8.4)**

Graph logarithmic functions. **(8.4)**

Use properties of logarithms. **(8.5)**

Solve exponential and logarithmic equations. **(8.6)**

Model data with exponential and power functions. **(8.7)**

Evaluate and graph logistic growth functions. **(8.8)**

Use exponential, logarithmic, and logistic growth functions to model real-life situations. **(8.1–8.8)**

Why did you learn it?

Estimate wind energy generated by turbines. **(p. 470)**
Find the depreciated value of a car. **(p. 476)**
Find the number of endangered species. **(p. 482)**

Find air pressure on Mount Everest. **(p. 484)**
Approximate distance traveled by a tornado. **(p. 491)**

Estimate the average diameter of sand particles for a beach with given slope. **(p. 489)**

Compare loudness of sounds. **(p. 495)**

Use Newton's law of cooling. **(p. 502)**

Model the number of U.S. stamps issued. **(p. 515)**

Model the height of a sunflower. **(p. 519)**

Model a telescope's limiting magnitude. **(p. 507)**

How does Chapter 8 fit into the BIGGER PICTURE of algebra?

In Chapter 2 you began your study of functions and learned that quantities that increase by the same *amount* over equal periods of time are modeled by linear functions. In Chapter 8 you saw that quantities that increase by the same *percent* over equal periods of time are modeled by exponential functions.

Exponential functions and logarithmic functions are two important "families" of functions. They model many real-life situations, and they are used in advanced mathematics topics such as calculus and probability.

STUDY STRATEGY

How did you study with a group?

Here is an example of a summary prepared for Lesson 8.4 and presented to the group, following the **Study Strategy** on page 464.

Study Group

Lesson 8.4 Summary

Definition of logarithm: $\log_b y = x$ if and only if $b^x = y$

Common logarithm (base 10): $\log_{10} x = \log x$

Natural logarithm (base e): $\log_e x = \ln x$

Inverse functions: $f(x) = b^x$ (exponential) and
$g(x) = \log_b x$ (logarithmic)

Graph of logarithmic function $f(x) = \log_b (x - h) + k$:
asymptote $x = h$; domain $x > h$; range all real
numbers; up $b > 0$; down $0 < b < 1$

- exponential function, p. 465
- base of an exponential function, p. 465
- asymptote, p. 465
- exponential growth function, p. 466
- growth factor, p. 467

- exponential decay function, p. 474
- decay factor, p. 476
- natural base e, or Euler number, p. 480
- logarithm of y with base b, p. 486

- common logarithm, p. 487
- natural logarithm, p. 487
- change-of-base formula, p. 494
- logistic growth function, p. 517

8.1   **EXPONENTIAL GROWTH**

Examples on pp. 465–468

> **EXAMPLE** An exponential growth function has the form $y = ab^x$ with $a > 0$ and $b > 1$.
>
> To graph $y = 2 \cdot 5^{x+2} - 4$, first lightly sketch the graph of $y = 2 \cdot 5^x$, which passes through $(0, 2)$ and $(1, 10)$. Then translate the graph 2 units to the left and 4 units down. The graph passes through $(-2, -2)$ and $(-1, 6)$. The asymptote is the line $y = -4$. The domain is all real numbers, and the range is $y > -4$.

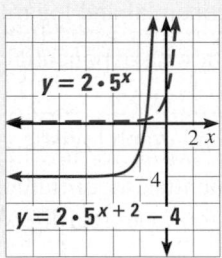

Graph the function. State the domain and range.

1. $y = -2^x + 4$ **2.** $y = 3 \cdot 2^x$ **3.** $y = 5 \cdot 3^{x-2}$ **4.** $y = 4^{x+3} - 1$

8.2   **EXPONENTIAL DECAY**

Examples on pp. 474–476

> **EXAMPLE** An exponential decay function has the form $y = ab^x$ with $a > 0$ and $0 < b < 1$.
>
> To graph $y = 4\left(\frac{1}{3}\right)^x$, plot $(0, 4)$ and $\left(1, \frac{4}{3}\right)$. From *right* to *left* draw a curve that begins just above the x-axis, passes through the two points, and moves up. The asymptote is the line $y = 0$. The domain is all real numbers, and the range is $y > 0$.

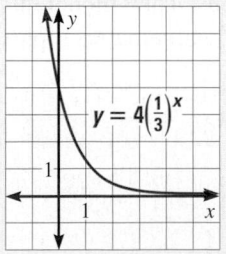

Tell whether the function represents *exponential growth* or *exponential decay*.

5. $f(x) = 5\left(\frac{3}{4}\right)^x$ **6.** $f(x) = 2\left(\frac{5}{4}\right)^x$ **7.** $f(x) = 3(6)^{-x}$ **8.** $f(x) = 4(3)^x$

Graph the function. State the domain and range.

9. $y = \left(\frac{1}{4}\right)^x$ **10.** $y = 2\left(\frac{3}{5}\right)^{x-1}$ **11.** $y = \left(\frac{1}{2}\right)^x - 5$ **12.** $y = -3\left(\frac{3}{4}\right)^x + 2$

QUANTITATIVE COMPARISON In Exercises 11 and 12, choose the statement that is true about the given quantities.

    Ⓐ The quantity in column A is greater.

    Ⓑ The quantity in column B is greater.

    Ⓒ The two quantities are equal.

    Ⓓ The relationship cannot be determined from the given information.

	Column A	Column B
11.	$\log 10{,}000$	$\ln e^4$
12.	$\log_2 4$	$\log_4 2$

13. **MULTI-STEP PROBLEM** You are considering two job offers. The first offer is a salary of $32,000 with a $550 annual raise. The other offer is a salary of $29,500 with a 4% annual raise.

   a. Write a linear model for the total salary with the first offer as a function of the number t of years.

   b. Write an exponential model for the total salary with the other offer as a function of the number t of years.

   c. Graph the functions in the same coordinate plane with domain $0 \le t \le 8$. Find the point of intersection of the two graphs and tell what it represents.

   d. *Writing* Explain the difference in the salaries over time.

14. **MULTI-STEP PROBLEM** The table gives the weight w (in pounds) of an average girl for the first five years of life where t is her age in months. ▶ Source: *Your Baby & Child*

t	2	4	6	8	10	12	24	36	48	60
w	10.5	13.5	16.0	18.5	20.0	21.5	27.5	31.5	35.5	39.0

   a. Draw a scatter plot of $\ln w$ versus t.

   b. Draw a scatter plot of $\ln w$ versus $\ln t$.

   c. Analyze your scatter plots and decide whether an exponential model or a power model is a better fit for the original data. Explain your choice.

   d. Using your answer from part (c), find a model for the data. Check your model by using the regression feature of a graphing calculator.

   e. Use your model to estimate a girl's weight at $1\frac{1}{2}$, $2\frac{1}{2}$, $3\frac{1}{2}$, and $4\frac{1}{2}$ years old.

15. **MULTI-STEP PROBLEM** Use the function $f(x) = \dfrac{5}{1 + 9e^{-x}}$.

   a. Find $f(-1)$, $f(0)$, and $f(2)$.

   b. Sketch a graph of the function.

   c. Identify the asymptotes, y-intercept, and point of maximum growth.

   d. Write and solve an equation to find the value of x when $f(x)$ equals 4. Label this point on your graph.

   e. *Writing* Describe how the growth represented by this function changes over time.

RATIONAL EQUATIONS AND FUNCTIONS

▶ *How does volume and surface area affect a skydiver's falling speed?*

APPLICATION: Skydiving

How fast a skydiver falls depends on both the volume and the cross-sectional surface area of the skydiver. Different falling positions result in different ratios of volume to cross-sectional surface area: the larger the ratio, the greater the skydiver's falling speed.

Think & Discuss

The table below gives the volume and cross-sectional surface area for a 70 inch tall skydiver in each of three different positions.

Position	Volume (in.^{3})	Cross-sectional surface area (in.^{2})
Face-to-Earth	13,000	1300
Sitting	13,000	800
Headfirst	13,000	350

1. Find the ratio of volume to cross-sectional surface area for the skydiver in each of the three positions.

2. In which position will the skydiver have the greatest falling speed? Explain.

Learn More About It

You will use a geometric model to write a rational expression for the ratio of a skydiver's volume to his or her cross-sectional surface area in Example 8 on p. 557 and in Ex. 15 on p. 558.

 APPLICATION LINK Visit www.mcdougallittell.com for more information on skydiving.

Study Guide

PREVIEW

What's the chapter about?

Chapter 9 is about **rational expressions, functions, and equations**. In Chapter 9 you'll learn

- how to simplify and perform operations with rational expressions.
- how to graph rational functions and solve rational equations.
- how to use variation models and rational models in real-life situations.

KEY VOCABULARY

▶ **Review**
- rational numbers, p. 3
- *x*-intercept, p. 84
- direct variation, p. 94
- zero of a function, p. 259

- degree of a polynomial function, p. 329
- asymptote, p. 465

▶ **New**
- inverse variation, p. 534
- joint variation, p. 536

- rational function, p. 540
- hyperbola, p. 540
- simplified form of a rational expression, p. 554
- complex fraction, p. 564

PREPARE

Are you ready for the chapter?

SKILL REVIEW Do these exercises to review key skills that you'll apply in this chapter. See the given **reference page** if there is something you don't understand.

STUDENT HELP

▶ **Study Tip**
"Student Help" boxes throughout the chapter give you study tips and tell you where to look for extra help in this book and on the Internet.

The variables *x* and *y* vary directly. Write an equation that relates the variables.
(Review Example 6, p. 94)

1. $x = 2, y = 5$ **2.** $x = 1, y = 0.1$ **3.** $x = 8, y = -2$ **4.** $x = -3, y = 12$

Multiply the polynomials. (Review Example 5, p. 13; Example 4, p. 339)

5. $5(3x - 1)$ **6.** $(x - 1)(x + 4)^2$ **7.** $-x(x^2 - 5)$ **8.** $x(x - 1)(x + 8)$

Factor the polynomial. (Review Examples 1–4, pp. 256 and 257; Examples 1–3, p. 346)

9. $x^2 - 6x + 9$ **10.** $4x^3 - 4$ **11.** $8x^3 - 162x$ **12.** $6x^2 + 7x - 5$

Find all the real zeros of the function. (Review Example 7, p. 259; Example 4, p. 354; Example 1, p. 359)

13. $y = x^2 + 2x$ **14.** $y = x^2 + 2x - 15$ **15.** $y = x^3 - 2x^2 - 7x - 4$

STUDY STRATEGY

Here's a study strategy!

Dictionary of Functions

Make a dictionary of all the types of functions you have learned in this course. For each entry, include the general form of the function and an example of the function and its graph. Continue to add entries as you work through this chapter. Use your dictionary as a study and reference tool.

⊙ ACTIVITY 9.1

Developing Concepts

GROUP ACTIVITY
Work with a partner.

MATERIALS
• tape measure or meter stick
• centimeter ruler
• masking tape

Investigating Inverse Variation

▶ **QUESTION** What is the relationship between the distance you are standing from your partner and the apparent height of your partner?

▶ **EXPLORING THE CONCEPT**

1 Have your partner stand with his or her back against a wall. Place the end of a tape measure against the wall and between your partner's feet. Use masking tape to mark off distances of 3 meters, 4 meters, . . . , 9 meters from the wall.

2 Stand facing your partner, with your toes just touching the 3 meter mark. Hold a centimeter ruler at arm's length and line up the "0" end of the ruler with the top of your partner's head. Measure (to the nearest centimeter) the apparent height of your partner at this distance.

3 Repeat **Step 2** for each of the marked distances and record your results in a table like the one shown.

Distance (m)	3	4	5	6	7	8	9
Apparent height (cm)	?	?	?	?	?	?	?

▶ **DRAWING CONCLUSIONS**

1. Does apparent height vary directly with distance? Justify your answer mathematically.

2. Multiply the paired values of distance and apparent height together. What do you notice?

3. Based on your results from Exercise 2, write an equation relating distance and apparent height.

4. Use your equation from Exercise 3 to predict your partner's apparent height at a distance not listed in your table. Test your prediction by standing that distance from your partner and measuring his or her apparent height. How close was your prediction?

9.1

Inverse and Joint Variation

What you should learn

GOAL 1 Write and use
inverse variation models, as
applied in **Example 4**.

GOAL 2 Write and use joint
variation models, as applied
in **Example 6**.

Why you should learn it

▼ To solve **real-life**
problems, such as finding the
speed of a whirlpool's current
in **Example 3**.

In Lesson 2.4 you learned that two variables x and y show direct variation if $y = kx$ for some nonzero constant k. Another type of variation is called *inverse variation*. Two variables x and y show **inverse variation** if they are related as follows:

$$y = \frac{k}{x}, \; k \neq 0$$

The nonzero constant k is called the **constant of variation**, and y is said to *vary inversely* with x.

EXAMPLE 1 *Classifying Direct and Inverse Variation*

Tell whether x and y show *direct variation*, *inverse variation*, or *neither*.

GIVEN EQUATION	REWRITTEN EQUATION	TYPE OF VARIATION
a. $\frac{y}{5} = x$	$y = 5x$	Direct
b. $y = x + 2$		Neither
c. $xy = 4$	$y = \frac{4}{x}$	Inverse

EXAMPLE 2 *Writing an Inverse Variation Equation*

The variables x and y vary inversely, and $y = 8$ when $x = 3$.

  a. Write an equation that relates x and y.

  b. Find y when $x = -4$.

SOLUTION

  a. Use the given values of x and y to find the constant of variation.

$$y = \frac{k}{x} \qquad \text{Write general equation for inverse variation.}$$

$$8 = \frac{k}{3} \qquad \text{Substitute 8 for } y \text{ and 3 for } x.$$

$$24 = k \qquad \text{Solve for } k.$$

  ▶ The inverse variation equation is $y = \dfrac{24}{x}$.

  b. When $x = -4$, the value of y is:

$$y = \frac{24}{-4}$$

$$= -6$$

EXAMPLE 3 *Writing an Inverse Variation Model*

Oceanography

The speed of the current in a whirlpool varies inversely with the distance from the whirlpool's center. The Lofoten Maelstrom is a whirlpool located off the coast of Norway. At a distance of 3 kilometers (3000 meters) from the center, the speed of the current is about 0.1 meter per second. Describe the change in the speed of the current as you move closer to the whirlpool's center.

SOLUTION

First write an inverse variation model relating distance from center d and speed s.

$$s = \frac{k}{d}$$ **Model for inverse variation**

$$0.1 = \frac{k}{3000}$$ **Substitute 0.1 for s and 3000 for d.**

$$300 = k$$ **Solve for k.**

The model is $s = \frac{300}{d}$. The table shows some speeds for different values of d.

Distance from center (meters), d	2000	1500	500	250	50
Speed (meters per second), s	0.15	0.2	0.6	1.2	6

▶ From the table you can see that the speed of the current increases as you move closer to the whirlpool's center.

· · · · · · · · · ·

The equation for inverse variation can be rewritten as $xy = k$. This tells you that a set of data pairs (x, y) shows inverse variation if the products xy are constant or approximately constant.

EXAMPLE 4 *Checking Data for Inverse Variation*

BIOLOGY CONNECTION The table compares the wing flapping rate r (in beats per second) to the wing length l (in centimeters) for several birds. Do these data show inverse variation? If so, find a model for the relationship between r and l.

Bird	r (beats per second)	l (cm)
Carrion crow	3.6	32.5
Common scoter	5.0	23.5
Great crested grebe	6.3	18.7
Curlew	4.0	29.2
Lesser black-backed gull	2.8	42.2

▶ Source: *Smithsonian Miscellaneous Collections*

**COMMON
SCOTER** The common scoter migrates from the Quebec/Labrador border in Canada to coastal cities such as Portland, Maine, and Galveston, Texas. To reach its winter destination, the scoter will travel up to 2150 miles.

SOLUTION

Each product rl is approximately equal to 117. For instance, $(3.6)(32.5) = 117$ and $(5.0)(23.5) = 117.5$. So, the data do show inverse variation. A model for the relationship between wing flapping rate and wing length is $r = \frac{117}{l}$.

GOAL 2 USING JOINT VARIATION

STUDENT HELP

▶ **Look Back**
For help with direct variation, see p. 94.

Joint variation occurs when a quantity varies directly as the product of *two or more* other quantities. For instance, if $z = kxy$ where $k \neq 0$, then z varies jointly with x and y. Other types of variation are also possible, as illustrated in the following example.

EXAMPLE 5 *Comparing Different Types of Variation*

Write an equation for the given relationship.

RELATIONSHIP	EQUATION
a. y varies directly with x.	$y = kx$
b. y varies inversely with x.	$y = \dfrac{k}{x}$
c. z varies jointly with x and y.	$z = kxy$
d. y varies inversely with the square of x.	$y = \dfrac{k}{x^2}$
e. z varies directly with y and inversely with x.	$z = \dfrac{ky}{x}$

EXAMPLE 6 *Writing a Variation Model*

SCIENCE CONNECTION The *law of universal gravitation* states that the gravitational force F (in newtons) between two objects varies jointly with their masses m_1 and m_2 (in kilograms) and inversely with the square of the distance d (in meters) between the two objects. The constant of variation is denoted by G and is called the *universal gravitational constant*.

a. Write an equation for the law of universal gravitation.

b. Estimate the universal gravitational constant. Use the Earth and sun facts given at the right.

> Mass of Earth:
> $m_1 = 5.98 \times 10^{24}$ kg
>
> Mass of sun:
> $m_2 = 1.99 \times 10^{30}$ kg
>
> Mean distance between Earth and sun:
> $d = 1.50 \times 10^{11}$ m
>
> Force between Earth and sun:
> $F = 3.53 \times 10^{22}$ N

SOLUTION

a. $F = \dfrac{Gm_1 m_2}{d^2}$

b. Substitute the given values and solve for G.

$$F = \frac{Gm_1 m_2}{d^2}$$

$$3.53 \times 10^{22} = \frac{G(5.98 \times 10^{24})(1.99 \times 10^{30})}{(1.50 \times 10^{11})^2}$$

$$3.53 \times 10^{22} \approx G(5.29 \times 10^{32})$$

$$6.67 \times 10^{-11} \approx G$$

▶ The universal gravitational constant is about $6.67 \times 10^{-11} \dfrac{\text{N} \cdot \text{m}^2}{\text{kg}^2}$.

FOCUS ON
APPLICATIONS

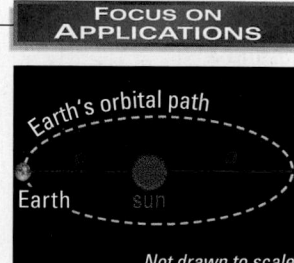

Earth's orbital path

Earth   sun

Not drawn to scale

EARTH AND SUN
Earth's orbit around the sun is elliptical, so its distance from the sun varies. The shortest distance p is 1.47×10^{11} meters and the longest distance a is 1.52×10^{11} meters.

APPLICATION LINK
www.mcdougallittell.com

GUIDED PRACTICE

Vocabulary Check ✔

1. Complete this statement: If w varies directly as the product of x, y, and z, then w varies _?_ with x, y, and z.

Concept Check ✔

2. How can you tell whether a set of data pairs (x, y) shows inverse variation?

3. Suppose z varies jointly with x and y. What can you say about $\frac{z}{xy}$?

Skill Check ✔

Tell whether x and y show *direct variation, inverse variation,* or *neither.*

4. $xy = \frac{1}{4}$

5. $\frac{x}{y} = 5$

6. $y = x - 3$

7. $x = \frac{7}{y}$

8. $\frac{y}{x} = 12$

9. $\frac{1}{2}xy = 9$

10. $y = \frac{1}{x}$

11. $2x + y = 4$

Tell whether x varies jointly with y and z.

12. $x = 15yz$

13. $\frac{x}{z} = 0.5y$

14. $xy = 4z$

15. $x = \frac{yz}{2}$

16. $x = \frac{3z}{y}$

17. $2yz = 7x$

18. $\frac{x}{y} = 17z$

19. $5x = 4yz$

20. 🌐 **TOOLS** The force F needed to loosen a bolt with a wrench varies inversely with the length l of the handle. Write an equation relating F and l, given that 250 pounds of force must be exerted to loosen a bolt when using a wrench with a handle 6 inches long. How much force must be exerted when using a wrench with a handle 24 inches long?

PRACTICE AND APPLICATIONS

STUDENT HELP

▶ **Extra Practice**
to help you master
skills is on p. 952.

DETERMINING VARIATION Tell whether x and y show *direct variation, inverse variation,* or *neither.*

21. $xy = 10$

22. $xy = \frac{1}{10}$

23. $y = x - 1$

24. $\frac{y}{9} = x$

25. $x = \frac{5}{y}$

26. $3x = y$

27. $x = 5y$

28. $x + y = 2.5$

INVERSE VARIATION MODELS The variables x and y vary inversely. Use the given values to write an equation relating x and y. Then find y when $x = 2$.

29. $x = 5, y = -2$

30. $x = 4, y = 8$

31. $x = 7, y = 1$

32. $x = \frac{1}{2}, y = 10$

33. $x = -\frac{2}{3}, y = 6$

34. $x = \frac{3}{4}, y = \frac{3}{8}$

STUDENT HELP

▶ **HOMEWORK HELP**
Example 1: Exs. 21–28
Example 2: Exs. 29–34
Example 3: Exs. 51–54
Example 4: Exs. 35–38,
            48, 49
Example 5: Exs. 45–47
Example 6: Exs. 55–58

INTERPRETING DATA Determine whether x and y show *direct variation, inverse variation,* or *neither.*

35.

x	y
1.5	20
2.5	12
4	7.5
5	6

36.

x	y
31	217
20	140
17	119
12	84

37.

x	y
3	36
7	105
5	50
16	48

38.

x	y
4	16
5	12.8
1.6	40
20	3.2

JOINT VARIATION MODELS The variable *z* varies jointly with *x* and *y*. Use the given values to write an equation relating *x*, *y*, and *z*. Then find *z* when $x = -4$ and $y = 7$.

39. $x = 3, y = 8, z = 6$

40. $x = -12, y = 4, z = 2$

41. $x = 1, y = \frac{1}{3}, z = 5$

42. $x = -6, y = 3, z = \frac{2}{5}$

43. $x = \frac{5}{6}, y = \frac{3}{10}, z = 8$

44. $x = \frac{3}{8}, y = \frac{16}{17}, z = \frac{3}{2}$

STUDENT HELP

HOMEWORK HELP
Visit our Web site
www.mcdougallittell.com
for help with Exs. 45–47.

WRITING EQUATIONS Write an equation for the given relationship.

45. *x* varies inversely with *y* and directly with *z*.

46. *y* varies jointly with *z* and the square root of *x*.

47. *w* varies inversely with *x* and jointly with *y* and *z*.

HOME REPAIR In Exercises 48–50, use the following information.
On some tubes of caulking, the diameter of the circular nozzle opening can be adjusted to produce lines of varying thickness. The table shows the length *l* of caulking obtained from a tube when the nozzle opening has diameter *d* and cross-sectional area *A*.

d (in.)	*A* (in.²)	*l* (in.)
$\frac{1}{8}$	$\frac{\pi}{256}$	1440
$\frac{1}{4}$	$\frac{\pi}{64}$	360
$\frac{3}{8}$	$\frac{9\pi}{256}$	160
$\frac{1}{2}$	$\frac{\pi}{16}$	90

48. Determine whether *l* varies inversely with *d*. If so, write an equation relating *l* and *d*.

49. Determine whether *l* varies inversely with *A*. If so, write an equation relating *l* and *A*.

50. Find the length of caulking you get from a tube whose nozzle opening has a diameter of $\frac{3}{4}$ inch.

ASTRONOMY In Exercises 51–53, use the following information.
A star's diameter *D* (as a multiple of the sun's diameter) varies directly with the square root of the star's luminosity *L* (as a multiple of the sun's luminosity) and inversely with the square of the star's temperature *T* (in kelvins).

51. Write an equation relating *D*, *L*, *T*, and a constant *k*.

52. The luminosity of Polaris is 10,000 times the luminosity of the sun. The surface temperature of Polaris is about 5800 kelvins. Using $k = 33,640,000$, find how the diameter of Polaris compares with the diameter of the sun.

53. The sun's diameter is 1,390,000 kilometers. What is the diameter of Polaris?

54. **INTENSITY OF SOUND** The intensity *I* of a sound (in watts per square meter) varies inversely with the square of the distance *d* (in meters) from the sound's source. At a distance of 1 meter from the stage, the intensity of the sound at a rock concert is about 10 watts per square meter. Write an equation relating *I* and *d*. If you are sitting 15 meters back from the stage, what is the intensity of the sound you hear?

55. SCIENCE ▸ CONNECTION   The work *W* (in joules) done when lifting an object varies jointly with the mass *m* (in kilograms) of the object and the height *h* (in meters) that the object is lifted. The work done when a 120 kilogram object is lifted 1.8 meters is 2116.8 joules. Write an equation that relates *W*, *m*, and *h*. How much work is done when lifting a 100 kilogram object 1.5 meters?

HEAT LOSS In Exercises 56 and 57, use the following information.
The heat loss h (in watts) through a single-pane glass window varies jointly with the window's area A (in square meters) and the difference between the inside and outside temperatures d (in kelvins).

56. Write an equation relating h, A, d, and a constant k.

57. A single-pane window with an area of 1 square meter and a temperature difference of 1 kelvin has a heat loss of 5.7 watts. What is the heat loss through a single-pane window with an area of 2.5 square meters and a temperature difference of 20 kelvins?

58. **GEOMETRY** ▶ **CONNECTION** The area of a trapezoid varies jointly with the height and the sum of the lengths of the bases. When the sum of the lengths of the bases is 18 inches and the height is 4 inches, the area is 36 square inches. Find a formula for the area of a trapezoid.

Test Preparation

59. **MULTI-STEP PROBLEM** The load P (in pounds) that can be safely supported by a horizontal beam varies jointly with the width W (in feet) of the beam and the square of its depth D (in feet), and inversely with its length L (in feet).

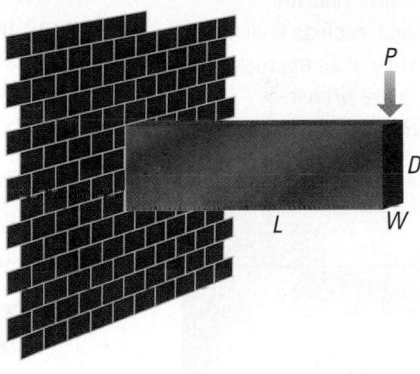

a. How does P change when the width and length of the beam are doubled?

b. How does P change when the width and depth of the beam are doubled?

c. How does P change when all three dimensions are doubled?

d. *Writing* Describe several ways a beam can be modified if the safe load it is required to support is increased by a factor of 4.

★ **Challenge**

60. **LOGICAL REASONING** Suppose x varies inversely with y and y varies inversely with z. How does x vary with z? Justify your answer algebraically.

MIXED REVIEW

SQUARE ROOT FUNCTIONS Graph the function. Then state the domain and range. **(Review 7.5 for 9.2)**

61. $y = \sqrt{x + 2}$ **62.** $y = \sqrt{x} - 4$ **63.** $y = \sqrt{x + 1} - 3$

SOLVING RADICAL EQUATIONS Solve the equation. Check for extraneous solutions. **(Review 7.6)**

64. $\sqrt{x} = 22$ **65.** $\sqrt[4]{2x} + 2 = 6$ **66.** $x^{1/3} - 7 = 0$

67. $\sqrt[3]{x + 12} = 5$ **68.** $(x - 2)^{3/2} = -8$ **69.** $\sqrt{3x + 1} = \sqrt{x + 15}$

70. **COLLEGE ADMISSION** The number of admission applications received by a college was 1152 in 1990 and increased 5% per year until 1998. **(Review 8.1 for 9.2)**

a. Write a model giving the number A of applications t years after 1990.

b. Graph the model. Use the graph to estimate the year in which there were 1400 applications.

9.2 Graphing Simple Rational Functions

What you should learn

GOAL 1 Graph simple rational functions.

GOAL 2 Use the graph of a rational function to solve **real-life** problems, such as finding the average cost per calendar in **Example 3**.

Why you should learn it

▼ To solve **real-life** problems, such as finding the frequency of an approaching ambulance siren in **Exs. 47 and 48**.

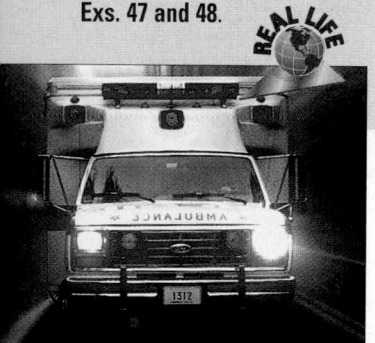

GOAL 1 GRAPHING A SIMPLE RATIONAL FUNCTION

A **rational function** is a function of the form

$$f(x) = \frac{p(x)}{q(x)}$$

where $p(x)$ and $q(x)$ are polynomials and $q(x) \neq 0$. In this lesson you will learn to graph rational functions for which $p(x)$ and $q(x)$ are linear. For instance, consider the following rational function:

$$y = \frac{1}{x}$$

The graph of this function is called a **hyperbola** and is shown below. Notice the following properties.

• The x-axis is a horizontal asymptote.

• The y-axis is a vertical asymptote.

• The domain and range are all nonzero real numbers.

• The graph has two symmetrical parts called **branches**. For each point (x, y) on one branch, there is a corresponding point $(-x, -y)$ on the other branch.

x	y
-4	$-\frac{1}{4}$
-3	$-\frac{1}{3}$
-2	$-\frac{1}{2}$
-1	-1
$-\frac{1}{2}$	-2

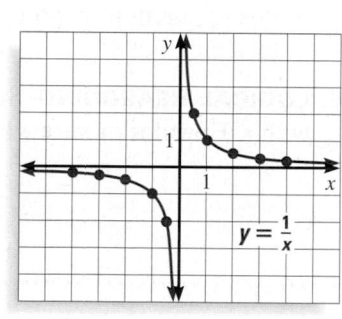

x	y
4	$\frac{1}{4}$
3	$\frac{1}{3}$
2	$\frac{1}{2}$
1	1
$\frac{1}{2}$	2

● ACTIVITY

Developing Concepts

Investigating Graphs of Rational Functions

1 Graph each function.

   a. $y = \frac{2}{x}$ **b.** $y = \frac{3}{x}$ **c.** $y = \frac{-1}{x}$ **d.** $y = \frac{-2}{x}$

2 Use the graphs to describe how the sign of a affects the graph of $y = \frac{a}{x}$.

3 Use the graphs to describe how $|a|$ affects the graph of $y = \frac{a}{x}$.

All rational functions of the form $y = \dfrac{a}{x - h} + k$ have graphs that are hyperbolas with asymptotes at $x = h$ and $y = k$. To draw the graph, plot a couple of points on each side of the vertical asymptote. Then draw the two branches of the hyperbola that approach the asymptotes and pass through the plotted points.

EXAMPLE 1 *Graphing a Rational Function*

Graph $y = \dfrac{-2}{x + 3} - 1$. State the domain and range.

STUDENT HELP

▶ **Look Back**
For help with asymptotes, see p. 465.

SOLUTION

Draw the asymptotes $x = -3$ and $y = -1$.

Plot two points to the left of the vertical asymptote, such as $(-4, 1)$ and $(-5, 0)$, and two points to the right, such as $(-1, -2)$ and $\left(0, -\dfrac{5}{3}\right)$.

Use the asymptotes and plotted points to draw the branches of the hyperbola.

The domain is all real numbers except -3, and the range is all real numbers except -1.

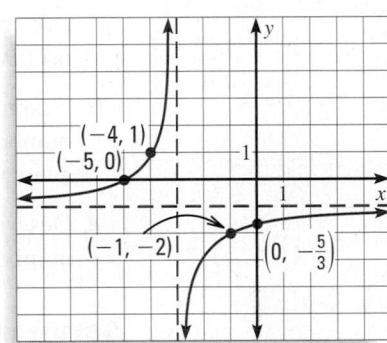

· · · · · · · · · ·

All rational functions of the form $y = \dfrac{ax + b}{cx + d}$ also have graphs that are hyperbolas. The vertical asymptote occurs at the x-value that makes the denominator zero. The horizontal asymptote is the line $y = \dfrac{a}{c}$.

EXAMPLE 2 *Graphing a Rational Function*

Graph $y = \dfrac{x + 1}{2x - 4}$. State the domain and range.

STUDENT HELP

HOMEWORK HELP
Visit our Web site
www.mcdougallittell.com
for extra examples.

SOLUTION

Draw the asymptotes. Solve $2x - 4 = 0$ for x to find the vertical asymptote $x = 2$. The horizontal asymptote is the line $y = \dfrac{a}{c} = \dfrac{1}{2}$.

Plot two points to the left of the vertical asymptote, such as $\left(0, -\dfrac{1}{4}\right)$ and $(1, -1)$, and two points to the right, such as $(3, 2)$ and $\left(4, \dfrac{5}{4}\right)$.

Use the asymptotes and plotted points to draw the branches of the hyperbola.

The domain is all real numbers except 2, and the range is all real numbers except $\dfrac{1}{2}$.

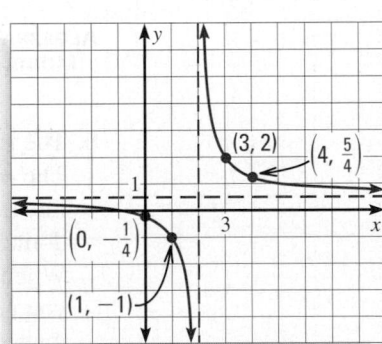

REAL LIFE
Business

EXAMPLE 3 *Writing a Rational Model*

For a fundraising project, your math club is publishing a fractal art calendar. The cost of the digital images and the permission to use them is $850. In addition to these "one-time" charges, the *unit cost* of printing each calendar is $3.25.

January

S	M	T	W	T	F	S
		1	2	3	4	5
6	7	8	9	10	11	12
13	14	15	16	17	18	19
20	21	22	23	24	25	26
27	28	29	30	31		

  a. Write a model that gives the average cost per calendar as a function of the number of calendars printed.

  b. Graph the model and use the graph to estimate the number of calendars you need to print before the average cost drops to $5 per calendar.

  c. Describe what happens to the average cost as the number of calendars printed increases.

SOLUTION

  a. The average cost is the total cost of making the calendars divided by the number of calendars printed.

PROBLEM SOLVING STRATEGY

VERBAL MODEL

$$\boxed{\text{Average cost}} = \frac{\boxed{\text{One-time charges}} + \boxed{\text{Unit cost}} \cdot \boxed{\text{Number printed}}}{\boxed{\text{Number printed}}}$$

LABELS

Average cost = A (dollars per calendar)

One-time charges = **850**   (dollars)

Unit cost = **3.25**   (dollars per calendar)

Number printed = x (calendars)

ALGEBRAIC MODEL

$$A = \frac{850 + 3.25\,x}{x}$$

  b. The graph of the model is shown at the right. The *A*-axis is the vertical asymptote and the line $A = 3.25$ is the horizontal asymptote. The domain is $x > 0$ and the range is $A > 3.25$. When $A = 5$ the value of x is about 500. So, you need to print about 500 calendars before the average cost drops to $5 per calendar.

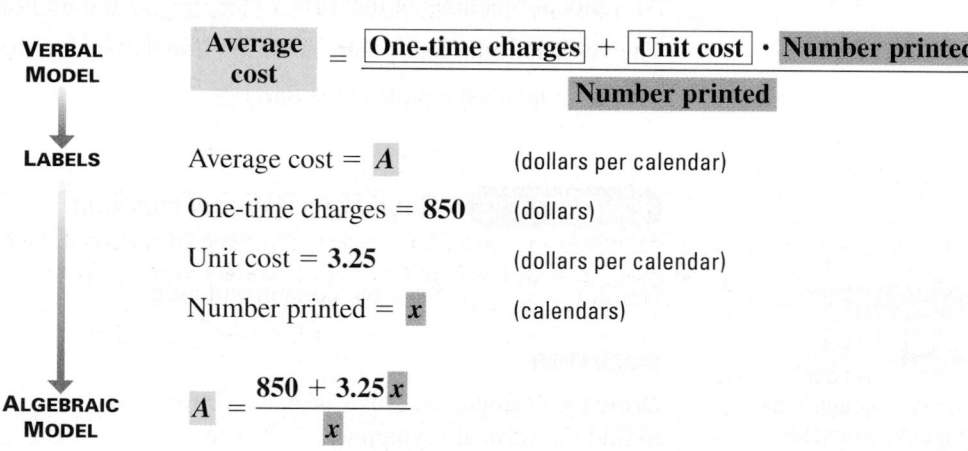

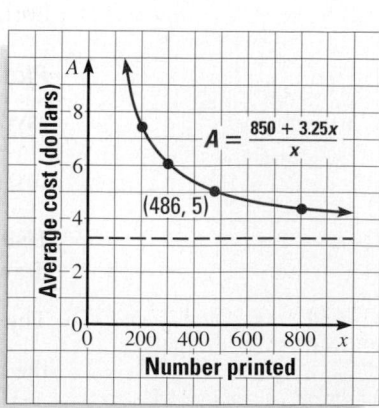

  c. As the number of calendars printed increases, the average cost per calendar gets closer and closer to $3.25. For instance, when $x = 5000$ the average cost is $3.42, and when $x = 10,000$ the average cost is $3.34.

GUIDED PRACTICE

Vocabulary Check ✓

1. Complete this statement: The graph of a function of the form $y = \dfrac{a}{x - h} + k$ is called a(n) __?__.

Concept Check ✓

2. **ERROR ANALYSIS** Explain why the graph shown is not the graph of $y = \dfrac{6}{x + 3} + 7$.

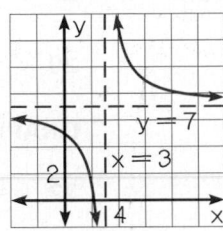

3. If the graph of a rational function is a hyperbola with the x-axis and the y-axis as asymptotes, what is the domain of the function? What is the range?

Skill Check ✓ **Identify the horizontal and vertical asymptotes of the graph of the function.**

4. $y = \dfrac{2}{x - 3} + 4$ 5. $y = \dfrac{2x + 3}{x + 4}$ 6. $y = \dfrac{x - 3}{x + 3}$

7. $y = \dfrac{x + 5}{2x - 4}$ 8. $y = \dfrac{3}{x + 8} - 10$ 9. $y = \dfrac{-4}{x - 6} - 5$

10. 🌎 **CALENDAR FUNDRAISER** Look back at Example 3 on page 542. Suppose you decide to generate your own fractals on a computer to save money. The cost for the software (a "one-time" cost) is $125. Write a model that gives the average cost per calendar as a function of the number of calendars printed. Graph the model and use the graph to estimate the number of calendars you need to print before the average cost drops to $5 per calendar.

PRACTICE AND APPLICATIONS

STUDENT HELP

▶ **Extra Practice**
to help you master
skills is on p. 952.

IDENTIFYING ASYMPTOTES Identify the horizontal and vertical asymptotes of the graph of the function. Then state the domain and range.

11. $y = \dfrac{3}{x} + 2$ 12. $y = \dfrac{4}{x - 3} + 2$ 13. $y = \dfrac{-2}{x + 3} - 2$

14. $y = \dfrac{x + 2}{x - 3}$ 15. $y = \dfrac{2x + 2}{3x + 1}$ 16. $y = \dfrac{-3x + 2}{-4x - 5}$

17. $y = \dfrac{-22}{x + 43} - 17$ 18. $y = \dfrac{34x - 2}{16x + 4}$ 19. $y = \dfrac{4}{x - 6} + 19$

MATCHING GRAPHS Match the function with its graph.

20. $y = \dfrac{3}{x - 2} + 3$ 21. $y = \dfrac{-3}{x - 2} + 3$ 22. $y = \dfrac{x + 2}{x + 3}$

STUDENT HELP

▶ **HOMEWORK HELP**
Example 1: Exs. 11–31
Example 2: Exs. 11–22,
          32–40
Example 3: Exs. 42–48

A. 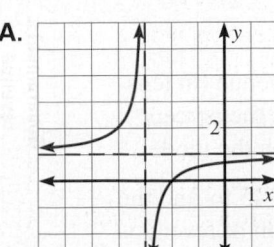   B. 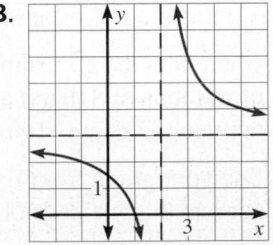   C.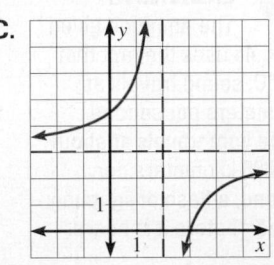

GRAPHING FUNCTIONS Graph the function. State the domain and range.

23. $y = \dfrac{4}{x}$

24. $y = \dfrac{3}{x - 3} + 1$

25. $y = \dfrac{-4}{x + 5} - 8$

26. $y = \dfrac{1}{x - 7} + 3$

27. $y = \dfrac{6}{x + 2} - 6$

28. $y = \dfrac{5}{x} + 4$

29. $y = \dfrac{1}{4x + 12} - 2$

30. $y = \dfrac{3}{2x}$

31. $y = \dfrac{4}{3x - 6} + 5$

GRAPHING FUNCTIONS Graph the function. State the domain and range.

32. $y = \dfrac{x + 2}{x + 3}$

33. $y = \dfrac{x}{4x + 3}$

34. $y = \dfrac{x - 7}{3x - 8}$

35. $y = \dfrac{9x + 1}{3x - 2}$

36. $y = \dfrac{-3x + 10}{4x - 12}$

37. $y = \dfrac{5x + 2}{4x}$

38. $y = \dfrac{3x}{2x - 4}$

39. $y = \dfrac{7x}{-x - 15}$

40. $y = \dfrac{-14x - 4}{2x - 1}$

41. CRITICAL THINKING Write a rational function that has the vertical asymptote $x = -4$ and the horizontal asymptote $y = 3$.

🌐 **RACQUETBALL** In Exercises 42 and 43, use the following information.
You've paid $120 for a membership to a racquetball club. Court time is $5 per hour.

42. Write a model that represents your average cost per hour of court time as a function of the number of hours played. Graph the model. What is an equation of the horizontal asymptote and what does the asymptote represent?

43. Suppose that you can play racquetball at the YMCA for $9 per hour without being a member. How many hours would you have to play at the racquetball club before your average cost per hour of court time is less than $9?

44. 🌐 **LIGHTNING** Air temperature affects how long it takes sound to travel a given distance. The time it takes for sound to travel one kilometer can be modeled by

$$t = \dfrac{1000}{0.6T + 331}$$

where t is the time (in seconds) and T is the temperature (in degrees Celsius). You are 1 kilometer from a lightning strike and it takes you exactly 3 seconds to hear the sound of thunder. Use a graph to find the approximate air temperature. (*Hint:* Use tick marks that are 0.1 unit apart on the t-axis.)

🌐 **ECONOMICS** In Exercises 45 and 46, use the following information.
Economist Arthur Laffer argues that beyond a certain percent p_m, increased taxes will produce less government revenue. His theory is illustrated in the graph below.

45. Using Laffer's theory, an economist models the revenue generated by one kind of tax by

$$R = \dfrac{80p - 8000}{p - 110}$$

where R is the government revenue (in tens of millions of dollars) and p is the percent tax rate ($55 \le p \le 100$). Graph the model.

46. Use your graph from Exercise 45 to find the tax rate that yields $600 million of revenue.

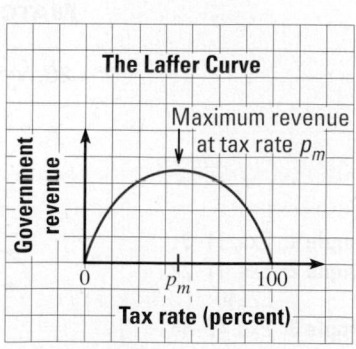

The Laffer Curve

Maximum revenue at tax rate p_m

Government revenue

0   p_m 100

Tax rate (percent)

DOPPLER EFFECT In Exercises 47 and 48, use the following information.
When the source of a sound is moving relative to a stationary listener, the frequency f_l (in hertz) heard by the listener is different from the frequency f_s (in hertz) of the sound at its source. An equation for the frequency heard by the listener is

$$f_l = \frac{740 f_s}{740 - r}$$

where r is the speed (in miles per hour) of the sound source relative to the listener.

47. The sound of an ambulance siren has a frequency of about 2000 hertz. You are standing on the sidewalk as an ambulance approaches with its siren on. Write the frequency that you hear as a function of the ambulance's speed.

48. Graph the function from Exercise 47 for $0 \le r \le 60$. What happens to the frequency you hear as the value of r increases?

49. *Writing* In what line(s) is the graph of $y = \frac{1}{x}$ symmetric? What does this symmetry tell you about the inverse of the function $f(x) = \frac{1}{x}$?

Test Preparation

50. **MULTIPLE CHOICE** What are the asymptotes of the graph of $y = \frac{-73}{x - 141} + 27$?

   Ⓐ $x = 141, y = 27$ Ⓑ $x = -141, y = 27$ Ⓒ $x = -73, y = 27$

   Ⓓ $x = -73, y = 141$ Ⓔ None of these

51. **MULTIPLE CHOICE** Which of the following is a function whose domain and range are all *nonzero* real numbers?

   Ⓐ $f(x) = \frac{x}{2x + 1}$ Ⓑ $f(x) = \frac{2x - 1}{3x - 2}$ Ⓒ $f(x) = \frac{1}{x} + 1$

   Ⓓ $f(x) = \frac{x - 2}{x}$ Ⓔ None of these

★ **Challenge**

52. **EQUIVALENT FORMS** Show algebraically that the function $f(x) = \frac{3}{x - 5} + 10$ and the function $g(x) = \frac{10x - 47}{x - 5}$ are equivalent.

MIXED REVIEW

GRAPHING POLYNOMIALS Graph the polynomial function. (Review 6.2 for 9.3)

53. $f(x) = 3x^5$ 54. $f(x) = 4 - 2x^3$ 55. $f(x) = x^6 - 1$

56. $f(x) = 4x^4 + 1$ 57. $f(x) = 6x^7$ 58. $f(x) = x^3 - 5$

FACTORING Factor the polynomial. (Review 6.4 for 9.3)

59. $8x^3 - 125$ 60. $3x^3 + 81$ 61. $x^3 + 3x^2 + 3x + 9$

62. $5x^3 + 10x^2 + x + 2$ 63. $81x^4 - 1$ 64. $4x^4 - 4x^2 - 120$

SIMPLIFYING EXPRESSIONS Simplify the expression. (Review 8.3)

65. $\frac{e^x}{5e}$ 66. $7e^{-5}e^8$ 67. $e^x e^{4x + 1}$

68. $\frac{6e^x}{e^{6x}}$ 69. $e^4 e^{2x} e^{-3x}$ 70. $e^3 e^{-5}$

▶ ACTIVITY 9.2

Using Technology

Graphing Rational Functions

You can use a graphing calculator to graph rational functions.

▶ EXAMPLE

Use a graphing calculator to graph $y = \dfrac{x + 2}{x - 2}$.

▶ SOLUTION

Begin by entering the function, using parentheses as shown.

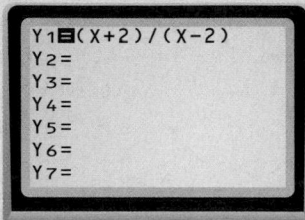

Most graphing calculators have two graphing modes: *Connected* mode and *Dot* mode. The graphs below show the function graphed in each mode.

Notice that the graph on the left has a vertical line at approximately $x = 2$. This line is *not* part of the graph—it is simply the graphing calculator's attempt at connecting the two branches of the graph.

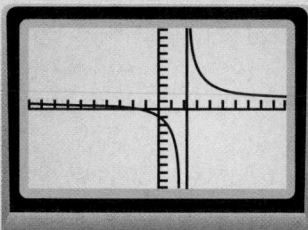

Connected mode

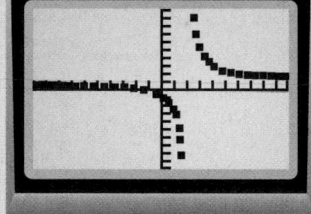

Dot mode

Be sure to choose a viewing window that shows all of the important characteristics of the graph. For instance, in the graph shown at the right, the viewing window is inadequate because it does not show the two branches of the graph of the rational function.

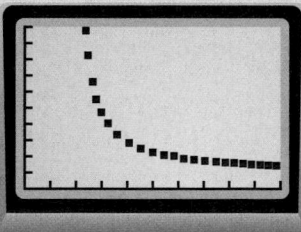

▶ EXERCISES

Use a graphing calculator to graph the rational function. Choose a viewing window that displays the important characteristics of the graph.

1. $y = \dfrac{7}{x} + 3$

2. $y = 9 - \dfrac{5}{x}$

3. $y = 5 + \dfrac{3}{x - 6}$

4. $y = \dfrac{4}{x} + 6$

5. $y = \dfrac{x - 5}{x + 1}$

6. $y = \dfrac{8 - 5x}{x - 5}$

7. 🌐 **DELIVERY CHARGES** You and your friends order pizza and have it delivered to your house. The restaurant charges $8 per pizza plus a $2 delivery fee. Write a model that gives the average cost per pizza as a function of the number of pizzas ordered. Graph the model. Describe what happens to the average cost as the number of pizzas ordered increases.

9.3
Graphing General Rational Functions

What you should learn

GOAL 1 Graph general rational functions.

GOAL 2 Use the graph of a rational function to solve **real-life** problems, such as determining the efficiency of packaging in **Example 4**.

Why you should learn it

▼ To solve **real-life** problems, such as finding the energy expenditure of a parakeet in **Ex. 39**.

GOAL 1 GRAPHING RATIONAL FUNCTIONS

In Lesson 9.2 you learned how to graph rational functions of the form

$$f(x) = \frac{p(x)}{q(x)}$$

for which $p(x)$ and $q(x)$ are linear polynomials and $q(x) \neq 0$. In this lesson you will learn how to graph rational functions for which $p(x)$ and $q(x)$ may be higher-degree polynomials.

CONCEPT SUMMARY

GRAPHS OF RATIONAL FUNCTIONS

Let $p(x)$ and $q(x)$ be polynomials with no common factors other than 1. The graph of the rational function

$$f(x) = \frac{p(x)}{q(x)} = \frac{a_m x^m + a_{m-1} x^{m-1} + \cdots + a_1 x + a_0}{b_n x^n + b_{n-1} x^{n-1} + \cdots + b_1 x + b_0}$$

has the following characteristics.

1. The x-intercepts of the graph of f are the real zeros of $p(x)$.

2. The graph of f has a vertical asymptote at each real zero of $q(x)$.

3. The graph of f has at most one horizontal asymptote.

   • If $m < n$, the line $y = 0$ is a horizontal asymptote.

   • If $m = n$, the line $y = \dfrac{a_m}{b_n}$ is a horizontal asymptote.

   • If $m > n$, the graph has no horizontal asymptote. The graph's end behavior is the same as the graph of $y = \dfrac{a_m}{b_n} x^{m-n}$.

EXAMPLE 1   *Graphing a Rational Function (m < n)*

Graph $y = \dfrac{4}{x^2 + 1}$. State the domain and range.

SOLUTION

The numerator has no zeros, so there is no x-intercept. The denominator has no real zeros, so there is no vertical asymptote. The degree of the numerator (0) is less than the degree of the denominator (2), so the line $y = 0$ (the x-axis) is a horizontal asymptote. The *bell-shaped* graph passes through the points $(-3, 0.4)$, $(-1, 2)$, $(0, 4)$, $(1, 2)$, and $(3, 0.4)$. The domain is all real numbers, and the range is $0 < y \leq 4$.

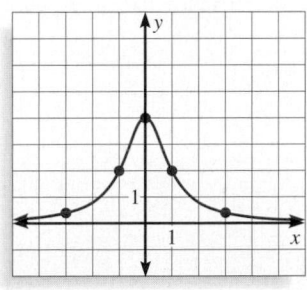

EXAMPLE 2 *Graphing a Rational Function (m = n)*

Graph $y = \dfrac{3x^2}{x^2 - 4}$.

STUDENT HELP

▶ **Look Back**
For help with finding zeros, see p. 259.

SOLUTION

The numerator has 0 as its only zero, so the graph has one x-intercept at $(0, 0)$. The denominator can be factored as $(x + 2)(x - 2)$, so the denominator has zeros -2 and 2. This implies that the lines $x = -2$ and $x = 2$ are vertical asymptotes of the graph. The degree of the numerator (2) is equal to the degree of the denominator (2), so the horizontal asymptote is $y = \dfrac{a_m}{b_n} = 3$. To draw the graph, plot points between and beyond the vertical asymptotes.

To the left of $x = -2$

x	y
−4	4
−3	5.4

Between $x = -2$ and $x = 2$

x	y
−1	−1
0	0
1	−1

To the right of $x = 2$

x	y
3	5.4
4	4

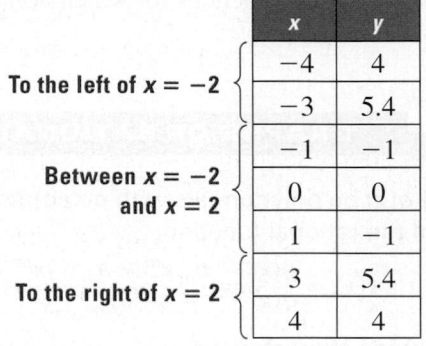
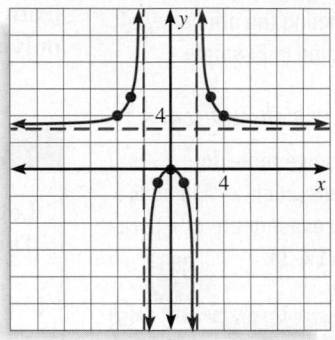

EXAMPLE 3 *Graphing a Rational Function (m > n)*

Graph $y = \dfrac{x^2 - 2x - 3}{x + 4}$.

SOLUTION

The numerator can be factored as $(x - 3)(x + 1)$, so the x-intercepts of the graph are 3 and -1. The only zero of the denominator is -4, so the only vertical asymptote is $x = -4$. The degree of the numerator (2) is greater than the degree of the denominator (1), so there is no horizontal asymptote and the end behavior of the graph of f is the same as the end behavior of the graph of $y = x^{2-1} = x$. To draw the graph, plot points to the left and right of the vertical asymptote.

To the left of $x = -4$

x	y
−12	−20.6
−9	−19.2
−6	−22.5

To the right of $x = -4$

x	y
−2	2.5
0	−0.75
2	−0.5
4	0.63
6	2.1

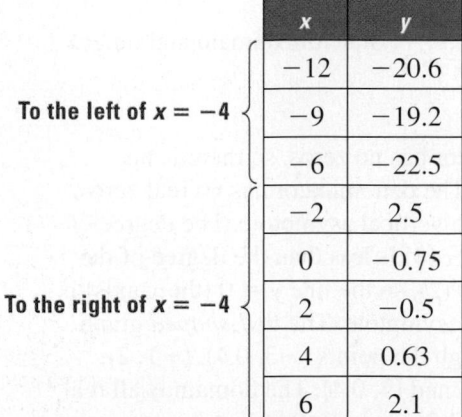
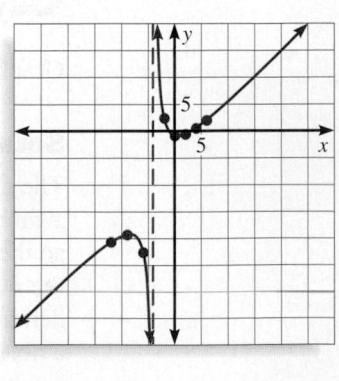

Manufacturers often want to package their products in a way that uses the least amount of packaging material. Finding the most efficient packaging sometimes involves finding a local minimum of a rational function.

Manufacturing

EXAMPLE 4 *Finding a Local Minimum*

 A standard beverage can has a volume of 355 cubic centimeters.

a. Find the dimensions of the can that has this volume and uses the least amount of material possible.

b. Compare your result with the dimensions of an actual beverage can, which has a radius of 3.1 centimeters and a height of 11.8 centimeters.

SOLUTION

STUDENT HELP

► **Look Back**
For help with rewriting an equation with more than one variable, see p. 26.

a. The volume must be 355 cubic centimeters, so you can write the height h of each possible can in terms of its radius r.

$$V = \pi r^2 h \qquad \text{Formula for volume of cylinder}$$

$$355 = \pi r^2 h \qquad \text{Substitute 355 for } V.$$

$$\frac{355}{\pi r^2} = h \qquad \text{Solve for } h.$$

Using the least amount of material is equivalent to having a minimum surface area S. You can find the minimum surface area by writing its formula in terms of a single variable and graphing the result.

$$S = 2\pi r^2 + 2\pi r h \qquad \text{Formula for surface area of cylinder}$$

$$= 2\pi r^2 + 2\pi r \left(\frac{355}{\pi r^2} \right) \qquad \text{Substitute for } h.$$

$$= 2\pi r^2 + \frac{710}{r} \qquad \text{Simplify.}$$

Graph the function for the surface area S using a graphing calculator. Then use the *Minimum* feature to find the minimum value of S. When you do this, you get a minimum value of about 278, which occurs when $r \approx 3.84$ centimeters and

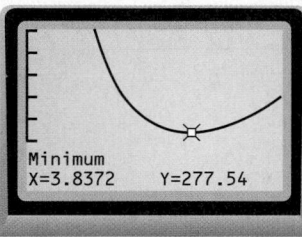
Minimum
X=3.8372   Y=277.54

$$h \approx \frac{355}{\pi(3.84)^2} \approx 7.66 \text{ centimeters.}$$

b. An actual beverage can is taller and narrower than the can with minimal surface area—probably to make it easier to hold the can in one hand.

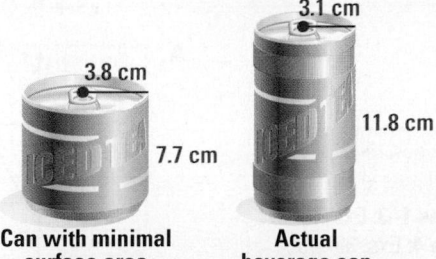

3.8 cm

7.7 cm

3.1 cm

11.8 cm

Can with minimal surface area   **Actual beverage can**

GUIDED PRACTICE

Vocabulary Check ✓

1. Let $f(x) = \dfrac{p(x)}{q(x)}$ where $p(x)$ and $q(x)$ are polynomials with no common factors other than 1. Complete this statement: The line $y = 0$ is a horizontal asymptote of the graph of f when the degree of $q(x)$ is _?_ the degree of $p(x)$.

Concept Check ✓

2. Let $f(x) = \dfrac{p(x)}{q(x)}$ where $p(x)$ and $q(x)$ are polynomials with no common factors other than 1. Describe how to find the x-intercepts and the vertical asymptotes of the graph of f.

3. Let $f(x) = \dfrac{p(x)}{q(x)}$ where $p(x)$ and $q(x)$ are both cubic polynomials with no common factors other than 1. The leading coefficient of $p(x)$ is 8 and the leading coefficient of $q(x)$ is 2. Describe the end behavior of the graph of f.

Skill Check ✓

Graph the function.

4. $y = \dfrac{6}{x^2 + 3}$

5. $y = \dfrac{x^2 - 4}{x + 1}$

6. $y = \dfrac{x^2 - 7}{x^2 + 2}$

7. $y = \dfrac{x^3}{x^2 + 7}$

8. $y = \dfrac{2x^2}{x^2 - 1}$

9. $y = \dfrac{x}{x^2 - 16}$

10. 🌐 **SOUP CANS** The can for a popular brand of soup has a volume of about 342 cubic centimeters. Find the dimensions of the can with this volume that uses the least metal possible. Compare these dimensions with the dimensions of the actual can, which has a radius of 3.3 centimeters and a height of 10 centimeters.

PRACTICE AND APPLICATIONS

STUDENT HELP

▶ **Extra Practice**
to help you master
skills is on p. 952.

ANALYZING GRAPHS Identify the x-intercepts and vertical asymptotes of the graph of the function.

11. $y = \dfrac{x}{x^2 - 9}$

12. $y = \dfrac{2x^2 + 3}{x - 1}$

13. $y = \dfrac{2x^2 - 9x - 5}{x^2 - 16}$

14. $y = \dfrac{2x + 3}{x^3}$

15. $y = \dfrac{x^2 + 4x - 5}{x - 6}$

16. $y = \dfrac{3x^2 - 13x + 10}{x^2 + 8}$

17. $y = \dfrac{2x + 8}{3x^2 - 9}$

18. $y = \dfrac{2x^2 + x}{x^2 + 1}$

19. $y = \dfrac{x^3 - 27}{2x}$

MATCHING GRAPHS Match the function with its graph.

20. $y = \dfrac{x^2 - 7}{x^2 + 2}$

21. $y = \dfrac{-8}{x^2 - 4}$

22. $y = \dfrac{x^3}{x^2 - 4}$

STUDENT HELP

▶ **HOMEWORK HELP**
Examples 1–3: Exs. 11–37
Example 4: Exs. 38–45

A.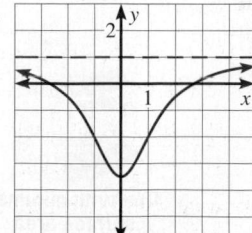

B.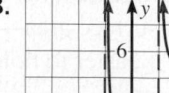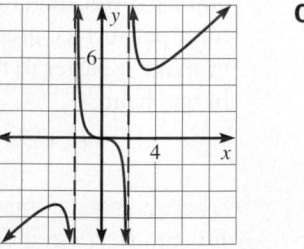

C.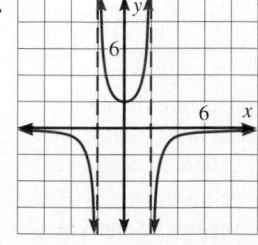

MATCHING GRAPHS Match the function with its graph.

23. $y = \dfrac{3}{x^3 - 27}$ **24.** $y = \dfrac{-x^3}{x^2 + 9}$ **25.** $y = \dfrac{x^2 + 4x}{2x - 1}$

A. 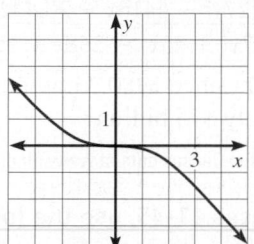   **B.** 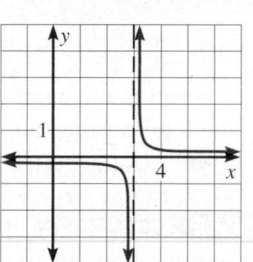   **C.**

GRAPHING FUNCTIONS Graph the function.

26. $y = \dfrac{2x^2 - 3}{x + 2}$ **27.** $y = \dfrac{-24}{x^2 + 8}$ **28.** $y = \dfrac{x^2 - 4}{x^2 + 3}$

29. $y = \dfrac{4x + 1}{x^2 - 1}$ **30.** $y = \dfrac{2x^2 + 3x + 1}{x^2 - 5x + 4}$ **31.** $y = \dfrac{-2x^2}{3x + 6}$

32. $y = \dfrac{3x^3 + 1}{4x^3 - 32}$ **33.** $y = \dfrac{x^2 - 11x - 12}{x^3 + 27}$ **34.** $y = \dfrac{4 - x}{5x^2 - 4x - 1}$

35. $y = \dfrac{-4x^2}{x^2 - 16}$ **36.** $y = \dfrac{x^2 - 9x + 20}{2x}$ **37.** $y = \dfrac{x^3 + 5x^2 - 1}{x^2 - 4x}$

38. 🌐 **GARDEN FENCING** Suppose you want to make a rectangular garden with an area of 200 square feet. You want to use the side of your house for one side of the garden and use fencing for the other three sides. Find the dimensions of the garden that minimize the length of fencing needed.

🖩 **GRAPHING MODELS** In Exercises 39–45, you may find it helpful to use a graphing calculator to graph the models.

39. 🌐 **ENERGY EXPENDITURE** The total energy expenditure E (in joules per gram mass per kilometer) of a typical budgerigar parakeet can be modeled by

$$E = \dfrac{0.31v^2 - 21.7v + 471.75}{v}$$

where v is the speed of the bird (in kilometers per hour). Graph the model. What speed minimizes a budgerigar's energy expenditure?
▶ Source: *Introduction to Mathematics for Life Scientists*

40. 🌐 **OCEANOGRAPHY** The mean temperature T (in degrees Celsius) of the Atlantic Ocean between latitudes 40°N and 40°S can be modeled by

$$T = \dfrac{17,800d + 20,000}{3d^2 + 740d + 1000}$$

where d is the depth (in meters). Graph the model. Use your graph to estimate the depth at which the mean temperature is 4°C.
▶ Source: *Practical Handbook of Marine Science*

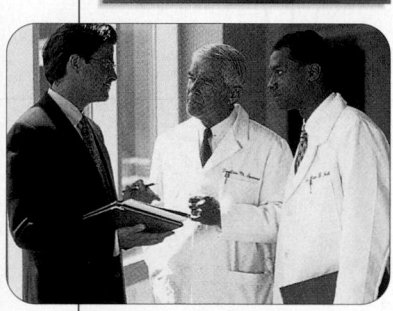
41. 🌐 **HOSPITAL COSTS** For 1985 to 1995, the average daily cost per patient C (in dollars) at community hospitals in the United States can be modeled by

$$C = \dfrac{-22,407x + 462,048}{5x^2 - 122x + 1000}$$

where x is the number of years since 1985. Graph the model. Would you use this model to predict patient costs in 2005? Explain. ▶ Source: *Hospital Statistics*

42. 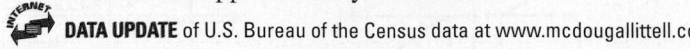 **AUTOMOTIVE INDUSTRY** For 1980 to 1995, the total revenue R (in billions of dollars) from parking and automotive service and repair in the United States can be modeled by

$$R = \frac{427x^2 - 6416x + 30{,}432}{-0.7x^3 + 25x^2 - 268x + 1000}$$

where x is the number of years since 1980. Graph the model. In what year was the total revenue approximately $75 billion?

DATA UPDATE of U.S. Bureau of the Census data at www.mcdougallittell.com

SCIENCE **CONNECTION** **In Exercises 43–45, use the following information.**
The acceleration due to gravity g' (in meters per second squared) of a falling object at the moment it is dropped is given by the function

$$g' = \frac{3.99 \times 10^{14}}{h^2 + (1.28 \times 10^7)h + 4.07 \times 10^{13}}$$

where h is the object's altitude (in meters) above sea level.

43. Graph the function.

44. What is the acceleration due to gravity for an object dropped at an altitude of 5000 kilometers?

45. Describe what happens to g' as h increases.

46. CRITICAL THINKING Give an example of a rational function whose graph has two vertical asymptotes: $x = 2$ and $x = 7$.

Test Preparation

47. MULTIPLE CHOICE What is the horizontal asymptote of the graph of the following function?

$$y = \frac{10x^2 - 1}{x^3 + 8}$$

    A $y = -10$ **B** $y = 0$ **C** $y = 2$

    D $y = 10$ **E** No horizontal asymptote

48. MULTIPLE CHOICE Which of the following functions is graphed?

    A $y = \dfrac{-5x^2}{x^2 + 9}$ **B** $y = \dfrac{5x^2}{x^2 - 9}$

    C $y = \dfrac{5x^2}{x^2 + 9}$ **D** $y = \dfrac{-5x^2}{x^2 - 9}$

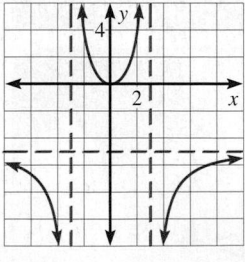

★ Challenge

49. Consider the following two functions:

$$f(x) = \frac{(x + 1)(x + 2)}{(x - 3)(x - 5)} \quad \text{and} \quad g(x) = \frac{(x + 2)(x - 3)}{(x - 3)(x - 5)}$$

Notice that the numerator and denominator of g have a common factor of $x - 3$.

   a. Make a table of values for each function from $x = 2.95$ to $x = 3.05$ in increments of 0.01.

   b. Use your table of values to graph each function for $2.95 \le x \le 3.05$.

   c. As x approaches 3, what happens to the graph of $f(x)$? to the graph of $g(x)$?

   d. What do you think is true about the graph of a function $g(x) = \dfrac{p(x)}{q(x)}$ where $p(x)$ and $q(x)$ have a common factor $x - k$?

SIMPLIFYING ALGEBRAIC EXPRESSIONS Simplify the expression. Tell which properties of exponents you used. (Review 6.1 for 9.4)

50. $\dfrac{x^{-3}y}{xy^4}$

51. $\dfrac{x^6y^5}{xy}$

52. $\dfrac{3x^3y^3}{6x^{-1}y}$

53. $\dfrac{12x^5y^{-2}}{3x^{-2}y^5}$

54. $\left(\dfrac{x^2y^2}{x^3y}\right)^2$

55. $\left(\dfrac{5x^3}{25xy^2}\right)^3$

JOINT VARIATION MODELS The variable z varies jointly with x and y. Use the given values to write an equation relating x, y, and z. Then find z when $x = -3$ and $y = 2$. (Review 9.1)

56. $x = 3, y = -6, z = 2$

57. $x = -5, y = 2, z = \dfrac{3}{4}$

58. $x = -8, y = 4, z = \dfrac{8}{3}$

59. $x = 1, y = \dfrac{1}{2}, z = 4$

VERIFYING INVERSES Verify that f and g are inverse functions. (Review 7.4)

60. $f(x) = \dfrac{1}{2}x - 3, g(x) = 2x + 6$

61. $f(x) = -3x + 2, g(x) = -\dfrac{1}{3}x + \dfrac{2}{3}$

62. $f(x) = 5x^3 + 2, g(x) = \left(\dfrac{x-2}{5}\right)^{1/3}$

63. $f(x) = 16x^4, x \ge 0; g(x) = \dfrac{\sqrt[4]{x}}{2}$

Quiz 1

Self-Test for Lessons 9.1–9.3

The variables x and y vary inversely. Use the given values to write an equation relating x and y. Then find y when $x = -3$. (Lesson 9.1)

1. $x = 6, y = -2$

2. $x = 11, y = 6$

3. $x = \dfrac{1}{5}, y = 30$

The variable x varies jointly with y and z. Use the given values to write an equation relating x, y, and z. Then find y when $x = 4$ and $z = 1$. (Lesson 9.1)

4. $x = 5, y = -5, z = 6$

5. $x = 12, y = 6, z = \dfrac{1}{2}$

6. $x = -10, y = 2, z = 4$

Graph the function. (Lessons 9.2 and 9.3)

7. $y = \dfrac{10}{x}$

8. $y = \dfrac{2}{x+9} - 7$

9. $y = \dfrac{3x+5}{2x-11}$

10. $y = \dfrac{6x}{x^2-36}$

11. $y = \dfrac{3x^2}{x^2-25}$

12. $y = \dfrac{x^2-4x-5}{x+2}$

13. 🌎 **HOTEL REVENUE** For 1980 to 1995, the total revenue R (in billions of dollars) from hotels and motels in the United States can be modeled by

$$R = \dfrac{2.76x + 26.88}{-0.01x + 1}$$

where x is the number of years since 1980. Graph the model. Use your graph to find the year in which the total revenue from hotels and motels was approximately $68 billion. (Lesson 9.2)

Multiplying and Dividing Rational Expressions

What you should learn

GOAL 1 Multiply and divide rational expressions.

GOAL 2 Use rational expressions to model **real-life** quantities, such as the heat generated by a runner in **Exs. 50 and 51**.

Why you should learn it

▼ To solve **real-life** problems, such as finding the average number of acres per farm in **Exs. 52 and 53.**

GOAL 1 WORKING WITH RATIONAL EXPRESSIONS

A rational expression is in **simplified form** provided its numerator and denominator have no common factors (other than ± 1). To simplify a rational expression, apply the following property.

SIMPLIFYING RATIONAL EXPRESSIONS

Let a, b, and c be nonzero real numbers or variable expressions. Then the following property applies:

$$\frac{a\cancel{c}}{b\cancel{c}} = \frac{a}{b} \qquad \text{Divide out common factor } c.$$

Simplifying a rational expression usually requires two steps. First, factor the numerator and denominator. Then, divide out any factors that are common to both the numerator and denominator. Here is an example:

$$\frac{x^2 + 5x}{x^2} = \frac{x(x + 5)}{x \cdot x} = \frac{x + 5}{x}$$

Notice that you can divide out common factors in the second expression above, but you cannot divide out like terms in the third expression.

EXAMPLE 1 *Simplifying a Rational Expression*

Simplify: $\dfrac{x^2 - 4x - 12}{x^2 - 4}$

SOLUTION

$$\frac{x^2 - 4x - 12}{x^2 - 4} = \frac{(x + 2)(x - 6)}{(x + 2)(x - 2)} \qquad \text{Factor numerator and denominator.}$$

$$= \frac{\cancel{(x + 2)}(x - 6)}{\cancel{(x + 2)}(x - 2)} \qquad \text{Divide out common factor.}$$

$$= \frac{x - 6}{x - 2} \qquad \text{Simplified form}$$

· · · · · · · · · ·

The rule for multiplying rational expressions is the same as the rule for multiplying numerical fractions: multiply numerators, multiply denominators, and write the new fraction in simplified form.

$$\frac{a}{b} \cdot \frac{c}{d} = \frac{ac}{bd} \longleftarrow \text{ Simplify } \frac{ac}{bd} \text{ if possible.}$$

EXAMPLE 2 *Multiplying Rational Expressions Involving Monomials*

Multiply: $\dfrac{5x^2y}{2xy^3} \cdot \dfrac{6x^3y^2}{10y}$

SOLUTION

$$\dfrac{5x^2y}{2xy^3} \cdot \dfrac{6x^3y^2}{10y} = \dfrac{30x^5y^3}{20xy^4}$$ **Multiply numerators and denominators.**

$$= \dfrac{3 \cdot \cancel{10} \cdot \cancel{x} \cdot x^4 \cdot \cancel{y^3}}{2 \cdot \cancel{10} \cdot \cancel{x} \cdot y \cdot \cancel{y^3}}$$ **Factor and divide out common factors.**

$$= \dfrac{3x^4}{2y}$$ **Simplified form**

EXAMPLE 3 *Multiplying Rational Expressions Involving Polynomials*

Multiply: $\dfrac{4x - 4x^2}{x^2 + 2x - 3} \cdot \dfrac{x^2 + x - 6}{4x}$

SOLUTION

$$\dfrac{4x - 4x^2}{x^2 + 2x - 3} \cdot \dfrac{x^2 + x - 6}{4x}$$

$$= \dfrac{4x(1 - x)}{(x - 1)(x + 3)} \cdot \dfrac{(x + 3)(x - 2)}{4x}$$ **Factor numerators and denominators.**

$$= \dfrac{4x(1 - x)(x + 3)(x - 2)}{(x - 1)(x + 3)(4x)}$$ **Multiply numerators and denominators.**

$$= \dfrac{4x(-1)(x - 1)(x + 3)(x - 2)}{(x - 1)(x + 3)(4x)}$$ **Rewrite (1 − x) as (−1)(x − 1).**

$$= \dfrac{4x(-1)\cancel{(x-1)}\cancel{(x+3)}(x - 2)}{\cancel{(x-1)}\cancel{(x+3)}\cancel{(4x)}}$$ **Divide out common factors.**

$$= -x + 2$$ **Simplified form**

EXAMPLE 4 *Multiplying by a Polynomial*

Multiply: $\dfrac{x + 3}{8x^3 - 1} \cdot (4x^2 + 2x + 1)$

STUDENT HELP

▶ **Look Back**
For help with factoring a
difference of two cubes,
see p. 345.

SOLUTION

$$\dfrac{x + 3}{8x^3 - 1} \cdot (4x^2 + 2x + 1)$$

$$= \dfrac{x + 3}{8x^3 - 1} \cdot \dfrac{4x^2 + 2x + 1}{1}$$ **Write polynomial as rational expression.**

$$= \dfrac{(x + 3)(4x^2 + 2x + 1)}{(2x - 1)(4x^2 + 2x + 1)}$$ **Factor and multiply numerators and denominators.**

$$= \dfrac{(x + 3)\cancel{(4x^2 + 2x + 1)}}{(2x - 1)\cancel{(4x^2 + 2x + 1)}}$$ **Divide out common factors.**

$$= \dfrac{x + 3}{2x - 1}$$ **Simplified form**

To divide one rational expression by another, multiply the first expression by the reciprocal of the second expression.

$$\frac{a}{b} \div \frac{c}{d} = \frac{a}{b} \cdot \frac{d}{c} = \frac{ad}{bc} \;\longleftarrow\; \text{Simplify } \frac{ad}{bc} \text{ if possible.}$$

EXAMPLE 5 — *Dividing Rational Expressions*

Divide: $\dfrac{5x}{3x - 12} \div \dfrac{x^2 - 2x}{x^2 - 6x + 8}$

SOLUTION

$$\frac{5x}{3x - 12} \div \frac{x^2 - 2x}{x^2 - 6x + 8} = \frac{5x}{3x - 12} \cdot \frac{x^2 - 6x + 8}{x^2 - 2x} \qquad \text{Multiply by reciprocal.}$$

$$= \frac{5x}{3(x - 4)} \cdot \frac{(x - 2)(x - 4)}{x(x - 2)} \qquad \text{Factor.}$$

$$= \frac{5x\cancel{(x-2)}\cancel{(x-4)}}{3\cancel{(x-4)}\cancel{(x)}\cancel{(x-2)}} \qquad \text{Divide out common factors.}$$

$$= \frac{5}{3} \qquad \text{Simplified form}$$

EXAMPLE 6 — *Dividing by a Polynomial*

Divide: $\dfrac{6x^2 + 7x - 3}{6x^2} \div (2x^2 + 3x)$

SOLUTION

$$\frac{6x^2 + 7x - 3}{6x^2} \div (2x^2 + 3x) = \frac{6x^2 + 7x - 3}{6x^2} \cdot \frac{1}{2x^2 + 3x}$$

$$= \frac{(3x - 1)(2x + 3)}{6x^2} \cdot \frac{1}{x(2x + 3)}$$

$$= \frac{(3x - 1)\cancel{(2x + 3)}}{(6x^2)(x)\cancel{(2x + 3)}}$$

$$= \frac{3x - 1}{6x^3}$$

EXAMPLE 7 — *Multiplying and Dividing*

Simplify: $\dfrac{x}{x + 5} \cdot (3x - 5) \div \dfrac{9x^2 - 25}{x + 5}$

SOLUTION

$$\frac{x}{x + 5} \cdot (3x - 5) \div \frac{9x^2 - 25}{x + 5} = \frac{x}{x + 5} \cdot \frac{3x - 5}{1} \cdot \frac{x + 5}{9x^2 - 25}$$

$$= \frac{x\cancel{(3x - 5)}\cancel{(x + 5)}}{\cancel{(x + 5)}\cancel{(3x - 5)}(3x + 5)}$$

$$= \frac{x}{3x + 5}$$

GOAL 2 **USING RATIONAL EXPRESSIONS IN REAL LIFE**

EXAMPLE 8 *Writing and Simplifying a Rational Model*

SKYDIVING A falling skydiver accelerates until reaching a constant falling speed, called the *terminal velocity*. Because of air resistance, the ratio of a skydiver's volume to his or her cross-sectional surface area affects the terminal velocity: the larger the ratio, the greater the terminal velocity.

a. The diagram shows a simplified geometric model of a skydiver with maximum cross-sectional surface area. Use the diagram to write a model for the ratio of volume to cross-sectional surface area for a skydiver.

b. Use the result of part (a) to compare the terminal velocities of two skydivers: one who is 60 inches tall and one who is 72 inches tall.

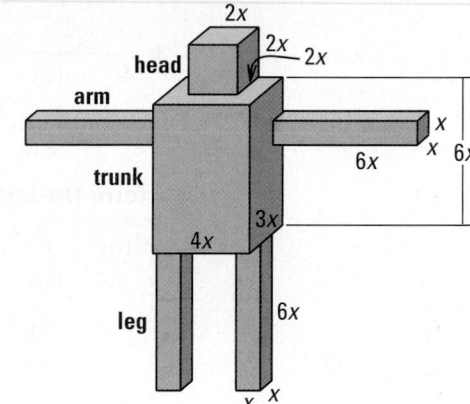

SOLUTION

a. The volume and cross-sectional surface area of each part of the skydiver are given in the table below. (Assume that the front side of the skydiver's body is parallel with the ground when falling.)

Body part	Volume	Cross-sectional surface area
Arm or leg	$V = 6x^3$	$S = 6x(x) = 6x^2$
Head	$V = 8x^3$	$S = 2x(2x) = 4x^2$
Trunk	$V = 72x^3$	$S = 6x(4x) = 24x^2$

Using these volumes and cross-sectional surface areas, you can write the ratio as:

$$\frac{\text{Volume}}{\text{Surface area}} = \frac{4(6x^3) + 8x^3 + 72x^3}{4(6x^2) + 4x^2 + 24x^2}$$

$$= \frac{104x^3}{52x^2}$$

$$= 2x$$

b. The overall height of the geometric model is $14x$. For the skydiver whose height is 60 inches, $14x = 60$, so $x \approx 4.3$. For the skydiver whose height is 72 inches, $14x = 72$, so $x \approx 5.1$. The ratio of volume to cross-sectional surface area for each skydiver is:

60 inch skydiver: $\dfrac{\text{Volume}}{\text{Surface area}} = 2x \approx 2(4.3) = 8.6$

72 inch skydiver: $\dfrac{\text{Volume}}{\text{Surface area}} = 2x \approx 2(5.1) = 10.2$

▶ The taller skydiver has the greater terminal velocity.

GUIDED PRACTICE

Vocabulary Check ✓

1. Explain how you know when a rational expression is in simplified form.

Concept Check ✓

2. **ERROR ANALYSIS** Explain what is wrong with the simplification of the rational expression shown.

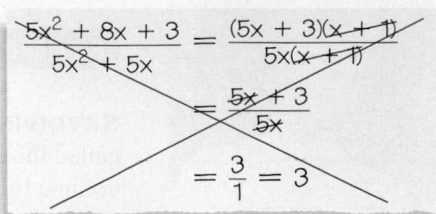

$$\frac{5x^2 + 8x + 3}{5x^2 + 5x} = \frac{(5x + 3)(x + 1)}{5x(x + 1)}$$
$$= \frac{5x + 3}{5x}$$
$$= \frac{3}{1} = 3$$

Skill Check ✓

If possible, simplify the rational expression.

3. $\dfrac{4x^2}{4x^3 + 12x}$

4. $\dfrac{x^2 + 4x - 5}{x^2 - 1}$

5. $\dfrac{x^2 + 10x - 4}{x^2 + 10x}$

6. $\dfrac{6x^2 - 4x - 3}{3x^2 + x}$

7. $\dfrac{x^2 - 9}{2x + 1}$

8. $\dfrac{2x^3 - 32x}{x^2 + 8x + 16}$

Perform the indicated operation. Simplify the result.

9. $\dfrac{16x^3}{5y^9} \cdot \dfrac{x^5y^8}{80x^3y}$

10. $\dfrac{7x^4y^3}{5xy} \cdot \dfrac{2x^7}{21y^5}$

11. $\dfrac{x^2 + x - 6}{2x^2} \cdot \dfrac{2x + 8}{x^2 + 7x + 12}$

12. $\dfrac{144}{4xy} \div \dfrac{54y^3}{3x^3y}$

13. $\dfrac{16xy}{3x^5y^5} \div \dfrac{8x^2}{9xy^7}$

14. $\dfrac{5x^2 + 10x}{x^2 - x - 6} \div \dfrac{15x^3 + 45x^2}{x^2 - 9}$

15. 🌐 **SKYDIVING** Look back at Example 8 on page 557. Some skydivers wear "wings" to increase their surface area. Suppose a skydiver who is 65 inches tall is wearing wings that add $18x^2$ of surface area and an insignificant amount of volume. Calculate the skydiver's volume to surface area ratio with and without the wings.

PRACTICE AND APPLICATIONS

STUDENT HELP

→ **Extra Practice**
to help you master
skills is on p. 953.

SIMPLIFYING **If possible, simplify the rational expression.**

16. $\dfrac{3x^3}{12x^2 + 9x}$

17. $\dfrac{x^2 - x - 6}{x^2 + 8x + 16}$

18. $\dfrac{x^2 - 3x + 2}{x^2 + 5x - 6}$

19. $\dfrac{x^2 + 2x - 4}{x^2 + x - 6}$

20. $\dfrac{x^2 - 2x - 3}{x^2 - 7x + 12}$

21. $\dfrac{3x^2 - 3x - 6}{x^2 - 4}$

22. $\dfrac{x - 2}{x^3 - 8}$

23. $\dfrac{x^3 - 27}{x^3 + 3x^2 + 9x}$

24. $\dfrac{x^2 + 6x + 9}{x^2 - 9}$

25. $\dfrac{15x^2 - 8x - 18}{-20x^2 + 14x + 12}$

26. $\dfrac{x^3 - 2x^2 + x - 2}{3x^2 - 3x - 8}$

27. $\dfrac{x^3 + 3x^2 - 2x - 6}{x^3 + 27}$

MULTIPLYING **Multiply the rational expressions. Simplify the result.**

STUDENT HELP

→ **HOMEWORK HELP**
Example 1: Exs. 16–27
Examples 2–4: Exs. 28–35,
44–49
Examples 5–7: Exs. 36–49
Example 8: Exs. 50–55

28. $\dfrac{4xy^3}{x^2y} \cdot \dfrac{y}{8x}$

29. $\dfrac{80x^4}{y^3} \cdot \dfrac{xy}{5x^2}$

30. $\dfrac{2x^2 - 10}{x + 1} \cdot \dfrac{x + 2}{3x^2 - 15}$

31. $\dfrac{x - 3}{2x - 8} \cdot \dfrac{6x^2 - 96}{x^2 - 9}$

32. $\dfrac{x^2 - x - 6}{4x^3} \cdot \dfrac{x + 1}{x^2 + 5x + 6}$

33. $\dfrac{2x^2 - 2}{x^2 - 6x - 7} \cdot (x^2 - 10x + 21)$

34. $\dfrac{x^3 + 5x^2 - x - 5}{x^2 - 25} \cdot (x + 1)$

35. $\dfrac{x - 3}{-x^3 + 3x^2} \cdot (x^2 + 2x + 1)$

DIVIDING Divide the rational expressions. Simplify the result.

36. $\dfrac{32x^3y}{y^9} \div \dfrac{8x^4}{y^6}$

37. $\dfrac{2xyz}{x^2z^2} \div \dfrac{6y^3}{3xz}$

38. $\dfrac{3x^2 + x - 2}{x^2 + 3x + 2} \div \dfrac{2x}{x + 2}$

39. $\dfrac{x^2 - 14x + 48}{x^2 - 6x} \div (3x - 24)$

40. $\dfrac{2x^2 - 12x}{x^2 - 7x + 6} \div \dfrac{2x}{3x - 3}$

41. $\dfrac{x^2 + 8x + 16}{x + 2} \div \dfrac{x^2 + 6x + 8}{x^2 - 4}$

42. $\dfrac{x^2 + 6x - 7}{3x^2} \div \dfrac{x + 7}{6x}$

43. $(x^2 + 6x - 27) \div \dfrac{3x^2 + 27x}{x + 5}$

COMBINED OPERATIONS Perform the indicated operations. Simplify the result.

44. $(x - 5) \div \dfrac{x^2 - 11x + 30}{x^2 + 7x + 12} \cdot (x - 6)$

45. $\dfrac{x^2 - x - 12}{8x^2} \div \dfrac{x^3 + 3x^2}{8x^3 - 2x^2} \div \dfrac{4x - 1}{x + 2}$

46. $\dfrac{x^2 + 11x}{x - 2} \div (3x^2 + 6x) \cdot \dfrac{x^2 - 4}{x + 11}$

47. $\dfrac{2x^2 + x - 15}{2x^2 - 11x - 21} \cdot (6x + 9) \div \dfrac{2x - 5}{3x - 21}$

48. $(x^3 + 8) \cdot \dfrac{x - 2}{x^2 - 2x + 4} \div \dfrac{x^2 - 4}{x - 6}$

49. $\dfrac{x^2 + 12x + 20}{4x^2 - 9} \cdot \dfrac{6x^3 - 9x^2}{x^3 + 10x^2} \cdot (2x + 3)$

 **HEAT GENERATION** In Exercises 50 and 51, use the following information.
Almost all of the energy generated by a long-distance runner is released in the form of heat. The rate of heat generation h_g and the rate of heat released h_r for a runner of height H can be modeled by

$$h_g = k_1 H^3 V^2 \qquad \text{and} \qquad h_r = k_2 H^2$$

where k_1 and k_2 are constants and V is the runner's speed.

50. Write the ratio of heat generated to heat released.

51. When the ratio of heat generated to heat released equals 1, how is height related to velocity? Does this mean that a taller or a shorter runner has an advantage?

FARMLAND In Exercises 52 and 53, use the following information.
From 1987 to 1996, the total acres of farmland L (in millions) and the total number of farms F (in hundreds of thousands) in the United States can be modeled by

$$L = \dfrac{43.3t + 999}{0.0482t + 1} \qquad \text{and} \qquad F = \dfrac{0.101t^2 + 2.20}{0.0500t^2 + 1}$$

where t represents the number of years since 1987. ▶ Source: U.S. Bureau of the Census

52. Write a model for the average number of acres A per farm as a function of the year.

53. What was the average number of acres per farm in 1993?

WEIGHT IN GOLD In Exercises 54 and 55, use the following information.
From 1990 to 1996, the price P of gold (in dollars per ounce) and the weight W of gold mined (in millions of ounces) in the United States can be modeled by

$$P = \dfrac{53.4t^2 - 243t + 385}{0.00146t^3 + 0.122t^2 - 0.586t + 1}$$

$$W = -0.0112t^5 + 0.193t^4 - 1.17t^3 + 2.82t^2 - 1.76t + 10.4$$

where t represents the number of years since 1990. ▶ Source: U.S. Bureau of the Census

54. Write a model for the total value V of gold mined as a function of the year.

55. What was the total value of gold mined in the United States in 1994?

56. 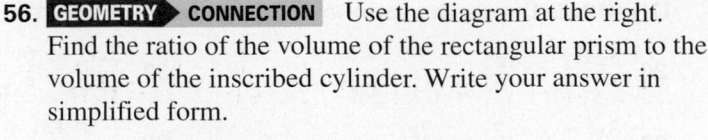 GEOMETRY CONNECTION Use the diagram at the right. Find the ratio of the volume of the rectangular prism to the volume of the inscribed cylinder. Write your answer in simplified form.

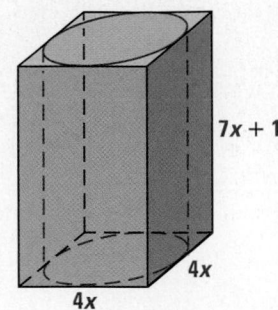

Test
Preparation

57. MULTI-STEP PROBLEM The surface area S and the volume V of a tin can are given by $S = 2\pi r^2 + 2\pi rh$ and $V = \pi r^2 h$ where r is the radius of the can and h is the height of the can. One measure of the *efficiency* of a tin can is the ratio of its surface area to its volume.

a. Find a general formula (in simplified form) for the ratio $\frac{S}{V}$.

b. Find the efficiency of a can when $h = 2r$.

c. Calculate the efficiency of each can.

• A soup can with $r = 2\frac{5}{8}$ inches and $h = 3\frac{7}{8}$ inches.

• A 2 pound coffee can with $r = 5\frac{1}{8}$ inches and $h = 6\frac{1}{2}$ inches.

• A 3 pound coffee can with $r = 6\frac{3}{16}$ inches and $h = 7$ inches.

d. *Writing* Rank the three cans in part (c) by efficiency (most efficient to least efficient). Explain your rankings.

★ **Challenge**

58. Find two rational functions $f(x)$ and $g(x)$ such that $f(x) \cdot g(x) = x^2$ and $\dfrac{f(x)}{g(x)} = \dfrac{(x-1)^2}{(x+2)^2}$.

59. Find two rational functions $f(x)$ and $g(x)$ such that $f(x) \cdot g(x) = x - 1$ and $\dfrac{f(x)}{g(x)} = \dfrac{(x+1)^2(x-1)}{x^4}$.

EXTRA CHALLENGE
www.mcdougallittell.com

MIXED REVIEW

GCFs AND LCMs Find the greatest common factor and least common multiple of each pair of numbers. (Skills Review, p. 908)

60. 96, 160 **61.** 120, 165 **62.** 48, 108

63. 72, 84 **64.** 238, 51 **65.** 480, 600

MULTIPLYING POLYNOMIALS Find the product. (Review 6.3 for 9.5)

66. $x(x^2 + 7x - 1)$ **67.** $(x + 7)(x - 1)$ **68.** $(x + 10)(x - 3)$

69. $(x + 3)(x^2 + 3x + 2)$ **70.** $(2x - 2)(x^3 - 4x^2)$ **71.** $x(x^2 - 4)(5 - 6x^3)$

BICYCLE DEPRECIATION In Exercises 72 and 73, use the following information. You bought a new mountain bike for $800. The value of the bike decreases by about 14% each year. (Review 8.2)

72. Write an exponential decay model for the value of the bike. Use the model to estimate the value after 4 years.

73. Graph the model. Use the graph to estimate when the bike will be worth $300.

● ACTIVITY 9.4

Using Technology

Operations with Rational Expressions

You have learned how to simplify rational expressions and how to multiply and divide rational expressions. You can use a graphing calculator to verify the results of these operations numerically and graphically.

▶ EXAMPLE

Simplify $\dfrac{x^2 + 3x - 10}{x^2 - 5x + 6}$. Use a graphing calculator to verify the results numerically and graphically.

▶ SOLUTION

You can simplify the rational expression as follows.

$$\frac{x^2 + 3x - 10}{x^2 - 5x + 6} = \frac{(x-2)(x+5)}{(x-2)(x-3)} = \frac{x+5}{x-3}$$

① Enter the original expression as y_1 and the simplified result as y_2. Use the *Path* style for y_2.

② Use the *Table* feature to examine corresponding values of the two expressions.

③ Put your calculator in *Connected* mode. Display your graphs in the standard viewing window.

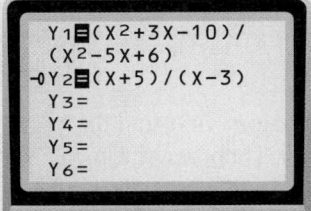

```
Y1=(X²+3X-10)/
(X²-5X+6)
↝Y2=(X+5)/(X-3)
Y3=
Y4=
Y5=
Y6=
```

Remember to use parentheses correctly.

X	Y1	Y2
0	-1.667	-1.667
1	-3	-3
2	ERROR	-7
3	ERROR	ERROR
4	9	9
X=0		

Why is only y_1 undefined at $x = 2$?

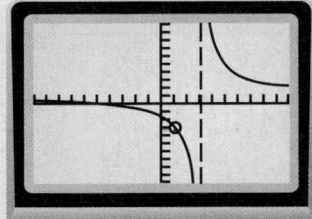

The *Path* style shows the graph of y_2 being drawn even though it coincides with the graph of y_1.

The graphing calculator allows you to check your solution in two ways. If the two expressions are equivalent, the values of y_1 and y_2 will be the same in the table *except where a common factor has been divided out*. Also, the graphs of the two expressions will coincide.

▶ EXERCISES

Simplify the expression. Use a graphing calculator to verify the result numerically and graphically.

1. $\dfrac{x^2 - 3x}{x^2 + x - 12}$

2. $\dfrac{2x^2 - 10x}{x^2 - 4x - 5}$

3. $\dfrac{x^2 + x - 6}{x^2 + 4x + 3}$

Perform the indicated operation and simplify. Use a graphing calculator to verify the result numerically and graphically.

4. $\dfrac{x - 1}{2x^2} \cdot \dfrac{x + 2}{x - 1}$

5. $\dfrac{2x^2 - 10x}{3x + 3} \div \dfrac{x - 5}{x + 1}$

6. $\dfrac{x^2 - x - 12}{x^2 + 6x + 6} \cdot \dfrac{x^2 + 3x + 2}{x^2 + 5x + 6}$

STUDENT HELP

INTERNET **KEYSTROKE HELP**

See keystrokes for several models of calculators at www.mcdougallittell.com

Addition, Subtraction, and Complex Fractions

What you should learn

GOAL 1 Add and subtract rational expressions, as applied in **Example 4**.

GOAL 2 Simplify complex fractions, as applied in **Example 6**.

Why you should learn it

▼ To solve **real-life** problems, such as modeling the total number of male college graduates in **Ex. 47**.

GOAL 1 WORKING WITH RATIONAL EXPRESSIONS

As with numerical fractions, the procedure used to add (or subtract) two rational expressions depends upon whether the expressions have *like* or *unlike* denominators.

To add (or subtract) two rational expressions with *like* denominators, simply add (or subtract) their numerators and place the result over the common denominator.

EXAMPLE 1 *Adding and Subtracting with Like Denominators*

Perform the indicated operation.

a. $\dfrac{4}{3x} + \dfrac{5}{3x}$

b. $\dfrac{2x}{x+3} - \dfrac{4}{x+3}$

SOLUTION

a. $\dfrac{4}{3x} + \dfrac{5}{3x} = \dfrac{4+5}{3x} = \dfrac{9}{3x} = \dfrac{3}{x}$ **Add numerators and simplify expression.**

b. $\dfrac{2x}{x+3} - \dfrac{4}{x+3} = \dfrac{2x-4}{x+3}$ **Subtract numerators.**

· · · · · · · · · ·

To add (or subtract) rational expressions with *unlike* denominators, first find the least common denominator (LCD) of the rational expressions. Then, rewrite each expression as an equivalent rational expression using the LCD and proceed as with rational expressions with like denominators.

EXAMPLE 2 *Adding with Unlike Denominators*

Add: $\dfrac{5}{6x^2} + \dfrac{x}{4x^2 - 12x}$

SOLUTION

First find the least common denominator of $\dfrac{5}{6x^2}$ and $\dfrac{x}{4x^2 - 12x}$.

It helps to factor each denominator: $6x^2 = 6 \cdot x \cdot x$ and $4x^2 - 12x = 4 \cdot x \cdot (x - 3)$.

The LCD is $12x^2(x - 3)$. Use this to rewrite each expression.

$$\frac{5}{6x^2} + \frac{x}{4x^2 - 12x} = \frac{5}{6x^2} + \frac{x}{4x(x-3)} = \frac{5[2(x-3)]}{6x^2[2(x-3)]} + \frac{x(3x)}{4x(x-3)(3x)}$$

$$= \frac{10x - 30}{12x^2(x-3)} + \frac{3x^2}{12x^2(x-3)}$$

$$= \frac{3x^2 + 10x - 30}{12x^2(x-3)}$$

STUDENT HELP

► **Skills Review**
For help with LCDs, see p. 908.

EXAMPLE 3 *Subtracting With Unlike Denominators*

Subtract: $\dfrac{x+1}{x^2+4x+4} - \dfrac{2}{x^2-4}$

STUDENT HELP

▸ **Look Back**
For help with multiplying polynomials, see p. 338.

SOLUTION

$$\frac{x+1}{x^2+4x+4} - \frac{2}{x^2-4} = \frac{x+1}{(x+2)^2} - \frac{2}{(x-2)(x+2)}$$

$$= \frac{(x+1)(x-2)}{(x+2)^2(x-2)} - \frac{2(x+2)}{(x-2)(x+2)(x+2)}$$

$$= \frac{x^2-x-2-(2x+4)}{(x+2)^2(x-2)}$$

$$= \frac{x^2-3x-6}{(x+2)^2(x-2)}$$

Statistics

EXAMPLE 4 *Adding Rational Models*

The distribution of heights for American men and women aged 20–29 can be modeled by

$$y_1 = \frac{0.143}{1+0.008(x-70)^4} \qquad \text{American men's heights}$$

$$y_2 = \frac{0.143}{1+0.008(x-64)^4} \qquad \text{American women's heights}$$

where x is the height (in inches) and y is the percent (in decimal form) of adults aged 20–29 whose height is $x \pm 0.5$ inches. ▸ Source: *Statistical Abstract of the United States*

a. Graph each model. What is the most common height for men aged 20–29? What is the most common height for women aged 20–29?

b. Write a model that shows the distribution of the heights of *all* adults aged 20–29. Graph the model and find the most common height.

SOLUTION

a. From the graphing calculator screen shown at the top right, you can see that the most common height for men is 70 inches (14.3%). The second most common heights are 69 inches and 71 inches (14.2% each). For women, the curve has the same shape, but is shifted to the left so that the most common height is 64 inches. The second most common heights are 63 inches and 65 inches.

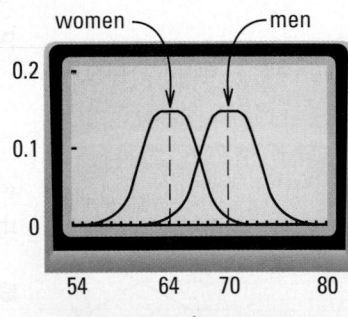

b. To find a model for the distribution of all adults aged 20–29, add the two models and divide by 2.

$$y = \frac{1}{2}\left[\frac{0.143}{1+0.008(x-70)^4} + \frac{0.143}{1+0.008(x-64)^4}\right]$$

From the graph shown at the bottom right, you can see that the most common height is 67 inches.

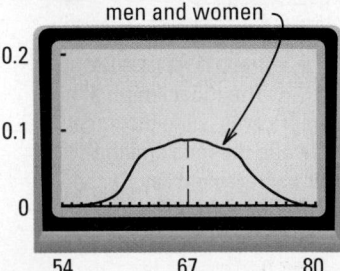

9.5 *Addition, Subtraction, and Complex Fractions* **563**

SIMPLIFYING COMPLEX FRACTIONS

A **complex fraction** is a fraction that contains a fraction in its numerator or denominator. To simplify a complex fraction, write its numerator and its denominator as single fractions. Then divide by multiplying by the reciprocal of the denominator.

EXAMPLE 5 *Simplifying a Complex Fraction*

STUDENT HELP

HOMEWORK HELP
Visit our Web site
www.mcdougallittell.com
for extra examples.

Simplify: $\dfrac{\dfrac{2}{x+2}}{\dfrac{1}{x+2}+\dfrac{2}{x}}$

SOLUTION

$$\dfrac{\dfrac{2}{x+2}}{\dfrac{1}{x+2}+\dfrac{2}{x}} = \dfrac{\dfrac{2}{x+2}}{\dfrac{3x+4}{x(x+2)}} \qquad \textbf{Add fractions in denominator.}$$

$$= \dfrac{2}{x+2} \cdot \dfrac{x(x+2)}{3x+4} \qquad \textbf{Multiply by reciprocal.}$$

$$= \dfrac{2x\cancel{(x+2)}}{\cancel{(x+2)}(3x+4)} \qquad \textbf{Divide out common factor.}$$

$$= \dfrac{2x}{3x+4} \qquad \textbf{Write in simplified form.}$$

. . . .

Another way to simplify a complex fraction is to multiply the numerator and denominator by the least common denominator of *every* fraction in the numerator and denominator.

EXAMPLE 6 *Simplifying a Complex Fraction*

PHOTOGRAPHY The focal length f of a thin camera lens is given by

$$f = \dfrac{1}{\dfrac{1}{p}+\dfrac{1}{q}}$$

where p is the distance between an object being photographed and the lens and q is the distance between the lens and the film. Simplify the complex fraction.

SOLUTION

$$f = \dfrac{1}{\dfrac{1}{p}+\dfrac{1}{q}} \qquad \textbf{Write equation.}$$

$$= \dfrac{pq}{pq} \cdot \dfrac{1}{\dfrac{1}{p}+\dfrac{1}{q}} \qquad \textbf{Multiply numerator and denominator by } pq.$$

$$= \dfrac{pq}{q+p} \qquad \textbf{Simplify.}$$

FOCUS ON APPLICATIONS

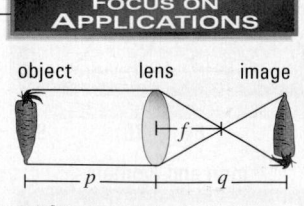
object   lens   image

PHOTOGRAPHY
The focal length of a camera lens is the distance between the lens and the point where light rays converge after passing through the lens.

GUIDED PRACTICE

Vocabulary Check ✓

1. Give two examples of a complex fraction.

Concept Check ✓

2. How is adding (or subtracting) rational expressions similar to adding (or subtracting) numerical fractions?

3. Describe two ways to simplify a complex fraction.

4. Why isn't $(x + 1)^3$ the LCD of $\dfrac{1}{x + 1}$ and $\dfrac{1}{(x + 1)^2}$? What is the LCD?

Skill Check ✓ **Perform the indicated operation and simplify.**

5. $\dfrac{2x}{x + 5} + \dfrac{7}{x + 5}$

6. $\dfrac{7}{5x} + \dfrac{8}{3x}$

7. $\dfrac{x}{x - 4} - \dfrac{6}{x + 3}$

Simplify the complex fraction.

8. $\dfrac{\dfrac{x}{5} + 4}{8 + \dfrac{1}{x}}$

9. $\dfrac{\dfrac{x + 2}{5} - 5}{8 + \dfrac{4}{x}}$

10. $\dfrac{\dfrac{15}{2x + 2}}{\dfrac{6}{x} - \dfrac{1}{2}}$

11. 🌐 **FINANCE** For a loan paid back over t years, the monthly payment is given by $M = \dfrac{Pi}{1 - \left(\dfrac{1}{1 + i}\right)^{12t}}$ where P is the principal and i is the annual interest rate. Show that this formula is equivalent to $M = \dfrac{Pi(1 + i)^{12t}}{(1 + i)^{12t} - 1}$.

PRACTICE AND APPLICATIONS

STUDENT HELP

▶ **Extra Practice**
to help you master
skills is on p. 953.

OPERATIONS WITH LIKE DENOMINATORS **Perform the indicated operation and simplify.**

12. $\dfrac{7}{6x} + \dfrac{11}{6x}$

13. $\dfrac{23}{10x^2} - \dfrac{x}{10x^2}$

14. $\dfrac{4x}{x + 1} - \dfrac{3}{x + 1}$

15. $\dfrac{5x^2}{x + 8} + \dfrac{5x}{x + 8}$

16. $\dfrac{6x^2}{x - 2} - \dfrac{12x}{x - 2}$

17. $\dfrac{x}{x^2 - 5x} - \dfrac{5}{x^2 - 5x}$

FINDING LCDS **Find the least common denominator.**

18. $\dfrac{14}{4(x + 1)}, \dfrac{7}{4x}$

19. $\dfrac{4}{21x^2}, \dfrac{x}{3x^2 - 15x}$

20. $\dfrac{5x + 2}{4x^2 - 1}, \dfrac{3}{x}, \dfrac{9x}{2x + 1}$

21. $\dfrac{1}{x(x - 6)}, \dfrac{12}{x^2 - 3x - 18}$

STUDENT HELP

▶ **HOMEWORK HELP**
Example 1: Exs. 12–17
Examples 2, 3: Exs. 18–23,
        26–37
Example 4: Exs. 47–51
Example 5: Exs. 38–46
Example 6: Exs. 52, 53

22. $\dfrac{3x + 1}{x(x - 7)}, \dfrac{3}{x^2 - 6x - 7}$

23. $\dfrac{1}{x^2 - 3x - 28}, \dfrac{x}{x^2 + 6x + 8}$

LOGICAL REASONING **Tell whether the statement is *always true, sometimes true*, or *never true*. Explain your reasoning.**

24. The LCD of two rational expressions is the product of the denominators.

25. The LCD of two rational expressions will have a degree greater than or equal to that of the denominator with the higher degree.

STUDENT HELP

▶ **Look Back**
For help with the negative exponents in Exs. 41 and 42, see p. 323.

OPERATIONS WITH UNLIKE DENOMINATORS Perform the indicated operation(s) and simplify.

26. $\dfrac{6}{4x^2} + \dfrac{2}{5x}$

27. $-\dfrac{4}{7x} - \dfrac{5}{3x}$

28. $\dfrac{7}{6(x-2)} - \dfrac{x+3}{6x}$

29. $\dfrac{6x+1}{x^2-9} + \dfrac{4}{x-3}$

30. $\dfrac{10}{x^2-5x-14} + \dfrac{2}{x-7}$

31. $\dfrac{5x-1}{x^2+2x-8} - \dfrac{6}{x+4}$

32. $\dfrac{4x^2}{3x+5} - \dfrac{10}{x+8}$

33. $\dfrac{2-5x}{x-10} + \dfrac{1}{3x+2}$

34. $\dfrac{x^2+x-3}{x^2-12x+32} + \dfrac{3x}{x-8}$

35. $\dfrac{2x+1}{x^2+8x+16} - \dfrac{3}{x^2-16}$

36. $\dfrac{4x}{x+1} + \dfrac{5}{2x-3} - \dfrac{4}{x}$

37. $\dfrac{10x}{3x^2-3} + \dfrac{4}{x-1} + \dfrac{5}{6x}$

SIMPLIFYING COMPLEX FRACTIONS Simplify the complex fraction.

38. $\dfrac{\frac{x}{2}-5}{6+\frac{3}{x}}$

39. $\dfrac{\frac{20}{x+1}}{\frac{1}{4}-\frac{7}{x+1}}$

40. $\dfrac{\frac{1}{2x^2-2}}{\frac{2}{x+1}+\frac{x}{x^2-2x-3}}$

41. $\dfrac{\frac{1}{x}-\frac{x}{x^{-1}+1}}{\frac{3}{x}}$

42. $\dfrac{\frac{1-x}{x^4}}{x^{-2}-\frac{2}{x^3+x^2}}$

43. $\dfrac{\frac{1}{4x+3}-\frac{5}{3(4x+3)}}{\frac{x}{4x+3}}$

44. $\dfrac{\frac{4}{x^2-9}+\frac{2}{x-3}}{\frac{1}{x+3}+\frac{1}{x-3}}$

45. $\dfrac{\frac{1}{x^3+64}}{\frac{5}{x^2-16}-\frac{2}{3x^2+12x}}$

46. $\dfrac{\frac{3}{2x^2+6x+18}+\frac{x}{x^3-27}}{\frac{5x}{3x-9}-\frac{3}{x-3}}$

47. 🌐 **COLLEGE GRADUATES** From the 1984–85 school year through the 1993–94 school year, the number of female college graduates F and the total number of college graduates G in the United States can be modeled by

$$F = \dfrac{-19{,}600t + 493{,}000}{-0.0580t + 1} \qquad \text{and} \qquad G = \dfrac{7560t^2 + 978{,}000}{0.00418t^2 + 1}$$

where t is the number of school years since the 1984–85 school year. Write a model for the number of male college graduates. ▶ Source: U.S. Department of Education

🖩 **DRUG ABSORPTION** In Exercises 48–51, use the following information.
The amount A (in milligrams) of an oral drug, such as aspirin, in a person's bloodstream can be modeled by

$$A = \dfrac{391t^2 + 0.112}{0.218t^4 + 0.991t^2 + 1}$$

where t is the time (in hours) after one dose is taken. ▶ Source: Drug Disposition in Humans

48. Graph the equation using a graphing calculator.

49. A second dose of the drug is taken 1 hour after the first dose. Write an equation to model the amount of the second dose in the bloodstream.

50. Write and graph a model for the total amount of the drug in the bloodstream after the second dose is taken.

51. About how long after the second dose has been taken is the greatest amount of the drug in the bloodstream?

FOCUS ON CAREERS

PHARMACIST
In addition to mixing and dispensing prescription drugs, pharmacists advise patients and physicians on the use of medications. This includes warning of possible side effects and recommending drug dosages, as discussed in Exs. 48–51.

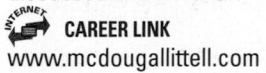
CAREER LINK
www.mcdougallittell.com

ELECTRONICS In Exercises 52 and 53, use the following information.
If three resistors in a parallel circuit have resistances R_1, R_2, and R_3 (all in ohms), then the total resistance R_t (in ohms) is given by this formula:

$$R_t = \dfrac{1}{\dfrac{1}{R_1} + \dfrac{1}{R_2} + \dfrac{1}{R_3}}$$

52. Simplify the complex fraction.

53. You have three resistors in a parallel circuit with resistances 6 ohms, 12 ohms, and 24 ohms. What is the total resistance of the circuit?

Test Preparation

54. ⬛ **MULTI-STEP PROBLEM** From 1988 through 1997, the total dollar value V (in millions of dollars) of the United States sound-recording industry can be modeled by

$$V = \dfrac{5783 + 1134t}{1 + 0.025t}$$

where t represents the number of years since 1988.
▶ Source: Recording Industry Association of America

a. Calculate the percent change in dollar value from 1988 to 1989.

b. Develop a general formula for the percent change in dollar value from year t to year $t + 1$.

c. Enter the formula into a graphing calculator or spreadsheet. Observe the changes from year to year for 1988 through 1997. Describe what you observe from the data.

★ Challenge

CRITICAL THINKING In Exercises 55 and 56, use the following expressions.

$$2 + \dfrac{1}{1 + \dfrac{1}{2}}, \quad 2 + \dfrac{1}{1 + \dfrac{1}{2 + \dfrac{2}{3}}}, \quad 2 + \dfrac{1}{1 + \dfrac{1}{2 + \dfrac{2}{3 + \dfrac{3}{4}}}}$$

55. The expressions form a pattern. Continue the pattern two more times. Then simplify all five expressions.

EXTRA CHALLENGE
www.mcdougallittell.com

56. The expressions are getting closer and closer to some value. What is it?

MIXED REVIEW

SOLVING LINEAR EQUATIONS Solve the equation. (Review 1.3 for 9.6)

57. $\frac{1}{2}x - 7 = 5$

58. $6 - \frac{1}{10}x = -1$

59. $\frac{3}{4}x + \frac{1}{2} = x - \frac{5}{6}$

60. $\frac{3}{8}x + 4 = -8$

61. $-\frac{1}{12}x - 3 = \frac{5}{2}$

62. $2 = -\frac{4}{3}x + 10$

63. $-5x - \frac{3}{4}x = \frac{51}{2}$

64. $2x + \frac{7}{8}x = -23$

65. $x = 12 + \frac{5}{6}x$

SOLVING QUADRATIC EQUATIONS Solve the equation. (Review 5.2, 5.3 for 9.6)

66. $x^2 - 5x - 24 = 0$

67. $5x^2 - 8 = 4(x^2 + 3)$

68. $6x^2 + 13x - 5 = 0$

69. $3(x - 5)^2 = 27$

70. $2(x + 7)^2 - 1 = 49$

71. $2x(x + 6) = 7 - x$

9.6

Solving Rational Equations

What you should learn

GOAL 1 Solve rational equations.

GOAL 2 Use rational equations to solve **real-life** problems, such as finding how to dilute an acid solution in **Example 5**.

Why you should learn it

▼ To solve **real-life** problems, such as finding the year in which a certain amount of rodeo prize money was earned in **Example 6**.

GOAL 1 SOLVING A RATIONAL EQUATION

To solve a rational equation, multiply each term on both sides of the equation by the LCD of the terms. Simplify and solve the resulting polynomial equation.

EXAMPLE 1 An Equation with One Solution

Solve: $\dfrac{4}{x} + \dfrac{5}{2} = -\dfrac{11}{x}$

SOLUTION

The least common denominator is $2x$.

$$\dfrac{4}{x} + \dfrac{5}{2} = -\dfrac{11}{x} \qquad \text{Write original equation.}$$

$$2x\left(\dfrac{4}{x} + \dfrac{5}{2}\right) = 2x\left(-\dfrac{11}{x}\right) \qquad \text{Multiply each side by } 2x.$$

$$8 + 5x = -22 \qquad \text{Simplify.}$$

$$5x = -30 \qquad \text{Subtract 8 from each side.}$$

$$x = -6 \qquad \text{Divide each side by 5.}$$

▶ The solution is -6. Check this in the original equation.

EXAMPLE 2 An Equation with an Extraneous Solution

Solve: $\dfrac{5x}{x-2} = 7 + \dfrac{10}{x-2}$

SOLUTION

The least common denominator is $x - 2$.

$$\dfrac{5x}{x-2} = 7 + \dfrac{10}{x-2}$$

$$(x-2) \cdot \dfrac{5x}{x-2} = (x-2) \cdot 7 + (x-2) \cdot \dfrac{10}{x-2}$$

$$5x = 7(x-2) + 10$$

$$5x = 7x - 4$$

$$x = 2$$

STUDENT HELP

HOMEWORK HELP
Visit our Web site
www.mcdougallittell.com
for extra examples.

▶ The solution appears to be 2. After checking it in the original equation, however, you can conclude that 2 is an extraneous solution because it leads to division by zero. So, the original equation has no solution.

EXAMPLE 3 *An Equation with Two Solutions*

Solve: $\dfrac{4x+1}{x+1} = \dfrac{12}{x^2-1} + 3$

SOLUTION

Write each denominator in factored form. The LCD is $(x+1)(x-1)$.

$$\frac{4x+1}{x+1} = \frac{12}{(x+1)(x-1)} + 3$$

$$(x+1)(x-1)\cdot\frac{4x+1}{x+1} = (x+1)(x-1)\cdot\frac{12}{(x+1)(x-1)} + (x+1)(x-1)\cdot 3$$

$$(x-1)(4x+1) = 12 + 3(x+1)(x-1)$$

$$4x^2 - 3x - 1 = 12 + 3x^2 - 3$$

$$x^2 - 3x - 10 = 0$$

$$(x+2)(x-5) = 0$$

$$x + 2 = 0 \quad \text{or} \quad x - 5 = 0$$

$$x = -2 \quad \text{or} \quad x = 5$$

▶ The solutions are -2 and 5. Check these in the original equation.

. . . .

You can use cross multiplying to solve a simple rational equation for which each side of the equation is a single rational expression.

EXAMPLE 4 *Solving an Equation by Cross Multiplying*

Solve: $\dfrac{2}{x^2-x} = \dfrac{1}{x-1}$

SOLUTION

$\dfrac{2}{x^2-x} = \dfrac{1}{x-1}$	**Write original equation.**
$2(x-1) = 1(x^2-x)$	**Cross multiply.**
$2x - 2 = x^2 - x$	**Simplify.**
$0 = x^2 - 3x + 2$	**Write in standard form.**
$0 = (x-2)(x-1)$	**Factor.**
$x = 2 \text{ or } x = 1$	**Zero product property**

▶ The solutions appear to be 2 and 1. After checking them in the original equation, however, you see that the only solution is 2. The apparent solution $x = 1$ is extraneous. A graphic check shows that the graphs of the left and right sides of the equation, $y = \dfrac{2}{x^2-x}$ and $y = \dfrac{1}{x-1}$, intersect only at $x = 2$. At $x = 1$, the graphs have a common vertical asymptote.

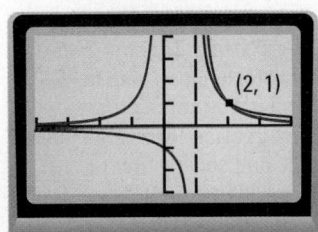

GOAL 2 **USING RATIONAL EQUATIONS IN REAL LIFE**

EXAMPLE 5 *Writing and Using a Rational Model*

CHEMISTRY You have 0.2 liter of an acid solution whose acid concentration is 16 moles per liter. You want to dilute the solution with water so that its acid concentration is only 12 moles per liter. How much water should you add to the solution?

SOLUTION

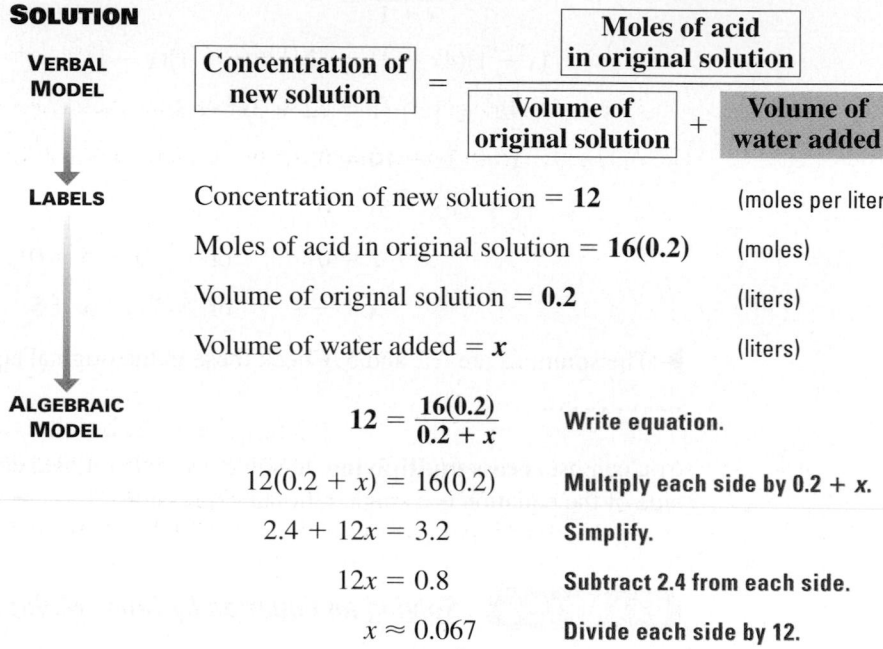

REAL LIFE **CHEMICAL ENGRAVING**
Acid mixtures are used to engrave, or *etch*, electronic circuits on silicon wafers. A wafer like the one shown above can be cut into as many as 1000 computer chips.

VERBAL MODEL

$$\boxed{\text{Concentration of new solution}} = \frac{\boxed{\text{Moles of acid in original solution}}}{\boxed{\text{Volume of original solution}} + \boxed{\text{Volume of water added}}}$$

LABELS

Concentration of new solution = **12** (moles per liter)

Moles of acid in original solution = **16(0.2)** (moles)

Volume of original solution = **0.2** (liters)

Volume of water added = **x** (liters)

ALGEBRAIC MODEL

$$12 = \frac{16(0.2)}{0.2 + x}$$ **Write equation.**

$$12(0.2 + x) = 16(0.2)$$ **Multiply each side by 0.2 + x.**

$$2.4 + 12x = 3.2$$ **Simplify.**

$$12x = 0.8$$ **Subtract 2.4 from each side.**

$$x \approx 0.067$$ **Divide each side by 12.**

▶ You should add about 0.067 liter, or 67 milliliters, of water.

EXAMPLE 6 *Using a Rational Model*

 RODEOS From 1980 through 1997, the total prize money *P* (in millions of dollars) at Professional Rodeo Cowboys Association events can be modeled by

$$P = \frac{380t + 5}{-t^2 + 31t + 1}$$

where *t* represents the number of years since 1980. During which year was the total prize money about \$20 million? ▶ Source: Professional Rodeo Cowboys Association

STUDENT HELP

▶ **Study Tip**
Example 6 can also be solved by setting the expression for *P* equal to 20 and solving the resulting equation algebraically.

SOLUTION

Use a graphing calculator to graph the equation $y = \dfrac{380x + 5}{-x^2 + 31x + 1}$. Then graph the line *y* = 20.

Use the *Intersect* feature to find the value of *x* that gives a *y*-value of 20. As shown at the right, this value is *x* ≈ 12. So, the total prize money was about \$20 million 12 years after 1980, in 1992.

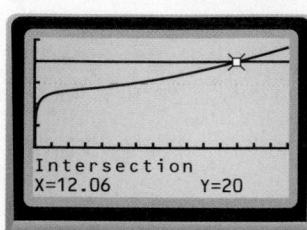

GUIDED PRACTICE

Vocabulary Check ✓

1. Give an example of a rational equation that can be solved using cross multiplication.

Concept Check ✓

2. A student solved the equation $\frac{2}{x-3} = \frac{x}{x-3}$ and got the solutions 2 and 3. Which, if either, of these is extraneous? Explain how you know.

3. Describe two methods that can be used to solve a rational equation. Which method can always be used? Why?

4. Solve the equation $\frac{1}{x} = \frac{2}{x^2}$. Check the apparent solutions graphically. Explain how a graph can help you identify actual and extraneous solutions.

Skill Check ✓   **Solve the equation using any method. Check each solution.**

5. $\frac{7}{x} + \frac{3}{4} = \frac{5}{x}$

6. $\frac{x-2}{6} = \frac{x-2}{x-1}$

7. $3x + \frac{x}{3} = 5$

8. $\frac{x}{x-3} = 2 - \frac{2}{x-3}$

9. $\frac{5}{x-3} = \frac{2x}{x^2-9}$

10. $\frac{5x}{x-1} + 5 = \frac{15}{x-1}$

11. $\frac{2x}{x+3} = \frac{3x}{x-3}$

12. $\frac{2x}{x-4} = \frac{8}{x-4} + 3$

13. $\frac{2x}{2x+4} = \frac{3x}{x+2}$

14. 🌐 **BASKETBALL STATISTICS** So far in the basketball season you have made 12 free throws out of the 20 free throws you have attempted, for a free-throw shooting percentage of 60%. How many consecutive free-throw shots would you have to make to raise your free-throw shooting percentage to 80%?

PRACTICE AND APPLICATIONS

STUDENT HELP

► **Extra Practice**
to help you master
skills is on p. 953.

CHECKING SOLUTIONS Determine whether the given *x*-value is a solution of the equation.

15. $\frac{2x-3}{x+3} = \frac{3x}{x+4}$; $x = -1$

16. $\frac{x}{2x+1} = \frac{5}{4-x}$; $x = -1$

17. $\frac{4x-3}{x-4} + 1 = \frac{x}{x-3}$; $x = 2$

18. $\frac{3x}{x-6} = 5 + \frac{18}{x-6}$; $x = 6$

19. $\frac{x}{x-3} = \frac{6}{x-3}$; $x = 6$

20. $\frac{2}{x(x+2)} + \frac{3}{x} = \frac{4}{x-2}$; $x = 2$

LEAST COMMON DENOMINATOR Solve the equation by using the LCD. Check each solution.

STUDENT HELP

► **HOMEWORK HELP**
Examples 1–3: Exs. 15–32,
42–50
Example 4: Exs. 15, 16, 19,
33–50
Examples 5, 6: Exs. 54–59

21. $\frac{3}{2} + \frac{1}{x} = 2$

22. $\frac{3}{x} + x = 4$

23. $\frac{3}{2x} - \frac{9}{2} = 6x$

24. $\frac{8}{x+2} + \frac{8}{2} = 5$

25. $\frac{3x}{x+1} + \frac{6}{2x} = \frac{7}{x}$

26. $\frac{2}{3x} + \frac{2}{3} = \frac{8}{x+6}$

27. $\frac{6x}{x+4} + 4 = \frac{2x+2}{x-1}$

28. $\frac{x-3}{x-4} + 4 = \frac{3x}{x}$

29. $\frac{7x+1}{2x+5} + 1 = \frac{10x-3}{3x}$

30. $\frac{10}{x^2-2x} + \frac{4}{x} = \frac{5}{x-2}$

31. $\frac{4(x-1)}{x-1} = \frac{2x-2}{x+1}$

32. $\frac{2(x+7)}{x+4} - 2 = \frac{2x+20}{2x+8}$

CROSS MULTIPLYING Solve the equation by cross multiplying. Check each solution.

33. $\dfrac{3}{4x} = \dfrac{5}{x + 2}$

34. $\dfrac{-3}{x + 1} = \dfrac{4}{x - 1}$

35. $\dfrac{x}{x^2 - 8} = \dfrac{2}{x}$

36. $\dfrac{x}{2x + 7} = \dfrac{x - 5}{x - 1}$

37. $\dfrac{-2}{x - 1} = \dfrac{x - 8}{x + 1}$

38. $\dfrac{2(x - 2)}{x^2 - 10x + 16} = \dfrac{2}{x + 2}$

39. $\dfrac{8(x - 1)}{x^2 - 4} = \dfrac{4}{x - 2}$

40. $\dfrac{x^2 - 3}{x + 2} = \dfrac{x - 3}{2}$

41. $\dfrac{-1}{x - 3} = \dfrac{x - 4}{x^2 - 27}$

CHOOSING A METHOD Solve the equation using any method. Check each solution.

42. $\dfrac{x - 2}{x + 2} = \dfrac{3}{x}$

43. $\dfrac{3}{x + 2} = \dfrac{6}{x - 1}$

44. $\dfrac{3x}{x + 1} = \dfrac{12}{x^2 - 1} + 2$

45. $\dfrac{3x + 6}{x^2 - 4} = \dfrac{x + 1}{x - 2}$

46. $\dfrac{x - 4}{x} = \dfrac{6}{x^2 - 3x}$

47. $\dfrac{2x}{4 - x} = \dfrac{x^2}{x - 4}$

48. $\dfrac{2x}{x - 3} = \dfrac{3x}{x^2 - 9} + 2$

49. $\dfrac{x}{2x - 6} = \dfrac{2}{x - 4}$

50. $\dfrac{2}{x + 1} + \dfrac{x}{x - 1} = \dfrac{2}{x^2 - 1}$

LOGICAL REASONING In Exercises 51–53, *a* is a nonzero real number. Tell whether the algebraic statement is *always true*, *sometimes true*, or *never true*. Explain your reasoning.

51. For the equation $\dfrac{1}{x - a} = \dfrac{x}{x - a}$, $x = a$ is an extraneous solution.

52. The equation $\dfrac{3}{x - a} = \dfrac{x}{x - a}$ has exactly one solution.

53. The equation $\dfrac{1}{x - a} = \dfrac{2}{x + a} + \dfrac{2a}{x^2 - a^2}$ has no solution.

54. 🌎 **FOOTBALL STATISTICS** At the end of the 1998 season, the National Football League's all-time leading passer during regular season play was Dan Marino with 4763 completed passes out of 7989 attempts. In his debut 1998 season, Peyton Manning made 326 completed passes out of 575 attempts. How many consecutive completed passes would Peyton Manning have to make to equal Dan Marino's pass completion percentage?

    ⚡ **DATA UPDATE** of National Football League data at www.mcdougallittell.com

55. 🌎 **PHONE CARDS** A telephone company offers you an opportunity to sell prepaid, 30 minute long-distance phone cards. You will have to pay the company a one-time setup fee of $200. Each phone card will cost you $5.70. How many cards would you have to sell before your average total cost per card falls to $8?

56. 🌎 **RIVER CURRENT** It takes a paddle boat 53 minutes to travel 5 miles up a river and 5 miles back, going at a steady speed of 12 miles per hour (with respect to the water). Find the speed of the current.

57. BIOLOGY CONNECTION The number *f* of flies eaten by a praying mantis in 8 hours can be modeled by

$$f = \dfrac{26.6d}{d + 0.0017}$$

where *d* is the density of flies available (in flies per cubic centimeter). Approximate the density of flies (in flies per cubic *meter*) when a praying mantis eats 15 flies in 8 hours. (*Hint:* There are 1,000,000 cm³ in 1 m³.) ▶ Source: *Biology by Numbers*

The praying mantis blends in with its environment.

 **FUEL EFFICIENCY In Exercises 58 and 59, use the following information.**
The cost of fueling your car for one year can be calculated using this equation:

$$\text{Fuel cost for one year} = \frac{\text{Miles driven} \times \text{Price per gallon of fuel}}{\text{Fuel efficiency rate}}$$

58. Last year you drove 9000 miles, paid $1.10 per gallon of gasoline, and spent a total of $412.50 on gasoline. What is the fuel efficiency rate of your car?

59. How much would you have saved if your car's fuel efficiency rate were 25 miles per gallon?

Test Preparation

QUANTITATIVE COMPARISON In Exercises 60 and 61, choose the statement below that is true about the given quantities.

(A) The quantity in column A is greater.

(B) The quantity in column B is greater.

(C) The two quantities are equal.

(D) The relationship cannot be determined from the given information.

	Column A	Column B
60.	The solution of $\dfrac{x^3 + 1}{x} = 2x^2$	The solution of $\dfrac{-2}{x+3} = \dfrac{4}{x-2}$
61.	The solution of $\dfrac{1}{x} + 3 = \dfrac{9}{2x}$	The solution of $\dfrac{1}{2} + \dfrac{3}{x} = \dfrac{43}{14}$

★ **Challenge**

62. **SCIENCE CONNECTION** You have 0.5 liter of an acid solution whose acid concentration is 16 moles per liter. To decrease the acid concentration to 12 moles per liter, you plan to add a certain amount of a second acid solution whose acid concentration is only 10 moles per liter. How many liters of the second acid solution should you add?

EXTRA CHALLENGE
www.mcdougallittell.com

MIXED REVIEW

SLOPES OF LINES Find the slope of a line parallel to the given line and the slope of a line perpendicular to the given line. (Review 2.4 for 10.1)

63. $y = x + 3$

64. $y = 3x - 4$

65. $y = -\dfrac{2}{3}x + 15$

66. $y + 3 = 3x + 2$

67. $2y - x = 7$

68. $4x - 3y = 17$

PROPERTIES OF SQUARE ROOTS Simplify the expression. (Review 5.3 for 10.1)

69. $\sqrt{48}$

70. $\sqrt{18}$

71. $\sqrt{108}$

72. $\sqrt{432}$

73. $\sqrt{6} \cdot \sqrt{45}$

74. $\sqrt{\dfrac{16}{72}}$

75. $\sqrt{75} \cdot \sqrt{3}$

76. $\sqrt{\dfrac{8}{49}}$

77.  **GEOLOGY** You can find the pH of a soil by using the formula

$$\text{pH} = -\log[\text{H}^+]$$

where $[\text{H}^+]$ is the soil's hydrogen ion concentration (in moles per liter). Find the pH of a layer of soil that has a hydrogen ion concentration of 1.6×10^{-7} moles per liter. **(Review 8.4)**

Perform the indicated operation and simplify. (Lessons 9.4 and 9.5)

1. $\dfrac{3x^3y}{2xy^2} \cdot \dfrac{10x^4y^2}{9x}$

2. $\dfrac{x^2 - 3x - 40}{5x} \div (x + 5)$

3. $\dfrac{18x}{x^2 - 5x - 36} + \dfrac{2x}{x + 4}$

4. $\dfrac{8x^2}{25x^2 - 36} - \dfrac{1}{10x + 12}$

Simplify the complex fraction. (Lesson 9.5)

5. $\dfrac{\dfrac{8}{x} + 11}{\dfrac{1}{6x} - 1}$

6. $\dfrac{36 - \dfrac{1}{x^2}}{\dfrac{1}{6x^2} - 6}$

7. $\dfrac{\dfrac{2}{x^2 - 1} - \dfrac{1}{x + 1}}{\dfrac{1}{12x^2 - 3}}$

8. $\dfrac{\dfrac{1}{x - 5} - \dfrac{x}{x^2 - 25}}{\dfrac{5}{2x}}$

9. 🌐 **AVERAGE COST** You bought a potholder weaving frame for $10. A bag of potholder material costs $4 and contains enough material to make a dozen potholders. How many dozens of potholders must you make before your average total cost per dozen falls to $4.50? (Lesson 9.6)

MATH & History

Deep Water Diving

APPLICATION LINK
www.mcdougallittell.com

THEN

IN 1530 the invention of the diving bell provided the first effective means of breathing underwater. Like many other diving devices, a diving bell uses air that is compressed by the pressure of the water. Because oxygen under high pressure (at great depths) can have toxic effects on the body, the percent of oxygen in the air must be adjusted. The recommended percent p of oxygen (by volume) in the air that a diver breathes is

$$p = \frac{660}{d + 33}$$

where d is the depth (in feet) at which the diver is working.

1. Graph the equation.

2. At what depth is the recommended percent of oxygen 5%?

3. What value does the recommended percent of oxygen approach as a diver's depth increases?

NOW

TODAY diving technology makes it easier for scientists like Dr. Sylvia Earle to study ocean life. Using one-person submarines, Earle has undertaken a five-year study of marine sanctuaries.

Sylvia Earle, marine biologist.

1530

The diving bell is invented. It is open to the water at the bottom and traps air at the top.

Augustus Siebe invents the closed hard-hat diving suit.

1837

1930

William Beebe descends 1426 feet in a bathysphere.

1979

Sylvia Earle walks untethered on the ocean floor at a record depth of 1250 feet.

Chapter Summary

WHAT did you learn?

Write and use variation models.
- inverse variation **(9.1)**
- joint variation **(9.1)**

Graph rational functions.
- simple rational functions **(9.2)**

- general rational functions **(9.3)**

Perform operations with rational expressions.
- multiply and divide **(9.4)**
- add and subtract **(9.5)**

Simplify complex fractions. **(9.5)**

Solve rational equations. **(9.6)**

Use rational models to solve real-life problems. **(9.1–9.6)**

WHY did you learn it?

Find the speed of a whirlpool's current. **(p. 535)**
Find the heat loss through a window. **(p. 539)**

Describe the frequency of an approaching ambulance siren. **(p. 545)**
Find the energy expenditure of a parakeet. **(p. 551)**

Compare the velocities of two skydivers. **(p. 557)**
Write a model for the number of male college graduates in the United States. **(p. 566)**

Write a simplified model for the focal length of a camera lens. **(p. 564)**

Find the amount of water to add when diluting an acid solution. **(p. 570)**

Find the year in which a certain amount of rodeo prize money was earned. **(p. 570)**

How does Chapter 9 fit into the BIGGER PICTURE of algebra?

In Chapter 9 you studied rational functions. A rational function is the ratio of two polynomial functions, which you studied in Chapter 2 (linear functions), Chapter 5 (quadratic functions), and Chapter 6 (polynomial functions).

A hyperbola is the graph of one important type of rational function. In the next chapter you will learn more about hyperbolas, parabolas, circles, and ellipses, which together are called the conic sections.

STUDY STRATEGY

How did you make and use a dictionary of functions?

Here is an example of one entry in a dictionary of functions, following the **Study Strategy** on page 532.

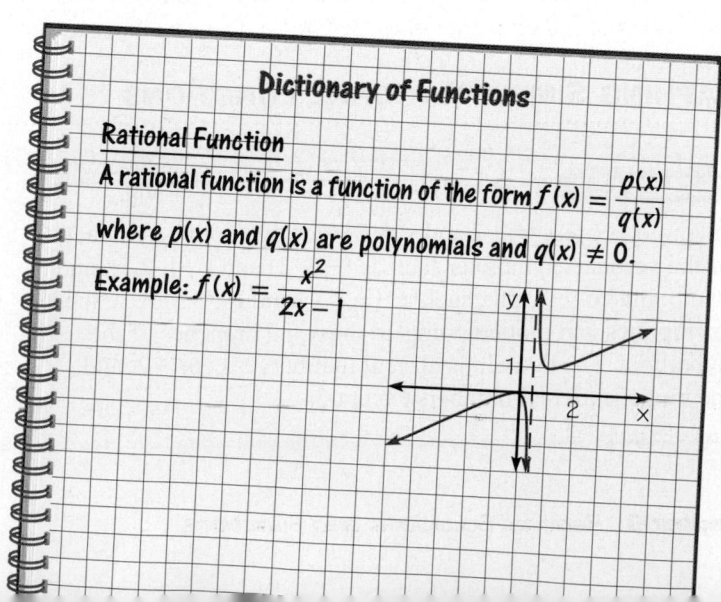

Dictionary of Functions

Rational Function

A rational function is a function of the form $f(x) = \dfrac{p(x)}{q(x)}$ where $p(x)$ and $q(x)$ are polynomials and $q(x) \neq 0$.

Example: $f(x) = \dfrac{x^2}{2x-1}$

Chapter Review

- inverse variation, p. 534
- constant of variation, p. 534
- joint variation, p. 536
- rational function, p. 540
- hyperbola, p. 540
- branches of a hyperbola, p. 540
- simplified form of a rational expression, p. 554
- complex fraction, p. 564
- cross multiplying, p. 569

9.1 INVERSE AND JOINT VARIATION

Examples on pp. 534–536

EXAMPLES You can write an inverse or joint variation equation using a general equation for the variation and given values of the variables.

Inverse variation: $x = 5, y = 4$

$y = \dfrac{k}{x}$ *y* varies inversely with *x*.

$4 = \dfrac{k}{5}$ Substitute for *x* and *y*.

$20 - k$ Solve for *k*.

The inverse variation equation is $y = \dfrac{20}{x}$.

Joint variation: $x = 3, y = 8, z = 30$

$z = kxy$ *z* varies jointly with *x* and *y*.

$30 = k(3)(8)$ Substitute for *x*, *y*, and *z*.

$30 = 24k$ Multiply.

$k = \dfrac{30}{24} = \dfrac{5}{4}$ Solve for *k*.

The joint variation equation is $z = \dfrac{5}{4}xy$.

The variables *x* and *y* vary inversely. Use the given values to write an equation relating *x* and *y*. Then find *y* when *x* = 2.

1. $x = 1, y = 5$ **2.** $x = 15, y = \dfrac{2}{3}$ **3.** $x = \dfrac{1}{4}, y = 8$ **4.** $x = -2, y = 2$

The variable *z* varies jointly with *x* and *y*. Use the given values to write an equation relating *x*, *y*, and *z*. Then find *z* when *x* = 5 and *y* = −6.

5. $x = 1, y = 12, z = 4$ **6.** $x = 6, y = 8, z = -6$ **7.** $x = \dfrac{3}{4}, y = 4, z = 9$

9.2 GRAPHING SIMPLE RATIONAL FUNCTIONS

Examples on pp. 540–542

EXAMPLE 1 To graph $y = \dfrac{1}{x + 2} + 3$, note that the asymptotes are $x = -2$ and $y = 3$. Plot two points to the left of the vertical asymptote, such as $(-3, 2)$ and $(-4, 2.5)$, and two points to the right, such as $(-1, 4)$ and $(0, 3.5)$. Use the asymptotes and plotted points to draw the branches of the hyperbola. The domain is all real numbers except −2, and the range is all real numbers except 3.

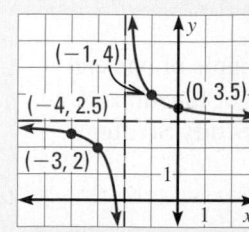

EXAMPLE 2 To graph $y = \dfrac{x+1}{x-3}$, note that when the denominator equals zero, $x = 3$. So the vertical asymptote is $x = 3$. The
horizontal asymptote, which occurs at the ratio of the x-coefficients,
is $y = 1$. Plot some points to the left and right of the vertical
asymptote. Use the asymptotes and plotted points to draw the
branches of the hyperbola. The domain is all real numbers except 3,
and the range is all real numbers except 1.

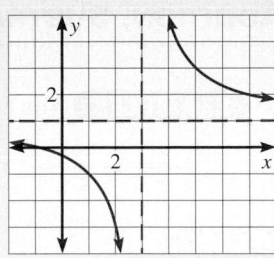

Graph the function. State the domain and range.

8. $y = \dfrac{3}{x-5}$
9. $y = \dfrac{1}{x+4} + 2$
10. $y = \dfrac{-6x}{x+2}$
11. $y = \dfrac{2x+5}{x-1}$

9.3 **GRAPHING GENERAL RATIONAL FUNCTIONS**

Examples on pp. 547–549

EXAMPLE To graph $y = \dfrac{3x^2}{x+2}$, note that the numerator has 0 as its only real zero,
so the graph has one x-intercept at $(0, 0)$. The only zero of the denominator is -2, so the
only vertical asymptote is $x = -2$. The degree of the numerator is greater than the
degree of the denominator, so there is no horizontal asymptote.

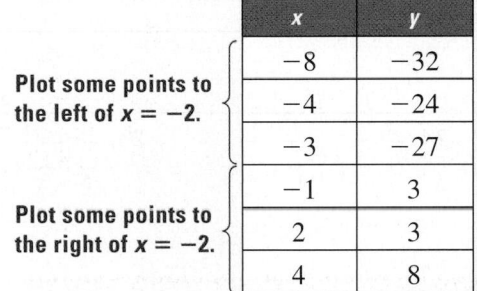

Plot some points to the left of $x = -2$.

x	y
−8	−32
−4	−24
−3	−27
−1	3
2	3
4	8

Plot some points to the right of $x = -2$.

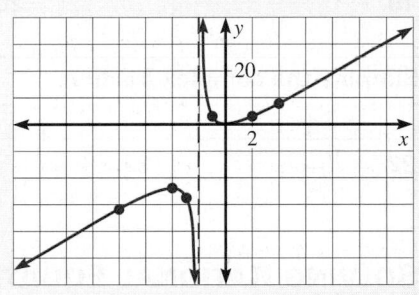

Graph the function.

12. $y = \dfrac{3x^2+1}{x^2-1}$
13. $y = \dfrac{x^3}{10}$
14. $y = \dfrac{x}{x^2-4}$
15. $y = \dfrac{3x^2-4x+1}{x^2-2x-3}$

9.4 **MULTIPLYING AND DIVIDING RATIONAL EXPRESSIONS**

Examples on pp. 554–557

EXAMPLE Dividing rational expressions is like dividing numerical fractions.

$$\frac{x^2-9}{5(x+2)} \div \frac{x-3}{5(x^2-4)} = \frac{x^2-9}{5(x+2)} \cdot \frac{5(x^2-4)}{x-3}$$ **Multiply by reciprocal.**

$$= \frac{(x+3)(x-3)(5)(x+2)(x-2)}{5(x+2)(x-3)}$$ **Factor and divide out common factors.**

$$= (x+3)(x-2)$$ **Simplified form**

Perform the indicated operation(s). Simplify the result.

16. $\dfrac{x^2-3x}{4x^2-8x} \cdot (4x^2-16)$
17. $5x \div \dfrac{1}{x-6} \cdot \dfrac{x^2-9}{x}$
18. $\dfrac{x^2-2x-3}{x+1} \div \dfrac{x^2+x-12}{x^2} - 1$

ADDITION, SUBTRACTION, AND COMPLEX FRACTIONS

Examples on pp. 562–564

EXAMPLES You can use the LCD to add or subtract rational expressions.

$$\frac{3}{x-3} - \frac{5}{x+2} = \frac{3(x+2)}{(x-3)(x+2)} - \frac{5(x-3)}{(x-3)(x+2)}$$ **Rewrite each expression using the LCD.**

$$= \frac{3(x+2) - 5(x-3)}{(x-3)(x+2)}$$ **Subtract.**

$$= \frac{3x + 6 - 5x + 15}{(x-3)(x+2)}$$ **Multiply.**

$$= \frac{-2x + 21}{(x-3)(x+2)}$$ **Simplified form**

To simplify a complex fraction, divide the numerator by the denominator.

$$\frac{\frac{2}{x} + 4}{\frac{2x+1}{5x^2}} = \frac{\frac{2+4x}{x}}{\frac{2x+1}{5x^2}} = \frac{2+4x}{x} \cdot \frac{5x^2}{2x+1} = \frac{2(1+2x)(5x^2)}{x(2x+1)} = 10x$$

Perform the indicated operation(s) and simplify.

19. $\dfrac{5}{x^2(x-2)} + \dfrac{x}{x-2}$

20. $\dfrac{x+5}{x-5} - \dfrac{3}{x+5}$

21. $\dfrac{x-2}{5x(x-1)} + \dfrac{1}{x-1} - \dfrac{3x+2}{x^2+4x-5}$

Simplify the complex fraction.

22. $\dfrac{\frac{x+3}{6}}{1 + \frac{x}{3}}$

23. $\dfrac{\frac{x}{2} - 4}{9 + \frac{2}{x}}$

24. $\dfrac{\frac{1}{x+1} + \frac{1}{x-1}}{\frac{x}{x+1}}$

25. $\dfrac{\frac{4}{5-x}}{\frac{2}{5-x} + \frac{1}{3x-15}}$

SOLVING RATIONAL EQUATIONS

Examples on pp. 568–570

EXAMPLES You can solve rational equations by multiplying each side of the equation by the LCD of the terms. If each side of the equation is a single rational expression, you can use cross multiplying. Check for extraneous solutions.

$$\frac{4}{x} + \frac{3}{2x} = 11$$

$$\frac{2}{3x+6} = \frac{x+2}{x^2-10}$$

$$(2x)\frac{4}{x} + (2x)\frac{3}{2x} = (2x)11 \quad \text{**Multiply each side by 2x.**}$$

$$2(x^2 - 10) = (x+2)(3x+6) \quad \text{**Cross multiply.**}$$

$$8 + 3 = 22x$$

$$2x^2 - 20 = 3x^2 + 12x + 12$$

$$0 = x^2 + 12x + 32$$

$$x = \frac{1}{2}$$

$$0 = (x+8)(x+4)$$

$$x = -8 \text{ or } x = -4$$

Solve the equation using any method. Check each solution.

26. $\dfrac{x}{x-1} = \dfrac{2x+10}{x+11}$

27. $\dfrac{x+3}{x} - 1 = \dfrac{1}{x-1}$

28. $\dfrac{2}{x-2} - \dfrac{2x}{3} = \dfrac{x-3}{3}$

29. $\dfrac{3x+2}{x+1} = 2 - \dfrac{2x+3}{x+1}$

30. $\dfrac{2}{x-6} = \dfrac{-5}{x+1}$

31. $1 + \dfrac{3}{x-3} = \dfrac{4}{x^2-9}$

Chapter Test

The variables x and y vary inversely. Use the given values to write an equation relating x and y. Then find y when $x = 3$.

1. $x = -4, y = 9$

2. $x = \frac{1}{2}, y = 5$

3. $x = 12, y = \frac{2}{3}$

4. $x = 6, y = -1$

The variable z varies jointly with x and y. Use the given values to write an equation relating x, y, and z. Then find z when $x = -2$ and $y = 4$.

5. $x = 5, y = 4, z = 2$

6. $x = -3, y = 2, z = 18$

7. $x = \frac{1}{3}, y = \frac{3}{4}, z = \frac{5}{2}$

Graph the function.

8. $y = \dfrac{-1}{x+1} - 2$

9. $y = \dfrac{4}{x-2}$

10. $y = \dfrac{x}{2x+5}$

11. $y = \dfrac{4x-3}{x-4}$

12. $y = \dfrac{6}{x^2+4}$

13. $y = \dfrac{-3x^2}{2x-1}$

14. $y = \dfrac{x^2-2}{x^2-9}$

15. $y = \dfrac{x^2-2x+15}{x+1}$

Perform the indicated operation. Simplify the result.

16. $\dfrac{x^2-4}{x+3} \cdot \dfrac{x^2+4x+3}{2x-4}$

17. $\dfrac{4x-8}{x^2-3x+2} \div \dfrac{3x-6}{x-1}$

18. $\dfrac{x+4}{x^2-25} \cdot (x^2+3x-10)$

19. $\dfrac{5}{6x} + \dfrac{7}{18x}$

20. $\dfrac{x-1}{x-2} - \dfrac{x-4}{x+1}$

21. $\dfrac{3x}{x^2-10x+21} + \dfrac{5}{x-3}$

Simplify the complex fraction.

22. $\dfrac{1 + \dfrac{3}{x}}{2 - \dfrac{5}{x^2}}$

23. $\dfrac{\dfrac{4+x}{10}}{\dfrac{x^2-16}{8}}$

24. $\dfrac{\dfrac{2}{x-1} + 5}{\dfrac{x}{3}}$

25. $\dfrac{36}{\dfrac{1}{x} + \dfrac{7}{2x}}$

Solve the equation using any method. Check each solution.

26. $\dfrac{9}{x} + \dfrac{11}{5} = \dfrac{31}{x}$

27. $\dfrac{-15}{x} = \dfrac{x+16}{4}$

28. $\dfrac{8}{x+3} = \dfrac{5}{x-3}$

29. $\dfrac{4x}{x+3} = \dfrac{37}{x^2-9} - 3$

30. **SCIENCE** **CONNECTION** A lever pivots on a support called a *fulcrum*. For a balanced lever, the distance d (in feet) an object is from the fulcrum varies inversely with the object's weight w (in pounds). An object weighing 140 pounds is placed 6 feet from a fulcrum. How far from the fulcrum must a 112 pound object be placed to balance the lever?

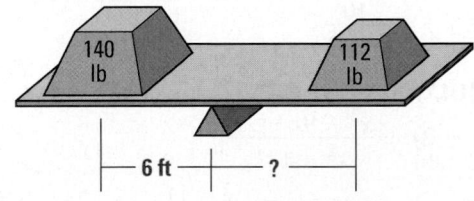

31. **GEOMETRY** **CONNECTION** A sphere with radius r is inscribed in a cube as shown. Find the ratio of the volume of the cube to the volume of the sphere. Write your answer in simplified form.

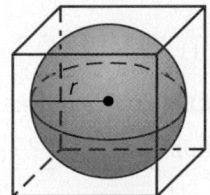

32. **STARTING A BUSINESS** You start a small bee-keeping business, spending $500 for equipment and bees. You figure it will cost $1.25 per pound to collect, clean, bottle, and label the honey. How many pounds of honey must you produce before your average cost per pound is $1.79?

Chapter Standardized Test

▶ **TEST-TAKING STRATEGY** During a test, draw graphs and figures in your test booklet to help you solve problems. Even though you must keep your answer sheet neat, you can make any kind of mark you want in your test booklet.

1. **MULTIPLE CHOICE** The variable x varies inversely with y. When $x = 6$, $y = 6.5$. Which equation relates x and y?

   Ⓐ $xy = 39$ Ⓑ $xy = 11.5$ Ⓒ $xy = \frac{1}{2}$

   Ⓓ $y = \frac{1}{2}x$ Ⓔ $y = 39x$

2. **MULTIPLE CHOICE** The variable z varies jointly with x and y. When $x = 6$ and $y = \frac{1}{3}$, $z = 30$. Which equation relates x, y, and z?

   Ⓐ $z = 30xy$ Ⓑ $30 = xyz$ Ⓒ $z = 15xy$

   Ⓓ $z = \frac{1}{30}xy$ Ⓔ $z = \frac{1}{15}xy$

3. **MULTIPLE CHOICE** Which function is graphed?

   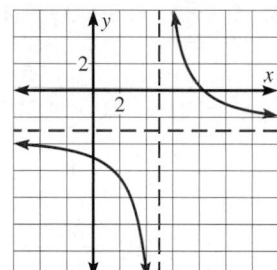

   Ⓐ $y = \frac{10}{x + 5} - 3$ Ⓑ $y = \frac{10}{x - 5} - 3$

   Ⓒ $y = \frac{10}{x + 5} + 3$ Ⓓ $y = \frac{10}{x - 5} + 3$

   Ⓔ $y = \frac{10}{x - 5}$

4. **MULTIPLE CHOICE** What is the quotient
   $(x + 2) \div \frac{x^2 - 9x - 22}{x^2 - 121}$?

   Ⓐ $x + 11$ Ⓑ $\frac{x + 11}{x + 2}$ Ⓒ $\frac{x + 2}{x + 11}$

   Ⓓ $\frac{x + 2}{x - 11}$ Ⓔ $x + 2$

5. **MULTIPLE CHOICE** What are all the solutions of the equation $\frac{-10}{x - 9} = \frac{x}{2}$?

   Ⓐ $-4, -5$ Ⓑ $4, -5$ Ⓒ 4

   Ⓓ 5 Ⓔ $4, 5$

6. **MULTIPLE CHOICE** Which function is graphed?

   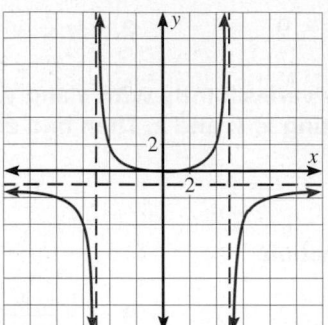

   Ⓐ $y = \frac{-x^2}{x^2 - 25}$ Ⓑ $y = \frac{-3x^2}{x^2 - 16}$

   Ⓒ $y = \frac{-3x^2}{x^2 - 25}$ Ⓓ $y = \frac{3x^2}{x^2 - 25}$

   Ⓔ $y = \frac{-3x^2}{x^2 + 25}$

7. **MULTIPLE CHOICE** What is the difference
   $\frac{8x - 3}{x^2 + 2x - 35} - \frac{7}{x^2 - 25}$?

   Ⓐ $\frac{2(4x^2 + 15x - 17)}{(x^2 + 2x - 35)(x + 5)}$

   Ⓑ $\frac{2(4x^2 + 15x + 32)}{(x^2 + 2x - 35)(x + 5)}$

   Ⓒ $\frac{2(4x^2 + 15x + 17)}{(x^2 + 2x - 35)(x + 5)}$

   Ⓓ $\frac{2(4x^2 + 15x - 32)}{(x^2 + 2x - 35)(x + 5)}$

   Ⓔ $\frac{2(4x^2 + 15x - 32)}{(x^2 + 2x - 35)(x^2 - 25)}$

8. **MULTIPLE CHOICE** What is the simplified form of the following complex fraction?

   $$\frac{\dfrac{10}{x + 1}}{\dfrac{1}{2} + \dfrac{3}{x + 1}}$$

   Ⓐ $\frac{20x}{x + 7}$ Ⓑ $\frac{20}{x + 7}$ Ⓒ $\frac{10}{x + 7}$

   Ⓓ $\frac{10(x + 7)}{x + 1}$ Ⓔ 20

9. **QUANTITATIVE COMPARISON** Choose the statement that is true about the given quantities.

   (A) The quantity in column A is greater.

   (B) The quantity in column B is greater.

   (C) The two quantities are equal.

   (D) The relationship cannot be determined from the given information.

Column A	Column B
The solution of $\dfrac{x-4}{x+1} = \dfrac{7}{2}$	The solution of $\dfrac{5}{x} - \dfrac{8}{3} = \dfrac{1}{12x}$

10. **MULTI-STEP PROBLEM** For parts (a)–(d), graph the function and identify the point at which the horizontal and vertical asymptotes intersect.

    a. $y = \dfrac{2}{x}$ **b.** $y = \dfrac{2}{x-1} + 3$ **c.** $y = \dfrac{2}{x-1} - 3$ **d.** $y = \dfrac{2}{x+1} + 3$

    e. Use your answers to parts (a)–(d) to predict the point of intersection of the asymptotes of the graph of $y = \dfrac{2}{x+1} - 3$. Check your prediction by graphing.

    f. **CRITICAL THINKING** Generalize your results for any function of the form $y = \dfrac{a}{x-h} + k$.

11. **MULTI-STEP PROBLEM** Three tennis balls fit tightly in a can as shown. Recall that the formula for the volume of a cylinder is $V = \pi r^2 h$ and the formula for the volume of a sphere is $V = \dfrac{4}{3}\pi r^3$.

    a. Write an expression for the height of the can, h, in terms of r. Rewrite the formula for the volume of a cylinder with r as the only variable.

    b. Find the ratio of the volume of the three tennis balls to the volume of the can.

    c. *Writing* Do you think using a cylindrical can is an efficient way of packaging tennis balls? Explain your reasoning.

12. **MULTI-STEP PROBLEM** The length l and width w of a *golden rectangle* satisfy the equation $\dfrac{l}{w} = \dfrac{l+w}{l}$. The ratio $\dfrac{l}{w}$ is called the *golden ratio*. For centuries, golden rectangles have been known to be very pleasing to the human eye.

    a. Rewrite the right side of the equation as a complex fraction by dividing each term of the numerator and denominator by w.

    b. Let g represent the golden ratio, so $g = \dfrac{l}{w}$. Substitute g for each occurrence of $\dfrac{l}{w}$ in the equation from part (a) and simplify the equation.

    c. Solve the equation from part (b) for g. (*Hint:* Use the quadratic formula.) Write an exact value and an approximate value for the golden ratio.

    d. **GEOMETRY > CONNECTION** Use a ruler or graph paper to draw an accurate golden rectangle of any size. Label the dimensions of your rectangle.

Cumulative Practice

Solve the equation for y. (1.4)

1. $6x - 2y = 7$

2. $-\dfrac{3}{4}x - y = 9$

3. $\dfrac{1}{3}x + \dfrac{2}{5}y = 10$

4. $xy + 5x = -4$

Tell whether the lines are *parallel*, *perpendicular*, or *neither*. (2.2)

5. Line 1: through $(2, 1)$ and $(-6, 1)$
Line 2: through $(0, -3)$ and $(-2, -3)$

6. Line 1: through $(-1, 1)$ and $(5, -1)$
Line 2: through $(2, 5)$ and $(3, 2)$

Graph the system of linear inequalities. (3.3)

7. $y < x + 3$
$y \geq -2x + 1$

8. $y < \dfrac{1}{2}x$
$y + 5 > \dfrac{1}{2}x$

9. $x \geq 0$
$2x + 3y < 12$
$x - 6y < 6$

10. $x \geq -2$
$x \leq 3$
$y \geq 0$
$y \leq 4$

Perform the indicated operation, if possible. If not possible, state the reason. (4.1, 4.2)

11. $\begin{bmatrix} 10 & 3 \\ -6 & -1 \end{bmatrix} - \begin{bmatrix} -2 & 5 \\ 6 & -3 \end{bmatrix}$

12. $3\begin{bmatrix} 1 & 0 & 6 \\ -3 & 5 & -2 \\ 2 & 8 & -1 \end{bmatrix}$

13. $\begin{bmatrix} 1 & -1 & -2 \\ 4 & 3 & -5 \end{bmatrix}\begin{bmatrix} 0 & 4 \\ 4 & 8 \\ -1 & 2 \end{bmatrix}$

Plot the numbers in the same complex plane and find their absolute values. (5.4)

14. $1 + 4i$

15. $-2 + i$

16. $-i$

17. 6

18. $-1 - 3i$

19. $3 - 5i$

Find all the zeros of the polynomial function. (6.6, 6.7)

20. $f(x) = x^3 + 2x^2 - 11x - 12$

21. $f(x) = x^3 - 5x^2 + 5x - 25$

22. $f(x) = x^4 - 81$

Simplify the expression. Assume all variables are positive. (6.1, 7.2, 8.3)

23. $\dfrac{3x^5}{5y} \cdot \dfrac{xy}{2x^2}$

24. $\left(-6x^{-2}y\right)^{-2}$

25. $\sqrt[4]{16a^4b^5c}$

26. $\left(9x^6\right)^{3/2}$

27. $\left(\dfrac{1}{2}e^{-2}\right)^3$

28. $\dfrac{100e^{6x}}{24e^{4x}}$

Evaluate the expression without using a calculator. (7.1, 8.4)

29. $\sqrt[6]{64}$

30. $-\left(100^{3/2}\right)$

31. $125^{-1/3}$

32. $\log_2 \dfrac{1}{32}$

33. $\log_7 \sqrt{7}$

34. $\log 0.1$

Perform the indicated operation and state the domain. (7.3)

35. $f - g$; $f(x) = 2x - 7$, $g(x) = x^2 - 20$

36. $f \cdot g$; $f(x) = 3x^{1/4}$, $g(x) = -x^{5/4}$

37. $f(g(x))$; $f(x) = x - 10$, $g(x) = -2x^2 - 5$

38. $g(f(x))$; $f(x) = x + 6$, $g(x) = x^2 - 7x + 3$

Find the inverse of the function. (7.4, 8.4)

39. $f(x) = \dfrac{1}{2}x - 6$

40. $f(x) = x^2 + 1$, $x \geq 0$

41. $f(x) = \log_5 x$

42. $f(x) = \ln 3x$

Condense the expression. (8.5)

43. $\log 3 + 2 \log x + 3 \log y$

44. $\log_7 4 + \log_7 y - 2 \log_7 3$

45. $2(\ln x + \ln y)$

Graph the function. (7.5, 8.1–8.4, 8.8, 9.2, 9.3)

46. $y = \sqrt{x + 12}$

47. $y = 2x^{1/3} - 3$

48. $y = 3\left(\dfrac{4}{3}\right)^x$

49. $y = 3\left(\dfrac{1}{2}\right)^{x + 2}$

50. $y = e^x - 5$

51. $y = \log(x - 1)$

52. $y = \ln x - 2$

53. $y = \dfrac{2}{1 + e^{-3x}}$

54. $y = \dfrac{5}{x - 2} - 1$

55. $y = \dfrac{x - 4}{2x + 1}$

56. $y = \dfrac{13}{x^2 - 4}$

57. $y = \dfrac{3x^2 + 5x - 2}{x - 1}$

Solve the equation. Check each solution. (7.6, 8.6, 8.8, 9.6)

58. $2\sqrt{x + 5} = 18$

59. $\dfrac{1}{8}(x - 6)^{3/2} = 1$

60. $2^{5x} = 8^{x + 6}$

61. $4 \log_3 (-2x) = 10$

62. $2 \ln x + 5 = 7$

63. $\dfrac{5}{1 + 2e^{-x}} = 4$

64. $\dfrac{5}{2x - 3} = \dfrac{2x}{x + 4}$

65. $\dfrac{1}{x - 2} - \dfrac{4}{x^2 - 4} = 5$

Write an exponential function of the form $y = ab^x$ whose graph passes through the given points. (8.7)

66. $(1, 2), (3, 10)$

67. $(5, 5), (6, 10)$

68. $(2, 4), (4, 8)$

69. $(0.5, 1), (5, 12)$

Write a power function of the form $y = ax^b$ whose graph passes through the given points. (8.7)

70. $(1, 1), (3, 9)$

71. $(2, 3), (10, 12)$

72. $(4, 1), (8, 7)$

73. $(0.1, 1), (2, 2)$

Perform the indicated operations. Simplify the result. (9.4, 9.5)

74. $\dfrac{3x^2 y}{x - 2} \cdot \dfrac{x^2 + x - 6}{3x - 6} \div (x^2 - 4)$

75. $\dfrac{6x}{3x + 1} + \dfrac{9}{2x} - \dfrac{x + 1}{x - 1}$

76. **FOOTBALL** The circumference of a standard football can vary from $20\dfrac{3}{4}$ inches to $21\dfrac{1}{4}$ inches around the middle and from $27\dfrac{3}{4}$ inches to $28\dfrac{1}{2}$ inches around the length of the football. Write two absolute value inequalities that describe the possible circumferences C_m and C_ℓ of a football. (1.7)

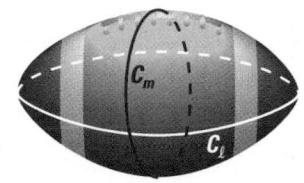

77. **WISHING WELL** A stone is dropped into a deep wishing well. The water level of the well is 200 feet below the top of the well. After how many seconds will the stone hit the water? (5.3)

HOME RUNS In Exercises 78–80, use the following data set of number of home runs hit by each member of the Chicago Cubs in the 1998 baseball season. (7.7)

    8, 1, 17, 66, 1, 1, 8, 14, 8, 2, 0, 9, 23, 31, 0, 5, 7, 4, 0, 0, 2, 1, 0

78. Find the mean, median, mode, range, and standard deviation of the data set.

79. Draw a box-and-whisker plot of the data set.

80. Make a frequency distribution of the data set. Use four intervals beginning with $1-10$. Then draw a histogram of the data set.

SCIENCE ▸ CONNECTION **In Exercises 81 and 82, use the following information.**
The electrical force f (in newtons) between two charged particles varies jointly with the electric charges q_1 and q_2 (in coulombs) of the particles and inversely with the square of the distance r (in meters) between the particles. (9.1)

81. Write an equation relating f, q_1, q_2, r, and a constant k.

82. Using $k = 8{,}987{,}760{,}000$, find the electrical force between a 2 coulomb charged particle and a 3 coulomb charged particle if the two particles are 2 meters apart.

Mathematical Models of Learning

OBJECTIVE Graph data about learning time and fit a model to the data.

Materials: simple puzzle, timer

When you were first learning to read, a page in a children's book might have taken you several minutes to work through. Now when reading a book to a small child, you can read an entire page easily. How did the time needed to read a page change as you got older and better at reading?

Many scientists study learning. Some study which environments seem to promote learning and which hinder it. Some study which parts of the brain are active when people learn a new skill and which are active when they practice old ones. Others explore how learning changes over time. In this project you will measure the time it takes to do a task as it becomes more familiar to you. You will then fit a model to your data.

INVESTIGATION

1. Find or create a simple task for someone to learn. The task should not take too long to complete and should gradually get easier with practice. Note, a brainteaser puzzle that is very difficult until you realize the trick and then is very easy will not show a gradual increase in performance. A task that is too easy will show only a slight variation in performance.

   Possible tasks include: assembling a small puzzle, such as a 10–30 piece jigsaw puzzle; putting 20 index cards with words on them in alphabetical order; solving 15 arithmetic problems involving order of operations where the same problems are in a different order each time; arranging shapes to match a given pattern.

2. Choose a partner as a test subject. Explain to your partner how to do the task you chose. Administer the task to your partner and then measure the time your partner takes to complete the task. Record the data in a table like the one on the right. Repeat the process nine times.

3. Make a scatter plot of your data.

4. So far in this book you have studied linear, quadratic, polynomial, power, radical, exponential, logarithmic, and rational functions. Find a mathematical model that is one of these types of functions to fit your data.

Task number	Time
1	?
2	?
3	?
4	?
5	?
6	?
7	?
8	?
9	?
10	?

PRESENT YOUR RESULTS

Write a report to present your results.

- Begin with a description of the learning task you used and explain how you chose it.

- Include your table of data, your graph, and your mathematical model.

- Explain how you chose the type of function to model your data.

- Explain how you obtained your model.

- Write a description of your data and what they show.

Extend your results.

- Recruit a second partner and repeat the experiment.

- Find a mathematical model to describe the learning time for the new data.

- Do you get the same or different results this time? Explain why you might expect similar or different results. (For example, you might obtain similar results because both subjects are juniors in high school who like word puzzles. You might obtain different results because one subject is several years younger than the other.)

EXTENSION

You have measured the times it takes to perform an increasingly familiar task. Now you will measure the times it takes to perform an increasingly complicated task.

Possible tasks include: assembling a puzzle cut out of paper with 2 pieces, then one with 4 pieces, then one with 8 pieces, and so on; arranging index cards with words on them in alphabetical order, first doing 5 cards, then 10 cards, then 15 cards, and so on; finding the ace of spades in a deck with 4 cards, then 8 cards, and so on.

Choose a task and recruit a volunteer to help you. Measure the times it takes your volunteer to complete the task 10 times at increasing levels of difficulty. Record the data in a table, make a scatter plot of the data, and then find a mathematical model to fit your data.

QUADRATIC RELATIONS AND CONIC SECTIONS

▶ *What shape does a telescope mirror have?*

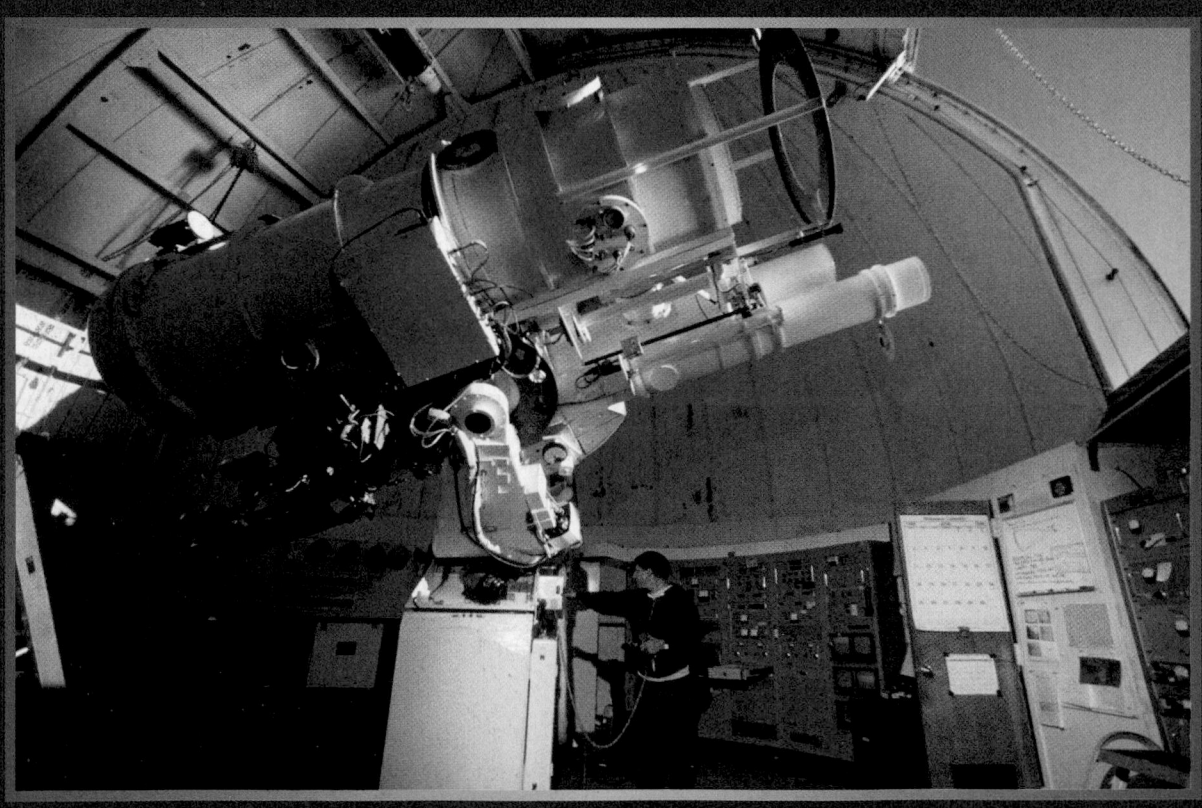

APPLICATION: Telescopes

Using powerful telescopes like the Hubble telescope, astronomers have discovered planets that exist outside our solar system. By examining the wobble in a star's motion, astronomers can detect the presence of one or more planets orbiting that star. The challenge is to see the planets, but that would require a telescope with a mirror 100 meters in diameter, 10 times larger than any existing telescope.

Think & Discuss

The diagram shows a cross section of a mirror from a telescope at the Big Bear Solar Observatory in California. An equation for the surface of the mirror, based on the coordinate system shown, is $y = \dfrac{x^2}{1040}$ where x and y are measured in centimeters.

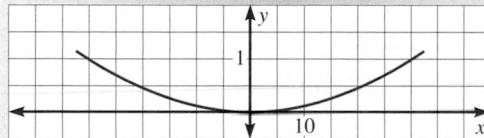

1. What shape is the cross section of the mirror?

2. The mirror has a diameter of 65 cm. What is the depth of the mirror? How did you get your answer?

Learn More About It

In Exercise 67 on p. 630 you will use your knowledge of conic sections to determine what shape a telescope's mirrors have.

 APPLICATION LINK Visit www.mcdougallittell.com for more information about telescopes.

Study Guide

What's the chapter about?

Chapter 10 is about **conic sections**. The four conic sections are parabolas, circles, ellipses, and hyperbolas. In Chapter 10 you'll learn

- how to use the distance and midpoint formulas.
- how to graph and write equations of conics, and how to classify conics.
- how to solve systems of quadratic equations.

KEY VOCABULARY

▶ **Review**
- parabola, p. 249
- hyperbola, p. 540

▶ **New**
- distance formula, p. 589

- midpoint formula, p. 590
- circle, p. 601
- ellipse, p. 609
- hyperbola, p. 615
- conic sections, p. 623

- general second-degree equation, p. 626
- discriminant, p. 626

Are you ready for the chapter?

SKILL REVIEW Do these exercises to review key skills that you'll apply in this chapter. See the given **reference page** if there is something you don't understand.

Write an equation of the line that passes through the given point and has the given slope. (Review Example 2, p. 92)

1. $(0, 4)$, $m = 2$
2. $(2, -2)$, $m = \frac{1}{3}$
3. $(-4, 1)$, $m = -\frac{3}{4}$

Solve the system using any algebraic method. (Review Examples 1–3, pp. 148–150)

4. $x + 2y = 8$
$3x - y = 3$

5. $2x + y = 3$
$3x + y = 2$

6. $4x - y = 7$
$5x - 2y = 2$

Graph the function. Label the vertex and axis of symmetry.
(Review Examples 1–3, pp. 250 and 251)

7. $y = x^2 + 4$
8. $y = -3x^2$
9. $y = 2(x - 3)^2 - 1$

Solve the equation by completing the square. (Review Examples 2 and 3, p. 283)

10. $x^2 + 8x + 14 = 0$
11. $5x^2 + 15x = -25$
12. $x^2 - 2x = -8x + 14$

Here's a
study strategy!

Dictionary of Graphs

Make a dictionary of graphs to use as a reference tool. Draw and label an example of each conic. Note the important characteristics of the conic, and write the conic's equation. Expand your dictionary to include all the types of graphs you have learned and continue to learn in this course.

The Distance and Midpoint Formulas

To find the distance d between $A(x_1, y_1)$ and $B(x_2, y_2)$, you can apply the Pythagorean theorem to right triangle ABC.

$$(AB)^2 = (AC)^2 + (BC)^2$$

$$d^2 = (x_2 - x_1)^2 + (y_2 - y_1)^2$$

$$d = \sqrt{(x_2 - x_1)^2 + (y_2 - y_1)^2}$$

The third equation is called the **distance formula**.

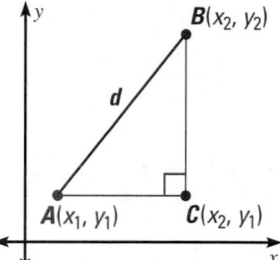

THE DISTANCE FORMULA

The distance d between the points (x_1, y_1) and (x_2, y_2) is as follows:

$$d = \sqrt{(x_2 - x_1)^2 + (y_2 - y_1)^2}$$

EXAMPLE 1 *Finding the Distance Between Two Points*

Find the distance between $(-2, 5)$ and $(3, -1)$.

SOLUTION

Let $(x_1, y_1) = (-2, 5)$ and $(x_2, y_2) = (3, -1)$.

$d = \sqrt{(x_2 - x_1)^2 + (y_2 - y_1)^2}$	Use distance formula.
$= \sqrt{(3 - (-2))^2 + (-1 - 5)^2}$	Substitute.
$= \sqrt{25 + 36}$	Simplify.
$= \sqrt{61} \approx 7.81$	Use a calculator.

EXAMPLE 2 *Classifying a Triangle Using the Distance Formula*

Classify $\triangle ABC$ as *scalene*, *isosceles*, or *equilateral*.

SOLUTION

$$AB = \sqrt{(6 - 4)^2 + (1 - 6)^2} = \sqrt{29}$$

$$BC = \sqrt{(1 - 6)^2 + (3 - 1)^2} = \sqrt{29}$$

$$AC = \sqrt{(1 - 4)^2 + (3 - 6)^2} = 3\sqrt{2}$$

▶ Because $AB = BC$, $\triangle ABC$ is isosceles.

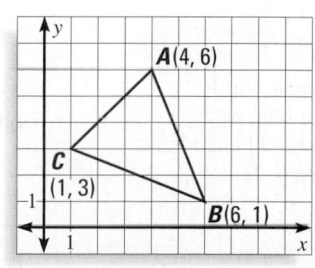

Another formula involving two points in a coordinate plane is the **midpoint formula**. Recall that the midpoint of a segment is the point on the segment that is equidistant from the two endpoints.

THE MIDPOINT FORMULA

The midpoint of the line segment joining $A(x_1, y_1)$ and $B(x_2, y_2)$ is as follows:

$$M\left(\frac{x_1 + x_2}{2}, \frac{y_1 + y_2}{2}\right)$$

Each coordinate of M is the mean of the corresponding coordinates of A and B.

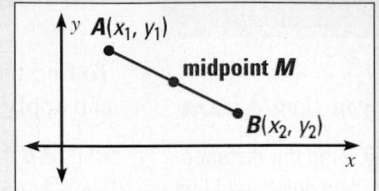

EXAMPLE 3 *Finding the Midpoint of a Segment*

Find the midpoint of the line segment joining $(-7, 1)$ and $(-2, 5)$.

SOLUTION

Let $(x_1, y_1) = (-7, 1)$ and $(x_2, y_2) = (-2, 5)$.

$$\left(\frac{x_1 + x_2}{2}, \frac{y_1 + y_2}{2}\right) = \left(\frac{-7 + (-2)}{2}, \frac{1 + 5}{2}\right)$$

$$= \left(-\frac{9}{2}, 3\right)$$

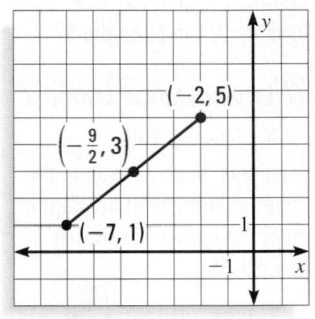

EXAMPLE 4 *Finding a Perpendicular Bisector*

Write an equation for the perpendicular bisector of the line segment joining $A(-1, 4)$ and $B(5, 2)$.

SOLUTION

First find the midpoint of the line segment:

$$\left(\frac{x_1 + x_2}{2}, \frac{y_1 + y_2}{2}\right) = \left(\frac{-1 + 5}{2}, \frac{4 + 2}{2}\right) = (2, 3)$$

Then find the slope of $\overline{AB}$:

$$m = \frac{y_2 - y_1}{x_2 - x_1} = \frac{2 - 4}{5 - (-1)} = \frac{-2}{6} = -\frac{1}{3}$$

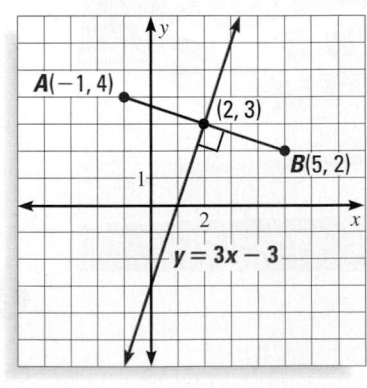

STUDENT HELP

► **Look Back**
For help with perpendicular lines, see p. 92.

The slope of the perpendicular bisector is the negative reciprocal of $-\frac{1}{3}$, or $m\perp = 3$.

Since you know the **slope** of the perpendicular bisector and a **point** that the bisector passes through, you can use the point-slope form to write its equation.

$$y - 3 = 3(x - 2)$$

$$y = 3x - 3$$

▶ An equation for the perpendicular bisector of $\overline{AB}$ is $y = 3x - 3$.

Recall from geometry that the perpendicular bisector of a chord of a circle passes through the center of the circle. Using this theorem, you can find the center of a circle given three points on the circle.

EXAMPLE 5 *Using the Distance and Midpoint Formulas in Real Life*

ARCHEOLOGY While on an archeological dig, you discover a piece of a broken dish. To estimate the original diameter of the dish, you lay the piece on a coordinate plane and mark three points on the circular edge, as shown. Use these points to find the diameter of the dish. (Each unit in the coordinate plane represents 1 inch.)

SOLUTION

Use the method illustrated in Example 4 to find the perpendicular bisectors of $\overline{AO}$ and $\overline{OB}$.

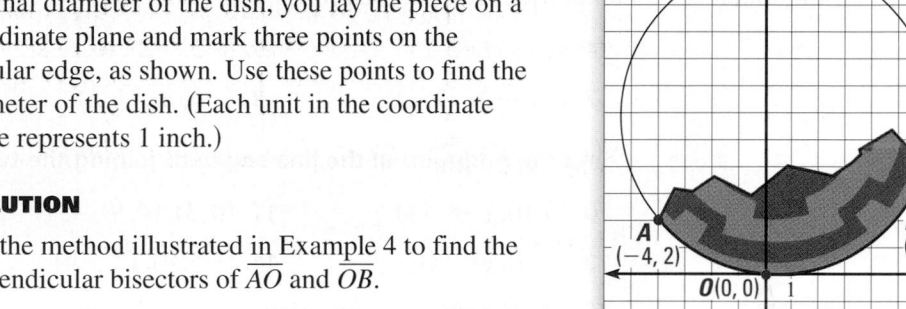

$y = 2x + 5$ **Perpendicular bisector of $\overline{AO}$**

$y = -\dfrac{3}{2}x + \dfrac{13}{2}$ **Perpendicular bisector of $\overline{OB}$**

Both bisectors pass through the circle's center. Therefore, the center of the circle is the solution of the system formed by these two equations.

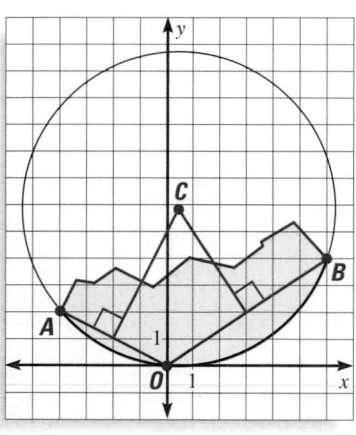

$y = 2x + 5$ **Write first equation.**

$-\dfrac{3}{2}x + \dfrac{13}{2} = 2x + 5$ **Substitute for *y*.**

$-3x + 13 = 4x + 10$ **Multiply each side by 2.**

$-7x = -3$ **Simplify.**

$x = \dfrac{3}{7}$ **Divide each side by −7.**

$y = 2\left(\dfrac{3}{7}\right) + 5$ **Substitute the *x*-value into the first equation.**

$y = \dfrac{41}{7}$ **Simplify.**

STUDENT HELP

→ **Look Back**
For help with solving systems, see p. 148.

The center of the circle is $C\left(\dfrac{3}{7}, \dfrac{41}{7}\right)$. The radius of the circle is the distance between C and any of the three given points.

$$CO = \sqrt{\left(0 - \dfrac{3}{7}\right)^2 + \left(0 - \dfrac{41}{7}\right)^2}$$

$$= \sqrt{\dfrac{1690}{49}}$$

$$\approx 5.87$$

▶ The dish had a diameter of about $2(5.87) = 11.74$ inches.

ARCHEOLOGISTS use grids to systematically explore a site. By labeling the grid squares, they can record where each artifact is found.

GUIDED PRACTICE

Vocabulary Check ✔ **1.** State the distance and midpoint formulas.

Concept Check ✔ **2.** Look back at Example 1. Find the distance between $(-2, 5)$ and $(3, -1)$, but this time letting $(x_1, y_1) = (3, -1)$ and $(x_2, y_2) = (-2, 5)$. How are the calculations different? Do you get the same answer?

3. a. Write a formula for the distance between a point (x, y) and the origin.

b. Write a formula for the midpoint of the segment joining a point (x, y) and the origin.

Skill Check ✔ **Find the distance between the two points.**

4. $(2, -1), (2, 3)$ **5.** $(-5, -2), (0, -2)$ **6.** $(0, 6), (4, 9)$

7. $(10, -2), (7, 4)$ **8.** $(-3, 8), (5, 6)$ **9.** $(6, -1), (-9, 8)$

Find the midpoint of the line segment joining the two points.

10. $(0, 0), (-8, 14)$ **11.** $(0, 3), (4, 9)$ **12.** $(1, -2), (1, 6)$

13. $(1, 3), (3, 11)$ **14.** $(-5, 4), (2, -4)$ **15.** $(-1, 5), (-8, -6)$

16. 🌐 **HIKING** You are going on a two-day hike. The map at the right shows the trails you plan to follow. (Each unit represents 1 mile.)

a. You hike from the lodge to point A and decide that you will hike to the midpoint of $\overline{AB}$ before you camp for the night. At what point in the plane will you be camping?

b. How far will you hike each day?

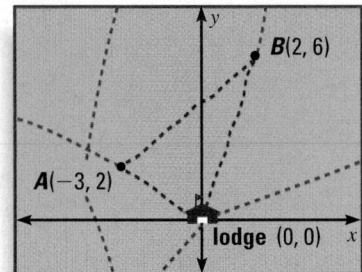

PRACTICE AND APPLICATIONS

STUDENT HELP

▶ **Extra Practice**
to help you master skills is on p. 953.

USING THE FORMULAS Find the distance between the two points. Then find the midpoint of the line segment joining the two points.

17. $(0, 0), (3, 4)$ **18.** $(0, 0), (4, 12)$ **19.** $(0, 4), (8, -3)$

20. $(-2, 8), (6, 0)$ **21.** $(-3, -1), (7, 4)$ **22.** $(9, -2), (3, 6)$

23. $(-5, -8), (1, 6)$ **24.** $(-2, 10), (10, -2)$ **25.** $(8, 3), (2, -1)$

26. $(-10, -15), (12, 18)$ **27.** $(-3.5, 1.2), (6, -3.8)$ **28.** $(6.3, -9), (1.3, -8.5)$

29. $(-7, 2), \left(-\frac{11}{2}, 4\right)$ **30.** $\left(\frac{2}{3}, -\frac{11}{4}\right), \left(-\frac{7}{2}, -\frac{11}{2}\right)$ **31.** $\left(-\frac{3}{4}, 2\right), \left(5, -\frac{7}{4}\right)$

STUDENT HELP

▶ **HOMEWORK HELP**
Example 1: Exs. 17–31, 47–50
Example 2: Exs. 32–40
Example 3: Exs. 17–31
Example 4: Exs. 41–46
Example 5: Exs. 51–58

GEOMETRY ▶ CONNECTION The vertices of a triangle are given. Classify the triangle as *scalene, isosceles,* or *equilateral.*

32. $(2, 0), (0, 8), (-2, 0)$ **33.** $(4, 1), (1, -2), (6, -4)$ **34.** $(1, 9), (-4, 2), (4, 2)$

35. $(2, 5), (8, 2), (4, -1)$ **36.** $(5, -1), (-4, 0), (3, 5)$ **37.** $(4, 4), (8, 1), (6, -5)$

38. $(0, -3), (3, 5), (-5, 2)$ **39.** $(1, 1), (-4, 0), (-2, 5)$ **40.** $(2, 4), (3, -2), (-1, 1)$

FINDING EQUATIONS Write an equation for the perpendicular bisector of the line segment joining the two points.

41. $(2, 2), (6, 14)$ **42.** $(0, 0), (-8, -10)$ **43.** $(0, -6), (-4, 9)$

44. $(3, -7), (-3, 1)$ **45.** $(-3, -7.2), (-4.2, 1.8)$ **46.** $\left(\frac{3}{2}, -6\right), (-3, 1)$

FINDING A COORDINATE Use the given distance *d* between the two points to solve for *x*.

47. $(0, 1), (x, 4); d = \sqrt{34}$ **48.** $(1, 3), (-6, x); d = \sqrt{74}$

49. $(x, -10), (-8, 4); d = 7\sqrt{5}$ **50.** $(0.5, x), (7, 2); d = 8.5$

STUDENT HELP

HOMEWORK HELP
Visit our Web site
www.mcdougallittell.com
for help with problem
solving in Exs. 51 and 52.

🌐 **URBAN PLANNING** In Exercises 51 and 52, use the following information.
You are designing a city park like the one shown at the right. You want the park to have two fountains so that each fountain is equidistant from four of the six park entrances. The labeled points shown in the coordinate plane represent the park entrances.

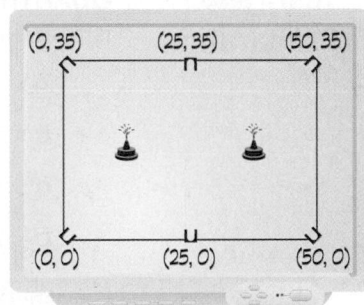

51. Where should the fountains be placed?

52. How far apart should the fountains be placed?

🌐 **HELICOPTER RESCUE** In Exercises 53–56, use the following information to find the distance a medical helicopter would have to travel to St. John's Hospital from each highway intersection.
The Highway Department of Sangamon County in Illinois uses a map with a coordinate plane whose origin represents downtown Springfield. Each unit represents one mile and the letters N, S, E, and W are used to indicate the direction. For example, 3E 5S corresponds to $(3, -5)$, a point 3 miles east and 5 miles south of downtown Springfield. St. John's Hospital is located at 1E 0, or $(1, 0)$.

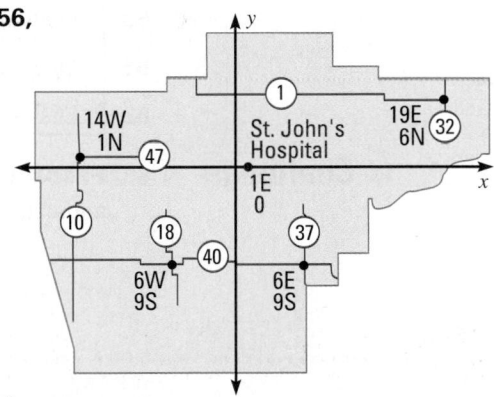

53. Rt. 1–Rt. 32 intersection at 19E 6N   **54.** Rt. 37–Rt. 40 intersection at 6E 9S

55. Rt. 18–Rt. 40 intersection at 6W 9S   **56.** Rt. 10–Rt. 47 intersection at 14W 1N

FOCUS ON CAREERS

ACCIDENT RECONSTRUC-TIONIST An accident reconstructionist uses physical evidence, such as skid marks, to determine how accidents occurred.

CAREER LINK
www.mcdougallittell.com

57. 🌐 **ACCIDENT RECONSTRUCTION** When a car makes a fast, sharp turn, an accident reconstructionist can use the car's skid mark to determine its speed. The equation $v = \sqrt{ar}$ gives the car's speed *v* (in meters per second) as a function of the radius *r* of the circle (in meters) along which the car was traveling. The constant *a* (measured in meters per second squared) varies depending on road conditions. Find the radius of the skid mark shown below. Then use the given equation and 6.86 for *a* to find how fast the car was going.
▶ Source: *Mathematical Modeling*

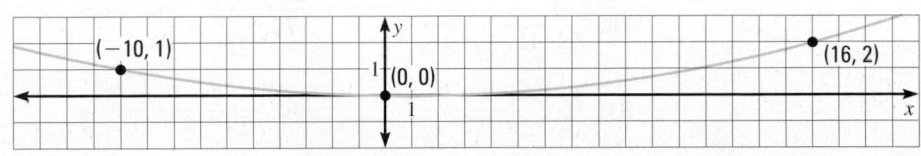

58. **STATISTICS ▶ CONNECTION** A physician uses many tests to evaluate a patient's condition. Some of these tests yield numerical results. In these cases, the physician can treat two test results as an ordered pair and use the distance formula to determine how close to average the patient is. In the table below the serum creatinine (C) and systolic blood pressure (P) for several patients are given. Tell how far from normal each patient is, where normal is represented by the ordered pair $(C, P) = (1, 127)$.

C	2	5	1	7	3	4	1
P	120	127	140	115	112	125	130

Test Preparation

QUANTITATIVE COMPARISON In Exercises 59–62, choose the statement that is true about the given quantities.

  Ⓐ The quantity in column A is greater.

  Ⓑ The quantity in column B is greater.

  Ⓒ The two quantities are equal.

  Ⓓ The relationship cannot be determined from the given information.

	Column A	Column B
59.	Distance between $(0, 7)$ and $(1, -1)$	Distance between $(9, 2)$ and $(3, 8)$
60.	Distance between $(-5, -2)$ and $(5, 2)$	Distance between $(-5, 5)$ and $(2, -2)$
61.	Distance between $(-3, 0)$ and $(2, -4)$	Distance between $(7, 6)$ and $(1, 5)$
62.	Distance between $(2, -5)$ and $(1, 6)$	Distance between $(0, 8)$ and $(6, 0)$

★ **Challenge**

63. **FINDING A FORMULA** Find formulas for the distance between a point (x, y) and each of the following: **(a)** a horizontal line $y = k$ and **(b)** a vertical line $x = h$.

MIXED REVIEW

GRAPHING FUNCTIONS Graph the quadratic function. (Review 5.1 for 10.2)

64. $y = 4x^2$ **65.** $y = 3x^2$ **66.** $y = -3x^2$ **67.** $y = -2x^2$

68. $y = \frac{1}{3}x^2$ **69.** $y = -\frac{2}{3}x^2$ **70.** $y = -\frac{3}{4}x^2$ **71.** $y = \frac{5}{6}x^2$

SOLVING EQUATIONS Solve the equation. Check for extraneous solutions. (Review 7.6)

72. $x^{2/3} + 13 = 17$ **73.** $\sqrt{x + 100} = 25$ **74.** $\sqrt{2x} = x - 4$

75. $\sqrt{x + 2} = \sqrt{3x}$ **76.** $2\sqrt[3]{3x} = 6$ **77.** $-2x^{3/2} = -8$

OPERATIONS WITH RATIONAL EXPRESSIONS Perform the indicated operation and simplify. (Review 9.5)

78. $\dfrac{2}{x + 1} - \dfrac{x}{x^2 - 1}$ **79.** $\dfrac{4}{2x^2} + \dfrac{1}{3x}$ **80.** $\dfrac{11}{4(x - 5)} - \dfrac{x + 1}{4x}$

81. $\dfrac{3x}{x^2} - \dfrac{x - 1}{x + 3}$ **82.** $\dfrac{2}{3x + 2} + \dfrac{5x^2}{x - 4}$ **83.** $\dfrac{1 - 3x}{x - 6} + \dfrac{2}{2x + 1}$

Parabolas

GOAL 1 GRAPHING AND WRITING EQUATIONS OF PARABOLAS

You already know that the graph of $y = ax^2$ is a parabola whose vertex $(0, 0)$ lies on its axis of symmetry $x = 0$. Every parabola has the property that any point on it is equidistant from a point called the **focus** and a line called the **directrix**.

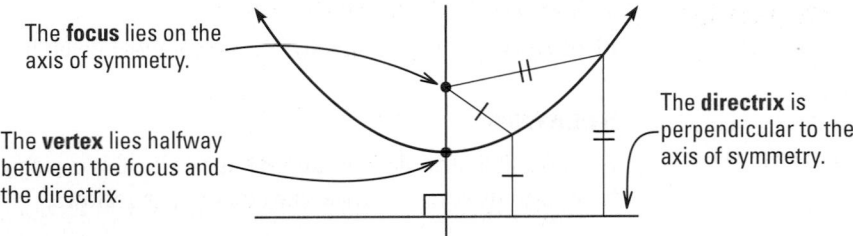

The **focus** lies on the axis of symmetry.

The **vertex** lies halfway between the focus and the directrix.

The **directrix** is perpendicular to the axis of symmetry.

In Chapter 5 you saw parabolas that have a vertical axis of symmetry and open up or down. In this lesson you will also work with parabolas that have a horizontal axis of symmetry and open left or right. In the four cases shown below, the focus and the directrix each lie $|p|$ units from the vertex.

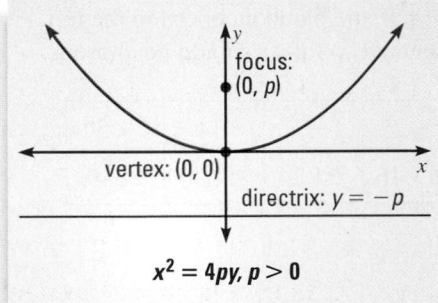

focus: $(0, p)$

vertex: $(0, 0)$

directrix: $y = -p$

$x^2 = 4py, p > 0$

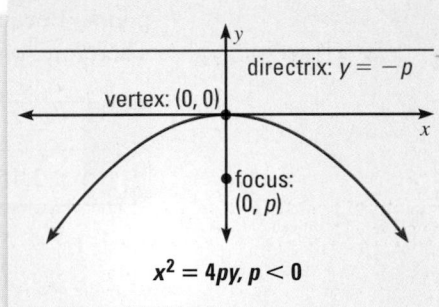

directrix: $y = -p$

vertex: $(0, 0)$

focus: $(0, p)$

$x^2 = 4py, p < 0$

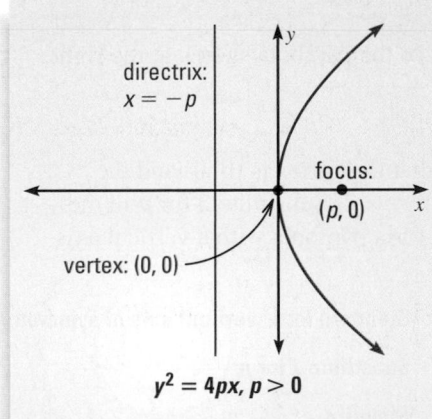

directrix: $x = -p$

focus: $(p, 0)$

vertex: $(0, 0)$

$y^2 = 4px, p > 0$

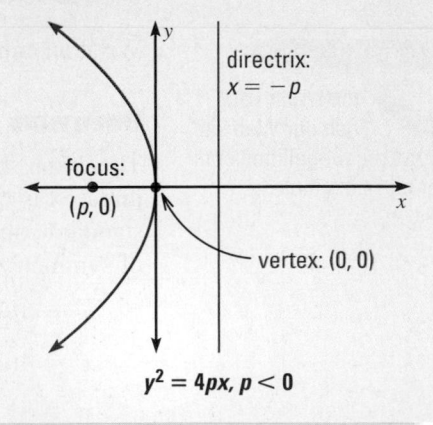

focus: $(p, 0)$

directrix: $x = -p$

vertex: $(0, 0)$

$y^2 = 4px, p < 0$

Characteristics of the parabolas shown above are given on the next page.

STANDARD EQUATION OF A PARABOLA (VERTEX AT ORIGIN)

The standard form of the equation of a parabola with vertex at (0, 0) is as follows.

EQUATION	FOCUS	DIRECTRIX	AXIS OF SYMMETRY
$x^2 = 4py$	$(0, p)$	$y = -p$	Vertical ($x = 0$)
$y^2 = 4px$	$(p, 0)$	$x = -p$	Horizontal ($y = 0$)

EXAMPLE 1   *Graphing an Equation of a Parabola*

STUDENT HELP

➡ **Look Back**
For help with drawing parabolas, see p. 249.

Identify the focus and directrix of the parabola given by $x = -\frac{1}{6}y^2$. Draw the parabola.

SOLUTION

Because the variable y is squared, the axis of symmetry is horizontal. To find the focus and directrix, rewrite the equation as follows.

$$x = -\frac{1}{6}y^2 \qquad \text{Write original equation.}$$

$$-6x = y^2 \qquad \text{Multiply each side by } -6.$$

Since $4p = -6$, you know $p = -\frac{3}{2}$. The focus is

$(p, 0) = \left(-\frac{3}{2}, 0\right)$ and the directrix is $x = -p = \frac{3}{2}$.

To draw the parabola, make a table of values and plot points. Because $p < 0$, the parabola opens to the left. Therefore, only negative x-values should be chosen.

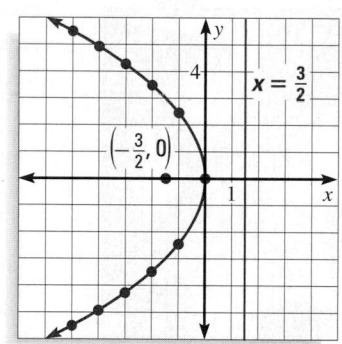

x	-1	-2	-3	-4	-5
y	± 2.45	± 3.46	± 4.24	± 4.90	± 5.48

EXAMPLE 2   *Writing an Equation of a Parabola*

STUDENT HELP

🌐 **HOMEWORK HELP**
Visit our Web site
www.mcdougallittell.com
for extra examples.

Write an equation of the parabola shown at the right.

SOLUTION

The graph shows that the vertex is (0, 0) and the directrix is $y = -p = -2$. Substitute **2** for p in the standard equation for a parabola with a vertical axis of symmetry.

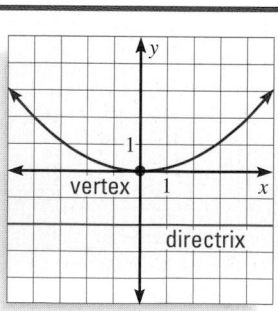

$$x^2 = 4py \qquad \text{Standard form, vertical axis of symmetry}$$

$$x^2 = 4(\mathbf{2})y \qquad \text{Substitute 2 for } p.$$

$$x^2 = 8y \qquad \text{Simplify.}$$

✓**CHECK** You can check this result by solving the equation for y to get $y = \frac{1}{8}x^2$ and graphing the equation using a graphing calculator.

GOAL 2 USING PARABOLAS IN REAL LIFE

Parabolic reflectors have cross sections that are parabolas. A special property of any parabolic reflector is that all incoming rays parallel to the axis of symmetry that hit the reflector are directed to the focus (Figure 1). Similarly, rays emitted from the focus that hit the reflector are directed in rays parallel to the axis of symmetry (Figure 2). These properties are the reason satellite dishes and flashlights are parabolic.

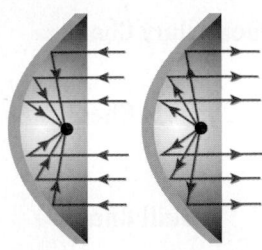

Figure 1   **Figure 2**

EXAMPLE 3   *Modeling a Parabolic Reflector*

SOLAR ENERGY Sunfire is a glass parabola used to collect solar energy. The sun's rays are reflected from the mirrors toward two boilers located at the focus of the parabola. When heated, the boilers produce steam that powers an alternator to produce electricity.

Sunfire

a. Write an equation for Sunfire's cross section.

b. How deep is the dish?

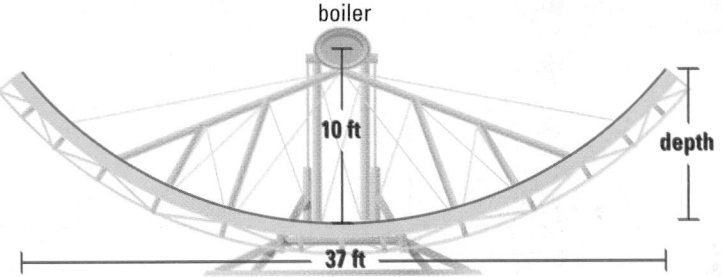

boiler

10 ft

depth

37 ft

SOLUTION

a. The boilers are 10 feet above the vertex of the dish. Because the boilers are at the focus and the focus is p units from the vertex, you can conclude that $p = 10$.

Assuming the vertex is at the origin, an equation for the parabolic cross section is as follows:

$x^2 = 4py$ **Standard form, vertical axis of symmetry**

$x^2 = 4(\mathbf{10})y$ **Substitute 10 for p.**

$x^2 = 40y$ **Simplify.**

b. The dish extends $\frac{37}{2} = 18.5$ feet on either side of the origin. To find the depth of the dish, substitute **18.5** for x in the equation from part (a).

$x^2 = 40y$ **Equation for the cross section**

$(\mathbf{18.5})^2 = 40y$ **Substitute 18.5 for x.**

$8.6 \approx y$ **Solve for y.**

▶ The dish is about 8.6 feet deep.

GUIDED PRACTICE

Vocabulary Check ✓

1. Complete this statement: A parabola is the set of points equidistant from a point called the ? and a line called the ? .

Concept Check ✓

2. How does the graph of $x = ay^2$ differ from the graph of $y = ax^2$?

3. Knowing the value of a in $y = ax^2$, how can you find the focus and directrix?

Skill Check ✓

Graph the equation. Identify the focus and directrix of the parabola.

4. $x^2 = 4y$ 5. $y = -5x^2$ 6. $-12x = y^2$

7. $8y^2 = x$ 8. $-6x = y^2$ 9. $x^2 = 2y$

Write the standard form of the equation of the parabola with the given focus or directrix and vertex at (0, 0).

10. focus: $(0, 3)$ 11. focus: $(5, 0)$ 12. focus: $(-6, 0)$

13. directrix: $x = 4$ 14. directrix: $x = -1$ 15. directrix: $y = 8$

PRACTICE AND APPLICATIONS

STUDENT HELP

▶ **Extra Practice**
to help you master
skills is on p. 953.

MATCHING Match the equation with its graph.

16. $y^2 = 4x$ 17. $x^2 = -4y$ 18. $x^2 = 4y$

19. $y^2 = -4x$ 20. $y^2 = \frac{1}{4}x$ 21. $x^2 = \frac{1}{4}y$

A. 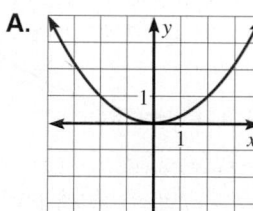   **B.** 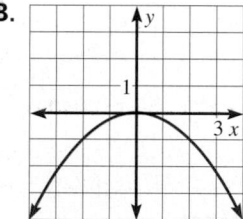   **C.**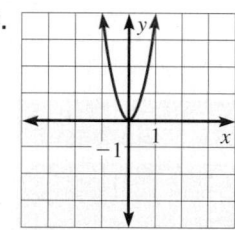

D. 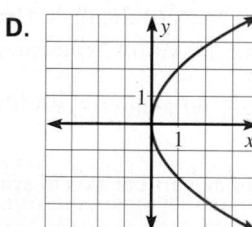   **E.** 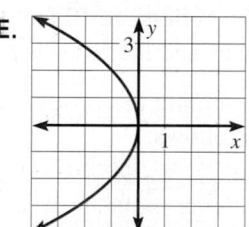   **F.**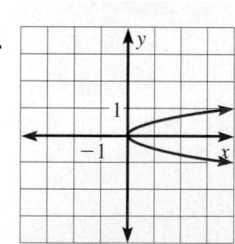

DIRECTION Tell whether the parabola opens *up, down, left,* or *right*.

22. $y = -3x^2$ 23. $-9x^2 = 2y$ 24. $2y^2 = -6x$ 25. $x = 7y^2$

26. $x^2 = 16y$ 27. $-3y^2 = 8x$ 28. $-5x = -y^2$ 29. $x^2 = \frac{4}{3}y$

STUDENT HELP

▶ **HOMEWORK HELP**
Example 1: Exs. 16–53
Example 2: Exs. 54–77
Example 3: Exs. 78–81

FOCUS AND DIRECTRIX Identify the focus and directrix of the parabola.

30. $3x^2 = -y$ 31. $2y^2 = x$ 32. $x^2 = 8y$ 33. $y^2 = -10x$

34. $y^2 = -16x$ 35. $x^2 = -36y$ 36. $-4x + 9y^2 = 0$ 37. $-28y + x^2 = 0$

GRAPHING Graph the equation. Identify the focus and directrix of the parabola.

38. $y^2 = 12x$ **39.** $x^2 = -6y$ **40.** $y^2 = -2x$ **41.** $y^2 = 24x$

42. $x^2 = 8y$ **43.** $y^2 = -14x$ **44.** $x^2 = -20y$ **45.** $x^2 = 18y$

46. $x^2 = -4y$ **47.** $x^2 = 16y$ **48.** $y^2 = 9x$ **49.** $y^2 = -3x$

50. $x^2 - 40y = 0$ **51.** $x + \frac{1}{20}y^2 = 0$ **52.** $3x^2 = 4y$ **53.** $x - \frac{1}{8}y^2 = 0$

WRITING EQUATIONS Write the standard form of the equation of the parabola with the given focus and vertex at (0, 0).

54. $(4, 0)$ **55.** $(-2, 0)$ **56.** $(-3, 0)$ **57.** $(0, 1)$

58. $(0, 4)$ **59.** $(0, -3)$ **60.** $(0, -4)$ **61.** $(-5, 0)$

62. $\left(-\frac{1}{4}, 0\right)$ **63.** $\left(0, -\frac{3}{8}\right)$ **64.** $\left(0, \frac{1}{2}\right)$ **65.** $\left(\frac{5}{12}, 0\right)$

WRITING EQUATIONS Write the standard form of the equation of the parabola with the given directrix and vertex at (0, 0).

66. $y = 2$ **67.** $y = -3$ **68.** $x = -4$ **69.** $x = 6$

70. $x = -5$ **71.** $y = -1$ **72.** $x = 2$ **73.** $y = 4$

74. $x = -\frac{1}{2}$ **75.** $x = \frac{3}{4}$ **76.** $y = \frac{5}{8}$ **77.** $y = -\frac{1}{12}$

78. 🌐 **COMMUNICATIONS** The cross section of a television antenna dish is a parabola. For the dish at the right, the receiver is located at the focus, 4 feet above the vertex. Find an equation for the cross section of the dish. (Assume the vertex is at the origin.) If the dish is 8 feet wide, how deep is it?

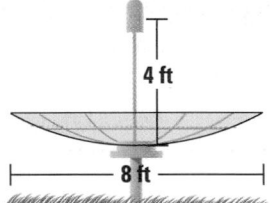
4 ft
8 ft

79. 🌐 **AUTOMOTIVE ENGINEERING** The filament of a lightbulb is a thin wire that glows when electricity passes through it. The filament of a car headlight is at the focus of a parabolic reflector, which sends light out in a straight beam. Given that the filament is 1.5 inches from the vertex, find an equation for the cross section of the reflector. If the reflector is 7 inches wide, how deep is it?

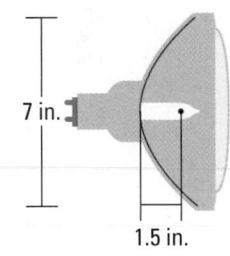
7 in.
1.5 in.

80. **HISTORY CONNECTION** In the drawing shown at the left, the rays of the sun are lighting a candle. If the candle flame is 12 inches from the back of the parabolic reflector and the reflector is 6 inches deep, then what is the diameter of the reflector?

81. 🌐 **CAMPING** You can make a solar hot dog cooker using foil-lined cardboard shaped as a parabolic trough. The drawing at the right shows how to suspend a hot dog with a wire through the focus of each end piece. If the trough is 12 inches wide and 4 inches deep, how far from the bottom should the wire be placed?

▶ Source: *Boys' Life*

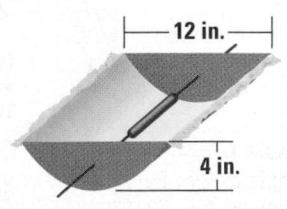
12 in.
4 in.

82. *Writing* For an equation of the form $y = ax^2$, discuss what effect increasing $|a|$ has on the focus and directrix.

83. MULTI-STEP PROBLEM A flashlight has a parabolic reflector. An equation for the cross section of the reflector is $y^2 = \frac{32}{7}x$. The depth of the reflector is $\frac{3}{2}$ inches.

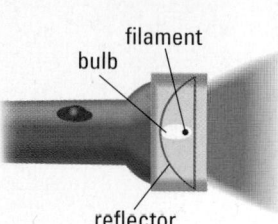

filament
bulb
reflector

    a. *Writing* Explain why the value of p must be less than the depth of the reflector of a flashlight.

    b. How wide is the beam of light projected by the flashlight?

    c. Write an equation for the cross section of a reflector having the same depth but a wider beam than the flashlight shown. How wide is the beam of the new reflector?

    d. Write an equation for the cross section of a reflector having the same depth but a narrower beam than the flashlight shown. How wide is the beam of the new reflector?

★ **Challenge**

EXTRA CHALLENGE
www.mcdougallittell.com

84. **GEOMETRY** **CONNECTION** The *latus rectum* of a parabola is the line segment that is parallel to the directrix, passes through the focus, and has endpoints that lie on the parabola. Find the length of the latus rectum of a parabola given by $x^2 = 4py$.

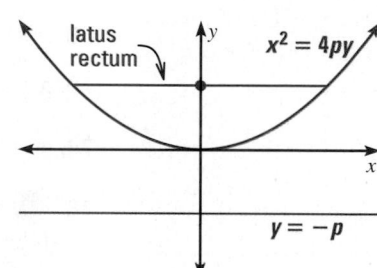

latus rectum

$x^2 = 4py$

$y = -p$

MIXED REVIEW

LOGARITHMIC AND EXPONENTIAL EQUATIONS Solve the equation. Check for extraneous solutions. **(Review 8.6)**

85. $8^{5x} = 16^{2x + 1}$ **86.** $3^x = 15$ **87.** $5^x = 7$

88. $10^{3x + 1} + 4 = 33$ **89.** $\log_7 (3x - 5) = \log_7 8x$ **90.** $\log_3 (4x - 3) = 3$

OPERATIONS WITH RATIONAL EXPRESSIONS Perform the indicated operation and simplify. **(Review 9.4 and 9.5)**

91. $\dfrac{3xy^3}{x^3y} \cdot \dfrac{y}{6x}$ **92.** $\dfrac{3xy^3}{2x} \div \dfrac{2xy^3}{3x}$ **93.** $\dfrac{x^2 - 9}{x^2 - x - 6} \cdot (x + 2)$

94. $\dfrac{-3x}{x + 2} + \dfrac{4x}{x - 1}$ **95.** $\dfrac{x + 1}{6x^2} - \dfrac{x + 1}{6x^2 + 6x}$ **96.** $\dfrac{x^2 - 3x + 2}{x - 1} - \dfrac{x^2 - 4}{x - 2}$

FINDING A DISTANCE Find the distance between the two points. **(Review 10.1 for 10.3)**

97. $(3, 4), (6, 7)$ **98.** $(-3, 7), (-7, 3)$ **99.** $(18, -4), (-2, 9)$

100. $(3.7, 5.1), (2, 5)$ **101.** $(-9, -31), (8, 7)$ **102.** $(8.8, 3.3), (1.2, 6)$

103. 🌎 **CONSUMER ECONOMICS** The amount A (in dollars) you pay for grapes varies directly with the amount P (in pounds) that you buy. Suppose you buy $1\frac{1}{2}$ pounds for \$2.25. Write a linear model that gives A as a function of P. **(Review 2.4)**

10.3

Circles

GOAL 1 GRAPHING AND WRITING EQUATIONS OF CIRCLES

What you should learn

GOAL 1 Graph and write equations of circles.

GOAL 2 Use circles to solve **real-life** problems, such as determining whether you are affected by an earthquake in **Ex. 81**.

Why you should learn it

▼ To model **real-life** situations with circular models, such as the region lit by a lighthouse beam in **Example 4**.

A **circle** is the set of all points (x, y) that are equidistant from a fixed point, called the **center** of the circle. The distance r between the center and any point (x, y) on the circle is the **radius**.

The distance formula can be used to obtain an equation of the circle whose center is the origin and whose radius is r. Because the distance between any point (x, y) on the circle and the center $(0, 0)$ is r, you can write the following.

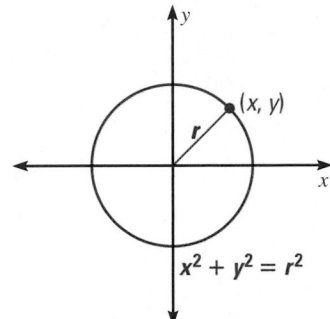

$$\sqrt{(x - 0)^2 + (y - 0)^2} = r \qquad \textbf{Distance formula}$$

$$(x - 0)^2 + (y - 0)^2 = r^2 \qquad \textbf{Square both sides.}$$

$$x^2 + y^2 = r^2 \qquad \textbf{Simplify.}$$

STANDARD EQUATION OF A CIRCLE (CENTER AT ORIGIN)

The **standard form of the equation of a circle** with center at (0, 0) and radius r is as follows:

$$x^2 + y^2 = r^2$$

EXAMPLE A circle with center at (0, 0) and radius 3 has equation $x^2 + y^2 = 9$.

EXAMPLE 1 Graphing an Equation of a Circle

Draw the circle given by $y^2 = 25 - x^2$.

SOLUTION

Write the equation in standard form.

$$y^2 = 25 - x^2 \qquad \textbf{Original equation}$$

$$x^2 + y^2 = 25 \qquad \textbf{Add } x^2 \textbf{ to each side.}$$

In this form you can see that the graph is a circle whose center is the origin and whose radius is $r = \sqrt{25} = 5$.

Plot several points that are 5 units from the origin. The points $(0, 5)$, $(5, 0)$, $(0, -5)$, and $(-5, 0)$ are most convenient.

Draw a circle that passes through the four points.

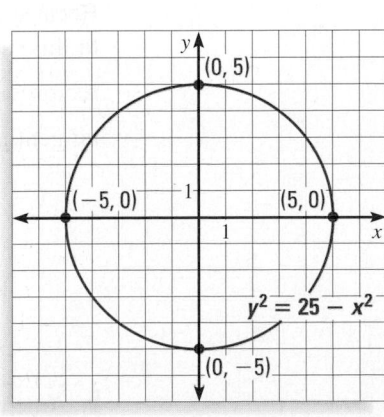

EXAMPLE 2   *Writing an Equation of a Circle*

STUDENT HELP

HOMEWORK HELP
Visit our Web site
www.mcdougallittell.com
for extra examples.

The point (1, 4) is on a circle whose center is the origin. Write the standard form of the equation of the circle.

SOLUTION

Because the point (1, 4) is on the circle, the radius of the circle must be the distance between the center and the point (1, 4).

$$r = \sqrt{(1-0)^2 + (4-0)^2}$$ **Use the distance formula.**

$$= \sqrt{1 + 16}$$ **Simplify.**

$$= \sqrt{17}$$

Knowing that the radius is $\sqrt{17}$, you can use the standard form to find an equation of the circle.

$$x^2 + y^2 = r^2$$ **Standard form**

$$x^2 + y^2 = \left(\sqrt{17}\right)^2$$ **Substitute $\sqrt{17}$ for r.**

$$x^2 + y^2 = 17$$ **Simplify.**

· · · · · · · · ·

STUDENT HELP

▸ **Study Tip**
In mathematics the term radius is used in two ways. As defined on the previous page, it is the distance from the center of a circle to a point on the circle. It can also refer to the line segment that connects the center to a point on the circle.

A theorem in geometry states that a line tangent to a circle is perpendicular to the circle's radius at the point of tangency. In the diagram, $\overleftrightarrow{AB}$ is tangent to the circle with center C at the point of tangency B, so $\overleftrightarrow{AB} \perp BC$. This property of circles is used in the next example.

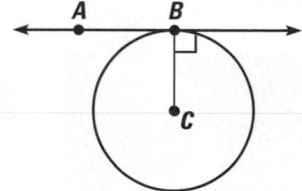

EXAMPLE 3   *Finding a Tangent Line*

Write an equation of the line that is tangent to the circle $x^2 + y^2 = 13$ at (2, 3).

SOLUTION

The slope of the radius through the point (2, 3) is:

$$m = \frac{3-0}{2-0} = \frac{3}{2}$$

Because the tangent line at **(2, 3)** is perpendicular to this radius, its slope must be the negative reciprocal of $\frac{3}{2}$, or $-\frac{2}{3}$. So, an equation of the tangent line is as follows.

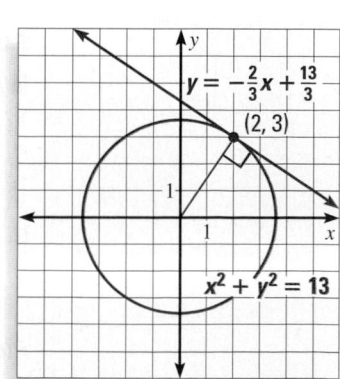

$$y - 3 = -\frac{2}{3}(x - 2)$$ **Point-slope form**

$$y - 3 = -\frac{2}{3}x + \frac{4}{3}$$ **Distributive property**

$$y = -\frac{2}{3}x + \frac{13}{3}$$ **Add 3 to each side.**

▸ An equation of the tangent line is $y = -\frac{2}{3}x + \frac{13}{3}$.

THE PHAROS OF ALEXANDRIA
was a lighthouse built in Egypt in about 280 B.C. One of the Seven Wonders of the World, it was said to be over 440 feet tall. It stood for nearly 1400 years.

GOAL 2 **USING CIRCLES IN REAL LIFE**

The regions inside and outside the circle $x^2 + y^2 = r^2$ can be described by inequalities.

Region inside circle: $x^2 + y^2 < r^2$

Region outside circle: $x^2 + y^2 > r^2$

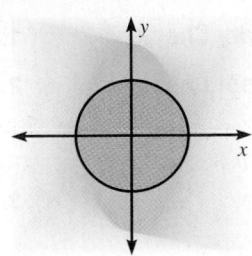

EXAMPLE 4 *Using a Circular Model*

OCEAN NAVIGATION The beam of a lighthouse can be seen for up to 20 miles. You are on a ship that is 10 miles east and 16 miles north of the lighthouse.

a. Write an inequality to describe the region lit by the lighthouse beam.

b. Can you see the lighthouse beam?

SOLUTION

a. As shown at the right the lighthouse beam can be seen from all points that satisfy this inequality:

$$x^2 + y^2 < 20^2$$

b. Substitute the coordinates of the ship into the inequality you wrote in part (a).

$$x^2 + y^2 < 20^2 \qquad \textbf{Inequality from part (a)}$$
$$10^2 + 16^2 \overset{?}{<} 20^2 \qquad \textbf{Substitute for } \textbf{\textit{x}} \textbf{ and } \textbf{\textit{y}}.$$
$$100 + 256 \overset{?}{<} 400 \qquad \textbf{Simplify.}$$
$$356 < 400 \; \checkmark \qquad \textbf{The inequality is true.}$$

▶ You can see the beam from the ship.

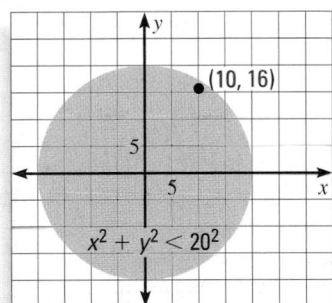

In the diagram above, the origin represents the lighthouse and the positive *y*-axis represents north.

EXAMPLE 5 *Using a Circular Model*

OCEAN NAVIGATION Your ship in Example 4 is traveling due south. For how many more miles will you be able to see the beam?

SOLUTION

When the ship exits the region lit by the beam, it will be at a point on the circle $x^2 + y^2 = 20^2$. Furthermore, its *x*-coordinate will be 10 and its *y*-coordinate will be negative. Find the point $(\mathbf{10}, y)$ where $y < 0$ on the circle $x^2 + y^2 = 20^2$.

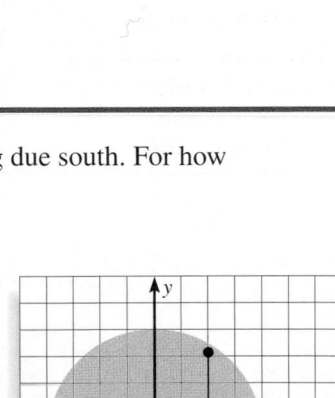

$$x^2 + y^2 = 20^2 \qquad \textbf{Equation for the boundary}$$
$$10^2 + y^2 = 20^2 \qquad \textbf{Substitute 10 for } \textbf{\textit{x}}.$$
$$y = \pm\sqrt{300} \approx \pm 17.3 \qquad \textbf{Solve for } \textbf{\textit{y}}.$$

▶ Since $y < 0$, $y \approx -17.3$. The beam will be in view as the ship travels from $(10, 16)$ to $(10, -17.3)$, a distance of $|16 - (-17.3)| = 33.3$ miles.

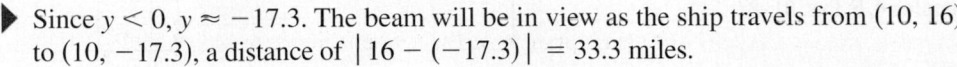

GUIDED PRACTICE

Vocabulary Check ✔

1. State the definition of a circle.

Concept Check ✔

2. LOGICAL REASONING Tell whether the following statement is *always true*, *sometimes true*, or *never true*: For a given circle and a given x-coordinate, there are two points on the circle with that x-coordinate.

3. How is the slope of a line tangent to a circle related to the slope of the radius at the point of tangency?

4. ERROR ANALYSIS A student was asked to write an equation of a circle with its center at the origin and a radius of 4. The student wrote the following equation:

$$x^2 + y^2 = 4$$

What did the student do wrong? Write the correct equation.

Skill Check ✔

Write the standard form of the equation of the circle that passes through the given point and whose center is the origin.

5. $(4, 0)$ **6.** $(0, -2)$ **7.** $(-8, 6)$ **8.** $(-5, -12)$

9. $(6, -9)$ **10.** $(3, 1)$ **11.** $(-5, -5)$ **12.** $(-2, 4)$

Graph the equation. Give the radius of the circle.

13. $x^2 + y^2 = 36$ **14.** $x^2 + y^2 = 81$ **15.** $x^2 + y^2 = 32$

16. $x^2 + y^2 = 12$ **17.** $36x^2 + 36y^2 = 144$ **18.** $9x^2 + 9y^2 = 162$

19. 🌐 **SHOT PUT** A person throws a shot put from a circle that has a diameter of 7 feet. Write the standard form of the equation of the shot put circle if the center is the origin.

PRACTICE AND APPLICATIONS

STUDENT HELP

▶ **Extra Practice**
to help you master
skills is on p. 954.

MATCHING GRAPHS Match the equation with its graph.

20. $x^2 + y^2 = 16$ **21.** $x^2 + y^2 = 5$ **22.** $x^2 + y^2 = 4$

23. $x^2 + y^2 = 25$ **24.** $x^2 + y^2 = 100$ **25.** $x^2 + y^2 = 10$

A. 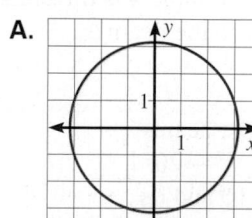   **B.** 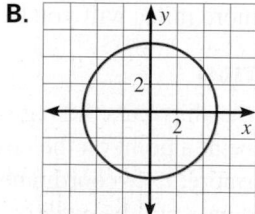   **C.**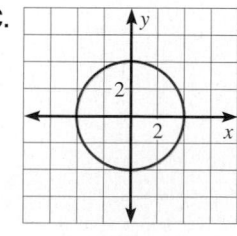

STUDENT HELP

▶ **HOMEWORK HELP**
Example 1: Exs. 20–46
Example 2: Exs. 47–70
Example 3: Exs. 71–79
Examples 4, 5: Exs. 81–87

D. 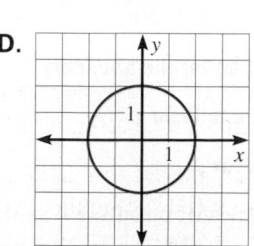   **E.** 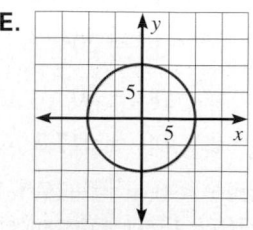   **F.**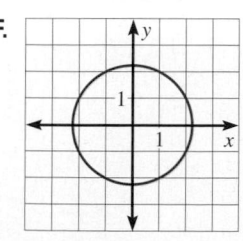

GRAPHING Graph the equation. Give the radius of the circle.

26. $x^2 + y^2 = 1$ **27.** $x^2 + y^2 = 49$ **28.** $x^2 + y^2 = 64$

29. $x^2 + y^2 = 20$ **30.** $x^2 + y^2 = 8$ **31.** $x^2 + y^2 = 10$

32. $x^2 + y^2 = 3$ **33.** $5x^2 + 5y^2 = 80$ **34.** $24x^2 + 24y^2 = 96$

35. $8x^2 + 8y^2 = 192$ **36.** $9x^2 + 9y^2 = 135$ **37.** $4x^2 + 4y^2 = 52$

GRAPHING In Exercises 38–46, the equations of both circles and parabolas are given. Graph the equation.

38. $x^2 + y^2 = 11$ **39.** $x^2 + y^2 = 1$ **40.** $x^2 + y = 0$

41. $\frac{1}{4}x^2 + \frac{1}{4}y^2 = 16$ **42.** $4x^2 + y = 0$ **43.** $9x^2 + 9y^2 = 441$

44. $-2x + 9y^2 = 0$ **45.** $\frac{3}{8}x^2 + \frac{3}{8}y^2 = 6$ **46.** $x^2 + 12y = 0$

WRITING EQUATIONS Write the standard form of the equation of the circle with the given radius and whose center is the origin.

47. 3   **48.** 9   **49.** 6   **50.** 11

51. $\sqrt{7}$ **52.** $\sqrt{30}$ **53.** $\sqrt{11}$ **54.** $\sqrt{21}$

55. $5\sqrt{6}$ **56.** $4\sqrt{5}$ **57.** $2\sqrt{7}$ **58.** $3\sqrt{3}$

WRITING EQUATIONS Write the standard form of the equation of the circle that passes through the given point and whose center is the origin.

59. $(0, -10)$ **60.** $(8, 0)$ **61.** $(-3, -4)$ **62.** $(-4, -1)$

63. $(5, -3)$ **64.** $(-6, 4)$ **65.** $(-6, 1)$ **66.** $(-1, -9)$

67. $(7, -4)$ **68.** $(10, 2)$ **69.** $(5, 8)$ **70.** $(2, -12)$

FINDING TANGENT LINES The equation of a circle and a point on the circle is given. Write an equation of the line that is tangent to the circle at that point.

71. $x^2 + y^2 = 10$; $(1, 3)$ **72.** $x^2 + y^2 = 5$; $(2, 1)$

73. $x^2 + y^2 = 41$; $(-4, -5)$ **74.** $x^2 + y^2 = 145$; $(12, 1)$

75. $x^2 + y^2 = 65$; $(-8, 1)$ **76.** $x^2 + y^2 = 40$; $(-2, 6)$

77. $x^2 + y^2 = 244$; $(-10, -12)$ **78.** $x^2 + y^2 = \frac{257}{4}$; $\left(\frac{1}{2}, -8\right)$

79. **CRITICAL THINKING** Look back at Example 3. Find an equation of the line that is tangent to the circle at the point $(2, -3)$. Describe how the line is geometrically related to the line found in Example 3.

80. *Writing* Describe how the equation of a circle is related to the Pythagorean theorem. Include a diagram to illustrate the relationship.

81. 🌐 **EARTHQUAKES** Suppose an earthquake can be felt up to 80 miles from its epicenter. You are located at a point 60 miles west and 45 miles south of the epicenter. Do you feel the earthquake? If so, how many miles south would you have to travel to be out of the range of the earthquake?

82. 🌐 **DESERT IRRIGATION** A circular field has an area of about 2,400,000 square yards. Write an equation that represents the boundary of the field. Let $(0, 0)$ represent the center of the field.

➤ **REAL LIFE IRRIGATION** This irrigation project in Colorado enables farmers to raise crops in the desert. Water from deep wells is pumped to sprinklers that rotate, forming circular patterns.

83. 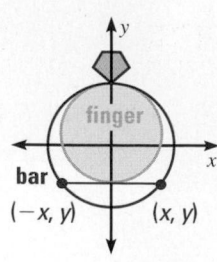 **RESIZING A RING** One way to resize a ring is to fit a bar
into the ring, as shown. Suppose a ring that is 20 millimeters
in diameter has to be resized to fit a finger 16 millimeters in
diameter. What is the length of the bar that should be inserted
in order to make the ring fit the finger? (*Hint:* Write an
equation of the ring, assuming it is centered at the origin.
Determine what the *y*-coordinate of the bar must be and then
substitute this coordinate into the equation to find *x*.)

84. **LIFEGUARD** You are a lifeguard at a pond. The pond is a circle with a
diameter of 360 feet. You want to rope off a section of the pond for swimming.
If you want the rope to form a chord of the circle and have a maximum distance
of 45 feet from shore, approximately how long will you need the rope to be?

85. **PHYSICAL THERAPY** A tilt-board
is a physical therapy device that a person
rocks back and forth on. Suppose the
ends of a tilt-board are part of a
circle with a radius of 30 inches.
If the tilt-board has a depth of
6 inches, how wide is it?

▶ Source: Steps to Follow

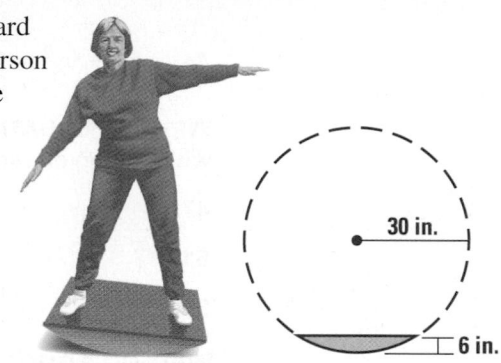

30 in.

6 in.

AIR TRAFFIC CONTROL In Exercises 86 and 87, use the following information.
An air traffic control tower can detect airplanes up to 50 miles away. You are in an
airplane 42 miles east and 43 miles south of the control tower.

86. Write an inequality that describes the region in which planes can be detected by
the control tower. Can the control tower detect your plane on its radar?

87. Suppose a jet is 35 miles west and 66 miles north of the control tower and is
traveling due south at a speed of 500 miles per hour. After how many minutes
will the jet appear on the control tower's radar?

Test
Preparation

88. **MULTIPLE CHOICE** What is the equation of the line that is tangent to the circle
$x^2 + y^2 = 53$ at the point $(7, 2)$?

Ⓐ $y = -\frac{7}{2}x + \frac{45}{2}$ Ⓑ $y = -\frac{7}{2}x + \frac{53}{2}$

Ⓒ $y = \frac{7}{2}x - \frac{45}{2}$ Ⓓ $y = -\frac{7}{2}x - \frac{45}{2}$

89. **MULTIPLE CHOICE** Suppose a signal from a television transmitter tower can be
received up to 150 miles away. The following points represent the locations of
houses near the transmitter tower with the origin representing the tower. Which
point is *not* within the range of the tower?

Ⓐ $(120, 20)$ Ⓑ $(40, 140)$ Ⓒ $(105, 120)$ Ⓓ $(10, 148)$

★ **Challenge**

90. **ESTIMATING AREA** The *segment* of a circle
is the region bounded by a chord and an arc.
Estimate the area of the shaded segment by
finding the area of $\triangle ABC$ and the area of
$\triangle ABD$, given that $\overline{AD}$ and $\overline{BD}$ are tangent to
the circle.

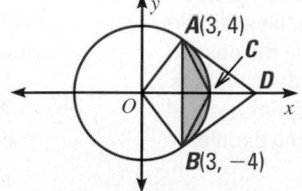

A(3, 4)
C
D
O
B(3, −4)

MIXED REVIEW

SOLVING SYSTEMS Solve the system using any algebraic method.
(Review 3.2)

91. $x - 9y = 25$
$6x - 5y = 3$

92. $9x - y = 8$
$3x + 10y = -49$

93. $2x - 3y = 2$
$-7x + 4y = 6$

94. $8x - 5y = 4$
$2x + y = 1$

95. $-x + 5y = 3$
$4x - 9y = 10$

96. $-9x + 4y = 15$
$3x + 2y = 5$

COMPOSITION OF FUNCTIONS Find $f(g(x))$ and $g(f(x))$. (Review 7.3)

97. $f(x) = x + 1$ and $g(x) = 2x$

98. $f(x) = 4x + 1$ and $g(x) = x - 5$

99. $f(x) = -x^2 - 1$ and $g(x) = x + 5$

100. $f(x) = x^2 - 7$ and $g(x) = 3x + 1$

GRAPHING FUNCTIONS Graph the function. (Review 8.1)

101. $y = \frac{1}{4} \cdot 5^x$

102. $y = -\left(\frac{5}{3}\right)^x$

103. $y = 4 \cdot 3^{x-1} - 7$

104. $y = 3 \cdot 2^{x-4}$

105. $y = 2^{x+3} - 1$

106. $y = \frac{1}{4} \cdot 8^{x+1}$

🌐 **BABYSITTING** In Exercises 107 and 108, use the following information.
In June you babysit 35 hours for the Johnsons and 52 hours for the Martins. In July you babysit 112 hours for the Johnsons and 40 hours for the Martins. In August you babysit 95 hours for the Johnsons and 63 hours for the Martins. (Review 4.1)

107. Use a matrix to organize the information.

108. You charge $6 per hour for babysitting. Using your matrix from Exercise 107, write a matrix that shows how much you earned over the summer vacation.

QUIZ 1

Find the distance between the two points. Then find the midpoint of the line segment joining the two points. (Lesson 10.1)

1. $(0, 0), (8, 6)$

2. $(3, 3), (-3, -3)$

3. $(-2, 7), (4, -10)$

4. $(3, -7), (-5, -9)$

5. $(8, 6), (-4, 4)$

6. $(-1, -13), (11, 15)$

Draw the parabola. Identify the focus and directrix. (Lesson 10.2)

7. $y^2 = 6x$

8. $3y = x^2$

9. $-x^2 = 5y$

10. $-4y^2 = 6x$

11. $3x^2 = 7y$

12. $\frac{1}{2}x = 2y^2$

13. $x + \frac{1}{8}y^2 = 0$

14. $-x^2 - 12y = 0$

Write the standard form of the equation of the circle that passes through the given point and whose center is the origin. (Lesson 10.3)

15. $(0, 3)$

16. $(-5, 0)$

17. $(4, 7)$

18. $(-2, -5)$

19. $(-1, 9)$

20. $(6, -3)$

21. $(6, -6)$

22. $(-7, 8)$

23. 🌐 **RADIO SIGNALS** The signals of a radio station can be received up to 65 miles away. Your house is 35 miles east and 56 miles south of the radio station. Can you receive the radio station's signals? Explain. (Lesson 10.3)

▶ ACTIVITY 10.3

Using Technology

Graphing Circles

When you use a graphing calculator to draw a circle, you need to remember two things. First, most graphing calculators cannot directly graph equations such as $x^2 + y^2 = 36$ because they are not functions. Second, to obtain a graph with true perspective (in which a circle looks like a circle) you must use a "square setting."

▶ EXAMPLE

Use a graphing calculator to draw the graph of $x^2 + y^2 = 36$.

▶ SOLUTION

1 Begin by solving the equation for y.

$$x^2 + y^2 = 36$$

$$y^2 = 36 - x^2$$

$$y = \pm\sqrt{36 - x^2}$$

Enter the two equations into the graphing calculator.

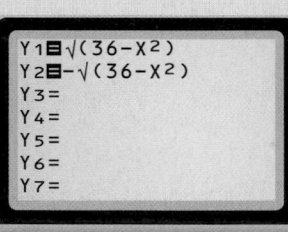

2 Next set the viewing window so that it has a "square setting." On some graphing calculators you can select a square setting, such as "ZSquare." On a graphing calculator whose viewing window's height is two thirds its width, you can obtain a "square setting" by choosing maximum and minimum values that satisfy this equation:

$$\frac{\text{Ymax} - \text{Ymin}}{\text{Xmax} - \text{Xmin}} = \frac{2}{3}$$

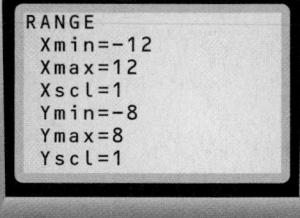

3 The graph is shown at the right. (Some calculators may not connect the ends of the two graphs.)

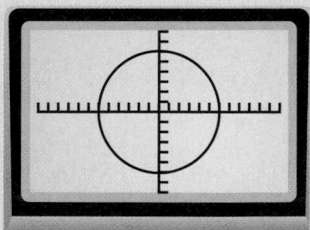

STUDENT HELP

KEYSTROKE HELP

See keystrokes for several models of calculators at www.mcdougallittell.com

▶ EXERCISES

Use a graphing calculator to graph the equation. Write the setting of the viewing window that you used and verify that it is a square setting.

1. $x^2 + y^2 = 121$ 2. $x^2 + y^2 = 50$ 3. $x^2 + y^2 = 484$

4. $5x^2 + 5y^2 = 120$ 5. $x^2 + y^2 = \frac{16}{9}$ 6. $\frac{1}{2}x^2 + \frac{1}{2}y^2 = 72$

7. $\frac{4}{5}x^2 + \frac{4}{5}y^2 = 20$ 8. $9x^2 + 9y^2 = 4$ 9. $125x^2 + 125y^2 = 1000$

10.4

Ellipses

What you should learn

GOAL 1 Graph and write equations of ellipses.

GOAL 2 Use ellipses in **real-life** situations, such as modeling the orbit of Mars in **Example 4**.

Why you should learn it

▼ To solve **real-life** problems, such as finding the area of an elliptical Australian football field in **Exs. 73–75**.

GOAL 1 GRAPHING AND WRITING EQUATIONS OF ELLIPSES

An **ellipse** is the set of all points P such that the sum of the distances between P and two distinct fixed points, called the **foci**, is a constant.

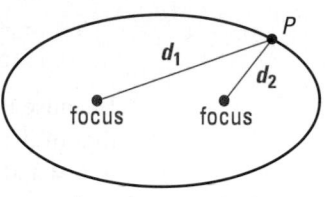

$d_1 + d_2 = \text{constant}$

The line through the foci intersects the ellipse at two points, the **vertices**. The line segment joining the vertices is the **major axis**, and its midpoint is the **center** of the ellipse. The line perpendicular to the major axis at the center intersects the ellipse at two points called the **co-vertices**. The line segment that joins these points is the **minor axis** of the ellipse. The two types of ellipses we will discuss are those with a horizontal major axis and those with a vertical major axis.

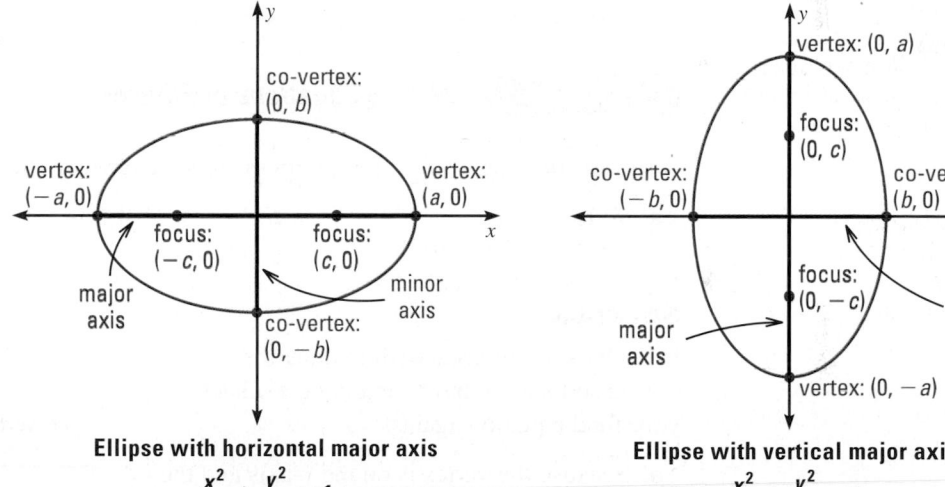

Ellipse with horizontal major axis

$$\frac{x^2}{a^2} + \frac{y^2}{b^2} = 1$$

Ellipse with vertical major axis

$$\frac{x^2}{b^2} + \frac{y^2}{a^2} = 1$$

CHARACTERISTICS OF AN ELLIPSE (CENTER AT ORIGIN)

The **standard form of the equation of an ellipse** with center at (0, 0) and major and minor axes of lengths $2a$ and $2b$, where $a > b > 0$, is as follows.

EQUATION	MAJOR AXIS	VERTICES	CO-VERTICES
$\dfrac{x^2}{a^2} + \dfrac{y^2}{b^2} = 1$	Horizontal	$(\pm a, 0)$	$(0, \pm b)$
$\dfrac{x^2}{b^2} + \dfrac{y^2}{a^2} = 1$	Vertical	$(0, \pm a)$	$(\pm b, 0)$

The foci of the ellipse lie on the major axis, c units from the center where $c^2 = a^2 - b^2$.

EXAMPLE 1 *Graphing an Equation of an Ellipse*

Draw the ellipse given by $9x^2 + 16y^2 = 144$. Identify the foci.

SOLUTION

First rewrite the equation in standard form.

$$\frac{9x^2}{144} + \frac{16y^2}{144} = \frac{144}{144} \qquad \textbf{Divide each side by 144.}$$

$$\frac{x^2}{16} + \frac{y^2}{9} = 1 \qquad \textbf{Simplify.}$$

Because the denominator of the x^2-term is greater than that of the y^2-term, the major axis is horizontal. So, $a = 4$ and $b = 3$. Plot the vertices and co-vertices. Then draw the ellipse that passes through these four points.

The foci are at $(c, 0)$ and $(-c, 0)$. To find the value of c, use the equation $c^2 = a^2 - b^2$.

$$c^2 = 4^2 - 3^2 = 16 - 9 = 7$$

$$c = \sqrt{7}$$

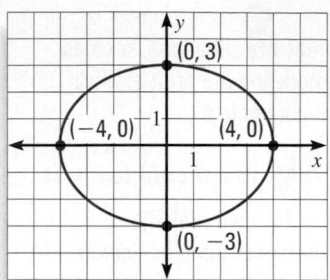

▶ The foci are at $\left(\sqrt{7}, 0\right)$ and $\left(-\sqrt{7}, 0\right)$.

STUDENT HELP

HOMEWORK HELP
Visit our Web site
www.mcdougallittell.com
for extra examples.

EXAMPLE 2 *Writing Equations of Ellipses*

Write an equation of the ellipse with the given characteristics and center at $(0, 0)$.

   a. Vertex: $(0, 7)$ **b.** Vertex: $(-4, 0)$
       Co-vertex: $(-6, 0)$ Focus: $(2, 0)$

SOLUTION

In each case, you may wish to draw the ellipse so that you have something to check your final equation against.

a. Because the vertex is on the y-axis and the co-vertex is on the x-axis, the major axis is vertical with $a = 7$ and $b = 6$.

▶ An equation is $\dfrac{x^2}{36} + \dfrac{y^2}{49} = 1$.

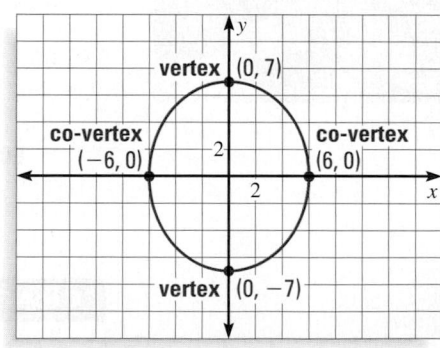

b. Because the vertex and focus are points on a horizontal line, the major axis is horizontal with $a = 4$ and $c = 2$. To find b, use the equation $c^2 = a^2 - b^2$.

$$2^2 = 4^2 - b^2$$

$$b^2 = 16 - 4 = 12$$

$$b = 2\sqrt{3}$$

▶ An equation is $\dfrac{x^2}{16} + \dfrac{y^2}{12} = 1$.

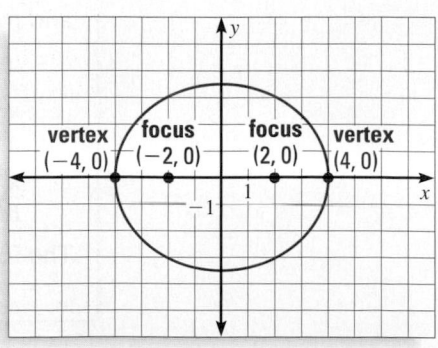

Both man-made objects, such as The Ellipse at the White House, and natural phenomena, such as the orbits of planets, involve ellipses.

Landscaping

EXAMPLE 3 *Finding the Area of an Ellipse*

A portion of the White House lawn is called The Ellipse. It is 1060 feet long and 890 feet wide.

a. Write an equation of The Ellipse.

b. The area of an ellipse is $A = \pi ab$. What is the area of The Ellipse at the White House?

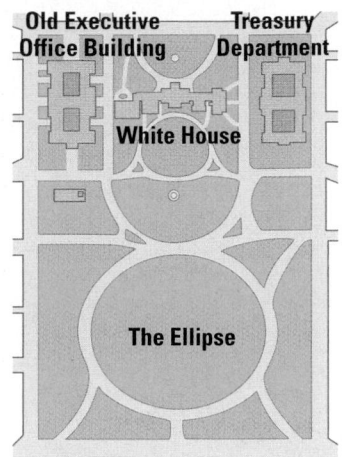

SOLUTION

a. The major axis is horizontal with
$$a = \frac{1060}{2} = 530 \text{ and } b = \frac{890}{2} = 445.$$

▶ An equation is $\dfrac{x^2}{530^2} + \dfrac{y^2}{445^2} = 1$.

b. The area is $A = \pi(530)(445) \approx 741{,}000$ square feet.

Astronomy

EXAMPLE 4 *Modeling with an Ellipse*

In its elliptical orbit, Mercury ranges from 46.04 million kilometers to 69.86 million kilometers from the center of the sun. The center of the sun is a focus of the orbit. Write an equation of the orbit.

SOLUTION

Using the diagram shown, you can write a system of linear equations involving *a* and *c*.

$$a - c = 46.04$$

$$a + c = 69.86$$

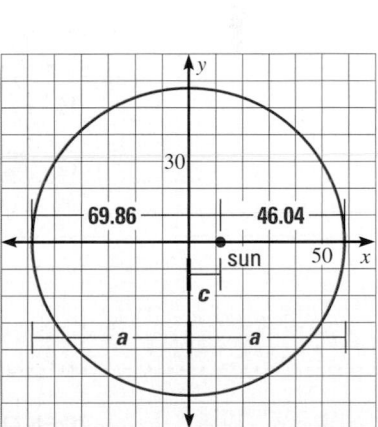

Adding the two equations gives $2a = 115.9$, so $a = \mathbf{57.95}$. Substituting this *a*-value into the second equation gives $57.95 + c = 69.86$, so $c = \mathbf{11.91}$.

From the relationship $c^2 = a^2 - b^2$, you can conclude the following:

$$b = \sqrt{a^2 - c^2}$$
$$= \sqrt{(\mathbf{57.95})^2 - (\mathbf{11.91})^2}$$
$$\approx 56.71$$

▶ An equation of the elliptical orbit is $\dfrac{x^2}{(57.95)^2} + \dfrac{y^2}{(56.71)^2} = 1$ where *x* and *y* are in millions of kilometers.

GUIDED PRACTICE

Vocabulary Check ✓

1. Complete each statement using the ellipse shown.

    a. The points $(-5, 0)$ and $(5, 0)$ are called the ? .

    b. The points $(0, -4)$ and $(0, 4)$ are called the ? .

    c. The points $(-3, 0)$ and $(3, 0)$ are called the ? .

    d. The segment with endpoints $(-5, 0)$ and $(5, 0)$ is called the ? .

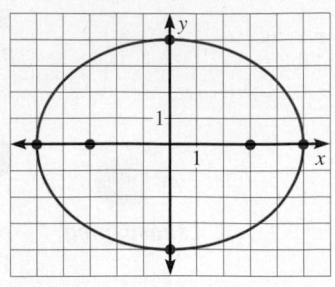

Ex. 1

Concept Check ✓

2. How can you tell from the equation of an ellipse whether the major axis is horizontal or vertical?

3. Explain how to find the foci of an ellipse given the coordinates of its vertices and co-vertices.

4. **ERROR ANALYSIS** A student was asked to write an equation of the ellipse shown at the right.

    The student wrote the equation $\frac{x^2}{4} + \frac{y^2}{9} = 1$.

    What did the student do wrong? What is the correct equation?

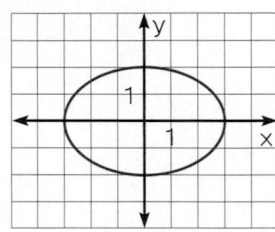

Ex. 4

Skill Check ✓

Write an equation of the ellipse with the given characteristics and center at (0, 0).

5. Vertex: $(0, 5)$
   Co-vertex: $(-4, 0)$

6. Vertex: $(9, 0)$
   Co-vertex: $(0, 2)$

7. Vertex: $(-7, 0)$
   Focus: $\left(-2\sqrt{10}, 0\right)$

8. Vertex: $(0, 13)$
   Focus: $(0, -5)$

9. Co-vertex: $\left(\sqrt{91}, 0\right)$
   Focus: $(0, 3)$

10. Co-vertex: $\left(0, \sqrt{33}\right)$
    Focus: $(4, 0)$

Draw the ellipse.

11. $\frac{x^2}{49} + \frac{y^2}{25} = 1$

12. $\frac{x^2}{9} + \frac{y^2}{16} = 1$

13. $\frac{x^2}{30} + \frac{y^2}{4} = 1$

14. $\frac{x^2}{64} + \frac{y^2}{45} = 1$

15. $75x^2 + 36y^2 = 2700$

16. $81x^2 + 63y^2 = 5103$

17. 🌐 **GARDEN** An elliptical garden is 10 feet long and 6 feet wide. Write an equation for the garden. Then graph the equation. Label the vertices, co-vertices, and foci. Assume that the major axis of the garden is horizontal.

PRACTICE AND APPLICATIONS

STUDENT HELP

▶ **Extra Practice**
to help you master
skills is on p. 954.

IDENTIFYING PARTS Write the equation in standard form (if not already). Then identify the vertices, co-vertices, and foci of the ellipse.

18. $\frac{x^2}{25} + \frac{y^2}{16} = 1$

19. $\frac{x^2}{121} + \frac{y^2}{100} = 1$

20. $\frac{x^2}{4} + \frac{y^2}{9} = 1$

21. $\frac{x^2}{9} + \frac{y^2}{25} = 1$

22. $\frac{x^2}{12} + \frac{y^2}{36} = 1$

23. $\frac{x^2}{28} + \frac{y^2}{20} = 1$

24. $16x^2 + y^2 = 16$

25. $49x^2 + 4y^2 = 196$

26. $9x^2 + 100y^2 = 900$

27. $x^2 + 10y^2 = 10$

28. $10x^2 + 25y^2 = 250$

29. $25x^2 + 15y^2 = 375$

STUDENT HELP

▶ **HOMEWORK HELP**
Example 1: Exs. 18–50
Example 2: Exs. 51–68
Examples 3, 4: Exs. 69–75

GRAPHING Graph the equation. Then identify the vertices, co-vertices, and foci of the ellipse.

30. $\dfrac{x^2}{16} + \dfrac{y^2}{36} = 1$

31. $\dfrac{x^2}{4} + \dfrac{y^2}{49} = 1$

32. $\dfrac{x^2}{36} + \dfrac{y^2}{64} = 1$

33. $\dfrac{x^2}{49} + \dfrac{y^2}{144} = 1$

34. $\dfrac{x^2}{196} + \dfrac{y^2}{100} = 1$

35. $\dfrac{x^2}{256} + \dfrac{y^2}{36} = 1$

36. $\dfrac{x^2}{225} + \dfrac{y^2}{81} = 1$

37. $\dfrac{x^2}{121} + \dfrac{y^2}{169} = 1$

38. $\dfrac{x^2}{144} + \dfrac{y^2}{400} = 1$

39. $\dfrac{x^2}{49} + \dfrac{y^2}{64} = 1$

40. $\dfrac{x^2}{4} + y^2 = 100$

41. $\dfrac{x^2}{4} + \dfrac{y^2}{25} = \dfrac{1}{4}$

GRAPHING In Exercises 42–50, the equations of parabolas, circles, and ellipses are given. Graph the equation.

42. $x^2 + y^2 = 33^2$

43. $64x^2 + 25y^2 = 1600$

44. $24y + x^2 = 0$

45. $72x^2 = 144y$

46. $24x^2 + 24y^2 = 96$

47. $\dfrac{x^2}{81} + \dfrac{4y}{9} = 1$

48. $\dfrac{3x^2}{12} + \dfrac{5y^2}{500} = 1$

49. $\dfrac{x^2}{36} + \dfrac{y^2}{36} = 4$

50. $5x^2 + 9y^2 = 45$

WRITING EQUATIONS Write an equation of the ellipse with the given characteristics and center at (0, 0).

51. Vertex: (0, 6)
Co-vertex: (5, 0)

52. Vertex: (0, 6)
Co-vertex: (−2, 0)

53. Vertex: (−4, 0)
Co-vertex: (0, 3)

54. Vertex: (0, −7)
Co-vertex: (−1, 0)

55. Vertex: (9, 0)
Co-vertex: (0, −8)

56. Vertex: (10, 0)
Co-vertex: (0, 4)

57. Vertex: (0, 7)
Focus: (0, 3)

58. Vertex: (−5, 0)
Focus: $(2\sqrt{6}, 0)$

59. Vertex: (0, 8)
Focus: $(0, -4\sqrt{3})$

60. Vertex: (15, 0)
Focus: (12, 0)

61. Vertex: (5, 0)
Focus: (−3, 0)

62. Vertex: (0, −30)
Focus: (0, 20)

63. Co-vertex: $(\sqrt{55}, 0)$
Focus: (0, −3)

64. Co-vertex: $(0, -\sqrt{3})$
Focus: (−1, 0)

65. Co-vertex: $(-2\sqrt{10}, 0)$
Focus: (0, 9)

66. Co-vertex: $(0, -3\sqrt{3})$
Focus: (3, 0)

67. Co-vertex: $(5\sqrt{11}, 0)$
Focus: (0, −7)

68. Co-vertex: $(0, -\sqrt{77})$
Focus: (−2, 0)

🌐 **WHISPERING GALLERY** In Exercises 69–71, use the following information.

Statuary Hall is an elliptical room in the United States Capitol in Washington, D.C. The room is also called the Whispering Gallery because a person standing at one focus of the room can hear even a whisper spoken by a person standing at the other focus. This occurs because any sound that is emitted from one focus of an ellipse will reflect off the side of the ellipse to the other focus. Statuary Hall is 46 feet wide and 97 feet long.

69. Find an equation that models the shape of the room.

70. How far apart are the two foci?

71. What is the area of the floor of the room?

72.  **SPACE EXPLORATION** The first artificial satellite to orbit Earth was Sputnik I, launched by the Soviet Union in 1957. The orbit was an ellipse with Earth's center as one focus. The orbit's highest point above Earth's surface was 583 miles, and its lowest point was 132 miles. Find an equation of the orbit. (Use 4000 miles as the radius of Earth.) Graph your equation.

 **AUSTRALIAN FOOTBALL In Exercises 73–75, use the information below.**
Australian football is played on an elliptical field. The official rules state that the field must be between 135 and 185 meters long and between 110 and 155 meters wide. ▶ Source: The Australian News Network

73. Write an equation for the largest allowable playing field.

74. Write an equation for the smallest allowable playing field.

75. Write an inequality that describes the possible areas of an Australian football field.

Test Preparation

76. MULTI-STEP PROBLEM A tour boat travels between two islands that are 12 miles apart. For a trip between the islands, there is enough fuel for a 20-mile tour.

   a. *Writing* The region in which the boat can travel is bounded by an ellipse. Explain why this is so.

   b. Let $(0, 0)$ represent the center of the ellipse. Find the coordinates of each island.

   c. Suppose the boat travels from one island, straight past the other island to the vertex of the ellipse, and back to the second island. How many miles does the boat travel? Use your answer to find the coordinates of the vertex.

   d. Use your answers to parts (b) and (c) to write an equation for the ellipse that bounds the region the boat can travel in.

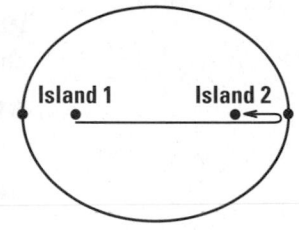

★ **Challenge**

77. LOGICAL REASONING Show that $c^2 = a^2 - b^2$ for any ellipse given by the equation $\dfrac{x^2}{a^2} + \dfrac{y^2}{b^2} = 1$ with foci at $(c, 0)$ and $(-c, 0)$.

MIXED REVIEW

RATIONAL EXPONENTS Evaluate the expression without using a calculator. (Review 7.1)

78. $125^{2/3}$ **79.** $-8^{5/3}$ **80.** $4^{5/2}$ **81.** $27^{-2/6}$

82. $4^{7/2}$ **83.** $81^{3/4}$ **84.** $64^{-2/3}$ **85.** $32^{4/5}$

INVERSE VARIATION The variables x and y vary inversely. Use the given values to write an equation relating x and y. (Review 9.1)

86. $x = 3, y = -2$ **87.** $x = 4, y = 6$ **88.** $x = 5, y = 1$

89. $x = 8, y = 9$ **90.** $x = 9, y = 2$ **91.** $x = 0.5, y = 24$

GRAPHING Graph the function. State the domain and range. (Review 9.2 for 10.5)

92. $f(x) = \dfrac{9}{x}$ **93.** $f(x) = -\dfrac{9}{x}$ **94.** $f(x) = \dfrac{12}{x}$

95. $f(x) = \dfrac{24}{x}$ **96.** $f(x) = \dfrac{10}{x - 2}$ **97.** $f(x) = \dfrac{4}{x + 3}$

10.5

Hyperbolas

What you should learn

GOAL 1 Graph and write equations of hyperbolas.

GOAL 2 Use hyperbolas to solve **real-life** problems, such as modeling a sundial in **Exs. 64–66**.

Why you should learn it

▼ To model **real-life** objects, such as a sculpture in **Example 4**.

GOAL 1 GRAPHING AND WRITING EQUATIONS OF HYPERBOLAS

The definition of a hyperbola is similar to that of an ellipse. For an ellipse, recall that the *sum* of the distances between a point on the ellipse and the two foci is constant. For a hyperbola, the *difference* is constant.

A **hyperbola** is the set of all points P such that the difference of the distances from P to two fixed points, called the **foci**, is constant. The line through the foci intersects the hyperbola at two points, the **vertices**. The line segment joining the vertices is the **transverse axis**, and its midpoint is the **center** of the hyperbola. A hyperbola has two branches and two asymptotes. The asymptotes contain the diagonals of a rectangle centered at the hyperbola's center, as shown below.

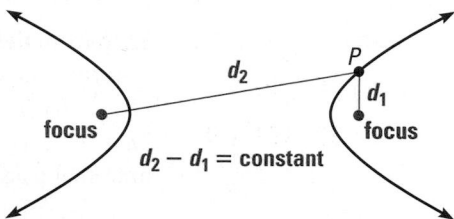

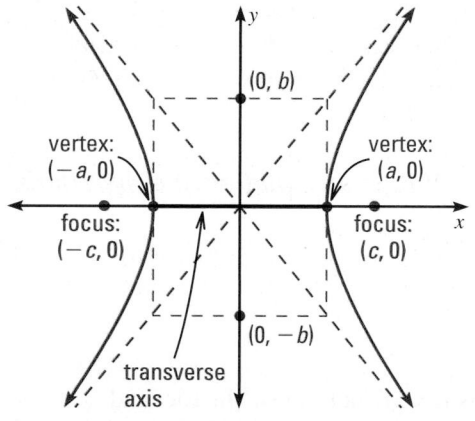

Hyperbola with horizontal transverse axis
$$\frac{x^2}{a^2} - \frac{y^2}{b^2} = 1$$

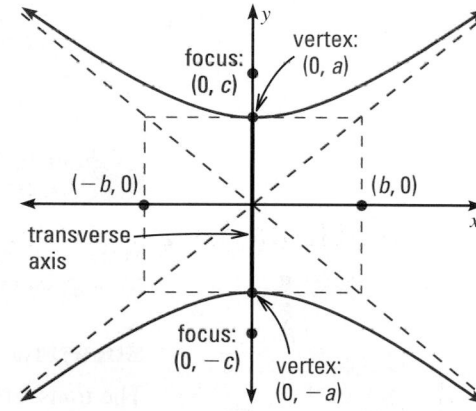

Hyperbola with vertical transverse axis
$$\frac{y^2}{a^2} - \frac{x^2}{b^2} = 1$$

CHARACTERISTICS OF A HYPERBOLA (CENTER AT ORIGIN)

The **standard form of the equation of a hyperbola** with center at (0, 0) is as follows.

EQUATION	TRANSVERSE AXIS	ASYMPTOTES	VERTICES
$\dfrac{x^2}{a^2} - \dfrac{y^2}{b^2} = 1$	Horizontal	$y = \pm\dfrac{b}{a}x$	$(\pm a, 0)$
$\dfrac{y^2}{a^2} - \dfrac{x^2}{b^2} = 1$	Vertical	$y = \pm\dfrac{a}{b}x$	$(0, \pm a)$

The foci of the hyperbola lie on the transverse axis, c units from the center where $c^2 = a^2 + b^2$.

EXAMPLE 1 *Graphing an Equation of a Hyperbola*

Draw the hyperbola given by $4x^2 - 9y^2 = 36$.

SOLUTION

First rewrite the equation in standard form.

$4x^2 - 9y^2 = 36$ **Write original equation.**

$\dfrac{4x^2}{36} - \dfrac{9y^2}{36} = \dfrac{36}{36}$ **Divide each side by 36.**

$\dfrac{x^2}{9} - \dfrac{y^2}{4} = 1$ **Simplify.**

Note from the equation that $a^2 = 9$ and $b^2 = 4$, so $a = 3$ and $b = 2$. Because the x^2-term is positive, the transverse axis is horizontal and the vertices are at $(-3, 0)$ and $(3, 0)$. To draw the hyperbola, first draw a rectangle that is centered at the origin, $2a = 6$ units wide and $2b = 4$ units high. Then show the asymptotes by drawing the lines that pass through opposite corners of the rectangle. Finally, draw the hyperbola.

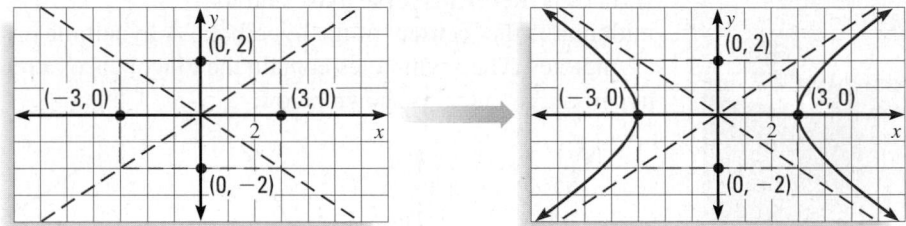

EXAMPLE 2 *Writing an Equation of a Hyperbola*

Write an equation of the hyperbola with foci at $(0, -3)$ and $(0, 3)$ and vertices at $(0, -2)$ and $(0, 2)$.

SOLUTION

The transverse axis is vertical because the foci and vertices lie on the y-axis. The center is the origin because the foci and the vertices are equidistant from the origin. Since the foci are each 3 units from the center, $c = 3$. Similarly, because the vertices are each 2 units from the center, $a = 2$.

You can use these values of a and c to find b.

$b^2 = c^2 - a^2$

$b^2 = 3^2 - 2^2 = 9 - 4 = 5$

$b = \sqrt{5}$

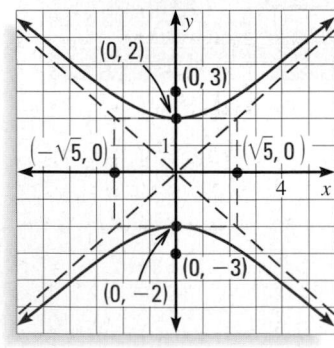

Because the transverse axis is vertical, the standard form of the equation is as follows.

$\dfrac{y^2}{2^2} - \dfrac{x^2}{(\sqrt{5})^2} = 1$ **Substitute 2 for a and $\sqrt{5}$ for b.**

$\dfrac{y^2}{4} - \dfrac{x^2}{5} = 1$ **Simplify.**

EXAMPLE 3 *Using a Real-Life Hyperbola*

PHOTOGRAPHY A hyperbolic mirror can be used to take panoramic photographs. A camera is pointed toward the vertex of the mirror and is positioned so that the lens is at one focus of the mirror. An equation for the cross section of the mirror is $\dfrac{y^2}{16} - \dfrac{x^2}{9} = 1$ where x and y are measured in inches. How far from the mirror is the lens?

SOLUTION

Notice from the equation that $a^2 = 16$ and $b^2 = 9$, so $a = 4$ and $b = 3$. Use these values and the equation $c^2 = a^2 + b^2$ to find the value of c.

$c^2 = a^2 + b^2$	**Equation relating a, b, and c**
$c^2 = 16 + 9 = 25$	**Substitute for a and b and simplify.**
$c = 5$	**Solve for c.**

Since $a = 4$ and $c = 5$, the vertices are at $(0, -4)$ and $(0, 4)$ and the foci are at $(0, -5)$ and $(0, 5)$. The camera is below the mirror, so the lens is at $(0, -5)$ and the vertex of the mirror is at $(0, 4)$. The distance between these points is $4 - (-5) = 9$.

▶ The lens is 9 inches from the mirror.

> **PANORAMIC CAMERAS**
> A panoramic photograph taken with the camera shown above gives a 360° view of a scene.
>
> **APPLICATION LINK**
> www.mcdougallittell.com

Sculpture

EXAMPLE 4 *Modeling with a Hyperbola*

The diagram at the right shows the hyperbolic cross section of a sculpture located at the Fermi National Accelerator Laboratory in Batavia, Illinois.

  a. Write an equation that models the curved sides of the sculpture.

  b. At a height of 5 feet, how wide is the sculpture? (Each unit in the coordinate plane represents 1 foot.)

SOLUTION

  a. From the diagram you can see that the transverse axis is horizontal and $a = 1$. So the equation has this form:

  $$\frac{x^2}{1^2} - \frac{y^2}{b^2} = 1$$

  Because the hyperbola passes through the point $(2, 13)$, you can substitute $x = 2$ and $y = 13$ into the equation and solve for b. When you do this, you obtain $b \approx 7.5$.

  ▶ An equation of the hyperbola is $\dfrac{x^2}{1^2} - \dfrac{y^2}{(7.5)^2} = 1$.

  b. At a height of 5 feet above the ground, $y = -8$. To find the width of the sculpture, substitute this value into the equation and solve for x. You get $x \approx 1.46$.

  ▶ At a height of 5 feet, the width is $2x \approx 2.92$ feet.

GUIDED PRACTICE

Vocabulary Check ✓

1. Complete these statements: The points $(0, -2)$ and $(0, 2)$ in the graph at the right are the _?_ of the hyperbola. The segment joining these two points is the _?_ .

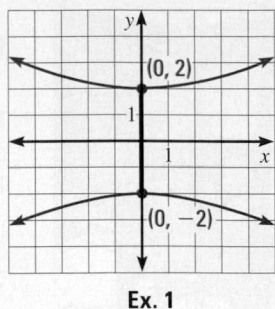

Ex. 1

Concept Check ✓

2. How are the definitions of ellipse and hyperbola alike? How are they different?

3. How do the asymptotes of a hyperbola help you draw the hyperbola?

Skill Check ✓

Graph the equation. Identify the foci and asymptotes.

4. $\dfrac{x^2}{49} - \dfrac{y^2}{81} = 1$

5. $\dfrac{y^2}{100} - \dfrac{x^2}{75} = 1$

6. $\dfrac{x^2}{64} - y^2 = 1$

7. $36x^2 - 4y^2 = 144$

8. $12y^2 - 25x^2 = 300$

9. $y^2 - 9x^2 = 9$

Write an equation of the hyperbola with the given foci and vertices.

10. Foci: $(0, -5)$, $(0, 5)$
    Vertices: $(0, -3)$, $(0, 3)$

11. Foci: $(-8, 0)$, $(8, 0)$
    Vertices: $(-7, 0)$, $(7, 0)$

12. Foci: $\left(-\sqrt{34}, 0\right)$, $\left(\sqrt{34}, 0\right)$
    Vertices: $(-5, 0)$, $(5, 0)$

13. Foci: $(0, -9)$, $(0, 9)$
    Vertices: $\left(0, -3\sqrt{5}\right)$, $\left(0, 3\sqrt{5}\right)$

14. 🌐 **PHOTOGRAPHY** Look back at Example 3. Suppose a mirror has a cross section modeled by the equation $\dfrac{x^2}{25} - \dfrac{y^2}{9} = 1$ where x and y are measured in inches. If you place a camera with its lens at the focus, how far is the lens from the vertex of the mirror?

PRACTICE AND APPLICATIONS

STUDENT HELP

▶ **Extra Practice**
to help you master
skills is on p. 954.

MATCHING Match the equation with its graph.

15. $\dfrac{x^2}{16} - \dfrac{y^2}{4} = 1$

16. $\dfrac{y^2}{4} - \dfrac{x^2}{2} = 1$

17. $\dfrac{y^2}{16} - \dfrac{x^2}{4} = 1$

18. $\dfrac{x^2}{4} - \dfrac{y^2}{2} = 1$

A.
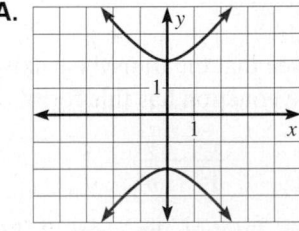

B.
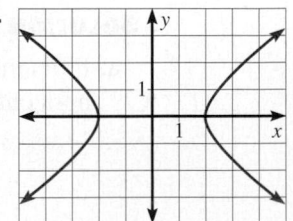

STUDENT HELP

▶ **HOMEWORK HELP**
Example 1: Exs. 15–55
Example 2: Exs. 56–63
Example 3: Ex. 67
Example 4: Exs. 64–66

C.
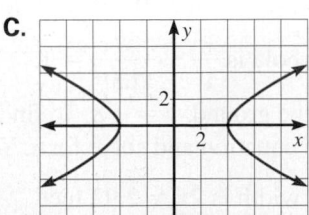

D.
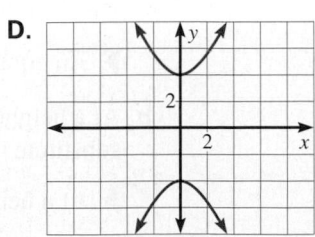

STANDARD FORM Write the equation of the hyperbola in standard form.

19. $36x^2 - 9y^2 = 324$ **20.** $y^2 - 81x^2 = 81$ **21.** $36y^2 - 4x^2 = 9$

22. $16y^2 - 36x^2 + 9 = 0$ **23.** $y^2 - \dfrac{x^2}{36} = 4$ **24.** $\dfrac{x^2}{9} - \dfrac{4y^2}{9} = 9$

IDENTIFYING PARTS Identify the vertices and foci of the hyperbola.

25. $\dfrac{x^2}{9} - \dfrac{y^2}{64} = 1$ **26.** $\dfrac{y^2}{49} - x^2 = 1$ **27.** $\dfrac{x^2}{121} - \dfrac{y^2}{4} = 1$

28. $4y^2 - 81x^2 = 324$ **29.** $25y^2 - 4x^2 = 100$ **30.** $36x^2 - 10y^2 = 360$

GRAPHING Graph the equation. Identify the foci and asymptotes.

31. $\dfrac{x^2}{25} - \dfrac{y^2}{121} = 1$ **32.** $\dfrac{x^2}{36} - y^2 = 1$ **33.** $\dfrac{y^2}{25} - \dfrac{x^2}{49} = 1$

34. $\dfrac{y^2}{9} - \dfrac{x^2}{100} = 1$ **35.** $\dfrac{x^2}{169} - \dfrac{y^2}{16} = 1$ **36.** $\dfrac{y^2}{64} - x^2 = 1$

37. $\dfrac{16x^2}{25} - \dfrac{y^2}{81} = 1$ **38.** $\dfrac{x^2}{144} - \dfrac{y^2}{121} = 1$ **39.** $\dfrac{x^2}{64} - \dfrac{9y^2}{4} = 1$

40. $\dfrac{y^2}{25} - \dfrac{x^2}{16} = 16$ **41.** $100x^2 - 81y^2 = 8100$ **42.** $x^2 - 9y^2 = 25$

GRAPHING HYPERBOLAS Use a graphing calculator to graph the equation. Tell what two equations you entered into the calculator.

43. $\dfrac{y^2}{144} - \dfrac{x^2}{100} = 1$ **44.** $\dfrac{x^2}{16} - \dfrac{y^2}{25} = 1$ **45.** $\dfrac{x^2}{42.25} - \dfrac{y^2}{72.25} = 1$

46. $\dfrac{y^2}{2.73} - \dfrac{x^2}{3.58} = 1$ **47.** $\dfrac{x^2}{10.1} - \dfrac{y^2}{22.3} = 1$ **48.** $1.2x^2 - 8.5y^2 = 4.6$

49. CRITICAL THINKING Suppose you tried to graph an equation of a hyperbola on a graphing calculator. You enter one function correctly, but you forget to enter the other function. Sketch what your graph might look like if the transverse axis is horizontal. Then sketch what your graph might look like if the transverse axis is vertical.

GRAPHING CONIC SECTIONS In Exercises 50–55, the equations of parabolas, circles, ellipses, and hyperbolas are given. Graph the equation.

50. $\dfrac{x^2}{169} - \dfrac{y^2}{25} = 1$ **51.** $x^2 + y^2 = 30$ **52.** $\dfrac{y^2}{9} - \dfrac{x^2}{64} = 1$

53. $x^2 = 15y$ **54.** $\dfrac{x^2}{196} + \dfrac{y^2}{256} = 1$ **55.** $14x^2 + 14y^2 = 126$

WRITING EQUATIONS Write an equation of the hyperbola with the given foci and vertices.

56. Foci: $(0, -13), (0, 13)$
Vertices: $(0, -5), (0, 5)$

57. Foci: $(-8, 0), (8, 0)$
Vertices: $(-6, 0), (6, 0)$

58. Foci: $(-4, 0), (4, 0)$
Vertices: $(-1, 0), (1, 0)$

59. Foci: $(-6, 0), (6, 0)$
Vertices: $(-5, 0), (5, 0)$

60. Foci: $(0, -7), (0, 7)$
Vertices: $(0, -3), (0, 3)$

61. Foci: $(0, -9), (0, 9)$
Vertices: $(0, -8), (0, 8)$

62. Foci: $(-8, 0), (8, 0)$
Vertices: $\left(-4\sqrt{3}, 0\right), \left(4\sqrt{3}, 0\right)$

63. Foci: $\left(0, -5\sqrt{6}\right), \left(0, 5\sqrt{6}\right)$
Vertices: $(0, -4), (0, 4)$

SUNDIAL The
Richard D. Swensen
sundial, located at the
University of Wisconsin –
River Falls, gives the correct
time to the minute.

APPLICATION LINK
www.mcdougallittell.com

SUNDIAL **In Exercises 64–66, use the following information.**
The sundial at the left was designed by Professor John Shepherd. The shadow of the *gnomon* traces a hyperbola throughout the day. Aluminum rods form the hyperbolas traced on the summer solstice, June 21, and the winter solstice, December 21.

64. One focus of the summer solstice hyperbola is 207 inches above the ground. The vertex of the aluminum branch is 266 inches above the ground. If the *x*-axis is 355 inches above the ground and the center of the hyperbola is at the origin, write an equation for the summer solstice hyperbola.

65. One focus of the winter solstice hyperbola is 419 inches above the ground. The vertex of the aluminum branch is 387 inches above the ground and the center of the hyperbola is at the origin. If the *x*-axis is 355 inches above the ground, write an equation for the winter solstice hyperbola.

66. Use your equations from Exercises 64 and 65 to draw the lower branch of the summer solstice hyperbola and the upper branch of the winter solstice hyperbola.

67. **AERONAUTICS** When an airplane travels faster than the speed of sound, the sound waves form a cone behind the airplane. If the airplane is flying parallel to the ground, the sound waves intersect the ground in a hyperbola with the airplane directly above its center. A sonic boom is heard along the hyperbola. If you hear a sonic boom that is audible along a hyperbola with the equation $\frac{x^2}{100} - \frac{y^2}{4} = 1$ where x and y are measured in miles, what is the shortest horizontal distance you could be to the airplane?

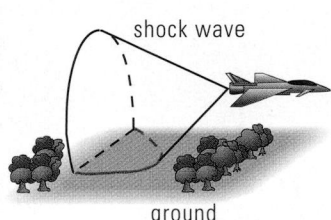

shock wave

ground

Test Preparation

68. **MULTI-STEP PROBLEM** Suppose you are making a ring out of clay for a necklace. If you have a fixed volume of clay and you want the ring to have a certain thickness, the area of the ring becomes fixed. However, you can still vary the inner radius x and the outer radius y.

a. Suppose you want to make a ring with an area of 2 square inches. Write an equation relating x and y.

b. Find three coordinate pairs (x, y) that satisfy the relationship from part (a). Then find the width of the ring, $y - x$, for each coordinate pair.

c. *Writing* How does the width of the ring, $y - x$, change as x and y both increase? Explain why this makes sense.

fixed

★ Challenge

69. Use the diagram at the right to show that $\left| d_2 - d_1 \right| = 2a$.

70. **LOCATING AN EXPLOSION** Two microphones, 1 mile apart, record an explosion. Microphone A receives the sound 2 seconds after Microphone B. Is this enough information to decide where the sound came from? Use the fact that sound travels at 1100 feet per second.

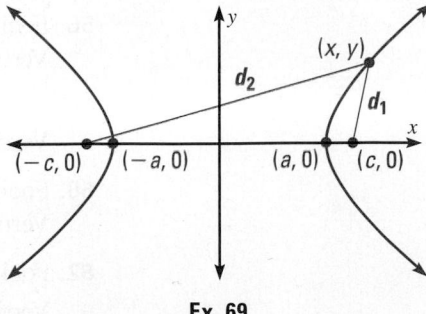

Ex. 69

MIXED REVIEW

GRAPHING FUNCTIONS Graph the function. (Review 2.8, 5.1 for 10.6)

71. $y = 2|x + 4| + 1$ **72.** $y = |x - 4| + 5$ **73.** $y = -|x - 6| - 8$

74. $y = 3(x - 1)^2 + 7$ **75.** $y = -2(x - 3)^2 - 6$ **76.** $y = \frac{1}{2}(x + 4)^2 + 5$

WRITING FUNCTIONS Write a polynomial function of least degree that has real coefficients, the given zeros, and a leading coefficient of 1. (Review 6.7)

77. $3, 1, 2$ **78.** $-7, -1, 3$ **79.** $6, -2, 2$

80. $-6, 4, 2$ **81.** $5, i, -i$ **82.** $3, -3, 2i$

EVALUATING LOGARITHMIC EXPRESSIONS Evaluate the expression without using a calculator. (Review 8.4)

83. $\log 10{,}000$ **84.** $\log_3 27$ **85.** $\log_5 625$ **86.** $\log_2 128$

87. $\log_4 64$ **88.** $\log_3 243$ **89.** $\log_6 216$ **90.** $\log_{100} 100{,}000{,}000$

91. 🌐 **TEST SCORES** Find the mean, median, mode(s), and range of the following set of test scores. (Review 7.7)

$$63, 67, 72, 75, 77, 78, 81, 81, 85, 86, 89, 89, 91, 92, 99$$

QUIZ 2

Self-Test for Lessons 10.4 and 10.5

Write an equation of the ellipse with the given characteristics and center at (0, 0). **(Lesson 10.4)**

1. Vertex: $(0, 7)$
Co-vertex: $(-3, 0)$

2. Vertex: $(-6, 0)$
Co-vertex: $(0, -1)$

3. Vertex: $(-10, 0)$
Focus: $(6, 0)$

4. Vertex: $(0, 5)$
Focus: $(0, \sqrt{17})$

5. Co-vertex: $(0, 2\sqrt{3})$
Focus: $(-\sqrt{3}, 0)$

6. Co-vertex: $(-9, 0)$
Focus: $(0, 4)$

Graph the equation. Identify the vertices, co-vertices, and foci. **(Lesson 10.4)**

7. $\dfrac{x^2}{4} + \dfrac{y^2}{49} = 1$ **8.** $\dfrac{x^2}{6} + y^2 = 1$ **9.** $x^2 + 9y^2 = 36$

Write an equation of the hyperbola with the given characteristics. **(Lesson 10.5)**

10. Foci: $(0, -8), (0, 8)$
Vertices: $(0, -5), (0, 5)$

11. Foci: $(-3, 0), (3, 0)$
Vertices: $(-1, 0), (1, 0)$

12. Foci: $(-6, 0), (6, 0)$
Vertices: $(-4, 0), (4, 0)$

13. Foci: $(0, -2\sqrt{5}), (0, 2\sqrt{5})$
Vertices: $(0, -4), (0, 4)$

Graph the equation. Identify the vertices, foci, and asymptotes. **(Lesson 10.5)**

14. $\dfrac{y^2}{25} - \dfrac{x^2}{36} = 1$ **15.** $8y^2 - 20x^2 = 160$ **16.** $18x^2 - 4y^2 = 36$

17. 🌐 **SPACE EXPLORATION** Suppose a satellite's orbit is an ellipse with Earth's center at one focus. If the satellite's least distance from Earth's surface is 150 miles and its greatest distance from Earth's surface is 600 miles, write an equation for the ellipse. (Use 4000 miles as Earth's radius.) **(Lesson 10.4)**

▶ ACTIVITY 10.6

Developing Concepts

GROUP ACTIVITY
Work with a partner.

MATERIALS
• flashlight
• graph paper
• pencil

Exploring Conic Sections

▶ **QUESTION** How do a plane and a double-napped cone intersect to form different conic sections?

▶ **EXPLORING THE CONCEPT** The reason that parabolas, circles, ellipses, and hyperbolas are called *conics* or *conic sections* is that each can be formed by the intersection of a plane and a double-napped cone, as shown below.

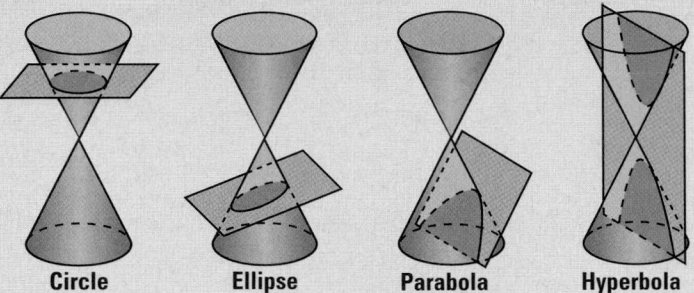

| Circle | Ellipse | Parabola | Hyperbola |

The beam of light from a flashlight is a cone. When the light hits a flat surface such as a wall, the edge of the beam of light forms a conic section.

Work in a group to find an equation of a conic formed by a flashlight beam.

① On a piece of graph paper, draw *x*- and *y*-axes to make a coordinate plane.

② Tape the paper to a wall.

③ Aim a flashlight perpendicular to the paper so that the light forms a circle. Move the flashlight so that the circle is centered on the origin of the coordinate plane.

④ Holding the flashlight very still, trace the circle on the graph paper. Find the radius of the circle and use it to write the standard form of the equation of the circle.

⑤ Aim the flashlight at the paper to form an ellipse with a vertical major axis and center at the origin. Trace the ellipse and find the standard form of its equation.

▶ **DRAWING CONCLUSIONS**

1. Compare the equation of your circle with the equations found by other groups. Are your equations all the same? Why or why not?

2. Compare the equation of your ellipse with the equations found by other groups. Are your equations all the same? Why or why not?

10.6 Graphing and Classifying Conics

What you should learn

GOAL 1 Write and graph an equation of a parabola with its vertex at (h, k) and an equation of a circle, ellipse, or hyperbola with its center at (h, k).

GOAL 2 Classify a conic using its equation, as applied in **Example 8**.

Why you should learn it

▼ To model **real-life** situations involving more than one conic, such as the circles that an ice skater uses to practice figure eights in **Ex. 64**.

GOAL 1 WRITING AND GRAPHING EQUATIONS OF CONICS

Parabolas, circles, ellipses, and hyperbolas are all curves that are formed by the intersection of a plane and a double-napped cone. Therefore, these shapes are called **conic sections** or simply **conics**.

In previous lessons you studied equations of parabolas with vertices at the origin and equations of circles, ellipses, and hyperbolas with centers at the origin. In this lesson you will study equations of conics that have been translated in the coordinate plane.

STANDARD FORM OF EQUATIONS OF TRANSLATED CONICS

In the following equations the point (h, k) is the *vertex* of the parabola and the *center* of the other conics.

CIRCLE $(x - h)^2 + (y - k)^2 = r^2$

	Horizontal axis	**Vertical axis**
PARABOLA	$(y - k)^2 = 4p(x - h)$	$(x - h)^2 = 4p(y - k)$
ELLIPSE	$\dfrac{(x - h)^2}{a^2} + \dfrac{(y - k)^2}{b^2} = 1$	$\dfrac{(x - h)^2}{b^2} + \dfrac{(y - k)^2}{a^2} = 1$
HYPERBOLA	$\dfrac{(x - h)^2}{a^2} - \dfrac{(y - k)^2}{b^2} = 1$	$\dfrac{(y - k)^2}{a^2} - \dfrac{(x - h)^2}{b^2} = 1$

EXAMPLE 1 *Writing an Equation of a Translated Parabola*

Write an equation of the parabola whose vertex is at $(-2, 1)$ and whose focus is at $(-3, 1)$.

SOLUTION

Choose form: Begin by sketching the parabola, as shown. Because the parabola opens to the left, it has the form

$$(y - k)^2 = 4p(x - h)$$

where $p < 0$.

Find h and k: The vertex is at $(-2, 1)$, so $h = -2$ and $k = 1$.

Find p: The distance between the vertex $(-2, 1)$ and the focus $(-3, 1)$ is

$$|p| = \sqrt{(-3 - (-2))^2 + (1 - 1)^2} = 1$$

so $p = 1$ or $p = -1$. Since $p < 0$, $p = -1$.

▶ The standard form of the equation is $(y - 1)^2 = -4(x + 2)$.

EXAMPLE 2 *Graphing the Equation of a Translated Circle*

Graph $(x - 3)^2 + (y + 2)^2 = 16$.

SOLUTION

Compare the given equation to the standard form of the equation of a circle:

$$(x - h)^2 + (y - k)^2 = r^2$$

You can see that the graph is a circle with center at $(h, k) = (3, -2)$ and radius $r = 4$.

Plot the center.

Plot several points that are each **4** units from the center:

$(3 + 4, -2) = (7, -2)$

$(3 - 4, -2) = (-1, -2)$

$(3, -2 + 4) = (3, 2)$

$(3, -2 - 4) = (3, -6)$

Draw a circle through the points.

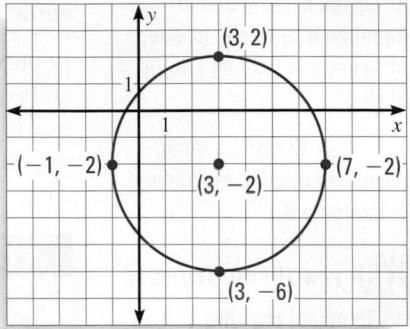

EXAMPLE 3 *Writing an Equation of a Translated Ellipse*

Write an equation of the ellipse with foci at $(3, 5)$ and $(3, -1)$ and vertices at $(3, 6)$ and $(3, -2)$.

SOLUTION

Plot the given points and make a rough sketch. The ellipse has a vertical major axis, so its equation is of this form:

$$\frac{(x - h)^2}{b^2} + \frac{(y - k)^2}{a^2} = 1$$

Find the center: The center is halfway between the vertices.

$$(h, k) = \left(\frac{3 + 3}{2}, \frac{6 + (-2)}{2} \right) = (3, 2)$$

Find a: The value of a is the distance between the vertex and the center.

$$a = \sqrt{(3 - 3)^2 + (6 - 2)^2} = \sqrt{0 + 4^2} = 4$$

Find c: The value of c is the distance between the focus and the center.

$$c = \sqrt{(3 - 3)^2 + (5 - 2)^2} = \sqrt{0 + 3^2} = 3$$

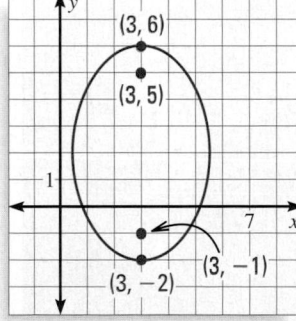

Find b: Substitute the values of a and c into the equation $b^2 = a^2 - c^2$.

$$b^2 = 4^2 - 3^2$$

$$b^2 = 7$$

$$b = \sqrt{7}$$

▶ The standard form of the equation is $\dfrac{(x - 3)^2}{7} + \dfrac{(y - 2)^2}{16} = 1$.

EXAMPLE 4 *Graphing the Equation of a Translated Hyperbola*

Graph $(y + 1)^2 - \dfrac{(x + 1)^2}{4} = 1$.

SOLUTION

The y^2-term is positive, so the transverse axis is vertical.
Since $a^2 = 1$ and $b^2 = 4$, you know that $a = 1$ and $b = 2$.

Plot the center at $(h, k) = (-1, -1)$. Plot the vertices
1 unit above and below the center at $(-1, 0)$ and $(-1, -2)$.

Draw a rectangle that is centered at $(-1, -1)$ and is
$2a = 2$ units high and $2b = 4$ units wide.

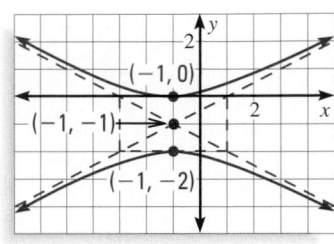

Draw the asymptotes through the corners of the rectangle.

Draw the hyperbola so that it passes through the vertices and approaches the asymptotes.

EXAMPLE 5 *Using Circular Models*

COMMUNICATIONS A cellular phone transmission tower located 10 miles west and 5 miles north of your house has a range of 20 miles. A second tower, 5 miles east and 10 miles south of your house, has a range of 15 miles.

  a. Write an inequality that describes each tower's range.

  b. Do the two regions covered by the towers overlap?

SOLUTION

  a. Let the origin represent your house. The first tower is at $(-10, 5)$ and the boundary of its range is a circle with radius 20. Substitute -10 for h, 5 for k, and 20 for r into the standard form of the equation of a circle.

$$(x - h)^2 + (y - k)^2 = r^2 \qquad \textbf{Standard form of a circle}$$

$$(x + 10)^2 + (y - 5)^2 < 400 \qquad \textbf{Region inside the circle}$$

The second tower is at $(5, -10)$. The boundary of its range is a circle with radius 15.

$$(x - h)^2 + (y - k)^2 = r^2 \qquad \textbf{Standard form of a circle}$$

$$(x - 5)^2 + (y + 10)^2 < 225 \qquad \textbf{Region inside the circle}$$

  b. One way to tell if the regions overlap is to graph the inequalities. You can see that the regions do overlap.

You can also check whether the distance between the two towers is less than the sum of the ranges.

$$\sqrt{(-10 - 5)^2 + (5 - (-10))^2} \stackrel{?}{<} 20 + 15$$

$$15\sqrt{2} \stackrel{?}{<} 35$$

$$21.2 < 35 \checkmark$$

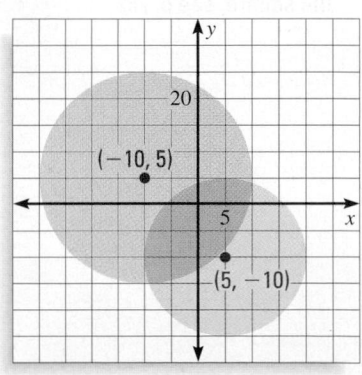

▶ The regions do overlap.

FOCUS ON
APPLICATIONS

CELLULAR
PHONES work only
when there is a transmission
tower nearby to retrieve the
signal. Because of the need
for many towers, they are
often designed to blend in
with the environment.

GOAL 2 CLASSIFYING A CONIC FROM ITS EQUATION

The equation of any conic can be written in the form

$$Ax^2 + Bxy + Cy^2 + Dx + Ey + F = 0$$

which is called a **general second-degree equation** in x and y. The expression $B^2 - 4AC$ is called the **discriminant** of the equation and can be used to determine which type of conic the equation represents.

CONCEPT SUMMARY   **CLASSIFYING CONICS**

If the graph of $Ax^2 + Bxy + Cy^2 + Dx + Ey + F = 0$ is a conic, then the type of conic can be determined as follows.

DISCRIMINANT	TYPE OF CONIC
$B^2 - 4AC < 0$, $B = 0$, and $A = C$	Circle
$B^2 - 4AC < 0$ and either $B \neq 0$ or $A \neq C$	Ellipse
$B^2 - 4AC = 0$	Parabola
$B^2 - 4AC > 0$	Hyperbola

If $B = 0$, each axis of the conic is horizontal or vertical. If $B \neq 0$, the axes are neither horizontal nor vertical.

EXAMPLE 6 *Classifying a Conic*

a. Classify the conic given by $2x^2 + y^2 - 4x - 4 = 0$.

b. Graph the equation in part (a).

SOLUTION

a. Since $A = 2$, $B = 0$, and $C = 1$, the value of the discriminant is as follows:

$$B^2 - 4AC = 0^2 - 4(2)(1) = -8$$

▶ Because $B^2 - 4AC < 0$ and $A \neq C$, the graph is an ellipse.

STUDENT HELP

▶ **Look Back**
For help with completing the square, see p. 282.

b. To graph the ellipse, first complete the square as follows.

$$2x^2 + y^2 - 4x - 4 = 0$$
$$(2x^2 - 4x) + y^2 = 4$$
$$2(x^2 - 2x) + y^2 = 4$$
$$2(x^2 - 2x + \underline{\ ?\ }) + y^2 = 4 + 2(\underline{\ ?\ })$$
$$2(x^2 - 2x + \mathbf{1}) + y^2 = 4 + 2(\mathbf{1})$$
$$2(x - 1)^2 + y^2 = 6$$
$$\frac{(x - 1)^2}{3} + \frac{y^2}{6} = 1$$

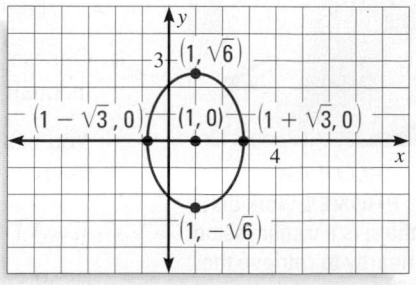

By comparing this equation to $\dfrac{(x - h)^2}{b^2} + \dfrac{(y - k)^2}{a^2} = 1$, you can see that $h = 1$, $k = 0$, $a = \sqrt{6}$, and $b = \sqrt{3}$. Use these facts to draw the ellipse.

EXAMPLE 7 *Classifying a Conic*

a. Classify the conic given by $4x^2 - 9y^2 + 32x - 144y - 548 = 0$.

b. Graph the equation in part (a).

SOLUTION

a. Since $A = 4$, $B = 0$, and $C = -9$, the value of the discriminant is as follows:

$$B^2 - 4AC = 0^2 - 4(4)(-9) = 144$$

▶ Because $B^2 - 4AC > 0$, the graph is a hyperbola.

b. To graph the hyperbola, first complete the square as follows.

$$4x^2 - 9y^2 + 32x - 144y - 548 = 0$$

$$(4x^2 + 32x) - (9y^2 + 144y) = 548$$

$$4(x^2 + 8x + \underline{\textbf{?}}) - 9(y^2 + 16y + \underline{\textbf{?}}) = 548 + 4(\underline{\textbf{?}}) - 9(\underline{\textbf{?}})$$

$$4(x^2 + 8x + \textbf{16}) - 9(y^2 + 16y + \textbf{64}) = 548 + 4(\textbf{16}) - 9(\textbf{64})$$

$$4(x + 4)^2 - 9(y + 8)^2 = 36$$

$$\frac{(x + 4)^2}{3^2} - \frac{(y + 8)^2}{2^2} = 1$$

By comparing this equation to $\dfrac{(x - h)^2}{a^2} - \dfrac{(y - k)^2}{b^2} = 1$, you can see that $h = -4$,

$k = -8$, $a = 3$, and $b = 2$.

To draw the hyperbola, plot the center at
$(\textbf{h, k}) = (\textbf{−4, −8})$ and the vertices at $(\textbf{−7, −8})$
and $(\textbf{−1, −8})$. Draw a rectangle $2a = 6$ units
wide and $2b = 4$ units high and centered at
$(\textbf{−4, −8})$. Draw the asymptotes through the
corners of the rectangle. Then draw the
hyperbola so that it passes through the vertices
and approaches the asymptotes.

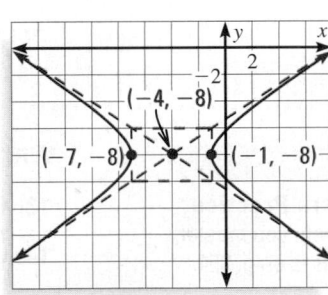

EXAMPLE 8 *Classifying Conics in Real Life*

Astronomy

The diagram at the right shows the mirrors in
a Cassegrain telescope. The equations of the
two mirrors are given below. Classify each
mirror as parabolic, elliptical, or hyperbolic.

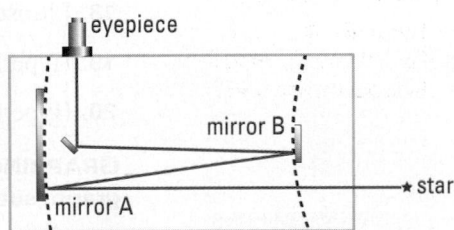

a. Mirror A: $y^2 - 72x - 450 = 0$

b. Mirror B: $88.4x^2 - 49.7y^2 - 4390 = 0$

SOLUTION

EQUATION	$B^2 - 4AC$	TYPE OF MIRROR
a. $y^2 - 72x - 450 = 0$	$0^2 - 4(0)(1) = 0$	Parabolic
b. $88.4x^2 - 49.7y^2 - 4390 = 0$	$0^2 - 4(88.4)(-49.7) > 0$	Hyperbolic

GUIDED PRACTICE

Vocabulary Check ✔

1. Explain why circles, ellipses, parabolas, and hyperbolas are called conic sections.

Concept Check ✔

2. How are the graphs of $x^2 + y^2 = 25$ and $(x - 1)^2 + (y + 2)^2 = 25$ alike? How are they different?

3. How can the discriminant $B^2 - 4AC$ be used to classify the graph of $Ax^2 + Bxy + Cy^2 + Dx + Ey + F = 0$?

Skill Check ✔ **Write an equation for the conic section.**

4. Circle with center at $(4, -1)$ and radius 7

5. Ellipse with foci at $(2, -4)$ and $(5, -4)$ and vertices at $(-1, -4)$ and $(8, -4)$

6. Parabola with vertex at $(3, -2)$ and focus at $(3, -4)$

7. Hyperbola with foci at $(5, 2)$ and $(5, -6)$ and vertices at $(5, 0)$ and $(5, -4)$

Classify the conic section.

8. $x^2 + 2x - 4y + 4 = 0$

9. $3x^2 - 5y^2 - 6x + y - 2 = 0$

10. $x^2 + y^2 + 7x - 4y - 8 = 0$

11. $-5x^2 - 2y^2 + x - 3y + 1 = 0$

12. 🌐 **COMMUNICATIONS** Look back at Example 5. Suppose there is a tower 25 miles east and 30 miles north of your house with a range of 25 miles. Does the region covered by this tower overlap the regions covered by the two towers in Example 5? Illustrate your answer with a graph.

PRACTICE AND APPLICATIONS

STUDENT HELP

➡ **Extra Practice**
to help you master
skills is on p. 954.

WRITING EQUATIONS **Write an equation for the conic section.**

13. Circle with center at $(9, 3)$ and radius 4

14. Circle with center at $(-4, 2)$ and radius 3

15. Parabola with vertex at $(1, -2)$ and focus at $(1, 1)$

16. Parabola with vertex at $(-3, 1)$ and directrix $x = -8$

17. Ellipse with vertices at $(2, -3)$ and $(2, 6)$ and foci at $(2, 0)$ and $(2, 3)$

18. Ellipse with vertices at $(-2, 2)$ and $(4, 2)$ and co-vertices at $(1, 1)$ and $(1, 3)$

19. Hyperbola with vertices at $(5, -4)$ and $(5, 4)$ and foci at $(5, -6)$ and $(5, 6)$

20. Hyperbola with vertices at $(-4, 2)$ and $(1, 2)$ and foci at $(-7, 2)$ and $(4, 2)$

GRAPHING **Graph the equation. Identify the important characteristics of the graph, such as the center, vertices, and foci.**

STUDENT HELP

➡ **HOMEWORK HELP**
Examples 1, 3: Exs. 13–20
Examples 2, 4: Exs. 21–28
Example 5: Exs. 63, 64
Examples 6, 7: Exs. 29–62
Example 8: Exs. 65–67

21. $(x - 6)^2 + (y - 2)^2 = 4$

22. $(x + 7)^2 = 12(y - 3)$

23. $\dfrac{(y - 8)^2}{16} - \dfrac{(x + 3)^2}{4} = 1$

24. $\dfrac{(x - 3)^2}{25} + \dfrac{(y + 6)^2}{49} = 1$

25. $\dfrac{(x + 1)^2}{16} + \dfrac{y^2}{9} = 1$

26. $\dfrac{x^2}{16} - (y + 4)^2 = 1$

27. $(x + 7)^2 + (y - 1)^2 = 1$

28. $(y - 4)^2 = 3(x + 2)$

CLASSIFYING Classify the conic section.

29. $9x^2 + 4y^2 + 36x - 24y + 36 = 0$

30. $x^2 - 4y^2 + 3x - 26y - 30 = 0$

31. $4x^2 - 9y^2 + 18y + 3x = 0$

32. $x^2 + y^2 - 10x - 2y + 10 = 0$

33. $36x^2 + 16y^2 - 25x + 22y + 2 = 0$

34. $4x^2 + 4y^2 - 16x + 4y - 60 = 0$

35. $9y^2 - x^2 + 2x + 54y + 62 = 0$

36. $16x^2 + 25y^2 - 18x - 20y + 8 = 0$

37. $x^2 - 2x + 8y + 9 = 0$

38. $2y^2 - 8y - 4x + 10 = 0$

39. $12x^2 + 20y^2 - 12x + 40y - 37 = 0$

40. $9x^2 - y^2 + 54x + 10y + 55 = 0$

41. $x^2 + y^2 - 4x - 2y - 4 = 0$

42. $16x^2 + 9y^2 + 24x - 36y + 23 = 0$

43. $16y^2 - x^2 + 2x + 64y + 63 = 0$

44. $x^2 - 4x + 16y + 17 = 0$

MATCHING Match the equation with its graph.

45. $9x^2 - 4y^2 + 36x - 24y - 36 = 0$

46. $y^2 - 2y - 4x + 9 = 0$

47. $9x^2 + 4y^2 + 36x + 24y + 36 = 0$

48. $y^2 - x^2 + 6y + 4x + 4 = 0$

49. $4x^2 + 9y^2 - 16x + 54y + 61 = 0$

50. $x^2 + y^2 - 4x + 6y + 4 = 0$

A.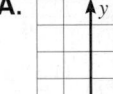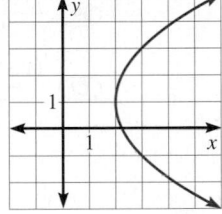

B.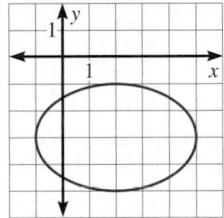

C.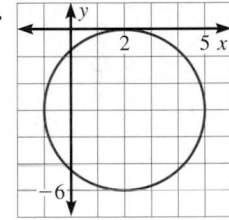

D.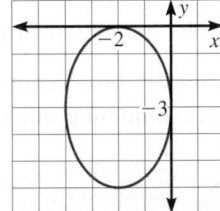

E.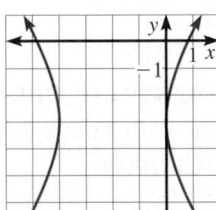

F.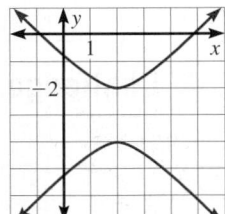

CLASSIFYING AND GRAPHING Classify the conic section and write its equation in standard form. Then graph the equation.

51. $y^2 - 12y + 4x + 4 = 0$

52. $x^2 + y^2 - 6x - 8y + 24 = 0$

53. $9x^2 - y^2 - 72x + 8y + 119 = 0$

54. $4x^2 + y^2 - 48x - 4y + 48 = 0$

55. $x^2 + 4y^2 - 2x - 8y + 1 = 0$

56. $x^2 + y^2 - 12x - 24y + 36 = 0$

57. $16x^2 - y^2 + 16y - 128 = 0$

58. $x^2 + 9y^2 + 8x + 4y + 7 = 0$

59. $x^2 + y^2 - 12x - 12y + 36 = 0$

60. $y^2 - 2x - 20y + 94 = 0$

61. $x^2 + 4x - 8y + 12 = 0$

62. $-9x^2 + 4y^2 - 36x - 16y - 164 = 0$

63. 🌐 **WHISPER DISHES** The whisper dish shown at the left can be seen at the Thronateeska Discovery Center in Albany, Georgia. Two dishes are positioned so that their vertices are 50 feet apart. The focus of each dish is 3 feet from its vertex. Write equations for the cross sections of the dishes so that the vertex of one dish is at the origin and the vertex of the other dish is on the positive *x*-axis.

64.  **FIGURE SKATING** To practice making a figure eight, a figure skater will skate along two circles etched in the ice. Write equations for two externally tangent circles that are each 6 feet in diameter so that the center of one circle is at the origin and the center of the other circle is on the positive *y*-axis.

65. VISUAL THINKING A new crayon has a cone-shaped tip. When it is used for the first time, a flat spot is worn on the tip. The edge of the flat spot is a conic section, as shown. What type(s) of conic could it be?

conic section

66. VISUAL THINKING When a pencil is sharpened the tip becomes a cone. On a pencil with flat sides, the intersection of the cone with each flat side is a conic section. What type of conic is it?

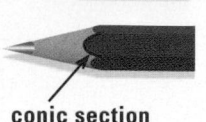

conic section

67.  **ASTRONOMY** A Gregorian telescope contains two mirrors whose cross sections can be modeled by the equations $405x^2 + 729y^2 - 295{,}245 = 0$ and $-120y^2 - 1440x = 0$. What types of mirrors are they?

Test Preparation

68. MULTIPLE CHOICE Which of the following is an equation of the hyperbola with vertices at $(3, 5)$ and $(3, -1)$ and foci at $(3, 7)$ and $(3, -3)$?

Ⓐ $\dfrac{(x-3)^2}{25} - \dfrac{(y-2)^2}{9} = 1$

Ⓑ $\dfrac{(y-2)^2}{9} - \dfrac{(x-3)^2}{25} = 1$

Ⓒ $\dfrac{(y-2)^2}{9} - \dfrac{(x-3)^2}{7} = 1$

Ⓓ $\dfrac{(x-3)^2}{9} - \dfrac{(y-2)^2}{16} = 1$

Ⓔ $\dfrac{(y-2)^2}{9} - \dfrac{(x-3)^2}{16} = 1$

69. MULTIPLE CHOICE What conic does $25x^2 + y^2 - 100x - 2y + 76 = 0$ represent?

Ⓐ Parabola   **Ⓑ** Circle   **Ⓒ** Ellipse

Ⓓ Hyperbola   **Ⓔ** Not enough information

 ★ **Challenge**

70. DEGENERATE CONICS A *degenerate* conic occurs when the intersection of a plane with a double-napped cone is something other than a parabola, circle, ellipse, or hyperbola.

a. Imagine a plane perpendicular to the axis of a double-napped cone. As the plane passes through the cone, the intersection is a circle whose radius decreases and then increases. At what point is the intersection something other than a circle? What is the intersection?

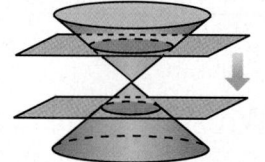

b. Imagine a plane parallel to the axis of a double-napped cone. As the plane passes through the cone, the intersection is a hyperbola whose vertices get closer together and then farther apart. At what point is the intersection something other than a hyperbola? What is the intersection?

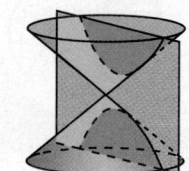

c. Imagine a plane parallel to the nappe passing through a double-napped cone. As the plane passes through the cone, the intersection is a parabola that gets narrower and then flips and gets wider. At what point is the intersection something other than a parabola? What is the intersection?

nappe

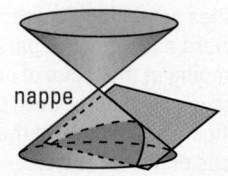

EXTRA CHALLENGE
▶ www.mcdougallittell.com

MIXED REVIEW

71. $x - y = 10$
$3x - 2y = 25$

72. $4x + 3y = 1$
$-3x - 6y = 3$

73. $4x + y = 2$
$6x + 3y = 0$

74. $2x - 3y = 0$
$x + 6y = 14$

75. $23x = 68$
$x + 3y = 19$

76. $x = y$
$123x - 18y = 17$

EVALUATING LOGARITHMIC EXPRESSIONS Evaluate the expression. (Review 8.4)

77. $\log_7 7^5$

78. $\log_4 64$

79. $\log_5 1$

80. $\log_{1/3} 9$

81. $\log_{25} 625$

82. $\log 0.0001$

SOLVING EQUATIONS Solve the equation. (Review 8.8)

83. $\dfrac{40}{1 + 6e^{-4x}} = 20$

84. $\dfrac{10}{1 + 9e^{-2x}} = 1$

85. $\dfrac{8}{1 + 8e^{-x}} = 7$

86. $\dfrac{15}{1 + 3e^{-6x}} = 3$

87. $\dfrac{24}{1 + 5e^{-4x}} = 9$

88. $\dfrac{9}{1 + 2e^{-3x}} = 7$

MATH & History

History of Conic Sections

APPLICATION LINK
www.mcdougallittell.com

THEN

IN 200 B.C. conic sections were studied thoroughly for the first time by a Greek mathematician named Apollonius. Six hundred years later, the Egyptian mathematician Hypatia simplified the works of Apollonius, making it accessible to many more people. For centuries, conics were studied and appreciated only for their mathematical beauty rather than for their occurrence in nature or practical use.

NOW

TODAY astronomers know that the paths of celestial objects, such as planets and comets, are conic sections. For example, a comet's path can be parabolic, hyperbolic, or elliptical.

Tell what type of path each comet follows. Which comet(s) will pass by the sun more than once?

1. $3550x^2 + 14{,}200x + 7100y - 13{,}050 = 0$

2. $2200x^2 + 4600y^2 - 13{,}200x - 18{,}400y + 12{,}900 = 0$

3. $5000x^2 - 6500y^2 + 20{,}000x - 52{,}000y - 695{,}000 = 0$

Hypatia simplifies
Apollonius' *Conics.*

A.D. 400

Debra Fischer
discovers two planets.

1999

1609

200 B.C.

Apollonius studies
conic sections.

Johannes Kepler discovers that
the planets' orbits are elliptical.

Solving Quadratic Systems

What you should learn

GOAL 1 Solve systems of quadratic equations.

GOAL 2 Use quadratic systems to solve **real-life** problems, such as determining when one car will catch up to another in **Ex. 58**.

Why you should learn it

▼ To model **real-life** situations with quadratic systems, such as finding the epicenter of an earthquake in **Example 4**.

GOAL 1 SOLVING A SYSTEM OF EQUATIONS

In Lesson 3.2 you studied two algebraic techniques for solving a system of linear equations. You can use the same techniques (substitution and linear combination) to solve quadratic systems.

EXAMPLE 1 *Finding Points of Intersection*

Find the points of intersection of the graphs of $x^2 + y^2 = 13$ and $y = x + 1$.

SOLUTION

To find the points of intersection, substitute $x + 1$ for y in the equation of the circle.

$x^2 + y^2 = 13$	**Equation of circle**
$x^2 + (x + 1)^2 = 13$	**Substitute $x + 1$ for y.**
$x^2 + x^2 + 2x + 1 = 13$	**Expand the power.**
$2x^2 + 2x - 12 = 0$	**Combine like terms.**
$2(x - 2)(x + 3) = 0$	**Factor.**
$x = 2$ or $x = -3$	**Zero product property**

You now know the x-coordinates of the points of intersection. To find the y-coordinates, substitute $x = 2$ and $x = -3$ into the linear equation and solve for y.

▶ The points of intersection are $(2, 3)$ and $(-3, -2)$.

✓ **CHECK** You can check your answer algebraically by substituting the coordinates of the points into each equation. Another way to check your answer is to graph the two equations. You can see from the graph shown that the line and the circle intersect in two points, at $(2, 3)$ and at $(-3, -2)$.

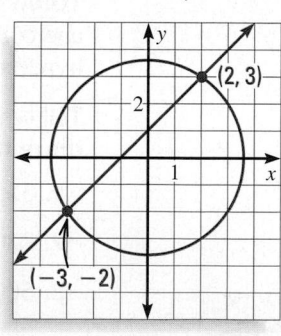

▶ ACTIVITY

Developing Concepts

Investigating Points of Intersection

The circle and line in Example 1 intersect in two points. A circle and a line can also intersect in one point or no points. Sketch examples to illustrate the different numbers of points of intersection that the following graphs can have.

a. Circle and parabola

b. Ellipse and hyperbola

c. Circle and ellipse

d. Hyperbola and line

STUDENT HELP

▶ **Look Back**
For help with solving systems, see p. 148.

EXAMPLE 2 **Solving a System by Substitution**

Find the points of intersection of the graphs in the system.

$$x^2 + 4y^2 - 4 = 0 \qquad \textbf{Equation 1}$$

$$-2y^2 + x + 2 = 0 \qquad \textbf{Equation 2}$$

SOLUTION

Because Equation 2 has no x^2-term, solve that equation for x.

$$-2y^2 + x + 2 = 0$$

$$x = 2y^2 - 2$$

Next, substitute $2y^2 - 2$ for x in Equation 1 and solve for y.

$x^2 + 4y^2 - 4 = 0$	**Equation 1**
$(2y^2 - 2)^2 + 4y^2 - 4 = 0$	**Substitute for x.**
$4y^4 - 8y^2 + 4 + 4y^2 - 4 = 0$	**Expand the power.**
$4y^4 - 4y^2 = 0$	**Combine like terms.**
$4y^2(y^2 - 1) = 0$	**Factor common monomial.**
$4y^2(y - 1)(y + 1) = 0$	**Difference of squares.**
$y = 0, y = 1, \text{ or } y = -1$	**Zero product property**

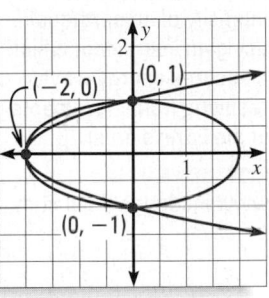

STUDENT HELP

Look Back
For help with factoring, see p. 256.

The corresponding x-values are $x = -2$, $x = 0$, and $x = 0$.

▶ The graphs intersect at $(-2, 0)$, $(0, 1)$, and $(0, -1)$, as shown.

EXAMPLE 3 **Solving a System by Linear Combination**

Find the points of intersection of the graphs in the system.

$$x^2 + y^2 - 16x + 39 = 0 \qquad \textbf{Equation 1}$$

$$x^2 - y^2 - 9 = 0 \qquad \textbf{Equation 2}$$

SOLUTION

You can eliminate the y^2-term by adding the two equations. The resulting equation can be solved for x because it contains no other variables.

$$x^2 + y^2 - 16x + 39 = 0$$

$$\underline{x^2 - y^2 \qquad - 9 = 0}$$

$2x^2 \qquad - 16x + 30 = 0$	**Add.**
$2(x - 3)(x - 5) = 0$	**Factor.**
$x = 3 \text{ or } x = 5$	**Zero product property**

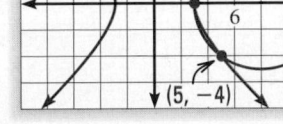

The corresponding y-values are $y = 0$ and $y = \pm 4$.

▶ The graphs intersect at $(3, 0)$, $(5, 4)$, and $(5, -4)$, as shown.

GOAL 2 SOLVING QUADRATIC SYSTEMS IN REAL LIFE

EXAMPLE 4 *Solving a System of Quadratic Models*

SEISMOLOGY A seismograph measures the intensity of an earthquake. Although a seismograph can determine the distance to the earthquake's epicenter, it cannot determine in what direction the epicenter is located. Use the following information from three seismographs to find an earthquake's epicenter.

Location 1: 500 miles from the epicenter

Location 2: 100 miles west and 400 miles south of Location 1
400 miles from the epicenter

Location 3: 300 miles east and 600 miles south of Location 1
200 miles from the epicenter

SOLUTION

Let each unit represent 100 miles. If Location 1 is at $(0, 0)$, then Location 2 is at $(-1, -4)$ and Location 3 is at $(3, -6)$. Write the equation of each circle.

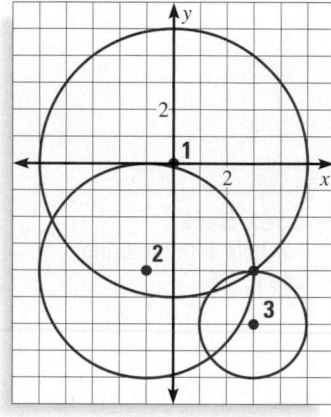

Location 1: $x^2 + y^2 = 25$

Location 2: $(x + 1)^2 + (y + 4)^2 = 16$, or
$x^2 + 2x + 1 + y^2 + 8y + 16 = 16$

Location 3: $(x - 3)^2 + (y + 6)^2 = 4$, or
$x^2 - 6x + 9 + y^2 + 12y + 36 = 4$

Subtract the equation for Location 1 from the equation for Location 2.

$$
\begin{aligned}
x^2 + 2x + 1 + y^2 + 8y + 16 &= 16 \\
- (x^2 + y^2 &= 25) \\
\hline
2x + 8y + 17 &= -9 \\
2x + 8y &= -26, \text{ or } x + 4y = -13
\end{aligned}
$$

Then subtract the equation for Location 1 from the equation for Location 3.

$$
\begin{aligned}
x^2 - 6x + 9 + y^2 + 12y + 36 &= 4 \\
- (x^2 + y^2 &= 25) \\
\hline
-6x + 12y + 45 &= -21 \\
-6x + 12y &= -66, \text{ or } -x + 2y = -11
\end{aligned}
$$

You are left with two linear equations. Solve this linear system to find the epicenter.

$$
\begin{aligned}
x + 4y &= -13 \\
-x + 2y &= -11 \\
\hline
6y &= -24 \\
y &= -4 \\
x &= 3
\end{aligned}
$$

▶ The epicenter of the earthquake is 300 miles east and 400 miles south of Location 1.

GUIDED PRACTICE

Vocabulary Check ✓

1. Complete this statement: The equations $x^2 + 3y^2 - 2y = 4$ and $x^2 + y^2 = 5$ are an example of a(n) _?_ system.

Concept Check ✓

2. Sketch an example of a circle and a line intersecting in a single point.

3. Explain what method you would use to find the points of intersection of the graphs in the following system. Do not solve the system.

$$4x^2 + y^2 - 16x = 0 \qquad \textbf{Equation 1}$$

$$x^2 - y^2 + 7 = 0 \qquad \textbf{Equation 2}$$

Skill Check ✓

Find the points of intersection, if any, of the graphs in the system.

4. $x^2 + y^2 = 17$
$y = x + 3$

5. $x^2 + y^2 + 8x - 20y + 7 = 0$
$x^2 + 9y^2 + 8x + 4y + 7 = 0$

6. $x^2 + y^2 - 3x = 8$
$2x^2 - y^2 = 10$

7. $x^2 - 2x + 2y + 2 = 0$
$-x^2 + 2x - y + 3 = 0$

8. 🌎 **SEISMOLOGY** Look back at Example 4. Why are three (not just two) seismographs needed to determine the location of the epicenter?

PRACTICE AND APPLICATIONS

STUDENT HELP

➤ **Extra Practice**
to help you master
skills is on p. 955.

CHECKING POINTS OF INTERSECTION Determine whether the given point is a point of intersection of the graphs in the system.

9. $x^2 + y^2 = 25$
$y = -3$
Point: $(-3, 4)$

10. $x^2 + y^2 = 41$
$y = -x - 1$
Point: $(4, -5)$

11. $x^2 + 4x - 4y - 16 = 0$
$-2x + y + 1 = 0$
Point: $(6, 11)$

12. $3x^2 - 5y^2 + 2y = 45$
$y = 2x + 10$
Point: $(-3, 4)$

13. $2x^2 - 4y = 22$
$y = -2x + 3$
Point: $(-5, 7)$

14. $6x^2 - 5x + 8y^2 + y = 23$
$y = x - 1$
Point: $(2, 1)$

SOLVING SYSTEMS Find the points of intersection, if any, of the graphs in the system.

15. $x^2 - y = 5$
$-3x + y = -7$

16. $x^2 + y^2 = 18$
$x - y = 0$

17. $-3x^2 + y^2 = 9$
$-2x + y = 0$

18. $9x^2 + 4y^2 = 36$
$-x + y = -4$

19. $x^2 + y^2 = 5$
$y = -2x$

20. $x + 2y^2 = -6$
$x + 8y = 0$

21. $5x^2 + 3y^2 = 17$
$-x + y = -1$

22. $4x^2 - 5y^2 = 16$
$3x + y = 6$

23. $2x^2 + 2y^2 = 15$
$x + 2y = 6$

STUDENT HELP

➤ **HOMEWORK HELP**
Example 1: Exs. 9–32
Examples 2, 3: Exs. 33–51
Example 4: Exs. 52–55,
58–63

24. $x^2 + y^2 = 1$
$x + y = -1$

25. $x^2 + y^2 = 20$
$y = x - 4$

26. $x^2 + y^2 = 5$
$y = 3x + 5$

27. $x^2 = 6y$
$y = -x$

28. $x^2 + y^2 = 9$
$x - 3y = 3$

29. $x^2 + y^2 = 7$
$y = x - 7$

30. $y^2 - 2x^2 = 6$
$y = -2x$

31. $6x^2 + 3y^2 = 12$
$y = -x + 2$

32. $3x^2 - y^2 = -6$
$y = 2x + 1$

SOLVING SYSTEMS Find the points of intersection, if any, of the graphs in the system.

33. $x^2 + y^2 = 16$
$x^2 - 5y = 5$

34. $-3x^2 + y^2 - 3x = 0$
$x^2 - y^2 + 27 = 0$

35. $-x^2 + y^2 + 10 = 0$
$-3y^2 + x + 1 = 0$

36. $x^2 + 2y^2 - 10 = 0$
$4y^2 + x + 4 = 0$

37. $y^2 = 16x$
$4x - y = -24$

38. $10y = x^2$
$x^2 - 6 = -2y$

39. $y^2 + x = 2$
$3x + y = 8$

40. $x^2 - 16y^2 = 16$
$x^2 + y^2 = 9$

41. $x^2 + y^2 = 81$
$x + y = 0$

42. $16x^2 - y^2 + 16y - 128 = 0$
$y^2 - 48x - 16y - 32 = 0$

43. $x^2 - y^2 - 8x + 8y - 24 = 0$
$x^2 + y^2 - 8x - 8y + 24 = 0$

44. $x^2 + 4y^2 - 4x - 8y + 4 = 0$
$x^2 + 4y - 4 = 0$

45. $4x^2 - 56x + 9y^2 + 160 = 0$
$4x^2 + y^2 - 64 = 0$

46. $x^2 + y^2 - 16x + 39 = 0$
$x^2 - y^2 - 9 = 0$

47. $x^2 - 4y^2 - 20x - 64y - 172 = 0$
$4x^2 + y^2 - 80x + 16y + 400 = 0$

48. $x^2 - 2x + 4 + y^2 - 10 = 0$
$2y^2 - x + 3 = 0$

49. $4x^2 - y^2 - 8x + 6y - 9 = 0$
$2x^2 - 3y^2 + 4x + 18y - 43 = 0$

50. $10x^2 - 25y^2 - 100x = -160$
$y^2 - 2x + 16 = 0$

51. $x^2 - y - 4 = 0$
$x^2 + 3y^2 - 4y - 10 = 0$

SYSTEMS OF THREE EQUATIONS Find the points, if any, that the graphs of all three equations have in common.

52. $x^2 + y^2 + 8x + 7 = 0$
$x^2 + y^2 + 4x + 4y - 5 = 0$
$x^2 + y^2 = 1$

53. $x^2 + y^2 - 8 = 0$
$x^2 + y^2 - 3x + y = 0$
$2x^2 + 2y^2 - 5x - 10 = 0$

54. $x^2 + 3y^2 = 16$
$3x^2 + y^2 = 16$
$y = -x$

55. $x^2 + y^2 - 4x - 4y = 26$
$x^2 + y^2 - 4x = 54$
$y = 3x - 8$

56. CRITICAL THINKING Suppose a line intersects a circle whose center is at the origin, and the line passes through the origin. If you know one of the points of intersection, how do you know what the other point of intersection is without solving the system algebraically?

57. LOGICAL REASONING Sketch examples to illustrate the different numbers of points of intersection that a circle and an ellipse can have if both are centered at the origin.

58.  **LAW ENFORCEMENT** Suppose a car is traveling down the highway at a constant rate of 60 miles per hour. It passes a police car parked at the side of the road. To catch up to the car, the police officer accelerates at a constant rate. The distance d (in miles) the police car has traveled as a function of time t (in hours) since the other car has passed it is given by $d = 3600t^2$. Write and solve a system of equations to calculate how long it takes the police car to catch up to the other car.

59. **COMMUNICATIONS** The range of a radio station is bounded by a circle given by the following equation:

$$x^2 + y^2 - 1620 = 0$$

A straight highway can be modeled by the following equation:

$$y = -\frac{1}{3}x + 30$$

Find the length of the highway that lies within the range of the radio station.

60. 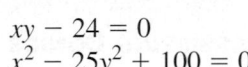 **BUS BOUNDARY** To be eligible to ride the school bus to East High School, a student must live at least 1 mile from the school. How long is the portion of Clark Street for which the residents are not eligible to ride the school bus? (Use a coordinate plane in which the school is at $(0, 0)$ and each unit represents one mile.)

STUDENT HELP

HOMEWORK HELP
Visit our Web site
www.mcdougallittell.com
for help with problem
solving in Exs. 60–62.

61. 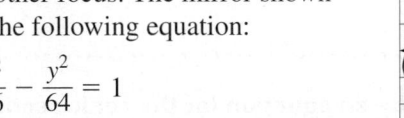 **NAVIGATION** LORAN (Long-Distance Radio Navigation) uses synchronized pulses sent out by pairs of transmitting stations. By calculating the difference in the times of arrival of the pulses from two stations, the LORAN equipment on a ship locates the ship on a hyperbola. By doing the same thing with a second pair of stations, LORAN locates the ship at the intersection of two hyperbolas. Suppose LORAN equipment indicates that a ship's location is the point of intersection of the graphs in the following system:

$$xy - 24 = 0$$
$$x^2 - 25y^2 + 100 = 0$$

Find the ship's location given that it is north and east of the origin.

62. 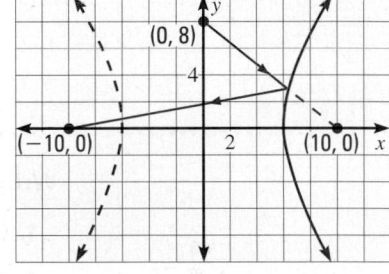 **HYPERBOLIC MIRROR** In a hyperbolic mirror, light rays directed to one focus will be reflected to the other focus. The mirror shown at the right has the following equation:

$$\frac{x^2}{36} - \frac{y^2}{64} = 1$$

At which point on the mirror will light from the point $(0, 8)$ be reflected to the focus at $(-10, 0)$?

63.  **EARTHQUAKES** An earthquake occurred in Peru on April 18, 1993. Use the following information to approximate the location of the epicenter.
▶ Source: U.S. Department of the Interior Geological Survey

Location 1: (Cayambe, Ecuador) The epicenter was 1300 kilometers away.

Location 2: (Cocohabamba, Bolivia, 1200 kilometers east and 1900 kilometers south of Cayambe) The epicenter was 1300 kilometers away.

Location 3: (Cerro El Oso, Venezuela, 1100 kilometers east and 1000 kilometers north of Cayambe) The epicenter was 2500 kilometers away.

Test Preparation

64. MULTIPLE CHOICE How many points of intersection do the equations $x^2 + y^2 = 6$ and $2x^2 + 4y^2 = 7$ have?

Ⓐ 0 　　 Ⓑ 1 　　 Ⓒ 2 　　 Ⓓ 3 　　 Ⓔ 4

65. MULTIPLE CHOICE Which of the following is a point of intersection of the graphs of $25x^2 + 36y^2 - 900 = 0$ and $-2x^2 + y + 5 = 0$?

Ⓐ $(-5, 0)$ 　　 Ⓑ $(0, 5)$ 　　 Ⓒ $(2, 5)$ 　　 Ⓓ $(1, 5)$ 　　 Ⓔ $(0, -5)$

★ Challenge

66. CRITICAL THINKING Write equations for three different conics that all intersect at the point $(-4, 6)$.

EVALUATING EXPRESSIONS Evaluate the expression for the given value of *x*.
(Review 1.2 for 11.1)

67. $2x + 5$ when $x = 4$

68. $\dfrac{1}{x^3} - 1$ when $x = 2$

69. $(-2)^{x-1}$ when $x = 5$

70. $\dfrac{3}{(-3)^{x-2}}$ when $x = 4$

WRITING FUNCTIONS Write a polynomial function of least degree that has
real coefficients, the given zeros, and a leading coefficient of 1. (Review 6.7)

71. $3, -3, 1$

72. $0, 2, 2, 4$

73. $2i, -2i$

74. $3 + i, 3 - i$

75. $2, -1, -1 - i$

76. $-2, -3, i, i$

GRAPHING Graph the function. Then state the domain and range. (Review 7.5)

77. $f(x) = \sqrt{2x + 3}$

78. $f(x) = 5\sqrt{x - 8}$

79. $f(x) = -(x + 4)^{1/2} + 2$

80. $f(x) = -3\sqrt[3]{x + 1}$

81. $f(x) = \sqrt[3]{4x + 1} + 2$

82. $f(x) = 5(x - 1)^{1/3}$

CLASSIFYING CONICS Classify the conic section. (Review 10.6)

83. $3x^2 + y^2 + 2x + 2y = 0$

84. $4x^2 - y^2 - 8x + 4y - 9 = 0$

85. $x^2 + 6x - 2y + 13 = 0$

86. $x^2 + y^2 - 2x + 6y + 9 = 0$

QUIZ 3

Self-Test for Lessons 10.6 and 10.7

Write an equation for the conic section. (Lesson 10.6)

1. Circle with center at $(-3, -5)$ and radius 8

2. Ellipse with vertices at $(-7, 2)$ and $(6, 2)$ and foci at $(4, 2)$ and $(-5, 2)$

3. Parabola with vertex at $(4, -1)$ and focus at $(7, -1)$

4. Hyperbola with foci at $(2, -1)$ and $(2, 8)$ and vertices at $(2, 3)$ and $(2, 4)$

Classify the conic section. (Lesson 10.6)

5. $x^2 + 4y^2 - 8x + 3y + 12 = 0$

6. $-3x^2 - 3y^2 + 6x + 4y + 1 = 0$

7. $-2y^2 + x + 5y + 26 = 0$

8. $-6x^2 + 4y^2 + 2x + 9 = 0$

Find the points of intersection, if any, of the graphs in the system. (Lesson 10.7)

9. $3x^2 - 4x - y + 2 = 0$
$y = -5x + 4$

10. $-x^2 + y^2 + 4x - 6y + 4 = 0$
$x^2 + y^2 - 4x - 6y + 12 = 0$

11. $x^2 + y^2 + 4y - 12 = 0$
$x^2 - 16y^2 - 64y - 80 = 0$

12. $y^2 - 6x - 2y - 3 = 0$
$2y^2 - 4y + x + 6 = 0$

13. 🌐 **SEISMOLOGY** A seismograph records the epicenter of an earthquake 50 miles away. A second seismograph, 50 miles west and 35 miles north of the first, records the epicenter as being 35 miles away. A third seismograph, 80 miles due west of the first, records the epicenter 30 miles away. Where was the earthquake's epicenter in relation to the first seismograph? **(Lesson 10.7)**

<u>*What*</u> *you should learn*

GOAL Find the eccentricity of a conic section.

<u>*Why*</u> *you should learn it*

▼ To write equations for **real-life** conics, such as the moon's orbit in **Example 3**.

Earth, as seen from the moon

Eccentricity of Conic Sections

Some ellipses are more oval than others. In an ellipse that is nearly circular, the ratio $c{:}a$ is close to 0. In a more oval ellipse, $c{:}a$ is close to 1. This ratio is called the **eccentricity** of the ellipse. Every conic has an eccentricity e associated with it.

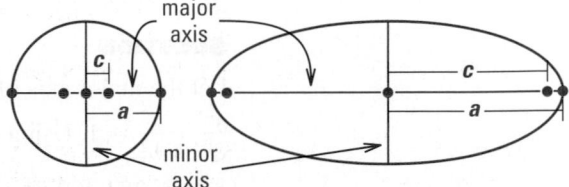

CONCEPT SUMMARY — **ECCENTRICITY OF CONIC SECTIONS**

Let c be the distance from each focus to the center of the conic section, and let a be the distance from each vertex to the center.

- The eccentricity of an ellipse is $e = \frac{c}{a}$, and $0 < e < 1$.

- The eccentricity of a hyperbola is $e = \frac{c}{a}$, and $e > 1$.

- The eccentricity of a parabola is $e = 1$.

- The eccentricity of a circle is $e = 0$.

EXAMPLE 1 *Finding Eccentricity*

Find the eccentricity of the conic section described by the equation.

a. $(x + 2)^2 = 4(y - 1)$ **b.** $25(x + 2)^2 - 36(y - 1)^2 = 900$

SOLUTION

a. This equation describes a parabola. By definition, the eccentricity is $e = 1$.

b. This equation describes a hyperbola with $a = \sqrt{36} = 6$, $b = \sqrt{25} = 5$, and $c = \sqrt{a^2 + b^2} = \sqrt{61}$. The eccentricity is $e = \frac{c}{a} = \frac{\sqrt{61}}{6} \approx 1.302$.

EXAMPLE 2 *Using Eccentricity to Write an Equation*

Find an equation of the hyperbola with center $(3, -5)$, vertex $(9, -5)$, and $e = 2$.

SOLUTION

Use the form $\frac{(x - h)^2}{a^2} - \frac{(y - k)^2}{b^2} = 1$. The vertex lies $9 - 3 = 6$ units from the center, so $a = 6$. Because $e = \frac{c}{a} = 2$, you know that $\frac{c}{6} = 2$, or $c = 12$. Therefore, $b^2 = c^2 - a^2 = 144 - 36 = 108$. The equation is $\frac{(x - 3)^2}{36} - \frac{(y + 5)^2}{108} = 1$.

EXAMPLE 3 *Using Eccentricity to Write a Model*

The moon orbits Earth in an elliptical path with the center of Earth at one focus. The eccentricity of the orbit is $e = 0.055$ and the length of the major axis is about 768,800 kilometers. Find an equation of the moon's orbit.

SOLUTION

Let the major axis of the ellipse be horizontal. The equation of the orbit has the form $\dfrac{x^2}{a^2} + \dfrac{y^2}{b^2} = 1$. Using the length of the major axis, you know that $2a = 768,800$, or $a \approx 384,400$. Because $e = \dfrac{c}{a}$, you know that $0.055 = \dfrac{c}{384,400}$, or $c \approx 21,142$ and $b = \sqrt{a^2 - c^2} = \sqrt{384,400^2 - 21,142^2} = \sqrt{1.47 \times 10^{11}} \approx 383,800$. The

equation of the moon's orbit is $\dfrac{x^2}{384,400^2} + \dfrac{y^2}{383,800^2} = 1$ where x and y are measured in kilometers.

EXERCISES

Find the eccentricity of the conic section.

1. $3x^2 - 5x + y + 20 = 0$

2. $25(x - 3)^2 + 9(y + 6)^2 = 225$

3. $x^2 + 16(y - 4)^2 = 16$

4. $\dfrac{(x - 3)^2}{8} + \dfrac{(y - 5)^2}{8} = 8$

5. $\dfrac{(x + 6)^2}{25} - \dfrac{(y - 6)^2}{100} = 1$

6. $\dfrac{(x + 2)^2}{49} + \dfrac{(y + 2)^2}{16} = 1$

7. $4(x + 1)^2 - 8(y - 2)^2 = 16$

8. $(x - 4)^2 - (y - 3)^2 = 1$

Write an equation of the conic section.

9. Ellipse with vertices at $(-5, -1)$ and $(5, -1)$, and $e = 0.6$

10. Ellipse with foci at $(2, -4)$ and $(2, 4)$, and $e = 0.5$

11. Ellipse with center at $(2, 0)$, focus at $(2, 2)$, and $e = 0.25$

12. Ellipse with center at $(0, 6)$, vertex at $(3, 6)$, and $e = 0.1$

13. Hyperbola with foci at $(3, -7)$ and $(3, 9)$, and $e = 3$

14. Hyperbola with vertices at $(-10, 4)$ and $(-2, 4)$, and $e = 2.4$

15. Hyperbola with center at $(3, 2)$, vertex at $(3, 5)$, and $e = 1.9$

16. Hyperbola with center at $(-1, 2)$, focus at $(4, 2)$, and $e = 5$

17. 🌎 **ASTRONOMY** Mercury orbits the sun in an elliptical path with the center of the sun at one focus. The eccentricity of Mercury's orbit is $e = 0.2056$. The length of the major axis of the orbit is 72 million miles. Find an equation of Mercury's orbit.

18. 🌎 **ASTRONOMY** Mars orbits the sun in an elliptical path with the center of the sun at one focus. The eccentricity of Mars' orbit is $e = 0.0932$. The *perihelion* of Mars' orbit is the point where the planet is closest to the sun. At the perihelion, Mars' distance from the sun is 128.4 million miles. Find an equation of Mars' orbit.

19. *Writing* Explain why the definition of eccentricity for ellipses and hyperbolas implies that $0 < e < 1$ for an ellipse and $e > 1$ for a hyperbola.

Chapter Summary

WHAT did you learn?

Find the distance between two points. **(10.1)**

Find the midpoint of the line segment connecting two points. **(10.1)**

Use distance and midpoint formulas in real-life situations. **(10.1)**

Graph and write equations of conics.
- parabolas **(10.2, 10.6)**
- circles **(10.3, 10.6)**
- ellipses **(10.4, 10.6)**

- hyperbolas **(10.5, 10.6)**

Classify a conic using its equation. **(10.6)**

Solve systems of quadratic equations. **(10.7)**

Use conics to solve real-life problems. **(10.2–10.7)**

WHY did you learn it?

Find the distance a medical helicopter must travel. **(p. 593)**

Find the diameter of a broken dish. **(p. 591)**

Design a city park. **(p. 593)**

Model a solar energy collector. **(p. 597)**
Model the region lit by a lighthouse. **(p. 603)**
Model the shape of an Australian football field. **(p. 614)**

Model the curved sides of a sculpture. **(p. 617)**

Classify mirrors in a Cassegrain telescope. **(p. 627)**

Find the epicenter of an earthquake. **(p. 634)**

Find the area of The Ellipse at the White House. **(p. 611)**

How does Chapter 10 fit into the BIGGER PICTURE of algebra?

In Chapter 5 you studied parabolas as graphs of quadratic functions, and in Chapter 9 you studied hyperbolas as graphs of rational functions. In a previous course you studied circles, and possibly ellipses, in the context of geometry. In Chapter 10 you studied all four conic sections (parabolas, hyperbolas, circles, and ellipses) as graphs of equations of the form $Ax^2 + Bxy + Cy^2 + Dx + Ey + F = 0$.

The conic sections are an important part of your study of algebra and geometry because they have many different real-life applications.

STUDY STRATEGY

How did you make and use a dictionary of graphs?

Here is an example of one entry for your dictionary of graphs, following the **Study Strategy** on page 588.

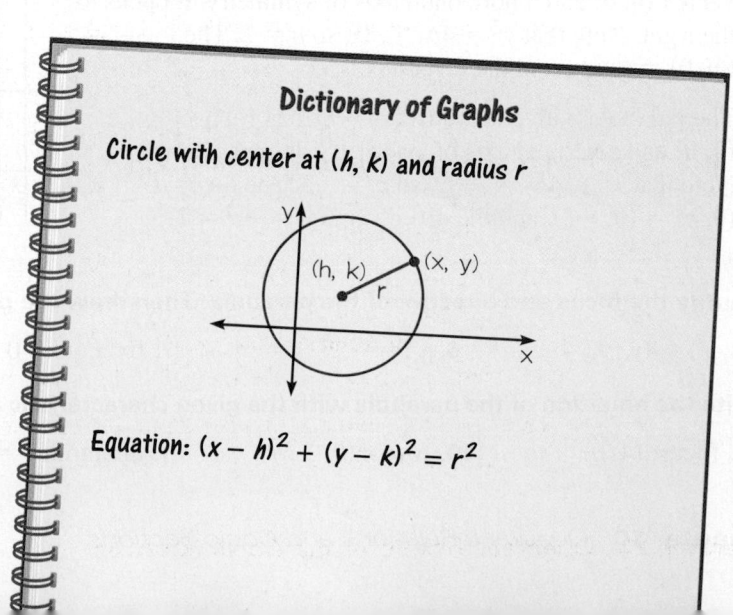

Dictionary of Graphs

Circle with center at (h, k) and radius r

Equation: $(x - h)^2 + (y - k)^2 = r^2$

Chapter Review

- distance formula, p. 589
- midpoint formula, p. 590
- focus, p. 595, 609, 615
- directrix, p. 595
- circle, p. 601
- center, p. 601, 609, 615

- radius, p. 601
- equation of a circle, p. 601
- ellipse, p. 609
- vertex, p. 609, 615
- major axis, p. 609

- co-vertex, p. 609
- minor axis, p. 609
- equation of an ellipse, p. 609
- hyperbola, p. 615
- transverse axis, p. 615

- equation of a hyperbola, p. 615
- conic sections, p. 623
- general second-degree equation, p. 626
- discriminant, p. 626

10.1 THE DISTANCE AND MIDPOINT FORMULAS

Examples on pp. 589–591

EXAMPLES Let $A = (-2, 4)$ and $B = (2, -3)$.

$$\text{Distance between } A \text{ and } B = \sqrt{(x_2 - x_1)^2 + (y_2 - y_1)^2}$$
$$= \sqrt{(2 - (-2))^2 + (-3 - 4)^2}$$
$$= \sqrt{16 + 49} = \sqrt{65} \approx 8.06$$

$$\text{Midpoint of } \overline{AB} = M\left(\frac{x_1 + x_2}{2}, \frac{y_1 + y_2}{2}\right) = \left(\frac{(-2) + 2}{2}, \frac{4 + (-3)}{2}\right) = \left(0, \frac{1}{2}\right)$$

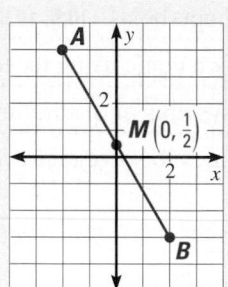

Find the distance between the two points. Then find the midpoint of the line segment connecting the two points.

1. $(-2, -3), (4, 2)$ **2.** $(-5, 4), (10, -3)$ **3.** $(0, 0), (-4, 4)$ **4.** $(-2, 0), (0, -8)$

10.2 PARABOLAS

Examples on pp. 595–597

EXAMPLES The parabola with equation $y^2 = 8x$ has **vertex $(0, 0)$** and a horizontal axis of symmetry. It opens to the right. Note that $y^2 = 4px = 8x$, so $p = 2$. The **focus** is $(p, 0) = (2, 0)$, and the **directrix** is $x = -p = -2$.

The parabola with equation $x^2 = -8y$ has **vertex $(0, 0)$** and a vertical axis of symmetry. It opens down. Note that $x^2 = 4py = -8y$, so $p = -2$. The **focus** is $(0, p) = (0, -2)$, and the **directrix** is $y = -p = 2$.

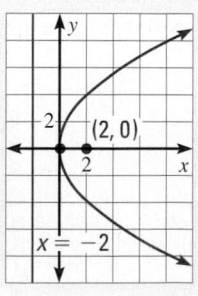 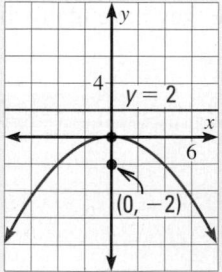

Identify the focus and directrix of the parabola. Then draw the parabola.

5. $x^2 = 4y$ **6.** $x^2 = -2y$ **7.** $6x + y^2 = 0$ **8.** $y^2 - 12x = 0$

Write the equation of the parabola with the given characteristic and vertex $(0, 0)$.

9. focus: $(4, 0)$ **10.** focus: $(0, -3)$ **11.** directrix: $y = -2$ **12.** directrix: $x = 1$

CIRCLES

Examples on pp. 601–603

> **EXAMPLE** The circle with equation $x^2 + y^2 = 9$ has center at $(0, 0)$ and radius $r = \sqrt{9} = 3$.
>
> Four points on the circle are $(3, 0)$, $(0, 3)$, $(-3, 0)$, and $(0, -3)$.

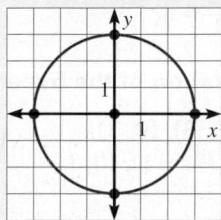

Graph the equation.

13. $x^2 + y^2 = 16$ **14.** $x^2 + y^2 = 64$ **15.** $x^2 + y^2 = 6$ **16.** $3x^2 + 3y^2 = 363$

Write the standard form of the equation of the circle that has the given radius or passes through the given point and whose center is the origin.

17. radius: 5   **18.** radius: $\sqrt{10}$ **19.** point: $(-2, 3)$ **20.** point: $(1, 8)$

ELLIPSES

Examples on pp. 609–611

> **EXAMPLE** The ellipse with equation $\dfrac{x^2}{9} + \dfrac{y^2}{4} = 1$ has a horizontal major axis because $9 > 4$.
>
> Since $\sqrt{9} = 3$, the vertices are at $(-3, 0)$ and $(3, 0)$.
>
> Since $\sqrt{4} = 2$, the co-vertices are at $(0, -2)$ and $(0, 2)$.
>
> Since $9 - 4 = 5$, the foci are at $(-\sqrt{5}, 0)$ and $(\sqrt{5}, 0)$.

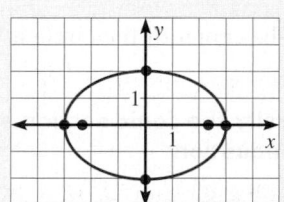

Graph the equation.

21. $4x^2 + 81y^2 = 324$ **22.** $-9x^2 - 4y^2 = -36$ **23.** $49x^2 + 36y^2 = 1764$

Write an equation of the ellipse with the given characteristics and center at (0, 0).

24. Vertex: $(0, 5)$, Co-vertex: $(1, 0)$ **25.** Vertex: $(4, 0)$, Focus: $(-3, 0)$

HYPERBOLAS

Examples on pp. 615–617

> **EXAMPLE** The hyperbola with equation $\dfrac{y^2}{4} - \dfrac{x^2}{9} = 1$ has a vertical transverse axis because the y^2-term is positive.
> Since $\sqrt{4} = 2$, vertices are $(0, -2)$ and $(0, 2)$.
> Since $4 + 9 = 13$, foci are $(0, -\sqrt{13})$ and $(0, \sqrt{13})$.
> Asymptotes are $y = \dfrac{2}{3}x$ and $y = -\dfrac{2}{3}x$.

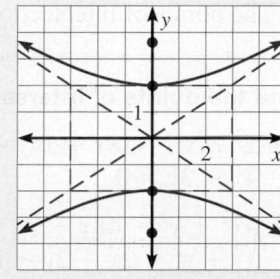

Graph the hyperbola.

26. $\dfrac{x^2}{100} - \dfrac{y^2}{64} = 1$ **27.** $16y^2 - 9x^2 = 144$ **28.** $y^2 - 4x^2 = 4$

Write an equation of the hyperbola with the given foci and vertices.

29. Foci: $(0, -3), (0, 3)$
    Vertices: $(0, -1), (0, 1)$

30. Foci: $(0, -4), (0, 4)$
    Vertices: $(0, -2), (0, 2)$

31. Foci: $(-5, 0), (5, 0)$
    Vertices: $(-3, 0), (3, 0)$

10.6   GRAPHING AND CLASSIFYING CONICS

Examples on pp. 623–627

> **EXAMPLE**   You can use the discriminant $B^2 - 4AC$ to classify a conic.
>
> For the equation $x^2 + y^2 - 6x + 2y + 6 = 0$, the discriminant is $B^2 - 4AC = 0^2 - 4(1)(1) = -4$. Because $B^2 - 4AC < 0$, $B = 0$, and $A = C$, the equation represents a circle.
>
> To graph the circle, complete the square as follows.
>
> $$x^2 + y^2 - 6x + 2y + 6 = 0$$
> $$(x^2 - 6x + \mathbf{9}) + (y^2 + 2y + \mathbf{1}) = -6 + \mathbf{9} + \mathbf{1}$$
> $$(x - 3)^2 + (y + 1)^2 = 4$$
>
> The center of the circle is at $(h, k) = (3, -1)$ and $r = \sqrt{4} = 2$.

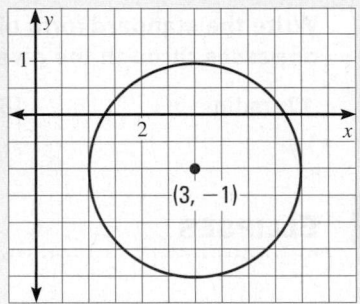

Classify the conic section and write its equation in standard form. Then graph the equation.

32. $x^2 + 8x - 8y + 16 = 0$ **33.** $x^2 + y^2 - 10x + 2y - 74 = 0$

34. $9x^2 + y^2 + 72x - 2y + 136 = 0$ **35.** $y^2 - 4x^2 - 18y - 8x + 76 = 0$

10.7   SOLVING QUADRATIC SYSTEMS

Examples on pp. 632–634

> **EXAMPLE**   You can solve systems of quadratic equations algebraically.
>
> $y^2 - 2x - 10y + 31 = 0$
> $x - y + 2 = 0$ **Solve the second equation for y: $y = x + 2$.**
>
> $(x + 2)^2 - 2x - 10(x + 2) + 31 = 0$ **Substitute into the first equation.**
>
> $x^2 - 8x + 15 = 0$, so $x = 3$ or $x = 5$.   **Simplify and solve.**
>
> The points of intersection of the graphs of the system are $(3, 5)$ and $(5, 7)$.

Find the points of intersection, if any, of the graphs in the system.

36. $x^2 + y^2 - 18x + 24y + 200 = 0$
    $4x + 3y = 0$

37. $5x^2 + 3x - 8y + 2 = 0$
    $3x + y - 6 = 0$

38. $4x^2 + y^2 - 48x - 2y + 129 = 0$
    $x^2 + y^2 - 2x - 2y - 7 = 0$

39. $9x^2 - 16y^2 + 18x + 153 = 0$
    $9x^2 + 16y^2 + 18x - 135 = 0$

Chapter Test

Find the distance between the two points. Then find the midpoint of the line segment connecting the two points.

1. $(1, 9)$, $(5, 3)$ **2.** $(-8, 3)$, $(4, 7)$ **3.** $(-4, -2)$, $(3, 10)$

4. $(-11, -5)$, $(-3, 7)$ **5.** $(-1, 6)$, $(2, 8)$ **6.** $(3, -2)$, $(4, 9)$

Graph the equation.

7. $x^2 + y^2 = 36$ **8.** $y^2 = 16x$ **9.** $9y^2 - 81x^2 = 729$

10. $25x^2 + 9y^2 = 225$ **11.** $(x - 4)^2 = y + 7$ **12.** $(x - 3)^2 + (y + 2)^2 = 1$

13. $\dfrac{(x + 6)^2}{4} + \dfrac{(y - 7)^2}{1} = 1$ **14.** $\dfrac{(x - 4)^2}{16} - \dfrac{(y + 4)^2}{16} = 1$ **15.** $\dfrac{(y + 2)^2}{4} - \dfrac{(x + 1)^2}{16} = 1$

Write an equation for the conic section.

16. Parabola with vertex at $(0, 0)$ and directrix $x = 5$

17. Parabola with vertex at $(3, -6)$ and focus at $(3, -4)$

18. Circle with center at $(0, 0)$ and passing through $(4, 6)$

19. Circle with center at $(-8, 3)$ and radius 5

20. Ellipse with center at $(0, 0)$, vertex at $(4, 0)$, and co-vertex at $(0, 2)$

21. Ellipse with vertices at $(3, -5)$ and $(3, -1)$ and foci at $(3, -4)$ and $(3, -2)$

22. Hyperbola with vertices at $(-7, 0)$ and $(7, 0)$ and foci at $(-9, 0)$ and $(9, 0)$

23. Hyperbola with vertex at $(4, 2)$, focus at $(4, 4)$, and center at $(4, -1)$

Classify the conic section and write its equation in standard form.

24. $x^2 + 4y^2 - 2x - 3 = 0$ **25.** $2x^2 + 20x - y + 41 = 0$ **26.** $5x^2 - 3y^2 - 30 = 0$

27. $x^2 + y^2 - 12x + 4y + 31 = 0$ **28.** $y^2 - 8x - 4y + 4 = 0$ **29.** $-x^2 + y^2 - 6x - 6y - 4 = 0$

30. $x^2 - 8x + 4y + 16 = 0$ **31.** $3x^2 + 3y^2 - 30x + 59 = 0$ **32.** $x^2 + 2y^2 - 8x + 7 = 0$

33. $4x^2 - y^2 + 16x + 6y - 3 = 0$ **34.** $3x^2 + y^2 - 4y + 3 = 0$ **35.** $x^2 + y^2 - 2x + 10y + 1 = 0$

Find the points of intersection, if any, of the graphs in the system.

36. $x^2 + y^2 = 64$
$x - 2y = 17$

37. $x^2 + y^2 = 20$
$x^2 + 4y^2 - 2x - 2 = 0$

38. $x^2 = 8y$
$x^2 = 2y + 12$

39. 🌐 **ARCHITECTURE** The Royal Albert Hall in London is nearly elliptical in shape, about 230 feet long and 200 feet wide. Write an equation for the shape of the hall, assuming its center is at $(0, 0)$. Then graph the equation.

40. 🌐 **SEARCH TEAM** A search team of three members splits to search an area in the woods. Each member carries a family service radio with a circular range of 3 miles. They agree to communicate from their bases every hour. One member sets up base 2 miles north of the first member. Where should the other member set up base to be as far east as possible but within range of communication?

Chapter Standardized Test

▶ **TEST-TAKING STRATEGY** During the test, do not worry excessively about how much time you have left. Concentrate on the question in front of you.

1. **MULTIPLE CHOICE** What is the midpoint of the line segment connecting points $(0, 0)$ and $(-8, 2)$?

   (A) $(-4, 1)$ **(B)** $(4, 1)$ **(C)** $(4, -1)$

   (D) $(1, 4)$ **(E)** $(1, -4)$

2. **MULTIPLE CHOICE** Which equation represents the perpendicular bisector of the line segment connecting points $(-7, 1)$ and $(9, 13)$?

   (A) $y = -\frac{4}{3}x + \frac{25}{3}$ **(B)** $y = \frac{3}{4}x + \frac{25}{4}$

   (C) $y = \frac{4}{3}x + \frac{25}{3}$ **(D)** $y = \frac{4}{3}x + \frac{17}{3}$

   (E) $y = -\frac{4}{3}x + \frac{17}{3}$

3. **MULTIPLE CHOICE** Which equation is graphed?

   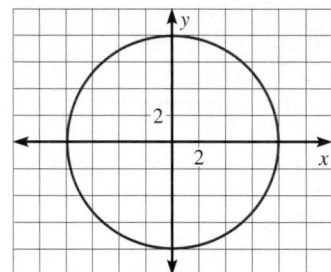

   (A) $x^2 + y^2 = 8$ **(B)** $x^2 - y^2 = 8$

   (C) $x^2 + y^2 = 16$ **(D)** $9x^2 + 9y^2 = 576$

   (E) $9x^2 - 9y^2 = 576$

4. **MULTIPLE CHOICE** What is the standard form of the ellipse with center at $(0, 0)$, vertex at $(0, 9)$, and co-vertex at $(4, 0)$?

   (A) $\frac{x^2}{9} + \frac{y^2}{4} = 1$ **(B)** $\frac{x^2}{4} + \frac{y^2}{9} = 1$

   (C) $\frac{x^2}{81} + \frac{y^2}{16} = 1$ **(D)** $\frac{x^2}{16} + \frac{y^2}{81} = 1$

   (E) $\frac{x^2}{2} + \frac{y^2}{3} = 1$

5. **MULTIPLE CHOICE** What is the focus of the parabola with equation $2x^2 = -120y$?

   (A) $(0, 60)$ **(B)** $(0, 15)$ **(C)** $(0, -60)$

   (D) $(0, 12)$ **(E)** $(0, -15)$

6. **MULTIPLE CHOICE** What is the directrix of the parabola with equation $y^2 = 24x$?

   (A) $x = 6$ **(B)** $x = -6$ **(C)** $x = 24$

   (D) $y = 6$ **(E)** $y = -6$

7. **MULTIPLE CHOICE** Which graph represents the equation $\frac{y^2}{25} - \frac{x^2}{9} = 1$?

   (A) 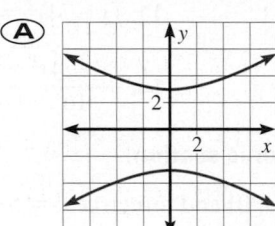   **(B)**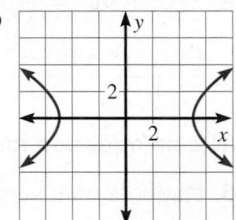

   (C) 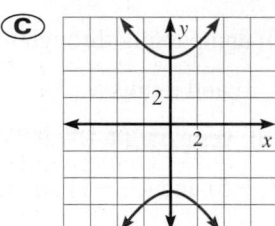   **(D)**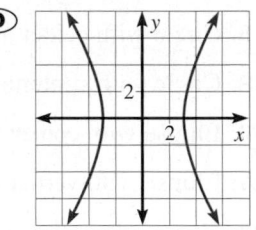

   (E)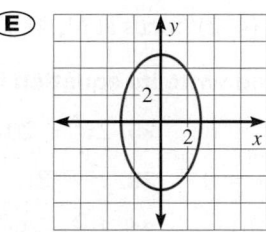

8. **MULTIPLE CHOICE** What conic does the equation $x^2 - 5x + 10y + 11 = 0$ represent?

   (A) circle   **(B)** ellipse

   (C) hyperbola   **(D)** parabola

   (E) none of the above

9. **MULTIPLE CHOICE** What point is the intersection of the graphs of $x^2 + y^2 = 41$ and $y = 3x - 7$?

   (A) $(-4, -4)$ **(B)** $(4, 5)$ **(C)** $(5, 8)$

   (D) $(3, 2)$ **(E)** $(-4, -19)$

QUANTITATIVE COMPARISON In Exercises 10 and 11, choose the statement that is true about the given quantities.

    Ⓐ The quantity in column A is greater.

    Ⓑ The quantity in column B is greater.

    Ⓒ The two quantities are equal.

    Ⓓ The relationship cannot be determined from the given information.

	Column A	Column B
10.	Distance between $(3, -2)$ and $(-5, 7)$	Distance between $(-8, -1)$ and $(0, 8)$
11.	Discriminant of $x^2 + y^2 - 6x + 1 = 0$	Discriminant of $3x^2 + y^2 - 2y + 5 = 0$

12. **MULTI-STEP PROBLEM** Let $(0, 0)$ represent a water fountain located in a city park. Each day Jane runs through the park along a path given by the equation $x^2 + y^2 - 200x - 52{,}500 = 0$ where x and y are measured in meters.

  a. *Writing* What type of conic is Jane's path? How do you know?

  b. Write the equation of the conic in standard form. Then graph the equation.

  c. After her run, Jane walks to the water fountain. If Jane stops running at $(-100, 150)$, how far must she walk for a drink of water?

13. **MULTI-STEP PROBLEM** The Mars Global Surveyor spacecraft followed an elliptical path with the center of Mars at one focus. The spacecraft's initial orbit had a low point of 262 kilometers above the northern hemisphere and a high point of 54,026 kilometers above the southern hemisphere. ▶ Source: NASA

  a. *Writing* The radius of Mars is approximately 5400 kilometers. If $(0, 0)$ represents the center of Mars and the positive y-axis represents north, what are the coordinates of the other focus of the orbit? How do you know?

  b. Write an equation for the spacecraft's initial orbit around Mars.

  c. In February, 1999, the spacecraft reached a nearly circular orbit, 410 kilometers above the surface of Mars. Write and graph an equation of the orbit.

14. **MULTI-STEP PROBLEM** Sara Peters is a mail carrier for a post office that receives mail for everyone living within a radius of 5 miles. Her route covers the portions of Anderson Road and Murphy Road that pass through this region.

  a. Assume that the post office is located at the point $(0, 0)$. Write an equation for the circle that bounds the region where the mail is delivered.

  b. Assuming Anderson Road follows one branch of a hyperbolic path given by $x^2 - y^2 - 4x - 23 = 0$, graph Anderson Road and the circular region where Sara delivers mail.

  c. *Writing* If Sara begins delivery on Anderson Road at the point $(-4, -3)$, where on Anderson Road does she end delivery? How do you know?

  d. Sara finishes delivering on Anderson Road at the point where it intersects both the circular boundary and Murphy Road. At the intersection, she begins delivering on Murphy Road which is a straight road that cuts through the center of the circular region past the post office. Find the equation that represents Murphy Road. Where does Sara Peters end delivery on Murphy Road?

SEQUENCES AND SERIES

▶ *How is a fractal formed?*

APPLICATION: *Fractals*

Have you ever noticed how a fern leaf looks like a miniature version of the fern? When the parts of an object are similar to the whole object, the object is called *self-similar*. A *fractal* is a complex shape that basically looks the same at different levels of magnification and is generally self-similar.

Think & Discuss

The diagram shows the first three stages in the growth of a fractal plant.

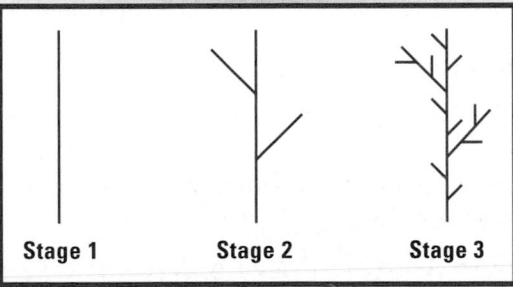

Stage 1   Stage 2   Stage 3

1. Draw the next stage in the growth process.
2. Describe in words how the fractal plant changes from one stage to the next.
3. What could you do to make the fractal plant look even more realistic?

Learn More About It

You will find the number of branches in a fractal tree in Exercise 45 on p. 685.

APPLICATION LINK Visit www.mcdougallittell.com for more information about fractals.

Study Guide

What's the chapter about?

Chapter 11 is about **sequences and series**. In Chapter 11 you'll learn

- how to find terms of sequences and write algebraic rules to define sequences.

- how to use summation notation and find sums of arithmetic and geometric series.

KEY VOCABULARY

▶ **Review**
- integers, p. 3
- finite differences, p. 380

▶ **New**
- terms of a sequence, p. 651
- sequence, p. 651

- finite sequence, p. 651
- infinite sequence, p. 651
- series, p. 653
- summation notation, p. 653
- arithmetic sequence, p. 659
- common difference, p. 659

- arithmetic series, p. 661
- geometric sequence, p. 666
- common ratio, p. 666
- geometric series, p. 668
- explicit rule, p. 681
- recursive rule, p. 681

Are you ready for the chapter?

SKILL REVIEW Do these exercises to review key skills that you'll apply in this chapter. See the given **reference page** if there is something you don't understand.

Write the given phrase as an algebraic expression. (Skills Review, p. 929)

1. 4 more than a number   **2.** 3 times a number   **3.** half of a number

Evaluate the expression. (Review Example 3, p. 12)

4. $3x - 7$ when $x = 3$ **5.** $\dfrac{x}{x+1}$ when $x = 8$ **6.** $3(2)^{n-1}$ when $n = 4$

Show that the nth-order finite differences for the function of degree n are nonzero and constant. (Review Example 2, p. 380)

7. $f(x) = -3x^2 + 3$ **8.** $f(x) = x^3 + 2x^2$ **9.** $f(x) = x^4 - 5x + 1$

Solve the equation. (Review Example 3, p. 502; Example 4, p. 569)

10. $4^x = 16{,}384$ **11.** $2^{x-1} = 32$ **12.** $10 = \dfrac{5}{1-x}$ **13.** $24 = \dfrac{2}{1+x}$

▶ **Study Tip**
"Student Help" boxes throughout the chapter give you study tips and tell you where to look for extra help in this book and on the Internet.

Here's a study strategy!

Learn by Teaching

Explain to a teacher, friend, or family member how to do an important skill in this chapter. Show an example and use words to describe your steps.

You can use a variation of this strategy when you are alone, too. Talk to yourself and explain your reasoning as you work toward an answer.

What you should learn

GOAL 1 Use and write sequences.

GOAL 2 Use summation notation to write series and find sums of series, as applied in **Example 6**.

Why you should learn it

▼ To model **real-life** situations, such as building a roof frame in **Exs. 65 and 66**.

GOAL 1 USING AND WRITING SEQUENCES

Saying that a collection of objects is listed "in sequence" means that the collection is ordered so that it has a first member, a second member, a third member, and so on. Below are two examples of sequences of numbers. The numbers in the sequences are called **terms**.

SEQUENCE 1:	SEQUENCE 2:
3, 6, 9, 12, 15	3, 6, 9, 12, 15, . . .

You can think of a **sequence** as a function whose domain is a set of consecutive integers. If a domain is not specified, it is understood that the domain starts with 1.

DOMAIN: 1   2   3   4   5   The domain gives the relative position of each term: 1st, 2nd, 3rd, and so on.

RANGE: 3   6   9   12   15   The range gives the terms of the sequence.

Sequence 1 above is a **finite sequence** because it has a last term. Sequence 2 is an **infinite sequence** because it continues without stopping. Both sequences have the general rule $a_n = 3n$ where a_n represents the nth term of the sequence. The general rule can also be written using function notation: $f(n) = 3n$.

EXAMPLE 1   *Writing Terms of Sequences*

Write the first six terms of the sequence.

a. $a_n = 2n + 3$ **b.** $f(n) = (-2)^{n-1}$

SOLUTION

a. $a_1 = 2(1) + 3 = 5$ **1st term**

$a_2 = 2(2) + 3 = 7$ **2nd term**

$a_3 = 2(3) + 3 = 9$ **3rd term**

$a_4 = 2(4) + 3 = 11$ **4th term**

$a_5 = 2(5) + 3 = 13$ **5th term**

$a_6 = 2(6) + 3 = 15$ **6th term**

b. $f(1) = (-2)^{1-1} = 1$ **1st term**

$f(2) = (-2)^{2-1} = -2$ **2nd term**

$f(3) = (-2)^{3-1} = 4$ **3rd term**

$f(4) = (-2)^{4-1} = -8$ **4th term**

$f(5) = (-2)^{5-1} = 16$ **5th term**

$f(6) = (-2)^{6-1} = -32$ **6th term**

STUDENT HELP

↳ **Look Back**
For help with evaluating expressions, see p. 12.

If the terms of a sequence have a recognizable pattern, then you may be able to write a rule for the *n*th term of the sequence.

EXAMPLE 2 Writing Rules for Sequences

For each sequence, describe the pattern, write the next term, and write a rule for the *n*th term.

a. $-\dfrac{1}{3}, \dfrac{1}{9}, -\dfrac{1}{27}, \dfrac{1}{81}, \ldots$ **b.** $2, 6, 12, 20, \ldots$

SOLUTION

a. You can write the terms as $\left(-\dfrac{1}{3}\right)^1, \left(-\dfrac{1}{3}\right)^2, \left(-\dfrac{1}{3}\right)^3, \left(-\dfrac{1}{3}\right)^4, \ldots$.

The next term is $a_5 = \left(-\dfrac{1}{3}\right)^5 = -\dfrac{1}{243}$. A rule for the *n*th term is $a_n = \left(-\dfrac{1}{3}\right)^n$.

b. You can write the terms as $1(2), 2(3), 3(4), 4(5), \ldots$.

The next term is $f(5) = 5(6) = 30$. A rule for the *n*th term is $f(n) = n(n + 1)$.

· · · · · · · · · ·

You can graph a sequence by letting the horizontal axis represent the position numbers (the domain) and the vertical axis represent the terms (the range).

EXAMPLE 3 Graphing a Sequence

You work in the produce department of a grocery store and are stacking oranges in the shape of a square pyramid with 10 layers.

a. Write a rule for the number of oranges in each layer.

b. Graph the sequence.

SOLUTION

a. The diagram below shows the first three layers of the stack. Let a_n represent the number of oranges in layer *n*.

n	1	2	3
	●	●●	●●●
a_n	$1 = 1^2$	$4 = 2^2$	$9 = 3^2$

From the diagram, you can see that $a_n = n^2$.

b. Plot the points $(1, 1), (2, 4), (3, 9), \ldots,$ $(10, 100)$. The graph is shown at the right.

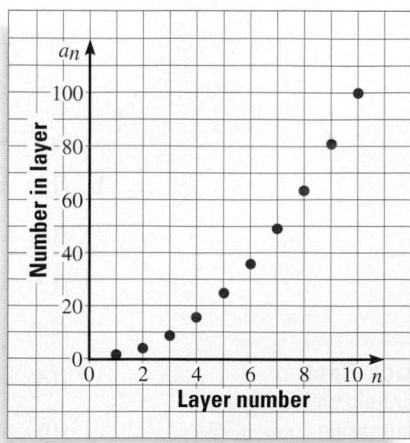

STUDENT HELP

→ **Study Tip**
If you are given only the first several terms of a sequence, there is no *single* rule for the *n*th term. For instance, the sequence $2, 4, 8, \ldots$ can be given by $a_n = 2^n$ or $a_n = n^2 - n + 2$.

STUDENT HELP

→ **Study Tip**
Although the plotted points in part (b) of Example 3 follow a curve, do *not* draw the curve because the sequence is defined only for integer values of *n*.

When the terms of a sequence are added, the resulting expression is a **series**. A series can be infinite or finite.

FINITE SEQUENCE	**INFINITE SEQUENCE**
3, 6, 9, 12, 15	3, 6, 9, 12, 15, . . .
FINITE SERIES	**INFINITE SERIES**
3 + 6 + 9 + 12 + 15	3 + 6 + 9 + 12 + 15 + · · ·

You can use **summation notation** to write a series. For example, for the finite series shown above, you can write

$$3 + 6 + 9 + 12 + 15 = \sum_{i=1}^{5} 3i$$

where i is the *index of summation*, 1 is the *lower limit of summation*, and 5 is the *upper limit of summation*. In this case the summation notation is read as "the sum from i equals 1 to 5 of $3i$." Summation notation is also called **sigma notation** because it uses the uppercase Greek letter *sigma*, written Σ.

Summation notation for an infinite series is similar to that for a finite series. For example, for the infinite series shown above, you can write:

$$3 + 6 + 9 + 12 + 15 + \cdots = \sum_{i=1}^{\infty} 3i$$

The infinity symbol, ∞, indicates that the series continues without end.

EXAMPLE 4 *Writing Series with Summation Notation*

Write each series with summation notation.

a. $5 + 10 + 15 + \cdots + 100$ **b.** $\dfrac{1}{2} + \dfrac{2}{3} + \dfrac{3}{4} + \dfrac{4}{5} + \cdots$

SOLUTION

a. Notice that the first term is 5(1), the second is 5(2), the third is 5(3), and the last is 5(20). So, the terms of the series can be written as:

$$a_i = 5i \text{ where } i = 1, 2, 3, \ldots, 20$$

▶ The summation notation for the series is $\displaystyle\sum_{i=1}^{20} 5i$.

b. Notice that for each term the denominator of the fraction is 1 more than the numerator. So, the terms of the series can be written as:

$$a_i = \frac{i}{i+1} \text{ where } i = 1, 2, 3, 4, \ldots$$

▶ The summation notation for the series is $\displaystyle\sum_{i=1}^{\infty} \frac{i}{i+1}$.

· · · · · · · · · ·

The index of summation does not have to be i — any letter can be used. Also, the index does not have to begin at 1. For instance, in part (b) of Example 5 on the next page, the index begins at 3.

EXAMPLE 5 *Using Summation Notation*

Find the sum of the series.

a. $\displaystyle\sum_{i=1}^{6} 2i = 2(1) + 2(2) + 2(3) + 2(4) + 2(5) + 2(6)$

$\qquad\qquad = 2(1 + 2 + 3 + 4 + 5 + 6)$

$\qquad\qquad = 2(21)$

$\qquad\qquad = 42$

b. $\displaystyle\sum_{k=3}^{6} \left(2 + k^2\right) = \left(2 + 3^2\right) + \left(2 + 4^2\right) + \left(2 + 5^2\right) + \left(2 + 6^2\right)$

$\qquad\qquad\qquad = 11 + 18 + 27 + 38$

$\qquad\qquad\qquad = 94$

· · · · · · · · · ·

The sum of the terms of a finite sequence can be found by simply adding the terms. For sequences with many terms, however, adding the terms can be tedious. Formulas for finding the sum of the terms of three special types of sequences are given below.

CONCEPT SUMMARY | **FORMULAS FOR SPECIAL SERIES**

1. $\displaystyle\sum_{i=1}^{n} 1 = n$ **2.** $\displaystyle\sum_{i=1}^{n} i = \frac{n(n+1)}{2}$ **3.** $\displaystyle\sum_{i=1}^{n} i^2 = \frac{n(n+1)(2n+1)}{6}$

In words, the first formula gives the sum of *n* 1's. The second formula gives the sum of the positive integers from 1 to *n*. The third formula gives the sum of the squares of the positive integers from 1 to *n*.

EXAMPLE 6 *Using a Formula for a Sum*

RETAIL DISPLAYS How many oranges are in the stack in Example 3?

SOLUTION

From Example 3 you know that the *i*th term of the series is given by $a_i = i^2$, where $i = 1, 2, 3, \ldots, 10$. Using summation notation and the third formula listed above, you can find the total number of oranges as follows.

$$\sum_{i=1}^{10} i^2 = 1^2 + 2^2 + \cdots + 10^2$$

$$= \frac{10(10 + 1)(2 \cdot 10 + 1)}{6}$$

$$= \frac{10(11)(21)}{6}$$

$$= 385$$

▸ There are 385 oranges in the stack. Check this by actually adding the number of oranges in each of the ten layers.

GUIDED PRACTICE

Vocabulary Check ✓

1. Explain the difference between a sequence and a series.

Concept Check ✓

2. Answer the following questions about the series $\sum_{k=3}^{10} (k + 2)$.

    a. In words, how do you read the summation notation?

    b. What is the index of summation?

    c. What is the lower limit of summation?

    d. What is the upper limit of summation?

Skill Check ✓

Write the first six terms of the sequence.

3. $a_n = 2n$ **4.** $a_n = 6 - n$ **5.** $a_n = 3n + 1$ **6.** $f(n) = 2^{n+3}$

7. Find the sum of the series in Exercise 2.

8. 🌐 **STACKING** Find the total number of oranges in the stack in Example 3 if there are 12 layers.

PRACTICE AND APPLICATIONS

► **Extra Practice**
to help you master
skills is on p. 955.

WRITING TERMS Write the first six terms of the sequence.

9. $a_n = n + 1$ **10.** $a_n = n^2$ **11.** $a_n = 3 - n$ **12.** $a_n = n^3 - 1$

13. $a_n = (n + 1)^2$ **14.** $a_n = (-n)^3$ **15.** $a_n = n^2 + 3$ **16.** $a_n = (n - 1)^2$

17. $f(n) = \dfrac{n}{n + 1}$ **18.** $f(n) = \dfrac{n^2}{2n}$ **19.** $f(n) = \dfrac{n + 2}{2n}$ **20.** $f(n) = \dfrac{3}{-n}$

WRITING RULES Write the next term in the sequence. Then write a rule for the *n*th term.

21. $1, 3, 5, 7, \ldots$ **22.** $1, 10, 100, 1000, \ldots$ **23.** $2, -4, 8, -10, 14, \ldots$

24. $-5, 10, -15, 20, \ldots$ **25.** $-\dfrac{1}{2}, -\dfrac{1}{4}, -\dfrac{1}{6}, -\dfrac{1}{8}, \ldots$ **26.** $\dfrac{1}{4}, \dfrac{2}{5}, \dfrac{3}{6}, \dfrac{4}{7}, \dfrac{5}{8}, \ldots$

27. $\dfrac{1}{3}, \dfrac{2}{3}, \dfrac{3}{3}, \dfrac{4}{3}, \dfrac{5}{3}, \ldots$ **28.** $\dfrac{1}{20}, \dfrac{2}{30}, \dfrac{3}{40}, \dfrac{4}{50}, \ldots$ **29.** $1.9, 2.7, 3.5, 4.3, 5.1, \ldots$

GRAPHING SEQUENCES Graph the sequence.

30. $1, 4, 7, 10, \ldots, 28$ **31.** $3, 6, 12, 21, 33, 48$ **32.** $-1, -6, -11, -16, -21$

33. $1, 4, 9, 16, 25, 36$ **34.** $\dfrac{1}{9}, \dfrac{2}{8}, \dfrac{3}{7}, \dfrac{4}{6}, \ldots, \dfrac{9}{1}$ **35.** $3, -6, 9, -12, \ldots, -36$

WRITING SUMMATION NOTATION Write the series with summation notation.

36. $1 + 5 + 9 + 13 + 17$ **37.** $4 + 8 + 12 + 16 + 20$

38. $-3 + 3 + 9 + 15 + 21 + \cdots$ **39.** $1 - 2 + 3 - 4 + 5 - \cdots$

40. $-7 - 8 - 9 - 10 - 11$ **41.** $\dfrac{5}{6} + \dfrac{6}{7} + \dfrac{7}{8} + \dfrac{8}{9} + \cdots$

42. $1 + 0.1 + 0.01 + 0.001$ **43.** $1 + 4 + 9 + 16 + 25 + 36$

USING SUMMATION NOTATION Find the sum of the series.

44. $\sum_{i=1}^{6} 3i$　　　**45.** $\sum_{i=0}^{5} 12i$　　　**46.** $\sum_{n=0}^{4} n^2$　　　**47.** $\sum_{n=1}^{3} 4n^3$

48. $\sum_{k=1}^{5} (k^2 - 1)$　　**49.** $\sum_{n=0}^{4} (2n^2 + 1)$　　**50.** $\sum_{k=1}^{4} k(k+2)$　　**51.** $\sum_{n=2}^{10} \frac{2}{n}$

52. $\sum_{n=2}^{12} \frac{1}{n-1}$　　**53.** $\sum_{n=1}^{5} \frac{n}{n+1}$　　**54.** $\sum_{i=2}^{6} \frac{i}{i-1}$　　**55.** $\sum_{n=1}^{\infty} \left(\frac{n}{n^2} - \frac{1}{n} \right)$

USING FORMULAS Use one of the formulas for special series to find the sum of the series.

56. $\sum_{i=1}^{42} 1$　　　**57.** $\sum_{n=1}^{5} n$　　　**58.** $\sum_{i=1}^{18} i$　　　**59.** $\sum_{k=1}^{20} k$

60. $\sum_{n=1}^{6} n^2$　　　**61.** $\sum_{i=1}^{10} i^2$　　　**62.** $\sum_{i=1}^{12} i^2$　　　**63.** $\sum_{k=1}^{35} k^2$

64. **GEOMETRY CONNECTION** The degree measurement d_n in each angle at the tips of the six n-pointed stars shown at the right is given by:

$$d_n = \frac{180(n-4)}{n}, n \geq 5$$

Write the first six terms of the sequence.

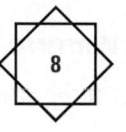 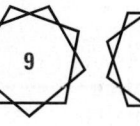 

🌐 **CARPENTRY In Exercises 65 and 66, use the following information.**
The diagram shows part of a roof frame. The length (in feet) of each vertical support is given below the support. These lengths form an arithmetic sequence from each end to the middle.

65. Find the total length of the vertical supports from one end to the middle.

66. Use your result from Exercise 65 to find the total length of the vertical supports from end to end.

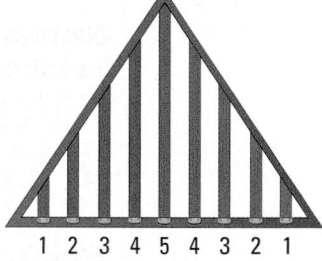

1 2 3 4 5 4 3 2 1

67. 🌐 **TOWER OF HANOI** In the puzzle called the Tower of Hanoi, the object is to use a series of moves to take the rings from one peg and stack them in order on another peg. A move consists of moving exactly one ring, and no ring may be placed on top of a smaller ring. The minimum number of moves required to move n rings is 1 for 1 ring, 3 for 2 rings, 7 for 3 rings, 15 for 4 rings, and 31 for 5 rings. Find a formula for the sequence. What is the minimum number of moves required to move 6 rings?

68. 🌐 **PYRAMID STACK** Suppose you are stacking tennis balls in a pyramid as a display at a sports store. If the base is an equilateral triangle, then the number a_n of balls per layer would be $a_n = \frac{1}{2}n^2 + \frac{1}{2}n$ where $n = 1$ represents the top layer. How many balls are in the fifth layer? How many balls are in a stack with 5 layers?

QUANTITATIVE COMPARISON In Exercises 69 and 70, choose the statement that is true about the given quantities.

- Ⓐ The quantity in column A is greater.
- Ⓑ The quantity in column B is greater.
- Ⓒ The two quantities are equal.
- Ⓓ The relationship cannot be determined from the given information.

	Column A	Column B
69.	The fifth term of the sequence $a_n = n^2 + 1$	$\sum\limits_{n=1}^{5} (n^2 + 1)$
70.	The first term of the sequence $a_n = 5 - n$	$\sum\limits_{n=4}^{8} (5 - n)$

★ **Challenge**

71. LOGICAL REASONING Tell whether the statement about summation notation is *true* or *false*. If the statement is true, prove it. If the statement is false, give a counterexample.

a. $\sum\limits_{i=1}^{n} ka_i = k \sum\limits_{i=1}^{n} a_i$ **b.** $\sum\limits_{i=1}^{n} (a_i + b_i) = \sum\limits_{i=1}^{n} a_i + \sum\limits_{i=1}^{n} b_i$

c. $\sum\limits_{i=1}^{n} a_i b_i = \left(\sum\limits_{i=1}^{n} a_i \right)\left(\sum\limits_{i=1}^{n} b_i \right)$ **d.** $\sum\limits_{i=1}^{n} (a_i)^k = \left(\sum\limits_{i=1}^{n} a_i \right)^k$

EXTRA CHALLENGE
www.mcdougallittell.com

72. Using the true statements from Exercise 71 and the special formulas from page 654, find a formula for the number of balls in *n* layers of the pyramid in Exercise 68.

MIXED REVIEW

SOLVING EQUATIONS Solve the equation. Check your solution.
(Review 1.3 for 11.2)

73. $17 = 3x + 5$ **74.** $18 = -7 + x$ **75.** $15 = -1 + 8x$

76. $9 = 4 - 5x$ **77.** $5 = 6 - 2x$ **78.** $24 = 10 + 7x$

FINDING EXPONENTIAL MODELS Use the table of values to draw a scatter plot of ln *y* versus *x*. Then find an exponential model for the data. (Review 8.7)

79.

x	1	2	3	4	5	6	7	8	9
y	5	10	20	40	80	160	320	640	1280

80.

x	1	2	3	4	5	6	7	8
y	3.2	9.6	28.8	86.4	259.2	777.6	2332.8	6998.4

FINDING THE DISTANCE Find the distance between the points. (Review 10.1)

81. $(0, 0), (-4, -6)$ **82.** $(1, 4), (-3, -9)$ **83.** $(5, 2), (-1, 8)$

84. $(9, -1), (2, 9)$ **85.** $(3, -3), (11, -4)$ **86.** $(10, 30), (40, -20)$

Working with Sequences

You can use a graphing calculator to find the terms of a sequence, graph a sequence, and find the sum of a series.

▶ **EXAMPLE**

Use a graphing calculator to perform the following.

- Find the first eight terms of the sequence $a_n = 3n - 1$.

- Graph the sequence.

- Find the sum of the first eight terms of the sequence.

▶ **SOLUTION**

1 Put the graphing calculator in *Sequence* mode and *Dot* mode. Enter the sequence. Note that the calculator uses $u(n)$ rather than a_n.

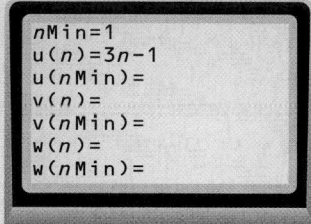

2 Use the *Table* feature to view the terms of the sequence. The first eight terms are 2, 5, 8, 11, 14, 17, 20, and 23.

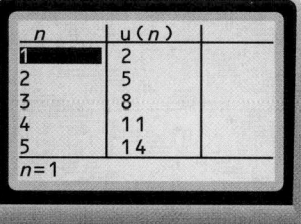

3 Set the viewing window so that $1 \leq n \leq 8$, $1 \leq x \leq 8$, and $0 \leq y \leq 25$. Graph the sequence. Use the *Trace* feature to view the terms of the sequence.

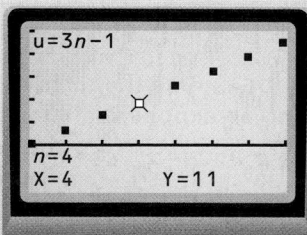

4 Use the *Summation* feature to find the sum of the first eight terms of the sequence. The screen shows that the sum is 100.

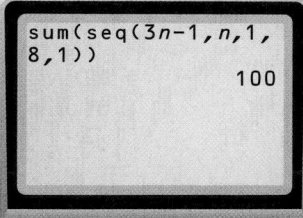

▶ **EXERCISES**

Use a graphing calculator to (a) find the first ten terms of the sequence, (b) graph the sequence, and (c) find the sum of the first ten terms of the sequence.

1. $a_n = 2n + 3$ **2.** $a_n = 4(n + 1)$ **3.** $a_n = 50 - 2n$

4. $a_n = 2^{n-1}$ **5.** $a_n = \left(\frac{1}{2}\right)^n$ **6.** $a_n = 2 + n^2$

7. $a_n = 3 \cdot 4^{n-2}$ **8.** $a_n = 10^n + 2$ **9.** $a_n = \frac{1}{3} + n^3$

11.2 Arithmetic Sequences and Series

What you should learn

GOAL 1 Write rules for arithmetic sequences and find sums of arithmetic series.

GOAL 2 Use arithmetic sequences and series in **real-life** problems, such as finding the number of cells in a honeycomb in **Ex. 57**.

Why you should learn it

▼ To solve **real-life** problems, such as finding the number of seats in a concert hall in **Example 7**.

GOAL 1 USING ARITHMETIC SEQUENCES AND SERIES

In an **arithmetic sequence**, the difference between consecutive terms is constant. The constant difference is called the **common difference** and is denoted by d.

EXAMPLE 1 Identifying Arithmetic Sequences

Decide whether each sequence is arithmetic.

a. $-3, 1, 5, 9, 13, \ldots$ **b.** $2, 5, 10, 17, 26, \ldots$

SOLUTION

To decide whether a sequence is arithmetic, find the differences of consecutive terms.

a. $a_2 - a_1 = 1 - (-3) = 4$ **b.** $a_2 - a_1 = 5 - 2 = 3$

$a_3 - a_2 = 5 - 1 = 4$ $a_3 - a_2 = 10 - 5 = 5$

$a_4 - a_3 = 9 - 5 = 4$ $a_4 - a_3 = 17 - 10 = 7$

$a_5 - a_4 = 13 - 9 = 4$ $a_5 - a_4 = 26 - 17 = 9$

Each difference is 4, so the sequence is arithmetic.

The differences are not constant, so the sequence is not arithmetic.

RULE FOR AN ARITHMETIC SEQUENCE

The nth term of an arithmetic sequence with first term a_1 and common difference d is given by:

$$a_n = a_1 + (n - 1)d$$

EXAMPLE 2 Writing a Rule for the nth Term

Write a rule for the nth term of the sequence $50, 44, 38, 32, \ldots$. Then find a_{20}.

SOLUTION

The sequence is arithmetic with first term $a_1 = 50$ and common difference $d = 44 - 50 = -6$. So, a rule for the nth term is:

$a_n = a_1 + (n - 1)d$ **Write general rule.**

$= 50 + (n - 1)(-6)$ **Substitute for a_1 and d.**

$= 56 - 6n$ **Simplify.**

The 20th term is $a_{20} = 56 - 6(20) = -64$.

EXAMPLE 3   *Finding the nth Term Given a Term and the Common Difference*

One term of an arithmetic sequence is $a_{13} = 30$. The common difference is $d = \frac{3}{2}$.

a. Write a rule for the nth term.   **b.** Graph the sequence.

SOLUTION

a. Begin by finding the first term as follows.

$a_n = a_1 + (n - 1)d$	**Write rule for *n*th term.**
$a_{13} = a_1 + (13 - 1)d$	**Substitute 13 for *n*.**
$30 = a_1 + 12\left(\dfrac{3}{2}\right)$	**Substitute for a_{13} and *d*.**
$12 = a_1$	**Solve for a_1.**

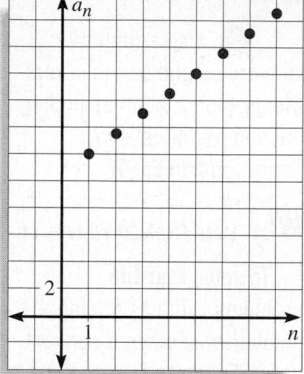

So, a rule for the nth term is:

$a_n = a_1 + (n - 1)d$	**Write general rule.**
$\quad = 12 + (n - 1)\dfrac{3}{2}$	**Substitute for a_1 and *d*.**
$\quad = \dfrac{21}{2} + \dfrac{3}{2}n$	**Simplify.**

b. The graph is shown at the right. Notice that the points lie on a line. This is true for *any* arithmetic sequence.

EXAMPLE 4   *Finding the nth Term Given Two Terms*

Two terms of an arithmetic sequence are $a_6 = 10$ and $a_{21} = 55$.

a. Find a rule for the nth term.   **b.** Find the value of n for which $a_n = 40$.

SOLUTION

a. *Write* a system of equations using $a_n = a_1 + (n - 1)d$ and substituting 21 for n (Equation 1) and then 6 for n (Equation 2).

$a_{21} = a_1 + (21 - 1)d$	$\longrightarrow \quad 55 = a_1 + 20d$	**Equation 1**
$a_6 = a_1 + (6 - 1)d$	$\longrightarrow \quad \underline{10 = a_1 + 5d}$	**Equation 2**
Solve the system.	$45 = 15d$	**Subtract equations.**
	$3 = d$	**Solve for *d*.**
	$55 = a_1 + 20(3)$	**Substitute for *d*.**
	$-5 = a_1$	**Solve for a_1.**

Find a rule for a_n.	$a_n = a_1 + (n - 1)d$	**Write general rule.**
	$a_n = -5 + (n - 1)3$	**Substitute for a_1 and *d*.**
	$a_n = -8 + 3n$	**Simplify.**

b.

$a_n = -8 + 3n$	**Use the rule for a_n from part (a).**
$40 = -8 + 3n$	**Substitute 40 for a_n.**
$16 = n$	**Solve for *n*.**

The expression formed by adding the terms of an arithmetic sequence is called an **arithmetic series**. The sum of the first n terms of an arithmetic series is denoted by S_n. To find a rule for S_n, you can write S_n in two different ways and add the results.

$$S_n = a_1 \qquad + (a_1 + d) \ + (a_1 + 2d) + \cdots + a_n$$
$$S_n = a_n \qquad + (a_n - d) \ + (a_n - 2d) + \cdots + a_1$$
$$\overline{2S_n = (a_1 + a_n) + (a_1 + a_n) + (a_1 + a_n) + \cdots + (a_1 + a_n)}$$

You can conclude that $2S_n = n(a_1 + a_n)$, which leads to the following result.

THE SUM OF A FINITE ARITHMETIC SERIES

The sum of the first n terms of an arithmetic series is:

$$S_n = n\left(\frac{a_1 + a_n}{2}\right)$$

In words, S_n is the mean of the first and nth terms, multiplied by the number of terms.

EXAMPLE 5   *Finding a Sum*

Consider the arithmetic series $4 + 7 + 10 + 13 + 16 + 19 + \cdots$.

a. Find the sum of the first 30 terms.   **b.** Find n such that $S_n = 175$.

SOLUTION

a. To begin, notice that $a_1 = 4$ and $d = 3$. So, a formula for the nth term is:

$$a_n = a_1 + (n - 1)d \qquad \text{Write rule for the } n\text{th term.}$$
$$= 4 + (n - 1)3 \qquad \text{Substitute for } a_1 \text{ and } d.$$
$$= 1 + 3n \qquad \text{Simplify.}$$

The 30th term is $a_{30} = 1 + 3(30) = 91$. So, the sum of the first 30 terms is:

$$S_{30} = 30\left(\frac{a_1 + a_{30}}{2}\right) \qquad \text{Write rule for } S_{30}.$$
$$= 30\left(\frac{4 + 91}{2}\right) \qquad \text{Substitute for } a_1 \text{ and } a_{30}.$$
$$= 1425 \qquad \text{Simplify.}$$

▶ The sum of the first 30 terms is 1425.

STUDENT HELP

Look Back
For help with quadratic equations, see p. 256.

b.
$$n\left(\frac{4 + (1 + 3n)}{2}\right) = 175 \qquad \text{Use rule for } S_n.$$
$$5n + 3n^2 = 350 \qquad \text{Multiply each side by 2.}$$
$$3n^2 + 5n - 350 = 0 \qquad \text{Write in standard form.}$$
$$(3n + 35)(n - 10) = 0 \qquad \text{Factor.}$$
$$n = 10 \qquad \text{Choose positive solution.}$$

▶ So, $S_n = 175$ when $n = 10$.

GOAL 2 **ARITHMETIC SEQUENCES AND SERIES IN REAL LIFE**

EXAMPLE 6 *Writing an Arithmetic Sequence*

SEATING CAPACITY The first row of a concert hall has 25 seats, and each row after the first has one more seat than the row before it. There are 32 rows of seats.

a. Write a rule for the number of seats in the nth row.

b. Thirty-five students from a class want to sit in the same row. How close to the front can they sit?

SOLUTION

a. Use $a_1 = 25$ and $d = 1$ to write a rule for a_n.

$$a_n = a_1 + (n - 1)d = 25 + (n - 1)(1) = 24 + n$$

b. Using the rule $a_n = 24 + n$, let $a_n = 35$ and solve for n.

$35 = 24 + n$ **Substitute for a_n.**

$11 = n$ **Solve for n.**

▶ The class can sit in the 11th row.

Seating Capacity

EXAMPLE 7 *Finding the Sum of an Arithmetic Series*

Use the information about the concert hall in Example 6.

a. What is the total number of seats in the concert hall?

b. Suppose 12 more rows of seats are built (where each row has one more seat than the row before it). How many additional seats will the concert hall have?

SOLUTION

a. Find the sum of an arithmetic series with $a_1 = 25$ and $a_{32} = 24 + 32 = 56$.

$$S_{32} = 32\left(\frac{a_1 + a_{32}}{2}\right)$$ **Write rule for S_{32}.**

$$= 32\left(\frac{25 + 56}{2}\right) = 1296$$ **Substitute for a_1 and a_{32}.**

▶ There are 1296 seats in the concert hall.

b. The expanded concert hall has $32 + 12 = 44$ rows of seats. Because $a_{44} = 24 + 44 = 68$, the *total* number of seats in the expanded hall is:

$$S_{44} = 44\left(\frac{a_1 + a_{44}}{2}\right)$$ **Write rule for S_{44}.**

$$= 44\left(\frac{25 + 68}{2}\right) = 2046$$ **Substitute for a_1 and a_{44}.**

▶ The number of *additional* seats is $S_{44} - S_{32} = 2046 - 1296 = 750$.

GUIDED PRACTICE

Vocabulary Check ✔

1. Complete this statement: The expression formed by adding the terms of an arithmetic sequence is called a(n) __?__.

Concept Check ✔

2. What is the difference between an arithmetic sequence and an arithmetic series?

3. Explain how to find the sum of the first n terms of an arithmetic series.

Skill Check ✔

Write a rule for the nth term of the arithmetic sequence.

4. $d = 2, a_1 = 5$
5. $d = -3, a_2 = 18$
6. $d = \frac{1}{2}, a_5 = 20$

7. $a_8 = 12, a_{15} = 61$
8. $a_5 = 10, a_{12} = 24$
9. $a_{10} = 8, a_{16} = 32$

Find the sum of the first 10 terms of the arithmetic series.

10. $2 + 6 + 10 + 14 + 18 + \cdots$
11. $3 + \frac{7}{2} + 4 + \frac{9}{2} + 5 + \cdots$

12. $6 + 3 + 0 + (-3) + (-6) + \cdots$
13. $0.7 + 1.9 + 3.1 + 4.3 + 5.5 + \cdots$

14. 🌐 **MOVIE THEATER** Suppose a movie theater has 42 rows of seats and there are 29 seats in the first row. Each row after the first has two more seats than the row before it. How many seats are in the theater?

PRACTICE AND APPLICATIONS

STUDENT HELP

→ **Extra Practice**
to help you master
skills is on p. 955.

IDENTIFYING ARITHMETIC SEQUENCES Decide whether the sequence is arithmetic. Explain why or why not.

15. $14, 11, 8, 5, 2, \ldots$
16. $1, 3, 9, 27, 81, \ldots$
17. $-5, -7, -11, -13, -15, \ldots$

18. $0.5, 1, 1.5, 2, 2.5, \ldots$
19. $\frac{1}{5}, \frac{2}{5}, \frac{4}{5}, \frac{8}{5}, \frac{16}{5}, \ldots$
20. $-\frac{5}{3}, -1, -\frac{1}{3}, \frac{1}{3}, 1, \ldots$

WRITING TERMS Write a rule for the nth term of the arithmetic sequence. Then find a_{25}.

21. $1, 3, 5, 7, 9, \ldots$
22. $6, 14, 22, 30, 38, \ldots$
23. $9, 23, 37, 51, 65, \ldots$

24. $-1, 0, 1, 2, 3, \ldots$
25. $4, 1, -2, -5, -8, \ldots$
26. $\frac{1}{2}, 3, \frac{11}{2}, 8, \frac{21}{2}, \ldots$

27. $\frac{11}{2}, \frac{25}{6}, \frac{17}{6}, \frac{3}{2}, \frac{1}{6}, \ldots$
28. $\frac{5}{2}, \frac{11}{6}, \frac{7}{6}, \frac{1}{2}, -\frac{1}{6}, \ldots$
29. $1.6, 4, 6.4, 8.8, 11.2, \ldots$

WRITING RULES Write a rule for the nth term of the arithmetic sequence.

30. $d = 4, a_{14} = 46$
31. $d = -12, a_1 = 80$
32. $d = \frac{5}{3}, a_8 = 24$

STUDENT HELP

→ **HOMEWORK HELP**
Example 1: Exs. 15–20
Example 2: Exs. 21–29
Example 3: Exs. 30–32, 34, 38–44
Example 4: Exs. 33, 35–37
Example 5: Exs. 45–56
Examples 6, 7: Exs. 57–60

33. $a_5 = 17, a_{15} = 77$
34. $d = -6, a_{12} = -4$
35. $a_2 = -28, a_{20} = 52$

36. $a_1 = -2, a_9 = -\frac{1}{6}$
37. $a_7 = 34, a_{18} = 122$
38. $d = -4.1, a_{16} = 48.2$

GRAPHING SEQUENCES Graph the arithmetic sequence.

39. $a_n = 7 + 2n$
40. $a_n = -3 + 5n$
41. $a_n = 5 - 2n$

42. $a_n = 2 - \frac{1}{3}n$
43. $a_n = 4 - \frac{1}{2}n$
44. $a_n = -0.25 + 0.45n$

FINDING SUMS For part (a), find the sum of the first *n* terms of the arithmetic series. For part (b), find *n* for the given sum S_n.

45. $3 + 8 + 13 + 18 + 23 + \cdots$

   a. $n = 20$ **b.** $S_n = 366$

46. $50 + 42 + 34 + 26 + 18 + \cdots$

   a. $n = 40$ **b.** $S_n = 182$

47. $-10 + (-5) + 0 + 5 + 10 + \cdots$

   a. $n = 19$ **b.** $S_n = 375$

48. $34 + 31 + 28 + 25 + 22 + \cdots$

   a. $n = 32$ **b.** $S_n = -12$

49. $2 + 9 + 16 + 23 + 30 + \cdots$

   a. $n = 68$ **b.** $S_n = 1661$

50. $2 + 16 + 30 + 44 + 58 + \cdots$

   a. $n = 24$ **b.** $S_n = 2178$

USING SUMMATION NOTATION Find the sum of the series.

51. $\displaystyle\sum_{i=1}^{20} (3 + 5i)$

52. $\displaystyle\sum_{i=1}^{34} (1 + 8i)$

53. $\displaystyle\sum_{i=1}^{15} (-10 - 3i)$

54. $\displaystyle\sum_{i=1}^{22} \left(6 - \frac{3}{4}i\right)$

55. $\displaystyle\sum_{i=1}^{45} (11 + 4i)$

56. $\displaystyle\sum_{i=1}^{18} (8.1 + 4.4i)$

57. 🌐 **HONEYCOMBS** Domestic bees make their honeycomb by starting with a single hexagonal cell, then forming ring after ring of hexagonal cells around the initial cell, as shown. The numbers of cells in successive rings form an arithmetic sequence.

▶ Source: USDA's Carl Hayden Bee Research Lab

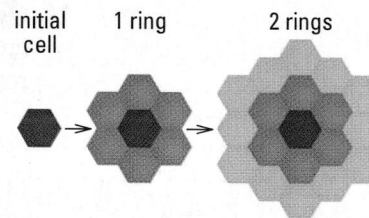

initial cell   1 ring   2 rings

   a. Write a rule for the number of cells in the *n*th ring.

   b. What is the total number of cells in the honeycomb after the 9th ring is formed? (*Hint:* Do not forget to count the initial cell.)

58. 🌐 **STACKING LOGS** Logs are stacked in a pile, as shown at the right. The bottom row has 21 logs and the top row has 15 logs. Each row has one less log than the row below it. How many logs are in the pile?

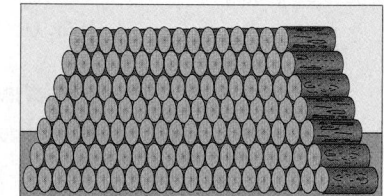

59. 🌐 **QUILTING** A quilt is made up of strips of cloth, starting with an inner square surrounded by rectangles to form successively larger squares. The inner square and all rectangles have a width of 1 foot. Write an expression using summation notation that gives the sum of the areas of all the strips of cloth used to make the quilt shown. Then evaluate the expression.

60. 🌐 **SEATING REVENUE** Suppose each seat in rows 1 through 11 of the concert hall in Example 6 costs $24, each seat in rows 12 through 22 costs $18, and each seat in rows 23 through 32 costs $12. How much money does the concert hall take in for a sold-out event?

61. *Writing* Compare the graphs of $a_n = 2n + 1$ where *n* is a positive integer and $f(x) = 2x + 1$ where *x* is a real number. Discuss how the graph of an arithmetic sequence is similar to and different from the graph of a linear function.

62. MULTI-STEP PROBLEM A paper manufacturer sells paper rolled onto cardboard dowels. The thickness of the paper is 0.004 inch. The diameter of a dowel is 3 inches, and the total diameter of a roll is 7 inches.

n	d_n (in.)	l_n (in.)
1	3	3π
2	?	?
3	?	?
4	?	?

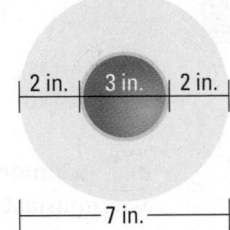

2 in. | 3 in. | 2 in.

7 in.

a. Let n be the number of times the paper is wrapped around the dowel, let d_n be the diameter of the roll just before the nth wrap, and let l_n be the length of paper added in the nth wrap. Copy and complete the table.

b. What can you say about the sequence $l_1, l_2, l_3, l_4, \ldots$? Write a formula for the nth term of the sequence.

c. Find the number of times the paper must be wrapped around the dowel to create a roll with a 7 inch diameter. Use your answer and the formula from part (b) to find the length of paper in a roll with a 7 inch diameter.

d. LOGICAL REASONING Suppose a roll with a 7 inch diameter costs $15. How much would you expect to pay for a roll with an 11 inch diameter whose dowel also has a diameter of 3 inches? Explain your reasoning and any assumptions you make.

 **Challenge**

63. AHMES PAPYRUS One of the major sources of our knowledge of Egyptian mathematics is the Ahmes papyrus (also known as the Rhind papyrus), which is a scroll copied in 1650 B.C. by an Egyptian scribe. The following problem is from the Ahmes papyrus.

Divide 10 hekats of barley among 10 men so that the common difference is $\frac{1}{8}$ of a hekat of barley.

Use what you know about arithmetic sequences and series to solve the problem.

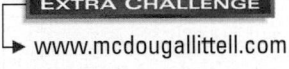
EXTRA CHALLENGE
www.mcdougallittell.com

MIXED REVIEW

SOLVING RATIONAL EXPONENT EQUATIONS Solve the equation.
(Review 7.6 for 11.3)

64. $x^{1/2} = 5$ **65.** $2x^{3/4} = 54$ **66.** $x^{2/3} + 10 = 19$

67. $(8x)^{1/2} + 6 = 0$ **68.** $x^{1/3} - 11 = 0$ **69.** $(2x)^{1/2} = x - 4$

SOLVING EXPONENTIAL EQUATIONS Solve the exponential equation.
(Review 8.6 for 11.3)

70. $2^x = 4.5$ **71.** $4^x - 3 = 5$ **72.** $10^{3x} + 7 = 15$

73. $6^x - 5 = 1$ **74.** $25^x - 28 = 97$ **75.** $5(2)^{2x} - 4 = 13$

GRAPHING EQUATIONS Graph the equation. **(Review 10.3)**

76. $x^2 + y^2 = 9$ **77.** $x^2 + y^2 = 24$ **78.** $x^2 + y^2 = 64$

79. $6x^2 + 6y^2 = 150$ **80.** $\frac{1}{2}x^2 + \frac{1}{2}y^2 = 4$ **81.** $20x^2 + 20y^2 = 400$

11.3 Geometric Sequences and Series

What you should learn

GOAL 1 Write rules for geometric sequences and find sums of geometric series.

GOAL 2 Use geometric sequences and series to model **real-life** quantities, such as monthly bills for cellular telephone service in **Example 6**.

Why you should learn it

▼ To solve **real-life** problems, such as finding the number of tennis matches played in **Exs. 70 and 71**.

GOAL 1 USING GEOMETRIC SEQUENCES AND SERIES

In a **geometric sequence**, the ratio of any term to the previous term is constant. This constant ratio is called the **common ratio** and is denoted by r.

EXAMPLE 1 Identifying Geometric Sequences

Decide whether each sequence is geometric.

a. 1, 2, 6, 24, 120, . . .   **b.** 81, 27, 9, 3, 1, . . .

SOLUTION

To decide whether a sequence is geometric, find the ratios of consecutive terms.

a. $\dfrac{a_2}{a_1} = \dfrac{2}{1} = 2$ $\dfrac{a_3}{a_2} = \dfrac{6}{2} = 3$ $\dfrac{a_4}{a_3} = \dfrac{24}{6} = 4$ $\dfrac{a_5}{a_4} = \dfrac{120}{24} = 5$

▶ The ratios are different, so the sequence is not geometric.

b. $\dfrac{a_2}{a_1} = \dfrac{27}{81} = \dfrac{1}{3}$ $\dfrac{a_3}{a_2} = \dfrac{9}{27} = \dfrac{1}{3}$ $\dfrac{a_4}{a_3} = \dfrac{3}{9} = \dfrac{1}{3}$ $\dfrac{a_5}{a_4} = \dfrac{1}{3}$

▶ The ratios are the same, so the sequence is geometric.

RULE FOR A GEOMETRIC SEQUENCE

The nth term of a geometric sequence with first term a_1 and common ratio r is given by:

$$a_n = a_1 r^{n-1}$$

EXAMPLE 2 Writing a Rule for the nth Term

Write a rule for the nth term of the sequence $-8, -12, -18, -27, \ldots$. Then find a_8.

SOLUTION

The sequence is geometric with first term $a_1 = -8$ and common ratio $r = \dfrac{-12}{-8} = \dfrac{3}{2}$. So, a rule for the nth term is:

$a_n = a_1 r^{n-1}$ **Write general rule.**

$= -8\left(\dfrac{3}{2}\right)^{n-1}$ **Substitute for a_1 and r.**

The 8th term is $a_8 = -8\left(\dfrac{3}{2}\right)^{8-1} = -\dfrac{2187}{16}$.

EXAMPLE 3 **Finding the nth Term Given a Term and the Common Ratio**

One term of a geometric sequence is $a_3 = 5$. The common ratio is $r = 2$.

  a. Write a rule for the nth term.   **b.** Graph the sequence.

SOLUTION

  a. Begin by finding the first term as follows.

$$a_n = a_1 r^{n-1}$$ **Write general rule.**

$$a_3 = a_1 r^{3-1}$$ **Substitute 3 for n.**

$$5 = a_1 (2)^2$$ **Substitute for a_3 and r.**

$$1.25 = a_1$$ **Solve for a_1.**

So, a rule for the nth term is:

$$a_n = a_1 r^{n-1}$$ **Write general rule.**

$$= 1.25(2)^{n-1}$$ **Substitute for a_1 and r.**

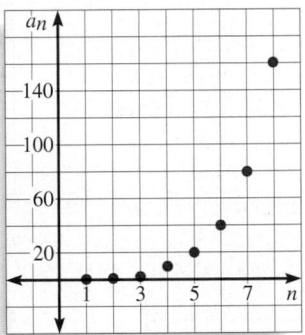

  b. The graph is shown at the right. Notice that the points lie on an exponential curve. This is true for *any* geometric sequence with $r > 0$.

EXAMPLE 4 **Finding the nth Term Given Two Terms**

Two terms of a geometric sequence are $a_2 = 45$ and $a_5 = -1215$. Find a rule for the nth term.

SOLUTION

Write a system of equations using $a_n = a_1 r^{n-1}$ and substituting 2 for n (Equation 1) and then 5 for n (Equation 2).

$$a_2 = a_1 r^{2-1} \longrightarrow 45 = a_1 r$$ **Equation 1**

$$a_5 = a_1 r^{5-1} \longrightarrow -1215 = a_1 r^4$$ **Equation 2**

Solve the system. $$\frac{45}{r} = a_1$$ **Solve Equation 1 for a_1.**

$$-1215 = \frac{45}{r}(r^4)$$ **Substitute for a_1 in Equation 2.**

$$-1215 = 45r^3$$ **Simplify.**

$$-27 = r^3$$ **Divide each side by 45.**

$$-3 = r$$ **Take the cube root of each side.**

$$45 = a_1(-3)$$ **Substitute for r in Equation 1.**

$$-15 = a_1$$ **Solve for a_1.**

Find a rule for a_n. $$a_n = a_1 r^{n-1}$$ **Write general rule.**

$$a_n = -15(-3)^{n-1}$$ **Substitute for a_1 and r.**

▶ A rule for the nth term is $a_n = -15(-3)^{n-1}$.

The expression formed by adding the terms of a geometric sequence is called a **geometric series**. As with an arithmetic series, the sum of the first n terms of a geometric series is denoted by S_n. You can develop a rule for S_n as follows.

$$
\begin{array}{l}
S_n = a_1 + a_1 r + a_1 r^2 + a_1 r^3 + \cdots + a_1 r^{n-1} \\
\underline{-rS_n = \quad\quad - a_1 r - a_1 r^2 - a_1 r^3 - \cdots - a_1 r^{n-1} - a_1 r^n} \\
S_n(1 - r) = a_1 \quad\quad\quad\quad\quad\quad\quad\quad\quad\quad\quad\quad\quad\quad - a_1 r^n
\end{array}
$$

Therefore, $S_n(1 - r) = a_1(1 - r^n)$. If $r \neq 1$, you can divide both sides of this equation by $1 - r$ to obtain the following rule for S_n.

THE SUM OF A FINITE GEOMETRIC SERIES

The sum S_n of the first n terms of a geometric series with common ratio $r \neq 1$ is:

$$S_n = a_1\left(\frac{1 - r^n}{1 - r}\right)$$

EXAMPLE 5 *Finding a Sum*

STUDENT HELP

HOMEWORK HELP
Visit our Web site
www.mcdougallittell.com
for extra examples.

Consider the geometric series $1 + 5 + 25 + 125 + 625 + \cdots$.

a. Find the sum of the first 10 terms.   **b.** Find n such that $S_n = 3906$.

SOLUTION

a. To begin, notice that $a_1 = 1$ and $r = 5$. Therefore:

$$S_{10} = a_1\left(\frac{1 - r^{10}}{1 - r}\right) \quad\quad \textbf{Write rule for } \boldsymbol{S_{10}}.$$

$$= 1\left(\frac{1 - 5^{10}}{1 - 5}\right) \quad\quad \textbf{Substitute for } \boldsymbol{a_1} \textbf{ and } \boldsymbol{r}.$$

$$= 2{,}441{,}406 \quad\quad \textbf{Simplify.}$$

▶ The sum of the first 10 terms is 2,441,406.

b. $a_1\left(\dfrac{1 - r^n}{1 - r}\right) = S_n \quad\quad \textbf{Write general rule.}$

$1\left(\dfrac{1 - 5^n}{1 - 5}\right) = 3906 \quad\quad \textbf{Substitute for } \boldsymbol{a_1}, \boldsymbol{r}, \textbf{ and } \boldsymbol{S_n}.$

$\dfrac{1 - 5^n}{-4} = 3906 \quad\quad \textbf{Simplify.}$

$1 - 5^n = -15{,}624 \quad\quad \textbf{Multiply each side by } \boldsymbol{-4}.$

$-5^n = -15{,}625 \quad\quad \textbf{Subtract 1 from each side.}$

$5^n = 15{,}625 \quad\quad \textbf{Divide each side by } \boldsymbol{-1}.$

$n = \dfrac{\log 15{,}625}{\log 5} = 6 \quad\quad \textbf{Solve for } \boldsymbol{n}.$

STUDENT HELP

▶ **Look Back**
For help with logarithmic equations, see p. 501.

▶ So, $S_n = 3906$ when $n = 6$.

GOAL 2 GEOMETRIC SEQUENCES AND SERIES IN REAL LIFE

EXAMPLE 6 *Writing a Geometric Sequence*

CELLULAR TELEPHONES In 1990 the average monthly bill for cellular telephone service in the United States was $80.90. From 1990 through 1997, the average monthly bill decreased by about 8.6% per year. ▶ Source: *Statistical Abstract of the United States*

a. Write a rule for the average monthly cellular telephone bill a_n (in dollars) in terms of the year. Let $n = 1$ represent 1990.

b. What was the average monthly cellular telephone bill in 1993?

c. When did the average monthly cellular telephone bill fall to $50?

SOLUTION

a. Because the average monthly bill decreased by the same percent each year, the average monthly bills from year to year form a geometric sequence. Use $a_1 = 80.9$ and $r = 1 - 0.086 = 0.914$. A rule for the average monthly bill is:

$$a_n = 80.9(0.914)^{n-1}$$

b. In 1993, $n = 4$. So, the average monthly bill was $a_4 = 80.9(0.914)^3 \approx \$61.77$.

c. You want to find n such that $a_n = 50$.

$80.9(0.914)^{n-1} = 50$	**Write equation using rule for a_n.**
$(0.914)^{n-1} \approx 0.618$	**Divide each side by 80.9.**
$n - 1 \approx \dfrac{\log 0.618}{\log 0.914} \approx 5.35$	**Solve for $n - 1$.**
$n \approx 6$	**Solve for n.**

The average monthly cellular telephone bill reached $50 in 1995 (when $n = 6$).

EXAMPLE 7 *Finding the Sum of a Geometric Series*

Cellular Phones

Use the model for the average monthly cellular telephone bill in Example 6. On average, what did a person pay for cellular telephone service during 1990–1997?

SOLUTION

Because the model $a_n = 80.9(0.914)^{n-1}$ gives the average *monthly* bill, the model $b_n = 12(80.9)(0.914)^{n-1} = 970.8(0.914)^{n-1}$ gives the average *annual* bill. Using $a_1 = 970.8$ and $r = 0.914$, you can estimate a person's total cost for cellular telephone service during the 8 year period 1990–1997 to be:

$S_8 = a_1\left(\dfrac{1 - r^8}{1 - r}\right)$	**Write rule for S_8.**
$= 970.8\left(\dfrac{1 - (0.914)^8}{1 - 0.914}\right)$	**Substitute for a_1 and r.**
≈ 5790	**Simplify.**

▶ A person paid about $5790 for cellular telephone service during 1990–1997.

**CELLULAR
TELEPHONES**
In 1990 there were about 5 million cellular phone subscribers. By 1997 the number had grown to over 55 million.

APPLICATION LINK
www.mcdougallittell.com

STUDENT HELP

DATA UPDATE
Visit our Web site
www.mcdougallittell.com

GUIDED PRACTICE

Vocabulary Check ✓

1. Complete this statement: The constant ratio in a geometric sequence is called the
   _?_ ratio and is denoted by _?_ .

Concept Check ✓

2. What makes a sequence geometric?

3. State the rule for the sum of the first n terms of a geometric series.

Skill Check ✓

Find the common ratio of the geometric sequence.

4. 4, 12, 36, 108, 324, . . .   5. 1, 6, 36, 216, 1296, . . .   6. 2, −6, 18, −54, 162, . . .

7. 7, 14, 28, 56, 128, . . .   8. 64, −32, 16, −8, 4, . . .   9. $10, 5, \frac{5}{2}, \frac{5}{4}, \frac{5}{8}, \ldots$

Write the next term and find a rule for the nth term of the geometric sequence.

10. 1, 3, 9, 27, . . .   11. 2, 8, 32, 128, . . .   12. 1, −6, 36, −216, . . .

13. 375, −75, 15, −3, . . .   14. $\frac{1}{2}, \frac{1}{4}, \frac{1}{8}, \frac{1}{16}, \ldots$ 15. $-28, 14, -7, \frac{7}{2}, -\frac{7}{4}, \ldots$

Write a rule for the nth term of the geometric sequence.

16. $r = 3, a_1 = 2$ 17. $r = -2, a_1 = 6$ 18. $r = -3, a_1 = 12$

19. $a_1 = \frac{1}{4}, a_3 = 6$ 20. $a_2 = 5, a_4 = \frac{1}{5}$ 21. $a_2 = 28, a_5 = -1792$

22. Find the sum of the first 8 terms of the geometric series $1 + 8 + 64 + 512 + \cdots$.

23. 🌐 **CELLULAR PHONES** Use the model from Example 6 to find the average
    monthly bill for cellular telephone service in 1997.

PRACTICE AND APPLICATIONS

STUDENT HELP

▶ **Extra Practice**
to help you master
skills is on p. 955.

CLASSIFYING SEQUENCES Decide whether the sequence is *arithmetic*,
geometric, or *neither*. Explain your answer.

24. 6, 24, 96, 384, . . .   25. 1, 3, 7, 13, . . .   26. 4, 13, 22, 31, . . .

27. 3, −1, −5, −9, . . .   28. −11, −7, −3, 1, . . .   29. $\frac{1}{2}, \frac{3}{2}, \frac{9}{2}, \frac{27}{2}, \ldots$

30. $\frac{1}{3}, \frac{2}{3}, 1, \frac{4}{3}, \ldots$ 31. $-\frac{3}{4}, \frac{1}{8}, -\frac{1}{16}, \frac{3}{32}, \ldots$ 32. $-\frac{3}{5}, \frac{4}{25}, \frac{5}{125}, \frac{6}{625}, \ldots$

FINDING COMMON RATIOS Find the common ratio of the geometric sequence.

STUDENT HELP

▶ **HOMEWORK HELP**
Example 1: Exs. 24–32
Example 2: Exs. 33–44
Example 3: Exs. 45–49,
   54–59
Example 4: Exs. 50–53
Example 5: Exs. 60–69
Examples 6, 7: Exs. 70–79

33. 1, 4, 16, 64, . . .   34. 3, 6, 12, 24, . . .   35. −3, 6, −12, 24, . . .

36. 5, 40, 320, 2560, . . .   37. 136, 68, 34, 17, . . .   38. $-\frac{1}{4}, \frac{1}{8}, -\frac{1}{16}, \frac{1}{32}, \ldots$

WRITING TERMS Write a rule for the nth term of the geometric sequence.
Then find a_6.

39. 1, −4, 16, −64, . . .   40. 5, 10, 20, 40, . . .   41. 2, 14, 98, 686, . . .

42. 6, −30, 150, −750, . . .   43. $5, -\frac{5}{3}, \frac{5}{9}, -\frac{5}{27}, \ldots$ 44. $2, \frac{4}{3}, \frac{8}{9}, \frac{16}{27}, \ldots$

WRITING RULES Write a rule for the *n*th term of the geometric sequence.

45. $r = 3$, $a_1 = 4$

46. $r = \frac{1}{3}$, $a_1 = 45$

47. $r = 6$, $a_3 = 72$

48. $r = \frac{1}{8}$, $a_1 = 4$

49. $r = 8$, $a_1 = -2$

50. $a_1 = -\frac{1}{2}$, $a_4 = -16$

51. $a_3 = 10$, $a_6 = 300$

52. $a_2 = -20$, $a_4 = -5$

53. $a_2 = -30$, $a_5 = 3750$

GRAPHING SEQUENCES Graph the geometric sequence.

54. $a_n = 4(2)^{n-1}$

55. $a_n = 3(5)^{n-1}$

56. $a_n = 2(3)^{n-1}$

57. $a_n = 8(3)^{n-1}$

58. $a_n = 5\left(\frac{1}{2}\right)^{n-1}$

59. $a_n = 4\left(\frac{3}{2}\right)^{n-1}$

FINDING SUMS For part (a), find the sum of the first *n* terms of the geometric series. For part (b), find *n* for the given sum S_n.

60. $1 + 4 + 16 + 64 + \cdots$
    a. $n = 14$ **b.** $S_n = 341$

61. $1 + 9 + 81 + 729 + \cdots$
    a. $n = 10$ **b.** $S_n = 820$

62. $7 + (-21) + 63 + (-189) + \cdots$
    a. $n = 18$ **b.** $S_n = 3829$

63. $-90 + 30 + (-10) + \frac{10}{3} + \cdots$
    a. $n = 16$ **b.** $S_n = -66.67$

USING SUMMATION NOTATION Find the sum of the series.

64. $\sum_{i=1}^{10} 6(2)^{i-1}$

65. $\sum_{i=1}^{8} 5(4)^{i-1}$

66. $\sum_{i=0}^{9} 12\left(-\frac{1}{2}\right)^{i}$

67. $\sum_{i=1}^{10} 8\left(\frac{3}{4}\right)^{i-1}$

68. $\sum_{i=0}^{6} 4\left(\frac{3}{2}\right)^{i}$

69. $\sum_{i=1}^{12} (-2)^{i-1}$

TENNIS In Exercises 70 and 71, use the following information.
The men's U.S. Open tennis tournament is held annually in Flushing Meadow in New York City. In the first round of the tournament, 64 matches are played. In each successive round, the number of matches played decreases by one half.
▶ Source: United States Tennis Association

70. Find a rule for the number of matches played in the *n*th round. For what values of *n* does your rule make sense?

71. Find the total number of matches played in the men's U.S. Open tennis tournament.

COMPUTER SCIENCE In Exercises 72 and 73, use the following information.
When a computer must find an item in an ordered list of data (such as an alphabetical list of names), it may be programmed to perform a *binary search*. This search technique involves jumping to the middle of the list and deciding whether the item is there. If not, the computer decides whether the item comes before or after the middle. Half of the list is then ignored on the next pass through the list, and the computer jumps to the middle of the remaining list. This is repeated until the item is found.

72. An ordered list contains 1024 items. Find a rule for the number of items remaining after the *n*th pass through the list.

73. In the worst case, the item to be found is the only one left in the list after *n* passes through the list. What is the worst-case value of *n* for a binary search of a list with 1024 items?

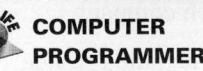

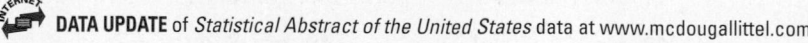 **PAGER SALES** In Exercises 74–77, use the following information.

In 1990 factory sales of pagers in the United States totaled $118 million. From 1990 through 1996, the sales increased by about 20% per year.

DATA UPDATE of *Statistical Abstract of the United States* data at www.mcdougallittel.com.

74. Write a rule for pager sales a_n (in millions of dollars) in terms of the year. Let $n = 1$ represent 1990.

75. What did factory sales of pagers total in 1992?

76. When did factory sales of pagers reach $300 million?

77. What was the total of factory sales of pagers for the period 1990–1996?

SIERPINSKI TRIANGLE In Exercises 78 and 79, use the following information.

The *Sierpinski triangle* is a design using equilateral triangles. The process involves removing smaller triangles from larger triangles by joining the midpoints of the sides of the larger triangles as shown below. Assume that the initial triangle is equilateral with sides 1 unit long.

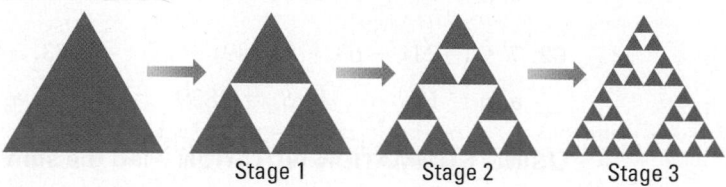

Stage 1   Stage 2   Stage 3

78. Let a_n be the number of triangles removed at the nth stage. Find a rule for a_n. Then find the total number of triangles removed through the 10th stage.

79. Let b_n be the remaining area of the original triangle at the nth stage. Find a rule for b_n. Then find the remaining area of the original triangle at the 15th stage.

80. *Writing* Compare the graphs of $a_n = 4(2)^{n-1}$ where n is a positive integer and $f(x) = 4(2)^{x-1}$ where x is a real number. Discuss how the graph of a geometric sequence with $r > 0$ is similar to and different from the graph of an exponential function.

Test Preparation

81. **MULTI-STEP PROBLEM** Suppose two computer companies, Company A and Company B, opened in 1991. The revenues of Company A increased arithmetically through 2000, while the revenues of Company B increased geometrically through 2000. In 1996 the revenue of Company A was $523.7 million. In 1996 the revenue of Company B was $65.6 million.

a. The revenues of Company A have a common difference of 55.5. The revenues of Company B have a common ratio of 2. Find a rule for the revenues in the nth year of each company. Let a_1 represent 1991.

b. Graph each sequence from part (a).

c. Find the sum of the revenues from 1991 through 2000 for each company.

d. *Writing* Use a graphing calculator or spreadsheet to find when the revenue of Company B is greater than the revenue of Company A. Write a brief paragraph explaining which company you would rather own. Be sure to refer to your graphs from part (b).

★ **Challenge**

82. **WORKING WITH FRACTIONS** Using the rule for the sum of the first n terms of a geometric series, write the polynomial as a rational expression.

a. $1 + x + x^2 + x^3 + x^4$ **b.** $3x + 6x^3 + 12x^5 + 24x^7$

MIXED REVIEW

ORDERING NUMBERS Plot the numbers on a number line. Write the numbers in increasing order. **(Review 1.1 for 11.4)**

83. $\frac{3}{2}, \frac{2}{5}, \frac{7}{6}, 1, \frac{6}{7}$

84. $\sqrt{5}, 2, -\frac{1}{5}, 0, 3$

85. $-\frac{5}{2}, -1, 1.5, -3.2, -2$

SOLVING ALGEBRAICALLY Solve the inequality algebraically. **(Review 5.7)**

86. $x^2 + x - 2 \geq 0$

87. $x^2 - 6x - 7 \leq 0$

88. $x^2 < 36$

89. $-x^2 - 8x < 20$

90. $3x^2 - 9x + 6 > 0$

91. $\frac{1}{2}x^2 + 5x \leq -12$

SOLVING EQUATIONS Solve using any method. Check each solution. **(Review 9.6 for 11.4)**

92. $\frac{3}{1+x} = 8$

93. $\frac{4}{1-x} = 10$

94. $\frac{-12}{x+4} = -x$

95. $-\frac{24}{x} - x = 11$

96. $\frac{x}{x-8} = \frac{x}{24}$

97. $x + 10 = \frac{x^2}{x-5}$

QUIZ 1

Self-Test for Lessons 11.1–11.3

Write the next term in the sequence. Then write a rule for the nth term. **(Lesson 11.1)**

1. $0, 2, 4, 6, \ldots$

2. $3, 9, 27, 81, \ldots$

3. $\frac{1}{5}, -\frac{1}{10}, \frac{1}{20}, -\frac{1}{40}, \ldots$

Find the sum of the series. **(Lesson 11.1)**

4. $\sum_{k=0}^{4} k^4$

5. $\sum_{m=1}^{6} (m^2 + 5)$

6. $\sum_{n=1}^{5} (n^3 - 1)$

Write a rule for the nth term of the arithmetic sequence. Then find a_{12}. **(Lesson 11.2)**

7. $1, 5, 9, 13, \ldots$

8. $34, 25, 16, 7, -2, \ldots$

9. $\frac{1}{2}, 1, \frac{3}{2}, 2, \ldots$

10. Find the sum of the first 30 terms of the arithmetic series $1.4 + 2.9 + 4.4 + 5.9 + 7.4 + \cdots$. **(Lesson 11.2)**

Write a rule for the nth term of the geometric sequence. Then find a_{15}. **(Lesson 11.3)**

11. $2, 10, 50, 250, \ldots$

12. $-3, 12, -48, 192, \ldots$

13. $12, 4, \frac{4}{3}, \frac{4}{9}, \ldots$

14. **FAMILY TREE** A portion of John's parental family tree is shown at the right. Find a rule for the number of people in the nth generation. If 10 generations of his family have lived in this country, how many people is this? **(Lesson 11.3)**

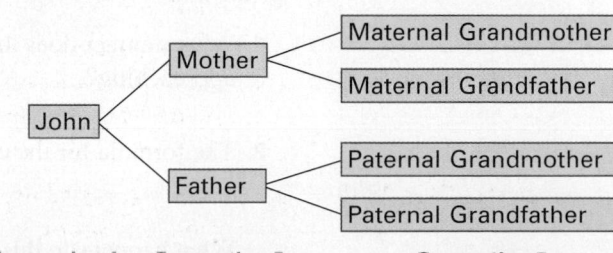

Generation 1   Generation 2   Generation 3

▶ ACTIVITY 11.4

Developing Concepts

Investigating an Infinite Geometric Series

GROUP ACTIVITY
Work in a small group.

MATERIALS
• scissors
• piece of paper

▶ **QUESTION** What is the sum of an infinite geometric series?

▶ **EXPLORING THE CONCEPT**

You can illustrate an infinite geometric series by cutting a piece of paper into smaller and smaller pieces. Start with a square piece of paper. Define the area of the paper to be 1 square unit.

1 Fold the paper in half and cut along the fold. Place one half on a desktop and hold the remaining half.

2 Fold the piece of paper you are holding in half and cut along the fold. Place one half on the desktop and hold the remaining half.

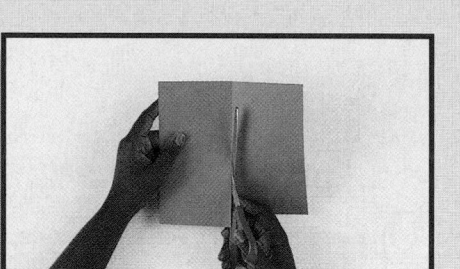

3 Repeat **Steps 1 and 2** until you find it too difficult to fold and cut the piece of paper you are holding.

4 The first piece of paper you placed on the desktop has an area of $\frac{1}{2}$ square unit. The second piece of paper has an area of $\frac{1}{4}$ square unit. Write the areas of the next three pieces of paper. Explain why these areas form a geometric sequence.

5 Copy and complete the table by recording the number of pieces of paper on the desktop and the combined area of the pieces at each step.

Number of pieces on desktop	1	2	3	4	5	...
Combined area of pieces	$\frac{1}{2}$	$\frac{1}{2} + \frac{1}{4} = ?$	?	?	?	...

▶ **DRAWING CONCLUSIONS**

1. What number does the combined area of the pieces of paper appear to be approaching?

2. The formula for the combined area after n cuts is $A_n = \frac{1}{2}\left(\dfrac{1 - \left(\frac{1}{2}\right)^n}{1 - \frac{1}{2}} \right)$.

   What happens to this formula as $n \to \infty$? (*Hint:* The only term with n in it, $\left(\frac{1}{2}\right)^n$, approaches 0 as $n \to \infty$.)

11.4

Infinite Geometric Series

What you should learn

GOAL 1 Find sums of infinite geometric series.

GOAL 2 Use infinite geometric series as models of **real-life** situations, such as the distance traveled by a bouncing ball in **Example 4**.

Why you should learn it

▼ To solve **real-life** problems, such as finding the spending generated by tourists in Malaysia in **Exs. 50 and 51**.

GOAL 1 USING INFINITE GEOMETRIC SERIES

Consider the following infinite geometric series:

$$\frac{1}{2} + \frac{1}{4} + \frac{1}{8} + \frac{1}{16} + \frac{1}{32} + \cdots$$

Even though this series has infinitely many terms, it has a finite sum! To see this, compute and graph the sum of the first n terms for several values of n.

$$S_1 = \frac{1}{2} = 0.5$$

$$S_2 = \frac{1}{2} + \frac{1}{4} = 0.75$$

$$S_3 = \frac{1}{2} + \frac{1}{4} + \frac{1}{8} \approx 0.88$$

$$S_4 = \frac{1}{2} + \frac{1}{4} + \frac{1}{8} + \frac{1}{16} \approx 0.94$$

$$S_5 = \frac{1}{2} + \frac{1}{4} + \frac{1}{8} + \frac{1}{16} + \frac{1}{32} \approx 0.97$$

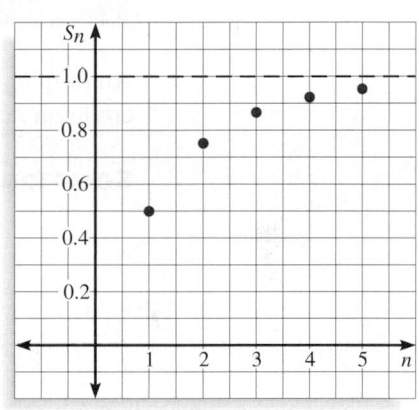

Notice that S_n appears to be approaching 1 as n increases. To see why this makes sense, consider the rule for S_n:

$$S_n = a_1\left(\frac{1 - r^n}{1 - r}\right) = \frac{1}{2}\left(\frac{1 - \left(\frac{1}{2}\right)^n}{1 - \frac{1}{2}}\right) = 1 - \left(\frac{1}{2}\right)^n$$

As n increases, $\left(\frac{1}{2}\right)^n$ gets closer and closer to 0, which means that S_n gets closer and closer to 1. The same is true for r^n provided r is between -1 and 1. Therefore, the formula for the sum of a *finite* geometric series, $S_n = a_1\left(\frac{1 - r^n}{1 - r}\right)$, approaches the formula below as n increases.

THE SUM OF AN INFINITE GEOMETRIC SERIES

The sum of an infinite geometric series with first term a_1 and common ratio r is given by

$$S = \frac{a_1}{1 - r}$$

provided $|r| < 1$. If $|r| \geq 1$, the series has no sum.

For the series described above, the sum is $S = \dfrac{\frac{1}{2}}{1 - \frac{1}{2}} = 1$, as expected.

EXAMPLE 1 *Finding Sums of Infinite Geometric Series*

Find the sum of the infinite geometric series.

a. $\displaystyle\sum_{i=1}^{\infty} 3(0.7)^{i-1}$

b. $1 - \dfrac{1}{4} + \dfrac{1}{16} - \dfrac{1}{64} + \cdots$

SOLUTION

a. For this series, $a_1 = 3$ and $r = 0.7$.

$$S = \frac{a_1}{1-r} = \frac{3}{1-0.7} = 10$$

b. For this series, $a_1 = 1$ and $r = -\dfrac{1}{4}$.

$$S = \frac{a_1}{1-r} = \frac{1}{1-\left(-\frac{1}{4}\right)} = \frac{4}{5}$$

EXAMPLE 2 *Finding the Common Ratio*

An infinite geometric series with first term $a_1 = 4$ has a sum of 10. What is the common ratio of the series?

SOLUTION

$$S = \frac{a_1}{1-r} \qquad \text{Write rule for sum.}$$

$$10 = \frac{4}{1-r} \qquad \text{Substitute for } S \text{ and } a_1.$$

$$10(1-r) = 4 \qquad \text{Multiply each side by } 1-r.$$

$$1 - r = \frac{2}{5} \qquad \text{Divide each side by 10.}$$

$$r = \frac{3}{5} \qquad \text{Solve for } r.$$

▶ The common ratio is $r = \dfrac{3}{5}$.

EXAMPLE 3 *Writing a Repeating Decimal as a Fraction*

Write $0.181818\ldots$ as a fraction.

SOLUTION

$$0.181818\ldots = 18(0.01) + 18(0.01)^2 + 18(0.01)^3 + \cdots$$

$$= \frac{a_1}{1-r} \qquad \text{Write rule for sum.}$$

$$= \frac{18(0.01)}{1-0.01} \qquad \text{Substitute for } a_1 \text{ and } r.$$

$$= \frac{18}{99} \qquad \text{Write as a quotient of integers.}$$

$$= \frac{2}{11} \qquad \text{Simplify.}$$

STUDENT HELP

▶ **Study Tip**
You can check the result
in Example 3 by dividing
2 by 11 on a calculator.

▶ The repeating decimal $0.181818\ldots$ is $\dfrac{2}{11}$ as a fraction.

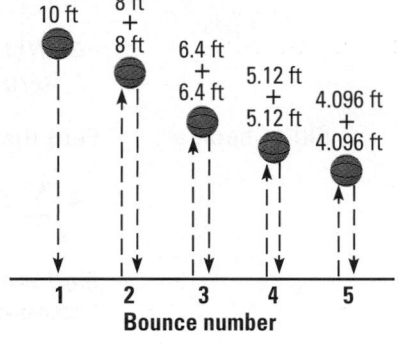

GOAL 2 **INFINITE GEOMETRIC SERIES IN REAL LIFE**

EXAMPLE 4 *Using an Infinite Series as a Model*

BALL BOUNCE A ball is dropped from a height of 10 feet. Each time it hits the ground, it bounces to 80% of its previous height.

a. Find the total distance traveled by the ball.

b. On which bounce will the ball have traveled 85% of its total distance?

SOLUTION

a. The total distance traveled by the ball is:

$$d = \underbrace{10}_{\text{down}} + \underbrace{10(0.8)}_{\text{up}} + \underbrace{10(0.8)}_{\text{down}} + \underbrace{10(0.8)^2}_{\text{up}} + \underbrace{10(0.8)^2}_{\text{down}} + \underbrace{10(0.8)^3}_{\text{up}} + \cdots$$

$$= 10 + 2[10(0.8)] + 2[10(0.8)^2] + 2[10(0.8)^3] + \cdots$$

$$= 10 + 20(0.8) + 20(0.8)^2 + 20(0.8)^3 + \cdots$$

$$= 10 + \frac{20(0.8)}{1 - 0.8} \qquad \text{Excluding first term, find sum of series.}$$

$$= 10 + 80 \qquad \text{Simplify fraction.}$$

$$= 90 \qquad \text{Simplify.}$$

▶ The ball travels a total distance of 90 feet.

b. Let n be the number of up-and-down bounces. The distance d_n the ball travels is:

$$d_n = 10 + \underbrace{20(0.8)\left(\frac{1 - (0.8)^n}{1 - 0.8}\right)}_{} \qquad \text{Write rule for } d_n.$$

down-only distance   sum of n up-and-down bounces

$$0.85(90) = 10 + 20(0.8)\left(\frac{1 - (0.8)^n}{1 - 0.8}\right) \qquad \text{Substitute for } d_n.$$

$$76.5 = 10 + 16\left(\frac{1 - (0.8)^n}{1 - 0.8}\right) \qquad \text{Simplify.}$$

$$4.156 \approx \frac{1 - (0.8)^n}{0.2} \qquad \text{Isolate fraction.}$$

$$0.831 \approx 1 - (0.8)^n \qquad \text{Multiply each side by 0.2.}$$

$$(0.8)^n \approx 0.169 \qquad \text{Isolate exponential expression.}$$

$$n \approx \frac{\log 0.169}{\log 0.8} \approx 7.97 \qquad \text{Solve for } n.$$

▶ The ball travels 85% of its total distance after about 8 up-and-down bounces, or after 9 bounces including the first down-only bounce.

GUIDED PRACTICE

1. Complete this statement: A(n) _?_ geometric series has infinitely many terms.

2. Under what conditions will $\displaystyle\sum_{i=1}^{\infty} a_1 r^{i-1}$ have a sum?

3. What two things do you need to know to find the sum of an infinite geometric series?

Find the sum of the infinite geometric series.

4. $\displaystyle\sum_{n=1}^{\infty} 5\left(\frac{1}{4}\right)^{n-1}$

5. $-2 + \dfrac{1}{2} - \dfrac{1}{8} + \dfrac{1}{32} - \cdots$

Find the common ratio of the infinite geometric series with the given sum and first term.

6. $S = 6, a_1 = 1$

7. $S = 12, a_1 = 2$

8. $S = 10\frac{1}{2}, a_1 = \frac{1}{2}$

Write the repeating decimal as a fraction.

9. $0.555\ldots$

10. $0.1212\ldots$

11. $245.245245\ldots$

12. **BALL BOUNCE** A ball is dropped from a height of 5 feet. Each time it hits the ground, it bounces one half of its previous height.

    a. Find the total distance traveled by the ball.

    b. On which bounce will the ball have traveled 75% of its total distance?

PRACTICE AND APPLICATIONS

STUDENT HELP

↳ **Extra Practice**
to help you master
skills is on p. 956.

IDENTIFYING A SUM Decide whether the infinite geometric series has a sum. Explain why or why not.

13. $\displaystyle\sum_{n=1}^{\infty} 3\left(\frac{3}{2}\right)^{n-1}$

14. $\displaystyle\sum_{n=0}^{\infty} -5\left(\frac{1}{5}\right)^{n}$

15. $\displaystyle\sum_{n=1}^{\infty} \frac{3}{2}\left(\frac{1}{3}\right)^{n-1}$

16. $\displaystyle\sum_{n=0}^{\infty} \frac{1}{4}\left(\frac{4}{3}\right)^{n}$

FINDING SUMS Find the sum of the infinite geometric series if it has one.

17. $\displaystyle\sum_{n=0}^{\infty} \left(\frac{1}{2}\right)^{n}$

18. $\displaystyle\sum_{n=0}^{\infty} 3\left(\frac{2}{3}\right)^{n}$

19. $\displaystyle\sum_{n=1}^{\infty} \left(-\frac{1}{2}\right)^{n-1}$

20. $\displaystyle\sum_{n=0}^{\infty} \frac{2}{7}(2)^{n}$

21. $\displaystyle\sum_{n=0}^{\infty} 4\left(\frac{1}{4}\right)^{n}$

22. $\displaystyle\sum_{n=1}^{\infty} \left(\frac{1}{10}\right)^{n-1}$

23. $\displaystyle\sum_{n=0}^{\infty} 2\left(\frac{6}{5}\right)^{n}$

24. $\displaystyle\sum_{n=0}^{\infty} 4\left(\frac{3}{7}\right)^{n}$

25. $\displaystyle\sum_{n=0}^{\infty} -\frac{1}{8}\left(-\frac{1}{2}\right)^{n}$

26. $\displaystyle\sum_{n=1}^{\infty} \frac{1}{2}\left(-\frac{2}{5}\right)^{n-1}$

27. $\displaystyle\sum_{n=0}^{\infty} \frac{1}{12}\left(-\frac{3}{25}\right)^{n}$

28. $\displaystyle\sum_{n=1}^{\infty} -\left(-\frac{2}{11}\right)^{n-1}$

STUDENT HELP

↳ **HOMEWORK HELP**
Example 1: Exs. 13–28
Example 2: Exs. 29–37
Example 3: Exs. 38–46
Example 4: Exs. 47–51

FINDING COMMON RATIOS Find the common ratio of the infinite geometric series with the given sum and first term.

29. $S = 4, a_1 = 1$

30. $S = 10, a_1 = 1$

31. $S = 12, a_1 = 3$

32. $S = 8, a_1 = 2$

33. $S = 6, a_1 = 2$

34. $S = 50, a_1 = 4$

35. $S = -\dfrac{1}{9}, a_1 = -\dfrac{1}{6}$

36. $S = -\dfrac{11}{13}, a_1 = -1$

37. $S = 2\dfrac{2}{9}, a_1 = 4$

WRITING REPEATING DECIMALS Write the repeating decimal as a fraction.

38. 0.444 . . .   **39.** 0.777 . . .   **40.** 0.999 . . .

41. 0.5151 . . .   **42.** 0.2323 . . .   **43.** 0.1616 . . .

44. 63.6363 . . .   **45.** 120.120120 . . .   **46.** 297.297297 . . .

47. 🌐 **PENDULUM** A pendulum is released to swing freely. On the first swing, the pendulum travels a distance of 18 inches. On each successive swing, the pendulum travels 90% of the distance of the previous swing. What is the total distance the pendulum swings? After how many swings has the pendulum traveled 80% of its total distance?

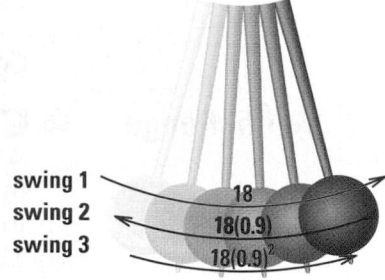

swing 1 — 18
swing 2 — 18(0.9)
swing 3 — 18(0.9)²

48. 🌐 **WINDOWS** Some types of windows are constructed with two parallel panes of glass, each of which reflects half of the sunlight that hits it from either side. The other half of the sunlight passes through the pane. How much of the sunlight will pass through *both* panes?

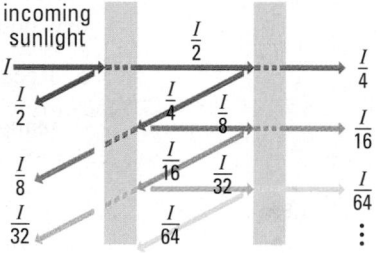

49. 🌐 **ZENO'S PARADOX** Can the Greek hero Achilles, running at 20 feet per second, ever catch a tortoise, starting 20 feet away and running at 10 feet per second? The Greek mathematician Zeno said no. He reasoned as follows:

- When Achilles runs 20 feet the tortoise will be in a new spot, 10 feet away.

- Then, when Achilles gets to that spot, the tortoise will be 5 feet away.

- Achilles will keep cutting the distance in half but will never catch the tortoise.

In actuality, looking at the race as Zeno did, you can see that both the distances and the times required to achieve them form infinite geometric series. Using the table, show that both series have finite sums. What do these sums represent?

Distance (ft)	20	10	5	2.5	1.25	0.625	. . .
Time (sec)	1	0.5	0.25	0.125	0.0625	0.03125	. . .

🌐 **TOURISM** In Exercises 50 and 51, use the following information.
In 1974 the Malaysian Tourist Development Corporation studied the economic impact of distributing tourist brochures. It was estimated that M$4.72 ("M$" means Malaysian dollars) in additional money was spent by tourists for every brochure distributed in the capital city of Kuala Lumpur. It was also estimated that for each M$1 spent on goods or services, 80.5% of that would be re-spent, creating a "multiplier" effect. (That is, each Malaysian dollar spent would lead to total spending of M$1 + (0.805)M$1 + (0.805)(0.805)M$1 + (0.805)(0.805)(0.805)M$1 + · · · .)

50. What total spending was generated by a tourist spending M$1 in 1974?

51. How much total spending would be generated by the average tourist who received a brochure?

52. LOGICAL REASONING Find two different infinite geometric series whose sum is 3.

53. MULTIPLE CHOICE An infinite geometric series with first term $a_1 = 24$ has a sum of 48. What is the common ratio of the series?

  Ⓐ $r = 1$ Ⓑ $r = \frac{1}{2}$ Ⓒ $r = 2$ Ⓓ $r = \frac{1}{24}$ Ⓔ $r = \frac{3}{8}$

54. MULTIPLE CHOICE The repeating decimal 18.181818 . . . is equivalent to what fraction?

  Ⓐ $\frac{891}{50}$ Ⓑ $\frac{2}{11}$ Ⓒ $\frac{181}{9}$ Ⓓ $\frac{200}{11}$ Ⓔ $\frac{1783}{99}$

★ Challenge

55. **GEOMETRY** **CONNECTION**

A *Koch snowflake* is created by starting with an equilateral triangle with sides 1 unit long. Then, on the middle third of each side of the triangle, a new equilateral triangle is constructed. This process is repeated as shown.

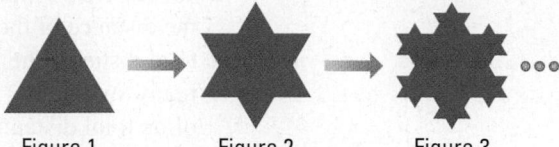

Figure 1   Figure 2   Figure 3

a. Recall that the area of an equilateral triangle with side length s can be found using the formula $A = \dfrac{s^2 \sqrt{3}}{4}$. Use this formula to complete the table below.

	Figure 1	Figure 2	Figure 3	Figure 4	. . .	Figure n
Number of new triangles	1	3	?	?	. . .	?
Area of each new triangle	$\frac{\sqrt{3}}{4}$	$\frac{\sqrt{3}}{36}$	?	?	. . .	?
Total new area	$\frac{\sqrt{3}}{4}$	$\frac{\sqrt{3}}{12}$	?	?	. . .	?

EXTRA CHALLENGE
www.mcdougallittell.com

b. What is the total area of the Koch snowflake? (*Hint:* Add up the entries in the last row of the table.)

MIXED REVIEW

IDENTIFYING ASYMPTOTES Identify the horizontal and vertical asymptotes. State the domain and range of the function. **(Review 9.2)**

56. $f(x) = \dfrac{5}{x}$

57. $f(x) = -\dfrac{5}{x}$

58. $f(x) = \dfrac{7}{x} - 3$

59. $f(x) = \dfrac{x - 5}{x + 7}$

60. $f(x) = \dfrac{4x + 3}{-2x + 17}$

61. $f(x) = \dfrac{2.2x + 3.1}{x - 0.7}$

GRAPHING Graph the equation. **(Review 10.4)**

62. $\dfrac{x^2}{4} + \dfrac{y^2}{16} = 1$

63. $\dfrac{25x^2}{4} + \dfrac{25y^2}{9} = 1$

64. $\dfrac{x^2}{16} + y^2 = 1$

WRITING RULES Write a rule for the nth term of the sequence. Recall that d is the common difference of an arithmetic sequence and r is the common ratio of a geometric sequence. **(Review 11.2, 11.3 for 11.5)**

65. $d = 4, a_1 = 1$

66. $d = 8, a_1 = -2$

67. $d = -2, a_2 = 9$

68. $r = 2, a_3 = -20$

69. $r = 0.5, a_1 = 4$

70. $r = 0.875, a_1 = -10$

11.5

Recursive Rules for Sequences

GOAL 1 Evaluate and write recursive rules for sequences.

GOAL 2 Use recursive rules to solve **real-life** problems, such as finding the number of fish in a lake in **Example 5**.

Why you should learn it

▼ To model **real-life** quantities, such as the number of trees on a tree farm in **Exs. 49 and 50**.

GOAL 1 USING RECURSIVE RULES FOR SEQUENCES

So far in this chapter you have worked with *explicit rules* for the *n*th term of a sequence, such as $a_n = 3n - 2$ and $a_n = 3(2)^n$. An **explicit rule** gives a_n as a function of the term's position number *n* in the sequence.

In this lesson you will learn another way to define a sequence—by a *recursive rule*. A **recursive rule** gives the beginning term or terms of a sequence and then a *recursive equation* that tells how a_n is related to one or more preceding terms.

EXAMPLE 1 *Evaluating Recursive Rules*

Write the first five terms of the sequence.

a. *Factorial numbers*: $a_0 = 1, a_n = n \cdot a_{n-1}$

b. *Fibonacci sequence*: $a_1 = 1, a_2 = 1, a_n = a_{n-2} + a_{n-1}$

SOLUTION

a. $a_0 = 1$

$a_1 = 1 \cdot a_0 = 1 \cdot 1 = 1$

$a_2 = 2 \cdot a_1 = 2 \cdot 1 = 2$

$a_3 = 3 \cdot a_2 = 3 \cdot 2 = 6$

$a_4 = 4 \cdot a_3 = 4 \cdot 6 = 24$

b. $a_1 = 1$

$a_2 = 1$

$a_3 = a_1 + a_2 = 1 + 1 = 2$

$a_4 = a_2 + a_3 = 1 + 2 = 3$

$a_5 = a_3 + a_4 = 2 + 3 = 5$

· · · · · · · · · ·

The factorial numbers in part (a) of Example 1 are denoted by a special symbol, !, called a **factorial** symbol. The expression *n*! is read "*n* factorial" and represents the product of all integers from 1 to *n*. Here are several factorial values.

$0! = 1$ (by definition) $1! = 1$ $2! = 2 \cdot 1 = 2$

$3! = 3 \cdot 2 \cdot 1 = 6$ $4! = 4 \cdot 3 \cdot 2 \cdot 1 = 24$ $5! = 5 \cdot 4 \cdot 3 \cdot 2 \cdot 1 = 120$

● ACTIVITY

Developing Concepts

Investigating Recursive Rules

① Find the first five terms of each sequence.

a. $a_1 = 3$

$a_n = a_{n-1} + 5$

b. $a_1 = 3$

$a_n = 2a_{n-1}$

② Based on the lists of terms you found in **Step 1**, what type of sequence is the sequence in part (a)? in part (b)?

EXAMPLE 2 *Writing a Recursive Rule for an Arithmetic Sequence*

Write the indicated rule for the arithmetic sequence with $a_1 = 4$ and $d = 3$.

a. an explicit rule

b. a recursive rule

SOLUTION

a. From Lesson 11.2 you know that an explicit rule for the nth term of the arithmetic sequence is:

$$a_n = a_1 + (n - 1)d \qquad \text{General explicit rule for } a_n$$

$$= 4 + (n - 1)3 \qquad \text{Substitute for } a_1 \text{ and } d.$$

$$= 1 + 3n \qquad \text{Simplify.}$$

b. To find the recursive equation, use the fact that you can obtain a_n by adding the common difference d to the previous term.

$$a_n = a_{n-1} + d \qquad \text{General recursive rule for } a_n$$

$$= a_{n-1} + 3 \qquad \text{Substitute for } d.$$

A recursive rule for the sequence is $a_1 = 4$, $a_n = a_{n-1} + 3$.

EXAMPLE 3 *Writing a Recursive Rule for a Geometric Sequence*

Write the indicated rule for the geometric sequence with $a_1 = 3$ and $r = 0.1$.

a. an explicit rule

b. a recursive rule

SOLUTION

a. From Lesson 11.3 you know that an explicit rule for the nth term of the geometric sequence is:

$$a_n = a_1 r^{n-1} \qquad \text{General explicit rule for } a_n$$

$$= 3(0.1)^{n-1} \qquad \text{Substitute for } a_1 \text{ and } r.$$

b. To write a recursive rule, use the fact that you can obtain a_n by multiplying the previous term by r.

$$a_n = r \cdot a_{n-1} \qquad \text{General recursive rule for } a_n$$

$$= (0.1)a_{n-1} \qquad \text{Substitute for } r.$$

A recursive rule for the sequence is $a_1 = 3$, $a_n = (0.1)a_{n-1}$.

EXAMPLE 4 *Writing a Recursive Rule*

Write a recursive rule for the sequence 1, 2, 2, 4, 8, 32, ...

SOLUTION

Beginning with the third term in the sequence, each term is the product of the two previous terms. Therefore, a recursive rule is given by:

$$a_1 = 1, \ a_2 = 2, \ a_n = a_{n-2} \cdot a_{n-1}$$

GOAL 2 USING RECURSIVE RULES IN REAL LIFE

EXAMPLE 5 *Using a Recursive Rule*

FISH A lake initially contains 5200 fish. Each year the population declines 30% due to fishing and other causes, and the lake is restocked with 400 fish.

a. Write a recursive rule for the number a_n of fish at the beginning of the nth year. How many fish are in the lake at the beginning of the fifth year?

b. What happens to the population of fish in the lake over time?

SOLUTION

a. Because the population declines 30% each year, 70% of the fish remain in the lake from one year to the next, and new fish are added.

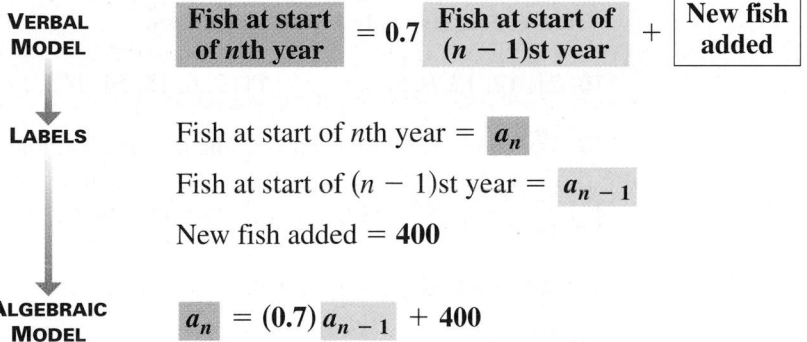

**VERBAL
MODEL** | Fish at start of nth year | = 0.7 | Fish at start of $(n-1)$st year | + | New fish added |

LABELS   Fish at start of nth year = a_n

Fish at start of $(n-1)$st year = a_{n-1}

New fish added = **400**

**ALGEBRAIC
MODEL** $a_n = (0.7)a_{n-1} + 400$

A recursive rule is:

$a_1 = 5200, a_n = (0.7)a_{n-1} + 400$

You can use a graphing calculator to find a_5, the number of fish in the lake at the beginning of the fifth year. Enter the number of fish at the beginning of the first year, which is $a_1 = 5200$. Then enter the rule $0.7 \times$ Ans $+ 400$ to find a_2. Press ENTER three more times to find $a_5 \approx 2262$.

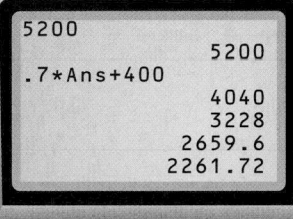

▶ There are about 2262 fish in the lake at the beginning of the fifth year.

b. To determine what happens to the lake's fish population over time, continue pressing ENTER on the calculator. The calculator screen at the right shows the fish populations for years 44–50. Observe that the numbers approach about 1333.

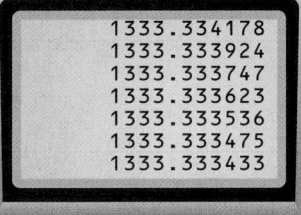

▶ Over time, the population of fish in the lake stabilizes at about 1333 fish.

GUIDED PRACTICE

Vocabulary Check ✓

1. Complete this statement: The expression ? represents the product of all integers from 1 to *n*.

Concept Check ✓

2. Explain the difference between an explicit rule for a sequence and a recursive rule for a sequence.

3. Give an example of an explicit rule for a sequence and a recursive rule for a sequence.

Skill Check ✓

Write the first five terms of the sequence.

4. $a_1 = 1$
$a_n = a_{n-1} + 1$

5. $a_1 = 2$
$a_n = 4a_{n-1}$

6. $a_0 = 1$
$a_n = a_{n-1} - 2$

7. $a_1 = -1$
$a_n = -3a_{n-1}$

8. $a_1 = 2$
$a_n = 2a_{n-1} - 3$

9. $a_0 = 3$
$a_n = (a_{n-1})^2 + 1$

Write a recursive rule for the sequence.

10. 21, 17, 13, 9, 5, . . .

11. 2, 6, 18, 54, 162, . . .

12. $\frac{1}{2}, \frac{1}{4}, \frac{1}{8}, \frac{1}{16}, \frac{1}{32}, \ldots$

13. 🌐 **FISH** Suppose each year the lake in Example 5 is restocked with 750 fish. How many fish are in the lake at the beginning of the fifth year?

PRACTICE AND APPLICATIONS

STUDENT HELP

▶ **Extra Practice**
to help you master
skills is on p. 956.

WRITING TERMS Write the first five terms of the sequence.

14. $a_0 = 1$
$a_n = a_{n-1} + 4$

15. $a_1 = 4$
$a_n = n + a_{n-1} + 6$

16. $a_0 = 0$
$a_n = a_{n-1} - n^2$

17. $a_0 = -4$
$a_n = a_{n-1} - 8$

18. $a_1 = 2$
$a_n = (a_{n-1})^2 + 2$

19. $a_0 = 5$
$a_n = n^2 - a_{n-1}$

20. $a_1 = 10$
$a_n = 3a_{n-1}$

21. $a_0 = 2$
$a_n = n^2 + 2n - a_{n-1}$

22. $a_0 = 3$
$a_n = (a_{n-1})^2 - 2$

23. $a_0 = 48$
$a_n = \frac{1}{2}a_{n-1} + 2$

24. $a_0 = 4, a_1 = 2$
$a_n = a_{n-1} - a_{n-2}$

25. $a_1 = 1, a_2 = 3$
$a_n = a_{n-1} \cdot a_{n-2}$

WRITING RULES Write an explicit rule and a recursive rule for the sequence.
(Recall that *d* is the common difference of an arithmetic sequence and *r* is the
common ratio of a geometric sequence.)

STUDENT HELP

▶ **HOMEWORK HELP**
Example 1: Exs. 14–25
Examples 2, 3: Exs. 26–34
Example 4: Exs. 35–43
Example 5: Exs. 44–54

26. $a_1 = 2$
$r = 10$

27. $a_1 = 3$
$d = 10$

28. $a_1 = 10$
$r = 2$

29. $a_1 = 5$
$d = 3$

30. $a_1 = 0$
$d = -1$

31. $a_1 = 5$
$r = 2.5$

32. $a_1 = 14$
$d = \frac{1}{2}$

33. $a_1 = \frac{1}{2}$
$r = 4$

34. $a_1 = -1$
$d = -\frac{3}{2}$

WRITING RULES Write a recursive rule for the sequence. The sequence may be arithmetic, geometric, or neither.

35. 1, 7, 13, 19, . . .   **36.** 66, 33, 16.5, 8.25, . . .   **37.** 41, 32, 23, 14, . . .

38. 3, 8, 63, 3968, . . .   **39.** 33, 11, $\frac{11}{3}$, $\frac{11}{9}$, . . .   **40.** 7.2, 3.2, -0.8, -4.8, . . .

41. 2, 5, 10, 50, 500, . . .   **42.** 6, $6\sqrt{2}$, 12, $12\sqrt{2}$, . . .   **43.** 48, 4.8, 0.48, 0.048, . . .

44. 🌎 **ON LAYAWAY** Suppose you buy a $500 camcorder on layaway by making a down payment of $150 and then paying $25 per month. Write a recursive rule for the total amount of money paid on the camcorder at the beginning of the nth month. How much will you have left to pay on the camcorder at the beginning of the twelfth month?

🌀 **FRACTAL TREE** In Exercises 45 and 46, use the following information.
A fractal tree starts with a single branch (the trunk). At each stage the new branches from the previous stage each grow two more branches, as shown.

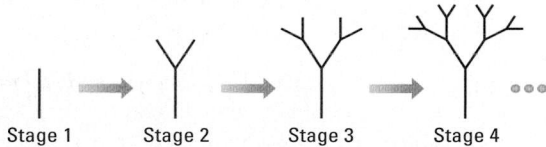

Stage 1   Stage 2   Stage 3   Stage 4

45. List the number of new branches in each of the first seven stages. What type of sequence do these numbers form?

46. Write an explicit rule and a recursive rule for the sequence in Exercise 45.

📱 **POOL CARE** In Exercises 47 and 48, use the following information.
You have just bought a new swimming pool and need to add chlorine to the water. You add 32 ounces of chlorine the first week and 14 ounces every week thereafter. Each week 40% of the chlorine in the pool evaporates.

47. Write a recursive rule for the amount of chlorine in the pool each week. How much chlorine is in the pool at the beginning of the sixth week?

48. What happens to the amount of chlorine after an extended period of time?

📱 **TREE FARM** In Exercises 49 and 50, use the following information.
Suppose a tree farm initially has 9000 trees. Each year 10% of the trees are harvested and 800 seedlings are planted.

49. Write a recursive rule for the number of trees on the tree farm at the beginning of the nth year. How many trees remain at the beginning of the fourth year?

50. What happens to the number of trees after an extended period of time?

🌎 **DOSAGE** In Exercises 51–54, use the following information.
A person repeatedly takes 20 milligrams of a prescribed drug every four hours. Suppose that 30% of the drug is removed from the bloodstream every four hours.

51. Write a recursive rule for the amount of the drug in the bloodstream after n doses.

52. What value does the drug level in the person's body approach after an extended period of time? This value is called the *maintenance level*.

53. Suppose the first dosage is doubled (to 40 milligrams), but the normal dosage is taken thereafter. Does the maintenance level from Exercise 52 change?

54. Suppose every dosage is doubled. Does the maintenance level double as well?

55. CRITICAL THINKING Give an example of a sequence in which each term after the third term is a function of the three terms preceding it. Write a recursive rule for the sequence and find the first 8 terms.

Test
Preparation

56. MULTIPLE CHOICE What is the fifth term of the sequence whose first term is $a_1 = 10$ and whose nth term is $a_n = 2a_{n-1} + 9$?

    Ⓐ 67   Ⓑ 143   Ⓒ 286   Ⓓ 295   Ⓔ 599

57. MULTIPLE CHOICE What is a recursive equation for the sequence $4, -6.6, 10.89, -17.9685, \ldots$?

    Ⓐ $a_n = (-2.6)a_{n-1}$ Ⓑ $a_n = (-1.65)a_{n-1}$

    Ⓒ $a_n = (2.6)a_{n-1}$ Ⓓ $a_n = (1.65)a_{n-1}$

★ **Challenge**

58. PIECEWISE-DEFINED SEQUENCE You can define a sequence using a piecewise rule. The following is an example of a piecewise-defined sequence.

$$a_1 = 7, a_n = \begin{cases} \dfrac{a_{n-1}}{2}, & \text{if } a_{n-1} \text{ is even} \\ 3a_{n-1} + 1, & \text{if } a_{n-1} \text{ is odd} \end{cases}$$

    a. Write the first ten terms of the sequence.

    b. LOGICAL REASONING Choose three different values for a_1 (other than $a_1 = 7$). For each value of a_1, find the first ten terms of the sequence. What conclusions can you make about the behavior of this sequence?

EXTRA CHALLENGE
www.mcdougallittell.com

MIXED REVIEW

EVALUATING POWERS Evaluate the power. (Review 1.2 for 12.1)

59. 2^5 **60.** 6^4 **61.** 8^4 **62.** 12^3

63. 26^3 **64.** 10^5 **65.** 18^3 **66.** 3^7

OPERATIONS WITH RATIONAL EXPRESSIONS Perform the indicated operation and simplify. (Review 9.5)

67. $\dfrac{3}{5x} + \dfrac{3}{7x}$ **68.** $\dfrac{-2}{7x} - \dfrac{5}{3x}$ **69.** $\dfrac{x+1}{x^2-9} - \dfrac{5}{x-3}$

70. $\dfrac{2x^2}{3x+5} - \dfrac{14}{x+7}$ **71.** $\dfrac{4x+1}{x^2-4} - \dfrac{3}{x-2}$ **72.** $\dfrac{x^2-1}{x+2} - \dfrac{3}{x+1}$

FINDING POINTS OF INTERSECTION Find the points of intersection, if any, of the graphs in the system. (Review 10.7)

73. $x^2 + y^2 = 4$ **74.** $x^2 + y^2 = 25$ **75.** $x^2 + 4y^2 = 16$
     $2x + y = -1$ $y = x - 1$ $y = 3x + 1$

76. $x^2 + y^2 = 10$ **77.** $x^2 + y^2 = 30$ **78.** $16x^2 + y^2 = 32$
     $4x + y = 6$ $y = x + 2$ $\dfrac{1}{4}x - \dfrac{1}{2}y = 2$

WRITING TERMS Write the first six terms of the sequence. (Review 11.1)

79. $a_n = 8 - n$ **80.** $a_n = n^4$ **81.** $a_n = n^2 + 9$

82. $a_n = (n+3)^2$ **83.** $a_n = \dfrac{n}{n+4}$ **84.** $a_n = \dfrac{n+3}{n+1}$

Find the sum of the infinite geometric series if it has one. (Lesson 11.4)

1. $\displaystyle\sum_{n=0}^{\infty} 4\left(\frac{1}{9}\right)^{n}$ **2.** $\displaystyle\sum_{n=1}^{\infty} 5\left(-\frac{6}{7}\right)^{n-1}$ **3.** $\displaystyle\sum_{n=0}^{\infty} -\frac{3}{8}\left(\frac{4}{7}\right)^{n}$ **4.** $\displaystyle\sum_{n=0}^{\infty} \frac{4}{5}\left(\frac{5}{4}\right)^{n}$

Find the common ratio of the infinite geometric series with the given sum and first term. (Lesson 11.4)

5. $S = 5, a_1 = 1$ **6.** $S = 12, a_1 = 1$ **7.** $S = 24, a_1 = 3$

Write the repeating decimal as a fraction. (Lesson 11.4)

8. $0.888\ldots$ **9.** $0.1515\ldots$ **10.** $126.126126\ldots$

Write the first five terms of the sequence. (Lesson 11.5)

11. $a_1 = 5$
$a_n = a_{n-1} + 3$

12. $a_0 = 1$
$a_n = 4a_{n-1}$

13. $a_1 = 17$
$a_n = a_{n-1} + n$

14. $a_1 = 1, a_2 = 2$
$a_n = a_{n-1} - a_{n-2}$

15. $a_1 = 2, a_2 = 4$
$a_n = a_{n-1} \cdot a_{n-2}$

16. $a_1 = 10, a_2 = 10$
$a_n = a_{n-2} + a_{n-1}$

17. 🌐 **BALL BOUNCE** You drop a ball from a height of 8 feet. Each time it hits the ground, it bounces 40% of its previous height. Find the total distance traveled by the ball. (Lesson 11.4)

MATH & *History*

The Fibonacci Sequence

APPLICATION LINK
www.mcdougallittell.com

THEN

IN 1202 the mathematician Leonardo Fibonacci wrote *Liber Abaci* in which he proposed the following rabbit problem.

Begin with a pair of newborn rabbits that never die. When a pair of rabbits is two months old, it begins producing a new pair of rabbits each month.

Month	1	2	3	4	5	6	. . .
Pairs at start of month	1	1	2	3	5	8	. . .

This problem can be represented by a sequence, known as the Fibonacci sequence. The numbers that make up the sequence are called Fibonacci numbers. The ratio of two Fibonacci numbers approximates the same number, denoted by Φ. The Greeks called this number the golden ratio.

1. Draw a tree diagram to illustrate the sequence.

2. If the initial pair of rabbits produces their first pair of rabbits in January, how many pairs of rabbits will there be in December of that year? What happens to the rabbit population over time?

NOW

TODAY we know that Fibonacci numbers occur in nature, such as in the spiral patterns on the head of a sunflower or the surface of a pineapple.

2500 B.C.
Golden Section used in Great Pyramid.

Fibonacci develops sequence.
A.D. 1202

1999
Fibonacci numbers recognized in nature.

► **ACTIVITY 11.5**

Using Technology

Evaluating Recursive Rules

You can use a spreadsheet to evaluate a recursive rule.

► **EXAMPLE**

You owe $5000 to a credit card company that charges interest at a rate of 1.5% per month. Each month you make a payment of $100. Write a recursive rule for a_n, the balance of the account at the beginning of the nth month. How much will you still owe at the beginning of the 6th month? How long will it take to pay off the account?

► **SOLUTION**

STUDENT HELP

INTERNET **SOFTWARE HELP**

Visit our Web site www.mcdougallittell.com to see instructions for several software packages.

A recursive rule for the balance of the account each month is:

$$a_1 = 5000, \quad a_n = (1.015)a_{n-1} - 100$$

You can use a spreadsheet to find how much you owe at the start of each month.

❶ Enter a_1 into cell A1.

A1	X ✓	5000	
	A	**B**	**C**
1	5000		
2			
3			

❷ In cell A2, enter the recursive equation.

A2		=1.015*A1−100	
	A	**B**	**C**
1	5000		
2	4975		
3			

❸ Use the *Fill Down* feature to copy the recursive equation into the rest of the column.

A2		=1.015*A1−100	
	A	**B**	**C**
1	5000		
2	4975		
3	4949.625		
4	4923.869375		
5	4897.727416		
6	4871.193327		
7	4844.261227		

A95		=1.015*A94−100	
	A	**B**	**C**
89	488.4879425		
90	395.8152616		
91	301.7524905		
92	206.2787779		
93	109.3729595		
94	11.01355393		
95	−88.8212428		

► At the beginning of the 6th month you still owe $4871.19, and it will take about 94 months, or 7 years and 10 months, to pay off the account.

► **EXERCISES**

Use a spreadsheet to find the first twelve terms of the sequence.

1. $a_1 = 5100, a_n = (0.9)a_{n-1} - 125$ **2.** $a_1 = 6150, a_n = (0.82)a_{n-1} - 200$

3. $a_1 = 3500, a_n = (0.85)a_{n-1} - 50$ **4.** $a_1 = 7500, a_n = (0.775)a_{n-1} - 175$

5.  **FINANCE** You owe $8000 on a credit card with 1% monthly interest. If you pay $125 each month, how long will it take to pay off the account?

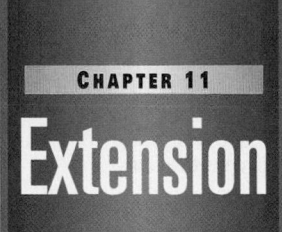

CHAPTER 11

Extension

Mathematical Induction

What you should learn

GOAL Use mathematical induction to prove statements about all positive integers.

In Lesson 11.1 you saw that the rule for the sum of the first n positive integers is:

$$\sum_{i=1}^{n} i = 1 + 2 + \cdots + n = \frac{n(n+1)}{2}$$

Statements like the one above about all positive integers can be proven using a method called *mathematical induction*.

MATHEMATICAL INDUCTION

To show that a statement is true for all positive integers n, perform these steps.

BASIS STEP: Show that the statement is true for $n = 1$.

INDUCTIVE STEP: Assume that the statement is true for $n = k$ where k is any positive integer. Show that this implies the statement is true for $n = k + 1$.

Mathematical induction works as follows. If you know from the basis step that a statement is true for $n = 1$, then the inductive step implies that it is true for $n = 2$, and therefore, for $n = 3$, and so on for all positive integers n.

EXAMPLE 1 *Using Mathematical Induction*

Use mathematical induction to prove that $1 + 2 + \cdots + n = \frac{n(n+1)}{2}$.

SOLUTION

Basis step: Check to see if the formula works for $n = 1$.

$$1 \stackrel{?}{=} \frac{(1)(1+1)}{2} \longrightarrow 1 = 1 \checkmark$$

Inductive step: Assume that $1 + 2 + \cdots + k = \frac{k(k+1)}{2}$.

Show that $1 + 2 + \cdots + k + (k+1) = \frac{(k+1)[(k+1)+1]}{2}$.

$$1 + 2 + \cdots + k = \frac{k(k+1)}{2} \qquad \text{Assume true for } k.$$

$$1 + 2 + \cdots + k + (k+1) = \frac{k(k+1)}{2} + (k+1) \qquad \text{Add } k+1 \text{ to each side.}$$

$$= \frac{k(k+1) + 2(k+1)}{2} \qquad \text{Add.}$$

$$= \frac{(k+1)(k+2)}{2} \qquad \text{Factor out } k+1.$$

$$= \frac{(k+1)[(k+1)+1]}{2} \qquad \text{Rewrite } k+2 \text{ as } (k+1)+1.$$

Therefore, $1 + 2 + \cdots + n = \frac{n(n+1)}{2}$ for all positive integers n.

EXAMPLE 2 *Using Mathematical Induction*

Let $a_n = 3a_{n-1} + 1$ with $a_1 = 1$. Use mathematical induction to prove that an explicit rule for the nth term is $a_n = \dfrac{3^n - 1}{2}$.

SOLUTION

Basis step: Check to see that the rule works for $n = 1$.

$$a_1 \overset{?}{=} \frac{3^1 - 1}{2} \implies 1 = 1 ✓$$

Inductive step: Assume that $a_k = \dfrac{3^k - 1}{2}$. Show that $a_{k+1} = \dfrac{3^{k+1} - 1}{2}$.

$$a_{k+1} = 3a_k + 1 \qquad \textbf{Definition of } a_n \textbf{ for } n = k+1$$

$$= 3\left(\frac{3^k - 1}{2}\right) + 1 \qquad \textbf{Substitute for } a_k.$$

$$= \frac{3^{k+1} - 3}{2} + 1 \qquad \textbf{Multiply.}$$

$$= \frac{3^{k+1} - 3 + 2}{2} \qquad \textbf{Add.}$$

$$= \frac{3^{k+1} - 1}{2} \qquad \textbf{Simplify.}$$

Therefore, an explicit rule for the nth term is $a_n = \dfrac{3^n - 1}{2}$ for all positive integers n.

EXERCISES

Use mathematical induction to prove the statement.

1. $\displaystyle\sum_{i=1}^{n} i^2 = \frac{n(n+1)(2n+1)}{6}$

2. $\displaystyle\sum_{i=1}^{n} (2i + 1) = n(n+2)$

3. $\displaystyle\sum_{i=1}^{n} a_1 r^{i-1} = a_1\left(\frac{1 - r^n}{1 - r}\right)$

4. $\displaystyle\sum_{i=1}^{n} (2i)^2 = \frac{2n(n+1)(2n+1)}{3}$

5. $\displaystyle\sum_{i=1}^{n} 5^i = \frac{5^{n+1} - 5}{4}$

6. $\displaystyle\sum_{i=1}^{n} \left(\frac{1}{2}\right)^i = 1 - \left(\frac{1}{2}\right)^n$

7. **GEOMETRY** **CONNECTION** The numbers 1, 5, 12, 22, 35, 51, . . . are called *pentagonal numbers* because they represent the numbers of dots used to make pentagons, as shown at the right. Prove that the nth pentagonal number P_n is given by:

$$P_n = \frac{n(3n - 1)}{2}$$

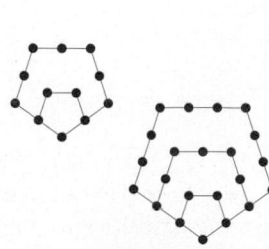

8. **LOGICAL REASONING** Let $f_1, f_2, \ldots, f_n, \ldots$ be the Fibonacci sequence. Prove that
$$f_1 + f_2 + \cdots + f_n = f_{n+2} - 1.$$

Chapter Summary

WHAT did you learn?

Use summation notation to write a series. **(11.1)**

Find terms of sequences.
- defined by explicit rules **(11.1)**
- defined by recursive rules **(11.5)**

Graph and classify sequences. **(11.1–11.3)**

Write rules for *n*th terms of sequences.
- given some terms **(11.1–11.3)**

- arithmetic sequences **(11.2)**
- geometric sequences **(11.3)**

Find sums of series.
- by adding terms or using formulas **(11.1)**
- finite arithmetic series **(11.2)**
- finite geometric series **(11.3)**
- infinite geometric series **(11.4)**

Write recursive rules for sequences. **(11.5)**

Use sequences and series to solve real-life problems. **(11.1–11.5)**

WHY did you learn it?

Express the number of oranges in a stack. **(p. 654)**

Find angle measures at the tips of a star. **(p. 656)**
Find the number of fish in a stocked lake. **(p. 683)**

Compare the revenues of two companies. **(p. 672)**

Model the minimum number of moves in the Tower of Hanoi puzzle. **(p. 656)**

Model the number of seats in a concert hall. **(p. 662)**
Model the number of matches in a tennis tournament. **(p. 671)**

Find the number of tennis balls in a stack. **(p. 656)**
Find the number of cells in a honeycomb. **(p. 664)**
Find the cost of cellular telephone service. **(p. 669)**
Find the amount of money spent by tourists who receive a tourist brochure. **(p. 679)**

Model the number of trees on a tree farm. **(p. 685)**

Find the total length of the vertical supports used to build a roof. **(p. 656)**

How does Chapter 11 fit into the BIGGER PICTURE of algebra?

Since elementary school you have studied number patterns (sequences). Now you can use algebra to write and use rules for sequences and series. An arithmetic sequence has a common difference, so it is similar to a linear function. A geometric sequence has a common ratio, so it is similar to an exponential function. Recursive rules are used in computer programs and in spreadsheet formulas.

STUDY STRATEGY

How did you learn by teaching?

Here is an example of an explanation given by one student to another, following the **Study Strategy** on page 650.

Learn by Teaching

Write a rule for the *n*th term of this sequence:
2, 7, 12, 17, . . .

"First look for a common difference or a common ratio. $7 - 2 = 5$, $12 - 7 = 5$, and $17 - 12 = 5$, so the common difference is 5. So $5n$ will be part of the rule. If $n = 1$, $5n = 5$. But the first term is 2, which is 3 less than 5, so we need to subtract 3. Let's try $5n - 3$ and see if it works. $5(1) - 3 = 2$, $5(2) - 3 = 7$, $5(3) - 3 = 12$, and $5(4) - 3 = 17$. Yes, it works. So the rule is $a_n = 5n - 3$."

Chapter Review

- terms of a sequence, p. 651
- sequence, p. 651
- finite sequence, p. 651
- infinite sequence, p. 651
- series, p. 653
- summation notation, p. 653

- sigma notation, p. 653
- arithmetic sequence, p. 659
- common difference, p. 659
- arithmetic series, p. 661
- geometric sequence, p. 666

- common ratio, p. 666
- geometric series, p. 668
- explicit rule, p. 681
- recursive rule, p. 681
- factorial, p. 681

11.1 **AN INTRODUCTION TO SEQUENCES AND SERIES**

Examples on pp. 651–654

> **EXAMPLES** You can find the first four terms of the sequence $a_n = 3n - 7$.
>
> $a_1 = 3(1) - 7 = -4$ ◄── first term
>
> $a_2 = 3(2) - 7 = -1$ ◄── second term
>
> $a_3 = 3(3) - 7 = 2$ ◄── third term
>
> $a_4 = 3(4) - 7 = 5$ ◄── fourth term
>
> The *sequence* defined by $a_n = 3n - 7$ is $-4, -1, 2, 5, \ldots$.
>
> The associated *series* is the sum of the terms of the sequence: $(-4) + (-1) + 2 + 5 + \cdots$.
>
> You can use summation notation to write the series $2 + 4 + 6 + 8 + 10$ as $\sum_{i=1}^{5} 2i$.
>
> You can find the sum of a series by adding the terms or by using formulas for special series.
>
> The sum of the series $\sum_{i=1}^{22} i^2$ is $\dfrac{n(n+1)(2n+1)}{6} = \dfrac{22(22+1)(2(22)+1)}{6} = 3795$.

Write the first six terms of the sequence.

1. $a_n = n^2 + 5$ **2.** $a_n = (n+1)^3$ **3.** $a_n = 6 - 2n$ **4.** $a_n = \dfrac{n}{n+3}$

Write the next term in the sequence. Then write a formula for the nth term.

5. $2, 4, 6, 8, \ldots$ **6.** $-3, 6, -12, 24, \ldots$ **7.** $\dfrac{1}{3}, \dfrac{1}{9}, \dfrac{1}{27}, \dfrac{1}{81}, \ldots$

Write the series with summation notation.

8. $4 + 8 + 12 + 16$ **9.** $1 + 2 + 3 + 4 + \cdots$ **10.** $0 + 3 + 6 + 9 + 12$

Find the sum of the series.

11. $\sum_{n=1}^{25} n^2$ **12.** $\sum_{n=4}^{10} n(2n-1)$ **13.** $\sum_{i=1}^{12} i$ **14.** $\sum_{k=1}^{30} 4$

Examples on pp. 659–662

EXAMPLES The sequence 4, 7, 10, 13, 16, . . . is an arithmetic sequence because the difference between consecutive terms is constant:

$$7 - 4 = 3 \qquad 10 - 7 = 3 \qquad 13 - 10 = 3 \qquad 16 - 13 = 3$$

The common difference is 3, so $d = 3$.

A rule for the nth term of this arithmetic sequence is:

$$a_n = a_1 + (n - 1)d = 4 + (n - 1)3 = 3n + 1$$

The sum of the first 20 terms of this arithmetic series is:

$$S_{20} = 20\left(\frac{a_1 + a_{20}}{2}\right) = 20\left(\frac{4 + 61}{2}\right) = 650$$

Write a rule for the nth term of the arithmetic sequence.

15. 1, 7, 13, 19, 25, . . .
16. 4, 6, 8, 10, 12, . . .
17. 3.5, 3, 2.5, 2, 1.5, . . .

18. $d = 5, a_1 = 13$
19. $d = -2, a_9 = 3$
20. $a_4 = 20, a_{13} = 65$

Find the sum of the first n terms of the arithmetic series.

21. $8 + 20 + 32 + 44 + \cdots; n = 14$
22. $(-6) + (-2) + 2 + 6 + \cdots; n = 20$

23. $0.5 + 0.9 + 1.3 + 1.7 + \cdots; n = 54$
24. $(-12) + (-8) + (-4) + 0 + \cdots; n = 40$

Examples on pp. 666–669

EXAMPLES The sequence 5, 15, 45, 135, 405, . . . is a geometric sequence because the ratio of any term to the previous term is constant:

$$\frac{15}{5} = 3 \qquad \frac{45}{15} = 3 \qquad \frac{135}{45} = 3 \qquad \frac{405}{135} = 3$$

The common ratio is 3, so $r = 3$.

A rule for the nth term of this geometric sequence is:

$$a_n = a_1 r^{n-1} = 5(3)^{n-1}$$

The sum of the first 8 terms of this geometric series is:

$$S_8 = a_1\left(\frac{1 - r^8}{1 - r}\right) = 5\left(\frac{1 - 3^8}{1 - 3}\right) = 16{,}400$$

Write a rule for the nth term of the geometric sequence.

25. 64, 32, 16, 8, 4, . . .
26. 6, 12, 24, 48, . . .
27. 200, 20, 2, 0.2, 0.02, . . .

28. $r = 3, a_1 = 6$
29. $r = -\frac{1}{4}, a_4 = 1$
30. $a_2 = 50, a_6 = 0.005$

Find the sum of the series.

31. $\displaystyle\sum_{i=1}^{5} 16(2)^{i-1}$
32. $\displaystyle\sum_{i=1}^{10} 20(0.2)^{i-1}$
33. $\displaystyle\sum_{i=0}^{6} 10\left(\frac{1}{2}\right)^{i}$
34. $\displaystyle\sum_{i=1}^{8} 2\left(\frac{3}{5}\right)^{i-1}$

EXAMPLES You can find the sum of the infinite geometric series

$\sum_{n=1}^{\infty} 4\left(\frac{3}{5}\right)^{n-1}$ because $|r| = \left|\frac{3}{5}\right| < 1$: $S = \frac{a_1}{1-r} = \frac{4}{1-\frac{3}{5}} = 10$.

The infinite geometric series $\sum_{n=1}^{\infty} \frac{1}{2}(5)^{n-1}$ has no sum because $|r| = |5| \geq 1$.

Find the sum of the infinite geometric series.

35. $\sum_{n=1}^{\infty} 15\left(\frac{2}{9}\right)^{n-1}$ **36.** $\sum_{n=1}^{\infty} 3\left(\frac{3}{4}\right)^{n-1}$ **37.** $\sum_{n=1}^{\infty} 5(0.8)^{n-1}$ **38.** $\sum_{n=1}^{\infty} 4(-0.2)^{n-1}$

Find the common ratio of the infinite geometric series with the given sum and first term.

39. $S = 18, a_1 = 12$ **40.** $S = 2, a_1 = 0.5$ **41.** $S = 20, a_1 = 4$ **42.** $S = -5, a_1 = -2$

43. $S = -10, a_1 = -3$ **44.** $S = 6, a_1 = \frac{1}{3}$ **45.** $S = \frac{1}{4}, a_1 = \frac{1}{16}$ **46.** $S = 3\frac{1}{3}, a_1 = 6$

Write the repeating decimal as a fraction.

47. $0.222\ldots$ **48.** $0.4545\ldots$ **49.** $39.3939\ldots$ **50.** $0.001001\ldots$

EXAMPLES You can find the first five terms of the sequence defined by the recursive rule $a_1 = 3$, $a_n = a_{n-1} + n + 6$.

$a_1 = 3$ ◀——first term

$a_2 = a_{n-1} + n + 6 = a_1 + 2 + 6 = 3 + 2 + 6 = 11$ ◀——second term

$a_3 = a_{n-1} + n + 6 = a_2 + 3 + 6 = 11 + 3 + 6 = 20$ ◀——third term

$a_4 = a_{n-1} + n + 6 = a_3 + 4 + 6 = 20 + 4 + 6 = 30$ ◀——fourth term

$a_5 = a_{n-1} + n + 6 = a_4 + 5 + 6 = 30 + 5 + 6 = 41$ ◀——fifth term

The sequence is 3, 11, 20, 30, 41, ...

A recursive formula for the sequence 1, 5, 14, 30, . . . is $a_1 = 1$, $a_n = a_{n-1} + n^2$.

Write the first six terms of the sequence.

51. $a_1 = 10$ **52.** $a_1 = 1$ **53.** $a_1 = 2$ **54.** $a_1 = -1$
$a_n = 4a_{n-1}$ $a_n = n \cdot a_{n-1}$ $a_n = a_{n-1} - n$ $a_n = (a_{n-1})^2 + 3$

Write a recursive rule for the sequence. The sequence may be arithmetic, geometric, or neither.

55. 7, 14, 28, 56, 112, . . .   **56.** 4, 8, 13, 19, 26, . . .   **57.** 1, 6, 11, 16, 21, . . .

58. 200, 100, 50, 25, . . .   **59.** 1, 2, 5, 26, 677, . . .   **60.** $-2, -6, -12, -20, \ldots$

Chapter Test

Tell whether the sequence is *arithmetic*, *geometric*, or *neither*. Explain your answer.

1. $-5, -3, -1, 1, \ldots$

2. $-4, -2, 2, 4, \ldots$

3. $12, 6, 3, \dfrac{3}{2}, \ldots$

4. $\dfrac{1}{3}, 1, 3, 9, \ldots$

Write the first six terms of the sequence.

5. $a_n = n^2 + 1$

6. $a_n = 3n - 5$

7. $a_1 = 4$
$a_n = n + a_{n-1}$

8. $a_1 = 1$
$a_n = 2a_{n-1}$

Write the next term of the sequence, and then write a rule for the *n*th term.

9. $2, 4, 8, 16, \ldots$

10. $4, 9, 14, 19, \ldots$

11. $2, 10, 50, 250, \ldots$

12. $-9, -10, -11, -12, \ldots$

13. $5, -\dfrac{5}{2}, \dfrac{5}{4}, -\dfrac{5}{8}, \ldots$

14. $\dfrac{2}{3}, \dfrac{3}{4}, \dfrac{4}{5}, \dfrac{5}{6}, \ldots$

15. $\dfrac{3}{2}, \dfrac{4}{4}, \dfrac{5}{6}, \dfrac{6}{8}, \ldots$

16. $1.1, 2.2, 3.3, 4.4, \ldots$

Write a recursive rule for the sequence. (Recall that *d* is the common difference of an arithmetic sequence and *r* is the common ratio of a geometric sequence.)

17. $r = 0.3, a_1 = 4$

18. $d = 4, a_1 = 1$

19. $40, 20, 10, 5, \ldots$

20. $2, 8, 18, 32, 50, \ldots$

Find the sum of the series.

21. $\displaystyle\sum_{i=1}^{100} i$

22. $\displaystyle\sum_{i=2}^{5} \dfrac{1}{2}i^2$

23. $\displaystyle\sum_{i=1}^{6} (i - 10)$

24. $\displaystyle\sum_{i=1}^{20} (3i + 2)$

25. $\displaystyle\sum_{i=1}^{5} 7(-2)^{i-1}$

26. $\displaystyle\sum_{i=0}^{9} 5\left(\dfrac{1}{4}\right)^i$

27. $\displaystyle\sum_{i=1}^{\infty} 64\left(-\dfrac{1}{2}\right)^{i-1}$

28. $\displaystyle\sum_{i=1}^{\infty} 100\left(\dfrac{7}{10}\right)^{i-1}$

29. Find the sum of the first 30 terms of the arithmetic sequence $3, 7, 11, 15, \ldots$.

30. Find the sum of the infinite geometric series $2 + 1 + 0.5 + 0.25 + \cdots$.

31. Write the series $1 + 3 + 5 + 7 + 9 + 11$ with summation notation.

32. Write the repeating decimal $0.7575 \ldots$ as a fraction.

33. **FALLING OBJECT** An object is dropped from an airplane. During the first second, the object falls 4.9 meters. During the second second, it falls 14.7 meters. During the third second, it falls 24.5 meters. During the fourth second, it falls 34.3 meters. If this pattern continues, how far will the object fall during the tenth second? Find the total distance the object will fall after 10 seconds.

34. **CELL DIVISION** In early growth of an embryo, a human cell divides into two cells, each of which divides into two cells, and so on. The number a_n of new cells formed after the *n*th division is $a_n = 2^{n-1}$. Find the sum of the first 9 terms of the series to find the total number of new cells after the 8th division.

35. **SPRING** The length of the first loop of a spring is 20 inches. The length of the second loop is $\dfrac{9}{10}$ of the length of the first loop. The length of the third loop is $\dfrac{9}{10}$ of the length of the second loop, and so on. If the spring could have infinitely many loops, would its length be finite? If so, find the length.

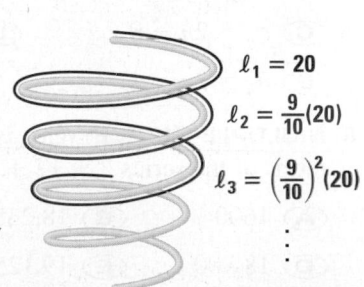

$\ell_1 = 20$

$\ell_2 = \dfrac{9}{10}(20)$

$\ell_3 = \left(\dfrac{9}{10}\right)^2(20)$

Chapter Standardized Test

▶ **TEST-TAKING STRATEGY** If the answers to a question are formulas, substitute the given numbers into the formulas to test the possible answers.

1. MULTIPLE CHOICE What is the next term in the sequence 1, 4, 9, 16, 25, . . .?

- Ⓐ 34
- Ⓑ 35
- Ⓒ 36
- Ⓓ 38
- Ⓔ 39

2. MULTIPLE CHOICE Which series is represented by
$$\sum_{i=1}^{4} (4i - 2)?$$

- Ⓐ $2 + 6 + 10 + 14$
- Ⓑ $-2 + 2 + 6 + 10$
- Ⓒ $4 + 8 + 12 + 16$
- Ⓓ $6 + 10 + 14 + 18$
- Ⓔ $2 + 6 + 10 + 14 + \cdots$

3. MULTIPLE CHOICE What type of series is $32 + 16 + 8 + 4 + 2 + 1$?

- Ⓐ Finite arithmetic series
- Ⓑ Finite geometric series
- Ⓒ Infinite arithmetic series
- Ⓓ Infinite geometric series
- Ⓔ None of these

4. MULTIPLE CHOICE What is the sum of the series
$$\sum_{n=0}^{5} (n^3 + 3)?$$

- Ⓐ 128
- Ⓑ 131
- Ⓒ 240
- Ⓓ 242
- Ⓔ 243

5. MULTIPLE CHOICE What is a rule for the nth term of the arithmetic sequence with $a_{14} = 9$ and common difference $d = 2$?

- Ⓐ $a_n = 2n + 7$
- Ⓑ $a_n = 2n + 11$
- Ⓒ $a_n = 2n - 9$
- Ⓓ $a_n = 2n - 15$
- Ⓔ $a_n = 2n - 19$

6. MULTIPLE CHOICE What is the sum of the first 50 terms of the series $2 + 17 + 32 + 47 + \cdots$?

- Ⓐ 1600
- Ⓑ 18,235
- Ⓒ 18,475
- Ⓓ 18,800
- Ⓔ 19,125

7. MULTIPLE CHOICE What is a rule for the nth term of the geometric sequence with $a_3 = -12$ and common ratio $r = 3$?

- Ⓐ $a_n = -\frac{4}{3}(3)^{n-1}$
- Ⓑ $a_n = -4(3)^{n-1}$
- Ⓒ $a_n = -\frac{3}{4}(3)^{n-1}$
- Ⓓ $a_n = -\frac{1}{3}(3)^{n-1}$
- Ⓔ $a_n = 4(3)^{n-1}$

8. MULTIPLE CHOICE What is the sum of the series
$$\sum_{i=0}^{9} 20\left(\frac{1}{2}\right)^i?$$

- Ⓐ ≈ 11.74
- Ⓑ ≈ 13.30
- Ⓒ ≈ 13.32
- Ⓓ ≈ 39.96
- Ⓔ ≈ 29.97

9. MULTIPLE CHOICE What is the sum of the series
$$\sum_{i=1}^{\infty} 5(1.2)^{i-1}?$$

- Ⓐ -30
- Ⓑ -25
- Ⓒ 25
- Ⓓ 30
- Ⓔ The series has no sum.

10. MULTIPLE CHOICE Which fraction is equivalent to the repeating decimal 0.3838 . . .?

- Ⓐ $\frac{3}{10}$
- Ⓑ $\frac{3}{8}$
- Ⓒ $\frac{38}{100}$
- Ⓓ $\frac{383}{1000}$
- Ⓔ $\frac{38}{99}$

11. MULTIPLE CHOICE What is a recursive rule for the sequence 2, 6, 18, 54, . . .?

- Ⓐ $a_n = 2(3)^{n-1}$
- Ⓑ $a_n = 3(2)^{n-1}$
- Ⓒ $a_1 = 2, a_n = a_{n-1} + 4$
- Ⓓ $a_1 = 2, a_n = 3a_{n-1}$
- Ⓔ $a_1 = 3, a_n = 2a_{n-1}$

12. MULTIPLE CHOICE What is the fourth term of the sequence defined by the recursive rule $a_1 = 3, a_n = n + a_{n-1} - 7$?

- Ⓐ -1
- Ⓑ -6
- Ⓒ -9
- Ⓓ -10
- Ⓔ -11

QUANTITATIVE COMPARISON In Exercises 13 and 14, choose the statement
that is true about the given quantities.

(A) The quantity in column A is greater.

(B) The quantity in column B is greater.

(C) The two quantities are equal.

(D) The relationship cannot be determined from the given information.

	Column A	Column B
13.	The tenth term of the sequence defined by $a_n = 7 - 2n$	$\sum_{n=1}^{10} (7 - 2n)$
14.	$n!$ when n is an integer greater than 1	n^n when n is an integer greater than 1

15. 🌐 **MULTI-STEP PROBLEM** Use the pattern of checkerboard quilts at the right.

   a. What does n represent in each quilt?

   b. What does a_n represent in each quilt?

   c. Draw the next four quilts in the pattern.

   d. Complete a table that gives n and a_n for $n = 1, 2, 3, 4, 5, 6, 7, 8$.

   e. Use the rule $a_n = \dfrac{n^2}{2} + \dfrac{1}{4}[1 - (-1)^n]$ to find a_n for $n = 1, 2, 3, 4, 5, 6, 7, 8$.
   Compare with the results in your table. What can you conclude about the
   sequence defined by this rule?

$n = 1$
$a_1 = 1$

$n = 2$
$a_2 = 2$

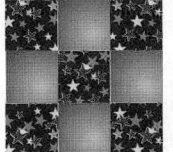
$n = 3$
$a_3 = 5$

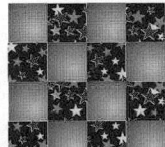
$n = 4$
$a_4 = 8$

16. MULTI-STEP PROBLEM Use the series $4 + 7 + 10 + 13 + 16 + 19 + 22 + 25$.

   a. Use a formula to find the sum of the series. Show your work.

   b. Find the sum of the series without using a formula. Explain your method.

   c. Write the series with summation notation. Use 1 as the lower limit of
   summation.

   d. Write the series with summation notation. Use 0 as the lower limit of
   summation.

   e. Write the series with summation notation. Use 4 as the lower limit of
   summation.

   f. *Writing* Compare your answers to parts (c), (d), and (e). Describe any
   similarities and differences. Which of these ways do you prefer to write the
   series? Explain your answer.

17. MULTI-STEP PROBLEM Use the sequence $100, 50, 25, 12.5, \ldots$.

   a. Is this sequence arithmetic, geometric, or neither? Is it finite or infinite?

   b. Write the next three terms of the sequence.

   c. Graph the sequence. Describe the curve on which the points lie.

   d. Write an explicit rule for the nth term of the sequence.

   e. Write a recursive rule for the sequence.

   f. Find the twelfth term of the sequence. Which rule from parts (d) and (e) did
   you use? Explain your choice.

PROBABILITY AND STATISTICS

▶ *In how many ways can you attend part of a summer concert series?*

APPLICATION: Concerts

*M*any cities offer summer concert series. Some have municipal bands that tour the city and play at different parks throughout the summer. Other cities have outdoor theaters where a variety of professional musicians can come to perform concerts.

Think & Discuss

Summer Concert Series

June 5th	June 19th
Music by Beethoven	Music by Mozart
July 3rd	**July 17th**
Music by Dvorak	Music by Brahms
August 7th	**August 21st**
Music by Strauss	Music by Tchaikovsky

1. Suppose you plan to attend exactly two of the concerts. Make a list of the possible choices of two concerts you can attend. How many choices do you have?

2. Suppose you plan to attend either one or two of the concerts. How many choices do you have?

Learn More About It

You will find the number of different combinations of concerts you can attend in Exercise 54 on p. 713.

 APPLICATION LINK Visit www.mcdougallittell.com for more information about concerts.

Study Guide

PREVIEW

What's the chapter about?

Chapter 12 is about **probability and statistics**. In Chapter 12 you'll learn

- how to count the number of ways an event can happen.
- how to calculate and use probabilities.
- how to use binomial and normal distributions.

KEY VOCABULARY

▶ **Review**
- binomial, p. 256
- mean, p. 445
- standard deviation, p. 446
- factorial, p. 681

▶ **New**
- permutation, p. 703
- combination, p. 708
- binomial theorem, p. 710
- probability, p. 716
- compound event, p. 724

- complement, p. 726
- independent events, p. 730
- dependent events, p. 732
- binomial distribution, p. 739
- hypothesis testing, p. 741
- normal distribution, p. 746

PREPARE

Are you ready for the chapter?

SKILL REVIEW Do these exercises to review key skills that you'll apply in this chapter. See the given **reference page** if there is something you don't understand.

Write the following as a decimal and as a percent. (Skills Review, p. 906)

1. $\frac{1}{2}$ **2.** $\frac{1}{5}$ **3.** $\frac{3}{20}$ **4.** $\frac{12}{25}$ **5.** $\frac{7}{36}$ **6.** $\frac{15}{32}$

Find the area of the figure. (Skills Review, p. 914)

7.
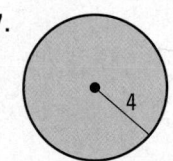

8.
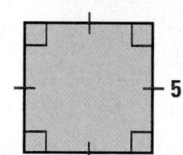

9.
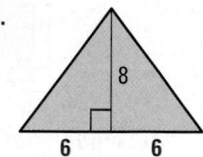

Solve the exponential equation. (Review Examples 2 and 3, pp. 501 and 502)

10. $10^x = 0.5$ **11.** $(0.5)^x + 3 = 3.75$ **12.** $1 - 9^x = 0.25$

STUDY STRATEGY

Here's a study strategy!

Connect to Your Life

Note real examples from your life that use the mathematics in this chapter. As you read the examples given in the textbook, listen to a teacher's explanation, and do the homework problems, think of problems in your own life that can be solved the same way. This will help you to understand and use the concepts you are learning.

The Fundamental Counting Principle and Permutations

What you should learn

GOAL 1 Use the funda-mental counting principle to count the number of ways an event can happen.

GOAL 2 Use permutations to count the number of ways an event can happen, as applied in **Ex. 62**.

Why you should learn it

▼ To find the number of ways a **real-life** event can happen, such as the number of ways skiers can finish in an aerial competition in **Example 3**.

GOAL 1 THE FUNDAMENTAL COUNTING PRINCIPLE

In many real-life problems you want to count the number of possibilities. For instance, suppose you own a small deli. You offer 4 types of meat (ham, turkey, roast beef, and pastrami) and 3 types of bread (white, wheat, and rye). How many choices do your customers have for a meat sandwich?

One way to answer this question is to use a *tree diagram*, as shown below. From the list on the right you can see that there are 12 choices.

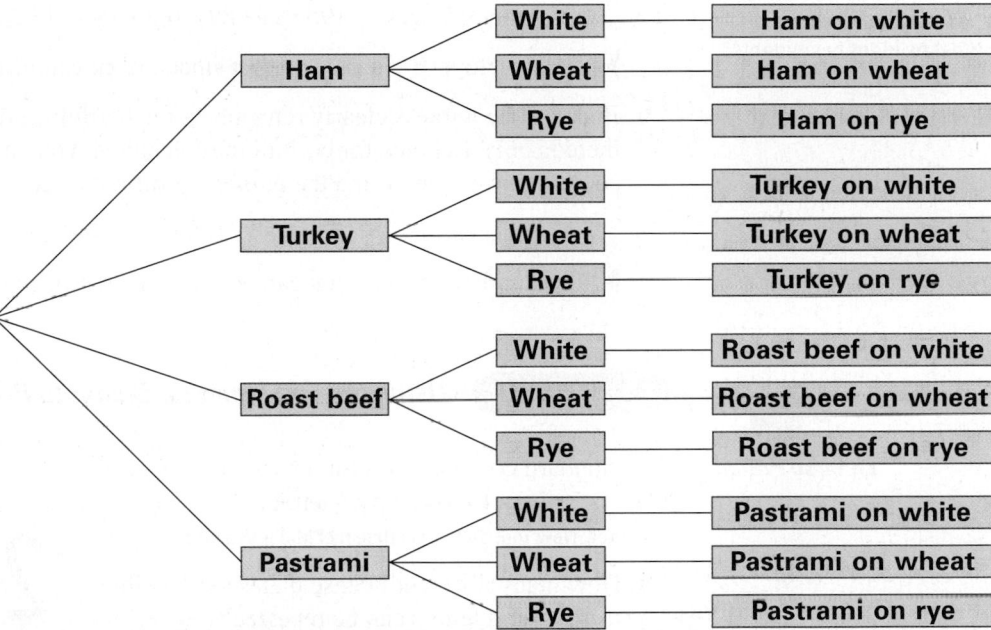

Another way to count the number of possible sandwiches is to use the *fundamental counting principle*. Because you have 4 choices for meat and 3 choices for bread, the total number of choices is 4 · 3 = 12.

FUNDAMENTAL COUNTING PRINCIPLE

TWO EVENTS If one event can occur in *m* ways and another event can occur in *n* ways, then the number of ways that *both* events can occur is *m* · *n*.

For instance, if one event can occur in 2 ways and another event can occur in 5 ways, then both events can occur in 2 · 5 = 10 ways.

THREE OR MORE EVENTS The fundamental counting principle can be extended to three or more events. For example, if three events can occur in *m, n,* and *p* ways, then the number of ways that *all* three events can occur is *m* · *n* · *p*.

For instance, if three events can occur in 2, 5, and 7 ways, then all three events can occur in 2 · 5 · 7 = 70 ways.

EXAMPLE 1 *Using the Fundamental Counting Principle*

CRIMINOLOGY Police use photographs of various facial features to help witnesses identify suspects. One basic identification kit contains 195 hairlines, 99 eyes and eyebrows, 89 noses, 105 mouths, and 74 chins and cheeks.
▶ Source: *Readers' Digest: How In The World?*

  a. The developer of the identification kit claims that it can produce billions of different faces. Is this claim correct?

  b. A witness can clearly remember the hairline and the eyes and eyebrows of a suspect. How many different faces can be produced with this information?

SOLUTION

  a. You can use the fundamental counting principle to find the total number of different faces.

    Number of faces = $195 \cdot 99 \cdot 89 \cdot 105 \cdot 74 = 13,349,986,650$

    ▶ The developer's claim is correct since the kit can produce over 13 billion faces.

  b. Because the witness clearly remembers the hairline and the eyes and eyebrows, there is only 1 choice for each of these features. You can use the fundamental counting principle to find the number of different faces.

    Number of faces = $1 \cdot 1 \cdot 89 \cdot 105 \cdot 74 = 691,530$

    ▶ The number of faces that can be produced has been reduced to 691,530.

License Plates

EXAMPLE 2 *Using the Fundamental Counting Principle with Repetition*

The standard configuration for a New York license plate is 3 digits followed by 3 letters.
▶ Source: New York State Department of Motor Vehicles

  a. How many different license plates are possible if digits and letters can be repeated?

  b. How many different license plates are possible if digits and letters cannot be repeated?

NEW YORK
234 ABC

SOLUTION

  a. There are 10 choices for each digit and 26 choices for each letter. You can use the fundamental counting principle to find the number of different plates.

    Number of plates = $10 \cdot 10 \cdot 10 \cdot 26 \cdot 26 \cdot 26 = 17,576,000$

    ▶ The number of different license plates is 17,576,000.

  b. If you cannot repeat digits there are still 10 choices for the first digit, but then only 9 remaining choices for the second digit and only 8 remaining choices for the third digit. Similarly, there are 26 choices for the first letter, 25 choices for the second letter, and 24 choices for the third letter. You can use the fundamental counting principle to find the number of different plates.

    Number of plates = $10 \cdot 9 \cdot 8 \cdot 26 \cdot 25 \cdot 24 = 11,232,000$

    ▶ The number of different license plates is 11,232,000.

GOAL 2 USING PERMUTATIONS

STUDENT HELP

→ **Study Tip**
Recall from Lesson 11.5 that $n!$ is read as "n factorial." Also note that $0! = 1$ and $1! = 1$.

An ordering of n objects is a **permutation** of the objects. For instance, there are six permutations of the letters A, B, and C: ABC, ACB, BAC, BCA, CAB, CBA.

The fundamental counting principle can be used to determine the number of permutations of n objects. For instance, you can find the number of ways you can arrange the letters A, B, and C by multiplying. There are 3 choices for the first letter, 2 choices for the second letter, and 1 choice for the third letter, so there are $3 \cdot 2 \cdot 1 = 6$ ways to arrange the letters.

In general, the number of permutations of n distinct objects is:

$$n! = n \cdot (n - 1) \cdot (n - 2) \cdot \ldots \cdot 3 \cdot 2 \cdot 1$$

Sports

EXAMPLE 3 *Finding the Number of Permutations*

Twelve skiers are competing in the final round of the Olympic freestyle skiing aerial competition.

a. In how many different ways can the skiers finish the competition? (Assume there are no ties.)

b. In how many different ways can 3 of the skiers finish first, second, and third to win the gold, silver, and bronze medals?

SOLUTION

a. There are 12! different ways that the skiers can finish the competition.

$$12! = 12 \cdot 11 \cdot 10 \cdot 9 \cdot 8 \cdot 7 \cdot 6 \cdot 5 \cdot 4 \cdot 3 \cdot 2 \cdot 1 = 479,001,600$$

b. Any of the 12 skiers can finish first, then any of the remaining 11 skiers can finish second, and finally any of the remaining 10 skiers can finish third. So, the number of ways that the skiers can win the medals is:

$$12 \cdot 11 \cdot 10 = 1320$$

· · · · · · · · · ·

STUDENT HELP

→ ⟳ **KEYSTROKE HELP**
Visit our Web site www.mcdougallittell.com to see keystrokes for several models of calculators.

Some calculators have special keys to evaluate factorials. The solution to Example 3 is shown.

The number in part (b) of Example 3 is called the number of permutations of 12 objects taken 3 at a time, is denoted by $_{12}P_3$, and is given by $\dfrac{12!}{(12 - 3)!}$.

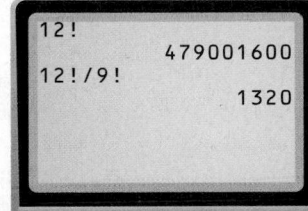

```
12!
                     479001600
12!/9!
                          1320
```

STUDENT HELP

→ **Derivations**
For a derivation of the formula for the permutation of n objects taken r at a time, see p. 899.

PERMUTATIONS OF *n* OBJECTS TAKEN *r* AT A TIME

The number of permutations of r objects taken from a group of n distinct objects is denoted by $_nP_r$ and is given by:

$$_nP_r = \frac{n!}{(n - r)!}$$

College Visits

EXAMPLE 4   *Finding Permutations of n Objects Taken r at a Time*

You are considering 10 different colleges. Before you decide to apply to the colleges, you want to visit some or all of them. In how many orders can you visit (**a**) 6 of the colleges and (**b**) all 10 colleges?

SOLUTION

a. The number of permutations of 10 objects taken 6 at a time is:

$$_{10}P_6 = \frac{10!}{(10-6)!} = \frac{10!}{4!} = \frac{3,628,800}{24} = 151,200$$

b. The number of permutations of 10 objects taken 10 at a time is:

$$_{10}P_{10} = \frac{10!}{(10-10)!} = \frac{10!}{0!} = 10! = 3,628,800$$

· · · · · · · · ·

STUDENT HELP

KEYSTROKE HELP
Visit our Web site
www.mcdougallittell.com
to see keystrokes for
several models of
calculators.

Some calculators have special keys that are programmed to evaluate $_nP_r$. The solution to Example 4 is shown.

So far you have been finding permutations of *distinct* objects. If some of the objects are repeated, then some of the permutations are not distinguishable. For instance, of the six ways to order the letters M, O, and M—

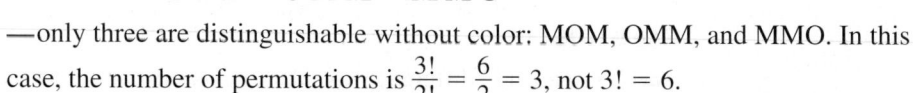

$$\textbf{MOM} \quad \textbf{OMM} \quad \textbf{MMO}$$

$$\textbf{MOM} \quad \textbf{OMM} \quad \textbf{MMO}$$

—only three are distinguishable without color: MOM, OMM, and MMO. In this case, the number of permutations is $\frac{3!}{2!} = \frac{6}{2} = 3$, not $3! = 6$.

PERMUTATIONS WITH REPETITION

The number of distinguishable permutations of *n* objects where one object is repeated q_1 times, another is repeated q_2 times, and so on is:

$$\frac{n!}{q_1! \cdot q_2! \cdot \ldots \cdot q_k!}$$

EXAMPLE 5   *Finding Permutations with Repetition*

Find the number of distinguishable permutations of the letters in (**a**) OHIO and (**b**) MISSISSIPPI.

SOLUTION

a. OHIO has 4 letters of which O is repeated 2 times. So, the number of distinguishable permutations is $\frac{4!}{2!} = \frac{24}{2} = 12$.

b. MISSISSIPPI has 11 letters of which I is repeated 4 times, S is repeated 4 times, and P is repeated 2 times. So, the number of distinguishable permutations is $\frac{11!}{4! \cdot 4! \cdot 2!} = \frac{39,916,800}{24 \cdot 24 \cdot 2} = 34,650$.

GUIDED PRACTICE

Vocabulary Check ✓

1. What is a permutation of n objects?

Concept Check ✓

2. Explain how the fundamental counting principle can be used to justify the formula for the number of permutations of n distinct objects.

3. Rita found the number of distinguishable permutations of the letters in OHIO by evaluating the expression $\frac{4!}{2! \cdot 1! \cdot 1!}$. Does this method give the same answer as in part (a) of Example 5? Explain.

4. ERROR ANALYSIS Explain the error in calculating how many three-digit numbers from 000 to 999 have only even digits.

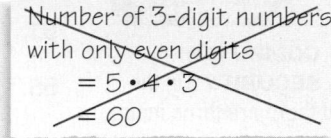

Number of 3-digit numbers with only even digits
$= 5 \cdot 4 \cdot 3$
$= 60$

Skill Check ✓

Find the number of permutations of n distinct objects.

5. $n = 2$ **6.** $n = 6$ **7.** $n = 1$ **8.** $n = 4$

Find the number of permutations of n objects taken r at a time.

9. $n = 6, r = 3$ **10.** $n = 5, r = 1$ **11.** $n = 3, r = 3$ **12.** $n = 10, r = 2$

Find the number of permutations of n objects where one or more objects are repeated the given number of times.

13. 7 objects with one object repeated 4 times

14. 5 objects with one object repeated 3 times and a second object repeated 2 times

PRACTICE AND APPLICATIONS

STUDENT HELP

▶ **Extra Practice**
to help you master skills is on p. 956.

FUNDAMENTAL COUNTING PRINCIPLE Each event can occur in the given number of ways. Find the number of ways all of the events can occur.

15. Event 1: 1 way, Event 2: 3 ways

16. Event 1: 3 ways, Event 2: 5 ways

17. Event 1: 2 ways, Event 2: 4 ways, Event 3: 5 ways

18. Event 1: 4 ways, Event 2: 6 ways, Event 3: 9 ways, Event 4: 7 ways

LICENSE PLATES For the given configuration, determine how many different license plates are possible if (a) digits and letters can be repeated, and (b) digits and letters cannot be repeated.

19. 3 letters followed by 3 digits

20. 2 digits followed by 4 letters

21. 4 digits followed by 2 letters

22. 5 letters followed by 1 digit

STUDENT HELP

▶ **HOMEWORK HELP**
Example 1: Exs. 15–18, 55, 56
Example 2: Exs. 19–22, 57
Example 3: Exs. 23–30, 39–46, 59, 60
Example 4: Exs. 31–38, 61
Example 5: Exs. 47–54, 62, 63

FACTORIALS Evaluate the factorial.

23. 8!   **24.** 5!   **25.** 10!   **26.** 9!

27. 0!   **28.** 7!   **29.** 3!   **30.** 12!

PERMUTATIONS Find the number of permutations.

31. $_3P_3$ **32.** $_5P_2$ **33.** $_2P_1$ **34.** $_7P_6$

35. $_8P_5$ **36.** $_9P_4$ **37.** $_{12}P_3$ **38.** $_{16}P_0$

PERMUTATIONS WITHOUT REPETITION Find the number of distinguishable permutations of the letters in the word.

39. HI   **40.** JET   **41.** IOWA   **42.** TEXAS

43. PENCIL   **44.** FLORIDA   **45.** MAGNETIC   **46.** GOLDFINCH

PERMUTATIONS WITH REPETITION Find the number of distinguishable permutations of the letters in the word.

47. DAD   **48.** PUPPY   **49.** OREGON   **50.** LETTER

51. ALGEBRA   **52.** ALABAMA   **53.** MISSOURI   **54.** CONNECTICUT

55. 🌐 **STEREO** You are going to set up a stereo system by purchasing separate components. In your price range you find 5 different receivers, 8 different compact disc players, and 12 different speaker systems. If you want one of each of these components, how many different stereo systems are possible?

56. 🌐 **PIZZA** A pizza shop runs a special where you can buy a large pizza with one cheese, one vegetable, and one meat for $9.00. You have a choice of 7 cheeses, 11 vegetables, and 6 meats. Additionally, you have a choice of 3 crusts and 2 sauces. How many different variations of the pizza special are possible?

57. 🌐 **COMPUTER SECURITY** To keep computer files secure, many programs require the user to enter a password. The shortest allowable passwords are typically six characters long and can contain both numbers and letters. How many six-character passwords are possible if (**a**) characters can be repeated and (**b**) characters cannot be repeated?

58. **CRITICAL THINKING** Simplify the formula for $_nP_r$ when $r = 0$. Explain why this result makes sense.

59. 🌐 **CLASS SEATING** A particular classroom has 24 seats and 24 students. Assuming the seats are not moved, how many different seating arrangements are possible? Write your answer in scientific notation.

60. 🌐 **RINGING BELLS** "Ringing the changes" is a process where the bells in a tower are rung in all possible permutations. Westminster Abbey has 10 bells in its tower. In how many ways can its bells be rung?

61. 🌐 **PLAY AUDITIONS** Auditions are being held for the play shown. How many ways can the roles be assigned if (**a**) 6 people audition and (**b**) 9 people audition?

62. 🌐 **WINDOW DISPLAY** A music store wants to display 3 identical keyboards, 2 identical trumpets, and 2 identical guitars in its store window. How many distinguishable displays are possible?

63. 🌐 **DOG SHOW** In a dog show how many ways can 3 Chihuahuas, 5 Labradors, 4 poodles, and 3 beagles line up in front of the judges if the dogs of the same breed are considered identical?

the **Drama Club**

is holding
Open Auditions
for parts in a one-act play
Parts available:

Student A	Teacher
Student B	Librarian
Principal	Coach

64. **CRITICAL THINKING** Find the number of permutations of n objects taken $n - 1$ at a time for any positive integer n. Compare this answer with the number of permutations of all n objects. Does this make sense? Explain.

QUANTITATIVE COMPARISON In Exercises 65 and 66, choose the statement that is true about the given quantities.

Ⓐ The quantity in column A is greater.

Ⓑ The quantity in column B is greater.

Ⓒ The two quantities are equal.

Ⓓ The relationship cannot be determined from the given information.

	Column A	Column B
65.	$_5P_1$	$5!$
66.	The number of permutations of 12 objects taken 7 at a time	The number of permutations of 12 objects, one of which is repeated 5 times

★ **Challenge**

67. CIRCULAR PERMUTATIONS You have learned that $n!$ represents the number of ways that n objects can be placed in a *linear* order, where it matters which object is placed first. Now consider *circular* permutations, where objects are placed in a circle so it does *not* matter which object is placed first. Find a formula for the number of permutations of n objects placed in clockwise order around a circle when only the relative order of the objects matters. Explain how you derived your formula.

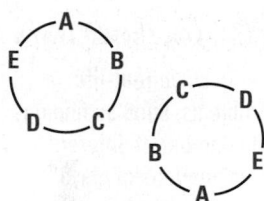

This is the same permutation.

MIXED REVIEW

SPECIAL PRODUCTS Find the product. **(Review 6.3 for 12.2)**

68. $(x + 9)(x - 9)$ **69.** $(x^2 + 2)^2$ **70.** $(2x - 1)^3$

71. $(4x + 5)(4x - 5)$ **72.** $(2y + 3x)^2$ **73.** $(8y - x)^2$

GRAPHING Graph the equation of the parabola. **(Review 10.2)**

74. $y^2 = 8x$ **75.** $x^2 = -10y$ **76.** $y^2 = -4x$

77. $x^2 = 26y$ **78.** $x + 14y^2 = 0$ **79.** $y - 2x^2 = 0$

FINDING SUMS Find the sum of the infinite geometric series if there is one. **(Review 11.4)**

80. $\displaystyle\sum_{n=0}^{\infty} 3\left(\frac{1}{2}\right)^n$ **81.** $\displaystyle\sum_{n=0}^{\infty} -4\left(\frac{1}{4}\right)^n$ **82.** $\displaystyle\sum_{n=0}^{\infty} 2\left(\frac{2}{3}\right)^n$

83. $\displaystyle\sum_{n=1}^{\infty} 2\left(\frac{7}{5}\right)^{n-1}$ **84.** $\displaystyle\sum_{n=0}^{\infty} -5\left(\frac{1}{8}\right)^n$ **85.** $\displaystyle\sum_{n=1}^{\infty} \frac{1}{2}(0.3)^{n-1}$

86. **SCIENCE CONNECTION** Ohm's law states that the resistance R (in ohms) of a conductor varies directly with the potential difference V (in volts) between two points and inversely with the current I (in amperes). The constant of variation is 1. What is the resistance of a light bulb if there is a current of 0.80 ampere when the potential difference across the bulb is 120 volts? **(Review 9.1)**

12.2

Combinations and the Binomial Theorem

What you should learn

GOAL 1 Use combinations to count the number of ways an event can happen, as applied in **Ex. 55**.

GOAL 2 Use the binomial theorem to expand a binomial that is raised to a power.

Why you should learn it

▼ To solve **real-life** problems, such as finding the number of different combinations of plays you can attend in **Example 3**.

GOAL 1 USING COMBINATIONS

In Lesson 12.1 you learned that order is important for some counting problems. For other counting problems, order is not important. For instance, in most card games the order in which your cards are dealt is not important. After your cards are dealt, reordering them does not change your card hand. These unordered groupings are called *combinations*. A **combination** is a selection of r objects from a group of n objects where the order is not important.

COMBINATIONS OF n OBJECTS TAKEN r AT A TIME

The number of combinations of r objects taken from a group of n distinct objects is denoted by $_nC_r$ and is given by:

$$_nC_r = \frac{n!}{(n-r)! \cdot r!}$$

For instance, the number of combinations of 2 objects taken from a group of 5 objects is $_5C_2 = \frac{5!}{3! \cdot 2!} = 10$.

EXAMPLE 1 Finding Combinations

A standard deck of 52 playing cards has 4 suits with 13 different cards in each suit as shown.

a. If the order in which the cards are dealt is not important, how many different 5-card hands are possible?

b. In how many of these hands are all five cards of the same suit?

Standard 52-Card Deck

K ♠	K ♣	K ♦	K ♥
Q ♠	Q ♣	Q ♦	Q ♥
J ♠	J ♣	J ♦	J ♥
10 ♠	10 ♣	10 ♦	10 ♥
9 ♠	9 ♣	9 ♦	9 ♥
8 ♠	8 ♣	8 ♦	8 ♥
7 ♠	7 ♣	7 ♦	7 ♥
6 ♠	6 ♣	6 ♦	6 ♥
5 ♠	5 ♣	5 ♦	5 ♥
4 ♠	4 ♣	4 ♦	4 ♥
3 ♠	3 ♣	3 ♦	3 ♥
2 ♠	2 ♣	2 ♦	2 ♥
A ♠	A ♣	A ♦	A ♥

SOLUTION

a. The number of ways to choose 5 cards from a deck of 52 cards is:

$$_{52}C_5 = \frac{52!}{47! \cdot 5!}$$

$$= \frac{52 \cdot 51 \cdot 50 \cdot 49 \cdot 48 \cdot \cancel{47!}}{\cancel{47!} \cdot 5!}$$

$$= 2{,}598{,}960$$

b. For all five cards to be the same suit, you need to choose 1 of the 4 suits and then 5 of the 13 cards in the suit. So, the number of possible hands is:

$$_4C_1 \cdot {}_{13}C_5 = \frac{4!}{3! \cdot 1!} \cdot \frac{13!}{8! \cdot 5!} = \frac{4 \cdot \cancel{3!}}{\cancel{3!} \cdot 1!} \cdot \frac{13 \cdot 12 \cdot 11 \cdot 10 \cdot 9 \cdot \cancel{8!}}{\cancel{8!} \cdot 5!} = 5148$$

When finding the number of ways both an event *A and* an event *B* can occur, you need to multiply (as you did in part (b) of Example 1). When finding the number of ways that an event *A or* an event *B* can occur, you add instead.

Menu Choices

EXAMPLE 2 *Deciding to Multiply or Add*

A restaurant serves omelets that can be ordered with any of the ingredients shown.

a. Suppose you want *exactly* 2 vegetarian ingredients and 1 meat ingredient in your omelet. How many different types of omelets can you order?

b. Suppose you can afford *at most* 3 ingredients in your omelet. How many different types of omelets can you order?

Omelets $3.00	
(plus $.50 for each ingredient)	
Vegetarian	Meat
green pepper	ham
red pepper	bacon
onion	sausage
mushroom	steak
tomato	
cheese	

SOLUTION

a. You can choose 2 of 6 vegetarian ingredients and 1 of 4 meat ingredients. So, the number of possible omelets is:

$$_6C_2 \cdot {}_4C_1 = \frac{6!}{4! \cdot 2!} \cdot \frac{4!}{3! \cdot 1!} = 15 \cdot 4 = 60$$

b. You can order an omelet with 0, 1, 2, or 3 ingredients. Because there are 10 items to choose from, the number of possible omelets is:

$$_{10}C_0 + {}_{10}C_1 + {}_{10}C_2 + {}_{10}C_3 = 1 + 10 + 45 + 120 = 176$$

· · · · · · · · ·

STUDENT HELP

KEYSTROKE HELP
Visit our Web site
www.mcdougallittell.com
to see keystrokes for
several models of
calculators.

Some calculators have special keys to evaluate combinations. The solution to Example 2 is shown.

Counting problems that involve phrases like "at least" or "at most" are sometimes easier to solve by subtracting possibilities you do not want from the total number of possibilities.

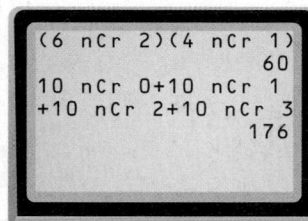

Theater

EXAMPLE 3 *Subtracting Instead of Adding*

A theater is staging a series of 12 different plays. You want to attend *at least* 3 of the plays. How many different combinations of plays can you attend?

SOLUTION

You want to attend 3 plays, or 4 plays, or 5 plays, and so on. So, the number of combinations of plays you can attend is $_{12}C_3 + {}_{12}C_4 + {}_{12}C_5 + \cdots + {}_{12}C_{12}$.

Instead of adding these combinations, it is easier to use the following reasoning. For each of the 12 plays, you can choose to attend or not attend the play, so there are 2^{12} total combinations. If you attend at least 3 plays you do not attend only 0, 1, or 2 plays. So, the number of ways you can attend at least 3 plays is:

$$2^{12} - \left({}_{12}C_0 + {}_{12}C_1 + {}_{12}C_2\right) = 4096 - (1 + 12 + 66) = 4017$$

► BLAISE PASCAL
developed his
arithmetic triangle in 1653.
The following year he and
fellow mathematician
Pierre Fermat outlined the
foundations of probability
theory.

GOAL 2 **USING THE BINOMIAL THEOREM**

If you arrange the values of $_nC_r$ in a triangular pattern in which each row corresponds to a value of n, you get what is called **Pascal's triangle**. It is named after the famous French mathematician Blaise Pascal (1623–1662).

$$
\begin{array}{ccccccc}
 & & & _0C_0 & & & \\
 & & _1C_0 & & _1C_1 & & \\
 & _2C_0 & & _2C_1 & & _2C_2 & \\
 _3C_0 & & _3C_1 & & _3C_2 & & _3C_3 \\
_4C_0 & _4C_1 & _4C_2 & _4C_3 & _4C_4 & & \\
_5C_0 & _5C_1 & _5C_2 & _5C_3 & _5C_4 & _5C_5 &
\end{array}
\qquad
\begin{array}{cccccc}
 & & 1 & & & \\
 & 1 & & 1 & & \\
 & 1 & 2 & 1 & & \\
 1 & 3 & 3 & 1 & & \\
1 & 4 & 6 & 4 & 1 & \\
1 & 5 & 10 & 10 & 5 & 1
\end{array}
$$

Pascal's triangle has many interesting patterns and properties. For instance, each number other than 1 is the sum of the two numbers directly above it.

> ▶ **ACTIVITY**
> **Developing Concepts**
>
> ## Investigating Pascal's Triangle
>
> **1** Expand each expression. Write the terms of each expanded expression so that the powers of a decrease.
>
>   **a.** $(a + b)^2$ **b.** $(a + b)^3$ **c.** $(a + b)^4$
>
> **2** Describe the relationship between the coefficients in parts (a), (b), and (c) of **Step 1** and the rows of Pascal's triangle.
>
> **3** Describe any patterns in the exponents of a and the exponents of b.

In the activity you may have discovered the following result, which is called the **binomial theorem**. This theorem describes the coefficients in the expansion of the binomial $a + b$ raised to the nth power.

THE BINOMIAL THEOREM

The binomial expansion of $(a + b)^n$ for any positive integer n is:

$$(a + b)^n = {_nC_0}a^n b^0 + {_nC_1}a^{n-1}b^1 + {_nC_2}a^{n-2}b^2 + \cdots + {_nC_n}a^0 b^n$$

$$= \sum_{r=0}^{n} {_nC_r}a^{n-r}b^r$$

EXAMPLE 4 *Expanding a Power of a Simple Binomial Sum*

STUDENT HELP

► **Study Tip**
You can calculate combinations using either Pascal's triangle or the formula on p. 708.

Expand $(x + 2)^4$.

SOLUTION

$$(x + 2)^4 = {_4C_0}x^4 2^0 + {_4C_1}x^3 2^1 + {_4C_2}x^2 2^2 + {_4C_3}x^1 2^3 + {_4C_4}x^0 2^4$$

$$= (1)(x^4)(1) + (4)(x^3)(2) + (6)(x^2)(4) + (4)(x)(8) + (1)(1)(16)$$

$$= x^4 + 8x^3 + 24x^2 + 32x + 16$$

EXAMPLE 5 **Expanding a Power of a Binomial Sum**

Expand $(u + v^2)^3$.

SOLUTION

$$(u + v^2)^3 = {}_3C_0u^3(v^2)^0 + {}_3C_1u^2(v^2)^1 + {}_3C_2u^1(v^2)^2 + {}_3C_3u^0(v^2)^3$$

$$= u^3 + 3u^2v^2 + 3uv^4 + v^6$$

· · · · · · · · · ·

To expand a power of a binomial difference, you can rewrite the binomial as a sum. The resulting expansion will have terms whose signs alternate between $+$ and $-$.

EXAMPLE 6 **Expanding a Power of a Simple Binomial Difference**

Expand $(x - y)^5$.

SOLUTION

$$(x - y)^5 = [x + (-y)]^5$$

$$= {}_5C_0x^5(-y)^0 + {}_5C_1x^4(-y)^1 + {}_5C_2x^3(-y)^2 + {}_5C_3x^2(-y)^3 +$$
$$\quad {}_5C_4x^1(-y)^4 + {}_5C_5x^0(-y)^5$$

$$= x^5 - 5x^4y + 10x^3y^2 - 10x^2y^3 + 5xy^4 - y^5$$

EXAMPLE 7 **Expanding a Power of a Binomial Difference**

Expand $(5 - 2a)^4$.

SOLUTION

$$(5 - 2a)^4 = [5 + (-2a)]^4$$

$$= {}_4C_05^4(-2a)^0 + {}_4C_15^3(-2a)^1 + {}_4C_25^2(-2a)^2 + {}_4C_35^1(-2a)^3 +$$
$$\quad {}_4C_45^0(-2a)^4$$

$$= (1)(625)(1) + (4)(125)(-2a) + (6)(25)(4a^2) + (4)(5)(-8a^3) +$$
$$\quad (1)(1)(16a^4)$$

$$= 625 - 1000a + 600a^2 - 160a^3 + 16a^4$$

EXAMPLE 8 **Finding a Coefficient in an Expansion**

Find the coefficient of x^4 in the expansion of $(2x - 3)^{12}$.

SOLUTION From the binomial theorem you know the following:

$$(2x - 3)^{12} = \sum_{r=0}^{12} {}_{12}C_r(2x)^{12-r}(-3)^r$$

The term that has x^4 is ${}_{12}C_8(2x)^4(-3)^8 = (495)(16x^4)(6561) = 51{,}963{,}120x^4$.

▶ The coefficient is $51{,}963{,}120$.

GUIDED PRACTICE

Vocabulary Check ✓

1. Explain the difference between a permutation and a combination.

Concept Check ✓

2. Describe a situation in which to find the total number of possibilities you would (**a**) add two combinations and (**b**) multiply two combinations.

3. Write the expansions for $(x + y)^4$ and $(x - y)^4$. How are they similar? How are they different?

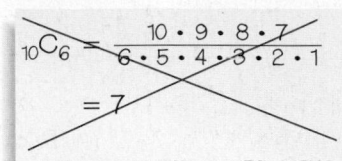

4. **ERROR ANALYSIS** What error was made in the calculation of $_{10}C_6$? Explain.

Skill Check ✓

Find the number of combinations of *n* objects taken *r* at a time.

5. $n = 8, r = 2$　　6. $n = 6, r = 5$　　7. $n = 5, r = 1$　　8. $n = 9, r = 9$

Expand the power of the binomial.

9. $(x + y)^3$　　10. $(x + 1)^4$　　11. $(2x + 4)^3$　　12. $(2x + 3y)^5$

13. $(x - y)^5$　　14. $(x - 2)^3$　　15. $(3x - 1)^4$　　16. $(4x - 4y)^3$

17. Complete this equation:

$$(x + 3y)^5 = x^5 + 15x^4y + 90x^3y^2 + \underline{?}\ x^2y^3 + 405xy^4 + \underline{?}\ y^5$$

PRACTICE AND APPLICATIONS

STUDENT HELP

▶ **Extra Practice**
to help you master
skills is on p. 956.

COMBINATIONS Find the number of combinations.

18. $_{10}C_2$　　19. $_8C_5$　　20. $_5C_2$　　21. $_8C_6$

22. $_{12}C_4$　　23. $_{12}C_{12}$　　24. $_{14}C_6$　　25. $_{11}C_3$

CARD HANDS In Exercises 26–30, find the number of possible 5-card hands that contain the cards specified.

26. 5 face cards (either kings, queens, or jacks)

27. 4 aces and 1 other card

28. 1 ace and 4 other cards (none of which are aces)

29. 2 aces and 3 kings

30. 4 of one kind (kings, queens, and so on) and 1 of a different kind

31. **PASCAL'S TRIANGLE** Copy Pascal's triangle on page 710 and add the rows for $n = 6$ and $n = 7$ to it.

STUDENT HELP

▶ HOMEWORK HELP
Example 1: Exs. 18–30,
　　　47, 48
Example 2: Exs. 49–52
Example 3: Exs. 53, 54
Examples 4–7: Exs. 31–43
Example 8: Exs. 44–46

PASCAL'S TRIANGLE Use the rows of Pascal's triangle from Exercise 31 to write the binomial expansion.

32. $(x + 4)^6$　　33. $(x - 3y)^6$　　34. $(x^2 + y)^7$　　35. $\left(2x - y^3\right)^7$

BINOMIAL THEOREM Use the binomial theorem to write the binomial expansion.

36. $(x - 2)^3$　　37. $(x + 4)^5$　　38. $(x + 3y)^4$　　39. $(2x - y)^6$

40. $(x^3 + 3)^5$　　41. $(3x^2 - 3)^4$　　42. $\left(2x - y^2\right)^7$　　43. $\left(x^3 + y^2\right)^3$

44. Find the coefficient of x^5 in the expansion of $(x - 3)^7$.

45. Find the coefficient of x^4 in the expansion of $(x + 2)^8$.

46. Find the coefficient of x^6 in the expansion of $(x^2 + 4)^{10}$.

47. 🌐 **NOVELS** Your English teacher has asked you to select 3 novels from a list of 10 to read as an independent project. In how many ways can you choose which books to read?

48. 🌐 **GAMES** Your friend is having a party and has 15 games to choose from. There is enough time to play 4 games. In how many ways can you choose which games to play?

49. 🌐 **CARS** You are buying a new car. There are 7 different colors to choose from and 10 different types of optional equipment you can buy. You can choose only 1 color for your car and can afford only 2 of the options. How many combinations are there for your car?

50. 🌐 **ART CONTEST** There are 6 artists each presenting 5 works of art in an art contest. The 4 works judged best will be displayed in a local gallery. In how many ways can these 4 works all be chosen from the same artist's collection?

51. **LOGICAL REASONING** Look back at Example 2. Suppose you can afford at most 7 ingredients. How many different types of omelets can you order?

52. 🌐 **AMUSEMENT PARKS** An amusement park has 20 different rides. You want to ride at least 15 of them. How many different combinations of rides can you go on?

53. 🌐 **FISH** From the list of different species of fish shown, an aquarium enthusiast is interested in knowing how compatible any group of 3 or more different species are. How many different combinations are there to consider?

54. 🌐 **CONCERTS** A summer concert series has 12 different performing artists. You decide to attend at least 4 of the concerts. How many different combinations of concerts can you attend?

On Sale This Month

Freshwater Tropical Fish

Neon Tetras	Black Mollies
Tiger Barbs	Zebra fish
Red Platys	Bala Sharks
Angelfish	Lyretails
Blue Gouramis	Catfish

CRITICAL THINKING Decide whether the problem requires combinations or permutations to find the answer. Then solve the problem.

55. 🌐 **MARCHING BAND** Eight members of a school marching band are auditioning for 3 drum major positions. In how many ways can students be chosen to be drum majors?

56. 🌐 **YEARBOOK** Your school yearbook has an editor-in-chief and an assistant editor-in-chief. The staff of the yearbook has 15 students. In how many ways can students be chosen for these 2 positions?

57. 🌐 **RELAY RACES** A relay race has 4 runners who run different parts of the race. There are 16 students on your track team. In how many ways can your coach select students to compete in the race?

58. 🌐 **COLLEGE COURSES** You must take 6 elective classes to meet your graduation requirements for college. There are 12 classes that you are interested in. In how many ways can you select your elective classes?

59. CRITICAL THINKING Write an equation that relates $_nP_r$ and $_nC_r$.

STACKING CUBES In Exercises 60–63, use the diagram shown which illustrates the different ways to stack four cubes.

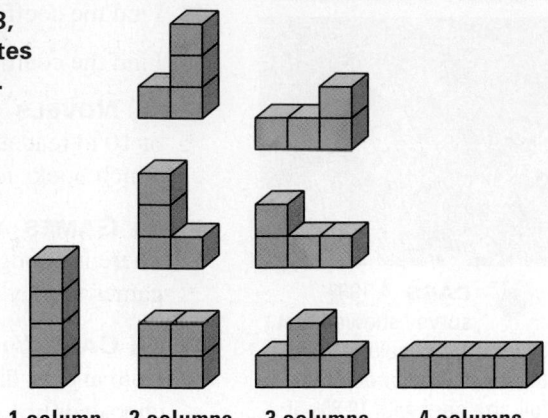

60. Sketch the different ways to stack three cubes.

61. Sketch the different ways to stack five cubes.

62. How does the number of ways to stack three, four, and five cubes relate to Pascal's triangle?

63. In how many different ways can you stack ten cubes?

1 column   2 columns   3 columns   4 columns

PASCAL'S TRIANGLE In Exercises 64–66, use the diagram of Pascal's triangle shown.

64. What is the sum of the numbers in row n of Pascal's triangle? Explain.

65. What is the sum of the numbers in rows 0 through 20 of Pascal's triangle?

66. LOGICAL REASONING Describe the pattern formed by the sums of the numbers along the diagonal segments of Pascal's triangle.

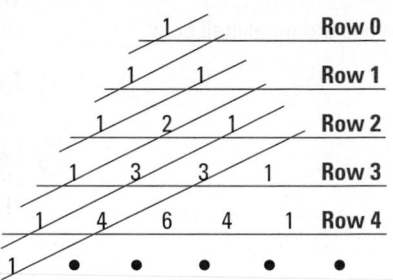

Test Preparation

67. MULTI-STEP PROBLEM A group of 20 high school students is volunteering to help elderly members of their community. Each student will be assigned a job based on requests received for help. There are 8 requests for raking leaves, 7 requests for running errands, and 5 requests for washing windows.

a. One way to count the number of possible job assignments is to find the number of permutations of 8 L's (for "leaves"), 7 E's (for "errands"), and 5 W's (for "windows"). Use this method to write the number of possible job assignments first as an expression involving factorials and then as a simple number.

b. Another way to count the number of possible job assignments is to first choose the 8 students who will rake leaves, then choose the 7 students who will run errands from the students who remain, and then choose the 5 students who will wash windows from the students who still remain. Use this method to write the number of possible job assignments first as an expression involving factorials and then as a simple number.

c. *Writing* How do the answers to parts (a) and (b) compare to each other? Explain why this makes sense.

★ **Challenge**   **COMBINATORIAL IDENTITIES** Verify the identity.

68. $_nC_0 = 1$

69. $_nC_n = 1$

70. $_nC_1 = {_nP_1}$

71. $_nC_r = {_nC_{n-r}}$

72. $_nC_r \cdot {_rC_m} = {_nC_m} \cdot {_{n-m}C_{r-m}}$

73. $_{n+1}C_r = {_nC_r} + {_nC_{r-1}}$

MIXED REVIEW

FINDING AREA Find the area of the figure. (Skills Review, p. 914)

74. Circle with radius 18 centimeters

75. Rectangle with sides 9.5 inches and 11.3 inches

76. Triangle with base 13 feet and height 9 feet

77. Trapezoid with bases 10 meters and 13 meters, and height 27 meters

GRAPHING Graph the equation of the hyperbola. (Review 10.5)

78. $\dfrac{x^2}{25} - \dfrac{y^2}{144} = 1$

79. $\dfrac{y^2}{100} - \dfrac{x^2}{36} = 1$

80. $x^2 - \dfrac{49y^2}{16} = 1$

81. $\dfrac{y^2}{4} - \dfrac{x^2}{9} = 9$

82. $64y^2 - x^2 = 64$

83. $9x^2 - 4y^2 = 144$

WRITING RULES Decide whether the sequence is arithmetic or geometric. Then write a rule for the nth term. (Review 11.2, 11.3)

84. 3, 9, 27, 81, 243, . . .

85. 3, 10, 17, 24, 31, . . .

86. 2, 10, 50, 250, 1250, . . .

87. 1, -2, 4, -8, 16, . . .

88. 8, 6, 4, 2, 0, . . .

89. -10, -5, 0, 5, 10, . . .

90. **POTTERY** A potter has 70 pounds of clay and 40 hours to make soup bowls and dinner plates to sell at a craft fair. A soup bowl uses 3 pounds of clay and a dinner plate uses 4 pounds of clay. It takes 3 hours to make a soup bowl and 1 hour to make a dinner plate. If the profit on a soup bowl is $25 and the profit on a dinner plate is $20, how many bowls and plates should the potter make in order to maximize profit? (Review 3.4)

QUIZ 1

Self-Test for Lessons 12.1 and 12.2

Find the number of distinguishable permutations of the letters in the word. (Lesson 12.1)

1. POP
2. JUNE
3. IDAHO
4. KANSAS

5. WYOMING
6. THURSDAY
7. SEPTEMBER
8. CALIFORNIA

Write the binomial expansion. (Lesson 12.2)

9. $(x + y)^6$

10. $(x + 2)^4$

11. $(x - 2y)^5$

12. $(3x - 4y)^3$

13. $(x^2 + 3y)^4$

14. $(4x^2 - 2)^6$

15. $(x^3 - y^3)^3$

16. $(2x^4 + 5y^2)^5$

17. Find the coefficient of x^3 in the expansion of $(x + 3)^5$. (Lesson 12.2)

18. Find the coefficient of y^4 in the expansion of $(5 - y^2)^3$. (Lesson 12.2)

19. **RESTAURANTS** You are eating dinner at a restaurant. The restaurant offers 6 appetizers, 12 main dishes, 6 side orders, and 8 desserts. If you order one of each of these, how many different dinners can you order? (Lesson 12.1)

20. **FLOWERS** You are buying a flower arrangement. The florist has 12 types of flowers and 6 types of vases. If you can afford exactly 3 types of flowers and need only 1 vase, how many different arrangements can you buy? (Lesson 12.2)

12.3

An Introduction to Probability

What you should learn

GOAL 1 Find theoretical and experimental probabilities.

GOAL 2 Find geometric probabilities, as applied in **Example 5**.

Why you should learn it

▼ To solve **real-life** problems, such as finding the probability that an archer hits the center of a target in **Ex. 46**.

GOAL 1 **THEORETICAL AND EXPERIMENTAL PROBABILITY**

The **probability** of an event is a number between 0 and 1 that indicates the likelihood the event will occur. An event that is certain to occur has a probability of 1. An event that *cannot* occur has a probability of 0. An event that is equally likely to occur or not occur has a probability of $\frac{1}{2}$.

P = 0
Event will not occur.

P = $\frac{1}{2}$
Event is equally likely to occur or not occur.

P = 1
Event is certain to occur.

There are two types of probability: *theoretical* and *experimental*. Theoretical probability is defined below and experimental probability is defined on page 717.

THE THEORETICAL PROBABILITY OF AN EVENT

When all outcomes are equally likely, the **theoretical probability** that an event A will occur is:

$$P(A) = \frac{\text{number of outcomes in } A}{\text{total number of outcomes}}$$

The theoretical probability of an event is often simply called the probability of the event.

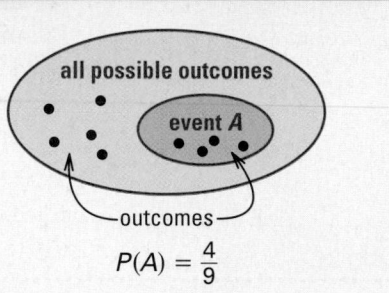

all possible outcomes

event A

outcomes

$P(A) = \frac{4}{9}$

EXAMPLE 1 *Finding Probabilities of Events*

You roll a six-sided die whose sides are numbered from 1 through 6. Find the probability of (**a**) rolling a 4, (**b**) rolling an odd number, and (**c**) rolling a number less than 7.

SOLUTION

a. Only one outcome corresponds to rolling a 4.

$$P(\text{rolling a 4}) = \frac{\text{number of ways to roll a 4}}{\text{number of ways to roll the die}} = \frac{1}{6}$$

b. Three outcomes correspond to rolling an odd number: rolling a 1, 3, or 5.

$$P(\text{rolling an odd number}) = \frac{\text{number of ways to roll an odd number}}{\text{number of ways to roll the die}} = \frac{3}{6} = \frac{1}{2}$$

c. All six outcomes correspond to rolling a number less than 7.

$$P(\text{rolling less than 7}) = \frac{\text{number of ways to roll less than 7}}{\text{number of ways to roll the die}} = \frac{6}{6} = 1$$

You can express a probability as a fraction, a decimal, or a percent. For instance, in part (b) of Example 1 the probability of rolling an odd number can be written as $\frac{1}{2}$, 0.5, or 50%.

EXAMPLE 2 *Probabilities Involving Permutations or Combinations*

You put a CD that has 8 songs in your CD player. You set the player to play the songs at random. The player plays all 8 songs without repeating any song.

   a. What is the probability that the songs are played in the same order they are listed on the CD?

   b. You have 4 favorite songs on the CD. What is the probability that 2 of your favorite songs are played first, in any order?

SOLUTION

STUDENT HELP

▶ **Skills Review**
For help with converting decimals, fractions, and percents, see p. 906.

   a. There are 8! different *permutations* of the 8 songs. Of these, only 1 is the order in which the songs are listed on the CD. So, the probability is:

$$P(\text{playing 8 in order}) = \frac{1}{8!} = \frac{1}{40,320} \approx 0.0000248$$

   b. There are $_8C_2$ different *combinations* of 2 songs. Of these, $_4C_2$ contain 2 of your favorite songs. So, the probability is:

$$P(\text{playing 2 favorites first}) = \frac{_4C_2}{_8C_2} = \frac{6}{28} = \frac{3}{14} \approx 0.214$$

· · · · · · · · · ·

Sometimes it is not possible or convenient to find the theoretical probability of an event. In such cases you may be able to calculate an **experimental probability** by performing an experiment, conducting a survey, or looking at the history of the event.

EXAMPLE 3 *Finding Experimental Probabilities*

In 1998 a survey asked Internet users for their ages. The results are shown in the bar graph. Find the experimental probability that a randomly selected Internet user is (**a**) at most 20 years old, and (**b**) at least 41 years old.

▶ Source: GVU's WWW User Surveys™

Internet Users

Age (years)	Number of users
Under 21	1636
21–40	6617
41–60	3693
61–80	491
Over 80	6

SOLUTION The number of people surveyed was $1636 + 6617 + 3693 + 491 + 6 = 12{,}443$.

   a. Of the people surveyed, 1636 are at most 20 years old. So, the probability is:

$$P(\text{user is at most 20}) = \frac{1636}{12{,}443} \approx 0.131$$

   b. Of the people surveyed, $3693 + 491 + 6 = 4190$ are at least 41 years old. So, the probability is:

$$P(\text{user is at least 41}) = \frac{4190}{12{,}443} \approx 0.337$$

GOAL 2 GEOMETRIC PROBABILITY

Some probabilities are found by calculating a ratio of two lengths, areas, or volumes. Such probabilities are called **geometric probabilities**.

EXAMPLE 4 *Using Area to Find Probability*

You throw a dart at the board shown. Your dart is equally likely to hit any point inside the square board. Are you more likely to get 10 points or 0 points?

SOLUTION

STUDENT HELP

Skills Review
For help with area, see p. 914.

The two probabilities are as follows.

$$P(10 \text{ points}) = \frac{\text{area of smallest circle}}{\text{area of entire board}}$$

$$= \frac{\pi \cdot 3^2}{18^2} = \frac{9\pi}{324} = \frac{\pi}{36} \approx 0.0873$$

$$P(0 \text{ points}) = \frac{\text{area outside largest circle}}{\text{area of entire board}}$$

$$= \frac{18^2 - (\pi \cdot 9^2)}{18^2} = \frac{324 - 81\pi}{324} = \frac{4 - \pi}{4} \approx 0.215$$

▶ You are more likely to get 0 points.

EXAMPLE 5 *Using Length to Find Probability*

Entertainment

You have recorded a 2 hour movie at the beginning of a videocassette that has 6 hours of recording time. Starting at a random location on the videocassette, your brother records a 30 minute television show. What is the probability that your brother's television show accidentally records over part of your movie?

SOLUTION

STUDENT HELP

HOMEWORK HELP
Visit our Web site www.mcdougallittell.com for extra examples.

You can think of the videocassette as a number line from 0 to 6. The movie can be represented as a line segment 2 units long and the television show as a line segment 0.5 unit long. Because you know the movie starts at the beginning of the videocassette, the number line is as shown.

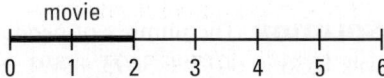
movie

If the 30 minute, or half hour, television show is to fit on the tape, it must start somewhere between 0 and 5.5. If it records over part of the movie, it must start somewhere between 0 and 2. So, the probability of recording over part of the movie is:

$$P(\text{recording over movie}) = \frac{\text{length where show will record over movie}}{\text{length where show will fit on tape}}$$

$$= \frac{2 - 0}{5.5 - 0} = \frac{2}{5.5} = \frac{4}{11} \approx 0.364$$

GUIDED PRACTICE

Vocabulary Check ✔

1. Complete this statement: A probability that involves length, area, or volume is called a(n) _?_ probability.

Concept Check ✔

2. $P(A) = 0.2$ and $P(B) = 0.6$. Which event is more likely to occur? Explain.

3. Explain the difference between theoretical probability and experimental probability. Give an example of each.

Skill Check ✔

A jar contains 2 red marbles, 3 blue marbles, and 1 green marble. Find the probability of randomly drawing the given type of marble.

4. a red marble

5. a green marble

6. a blue or a green marble

7. a red or a blue marble

Find the probability that a dart thrown at the given target will hit the shaded region. Assume the dart is equally likely to hit any point inside the target. The targets and regions within are either squares, circles, or triangles.

8.
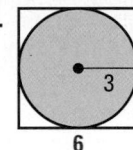
6

9.
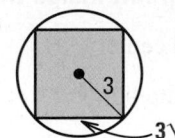
$3\sqrt{2}$

10.
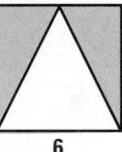
6

11. 🌎 **POPULATION** The bar graph shown gives the resident population (in thousands) of the United States in 1997. For a randomly selected person in the United States, find the probability of the given event.

🔗 **DATA UPDATE** of *Statistical Abstract of the United States* data at www.mcdougallittell.com

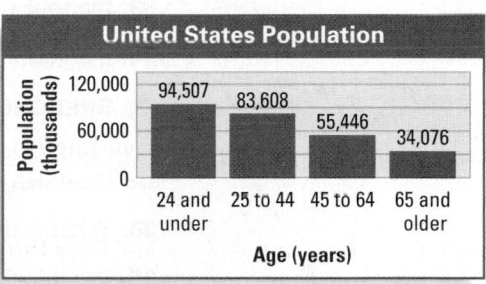

a. The person is 24 years old or under. b. The person is at least 45 years old.

PRACTICE AND APPLICATIONS

STUDENT HELP

▸ **Extra Practice**
to help you master skills is on p. 956.

CHOOSING NUMBERS You have an equally likely chance of choosing any integer from 1 through 20. Find the probability of the given event.

12. An odd number is chosen.

13. A number less than 7 is chosen.

14. A perfect square is chosen.

15. A prime number is chosen.

16. A multiple of 3 is chosen.

17. A factor of 240 is chosen.

CHOOSING CARDS A card is drawn randomly from a standard 52-card deck. Find the probability of drawing the given card.

STUDENT HELP

▸ **Look Back**
For help with a standard 52-card deck, see p. 708.

18. the ace of hearts

19. any ace

20. a diamond

21. a red card

22. a card other than 10

23. a face card (a king, queen, or jack)

STUDENT HELP

→ HOMEWORK HELP
Example 1: Exs. 12–23
Example 2: Exs. 35–40
Example 3: Exs. 24–29,
          41–43
Example 4: Exs. 30–34,
          46, 47
Example 5: Exs. 44, 45

ROLLING A DIE The results of rolling a six-sided die 120 times are shown. Use the table to find the experimental probability of each event. Also find the theoretical probability. How do the probabilities compare?

Results from Rolling a Die 120 Times						
Roll	1	2	3	4	5	6
Number of occurrences	15	18	20	17	24	26

24. rolling a 6

25. rolling a 3 or 4

26. rolling an odd number

27. rolling an even number

28. rolling a number greater than 2

29. rolling anything but a 1

GEOMETRY ▶ **CONNECTION** Find the probability that a dart thrown at the square target shown will hit the given region. Assume the dart is equally likely to hit any point inside the target.

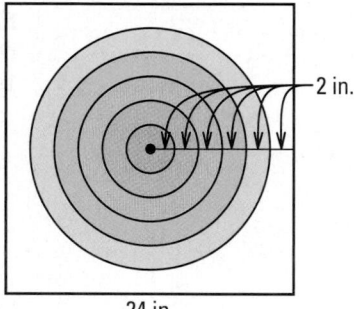

2 in.

24 in.

30. the red center

31. the white border

32. the red center or the white border

33. the four rings or the red center

34. the yellow or green ring

🌐 **SPEECHES** In Exercises 35 and 36, use the following information.

Your English teacher is drawing names to see who will give the first speech. There are 26 students in the class and 4 speeches will be given each day.

35. What is the probability that you will give your speech first?

36. What is the probability that you will give your speech on the first day?

🌐 **WORD GAMES** In Exercises 37 and 38, use the following information.

You and a friend are playing a word game that involves lettered tiles. The distribution of letters is shown at the right. At the start of the game you choose 7 letters.

Distribution of Letters			
A: 9	H: 2	O: 8	V: 2
B: 2	I: 9	P: 2	W: 2
C: 2	J: 1	Q: 1	X: 1
D: 4	K: 1	R: 6	Y: 2
E: 12	L: 4	S: 4	Z: 1
F: 2	M: 2	T: 6	Blank: 2
G: 3	N: 6	U: 4	

37. What is the probability that you will choose three vowels and four consonants? (Count "Y" as a vowel.)

38. What is the probability that you will choose the letters A, B, C, D, E, F, and G in order?

🌐 **LOTTERIES** In Exercises 39 and 40, find the probability of winning the lottery according to the given rules. Assume numbers are selected at random.

39. You must correctly select 6 out of 51 numbers. The order of the numbers is not important.

40. You must correctly select 3 numbers, each from 0 to 9. The order of the numbers is important.

41. 🌐 **MEDIA CONCERN** In a 1998 survey, parents were asked what media influence on their children most concerned them. The results are shown in the bar graph. Find the experimental probability that a randomly selected parent is most concerned about the given topic. ▶ Source: Annenberg Public Policy Center

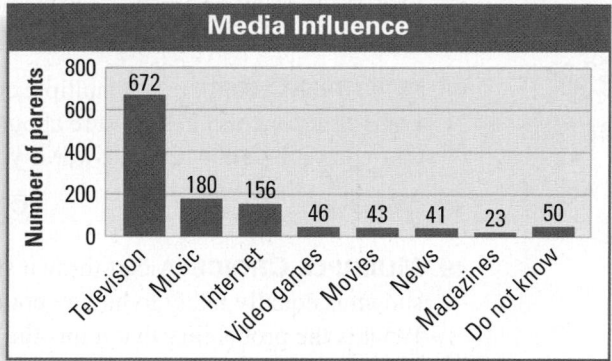

a. Television

b. Video games

42. **HISTORY CONNECTION** The table shows how many years the stock market gained or lost a given percent over a recent 17 year period based on the Dow Jones Industrial Average. Find the experimental probability of the given event.

Range	Lost more than 0%	Gained 0% to 9%	Gained 10% to 19%	Gained 20% to 29%	Gained more than 29%
Years	4	2	4	4	3

a. The stock market has a loss.

b. The stock market gains at least 10%.

43. **STATISTICS CONNECTION** The table shows how people in the United States got to work in 1990. For a randomly selected person in the United States, find the probability that the person chose the given type of transportation.

▶ Source: *The World Almanac*

a. Used public transportation

b. Drove to work (either in an automobile or on a motorcycle)

Means of transportation	Number
Automobile	99,592,932
Public transportation	6,069,589
Motorcycle	237,404
Bicycle	466,856
Other	5,297,468
None (work at home)	3,406,025

44. 🌐 **VIDEOCASSETTES** Look back at Example 5. Suppose you recorded your movie starting 1 hour into the videocassette. What is the probability that your brother's television show accidentally records over part of your movie?

45. 🌐 **CABLE INSTALLATION** You set up an appointment to have cable television installed between 12:00 P.M. and 4:00 P.M. The installer will wait 15 minutes if no one is home. Your cousin asks for a favor that would take you away from your home from 1:30 P.M. to 2:00 P.M. If you do the favor, what is the probability that you will miss the cable installer?

46. 🌐 **KYUDO** *Kyudo* is a form of Japanese archery. The most common target is shown. Find the probability that an arrow shot at the target will hit the center circle. Assume the arrow is equally likely to hit any point inside the target.

3.6 cm
1.5 cm
3.3 cm
3.0 cm
3.0 cm
3.6 cm

47. 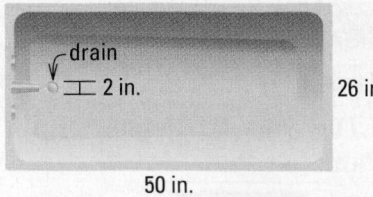 **CONTACT LENSES** You have just stepped into the tub to take a shower when one of your contact lenses falls out. (You have not yet turned on the shower.) Assuming that the lens is equally likely to land anywhere on or inside of the tub, what is the probability that it landed in the drain?

drain
2 in.
26 in.
50 in.

48. MULTIPLE CHOICE On a multiple choice question, you know that the answer is not B or D, but you are not sure about answers A, C, or E. What is the probability that you will get the right answer if you guess?

  A $\frac{1}{5}$ **B** $\frac{4}{5}$ **C** $\frac{1}{3}$ **D** $\frac{2}{3}$ **E** $\frac{3}{5}$

49. MULTIPLE CHOICE A dart thrown at the circular target shown is equally likely to hit any point inside the target. What is the probability that it hits the region outside the triangle?

5

  A 0.5   **B** 0.75   **C** 0.32

  D 0.47   **E** 0.68

★ **Challenge**

50. PROBABILITY Find the probability that the graph of $y = x^2 - 4x + c$ intersects the x-axis if c is a randomly chosen integer from 1 to 6.

MIXED REVIEW

DETERMINANTS Evaluate the determinant of the matrix. **(Review 4.3)**

51. $\begin{bmatrix} 2 & 7 \\ 5 & 9 \end{bmatrix}$ **52.** $\begin{bmatrix} 6 & 0 \\ 1 & -3 \end{bmatrix}$ **53.** $\begin{bmatrix} 3 & 8 \\ -2 & 1 \end{bmatrix}$

54. $\begin{bmatrix} 1 & 2 & 3 \\ 2 & 3 & 1 \\ 3 & 1 & 2 \end{bmatrix}$ **55.** $\begin{bmatrix} 0 & 1 & 5 \\ -3 & 4 & 7 \\ 2 & 1 & -4 \end{bmatrix}$ **56.** $\begin{bmatrix} -1 & -2 & 2 \\ 4 & 3 & -4 \\ 2 & 4 & 6 \end{bmatrix}$

MULTIPLYING Multiply the rational expressions. Simplify the result. **(Review 9.4)**

57. $\dfrac{6xy^2}{5x^3y} \cdot \dfrac{10y^4}{9xy}$ **58.** $\dfrac{x^2 + 3x + 2}{x^2 - x - 6} \cdot \dfrac{x^2 - 3x}{x^2 - x - 2}$

59. $\dfrac{25x^2 - 16}{5x - 4} \cdot \dfrac{x^2 - 4x - 21}{5x^3 - 31x^2 - 28x}$ **60.** $\dfrac{4x^2 - 12x}{27 - x^3} \cdot (x^2 + 3x + 9)$

WRITING TERMS Write the first five terms of the sequence. **(Review 11.5)**

61. $a_0 = 3$
$a_n = a_{n-1} + 7$

62. $a_0 = -1$
$a_n = 3 \cdot a_{n-1}$

63. $a_0 = 2$
$a_n = (a_{n-1})^3$

64. $a_0 = 1$
$a_1 = 1$
$a_n = a_{n-1} + a_{n-2}$

65. $a_0 = -2$
$a_1 = 0$
$a_n = a_{n-1} - a_{n-2}$

66. $a_0 = 1$
$a_1 = -2$
$a_n = a_{n-1} \cdot a_{n-2}$

67. 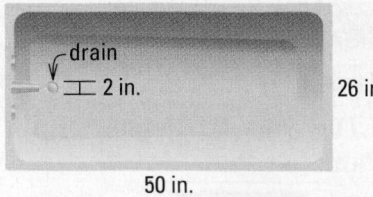 **TRADE SHOWS** You are attending a trade show that has booths from 20 different vendors. You hope to visit at least 5 of the booths. How many combinations of booths can you visit? **(Review 12.2 for 12.4)**

ACTIVITY 12.3

Using Technology

Generating Random Numbers

Most graphing calculators have a random number generator that you can use to perform probability experiments.

▶ **EXAMPLE**

Use the random number generator of a graphing calculator to simulate rolling a 6-sided die 120 times. Record the number of times you obtain 1, 2, 3, 4, 5, and 6.

▶ **SOLUTION**

1 In a list, enter randInt(1,6,120) to generate 120 random integers from 1 to 6.

2 Put the list in ascending order using the *Sort* feature. Scroll through the list to count and record the frequency of each number.

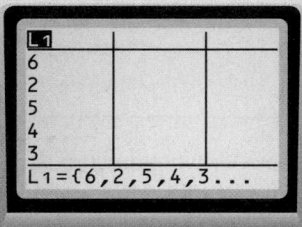

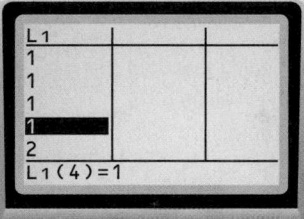

▶ **EXERCISES**

1. Copy and complete the table by performing the experiment above. What is the theoretical probability of rolling each number? What is the experimental probability? Do your experimental results agree with the theoretical results?

Number	1	2	3	4	5	6
Frequency	?	?	?	?	?	?

2. Copy and complete the table by simulating drawing 52 cards with replacement from a standard deck. Let 1 represent an ace, 2–10 represent the cards 2–10, 11 represent a jack, 12 represent a queen, and 13 represent a king. What is the theoretical probability of drawing each card? What is the experimental probability? Do your experimental results agree with the theoretical results?

Card	1	2	3	4	5	6	7	8	9	10	11	12	13
Frequency	?	?	?	?	?	?	?	?	?	?	?	?	?

3. Copy and complete the table by simulating tossing a coin 10, 20, 50, 100, and 200 times. Let 0 represent heads and 1 represent tails. For each number of trials record the number of heads and tails. As the number of trials increases, how do the experimental results compare with the theoretical results?

Number of trials	10	20	50	100	200
Number of heads	?	?	?	?	?
Number of tails	?	?	?	?	?

12.4

Probability of Compound Events

What you should learn

GOAL 1 Find probabilities of unions and intersections of two events.

GOAL 2 Use complements to find the probability of an event, as applied in **Example 5**.

Why you should learn it

▼ To solve **real-life** problems, such as finding the probability that friends will be in the same college dormitory in **Ex. 49**.

GOAL 1 PROBABILITIES OF UNIONS AND INTERSECTIONS

When you consider all the outcomes for either of two events *A* and *B*, you form the *union* of *A* and *B*. When you consider only the outcomes shared by both *A* and *B*, you form the *intersection* of *A* and *B*. The union or intersection of two events is called a **compound event**.

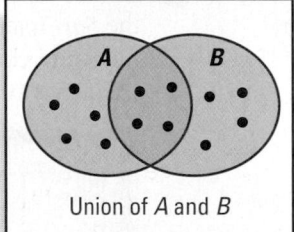

Union of *A* and *B*

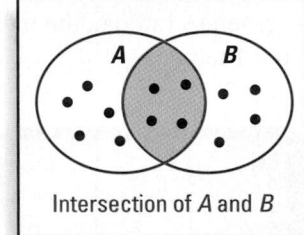

Intersection of *A* and *B*

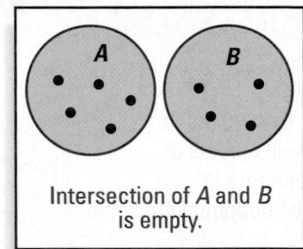

Intersection of *A* and *B* is empty.

To find *P*(*A* or *B*) you must consider what outcomes, if any, are in the intersection of *A* and *B*. If there are none, then *A* and *B* are **mutually exclusive events** and *P*(*A* or *B*) = *P*(*A*) + *P*(*B*). If *A* and *B* are not mutually exclusive, then the outcomes in the intersection of *A* and *B* are counted *twice* when *P*(*A*) and *P*(*B*) are added. So, *P*(*A* and *B*) must be subtracted *once* from the sum.

PROBABILITY OF COMPOUND EVENTS

If *A* and *B* are two events, then the probability of *A* or *B* is:

$$P(A \text{ or } B) = P(A) + P(B) - P(A \text{ and } B)$$

If *A* and *B* are mutually exclusive, then the probability of *A* or *B* is:

$$P(A \text{ or } B) = P(A) + P(B)$$

EXAMPLE 1 *Probability of Mutually Exclusive Events*

A card is randomly selected from a standard deck of 52 cards. What is the probability that it is an ace *or* a face card?

SOLUTION

Let event *A* be selecting an ace, and let event *B* be selecting a face card. Event *A* has 4 outcomes and event *B* has 12 outcomes. Because *A* and *B* are mutually exclusive, the probability is:

$$P(A \text{ or } B) = P(A) + P(B) = \frac{4}{52} + \frac{12}{52} = \frac{16}{52} = \frac{4}{13} \approx 0.308$$

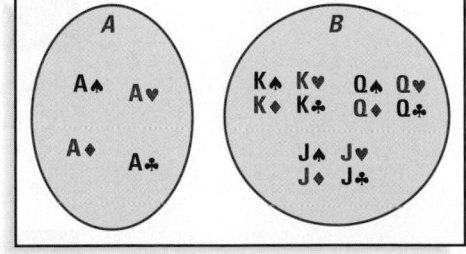

EXAMPLE 2 *Probability of a Compound Event*

A card is randomly selected from a standard deck of 52 cards. What is the probability that the card is a heart *or* a face card?

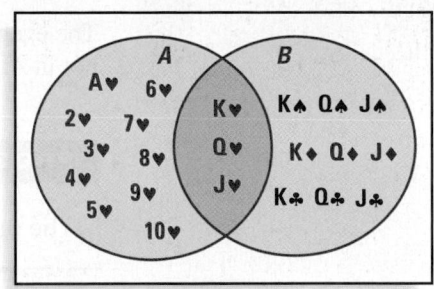

SOLUTION

Let event A be selecting a heart, and let event B be selecting a face card. Event A has 13 outcomes and event B has 12 outcomes. Of these, three outcomes are common to A and B. So, the probability of selecting a heart *or* a face card is:

$P(A \text{ or } B) = P(A) + P(B) - P(A \text{ and } B)$ Write general formula.

$\qquad = \dfrac{13}{52} + \dfrac{12}{52} - \dfrac{3}{52}$ Substitute known probabilities.

$\qquad = \dfrac{22}{52}$ Combine terms.

$\qquad = \dfrac{11}{26}$ Simplify.

$\qquad \approx 0.423$ Use a calculator.

EXAMPLE 3 *Using Intersection to Find Probability*

Last year a company paid overtime wages *or* hired temporary help during 9 months. Overtime wages were paid during 7 months and temporary help was hired during 4 months. At the end of the year, an auditor examines the accounting records and randomly selects one month to check the company's payroll. What is the probability that the auditor will select a month in which the company paid overtime wages *and* hired temporary help?

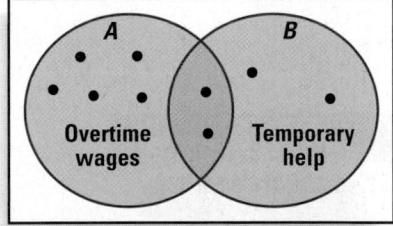

SOLUTION

Let event A represent paying overtime wages during a month, and let event B represent hiring temporary help during a month. From the given information you know that:

$$P(A) = \frac{7}{12}, P(B) = \frac{4}{12}, \text{ and } P(A \text{ or } B) = \frac{9}{12}$$

The probability that the auditor will select a month in which the company paid overtime wages *and* hired temporary help is $P(A \text{ and } B)$.

$P(A \text{ or } B) = P(A) + P(B) - P(A \text{ and } B)$ Write general formula.

$\dfrac{9}{12} = \dfrac{7}{12} + \dfrac{4}{12} - P(A \text{ and } B)$ Substitute known probabilities.

$P(A \text{ and } B) = \dfrac{7}{12} + \dfrac{4}{12} - \dfrac{9}{12}$ Solve for $P(A \text{ and } B)$.

$P(A \text{ and } B) = \dfrac{2}{12} = \dfrac{1}{6} \approx 0.167$ Simplify.

The event A', called the **complement** of event A, consists of all outcomes that are not in A. The notation A' is read as "A prime."

PROBABILITY OF THE COMPLEMENT OF AN EVENT

The probability of the complement of A is $P(A') = 1 - P(A)$.

EXAMPLE 4 *Probabilities of Complements*

STUDENT HELP

HOMEWORK HELP
Visit our Web site
www.mcdougallittell.com
for extra examples.

When two six-sided dice are tossed, there are 36 possible outcomes as shown. Find the probability of the given event.

a. The sum is not 8.

b. The sum is greater than or equal to 4.

SOLUTION

a. $P(\text{sum is not } 8) = 1 - P(\text{sum is } 8)$

$$= 1 - \frac{5}{36}$$

$$= \frac{31}{36}$$

$$\approx 0.861$$

b. $P(\text{sum} \geq 4) = 1 - P(\text{sum} < 4)$

$$= 1 - \frac{3}{36}$$

$$= \frac{33}{36}$$

$$= \frac{11}{12}$$

$$\approx 0.917$$

EXAMPLE 5 *Using a Complement in Real Life*

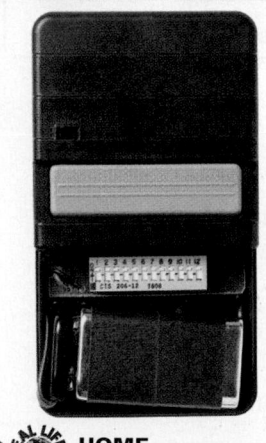

FOCUS ON APPLICATIONS

HOME ELECTRICS Four houses in a neighborhood have the same model of garage door opener. Each opener has 4096 possible transmitter codes. What is the probability that at least two of the four houses have the same code?

SOLUTION

The total number of ways to assign codes to the four openers is 4096^4. The number of ways to assign *different* codes to the four openers is $4096 \cdot 4095 \cdot 4094 \cdot 4093$. So, the probability that at least two of the four openers have the same code is:

$$P(\text{at least 2 are the same}) = 1 - P(\text{none are the same})$$

$$= 1 - \frac{4096 \cdot 4095 \cdot 4094 \cdot 4093}{4096^4}$$

$$\approx 1 - 0.99854$$

$$= 0.00146$$

HOME ELECTRONICS
One type of garage door opener has 12 switches that can be set in one of two positions (off or on) to create a code. So for this type of garage door opener, there are 2^{12}, or 4096, possible transmitter codes.

GUIDED PRACTICE

Vocabulary Check ✓

1. Describe what it means for two events to be mutually exclusive.

Concept Check ✓

2. Write a formula for computing $P(A \text{ or } B)$ that applies to *any* events A and B. How can you simplify this formula when A and B are mutually exclusive?

3. Are the events A and A' mutually exclusive? Explain.

Skill Check ✓

Events A and B are mutually exclusive. Find $P(A \text{ or } B)$.

4. $P(A) = 0.2$, $P(B) = 0.3$

5. $P(A) = 0.5$, $P(B) = 0.5$

6. $P(A) = \frac{3}{8}$, $P(B) = \frac{1}{8}$

7. $P(A) = \frac{1}{3}$, $P(B) = \frac{1}{4}$

Find $P(A \text{ or } B)$.

8. $P(A) = 0.5$, $P(B) = 0.4$, $P(A \text{ and } B) = 0.3$

9. $P(A) = \frac{2}{5}$, $P(B) = \frac{3}{5}$, $P(A \text{ and } B) = \frac{1}{5}$

Find $P(A \text{ and } B)$.

10. $P(A) = 0.7$, $P(B) = 0.2$, $P(A \text{ or } B) = 0.8$

11. $P(A) = \frac{5}{16}$, $P(B) = \frac{7}{16}$, $P(A \text{ or } B) = \frac{9}{16}$

Find $P(A')$.

12. $P(A) = 0.5$

13. $P(A) = 0.75$

14. $P(A) = \frac{1}{3}$

15. $P(A) = \frac{4}{7}$

PRACTICE AND APPLICATIONS

STUDENT HELP

▶ **Extra Practice**
to help you master
skills is on p. 957.

FINDING PROBABILITIES Find the indicated probability. State whether A and B are mutually exclusive.

16. $P(A) = 0.4$
$P(B) = 0.35$
$P(A \text{ or } B) = 0.5$
$P(A \text{ and } B) = \underline{?}$

17. $P(A) = 0.6$
$P(B) = 0.2$
$P(A \text{ or } B) = \underline{?}$
$P(A \text{ and } B) = 0.1$

18. $P(A) = 0.25$
$P(B) = \underline{?}$
$P(A \text{ or } B) = 0.70$
$P(A \text{ and } B) = 0$

19. $P(A) = \frac{13}{17}$
$P(B) = \underline{?}$
$P(A \text{ or } B) = \frac{14}{17}$
$P(A \text{ and } B) = \frac{6}{17}$

20. $P(A) = \frac{1}{3}$
$P(B) = \frac{1}{4}$
$P(A \text{ or } B) = \frac{7}{12}$
$P(A \text{ and } B) = \underline{?}$

21. $P(A) = \frac{3}{4}$
$P(B) = \frac{1}{3}$
$P(A \text{ or } B) = \underline{?}$
$P(A \text{ and } B) = \frac{1}{4}$

STUDENT HELP

▶ **HOMEWORK HELP**
Example 1: Exs. 16–24,
29–34, 42, 43
Example 2: Exs. 16–24,
29–34, 44, 45
Example 3: Exs. 16–24,
29–34, 46, 47
Example 4: Exs. 25–28,
35–40
Example 5: Exs. 48, 49

22. $P(A) = 5\%$
$P(B) = 29\%$
$P(A \text{ or } B) = \underline{?}$
$P(A \text{ and } B) = 0\%$

23. $P(A) = 30\%$
$P(B) = \underline{?}$
$P(A \text{ or } B) = 50\%$
$P(A \text{ and } B) = 10\%$

24. $P(A) = 16\%$
$P(B) = 24\%$
$P(A \text{ or } B) = 32\%$
$P(A \text{ and } B) = \underline{?}$

FINDING PROBABILITIES OF COMPLEMENTS Find $P(A')$.

25. $P(A) = 0.34$

26. $P(A) = 0$

27. $P(A) = \frac{3}{4}$

28. $P(A) = 1$

STUDENT HELP

→ **Look Back**
For help with a standard 52-card deck in Exs. 29–34, see p. 708.

→ **Look Back**
For help with simulations on a graphing calculator in Ex. 41, see p. 723.

CHOOSING CARDS A card is randomly drawn from a standard 52-card deck. Find the probability of the given event. (A face card is a king, queen, or jack.)

29. a queen and a heart
30. a queen or a heart
31. a heart or a diamond

32. a five or a six
33. a five and a six
34. a three or a face card

USING COMPLEMENTS Two six-sided dice are rolled. Find the probability of the given event. (Refer to Example 4 for a diagram of all possible outcomes.)

35. The sum is not 3.
36. The sum is greater than or equal to 5.

37. The sum is neither 3 nor 7.
38. The sum is less than or equal to 10.

39. The sum is greater than 2.
40. The sum is less than 8 or greater than 11.

41. **EXPERIMENTAL PROBABILITIES** Simulate rolling two dice 120 times. Use separate lists for the results of each die, and a third list for the sum. Record the frequency of each sum in a table. Find the experimental probabilities of the events in Exercises 35–40. How do your experimental results compare with the theoretical results?

42. **COMPANY MOVE** An employee of a large national company is promoted to management and will be moved within six months. The employee is told that there is a 33% probability of being moved to Denver, Colorado, and a 50% probability of being moved to Dallas, Texas. What is the probability that the employee will be moved to Dallas or Denver?

43. **CLASS ELECTIONS** You and your best friend are among several candidates running for class president. You estimate that there is a 40% chance you will win the election and a 35% chance your best friend will win. What is the probability that either you or your best friend wins the election?

44. **PARAKEETS** A pet store contains 35 light green parakeets (14 females and 21 males) and 44 sky blue parakeets (28 females and 16 males). You randomly choose one of the parakeets. What is the probability that it is a female or a sky blue parakeet?

45. **HONORS BANQUET** Of 162 students honored at an academic awards banquet, 48 won awards for mathematics and 78 won awards for English. Fourteen of these students won awards for both mathematics and English. One of the 162 students is chosen at random to be interviewed for a newspaper article. What is the probability that the student interviewed won an award for English or mathematics?

46. SCIENCE CONNECTION A tree in a forest is not growing properly. A botanist determines that there is an 85% probability the tree has a disease or is being damaged by insects, a 45% probability it has a disease, and a 50% probability it is being damaged by insects. What is the probability that the tree both has a disease and is being damaged by insects?

47. **RAIN** A weather forecaster says that the probability it will rain on Saturday or Sunday is 50%, the probability it will rain on Saturday is 20%, and the probability it will rain on Sunday is 40%. What is the probability that it will rain on both Saturday and Sunday?

48. **POTLUCK DINNER** The organizer of a potluck dinner sends 5 people a list of 8 different recipes and asks each person to bring one of the items on the list. If all 5 people randomly choose a recipe from the list, what is the probability that at least 2 will bring the same thing?

FOCUS ON CAREERS

→ **BOTANIST**
A botanist studies plants and their environment. Some botanists specialize in the causes and cures of plant illnesses, as discussed in Ex. 46.

CAREER LINK
www.mcdougallittell.com

49.  **CAMPUS HOUSING** Four high school friends will all be attending the same university next year. There are 14 dormitories on campus. Find the probability that at least 2 of the friends will be in the same dormitory.

50. CRITICAL THINKING What is the complement of A'? Explain.

51. **MULTI-STEP PROBLEM** Follow the steps below to explore a famous probability problem called the *birthday problem*.

a. Suppose that 5 people are chosen at random. Find the probability that at least two share the same birthday (Assume that there are 365 possible birthdays).

b. Suppose that 10 people are chosen at random. Find the probability that at least two of the people share the same birthday.

c. Generalize the results from parts (a) and (b) by writing a formula that gives the probability $P(n)$ that in a group of n people at least two people share the same birthday. (*Hint:* Use $_nP_r$ notation.)

d. **LOGICAL REASONING** Enter the formula for $P(n)$ from part (c) into a graphing calculator put in sequence mode. Use the *Table* feature to make a table of values for $P(n)$. How large must a group be if the probability that at least two of the people share the same birthday exceeds 50%?

Test Preparation

STUDENT HELP

KEYSTROKE HELP
Visit our Web site www.mcdougallittell.com to see keystrokes for several models of calculators.

★ Challenge

ODDS The odds in favor of an event occurring are the ratio of the probability that the event *will* occur to the probability that the event *will not* occur. The reciprocal of this ratio represents the odds *against* the event occurring.

52. Five marbles in a jar are green. The odds against choosing a green marble are "4 to 1." How many marbles are in the jar?

53. If a jar contains 4 red marbles and 7 blue marbles, what are the odds in favor of choosing a red marble? What are the odds against choosing a red marble?

54. Write a formula that converts the odds in favor of an event to the probability of the event.

55. Write a formula that converts the probability of an event to the odds in favor of the event.

EXTRA CHALLENGE
www.mcdougallittell.com

MIXED REVIEW

SOLVING EXPONENTIAL EQUATIONS Solve the equation. (Review 8.6 for 12.5)

56. $7^{2x} = 49^{16}$ **57.** $9^x = 3^{x+1}$ **58.** $2^{4x+8} = 32^{19}$

59. $5^x = 21$ **60.** $10^{3x-1} - 13 = 8$ **61.** $72 = 91e^{-0.023x} + 50$

WRITING EQUATIONS Write the standard form of the equation of the circle that passes through the given point and whose center is the origin. (Review 10.3)

62. $(0, 7)$ **63.** $(3, 4)$ **64.** $(-1, 6)$ **65.** $(8, -2)$

66. $(4, 4)$ **67.** $(3, 10)$ **68.** $(-4, -2)$ **69.** $(16, 0)$

LICENSE PLATES For the given configuration, determine how many different license plates are possible if (a) digits and letters can be repeated, and (b) digits and letters cannot be repeated. (Review 12.1 for 12.5)

70. 3 letters followed by 4 digits   **71.** 4 letters followed by 3 digits

Probability of Independent and Dependent Events

What you should learn

GOAL 1 Find the probability of independent events.

GOAL 2 Find the probability of dependent events, as applied in **Ex. 33**.

Why you should learn it

▼ To solve **real-life** problems, such as finding the probability that the Florida Marlins win three games in a row in **Example 2**.

GOAL 1 **PROBABILITIES OF INDEPENDENT EVENTS**

Two events are **independent** if the occurrence of one has no effect on the occurrence of the other. For instance, if a coin is tossed twice, the outcome of the first toss (heads or tails) has no effect on the outcome of the second toss.

PROBABILITY OF INDEPENDENT EVENTS

If A and B are independent events, then the probability that both A and B occur is $P(A \text{ and } B) = P(A) \cdot P(B)$.

EXAMPLE 1 *Probability of Two Independent Events*

You are playing a game that involves spinning the money wheel shown. During your turn you get to spin the wheel twice. What is the probability that you get more than $500 on your first spin and then go bankrupt on your second spin?

SOLUTION Let event A be getting more than $500 on the first spin, and let event B be going bankrupt on the second spin. The two events are independent. So, the probability is:

$$P(A \text{ and } B) = P(A) \cdot P(B) = \frac{8}{24} \cdot \frac{2}{24} = \frac{1}{36} \approx 0.028$$

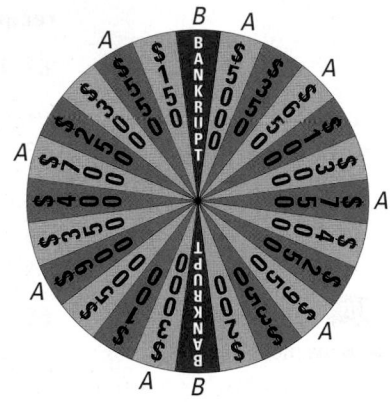

· · · · · · · · ·

The formula given above for the probability of two independent events can be extended to the probability of three or more independent events.

EXAMPLE 2 *Probability of Three Independent Events*

BASEBALL During the 1997 baseball season, the Florida Marlins won 5 out of 7 home games and 3 out of 7 away games against the San Francisco Giants. During the 1997 National League Division Series with the Giants, the Marlins played the first two games at home and the third game away. The Marlins won all three games. Estimate the probability of this happening. ▶ Source: The Florida Marlins

SOLUTION Let events A, B, and C be winning the first, second, and third games. The three events are independent and have experimental probabilities based on the regular season games. So, the probability of winning the first three games is:

$$P(A \text{ and } B \text{ and } C) = P(A) \cdot P(B) \cdot P(C) = \frac{5}{7} \cdot \frac{5}{7} \cdot \frac{3}{7} = \frac{75}{343} \approx 0.219$$

Trading Cards

EXAMPLE 3 *Using a Complement to Find a Probability*

You collect hockey trading cards. For one team there are 25 different cards in the set, and you have all of them except for the starting goalie card. To try and get this card, you buy 8 packs of 5 cards each. All cards in a pack are different and each of the cards is equally likely to be in a given pack. Find the probability that you will get at least one starting goalie card.

PATRICK ROY
MONTREAL CANADIENS

SOLUTION

In one pack the probability of *not* getting the starting goalie card is:

$$P(\text{no starting goalie}) = \frac{_{24}C_5}{_{25}C_5}$$

Buying packs of cards are independent events, so the probability of getting at least one starting goalie card in the 8 packs is:

$$P(\text{at least one starting goalie}) = 1 - P(\text{no starting goalie in any pack})$$

$$= 1 - \left(\frac{_{24}C_5}{_{25}C_5}\right)^8$$

$$\approx 0.832$$

Manufacturing

EXAMPLE 4 *Solving a Probability Equation*

A computer chip manufacturer has found that only 1 out of 1000 of its chips is defective. You are ordering a shipment of chips for the computer store where you work. How many chips can you order before the probability that at least one chip is defective reaches 50%?

SOLUTION

Let n be the number of chips you order. From the given information you know that $P(\text{chip is } not \text{ defective}) = \frac{999}{1000} = 0.999$. Use this probability and the fact that each chip ordered represents an independent event to find the value of n.

STUDENT HELP

↪ **Look Back**
For help with solving exponential equations, see p. 501.

$P(\text{at least one chip is defective}) = 0.5$	**Write given assumption.**
$1 - P(\text{no chips are defective}) = 0.5$	**Use complement.**
$1 - (0.999)^n = 0.5$	**Substitute known probability.**
$-(0.999)^n = -0.5$	**Subtract 1 from each side.**
$(0.999)^n = 0.5$	**Divide each side by –1.**
$n = \dfrac{\log 0.5}{\log 0.999}$	**Solve for n.**
$n \approx 693$	**Use a calculator.**

▶ If you order 693 chips, you have a 50% chance of getting a defective chip. Therefore, you can order 692 chips before the probability that at least one chip is defective reaches 50%.

GOAL 2 PROBABILITIES OF DEPENDENT EVENTS

Two events *A* and *B* are **dependent events** if the occurrence of one affects the occurrence of the other. The probability that *B* will occur given that *A* has occurred is called the **conditional probability** of *B* given *A* and is written $P(B \mid A)$.

PROBABILITY OF DEPENDENT EVENTS

If *A* and *B* are dependent events, then the probability that both *A* and *B* occur is $P(A \text{ and } B) = P(A) \cdot P(B \mid A)$.

Endangered Species

EXAMPLE 5 *Finding Conditional Probabilities*

The table shows the number of endangered and threatened animal species in the United States as of November 30, 1998. Find (**a**) the probability that a listed animal is a reptile and (**b**) the probability that an endangered animal is a reptile.

▶ Source: United States Fish and Wildlife Service

	Mammals	Birds	Reptiles	Amphibians	Other
Endangered	59	75	14	9	198
Threatened	8	15	21	7	69

SOLUTION

a. $P(\text{reptile}) = \dfrac{\text{number of reptiles}}{\text{total number of animals}} = \dfrac{35}{475} \approx 0.0737$

b. $P(\text{reptile} \mid \text{endangered}) = \dfrac{\text{number of endangered reptiles}}{\text{total number of endangered animals}}$

$\qquad\qquad\qquad = \dfrac{14}{355} \approx 0.0394$

EXAMPLE 6 *Comparing Dependent and Independent Events*

STUDENT HELP

↳ **Look Back**
For help with a standard 52-card deck, see p. 708.

You randomly select two cards from a standard 52-card deck. What is the probability that the first card is not a face card (a king, queen, or jack) and the second card is a face card if (**a**) you replace the first card before selecting the second, and (**b**) you do *not* replace the first card?

SOLUTION

a. If you replace the first card before selecting the second card, then *A* and *B* are independent events. So, the probability is:

$$P(A \text{ and } B) = P(A) \cdot P(B) = \frac{40}{52} \cdot \frac{12}{52} = \frac{30}{169} \approx 0.178$$

b. If you do *not* replace the first card before selecting the second card, then *A* and *B* are dependent events. So, the probability is:

$$P(A \text{ and } B) = P(A) \cdot P(B \mid A) = \frac{40}{52} \cdot \frac{12}{51} = \frac{40}{221} \approx 0.181$$

The formula for finding probabilities of dependent events can be extended to three or more events, as shown in Example 7.

Dining Out

EXAMPLE 7 *Probability of Three Dependent Events*

You and two friends go to a restaurant and order a sandwich. The menu has 10 types of sandwiches and each of you is equally likely to order any type. What is the probability that each of you orders a different type?

SOLUTION

Let event A be that you order a sandwich, event B be that one friend orders a different type, and event C be that your other friend orders a third type. These events are dependent. So, the probability that each of you orders a different type is:

$$P(A \text{ and } B \text{ and } C) = P(A) \cdot P(B|A) \cdot P(C|A \text{ and } B)$$

$$= \frac{10}{10} \cdot \frac{9}{10} \cdot \frac{8}{10}$$

$$= \frac{18}{25} = 0.72$$

STUDENT HELP

▶ **Study Tip**
You can also use the fundamental counting principle to find the probability in Example 7.

P(all different)

$= \dfrac{\text{no. of different orders}}{\text{no. of possible orders}}$

$= \dfrac{10 \cdot 9 \cdot 8}{10 \cdot 10 \cdot 10} = 0.72$

EXAMPLE 8 *Using a Tree Diagram to Find Conditional Probabilities*

HEALTH The American Diabetes Association estimates that 5.9% of Americans have diabetes. Suppose that a medical lab has developed a simple diagnostic test for diabetes that is 98% accurate for people who have the disease and 95% accurate for people who do not have it. If the medical lab gives the test to a randomly selected person, what is the probability that the diagnosis is correct?

SOLUTION

A probability tree diagram, where the probabilities are given along the branches, can help you see the different ways to obtain a correct diagnosis. Notice that the probabilities for all branches from the same point must sum to 1.

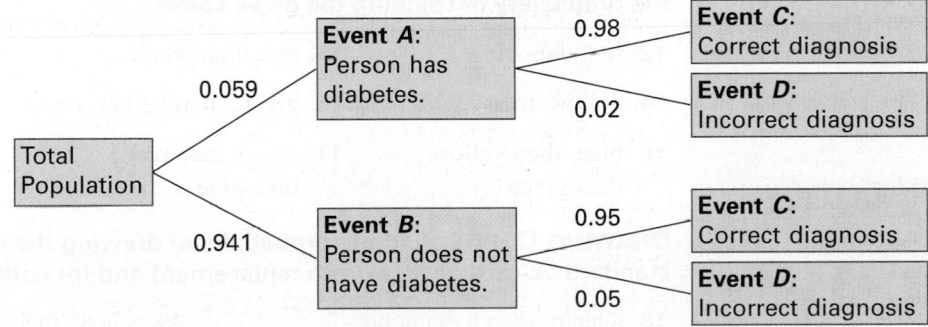

So, the probability that the diagnosis is correct is:

$$P(C) = P(A \text{ and } C) + P(B \text{ and } C) \qquad \text{Follow branches leading to } C.$$

$$= P(A) \cdot P(C|A) + P(B) \cdot P(C|B) \qquad \text{Use formula for dependent events.}$$

$$= (0.059)(0.98) + (0.941)(0.95) \qquad \text{Substitute.}$$

$$\approx 0.952 \qquad \text{Use a calculator.}$$

GUIDED PRACTICE

Vocabulary Check ✔
1. Explain the difference between dependent events and independent events, and give an example of each.

Concept Check ✔
2. If event *A* is drawing a queen from a deck of cards and event *B* is drawing a king from the remaining cards, are events *A* and *B* dependent or independent?

3. If event *A* is rolling a two on a six-sided die and event *B* is rolling a four on a different six-sided die, are events *A* and *B* dependent or independent?

Skill Check ✔ **Events *A* and *B* are independent. Find the indicated probability.**

4. $P(A) = 0.3$
   $P(B) = 0.9$
   $P(A \text{ and } B) = \underline{\ ?\ }$

5. $P(A) = \underline{\ ?\ }$
   $P(B) = 0.3$
   $P(A \text{ and } B) = 0.06$

6. $P(A) = 0.75$
   $P(B) = \underline{\ ?\ }$
   $P(A \text{ and } B) = 0.15$

Events *A* and *B* are dependent. Find the indicated probability.

7. $P(A) = 0.1$
   $P(B \mid A) = 0.8$
   $P(A \text{ and } B) = \underline{\ ?\ }$

8. $P(A) = \underline{\ ?\ }$
   $P(B \mid A) = 0.5$
   $P(A \text{ and } B) = 0.25$

9. $P(A) = 0.9$
   $P(B \mid A) = \underline{\ ?\ }$
   $P(A \text{ and } B) = 0.54$

 READING LIST In Exercises 10 and 11, use the following information.
Three friends are taking an English class that has a summer reading list. Each student is required to read one book from the list, which contains 3 biographies, 10 classics, and 5 historical novels.

10. Find the probability that the first friend chooses a biography, the second friend chooses a classic, and the third friend chooses a historical novel.

11. Find the probability that the three friends each choose a different classic.

PRACTICE AND APPLICATIONS

┌─ **STUDENT HELP** ─┐
▸ **Extra Practice**
to help you master
skills is on p. 957.

SPINNING A WHEEL You are playing a game that involves spinning the wheel shown. Find the probability of spinning the given colors.

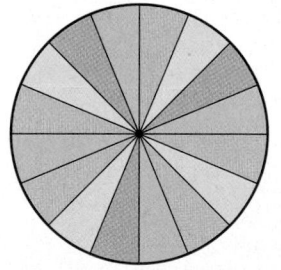

12. red, then blue

13. red, then green

14. yellow, then red

15. green, then yellow

16. blue, then yellow, then green

17. green, then red, then blue

┌─ **STUDENT HELP** ─┐
▸ **HOMEWORK HELP**
Example 1: Exs. 12–15
Example 2: Exs. 16, 17, 24, 25
Example 3: Exs. 26, 27
Example 4: Exs. 28, 29
Example 5: Exs. 30–32
Example 6: Exs. 18–21
Example 7: Exs. 22, 23, 33, 34
Example 8: Exs. 35, 36

DRAWING CARDS Find the probability of drawing the given cards from a standard 52-card deck (a) with replacement and (b) without replacement.

18. a heart, then a diamond

19. a jack, then a king

20. a 2, then a face card (K, Q, or J)

21. a face card (K, Q, or J), then a 2

22. an ace, then a 2, then a 3

23. a heart, then a diamond, then another heart

24. 🌐 **GAMES** You are playing a game that involves drawing three numbers from a hat. There are 25 pieces of paper numbered 1 to 25 in the hat. Each number is replaced after it is drawn. What is the probability that each number is greater than 20 or less than 4?

25.  **LAWN CARE** The owner of a one-man lawn mowing business owns three old and unreliable riding mowers. As long as one of the three is working he can stay productive. From past experience, one of the mowers is unusable 12 percent of the time, one 6 percent of the time, and one 20 percent of the time. Find the probability that all three mowers are unusable on a given day.

26.  **TRADING CARDS** You collect movie trading cards, which have different scenes from a movie. For one movie there are 90 different cards in the set, and you have all of them except the final scene. To try and get this card, you buy 10 packs of 8 cards each. All cards in a pack are different and each of the cards is equally likely to be in a given pack. Find the probability that you will get the final scene.

27.  **FREE THROWS** Chris Mullin of the Indiana Pacers led the National Basketball Association in free-throw percentage during the 1997–1998 season. He made 93.9% of his free-throw attempts. If he attempted 10 free throws in a game, what is the probability that he missed at least one? ▶ Source: NBA

28.  **MANUFACTURING** Look back at Example 4. Suppose the computer chip manufacturer has improved quality control so that only 1 out of 10,000 of its chips is defective. Now how many chips can you order before the probability that at least one chip is defective reaches 50%?

29.  **LOTTERY** To win a state lottery, a player must correctly match six different numbers from 1 to 42. If a computer randomly assigns six numbers per ticket, how many tickets would a person have to buy to have a 1% chance of winning?

STATISTICS ▶ **CONNECTION** **In Exercises 30 and 31, use the following information.**
The table, based on a Gallup Poll, shows the number of voters (in 1000's) by party affiliation who were expected to vote for Bill Clinton and Bob Dole in the 1996 Presidential election. ▶ Source: The Gallup Organization

	Democrat	Republican	Independent
Clinton	31,378	3,340	12,685
Dole	2,092	28,386	8,721

30. Find the probability that a randomly selected person voted for Clinton.

31. Find the probability that a randomly selected Democrat voted for Clinton.

32.  **TEACHERS** In the United States during the 1993–1994 school year, 39.6% of all male teachers and 26.1% of all female teachers had twenty years or more of full-time teaching experience. That year 694,000 males and 1,867,000 females were teachers. What is the probability that a randomly chosen teacher in the United States that year was a female with twenty years or more of full-time teaching experience?

 **DATA UPDATE** of *Statistical Abstract of the United States* data at www.mcdougallittell.com

33.  **COSTUMES** You and four of your friends go to the same store at different times to buy costumes for a costume party. There are 20 different costumes at the store, and the store has at least five duplicates of each costume. Find the probability that all five of you choose different costumes.

34.  **AIRPLANE MEALS** On a long flight an airline usually serves a meal. If there are 2 choices for the meal, what is the probability that all 6 people in the first row choose the same meal assuming choices are made independently?

STUDENT HELP

HOMEWORK HELP
Visit our Web site
www.mcdougallittell.com
for help with problem
solving in Ex. 29.

FOCUS ON CAREERS

TEACHER
In addition to teaching, teachers plan daily lessons and activities, assign and correct homework, and prepare and grade exams. They also monitor homerooms, study halls, and cafeterias, meet with parents, and supervise extracurricular activities.

CAREER LINK
www.mcdougallittell.com

35.  **RETIREMENT PLAN** At a particular company 64% of the employees are forty years old or over. Of those employees, 83% are enrolled in the company's retirement plan. Only 61% of the employees under forty years old are enrolled in the plan. Make a probability tree diagram and use it to find the probability that a randomly selected employee is enrolled in the company's retirement plan.

36.  **FOCUS TESTING** A company is focus testing a new type of fruit drink. The focus group is 47% male. Of the males in the group, 40% said they would buy the fruit drink, and of the females, 54% said they would buy the fruit drink. Make a probability tree diagram and use it to find the probability that a randomly selected person would buy the fruit drink.

Test Preparation

QUANTITATIVE COMPARISON In Exercises 37 and 38, choose the statement that is true about the given quantities. Assume a standard 52-card deck is used.

    Ⓐ The quantity in column A is greater.

    Ⓑ The quantity in column B is greater.

    Ⓒ The two quantities are equal.

    Ⓓ The relationship cannot be determined from the given information.

	Column A	Column B
37.	The probability of drawing at least one heart when drawing 4 times with replacement	The probability of drawing at least one heart when drawing 4 times without replacement
38.	The probability of not drawing any card twice when drawing 9 times with replacement	The probability of drawing any card 2 or more times when drawing 9 times with replacement

★ **Challenge**

39. CONDITIONAL PROBABILITY Using the data from Example 8, find the conditional probability that a randomly selected person has diabetes given that the person is diagnosed incorrectly.

MIXED REVIEW

HISTOGRAMS Using the given intervals, make a frequency distribution of the data set. Then draw a histogram of the data set. (Review 7.7 for 12.6)

40. Use five intervals beginning with 51–60.
    56, 68, 73, 79, 82, 82, 83, 85, 85, 87, 88, 89, 90, 90, 91, 93, 95, 100

41. Use four intervals beginning with 0.01–0.25.
    0.3, 0.3, 0.4, 0.4, 0.5, 0.6, 0.6, 0.6, 0.7, 0.9, 0.9, 0.9, 0.9, 0.9

SOLVING EQUATIONS Solve the equation. (Review 8.8)

42. $\dfrac{5}{1 + 2e^{-x}} = 4$ **43.** $\dfrac{10}{1 + 6e^{-x}} = 8$ **44.** $\dfrac{9}{1 + 3e^{-3x}} = 6$

45. $\dfrac{12}{1 + e^{-2x}} = 4$ **46.** $\dfrac{1}{1 + 3e^{-5x}} = \dfrac{1}{2}$ **47.** $\dfrac{70}{1 + 12e^{-10x}} = \dfrac{2}{9}$

BINOMIAL THEOREM Expand the power of the binomial. (Review 12.2 for 12.6)

48. $(x + 1)^5$ **49.** $(2x - 1)^7$ **50.** $(x - 3y)^4$ **51.** $(x - 1)^6$

A jar contains 6 blue marbles, 12 green marbles, and 7 yellow marbles. Find the probability of randomly drawing the given marble. (Lesson 12.3)

1. a green marble   2. a blue marble   3. a green or a blue marble

Find the probability that a dart thrown at the circular target shown will hit the given region. Assume the dart is equally likely to hit any point inside the target. (Lesson 12.3)

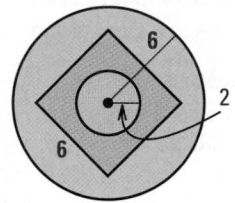

4. the center circle   5. outside the square

6. the area inside the square but outside the center circle

Find the indicated probability. (Lesson 12.4)

7. $P(A) = 0.7$
   $P(B) = 0.2$
   $P(A \text{ or } B) = \underline{\ ?\ }$
   $P(A \text{ and } B) = 0.1$

8. $P(A) = 0.5$
   $P(B) = 0.4$
   $P(A \text{ or } B) = 0.9$
   $P(A \text{ and } B) = \underline{\ ?\ }$

9. $P(A) = 0.25$
   $P(A') = \underline{\ ?\ }$

10. 🌐 **FRUIT** You and four friends are in line at lunch and are each selecting a piece of fruit to eat. If there are 5 types of fruit available, what is the probability that you each select a different type? **(Lesson 12.5)**

MATH & History   **Probability Theory**

APPLICATION LINK
www.mcdougallittell.com

THEN

IN 1654 Blaise Pascal and Pierre Fermat solved the first probability problem, which asked how to divide the stakes of an interrupted game of chance between two players of equal ability. Suppose Player A has 2 points, Player B has 1 point, and the game is won by the first player to score 4 out of a possible 7 points.

1. If the stakes are divided based on which player is closest to winning, what fraction of the stakes should each player receive?

2. If the stakes are divided based on the number of points each player has so far, what fraction of the stakes should each player receive?

3. What is the probability Player A will win the game? What is the probability Player B will win the game? Based on these probabilities, what fraction of the stakes should each player receive?

NOW

TODAY probability theory is used to decide more than just games of chance. Actuaries, for example, use probability theory to design financial plans, to calculate insurance rates, and to price corporate securities offerings.

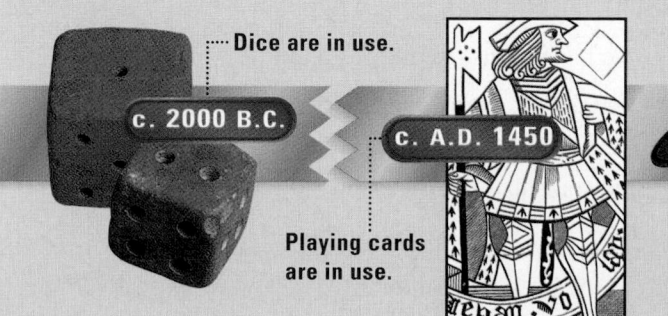

Dice are in use.

c. 2000 B.C.

Playing cards are in use.

c. A.D. 1450

1820

Probability theory is extended to astronomy.

Actuary is named the best job in America.

1995

JOB RANKINGS
1. ACTUARY
2. SOFTWARE ENGINEER
3. COMPUTER SYSTEMS ANALYST
4. ACCOUNTANT
5. PARALEGAL ASSISTANT
6. MATHEMATICIAN

● ACTIVITY 12.6

Developing Concepts

Investigating Binomial Distributions

▶ **QUESTION** What are the characteristics of a histogram that displays the results of a *binomial experiment*?

▶ **EXPLORING THE CONCEPT** Performing an Experiment

① Toss three coins and record the number of heads. Repeat this 25 times.

You can also use a random number generator on a graphing calculator to simulate the coin toss. Let 0 represent heads and let 1 represent tails.

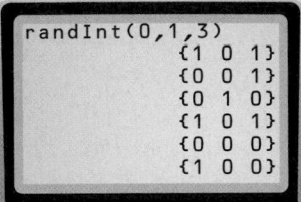

② Record the results for the entire class in a table like the one shown below.

Number of Heads			
0	1	2	3
ⅢⅢ ⅢⅢ ⅢⅢ	ⅢⅢ ⅢⅢ ⅢⅢ ⅢⅢ ⅢⅢ ⅢⅢ ⅢⅢ ⅢⅢ ⅢⅢ	ⅢⅢ ⅢⅢ ⅢⅢ ⅢⅢ ⅢⅢ ⅢⅢ ⅢⅢ ⅢⅢ ⅢⅢ ⅢⅢ Ⅰ	ⅢⅢ ⅢⅢ ⅢⅢ

③ Construct a histogram for the class results for the experiment.

▶ **EXPLORING THE CONCEPT** Calculating Theoretical Probabilities

④ Make a tree diagram of the results of tossing three coins simultaneously.

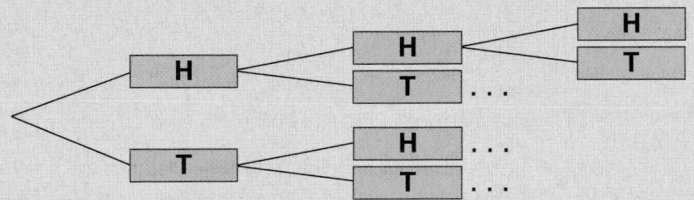

⑤ Calculate the theoretical probabilities of getting 0, 1, 2, or 3 heads.

⑥ Construct a histogram of the theoretical probabilities.

▶ **DRAWING CONCLUSIONS**

1. Compare the shapes of the two histograms from **Steps 3 and 6**.

2. Would the shape of the histogram from **Step 3** change if your class had conducted twice as many trials as it did? Explain.

3. Your friend has three weighted coins that land heads up 60% of the time and tails up 40% of the time. Suppose these coins are tossed 1000 times and the number of heads is recorded for each trial. Would a histogram constructed from the results have the same shape as the histograms from **Steps 3 and 6**? Explain.

12.6

Binomial Distributions

What you should learn

GOAL 1 Find binomial probabilities and analyze binomial distributions.

GOAL 2 Test a hypothesis, as applied in **Example 4**.

Why you should learn it

▼ To solve **real-life** problems, such as determining whether a computer manufacturer's claim is correct in **Ex. 46**.

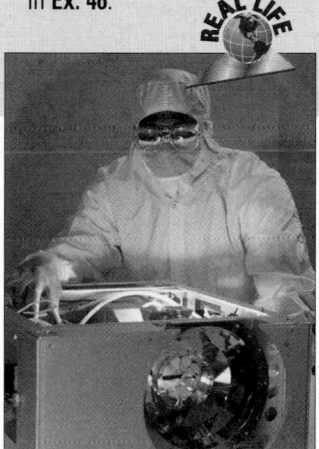

GOAL 1 FINDING BINOMIAL PROBABILITIES

There are many probability experiments in which the results of each trial can be reduced to two outcomes. If such an experiment satisfies the following conditions, then it is called a **binomial experiment**.

- There are n independent trials.

- Each trial has only two possible outcomes: success and failure.

- The probability of success is the same for each trial. This probability is denoted by p. The probability of failure is given by $1 - p$.

FINDING A BINOMIAL PROBABILITY

For a binomial experiment consisting of n trials, the probability of exactly k successes is

$$P(k \text{ successes}) = {}_nC_k p^k (1 - p)^{n-k}$$

where the probability of success on each trial is p.

EXAMPLE 1   *Finding a Binomial Probability*

UFOs According to a survey taken by *USA Today*, about 37% of adults believe that Unidentified Flying Objects (UFOs) really exist. Suppose you randomly survey 6 adults. What is the probability that exactly 2 of them believe that UFOs really exist?

Do UFOs Exist?

No or Do not know 63%

Yes 37%

SOLUTION

Let $p = 0.37$ be the probability that a randomly selected adult believes that UFOs really exist. By surveying 6 adults, you are conducting $n = 6$ independent trials. The probability of getting exactly $k = 2$ successes is:

$$P(k = 2) = {}_6C_2(0.37)^2(1 - 0.37)^{6-2}$$

$$= \frac{6!}{4! \cdot 2!}(0.37)^2(0.63)^4$$

$$\approx 0.323$$

▶ The probability that exactly 2 of the people surveyed believe that UFOs really exist is about 32%.

· · · · · · · · · ·

A **binomial distribution** shows the probabilities of all possible numbers of successes in a binomial experiment, as illustrated in Example 2 on the next page.

UFOs

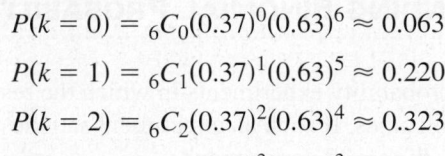

Draw a histogram of the binomial distribution for the survey in Example 1. Then find the probability that at most 2 of the people surveyed believe that UFOs really exist.

SOLUTION

STUDENT HELP

▸ **Study Tip**
You can check your calculations for a binomial distribution by adding all the probabilities. The sum should always be 1.

$$P(k = 0) = {}_6C_0(0.37)^0(0.63)^6 \approx 0.063$$

$$P(k = 1) = {}_6C_1(0.37)^1(0.63)^5 \approx 0.220$$

$$P(k = 2) = {}_6C_2(0.37)^2(0.63)^4 \approx 0.323$$

$$P(k = 3) = {}_6C_3(0.37)^3(0.63)^3 \approx 0.253$$

$$P(k = 4) = {}_6C_4(0.37)^4(0.63)^2 \approx 0.112$$

$$P(k = 5) = {}_6C_5(0.37)^5(0.63)^1 \approx 0.026$$

$$P(k = 6) = {}_6C_6(0.37)^6(0.63)^0 \approx 0.003$$

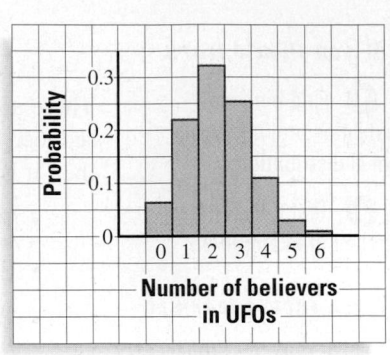

The probability of getting at most $k = 2$ successes is:

$$P(k \le 2) = P(2) + P(1) + P(0) \approx 0.323 + 0.220 + 0.063 = 0.606$$

▸ The probability that at most 2 of the people surveyed believe that UFOs really exist is about 61%.

EXAMPLE 3 *Interpreting a Binomial Distribution*

Egg Incubation

For a science project you are incubating 12 chicken eggs. The probability that a chick is female is 0.5. Draw a histogram of the binomial distribution based on the probability that exactly k of the chicks are female. Then find the most likely number of female chicks.

SOLUTION Begin by calculating each binomial probability using the formula $P(k) = {}_nC_k(0.5)^k(0.5)^{n-k} = {}_nC_k(0.5)^n$ as shown in the table. Then draw the histogram.

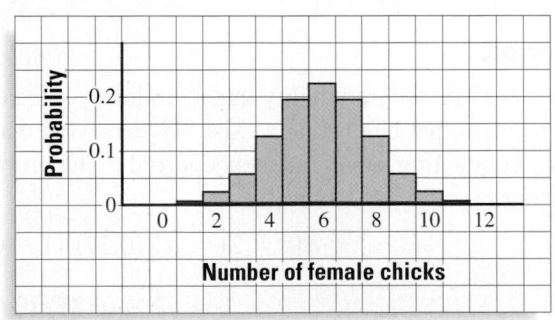

k	P(k)
0	0.000
1	0.003
2	0.016
3	0.054
4	0.121
5	0.193
6	0.226
7	0.193
8	0.121
9	0.054
10	0.016
11	0.003
12	0.000

The most likely number of female chicks is the value of k for which $P(k)$ is greatest. This probability is greatest for $k = 6$. So, the most likely number of female chicks is 6.

· · · · · · · · · ·

The distribution in Example 3 is **symmetric**, which means that the left half of the histogram is a mirror image of the right half. A distribution that is not symmetric is called **skewed**. The distribution in Example 2 is an example of a skewed distribution.

GOAL 2 TESTING HYPOTHESES

Example 1 presented the claim that 37% of adults believe that UFOs really exist. If you wanted to test this claim, you could use a procedure from statistics called **hypothesis testing**. Here are the basic steps.

HYPOTHESIS TESTING

STEP 1 State the hypothesis you are testing. The hypothesis should make a statement about some statistical measure (mean, standard deviation, or proportion) of a population.

STEP 2 Collect data from a random sample of the population and compute the statistical measure of the sample.

STEP 3 Assume that the hypothesis is true and calculate the resulting probability of obtaining the sample statistical measure *or a more extreme* sample statistical measure. If this probability is small, you should reject the hypothesis.

EXAMPLE 4 *Testing a Hypothesis*

UFOs To test the claim that 37% of adults believe UFOs really exist, you conduct a survey of 10 randomly selected adults. In your survey only 2 of the adults believe that UFOs really exist. Should you reject the claim? Explain.

SOLUTION

1 Assume the claim *37% of adults believe that UFOs really exist* is true.

2 Form the binomial distribution for the probability of selecting exactly k people out of 10 who believe that UFOs really exist.

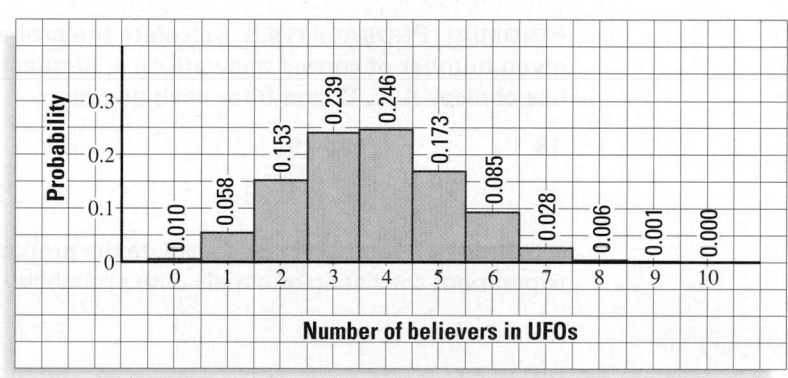

Number of believers in UFOs

3 Calculate the probability that you could randomly select 2 *or fewer* adults out of 10 who believe that UFOs really exist.

$$P(k \le 2) = 0.010 + 0.058 + 0.153 = 0.221$$

▶ If it is true that *37% of adults believe that UFOs really exist*, then there is a 22% probability of finding only 2 or fewer believers in a random sample of 10. With a probability this large, you should not reject the claim.

GUIDED PRACTICE

Vocabulary Check ✔

1. Explain the difference between a binomial experiment and a binomial distribution.

Concept Check ✔

2. You draw ten cards from a standard 52-card deck without replacement. Is this a binomial experiment? Explain.

3. Consider the binomial distribution shown. Is the distribution skewed or symmetric? Explain.

k	P(k)
0	0.0625
1	0.25
2	0.375
3	0.25
4	0.0625

Ex. 3

Skill Check ✔

Calculate the probability of *k* successes for a binomial experiment consisting of *n* trials with probability *p* of success on each trial.

4. $k = 7, n = 12, p = 0.7$

5. $k \le 3, n = 14, p = 0.45$

A binomial experiment consists of *n* trials with probability *p* of success on each trial. Draw a histogram of the binomial distribution that shows the probability of exactly *k* successes. Then find the most likely number of successes.

6. $n = 6, p = 0.5$

7. $n = 8, p = 0.33$

8. $n = 10, p = 0.25$

9. 🌎 **CLASS RINGS** You read an article that claims only 30% of graduating seniors will buy a class ring. To test this claim you survey 15 randomly selected seniors in your school and find that 4 are planning to buy class rings. Should you reject the claim? Explain. ▶ Source: *America by the Numbers*

PRACTICE AND APPLICATIONS

STUDENT HELP

▶ **Extra Practice**
to help you master skills is on p. 957.

CALCULATING PROBABILITIES Calculate the probability of tossing a coin 20 times and getting the given number of heads.

10. 1

11. 3

12. 5

13. 9

14. 10

15. 11

16. 15

17. 17

BINOMIAL PROBABILITIES Calculate the probability of randomly guessing the given number of correct answers on a 30-question multiple-choice exam that has choices A, B, C, and D for each question.

18. 0

19. 2

20. 5

21. 10

22. 15

23. 20

24. 25

25. 30

BINOMIAL DISTRIBUTIONS Calculate the probability of *k* successes for a binomial experiment consisting of *n* trials with probability *p* of success on each trial.

26. $k \ge 3, n = 5, p = 0.2$

27. $k \le 2, n = 6, p = 0.5$

28. $k \le 1, n = 9, p = 0.15$

29. $k \le 5, n = 12, p = 0.64$

STUDENT HELP

▶ **HOMEWORK HELP**
Example 1: Exs. 10–25, 36, 37
Example 2: Exs. 26–29, 38–41
Example 3: Exs. 30–35, 42–45
Example 4: Exs. 46–48

HISTOGRAMS A binomial experiment consists of *n* trials with probability *p* of success on each trial. Draw a histogram of the binomial distribution that shows the probability of exactly *k* successes. Then find the most likely number of successes.

30. $n = 2, p = 0.4$

31. $n = 4, p = 0.7$

32. $n = 5, p = 0.17$

33. $n = 8, p = 0.92$

34. $n = 9, p = 0.125$

35. $n = 12, p = 0.033$

36. COURT CASE In a particular court case, legal analysts determine from the evidence presented that there is about a 90% probability a juror will vote that the defendant is guilty. Find the probability that all 12 jurors vote that the defendant is guilty.

37. VIDEOCASSETTES A product-quality researcher runs a study on a particular brand of videocassette tape and discovers that on a random basis one out of 400 tapes is defective. Find the probability that you buy 20 of these tapes and exactly 2 are defective.

PUPPIES In Exercises 38 and 39, use the following information.
A dog gives birth to a litter of 8 puppies. Assume that the probability of a puppy being female is 0.5.

38. Draw a histogram of the binomial distribution for the number of female puppies in the litter.

39. What is the probability of having at least 5 female puppies?

EGGS In Exercises 40 and 41, use the following information.
A study states 34% of people prefer their eggs scrambled. You randomly select 7 people who had eggs for breakfast ▶ Source: *America by the Numbers*

40. Draw a histogram of the binomial distribution for the number of people who prefer their eggs scrambled.

41. What is the probability that at most 3 of these people prefer scrambled eggs?

BLOOD DRIVE In Exercises 42 and 43, use the following information.
A hospital is having a blood drive. The hospital is desperately in need of type O− blood, which 7% of the people in the United States have. Each hour at the hospital, an average of 12 people give blood. ▶ Source: American Red Cross

42. Draw a histogram of the binomial distribution for the number of people each hour who give type O− blood.

43. What is the most likely number of people each hour who give type O− blood?

WORK HOURS In Exercises 44 and 45, use the following information.
A recent survey found that 25% of women wish they had more flexible work hours. A small company has 24 female employees. ▶ Source: *America by the Numbers*

44. Draw a histogram of the binomial distribution for the number of female employees who want more flexible work hours.

45. At the small company, what is the most likely number of female employees who want more flexible work hours?

46. PERSONAL COMPUTERS A manufacturer of personal computers claims that under normal work use only 5% of its computers will fail to operate at some point in a month. A small business firm uses 30 of the manufacturer's computers under normal work use and has 2 failures in a month. Would you reject the manufacturer's claim? Explain.

47. STUDENT ATHLETES In an article about athletes at a particular college, a journalist claims that 75% of the athletes who were given scholarships would still be attending the college if they had not been given scholarships. Curious, a professor polls a random sample of 10 students with sports scholarships. Three of the students said they had plans to attend the college with or without a scholarship. Would you reject the journalist's claim? Explain.

48. 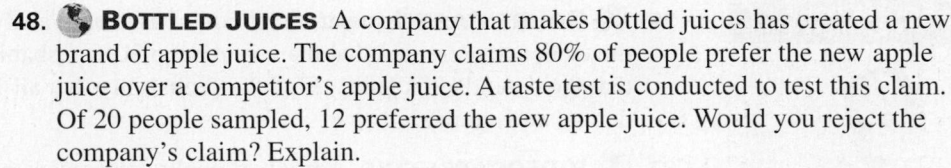 **BOTTLED JUICES** A company that makes bottled juices has created a new brand of apple juice. The company claims 80% of people prefer the new apple juice over a competitor's apple juice. A taste test is conducted to test this claim. Of 20 people sampled, 12 preferred the new apple juice. Would you reject the company's claim? Explain.

Test Preparation

49. **MULTIPLE CHOICE** A baseball player's batting average is .310. What is the probability that the player will get 3 or more hits in a game in which the player has 5 official at-bats?

    Ⓐ 0.500   Ⓑ 0.142   Ⓒ 0.035   Ⓓ 0.177   Ⓔ 0.600

50. **MULTIPLE CHOICE** Based on sales figures it is assumed that 60% of the students in a particular high school prefer Beverage A to Beverage B. In a survey of 10 randomly selected students, 3 preferred Beverage A. What is the probability of obtaining this sample result *or a more extreme* sample result?

    Ⓐ 0.947   Ⓑ 0.043   Ⓒ 0.055   Ⓓ 0.300   Ⓔ 0.200

★ **Challenge**

51. **FINDING A FORMULA** The mean of a binomial distribution is the sum of the products of the numbers of successes and the corresponding probabilities. Mathematically, the mean can be represented by:

$$\sum_{k=0}^{n} k \cdot P(k)$$

Find the mean of the binomial distribution in Example 2. Then divide the mean by n. What significance does this number have relative to the probability of success on any trial? Use this result to find a simpler formula for the mean of a binomial distribution.

EXTRA CHALLENGE
→ www.mcdougallittell.com

MIXED REVIEW

MEASURES OF DISPERSION Find the range and standard deviation of the data set. **(Review 7.7 for 12.7)**

52. 8, 9, 9, 9, 10

53. 16, 18, 19, 21, 25, 27, 27

54. 1.2, 1.3, 1.4, 1.7, 1.8

55. 81, 87, 88, 91, 99, 100

SOLVING SYSTEMS Find the points of intersection, if any, of the graphs in the system. **(Review 10.7)**

56. $x^2 + y^2 = 1$
$y = x$

57. $x^2 + y^2 = 74$
$x - y = -2$

58. $x^2 + 4y^2 = 1$
$y = x + 1$

59. $5x^2 + y^2 = 10$
$x^2 + y^2 = 9$

60. $x^2 - y^2 = 49$
$y = 7$

61. $2x^2 - 3y^2 = 6$
$y = 3x + 1$

WRITING RULES Write a recursive rule for the sequence. The sequence may be arithmetic, geometric, or neither. **(Review 11.5)**

62. 3, 5, 9, 15, . . .

63. 4, 40, 400, 4000, . . .

64. 80, 60, 40, 20, . . .

65. 1, 3, 3, 9, . . .

66. 160, 40, 10, 2.5, . . .

67. 1, 2, 3, 5, . . .

68. **GEOMETRY CONNECTION** The radius r of a sphere can be approximated by $r = 0.62\sqrt[3]{V}$ where V is the volume of the sphere. Graph the model. Then determine the volume of a sphere with a radius of 3 inches. **(Lesson 7.5)**

ACTIVITY 12.6

Using Technology

Constructing a Binomial Distribution

Some calculators have a binomial probability distribution function that you can use to calculate binomial probabilities.

▶ **EXAMPLE**

According to a survey, oatmeal is found in 80% of all United States households. Suppose you survey 7 households at random. Draw a histogram of the binomial distribution showing the probability that oatmeal is found in exactly k households.

▶ **SOLUTION**

Let $p = 0.8$ be the probability that a household has oatmeal.

1 Enter the k-values 0 through 7 into a list on your graphing calculator.

2 Enter the binomial probability command to generate $P(k)$ for all eight k-values. Store the results in a second list.

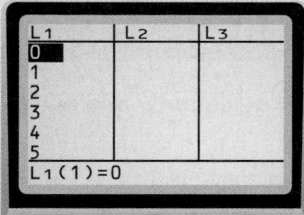

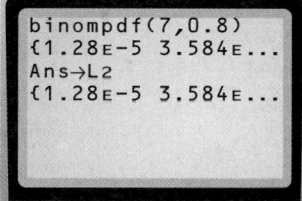

3 To set up the histogram, let the x-values be the k-values stored in List 1, and let the frequencies be the values of $P(k)$ stored in List 2.

4 To draw the histogram shown, set the viewing window so that $-0.5 \le x \le 7.5$ with a scale of 1 and $0 \le y \le 0.5$ with a scale of 0.1.

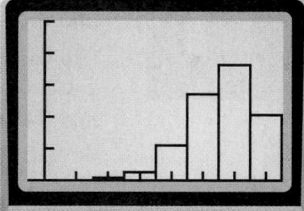

▶ **EXERCISES**

1. Suppose you conduct a survey similar to the one described in the example, except that you survey 14 households at random. Draw a histogram of the binomial distribution showing the probability that oatmeal is found in exactly k households.

2. According to a survey, 21% of teachers in kindergarten through grade 6 use the Internet with their students. You survey 10 teachers of kindergarten through grade 6 at random. Draw a histogram of the binomial distribution showing the probability that exactly k teachers use the Internet with their students.

Normal Distributions

GOAL **1** USING NORMAL DISTRIBUTIONS

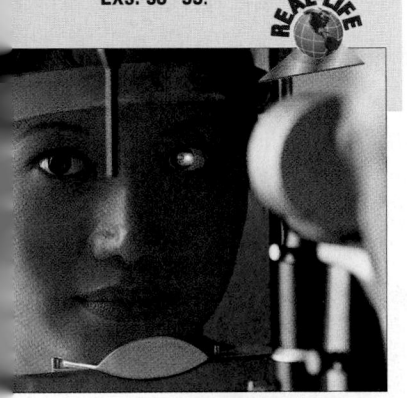

As statisticians began to study binomial distributions consisting of n trials with
probability P of success on each trial, they discovered that when np and $n(1 - p)$
are both greater than or equal to five, the distributions all resemble one another.
Here are two examples.

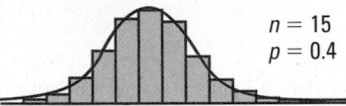

$n = 15$
$p = 0.4$

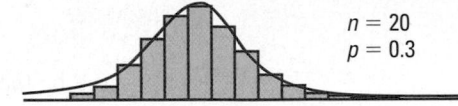

$n = 20$
$p = 0.3$

In both cases the binomial distribution can be approximated by a smooth,
symmetrical, bell-shaped curve called a **normal curve**. Areas under this curve
represent probabilities from **normal distributions**.

**CONCEPT
SUMMARY**   AREAS UNDER A NORMAL CURVE

The mean $\overline{x}$ and standard deviation σ of a normal distribution determine the
following areas.

- The total area under the curve is 1.
- 68% of the area lies within 1 standard deviation of the mean.
- 95% of the area lies within 2 standard deviations of the mean.
- 99.7% of the area lies within 3 standard deviations of the mean.

From the second bulleted statement above
and the symmetry of a normal curve, you
can deduce that 34% of the area lies within
1 standard deviation to the left of the mean,
and 34% of the area lies within 1 standard
deviation to the right of the mean. The
diagram shows other partial areas
(expressed as decimals rather than percents)
based on the properties of a normal curve.

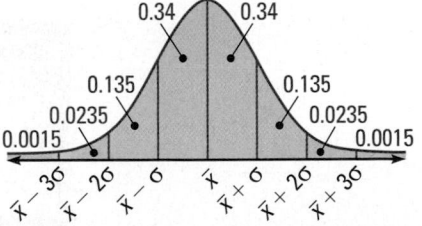

You can interpret these areas as probabilities.
In a normal distribution, the probability that
a randomly chosen x-value is between a and
b is given by the area under the normal curve
between a and b. For instance, the probability
that a randomly selected x-value is between 1
and 2 standard deviations to the right of the
mean is:

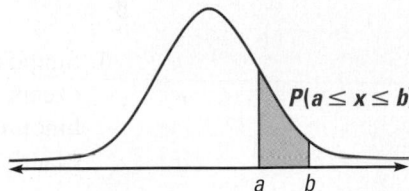

$$P(\overline{x} + \sigma \le x \le \overline{x} + 2\sigma) = 0.135$$

Many real-life distributions are normal or approximately normal.

EXAMPLE 1 *Using a Normal Distribution*

A survey shows that the time spent by shoppers in supermarkets is normally distributed with a mean of 45 minutes and a standard deviation of 12 minutes.

a. What percent of the shoppers at a supermarket will spend between 33 and 57 minutes in the supermarket?

b. What is the probability that a randomly chosen shopper will spend between 45 and 69 minutes in the supermarket?

SOLUTION

STUDENT HELP

↳ **Study Tip**
When calculating probabilities using a normal distribution, refer to the diagram below the property box on p. 746.

a. The given times of 33 minutes and 57 minutes represent one standard deviation on either side of the mean, as shown below. So, 68% of the shoppers will spend between 33 and 57 minutes in the supermarket.

b. The time of 45 minutes is the mean and the time of 69 minutes is two standard deviations to the right of the mean, as shown below. So, the probability that a randomly chosen shopper will spend between 45 and 69 minutes in the supermarket is 0.475.

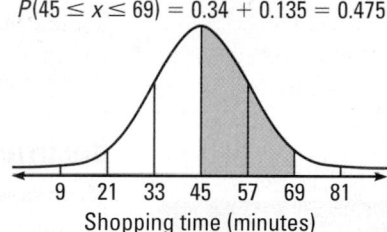

EXAMPLE 2 *Using a Normal Distribution (Compound Event)*

According to a survey by the National Center for Health Statistics, the heights of adult men in the United States are normally distributed with a mean of 69 inches and a standard deviation of 2.75 inches. If you randomly choose 3 adult men, what is the probability that all three are 71.75 inches or taller?

SOLUTION

A height of 71.75 inches is one standard deviation to the right of the mean, as shown. The probability of randomly selecting a man who is this height or taller is:

$$P(x \geq 71.75) = 0.135 + 0.0235 + 0.0015$$

$$= 0.16$$

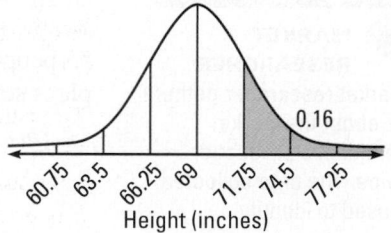

Randomly choosing men are independent events, so the probability that all three randomly chosen men are 71.75 inches or taller is:

$$P(\text{all are 71.75 inches or taller}) = (0.16)^3$$

$$\approx 0.00410$$

GOAL 2 APPROXIMATING BINOMIAL DISTRIBUTIONS

When n is large it can be tedious to compute binomial probabilities using the formula $P(k) = {}_nC_kp^k(1-p)^{n-k}$. In such cases you may be able to use a normal distribution to approximate a binomial distribution.

NORMAL APPROXIMATION OF A BINOMIAL DISTRIBUTION

Consider the binomial distribution consisting of n trials with probability p of success on each trial. If $np \geq 5$ and $n(1-p) \geq 5$, then the binomial distribution can be approximated by a normal distribution with a mean of

$$\overline{x} = np$$

and a standard deviation of

$$\sigma = \sqrt{np(1-p)}.$$

EXAMPLE 3   *Finding a Binomial Probability*

SURVEYS According to a survey conducted by the Harris Poll, 29% of adults in the United States say that they or someone in their family plays soccer regularly. You are conducting a random survey of 238 adults. What is the probability that you will find at most 55 adults who come from a family in which someone plays soccer regularly?

SOLUTION

To answer the question using the binomial probability formula, you would have to calculate the following:

$$P(x \leq 55) = P(0) + P(1) + P(2) + \cdots + P(55)$$

This would be tedious. Instead you can approximate the answer with a normal distribution having a mean of

$$\overline{x} = np = 238(0.29) \approx 69$$

and a standard deviation of

$$\sigma = \sqrt{np(1-p)} = \sqrt{238(0.29)(0.71)} \approx 7.$$

For this normal distribution, 55 is two standard deviations to the left of the mean. So, the probability that you will find at most 55 people from families in which someone plays soccer regularly is:

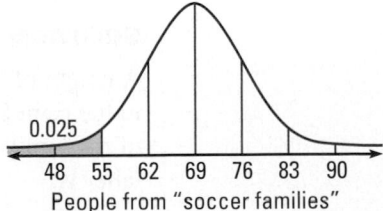

0.025

People from "soccer families"

$$P(x \leq 55) \approx 0.0015 + 0.0235$$

$$= 0.025$$

• • • • • • • • • •

If you had instead used the binomial probability formula in Example 3, you would have found the actual binomial probability to be approximately 0.0249. So, you can see that the normal approximation is a very good approximation.

FOCUS ON CAREERS

MARKET RESEARCHER

A market researcher gathers data about the market potential of a product or service. The data collected are used to identify opportunities to improve a company's success in the marketplace.

CAREER LINK
www.mcdougallittell.com

GUIDED PRACTICE

Vocabulary Check ✓

1. Complete this statement: A(n) _?_ can be used to approximate a binomial distribution when np and $n(1 - p)$ are both greater than or equal to 5.

Concept Check ✓

2. A normal curve is symmetric about what x-value?

3. What percent of the area under a normal curve lies within 1 standard deviation of the mean? within 2 standard deviations of the mean? within 3 standard deviations of the mean?

Skill Check ✓

A normal distribution has a mean of 10 and a standard deviation of 1. Find the probability that a randomly selected x-value is in the given interval.

4. between 8 and 12   5. between 7 and 13   6. between 8 and 11

7. at most 10   8. at least 12   9. at most 9

Find the mean and standard deviation of a normal distribution that approximates a binomial distribution consisting of n trials with probability p of success on each trial.

10. $n = 10, p = 0.5$ 11. $n = 17, p = 0.3$ 12. $n = 28, p = 0.2$

13. $n = 20, p = 0.25$ 14. $n = 12, p = 0.42$ 15. $n = 30, p = 0.17$

🌎 **COLORBLINDNESS** In Exercises 16–18, use the fact that approximately 2% of people are colorblind, and consider a class of 460 students.

16. What is the probability that 15 or fewer students are colorblind?

17. What is the probability that 12 or more students are colorblind?

18. What is the probability that between 6 and 18 students are colorblind?

PRACTICE AND APPLICATIONS

STUDENT HELP

▶ **Extra Practice**
to help you master
skills is on p. 957.

USING A NORMAL CURVE Give the percent of the area under a normal curve represented by the shaded region.

19.

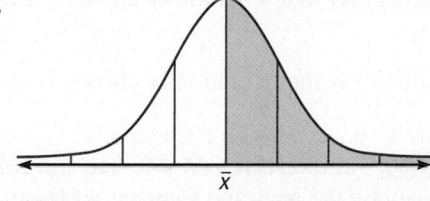

20.

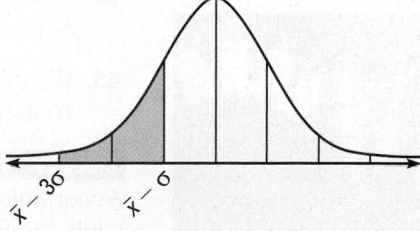

STUDENT HELP

▶ **HOMEWORK HELP**
Example 1: Exs. 19–28,
          38–43
Example 2: Exs. 29–31,
          44–49
Example 3: Exs. 32–37,
          50–55

21.

22.

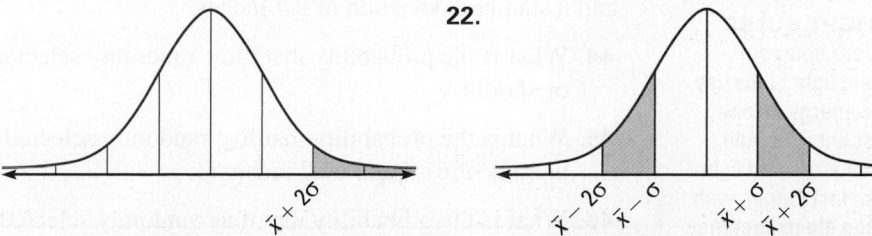

NORMAL DISTRIBUTIONS A normal distribution has a mean of 22 and a standard deviation of 3. Find the probability that a randomly selected x-value is in the given interval.

23. between 19 and 25   **24.** between 13 and 22   **25.** between 16 and 31

26. at most 25   **27.** at least 19   **28.** at most 28

FINDING PROBABILITIES A normal distribution has a mean of 64 and a standard deviation of 7. Find the given probability.

29. three randomly selected x-values are all 71 or greater

30. four randomly selected x-values are all 50 or less

31. two randomly selected x-values are both between 57 and 78

APPROXIMATING BINOMIAL DISTRIBUTIONS Find the mean and standard deviation of a normal distribution that approximates a binomial distribution consisting of n trials with probability p of success on each trial.

32. $n = 18, p = 0.7$ **33.** $n = 50, p = 0.1$ **34.** $n = 32, p = 0.8$

35. $n = 49, p = 0.12$ **36.** $n = 24, p = 0.67$ **37.** $n = 140, p = 0.06$

 DRIVE-THROUGH In Exercises 38–40, use the following information.
A certain bank is busiest during the Friday evening rush hours from 3:00 P.M. until 6:00 P.M. During these hours the waiting time for drive-through customers is normally distributed with a mean of 8 minutes and a standard deviation of 2 minutes.

38. What percent of drive-through customers will wait for 10 minutes or longer during the Friday evening rush hours?

39. What is the probability that a customer will wait between 4 and 12 minutes during the Friday evening rush hours?

40. What is the probability that a customer will wait 2 minutes or less during the Friday evening rush hours?

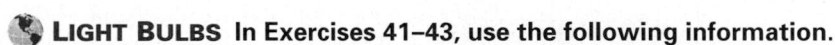 **LIGHT BULBS** In Exercises 41–43, use the following information.
A company produces light bulbs having a life expectancy that is normally distributed with a mean of 1000 hours and a standard deviation of 50 hours.

41. What percent of the bulbs will last for 1000 hours or more?

42. What is the probability that a randomly chosen bulb will burn out in 900 hours or less?

43. What is the probability that a randomly chosen bulb will last between 850 and 1050 hours?

BIOLOGY ⟩ **CONNECTION** In Exercises 44–46, use the following information.
According to a survey by the National Center for Health Statistics, the heights of adult women in the United States are normally distributed with a mean of 64 inches and a standard deviation of 2.7 inches.

44. What is the probability that three randomly selected women are all 58.6 inches or shorter?

45. What is the probability that five randomly selected women are all between the heights of 61.3 and 66.7 inches?

46. What is the probability that four randomly selected women are all 72.1 inches or taller?

STUDENT HELP

INTERNET
HOMEWORK HELP
Visit our Web site
www.mcdougallittell.com
for help with problem
solving in Exs. 47–49.

🌎 **SAT SCORES** In Exercises 47–49, use the following information.

In 1998 scores on the mathematics section of the SAT (Scholastic Aptitude Test) were normally distributed with a mean of 512 and a standard deviation of 112. Scores on the English section of the SAT were normally distributed with a mean of 505 and a standard deviation of 111. ➡️ **DATA UPDATE** of SAT data at www.mcdougallittell.com

47. What is the probability that a randomly chosen student who took the SAT in 1998 scored at least 736 on the mathematics section and at least 727 on the English section? Assume the scores are independent.

48. What is the probability that five randomly chosen students who took the SAT in 1998 all scored at most 394 on the English section?

49. What is the probability that two randomly chosen students who took the SAT in 1998 both scored between 400 and 624 on the mathematics section?

🌎 **LEFT-HANDEDNESS** In Exercises 50–52, use the fact that approximately 9% of people are left-handed, and consider a high school with 1221 students.

50. What is the probability that at least 140 students are left-handed?

51. What is the probability that at most 100 students are left-handed?

52. What is the probability that between 80 and 130 students are left-handed?

🌎 **MYOPIA** In Exercises 53–55, use the fact that myopia, or nearsightedness, is a condition that affects approximately 25% of the adult population in the United States, and consider a random sample of 192 people.

53. What is the probability that 42 or more people are nearsighted?

54. What is the probability that between 36 and 60 people are nearsighted?

55. What is the probability that 66 or fewer people are nearsighted?

Test Preparation

56. MULTI-STEP PROBLEM In 1998 Ben took both the SAT (Scholastic Aptitude Test) and the ACT (American College Test). On the mathematics section of the SAT, he earned a score of 624. On the mathematics section of the ACT, he earned a score of 31. For the SAT the mean was 512 and the standard deviation was 112. For the ACT the mean was 21 and the standard deviation was 5.

　a. What percent of students did Ben outscore on the math section of the SAT?

　b. What percent of students did Ben outscore on the math section of the ACT?

　c. On which exam did Ben score better?

　d. *Writing* Explain how you could translate ACT scores such as 15, 20, 25, and 30 into equivalent SAT scores if you know the mean and standard deviation of each exam.

★ **Challenge**

57. 🖩 **NORMAL CURVE** A normal curve is defined by an equation whose general form is as follows:

$$y = \frac{1}{\sigma\sqrt{2\pi}}\, e^{-\frac{1}{2}\left(\frac{x - \bar{x}}{\sigma}\right)^2}$$

Use a graphing calculator to draw a histogram of a binomial distribution consisting of $n = 20$ trials with probability $p = 0.5$ of success. Also graph the normal curve that approximates this binomial distribution. Then graph other binomial distributions and normal curves in which you change p but leave n constant. When is the normal curve a good approximation of a binomial distribution and when is it a poor approximation? Why?

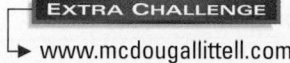
EXTRA CHALLENGE
www.mcdougallittell.com

EVALUATING EXPRESSIONS Evaluate the expression without using a calculator. (Review 7.1 for 13.1)

58. $9^{3/2}$

59. $256^{3/4}$

60. $49^{-1/2}$

61. $\sqrt[3]{125}$

62. $\sqrt{81}$

63. $\left(\sqrt[4]{625}\right)^2$

IDENTIFYING PARTS Write the equation of the ellipse in standard form (if not already). Then identify the vertices, co-vertices, and foci of the ellipse. (Review 10.4)

64. $\dfrac{x^2}{4} + \dfrac{y^2}{16} = 1$

65. $\dfrac{x^2}{144} + \dfrac{y^2}{169} = 1$

66. $\dfrac{x^2}{5} + \dfrac{y^2}{10} = 1$

67. $\dfrac{x^2}{6} + \dfrac{y^2}{21} = 1$

68. $4x^2 + 9y^2 = 36$

69. $10x^2 + 7y^2 = 70$

USING COMPLEMENTS Two six-sided dice are rolled. Find the probability of the given event. (Review 12.4)

70. The sum is not 4.

71. The sum is less than or equal to 10.

72. The sum is not 3 or 12.

73. The sum is greater than 3.

QUIZ 3

Self-Test for Lessons 12.6 and 12.7

Calculate the probability of rolling a six-sided die 50 times and getting the given number of ones. (Lesson 12.6)

1. 0

2. 1

3. 8

4. 17

5. 25

6. 33

7. 42

8. 50

A binomial experiment consists of n trials with probability p of success on each trial. Draw a histogram of the binomial distribution that shows the probability of exactly k successes. Then find the most likely number of successes. (Lesson 12.6)

9. $n = 4, p = 0.3$

10. $n = 7, p = 0.5$

11. $n = 8, p = 0.6$

12. $n = 10, p = 0.33$

13. $n = 12, p = 0.48$

14. $n = 15, p = 0.21$

A normal distribution has a mean of 62 and a standard deviation of 4. Find the probability that a randomly selected x-value is in the given interval. (Lesson 12.7)

15. between 58 and 66

16. between 62 and 74

17. between 50 and 70

18. 62 or greater

19. 58 or less

20. 50 or less

21. 🌎 **WELL-BEING** A survey that asked people in the United States about their feelings of personal well-being found that 85% are generally happy. To test this finding you survey 26 people at random and find that 19 consider themselves generally happy. Would you reject the survey's findings? Explain. (Lesson 12.6)

22. 🌎 **DRINKING WATER** Approximately 64% of people in the United States think that the nation's water supply is safe to drink. A town has 625 people. What is the probability that 400 or more people think that the nation's water supply is safe to drink? (Lesson 12.7)

Extension

Expected Value

What you should learn

GOAL Find expected values of collections of outcomes.

Why you should learn it

▼ To solve **real-life** problems, such as finding the expected value of insurance coverage in **Example 2**.

Suppose you and a friend are playing a game. You flip a coin. If the coin lands heads up, then your friend scores 1 point and you lose 1 point. If the coin lands tails up, then you score 1 point and your friend loses 1 point. After playing the game many times, would you expect to have more, fewer, or the same number of points as when you started? The answer is that you should expect to end up with about the same number of points. You can expect to lose a point about half the time and win a point about half the time. Therefore, the *expected value* for this game is 0.

EXPECTED VALUE

A collection of outcomes is partitioned into *n* events, no two of which have any outcomes in common. The probabilities of the *n* events occurring are $p_1, p_2, p_3, \ldots, p_n$ where $p_1 + p_2 + p_3 + \cdots + p_n = 1$. The values of the *n* events are $x_1, x_2, x_3, \ldots, x_n$. The **expected value** *V* of the collection of outcomes is the sum of the products of the events' probabilities and their values.

$$V = p_1x_1 + p_2x_2 + p_3x_3 + \cdots + p_nx_n$$

EXAMPLE 1 *Finding the Expected Value of a Game*

You and a friend each flip a coin. If both coins land heads up, then your friend scores 3 points and you lose 3 points. If one or both of the coins land tails up, then you score 1 point and your friend loses 1 point. What is the expected value of the game from your point of view?

SOLUTION

When two coins are tossed, four outcomes are possible: HH, HT, TH, and TT. Let event *A* be HH and event *B* be HT, TH, and TT. Note that all possible outcomes are listed, but no outcome is listed twice. The probabilities of the events are:

$$P(A) = \frac{1}{4} \qquad\qquad P(B) = \frac{3}{4}$$

From your point of view the values of the events are:

value of event $A = -3$ value of event $B = 1$

Therefore, the expected value of the game is:

$$V = \frac{1}{4}(-3) + \frac{3}{4}(1) = 0$$

. . . .

If the expected value of the game is 0, as in Example 1, then the game is called a **fair game**.

EXAMPLE 2 *Finding an Expected Value in Real Life*

In 1996 there were 124,600,000 cars in use in the United States. That year there were 13,300,000 automobile accidents. The average premium paid in 1996 for automobile collision insurance was $685 per car, and the average automobile collision claim paid by insurance companies was $2100 per car. What was the expected value of insurance coverage for a car with collision insurance in 1996?

SOLUTION

STUDENT HELP

HOMEWORK HELP
Visit our Web site
www.mcdougallittell.com
for extra examples.

Let event A be having an automobile accident and event B be not having an automobile accident. Note that events A and B are mutually exclusive and that $B = A'$, so all outcomes are accounted for but no outcome is counted twice. The probabilities of the events are:

$$P(A) = \frac{13,300,000}{124,600,000} \approx 0.107 \qquad P(B) = 1 - P(A) \approx 1 - 0.107 = 0.893$$

You can calculate the values of the events as follows. If an insured car had an accident, the owner paid an average of $685 and received an average of $2100. If a car did not have an accident, the owner only paid an average of $685. So, the values of the events for an insured person are:

value of event $A = -685 + 2100 = 1415$ value of event $B = -685$

Therefore, the expected value of insurance coverage was:

$$V \approx 0.107(1415) + 0.893(-685) \approx -\$460$$

EXERCISES

EXPECTED VALUE In Exercises 1 and 2, consider a game in which two people each choose an integer from 1 to 3. Find the expected value of the game for each player. Is the game fair? (*Hint:* There may be more than two events to consider.)

1. If the two numbers are equal, then no points are received. If the numbers differ by one, then the player with the higher number wins 1 point and the other player loses 1 point. If the numbers differ by two, then the player with the lower number wins 1 point and the other player loses 1 point.

2. If the sum of the two numbers is odd, then player A loses that sum of points and player B wins that sum. If the sum of the two numbers is even, then player B loses 4 points and player A wins 4 points.

3. 🌐 **LOTTERY** To win a certain state's weekly lottery, you must match 5 different numbers chosen from the integers 1 to 49 plus an additional number chosen from the integers 1 to 42. You purchase a ticket for $1. If the jackpot for that week is $45,000,000, what is the expected value of your ticket?

4. 🌐 **CONTESTS** A fast-food restaurant chain is having a contest with five prizes. No purchase is necessary to enter. What is the expected value of a contest ticket?

Prize	Value	Probability of winning
Gift certificate	$5	0.0002
Home theater system	$3,000	0.0000004
Hawaiian vacation	$7,000	0.00000008
Car	$50,000	0.000000003
Cash	$1,000,000	0.000000002

Chapter Summary

WHAT did you learn?

Count the number of ways an event can happen.
- using the fundamental counting principle **(12.1)**
- using permutations **(12.1)**

- using combinations **(12.2)**

Expand a binomial that is raised to a power. **(12.2)**

Find theoretical, experimental, and geometric probabilities. **(12.3)**

Find probabilities of unions and intersections of two events. **(12.4)**

Use complements to find probabilities. **(12.4)**

Find probabilities of independent and dependent events. **(12.5)**

Find binomial probabilities and analyze binomial distributions. **(12.6)**

Test a hypothesis. **(12.6)**

Use normal distributions to calculate probabilities and to approximate binomial distributions. **(12.7)**

Use probability and statistics to solve real-life problems. **(12.1–12.7)**

WHY did you learn it?

Find the number of possible license plates. **(p. 702)**

Find the number of ways skiers can finish in an Olympic event. **(p. 703)**

Find the number of combinations of plays you can attend. **(p. 709)**

Apply Pascal's triangle to algebra. **(p. 710)**

Find the probability that an archer hits the center of a target. **(p. 721)**

Find the probability that it will rain on both Saturday and Sunday. **(p. 728)**

Find the probability that friends will be in the same college dormitory. **(p. 729)**

Find the probability that a baseball team wins three games in a row. **(p. 730)**

Find the most likely number of people who will give type O− blood. **(p. 743)**

Test the claim that only 5% of computers will fail in a month. **(p. 743)**

Find the probability that certain numbers of patients are nearsighted. **(p. 751)**

Find the probability of winning a lottery. **(p. 720)**

How does Chapter 12 fit into the BIGGER PICTURE of algebra?

In this chapter you saw how algebra is used in probability and statistics. In fact, every branch of mathematics uses algebra. You can use what you have learned in this and other chapters to make everyday decisions.

STUDY STRATEGY

How did you connect to your life?

Here is an example of a connection, following the **Study Strategy** on page 700.

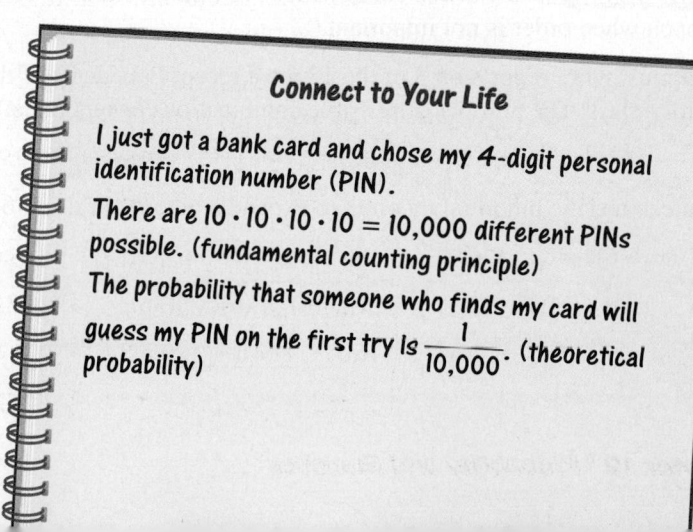

Connect to Your Life

I just got a bank card and chose my 4-digit personal identification number (PIN).

There are $10 \cdot 10 \cdot 10 \cdot 10 = 10{,}000$ different PINs possible. (fundamental counting principle)

The probability that someone who finds my card will guess my PIN on the first try is $\frac{1}{10{,}000}$. (theoretical probability)

VOCABULARY

- permutation, p. 703
- combination, p. 708
- Pascal's triangle, p. 710
- binomial theorem, p. 710
- probability, p. 716
- theoretical probability, p. 716

- experimental probability, p. 717
- geometric probability, p. 718
- compound event, p. 724
- mutually exclusive events, p. 724
- complement, p. 726

- independent events, p. 730
- dependent events, p. 732
- conditional probability, p. 732
- binomial experiment, p. 739
- binomial distribution, p. 739
- symmetric distribution, p. 740

- skewed distribution, p. 740
- hypothesis testing, p. 741
- normal curve, p. 746
- normal distribution, p. 746
- expected value, p. 753
- fair game, p. 753

12.1 **THE FUNDAMENTAL COUNTING PRINCIPLE AND PERMUTATIONS**

Examples on pp. 701–704

EXAMPLES You can use the fundamental counting principle and permutations to count the number of ways an event can happen.

The number of possible outfits you can make with 2 pairs of jeans and 5 shirts is:

$$2 \cdot 5 = 10 \text{ outfits}$$

The number of ways 4 members from a family of 5 can line up for a photo is:

$$_5P_4 = \frac{5!}{(5-4)!} = \frac{5!}{1!} = \frac{120}{1} = 120$$

1. How many different 5-digit zip codes are there if any of the digits 0–9 can be used?

2. How many different ways can 4 friends stand in a cafeteria line?

Find the number of permutations.

3. $_6P_6$ **4.** $_8P_4$ **5.** $_5P_1$ **6.** $_9P_3$ **7.** $_{10}P_6$ **8.** $_4P_4$

12.2 **COMBINATIONS AND THE BINOMIAL THEOREM**

Examples on pp. 708–711

EXAMPLES You can use combinations to find the number of ways an event can happen when order is not important.

You must write reports on 3 of the 12 most recent Presidents of the United States for history class. The number of possible combinations of reports is:

$$_{12}C_3 = \frac{12!}{9! \cdot 3!} = \frac{12 \cdot 11 \cdot 10 \cdot 9!}{9! \cdot 3!} = \frac{1320}{6} = 220$$

You can use the binomial theorem to expand a binomial raised to a power.

$$(x + 6)^4 = {}_4C_0x^46^0 + {}_4C_1x^36^1 + {}_4C_2x^26^2 + {}_4C_3x^16^3 + {}_4C_4x^06^4$$

$$= (1)(x^4)(1) + (4)(x^3)(6) + (6)(x^2)(36) + (4)(x)(216) + (1)(1)(1296)$$

$$= x^4 + 24x^3 + 216x^2 + 864x + 1296$$

Find the number of combinations.

9. $_9C_2$ **10.** $_7C_1$ **11.** $_5C_3$ **12.** $_8C_7$ **13.** $_{10}C_{10}$ **14.** $_{13}C_5$

Use the binomial theorem to write the binomial expansion.

15. $(x + 4)^3$ **16.** $(x - 10)^5$ **17.** $(x - 3y)^7$ **18.** $(2x + y^2)^4$

12.3   AN INTRODUCTION TO PROBABILITY

Examples on pp. 716–718

> **EXAMPLES** You can find the probability that an event will occur.
>
> You toss two six-sided dice. The *theoretical* probability that the sum of the dice is 4 is
> $$\frac{\text{number of ways sum can be 4}}{\text{number of possible outcomes}} = \frac{3}{36} = \frac{1}{12}.$$
>
> You toss two 6-sided dice 100 times and record 8 times that the sum is 4. The *experimental* probability that the sum of the dice is 4 is
> $$\frac{\text{number of times sum is 4}}{\text{number of times dice are tossed}} = \frac{8}{100} = \frac{2}{25}.$$
>
> A dart thrown at the square target shown is equally likely to hit any point inside the target. The *geometric* probability that the dart hits the shaded square is $\dfrac{\text{area of shaded square}}{\text{area of entire target}} = \dfrac{4}{16} = \dfrac{1}{4}.$
>
>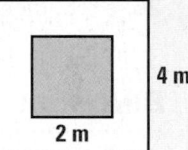
> 4 m   2 m

You toss a coin 3 times. Find the probability of the given event.

19. You toss exactly 1 tail.   **20.** You toss at least 1 tail.

21. You toss a coin 200 times and get heads 90 times. Find the experimental probability of getting heads. Compare this with the theoretical probability.

22. What is the probability that a dart hits the unshaded region of the target above?

12.4   PROBABILITY OF COMPOUND EVENTS

Examples on pp. 724–726

> **EXAMPLES** You can find the probability that compound events will occur and the probability that the complement of an event will occur.
>
> If A and B are two events and $P(A) = \dfrac{3}{4}$, $P(B) = \dfrac{2}{5}$, and $P(A \text{ and } B) = \dfrac{1}{4}$,
>
> then $P(A \text{ or } B) = P(A) + P(B) - P(A \text{ and } B) = \dfrac{3}{4} + \dfrac{2}{5} - \dfrac{1}{4} = \dfrac{18}{20} = \dfrac{9}{10}.$
>
> The probability of the complement of A is $P(A') = 1 - P(A) = 1 - \dfrac{3}{4} = \dfrac{1}{4}.$

Find the indicated probability.

23. $P(A) = 0.25$, $P(B) = 0.2$, $P(A \text{ and } B) = 0.15$, $P(A \text{ or } B) = \underline{\ ?\ }$

24. $P(A) = \dfrac{2}{5}$, $P(B) = \dfrac{1}{10}$, $P(A \text{ and } B) = \underline{\ ?\ }$, $P(A \text{ or } B) = \dfrac{1}{2}$

25. $P(A) = 99\%$, $P(A') = \underline{\ ?\ }$

PROBABILITY OF INDEPENDENT AND DEPENDENT EVENTS

Examples on
pp. 730–733

> **EXAMPLES** You can find the probability that independent events will occur and the probability that dependent events will occur.
>
> Nine slips of paper numbered 1–9 are placed in a hat. You randomly draw two slips. What is the probability that the first number is odd (A) and the second is even (B)?
>
> If you replace the first slip of paper before selecting the second, A and B are *independent* events, and $P(A \text{ and } B) = P(A) \cdot P(B) = \frac{5}{9} \cdot \frac{4}{9} = \frac{20}{81} \approx 0.247$.
>
> If you do not replace the first slip of paper before selecting the second, A and B are *dependent* events, and $P(A \text{ and } B) = P(A) \cdot P(B \mid A) = \frac{5}{9} \cdot \frac{4}{8} = \frac{20}{72} = \frac{5}{18} \approx 0.278$.

Find the probability of randomly drawing the given marbles from a bag of 4 red, 6 green, and 2 blue marbles (a) with replacement and (b) without replacement.

26. a red, then a green   **27.** a blue, then a red   **28.** a red, then a red

BINOMIAL DISTRIBUTIONS

Examples on
pp. 739–741

> **EXAMPLE** You can find the probability of getting exactly k successes for a binomial experiment.
>
> The probability of tossing a coin 10 times and getting exactly 7 heads is:
>
> $$P(k = 7) = {}_{10}C_7(0.5)^7(1 - 0.5)^3 = \frac{10!}{3! \cdot 7!}(0.5)^7(0.5)^3 \approx 0.117$$

Calculate the probability of tossing a coin 10 times and getting the given number of tails.

29. 3   **30.** 5   **31.** 9   **32.** 6   **33.** 1   **34.** 10

NORMAL DISTRIBUTIONS

Examples on
pp. 746–748

> **EXAMPLE** You can use normal distributions to approximate binomial distributions.
>
> In 1990 about 1 in 43 births resulted in twins. If a town had 2157 births that year, what is the probability that between 29 and 50 of them were twins?
>
> $$\bar{x} = np = 2157\left(\frac{1}{43}\right) \approx 50 \text{ and } \sigma = \sqrt{np(1 - p)} = \sqrt{(2157)\left(\frac{1}{43}\right)\left(\frac{42}{43}\right)} \approx 7$$
>
> So, $P(29 \le x \le 50) = P(\bar{x} - 3\sigma \le x \le \bar{x}) = 0.0235 + 0.135 + 0.34 = 0.4985$, referring to the diagram on page 746.

A binomial distribution consists of 100 trials with probability 0.9 of success. Approximate the probability of getting the given numbers of successes.

35. between 87 and 93   **36.** greater than 90   **37.** less than 84   **38.** between 81 and 84

12

Chapter Test

Find the number of permutations or combinations.

1. $_4P_3$ **2.** $_{11}P_5$ **3.** $_{14}P_2$ **4.** $_9C_6$ **5.** $_{17}C_3$ **6.** $_5C_4$

7. Find the number of distinguishable permutations of the letters in MONTANA.

Expand the power of the binomial.

8. $(x + 4)^6$ **9.** $(2x - 2)^5$ **10.** $(x + 8)^3$ **11.** $(x^2 + 1)^4$ **12.** $(x + y^2)^5$ **13.** $(3x - y)^3$

A card is drawn randomly from a standard 52-card deck. Find the probability of drawing the given card. (For a listing of the deck, see page. 708.)

14. a black card **15.** an ace **16.** a black ace **17.** a king **18.** a heart **19.** the king of hearts

Find the indicated probability.

20. $P(A) = 80\%$
$P(B) = 20\%$
$P(A \text{ or } B) = 100\%$
$P(A \text{ and } B) = \underline{?}$

21. $P(A) = \underline{?}$
$P(B) = 0.7$
$P(A \text{ or } B) = 0.82$
$P(A \text{ and } B) = 0.05$

22. $P(A) = \frac{1}{4}$
$P(A') = \underline{?}$

23. A and B are independent events.
$P(A) = 0.25$
$P(B) = 0.75$
$P(A \text{ and } B) = \underline{?}$

24. A and B are dependent events.
$P(A) = 30\%$
$P(B \mid A) = 40\%$
$P(A \text{ and } B) = \underline{?}$

25. A and B are dependent events.
$P(A) = \underline{?}$
$P(B \mid A) = 0.8$
$P(A \text{ and } B) = 0.32$

26. Calculate the probability of randomly guessing at least 7 correct answers on a 10-question true-or-false quiz to get a passing grade.

27. What percent of the area under a normal curve lies within 1 standard deviation of the mean? What percent lies within 2 standard deviations of the mean?

28. **SCHOOL SHIRTS** A school shirt is available either long-sleeved or short-sleeved, in sizes small, medium, large, or extra large, and in one of two colors. How many different choices for a school shirt are there?

29. **SUPREME COURT** The Supreme Court of the United States has 9 justices. On a certain case the justices voted 5 to 4 in favor of the defendant. In how many ways could this have happened?

30. **ASTRONOMY** The surface area of Earth is about 197 million square miles. The land area is about 57 million square miles and the rest is water. What is the probability that a meteorite falling to Earth will hit land? What is the probability that it will hit water?

31. **EMPLOYMENT AGENCY** A temporary employment agency claims that it has a "no-show" rate of 1 out of 1000 workers. If fewer employees show up for a job than are requested, the difference is the number of "no-shows." A company hires the employment agency to supply 200 workers and only 198 show up. Would you reject the agency's claim about its "no-show" rate? Explain.

32. **HEALTH** Health officials who have studied a particular virus say that 50% of all Americans have had the virus. If a random sample of 144 people is taken, what is the probability that fewer than 60 have had the virus?

Chapter Standardized Test

● **TEST-TAKING STRATEGY** Do not panic if you run out of time before answering all of the questions. You can still receive a high score on the SAT without answering every question.

1. **MULTIPLE CHOICE** In how many ways can a president and vice president be selected from a club of 20 students?

   (A) 20   (B) 39   (C) 40

   (D) 380   (E) 400

2. **MULTIPLE CHOICE** In how many ways can 2 co-chairs be selected from a club of 20 students?

   (A) 10   (B) 39   (C) 40

   (D) 190   (E) 380

3. **MULTIPLE CHOICE** What is the coefficient of x^5 in the expansion of $(2x + 5)^8$?

   (A) 6   (B) 56   (C) 240

   (D) 1792   (E) 224,000

4. **MULTIPLE CHOICE** You have an equally likely chance of choosing any number from 1 to 10. What is the probability that you choose a number greater than 6?

   (A) $\frac{1}{10}$ (B) $\frac{2}{5}$ (C) $\frac{1}{2}$

   (D) $\frac{3}{5}$ (E) $\frac{2}{3}$

5. **MULTIPLE CHOICE** A dart thrown at the square target shown is equally likely to hit anywhere inside the target. What is the probability that the dart hits the shaded semicircle?

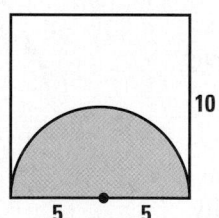

   (A) $\frac{\pi}{20}$ (B) $\frac{\pi}{10}$ (C) $\frac{\pi}{8}$

   (D) $\frac{\pi}{4}$ (E) $\frac{\pi}{2}$

6. **MULTIPLE CHOICE** $P(A) = 0.7$, $P(B) = 0.23$, and $P(A \text{ and } B) = 0.1$. What is $P(A \text{ or } B)$?

   (A) 0.13   (B) 0.47   (C) 0.6

   (D) 0.83   (E) 0.93

7. **MULTIPLE CHOICE** A mother makes a list of 5 gift ideas for Mother's Day and gives the list to each of her 5 children. If each child buys one gift on the list at random, what is the probability that at least 2 of the gifts are the same?

   (A) 25%   (B) 50%   (C) 75%

   (D) 96%   (E) 100%

8. **MULTIPLE CHOICE** Events A and B are independent, $P(A) = 0.8$, and $P(B) = 0.7$. What is $P(A \text{ and } B)$?

   (A) 1.5   (B) 0.75   (C) 0.56

   (D) 0.28   (E) 0.1

9. **MULTIPLE CHOICE** Events A and B are dependent, $P(A) = 50\%$, and $P(B \mid A) = 50\%$. What is $P(A \text{ and } B)$?

   (A) 25%   (B) 30%   (C) 50%

   (D) 75%   (E) 100%

10. **MULTIPLE CHOICE** What is the probability that in a family with 5 children exactly 2 are girls? Assume a boy and a girl are equally likely.

   (A) $\frac{1}{16}$ (B) $\frac{5}{32}$ (C) $\frac{1}{5}$

   (D) $\frac{5}{16}$ (E) $\frac{2}{5}$

11. **MULTIPLE CHOICE** The time that it takes for a fire department to arrive at a particular address on an emergency call is normally distributed with a mean of 6 minutes and a standard deviation of 1 minute. What is the probability that the fire department takes longer than 8 minutes to arrive at a particular address on an emergency call?

   (A) 0.015   (B) 0.025   (C) 0.05

   (D) 0.235   (E) 0.5

12. **MULTIPLE CHOICE** What is the standard deviation of the normal distribution that approximates a binomial distribution consisting of 119 trials with probability 0.7 of success?

   (A) ≈ 0.8   (B) ≈ 5   (C) ≈ 6

   (D) ≈ 7   (E) ≈ 11

Ⓐ The quantity in column A is greater.

Ⓑ The quantity in column B is greater.

Ⓒ The two quantities are equal.

Ⓓ The relationship cannot be determined from the given information.

	Column A	Column B
13.	The number of ways 4 books can be arranged on a bookshelf	The number of ways 4 books can be chosen from a set of 6 books
14.	$_{12}C_7$	$_{12}C_5$

15. **MULTI-STEP PROBLEM** You and a friend are taking part in a fundraiser walk. You both agree to arrive for registration between 8:00 A.M. and 8:30 A.M. You will wait for each other at the registration table for up to 10 minutes.

   a. Let x be the number of minutes after 8:00 A.M. that you arrive, and let y be the number of minutes after 8:00 A.M. that your friend arrives. Let $x = 0$ and $y = 0$ represent 8:00 A.M. Write inequalities representing the time intervals in which you and your friend will arrive.

   b. If you and your friend are to meet, the difference between your arrival times must not exceed 10 minutes. Write two inequalities that show this fact.

   c. Graph your inequalities from part (a) showing the times in which you and your friend will arrive. In the same coordinate plane, graph your inequalities from part (b) showing the times you and your friend could meet.

   d. Using your graph from part (c), find the probability that you and your friend will meet at the registration table.

16. **MULTI-STEP PROBLEM** The *standard normal distribution* has a mean of 0 and a standard deviation of 1. To convert an x-value from a normal distribution with a mean of $\bar{x}$ and a standard deviation of σ to a z-value from a standard normal distribution, use this formula:

$$z = \frac{x - \bar{x}}{\sigma}$$

A z-value gives the number of standard deviations an x-value is from the mean $\bar{x}$. You can use z-values to compare x-values from different normal distributions.

   a. The scores of your class on a test have a mean of 70 and a standard deviation of 8. If your score on the test is x_{old}, what is your corresponding z-value?

   b. Your teacher wants to recenter the scores so that they have a mean of 85 and a standard deviation of 5, but does not want to change the z-value of any score. If your new score is to be x_{new}, what is your corresponding z-value?

   c. Set the formulas for the z-values from parts (a) and (b) equal to each other to get an equation in terms of x_{old} and x_{new}. Solve this equation for x_{new}.

   d. If your score was 70, what is your new score? Does this make sense? Explain.

   e. What percent of your class would originally have had scores between 54 and 78? What will be the new range of scores for this part of the class? How can you answer this question without using the formula from part (c)?

Cumulative Practice

Solve the equation. (1.3, 1.7, 5.2–5.6, 6.4, 7.6, 8.6, 9.6)

1. $-4x + 5 = 33$

2. $\frac{1}{4}(x - 7) = 2$

3. $|x - 3| = 11$

4. $|8 - 3x| = 1$

5. $x^2 + 7x + 10 = 0$

6. $5x^2 - 13 = 32$

7. $-x^2 = 16$

8. $x^2 + 6x - 5 = 0$

9. $4x^2 - x + 1 = 0$

10. $x^3 - 27 = 0$

11. $x^3 + x^2 - 4x = 4$

12. $\sqrt{x + 5} = 7$

13. $8(x - 3)^{3/2} = 1$

14. $4^{x + 1} = 64$

15. $\log 4x = 2$

16. $\frac{1}{x - 4} = \frac{6}{x + 6}$

Graph in a three-dimensional coordinate system. (3.5)

17. $(0, 4, 1)$

18. $(3, -2, -1)$

19. $4x + 4y - z = 8$

20. $2x + 6y + 4z = 12$

Evaluate the determinant of the matrix. (4.3)

21. $\begin{bmatrix} 4 & -2 \\ -1 & 5 \end{bmatrix}$

22. $\begin{bmatrix} -3 & 10 \\ -6 & 3 \end{bmatrix}$

23. $\begin{bmatrix} 3 & -2 & 4 \\ -1 & 5 & 0 \\ 0 & 2 & 1 \end{bmatrix}$

24. $\begin{bmatrix} -5 & -1 & 4 \\ 1 & 0 & 6 \\ 1 & 3 & 0 \end{bmatrix}$

The variables *x* and *y* vary inversely. Use the given values to write an equation relating *x* and *y*. Then find *y* when *x* = 2. (9.1)

25. $x = -2, y = 20$

26. $x = \frac{1}{3}, y = 9$

27. $x = 20, y = -\frac{4}{5}$

28. $x = 1, y = 4$

The variable *z* varies jointly with *x* and *y*. Use the given values to write an equation relating *x*, *y*, and *z*. Then find *z* when *x* = −1 and *y* = 5. (9.1)

29. $x = 2, y = 3, z = -4$

30. $x = -2, y = 6, z = 24$

31. $x = \frac{1}{2}, y = \frac{1}{4}, z = \frac{3}{8}$

Find the distance between the two points. Then find the midpoint of the line segment connecting the two points. (10.1)

32. $(0, 0), (-9, 2)$

33. $(0, 8), (5, 0)$

34. $(-5, 14), (3, -8)$

35. $(-2, -3), (5, 1)$

Graph the conic section. (10.2–10.6)

36. $\frac{y^2}{121} - \frac{x^2}{49} = 1$

37. $x^2 + y^2 = 16$

38. $\frac{x^2}{81} + \frac{y^2}{36} = 1$

39. $(y + 4)^2 = x - 1$

Write an equation of the conic section. (10.2–10.6)

40. Parabola with vertex at $(0, 0)$ and directrix $y = -2$

41. Circle with center at $(2, -2)$ and radius 3

42. Ellipse with center at $(0, 0)$, vertex at $(8, 0)$, and co-vertex at $(0, 5)$

43. Hyperbola with vertices at $(0, 2)$ and $(0, -2)$ and foci at $(0, 3)$ and $(0, -3)$

Find the point(s) of intersection, if any, of the graphs in the system. (10.7)

44. $16x^2 + y^2 - 24y + 80 = 0$
$16x^2 + 25y^2 - 400 = 0$

45. $x^2 + y^2 + 36x - 10y + 324 = 0$
$x^2 + y^2 + 36x - 20y + 324 = 0$

46. $x^2 + y^2 - 4x + 2y = 20$
$y^2 - 5x + 34 = 0$

47. $x^2 - y - 2 = 0$
$x^2 + 4y^2 - 3y - 4 = 0$

Tell whether the sequence is *arithmetic, geometric,* or *neither.* Explain your answer. (11.2, 11.3)

48. $-7, -1, 5, 11, \ldots$ **49.** $7, 21, 63, 189, \ldots$ **50.** $2, 3, 6, 11, \ldots$ **51.** $1, 0.1, 0.01, 0.001, \ldots$

Write the first five terms of the sequence. (11.1, 11.5)

52. $a_n = 5n - 2$

53. $a_n = 10 - n^2$

54. $a_1 = 5$
$a_n = a_{n-1} + 6$

55. $a_1 = 1$
$a_n = a_{n-1} + n^2$

Write an explicit rule and a recursive rule for the sequence. (Recall that *d* is the common difference of an arithmetic sequence and *r* is the common ratio of a geometric sequence.) (11.2, 11.3, 11.5)

56. $r = 2, a_1 = 5$

57. $d = -6, a_1 = 1$

58. $3, 5, 7, 9, \ldots$

59. $243, 81, 27, 9, \ldots$

Find the sum of the series. (11.1–11.4)

60. $\sum\limits_{i=1}^{40} i$

61. $\sum\limits_{i=1}^{5} (7 + i)$

62. $\sum\limits_{i=1}^{6} \left(\dfrac{3}{4}\right)^{i-1}$

63. $\sum\limits_{i=1}^{\infty} 8\left(\dfrac{1}{2}\right)^{i-1}$

Find the given number of permutations or combinations. (12.1, 12.2)

64. $_8P_5$ **65.** $_6P_6$ **66.** $_{20}P_2$ **67.** $_8C_4$ **68.** $_5C_5$ **69.** $_7C_2$

Use the binomial theorem to write the binomial expansion. (12.2)

70. $(x + 4)^5$ **71.** $(2x + 5)^3$ **72.** $(x + y)^6$ **73.** $(3x - 1)^4$ **74.** $(x + 2)^4$ **75.** $(x^2 - 4)^3$

Find the indicated probability. (12.4, 12.5)

76. $P(A) = 0.3$
$P(B) = 0.5$
$P(A \text{ or } B) = 0.75$
$P(A \text{ and } B) = \underline{?}$

77. *A* and *B* are dependent events.
$P(B \mid A) = 0.5$
$P(A) = 0.4$
$P(A \text{ and } B) = \underline{?}$

78. *A* and *B* are independent events.
$P(A) = 90\%$
$P(B) = 10\%$
$P(A \text{ and } B) = \underline{?}$

Calculate the probability of tossing a coin 5 times and getting exactly the given number of tails. (12.6)

79. 0 **80.** 1 **81.** 2 **82.** 3 **83.** 4 **84.** 5

85. **OVERNIGHT DELIVERY** The table at the right gives a company's overnight delivery charges for packages up to 10 pounds. Write and graph a piecewise function for this situation. **(2.7)**

86. **EARNING INTEREST** You deposit $1000 in an account that pays 4% annual interest compounded monthly. What is the balance after 5 years? **(8.1)**

87. **FISH POPULATION** A lake initially contains 7000 fish. Each year the population declines 20% and the lake is restocked with 1000 new fish. Write a recursive rule for the number of fish in the lake after *n* years. What happens to the population of fish in the lake over time? **(11.5)**

88. **PASSWORD** You need to select a four-character password for a computer account. Any digit 0–9 and any letter A–Z can be used for a character, and digits and letters can be repeated. How many possible passwords are there? **(12.1)**

89. **CLASS CLUB** A high school club has 10 members. The faculty advisor selects members at random to fill leadership positions for president, vice president, treasurer, and secretary. Find the probability that Mark, one of the club members, is selected for a leadership position. **(12.3)**

Package weight (lb)	Delivery charge ($)
0.5	11.75
1	14.00
2	15.75
3	18.50
4	21.25
5	24.00
6	26.25
7	28.00
8	30.25
9	31.00
10	32.75

Monte Carlo Methods

OBJECTIVE Use a Monte Carlo method to estimate the area of an ellipse.

Materials: graph paper, calculator or computer

Some situations are too complex to be conveniently modeled by equations, graphs, or other standard mathematical tools. Even many simple-sounding problems, such as finding the average wait in line at an ATM machine, can be difficult to solve using traditional mathematics.

To solve such problems, you can often use *Monte Carlo* methods. A Monte Carlo method uses simulations based on random processes to model a real-life situation. The outcomes of these simulations are used to predict the outcomes of the real-life situation and to solve problems requiring knowledge of these outcomes. In this project you will estimate the area of an ellipse with a Monte Carlo method.

INVESTIGATION

1. An ellipse with a horizontal major axis and center $(0, 0)$ has an equation of the form $\frac{x^2}{a^2} + \frac{y^2}{b^2} = 1$. Write an inequality that must be satisfied if a point (x, y) is on or inside the ellipse (that is, (x, y) is part of the region bounded by the ellipse).

2. Write an equation for a particular ellipse with a horizontal major axis and center $(0, 0)$. Choose integer values of a and b so that the equation will be easy to work with. Graph your equation.

3. On the graph, draw a rectangle extending horizontally from $-a$ to a and vertically from $-b$ to b that will contain your ellipse. An example is shown below.

4. Use a random number generator on a calculator or computer to generate 20 points (x, y) where $-a \le x \le a$ and $-b \le y \le b$. Check if each point satisfies your inequality from **Step 1**. Make a table to keep track of your results.

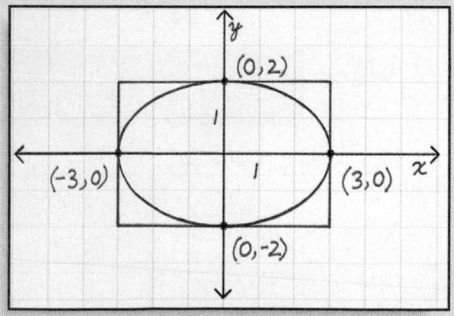

Point (x, y)	On or inside ellipse?
$(-1.2, 0)$	Yes
$(2.6, 1.9)$	No

5. Use your table to find the ratio of the number of points on or inside the ellipse to the number of points on or inside the rectangle. To estimate the area of the ellipse, multiply the area of the rectangle by this ratio.

6. Use the formula for the area of an ellipse to find the actual area. Compare this with the area you found in **Step 5**. (*Hint:* See page 611 for help with the formula for the area of an ellipse.)

7. Repeat **Steps 4 and 5** using simulations with 10, 50, and 100 randomly generated points. Make a conjecture about the relationship between the number of points generated and the accuracy of your estimate for the ellipse's area.

PRESENT YOUR RESULTS

Write a report to present your results.

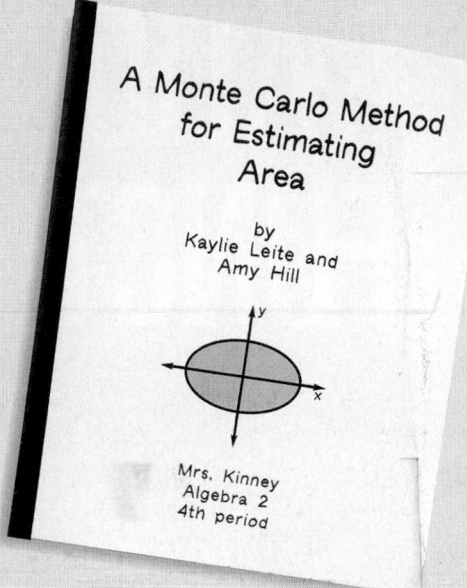

- Explain how you used a Monte Carlo method to estimate the area of an ellipse.

- Is using the Monte Carlo method the same as calculating the area of the ellipse directly? Explain any differences.

- Explain why you estimated the area of the ellipse by multiplying the area of the rectangle by the ratio of the points on or inside the ellipse to those on or inside the rectangle.

- Include your graph.

- Include your table.

- Let n be the number of points used to estimate the area of the ellipse, and let a_n be a sequence defined as follows:

$$a_n = |\text{estimated area} - \text{actual area}|$$

Use your results from the investigation to graph the sequence defined by a_n for $n = 10, 25, 50,$ and $100.$ Describe what your graph shows.

- Modify the Monte Carlo method so that you generate random points only in the first quadrant. Explain how you can use these points and the ellipse's symmetry to estimate the entire area of the ellipse.

Now estimate the area of your ellipse using this method:

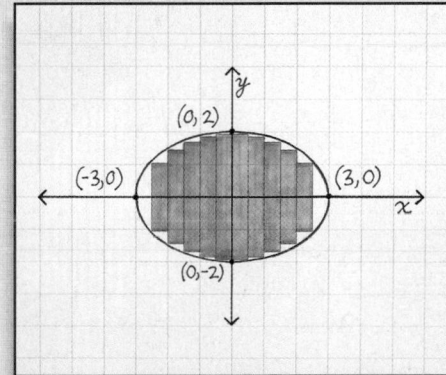

- Copy the ellipse you drew. Sketch small rectangles to fill it, as shown.

- Find the area of each rectangle. Add these areas together to estimate the area of the ellipse.

- Compare the areas given by this method and the Monte Carlo method. How would you make this method more accurate?

EXTENSION

Modify your Monte Carlo method to estimate the area of a region bounded (at least in part) by a different conic section. For example, you could estimate the area of a region bounded by one branch of a hyperbola and a line that intersects the branch in two points.

TRIGONOMETRIC RATIOS AND FUNCTIONS

How can you find the width of the opening between two halves of a bridge?

APPLICATION: Drawbridges

The Chicago River System has 52 movable bridges, more than any other city in the world. One type of moveable bridge is a double-leaf drawbridge, a series of which are shown open in the photo at the left and closed in the photo at the right.

Think & Discuss

The diagram below gives the dimensions for a double-leaf drawbridge. Each leaf of the bridge is 65 feet long and has a maximum opening angle of 60°. For a 30°-60°-90° triangle, the ratio of the lengths of the sides, from shortest to longest, is $1 : \sqrt{3} : 2$.

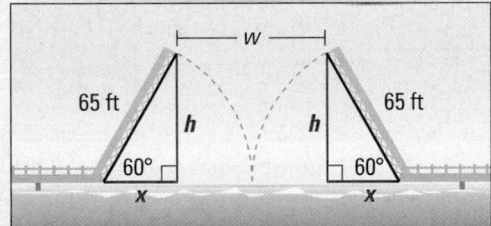

1. Find the height h to which the end of each leaf is lifted.

2. What is the maximum width w that a boat could have at the height of the opening and still fit through the opening? (*Hint:* Use the fact that $2x + w = 130$.)

Learn More About It

You will find the angle at which a drawbridge must open to allow a ship to pass in Ex. 56 on p. 796.

APPLICATION LINK Visit www.mcdougallittell.com for more information on drawbridges.

PREVIEW

What's the chapter about?

Chapter 13 is about **trigonometry**. In Chapter 13 you'll learn

- how to evaluate trigonometric functions and inverse trigonometric functions.
- how to find side lengths, angle measures, and areas of triangles.
- how to use parametric equations.

KEY VOCABULARY

▶ **Review**
- reciprocal, p. 5
- inverse functions, p. 422

▶ **New**
- sine, p. 769
- cosine, p. 769

- tangent, p. 769
- cosecant, p. 769
- secant, p. 769
- cotangent, p. 769
- radian, p. 777
- sector, p. 779

- inverse sine, p. 792
- inverse cosine, p. 792
- inverse tangent, p. 792
- law of sines, p. 799
- law of cosines, p. 807
- parametric equations, p. 813

PREPARE

Are you ready for the chapter?

SKILL REVIEW Do these exercises to review key skills that you'll apply in this chapter. See the given **reference page** if there is something you don't understand.

Find the missing side length. (Skills Review, p. 917)

1.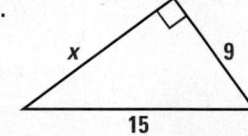

2.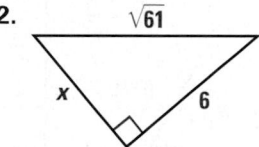

3.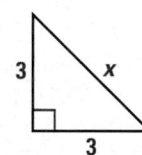

Simplify the expression. (Review Example 1, p. 264)

4. $\sqrt{96}$ 5. $\sqrt{18}$ 6. $\sqrt{200}$ 7. $\dfrac{2}{\sqrt{2}}$ 8. $\dfrac{2}{\sqrt{3}}$ 9. $\sqrt{\dfrac{3}{4}}$

Solve the equation. (Review Example 4, p. 569)

10. $\dfrac{3}{x} = \dfrac{6}{x-1}$ 11. $\dfrac{4x}{5} = \dfrac{5}{x}$ 12. $\dfrac{7}{4} = \dfrac{x}{8}$ 13. $\dfrac{x+3}{x} = \dfrac{7}{10}$

STUDY
STRATEGY

Here's a study strategy!

Draw Diagrams

Drawing a diagram can help you figure out how to solve a problem from the given information. A diagram can help you with almost every problem (not just word problems) in this chapter. Whenever you are given lengths, angle measures, points, or ratios, try drawing and labeling a diagram.

13.1

Right Triangle Trigonometry

What you should learn

GOAL 1 Use trigonometric relationships to evaluate trigonometric functions of acute angles.

GOAL 2 Use trigonometric functions to solve **real-life** problems, such as finding the altitude of a kite in **Example 4**.

Why you should learn it

▼ To solve **real-life** problems, such as finding the length of a zip-line at a ropes course in **Ex. 50**.

GOAL 1 EVALUATING TRIGONOMETRIC FUNCTIONS

Consider a right triangle, one of whose acute angles is θ (the Greek letter *theta*). The three sides of the triangle are the *hypotenuse*, the side *opposite* θ, and the side *adjacent* to θ.

Ratios of a right triangle's three sides are used to define the six trigonometric functions: **sine**, **cosine**, **tangent**, **cosecant**, **secant**, and **cotangent**. These six functions are abbreviated sin, cos, tan, csc, sec, and cot, respectively.

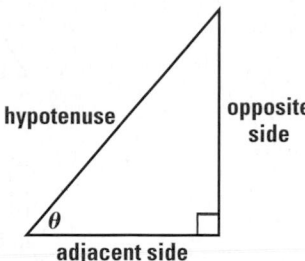

RIGHT TRIANGLE DEFINITION OF TRIGONOMETRIC FUNCTIONS

Let θ be an acute angle of a right triangle. The six trigonometric functions of θ are defined as follows.

$$\sin \theta = \frac{\text{opp}}{\text{hyp}} \qquad \cos \theta = \frac{\text{adj}}{\text{hyp}} \qquad \tan \theta = \frac{\text{opp}}{\text{adj}}$$

$$\csc \theta = \frac{\text{hyp}}{\text{opp}} \qquad \sec \theta = \frac{\text{hyp}}{\text{adj}} \qquad \cot \theta = \frac{\text{adj}}{\text{opp}}$$

The abbreviations *opp, adj,* and *hyp* represent the lengths of the three sides of the right triangle. Note that the ratios in the second row are the reciprocals of the ratios in the first row. That is:

$$\csc \theta = \frac{1}{\sin \theta} \qquad \sec \theta = \frac{1}{\cos \theta} \qquad \cot \theta = \frac{1}{\tan \theta}$$

EXAMPLE 1 Evaluating Trigonometric Functions

Evaluate the six trigonometric functions of the angle θ shown in the right triangle.

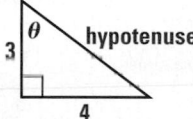

SOLUTION

From the Pythagorean theorem, the length of the hypotenuse is:

$$\sqrt{3^2 + 4^2} = \sqrt{25} = 5$$

Using adj = 3, opp = 4, and hyp = 5, you can write the following.

$$\sin \theta = \frac{\text{opp}}{\text{hyp}} = \frac{4}{5} \qquad \cos \theta = \frac{\text{adj}}{\text{hyp}} = \frac{3}{5} \qquad \tan \theta = \frac{\text{opp}}{\text{adj}} = \frac{4}{3}$$

$$\csc \theta = \frac{\text{hyp}}{\text{opp}} = \frac{5}{4} \qquad \sec \theta = \frac{\text{hyp}}{\text{adj}} = \frac{5}{3} \qquad \cot \theta = \frac{\text{adj}}{\text{opp}} = \frac{3}{4}$$

STUDENT HELP

▶ **Skills Review**
For help with the Pythagorean theorem, see p. 917.

The angles 30°, 45°, and 60° occur frequently in trigonometry. The table below gives the values of the six trigonometric functions for these angles. To remember these values, you may find it easier to draw the triangles shown, rather than memorize the table.

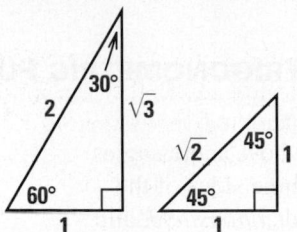

θ	$\sin \theta$	$\cos \theta$	$\tan \theta$	$\csc \theta$	$\sec \theta$	$\cot \theta$
30°	$\dfrac{1}{2}$	$\dfrac{\sqrt{3}}{2}$	$\dfrac{\sqrt{3}}{3}$	2	$\dfrac{2\sqrt{3}}{3}$	$\sqrt{3}$
45°	$\dfrac{\sqrt{2}}{2}$	$\dfrac{\sqrt{2}}{2}$	1	$\sqrt{2}$	$\sqrt{2}$	1
60°	$\dfrac{\sqrt{3}}{2}$	$\dfrac{1}{2}$	$\sqrt{3}$	$\dfrac{2\sqrt{3}}{3}$	2	$\dfrac{\sqrt{3}}{3}$

Trigonometric functions can be used to find a missing side length or angle measure of a right triangle. Finding *all* missing side lengths and angle measures is called **solving a right triangle**.

EXAMPLE 2 *Finding a Missing Side Length of a Right Triangle*

Find the value of x for the right triangle shown.

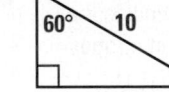

SOLUTION

Write an equation using a trigonometric function that involves the ratio of x and 10. Solve the equation for x.

$$\sin 60° = \frac{\text{opp}}{\text{hyp}}$$ **Write trigonometric equation.**

$$\frac{\sqrt{3}}{2} = \frac{x}{10}$$ **Substitute.**

$$5\sqrt{3} = x$$ **Multiply each side by 10.**

▶ The length of the side is $x = 5\sqrt{3} \approx 8.66$.

· · · · · · · · · ·

You can use a calculator to evaluate trigonometric functions of *any* angle, not just 30°, 45°, and 60°. Use the keys $\boxed{\text{SIN}}$, $\boxed{\text{COS}}$, and $\boxed{\text{TAN}}$ for sine, cosine, and tangent. Use these keys and the reciprocal key for cosecant, secant, and cotangent. Before using the calculator be sure it is set in degree mode.

EXAMPLE 3 *Using a Calculator to Solve a Right Triangle*

Solve $\triangle ABC$.

SOLUTION

Because the triangle is a right triangle, A and B are complementary angles, so $B = 90° - 19° = 71°$.

$$\frac{a}{13} = \tan 19° \approx 0.3443 \qquad \frac{c}{13} = \sec 19° = \frac{1}{\cos 19°} \approx 1.058$$

$$a \approx 4.48 \qquad\qquad\qquad c \approx 13.8$$

KITE FLYING
In the late 1800s and early 1900s, kites were used to lift weather instruments. In 1919 the German Weather Bureau set a kite-flying record. Eight kites on a single line, like those pictured above, were flown at an altitude of 9740 meters.

GOAL 2 **USING TRIGONOMETRY IN REAL LIFE**

EXAMPLE 4 *Finding the Altitude of a Kite*

KITE FLYING Wind speed affects the angle at which a kite flies. The table at the right shows the angle the kite line makes with a line parallel to the ground for several different wind speeds. You are flying a kite 4 feet above the ground and are using 500 feet of line. At what altitude is the kite flying if the wind speed is 35 miles per hour?

Wind speed (miles per hour)	Angle of kite line (degrees)
25	70
30	60
35	48
40	29
45	0

SOLUTION

At a wind speed of 35 miles per hour, the angle the kite line makes with a line parallel to the ground is 48°. Write an equation using a trigonometric function that involves the ratio of the distance d and 500.

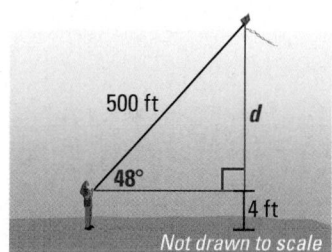

$$\sin 48° = \frac{d}{500} \qquad \textbf{Write trigonometric equation.}$$

$$0.7431 \approx \frac{d}{500} \qquad \textbf{Simplify.}$$

$$372 \approx d \qquad \textbf{Solve for } d.$$

▶ When you add 4 feet for the height at which you are holding the kite line, the kite's altitude is about 376 feet.

· · · · · · · · · ·

In Example 4 the angle the kite line makes with a line parallel to the ground is the **angle of elevation**. At the height of the kite, the angle from a line parallel to the ground to the kite line is the **angle of depression**. These two angles have the same measure.

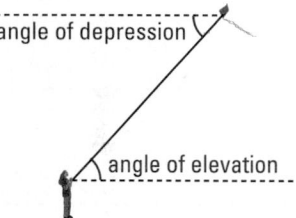

EXAMPLE 5 *Finding the Distance to an Airport*

An airplane flying at an altitude of 30,000 feet is headed toward an airport. To guide the airplane to a safe landing, the airport's landing system sends radar signals from the runway to the airplane at a 10° angle of elevation. How far is the airplane (measured along the ground) from the airport runway?

SOLUTION

Begin by drawing a diagram.

$$\frac{x}{30,000} = \cot 10° = \frac{1}{\tan 10°} \approx 5.671$$

$$x \approx 170,100$$

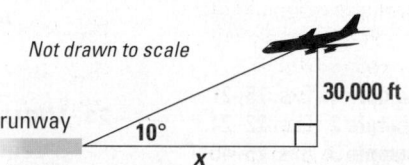

▶ The plane is about 170,100 feet (or 32.2 miles) from the airport.

GUIDED PRACTICE

Vocabulary Check ✔

1. Explain what it means to solve a right triangle.

Concept Check ✔

2. Given a 30°-60°-90° triangle with only the measures of the angles labeled, can you find the lengths of any of the sides? Explain.

3. If you are given a right triangle with an acute angle θ, what two trigonometric functions of θ can you calculate using the lengths of the hypotenuse and the side opposite θ?

4. For which acute angle θ is $\cos \theta = \dfrac{\sqrt{3}}{2}$?

Skill Check ✔

Evaluate the six trigonometric functions of the angle θ.

5.

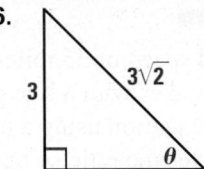

6.

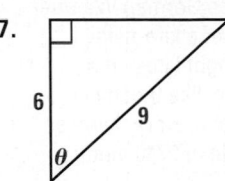

7.

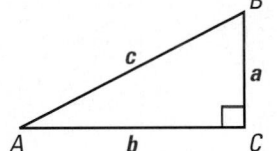

Solve △ABC using the diagram at the right and the given measurements.

8. $A = 20°$, $a = 12$

9. $A = 75°$, $c = 20$

10. $B = 40°$, $c = 5$

11. $A = 62°$, $b = 30$

12. $B = 63°$, $a = 15$

13. $B = 15°$, $b = 42$

14. 🌐 **KITE FLYING** Look back at Example 4 on page 771. Suppose you are flying a kite 4 feet above the ground on a line that is 300 feet long. If the wind speed is 30 miles per hour, what is the altitude of the kite?

PRACTICE AND APPLICATIONS

STUDENT HELP

➤ **Extra Practice**
to help you master
skills is on p. 957.

EVALUATING FUNCTIONS Evaluate the six trigonometric functions of the angle θ.

15.

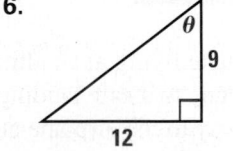

16.

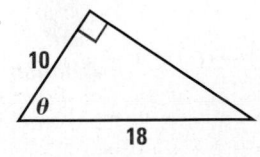

17.

18.

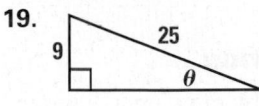

19.

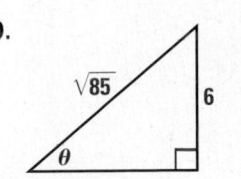

20.

STUDENT HELP

➤ **HOMEWORK HELP**
Example 1: Exs. 15–21
Example 2: Exs. 22–24
Example 3: Exs. 25–40
Examples 4, 5: Exs. 43–50

21. **VISUAL THINKING** The lengths of the sides of a right triangle are 5 centimeters, 12 centimeters, and 13 centimeters. Sketch the triangle. Let θ represent the angle that is opposite the side whose length is 5 centimeters. Evaluate the six trigonometric functions of θ.

FINDING SIDE LENGTHS Find the missing side lengths *x* and *y*.

22.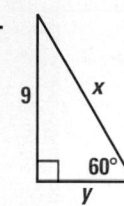

23.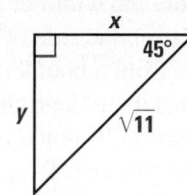

24.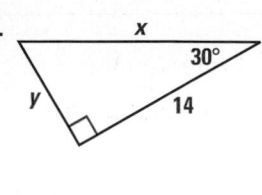

EVALUATING FUNCTIONS Use a calculator to evaluate the trigonometric function. Round the result to four decimal places.

25. sin 14° **26.** cos 31° **27.** tan 59° **28.** sec 23°

29. csc 80° **30.** cot 36° **31.** csc 6° **32.** cot 11°

SOLVING TRIANGLES Solve △*ABC* using the diagram and the given measurements.

33. $B = 24°$, $a = 8$ **34.** $A = 37°$, $c = 22$

35. $A = 19°$, $b = 4$ **36.** $B = 41°$, $c = 18$

37. $A = 29°$, $b = 21$ **38.** $B = 56°$, $a = 6.8$

39. $B = 65°$, $c = 12$ **40.** $A = 70°$, $c = 30$

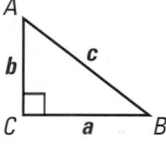

GEOMETRY CONNECTION Find the area of the regular polygon with point *P* at its center.

41.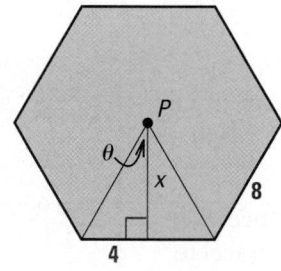

42.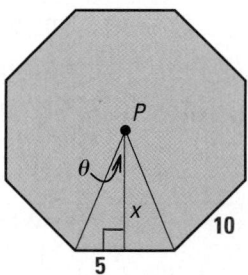

DUQUESNE INCLINE In Exercises 43 and 44, use the following information. The track of the Duquesne Incline is about 800 feet long and the angle of elevation is 30°. The average speed of the cable cars is about 320 feet per minute.

43. How high does the Duquesne Incline rise?

44. What is the vertical speed of the cable cars (in feet per minute)?

45. **SKI SLOPE** A ski slope at a mountain has an angle of elevation of 25.2°. The vertical height of the slope is 1808 feet. How long is the ski slope?

46. **BOARDING A SHIP** A gangplank is a narrow ramp used for boarding or leaving a ship. The maximum safe angle of elevation for a gangplank is 20°. Suppose a gangplank is 10 feet long. What is the closest a ship can come to the dock for the gangplank to be used?

47. **JIN MAO BUILDING** You are standing 75 meters from the base of the Jin Mao Building in Shanghai, China. You estimate that the angle of elevation to the top of the building is 80°. What is the approximate height of the building? Suppose one of your friends is at the top of the building. What is the distance between you and your friend?

48. 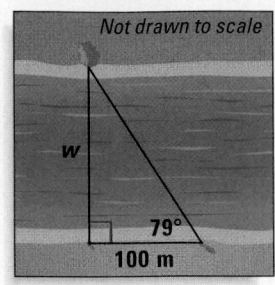 **MEASURING RIVER WIDTH** To measure the width of a river you plant a stake on one side of the river, directly across from a boulder. You then walk 100 meters to the right of the stake and measure a 79° angle between the stake and the boulder. What is the width w of the river?

49. **MOUNT COOK** You are climbing Mount Cook in New Zealand. You are below the mountain's peak at an altitude of 8580 feet. Using surveying instruments, you measure the angle of elevation to the peak to be 30.5°. The distance (along the face of the mountain) between you and the peak is 7426 feet. What is the altitude of the peak?

50. **ROPES COURSE** You are designing a zip-line for a ropes course at a summer camp. A zip-line is a cable to which people can attach their safety harnesses and slide down to the ground. You want to attach one end of the cable to a pole 50 feet high and the other end to a pole 5 feet high. The maximum safe angle of elevation for the zip-line is 25°. Calculate the minimum length x of cable needed.

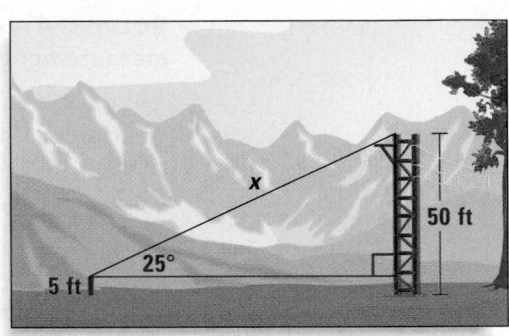

Test Preparation

51. **MULTI-STEP PROBLEM** You are a surveyor in a helicopter and are trying to determine the width of an island, as illustrated at the right.

    a. What is the shortest distance d the helicopter would have to travel to land on the island?

    b. What is the horizontal distance x that the helicopter has to travel before it is directly over the nearer end of the island?

    c. *Writing* Find the width w of the island. Explain the process you used to find your answer.

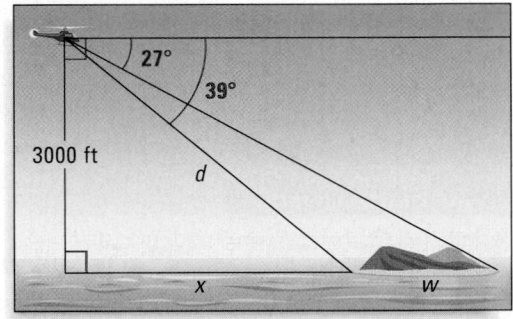

★ Challenge

ANALYZING SIMILAR TRIANGLES In Exercises 52–54, use the diagram below.

52. Explain why $\triangle ABC$, $\triangle ADE$, and $\triangle AFG$ are similar triangles.

53. What does similarity imply about the ratios $\frac{BC}{AB}$, $\frac{DE}{AD}$, and $\frac{FG}{AF}$? Does the value of $\sin A$ depend on which triangle from Exercise 52 is used to calculate it? Would the value of $\sin A$ change if it were found using a different right triangle that is similar to the three given triangles?

STUDENT HELP

▶ **Skills Review**
For help with similar triangles, see p. 923.

54. Do your observations about $\sin A$ also apply to the other five trigonometric functions? Explain.

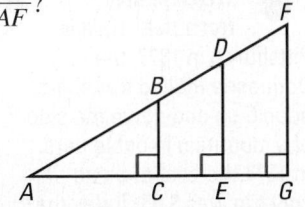

UNIT ANALYSIS Find the product. Give the answer with the appropriate unit of measure. **(Review 1.1 for 13.2)**

55. $(3.5 \text{ hours}) \cdot \dfrac{45 \text{ miles}}{1 \text{ hour}}$

56. $(500 \text{ dollars}) \cdot \dfrac{12.2 \text{ schillings}}{1 \text{ dollar}}$

57. $\dfrac{3 \text{ dollars}}{1 \text{ square foot}} \cdot (1222 \text{ square feet})$

58. $(12 \text{ seconds}) \cdot \dfrac{254 \text{ feet}}{1 \text{ second}}$

CLASSIFYING Classify the conic section. **(Review 10.6)**

59. $y^2 - 16x - 14y + 17 = 0$

60. $25x^2 + y^2 - 100x - 2y + 76 = 0$

61. $x^2 + y^2 = 25$

62. $x^2 - y^2 = 100$

63. 🌐 **ESSAY TOPICS** For a homework assignment you have to choose from 15 possible topics on which to write an essay. If all of the topics are equally interesting, what is the probability that you and your five friends will all choose different topics? **(Review 12.5)**

 **MATH & History**

Columbus's Voyage

 **APPLICATION LINK**
www.mcdougallittell.com

THEN

IN 1492 Christopher Columbus set sail west from the Canary Islands intending to reach Japan. Due to miscalculations of Earth's circumference and the relative location of Japan, he instead sailed to the New World.

Columbus believed the distance west from the Canary Islands to Japan to be $\frac{1}{6}$ the circumference of Earth at that latitude. He supposed Earth's radius at the equator to be about 2865 miles.

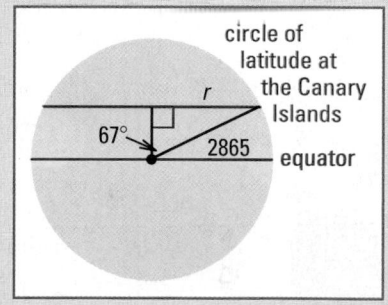

circle of latitude at the Canary Islands

67°   *r*   2865   equator

1. Use the diagram at the right to calculate what Columbus believed to be the radius *r* of Earth at the latitude of the Canary Islands.

2. Use your answer to Exercise 1 to calculate the distance west from the Canary Islands that Columbus believed he would find Japan.

3. Use reference materials to find the true distance west from the Canary Islands to Japan. How far off were Columbus's calculations?

NOW

TODAY aerial photography and computers are used to make maps. Accurate maps in combination with satellite-based navigation make travel a more exact science.

The oldest existing map was made on a clay tablet in Babylonia.

2500 B.C.

A.D. 150

Influential map maker Claudius Ptolemy wrote his eight-volume *Geography*.

1492

Columbus sails to the Bahama Islands and Cuba, intending to reach Japan.

1999

The Landsat 7 satellite was launched.

General Angles and Radian Measure

GOAL 1 **ANGLES IN STANDARD POSITION**

In Lesson 13.1 you worked only with acute angles (angles measuring between 0° and 90°). In this lesson you will study angles whose measures can be any real numbers.

Recall that an angle is formed by two rays that have a common endpoint, called the vertex. You can generate any angle by fixing one ray, called the **initial side,** and rotating the other ray, called the **terminal side,** about the vertex. In a coordinate plane, an angle whose vertex is at the origin and whose initial side is the positive *x*-axis is in **standard position.**

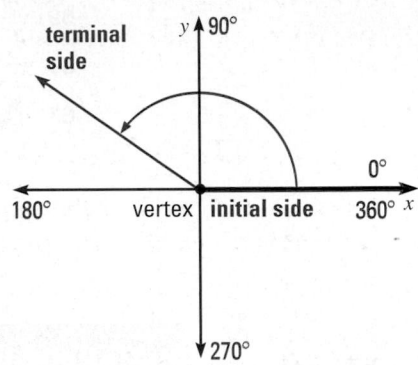

The measure of an angle is determined by the amount and direction of rotation from the initial side to the terminal side. The angle measure is positive if the rotation is counterclockwise, and negative if the rotation is clockwise. The terminal side of an angle can make more than one complete rotation.

EXAMPLE 1 *Drawing Angles in Standard Position*

Draw an angle with the given measure in standard position. Then tell in which quadrant the terminal side lies.

    a. 210°   **b.** −45°   **c.** 510°

SOLUTION

a. Use the fact that 210° = 180° + 30°. So, the terminal side is 30° counterclockwise past the negative *x*-axis.

b. Because −45° is negative, the terminal side is 45° clockwise from the positive *x*-axis.

c. Use the fact that 510° = 360° + 150°. So, the terminal side makes one complete revolution counterclockwise and continues another 150°.

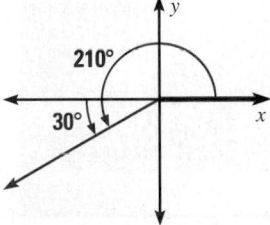

Terminal side in Quadrant III

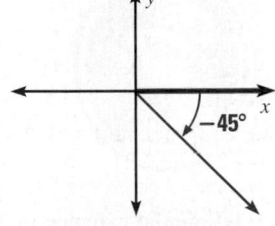

Terminal side in Quadrant IV

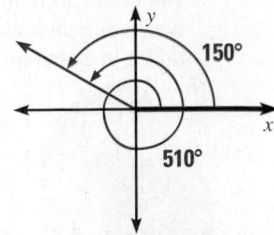

Terminal side in Quadrant II

In Example 1 the angles 510° and 150° are *coterminal*. Two angles in standard position are **coterminal** if their terminal sides coincide. An angle coterminal with a given angle can be found by adding or subtracting multiples of 360°.

STUDENT HELP

HOMEWORK HELP
Visit our Web site
www.mcdougallittell.com
for extra examples.

EXAMPLE 2 *Finding Coterminal Angles*

Find one positive angle and one negative angle that are coterminal with (**a**) −60° and (**b**) 495°.

SOLUTION

There are many such angles, depending on what multiple of 360° is added or subtracted.

a. Positive coterminal angle: −60° + 360° = 300°
Negative coterminal angle: −60° − 360° = −420°

b. Positive coterminal angle: 495° − 360° = 135°
Negative coterminal angle: 495° − 2(360°) = −225°

· · · · · · · · ·

So far, all the angles you have worked with have been measured in degrees. You can also measure angles in *radians*. To define a radian, consider a circle with radius *r* centered at the origin. One **radian** is the measure of an angle in standard position whose terminal side intercepts an arc of length *r*.

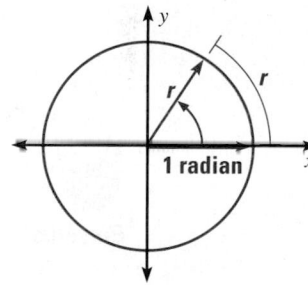

Because the circumference of a circle is $2\pi r$, there are 2π radians in a full circle. Degree measure and radian measure are therefore related by the equation $360° = 2\pi$ radians, or $180° = \pi$ radians.

The diagram shows equivalent radian and degree measures for special angles from 0° to 360° (0 radians to 2π radians).

STUDENT HELP

Study Tip
When no units of angle measure are specified, radian measure is implied. For instance, $\theta = 2$ means that $\theta = 2$ radians.

You may find it helpful to memorize the equivalent degree and radian measures of special angles in the first quadrant and for $90° = \frac{\pi}{2}$ radians. All other special angles are just multiples of these angles.

You can use the following rules to convert degrees to radians and radians to degrees.

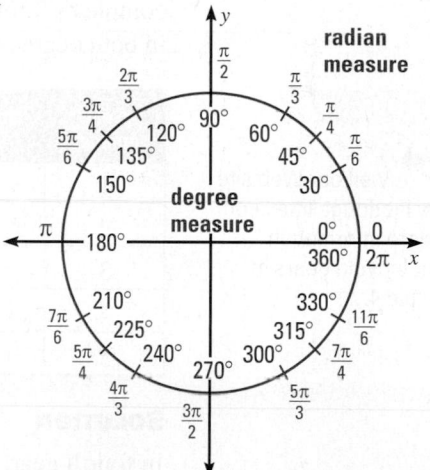

CONVERSIONS BETWEEN DEGREES AND RADIANS

• To rewrite a degree measure in radians, multiply by $\frac{\pi \text{ radians}}{180°}$.

• To rewrite a radian measure in degrees, multiply by $\frac{180°}{\pi \text{ radians}}$.

EXAMPLE 3 **Converting Between Degrees and Radians**

a. Convert 110° to radians.   **b.** Convert $-\dfrac{\pi}{9}$ radians to degrees.

SOLUTION

a. $110° = 110°\left(\dfrac{\pi \text{ radians}}{180°}\right)$

$\qquad = \dfrac{11\pi}{18}$ radians

✔ **CHECK** Check that your answer is reasonable:

The angle 110° is between the special angles 90° and 120°. The angle $\dfrac{11\pi}{18}$ is between the same special angles: $\dfrac{\pi}{2} = \dfrac{9\pi}{18}$ and $\dfrac{2\pi}{3} = \dfrac{12\pi}{18}$.

b. $-\dfrac{\pi}{9} = \left(-\dfrac{\pi}{9} \text{ radians}\right)\left(\dfrac{180°}{\pi \text{ radians}}\right)$

$\qquad = -20°$

✔ **CHECK** Check that your answer is reasonable:

The angle $-\dfrac{\pi}{9}$ is between the special angles 0 and $-\dfrac{\pi}{6}$. The angle $-20°$ is between the same special angles: 0° and $-30°$.

Bicycles

EXAMPLE 4 **Measuring an Angle for a Bicycle**

A bicycle's *gear ratio* is the number of times the freewheel turns for every one turn of the chainwheel. The table shows the number of teeth in the freewheel and chainwheel for the first 5 gears on an 18-speed touring bicycle. In fourth gear, if the chainwheel completes 3 rotations, through what angle does the freewheel turn? Give your answer in both degrees and radians. ▶ Source: *The All New Complete Book of Bicycling*

Gear number	Number of teeth in freewheel	Number of teeth in chainwheel
1	32	24
2	26	24
3	22	24
4	32	40
5	19	24

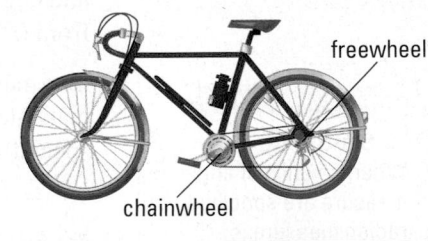

freewheel

chainwheel

SOLUTION

In fourth gear, the gear ratio is $\dfrac{40}{32}$. For every one turn of the chainwheel in this gear, the freewheel makes 1.25 rotations. The measure of the angle θ through which the freewheel turns when the chainwheel completes 3 rotations is:

$$\theta = (3.75 \text{ rotations})\left(\dfrac{360°}{1 \text{ rotation}}\right) = 1350°$$

To find the angle measure in radians, multiply by $\dfrac{\pi \text{ radians}}{180°}$:

$$\theta = 1350°\left(\dfrac{\pi \text{ radians}}{180°}\right) = \dfrac{15\pi}{2} \text{ radians}$$

GOAL 2 ARC LENGTHS AND AREAS OF SECTORS

A **sector** is a region of a circle that is bounded by two radii and an arc of the circle. The **central angle** θ of a sector is the angle formed by the two radii. There are simple formulas for the arc length and area of a sector when the central angle is measured in radians.

STUDENT HELP

▶ **Derivations**
For a derivation of the formula for arc length, see p. 900.

ARC LENGTH AND AREA OF A SECTOR

The arc length s and area A of a sector with radius r and central angle θ (measured in radians) are as follows.

Arc length: $s = r\theta$

Area: $A = \dfrac{1}{2}r^2\theta$

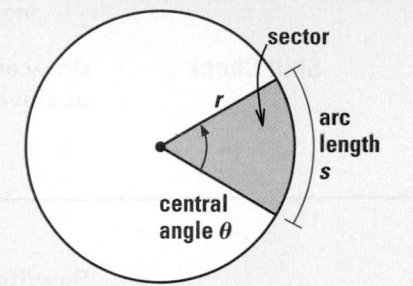

EXAMPLE 5 *Finding Arc Length and Area*

Find the arc length and area of a sector with a radius of 9 cm and a central angle of 60°.

SOLUTION

First convert the angle measure to radians.

$$\theta = 60° \left(\frac{\pi \text{ radians}}{180°} \right) = \frac{\pi}{3} \text{ radians}$$

Then use the formulas for arc length and area.

$$\text{Arc length: } s = r\theta = 9\left(\frac{\pi}{3}\right) = 3\pi \text{ centimeters}$$

$$\text{Area: } A = \frac{1}{2}r^2\theta = \frac{1}{2}(9^2)\left(\frac{\pi}{3}\right) = \frac{27\pi}{2} \text{ square centimeters}$$

EXAMPLE 6 *Finding an Angle and Arc Length*

SPACE NEEDLE Read the photo caption at the left. You go to dinner at the Space Needle and sit at a window table at 6:42 P.M. Your dinner ends at 8:18 P.M. Through what angle do you rotate during your stay? How many feet do you revolve?

SOLUTION

You spend 96 minutes at dinner. Because the Space Needle makes one complete revolution every 60 minutes, your angle of rotation is:

$$\theta = \frac{96}{60}(2\pi) = \frac{16\pi}{5} \text{ radians}$$

Because the radius is 47.25 feet, you move through an arc length of:

$$s = r\theta = 47.25\left(\frac{16\pi}{5}\right) \approx 475 \text{ feet}$$

FOCUS ON APPLICATIONS

SPACE NEEDLE The restaurant at the top of the Space Needle in Seattle, Washington, is circular and has a radius of 47.25 feet. The dining part of the restaurant (by the windows) revolves, making about one complete revolution per hour.

GUIDED PRACTICE

Vocabulary Check ✓

Concept Check ✓

1. In your own words, describe what a radian is.

2. **ERROR ANALYSIS** An error has been made in finding the area of a sector with a radius of 5 inches and a central angle of 25°. Find and correct the error.

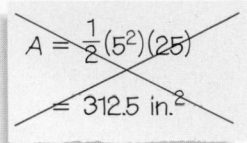

$$A = \frac{1}{2}(5^2)(25)$$
$$= 312.5 \text{ in.}^2$$

3. How does the sign of an angle's measure determine its direction of rotation?

4. A circle has radius r. What is the length of the arc corresponding to a central angle of π radians?

Skill Check ✓

Draw an angle with the given measure in standard position. Then find one positive and one negative coterminal angle.

5. 60°

6. −45°

7. $\frac{7\pi}{4}$

8. 300°

9. $-\frac{3\pi}{2}$

10. $\frac{7\pi}{8}$

11. 150°

12. $-\frac{5\pi}{4}$

Rewrite each degree measure in radians and each radian measure in degrees.

13. 30°

14. 100°

15. 260°

16. −320°

17. $\frac{7\pi}{4}$

18. $\frac{18\pi}{4}$

19. $\frac{\pi}{12}$

20. $-\frac{5\pi}{2}$

Find the arc length and area of a sector with the given radius r and central angle θ.

21. $r = 4$ in., $\theta = 55°$

22. $r = 5$ m, $\theta = 135°$

23. $r = 2$ cm, $\theta = 85°$

24. 🌎 **SPACE NEEDLE** Recall from Example 6 on page 779 that the circular restaurant at the Space Needle has a radius of 47.25 feet and rotates about once per hour. If you are seated at a window table from 6:00 P.M. to 8:10 P.M., through what angle do you rotate? How many feet do you revolve?

PRACTICE AND APPLICATIONS

STUDENT HELP

▶ **Extra Practice**
to help you master skills is on p. 958.

VISUAL THINKING Match the angle measure with the angle.

25. −210°

26. 420°

27. $-\frac{13\pi}{3}$

A.

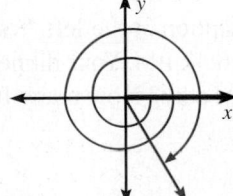

B.

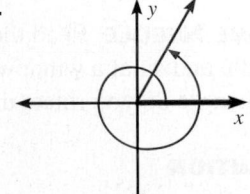

C.

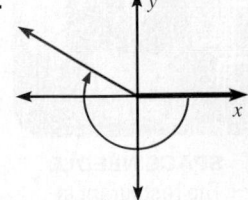

DRAWING ANGLES Draw an angle with the given measure in standard position.

28. 144°

29. $\frac{2\pi}{9}$

30. −15°

31. $-\frac{7\pi}{6}$

32. $\frac{19\pi}{12}$

33. 1620°

34. −5π

35. $-\frac{13\pi}{4}$

STUDENT HELP

▶ **HOMEWORK HELP**
Example 1: Exs. 25–35
Example 2: Exs. 36–43
Example 3: Exs. 44–59
Example 4: Exs. 77–81
Example 5: Exs. 60–68
Example 6: Exs. 82–88

FINDING COTERMINAL ANGLES Find one positive angle and one negative angle coterminal with the given angle.

36. $55°$

37. $210°$

38. $420°$

39. $780°$

40. $\dfrac{13\pi}{2}$

41. $\dfrac{17\pi}{4}$

42. $\dfrac{24\pi}{7}$

43. $\dfrac{16\pi}{3}$

CONVERTING MEASURES Rewrite each degree measure in radians and each radian measure in degrees.

44. $25°$

45. $225°$

46. $160°$

47. $45°$

48. $-110°$

49. $325°$

50. $400°$

51. $-290°$

52. $\dfrac{7\pi}{3}$

53. $-\dfrac{9\pi}{2}$

54. $\dfrac{\pi}{10}$

55. $-\dfrac{5\pi}{12}$

56. $\dfrac{7\pi}{15}$

57. $-\dfrac{15\pi}{4}$

58. $-\dfrac{5\pi}{6}$

59. $\dfrac{8\pi}{5}$

FINDING ARC LENGTH AND AREA Find the arc length and area of a sector with the given radius r and central angle θ.

60. $r = 3$ in., $\theta = \dfrac{\pi}{4}$

61. $r = 3$ ft, $\theta = \dfrac{\pi}{18}$

62. $r = 2$ cm, $\theta = \dfrac{9\pi}{20}$

63. $r = 12$ in., $\theta = 90°$

64. $r = 5$ m, $\theta = 120°$

65. $r = 15$ mm, $\theta = 175°$

66. $r = 4$ ft, $\theta = 200°$

67. $r = 16$ cm, $\theta = 50°$

68. $r = 20$ ft, $\theta = 270°$

EVALUATING FUNCTIONS Evaluate the trigonometric function using a calculator if necessary. If possible, give an exact answer.

69. $\sin \dfrac{\pi}{6}$

70. $\cos \dfrac{\pi}{4}$

71. $\tan \dfrac{\pi}{3}$

72. $\cos \dfrac{4\pi}{11}$

73. $\cot \dfrac{\pi}{5}$

74. $\sec \dfrac{\pi}{8}$

75. $\sin \dfrac{2\pi}{9}$

76. $\csc \dfrac{3\pi}{10}$

🌐 **FIGURE SKATING** In Exercises 77–79, use the following information.
The number of revolutions made by a figure skater for each type of Axel jump is given. Determine the measure of the angle generated as the skater performs the jump. Give the answer in both degrees and radians.

77. Single Axel: $1\frac{1}{2}$

78. Double Axel: $2\frac{1}{2}$

79. Triple Axel: $3\frac{1}{2}$

80. 🌐 **TIME IN SCHOOL** You are in school from 8:00 A.M. to 3:00 P.M. Draw a diagram that shows the number of rotations completed by the minute hand of a clock during this time. Find the measure of the angle generated by the minute hand. Give the answer in both degrees and radians.

81. 🌐 **BICYCLE GEARS** Look back at Example 4 on page 778. In fifth gear, if the bicycle's chainwheel completes 4 rotations, through what angle does the freewheel turn? Give your answer in both degrees and radians.

82. 🌐 **FARMING TECHNOLOGY** A sprinkler system on a farm rotates $140°$ and sprays water up to 35 meters. Draw a diagram that shows the region that can be irrigated with the sprinkler. Then find the area of the region.

83. 🌐 **WINDSHIELD WIPERS** A car's rear windshield wiper rotates $120°$ as shown. Find the area covered by the wiper.

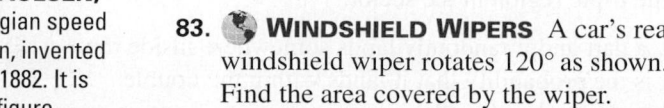

FOCUS ON PEOPLE

AXEL PAULSEN, a Norwegian speed skating champion, invented the Axel jump in 1882. It is the only jump in figure skating that requires taking off from a forward position.

🌐 **SPIRAL STAIRS** In Exercises 84–86, use the following information.
A spiral staircase has 13 steps. Each step is a sector with a radius of 36 inches and a central angle of $\frac{\pi}{7}$.

84. What is the length of the arc formed by the outer edge of each step?

85. Through what angle would you rotate by climbing the stairs? Include a fourteenth turn for stepping up on the landing.

86. How many square inches of carpeting would you need to cover the 13 steps?

🌐 **SNOW CONES** In Exercises 87 and 88, use the following information.
You are starting a business selling homemade snow cones in paper cups. You cut out a paper cup in the shape of a sector.

87. The sector has a central angle of 60° and a radius of 5 inches. When you shape the sector into a cone without overlapping edges, what will the cone's diameter be?

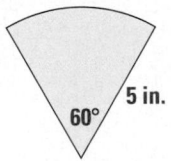

88. Suppose you want to make a cone that has a diameter of 4 inches and a slant height of 6 inches. What should the radius and central angle of the sector be?

Test Preparation

QUANTITATIVE COMPARISON In Exercises 89 and 90, choose the statement that is true about the given quantities.

    Ⓐ The quantity in column A is greater.

    Ⓑ The quantity in column B is greater.

    Ⓒ The two quantities are equal.

    Ⓓ The relationship cannot be determined from the given information.

	Column A	Column B
89.	Arc length of a sector with $r = 2$ inches and $\theta = 45°$	Arc length of a sector with $r = 2.5$ inches and $\theta = \frac{\pi}{5}$
90.	Area of a sector with $r = 2$ inches and $\theta = 45°$	Area of a sector with $r = 2.5$ inches and $\theta = \frac{\pi}{5}$

★ **Challenge**

🌐 **DARTS** In Exercises 91 and 92, use the following information.
A dart board is divided into 20 sectors. Each sector is worth a point value from 1 to 20 and has shaded regions that double or triple this value. The 20 point sector is shown at the right.

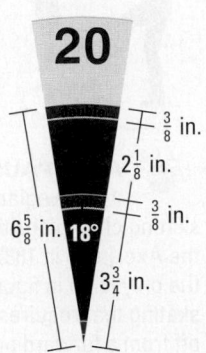

91. Find the area of the sector. Then find the areas of the double region and the triple region in the sector.

92. If you throw a dart and it randomly lands somewhere inside the sector, what is the probability that it lands within the double region? within the triple region?

PROPERTIES OF SQUARE ROOTS Simplify the expression. **(Review 5.3 for 13.3)**

93. $\sqrt{275}$ **94.** $\sqrt{1216}$ **95.** $\sqrt{8} \cdot \sqrt{32}$ **96.** $\sqrt{18} \cdot \sqrt{24}$

97. $\sqrt{\dfrac{7}{16}}$ **98.** $\sqrt{\dfrac{11}{36}}$ **99.** $\dfrac{\sqrt{8}}{\sqrt{7}}$ **100.** $\dfrac{\sqrt{12}}{\sqrt{5}}$

EVALUATING EXPRESSIONS Evaluate the expression $\dfrac{x^2}{2y + 5}$ for the given values of x and y. **(Review 1.2 for 13.3)**

101. $x = 6, y = 11$ **102.** $x = 3, y = -3$ **103.** $x = 12, y = 15$

104. $x = -1, y = -5$ **105.** $x = -10, y = 16$ **106.** $x = -20, y = -25$

WRITING EQUATIONS Write the standard form of the equation of the parabola with the given focus and vertex at **(0, 0)**. **(Review 10.2)**

107. $(5, 0)$ **108.** $(-3, 0)$ **109.** $(6, 0)$

110. $(0, -12)$ **111.** $(0, -4.4)$ **112.** $(0, 15)$

QUIZ 1

Self-Test for Lessons 13.1 and 13.2

Evaluate the six trigonometric functions of θ. **(Lesson 13.1)**

1. 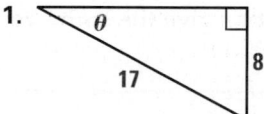 **2.** 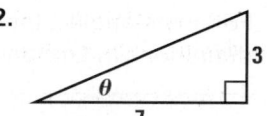 **3.**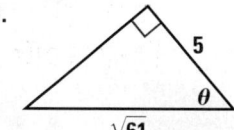

Solve △*ABC* using the diagram at the right and the given measurements. **(Lesson 13.1)**

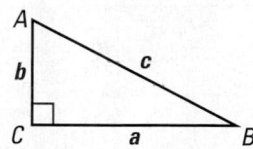

4. $B = 50°, a = 18$ **5.** $A = 33°, c = 12$

6. $A = 10°, a = 3$ **7.** $B = 71°, c = 2.3$

Find one positive angle and one negative angle coterminal with the given angle. **(Lesson 13.2)**

8. $25°$ **9.** $-\dfrac{14\pi}{3}$ **10.** $\dfrac{33\pi}{4}$ **11.** $-6200°$

Find the arc length and area of a sector with the given radius *r* and central angle θ. **(Lesson 13.2)**

12. $r = 6 \text{ m}, \theta = \dfrac{\pi}{3}$ **13.** $r = 2 \text{ ft}, \theta = \dfrac{5\pi}{6}$ **14.** $r = 8 \text{ cm}, \theta = 20°$

15. $r = 22 \text{ in.}, \theta = 220°$ **16.** $r = 5 \text{ ft}, \theta = 75°$ **17.** $r = 12 \text{ mm}, \theta = 160°$

18. 🌏 **THE BEST DEAL** Decide which of the two pizza slices shown is the best deal. Explain your reasoning. **(Lesson 13.2)**

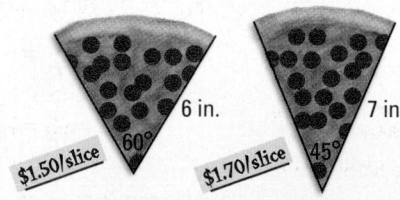

13.3 Trigonometric Functions of Any Angle

What you should learn

GOAL 1 Evaluate trigonometric functions of any angle.

GOAL 2 Use trigonometric functions to solve **real-life** problems, such as finding the distance a soccer ball is kicked in **Ex. 71**.

Why you should learn it

▼ To solve **real-life** problems, such as finding distances for a marching band on a football field in **Example 6**.

GOAL 1 EVALUATING TRIGONOMETRIC FUNCTIONS

In Lesson 13.1 you learned how to evaluate trigonometric functions of an acute angle. In this lesson you will learn to evaluate trigonometric functions of *any* angle.

GENERAL DEFINITION OF TRIGONOMETRIC FUNCTIONS

Let θ be an angle in standard position and (x, y) be any point (except the origin) on the terminal side of θ. The six trigonometric functions of θ are defined as follows.

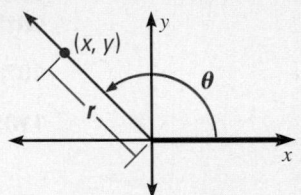

$$\sin \theta = \frac{y}{r} \qquad \csc \theta = \frac{r}{y}, \; y \neq 0$$

$$\cos \theta = \frac{x}{r} \qquad \sec \theta = \frac{r}{x}, \; x \neq 0$$

$$\tan \theta = \frac{y}{x}, \; x \neq 0 \qquad \cot \theta = \frac{x}{y}, \; y \neq 0$$

Pythagorean theorem gives
$$r = \sqrt{x^2 + y^2}.$$

For acute angles, these definitions give the same values as those given by the definitions in Lesson 13.1.

EXAMPLE 1 *Evaluating Trigonometric Functions Given a Point*

Let $(3, -4)$ be a point on the terminal side of an angle θ in standard position. Evaluate the six trigonometric functions of θ.

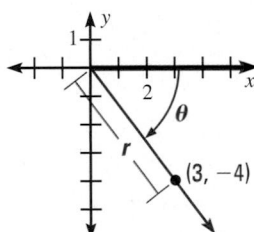

SOLUTION

Use the Pythagorean theorem to find the value of r.

$$r = \sqrt{x^2 + y^2}$$
$$= \sqrt{3^2 + (-4)^2}$$
$$= \sqrt{25}$$
$$= 5$$

Using $x = 3$, $y = -4$, and $r = 5$, you can write the following.

$$\sin \theta = \frac{y}{r} = -\frac{4}{5} \qquad \csc \theta = \frac{r}{y} = -\frac{5}{4}$$

$$\cos \theta = \frac{x}{r} = \frac{3}{5} \qquad \sec \theta = \frac{r}{x} = \frac{5}{3}$$

$$\tan \theta = \frac{y}{x} = -\frac{4}{3} \qquad \cot \theta = \frac{x}{y} = -\frac{3}{4}$$

If the terminal side of θ lies on an axis, then θ is a **quadrantal angle**. The diagrams below show the values of x and y for the quadrantal angles 0°, 90°, 180°, and 270°.

0° or 0 radians

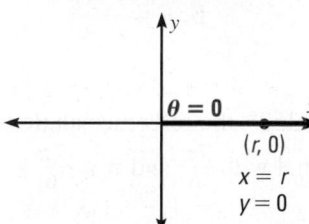

90° or $\frac{\pi}{2}$ radians

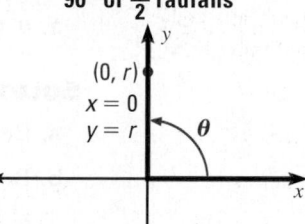

180° or π radians

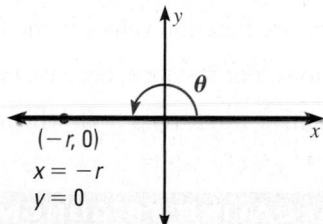

270° or $\frac{3\pi}{2}$ radians

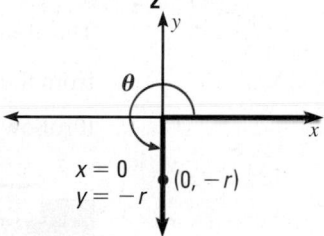

EXAMPLE 2   *Trigonometric Functions of a Quadrantal Angle*

Evaluate the six trigonometric functions of $\theta = 180°$.

SOLUTION

When $\theta = 180°$, $x = -r$ and $y = 0$. The six trigonometric functions of θ are as follows.

$$\sin \theta = \frac{y}{r} = \frac{0}{r} = 0 \qquad\qquad \csc \theta = \frac{r}{y} = \frac{r}{0} = \text{undefined}$$

$$\cos \theta = \frac{x}{r} = \frac{-r}{r} = -1 \qquad\qquad \sec \theta = \frac{r}{x} = \frac{r}{-r} = -1$$

$$\tan \theta = \frac{y}{x} = \frac{0}{-r} = 0 \qquad\qquad \cot \theta = \frac{x}{y} = \frac{-r}{0} = \text{undefined}$$

· · · · · · · · ·

The values of trigonometric functions of angles greater than 90° (or less than 0°) can be found using corresponding acute angles called *reference angles*. Let θ be an angle in standard position. Its **reference angle** is the acute angle θ' (read *theta prime*) formed by the terminal side of θ and the x-axis. The relationship between θ and θ' is given below for nonquadrantal angles θ such that $90° < \theta < 360°$ $\left(\frac{\pi}{2} < \theta < 2\pi \right)$.

90° < θ < 180°;

$\frac{\pi}{2} < \theta < \pi$

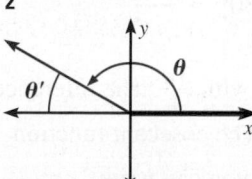

180° < θ < 270°;

$\pi < \theta < \frac{3\pi}{2}$

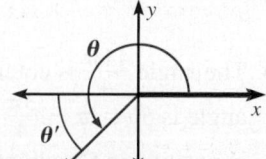

270° < θ < 360°;

$\frac{3\pi}{2} < \theta < 2\pi$

Degrees: $\theta' = 180° - \theta$
Radians: $\theta' = \pi - \theta$

Degrees: $\theta' = \theta - 180°$
Radians: $\theta' = \theta - \pi$

Degrees: $\theta' = 360° - \theta$
Radians: $\theta' = 2\pi - \theta$

EXAMPLE 3 *Finding Reference Angles*

Find the reference angle θ' for each angle θ.

   a. $\theta = 320°$ **b.** $\theta = -\dfrac{5\pi}{6}$

SOLUTION

   a. Because $270° < \theta < 360°$, the reference angle is $\theta' = 360° - 320° = 40°$.

   b. Because θ is coterminal with $\dfrac{7\pi}{6}$ and $\pi < \dfrac{7\pi}{6} < \dfrac{3\pi}{2}$, the reference angle

   is $\theta' = \dfrac{7\pi}{6} - \pi = \dfrac{\pi}{6}$.

· · · · · · · · · ·

The signs of the trigonometric function values in the four quadrants can be determined from the function definitions. For instance, because $\cos \theta = \dfrac{x}{r}$ and r is always positive, it follows that $\cos \theta$ is positive wherever $x > 0$, which is in Quadrants I and IV.

CONCEPT SUMMARY   **EVALUATING TRIGONOMETRIC FUNCTIONS**

Use these steps to evaluate a trigonometric function of any angle θ.

❶ Find the reference angle θ'.

❷ Evaluate the trigonometric function for the angle θ'.

❸ Use the quadrant in which θ lies to determine the sign of the trigonometric function value of θ. (See the diagram at the right.)

Signs of Function Values

Quadrant II	Quadrant I
$\sin \theta$, $\csc \theta$: $+$	$\sin \theta$, $\csc \theta$: $+$
$\cos \theta$, $\sec \theta$: $-$	$\cos \theta$, $\sec \theta$: $+$
$\tan \theta$, $\cot \theta$: $-$	$\tan \theta$, $\cot \theta$: $+$
Quadrant III	Quadrant IV
$\sin \theta$, $\csc \theta$: $-$	$\sin \theta$, $\csc \theta$: $-$
$\cos \theta$, $\sec \theta$: $-$	$\cos \theta$, $\sec \theta$: $+$
$\tan \theta$, $\cot \theta$: $+$	$\tan \theta$, $\cot \theta$: $-$

EXAMPLE 4 *Using Reference Angles to Evaluate Trigonometric Functions*

Evaluate **(a)** $\tan(-210°)$ and **(b)** $\csc \dfrac{11\pi}{4}$.

SOLUTION

   a. The angle $-210°$ is coterminal with $150°$. The reference angle is $\theta' = 180° - 150° = 30°$. The tangent function is negative in Quadrant II, so you can write:

$$\tan(-210°) = -\tan 30° = -\dfrac{\sqrt{3}}{3}$$

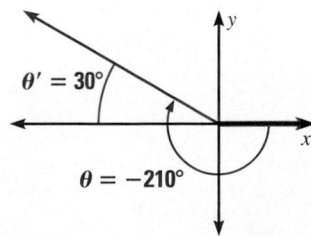

   b. The angle $\dfrac{11\pi}{4}$ is coterminal with $\dfrac{3\pi}{4}$. The reference angle is $\theta' = \pi - \dfrac{3\pi}{4} = \dfrac{\pi}{4}$. The cosecant function is positive in Quadrant II, so you can write:

$$\csc \dfrac{11\pi}{4} = \csc \dfrac{\pi}{4} = \sqrt{2}$$

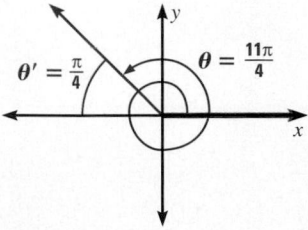

GOAL 2 **USING TRIGONOMETRIC FUNCTIONS IN REAL LIFE**

EXAMPLE 5 *Calculating Projectile Distance*

GOLF The horizontal distance d (in feet) traveled by a projectile with an initial speed v (in feet per second) is given by

$$d = \frac{v^2}{32} \sin 2\theta$$

where θ is the angle at which the projectile is launched. Estimate the horizontal distance traveled by a golf ball that is hit at an angle of $50°$ with an initial speed of 105 feet per second. (This model neglects air resistance and wind conditions. It also assumes that the projectile's starting and ending heights are the same.)

SOLUTION

The horizontal distance given by the model is:

$$d = \frac{v^2}{32} \sin 2\theta \qquad \textbf{Write distance model.}$$

$$= \frac{105^2}{32} \sin (2 \cdot \mathbf{50°}) \approx 339 \text{ feet} \qquad \textbf{Substitute and use a calculator.}$$

▶ The golf ball travels a horizontal distance of about 339 feet.

Marching Band

EXAMPLE 6 *Modeling with Trigonometric Functions*

Your school's marching band is performing at halftime during a football game. In the last formation, the band members form a circle 100 feet wide in the center of the field. Your starting position is 100 feet from the goal line, where you will exit the field. How far from the goal line will you be after you have marched $300°$ around the circle?

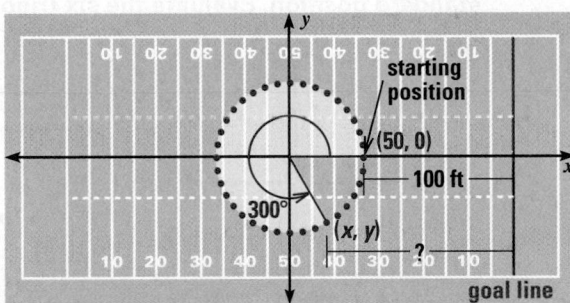

SOLUTION

The radius of the circle is $r = 50$. So, you can write:

$$\cos 300° = \frac{x}{r} \qquad \textbf{Use definition of cosine.}$$

$$\frac{1}{2} = \frac{x}{50} \qquad \textbf{Substitute.}$$

$$25 = x \qquad \textbf{Solve for } x.$$

▶ You will be $100 + (50 - 25) = 125$ feet from the goal line.

Next to image 1:

GOLF BALLS
The dimples on a golf ball create pockets of air turbulence that keep the ball in the air for a longer period of time than if the ball were smooth. The longest drive of a golf ball on record is 473 yards, 2 feet, 6 inches.

DATA UPDATE
www.mcdougallittell.com

GUIDED PRACTICE

Vocabulary Check ✓

Concept Check ✓

1. Define the terms quadrantal angle and reference angle.

2. Given an angle θ in Quadrant III, explain how you can use a reference angle to find sin θ.

3. Explain why tan 270° is undefined.

4. In which quadrant(s) must θ lie for cos θ to be positive?

Skill Check ✓

5. Let (−4, −5) be a point on the terminal side of an angle θ in standard position. Evaluate the six trigonometric functions of θ.

Sketch the angle. Then find its reference angle.

6. $\dfrac{7\pi}{4}$ **7.** −120°   **8.** $\dfrac{7\pi}{8}$ **9.** 390°

10. $-\dfrac{2\pi}{3}$ **11.** −370°   **12.** $\dfrac{2\pi}{3}$ **13.** 230°

Evaluate the function without using a calculator.

14. $\cos\left(-\dfrac{4\pi}{3}\right)$ **15.** tan 240°   **16.** $\sin\dfrac{7\pi}{4}$ **17.** csc (−225°)

18. $\cot\left(-\dfrac{3\pi}{4}\right)$ **19.** cos 240°   **20.** $\sec\dfrac{11\pi}{6}$ **21.** $\tan\dfrac{5\pi}{6}$

22. 🌐 **MARCHING BAND** Look back at Example 6 on page 787. Suppose you marched 135° around the circle from the same starting position. How far from the goal line would you be?

PRACTICE AND APPLICATIONS

STUDENT HELP

▶ **Extra Practice**
to help you master skills is on p. 958.

USING A POINT Use the given point on the terminal side of an angle θ in standard position. Evaluate the six trigonometric functions of θ.

23.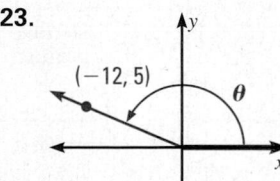
24.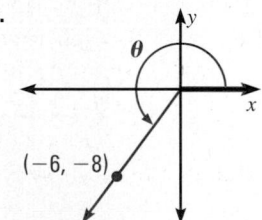
25.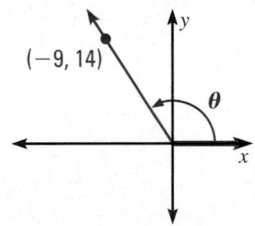

26. (−12, −15)   **27.** (−1, 1)   **28.** (15, −8)   **29.** (6, −9)

30. (7, 10)   **31.** $\left(1, -\sqrt{3}\right)$ **32.** (−3, −4)   **33.** $\left(-15, 5\sqrt{7}\right)$

QUADRANTAL ANGLES Evaluate the six trigonometric functions of θ.

34. θ = 90°   **35.** θ = 270°   **36.** θ = 0°

FINDING REFERENCE ANGLES Sketch the angle. Then find its reference angle.

37. 240°   **38.** −515°   **39.** −170°   **40.** 315°

41. −440°   **42.** $-\dfrac{3\pi}{4}$ **43.** $\dfrac{25\pi}{4}$ **44.** $-\dfrac{11\pi}{3}$

STUDENT HELP

▶ **HOMEWORK HELP**

Example 1: Exs. 23–33
Example 2: Exs. 34–36
Example 3: Exs. 37–44
Example 4: Exs. 45–60
Example 5: Exs. 69–71
Example 6: Exs. 72–76

EVALUATING FUNCTIONS Evaluate the function without using a calculator.

45. $\cos 315°$ **46.** $\cos (-210°)$ **47.** $\csc (-240°)$ **48.** $\tan 210°$

49. $\sec 780°$ **50.** $\sin 225°$ **51.** $\cos (-225°)$ **52.** $\tan (-120°)$

53. $\cot \dfrac{11\pi}{6}$ **54.** $\sec \dfrac{9\pi}{4}$ **55.** $\sin \left(-\dfrac{5\pi}{6}\right)$ **56.** $\cos \dfrac{5\pi}{3}$

57. $\sin \left(-\dfrac{17\pi}{6}\right)$ **58.** $\sec \dfrac{23\pi}{6}$ **59.** $\csc \dfrac{17\pi}{3}$ **60.** $\cot \left(-\dfrac{13\pi}{4}\right)$

STUDENT HELP

→ **Study Tip**
Make sure your calculator is in radian mode when finding trigonometric functions of angles measured in radians.

USING A CALCULATOR Use a calculator to evaluate the function. Round the result to four decimal places.

61. $\sec 137°$ **62.** $\cot 400°$ **63.** $\sin (-10°)$ **64.** $\csc 540°$

65. $\cot \left(-\dfrac{4\pi}{5}\right)$ **66.** $\sec \dfrac{11\pi}{2}$ **67.** $\cos \dfrac{6\pi}{5}$ **68.** $\csc \dfrac{23\pi}{8}$

69. 🌐 **SKATEBOARDING** A skateboarder is setting up two ramps for a jump as shown. He wants to jump off one ramp and land on the other. If the ramps are placed 5 feet apart, at what speed must the skateboarder launch off the first ramp to land on the second ramp?

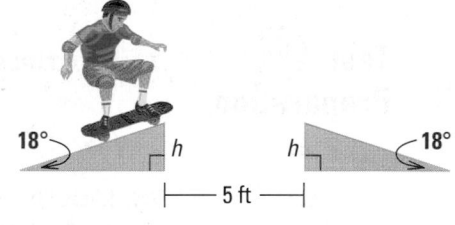

70. 🌐 **VOLLEYBALL** While playing a game of volleyball, you set the ball to your teammate. You hit the ball with an initial speed of 24 feet per second at an angle of 70°. About how far away should your teammate be to receive your set?

71. 🌐 **SOCCER** You and a friend are playing soccer. Both of you kick the ball with an initial speed of 42 feet per second. Your kick was projected at an angle of 45° and your friend's kick was projected at an angle of 60°. About how much farther will your soccer ball go than your friend's soccer ball?

72. 🌐 **FERRIS WHEEL** The largest Ferris wheel in operation is the Cosmolock 21 at Yokohama City, Japan. It has a diameter of 328 feet. Passengers board the cars at the bottom of the wheel, about 16.5 feet above the ground. Imagine that you have boarded the Cosmolock 21. The wheel rotates 312° and then stops. How high above the ground are you?

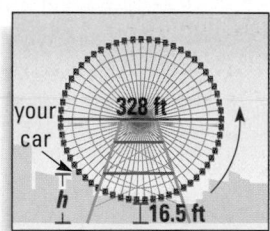

FOCUS ON CAREERS

→ **CARTOGRAPHER**
Cartographers compile information from aerial photographs and satellite data to map Earth's surface. A map's circles of latitude and longitude, as discussed in Exs. 73 and 74, are used to describe location.

CAREER LINK
www.mcdougallittell.com

SOCIAL STUDIES **CONNECTION** In Exercises 73 and 74, use the information below.
The Tropic of Cancer is the circle of latitude farthest north of the equator where the sun can appear directly overhead. It lies 23.5° north of the equator, as shown below.

73. Find the circumference of the Tropic of Cancer using 3960 miles as Earth's approximate radius.

74. What is the distance between two points that lie directly across from each other (through the axis) on the Tropic of Cancer?

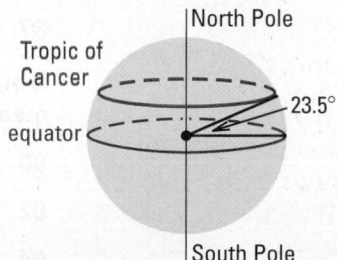

13.3 *Trigonometric Functions of Any Angle*   **789**

STUDENT HELP

► **Look Back**
For help with the distance
formula, see p. 589.

SCIENCE CONNECTION In Exercises 75 and 76, use the following information.
When two atoms in a molecule are bonded to a common atom, chemists are
interested in both the bond angle and the bond length. A water molecule (H_2O) is
made up of two hydrogen atoms bonded to an oxygen atom. The diagram below
shows a coordinate plane superimposed on a cross section of a water molecule.

75. In the diagram, coordinates are given in
    picometers (pm). (Note: 1 pm $= 10^{-12}$ m).
    If the center of one hydrogen atom has
    coordinates (96, 0), find the coordinates
    (x, y) of the center of the other hydrogen
    atom.

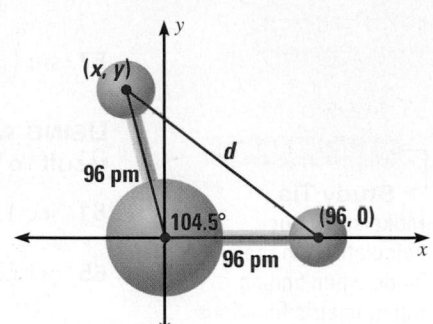

76. Use your answer to Exercise 75 and the
    distance formula to find the distance d
    (in picometers) between the centers of
    the two hydrogen atoms.

Test Preparation

77. **MULTIPLE CHOICE** What is the value of $\sec\left(\frac{40\pi}{3}\right)$?

   (A) -2 (B) $-\sqrt{2}$ (C) $-\frac{\sqrt{2}}{2}$ (D) $-\frac{1}{2}$ (E) $\sqrt{2}$

78. **MULTIPLE CHOICE** What is the approximate horizontal distance traveled by a
    football that is kicked at an angle of $40°$ with an initial speed of 70 feet per
    second?

   (A) 98 feet   (B) 142 feet   (C) 151 feet   (D) 157 feet   (E) 280 feet

★ **Challenge**

79. **CRITICAL THINKING** If θ is an angle in Quadrant II and $\tan\theta = -2$, find the
    values of the other five trigonometric functions of θ.

80. **CRITICAL THINKING** If θ is an angle in Quadrant III and $\cos\theta = -0.64$, find
    the values of the other five trigonometric functions of θ.

MIXED REVIEW

HORIZONTAL LINE TEST Graph the function. Then use the graph to determine
whether the inverse of f is a function. (Review 7.4 for 13.4)

81. $f(x) = x - 3$ 82. $f(x) = 4x + 5$ 83. $f(x) = 5x^2$

84. $f(x) = 5x^3$ 85. $f(x) = 3x^2 - 7$ 86. $f(x) = -|x + 2|$

CHOOSING CARDS A card is randomly drawn from a standard 52-card deck.
Find the probability of the given event. (A face card is a king, queen, or jack.)
(Review 12.4)

87. a king and a diamond   88. a jack or a club   89. a ten or a face card

SOLVING TRIANGLES Solve $\triangle ABC$ using the diagram and the given
measurements. (Review 13.1)

90. $A = 62°$, $b = 5$ 91. $B = 20°$, $c = 22$

92. $B = 31°$, $a = 17$ 93. $A = 50°$, $c = 3$

94. $B = 75°$, $b = 34$ 95. $A = 83°$, $a = 50$

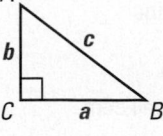

● ACTIVITY 13.4

Developing Concepts

Investigating Inverse Trigonometric Functions

GROUP ACTIVITY
Work in a small group.

MATERIALS
• paper
• pencil

▶ **QUESTION** Do the trigonometric functions sine, cosine, and tangent have inverses that are also functions?

▶ **EXPLORING THE CONCEPT**

① Copy and complete the table to find the value of $f(x) = x^2$ for each of the given x-values.

x	−4	−3	−2	−1	0	1	2	3	4
$f(x) = x^2$	?	?	?	?	?	?	?	?	?

② For a function to have an inverse, it must be true that no two values of x are paired with the same value of y. Use your completed table to explain why the function $f(x) = x^2$ does not have an inverse on the domain $-4 \le x \le 4$.

③ Restrict the domain of $f(x) = x^2$ so that it does have an inverse. Explain why you chose the domain you did.

④ Copy and complete the table to find the values of $f(\theta) = \sin \theta$, $g(\theta) = \cos \theta$, and $h(\theta) = \tan \theta$ for each of the given values of θ.

θ	$-\pi$	$-\dfrac{3\pi}{4}$	$-\dfrac{\pi}{2}$	$-\dfrac{\pi}{4}$	0	$\dfrac{\pi}{4}$	$\dfrac{\pi}{2}$	$\dfrac{3\pi}{4}$	π
$f(\theta) = \sin \theta$	?	?	?	?	?	?	?	?	?
$g(\theta) = \cos \theta$	?	?	?	?	?	?	?	?	?
$h(\theta) = \tan \theta$	?	?	?	?	?	?	?	?	?

⑤ Use the table to explain why $f(\theta) = \sin \theta$ does not have an inverse on the domain $-\pi \le \theta \le \pi$.

⑥ Does $g(\theta) = \cos \theta$ have an inverse on the domain $-\pi \le \theta \le \pi$? Explain why or why not.

⑦ Does $h(\theta) = \tan \theta$ have an inverse on the domain $-\pi \le \theta \le \pi$? Explain why or why not.

▶ **DRAWING CONCLUSIONS**

1. Use the table you completed in **Step 4** to choose a restricted domain for which $f(\theta) = \sin \theta$ does have an inverse. Explain how you made your choice.

2. Write a restricted domain for which $g(\theta) = \cos \theta$ has an inverse. Explain how you chose the domain.

3. Write a restricted domain for which $h(\theta) = \tan \theta$ has an inverse. Explain how you chose the domain.

4. Are the domains that you wrote in Exercises 1–3 the *only* domains for which the trigonometric functions have inverses? Explain.

13.4 Inverse Trigonometric Functions

What you should learn

GOAL 1 Evaluate inverse trigonometric functions.

GOAL 2 Use inverse trigonometric functions to solve **real-life** problems, such as finding an angle of repose in **Example 4**.

Why you should learn it

▼ To solve **real-life** problems, such as finding the angle at which to set the arm of a crane in **Example 5**.

GOAL 1 EVALUATING AN INVERSE TRIGONOMETRIC FUNCTION

In the first three lessons of this chapter, you learned to evaluate trigonometric functions of a given angle. In this lesson you will study the reverse problem—finding angles that correspond to a given value of a trigonometric function.

Suppose you were asked to find an angle θ whose sine is 0.5. After thinking about the problem for a while, you would probably realize that there are *many* such angles. For instance, the angles

$$\frac{\pi}{6}, \frac{5\pi}{6}, \frac{13\pi}{6}, \frac{17\pi}{6}, \text{ and } -\frac{7\pi}{6}$$

all have a sine value of 0.5. (Try checking this with a calculator.) Of these, the value of the *inverse sine function* at 0.5 is defined to be $\frac{\pi}{6}$. General definitions of inverse sine, inverse cosine, and inverse tangent are given below.

INVERSE TRIGONOMETRIC FUNCTIONS

- If $-1 \leq a \leq 1$, then the **inverse sine** of a is $\sin^{-1} a = \theta$ where $\sin \theta = a$ and $-\frac{\pi}{2} \leq \theta \leq \frac{\pi}{2}$ (or $-90° \leq \theta \leq 90°$).

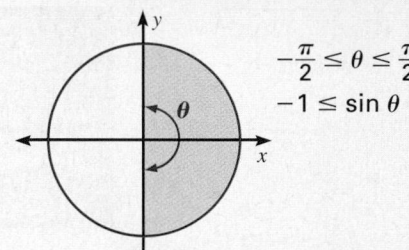

- If $-1 \leq a \leq 1$, then the **inverse cosine** of a is $\cos^{-1} a = \theta$ where $\cos \theta = a$ and $0 \leq \theta \leq \pi$ (or $0° \leq \theta \leq 180°$).

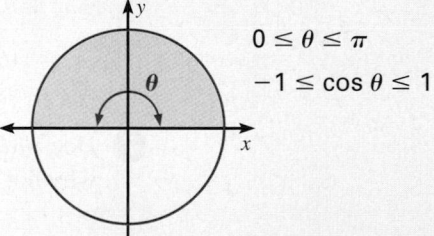

- If a is any real number, then the **inverse tangent** of a is $\tan^{-1} a = \theta$ where $\tan \theta = a$ and $-\frac{\pi}{2} < \theta < \frac{\pi}{2}$ (or $-90° < \theta < 90°$).

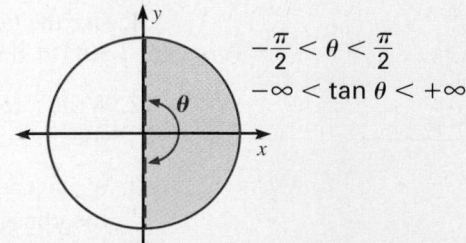

EXAMPLE 1   *Evaluating Inverse Trigonometric Functions*

Evaluate the expression in both radians and degrees.

a. $\sin^{-1} \dfrac{\sqrt{3}}{2}$ **b.** $\cos^{-1} 2$ **c.** $\tan^{-1}(-1)$

SOLUTION

a. When $-\dfrac{\pi}{2} \le \theta \le \dfrac{\pi}{2}$, or $-90° \le \theta \le 90°$, the angle whose sine is $\dfrac{\sqrt{3}}{2}$ is:

$$\theta = \sin^{-1}\dfrac{\sqrt{3}}{2} = \dfrac{\pi}{3} \qquad \text{or} \qquad \theta = \sin^{-1}\dfrac{\sqrt{3}}{2} = 60°$$

b. There is no angle whose cosine is 2. So, $\cos^{-1} 2$ is undefined.

c. When $-\dfrac{\pi}{2} < \theta < \dfrac{\pi}{2}$, or $-90° < \theta < 90°$, the angle whose tangent is -1 is:

$$\theta = \tan^{-1}(-1) = -\dfrac{\pi}{4} \qquad \text{or} \qquad \theta = \tan^{-1}(-1) = -45°$$

EXAMPLE 2   *Finding an Angle Measure*

Find the measure of the angle θ for the triangle shown.

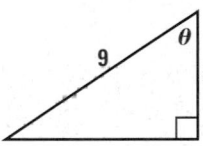

SOLUTION

In the right triangle, you are given the adjacent side and the hypotenuse. You can write:

$$\cos \theta = \dfrac{\text{adj}}{\text{hyp}} = \dfrac{5}{9}$$

This equation is asking you to find the acute angle whose cosine is $\dfrac{5}{9}$. Use a calculator to find the measure of θ.

$$\theta = \cos^{-1}\dfrac{5}{9} \approx 0.982 \text{ radians} \qquad \text{or} \qquad \theta = \cos^{-1}\dfrac{5}{9} \approx 56.3°$$

EXAMPLE 3   *Solving a Trigonometric Equation*

Solve the equation $\sin \theta = -\dfrac{1}{4}$ where $180° < \theta < 270°$.

SOLUTION

In the interval $-90° < \theta < 90°$, the angle whose sine is $-\dfrac{1}{4}$ is $\sin^{-1}\left(-\dfrac{1}{4}\right) \approx -14.5°$. This angle is in Quadrant IV as shown. In Quadrant III (where $180° < \theta < 270°$), the angle that has the same sine value is:

$$\theta \approx 180° + 14.5° = 194.5°$$

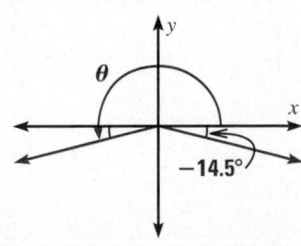

✔ **CHECK**   Use a calculator to check the answer.

$$\sin 194.5° \approx -0.25 \quad ✔$$

GOAL 2 **USING INVERSE TRIGONOMETRIC FUNCTIONS IN REAL LIFE**

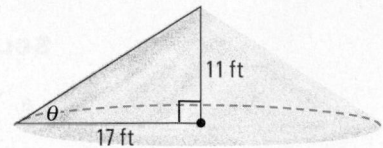

EXAMPLE 4 *Writing and Solving a Trigonometric Equation*

ROCK SALT Different types of granular substances naturally settle at different angles when stored in cone-shaped piles. This angle θ is called the *angle of repose*. When rock salt is stored in a cone-shaped pile 11 feet high, the diameter of the pile's base is about 34 feet. ▶ Source: Bulk-Store Structures, Inc.

a. Find the angle of repose for rock salt.

b. How tall is a pile of rock salt that has a base diameter of 50 feet?

ROCK SALT Each year about 9 million tons of rock salt are poured on highways in North America to melt ice. Although rock salt is the best deicing material, it also eats away at cars and road surfaces.

SOLUTION

a. In the right triangle shown inside the cone, you are given the opposite side and the adjacent side. You can write:

$$\tan \theta = \frac{\text{opp}}{\text{adj}} = \frac{11}{17}$$

This equation is asking you to find the acute angle whose tangent is $\frac{11}{17}$.

$$\theta = \tan^{-1} \frac{11}{17} \approx 32.9°$$

▶ The angle of repose for rock salt is about 32.9°.

b. The pile of rock salt has a base radius of 25 feet. From part (a) you know that the angle of repose for rock salt is about 32.9°. To find the height h (in feet) of the pile you can write:

$$\tan 32.9° = \frac{h}{25}$$

$$h = 25 \tan 32.9°$$

$$\approx 16.2$$

▶ The pile of rock salt is about 16.2 feet tall.

EXAMPLE 5 *Writing and Solving a Trigonometric Equation*

Construction

A crane has a 200 foot arm whose lower end is 5 feet off the ground. The arm has to reach the top of a building 130 feet high. At what angle θ should the arm be set?

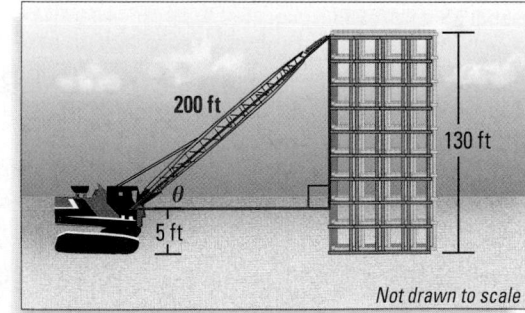

SOLUTION

In the right triangle in the diagram, you know the opposite side and the hypotenuse. You can write:

$$\sin \theta = \frac{\text{opp}}{\text{hyp}} = \frac{130 - 5}{200} = \frac{5}{8}$$

This equation is asking you to find the acute angle whose sine is $\frac{5}{8}$.

$$\theta = \sin^{-1} \frac{5}{8} \approx 38.7°$$

▶ The crane's arm should be set at an acute angle of about 38.7°.

GUIDED PRACTICE

Vocabulary Check ✓

1. Complete this statement: The __?__ sine of 1 equals $\frac{\pi}{2}$, or 90°.

Concept Check ✓

2. Explain why the domain of $y = \cos \theta$ cannot be restricted to $-\frac{\pi}{2} \le \theta \le \frac{\pi}{2}$ if the inverse is to be a function.

3. Explain why $\tan^{-1} 3$ is defined, but $\cos^{-1} 3$ is undefined.

4. **ERROR ANALYSIS** A student needed to find an angle θ in Quadrant III such that $\sin \theta = -0.3221$. She used a calculator to find that $\sin^{-1}(-0.3221) \approx -18.8°$. Then she added this result to 180° to get an answer of $\theta = 161.2°$. What did she do wrong?

Skill Check ✓

Evaluate the expression without using a calculator.

5. $\tan^{-1} \sqrt{3}$
6. $\cos^{-1} \frac{\sqrt{2}}{2}$
7. $\sin^{-1} \frac{1}{2}$
8. $\cos^{-1}\left(-\frac{1}{2}\right)$

Use a calculator to evaluate the expression in both radians and degrees. Round to three significant digits.

9. $\tan^{-1} 3.9$
10. $\cos^{-1}(-0.94)$
11. $\cos^{-1} 0.34$
12. $\sin^{-1}(-0.4)$

Solve the equation for θ. Round to three significant digits.

13. $\sin \theta = -0.35;\ 180° < \theta < 270°$
14. $\tan \theta = 2.4;\ 180° < \theta < 270°$

15. $\cos \theta = 0.43;\ 270° < \theta < 360°$
16. $\sin \theta = 0.8;\ 90° < \theta < 180°$

17. 🌐 **CONSTRUCTION** A crane has a 150 foot arm whose lower end is 4 feet off the ground. The arm has to reach the top of a building 105 feet high. At what angle should the crane's arm be set?

PRACTICE AND APPLICATIONS

STUDENT HELP

▶ **Extra Practice**
to help you master
skills is on p. 958.

EVALUATING EXPRESSIONS Evaluate the expression without using a calculator. Give your answer in both radians and degrees.

18. $\sin^{-1} \frac{\sqrt{2}}{2}$
19. $\cos^{-1} \frac{1}{2}$
20. $\tan^{-1} 1$
21. $\sin^{-1} 0$

22. $\cos^{-1}(-1)$
23. $\sin^{-1}(-1)$
24. $\tan^{-1}\left(-\frac{\sqrt{3}}{3}\right)$
25. $\cos^{-1}\left(-\frac{\sqrt{3}}{2}\right)$

FINDING ANGLES Find the measure of the angle θ. Round to three significant digits.

26.
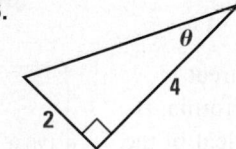

27.
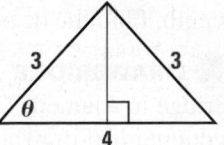

28.
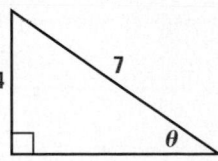

STUDENT HELP

▶ **HOMEWORK HELP**
Example 1: Exs. 18–25,
32–43
Example 2: Exs. 26–43
Example 3: Exs. 44–51
Examples 4, 5: Exs. 52–57

29.
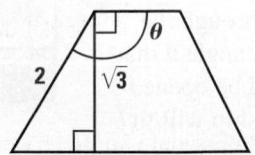

30.
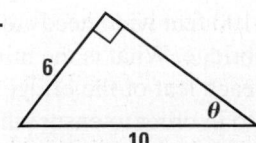

31.
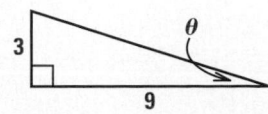

EVALUATING EXPRESSIONS Use a calculator to evaluate the expression in both radians and degrees. Round to three significant digits.

32. $\tan^{-1} 3.9$ **33.** $\cos^{-1} 0.24$ **34.** $\cos^{-1} 0.34$ **35.** $\sin^{-1} 0.75$

36. $\sin^{-1} (-0.4)$ **37.** $\cos^{-1} (-0.6)$ **38.** $\tan^{-1} (-0.2)$ **39.** $\tan^{-1} 2.25$

40. $\cos^{-1} (-0.8)$ **41.** $\sin^{-1} 0.99$ **42.** $\tan^{-1} 12$ **43.** $\cos^{-1} 0.55$

STUDENT HELP

HOMEWORK HELP
Visit our Web site
www.mcdougallittell.com
for help with Exs. 44–51.

SOLVING EQUATIONS Solve the equation for θ. Round to three significant digits.

44. $\sin \theta = -0.35$; $180° < \theta < 270°$ **45.** $\tan \theta = 2.4$; $180° < \theta < 270°$

46. $\cos \theta = 0.43$; $270° < \theta < 360°$ **47.** $\sin \theta = 0.8$; $90° < \theta < 180°$

48. $\tan \theta = -2.1$; $90° < \theta < 180°$ **49.** $\cos \theta = -0.72$; $180° < \theta < 270°$

50. $\sin \theta = 0.2$; $90° < \theta < 180°$ **51.** $\tan \theta = 0.9$; $180° < \theta < 270°$

52. 🌐 **SWIMMING POOL** The swimming pool shown in cross section at the right ranges in depth from 3 feet at the shallow end to 8 feet at the deep end. Find the angle of depression θ between the shallow end and the deep end.

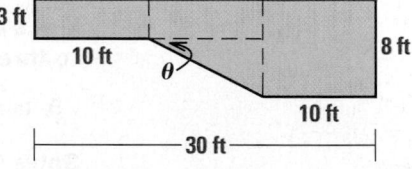

53. 🌐 **DUMP TRUCK** The dump truck shown has a 10 foot bed. When tilted at its maximum angle, the bed reaches a height of 7 feet above its original position. What is the maximum angle θ that the truck bed can tilt?

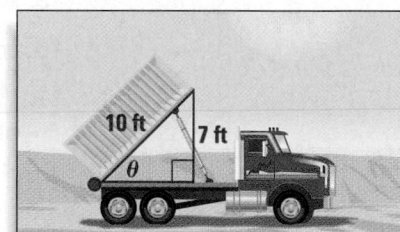

54. 🌐 **GRANULAR ANGLE OF REPOSE** Look back at Example 4 on page 794. When whole corn is stored in a cone-shaped pile 20 feet high, the diameter of the pile's base is about 82 feet. Find the angle of repose for whole corn.

55. 🌐 **ROAD DESIGN** Curves that connect two straight sections of a road are often constructed as arcs of circles. In the diagram, θ is the central angle of a circular arc that has a radius of 225 feet. Each radius line shown is perpendicular to one of the straight sections. The straight sections are therefore tangent to the arc. The extension of each straight section to their point of intersection is 158 feet in length. Find the degree measure of θ.

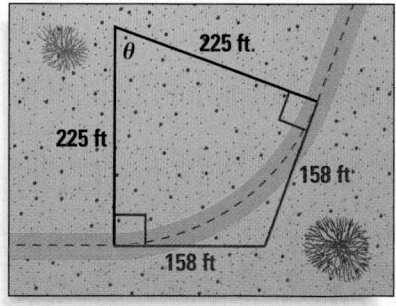

56. 🌐 **DRAWBRIDGE** The Park Street Bridge in Alameda County, California, is a double-leaf drawbridge. Each leaf of the bridge is 120 feet long. A ship that is 100 feet wide needs to pass through the bridge. What is the minimum angle θ that each leaf of the bridge should be opened to in order to ensure that the ship will fit?

▶ Source: Alameda County Drawbridges

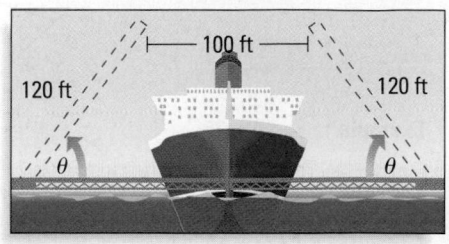

57. RACEWAY Suppose you are at a raceway and are sitting on the straightaway, 100 feet from the center of the track. If a car traveling 145 miles per hour passes directly in front of you, at what angle do you have to turn your head to see the car t seconds later? Assume that the car is still on the straightaway and is traveling at a constant speed. (*Hint:* First convert 145 miles per hour to a speed v in feet per second. The expression vt represents the distance in feet traveled by the car.)

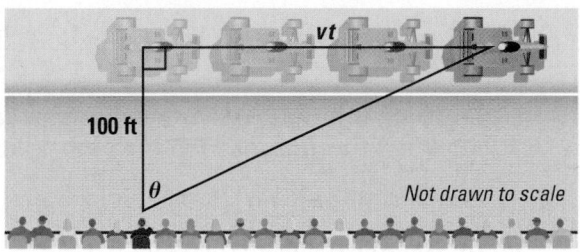

100 ft

θ

Not drawn to scale

GEOMETRY CONNECTION **In Exercises 58–62, use the following information.**
Consider a line with positive slope m that makes an angle θ with the x-axis (measuring counterclockwise from the x-axis).

58. Find the slope m of the line $y = 3x - 2$.

59. Find θ for the line $y = 3x - 2$.

60. CRITICAL THINKING How could you have found θ for the line $y = 3x - 2$ by using the slope m of the line? Write an equation relating θ and m.

61. Find an equation of the line that makes an angle of 58° with the x-axis and whose y-intercept is 3.

62. Find an equation of the line that makes an angle of 35° with the x-axis and whose x-intercept is 4.

Test Preparation

63. MULTI-STEP PROBLEM If you stand in shallow water and look at an object below the surface of the water, the object will look farther away from you than it really is. This is because when light rays pass between air and water, the water *refracts*, or bends, the light rays. The *index of refraction* for seawater is 1.341. This is the ratio of the sine of θ_1 to the sine of θ_2 for angles θ_1 and θ_2 below.

a. You are standing in seawater that is 2 feet deep and are looking at a shell at angle $\theta_1 = 60°$ (measured from a line perpendicular to the surface of the water). Find θ_2.

b. Find the distances x and y.

c. Find the distance d between where the shell is and where it appears to be.

d. *Writing* What happens to d as you move closer to the shell? Explain your reasoning.

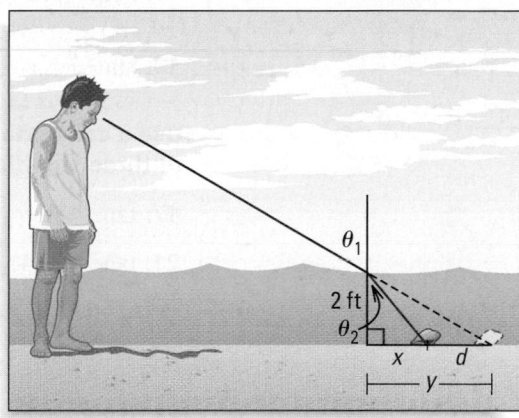

θ_1

2 ft

θ_2

x d

y

★ Challenge

64. LENGTH OF A PULLEY BELT Find the length of the pulley belt shown at the right. (*Hint:* Partition the belt into four parts: the two straight segments, the arc around the small wheel, and the arc around the large wheel.)

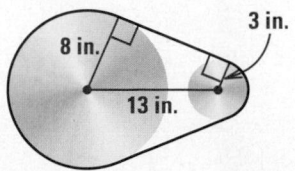

3 in.

8 in.

13 in.

SOLVING EQUATIONS Solve the rational equation. Check for extraneous solutions. (Review 9.6 for 13.5)

65. $\dfrac{6}{x} = \dfrac{7}{x + 3}$

66. $\dfrac{3}{x - 3} = \dfrac{7}{x}$

67. $\dfrac{-1}{4 + x} = \dfrac{6}{2x}$

68. $\dfrac{3}{x + 3} + 7 = \dfrac{-4}{x + 3}$

69. $\dfrac{1}{x + 2} = \dfrac{x}{2x + 9}$

70. $\dfrac{3x}{x - 2} = 2 + \dfrac{6}{x - 2}$

CHOOSING NUMBERS You have an equally likely chance of choosing any number 1 through 30. Find the probability of the given event. (Review 12.3)

71. A multiple of 5 is chosen.

72. A prime number is chosen.

73. An even number is chosen.

74. A factor of 90 is chosen.

75. A number less than 12 is chosen.

76. A number greater than 23 is chosen.

EVALUATING FUNCTIONS Use a calculator to evaluate the function. Round to four decimal places. (Review 13.3 for 13.5)

77. $\sin 27°$

78. $\sin \dfrac{23\pi}{8}$

79. $\cos 67°$

80. $\sec \dfrac{53\pi}{9}$

81. $\tan 192°$

82. $\csc 219°$

QUIZ 2

Self-Test for Lessons 13.3 and 13.4

Use the given point on the terminal side of an angle θ in standard position. Evaluate the six trigonometric functions of θ. (Lesson 13.3)

1. $(-9, -16)$

2. $(7, -2)$

3. $(-1, 5)$

4. $(6, -11)$

5. $(3, 6)$

6. $(-12, 3)$

7. $(9, -5)$

8. $(-7, -8)$

Evaluate the function without using a calculator. (Lesson 13.3)

9. $\sin(-135°)$

10. $\tan \dfrac{8\pi}{3}$

11. $\cos(-420°)$

12. $\tan\left(-\dfrac{2\pi}{3}\right)$

13. $\sin \dfrac{5\pi}{3}$

14. $\cos 870°$

15. $\tan(-30°)$

16. $\sin \dfrac{23\pi}{6}$

Use a calculator to evaluate the expression in both radians and degrees. Round to three significant digits. (Lesson 13.4)

17. $\tan^{-1} 2.3$

18. $\sin^{-1}(-0.6)$

19. $\cos^{-1} 0.95$

20. $\sin^{-1} 0.23$

21. $\tan^{-1}(-4)$

22. $\cos^{-1}(-0.8)$

23. $\sin^{-1} 0.1$

24. $\tan^{-1} 10$

Solve the equation for θ. Round to three significant digits. (Lesson 13.4)

25. $\sin \theta = 0.25;\ 90° < \theta < 180°$

26. $\cos \theta = 0.21;\ 270° < \theta < 360°$

27. $\tan \theta = 7;\ 180° < \theta < 270°$

28. $\sin \theta = -0.44;\ 180° < \theta < 270°$

29. $\cos \theta = -0.3;\ 180° < \theta < 270°$

30. $\tan \theta = -4.5;\ 90° < \theta < 180°$

31. 🌐 **LACROSSE** A lacrosse player throws a ball at an angle of 55° and at an initial speed of 40 feet per second. How far away should her teammate be to catch the ball at the same height from which it was thrown? (Lesson 13.3)

13.5

The Law of Sines

What you should learn

GOAL 1 Use the law of sines to find the sides and angles of a triangle.

GOAL 2 Find the area of any triangle, as applied in **Example 6**.

Why you should learn it

▼ To solve **real-life** problems, such as finding the distance between the Empire State Building and the Statue of Liberty in **Ex. 60**.

GOAL 1 USING THE LAW OF SINES

In Lesson 13.1 you learned how to solve right triangles. To solve a triangle with no right angle, you need to know the measure of at least one side and any two other parts of the triangle. This breaks down into four possible cases.

1. Two angles and any side (AAS or ASA)

2. Two sides and an angle opposite one of them (SSA)

3. Three sides (SSS)

4. Two sides and their included angle (SAS)

The first two cases can be solved using the **law of sines**. The last two cases require the law of cosines, which you will study in Lesson 13.6.

LAW OF SINES

If $\triangle ABC$ has sides of length a, b, and c as shown, then:

$$\frac{\sin A}{a} = \frac{\sin B}{b} = \frac{\sin C}{c}$$

An equivalent form is $\frac{a}{\sin A} = \frac{b}{\sin B} = \frac{c}{\sin C}$.

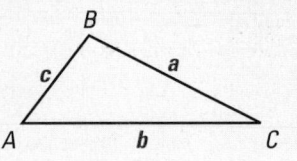

EXAMPLE 1 The AAS or ASA Case

Solve $\triangle ABC$ with $C = 103°$, $B = 28°$, and $b = 26$ feet.

SOLUTION

You can find the third angle of $\triangle ABC$ as follows.

$$A = 180° - 103° - 28° = 49°$$

By the law of sines you can write:

$$\frac{a}{\sin 49°} = \frac{26}{\sin 28°} = \frac{c}{\sin 103°}$$

You can then solve for a and c as follows.

$\dfrac{a}{\sin 49°} = \dfrac{26}{\sin 28°}$	**Write two equations, each with one variable.**	$\dfrac{c}{\sin 103°} = \dfrac{26}{\sin 28°}$
$a = \dfrac{26 \sin 49°}{\sin 28°}$	**Solve for the variable.**	$c = \dfrac{26 \sin 103°}{\sin 28°}$
$a \approx 41.8$ feet	**Use a calculator.**	$c \approx 54.0$ feet

---

STUDENT HELP

▶ **Derivations**
For a derivation of the law of sines, see p. 900.

Two angles and one side (AAS or ASA) determine exactly one triangle. Two sides and an angle opposite one of those sides (SSA) may determine no triangle, one triangle, or two triangles. The SSA case is called the *ambiguous case*.

POSSIBLE TRIANGLES IN THE SSA CASE

Consider a triangle in which you are given *a*, *b*, and *A*.

A IS OBTUSE.

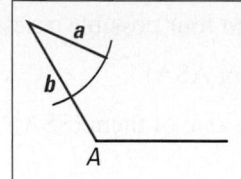

$a \le b$
No triangle

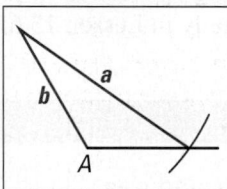

$a > b$
One triangle

A IS ACUTE.

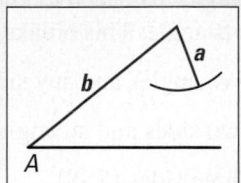

$b \sin A > a$
No triangle

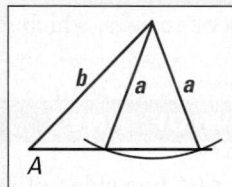

$b \sin A < a < b$
Two triangles

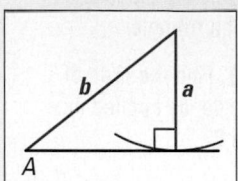

$b \sin A = a$
One triangle

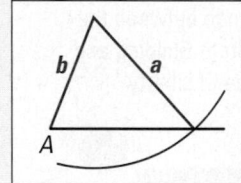

$a > b$
One triangle

EXAMPLE 2 *The SSA Case—One Triangle*

Solve $\triangle ABC$ with $C = 122°$, $a = 12$ cm, and $c = 18$ cm.

STUDENT HELP

▸ **Look Back**
For help with solving rational equations, see p. 569.

SOLUTION

First make a sketch. Because *C* is obtuse and the side opposite *C* is longer than the given adjacent side, you know that only one triangle can be formed. Use the law of sines to find *A*.

$$\frac{\sin A}{12} = \frac{\sin 122°}{18} \qquad \textbf{Law of sines}$$

$$\sin A = \frac{12 \sin 122°}{18} \qquad \textbf{Multiply each side by 12.}$$

$$\sin A \approx 0.5654 \qquad \textbf{Use a calculator.}$$

$$A \approx 34.4° \qquad \textbf{Use inverse sine function.}$$

You then know that $B \approx 180° - 122° - 34.4° = 23.6°$. Use the law of sines again to find the remaining side length *b* of the triangle.

$$\frac{b}{\sin 23.6°} = \frac{18}{\sin 122°}$$

$$b = \frac{18 \sin 23.6°}{\sin 122°} \approx 8.5 \text{ centimeters}$$

EXAMPLE 3 **The SSA Case—No Triangle**

Solve △*ABC* with *a* = 4 inches, *b* = 2.5 inches, and *B* = 58°.

SOLUTION

Begin by drawing a horizontal line. On one end form a 58° angle (*B*) and draw a segment ($\overline{BC}$) 4 inches long. At vertex *C*, use a compass to draw an arc of radius 2.5 inches. This arc does not intersect the horizontal line, so it is not possible to draw the indicated triangle.

You can see that *b* needs to be at least 4 sin 58° ≈ 3.39 inches long to reach the horizontal side and form a triangle.

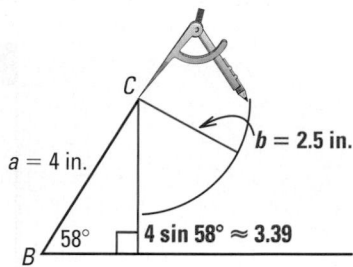

EXAMPLE 4 **The SSA Case—Two Triangles**

ASTRONOMY At certain times during the year, you can see Venus in the morning sky. The distance between Venus and the sun is approximately 67 million miles. The distance between Earth and the sun is approximately 93 million miles. Estimate the distance between Venus and Earth if the observed angle between the sun and Venus is 34°.

SOLUTION

Venus's distance from the sun, *e* = 67, is greater than *v* sin *E* = 93 sin 34° ≈ 52 and less than Earth's distance from the sun, *v* = 93. Therefore, two possible triangles can be formed. Draw diagrams as shown. Use the law of sines to find the possible measures of *V*.

$$\frac{\sin 34°}{67} = \frac{\sin V}{93}$$

$$\sin V = \frac{93 \sin 34°}{67}$$

$$\sin V \approx 0.7762$$

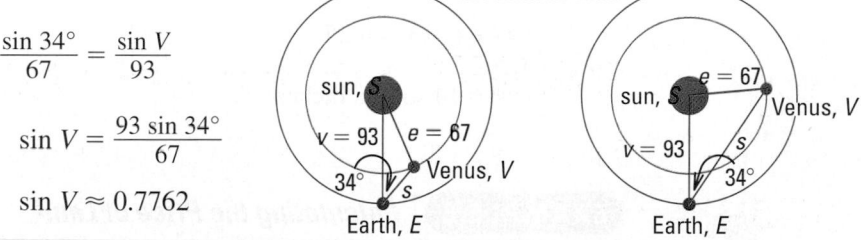

Not drawn to scale

There are two angles between 0° and 180° for which sin *V* ≈ 0.7762. Use your calculator to find the angle between 0° and 90°: sin⁻¹ 0.7762 ≈ 50.9°. To find the second angle, subtract the angle given by your calculator from 180°: 180° − 50.9° = 129.1°. So, *V* ≈ 50.9° or *V* ≈ 129.1°.

Because the sum of the angle measures in a triangle equals 180°, you know that *S* ≈ 95.1° when *V* ≈ 50.9° or *S* ≈ 16.9° when *V* ≈ 129.1°. Finally, use the law of sines again to find the side length *s*.

$$\frac{s}{\sin 95.1°} = \frac{67}{\sin 34°}$$

$$s = \frac{67 \sin 95.1°}{\sin 34°}$$

$$\approx 119$$

$$\frac{s}{\sin 16.9°} = \frac{67}{\sin 34°}$$

$$s = \frac{67 \sin 16.9°}{\sin 34°}$$

$$\approx 34.8$$

▶ The approximate distance between Venus and Earth is either 119 million miles or 34.8 million miles.

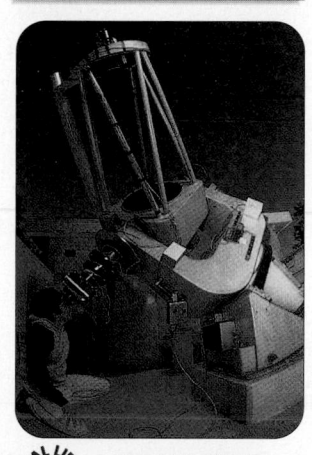

FOCUS ON CAREERS

ASTRONOMER
Astronomers study energy, matter, and natural processes throughout the universe. A doctoral degree and an aptitude for physics and mathematics are needed to become an astronomer.

CAREER LINK
www.mcdougallittell.com

GOAL 2 FINDING THE AREA OF A TRIANGLE

You can find the area of any triangle if you know the lengths of two sides and the measure of the included angle.

AREA OF A TRIANGLE

The area of any triangle is given by one half the product of the lengths of two sides times the sine of their included angle. For △*ABC* shown, there are three ways to calculate the area:

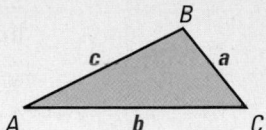

$$\text{Area} = \frac{1}{2}bc \sin A \qquad \text{Area} = \frac{1}{2}ac \sin B \qquad \text{Area} = \frac{1}{2}ab \sin C$$

EXAMPLE 5   *Finding a Triangle's Area*

Find the area of △*ABC*.

SOLUTION

Use the appropriate formula for the area of a triangle.

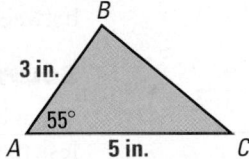

$$\text{Area} = \frac{1}{2}bc \sin A$$

$$= \frac{1}{2}(5)(3) \sin 55°$$

$$\approx 6.14 \text{ square inches}$$

Real Estate

EXAMPLE 6   *Calculating the Price of Land*

You are buying the triangular piece of land shown. The price of the land is $2000 per acre (1 acre = 4840 square yards). How much does the land cost?

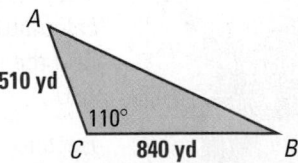

SOLUTION

The area of the land is:

$$\text{Area} = \frac{1}{2}ab \sin C$$

$$= \frac{1}{2}(840)(510) \sin 110°$$

$$\approx 201{,}000 \text{ square yards}$$

▶ The property contains 201,000 ÷ 4840 ≈ 41.5 acres. At $2000 per acre, the price of the land is about (2000)(41.5) = $83,000.

GUIDED PRACTICE

Vocabulary Check ✓ 1. What is the SSA case called? Why is it called this?

Concept Check ✓ 2. Which two of the following cases can be solved using the law of sines?

    A. SSS   **B.** SSA   **C.** AAS or ASA   **D.** SAS

3. Suppose a, b, and A are given for $\triangle ABC$ where $A < 90°$. Under what conditions would you have no triangle? one triangle? two triangles?

Skill Check ✓ **Decide whether the given measurements can form exactly *one triangle*, exactly *two triangles*, or *no triangle*. (You do not need to solve the triangle.)**

4. $C = 65°$, $c = 44$, $b = 32$ 5. $A = 140°$, $a = 5$, $c = 7$

6. $A = 18°$, $a = 16$, $c = 10$ 7. $A = 70°$, $a = 155$, $c = 160$

Solve $\triangle ABC$.

8. 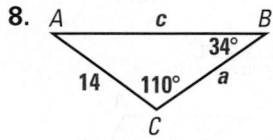   9. 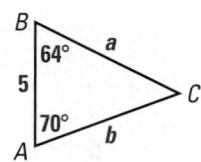   10.

Find the area of the triangle with the given side lengths and included angle.

11. $b = 2$, $c = 3$, $A = 47°$ 12. $a = 23$, $b = 15$, $C = 51°$

13. $a = 13$, $c = 24$, $B = 127°$ 14. $b = 12$, $c = 17$, $A = 103°$

15. 🌎 **REAL ESTATE** Suppose you are buying the triangular piece of land shown. The price of the land is $2200 per acre (1 acre = 4840 square yards). How much does the land cost?

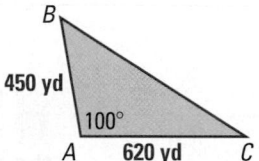

PRACTICE AND APPLICATIONS

STUDENT HELP

▸ **Extra Practice**
to help you master skills is on p. 958.

NUMBER OF SOLUTIONS Decide whether the given measurements can form exactly *one triangle*, exactly *two triangles*, or *no triangle*.

16. $C = 65°$, $c = 44$, $b = 32$ 17. $A = 140°$, $a = 5$, $c = 7$

18. $A = 18°$, $a = 16$, $c = 10$ 19. $A = 70°$, $a = 155$, $c = 160$

20. $C = 160°$, $c = 12$, $b = 15$ 21. $B = 105°$, $b = 11$, $a = 5$

22. $B = 56°$, $b = 13$, $a = 14$ 23. $C = 25°$, $c = 6$, $b = 20$

STUDENT HELP

▸ **HOMEWORK HELP**
Examples 1–3: Exs. 16–36
Example 4: Exs. 16–36, 56–62
Example 5: Exs. 37–52
Example 6: Exs. 63–67

SOLVING TRIANGLES Solve $\triangle ABC$.

24. 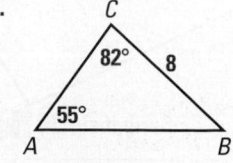   25. 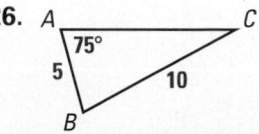   26.

STUDENT HELP

INTERNET HOMEWORK HELP
Visit our Web site
www.mcdougallittell.com
for help with Exs. 27–36.

SOLVING TRIANGLES Solve △*ABC*. (*Hint:* Some of the "triangles" have no solution and some have two solutions.)

27. $B = 60°$, $b = 30$, $c = 20$ **28.** $B = 110°$, $C = 30°$, $a = 15$

29. $B = 130°$, $a = 10$, $b = 8$ **30.** $A = 20°$, $a = 10$, $c = 11$

31. $C = 95°$, $a = 8$, $c = 9$ **32.** $A = 70°$, $B = 60°$, $c = 25$

33. $C = 16°$, $b = 92$, $c = 32$ **34.** $A = 10°$, $C = 130°$, $b = 5$

35. $B = 35°$, $a = 12$, $b = 26$ **36.** $C = 145°$, $b = 5$, $c = 9$

FINDING AREA Find the area of the triangle with the given side lengths and included angle.

37. $B = 25°$, $a = 17$, $c = 33$ **38.** $C = 130°$, $a = 21$, $b = 17$

39. $C = 120°$, $a = 8$, $b = 5$ **40.** $A = 85°$, $b = 11$, $c = 18$

41. $A = 75°$, $b = 16$, $c = 21$ **42.** $B = 110°$, $a = 11$, $c = 24$

43. $C = 125°$, $a = 3$, $b = 8$ **44.** $B = 29°$, $a = 13$, $c = 13$

45. $B = 96°$, $a = 15$, $c = 9$ **46.** $A = 32°$, $b = 10$, $c = 12$

FINDING AREA Find the area of △*ABC*.

47. 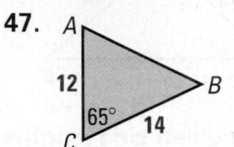   **48.** 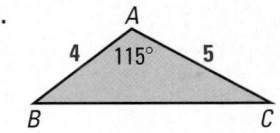   **49.**

50. 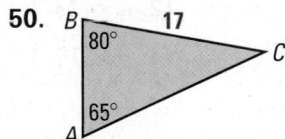   **51.** 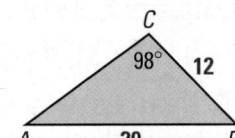   **52.**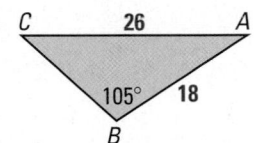

FINDING A PATTERN In Exercises 53–55, use a graphing calculator to explore how the angle measure between two sides of a triangle affects the area of the triangle.

53. Choose a fixed length for each of two sides of a triangle. Let x represent the measure of the included angle. Enter an equation for the area of this triangle into the calculator.

54. Use the *Table* feature to look at the y-values for $0° < x < 180°$. Does area always increase for increasing values of x? Explain.

55. What value of x maximizes area?

56. 🌐 **AQUEDUCT** A reservoir supplies water through an aqueduct to Springfield, which is 15 miles from the reservoir at 25° south of east. A pumping station at Springfield pumps water 7.5 miles to Centerville, which is due east from the reservoir. Plans have been made to build an aqueduct directly from the reservoir to Centerville. How long will the aqueduct be?

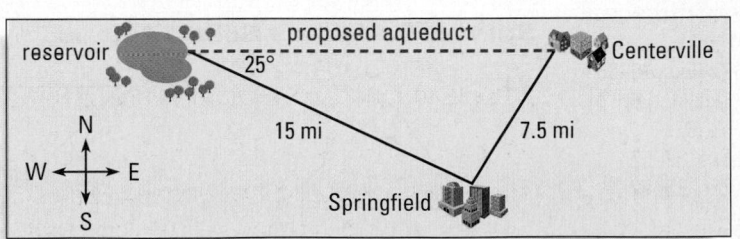

In Exercises 57–59, use the following information.

In 1802 Captain William Lambton began what is known as the Great Trigonometrical Survey of India. Lambton and his company systematically divided India into triangles. They used trigonometry to find unknown distances from a known distance they measured, called a *baseline*. The map below shows a section of the Great Trigonometrical Survey of India.

57. Use the given measurements to find the distance between Júin and Amsot.

58. Find the distance between Júin and Rámpúr.

59. *Writing* How could you find the distance from Shí to Dádú? Explain.

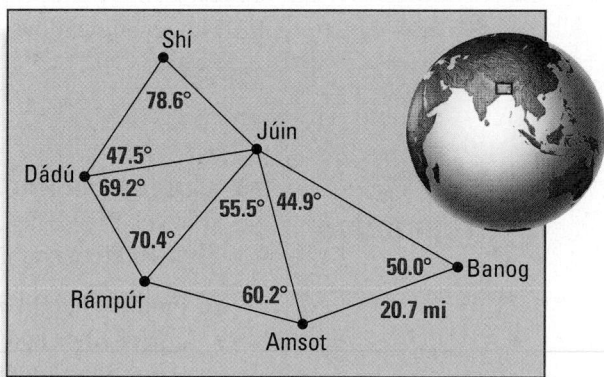

60. **NEW YORK CITY** You are on the observation deck of the Empire State Building looking at the Chrysler Building. When you turn about 145° you see the Statue of Liberty. You know that the Chrysler Building and the Empire State Building are about 0.6 mile apart and that the Chrysler Building is about 5.7 miles from the Statue of Liberty. Find the approximate distance between the Empire State Building and the Statue of Liberty.

ART CONNECTION In Exercises 61 and 62, use the following information.

You are creating a sculpture for an art show at your school. One 50 inch wooden beam makes an angle of 70° with the base of your sculpture. You have another wooden beam 48 inches long that you would like to attach to the top of the 50 inch beam and to the base of the sculpture, as shown below.

61. Find all possible angles θ that the 48 inch beam can make with the 50 inch beam.

62. Find all possible distances d that the bottom of the 48 inch beam can be from the left end of the base.

63. **HANG GLIDER** A hang glider is shown at the right. Use the given nose angle and wing measurements to approximate the area of the sail.

COURTYARD In Exercises 64 and 65, use the following information.

You are seeding a triangular courtyard. One side of the courtyard is 52 feet long and another side is 46 feet long. The angle opposite the 52 foot side is 65°.

64. How long is the third side of the courtyard?

65. One bag of grass seed covers an area of 50 square feet. How many bags of grass seed will you need to cover the courtyard?

BUYING PAINT In Exercises 66 and 67, use the following information.
You plan to paint the side of the house shown below. One gallon of paint will cover an area of 400 square feet.

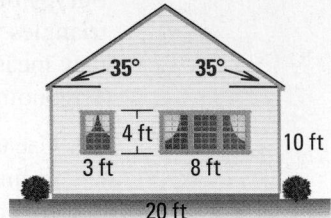

66. Find the area to be painted. Do not include the window area.

67. How many gallons of paint do you need?

68. **MULTI-STEP PROBLEM** You are at an unknown distance d from a mountain, as shown below. The angle of elevation to the top of the mountain is 65°. You step back 100 feet and measure the angle of elevation to be 60°.

   a. Find the height h of the mountain using the law of sines and right triangle trigonometry. (*Hint:* First find θ.)

   b. Find the height h of the mountain using a system of equations. Set up one tangent equation involving the ratio of d and h, and another tangent equation involving the ratio of $100 + d$ and h, and then solve the system.

   c. *Writing* Which method was easier for you to use? Explain.

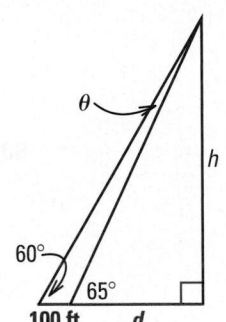

★ Challenge

69. **DERIVING FORMULAS** Using the triangle shown at the right as a reference, derive the formulas for the area of a triangle given in the property box on page 802. Then show how to derive the law of sines using the area formulas.

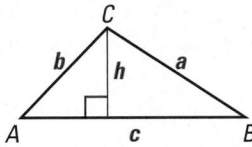

MIXED REVIEW

COMBINING EXPRESSIONS Perform the indicated operations. (Review 7.2 for 13.6)

70. $5\sqrt{11} + \sqrt{11} - 9\sqrt{11}$

71. $2\sqrt{12} + 5\sqrt{12} + 3\sqrt{27}$

72. $\sqrt{125} - 7\sqrt{45} + 10\sqrt{40}$

73. $\sqrt{7} + 5\sqrt{63} - 2\sqrt{112}$

74. $2\sqrt{486} - 5\sqrt{54} - 2\sqrt{150}$

75. $\sqrt{72} + 6\sqrt{98} - 10\sqrt{8}$

FINDING COSINE VALUES Use a calculator to evaluate the trigonometric function. Round the result to four decimal places. (Review 13.1, 13.3 for 13.6)

76. $\cos 52°$

77. $\cos \dfrac{12\pi}{5}$

78. $\cos \dfrac{9\pi}{5}$

79. $\cos \dfrac{10\pi}{7}$

80. $\cos 20°$

81. $\cos 305°$

82. $\cos (-200°)$

83. $\cos 5°$

84. **CAR HEADLIGHTS** In Massachusetts the low-beam headlights of cars are set to focus down 4 inches at a distance of 10 feet. At what angle θ are the beams directed? **(Review 13.4)**

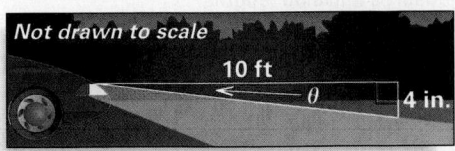

The Law of Cosines

GOAL 1 USING THE LAW OF COSINES

You have not yet solved triangles for which two sides and the included angle (SAS) or three sides (SSS) are given. You can solve both of these cases using the **law of cosines**.

LAW OF COSINES

If $\triangle ABC$ has sides of length a, b, and c as shown, then:
$$a^2 = b^2 + c^2 - 2bc \cos A$$
$$b^2 = a^2 + c^2 - 2ac \cos B$$
$$c^2 = a^2 + b^2 - 2ab \cos C$$

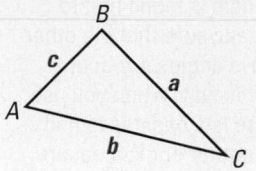

EXAMPLE 1 *The SAS Case*

Solve $\triangle ABC$ with $a = 12$, $c = 16$, and $B = 38°$.

SOLUTION

Begin by using the law of cosines to find the length b of the third side.

$b^2 = a^2 + c^2 - 2ac \cos B$	**Write law of cosines.**
$b^2 = 12^2 + 16^2 - 2(12)(16) \cos 38°$	**Substitute for *a*, *c*, and *B*.**
$b^2 \approx 97.4$	**Simplify.**
$b \approx \sqrt{97.4} \approx 9.87$	**Take square root.**

Now that you know all three sides and one angle, you can use the law of cosines *or* the law of sines to find a second angle.

$\dfrac{\sin A}{a} = \dfrac{\sin B}{b}$	**Write law of sines.**
$\dfrac{\sin A}{12} = \dfrac{\sin 38°}{9.87}$	**Substitute for *a*, *b*, and *B*.**
$\sin A = \dfrac{12 \sin 38°}{9.87}$	**Multiply each side by 12.**
$\sin A \approx 0.7485$	**Simplify.**
$A \approx \sin^{-1} 0.7485 \approx 48.5°$	**Use inverse sine.**

You can find the third angle as follows.

$$C \approx 180° - 38° - 48.5° = 93.5°$$

For a derivation of the law of cosines, see p. 901.

EXAMPLE 2 *The SSS Case*

Solve $\triangle ABC$ with $a = 8$ feet, $b = 18$ feet, and $c = 13$ feet.

SOLUTION

First find the angle opposite the longest side, $\overline{AC}$.
Using the law of cosines, you can write:

$$\cos B = \frac{a^2 + c^2 - b^2}{2ac} = \frac{8^2 + 13^2 - 18^2}{2(8)(13)} = -0.4375$$

Using the inverse cosine function, you can find the measure of obtuse angle B:

$$B = \cos^{-1}(-0.4375) \approx 115.9°$$

Now use the law of sines to find A.

$\dfrac{\sin A}{a} = \dfrac{\sin B}{b}$	**Write law of sines.**
$\dfrac{\sin A}{8} = \dfrac{\sin 115.9°}{18}$	**Substitute.**
$\sin A = \dfrac{8 \sin 115.9°}{18}$	**Multiply each side by 8.**
$\sin A \approx 0.3998$	**Simplify.**
$A \approx \sin^{-1} 0.3998 \approx 23.6°$	**Use inverse sine.**

Finally, you can find the measure of angle C:

$$C \approx 180° - 23.6° - 115.9° = 40.5°$$

> **STUDENT HELP**
>
> ▶ **Study Tip**
> In Example 2 the largest angle is found first to make sure that the other two angles are acute. This way, when you use the law of sines to find another angle measure, you will know that it is between 0° and 90°.

REAL LIFE
Softball

EXAMPLE 3 *The SAS Case*

The pitcher's mound on a softball field is 46 feet from home plate. The distance between the bases is 60 feet. How far is the pitcher's mound from first base?

SOLUTION

Begin by forming $\triangle HPF$. In this triangle you know that $H = 45°$ because the line HP bisects the right angle at home plate. From the given information you know that $f = 46$ and $p = 60$. Using the law of cosines, you can solve for h.

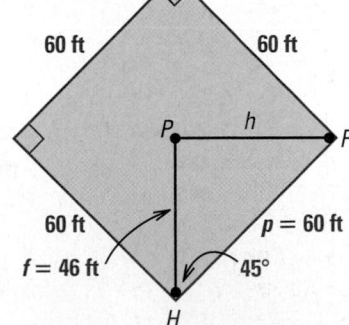

$h^2 = f^2 + p^2 - 2fp \cos H$	**Write law of cosines.**
$h^2 = 46^2 + 60^2 - 2(46)(60) \cos 45°$	**Substitute for f, p, and H.**
$h^2 \approx 1812.8$	**Simplify.**
$h \approx \sqrt{1812.8}$	**Take square root.**
≈ 42.6 feet	**Simplify.**

▶ The distance between the pitcher's mound and first base is about 42.6 feet.

GOAL 2 USING HERON'S FORMULA

The law of cosines can be used to establish the following formula for the area of a triangle. This formula is credited to the Greek mathematician Heron (circa A.D. 100).

HERON'S AREA FORMULA

The area of the triangle with sides of length *a, b,* and *c* is

$$\text{Area} = \sqrt{s(s - a)(s - b)(s - c)}$$

where $s = \frac{1}{2}(a + b + c)$. The variable *s* is called the *semiperimeter*, or half-perimeter, of the triangle.

EXAMPLE 4 *Finding the Area of a Triangle*

Find the area of △*ABC*.

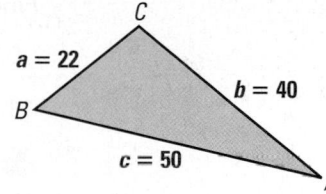

SOLUTION

Begin by finding the semiperimeter.

$$s = \frac{1}{2}(a + b + c) = \frac{1}{2}(22 + 40 + 50) = 56$$

Now use Heron's formula to find the area of △*ABC*:

$$\begin{aligned}\text{Area} &= \sqrt{s(s - a)(s - b)(s - c)} \\ &= \sqrt{56(56 - 22)(56 - 40)(56 - 50)} \\ &= \sqrt{182{,}784} \approx 428 \text{ square units}\end{aligned}$$

STUDENT HELP

▶ **Look Back**
For help with simplifying radical expressions, see p. 264.

EXAMPLE 5 *Finding the Volume of a Building*

LANDAU BUILDING The dimensions of the Landau Building are given at the right. Find the volume of the building.

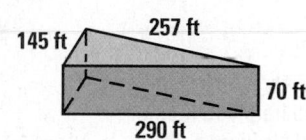

SOLUTION

Begin by finding the area of the base. The semiperimeter of the base is:

$$s = \frac{1}{2}(a + b + c) = \frac{1}{2}(145 + 257 + 290) = 346$$

So, the area of the base is:

$$\begin{aligned}\text{Area} &= \sqrt{s(s - a)(s - b)(s - c)} \\ &= \sqrt{346(346 - 145)(346 - 257)(346 - 290)} \\ &\approx 18{,}600 \text{ square feet}\end{aligned}$$

To find the volume, multiply this area by the building's height:

$$\text{Volume} = (\text{Area of base})(\text{Height}) \approx (18{,}600)(70) = 1{,}302{,}000 \text{ cubic feet}$$

GUIDED PRACTICE

Vocabulary Check ✔

1. Complete this statement: In a triangle with sides of length a, b, and c, $\frac{1}{2}(a + b + c)$ is called the __?__ .

Concept Check ✔

2. For each case, tell whether you would use the *law of sines* or the *law of cosines* to solve the triangle.

   a. SSS   **b.** SSA   **c.** SAS   **d.** ASA   **e.** AAS

3. If when using the law of cosines to find angle A in $\triangle ABC$, you get $\cos A < 0$, what type of angle is A?

4. Express Heron's formula in words.

Skill Check ✔

Solve $\triangle ABC$.

5. $B = 20°$, $a = 120$, $c = 100$ 6. $C = 95°$, $a = 10$, $b = 12$

7. $a = 25$, $b = 11$, $c = 24$ 8. $a = 2$, $b = 4$, $c = 5$

Find the area of $\triangle ABC$ having the given side lengths.

9. $a = 25$, $b = 60$, $c = 45$ 10. $a = 9$, $b = 4$, $c = 11$

11. $a = 100$, $b = 55$, $c = 61$ 12. $a = 5$, $b = 27$, $c = 29$

🌐 **BASEBALL** **In Exercises 13 and 14, use the following information.**
The pitcher's mound on a baseball field is 60.5 feet from home plate. The distance between the bases is 90 feet.

13. How far is the pitcher's mound from first base?

14. Using Heron's formula, find the area of the triangle formed by the pitcher's mound, home plate, and first base.

PRACTICE AND APPLICATIONS

STUDENT HELP

▶ **Extra Practice**
to help you master
skills is on p. 959.

SOLVING TRIANGLES **Solve $\triangle ABC$.**

15.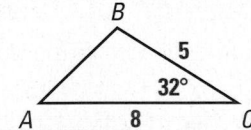

16.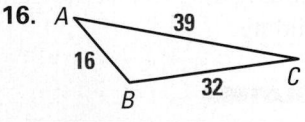

17.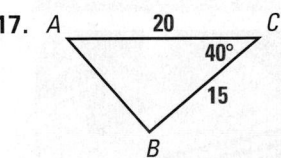

SOLVING TRIANGLES **Solve $\triangle ABC$.**

18. $B = 20°$, $a = 120$, $c = 100$ 19. $C = 95°$, $a = 10$, $b = 12$

20. $a = 25$, $b = 11$, $c = 24$ 21. $a = 2$, $b = 4$, $c = 5$

22. $A = 78°$, $b = 2$, $c = 4$ 23. $A = 60°$, $b = 30$, $c = 28$

24. $B = 45°$, $a = 11$, $c = 22$ 25. $C = 30°$, $a = 20$, $b = 20$

26. $a = 9$, $b = 3$, $c = 11$ 27. $B = 15°$, $a = 12$, $c = 6$

28. $a = 25$, $b = 26$, $c = 5$ 29. $a = 47$, $b = 30$, $c = 62$

STUDENT HELP

▶ **HOMEWORK HELP**
Examples 1, 2: Exs. 15–37
Example 3: Exs. 50, 51
Example 4: Exs. 38–48
Example 5: Exs. 52–54

STUDENT HELP

HOMEWORK HELP
Visit our Web site
www.mcdougallittell.com
for help with Exs. 30–37.

CHOOSING A METHOD Use the law of sines, the law of cosines, or the Pythagorean theorem to solve △*ABC*.

30. $A = 96°, B = 39°, b = 13$

31. $B = 80°, C = 30°, b = 34$

32. $A = 34°, b = 17, c = 48$

33. $C = 104°, b = 11, c = 32$

34. $A = 48°, B = 51°, c = 36$

35. $a = 48, b = 51, c = 36$

36. $B = 10°, b = 5, c = 25$

37. $C = 90°, a = 4, b = 11$

FINDING AREA Find the area of △*ABC*.

38.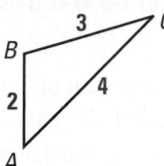

39.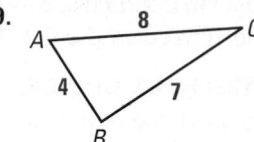

40.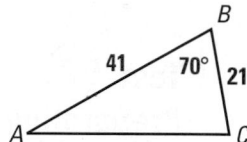

FINDING AREA Find the area of △*ABC* having the given side lengths.

41. $a = 15, b = 20, c = 25$

42. $a = 13, b = 10, c = 4$

43. $a = 75, b = 68, c = 72$

44. $a = 3, b = 19, c = 21$

45. $a = 4, b = 2, c = 4$

46. $a = 20, b = 21, c = 37$

47. $a = 8, b = 8, c = 8$

48. $a = 18, b = 15, c = 10$

49. CRITICAL THINKING Explain why the Pythagorean theorem is a special case of the law of cosines.

50. TRAPEZE ARTISTS The diagram shows the path of two trapeze artists who are both 5 feet long when hanging by their knees. The "flyer" on the left bar is preparing to make hand-to-hand contact with the "catcher" on the right bar. At what angle θ will the two meet? ▶ Source: Trapeze Arts, Inc.

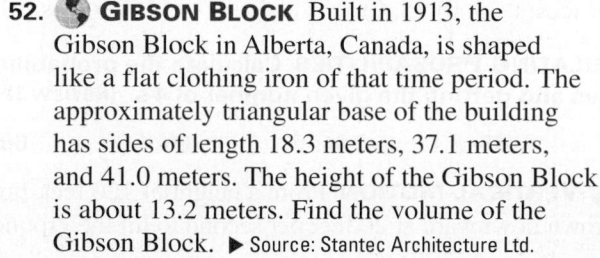

51. SURVEYING You are a surveyor measuring the width of a pond from point *A* to point *B*, as shown. You set up your transit at point *C* and measure an angle of 73°. You also measure the distance from point *C* to points *A* and *B*, getting 56 feet and 68 feet, respectively. What is the width of the pond?

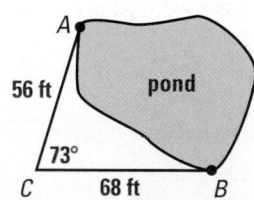

52. GIBSON BLOCK Built in 1913, the Gibson Block in Alberta, Canada, is shaped like a flat clothing iron of that time period. The approximately triangular base of the building has sides of length 18.3 meters, 37.1 meters, and 41.0 meters. The height of the Gibson Block is about 13.2 meters. Find the volume of the Gibson Block. ▶ Source: Stantec Architecture Ltd.

53. 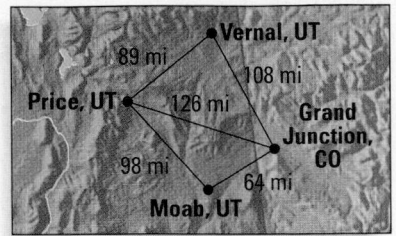 **DINOSAUR DIAMOND** In Utah and
Colorado, an area called the Dinosaur Diamond
is known for containing many dinosaur fossils.
The map at the right shows the towns at the four
vertices of the diamond. Use the given distances
to find the area of the Dinosaur Diamond.
▶ *Source: Dinomation*

54. 🌍 **FERTILIZER** A farmer has a triangular field with sides that are 240 feet,
300 feet, and 360 feet long. He wants to apply fall fertilizer to the field. If it takes
one 40 pound bag of fertilizer to cover 6000 square feet, how many bags does he
need to cover the field?

**Test
Preparation**

55. MULTIPLE CHOICE Two airplanes leave an airport at the same time, the first
headed due north and the second headed 37° east of north. At 2:00 P.M. the first
airplane is 250 miles from the airport and the second airplane is 316 miles from
the airport. How far apart are the two airplanes?

Ⓐ about 190 miles   Ⓑ about 210 miles   Ⓒ about 200 miles

Ⓓ about 310 miles   Ⓔ about 165 miles

56. MULTIPLE CHOICE Find the area of a triangle with sides of length 37 feet,
23 feet, and 42 feet.

Ⓐ about 189 ft^2 Ⓑ about 134 ft^2 Ⓒ about 477 ft^2

Ⓓ about 424 ft^2 Ⓔ about 777 ft^2

★ **Challenge**

57. 🔦 **MIRRORS** In the diagram, a beam of
light is directed at the blue mirror, reflected
to the red mirror, and then reflected back
to the blue mirror. Find the distance *PT* that
the light travels from the red mirror back
to the blue mirror given that *OQ* = 6 feet
and *OP* = 4.7 feet. (*Hint:* You will need
to find θ. To do this, find $\angle OPQ$ and use
the fact that $2\theta + m\angle TPQ = 180°$.)

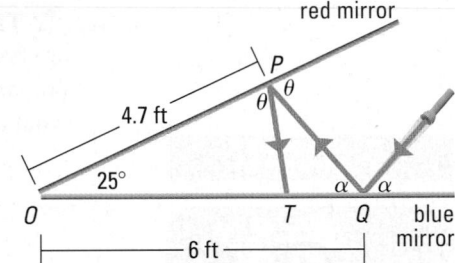

EXTRA CHALLENGE
↳ www.mcdougallittell.com

MIXED REVIEW

WRITING EQUATIONS Write an equation of the hyperbola with the given foci
and vertices. (Review 10.5)

58. Foci: $(-7, 0)$, $(7, 0)$
Vertices: $(-2, 0)$, $(2, 0)$

59. Foci: $(0, -11)$, $(0, 11)$
Vertices: $(0, -3)$, $(0, 3)$

60. Foci: $(-9, 0)$, $(9, 0)$
Vertices: $(-5, 0)$, $(5, 0)$

61. Foci: $\left(0, -2\sqrt{5}\right)$, $\left(0, 2\sqrt{5}\right)$
Vertices: $(0, -1)$, $(0, 1)$

CALCULATING PROBABILITIES Calculate the probability of rolling a die
30 times and getting the given number of 4's. (Review 12.6)

62. 1   **63.** 3   **64.** 5   **65.** 6   **66.** 8   **67.** 10

68. 🏀 **VERTICAL MOTION** From a height of 120 feet, how long does it take a ball
thrown downward at 20 feet per second to hit the ground? (Review 5.6 for 13.7)

Parametric Equations and Projectile Motion

GOAL 1 USING PARAMETRIC EQUATIONS

> **ACTIVITY**
>
> **Developing Concepts**
>
> ### Investigating Linear Motion
>
> Suppose an ant starts at one corner of a picnic tablecloth and moves in a straight line, as shown. The ant's position (x, y) relative to the edges of the tablecloth is given for different times t (in seconds).
>
> **1** Write two equations: one that gives the ant's horizontal position x as a function of t, and one that gives the ant's vertical position y as a function of t.
>
> **2** What is the ant's position after 5 seconds?
>
> **3** How long will it take the ant to reach an edge of the tablecloth?

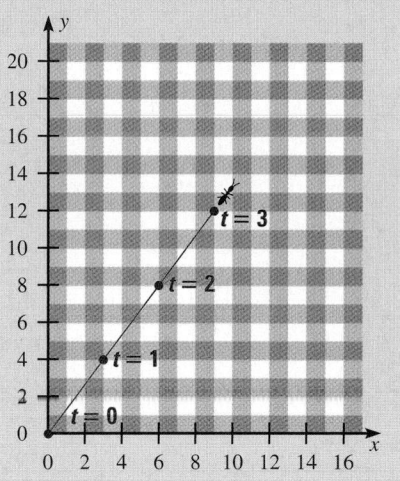

In the investigation you wrote a pair of equations that expressed x and y in terms of a third variable t. These equations, $x = f(t)$ and $y = g(t)$, are called **parametric equations,** and t is called the **parameter**.

EXAMPLE 1 *Graphing a Set of Parametric Equations*

Graph $x = 3t - 12$ and $y = -2t + 3$ for $0 \le t \le 5$.

SOLUTION

Begin by making a table of values.

t	0	1	2	3	4	5
x	-12	-9	-6	-3	0	3
y	3	1	-1	-3	-5	-7

Plot the points (x, y) given in the table:

$(-12, 3), (-9, 1), (-6, -1),$
$(-3, -3), (0, -5), (3, -7)$

Then connect the points with a line segment as shown.

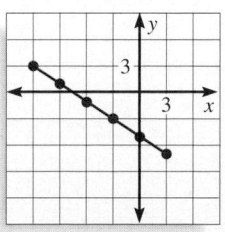

EXAMPLE 2 *Eliminating the Parameter*

Write an xy-equation for the parametric equations in Example 1: $x = 3t - 12$ and $y = -2t + 3$ for $0 \le t \le 5$. State the domain for the equation.

SOLUTION

First solve one of the parametric equations for t.

$x = 3t - 12$	**Write original equation.**
$x + 12 = 3t$	**Add 12 to each side.**
$\frac{1}{3}x + 4 = t$	**Multiply each side by $\frac{1}{3}$.**

Then substitute for t in the other parametric equation.

$y = -2t + 3$	**Write original equation.**
$y = -2\left(\frac{1}{3}x + 4\right) + 3$	**Substitute for t.**
$y = -\frac{2}{3}x - 5$	**Simplify.**

This process is called *eliminating the parameter* because the parameter t is not in the final equation. When $t = 0$, $x = -12$ and when $t = 5$, $x = 3$. So, the domain of the xy-equation is $-12 \le x \le 3$.

· · · · · · · · · ·

Consider an object that is moving with constant speed v along a straight line that makes an angle θ measured counterclockwise from a line parallel to the x-axis. The position of the object at any time t can be represented by the parametric equations

$$x = (v \cos \theta)t + x_0$$
$$y = (v \sin \theta)t + y_0$$

where (x_0, y_0) is the object's location when $t = 0$.

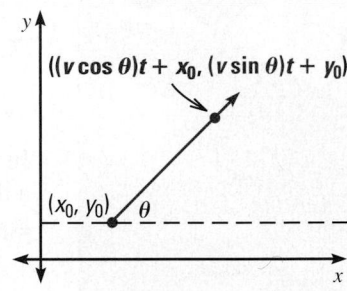

Aviation

EXAMPLE 3 *Modeling Linear Motion*

Write a set of parametric equations for the airplane shown, given that its speed is 306 feet per second.

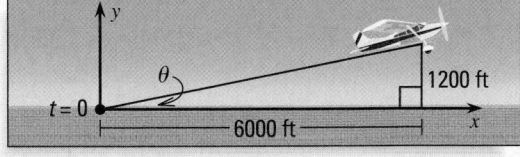

SOLUTION

The angle of elevation is $\theta = \tan^{-1}\left(\frac{1200}{6000}\right) \approx 11.3°$.

Using $v = 306$, $\theta = 11.3°$, and $(x_0, y_0) = (0, 0)$, you can write the following.

$x = (v \cos \theta)t + x_0$	and	$y = (v \sin \theta)t + y_0$
$x \approx (306 \cos 11.3°)t + 0$		$y \approx (306 \sin 11.3°)t + 0$
$\approx 300t$		$\approx 60t$

Chapter 13 *Trigonometric Ratios and Functions*

GOAL 2 MODELING PROJECTILE MOTION

Parametric equations can also be used to model nonlinear motion in a plane. For instance, consider an object that is projected into the air at an angle θ with an initial speed v. The object's parabolic path can be modeled with the parametric equations

$$x = (v \cos \theta)t + x_0$$

$$y = -\frac{1}{2}gt^2 + (v \sin \theta)t + y_0$$

where (x_0, y_0) is the object's location when $t = 0$. The constant g is the acceleration due to gravity. Its value is 32 ft/sec² or 9.8 m/sec². (Note that this model neglects air resistance.)

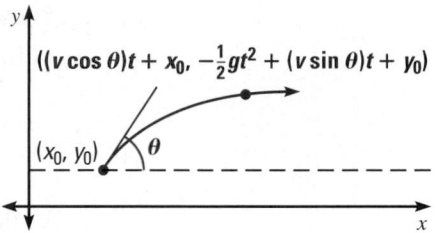

EXAMPLE 4 *Modeling Projectile Motion*

PUMPKIN TOSSING In a pumpkin tossing contest in Morton, Illinois, a contestant won the catapult competition by using two telephone poles, huge rubber bands, and a power winch. Suppose the pumpkin was launched with an initial speed of 125 feet per second, at an angle of 45°, and from an initial height of 25 feet.

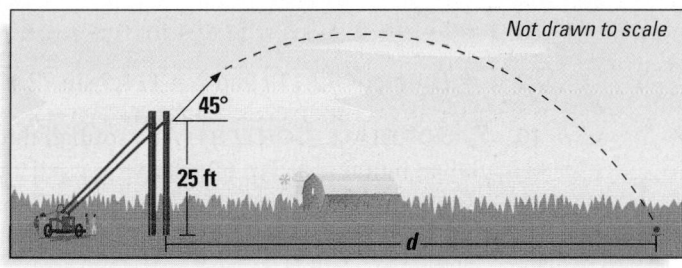

a. Write a set of parametric equations for the motion of the pumpkin.

b. Use the equations to find how far the pumpkin traveled.

SOLUTION

a. Using $v = 125$ ft/sec, $\theta = 45°$, and $(x_0, y_0) = (0, 25)$, you can write the following.

$$x = (v \cos \theta)t + x_0 \qquad \text{and} \qquad y = -\frac{1}{2}gt^2 + (v \sin \theta)t + y_0$$

$$\approx 88.4t \qquad\qquad\qquad \approx -16t^2 + 88.4t + 25$$

b. The pumpkin hits the ground when $y = 0$.

$-16t^2 + 88.4t + 25 = y$	**Write parametric equation for y.**
$-16t^2 + 88.4t + 25 = 0$	**Substitute 0 for y.**
$t = \dfrac{-88.4 \pm \sqrt{(88.4)^2 - 4(-16)(25)}}{2(-16)}$	**Use the quadratic formula to find t.**
$t \approx 5.8$ seconds	**Simplify and choose positive t-value.**

STUDENT HELP

Look Back
For help with the quadratic formula, see p. 291.

When $t = 5.8$ seconds, the pumpkin's location will have an x-value of $x = (88.4)(5.8) \approx 513$ feet. So, the pumpkin traveled about 513 feet.

GUIDED PRACTICE

Vocabulary Check ✓

1. Complete this statement: Parametric equations express variables like x and y in terms of another variable such as t. In this case, t is called the ? .

Concept Check ✓

2. For an object moving in a straight line at a constant speed v, what do you need to know in order to write parametric equations describing the object's motion?

3. In this lesson you studied two parametric models for describing motion:

$$x = (v \cos \theta)t + x_0 \qquad \text{and} \qquad x = (v \cos \theta)t + x_0$$
$$y = (v \sin \theta)t + y_0 \qquad\qquad\qquad y = -\frac{1}{2}gt^2 + (v \sin \theta)t + y_0$$

Under what circumstances would you use each model?

Skill Check ✓

Graph the parametric equations.

4. $x = 2t$ and $y = t$ for $0 \le t \le 4$

5. $x = 3t + 4$ and $y = t - 3$ for $0 \le t \le 5$

6. $x = (20 \cos 60°)t$ and $y = (20 \sin 60°)t$ for $2 \le t \le 6$

Write an *xy*-equation for the parametric equations. State the domain.

7. $x = 7t$ and $y = 3t - 2$ for $0 \le t \le 5$

8. $x = -4t + 2$ and $y = 5t - 4$ for $0 \le t \le 6$

9. $x = (11.5 \cos 72.1°)t$ and $y = (11.5 \sin 72.1°)t + 3$ for $0 \le t \le 10$

10. 🌏 **SOFTBALL CONTEST** At a softball throwing contest, you throw a softball with an initial speed of 60 feet per second, at an angle of 50°, and from an initial height of 5.5 feet. Write parametric equations for the softball's motion.

PRACTICE AND APPLICATIONS

STUDENT HELP

▶ **Extra Practice**
to help you master
skills is on p. 959.

GRAPHING **Graph the parametric equations.**

11. $x = 2t - 2$ and $y = -t + 3$ for $0 \le t \le 5$

12. $x = 5 - 5t$ and $y = 3t - 2$ for $0 \le t \le 5$

13. $x = 2t - 6$ and $y = t - 3$ for $3 \le t \le 8$

14. $x = 30t + 10$ and $y = 60t - 20$ for $0 \le t \le 4$

15. $x = (80.6 \cos 7.1°)t$ and $y = (80.6 \sin 7.1°)t$ for $0 \le t \le 5$

ELIMINATING THE PARAMETER **Write an *xy*-equation for the parametric equations. State the domain.**

16. $x = 2t$ and $y = -4t$ for $0 \le t \le 5$

STUDENT HELP

▶ **HOMEWORK HELP**
Example 1: Exs. 11–15
Example 2: Exs. 16–20
Example 3: Exs. 24–32
Example 4: Exs. 33–40

17. $x = t + 1$ and $y = 2t - 3$ for $0 \le t \le 5$

18. $x = 3t + 6$ and $y = 5t - 1$ for $0 \le t \le 20$

19. $x = (14.14 \cos 45°)t$ and $y = (14.14 \sin 45°)t$ for $0 \le t \le 10$

20. $x = (111.8 \cos 63.43°)t$ and $y = (111.8 \sin 63.43°)t$ for $0 \le t \le 10$

DESCRIBING LINEAR MOTION Use the given information to write parametric equations describing the linear motion.

21. An object is at $(0, 0)$ at time $t = 0$ and then at $(19, 57)$ at time $t = 3$.

22. An object is at $(18, 8)$ at time $t = 4$ and then at $(40.8, 19.0)$ at time $t = 9$.

23. An object is at $(3, 2)$ at time $t = 0$ and then at $(14.3, 66.1)$ at time $t = 5$.

24. 🌎 **ROWBOAT** You are trying to row a boat due east across a river that is 0.75 mile wide and flows due south. You reach the other side in 15 minutes, but the current has pulled you 1 mile downstream. Write a set of parametric equations to describe the path you traveled. Then write an *xy*-equation for the parametric equations. State the domain of the *xy*-equation.

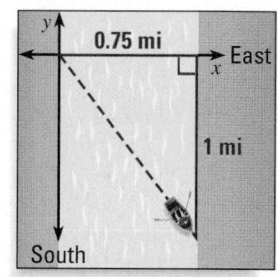

25. 🌎 **BIKE PATH** A bike trail connects Park Street and Main Street as shown. You enter the trail 2 miles from the intersection of the streets and bike at a speed of 10 miles per hour. You reach Main Street 1.5 miles from the intersection. Write a set of parametric equations to describe your path.

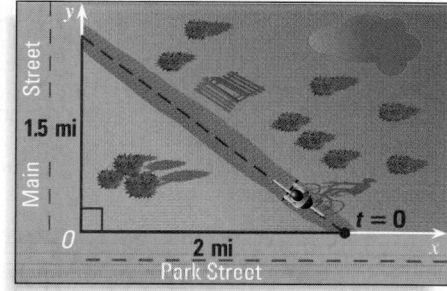

🌎 **SWIMMING** In Exercises 26–28, use the following information.
You are swimming in a race across a lake and back. Swimmers must swim to, and then back from, a buoy placed 2640 feet from the center of the start/finish line. You start the race 100 feet from the center of the start/finish line as shown.

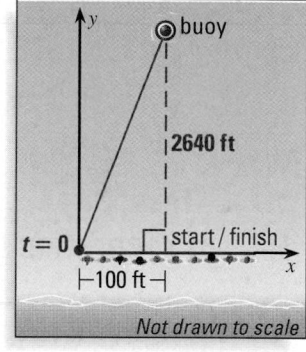

26. You swim to the buoy at a steady rate of 0.7 foot per second. Write a set of parametric equations for your path.

27. Use the equations to determine how long it takes you to reach the buoy.

28. If you continue to swim at a steady rate of 0.7 foot per second straight back to the center of the start/finish line, how long will it take you to complete the race?

🌎 **LANDING A PLANE** In Exercises 29–32, use the following information.
You are flying in a small airplane at an altitude of 10,000 feet. When you descend to land the plane, your horizontal air speed will be 260 feet per second (177 miles per hour) and your rate of descent will be 30 feet per second.

29. Write a set of parametric equations for the plane's descent.

30. What is the angle of descent?

31. How long will it take for the plane to land?

32. How far from the airport should you begin the descent?

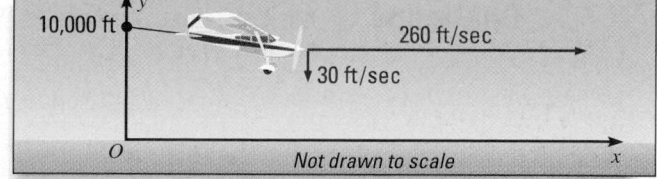

🌐 **WATER SKIING** In Exercises 33–35, use the following information.
A water skier jumps off a ramp at a speed of 17.9 meters per second. The ramp's angle of elevation is 14.3°, and the height of the end of the ramp above the surface of the water is 1.71 meters. ▶ Source: American Water Ski Association

33. Write a set of parametric equations for the water skier's jump.

34. For how many seconds is the water skier in the air?

35. How far from the ramp does the water skier land?

🌐 **LEAPING DOLPHIN** In Exercises 36–38, use the following information.
A dolphin is performing in a show at an oceanic park and makes a leap out of the water. The dolphin leaves the water traveling at a speed of 32 feet per second and at an angle of 48° with the surface of the water.

36. Write a set of parametric equations for the dolphin's motion.

37. For how many seconds is the dolphin in the air?

38. How far across the water does the dolphin travel in the air?

🌐 **SHOT PUT** In Exercises 39 and 40, use the following information.
A shot put is thrown a distance of 54.5 feet at a high school track and field meet. The shot put was released from a height of 6 feet and at an angle of 43°.

39. Write a set of parametric equations for the path of the shot put.

40. Use the equations to determine the speed of the shot put at the time of release.

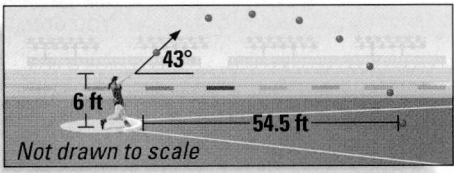

Not drawn to scale

Test Preparation

41. MULTIPLE CHOICE Which equation is an xy-equation for the parametric equations $x = 3t + 12$ and $y = 12t - 8$ where $0 \le t \le 20$?

Ⓐ $y = 9x + 4; 0 \le x \le 20$

Ⓑ $y = 36x + 132; -8 \le x \le 132$

Ⓒ $y = 4x - 56; 12 \le x \le 72$

Ⓓ $y = 15x + 4; 4 \le x \le 304$

42. MULTIPLE CHOICE An airplane takes off at an angle of 10.6° with the ground and travels at a constant speed of 324 miles per hour. Which set of parametric equations describes the airplane's ascent?

Ⓐ $x = 4670t, y = 874t$

Ⓑ $x = 318t, y = 60t$

Ⓒ $x = 5000t, y = 80t$

Ⓓ $x = 800t, y = 150t$

★ **Challenge**

43. CRITICAL THINKING Write the following pairs of equations in the form $y = f(x)$.

$$x = (v \cos \theta)t + x_0 \qquad\qquad x = (v \cos \theta)t + x_0$$
$$y = (v \sin \theta)t + y_0 \qquad\qquad y = -\frac{1}{2}gt^2 + (v \sin \theta)t + y_0$$

In which case is the path of the moving object *not* affected by changing the speed v? Explain why this makes sense.

GRAPHING Graph the function. (Review 5.1, 7.5, 8.1 for 14.1)

44. $y = 9x^2$

45. $y = -10x^2$

46. $y = 7\sqrt{x}$

47. $y = -6\sqrt{x}$

48. $y = 7 \cdot 2^x$

49. $y = -\dfrac{3}{4} \cdot 3^x$

FINDING SUMS Find the sum of the series. (Review 11.1, 11.4)

50. $\displaystyle\sum_{i=1}^{10} -3i$

51. $\displaystyle\sum_{i=1}^{27} i^2$

52. $\displaystyle\sum_{n=1}^{\infty} 20\left(\dfrac{4}{5}\right)^{n-1}$

53. $\displaystyle\sum_{n=1}^{\infty} -\dfrac{1}{6}\left(-\dfrac{1}{2}\right)^{n-1}$

NORMAL DISTRIBUTIONS Find the probability that a randomly selected *x*-value is in the given interval. (Review 12.7)

54. to the left of the mean

55. between the mean and 1 standard deviation to the left of the mean

56. between 2 and 3 standard deviations from the mean

57. more than 3 standard deviations to the right of the mean

QUIZ 3

Self-Test for Lessons 13.5–13.7

Solve △*ABC*. (Lessons 13.5 and 13.6)

1. $B = 70°, b = 30, c = 25$

2. $B = 10°, C = 100°, a = 15$

3. $A = 40°, B = 110°, b = 30$

4. $A = 122°, a = 9, c = 13$

5. $a = 45, b = 32, c = 24$

6. $A = 107°, b = 15, c = 28$

Find the area of △*ABC*. (Lessons 13.5 and 13.6)

7. $B = 95°, a = 12, c = 30$

8. $C = 103°, a = 41, b = 25$

9. $A = 117°, b = 16, c = 8$

10. $a = 7, b = 7, c = 5$

11. $a = 89, b = 55, c = 71$

12. $a = 40, b = 21, c = 32$

Graph the parametric equations. (Lesson 13.7)

13. $x = 4 - 2t$ and $y = 3t + 1$ for $0 \le t \le 5$

14. $x = 2t - 5$ and $y = 4t - 3$ for $3 \le t \le 7$

15. $x = (10.5 \cos 45°)t$ and $y = (10.5 \sin 45°)t + 4$ for $0 \le t \le 5$

Write an *xy*-equation for the parametric equations. State the domain. (Lesson 13.7)

16. $x = -5t + 3$ and $y = t - 6$ for $0 \le t \le 5$

17. $x = (10 \cos 35°)t$ and $y = (10 \sin 35°)t$ for $0 \le t \le 30$

18. **SOCCER** You are a goalie in a soccer game. You save the ball and then drop kick it as far as you can down the field. Your kick has an initial speed of 26 feet per second and starts at a height of 2 feet. If you kick the ball at an angle of 45°, how far down the field does the ball hit the ground? (Lesson 13.7)

ACTIVITY 13.7

Using Technology

Graphing Parametric Equations

You can use a graphing calculator to graph a set of parametric equations.

▶ EXAMPLE

At a driving range, you hit a golf ball at ground level with an initial speed of 120 feet per second and at an angle of 45°. Use a graphing calculator to graph a set of parametric equations that describe the path of the ball. Then use the graphing calculator to estimate how far the ball travels.

▶ SOLUTION

Assume that $x_0 = 0$ and $y_0 = 0$. The parametric equations that describe the path of the golf ball are as follows.

$$x = (v \cos \theta)t + x_0 \qquad\qquad y = -\frac{1}{2}gt^2 + (v \sin \theta)t + y_0$$

$$\approx 84.9t \qquad\qquad\qquad\qquad \approx -16t^2 + 84.9t$$

❶ Put your calculator in *Parametric* mode.

❷ Enter the parametric equations.

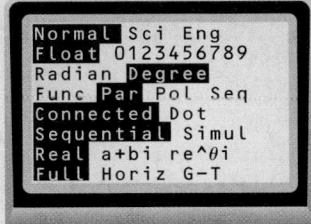

❸ Set the viewing window so that $0 \le t \le 10$, $0 \le x \le 500$, and $-50 \le y \le 150$.

❹ Graph the parametric equations. Use the graphing calculator's *Trace* feature to find the value of x when $y = 0$.

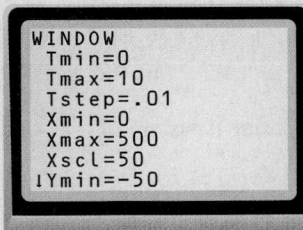
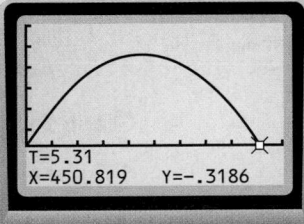

▶ An estimate of the distance the ball travels is about 450 feet, or 150 yards.

▶ EXERCISES

1. Graph a set of parametric equations that describe the path of the golf ball in the example when it is hit at different angles. Copy and complete the table.

Angle, θ	30°	35°	40°	50°	55°	60°
Horizontal distance (ft), x	?	?	?	?	?	?

2. At what angle should you hit the ball so that it travels the maximum horizontal distance? Explain.

Chapter Summary

WHAT did you learn?

Evaluate trigonometric functions.
- of acute angles **(13.1)**
- of any angle **(13.3)**

Find the sides and angles of a triangle.
- solve right triangles **(13.1)**
- use the law of sines **(13.5)**
- use the law of cosines **(13.6)**

Measure angles using degree measure and radian measure. **(13.2)**

Find arc lengths and areas of sectors. **(13.2)**

Evaluate inverse trigonometric functions. **(13.4)**

Find the area of a triangle.
- using two sides and the included angle **(13.5)**

- using Heron's formula **(13.6)**

Use parametric equations to model linear or projectile motion. **(13.7)**

Use trigonometric and inverse trigonometric functions to solve real-life problems. **(13.1, 13.3–13.7)**

WHY did you learn it?

Find the altitude of a kite. **(p. 771)**
Find the horizontal distance traveled by a golf ball. **(p. 787)**

Find the length of a zip-line at a ropes course. **(p. 774)**
Find the distance between two buildings. **(p. 805)**
Find the angle at which two trapeze artists meet. **(p. 811)**

Find the angle generated by a figure skater performing a jump. **(p. 781)**

Find the area irrigated by a rotating sprinkler. **(p. 781)**

Find the angle at which to set the arm of a crane. **(p. 794)**

Find the amount of paint needed for the side of a house. **(p. 806)**
Find the area of the Dinosaur Diamond. **(p. 812)**

Model the path of a leaping dolphin. **(p. 818)**

Find distances for a marching band on a football field. **(p. 787)**

How does Chapter 13 fit into the BIGGER PICTURE of algebra?

Trigonometry is closely tied to both algebra and geometry. In this chapter you studied trigonometric functions of *angles*, defined by ratios of side lengths of right triangles.

In the next chapter you will study trigonometric functions of *real numbers*, used to model periodic behavior. You will see even more connections between trigonometry and algebra as you graph trigonometric functions in a coordinate plane.

STUDY STRATEGY

How did you draw diagrams?

Here is an example of a diagram drawn for Exercise 22 on page 810, following the **Study Strategy** on page 768.

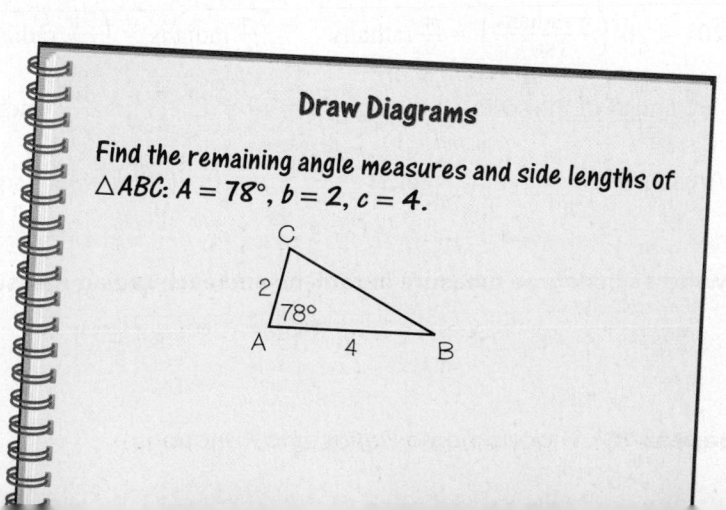

Draw Diagrams

Find the remaining angle measures and side lengths of $\triangle ABC$: $A = 78°$, $b = 2$, $c = 4$.

• sine, p. 769
• cosine, p. 769
• tangent, p. 769
• cosecant, p. 769
• secant, p. 769
• cotangent, p. 769
• solving a right triangle, p. 770

• angle of elevation, p. 771
• angle of depression, p. 771
• initial side of an angle, p. 776
• terminal side of an angle, p. 776
• standard position, p. 776
• coterminal angles, p. 777

• radian, p. 777
• sector, p. 779
• central angle, p. 779
• quadrantal angle, p. 785
• reference angle, p. 785
• inverse sine, p. 792

• inverse cosine, p. 792
• inverse tangent, p. 792
• law of sines, p. 799
• law of cosines, p. 807
• parametric equations, p. 813
• parameter, p. 813

13.1 RIGHT TRIANGLE TRIGONOMETRY

Examples on pp. 769–771

EXAMPLE You can evaluate the six trigonometric functions of θ for the triangle shown. First find the hypotenuse length: $\sqrt{5^2 + 12^2} = \sqrt{169} = 13$.

$$\sin \theta = \frac{\text{opp}}{\text{hyp}} = \frac{12}{13} \qquad \cos \theta = \frac{\text{adj}}{\text{hyp}} = \frac{5}{13} \qquad \tan \theta = \frac{\text{opp}}{\text{adj}} = \frac{12}{5}$$

$$\csc \theta = \frac{\text{hyp}}{\text{opp}} = \frac{13}{12} \qquad \sec \theta = \frac{\text{hyp}}{\text{adj}} = \frac{13}{5} \qquad \cot \theta = \frac{\text{adj}}{\text{opp}} = \frac{5}{12}$$

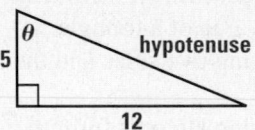

Evaluate the six trigonometric functions of θ.

1. 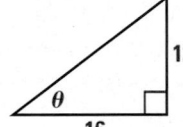   **2.** 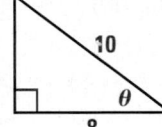   **3.** 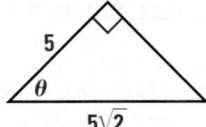   **4.**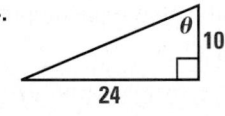

13.2 GENERAL ANGLES AND RADIAN MEASURE

Examples on pp. 776–779

EXAMPLES You can measure angles using degree measure or radian measure.

$$20° = 20°\left(\frac{\pi \text{ radians}}{180°}\right) = \frac{\pi}{9} \text{ radians} \qquad \frac{7\pi}{6} \text{ radians} = \left(\frac{7\pi}{6} \text{ radians}\right)\left(\frac{180°}{\pi \text{ radians}}\right) = 210°$$

Arc length of the sector at the right: $s = r\theta = 8\left(\frac{2\pi}{3}\right) = \frac{16\pi}{3}$ inches

Area of the sector at the right: $A = \frac{1}{2}r^2\theta = \frac{1}{2}(8^2)\left(\frac{2\pi}{3}\right) = \frac{64\pi}{3}$ square inches

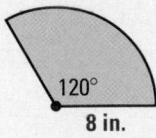

Rewrite each degree measure in radians and each radian measure in degrees.

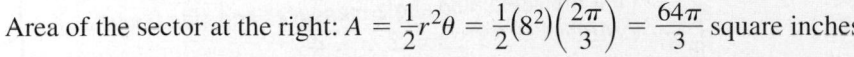

5. $30°$ **6.** $225°$ **7.** $-15°$ **8.** $\dfrac{3\pi}{4}$ **9.** $\dfrac{5\pi}{3}$ **10.** $\dfrac{\pi}{3}$

Find the arc length and area of a sector with the given radius *r* and central angle θ.

11. $r = 5$ ft, $\theta = \dfrac{\pi}{2}$ **12.** $r = 12$ in., $\theta = 25°$ **13.** $r = 16$ cm, $\theta = 210°$

13.3 **TRIGONOMETRIC FUNCTIONS OF ANY ANGLE**

Examples on pp. 784–787

EXAMPLE You can evaluate the six trigonometric functions of θ = 240° using a reference angle: $\theta' = \theta - 180° = 240° - 180° = 60°$.

$$\sin 240° = -\sin 60° = -\frac{\sqrt{3}}{2} \qquad \csc 240° = -\csc 60° = -\frac{2\sqrt{3}}{3}$$

$$\cos 240° = -\cos 60° = -\frac{1}{2} \qquad \sec 240° = -\sec 60° = -2$$

$$\tan 240° = +\tan 60° = \sqrt{3} \qquad \cot 240° = +\cot 60° = \frac{\sqrt{3}}{3}$$

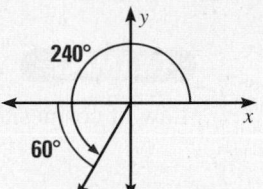

Evaluate the function without using a calculator.

14. $\tan \dfrac{11\pi}{4}$ **15.** $\cos \dfrac{11\pi}{6}$ **16.** $\sec 225°$ **17.** $\sin 390°$ **18.** $\csc(-120°)$

13.4 **INVERSE TRIGONOMETRIC FUNCTIONS**

Examples on pp. 792–794

EXAMPLE You can find an angle within a certain range that corresponds to a given value of a trigonometric function.

To find $\cos^{-1}\left(-\dfrac{\sqrt{2}}{2}\right)$, find θ so that $\cos\theta = -\dfrac{\sqrt{2}}{2}$ and $0° \leq \theta \leq 180°$.

So, $\theta = \cos^{-1}\left(-\dfrac{\sqrt{2}}{2}\right) = 135°\left(\text{or } \dfrac{3\pi}{4} \text{ radians}\right)$.

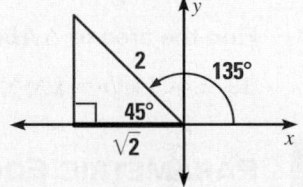

Evaluate the expression without using a calculator. Give your answer in both radians and degrees.

19. $\sin^{-1}\dfrac{\sqrt{2}}{2}$ **20.** $\tan^{-1}\dfrac{\sqrt{3}}{3}$ **21.** $\cos^{-1}0$ **22.** $\tan^{-1}(-1)$ **23.** $\cos^{-1}\left(-\dfrac{1}{2}\right)$

13.5 **THE LAW OF SINES**

Examples on pp. 799–802

EXAMPLE You can solve the triangle shown using the law of sines.

The measure of the third angle is: $B = 180° - 105° - 48° = 27°$.

$$\frac{a}{\sin 105°} = \frac{12}{\sin 27°} \qquad\qquad \frac{c}{\sin 48°} = \frac{12}{\sin 27°}$$

$$a = \frac{12 \sin 105°}{\sin 27°} \approx 25.5 \qquad\qquad c = \frac{12 \sin 48°}{\sin 27°} \approx 19.6$$

Area of this triangle $= \dfrac{1}{2}bc \sin A = \dfrac{1}{2}(12)(19.6) \sin 105° \approx 114$ square units

Solve △*ABC*. (*Hint:* Some of the "triangles" may have no solution and some may have two.)

24. $A = 45°, B = 60°, c = 44$ **25.** $B = 18°, b = 12, a = 19$ **26.** $C = 140°, c = 40, b = 20$

Find the area of the triangle with the given side lengths and included angle.

27. $C = 35°, b = 10, a = 22$ **28.** $A = 110°, b = 8, c = 7$ **29.** $B = 25°, a = 15, c = 31$

13.6 THE LAW OF COSINES

Examples on pp. 807–809

> **EXAMPLE** You can solve the triangle below using the law of cosines.
>
> Law of cosines: $b^2 = 35^2 + 37^2 - 2(35)(37) \cos 25° \approx 247$
>
> $$b \approx 15.7$$
>
> Law of sines: $\dfrac{\sin A}{35} \approx \dfrac{\sin 25°}{15.7}$, $\sin A \approx \dfrac{35 \sin 25°}{15.7}$, $A \approx 70.4°$
>
> $C \approx 180° - 25° - 70.4° = 84.6°$
>
> You can use Heron's formula to find the area of this triangle:
>
> $s \approx \dfrac{1}{2}(35 + 15.7 + 37) \approx 44$, so area $\approx \sqrt{44(44 - 35)(44 - 15.7)(44 - 37)} \approx 280$ square units

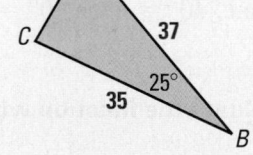

Solve △*ABC*.

30. $a = 25, b = 18, c = 28$ **31.** $a = 6, b = 11, c = 14$ **32.** $B = 30°, a = 80, c = 70$

Find the area of △*ABC* having the given side lengths.

33. $a = 11, b = 2, c = 12$ **34.** $a = 4, b = 24, c = 26$ **35.** $a = 15, b = 8, c = 21$

13.7 PARAMETRIC EQUATIONS AND PROJECTILE MOTION

Examples on pp. 813–815

> **EXAMPLE** You can graph the parametric equations $x = -3t$ and $y = -t$ for $0 \le t \le 3$. Make a table of values, plot the points (x, y), and connect the points.
>
> | *t* | 0 | 1 | 2 | 3 |
> |---|---|---|---|---|
> | *x* | 0 | −3 | −6 | −9 |
> | *y* | 0 | −1 | −2 | −3 |
>
>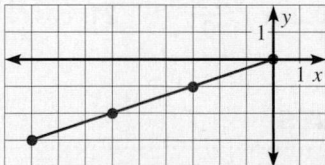
>
> To write an *xy*-equation for these parametric equations, solve the first equation for *t*:
>
> $t = -\dfrac{1}{3}x$. Substitute into the second equation: $y = \dfrac{1}{3}x$. The domain is $-9 \le x \le 0$.

Graph the parametric equations.

36. $x = 3t + 1$ and $y = 3t + 6$ for $0 \le t \le 5$ **37.** $x = 2t + 4$ and $y = -4t + 2$ for $2 \le t \le 5$

Write an *xy*-equation for the parametric equations. State the domain.

38. $x = 5t$ and $y = t + 7$ for $0 \le t \le 20$ **39.** $x = 2t - 3$ and $y = -4t + 5$ for $0 \le t \le 8$

APPLICATION: Ferris Wheels

The Texas State Fair is home to America's tallest Ferris wheel. The Ferris wheel takes riders to a height of 212 feet and has a diameter of about 203 feet. The maximum speed of the Ferris wheel is 1.5 rotations per minute.

Think & Discuss

The graph below shows a person's height (in feet) above the ground while riding the Ferris wheel at maximum speed. Use the graph to answer the questions below.

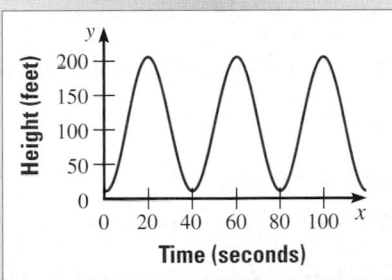

1. How many seconds does it take to reach the maximum height from the minimum height?

2. How long does it take to complete one revolution?

3. How would the graph change if the Ferris wheel rotated faster? if the Ferris wheel had a smaller diameter?

Learn More About It

In Example 5 on p. 842 you will use trigonometric functions to model a person's height above the ground while riding a Ferris wheel.

APPLICATION LINK Visit www.mcdougallittell.com for more information about Ferris wheels.

Study Guide

What's the chapter about?

Chapter 14 is about **trigonometry**. In Chapter 14 you'll learn

- how to graph trigonometric functions and transformations of trigonometric graphs.
- how to use trigonometric identities and solve trigonometric equations.
- how to write and use trigonometric models.

KEY VOCABULARY

▶ **Review**
- identity, p. 13
- domain, p. 67
- range, p. 67
- *x*-intercept, p. 84
- quadratic form, p. 346

- local maximum, p. 374
- local minimum, p. 374
- asymptote, p. 465
- sine, p. 769
- cosine, p. 769
- tangent, p. 769

▶ **New**
- periodic function, p. 831
- cycle, p. 831
- period, p. 831
- amplitude, p. 831
- trigonometric identities, p. 848

Are you ready for the chapter?

SKILL REVIEW Do these exercises to review key skills that you'll apply in this chapter. See the given **reference page** if there is something you don't understand.

▶ **Study Tip**
"Student Help" boxes throughout the chapter give you study tips and tell you where to look for extra help in this book and on the Internet.

Graph the function. (Review Example 1, p. 123; Example 2, p. 250; Example 2, p. 624)

1. $y = -|x + 2| - 4$ **2.** $y = 2(x + 2)^2 + 3$ **3.** $(x + 4)^2 + (y - 1)^2 = 9$

Solve the equation. (Review Example 5, p. 258; Example 1, p. 291)

4. $x^2 + 7x - 8 = 0$ **5.** $9x^2 - 25 = 0$ **6.** $3x^2 - x - 5 = 0$

Evaluate the function without using a calculator. (Review Example 4, p. 786)

7. $\sin 60°$ **8.** $\tan 30°$ **9.** $\cos \dfrac{\pi}{4}$ **10.** $\sin \pi$

Evaluate the expression without using a calculator. Give your answer in both radians and degrees. (Review Example 1, p. 793)

11. $\sin^{-1} \dfrac{\sqrt{2}}{2}$ **12.** $\cos^{-1} \dfrac{\sqrt{3}}{2}$ **13.** $\cos^{-1} 0$ **14.** $\tan^{-1} \left(-\sqrt{3}\right)$

Here's a study strategy!

Multiple Methods

There is often more than one way to do an exercise. Multiple methods can help in three situations. (1) If you get stuck using one method, try another. (2) Do an exercise more than one way to reinforce your understanding. (3) Check your work by using a different method.

14.1

Graphing Sine, Cosine, and Tangent Functions

What you should learn

GOAL 1 Graph sine and cosine functions, as applied in **Example 3**.

GOAL 2 Graph tangent functions.

Why you should learn it

▼ To model repeating **real-life** patterns, such as the vibrations of a tuning fork in **Ex. 52**.

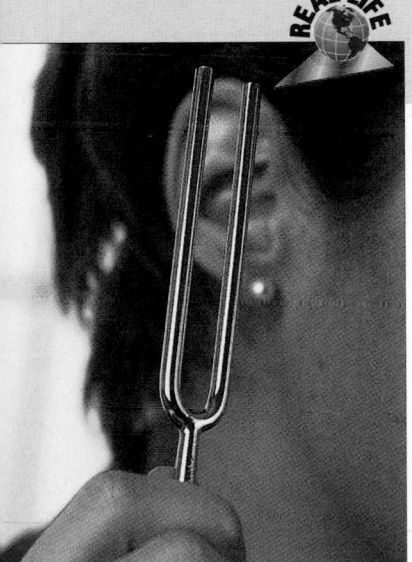

GOAL 1 GRAPHING SINE AND COSINE FUNCTIONS

In this lesson you will learn to graph functions of the form $y = a \sin bx$ and $y = a \cos bx$ where a and b are positive constants and x is in radian measure. The graphs of all sine and cosine functions are related to the graphs of

$$y = \sin x \qquad \text{and} \qquad y = \cos x$$

which are shown below.

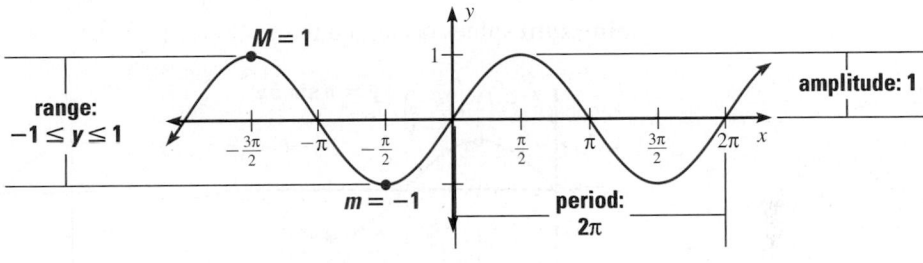

Graph of y = sin x

Graph of y = cos x

The functions $y = \sin x$ and $y = \cos x$ have the following characteristics.

1. The *domain* of each function is all real numbers.

2. The *range* of each function is $-1 \le y \le 1$.

3. Each function is **periodic**, which means that its graph has a repeating pattern that continues indefinitely. The shortest repeating portion is called a **cycle**. The horizontal length of each cycle is called the **period**. Each graph shown above has a period of 2π.

4. The maximum value of $y = \sin x$ is $M = 1$ and occurs when $x = \frac{\pi}{2} + 2n\pi$ where n is any integer. The maximum value of $y = \cos x$ is also $M = 1$ and occurs when $x = 2n\pi$ where n is any integer.

5. The minimum value of $y = \sin x$ is $m = -1$ and occurs when $x = \frac{3\pi}{2} + 2n\pi$ where n is any integer. The minimum value of $y = \cos x$ is also $m = -1$ and occurs when $x = (2n + 1)\pi$ where n is any integer.

6. The **amplitude** of each function's graph is $\frac{1}{2}(M - m) = 1$.

CHARACTERISTICS OF $Y = A$ SIN BX AND $Y = A$ COS BX

The amplitude and period of the graphs of $y = a \sin bx$ and $y = a \cos bx$, where a and b are nonzero real numbers, are as follows:

$$\text{amplitude} = |a| \qquad \text{and} \qquad \text{period} = \frac{2\pi}{|b|}$$

Examples The graph of $y = 2 \sin 4x$ has amplitude 2 and period $\frac{2\pi}{4} = \frac{\pi}{2}$.

The graph of $y = \frac{1}{3} \cos 2\pi x$ has amplitude $\frac{1}{3}$ and period $\frac{2\pi}{2\pi} = 1$.

For $a > 0$ and $b > 0$, the graphs of $y = a \sin bx$ and $y = a \cos bx$ each have five key x-values on the interval $0 \le x \le \frac{2\pi}{b}$: the x-values at which the **maximum** and **minimum** values occur and the **x-intercepts**.

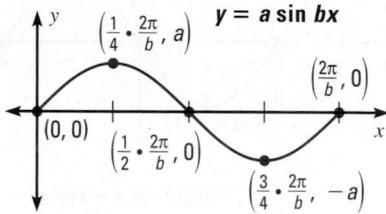
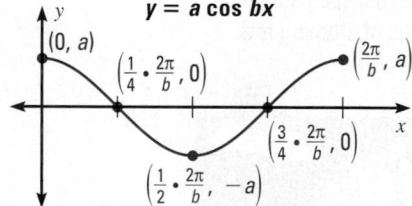

EXAMPLE 1 *Graphing Sine and Cosine Functions*

Graph the function.

   a. $y = 2 \sin x$ **b.** $y = \cos 2x$

SOLUTION

a. The amplitude is $a = 2$ and the period is $\frac{2\pi}{b} = \frac{2\pi}{1} = 2\pi$. The five key points are:

    Intercepts: $(0, 0)$; $(2\pi, 0)$;

$$\left(\frac{1}{2} \cdot 2\pi, 0\right) = (\pi, 0)$$

    Maximum: $\left(\frac{1}{4} \cdot 2\pi, 2\right) = \left(\frac{\pi}{2}, 2\right)$

    Minimum: $\left(\frac{3}{4} \cdot 2\pi, -2\right) = \left(\frac{3\pi}{2}, -2\right)$

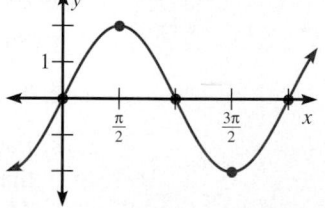

STUDENT HELP

Study Tip
In Example 1 notice how changes in *a* and *b* affect the graphs of $y = a \sin bx$ and $y = a \cos bx$. When the value of *a* increases, the amplitude is greater. When the value of *b* increases, the period is shorter.

b. The amplitude is $a = 1$ and the period is $\frac{2\pi}{b} = \frac{2\pi}{2} = \pi$. The five key points are:

    Intercepts: $\left(\frac{1}{4} \cdot \pi, 0\right) = \left(\frac{\pi}{4}, 0\right)$;

$$\left(\frac{3}{4} \cdot \pi, 0\right) = \left(\frac{3\pi}{4}, 0\right)$$

    Maximums: $(0, 1)$; $(\pi, 1)$

    Minimum: $\left(\frac{1}{2} \cdot \pi, -1\right) = \left(\frac{\pi}{2}, -1\right)$

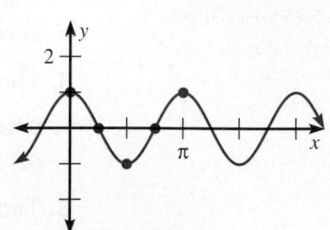

EXAMPLE 2 Graphing a Cosine Function

Graph $y = \frac{1}{3} \cos \pi x$.

SOLUTION

The amplitude is $a = \frac{1}{3}$ and the period is $\frac{2\pi}{b} = \frac{2\pi}{\pi} = 2$. The five key points are:

Intercepts: $\left(\frac{1}{4} \cdot 2, 0\right) = \left(\frac{1}{2}, 0\right)$;

$\left(\frac{3}{4} \cdot 2, 0\right) = \left(\frac{3}{2}, 0\right)$

Maximums: $\left(0, \frac{1}{3}\right)$; $\left(2, \frac{1}{3}\right)$

Minimum: $\left(\frac{1}{2} \cdot 2, -\frac{1}{3}\right) = \left(1, -\frac{1}{3}\right)$

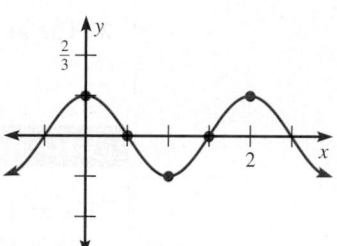

. . . .

The periodic nature of trigonometric functions is useful for modeling *oscillating* motions or repeating patterns that occur in real life. Some examples are sound waves, the motion of a pendulum or a spring, and seasons of the year. In such applications, the reciprocal of the period is called the **frequency.** The frequency gives the number of cycles per unit of time.

EXAMPLE 3 Modeling with a Sine Function

MUSIC When you strike a tuning fork, the vibrations cause changes in the pressure of the surrounding air. A middle-A tuning fork vibrates with frequency $f = 440$ hertz (cycles per second). You strike a middle-A tuning fork with a force that produces a maximum pressure of 0.1 pascal.

a. Write a sine model that gives the pressure P as a function of time t (in seconds).

b. Graph the model.

SOLUTION

a. In the model $P = a \sin bt$, the maximum pressure P is 0.1, so $a = 0.1$. You can use the frequency to find the value of b.

$$\text{frequency} = \frac{1}{\text{period}} \implies 440 = \frac{b}{2\pi}$$
$$880\pi = b$$

▶ The pressure as a function of time is given by $P = 0.1 \sin 880\pi t$.

b. The amplitude is $a = 0.1$ and the period is $\frac{1}{f} = \frac{1}{440}$. The five key points are:

Intercepts: $(0, 0)$; $\left(\frac{1}{440}, 0\right)$;

$\left(\frac{1}{2} \cdot \frac{1}{440}, 0\right) = \left(\frac{1}{880}, 0\right)$

Maximum: $\left(\frac{1}{4} \cdot \frac{1}{440}, 0.1\right) = \left(\frac{1}{1760}, 0.1\right)$

Minimum: $\left(\frac{3}{4} \cdot \frac{1}{440}, -0.1\right) = \left(\frac{3}{1760}, -0.1\right)$

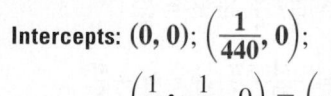

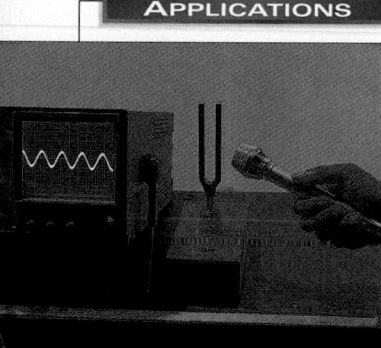

GOAL 2 GRAPHING TANGENT FUNCTIONS

The graph of $y = \tan x$ has the following characteristics.

1. The domain is all real numbers except odd multiples of $\frac{\pi}{2}$. At odd multiples of $\frac{\pi}{2}$, the graph has vertical asymptotes.

2. The range is all real numbers.

3. The graph has a period of π.

CHARACTERISTICS OF Y = A TAN BX

If a and b are nonzero real numbers, the graph of $y = a \tan bx$ has these characteristics:

- The period is $\dfrac{\pi}{|b|}$.

- There are vertical asymptotes at odd multiples of $\dfrac{\pi}{2|b|}$.

Example   The graph of $y = 5 \tan 3x$ has period $\frac{\pi}{3}$ and asymptotes at $x = (2n + 1)\dfrac{\pi}{2(3)} = \dfrac{\pi}{6} + \dfrac{n\pi}{3}$ where n is any integer.

The graph at the right shows five key x-values that can help you sketch the graph of $y = a \tan bx$ for $a > 0$ and $b > 0$. These are the **x-intercept**, the x-values where the **asymptotes** occur, and the x-values **halfway between** the x-intercept and the asymptotes. At each halfway point, the function's value is either a or $-a$.

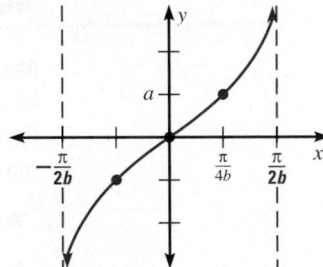

EXAMPLE 4   *Graphing a Tangent Function*

Graph $y = \frac{3}{2} \tan 4x$.

SOLUTION

The period is $\dfrac{\pi}{b} = \dfrac{\pi}{4}$.

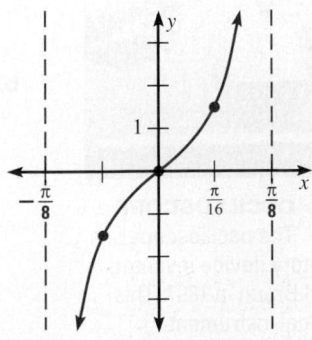

Intercept:	$(0, 0)$
Asymptotes:	$x = \frac{1}{2} \cdot \frac{\pi}{4}$, or $x = \frac{\pi}{8}$;
	$x = -\frac{1}{2} \cdot \frac{\pi}{4}$, or $x = -\frac{\pi}{8}$
Halfway points:	$\left(\frac{1}{4} \cdot \frac{\pi}{4}, \frac{3}{2}\right) = \left(\frac{\pi}{16}, \frac{3}{2}\right)$;
	$\left(-\frac{1}{4} \cdot \frac{\pi}{4}, -\frac{3}{2}\right) = \left(-\frac{\pi}{16}, -\frac{3}{2}\right)$

GUIDED PRACTICE

Vocabulary Check ✓

1. Define the terms cycle and period.

Concept Check ✓

2. What are the domain and range of $y = a \sin bx$, $y = a \cos bx$, and $y = a \tan bx$?

3. Consider the two functions $y = 4 \sin \frac{x}{3}$ and $y = \frac{1}{3} \sin 4x$. Which function has the greater amplitude? Which function has the longer period?

Skill Check ✓

Find the amplitude and period of the function.

4. $y = 6 \sin x$

5. $y = 3 \cos \pi x$

6. $y = \frac{1}{4} \cos 3x$

7. $y = \frac{2}{3} \sin \frac{\pi}{3}x$

8. $y = 5 \sin 3\pi x$

9. $y = \cos \frac{x}{2}$

Graph the function.

10. $y = 3 \sin x$

11. $y = \cos 4x$

12. $y = \tan 3x$

13. $y = \frac{1}{4} \sin \pi x$

14. $y = 5 \cos \frac{2}{3}x$

15. $y = 2 \tan 4x$

16. 🌐 **PENDULUMS** The motion of a certain pendulum can be modeled by the function

$$d = 4 \cos 8\pi t$$

where d is the pendulum's horizontal displacement (in inches) relative to its position at rest and t is the time (in seconds). Graph the function. How far horizontally does the pendulum travel from its original position?

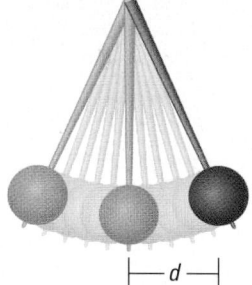

PRACTICE AND APPLICATIONS

STUDENT HELP

▸ **Extra Practice**
to help you master
skills is on p. 959.

MATCHING GRAPHS Match the function with its graph.

17. $y = 2 \sin \frac{1}{2}x$

18. $y = 2 \cos \frac{1}{2}x$

19. $y = 2 \sin 2x$

20. $y = 2 \tan \frac{1}{2}x$

21. $y = 2 \cos 2x$

22. $y = 2 \tan 2x$

A.

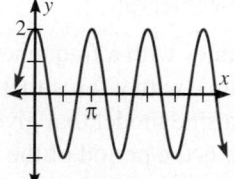

B.

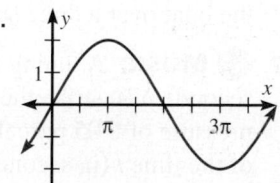

C.

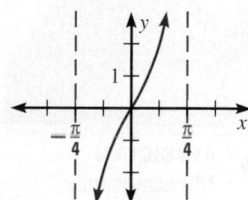

STUDENT HELP

▸ **HOMEWORK HELP**
Examples 1, 2: Exs. 17–49
Example 3: Exs. 51–55
Example 4: Exs. 17–22,
        32–43

D.

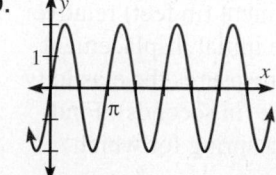

E.

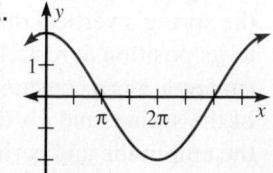

F.

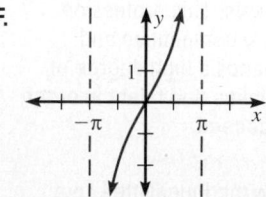

ANALYZING FUNCTIONS In Exercises 23–31, find the amplitude and period of the graph of the function.

23.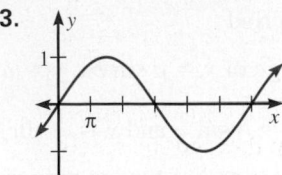

24.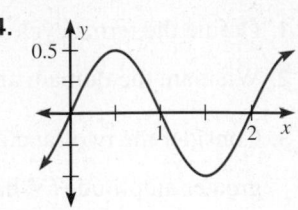

25.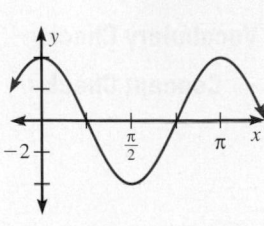

26. $y = \frac{1}{2} \cos \pi x$

27. $y = \sin 2x$

28. $y = 3 \cos \frac{1}{4}x$

29. $y = 5 \cos \frac{1}{2}x$

30. $y = 2 \sin \frac{1}{2}\pi x$

31. $y = \frac{1}{3} \sin 4\pi x$

GRAPHING Draw one cycle of the function's graph.

32. $y = \sin \frac{1}{4}x$

33. $y = \cos \frac{1}{5}x$

34. $y = \frac{1}{4} \tan \pi x$

35. $y = \frac{1}{4} \sin x$

36. $y = 4 \cos x$

37. $y = 4 \tan 2x$

38. $y = 3 \cos 2x$

39. $y = 8 \sin x$

40. $y = 2 \tan \frac{1}{3}x$

41. $y = \frac{1}{2} \sin \frac{1}{4}\pi x$

42. $y = \tan 4\pi x$

43. $y = 2 \cos 6\pi x$

WRITING EQUATIONS Write an equation of the form $y = a \sin bx$, where $a > 0$ and $b > 0$, so that the graph has the given amplitude and period.

44. Amplitude: 1
    Period: 5

45. Amplitude: 10
    Period: 4

46. Amplitude: 2
    Period: 2π

47. Amplitude: $\frac{1}{2}$
    Period: 3π

48. Amplitude: 4
    Period: $\frac{\pi}{6}$

49. Amplitude: 3
    Period: $\frac{1}{2}$

50. **LOGICAL REASONING** Use the fact that the frequency of a periodic function's graph is the reciprocal of the period to show that an oscillating motion with maximum displacement a and frequency f can be modeled by $y = a \sin 2\pi f t$ or $y = a \cos 2\pi f t$.

51. **BOATING** The displacement d (in feet) of a boat's water line above sea level as it moves over waves can be modeled by the function

$$d = 2 \sin 2\pi t$$

where t is the time (in seconds). Graph the height of the boat over a three second time interval.

52. **MUSIC** A tuning fork vibrates with a frequency of 220 hertz (cycles per second). You strike the tuning fork with a force that produces a maximum pressure of 0.05 pascal. Write a sine model that gives the pressure P as a function of the time t (in seconds). What is the period of the sound wave?

53. **SPRING MOTION** The motion of a simple spring can be modeled by $y = A \cos kt$ where y is the spring's vertical displacement (in feet) relative to its position at rest, A is the initial displacement (in feet), k is a constant that measures the elasticity of the spring, and t is the time (in seconds). Find the amplitude and period of a spring for which $A = 0.5$ foot and $k = 6$.

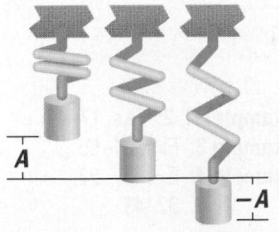

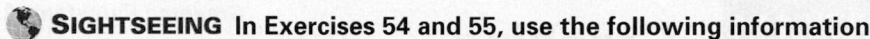

SIGHTSEEING In Exercises 54 and 55, use the following information.

Suppose you are standing 100 feet away from the base of the Statue of Liberty with a video camera. As you videotape the statue, you pan up the side of the statue at 5° per second.

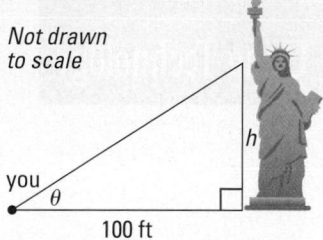

Not drawn to scale

54. Write and graph an equation that gives the height h of the part of the statue seen through the video camera as a function of the time t.

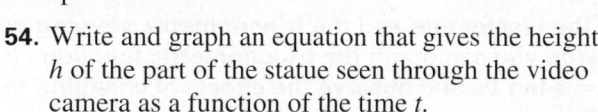

you θ

100 ft

55. Find the change in height from $t = 0$ to $t = 1$, from $t = 1$ to $t = 2$, and from $t = 2$ to $t = 3$. Briefly explain what happens to h as t increases.

Test Preparation

56. **MULTIPLE CHOICE** Which function represents the graph shown?

Ⓐ $y = \frac{1}{2}\tan 5x$ Ⓑ $y = 5\tan \frac{1}{2}x$

Ⓒ $y = \tan 5x$ Ⓓ $y = 5\tan 2x$

Ⓔ $y = 5\tan \frac{1}{8}x$

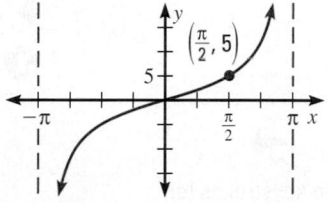

$\left(\frac{\pi}{2}, 5\right)$

57. **MULTIPLE CHOICE** Which of the following is an x-intercept of the graph of $y = \frac{1}{3}\sin \frac{\pi}{4}x$?

Ⓐ 4   Ⓑ 2   Ⓒ -6 Ⓓ 1   Ⓔ 4π

★ Challenge

SKETCHING GRAPHS Sketch the graph of the function by plotting points. Then state the function's domain, range, and period.

58. $y = \csc x$ 59. $y = \sec x$ 60. $y = \cot x$

MIXED REVIEW

GRAPHING Graph the quadratic function. Label the vertex and axis of symmetry. (Review 5.1 for 14.2)

61. $y = 2(x - 5)^2 + 4$ 62. $y = -(x - 3)^2 - 7$ 63. $y = 4(x + 2)^2 - 1$

64. $y = -3(x + 1)^2 + 6$ 65. $y = \frac{3}{4}(x - 1)^2 - 2$ 66. $y = 10(x + 4)^2 + 3$

CALCULATING PROBABILITY Find the probability of drawing the given numbers if the integers 1 through 30 are placed in a hat and drawn randomly without replacement. (Review 12.5)

67. an even number, then an odd number   68. the number 30, then an odd number

69. a multiple of 4, then an odd number   70. the number 19, then the number 20

FINDING REFERENCE ANGLES Sketch the angle. Then find its reference angle. (Review 13.3)

71. $220°$ 72. $-155°$ 73. $280°$ 74. $-510°$

75. $\frac{35\pi}{3}$ 76. $\frac{21\pi}{4}$ 77. $-\frac{17\pi}{6}$ 78. $-\frac{5\pi}{8}$

79. **PERSONAL FINANCE** You deposit $1000 in an account that pays 1.5% annual interest compounded continuously. How long will it take for the balance to double? (Review 8.6)

⊙ ACTIVITY 14.1

Using Technology

Graphing Trigonometric Functions

Using the *List* feature and the trigonometric viewing window of a graphing calculator, you can graph the trigonometric functions $y = a \sin bx$, $y = a \cos bx$, and $y = a \tan bx$ and observe the effects of changing the values of a and b.

▶ **EXAMPLE**

Graph $y = a \sin x$ for $a = 1, 2,$ and 4.

▶ **SOLUTION**

❶ Use the graphing calculator's *List* feature to enter the function as $y_1 = \{1, 2, 4\} \sin x$. This represents the three functions $y = \sin x$, $y = 2 \sin x$, and $y = 4 \sin x$.

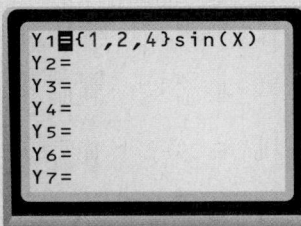

❷ Select the trigonometric viewing window. In this window, each tick mark on the x-axis represents $\dfrac{\pi}{2}$ and each tick mark on the y-axis represents 1.

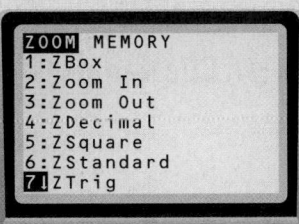

❸ If the functions you graph have amplitudes much greater than 1 or periods longer than 4π, you may need to change the parameters of the viewing window. Then you can use the *Maximum*, *Minimum*, and *Zero* features to find the amplitude and the period of each function.

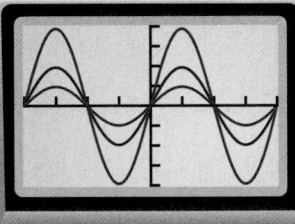

▶ **EXERCISES**

Use a graphing calculator's *List* feature to graph the functions for the given values of *a* in the same trigonometric viewing window. Find the amplitude and the period of each function's graph.

1. $y = a \sin x$ for $a = \dfrac{1}{3}, 3, 9$

2. $y = a \sin x$ for $a = 10, 20, 40$

3. $y = a \cos x$ for $a = \dfrac{1}{2}, 1, 2$

4. $y = a \cos x$ for $a = 1, 2, 4$

Use a graphing calculator's *List* feature to graph the functions for the given values of *b* in the same trigonometric viewing window. Find the amplitude and the period of each function's graph.

5. $y = \sin bx$ for $b = 1, 2, 4$

6. $y = \sin bx$ for $b = \dfrac{1}{3}, 1, 3$

7. $y = \cos bx$ for $b = \dfrac{1}{2}, 1, 2$

8. $y = \cos bx$ for $b = \dfrac{1}{3}, 1, 3$

Translating and Reflecting Trigonometric Graphs

GROUP ACTIVITY
Work with a partner.

MATERIALS
graphing calculator

► **QUESTION** How can you graph reflections and horizontal and vertical translations of graphs of trigonometric functions?

► **EXPLORING THE CONCEPT**

1 Use a graphing calculator to graph each pair of functions in the same viewing window. How are the graphs geometrically related?

a. $y = \cos x$

$y = -\cos x$

b. $y = 2 \sin x$

$y = -2 \sin x$

c. $y = \frac{3}{5} \sin 3x$

$y = -\frac{3}{5} \sin 3x$

2 Use a graphing calculator to graph each pair of functions in the same viewing window. How are the graphs geometrically related?

a. $y = \cos x$

$y = \cos \left(x - \frac{\pi}{2} \right)$

b. $y = 2 \sin x$

$y = 2 \sin \left(x + \frac{\pi}{2} \right)$

c. $y = \sin 3x$

$y = \sin 3(x + \pi)$

3 Use a graphing calculator to graph each pair of functions in the same viewing window. How are the graphs geometrically related?

a. $y = \cos x$

$y = \cos x + 1$

b. $y = 2 \sin x$

$y = 2 \sin x - 1$

c. $y = \frac{1}{4} \sin 3x$

$y = \frac{1}{4} \sin 3x - 2$

► **DRAWING CONCLUSIONS**

1. Predict what the graph of each function looks like by making a sketch. Check your prediction by graphing the function on a graphing calculator.

a. $y = -3 \cos x$

b. $y = \sin \left(x + \frac{3\pi}{4} \right)$

c. $y = \sin x - 4$

2. Predict what the graph of each function looks like by making a sketch. Check your prediction by graphing the function on a graphing calculator.

a. $y = -\frac{1}{2} \cos x - 2$

b. $y = -3 \cos (x + \pi)$

c. $y = 2 \sin (x - \pi) + 3$

d. $y = -4 \sin \left(x - \frac{\pi}{4} \right) - 6$

3. CRITICAL THINKING Use the following phrases to describe how the graph of each function in parts (a)–(d) is related to the graph of $y = \sin x$.

• shifted up 1 unit

• shifted down 1 unit

• shifted left 1 unit

• shifted right 1 unit

• reflected in a horizontal line

a. $y = \sin (x - 1) + 1$

b. $y = -\sin (x - 1) - 1$

c. $y = -\sin (x + 1) + 1$

d. $y = \sin (x + 1) - 1$

Translations and Reflections of Trigonometric Graphs

What you should learn

GOAL 1 Graph translations and reflections of sine and cosine graphs.

GOAL 2 Graph translations and reflections of tangent graphs, as applied in **Ex. 61**.

Why you should learn it

▼ To model **real-life** quantities, such as the height above the ground of a person rappelling down a cliff in **Example 7**.

GOAL 1 GRAPHING SINE AND COSINE FUNCTIONS

In previous chapters you learned that the graph of $y = a \cdot f(x - h) + k$ is related to the graph of $y = |a| \cdot f(x)$ by horizontal and vertical translations and by a reflection when a is negative. This also applies to sine, cosine, and tangent functions.

TRANSFORMATIONS OF SINE AND COSINE GRAPHS

To obtain the graph of

$$y = a \sin b(x - h) + k \qquad \text{or} \qquad y = a \cos b(x - h) + k,$$

transform the graph of $y = |a| \sin bx$ or $y = |a| \cos bx$ as follows.

VERTICAL SHIFT Shift the graph k units vertically.

HORIZONTAL SHIFT Shift the graph h units horizontally.

REFLECTION If $a < 0$, reflect the graph in the line $y = k$ after any vertical and horizontal shifts have been performed.

EXAMPLE 1 *Graphing a Vertical Translation*

Graph $y = -2 + 3 \sin 4x$.

SOLUTION

Because the graph is a transformation of the graph of $y = 3 \sin 4x$, the amplitude is **3** and the period is $\frac{2\pi}{4} = \frac{\pi}{2}$. By comparing the given equation to the general equation $y = a \sin b(x - h) + k$, you can see that $h = 0$, $k = -2$, and $a > 0$. Therefore, translate the graph of $y = 3 \sin 4x$ **down 2 units**.

The graph oscillates **3 units** up and down from its center line $y = -2$. Therefore, the maximum value of the function is $-2 + 3 = 1$ and the minimum value of the function is $-2 - 3 = -5$.

The five key points are:

On $y = k$: $(0, -2)$; $\left(\frac{\pi}{4}, -2\right)$; $\left(\frac{\pi}{2}, -2\right)$

Maximum: $\left(\frac{\pi}{8}, 1\right)$

Minimum: $\left(\frac{3\pi}{8}, -5\right)$

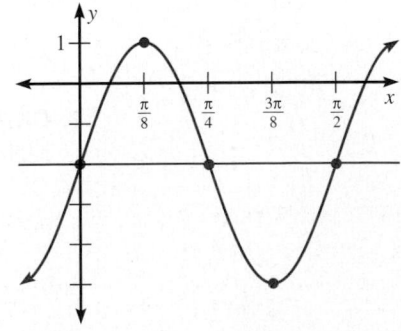

✓ **CHECK** You can check your graph with a graphing calculator. Use the *Maximum*, *Minimum*, and *Intersect* features to check the key points.

EXAMPLE 2 *Graphing a Horizontal Translation*

Graph $y = 2 \cos \frac{2}{3}\left(x - \frac{\pi}{4}\right)$.

SOLUTION

Because the graph is a transformation of the graph of $y = 2 \cos \frac{2}{3}x$, the amplitude is 2 and the period is $\frac{2\pi}{\frac{2}{3}} = 3\pi$. By comparing the given equation to the general equation $y = a \cos b(x - h) + k$, you can see that $h = \frac{\pi}{4}$, $k = 0$, and $a > 0$. Therefore, translate the graph of $y = 2 \cos \frac{2}{3}x$ **right** $\frac{\pi}{4}$ **unit**. (Notice that the maximum occurs $\frac{\pi}{4}$ unit to the right of the *y*-axis.)

The five key points are:

On *y* = *k*: $\left(\left(\frac{1}{4} \cdot 3\pi\right) + \frac{\pi}{4}, 0\right) = (\pi, 0);$

$\left(\left(\frac{3}{4} \cdot 3\pi\right) + \frac{\pi}{4}, 0\right) = \left(\frac{5\pi}{2}, 0\right)$

Maximums: $\left(0 + \frac{\pi}{4}, 2\right) = \left(\frac{\pi}{4}, 2\right);$

$\left(3\pi + \frac{\pi}{4}, 2\right) = \left(\frac{13\pi}{4}, 2\right)$

Minimum: $\left(\left(\frac{1}{2} \cdot 3\pi\right) + \frac{\pi}{4}, -2\right) = \left(\frac{7\pi}{4}, -2\right)$

EXAMPLE 3 *Graphing a Reflection*

Graph $y = -3 \sin x$.

SOLUTION

Because the graph is a reflection of the graph of $y = 3 \sin x$, the amplitude is 3 and the period is 2π. When you plot the five key points on the graph, note that the intercepts are the same as they are for the graph of $y = 3 \sin x$. However, when the graph is reflected in the *x*-axis, the **maximum** becomes a **minimum** and the **minimum** becomes a **maximum**.

The five key points are:

On *y* = *k*: $(0, 0); (2\pi, 0);$

$\left(\frac{1}{2} \cdot 2\pi, 0\right) = (\pi, 0)$

Minimum: $\left(\frac{1}{4} \cdot 2\pi, -3\right) = \left(\frac{\pi}{2}, -3\right)$

Maximum: $\left(\frac{3}{4} \cdot 2\pi, 3\right) = \left(\frac{3\pi}{2}, 3\right)$

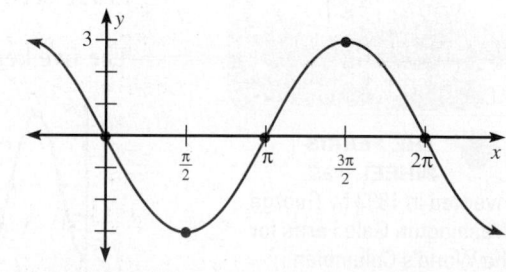

· · · · · · · · · ·

The next example shows how to graph a function when multiple transformations are involved.

EXAMPLE 4 *Combining a Translation and a Reflection*

Graph $y = -\frac{1}{2} \cos (2x + 3\pi) + 1$.

SOLUTION

Begin by rewriting the function in the form $y = a \cos b(x - h) + k$:

$$y = -\frac{1}{2} \cos (2x + 3\pi) + 1 = -\frac{1}{2} \cos 2\left[x - \left(-\frac{3\pi}{2}\right)\right] + 1$$

The amplitude is $\frac{1}{2}$ and the period is $\frac{2\pi}{2} = \pi$. Since $h = -\frac{3\pi}{2}$, $k = 1$, and $a < 0$, the

graph of $y = \frac{1}{2} \cos 2x$ is shifted **left $\frac{3\pi}{2}$ units** and **up 1 unit**, and then reflected in the

line $y = 1$. The five key points are:

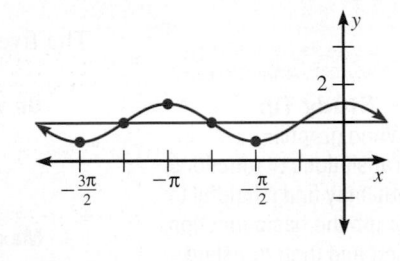

On y = k: $\left(\left(\frac{1}{4} \cdot \pi\right) - \frac{3\pi}{2}, 1\right) = \left(-\frac{5\pi}{4}, 1\right);$
$\left(\left(\frac{3}{4} \cdot \pi\right) - \frac{3\pi}{2}, 1\right) = \left(-\frac{3\pi}{4}, 1\right)$

Minimums: $\left(0 - \frac{3\pi}{2}, 1 - \frac{1}{2}\right) = \left(-\frac{3\pi}{2}, \frac{1}{2}\right);$
$\left(\pi - \frac{3\pi}{2}, 1 - \frac{1}{2}\right) = \left(-\frac{\pi}{2}, \frac{1}{2}\right)$

Maximum: $\left(\left(\frac{1}{2} \cdot \pi\right) - \frac{3\pi}{2}, 1 + \frac{1}{2}\right) = \left(-\pi, \frac{3}{2}\right)$

EXAMPLE 5 *Modeling Circular Motion*

FERRIS WHEEL You are riding a Ferris wheel. Your height h (in feet) above the ground at any time t (in seconds) can be modeled by the following equation:

$$h = 25 \sin \frac{\pi}{15}\left(t - 7.5\right) + 30$$

The Ferris wheel turns for 135 seconds before it stops to let the first passengers off.

a. Graph your height above the ground as a function of time.

b. What are your minimum and maximum heights above the ground?

SOLUTION

a. The amplitude is 25 and the period is $\frac{2\pi}{\frac{\pi}{15}} = 30$. The wheel turns $\frac{135}{30} = 4.5$ times

in 135 seconds, so the graph shows 4.5 cycles.

The five key points are (7.5, 30), (15, 55), (22.5, 30), (30, 5), and (37.5, 30).

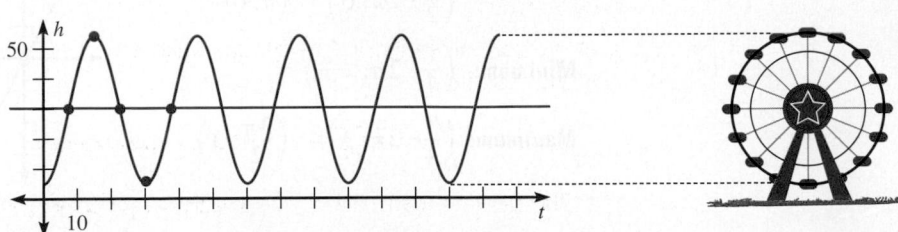

b. Since the amplitude is **25** and the graph is shifted **up 30 units**, the maximum height is **30 + 25** = 55 feet and the minimum height is **30 − 25** = 5 feet.

GOAL 2 GRAPHING TANGENT FUNCTIONS

Graphing tangent functions using translations and reflections is similar to graphing sine and cosine functions.

TRANSFORMATIONS OF TANGENT GRAPHS

To obtain the graph of $y = a \tan b(x - h) + k$, transform the graph of $y = |a| \tan bx$ as follows.

- Shift the graph k units vertically and h units horizontally.
- Then, if $a < 0$, reflect the graph in the line $y = k$.

EXAMPLE 6 *Combining a Translation and a Reflection*

Graph $y = -2 \tan\left(x + \dfrac{\pi}{4}\right)$.

SOLUTION

The graph is a transformation of the graph of $y = 2 \tan x$, so the period is π. By comparing the given equation to $y = a \tan b(x - h) + k$, you can see that $h = -\dfrac{\pi}{4}$, $k = 0$, and $a < 0$. Therefore, translate the graph of $y = 2 \tan x$ left $\dfrac{\pi}{4}$ unit and then reflect it in the x-axis.

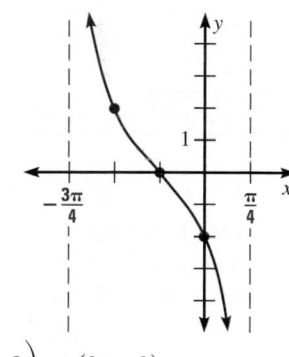

Asymptotes: $x = -\dfrac{\pi}{2 \cdot 1} - \dfrac{\pi}{4} = -\dfrac{3\pi}{4}$; $x = \dfrac{\pi}{2 \cdot 1} - \dfrac{\pi}{4} = \dfrac{\pi}{4}$

On $y = k$: $(h, k) = \left(-\dfrac{\pi}{4}, 0\right)$

Halfway points: $\left(-\dfrac{\pi}{4 \cdot 1} - \dfrac{\pi}{4}, 2\right) = \left(-\dfrac{\pi}{2}, 2\right)$; $\left(\dfrac{\pi}{4 \cdot 1} - \dfrac{\pi}{4}, -2\right) = (0, -2)$

Rappelling

EXAMPLE 7 *Modeling with a Tangent Function*

You are standing 200 feet from the base of a 180 foot cliff. Your friend is rappelling down the cliff. Write and graph a model for your friend's distance d from the top as a function of her angle of elevation θ.

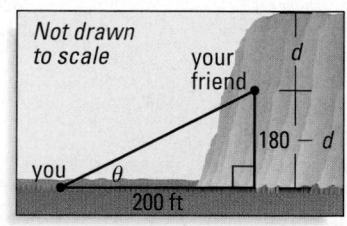

SOLUTION

Use the tangent function to write an equation relating d and θ.

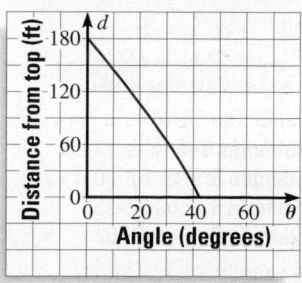

$\tan \theta = \dfrac{\text{opp}}{\text{adj}} = \dfrac{180 - d}{200}$ **Definition of tangent**

$200 \tan \theta = 180 - d$ **Multiply each side by 200.**

$d = -200 \tan \theta + 180$ **Solve for d.**

14.2 *Translations and Reflections of Trigonometric Graphs*   **843**

GUIDED PRACTICE

Vocabulary Check ✓

1. Complete this statement: A(n) _?_ shifts a graph horizontally or vertically.

Concept Check ✓

2. How is the graph of $y = -2 \cos 3x$ related to the graph of $y = 2 \cos 3x$?

3. How is the graph of $y = \tan 2(x - \pi)$ related to the graph of $y = \tan 2x$?

Skill Check ✓

State whether the graph of the function is a *vertical shift*, a *horizontal shift*, and/or a *reflection* of the graph of $y = 4 \cos 2x$.

4. $y = 3 + 4 \cos 2x$

5. $y = 4 \cos (2x + 1)$

6. $y = -4 \cos 2x$

7. $y = 4 \cos 2(x + 1)$

8. $y = 4 \cos (2x - 1) + 3$

9. $y = -3 - 4 \cos 2x$

Graph the function.

10. $y = 3 \sin (x + \pi)$

11. $y = -2 \cos x + 1$

12. $y = 2 \tan (x - \pi)$

13. $y = -\sin \pi(x - 2) + 3$

14. $y = 4 \cos 2(x - \pi) + 1$

15. $y = 5 - \tan 2(x - \pi)$

16. 🧗 **RAPPELLING** Look back at Example 7. Suppose the cliff is 250 feet high and you are 150 feet from the base. Write and graph an equation that gives your friend's distance from the top as a function of her angle of elevation.

PRACTICE AND APPLICATIONS

STUDENT HELP

➤ **Extra Practice**
to help you master
skills is on p. 959.

TRANSFORMING GRAPHS Describe how the graph of $y = \sin x$ or $y = \cos x$ can be transformed to produce the graph of the given function.

17. $y = 2 + \sin x$

18. $y = 5 - \cos x$

19. $y = -2 + \cos x$

20. $y = \cos \left(x + \dfrac{\pi}{2}\right)$

21. $y = -\sin (x + \pi)$

22. $y = \sin \left(x - \dfrac{\pi}{2}\right)$

23. $y = 5 - \cos \left(x - \dfrac{\pi}{4}\right)$

24. $y = -2 - \sin (x - \pi)$

25. $y = 3 + \cos \left(x + \dfrac{3\pi}{4}\right)$

MATCHING Match the function with its graph.

26. $y = -2 + \sin (2x + \pi)$

27. $y = -\sin (x + \pi)$

28. $y = -3 + \cos x$

29. $y = \cos \left(x + \dfrac{\pi}{2}\right)$

30. $y = 1 + \sin \dfrac{1}{2}x$

31. $y = 1 + 2 \cos \left(\dfrac{1}{2}x + \dfrac{\pi}{2}\right)$

A.
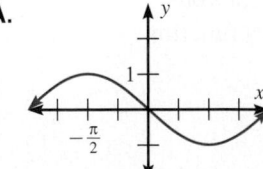

B.
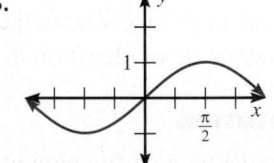

C.
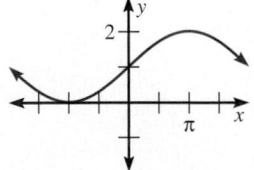

STUDENT HELP

➤ **HOMEWORK HELP**
Examples 1–4: Exs. 17–55
Example 5: Exs. 57–60
Example 6: Exs. 32–55
Example 7: Exs. 61, 62

D.
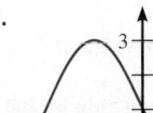

E.
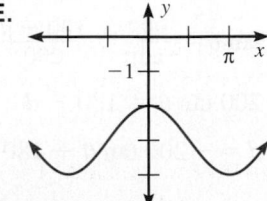

F.
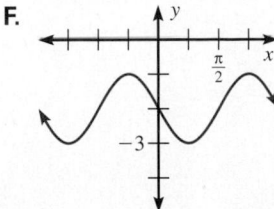

GRAPHING Graph the function.

32. $y = 2 + \sin\frac{1}{2}x$ **33.** $y = \cos\left(x - \frac{\pi}{2}\right)$ **34.** $y = -4\sin\frac{1}{4}x$

35. $y = 1 + \cos(x + \pi)$ **36.** $y = -1 + \cos(x - \pi)$ **37.** $y = 2 + 3\sin(4x + \pi)$

38. $y = -4 + \sin 2x$ **39.** $y = 1 + 5\cos(x - \pi)$ **40.** $y = 2 - \sin x$

41. $y = \sin\left(x - \frac{3\pi}{2}\right) - 2$ **42.** $y = \cos\left(2x + \frac{\pi}{2}\right) - 2$ **43.** $y = 6 + 4\cos\left(x - \frac{\pi}{2}\right)$

44. $y = \frac{1}{2}\tan x$ **45.** $y = 2 - \tan\left(x + \frac{\pi}{2}\right)$ **46.** $y = 2\tan\left(x - \frac{\pi}{2}\right)$

47. $y = -1 + \tan 2x$ **48.** $y = 3 + \tan(x - \pi)$ **49.** $y = 1 + \frac{1}{2}\tan\left(2x - \frac{\pi}{4}\right)$

WRITING EQUATIONS In Exercises 50–55, write an equation of the graph described.

50. The graph of $y = \sin 2\pi x$ translated down 5 units and right 2 units

51. The graph of $y = 3\cos x$ translated up 3 units and left π units

52. The graph of $y = 5\tan 4x$ translated left $\frac{\pi}{4}$ unit and then reflected in the *x*-axis

53. The graph of $y = \frac{1}{3}\sin 6x$ translated down 1 unit and then reflected in the line $y = -1$

54. The graph of $y = \frac{1}{2}\cos \pi x$ translated down $\frac{3}{2}$ units and left 1 unit, and then reflected in the line $y = -\frac{3}{2}$

55. The graph of $y = 4\tan\frac{\pi}{2}x$ translated up 6 units and right $\frac{1}{2}$ unit, and then reflected in the line $y = 6$

56. CRITICAL THINKING Explain how the graph of $y = \sin x$ can be translated to become the graph of $y = \cos x$.

57. HEIGHT OF A SWING A swing's height h (in feet) above the ground is
$$h = -8\cos\theta + 10$$
where the pivot is 10 feet above the ground, the rope is 8 feet long, and θ is the angle that the rope makes with the vertical. Graph the function. What is the height of the swing when θ is 45°?

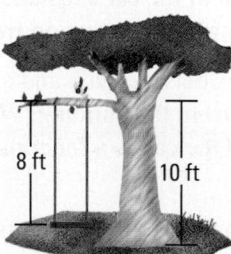
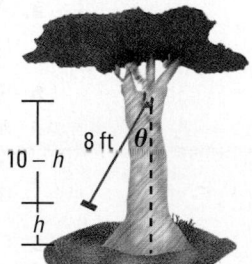

58. BLOOD PRESSURE The pressure P (in millimeters of mercury) against the walls of the blood vessels of a certain person is given by
$$P = 100 - 20\cos\frac{8\pi}{3}t$$
where t is the time (in seconds). Graph the function. If one cycle is equivalent to one heartbeat, what is the person's pulse rate in heartbeats per minute?

ANIMAL POPULATIONS In Exercises 59 and 60, use the following information.

Biologists use sine and cosine functions to model oscillations in predator and prey populations. The population R of rabbits and the population C of coyotes in a particular region can be modeled by

$$R = 25{,}000 + 15{,}000 \cos \frac{\pi}{12}t$$

$$C = 5000 + 2000 \sin \frac{\pi}{12}t$$

where t is the time in months.

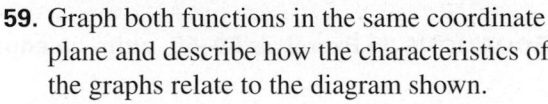

Rabbit population increases.

Coyote population decreases.

Rabbit population decreases.

Coyote population increases.

59. Graph both functions in the same coordinate plane and describe how the characteristics of the graphs relate to the diagram shown.

60. LOGICAL REASONING Look at the diagram above. Explain why each step leads to the next.

61. **AMUSEMENT PARK** At an amusement park you watch your friend on a ride that simulates a free fall. You are standing 250 feet from the base of the ride and the ride is 100 feet tall. Write an equation that gives the distance d (in feet) that your friend has fallen as a function of the angle of elevation θ. State the domain of the function. Then graph the function.

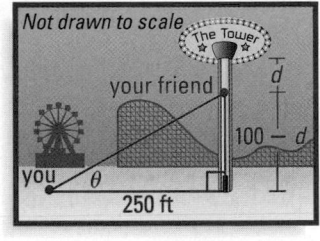

Not drawn to scale

The Tower

your friend

d

$100 - d$

you θ

250 ft

62. **WINDOW WASHERS** You are standing 80 feet from a 300 foot building, watching as a window washer lowers himself to the ground. Write an equation that gives the window washer's distance d (in feet) from the top of the building as a function of the angle of elevation θ. State the domain of the function. Then graph the function.

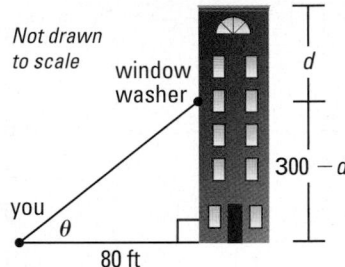

Not drawn to scale

window washer

d

$300 - d$

you θ

80 ft

Test Preparation

63. MULTI-STEP PROBLEM You are at the top of a 120 foot building that straddles a road. You are looking down at a car traveling straight toward the building.

a. Write an equation of the car's distance from the base of the building as a function of the angle of depression from you to the car.

b. Suppose the car is between you and a large road sign that you know is one mile (5280 feet) from the building. Write an equation for the distance between the road sign and the car as a function of the angle of depression from you to the car.

c. Graph the functions you wrote in parts (a) and (b) in the same coordinate plane.

d. *Writing* Describe how the graphs you drew in part (c) are geometrically related.

★ **Challenge**

64. **FERRIS WHEEL** Suppose a Ferris wheel has a radius of 20 feet and operates at a speed of 3 revolutions per minute. The bottom car is 4 feet above the ground. Write a model for the height of a person above the ground whose height when $t = 0$ is $h = 44$.

MIXED REVIEW

CLASSIFYING CONICS Classify the conic section and write its equation in standard form. (Review 10.6 for 14.3)

65. $36x^2 + 25y^2 - 900 = 0$ **66.** $9x^2 - 16y^2 - 144 = 0$

67. $10x^2 + 10y^2 - 250 = 0$ **68.** $100x^2 + 81y^2 - 100 = 0$

COMBINATIONS Find the number of combinations. (Review 12.2)

69. $_8C_7$ **70.** $_{142}C_1$ **71.** $_{10}C_3$ **72.** $_{14}C_5$

73. $_5C_3$ **74.** $_6C_2$ **75.** $_7C_6$ **76.** $_{100}C_2$

EVALUATING FUNCTIONS Evaluate the six trigonometric functions of the angle θ. (Review 13.1 for 14.3)

77. 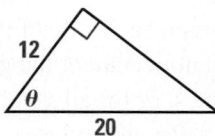   **78.** 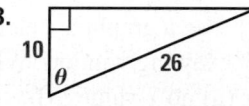   **79.**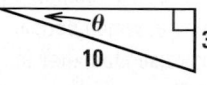

80. 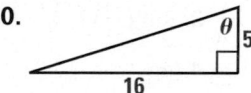   **81.** 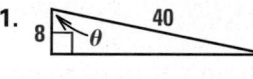   **82.**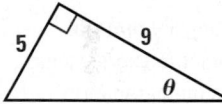

83. **BOX LUNCHES** You have made eight different lunches for eight people. How many different ways can you distribute the lunches? (Review 12.1)

QUIZ 1

Self-Test for Lessons 14.1 and 14.2

Find the amplitude and period of the function. (Lesson 14.1)

1. $y = \frac{5}{2}\sin 7x$ **2.** $y = \cos 2x$ **3.** $y = \sin \frac{\pi}{2}x$

4. $y = \frac{1}{4}\sin 2\pi x$ **5.** $y = 3\cos \pi x$ **6.** $y = 4\cos \frac{3\pi}{2}x$

7. $y = \frac{7}{3}\cos 4x$ **8.** $y = \frac{1}{3}\sin x$ **9.** $y = 6\sin \frac{1}{8}x$

Graph the function. (Lessons 14.1, 14.2)

10. $y = 2\sin \pi x$ **11.** $y = \frac{3}{2}\cos \frac{1}{2}\pi x$ **12.** $y = -\sin 2x$

13. $y = 4\tan \frac{1}{2}x$ **14.** $y = -4 + 2\sin 3x$ **15.** $y = 3\tan 2(x + \pi)$

16. $y = -3\cos(x + \pi)$ **17.** $y = -2 + \cos \frac{1}{2}(x - \pi)$ **18.** $y = 2 - 5\tan\left(x + \frac{\pi}{3}\right)$

19. **GLASS ELEVATOR** You are standing 120 feet from the base of a 260 foot building. You are looking at your friend who is going up the side of the building in a glass elevator. Write and graph a function that gives your friend's distance d (in feet) above the ground as a function of her angle of elevation θ. What is her angle of elevation when she is 70 feet above the ground? (Lesson 14.2)

14.3

Verifying Trigonometric Identities

What you should learn

GOAL 1 Use trigonometric identities to simplify trigonometric expressions and to verify other identities.

GOAL 2 Use trigonometric identities to solve **real-life** problems, such as comparing the speeds at which people pedal exercise machines in **Example 7**.

Why you should learn it

▼ To simplify **real-life** trigonometric expressions, such as the parametric equations that describe a carousel's motion in **Ex. 65**.

GOAL 1 USING TRIGONOMETRIC IDENTITIES

In this lesson you will use *trigonometric identities* to evaluate trigonometric functions, simplify trigonometric expressions, and verify other identities.

▶ **ACTIVITY**

Developing Concepts

Investigating Trigonometric Identities

Use a graphing calculator to graph each side of the equation in the same viewing window. What do you notice about the graphs? Is the equation true for **(a)** no *x*-values, **(b)** some *x*-values, or **(c)** all *x*-values? (Set your calculator in radian mode and use $-2\pi \le x \le 2\pi$ and $-2 \le y \le 2$.)

1. $\sin^2 x + \cos^2 x = 1$ 2. $\sin(-x) = -\sin x$

3. $\sin x = -\cos x$ 4. $\cos x = 1.5$

In the activity you may have discovered that some trigonometric equations are true for all values of *x* (in their domain). Such equations are called **trigonometric identities**. In Lesson 13.1 you used reciprocal identities to find the values of the cosecant, secant, and cotangent functions. These and other fundamental identities are listed below.

FUNDAMENTAL TRIGONOMETRIC IDENTITIES

RECIPROCAL IDENTITIES

$$\csc \theta = \frac{1}{\sin \theta} \qquad \sec \theta = \frac{1}{\cos \theta} \qquad \cot \theta = \frac{1}{\tan \theta}$$

TANGENT AND COTANGENT IDENTITIES

$$\tan \theta = \frac{\sin \theta}{\cos \theta} \qquad \cot \theta = \frac{\cos \theta}{\sin \theta}$$

PYTHAGOREAN IDENTITIES

$$\sin^2 \theta + \cos^2 \theta = 1 \qquad 1 + \tan^2 \theta = \sec^2 \theta \qquad 1 + \cot^2 \theta = \csc^2 \theta$$

COFUNCTION IDENTITIES

$$\sin\left(\frac{\pi}{2} - \theta\right) = \cos \theta \qquad \cos\left(\frac{\pi}{2} - \theta\right) = \sin \theta \qquad \tan\left(\frac{\pi}{2} - \theta\right) = \cot \theta$$

NEGATIVE ANGLE IDENTITIES

$$\sin(-\theta) = -\sin \theta \qquad \cos(-\theta) = \cos \theta \qquad \tan(-\theta) = -\tan \theta$$

EXAMPLE 1 **Finding Trigonometric Values**

Given that $\sin \theta = \frac{3}{5}$ and $\frac{\pi}{2} < \theta < \pi$, find the values of the other five trigonometric functions of θ.

SOLUTION

Begin by finding $\cos \theta$.

$$\sin^2 \theta + \cos^2 \theta = 1 \qquad \text{Write Pythagorean identity.}$$

$$\left(\frac{3}{5}\right)^2 + \cos^2 \theta = 1 \qquad \text{Substitute } \frac{3}{5} \text{ for } \sin \theta.$$

$$\cos^2 \theta = 1 - \left(\frac{3}{5}\right)^2 \qquad \text{Subtract } \left(\frac{3}{5}\right)^2 \text{ from each side.}$$

$$\cos^2 \theta = \frac{16}{25} \qquad \text{Simplify.}$$

$$\cos \theta = \pm\frac{4}{5} \qquad \text{Take square roots of each side.}$$

$$\cos \theta = -\frac{4}{5} \qquad \text{Because } \theta \text{ is in Quadrant II, } \cos \theta \text{ is negative.}$$

Now, knowing $\sin \theta$ and $\cos \theta$, you can find the values of the other four trigonometric functions.

$$\tan \theta = \frac{\sin \theta}{\cos \theta} = \frac{\frac{3}{5}}{-\frac{4}{5}} = -\frac{3}{4} \qquad\qquad \cot \theta = \frac{\cos \theta}{\sin \theta} = \frac{-\frac{4}{5}}{\frac{3}{5}} = -\frac{4}{3}$$

$$\csc \theta = \frac{1}{\sin \theta} = \frac{1}{\frac{3}{5}} = \frac{5}{3} \qquad\qquad \sec \theta = \frac{1}{\cos \theta} = \frac{1}{-\frac{4}{5}} = -\frac{5}{4}$$

EXAMPLE 2 **_Simplifying a Trigonometric Expression_**

Simplify the expression $\sec \theta \tan^2 \theta + \sec \theta$.

SOLUTION

$$\sec \theta \tan^2 \theta + \sec \theta = \sec \theta (\sec^2 \theta - 1) + \sec \theta \qquad \text{Pythagorean identity}$$

$$= \sec^3 \theta - \sec \theta + \sec \theta \qquad \text{Distributive property}$$

$$= \sec^3 \theta \qquad \text{Simplify.}$$

EXAMPLE 3 **_Simplifying a Trigonometric Expression_**

Simplify the expression $\cos\left(\frac{\pi}{2} - x\right) \cot x$.

SOLUTION

$$\cos\left(\frac{\pi}{2} - x\right) \cot x = \sin x \cot x \qquad \text{Cofunction identity}$$

$$= \sin x \left(\frac{\cos x}{\sin x}\right) \qquad \text{Cotangent identity}$$

$$= \cos x \qquad \text{Simplify.}$$

You can use the fundamental identities on page 848 to *verify* new trigonometric identities. A *verification* of an identity is a chain of equivalent expressions showing that one side of the identity is equal to the other side. When verifying an identity, begin with the expression from one side and manipulate it algebraically until it is identical to the other side.

EXAMPLE 4 *Verifying a Trigonometric Identity*

Verify the identity $\cot(-\theta) = -\cot\theta$.

SOLUTION

$$\cot(-\theta) = \frac{\cos(-\theta)}{\sin(-\theta)} \qquad \text{Cotangent identity}$$

$$= \frac{\cos\theta}{-\sin\theta} \qquad \text{Negative angle identities}$$

$$= -\cot\theta \qquad \text{Cotangent identity}$$

STUDENT HELP

↳ **Study Tip**
Verifying an identity is *not* the same as solving an equation. When verifying an identity you should *not* use any properties of equality, such as adding the same number or expression to both sides.

EXAMPLE 5 *Verifying a Trigonometric Identity*

Verify the identity $\dfrac{\cot^2 x}{\csc x} = \csc x - \sin x$.

SOLUTION

$$\frac{\cot^2 x}{\csc x} = \frac{\csc^2 x - 1}{\csc x} \qquad \text{Pythagorean identity}$$

$$= \frac{\csc^2 x}{\csc x} - \frac{1}{\csc x} \qquad \text{Write as separate fractions.}$$

$$= \csc x - \frac{1}{\csc x} \qquad \text{Simplify.}$$

$$= \csc x - \sin x \qquad \text{Reciprocal identity}$$

EXAMPLE 6 *Verifying a Trigonometric Identity*

Verify the identity $\dfrac{\sin x}{1 - \cos x} = \dfrac{1 + \cos x}{\sin x}$.

SOLUTION

$$\frac{\sin x}{1 - \cos x} = \frac{\sin x\,(1 + \cos x)}{(1 - \cos x)(1 + \cos x)} \qquad \text{Multiply by } \frac{1 + \cos x}{1 + \cos x}.$$

$$= \frac{\sin x\,(1 + \cos x)}{1 - \cos^2 x} \qquad \text{Simplify denominator.}$$

$$= \frac{\sin x\,(1 + \cos x)}{\sin^2 x} \qquad \text{Pythagorean identity}$$

$$= \frac{1 + \cos x}{\sin x} \qquad \text{Simplify.}$$

STUDENT HELP

↳ **Study Tip**
In Example 6, notice how multiplying by an expression equal to 1 allows you to write an expression in an equivalent form.

In Lesson 13.7 you learned that parametric equations can be used to describe linear and parabolic motion. They can be used to describe other types of motion as well.

EXAMPLE 7 *Using Parametric Equations in Real Life*

PHYSICAL FITNESS You and Sara are riding exercise machines that involve pedaling. The following parametric equations describe the motion of your feet and Sara's feet:

YOU:	SARA:
$x = 8 \cos 4\pi t$	$x = 10 \cos 2\pi t$
$y = 8 \sin 4\pi t$	$y = 6 \sin 2\pi t$

In each case, x and y are measured in inches and t is measured in seconds.

   a. Describe the paths followed by your feet and Sara's feet.

   b. Who is pedaling faster (in revolutions per second)?

SOLUTION

   a. Use the Pythagorean identity $\sin^2 \theta + \cos^2 \theta = 1$ to eliminate the parameter t.

YOU:	SARA:	
$\dfrac{x}{8} = \cos 4\pi t$	$\dfrac{x}{10} = \cos 2\pi t$	Isolate the cosine.
$\dfrac{y}{8} = \sin 4\pi t$	$\dfrac{y}{6} = \sin 2\pi t$	Isolate the sine.
$\cos^2 4\pi t + \sin^2 4\pi t = 1$	$\cos^2 2\pi t + \sin^2 2\pi t = 1$	Pythagorean identity
$\left(\dfrac{x}{8}\right)^2 + \left(\dfrac{y}{8}\right)^2 = 1$	$\left(\dfrac{x}{10}\right)^2 + \left(\dfrac{y}{6}\right)^2 = 1$	Substitute.
$x^2 + y^2 = 64$	$\dfrac{x^2}{100} + \dfrac{y^2}{36} = 1$	Simplify.

   ▶ Your feet follow a circle with a radius of 8 inches. Sara's feet follow an ellipse whose major axis is 20 inches long and whose minor axis is 12 inches long.

   b. The number of revolutions per second for you and Sara is the reciprocal of the common period of the corresponding parametric functions.

YOU:	SARA:
$\dfrac{1}{\frac{2\pi}{4\pi}} = \dfrac{1}{\frac{1}{2}} = 2$	$\dfrac{1}{\frac{2\pi}{2\pi}} = \dfrac{1}{1} = 1$

   ▶ In one second, your feet travel around 2 times and Sara's feet travel around 1 time. So, you are pedaling faster.

✓ **CHECK** To check your results, set a graphing calculator to parametric, radian, and simultaneous modes. Enter both sets of parametric equations with $0 \le t \le 1$ and a t-step of 0.01. As the paths are graphed, you can see that your path is traced faster.

Vocabulary Check ✓

1. What is a trigonometric identity?

Concept Check ✓

2. Is $\sec(-\theta)$ equal to $\sec \theta$ or $-\sec \theta$? How do you know?

3. Verify the identity $1 - \sin^2 x \cot^2 x = \sin^2 x$. Is there more than one way to verify the identity? If so, tell which way you think is easier and why.

4. **ERROR ANALYSIS** Describe what is wrong with the simplification shown.

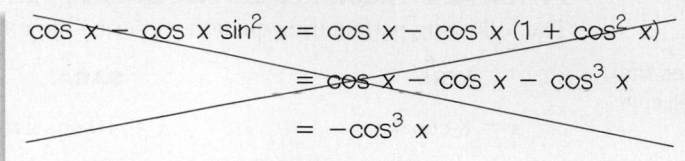

$$\cos x - \cos x \sin^2 x = \cos x - \cos x (1 + \cos^2 x)$$
$$= \cos x - \cos x - \cos^3 x$$
$$= -\cos^3 x$$

Skill Check ✓

Find the values of the other five trigonometric functions of θ.

5. $\cos \theta = -\dfrac{3}{5}, \dfrac{\pi}{2} < \theta < \pi$

6. $\tan \theta = \dfrac{2}{3}, 0 < \theta < \dfrac{\pi}{2}$

7. $\sec \theta = \dfrac{4}{3}, \dfrac{3\pi}{2} < \theta < 2\pi$

8. $\sin \theta = -\dfrac{1}{2}, \pi < \theta < \dfrac{3\pi}{2}$

Simplify the expression.

9. $\dfrac{(\sec x + 1)(\sec x - 1)}{\tan x}$

10. $\sin\left(\dfrac{\pi}{2} - x\right) \sec x$

11. $\cos^2\left(\dfrac{\pi}{2} - x\right) + \cos^2(-x)$

Verify the identity.

12. $\dfrac{1}{\sin(-x)} = -\csc x$

13. $\cot x \tan(-x) = -1$

14. $\csc x \tan x = \sec x$

15. 🌐 **PHYSICAL FITNESS** Look back at Example 7 on page 851. Suppose your friend Pete starts riding another machine that involves pedaling. The motion of his feet is described by the equations $x = 10 \cos \dfrac{5\pi}{2} t$ and $y = 6 \sin \dfrac{5\pi}{2} t$. What type of path are his feet following?

PRACTICE AND APPLICATIONS

STUDENT HELP

▶ **Extra Practice**
to help you master
skills is on p. 959.

FINDING VALUES Find the values of the other five trigonometric functions of θ.

16. $\cos \theta = \dfrac{1}{\sqrt{5}}, 0 < \theta < \dfrac{\pi}{2}$

17. $\tan \theta = \dfrac{3}{8}, 0 < \theta < \dfrac{\pi}{2}$

18. $\sin \theta = \dfrac{5}{6}, 0 < \theta < \dfrac{\pi}{2}$

19. $\sin \theta = \dfrac{3}{5}, \dfrac{\pi}{2} < \theta < \pi$

20. $\cot \theta = -\dfrac{9}{4}, \dfrac{3\pi}{2} < \theta < 2\pi$

21. $\cos \theta = -\dfrac{11}{12}, \dfrac{\pi}{2} < \theta < \pi$

22. $\csc \theta = \dfrac{7}{5}, 0 < \theta < \dfrac{\pi}{2}$

23. $\sec \theta = -\dfrac{10}{3}, \pi < \theta < \dfrac{3\pi}{2}$

24. $\tan \theta = -\dfrac{1}{6}, \dfrac{\pi}{2} < \theta < \pi$

25. $\sec \theta = 2, \dfrac{3\pi}{2} < \theta < 2\pi$

26. $\csc \theta = -\dfrac{5}{3}, \pi < \theta < \dfrac{3\pi}{2}$

27. $\cot \theta = -\sqrt{3}, \dfrac{3\pi}{2} < \theta < 2\pi$

SIMPLIFYING EXPRESSIONS Simplify the expression.

28. $\cot x \sec x$

29. $\dfrac{\cos(-x)}{\sin(-x)}$

30. $\sec x \cos(-x) - \sin^2 x$

31. $\sin x (1 + \cot^2 x)$

32. $1 - \sin^2\left(\dfrac{\pi}{2} - x\right)$

33. $\dfrac{\tan\left(\dfrac{\pi}{2} - x\right)}{\csc x}$

34. $\cos\left(\dfrac{\pi}{2} - x\right)\csc x$

35. $\dfrac{\sin(-x)}{\csc x} + \cos^2(-x)$

36. $\dfrac{\cos^2 x \tan^2(-x) - 1}{\cos^2 x}$

37. $\sec^2 x - \tan^2 x$

38. $\dfrac{\tan\left(\dfrac{\pi}{2} - x\right)\sec x}{1 - \csc^2 x}$

39. $\dfrac{\cos\left(\dfrac{\pi}{2} - x\right) - 1}{1 + \sin(-x)}$

40. $\dfrac{\cot x \cos x}{\tan(-x)\sin\left(\dfrac{\pi}{2} - x\right)}$

41. $\dfrac{\sec x \sin x + \cos\left(\dfrac{\pi}{2} - x\right)}{1 + \sec x}$

42. $\cot^2 x + \sin^2 x + \cos^2(-x)$

43. $\tan\left(\dfrac{\pi}{2} - x\right)\cot x - \csc^2 x$

VERIFYING IDENTITIES Verify the identity.

44. $\cos x \sec x = 1$

45. $\tan x \csc x \cos x = 1$

46. $\cos\left(\dfrac{\pi}{2} - x\right)\cot x = \cos x$

47. $2 - \sec^2 x = 1 - \tan^2 x$

48. $\sin x + \cos x \cot x = \csc x$

49. $\dfrac{\cos^2 x + \sin^2 x}{1 + \tan^2 x} = \cos^2 x$

50. $\dfrac{\sin^2(-x)}{\tan^2 x} = \cos^2 x$

51. $\dfrac{\sin\left(\dfrac{\pi}{2} - x\right) - 1}{1 - \cos(-x)} = -1$

52. $\dfrac{1 + \sin x}{\cos x} + \dfrac{\cos x}{1 + \sin x} = 2\sec x$

53. $\dfrac{\cos(-x)}{1 + \sin(-x)} = \sec x + \tan x$

IDENTIFYING CONICS Use a graphing calculator set in parametric mode to graph the parametric equations. Use a trigonometric identity to determine whether the graph is *a circle, an ellipse,* or *a hyperbola.* (Use a square viewing window.)

54. $x = 6\cos t,\ y = 6\sin t$

55. $x = 5\sec t,\ y = \tan t$

56. $x = 2\cos t,\ y = 3\sin t$

57. $x = 8\cos \pi t,\ y = 8\sin \pi t$

58. $x = 2\cot 2t,\ y = 3\csc 2t$

59. $x = \cos\dfrac{t}{2},\ y = 4\sin\dfrac{t}{2}$

60. CRITICAL THINKING A function f is *odd* if $f(-x) = -f(x)$. A function f is *even* if $f(-x) = f(x)$. Which of the six trigonometric functions are odd? Which of them are even?

61. 🌐 **SHADOW OF A SUNDIAL** The length s of a shadow cast by a vertical *gnomon* (column or shaft on a sundial) of height h when the angle of the sun above the horizon is θ can be modeled by this equation:

$$s = \dfrac{h\sin(90° - \theta)}{\sin\theta}$$

This equation was developed by Abu Abdullah al-Battani (circa A.D. 920). Show that the equation is equivalent to $s = h\cot\theta$. ► Source: *Trigonometric Delights*

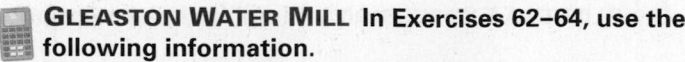

GLEASTON WATER MILL In Exercises 62–64, use the following information.

Suppose you have constructed a working scale model of the water wheel at the Gleaston Water Mill. The parametric equations that describe the motion of one of the paddles on each of the water wheels are as follows.

Actual waterwheel:	Scale model:
$x = 9 \cos 8\pi t$	$x = 0.5 \cos 15\pi t$
$y = 9 \sin 8\pi t$	$y = 0.5 \sin 15\pi t$

In each case, x and y are measured in feet and t is measured in minutes.

62. Use a graphing calculator to graph both sets of parametric equations.

63. How is your scale model different from the actual waterwheel?

64. How many revolutions does each wheel make in 5 minutes?

Test Preparation

65. MULTI-STEP PROBLEM The Dentzel Carousel in Glen Echo Park near Washington, D.C., is one of about 135 functioning antique carousels in the United States. The platform of the carousel is about 48 feet in diameter and makes about 5 revolutions per minute. ▶ Source: National Park Service

 a. Find parametric equations that describe the ride's motion.

 b. Suppose the platform of the carousel had a diameter of 38 feet and made about 4.5 revolutions per minute. Find parametric equations that would describe the ride's motion.

 c. *Writing* How are the parametric equations affected when the speed is changed? How are the equations affected when the diameter is changed?

★ Challenge

66. Use the definitions of sine and cosine from Lesson 13.3 to derive the Pythagorean identity $\sin^2 \theta + \cos^2 \theta = 1$.

67. Use the Pythagorean identity $\sin^2 \theta + \cos^2 \theta = 1$ to derive the other Pythagorean identities, $1 + \tan^2 \theta = \sec^2 \theta$ and $1 + \cot^2 \theta = \csc^2 \theta$.

MIXED REVIEW

QUADRATIC EQUATIONS Solve the equation by factoring. (Review 5.2 for 14.4)

68. $x^2 - 5x - 14 = 0$ **69.** $x^2 + 5x - 36 = 0$ **70.** $x^2 - 19x + 88 = 0$

71. $2x^2 - 7x - 15 = 0$ **72.** $36x^2 - 16 = 0$ **73.** $9x^2 - 1 = 0$

EVALUATING EXPRESSIONS Evaluate the expression without using a calculator. Give your answer in both radians and degrees. (Review 13.4 for 14.4)

74. $\cos^{-1} \dfrac{\sqrt{2}}{2}$ **75.** $\tan^{-1} \sqrt{3}$ **76.** $\sin^{-1} \left(-\dfrac{\sqrt{3}}{2}\right)$

77. $\sin^{-1} \dfrac{1}{2}$ **78.** $\tan^{-1} (-1)$ **79.** $\cos^{-1} \left(-\dfrac{1}{2}\right)$

GRAPHING Draw one cycle of the function's graph. (Review 14.1)

80. $y = 4 \sin x$ **81.** $y = 2 \cos x$ **82.** $y = \tan 4\pi x$

83. $y = 3 \tan \pi x$ **84.** $y = 5 \cos 2x$ **85.** $y = 10 \sin 4x$

Solving Trigonometric Equations

What you should learn

GOAL 1 Solve a trigonometric equation.

GOAL 2 Solve **real-life** trigonometric equations, such as an equation for the number of hours of daylight in Prescott, Arizona, in **Example 6**.

Why you should learn it

▼ To solve many types of **real-life** problems, such as finding the position of the sun at sunrise in **Ex. 58**.

GOAL 1 SOLVING A TRIGONOMETRIC EQUATION

In Lesson 14.3 you verified trigonometric identities. In this lesson you will solve trigonometric equations. To see the difference, consider the following equations:

$$\sin^2 x + \cos^2 x = 1 \qquad \textbf{Equation 1}$$

$$\sin x = 1 \qquad \textbf{Equation 2}$$

Equation 1 is an identity because it is true for all real values of x. Equation 2, however, is true only for some values of x. When you find these values, you are solving the equation.

EXAMPLE 1 *Solving a Trigonometric Equation*

Solve $2 \sin x - 1 = 0$.

SOLUTION

First isolate $\sin x$ on one side of the equation.

$2 \sin x - 1 = 0$	**Write original equation.**
$2 \sin x = 1$	**Add 1 to each side.**
$\sin x = \dfrac{1}{2}$	**Divide each side by 2.**

One solution of $\sin x = \dfrac{1}{2}$ in the interval $0 \le x < 2\pi$ is $x = \sin^{-1} \dfrac{1}{2} = \dfrac{\pi}{6}$. Another

such solution is $x = \pi - \dfrac{\pi}{6} = \dfrac{5\pi}{6}$.

Moreover, because $y = \sin x$ is a periodic function, there are infinitely many other solutions. You can write the general solution as

$$x = \frac{\pi}{6} + 2n\pi \qquad \text{or} \qquad x = \frac{5\pi}{6} + 2n\pi$$

where n is any integer.

✓ **CHECK** You can check your answer graphically. Graph $y = \sin x$ and $y = \dfrac{1}{2}$ in the same coordinate plane and find the points where the graphs intersect.

You can see that there are infinitely many such points.

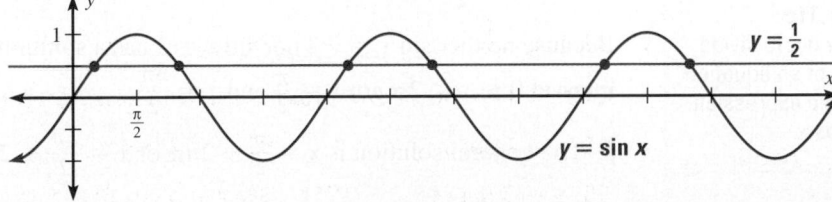

STUDENT HELP

▶ **Look Back**
For help with inverse trigonometric functions, see p. 792.

EXAMPLE 2 *Solving a Trigonometric Equation in an Interval*

Solve $4 \tan^2 x - 1 = 0$ in the interval $0 \le x < 2\pi$.

SOLUTION

$$4 \tan^2 x - 1 = 0 \qquad \text{Write original equation.}$$

$$4 \tan^2 x = 1 \qquad \text{Add 1 to each side.}$$

$$\tan^2 x = \frac{1}{4} \qquad \text{Divide each side by 4.}$$

$$\tan x = \pm\frac{1}{2} \qquad \text{Take square roots of each side.}$$

Use a calculator to find values of x for which $\tan x = \pm\frac{1}{2}$, as shown at the right.

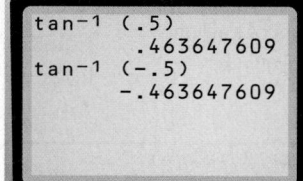

The general solution of the equation is

$$x \approx 0.464 + n\pi$$

or

$$x \approx -0.464 + n\pi$$

where n is any integer. The solutions that are in the interval $0 \le x < 2\pi$ are:

$x \approx 0.464$ $x \approx 0.464 + \pi \approx 3.61$

$x \approx -0.464 + \pi \approx 2.628$ $x \approx -0.464 + 2\pi \approx 5.82$

✓ **CHECK** Check these solutions by substituting them back into the original equation.

> **STUDENT HELP**
>
> ▶ **Study Tip**
> Note that to find the general solution of a trigonometric equation, you must add multiples of the period to the solutions in one cycle.

EXAMPLE 3 *Factoring to Solve a Trigonometric Equation*

Solve $\sin^2 x \cos x = 4 \cos x$.

SOLUTION

$$\sin^2 x \cos x = 4 \cos x \qquad \text{Write original equation.}$$

$$\sin^2 x \cos x - 4 \cos x = 0 \qquad \text{Subtract 4 cos } x \text{ from each side.}$$

$$\cos x\,(\sin^2 x - 4) = 0 \qquad \text{Factor out cos } x.$$

$$\cos x\,(\sin x + 2)(\sin x - 2) = 0 \qquad \text{Factor difference of squares.}$$

Set each factor equal to 0 and solve for x, if possible.

$\cos x = 0$ $\sin x + 2 = 0$ $\sin x - 2 = 0$

$x = \dfrac{\pi}{2}$ or $x = \dfrac{3\pi}{2}$ $\sin x = -2$ $\sin x = 2$

Because neither $\sin x = -2$ nor $\sin x = 2$ has a solution, the only solutions in the interval $0 \le x < 2\pi$ are $x = \dfrac{\pi}{2}$ and $x = \dfrac{3\pi}{2}$.

▶ The general solution is $x = \dfrac{\pi}{2} + 2n\pi$ or $x = \dfrac{3\pi}{2} + 2n\pi$ where n is any integer.

> **STUDENT HELP**
>
> ▶ **Study Tip**
> Remember not to divide both sides of an equation by a variable expression, such as cos x.

EXAMPLE 4 **Using the Quadratic Formula**

Solve $\cos^2 x - 4\cos x + 1 = 0$ in the interval $0 \le x \le \pi$.

SOLUTION

STUDENT HELP

Look Back
For help with the quadratic formula, see p. 291.

Since the equation is in the form $au^2 + bu + c = 0$, you can use the quadratic formula to solve for $u = \cos x$.

$\cos^2 x - 4\cos x + 1 = 0$	**Write original equation.**
$\cos x = \dfrac{4 \pm \sqrt{(-4)^2 - 4(1)(1)}}{2(1)}$	**Quadratic formula**
$= \dfrac{4 \pm \sqrt{12}}{2} = 2 \pm \sqrt{3}$	**Simplify.**
$\approx 3.73 \text{ or } 0.268$	**Use a calculator.**
$x \approx \cos^{-1} 3.73 \quad \text{or} \quad x \approx \cos^{-1} 0.268$	**Use inverse cosine.**
$\text{No solution} \qquad\qquad \approx 1.30$	**Use a calculator if possible.**

▶ In the interval $0 \le x \le \pi$, the only solution is $x \approx 1.30$. Check this in the original equation.

· · · · · · · · · ·

When solving a trigonometric equation, it is possible to obtain extraneous solutions. Therefore, you should always check your solutions in the original equation.

EXAMPLE 5 **An Equation with Extraneous Solutions**

STUDENT HELP

HOMEWORK HELP
Visit our Web site
www.mcdougallittell.com
for extra examples.

Solve $1 - \cos x = \sqrt{3}\,\sin x$ in the interval $0 \le x < 2\pi$.

SOLUTION

$1 - \cos x = \sqrt{3}\,\sin x$	**Write original equation.**
$(1 - \cos x)^2 = (\sqrt{3}\,\sin x)^2$	**Square both sides.**
$1 - 2\cos x + \cos^2 x = 3\sin^2 x$	**Multiply.**
$1 - 2\cos x + \cos^2 x = 3(1 - \cos^2 x)$	**Pythagorean identity**
$4\cos^2 x - 2\cos x - 2 = 0$	**Quadratic form**
$2\cos^2 x - \cos x - 1 = 0$	**Divide each side by 2.**
$(2\cos x + 1)(\cos x - 1) = 0$	**Factor.**
$2\cos x + 1 = 0 \quad \text{or} \quad \cos x - 1 = 0$	**Zero product property**
$\cos x = -\dfrac{1}{2} \qquad\qquad \cos x = 1$	**Solve for cos x.**
$x = \dfrac{2\pi}{3} \;\text{ or }\; x = \dfrac{4\pi}{3} \qquad\qquad x = 0$	**Solve for x.**

▶ The apparent solution $x = \dfrac{4\pi}{3}$ does not check in the original equation. The only solutions in the interval $0 \le x < 2\pi$ are $x = 0$ and $x = \dfrac{2\pi}{3}$.

GOAL 2 **SOLVING TRIGONOMETRIC EQUATIONS IN REAL LIFE**

EXAMPLE 6 *Solving a Real-Life Trigonometric Equation*

METEOROLOGY The number h of hours of sunlight per day in Prescott, Arizona, can be modeled by

$$h = 2.325 \sin \frac{\pi}{6}(t - 2.667) + 12.155$$

where t is measured in months and $t = 0$ represents January 1. On which days of the year are there 13 hours of sunlight in Prescott? ▶ Source: Gale Research Company

SOLUTION

Method 1 Substitute 13 for h in the model and solve for t.

$$2.325 \sin \frac{\pi}{6}(t - 2.667) + 12.155 = 13$$

$$2.325 \sin \frac{\pi}{6}(t - 2.667) = 0.845$$

$$\sin \frac{\pi}{6}(t - 2.667) \approx 0.363$$

$$\frac{\pi}{6}(t - 2.667) \approx \sin^{-1}(0.363) \quad \text{or} \quad \frac{\pi}{6}(t - 2.667) \approx \pi - \sin^{-1}(0.363)$$

$$\frac{\pi}{6}(t - 2.667) \approx 0.371 \qquad\qquad \frac{\pi}{6}(t - 2.667) \approx \pi - 0.371 \approx 2.771$$

$$t - 2.667 \approx 0.709 \qquad\qquad t - 2.667 \approx 5.292$$

$$t \approx 3.38 \qquad\qquad\qquad t \approx 7.96$$

▶ The time $t = 3.38$ represents 3 full months plus $(0.38)(30) \approx 11$ days, or April 11. Likewise, the time $t = 7.96$ represents 7 full months plus $(0.96)(31) \approx 30$ days, or August 30. (Notice that these two days occur about 70 days before and after June 21, which is the date of the summer solstice, the longest day of the year.)

Method 2 Use a graphing calculator. Graph the equations

$$y = 2.325 \sin \frac{\pi}{6}(x - 2.667) + 12.155$$

$$y = 13$$

in the same viewing window. Then use the *Intersect* feature to find the points of intersection.

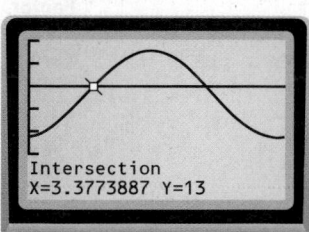

Intersection
X=3.3773887 Y=13

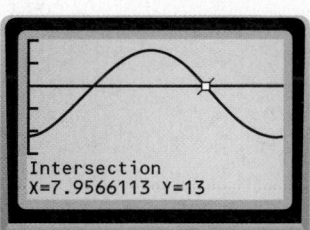

Intersection
X=7.9566113 Y=13

▶ From the screens above, you can see that $t \approx 3.38$ or $t \approx 7.96$. The time $t = 3.38$ is about April 11, and the time $t = 7.96$ is about August 30.

Vocabulary Check ✓

1. What is the difference between a trigonometric equation and a trigonometric identity?

Concept Check ✓

2. Name several techniques for solving trigonometric equations.

3. **ERROR ANALYSIS** Describe the error(s) in the calculations shown.

$$\cos^2 x = \tfrac{1}{2} \cos x$$

$$\cos x = \tfrac{1}{2}$$

$$x = \tfrac{\pi}{3} \text{ or } x = \tfrac{5\pi}{3} \qquad \text{Solution for } 0 \le x < 2\pi$$

$$x = \tfrac{\pi}{3} + 2\pi \text{ or } x = \tfrac{5\pi}{3} + 2\pi \quad \text{General solution}$$

Skill Check ✓

Solve the equation in the interval $0 \le x < 2\pi$.

4. $2 \cos x + 4 = 5$

5. $3 \sec^2 x - 4 = 0$

6. $\tan^2 x = \cos x \tan^2 x$

7. $5 \cos x - \sqrt{3} = 3 \cos x$

Find the general solution of the equation.

8. $3 \csc x + 5 = 0$

9. $4 \sin x = \sqrt{3}$

10. $1 + \tan^2 x = 6 - 2 \sec^2 x$

11. $2 - 2 \cos^2 x = 5 \sin x + 3$

12. 🌐 **METEOROLOGY** Look back at the model in Example 6 on page 858. On which days of the year are there 10 hours of sunlight in Prescott, Arizona?

PRACTICE AND APPLICATIONS

STUDENT HELP

▶ **Extra Practice**
to help you master
skills is on p. 960.

CHECKING SOLUTIONS Verify that the given x-value is a solution of the equation.

13. $5 + 4 \cos x - 1 = 0, x = \pi$

14. $\csc x - 2 = 0, x = \dfrac{5\pi}{6}$

15. $4 \cos^2 x - 3 = 0, x = \dfrac{\pi}{6}$

16. $3 \tan^3 x - 3 = 0, x = \dfrac{\pi}{4}$

17. $2 \sin^4 x - \sin^2 x = 0, x = \dfrac{5\pi}{4}$

18. $2 \cot^4 x - \cot^2 x - 15 = 0, x = \dfrac{13\pi}{6}$

SOLVING Find the general solution of the equation.

19. $2 \cos x - 1 = 0$

20. $3 \tan x - \sqrt{3} = 0$

21. $\sin x = \sin (-x) + 1$

22. $4 \cos x = 2 \cos x + 1$

STUDENT HELP

▶ **HOMEWORK HELP**
Examples 1, 3: Exs. 13–32
Examples 2, 4, 5:
 Exs. 13–18, 33–56
Example 6: Exs. 57–59

23. $4 \sin^2 x - 2 = 0$

24. $9 \tan^2 x - 3 = 0$

25. $\sin x \cos x - 2 \cos x = 0$

26. $\sqrt{2} \cos x \sin x - \cos x = 0$

27. $2 \sin^2 x - \sin x = 1$

28. $0 = \cos^2 x - 5 \cos x + 1$

29. $1 - \sin x = \sqrt{3} \cos x$

30. $\sqrt{\sin x} = 2 \sin x - 1$

31. $\cos x - 1 = -\cos x$

32. $6 \sin x = \sin x + 3$

SOLVING Solve the equation in the interval $0 \le x < 2\pi$. Check your solutions.

33. $5 \cos x - 3 = 0$

34. $3 \sin x = \sin x - 1$

35. $\tan^2 x - 3 = 0$

36. $10 \tan x - 5 = 0$

37. $2 \cos^2 x - \sin x - 1 = 0$

38. $\cos^3 x = \cos x$

39. $\sec^2 x - 2 = 0$

40. $\tan^2 x = \sin x \sec x$

41. $2 \cos x = \sec x$

42. $\cos x \csc^2 x + 3 \cos x = 7 \cos x$

APPROXIMATING SOLUTIONS Use a graphing calculator to approximate the solutions of the equation in the interval $0 \le x < 2\pi$.

43. $3 \tan x + 1 = 13$

44. $8 \cos x + 3 = 4$

45. $4 \sin x = -2 \sin x - 5$

46. $3 \sin x + 5 \cos x = 4$

FINDING INTERCEPTS Find the *x*-intercepts of the graph of the given function in the interval $0 \le x < 2\pi$.

47. $y = 2 \sin x + 1$

48. $y = 2 \tan^2 x - 6$

49. $y = \sec^2 x - 1$

50. $y = -3 \cos x + \sin x$

FINDING INTERSECTION POINTS Find the points of intersection of the graphs of the given functions in the interval $0 \le x < 2\pi$.

51. $y = \sqrt{3} \tan^2 x$
$y = \sqrt{3} - 2 \tan x$

52. $y = 9 \cos^2 x$
$y = \cos^2 x + 8 \cos x - 2$

53. $y = \tan x \sin x$
$y = \cos x$

54. $y = \sin^2 x$
$y = 2 \sin x - 1$

55. $y = 2 - \sin x \tan x$
$y = \cos x$

56. $y = 4 \cos^2 x$
$y = 4 \cos x - 1$

57. 🌎 **OCEAN TIDES** The *tide*, or depth of the ocean near the shore, changes throughout the day. The depth of the Bay of Fundy can be modeled by

$$d = 35 - 28 \cos \frac{\pi}{6.2} t$$

where *d* is the water depth in feet and *t* is the time in hours. Consider a day in which $t = 0$ represents 12:00 A.M. For that day, when do the high and low tides occur? At what time(s) is the water depth $3\frac{1}{2}$ feet?

58. 🖩 **POSITION OF THE SUN** Cheyenne, Wyoming, has a latitude of 41°N. At this latitude, the position of the sun at sunrise can be modeled by

$$D = 31 \sin\left(\frac{2\pi}{365} t - 1.4\right)$$

where *t* is the time in days and $t = 1$ represents January 1. In this model, *D* represents the number of degrees north or south of due east that the sun rises. Use a graphing calculator to determine the days that the sun is more than 20° north of due east at sunrise.

59. 🌎 **METEOROLOGY** A model for the average daily temperature *T* (in degrees Fahrenheit) in Kansas City, Missouri, is given by

$$T = 54 + 25.2 \sin\left(\frac{2\pi}{12} t + 4.3\right)$$

where *t* is measured in months and $t = 0$ represents January 1. What months have average daily temperatures higher than 70°F? Do any months have average daily temperatures below 20°F? ▶ Source: National Climatic Data Center

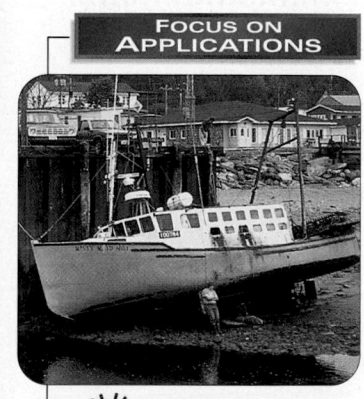

60. MULTIPLE CHOICE What is the general solution of the equation $\cos x + \sqrt{2} = -\cos x$? Assume n is an integer.

Ⓐ $x = \dfrac{\pi}{4} + 2n\pi$

Ⓑ $x = \dfrac{\pi}{4} + 2n\pi$ or $x = \dfrac{7\pi}{4} + 2n\pi$

Ⓒ $x = \dfrac{3\pi}{4} + 2n\pi$

Ⓓ $x = \dfrac{3\pi}{4} + 2n\pi$ or $x = \dfrac{5\pi}{4} + 2n\pi$

Ⓔ $x = \dfrac{3\pi}{4} + n\pi$ or $x = \dfrac{5\pi}{4} + n\pi$

61. MULTIPLE CHOICE Find the points of intersection of the graphs of $y = 2 + \sin x$ and $y = 3 - \sin x$ in the interval $0 \le x < 2\pi$.

Ⓐ $\left(\dfrac{\pi}{6}, \dfrac{5}{2}\right), \left(\dfrac{5\pi}{6}, \dfrac{5}{2}\right)$

Ⓑ $\left(\dfrac{\pi}{6}, \dfrac{1}{2}\right), \left(\dfrac{5\pi}{6}, \dfrac{1}{2}\right)$

Ⓒ $\left(\dfrac{\pi}{3}, \dfrac{5}{2}\right), \left(\dfrac{4\pi}{3}, \dfrac{5}{2}\right)$

Ⓓ $\left(\dfrac{\pi}{3}, \dfrac{1}{2}\right), \left(\dfrac{4\pi}{3}, \dfrac{1}{2}\right)$

Ⓔ $\left(\dfrac{\pi}{6}, \dfrac{5}{2}\right), \left(\dfrac{11\pi}{6}, \dfrac{5}{2}\right)$

★ **Challenge**

MATRICES In Exercises 62 and 63, use the following information.
Matrix multiplication can be used to rotate a point (x, y) counter clockwise about the origin through an angle θ. The coordinates of the resulting point (x', y') are determined by the following matrix equation:

$$\begin{bmatrix} \cos \theta & -\sin \theta \\ \sin \theta & \cos \theta \end{bmatrix} \begin{bmatrix} x \\ y \end{bmatrix} = \begin{bmatrix} x' \\ y' \end{bmatrix}$$

62. The point $(4, 1)$ is rotated counter clockwise about the origin through an angle of $\dfrac{\pi}{3}$. What are the coordinates of the resulting point?

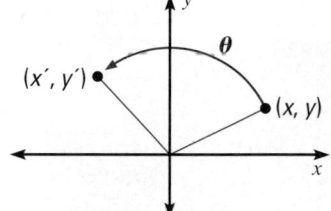

EXTRA CHALLENGE
www.mcdougallittell.com

63. Through what angle θ must the point $(2, 4)$ be rotated to produce $(x', y') = \left(-2 + \sqrt{3}, 1 + 2\sqrt{3}\right)$?

MIXED REVIEW

USING COMPLEMENTS Two six-sided dice are rolled. Find the probability of the given event. (Review 12.4)

64. The sum is less than or equal to 10.

65. The sum is not 4.

66. The sum is not 2 or 12.

67. The sum is greater than 3.

GRAPHING Graph the function. (Review 14.1, 14.2 for 14.5)

68. $y = \sin 3x$

69. $y = 2 \cos 4x$

70. $y = 10 \sin 2x$

71. $y = 3 \cos \dfrac{1}{2}x$

72. $y = \dfrac{1}{4} \tan x$

73. $y = 3 \tan \dfrac{1}{2}x - 2$

74. $y = \cos \dfrac{1}{2}x + \pi$

75. $y = 3 + \tan \left(x - \dfrac{3\pi}{2}\right)$

76. $y = -\sin 3\pi(x + 4) + 1$

77. 🌐 **SURVEYING** Suppose you are trying to determine the width w of a small pond. You stand at a point 43 feet from one end of the pond and 50 feet from the other end. The angle formed by your lines of sight to each end of the pond measures $45°$. How wide is the pond? **(Review 13.6)**

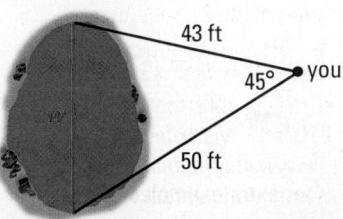

Modeling with Trigonometric Functions

What you should learn

GOAL 1 Model data with a sine or cosine function.

GOAL 2 Use technology to write a trigonometric model, as applied in **Example 4**.

Why you should learn it

▼ To model many types of **real-life** quantities, such as the temperature inside and outside an igloo in **Ex. 30**.

Graphs of sine and cosine functions are called *sinusoids*. When you write a sine or cosine function for a sinusoid, you need to find the values of a, $b > 0$, h, and k for

$$y = a \sin b(x - h) + k \qquad \text{or} \qquad y = a \cos b(x - h) + k$$

where $|a|$ is the amplitude, $\frac{2\pi}{b}$ is the period, h is the horizontal shift, and k is the vertical shift.

EXAMPLE 1 *Writing Trigonometric Functions*

Write a function for the sinusoid.

a.

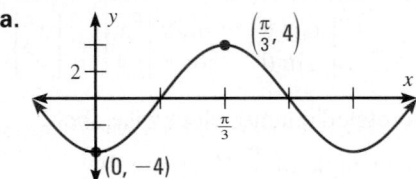

b.

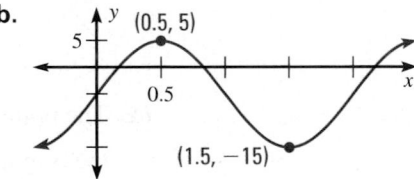

SOLUTION

a. Since the maximum and minimum values of the function occur at points equidistant from the x-axis, the curve has no vertical shift. And because the minimum occurs on the y-axis, the graph is a reflection of a cosine curve with no horizontal shift. Therefore, the function has the form $y = a \cos bx$.

The period is $\frac{2\pi}{b} = \frac{2\pi}{3}$, so $b = 3$.

The amplitude is $|a| = 4$. Since the graph is a reflection, $a = -4$.

▶ The function is $y = -4 \cos 3x$.

b. Since the maximum and minimum values of the function do *not* occur at points equidistant from the x-axis, the curve has a vertical shift. To find the value of k, add the maximum and minimum values and divide by 2:

$$k = \frac{M + m}{2} = \frac{5 + (-15)}{2} = \frac{-10}{2} = -5$$

Because the graph crosses the y-axis at $y = k$, the graph is a sine curve with no horizontal shift. Therefore, the function has the form $y = a \sin bx - 5$.

The period is $\frac{2\pi}{b} = 2$, so $b = \pi$.

The amplitude is $|a| = \frac{M - m}{2} = \frac{5 - (-15)}{2} = \frac{20}{2} = 10$.

Since the graph is not a reflection, $a = 10 > 0$.

▶ The function is $y = 10 \sin \pi x - 5$.

Meteorology

EXAMPLE 2 *Modeling a Sinusoid*

Write a trigonometric model for the average daily temperature in Birmingham, Alabama. ▶ Source: National Climatic Data Center

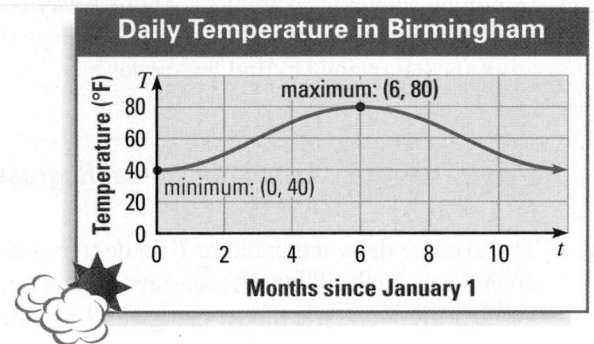

SOLUTION

Notice that the graph crosses the T-axis at the minimum point. So if you model the temperature curve with a cosine function, there is a reflection but no horizontal shift. The mean of the maximum and minimum values is 60, so there is a vertical shift of $k = 60$.

The period is $\frac{2\pi}{b} = 12$, so $b = \frac{\pi}{6}$.

The amplitude is $|a| = 20$, and because the graph is a reflection it follows that $a = -20$.

▶ The model is $T = -20 \cos \frac{\pi}{6}t + 60$ where t is measured in months and $t = 0$ represents January 1.

Ferris Wheel

EXAMPLE 3 *Modeling Circular Motion*

A Ferris wheel with a radius of 25 feet is rotating at a rate of 3 revolutions per minute. When $t = 0$, a chair starts at the lowest point on the wheel, which is 5 feet above the ground. Write a model for the height h (in feet) of the chair as a function of the time t (in seconds).

SOLUTION

When the chair is at the bottom of the Ferris wheel, it is 5 feet above the ground, so $m = 5$. When it is at the top, it is $5 + 2(25) = 55$ feet above the ground, so $M = 55$.

The vertical shift for the model is $k = \frac{M + m}{2} = \frac{55 + 5}{2} = \frac{60}{2} = 30$.

When $t = 0$, the height is at its minimum, so the model is a cosine function with $a < 0$ and no horizontal shift.

The amplitude is $|a| = \frac{M - m}{2} = \frac{55 - 5}{2} = \frac{50}{2} = 25$. Because $a < 0$ it follows that $a = -25$.

Since the Ferris wheel is rotating at 3 revolutions per minute, it completes one revolution in 20 seconds. The period is $\frac{2\pi}{b} = 20$, so $b = \frac{\pi}{10}$.

▶ A model for the height of the chair as a function of time is $h = -25 \cos \frac{\pi}{10}t + 30$.

There are two ways you can model a set of data points whose scatter plot appears sinusoidal. One way is to estimate the minimum and maximum values and use the technique shown in Example 2. Another way is to use a graphing calculator that has a sinusoidal regression feature. The advantage of the second method is that it uses all of the data points to find the model.

REAL LIFE

Meteorology

EXAMPLE 4   *Using Sinusoidal Regression*

The average daily temperature T (in degrees Fahrenheit) in Fairbanks, Alaska, is given in the table. Time t is measured in months, with $t = 0$ representing January 1. Write a trigonometric model that gives T as a function of t.

t	0.5	1.5	2.5	3.5	4.5	5.5	6.5	7.5	8.5	9.5	10.5	11.5
T	−10.1	−3.6	11.0	30.7	48.6	59.8	62.5	56.8	45.5	25.1	2.7	−6.5

▶ Source: National Climatic Data Center

SOLUTION

Begin by entering the data in a graphing calculator and drawing a scatter plot.

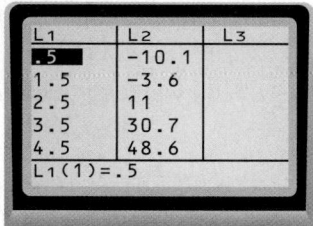

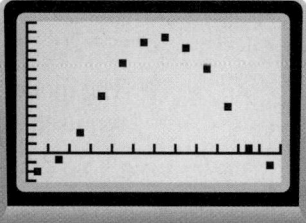

❶ Enter the data.

❷ Draw a scatter plot.

Because the scatter plot appears sinusoidal, you can fit the data with a sine function to get the following model:

$$T = 37.4 \sin (0.518t - 1.72) + 26.5$$

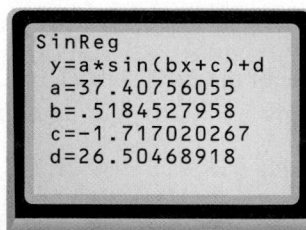

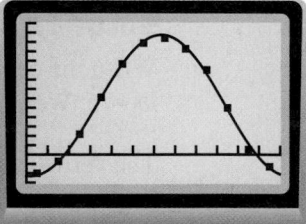

❸ Perform a sinusoidal regression.

❹ Graph the model and the data in the same viewing window.

After obtaining the model, you should graph it in the same viewing window as the scatter plot to see how well the model fits the data. In this case, the model is a good fit.

✓**CHECK** As a check on the reasonableness of the model, notice that the period is $\frac{2\pi}{0.518} \approx 12$, which is the number of months in a year.

GUIDED PRACTICE

Vocabulary Check ✓

1. Complete this statement: Graphs of sine and cosine functions are called ___?___.

Concept Check ✓

2. Which two points are most useful when writing a sinusoidal model for a given graph or set of data? Explain.

3. Describe a characteristic of a sinusoidal graph that you would model with a cosine function rather than a sine function.

Skill Check ✓

Write a function for the sinusoid.

4.

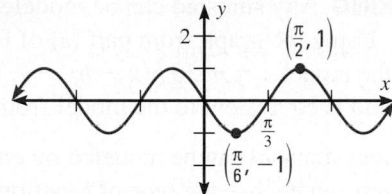

5.

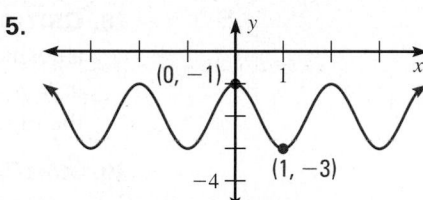

Write a function for the sinusoid with maximum at *A* and minimum at *B*.

6. $A(0, 8)$, $B(\pi, -2)$ **7.** $A(\pi, 10)$, $B(3\pi, 4)$ **8.** $A(6, 5)$, $B(2, 1)$

9. 🌐 **FERRIS WHEEL** Look back at Example 3. Suppose the Ferris wheel rotates at a rate of 4 revolutions per minute and has a radius of 20 feet. Write a model for the height h (in feet) of the chair as a function of the time t (in seconds).

PRACTICE AND APPLICATIONS

STUDENT HELP

▸ **Extra Practice**
to help you master
skills is on p. 960.

WRITING FUNCTIONS Write a function for the sinusoid.

10.

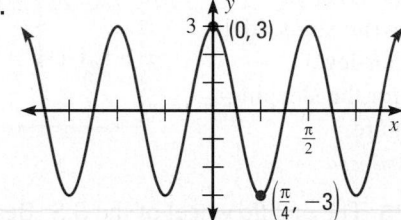

11.

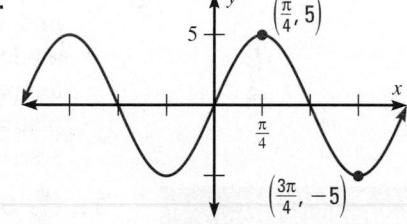

12.

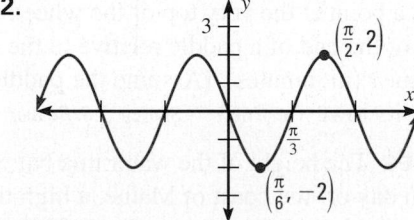

13.

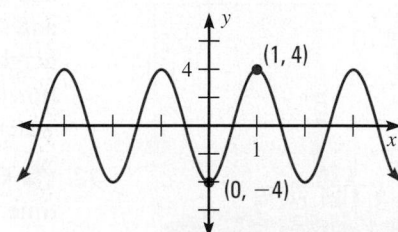

STUDENT HELP

▸ **HOMEWORK HELP**
Example 1: Exs. 10–27
Example 2: Exs. 30, 32
Example 3: Exs. 31, 33
Example 4: Exs. 34, 35

14.

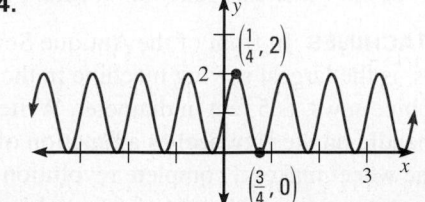

15.

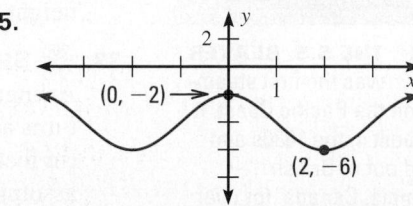

WRITING TRIGONOMETRIC FUNCTIONS Write a function for the sinusoid with maximum at *A* and minimum at *B*.

16. $A(0, 3), B(2\pi, -3)$ **17.** $A(\pi, 8), B(3\pi, -8)$ **18.** $A(9\pi, 1), B(3\pi, -5)$

19. $A\left(\dfrac{\pi}{3}, 4\right), B(0, 2)$ **20.** $A(2, 6), B(6, 0)$ **21.** $A(3, 7), B(1, -3)$

22. $A\left(\dfrac{2\pi}{3}, 9\right), B(2\pi, 5)$ **23.** $A\left(\dfrac{\pi}{6}, 11\right), B(0, -1)$ **24.** $A(0, 5), B(4, -13)$

25. $A(0, 0), B(3\pi, -8)$ **26.** $A(6, 2), B(0, -4)$ **27.** $A\left(\dfrac{\pi}{4}, -2\right), B\left(\dfrac{\pi}{12}, -6\right)$

28. CRITICAL THINKING Any sinusoid can be modeled by either a sine function or a cosine function. Using the graph from part (a) of Example 1, find the values of *a*, *b*, *h*, and *k* for the model $y = a \sin b(x - h) + k$. Use identities to show that the model you found is equivalent to the model from part (a) of Example 1.

29. *Writing* Since any sinusoid can be modeled by either a sine function or a cosine function, you can choose the type of function that is more convenient. For a sinusoid whose *y*-intercept occurs halfway between the maximum and minimum values of the function, tell which type of function you would use to model the graph. Explain your answer.

30. 🌐 **CLIMATE CONTROL** Eskimos use igloos as temporary shelter from harsh winter weather. The graph shows the temperatures inside and outside an igloo throughout a typical winter day. Write a sinusoidal model for the outside temperature *T* (in degrees Fahrenheit) as a function of the time of day *t* (in hours since midnight). Then write sinusoidal models for the floor-level temperature and for the sleeping-platform temperature.

▶ Source: *Scientific American*

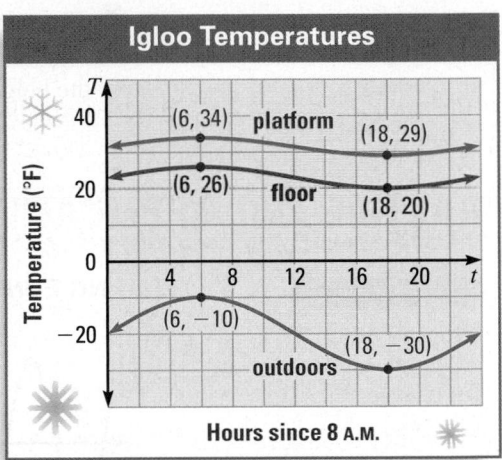

Igloo Temperatures

31. 🌐 **STEAMSHIPS** The paddle wheel of the S.S. Beaver was 13 feet in diameter and revolved 30 times per minute when moving at top speed. Using this speed and starting from a point at the very top of the wheel, write a model for the height *h* (in feet) of the end of a paddle relative to the water's surface as a function of the time *t* (in minutes). (Assume the paddle is 2 feet below the water's surface at its lowest point.) ▶ Source: *S.S. Beaver: The Ship That Saved the West*

32. 🌐 **OCEAN TIDES** The height of the water in a bay varies sinusoidally over time. On a certain day off the coast of Maine, a high tide of 10 feet occurred at 5:00 A.M. and a low tide of 2 feet occurred at 1:00 P.M. Write a model for the height *h* (in feet) of the water as a function of time *t* (in hours since midnight).

33. 🌐 **SEWING MACHINES** In front of the Antique Sewing Machine Museum in Arlington, Texas, is the largest sewing machine in the world. The *flywheel*, which turns as the machine sews, is 5 feet in diameter. Write a model for the height *h* (in feet) of the handle on the flywheel as a function of the time *t* (in seconds), assuming that the wheel makes a complete revolution every 2 seconds and that the handle starts at its minimum height of 4 feet above the ground.

34. 🌐 **METEOROLOGY** The average daily temperature T (in degrees Fahrenheit) in Moline, Illinois, is given in the table. Time t is measured in months, with $t = 0$ representing January 1. Find a model for the data. ▶ Source: National Climatic Data Center

t	0.5	1.5	2.5	3.5	4.5	5.5	6.5	7.5	8.5	9.5	10.5	11.5
T	19.9	24.8	37.4	50.4	61.4	71.1	75.2	72.7	64.7	53.0	39.6	25.4

35. 🌐 **HEATING DEGREE-DAYS** For any given day, the number of degrees that the average temperature is below 65°F is called the *degree-days* for that day. This figure is used to calculate how much is spent on heating. The table below gives the total number T of degree-days for each month t in Dubuque, Iowa, with $t = 1$ representing January. Find a model for the data. ▶ Source: *Workshop Math*

t	1	2	3	4	5	6	7	8	9	10	11	12
T	1420	1204	1026	546	260	78	12	31	156	450	906	1287

Test
Preparation

36. MULTIPLE CHOICE During one cycle, a sinusoid has a minimum at $(18, 44)$ and a maximum at $(30, 68)$. What is the amplitude of this sinusoid?

  Ⓐ 6　　　　Ⓑ 12　　　　Ⓒ 22　　　　Ⓓ 24　　　　Ⓔ 48

37. MULTIPLE CHOICE During one cycle, a sinusoid has a maximum at $(4, 12)$ and a minimum at $(12, -2)$. What is the period of this sinusoid?

  Ⓐ 8　　　　Ⓑ 8π　　　　Ⓒ 16　　　　Ⓓ 16π　　　　Ⓔ 32

★ Challenge

38. FINDING A FUNCTION Write a sinusoidal function whose graph has a minimum at $(\pi, 4)$ and a maximum at $\left(\dfrac{\pi}{2}, 7\right)$.

MIXED REVIEW

FINDING PROBABILITY Two six-sided dice are rolled. Find the probability of the given event. (Review 12.4)

39. The sum is 3.　　　　**40.** The sum is 6.　　　　**41.** The sum is 12.

42. The sum is odd.　　　　**43.** The sum is 5 or 6.　　　　**44.** The sum is less than 7.

EVALUATING FUNCTIONS Evaluate the function without using a calculator. (Review 13.3 for 14.6)

45. $\cos(-225°)$　　　　**46.** $\cos 240°$　　　　**47.** $\sin(-30°)$

48. $\tan 330°$　　　　**49.** $\tan\left(-\dfrac{7\pi}{6}\right)$　　　　**50.** $\sin\dfrac{5\pi}{4}$

FINDING AREA Find the area of $\triangle ABC$ having the given side lengths. (Review 13.6)

51. $a = 3, b = 8, c = 10$　　　　**52.** $a = 12, b = 20, c = 25$

53. $a = 5, b = 9, c = 11$　　　　**54.** $a = 4, b = 6, c = 7$

55. $a = 6, b = 11, c = 14$　　　　**56.** $a = 8, b = 13, c = 20$

Simplify the expression. (Lesson 14.3)

1. $\tan\left(\dfrac{\pi}{2} - x\right) \sec x$ **2.** $1 - \sin^2 x + \dfrac{\cos x}{\sec x}$ **3.** $\cos(-x) \cos\left(\dfrac{\pi}{2} - x\right)$

Find the general solution of the equation. (Lesson 14.4)

4. $4\cos^2 x - 3 = 0$ **5.** $3\sin^2 x - 8\sin x = 3$ **6.** $\sqrt{3}\tan^2 x + 4\tan x = -\sqrt{3}$

Write a function for the sinusoid with maximum at *A* and minimum at *B*.
(Lesson 14.5)

7. $A\left(\dfrac{3\pi}{4}, 5\right), B\left(\dfrac{\pi}{4}, -5\right)$ **8.** $A(0, 3), B(3\pi, 1)$ **9.** $A(\pi, 6), B(0, 2)$

10. **METEOROLOGY** The average daily temperature T (in degrees Fahrenheit) in Detroit, Michigan, is given in the table. Time t is measured in months, with $t = 0$ representing January 1. Find a model for the data. **(Lesson 14.5)**

t	0.5	1.5	2.5	3.5	4.5	5.5	6.5	7.5	8.5	9.5	10.5	11.5
T	22.9	25.4	35.7	47.3	58.4	67.6	72.3	70.5	63.2	51.2	40.2	28.3

MATH & History

Music and Math

APPLICATION LINK
www.mcdougallittell.com

THEN

MUSIC AND MATH have been studied together for many centuries. For instance, 2500 years ago Pythagoras discovered that when the ratio of the lengths of two strings is a whole number, plucking the strings produces harmonious tones.

NOW

TODAY we know that musical notes can be modeled by sine functions. The function $y = \sin 2\pi f x$ models a note with frequency f (in hertz) where x represents the length of time (in seconds) that the note is played. By adding the functions modeling two different notes, you can analyze the sound that occurs when the notes are played together.

1. Write functions that model notes with frequencies 10 hertz, 11 hertz, 12 hertz, 13 hertz, 14 hertz, and 15 hertz.

2. Use a graphing calculator to graph the sum of the models for 10 hertz and 15 hertz. How many cycles of the function occur in 1 second?

3. How many cycles per second are there in the function that describes what you hear when notes with frequencies of 10 and 14 hertz are played together? 10 and 13 hertz? 10 and 12 hertz?

Harps first appeared.

First piano built.

c. 3000 B.C. **c. A.D. 700** **1709** **1964**

The lyre is introduced.

Synthesizer invented.

14.6

Using Sum and Difference Formulas

What you should learn

GOAL 1 Evaluate trigonometric functions of the sum or difference of two angles.

GOAL 2 Use sum and difference formulas to solve **real-life** problems, such as determining when pistons in a car engine are at the same height in **Example 6**.

Why you should learn it

▼ To model **real-life** quantities, such as the size of an object in an aerial photograph in **Ex. 58**.

GOAL 1 SUM AND DIFFERENCE FORMULAS

In this lesson you will study formulas that allow you to evaluate trigonometric functions of the sum or difference of two angles.

SUM AND DIFFERENCE FORMULAS

SUM FORMULAS

$\sin (u + v) = \sin u \cos v + \cos u \sin v$

$\cos (u + v) = \cos u \cos v - \sin u \sin v$

$\tan (u + v) = \dfrac{\tan u + \tan v}{1 - \tan u \tan v}$

DIFFERENCE FORMULAS

$\sin (u - v) = \sin u \cos v - \cos u \sin v$

$\cos (u - v) = \cos u \cos v + \sin u \sin v$

$\tan (u - v) = \dfrac{\tan u - \tan v}{1 + \tan u \tan v}$

In general, $\sin (u + v) \neq \sin u + \sin v$. Similar statements can be made for the other trigonometric functions of sums and differences.

EXAMPLE 1 *Evaluating a Trigonometric Expression*

Find the exact value of **(a)** $\cos 75°$ and **(b)** $\tan \dfrac{\pi}{12}$.

SOLUTION

a. $\cos 75° = \cos (45° + 30°)$ **Substitute 45° + 30° for 75°.**

$\qquad = \cos 45° \cos 30° - \sin 45° \sin 30°$ **Sum formula for cosine**

$\qquad = \dfrac{\sqrt{2}}{2}\left(\dfrac{\sqrt{3}}{2}\right) - \dfrac{\sqrt{2}}{2}\left(\dfrac{1}{2}\right)$ **Evaluate.**

$\qquad = \dfrac{\sqrt{6} - \sqrt{2}}{4}$ **Simplify.**

b. $\tan \dfrac{\pi}{12} = \tan \left(\dfrac{\pi}{3} - \dfrac{\pi}{4}\right)$ **Substitute $\dfrac{\pi}{3} - \dfrac{\pi}{4}$ for $\dfrac{\pi}{12}$.**

$\qquad = \dfrac{\tan \dfrac{\pi}{3} - \tan \dfrac{\pi}{4}}{1 + \tan \dfrac{\pi}{3} \tan \dfrac{\pi}{4}}$ **Difference formula for tangent**

$\qquad = \dfrac{\sqrt{3} - 1}{1 + (\sqrt{3})(1)}$ **Evaluate.**

$\qquad = 2 - \sqrt{3}$ **Simplify.**

✓ **CHECK** Try checking these results with a calculator. For instance, evaluate $\cos 75°$ and $\dfrac{\sqrt{6} - \sqrt{2}}{4}$ to see that both have the same value.

EXAMPLE 2 *Using a Difference Formula*

Find $\sin (u - v)$ given that $\sin u = -\frac{3}{5}$ with $\pi < u < \frac{3\pi}{2}$ and $\cos v = \frac{12}{13}$ with $0 < v < \frac{\pi}{2}$.

SOLUTION

Using a Pythagorean identity and quadrant signs gives $\cos u = -\frac{4}{5}$ and $\sin v = \frac{5}{13}$.

$\sin (u - v) = \sin u \cos v - \cos u \sin v$ **Difference formula for sine**

$= -\frac{3}{5}\left(\frac{12}{13}\right) - \left(-\frac{4}{5}\right)\left(\frac{5}{13}\right)$ **Substitute.**

$= -\frac{16}{65}$ **Simplify.**

EXAMPLE 3 *Simplifying an Expression*

Simplify the expression $\cos (x - \pi)$.

SOLUTION

$\cos (x - \pi) = \cos x \cos \pi + \sin x \sin \pi$ **Difference formula for cosine**

$= (\cos x)(-1) + (\sin x)(0)$ **Evaluate.**

$= -\cos x$ **Simplify.**

EXAMPLE 4 *Solving a Trigonometric Equation*

Solve $\sin \left(x + \frac{\pi}{4}\right) + 1 = \sin \left(\frac{\pi}{4} - x\right)$ for $0 \le x < 2\pi$.

SOLUTION

$\sin \left(x + \frac{\pi}{4}\right) + 1 = \sin \left(\frac{\pi}{4} - x\right)$ **Write original equation.**

$\sin x \cos \frac{\pi}{4} + \cos x \sin \frac{\pi}{4} + 1 = \sin \frac{\pi}{4} \cos x - \cos \frac{\pi}{4} \sin x$ **Use formulas.**

$\sin x \cos \frac{\pi}{4} + \cos x \sin \frac{\pi}{4} + 1 = \cos x \sin \frac{\pi}{4} - \sin x \cos \frac{\pi}{4}$ **Commutative property**

$2 \sin x \cos \frac{\pi}{4} = -1$ **Simplify.**

$2(\sin x)\left(\frac{\sqrt{2}}{2}\right) = -1$ **Evaluate.**

$\sin x = -\frac{1}{\sqrt{2}} = -\frac{\sqrt{2}}{2}$ **Solve for sin x.**

▶ In the interval $0 \le x < 2\pi$, the solutions are $x = \frac{5\pi}{4}$ and $x = \frac{7\pi}{4}$.

✓**CHECK** You can check the solutions with a graphing calculator by graphing each side of the original equation and using the *Intersect* feature to determine the *x*-values for which the expressions are equal.

Chapter 14 *Trigonometric Graphs, Identities, and Equations*

Biomechanics

EXAMPLE 5 *Simplifying a Real-Life Formula*

The force F (in pounds) on a person's back when he or she bends over at an angle θ is

$$F = \frac{0.6W \sin(\theta + 90°)}{\sin 12°}$$

where W is the person's weight (in pounds).
Simplify this formula.

SOLUTION

Begin by expanding $\sin(\theta + 90°)$.

$$F = \frac{0.6W \sin(\theta + 90°)}{\sin 12°} \approx \frac{0.6W(\sin\theta \cos 90° + \cos\theta \sin 90°)}{0.208}$$

$$= \left(\frac{0.6}{0.208}\right) W \left[(\sin\theta)(0) + (\cos\theta)(1)\right] \approx 2.88W \cos\theta$$

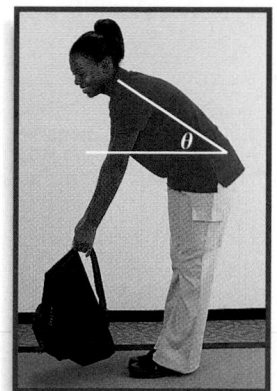

EXAMPLE 6 *Solving a Trigonometric Equation in Real Life*

AUTOMOTIVE ENGINEERING The heights h (in inches) of
pistons 1 and 2 in an automobile engine can be modeled by

$$h_1 = 3.75 \sin 733t + 7.5 \quad \text{and} \quad h_2 = 3.75 \sin 733\left(t + \frac{4\pi}{3}\right) + 7.5$$

where t is measured in seconds. How often are these two
pistons at the same height?

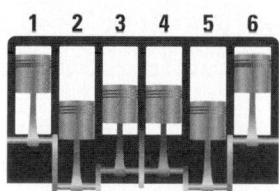

SOLUTION

Let $h_1 = h_2$ and solve for t.

$$3.75 \sin 733t + 7.5 = 3.75 \sin 733\left(t + \frac{4\pi}{3}\right) + 7.5$$

$$\sin 733t = \sin 733t \cos\frac{2932\pi}{3} + \cos 733t \sin\frac{2932\pi}{3}$$

$$\sin 733t = (\sin 733t)\left(-\frac{1}{2}\right) + (\cos 733t)\left(-\frac{\sqrt{3}}{2}\right)$$

$$\frac{3}{2} \sin 733t = -\frac{\sqrt{3}}{2} \cos 733t$$

$$\tan 733t = -\frac{\sqrt{3}}{3}$$

$$733t = \tan^{-1}\left(-\frac{\sqrt{3}}{3}\right) + n\pi$$

$$733t = -\frac{\pi}{6} + n\pi$$

$$t = -\frac{\pi}{4398} + \frac{n\pi}{733}$$

▶ The heights are equal once every $\frac{\pi}{733}$ second. So in one second,
the heights are equal the following number of times: $1 \div \frac{\pi}{733} = \frac{733}{\pi} \approx 233.3$.

GUIDED PRACTICE

Vocabulary Check ✔

1. Give the sum and difference formulas for sine, cosine, and tangent.

Concept Check ✔

2. Fill in the blanks for each of the following equations.

    a. $\sin(45° - 30°) = \sin \underline{\ ?\ } \cos 30° - \cos 45° \sin \underline{\ ?\ }$

    b. $\tan(90° + 60°) = \dfrac{\underline{\ ?\ } + \tan 60°}{1 - \tan 90° \ \underline{\ ?\ }}$

3. Explain how you can evaluate $\tan 105°$ using either the sum or difference formula for tangent.

Skill Check ✔

Find the exact value of the expression.

4. $\cos 105°$ **5.** $\sin 15°$ **6.** $\tan 75°$

7. $\cos \dfrac{11\pi}{12}$ **8.** $\sin \dfrac{23\pi}{12}$ **9.** $\tan \dfrac{7\pi}{12}$

Solve the equation for $0 \le x < 2\pi$.

10. $2\sin\left(x + \dfrac{\pi}{3}\right) = \tan \dfrac{\pi}{3}$ **11.** $\tan\left(x + \dfrac{\pi}{6}\right) = \tan\left(x + \dfrac{\pi}{4}\right)$

12. $\cos\left(x - \dfrac{\pi}{6}\right) = 1 + \cos\left(x + \dfrac{\pi}{6}\right)$ **13.** $\sin\left(x - \dfrac{4\pi}{3}\right) = 2\sin\left(x - \dfrac{\pi}{3}\right)$

14. $4\sin(x + \pi) = 2\cos\left(x + \dfrac{\pi}{2}\right) + 2$ **15.** $-\cos x = 1 + 2\cos(x - \pi)$

16. 🌐 **AUTOMOTIVE ENGINEERING** Look back at Example 6 on page 871. The height h_3 of piston 3 in the same engine can be modeled by

$$h_3 = 3.75 \sin 733\left(t + \dfrac{2\pi}{3}\right) + 7.5$$

where t is measured in seconds. How often is piston 3 the same height as piston 2?

PRACTICE AND APPLICATIONS

STUDENT HELP

▶ **Extra Practice**
to help you master
skills is on p. 960.

FINDING VALUES **Find the exact value of the expression.**

17. $\cos 210°$ **18.** $\tan 195°$ **19.** $\tan 225°$

20. $\sin(-15°)$ **21.** $\cos(-225°)$ **22.** $\sin 165°$

23. $\tan \dfrac{11\pi}{12}$ **24.** $\cos \dfrac{17\pi}{12}$ **25.** $\sin\left(-\dfrac{11\pi}{12}\right)$

26. $\cos \dfrac{\pi}{12}$ **27.** $\tan\left(-\dfrac{5\pi}{12}\right)$ **28.** $\sin \dfrac{5\pi}{12}$

STUDENT HELP

▶ **HOMEWORK HELP**
Example 1: Exs. 17–28
Example 2: Exs. 29–40
Example 3: Exs. 41–48
Example 4: Exs. 49–54
Examples 5, 6: Exs. 57–59

EVALUATING EXPRESSIONS **Evaluate the expression given $\cos u = \dfrac{4}{7}$ with $0 < u < \dfrac{\pi}{2}$ and $\sin v = -\dfrac{9}{10}$ with $\pi < v < \dfrac{3\pi}{2}$.**

29. $\sin(u + v)$ **30.** $\cos(u + v)$ **31.** $\tan(u + v)$

32. $\sin(u - v)$ **33.** $\cos(u - v)$ **34.** $\tan(u - v)$

EVALUATING EXPRESSIONS Evaluate the expression given that $\sin u = \frac{3}{5}$ with $\frac{\pi}{2} < u < \pi$ and $\cos v = -\frac{5}{6}$ with $\pi < v < \frac{3\pi}{2}$.

35. $\sin (u + v)$ 36. $\cos (u + v)$ 37. $\tan (u + v)$

38. $\sin (u - v)$ 39. $\cos (u - v)$ 40. $\tan (u - v)$

SIMPLIFYING EXPRESSIONS Simplify the expression.

41. $\tan (x - 2\pi)$ 42. $\tan (x + \pi)$ 43. $\sin (x + \pi)$ 44. $\cos (x + \pi)$

45. $\sin \left(x - \frac{\pi}{2} \right)$ 46. $\cos \left(x + \frac{3\pi}{2} \right)$ 47. $\cos \left(x + \frac{\pi}{2} \right)$ 48. $\sin \left(x - \frac{3\pi}{2} \right)$

SOLVING TRIGONOMETRIC EQUATIONS Solve the equation for $0 \le x < 2\pi$.

49. $\cos \left(x + \frac{\pi}{6} \right) - 1 = \cos \left(x - \frac{\pi}{6} \right)$ 50. $\sin \left(x + \frac{3\pi}{4} \right) + \sin \left(x - \frac{3\pi}{4} \right) = 1$

51. $\sin \left(x + \frac{\pi}{6} \right) + \sin \left(x - \frac{\pi}{6} \right) = 0$ 52. $\cos \left(x + \frac{\pi}{3} \right) + \cos \left(x - \frac{\pi}{3} \right) = 1$

53. $\tan (x + \pi) + 2 \sin (x + \pi) = 0$ 54. $\tan (x + \pi) + \cos \left(x + \frac{\pi}{2} \right) = 0$

GEOMETRY CONNECTION In Exercises 55 and 56, use the following information.
In the figure shown, the acute angle of intersection, $\theta_2 - \theta_1$, of two lines with slopes m_1 and m_2 is given by:

$$\tan (\theta_2 - \theta_1) = \frac{m_2 - m_1}{1 + m_1 m_2}$$

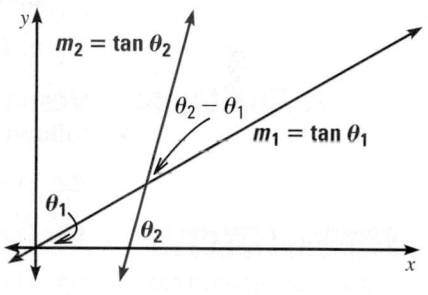

55. Find the acute angle of intersection of the lines $y = \frac{1}{2}x + 3$ and $y = 2x - 3$.

56. Find the acute angle of intersection of the lines $y = x + 2$ and $y = 3x + 1$.

57. **SOUND WAVES** The pressure P of sound waves on a person's eardrum can be modeled by

$$P = \frac{a}{r} \cos \left(\frac{2\pi r}{l} - 1100t \right)$$

where a is the maximum sound pressure (in pounds per square foot) at the source, r is the distance (in feet) from the source, l is the length (in feet) of the sound wave, and t is the time (in seconds). Simplify this formula when $r = 16$ feet, $l = 4$ feet, and $a = 0.4$ pound per square foot.

58. **AERIAL PHOTOGRAPHY** You are at a height h taking aerial photographs. The ratio of the length WQ of the image to the length NA of the actual object is

$$\frac{WQ}{NA} = \frac{f \tan (\theta - t) + f \tan t}{h \tan \theta}$$

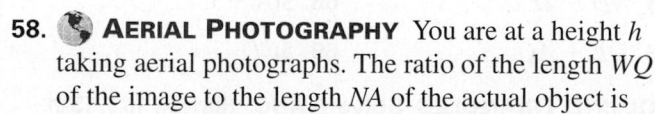

where f is the focal length of the camera, θ is the angle with the vertical made by the line from the camera to point A and t is the tilt angle of the film. Use the difference formula for tangent to simplify the ratio. Then show that $\frac{WQ}{NA} = \frac{f}{h}$ when $t = 0$.

▶ Source: *Math Applied to Space Science*

59.  **FERRIS WHEEL** The heights h (in feet) of two people in different seats on a Ferris wheel can be modeled by

$$h_1 = 28 \cos 10t + 38 \qquad \text{and} \qquad h_2 = 28 \cos 10\left(t - \frac{\pi}{6}\right) + 38$$

where t is the time (in minutes). When are the two people at the same height?

60. CRITICAL THINKING You can write the sum and difference formulas for cosine as a single equation: $\cos (u \pm v) = \cos u \cos v \mp \sin u \sin v$. Explain why the symbol $\pm$ is used on the left side, but the symbol $\mp$ is used on the right side. Then use the symbols $\pm$ and $\mp$ to write the sum and difference formulas for sine and tangent as single equations.

61.  **MULTI-STEP PROBLEM** Suppose two middle-A tuning forks are struck at different times so that their vibrations are slightly out of phase. The combined pressure change P (in pascals) caused by the forks at time t (in seconds) is:

$$P = 3 \sin 880\pi t + 4 \cos 880\pi t$$

a. Graph the equation on a graphing calculator using a viewing window of $0 \le x \le 0.5$ and $-6 \le y \le 6$. What do you observe about the graph?

b. Write the given model in the form $y = a \cos b(x - h)$.

c. Graph the model from part (b) to confirm that the graphs are the same.

★ **Challenge**

VERIFYING FORMULAS Use the difference formula for cosine to verify the following formulas.

62. The sum formula for cosine, by replacing v with $-v$

63. The difference formula for tangent, by using the identity $\tan \theta = \dfrac{\sin \theta}{\cos \theta}$

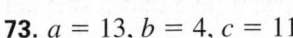
www.mcdougallittell.com

64. The difference formula for sine, by using a cofunction identity

MIXED REVIEW

SIMPLIFYING EXPRESSIONS Using the given matrices, simplify the expression. (Review 4.2)

$$A = \begin{bmatrix} 2 & 3 \\ -1 & -2 \end{bmatrix}, B = \begin{bmatrix} -1 \\ 3 \end{bmatrix}, C = \begin{bmatrix} 2 & 0 \\ -4 & 1 \end{bmatrix}, D = \begin{bmatrix} 3 & 1 & -1 \\ -2 & 0 & 2 \end{bmatrix}, E = \begin{bmatrix} 3 & 1 \\ -1 & 2 \\ 0 & -2 \end{bmatrix}$$

65. $AD + D$

66. $3(A + C)$

67. $-2AB + B$

68. $DE + AC$

69. $5CD$

70. $AD - CD$

SOLVING TRIANGLES Solve $\triangle ABC$. (Review 13.5, 13.6)

71. $A = 18°, B = 28°, b = 100$

72. $A = 60°, C = 95°, c = 5$

73. $a = 13, b = 4, c = 11$

74. $a = 2, b = 2.5, c = 3$

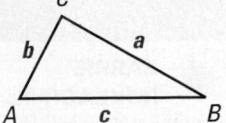

SOLVING TRIGONOMETRIC EQUATIONS Solve the equation in the interval $0 \le x < 2\pi$. (Review 14.4 for 14.7)

75. $\tan x + \sqrt{3} = 0$

76. $4 \cos^2 x - 3 = 0$

77. $8 \tan x + 8 = 0$

78. $-5 + 8 \cos x = -1$

Using Double- and Half-Angle Formulas

What you should learn

GOAL 1 Evaluate expressions using double- and half-angle formulas.

GOAL 2 Use double- and half-angle formulas to solve **real-life** problems, such as finding the mach number for an airplane in **Ex. 70**.

Why you should learn it

▼ To model **real-life** situations with double- and half-angle relationships, such as kicking a football in **Example 8**.

GOAL 1 DOUBLE- AND HALF-ANGLE FORMULAS

In this lesson you will use formulas for double angles (angles of measure $2u$) and half angles $\left(\text{angles of measure } \dfrac{u}{2}\right)$. The three formulas for $\cos 2u$ below are equivalent, as are the two formulas for $\tan \dfrac{u}{2}$. Use whichever formula is most convenient for solving a problem.

DOUBLE-ANGLE AND HALF-ANGLE FORMULAS

DOUBLE-ANGLE FORMULAS

$$\cos 2u = \cos^2 u - \sin^2 u \qquad \sin 2u = 2 \sin u \cos u$$

$$\cos 2u = 2 \cos^2 u - 1 \qquad \tan 2u = \frac{2 \tan u}{1 - \tan^2 u}$$

$$\cos 2u = 1 - 2 \sin^2 u$$

HALF-ANGLE FORMULAS

$$\sin \frac{u}{2} = \pm\sqrt{\frac{1 - \cos u}{2}} \qquad \tan \frac{u}{2} = \frac{1 - \cos u}{\sin u}$$

$$\cos \frac{u}{2} = \pm\sqrt{\frac{1 + \cos u}{2}} \qquad \tan \frac{u}{2} = \frac{\sin u}{1 + \cos u}$$

The signs of $\sin \dfrac{u}{2}$ and $\cos \dfrac{u}{2}$ depend on the quadrant in which $\dfrac{u}{2}$ lies.

EXAMPLE 1 *Evaluating Trigonometric Expressions*

Find the exact value of **(a)** $\tan \dfrac{\pi}{8}$ and **(b)** $\cos 105°$.

SOLUTION

a. Use the fact that $\dfrac{\pi}{8}$ is half of $\dfrac{\pi}{4}$.

$$\tan \frac{\pi}{8} = \tan \frac{1}{2}\left(\frac{\pi}{4}\right) = \frac{1 - \cos \frac{\pi}{4}}{\sin \frac{\pi}{4}} = \frac{1 - \frac{\sqrt{2}}{2}}{\frac{\sqrt{2}}{2}} = \frac{2 - \sqrt{2}}{\sqrt{2}} = \sqrt{2} - 1$$

b. Use the fact that $105°$ is half of $210°$ and that cosine is negative in Quadrant II.

$$\cos 105° = \cos \frac{1}{2}(210°) = -\sqrt{\frac{1 + \cos 210°}{2}}$$

$$= -\sqrt{\frac{1 + \left(-\frac{\sqrt{3}}{2}\right)}{2}} = -\sqrt{\frac{2 - \sqrt{3}}{4}} = -\frac{\sqrt{2 - \sqrt{3}}}{2}$$

STUDENT HELP

▶ **Study Tip**
In Example 1 note that, in general, $\tan \dfrac{u}{2} \neq \dfrac{1}{2} \tan u$. Similar statements can be made for the other trigonometric functions of double and half angles.

Study Tip
Because $\pi < u < \frac{3\pi}{2}$ in Example 2, you can multiply through the inequality by $\frac{1}{2}$ to get $\frac{\pi}{2} < \frac{u}{2} < \frac{3\pi}{4}$, so $\frac{u}{2}$ is in Quadrant II.

EXAMPLE 2 *Evaluating Trigonometric Expressions*

Given $\cos u = -\frac{3}{5}$ with $\pi < u < \frac{3\pi}{2}$, find the following.

a. $\sin 2u$ **b.** $\sin \frac{u}{2}$

SOLUTION

a. Use a Pythagorean identity to conclude that $\sin u = -\frac{4}{5}$.

$$\sin 2u = 2 \sin u \cos u$$
$$= 2\left(-\frac{4}{5}\right)\left(-\frac{3}{5}\right) = \frac{24}{25}$$

b. Because $\frac{u}{2}$ is in Quadrant II, $\sin \frac{u}{2}$ is positive.

$$\sin \frac{u}{2} = \sqrt{\frac{1 - \cos u}{2}} = \sqrt{\frac{1 - \left(-\frac{3}{5}\right)}{2}} = \sqrt{\frac{4}{5}} = \frac{2\sqrt{5}}{5}$$

EXAMPLE 3 *Simplifying a Trigonometric Expression*

Simplify $\dfrac{\cos 2\theta}{\sin \theta + \cos \theta}$.

SOLUTION

$$\frac{\cos 2\theta}{\sin \theta + \cos \theta} = \frac{\cos^2 \theta - \sin^2 \theta}{\sin \theta + \cos \theta}$$ **Use a double-angle formula.**

$$= \frac{(\cos \theta - \sin \theta)(\cos \theta + \sin \theta)}{\sin \theta + \cos \theta}$$ **Factor difference of squares.**

$$= \cos \theta - \sin \theta$$ **Simplify.**

Study Tip
Because there are three formulas for $\cos 2u$, you will want to choose the one that allows you to simplify the expression in which $\cos 2u$ appears, as illustrated in Example 3.

EXAMPLE 4 *Verifying a Trigonometric Identity*

Verify the identity $\sin 3x = 3 \sin x - 4 \sin^3 x$.

SOLUTION

$$\sin 3x = \sin (2x + x)$$ **Rewrite $\sin 3x$ as $\sin (2x + x)$.**

$$= \sin 2x \cos x + \cos 2x \sin x$$ **Use a sum formula.**

$$= (2 \sin x \cos x) \cos x + (1 - 2 \sin^2 x) \sin x$$ **Use double-angle formulas.**

$$= 2 \sin x \cos^2 x + \sin x - 2 \sin^3 x$$ **Multiply.**

$$= 2 \sin x (1 - \sin^2 x) + \sin x - 2 \sin^3 x$$ **Use a Pythagorean identity.**

$$= 2 \sin x - 2 \sin^3 x + \sin x - 2 \sin^3 x$$ **Distributive property**

$$= 3 \sin x - 4 \sin^3 x$$ **Combine like terms.**

EXAMPLE 5 *Solving a Trigonometric Equation*

Solve $\tan 2x + \tan x = 0$ for $0 \le x < 2\pi$.

SOLUTION

$\tan 2x + \tan x = 0$	**Write original equation.**
$\dfrac{2 \tan x}{1 - \tan^2 x} + \tan x = 0$	**Use a double-angle formula.**
$2 \tan x + \tan x \,(1 - \tan^2 x) = 0$	**Multiply each side by $1 - \tan^2 x$.**
$2 \tan x + \tan x - \tan^3 x = 0$	**Distributive property.**
$3 \tan x - \tan^3 x = 0$	**Combine like terms.**
$\tan x \,(3 - \tan^2 x) = 0$	**Factor.**

Set each factor equal to 0 and solve for x.

$$\tan x = 0 \qquad\qquad \text{or} \qquad\qquad 3 - \tan^2 x = 0$$
$$x = 0,\ \pi \qquad\qquad\qquad\qquad\qquad 3 = \tan^2 x$$
$$\pm\sqrt{3} = \tan x$$
$$x = \frac{\pi}{3}, \frac{2\pi}{3}, \frac{4\pi}{3}, \frac{5\pi}{3}$$

✓**CHECK** You can use a graphing calculator to check the solutions. Graph the following function:

$$y = \tan 2x + \tan x$$

Then use the *Zero* feature to find the x-values for which $y = 0$.

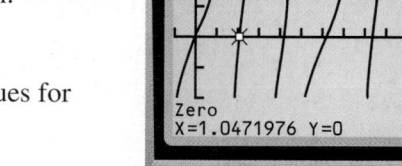

Some equations that involve double or half angles can be solved directly—without resorting to double- or half-angle formulas.

EXAMPLE 6 *Solving a Trigonometric Equation*

Solve $2 \cos \frac{x}{2} + 1 = 0$.

SOLUTION

$2 \cos \frac{x}{2} + 1 = 0$	**Write original equation.**
$2 \cos \frac{x}{2} = -1$	**Subtract 1 from each side.**
$\cos \frac{x}{2} = -\frac{1}{2}$	**Divide each side by 2.**
$\dfrac{x}{2} = \dfrac{2\pi}{3} + 2n\pi \quad \text{or} \quad \dfrac{4\pi}{3} + 2n\pi$	**General solution for $\frac{x}{2}$**
$x = \dfrac{4\pi}{3} + 4n\pi \quad \text{or} \quad \dfrac{8\pi}{3} + 4n\pi$	**General solution for x**

The path traveled by an object that is projected at an initial height of h_0 feet, an initial speed of v feet per second, and an initial angle θ is given by

$$y = -\frac{16}{v^2 \cos^2 \theta}x^2 + (\tan \theta)x + h_0$$

where x and y are measured in feet. (This model neglects air resistance.)

EXAMPLE 7 *Simplifying a Trigonometric Model*

SPORTS Find the horizontal distance traveled by a football kicked from ground level ($h_0 = 0$) at speed v and angle θ.

Not drawn to scale

SOLUTION

Using the model above with $h_0 = 0$, set y equal to 0 and solve for x.

$-\dfrac{16}{v^2 \cos^2 \theta}x^2 + (\tan \theta)x = 0$	**Let $y = 0$.**
$(-x)\left(\dfrac{16}{v^2 \cos^2 \theta}x - \tan \theta\right) = 0$	**Factor.**
$\dfrac{16}{v^2 \cos^2 \theta}x - \tan \theta = 0$	**Zero product property (Ignore $-x = 0$.)**
$\dfrac{16}{v^2 \cos^2 \theta}x = \tan \theta$	**Add $\tan \theta$ to each side.**
$x = \dfrac{1}{16}v^2 \cos^2 \theta \tan \theta$	**Multiply each side by $\frac{1}{16}v^2 \cos^2 \theta$.**
$x = \dfrac{1}{16}v^2 \cos \theta \sin \theta$	**Use $\cos \theta \tan \theta = \sin \theta$.**
$x = \dfrac{1}{32}v^2 (2 \cos \theta \sin \theta)$	**Rewrite $\frac{1}{16}$ as $\frac{1}{32} \cdot 2$.**
$x = \dfrac{1}{32}v^2 \sin 2\theta$	**Use a double-angle formula.**

EXAMPLE 8 *Using a Trigonometric Model*

REAL LIFE **FIELD GOALS** The longest professional field goal was 63 yards, made by Tom Dempsy in 1970. This record was tied by Jason Elam during the 1998–1999 season.

APPLICATION LINK
www.mcdougallittell.com

SPORTS You are kicking a football from ground level with an initial speed of 80 feet per second. Can you make the ball travel 200 feet?

SOLUTION

$200 = \dfrac{1}{32}(80)^2 \sin 2\theta$	**Substitute for x and v in the formula from Example 7.**
$1 = \sin 2\theta$	**Divide each side by $\frac{1}{32}(80)^2 = 200$.**
$90° = 2\theta$	**$\sin^{-1} 1 = 90°$**
$45° = \theta$	**Solve for θ.**

▶ You can make the football travel 200 feet if you kick it at an angle of 45°.

GUIDED PRACTICE

Vocabulary Check ✓

1. Complete this statement: $\sin 2u = 2 \sin u \cos u$ is called the __?__ formula for sine.

Concept Check ✓

2. Suppose you want to simplify $\dfrac{\cos 2\theta - \cos \theta}{\cos \theta - 1}$. Which double-angle formula for cosine would you use to rewrite $\cos 2\theta$? Explain.

3. **ERROR ANALYSIS** Explain what is wrong in the calculations shown below.

a.
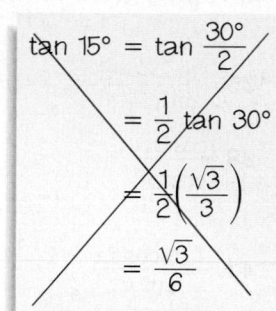

$$\tan 15° = \tan \frac{30°}{2}$$
$$= \frac{1}{2} \tan 30°$$
$$= \frac{1}{2}\left(\frac{\sqrt{3}}{3}\right)$$
$$= \frac{\sqrt{3}}{6}$$

b.
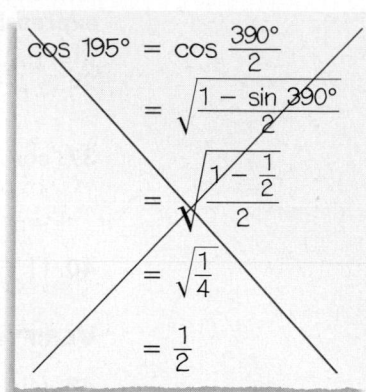

$$\cos 195° = \cos \frac{390°}{2}$$
$$= \sqrt{\frac{1 - \sin 390°}{2}}$$
$$= \sqrt{\frac{1 - \frac{1}{2}}{2}}$$
$$= \sqrt{\frac{1}{4}}$$
$$= \frac{1}{2}$$

Skill Check ✓

Given $\tan u = \dfrac{2}{5}$ with $\pi < u < \dfrac{3\pi}{2}$, find the exact value of the expression.

4. $\sin \dfrac{u}{2}$

5. $\cos \dfrac{u}{2}$

6. $\tan \dfrac{u}{2}$

7. $\sin 2u$

8. $\cos 2u$

9. $\tan 2u$

Simplify the expression.

10. $\cos^2 x - 2 \cos 2x + 1$

11. $\sin 2x \tan \dfrac{x}{2}$

12. $\sin^2 x + \sin 2x + \cos^2 x$

13. $\dfrac{\tan 2x}{\sec^2 x}$

14. $\sin \dfrac{x}{2} \cos \dfrac{x}{2}$

15. $\cos 2x \cot^2 x - \cot^2 x$

16. 🌐 **FOOTBALL** Look back at Example 8 on page 878. Through what range of angles can you kick the football to make it travel at least 150 feet?

PRACTICE AND APPLICATIONS

STUDENT HELP

▶ **Extra Practice**
to help you master
skills is on p. 960.

EVALUATING TRIGONOMETRIC EXPRESSIONS Find the exact value of the expression.

17. $\tan 15°$

18. $\sin 22.5°$

19. $\tan (-22.5°)$

20. $\cos 67.5°$

21. $\tan (-75°)$

22. $\cos \dfrac{7\pi}{8}$

23. $\sin -\dfrac{7\pi}{12}$

24. $\cos -\dfrac{5\pi}{12}$

25. $\sin \dfrac{\pi}{12}$

HALF-ANGLE FORMULAS Find the exact values of $\sin \dfrac{u}{2}$, $\cos \dfrac{u}{2}$, and $\tan \dfrac{u}{2}$.

26. $\cos u = \dfrac{3}{5}, 0 < u < \dfrac{\pi}{2}$

27. $\cos u = \dfrac{2}{3}, \dfrac{3\pi}{2} < u < 2\pi$

28. $\sin u = \dfrac{9}{10}, \dfrac{\pi}{2} < u < \pi$

29. $\sin u = -\dfrac{4}{5}, \dfrac{3\pi}{2} < u < 2\pi$

STUDENT HELP

► HOMEWORK HELP
Example 1: Exs. 17–25
Example 2: Exs. 26–33
Example 3: Exs. 34–42
Example 4: Exs. 43–50
Examples 5, 6: Exs. 51–65
Examples 7, 8: Exs. 69–73

DOUBLE-ANGLE FORMULAS Find the exact values of sin 2x, cos 2x, and tan 2x.

30. $\tan x = 2, 0 < x < \dfrac{\pi}{2}$

31. $\tan x = -\dfrac{1}{2}, -\dfrac{\pi}{2} < x < 0$

32. $\cos x = -\dfrac{1}{3}, \pi < x < \dfrac{3\pi}{2}$

33. $\sin x = -\dfrac{3}{5}, \dfrac{3\pi}{2} < x < 2\pi$

SIMPLIFYING TRIGONOMETRIC EXPRESSIONS Rewrite the expression without double angles or half angles, given that $0 < x < \dfrac{\pi}{2}$. Then simplify the expression.

34. $\sqrt{2 + 2\cos x}\left(\cos \dfrac{x}{2}\right)$

35. $\dfrac{\sin 2x}{\sin x}$

36. $\tan 2x\,(1 + \tan x)$

37. $\cos 2x - 3\sin^2 x$

38. $\dfrac{\cos 2x}{\cos^2 x}$

39. $\left(\dfrac{\sin x}{1 - \cos^2 x}\right)\tan \dfrac{x}{2}$

40. $(1 + \cos x)^2 \tan \dfrac{x}{2}$

41. $\dfrac{1 + \cos 2x}{\cot x}$

42. $\dfrac{\sin \frac{x}{2}\tan \frac{x}{2}}{1 - \cos x}$

VERIFYING IDENTITIES Verify the identity.

43. $(\sin x + \cos x)^2 = 1 + \sin 2x$

44. $1 + \cos 10x = 2\cos^2 5x$

45. $\cos \theta + 2\sin^2 \dfrac{\theta}{2} = 1$

46. $\sin \dfrac{\theta}{3}\cos \dfrac{\theta}{3} = \dfrac{1}{2}\sin \dfrac{2\theta}{3}$

47. $\cos 3x = \cos^3 x - 3\sin^2 x \cos x$

48. $\sin 4\theta = 4\sin \theta \cos \theta\,(1 - 2\sin^2 \theta)$

49. $\cos^2 2x - \sin^2 2x = \cos 4x$

50. $\cot \theta + \tan \theta = 2\csc 2\theta$

SOLVING TRIGONOMETRIC EQUATIONS Solve the equation for $0 \le x < 2\pi$.

51. $\sin \dfrac{1}{2}x = -1$

52. $\cos x - \cos \dfrac{1}{2}x = 0$

53. $\sin 2x \cos x = \sin x$

54. $\cos 2x = -2\cos^2 x$

55. $\tan 2x - \tan x = 0$

56. $\sin \dfrac{x}{2} + \cos x = 1$

57. $\tan 2x = \dfrac{\cos 2x}{2}$

58. $\tan \dfrac{x}{2} = \sin x$

59. $\dfrac{\cos 2x}{\cos^2 x} = 1$

FINDING GENERAL SOLUTIONS Find the general solution of the equation.

60. $\cos 2x = -1$

61. $\sin 2x + \sin x = 0$

62. $\cos 2x - \cos x = 0$

63. $\cos \dfrac{x}{2} - \sin x = 0$

64. $\sin \dfrac{x}{2} + \cos x = 0$

65. $\cos 2x = 3\sin x + 2$

66. **LOGICAL REASONING** Show that the three double-angle formulas for cosine are equivalent.

67. **LOGICAL REASONING** Show that the two half-angle formulas for tangent are equivalent.

68. *Writing* Use the formula at the top of page 878 to explain why the projection angle that maximizes the distance a projectile travels is $\theta = 45°$ when $h_0 = 0$.

69. 🌎 **PROJECTILE HEIGHT** Find a formula for the maximum height of an object projected from ground level at speed v and angle θ. To do this, find half of the horizontal distance $\dfrac{1}{32}v^2 \sin 2\theta$ and then substitute it for x in the general model for the path of a projectile (where $h_0 = 0$) at the top of page 878.

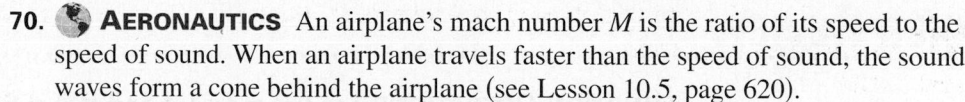

MACHU PICCHU is an ancient Incan city discovered by Hiram Bingham in 1911 and located in the Andes Mountains near Cuzco, Peru. The site consists of 5 square miles of terraced gardens linked by 3000 steps.

70. 🌐 **AERONAUTICS** An airplane's mach number M is the ratio of its speed to the speed of sound. When an airplane travels faster than the speed of sound, the sound waves form a cone behind the airplane (see Lesson 10.5, page 620).

The mach number is related to the apex angle θ of the cone by $\sin \frac{\theta}{2} = \frac{1}{M}$. Find the angle θ that corresponds to a mach number of 4.5.

🌐 **INCA DWELLING** **In Exercises 71 and 72, use the following information.**
Shown below is a drawing of an Inca dwelling found in Machu Picchu, about 50 miles northwest of Cuzco, Peru. All that remains of the ancient city today are stone ruins.

71. Express the area of the triangular portion of the side of the dwelling as a function of $\sin \frac{\theta}{2}$ and $\cos \frac{\theta}{2}$.

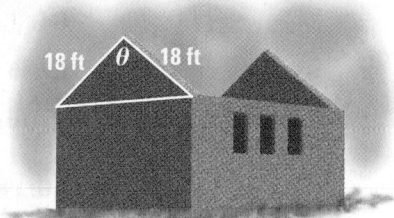

72. Express the area found in Exercise 71 as a function of $\sin \theta$. Then solve for θ assuming that the area is 132 square feet.

73. 🌐 **OPTICS** The index of refraction n of a transparent material is the ratio of the speed of light in a vacuum to the speed of light in the material. Some common materials and their indices are air (1.00), water (1.33), and glass (1.5). Triangular prisms are often used to measure the index of refraction based on this formula:

$$n = \frac{\sin\left(\frac{\theta}{2} + \frac{\alpha}{2}\right)}{\sin \frac{\theta}{2}}$$

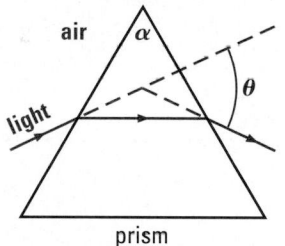

For the prism shown, $\alpha = 60°$. Write the index of refraction as a function of $\cot \frac{\theta}{2}$. Then find θ if the prism is made of glass.

Test Preparation

QUANTITATIVE COMPARISON **In Exercises 74–76, choose the statement that is true about the given quantities.**

(A) The quantity in column A is greater.

(B) The quantity in column B is greater.

(C) The two quantities are equal.

(D) The relationship cannot be determined from the given information.

	Column A	Column B
74.	$\sin x$, with $45° < x < 90°$	$\sin 2x$
75.	$\cos x$, with $90° < x < 135°$	$\cos 2x$
76.	$\tan x$, with $45° < x < 90°$	$\tan 2x$

★ **Challenge**

77. DERIVING FORMULAS Use the diagram shown at the right to derive the formulas for $\sin \frac{\theta}{2}$, $\cos \frac{\theta}{2}$, and $\tan \frac{\theta}{2}$ when θ is an acute angle.

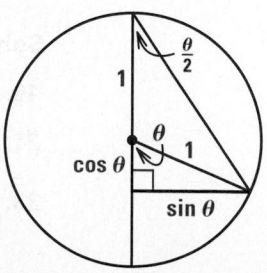

FUNCTION OPERATIONS Let $f(x) = 4x + 1$ and $g(x) = 6x$. Perform the indicated operation and state the domain. (Review 7.3)

78. $f(x) + g(x)$ **79.** $f(x) - g(x)$ **80.** $f(x) \cdot g(x)$

81. $f(x) \div g(x)$ **82.** $f(g(x))$ **83.** $g(f(x))$

CALCULATING PROBABILITIES Calculate the probability of rolling a die 30 times and getting the given number of 4's. (Review 12.6)

84. 1   **85.** 3   **86.** 5

87. 6   **88.** 8   **89.** 10

SIMPLIFYING EXPRESSIONS Simplify the expression. (Review 14.6)

90. $\cos\left(x - \dfrac{3\pi}{2}\right)$ **91.** $\sin(x - \pi)$ **92.** $\tan\left(x - \dfrac{\pi}{3}\right)$

93. $\cos(x - \pi)$ **94.** $\sin\left(x + \dfrac{\pi}{2}\right)$ **95.** $\tan\left(x + \dfrac{\pi}{4}\right)$

96. 🚚 **MOVING** The truck you have rented for moving your furniture has a ramp. If the ramp is 20 feet long and the back of the truck is 3 feet above the ground, at what angle does the ramp meet the ground? (Review 13.4)

QUIZ 3

Self-Test for Lessons 14.6 and 14.7

Find the exact value of the expression. (Lesson 14.6)

1. $\sin 105°$ **2.** $\cos 285°$ **3.** $\tan 165°$

4. $\sin \dfrac{17\pi}{12}$ **5.** $\cos \dfrac{13\pi}{12}$ **6.** $\tan\left(-\dfrac{\pi}{12}\right)$

Given $\sin u = \dfrac{1}{3}$ with $\dfrac{\pi}{2} < u < \pi$, find the exact value of the expression. (Lesson 14.7)

7. $\sin \dfrac{u}{2}$ **8.** $\cos \dfrac{u}{2}$ **9.** $\tan \dfrac{u}{2}$

10. $\sin 2u$ **11.** $\cos 2u$ **12.** $\tan 2u$

Simplify the expression. (Lessons 14.6, 14.7)

13. $\sin(x + 3\pi)$ **14.** $\cos(\pi - x)$ **15.** $\tan\left(x + \dfrac{\pi}{4}\right)$

16. $\dfrac{\sin 2x}{2\cos x}$ **17.** $2\cos^2 \dfrac{x}{2} - \cos x$ **18.** $\left(\dfrac{1 - \tan x}{2}\right)\tan 2x$

Solve the equation. (Lessons 14.6, 14.7)

19. $\sin 3x = 0.5$ **20.** $\cos 2x - \cos^2 x = 0$

21. $\sin(2x - \pi) = \sin x$ **22.** $\tan(-2x) = 1$

23. 🏌️ **GOLF** Use the formula $x = \dfrac{1}{32}v^2 \sin 2\theta$ to find the horizontal distance x (in feet) that a golf ball will travel when it is hit at an initial speed of 50 feet per second and at an angle of 40°. (Lesson 14.7)

Chapter Summary

WHAT did you learn?

Graph sine, cosine, and tangent functions. **(14.1)**

Graph translations and reflections of sine, cosine, and tangent graphs. **(14.2)**

Use trigonometric identities to simplify expressions. **(14.3)**

Verify identities that involve trigonometric expressions. **(14.3)**

Solve trigonometric equations. **(14.4, 14.6, 14.7)**

Write sine and cosine models for graphs and data. **(14.5)**

Use sum and difference formulas. **(14.6)**

Use double- and half-angle formulas. **(14.7)**

Use trigonometric functions to solve real-life problems. **(14.1–14.7)**

WHY did you learn it?

Graph the height of a boat moving over waves. **(p. 836)**

Graph the height of a person rappelling down a cliff. **(p. 843)**

Simplify the parametric equations that describe a carousel's motion. **(p. 854)**

Show that two equations modeling the shadow of a sundial are equivalent. **(p. 853)**

Solve an equation that models the position of the sun at sunrise. **(p. 860)**

Write models for temperatures inside and outside an igloo. **(p. 866)**

Relate the length of an image to the length of an actual object when taking aerial photographs. **(p. 873)**

Find the angle at which you should kick a football to make it travel a certain distance. **(p. 878)**

Model real-life patterns, such as the vibrations of a tuning fork. **(p. 833)**

How does Chapter 14 fit into the BIGGER PICTURE of algebra?

In Chapter 14 you continued your study of trigonometry, focusing more on algebra connections than geometry connections. You graphed trigonometric functions and studied characteristics of the graphs, just as you have done with other types of functions during this course.

In this chapter you saw how some algebraic skills are used in trigonometry, such as in solving a trigonometric equation in quadratic form. If you go on to study higher-level algebra, you will see how trigonometry is used in algebra, such as in finding the complex nth roots of a real number.

STUDY STRATEGY

How did you use multiple methods?

Here is an example of two methods used for Example 2 on page 849 following the **Study Strategy** on page 830.

Multiple Methods

(1) $\sec \theta \tan^2 \theta + \sec \theta = \sec \theta (\sec^2 \theta - 1) + \sec \theta$
$$= \sec^3 \theta - \sec \theta + \sec \theta$$
$$= \sec^3 \theta$$

(2) $\sec \theta \tan^2 \theta + \sec \theta = \sec \theta (\tan^2 \theta + 1)$
$$= \sec \theta (\sec^2 \theta)$$
$$= \sec^3 \theta$$

Chapter Review

- periodic function, p. 831
- cycle, p. 831
- period, p. 831
- amplitude, p. 831
- frequency, p. 833
- trigonometric identities, p. 848

14.1 GRAPHING SINE, COSINE, AND TANGENT FUNCTIONS

Examples on pp. 831–834

EXAMPLES You can graph a trigonometric function by identifying the characteristics and key points of the graph.

$y = 2 \sin 4x$

Amplitude $= |2| = 2$ Period $= \dfrac{2\pi}{|4|} = \dfrac{\pi}{2}$

Intercepts: $(0, 0);\ \left(\dfrac{\pi}{4}, 0\right);\ \left(\dfrac{\pi}{2}, 0\right)$

Maximum: $\left(\dfrac{\pi}{8}, 2\right)$ **Minimum:** $\left(\dfrac{3\pi}{8}, -2\right)$

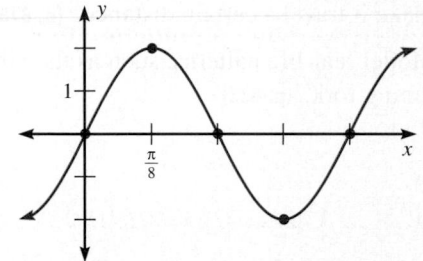

$y = \dfrac{1}{2} \tan 3x$

Period $= \dfrac{\pi}{|3|} = \dfrac{\pi}{3}$ **Intercept:** $(0, 0)$

Asymptotes: $x = \dfrac{\pi}{6},\ x = -\dfrac{\pi}{6}$

Halfway points: $\left(\dfrac{\pi}{12}, \dfrac{1}{2}\right);\ \left(-\dfrac{\pi}{12}, -\dfrac{1}{2}\right)$

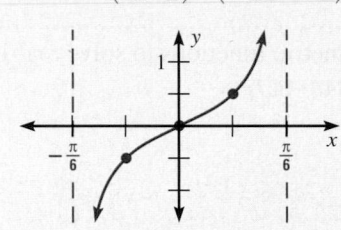

Draw one cycle of the function's graph.

1. $y = \sin \dfrac{1}{4}x$ 　　 **2.** $y = \dfrac{1}{2} \cos \pi x$ 　　 **3.** $y = \tan 2\pi x$ 　　 **4.** $y = 3 \tan \dfrac{2}{3}x$

14.2 TRANSLATIONS AND REFLECTIONS OF TRIGONOMETRIC GRAPHS

Examples on pp. 840–843

EXAMPLE To graph $y = 2 - 4 \cos 2\left(x + \dfrac{\pi}{4}\right)$, start with the graph of $y = 4 \cos 2x$.

Translate the graph **left $\dfrac{\pi}{4}$ units** and **up 2 units**, and reflect it in the line $y = 2$.

Amplitude $= |-4| = 4$ 　　　 Period $= \dfrac{2\pi}{|2|} = \pi$

On $y = 2$: $(0, 2);\ \left(\dfrac{\pi}{2}, 2\right)$

Maximum: $\left(\dfrac{\pi}{4}, 6\right)$ 　 **Minimums:** $\left(-\dfrac{\pi}{4}, -2\right);\ \left(\dfrac{3\pi}{4}, -2\right)$

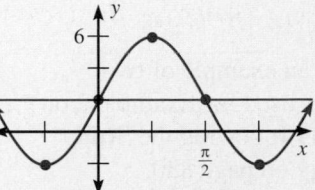

Graph the function.

5. $y = 5 \sin (2x + \pi)$ **6.** $y = -4 \cos (x - \pi)$ **7.** $y = 2 + \tan \left(\frac{1}{2}x + \pi\right)$

14.3   **VERIFYING TRIGONOMETRIC IDENTITIES**

Examples on pp. 848–851

> **EXAMPLE**   You can verify identities such as $\sin x + \cot x \cos x = \csc x$.
>
> $\sin x + \cot x \cos x = \sin x + \left(\dfrac{\cos x}{\sin x}\right) \cos x$ **Reciprocal identity**
>
> $\qquad\qquad\qquad\quad = \dfrac{\sin^2 x + \cos^2 x}{\sin x}$ **Write as one fraction.**
>
> $\qquad\qquad\qquad\quad = \dfrac{1}{\sin x}$ **Pythagorean identity**
>
> $\qquad\qquad\qquad\quad = \csc x$ **Reciprocal identity**

Simplify the expression.

8. $\tan (-x) \cos (-x)$ **9.** $\csc^2 (-x) \cos^2 \left(\dfrac{\pi}{2} - x\right)$ **10.** $\sin^2 \left(\dfrac{\pi}{2} - x\right) - 2 \sin^2 x + 1$

Verify the identity.

11. $\sin^2 (-x) = \dfrac{\tan^2 x}{\tan^2 x + 1}$ **12.** $1 - \cos^2 x = \tan^2 (-x) \cos^2 x$

14.4   **SOLVING TRIGONOMETRIC EQUATIONS**

Examples on pp. 855–858

> **EXAMPLE**   You can find the general solution of a trigonometric equation or just the solution(s) in an interval.
>
> $\qquad\qquad 3 \tan^2 x - 1 = 0$ **Write original equation.**
>
> $\qquad\qquad\quad 3 \tan^2 x = 1$ **Add 1 to each side.**
>
> $\qquad\qquad\qquad \tan^2 x = \dfrac{1}{3}$ **Divide each side by 3.**
>
> $\qquad\qquad\qquad\quad \tan x = \pm \dfrac{\sqrt{3}}{3}$ **Take square roots of each side.**
>
> There are two solutions in the interval $0 \le x < \pi$: $x = \dfrac{\pi}{6}$ and $x = \dfrac{5\pi}{6}$. The general
>
> solution of the equation is: $x = \dfrac{\pi}{6} + n\pi$ or $x = \dfrac{5\pi}{6} + n\pi$ where n is any integer.

Find the general solution of the equation.

13. $2 \sin^2 x \tan x = \tan x$ **14.** $\sec^2 x - 2 = 0$ **15.** $\cos 2x + 2 \sin^2 x - \sin x = 0$

16. $\tan^2 3x = 3$ **17.** $2 \sin x - 1 = 0$ **18.** $\sin x (\sin x + 1) = 0$

Chapter Review   **885**

MODELING WITH TRIGONOMETRIC FUNCTIONS

Examples on pp. 862–864

EXAMPLE You can write a model for the sinusoid at the right. Since the maximum and minimum values of the function do not occur at points equidistant from the *x*-axis, the curve has a vertical shift. To find the value of *k*, add the maximum and minimum values and divide by 2.

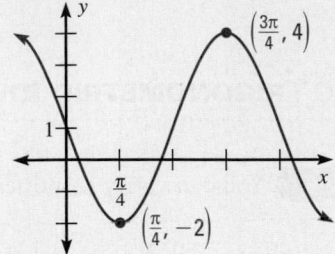

$$k = \frac{M + m}{2} = \frac{4 + (-2)}{2} = \frac{2}{2} = 1$$

The period is $\frac{2\pi}{b} = \pi$, so $b = 2$. Because the minimum occurs at $\frac{\pi}{4}$, the graph is a sine curve that involves a reflection but no horizontal shift. The amplitude is

$$|a| = \frac{M - m}{2} = \frac{4 - (-2)}{2} = 3.$$ Since $a < 0$, $a = -3$. The model is $y = 1 - 3 \sin 2x$.

Write a trigonometric function for the sinusoid with maximum at *A* and minimum at *B*.

19. $A\left(\frac{\pi}{2}, 2\right)$, $B\left(\frac{3\pi}{2}, -2\right)$ **20.** $A(0, 6)$, $B(2\pi, 0)$ **21.** $A(0, 1)$, $B\left(\frac{\pi}{2}, -1\right)$

USING SUM AND DIFFERENCE FORMULAS

Examples on pp. 869–871

EXAMPLE You can use formulas to evaluate trigonometric functions of the sum or difference of two angles.

$$\sin 105° = \sin (45° + 60°) = \sin 45° \cos 60° + \cos 45° \sin 60°$$
$$= \frac{\sqrt{2}}{2} \cdot \frac{1}{2} + \frac{\sqrt{2}}{2} \cdot \frac{\sqrt{3}}{2} = \frac{\sqrt{2} + \sqrt{6}}{4}$$

Find the exact value of the expression.

22. $\sin 150°$ **23.** $\cos 195°$ **24.** $\tan 15°$ **25.** $\tan \frac{7\pi}{12}$ **26.** $\cos \frac{13\pi}{12}$

USING DOUBLE- AND HALF-ANGLE FORMULAS

Examples on pp. 875–878

EXAMPLE You can use formulas to evaluate some trigonometric functions.

$$\tan \frac{\pi}{12} = \tan \left(\frac{1}{2} \cdot \frac{\pi}{6}\right) = \frac{1 - \cos \frac{\pi}{6}}{\sin \frac{\pi}{6}} = \frac{1 - \frac{\sqrt{3}}{2}}{\frac{1}{2}} = 2 - \sqrt{3}$$

Find the exact value of the expression.

27. $\tan 165°$ **28.** $\sin 67.5°$ **29.** $\cos \frac{5\pi}{8}$ **30.** $\cos \frac{\pi}{12}$ **31.** $\sin 6\pi$

Draw one cycle of the function's graph.

1. $y = 3 \cos \frac{1}{4}x$

2. $y = 4 \sin \frac{1}{2}\pi x$

3. $y = \frac{5}{2} \tan x$

4. $y = -2 \tan 2x$

5. $y = -3 + 2 \cos (x - \pi)$

6. $y = 1 - \cos x$

7. $y = 5 + \sin \frac{1}{2}x$

8. $y = 5 + 2 \tan (x + \pi)$

Simplify the expression.

9. $\cos \left(x - \frac{\pi}{2}\right)$

10. $\dfrac{\cos 2x + \sin^2 x}{\cos^2 x}$

11. $\dfrac{\tan 2x}{2 \tan x} - \dfrac{\sec^2 x}{1 - \tan^2 x}$

12. $\dfrac{4 \sin x \cos x - 2 \sin x \sec x}{2 \tan x}$

Verify the identity.

13. $-2 \cos^2 x \tan (-x) = \sin 2x$

14. $\tan \frac{x}{2} = \csc x - \cot x$

15. $\cos 3x = \cos^3 x - 3 \sin^2 x \cos x$

Solve the equation in the interval $0 \le x < 2\pi$. Check your solutions.

16. $-6 + 10 \cos x = -1$

17. $\tan^2 x - 2 \tan x + 1 = 0$

18. $\tan (x + \pi) + 2 \sin (x + \pi) = 0$

Find the general solution of the equation.

19. $4 - 3 \sec^2 x = 0$

20. $\cos x - \sin x \sin 2x = 0$

21. $\cos x \csc^2 x + 3 \cos x = 7 \cos x$

Find the exact value of the expression.

22. $\sin 345°$

23. $\tan 112.5°$

24. $\cos 375°$

25. $\tan \frac{13\pi}{12}$

26. $\sin \frac{\pi}{8}$

27. $\cos \frac{41\pi}{12}$

Find the amplitude and period of the graph. Then write a trigonometric function for the graph.

28.
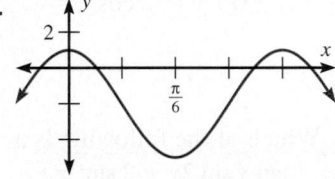

29.
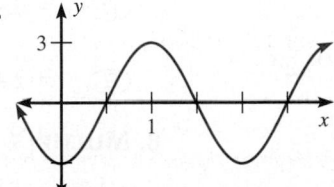

30.
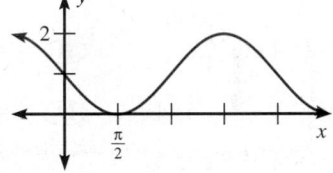

31. 🌐 **TIDES** The depth of the ocean at a swim buoy reaches a maximum of 6 feet at 3 A.M. and a minimum of 2 feet at 9 A.M. Write a trigonometric function that models the water depth y (in feet) as a function of time t (in hours). Assume that $t = 0$ represents 12:00 A.M.

32. 🖩 **TEMPERATURES** The average daily temperature T (in degrees Fahrenheit) in Baltimore, Maryland, is given in the table. The variable t is measured in months, with $t = 0$ representing January 1. Use a graphing calculator to write a trigonometric model for T as a function of t.

▶ Source: U.S. National Oceanic and Atmospheric Administration

t	0.5	1.5	2.5	3.5	4.5	5.5	6.5	7.5	8.5	9.5	10.5	11.5
T	75	79	87	94	98	101	104	105	100	92	87	77

Chapter Standardized Test

▶ **TEST-TAKING STRATEGY** Long-term preparation for the SAT can be done throughout your high school career and can improve your overall abilities. If you keep up with your homework, both your problem-solving abilities and your vocabulary will improve. This type of long-term preparation will definitely affect not only your SAT scores, but your overall future academic performance as well.

1. MULTIPLE CHOICE Which function is graphed?

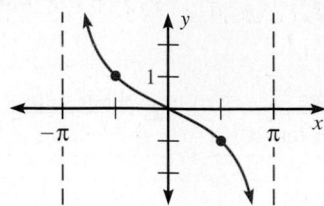

(**A**) $y = \tan 2x$ (**B**) $y = -\tan 2x$

(**C**) $y = \tan \frac{1}{2}x$ (**D**) $y = -\tan \frac{1}{2}x$

(**E**) $y = -2 \tan x$

2. MULTIPLE CHOICE Which function is graphed?

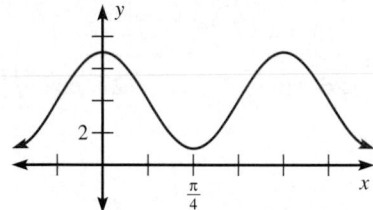

(**A**) $y = 4 \cos \frac{1}{4}x$ (**B**) $y = 3 + 4 \cos \frac{1}{4}x$

(**C**) $y = 3 + 4 \cos 4x$ (**D**) $y = 4 \cos 4x$

(**E**) $y = 4 + 3 \cos 4x$

3. MULTIPLE CHOICE What is the simplified form of $\sin^2 \left(\frac{\pi}{2} - x \right) \tan^2 x + \cos^2 (-x) + \tan^2 x$?

(**A**) $\sec^2 x$ (**B**) $2 \tan^2 x$ (**C**) $\csc^2 x$

(**D**) $1 + \sec^2 x$ (**E**) $\sin^2 x + \tan^2 x$

4. MULTIPLE CHOICE Which of the following is a solution of the equation $\tan^2 x \cos x = \cos x$?

(**A**) $x = 0$ (**B**) $x = \frac{\pi}{6}$ (**C**) $x = \frac{\pi}{2}$

(**D**) $x = \frac{5\pi}{6}$ (**E**) $x = \frac{5\pi}{4}$

5. MULTIPLE CHOICE What is the exact value of $\tan \frac{5\pi}{12}$?

(**A**) $3 - 2\sqrt{3}$ (**B**) $2 - \sqrt{3}$ (**C**) $\sqrt{3} - 1$

(**D**) $2 + \sqrt{3}$ (**E**) $2\sqrt{3} + 3$

6. MULTIPLE CHOICE Given that $\cos \theta = -\frac{3}{5}$ and $\pi < \theta < \frac{3\pi}{2}$, which of the following is true?

(**A**) $\tan \theta = \frac{3}{4}$ (**B**) $\csc \theta = \frac{5}{4}$

(**C**) $\sec \theta = \frac{5}{3}$ (**D**) $\tan \theta = -\frac{4}{3}$

(**E**) $\cot \theta = \frac{3}{4}$

7. MULTIPLE CHOICE What trigonometric function has a graph with maximum $(\pi, 2)$ and minimum $(3\pi, -2)$?

(**A**) $y = 2 \sin 2x$ (**B**) $y = 2 \cos 2x$

(**C**) $y = 2 \sin \frac{1}{2}x$ (**D**) $y = 2 \cos \frac{1}{2}x$

(**E**) $y = 2 \sin \frac{\pi}{2}x$

8. MULTIPLE CHOICE Which of the following is a solution of the equation $\frac{\tan x \sin 2x + 2 \sin^2 x}{-1 + 4 \sin x} = 1$?

(**A**) $x = 0$ (**B**) $x = \frac{5\pi}{6}$ (**C**) $x = \frac{11\pi}{6}$

(**D**) $x = \pi$ (**E**) There is no solution.

9. MULTIPLE CHOICE What is the simplified form of the expression $\dfrac{2 \sin x \tan \frac{x}{2}}{\cos \left(\frac{\pi}{2} - x \right) \sin (-x) + 1}$?

(**A**) $\frac{1 - \cos x}{\cos^2 x}$ (**B**) $2 \sec^2 x$

(**C**) $\frac{2 - 2 \cos x}{\cos^2 x}$ (**D**) $\frac{2}{\cos^2 x}$

(**E**) $\frac{2 \sin x}{\cos^2 x}$

QUANTITATIVE COMPARISON In Exercises 10 and 11, choose the statement that is true about the given quantities.

Ⓐ The quantity in column A is greater.

Ⓑ The quantity in column B is greater.

Ⓒ The two quantities are equal.

Ⓓ The relationship cannot be determined from the given information.

Column A	Column B
10. Amplitude of the graph of $y = -5 + 4 \sin 3\pi x$	Amplitude of the graph of $y = 3 - 5 \sin 2\pi x$
11. Period of the graph of $y = \tan 4\pi x$	Period of the graph of $y = 3 \tan 4x$

12. 🖩 **MULTI-STEP PROBLEM** The average daily time R of the sunrise and the average daily time S of the sunset for each month in Dallas, Texas, is given in the table. The variable t is measured in months, with $t = 0$ representing January 1.

t	0.5	1.5	2.5	3.5	4.5	5.5	6.5	7.5	8.5	9.5	10.5	11.5
R	7:29	7:10	6:37	5:58	5:29	5:20	5:31	5:51	6:11	6:32	6:58	7:21
S	17:45	18:12	18:36	18:58	19:20	19:36	19:35	19:11	18:33	17:54	17:27	17:24

a. Use a graphing calculator to find trigonometric models for R and S as functions of t. When entering the data into the calculator, you must convert the number of minutes into a fraction of an hour. For example, enter 7:27 as $7 + (27/60)$.

b. Graph the functions you found in part (a). Use a viewing window of $0 \le x \le 48$ and $0 \le y \le 24$. Describe the periods, amplitudes, and locations of local maximums and minimums. How are the functions alike? How are they different?

c. Let $D = S - R$. What does D represent?

d. Graph D in the same viewing window as R and S. How are the maximums and minimums of the three functions related? Explain the real-life significance of the relationships.

13. 🖩 **MULTI-STEP PROBLEM** The average number of daylight hours D_M in Great Falls, Michigan, is given in the table. The variable t is measured in months, with $t = 0$ representing January 1.

t	0.5	1.5	2.5	3.5	4.5	5.5	6.5	7.5	8.5	9.5	10.5	11.5
D_M	8:57	10:18	11:55	13:38	15:07	15:54	15:31	14:14	12:34	10:51	9:21	8:32

a. Use a calculator to find a trigonometric model for D_M as a function of t.

b. Use the table given in Exercise 12. Subtract each R-value from its corresponding S-value to find the average number of hours of sunlight a day for each month in Dallas. Use a graphing calculator to find a trigonometric model for the data as a function of t.

c. Graph the functions you found in parts (a) and (b). Use a viewing window of $0 \le x \le 48$ and $0 \le y \le 24$. Describe the periods, amplitudes, and locations of local maximums and minimums of the functions. How are the functions alike? How are they different? Do the graphs intersect? If so, where?

Cumulative Practice

Write an equation of the line with the given characteristics. (2.4)

1. slope: -2, y-intercept: 7

2. points: $(5, 0)$, $(-3, 2)$

3. vertical line through $(4, 2)$

Solve the system. (3.1, 3.2, 3.6, 4.3, 4.5, 10.7)

4. $x - 2y = 6$
$3x + y = 4$

5. $x + y + z = 10$
$-x + 2y - z = 2$
$3x - y + 4z = 10$

6. $x^2 + y^2 = 16$
$x^2 + y^2 - 6x - 8y + 16 = 0$

Solve the matrix equation. (4.4)

7. $\begin{bmatrix} 4 & 3 \\ -1 & -1 \end{bmatrix} X = \begin{bmatrix} 2 & -5 \\ 3 & -1 \end{bmatrix}$

8. $\begin{bmatrix} 5 & 3 \\ 7 & 4 \end{bmatrix} X = \begin{bmatrix} -1 & 6 \\ 2 & 0 \end{bmatrix}$

9. $\begin{bmatrix} 8 & -1 \\ -2 & 0 \end{bmatrix} X = \begin{bmatrix} 6 & 0 \\ 3 & -2 \end{bmatrix}$

Perform the indicated operations. (6.3, 6.5, 9.4, 9.5)

10. $(-2x^2 - x + 4) - (3x + 10)$

11. $(x - 4)(2x^2 + 3x - 1)$

12. $(x^3 - 5x + 6) \div (x - 2)$

13. $\dfrac{x + 6}{8x + 10} \div \dfrac{x^2 - 36}{2x}$

14. $\dfrac{6x}{x^2 + 3x - 10} + \dfrac{x - 4}{x - 2}$

15. $\dfrac{4x}{x - 7} - \dfrac{1}{x + 7}$

Evaluate the expression without using a calculator. (7.1, 8.4)

16. $8^{2/3}$

17. $125^{-1/3}$

18. $-9^{3/2}$

19. $\sqrt[5]{-1}$

20. $\sqrt[4]{10{,}000}$

21. $\log_2 \dfrac{1}{16}$

22. $\log_3 81$

23. $\ln e^7$

24. $\log 0.01$

25. $\log_5 1$

Find the distance between the two points. Then find the midpoint of the line segment connecting the two points. (10.1)

26. $(0, 0)$, $(3, -8)$

27. $(-5, 0)$, $(0, 2)$

28. $(-1, -4)$, $(2, 3)$

29. $(7, 4)$, $(0, -3)$

Write the next term of the sequence. Then write a rule for the nth term. (11.1–11.3)

30. $1, 4, 9, 16, \ldots$

31. $8, 4, 2, 1, \ldots$

32. $2, 6, 18, 54, \ldots$

33. $-6, -1, 4, 9, \ldots$

Find the sum of the series. (11.1–11.4)

34. $\displaystyle\sum_{i=1}^{10} 16$

35. $\displaystyle\sum_{i=1}^{5} (3i - 1)$

36. $\displaystyle\sum_{i=0}^{4} 1000\left(\dfrac{1}{2}\right)^i$

37. $\displaystyle\sum_{n=1}^{\infty} 2\left(-\dfrac{1}{3}\right)^{n-1}$

Find the number of permutations or combinations. (12.1, 12.2)

38. $_6P_5$

39. $_{10}P_2$

40. $_3P_3$

41. $_8C_1$

42. $_4C_2$

43. $_7C_4$

Find the arc length and area of a sector with the given radius r and central angle θ. (13.2)

44. $r = 11$ cm, $\theta = 80°$

45. $r = 6$ in., $\theta = 270°$

46. $r = 3$ ft, $\theta = 120°$

Evaluate the function without using a calculator. (13.3)

47. $\tan 390°$

48. $\sin(-45°)$

49. $\csc 90°$

50. $\cot\left(-\dfrac{3\pi}{4}\right)$

51. $\cos \dfrac{5\pi}{3}$

Evaluate the expression without using a calculator. Give your answer in both radians and degrees. (13.4)

52. $\cos^{-1} 0$ **53.** $\sin^{-1} \frac{1}{2}$ **54.** $\tan^{-1} 1$ **55.** $\cos^{-1}\left(-\frac{\sqrt{2}}{2}\right)$ **56.** $\tan^{-1}\left(-\sqrt{3}\right)$

Solve $\triangle ABC$. (13.5, 13.6)

57. $A = 65°, a = 7, b = 4$ **58.** $B = 110°, a = 3, c = 8$ **59.** $a = 10, b = 9, c = 4$

Find the area of $\triangle ABC$. (13.5, 13.6)

60. $A = 63°, c = 13, b = 20$ **61.** $C = 98°, a = 34, b = 20$ **62.** $a = 7, b = 4, c = 6$

Graph the parametric equations. Then write an xy-equation and state the domain. (13.7)

63. $x = \frac{1}{4}t + 1, y = t - 3$ for $0 \le t \le 4$ **64.** $x = -2t, y = t + 3$ for $1 \le t \le 5$

Graph the function. (14.1, 14.2)

65. $y = 5 \cos 2x$ **66.** $y = 4 \sin \frac{1}{3}\pi x$ **67.** $y = 5 + \sin 4x$ **68.** $y = -3 + \tan \frac{1}{2}x$

Simplify the expression. (14.3)

69. $\tan(-x) + \tan x \sec^2 x$ **70.** $\dfrac{\sin\left(\frac{\pi}{2} - x\right)}{\sin x}$ **71.** $\tan x \sec x - \csc x \sec^2 x$

Find the general solution of the equation. (14.4)

72. $3 \sin x = \sqrt{3} + 5 \sin x$ **73.** $2 \cos^2 \frac{x}{2} - 1 = 0$ **74.** $\cos x \sin^2 x - \cos x = 0$

Find the exact value of the expression. (14.6, 14.7)

75. $\sin 255°$ **76.** $\sin 157.5°$ **77.** $\tan 105°$ **78.** $\tan \dfrac{\pi}{12}$ **79.** $\cos \dfrac{13\pi}{12}$

80. FRACTAL GEOMETRY Tell whether $c = 1 + i$ is in the Mandelbrot set. Use absolute value to justify your answer. (5.4)

81. 🌐 **GIRLS BASKETBALL** The heights (in inches) of the girls chosen for the first team on PARADE's 23rd annual All-America High School Girls Basketball Team are listed below. Find the mean, median, mode(s), range, and standard deviation of the heights. Draw a box-and-whisker plot for the heights.
▶ Source: Parade Magazine (7.7)

$$76, 74, 76, 71, 72, 78, 66, 68, 74, 69$$

82. 🌐 **EQUAL GENDERS** What is the probability that a family with four children has exactly two girls and two boys in any order? Assume that having a girl and having a boy are equally likely events. (12.6)

83. 🌐 **RIALTO TOWER** Suppose you are looking at the Rialto Tower in Melbourne, Australia, which reaches a height of 794 feet. Your angle of elevation to the top of the building is 39.8°. How far are you from the base of the building?
▶ Source: Council on Tall Buildings and Urban Habitat (13.1)

84. 🌐 **BICYCLING** As you pedal up a hill, the pedals on your mountain bike make one revolution every two seconds. The maximum height of the pedal is 19 inches above the ground and the minimum height is 5 inches above the ground. Write a trigonometric model for the height H of the pedal as a function of time t. (14.1, 14.2)

The Mathematics of Music

OBJECTIVE Explore the relationship between music and trigonometric functions.

Materials: plastic or glass bottle, container of water, CBL, CBL microphone, TI-82 or TI-83 graphing calculator with cable to link to the CBL

Sound is a variation in pressure transmitted through air, water, or other matter. Sound travels as a wave. The sound of a pure note can be represented using a sine wave (or a cosine wave; recall that a cosine wave is just a sine wave shifted horizontally). More complicated sounds can be modeled by the sum of several sine waves.

The pitch of a sound wave is determined by the wave's frequency. The greater the frequency, the higher the pitch.

Note	middle C	D	E	F	G	A	B	C
Frequency (cycles/second)	262	294	330	349	392	440	494	523

INVESTIGATION

1. Fill a 12–20 ounce plastic or glass bottle almost to the top with water. Blow across the top and listen to the note produced. Pour a small amount of water out and repeat. Continue to remove water and blow notes until the bottle is empty. What happens to the frequency of the notes as the water level decreases? How can you tell?

2. Fill the bottle partway with water and blow across the top to create a note with constant pitch and volume. If you have trouble producing a steady stream of air, use a straw to blow across the bottle top. Use the CBL and the CBL microphone to collect the sound data and store it in the graphing calculator. Use the graphing calculator to graph the pressure of the sound as a function of time. The graph should resemble a sine wave.

3. Use the graph of the sound data to calculate the frequency of the note—the number of complete cycles in one second.

4. Write a sine function to describe the note.

5. Choose a note from the table. Try producing the note as follows: Adjust the water level in the bottle, blow across the top, and use the CBL and graphing calculator to find the frequency of the resulting note. Repeat this process until the frequency of the note you produce is approximately equal to the frequency of the note you chose from the table.

6. Write a sine function to describe the note you chose from the table.

PRESENT YOUR RESULTS

Write a report to present your results.

- Explain how you used the CBL.

- Explain how you found the frequency of a note from the note's sine wave.

- Explain how you wrote the sine functions in Exercises 4 and 6.

- Include a sketch of the water level in your bottle for both notes you produced in Exercises 2 and 5.

- Include a graph of the sine wave for each of the two notes.

- Consider including a recording of the notes you produced. You might repeat the experiment to produce several different notes.

- Describe how you used your knowledge of trigonometric functions in this project.

The Mathematics of Music

Laurie Hernandez
Paul Green
Algebra 2
Mrs. Cheung

EXTENSION

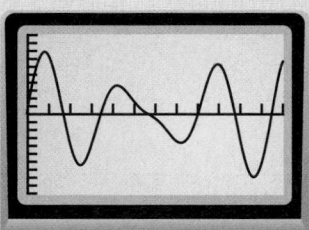

Choose a note to play and have a classmate also choose a note. Find sine functions $y = f(x)$ and $y = g(x)$ that model the two notes (as you did in Exercises 4 and 6 of the investigation). Then play the notes *simultaneously* and use the CBL and graphing calculator to graph the resulting sound wave. Compare this graph with the graph of $y = f(x) + g(x)$. What do you notice?

MUSIC CONNECTION

Bring in musical instruments and play a pure note on each. Use the CBL and graphing calculator to find the sine function that corresponds to each note. Observe what happens when you change the volume of the notes. Also, compare the sine waves for different instruments playing the same note.

Contents
of Student Resources

Derivations of Key Formulas

The derivations of various key formulas presented in this book are given below. Follow-up exercises allow you to understand the derivations better by applying them to specific situations and/or repeating them under different conditions.

The Quadratic Formula .... *Lesson 5.6, page 291*

You can derive the quadratic formula by completing the square for the general quadratic equation $ax^2 + bx + c = 0$ (where $a \neq 0$).

$ax^2 + bx + c = 0$	**Standard form of general equation**
$x^2 + \dfrac{b}{a}x + \dfrac{c}{a} = 0$	**Divide each side by a.**
$x^2 + \dfrac{b}{a}x = -\dfrac{c}{a}$	**Subtract $\dfrac{c}{a}$ from each side.**
$x^2 + \dfrac{b}{a}x + \left(\dfrac{b}{2a}\right)^2 = -\dfrac{c}{a} + \left(\dfrac{b}{2a}\right)^2$	**Complete the square by adding the square of half the coefficient of x to each side.**
$\left(x + \dfrac{b}{2a}\right)^2 = \dfrac{b^2 - 4ac}{4a^2}$	**Write the left side as the square of a binomial. Write the right side as a single fraction.**
$x + \dfrac{b}{2a} = \pm\sqrt{\dfrac{b^2 - 4ac}{4a^2}}$	**Take square roots of each side.**
$x = -\dfrac{b}{2a} \pm \sqrt{\dfrac{b^2 - 4ac}{4a^2}}$	**Subtract $\dfrac{b}{2a}$ from each side.**
$x = \dfrac{-b \pm \sqrt{b^2 - 4ac}}{2a}$	**Simplify.**

Exercises

1. Solve the quadratic equation $3x^2 + 5x + 2 = 0$ by completing the square and by using the quadratic formula. Check to see that you get the same solutions.

2. Derive a formula for the solution of a quadratic equation of the form $x^2 + mx + n = 0$. Check to see that your formula works for $x^2 - 4x + 3 = 0$.

3. Show that the function $f(x) = ax^2 + bx + c$ can be written in intercept form as

$$f(x) = a\left(x - \frac{-b + \sqrt{b^2 - 4ac}}{2a}\right)\left(x - \frac{-b - \sqrt{b^2 - 4ac}}{2a}\right)$$

by multiplying the factors in the intercept form and simplifying.

Equation of a Parabola .... *Lesson 10.2, page 596*

Using the geometric definition of a parabola and the distance formula (page 589), you can derive the equation of a parabola.

DEFINITION A parabola is the set of points (x, y) that are equidistant from a fixed line, called the *directrix*, and a fixed point, called the *focus*.

Equation of a Parabola (*continued*)

For $p > 0$, let the coordinates of the focus be $(0, p)$ and the equation of the directrix be $y = -p$ as in the diagram shown. Notice that $(0, 0)$ is p units from the focus and also p units from the directrix. Therefore, $(0, 0)$ is a point on the parabola.

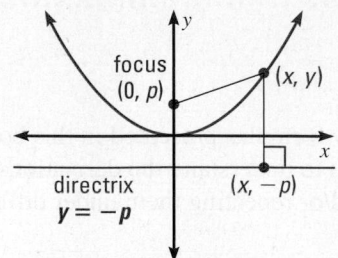

For any point (x, y) on the parabola:

$$\begin{array}{ll}
\dfrac{\text{distance between}}{(x,\,y)\text{ and }(0,\,p)} = \dfrac{\text{distance between}}{(x,\,y)\text{ and } y = -p} & \textbf{Definition of a parabola} \\[2ex]
\sqrt{(x-0)^2 + (y-p)^2} = \sqrt{(x-x)^2 + (y-(-p))^2} & \textbf{Distance formula} \\[2ex]
\sqrt{x^2 + (y-p)^2} = \sqrt{(y+p)^2} & \textbf{Simplify.} \\[2ex]
x^2 + (y-p)^2 = (y+p)^2 & \textbf{Square each side.} \\[2ex]
x^2 + y^2 - 2py + p^2 = y^2 + 2py + p^2 & \textbf{Multiply.} \\[2ex]
x^2 = 4py & \textbf{Subtract } y^2 - 2py + p^2 \textbf{ from each side.}
\end{array}$$

In the preceding derivation, p was assumed to be positive. If p were negative, the focus would be below the x-axis and the directrix would be above it, as shown. There would be no change in the derivation, however, so the equation $x^2 = 4py$ describes a parabola that opens up when $p > 0$ and a parabola that opens down when $p < 0$.

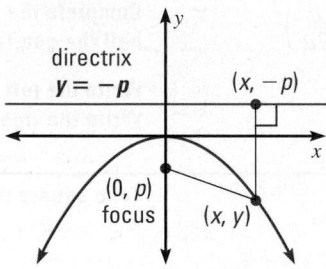

Exercises

1. Derive an equation for the set of all points (x, y) that are the same distance from $(0, 5)$ as they are from $y = -5$. Compare your work with each step of the derivation shown above.

2. Show that $y^2 = 4px$ describes a parabola that opens to the right when $p > 0$ and a parabola that opens to the left when $p < 0$.

Equation of an Ellipse .... *Lesson 10.4, page 609*

Using the geometric definition of an ellipse and the distance formula (page 589), you can derive the equation of an ellipse.

DEFINITION An ellipse is the set of points (x, y) such that the sum of the distances between (x, y) and two distinct points, called the *foci*, is constant.

Let the foci have coordinates $(-c, 0)$ and $(c, 0)$, and let $(0, b)$ be the point where the ellipse intersects the positive y-axis. Let the distance between $(0, b)$ and each focus be a. Then the sum of the distances from any point (x, y) on the ellipse to the two foci must be $2a$.

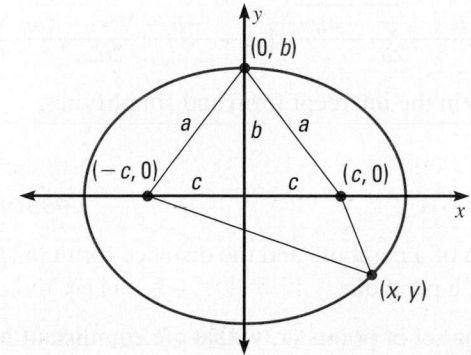

$$\text{distance between} \atop (x, y) \text{ and } (-c, 0)} \quad + \quad {\text{distance between} \atop (x, y) \text{ and } (c, 0)} = 2a$$

Definition of an ellipse

$$\sqrt{(x - (-c))^2 + (y - 0)^2} + \sqrt{(x - c)^2 + (y - 0)^2} = 2a$$

Distance formula

$$\sqrt{(x + c)^2 + y^2} + \sqrt{(x - c)^2 + y^2} = 2a$$

Simplify.

$$\sqrt{(x + c)^2 + y^2} = 2a - \sqrt{(x - c)^2 + y^2}$$

Subtract $\sqrt{(x - c)^2 + y^2}$ from each side.

At this point, square each side of the equation twice to eliminate the two radicals.

$$(x + c)^2 + y^2 = 4a^2 - 4a\sqrt{(x - c)^2 + y^2} + (x - c)^2 + y^2$$

Square each side.

$$4cx = 4a^2 - 4a\sqrt{(x - c)^2 + y^2}$$

Subtract $(x - c)^2 + y^2$ from each side, and simplify.

$$cx - a^2 = -a\sqrt{(x - c)^2 + y^2}$$

Subtract $4a^2$ from each side, and divide each side by 4.

$$c^2x^2 - 2a^2cx + a^4 = a^2\left[(x - c)^2 + y^2\right]$$

Square each side again.

$$c^2x^2 - 2a^2cx + a^4 = a^2x^2 - 2a^2cx + a^2c^2 + a^2y^2$$

Multiply.

$$a^4 = a^2x^2 - c^2x^2 + a^2c^2 + a^2y^2$$

Subtract $c^2x^2 - 2a^2cx$ from each side.

$$a^2(a^2 - c^2) = (a^2 - c^2)x^2 + a^2y^2$$

Subtract a^2c^2 from each side, and factor.

Since a, b, and c are the lengths of the sides of a right triangle (see diagram on previous page), you have $a^2 = b^2 + c^2$, or $a^2 - c^2 = b^2$, by the Pythagorean theorem. Therefore:

$$a^2b^2 = b^2x^2 + a^2y^2$$

Substitute b^2 for $a^2 - c^2$.

$$1 = \frac{x^2}{a^2} + \frac{y^2}{b^2}$$

Divide each side by a^2b^2.

You now have the equation of an ellipse whose center is $(0, 0)$. You know that the length of the vertical axis of the ellipse—the distance between $(0, b)$ and $(0, -b)$—is $2b$. But what is the length of the other axis?

Let $(d, 0)$ be the intersection of the ellipse with the positive x-axis as shown. Then the distance between $(d, 0)$ and $(-c, 0)$ plus the distance between $(d, 0)$ and $(c, 0)$ is $2a$. That is:

$$[c + c + (d - c)] + (d - c) = 2a$$

$$2d = 2a$$

$$d = a$$

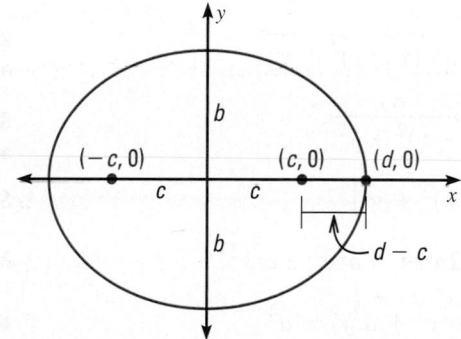

Therefore, the ellipse intersects the x-axis at $(-a, 0)$ and $(a, 0)$, and the length of the horizontal axis of the ellipse is $2a$.

Exercises

1. Derive an equation for the set of all points (x, y) such that the sum of the distances between (x, y) and the two points $(-3, 0)$ and $(3, 0)$ is 10. Compare your work with each step of the derivation shown above.

2. Show that the equation $\dfrac{x^2}{b^2} + \dfrac{y^2}{a^2} = 1$ describes an ellipse where the two foci have coordinates $(0, -c)$ and $(0, c)$ and where $(b, 0)$ is the point where the ellipse intersects the positive x-axis. (Let the distance between $(b, 0)$ and each focus be a.)

Equation of a Hyperbola .... *Lesson 10.5, page 615*

Using the geometric definition of a hyperbola and the distance formula (page 589), you can derive the equation of a hyperbola.

DEFINITION A hyperbola is the set of points (x, y) such that the difference of the distances between (x, y) and two distinct points, called the *foci*, is constant.

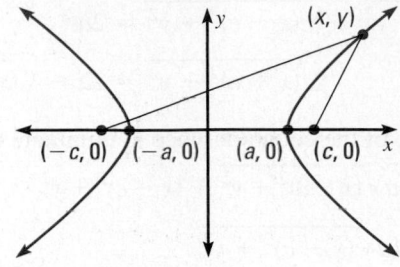

Let the two foci have coordinates $(-c, 0)$ and $(c, 0)$ where $c > 0$, and let the coordinates of the points, called the *vertices*, where the hyperbola intersects the x-axis have coordinates $(-a, 0)$ and $(a, 0)$ where $a > 0$.

The distance between either focus and the vertex farther from it is $c + a$, while the distance between either focus and the vertex closer to it is $c - a$. The difference in the distances is $c + a - (c - a) = 2a$ or $c - a - (c + a) = -2a$. Therefore, $\pm 2a$ is the common difference in the distances to the foci from any point on the hyperbola.

$\dfrac{\text{distance between}}{(x, y) \text{ and } (-c, 0)} - \dfrac{\text{distance between}}{(x, y) \text{ and } (c, 0)} = \pm 2a$	**Definition of a hyperbola**
$\sqrt{(x - (-c))^2 + (y - 0)^2} - \sqrt{(x - c)^2 + (y - 0)^2} = \pm 2a$	**Distance formula**
$\sqrt{(x + c)^2 + y^2} - \sqrt{(x - c)^2 + y^2} = \pm 2a$	**Simplify.**
$\sqrt{(x + c)^2 + y^2} = \pm 2a + \sqrt{(x - c)^2 + y^2}$	**Add $\sqrt{(x - c)^2 + y^2}$ to each side.**

At this point, square each side of the equation twice to eliminate the two radicals.

$(x + c)^2 + y^2 = 4a^2 \pm 4a\sqrt{(x - c)^2 + y^2} + (x - c)^2 + y^2$	**Square each side.**
$4cx = 4a^2 \pm 4a\sqrt{(x - c)^2 + y^2}$	**Subtract $(x - c)^2 + y^2$ from each side, and simplify.**
$cx - a^2 = \pm a\sqrt{(x - c)^2 + y^2}$	**Subtract $4a^2$ from each side, and divide each side by 4.**
$c^2x^2 - 2a^2cx + a^4 = a^2\left[(x - c)^2 + y^2\right]$	**Square each side again.**
$c^2x^2 - 2a^2cx + a^4 = a^2x^2 - 2a^2cx + a^2c^2 + a^2y^2$	**Multiply.**
$c^2x^2 = a^2x^2 + a^2c^2 + a^2y^2 - a^4$	**Subtract $-2a^2cx + a^4$ from each side.**
$(c^2 - a^2)x^2 - a^2y^2 = a^2(c^2 - a^2)$	**Subtract $a^2x^2 + a^2y^2$ from each side, and factor.**

By drawing perpendiculars to the x-axis at the vertices, you can form right triangles each having one leg (along the x-axis) of length a and a hypotenuse of length c as shown at the top of the next page. Let b be the length of the other leg. Then $a^2 + b^2 = c^2$, or $b^2 = c^2 - a^2$, by the Pythagorean theorem. Therefore:

$b^2x^2 - a^2y^2 = a^2b^2$	**Substitute b^2 for $c^2 - a^2$.**
$\dfrac{x^2}{a^2} - \dfrac{y^2}{b^2} = 1$	**Divide each side by a^2b^2.**

You now have the equation of a hyperbola whose center is (0, 0). The lines that contain the hypotenuses of the right triangles have equations $y = \pm\frac{b}{a}x$. To see that these lines are asymptotes of the hyperbola, solve the equation of the hyperbola for y:

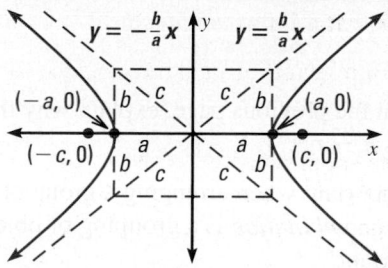

$$\frac{x^2}{a^2} - \frac{y^2}{b^2} = 1$$ **Equation of a hyperbola**

$$b^2x^2 - a^2y^2 = a^2b^2$$ **Multiply each side by a^2b^2.**

$$-a^2y^2 = a^2b^2 - b^2x^2$$ **Subtract b^2x^2 from each side.**

$$y^2 = \frac{b^2}{a^2}x^2 - b^2$$ **Divide each side by $-a^2$.**

$$y^2 = \frac{b^2}{a^2}(x^2 - a^2)$$ **Factor out $\frac{b^2}{a^2}$.**

$$y = \pm\frac{b}{a}\sqrt{x^2 - a^2}$$ **Take square roots of each side.**

As $x \to +\infty$, the value of x^2 becomes much greater than the value of a^2 (a constant) so that $\sqrt{x^2 - a^2} \to \sqrt{x^2} = x$. Therefore, the graph of $y = \pm\frac{b}{a}\sqrt{x^2 - a^2}$ approaches the graph of $y = \pm\frac{b}{a}x$ as $x \to +\infty$. You can make a similar argument for $x \to -\infty$.

Exercises

1. Derive an equation for the set of all points (x, y) such that the difference of the distances between (x, y) and the two points $(-5, 0)$ and $(5, 0)$ is ± 8. Compare your work with each step of the derivation shown on the previous page.

2. Show that the equation $\frac{y^2}{a^2} - \frac{x^2}{b^2} = 1$ describes a hyperbola where the two foci have coordinates $(0, -c)$ and $(0, c)$ and where the hyperbola intersects the y-axis at $(0, -a)$ and $(0, a)$.

Permutations of *n* Objects Taken *r* at a Time .... *Lesson 12.1, page 703*

Using the fundamental counting principle (page 701) and the definition of factorial (page 681), you can derive the formula for the number of permutations of *n* objects taken *r* at a time.

Number of permutations	=	Number of ways to choose 1st object	·	Number of ways to choose 2nd object	·	Number of ways to choose 3rd object	· . . . ·	Number of ways to choose *r*th object

$$_nP_r = n \cdot (n - 1) \cdot (n - 2) \cdot \ldots \cdot (n - r + 1)$$

$$= \frac{n \cdot (n - 1) \cdot (n - 2) \cdot \ldots \cdot (n - r + 1) \cdot (n - r) \cdot (n - r - 1) \cdot \ldots \cdot 2 \cdot 1}{(n - r) \cdot (n - r - 1) \cdot \ldots \cdot 2 \cdot 1}$$ **Multiply and divide by $(n - r)!$.**

$$= \frac{n!}{(n - r)!}$$ **Definition of factorial**

Permutations of n Objects Taken r at a Time (continued)

Exercises

1. In the derivation shown on the previous page, explain why the number of ways to choose the rth object is $n - r + 1$.

2. You know that order is important when arranging a group of objects. You will learn in Lesson 12.2 that a *combination* is a grouping of objects where the order of the objects is not important.

  a. For any group of r objects, how many ways are there of arranging the objects?

  b. Let $_nC_r$ denote the number of combinations of n objects taken r at a time. Use your answer from part (a) to write $_nP_r$ in terms of $_nC_r$. (That is, complete this statement: $_nP_r = (\underline{\ ?\ })(_nC_r)$ because for each combination of r objects there are $\underline{\ ?\ }$ permutations of those objects.)

  c. Using the equation from part (b) and the formula for $_nP_r$, derive a formula for $_nC_r$ in terms of n and r. (This is the formula given on page 708.)

Formula for Arc Length .... *Lesson 13.2, page 779*

By using the circumference and radian measure of a circle (page 777), you can write a proportion to derive the formula for the length of a circular arc.

Let r be the radius of a circle, and let θ be the radian measure of a central angle that intercepts an arc of length s. Knowing that the circumference of the circle is $2\pi r$ and that there are 2π radians in a full circle, you can write the following proportion:

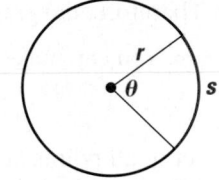

$$\frac{\text{length of arc}}{\text{circumference of circle}} = \frac{\text{radian measure of central angle}}{\text{radian measure of full circle}}$$ **Write a proportion.**

$$\frac{s}{2\pi r} = \frac{\theta}{2\pi}$$ **Substitute.**

$$s = r\theta$$ **Multiply each side by $2\pi r$.**

So, the length of the arc is just the product of the circle's radius and the radian measure of the central angle that intercepts the arc.

Exercises

1. Show that the arc length formula gives a correct result for a semicircular arc.

2. Derive the formula for the area of a sector formed by a central angle θ (measured in radians) in a circle of radius r. Your derivation should involve setting up and solving a proportion, as above.

The Law of Sines .... *Lesson 13.5, page 799*

By using the right triangle definition of sine (page 769), you can derive the law of sines, which applies to any triangle.

Let a, b, and c be the lengths of the sides of $\triangle ABC$ as shown. Introduce altitude $\overline{CD}$ having length h.

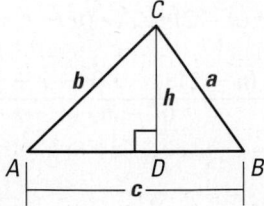

From right $\triangle ACD$ you have $\sin A = \dfrac{h}{b}$, or $h = b \sin A$, by the definition of sine.

Likewise, from right $\triangle BCD$ you have $\sin B = \dfrac{h}{a}$, or $h = a \sin B$, also by the definition of sine. Therefore:

$$b \sin A = a \sin B \qquad \text{\textbf{Equate expressions for } h.}$$

$$\dfrac{\sin A}{a} = \dfrac{\sin B}{b} \qquad \text{\textbf{Divide each side by } ab.}$$

This establishes one of the three equalities from the law of sines.

Exercises

1. Introduce a different altitude in $\triangle ABC$ and derive another equality from the law of sines. How does this result, combined with the one above, imply the third equality from the law of sines?

2. Derive the three formulas for the area of a triangle given on page 802 using an argument similar to the one above for the law of sines.

The Law of Cosines   ....   *Lesson 13.6, page 807*

By using the Pythagorean theorem and the right triangle definition of cosine (page 769), you can derive the law of cosines, which applies to any triangle.

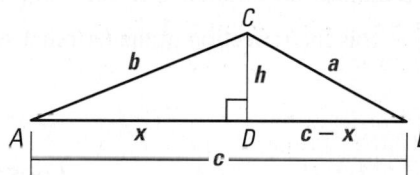

Let a, b, and c be the lengths of the sides of $\triangle ABC$ as shown. Introduce altitude $\overline{CD}$ having length h.

Let $AD = x$; it follows that $DB = c - x$. Use the Pythagorean theorem to find two different expressions for h^2:

RIGHT $\triangle BCD$	**RIGHT $\triangle ACD$**
$h^2 + (c - x)^2 = a^2$	$x^2 + h^2 = b^2$
$\qquad h^2 = a^2 - (c - x)^2$	$\qquad h^2 = b^2 - x^2$

Therefore:

$$a^2 - (c - x)^2 = b^2 - x^2 \qquad \text{\textbf{Equate expressions for } } h^2.$$

$$a^2 - c^2 + 2cx - x^2 = b^2 - x^2 \qquad \text{\textbf{Multiply.}}$$

$$a^2 = b^2 + c^2 - 2cx \qquad \text{\textbf{Add } } c^2 - 2cx + x^2 \text{ \textbf{to each side.}}$$

From right $\triangle ACD$ you have $\cos A = \dfrac{x}{b}$, or $x = b \cos A$, by the definition of cosine. Therefore:

$$a^2 = b^2 + c^2 - 2c(b \cos A) \qquad \text{\textbf{Substitute } } b \cos A \text{ \textbf{for } } x.$$

$$a^2 = b^2 + c^2 - 2bc \cos A \qquad \text{\textbf{Commutative property of multiplication}}$$

This establishes one of the three forms of the law of cosines.

Exercises

1. Using a different altitude in $\triangle ABC$, derive another form of the law of cosines.

2. Solve $a^2 = b^2 + c^2 - 2bc \cos A$ for $\cos A$.

Negative Angle Identities ⋯⋯⋯⋯⋯⋯⋯⋯⋯ *Lesson 14.3, page 848*

By using a geometric argument, you can establish the negative angle identities.

Draw an angle θ in standard position. Let $P(a, b)$ be a point (other than the origin) on the terminal side of θ. The angle $-\theta$ has the same amount of rotation as θ but the direction of rotation is clockwise rather than counterclockwise from the positive x-axis. The terminal side of $-\theta$ is therefore a reflection of the terminal side of θ in the x-axis. This means that the point $P'(a, -b)$ is on the terminal side of $-\theta$. If r is the distance $OP = OP'$, then by the definition of sine (see page 784) you have:

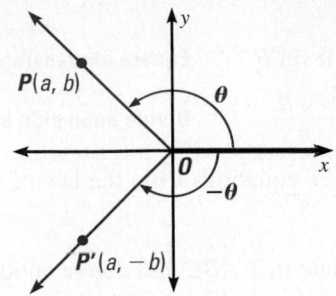

$$\sin(-\theta) = \frac{-b}{r} = -\frac{b}{r} = -\sin \theta$$

Exercises

1. Continue the argument presented above to establish the identities $\cos(-\theta) = \cos \theta$ and $\tan(-\theta) = -\tan \theta$.

2. Use a geometric argument to establish the cofunction identity $\sin\left(\frac{\pi}{2} - \theta\right) = \cos \theta$.

   (*Hint:* The terminal side of $\frac{\pi}{2} - \theta$ is the reflection of the terminal side of θ in the line $y = x$.)

The Difference Formula for Cosine ⋯⋯⋯⋯ *Lesson 14.6, page 869*

By using the right triangle definitions of sine and cosine (page 769), the distance formula (page 589), the law of cosines (page 807), and a Pythagorean identity (page 848), you can derive the difference formula for cosine.

Draw two angles in standard position. Let v be the measure of the smaller angle and u be the measure of the larger angle. Choose points P and Q on the terminal sides of the angles so that the points are each 1 unit from the origin.

Draw perpendiculars from P and Q to the x-axis, and let R and S be the points of intersection of the perpendiculars with the x-axis. Since $\triangle PRO$ and $\triangle QSO$ are right triangles, the lengths of their legs are $\sin u$ and $\cos u$ (for $\triangle PRO$) and $\sin v$ and $\cos v$ (for $\triangle QSO$) by the right triangle definitions of sine and cosine. Therefore, the coordinates of P are $(\cos u, \sin u)$, and the coordinates of Q are $(\cos v, \sin v)$.

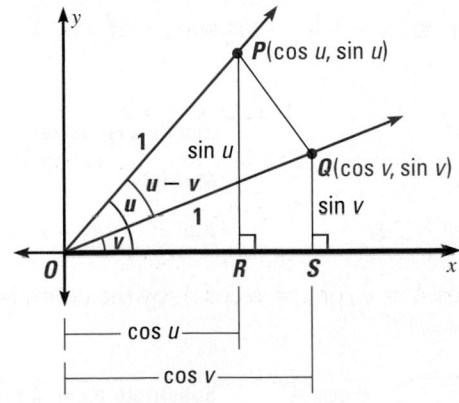

By the distance formula, you have:

$$PQ = \sqrt{(\cos u - \cos v)^2 + (\sin u - \sin v)^2},$$

or $PQ^2 = (\cos u - \cos v)^2 + (\sin u - \sin v)^2$.

By the law of cosines applied to $\triangle PQO$, you have:

$$PQ^2 = 1^2 + 1^2 - 2(1)(1) \cos(u - v)$$

Equating the two expressions for PQ^2, using a Pythagorean identity, and solving for $\cos(u - v)$, you have:

$$2 - 2\cos(u - v) = (\cos u - \cos v)^2 + (\sin u - \sin v)^2$$

$$2 - 2\cos(u - v) = \cos^2 u - 2\cos u \cos v + \cos^2 v + \sin^2 u - 2\sin u \sin v + \sin^2 v$$

$$2 - 2\cos(u - v) = (\cos^2 u + \sin^2 u) + (\cos^2 v + \sin^2 v) - 2(\cos u \cos v + \sin u \sin v)$$

$$2 - 2\cos(u - v) = 1 + 1 - 2(\cos u \cos v + \sin u \sin v)$$

$$-2\cos(u - v) = -2(\cos u \cos v + \sin u \sin v)$$

$$\cos(u - v) = \cos u \cos v + \sin u \sin v$$

The same argument can be used for angles in any quadrants, not just Quadrant I. You can verify the cofunction identities (page 848) using the difference formula for cosine. And you can in turn derive the other sum and difference formulas on page 869 using the difference formula for cosine and the cofunction and negative angle identities (for example, see Exercises 62–64 on page 874).

Exercises

1. a. Verify the cofunction identity $\cos\left(\dfrac{\pi}{2} - \theta\right) = \sin\theta$ using the difference formula for cosine.

b. Use the cofunction identity from part (a) to verify $\sin\left(\dfrac{\pi}{2} - \theta\right) = \cos\theta$.

2. Use the cofunction identities from Exercise 1 to derive the sum formula for sine. Begin by writing $\sin(u + v) = \cos\left(\dfrac{\pi}{2} - (u + v)\right) = \cos\left(\left(\dfrac{\pi}{2} - u\right) - v\right)$.

3. Use the sum formula for sine (see Exercise 2) and the negative angle identities to derive the difference formula for sine.

The Double- and Half-Angle Formulas .... *Lesson 14.7, page 875*

The double-angle formulas are obtained directly from the sum formulas, and the half-angle formulas are obtained directly from the double-angle formulas.

To establish one of the double-angle formulas for cosine, simply let $v = u$ in the sum formula for cosine:

$\cos 2u = \cos(u + u)$	**Write 2*u* as a sum.**
$= \cos u \cos u - \sin u \sin u$	**Use sum formula for cosine.**
$= \cos^2 u - \sin^2 u$	**Simplify.**

The other variations of the double-angle formula for cosine are obtained using the Pythagorean identity $\sin^2 u + \cos^2 u = 1$. For instance, replace $\cos^2 u$ with $1 - \sin^2 u$ in $\cos 2u = \cos^2 u - \sin^2 u$ to obtain:

$\cos 2u = (1 - \sin^2 u) - \sin^2 u$	**Substitute.**
$= 1 - 2\sin^2 u$	**Simplify.**

Likewise, replace $\sin^2 u$ with $1 - \cos^2 u$ in $\cos 2u = \cos^2 u - \sin^2 u$ to obtain:

$\cos 2u = \cos^2 u - (1 - \cos^2 u)$	**Substitute.**
$= \cos^2 u - 1 + \cos^2 u$	**Distribute.**
$= 2\cos^2 u - 1$	**Simplify.**

The Double- and Half-Angle Formulas (*continued*)

To establish the half-angle formula for cosine, use the double-angle formula
$\cos 2\theta = 2 \cos^2 \theta - 1$:

$$\cos 2\theta = 2 \cos^2 \theta - 1 \qquad \textbf{Double-angle formula for cosine}$$

$$\cos 2\left(\frac{u}{2}\right) = 2 \cos^2 \frac{u}{2} - 1 \qquad \textbf{Substitute } \tfrac{u}{2} \textbf{ for } \theta.$$

$$\cos u = 2 \cos^2 \frac{u}{2} - 1 \qquad \textbf{Simplify.}$$

$$1 + \cos u = 2 \cos^2 \frac{u}{2} \qquad \textbf{Add 1 to each side.}$$

$$\frac{1 + \cos u}{2} = \cos^2 \frac{u}{2} \qquad \textbf{Divide each side by 2.}$$

$$\pm \sqrt{\frac{1 + \cos u}{2}} = \cos \frac{u}{2} \qquad \textbf{Take square roots of each side.}$$

Exercises

1. Use the sum formula for sine to establish the double-angle formula for sine.

2. Use the double-angle formula $\cos 2\theta = 1 - 2 \sin^2 \theta$ to establish the half-angle formula for sine.

Skills Review Handbook

▶ Real Numbers
OPERATIONS WITH SIGNED NUMBERS

When adding signed numbers, you may find using a number line helpful. When subtracting signed numbers, remember that you can add the opposite because $a - b = a + (-b)$.

EXAMPLE Simplify the expression.

a. $3 + (-5)$

b. $(-2) - (-1)$

SOLUTION

a. $3 + (-5) = -2$

b. $(-2) - (-1) = -2 + 1$

$$= -1$$

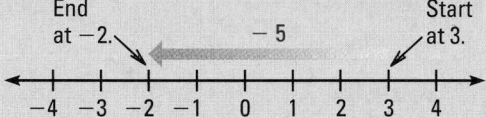 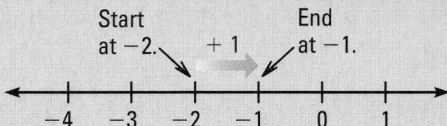

When multiplying and dividing signed numbers, use the following rules.

• Two positive numbers have a positive product or dividend.

• Two negative numbers have a positive product or dividend.

• A positive number and a negative number have a negative product or dividend.

EXAMPLE Perform the operation.

a. $3 \cdot 5$ **b.** $(-4) \cdot (-3)$ **c.** $(-6) \div (-2)$ **d.** $(-4) \div 2$ **e.** $2 \cdot (-5)$

SOLUTION

a. $3 \cdot 5 = 15$ **b.** $(-4) \cdot (-3) = 12$ **c.** $(-6) \div (-2) = 3$ **d.** $(-4) \div 2 = -2$ **e.** $2 \cdot (-5) = -10$

PRACTICE

Simplify the expression.

1. $1 + (-3)$ **2.** $3 + 12$ **3.** $(-4) + 4$ **4.** $(-8) + (-3)$

5. $7 + (-8)$ **6.** $(-3) + (-9)$ **7.** $(-4) + 10$ **8.** $4 + (-12)$

9. $6 + (-16)$ **10.** $(-18) + 2$ **11.** $(-13) + (-8)$ **12.** $(-3) + (-22)$

13. $8 - 2$ **14.** $(-5) - 8$ **15.** $1 - 5$ **16.** $0 - (-3)$

17. $7 - (-2)$ **18.** $(-8) - (-8)$ **19.** $6 - 11$ **20.** $(-1) - 4$

21. $(-2) - 1$ **22.** $(-11) - (-3)$ **23.** $12 - (-3)$ **24.** $(-11) - (-5)$

Simplify the expression.

25. $8 \cdot 3$ **26.** $(-7) \cdot 2$ **27.** $4 \cdot (-6)$ **28.** $(-3) \cdot (-3)$

29. $(-6) \cdot (-5)$ **30.** $2 \cdot (-3)$ **31.** $5 \cdot 5$ **32.** $(-9) \cdot 2$

33. $5 \div (-1)$ **34.** $(-9) \div (-3)$ **35.** $16 \div 2$ **36.** $(-4) \div 4$

37. $(-36) \div 9$ **38.** $21 \div (-7)$ **39.** $(-12) \div (-4)$ **40.** $(-36) \div (-3)$

Perform the indicated operation.

41. $(-5) \cdot 4$ **42.** $3 - (-4)$ **43.** $(-9) + 7$ **44.** $27 \div 3$

45. $(-30) \div 10$ **46.** $45 + (-5)$ **47.** $17 - (-12)$ **48.** $(-8) \cdot (-6)$

49. $14 \div (-2)$ **50.** $(-5) + 4$ **51.** $(-9) \cdot (-15)$ **52.** $(-20) - 12$

53. $(-42) - (-7)$ **54.** $7 \cdot (-3)$ **55.** $18 \div (-6)$ **56.** $(-13) + (-6)$

57. $(-11) + 18$ **58.** $12 \cdot (-8)$ **59.** $(-14) - (-7)$ **60.** $(-24) \div (-3)$

61. $63 \div (-7)$ **62.** $(-7) - (-26)$ **63.** $-12 \cdot (-11)$ **64.** $(-27) + (-15)$

CONVERTING DECIMALS, FRACTIONS, AND PERCENTS

Percent means "per hundred." It is a ratio (see page 910) that compares a number to 100.

EXAMPLE   Write as a percent.

a. 0.3 **b.** $\dfrac{4}{5}$ **c.** 1.6

SOLUTION

a. $0.3 = \dfrac{3}{10} = \dfrac{30}{100} = 30\%$ **b.** $\dfrac{4}{5} = \dfrac{4 \cdot 20}{5 \cdot 20} = \dfrac{80}{100} = 80\%$ **c.** $1.6 = 1\dfrac{6}{10} = \dfrac{16}{10} = \dfrac{160}{100} = 160\%$

EXAMPLE   Write as a decimal.

a. 66% **b.** $\dfrac{17}{25}$ **c.** 125%

SOLUTION

a. $66\% = \dfrac{66}{100} = 0.66$ **b.** $\dfrac{17}{25} = 17 \div 25 = 0.68$ **c.** $125\% = \dfrac{125}{100} = 1.25$

PRACTICE

Write as a percent.

1. 0.20 **2.** 0.15 **3.** 0.55 **4.** 1.34 **5.** 0.87

6. $\dfrac{9}{10}$ **7.** $\dfrac{2}{5}$ **8.** $\dfrac{15}{50}$ **9.** $\dfrac{3}{5}$ **10.** $\dfrac{21}{20}$

Write as a decimal.

11. 50% **12.** 120% **13.** 2% **14.** 85% **15.** 40%

16. $\dfrac{3}{5}$ **17.** $\dfrac{9}{25}$ **18.** $\dfrac{11}{20}$ **19.** $\dfrac{75}{50}$ **20.** $\dfrac{9}{10}$

CALCULATING PERCENTS

To calculate a percent of a number, write the percent as a fraction or decimal and multiply.

EXAMPLE   **a.** Find 14% of 150.   **b.** Find 80% of 200.

SOLUTION   **a.** 14% of 150 $= \frac{14}{100}(150) = 21$ **b.** 80% of 200 $= 0.8 \cdot 200 = 160$

To find the percent one number is of another, divide.

EXAMPLE   **a.** What percent is 2 of 8?   **b.** What percent is 12 of 9?

SOLUTION   **a.** $\frac{2}{8} = 0.25 = 25\%$ **b.** $\frac{12}{9} = 1.\overline{3} = 133\frac{1}{3}\%$

To find a percent increase or decrease, find the difference between the two numbers and divide by the first number.

EXAMPLE   A television is marked down from $500 to $400. Find the percent increase or decrease.

SOLUTION   Percent change in price $= \dfrac{\text{New price} - \text{Old price}}{\text{Old price}} = \dfrac{400 - 500}{500} = \dfrac{-100}{500} = \dfrac{-20}{100} = -20\%$

▶ The negative sign indicates that the percent change is a decrease. Therefore, the price of a television decreased 20%.

PRACTICE

Find the number.

1. 15% of 20   **2.** 50% of $\frac{2}{3}$ **3.** 10% of 3   **4.** 20% of $\frac{1}{2}$

5. 60% of 50   **6.** 12% of 18.5   **7.** 9% of 6   **8.** 2% of 100

9. 100% of 12   **10.** 25% of $\frac{3}{5}$ **11.** 1% of $\frac{3}{8}$ **12.** 85% of $\frac{1}{10}$

13. 5% of 0.5   **14.** 20% of 90   **15.** 10% of 0.84   **16.** 38% of 16

17. 200% of 7   **18.** 33% of 15   **19.** 0.5% of 1   **20.** 125% of 1.2

Find the answer.

21. What percent is 15 of 30?   **22.** What percent is 3 of 12?   **23.** What percent is 10 of 10?

24. What percent is 1 of 20?   **25.** What percent is 14 of 40?   **26.** What percent is 300 of 200?

27. What percent is 4 of 18?   **28.** What percent is 6 of 16?   **29.** What percent is 2 of 85?

30. What percent is 4 of 100?   **31.** What percent is 8 of 40?   **32.** What percent is 90 of 50?

33. What percent is 0.4 of 200?   **34.** What percent is 80 of 5?   **35.** What percent is 0.22 of 50?

Find the percent increase or decrease.

36. 50 votes increased to 200 votes

37. $80 decreased to $56

38. 300 fish increased to 360 fish

39. $400 increased to $600

40. 15 feet decreased to 12 feet

41. 4500 units sold increased to 4800 units sold

42. 100 students increased to 108 students

43. A 40 minute run decreased to a 35 minute run

FACTORS AND MULTIPLES

Factors are numbers or variable expressions that are multiplied together. A **prime number** is a whole number greater than 1 that has exactly two factors, itself and 1. To write the **prime factorization** of a number, write the number as a product of prime numbers.

Prime numbers less than 100
2, 3, 5, 7, 11, 13, 17, 19, 23, 29, 31, 37, 41, 43, 47, 53, 59, 61, 67, 71, 73, 79, 83, 89, 97

EXAMPLE   Write the prime factorization of 24.

SOLUTION   Use a tree diagram:

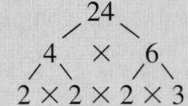

Write 24 as a product.

Write 4 and 6 as products.

A **common factor** of two whole numbers is a whole number that is a factor of each number. The **greatest common factor (GCF)** of two whole numbers is the greatest whole number that is a factor of each number. The **least common multiple (LCM)** of two whole numbers is the smallest whole number (other than zero) that is a multiple of each number.

EXAMPLE   What is the greatest common factor of 16 and 24?

SOLUTION

Method 1

Make a list of each number's factors.

16: **1**, **2**, **4**, **8**, 16
24: **1**, **2**, 3, **4**, 6, **8**, 12, 24

The common factors are 1, 2, 4, and 8. The GCF of 16 and 24 is 8.

Method 2

The GCF of two whole numbers is equal to the product of all common prime factors of the numbers.

16 = **2 · 2 · 2** · 2   Prime factorization of 16
24 = **2 · 2 · 2** · 3   Prime factorization of 24

The common prime factors are 2, 2, and 2, so the GCF of 16 and 24 is 2 · 2 · 2, or 8.

EXAMPLE   What is the least common multiple of 16 and 24?

SOLUTION

Method 1

Make a list of each number's multiples.

Multiples of 16: 16, 32, **48**, 64, . . .
Multiples of 24: 24, **48**, 72, . . .

The LCM of 16 and 24 is 48.

Method 2

The LCM of two whole numbers is the product of the highest power of each prime number that appears in the factorization of either number.

$16 = 2^4$ Prime factorization of 16
$24 = 2^3 \cdot 3$ Prime factorization of 24

The LCM of 16 and 24 is $2^4 \cdot 3 = 48$.

The **least common denominator (LCD)** of two fractions is the least common multiple of the denominators. To add or subtract two fractions with unlike denominators, first write equivalent fractions using the LCD, then add or subtract the numerators.

EXAMPLE Add: $\dfrac{3}{16} + \dfrac{7}{24}$

SOLUTION The LCD is 48. Rewrite fractions: $\dfrac{3}{16} = \dfrac{3 \cdot 3}{16 \cdot 3} = \dfrac{9}{48}$ and $\dfrac{7}{24} = \dfrac{7 \cdot 2}{24 \cdot 2} = \dfrac{14}{48}$

Add the rewritten fractions: $\dfrac{9}{48} + \dfrac{14}{48} = \dfrac{23}{48}$

PRACTICE

Write the prime factorization of the number. If the number is prime, write *prime*.

1. 8   **2.** 100   **3.** 64   **4.** 21   **5.** 17

6. 9   **7.** 12   **8.** 56   **9.** 22   **10.** 50

11. 41   **12.** 30   **13.** 31   **14.** 46   **15.** 25

Give the greatest common factor (GCF) and least common multiple (LCM) of the pair of numbers.

16. 15, 25   **17.** 4, 7   **18.** 10, 15   **19.** 20, 6   **20.** 3, 13

21. 20, 40   **22.** 12, 9   **23.** 18, 24   **24.** 8, 10   **25.** 48, 36

26. 4, 6   **27.** 2, 3   **28.** 22, 11   **29.** 6, 18   **30.** 45, 25

Find the least common denominator.

31. $\dfrac{7}{48}, \dfrac{5}{24}$ **32.** $\dfrac{3}{7}, \dfrac{5}{6}$ **33.** $\dfrac{3}{13}, \dfrac{1}{2}$ **34.** $\dfrac{7}{2}, \dfrac{3}{4}$ **35.** $\dfrac{6}{10}, \dfrac{5}{2}$

36. $\dfrac{1}{3}, \dfrac{7}{8}$ **37.** $\dfrac{5}{6}, \dfrac{11}{12}$ **38.** $\dfrac{3}{10}, \dfrac{17}{30}$ **39.** $\dfrac{7}{15}, \dfrac{7}{12}$ **40.** $\dfrac{7}{4}, \dfrac{3}{5}$

41. $\dfrac{5}{6}, \dfrac{3}{4}, \dfrac{1}{2}$ **42.** $\dfrac{2}{3}, \dfrac{5}{12}, \dfrac{4}{9}$ **43.** $\dfrac{7}{8}, \dfrac{5}{6}, \dfrac{4}{5}$ **44.** $\dfrac{1}{2}, \dfrac{1}{4}, \dfrac{1}{5}$ **45.** $\dfrac{8}{12}, \dfrac{6}{4}$

46. $\dfrac{2}{11}, \dfrac{4}{9}, \dfrac{5}{3}$ **47.** $\dfrac{5}{6}, \dfrac{11}{20}, \dfrac{14}{15}$ **48.** $\dfrac{4}{7}, \dfrac{3}{4}, \dfrac{1}{28}$ **49.** $\dfrac{1}{5}, \dfrac{5}{12}, \dfrac{1}{4}$ **50.** $\dfrac{5}{3}, \dfrac{1}{2}$

Perform the indicated operation(s). Simplify the result.

51. $\dfrac{3}{8} + \dfrac{5}{12}$ **52.** $\dfrac{7}{4} - \dfrac{1}{12}$ **53.** $-\dfrac{3}{4} - \dfrac{1}{2}$ **54.** $\dfrac{7}{8} - \dfrac{1}{2}$

55. $\dfrac{2}{5} - \dfrac{1}{3} - \dfrac{1}{6}$ **56.** $\dfrac{8}{9} + \dfrac{2}{3} + \dfrac{1}{2}$ **57.** $\dfrac{5}{16} + \dfrac{2}{5} - \dfrac{3}{10}$ **58.** $\dfrac{4}{9} + \dfrac{2}{3}$

59. $\dfrac{1}{2} + \dfrac{1}{3} + \dfrac{1}{4}$ **60.** $-\dfrac{5}{24} + \dfrac{2}{3} - \dfrac{1}{6}$ **61.** $\dfrac{9}{11} - \dfrac{5}{3} - \dfrac{5}{6}$ **62.** $-\dfrac{6}{7} - \dfrac{2}{14}$

63. $\dfrac{2}{6} - \dfrac{1}{3} + \dfrac{1}{2}$ **64.** $\dfrac{2}{8} - \dfrac{3}{4} + \dfrac{1}{2}$ **65.** $-\dfrac{3}{12} + \dfrac{4}{10} - \dfrac{1}{5}$ **66.** $\dfrac{1}{3} + \dfrac{5}{6} - \dfrac{2}{9}$

67. $\dfrac{3}{2} - \dfrac{4}{8} + \dfrac{1}{6}$ **68.** $\dfrac{1}{12} - \dfrac{5}{6} + \dfrac{4}{9}$ **69.** $\dfrac{7}{15} - \dfrac{4}{5} + \dfrac{2}{3}$ **70.** $\dfrac{1}{2} - \dfrac{8}{10} + \dfrac{5}{4}$

WRITING RATIOS AND SOLVING PROPORTIONS

A *ratio* compares two numbers using division. If a and b are two quantities measured in the same units, then the **ratio of a to b** can be written in three ways:

a to b $\qquad\qquad\qquad$ $a : b$ $\qquad\qquad\qquad$ $\dfrac{a}{b}$

EXAMPLE Write the ratio 4 to 3 in two other ways.

SOLUTION $4 : 3$ $\qquad$ $\dfrac{4}{3}$

To write a ratio in lowest terms, divide out any common factors.

EXAMPLE Write the ratio 12 to 18 in lowest terms.

SOLUTION 6 is the greatest common factor, so divide each number by 6.

▶ In lowest terms, the ratio 12 to 18 is 2 to 3.

A **proportion** is an equation stating that two ratios are equivalent. If a proportion contains a variable, you can cross multiply to solve for the variable.

EXAMPLE Solve the proportion $\dfrac{5}{6} = \dfrac{10}{x}$.

SOLUTION

$\dfrac{5}{6} = \dfrac{10}{x}$	**Rewrite proportion.**
$5 \cdot x = 6 \cdot 10$	**Cross multiply.**
$5x = 60$	**Simplify.**
$x = 12$	**Solve for *x*.**

PRACTICE

Write the ratio in two other ways.

1. 4 to 5 $\qquad$ **2.** $1 : 1$ $\qquad$ **3.** 2 to 6 $\qquad$ **4.** $3 : 5$

5. $\dfrac{1}{5}$ $\qquad$ **6.** 10 to 1 $\qquad$ **7.** $\dfrac{8}{5}$ $\qquad$ **8.** $5 : 4$

9. $3 : 1$ $\qquad$ **10.** $\dfrac{2}{3}$ $\qquad$ **11.** $\dfrac{3}{4}$ $\qquad$ **12.** 6 to 3

Write the ratio in lowest terms.

13. 2 to 8 $\qquad$ **14.** $5 : 10$ $\qquad$ **15.** $4 : 16$ $\qquad$ **16.** 80 to 100

17. $\dfrac{2}{10}$ $\qquad$ **18.** $\dfrac{3}{27}$ $\qquad$ **19.** 25 to 15 $\qquad$ **20.** $9 : 3$

21. $\dfrac{12}{20}$ $\qquad$ **22.** $4 : 24$ $\qquad$ **23.** $\dfrac{24}{18}$ $\qquad$ **24.** $20 : 35$

Solve the proportion.

25. $\dfrac{x}{4} = \dfrac{2}{8}$

26. $\dfrac{5}{7} = \dfrac{a}{28}$

27. $\dfrac{6}{b} = \dfrac{3}{8}$

28. $\dfrac{20}{4} = \dfrac{10}{y}$

29. $\dfrac{2}{1} = \dfrac{6}{c}$

30. $\dfrac{5}{4} = \dfrac{x}{10}$

31. $\dfrac{3}{7} = \dfrac{9}{b}$

32. $\dfrac{36}{r} = \dfrac{12}{3}$

33. $\dfrac{p}{2} = \dfrac{5}{2}$

34. $\dfrac{8}{5} = \dfrac{w}{25}$

35. $\dfrac{9}{4} = \dfrac{k}{12}$

36. $\dfrac{n}{3} = \dfrac{3}{1}$

37. $\dfrac{2}{11} = \dfrac{x}{99}$

38. $\dfrac{80}{48} = \dfrac{10}{s}$

39. $\dfrac{z}{5} = \dfrac{8}{2}$

40. $\dfrac{1}{8} = \dfrac{5}{j}$

41. $\dfrac{16}{3} = \dfrac{2a}{6}$

42. $\dfrac{c}{15} = \dfrac{4}{3}$

43. $\dfrac{60}{40} = \dfrac{12}{m}$

44. $\dfrac{3x}{4} = \dfrac{27}{12}$

45. $\dfrac{2}{9} = \dfrac{y}{27}$

46. $\dfrac{13}{w} = \dfrac{39}{9}$

47. $\dfrac{x}{20} = \dfrac{3}{60}$

48. $\dfrac{x}{3} = \dfrac{40}{6}$

SIGNIFICANT DIGITS

Significant digits indicate how precisely a number is known. Use the following guidelines to determine the number of significant digits.

- All nonzero digits are significant.
- All zeros that appear between two nonzero digits are significant.
- For a decimal, all zeros that appear after the last nonzero digit are significant. For a whole number, you cannot tell whether any zeros after the last nonzero digit are significant, so you should assume that they are not significant (unless you know otherwise).

Sometimes calculations involve measurements that have various numbers of significant digits. In this case, a general rule is to carry all digits through the calculation and then round the result to the same number of significant digits as the measurement with the *fewest* number of significant digits.

EXAMPLE Add: $76.33 + 22.0 + 1500$

SOLUTION Of the three numbers, 1500 has the fewest number of significant digits. Add all three numbers, then round the sum to two significant digits.

$$76.33 + 22.0 + 1500 = 1598.33$$
$$\approx 1600$$

EXAMPLE Perform the indicated operation.

a. $0.004 \cdot 3.22$

b. $374{,}039.8 \div 305$

SOLUTION **a.** Since the zeros before the 4 in 0.004 are not significant, round the answer to one significant digit.

$$0.004 \cdot 3.22 = 0.01288$$
$$\approx 0.01$$

b. Since the zero between the 3 and the 5 in 305 is significant, round the answer to three significant digits.

$$374{,}039.8 \div 305 = 1226.36$$
$$\approx 1230$$

Note that some units, such as number of people, cannot be divided into fractional parts. In that case, use the significant digits of the other numbers to round the answer.

EXAMPLE A bill of $98.80 is divided among 8 people. How much does each person pay?

SOLUTION The number of people is exact, so the fact that it is a one-digit number is irrelevant. Use the significant digits for the money to round your answer.

$$\$98.80 \div 8 = \$12.35$$

▶ Each person should pay $12.35.

PRACTICE

Simplify the expression. Write your answer with the appropriate number of significant digits.

1. $8244 + 3.6$
2. $-25 - 3$
3. $2.50 \cdot 3.80$

4. $0.95 \div 4.25$
5. $30.82 - 2.6690$
6. $16 \div 7$

7. $700 + 20$
8. $60 \div 24$
9. $50 \div 4.5$

10. $2.64 + 3.0008$
11. $38.25 \div 52$
12. $6 - 3.4$

13. $5.0 - 1.8$
14. $0.74 \cdot 2.15$
15. $25.000 \div 25$

16. $13.36 + 40.58$
17. $200 - 3.5$
18. $40 \div 0.368$

19. $14.85 + 5.00 + 4.8$
20. $0.0036 + 0.017 + 0.0249$
21. $23.89 - 2.5 - 3.74$

22. $100 - 21 - 2.9 - 3.62$
23. $27.5 \cdot 9.8 \cdot 0.332$
24. $0.783 \cdot 2.11 \cdot 4.51$

25. $2.48 \cdot 16.4 \div 56.25$
26. $42.6 \cdot 2.05 \div 0.0068$
27. $60 \div (52.4 \cdot 20)$

28. $388 \cdot 16 \cdot 108 \cdot 27$
29. $13,720 + 2800 - 513$
30. $(200 \cdot 45) \div (36 \cdot 15)$

Perform the calculation. Write your answer with the appropriate number of significant digits.

31. $1.50 per card • 5 cards
32. 324 pens ÷ 36 students
33. $39.95 per sweater • 6 sweaters

34. $.40 per orange • 10 oranges
35. 89 miles ÷ 6.8 gallons
36. 282 books ÷ 47 students

37. 101 gallons of milk + 8.75 gallons of milk − 6.9 gallons of milk

38. 210 pounds of sand − 16.25 pounds of sand − 1.5 pounds of sand

39. 20.3 milliliters of water + 1.08 milliliters of hydrochloric acid

40. 8.0 liters of juice − 5 liters of juice

41. 38,050 computers ÷ 52 computer stores

42. 3000 kilogram car + 65.50 kilogram passenger + 2.37 kilogram groceries

43. 13.2 milligrams of rice + 0.015 milligram of saffron + 1.25 milligrams of salt

44. 325 milligrams of Vitamin C + 5.50 milligrams of Vitamin C − 24.3 milligrams of Vitamin C

45. 7.55 inches of rain in March + 12.25 inches of rain in April + 6.08 inches of rain in May

SCIENTIFIC NOTATION

Numbers written in scientific notation have the form $c \times 10^n$ where $1 \le c < 10$ and n is an integer. Recall that $10^0 = 1$.

EXAMPLE   Write each number in scientific notation.

    a. 721,000,000   **b.** 0.001046

SOLUTION   **a.** Move the decimal point 8 places to the left.

         $721,000,000 = 7.21 \times 10^8$

    b. Move the decimal point three places to the right.

         $0.001046 = 1.046 \times 10^{-3}$

EXAMPLE   Write each number in standard form.

    a. 5.23×10^7 **b.** 2.600×10^{-4}

SOLUTION   **a.** Move the decimal point 7 places to the right.

         $5.23 \times 10^7 = 52,300,000$

    b. Move the decimal point 4 places to the left. Note that 4 significant digits are kept.

         $2.600 \times 10^{-4} = 0.0002600$

PRACTICE

Write each number in scientific notation.

1. 0.4	**2.** 0.34	**3.** 0.09	**4.** 30.58
5. 4	**6.** 0.0000000025	**7.** 0.0000926	**8.** 4,983,200,000
9. 211.111	**10.** 4193	**11.** 0.005	**12.** 21,040
13. 98,400	**14.** 0.00002	**15.** 204.89	**16.** 295
17. 0.00037	**18.** 0.2000	**19.** 59.8	**20.** 5,000,000
21. 23,085,600	**22.** 0.0000004	**23.** 0.000100	**24.** 0.101001

Write each number in standard form.

25. 9×10^2	**26.** 2.52×10^{-1}	**27.** 3.1×10^3
28. 6×10^5	**29.** 2.90×10^{-1}	**30.** 9.1×10^0
31. 1.001×10^4	**32.** 5.273×10^{-3}	**33.** 7.926×10^6
34. 8.13×10^{-1}	**35.** 3.84×10^{-4}	**36.** 4.6000×10^8
37. 3.7×10^{-5}	**38.** 1.11×10^{-2}	**39.** 4.9831×10^{-3}
40. 7.05×10^{-7}	**41.** 3.9502×10^5	**42.** 1.0063×10^0
43. 2.64095×10^3	**44.** 3.03×10^{-7}	**45.** 4.55×10^{-4}
46. 5.0×10^3	**47.** 5.9438×10^{-2}	**48.** 6.105×10^{-6}

▶ GEOMETRY
PERIMETER, AREA, AND VOLUME

The **perimeter** of a two-dimensional figure is the sum of the lengths of the edges, or the distance around the figure.

EXAMPLE Find the perimeter of the figure.

a.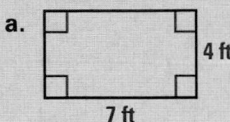

b.
```
        2 cm
1 cm  ┌────┐ 1.5 cm
      └─────┘
        2 cm
```

SOLUTION

a. $4 + 4 + 7 + 7 = 22$

  ▶ The perimeter is 22 feet.

b. $2 + 1.5 + 2 + 1 = 6.5$

  ▶ The perimeter is 6.5 cm.

The perimeter of a circle, called its **circumference,** is the distance around the circle. The formula for circumference is $C = 2\pi r$ where r is the **radius.** Because the **diameter** is twice the radius, the formula for circumference can also be written as $C = \pi d$ where d is the diameter.

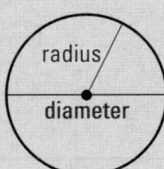

EXAMPLE Find the circumference of the circle with radius 3 inches.

SOLUTION $C = 2\pi r = 2\pi(3) = 6\pi \approx 6(3.14) = 18.84$

  ▶ The circumference is 6π inches or about 18.84 inches.

EXAMPLE Find the circumference of the circle with diameter 4 meters.

SOLUTION $C = \pi d = \pi(4) = 4\pi \approx 4(3.14) = 12.56$

  ▶ The circumference is 4π meters or about 12.56 meters.

The **area** of a two-dimensional figure is the number of square units enclosed within the boundary of the figure.

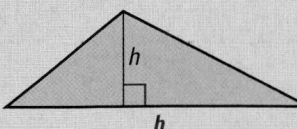

Area of a triangle: $A = \frac{1}{2}bh$

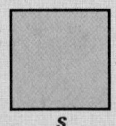

Area of a square: $A = s^2$

Area of a rectangle: $A = \ell w$

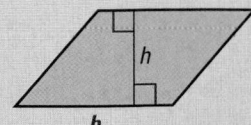

Area of a parallelogram: $A = bh$

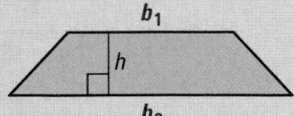

Area of a trapezoid: $A = \frac{1}{2}(b_1 + b_2)h$

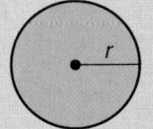

Area of a circle: $A = \pi r^2$

EXAMPLE Find the area of the figure.

a.

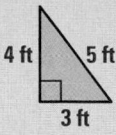

4 ft 5 ft

3 ft

b.

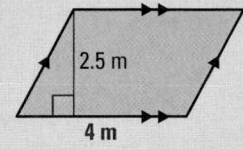

2.5 m

4 m

c.

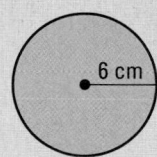

6 cm

SOLUTION

a. $A = \frac{1}{2}bh$

$= \frac{1}{2}(3)(4)$

$= 6$ square feet

b. $A = bh$

$= (4)(2.5)$

$= 10$ square meters

c. $A = \pi r^2$

$= \pi(6)^2$

$= 36\pi$

≈ 113 square centimeters

A **prism** is a three-dimensional figure with two congruent faces, called *bases*, that lie in parallel planes. The **surface area** of a prism is the sum of the areas of all the faces of the prism. Surface area is measured in square units.

EXAMPLE Find the surface area of the prism or cylinder.

a.

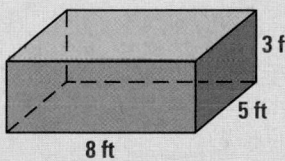

3 ft

5 ft

8 ft

b.

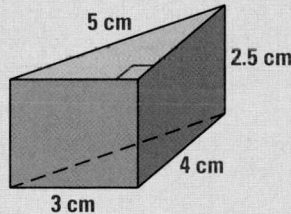

5 cm

2.5 cm

4 cm

3 cm

c.

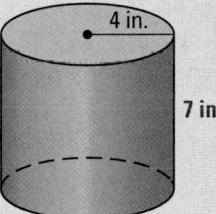

4 in.

7 in.

SOLUTION

a. A rectangular prism has three pairs of identical rectangular faces.

Surface area $= 2(8 \cdot 5) + 2(8 \cdot 3) + 2(5 \cdot 3)$

$= 80 + 48 + 30$

$= 158$

▶ The prism has a surface area of 158 square feet.

b. Surface area $=$ area of bases $+$ area of faces

$= 2\left[\frac{1}{2}(3)(4)\right] + (2.5)(3) + (2.5)(4) + (2.5)(5)$

$= 12 + 7.5 + 10 + 12.5$

$= 42$

▶ The prism has a surface area of 42 square centimeters.

c. Surface area $=$ area of bases $+$ (circumference)(height)

$= 2(\pi r^2) + (2\pi r)(h)$

$= 2[\pi(4)^2] + [2\pi(4)](7)$

$= 32\pi + 56\pi$

$= 88\pi$

≈ 276

▶ The cylinder has a surface area of about 276 square inches.

The **volume** of a solid is a measure of how much it will hold and is measured in cubic units. The volume of a prism is calculated by multiplying the area of the base by the height.

EXAMPLE Find the volume of the three solids in the previous example.

SOLUTION

a. Volume $= (8 \cdot 5) \cdot 3$
    $= 120$

b. Volume $= \left(\frac{1}{2} \cdot 3 \cdot 4\right) \cdot 2.5$
    $= 15$

c. Volume $= \left[\pi(4)^2\right] \cdot 7$
    $= 112\pi$
    ≈ 352

▶ The prism has a volume of 120 ft³.

▶ The prism has a volume of 15 cm³.

▶ The cylinder has a volume of about 352 in.³

PRACTICE

Find the perimeter or circumference of the figure.

1.
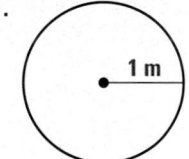

2.
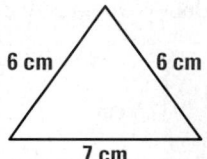

3.
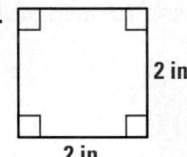

4.
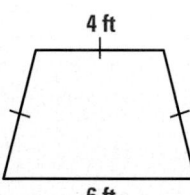

5.
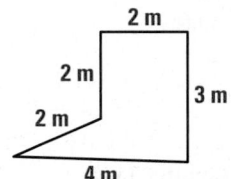

6.
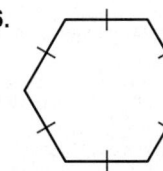

7. A square 3 ft on each side

8. A circle with diameter 10 in.

9. A rectangle with sides of 4 cm and 7 cm

10. A regular pentagon with side length 2.5 m

11. A triangle with sides of length 8 cm, 3 cm, and 7 cm

12. A parallelogram with sides 3.5 m and 5.8 m

13. A circle with a diameter of 22 in.

14. A rectangle with sides of 5 ft and 8 ft

Find the area of the figure.

15.
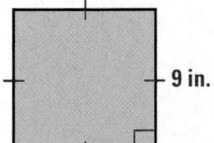

16.
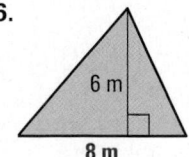

17.
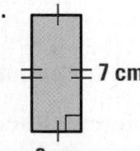

18.
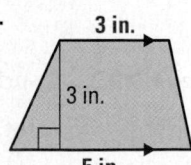

19. A trapezoid with bases 4 in. and 8 in. and height 4 in.

20. A square with side length 7 ft

21. A circle with radius 0.5 in.

22. A parallelogram with height 6 m and base 9 m

23. A 2 mi by 6 mi rectangle

24. A circle with radius 9 mm

25. A triangle with a base of 5 in. and height of 4 in.

26. A circle with a radius of 10 ft

Find the surface area of the prism or cylinder.

27.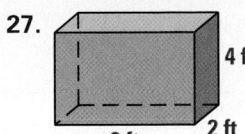
4 ft
2 ft
6 ft

28.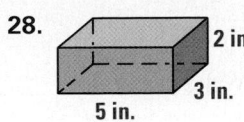
2 in.
3 in.
5 in.

29.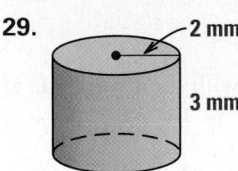
2 mm
3 mm

30.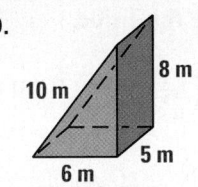
8 m
10 m
5 m
6 m

31. A cylinder with radius 2 in. and height 14 in.   **32.** A cube with side length 3 cm

33. A rectangular prism 4 cm by 6 cm by 12 cm   **34.** A cylinder with a radius of 50 ft and height of 200 ft

Find the volume of the prism or cylinder.

35.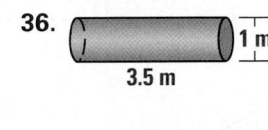
10 cm
10 cm
10 cm

36.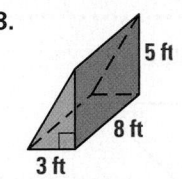
1 m
3.5 m

37.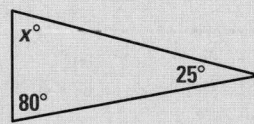
$1\frac{1}{2}$ yd
2 yd
4 yd

38.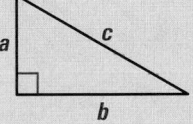
5 ft
8 ft
3 ft

39. A rectangular prism 1 ft by 1 ft by 5 ft   **40.** A cube 8 in. on each side

41. A cylinder with diameter 9 in. and height 2 in.   **42.** A rectangular prism with base 12.8 m^2 and height 3 m

TRIANGLE RELATIONSHIPS

The sum of the angles of a triangle is 180°.

EXAMPLE   Find the value of x.

SOLUTION $180° = 25° + 80° + x$

$x = 75°$

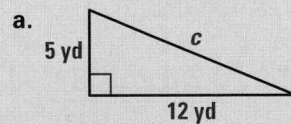
$x°$
80°
25°

The **Pythagorean theorem** states that in a right triangle with legs of length a and b and hypotenuse of length c, $c^2 = a^2 + b^2$.

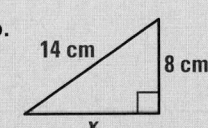
a
c
b

EXAMPLE   Find the length of the unknown side.

a.
5 yd
c
12 yd

b.
14 cm
8 cm
x

SOLUTION

a. $5^2 + 12^2 = c^2$
  $25 + 144 = c^2$
  $169 = c^2$
  $c = 13$
  ▶ The hypotenuse is 13 yards long.

b. $8^2 + x^2 = 14^2$
  $64 + x^2 = 196$
  $x^2 = 132$
  $x \approx 11.5$
  ▶ The length of the second leg is about 11.5 centimeters.

The sum of the lengths of the two shorter sides of a triangle must be greater than the length of the third side.

EXAMPLE Can you form a triangle with the given side lengths? Write *yes* or *no*.

a. 2, 3, 8   b. 9, 11, 19   c. 3, 18, 21

SOLUTION

a. No, because $2 + 3 < 8$.   b. Yes, because $9 + 11 > 19$.   c. No, because $18 + 3 = 21$.

PRACTICE

Find the value of *x*.

1.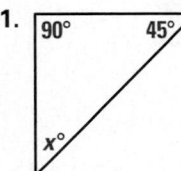

2.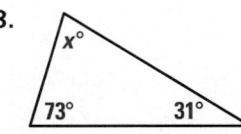

3.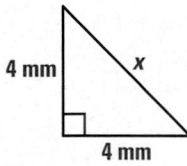

4.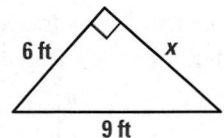

5. A triangle with angles $x°$, 5°, and 10°

6. A triangle with angles $x°$, 48°, and 22°

7. A triangle with angles $x°$, 38°, and 82°

8. A triangle with angles $x°$, 25°, and 63°

Can a triangle have the following angle measures? Write *yes* or *no*.

9. 60°, 60°, 60°   **10.** 136°, 19°, 45°   **11.** 112°, 15°, 43°   **12.** 45°, 67°, 68°

13. 47°, 90°, 23°   **14.** 59°, 60°, 61°   **15.** 31°, 78°, 91°   **16.** 25°, 30°, 125°

17. 160°, 5°, 5°   **18.** 55°, 75°, 60°   **19.** 40°, 50°, 90°   **20.** 113°, 14°, 53°

21. 17°, 52°, 111°   **22.** 20°, 140°, 20°   **23.** 70°, 60°, 50°   **24.** 43°, 56°, 101°

Find the length of the unknown side.

25.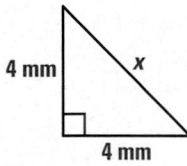

26.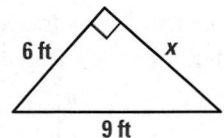

27.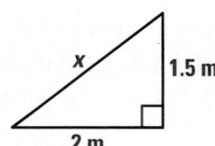

28.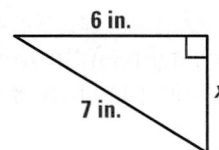

29.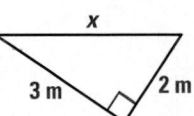

30.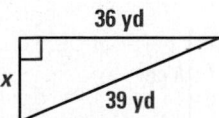

31.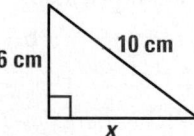

32.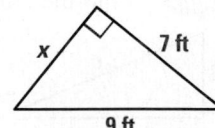

33. A right triangle with two sides 5 in. long

34. A right triangle with one side 8 ft and hypotenuse 10 ft

Can you form a triangle with the given side lengths? Write *yes* or *no*.

35. 8, 3, 7   **36.** 10, 10, 10   **37.** 16, 5, 11   **38.** 3, 6, 8

39. 4, 4, 5   **40.** 2, 5, 2   **41.** 6, 5, 4   **42.** 17, 9, 8

43. 85, 19, 51   **44.** 12, 7, 4   **45.** 10, 24, 26   **46.** 46, 22, 17

SYMMETRY

A figure has **line symmetry** if it can be divided by a line into two parts, each of which is the mirror image of the other. The line that divides the figure into two parts is called the **line of symmetry**.

EXAMPLE Identify the lines of symmetry in the figure.

a.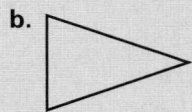

b.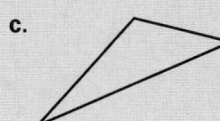

c.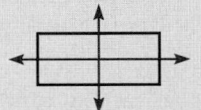

SOLUTION a. This figure has a vertical line of symmetry and a horizontal line of symmetry.

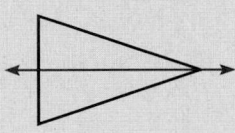

b. This figure has a horizontal line of symmetry.

c. This figure is not symmetric. It has no line of symmetry.

A figure has **rotational symmetry** if it coincides with itself after rotating 180° or less, either clockwise or counterclockwise, about a point. The point of rotation is usually the center of the figure.

EXAMPLE Identify any rotational symmetry in the figure.

a.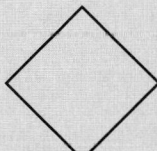

b.

c.

SOLUTION a. This figure has rotational symmetry. It will coincide with itself after being rotated 90° or 180° in either direction. Notice that the point of rotation is located at the center of the figure.

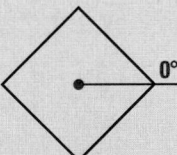 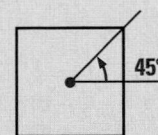 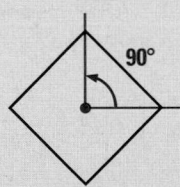

b. This figure has rotational symmetry. It will coincide with itself after being rotated 45°, 90°, 135°, or 180° in either direction. The point of rotation is located at the center of the figure.

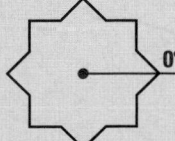 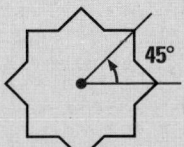

c. This figure has no rotational symmetry.

EXAMPLE The figure at the right has line symmetry.
Find the coordinates of point *A*.

SOLUTION The line of symmetry is $x = 1$. Point $(3, 4)$ is
2 units to the right of the line of symmetry so
A must be an equal distance to the left.
Therefore, *A* is at $(-1, 4)$.

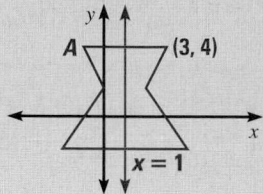

PRACTICE

**State whether the figure has line symmetry or rotational symmetry.
Then identify the line(s) of symmetry or the angle of rotation.**

1.

2.

3.
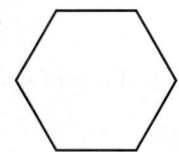

4.
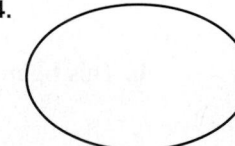

5.

6.
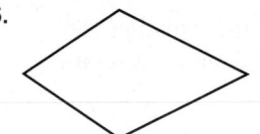

7.

8.
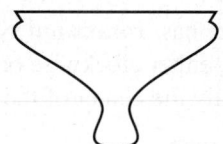

**The figure is symmetric. The line of symmetry is shown in red. Find the
coordinates of point *A*.**

9.
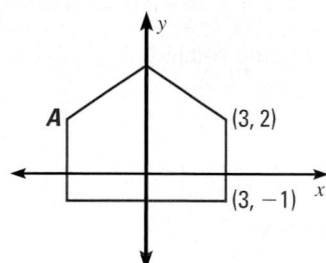

10.
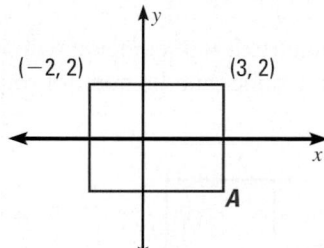

11.
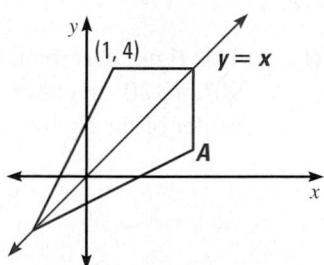

12.
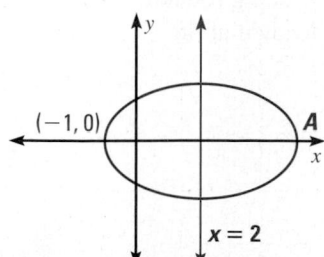

13.
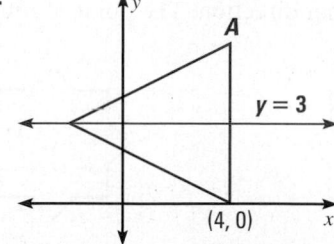

14.
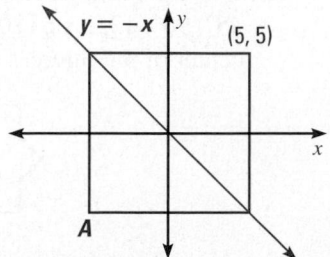

TRANSFORMATIONS

A **transformation** is a change made to the size or position of a figure. A **translation** is a transformation that slides every point of a figure the same distance in the same direction while preserving its size and orientation.

EXAMPLE Translate $\overline{AB}$ 2 units to the left and 5 units up.

SOLUTION To shift $\overline{AB}$ left 2 units, subtract 2 from each x-coordinate. To shift $\overline{AB}$ up 5 units, add 5 to each y-coordinate. You can describe this transformation as $\overline{AB}$ *is mapped onto* $\overline{A'B'}$, written symbolically as $\overline{AB} \rightarrow \overline{A'B'}$. In particular:

$$A(3, 0) \rightarrow A'(1, 5)$$
$$B(8, 2) \rightarrow B'(6, 7)$$

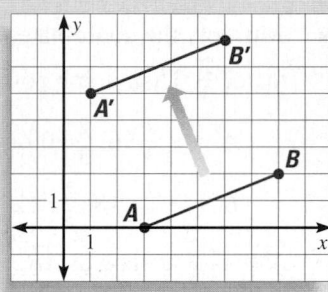

A **reflection** is a transformation in which each point of a figure has an image that is the same distance from the **line of reflection** as the original point but on the opposite side. A reflection preserves the size of a figure but not its orientation.

EXAMPLE **a.** Reflect the blue triangle over the x-axis. **b.** Reflect the blue kite over the y-axis.

SOLUTION **a.**

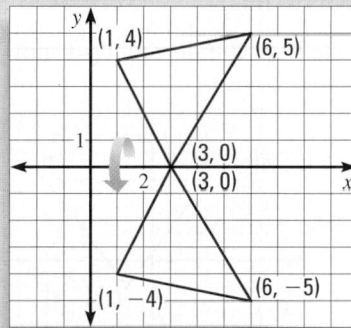

Change each y-coordinate to its opposite.

b.

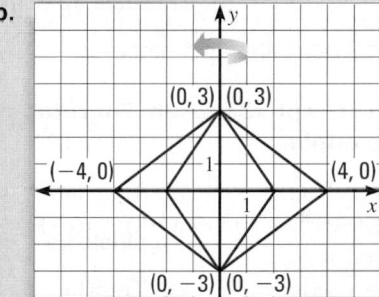

Change each x-coordinate to its opposite.

A **rotation** is a transformation in which every point moves along a circular path around a fixed point. Rotations preserve both size and orientation.

EXAMPLE Rotate the blue quadrilateral 270° about the origin.

SOLUTION When a point (x, y) is rotated counterclockwise around the origin use the following patterns:

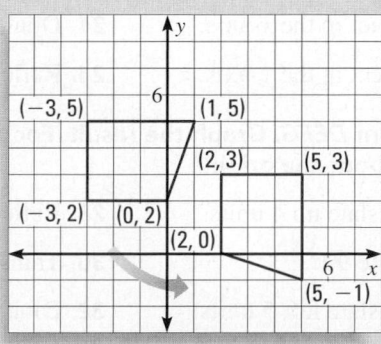

90° rotation:	$A(x, y) \rightarrow A'(-y, x)$
180° rotation:	$A(x, y) \rightarrow A'(-x, -y)$
270° rotation:	$A(x, y) \rightarrow A'(y, -x)$

In this case, use the pattern for a 270° rotation about the origin. So, $(-3, 5) \rightarrow (5, 3)$, $(-3, 2) \rightarrow (2, 3)$, $(0, 2) \rightarrow (2, 0)$, and $(1, 5) \rightarrow (5, -1)$.

A **dilation** is a transformation in which every point of a figure is multiplied by a **scale factor** to create a similar image (see page 923). Dilations preserve the orientation of the original figure while enlarging or reducing the size.

EXAMPLE Dilate $\overline{AB}$ by a scale factor of $\frac{2}{3}$.

SOLUTION Multiply the coordinates of A and B by the scale factor $\frac{2}{3}$. Then graph points A' and B'.

$$A' = \left(\frac{2}{3} \cdot 6, \frac{2}{3} \cdot 0\right) = (4, 0)$$

$$B' = \left(\frac{2}{3} \cdot 18, \frac{2}{3} \cdot 12\right) = (12, 8)$$

$\overline{A'B'}$ is $\frac{2}{3}$ as long as $\overline{AB}$.

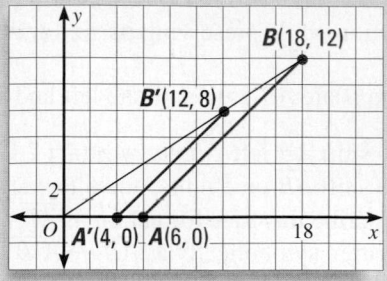

PRACTICE

Give the coordinates of $A(3, -6)$ after the following transformations. For rotations, rotate about the origin.

1. Reflect in y-axis. **2.** Dilate by $\frac{2}{3}$. **3.** Dilate by $\frac{3}{2}$. **4.** Translate left 6 units.

5. Rotate 90°. **6.** Translate up 6 units. **7.** Reflect in x-axis. **8.** Rotate 180°.

9. Translate left 3 units and up 5 units. **10.** Translate right 2 units and up 1 unit.

Transform △ABC. Graph the result. For rotations, rotate about the origin.

11. Translate down 1 unit. **12.** Translate left 3 units.

13. Rotate 180°. **14.** Dilate by $\frac{1}{4}$.

15. Reflect in the x-axis. **16.** Translate right 2 units.

17. Dilate by 3. **18.** Rotate 90°.

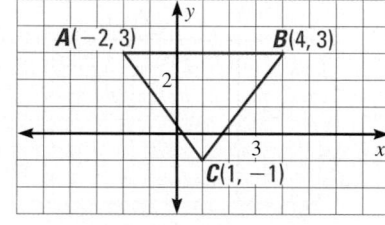

Transform MNOP. Graph the result. For rotations, rotate about the origin.

19. Dilate by $\frac{1}{2}$. **20.** Translate left 1 unit and down 2 units.

21. Rotate 270°. **22.** Translate down 4 units.

23. Reflect in the x-axis. **24.** Dilate by $\frac{5}{2}$.

25. Reflect in the y-axis. **26.** Reflect in the line $y = x$.

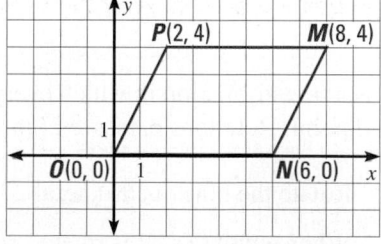

Transform DEFG. Graph the result. For rotations, rotate about the origin.

27. Translate up 4 units. **28.** Reflect in the y-axis.

29. Rotate 90°. **30.** Translate right 9 units.

31. Translate left 5 units. **32.** Dilate by 4.

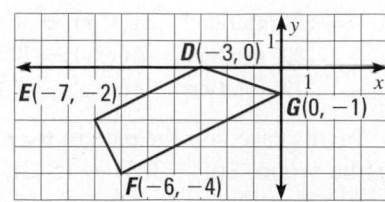

SIMILAR FIGURES

Two figures are **congruent** if they are exactly the same shape and the same size. Triangles *ABC* and *DEF* are congruent. Corresponding angles are marked with the same symbol.

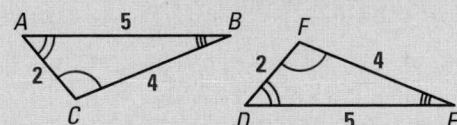

Two figures are **similar** if corresponding angles are congruent and the lengths of corresponding sides are in proportion.

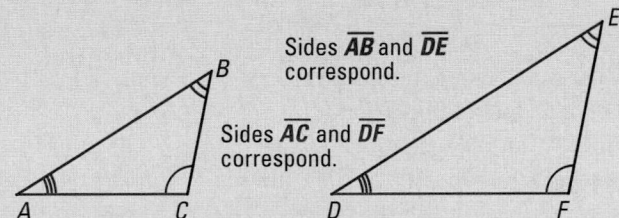

Sides $\overline{AB}$ and $\overline{DE}$ correspond.

Sides $\overline{AC}$ and $\overline{DF}$ correspond.

The ratios of the lengths of corresponding sides of similar figures are equal.

For example, in the similar triangles above, $\dfrac{AB}{DE} = \dfrac{AC}{DF} = \dfrac{BC}{EF}$.

EXAMPLE   The two polygons are similar. Find the values of *x* and *y*.

SOLUTION   Write and solve a proportion to find each unknown length.

$$\frac{AB}{EF} = \frac{CD}{GH} \quad \text{and} \quad \frac{AD}{EH} = \frac{BC}{FG}$$

$$\frac{6}{4} = \frac{6}{x} \qquad\qquad \frac{9}{6} = \frac{4}{y}$$

$$6x = 24 \qquad\qquad 9y = 24$$

$$x = 4 \qquad\qquad y = 2\frac{2}{3}$$

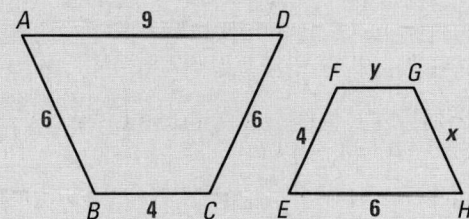

PRACTICE

The two polygons are similar. Find the value of x.

1.
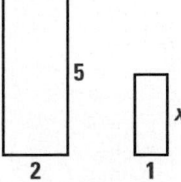

2.
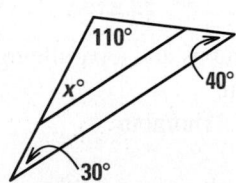

3.
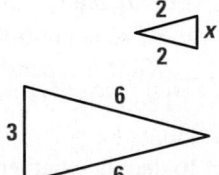

4.
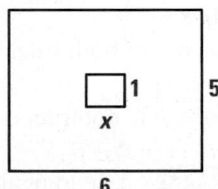

5.
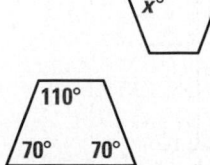

6.
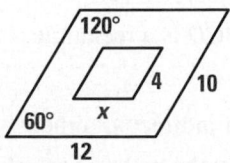

7.
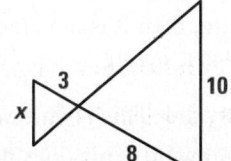

8.
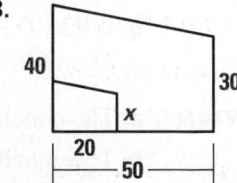

▶ Logical Reasoning
LOGICAL ARGUMENT

A logical argument has two given statements, called **premises**, and a statement, called a **conclusion**, that follows them.

If a figure is a rhombus, then it is a parallelogram.	Premise
JKLM is a rhombus.	Premise
Therefore, JKLM is a parallelogram.	Conclusion

There are five types of logical arguments that can be made using these statements. Arguments that use these patterns correctly will have a **valid conclusion**. Arguments that use these patterns incorrectly will have an **invalid conclusion**. The letters p and q are often used to write an argument symbolically. In the examples below, p and q are given the following meanings.

p: a figure is a rhombus
q: a figure is a parallelogram

Direct Argument
If p is true, then q is true.
p is true.
Therefore, q is true.

Example:
If *JKLM* is a rhombus, then it is a parallelogram.
JKLM is a rhombus.
Therefore, *JKLM* is a parallelogram.

Indirect Argument
If p is true, then q is true.
q is not true.
Therefore, p is not true.

Example:
If *JKLM* is a rhombus, then it is a parallelogram.
JKLM is not a parallelogram.
Therefore, *JKLM* is not a rhombus.

Chain Rule
If p is true, then q is true.
If q is true, then r is true.
Therefore, if p, then r.

Example:
If *JKLM* is a rhombus, then it is a parallelogram.
If *JKLM* is a parallelogram, then it is a quadrilateral.
Therefore, if *JKLM* is a rhombus, then it is a quadrilateral.

***Or* Rule**
p is true or q is true.
p is not true.
Therefore, q is true.

Example:
JKLM is a rhombus or a parallelogram.
JKLM is not a rhombus.
Therefore, *JKLM* is a parallelogram.

***And* Rule**
p and q are not both true.
But q is true.
Therefore, p is not true.

Example:
JKLM is not both a rhombus and a parallelogram.
JKLM is a parallelogram.
Therefore, *JKLM* is not a rhombus.

EXAMPLE   Use logical reasoning to decide whether the conclusion is *valid* or *invalid*. State the type of logical argument used to arrive at the conclusion.

     a. If $x = 2$, then $3x - 1 = 5$. $3x - 1 \neq 5$. Therefore, $x \neq 2$.

     b. If *ABCD* is a square, then it is a rectangle. *ABCD* is a rectangle. Therefore, *ABCD* is a square.

SOLUTION   **a.** The conclusion is valid. This is an example of indirect argument.

     b. The conclusion is invalid. This does not follow the pattern for a direct argument.

A compound statement has two or more parts joined by *or* or *and*. For an *and* statement to be true, each part must be true. For an *or* statement to be true, at least one part must be true.

EXAMPLE Tell whether the compound statement is *true* or *false*.
   a. $2 < 3$ and $1 < 2$
   b. $8 > 7$ and $7 > 9$
   c. $-2 < 1$ or $-1 < 1$
   d. $2 > 3$ or $1 > 2$

SOLUTION **a.** True; both parts are true.
   b. False; only one part is true, but both must be true for *and*.
   c. True; at least one part is true, as required for *or*.
   d. False; no part is true.

PRACTICE

Use logical reasoning to decide whether the conclusion is *valid* or *invalid*. State the type of logical argument used to arrive at the conclusion.

1. If Harold can drive, he has a license.
   If Harold has a license, he is at least 16.
   Therefore, if Harold is at least 16, he can drive.

2. If triangle *ABC* is equilateral, it is also isosceles.
   Triangle *ABC* is equilateral.
   Therefore, triangle *ABC* is isosceles.

3. John is in his room or John is in the kitchen.
   John is not in the kitchen.
   Therefore, John is in his room.

4. If Grace is 19, her twin brother Michael is also 19.
   Michael is 17.
   Therefore, Grace is not 19.

5. If $x = 4$, then $y = 1$.
   If $y = 1$, then $z = 8$.
   Therefore, if $x = 4$, then $z = 8$.

6. If an animal has a backbone, it is a vertebrate.
   A horse has a backbone.
   Therefore, a horse is a vertebrate.

7. If $x = 2$, then $2x = 4$.
   $2x = 6$.
   Therefore, $x = 2$.

8. If an apple is a Granny Smith, it is green.
   The apple is green.
   Therefore, the apple is a Granny Smith.

9. It is impossible for my watch to be right and that we are late. We are late.
   Therefore, my watch cannot be right.

10. Triangle *ABC* is equilateral or scalene.
   Triangle *ABC* is not scalene.
   Therefore, triangle *ABC* is not equilateral.

State whether each compound statement is *true* or *false*.

11. $1 < 2$ and $8 \geq 5$

12. $5 < 1$ or $3 < 4$

13. $-6 \geq -6$ or $3 < -3$

14. $2 \leq 5$ and $2 \leq 1$

15. $-8 < 5$ and $-5 < 8$

16. $3 < 1$ or $3 < -1$

17. $4 = 4$ or $4 = 5$ or $4 = -4$

18. $-1 < 1$ and $1 \geq 0$ and $-1 < 0$

19. $8 < 9$ and $9 < 14$ and $14 < 20$

20. $3 > 4$ or $3 > 7$ or $3 > 6$

21. $-10 < -8$ and $-7 < -4$ and $7 > 4$

22. $-15 < -35$ or $0 \geq 1$ or $26 \geq 26$

23. $159 \leq 100$ or $100 < 159$

24. $47 \leq 48$ and $48 < 49$ and $49 > 47$

25. $95 \neq 95$ or $95 > -96$ or $95 > 94$

26. $5 \cdot 6 = 30$ or $-6 \cdot 5 = 30$

IF-THEN STATEMENTS

The **conditional** statement "if p, then q" has a **hypothesis** p and a **conclusion** q.

> **EXAMPLE** Identify the hypothesis and conclusion.
> **a.** $y = 6$ when $x = 5$. **b.** Raspberries are a red fruit.

SOLUTION Rewrite the statement as an if-then statement.

> **a.** If $x = 5$, then $y = 6$. **b.** If a fruit is a raspberry, then the fruit is red.
> Hypothesis: $x = 5$ Hypothesis: a fruit is a raspberry
> Conclusion: $y = 6$ Conclusion: the fruit is red

The **converse** of the **conditional** statement "if p, then q" is "if q, then p."

> **EXAMPLE** Give the converse of each statement. State whether the converse is *true* or *false*.
> **a.** If $x = 8$, then $2x = 16$. **b.** If a fruit is a raspberry, then the fruit is red.

SOLUTION Reverse the hypothesis and conclusion of each statement.

> **a.** If $2x = 16$, then $x = 8$. True **b.** If a fruit is red, then the fruit is a raspberry. False

When a conditional statement and its converse are combined by "if and only if," the resulting statement is called a **biconditional statement**. The biconditional "*p if and only if q*" is true only when the conditional "if p, then q" and its converse "if q, then p" are *both* true.

> **EXAMPLE** Tell whether the statement is *true* or *false*. If false, tell why.
>
> **a.** A parallelogram is a rectangle if and only if it has four right angles.
>
> **b.** A triangle is an equilateral triangle if and only if it has two equal sides.

SOLUTION **a.** True

> **b.** False. It is true that an equilateral triangle has two equal sides
> (it has three), but not that a triangle with two equal sides must be
> equilateral (for example, a 5-5-2 triangle).

PRACTICE

Rewrite the statement as an if-then statement.

1. The rain in Spain falls on the plain.

2. A rhombus is a parallelogram with four equal sides.

3. $3x^2 = 48$ when $x = 4$.

4. The area of a square is given by the formula $A = s^2$.

5. You can go out tonight if you finish cleaning.

6. Luis will earn $50 for baby-sitting 12 hours.

7. $y = 16$ when $x = 3$.

8. Corresponding angles of similar figures are congruent.

9. A square is a rectangle with four equal sides.

10. He earns a bonus for sales over $10,000 each month.

11. The graph of $y = x^2$ is a parabola.

12. The circumference of a circle is π times the diameter.

Give the converse of each statement. State whether the converse is *true* or *false*.

13. If $x = 4$, then $x^2 = 16$.

14. If you live in Ohio, then you live in the United States.

15. If a line is vertical, then its slope is undefined.

16. If an animal is a pigeon, then it is a bird.

17. If a figure has two pairs of opposite congruent sides, then it is a parallelogram.

18. If you add two odd numbers, then the answer will be an even number.

19. If you are in Minnesota in January, then you will be cold.

20. If an animal is a dog, then it has four legs.

21. If Margot won the election, then she got more votes than her opponent.

22. If a triangle has three sides of different lengths, then it is a scalene triangle.

23. If a convex polygon has five equal sides, then it is a regular pentagon.

24. If $x = 3$, then $x - 2 = 1$.

Determine whether the statement is *true* or *false*. If false, tell why.

25. A figure is a square if and only if it has four equal sides.

26. Eric will win the election if and only if he receives 60% of the vote.

27. $x^2 = 25$ if and only if $x = -5$.

28. A quadrilateral is a trapezoid if and only if it has exactly one pair of parallel opposite sides.

29. $2x + 6 = 6$ if and only if $x = 0$.

30. An animal is a cat if and only if it is a mammal.

31. Corresponding angles of figures are congruent if and only if the figures are similar.

32. A triangle is isosceles if and only if it has two equal angles.

33. Your team wins at basketball if and only if your team scores more points than your opponents.

34. $x^3 = 8$ if and only if $x = 2$.

35. You are north of the equator if and only if you are in the northern hemisphere.

36. A polygon is a decagon if and only if it has 10 sides.

COUNTEREXAMPLES

A **counterexample** disproves a logical statement.

EXAMPLE   Is it true that when $|a| < |b|$, $a < b$?

SOLUTION   No, because when $a = 1$ and $b = -2$, $|a| < |b|$, but $a > b$.

PRACTICE

Determine whether each statement is *true* or *false*. If false, give a counterexample.

1. If a quadrilateral is a parallelogram, then it is a rectangle.

2. If Joe has $5, then he earned it mowing lawns.

3. If the last digit of a number is 6, then it is divisible by 3.

4. If a triangle is equilateral, then it is equiangular.

5. If a triangle contains a 90° angle, then it contains another 90° angle.

6. If a parallelogram has four right angles, then it is a square.

7. If an animal is black, then it is a dog.

8. If you live in California, then you live in the Pacific time zone.

9. If two lines are perpendicular, then they form right angles.

10. If two lines in the same plane are intersected by a transversal and alternate interior angles are equal in measure, then the lines are parallel.

11. If $a > 0$, then $3a - 4 > 0$.

12. If $a < b$, then $2a < 2b$.

13. If $c = d$, then $c - 2 = d - 2$.

14. If $x > 0$, then $x^2 > x$.

15. If $x \leq 0$, then $x^2 \geq x$.

16. If $x \leq 0$, then $2x^2 \geq -4x$.

JUSTIFY REASONING

Algebraic reasoning can be justified using the postulates of algebra.

Postulates of Algebra	Statement of Postulate	Example
ADDITION/SUBTRACTION PROPERTY OF EQUALITY	If the same number is added to (or subtracted from) equal numbers, then the sums (differences) are equal.	$x - 2 = 4$ $x - 2 + 2 = 4 + 2$
MULTIPLICATION/DIVISION PROPERTY OF EQUALITY	If equal numbers are multiplied by (or divided by) the same number, then the products (quotients) are equal.	$3x = -9$ $\dfrac{3x}{3} = \dfrac{-9}{3}$
SUBSTITUTION PROPERTY	If values are equal, then one value may be substituted for the other.	$x = y - 1$ and $x = 2$ $2 = y - 1$
DISTRIBUTIVE PROPERTY	$a(b + c) = ab + ac$	$3(2x - 1) = 3(2x) + 3(-1)$

You may also use algebraic definitions, such as the definition of raising to a power, to justify algebraic reasoning.

EXAMPLE   Solve the equation $2x + 5 = 3$ and justify each step.

SOLUTION

$2x + 5 = 3$	Given
$2x = -2$	Subtraction property of equality
$x = -1$	Division property of equality

PRACTICE

Identify the property that justifies the statement.

1. If $2x = 8$, then $x = 4$.

2. If $4x - 1 = 7$, then $4x = 8$.

3. If $\frac{4}{5}x = 8$, then $4x = 40$.

4. If $x^2 = 36$, then $x = 6$ or $x = -6$.

5. If $3x = 9$, then $3x + 2 = 11$.

6. If $3x^2 - 6 = 21$, then $x^2 - 2 = 7$.

7. If $x = 4$, then $3x = 12$.

8. If $x(2x - 3) = 7$, then $2x^2 - 3x = 7$.

9. If $\sqrt{x} = 4$, then $x = 16$.

10. If $-5x = 0$, then $x = 0$.

11. If $4x + 7 = 9$, then $4x = 2$.

12. If $x^5 - 1 = 0$, then $x^5 = 1$.

13. If $\frac{1}{6}x = \frac{2}{3}$, then $x = 4$.

14. If $\sqrt{x} = \frac{3}{4}$, then $x = \frac{9}{16}$.

15. If $6 = x - 1$, then $x = 7$.

16. If $4(2x + 2) = 12$, then $2x + 2 = 3$.

17. If $\frac{2x}{9} = 3$, then $2x = 27$.

18. If $2 + x = 5$, then $1 + x = 4$.

19. If $2(3 - 5x) = 1$, then $6 - 10x = 1$.

20. If $6x = 1$, then $6x - 3 = -2$.

Solve each equation for x and justify each step of the solution.

21. $9x = 27$

22. $8 + x = 8$

23. $\frac{x}{2} + 5 = 0$

24. $2(3 - x) = 1$

25. $\frac{5x}{2} - 2 = -5$

26. $3x - 8 = 13$

27. $\frac{3x}{4} = 6$

28. $6 = \frac{1}{2}(x - 2)$

▶ Problem Solving
TRANSLATING PHRASES INTO ALGEBRAIC EXPRESSIONS

To solve a problem algebraically, you often must translate a phrase into an algebraic expression.

EXAMPLE Write the given phrase as an algebraic expression.

a. 3 less than a number   **b.** twice a number   **c.** the quotient of x and y

SOLUTION **a.** "Less than" indicates subtraction:

$x - 3$

b. "Twice" indicates multiplication by 2:

$2x$

c. "Quotient of" indicates division:

$\frac{x}{y}$

EXAMPLE Write an algebraic expression to answer the question.

a. You buy x pounds of apples at \$1.49 per pound. How much do you spend?

b. You have x dollars and spend \$17.38 on dinner. How much do you have left?

SOLUTION **a.** The amount you spent is the product of the number of pounds of apples and the price per pound:

$1.49x$

b. The amount you have left is the difference between the amount you had before dinner and the cost of the dinner:

$x - 17.38$

PRACTICE

Write the given phrase as an algebraic expression.

1. 8 more than a number

2. 3 times a number

3. a number minus 49

4. a number divided by 100

5. a number multiplied by 7

6. one sixth of a number

7. $\frac{3}{4}$ of a number

8. $\frac{7}{8}$ more than a number

9. 90% of a number

10. 5 times a number

11. 4 less than a number

12. the cube of a number

13. 3 more than a number, all divided by 2

14. the square root of the product of 8 and a number

Write an expression to answer the question.

15. A triangle has base b and height 6. What is its area?

16. Violet pays $50 for a membership fee and $25 per dress rental. How much does she spend altogether for x rentals?

17. Serge has $67.39. He spends x dollars for a new book. How much does he have left?

18. How much is 4.5% sales tax on an item that costs x dollars?

19. You bicycle at x miles per hour for 2.5 hours. How far do you go?

20. You buy s sandwiches at $4.25 apiece and d drinks at $1 apiece. How much do you spend all together?

ADDITIONAL PROBLEM SOLVING STRATEGIES

When solving mathematical or real-life problems, you will find that different strategies are appropriate for different types of problems. Refer to Lesson 1.5 for examples of problem solving based on the strategies *use a verbal model*, *draw a diagram*, *look for a pattern*, and *guess, check, and revise*.

Make a List or Table

An organized list or table is helpful when enumerating possibilities.

EXAMPLE Andrea, Brian, and Colleen are going to have their picture taken. In how many ways can the three friends line up for the picture?

SOLUTION You may find a tree diagram useful in listing the possibilities.

PERSON ON LEFT	PERSON IN MIDDLE	PERSON ON RIGHT	POSSIBLE ARRANGEMENT
Andrea	Brian	Colleen	Andrea, Brian, Colleen
Andrea	Colleen	Brian	Andrea, Colleen, Brian
Brian	Andrea	Colleen	Brian, Andrea, Colleen
Brian	Colleen	Andrea	Brian, Colleen, Andrea
Colleen	Andrea	Brian	Colleen, Andrea, Brian
Colleen	Brian	Andrea	Colleen, Brian, Andrea

▶ There are six ways that the three friends can line up for the picture.

Use a Formula

You may be given a formula or know one that applies to the situation.

EXAMPLE Carol biked 25 kilometers in 2 hours. What was her average speed?

SOLUTION The formula for speed is $s = \dfrac{d}{t}$ where s is speed, d is distance, and t is time.

$$s = \frac{d}{t} = \frac{25\ \text{km}}{2\ \text{h}} = 12.5$$

▶ Carol's average speed was 12.5 kilometers per hour.

Break into Simpler Parts

You may want to break a difficult problem into more easily managed parts or cases. Be sure the parts or cases are *mutually exclusive* (that is, they do not overlap) and *collectively exhaustive* (that is, they cover all the possibilities).

EXAMPLE Find the area of the pentagon shown at the right.

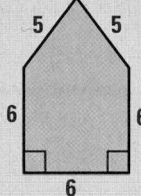

SOLUTION Break the figure into a square and two right triangles as shown at the bottom right. Using the Pythagorean theorem, you find that the length of the leg shared by the two triangles is 4 units.

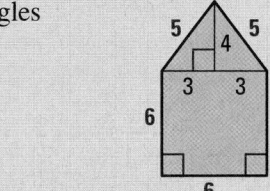

Area of pentagon = area of square + area of triangles

$$= 6^2 + 2\left[\frac{1}{2}(3)(4)\right]$$

$$= 36 + 12$$

$$= 48$$

▶ The area of the pentagon is 48 square units.

Solve a Simpler Problem

You may try solving simpler problems and looking for a pattern in their solutions.

EXAMPLE When 15 diameters are drawn in a circle, into how many wedges is the circle divided?

SOLUTION Look for a pattern in the number of wedges when 1, 2, 3, and 4 diameters are drawn in a circle.

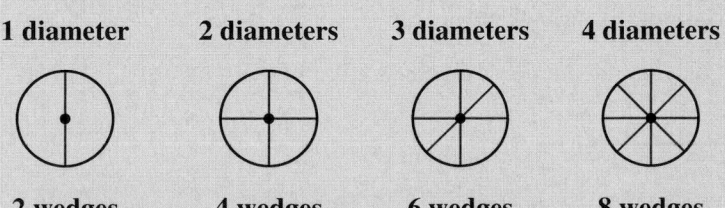

1 diameter	2 diameters	3 diameters	4 diameters
2 wedges	4 wedges	6 wedges	8 wedges

▶ The number of wedges is always twice the number of diameters. So, when 15 diameters are drawn in a circle, the circle is divided into 30 wedges.

PRACTICE

Use a list or table to solve the problem.

1. A frozen yogurt stand offers walnuts, peanuts, sprinkles, chocolate chips, and toffee bits as toppings. How many combinations of two different toppings are possible?

2. Kyle packs 4 pairs of pants and 6 shirts for a trip. How many different outfits are possible?

3. At a small theater, tickets for adults cost $12 and tickets for children cost $8. At one performance ticket sales were $480. How many people may have attended the performance?

Use a formula to solve the problem.

4. What is the area of a trapezoid with base lengths 7 inches and 11 inches and height 3 inches?

5. The formula $s = 32t$ gives the speed s (in feet per second) of an object falling without air resistance after t seconds have elapsed. How fast is a rock falling after 4 seconds?

6. You took two trips in your new car. The first trip covered 136 miles and used 6.4 gallons of gas. The second trip covered 285 miles and used 12.5 gallons of gas. On which trip did you get better gas mileage?

Solve the problem by breaking it into simpler parts or cases.

7. You throw three darts at the target shown. All three darts hit the target, and your score is the sum of the points that correspond to the regions where the darts land. What are the possibilities for your score?

8. A painter is stenciling numbers, starting with 1, on the parking spaces in a parking lot. If there are 200 spaces, how many times does the painter stencil the digit 7?

9. In a best-of-five series, the first team to win three games wins the series. How many ways are there for a team to win a best-of-five series?

10. Find the area of the figure.

a.
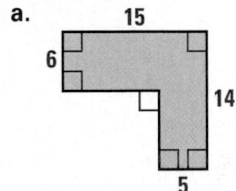

b.
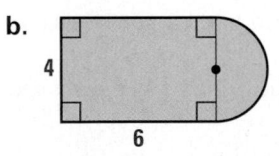

c.
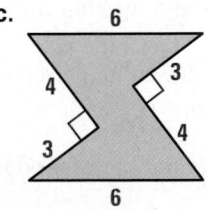

d.
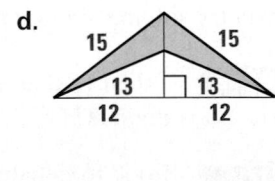

Solve the problem by first solving simpler problems.

11. By moving only up and to the right, find the number of paths that lead from point A to point B on the grid shown.

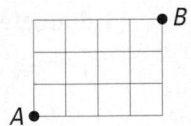

12. How many diagonals does a convex polygon with 12 sides have?

13. How many squares of any integral size can you draw on an 8×8 grid?

14. Without using a calculator, find the value of $(100,000,001)^2$.

▶ Graphing
POINTS IN THE COORDINATE PLANE

A **coordinate plane** is divided into four regions by the x-axis and y-axis. Each region is called a **quadrant**. A point in a coordinate plane can be represented by an **ordered pair** of numbers. The **x-coordinate** gives the horizontal position of the point. The **y-coordinate** gives the vertical position of the point. You can tell which quadrant a point is in by looking at the signs of its coordinates.

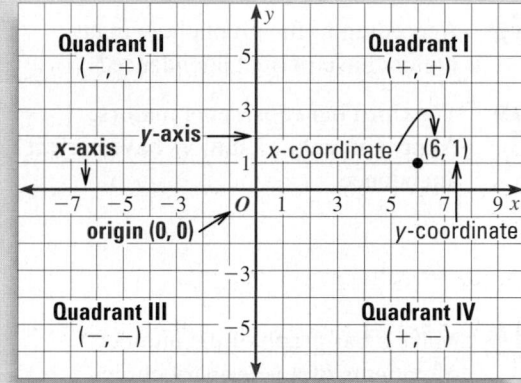

EXAMPLE   Graph the point $(4, -1)$. What quadrant is it in?

SOLUTION   To graph the point, start at the origin and move 4 units to the right and 1 unit down.

$(4, -1)$ is in Quadrant IV.

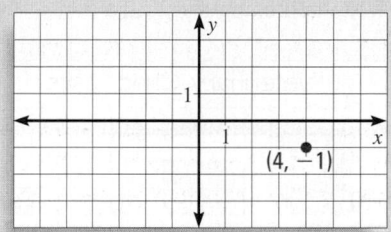

PRACTICE

Graph the point in a coordinate plane.

1. $A(3, 4)$ **2.** $B(0, -4)$ **3.** $C(3, -1)$ **4.** $D(-4, 5)$

5. $E(-1, -1)$ **6.** $F(1, 1)$ **7.** $G(-6, -6)$ **8.** $H(0, 2)$

9. $J(1, 5)$ **10.** $K(-1, 0)$ **11.** $L(5, -2)$ **12.** $M(-2, -4)$

13. $N(0, 5)$ **14.** $P(-3, 2)$ **15.** $Q(3, 0)$ **16.** $R(-1, -3)$

Give the coordinates and quadrant of each of the following points.

17. A **18.** B **19.** C

20. D **21.** E **22.** F

23. G **24.** H **25.** J

26. K **27.** L **28.** M

29. N **30.** O **31.** P

32. Q **33.** R **34.** S

35. T **36.** U **37.** V

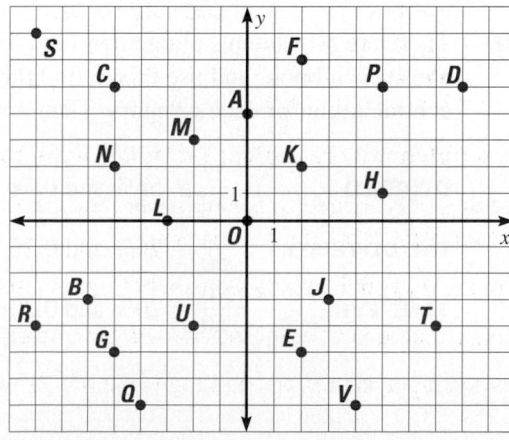

BAR, CIRCLE, AND LINE GRAPHS

A **bar graph** is used to represent data that fall into distinct categories.

EXAMPLE According to the graph, how many juniors have perfect attendance?

SOLUTION The third bar represents juniors. Approximately 13 juniors have perfect attendance.

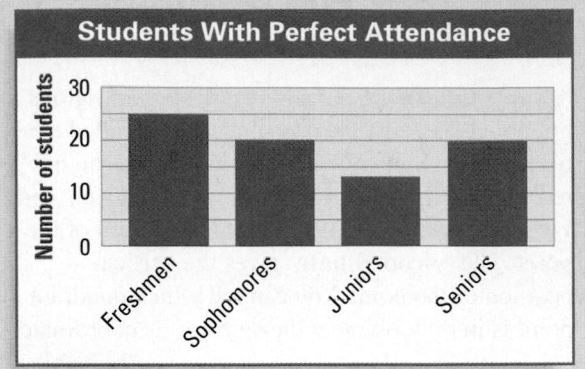

Students With Perfect Attendance

EXAMPLE Make a bar graph of the number of patients of a veterinary clinic. Represent each category with a bar.

Patients	Cats	Dogs	Birds	Hamsters
Visits	15	10	3	5

SOLUTION

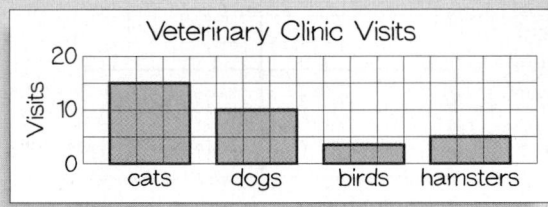

A **circle graph** is used to show parts of a whole.

EXAMPLE According to the graph, for what category do students spend the most money? the least money?

SOLUTION Students spend the most money on entertainment and the least money on snacks.

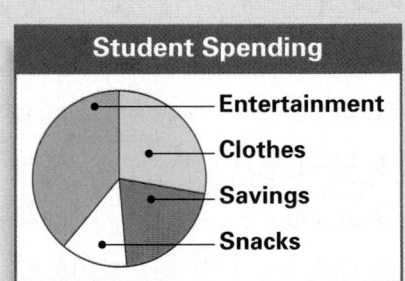

Student Spending
- Entertainment
- Clothes
- Savings
- Snacks

EXAMPLE Make a circle graph of the favorite books that students read in English class this year.

SOLUTION There are 50 students altogether. Find the percent who chose each book, and use this to find the measure of the central angle for each category. Then draw the circle graph.

Favorite Book	Students
Othello	27
The Odyssey	13
Jane Eyre	10

OTHELLO $\frac{27}{50} = 54\%$ and $0.54 \cdot 360° \approx 194°$

THE ODYSSEY $\frac{13}{50} = 26\%$ and $0.26 \cdot 360° \approx 94°$

JANE EYRE $\frac{10}{50} = 20\%$ and $0.20 \cdot 360° = 72°$

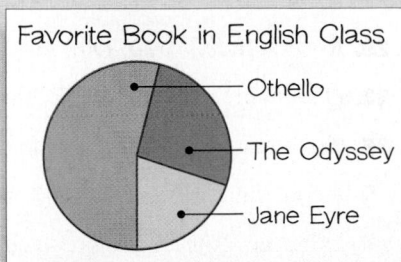

Favorite Book in English Class
- Othello
- The Odyssey
- Jane Eyre

A **line graph** is often used to show change over time.

EXAMPLE Make a line graph of the number of scholarship awards given.

Year	1998	1999	2000	2001	2002
Awards	6	7	4	8	7

SOLUTION Graph the data in the table. Connect the data points from year to year.

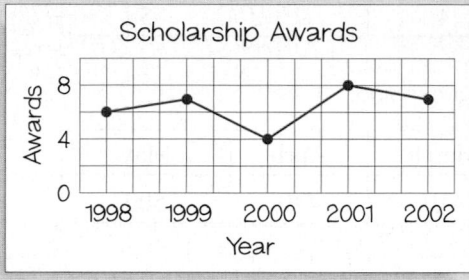

EXAMPLE According to the graph, how many juniors took AP English in 1999?

SOLUTION Find 1999 on the time axis, move up to the graph, and then move over to the student axis. Eleven juniors took AP English in 1999.

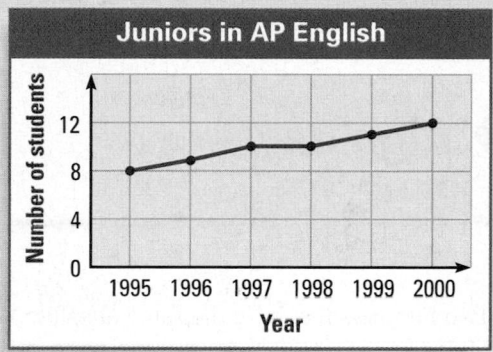

PRACTICE

Use the graphs to answer the questions.

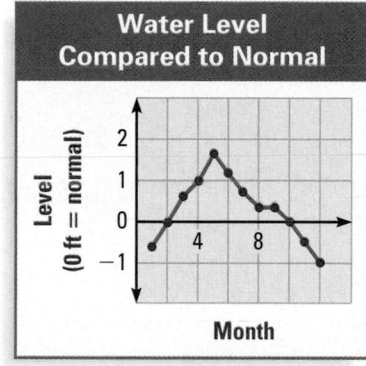

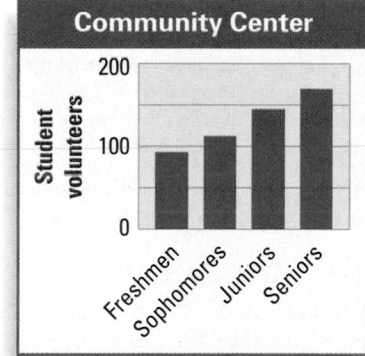

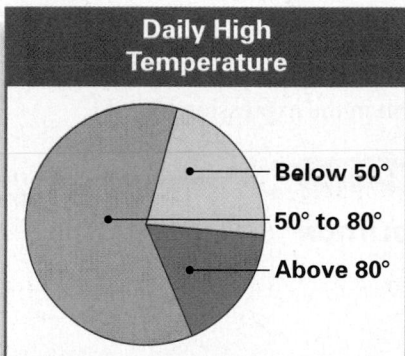

1. What was the water level in June?

2. In what month was water level lowest?

3. How many sophomores volunteer at the community center?

4. How many more juniors than sophomores volunteer at the community center?

5. About what percent of the year is the average daily temperature above 80°?

6. Does the temperature graph support the statement that during most of the year the average temperature is above 50°?

7. Make a bar graph to represent choices of college majors.

College majors	English	History	Mathematics	Biology	Economics
Number of students	65	37	40	70	45

8. Make a circle graph to represent the favorite sports of students in a class.

Favorite sports	Basketball	Baseball	Hockey	Soccer	Swimming
Number of students	16	10	4	7	5

9. Make a line graph to represent the number of visitors to a city zoo.

Month	January	February	March	April	May
Number of visitors	450	400	410	470	500

▶ Algebra
OPPOSITES

Two numbers that have the same absolute value but opposite signs are **opposites**.
Multiplication by -1 changes a number to its opposite.

EXAMPLE Find the opposite of the number.

   a. 13   **b.** -4

SOLUTION   **a.** $13(-1) = -13$ **b.** $(-4)(-1) = 4$

To find the opposite of an expression, use the distributive property to multiply each
term in the expression by -1.

EXAMPLE   Simplify the expression $-(3 - 2x)$.

SOLUTION $-(3 - 2x) = -1(3 - 2x) = (-1)(3) + (-1)(-2x)$
$$= -3 + 2x$$

PRACTICE

Find the opposite of the number.

1. 3   **2.** -27 **3.** 150   **4.** -13

5. 4.3   **6.** -9.28 **7.** $\frac{3}{5}$ **8.** $-\frac{1}{2}$

Simplify the expression.

9. $-(2a + b)$ **10.** $-(y - x)$ **11.** $-(a - b - c)$ **12.** $-(2y - 3x)$

13. $-(2 + x)$ **14.** $-(-3 - 11x)$ **15.** $-(4x - 1)$ **16.** $-(-x + 13)$

Simplify the expression.

17. $-(x^2 + 2x - 4)$ **18.** $-(x - (-2y))$ **19.** $-x - (3y + x)$ **20.** $-(-(x - y + 3))$

21. $-(3x - y + 11z)$ **22.** $x - (7y - 4x)$ **23.** $-9(-4x + 6y)$ **24.** $5x - (-(x - y))$

25. $-(2x + 7y) + 3x$ **26.** $4x - (-x + y)$ **27.** $a - (3b + 2a) + 6b$ **28.** $-2(-x + 3y - 6)$

MULTIPLYING BINOMIALS

A **binomial** is an expression that has two terms. You may find using a geometric model helpful when multiplying two binomials.

EXAMPLE   Simplify $(x + 1)(x + 2)$.

SOLUTION   Draw a rectangle and divide the width and length into two parts: x and 1 for the width, and x and 2 for the length. Divide the rectangle into four regions and find the area of each region. The product of $x + 1$ and $x + 2$ is the sum of the areas of the four regions.

$$(x + 1)(x + 2) = x^2 + 2x + x + 2$$
$$= x^2 + 3x + 2$$

The **FOIL** method can also be used to multiply two binomials. **FOIL** stands for **F**irst, **O**uter, **I**nner, and **L**ast, which is the order in which you multiply terms.

$$
\begin{array}{cccc}
\mathbf{F} & \mathbf{O} & \mathbf{I} & \mathbf{L}
\end{array}
$$
$$(2x + 3)(x - 1) = 2x(x) + 2x(-1) + 3(x) + 3(-1)$$
$$= 2x^2 - 2x + 3x - 3$$
$$= 2x^2 + x - 3$$

EXAMPLE   Simplify $(3x + 2)(x - 1)$.

SOLUTION $(3x + 2)(x - 1) = 3x \cdot x + 3x \cdot (-1) + 2 \cdot x + 2 \cdot (-1)$ **Multiply using FOIL.**
$$= 3x^2 - 3x + 2x - 2$$ **Simplify.**
$$= 3x^2 - x - 2$$ **Combine like terms**

PRACTICE

Simplify.

1. $(x + 1)(x + 1)$ **2.** $(2 - 4x)(1 + 2x)$ **3.** $(4x + 1)(2 + x)$

4. $(3x + 2)(x - 1)$ **5.** $(1 - 2x)(x + 3)$ **6.** $(-2x + 1)(3x - 4)$

7. $(2x - 5)(2x + 5)$ **8.** $(6x + 3)(1 - x)$ **9.** $(5x + 3)(x - 2)$

10. $(a + 1)(b + 1)$ **11.** $(y + 3)(2y - 3)$ **12.** $(-x + 2)(-3x - 2)$

13. $(a + b)(c + d)$ **14.** $(x + 2)(x + 3)$ **15.** $(2x - 1)(-2x - 1)$

16. $(x + 2)(2x - y)$ **17.** $(x - y)(x + y)$ **18.** $(3y - a)(y + 3a)$

19. $(3x + 5)(x - 2)$ **20.** $(x + 0)(x - 1)$ **21.** $(-4x + 12)(3x + 8)$

FACTORING

To factor a polynomial of the form $x^2 + bx + c$, you may find a geometric model helpful.

As when multiplying binomials, draw a rectangle and divide the width and length into two parts: x and m for the width, and x and n for the length. Divide the rectangle into four regions and find the area of each region. You can see that m and n must be factors of c and that the sum of m and n must be equal to b.

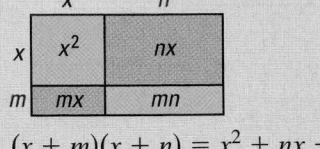

$$(x + m)(x + n) = x^2 + \underbrace{nx + mx}_{bx} + \underbrace{mn}_{c}$$
$$= x^2 + \quad bx \quad + c$$

EXAMPLE Factor $x^2 + 5x + 4$.

SOLUTION

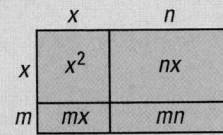

The integral factors of 4 are 1 and 4, -1 and -4, 2 and 2, and -2 and -2. Since $1x + 4x = 5x$, $m = 1$ and $n = 4$.

You want $mx + nx = 5x$ and $mn = 4$.

$x^2 + 5x + 4 = (x + 1)(x + 4)$

You can factor polynomials of the form $x^2 + bx + c$ without using a geometric model by listing the factors of c and finding the pair of factors that has a sum equal to b.

EXAMPLE Factor $x^2 - 2x - 15$.

SOLUTION You want $x^2 - 2x - 15 = (x + m)(x + n)$ where $mn = -15$ and $m + n = -2$.

Factors of -15	$1, -15$	$-1, 15$	$3, -5$	$-3, 5$
Sum of factors ($m + n$)	-14	14	-2	2

▶ The table shows that the values of m and n you want are $m = 3$ and $n = -5$. So, $x^2 - 2x - 15 = (x + 3)(x - 5)$.

PRACTICE

Factor.

1. $x^2 + 5x + 6$

2. $x^2 + 7x + 10$

3. $x^2 + 9x + 20$

4. $x^2 - 7x + 10$

5. $x^2 + 6x + 9$

6. $x^2 - 10x + 21$

7. $x^2 - 5x - 24$

8. $x^2 + 3x - 28$

9. $x^2 + 3x + 2$

10. $x^2 - 4x - 12$

11. $x^2 + x - 6$

12. $x^2 + 6x - 16$

13. $x^2 + 14x + 49$

14. $x^2 + 5x - 6$

15. $x^2 - 8x - 20$

16. $x^2 + 9x - 36$

17. $x^2 - 18x + 81$

18. $x^2 + 5x + 4$

19. $x^2 - 8x + 15$

20. $x^2 + 10x + 9$

21. $x^2 - 21x + 80$

22. $x^2 - 4x - 5$

23. $x^2 - 3x - 4$

24. $x^2 + 8x + 12$

25. $x^2 - 9x + 20$

26. $x^2 + 8x + 16$

27. $x^2 + 10x + 25$

28. $x^2 + x - 30$

29. $x^2 + 6x + 8$

30. $x^2 + 4x - 21$

LEAST COMMON DENOMINATOR

To add or subtract rational expressions with unlike denominators, first find the **least common denominator (LCD)** of the original rational expressions. To find the least common denominator of two rational expressions, follow these steps.

❶ Factor each denominator. If a constant factor is negative, multiply the numerator and denominator of the expression by -1.

❷ Find the *least common multiple* (*LCM*) of the constant factors in the factored denominators. (For help with LCM, see page 908.)

❸ For each different variable factor that appears in any denominator, write the factor as many times as it appears in the denominator having the greatest number of that factor.

❹ Write the LCD as the product of the results of Steps 2 and 3.

EXAMPLE   Find the LCD of the pair of rational expressions.

a. $\dfrac{5}{6x^2}, \dfrac{x}{4x^2 - 12x}$

b. $\dfrac{x + 1}{x^2 + 4x + 4}, \dfrac{2}{x^2 - 4}$

SOLUTION

a. **❶** $6x^2 = 6 \cdot x \cdot x$

$4x^2 - 12x = 4 \cdot x \cdot (x - 3)$

❷ LCM of 6 and 4 is 12.

❸ LCM of variable factors is $x \cdot x \cdot (x - 3)$.

❹ LCD is $12x^2(x - 3)$.

▶ LCD of $\dfrac{5}{6x^2}$ and $\dfrac{x}{4x^2 - 12x}$ is $12x^2(x - 3)$.

b. **❶** $x^2 + 4x + 4 = (x + 2) \cdot (x + 2)$

$x^2 - 4 = (x + 2) \cdot (x - 2)$

❷ LCM of 1 and 1 is 1.

❸ LCM of variable factors is $(x + 2) \cdot (x + 2) \cdot (x - 2)$.

❹ LCD is $(x + 2)^2(x - 2)$.

▶ LCD of $\dfrac{x + 1}{x^2 + 4x + 4}$ and $\dfrac{2}{x^2 - 4}$ is $(x + 2)^2(x - 2)$.

PRACTICE

Find the least common denominator of the pair of rational expressions.

1. $\dfrac{1}{2x}, \dfrac{1}{2}$

2. $\dfrac{1}{3y}, \dfrac{3}{-4y}$

3. $\dfrac{2}{45k}, \dfrac{-1}{30k^2}$

4. $\dfrac{9}{z(z + 1)}, \dfrac{15}{z^3}$

5. $\dfrac{4}{6x}, \dfrac{6}{2y}$

6. $\dfrac{5}{12a}, \dfrac{a}{9}$

7. $\dfrac{10}{3z}, \dfrac{1}{z^2}$

8. $\dfrac{-4}{9k}, \dfrac{1}{3k^2}$

9. $\dfrac{b}{b - 1}, \dfrac{3}{(b + 1)^2}$

10. $\dfrac{7}{12d}, \dfrac{d + 4}{-12d^2}$

11. $\dfrac{-3n + 4}{2n + 4}, \dfrac{5}{n + 2}$

12. $\dfrac{w}{w + 9}, \dfrac{w - 1}{w^2 + 18w + 81}$

13. $\dfrac{x - 11}{6 + 9x}, \dfrac{-x + 11}{18x + 12}$

14. $\dfrac{5g}{3g^3 - 21}, \dfrac{g^3 + 3}{2g^3 - 14}$

15. $\dfrac{h}{20 - 15h}, \dfrac{9h}{6h - 8}$

16. $\dfrac{7 - q^2}{q - 8q^3}, \dfrac{5q^2}{24q^3 - 3q}$

17. $\dfrac{7e}{6 - 10e}, \dfrac{e + 9}{12 - 20e}$

18. $\dfrac{4x}{5x^3 - 20x}, \dfrac{9 - x}{4x - x^3}$

19. $\dfrac{12c + 1}{c^3 - 4c^2}, \dfrac{c^3 - 3}{c^2 - c^3}$

20. $\dfrac{5}{6 - 2p^5}, \dfrac{7}{-2p^5 + 6}$

21. $\dfrac{7}{36x^2}, \dfrac{11}{-9x}$

22. $\dfrac{16}{x - 5}, \dfrac{6}{7x - 35}$

23. $\dfrac{x + 4}{3x^2 + 2x}, \dfrac{6}{3x + 2}$

24. $\dfrac{6x + 9}{2x^3 + 5x^2}, \dfrac{15}{-4x^2}$

Extra Practice

CHAPTER 1

Graph the numbers on a number line. Then write the numbers in increasing order. (Lesson 1.1)

1. $-3, \sqrt{8}, \dfrac{4}{7}, -2.8, \dfrac{9}{5}$

2. $4, \dfrac{2}{3}, -\sqrt{6}, -\dfrac{2}{3}, 0$

3. $0.4, \dfrac{3}{5}, -1.6, 0, \sqrt{3}$

4. $-5, 0, -\dfrac{17}{3}, -\sqrt{5}, 1$

5. $3.4, 0.3, -\dfrac{2}{5}, \sqrt{5}, \dfrac{5}{2}$

6. $\sqrt{2}, 1.4, 1.5, 0.5, 1$

Identify the property shown. (Lesson 1.1)

7. $(3 + 7)5 = 5(3 + 7)$

8. $(19 \cdot 4) \cdot 4 = 19 \cdot (4 \cdot 4)$

9. $-6 + 6 = 0$

10. $2(13 + 11) = 2 \cdot 13 + 2 \cdot 11$

11. $150 + 11 = 11 + 150$

12. $(4 + 8) + 9 = 4 + (8 + 9)$

Evaluate the expression. (Lesson 1.2)

13. $4 + 7 - 8 \div 4$

14. $3 \cdot 9 - (15 - 7)$

15. $8 - (4 + 3)^2 + 5$

16. $2x - 8$ when $x = 6$

17. $x^3 - 5x$ when $x = 3$

18. $3 + 12x - x^2$ when $x = -2$

Simplify the expression. (Lesson 1.2)

19. $5x^2 - 3x + 7x^2 - 10x$

20. $7x - y + 9x - 2y$

21. $-3x^2 + 2x - 6x^2$

22. $4(x - 5) - 3(2x + 7)$

23. $2(x - 1) + 3(x + 2)$

24. $6(x - y) + 3(y + 2x)$

Solve the equation. Check your solution. (Lesson 1.3)

25. $3n - 4 = 17$

26. $m + 14 = 8 - 2m$

27. $5x + 17 = 2x - 10$

28. $-5(2x - 1) = 3(x + 4)$

29. $4.7a + 6.2 = -4.61$

30. $\dfrac{1}{3}(x - 6) = -\dfrac{2}{5}x + \dfrac{14}{15}$

Solve the equation for y. (Lesson 1.4)

31. $3x + 4y = 12$

32. $3y - 5x = -13$

33. $-6y + 7x = -9$

34. $3xy + x = 15$

35. $\dfrac{4}{5}x - 10y = -3$

36. $\dfrac{1}{3}x - \dfrac{2}{5}y = -10$

POSTAGE In Exercises 37–39, the cost of sending an overnight package from Speedy Air is $15.00 for the first pound and $3.00 for each additional pound. How much will it cost to send a 7 pound package? Use the following verbal model. (**Lesson 1.5**)

$$\boxed{\begin{array}{c}\text{Total} \\ \text{cost}\end{array}} = \boxed{\begin{array}{c}\text{Cost of} \\ \text{first pound}\end{array}} + \boxed{\begin{array}{c}\text{Cost per pound of} \\ \text{additional pounds}\end{array}} \cdot \boxed{\begin{array}{c}\text{Number of} \\ \text{additional pounds}\end{array}}$$

37. Assign labels to the parts of the verbal model.

38. Use the labels to translate the verbal model into an algebraic model.

39. Solve the algebraic model. Answer the question.

40. **SCHOOL BAND** The school band is planning a carnival to raise money. They plan to sell 500 tickets. Adult tickets will be $4.50 and student tickets will be $2.50. They need to collect $1650 in ticket sales to meet their goal. How many adult and student tickets do they need to sell? (**Lesson 1.5**)

Solve the inequality. Then graph your solution. (Lesson 1.6)

41. $3x + 7 > 28$

42. $-m - 3 < 3m + 5$

43. $2.3x - 5.9 > -1.3$

44. $-7(n + 3) \geq 0$

45. $4 \leq x + 2 \leq 12$

46. $-6 \leq 3x + 2 \leq 11$

47. $6x + 4 < 22$ or $5x - 8 \geq 32$

48. $5n + 16 \leq 31$ or $8 + 4n > 48$

49. $3x - 7 \leq 16$ or $2x - 1 > 23$

Solve the equation. (Lesson 1.7)

50. $|x + 3| = 6$

51. $|2x - 6| = 50$

52. $|x - 7| = 3$

53. $|10x - 73| = 29$

54. $|9 - 3x| = 15$

55. $|20 - 7x| = 42$

56. $\left|\frac{1}{4}x + 5\right| = 21$

57. $\left|\frac{1}{2}x - 1\right| = 0$

58. $\left|10 + \frac{1}{3}x\right| = 16$

Solve the inequality. Then graph the solution. (Lesson 1.7)

59. $|x + 3| > 4$

60. $|4 - 8x| \geq 100$

61. $|7x + 7| < 14$

62. $|y + 8| \leq 15$

63. $|2y - 5| < 1$

64. $|2a - 6| > 0$

65. $|3x + 1| \geq 16$

66. $|4a + 7| \leq 13$

67. $|-2y + 3| > 5$

CHAPTER 2

Use a mapping diagram to represent the relation. Then tell whether the relation is a function. (Lesson 2.1)

1.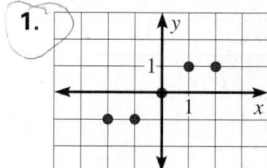

2.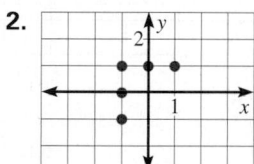

3.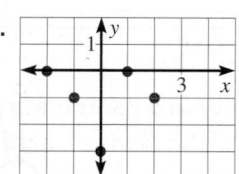

Evaluate the function when $x = -2$. (Lesson 2.1)

4. $f(x) = x + 17$

5. $f(x) = -x + 3$

6. $f(x) = -5 + 8x$

7. $f(x) = -x - 48$

8. $f(x) = |x + 3| - 9$

9. $f(x) = 2x^3 - 7x^2 + 8$

Tell whether the lines are *parallel*, *perpendicular*, or *neither*. (Lesson 2.2)

10. Line 1: through $(3, 4)$ and $(1, 6)$
Line 2: through $(-1, 0)$ and $(3, 5)$

11. Line 1: through $(1, 5)$ and $(-4, -5)$
Line 2: through $(-1, -9)$ and $(2, -3)$

12. Line 1: through $(-6, 7)$ and $(-3, 6)$
Line 2: through $(-1, -9)$ and $(1, -3)$

13. Line 1: through $(0, 0)$ and $(5, 2)$
Line 2: through $(0, -4)$ and $(-2, 1)$

14. Line 1: through $(1, 8)$ and $(-3, -4)$
Line 2: through $(-2, -5)$ and $(3, 5)$

15. Line 1: through $(0, -2)$ and $(2, -2.5)$
Line 2: through $(-4, 6)$ and $(0, 5)$

Draw the line with the given slope and *y*-intercept. (Lesson 2.3)

16. $m = 2, b = -4$

17. $m = 0, b = 4$

18. $m = -3, b = -2$

19. $m = -1, b = 0$

20. $m = \frac{1}{2}, b = 2$

21. $m = -\frac{4}{5}, b = -1$

Find the slope and *y*-intercept of the line. (Lesson 2.3)

22. $y = 2x$

23. $x = -1$

24. $y = 5$

25. $y = 2x - 5$

26. $y = 3x + 7$

27. $-2x + y = 10$

28. $5x - y = 12$

29. $x - 3y = -8$

Graph the equation. (Lesson 2.3)

30. $y = 3x$

31. $y = -2x - 4$

32. $y = 5x - 5$

33. $y = -x - 3$

34. $y = 2x - \dfrac{1}{4}$

35. $y = \dfrac{3}{8}x$

36. $y = \dfrac{3}{5}x + 2$

37. $y = -\dfrac{1}{2}x + 1$

Write an equation of a line that has the given properties. (Lesson 2.4)

38. slope: 2, y-intercept: -4

39. slope: 0, y-intercept: 2

40. slope: $\dfrac{4}{5}$, y-intercept: 5

41. slope: 2, passes through $(1, -3)$

42. slope: $\dfrac{1}{2}$, passes through $(-1, -1)$

43. slope: $-\dfrac{5}{2}$, passes through $(3, -4)$

44. passes through $(1, -6)$ and $(4, -3)$

45. passes through $(-3, 3)$ and $(2, -7)$

46. passes through $(-5, 3)$ and $(5, -3)$

47. passes through $(2, 6)$ and $(-7, 6)$

48. FLYING TIME The table below gives the distance (in miles) and flying time (in hours) to Atlanta, Georgia, from various U.S. cities. Draw a scatter plot of the data and approximate an equation of the best-fitting line. Then predict the flying time for a city that is 900 miles from Atlanta. **(Lesson 2.5)**

	Mobile	Little Rock	Chicago	Dallas	Austin	Colorado Springs	Denver	Los Angeles
Distance	302	459	585	717	817	1185	1204	1944
Time	2.23	2.5	2.82	3.03	3.2	4.83	4.92	7.33

Graph the inequality in a coordinate plane. (Lesson 2.6)

49. $y \geq 2$

50. $x < 3.6$

51. $x > -3$

52. $3x > 12$

53. $-2y \leq 8$

54. $y > 2.5$

55. $y < x - 2$

56. $y \geq 3x + 4$

57. $y > 4x - 7$

58. $y \leq 2x + 3$

59. $6x + 12y \leq -24$

60. $\dfrac{1}{2}x + \dfrac{3}{4}y > 0$

Evaluate the function for the given value of x. $f(x) = \begin{cases} 3x + 2, & \text{if } x \leq 1 \\ x + 4, & \text{if } x > 1 \end{cases}$
(Lesson 2.7)

61. $f(-2)$

62. $f(1)$

63. $f(5)$

64. $f(-1)$

65. $f(0)$

Graph the function. (Lesson 2.7)

66. $f(x) = \begin{cases} \dfrac{1}{2}x - 5, & \text{if } x < -2 \\ 5x + 4, & \text{if } x \geq -2 \end{cases}$

67. $f(x) = \begin{cases} -1, & \text{if } x < 0 \\ 1, & \text{if } 0 \leq x < 3 \\ 3, & \text{if } x \geq 3 \end{cases}$

Graph the function. Then identify the vertex, tell whether the graph opens up or down, and tell whether the graph is *wider*, *narrower*, or the *same width* as the graph of $y = |x|$. (Lesson 2.8)

68. $y = |x| - 4$

69. $y = 2|x| + 5$

70. $y = -|x| + 1$

71. $y = |x + 3|$

72. $y = -2|x|$

73. $y = 3|x| - 4$

74. $y = |1 - x| + 3$

75. $y = \dfrac{1}{2}|x| + 2$

76. $y = \dfrac{1}{3}|x|$

CHAPTER 3

Check whether the ordered pair is a solution of the system. (Lesson 3.1)

1. $(2, 1)$
$3x - 2y = 4$
$-2x + 2y = 3$

2. $(0, 5)$
$5x + y = 5$
$9x - 4y = -20$

3. $(-3, -2)$
$-7x + 12y = -22$
$-4x + y = 10$

4. $(-1, -8)$
$10x + 5y = -50$
$3x - 7y = 53$

Graph the linear system and tell how many solutions it has. If there is exactly one solution, estimate the solution and check it algebraically. (Lesson 3.1)

5. $y = 3$
$x + y = 7$

6. $3x + y = 10$
$y = 2x - 5$

7. $y = 2x - 5$
$6x - 3y = 15$

8. $2x - y = 4$
$5x + 2y = 17$

9. $5x - y = 7$
$y = 5x + 6$

10. $y = \frac{1}{3}x - 4$
$y = \frac{1}{3}x + 9$

11. $\frac{1}{2}x + 3y = 2$
$\frac{1}{5}x - 2y = -4$

12. $\frac{1}{3}x + y = 0$
$\frac{1}{6}x - 4y = 9$

Solve the system using any algebraic method. (Lesson 3.2)

13. $3x - 2y = 4$
$-2x + 2y = 3$

14. $5x + y = 5$
$9x - 4y = -20$

15. $12x - 7y = -22$
$-4x + y = 10$

16. $8x - y = 1$
$-x + 4y = 27$

17. $y = 2x - 4$
$-2y = x - 2$

18. $x + 2y = 5$
$-2x + 3y = -3$

19. $x - y = 1$
$9x - 8y = 0$

20. $-2x + 3y = 10$
$5x + 6y = -16$

Graph the system of linear inequalities. (Lesson 3.3)

21. $x > -6$
$y < x + 4$

22. $y \geq 2x + 3$
$y < -3x + 5$

23. $x + y \geq -2$
$-4x + y \leq -5$

24. $2x - y > 1$
$-5x + y \leq 4$

25. $x > 3$
$y < -10$
$x + y < 7$

26. $3x + y < -4$
$y \geq 2x + 1$
$-x + y < 4$

27. $x < -10$
$y < 3$
$y \geq x + 5$
$y \leq -x - 8$

28. $x > 1$
$y < 5$
$y \geq x + 2$
$y \leq -x + 5$

Find the minimum and maximum values of the objective function subject to the given constraints. (Lesson 3.4)

29. Objective function:
$C = 4x + 5y$

Constraints:
$x \geq 0$
$y \leq 4$
$x \leq 7$
$y \geq -5$

30. Objective function:
$C = x + 3y$

Constraints:
$x \leq 0$
$x \geq -4$
$y \geq 3$
$y \leq -2x + 5$

31. Objective Function:
$C = 5x - 3y$

Constraints:
$x \geq 0$
$y \geq 0$
$y \leq -x + 9$
$x \leq 5$

Sketch the graph of the equation. Label the points where the graph crosses the x-, y-, and z-axes. (Lesson 3.5)

32. $x + y + z = 10$

33. $3x + y + 2z = 12$

34. $4x + 5y + 2z = 20$

35. $5x + 5y + 3z = 15$

36. $6x - 4y + 3z = 16$

37. $3x + 5y + z = -9$

Write the linear equation as a function of x and y. Then evaluate the function for the given values. (Lesson 3.5)

38. $3x + 2y + 4z = 12$, $f(2, 3)$

39. $x + y + 3z = 9$, $f(-3, 3)$

40. $9x + 6y - 18z = 12$, $f\left(-\frac{1}{3}, 2\right)$

41. $-2x + 5y - 2z = 10$, $f(1, 4)$

42. $8x - y - z = 16$, $f\left(-\frac{1}{4}, -8\right)$

43. $-x + 4y + 7z = -31$, $f\left(5, \frac{1}{2}\right)$

Solve the system using any algebraic method. (Lesson 3.6)

44. $3x + 2y = 12$
$2y - 5z = 1$
$x + y + z = 6$

45. $2x + y = -2$
$-x + 3y - 4z = -26$
$5x - 6y + z = 17$

46. $x + y + z = 3$
$3x + 3y + 3z = 10$
$x - 3y + 4z = 6$

47. $-2x + 3y + z = 20$
$7x - 5y + 3z = -35$
$4x + 4y + 4z = 12$

48. $x + y + z = 3$
$x + y - z = 3$
$2x + 2y + z = 6$

49. $2x - 4y - z = -18$
$-6x - 3y + 2z = 2$
$4x + y - 6z = -37$

50. APPLES You have $20.75 to spend on picking 15 pounds of three different types of apples in an orchard. The Red Rome apples cost $1.29 per pound, the Granny Smith apples cost $1.49 per pound, and the Empire apples cost $1.09 per pound. You want twice as many Granny Smith apples as the other two kinds combined. How many pounds of each type of apples should you buy? (Lesson 3.6)

CHAPTER 4

Perform the indicated operation. (Lesson 4.1)

1. $\begin{bmatrix} 3 & 6 \\ -4 & -2 \end{bmatrix} + \begin{bmatrix} 1 & -4 \\ 0 & 6 \end{bmatrix}$

2. $\begin{bmatrix} -6 & 5 \\ 7 & 9 \end{bmatrix} + \begin{bmatrix} 1 & 0 \\ 3 & -1 \end{bmatrix}$

3. $\begin{bmatrix} -1 & 3 & 5 \\ -2 & 6 & -3 \end{bmatrix} + \begin{bmatrix} 0 & -4 & 2 \\ 3 & -6 & -1 \end{bmatrix}$

4. $\begin{bmatrix} 2 & -3 \\ 3 & 4 \\ 4 & 5 \end{bmatrix} - \begin{bmatrix} 9 & -3 \\ -2 & 5 \\ 0 & 4 \end{bmatrix}$

5. $\begin{bmatrix} 4 & \frac{2}{5} \\ 6 & \frac{1}{3} \end{bmatrix} - \begin{bmatrix} \frac{1}{3} & \frac{1}{5} \\ 1 & \frac{2}{3} \end{bmatrix}$

6. $-6\begin{bmatrix} 2 & -1 & 0 \\ -3 & 4 & 7 \end{bmatrix}$

7. $2\begin{bmatrix} 4 & 0 \\ 1 & 3 \end{bmatrix} + 3\begin{bmatrix} -1 & -2 \\ 5 & 7 \end{bmatrix}$

8. $5\begin{bmatrix} -2 & 0 & 1 \\ -3 & 7 & 4 \end{bmatrix} - \begin{bmatrix} 7 & 7 & 8 \\ 3 & 6 & 0 \end{bmatrix}$

9. $\frac{1}{2}\begin{bmatrix} 5.2 & 7.4 & 9.8 \\ 4.6 & 6.8 & 8.4 \end{bmatrix}$

Find the product. If it is not defined, state the reason. (Lesson 4.2)

10. $\begin{bmatrix} 2 & -6 \\ 3 & 1 \end{bmatrix}\begin{bmatrix} 0 & 4 \\ -1 & -5 \end{bmatrix}$

11. $\begin{bmatrix} 1.6 & 3 & 9 \end{bmatrix}\begin{bmatrix} 2 \\ 6.4 \\ -2 \end{bmatrix}$

12. $\begin{bmatrix} -8 & 0 & 5 \\ 3 & 6 & 7 \end{bmatrix}\begin{bmatrix} 4 & -3 & 9 \\ 8 & 6 & 9 \end{bmatrix}$

13. $\begin{bmatrix} -4 & 4.5 & 3.8 \\ 2 & 1.7 & 7.5 \end{bmatrix}\begin{bmatrix} 9 & 8 \\ 6.1 & 4.3 \\ 5.1 & 0 \end{bmatrix}$

14. $\begin{bmatrix} -3.0 & 10 \\ 0 & -4 \\ -2.0 & 0.3 \end{bmatrix}\begin{bmatrix} 0 & -1 \\ 0.5 & -1.8 \end{bmatrix}$

15. $\begin{bmatrix} 5 & 1 & 5 \\ -3 & 0 & 6 \\ -3 & -8 & 11 \end{bmatrix}\begin{bmatrix} 6 & 5 & 12 \\ -4 & -2 & -3 \\ -8 & 2 & 0 \end{bmatrix}$

BEVERAGE MACHINE In Exercises 16–18, you refill the beverage machines at work and you record the money received as income from each machine every day. There are three machines with four types of beverages. Juice is $.85, fruit punch is $.75, lemonade is $.65, and water is $.60. The matrix shows how many of each item were sold today. (Lesson 4.2)

	J	FP	L	W
MACHINE 1	12	13	18	14
MACHINE 2	15	15	21	22
MACHINE 3	8	16	9	33

16. Write the matrix that gives the price of each item.

17. Use matrix multiplication to determine how much money is in each machine.

18. Which machine has the most money?

Evaluate the determinant of the matrix. (Lesson 4.3)

19. $\begin{bmatrix} 4 & -3 \\ 7 & 2 \end{bmatrix}$

20. $\begin{bmatrix} 0 & 6 \\ 1 & -4 \end{bmatrix}$

21. $\begin{bmatrix} -3 & 5 \\ 9 & 2 \end{bmatrix}$

22. $\begin{bmatrix} 6 & 3 & 1 \\ 0 & 0 & -1 \\ 13 & 9 & 12 \end{bmatrix}$

23. $\begin{bmatrix} 21 & 7 & 2 \\ -6 & 10 & 9 \\ 1 & 0 & 3 \end{bmatrix}$

24. $\begin{bmatrix} -9 & 5 & -6 \\ 0 & 3 & 10 \\ -10 & 17 & 4 \end{bmatrix}$

Use Cramer's rule to solve the linear system. (Lesson 4.3)

25. $3x + y = 3$
$4x + 5y = -7$

26. $4x + 5y = 30$
$-3x - 3y = -9$

27. $8x - 10y = -8$
$9x + 2y = -62$

28. $2x + z = 6$
$3x - 2y + 4z = 13$
$-y - 3z = -15$

29. $x + y + 2z = 0$
$2x - 6y + 5z = 6$
$-x + 3y - 7z = 6$

30. $3x + 4y + 2z = 12$
$-2x - 3y - 4z = -12$
$5x + 5y + 6z = 8$

Find the inverse of the matrix. (Lesson 4.4)

31. $\begin{bmatrix} 4 & 3 \\ 7 & 6 \end{bmatrix}$

32. $\begin{bmatrix} 0 & 6 \\ 1 & -4 \end{bmatrix}$

33. $\begin{bmatrix} -3 & 6 \\ 1 & 2 \end{bmatrix}$

34. $\begin{bmatrix} -1 & 7 \\ 2 & -5 \end{bmatrix}$

35. $\begin{bmatrix} 1 & 2 \\ 4 & -8 \end{bmatrix}$

36. $\begin{bmatrix} 6 & 2 \\ -8 & 1 \end{bmatrix}$

37. $\begin{bmatrix} -9 & 7 \\ 4 & -3 \end{bmatrix}$

38. $\begin{bmatrix} 3 & -1 \\ -2 & 9 \end{bmatrix}$

Use an inverse matrix to solve the linear system. (Lesson 4.5)

39. $2x + 3y = 13$
$x - 5y = 0$

40. $-4x - 3y = -2$
$2x + y = 2$

41. $6x - 3y = -3$
$-4x + 7y = -3$

42. $5x + 2y = 8$
$-2x - 9y = 46$

43. $3x - 8y = 16$
$-2x + 5y = -10$

44. $-7x - 2y = -8$
$3x - 6y = 0$

45. $-5x - y = 2$
$10x + 3y = 1$

46. $-6x + 5y = -2$
$4x - 3y = 2$

47. Use the given inverse of the coefficient matrix to solve the linear system. **(Lesson 4.5)**

$x + 2z = 5$
$-2x + 3y + 4z = -8$
$2x - y + 2z = 10$

$A^{-1} = \begin{bmatrix} 5 & -1 & -3 \\ 6 & -1 & -4 \\ -2 & 0.5 & 1.5 \end{bmatrix}$

CHAPTER 5

Graph the quadratic function. Label the vertex and axis of symmetry. (Lesson 5.1)

1. $y = x^2 + 3x - 4$

2. $y = -2x^2 + x + 5$

3. $y = (x + 3)^2 - 4$

4. $y = (x + 1)(x - 4)$

5. $y = \frac{1}{2}(x - 4)^2 + 2$

6. $y = 3(x + 4)(x - 1)$

7. $y = (x + 8)(x - 3)$

8. $y = -\frac{1}{3}(x + 2)(x - 1)$

9. SWIMMING The drag force F (in pounds) of water on a swimmer can be modeled by $F = 1.35s^2$ where s is the swimmer's speed (in miles per hour). At what speed is the force minimized? **(Lesson 5.1)**

Factor the trinomial. If the trinomial cannot be factored, say so. (Lesson 5.2)

10. $x^2 + 8x + 15$

11. $m^2 - 9m + 20$

12. $3x^2 + 11x - 4$

13. $6x^2 + 5x - 6$

14. $9a^2 - 56a + 12$

15. $4u^2 - 4u - 35$

16. $n^2 - 49$

17. $x^2 - 10x + 25$

18. $16m^2 - 24m + 9$

19. $4x^2 - 2x - 20$

20. $3p^2 + 15p - 42$

21. $6x^2 + 13x - 25$

Solve the equation. (Lesson 5.2)

22. $x^2 + 10x + 21 = 0$　　**23.** $2x^2 - 13x - 7 = 0$　　**24.** $3x^2 - 24x - 27 = 0$　　**25.** $25m^2 - 20m + 4 = 0$

26. $x^2 - 8x = -15$　　**27.** $8k^2 + 5k = 2k^2 + 4$　　**28.** $10x^2 - 3x = -2x^2 + 36$　　**29.** $2(q^2 - 20) + 17q = -10q^2$

Write the quadratic function in intercept form and give the function's zeros.
(Lesson 5.2)

30. $y = x^2 + 10x + 9$　　**31.** $y = x^2 - 5x$　　　　**32.** $y = 2x^2 + 3x - 2$　　**33.** $y = 6x^2 - 24$

34. $y = 4x^2 - 12x + 8$　　**35.** $y = 5x^2 - 13x + 6$　　**36.** $y = 4x^2 + 22x + 24$　　**37.** $y = 7x^2 - 63$

Simplify the expression. (Lesson 5.3)

38. $\sqrt{32}$　　　　　　**39.** $\sqrt{125}$　　　　　**40.** $3\sqrt{27} \cdot \sqrt{3}$　　　**41.** $\sqrt{243}$

42. $\sqrt{15} \cdot \sqrt{3}$　　　**43.** $\sqrt{\dfrac{81}{125}}$　　　　**44.** $6\sqrt{5} \cdot \sqrt{5}$　　　**45.** $\sqrt{\dfrac{16}{25}}$

Solve the equation. (Lesson 5.3)

46. $x^2 = 144$　　　　**47.** $x^2 = 160$　　　　**48.** $2x^2 = 400$　　　**49.** $-4(x + 2)^2 = -20$

50. $\dfrac{x^2}{9} - 1 = 5$　　　**51.** $7x^2 = 175$　　　**52.** $x^2 - 100 = -82$　　**53.** $\dfrac{1}{3}(x - 4)^2 = 3$

Solve the equation. (Lesson 5.4)

54. $x^2 = -16$　　　**55.** $x^2 = -10$　　　**56.** $3x^2 = -27$　　　**57.** $5x^2 = -125$

58. $(y - 3)^2 = -49$　　**59.** $6x^2 = -216$　　**60.** $4(x + 5)^2 = -8$　　**61.** $-\dfrac{1}{4}(r + 1)^2 = 5$

Write the expression as a complex number in standard form. (Lesson 5.4)

62. $(3 + 5i) + (2 + i)$　　**63.** $(-6 + 4i) + (2 - 7i)$　　**64.** $(4 + 3i)^2$　　　　**65.** $(15 - 7i) - (15 - 7i)$

66. $i(5 + i)$　　　　**67.** $-2i(3 - 2i)$　　　**68.** $(9 - 2i)(9 + 2i)$　　**69.** $(9 - 5i) - (-2 + 6i)$

70. $(10 - 7i)^2$　　　**71.** $\dfrac{3}{5 + i}$　　　　**72.** $\dfrac{2i}{4 - i}$　　　**73.** $\dfrac{1 - i}{1 + i}$

Solve the equation by completing the square. (Lesson 5.5)

74. $x^2 - 6x = 7$　　　**75.** $x^2 - 4x + 8 = 0$　　**76.** $x^2 - 10x = 1$　　**77.** $m^2 + 2.6m - 3 = 0$

78. $2n^2 - 5n = 7$　　**79.** $3n^2 - 4n = 4$　　　**80.** $3y^2 + 2y = 5 - 4y$　　**81.** $5n^2 + 6n = 8$

82. VEGETABLE GARDEN You are planning to create a vegetable garden behind
your house. Your house will be one side of the rectangular garden, and the garden
will have a fence on its other sides. You bought 40 feet of fencing and enough
mulch to cover 140 square feet. If the back of the house is 30 feet wide, what
should the garden's dimensions be? (Lesson 5.5)

Use the quadratic formula to solve the equation. (Lesson 5.6)

83. $4x^2 + x = 3$　　　　**84.** $x^2 + 10x + 25 = 0$　　**85.** $x^2 + 3x - 8 = 0$

86. $x^2 - 4x + 5 = 0$　　　**87.** $7m^2 - 6m + 10 = 0$　　**88.** $2(m + 1)^2 = 3m + 7$

**Find the discriminant of the quadratic equation and give the number and type
of solutions of the equation.** (Lesson 5.6)

89. $x^2 + 7x + 12 = 0$　　　**90.** $x^2 - 8x + 16 = 0$　　　**91.** $5m^2 + 3m + 10 = 0$

92. $x^2 + 5x - 6 = 0$　　　**93.** $2x^2 - 4x + 7 = 0$　　　**94.** $4x^2 + 3x - 15 = 0$

Graph the inequality or system of inequalities. (Lesson 5.7)

95. $y \le 2x^2$

96. $y > x^2 - 4$

97. $y < -3x^2 + 2x + 4$

98. $y \le x^2 + 1$
  $y \ge x^2$

99. $y > x^2 - 4x + 4$
  $y < -x^2 + 5x - 3$

100. $y > x^2 + 3x - 5$
  $y < -2x^2 + 1$

Write a quadratic function in vertex form for the parabola whose graph has the given vertex and passes through the given point. (Lesson 5.8)

101.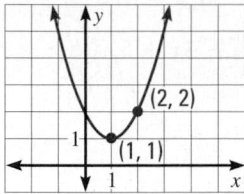

102.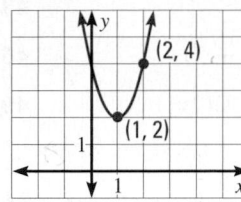

103.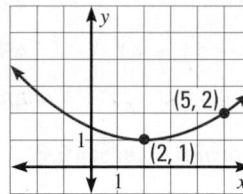

104. vertex: $(3, 0)$
  point: $(2, 1)$

105. vertex: $(-3, -5)$
  point: $(1, 27)$

106. vertex: $(-1, -4)$
  point: $(-2, -6)$

Write a quadratic function in intercept form whose graph has the given x-intercepts and passes through the given point. (Lesson 5.8)

107. x-intercepts: $2, 6$
  point: $(5, -3)$

108. x-intercepts: $-1, 3$
  point: $(2, 3)$

109. x-intercepts: $4, 0$
  point: $(1, -6)$

110. x-intercepts: $-2, 3$
  point: $(2, 1)$

111. x-intercepts: $1, 2$
  point: $(5, 9)$

112. x-intercepts: $-1, 4$
  point: $(0, -1)$

113. x-intercepts: $5, -2$
  point: $(2, 2)$

114. x-intercepts: $-3, -3$
  point: $(1, 48)$

CHAPTER 6

Evaluate the expression. Tell which properties of exponents you used. (Lesson 6.1)

1. $5^2 \cdot 5^2$

2. $(-4)^3(-4)$

3. $(2^3)^3$

4. 6^{-2}

5. $\left(\dfrac{4}{5}\right)^2$

6. $\left(\dfrac{3}{7}\right)^{-2}$

7. $8^0 \cdot 8^{-3}$

8. $\dfrac{3^{-2}}{3^{-4}}$

9. $\left(\dfrac{1}{6}\right)^3\left(\dfrac{1}{6}\right)^3$

10. $\left(\left(\dfrac{1}{3}\right)^2\right)^{-3}$

11. $\dfrac{6^3}{4^0 \cdot 6^2}$

12. $5^5 \cdot 5^0 \cdot 5^{-3}$

Simplify the expression. Tell which properties of exponents you used. (Lesson 6.1)

13. $(32x^2)^4$

14. $(x^2y^2)^{-3}$

15. $\dfrac{x^8}{x^5}$

16. $\dfrac{4x^4y^7}{8x^5y^3}$

17. $(6x^3y^4)^{-2}$

18. $-4(x^{-5}y^2)^2$

19. $(-3x^9y^3)^{-7}$

20. $(6x^{-3}y^{-1})^{-8}$

21. $(8(x^3y^4)^2)^{-2}$

22. $\dfrac{2x^{-3}y^{-5}}{3x^{-6}y^{-3}}$

23. $\dfrac{x^{10}}{3y^4} \cdot \dfrac{9x^2y^2}{x^4y^3}$

24. $\dfrac{15xy^4}{8x^3y^0} \cdot \dfrac{16x^5y^2}{5y^4}$

Use synthetic division to evaluate the polynomial function for the given value of x. (Lesson 6.2)

25. $f(x) = 2x^3 + 3x^2 - 5x + 1; x = 2$

26. $f(x) = 10x^3 - 5x^2 + 4; x = -1$

27. $f(x) = x^5 - 3x^3 - 2x; x = -2$

28. $f(x) = -x^4 + 7x - 12; x = 3$

Graph the polynomial function. (Lesson 6.2)

29. $f(x) = x^3$

30. $f(x) = x^4 + 1$

31. $f(x) = 3 - x^3$

32. $f(x) = x^4 - 3x$

33. $f(x) = -x^5 - 2$

34. $f(x) = x^5 + 2x^3 + 3$

Find the sum or difference. (Lesson 6.3)

35. $(2x^2 + 6x + 3) + (3x^2 + 4x + 4)$

36. $(4x - 3) + (3 - 8x)$

37. $(5x^3 - 2x^2 + 7) - (8x^2 - 11)$

38. $(9x^3 - 7x^2 + 8) + (-8x^3 + 5x^2 - 15)$

39. $(29x - 8) + (15x^3 + 9x^2 - 8)$

40. $(6x^3 - 7x^4 + 10x) - (4x^3 - 6x^2)$

Find the product of the polynomials. (Lesson 6.3)

41. $(x + 7)(x - 5)$

42. $(x - 3)^2$

43. $(5 - 3x)(x + 1)(x + 6)$

44. $(-x^3 - 3)(x^2 - 5x + 4)$

45. $6x(2x^3 - 4x^2 + 7)$

46. $(x + 12)(2x^2 - 3x + 5)$

47. $(2x + 8)^3$

48. $(x + 1)(3x + 3)(2x + 3)$

49. $(x + y)^3$

Factor the polynomial. (Lesson 6.4)

50. $x^3 - 27$

51. $2x^3 + 250$

52. $256x^5 - 81x^3$

53. $x^3 + 7x^2 + 15x + 9$

54. $x^3 - x^2 - 14x + 24$

55. $3x^3 - 24$

56. $x^3 + 5x^2 + 8x + 40$

57. $2x^3 + 18x^2 - 5x - 45$

58. $3x^5 + 6x^3 - 45x$

59. PACKAGING A factory needs a box that has a volume of 6 cubic inches. The width should be 1 inch less than the height and the length should be 3 inches greater than the height. What should the dimensions of the box be? (Lesson 6.4)

Divide. Use synthetic division when possible. (Lesson 6.5)

60. $(x^3 - 2x^2 - 8x + 5) \div (x - 1)$

61. $(x^3 - 10x^2 + 27x - 12) \div (x - 4)$

62. $(5x^2 - 6) \div (x - 2)$

63. $(3x^4 - 17x^3 + 13x^2 - 24x + 16) \div (x + 4)$

64. $(x^4 + x^3 - 3x - 3) \div (x + 1)$

65. $(4x^4 - 5x^3 + 2x^2 - x + 5) \div (x - 2)$

Find all the real zeros of the polynomial function. (Lesson 6.6)

66. $f(x) = x^3 - 2x^2 - 11x + 12$

67. $f(x) = x^4 + 5x^3 + 10x^2 + 20x + 24$

68. $f(x) = 2x^3 - 3x^2 - 23x + 12$

69. $f(x) = x^5 + x^4 + 3x^3 - 8x^2 - 8x - 24$

70. $f(x) = 3x^4 - 5x^3 - 5x^2 + 5x + 2$

71. $f(x) = 16x^3 + 80x^2 + x + 5$

Find all the zeros of the polynomial function. (Lesson 6.7)

72. $f(x) = x^3 - x^2 + 4x - 4$

73. $f(x) = x^4 - 7x^3 + 17x^2 - 17x + 6$

74. $f(x) = x^3 + x^2 + 9x + 9$

75. $f(x) = x^4 + 2x^3 - 12x^2 - 40x - 32$

76. $f(x) = x^3 - 7x^2 - x + 7$

77. $f(x) = x^4 - 6x^2 + 5$

Write a polynomial function of least degree that has real coefficients, the given zeros, and a leading coefficient of 1. (Lesson 6.7)

78. $3, 1, 5$

79. $-1, -2, -2$

80. $4, 6, -7$

81. $i, -i, 3$

82. $i, -4i, 4i$

83. $2, 1 + i$

84. $6i, 6i$

85. $3, -2, -1 + i$

86. $4 - i, 5 - i, 2$

87. $2 + i, 6i$

88. $2, 2, 3 - i$

89. $5, -5, -6i, 5i$

Graph the function. (Lesson 6.8)

90. $f(x) = (x + 3)(x - 4)(x + 1)$

91. $f(x) = 3(x - 3)(x + 1)^3$

92. $f(x) = -(x - 1)(x + 1)(x - 5)$

93. $f(x) = 2(x - 1)(x + 4)^2$

94. $f(x) = 2(x - 3)(x + 2)^2$

95. $f(x) = -3(x + 1)(x - 1)(x - 2)$

96. $f(x) = 2(x - 1)(x + 2)^3$

97. $f(x) = 5(x + 3)(x - 2)^2$

98. $f(x) = 2(x - 1)(x - 2)(x + 3)$

Find a polynomial that fits the data. (Lesson 6.9)

99.

x	1	2	3	4	5	6
$f(x)$	2	5	9	14	20	27

100.

x	1	2	3	4	5	6
$f(x)$	5	16	43	92	169	280

101.

x	1	2	3	4	5	6
$f(x)$	3	3	9	27	63	123

102.

x	1	2	3	4	5	6
$f(x)$	3	15	55	141	291	523

CHAPTER 7

Evaluate the expression without using a calculator. (Lesson 7.1)

1. $\sqrt[3]{27}$

2. $\sqrt[3]{-125}$

3. $16^{-1/2}$

4. $64^{2/3}$

5. $-\left(25^{3/2}\right)$

6. $-\left(243^{3/5}\right)$

7. $\left(\sqrt[4]{81}\right)^{-2}$

8. $\sqrt[5]{32}$

9. $8^{1/3}$

10. $(-216)^{-1/3}$

11. $\left(\sqrt[3]{64}\right)^{1/2}$

12. $\left(\sqrt[3]{729}\right)^{1/2}$

Simplify the expression. (Lesson 7.2)

13. $5^{1/4} \cdot 5^{3/4}$

14. $\left(3^{1/3}\right)^{2/5}$

15. $2^{1/4} \cdot 8^{1/4}$

16. $\dfrac{12^{3/5}}{12^{1/5}}$

17. $\dfrac{80^{1/2}}{16^{1/2}}$

18. $\sqrt{25} \cdot \sqrt[3]{25}$

19. $\left(\sqrt[3]{7} \cdot \sqrt[4]{7}\right)^2$

20. $\dfrac{\sqrt{10}}{\sqrt[4]{10}}$

Simplify the expression. Assume all variables are positive. (Lesson 7.2)

21. $x^{1/2} \cdot x^{1/5}$

22. $\left(x^3\right)^{1/2}$

23. $\sqrt[4]{81x^6 y^8}$

24. $\sqrt{\dfrac{16x^4 y^5}{25z^4}}$

25. $\dfrac{\sqrt[3]{x} \cdot \sqrt{x^3}}{\sqrt{16x^{12}}}$

26. $\dfrac{\sqrt[5]{x^4}}{\sqrt[8]{x^3}}$

27. $\sqrt[3]{\dfrac{8x^6 y^{12}}{27}}$

28. $\sqrt[6]{9xy^6} \cdot \sqrt[6]{6x^{12}}$

Let $f(x) = x^2 - 4x + 5$ and $g(x) = x^2 - 9$. Perform the indicated operation and state the domain. (Lesson 7.3)

29. $f(x) + g(x)$

30. $f(x) - g(x)$

31. $g(x) + f(x)$

32. $g(x) - f(x)$

33. $f(x) + f(x)$

34. $f(x) - f(x)$

35. $g(x) + g(x)$

36. $g(x) - g(x)$

Let $f(x) = 3x^{1/3}$ and $g(x) = x^{1/2}$. Perform the indicated operation and state the domain. (Lesson 7.3)

37. $f(x) \cdot g(x)$

38. $\dfrac{f(x)}{g(x)}$

39. $g(x) \cdot f(x)$

40. $\dfrac{g(x)}{f(x)}$

41. $f(g(x))$

42. $g(f(x))$

43. $f(f(x))$

44. $g(g(x))$

Find the inverse function. (Lesson 7.4)

45. $f(x) = 3x + 1$

46. $f(x) = -2x - 1$

47. $f(x) = -x - 4$

48. $f(x) = 5x - 7$

49. $f(x) = 2x + 3$

50. $f(x) = -4x - 5$

51. $f(x) = \dfrac{1}{2}x - 4$

52. $f(x) = 3x^3 + 2$

53. $f(x) = -\dfrac{1}{3}x + 5$

54. $f(x) = 2x^4; x \geq 0$

55. $f(x) = x^4 - \dfrac{1}{8}; x \geq 0$

56. $f(x) = \dfrac{1}{2}x^2 - 5; x \geq 0$

57. **AREA** The area A of a circular object is $A = \pi r^2$ where r is the radius of the object. Find r in terms of A. (Lesson 7.4)

Graph the function. Then state the domain and range. (Lesson 7.5)

58. $y = 2\sqrt{x}$

59. $y = \frac{1}{4}\sqrt{x}$

60. $y = \sqrt{x - 4}$

61. $y = (x + 5)^{1/2}$

62. $y = 6\sqrt{x + 5}$

63. $y = \sqrt[3]{x} + 1$

64. $y = 3\sqrt[3]{x + 1}$

65. $y = 4\sqrt[3]{x - 12} + 3$

66. $y = \frac{1}{2}\sqrt{x + 2}$

67. $y = \sqrt[3]{x - 5} + 1$

68. $y = \frac{1}{3}\sqrt[3]{x - 8} - 5$

69. $y = -2(x + 2)^{1/3} - 4$

Solve the equation. Check for extraneous solutions. (Lesson 7.6)

70. $x^{1/4} = \frac{1}{256}$

71. $x^{1/4} - 81 = 0$

72. $2(x + 1)^{2/3} = 6$

73. $\sqrt{x} + 1 = \frac{1}{16}$

74. $x^{2/3} = 16$

75. $\sqrt[3]{x} + 4 = 2$

76. $\sqrt{11x + 3} = 2x$

77. $\sqrt{x - 13} = 2\sqrt{x + 7}$

78. $\sqrt{5x + 1} = x - 4$

79. $\sqrt{x + 3} = \sqrt{2x - 7}$

80. $2\sqrt{x - 2} = \sqrt{x}$

81. $4\sqrt{3x - 7} = 2\sqrt{-x + 73}$

Find the mean, median, mode, range, and standard deviation of the data set.
(Lesson 7.7)

82. 8, 9, 9, 10, 11, 10, 12, 8, 9, 11

83. 52, 56, 57, 58, 58, 73, 55, 58, 57, 58

84. 2.3, 2.7, 2.8, 2.8, 2.8, 4.7, 4.9, 5.2

85. 21.4, 18.6, 15.3, 62, 21.9, 18.6, 21.3

CHAPTER 8

Graph the function. State the domain and range. (Lesson 8.1)

1. $y = 3^x$

2. $y = 3 \cdot 4^x$

3. $y = 5(1.5)^x$

4. $y = 4(2)^x$

5. $y = 2 \cdot 7^{x - 1}$

6. $y = -\frac{1}{2}(2.5)^x$

7. $y = 3^{x - 1}$

8. $y = 3^{x - 2} + 1$

9. $y = 2^{x - 2} + 4$

10. $y = 4 \cdot 5^{x - 1} - 2$

11. $y = 3 \cdot 2^{x + 2}$

12. $y = 5 \cdot 2^{x - 3}$

Graph the function. State the domain and range. (Lesson 8.2)

13. $y = \left(\frac{1}{2}\right)^x$

14. $y = 2\left(\frac{1}{3}\right)^x$

15. $y = -3\left(\frac{1}{4}\right)^x$

16. $y = -\left(\frac{1}{5}\right)^x$

17. $y = (0.25)^x$

18. $y = -2\left(\frac{1}{4}\right)^x - 1$

19. $y = \left(\frac{2}{3}\right)^x + 3$

20. $y = -5\left(\frac{1}{2}\right)^x$

Simplify the expression. (Lesson 8.3)

21. $e^4 \cdot e^3$

22. $e^{-6} \cdot e^7$

23. $4e^{3x} \cdot 4e^{3x}$

24. $\left(7e^{-x}\right)^{-2}$

25. $\frac{10e^x}{e^{3x}}$

26. $\sqrt[3]{64e^{6x}}$

27. $e^{2x} \cdot e^{4x - 1}$

28. $\frac{e^x}{5e}$

29. $\frac{20e^{4x}}{5e}$

30. $\left(6e^{-2x}\right)^3$

31. $\sqrt{16e^{8x}}$

32. $\left(\frac{1}{3}e^{-3}\right)^{-3}$

Graph the function. State the domain and range. (Lesson 8.3)

33. $y = e^{0.5x}$

34. $y = e^{-0.75x}$

35. $y = 2e^{-(x - 1)}$

36. $y = 0.5e^{-x}$

37. $y = \frac{1}{2}e^{x - 3} + 1$

38. $y = 3e^{x - 2} - 4$

39. $y = \frac{1}{3}e^{-2(x - 1)} - 2$

40. $y = 0.1e^{2x} - 3$

41. MOUNT FUJI The relationship between air pressure and altitude can be modeled by
$P = 14.7e^{-0.00004h}$ where P is the air pressure (in pounds per square inch) and h is
the altitude (in feet above sea level). Mount Fuji in Japan rises to a height of 12,388
feet above sea level. What is the air pressure at the peak of Mount Fuji? (**Lesson 8.3**)

Evaluate the expression without using a calculator. (Lesson 8.4)

42. $\log_2 16$ **43.** $\log_5 25$ **44.** $\log_{11} 1$ **45.** $\log_{1/4} 2$

46. $\log_3 3^{-2.16}$ **47.** $\log_7 343$ **48.** $\log_{29} 29$ **49.** $\log_9 9^3$

Find the inverse of the function. (Lesson 8.4)

50. $y = \log_4 x$ **51.** $y = \log_{1/3} x$ **52.** $y = \log_6 36^x$

53. $y = \ln 3x$ **54.** $y = \ln (x + 1)$ **55.** $y = \ln (x - 3)$

Graph the function. State the domain and range. (Lesson 8.4)

56. $y = \log_3 x$ **57.** $y = \ln x - 2$ **58.** $y = \log x + 4$ **59.** $y = \ln (x - 3)$

60. $y = \log_5 (x + 2)$ **61.** $y = \ln x + 7$ **62.** $y = \log_{1/2} x + 1$ **63.** $y = \log_5 x + 2$

Use a property of logarithms to evaluate the expression. (Lesson 8.5)

64. $\log_2 (4 \cdot 8)$ **65.** $\ln e^3$ **66.** $\log_2 8^2$ **67.** $\log_6 216$

68. $\log \dfrac{1}{100}$ **69.** $\ln \dfrac{1}{e^5}$ **70.** $\log 0.001$ **71.** $\log_3 27^2$

Expand the expression. (Lesson 8.5)

72. $\log_3 9x$ **73.** $\log 3x^4$ **74.** $\log_6 x^5$ **75.** $\ln 15x$

76. $\log_7 49x^2$ **77.** $\log \sqrt{9x}$ **78.** $\ln x^{1/3}y^4$ **79.** $\log x^2 y^3 z^4$

Condense the expression. (Lesson 8.5)

80. $\log_4 7 + \log_4 10 - \log_4 2$ **81.** $4 \ln x + 6 \ln y + 3 \ln z$ **82.** $5 \log_4 3 + 6 \log_4 x + 7 \log_4 y$

83. $\dfrac{1}{4}(\ln 9 - \ln x) + \dfrac{1}{4} \ln 3$ **84.** $6(\ln 3 + \ln x) + \dfrac{1}{4} \ln 3$ **85.** $3(\log_5 10 - \log_5 2) + \dfrac{1}{2} \log_5 \dfrac{1}{100}$

Solve the equation. Check for extraneous solutions. (Lesson 8.6)

86. $3^x = 10$ **87.** $4^x - 3 = 11$ **88.** $3^{x+2} = 9^{x+1}$ **89.** $10^x + 4 = 10$

90. $\ln 8x = 4$ **91.** $\ln (5 - x) = 12$ **92.** $\log_3 x = 4$ **93.** $\log_5 (2x + 10) = \log_5 4x$

Write an exponential function of the form $y = ab^x$ whose graph passes through the given points. (Lesson 8.7)

94. $(2, 18), (1, 6)$ **95.** $(0, 0.5), (3, 4)$ **96.** $(-1, 6), (1, 0.5)$ **97.** $(-2, 0.01), (1, 1.25)$

98. $(3, 9), \left(8, \dfrac{25}{4}\right)$ **99.** $\left(-1, \dfrac{1}{4}\right), \left(2, \dfrac{3}{8}\right)$ **100.** $(2, 27), \left(-2, \dfrac{1}{3}\right)$ **101.** $(1, -8), (0, -2)$

102. EXPANDING BUSINESS The table below shows the number s of stores owned by a company from 1987 to 1998 where t represents the number of years since 1987. Find an exponential model for the data. Then use the model to predict how many more stores there will be in 2006. **(Lesson 8.7)**

t	0	1	2	3	4	5	6	7	8	9	10	11
s	17	33	55	84	116	165	272	425	676	1015	1412	1900

Write a power function of the form $y = ax^b$ whose graph passes through the given points. (Lesson 8.7)

103. $(-2, -8), (3, 27)$ **104.** $(1, 5), (4, 10)$ **105.** $(1, 2), (4, 4)$ **106.** $(2, 4), (3, 37)$

107. $(-1, -3), (3, 81)$ **108.** $(2, 1), (6, 9)$ **109.** $(-1, 0.5), (4, 8)$ **110.** $(-5, -8), (-10, -32)$

Evaluate the function $f(x) = \dfrac{6}{1 + 4e^{-x}}$ for the given value of x. (Lesson 8.8)

111. $f(1)$
112. $f(2)$
113. $f(-2)$
114. $f(3)$

115. $f(0)$
116. $f(4.1)$
117. $f(-0.6)$
118. $f\left(\dfrac{1}{4}\right)$

Graph the function. Identify the asymptotes, y-intercept, and the point of maximum growth. (Lesson 8.8)

119. $y = \dfrac{1}{1 + 3e^{-2x}}$
120. $y = \dfrac{1}{1 + 2e^{-0.5x}}$
121. $y = \dfrac{2}{1 + e^{-x}}$
122. $y = \dfrac{5}{1 + e^{-2x}}$

123. $y = \dfrac{3}{1 + 2e^{-4x}}$
124. $y = \dfrac{4}{1 + e^{-1.04x}}$
125. $y = \dfrac{5}{1 + 6e^{-2.5x}}$
126. $y = \dfrac{8}{1 + 2e^{-0.4x}}$

CHAPTER 9

The variables x and y vary inversely. Use the given values to write an equation relating x and y. Then find y when $x = 4$. (Lesson 9.1)

1. $x = 3, y = 6$
2. $x = 2, y = 8$
3. $x = -1, y = 4$
4. $x = 2, y = 6$

5. $x = -\dfrac{1}{3}, y = 9$
6. $x = \dfrac{1}{2}, y = 6$
7. $x = \dfrac{1}{2}, y = \dfrac{1}{8}$
8. $x = \dfrac{2}{5}, y = \dfrac{1}{10}$

The variable z varies jointly with x and y. Use the given values to write an equation relating x, y, and z. Then find z when $x = 4$ and $y = 7$. (Lesson 9.1)

9. $x = 2, y = 3, z = 6$
10. $x = -3, y = 6, z = 18$
11. $x = 10, y = -15, z = 5$

12. $x = -1, y = 2, z = 4$
13. $x = \dfrac{3}{4}, y = \dfrac{1}{2}, z = 8$
14. $x = \dfrac{1}{5}, y = \dfrac{7}{8}, z = \dfrac{1}{2}$

Graph the function. State the domain and range. (Lesson 9.2)

15. $y = \dfrac{3}{x}$
16. $y = \dfrac{2}{x - 3} + 1$
17. $y = \dfrac{5}{2x + 1} - 4$
18. $y = \dfrac{x + 1}{x + 6}$

19. $y = \dfrac{x - 2}{x + 1}$
20. $y = \dfrac{x + 3}{x + 4}$
21. $y = \dfrac{x}{2x - 5}$
22. $y = \dfrac{4x}{-x - 3}$

FUNDRAISER In Exercises 23–25, your school is publishing a calendar to raise money for a local charity. The total cost of using the photos in the calendar is \$710. In addition to this "one-time" charge, the unit cost of printing each calendar is \$4.50. (Lesson 9.2)

23. Write a model that gives the average cost per calendar as a function of the number of calendars printed.

24. Graph the model and use the graph to estimate the number of calendars you need to print before the average cost decreases to \$6 per calendar.

25. Describe what happens to the average cost as the number of calendars printed increases.

Graph the function. (Lesson 9.3)

26. $y = \dfrac{2x^2 + 1}{x + 3}$
27. $y = \dfrac{7}{x^2 + 5}$
28. $y = \dfrac{x^2 + 9}{x^2 + 2}$
29. $y = \dfrac{x^2 - 5x - 6}{x - 6}$

30. $y = \dfrac{5 - x}{3x^2 - 2x + 1}$
31. $y = \dfrac{x^2 + 8x + 15}{2x}$
32. $y = \dfrac{-3x^2}{x^2 - 9}$
33. $y = \dfrac{x^2 - 3x - 10}{2x}$

Perform the indicated operation. Simplify the result. (Lesson 9.4)

34. $\dfrac{3xy^5}{x^2y^3} \cdot \dfrac{y^2}{6x}$

35. $\dfrac{20x^5}{y^2} \cdot \dfrac{x^2y^2}{10x^3}$

36. $\dfrac{x^2 - 4}{x - 3} \cdot \dfrac{x + 2}{8x - 16}$

37. $\dfrac{x^3 + 3x^2}{2x} \cdot \dfrac{5x^3}{x^2 + 5x + 6}$

38. $\dfrac{7x^2 - 14x}{x^3} \div \dfrac{5x - 10}{x^5}$

39. $\dfrac{x^2 - x - 20}{x + 4} \cdot \dfrac{x - 3}{x^2 - 2x - 15}$

40. $(x^2 + 5x - 36) \div \dfrac{5x^2 + 45x}{x - 6}$

41. $(x^3 + 8) \cdot \dfrac{6x^3 - 9x^2}{3x^3 - 12x}$

42. $\dfrac{x^2 + 2x - 35}{x^2 - 7x + 12} \div \dfrac{x^2 - 13x + 40}{3x^2 - 12x}$

Perform the indicated operation and simplify. (Lesson 9.5)

43. $\dfrac{3}{5x} + \dfrac{9}{5x}$

44. $\dfrac{15}{6x^2} - \dfrac{8}{6x^2}$

45. $\dfrac{4}{3x} + \dfrac{2}{5x}$

46. $\dfrac{3}{2(x - 1)} + \dfrac{x + 1}{4}$

47. $\dfrac{2x + 1}{x^2 - 4} + \dfrac{5}{x - 2}$

48. $\dfrac{4 - 9x}{x + 5} + \dfrac{1}{2x - 1}$

49. $\dfrac{7}{x^2 + 8x + 15} - \dfrac{3}{x + 5}$

50. $\dfrac{8x - 1}{x^2 + x - 6} - \dfrac{4}{x - 2}$

Simplify the complex fraction. (Lesson 9.5)

51. $\dfrac{\dfrac{4}{x} - 4}{2 + \dfrac{1}{x}}$

52. $\dfrac{\dfrac{9}{x + 1}}{\dfrac{1}{3} - \dfrac{6}{x + 1}}$

53. $\dfrac{\dfrac{7}{5x + 2} - \dfrac{3}{2(5x + 2)}}{\dfrac{x^2}{5x + 2}}$

54. $\dfrac{\dfrac{2}{3x^2 - 3}}{\dfrac{1}{x + 1} + \dfrac{3x}{x^2 - 2x - 3}}$

55. $\dfrac{\dfrac{2}{3x - 1} - \dfrac{5}{4(3x + 1)}}{\dfrac{x}{9x^2 - 1}}$

56. $\dfrac{\dfrac{2}{x^2 - 4} + \dfrac{1}{x - 2}}{\dfrac{5}{x - 2} + \dfrac{3}{x + 2}}$

57. $\dfrac{\dfrac{8}{x^2 - 49}}{\dfrac{5}{3x^2 - 21x} - \dfrac{6}{x - 7}}$

58. $\dfrac{\dfrac{2}{3x^2 + 6x + 12} + \dfrac{x}{x^3 - 8}}{\dfrac{3x}{2x^2 + 4} - \dfrac{x - 2}{4x^2 + 8}}$

Solve the equation using any method. Check each solution. (Lesson 9.6)

59. $\dfrac{7}{x} + \dfrac{1}{2} = 4$

60. $\dfrac{x}{4} + \dfrac{1}{2} = 5$

61. $\dfrac{4}{x} + \dfrac{1}{3} = 10$

62. $\dfrac{1}{2x} + \dfrac{x}{3} = 7$

63. $\dfrac{-2}{x + 3} = \dfrac{1}{x + 1}$

64. $\dfrac{4}{x + 2} = \dfrac{-3}{x - 3}$

65. $\dfrac{-4}{x + 1} = \dfrac{2}{x - 1}$

66. $\dfrac{3}{x + 4} = \dfrac{9}{x - 2}$

67. $\dfrac{4x}{x - 1} = \dfrac{x}{x^2 - 1}$

68. $\dfrac{5x}{10 - x} = \dfrac{x^2}{x - 10}$

69. $\dfrac{3}{x^2 - 9} = \dfrac{6}{x + 3}$

70. $\dfrac{3}{x^2 - 4} = \dfrac{2}{x + 2} + \dfrac{x}{x - 2}$

CHAPTER 10

Find the distance between the two points. Then find the midpoint of the line segment joining the two points. (Lesson 10.1)

1. $(0, 0), (6, 8)$

2. $(0, 5), (-2, 0)$

3. $(-4, -2), (1, -5)$

4. $(3, 3), (3, 6)$

5. $(4.5, 2), (1.5, 6)$

6. $(-3, 5), \left(\dfrac{1}{2}, 6\right)$

7. $(-5, 2.3), (-3, 4.7)$

8. $\left(-\dfrac{1}{4}, 6\right), \left(8, -\dfrac{3}{4}\right)$

Graph the equation. Identify the focus and directrix of the parabola. (Lesson 10.2)

9. $y^2 = 10x$

10. $x^2 = -4y$

11. $y^2 = -6x$

12. $y^2 = 11x$

13. $x^2 - 16y = 0$

14. $6x^2 = 5y$

15. $x - \dfrac{1}{8}y^2 = 0$

16. $x + \dfrac{1}{10}y^2 = 0$

Write the standard form of the equation of the parabola with the given focus or directrix and vertex at (0, 0). (Lesson 10.2)

17. $(3, 0)$

18. $(0, -4)$

19. $\left(\dfrac{1}{2}, 0\right)$

20. $\left(0, -\dfrac{1}{8}\right)$

21. $y = 6$

22. $x = -2$

23. $y = \dfrac{3}{4}$

24. $x = -\dfrac{7}{8}$

Graph the equation. (Lesson 10.3)

25. $x^2 + y^2 = 4$ **26.** $x^2 + y^2 = 36$ **27.** $x^2 + y^2 = 12$ **28.** $2x^2 + 2y^2 = 98$

29. $6x^2 + 6y^2 = 54$ **30.** $5x^2 + 5y^2 = 120$ **31.** $9x^2 + 9y^2 = 126$ **32.** $15x^2 + 15y^2 = 300$

Write the standard form of the equation of the circle that has the given radius or passes through the given point and whose center is the origin. (Lesson 10.3)

33. $r = 4$ **34.** $r = 8$ **35.** $r = \sqrt{13}$ **36.** $r = 2\sqrt{5}$

37. $(0, 6)$ **38.** $(-4, 1)$ **39.** $(2, 5)$ **40.** $(-6, -2)$

OCEAN NAVIGATION In Exercises 41 and 42, the beam of a lighthouse can be seen for up to 10 miles. You are on a ship that is 5 miles east and 7 miles north of the lighthouse. (Lesson 10.3)

41. Write an inequality to describe the region lit by the lighthouse beam.

42. Can you see the lighthouse beam from the ship?

Graph the equation. Then identify the vertices, co-vertices, and foci of the ellipse. (Lesson 10.4)

43. $\dfrac{x^2}{9} + \dfrac{y^2}{16} = 1$ **44.** $\dfrac{x^2}{81} + \dfrac{y^2}{36} = 1$ **45.** $\dfrac{x^2}{25} + \dfrac{y^2}{49} = 1$ **46.** $\dfrac{x^2}{25} + \dfrac{y^2}{144} = 1$

47. $\dfrac{x^2}{169} + \dfrac{y^2}{225} = 1$ **48.** $x^2 + \dfrac{y^2}{4} = 1$ **49.** $\dfrac{x^2}{16} + y^2 = 4$ **50.** $\dfrac{x^2}{4} + y^2 = 81$

Write an equation of the ellipse with the given characteristics and center at (0, 0). (Lesson 10.4)

51. Vertex: $(0, 8)$
Co-vertex: $(4, 0)$

52. Vertex: $(5, 0)$
Co-vertex: $(0, -3)$

53. Vertex: $(-7, 0)$
Co-vertex: $(0, -2)$

54. Vertex: $(-2, 0)$
Focus: $(-\sqrt{3}, 0)$

55. Vertex: $(16, 0)$
Focus: $(2\sqrt{39}, 0)$

56. Vertex: $(0, 13)$
Focus: $(0, 12)$

57. Co-vertex: $(-2, 0)$
Focus: $(0, 2\sqrt{99})$

58. Co-vertex: $(0, -3)$
Focus: $(-\sqrt{7}, 0)$

Graph the equation. Identify the foci and asymptotes. (Lesson 10.5)

59. $\dfrac{x^2}{49} - \dfrac{y^2}{64} = 1$ **60.** $\dfrac{x^2}{25} - y^2 = 1$ **61.** $\dfrac{x^2}{10} - \dfrac{y^2}{6} = 1$ **62.** $\dfrac{x^2}{81} - \dfrac{y^2}{25} = 1$

63. $\dfrac{y^2}{36} - x^2 = 1$ **64.** $y^2 - 25x^2 = 25$ **65.** $x^2 - 16y^2 = 144$ **66.** $100x^2 - 49y^2 = 4900$

Write an equation for the conic section. (Lesson 10.6)

67. Circle with center at $(3, 4)$ and radius 5

68. Parabola with vertex at $(2, -1)$ and focus at $(2, 1)$

69. Circle with center at $(2, -5)$ and radius 7

70. Parabola with vertex at $(-2, 5)$ and focus at $(3, 5)$

71. Ellipse with vertices at $(-2, 3)$ and $(8, 3)$ and foci at $(-1, 3)$ and $(7, 3)$

72. Ellipse with vertices at $(-9, 1)$ and $(5, 1)$ and co-vertices at $(-2, 6)$ and $(-2, -4)$

73. Hyperbola with vertices at $(5, 6)$ and $(-1, 6)$ and foci at $(-2, 6)$ and $(6, 6)$

74. Hyperbola with vertices at $(4, -2)$ and $(4, -6)$ and foci at $(4, 1)$ and $(4, -9)$

Classify the conic section. (Lesson 10.6)

75. $x^2 - 3y + 10 = 0$ **76.** $8x^2 + 8y^2 + 64x + 32y - 160 = 0$

77. $16x^2 - 9y^2 + 96x + 18y - 135 = 0$ **78.** $25x^2 + 16y^2 + 100x - 128y - 44 = 0$

Find the points of intersection, if any, of the graphs in the system. (Lesson 10.7)

79. $x^2 + y^2 = 20$
$x - y = -2$

80. $x^2 - y = 3$
$2x - y = -12$

81. $x^2 + y^2 = 6$
$x - y = 5$

82. $4x^2 + y^2 = 16$
$y = x - 2$

83. $x^2 - y^2 = 9$
$y = 2x - 6$

84. $2x^2 + y^2 = 10$
$y = x - 3$

85. $x^2 + y^2 = 8$
$\frac{1}{4}x + \frac{1}{2}y = \frac{1}{2}$

86. $5x^2 + 4y^2 = 12$
$y = \frac{1}{3}x + 1$

CHAPTER 11

Write the next term in the sequence. Then write a rule for the nth term. (Lesson 11.1)

1. $2, 5, 8, 11, \ldots$

2. $5, 10, 20, 40, \ldots$

3. $3, -1, -5, -9, \ldots$

4. $\frac{1}{3}, 1, \frac{5}{3}, \frac{7}{3}, \ldots$

5. $-1, 4, -16, 64, \ldots$

6. $\frac{2}{3}, \frac{3}{6}, \frac{4}{9}, \frac{5}{12}, \ldots$

7. $\frac{1}{4}, \frac{1}{16}, \frac{1}{64}, \frac{1}{256}, \ldots$

8. $\frac{1}{3}, 3, 27, 243, \ldots$

Find the sum of the series. (Lesson 11.1)

9. $\displaystyle\sum_{i=1}^{8} 2i$

10. $\displaystyle\sum_{i=1}^{4} (6i + 1)$

11. $\displaystyle\sum_{i=0}^{5} i^2$

12. $\displaystyle\sum_{k=1}^{7} 3k^2$

13. $\displaystyle\sum_{n=2}^{6} n^3$

14. $\displaystyle\sum_{n=1}^{3} \frac{n}{n+1}$

15. $\displaystyle\sum_{k=1}^{6} \frac{k+1}{k}$

16. $\displaystyle\sum_{k=4}^{8} k(k-1)$

Write a rule for the nth term of the arithmetic sequence. Then find a_{10}. (Lesson 11.2)

17. $1, 4, 7, 10, 13, \ldots$

18. $-3, 2, 7, 12, 17, \ldots$

19. $8, -2, -12, -22, -32, \ldots$

20. $2.4, 3.5, 4.6, 5.7, \ldots$

21. $\frac{9}{4}, \frac{7}{4}, \frac{5}{4}, \frac{3}{4}, \frac{1}{4}, \ldots$

22. $d = 3, a_1 = 3.5$

23. $d = -2, a_4 = 0$

24. $d = 1.75, a_6 = 10.75$

25. $a_1 = -5, a_8 = 23$

SEATING CAPACITY In Exercises 26 and 27, the first row of a concert hall has 20 seats, and each row after the first has one more seat than the row before it. There are 30 rows of seats. (Lesson 11.2)

26. Write a rule for the number of seats in the nth row.

27. Forty students from a class want to sit in the same row. How close to the front can they sit?

Write a rule for the nth term of the geometric sequence. Then find a_8. (Lesson 11.3)

28. $3, 6, 12, 24, \ldots$

29. $-1, -\frac{1}{2}, -\frac{1}{4}, -\frac{1}{8}, \ldots$

30. $6, 42, 294, 2058, \ldots$

31. $-10, 1, -\frac{1}{10}, \frac{1}{100}, \ldots$

32. $r = 3, a_1 = 3$

33. $r = 6, a_2 = -18$

34. $r = 9, a_1 = -27$

35. $a_1 = 150, a_3 = 6$

36. $a_2 = 20, a_6 = 5120$

Find the sum of the first n terms of the geometric series. (Lesson 11.3)

37. $1 + 5 + 25 + 125 + \cdots$
$n = 12$

38. $5 + 10 + 20 + 40 + \cdots$
$n = 10$

39. $4 + (-12) + 36 + (-108) + \cdots$
$n = 6$

40. $100 + 50 + 25 + \frac{25}{2} + \cdots$
$n = 8$

41. $60 + 10 + \frac{10}{6} + \frac{10}{36} + \cdots$
$n = 10$

42. $6 + (-12) + 24 + (-48) + \cdots$
$n = 7$

Find the sum of the infinite geometric series if it has one. (Lesson 11.4)

43. $\displaystyle\sum_{n=0}^{\infty}\left(\frac{1}{3}\right)^{n}$

44. $\displaystyle\sum_{n=1}^{\infty}2\left(\frac{1}{2}\right)^{n}$

45. $\displaystyle\sum_{n=0}^{\infty}\frac{4}{5}(3)^{n}$

46. $\displaystyle\sum_{n=1}^{\infty}2\left(\frac{1}{5}\right)^{n}$

47. $\displaystyle\sum_{n=0}^{\infty}3\left(\frac{7}{6}\right)^{n}$

48. $\displaystyle\sum_{n=0}^{\infty}\left(\frac{1}{8}\right)^{n-1}$

49. $\displaystyle\sum_{n=1}^{\infty}\frac{1}{3}\left(-\frac{1}{5}\right)^{n}$

50. $\displaystyle\sum_{n=0}^{\infty}\left(-\frac{1}{4}\right)^{n-1}$

Write a recursive rule for the sequence. The sequence may be arithmetic, geometric, or neither. (Lesson 11.5)

51. $2, 6, 10, 14, \ldots$

52. $77, 11, \frac{11}{7}, \frac{11}{49}, \ldots$

53. $2, 7, 22, 67, 202, \ldots$

54. $11.6, 10.1, 8.6, 7.1, \ldots$

55. $-6, -9, 54, -486, \ldots$

56. $8, 8\sqrt{3}, 24, 24\sqrt{3}, \ldots$

CHAPTER 12

Each event can occur in the given number of ways. Find the number of ways all of the events can occur. (Lesson 12.1)

1. Event 1: 2 ways, Event 2: 1 way

2. Event 1: 2 ways, Event 2: 3 ways, Event 3: 4 ways

3. Event 1: 3 ways, Event 2: 4 ways

4. Event 1: 3 ways, Event 2: 3 ways, Event 3: 6 ways, Event 4: 5 ways

5. FOOD At your school cafeteria you can order a taco with one meat filling and one cheese filling. You have a choice of 3 meats and 4 cheeses. How many ways can you order a taco with meat and cheese? **(Lesson 12.1)**

Find the number of distinguishable permutations of the letters in the word. (Lesson 12.1)

6. MATH

7. DOG

8. HELLO

9. MAINE

10. SCHOOL

11. STATISTICS

12. GEOMETRY

13. SISTERS

Find the number of combinations. (Lesson 12.2)

14. $_{10}C_{3}$

15. $_{6}C_{2}$

16. $_{11}C_{5}$

17. $_{8}C_{8}$

18. $_{15}C_{4}$

19. $_{1}C_{1}$

20. $_{9}C_{8}$

21. $_{20}C_{3}$

Expand the binomial. (Lesson 12.2)

22. $(x+3)^{4}$

23. $(x+y)^{7}$

24. $(2x-y)^{5}$

25. $(x^{2}+2y)^{6}$

26. $(x^{4}+4)^{3}$

27. $(3x^{2}-5)^{5}$

28. $(3x-y^{2})^{4}$

29. $(x^{3}+y^{3})^{3}$

A card is drawn randomly from a standard 52-card deck. Find the probability of drawing the given card. (Lesson 12.3)

30. ace of diamonds

31. any king

32. a club

33. a red card

34. a card other than 7

35. a face card (king, queen, jack)

The results of rolling a six-sided die 200 times are shown in the table below. Use the table to find the experimental probability of each event. (Lesson 12.3)

Roll on die	1	2	3	4	5	6
Number of occurrences	20	40	33	37	34	36

36. rolling a 1

37. rolling an even number

38. rolling a number greater than 1

39. rolling an odd number

40. rolling a 5 or a 6

41. rolling a number other than 2 or 3

Find the probability that the spinner will stop on a given region. (Lesson 12.3)

42. 1

43. 3

44. even

45. odd

46. blue

47. yellow

Find the indicated probability. State whether A and B are mutually exclusive. (Lesson 12.4)

48. $P(A) = 0.3$
$P(B) = 0.55$
$P(A \text{ or } B) = 0.85$
$P(A \text{ and } B) = \underline{\ ?\ }$

49. $P(A) = 0.4$
$P(B) = 0.2$
$P(A \text{ or } B) = \underline{\ ?\ }$
$P(A \text{ and } B) = 0.1$

50. $P(A) = \frac{8}{15}$
$P(B) = \underline{\ ?\ }$
$P(A \text{ or } B) = \frac{12}{15}$
$P(A \text{ and } B) = 0$

51. $P(A) = 6\%$
$P(B) = 37\%$
$P(A \text{ or } B) = \underline{\ ?\ }$
$P(A \text{ and } B) = 0\%$

52. $P(A) = 40\%$
$P(B) = \underline{\ ?\ }$
$P(A \text{ or } B) = 12\%$
$P(A \text{ and } B) = 60\%$

53. $P(A) = 38\%$
$P(B) = 6\%$
$P(A \text{ or } B) = 40\%$
$P(A \text{ and } B) = \underline{\ ?\ }$

Find $P(A')$. (Lesson 12.4)

54. $P(A) = \frac{1}{2}$

55. $P(A) = 0$

56. $P(A) = 1$

57. $P(A) = \frac{3}{4}$

58. $P(A) = 0.6$

59. $P(A) = 0.2$

60. $P(A) = \frac{1}{12}$

61. $P(A) = \frac{15}{16}$

You are drawing marbles from a bag. There are 6 green, 4 yellow, and 5 blue marbles. Find the probability for the event if you replace the marble after each draw. (Lesson 12.5)

62. blue, then blue

63. green, then yellow

64. blue, then green

65. yellow, then blue

66. green, then green

67. yellow, then green

68. blue, then yellow

69. green, then blue

Calculate the probability of rolling a six-sided die 10 times and getting the given result. (Lesson 12.6)

70. exactly 3 sixes

71. exactly 4 ones

72. all odd numbers

73. exactly 3 evens

74. no odd numbers

75. exactly 6 threes

76. exactly 7 fives

77. 8 rolls greater than four

A normal distribution has a mean of 36 and a standard deviation of 5. Find the probability that a randomly selected x-value is in the given interval. (Lesson 12.7)

78. between 31 and 41

79. between 21 and 36

80. between 31 and 46

81. less than 41

82. greater than 26

83. less than 51

84. between 21 and 46

85. greater than 36

CHAPTER 13

Evaluate the six trigonometric functions of the angle θ. (Lesson 13.1)

1.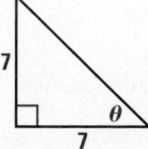

2.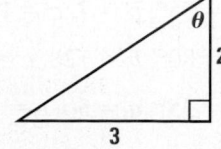

3.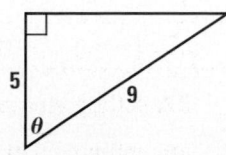

4.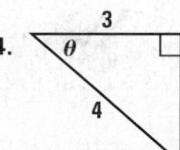

Find one positive angle and one negative angle coterminal with the given angle. (Lesson 13.2)

5. 35°

6. −70°

7. 125°

8. 2°

9. −45°

10. 315°

11. 585°

12. 600°

13. $\dfrac{2\pi}{3}$

14. $\dfrac{11\pi}{2}$

15. $\dfrac{16\pi}{5}$

16. $\dfrac{7\pi}{13}$

Find the arc length and area of a sector with the given radius *r* and central angle θ. (Lesson 13.2)

17. $r = 4$ in., $\theta = 60°$

18. $r = 7$ ft, $\theta = 37°$

19. $r = 14$ cm, $\theta = 135°$

20. $r = 120$ m, $\theta = 167°$

21. $r = 9$ cm, $\theta = 4°$

22. $r = 28$ in., $\theta = 210°$

Use the given point on the terminal side of an angle θ in standard position. Evaluate the six trigonometric functions of θ. (Lesson 13.3)

23. $(4, 5)$

24. $(4, -1)$

25. $(-2, -6)$

26. $\left(-12, \sqrt{3}\right)$

27. $(6, 3)$

28. $(5, -12)$

29. $\left(3\sqrt{7}, -2\right)$

30. $\left(\sqrt{2}, \sqrt{2}\right)$

31. $(3, -5)$

32. $(7, -8)$

33. $(-3, 6)$

34. $\left(\sqrt{5}, 3\right)$

Evaluate the function without using a calculator. (Lesson 13.3)

35. $\sin(-390°)$

36. $\sec 120°$

37. $\cos 315°$

38. $\tan(-150°)$

39. $\cos \dfrac{7\pi}{4}$

40. $\tan \dfrac{7\pi}{6}$

41. $\sin\left(-\dfrac{2\pi}{3}\right)$

42. $\csc \dfrac{13\pi}{4}$

Evaluate the expression without using a calculator. Give your answer in both radians and degrees. (Lesson 13.4)

43. $\tan^{-1}(-1)$

44. $\cos^{-1} 0$

45. $\sin^{-1}\left(-\dfrac{1}{2}\right)$

46. $\cos^{-1}\left(-\dfrac{\sqrt{2}}{2}\right)$

47. $\tan^{-1}\dfrac{\sqrt{3}}{3}$

48. $\sin^{-1}\dfrac{1}{2}$

49. $\tan^{-1}\sqrt{3}$

50. $\sin^{-1}\dfrac{\sqrt{3}}{2}$

51. PLAYGROUND EQUIPMENT Two slides 12 feet long will be installed at the local playground. At what angle to the ground should the first slide be set if the top of the slide is 8 feet off the ground? At what angle should the top of the second slide be set if the slide must fit into a space that is only 6 feet wide? **(Lesson 13.4)**

Solve △ABC. (Lesson 13.5)

52.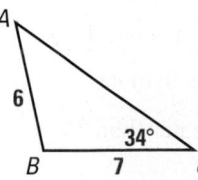

53.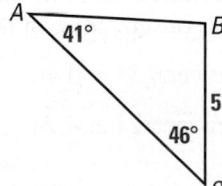

54.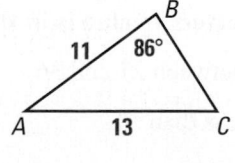

55.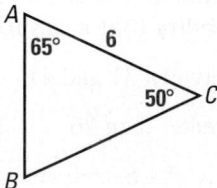

Find the area of the triangle with the given side lengths and included angle. (Lesson 13.5)

56. $C = 120°$, $a = 12$, $b = 20$

57. $A = 55°$, $b = 7$, $c = 12$

58. $B = 30°$, $a = 18$, $c = 13$

59. $A = 80°$, $b = 120$, $c = 70$

60. $C = 20°$, $a = 10$, $b = 16$

61. $B = 35°$, $a = 50$, $c = 120$

Find the area of △ABC. (Lesson 13.6)

62.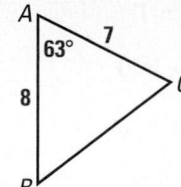

63.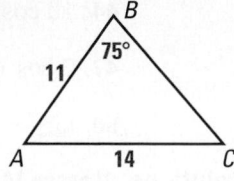

64.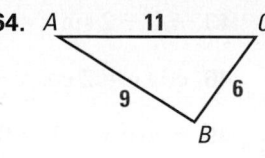

65.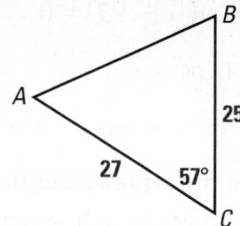

Write an *xy*-equation for the parametric equations. State the domain.
(Lesson 13.7)

66. $x = 12t - 5$ and $y = 10t - 3$ for $0 \le t \le 60$

67. $x = 42t - 7$ and $y = 21t - 7$ for $0 \le t \le 128$

68. $x = (17.54 \sin 20°)t$ and $y = 3t$ for $0 \le t \le 24$

69. $x = (10 \cos 1°)t$ and $y = (10 \cos 1°)t$ for $0 \le t \le 50$

CHAPTER 14

Find the amplitude and period of the graph of the function. (Lesson 14.1)

1. $y = 6 \sin \frac{1}{2}x$

2. $y = 2 \sin \frac{1}{8}x$

3. $y = \frac{1}{7} \cos \pi x$

4. $y = \frac{1}{2} \cos 2\pi x$

5. $y = \sin 2\pi x$

6. $y = \frac{1}{3} \cos \frac{1}{12}x$

7. $y = \frac{2}{5} \cos \frac{1}{4}x$

8. $y = \frac{1}{3} \sin \frac{1}{2}\pi x$

Draw one cycle of the function's graph. (Lesson 14.1)

9. $y = 3 \sin 2x$

10. $y = \frac{1}{2} \cos 5x$

11. $y = 2 \cos \pi x$

12. $y = 3 \sin 2\pi x$

13. $y = 5 \tan 2x$

14. $y = 5 \tan \frac{1}{6}x$

15. $y = 7 \cos 2\pi x$

16. $y = \frac{1}{3} \sin 3\pi x$

Describe how the graph of $y = \sin x$ or $y = \cos x$ can be transformed to produce the graph of the given function. (Lesson 14.2)

17. $y = 3 + \cos x$

18. $y = 7 + \cos x$

19. $y = 4 - \cos x$

20. $y = \sin (x - \pi)$

21. $y = \cos (x - \pi)$

22. $y = \sin \left(x + \frac{\pi}{4}\right)$

23. $y = \cos \left(x - \frac{\pi}{2}\right)$

24. $y = -1 - \sin \left(x + \frac{3\pi}{4}\right)$

Graph the function. (Lesson 14.2)

25. $y = 2 + \cos (x + \pi)$

26. $y = 1 - \tan \left(x + \frac{\pi}{2}\right)$

27. $y = 1 + \sin (x + \pi)$

28. $y = 1 + \sin \left(\frac{1}{2}x + \frac{3\pi}{4}\right)$

29. $y = -2 + \tan x$

30. $y = -2 \sin \frac{1}{2}x$

31. $y = \cos \left(x - \frac{3\pi}{2}\right)$

32. $y = 2 - \tan (x - \pi)$

Simplify the expression. (Lesson 14.3)

33. $\csc x \tan x$

34. $\sin \left(\frac{\pi}{2} - x\right) \tan (-x)$

35. $1 - \sin \left(\frac{\pi}{2} - x\right) \cos x$

36. $\dfrac{\sin^2 (-x)}{\sec^2 x - 1} - \dfrac{1}{\tan^2 x + 1}$

37. $\dfrac{\sin (-x)}{-\tan x}$

38. $\dfrac{\cos^4 x + \sin^2 x \cos^2 x + \sin^2 x}{\cos^2 x}$

39. $\dfrac{\sin x}{1 + \cos x} + \dfrac{1 + \cos x}{\sin x}$

40. $\dfrac{\sec x - \cos x}{\tan^2 x}$

41. $\dfrac{\cos x \sin^2 x - \cos x}{\cos x \cot x}$

Find the general solution of the equation. (Lesson 14.4)

42. $2 \sin x - \sqrt{3} = 0$

43. $-1 - 2 \sin x = 0$

44. $10 \cos x = 9 \cos x + 1$

45. $4 \cos^2 x - 1 = 0$

46. $\cos x = 2 \cos x + 1$

47. $2 \cos x \sin x + \sin x = 0$

48. $\cos^2 x = \tan x - \sin^2 x$

49. $6 \cos^2 x - 3 = 0$

50. $\tan^2 x - 2 \tan x + 1 = 0$

Solve the equation in the interval $0 \le x < 2\pi$. Check your solutions. (Lesson 14.4)

51. $2 \tan^2 x - 1 = 0$

52. $\sec^2 x - 4 = 0$

53. $2 \sin x = \sin x - 1$

54. $\sin^3 x = \sin x$

55. $4 \cos x - 2 = 0$

56. $6 \cos x = 3 \sec x$

57. $2 \tan^2 x = \sin x \sec x$

58. $1 - \sin x = \sqrt{2} \cos x$

59. $\cos^2 x \sin x = 3 \sin x$

Write a trigonometric function for the sinusoid with maximum at A and minimum at B. (Lesson 14.5)

60. $A(0, 10), B(2\pi, 2)$

61. $A(-\pi, 2), B(\pi, 1)$

62. $A(-2, 7), B(0, 1)$

63. $A\left(\dfrac{\pi}{3}, 0\right), B(0, -8)$

64. $A(0, 0), B(\pi, -1)$

65. $A(1, 23), B(2, 21)$

66. **CARNIVAL RIDE** You and your friend are riding on a Ferris wheel with a diameter of 30 feet. When $t = 0$, your chair starts at the lowest point on the wheel, which is 6 feet above the ground. If the Ferris wheel is rotating at a rate of 4 revolutions per minute, write a model for the height h (in feet) of the chair as a function of the time t (in seconds). (Lesson 14.5)

Find the exact value of the expression. (Lesson 14.6)

67. $\sin 225°$

68. $\cos (-15°)$

69. $\cos 195°$

70. $\sin 555°$

71. $\tan \left(-\dfrac{\pi}{12}\right)$

72. $\sin \dfrac{19\pi}{2}$

73. $\tan \dfrac{7\pi}{6}$

74. $\sin \dfrac{\pi}{12}$

Evaluate the expression given $\sin u = \dfrac{2}{3}$ with $0 < u < \dfrac{\pi}{2}$ and $\cos v = -\dfrac{2}{7}$ with $\pi < v < \dfrac{3\pi}{2}$. (Lesson 14.6)

75. $\sin (u + v)$

76. $\cos (u + v)$

77. $\tan (u + v)$

78. $\sin (u - v)$

79. $\cos (u - v)$

80. $\tan (u - v)$

81. $\sin (v - u)$

82. $\cos (v - u)$

Find the exact value of the expression. (Lesson 14.7)

83. $\tan 105°$

84. $\sin (-22.5°)$

85. $\cos (-112.5°)$

86. $\cos 165°$

87. $\sin \dfrac{7\pi}{8}$

88. $\cos \left(-\dfrac{\pi}{8}\right)$

89. $\tan (-75°)$

90. $\cos \left(-\dfrac{7\pi}{8}\right)$

91. $\sin 67.5°$

92. $\tan 22.5°$

93. $\cos 105°$

94. $\sin (-112.5°)$

Find the exact values of sin 2x, cos 2x, and tan 2x. (Lesson 14.7)

95. $\cos x = \dfrac{9}{10}, 0 < x < \dfrac{\pi}{2}$

96. $\sin x = \dfrac{4}{5}, \dfrac{\pi}{2} < x < \pi$

97. $\sin x = \dfrac{3}{5}, 0 < x < \dfrac{\pi}{2}$

98. $\sin x = \dfrac{5}{8}, \dfrac{\pi}{2} < x < \pi$

99. $\cos x = \dfrac{11}{12}, 0 < x < \dfrac{\pi}{2}$

100. $\cos x = \dfrac{4}{5}, \dfrac{3\pi}{2} < x < 2\pi$

101. $\sin x = -\dfrac{4}{5}, \dfrac{3\pi}{2} < x < 2\pi$

102. $\cos x = \dfrac{3}{4}, 0 < x < \dfrac{\pi}{2}$

103. $\sin x = \dfrac{2}{3}, \dfrac{3\pi}{2} < x < 2\pi$

Table of Symbols

Symbol		Page
$\ldots$	and so on	3
$\approx$	is approximately equal to	3
$<$	is less than	4
$>$	is greater than	4
$\leq$	is less than or equal to	4
$\geq$	is greater than or equal to	4
$\cdot$	multiplication, times	5
$-a$	opposite of a	5
$\dfrac{1}{a}$	reciprocal of a, $a \neq 0$	5
$\neq$	not equal to	5
π	pi; irrational number ≈ 3.14	28
$\lvert x \rvert$	absolute value of x	50
(x, y)	ordered pair	67
$f(x)$	f of x, or the value of f at x	69
m	slope	75
x_1	x sub 1	75
$[\![x]\!]$	greatest integer less than or equal to x	115
(x, y, z)	ordered triple	170
$f(x, y)$	function of two variables	171
$\begin{bmatrix} 1 & 0 \\ 0 & 1 \end{bmatrix}$	matrix	199
$\lvert A \rvert$	determinant of matrix A	214
A^{-1}	inverse of matrix A	223
$\sqrt{a}$	the nonnegative square root of a	264
i	imaginary unit equal to $\sqrt{-1}$	272
$\lvert z \rvert$	absolute value of complex number z	275
$+\infty$	positive infinity	331
$-\infty$	negative infinity	331
$x \rightarrow +\infty$	x approaches positive infinity	331

Symbol		Page
$f(x) \rightarrow +\infty$	f of x approaches positive infinity	331
$\sqrt[n]{a}$	nth root of a	401
f^{-1}	inverse of function f	423
$\bar{x}$	x-bar; the mean of a data set	445
σ	sigma; the standard deviation of a data set	446
e	irrational number ≈ 2.718	480
$\log_b y$	base-b logarithm of y	486
$\log x$	base-10 logarithm of x	487
$\ln x$	base-e logarithm of x	487
Σ	summation	653
S_n	sum of the first n terms of an arithmetic or geometric series	661, 668
$n!$	n factorial; number of permutations of n objects	703
$_nP_r$	number of permutations of r objects from n distinct objects	703
$_nC_r$	number of combinations of r objects from n distinct objects	708
$P(A)$	probability of event A	716
$P(B \mid A)$	probability of event B given that event A has occurred	732
θ	theta; name of an angle, or measure of an angle	769
$\sin$	sine	769
$\cos$	cosine	769
$\tan$	tangent	769
$\csc$	cosecant	769
$\sec$	secant	769
$\cot$	cotangent	769
$\sin^{-1}$	inverse sine	792
$\cos^{-1}$	inverse cosine	792
$\tan^{-1}$	inverse tangent	792

Table of Measures

Time

60 seconds (sec) = 1 minute (min)	$\left.\begin{array}{r}365 \text{ days} \\ 52 \text{ weeks (approx.)} \\ 12 \text{ months}\end{array}\right\}$ = 1 year
60 minutes = 1 hour (h)	
24 hours = 1 day	10 years = 1 decade
7 days = 1 week	100 years = 1 century
4 weeks (approx.) = 1 month	

Metric

Length

10 millimeters (mm) = 1 centimeter (cm)

$\left.\begin{array}{r}100 \text{ cm} \\ 1000 \text{ mm}\end{array}\right\}$ = 1 meter (m)

1000 m = 1 kilometer (km)

Area

100 square millimeters = 1 square centimeter
(mm^2)   (cm^2)

10,000 cm^2 = 1 square meter (m^2)

10,000 m^2 = 1 hectare (ha)

Volume

1000 cubic millimeters = 1 cubic centimeter
(mm^3)   (cm^3)

1,000,000 cm^3 = 1 cubic meter (m^3)

Liquid Capacity

$\left.\begin{array}{r}1000 \text{ milliliters (mL)} \\ 10 \text{ deciliters (dL)}\end{array}\right\}$ = 1 liter (L)

1000 L = 1 kiloliter (kL)

Mass

1000 milligrams (mg) = 1 gram (g)

1000 g = 1 kilogram (kg)

1000 kg = 1 metric ton (t)

Temperature — Degrees Celsius (°C)

0°C = freezing point of water

37°C = normal body temperature

100°C = boiling point of water

United States Customary

Length

12 inches (in.) = 1 foot (ft)

$\left.\begin{array}{r}36 \text{ in.} \\ 3 \text{ ft}\end{array}\right\}$ = 1 yard (yd)

$\left.\begin{array}{r}5280 \text{ ft} \\ 1760 \text{ yd}\end{array}\right\}$ = 1 mile (mi)

Area

144 square inches (in.^{2}) = 1 square foot (ft^2)

9 ft^2 = 1 square yard (yd^2)

$\left.\begin{array}{r}43,560 \text{ ft}^2 \\ 4840 \text{ yd}^2\end{array}\right\}$ = 1 acre (A)

Volume

1728 cubic inches (in.^{3}) = 1 cubic foot (ft^3)

27 ft^3 = 1 cubic yard (yd^3)

Liquid Capacity

8 fluid ounces (fl oz) = 1 cup (c)

2 c = 1 pint (pt)

2 pt = 1 quart (qt)

4 qt = 1 gallon (gal)

Weight

16 ounces (oz) = 1 pound (lb)

2000 lb = 1 ton (t)

Temperature — Degrees Fahrenheit (°F)

32°F = freezing point of water

98.6°F = normal body temperature

212°F = boiling point of water

Table of Formulas

Formulas from Coordinate Geometry

Slope of a line	$m = \dfrac{y_2 - y_1}{x_2 - x_1}$ where m is the slope of the nonvertical line through (x_1, y_1) and (x_2, y_2)
Parallel and perpendicular lines	If line l_1 has slope m_1 and line l_2 has slope m_2, then: $$l_1 \parallel l_2 \text{ if and only if } m_1 = m_2$$ $$l_1 \perp l_2 \text{ if and only if } m_1 = -\frac{1}{m_2} \text{ or } m_1 m_2 = -1$$
Distance formula	$d = \sqrt{(x_2 - x_1)^2 + (y_2 - y_1)^2}$ where d is the distance between points (x_1, y_1) and (x_2, y_2)
Midpoint formula	$M\left(\dfrac{x_1 + x_2}{2}, \dfrac{y_1 + y_2}{2}\right)$ is the midpoint of the line segment joining points (x_1, y_1) and (x_2, y_2)

Formulas from Matrix Algebra

Determinant of a 2×2 matrix	$\det \begin{bmatrix} a & b \\ c & d \end{bmatrix} = ad - cb$
Determinant of a 3×3 matrix	$\det \begin{bmatrix} a & b & c \\ d & e & f \\ g & h & i \end{bmatrix} = (aei + bfg + cdh) - (gec + hfa + idb)$
Area of a triangle	The area of a triangle with vertices (x_1, y_1), (x_2, y_2), and (x_3, y_3) is given by $$\text{Area} = \pm\frac{1}{2}\begin{vmatrix} x_1 & y_1 & 1 \\ x_2 & y_2 & 1 \\ x_3 & y_3 & 1 \end{vmatrix}$$ where the appropriate sign $(\pm)$ should be chosen to yield a positive value.
Cramer's rule	Let $A = \begin{bmatrix} a & b \\ c & d \end{bmatrix}$ be the coefficient matrix of this linear system: $$ax + by = e$$ $$cx + dy = f$$ If $\det A \neq 0$, then the system has exactly one solution. The solution is: $$x = \frac{\begin{vmatrix} e & b \\ f & d \end{vmatrix}}{\det A} \quad \text{and} \quad y = \frac{\begin{vmatrix} a & e \\ c & f \end{vmatrix}}{\det A}$$ Cramer's rule can be extended to a linear system of 3 equations in 3 variables.
Inverse of a 2×2 matrix	The inverse of the matrix $A = \begin{bmatrix} a & b \\ c & d \end{bmatrix}$ is $$A^{-1} = \frac{1}{|A|}\begin{bmatrix} d & -b \\ -c & a \end{bmatrix} = \frac{1}{ad - cb}\begin{bmatrix} d & -b \\ -c & a \end{bmatrix}$$ provided $ad - cb \neq 0$.

Formulas and Theorems from Algebra

Special product patterns	**Sum and difference:** $(a + b)(a - b) = a^2 - b^2$
	 Square of a binomial: $(a + b)^2 = a^2 + 2ab + b^2$
	                             $(a - b)^2 = a^2 - 2ab + b^2$
	 Cube of a binomial: $(a + b)^3 = a^3 + 3a^2b + 3ab^2 + b^3$
	                             $(a - b)^3 = a^3 - 3a^2b + 3ab^2 - b^3$

Special factoring patterns	Each of the patterns above can be read from right to left as a factoring pattern. In addition, there are two other special factoring patterns: **Sum of two cubes:** $a^3 + b^3 = (a + b)(a^2 - ab + b^2)$ **Difference of two cubes:** $a^3 - b^3 = (a - b)(a^2 + ab + b^2)$
Quadratic formula	$x = \dfrac{-b \pm \sqrt{b^2 - 4ac}}{2a}$ where x is a solution of $ax^2 + bx + c = 0$ and a, b, and c are real numbers such that $a \neq 0$
Discriminant of a quadratic equation	The expression $b^2 - 4ac$ is called the discriminant of the associated equation $ax^2 + bx + c = 0$. The value of the discriminant can be positive, zero, or negative, which corresponds to an equation having two real solutions, one real solution, or two imaginary solutions, respectively.
Remainder theorem	If a polynomial $f(x)$ is divided by $x - k$, then the remainder is $r = f(k)$.
Factor theorem	A polynomial $f(x)$ has a factor $x - k$ if and only if $f(k) = 0$.
Rational zero theorem	If $f(x) = a_n x^n + \cdots + a_1 x + a_0$ has *integer* coefficients, then every rational zero of f has this form: $$\frac{p}{q} = \frac{\text{factor of constant term } a_0}{\text{factor of leading coefficient } a_n}$$
Fundamental theorem of algebra	If $f(x)$ is a polynomial of degree n where $n > 0$, then the equation $f(x) = 0$ has at least one solution in the set of complex numbers.

Formulas from Statistics

Mean of a data set	$\bar{x} = \dfrac{x_1 + x_2 + \cdots + x_n}{n}$ where $\bar{x}$ (read "x-bar") is the mean of the data $x_1, x_2, \ldots, x_n$
Standard deviation of a data set	$\sigma = \sqrt{\dfrac{(x_1 - \bar{x})^2 + (x_2 - \bar{x})^2 + \cdots + (x_n - \bar{x})^2}{n}}$ where σ (read "sigma") is the standard deviation of the data $x_1, x_2, \ldots, x_n$
Areas under a normal curve	The mean $\bar{x}$ and standard deviation σ of a normal distribution determine the following areas under the corresponding normal curve. • The total area under the curve is 1. • 68% of the area lies within 1 standard deviation of the mean. • 95% of the area lies within 2 standard deviations of the mean. • 99.7% of the area lies within 3 standard deviations of the mean.
Normal approximation of a binomial distribution	Consider the binomial distribution consisting of n trials with a probability p of success on each trial. If $np \geq 5$ and $n(1 - p) \geq 5$, then the binomial distribution can be approximated by a normal distribution with a mean of $\bar{x} = np$ and a standard deviation of $\sigma = \sqrt{np(1 - p)}$.

Formulas for Sequences and Series

Explicit rule for an arithmetic sequence	The nth term of an arithmetic sequence with first term a_1 and common difference d is: $$a_n = a_1 + (n-1)d$$
Explicit rule for a geometric sequence	The nth term of a geometric sequence with first term a_1 and common ratio r is: $$a_n = a_1 r^{n-1}$$
Sum of a finite arithmetic series	The sum of the first n terms of an arithmetic series is: $$S_n = n\left(\frac{a_1 + a_n}{2}\right)$$
Sum of a finite geometric series	The sum of the first n terms of a geometric series with common ratio $r \neq 1$ is: $$S_n = a_1\left(\frac{1 - r^n}{1 - r}\right)$$
Sum of an infinite geometric series	The sum of an infinite geometric series with first term a_1 and common ratio r is $$S = \frac{a_1}{1 - r}$$ provided $\lvert r \rvert < 1$. If $\lvert r \rvert \geq 1$, the series has no sum.
Formulas for sums of special series	1. $\displaystyle\sum_{i=1}^{n} 1 = n$ 2. $\displaystyle\sum_{i=1}^{n} i = \frac{n(n+1)}{2}$ 3. $\displaystyle\sum_{i=1}^{n} i^2 = \frac{n(n+1)(2n+1)}{6}$

Formulas from Combinatorics

Fundamental counting principle	If one event can occur in m ways and another event can occur in n ways, then the number of ways that *both* events can occur is $m \cdot n$.
Permutations of n objects taken r at a time	The number of permutations of r objects taken from a group of n distinct objects is denoted by $_nP_r$ and is given by: $$_nP_r = \frac{n!}{(n-r)!}$$
Permutations with repetition	The number of distinguishable permutations of n objects where one object is repeated q_1 times, another is repeated q_2 times, and so on is: $$\frac{n!}{q_1! \cdot q_2! \cdot \ldots \cdot q_k!}$$
Combinations of n objects taken r at a time	The number of combinations of r objects taken from a group of n distinct objects is denoted by $_nC_r$ and is given by: $$_nC_r = \frac{n!}{(n-r)! \cdot r!}$$
Pascal's triangle	If you arrange the values of $_nC_r$ in a triangular pattern in which each row corresponds to a value of n, you get what is called Pascal's triangle. $_0C_0$ 1 $_1C_0 \quad _1C_1$ 1 1 $_2C_0 \quad _2C_1 \quad _2C_2$ 1 2 1 $_3C_0 \quad _3C_1 \quad _3C_2 \quad _3C_3$ 1 3 3 1 $_4C_0 \quad _4C_1 \quad _4C_2 \quad _4C_3 \quad _4C_4$ 1 4 6 4 1
Binomial theorem	The binomial expansion of $(a + b)^n$ for any positive integer n is: $$(a+b)^n = {_nC_0}a^n b^0 + {_nC_1}a^{n-1}b^1 + {_nC_2}a^{n-2}b^2 + \cdots + {_nC_n}a^0 b^n$$ $$= \sum_{r=0}^{n} {_nC_r}a^{n-r}b^r$$

Formulas from Probability

Theoretical probability of an event	When all outcomes are equally likely, the theoretical probability that an event A will occur is: $$P(A) = \frac{\text{number of outcomes in } A}{\text{total number of outcomes}}$$
Probability of compound events	If A and B are two events, then the probability of A or B is: $$P(A \text{ or } B) = P(A) + P(B) - P(A \text{ and } B)$$ If A and B are mutually exclusive, then the probability of A or B is: $$P(A \text{ or } B) = P(A) + P(B)$$
Probability of the complement of an event	The probability of the complement of event A, denoted A', is: $$P(A') = 1 - P(A)$$
Probability of independent events	If A and B are independent, then the probability that both A and B occur is: $$P(A \text{ and } B) = P(A) \cdot P(B)$$
Probability of dependent events	If A and B are dependent, then the probability that both A and B occur is: $$P(A \text{ and } B) = P(A) \cdot P(B \mid A)$$
Binomial probabilities	For a binomial experiment consisting of n trials where the probability of success on each trial is p, the probability of exactly k successes is: $$P(k \text{ successes}) = {}_nC_k p^k (1 - p)^{n - k}$$

Formulas and Identities from Trigonometry

Conversion between degrees and radians	To rewrite a degree measure in radians, multiply by $\frac{\pi \text{ radians}}{180°}$. To rewrite a radian measure in degrees, multiply by $\frac{180°}{\pi \text{ radians}}$.
Definition of trigonometric functions	Let θ be an angle in standard position and (x, y) be any point (except the origin) on the terminal side of θ. Let $r = \sqrt{x^2 + y^2}$. Then the six trigonometric functions of θ are: $$\sin \theta = \frac{y}{r} \qquad \cos \theta = \frac{x}{r} \qquad \tan \theta = \frac{y}{x}, x \neq 0$$ $$\csc \theta = \frac{r}{y}, y \neq 0 \qquad \sec \theta = \frac{r}{x}, x \neq 0 \qquad \cot \theta = \frac{x}{y}, y \neq 0$$
Law of sines	If $\triangle ABC$ has sides of length a, b, and c, then: $$\frac{\sin A}{a} = \frac{\sin B}{b} = \frac{\sin C}{c}$$
Area of a triangle (given two sides and the included angle)	If $\triangle ABC$ has sides of length a, b, and c, then the area is: $$\text{Area} = \frac{1}{2}bc \sin A \qquad \text{Area} = \frac{1}{2}ac \sin B \qquad \text{Area} = \frac{1}{2}ab \sin C$$
Law of cosines	If $\triangle ABC$ has sides of length a, b, and c, then: $$a^2 = b^2 + c^2 - 2bc \cos A$$ $$b^2 = a^2 + c^2 - 2ac \cos B$$ $$c^2 = a^2 + b^2 - 2ab \cos C$$

Formulas and Identities from Trigonometry (continued)

Heron's area formula	The area of the triangle with sides of length a, b, and c is $$\text{Area} = \sqrt{s(s-a)(s-b)(s-c)}$$ where $s = \frac{1}{2}(a+b+c)$.
Reciprocal identities	$\csc\theta = \dfrac{1}{\sin\theta}$ $\sec\theta = \dfrac{1}{\cos\theta}$ $\cot\theta = \dfrac{1}{\tan\theta}$
Tangent and cotangent identities	$\tan\theta = \dfrac{\sin\theta}{\cos\theta}$ $\cot\theta = \dfrac{\cos\theta}{\sin\theta}$
Pythagorean identities	$\sin^2\theta + \cos^2\theta = 1$ $1 + \tan^2\theta = \sec^2\theta$ $1 + \cot^2\theta = \csc^2\theta$
Cofunction identities	$\sin\left(\dfrac{\pi}{2} - \theta\right) = \cos\theta$ $\cos\left(\dfrac{\pi}{2} - \theta\right) = \sin\theta$ $\tan\left(\dfrac{\pi}{2} - \theta\right) = \cot\theta$
Negative angle identities	$\sin(-\theta) = -\sin\theta$ $\cos(-\theta) = \cos\theta$ $\tan(-\theta) = -\tan\theta$
Sum formulas	$$\sin(u+v) = \sin u \cos v + \cos u \sin v$$ $$\cos(u+v) = \cos u \cos v - \sin u \sin v$$ $$\tan(u+v) = \frac{\tan u + \tan v}{1 - \tan u \tan v}$$
Difference formulas	$$\sin(u-v) = \sin u \cos v - \cos u \sin v$$ $$\cos(u-v) = \cos u \cos v + \sin u \sin v$$ $$\tan(u-v) = \frac{\tan u - \tan v}{1 + \tan u \tan v}$$
Double-angle formulas	$\cos 2u = \cos^2 u - \sin^2 u$ $\sin 2u = 2\sin u \cos u$ $\cos 2u = 2\cos^2 u - 1$ $\tan 2u = \dfrac{2\tan u}{1 - \tan^2 u}$ $\cos 2u = 1 - 2\sin^2 u$
Half-angle formulas	$\sin\dfrac{u}{2} = \pm\sqrt{\dfrac{1-\cos u}{2}}$ $\tan\dfrac{u}{2} = \dfrac{1-\cos u}{\sin u}$ $\cos\dfrac{u}{2} = \pm\sqrt{\dfrac{1+\cos u}{2}}$ $\tan\dfrac{u}{2} = \dfrac{\sin u}{1+\cos u}$ The signs of $\sin\dfrac{u}{2}$ and $\cos\dfrac{u}{2}$ depend on the quadrant in which $\dfrac{u}{2}$ lies.

Formulas from Mathematical Modeling

Projectile motion	**Height as a function of time:** $h = -16t^2 + v_0 t + h_0$ where h is the height (in feet) of the object t seconds after launch, h_0 is the object's initial height, and v_0 is the object's initial vertical velocity (in feet per second) **Parametric equations for a projectile's path:** $x = (v\cos\theta)t + x_0$ and $y = -\frac{1}{2}gt^2 + (v\sin\theta)t + y_0$ where θ is the angle at which the projectile is launched, v is the initial speed, and (x_0, y_0) is the projectile's location at time $t = 0$. (The constant g is the acceleration due to gravity; its value is 32 ft/sec^2 or 9.8 m/sec^2.)
Compound interest	**Compounded n times per year:** $A = P\left(1 + \dfrac{r}{n}\right)^{nt}$ where A is the amount in the account after t years, P is the initial deposit (called the principal), and r is the annual interest rate (expressed as a decimal) **Compounded continuously:** $A = Pe^{rt}$ where A is the amount in the account after t years, P is the initial deposit (called the principal), and r is the annual interest rate (expressed as a decimal)

Formulas from Geometry

Basic geometric figures	See page 914 for area formulas for basic two-dimensional geometric figures.
Area of an equilateral triangle	Area $= \frac{\sqrt{3}}{4}s^2$ where s is the length of a side
Arc length and area of a sector	Arc length $= r\theta$ where r is the radius and θ is the radian measure of the central angle that intercepts the arc Area $= \frac{1}{2}r^2\theta$
Area of an ellipse	Area $= \pi ab$ where a and b are half the lengths of the major and minor axes of the ellipse
Volume and surface area of a right rectangular prism	Volume $= \ell wh$ where ℓ is the length, w is the width, and h is the height Surface area $= 2(\ell w + wh + \ell h)$
Volume and surface area of a right cylinder	Volume $= \pi r^2 h$ where r is the base radius and h is the height Lateral surface area $= 2\pi rh$ Surface area $= 2\pi r^2 + 2\pi rh$
Volume and surface area of a right regular pyramid	Volume $= \frac{1}{3}Bh$ where B is the area of the base and h is the height Lateral surface area $= \frac{1}{2}n\ell s$ where n is the number of sides on the base, l is the length of a side of the base, and s is the slant height Surface area $= B + \frac{1}{2}n\ell s$
Volume and surface area of a right circular cone	Volume $= \frac{1}{3}\pi r^2 h$ where r is the base radius and h is the height Lateral surface area $= \pi rs$ where s is the slant height Surface area $= \pi r^2 + \pi rs$
Volume and surface area of a sphere	Volume $= \frac{4}{3}\pi r^3$ where r is the radius Surface area $= 4\pi r^2$

Table of Properties

Properties of Real Numbers

Let a, b, and c be real numbers.

	Addition	**Multiplication**
Closure Property	$a + b$ is a real number.	ab is a real number.
Commutative Property	$a + b = b + a$	$ab = ba$
Associative Property	$(a + b) + c = a + (b + c)$	$(ab)c = a(bc)$
Identity Property	$a + 0 = a, 0 + a = a$	$a \cdot 1 = a, 1 \cdot a = a$
Inverse Property	$a + (-a) = 0$	$a \cdot \dfrac{1}{a} = 1, a \neq 0$

Distributive Property

The distributive property involves both addition and multiplication:
$$a(b + c) = ab + ac$$

Zero Product Property

Let A and B be real numbers or algebraic expressions. If $AB = 0$, then $A = 0$ or $B = 0$.

Properties of Matrices

Let A, B, and C be matrices, and let c be a scalar.

Associative Property of Addition $\qquad (A + B) + C = A + (B + C)$

Commutative Property of Addition $\qquad A + B = B + A$

Distributive Property of Addition $\qquad c(A + B) = cA + cB$

Distributive Property of Subtraction $\qquad c(A - B) = cA - cB$

Associative Property of Matrix Multiplication $\qquad (AB)C = A(BC)$

Left Distributive Property of Matrix Multiplication $\qquad A(B + C) = AB + AC$

Right Distributive Property of Matrix Multiplication $\qquad (A + B)C = AC + BC$

Associative Property of Scalar Multiplication $\qquad c(AB) = (cA)B = A(cB)$

Multiplicative Identity $\qquad$ An $n \times n$ matrix with 1's on the main diagonal and 0's elsewhere is an identity matrix, denoted I. For any $n \times n$ matrix A, $AI = IA = A$.

Inverse Matrices $\qquad$ If the determinant of an $n \times n$ matrix A is nonzero, then A has an inverse, denoted A^{-1}, such that $AA^{-1} = A^{-1}A = I$.

Properties of Exponents

Let a and b be real numbers, and let m and n be integers.

Product of Powers Property $\qquad a^m \cdot a^n = a^{m+n}$

Power of a Power Property $\qquad (a^m)^n = a^{mn}$

Power of a Product Property $\qquad (ab)^m = a^m b^m$

Negative Exponent Property $\qquad a^{-m} = \dfrac{1}{a^m}, a \neq 0$

Zero Exponent Property $\qquad a^0 = 1, a \neq 0$

Quotient of Powers Property $\qquad \dfrac{a^m}{a^n} = a^{m-n}, a \neq 0$

Power of a Quotient Property $\qquad \left(\dfrac{a}{b}\right)^m = \dfrac{a^m}{b^m}, b \neq 0$

Properties of Radicals and Rational Exponents

Number of Real nth Roots	Let n be an integer greater than 1, and let a be a real number. • If n is odd, then a has one real nth root: $\sqrt[n]{a} = a^{1/n}$ • If n is even and $a > 0$, then a has two real nth roots: $\pm\sqrt[n]{a} = \pm a^{1/n}$ • If n is even and $a = 0$, then a has one nth root: $\sqrt[n]{0} = 0^{1/n} = 0$ • If n is even and $a < 0$, then a has no real nth roots.
Radicals and Rational Exponents	Let $a^{1/n}$ be an nth root of a, and let m be a positive integer. • $a^{m/n} = \left(a^{1/n}\right)^m = \left(\sqrt[n]{a}\right)^m$ • $a^{-m/n} = \dfrac{1}{a^{m/n}} = \dfrac{1}{\left(a^{1/n}\right)^m} = \dfrac{1}{\left(\sqrt[n]{a}\right)^m}, a \neq 0$
Properties of Rational Exponents	All of the properties of exponents listed on the previous page apply to rational exponents as well as integer exponents.
Product and Quotient Properties of Radicals	Let n be an integer greater than 1, and let a and b be positive real numbers. Then: $$\sqrt[n]{a \cdot b} = \sqrt[n]{a} \cdot \sqrt[n]{b} \quad \text{and} \quad \sqrt[n]{\frac{a}{b}} = \frac{\sqrt[n]{a}}{\sqrt[n]{b}}$$

Properties of Logarithms

	Let b, c, x, y, u, and v be positive real numbers such that $b \neq 1$ and $c \neq 1$.
Logarithms and Exponents	$\log_b y = x$ if and only if $b^x = y$
Special Logarithm Values	$\log_b 1 = 0$ because $b^0 = 1$ and $\log_b b = 1$ because $b^1 = b$
Common and Natural Logarithms	$\log_{10} x = \log x$ and $\log_e x = \ln x$
Product Property of Logarithms	$\log_b uv = \log_b u + \log_b v$
Quotient Property of Logarithms	$\log_b \dfrac{u}{v} = \log_b u - \log_b v$
Power Property of Logarithms	$\log_b u^n = n \log_b u$
Change of Base	$\log_c u = \dfrac{\log_b u}{\log_b c}$

Properties of Functions

Operations on Functions	Let f and g be any two functions. A new function h can be defined using any of the following operations: **Addition:** $\quad h(x) = f(x) + g(x)$ **Subtraction:** $\quad h(x) = f(x) - g(x)$ **Multiplication:** $\quad h(x) = f(x) \cdot g(x)$ **Division:** $\quad h(x) = \dfrac{f(x)}{g(x)}$ **Composition:** $\quad h(x) = f(g(x))$ For addition, subtraction, multiplication, and division, the domain of h consists of the x-values that are in the domains of both f and g. Additionally, the domain of a quotient does not include x-values for which $g(x) = 0$. For composition, the domain of h is the set of all x-values such that x is in the domain of g and $g(x)$ is in the domain of f.
Inverse Functions	Functions f and g are inverses of each other provided: $$f(g(x)) = x \quad \text{and} \quad g(f(x)) = x$$

Mixed Problem Solving

CHAPTER 1

1. BANKING The table below shows the balance in a checking account on the first day of each month for one year. List the dollar amounts in increasing order. **(Lesson 1.1)**

Jan	Feb	Mar	Apr	May	June
$55	−$20	$15	$62	$47	−$38
July	**Aug**	**Sept**	**Oct**	**Nov**	**Dec**
−$27	$11	$85	$36	$12	−$10

2. INTELLIGENCE QUOTIENT An *Intelligence Quotient,* or IQ, is sometimes used to evaluate a person's intelligence potential. You can find a person's IQ by multiplying the quotient of the person's mental age and the person's chronological age by 100. Write an algebraic expression for finding a person's IQ. What is the IQ of a person whose mental age is 18 and whose chronological age is 16? **(Lesson 1.2)**

3. COMMISSION At a clothing store, sales associates are paid an hourly rate of $7 and receive a 3% commission on sales. A sales associate works 30 hours one week and earns a total of $243. How much did the sales associate sell that week? **(Lesson 1.3)**

4. PRODUCE SALES A farmer makes a profit of $.06 per pound of potatoes and $.08 per pound of carrots, and always produces twice as many pounds of potatoes as carrots. Last year the farmer produced 192,000 pounds of potatoes and 96,000 pounds of carrots. This year the farmer wants to make a profit of $24,000. By what percent should the farmer increase his production of potatoes and carrots? **(Lesson 1.3)**

5. SIMPLE INTEREST The formula for simple interest is $I = Prt$ where I is the interest, P is the principal, r is the rate (written as a decimal) and t is the time (in years). You deposit $4000 into a savings account that pays a simple annual interest rate of 2%. Solve the simple interest formula for t. Then find how many years will it take to earn $500 in interest. **(Lesson 1.4)**

6. PHYSICS Newton's second law states that a force F acting on an object equals the mass of the object m times the acceleration a. Force is measured in Newtons. One Newton is equal to $1\frac{kg \cdot m}{sec^2}$. A force of 60 Newtons acts on an object and produces an acceleration of 3 meters per second squared. What is the mass of the object? **(Lesson 1.5)**

7. SUMMER JOB You work 35 hours per week for a landscaping company during the summer. You earn $7 per hour for office work and $8 per hour for outside work. You earn $250 one week. How many hours did you work outside that week? **(Lesson 1.5)**

8. BOTANY A botanist received a sample of a certain species of a flower from her colleague in Africa. The botanist's colleague advised her to keep the flower in the temperature range of 35°C to 40°C. Write this temperature range as a compound inequality in degrees Fahrenheit. **(Lesson 1.6)**

9. GRADES A student's scores on the first four out of five tests are given in the table below. In order to achieve a final grade of A, the student needs a test average of 90 or greater. What scores could the student earn on the fifth test to achieve a final grade of A? **(Lesson 1.6)**

Test 1	88
Test 2	89
Test 3	93
Test 4	87
Test 5	?

10. DANCE COMPANY To be a member of a certain dance company, you must be between 66 inches and 69 inches tall when standing in stocking feet. Write an absolute value inequality that describes the acceptable heights for the members of the dance company. **(Lesson 1.7)**

CHAPTER 2

1. **WEIGHT ON THE MOON** A person's weight on the moon m (in pounds) can be modeled by $m = \frac{w}{6}$, where w is the person's weight (in pounds) on Earth. Graph the function. If a person weighs 150 pounds on Earth, about how much would the person weigh on the moon? **(Lesson 2.1)**

2. **STAIRCASE** A pull-down staircase for an attic is designed to have a slope of about 2. Find the horizontal distance x that a pull-down staircase would take up, given that the distance from the floor to the ceiling is 10 feet. **(Lesson 2.2)**

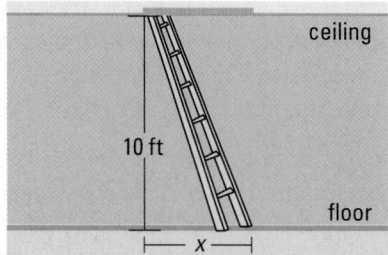

CALLING RATES In Exercises 3–5, use the following information. **(Lesson 2.3)**
A phone company charges $.30 for the first minute of a long-distance call and $.05 for each additional minute.

3. Write an equation that models the cost of a long-distance phone call that lasts more than one minute.

4. Graph the equation.

5. How many minutes can you talk for $2?

PROFIT In Exercises 6 and 7, use the following information. **(Lesson 2.4)**
A company experienced a linear growth in profit from 1990 through 1999. The company's profit was $32,000 in 1990 and $87,000 in 1999.

6. Find the company's average annual rate of increase in profit.

7. Write a linear model for the company's profit at any given time between 1990 and 1999.

8. If the company continued to experience the same kind of profit in years beyond 1999, predict the company's profit in 2005.

COMMUTER TRAIN In Exercises 9 and 10, use the following information. **(Lesson 2.5)**
The table below gives the time t (in minutes) and the distance d (in miles) a commuter train must travel to get to a city from each of several train stations along its route.

t	45.5	41	34.5	31	27	9.5	4
d	26	24	20	19	17	5	3

9. Draw a scatter plot of the data. Then approximate the best-fitting line for the data.

10. Predict the time it would take the same train to travel 35 miles from a station.

VIDEO RENTAL STORE In Exercises 11 and 12, use the following information. **(Lesson 2.6)**
You have a $30 gift card for a video rental store. It costs $4.50 to rent a movie and $5.50 to rent a video game.

11. Write and graph an inequality that represents the numbers of movies and video games you can rent.

12. Give three possible combinations of the numbers of movies and video games you can rent.

13. **WATER RATES** For a certain city, the cost C for water is given by the following function, where g is the number of gallons consumed (in thousands):

$$C(g) = \begin{cases} 1.48g + 3.2 & \text{if } 0 \le g \le 22 \\ 1.78g - 3.4 & \text{if } g > 22 \end{cases}$$

Graph the function. Then find the total cost for 31,000 gallons of water. **(Lesson 2.7)**

BOOK SALES In Exercises 14 and 15, use the following information. **(Lesson 2.8)**
The number of copies of a new book sold s (in hundreds) increases steadily for a while and then decreases as given by the function $s = -3\,|t - 29| + 112$ where t is the time (in weeks).

14. Graph the function.

15. What was the maximum number of copies sold in one week?

CHAPTER 3

1. PHONE BILL Your family pays different rates for long-distance phone calls made during the night and during the day. Daytime calls cost $.12 per minute. Nighttime calls cost $.07 per minute. Your family used 425 minutes this month, and the total bill (excluding base fees) was $36. How many daytime minutes did your family use? Use a verbal model to write a system of linear equations. Graph and solve the system. **(Lesson 3.1)**

MOVIE THEATER In Exercises 2 and 3, use the following information. **(Lesson 3.2)**
A movie theater charges $9 for an adult's ticket and $6 for a child's ticket. One Friday night the theater sold a total of 848 tickets for $6711.

2. How many tickets of each type were sold?

3. How much money did the theater make on each type of ticket?

4. FUNDRAISING Your student government is planning a sale of donated used books and CDs to raise money for a local charity. You have 200 books and 160 CDs. Each book will cost $4 and each CD will cost $6. Use the information below to write and graph a system of linear inequalities for the possible numbers of books and CDs sold. **(Lesson 3.3)**

> **Fundraiser on Saturday in the gym**
>
> - Buy used books and CDs.
> - All proceeds to benefit local charity.
> - Please help us raise at least $200.

5. GARDEN DESIGN You are designing a rectangular garden that is to be enclosed by a fence. The fence can be no longer than 500 feet. The length of the garden must be greater than 50 feet, and the width of the garden must be greater than 25 feet. Let l be the length of the garden and let w be the width of the garden. Write and graph a system of linear inequalities to describe the possible lengths and widths of the garden. **(Lesson 3.3)**

6. RUNNING You are training for a running race. You want to consume at least 300 grams of carbohydrates per day, but no more than 2000 calories. You are considering how you can meet these requirements by eating only pasta and lentils. Lentils cost $.79 per cup and pasta costs $.25 per cup. How many cups of lentils and how many cups of pasta should you buy to minimize cost while satisfying your nutritional requirements? **(Lesson 3.4)**

Contents	1 cup pasta	1 cup lentils
Calories	160	200
Carbohydrates (grams)	30	30

PAINTING In Exercises 7–9, use the following information. **(Lesson 3.5)**
You are hired to paint the exterior of a house. The cost of siding paint is $16 per gallon and the cost of trim paint is $14 per gallon. The painting equipment costs $26.

7. Write a model for the total cost of the project as a function of the number of gallons of siding paint and the number of gallons of trim paint you buy.

8. Evaluate the model for 10 gallons of siding paint and 3 gallons of trim paint.

9. Make a table that shows the total cost for several different numbers of gallons.

BASEBALL GAME In Exercises 10 and 11, use the following information. **(Lesson 3.6)**
You and two friends are at a baseball game together. You each buy concessions from a vendor. You buy one drink, one hot dog, and one bag of peanuts for $7.75. Tim buys one drink and two hot dogs for $6.25. Meg buys one hot dog and one bag of peanuts for $5.50.

10. Write a system of equations to represent the given information.

11. What is the price of each item purchased?

CHAPTER 4

PRODUCT SHIPPING In Exercises 1–3, use the following information. (Lesson 4.1, 4.2)

A company produces printers and fax machines. Both machines come in models A, B, and C. The matrices below show the company's shipping totals in 2002.

Units Shipped to Europe

	A	B	C
Printers	1200	1800	1500
Fax machines	2400	2800	2500

Units Shipped to Asia

	A	B	C
Printers	240	380	280
Fax machines	120	480	300

1. Write a matrix that shows the total numbers of units shipped to Europe and Asia.

2. The company shipped twice as many units to Asia in 2003 as in 2002. Write a matrix that shows the units shipped to Asia in 2003.

3. For both printers and fax machines, the shipping cost of model A is $2, the shipping cost of model B is $2.50, and the shipping cost of model C is $3. Use matrix multiplication to find the total cost of shipping to Europe for each model of printer and fax machine in 2002.

4. TRAY WEIGHT A server makes three trips from the kitchen carrying heavy trays. The matrix below shows the contents of each tray. Each entree weighs 3 pounds, each salad weighs 1.5 pounds, and each drink weighs 2 pounds. Use matrix multiplication to find the total weight carried on each tray. **(Lesson 4.2)**

Trays

	A	B	C
Entrees	2	4	3
Salads	4	2	1
Drinks	4	2	2

5. THEATER The total cost of theater tickets for 3 adults and 5 children is $120. The total cost of theater tickets for 5 adults and 3 children is $136. Use a linear system and Cramer's rule to find the price of one adult's ticket and the price of one child's ticket. **(Lesson 4.3)**

6. SCULPTURE You are constructing a wooden sculpture for an art class. You cut a triangle from a larger piece of wood as shown below. The coordinates given are measured in inches. Find the area of the triangle. **(Lesson 4.3)**

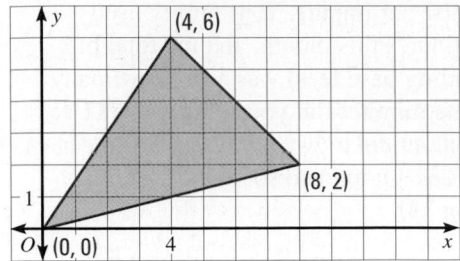

CRYPTOGRAPHY In Exercises 7–9, use the code below. A blank space is represented by the number 0. (Lesson 4.4)

E = 7	H = 3	M = 10	N = 8	O = 2
P = 9	R = 5	U = 1	V = 4	Y = 6

7. Convert the message HURRY UP to row matrices.

8. Use matrix A below to encode the message HURRY UP.

$$A = \begin{bmatrix} -2 & -1 \\ 1 & 1 \end{bmatrix}$$

9. Use the inverse of the matrix A to decode the following message.

$$-18, -8, -1, 3, 2, 2, -16, -8$$

10. COINS In a collection of nickels and dimes, there are 115 coins. The total value of the coins is $8.25. Use an inverse matrix to determine how many nickels and how many dimes are in the collection. **(Lesson 4.5)**

11. BANQUET HALL A banquet hall contains square, hexagonal, and octagonal tables. There are a total of 12 tables, and no table has an empty seat. Square tables seat 4 people, hexagonal tables seat 6 people, and octagonal tables seat 8 people. The number of square tables is two less than the total number of octagonal and hexagonal tables. There are 68 people at the banquet. Use an inverse matrix and a graphing calculator to find the number of tables of each size. **(Lesson 4.5)**

CHAPTER 5

1. **CABLES** A cable is suspended between the tops of two poles that are both 12 feet tall. The cable forms a parabola modeled by the equation $y = \frac{4}{625}(x - 25)^2 + 8$ where x and y are measured in feet. Use a graph to find the distance between the two poles. **(Lesson 5.1)**

2. **PICTURE FRAME** You are making a frame for a picture that is 3 inches by 4 inches. You have 18 square inches of material for the frame. You want all sides of the frame to have the same width. What should the width of the frame be? **(Lesson 5.2)**

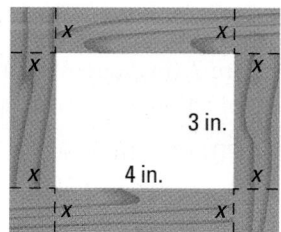

3 in.

4 in.

3. **FALLING OBJECT** A button accidentally falls off of a shirtsleeve and drops from the top of a building that is 784 feet tall. How many seconds will it take for the button to hit the ground? **(Lesson 5.3)**

ELECTRICAL CIRCUITS In Exercises 4 and 5, use the following information. (Lesson 5.4)
The resistance to the flow of electrical current in a circuit is called *impedance*. The equation $V = IZ$ relates the voltage of a circuit V (in volts) to the impedance Z (in ohms) and the current I (in amperes).

4. The current of a circuit is $6 + 3i$ amperes, and the impedance is $5 - 2i$ ohms. What is the voltage of the circuit?

5. What is the impedance for a current of $8 + 4i$ amperes in a 120 volt circuit? Write your answer in standard form.

6. **COMPANY PROFITS** The profits of a company from 1992 to 2001 can be modeled by $P = 100t^2 - 20t + 55,000$ where t is the number of years since 1992. Predict the year in which the profits of the company will be $69,160. **(Lesson 5.5)**

7. **TENNIS** You throw a tennis ball into the air in order to serve the ball. The tennis ball leaves your hand 6 feet above the ground and has an initial velocity of 50 feet per second. You hit the ball when it falls back to a height of 7 feet. For how long was the ball in the air? **(Lesson 5.6)**

8. **WEB TRAFFIC** The number of visitors to a certain Web site increases weekly. A Web site monitor develops the formula $\frac{T}{1000} = d^2 - 8d + 32$ for the average number of visitors T in week d of the Web site's first year. During what week will the average number of visitors reach 50,000? **(Lesson 5.6)**

9. **POTTERY** You are making a cylindrical clay pencil holder. So that you have enough space to paint the outside of the pencil holder, you want the outer surface area to be at least 35 square inches. You want the height of the pencil holder to be 4 inches. What values can you use for the radius of the pencil holder? (*Hint:* Because the pencil holder has no lid, include the area of only one base in your calculation of the surface area.) **(Lesson 5.7)**

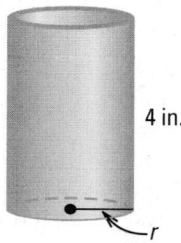

4 in.

r

SCHOOL ENROLLMENT In Exercises 10 and 11, use the following information. (Lesson 5.8)
The table below gives the annual enrollment E at a school t years after 1990.

t	1	2	3	4	5	6
E	525	492	498	521	534	582

10. Make a scatter plot of the data and draw the parabola you think best fits the data.

11. Write and solve a system of linear equations to find a quadratic model for the data.

CHAPTER 6

1. **ASTRONOMY** The radius of Mars is about one half the radius of Earth. What fraction of Earth's volume is Mars's volume? **(Lesson 6.1)**

2. **ASTRONOMY** The distance from Neptune to Earth is about 4.3×10^9 kilometers. The distance from Mars to Earth is about 5.5×10^7 kilometers. About how many times farther is Neptune from Earth than Mars is from Earth? **(Lesson 6.1)**

3. **MOVIES** The monthly revenue R (in millions of dollars) earned by a certain movie from January 2002 to September 2002 can be modeled by

$$R = 0.025t^3 - t^2 + 7t + 14$$

where t is the number of months since January 2002. What was the monthly revenue in April 2002? **(Lesson 6.2)**

4. **SCHOOL POPULATION** The number of students in each class in a high school from 1995 to 2000 can be modeled by

Freshman: $y = x^2 + 2x + 97$

Sophomore: $y = x^2 + 3x + 77$

Junior: $y = x^2 + x + 81$

Senior: $y = x^2 + x + 43$

where x is the number of students and y is the number of years since 1995. Find a model for the total number of students in the high school. **(Lesson 6.3)**

5. **GIFT BOXES** A department store purchases gift boxes that each have a volume of 256 cubic inches. The width of each box is 4 inches less than the length. The height is twice the width. Find the dimensions of a gift box. **(Lesson 6.4)**

6. **ORANGE GROVE** The area A (in square feet) and the length L (in feet) of a rectangular orange grove can be modeled by

$$A = 1.5x^2 + 36x \quad \text{and} \quad L = x + 24$$

where x is the number of orange trees in the grove. Find a model for the width of the orange grove. **(Lesson 6.5)**

7. **ICE SCULPTURE** As part of an ice sculpture, an artist wants to build an ice cone that has a volume of 24π cubic feet. The artist wants the height of the cone to be 2 feet longer than the diameter of the base. What should the diameter and the height of the cone be? **(Lesson 6.6)**

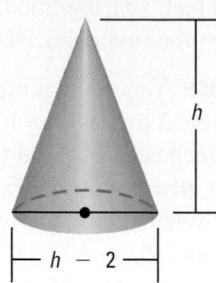

8. **BODY TEMPERATURE** Suppose a patient's body temperature T (in degrees Fahrenheit) during a viral infection can be modeled by

$$T = -0.001x^3 - 0.1x + 103$$

where x is the number of days since the infection began. After about how many days does the patient's temperature drop to $100°F$? **(Lesson 6.7)**

9. **COAT SALES** The number of coats sold at a department store during one year can be modeled by

$$f(x) = 0.627x^3 - 6.32x^2 - 4.06x + 125$$

where x is the number of months and $x = 1$ represents January. In what month were sales at a minimum? **(Lesson 6.8)**

10. **SALARIES** The table shows the salary y (in thousands of dollars) of a bank employee between 1993 and 2002. Find a polynomial model for the data. Then predict the employee's salary in 2005. **(Lesson 6.9)**

t	1993	1994	1995	1996	1997
y	33	38	43	46	48
t	1998	1999	2000	2001	2002
y	49	49	50	55	56

CHAPTER 7

1. **ASTRONOMY** Phoebe is a satellite that orbits Saturn. Phoebe is roughly spherical in shape and has a volume of approximately 5,580,000 cubic kilometers. The formula for the volume of a sphere is $V = \frac{4}{3}\pi r^3$ where r is the radius of the sphere. Find the approximate radius of Phoebe. **(Lesson 7.1)**

BIOLOGY In Exercises 2 and 3, use the following information. **(Lesson 7.2)**
The surface area S (in square centimeters) of a large dog's body can be approximated by the model $S = 11.2m^{2/3}$ where m is the mass (in grams) of the dog.

2. Approximate the surface area of a dog that has a mass of 9 kilograms (9×10^3 grams).

3. Dog A has a mass that is 5 times the mass of dog B. What is the ratio of the surface area of dog A to the surface area of dog B?

GEOMETRY In Exercises 4 and 5, use the following information. **(Lesson 7.3)**
The functions below show how the circumference c (in centimeters) of a circle is related to the radius of the circle r (in centimeters), and how the area a (in square centimeters) of the rectangle is related to c.

$$c(r) = 2\pi r \qquad a(c) = \frac{c^2}{2\pi}$$

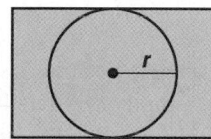

4. Use composition of functions to find the relationship between the radius of the circle and the area of the rectangle.

5. Find the area of the rectangle when the radius of the circle is 5 centimeters.

6. **WIND POWER** The power of wind W (in watts per square meter) can be modeled by the function $W = 0.6125s^3$ where s is the wind's speed (in meters per second). Find the inverse of the function. Then find the speed of wind with a power of 132.3 watts per square meter. **(Lesson 7.4)**

7. **FREE FALL** The time t (in seconds) it takes a dropped object to reach the ground can be modeled by $t = \frac{1}{4}\sqrt{h}$ where h is the height (in feet) from which the object is dropped. Graph the model. Then determine from what height you must drop an object so that it falls for 1.5 seconds. **(Lesson 7.5)**

8. **PENDULUMS** The period of a pendulum is the time it takes the pendulum to complete one swing. The period p (in seconds) can be modeled by $p = 2\pi\sqrt{\frac{l}{32}}$ where l is the pendulum's length (in feet). What is the length of a pendulum with a period of 3 seconds? **(Lesson 7.6)**

9. **SHIP POWER** The power p (in horsepower) that a ship needs can be modeled by $p = \dfrac{d^{2/3} \cdot s^3}{c}$ where d is the ship's displacement (in tons), s is the normal speed (in knots), and c is the Admiralty coefficient. A ship's power is 81,000 horsepower, its normal speed is 30 knots, and its Admiralty coefficient is 300. What is the ship's displacement? **(Lesson 7.6)**

BASEBALL In Exercises 10 and 11, use the table below which gives the home run totals of fourteen Major League Baseball teams for the 2002 season. **(Lesson 7.7)**

Team Home Run Totals (2002 Season)
165, 152, 164, 177, 200, 223, 146, 205, 139, 198, 152, 175, 165, 152

10. Find the mean, median, and mode of the data.

11. Find the standard deviation of the data.

12. **REPTILES** The table below shows the numbers of threatened reptile species in countries of Central America, South America, and the Caribbean. Draw a box-and-whisker plot of the data set. **(Lesson 7.7)**

Threatened Reptile Species
5, 7, 7, 10, 6, 9, 6, 7, 8, 18, 7, 7, 5, 5, 3, 15, 1, 15, 12, 8, 3, 9, 6, 0, 14

CHAPTER 8

1. **ACCOUNT BALANCE** You deposit $2000 in an account that pays 5% annual interest. Find the balance after 3 years if the interest is compounded quarterly. **(Lesson 8.1)**

2. **POPULATION** The population of a certain town increases by about 2% each year. If the population of the town is 3560 in 2002, predict the population in 2006. **(Lesson 8.1)**

SAILBOATS In Exercises 3–5, use the following information. (Lesson 8.2)
You buy a new sailboat for $15,000. The value of the boat decreases by 11% each year.

3. Write an exponential decay model for the value of the sailboat. Use the model to determine the value after 5 years.

4. Graph the model.

5. Use the graph to estimate when the sailboat will have a value of about $10,000.

6. **CONTINUOUS COMPOUNDING** You deposit $1800 in bank A that pays 6% annual interest compounded continuously and deposit $1200 in bank B that pays 8% annual interest compounded continuously. What is the balance of each account after 10 years? **(Lesson 8.3)**

7. **HURRICANES** Once a hurricane reaches land, the wind speed s (in knots) within the hurricane is related to the time t (in hours) the hurricane remains over land. For one particular hurricane, this relationship is given by:

$$s = -57.1 \log t + 121$$

Graph the model. About how long after the hurricane reached land was the wind speed about 60 knots? **(Lesson 8.4)**

8. **PH MEASUREMENT** The pH of a solution is given by

$$pH = -\log[H^+]$$

where $[H^+]$ is the solution's hydrogen ion concentration (in moles per liter). Find the pH of a solution whose hydrogen ion concentration is 1×10^{-7} mole per liter. **(Lesson 8.4)**

9. **SOUND INTENSITY** The loudness L (in decibels) produced by a sound is related to the intensity I of the sound (in watts per square meter) by the equation

$$L = 10 \log \frac{I}{I_0}$$

where I_0 is an intensity of 10^{-12} watt per square meter, the faintest sound that can be heard by humans. Use the equation to find the difference in the loudness of a hair dryer with an intensity of 10^{-4} watt per square meter and an air conditioning unit with an intensity of 10^{-6} watt per square meter. **(Lesson 8.5)**

10. **RADIOACTIVE DECAY** You have 30 grams of cobalt-60 that decays 12% per year. How many years will it take for half the original amount to decay? **(Lesson 8.6)**

BASEBALL In Exercises 11 and 12, use the following information. (Lesson 8.7)
The table gives the average salary S (in millions of dollars) of a professional baseball player from 1998 to 2002 where t is the number of years since 1998.

t	0	1	2	3	4
S	1.441	1.720	1.988	2.264	2.383

11. Draw a scatter plot of ln S versus t. Is an exponential model a good fit for the original data?

12. Find an exponential model for the original data.

13. **CHILD DEVELOPMENT** For the first 36 months of life, the body weight W (in pounds) of male babies in the 50th percentile (the median weight for all male babies) can be modeled by

$$W = \frac{30.4}{1 + 1.99e^{-0.144t}}$$

where t is the number of months since birth. Graph the model. At about what age will a male baby in the 50th percentile weigh 20 pounds? **(Lesson 8.8)**

CHAPTER 9

GAS LAWS In Exercises 1 and 2, use the following information. (Lesson 9.1)

According to Boyle's Law, the volume V of a gas varies inversely with the pressure P of a gas, as long as the temperature of the gas remains constant. According to Charles's Law, the volume V of a gas varies directly with the absolute temperature T of the gas (in kelvins), as long as the pressure of the gas remains constant.

1. Write an equation relating V, P, and a constant k when temperature is constant. Find the value of k for 3.1 cubic meters of a gas at a pressure of 1.3 atmospheres.

2. Write an equation that that relates V, T, and a constant k when pressure is constant. Find the value of k for 4.8 liters of a gas at a temperature of 320 kelvins.

INTERNET SERVICE In Exercises 3 and 4, use the advertisement shown below. (Lesson 9.2)

> **Low Cost Internet Access**
> Low monthly fee of $8.
> Just $.40 per hour of high-speed access.
> Order NOW!

3. Write a model that represents the average cost per hour of Internet access as a function of the number of hours of use per month. Graph the model.

4. A second Internet provider offers service for $1 per hour of access with no monthly fee. If you subscribe to the plan in the advertisement above, how many hours of Internet access would you have to use to make your average cost per hour less than $1?

5. **PACKAGING** A packaging company has been asked to design a box that has a volume of 100 cubic inches. The length of the box must be twice the width of the box. Find the dimensions of the box that minimize the material needed to make the box. **(Lesson 9.3)**

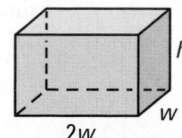

EDUCATION COSTS In Exercises 6 and 7, use the following information. (Lesson 9.4)

In one city from the 1990–91 school year through the 2001–02 school year, the number of students S and the cost of education per student C (in dollars) can be modeled by

$$S = \frac{50t + 9000}{0.005t + 1} \quad \text{and} \quad C = \frac{12t + 6300}{0.003t^2 + 1}$$

where t is the number of years since the 1990–91 school year.

6. Write a model for the total cost of education for students in the city.

7. What was the total cost of education for students in the 1996–97 school year?

8. **GEOMETRY** Use the diagram below. Find the ratio of the volume of the square pyramid to the volume of the inscribed cone. Write your answer in simplified form. **(Lesson 9.4)**

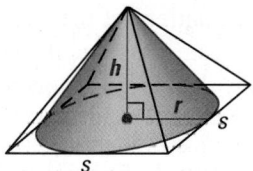

RESISTANCE In Exercises 9 and 10, use the following information. (Lesson 9.5)

Four resistors in a parallel circuit have resistances R_1, R_2, R_3, and R_4 (all in ohms). The total resistance R_t (in ohms) is given by this formula:

$$R_t = \frac{1}{\frac{1}{R_1} + \frac{1}{R_2} + \frac{1}{R_3} + \frac{1}{R_4}}$$

9. Simplify the complex fraction.

10. You have four resistors in a parallel circuit with resistances 5 ohms, 8 ohms, 15 ohms, and 12 ohms. What is the total resistance?

11. **BASEBALL** An Earned Run Average (ERA) is the average number of earned runs a pitcher gives up in 9 innings of baseball. ERA is nine times the number of earned runs divided by the number of innings pitched. If a pitcher has given up 20 runs in 80 innings, how many more innings must he pitch without giving up a run in order to have an ERA of 2.00? **(Lesson 9.6)**

CHAPTER 10

1. **WALKING** You plan to walk along a path at a local park. Quadrilateral $ABCD$ represents the path that you plan to follow. Find the length of the path. Two units in the coordinate plane represent 1 mile. **(Lesson 10.1)**

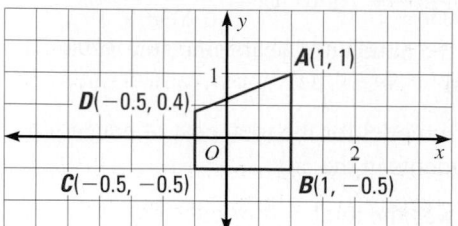

2. **RADIO TELESCOPES** A radio telescope is a large dish that astronomers use to collect data from space. The cross section of a radio telescope dish is a parabola. The receiver is located at the focus, 6.125 meters above the vertex. Find an equation for the cross section of the telescope dish. (Assume the vertex is at the origin.) If the dish is 14 meters wide, how deep is it? **(Lesson 10.2)**

SCHOOL BUS ROUTES In Exercises 3 and 4, use the following information. **(Lesson 10.3)**
Students living within 1 mile of the high school in your town are not eligible to ride a school bus to school.

3. Write an inequality to describe the region for which students are not eligible to ride a school bus. Let $(0, 0)$ represent the location of the high school.

4. Your house is located 1.5 miles east and 1 mile south of the school. Tell whether you are eligible to ride a school bus to school.

5. **SPRINKLERS** A lawn sprinkler waters a circular region of grass with an area of 2000 square feet. Write an equation that represents the boundary of the watered region of grass. Let $(0, 0)$ represent the location of the sprinkler. **(Lesson 10.3)**

6. **PLANETARY ORBITS** In its elliptical orbit, Mars ranges from 206.6 million kilometers to 249.2 million kilometers from the center of the sun. The center of the sun is a focus of the orbit. Write an equation of the orbit. **(Lesson 10.4)**

COFFEE TABLES In Exercises 7–9, use the following information. **(Lesson 10.4)**
The surface of a coffee table is shaped like an ellipse. It is 20 inches wide and 40 inches long.

7. Write an equation that models the shape of the surface of the coffee table.

8. How far apart are the two foci?

9. The area of an ellipse is given by the formula $A = \pi ab$. What is the area of the surface of the table?

HOURGLASSES In Exercises 10 and 11, use the following information. **(Lesson 10.5)**
The diagram below shows the hyperbolic cross section of an hourglass. Each unit in the coordinate plane represents 1 inch.

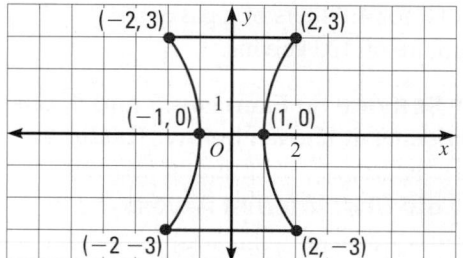

10. Write an equation that models the curved sides of the hourglass.

11. At a height of 1.5 inches, how wide is the hourglass?

12. **AIRCRAFT ALTITUDES** The KC-135 is an aircraft that flies in arcs to produce a weightless environment. At the top of each arc, passengers experience about 25 seconds of weightlessness. The altitude y, in feet, of the aircraft during part of an arc after x seconds can be modeled by the equation $15x^2 - 923x + y - 18,659 = 0$. What type of conic is it? **(Lesson 10.6)**

13. **COMMUNICATIONS** The range (in miles) of a cellular telephone tower is bounded by a circle given by the equation $x^2 + y^2 = 178$. A straight highway can be modeled by the equation $y = x + 10$. Find the length of the highway that lies within the range of the cellular telephone tower. **(Lesson 10.7)**

CHAPTER 11

1. **ANGLE MEASURES** The degree measure d_n of an interior angle of a regular polygon with n sides is given by:

$$d_n = \frac{180(n-2)}{n},\ n \geq 3$$

Copy and complete the table below using the terms of the sequence. **(Lesson 11.1)**

Regular polygon	Number of sides (n)	Interior angle measure
triangle	?	?
quadrilateral	?	?
pentagon	?	?
hexagon	?	?
heptagon	?	?
octagon	?	?

AUDITORIUM In Exercises 2–5, use the following information. **(Lesson 11.2)**
An auditorium has 25 rows of seats. There are 16 seats in the first row, and each row after the first has 4 more seats than the row before it.

2. Write a rule for the number of seats in the nth row.

3. A group of 40 people want to sit in the same row. How close to the front can they sit?

4. What is the total number of seats in the auditorium?

5. During a renovation, 8 rows of seats are added to the back of the auditorium. (Each row has 4 more seats than the row before it.) How many additional seats are added?

AUDITIONS In Exercises 6 and 7, use the following information. **(Lesson 11.3)**
Several rounds of auditions are being held to cast the three main parts in a musical production. There were 3072 actors at the first round of auditions. In each successive round of auditions, one fourth of the actors from the previous round remain.

6. Find a rule for the number of actors in the nth round of auditions.

7. For what values of n does your rule make sense?

BACTERIA In Exercises 8 and 9, use the following information. **(Lesson 11.3)**
The number of bacteria in a petri dish doubles each hour. Initially there are 2.4×10^{18} bacteria in the petri dish.

8. Find a rule for the total number of bacteria after n hours.

9. Find the total number of bacteria in the dish after 8 hours. Write your answer in scientific notation.

BOUNCING BALL In Exercises 10 and 11, use the following information. **(Lesson 11.4)**
A ball drops from a height of 12 feet. Each time it hits the ground, it bounces to 70% of its previous height.

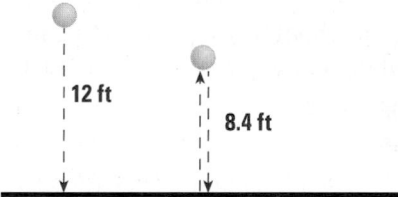

12 ft

8.4 ft

10. Find the total distance traveled by the ball.

11. On which bounce will the ball have traveled 90% of its total distance?

12. **DOG POPULATION** A town's dog population increases at a rate of about 4% per year. In 2000, there were a total of 1050 dogs in the town. Let $n = 1$ represent the dog population in 2000. Write an explicit and a recursive rule for the town's dog population in terms of the year. **(Lesson 11.5)**

SAVING MONEY In Exercises 13 and 14, use the following information. **(Lesson 11.5)**
You keep $120 in a jar in your room. Each week, you allow yourself to spend 5% of the money in the jar. You also add $5 to the jar every week.

13. Write a recursive rule for the amount of money in the jar after n weeks. How much money is in the jar after 10 weeks?

14. Use a graphing calculator to determine what happens to the amount of money in the jar over time.

CHAPTER 12

BANKING In Exercises 1 and 2, use the following information. (Lesson 12.1)

You are given a random four-digit personal identification number (PIN) to use with your bank card. Each of the digits is a whole number from 0 to 9.

1. How many different four-digit PINs are possible if the digits can be repeated?

2. How many different four-digit PINs are possible if the digits cannot be repeated?

MUSIC In Exercises 3 and 4, decide whether the problem requires permutations or combinations to find the answer. Then solve the problem. (Lessons 12.1, 12.2)

3. There are 15 school bands participating in a competition. In how many ways can first, second, and third places be awarded?

4. You want to buy 9 CDs at a music store. However, you have enough money for only 3 CDs. In how many ways can you select 3 of the CDs to buy?

5. **GEOMETRY** The target below is a circle enclosed by a rectangle. Find the probability that a dart thrown at the target will hit the shaded region. Assume that the dart is equally likely to hit any point inside the target. (Lesson 12.3)

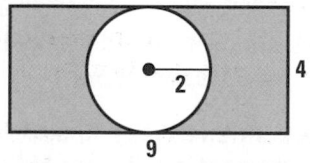

CHOOSING CARDS In Exercises 6–9, a card is randomly drawn from a standard 52-card deck. Find the probability of the event. (Lesson 12.4)

6. a four or a nine

7. a five or a diamond

8. a seven and a heart

9. a club or a heart

STUDENTS In Exercises 10 and 11, use the table below, which shows the male and female students at a school. (Lesson 12.5)

	Male	Female
Freshman	97	103
Sophomore	92	84
Junior	95	93
Senior	93	97

10. Find the probability that a randomly selected student is a freshman.

11. Find the probability that a randomly selected junior is a male student.

12. **SOCKS** A drawer contains 11 pairs of white socks and 9 pairs of gray socks. You randomly select 3 pairs of socks from the drawer. Find the probability that the 3 pairs that you selected are white. (Lesson 12.5)

TESTS In Exercises 13 and 14, use the following information. (Lesson 12.6)

Your chemistry test has 6 multiple choice questions, and each question has 4 choices. Suppose you randomly select the answer to each multiple choice question. Assume that the probability of answering a multiple choice question correctly is 0.25.

13. Draw a histogram of the binomial distribution for the number of multiple choice questions answered correctly.

14. What is the probability of answering at least 4 of the multiple choice questions correctly?

GARDENS In Exercises 15 and 16, use the following information. (Lesson 12.7)

The heights of the day lilies in a garden are normally distributed with a mean of 33 inches and a standard deviation of 3 inches.

15. What percent of the day lilies have heights between 27 inches and 36 inches?

16. You randomly select two day lilies in the garden. What is the probability that the day lilies have a height of 30 inches or less?

CHAPTER 13

1. ESCALATORS An escalator connects two levels of a shopping mall. The escalator rises 66 feet at a 30° angle, as shown below. Find the distance *d* that a person travels on the escalator. **(Lesson 13.1)**

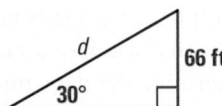

2. FERRIS WHEELS A Ferris wheel with a radius of 83 feet takes 40 seconds to complete one rotation. After you ride the Ferris wheel for 54 seconds, it stops to let more passengers on. Through what angle did you rotate? Give the answer in both degrees and radians. **(Lesson 13.2)**

FOOTBALL In Exercises 3–5, use the following information. **(Lesson 13.3)**
The horizontal distance *d* (in feet) traveled by a projectile with an initial speed *v* (in feet per second) is given by $d = \dfrac{v^2}{32} \sin 2\theta$, where θ is the angle at which the projectile is launched.

3. Estimate the horizontal distance traveled by a football that is kicked at an angle of 60° with an initial speed of 62 feet per second.

4. Estimate the horizontal distance traveled by a football that is kicked at an angle of 45° with an initial speed of 70 feet per second.

5. Estimate the horizontal distance traveled by a football that is kicked at an angle of 55° with an initial speed of 50 feet per second.

6. WHEAT Different types of granular substances naturally settle at different angles when stored in cone-shaped piles. The angle θ is called the angle of repose. The diagram below shows granular wheat stored in a cone-shaped pile. Find the angle of repose. **(Lesson 13.4)**

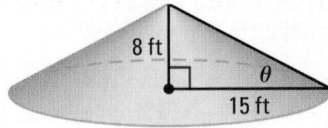

7. LOCATING A FIRE Two fire towers *A* and *B* are located 12 miles apart, as shown below. Use the information in the diagram to find the distance of the fire from each tower. **(Lesson 13.5)**

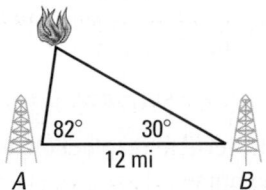

8. LONG JUMP The diagram below shows the position of a jumper's leg at the take off phase of a long jump. The angle θ of the jumper's knee at the take off phase should be between 165° and 170°. Is the angle of the jumper's knee in this range? Explain. **(Lesson 13.6)**

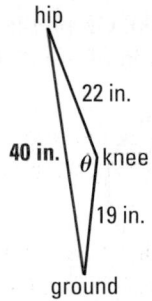

9. GARDENS A triangular garden has side lengths that are 12 feet, 9 feet, and 5 feet long. Find the area of the garden. **(Lesson 13.6)**

MARBLE ROLLER COASTER In Exercises 10 and 11, use the following information. **(Lesson 13.7)**
Your physics class is constructing a marble roller coaster. At the end of the track, the marble should project off a jump and land in a cup. Suppose the marble is projected with an initial speed of 14 feet per second, at an angle of 55°, and from an initial height of 0.8 feet.

10. Write a set of parametric equations for the motion of the marble.

11. Use the equations from Exercise 10 to find how far from the jump to place the cup.

CHAPTER 14

1. **MERRY-GO-ROUND** A wooden horse on a merry-go-round moves 6 inches above and 6 inches below its center position. It takes the horse 3 seconds to make 1 complete up-and-down movement. The motion of the horse can be modeled by the function

$$d = 6 \sin \frac{2}{3} \pi t$$

   where d is the vertical displacement (in inches) of the horse relative to its center position and t is the time (in seconds). Graph the function over a 12 second time interval. **(Lesson 14.1)**

2. **BICYCLE** You put a reflector on the spoke of your bicycle wheel. As you ride the bicycle, the reflector's height h (in inches) above the ground is $h = 13.5 + 13.5 \sin 2\pi t$, where t is the time (in seconds). Graph the height of the reflector as a function of time. **(Lesson 14.2)**

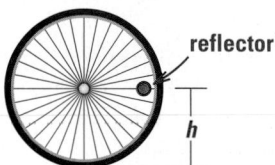
reflector

h

3. **ELEVATOR** You stand 25 meters away from a glass elevator that descends from 50 meters above the ground. Write and graph a model for the distance d (in meters) that the elevator has descended as a function of its angle of elevation θ. **(Lesson 14.2)**

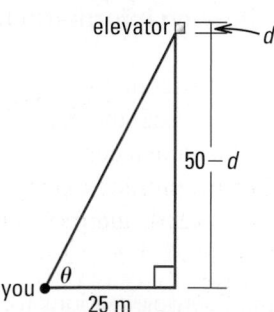
elevator
d
$50 - d$
you
θ
25 m

4. **RUNNING** The path a runner takes around a lake can be described by the equations $y = \frac{1}{2} \sin 2\pi t$ and $x = \cos 2\pi t$, where x and y are measured in feet and t is measured in hours. Describe the path followed by the runner. **(Lesson 14.3)**

5. **POSITION OF THE SUN** Houston, Texas, has a latitude of 30°N. At this latitude, the position of the sun at sunrise can be modeled by

$$D = 27 \sin \left(\frac{2\pi}{365} t - 1.3 \right)$$

   where t is the time in days and $t = 1$ represents January 1. In this model, D represents the number of degrees north of due east that the sun rises. Use a graphing calculator to determine the days that the sun is more than 23° north of due east at sunrise in Houston, Texas. **(Lesson 14.4)**

6. **SNOWFALL** The table below gives the average snowfall S (in inches) for each month m at Mount Washington in New Hampshire, with $m = 1$ representing January. Find a model for the data. **(Lesson 14.5)**

m	1	2	3	4	5	6
S	40.1	40.7	42.5	30.9	10.3	1.2
m	7	8	9	10	11	12
S	0	0.1	1.9	11.8	40.4	42.6

7. **REFRACTION** A beam of light passes through water at an angle of $\frac{\pi}{2}$ radians. The light then passes through oil at an angle α radians more than $\frac{\pi}{2}$. The refraction index of water N_1 is 1.33. The refraction index of oil N_2 is 1.51. The refraction index of the oil and water are related to the angle of the light beam by the equation $N_1 \sin \frac{\pi}{2} = N_2 \sin \left(\frac{\pi}{2} + \alpha \right)$. Simplify the equation and find the value of α. **(Lesson 14.6)**

8. **WINDOW** Express the area of the triangular window as a function of $\sin \frac{\theta}{2}$ and $\cos \frac{\theta}{2}$. Simplify the function. Then solve for θ assuming that the area is 200 square inches. **(Lesson 14.7)**

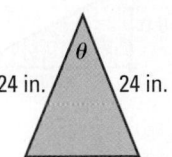
θ
24 in.   24 in.

Appendix 1

Transformations of Functions

GOAL *Identify the effects of transformations on the graphs of quadratic, exponential, absolute value, and radical functions.*

Sometimes a basic function can be related to other functions through transformations. In such instances, the basic function is called a **parent function**.

In general, a related graph is called a *translation* of a parent graph $y = f(x)$ if the related graph can be given by an equation of the form $y - k = f(x - h)$. For example, the parent graph $y = |x|$ is shown below translated vertically and horizontally. Notice that subtracting a positive number from one of the variables moves the graph that number of units *in a positive direction* parallel to the axis of the variable.

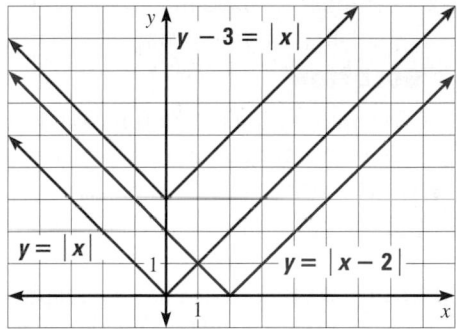

EXAMPLE 1 *Graphing a Function Using a Parent Function*

Graph the function by translating the graph of its parent function.

a. $y = 2^{x-3}$

b. $y - 2 = (x + 1)^2$

SOLUTION

To find the parent function, think of the given function with any added or subtracted constants removed.

a. The parent function is $y = 2^x$. Translate the graph of the parent function 3 units to the right.

b. The parent function is $y = x^2$. Translate the graph of the parent function 2 units up and 1 unit to the left.

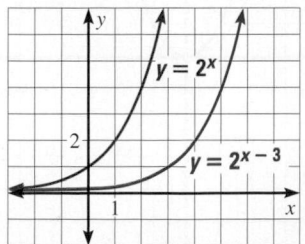

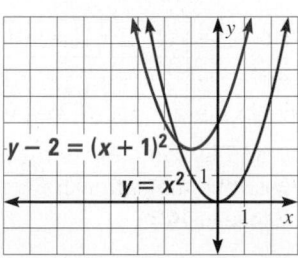

In Example 1 you identified the parent function in order to draw the graph of a related function. You can also do the reverse. Given the graph of a related function, you can write the function represented by the graph by first identifying the parent function.

EXAMPLE 2 *Writing a Function Using a Parent Function*

Tell whether the function represented by the graph has a parent function of $y = |x|$, $y = \sqrt{x}$, $y = x^2$, or $y = 2^x$. Write the function represented by the graph, using the graph of the parent function.

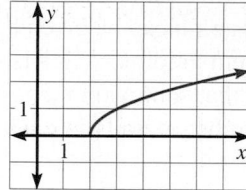

SOLUTION

First identify the parent function. Because the shape of the graph is that of a square-root graph, the parent function is $y = \sqrt{x}$. The graph is translated 2 units to the right, so the function is $y = \sqrt{x - 2}$.

· · · · · · · · · ·

DILATIONS You can use the graph of a parent function $y = f(x)$ to sketch the graph of the related function $y = a \cdot f(x)$, where a is nonzero.

· If $|a| > 1$, the graph is stretched vertically.

· If $|a| < 1$, the graph is shrunk vertically.

The transformations described above are called *dilations*. If $a = -1$, the graph of $y = a \cdot f(x)$ is the mirror image of the graph of $y = f(x)$ across the x-axis. This type of transformation is called a *reflection* in the x-axis. If $a < 0$ and $a \neq -1$, you have a combination of a dilation and a reflection. The following graph shows the parent graph $y = x^2$, the dilations $y = 2x^2$ and $y = \frac{1}{2}x^2$, and the reflection $y = -x^2$.

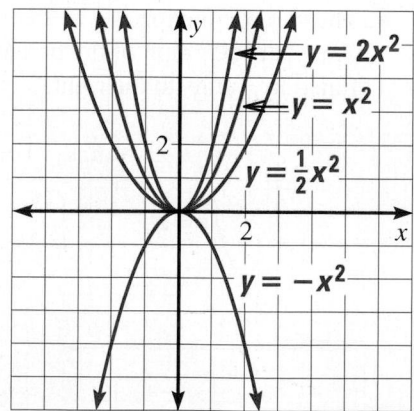

EXAMPLE 3 **Sketching the Graph of a Dilated Function**

Sketch the graph of the function, using the graph of its parent function.

a. $y = 4 \cdot 3^x$

b. $y = -\frac{1}{3}|x|$

SOLUTION

a. First graph the parent function, $y = 3^x$. Then identify several key points, such as $(0, 1)$ and $(1, 3)$. Since $|4| > 1$, increase the y-coordinate of each key point by a factor of 4. Plot and connect the new points.

b. First graph the parent function, $y = |x|$. Identify several key points on the graph of the parent function, such as $(-3, 3)$, $(0, 0)$, and $(3, 3)$. Since $\left|-\frac{1}{3}\right| < 1$ and $-\frac{1}{3} < 0$, decrease the y-coordinate of each key point by a factor of $\frac{1}{3}$ and reflect the points in the x-axis. Plot and connect the new points.

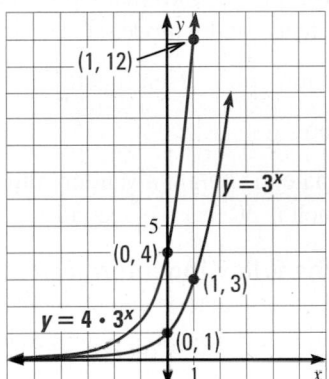

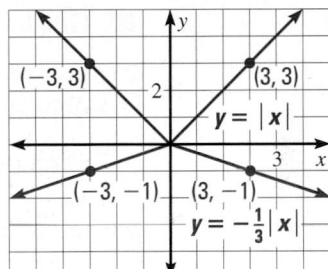

EXERCISES

Graph the function.

1. $y = (x + 3)^2$

2. $y - 4 = \sqrt{x + 2}$

3. $y + 1 = |x - 4|$

4. $y - 3 = \sqrt{x - 1}$

5. $y = 3|x|$

6. $y = -4^x$

7. $y = \frac{1}{4}(x - 1)^2$

8. $y = -\frac{1}{2}|x|$

9. $y = 2 \cdot 3^{x + 1}$

Tell whether the graph has a parent function of $y = |x|$, $y = \sqrt{x}$, $y = x^2$, or $y = 2^x$. Then write the function represented by the graph.

10.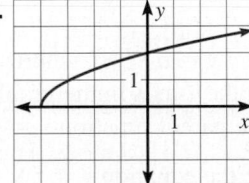

11.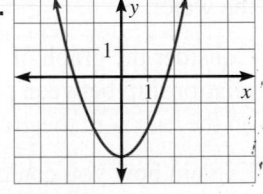

12.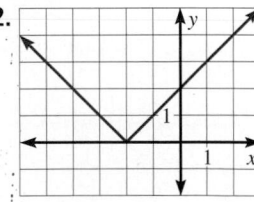

13.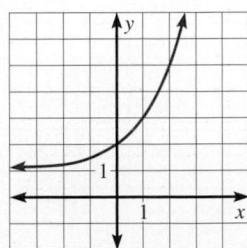

14.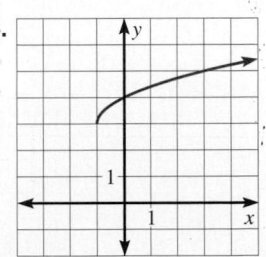

15.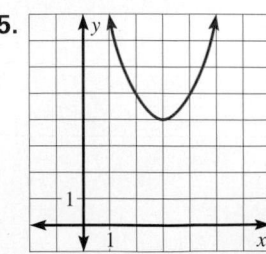

The graph of a function $y = f(x)$ is given. Graph the related function given. (*Hint:* First draw the translation of several key points on the graph.)

16.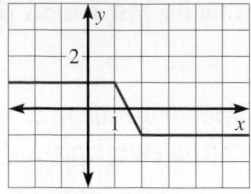

Related function:
$y - 2 = f(x)$

17.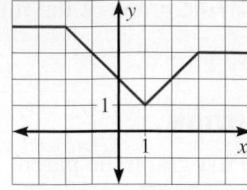

Related function:
$y = f(x + 3)$

18.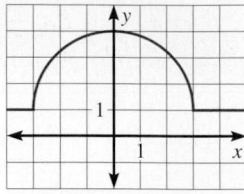

Related function:
$y + 4 = f(x - 1)$

In Exercises 19–21, use the following information.
The running velocity v (in feet per second) that a pole vaulter must reach at launch in order to vault a height h (in feet) can be modeled by $v = 8\sqrt{h}$.

19. What is the parent function of the given function?

20. Graph the given function.

21. Use your graph to estimate the height a vaulter could vault if the vaulter's running velocity at launch is 30 feet per second.

In Exercises 22–24, use the following information.
The total population b of a certain bacteria can be modeled by $b = 500 \cdot 2^t$, where t is the number of times the bacteria population doubles.

22. What is the parent function of the given function?

23. Graph the given function.

24. Use your graph to estimate the number of times the bacteria population needs to double to reach a total population of 10,000.

In Exercises 25–27, use the following information.
A stone is dropped from a bridge that is 60 feet above the water below. The height h (in feet) of the stone above the water after t seconds can be modeled by $h = -16t^2 + 60$.

25. What is the parent function of the given function?

26. Graph the given function.

27. Use your graph to estimate the number of seconds it takes for the stone to hit the water.

28. Consider the graph of a function $y = a \cdot f(x)$, where a is nonzero. What is the relationship between points on the x-axis in the graph of $y = a \cdot f(x)$ and points on the x-axis in the graph of the parent function $y = f(x)$?

29. Explain how you could rewrite the equation $y = 5\sqrt{4x - 8} + 1$ so that it is in the form $y - k = a\sqrt{x - h}$.

Modeling Data with Functions

GOAL *Model data using linear, quadratic, or exponential functions; estimate the correlation coefficient for a set of data.*

Data can sometimes be modeled by a function. Drawing a scatter plot of the data can help you recognize the type of function that best models the data. You can then use one of the regression features on a graphing calculator to find and graph an equation of the best-fitting model.

EXAMPLE 1 *Choosing a Model for Data*

Use a graphing calculator to draw a scatter plot of the data. Then tell whether a *linear*, *quadratic*, or *exponential* function would best model the data.

a. Average total cost y of a year of college, where $x = 3$ represents 1993:

x	3	4	5	6	7	8	9	10
y	7931	8306	8800	9206	9588	10,076	10,444	10,876

b. Number of customers y in a restaurant each hour, where $x = 3$ represents 3 P.M.:

x	3	4	5	6	7	8	9	10
y	15	30	40	50	45	42	31	18

c. Population y of bacteria in a petri dish after x hours:

x	1	2	3	4	5	6
y	3	15	35	80	300	740

SOLUTION

a.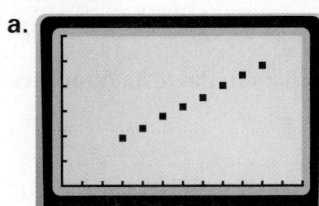

The points lie nearly in a straight line. This suggests a linear model.

b.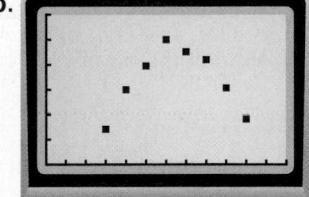

The points show a parabolic trend. This suggests a quadratic model.

c.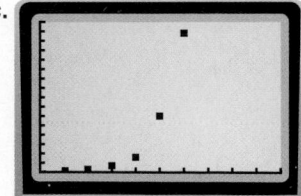

The points lie in a curve that seems to have an asymptote. This suggests an exponential model.

EXAMPLE 2 Finding a Model for Data

Find and graph an equation of the best-fitting model for each data set in Example 1.

SOLUTION

Perform the chosen type of regression on a graphing calculator. Round the values to three significant digits. Then graph the model with the data.

a.

 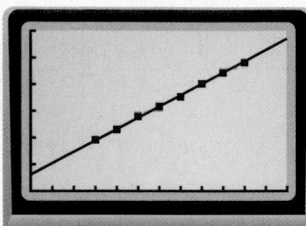

The linear regression equation is $y = 423x + 6660$.

b.

 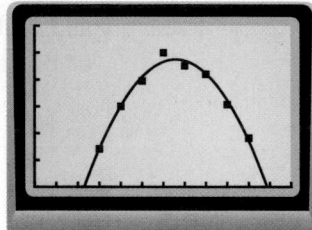

The quadratic regression equation is $y = -2.55x^2 + 33.5x - 62.7$.

c.

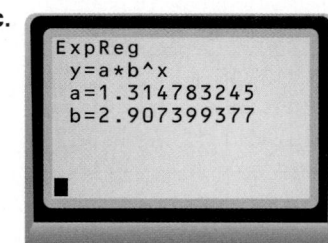 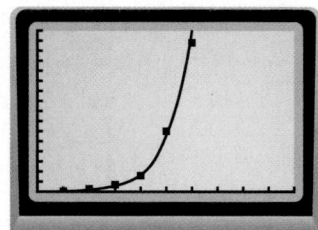

The exponential regression equation is $y = 1.31 \cdot 2.91^x$.

EXAMPLE 3 Using a Model to Make Predictions

Use the models in parts (a) and (b) of Example 2.

a. Predict the average total cost of a year of college in 2007.

b. Predict the number of customers in the restaurant at 6:30 P.M.

SOLUTION

a. Substituting 17 for x in the model $y = 423x + 6660$ gives $y = 13,851$. You can predict that in 2007 the average total cost of a year of college will be about $13,900.

b. Substituting 6.5 for x in the model $y = -2.55x^2 + 33.5x - 62.7$ gives $y = 47.3125$. You can estimate that at 6:30 P.M., there were 47 customers in the restaurant.

STUDENT HELP

▶ **Look Back**
For help with linear, quadratic, and exponential regression, see pp. 107, 308, and 510.

The **correlation coefficient** r for a set of paired data is a measure of how well a linear function models the data. If all of the graphed data pairs lie exactly on a line with a positive slope, the correlation coefficient is 1. If all of the graphed data pairs lie exactly on a line with a negative slope, the correlation coefficient is −1. If the graphed data pairs tend not to lie on any line, the correlation coefficient is close to 0.

EXAMPLE 4 *Estimating a Correlation Coefficient*

Estimate the correlation coefficient for the data.

a. 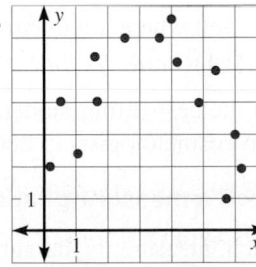 b. 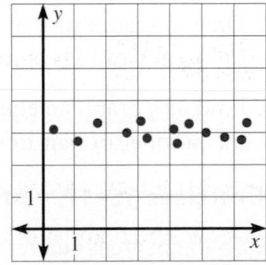 c.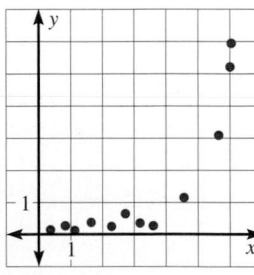

SOLUTION

a. The scatter plot shows a weak negative correlation, so r is between 0 and −1, but not too close to either one. An estimate is $r = -0.5$.
(Actual value: $r \approx -0.56153$)

b. The scatter plot does not seem to show a correlation, so an estimate is $r = 0$.
(Actual value: $r \approx 0.01926$)

c. The scatter plot shows a strong positive correlation. An estimate is $r = 0.9$.
(Actual value: $r \approx 0.96019$)

EXERCISES

Tell whether a *linear*, *quadratic*, or *exponential* function would best model the data.

1. 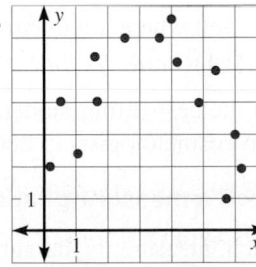 2. 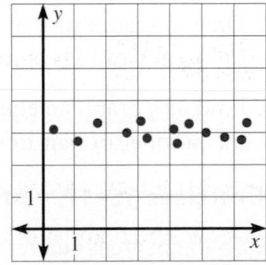 3.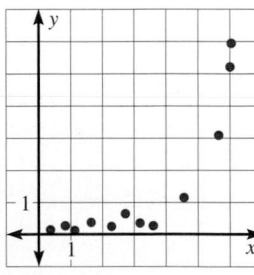

4. 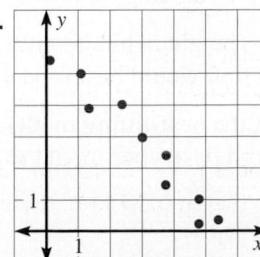 5. 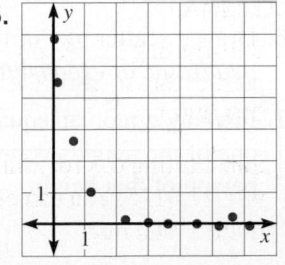 6.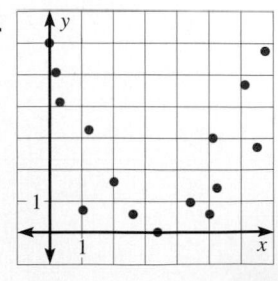

Use a graphing calculator to find an equation of the best-fitting model for each data set. Then graph the model with the data.

7.

x	3	4	5	6	7	8	9	10
y	1.6	3	6	13	26	51	102	205

8.

x	2	7	9	13	17	20	25
y	34	37	38	37	36	32	26

9.

x	4	8	12	16	20	24	28	32
y	24	28	30	32	36	39	43	45

Estimate the correlation coefficient for the data.

10. 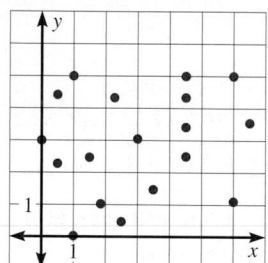   **11.** 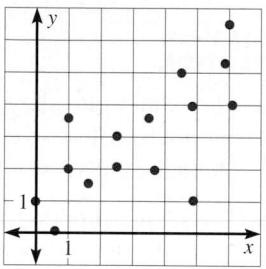   **12.**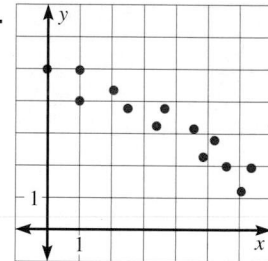

In Exercises 13 and 14, use the table below which gives the number *y* (in thousands) of hairdressers and cosmetologists in the United States from 1995 through 2000, where *x* = 5 represents 1995.

x	5	6	7	8	9	10
y	750	737	748	763	784	820

13. Draw a scatter plot of the data. Tell whether a *linear*, *quadratic*, or *exponential* function would best model the data.

14. Find and graph an equation of the best-fitting model. Use your model to predict the number of hairdressers and cosmetologists in 2005.

In Exercises 15–17, you will need a measuring tape.

15. To the nearest quarter of an inch, measure the heights and hip heights (the top of the hip to the floor) of 10 people standing barefoot.

16. Draw a scatter plot of the data (height *x*, hip height *y*). Tell whether a *linear*, *quadratic*, or *exponential* function would best model the data.

17. Find and graph an equation of the best-fitting model. Choose a height that is not one of the heights you measured. Use your model to predict the hip height of a person of that height.

Appendix 3

Collecting Data

GOAL *Use simulations and surveys to collect data; identify biased samples.*

One way to collect data about people or objects is by performing a *simulation*. A **simulation** is an experiment that models a real-life situation.

EXAMPLE 1 *Performing a Simulation*

A movie theater is giving away a prize card with every ticket purchase. Each card allows the holder to get one of six different concession stand items. If you are equally likely to receive each of the cards, how many tickets would you need to buy in order to receive at least one of each type of prize card?

SOLUTION

Perform a simulation by using a number cube. Let each number on the cube represent a different type of prize card.

1. Roll the number cube. Record the result in a tally chart.

2. Continue rolling and recording until you have at least one tally mark for each prize card.

3. Count the total number of tickets purchased.

▶ The results suggest that you would need to purchase about 16 tickets. Repeating the simulation and combining the results by calculating the mean of the numbers of tickets purchased would give a more accurate estimate.

Prize card	Number of tickets
1	I
2	JHT I
3	III
4	IIII
5	I
6	I

· · · · · · · · · ·

Another way to collect data is by conducting a survey. A **population** is a group of people or objects that you want information about. When it is difficult to survey an entire population, a **sample**, or part of the population, is surveyed. An **unbiased sample** is representative of the population you want information about. A **biased sample** overrepresents or underrepresents part of the population.

EXAMPLE 2 *Identifying a Biased Sample*

A survey is being conducted to decide on a yearbook theme. Students can choose from a sports theme or a music theme. Tell whether the given sample is *biased* or *unbiased*.

a. Students on the volleyball team

b. Students in line in the cafeteria

SOLUTION

a. The sample is biased because students on the volleyball team are more likely to want a sports theme.

b. The sample is unbiased because a wide range of students will be surveyed.

In a simulation, such as the one in Example 1, the results are more accurate if you increase the number of times you perform the simulation. Similarly, as the size of a sample increases, the sample will more accurately represent the population.

Because a sample is an approximation of an entire population, the results of a survey may not be exact. A **margin of sampling error** is a percent that indicates an interval that is likely, but not certain, to contain the exact result.

MARGIN OF SAMPLING ERROR

For a random sample of size n, taken from a large population, the margin of sampling error S can be approximated by this formula:

$$S \approx \frac{1}{\sqrt{n}}$$

EXAMPLE 3   *Finding a Margin of Sampling Error*

In a survey of 1600 voters, 51% said they voted for candidate A.

a. What is the margin of sampling error for the survey?

b. Give an interval that is likely to contain the exact percent of all voters who voted for candidate A.

SOLUTION

a. Use the formula for the margin of sampling error.

$$S \approx \frac{1}{\sqrt{n}}$$ **Write margin of sampling error formula.**

$$\approx \frac{1}{\sqrt{1600}}$$ **Substitute 1600 for n.**

$$\approx 0.025$$ **Simplify.**

▶ The margin of sampling error is about 2.5%.

b. To find the interval, take the percent of people in the sample who voted for candidate A, 51%, and subtract and add the margin of sampling error, 2.5%.

51% − 2.5% = 48.5%   51% + 2.5% = 53.5%

47% 48% 49% 50% 51% 52% 53% 54% 55%

▶ It is likely that the exact percent of all voters who voted for candidate A is between 48.5% and 53.5%.

EXAMPLE 4 *Using a Margin of Sampling Error*

In a school survey, 18% of students named root beer as their favorite soda. If the margin of sampling error is 5%, how many students were surveyed?

SOLUTION

To answer the question, use the formula for the margin of sampling error.

$$S \approx \frac{1}{\sqrt{n}}$$ **Write margin of sampling error formula.**

$$0.05 \approx \frac{1}{\sqrt{n}}$$ **Substitute 0.05 for *S*.**

$$0.05\sqrt{n} \approx 1$$ **Cross multiply.**

$$n \approx 400$$ **Solve for *n*.**

▶ There were about 400 students surveyed.

EXERCISES

In Exercises 1 and 2, refer to Example 1 on page 993.

1. Repeat the simulation in Example 1 an additional 9 times. Find the mean of the total number of tickets for the 10 simulation results.

2. How does your answer to Exercise 1 compare with the results of the simulation in Example 1? Which of the results do you think is a more accurate approximation of the number of tickets you would have to buy to receive at least one of each type of prize card? Explain.

A survey of people's favorite animals is being conducted. Tell whether the sample is *biased* or *unbiased*. Explain your reasoning.

3. People at a dog show

4. People at a pet store

5. Every twentieth person listed in the phone book

A survey of students' favorite school subjects is being conducted. Tell whether the sample is *biased* or *unbiased*. Explain your reasoning.

6. Students from the math club

7. Every fifth student that enters the school

8. Every other student in the French club

9. Suppose you want to conduct a survey to find out how many books the average student reads in one year. Describe a biased sample and an unbiased sample that you could survey.

10. Ask both samples that you named in Exercise 9 the following survey question: "How many books have you read in the past year?" Compare your results.

Find the margin of sampling error for a survey with the given sample size. Round your answer to the nearest tenth of a percent.

11. 330   **12.** 10,000   **13.** 575

14. 1000   **15.** 2250   **16.** 900

Find the smallest sample size required for the given margin of sampling error. Round your answer to the nearest whole number.

17. 4%   **18.** 6%   **19.** 3.5%

20. 2.8%   **21.** 5.2%   **22.** 1.5%

In Exercises 23–25, design and perform a simulation to answer the question. Perform the simulation at least 10 times. (*Hint:* You may want to consider using a coin, a number cube, or index cards in a paper bag.)

23. You are playing a game of chance in which you are equally likely to win or lose. About how many times would you have to play the game in order to win at least once and lose at least once?

24. A gumball machine contains pink, blue, and white gumballs. There are twice as many pink gumballs as blue gumballs, and three times as many blue gumballs as white gumballs. If gumballs are randomly dispensed from the machine, what is the experimental probability of getting a blue gumball?

25. A brand of cereal has one of five different colored toy cars in each box. There are equal numbers of the blue, yellow, silver, and green cars. There are twice as many red cars as there are blue cars. Assuming the cars are randomly placed in boxes of cereal, about how many boxes would you have to buy in order to obtain at least one of each kind of car?

In Exercises 26–28, a survey reported that 15%, or 315 students, prefer having gym class during the last period of the day.

26. How many students were surveyed?

27. What is the margin of sampling error? Round your answer to the nearest tenth of a percent.

28. Give an interval that is likely to contain the exact percent of all students who prefer to have gym class during the last period.

In Exercises 29–32, a survey reported that 235 of the 500 voters in a sample voted for candidate A and the rest voted for candidate B.

29. What percent of the voters in the sample voted for candidate A? What percent of the voters in the sample voted for candidate B?

30. What is the margin of sampling error? Round your answer to the nearest tenth of a percent.

31. For each candidate, give an interval that is likely to contain the exact percent of all voters who voted for the candidate.

32. Based on your answer from Exercise 31, can you determine which candidate won? Explain.

33. What happens to the margin of sampling error as sample size increases? Give an example to support your answer.

Displaying and Analyzing Data

GOAL *Display data in appropriate graphs; describe the effect of outliers.*

Different data displays emphasize different aspects of data. Think about what you want to emphasize about a set of data before you choose a display.

Type of Display	How Data is Shown
Circle graph	Shows data as parts of a whole
Histogram and bar graph	Compares data in different categories
Line graph	Shows data that change over time
Box-and-whisker plot	Shows the spread of data
Stem-and-leaf plot	Shows how data are clustered

EXAMPLE 1 *Choosing a Data Display*

For parts (a) and (b), use the table below which gives the areas of the Great Lakes.

Lake	Erie	Huron	Michigan	Ontario	Superior
Area (square miles)	9940	23,010	22,400	7540	31,820

a. Create a data display that compares the area of Lake Superior to the area of Lake Erie.

b. Create a data display that compares the combined areas of Lake Huron and Lake Michigan to the total area of the Great Lakes.

SOLUTION

a. Because you want to compare two categories of data, make a bar graph.

You can see that the area of Lake Superior is more than three times the area of Lake Erie.

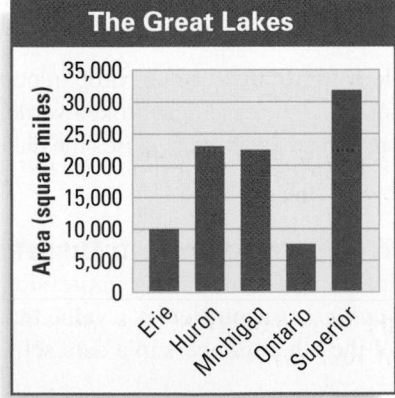

b. Because you want to compare a part to a whole, make a circle graph.

You can see that combined, Lake Huron and Lake Michigan make up about half of the total area of the Great Lakes.

MISLEADING GRAPHS The way that a graph is drawn can sometimes give a misleading impression of data. Watch out for things like broken scales, collapsed data categories, and the scaled dimensions of objects that represent categories of data.

EXAMPLE 2 *Identifying Misleading Graphs*

Tell how the graph could potentially be misleading.

a.

Type of music	Percent of sales
Classical	7%
Country	16%
Jazz	5%
Oldies	5%
Pop	13%
Rap	15%
R&B	12%
Rock	27%

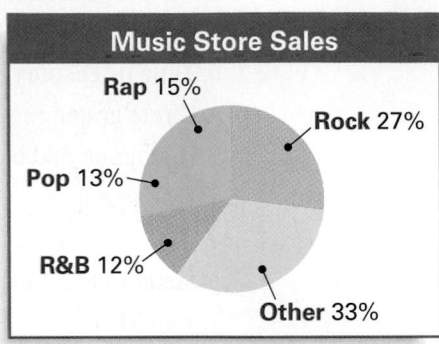

b.

Year	Population of Allentown, PA (thousands)
1970	110
1980	104
1990	105
2000	107

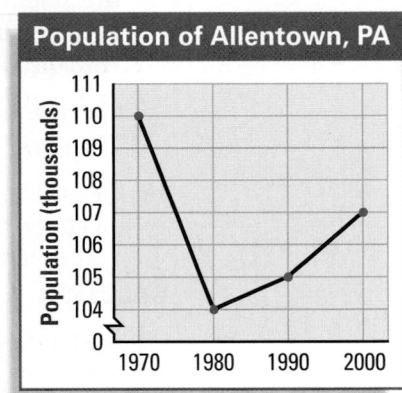

SOLUTION

a. It appears as if rap music is the second highest in music sales, but this is not really the case. The "other" category hides the fact that country music makes up 16% of sales.

b. It appears as if Allentown, PA, had a huge drop in population between 1970 and 1980, but this is not really the case. The broken vertical scale causes the numbers on the scale to be more spread out, which causes the data values to look further apart.

· · · · · · · · · ·

MEASURES OF CENTRAL TENDENCY AND DISPERSION Measures of central tendency and dispersion can give misleading impressions of a data set if the data set contains one or more *outliers*. An **outlier** is a value that is much greater than or much less than most of the other numbers in a data set.

EXAMPLE 3 *Examining the Effect of Outliers*

A city's high temperatures, in degrees Fahrenheit, during a 14-day period were 36, 37, 36, 34, 33, 30, 30, 32, 31, 31, 32, 32, 33, and 35.

  a. Calculate the mean, median, mode, range, and standard deviation of the data.

  b. On the 15th day, the temperature was 49°F. Calculate the new mean, median, mode, range, and standard deviation.

  c. Of the mean, median, and mode, which measure of central tendency is affected the most by the additional temperature? the least?

  d. What effect does an outlier have on range and standard deviation?

SOLUTION

  a. Mean: $\bar{x} = \dfrac{30 + 30 + \ldots + 37}{14} = \dfrac{462}{14} = 33$ **Median:** 32.5 **Mode:** 32 **Range:** 7

    Std. Dev.: $\sigma = \sqrt{\dfrac{(30-33)^2 + (30-33)^2 + \ldots + (37-33)^2}{14}} = \sqrt{\dfrac{68}{14}} \approx 2.2$

  b. Mean: $\bar{x} = \dfrac{30 + 30 + \ldots + 49}{15} = \dfrac{511}{15} \approx 34.1$ **Median:** 33 **Mode:** 32 **Range:** 19

    Std. Dev.: $\sigma \approx \sqrt{\dfrac{(30-34.1)^2 + (30-34.1)^2 + \ldots + (49-34.1)^2}{15}} = \sqrt{\dfrac{300.54}{15}} \approx 4.5$

  c. The mean is affected the most by the additional temperature. The mode is affected the least by the additional temperature.

  d. The range and the standard deviation increase with the addition of an outlier.

EXERCISES
• •

  1. The table below shows the number of farms in the United States from 1995 through 2000. Draw a data display that shows how the number of farms changed from year to year.

Year	1995	1996	1997	1998	1999	2000
Number of farms (thousands)	2196	2191	2191	2191	2192	2172

  2. The table below shows the cost of airmailing a 4-ounce letter from the United States to four different countries in 2000. Draw a data display that shows how the costs of mailing to Canada, Mexico, and Spain compare to the cost of mailing to Japan. The cost of mailing to which country is about half of the cost of mailing to Japan?

Country	Canada	Mexico	Spain	Japan
Cost (dollars)	$1.35	$1.65	$3.20	$3.50

In Exercises 3 and 4, use the following prices (in dollars) of CDs in a sale bin at a music store.

3.99, 10.99, 14.99, 4.99, 8.99, 15.99, 10.99, 5.99, 12.99, 8.99, 11.99, 17.99

3. Draw a data display that can be used to visually compare the number of CDs that cost between $1.00 and $5.99 to the number of CDs that cost between $16.00 and $20.99. How do these two categories compare?

4. Draw a data display that can be used to find the range of the upper half of the prices. Then find the range of the upper half of the prices.

Tell how the graph could potentially be misleading. Then redraw the graph so that it is not misleading.

5.

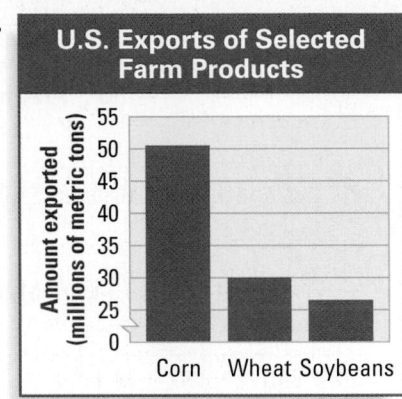

6.

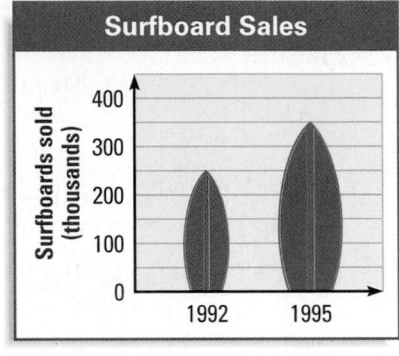

In Exercises 7–10, use the following data:

29, 64, 22, 25, 3, 35, 29, 22, 29, 32, 7

7. Calculate the mean, median, mode, range, and standard deviation.

8. Which data values would you consider to be outliers? Explain.

9. Calculate the mean, median, mode, range, and standard deviation for the data without the outliers you identified in Exercise 8.

10. Of the mean, median, or mode, which measure of central tendency would you use to describe the original set of data? Why?

In Exercises 11–14, use the following data:

x	3	1	2	6	2	7	4	5	6	3	7	5	4
y	6	6	7	3	5	8	4	4	2	4	2	5	6

STUDENT HELP

▶ **Look Back**
For help with linear regression, see p. 107.

11. Use a graphing calculator to draw a scatter plot of the data. Then use linear regression to find and graph an equation of the best-fitting line.

12. What are the outlier(s) of the data set? Remove the outlier(s) from the data set and redraw the scatter plot.

13. Find and graph an equation of the best-fitting line for the new data set.

14. Explain how removing the outlier(s) from the data set affected the equation of the best-fitting line.

Glossary

A

absolute value of a complex number (p. 275) If $z = a + bi$, then the absolute value of z, denoted $|z|$, is a nonnegative real number defined as $|z| = \sqrt{a^2 + b^2}$. Geometrically, the absolute value of a complex number is the number's distance from the origin in the complex plane.

absolute value of a real number (p. 50) The distance the number is from 0 on a number line. The absolute value of a number x is written $|x|$.

algebraic expression (p. 12) An expression with variables.

algebraic model (p. 33) A mathematical statement that represents a real-life problem.

amplitude (p. 831) The amplitude of the graph of a sine or cosine function is $\frac{1}{2}(M - m)$ where M is the maximum value of the function and m is the minimum value of the function.

angle of depression (p. 771) The angle from a horizontal line through an object A to a line connecting object A and a lower object B.

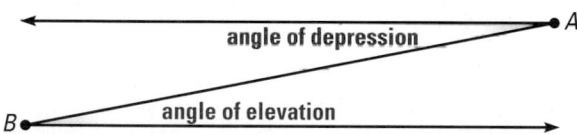

angle of elevation (p. 771) The angle from a horizontal line through an object B to a line connecting B and a higher object A.

arithmetic sequence (p. 659) A sequence in which the difference between consecutive terms is constant.

arithmetic series (p. 661) The expression formed by adding the terms of an arithmetic sequence.

asymptote (p. 465) A line that a graph approaches as you move away from the origin.

augmented matrix (p. 237) A matrix containing the coefficient matrix and the matrix of constants for a system of linear equations. The augmented matrix of the linear system $ax + by = e, cx + dy = f$ is $\begin{bmatrix} a & e \vdots d \\ b & c \vdots f \end{bmatrix}$.

axis of symmetry of a parabola (pp. 249, 595) The line perpendicular to the parabola's directrix and passing through its focus. In particular, the axis of symmetry is the vertical line through the vertex of the graph of a quadratic function.

B

base of an exponential function (p. 465) *See* exponential function.

base of a power (p. 11) The number in a power that is used as a factor. The base of the expression 2^5 is the number 2. *See also* exponent *and* power.

best-fitting quadratic model (p. 308) The model given by performing quadratic regression on a graphing calculator, which uses all the data points entered.

binomial (p. 256) An expression with two terms, such as $x + 3$.

binomial distribution (p. 739) The set of probabilities of all possible numbers of successes in a binomial experiment.

binomial experiment (p. 739) An experiment that satisfies the following three conditions. (1) There are n independent trials. (2) Each trial has only two possible outcomes, success and failure. (3) The probability of success is the same for each trial. This probability is denoted by p. The probability of failure is given by $1 - p$.

binomial theorem (p. 710) The binomial expansion of $(a + b)^n$ for any positive integer n is $(a + b)^n = {}_nC_0a^nb^0 + {}_nC_1a^{n-1}b^1 + {}_nC_2a^{n-2}b^2 + \cdots + {}_nC_na^0b^n = \sum_{r=0}^{n} {}_nC_r a^{n-r}b^r$.

box-and-whisker plot (p. 447) A type of statistical graph in which a "box" encloses the middle half of the data set and "whiskers" extend to the minimum and maximum data values. An example is shown.

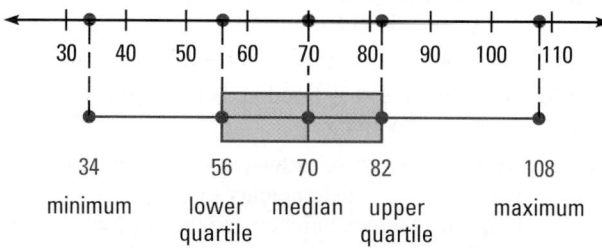

branches of a hyperbola (p. 540) Two symmetrical parts of a hyperbola. *See also* hyperbola.

C

center of a circle (p. 601) *See* circle.

center of a hyperbola (p. 615) The midpoint of the transverse axis of a hyperbola. *See also* hyperbola.

center of an ellipse (p. 609) The midpoint of the major axis of an ellipse. *See also* ellipse.

central angle of a sector (p. 779) An angle formed by two radii of a circle. *See also* sector.

circle (p. 601) The set of all points (x, y) that are equidistant from a fixed point, called the center of the circle. The distance r between the center of the circle and any point (x, y) on the circle is the radius.

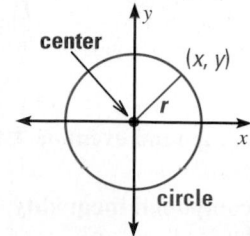

coefficient (p. 13) When a term is the product of a number and a power of a variable, such as $2x$ or $4x^3$, the number is the coefficient of the power. The coefficient of $2x$ is 2.

coefficient matrix (p. 216) The coefficient matrix of the linear system $ax + by = e$, $cx + dy = f$ is $\begin{bmatrix} a & b \\ c & d \end{bmatrix}$.

combination (p. 708) A selection of r objects from a group of n objects where the order is not important. The number of combinations of r objects taken from a group of n distinct objects is denoted $_nC_r$.

common difference (p. 659) The constant difference between consecutive terms of an arithmetic sequence.

common logarithm (p. 487) The logarithm with base 10. It is denoted by $\log_{10}$ or simply by log.

common ratio (p. 666) The constant ratio between consecutive terms of a geometric sequence.

complement (p. 726) The complement of event A, denoted A', consists of all outcomes that are not in A.

completing the square (p. 282) A process in which you write an expression of the form $x^2 + bx$ as the square of a binomial by adding the square of half the x-coefficient to the expression: $x^2 + bx + \left(\dfrac{b}{2}\right)^2 = \left(x + \dfrac{b}{2}\right)^2$. The process can be used to solve any quadratic equation.

complex conjugates (p. 274) Two complex numbers of the form $a + bi$ and $a - bi$. The product of complex conjugates is always a real number.

complex fraction (p. 564) A fraction that contains a fraction in its numerator or denominator.

complex number (p. 272) A number $a + bi$ where a and b are real numbers and i is the imaginary unit. The number a is the real part of the complex number, and the number bi is the imaginary part.

complex plane (p. 273) A coordinate plane where each point (a, b) represents a complex number $a + bi$. The complex plane has a horizontal real axis and a vertical imaginary axis.

composition (p. 416) The composition of the function f with the function g is $h(x) = f(g(x))$. The domain of h is the set of all x-values such that x is in the domain of g and $g(x)$ is in the domain of f.

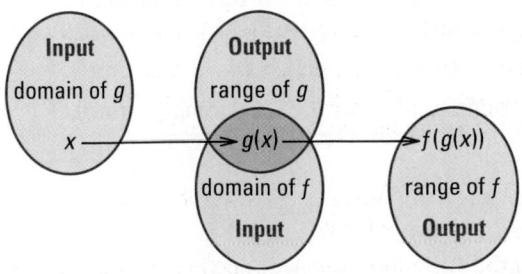

compound event (p. 724) The union or intersection of two events.

compound inequality (p. 43) Two simple inequalities joined by "and" or "or."

conditional probability (p. 732) The probability that event B will occur depending on whether event A has occurred. This is called the conditional probability of B given A and is written $P(B \mid A)$.

conic (p. 623) *See* conic section.

conic section (p. 623) A curve formed by the intersection of a plane and a double-napped cone. Examples include parabolas, circles, ellipses, and hyperbolas.

constant of variation (pp. 94, 534) The nonzero constant (usually denoted k) in a direct variation equation ($y = kx$), an inverse variation equation $\left(y = \dfrac{k}{x}\right)$, or a joint variation equation ($z = kxy$).

constant term (pp. 13, 329) A term that has no variable part, such as -4 or 2. *See also* polynomial function.

constraints (p. 163) In linear programming, the linear inequalities that form a system. *See also* linear programming.

coordinate (p. 3) The number that corresponds to a point on a number line.

coordinate plane (p. 67) A plane divided into four quadrants by the x-axis and the y-axis. It is used to plot ordered pairs of the form (x, y).

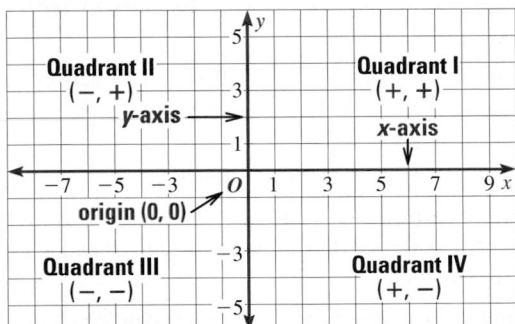

cosecant function (p. 769) If θ is an acute angle of a right triangle, the cosecant of θ is $\csc \theta = \dfrac{\text{hyp}}{\text{opp}}$ where *hyp* represents the length of the hypotenuse and *opp* represents the length of the side opposite θ.

cosine function (p. 769) If θ is an acute angle of a right triangle, the cosine of θ is $\cos \theta = \dfrac{\text{adj}}{\text{hyp}}$ where *adj* represents the length of the side adjacent to θ and *hyp* represents the length of the hypotenuse.

cotangent function (p. 769) If θ is an acute angle of a right triangle, the cotangent of θ is $\cot \theta = \dfrac{\text{adj}}{\text{opp}}$ where *adj* represents the length of the side adjacent to θ and *opp* represents the length of the side opposite θ.

coterminal angles (p. 777) Two angles in standard position with terminal sides that coincide.

co-vertices of an ellipse (p. 609) The points of intersection of an ellipse and the line perpendicular to the major axis at the center. *See also* ellipse.

Cramer's rule (p. 216) A method for solving a system of linear equations which uses determinants of matrices.

cross multiplying (p. 569) A method of solving a simple rational equation for which each side of the equation is a single rational expression. Equal products are formed by multiplying the numerator of each expression by the denominator of the other.

cubic function (p. 329) A polynomial function of degree 3.

cycle (p. 831) The shortest repeating portion of a periodic function.

D

decay factor (p. 476) The quantity $1 - r$ in the exponential decay model $y = a(1 - r)^t$ where a is the initial amount and r is the percent decrease expressed as a decimal.

degree of a polynomial (p. 329) *See* polynomial function.

dependent events (p. 732) Two events such that the occurrence of one affects the occurrence of the other. *See also* conditional probability.

dependent variable (p. 69) The output variable in an equation, which depends on the value of the input variable. *See also* independent variable.

determinant (p. 214) A real number associated with any square matrix A, denoted by det A or by $|A|$. The determinant of a 2×2 matrix is the difference of the products of the entries on the diagonals.

dimensions of a matrix (p. 199) The number m of rows of a matrix by the number n of columns of the matrix, written $m \times n$.

directrix of a parabola (p. 595) *See* parabola.

direct variation (p. 94) Two variables x and y show direct variation provided $y = kx$ where k is a nonzero constant.

discriminant of a general second-degree equation (p. 626) The expression $B^2 - 4AC$ for the equation $Ax^2 + Bxy + Cy^2 + Dx + Ey + F = 0$. Used to determine which type of conic the equation represents.

discriminant of a quadratic equation (p. 293) The expression $b^2 - 4ac$ for the quadratic equation $ax^2 + bx + c = 0$; also the expression under the radical sign in the quadratic formula. Used to find the number and type of solutions of a quadratic equation.

distance formula (p. 589) The distance d between the points (x_1, y_1) and (x_2, y_2) is $d = \sqrt{(x_2 - x_1)^2 + (y_2 - y_1)^2}$.

domain of a relation (p. 67) The set of input values for a relation.

E

eccentricity of a conic section (p. 639) The eccentricity of a hyperbola or an ellipse is $e = \frac{c}{a}$ where c is the distance from each focus to the center and a is the distance from each vertex to the center. The eccentricity of a parabola is $e = 1$. The eccentricity of a circle is $e = 0$.

ellipse (p. 609) The set of all points P such that the sum of the distances between P and two distinct fixed points, called foci, is a constant.

The ellipse shown below has a horizontal major axis.

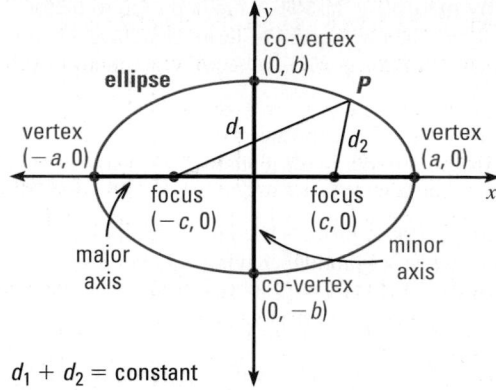

$d_1 + d_2 = $ constant

end behavior (p. 331) The behavior of the graph of a function as x approaches positive infinity or negative infinity.

entries of a matrix (p. 199) The numbers in a matrix.

equal matrices (p. 199) Matrices that have the same dimensions and equal entries in corresponding positions.

equation (p. 19) A statement in which two expressions are equal.

equation in two variables (p. 69) An equation such as $y = 2x - 7$.

equivalent algebraic expressions (p. 13) Expressions that have the same value for all values of their variable(s).

equivalent equations (p. 19) Equations that have the same solutions.

Euler number (p. 480) *See* natural base e.

expected value (p. 753) A collection of outcomes is partitioned into n events, no two of which have any outcomes in common. The probabilities of the n events occurring are $p_1, p_2, p_3, \ldots, p_n$ where $p_1 + p_2 + p_3 + \cdots + p_n = 1$. The values of the n events are $x_1, x_2, x_3, \ldots, x_n$. The expected value, V, of the collection of outcomes is the sum of the products of the events' probabilities and their values:
$$V = p_1x_1 + p_2x_2 + p_3x_3 + \cdots + p_nx_n.$$

experimental probability (p. 717) A calculation of the probability of an event based on performing an experiment, conducting a survey, or looking at the history of an event.

explicit rule (p. 681) A rule for a sequence that gives a_n as a function of the term's position number n in the sequence.

exponent (p. 11) The number in a power that represents the number of times the base is used as a factor. The exponent of the expression 2^5 is the number 5. *See also* base of a power *and* power.

exponential decay function (p. 474) A function of the form $f(x) = ab^x$ where $a > 0$ and $0 < b < 1$.

exponential function (p. 465) A function that involves the expression b^x where the base b is a positive number other than 1.

exponential growth function (p. 466) A function of the form $f(x) = ab^x$ where $a > 0$ and $b > 1$.

extraneous solution (p. 439) A solution of a transformed equation that is not a valid solution of the original equation.

factor by grouping (p. 346) A method used to factor some polynomials with pairs of terms that have a common monomial factor: $ra + rb + sa + sb = r(a + b) + s(a + b) = (r + s)(a + b)$.

factorial (p. 681) The expression $n!$ is read "n factorial" and represents the product of all integers from 1 to n. Example: $4! = 4 \cdot 3 \cdot 2 \cdot 1 = 24$.

factoring (p. 256) A process used to write a polynomial as a product of other polynomials having equal or lesser degree. Example: $x^2 + 8x + 15 = (x + 3)(x + 5)$.

fair game (p. 753) A game for which the expected value is 0.

feasible region (p. 163) In linear programming, the graph of the system of constraints. *See also* linear programming.

finite differences (p. 380) The first-order differences of a polynomial function $f(x)$ are found by subtracting function values for equally spaced x-values. The second-order differences are found by subtracting consecutive first-order differences. The third-order differences are found by subtracting consecutive second-order differences, and so on.

finite sequence (p. 651) A sequence that has a last term.

foci of a hyperbola (p. 615) *See* hyperbola.

foci of an ellipse (p. 609) *See* ellipse.

focus of a parabola (p. 595) *See* parabola.

frequency distribution (p. 448) A table that shows the frequencies for the intervals into which data are grouped.

frequency of a periodic function (p. 833) The reciprocal of the period. Frequency is the number of cycles per unit of time.

frequency of data values (p. 448) The number of data values in an interval. *See also* frequency distribution.

function (p. 67) A relation with exactly one output for each input.

function notation (p. 69) Use of the symbol $f(x)$ for the dependent variable of a function. For example, the linear function $y = mx + b$ can be written $f(x) = mx + b$.

function of two variables (p. 171) A relationship in which one variable depends on two other variables. A linear equation in x, y, and z can be written as a function of two variables by solving for z and then replacing z with $f(x, y)$.

general second-degree equation in x and y (p. 626) The form $Ax^2 + Bxy + Cy^2 + Dx + Ey + F = 0$.

geometric probability (p. 718) A type of probability found by calculating a ratio of two lengths, areas, or volumes.

geometric sequence (p. 666) A sequence in which the ratio of any term to the previous term is constant.

geometric series (p. 668) The expression formed by adding the terms of a geometric sequence.

graph of an equation in two variables (p. 69) The collection of all points (x, y) whose coordinates are solutions of the equation.

graph of an inequality in one variable (p. 41) All points on a real number line that correspond to solutions of the inequality.

graph of an inequality in two variables (p. 108) The graph of all solutions of the inequality.

graph of a real number (p. 3) The point on a number line that corresponds to a real number.

graph of a system of linear inequalities (p. 156) The graph of all solutions of the system.

growth factor (p. 467) The quantity $1 + r$ in the exponential growth model $y = a(1 + r)^t$ where a is the initial amount and r is the percent increase expressed as a decimal.

H

half-planes (p. 108) The two regions of a coordinate plane that are separated by the boundary line of an inequality. One region contains the points that are solutions of the inequality, and the other region contains the points that are not.

histogram (p. 448) A special type of bar graph in which data are grouped into intervals of equal width.

hyperbola (pp. 540, 615) The set of all points P such that the difference of the distances from P to two fixed points, called the foci, is constant. The hyperbola below has a horizontal transverse axis.

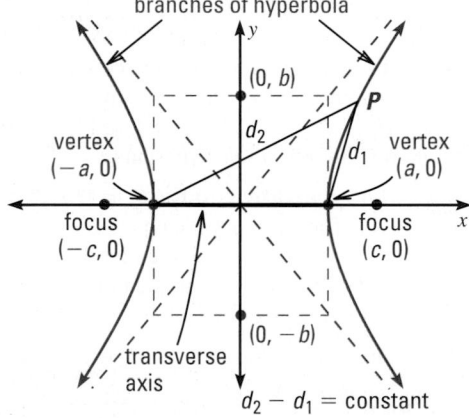

The graphs of rational functions of the form $y = \dfrac{a}{x - h} + k$ are hyperbolas.

hypothesis testing (p. 741) A three-step procedure from statistics for testing a claim. (1) State the hypothesis you are testing. The hypothesis should make a statement about some statistical measure (mean, standard deviation, or proportion) of a population. (2) Collect data from a random sample of the population and compute the statistical measure of the sample. (3) Assume that the hypothesis is true and calculate the resulting probability of obtaining the sample statistical measure or a more extreme sample statistical measure. If this probability is small, you should reject the hypothesis.

I

identity (p. 13) A statement such as $7x + 4x = 11x$ that equates two equivalent expressions.

identity matrix (p. 223) The $n \times n$ matrix that has 1's on the main diagonal and 0's elsewhere. The 2×2 identity matrix is $\begin{bmatrix} 1 & 0 \\ 0 & 1 \end{bmatrix}$.

imaginary number (p. 272) A complex number $a + bi$ where $b \neq 0$.

imaginary unit *i* (p. 272) The imaginary unit i is defined as $i = \sqrt{-1}$, so that $i^2 = -1$.

independent events (p. 730) Two events such that the occurrence of one has no effect on the occurrence of the other.

independent variable (p. 69) The input variable in an equation. *See also* dependent variable.

index of a radical (p. 401) The integer n (greater than 1) in the expression $\sqrt[n]{a}$.

infinite sequence (p. 651) A sequence that continues without stopping.

initial side of an angle (p. 776) You can generate any angle by fixing one ray, called the initial side, and rotating the other ray, called the terminal side, about the vertex.

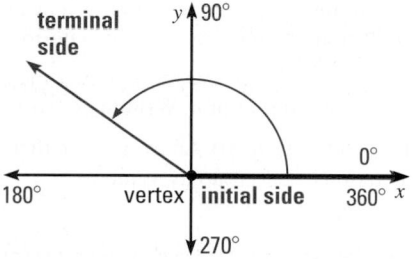

intercept form of a quadratic function (p. 250) The form $y = a(x - p)(x - q)$ where the x-intercepts of the graph are p and q and the axis of symmetry is halfway between $(p, 0)$ and $(q, 0)$.

inverse cosine function (p. 792) If $-1 \le a \le 1$, then the inverse cosine of a is $\cos^{-1} a = \theta$ where $\cos \theta = a$ and $0 \le \theta \le \pi$ (or $0° \le \theta \le 180°$).

inverse functions (p. 422) A relation and its inverse relation whenever both relations are functions. Functions f and g are inverses of each other provided $f(g(x)) = x$ and $g(f(x)) = x$. *See also* inverse relation.

inverse matrices (p. 223) Two $n \times n$ matrices are inverses of each other if their product (in both orders) is the $n \times n$ identity matrix. *See also* identity matrix.

inverse relation (p. 422) A relation that maps the output values of an original relation back to their original input values. The graph of an inverse relation is the reflection of the graph of the original relation, with $y = x$ as the line of reflection.

inverse sine function (p. 792) If $-1 \le a \le 1$, then the inverse sine of a is $\sin^{-1} a = \theta$ where $\sin \theta = a$ and $-\frac{\pi}{2} \le \theta \le \frac{\pi}{2}$ (or $-90° \le \theta \le 90°$).

inverse tangent function (p. 792) If a is any real number, then the inverse tangent of a is $\tan^{-1} a = \theta$ where $\tan \theta = a$ and $-\frac{\pi}{2} < \theta < \frac{\pi}{2}$ (or $-90° < \theta < 90°$).

inverse variation (p. 534) Two variables x and y show inverse variation provided $y = \frac{k}{x}$ where k is a nonzero constant.

J

joint variation (p. 536) A relationship that occurs when a quantity varies directly as the product of two or more other quantities. For instance, if $z = kxy$ where the constant $k \neq 0$, then z varies jointly with x and y.

L

law of cosines (p. 807) If $\triangle ABC$ has sides of length a, b, and c as shown below, then $a^2 = b^2 + c^2 - 2bc \cos A$, $b^2 = a^2 + c^2 - 2ac \cos B$, and $c^2 = a^2 + b^2 - 2ab \cos C$.

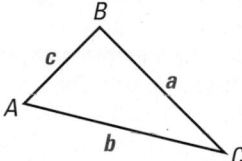

law of sines (p. 799) If $\triangle ABC$ has sides of length a, b, and c as shown above, then $\frac{\sin A}{a} = \frac{\sin B}{b} = \frac{\sin C}{c}$.

leading coefficient (p. 329) *See* polynomial function.

like radicals (p. 408) Two radical expressions that have the same index and the same radicand.

like terms (p. 13) Terms that have the same variable part, such as $3x^2$ and $-5x^2$.

linear equation in one variable (p. 19) An equation that can be written in the form $ax = b$ where a and b are constants and $a \neq 0$.

linear equation in three variables (p. 171) An equation of the form $ax + by + cz = d$ where x, y, and z are variables and a, b, and c are not all zero. The solution of a linear equation in three variables is an ordered triple (x, y, z), and the graph is a plane.

linear function (p. 69) A function of the form $y = mx + b$ where m and b are constants. The graph of a linear function is a line.

linear inequality in one variable (p. 41) An inequality such as $x \le 1$ or $2n - 3 > 9$. Note that an inequality symbol is placed between two expressions.

linear inequality in two variables (p. 108) An inequality that can be written in one of the following forms: $Ax + By < C$, $Ax + By \le C$, $Ax + By > C$, or $Ax + By \ge C$.

linear programming (p. 163) The process of optimizing a linear objective function subject to a system of linear inequalities called constraints. The graph of the system of constraints is called the feasible region.

local maximum (p. 374) The y-coordinate of a turning point of the graph of a function if the point is higher than all nearby points.

local minimum (p. 374) The y-coordinate of a turning point of the graph of a function if the point is lower than all nearby points.

logarithm of y with base b (p. 486) Let b and y be positive numbers with $b \neq 1$. The logarithm of y with base b is denoted by $\log_b y$ and is defined as $\log_b y = x$ if and only if $b^x = y$. The expression $\log_b y$ is read as "log base b of y."

logistic growth function (p. 517) A function of the form $y = \dfrac{c}{1 + ae^{-rx}}$ where a, c, and r are all positive constants. Used to model real-life quantities whose growth levels off because the rate of growth changes—from an increasing growth rate to a decreasing growth rate.

lower quartile (p. 447) The median of the lower half of a data set. *See also* box-and-whisker plot.

major axis of an ellipse (p. 609) The line segment joining the vertices of an ellipse. *See also* ellipse.

mathematical model (p. 12) A mathematical representation of a real-life situation.

matrix (p. 199) A rectangular arrangement of numbers in rows and columns.

matrix of constants (p. 230) The matrix of constants of the linear system $ax + by = e$, $cx + dy = f$ is $\begin{bmatrix} e \\ f \end{bmatrix}$.

matrix of variables (p. 230) The matrix of variables of the linear system $ax + by = e$, $cx + dy = f$ is $\begin{bmatrix} x \\ y \end{bmatrix}$.

mean (p. 445) The sum of n numbers divided by n. Also called *average*.

measures of central tendency (p. 445) Three commonly used statistics: the mean, the median, and the mode of a set of numbers.

measures of dispersion (p. 446) Commonly used statistics that tell you how spread out the data are. They include the range and the standard deviation.

median (p. 445) The middle number when n numbers are written in order. (If n is even, the median is the mean of the two middle numbers.)

midpoint formula (p. 590) The midpoint of the line segment joining $A(x_1, y_1)$ and $B(x_2, y_2)$ is $M\left(\dfrac{x_1 + x_2}{2}, \dfrac{y_1 + y_2}{2}\right)$. Each coordinate of M is the mean of the corresponding coordinates of A and B.

minor axis of an ellipse (p. 609) The line segment joining the co-vertices of an ellipse. *See also* ellipse.

mode (p. 445) The number or numbers that occur most frequently in a set of n numbers. There may be one mode, no mode, or more than one mode.

monomial (p. 257) An expression with one term, such as $7x$.

mutually exclusive events (p. 724) Events A and B are mutually exclusive if the intersection of A and B is empty.

natural base e (p. 480) An irrational number defined as follows: As n approaches $+\infty$, the value of $\left(1 + \dfrac{1}{n}\right)^n$ approaches $e \approx 2.718281828459$.

natural logarithm (p. 487) The logarithm with base e. It can be denoted by $\log_e$, but it is more often denoted by ln.

negative correlation (p. 100) The relationship between paired data when y tends to decrease as x increases, as shown by a scatter plot where the plotted points generally fall from left to right.

normal curve (p. 746) A smooth, symmetrical, bell-shaped curve that can model normal distributions and approximate some binomial distributions. *See also* normal distribution *and* binomial distribution.

normal distribution (p. 746) A distribution for which the mean and the standard deviation determine the following areas under a normal curve. (1) The total area under the curve is 1. (2) 68% of the area lies within 1 standard deviation of the mean. (3) 95% of the area lies within 2 standard deviations of the mean. (4) 99.7% of the area lies within 3 standard deviations of the mean. *See also* normal curve.

nth root of a (p. 401) For an integer n greater than 1, if $b^n = a$, then b is an nth root of a. Written as $\sqrt[n]{a}$.

numerical expression (p. 11) An expression that consists of numbers, operations, and grouping symbols.

objective function (p. 163) In linear programming, the linear function that is optimized. *See also* linear programming.

octants (p. 170) *See* three-dimensional coordinate system.

opposite (p. 5) The opposite, or additive inverse, of any number a is $-a$.

optimization (p. 163) A process in which you find the maximum or minimum value of some variable quantity. One type of optimization process is linear programming.

ordered pair (p. 67) A pair of numbers of the form (x, y) that represents a point in the coordinate plane.

ordered triple (p. 170) A set of three numbers of the form (x, y, z) that represents a point in space. *See also* three-dimensional coordinate system.

order of operations (p. 11) A set of rules that gives the order in which operations should be performed when evaluating expressions.

origin of a coordinate plane (p. 67) The point $(0, 0)$ where the x-axis and y-axis intersect on a coordinate plane. *See also* coordinate plane.

origin of a real number line (p. 3) The point labeled O on a real number line.

P.

parabola (pp. 249, 595) The set of all points equidistant from a point called the focus and a line called the directrix. The focus lies on the axis of symmetry, and the directrix is perpendicular to the axis of symmetry.

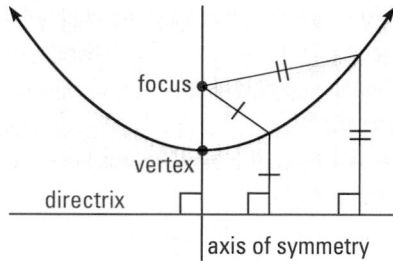

The graph of a quadratic function $y = ax^2 + bx + c$ is a parabola.

parallel lines (p. 77) Two lines in a plane that do not intersect.

parameter (p. 813) A variable, usually denoted t, upon which two other variables depend. *See also* parametric equations.

parametric equations (p. 813) Equations that express two variables in terms of a third variable, called the parameter.

Pascal's triangle (p. 710) An arrangement of the values of $_nC_r$ in a triangular pattern in which each row corresponds to a value of n. Each number other than 1 in Pascal's triangle is the sum of the two numbers directly above it.

$_0C_0$						1					
$_1C_0$	$_1C_1$					1		1			
$_2C_0$	$_2C_1$	$_2C_2$				1	2	1			
$_3C_0$	$_3C_1$	$_3C_2$	$_3C_3$			1	3	3	1		
$_4C_0$	$_4C_1$	$_4C_2$	$_4C_3$	$_4C_4$		1	4	6	4	1	
$_5C_0$	$_5C_1$	$_5C_2$	$_5C_3$	$_5C_4$	$_5C_5$	1	5	10	10	5	1

period (p. 831) The horizontal length of each cycle of a periodic function.

periodic function (p. 831) A function whose graph has a repeating pattern that continues indefinitely.

permutation (p. 703) An ordering of objects. The number of permutations of r objects taken from a group of n distinct objects is denoted $_nP_r$.

perpendicular lines (p. 77) Two lines in a plane that intersect to form a right angle.

piecewise function (p. 114) A function represented by a combination of equations, each corresponding to a part of the domain. Example: $f(x) = \begin{cases} 2x - 1, & \text{if } x \le 1 \\ 3x + 1, & \text{if } x > 1 \end{cases}$

polynomial function (p. 329) A function of the form $f(x) = a_nx^n + a_{n-1}x^{n-1} + \cdots + a_1x + a_0$ where $a_n \ne 0$, $a_0, a_1, a_2, \ldots a_n$ are real numbers, and the exponents are all whole numbers. For this polynomial function, a_n is the leading coefficient, a_0 is the constant term, and n is the degree.

polynomial long division (p. 352) A method used to divide polynomials similar to the way you divide numbers.

positive correlation (p. 100) The relationship between paired data when y tends to increase as x increases, as shown by a scatter plot where the plotted points generally rise from left to right.

power (p. 11) An expression such as 2^5, which represents $2 \cdot 2 \cdot 2 \cdot 2 \cdot 2 = 32$.

power function (p. 415) A function of the form $y = ax^b$ where a is a real number and b is a rational number.

probability (p. 716) A number between 0 and 1 that indicates the likelihood an event will occur.

pure imaginary number (p. 272) A complex number $a + bi$ where $a = 0$ and $b \ne 0$.

Q.

quadrantal angle (p. 785) An angle in standard position with its terminal side on an axis. Examples: $0°$, $90°$, $180°$, and $270°$.

quadrants (p. 67) The four regions that result when the x-axis and y-axis divide a coordinate plane. *See also* coordinate plane.

quadratic equation in one variable (p. 257) An equation that can be written in the form $ax^2 + bx + c = 0$ where $a \ne 0$.

quadratic form (p. 346) The form $au^2 + bu + c$ where u is any expression in x.

quadratic formula (p. 291) A formula that gives the solutions of any quadratic equation. If a, b, and c are real numbers with $a \ne 0$, the solutions of $ax^2 + bx + c = 0$ are $x = \dfrac{-b \pm \sqrt{b^2 - 4ac}}{2a}$.

quadratic function (p. 249) A function of the form $y = ax^2 + bx + c$ where $a \ne 0$.

quadratic inequality in one variable (p. 301) An inequality of the form $ax^2 + bx + c < 0$, $ax^2 + bx + c > 0$, $ax^2 + bx + c \le 0$, or $ax^2 + bx + c \ge 0$.

quadratic inequality in two variables (p. 299) An inequality of the form $y < ax^2 + bx + c$, $y > ax^2 + bx + c$, $y \le ax^2 + bx + c$, or $y \ge ax^2 + bx + c$.

quartic function (p. 329) A polynomial function of degree 4.

R.

radian (p. 777) In a circle with radius r and center at the origin, one radian is the measure of an angle in standard position whose terminal side intercepts an arc of length r.

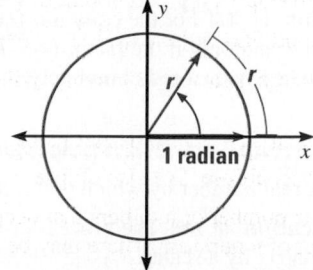

radical (p. 264) An expression of the form $\sqrt{s}$ or $\sqrt[n]{s}$ where s is a number or expression.

radical function (p. 431) A function that contains a radical, such as $y = \sqrt{x}$ or $y = \sqrt[3]{x}$.

radical symbol (p. 264) The symbol $\sqrt{}$ or $\sqrt[n]{}$, which denotes a square root or nth root, respectively.

radicand (p. 264) The number or expression beneath a radical sign. The radicand of $\sqrt{5}$ is 5 and the radicand of $\sqrt[3]{7x}$ is $7x$.

radius of a circle (p. 601) The distance from the center of a circle to a point on the circle, or the line segment that connects the center of a circle to a point on the circle. *See also* circle.

range of a relation (p. 67) The set of output values for a relation.

range of data values (p. 446) The difference between the greatest and least data values.

rational function (p. 540) A function of the form $f(x) = \dfrac{p(x)}{q(x)}$ where $p(x)$ and $q(x)$ are polynomials and $q(x) \neq 0$.

rationalizing the denominator (p. 265) The process of eliminating a radical in the denominator of a fraction by multiplying both the numerator and the denominator by an appropriate radical.

reciprocal (p. 5) The reciprocal, or multiplicative inverse, of any nonzero real number a is $\dfrac{1}{a}$.

recursive rule (p. 681) A rule for a sequence that gives the beginning term or terms of a sequence and then a recursive equation that tells how a_n is related to one or more preceding terms.

reference angle (p. 785) If θ is an angle in standard position, its reference angle is the acute angle θ' formed by the terminal side of θ and the x-axis. An example is shown.

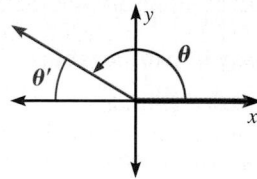

relation (p. 67) A mapping, or pairing, of input values with output values.

relatively no correlation (p. 100) The relationship between paired data when a scatter plot of the data shows no linear pattern.

repeated solution (p. 366) For the equation $f(x) = 0$, k is a repeated solution if and only if the factor $(x - k)$ has degree greater than 1 when f is factored completely.

S ....

scalar (p. 200) A real number by which you multiply a matrix.

scalar multiplication (p. 200) The process of multiplying each entry in a matrix by a scalar.

scatter plot (p. 100) A graph of ordered pairs used to determine whether there is a relationship between paired data.

scientific notation (p. 325) A number is expressed in scientific notation if it is in the form $c \times 10^n$ where $1 \leq c < 10$ and n is an integer.

secant function (p. 769) If θ is an acute angle of a right triangle, the secant of θ is $\sec \theta = \dfrac{\text{hyp}}{\text{adj}}$ where *hyp* represents the length of the hypotenuse and *adj* represents the length of the side adjacent to θ.

sector (p. 779) A region of a circle that is bounded by two radii and an arc of the circle.

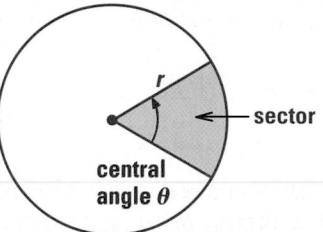

sequence (p. 651) A function whose domain is a set of consecutive integers. The domain gives the relative position of each term of the sequence: 1st, 2nd, 3rd, and so on. The range gives the terms of the sequence.

series (p. 653) The expression that results when the terms of a sequence are added.

sigma notation (p. 653) *See* summation notation.

simplest form of a radical (p. 408) A radical expression after you apply the properties of radicals, remove any perfect nth powers, and rationalize any denominators.

simplified form of a rational expression (p. 554) A rational expression in which the numerator and denominator have no common factors (other than ± 1).

sine function (p. 769) If θ is an acute angle of a right triangle, the sine of θ is $\sin \theta = \dfrac{\text{opp}}{\text{hyp}}$ where *opp* represents the length of the side opposite θ and *hyp* represents the length of the hypotenuse.

skewed distribution (p. 740) A distribution that is not symmetric. *See also* symmetric distribution.

slope (p. 75) The ratio of vertical change (the rise) to horizontal change (the run) for a nonvertical line. The slope of a nonvertical line passing through the points (x_1, y_1) and (x_2, y_2) is $m = \dfrac{y_2 - y_1}{x_2 - x_1} = \dfrac{\text{rise}}{\text{run}}$.

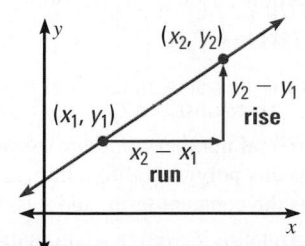

slope-intercept form (p. 82) A linear equation written in the form $y = mx + b$ where m is the slope and b is the y-intercept of the line.

solution of an equation in one variable (p. 19) A number that, when substituted for the variable, makes the equation a true statement.

solution of an equation in two variables (p. 69) An ordered pair (x, y) that makes the equation a true statement when the values of x and y are substituted in the equation.

solution of an inequality in one variable (p. 41) A value of the variable that makes the inequality true.

solution of an inequality in two variables (p. 108) An ordered pair (x, y) that, when x and y are substituted in the inequality, gives a true statement.

solution of a system of linear equations (p. 139) An ordered pair (x, y) that satisfies each equation of the system.

solution of a system of linear inequalities (p. 156) An ordered pair that is a solution of each inequality in the system.

solution of a system of three linear equations (p. 177) An ordered triple (x, y, z) that is a solution of all three equations of the system.

solving a right triangle (p. 770) Finding all missing side lengths and angle measures of a right triangle.

square root (p. 264) A number r is a square root of a number s if $r^2 = s$.

standard deviation (p. 446) The typical difference (or *deviation*) between the mean and a data value. The standard deviation σ of $x_1, x_2, \ldots, x_n$ is

$$\sigma = \sqrt{\frac{(x_1 - \bar{x})^2 + (x_2 - \bar{x})^2 + \cdots + (x_n - \bar{x})^2}{n}}.$$

standard form of a complex number (p. 272) The form $a + bi$ where a and b are real numbers and i is the imaginary unit.

standard form of a linear equation (p. 84) A linear equation written in the form $Ax + By = C$ where A and B are not both zero.

standard form of a polynomial function (p. 329) The form of a polynomial function when the terms are written in descending order of exponents from left to right.

standard form of a quadratic equation (p. 257) The form $ax^2 + bx + c = 0$ where $a \neq 0$.

standard form of a quadratic function (p. 250) The form $y = ax^2 + bx + c$ where $a \neq 0$.

standard form of the equation of a circle (pp. 601, 623) If a circle has center (h, k) and radius r, its equation is $(x - h)^2 + (y - k)^2 = r^2$. *See also* circle.

standard form of the equation of a hyperbola (p. 615) If a hyperbola has center (h, k), its equation is as follows:
$\frac{(x - h)^2}{a^2} - \frac{(y - k)^2}{b^2} = 1$ (horizontal transverse axis) or
$\frac{(y - k)^2}{a^2} - \frac{(x - h)^2}{b^2} = 1$ (vertical transverse axis).
See also hyperbola.

standard form of the equation of an ellipse (p. 609) If an ellipse has center (h, k) and major and minor axes of lengths $2a$ and $2b$, where $a > b > 0$, its equation is as follows:
$\frac{(x - h)^2}{a^2} + \frac{(y - k)^2}{b^2} = 1$ (horizontal major axis) or
$\frac{(x - h)^2}{b^2} + \frac{(y - k)^2}{a^2} = 1$ (vertical major axis). *See also* ellipse.

standard form of the equation of a parabola (pp. 596, 623) If a parabola has vertex (h, k), its equation is as follows:
$(y - k)^2 = 4p(x - h)$ (horizontal axis) or
$(x - h)^2 = 4p(y - k)$ (vertical axis).

standard position of an angle (p. 776) In a coordinate plane, the position of an angle whose vertex is at the origin and whose initial side is the positive x-axis. *See also* initial side of an angle.

statistics (p. 445) Numerical values used to summarize and compare sets of data.

step function (p. 115) A piecewise function whose graph resembles a set of stair steps. *See also* piecewise function.

summation notation (p. 653) Notation for a series that uses the uppercase Greek letter sigma, Σ. For example, you can write $3 + 6 + 9 + 12 + 15 = \sum_{i=1}^{5} 3i$ where i is the index of summation, 1 is the lower limit of summation, and 5 is the upper limit of summation.

symmetric distribution (p. 740) A distribution in which the left half of the histogram representing the distribution is a mirror image of the right half.

synthetic division (p. 353) A method used to divide a polynomial by an expression of the form $x - k$.

synthetic substitution (p. 330) A method used to evaluate a polynomial function.

system of linear inequalities in two variables (p. 156) A system made up of two linear inequalities in two variables. *See also* linear inequality in two variables.

system of three linear equations (p. 177) A system made up of three linear equations in three variables. *See also* linear equation in three variables.

system of two linear equations (p. 139) Two equations of the form $Ax + By = C$ and $Dx + Ey = F$ where x and y are variables, A and B are not both zero, and D and E are not both zero.

T

tangent function (p. 769) If θ is an acute angle of a right triangle, the tangent of θ is $\tan \theta = \frac{\text{opp}}{\text{adj}}$ where *opp* represents the length of the side opposite θ and *adj* represents the length of the side adjacent to θ.

terminal side of an angle (p. 776) *See* initial side of an angle.

terms of an expression (p. 13) The parts of an algebraic expression that are added together. The terms of $2x + 3$ are $2x$ and 3. The terms of $2x - 3 = 2x + (-3)$ are $2x$ and -3.

terms of a sequence (p. 651) For a sequence of numbers, the numbers in the sequence are called terms. *See also* sequence.

theoretical probability (p. 716) When all outcomes are equally likely, the theoretical probability that an event A will occur is $P(A) = \dfrac{\text{number of outcomes in } A}{\text{total number of outcomes}}$. The theoretical probability of an event is often simply called the probability of the event.

three-dimensional coordinate system (p. 170) A coordinate system determined by three mutually perpendicular axes. When taken pairwise, these axes form three coordinate planes that divide space into eight parts called octants. A point in space is represented by an ordered triple of the form (x, y, z). The ordered triples $(-5, 3, 4)$, $(0, 0, 0)$, and $(2, -2, -3)$ are plotted below.

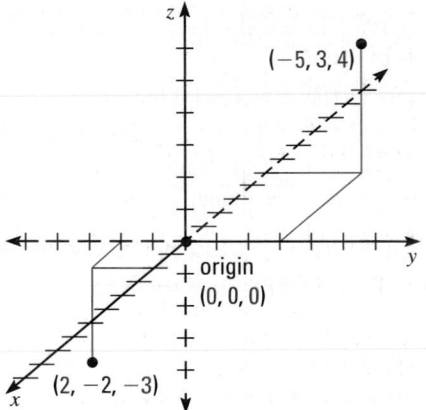

transverse axis of a hyperbola (p. 615) The line segment joining the vertices of a hyperbola. *See also* hyperbola.

trigonometric identity (p. 848) A trigonometric equation that is true for all domain values.

trinomial (p. 256) An expression with three terms, such as $x^2 + 8x + 15$.

U

upper quartile (p. 447) The median of the upper half of a data set. *See also* box-and-whisker plot.

V

value of an expression (p. 12) The result when the variables in an algebraic expression are replaced by numbers and the expression is simplified.

value of a variable (p. 12) Any number used to replace a variable.

variable (p. 12) A letter that is used to represent one or more numbers.

verbal model (p. 33) A word equation that represents a real-life problem.

vertex form of a quadratic function (p. 250) The form $y = a(x - h)^2 + k$ where the vertex of the graph is (h, k) and the axis of symmetry is $x = h$.

vertex of an absolute value graph (p. 122) The corner point of the graph of an absolute value function.

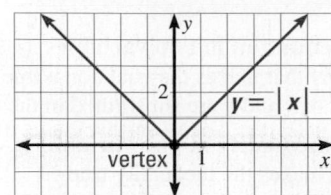

vertex of a parabola (pp. 249, 595) The point on a parabola that lies on the axis of symmetry. This point is the lowest or highest point on a parabola with a vertical axis of symmetry and the leftmost or rightmost point on a parabola with a horizontal axis of symmetry. *See also* parabola.

vertices of a hyperbola (p. 615) The points of intersection of a hyperbola and the line through the foci of the hyperbola. *See also* hyperbola.

vertices of an ellipse (p. 609) The points of intersection of an ellipse and the line through the foci of the ellipse. *See also* ellipse.

X

x-axis (p. 67) The horizontal axis in the coordinate plane. *See also* coordinate plane.

x-coordinate (p. 67) The first number in an ordered pair.

x-intercept of a line (p. 84) The x-coordinate of the point where a line intersects the x-axis. Given an equation of the line, it is the value of x when $y = 0$.

Y

y-axis (p. 67) The vertical axis in the coordinate plane. *See also* coordinate plane.

y-coordinate (p. 67) The second number in an ordered pair.

y-intercept (p. 82) If the graph of an equation intersects the y-axis at the point $(0, b)$, then the number b is the y-intercept of the graph. Given an equation of the graph, it is the value of y when $x = 0$.

Z

z-axis (p. 170) A vertical line through the origin and perpendicular to the xy-coordinate plane in a three-dimensional coordinate system. *See also* three-dimensional coordinate system.

zero of a function (p. 354) A number k is a zero of a function f if $f(k) = 0$.

English-to-Spanish Glossary

absolute value of a complex number (p. 275) **valor absoluto de un número complejo** Si $z = a + bi$, entonces el valor absoluto de z, escrito $|z|$, es un número no negativo definido $|z| = \sqrt{a^2 + b^2}$. Geométricamente, el valor absoluto de un número complejo es la distancia del número desde el origen en el plano complejo.

absolute value of a real number (p. 50) **valor absoluto de un número real** La distancia a la que está el número de 0 en una recta numérica. El valor absoluto del número x se escribe $|x|$.

algebraic expression (p. 12) **expresión algebraica** Una expresión con variables.

algebraic model (p. 33) **modelo algebraico** Un enunciado matemático que representa un problema de la vida real.

amplitude (p. 831) **amplitud** La amplitud de la gráfica de una función seno o coseno es $\frac{1}{2}(M - m)$, donde M es el máximo valor de la función y m es el mínimo valor de la función.

angle of depression (p. 771) **ángulo de depresión** El ángulo desde una recta horizontal a través de un objeto A hasta una recta que conecta el objeto A con un objeto B más abajo.

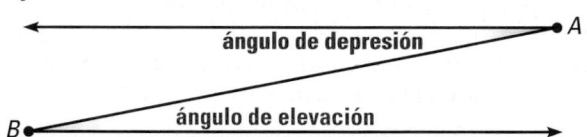

angle of elevation (p. 771) **ángulo de elevación** El ángulo desde una recta horizontal a través de un objeto B que conecta B con un objeto más arriba A.

arithmetic sequence (p. 659) **progresión aritmética** Una progresión en la que la diferencia entre términos consecutivos es constante.

arithmetic series (p. 661) **serie aritmética** La expresión formada al sumar los términos de una progresión aritmética.

asymptote (p. 465) **asíntota** Una recta a la que una gráfica se aproxima al alejarse del origen.

augmented matrix (p. 237) **matriz aumentada** Una matriz que contiene la matriz coeficiente y la matriz de constantes para un sistema de ecuaciones lineales. La matriz aumentada del sistema lineal

$ax + by = e, cx + dy = f$ es $\begin{bmatrix} a & e & \vdots & d \\ b & c & \vdots & f \end{bmatrix}$.

axis of symmetry of a parabola (pp. 249, 595) **eje de simetría de una parábola** La recta perpendicular a la directriz de la parábola que pasa por el foco. Específicamente, el eje de simetría es la recta vertical que atraviesa el vértice de la gráfica de una función cuadrática.

base of an exponential function (p. 465) **base de una función exponencial** *Ver* exponential function / función exponencial.

base of a power (p. 11) **base de una potencia** El número de una potencia que se usa como factor. La base de la expresión 2^5 es el número 2. *Ver también* exponent / exponente *y* power / potencia.

best-fitting quadratic model (p. 308) **modelo cuadrático que produce el mejor ajuste** El modelo que resulta de realizar una regresión cuadrática en una calculadora de gráficas y que contenga todos los puntos de datos entrados.

binomial (p. 256) **binomio** Una expresión con dos términos como $x + 3$.

binomial distribution (p. 739) **distribución binomial** El conjunto de probabilidades de todos los números posibles de casos favorables en un experimento binomial.

binomial experiment (p. 739) **experimento binomial** Un experimento que satisface las siguientes tres condiciones. (1) Hay n pruebas independientes. (2) Cada prueba tiene sólo dos casos posibles, favorable o desfavorable. (3) La probabilidad de favorable es igual para cada prueba. Esta probabilidad viene dada por p. La probabilidad de desfavorable viene dada por $1 - p$.

binomial theorem (p. 710) **teorema binomial** La expansión binomial de $(a + b)^n$ para cualquier número entero n es $(a + b)^n = {}_nC_0a^nb^0 + {}_nC_1a^{n-1}b^1 + {}_nC_2a^{n-2}b^2 + \cdots + {}_nC_na^0b^n = \sum_{r=0}^{n} {}_nC_ra^{n-r}b^r$.

box-and-whisker plot (p. 447) **gráfica de frecuencias acumuladas** Un tipo de gráfica de estadísticas en la que una caja encierra la mitad central del conjunto de datos y los segmentos se extienden hasta los valores mínimo y máximo. Se muestra un ejemplo.

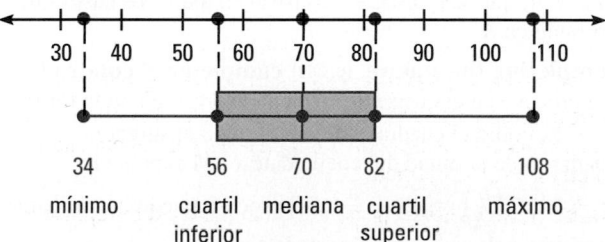

branches of a hyperbola (p. 540) **ramas de una hipérbola** Dos partes simétricas de una hipérbola. *Ver también* hyperbola / hipérbola.

C

center of a circle (p. 601) **centro de un círculo** *Ver* circle / círculo.

center of a hyperbola (p. 615) **centro de una hipérbola** El punto medio del eje transversal de una hipérbola. *Ver también* hyperbola / hipérbola.

center of an ellipse (p. 609) **centro de una elipse** El punto medio del eje mayor de una elipse. *Ver también* ellipse / elipse.

central angle of a sector (p. 779) **ángulo central de un sector** Un ángulo formado por dos radios de un círculo. *Ver también* sector / sector.

circle (p. 601) **círculo** El conjunto de todos los puntos (x, y) que están equidistantes de un punto fijo llamado centro del círculo. La distancia r entre el centro del círculo y cualquier punto (x, y) del círculo es el radio.

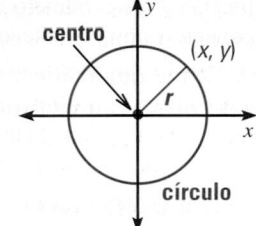

coefficient (p. 13) **coeficiente** Cuando un término es el producto de un número y una potencia de una variable, tal como $2x$ ó $4x^3$, el número es el coeficiente de la potencia. El coeficiente de $2x$ es 2.

coefficient matrix (p. 216) **matriz coeficiente** La matriz coeficiente del sistema lineal $ax + by = e$,
$cx + dy = f$ es $\begin{bmatrix} a & b \\ c & d \end{bmatrix}$.

combination (p. 708) **combinación** Una selección de r objetos de un grupo de n objetos donde el orden no importa. El número de combinaciones de r objetos tomados de un grupo de n objetos distintos se escribe $_nC_r$.

common difference (p. 659) **diferencia común** La diferencia constante entre términos consecutivos de una progresión aritmética.

common logarithm (p. 487) **logaritmo común** El logaritmo con base 10. Se escribe $\log_{10}$ o simplemente log.

common ratio (p. 666) **razón común** La razón constante entre términos consecutivos de una progresión geométrica.

complement (p. 726) **complemento** El complemento de suceso A, que se escribe A', consiste en todos los casos que no están en A.

completing the square (p. 282) **completar el cuadrado** Un proceso en el que se escribe una expresión con la forma $x^2 + bx$ como el cuadrado de un binomio al sumar el cuadrado de la mitad del coeficiente x a la expresión: $x^2 + bx + \left(\dfrac{b}{2}\right)^2 = \left(x + \dfrac{b}{2}\right)^2$. El proceso puede usarse para resolver cualquier ecuación cuadrática.

complex conjugates (p. 274) **números complejos conjugados** Dos números complejos de la forma $a + bi$ y $a - bi$. El producto de números complejos conjugados es siempre un número real.

complex fraction (p. 564) **fracción complejo** Una fracción que contiene una fracción en su numerador o denominador.

complex number (p. 272) **número complejo** Un número $a + bi$ donde a y b son números reales e i es la unidad imaginaria. El número a es la parte real del número complejo y el número bi es la parte imaginaria.

complex plane (p. 273) **plano complejo** Un plano de coordenadas donde cada punto (a, b) representa un número complejo $a + bi$. El plano complejo tiene una recta horizontal real y un eje vertical imaginario.

composition (p. 416) **composición** La composición de la función f con la función g es $h(x) = f(g(x))$. El dominio de h es el conjunto de todos los valores de x siendo que x está en el dominio de g y $g(x)$ está en el dominio de f.

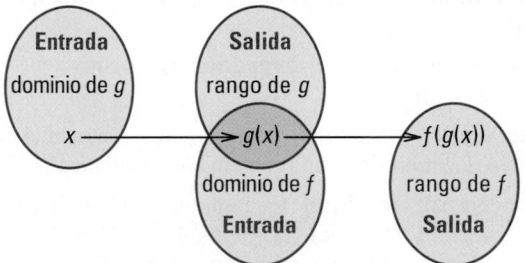

compound event (p. 724) **suceso compuesto** La unión o intersección de dos sucesos.

compound inequality (p. 43) **desigualdad compuesta** Dos desigualdades simples conectadas por "y" u "o".

conditional probability (p. 732) **probabilidad condicional** La probabilidad de que suceso B ocurra según si suceso A ocurre. Esto se llama la probabilidad condicional de B dado A. Se escribe $P(B \mid A)$.

conic (p. 623) **cónico** *Ver* conic section / sección cónica.

conic section (p. 623) **sección cónica** Una curva formada por la intersección de un plano y un cono doble. Ejemplos incluyen parábolas, círculos, elipses e hipérbolas.

constant of variation (pp. 94, 534) **constante de variación** La constante distinta a cero (usualmente denominada k) en una ecuación de variación directa ($y = kx$), en una ecuación de variación inversa $\left(y = \dfrac{k}{x}\right)$, o en una ecuación de variación conjunta ($z = kxy$).

constant term (pp. 13, 329) **término constante** Un término que no tiene una parte variable, tal como -4 ó 2. *Ver también* polynomial function / función polinómica.

constraints (p. 163) **restricciones** En la programación lineal, las desigualdades lineales que forman un sistema. *Ver también* linear programming / programación lineal.

coordinate (p. 3) **coordenada** El número que corresponde a un punto de una recta numérica.

coordinate plane (p. 67) **plano de coordenadas** Un plano dividido en cuatro cuadrantes por los ejes de x y de y. Se usa para marcar pares ordenados de la forma (x, y).

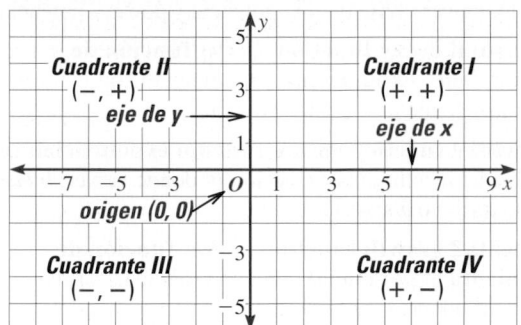

cosecant function (p. 769) **función cosecante** Si θ es un ángulo agudo de un triángulo rectángulo, la cosecante de θ es $\csc \theta = \dfrac{\text{hip}}{\text{op}}$, donde *hip* representa la longitud de la hipotenusa y *op* representa la longitud del lado opuesto a θ.

cosine function (p. 769) **función coseno** Si θ es un ángulo agudo de un triángulo rectángulo, el coseno de θ es $\cos \theta = \dfrac{\text{ady}}{\text{hip}}$, donde *ady* representa la longitud del lado adyacente a θ e *hip* representa la longitud de la hipotenusa.

cotangent function (p. 769) **función cotangente** Si θ es un ángulo agudo de un triángulo rectángulo, la cotangente de θ es $\cot \theta = \dfrac{\text{ady}}{\text{op}}$, donde *ady* representa la longitud del lado adyacente a θ y *op* representa la longitud del lado opuesto a θ.

coterminal angles (p. 777) **ángulos coterminales** Dos ángulos en posición normal con lados terminales que coinciden.

co-vertices of an ellipse (p. 609) **intersecciones de una elipse** Los puntos de intersección de una elipse y la recta perpendicular al eje mayor en su centro. *Ver también* ellipse / elipse.

Cramer's rule (p. 216) **regla de Cramer** Un método para resolver un sistema de ecuaciones lineales que usa las determinantes de matrices.

cross multiplying (p. 569) **efectuar los productos cruzados** Un método de resolver una ecuación racional simple en la que cada lado de la ecuación es una sola expresión racional. Se forman productos iguales al multiplicar el numerador de cada expresión por el denominador de la otra.

cubic function (p. 329) **función cúbica** Una función polinómica de grado 3.

cycle (p. 831) **ciclo** La parte más corta que se repite de una función periódica.

D

decay factor (p. 476) **factor de decrecimiento** La cantidad $1 - r$ del modelo de decrecimiento exponencial $y = a(1 - r)^t$, donde a es la cantidad inicial y r es el porcentaje de decrecimiento expresado en forma decimal.

degree of a polynomial (p. 329) **grado de un polinomio** *Ver* polynomial function / función polinómica.

dependent events (p. 732) **sucesos dependientes** Dos sucesos tales que la ocurrencia de uno afecta la ocurrencia del otro. *Ver también* conditional probability / probabilidad condicional.

dependent variable (p. 69) **variable dependiente** La variable de salida de una ecuación, que depende del valor de la variable de entrada. *Ver también* independent variable / variable independiente.

determinant (p. 214) **determinante** Un número real asociado con cualquier matriz cuadrada A, escrito det A o $|A|$. La determinante de una matriz 2×2 es la diferencia de los productos de las entradas de las diagonales.

dimensions of a matrix (p. 199) **dimensiones de una matriz** El número m de filas de una matriz por el número n de columnas de la matriz, escrito $m \times n$.

directrix of a parabola (p. 595) **directriz de una parábola** *Ver* parabola / parábola.

direct variation (p. 94) **variación directa** Dos variables x e y muestran variación directa con tal de que $y = kx$ donde k es una constante distinta a cero.

discriminant of a general second-degree equation (p. 626) **discriminante de una ecuación general de segundo grado** La expresión $B^2 - 4AC$ para la ecuación $Ax^2 + Bxy + Cy^2 + Dx + Ey + F = 0$. Se usa para determinar qué tipo de cónico representa la ecuación.

discriminant of a quadratic equation (p. 293) **discriminante de una ecuación cuadrática** La expresión $b^2 - 4ac$ para la ecuación cuadrática $ax^2 + bx + c = 0$; también la expresión bajo el signo radical de la fórmula cuadrática. Se usa para hallar el número y tipo de soluciones de una ecuación cuadrática.

distance formula (p. 589) **fórmula de la distancia** La distancia d entre los puntos (x_1, y_1) y (x_2, y_2) es $d = \sqrt{(x_2 - x_1)^2 + (y_2 - y_1)^2}$.

domain of a relation (p. 67) **dominio de una relación** El conjunto de valores de entrada para una relación.

E

eccentricity of a conic section (p. 639) **excentricidad de una sección cónica** La excentricidad de una hipérbola o elipse es $e = \dfrac{c}{a}$ donde c es la distancia de cada foco al centro y a es la distancia de cada vértice al centro. La excentricidad de una parábola es $e = 1$. La excentricidad de un círculo es $e = 0$.

ellipse (p. 609) **elipse** El conjunto de todos los puntos P en el que la suma de las distancias entre P y dos puntos fijos distantes, llamados focos, es una constante.

La elipse que se muestra abajo tiene un eje mayor horizontal.

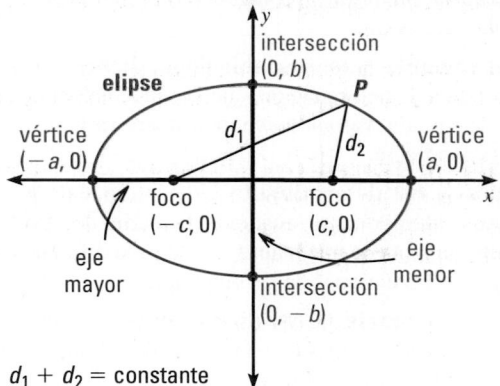

$d_1 + d_2 = $ constante

end behavior (p. 331) **comportamiento de una función** El comportamiento de la gráfica de una función al aproximarse x a la infinidad positiva o la infinidad negativa.

entries of a matrix (p. 199) **entradas de una matriz** Los números de una matriz.

equal matrices (p. 199) **matrices iguales** Matrices que tienen las mismas dimensiones y entradas iguales en posiciones correspondientes.

equation (p. 19) **ecuación** Un enunciado en el que dos expresiones son iguales.

equation in two variables (p. 69) **ecuación de dos variables** Una ecuación como $y = 2x - 7$.

equivalent algebraic expressions (p. 13) **expresiones algebraicas equivalentes** Expresiones que tienen el mismo valor para todos los valores de su variable o de sus variables.

equivalent equations (p. 19) **ecuaciones equivalentes** Ecuaciones que tienen las mismas soluciones.

Euler number (p. 480) **número de Euler** *Ver* natural base e / base natural e.

expected value (p. 753) **valor anticipado** Un conjunto de casos se divide en n sucesos, de los cuales no hay dos con casos en común. Las probabilidades de que ocurran los n sucesos son $p_1, p_2, p_3, \ldots, p_n$ donde $p_1 + p_2 + p_3 + \cdots + p_n = 1$. Los valores de los n sucesos son $x_1, x_2, x_3, \ldots, x_n$. El valor anticipado, V, del conjunto de casos es la suma de los productos de las probabilidades de los sucesos y sus valores:
$$V = p_1 x_1 + p_2 x_2 + p_3 x_3 + \cdots + p_n x_n.$$

experimental probability (p. 717) **probabilidad experimental** Un cálculo de la probabilidad de un suceso basado en realizar un experimento, llevar a cabo una encuesta o examinar la historia de un suceso.

explicit rule (p. 681) **regla explícita** Una regla para una progresión que da a_n como la función del número n de la posición del término en la secuencia.

exponent (p. 11) **exponente** El número de una potencia que representa el número de veces que se usa la base como factor. El exponente de la expresión 2^5 es el número 5. *Ver también* base of a power / base de una potencia y power / potencia.

exponential decay function (p. 474) **función de decrecimiento exponencial** Una función con la forma $f(x) = ab^x$ donde $a > 0$ y $0 < b < 1$.

exponential function (p. 465) **función exponencial** Una función que involucra la expresión b^x donde la base b es un número positivo distinto a 1.

exponential growth function (p. 466) **función de crecimiento exponencial** Una función de la forma $f(x) = ab^x$ donde $a > 0$ y $b > 1$.

extraneous solution (p. 439) **solución extraña** Una solución de una ecuación transformada que no es una solución válida de la ecuación original.

F

factor by grouping (p. 346) **factorizar por grupos** Un método usado para factorizar algunos polinomios con pares de términos que tienen un factor monomial común:
$$ra + rb + sa + sb = r(a + b) + s(a + b) = (r + s)(a + b).$$

factorial (p. 681) **factorial** La expresión $n!$ se lee "ene factorial" y representa el producto de todos los números enteros de 1 a n. Ejemplo: $4! = 4 \cdot 3 \cdot 2 \cdot 1 = 24$.

factoring (p. 256) **factorizar** Un proceso que se usa para escribir un polinomio como el producto de otros polinomios de igual o menor grado.

Ejemplo: $x^2 + 8x + 15 = (x + 3)(x + 5)$.

fair game (p. 753) **juego justo** Un juego en el que el valor anticipado es 0.

feasible region (p. 163) **región factible** En la programación lineal, la gráfica del sistema de restricciones. *Ver también* linear programming / programación lineal.

finite differences (p. 380) **diferencias finitas** Las diferencias de primer orden de una función polinómica $f(x)$ se hallan al restar valores de función para los valores de x equidistantes. Las diferencias de segundo orden se hallan al restar diferencias consecutivas de primer orden. Las diferencias de tercer orden se hallan al restar diferencias consecutivas de segundo orden, y así sucesivamente.

finite sequence (p. 651) **progresión finita** Una secuencia que tiene un término final.

foci of a hyperbola (p. 615) **focos de una hipérbola** *Ver* hyperbola / hipérbola.

foci of an ellipse (p. 609) **focos de una elipse** *Ver* ellipse / elipse.

focus of a parabola (p. 595) **foco de una parábola** *Ver* parabola / parábola.

frequency distribution (p. 448) **distribución de frecuencias** Una tabla que muestra las frecuencias de los intervalos en los que se agrupan los datos.

frequency of a periodic function (p. 833) **frecuencia de una función periódica** El recíproco del período. La frecuencia es el número de ciclos por unidad de tiempo.

frequency of data values (p. 448) **frecuencia de los valores** El número de valores de un intervalo. *Ver también* frequency distribution / distribución de frecuencias.

function (p. 67) **función** Una relación con exactamente una salida por cada entrada.

function notation (p. 69) **notación de función** El uso del símbolo $f(x)$ para la variable dependiente de una función. Por ejemplo, la función lineal $y = mx + b$ puede escribirse $f(x) = mx + b$.

function of two variables (p. 171) **función de dos variables** Una relación en la que una variable depende de dos variables más. Una ecuación lineal en x, y y z puede escribirse como una función de dos variables al resolver para z y luego reemplazar z por $f(x, y)$.

general second-degree equation in x and y (p. 626) **ecuación general de segundo grado en x e y** La forma $Ax^2 + Bxy + Cy^2 + Dx + Ey + F = 0$.

geometric probability (p. 718) **probabilidad geométrica** Un tipo de probabilidad hallada al calcular una razón de dos longitudes o áreas o volúmenes.

geometric sequence (p. 666) **progresión geométrica** Una progresión en la que la razón de cualquier término con el término anterior es constante.

geometric series (p. 668) **serie geométrica** La expresión que se forma al sumar los términos de una progresión geométrica.

graph of an equation in two variables (p. 69) **gráfica de una ecuación de dos variables** El conjunto de todos los puntos (x, y) cuyas coordenadas son soluciones de la ecuación.

graph of an inequality in one variable (p. 41) **gráfica de una desigualdad de una variable** Todos los puntos de una recta numérica real que corresponden a soluciones de la desigualdad.

graph of an inequality in two variables (p. 108) **gráfica de una desigualdad de dos variables** La gráfica de todas las soluciones de la desigualdad.

graph of a real number (p. 3) **gráfica de un número real** El punto de una recta numérica que corresponde a un número real.

graph of a system of linear inequalities (p. 156) **gráfica de un sistema de desigualdades lineales** La gráfica de todas las soluciones del sistema.

growth factor (p. 467) **factor de crecimiento** La cantidad $1 + r$ del modelo de crecimiento exponencial $y = a(1 + r)^t$ donde a es la cantidad inicial y r es el porcentaje de crecimiento expresado en forma decimal.

half-planes (p. 108) **semiplanos** Las dos regiones de un plano de coordenadas que están separadas por la recta limítrofe de una desigualdad. Una región contiene los puntos que son soluciones de la desigualdad y la otra región contiene los puntos que no lo son.

histogram (p. 448) **histograma** Un tipo de gráfica de barras especial en la que los datos se agrupan en intervalos de igual ancho.

hyperbola (pp. 540, 615) **hipérbola** El conjunto de todos los puntos P de manera que la diferencia de las distancias desde P a dos puntos fijos, llamados focos, es constante. La hipérbola que se muestra abajo tiene un eje transversal horizontal.

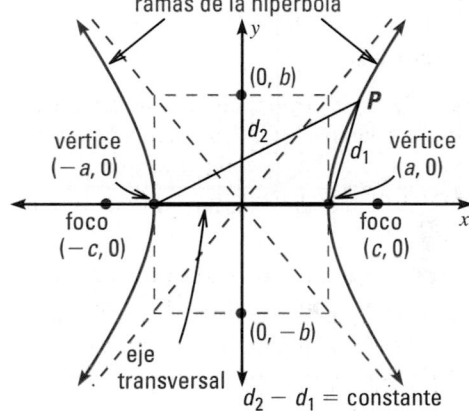

Las gráficas de funciones racionales de la forma $y = \dfrac{a}{x - h} + k$ son hipérbolas.

hypothesis testing (p. 741) **pruebas de hipótesis** Un procedimiento de la estadística de tres pasos para comprobar una aseveración. (1) Enunciar la hipótesis que se está probando. La hipótesis debe hacer un aseveración sobre alguna medida estadística (media, desviación estándar o proporción) de una población. (2) Reunir datos de una muestra aleatoria de la población y calcular la medida estadística de la muestra. (3) Asumir que la hipótesis es verdadera y calcular la probabilidad resultante de obtener la medida estadística de muestra o una medida más extrema. Si esta probabilidad es pequeña, se debe rechazar la hipótesis.

identity (p. 13) **identidad** Un enunciado como $7x + 4x = 11x$ que hace iguales dos expresiones equivalentes.

identity matrix (p. 223) **matriz de identidad** La matriz $n \times n$ que tiene los 1 en la diagonal principal y en otras partes los 0. La matriz 2×2 es $\begin{bmatrix} 1 & 0 \\ 0 & 1 \end{bmatrix}$.

imaginary number (p. 272) **número imaginario** Un número complejo $a + bi$ donde $b \neq 0$.

imaginary unit i (p. 272) **unidad imaginaria i** La unidad imaginaria i se define como $i = \sqrt{-1}$, de manera que $i^2 = -1$.

independent events (p. 730) **sucesos independientes** Dos sucesos que ocurren sin que la ocurrencia de uno afecte la ocurrencia del otro.

independent variable (p. 69) **variable independiente** La variable de entrada de una ecuación. *Ver también* dependent variable / variable dependiente.

index of a radical (p. 401) **índice de un radical** El número entero n (mayor que 1) de la expresión $\sqrt[n]{a}$.

infinite sequence (p. 651) **progresión infinita** Una progresión que sigue sin parar.

initial side of an angle (p. 776) **lado inicial de un ángulo** Se puede generar cualquier ángulo al fijar un rayo, llamado lado inicial, y rotar el otro rayo, llamado lado terminal, alrededor del vértice.

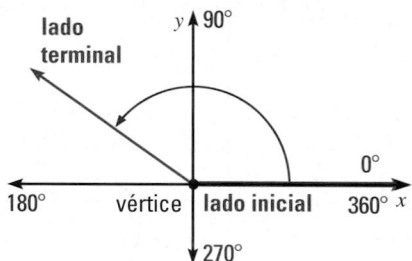

intercept form of a quadratic function (p. 250) **forma intercepto de una función cuadrática** La forma $y = a(x - p)(x - q)$ donde los interceptos en x son p y q y el eje de simetría está a mitad de camino entre $(p, 0)$ y $(q, 0)$.

inverse cosine function (p. 792) **función inversa de coseno** Si $-1 \leq a \leq 1$, entonces el coseno inverso de a es $\cos^{-1} a = \theta$ donde $\cos \theta = a$ y $0 \leq \theta \leq \pi$ (ó $0° \leq \theta \leq 180°$).

inverse functions (p. 422) **funciones inversas** Una relación y su relación inversa siempre que las dos relaciones sean funciones. Las funciones f y g son inversas una de otra con tal de que $f(g(x)) = x$ y $g(f(x)) = x$. *Ver también* inverse relation / relación inversa.

inverse matrices (p. 223) **matrices inversas** Dos matrices $n \times n$ son inversas una de otra si su producto (en ambos órdenes) es la matriz de identidad $n \times n$. *Ver también* identity matrix / matriz de identidad.

inverse relation (p. 422) **relación inversa** Una relación que transforma los valores de salida de una relación original en sus valores de entrada iniciales. La gráfica de una relación inversa es la reflexión de la gráfica de la relación original, con $y = x$ como eje de reflexión.

inverse sine function (p. 792) **función inversa de seno** Si $-1 \leq a \leq 1$, entonces el seno inverso de a es $\operatorname{sen}^{-1} a = \theta$ donde $\operatorname{sen} \theta = a$ y $-\frac{\pi}{2} \leq \theta \leq \frac{\pi}{2}$ (ó $-90° \leq \theta \leq 90°$).

inverse tangent function (p. 792) **función inversa de tangente** Si a es cualquier número real, entonces la tangente inversa de a es $\tan^{-1} a = \theta$ donde $\tan \theta = a$ y $-\frac{\pi}{2} < \theta < \frac{\pi}{2}$ (ó $-90° < \theta < 90°$).

inverse variation (p. 534) **variación inversa** Dos variables x e y muestran variación inversa con tal de que $y = \frac{k}{x}$ donde k es una constante distinta a cero.

joint variation (p. 536) **variación conjunta** Una relación que ocurre cuando una cantidad varía directamente como el producto de dos o más cantidades adicionales. Por ejemplo, si $z = kxy$ donde la constante $k \neq 0$, entonces z varía conjuntamente con x e y.

law of cosines (p. 807) **ley de los cosenos** Si $\triangle ABC$ tiene lados de longitud a, b y c, como se muestra, entonces
$a^2 = b^2 + c^2 - 2bc \cos A$,
$b^2 = a^2 + c^2 - 2ac \cos B$, y
$c^2 = a^2 + b^2 - 2ab \cos C$.

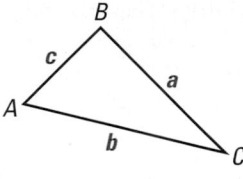

law of sines (p. 799) **ley de los senos** Si $\triangle ABC$ tiene lados de longitud a, b y c, como se muestra abajo, entonces $\frac{\operatorname{sen} A}{a} = \frac{\operatorname{sen} B}{b} = \frac{\operatorname{sen} C}{c}$.

leading coefficient (p. 329) **coeficiente inicial** *Ver* polynomial function / función polinómica.

like radicals (p. 408) **radicales semejantes** Dos expresiones radicales que tienen el mismo índice y el mismo radicando.

like terms (p. 13) **términos semejantes** Términos que tienen la misma parte variable, como $3x^2 y - 5x^2$.

linear equation in one variable (p. 19) **ecuación lineal de una variable** Una ecuación que puede escribirse en la forma $ax = b$ donde a y b son constantes y $a \neq 0$.

linear equation in three variables (p. 171) **ecuación lineal de tres variables** Una ecuación de la forma $ax + by + cz = d$ donde x, y y z son variables y a, b y c no son todos cero. La solución de una ecuación lineal de tres variables es una terna ordenada (x, y, z), y la gráfica es un plano.

linear function (p. 69) **función lineal** Una función de la forma $y = mx + b$ donde m y b son constantes. La gráfica de una función lineal es una recta.

linear inequality in one variable (p. 41) **desigualdad lineal de una variable** Una desigualdad como $x \leq 1$ ó $2n - 3 > 9$. Nótese que se coloca un signo de desigualdad entre las dos expresiones.

linear inequality in two variables (p. 108) **desigualdad lineal de dos variables** Una desigualdad que puede escribirse en una de las formas siguientes: $Ax + By < C$, $Ax + By \leq C$, $Ax + By > C$, o $Ax + By \geq C$.

linear programming (p. 163) **programación lineal** El proceso de optimizar una función objetiva lineal que está sujeto a un sistema de desigualdades lineales llamadas restricciones. La gráfica del sistema de restricciones se llama región factible.

local maximum (p. 374) **máximo local** La coordenada *y* del punto donde se curva la gráfica de una función si este punto se encuentra más alto que todos los puntos cercanos.

local minimum (p. 374) **mínimo local** La coordenada *y* del punto donde se curva la gráfica de una función si este punto se encuentra más bajo que todos los puntos cercanos.

logarithm of *y* with base *b* (p. 486) **logaritmo de *y* con base *b*** Sean *b* e *y* números positivos con $b \neq 1$. El logaritmo de *y* con base *b* se escribe $\log_b y$ y se define como $\log_b y = x$, si y sólo si, $b^x = y$. La expresión $\log_b y$ se lee "la base *b* logarítmica de *y*".

logistic growth function (p. 517) **función de crecimiento logístico** Una función de la forma $y = \dfrac{c}{1 + ae^{-rx}}$ donde *a*, *c* y *r* son constantes positivas. Se usa para representar cantidades de la vida real cuyo crecimiento se estabiliza debido a que la tasa de crecimiento cambia de una tasa de crecimiento a una tasa de decrecimiento.

lower quartile (p. 447) **cuartil inferior** La mediana de la mitad inferior de un conjunto de datos. *Ver también* box-and-whisker plot / gráfica de frecuencias acumuladas.

M

major axis of an ellipse (p. 609) **eje mayor de una elipse** El segmento de recta que une los vértices de una elipse. *Ver también* ellipse / elipse.

mathematical model (p. 12) **modelo matemático** Una representación matemática de una situación de la vida real.

matrix (p. 199) **matriz** Un arreglo rectangular de números en filas y columnas.

matrix of constants (p. 230) **matriz de constantes** La matriz de constantes del sistema lineal $ax + by = e, cx + dy = f$ es $\begin{bmatrix} e \\ f \end{bmatrix}$.

matrix of variables (p. 230) **matriz de variables** La matriz de variables del sistema lineal $ax + by = e, cx + dy = f$ es $\begin{bmatrix} x \\ y \end{bmatrix}$.

mean (p. 445) **media** La suma de *n* números dividido por *n*. También se llama *promedio*.

measures of central tendency (p. 445) **medidas de tendencia central** Tres estadísticas comunmente usadas: la media, la mediana y la moda de un conjunto de números.

measures of dispersion (p. 446) **medidas de dispersión** Estadísticas comúnmente usadas que indican lo dispersos que están los datos. Incluyen la gama y la desviación estándar.

median (p. 445) **mediana** El número del medio cuando *n* números se escriben en orden. (Si *n* es par, la mediana es la media de los dos números del medio.)

midpoint formula (p. 590) **fórmula del punto medio** El punto medio del segmento de recta que une $A(x_1, y_1)$ y $B(x_2, y_2)$ es $M\left(\dfrac{x_1 + x_2}{2}, \dfrac{y_1 + y_2}{2}\right)$. Cada coordenada de *M* es la media de las coordenadas correspondientes de *A* y *B*.

minor axis of an ellipse (p. 609) **eje menor de una elipse** El segmento de recta que une los covértices de una elipse. *Ver también* ellipse / elipse.

mode (p. 445) **moda** El número o los números que ocurren con mayor frecuencia en un conjunto *n* de números. Puede haber una moda, ninguna o más de una.

monomial (p. 257) **monomio** Una expresión con un término, tal como $7x$.

mutually exclusive events (p. 724) **sucesos mutuamente excluyentes** Sucesos *A* y *B* son mutuamente excluyentes si la intersección de *A* y *B* está vacía.

N

natural base *e* (p. 480) **base natural *e*** Un número irracional definido así: Al acercarse *n* a $+\infty$, el valor de $\left(1 + \dfrac{1}{n}\right)^n$ se acerca a $e \approx 2.718281828459$.

natural logarithm (p. 487) **logaritmo natural** El logaritmo con base *e*. Puede escribirse $\log_e$, pero suele escribirse ln.

negative correlation (p. 100) **correlación negativa** La relación entre datos emparejados cuando *y* tiende a disminuir mientras *x* aumenta, tal como se muestra en un diagrama de dispersión donde los puntos marcados suelen caer de izquierda a derecha.

normal curve (p. 746) **curva normal** Una curva lisa, simétrica y con forma de campana que puede representar la distribución normal y aproximar algunas distribuciones binomiales. *Ver también* normal distribution / distribución normal *y* binomial distribution / distribución binomial.

normal distribution (p. 746) **distribución normal** Una distribución en la que la mediana y la desviación estándar determinan las áreas siguientes bajo una curva normal. (1) El área total bajo la curva es 1. (2) El 68% del área se sitúa dentro de 1 desviación estándar de la media. (3) El 95% del área se sitúa dentro de 2 desviaciones estándares de la media. (4) El 99.7% del área se sitúa dentro de 3 desviaciones estándares de la media. *Ver también* normal curve / curva normal.

nth root of *a* (p. 401) **raíz enésima de *a*** Para un número entero *n* mayor que 1, si $b^n = a$, entonces *b* es una raíz n^a de *a*. Se escribe $\sqrt[n]{a}$.

numerical expression (p. 11) **expresión numérica** Una expresión que consiste de números, operaciones y signos de agrupación.

O

objective function (p. 163) **función objetivo** En la programación lineal, la función lineal que se optimiza. *Ver también* linear programming / programación lineal.

octants (p. 170) **octantes** *Ver* three-dimensional coordinate system / sistema de coordenadas en tres dimensiones.

opposite (p. 5) **opuesto** El opuesto o la inversa aditiva de cualquier número *a* es $-a$.

optimization (p. 163) **optimización** Un proceso en que se halla el valor máximo o mínimo de alguna cantidad variable. Un tipo de proceso de optimización es la programación lineal.

ordered pair (p. 67) **par ordenado** Un par de números de la forma (x, y) que representa un punto en el plano de coordenadas.

ordered triple (p. 170) **terna ordenada** Un conjunto de tres números de la forma (x, y, z) que representa un punto en el espacio. *Ver también* three-dimensional coordinate system / sistema de coordenadas en tres dimensiones.

order of operations (p. 11) **orden de las operaciones** Un conjunto de reglas que dicta el orden en el que deben realizarse las operaciones al evaluar expresiones.

origin of a coordinate plane (p. 67) **origen de un plano de coordenadas** El punto $(0, 0)$ donde el eje de x y el eje de y se cortan en un plano de coordenadas. *Ver también* coordinate plain / plano de coordenadas.

origin of a real number line (p. 3) **origen de una recta numérica real** El punto de una recta numérica real denominado O.

P ....

parabola (pp. 249, 595) **parábola** El conjunto de todos los puntos equidistantes de un punto llamado el foco y una recta llamada la directriz. El foco está situado en el eje de simetría y la directriz es perpendicular al eje de simetría.

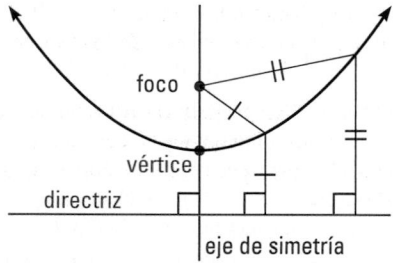

La gráfica de una función cuadrática $y = ax^2 + bx + c$ es una parábola.

parallel lines (p. 77) **rectas paralelas** Dos rectas de un plano que no se cortan.

parameter (p. 813) **parámetro** Una variable, generalmente denominada t de la que dependen dos otras variables . *Ver también* parametric equations / ecuaciones paramétricas.

parametric equations (p. 813) **ecuaciones paramétricas** Ecuaciones que expresan dos variables en términos de una tercera variable, llamada el parámetro.

Pascal's triangle (p. 710) **triángulo de Pascal** Un arreglo de los valores $_nC_r$ en un patrón triangular en el que cada fila corresponde a un valor de n. En un triángulo de Pascal cada número menos el 1 es la suma de los dos números directamente encima.

$_0C_0$						1				
$_1C_0$	$_1C_1$					1	1			
$_2C_0$	$_2C_1$	$_2C_2$				1	2	1		
$_3C_0$	$_3C_1$	$_3C_2$	$_3C_3$			1	3	3	1	
$_4C_0$	$_4C_1$	$_4C_2$	$_4C_3$	$_4C_4$		1	4	6	4	1
$_5C_0$	$_5C_1$	$_5C_2$	$_5C_3$	$_5C_4$	$_5C_5$	1	5	10	10	5	1

period (p. 831) **período** La longitud horizontal de cada ciclo de una función periódica.

periodic function (p. 831) **función periódica** Una función cuya gráfica tiene un patrón que se repite y que continúa indefinidamente.

permutation (p. 703) **permutación** Una ordenación de objetos. El número de permutaciones de r objetos tomados de un grupo de n objetos distintos se escribe $_nP_r$.

perpendicular lines (p. 77) **rectas perpendiculares** Dos rectas de un plano que se intersecan para formar un ángulo recto.

piecewise function (p. 114) **función definida a tramos** Una función representada por una combinación de ecuaciones, cada una de las cuales corresponde a una parte del dominio. Ejemplo: $f(x) = \begin{cases} 2x - 1, \text{ si } x \leq 1 \\ 3x + 1, \text{ si } x > 1 \end{cases}$.

polynomial function (p. 329) **función polinómica** Una función de la forma $f(x) = a_n x^n + a_{n-1} x^{n-1} + \cdots + a_1 x + a_0$ donde $a_n \neq 0$, $a_0, a_1, a_2, \ldots a_n$ son números reales y los exponentes son todos números enteros. Para esta función polinómica, a_n es el coeficiente inicial, a_0 es el término constante y n es el grado.

polynomial long division (p. 352) **división desarrollada polinómica** Un método que se usa para dividir polinomios semejante al método que se usa para dividir números.

positive correlation (p. 100) **correlación positiva** La relación entre pares de datos cuando y tiende a aumentar mientras x aumenta, como se muestra en un diagrama de dispersión donde los puntos marcados generalmente suben de izquierda a derecha.

power (p. 11) **potencia** Una expresión como 2^5, que representa $2 \cdot 2 \cdot 2 \cdot 2 \cdot 2 = 32$.

power function (p. 415) **función potencial** Una función de la forma $y = ax^b$ donde a es un número real y b es un número racional.

probability (p. 716) **probabilidad** Un número entre 0 y 1 que indica las probabilidades de que ocurra un suceso.

pure imaginary number (p. 272) **número imaginario puro** Un número complejo $a + bi$ donde $a = 0$ y $b \neq 0$.

Q...

quadrantal angle (p. 785) **ángulo cuadrantal** Un ángulo en una posición normal con su lado terminal en un eje. Ejemplos: 0°, 90°, 180° y 270°.

quadrants (p. 67) **cuadrantes** Las cuatro regiones que resultan cuando los ejes x e y dividen un plano de coordenadas. *Ver también* coordinate plane / plano de coordenadas.

quadratic equation in one variable (p. 257) **ecuación cuadrática de una variable** Una ecuación que puede escribirse en la forma $ax^2 + bx + c = 0$ donde $a \neq 0$.

quadratic form (p. 346) **forma cuadrática** La forma $au^2 + bu + c$ donde u es cualquier expresión en x.

quadratic formula (p. 291) **fórmula cuadrática** Una fórmula que da las soluciones de cualquier ecuación cuadrática. Si a, b y c son números reales con $a \neq 0$, las soluciones de $ax^2 + bx + c = 0$ son
$$x = \frac{-b \pm \sqrt{b^2 - 4ac}}{2a}.$$

quadratic function (p. 249) **función cuadrática** Una función de la forma $y = ax^2 + bx + c$ donde $a \neq 0$.

quadratic inequality in one variable (p. 301) **desigualdad cuadrática de una variable** Una desigualdad de la forma $ax^2 + bx + c < 0$, $ax^2 + bx + c > 0$, $ax^2 + bx + c \leq 0$, o $ax^2 + bx + c \geq 0$.

quadratic inequality in two variables (p. 299) **desigualdad cuadrática de dos variables** Una desigualdad de la forma
$y < ax^2 + bx + c$, $y > ax^2 + bx + c$,
$y \leq ax^2 + bx + c$, o $y \geq ax^2 + bx + c$.

quartic function (p. 329) **función cuártica** Una función polinómica de grado 4.

R...

radian (p. 777) **radián** En un círculo con radio r y centro en el origen, un radián es la medida de un ángulo en posición normal cuyo lado terminal intercepta un arco de longitud r.

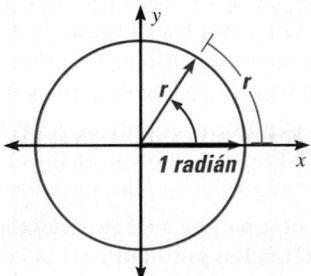

1 radián

radical (p. 264) **radical** Una expresión de la forma $\sqrt{s}$ o $\sqrt[n]{s}$ donde s es un número o una expresión.

radical function (p. 431) **función radical** Una función que contiene un radical, tal como $y = \sqrt{x}$ o $y = \sqrt[3]{x}$.

radical symbol (p. 264) **símbolo radical** El símbolo $\sqrt{\ }$ o $\sqrt[n]{\ }$, que significan respectivamente una raíz cuadrada o una enésima raíz.

radicand (p. 264) **radicando** El número o la expresión bajo el signo radical. El radicando de $\sqrt{5}$ es 5 y el radicando de $\sqrt[3]{7x}$ es $7x$.

radius of a circle (p. 601) **radio de un círculo** La distancia desde el centro de un círculo hasta un punto del círculo, o el segmento de recta que conecta el centro de un círculo con un punto del círculo. *Ver también* circle / círculo.

range of a relation (p. 67) **rango de una relación** El conjunto de valores de salida de una relación.

range of data values (p. 446) **rango de valores** La diferencia entre los valores mayores y menores.

rational function (p. 540) **función racional** Una función de la forma $f(x) = \dfrac{p(x)}{q(x)}$ donde $p(x)$ y $q(x)$ son polinomios y $q(x) \neq 0$.

rationalizing the denominator (p. 265) **racionalizar el denominador** El proceso de eliminar un radical en el denominador de una fracción al multiplicar ambos el numerador y el denominador por un radical apropiado.

reciprocal (p. 5) **recíproco** El recíproco o el inverso multiplicativo de cualquiera número real es $\dfrac{1}{a}$.

recursive rule (p. 681) **regla recursiva** Una regla para una progresión que da el primer término o los primeros términos de una progresión y luego una ecuación recursiva que indica cómo a_n se relaciona con uno o más de los términos anteriores.

reference angle (p. 785) **ángulo de referencia** Si θ es un ángulo en posición normal, su ángulo de referencia es el ángulo agudo θ' formado por el lado terminal de θ y el eje de x. Se da un ejemplo.

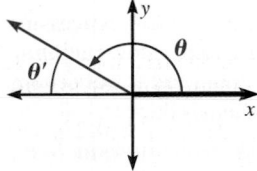

relation (p. 67) **relación** Un emparejamiento de valores de entrada con valores de salida.

relatively no correlation (p. 100) **correlación nula** Una relación entre datos emparejados cuando un diagrama de dispersión no indica un patrón lineal.

repeated solution (p. 366) **solución repetida** Para la ecuación $f(x) = 0$, k es una solución repetida si, y sólo si, el factor $(x - k)$ tiene un grado mayor que 1 cuando se factoriza f completamente.

S...

scalar (p. 200) **escalar** Un número real por el que se multiplica una matriz.

scalar multiplication (p. 200) **multiplicación escalar** El proceso de multiplicar cada entrada de una matriz por un escalar.

scatter plot (p. 100) **diagrama de dispersión / esparcimiento** Una gráfica de pares ordenados que se usa para determinar si hay una relación entre datos emparejados.

scientific notation (p. 325) **notación científica** Un número está expresado en notación científica si está en la forma $c \times 10^n$ donde $1 \le c < 10$ y n es un número entero.

secant function (p. 769) **función secante** Si θ es un ángulo agudo de un triángulo rectángulo, la secante de θ es $\sec \theta = \dfrac{\text{hip}}{\text{ady}}$, donde *hip* representa la longitud de la hipotenusa y *ady* representa la longitud del lado adyacente a θ.

sector (p. 779) **sector** Una región de un círculo limitado por dos radios y un arco del círculo.

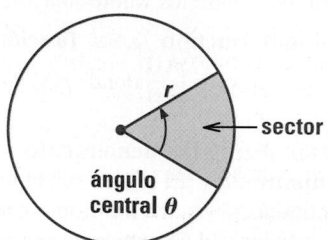

sequence (p. 651) **progresión** Una función cuyo dominio es un conjunto de números enteros consecutivos. El dominio da la posición relativa de cada término de la progresión: 1^a, 2^a, 3^a, y así sucesivamente.

series (p. 653) **serie** La expresión que resulta cuando se suman los términos de una secuencia.

sigma notation (p. 653) **notación sigma** *Ver* summation notation / notación de sumatoria.

simplest form of a radical (p. 408) **forma más simple de un radical** La expresión radical que resulta al aplicarse las propiedades de radicales, quitar los poderes enésimos perfectos y racionalizar los denominadores que haya.

simplified form of a rational expression (p. 554) **forma simplificada de una expresión racional** Una expresión racional en la que el numerador y el denominador no tienen factores comunes (además de ± 1).

sine function (p. 769) **función seno** Si θ es un ángulo agudo de un triángulo rectángulo, el seno de θ es $\text{sen } \theta = \dfrac{\text{op}}{\text{hip}}$ donde *op* representa la longitud del lado opuesto θ e *hip* representa la longitud de la hipotenusa.

skewed distribution (p. 740) **distribución asimétrica** Una distribución que no es simétrica. *Ver también* symmetric distribution / distribución simétrica.

slope (p. 75) **pendiente** La razón de cambio vertical (elevación) a cambio horizontal (avance) para una recta no vertical. La pendiente de una recta no vertical que pasa por los puntos (x_1, y_1) y (x_2, y_2) es $m = \dfrac{y_2 - y_1}{x_2 - x_1} = \dfrac{\text{elevación}}{\text{avance}}$.

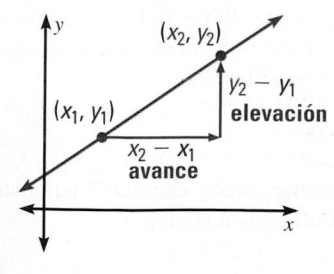

slope-intercept form (p. 82) **ecuación pendiente-intercepto de una recta** Una ecuación lineal escrita en la forma $y = mx + b$ donde m es la pendiente y b es el intercepto en y de la recta.

solution of an equation in one variable (p. 19) **solución de una ecuación de una variable** Un número que al sustituir a la variable hace la ecuación un enunciado verdadero.

solution of an equation in two variables (p. 69) **solución de una ecuación de dos variables** Un par ordenado (x, y) que hace la ecuación un enunciado verdadero cuando los valores de x e y se sustituyen en la ecuación.

solution of an inequality in one variable (p. 41) **solución de una desigualdad de una variable** Un valor de la variable que hace que la desigualdad sea verdadera.

solution of an inequality in two variables (p. 108) **solución de una desigualdad de dos variables** Un par ordenado (x, y) que resulta en un enunciado verdadero cuando x e y se sustituyen en la desigualdad.

solution of a system of linear equations (p. 139) **solución de un sistema de ecuaciones lineales** Un par ordenado (x, y) que satisface cada una de las ecuaciones del sistema.

solution of a system of linear inequalities (p. 156) **solución de un sistema de desigualdades lineales** Un par ordenado que es la solución de cada una de las desigualdades del sistema.

solution of a system of three linear equations (p. 177) **solución de un sistema de tres ecuaciones lineales** Una terna ordenada (x, y, z) que es la solución de las tres ecuaciones del sistema.

solving a right triangle (p. 770) **resolver un triángulo rectángulo** Hallar todas las longitudes y medidas de ángulo que faltan en un triángulo rectángulo.

square root (p. 264) **raíz cuadrada** Un número r es la raíz cuadrada de un número s si $r^2 = s$.

standard deviation (p. 446) **desviación estándar** La diferencia típica (o *desviación*) entre la media y un valor. La desviación estándar σ de $x_1, x_2, \ldots, x_n$ es
$$\sigma = \sqrt{\frac{(x_1 - \bar{x})^2 + (x_2 - \bar{x})^2 + \cdots + (x_n - \bar{x})^2}{n}}.$$

standard form of a complex number (p. 272) **forma general de un número complejo** La forma $a + bi$ donde a y b son números reales e i es la unidad imaginaria.

standard form of a linear equation (p. 84) **forma general de una ecuación lineal** Una ecuación lineal escrita en la forma $Ax + By = C$ donde A y B no son ambos cero.

standard form of a polynomial function (p. 329) **forma general de una función polinómica** La forma de una función polinómica cuando los términos se escriben en orden descendiente de los exponentes de izquierda a derecha.

standard form of a quadratic equation (p. 257) **forma general de una ecuación cuadrática** La forma $ax^2 + bx + c = 0$ donde $a \ne 0$.

standard form of a quadratic function (p. 250) **forma general de una función cuadrática** La forma $y = ax^2 + bx + c$ donde $a \ne 0$.

standard form of the equation of a circle (pp. 601, 623) **forma general de la ecuación de un círculo** Si un círculo tiene el centro (h, k) y el radio r, su ecuación es $(x - h)^2 + (y - k)^2 = r^2$. *Ver también* circle / círculo.

standard form of the equation of a hyperbola (p. 615) **forma general de la ecuación de una hipérbola** Si una hipérbola tiene el centro (h, k), su ecuación es así:
$$\frac{(x - h)^2}{a^2} - \frac{(y - k)^2}{b^2} = 1 \text{ (eje horizontal mayor) o}$$
$$\frac{(y - k)^2}{a^2} - \frac{(x - h)^2}{b^2} = 1 \text{ (eje vertical transversal).}$$
Ver también hyperbola / hipérbola.

standard form of the equation of an ellipse (p. 609) **forma general de la ecuación de una elipse** Si una elipse tiene el centro (h, k) y los ejes mayor y menor con longitudes $2a$ y $2b$, donde $a > b > 0$, su ecuación es así:
$$\frac{(x - h)^2}{a^2} + \frac{(y - k)^2}{b^2} = 1 \text{ (eje horizontal mayor) o}$$
$$\frac{(x - h)^2}{b^2} + \frac{(y - k)^2}{a^2} = 1 \text{ (eje vertical mayor).}$$
Ver también ellipse / elipse.

standard form of the equation of a parabola (pp. 596, 623) **forma general de la ecuación de una parábola** Si una parábola tiene el vértice (h, k), su ecuación es así:
$(y - k)^2 = 4p(x - h)$ (eje horizontal) o
$(x - h)^2 = 4p(y - k)$ (eje vertical).

standard position of an angle (p. 776) **posición normal de un ángulo** En un plano de coordenadas, la posición de un ángulo cuyo vértice está en el origen y cuyo lado inicial es el eje de x positivo. *Ver también* initial side of an angle / lado inicial de un ángulo.

statistics (p. 445) **estadística** Valores numéricos usados para resumir y comparar conjuntos de datos.

step function (p. 115) **función escalonada** Una función definida por tramos cuya gráfica se parece a una escalera de escalones. *Ver también* piecewise function / función definida por tramos.

summation notation (p. 653) **notación de sumatoria** La notación de una serie que usa la letra mayúscula griega sigma Σ. Por ejemplo, se puede escribir
$$3 + 6 + 9 + 12 + 15 = \sum_{i=1}^{5} 3i \text{ donde } i \text{ es el índice de la}$$
sumatoria, 1 es el límite inferior de la sumatoria y 5 es el límite superior de la sumatoria.

symmetric distribution (p. 740) **distribución simétrica** Una distribución en la que la mitad izquierda del histograma que representa la distribución es una imagen especular de la mitad derecha.

synthetic division (p. 353) **división sintética** Un método usado para dividir un polinomio por una expresión de la forma $x - k$.

synthetic substitution (p. 330) **sustitución sintética** Un método usado para elvaluar una función polinómica.

system of linear inequalities in two variables (p. 156) **sistema de desigualdades lineales de dos variables** Un sistema compuesto de dos desigualdades lineales de dos variables. *Ver también* linear inequality in two variables / desigualdad lineal de dos variables.

system of three linear equations (p. 177) **sistema de tres ecuaciones lineales** Un sistema compuesto de tres ecuaciones lineales de tres variables. *Ver también* linear equation in three variables / ecuación lineal de tres variables.

system of two linear equations (p. 139) **sistema de dos ecuaciones lineales** Dos ecuaciones de la forma $Ax + By = C$ y $Dx + Ey = F$ donde x e y son variables, A y B no son ambos cero y D y E no son ambos cero.

T

tangent function (p. 769) **función tangente** Si θ es un ángulo agudo de un triángulo rectángulo, la tangente de θ es $\tan \theta = \frac{\text{op}}{\text{ady}}$ donde *op* representa la longitud del lado opuesto y *ady* representa la longitud del lado adyacente a θ.

terminal side of an angle (p. 776) **lado terminal de un ángulo** *Ver* initial side of an angle / lado inicial de un ángulo.

terms of an expression (p. 13) **términos de una expresión** Las partes de una expresión algebraica que se suman. Los términos de $2x + 3$ son $2x$ y 3. Los términos de $2x - 3 = 2x + (-3)$ son $2x$ y -3.

terms of a sequence (p. 651) **términos de una progresión** Para una progresión de números, los números de la progresión se llaman términos. *Ver también* sequence / progresión.

theoretical probability (p. 716) **probabilidad teórica** Cuando todos los casos son igualmente probables, la probabilidad teórica de que suceso A ocurra es $P(A) = \frac{\text{número de casos en } A}{\text{número total de casos}}$. La probabilidad teórica de un suceso a menudo se llama simplemente la probabilidad de un suceso.

three-dimensional coordinate system (p. 170) **sistema de coordenadas en tres dimensiones** Un sistema de coordenadas determinado por tres ejes mutuamente perpendiculares. Cuando se toman por pares, estos ejes forman tres planos de coordenadas que dividen el espacio en ocho partes llamadas octantes. Un punto en el espacio se representa por una terna ordenada de la forma (x, y, z). Las ternas ordenadas $(-5, 3, 4)$, $(0, 0, 0)$ y $(2, -2, -3)$ se indican a la derecha.

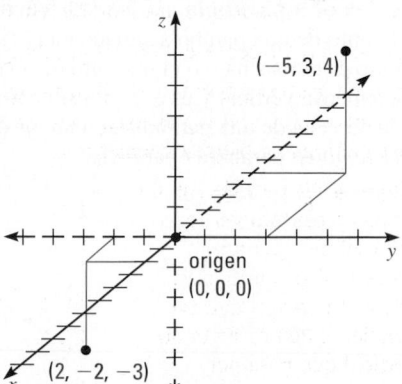

transverse axis of a hyperbola (p. 615) **eje transverso de una hipérbola** El segmento de recta que une los vértices de una hipérbola. *Ver también* hyperbola / hipérbola.

trigonometric identity (p. 848) **identidad trigonométrica** Una ecuación trigonométrica que es verdadera para todos los valores del dominio.

trinomial (p. 256) **trinomio** Una expresión con tres términos, tales como $x^2 + 8x + 15$.

U

upper quartile (p. 447) **cuartil superior** La mediana de la mitad superior de los datos de un conjunto. *Ver también* box-and-whisker plot / gráfica de frecuencias acumuladas.

V

value of an expression (p. 12) **valor de una expresión** El resultado cuando las variables de una expresión algebraica se reemplazan por números y se simplifica la expresión.

value of a variable (p. 12) **valor de una variable** Cualquier número usado para reemplazar una variable.

variable (p. 12) **variable** Una letra que se usa para representar uno o más números.

verbal model (p. 33) **modelo verbal** Una ecuación de palabras que representa un problema de la vida real.

vertex form of a quadratic function (p. 250) **forma vértice de una función cuadrática** La forma $y = a(x - h)^2 + k$ donde el vértice de la gráfica es (h, k) y el eje de simetría es $x = h$.

vertex of an absolute value graph (p. 122) **forma vértice de una gráfica de valor absoluto** El vértice de una gráfica de una función de valor absoluto.

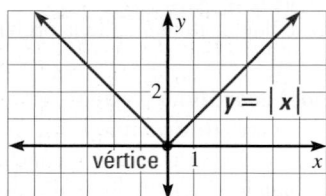

vertex of a parabola (pp. 249, 595) **vértice de una parábola** El punto de una parábola situado en el eje de simetría. Este punto es el más bajo o el más alto de una parábola con un eje de simetría vertical y es el punto situado más a la izquierda o a la derecha de una parábola con un eje de simetría horizontal. *Ver también* parabola / parábola.

vertices of a hyperbola (p. 615) **vértices de una hipérbola** Los puntos de intersección de una hipérbola y la recta que pasa por los focos de la hipérbola. *Ver también* hyperbola / hipérbola.

vertices of an ellipse (p. 609) **vértices de una elipse** Los puntos de intersección de una elipse y la recta que pasa por los focos de la elipse. *Ver también* ellipse / elipse.

X

x-axis (p. 67) **eje de x** El eje horizontal de un plano de coordenadas. *Ver también* coordinate plane / plano de coordenadas.

x-coordinate (p. 67) **coordenada x** El primer número de un par ordenado.

x-intercept of a line (p. 84) **intercepto en x de una recta** La coordenada x del punto donde una recta corta el eje de x. Dada una ecuación de la recta, es el valor de x cuando $y = 0$.

Y

y-axis (p. 67) **eje de y** El eje vertical de un plano de coordenadas. *Ver también* coordinate plane / plano de coordenadas.

y-coordinate (p. 67) **coordenada y** El segundo número de un par ordenado.

y-intercept (p. 82) **intercepto en y** Si la gráfica de una ecuación corta el eje de y en el punto $(0, b)$, entonces el número b es el intercepto en y de la gráfica. Dada la ecuación de la gráfica, es el valor de y cuando $x = 0$.

Z

z-axis (p. 170) **eje de z** Una recta vertical que pasa a través del origen y es perpendicular al plano de coordenadas xy en un sistema de coordenadas en tres dimensiones. *Ver también* three-dimensional coordinate system / sistema de coordenadas en tres dimensiones.

zero of a function (p. 354) **cero de una función** Un número k es un cero de una función f si $f(k) = 0$.

Index

by finding square roots, 264–270, 314

by graphing, 271

with the quadratic formula, 291–298

using the discriminant, 293

standard form of, 257

systems of, 632–637, 644

Quadratic expressions, factoring, 256–263

Quadratic form, 346

Quadratic formula, 291–298, 316

derivation of, 895

discriminant and, 293

trigonometric equations and, 857

Quadratic functions

graphing, 249–255, 314

intercept form of, 250, 251, 259, 306

maximum and minimum values of, 290

modeling with, 306–312, 316, 989–992

standard form of, 250–252, 307

vertex form of, 250–252, 285, 306

writing, 306–312

zeros of, 259

Quadratic inequalities

in one variable, 301–302, 316

system of, 300

in two variables, 299–300, 316

Quadratic regression, 308, 989–992

Quotient of powers property, 323, 407

Quotient property

of logarithms, 493

of square roots, 264

R

Radian

conversion to degrees, 777–778, 822–823

measure of an angle, 777–778, 822–823

Radical equations, solving, 437–443, 458

Radical functions, graphing, 431–436, 457, 995–998

Radicals, 264

adding, 408–409

index of, 401

notation, 264, 401

simplest form of, 264, 408

simplifying, 264–265, 407–413

subtracting, 408–409

Radicand, 264

Radius, of a circle, 601, 914

Random number generation, 723, 738

Range

of a data set, 446, 453, 999

of a function, 67

Rate, of change, 78

Rational equations, solving, 402–406, 568–573

Rational exponents, 401–406, 456

notation, 401–402

properties of, 407–413, 456

solving an equation with, 437

Rational expressions

adding, 562–563, 565–567, 578

dividing, 556–561, 577

evaluating, 402, 939

multiplying, 554–561, 577

simplifying, 554

subtracting, 562–563, 565–567, 578

Rational functions

graphing

general, 547–552, 577

simple, 540–546, 576–577

Rational numbers, definition of, 3

Rational zero theorem, 359

Rationalizing the denominator, 265

Ratios

common, 666

trigonometric, 769

writing, 910–911

Real axis, 273

Real numbers

calculating percents, 907–908

converting decimals, fractions, and percents, 906

graphing, 3

least common denominator, 908–909

nth roots, 401

operations with, 5–6, 58

signed numbers, 905–906

ordering, 4

properties of, 5

scalar, 200

scientific notation, 913

significant digits, 911–912

writing ratios and solving proportions, 910–911

Reasoning, *See* **Critical Thinking; Logical Reasoning**

Reciprocal, 5

Reciprocal identities, 848

Rectangle

area of, 28, 914

perimeter of, 28

Recursive rules, for sequences, 681–686, 694

Reference angle, 785–786

Reflections, 921

of trigonometric graphs, 839–846

Reflexive property of equality, 928

Relation, 67

inverse, 422

representing, 67

Remainder theorem, 353

Repeated solution, 366

Repeating decimal, 676

Reviews, *See also* **Assessment; Projects**

Chapter Review, 58–60, 130–132, 186–188, 240–242, 314–316, 388–390, 456–458, 524–526, 576–578, 642–644, 692–694, 756–758, 822–824, 884–886

Chapter Summary, 57, 129, 185, 239, 313, 387, 455, 523, 575, 641, 691, 755, 821, 883

Cumulative Practice, 192–193, 394–395, 582–583, 762–763, 890–891

Extra Practice, 940–960

Mixed Review, 10, 17, 24, 32, 39, 47, 56, 74, 81, 88, 98, 106, 113, 120, 128, 145, 155, 162, 168, 175, 184, 206, 213, 221, 229, 235, 255, 263, 269, 280, 289, 298, 305, 312, 328, 336, 344, 351, 358, 365, 371, 378, 386, 406, 414, 420, 429, 436, 444, 452, 472, 479, 485, 492, 499, 508, 516, 522, 539, 545, 553, 560, 567, 573, 594, 600, 607, 614, 621, 631, 638, 657, 665, 673, 680, 686, 707, 715, 722, 729, 736, 744, 752, 775, 783, 790, 798, 806, 812, 819, 837, 847, 854, 861, 867, 874, 882

Skill Review, 2, 66, 138, 198, 248, 322, 400, 464, 532, 588, 650, 700, 768, 830

Skills Review Handbook

Algebra, 936–939

Geometry, 914–923

Graphing, 933–936

Logical Reasoning, 924–929

Problem Solving, 929–932

Real Numbers, 905–913

436, 479, 507, 516, 522, 539, 560, 567, 600, 614, 620, 665, 672, 714, 729, 751, 774, 797, 806, 846, 854, 874

multiple choice, 39, 55, 88, 127, 162, 168, 213, 229, 263, 289, 343, 350, 358, 378, 443, 451, 472, 485, 498, 545, 552, 606, 630, 637, 680, 686, 722, 744, 790, 812, 818, 837, 861, 867

quantitative comparison, 16, 31, 74, 120, 154, 220, 280, 297, 364, 420, 428, 492, 573, 594, 657, 707, 736, 782, 881

Test-Taking Strategies, 62, 134, 190, 244, 318, 392, 460, 528, 580, 646, 696, 760, 826, 888

Theorems
binomial theorem, 710–714, 756
factor theorem, 354
fundamental theorem of algebra, 366–371
Pythagorean theorem, 917–918
rational zero theorem, 359
remainder theorem, 353

Theoretical probability, 716–717, 757

Third-order differences, 379

Three-dimensional coordinate system, 170

Transformations, 921–922
of absolute value inequalities, 51
of functions, 985–988
that produce equivalent equations, 19
that produce equivalent inequalities, 41
of trigonometric graphs, 839–846

Translations, 921
of trigonometric graphs, 839–846

Transverse axis, of a hyperbola, 615

Trapezoid, area of, 28, 914

Tree diagram
for finding conditional probability, 733
for finding theoretical probability, 738
fundamental counting principle and, 701

Triangles
AAS, 799
area of, 28, 215, 802–806, 809–812, 914, 915
Heron's area formula and, 809

law of cosines and, 807–812
law of sines and, 799–806
relationships, 917–919
right-triangle trigonometric, 769–774
SAS, 807, 808
semiperimeter of, 809
SSA, 800–801
SSS, 808

Triangular numbers, 380

Triangular pyramidal numbers, 381

Trigonometric equations, solving, 793–798, 855–861, 870–874, 877–881, 885

Trigonometric expressions
evaluating, 869–870, 872–873, 875–876, 879, 880
simplifying, 849, 854, 870, 873, 876, 879, 880

Trigonometric functions
of any angle, 784–790, 823
graphing, 831–838
inverse, 791–798, 823
modeling with, 862–867
of a quadrantal angle, 785
right triangle, 769–774, 822
writing, 862

Trigonometric identities, 848–854, 876, 885
verification of, 850, 853, 876, 885

Trinomials, 256, *See also* **Polynomials**
irreducible, 257
perfect square, 257

Turing, Alan, 226

Turning points, of a polynomial function, 374–378

dependent, 69
equations with more than one, 26–27, 69
independent, 69
on one side
of an equation, 19
of an inequality, 42
subscripts and, 27
value of, 12

Variation
constant of, 94, 534
direct, 94, 534
inverse, 533–535, 537–539, 576
joint, 536–539, 576

Venn diagram, compound events and, 724–725

Verbal model, 12, 13, 15, 21, 27, 33–39, 52, 60, 85, 93, 110, 141, 151, 172, 180, 232, 258, 347, 355, 361, 375, 417, 542, 570, 683

Verification, of trigonometric identities, 850, 853, 876

Vertex
of an ellipse, 609
of the graph of an absolute value function, 122
of the graph of a quadratic function, 249, 250
of a hyperbola, 615
of a parabola, 595, 642

Vertex form
of a quadratic function, 250–252, 285
writing, 306

Vertical asymptote, 540

Vertical line
graph of, 85
slope of, 76

Vertical line test, 68

Vertical translation, of trigonometric graphs, 839–840, 842–846

Visual Thinking, 96, 113, 119, 162, 254, 262, 278, 296, 406, 427, 428, 451, 514, 630, 772, 780, *See also* **Graphs; Manipulatives; Modeling; Multiple representations**

Volume, 916, *See also* **Formulas**

W

Whole numbers, 3

Credits

CORBIS/Catherine Karnow; **410** Stephen J. Krasemann/DRK Photo; **415** CORBIS/Tom Bean; **417** Joe McDonald/Animals Animals; **419** CORBIS/Jonathan Blair; **421** RMIP/Richard Haynes (all); **422** Michael Newman/PhotoEdit; **425** Frank Rossotto/The Stock Market; **427** CORBIS/Robert Maass; **428** Herb Segars/Animals Animals; **431** M. Colbeck/Animals Animals; **433** Courtesy of Chance Rides, Inc. (all); **435** CORBIS/Jim Sugar; **437** CORBIS/Nick Rains; Cordaiy Photo Library Ltd.; **440** CORBIS/James L. Amos; **442** Courtesy of Dr. Alexa Canady/The Detroit Medical Center (cl); Kathy Squires (br); **444** The Granger Collection (bl); Smithsonian Institution (bc); Courtesy of NOAA/National Geophysical Data Center (bcr); PMEL/NOAA, Seattle, Washington (br); **445** Todd Warshaw/Allsport; **447** The Detroit News, photograph by Robin Buckson; **450** William Taufic/The Stock Market; **462** Galen Rowell/Mountain Light; **463** Paul Souders/Tony Stone Images; **465** Alan G. Nelson/Animals Animals/Earth Scenes; **467** Mark Richards/PhotoEdit; **468** Gary Conner/PhotoEdit; **473** RMIP/Richard Haynes; **474** James Wilson/Woodfin Camp and Associates; **480** Michio Hoshino/Minden Pictures; **481** The Granger Collection; **482** Douglas Faulkner/Photo Researchers, Inc.; **484** Archive Photos; **486** Herb Segars/Animals Animals/Earth Scenes; **489** E.H. Degginger/Photo Researchers, Inc. (l); Richard Kolar/Earth Scenes (r); **491** A.T. Willett/Image Bank; **493** Uniphoto; **495** Stephen Frisch/Stock Boston; **497** RMIP/Richard Haynes; **498** Courtesy of Jean Young; **499** School Division, Houghton Mifflin Company (cr, br); Science & Society Picture Library (bl); Science Photo Library/Photo Researchers, Inc. (bcl); The Granger Collection (bcr); **498** Courtesy of Jean Young; **501** Phil Degginger/Animals Animals; **504** UPI/CORBIS/Bettmann; **507** Jerry Schad/Photo Researchers, Inc.; **509** Reproduced with permission from Hamilton Projects, Inc. and the U.S. Postal Service. Photo taken by School Division, Houghton Mifflin Company; **512** Science Photo Library/Photo Researchers, Inc.; **515** Akira Uchiyama/Photo Researchers, Inc.; **517** Richard B. Levine; **521** Mitch Kezar/Tony Stone Images; **530** Vandystadt/Photo Researchers, Inc.; **531** Superstock; **533** RMIP/Richard Haynes (all); **534** Françoise Sauze/SPL/Photo Researchers, Inc.; **535** Ian Beames/Ardea London Limited; **538** Mike Yamashita/Woodfin Camp and Associates; **540** Mug Shots/The Stock Market; **542** Gregory Sams/Photo Researchers, Inc.; **544** Keith Kent/Photo Researchers, Inc.; **547** Gerard Lacz/Peter Arnold, Inc.; **551** Feingersh/The Stock Market; **554** Jeremy Walker/Tony Stone Images; **557** Courtesy of Gregory Robertson; **559** Zane Williams/Tony Stone Images; **562** Chromosohm/Sohm/Photo Researchers, Inc.; **566** Bruce Ayres/Tony Stone Images; **568** Bob Daemmrich/Stock Boston; **570** Bill Gallery/Stock Boston; **572** John Marshall/Tony Stone Images; **574** Macduff Everton (cr); The Granger Collection (bl); CORBIS/Bettmann-UPI (bcl); John (New York) Tee-Van/National Geographic Image Collection (bcr); Charles Nicklin/Al Giddings Images (br); **584** Bob Daemmrich/Stock Boston; **585** RMIP/Richard Haynes (all); **586, 587** CORBIS/Roger Ressmeyer; **589** Richard Pasley/Stock Boston; **591** CORBIS/Lowell Georgia; **593** Brian G. Miller/Illinois State Police; **595** Ken Biggs/Tony Stone Images; **597** Sonia Balcer (tr); Douglas Kirkland (bl); **599** CORBIS/Bettmann; **601** CORBIS/Ron Watts; **603** Stock Montage, Inc.; **605** CORBIS/James L. Amos; **606** Peter Menzel/Stock Boston; **609** Gatha Ashvin/Leo de Wys Inc.; **613** David Burnett/Contact Press/PNI; **615** Fermilab Visual Media Services; **617** Photo courtesy of Carnegie Mellon University; **620** John P. Shepherd; **622** RMIP/Richard Haynes; **623** Nathan Bilow/Allsport; **625** Richard B. Levine; **629** courtesy, Thronateeska Heritage Center, Albany, Georgia; **631** Rev. Ronald Royer/Science Photo Library/Photo Researchers, Inc. (cr); CORBIS/Ruggero Vanni (bl); CORBIS/Bettmann (bcl); PhotoDisc, Inc. (frame bcl); courtesy, Debra Fischer, San Francisco State University (br); **632** Kevin Schafer/Allstock/PNI; **634** Andrew Rafkind/Tony Stone Images; **636** Spencer Grant III/Stock Boston; **640** courtesy, NASA; **648** (clockwise from left) Bruce Forster/Tony Stone Images; Craig Tuttle/The Stock Market; Daniel W. Gotshall/Visuals Unlimited; Gerben Oppermans/Tony Stone Images; **649** TC Nature/Animals Animals; **651** Lance Nelson/The Stock Market; **654** Bill Wood/University of Michigan, Photo Services Department; **656** RMIP/Richard Haynes; **659** Lincoln Russell/Stock Boston; **661** The Granger Collection; **662** CORBIS/Andrea Jemolo; **664** Stephen Frisch/Stock Boston; **666** Al Bello/Allsport; **669** Mike Yamashita/Woodfin Camp and Associates; **671** David Young-Wolff/PhotoEdit; **674** RMIP/Richard Haynes (all); **675** Jose Fuste Raga/The Stock Market; **677** Andy Washnik/The Stock Market; **679** Jon Feingersh/The Stock Market; **681** Mark Burnett/Stock Boston; **683** Bob Daemmrich/Tony Stone Images; **685** Peter Holden/Visuals Unlimited; **687** CORBIS/Larry Lee (bl); The Granger Collection (bc); Darrell Gulin/DRK Photo & CORBIS (montage, br); **698** Bill Gallery/Stock Boston; **699** CORBIS/Kevin Fleming; **701** Nathan Bilow/Allsport; **702** Richard Pasley/Stock Boston; **706** Bob Daemmrich/Stock Boston; **708** Bonnie Kamin/PhotoEdit; **710** The Granger Collection; **713** CORBIS/Kevin Fleming; **716** Paolo Negri/Tony Stone Images; **721** Carlin/Archive Photos; **724** Andy Levin/Photo Researchers, Inc.; **726** School Division, Houghton Mifflin Company; **728** Gary Retherford/Science Source/Photo Researchers, Inc.; **730** Andy Lyons/Allsport; **731** School Division, Houghton Mifflin Company; **735** Barros & Barros/The Image Bank; **737** National Museum, Karachi/E.T. Archive (bl); (Bibl. Imp., Paris.)/North Wind Picture Archives (bcl); World Perspectives/Tony Stone Images (bcr); **739** CORBIS/Richard T. Nowitz; **741** Photofest; **743** Betsy G. Reyneau/The Granger Collection; **746** Bruce Ayres/Tony Stone Images; **748** Bob Daemmrich/Stock Boston; **750** CORBIS/Roger Ressmeyer; **753** Tony Freeman/PhotoEdit; **766** Duvall/Liaison Agency; **767** Mark Segal/Tony Stone Images; **769** Amy C. Etra/PhotoEdit; **771** CORBIS/Richard Bickel; **773** Mark C. Burnett/Stock Boston; **775** CORBIS/Bettmann (bl, bcl); The Granger Collection (bcr); courtesy, NASA (br); **776** Matthew Stockman/Allsport; **779** Tom Dietrich/Tony Stone Images; **782** CORBIS/Kevin R. Morris; **784** Myrleen Ferguson/PhotoEdit; **787** Tom Young/The Stock Market; **789** David Sailors/The Stock Market; **792** Randy Masser/International Stock; **794** DiMaggio/The Stock Market; **797** Robert Laberge/Allsport; **799** Photodisc, Inc.; **801** Paul Souders/Tony Stone Images; **805** Linda Howard, *Centerpeace* 14'h x 24' w x 16' d, Aluminum, 1991, Bradley University, Peoria, Illinois; **807** Addison Geary/Stock Boston; **809** Landsman Photography/Courtesy of Pei Cobb Freed & Partners; **811** Bob Daemmrich/Stock Boston (l); Robert B. McGouey/Spectrum (r); **813** Stuart Westmorland/Tony Stone Images; **815** Courtesy of the Morton Punkin Chuckin' Contest; **817** Jeff Corwin/Tony Stone Images; **829, 830** Siegfried Lavda/Tony Stone Images; **831** Llewllyn/Uniphoto; **833** Leonard Lessin, FBPA/Photo Researchers, Inc.; **836** Mark Burnett/Stock Boston; **840** CORBIS/Galen Rowell; **842** The Granger Collection; **846** Hans Reinhard/Tony Stone Images (l); Alan D. Carey/Photo Researchers, Inc.(r); **848** CORBIS/The Purcell Team; **851** courtesy, Precor and EFX Elliptical Fitness Crosstrainer (all); **854** courtesy, Michael & Vicky Brereton/The Gleaston Water Mill (www.watermill.co.uk); **855** Jon Ortner/Tony Stone Images; **858** CORBIS/Tony Aruzza; **860** Jeff Greenberg/dMRp/Photo Researchers, Inc.; **862** CORBIS/Stuart Westmorland; **866** British Columbia Archives, A-00009; **868** PhotoDisc, Inc. (cr); CORBIS/Archivo Iconografico, S.A. (bl); Artville, LLC. (bcl, bcr); Bob Daemmrich/Stock Boston/PNI/PictureQuest (br); **869** Barrie Rokeach; **873** Jonathan Reichele/Barrie Rokeach; **871** Bob Daemmrich/Stock Boston; **875** Tim Davis/Photo Researchers, Inc.; **878** Michael Dwyer/Stock Boston; **881** Jeremy Horner/Tony Stone Images; **892** RMIP/Richard Haynes; **893** School Division, Houghton Mifflin Company (t); RMIP/Richard Haynes (b).

Illustration

Steve Cowden **606, 781**
Laurie O'Keefe **268**
School Division, Houghton Mifflin Company **597, 599, 600, 767, 774** (all), **778, 789, 796, 797** (t), **804, 805** (b), **811** (all), **812, 814, 815, 817, 818**
Doug Stevens **294** (all), **368, 797** (b)

Selected Answers

CHAPTER 1

SKILL REVIEW (p. 2) **1.** 11 **2.** −70 **3.** 8 **4.** 9 **5.** 24 **6.** −7
7. −10 **8.** −8 **9.** 60 units^2 **10.** 121 units^2 **11.** 165 units^2
12. 20.25π units^2, or about 63.6 units^2

1.1 PRACTICE (pp. 7–10)
5.
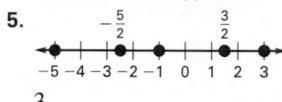
3
7.
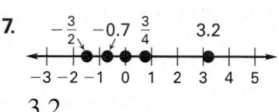
3.2
9. inverse property of addition **11.** commutative property
of multiplication **13.** inverse property of multiplication
15.

$;\dfrac{1}{2} > -5$ **17.** $2.3 > -0.6$

19.

21.

$-\dfrac{5}{3} < \sqrt{3}$ $-\dfrac{9}{4} > -3$

23. $\sqrt{5} > 2$ **25.** $\sqrt{8} > 2.5$ **27.** $-6, -3, -\dfrac{1}{2}, 2, \dfrac{13}{4}$

29.

$;-\dfrac{5}{2}, -\sqrt{5}, -\dfrac{1}{3}, 0, 3$

31. $-\sqrt{12}, -\dfrac{12}{5}, -1.5, 0, 0.3$ **33.** inverse property of addition
35. commutative property of multiplication **37.** identity
property of multiplication **39.** Yes; the associative
property of addition is true for all real numbers a, b, and c.
41. Yes; the associative property of multiplication is true
for all real numbers a, b, and c. **43.** $32 + (-7) = 25$
45. $-5 - 8 = -13$ **47.** $9 \cdot (-4) = -36$ **49.** $-5 \div \left(-\dfrac{1}{2}\right) = 10$
51. 13 ft **53.** $612.50 **55.** Honolulu, HI; New Orleans, LA;
Jackson, MS; Seattle-Tacoma, WA; Norfolk, VA;
Atlanta, GA; Detroit, MI; Milwaukee, WI; Albany, NY;
Helena, MT; three **57.** Yes; the result of performing the
given operations is 9, the check digit. **59.** Sky Central
Plaza: 352 yd, 12,672 in., 0.2 mi; Petronas Tower I: about
494.3 yd, 17,796 in., about 0.2809 mi **61.** yes **63.** $214
65. −15°F

1.1 MIXED REVIEW (p. 10) **69.** 63 **71.** −30 **73.** 19
75. −34 **77.** $x - 3$ **79.** $\dfrac{1}{4}x$ **81.** 10.5 in.^{2} **83.** 750 in.^{2}

1.2 PRACTICE (pp. 14–16) **7.** 5 **9.** 27 **11.** $9x + 9y$
13. $8x^2 - 8x$ **15.** 8^3 **17.** 5^n **19.** 256 **21.** −32 **23.** 125
25. 256 **27.** 24 **29.** 19 **31.** 0 **33.** −5 **35.** 125 **37.** −8
39. 76 **41.** $\dfrac{9}{5}$ **43.** $-\dfrac{5}{13}$ **45.** 16 **47.** $6x^2 - 28x$ **49.** $16n - 88$
51. $-5x - y$ **53.** $\dfrac{1}{2}n(n + 10)$; 1000 **55.** $(x + y)^2$; 289

57. about 1,200,000; about 238,000 **59.** $149 + 3.85(12)n$,
where n is the number of movies rented each month;
$426.20 **61.** $[4n + 8(3 - n)]15$, or $360 - 60n$, where n is
the number of hours spent walking; $240

1.2 MIXED REVIEW (p. 17) **69.** 20 **71.** 15 **73.** 105
75.
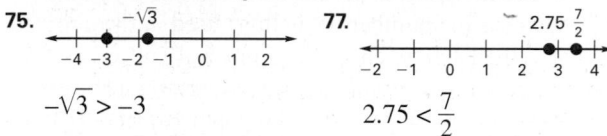
77.

$-\sqrt{3} > -3$ $2.75 < \dfrac{7}{2}$

79. inverse property of addition **81.** identity property of
multiplication **83.** $\dfrac{8}{7}$ **85.** $-\dfrac{4}{5}$ **87.** −9 **89.** $-\dfrac{1}{14}$

QUIZ 1 (p. 17)
1.

2.

$-2.5, -\dfrac{3}{4}, 0, 1, \dfrac{9}{2}$ $-1.5, -0.25, 0.8, \dfrac{15}{8}, \dfrac{10}{3}$

3. distributive property **4.** associative property of addition
5. 15 **6.** $-\dfrac{17}{3}$ **7.** −14 **8.** 76 **9.** −124 **10.** $8x - 11y + 4$
11. $2x - 10$ **12.** $-2x^2 + 5x - 6$ **13.** $-2x^2 + 14x$
14. $0.35n + 13.95(15 - n)$, or $209.25 - 13.60n$, where n is
the number of regular floppy disks bought

TECHNOLOGY ACTIVITY 1.2 (p. 18) **1.** $(-4)^2 - 5$; 11
3. $(1 + 4)^6$; 15,625 **5.** 4.32 **7.** 160.989 **9.** 7.833
11. 5912.099 **13.** 0.81

1.3 PRACTICE (pp. 22–24) **7.** 5 **9.** 5 **11.** $\dfrac{5}{4}$ **13.** −3 **15.** 28
17. Subtract 5 from each side. **19.** Multiply each side
by $-\dfrac{7}{4}$. **21.** Subtract 2 from each side; then multiply each
side by 3. **23.** 5 **25.** $\dfrac{7}{2}$ **27.** $\dfrac{4}{5}$ **29.** −1 **31.** 0 **33.** 4 **35.** $\dfrac{85}{12}$
37. 3.2 **39.** 7.5 **41.** length: 36, width: 14 **43.** −78.5°C
45. 5 h **47.** $635,000 **49.** 16.25 ft

1.3 MIXED REVIEW (p. 24) **57.** 25π in.^{2}, or about 78.5 in.^{2}
59. 49π in.^{2}, or about 154 in.^{2} **61.** 8 **63.** 21 **65.** 11
67. −28 **69.** $21 - 5x$ **71.** $7x - 6$ **73.** $x + 35$ **75.** $3x^2 - x + 11$
77. $4x^2 + 16x$

TECHNOLOGY ACTIVITY 1.3 (p. 25) **1.** False; $y_1 = y_2$ when
$x = -2$, not when $x = 2$. **3.** −2 **5.** 1 **7.** 1

1.4 PRACTICE (pp. 29–32) **5.** $y = \dfrac{5}{3}x - 3$ **7.** $y = -\dfrac{3}{20}x + 4$
9. $y = \dfrac{4}{3}x - 24$ **11.** 20 in. **13.** −1 **15.** $\dfrac{16}{9}$ **17.** $\dfrac{35}{3}$ **19.** 1
21. −4 **23.** $\dfrac{11}{2}$ **25.** $h = \dfrac{3V}{\pi r^2}$ **27.** $P = \dfrac{I}{rt}$ **29.** $b_2 = \dfrac{2A}{h} - b_1$
31. $h = \dfrac{S - 2\pi r^2}{2\pi r}$; $\dfrac{35 - 6\pi}{2\pi}$, or about 2.57 in. **33.** $L = \dfrac{T}{m} + 21$

35. $W \approx \dfrac{TR^2}{R^2 + A^2}$ **37.** $R = p_1V + p_2C$ **39.** *Sample answer:* 210 sun visors, 550 baseball caps; 490 sun visors, 430 baseball caps; 700 sun visors, 340 baseball caps

41. a. $A = \dfrac{\sqrt{3}}{4}b^2$ **b.** $A = \dfrac{\sqrt{3}}{3}h^2$

1.4 MIXED REVIEW (p. 32) 47. $30 - x$ **49.** $250 + x$ **51.** $2x$ **53.** 8736 h **55.** $4\dfrac{3}{8}$ L **57.** \$165 **59.** -6 **61.** 4 **63.** -7 **65.** 40 **67.** 3

1.5 PRACTICE (pp. 37–39) 3. The diagram helps you see how to express the numbers of gallons used in town in terms of x, the label given to the number of gallons used on the highway. **5.** water pressure = 2184 (lb/ft^2); pressure per ft of depth = 62.4 (lb/ft^2 per ft); depth = d (ft) **7.** 35 ft **9.** $547 = 32t$ **11.** about 17 h **13.** $80t = (180)(3)$ **15.** total calories = (calories/gram of fat)(number of grams of fat) + (calories/gram of protein)(number of grams of protein) + (calories/gram of carbohydrate)(number of grams of carbohydrate) **17.** 4.1 g **19.** Great Britain: 22.4 km, France: 15.5 km; Dec. 1, 1990 **21.** \$1.68 per page **23.** length: 135 ft, width: 105 ft **25.** 4.5 m **27.** 4 bounces

1.5 MIXED REVIEW (p. 39) 31. true **33.** false **35.** -55, -10, -5, -1, 4 **37.** -2.9, -2.1, -1.2, 2, 2.09 **39.** 2 **41.** $\dfrac{4}{7}$

QUIZ 2 (p. 40) 1. 4 **2.** -8 **3.** $\dfrac{17}{3}$ **4.** 160 **5.** $y = -\dfrac{3}{5}x + \dfrac{9}{5}$; $\dfrac{3}{5}$ **6.** $y = \dfrac{4}{3}x - \dfrac{14}{3}$; -2 **7.** $d_1 = \dfrac{2A}{d_2}$ **8.** 49 boxes

1.6 PRACTICE (pp. 45–47)

5. $x \geq 5$;

7. $x \leq 12$;

9. $x > 2$;

11.

13. C **15.** D **17.** F **19.** no **21.** no **23.** yes **25.** $x > 5$

27. $x \leq -11$;

29. $x < 6$;

31. $x > 3$; **33.** $x < 6$ **35.** $x < 0$

37. $5 \leq x \leq 18$ **39.** $-6 \leq n \leq -1$;

41. $-1 < x < 1$; **43.** $x \leq 3$ or $x \geq 6$;

45. $x < -5$ or $x > -0.52$; **47.** $0.5 \leq x < 2.5$

49. Your sales must be greater than or equal to \$5000.
51. Her score must be between 93 and 100, inclusive.
53. $184 \leq K \leq 242$ **55.** $c > 2.83$

1.6 MIXED REVIEW (p. 47) 61. associative property of multiplication **63.** commutative property of addition
65. $-\dfrac{10}{7}$ **67.** -1 **69.** $1\dfrac{1}{5}$ h, or 1 h 12 min

TECHNOLOGY ACTIVITY 1.6 (p. 48) 1. $x \leq 4$ **3.** $x > 3$ **5.** $x \leq -6$ **7.** $x < 2$ **9.** $x < 6$ **11.** $x \leq 9$ **13.** $x < -7$

1.7 PRACTICE (pp. 53–55) 5. yes **7.** no **9.** no **11.** $11 - 2x \leq -13$ or $11 - 2x \geq 13$ **13.** $-9 \leq x + 5 \leq 9$ **15.** $-18 < \dfrac{1}{4}x + 10 < 18$ **17.** $x - 8 = 11$ or $x - 8 = -11$ **19.** $6n + 1 = \dfrac{1}{2}$ or $6n + 1 = -\dfrac{1}{2}$ **21.** $2x + 1 = 5$ or $2x + 1 = -5$ **23.** $15 - 2x = 8$ or $15 - 2x = -8$ **25.** $\dfrac{2}{3}x - 9 = 18$ or $\dfrac{2}{3}x - 9 = -18$ **27.** no **29.** no **31.** yes **33.** 2, 3 **35.** 6, -1 **37.** $\dfrac{26}{7}$, $\dfrac{34}{7}$ **39.** 12, -18 **41.** $-15 \leq 3 + 4x \leq 15$ **43.** $-7 < 3x + 2 < 7$ **45.** $-18 \leq 8 - 3n \leq 18$

47. $-9 < x < 7$; 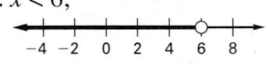 **49.** $x \leq 6$ or $x \geq 26$

51. $3 \leq x \leq 13$; **53.** $x < -\dfrac{4}{3}$ or $x > \dfrac{32}{3}$;

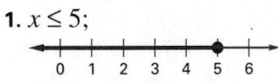 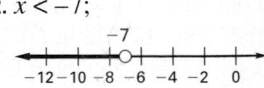

55. $x \leq -\dfrac{15}{2}$ or $x \geq \dfrac{1}{2}$;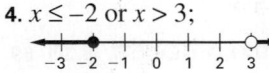

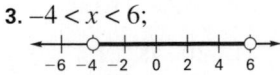

57. $-4 < x < \dfrac{18}{7}$ **59.** $-4 < x < 2$ **61.** $x < -3$ or $x > 7$ **63.** $x < 1$ or $x > 4$ **65.** $|p - 3.49| \leq 0.26$;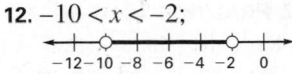

67. $|x - p| \leq \dfrac{3}{16}$; between $8\dfrac{15}{16}$ in. and $9\dfrac{5}{16}$ in., inclusive. **69.** $|t - 98.6| \leq 1$ **71.** 393.6 oz; 374.4 oz; $|c - 384| \leq 9.6$ **73.** volleyball: $|v - 270| > 10$, basketball: $|b - 625| > 25$, water polo: $|w - 425| > 25$, lacrosse: $|l - 145.5| > 3.5$, football: $|f - 14.5| > 0.5$ **75.** 2 L: $|c - 2000| > 9$, 1 L: $|c - 1000| > 5$, 500 mL: $|c - 500| > 2$

1.7 MIXED REVIEW (p. 56) 91. False; if $x = -7$, then $2x = 2(-7) = -14$, not 14. **93.** 21 **95.** -27 **97.** -14 **99.** 10 **101.** $x > \dfrac{1}{3}$ **103.** $x \geq -5$ **105.** $-14 < x < -2$

QUIZ 3 (p. 56)

1. $x \leq 5$; **2.** $x < -7$;

3. $-4 < x < 6$; **4.** $x \leq -2$ or $x > 3$;

5. -1, -9 **6.** 5, 1 **7.** -3, 15 **8.** 5, $-\dfrac{3}{2}$ **9.** $\dfrac{16}{3}$, -8 **10.** 1, 9

11. $y \leq -5$ or $y \geq 1$; **12.** $-10 < x < -2$;

13. $x < -4$ or $x > 10$;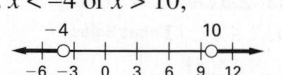

14. $1 \le y \le 4$;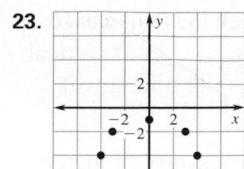

15. $x < 1$ or $x > 2$;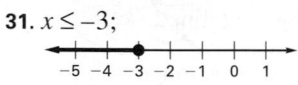

16. $x \le -\dfrac{9}{2}$ or $x \ge 2$;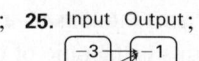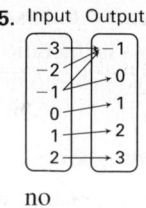

17. $20 \le e \le 28$; between 320 mi and 448 mi, inclusive

18. $|d - 30| \le 0.045$; between 29.955 mm and 30.045 mm, inclusive

CHAPTER 1 REVIEW (pp. 58–60)

1. ; $-\pi, -\sqrt{6}, -2, 0.2, \dfrac{6}{5}$

3. distributive property **5.** -18 **7.** 4 **9.** $5x + 4y$
11. $11x^2 - x$ **13.** -3 **15.** -32 **17.** 4 **19.** $y = 5x - 10$
21. $y = -0.2x + 7$ **23.** $y = \dfrac{5}{6}x + 2$ **25.** $l = \dfrac{P - 2w}{2}$
27. about 5 h 55 min **29.** $x > 8$;
31. $x \le -3$; **33.** $-2 \le y \le 2$;
35. $-5, 3$ **37.** $-\dfrac{8}{3}, 6$ **39.** $-2 < x < 7$

CHAPTER 2

SKILL REVIEW (p. 66)
1. 2 **2.** 2 **3.** 3 **4.** $y = -3x + 4$
5. $y = \dfrac{1}{2}x - 5$ **6.** $y = -\dfrac{5}{6}x - 10$ **7.** $x < \dfrac{9}{2}$ **8.** $y \ge -26$ **9.** $x < \dfrac{5}{2}$

2.1 PRACTICE (pp. 71–74)
5. 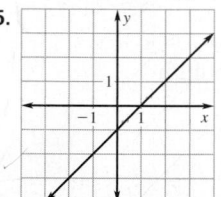 **9.**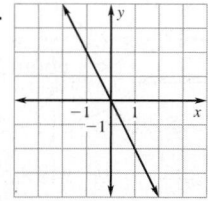

11. 3 **13.** 9 **15.** 1
17. domain: $0 \le t \le 8$; range: $0 \le g \le 16$;
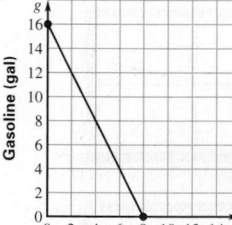

19. domain: $-1, 2, 5, 6$; range: $-2, 3$
21. domain: $1, 2, 3, 4$; range: $1, 2, 3, 4$

23. 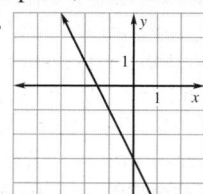 ; **25.** no **27.** yes

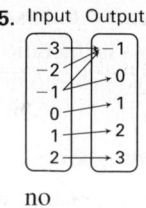 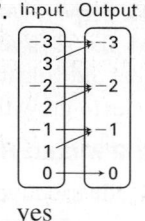

yes

29. If a relation is a function, then no vertical line intersects the graph of the relation at more than one point. If no vertical line intersects the graph of a relation at more than one point, then the relation is a function. **31.** yes

39. 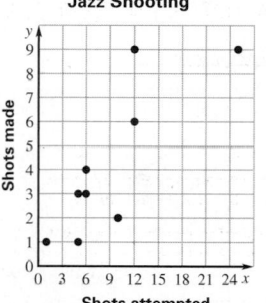 **41.**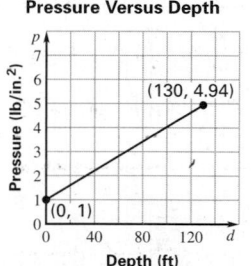

43. linear; -7 **45.** not linear; 1 **47.** not linear; -25
49. 125; the volume of a cube with sides of length 5 units
51. No. *Sample answer:* Not every age corresponds to exactly one place. For example, there were 24-year-olds with finishes of first and third.
53. domain: $1, 5, 6, 10, 12, 25$; range: $1, 2, 3, 4, 6, 9$;

Jazz Shooting

55. domain: $0 \le d \le 130$; range: $1 \le p \le 4\dfrac{31}{33}$;

Pressure Versus Depth

57. domain: $20\dfrac{7}{8} \le c \le 25$; range: $6\dfrac{5}{8} \le s \le 8$;

Cap Size

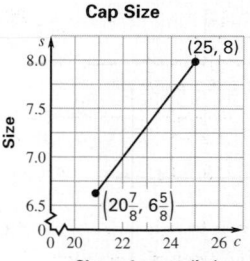

2.1 MIXED REVIEW (p. 74)
65. 1 **67.** $\dfrac{1}{2}$ **69.** $\dfrac{1}{4}$ **71.** -7.5
73. $-4\dfrac{11}{16}$ **75.** $-\dfrac{12}{11}$ **77.** yes **79.** yes **81.** yes

2.2 PRACTICE (pp. 79–81)
5. undefined; vertical **7.** -1; falls
9. 2; rises **11.** line 2 **13.** neither **15.** parallel **17.** 1
19. undefined **21.** 10; rises **23.** $\dfrac{1}{2}$; rises **25.** -1; falls
27. undefined; vertical **29.** $-\dfrac{1}{2}$; falls **31.** undefined; vertical **33.** C **35.** A **37.** line 1 **39.** line 2 **41.** parallel

43. perpendicular **45.** 6; dollars/h **47.** 3; in./year **49.** 10.75
51. 0.062 ft/year; this is the ratio of the number of vertical feet the volcano must grow to the length of time it will take to grow that high.

2.2 MIXED REVIEW (p. 81) **59.** additive inverse property
61. distributive property **63.** $15 - 8x$ **65.** $8 - \frac{4}{3}x$ **67.** $-8, -1$
69. $-1, \frac{5}{3}$ **71.** about $.45/oz

2.3 PRACTICE (pp. 86–88) **5.** $-2; -7$ **7.** x-intercept: 11;
y-intercept: -11 **9.** x-intercept: 3; y-intercept: -15 **17.** A

19. 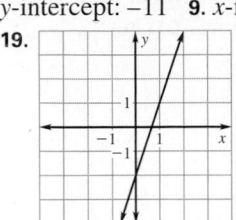 **23.**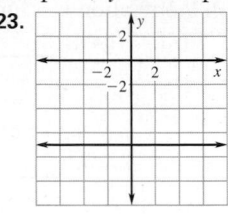

27. 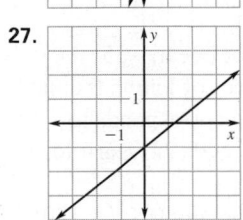 **29.**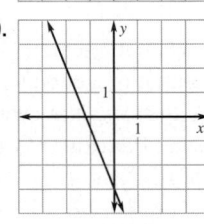

31. 6; 10 **33.** 0; 100 **35.** 4; -7 **37.** B **39.** A

41. 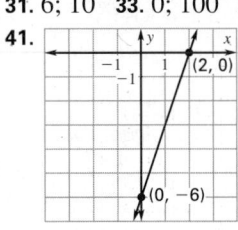 **45.**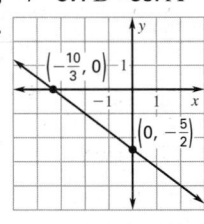

47. 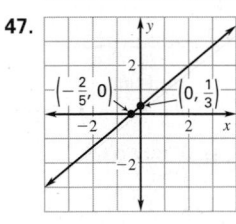 **51.**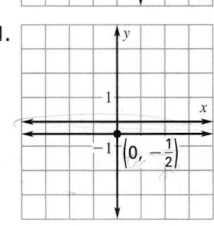

53.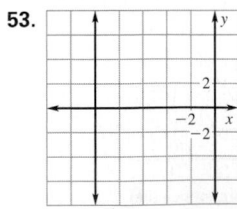

59.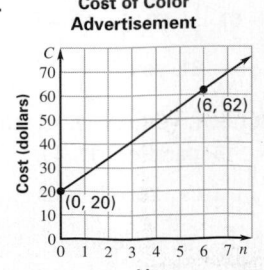

The slope, 7, represents the price of each line in the ad, while the intercept, 20, represents the initial cost of placing a colored ad.

61. $8w + 12x = 3464$;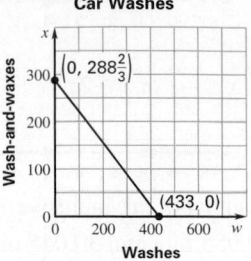

63. $2.5s + 6a = 7000$;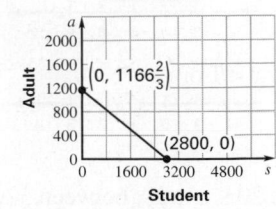

Sample answer:
1600 student tickets,
500 adult; 880 student,
800 adult; 400 student,
1000 adult

2.3 MIXED REVIEW (p. 88)
69. $x > -12$; 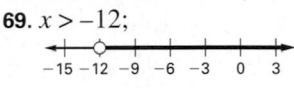   **71.** $x \le 45$;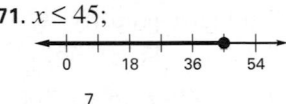

73. $x \le -7$ or $x \ge 7$;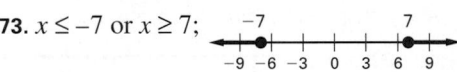

75. 12 **77.** 8 **79.** -16 **81.** $-\frac{6}{7}$ **83.** undefined **85.** -2

QUIZ 1 (p. 89) **1.** domain: $-2, -1, 0, 1, 2$; range: $-2, 1$;
function **2.** domain: 1, 2, 3, 4; range: 1, 2, 3, 4; not a
function **3.** domain: $-3, -1, 0, 1, 2$; range: $-3, -2, 0, 1$;
function **4.** -21 **5.** 139 **6.** perpendicular **7.** neither

8. 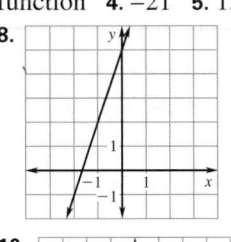 **9.**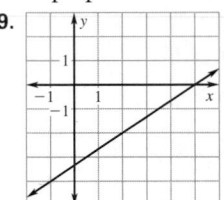

10. 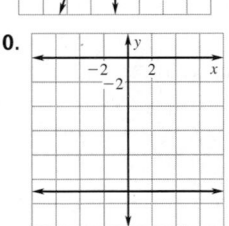 **11.** about 8.36 mi/h

TECHNOLOGY ACTIVITY 2.3 (p. 90)
1. 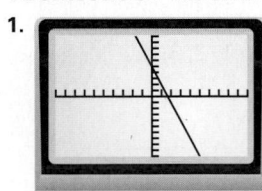 **3.**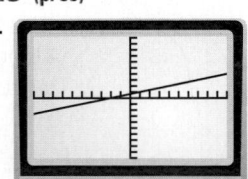

5. 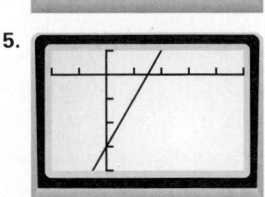 **7.**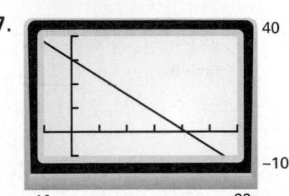

2.4 PRACTICE (pp. 95–98) **5.** $y = 2x - 4$ **7.** $y = -\frac{3}{4}x - \frac{21}{4}$

9. $y = \frac{2}{5}x + 2$ **11.** $y = 5x - 6$ **13.** $y = 5x - 3$ **15.** $y = -4x$

17. $y = \frac{3}{5}x + 6$ **19.** $y = 2x + 4$ **21.** $y = 5$ **23.** $y = -\frac{4}{3}x + 2$

25. $y = 2x - 3$ **27.** $x = 2$ **29.** $y = \frac{3}{2}x - \frac{1}{2}$ **31.** $y = -\frac{1}{2}x - \frac{15}{2}$

33. $y = -x + 8$ **35.** $y = 3x - 19$ **37.** $y = -\frac{7}{8}x + 1$

39. $y = x + 10$ **41.** $3 = -\frac{1}{2}(2) + b; 3 = -1 + b; b = 4$. The

equation is $y = -\frac{1}{2}x + 4$, the same as in Example 2. The

slope-intercept equation of a line is unique. **43.** $y = \frac{7}{2}x; 28$

45. $y = -3x; -24$ **47.** $y = \frac{1}{2}x; 4$ **49.** $y = \frac{1}{2}x; -10$

51. $y = \frac{1}{5}x; -25$ **53.** $y = \frac{1}{2}x; -10$ **55.** yes; $y = \frac{1}{2}x$

57. yes; $y = -x$ **59.** $P = 60,300t + 2,842,200; 4,289,400$

61. $s = 0.629t + 7.4$; about \$21.2 billion **63.** $h = \frac{1}{7}l; 38.5$ ft

65. $r = \frac{1}{240}t; 11$ min **67.** no

2.4 MIXED REVIEW (p. 98) **71.** $-7, 27$ **73.** $-10, -8$

75. $-\frac{38}{55}, \frac{8}{55}$ **77.** 14 **79.** 2 **81.** 0 **83.** -2 **85.** 1

87. 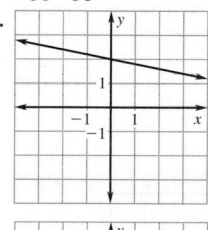 **91.**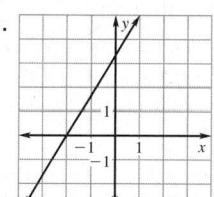

93.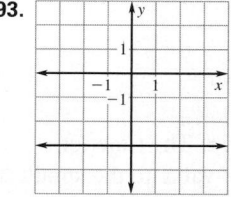

2.5 PRACTICE (pp. 103–105) **5.** about 1.4 m
7. *Sample answer:* about 8830 **9.** positive correlation
11. 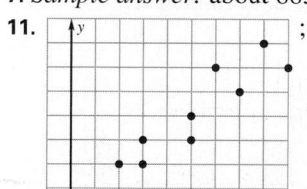 ; **13.** 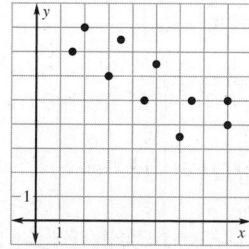 ;

positive correlation   negative correlation

15. *Sample answer:* List the data points so that the values of x are in increasing order. If the y-values mostly increase along with the x-values, there is a positive correlation. If the y-values mostly decrease as the x-values increase, there is a negative correlation. Otherwise, there is relatively no correlation. **17.** *Sample answer:* $y = -0.86x - 0.05$

19. 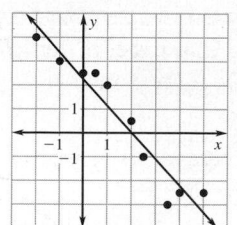 ; *Sample answer:*
$y = -1.11x + 2.27$
21. *Sample answer:*
$y = -0.73x + 2.47$

23. **Old Faithful Eruptions** ; positive correlation

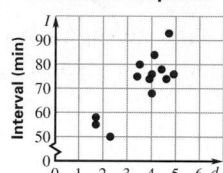

25. about 2290
27. about 84.3 years

2.5 MIXED REVIEW (p. 106)

31. $x < -\frac{11}{4}$; 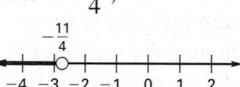   **33.** $x < 4$ or $x \geq 10$;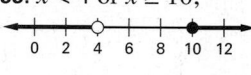

35. line 2 **37.** line 1 **39.**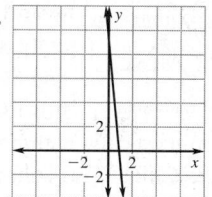

41. 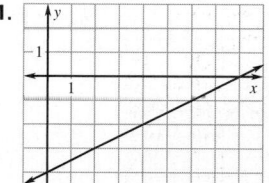   **43.**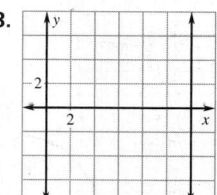

QUIZ 2 (p. 106) **1.** $y = \frac{2}{3}x + 6$ **2.** $y = 2x + 5$ **3.** $y = -\frac{1}{5}x - \frac{33}{5}$

4. $y = 2x - 4$ **5.** relatively no correlation **6.** negative correlation **7.** positive correlation **8.** $d = 1.3h; 4$ ft

9. **Heights of Children** ; *Sample answer:* $h = 6.63t + 71.5$

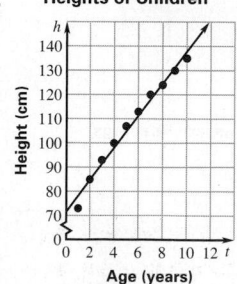

TECHNOLOGY ACTIVITY 2.5 (p. 107)
1. $y = 0.0028x + 0.32$;

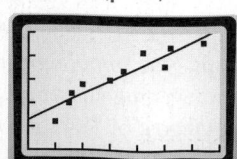

2.6 PRACTICE (pp. 111–113)

7. 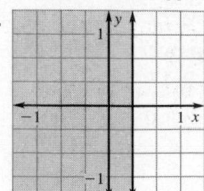 **9.**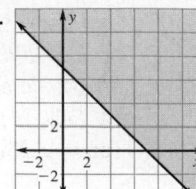

11.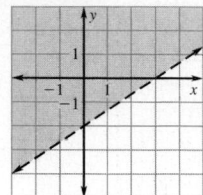

13. $0.16x + 0.75y \le 50;$

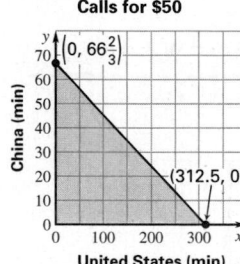

; One possible solution is to spend 50 min on calls to China and 78 min on calls in the United States, for a total cost of $49.98. Another solution would be to spend 50 min on calls within the United States and 56 min on calls to China; this uses exactly $50. A third solution is 100 min on calls within the United States and 45 min on calls to China. This solution uses a total of $49.75.

15. no; yes **17.** yes; no

21. 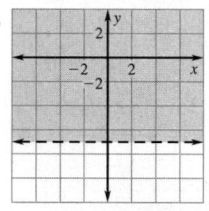 **23.** 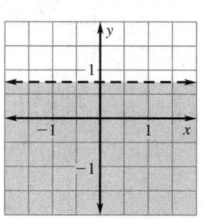 **25.** C

27. 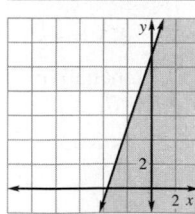 **31.** 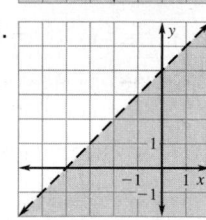 **33.** C
35. B

41. 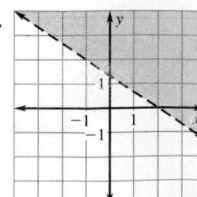 **45.** $y < 0.9x;$

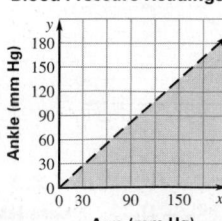

47. about 1.77 cups **49.** *Sample answer:* You can attend 5 matinees and no evening showings for a total of $22.50, 2 of each for a total cost of $24, or 3 evening showings at a cost of $22.50.

51. *Sample answer:* 9 touchdowns and no field goals for 63 points; 5 touchdowns and 1 field goal for 38 points; 2 touchdowns and 3 field goals for 23 points; 3 touchdowns and 3 field goals for 30 points; 4 touchdowns and 6 field goals for 46 points

2.6 MIXED REVIEW (p. 113)
57. 1.65×10^9 **59.** 6.7×10^{-4} **61.** 8.08×10^{-2}

63. 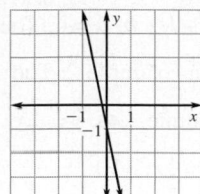 **67.**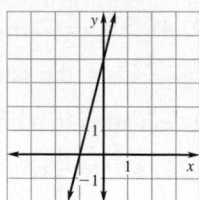

69. $y = -\dfrac{6}{5}x + 7$ **71.** $x = 3$ **73.** $y = -8$

2.7 PRACTICE (pp. 117–120) **5.** 27 **7.** 11
11. $f(x) = -\dfrac{4}{3}x + 6$, if $0 \le x < 3$, $f(x) = -\dfrac{2}{5}x + \dfrac{16}{5}$, if $3 \le x \le 8$ **13.** -21 **15.** -9 **17.** -9.5 **19.** -7

23. 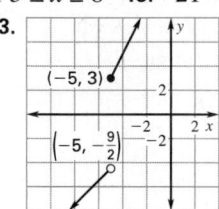 **25.**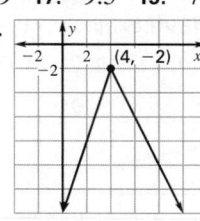

27. 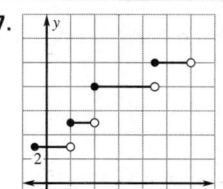 **29.**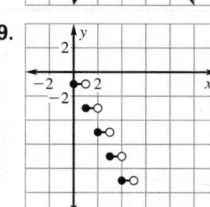

31. 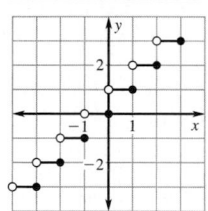 ; *Sample answer:* The function graphs each x-value to the smallest integer that is not less than it, giving a sort of upper limit to the x-values in each interval.

35. $f(x) = \begin{cases} x, & \text{if } x < 0 \text{ (or } x \le 0) \\ 2x, & \text{if } x \ge 0 \text{ (or } x > 0) \end{cases}$

37. $f(x) = \begin{cases} \dfrac{3}{2}x + \dfrac{9}{2}, & \text{if } x < -1 \\ -1, & \text{if } x \ge -1 \end{cases}$

39. $f(x) = \begin{cases} x + 2, & \text{if } x \le -1 \\ x + 3, & \text{if } -1 < x < 1 \\ x + 1, & \text{if } 1 \le x \end{cases}$

43. 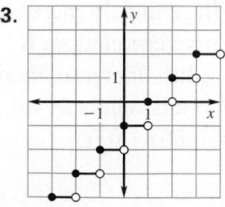 **45.**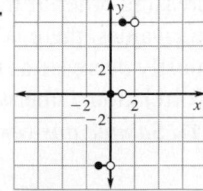

47. 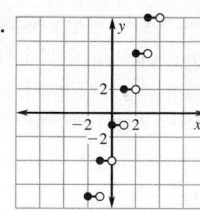 **49.**

51. domain: $0 < x \le 80$; range: 11.75, 15.75, 18.50, 21.25, 24.00 **53.** 450 photocopies cost more than 501 would.

55.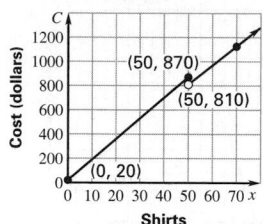

Charges

57. $1860 **59.** 15 in.

2.7 MIXED REVIEW (p. 120) **63.** $\frac{3}{2}$, -6 **65.** 6, 15 **67.** -12, 32

69. 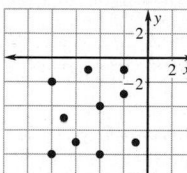 ; relatively no correlation

71. $n = -\frac{1}{40}T + 2.5$; 2.5 in.

TECHNOLOGY ACTIVITY 2.7 (p. 121)

1. 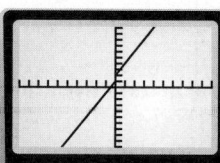 ; 6 **3.** 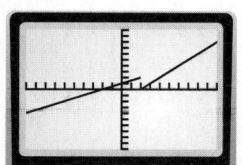 ; 2

5. 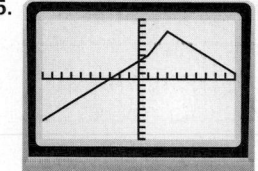 ; 6

2.8 PRACTICE (pp. 125–127)

5. ; **7.** 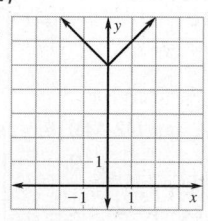 ;

(−5, 0); opens up; same width

(0, 5); opens up; same width

9. $\left(\frac{1}{2}, -14\right)$; opens down; same width

11. *Sample answer:* $y = -\frac{10}{7}\left|x - 3.5\right| + 5$; 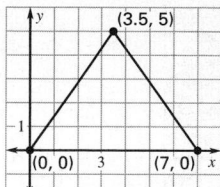 ; domain: $0 \le x \le 7$; range: $0 \le y \le 5$

13. C **15.** C **17.** B
19. (0, 9); opens up; same width
21. (−2, 11); opens down; same width

23. 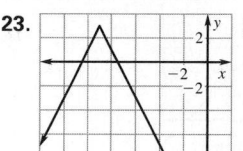 ; **25.** 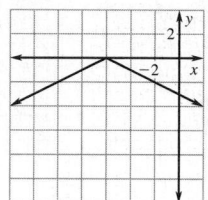 ;

(−9, 3); opens down; narrower

(−6, 0); opens down; wider

27. -23, -5 **29.** $-\frac{39}{7}$, $\frac{31}{7}$ **31.** -2.8125, 2.8125 **33.** 1.5, 4.5

35. $y = -\left|x - 3\right| + 1$ **37.** $y = 2\left|x + 1\right| - 1$

39. $y = -4\left|x\right| + 20$ **41.** 40,000

43. 2 h; 1 h after the rain started

45. after 2 measures and again after 6 measures

47. $y = 2\left|x - 2\right|$;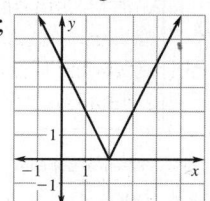

2.8 MIXED REVIEW (p. 128) **57.** $y = -3x - \frac{9}{2}$

61. 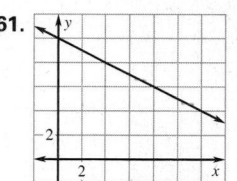 **63.**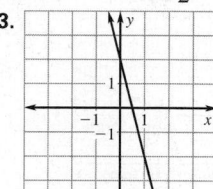

65. $y = 1.87x - 0.46$;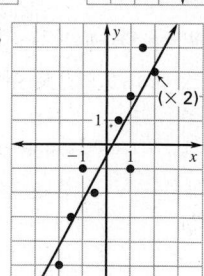

QUIZ 3 (p. 128)

1. 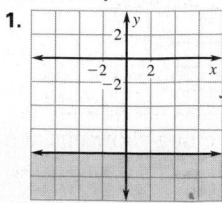 **2.**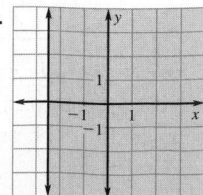

3.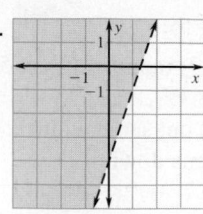

4.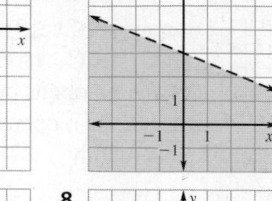

5. 7 **6.** 5

15.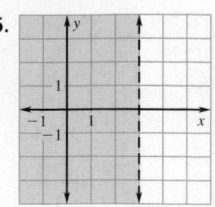

17.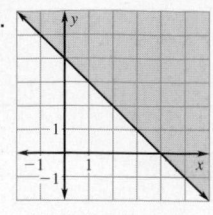

7.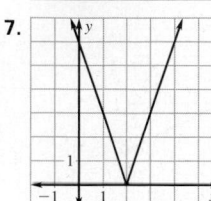

8.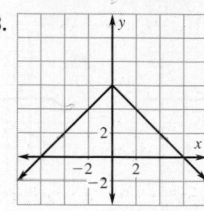

19.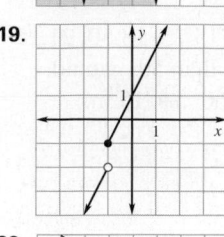

21.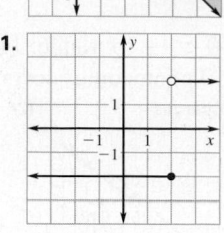

9.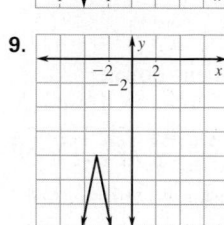

10. $y = \frac{3}{2}|x - 2|$

11. $y = -|x + 2| + 2$

12. $y = \frac{1}{3}|x + 1| + 2$

23.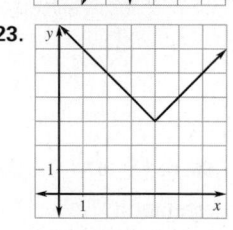

25.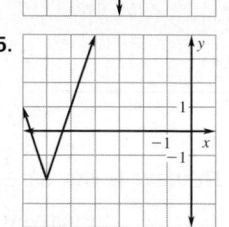

13. $2.5p + 1.25d \le 15$;

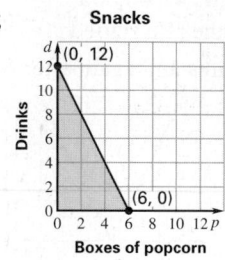

14. $f(x) = \begin{cases} 200, & \text{if } 0 < x \le 1000 \\ 0.2x, & \text{if } x > 1000 \end{cases}$; \$240

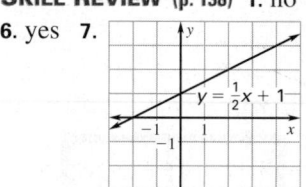

CHAPTER 2 REVIEW (pp. 130–132)

1. 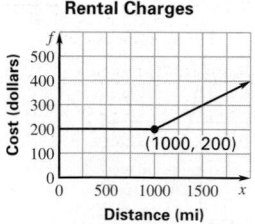 ; yes   **3.** $\frac{2}{3}$ **5.** -1

7.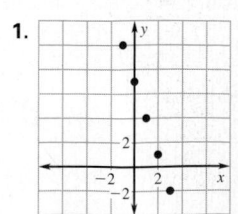

9.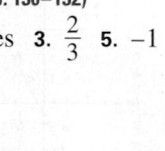

11. $y = -x + 2$ **13.** $y = 2x - 14$

CHAPTER 3

SKILL REVIEW (p. 138)   **1.** no   **2.** yes   **3.** yes   **4.** yes   **5.** no

6. yes   **7.** 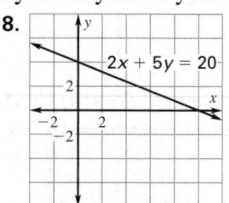   **8.**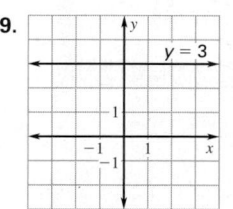

9. 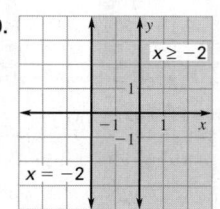   **10.**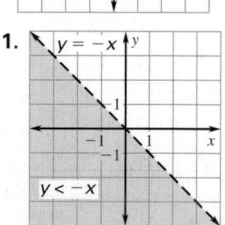

11. 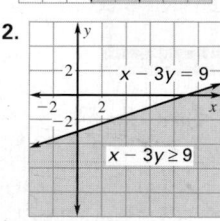   **12.**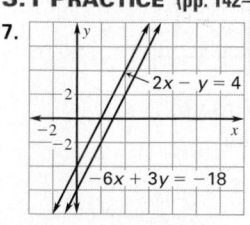

3.1 PRACTICE (pp. 142–145)   **5.** yes

7. 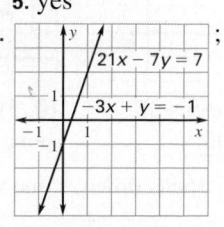 ;   **9.** ;

0   infinitely many

11. yes   **13.** no   **15.** yes   **17.** no   **19.** no

21.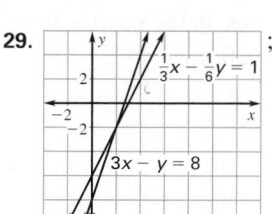

$(7, 1)$

23.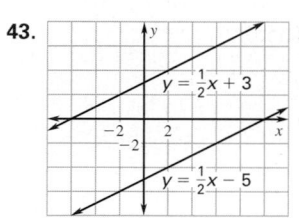

$(2, -4)$

29.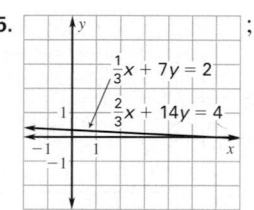

$(2, -2)$ **33.** no solution; the two lines are parallel and have no points in common   **35.** E; 1   **37.** B; infinitely many   **39.** A; 0

43.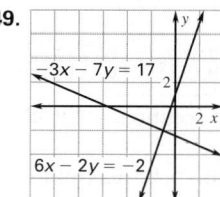

no solutions

45.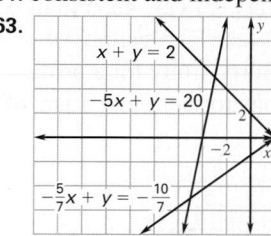

infinitely many solutions

49.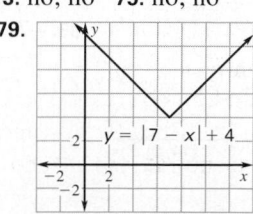

one solution; $(-1, -2)$ **55.** $l + m = 125$; $0.1l + 0.5m = 32.5$; buy 75 latex balloons and 50 mylar balloons.   **57.** $d + 1.25h = 6$; $720d + 1440h = 6480$; you can buy 4 high density disks and 1 double density disk.

59. Let f = the travel time in hours of the first bus; let s = the travel time in hours of the second bus; $f = s + \frac{1}{12}$; 10 miles from the airport; $30f = 40s$.

61. consistent and independent

63. ; a triangle; $(-3, 5)$, $(-5, -5)$, and $(2, 0)$; *Sample answer:* I graphed the lines carefully and found the apparent points of their intersections from the graph. It was easy to see that two of the lines had the same x-intercept, so that was one point. The other points I checked algebraically in the equations to make sure they were solutions.

MIXED REVIEW (p. 145)

67. 36   **69.** -0.3 **71.** -2 **73.** no; no   **75.** no; no

77.

79.

TECHNOLOGY ACTIVITY 3.1 (p. 146)

1. $(-1, 3)$ **3.** $\left(\frac{141}{19}, \frac{119}{19}\right)$, or about $(7.42, 6.26)$

5. $\left(-\frac{116}{21}, \frac{47}{21}\right)$, or about $(-5.52, 2.24)$

3.2 PRACTICE (pp. 152–154)   **5.** $(4, -1)$ **7.** $(6, 6)$ **9.** $(3, 4)$

11. $(4, -1)$ **13.** $(3, 3)$ **15.** $\left(0, \frac{5}{2}\right)$ **17.** $(-2.4, 10.2)$

19. $(3, -10)$ **21.** $(-2, 2)$ **23.** $\left(-\frac{11}{3}, -1\right)$ **25.** $\left(0, \frac{4}{5}\right)$

27. infinitely many solutions   **29.** $\left(\frac{1}{3}, 1\right)$ **31.** $\left(\frac{18}{41}, \frac{605}{82}\right)$, or about $(0.439, 7.378)$ **33.** no solution   **35.** $(-5, -2)$

37. $(5, 0)$ **39.** no solution   **41.** $\left(-\frac{69}{11}, \frac{65}{11}\right)$ **43.** $\left(-\frac{25}{4}, 2.5\right)$

45. $(20, 3)$ **47.** no solution   **49.** $(9, 6)$ **51.** $(2, 3)$ **53.** $(2, 2)$
55. \$12; *Sample answer:* let x = the cost per foot of the cable itself and y = the cost of one connector. Then $6x + 2y = 15.5$ and $3x + 2y = 10.25$. Subtracting the second equation from the first, find $x = 1.75$. Then a 4-foot cable with connectors will cost $10.25 + 1.75 = \$12$.   **57.** inline skating: 25 min; swimming: 15 min

59.

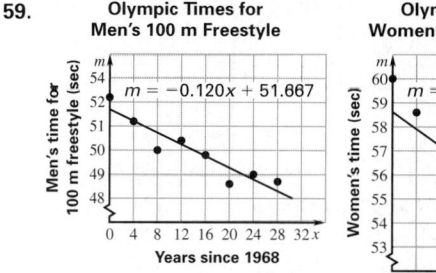
Olympic Times for Men's 100 m Freestyle

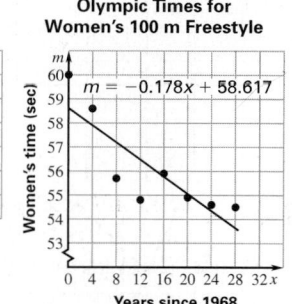
Olympic Times for Women's 100 m Freestyle

61. $(119.83, 37.288)$; 120 years after 1968, in the year 2088 summer olympics, the men's and women's times in the 100 m freestyle will both be about 37.3 sec.

3.2 MIXED REVIEW (p. 155)

67. $-8, -2$ **69.** $-\frac{3}{2}, 1$ **71.** $24, -4$ **73.** $y = 2x - 3$

75.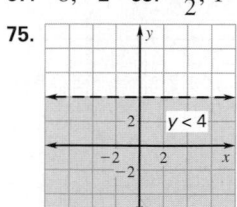

77.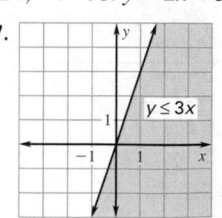

79.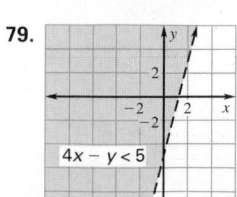

81. $12x + 25 \le 60$; $x \le \frac{35}{12}$

QUIZ 1 (p. 155) **1.** $(-2, 1)$ **2.** $(1, -3)$ **3.** no solutions
4. $\left(\frac{7}{3}, -\frac{8}{3}\right)$ **5.** $(1, 4)$ **6.** $(-1, -1)$ **7.** infinitely many
solutions **8.** 1 **9.** no solutions **10.** 1 **11.** 1 **12.** infinitely
many solutions **13.** $\left(-\frac{5}{4}, -\frac{15}{4}\right)$ **14.** $(6, 6)$ **15.** infinitely
many solutions **16.** $\left(-4, \frac{7}{2}\right)$ **17.** no solution **18.** $\left(-\frac{33}{29}, \frac{13}{29}\right)$
19. 371; 566

3.3 GUIDED PRACTICE (pp. 159–161) **5.** no **7.** yes

9.
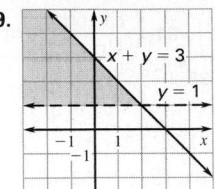

11. $18 \le x \le 55$; $60 \le y \le 74$;
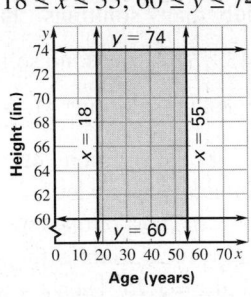

13. no **15.** *Sample answer:* $(13, 10)$ **17.** *Sample answer:* $(-2, -10)$ **19.** *Sample answer:* $(4, 2)$ **21.** C **23.** F **25.** A

27.
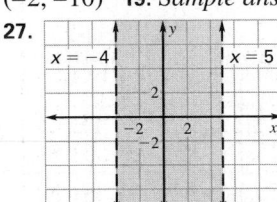

29.
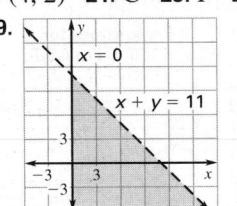

33.
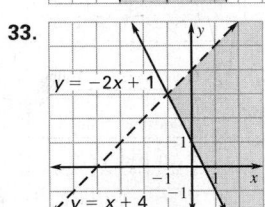

37.
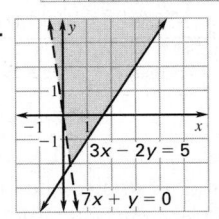

41.
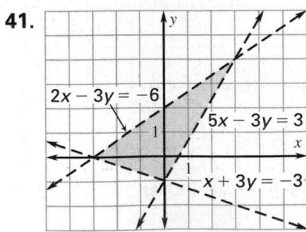

43.
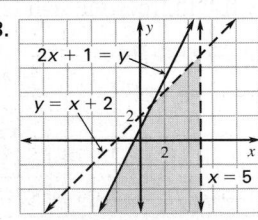

49.
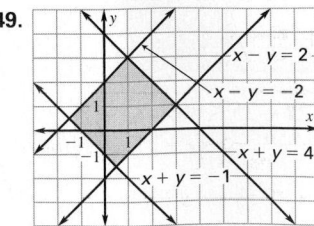

51. $7.4 \le p \le 7.6$, $1.0 \le c \le 1.5$;
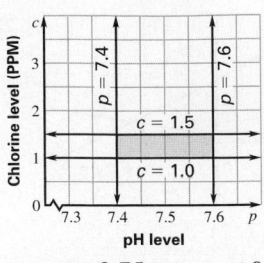

53.
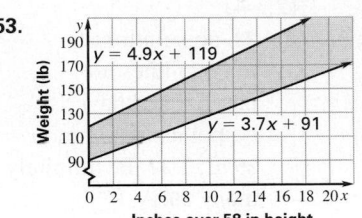

55. $0.75x \le y$; $y \le 0.9x$; $20 \le x \le 80$

57. $s > 205.5$; $j \le 262.5$; $s + j > 465.0$;
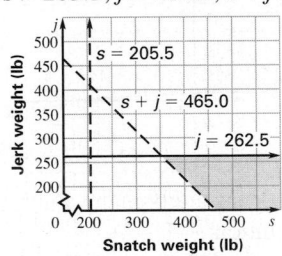

3.3 MIXED REVIEW (p. 162) **67.** 27 **69.** -13 **71.** relatively
no correlation **73.** $\left(\frac{58}{57}, -\frac{128}{57}\right)$ **75.** no solution **77.** $(-8, 2)$

3.4 PRACTICE (pp. 166–167) **5.** Minimum is 0; maximum
is 38. **7.** max of 31 at $(17, 3)$; min of -20 at $(0, 20)$
9. min of -40 at $(0, 40)$; max of 40 at $(40, 0)$ **11.** min of
10 at $(2, 1)$; no max—feasible region is unbounded.
13. min of 6 at $(2, 1)$; max of 29 at $(5, 6)$ **15.** min of 0 at
$(0, 0)$; max of 740 at $(60, 20)$ **17.** no min, since feasible
region is unbounded; max of 132 at $(15, 12)$ **19.** min of 6
at $(0, 2)$; max of 29 at $(5, 3)$ **21.** Make 37.5 gallons of
Orangeade and 31.25 gallons of Berry-fruity for a profit
of \$31.25. **23.** Make 14 jars of tomato sauce and 4 jars of
salsa for a profit of \$34.

3.4 MIXED REVIEW (p. 168)

29.
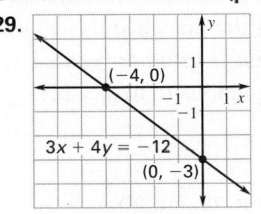

31.
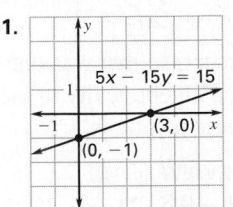

33.
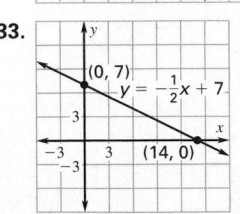

35. -7 **37.** -6 **39.** 35 **41.** 15

43.
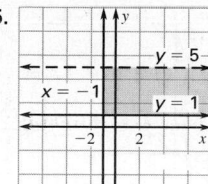

45.
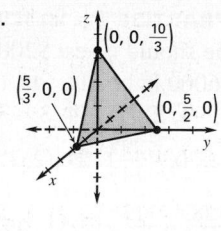

47.
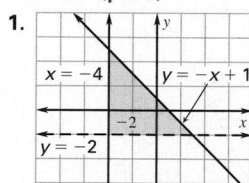

QUIZ 2 (p. 169)

1.
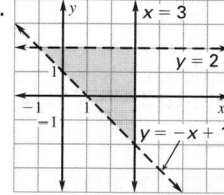

2.
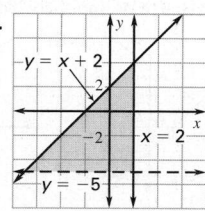

3.
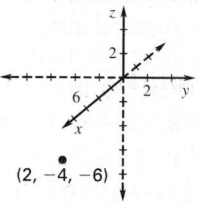

4. min of -18 at $(-4, 1)$; max of 2 at $(-2, 6)$ **5.** min of 19 at $(3, 2)$; max of 24 at $(4, 2)$ **6.** min of 0 at $(0, 0)$; max of 70 at $(14, 0)$ **7.** 6 small boxes and 6 large boxes

3.5 PRACTICE (pp. 173–174)

5.
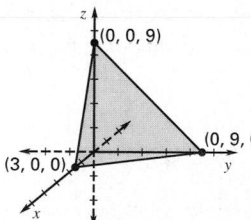

7.
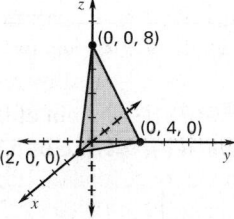

11.
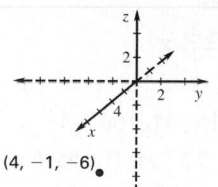

15. $f(x, y) = -2x - \frac{1}{2}y - 4; -17$

17. $C = 2.25r + 2.95p + 2.65; \$37.50$

19.
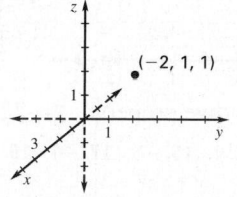

23.

27.
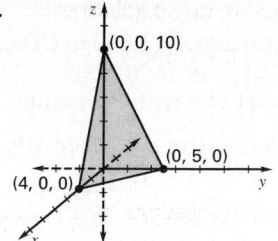

33.

37.
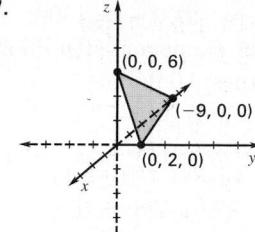

39. $f(x, y) = \frac{2}{5}x + y + 3; \frac{8}{5}$

41. $f(x, y) = -\frac{6}{5}x + \frac{3}{10}y + \frac{18}{5}; 12$

43. $f(x, y) = -\frac{1}{6}x - \frac{1}{4}y + \frac{1}{5}; \frac{1}{2}$

45. $f(x, y) = -\frac{1}{9}x + \frac{2}{3}y - \frac{4}{3}, \frac{121}{18}$ **47.** 60

49. $C = 1.5n + p + 16$; *Sample answer:*

Price of Pottery	Number of Colors				
	1	2	3	4	5
$8	$22.50	$27.00	$28.50	$30.00	$31.50
$18	$35.50	$37.00	$38.50	$40.00	$41.50
$28	$45.50	$47.00	$48.50	$50.00	$51.50
$38	$55.50	$57.00	$58.50	$60.00	$61.50
$48	$65.50	$67.00	$68.50	$70.00	$71.50

51. $C = 0.9e + 0.25s + 20; \$29.70$; *Sample answer:*

Number of Express Bus Trips	Number of Subway Trips				
	2	4	6	8	10
2	$22.30	$22.80	$23.30	$23.80	$24.30
4	$24.10	$24.60	$25.10	$25.60	$26.10
6	$25.90	$26.40	$26.90	$27.40	$27.90
8	$27.70	$28.20	$28.70	$29.20	$29.70
10	$29.50	$30.00	$30.50	$31.00	$31.50

3.5 MIXED REVIEW (p. 175)

57. $x \le 14$;

59. $x > -2$;

61. $18 \le x \le 21$;   **63.** neither

65. parallel **67.** $3.95r + 3.1p = 48.5; r + p = 14$; buy 6 red oak boards and 8 poplar boards.

TECHNOLOGY ACTIVITY 3.5 (p. 176) **1.** -14 **3.** 0.4 **5.** 21.6

3.6 PRACTICE (pp. 181-183) **5.** no **7.** no **9.** (5, −1, 1)
11. She should invest $2000 in savings, $12,000 in CDs, and $6000 in bonds. **13.** (2, 1, −1) **15.** (6, 0, −3)
17. (1, −4, 2) **19.** (4, 3, −3) **21.** (−3, 2, 5) **23.** (7, 3, 5)
25. $\left(-\frac{2}{7}, 0, -\frac{29}{14}\right)$ **27.** (2, 1, 2) **29.** (−1, 1, −1) **31.** (6, 6, −4)
33. $\left(\frac{128}{13}, -\frac{113}{26}, 13.5\right)$ **35.** $f + s + t = 20$; $5f + 3s + t = 68$; $s = f + t$; there were 7 first-place finishers, 10 second-place finishers, and 3 third-place finishers. **37.** $s + l = 1300$; $s + 2c = 1400$; $s + l + c = 1600$ **39.** Democrat: 50 million, Republican: 40 million, Other parties: 10 million
41. Sample answers are given.
a. $x + y + z = 3$; $2x − 2y + 5z = 23$; $4x + 3z = 1$
b. $x + y + z = 3$; $2x − 2y + 5z = 23$; $4x − 4y + 10z = 11$
c. $x + y + z = 3$; $2x − 2y + 5z = 23$; $3x − y + 6z = 26$

3.6 MIXED REVIEW (p. 184)
45. 11 **47.** 84 **49.** −16 **51.** $\frac{3}{10}$ **53.** $-\frac{9}{4}$
55. $x \leq −14.5$ or $x \geq 11.5$; **59.** $-\frac{29}{3} \leq x \leq \frac{31}{3}$;

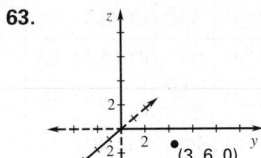

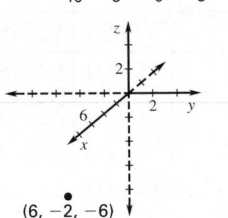

63.

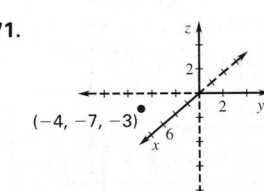

(3, 6, 0)

67.

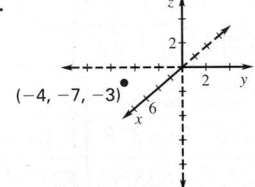

(6, −2, −6)

71.

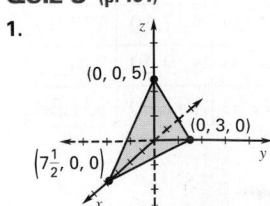

(−4, −7, −3)

QUIZ 3 (p. 184)
1.

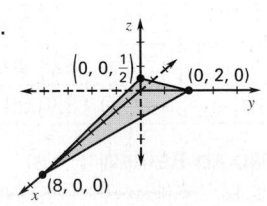

(0, 0, 5) (0, 3, 0) $\left(7\frac{1}{2}, 0, 0\right)$

2.

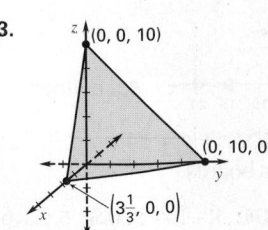

$\left(0, 0, \frac{1}{2}\right)$ (0, 2, 0) (8, 0, 0)

3.

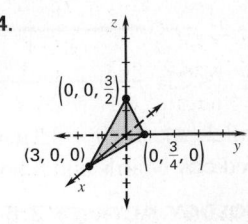

(0, 0, 10) (0, 10, 0) $\left(3\frac{1}{3}, 0, 0\right)$

4.

$\left(0, 0, \frac{3}{2}\right)$ (3, 0, 0) $\left(0, \frac{3}{4}, 0\right)$

5.

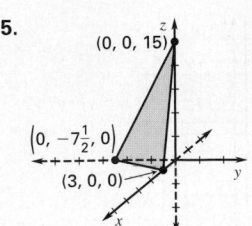

(0, 0, 15) $\left(0, -7\frac{1}{2}, 0\right)$ (3, 0, 0)

6.

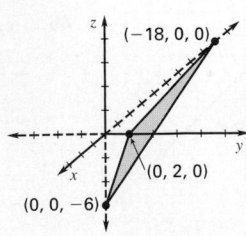

(−18, 0, 0) (0, 2, 0) (0, 0, −6)

7. $f(x, y) = \frac{1}{3}x - \frac{1}{6}y + 6$; $\frac{20}{3}$ **8.** $f(x, y) = \frac{1}{2}x + y + 2$; 4
9. $f(x, y) = 20x - 3y - 15$; 66 **10.** $f(x, y) = \frac{1}{3}x - \frac{1}{6}y + 4$; $\frac{41}{6}$
11. (5, 0, 0) **12.** (2, −4, −1) **13.** no solutions
14. 3 string players, 10 woodwinds, and 2 percussionists were selected.

CHAPTER 3 REVIEW (pp. 186−188)
1.

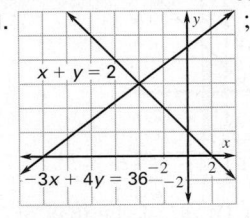

$x + y = 2$
$-3x + 4y = 36$
one solution; (−4, 6)

3.

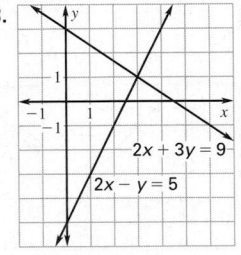

$2x + 3y = 9$
$2x − y = 5$
one solution; (3, 1)

5. (0, 6) **7.** (−2, −1)
9.

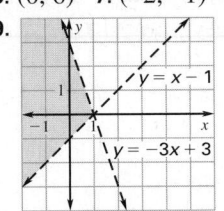

$y = x − 1$
$y = −3x + 3$

11.

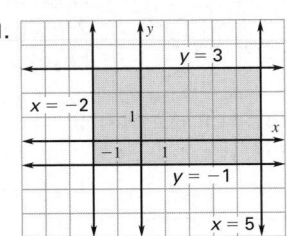

$y = 3$
$x = −2$
$y = −1$
$x = 5$

13. max of 50 at (10, 0); min of 0 at (0, 0)
15. max of 38 at (4, 9); min of 5 at (1, 0)
19.

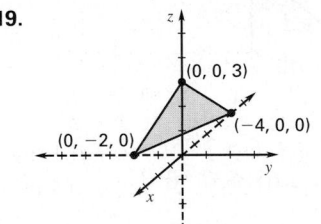

(0, 0, 3) (0, −2, 0) (−4, 0, 0)

21. $\left(-\frac{1}{2}, 1, 2\right)$

CUMULATIVE PRACTICE (pp. 192−193)
1. $-\frac{3}{2}, 0, 2\frac{3}{4}$; π, 4
5. distributive property **7.** −22 **9.** 16 **11.** $16a + 11$
13. $n^2 + 2n$ **15.** −8 **17.** −4 **19.** −10, 9.5 **21.** 10 **23.** $h = \frac{V}{\pi r^2}$

25. $x < 4$;

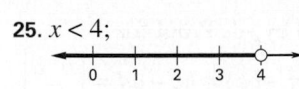

27. $x \le \frac{2}{3}$ or $x > 2$;

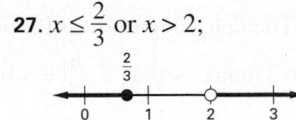

31. $-2 < x < 2$;

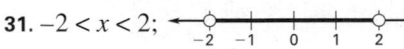

33.

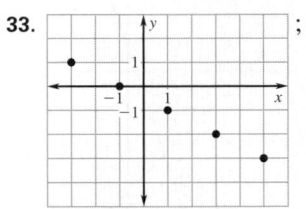

; yes **35.**

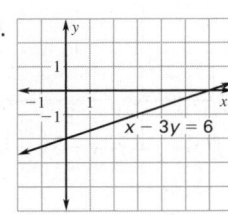

41.

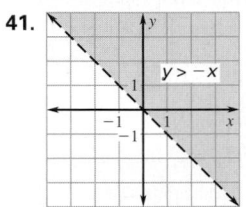

45.

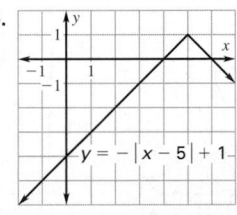

49.

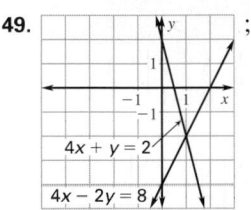

; **51.**

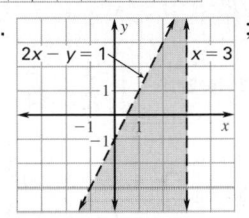

;

one solution at $(1, -2)$

Solution region is to the right of $2x - y = 1$ and to the left of $x = 3$.

53. perpendicular **55.** $y = -3x + 7$ **57.** $y = \frac{1}{2}x + 1$

59. 11 **61.** -4 **63.** 2 **65.** $(4, -1)$ **67.** $(0, -1, 5)$

69.

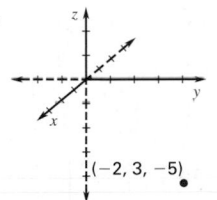

75.

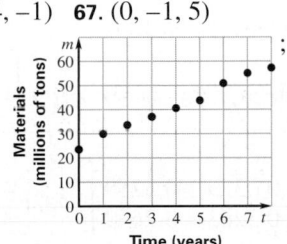

;

Sample answer: $y = 4.20t + 24.5$; about 83.3 million tons

77. Order 100 lb of vegetables and 50 lb of beef at a total cost of $228.50.

CHAPTER 4

SKILL REVIEW (p. 198) **1.** -1 **2.** -13 **3.** -14 **4.** 40
5. commutative property of multiplication **6.** commutative property of addition **7.** distributive property **8.** $(15, 3)$
9. $(-3, -10)$ **10.** $\left(\frac{112}{5}, -\frac{4}{5}\right)$ **11.** $(-2, -2)$

4.1 PRACTICE (pp. 203–205) **7.** $\begin{bmatrix} -7 & -12 & 12 \\ -5 & 12 & -10 \end{bmatrix}$

9. $\begin{bmatrix} -25 & -6 \\ -8 & 15 \end{bmatrix}$ **11.** not equal **13.** not equal **15.** $\begin{bmatrix} 4 & 1 \\ -12 & 4 \end{bmatrix}$

17. $\begin{bmatrix} -4 & -7 \\ 5 & 5 \end{bmatrix}$ **19.** $\begin{bmatrix} 5.3 & 12.2 \\ 2.8 & 10.4 \end{bmatrix}$ **21.** Not possible; the two matrices do not have the same dimensions.

23. $\begin{bmatrix} 4 & 12 & -28 \\ 16 & 0 & -24 \end{bmatrix}$ **25.** $\begin{bmatrix} 4 & 12 & 36 \\ -20 & 20 & 60 \\ -12 & -20 & -44 \end{bmatrix}$ **27.** $\begin{bmatrix} -1 & -1 & -2 \\ \frac{1}{8} & \frac{3}{11} & -5 \end{bmatrix}$

29. $\begin{bmatrix} 8 & -8 \\ 12 & -3 \\ -16 & 23 \end{bmatrix}$ **31.** $\begin{bmatrix} 22 & -30 \\ -22 & -18 \end{bmatrix}$ **33.** $x = -3$, $y = -8$

35. $x = -2$, $y = 44$ **37–41.** Matrices can also be written with the rows and columns switched.

	Before		After	
	Wins	Losses	Wins	Losses
37. Atlanta Braves	59	29	47	27
Seattle Mariners	37	51	39	34
Chicago Cubs	48	39	42	34

	1996	
	No. of units shipped (in mil)	$ Value (in mil)
39. CDs	20,779	$268,441
Cassettes	15,299	$122,329
Music Videos	45	$916

	1997	
	No. of units shipped (in mil)	$ Value (in mil)
CDs	26,277	$344,697
Cassettes	17,799	$144,645
Music Videos	70	$1,260

41. $\begin{bmatrix} 5,498 & \$76,256 \\ 2,500 & \$22,316 \\ 25 & \$344 \end{bmatrix}$ **43.** $2V + M$; $\begin{bmatrix} 146.8 & 148.4 \\ 146.1 & 147.8 \\ 146.8 & 148.4 \\ 146.2 & 148.1 \end{bmatrix}$

Percent of Population in 1991

	0–17	18–65	over 65
Northeast	4.8	12.6	2.8
Midwest	6.3	14.5	3.1
45. South	8.9	21.2	4.3
Mountain	1.6	3.4	0.6
Pacific	4.2	9.9	1.7

Percent of Population in 2010

	0–17	18–65	over 65
Northeast	4.2	11.4	2.5
Midwest	5.3	13.8	3.0
South	8.5	22.6	5.0
Mountain	1.7	4.2	0.9
Pacific	4.6	10.5	1.9

47. South: 18–65, over 65, Mountain: 0–17, 18–65, over 65, Pacific: 0–17, 18–65, over 65

4.1 MIXED REVIEW (p. 206)

51.

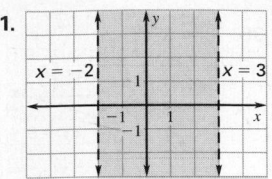

53. 20 **55.** 7 **57.** $\frac{5}{14}$

59. no, yes **61.** no, yes

63. *Sample answer:* (1, 2)

65. *Sample answer:* (5, 5)

TECHNOLOGY ACTIVITY 4.1 (p. 207)

1. $\begin{bmatrix} 6.6 & -6.1 \\ 15.33 & 1.72 \end{bmatrix}$ **3.** $\begin{bmatrix} 6.4666 & 1.6688 \\ 23.0503 & 7.301 \end{bmatrix}$

5. $\begin{bmatrix} -8 & -1 & 0 & -1 \\ -3 & -2 & -1 & 0 \end{bmatrix}$; none; Rock CDs, Country CDs, Easy Listening CDs, Rock tapes, Country tapes, Jazz tapes

4.2 PRACTICE (pp. 211–212) **5.** defined; 3×3

7. $\begin{bmatrix} 2 & 0 \\ -5 & -3 \end{bmatrix}$ **9.** $\begin{bmatrix} -9 & -3 \\ 7 & 2 \\ 2 & 1 \end{bmatrix}$ **11.** defined; 1×2

13. not defined **15.** defined; 3×1 **17.** [2] **19.** $\begin{bmatrix} 4 & 11 \\ 12 & 3 \end{bmatrix}$

21. Not defined; the number of columns in the left matrix (3) does not equal the number of rows in the right matrix (2).

23. $\begin{bmatrix} -1.3 \\ 0.9 \end{bmatrix}$ **25.** $\begin{bmatrix} -32 & 0 & 32 \\ 12 & -26 & 1 \\ 20 & -30 & -5 \end{bmatrix}$ **27.** $\begin{bmatrix} 16 & -16 \\ 16 & -8 \end{bmatrix}$

29. $\begin{bmatrix} 8 & -5 & 8 \\ -1 & 1 & 1 \\ 7 & -30 & -35 \end{bmatrix}$ **31.** $\begin{bmatrix} 0 & -30 \\ 12 & -51 \end{bmatrix}$ **33.** $x = 2, y = 8$

35. $\begin{bmatrix} 0.201 & 0.348 & 0.180 \\ 0.220 & 0.215 & 0.017 \\ 0.073 & 0.001 & 0.005 \\ 0.113 & 0.014 & 0.405 \end{bmatrix}$ **37.** Matrix B $\begin{bmatrix} 6 \\ 5 \\ 4 \end{bmatrix}$

39. Team 3; 62 points

4.2 MIXED REVIEW (p. 213) **45.** 180 m^2 **47.** 9π ft^2, or about 28.26 ft^2 **49.** $y = -\frac{1}{4}x + 4$ **51.** $y = 3x + 2$

53. $y = \frac{3}{2}x - 6$ **55.** (−7, 5) **57.** no solution **59.** (0, −5)

61. $\left(-\frac{49}{37}, -\frac{52}{37}\right)$

4.3 PRACTICE (pp. 218–220) **5.** −6 **7.** 28 **9.** (−5, 1)

11. 1750 in.^{2} **13.** 24 **15.** 63 **17.** −31 **19.** 24 **21.** −77

23. 360 **25.** 116 **27.** 81 **29.** −732 **31.** 6 **33.** 11 **35.** 6

37. (−2, −5) **39.** (4, −1) **41.** (6, 2) **43.** $\left(\frac{584}{11}, \frac{480}{11}\right)$

45. (0, 5, 4) **47.** $\left(-\frac{2}{3}, -34, -12\right)$ **49.** (4, 3, −2)

51. $\left(\frac{1}{11}, \frac{34}{11}, \frac{19}{11}\right)$ **53.** $\left(-\frac{1}{44}, -\frac{69}{22}, -\frac{481}{88}\right)$ **55.** 144 ft^2

57. 4 in.^{2} **59.** regular: \$1.03 per gal, premium: \$1.15 per gal

61. The determinant is multiplied by −1. Proof for 2×2 matrices: $-1\begin{vmatrix} a & b \\ c & d \end{vmatrix} = -1(ad - bc) = bc - ad = \begin{vmatrix} b & a \\ d & c \end{vmatrix}$

4.3 MIXED REVIEW (p. 221) **65.** −3 **67.** 4 **69.** $\frac{5}{4}$

71. 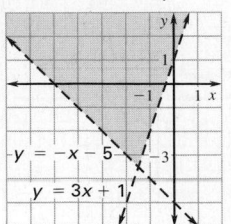 **73.**

75. 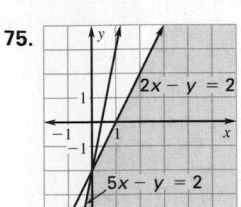 **77.** $\begin{bmatrix} -24 & 14 \\ 33 & -8 \end{bmatrix}$ **79.** $\begin{bmatrix} -104 & 35 \\ 32 & -4 \end{bmatrix}$

81. $\begin{bmatrix} 12 & 2.7 \\ 4 & 0.92 \end{bmatrix}$

QUIZ 1 (p. 221) **1.** $\begin{bmatrix} -5 & 4 & 15 \\ 2 & -14 & 1 \end{bmatrix}$ **2.** $\begin{bmatrix} -5 & -7 \\ 0 & -1 \end{bmatrix}$

3. $\begin{bmatrix} -2 & -2 \\ -18 & -12 \end{bmatrix}$ **4.** $\begin{bmatrix} -4 & -2 & 22 \\ 3 & -18 & 20 \\ -17 & -4 & 1 \end{bmatrix}$ **5.** $\begin{bmatrix} 26 & 56 \\ 22 & 42 \end{bmatrix}$

6. $\begin{bmatrix} 5 & -15 \\ 38 & -12 \end{bmatrix}$ **7.** 10 **8.** 0 **9.** 70 **10.** −15 **11.** (1, 2)

12. $\left(\frac{4}{9}, -\frac{13}{3}\right)$ **13.** $\left(2, \frac{1}{2}\right)$ **14.** $\left(\frac{5}{2}, 1, -\frac{3}{2}\right)$ **15.** $\left(\frac{7}{3}, 10, -\frac{4}{3}\right)$

16. (0, −4, 3) **17.** 12 ft^2

4.4 PRACTICE (pp. 227–228) **7.** $\begin{bmatrix} -\frac{1}{3} & -\frac{2}{3} \\ 0 & -1 \end{bmatrix}$ **9.** $\begin{bmatrix} \frac{2}{65} & -\frac{32}{65} \\ \frac{16}{65} & \frac{4}{65} \end{bmatrix}$

11. $\begin{bmatrix} -0.0329 & 0.3289 \\ 0.5263 & -0.2632 \end{bmatrix}$ **13.** $\begin{bmatrix} 4 & 5 \\ 3 & 4 \end{bmatrix}$ **15.** $\begin{bmatrix} -7 & 8 \\ 1 & -1 \end{bmatrix}$

17. $\begin{bmatrix} 1 & -2 \\ -3 & 7 \end{bmatrix}$ **19.** $\begin{bmatrix} 1 & \frac{7}{2} \\ -1 & -3 \end{bmatrix}$ **21.** $\begin{bmatrix} \frac{1}{2} & \frac{1}{2} \\ \frac{3}{2} & \frac{11}{6} \end{bmatrix}$ **23.** $\begin{bmatrix} 5 & -1.25 \\ -4 & 1.1 \end{bmatrix}$

25. $\begin{bmatrix} \frac{37}{25} & -\frac{1}{5} \\ -\frac{4}{5} & 0 \end{bmatrix}$ **27.** $\begin{bmatrix} -4 & 2 & -7 \\ 3 & -1 & 5 \end{bmatrix}$ **29.** $\begin{bmatrix} \frac{17}{5} & \frac{136}{5} \\ -\frac{8}{5} & -\frac{64}{5} \end{bmatrix}$

31. $\begin{bmatrix} 11 & -2 \\ 8 & -1.5 \end{bmatrix}$ **33.** no **35.** yes

37. $\begin{bmatrix} -0.0654 & -0.0131 & 0.1634 \\ 0.0131 & 0.2026 & -0.0327 \\ 0.1503 & -0.1699 & 0.1242 \end{bmatrix}$ **39.** $\begin{bmatrix} 12 & -7 & 3 \\ -20 & 12 & -5 \\ 1.5 & -1 & 0.5 \end{bmatrix}$

41. 39, 98, 26, 77, 20, 60, 13, 31, 23, 51

43. 36, −14, 16, 0, 125, −50, −26, 14, 10, 4, 24, −8, −95, 48

45. KARNAK TEMPLE **47.** THE GREAT SPHINX

49. a. $\begin{bmatrix} -1 & -4 & -2 \\ 1 & 2 & 3 \end{bmatrix}$; $\begin{bmatrix} -1 & -2 & -3 \\ -1 & -4 & -2 \end{bmatrix}$;

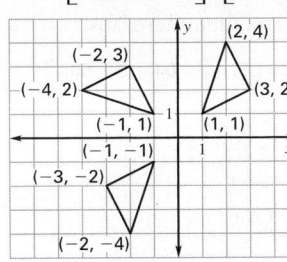

; 90° rotation

b. *Sample answer:* Find A^{-1} and then multiply AAT by A^{-1} on the left: $A^{-1}AAT = IAT = AT$. Now multiply AT by A^{-1} on the left: $A^{-1}AT = IT = T$.

4.4 MIXED REVIEW (p. 229)

55. all real numbers **57.** $(4, 0, -2)$ **59.** $\left(\dfrac{1}{2}, 4, \dfrac{1}{4}\right)$

61. Not possible; the matrices have different dimensions.

63. $\begin{bmatrix} 17 & -3 & -1 \\ 0 & 25 & 31 \end{bmatrix}$ **65.** $\begin{bmatrix} 2 & 5 & 1 \\ 3 & 4 & 8 \end{bmatrix}$

4.5 PRACTICE (pp. 233–235)

5. $\begin{bmatrix} 1 & 3 \\ 4 & -2 \end{bmatrix}\begin{bmatrix} x \\ y \end{bmatrix} = \begin{bmatrix} 9 \\ 7 \end{bmatrix}$ **7.** $(-5, 7)$ **9.** $\left(\dfrac{21}{13}, -\dfrac{2}{13}\right)$

11. $\begin{bmatrix} 1 & 1 \\ 3 & -4 \end{bmatrix}\begin{bmatrix} x \\ y \end{bmatrix} = \begin{bmatrix} 5 \\ 8 \end{bmatrix}$ **13.** $\begin{bmatrix} 5 & -3 \\ -4 & 2 \end{bmatrix}\begin{bmatrix} x \\ y \end{bmatrix} = \begin{bmatrix} 9 \\ 10 \end{bmatrix}$

15. $\begin{bmatrix} 1 & 8 \\ 4 & -5 \end{bmatrix}\begin{bmatrix} x \\ y \end{bmatrix} = \begin{bmatrix} 4 \\ -11 \end{bmatrix}$ **17.** $\begin{bmatrix} 1 & -4 & 5 \\ 2 & 1 & -7 \\ -4 & 5 & 2 \end{bmatrix}\begin{bmatrix} x \\ y \\ z \end{bmatrix} = \begin{bmatrix} -4 \\ -23 \\ 38 \end{bmatrix}$

19. $\begin{bmatrix} 0.5 & 3.1 & -0.2 \\ 1.2 & -2.5 & 0.7 \\ 0.3 & 4.8 & -4.3 \end{bmatrix}\begin{bmatrix} x \\ y \\ z \end{bmatrix} = \begin{bmatrix} 5.9 \\ 2.2 \\ 4.8 \end{bmatrix}$

21. $\begin{bmatrix} 0 & 8 & -10 \\ 0 & 6 & -12 \\ -9 & 0 & 5 \end{bmatrix}\begin{bmatrix} x \\ y \\ z \end{bmatrix} = \begin{bmatrix} -23 \\ 14 \\ 0 \end{bmatrix}$ **23.** $(5, -7)$ **25.** $(5, -9)$

27. $(1, -7)$ **29.** $(-1, -4)$ **31.** $(-3, -14)$ **33.** $(-61, 179, -83)$
35. $(4, 3, 1)$ **37.** $(2, 3, -2)$ **39.** $(3, -2, 6)$ **41.** 2239.8 g of A, 1313.6 g of B, 4067.6 g of C **43.** transformer: $10.00, wire: $.20 per ft, light: $1.00

4.5 MIXED REVIEW (p. 235) **47.** -2 **49.** $-\dfrac{19}{2}$ **51.** 5 **53.** -3

55.

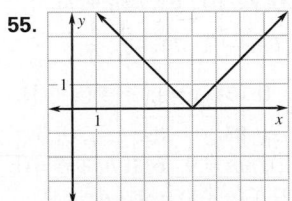

57.

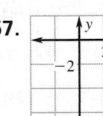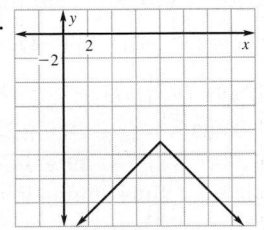

61. $\begin{bmatrix} 3 & 4 \\ 5 & 7 \end{bmatrix}$ **65.** $\begin{bmatrix} 1 & -2 \\ -\dfrac{3}{2} & \dfrac{7}{2} \end{bmatrix}$

QUIZ 2 (p. 236)

1. $\begin{bmatrix} 2 & -1 \\ -7 & 4 \end{bmatrix}$ **2.** $\begin{bmatrix} -3 & -5 \\ -4 & -7 \end{bmatrix}$ **3.** $\begin{bmatrix} -\dfrac{1}{3} & -\dfrac{1}{9} \\ -1 & -\dfrac{2}{3} \end{bmatrix}$ **4.** $\begin{bmatrix} \dfrac{7}{2} & -\dfrac{5}{2} \\ -4 & 3 \end{bmatrix}$

5. $(-1, 4)$ **6.** $(4, 3)$ **7.** $(3, -3)$ **8.** place setting: $35.50, serving set: $67.00

CHAPTER 4 EXTENSION (p. 238) **1.** $(-2, 5)$ **3.** $(-1, -4)$

5. $(4, -5)$ **7.** $(2, 1)$ **9.** $\left(0, \dfrac{1}{5}\right)$ **11.** $(16, -5, 2)$ **13.** $(-5, 2, 0)$
15. $(-16, 12, 10)$

CHAPTER 4 REVIEW (pp. 240–242)

1. $\begin{bmatrix} 15 & -5 \\ 1 & 5 \end{bmatrix}$ **3.** $\begin{bmatrix} 8 & 11 \\ 9 & 13 \\ 8 & 6 \end{bmatrix}$ **5.** $\begin{bmatrix} 8 & 12 & -2 \\ 20 & -10 & 4 \\ 0 & 22 & 2 \end{bmatrix}$ **7.** $x = -1, y = 10$

9. $x = -1, y = 5$ **11.** $\begin{bmatrix} -120 & -84 \\ 40 & 28 \end{bmatrix}$ **13.** $\begin{bmatrix} 17 & -29 & 64 \\ 18 & -36 & 72 \end{bmatrix}$

15. 12 **17.** 4 **19.** $(-1, -1)$ **21.** $(6, 0, -3)$

23. $\begin{bmatrix} \dfrac{3}{4} & -\dfrac{1}{2} \\ -\dfrac{1}{4} & \dfrac{1}{2} \end{bmatrix}$ **25.** $\begin{bmatrix} 1 & 1 \\ 5 & 6 \end{bmatrix}$ **27.** $\begin{bmatrix} -3 & -2 \\ 4 & 3 \end{bmatrix}$ **29.** $\left(\dfrac{5}{2}, \dfrac{3}{2}\right)$

31. $(4, 1, 0)$ **33.** $(-3, 2, 4)$

CHAPTER 5

SKILL REVIEW (p. 248) **1.** $\dfrac{5}{3}$ **2.** -3 **3.** 2

4.

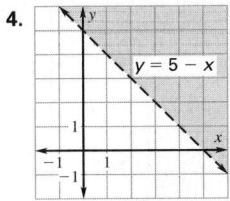

5.

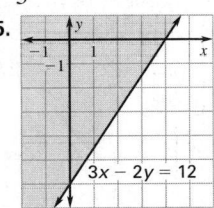

6.

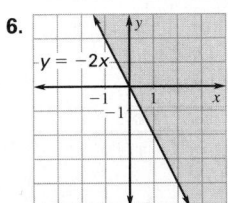

7.

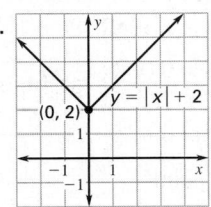

8.

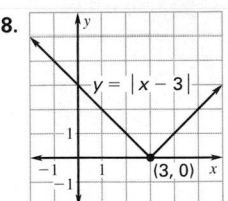

9.

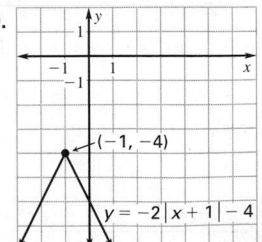

5.1 PRACTICE (pp. 253–254)

5.

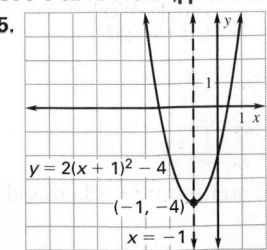

7.

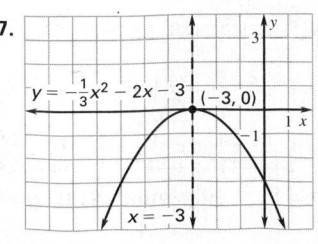

9.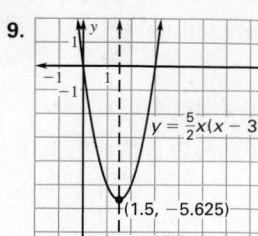

11. $y = -2x^2 - 2x + 24$

13. $y = -x^2 - 4x - 11$

15. $y = \frac{2}{3}x^2 - 12x + 50$

17. C **19.** B

21.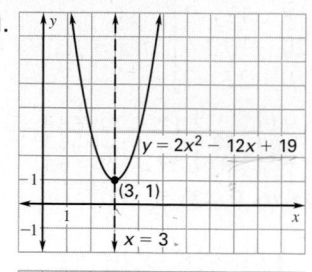

23.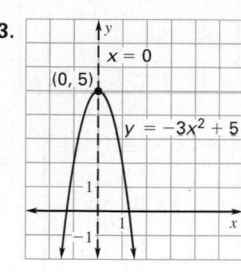

25.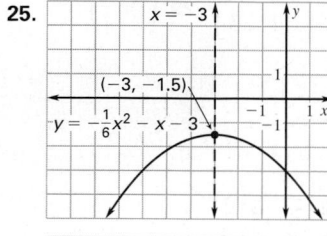

27. 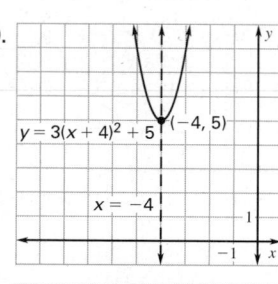   **29.**

31. 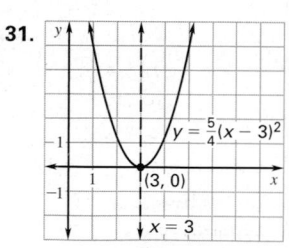   **33.**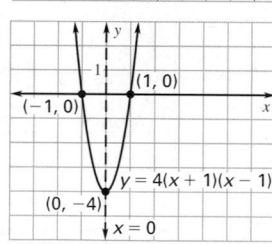

35.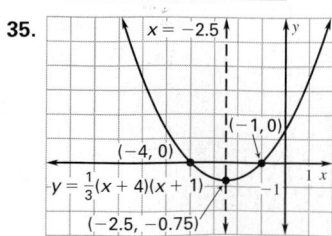

37.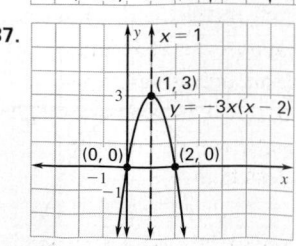

39. $y = -x^2 + x + 12$

41. $y = -3x^2 + 9x + 84$

43. $y = x^2 + 6x + 11$

45. $y = -6x^2 + 24x - 33$

47. $y = -81x^2 - 32x - 4$

49. $y = 32x^2 - 8x - 1$

51. about 3,090 revolutions per min; about 74.7 foot-pounds **53.** *Sample answer:* The energy use decreases until about 90 meters per minute and then increases.

5.1 MIXED REVIEW (p. 255) **57.** 2 **59.** −7 **61.** −5 **63.** 7 **65.** −3 **67.**

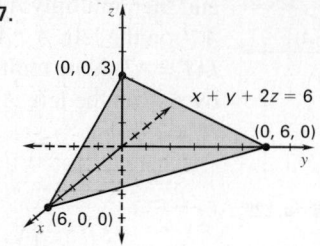

69.

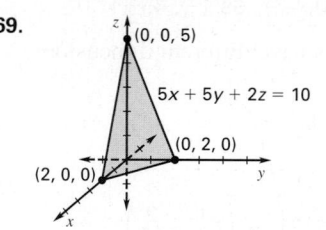

71.

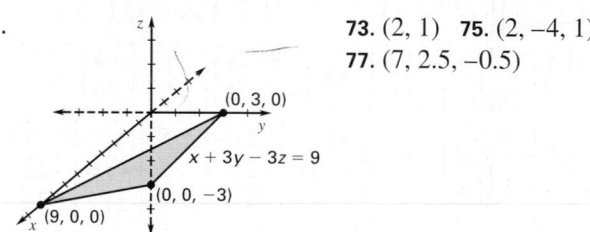

73. (2, 1) **75.** (2, −4, 1)

77. (7, 2.5, −0.5)

5.2 PRACTICE (pp. 260–262) **5.** $(2x + 3)(x - 1)$ **7.** $(y + 1)^2$

9. $q(q + 1)$ **11.** −2, 4 **13.** $-\frac{1}{2}, \frac{1}{2}$ **15.** 0, 6

17. $y = (x + 4)(x + 2)$; −4, −2 **19.** $y = (x + 5)^2$; −5

21. $y = (3x - 2)(x - 2)$; $\frac{2}{3}$, 2 **23.** $(x + 4)(x + 1)$

25. $(x + 5)(x + 8)$ **27.** $(x - 6)(x - 2)$ **29.** $(a + 5)(a - 2)$

31. $(c + 10)(c - 8)$ **33.** cannot be factored

35. $(2x + 1)(x + 3)$ **37.** $(4x + 3)(2x + 3)$ **39.** cannot be factored **41.** $(3k - 1)(k + 11)$ **43.** $(3n - 2)(6n + 7)$

45. $(3v - 7)(4v + 1)$ **47.** $(x - 5)(x + 5)$ **49.** $(x - 3)^2$

51. $(3s + 2)^2$ **53.** $(7 - 10a)(7 + 10a)$ **55.** $(9c + 11)^2$

57. $2(3x - 1)(3x + 1)$ **59.** $4(2y + 3)(y - 5)$ **61.** $u(u + 7)$

63. $-(v - 1)^2$ **65.** −1, 4 **67.** $\frac{3}{5}$, 2 **69.** −12 **71.** $-\frac{4}{9}, \frac{4}{9}$

73. −5, 6 **75.** $\frac{1}{4}$ **77.** −1, $\frac{8}{3}$ **79.** $-\frac{9}{2}$, 0 **81.** $y = (x + 4)(x + 3)$; −4, −3 **83.** $y = (x - 2)(x + 2)$; −2, 2 **85.** $y = x(x - 3)$; 0, 3

87. $y = -(x - 8)^2$; 8 **89. a.** $m + n = 0$, $mn = 9$ **b.** If $m + n = 0$, then $m = -n$. Substituting in $mn = 9$, $(-n)(n) = 9$, $-n^2 = 9$, and $n^2 = -9$. There is no number such that $n^2 = -9$. Therefore, $x^2 + 9$ is not factorable. **91.** 60 ft **93.** 7 **95.** 6 **97.** 2.5 ft **99.** $80; $12,800 **101.** about 70 mi; about 24 mi

5.2 MIXED REVIEW (p. 263) **107.** −4, 8 **109.** −2, 3.6 **111.** $-4 < x < 2$ **113.** $x < -3$ or $x > 11$

115.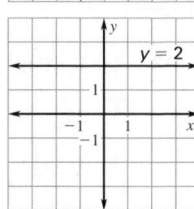

119.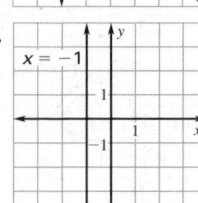

123.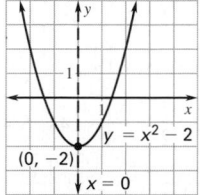

125.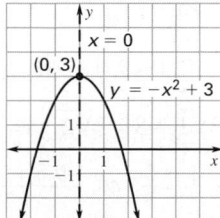

127.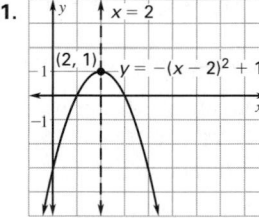

129.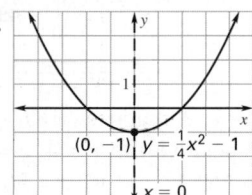

131.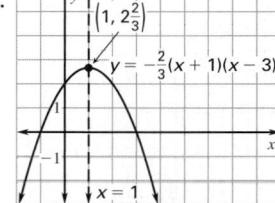

133.

135.

5.3 PRACTICE (pp. 267–268) **5.** $2\sqrt{3}$ **7.** 9 **9.** $\dfrac{\sqrt{7}}{3}$ **11.** $\dfrac{\sqrt{10}}{2}$
13. $-5, 5$ **15.** $-2\sqrt{3}, 2\sqrt{3}$ **17.** $-2\sqrt{7} - 8, 2\sqrt{7} - 8$
19. $3\sqrt{2}$ **21.** $3\sqrt{3}$ **23.** $6\sqrt{2}$ **25.** $7\sqrt{2}$ **27.** 14 **29.** 6
31. $2\sqrt{6}$ **33.** $12\sqrt{7}$ **35.** $\dfrac{1}{3}$ **37.** $\dfrac{6}{5}$ **39.** $\dfrac{\sqrt{3}}{4}$ **41.** $\dfrac{5\sqrt{3}}{6}$
43. $\dfrac{2\sqrt{3}}{3}$ **45.** $\dfrac{\sqrt{30}}{5}$ **47.** $\dfrac{\sqrt{14}}{4}$ **49.** $\dfrac{3\sqrt{10}}{8}$ **51.** $-11, 11$
53. $-6, 6$ **55.** $-5\sqrt{3}, 5\sqrt{3}$ **57.** $-10\sqrt{3}, 10\sqrt{3}$ **59.** $-12, 12$
61. $-6, 4$ **63.** $-3\sqrt{3} + 7, 3\sqrt{3} + 7$ **65.** $-1, 13$ **67.** $-2, 7$
69. about 3.3 sec **71.** Earth: 3.5 sec; Mars: 5.8 sec;
Jupiter: 2.2 sec; Neptune: 3.3 sec; Pluto: 13.8 sec
73. 16.2 in. by 21.6 in. **75. a.** about 60.6 sec **b.** 146 sec
c. *Sample answer:* The water drains more slowly as the
time increases.

5.3 MIXED REVIEW (p. 269) **77.** $(1, 2)$ **79.** $(-3, -5)$

81. $(6, -2)$ **83.** $\begin{bmatrix} 13 & -1 \\ -11 & 1 \end{bmatrix}$ **85.** $\begin{bmatrix} 81 & 57 \\ -40 & -31 \end{bmatrix}$

87. $y = x^2 - 9x + 8$ **89.** $y = 16x^2 - 81$
91. $y = 5x^2 + 60x + 168$

QUIZ 1 (p. 270)

1.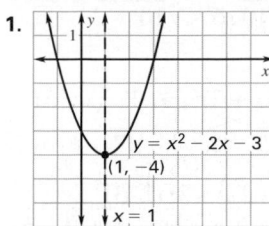

2.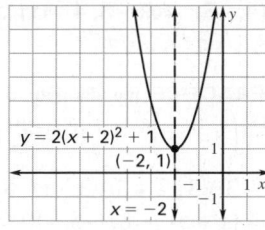

3.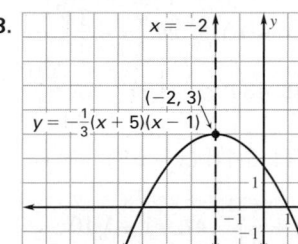

4. $-3, 9$ **5.** $-4, -\dfrac{5}{4}$ **6.** $\dfrac{1}{2}$
7. $3\sqrt{6}$ **8.** $14\sqrt{5}$
9. $\dfrac{6\sqrt{5}}{5}$ **10.** $\dfrac{2\sqrt{3}}{3}$
11. about 2.7 mi/h

TECHNOLOGY ACTIVITY 5.3 (p. 271) **1.** $-1.53, 1.53$
3. $-2.45, 2.45$ **5.** $-2.73, 0.73$ **7.** $-3.65, 1.65$
9. $48\pi = 6\pi r^2$; $r \approx 2.8$ in.

5.4 PRACTICE (pp. 277–279) **5.** $-2i\sqrt{2}, 2i\sqrt{2}$ **7.** $7 + 3i$
9. $9 - 5i$ **11.** $\sqrt{2}$ **13.** $\sqrt{13}$ **15.**
17. $-2i, 2i$ **19.** $-3i\sqrt{3}, 3i\sqrt{3}$
21. $-i\sqrt{3}, i\sqrt{3}$ **23.** $-i, i$
25. $2 + 4i, 2 - 4i$
27. $-3 - 2i\sqrt{14}, -3 + 2i\sqrt{14}$

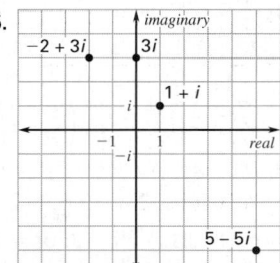

29–35 odd:

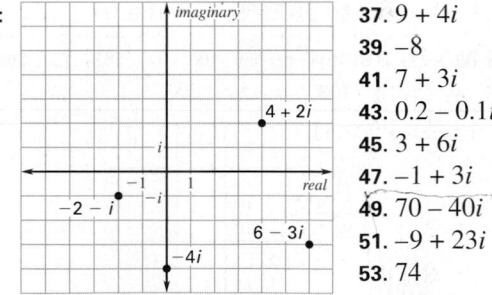

37. $9 + 4i$
39. -8
41. $7 + 3i$
43. $0.2 - 0.1i$
45. $3 + 6i$
47. $-1 + 3i$
49. $70 - 40i$
51. $-9 + 23i$
53. 74

55. $161 - 240i$ **57.** $-1 + i$ **59.** $\dfrac{4}{5} + \dfrac{3}{5}i$ **61.** $-\dfrac{87}{97} + \dfrac{26}{97}i$
63. $\dfrac{17}{19} - \dfrac{6\sqrt{2}}{19}i$ **65.** 13 **67.** $5\sqrt{2}$ **69.** $4\sqrt{5}$ **71.** 4

73. *Sample answer:* It does because the absolute values are
equal to or less than $N = 1$. **75.** *Sample answer:* It does not
because the absolute values become infinitely large.
77. *Sample answer:* It does not because the absolute values
become infinitely large. **79.** *Sample answer:* It does
because the absolute values are less than $N = 1$.

81. true
83. false; *Sample answer:* $(6 + 3i) + (-5 - 3i) = 1$, which is
not imaginary. **85.** true

87. true; true **89.** false; false **91.** false; false **95. a.** $2 - 2i$
b. $12 - 7i$ **c.** $8 - 4i$

5.4 MIXED REVIEW (p. 280) **101.** 11 **103.** 3 **105.** $(1, 2)$
107. $(4, -3)$ **109.** $-8, 4$ **111.** $5 + \sqrt{10}, 5 - \sqrt{10}$
113. $6 + \sqrt{7}, 6 - \sqrt{7}$

5.5 PRACTICE (pp. 286–289) **5.** $49; (x + 7)^2$ **7.** $25; (x - 5)^2$
9. $\dfrac{169}{4}; \left(x - \dfrac{13}{2}\right)^2$ **11.** $1 - \sqrt{5}, 1 + \sqrt{5}$ **13.** $-4 - \sqrt{7}, -4 + \sqrt{7}$
15. $2 - 3i\sqrt{3}, 2 + 3i\sqrt{3}$ **17.** $y = (x - 2)^2 + 3; (2, 3)$
19. $y = (x + 5)^2 - 8; (-5, -8)$ **21.** $y = 2(x + 1)^2 - 6; (-1, -6)$
23. $(x + 8)^2$ **25.** $(x - 12)^2$ **27.** $(x + 0.5)^2$ **29.** $\left(x - \dfrac{3}{2}\right)^2$
31. $\left(x - \dfrac{2}{9}\right)^2$ **33.** $81; (x + 9)^2$ **35.** $484; (x - 22)^2$ **37.** $\dfrac{121}{4};$
$\left(x - \dfrac{11}{2}\right)^2$ **39.** $\dfrac{225}{4}; \left(x + \dfrac{15}{2}\right)^2$ **41.** $8.41; (x - 2.9)^2$
43. $22.09; (x + 4.7)^2$ **45.** $\dfrac{25}{9}; \left(x + \dfrac{5}{3}\right)^2$ **47.** $-1 + \sqrt{10},$
$-1 - \sqrt{10}$ **49.** $-10 + 2i, -10 - 2i$ **51.** $3 - 2\sqrt{11}, 3 + 2\sqrt{11}$
53. $-0.9 - \sqrt{2.31}, -0.9 + \sqrt{2.31}$ **55.** $3 + \sqrt{2}, 3 - \sqrt{2}$
57. $-7 - i, -7 + i$ **59.** $\dfrac{5 - 2\sqrt{3}}{2}, \dfrac{5 + 2\sqrt{3}}{2}$ **61.** $\dfrac{-1 - i}{2}, \dfrac{-1 + i}{2}$
63. $-6, 2$ **65.** $-\dfrac{\sqrt{23}}{3}, \dfrac{\sqrt{23}}{3}$ **67.** $\dfrac{1 - i\sqrt{71}}{6}, \dfrac{1 + i\sqrt{71}}{6}$
69. $-1 - 4\sqrt{2}, -1 + 4\sqrt{2}$ **71.** $11 - 13i, 11 + 13i$
73. $y = (x - 3)^2 + 2; (3, 2)$ **75.** $y = (x + 8)^2 - 50; (-8, -50)$
77. $y = \left(x - \dfrac{3}{2}\right)^2 - \dfrac{17}{4}; \left(\dfrac{3}{2}, -\dfrac{17}{4}\right)$ **79.** $y = -(x - 10)^2 + 20;$
$(10, 20)$ **81.** $y = 3(x - 2)^2 - 11; (2, -11)$
83. $y = 1.4(x + 2)^2 - 2.6; (-2, -2.6)$ **85.** $-5 + 5\sqrt{5},$
or ≈ 6.18 **87.** $\sqrt{39} - 2$, or ≈ 4.24 **89.** $d = 0.08(30)^2 +$
$1.1(30) = 105$ ft; about 25.5 mi/h **91.** 45.50 ft; 161.16 ft
93. about 1 cm **95.** $507.5°$F; 3.91 Btu/ft^3

5.5 MIXED REVIEW (p. 289) **101.** 17 **103.** 52 **105.** 0
107. $y = 2x - 5$ **109.** $y = -5x - 25$
111. $y = \dfrac{1}{3}x + 7$ **113.**

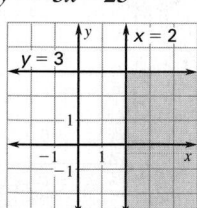

115.

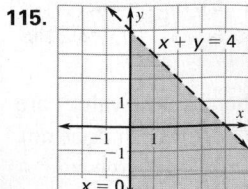

117.

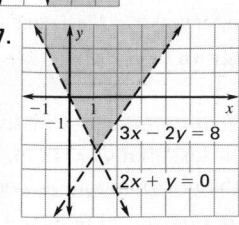

TECHNOLOGY ACTIVITY 5.5 (p. 290)
1–9 odd: Estimates may vary. **1.** minimum; -4.25; 2.5
3. minimum; 4; -3 **5.** maximum; 8.125; -0.75
7. minimum; 2.375; 3.75 **9.** maximum; 8.65; 2.29

5.6 PRACTICE (pp. 295–297)
5. $\dfrac{-1 + \sqrt{5}}{2}, \dfrac{-1 - \sqrt{5}}{2}$ **7.** $\dfrac{-1 + \sqrt{2}}{3}, \dfrac{-1 - \sqrt{2}}{3}$
9. $\dfrac{1}{2} + 3i, \dfrac{1}{2} - 3i$ **11.** -16; 2 imaginary **13.** -47; 2 imaginary
15. 261; 2 real **17.** $-2, 7$ **19.** $1 + \sqrt{5}, 1 - \sqrt{5}$ **21.** $-3 - 7i,$
$-3 + 7i$ **23.** $\dfrac{-3 + \sqrt{29}}{10}, \dfrac{-3 - \sqrt{29}}{10}$ **25.** $\dfrac{-1 + i\sqrt{7}}{4}, \dfrac{-1 - i\sqrt{7}}{4}$
27. $-1, \dfrac{9}{7}$ **29.** $\dfrac{-9 + \sqrt{33}}{8}, \dfrac{-9 - \sqrt{33}}{8}$ **31.** $-\dfrac{2}{5} + \dfrac{\sqrt{26}}{10},$
$-\dfrac{2}{5} - \dfrac{\sqrt{26}}{10}$ **33.** $-9, 11$ **35.** $4 + i\sqrt{19}, 4 - i\sqrt{19}$
37. $-8 + 3\sqrt{2}, -8 - 3\sqrt{2}$ **39.** $\dfrac{1}{2} + \dfrac{\sqrt{6}}{4}, \dfrac{1}{2} - \dfrac{\sqrt{6}}{4}$ **41.** $5 + \dfrac{i}{2},$
$5 - \dfrac{i}{2}$ **43.** $\dfrac{1}{3}, -\dfrac{5}{3}$ **45.** $\dfrac{-9.5 + \sqrt{218.17}}{7.8}, \dfrac{-9.5 - \sqrt{218.17}}{7.8}$
47. $\dfrac{3 + \sqrt{69}}{2}, \dfrac{3 - \sqrt{69}}{2}$ **49.** $2, 16$ **51.** $-4 + 3i, -4 - 3i$
53. $\dfrac{\sqrt{3}}{2}, -\dfrac{\sqrt{3}}{2}$ **55.** $-\dfrac{3}{2}, \dfrac{1}{7}$ **57.** 33; 2 real **59.** 160; 2 real
61. -7; 2 imaginary **63.** -19; 2 imaginary **65.** zero
67. positive **69.** $c < 4; c = 4; c > 4$ **71.** $c < 16; c = 16;$
$c > 16$ **73.** $c < 36; c = 36; c > 36$ **75.** about 2.56 sec
77. about 0.17 sec **79.** 1993

5.6 MIXED REVIEW (p. 298)
85. $x > 2$ **87.** $x \geq -13$ **89.** $3 \leq x \leq 8$
91.

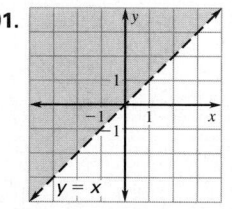

93.

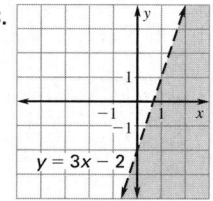

95.

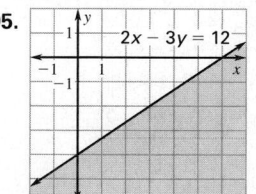

97.

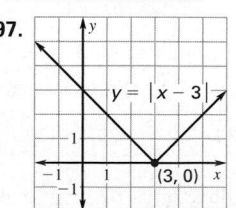

99.

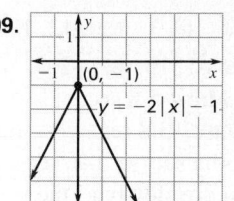

101.

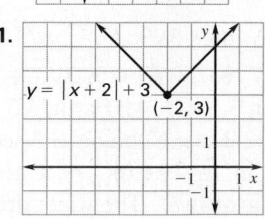

QUIZ 2 (p. 298) **1.** $5 + 16i$ **2.** $-4 + 10i$ **3.** $31 + 22i$

4. $\dfrac{1}{13} - \dfrac{8}{13}i$ **5–10.**

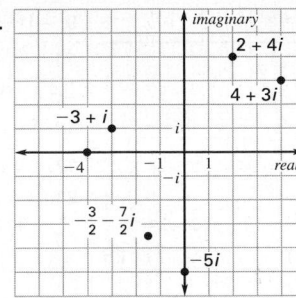

5. $2\sqrt{5}$ **6.** 5

7. $\sqrt{10}$ **8.** 5

9. 4 **10.** $\dfrac{\sqrt{58}}{2}$

11. $-4 + \sqrt{2}, -4 - \sqrt{2}$ **12.** $1 + 4i, 1 - 4i$ **13.** $5 + 3\sqrt{3}$,
$5 - 3\sqrt{3}$ **14.** $-2 + \dfrac{\sqrt{5}}{5}, -2 - \dfrac{\sqrt{5}}{5}$ **15.** $y = (x + 3)^2 - 8$

16. $y = (x - 9)^2 - 31$ **17.** $y = -2(x - 2)^2 + 1$ **18.** $-1 + \sqrt{11}$,
$-1 - \sqrt{11}$ **19.** $8 + 3i, 8 - 3i$ **20.** $\dfrac{3 + i\sqrt{7}}{2}, \dfrac{3 - i\sqrt{7}}{2}$

21. $\dfrac{-4 + 2\sqrt{6}}{5}, \dfrac{-4 - 2\sqrt{6}}{5}$ **22.** about 1 sec

5.7 PRACTICE (pp. 303–305)

5.

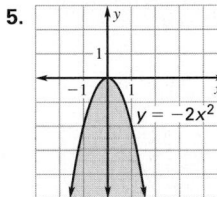

7.

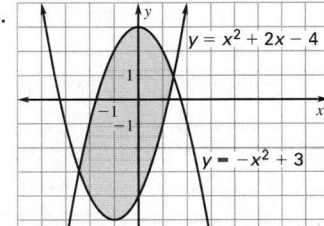

9.

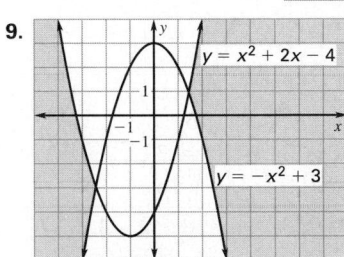

11. $x \le -2$ or $x \ge 2$
13. about 55.1 m and
447.3 m **15.** C

17.

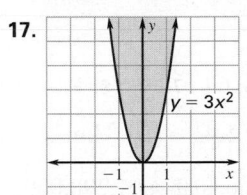

19.

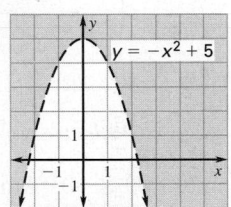

21.

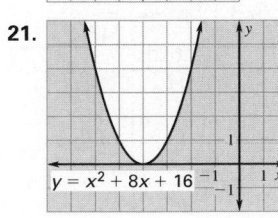

23.

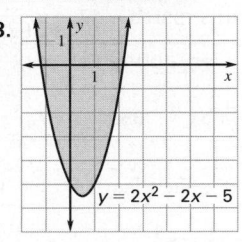

25.

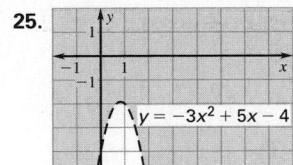

27.

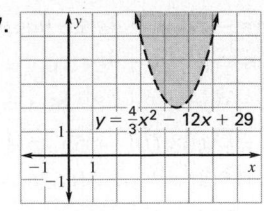

29.

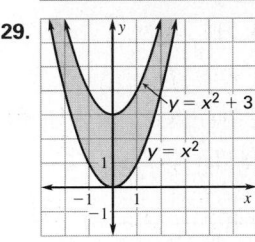

31.

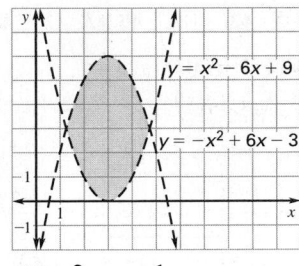

33.

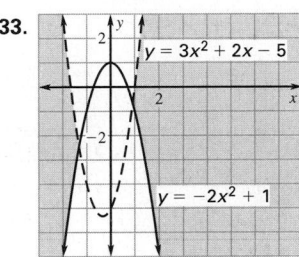

35. $-2 < x < 1$
37. $x \le -4$ or $x \ge 2$
39. $x \le -5.5$ or $x \ge -2.5$
41. $x \le -6$ or $x \ge 3$
43. $-\dfrac{5}{2} < x < \dfrac{5}{2}$
45. $x < -0.9$ or $x > 2.9$

47. Weight for Manila Rope Weight for Wire Rope

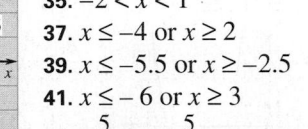

49. Healthy Weights ; $121 \le W \le 160$

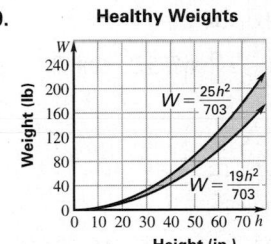

51. about 39 to 61 years old

5.7 MIXED REVIEW (p. 305) **55.** $y = 4x - 5$ **57.** $y = -\dfrac{11}{4} - \dfrac{1}{2}x$
59. $y = -9x$ **61.** $(2, 3, -4)$ **63.** -6 **65.** $6 - 5i$ **67.** $29 - 29i$
69. $\dfrac{6}{17} - \dfrac{7}{17}i$

5.8 PRACTICE (pp. 309–311) **3.** $y = -1(x - 1)^2 + 3$
5. $y = x^2 + 3x - 2$ **7.** $y = (x - 2)^2 - 2$ **9.** $y = -\dfrac{3}{4}(x - 1)^2$
11. $y = \dfrac{1}{3}(x + 4)^2 + 6$ **13.** $y = -3x^2$ **15.** $y = -\dfrac{3}{2}(x + 6)^2 - 7$
17. $y = 3(x + 2)(x - 1)$ **19.** $y = -1(x - 1)(x - 4)$
21. $y = 2(x + 1)(x - 6)$ **23.** $y = \dfrac{7}{5}(x - 3)(x - 9)$

25. $y = -x^2 + x + 4$ **27.** $y = -\frac{3}{4}x^2 - \frac{11}{4}x + 1$

29. $y = -x^2 + 5x - 2$ **31.** $y = -2x^2 - 4x + 9$

33. $y = \frac{5}{2}x^2 + 6x - 8$ **35.** $y = -0.00168(x - 0)(x - 24)$

37. $s = -0.0807p^2 + 55.2p + 330$;

$k = -0.0000609p^2 + 0.626p + 125$

5.8 MIXED REVIEW (p. 312)

41. 5 **43.** -182 **45.** $(3, -1)$ **47.** $(-4, 5)$

QUIZ 3 (p. 312)

1. 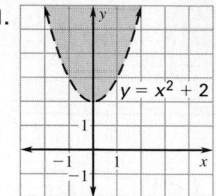 **2.**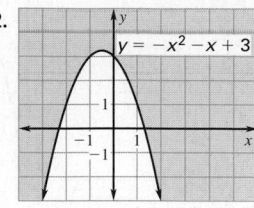

3. 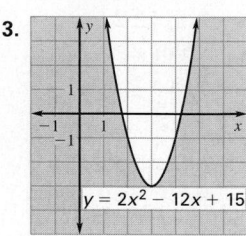 **4.**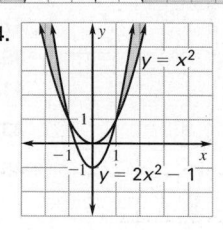

5.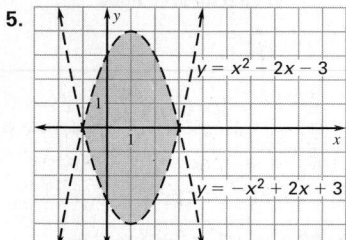

6.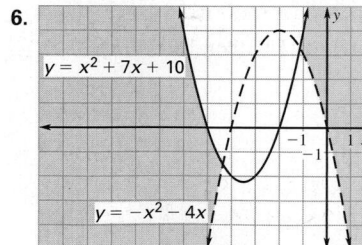

7. $y = 2(x - 5)^2 - 2$

8. $y = -1(x + 3)(x - 1)$

9. $y = \frac{3}{4}x^2 + x$

10. $0.00339N^2 + 0.00143N - 5.95 < 1000; 0 < N < 544$

CHAPTER 5 REVIEW (pp. 314-316)

1.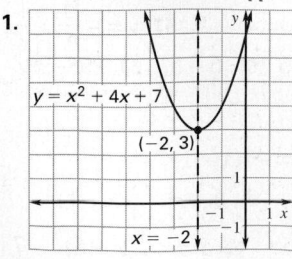

3.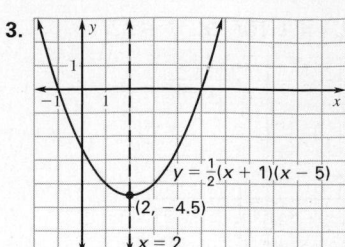

5. 4 **7.** $-3, \frac{5}{3}$

9. $-10, 10$

11. $-6 - 2\sqrt{10}$, $-6 + 2\sqrt{10}$

13. $5 + i$ **15.** $102 + 13i$

17. $3\sqrt{13}$ **19.** $5 + i, 5 - i$

21. $y = (x - 4)^2 + 1; (4, 1)$

23. $y = 4(x + 2)^2 + 7; (-2, 7)$ **25.** $-\frac{7}{18} - \frac{\sqrt{85}}{18}, -\frac{7}{18} + \frac{\sqrt{85}}{18}$

27. 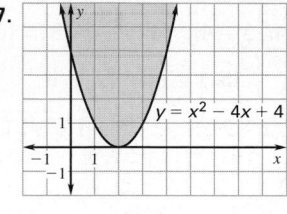 **29.**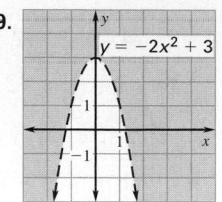

31. $x \leq \dfrac{-7 - \sqrt{33}}{4}$ or $x \geq \dfrac{-7 + \sqrt{33}}{4}$ **33.** $y = (x - 6)^2 + 1$

35. $y = 0.5x^2 + 1.5x - 4$

CHAPTER 6

SKILL REVIEW (p. 322) **1.** $3x^2 - x$ **2.** $-3x + 10$

3. $-5x^4 - 4x^3 + 7x^2$

4. 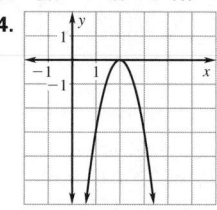 **5.**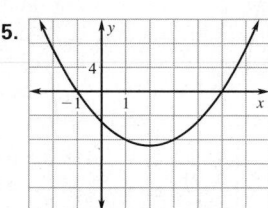

6.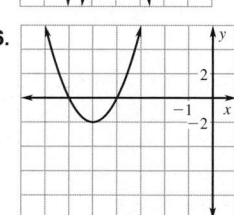

7. $y = x^2 - 2x - 6$

8. $y = 2x^2 + 16x + 32$

9. $y = -x^2 - 6x + 16$

10. $-9, 3$ **11.** -10 **12.** $-4, \frac{3}{2}$

6.1 PRACTICE (pp. 326–328) **3.** 216 **5.** 64 **7.** $\frac{25}{9}$ **9.** 1

11. $\dfrac{1}{16x^6}$ **13.** $3y^3$ **15.** sun's volume: 1.41×10^{18} km³;

Earth's volume: 1.09×10^{12} km³; ratio is about 1,298,000;

the results match. **17.** $\dfrac{1}{15,625}$ **19.** 262,144 **21.** $\dfrac{27}{343}$

23. $\dfrac{1}{121}$ **25.** 4096 **27.** 2048 **29.** $\dfrac{1}{6}$ **31.** $\dfrac{15,625}{64}$

33. $32,768x^{10}$ **35.** x^7 **37.** $\dfrac{1}{x^{12}y^{21}}$ **39.** $-\dfrac{3}{x^4}$ **41.** $\dfrac{y^3}{x^2}$

43. $\dfrac{1}{3}xy^2$ **45.** $-\dfrac{y^{12}}{9x^4}$ **47.** $3x^2y^2$ **49.** $A = 16\pi x^2$

51. $V = \dfrac{4}{81}\pi x^3$

53.

Country	Per capita GDP
France	2.13×10^4
Germany	2.24×10^4
Ireland	1.95×10^4
Luxembourg	3.24×10^4
The Netherlands	2.14×10^4
Sweden	2.00×10^4

55. about 7.48×10^3 days

65. 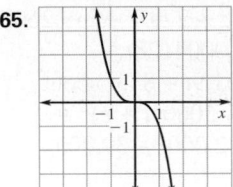 **67.**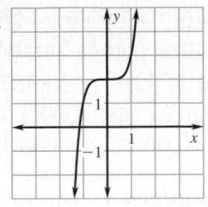

69. 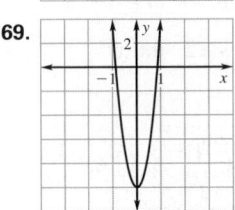 **71.**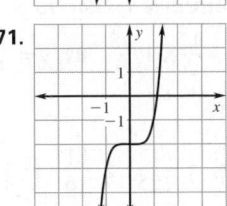

73. 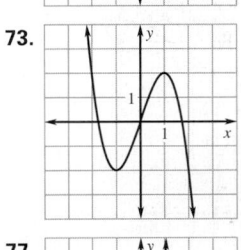 **75.**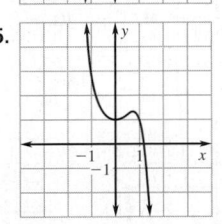

77. 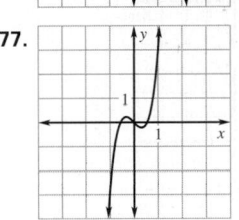 **79.**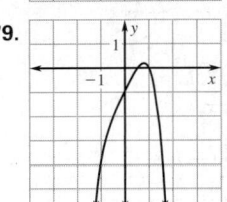

6.1 MIXED REVIEW (p. 328)

61. 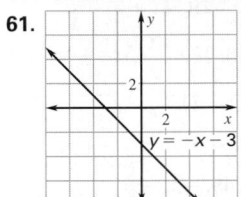 **63.**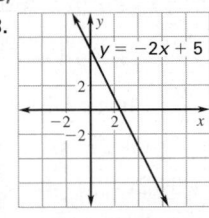

65. 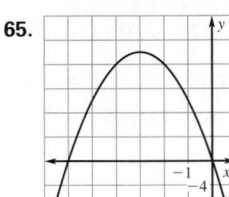 **67.**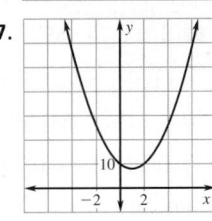

69. ± 4 **71.** $\pm\dfrac{4}{5}$ **73.** ± 1 **75.** $\pm\sqrt{5}$ **77.** $\pm\sqrt{3}$ **79.** $-3 + 4i$
81. $2 - 7i$ **83.** $26 + 12i$

6.2 PRACTICE (pp. 333–336)
5. no **7.** yes; -2
9. $f(x) \to +\infty$ as $x \to -\infty$ and $f(x) \to -\infty$ as $x \to +\infty$
11. $f(x) \to -\infty$ as $x \to -\infty$ and $f(x) \to +\infty$ as $x \to +\infty$
13. $f(x) \to -\infty$ as $x \to -\infty$ and $f(x) \to -\infty$ as $x \to +\infty$
15. yes; $f(x) = -5x + 12$, 1, linear, -5 **17.** yes;
$f(x) = x + \pi$, 1, linear, 1 **19.** no **21.** yes; $f(x) = x^2 - x + 1$,
2, quadratic, 1 **23.** yes; $f(x) = x^4 - x^3 + 36x^2$, 4, quartic, 1
25. yes; $f(x) = 3x^3$, 3, cubic, 3 **27.** 4 **29.** 36 **31.** 4 **33.** 2
35. 7930 **37.** 73 **39.** -91 **41.** -31 **43.** -7 **45.** 255

47.

Function	As $x \to -\infty$	As $x \to +\infty$
$f(x) = -5x^3$	$f(x) \to +\infty$	$f(x) \to -\infty$
$f(x) = -x^3 + 1$	$f(x) \to +\infty$	$f(x) \to -\infty$
$f(x) = 2x - 3x^3$	$f(x) \to +\infty$	$f(x) \to -\infty$
$f(x) = 2x^2 - x^3$	$f(x) \to +\infty$	$f(x) \to -\infty$

49. C **51.** B
53. $f(x) \to -\infty$ as $x \to -\infty$ and $f(x) \to -\infty$ as $x \to +\infty$
55. $f(x) \to -\infty$ as $x \to -\infty$ and $f(x) \to +\infty$ as $x \to +\infty$
57. $f(x) \to -\infty$ as $x \to -\infty$ and $f(x) \to -\infty$ as $x \to +\infty$
59. $f(x) \to +\infty$ as $x \to -\infty$ and $f(x) \to -\infty$ as $x \to +\infty$
61. $f(x) \to +\infty$ as $x \to -\infty$ and $f(x) \to +\infty$ as $x \to +\infty$
63. $f(x) \to +\infty$ as $x \to -\infty$ and $f(x) \to -\infty$ as $x \to +\infty$

81. about 4272.9 million ft^2 **83.** $f(x) \to -\infty$ as $x \to -\infty$ and
$f(x) \to -\infty$ as $x \to +\infty$; less; the graph will tend to go down
over time. **85.** $f(x) \to +\infty$ as $x \to -\infty$ and $f(x) \to +\infty$ as
$x \to +\infty$; more; the graph will tend to go up over time.

6.2 MIXED REVIEW (p. 336)
91. $7x$ **93.** $x^2 + 4x - 11$
95. $-x^2 - x + 2$ **97.** $y = -2x^2 - 2x + 60$ **99.** $y = 4x^2 -$
$24x + 12$ **101.** $y = -3x^2 + 30x - 72$ **103.** $\pm\sqrt{5}\,i$ **105.** $\pm\sqrt{3}\,i$
107. $\pm\dfrac{\sqrt{6}}{6}\,i$ **109.** $\pm\dfrac{\sqrt{10}}{2}\,i$

TECHNOLOGY ACTIVITY 6.2 (p. 337)
1–7. Ranges may vary.
1. $-10 \le x \le 10$, $-10 \le y \le 100$ **3.** $-5 \le x \le 5$, $-5 \le y \le 10$
5. $-5 \le x \le 5$, $0 \le y \le 20$ **7.** $0 \le x \le 16$, $0 \le y \le 300{,}000$

6.3 PRACTICE (pp. 341–343)
5. $2x^3 - 5x^2 - 3x + 6$
7. $-2x^2 + 4x - 2$ **9.** $4x^4 + 10x^3 + 27x^2 - 41x - 70$
11. $-27x^3 + 27x^2 - 9x + 1$ **13.** $11x^2 - 1$ **15.** $-7x + 7$
17. $-8x^3 - 4x^2 + x - 4$ **19.** $4x^2 - 6x - 21$ **21.** $-7x^3 - x^2 +$
$2x - 11$ **23.** $9x^3 - 3x^2 + 3x - 1$ **25.** $x^3 + 7x^2 + 8x + 14$
27. $x^3 + 6x^2 - 7x$ **29.** $-4x^3 + 32x^2 - 12x$ **31.** $x^2 - 11x + 28$
33. $x^3 - x^2 - 3x + 27$ **35.** $6x^4 + 13x^3 - 3x^2 + 5x$
37. $x^3 + 6x^2 - 46x + 99$ **39.** $x^4 + x^3 - 2x^2 + 2x - 2$
41. $3x^4 + 12x^3 + 7x^2 - 8x - 6$ **43.** $2x^4 + x^3 + 8x^2 - 3x + 4$
45. $x^3 - 67x + 126$ **47.** $-x^3 - 11x^2 - 23x + 35$
49. $3x^3 - 31x^2 + 32x + 36$ **51.** $6x^3 + 29x^2 + 21x + 4$
53. $x^2 - 49$ **55.** $64x^3 - 144x^2 + 108x - 27$ **57.** $x^4 - 12x^2 +$
36 **59.** $27x^3 + 189x^2 + 441x + 343$ **61.** $8x^3 + 36x^2y +$
$54xy^2 + 27y^3$ **63.** $V = 2x^3 + 5x^2 + 3x$

65. $y = -0.8246t^4 + 27.57t^3 - 268.42t^2 + 2797t + 219{,}260$; about 252 million people **67.** $W = -0.0004128t^5 - 0.03414t^4 + 1.3539t^3 - 12.8387t^2 + 51.9t + 833$; about 1,086,000 degrees **69.** $4000(1 + r)^3 + 5000(1 + r)^2 + 7000(1 + r)$; $10{,}000r^3 + 43{,}000r^2 + 72{,}000r + 39{,}000$

6.3 MIXED REVIEW (p. 344) **73.** ± 3 **75.** -8 **77.** $-\dfrac{3}{2}$, 5 **79.** $y = -\dfrac{6}{5}x^2 - \dfrac{12}{5}x + \dfrac{48}{5}$ **81.** $y = \dfrac{1}{3}x^2 - 12$ **83.** x^3 **85.** $-\dfrac{1}{25}$ **87.** $\dfrac{1}{2}x^4 y^{11}$

QUIZ 1 (p. 344) **1.** $\dfrac{1}{125}$ **2.** $\dfrac{81}{16}$ **3.** $\dfrac{25}{81}$ **4.** $\dfrac{1}{16}$ **5.** 1 **6.** $\dfrac{1}{648}$ **7.** $\dfrac{1}{25}$ **8.** $\dfrac{1}{9x^6 y^{12}}$ **9.** $\dfrac{x^7}{y^3}$ **10.** $\dfrac{x^3}{y}$ **11.** $\dfrac{y^6}{8x^3}$ **12.** $\dfrac{x^7}{y^7}$

13. 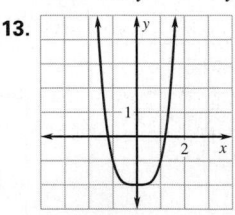 **14.**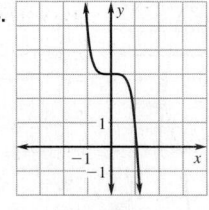

15. 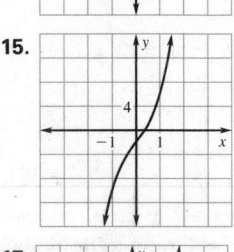 **16.**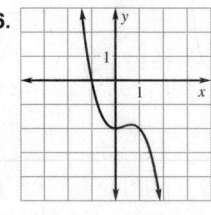

17. 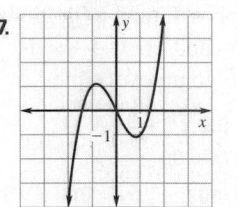 **18.**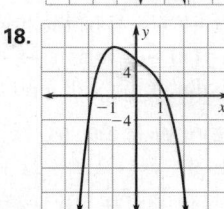

19. $7x^3 + 3x^2 + 7x - 3$ **20.** $3x^2 + 3x - 11$ **21.** $2x^2 + 18x - 2$ **22.** $x^3 + 3x^2 + 2x - 6$ **23.** $4x^3 + 19x^2 - 6x - 5$ **24.** $2x^3 + 3x^2 - 17x - 30$ **25.** $x^3 - 18x^2 + 108x - 216$ **26.** $4x^4 + 12x^2 + 9$ **27.** about 1.98×10^4 hours (about 825 days)

6.4 PRACTICE (pp. 348–350) **5.** $(x^2 + 5)(x^4 - 5x^2 + 25)$ **7.** $(x + 1)(x - 1)(x^2 + 1)$ **9.** $5(x - 4)(x^2 + 4x + 16)$ **11.** 3 **13.** $-2, \pm 3$ **15.** $\pm\dfrac{\sqrt{6}}{3}$ **17.** 1998 **19.** $3x^3$ **21.** $6x$ **23.** 1 **25.** $3x^3$ **27.** C **29.** F **31.** E **33.** $(x - 2)(x^2 + 2x + 4)$ **35.** $(6x + 1)(36x^2 - 6x + 1)$ **37.** $(10x + 3)(100x^2 - 30x + 9)$ **39.** $4(2x - 1)(4x^2 + 2x + 1)$ **41.** $(x + 1)(x^2 + 1)$ **43.** $(x + 3)(x^2 + 10)$ **45.** $(2x - 5)(x^2 + 9)$ **47.** $(x - 2)(3x^2 + 1)$ **49.** $(3x - 2)(x^2 - 3)$ **51.** $(x^2 + 1)(x^2 + 2)$ **53.** $(3x - 4)(3x + 4)(9x^2 + 16)$ **55.** $(x^2 + 2)(x^2 + 8)$ **57.** $2x^2(2x - 1)(2x + 1)(4x^2 + 1)$ **59.** $(2x^2 + 3)(9x - 1)$ **61.** $(2x + 1)(2x - 1)(x^2 + 10)$ **63.** $8(x - 2)(x^2 + 2x + 4)$ **65.** $3x(x - 2)(x^2 + 2x + 4)$ **67.** $x(3x^2 + 1)(x + 3)$ **69.** 0, 3 **71.** -3 **73.** $-7, 2$ **75.** $0, \pm 3$ **77.** $\dfrac{1}{2}$ **79.** 5 **81.** ± 1 **83.** none **85.** $0, \pm 2, \pm\sqrt{2}$ **87.** about 3.16 in. by 1.16 in. by 8.16 in.

89. 6 ft by 3 ft by 1 ft **91.** base: 5 ft by 5 ft, height: 30 ft

6.4 MIXED REVIEW (p. 351) **99.** $\dfrac{y^{11}}{6}$ **101.** y^4 **103.** 481

6.5 PRACTICE (pp. 356–358) **5.** $x^2 + x - 4 + \dfrac{14}{x + 4}$ **7.** $-x + 2 + \dfrac{-3x + 5}{x^2 - 1}$ **9.** $x^3 - 4x^2 + 1$ **11.** $x + 9 + \dfrac{16}{x - 2}$ **13.** $-2, -1$ **15.** $x + 9 + \dfrac{13}{x - 2}$ **17.** $2x - 5 + \dfrac{19}{x + 4}$ **19.** $x + 15 + \dfrac{147}{x - 10}$ **21.** $2x^2 + 2 + \dfrac{9}{x^2 - 1}$ **23.** $3x - 4 + \dfrac{5}{2x + 3}$ **25.** $5x^2 - x + 3$ **27.** $x^2 + 2x - 3 - \dfrac{12}{x - 2}$ **29.** $4x + 1 - \dfrac{5}{x + 1}$ **31.** $2x + 11 + \dfrac{30}{x - 2}$ **33.** $x - 4 + \dfrac{26}{x + 4}$ **35.** $10x^3 - 5x^2 + 9x - 9$ **37.** $2x^3 + x - \dfrac{3}{x - 3}$ **39.** $(x + 2)(x - 3)(x - 4)$ **41.** $(x - 10)(x - 4)(x + 2)$ **43.** $(x + 5)(x - 3)^2$ **45.** $(x - 1)(2x + 3)(2x - 3)$ **47.** $-\dfrac{1}{9}, 1$ **49.** $-5, -\dfrac{1}{2}$ **51.** $\dfrac{5 \pm \sqrt{17}}{2}$ **53.** $1 \pm i\sqrt{7}$ **55.** $3x - 10$ **57.** $(-2, 6), (-1, 5), (1, -3)$ **59.** $5x^3 - 3x^2 + 21x - 8$; I multiplied $5x^2 - 13x + 47$ by $x + 2$ and added -102. **61.** Answers may vary depending on rounding. $C = 0.0031x^2 + 0.1578x + 11.155 + \dfrac{6398}{8.4x - 580}$; about 144 million cars

6.5 MIXED REVIEW (p. 358) **67.** Both are solutions. **69.** $(1, 4)$ is a solution, but $(2, 0)$ is not a solution. **71.** $4 \pm \sqrt{13}$ **73.** $\dfrac{7 \pm \sqrt{33}}{8}$ **75.** $\dfrac{-1 \pm \sqrt{41}}{10}$ **77.** $\dfrac{-1 \pm i\sqrt{159}}{10}$ **79.** $-4x + 9$ **81.** $-14x^3 - 2x^2 + x + 4$ **83.** 82 guests

6.6 PRACTICE (pp. 362–364) **5.** $\pm 1, \pm 2, \pm 3, \pm 4, \pm 6, \pm 8, \pm 9, \pm 12, \pm 18, \pm 24, \pm 36, \pm 72$ **7.** $\pm 1, \pm 2, \pm 5, \pm 10, \pm\dfrac{1}{5}, \pm\dfrac{2}{5}$ **9.** $-4, -1, 1$ **11.** $-3, \dfrac{3}{2}, 2$ **13.** $-5, -1, 1$ **15.** $\pm 1, \pm 2, \pm 3, \pm 4, \pm 6, \pm 8, \pm 12, \pm 24$ **17.** $\pm\dfrac{1}{2}, \pm 1, \pm 2, \pm 4, \pm 8, \pm 16$ **19.** $\pm 1, \pm 2, \pm 5, \pm 10, \pm\dfrac{1}{2}, \pm\dfrac{5}{2}, \pm\dfrac{1}{3}, \pm\dfrac{2}{3}, \pm\dfrac{5}{3}, \pm\dfrac{10}{3}, \pm\dfrac{1}{6}, \pm\dfrac{5}{6}$ **21.** $\pm 1, \pm 3, \pm\dfrac{1}{2}, \pm\dfrac{3}{2}, \pm\dfrac{1}{4}, \pm\dfrac{3}{4}, \pm\dfrac{1}{8}, \pm\dfrac{3}{8}$ **23.** $-2, 2$ **25.** $-2, -1$ **27.** $-1, 1$ **29.** none **31.** $-2, -1, 1, 2$ **33.** $-3, 1, 10$ **35.** $-2, 4, 5$ **37.** $-4, 3, 6$ **39.** $-1, 2$ **41.** $-3, -2, 1, 3$ **43.** $-3, -2, 3$ **45.** $-1, \dfrac{3}{2}, \dfrac{5}{2}$ **47.** $-2, -1, 1$ **49.** $-1, \dfrac{3}{2}, 2$ **51.** $-4, \dfrac{1}{2}, 4$ **53.** $-\dfrac{5}{2}, 1$ **55.** $-1, 1$ **57.** $-2, -\dfrac{1}{2}, 2$ **59.** 1993 **61.** 2 in. by 2 in. by 5 in. **63.** 5 ft deep, 10 ft wide, 40 ft long

6.6 MIXED REVIEW (p. 365) **71.** 3 **73.** 1 **75.** 10 **77.** $y = -\dfrac{5}{9}(x + 3)(x - 3)$ **79.** $y = -2(x + 1)(x - 5)$ **81.** $y = -\dfrac{1}{63}(x + 12)(x + 6)$ **83.** $y = -\dfrac{1}{3}(x - 4)(x - 10)$ **85.** $y = (x + 1)(x + 9)$

QUIZ 2 (p. 365) **1.** $5(x + 3)(x^2 - 3x + 9)$ **2.** $6(x + 2)(x^2 + 2)$ **3.** $4x(x^2 + 2)(x^2 - 2)$ **4.** $(x^2 - 5)(3x - 1)$ **5.** $0, \pm 6$ **6.** $0, \dfrac{3}{2}$ **7.** $0, 3$ **8.** $-\dfrac{5}{2}, -2, 2$ **9.** $x + 11$ **10.** $x - \dfrac{10}{3} + \dfrac{80}{3(3x + 2)}$

11. $4x - 7 + \dfrac{11x - 11}{x^2 - 3}$ **12.** $12x^3 - 7x^2 + 10x - 10 + \dfrac{5}{x + 1}$

13. $x + \dfrac{2x^2 + 6x + 6}{x^3 - 3}$ **14.** $5x^3 - 23x^2 + 115x - 576 + \dfrac{2875}{x + 5}$

15. $\pm\sqrt{7},\ 4$ **16.** 2 **17.** $-5, -3, \dfrac{1}{2}$ **18.** $-6, \dfrac{1}{2}, 2$

19. 16 ft by 16 ft by 0.5 ft

6.7 PRACTICE (pp. 369–371)
5. $\pm\sqrt{3},\ \pm 2i$ **7.** $-1, 2, \pm 2i$
9. $f(x) = x^4 - 2x^3 + 2x^2 - 2x + 1$ **11.** $f(x) = x^5 - 3x^4 - 5x^3 + 15x^2 + 4x - 12$ **13.** $f(x) = x^4 + 32x^2 + 256$ **15.** yes
17. no **19.** yes **21.** $-3, -2, -1, 1$ **23.** $0, 1, 3$ **25.** $-5, -4, -1, 3$ **27.** $1, \pm 7i$ **29.** $-5, -1, \pm 3i$ **31.** $-2, 3, \pm i$ **33.** $-3, -1, 3, 4.5$ **35.** $f(x) = x^3 - 7x^2 + 14x - 8$ **37.** $f(x) = x^3 - 2x^2 - 33x + 90$ **39.** $f(x) = x^3 + 13x^2 + 50x + 56$ **41.** $f(x) = x^3 - 5x^2 + 9x - 45$ **43.** $f(x) = x^4 + 10x^2 + 9$ **45.** $f(x) = x^4 - 12x^3 + 53x^2 - 104x + 80$ **47.** $-2.09, 0.57, 2.51$ **49.** -0.47
51. $-1.27, 2.86$ **53.** $-0.75, 0.75$ **55.** 1988 **57.** Yes; there were 2 such years, 1988 and 1993, because the graph intersects the line $S = 2000$ when t is about 1.6 and when t is about 6.3. **59.** 1965

6.7 MIXED REVIEW (p. 371)

65.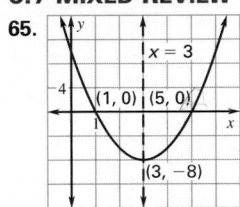

67.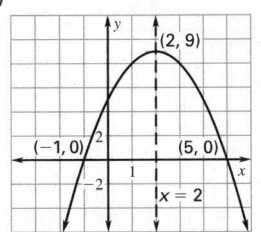

69.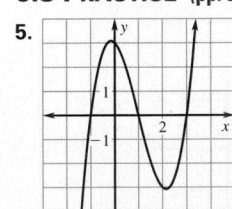

71.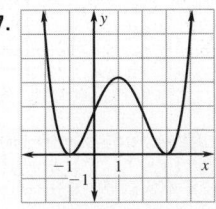

TECHNOLOGY ACTIVITY 6.7 (p. 372)
1. $-0.640, 1.135, 5.505$ **3.** 5 **5.** $-2.334, -0.742, 0.742, 2.334$
7. $-1.088, -0.668, 1.191$ **9.** $-7.349, 16.429, 30.921$; yes

6.8 PRACTICE (pp. 376–378)

5.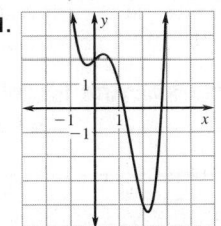

7.

9. x-intercepts: $-0.41, 1, 2.41$; local maximum: $(0.18, 1.09)$; local minimum: $(1.82, -1.09)$ **11.** x-intercepts: $0, 1, 1.51$; local maximums: $(-1.59, -3.23), (0.49, 1.35)$; local minimums: $(-1, -4), (1.30, -0.79)$

13.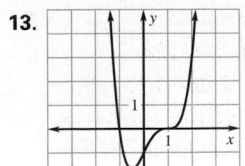

15.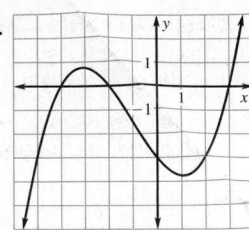

17.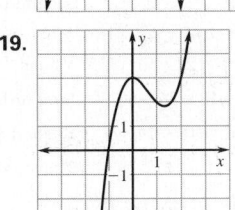

19.

21.

23. $(-0.5, 0.5)$ max, $(0.5, -0.3)$ min; $-0.9, 0, 0.6$; 3
25. $(-2, 1)$ min, $(0, 2)$ max; 1.4; 3
27. $(-2, -1)$ max, $(0, -2.2)$ min, $(1, -2)$ max; none; 4

29. x-intercepts: $-1.79, 0.11, 1.67$; local maximum: $(-1, 7)$; local minimum: $(1, -5)$ **31.** x-intercepts: $-2.83, 0, 2.83$; local maximums: $(-2, 4), (2, 4)$; local minimum: $(0, 0)$
33. x-intercepts: $-2, -1, 0, 1, 2$; local maximums: $(-1.64, 3.63), (0.54, 1.42)$; local minimums: $(-0.54, -1.42), (1.64, -3.63)$

35.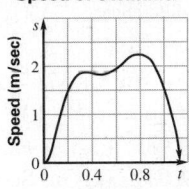

; at about $t = 0.8$ sec into the stroke
37. $l = \dfrac{600 - \pi r^2}{\pi r}$

39. 1600 ft^3; $r \approx 7.98$ ft, $l \approx 15.97$ ft, or about 16 ft long, 16 ft wide, and 8 ft high

6.8 MIXED REVIEW (p. 378) **45.** $y = 7x$ **47.** $y = \dfrac{1}{4}x$
49. $y = -\dfrac{3}{5}x$ **51.** yes; 4×1 **53.** no **55.** $y = -(x - 1)^2 + 4$
57. $y = \dfrac{5}{24}(x + 5)(x - 5)$ **59.** 10 in./day

6.9 PRACTICE (pp. 383–385)
5. $f(1)\ f(2)\ f(3)\ f(4)\ f(5)\ f(6)$

4	17	40	73	116	169	Values
13	23	33	43	53		First-order differences
10	10	10	10			Second-order differences

7. $f(1)\ f(2)\ f(3)\ f(4)\ f(5)\ f(6)$

3	20	87	264	635	1308	Values
17	67	177	371	673		First-order differences
50	110	194	302			Second-order differences
60	84	108				Third-order differences
24	24					Fourth-order differences

9. 3 **11.** $f(x) = -x^3 + 5x^2 + x + 1$ **13.** $d(n) = \dfrac{1}{2}n^2 - \dfrac{3}{2}n$

15. $f(x) = -\dfrac{1}{2}(x + 1)(x - 2)(x - 3)$ **17.** $f(x) = -\dfrac{1}{2}x(x + 1)(x + 2)$

19. $f(x) = -\frac{1}{4}(x-1)(x-3)(x+2)$

21. $f(x) = (x-3)(x-2)(x+1)$

23.
$f(1)\ f(2)\ f(3)\ f(4)\ f(5)\ f(6)$
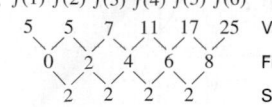
5	5	7	11	17	25	Values
	0	2	4	6	8	First-order differences
		2	2	2	2	Second-order differences

25.
$f(1)\ f(2)\ f(3)\ f(4)\ f(5)\ f(6)$
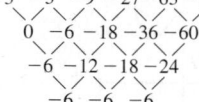
−3	−3	−9	−27	−63	−123	Values
	0	−6	−18	−36	−60	First-order differences
		−6	−12	−18	−24	Second-order differences
			−6	−6	−6	Third-order differences

27.
$f(1)\ f(2)\ f(3)\ f(4)\ f(5)\ f(6)$
−18	−8	102	432	1150	2472	Values
	10	110	330	718	1322	First-order differences
		100	220	388	604	Second-order differences
			120	168	216	Third-order differences
				48	48	Fourth-order differences

29.
$f(1)\ f(2)\ f(3)\ f(4)\ f(5)\ f(6)$
4	4	−36	−176	−500	−1116	Values
	0	−40	−140	−324	−616	First-order differences
		−40	−100	−184	−292	Second-order differences
			−60	−84	−108	Third-order differences
				−24	−24	Fourth-order differences

31.
$f(1)\ f(2)\ f(3)\ f(4)\ f(5)\ f(6)$
3	−2	−13	−30	−53	−82	Values
	−5	−11	−17	−23	−29	First-order differences
		−6	−6	−6	−6	Second-order differences

33. $f(x) = -3x^2 + 20x$ 35. $f(x) = x^3 - 4x^2 + x$

37. $f(x) = x^3 + 4x^2 - x - 2$ 39. $y = 2x^3 - 16x^2 + 37x - 25$

41. $f(x) = -x^3 + 10x^2 - 30x + 23$ 43. $f(x) = -x^4 + 13x^3 - 58x^2 + 104x - 58$ 47. $f(t) = 0.641t^3 - 4.93t^2 + 25.8t + 232$ where t is the number of years since 1989; 772,000 Girl Scouts

49. $y = 0.007t^3 - 0.740t^2 + 49.0t - 236$; about 101 sec

6.9 MIXED REVIEW (p. 386) 53. $\pm\frac{1}{2}$ 55. $\pm\frac{\sqrt{78}}{6}$ 57. $\pm\frac{\sqrt{2}}{2}$

59. $-3 \pm \sqrt{33}$ 61. $-2 \pm \frac{i\sqrt{6}}{2}$ 63. $3 \pm \frac{i\sqrt{15}}{3}$

65. $(3x+2)(9x^2 - 6x + 4)$ 67. $(2x-5)(4x^2 + 10x + 25)$

69. $8(x+3)(x^2 - 3x + 9)$ 71. $3(x+3)(x^2 - 3x + 9)$

QUIZ 3 (p. 386) 1. $-2.61, -0.74, 3.86$ 2. $-2, \frac{-1 \pm i\sqrt{3}}{2}$

3. $-1, 4, \pm i\sqrt{2}$ 4. $-\frac{3}{2}, -1, 1, 2$ 5. $y = x^3 + 2x^2 - 4x - 8$

6. $y = x^3 + 2x^2 - 3x$ 7. $y = x^3 - 8x^2 + 21x - 20$

8. $y = x^4 - 7x^3 + 11x^2 - 7x + 10$ 9. $y = x^3 - 8x^2 + 29x - 52$

10. $y = x^4 - 6x^3 + 18x^2 - 24x + 16$

11. local max $(0.79, 8.21)$, local min $(-2.12, -4.06)$

12. local max $(-0.50, 0.56)$, local min $(-1.62, -1)$, $(0.62, -1)$

13. local max $(2.42, 0.77)$, local min $(3.58, -0.77)$

14. local max $(-3, 0)$, local min $(-1.67, -1.19)$ 15. $f(x) = -\frac{1}{3}(x+2)(x+4)(x-2)$ 16. $f(x) = -\frac{1}{70}(x+1)(x-4)(x-2)$

17. $f(x) = x(x-3)(x-5)$ 18. $f(x) = 2(x-1)(x+3)(x+5)$

19. $f(x) = x^3 - 3x^2 + x - 4$ 20. $f(x) = x^3 - 4x^2 + 2x$

21. $N = -3.75x^3 + 50.9x^2 - 97.3x + 3210$ where x is the number of years since 1988

CHAPTER 6 REVIEW (pp. 388–390)

1. $\frac{96x^3}{y^3}$; negative exponent, power of a quotient, power of a product, and power of a power property

3. $-\frac{7}{2}x^3y^6$; quotient of powers property 5. 25

7. 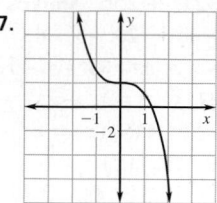 9.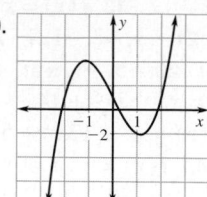

11. $x^3 - 2x^2 - 10x + 21$ 13. -4 15. $-3, -1, 1$

17. $x^2 + \frac{5}{2} + \frac{33}{2(2x-5)}$ 19. $-2, 1$

21. 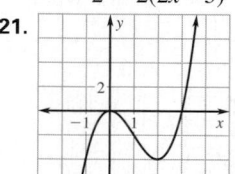 ; x-intercepts: 0, 3; local max: $(0, 0)$; local min: $(2, -4)$

23.
$f(1)\ f(2)\ f(3)\ f(4)\ f(5)\ f(6)$
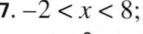
2	9	28	65	126	217	Values
	7	19	37	61	91	First-order differences
		12	18	24	30	Second-order differences
			6	6	6	Third-order differences

CUMULATIVE PRACTICE (pp. 394–395) 1. -5 3. $-4, 8$

5. $x < 3$;
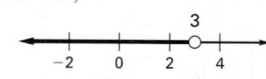

7. $-2 < x < 8$;
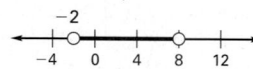

9. 0 11. 4

13. 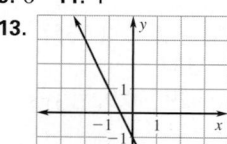 15.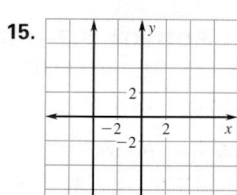

17. 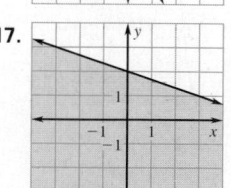 19.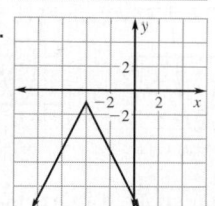

21. 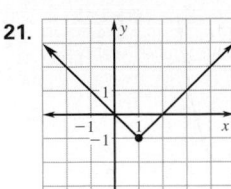 23. $y = -4x + 5$ 25. $(3, 5)$
27. $(1, 0, 3)$

31. 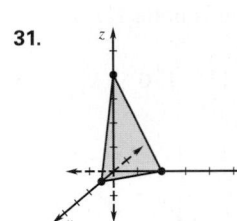 33. $\begin{bmatrix} -11 & 8 \\ 1 & -2 \end{bmatrix}$ 35. $\begin{bmatrix} 17 & -7 & -27 \\ 3 & -9 & 69 \end{bmatrix}$
37. 3   39. -55 41. $\begin{bmatrix} 7 & 2 \\ -4 & -1 \end{bmatrix}$
43. no inverse

45. 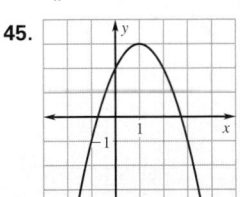   47.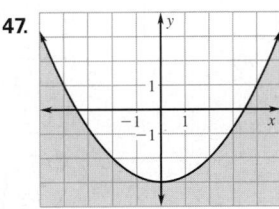

49. 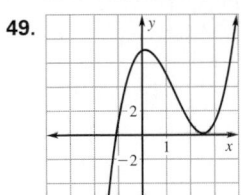   51.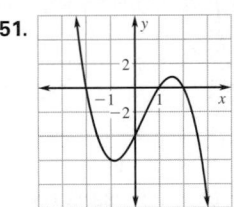

53. $\pm\sqrt{13}$ 55. $\pm 8i$ 57. $-10 \le x \le 10$ 59. $\pm 2, \pm 1$
61. $-2, \pm\dfrac{\sqrt6}{2}$ 63. $32 + 20i$ 65. $9 + 2i$ 67. $y = -(x+3)(x+2)$
69. $36x^2y^6$ 71. $\dfrac{16}{25}$ 73. $x^4 - 5x^3 + 11x^2 - 27x + 36$
75. $x^3 - 5x^2 + 18x - 36 + \dfrac{70}{x+2}$ 77. $\pm\sqrt5, \pm\sqrt5\,i$
79. $f(x) = (x+4)(x+1)(x-1)$ 81. $r = \dfrac{I}{Pt}, 5.5\%$
83. 8 min   85. about 5.45 h

CHAPTER 7

SKILL REVIEW (p. 400)   1. $y = \dfrac{3x-12}{2}$ 2. $y = 10 - 2x$
3. $y = \dfrac{x+1}{4}$ 4. $(x+7)(x+3)$ 5. $(x+9)(x-4)$
6. $2(x-3)(x-5)$ 7. $a^4b^4c^8$ 8. x^2 9. $\dfrac{x^4}{y^2}$ 10. $\dfrac{3x^3}{4y^6}$
11. $5x^3 - 40x^2$ 12. $9y^2 - 12y + 4$ 13. $7x^2 - 5x + 4$

7.1 PRACTICE (pp. 404–406)   5. -7 7. 25   9. -1 11. ± 10
13. $14^{1/4}$ 15. $5^{2/7}$ 17. $2^{11/8}$ 19. $\sqrt[4]{7}$ 21. $\left(\sqrt[5]{5}\right)^2$ 23. ± 10
25. -2 27. none   29. 4   31. -2 33. 1   35. 4   37. 0
39. 16   41. -7 43. 4   45. 0.56   47. 0.0019   49. 1.82
51. 0.087   53. 3   55. 0   57. -1.69 59. -9.24 61. ± 1.40
63. 1247.73 ft³/sec   65. 1.58 ft   67. about 37 species

7.1 MIXED REVIEW (p. 406)   73. $x = 3, y = -4$ 75. $x = \dfrac{16}{5}$,
$y = \dfrac{3}{10}$ 77. $x = \dfrac{13}{11}, y = -\dfrac{13}{11}$ 79. $\dfrac{1}{x^{15}}$; power of a power and

negative exponent properties   81. $\dfrac{5}{x^2}$; negative exponent and zero exponent properties
83. $\dfrac{1}{x^4y^2}$; negative exponent and power of a quotient properties   85. $4x^2y$; product of powers and quotient of powers properties   87. $-1, 2, 3, -5$ 89. $1, \pm 3i$

7.2 PRACTICE (pp. 411–413)   5. 3   7. 4   9. $\dfrac{2}{3}$ 11. $3\sqrt[7]{8}$
13. x^2 15. $2a^3$ 17. $\dfrac{x^2}{y}$ 19. $-4a^{1/5}$ 21. 1333.78 cm²
23. $5^{1/3}$ 25. 6   27. $5^{1/3}$ 29. $\dfrac{8}{5}$ 31. $5^{3/4}$ 33. $\dfrac{1}{64,000}$
35. 2   37. $6^7 = 279,936$ 39. $\dfrac{1}{2}$ 41. 3   43. $3\sqrt[5]{5}$ 45. $30\sqrt[4]{3}$
47. $\dfrac{2\sqrt[3]{3}}{3}$ 49. $\sqrt[15]{2}$ 51. $-2\sqrt[7]{5}$ 53. $3\sqrt{10}$ 55. $9\sqrt[4]{11}$
57. $y^{1/2}$ 59. $x^{5/4}$ 61. $\dfrac{x^3}{y}$ 63. $y^{5/3}$ 65. $\dfrac{x^{1/2}y}{z}$ 67. $\dfrac{1}{3y^2}$
69. $xy^2z^2\sqrt[4]{10xz^2}$ 71. $y^2z^2\sqrt{2xz}$ 73. $\dfrac{x\sqrt[3]{y}}{y}$ 75. $x^{1/35}$
77. $7x^{1/5}$ 79. $2x^3y^{1/3}$ 81. $(2x-1)y\sqrt[3]{3x^2}$ 83. y^2
85. $\dfrac{1}{4^{\sqrt7}}$ 87. $\dfrac{x}{y^2}$ 89. $-2xy^{\sqrt{11}}$ 91. $\dfrac{\sqrt3}{2}$ 93. 0.45 mm
95. Higher notes have frequencies twice as high as lower notes of the same letter.   97. $2^{2/3}$

7.2 MIXED REVIEW (p. 414)   101. $\dfrac{441}{4}, \left(x - \dfrac{21}{2}\right)^2$
103. $24.5025, (x + 4.95)^2$ 105. $\dfrac{1}{64}, \left(x - \dfrac{1}{8}\right)^2$
107. $8x^3 + 9x^2 + 52x + 1$ 109. $4x^2 + 28x + 49$
111. $(4x - 1) - \dfrac{2}{x+1}$ 113. $x^3 + 3x^2 + 15x + 5 + \dfrac{45}{x-5}$

QUIZ 1 (p. 414)   1. 4   2. $\dfrac{1}{8}$ 3. -3 4. 16   5. 1.58   6. ± 1.12
7. ± 1.90 8. -4.47 9. $4^{1/4}$ or $2^{1/2}$ 10. $\dfrac{2\sqrt[4]{27}}{3}$ 11. 4
12. $3\sqrt5$ 13. 7   14. $3\sqrt[5]{8}$ 15. $x^{11/12}$ 16. $x^{1/2}$ 17. $x^{1/4}y^{5/2}$
18. $xy\sqrt[3]{5y^2}$ 19. $\dfrac{6\sqrt{xy}}{y^2}$ 20. $2xy^{1/2}$ 21. about 30,000 horsepower   22. No; The surface area of the Labrador retriever is about 2.08 times the surface area of the Scottish terrier.

7.3 PRACTICE (pp. 418–420)   5. $5x - 1$; all real numbers
7. $4x^2 - 4x$; all real numbers   9. $4x - 4$; all real numbers
11. $g(f(x))$; The bonus is 0.02 times the amount over $200,000 $(x - 200,000)$, so calculate amount first and then take 2%.   13. $2x^2 - 5x + 4$; all real numbers   15. $2x^2 - 8$; all real numbers   17. $5x - 12$; all real numbers   19. 0; all real numbers   21. $6x^{7/6}$; nonnegative real numbers

23. $9x$; nonnegative real numbers   25. $\dfrac{3}{2x^{1/6}}$; positive real numbers   27. 1; positive real numbers   29. $2^{3/2}x^{-15/4}$; positive real numbers   31. $x^{9/16}$; nonnegative real numbers
33. $9x - 4$; all real numbers   35. $\dfrac{10x}{x+4}$; all real numbers

except -4 **37.** $10x + 4$; all real numbers   **39.** $x + 8$; all real numbers   **41.** $x^{1/2}$; nonnegative real numbers   **43.** $x^2 - x - 8$; all real numbers   **45.** $4x^3 - 16x^2$; all real numbers   **47.** $x - 5$; all real numbers except 0   **49.** $x^4 - 6x^2 + 10$; all real numbers   **51.** $81x - 20$; all real numbers   **53.** $r(w) = 220w^{-0.266}$; about 134 breaths per minute; about 18 breaths per minute; about 11 breaths per minute

7.3 MIXED REVIEW (p. 420)

69. $y = \dfrac{-2x - 8}{3}$ **71.** $y = \dfrac{5}{x}$ **73.** $y = \dfrac{c - ax}{b}$

75. 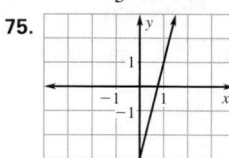   **77.**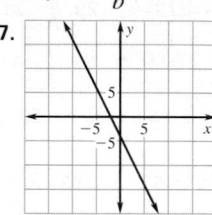

79. 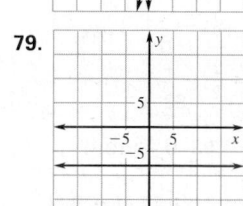   **81.** 3   **83.** $-6, -2$

7.4 PRACTICE (pp. 426–428)

5.

x	2	1	0	1	2
y	-4	-2	0	2	4

7. $y = \dfrac{x + 1}{2}$ **9.** Both compositions equal x.

11. $\dfrac{\sqrt[4]{27x}}{3}$ **13.** No; horizontal lines, such as $y = 0$, cross the graph more than once.   **15.**

x	0	3	-2	2	-1
y	1	-2	4	2	-2

17. $y = \dfrac{x + 3}{3}$

19. $y = -\dfrac{5}{4}(x - 11)$ **21.** $y = \dfrac{-x + 7}{12}$ **23.** $y = \dfrac{x + 13}{8}$

33. A   **35.** B   **37.** $f^{-1}(x) = \sqrt[6]{-x}$ **39.** $f^{-1}(x) = 2\sqrt[5]{x}$

41. $f^{-1}(x) = -\dfrac{2}{3}\sqrt{-x}$ **43.** $f^{-1}(x) = \sqrt[5]{-\dfrac{1}{2}x + \dfrac{1}{6}}$

45. $f^{-1}(x) = \sqrt[3]{\dfrac{5}{3}x + 15}$ **47.** $f^{-1}(x) = \sqrt[5]{6x - 4}$

49. 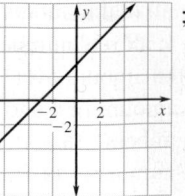 ;   **51.** 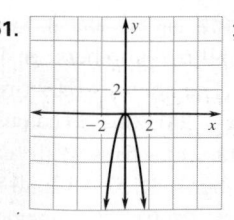 ;

Yes, inverse is a function.   No, inverse is not a function.

53. 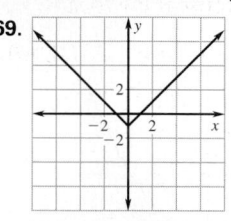 ;   **55.** 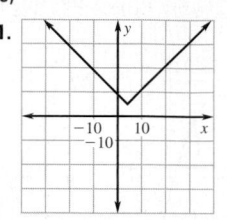 ;

Yes, inverse is a function.   No, inverse is not a function.

57. $D_{US} = 0.65677D_C$ **59.** $a = 200 - 1.11h$; 170

61. $l = \sqrt[3]{106723.59w}$; 41.69 cm

7.4 MIXED REVIEW (p. 429)

69. 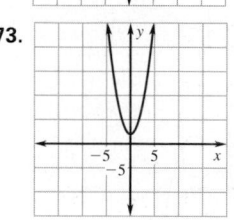   **71.**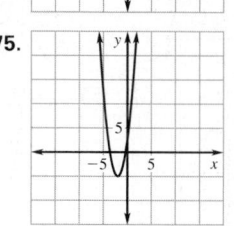

73. 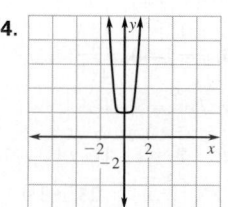 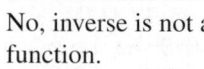   **75.**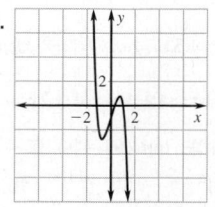

77. 2   **79.** $\dfrac{1}{5y}$ **81.** $5\sqrt[7]{5}$ **83.** $.65

QUIZ 2 (p. 429)

1. $f(x) + g(x) = 6x^2 + x^{1/2}$; nonnegative real numbers   **2.** $f(x) - g(x) = 6x^2 - 3x^{1/2}$; nonnegative real numbers   **3.** $f(x) \cdot g(x) = 2x(6x^{3/2} - 1)$; nonnegative real numbers   **4.** $\dfrac{f(x)}{g(x)} = 3x^{3/2} - \dfrac{1}{2}$; positive real numbers   **5.** $f(g(x)) = \dfrac{3}{x - 8}$; real numbers except 8   **6.** $g(f(x)) = \dfrac{3}{x} - 8$; real numbers except 0   **7.** $f(f(x)) = x$; real numbers except 0   **8.** $g(g(x)) = x - 16$; all real numbers   **9.** Both compositions equal x.   **10.** Both compositions equal x.

11. $f^{-1}(x) = x - 8$ **12.** $f^{-1}(x) = \dfrac{-\sqrt[4]{8x}}{2}$ **13.** $f^{-1}(x) = \sqrt[5]{6 - x}$

14. 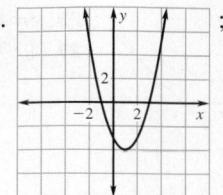 ;   **15.** ;

No, inverse is not a function.   No, inverse is not a function.

16. 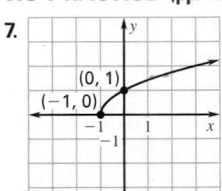 ; Yes, inverse is a function.
17. $A(t) = 0.36\pi t^2$; about 4.52 ft^2

TECHNOLOGY ACTIVITY 7.4 (p. 430) **1.** Yes; the inverse passes the vertical line test. **3.** Yes; the inverse passes the vertical line test. **5.** No; the inverse does not pass the vertical line test. **7.** Yes; the inverse passes the vertical line test. **9.** Yes; the inverse passes the vertical line test. **11.** No; the inverse does not pass the vertical line test.

7.5 PRACTICE (pp. 434–436) **5.** Shift the graph 10 units down.

7. 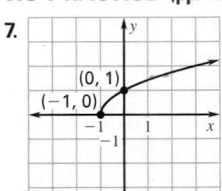 ; **9.** 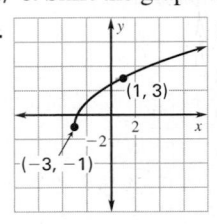 ;
$x \geq -1, y \geq 0$ $x \geq -3, y \geq -1$

11. 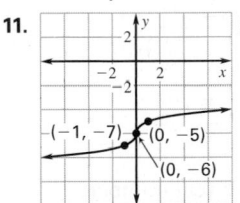 ; **13.** 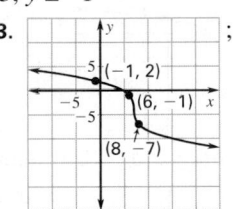 ;
x, y: all real numbers. x, y: all real numbers.
15. Shift graph 14 units left. **17.** Shift graph 10 units down.
19. B **21.** C

23. 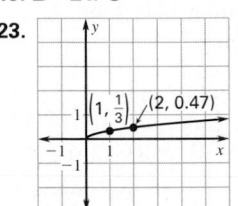 ; **25.** 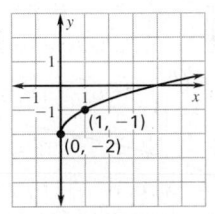 ;
$x \geq 0, y \geq 0$ $x \geq 0, y \geq -2$

27. 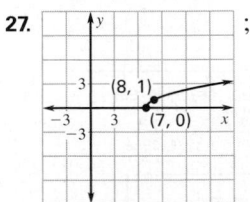 ; **29.** 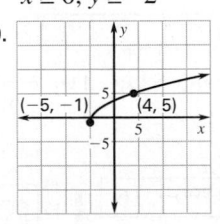 ;
$x \geq 7, y \geq 0$ $x \geq -5, y \geq -1$

31. 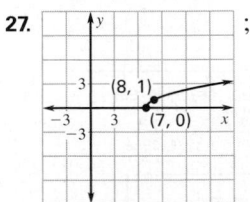 ; **33.** 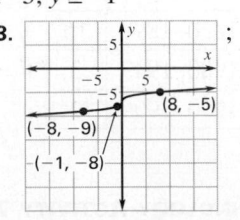 ;
x, y are all real numbers. x, y are all real numbers.

35. 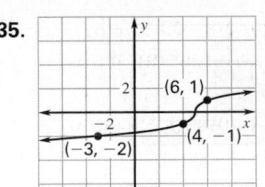 ; **37.** 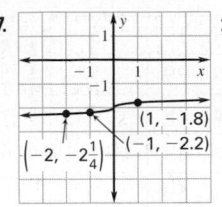 ;
x, y are all real numbers. x, y are all real numbers.

39. 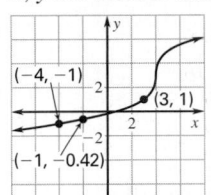 ; x, y are all real numbers.
47. 2.36 square units, **49.** 80.15 nautical miles

7.5 MIXED REVIEW (p. 436) **55.** $\pm\sqrt{10} - 7$ **57.** ± 6
59. $\dfrac{\pm\sqrt{33}}{2} + \dfrac{1}{4}$ **61.** $x^2 - 18xy + 81y^2$ **63.** $9x^2 - 24xy^4 + 16y^8$ **65.** $1 + 4x^2 + 4x^4$ **67.** $f(g(x)) = 2x - 5$; $g(f(x)) = 2x - 2$ **69.** $f(g(x)) = 9x^2 - 18x + 16$; $g(f(x)) = 3x^2 + 18$

7.6 PRACTICE (pp. 441–443) **5.** 1 **7.** 8 **9.** -5 **11.** $\dfrac{64}{3}$
13. 2, 3 **15.** no solution **17.** yes **19.** yes **21.** no **23.** 4
25. 27 **27.** 81 **29.** $\dfrac{11}{2}$ **31.** $\dfrac{406}{81}$ **33.** 216 **35.** 200
37. no solution **39.** $\dfrac{12}{7}$ **41.** 36 **43.** $-\dfrac{2}{3}$ **45.** 1, 3 **47.** 5
49. $-\dfrac{1}{6}$ **51.** no solution **53.** 5 **55.** -18.96296
57. $-0.\overline{17}$ or 0.10345 **59.** 11.099 **61.** no solution
63. 0.146 in. **65.** 1991 **67.** 34.078 mi/h **69.** 4.90

7.6 MIXED REVIEW (p. 444) **81.** 20 **83.** -78 **85.** 19
87. -0.95; no local maximums or minimums
89. $0, \pm 1.41$; $(-0.914, 4.08)$; $(0.914, -4.08)$

7.7 PRACTICE (pp. 449–451) **5.** 31
7. 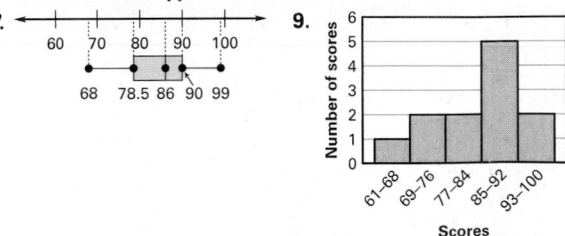 **9.**

11. 49.57, 47, 47 **13.** about 249, 230, 230 **15.** 0.356; 0.3; 0, 0.5 (two modes) **17.** 8, 2.73 **19.** 417, 143
21. 12.1, 3.82 **23.**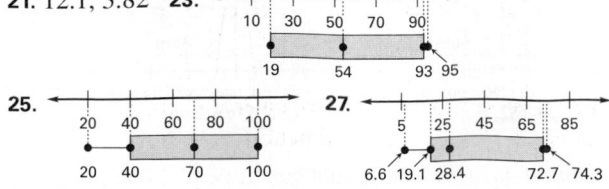

25. **27.**

29.

10–19	5
20–29	5
30–39	7
40–49	2
50–59	1

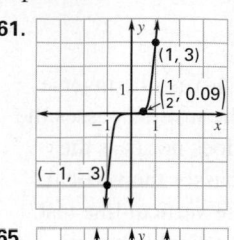

31.

0–0.4	0	4.0–4.4	1
0.5–0.9	0	4.5–4.9	1
1.0–1.4	0	5.0–5.4	2
1.5–1.9	0	5.5–5.9	2
2.0–2.4	6	6.0–6.4	1
2.5–2.9	0	6.5–6.9	1
3.0–3.4	0	7.0–7.4	1
3.5–3.9	0		

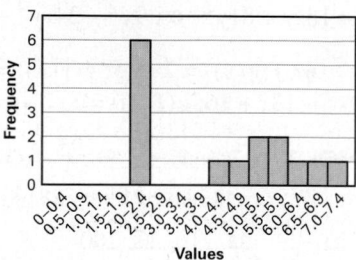

33. machine 1: 2.59, 2.59, none; machine 2: 2.59, 2.59, none
37. $645,000; $213,243.66 **39.** The mode is the most appropriate measure because it would indicate that most people have a positive opinion on the issue. Because the categories are not part of an ordered scale, means and medians are not meaningful.

41.

Age	Pres	VP
30–39	0	1
40–49	8	12
50–59	24	21
60–69	10	12
70–79	0	1

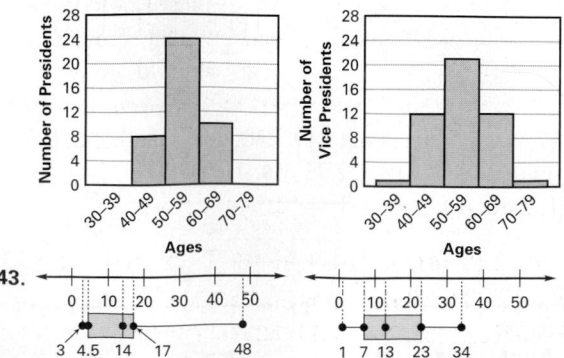

43.

45. *Sample answer:* You cannot conclude that one conference consistently has larger (or smaller) margins of victory than the other.

7.7 MIXED REVIEW (p. 452) **51.** 24 **53.** −326
55. 2187; product of powers **57.** $\frac{1}{4}$; product of powers, negative exponent **59.** $\frac{1}{100}$; zero exponent; negative exponent

61. 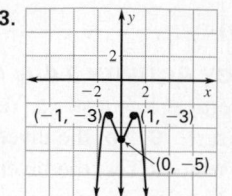 **63.**

65.

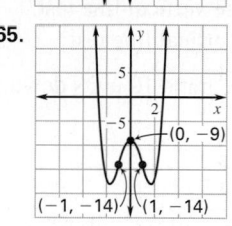

QUIZ 3 (p. 452)

1. ; **2.** ;

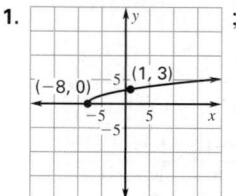

$x \geq -8,\ y \geq 0$ $x \geq -7,\ y \geq -2$

3. ; x and y are all real numbers.
4. 312.5
5. 6 (−1 is an extraneous solution.)
6. 0 **7.** 4.4, 5.5, 6, 9, 2.8
8. 23.9, 21, none, 31, 9.99

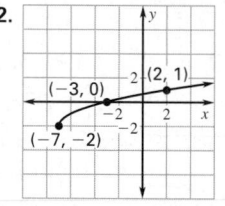

9. ; 4196 cubic units

10. 228.24 million km **11.**

12.

1750–1799	16
1800–1849	14
1850–1899	15
1900–1949	3
1950–1999	2

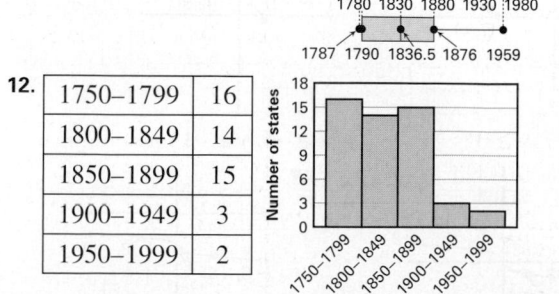

TECHNOLOGY ACTIVITY 7.7 (p. 454)
1. 17.3, 17.5, 22, 5.71 **5.** The second restaurant's

sandwiches have fewer calories than the sandwiches at the first restaurant. The histograms show that half of the sandwiches in the 1st restaurant contain over 500 calories while only 1 out of 10 sandwiches in the second restaurant contain over 500 calories.

CHAPTER 7 REVIEW (pp. 456–458) **1.** 2 **3.** $\frac{1}{243}$ **5.** -2

7. -1 **9.** $\frac{1}{25}$ **11.** $\frac{\sqrt[3]{2}}{5}$ **13.** $3x^{1/4}$ **15.** $xyz\sqrt[6]{6yz^4}$ **17.** $3x - 6$

17. $3x - 6$ **19.** $2x^2 - 8x + 8$ **21.** $2x - 8$ **23.** $f^{-1}(x) = (-x)^{1/4}$, $x \le 0$ **25.** Both compositions equal x.

27. 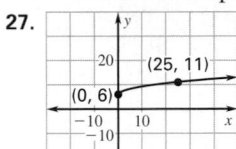 ; **29.** 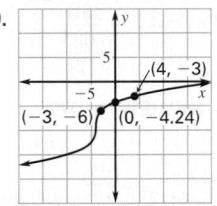 ;

$x \ge 0$; $y \ge 6$ x and y are all real numbers.
31. -3 **33.** 40.9, 42, 51, 42, 11.3

CHAPTER 8

SKILL REVIEW (p. 464) **1.** $\frac{1}{64}$ **2.** $\frac{1}{9}$ **3.** 1 **4.** -25 **5.** $\frac{2}{5}$

6. $f(x) \to -\infty$ as $x \to -\infty$; $f(x) \to +\infty$ as $x \to +\infty$
7. $f(x) \to -\infty$ as $x \to -\infty$; $f(x) \to -\infty$ as $x \to +\infty$
8. $f(x) \to +\infty$ as $x \to -\infty$; $f(x) \to +\infty$ as $x \to +\infty$
9. $f(x) \to +\infty$ as $x \to -\infty$; $f(x) \to -\infty$ as $x \to +\infty$
10. *Sample answer:* $y = 0.403x + 2.013$

8.1 PRACTICE (pp. 469–471)

5. 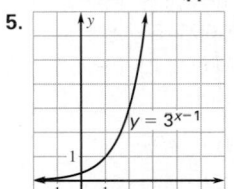 ; **7.** 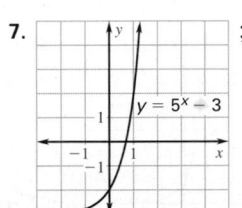 ;

domain: all real numbers;   domain: all real numbers;
range: all positive   range: $y > -3$
real numbers

9. 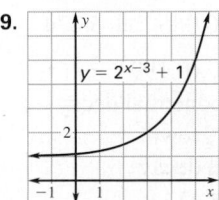 ; domain: all real numbers;
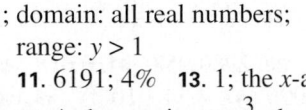 range: $y > 1$
11. 6191; 4% **13.** 1; the x-axis
15. 4; the x-axis **17.** $\frac{3}{2}$; the x-axis
19. C **21.** B **23.** F

25. 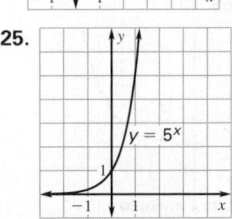 **27.**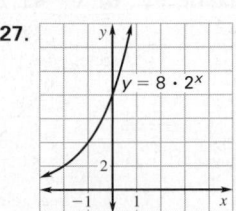

29. 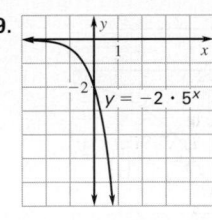 **31.**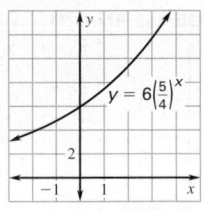

33. 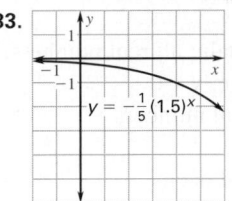 **35.** 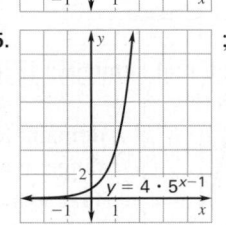 ;

domain: all real numbers;
range: $y > 0$

39. 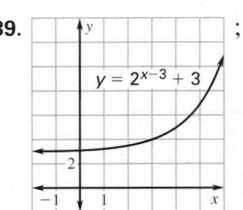 ; **41.** 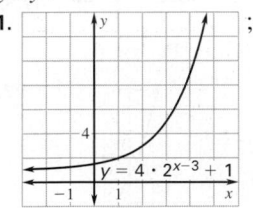 ;

domain: all real numbers;   domain: all real numbers;
range: $y > 3$ range: $y > 1$

43. 2.91 trillion ft^3; 1.07; 7% **45.** 8.03 trillion ft^3

47.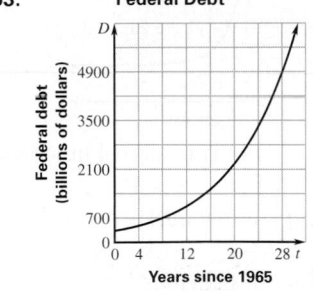
Average number of transistors (millions) vs. Years since 1971

49. $E = 5(1.59)^t$; about 32 gigawatt-hours
51. $t \approx 5.98$; near the end of 1985

53. Federal Debt
Federal debt (billions of dollars) vs. Years since 1965

55. a. $2600 **b.** $3041.63 **c.** ANS + ANS $\times$ 0.01; push "ENTER" four times. **d.** $3050.48; this is $8.85 more.
57. $A = 400(1.005)^{4t}$ where t is the number of years **59.** $1724.48
61. $1799.78 **63.** $2402.21

8.1 MIXED REVIEW (p. 472) **71.** $\frac{1}{8}$ **73.** $\frac{1}{32}$ **75.** $\frac{343}{1728}$

77. $\frac{16}{25}$ **79.** 2.18 **81.** -3 **83.** 3.16 **85.** 3 **87.** 3.04 **89.** 1.73
91. $4x^2 + 6x - 11$; all real numbers **93.** $24x^3 - 44x^2$; all real numbers **95.** $24x^2 - 11$; all real numbers
97. $\frac{6x - 11}{4x^2}$; all nonzero real numbers
99. $36x - 77$; all real numbers

8.2 PRACTICE (pp. 477–479)

5. 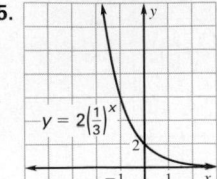 ;

7. 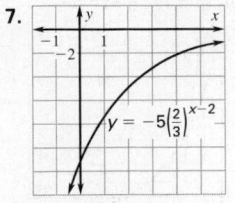 ;

domain: all real numbers; range: $y > 0$

domain: all real numbers; range: $y < 0$

9. 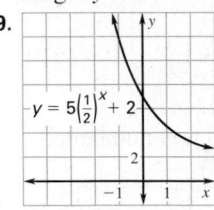 ; domain: all real numbers; range: $y > 2$

11. exponential decay
13. exponential decay
15. exponential growth
17. exponential decay

19. F **21.** D **23.** C

25.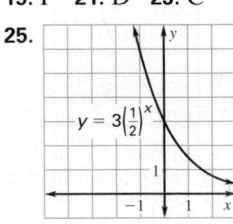

27.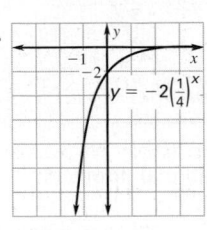

33.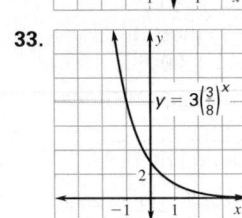

35. 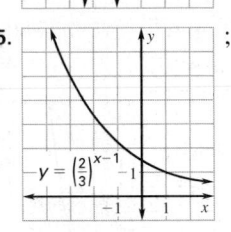 ;

domain: all real numbers; range: $y > 0$

37. 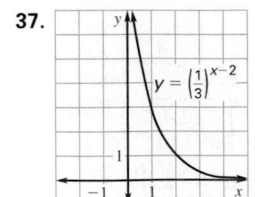 ;

39. 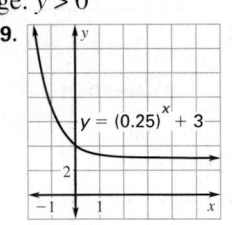 ;

domain: all real numbers; range: $y > 0$

domain: all real numbers; range: $y > 3$

41. 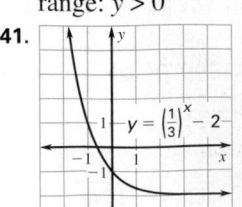 ; domain: all real numbers; range: $y > -2$

43. $V = 780(0.95)^t$
45. $i = 400(0.71)^h$
47. 265; 0.39; 61%
49. about 1988

51.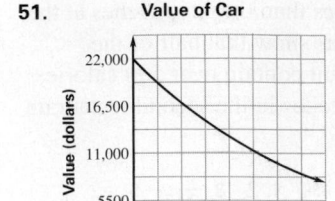

Value of Car

53. $V = 2100(0.5)^t$; $525
55. after about 22 months

57. a. $V = 18,354(0.83)^t$

b. $A(n) = \left(18,354 - \dfrac{280}{\frac{0.085}{12}} \right)\left(1 + \dfrac{0.085}{12} \right)^n + \dfrac{280}{\frac{0.085}{12}}$

8.2 MIXED REVIEW (p. 479)

59.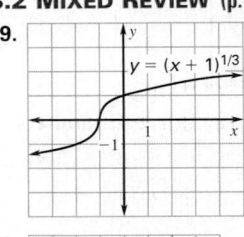

61.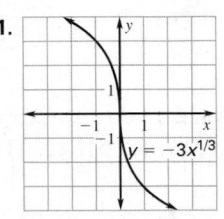

63.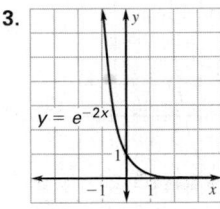

65. 16; 15; 15; 12
67. a. $2639.86 **b.** $2441.79

8.3 PRACTICE (pp. 483–485)

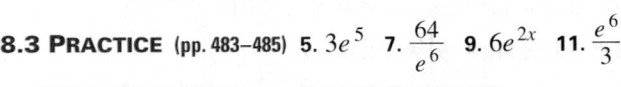

5. $3e^5$ **7.** $\dfrac{64}{e^6}$ **9.** $6e^{2x}$ **11.** $\dfrac{e^6}{3}$

13.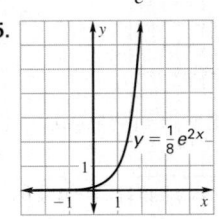

15.

17. e^6 **19.** $\dfrac{e^{3x}}{3}$ **21.** $3e^4$ **23.** e^{-2x+5} **25.** $\dfrac{1}{10,000e^x}$

27. $\dfrac{e^{x-1}}{2}$ **29.** $3e^{2x}$ **31.** $\dfrac{3}{2}e^{3x-1}$ **33.** 20.086 **35.** 5.474

37. 0.779 **39.** 2980.958 **41.** 0.018 **43.** −0.199
45. −178.096 **47.** $4.34 \cdot 10^{-20}$ **49.** exponential decay
51. exponential decay **53.** exponential growth
55. exponential growth **57.** exponential decay
59. exponential decay **61.** C **63.** F **65.** D

67. 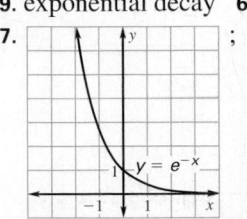 ;

73. 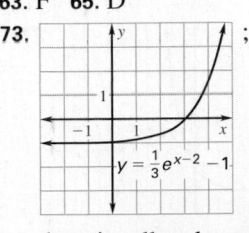 ;

domain: all real numbers; range: $y > 0$

domain: all real numbers; range: $y > -1$

75. 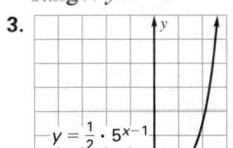 ; domain: all real numbers; range: $y > -2$

$y = 0.5e^{-2(x-1)} - 2$

77. $2650; $2652.25; $2653.41; $2654.19; $2654.59; *Sample answer:* The extra amount of interest earned with more and more compoundings decreases drastically, with the difference between compounding monthly and continuously being only 40¢, 0.016% of the amount initially invested. **79.** about 4.603 lb/in.^{2}

8.3 MIXED REVIEW (p. 485) **85.** $f^{-1}(x) = \dfrac{x-7}{6}$
87. $f^{-1}(x) = 2x + 20$ **89.** $f^{-1}(x) = -5x - 65$ **91.** 6.2 **93.** 2
95. no solution

QUIZ 1 (p. 485)

1. 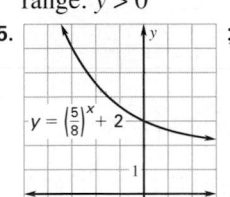 ;
$y = 4^x - 1$
domain: all real numbers; range: $y > -1$

2. 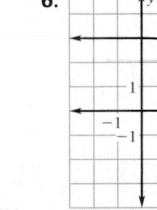 ;
$y = 3^{x+1} + 2$
domain: all real numbers; range: $y > 2$

3. ;
$y = \frac{1}{2} \cdot 5^{x-1}$
domain: all real numbers; range: $y > 0$

4. ;
$y = -2\left(\frac{1}{6}\right)^x$
domain: all real numbers; range: $y < 0$

5. ;
$y = \left(\frac{5}{8}\right)^x + 2$
domain: all real numbers; range: $y > 2$

6. ;
$y = -2 \cdot 6^{x-3} + 3$
domain: all real numbers; range: $y < 3$

7. $2e^7$ **8.** $4e^2$ **9.** $9e^{4x}$ **10.** $\dfrac{e^{12x}}{5^{4x}}$ **11.** $\dfrac{3}{4}e^{x-1}$ **12.** $\dfrac{6}{e^{4x}}$
13. $4e\sqrt{x}$ **14.** $5e^{2x}$ **15.**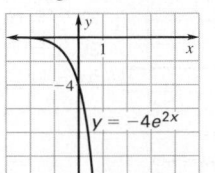
$y = -4e^{2x}$

16. 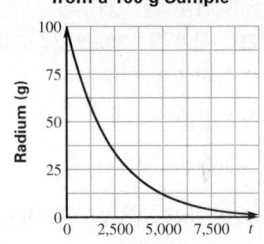 ; about 1.357 g

Amount of Radium Left from a 100 g Sample

8.4 PRACTICE (pp. 490–492) **5.** $3^2 = 9$ **7.** $\left(\dfrac{1}{2}\right)^{-2} = 4$ **9.** 6
11. 0 **13.** 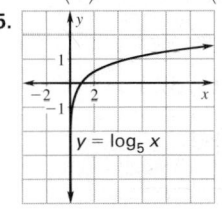 ; domain: $x > -1$; range: all real numbers
$y = \log_2(x+1) - 3$
15. about 0.316 mm
17. $5^{-1} = \dfrac{1}{5}$
19. $8^3 = 512$

21. $14^2 = 196$ **23.** $105^2 = 11{,}025$ **25.** 3 **27.** 1 **29.** 2
31. 4 **33.** -0.38 **35.** -2 **37.** 2.303 **39.** 0.571 **41.** -0.523
43. 0.544 **45.** 5.011 **47.** 3.114 **49.** x **51.** x **53.** x **55.** $3x$
57. $y = \left(\dfrac{1}{4}\right)^x$ **59.** $y = \left(\dfrac{1}{2}\right)^x$ **61.** $y = \dfrac{e^x}{6}$ **63.** $y = -2 + e^x$

65. 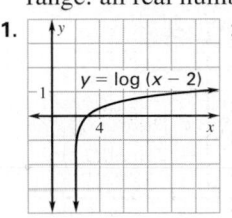 ;
$y = \log_5 x$
domain: $x > 0$; range: all real numbers

67. 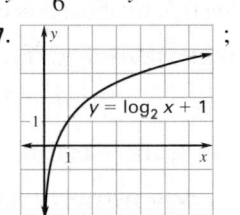 ;
$y = \log_2 x + 1$
domain: $x > 0$; range: all real numbers

71. 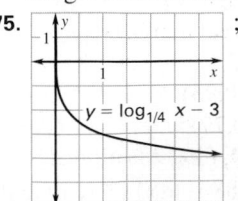 ;
$y = \log(x - 2)$
domain: $x > 2$; range: all real numbers

73. ;
$y = \log_5(x + 4)$
domain: $x > -4$; range: all real numbers

75. ; domain: $x > 0$; range: all real numbers
$y = \log_{1/4} x - 3$
77. a. 2.4 **b.** 3 **c.** 3.5
79. about 8 (7.9982…)
81. about 205 mi

8.4 MIXED REVIEW (p. 492) **93.** 3125 **95.** 7 **97.** $\dfrac{1}{6}$ **99.** 64
101. 16 **103.** $\dfrac{1}{16}$ **105.** $2x - 7 + \dfrac{27}{x+4}$ **107.** $4x + 3 - \dfrac{6x+9}{x^2+2}$
109. $y = -\dfrac{1}{6}x(x-2)(x+3)$ **111.** $y = \dfrac{1}{75}(x-4)(x-6)(x+4)$

5. 3   **7.** −1   **9.** 1.58   **11.** 7.2
13. about 26 decibels   **15.** −2   **17.** 3   **19.** −1   **21.** −6
23. 1.398   **25.** 2.097   **27.** 2.352   **29.** −0.477   **31.** $\ln 22 + \ln x$
33. $6 \log_6 x$ **35.** $2 \log_3 5$ **37.** $\ln 3 + \ln x + 3 \ln y$
39. $2 + 2 \log_8 x$ **41.** $\frac{5}{6} \log_3 12 + 9 \log_3 x$
43. $\ln 3 + 4 \ln y - 3 \ln x$ **45.** $1 + \frac{1}{2} \log_2 x$ **47.** $\ln 4$
49. $\log_{16} 1296$ **51.** $\log_4 128x^5 y^3$ **53.** $\log_3 2\sqrt{y}$ **55.** $\ln \dfrac{3}{x^2}$
57. $\log_5 \frac{1}{6}$ **59.** 1.277   **61.** 1.465   **63.** 1.226   **65.** 2.153
67. 1.774   **69.** 1.585   **71.** −0.529   **73.** 1.471

75.

f	s
1.414	1.000
2.000	2.000
2.828	3.000
4.000	4.000
5.657	5.000
8.000	6.000
11.314	7.000
16.000	8.000

; The first row of the table shows successive powers of $\sqrt{2}$, and the second row shows the integers, beginning with 1.
77. $E = 1.4 \log \dfrac{C_2}{C_1}$
79. about 1.089 kcal/g-molecule
81. about 95 decibels; between subway train and boiler shop
83. about 92 decibels
85. $10 \log 0.5$, or about 3 decibels less

93. y^{12} **95.** $9x^4$
97. $\dfrac{x^2}{y^2}$ **99.** $\dfrac{xy^8}{2}$ **101.** 7   **103.** 500   **105.** 6.14×10^{-6}
107. 3.581×10^{-3} **109.** 0.238   **111.** 1.773

TECHNOLOGY ACTIVITY 8.5 (p. 500)
Points may vary. Points given are sample responses.

1. 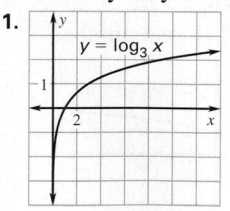   **7.**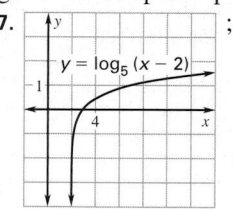
(1, 0); $x = 0$ (3, 0); $x = 2$

9. 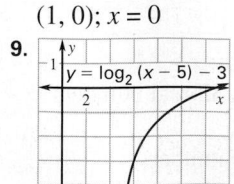 ; (6, −3); $x = 5$

13. *Sample answer:* The domain of $y = \log x$ is all real numbers greater than 0, while that of $y = \log |x|$ is all real numbers except 0. The graph of $y = \log |x|$ is the graph of $y = \log x$ and its reflection in the y-axis.

5. 1.292   **7.** 1   **9.** $\dfrac{\log 28 + 1}{3} \approx$
0.816   **11.** 1000   **13.** 39.121   **15.** $-1 + \dfrac{\sqrt{39}}{3} \approx 1.082$

17. $e^{\log_2 5x} \neq 5x$, since e^x and $\log_2 x$ are not inverse functions.   **19.** yes   **21.** no   **23.** yes   **25.** 1   **27.** $-\dfrac{7}{5}$ **29.** $\dfrac{16}{3}$
31. 3.907   **33.** $\dfrac{3}{2}$ **35.** $\dfrac{\log 5}{2} \approx 0.3495$ **37.** 1
39. $-\dfrac{1}{12} \log 94 \approx -0.164$ **41.** 20   **43.** 2   **45.** 2187   **47.** 2916
49. $-e^{7/2}$ **51.** $1 + \sqrt{1 + e} \approx 2.928$ **53.** no solution
55. $\dfrac{1}{3} e^5$ **57.** 47.158   **59.** no solution
63. a little over 9 years   **65.** about 27.7 years
67. Subantarctic: 8°; Antarctic intermediate: 4°; North Atlantic deep: 2°; Antarctic bottom: 0°   **69.** 100 mm

77. Lines may vary.;
$y = 0.305x + 1.780$ **79.** (4, 5)   **81.** (0, −6)   **83.** no solution
85. $(3x^2 + 4)(x - 2)$ **87.** $(x^2 + 5)(7x + 4)$

QUIZ 2 (p. 508)   **1.** 3   **2.** 4   **3.** 3   **4.** $y = e^x - 3$

5. 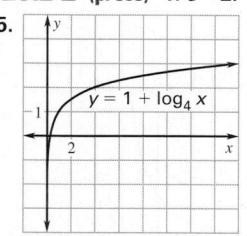 ;   **6.** 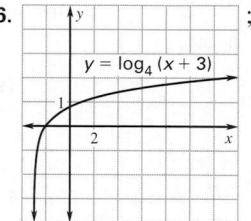 ;
domain: $x > 0$;   domain: $x > -3$;
range: all real numbers   range: all real numbers

7. 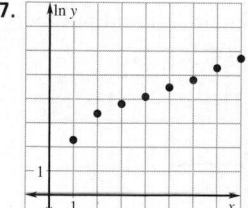 ; domain: $x > 2$;
range: all real numbers
8. 4   **9.** −1   **10.** 2
11. $\dfrac{1}{2} \log_4 x + 4 \log_4 y$
12. $\log_6 28x^3$ **13.** 2.230   **14.** $\ln 5$
15. $2^{28/3}$ **16.** no solution
17. about 87 billion ergs

5. $y = \dfrac{2}{9} \cdot 3^x$
7. $y = \dfrac{2704}{350} \left(\dfrac{35}{52}\right)^x$ **9.** $y = \dfrac{1}{\sqrt{3}} \left(\dfrac{\sqrt{3}}{2}\right)^x$ **11.** $y = 2x^2$
13. $y = 4x^{0.631}$ **15.** $y = 0.417x^{0.263}$ **17.** $y = \left(\dfrac{4}{3}\right) 3^x$
19. $y = \left(\dfrac{1}{512}\right) 4^x$ **21.** $y = 2^x$ **23.** $y = 7\left(\dfrac{2}{3}\right)^x$ **25.** $y = \left(\dfrac{1}{4}\right) 5^x$

27. ; *Sample answer:*
$y = 9.715(1.550)^x$
29. $y = 0.362x^{1.465}$
31. $y = 0.358x^{2.181}$
33. $y = 6.325x^{0.661}$
35. $y = 7.109x^{0.482}$
37. $y = 2.481x^{0.954}$

39. 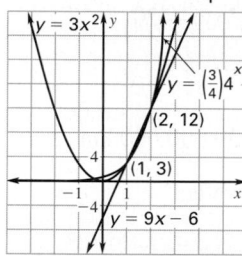 ; $y = 1.193x^{1.962}$

41. $y = 31,623(1.738)^x$

43. $y = 54.598e^x$

45. $y = 0.283x^{-0.48}$

47. $y = 2.664(0.0926)^x$

49. $y = 12.182(0.223)^x$

51. $y = x^{5/3}$

53. $y = 9x - 6$; $y = \frac{3}{4} \cdot 4^x$; $y = 3x^2$;

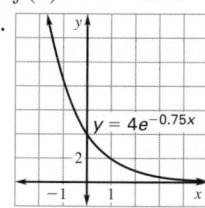 ; *Sample answer:* The linear function grows the slowest, the quadratic is in the middle, and the exponential function grows at the fastest rate.

55. a. yes **b.** $C = 250.31(1.104)^t$; about 35,232

57. a. yes **b.** $y = 2.022x^{-0.582}$; about 354,000

8.7 MIXED REVIEW (p. 516)

61. $f(x) \to +\infty$ as $x \to -\infty$; $f(x) \to -\infty$ as $x \to +\infty$

63. $f(x) \to -\infty$ as $x \to -\infty$; $f(x) \to -\infty$ as $x \to +\infty$

65. $f(x) \to +\infty$ as $x \to -\infty$; $f(x) \to +\infty$ as $x \to +\infty$

67.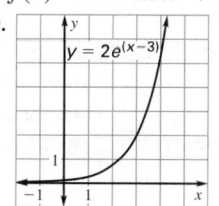

69.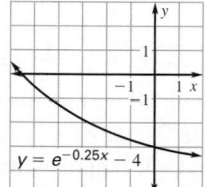

71.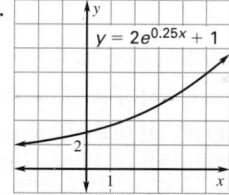

73.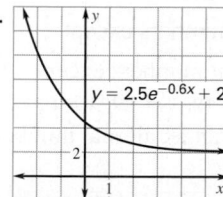

75.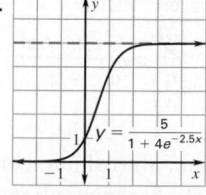

77. $\log 27$ **79.** $\ln \dfrac{x^2}{4}$

81. $\log_7 3840$

8.8 PRACTICE (pp. 520–522) **5.** 0.0438 **7.** 0.822

9. ; **11.** 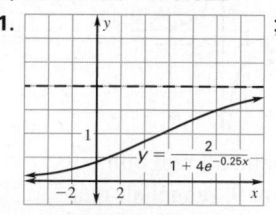 ;

x-axis and $y = 5$; 1; (0.555, 2.5)

x-axis and $y = 2$; $\dfrac{2}{5}$; (5.545, 1)

---

13. 0.693 **15.** $h = \dfrac{117}{1 + 18e^{-0.73t}}$ **17.** 6.090 **19.** 0.00578

21. 2.896 **23.** 0.835 **25.** A

27. 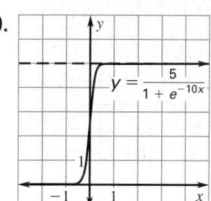 ; asymptotes: x-axis and $y = 1$; y-intercept: $\dfrac{1}{7}$; pt of max growth: $\left(1.792, \dfrac{1}{2}\right)$

29. 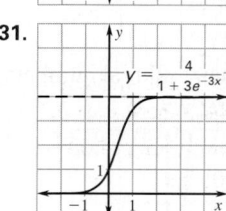 ; asymptotes: x-axis and $y = 5$; y-intercept: $\dfrac{5}{2}$; pt of max growth: $\left(0, \dfrac{5}{2}\right)$

31. 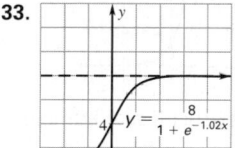 ; asymptotes: x-axis and $y = 4$; y-intercept: 1; pt of max growth: (0.366, 2)

33.  ; asymptotes: x-axis and $y = 8$; y-intercept: 4; pt of max growth: (0, 4)

37. $\dfrac{\ln 18}{4} \approx 0.723$ **39.** 1.741

41. 0.356 **43.** −3.942

45. during 1994

47. to approach 91.86 million households

49. 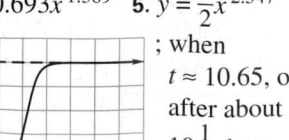 ; **51.** $y = \dfrac{721}{1 + 72e^{-0.526t}}$

1987

8.8 MIXED REVIEW (p. 522) **55.** $y = -2x$ **57.** $y = \dfrac{1}{8}x$

59. $y = 0.2x$ **61.** $y = 2.560(0.0872)^x$ **63.** $y = 0.0174x^{-0.75}$

QUIZ 3 (p. 522) **1.** $y = 1.191(1.587)^x$ **2.** $y = 9.541(1.677)^x$

3. $y = 0.936(1.573)^x$ **4.** $y = 10.693x^{1.389}$ **5.** $y = \dfrac{1}{2}x^{2.547}$

6. $y = 1.429x^{2.070}$ **7.** ; when $t \approx 10.65$, or after about $10\dfrac{1}{2}$ days

1. 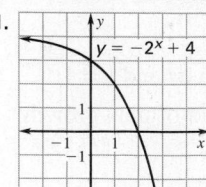 ;

domain: all real numbers;
range: $y < 4$

3. 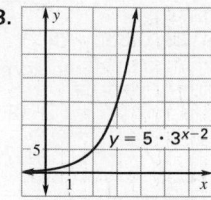 ;

domain: all real numbers;
range: $y > 0$

5. exponential decay **7.** exponential decay

9. 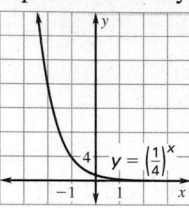 ;

domain: all real numbers;
range: $y > 0$

11. 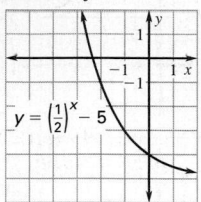 ;

domain: all real numbers;
range: $y > -5$

13. 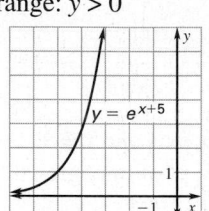 ;

domain: all real numbers;
range: $y > 0$

15. 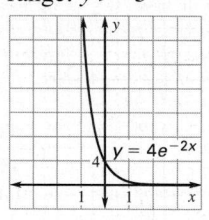 ;

domain: all real numbers;
range: $y > 0$

17. 3 **19.** -2

21. 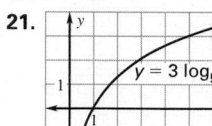 ;

domain: $x > 0$;
range: all real numbers

23. 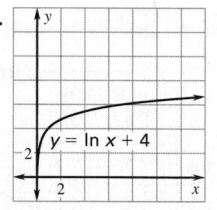 ;

domain: $x > 0$;
range: all real numbers

25. $\log_3 6 + \log_3 x + \log_3 y$ **27.** $\log 5 + 3 \log x$

29. $\ln \frac{9}{5}$ **31.** $\log 18$ **33.** -1.466 **35.** 160.49

37. $y = 3.9605(1.499)^x$ **39.** $y = 2.099x^{0.696}$

41. $y = 3.188x^{1.673}$

43. 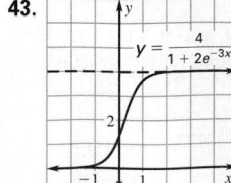 ; asymptotes: x-axis and $y = 4$;

y-intercept: $\frac{4}{3}$; pt of max growth:
$(0.231, 2)$

CHAPTER 9

SKILL REVIEW (p. 532) **1.** $y = \frac{5}{2}x$ **2.** $y = \frac{1}{10}x$

3. $y = -\frac{1}{4}x$ **4.** $y = -4x$ **5.** $15x - 5$ **6.** $x^3 + 7x^2 + 8x - 16$

7. $-x^3 + 5x$ **8.** $x^3 + 7x^2 - 8x$ **9.** $(x - 3)^2$

10. $4(x - 1)(x^2 + x + 1)$ **11.** $2x(2x - 9)(2x + 9)$

12. $(2x - 1)(3x + 5)$ **13.** $0, -2$ **14.** $-5, 3$ **15.** $-1, 4$

9.1 PRACTICE (pp. 537–539) **5.** direct variation **7.** inverse

variation **9.** inverse variation **11.** neither **13.** yes **15.** yes

17. yes **19.** yes **21.** inverse variation **23.** neither

25. inverse variation **27.** direct variation **29.** $y = -\frac{10}{x}; -5$

31. $y = \frac{7}{x}; 3.5$ **33.** $y = -\frac{4}{x}; -2$ **35.** inverse variation

37. neither **39.** $z = \frac{1}{4}xy; -7$ **41.** $z = 15xy; -420$

43. $z = 32xy; -896$ **45.** $x = \frac{kz}{y}$ **47.** $w = \frac{kyz}{x}$

49. yes; $l = \frac{45\pi}{8A}$ **51.** $D = \frac{k\sqrt{L}}{T^2}$ **53.** $139{,}000{,}000$ km

55. $W = \frac{49}{5}mh$; 1470 joules **57.** 285 watts

9.1 MIXED REVIEW (p. 539)

61. 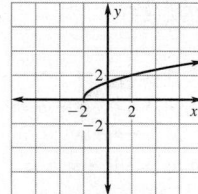 ; domain: all real numbers x
such that $x \geq -2$; range: all real
numbers y such that $y \geq 0$

63. 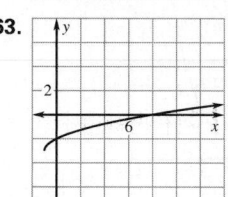 ; domain: all real numbers x
such that $x \geq -1$; range: all real
numbers y such that $y \geq -3$

65. 128 **67.** 113 **69.** 7

9.2 PRACTICE (pp. 543–545) **5.** $y = 2$; $x = -4$ **7.** $y = \frac{1}{2}$; $x = 2$

9. $y = -5$; $x = 6$ **11.** $y = 2$; $x = 0$; domain: all real numbers
except 0; range: all real numbers except 2 **13.** $y = -2$;
$x = -3$; domain: all real numbers except -3; range: all real
numbers except -2 **15.** $y = \frac{2}{3}$; $x = -\frac{1}{3}$; domain: all real
numbers except $-\frac{1}{3}$; range: all real numbers except $\frac{2}{3}$

17. $y = -17$; $x = -43$; domain: all real numbers except -43;
range: all real numbers except -17 **19.** $y = 19$; $x = 6$;
domain: all real numbers except 6; range: all real numbers
except 19 **21.** C

23. 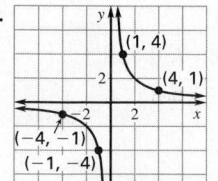 ;

domain: all real numbers
except 0; range: all real
numbers except 0

25. 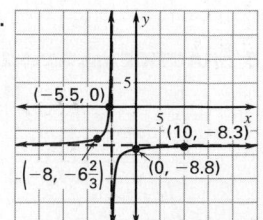 ;

domain: all real numbers
except -5; range: all real
numbers except -8

27. 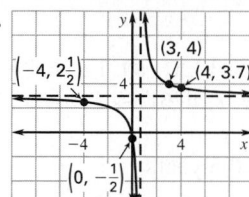 ;

domain: all real numbers except –2; range: all real numbers except –6

33. 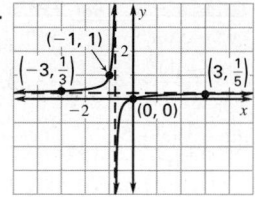 ;

domain: all real numbers except $-\frac{3}{4}$; range: all real numbers except $\frac{1}{4}$

35. 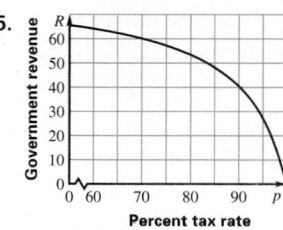 ; domain: all real numbers except $\frac{2}{3}$; range: all real numbers except 3

41. *Sample answer:*
$y = \frac{1}{x+4} + 3$ **43.** 30

45.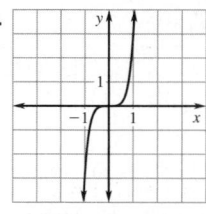
Government revenue vs. Percent tax rate

47. $f = \frac{1,480,000}{740 - r}$

9.2 MIXED REVIEW (p. 545)

53.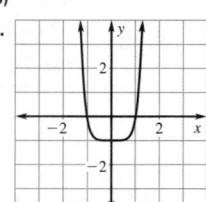

55.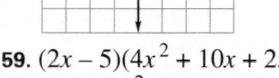

57.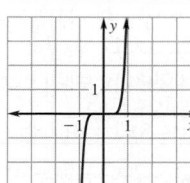

59. $(2x - 5)(4x^2 + 10x + 25)$
61. $(x + 3)(x^2 + 3)$
63. $(3x - 1)(3x + 1)(9x^2 + 1)$
65. $\frac{1}{5}e^{x-1}$ **67.** e^{5x+1}
69. e^{4-x}

TECHNOLOGY ACTIVITY 9.2 (p. 546)

7. $A = \frac{2 + 8n}{n}$;

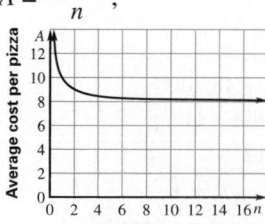
Average cost per pizza vs. Number of pizzas

The average cost approaches $8.

9.3 PRACTICE (pp. 550–552)

5.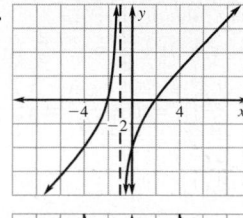

7.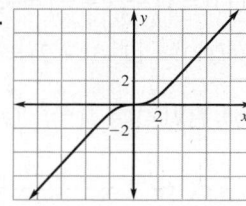

9.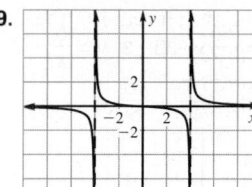

11. *x*-intercept: 0; vertical asymptotes: $x = -3$, $x = 3$
13. *x*-intercepts: $-\frac{1}{2}$, 5; vertical asymptotes: $x = -4$, $x = 4$
15. *x*-intercepts: –5, 1; vertical asymptote: $x = 6$
17. *x*-intercept: –4; vertical asymptotes: $x = -\sqrt{3}$, $x = \sqrt{3}$
19. *x*-intercept: 3; vertical asymptote: $x = 0$
21. C   **23.** B   **25.** C

27.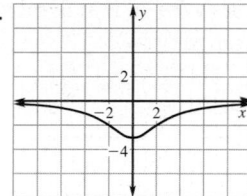

29.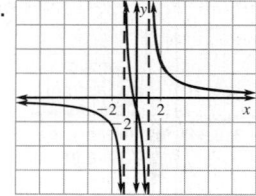

31.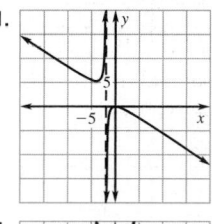

33.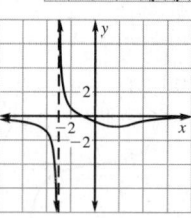

35.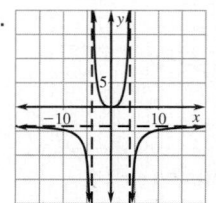

37.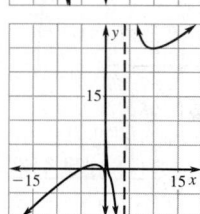

39. 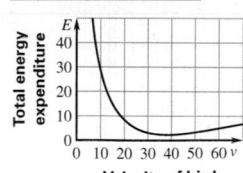 ;
Total energy expenditure vs. Velocity of bird

about 39 km/h

41. No; this model predicts an average daily cost close to zero after 2005, and this is not realistic.

43.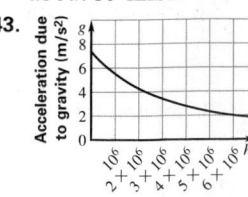
Acceleration due to gravity (m/s²) vs. Height (m)

45. g' decreases as h increases.

9.3 MIXED REVIEW (p. 553)   **51.** x^5y^4 **53.** $\frac{4x^7}{y^7}$ **55.** $\frac{x^6}{125y^6}$

57. $z = -\frac{3xy}{40}$; $\frac{9}{20}$ **59.** $z = 8xy$; –48

61. $f(g(x)) = f\left(-\dfrac{1}{3}x + \dfrac{2}{3}\right) = -3\left(-\dfrac{1}{3}x + \dfrac{2}{3}\right) + 2 = x - 2 +$

$2 = x$; $g(f(x)) = g(-3x + 2) = -\dfrac{1}{3}(-3x + 2) + \dfrac{2}{3} = x - \dfrac{2}{3} +$

$\dfrac{2}{3} = x$ **63.** $f(g(x)) = f\left(\dfrac{\sqrt[4]{x}}{2}\right) = 16\left(\dfrac{\sqrt[4]{x}}{2}\right)^4 = 16\left(\dfrac{x}{16}\right) = x$;

$g(f(x)) = g(16x^4) = \dfrac{\sqrt[4]{16x^4}}{2} = \dfrac{2x}{2} = x$

QUIZ 1 (p. 553) **1.** $y = -\dfrac{12}{x}$; 4 **2.** $y = \dfrac{66}{x}$; −22 **3.** $y = \dfrac{6}{x}$; −2

4. $x = -\dfrac{yz}{6}$; −24 **5.** $x = 4yz$; 1 **6.** $x = -\dfrac{5yz}{4}$; $-\dfrac{16}{5}$

7.
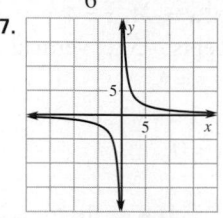
8.
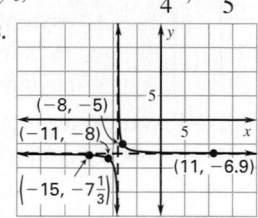

9.
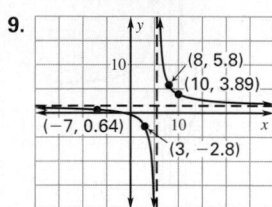

10.
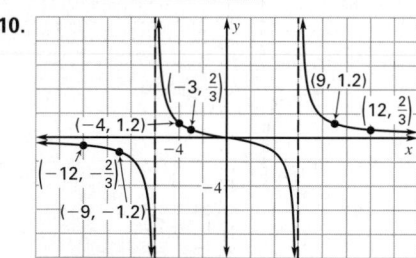

11.
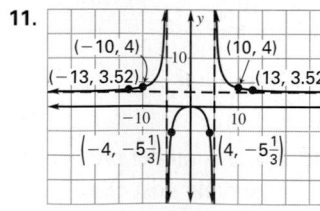
12.
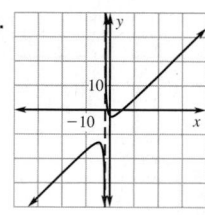

13.
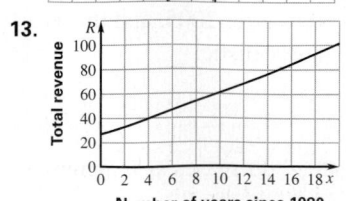
; 1992

9.4 PRACTICE (p. 558–560) **3.** $\dfrac{x}{x^2 + 3}$ **5.** not possible

7. not possible **9.** $\dfrac{x^5}{25y^2}$ **11.** $\dfrac{x-2}{x^2}$ **13.** $\dfrac{6y^3}{x^5}$

15. with: 6.9; without: 9.3 **17.** not possible

19. not possible **21.** $\dfrac{3(x+1)}{x+2}$ **23.** $\dfrac{x-3}{x}$ **25.** not possible

27. $\dfrac{x^2 - 2}{x^2 - 3x + 9}$ **29.** $\dfrac{16x^3}{y^2}$ **31.** $\dfrac{3(x+4)}{x+3}$ **33.** $2(x-1)(x-3)$

35. $\dfrac{-(x+1)^2}{x^2}$ **37.** $\dfrac{1}{y^2}$ **39.** $\dfrac{1}{3x}$ **41.** $\dfrac{(x+4)(x-2)}{x+2}$

43. $\dfrac{(x-3)(x+5)}{3x}$ **45.** $\dfrac{(x-4)(x+2)}{4x^2}$ **47.** $9(x+3)$

49. $3(x+2)$ **51.** $H = \dfrac{k_2}{k_1V^2}$ or HV^2 is a constant. A shorter

runner can run faster than a taller runner and still have
the heat being generated equal the heat being released,
so a shorter runner has an advantage. **53.** 468.5 acres
55. about $4,400 million

9.4 MIXED REVIEW (p. 560) **61.** 15; 1320 **63.** 12; 504
65. 120; 2400 **67.** $x^2 + 6x - 7$ **69.** $x^3 + 6x^2 + 11x + 6$
71. $-6x^6 + 24x^4 + 5x^3 - 20x$

73.
; in 6.5 years

**Number of years
since bike bought**

TECHNOLOGY ACTIVITY 9.4 (p. 561)

1. $\dfrac{x}{x+4}$ **3.** $\dfrac{x-2}{x+1}$ **5.** $\dfrac{2x}{3}$

9.5 PRACTICE (pp. 565–567)

5. $\dfrac{2x+7}{x+5}$ **7.** $\dfrac{x^2 - 3x + 24}{(x-4)(x+3)}$ **9.** $\dfrac{x(x-23)}{20(2x+1)}$

11. $\dfrac{Pi}{1 - \left(\dfrac{1}{1+i}\right)^{12t}} = \dfrac{Pi(1+i)^{12t}}{\left(1 - \left(\dfrac{1}{(1+i)^{12t}}\right)\right)(1+i)^{12t}} = \dfrac{Pi(1+i)^{12t}}{(1+i)^{12t} - 1}$

13. $\dfrac{23-x}{10x^2}$ **15.** $\dfrac{5x(x+1)}{x+8}$ **17.** $\dfrac{1}{x}$ **19.** $21x^2(x-5)$

21. $x(x+3)(x-6)$ **23.** $(x-7)(x+2)(x+4)$ **25.** Always;
each denominator must be a factor of the LCD, so the
LCD must have degree greater than or equal to each of the
separate denominators. **27.** $\dfrac{-47}{21x}$ **29.** $\dfrac{10x+13}{(x-3)(x+3)}$

31. $\dfrac{11-x}{(x-2)(x+4)}$ **33.** $\dfrac{-3(5x^2 + x + 2)}{(x-10)(3x+2)}$ **35.** $\dfrac{2(x^2 - 5x - 8)}{(x-4)(x+4)^2}$

37. $\dfrac{49x^2 + 24x - 5}{6x(x-1)(x+1)}$ **39.** $\dfrac{80}{x-27}$ **41.** $\dfrac{-(x^3 - x - 1)}{3(x+1)}$ **43.** $\dfrac{-2}{3x}$

45. $\dfrac{3x(x-4)}{(13x+8)(x^2 - 4x + 16)}$

47. $M = \dfrac{357t^3 + 5500t^2 - 37,100t + 485,000}{(0.00418t^2 + 1)(-0.0580t + 1)}$

49. $A = \dfrac{391(t-1)^2 + 0.112}{0.218(t-1)^4 + 0.991(t-1)^2 + 1}$

51. about 1.2 hours after the second dose **53.** $\dfrac{24}{7}$ ohms

9.5 MIXED REVIEW (p. 567) **57.** 24 **59.** $\dfrac{16}{3}$ **61.** −66

63. $-\dfrac{102}{23}$ **65.** 72 **67.** $\pm 2\sqrt{5}$ **69.** 2, 8 **71.** $-7, \dfrac{1}{2}$

9.6 PRACTICE (pp. 571–573) **5.** $-\dfrac{8}{3}$ **7.** $\dfrac{3}{2}$ **9.** -5 **11.** $-15, 0$

13. 0 **15.** no **17.** no **19.** yes **21.** 2 **23.** $-1, \dfrac{1}{4}$ **25.** $-\dfrac{2}{3}, 2$

27. $-\dfrac{3}{2}, 2$ **29.** $\dfrac{5}{7}, 3$ **31.** -3 **33.** $\dfrac{6}{17}$ **35.** $-4, 4$ **37.** $2, 5$

39. 4 **41.** $-\dfrac{3}{2}, 5$ **43.** -5 **45.** no solution **47.** $-2, 0$ **49.** $2, 6$

51. Always; when you solve by cross multiplying, you get $x = 1$ or $x = a$ and $x = a$ makes both fractions undefined.
53. Always; when you multiply each side of the equation by $x^2 - a^2$, you get $x = a$, making the fractions undefined.
55. 87 **57.** about 2198 flies/m^3 **59.** $16.50

9.6 MIXED REVIEW (p. 573) **63.** $1; -1$ **65.** $-\dfrac{2}{3}; \dfrac{3}{2}$ **67.** $\dfrac{1}{2}; -2$

69. $4\sqrt{3}$ **71.** $6\sqrt{3}$ **73.** $3\sqrt{30}$ **75.** 15 **77.** 6.796

QUIZ 2 (p. 574) **1.** $\dfrac{5x^5 y}{3}$ **2.** $\dfrac{x - 8}{5x}$ **3.** $\dfrac{2x^2}{(x-9)(x+4)}$

4. $\dfrac{16x^2 - 5x + 6}{2(5x-6)(5x+6)}$ **5.** $\dfrac{-6(11x+8)}{6x-1}$ **6.** -6

7. $\dfrac{-3(x-3)(2x-1)(2x+1)}{(x-1)(x+1)}$ **8.** $\dfrac{2x}{(x-5)(x+1)}$ **9.** 20 dozen

CHAPTER 9 REVIEW (pp. 576–578)

1. $y = \dfrac{5}{x}; 2.5$ **3.** $y = \dfrac{2}{x}; 1$ **5.** $z = \dfrac{1}{3}xy; -10$ **7.** $z = 3xy; -90$

9. 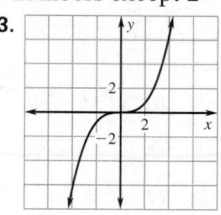 ;

11. 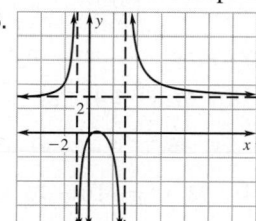 ;

domain: all real numbers; except -4; range: all real numbers except 2

domain: all real numbers; except 1; range: all real numbers except 2

13. 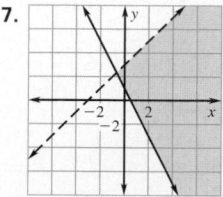 **15.**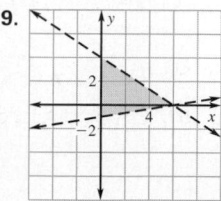

17. $5(x-6)(x+3)(x-3)$ **19.** $\dfrac{x^3 + 5}{x^2(x-2)}$

21. $\dfrac{-9x^2 + 18x - 10}{5x(x-1)(x+5)}$ **23.** $\dfrac{x(x-8)}{2(9x+2)}$ **25.** $\dfrac{12}{5}$

27. $\dfrac{3}{2}$ **29.** no solution **31.** $-4, 1$

CUMULATIVE PRACTICE (pp. 582–583)

1. $y = 3x - \dfrac{7}{2}$ **3.** $y = -\dfrac{5}{6}x + 25$ **5.** parallel

7. 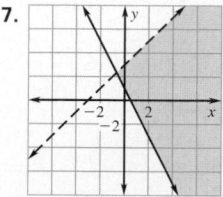 **9.**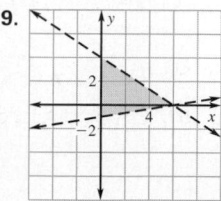

11. $\begin{bmatrix} 12 & -2 \\ -12 & 2 \end{bmatrix}$ **13.** $\begin{bmatrix} -2 & -8 \\ 17 & 30 \end{bmatrix}$

15–19.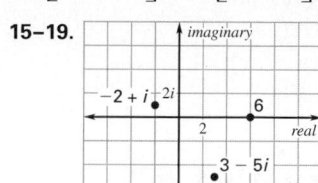

15. $\sqrt{5}$ **17.** 6 **19.** $\sqrt{34}$

21. 5 **23.** $\dfrac{3x^4}{10}$

25. $2ab\sqrt[4]{bc}$ **27.** $\dfrac{1}{8e^6}$

29. 2 **31.** $\dfrac{1}{5}$ **33.** $\dfrac{1}{2}$

35. $-x^2 + 2x + 13$; all real numbers
37. $-2x^2 - 15$; all real numbers **39.** $f^{-1}(x) = 2(x + 6)$
41. $f^{-1}(x) = 5^x$ **43.** $\log(3x^2 y^3)$ **45.** $\ln(x^2 y^2)$

47. 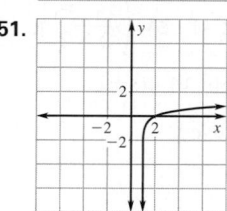 **49.**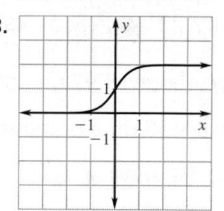

51. 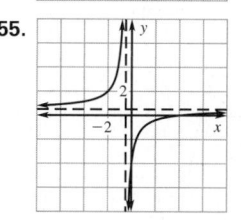 **53.**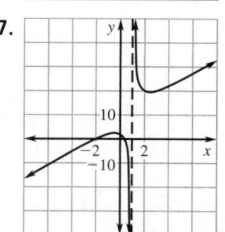

55. 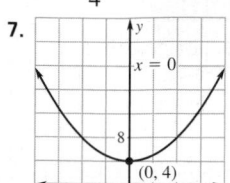 **57.**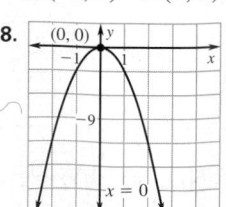

59. 10 **61.** $-\dfrac{9\sqrt{3}}{2}$ **63.** $\ln 8 \approx 2.079$ **65.** $-\dfrac{9}{5}$

67. $y = \dfrac{5}{32}(2)^x$ **69.** $y = 0.759(1.737)^x$ **71.** $y = 1.651x^{0.861}$

73. $y = 1.704x^{0.231}$ **75.** $\dfrac{6x^3 + 7x^2 - 20x - 9}{2x(x-1)(3x+1)}$

77. about 3.5 sec **81.** $f = \dfrac{kq_1 q_2}{r^2}$

CHAPTER 10

SKILL REVIEW (p. 588) **1.** $y = 2x + 4$ **2.** $y = \dfrac{1}{3}x - \dfrac{8}{3}$

3. $y = -\dfrac{3}{4}x - 2$ **4.** $(2, 3)$ **5.** $(-1, 5)$ **6.** $(4, 9)$

7. 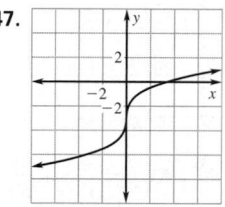 **8.**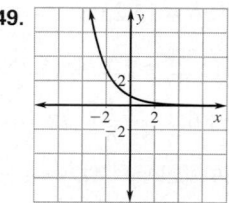

9.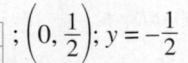

10. $-4 \pm \sqrt{2}$ **11.** $-\dfrac{3}{2} \pm \dfrac{\sqrt{11}}{2}i$

12. $-3 \pm \sqrt{23}$

10.1 Practice (pp. 592–594) **5.** 5 **7.** $3\sqrt{5} \approx 6.71$

9. $3\sqrt{34} \approx 17.49$ **11.** (2, 6) **13.** (2, 7) **15.** $\left(-\dfrac{9}{2}, -\dfrac{1}{2}\right)$

17. 5; $\left(\dfrac{3}{2}, 2\right)$ **19.** $\sqrt{113} \approx 10.63$; $\left(4, \dfrac{1}{2}\right)$ **21.** $5\sqrt{5} \approx 11.18$;

$\left(2, \dfrac{3}{2}\right)$ **23.** $2\sqrt{58} \approx 15.23$; $(-2, -1)$ **25.** $2\sqrt{13} \approx 7.21$;

(5, 1) **27.** $\sqrt{115.25} \approx 10.74$; (1.25, −1.3) **29.** 2.5; (−6.25, 3)

31. $\sqrt{\dfrac{377}{8}} \approx 6.86$; $\left(\dfrac{17}{8}, \dfrac{1}{8}\right)$ **33.** isosceles **35.** scalene

37. scalene **39.** scalene **41.** $y = -\dfrac{1}{3}x + \dfrac{28}{3}$ **43.** $y = \dfrac{4}{15}x + \dfrac{61}{30}$

45. $y = \dfrac{2}{15}x - 2.22$ **47.** −5; 5 **49.** −15; −1 **51.** $\left(\dfrac{25}{2}, \dfrac{35}{2}\right)$;

$\left(\dfrac{75}{2}, \dfrac{35}{2}\right)$ **53.** about 18.97 mi **55.** about 11.40 mi

57. r is about 58.56 m, v is about 20 m/sec.

10.1 Mixed Review (p. 594)

65. 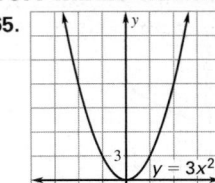 **67.**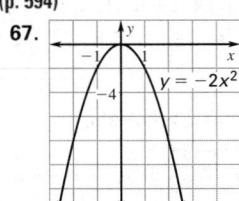

69. 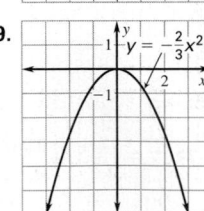 **71.**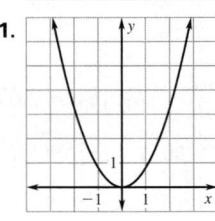

73. 525 **75.** 1 **77.** $4^{2/3} \approx 2.52$ **79.** $\dfrac{x+6}{3x^2}$ **81.** $\dfrac{-x^2 + 4x + 9}{x^2 + 3x}$

83. $\dfrac{-6x^2 + x - 11}{(x-6)(2x+1)}$

10.2 Practice (pp. 598–600)

5. 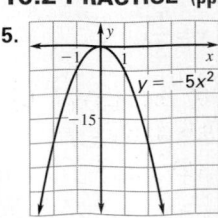 **7.**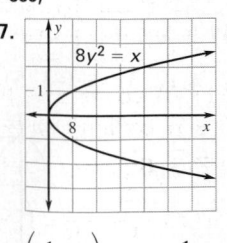

$\left(0, -\dfrac{1}{20}\right)$; $y = \dfrac{1}{20}$ $\left(\dfrac{1}{32}, 0\right)$; $x = -\dfrac{1}{32}$

9. 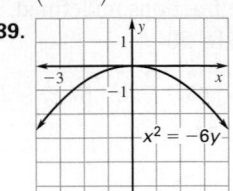 ; $\left(0, \dfrac{1}{2}\right)$; $y = -\dfrac{1}{2}$

11. $y^2 = 20x$ **13.** $y^2 = -16x$

15. $x^2 = -32y$ **17.** B **19.** E **21.** C

23. down **25.** right **27.** left **29.** up

31. $\left(\dfrac{1}{8}, 0\right)$; $x = -\dfrac{1}{8}$

33. $\left(-\dfrac{5}{2}, 0\right)$; $x = \dfrac{5}{2}$ **35.** (0, −9); $y = 9$ **37.** (0, 7); $y = -7$

39. 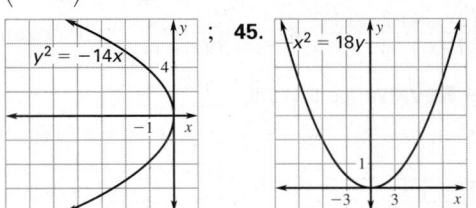 **41.** ;

$\left(0, -\dfrac{3}{2}\right)$; $y = \dfrac{3}{2}$ (6, 0); $x = -6$

43. 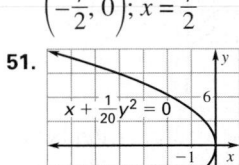 ; **45.** 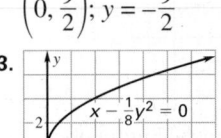 ;

$\left(-\dfrac{7}{2}, 0\right)$; $x = \dfrac{7}{2}$ $\left(0, \dfrac{9}{2}\right)$; $y = -\dfrac{9}{2}$

51. 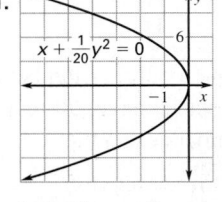 ; **53.** ;

(−5, 0); $x = 5$ (2, 0); $x = -2$

55. $y^2 = -8x$ **57.** $x^2 = 4y$ **59.** $x^2 = -12y$ **61.** $y^2 = -20x$

63. $x^2 = -\dfrac{3}{2}y$ **65.** $y^2 = \dfrac{5}{3}x$ **67.** $x^2 = 12y$ **69.** $y^2 = -24x$

71. $x^2 = 4y$ **73.** $x^2 = -16y$ **75.** $y^2 = -3x$ **77.** $x^2 = \dfrac{1}{3}y$

79. $y^2 = 6x$; 2.04 in. **81.** 2.25 in.

10.2 Mixed Review (p. 600) **85.** $\dfrac{4}{7}$ **87.** about 1.209

89. no solution **91.** $\dfrac{y^3}{2x^3}$ **93.** $x + 3$ **95.** $\dfrac{1}{6x^2}$

97. $3\sqrt{2} \approx 4.243$ **99.** $\sqrt{569} \approx 23.854$ **101.** $\sqrt{1733} \approx 41.629$

103. $A = 1.5p$

10.3 Practice (pp. 604–606) **5.** $x^2 + y^2 = 16$

7. $x^2 + y^2 = 100$ **9.** $x^2 + y^2 = 117$ **11.** $x^2 + y^2 = 50$

13. 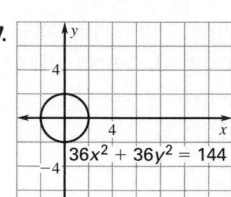 ; 6   **15.** 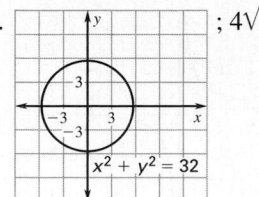 ; $4\sqrt{2}$

17. 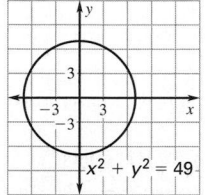 ; 2   **19.** $x^2 + y^2 = 12.25$
21. F   **23.** B   **25.** A

27. 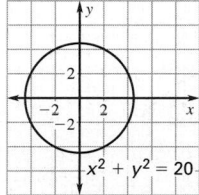 ;   **29.** 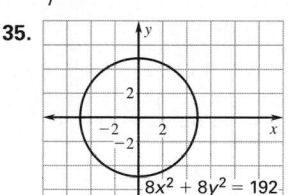 ;

7                                    $2\sqrt{5} \approx 4.47$

35. 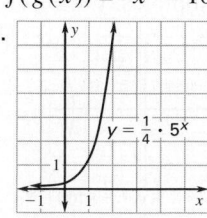 ;   **41.**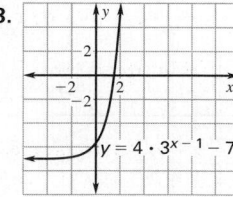

$2\sqrt{6} \approx 4.90$
47. $x^2 + y^2 = 9$ **49.** $x^2 + y^2 = 36$ **51.** $x^2 + y^2 = 7$
53. $x^2 + y^2 = 11$ **55.** $x^2 + y^2 = 150$ **57.** $x^2 + y^2 = 28$
59. $x^2 + y^2 = 100$ **61.** $x^2 + y^2 = 25$ **63.** $x^2 + y^2 = 34$
65. $x^2 + y^2 = 37$ **67.** $x^2 + y^2 = 65$ **69.** $x^2 + y^2 = 89$
71. $y = -\frac{1}{3}x + \frac{10}{3}$ **73.** $y = -\frac{4}{5}x - \frac{41}{5}$ **75.** $y = 8x + 65$
77. $y = -\frac{5}{6}x - \frac{61}{3}$ **79.** $y = \frac{2}{3}x - \frac{13}{3}$; they have opposite
slopes and intercepts.   **81.** yes; about 7.92 mi   **83.** 16 mm
85. 36 in.   **87.** about 3.6 min

10.3 MIXED REVIEW (p. 607)
91. $(-2, -3)$ **93.** $(-2, -2)$ **95.** $(7, 2)$
97. $f(g(x)) = 2x + 1$; $g(f(x)) = 2x + 2$
99. $f(g(x)) = -x^2 - 10x - 26$; $g(f(x)) = -x^2 + 4$
101. 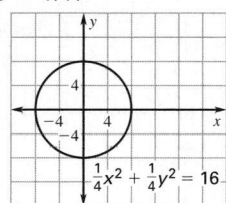   **103.**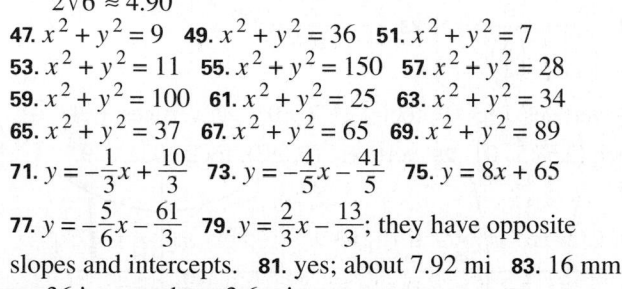

107. $\begin{bmatrix} 35 & 52 \\ 112 & 40 \\ 95 & 63 \end{bmatrix}$

QUIZ 1 (p. 607) **1.** 10; (4, 3) **2.** $6\sqrt{2} \approx 8.485$; (0, 0) **3.** $5\sqrt{13} \approx$
18.028; $\left(1, -\frac{3}{2}\right)$ **4.** $2\sqrt{17} \approx 8.246$; (-1, -8) **5.** $2\sqrt{37} \approx$
12.166; (2, 5)   **6.** $4\sqrt{58} \approx 30.463$; (5, 1)   **7.** $\left(\frac{3}{2}, 0\right)$; $x = -\frac{3}{2}$
8. $\left(0, \frac{3}{4}\right)$; $y = -\frac{3}{4}$ **9.** $\left(0, -\frac{5}{4}\right)$; $y = \frac{5}{4}$ **10.** $\left(-\frac{3}{8}, 0\right)$; $x = \frac{3}{8}$

11. 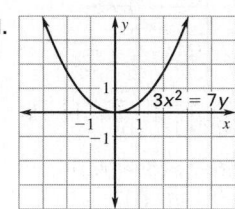 ; $\left(0, \frac{7}{12}\right)$; $y = -\frac{7}{12}$
12. $\left(\frac{1}{16}, 0\right)$; $x = -\frac{1}{16}$

13. 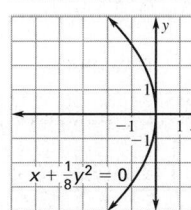 ; (-2, 0); $x = 2$
14. (0, -3); $y = 3$ **15.** $x^2 + y^2 = 9$
16. $x^2 + y^2 = 25$ **17.** $x^2 + y^2 = 65$
18. $x^2 + y^2 = 29$ **19.** $x^2 + y^2 = 82$
20. $x^2 + y^2 = 45$ **21.** $x^2 + y^2 = 72$
22. $x^2 + y^2 = 113$

23. no; $\sqrt{35^2 + 56^2} \approx 66$ mi

TECHNOLOGY ACTIVITY 10.3 (p. 608) 1–9: Sample answers
are given.   **1.** $-18 \le x \le 18$; $-12 \le y \le 12$ **3.** $-36 \le x \le 36$;
$-24 \le y \le 24$ **5.** $-3 \le x \le 3$; $-2 \le y \le 2$ **7.** $-9 \le x \le 9$;
$-6 \le y \le 6$ **9.** $-6 \le x \le 6$; $-4 \le y \le 4$

10.4 PRACTICE (pp. 612–614)
5. $\frac{x^2}{16} + \frac{y^2}{25} = 1$ **7.** $\frac{x^2}{49} + \frac{y^2}{9} = 1$ **9.** $\frac{x^2}{91} + \frac{y^2}{100} = 1$

11. 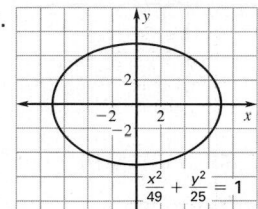   **15.**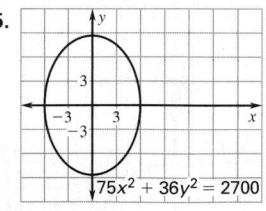

17. $\frac{x^2}{25} + \frac{y^2}{9} = 1$;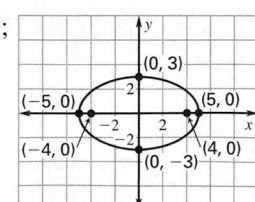

19. vertices: (±11, 0); co-vertices: (0, ±10); foci: $\left(\pm\sqrt{21}, 0\right)$
21. vertices: (0, ±5); co-vertices: (±3, 0); foci: (0, ±4)
23. vertices: $\left(\pm2\sqrt{7}, 0\right)$; co-vertices: $\left(0, \pm2\sqrt{5}\right)$;
foci: $\left(\pm2\sqrt{2}, 0\right)$ **25.** $\frac{x^2}{4} + \frac{y^2}{49} = 1$; vertices: (0, ±7);
co-vertices: (±2, 0); foci: $\left(0, \pm3\sqrt{5}\right)$ **27.** $\frac{x^2}{10} + y^2 = 1$;

vertices: $\left(\pm\sqrt{10}, 0\right)$; co-vertices: $(0, \pm1)$; foci: $(\pm3, 0)$

29. $\dfrac{x^2}{15} + \dfrac{y^2}{25} = 1$; vertices: $(0, \pm5)$; co-vertices: $\left(\pm\sqrt{15}, 0\right)$; foci: $\left(0, \pm\sqrt{10}\right)$

31. 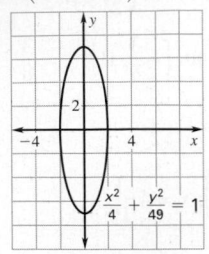 ; **35.** 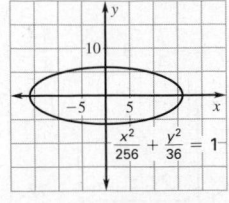 ;

vertices: $(0, \pm7)$; co-vertices: $(\pm2, 0)$; foci: $\left(0, \pm3\sqrt{5}\right)$

vertices: $(\pm16, 0)$; co-vertices: $(0, \pm6)$; foci: $\left(\pm2\sqrt{55}, 0\right)$

37. 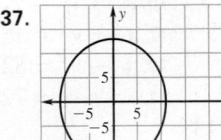 ; **41.** 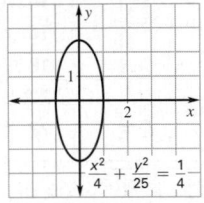 ;

vertices: $(0, \pm13)$; co-vertices: $(\pm11, 0)$; foci: $\left(0, \pm4\sqrt{3}\right)$

vertices: $(0, \pm2.5)$; co-vertices: $(\pm1, 0)$; foci: $\left(0, \pm\dfrac{\sqrt{21}}{2}\right)$

43. 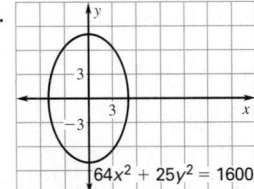 **45.**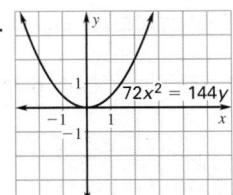

49.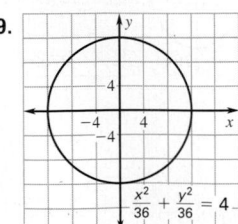

51. $\dfrac{x^2}{25} + \dfrac{y^2}{36} = 1$ **53.** $\dfrac{x^2}{16} + \dfrac{y^2}{9} = 1$

55. $\dfrac{x^2}{81} + \dfrac{y^2}{64} = 1$ **56.** $\dfrac{x^2}{100} + \dfrac{y^2}{16} = 1$

57. $\dfrac{x^2}{40} + \dfrac{y^2}{49} = 1$ **59.** $\dfrac{x^2}{16} + \dfrac{y^2}{64} = 1$

61. $\dfrac{x^2}{25} + \dfrac{y^2}{16} = 1$ **63.** $\dfrac{x^2}{55} + \dfrac{y^2}{64} = 1$

65. $\dfrac{x^2}{40} + \dfrac{y^2}{121} = 1$ **67.** $\dfrac{x^2}{275} + \dfrac{y^2}{324} = 1$ **69.** $\dfrac{x^2}{2352.25} + \dfrac{y^2}{529} = 1$

71. about 3500 ft^2 **73.** $\dfrac{x^2}{92.5^2} + \dfrac{y^2}{77.5^2} = 1$

75. $3710\pi \le A \le 7170\pi$

10.4 MIXED REVIEW (p. 614) **79.** -32 **81.** $\dfrac{1}{3}$ **83.** 27

85. 16 **87.** $y = \dfrac{24}{x}$ **89.** $y = \dfrac{72}{x}$ **91.** $y = \dfrac{12}{x}$

93. 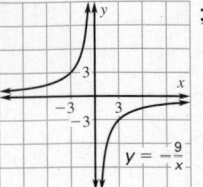 ; **97.** 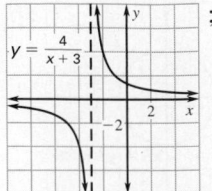 ;

domain: all real numbers except 0; range: all real numbers except 0

domain: all real numbers except -3; range: all real numbers except 0

10.5 PRACTICE (pp. 618–620)

5. 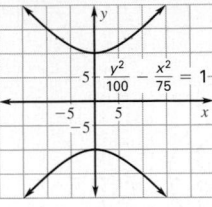 ; **7.** 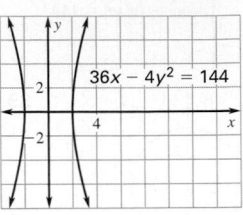 ;

foci: $\left(0, \pm5\sqrt{7}\right)$; asymptotes: $y = \pm\dfrac{2\sqrt{3}}{3}x$

foci: $\left(\pm2\sqrt{10}, 0\right)$; asymptotes: $y = \pm3x$

9. 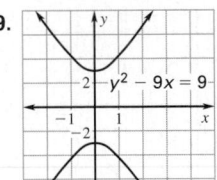 ; foci: $\left(0, \pm\sqrt{10}\right)$; asymptotes: $y = \pm3x$

11. $\dfrac{x^2}{49} - \dfrac{y^2}{15} = 1$ **13.** $\dfrac{y^2}{45} - \dfrac{x^2}{36} = 1$

15. C **17.** D **19.** $\dfrac{x^2}{9} - \dfrac{y^2}{36} = 1$

21. $\dfrac{y^2}{\left(\dfrac{1}{4}\right)} - \dfrac{x^2}{\left(\dfrac{9}{4}\right)} = 1$ **23.** $\dfrac{y^2}{4} - \dfrac{x^2}{144} = 1$

25. vertices: $(\pm3, 0)$; foci: $\left(\pm\sqrt{73}, 0\right)$ **27.** vertices: $(\pm11, 0)$; foci: $\left(\pm5\sqrt{5}, 0\right)$ **29.** vertices: $(0, \pm2)$; foci: $\left(0, \pm\sqrt{29}\right)$

31. 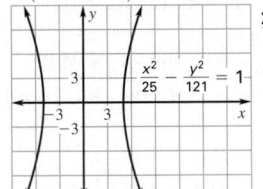 ; **33.** 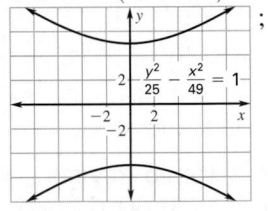 ;

foci: $\left(\pm\sqrt{146}, 0\right)$; asymptotes: $y = \pm\dfrac{11}{5}x$

foci: $\left(0, \pm\sqrt{74}\right)$; asymptotes: $y = \pm\dfrac{5}{7}x$

35. 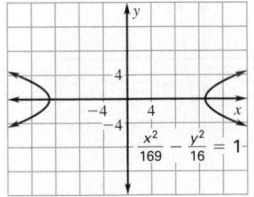 ; **41.** 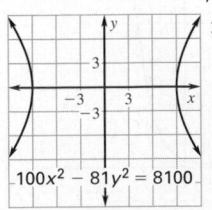 ;

foci: $\left(\pm\sqrt{185}, 0\right)$; asymptotes: $y = \pm\dfrac{4}{13}x$

foci: $\left(\pm\sqrt{181}, 0\right)$; asymptotes: $y = \pm\dfrac{10}{9}x$

43. $y = \pm \dfrac{6\sqrt{x^2 + 100}}{5}$ **45.** $y = \pm \dfrac{8.5\sqrt{x^2 - 42.25}}{6.5}$

47. $y = \pm \sqrt{\dfrac{22.3(x^2 - 10.1)}{10.1}}$

49. Sample answer:

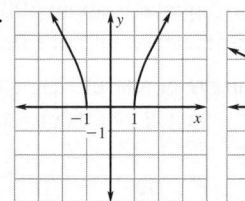 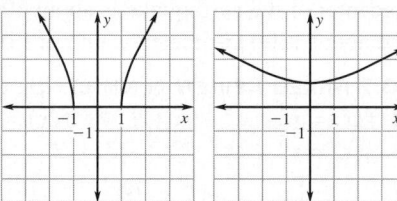

53. 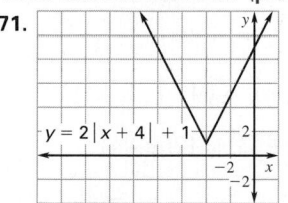 **55.**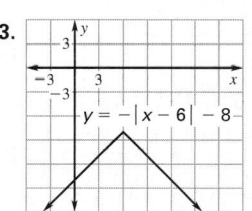

$x^2 = 15y$

$14x^2 + 14y^2 = 126$

57. $\dfrac{x^2}{36} - \dfrac{y^2}{28} = 1$ **59.** $\dfrac{x^2}{25} - \dfrac{y^2}{11} = 1$ **61.** $\dfrac{y^2}{64} - \dfrac{x^2}{17} = 1$

63. $\dfrac{y^2}{16} - \dfrac{x^2}{134} = 1$ **65.** $\dfrac{y^2}{1024} - \dfrac{x^2}{3070} = 1$ **67.** 10 mi

10.5 MIXED REVIEW (p. 621)

71. 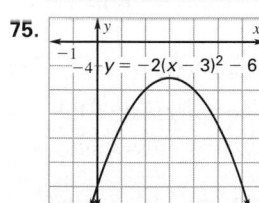 **73.**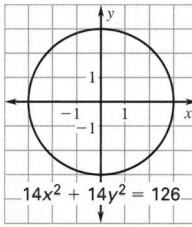

$y = 2|x + 4| + 1$

$y = -|x - 6| - 8$

75. 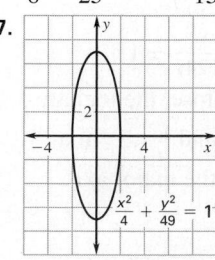 **77.** $f(x) = x^3 - 6x^2 + 11x - 6$
$y = -2(x - 3)^2 - 6$ **79.** $f(x) = x^3 - 6x^2 - 4x + 24$
81. $f(x) = x^3 - 5x^2 + x - 5$
83. 4 **85.** 4 **87.** 3 **89.** 3
91. mean: 81.67; median: 81; modes: 81, 89; range: 36

QUIZ 2 (p. 621)

1. $\dfrac{x^2}{9} + \dfrac{y^2}{49} = 1$ **2.** $\dfrac{x^2}{36} + y^2 = 1$ **3.** $\dfrac{x^2}{100} + \dfrac{y^2}{64} = 1$

4. $\dfrac{x^2}{8} + \dfrac{y^2}{25} = 1$ **5.** $\dfrac{x^2}{15} + \dfrac{y^2}{12} = 1$ **6.** $\dfrac{x^2}{81} + \dfrac{y^2}{97} = 1$

7. 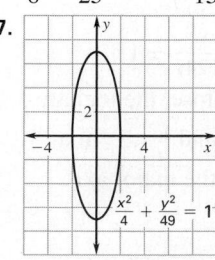 ; **8.** 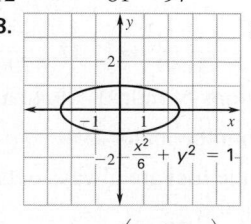 ;

$\dfrac{x^2}{4} + \dfrac{y^2}{49} = 1$

$\dfrac{x^2}{6} + y^2 = 1$

vertices: $(0, \pm 7)$;
co-vertices: $(\pm 2, 0)$;
foci: $\left(0, \pm 3\sqrt{5}\right)$

vertices: $\left(\pm\sqrt{6}, 0\right)$;
co-vertices: $(0, \pm 1)$;
foci: $\left(\pm\sqrt{5}, 0\right)$

9. 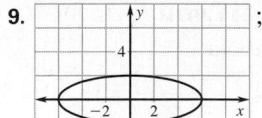 ; vertices: $(\pm 6, 0)$;
co-vertices: $(0, \pm 2)$; foci: $\left(\pm 4\sqrt{2}, 0\right)$

$x^2 + 9y^2 = 36$

10. $\dfrac{y^2}{25} - \dfrac{x^2}{39} = 1$ **11.** $x^2 - \dfrac{y^2}{8} = 1$

12. $\dfrac{x^2}{16} - \dfrac{y^2}{20} = 1$ **13.** $\dfrac{y^2}{16} - \dfrac{x^2}{4} = 1$

14. 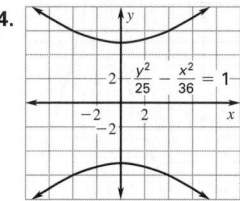 ; **15.** 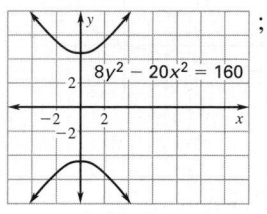 ;

$\dfrac{y^2}{25} - \dfrac{x^2}{36} = 1$

$8y^2 - 20x^2 = 160$

vertices: $(0, \pm 5)$;
foci: $\left(0, \pm\sqrt{61}\right)$;
asymptotes: $y = \pm\dfrac{5}{6}x$

vertices: $\left(0, \pm 2\sqrt{5}\right)$;
foci: $\left(0, \pm 2\sqrt{7}\right)$;
asymptotes: $y = \pm\dfrac{\sqrt{10}}{2}x$

16. 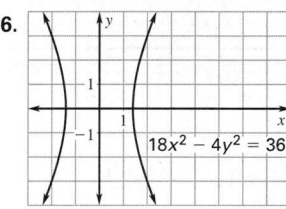 ; vertices: $\left(\pm\sqrt{2}, 0\right)$;
foci: $\left(\pm\sqrt{11}, 0\right)$;
asymptotes: $y = \pm\dfrac{3\sqrt{2}}{2}x$

$18x^2 - 4y^2 = 36$

17. $\dfrac{x^2}{4375^2} + \dfrac{y^2}{4369^2} = 1$

10.6 PRACTICE (pp. 628–630) **5.** $\dfrac{(x - 3.5)^2}{20.25} + \dfrac{(y + 4)^2}{18} = 1$

7. $\dfrac{(y + 2)^2}{4} - \dfrac{(x - 5)^2}{12} = 1$ **9.** hyperbola **11.** ellipse

13. $(x - 9)^2 + (y - 3)^2 = 16$ **15.** $(x - 1)^2 = 12(y + 2)$

17. $\dfrac{(x - 2)^2}{18} + \dfrac{(y - 1.5)^2}{20.25} = 1$ **19.** $\dfrac{y^2}{16} - \dfrac{(x - 5)^2}{20} = 1$

21. 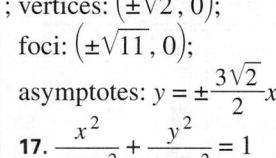 center: (6, 2);
points: (6, 4), (6, 0), (4, 2), (8, 2)

$(x - 6)^2 + (y - 2)^2 = 4$

23. 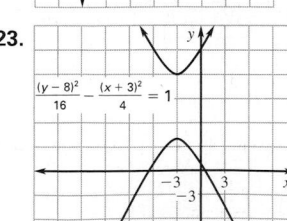 center $(-3, 8)$;
vertices: $(-3, 4)$, $(-3, 12)$;
foci: $\left(-3, 8 \pm 2\sqrt{5}\right)$

$\dfrac{(y - 8)^2}{16} - \dfrac{(x + 3)^2}{4} = 1$

25. 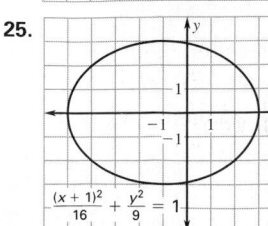 center $(-1, 0)$;
vertices: $(-5, 0)$, $(3, 0)$;
co-vertices: $(-1, -3)$, $(-1, 3)$;
foci: $\left(-1 \pm \sqrt{7}, 0\right)$

$\dfrac{(x + 1)^2}{16} + \dfrac{y^2}{9} = 1$

29. ellipse **31.** hyperbola
33. ellipse **35.** hyperbola
37. parabola **39.** ellipse

41. circle **43.** hyperbola **45.** E **47.** D **49.** B

51. parabola;
$(y - 6)^2 = -4(x - 8)$;

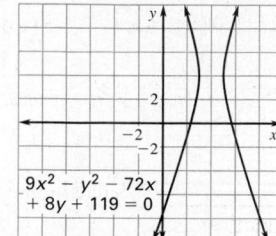

53. hyperbola;
$(x - 4)^2 - \dfrac{(y - 4)^2}{9} = 1$;

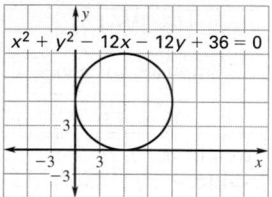

55. ellipse;
$\dfrac{(x - 1)^2}{4} + (y - 1)^2 = 1$;

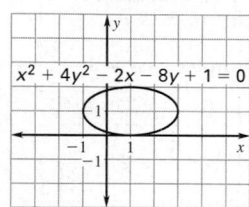

59. circle;
$(x - 6)^2 + (y - 6)^2 = 36$;

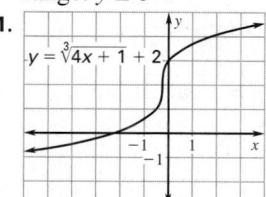

61. parabola;
$(x + 2)^2 = 8(y - 1)$;

63. $y^2 = 12x$; $y^2 = -12(x - 50)$ (x, y in ft)
65. ellipse
67. The first is elliptical, the second is parabolic.

10.6 MIXED REVIEW (p. 631) 71. $(5, -5)$ **73.** $(1, -2)$
75. $\left(\dfrac{68}{23}, \dfrac{123}{23}\right)$ **77.** 5 **79.** 0 **81.** 2 **83.** about 0.45
85. about 4.03 **87.** about 0.27

10.7 PRACTICE (pp. 635–637) 5. $(-1, 0)$, $(-7, 0)$ **7.** $(-2, -5)$, $(4, -5)$ **9.** no **11.** yes **13.** no **15.** $(1, -4)$, $(2, -1)$
17. $(3, 6)$, $(-3, -6)$ **19.** $(1, -2)$, $(-1, 2)$ **21.** $(-1, -2)$, $\left(\dfrac{7}{4}, \dfrac{3}{4}\right)$
23. $\left(\dfrac{6 - \sqrt{6}}{5}, \dfrac{24 + \sqrt{6}}{10}\right)$, $\left(\dfrac{6 + \sqrt{6}}{5}, \dfrac{24 - \sqrt{6}}{10}\right)$
25. $\left(2 + \sqrt{6}, \sqrt{6} - 2\right)$, $\left(2 - \sqrt{6}, -\sqrt{6} - 2\right)$
27. $(0, 0)$, $(-6, 6)$ **29.** none **31.** $(0, 2)$, $\left(\dfrac{4}{3}, \dfrac{2}{3}\right)$
33. $\left(\pm\sqrt{\dfrac{5\sqrt{69} - 15}{2}}, \dfrac{-5 + \sqrt{69}}{2}\right)$
35. $\left(\dfrac{1 + \sqrt{373}}{6}, \pm\sqrt{\dfrac{7 + \sqrt{373}}{18}}\right)$ **37.** none **39.** none
41. $\left(\dfrac{9\sqrt{2}}{2}, -\dfrac{9\sqrt{2}}{2}\right)$, $\left(-\dfrac{9\sqrt{2}}{2}, \dfrac{9\sqrt{2}}{2}\right)$ **43.** none **45.** $(4, 0)$

47. $(6, -8)$, $(14, -8)$ **49.** $(2, 3)$ **51.** $\left(\pm\sqrt{6}, 2\right)$, $\left(\pm\sqrt{3}, -1\right)$
53. no intersection **55.** $(5, 7)$ **59.** about 56.9 mi
61. $\left(4\sqrt{5}, \dfrac{6\sqrt{5}}{5}\right) \approx (8.9, 2.7)$ **63.** *Sample answer:* The epicenter of the earthquake is about 100 kilometers east and about 1300 kilometers south of Location 1.

10.7 MIXED REVIEW (p. 638) 67. 13 **69.** 16
71. $f(x) = x^3 - x^2 - 9x + 9$ **73.** $f(x) = x^2 + 4$
75. $f(x) = x^5 - 2x^3 - 2x^2 - 3x - 2$

77.
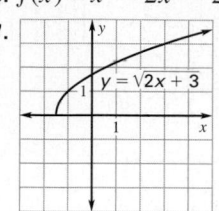
; **79.**
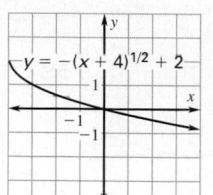
;

domain: $x \geq -\dfrac{3}{2}$;
range: $y \geq 0$

domain: $x \geq -4$;
range: $y \leq 2$

81.
; domain: all reals; range: all reals **83.** ellipse **85.** parabola

QUIZ 3 (p. 638) 1. $(x + 3)^2 + (y + 5)^2 = 64$
2. $\dfrac{(x + 0.5)^2}{42.25} + \dfrac{(y - 2)^2}{22} = 1$ **3.** $(y + 1)^2 = 12(x - 4)$
4. $\dfrac{(y - 3.5)^2}{0.25} - \dfrac{(x - 2)^2}{20} = 1$ **5.** ellipse **6.** circle **7.** parabola
8. hyperbola **9.** $\left(\dfrac{2}{3}, \dfrac{2}{3}\right)$, $(-1, 9)$ **10.** $(2, 2)$, $(2, 4)$
11. $(4, -2)$, $(-4, -2)$ **12.** none **13.** The epicenter of the earthquake is 50 mi due west of the first seismograph.

CHAPTER 10 EXTENSION (p. 640) 1. 1 **3.** $\dfrac{\sqrt{15}}{4} \approx 0.968$
5. $\sqrt{5} \approx 2.236$ **7.** $\dfrac{\sqrt{6}}{2} \approx 1.225$ **9.** $\dfrac{x^2}{25} + \dfrac{(y + 1)^2}{16} = 1$
11. $\dfrac{(x - 2)^2}{60} + \dfrac{y^2}{64} = 1$ **13.** $\dfrac{(y - 1)^2}{\left(\dfrac{64}{9}\right)} - \dfrac{(x - 3)^2}{\left(\dfrac{512}{9}\right)} = 1$
15. $\dfrac{(y - 2)^2}{9} - \dfrac{(x - 3)^2}{23.49} = 1$ **17.** $\dfrac{x^2}{1296} + \dfrac{y^2}{1241} = 1$
(x, y in millions of miles) **19.** In an ellipse, the foci are always within the major axis, so $c < a$ and $\dfrac{c}{a} < 1$. In a hyperbola, the foci are always outside the major axis, so $c > a$ and $\dfrac{c}{a} > 1$.

CHAPTER 10 REVIEW (pp. 642–644)

1. $\sqrt{61} \approx 7.81$; $\left(1, -\frac{1}{2}\right)$ **3.** $4\sqrt{2} \approx 5.66$; $(-2, 2)$

5. focus: $(0, 1)$;
directrix: $y = -1$;

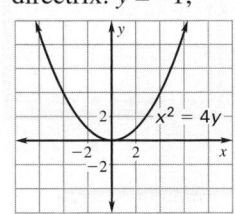

7. focus: $\left(-\frac{3}{2}, 0\right)$;
directrix: $x = \frac{3}{2}$;

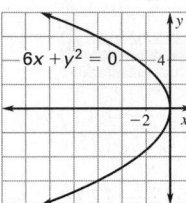

9. $y^2 = 16x$ **11.** $x^2 = 8y$

13.

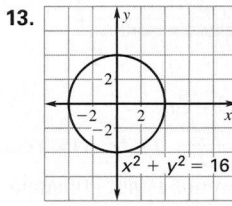

15.

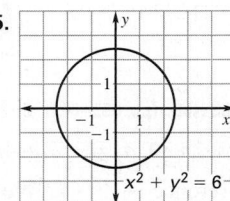

17. $x^2 + y^2 = 25$ **19.** $x^2 + y^2 = 13$

21.

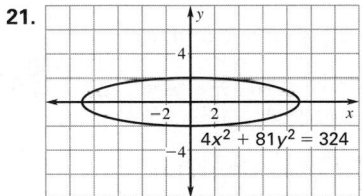

23.

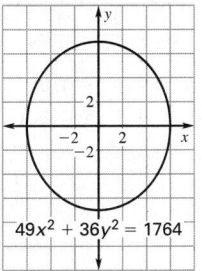

25. $\dfrac{x^2}{16} + \dfrac{y^2}{7} = 1$ **27.**

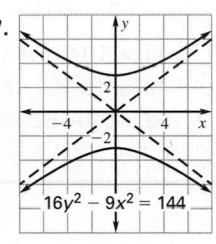

29. $y^2 - \dfrac{x^2}{8} = 1$

31. $\dfrac{x^2}{9} - \dfrac{y^2}{16} = 1$

33. circle; $(x - 5)^2 + (y + 1)^2 = 100$;

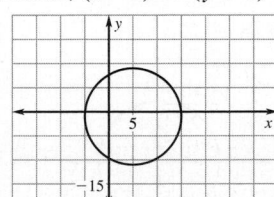

35. hyperbola;
$(y - 9)^2 - \dfrac{(x + 1)^2}{\left(\frac{1}{4}\right)} = 1$;

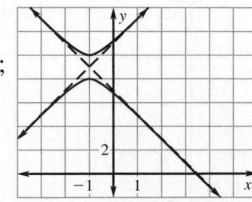

37. $\left(\dfrac{-27 - \sqrt{1649}}{10}, \dfrac{141 + 3\sqrt{1649}}{10}\right)$;

$\left(\dfrac{-27 + \sqrt{1649}}{10}, \dfrac{141 - 3\sqrt{1649}}{10}\right) \approx (-6.761, 26.28)$;
$(1.361, 1.918)$ **39.** $(-1, -3)$ and $(-1, 3)$

CHAPTER 11

SKILL REVIEW (p. 650) **1.** $n + 4$ **2.** $3n$ **3.** $\dfrac{n}{2}$ **4.** 2 **5.** $\dfrac{8}{9}$ **6.** 24

7.

	$f(0)$	$f(1)$	$f(2)$	$f(3)$	$f(4)$	$f(5)$	$f(6)$
function values	3	0	–9	–24	–45	–72	–105
1st order differences	–3	–9	–15	–21	–27	–33	
2nd order differences	–6	–6	–6	–6	–6		

8.

	$f(1)$	$f(2)$	$f(3)$	$f(4)$	$f(5)$	$f(6)$
function values	3	16	45	96	175	288
1st order differences	13	29	51	79	113	
2nd order differences	16	22	28	34		
3rd order differences	6	6	6			

9.

	$f(1)$	$f(2)$	$f(3)$	$f(4)$	$f(5)$	$f(6)$
function values	–3	7	67	237	601	1267
1st order differences	10	60	170	364	666	
2nd order differences	50	110	194	302		
3rd order differences	60	84	108			
4th order differences	24	24				

10. 7 **11.** 6 **12.** $\dfrac{1}{2}$ **13.** $-\dfrac{11}{12}$

11.1 PRACTICE (pp. 655–657) **3.** 2, 4, 6, 8, 10, 12 **5.** 4, 7, 10, 13, 16, 19 **7.** 68 **9.** 2, 3, 4, 5, 6, 7 **11.** 2, 1, 0, –1, –2, –3 **13.** 4, 9, 16, 25, 36, 49 **15.** 4, 7, 12, 19, 28, 39
17. $\dfrac{1}{2}, \dfrac{2}{3}, \dfrac{3}{4}, \dfrac{4}{5}, \dfrac{5}{6}, \dfrac{6}{7}$ **19.** $\dfrac{3}{2}, 1, \dfrac{5}{6}, \dfrac{3}{4}, \dfrac{7}{10}, \dfrac{2}{3}$ **21.** 9; $2n - 1$
23. –16; $a_n = 3n - 1$ if n is odd or $2 - 3n$ if n is even.
25. $-\dfrac{1}{10}$; $-\dfrac{1}{2n}$ **27.** 2; $\dfrac{n}{3}$ **29.** 5.9; $1.1 + 0.8n$

31.

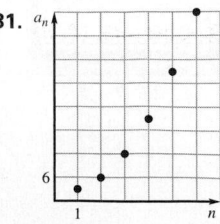

33.

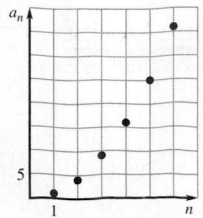

35.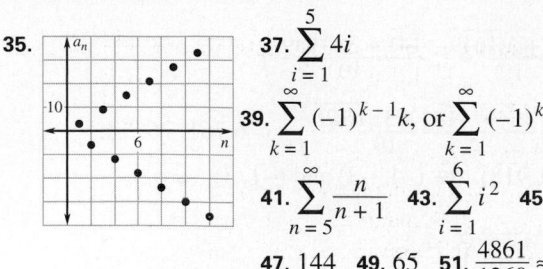

37. $\sum\limits_{i=1}^{5} 4i$

39. $\sum\limits_{k=1}^{\infty} (-1)^{k-1}k$, or $\sum\limits_{k=1}^{\infty} (-1)^{k+1}k$

41. $\sum\limits_{n=5}^{\infty} \dfrac{n}{n+1}$ **43.** $\sum\limits_{i=1}^{6} i^2$ **45.** 180

47. 144 **49.** 65 **51.** $\dfrac{4861}{1260} \approx 3.858$

53. 3.55 **55.** 0 **57.** 15 **59.** 210 **61.** 385 **63.** 14,910
65. 15 ft **67.** $2^n - 1$; 63 **69.** B

71. a. true; $\sum\limits_{i=1}^{n} ka_i = ka_1 + ka_2 + \ldots + ka_n =$

$k(a_1 + a_2 + \ldots + a_n) = k\sum\limits_{i=1}^{n} a_i$

b. true; $\sum\limits_{i=1}^{n} (a_i + b_i) = (a_1 + b_1) + (a_2 + b_2) + \ldots +$
$(a_n + b_n) = (a_1 + a_2 + \ldots + a_n) + (b_1 + b_2 + \ldots + b_n) =$
$\sum\limits_{i=1}^{n} a_i + \sum\limits_{i=1}^{n} b_i$

c. false; $\sum\limits_{i=1}^{4} i(i+1) = 1(2) + 2(3) + 3(4) + 4(5) =$

$2 + 6 + 12 + 20 = 40$, but $\sum\limits_{i=1}^{4} i = 10$ and $\sum\limits_{i=1}^{4} (i+1) = 14$
and $10 \times 14 = 140 \neq 40$.

d. false; $\sum\limits_{i=1}^{5} (i)^2 = 1 + 4 + 9 + 16 + 25 = 55$,

but $\left(\sum\limits_{i=1}^{5} i\right)^2 = 15^2 = 225$.

11.1 MIXED REVIEW (p. 657) **73.** 4 **75.** 2 **77.** $\dfrac{1}{2}$

79. $y = (2.5)2^x$;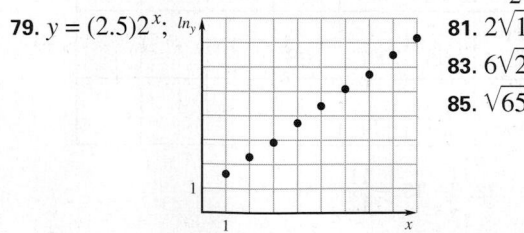

81. $2\sqrt{13} \approx 7.211$
83. $6\sqrt{2} \approx 8.485$
85. $\sqrt{65} \approx 8.062$

TECHNOLOGY ACTIVITY 11.1 (p. 658)
1. 5, 7, 9, 11, 13, 15, 17, 19, 21, 23; 140
3. 48, 46, 44, 42, 40, 38, 36, 34, 32, 30; 390

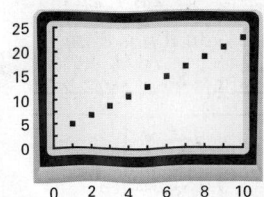
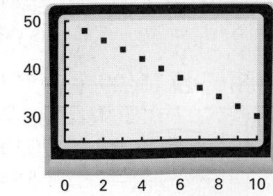

5. $\dfrac{1}{2}, \dfrac{1}{4}, \dfrac{1}{8}, \dfrac{1}{16}, \dfrac{1}{32}, \dfrac{1}{64}, \dfrac{1}{128},$
$\dfrac{1}{256}, \dfrac{1}{512}, \dfrac{1}{1024}; \dfrac{1023}{1024}$

7. $\dfrac{3}{4}$, 3, 12, 48, 192, 768, 3072, 12,288, 49,152, 196,608; 262,143.75

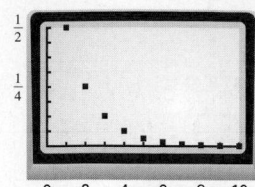
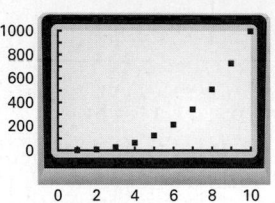

9. $\dfrac{4}{3}, 8\dfrac{1}{3}, 27\dfrac{1}{3}, 64\dfrac{1}{3}, 125\dfrac{1}{3},$
$216\dfrac{1}{3}, 343\dfrac{1}{3}, 512\dfrac{1}{3}, 729\dfrac{1}{3},$
$1000\dfrac{1}{3}; 3028\dfrac{1}{3}$

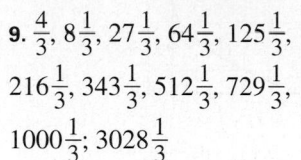

11.2 PRACTICE (pp. 663–664) **5.** $a_n = 24 - 3n$
7. $a_n = -44 + 7n$ **9.** $a_n = -32 + 4n$ **11.** $\dfrac{105}{2}$ **13.** 61 **15.** Yes; constant difference is –3. **17.** No; difference is not constant.
19. No; difference is not constant. **21.** $a_n = -1 + 2n$; 49
23. $a_n = -5 + 14n$; 345 **25.** $a_n = 7 - 3n$; –68
27. $a_n = \dfrac{41}{6} - \dfrac{4}{3}n$; $-\dfrac{53}{2}$ **29.** $a_n = -0.8 + 2.4n$; 59.2
31. $a_n = 92 - 12n$ **33.** $a_n = -13 + 6n$ **35.** $a_n = -\dfrac{332}{9} + \dfrac{40}{9}n$
37. $a_n = -22 + 8n$

39. 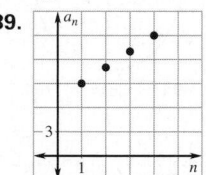 **41.**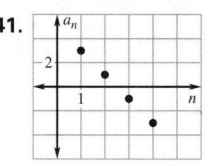

43.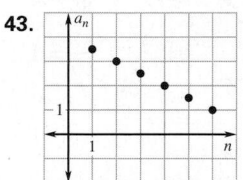

45. a. 1010 **b.** 12 **47. a.** 665 **b.** 15
49. a. 16,082 **b.** 22 **51.** 1110
53. –510 **55.** 4635 **57. a.** $a_n = 6n$
b. 271 **59.** $1 + 4\sum\limits_{i=1}^{4} 2i$; 81 ft^2

11.2 MIXED REVIEW (p. 665) **65.** 81 **67.** no solution **69.** 8
71. $\dfrac{3}{2}$ **73.** 1 **75.** $\log_4 3.4 \approx 0.8828$

77. 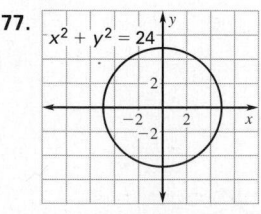 **79.**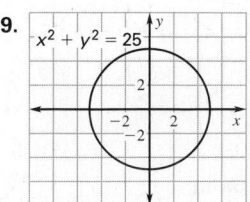

81.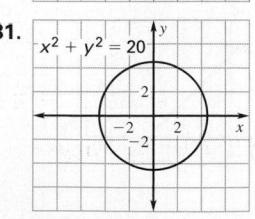

11.3 PRACTICE (pp. 670–672) **5.** 6 **7.** 2 **9.** $\frac{1}{2}$

11. 512; $2(4)^{n-1}$ **13.** 0.6; $375\left(-\frac{1}{5}\right)^{n-1}$ **15.** $\frac{7}{8}$; $\frac{-28}{(-2)^{n-1}}$

17. $6(-2)^{n-1}$ **19.** $\left(\frac{1}{4}\right)\left(2\sqrt{6}\right)^{n-1}$ **21.** $-7(-4)^{n-1}$

23. \$43.11 **25.** neither; no common ratio or difference
27. arithmetic; common difference of -4 **29.** geometric;
common ratio of 3 **31.** neither; no common ratio or
difference **33.** 4 **35.** -2 **37.** $\frac{1}{2}$ **39.** $(-4)^{n-1}$; -1024

41. $2(7)^{n-1}$; 33,614 **43.** $5\left(-\frac{1}{3}\right)^{n-1}$; $-\frac{5}{243}$ **45.** $4(3)^{n-1}$

47. $2(6)^{n-1}$ **49.** $-2(8)^{n-1}$ **51.** $\left(\frac{10}{\sqrt[3]{900}}\right)\left(\sqrt[3]{30}\right)^{n-1}$

53. $6(-5)^{n-1}$ **55.** 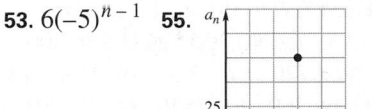 **57.**

59.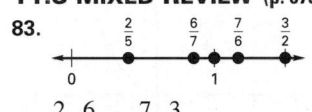
61. a. 435,848,050 **b.** 4
63. a. -67.5 **b.** 4 **65.** 109,225
67. 30.198 **69.** -1365 **71.** 127
73. 10 **75.** \$169.92 million

77. about \$1.524 billion **79.** $\left(\frac{\sqrt{3}}{4}\right)\left(\frac{3}{4}\right)^n$; 0.006

11.3 MIXED REVIEW (p. 673)
83. | $\frac{2}{5}$ | $\frac{6}{7}$ | $\frac{7}{6}$ | $\frac{3}{2}$ |
85. -3.2 $-\frac{5}{2}$ 1.5

$\frac{2}{5}, \frac{6}{7}, 1, \frac{7}{6}, \frac{3}{2}$

$-3.2, -\frac{5}{2}, -2, -1, 1.5$

87. $-1 \leq x \leq 7$ **89.** all real numbers **91.** $-6 \leq x \leq -4$
93. $\frac{3}{5}$ **95.** $-8, -3$ **97.** 10

QUIZ 1 (p. 673) **1.** 8; $2(n-1)$ **2.** 243; 3^n

3. $\frac{1}{80}$; $\left(\frac{1}{5}\right)\left(-\frac{1}{2}\right)^{n-1}$ **4.** 354 **5.** 121 **6.** 220 **7.** $-3+4n$; 45

8. $43-9n$; -65 **9.** $\frac{n}{2}$; 6 **10.** 694.5 **11.** $2(5)^{n-1}$;
12,207,031,250 **12.** $-3(-4)^{n-1}$; $-805,306,368$

13. $12\left(\frac{1}{3}\right)^{n-1}$; 2.509×10^{-6} **14.** 2^{n-1}; 1023

11.4 PRACTICE (pp. 678–679) **5.** $-\frac{8}{5}$ **7.** $\frac{5}{6}$ **9.** $\frac{5}{9}$

11. $\frac{245,000}{999}$ **13.** no; $|r| = \frac{3}{2}, \frac{3}{2} > 1$ **15.** yes; $|r| = \frac{1}{3}$,

$\frac{1}{3} < 1$ **17.** 2 **19.** $\frac{2}{3}$ **21.** $\frac{16}{3}$ **23.** no sum **25.** $-\frac{1}{12}$

27. $\frac{25}{336}$ **29.** $\frac{3}{4}$ **31.** $\frac{3}{4}$ **33.** $\frac{2}{3}$ **35.** $-\frac{1}{2}$ **37.** $-\frac{4}{5}$ **39.** $\frac{7}{9}$ **41.** $\frac{17}{33}$

43. $\frac{16}{99}$ **45.** $\frac{40,000}{333}$ **47.** 180 in. = 15 ft; after 16 swings

49. total distance $= \dfrac{20}{1-\frac{1}{2}} = 40$ ft; total time $= \dfrac{1}{1-\frac{1}{2}} = 2$ sec

51. about M\$24.21

11.4 MIXED REVIEW (p. 680)
57. x-axis; y-axis; domain: $x \neq 0$; range: $y \neq 0$
59. $y = 1$; $x = -7$; domain: $x \neq -7$; range: $y \neq 1$
61. $y = 2.2$; $x = 0.7$; domain: $x \neq 0.7$; range: $y \neq 2.2$

63. 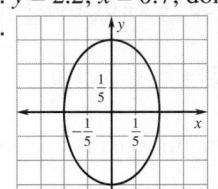 **65.** $-3+4n$ **67.** $13-2n$
69. $4\left(\frac{1}{2}\right)^{n-1}$

11.5 PRACTICE (pp. 684–685) **5.** 2, 8, 32, 128, 512
7. $-1, 3, -9, 27, -81$ **9.** 3; 10; 101; 10,202; 104,080,805
11. $a_1 = 2$; $a_n = (3)a_{n-1}$ **13.** about 3148 **15.** 4, 12, 21, 31,
42 **17.** $-4, -12, -20, -28, -36$ **19.** 5, -4, 8, 1, 15
21. 2, 1, 7, 8, 16 **23.** 48, 26, 15, 9.5, 6.75 **25.** 1, 3, 3, 9, 27
27. $-7+10n$; $a_1 = 3$; $a_n = a_{n-1} + 10$ **29.** $2+3n$; $a_1 = 5$;
$a_n = a_{n-1} + 3$ **31.** $5(2.5)^{n-1}$; $a_1 = 5$; $a_n = (2.5)a_{n-1}$

33. $\left(\frac{1}{2}\right)4^{n-1}$; $a_1 = \frac{1}{2}$; $a_n = (4)a_{n-1}$ **35.** $a_1 = 1$;

$a_n = a_{n-1} + 6$ **37.** $a_1 = 41$; $a_n = a_{n-1} - 9$ **39.** $a_1 = 33$;

$a_n = \dfrac{a_{n-1}}{3}$ **41.** $a_1 = 2$; $a_2 = 5$; $a_n = a_{n-1} \cdot a_{n-2}$

43. $a_1 = 48$; $a_n = \dfrac{a_{n-1}}{10}$ **45.** 1, 2, 4, 8, 16, 32, 64;

geometric **47.** $a_1 = 32$; $a_n = 0.6a_{n-1} + 14$; about 34.77 oz
49. $a_1 = 9000$; $a_n = (0.9)a_{n-1} + 800$; 8729,
51. $a_1 = 20$; $a_n = (0.7)a_{n-1} + 20$ **53.** no

11.5 MIXED REVIEW (p. 686) **59.** 32 **61.** 4096 **63.** 17,576
65. 5832 **67.** $\frac{36}{35x}$ **69.** $\frac{-(4x+14)}{x^2-9}$ **71.** $\frac{x-5}{x^2-4}$

73. $(-1.272, 1.544)$; $(0.472, -1.944)$ **75.** $(-0.980, -1.939)$;
$(0.331, 1.993)$ **77.** $(-4.742, -2.742)$; $(2.742, 4.742)$
79. 7, 6, 5, 4, 3, 2 **81.** 10, 13, 18, 25, 34, 45
83. $\frac{1}{5}, \frac{1}{3}, \frac{3}{7}, \frac{1}{2}, \frac{5}{9}, \frac{3}{5}$

QUIZ 2 (p. 687) **1.** $\frac{9}{2}$ **2.** $\frac{35}{13}$ **3.** $-\frac{7}{8}$ **4.** no sum **5.** $\frac{4}{5}$ **6.** $\frac{11}{12}$

7. $\frac{7}{8}$ **8.** $\frac{8}{9}$ **9.** $\frac{5}{33}$ **10.** $\frac{14,000}{111}$ **11.** 5, 8, 11, 14, 17 **12.** 1, 4,
16, 64, 256 **13.** 17, 19, 22, 26, 31 **14.** 1, 2, 1, -1, -2
15. 2, 4, 8, 32, 256 **16.** 10, 10, 20, 30, 50 **17.** $18\frac{2}{3}$ ft

TECHNOLOGY ACTIVITY 11.5 (p. 688) **1.** 5100, 4465,
3893.5, 3379.15, 2916.24, 2499.61, 2124.65, 1787.19,
1483.47, 1210.12, 964.11, 742.70
3. 3500, 2925, 2436.25, 2020.81, 1667.69, 1367.54,
1112.41, 895.55, 711.21, 554.53, 421.35, 308.15
5. 103 months or 8 years, 7 months

CHAPTER 11 EXTENSION (p. 689–690)

1. $\dfrac{1(1+1)(2 \cdot 1 + 1)}{6} = \dfrac{6}{6} = 1 = 1^2$, so the formula is true for

$n = 1$. Suppose $1^2 + 2^2 + \ldots k^2 = \dfrac{k(k+1)(2k+1)}{6}$. Then

$1^2 + 2^2 + \ldots k^2 + (k+1)^2 = \dfrac{k(k+1)(2k+1)}{6} + (k+1)^2 =$

$\dfrac{k(k+1)(2k+1) + 6(k+1)^2}{6} = \dfrac{(k+1)(2k^2 + k + 6k + 6)}{6} =$

$\dfrac{(k+1)(2k^2 + 7k + 6)}{6} = \dfrac{(k+1)(k+2)(2k+3)}{6} =$

$\dfrac{(k+1)[(k+1)+1][2(k+1)+1]}{6}$, and the formula is true for

$n = k + 1$. Therefore, the formula is true for all positive integers.

3. $\dfrac{a_1(1-r^1)}{1-r} = a_1 \cdot r^{1-1}$, so the statement is true for $n = 1$.

Assume it is true for $n = k$. Then $\displaystyle\sum_{i=1}^{k} a_1 r^{i-1} = \dfrac{a_1(1-r^k)}{1-r}$,

so $\displaystyle\sum_{i=1}^{k+1} a_1 r^{i-1} = \dfrac{a_1(1-r^k)}{1-r} + a_1 r^{k+1-1} =$

$\dfrac{a_1(1-r^k) + a_1(r^k)(1-r)}{1-r} = \dfrac{a_1[(1-r^k) + r^k(1-r)]}{1-r} =$

$\dfrac{a_1(1-r^{k+1})}{1-r}$, and the formula is true for $n = k + 1$.

Therefore, the formula is true for all positive integers.

5. $\dfrac{5^{1+1}-5}{4} = \dfrac{25-5}{4} = \dfrac{20}{4} = 5 = 5^1$, so the formula is

true for $n = 1$. Suppose the formula is true for $n = k$.

Then $\displaystyle\sum_{i=1}^{k} 5^i = \dfrac{5^{k+1}-5}{4}$. So $\displaystyle\sum_{i=1}^{k+1} 5^i = \dfrac{5^{k+1}-5}{4} + 5^{k+1} =$

$\dfrac{[(5^{k+1}-5) + 4(5^{k+1})]}{4} = \dfrac{5(5^{k+1})-5}{4} = \dfrac{5^{(k+1)+1}-5}{4}$, and

the formula is true for $n = k + 1$. Therefore, the formula is
true for all positive integers.

7. A recursive formula for the nth pentagonal number is

$P_n = P_{n-1} + 3n - 2$. $\dfrac{1(3 \cdot 1 - 1)}{2} = 1 = P_1$, so the formula is

true for $n = 1$. Suppose the formula is true for $n = k$. Then

$P_k = \dfrac{k(3k-1)}{2}$, so $P_{k+1} = \dfrac{k(3k-1)}{2} + 3(k+1) - 2 =$

$\dfrac{3k^2 - k + 6k + 6 - 4}{2} = \dfrac{3k^2 + 5k + 2}{2} = \dfrac{(k+1)(3k+2)}{2} =$

$\dfrac{(k+1)[3(k+1)-1]}{2}$, and the formula is true for $n = k + 1$.

Therefore, the formula is true for all positive integers.

CHAPTER 11 REVIEW (pp. 692–694)

1. 6, 9, 14, 21, 30, 41

3. 4, 2, 0, −2, −4, −6 **5.** 10; $2n$ **7.** $\dfrac{1}{243}$; $\left(\dfrac{1}{3}\right)^n$ **9.** $\displaystyle\sum_{i=1}^{\infty} i$

11. 5525 **13.** 78 **15.** $-5 + 6n$ **17.** $4 - \dfrac{1}{2}n$ **19.** $21 - 2n$

21. 1204 **23.** 599.4 **25.** $64\left(\dfrac{1}{2}\right)^{n-1}$ **27.** $200\left(\dfrac{1}{10}\right)^{n-1}$

29. $-64\left(-\dfrac{1}{4}\right)^{n-1}$ **31.** 496 **33.** 19.844 **35.** $\dfrac{135}{7}$ **37.** 25

39. $\dfrac{1}{3}$ **41.** $\dfrac{4}{5}$ **43.** $\dfrac{7}{10}$ **45.** $\dfrac{3}{4}$ **47.** $\dfrac{2}{9}$ **49.** $\dfrac{1300}{33}$ **51.** 10; 40;
160; 640; 2560; 10,240 **53.** 2, 0, −3, −7, −12, −18

55. $a_1 = 7$; $a_n = 2 \cdot a_{n-1}$ **57.** $a_1 = 1$; $a_n = a_{n-1} + 5$

59. $a_1 = 1$; $a_n = (a_{n-1})^2 + 1$

CHAPTER 12

SKILL REVIEW (p. 700) 1. 0.5, 50% **2.** 0.2, 20% **3.** 0.15,
15% **4.** 0.48, 48% **5.** 0.194, 19.4% **6.** 0.469, 46.9%
7. 50.27 **8.** 25 **9.** 48 **10.** −0.301 **11.** 0.415 **12.** −0.131

12.1 PRACTICE (pp. 705–707) 5. 2 **7.** 1 **9.** 120 **11.** 6
13. 210 **15.** 3 **17.** 40 **19. a.** 17,576,000 **b.** 11,232,000
21. a. 6,760,000 **b.** 3,276,000 **23.** 40,320 **25.** 3,628,800
27. 1 **29.** 6 **31.** 6 **33.** 2 **35.** 6720 **37.** 1320 **39.** 2 **41.** 24
43. 720 **45.** 40,320 **47.** 3 **49.** 360 **51.** 2520 **53.** 10,080
55. 480 **57. a.** 2,176,782,336 **b.** 1,402,410,240
59. 6.20×10^{23} **61. a.** 720 **b.** 60,480 **63.** 12,612,600

12.1 MIXED REVIEW (p. 707) 69. $x^4 + 4x^2 + 4$

71. $16x^2 - 25$ **73.** $64y^2 - 16xy + x^2$

75.

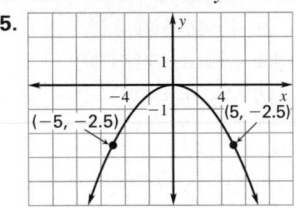

77. 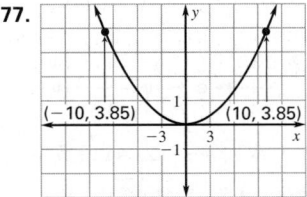 **79.**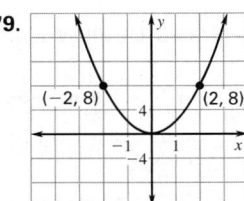

81. $-\dfrac{16}{3}$ **83.** no sum **85.** 0.714

12.2 PRACTICE (pp. 712–714) 5. 28 **7.** 5
9. $x^3 + 3x^2y + 3xy^2 + y^3$ **11.** $8x^3 + 48x^2 + 96x + 64$
13. $x^5 - 5x^4y + 10x^3y^2 - 10x^2y^3 + 5xy^4 - y^5$
15. $81x^4 - 108x^3 + 54x^2 - 12x + 1$ **17.** 270; 243
19. 56 **21.** 28 **23.** 1 **25.** 165 **27.** 48 **29.** 24

31.

```
                1
              1   1
            1   2   1
          1   3   3   1
        1   4   6   4   1
      1   5  10  10   5   1
    1   6  15  20  15   6   1
  1   7  21  35  35  21   7   1
```

33. $x^6 - 18x^5y + 135x^4y^2 - 540x^3y^3 + 1215x^2y^4 - 1458xy^5 + 729y^6$

35. $128x^7 - 448x^6y^3 + 672x^5y^6 - 560x^4y^9 + 280x^3y^{12} - 84x^2y^{15} + 14xy^{18} - y^{21}$ **37.** $x^5 + 20x^4 + 160x^3 + 640x^2 + 1280x + 1024$ **39.** $64x^6 - 192x^5y + 240x^4y^2 - 160x^3y^3 + 60x^2y^4 - 12xy^5 + y^6$ **41.** $81x^8 - 324x^6 + 486x^4 - 324x^2 + 81$ **43.** $x^9 + 3x^6y^2 + 3x^3y^4 + y^6$ **45.** 1120
47. 120 **49.** 315 **51.** 968 **53.** 968

61.

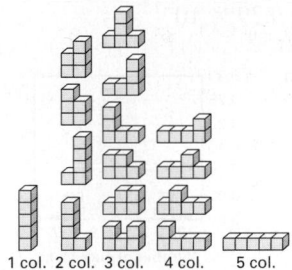

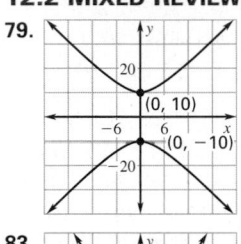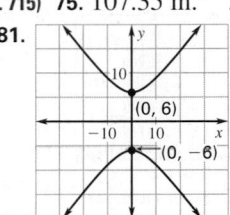

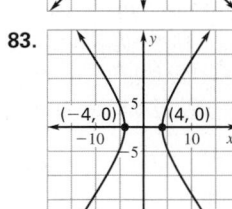

1 col. 2 col. 3 col. 4 col. 5 col.

63. 512 **65.** 2,097,151

1.

number	1	2	3	4	5	6
freq	19	24	20	16	20	21
theor prob	0.167	0.167	0.167	0.167	0.167	0.167
exp prob	0.158	0.200	0.167	0.133	0.167	0.175

The experimental and theoretical probabilities are close but not the same.

3.

trials	10	20	50	100	200
heads	4	13	32	52	100
tails	6	7	18	48	100

As the number of trials increases, the experimental results get closer to the theoretical results.

12.2 MIXED REVIEW (p. 715) **75.** 107.35 in.^{2} **77.** 310.5 m^2

79.

81.

83.

85. arithmetic; $-4 + 7n$
87. geometric; $(-2)^{n-1}$
89. arithmetic; $-15 + 5n$

QUIZ 1 (p. 715) **1.** 3 **2.** 24 **3.** 120 **4.** 180 **5.** 5040
6. 40,320 **7.** 60,480 **8.** 907,200 **9.** $x^6 + 6x^5y + 15x^4y^2 + 20x^3y^3 + 15x^2y^4 + 6xy^5 + y^6$ **10.** $x^4 + 8x^3 + 24x^2 + 32x + 16$ **11.** $x^5 - 10x^4y + 40x^3y^2 - 80x^2y^3 + 80xy^4 - 32y^5$ **12.** $27x^3 - 108x^2y + 144xy^2 - 64y^3$
13. $x^8 + 12x^6y + 54x^4y^2 + 108x^2y^3 + 81y^4$ **14.** $4096x^{12} - 12,288x^{10} + 15,360x^8 - 10,240x^6 + 3840x^4 - 768x^2 + 64$
15. $x^9 - 3x^6y^3 + 3x^3y^6 - y^9$ **16.** $32x^{20} + 400x^{16}y^2 + 2000x^{12}y^4 + 5000x^8y^6 + 6250x^4y^8 + 3125y^{10}$ **17.** 90
18. 15 **19.** 3456 **20.** 1320

12.3 PRACTICE (pp. 719–722) **5.** $\frac{1}{6}$ **7.** $\frac{5}{6}$ **9.** 0.637
11. a. 0.353 **b.** 0.334 **13.** 0.3 **15.** 0.4 **17.** 0.6
19. 0.0769 **21.** 0.5 **23.** 0.231

	theor prob	exp prob	
25.	0.333	0.308	The two probabilities are
27.	0.5	0.508	not exactly the same, but they are very similar in
29.	0.833	0.875	every case.

31. 0.455 **33.** 0.545 **35.** 0.0385 **37.** 0.262 **39.** 5.6×10^{-8}
41. a. 0.555 **b.** 0.0380 **43. a.** 0.0527 **b.** 0.868 **45.** 0.0625
47. 0.00242

12.3 MIXED REVIEW (p. 722) **51.** -17 **53.** 19 **55.** -53
57. $\frac{4y^4}{3x^3}$ **59.** $\frac{x+3}{x}$ **61.** 3, 10, 17, 24, 31 **63.** 2; 8; 512; 134,217,728; 2.418×10^{24} **65.** $-2, 0, 2, 2, 0$ **67.** 1,042,380

12.4 PRACTICE (pp. 727–729) **5.** 1 **7.** $\frac{7}{12}$ **9.** $\frac{4}{5}$ **11.** $\frac{3}{16}$
13. 0.25 **15.** $\frac{3}{7}$ **17.** 0.7; no **19.** $\frac{7}{17}$; no **21.** $\frac{5}{6}$; no
23. 30%; no **25.** 0.66 **27.** $\frac{1}{4}$ **29.** $\frac{1}{52}$ **31.** $\frac{1}{2}$ **33.** 0 **35.** $\frac{17}{18}$, or about 0.944 **37.** $\frac{7}{9}$, or about 0.778 **39.** $\frac{35}{36}$, or about 0.972
41. *Sample answers:* not 3: 0.933; ≥ 5: 0.825; not 3 or 7: 0.783; ≤ 10: 0.942; > 2: 0.983; < 8 or > 11: 0.600; The experimental results are very similar to the theoretical results. **43.** 0.75 **45.** 0.691 **47.** 0.1 **49.** 0.375

12.4 MIXED REVIEW (p. 729) **57.** 1 **59.** 1.892 **61.** 61.73
63. $x^2 + y^2 = 25$ **65.** $x^2 + y^2 = 68$ **67.** $x^2 + y^2 = 109$
69. $x^2 + y^2 = 256$ **71. a.** 456,976,000 **b.** 258,336,000

12.5 PRACTICE (pp. 734–736) **5.** 0.2 **7.** 0.08 **9.** 0.6
11. 0.123 **13.** 0.047 **15.** 0.078 **17.** 0.012 **19. a.** 0.0059
b. 0.0060 **21. a.** 0.0178 **b.** 0.0181 **23. a.** 0.0156
b. 0.0153 **25.** 0.00144 **27.** 0.467 **29.** at least 52,722 tickets
31. 0.937 **33.** 0.581 **35.** 0.751

12.5 MIXED REVIEW (p. 736)

41.

0.01–0.25	0
0.26–0.50	5
0.51–0.75	4
0.76–1.00	5

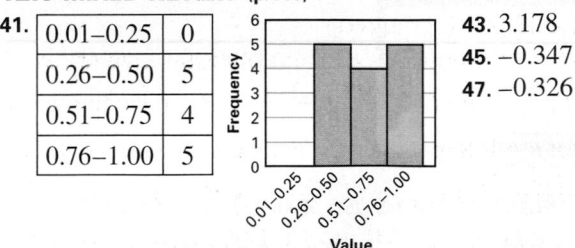

43. 3.178
45. -0.347
47. -0.326

49. $128x^7 - 448x^6 + 672x^5 - 560x^4 + 280x^3 - 84x^2 + 14x - 1$ **51.** $x^6 - 6x^5 + 15x^4 - 20x^3 + 15x^2 - 6x + 1$

QUIZ 2 (p. 737) **1.** $\frac{12}{25}$, or 0.48 **2.** $\frac{6}{25}$, or 0.24
3. $\frac{18}{25}$, or 0.72 **4.** 0.111 **5.** 0.682 **6.** 0.207 **7.** 0.8 **8.** 0
9. 0.75 **10.** 0.0384

SELECTED ANSWERS

12.6 PRACTICE (pp. 742–744) **5.** 0.063

7. 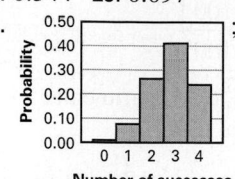 ; 2 **9.** No; the probability of 4 or fewer students buying rings is much greater than 0.1 if the claim is true. Therefore, you should not reject the claim.

11. 0.00109 **13.** 0.160 **15.** 0.160 **17.** 0.00109 **19.** 0.00863 **21.** 0.0909 **23.** 0.00000154 **25.** 8.67×10^{-19} **27.** 0.344 **29.** 0.097

31. 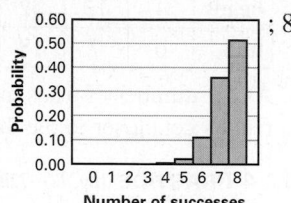 ; 3 **33.** ; 8

35. 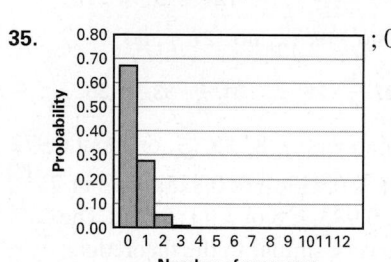 ; 0 **37.** 0.00114 **39.** 0.363 **41.** 0.816 **43.** 0 **45.** 6

47. Reject the claim because the probability that 3 or fewer students would have attended college anyway is 0.00351, which is much smaller than 0.01.

12.6 MIXED REVIEW (p. 744) **53.** 11, 4.155 **55.** 19, 6.708 **57.** $(-7, -5), (5, 7)$ **59.** $\left(\pm\frac{1}{2}, \pm\frac{\sqrt{35}}{2}\right)$ **61.** none **63.** $a_1 = 4, a_n = a_{n-1} \times 10$ **65.** $a_1 = 1, a_2 = 3, a_n = a_{n-1} \times a_{n-2}$ **67.** $a_1 = 1, a_2 = 2, a_n = a_{n-1} + a_{n-2}$

TECHNOLOGY ACTIVITY 12.6 (p. 745)

1.

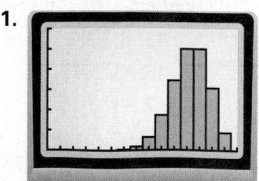

12.7 PRACTICE (pp. 749–751) **5.** 0.997 **7.** 0.5 **9.** 0.16 **11.** 5.1, 1.89 **13.** 5, 1.94 **15.** 5.1, 2.06 **17.** 0.16 **19.** 50% **21.** 2.5% **23.** 0.68 **25.** 0.9735 **27.** 0.84 **29.** 0.004096 **31.** 0.664 **33.** 5, 2.12 **35.** 5.88, 2.27 **37.** 8.4, 2.810 **39.** 0.95 **41.** 50% **43.** 0.839 **45.** 0.145 **47.** 0.000625 **49.** 0.462 **51.** 0.16 **53.** 0.84 **55.** 0.999

12.7 MIXED REVIEW (p. 752) **59.** 64 **61.** 5 **63.** 25 **65.** $(0, \pm13); (\pm12, 0); (0, \pm5)$ **67.** $\left(0, \pm\sqrt{21}\right); \left(\pm\sqrt{6}, 0\right);$ $\left(0, \pm\sqrt{15}\right)$ **69.** $\frac{x^2}{7} + \frac{y^2}{10} = 1; \left(0, \pm\sqrt{10}\right); \left(\pm\sqrt{7}, 0\right); (0, \pm\sqrt{3})$ **71.** $\frac{11}{12}$ **73.** $\frac{11}{12}$

QUIZ 3 (p. 752) **1.** 0.000110 **2.** 0.00110 **3.** 0.151

4. 0.0014 **5.** 4.66×10^{-8} **6.** 9.29×10^{-15} **7.** 2.59×10^{-25} **8.** 1.24×10^{-39}

9. 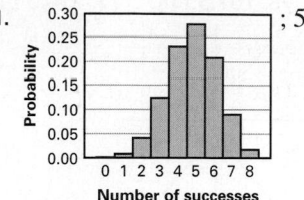 ; 1 **10.** 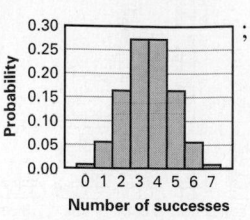 ;

3 and 4 are equally likely.

11. 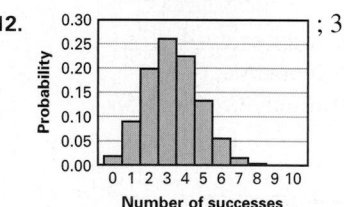 ; 5

12. 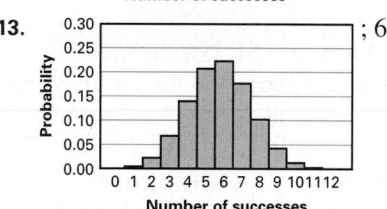 ; 3

13. 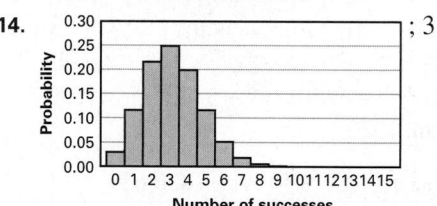 ; 6

14. ; 3

15. 0.68 **16.** 0.4985 **17.** 0.9735 **18.** 0.50 **19.** 0.16 **20.** 0.0015 **21.** Yes; there is a 0.083 chance of getting 19 or fewer out of 26 and 0.083 < 0.1, so reject the survey's findings. **22.** 0.50

CHAPTER 12 EXTENSION (p. 754) **1.** Player A expected value: $0 \cdot \frac{1}{3} + 1 \cdot \frac{1}{3} - 1 \cdot \frac{1}{3} = 0$; Player B expected value: $0 \cdot \frac{1}{3} - 1 \cdot \frac{1}{3} + 1 \cdot \frac{1}{3} = 0$; Yes, the game is fair. **3.** –$.44

CHAPTER 12 REVIEW (pp. 756–758) **1.** 100,000 **3.** 720 **5.** 5 **7.** 151,200 **9.** 36 **11.** 10 **13.** 1 **15.** $x^3 + 12x^2 + 48x + 64$ **17.** $x^7 - 21x^6y + 189x^5y^2 - 945x^4y^3 + 2835x^3y^4 - 5103x^2y^5 + 5103xy^6 - 2187y^7$ **19.** $\frac{3}{8}$ **21.** experimental probability = 0.45; theoretical probability = 0.50; you got slightly fewer heads than expected. **23.** 0.3 **25.** 1% **27. a.** 0.056 **b.** 0.0606 **29.** 0.117 **31.** 0.00977 **33.** 0.00977 **35.** 0.68 **37.** 0.025

CUMULATIVE PRACTICE (pp. 762–763) **1.** –7 **3.** 14, –8

5. $-2, -5$ **7.** $4i, -4i$ **9.** $\dfrac{1}{8} \pm \dfrac{\sqrt{15}}{8}i$ **11.** $-1, 2, -2$ **13.** 3.25

15. 25 **17.**

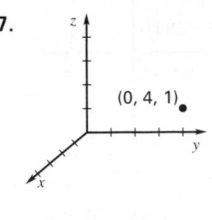

(0, 4, 1)

19.

(0, 2, 0)
(2, 0, 0)
(0, 0, −8)

21. 18 **23.** 5 **25.** $xy = -40; y = -20$ **27.** $xy = -16;$ $y = -8$ **29.** $z = -\dfrac{2}{3}xy; z = \dfrac{10}{3}$ **31.** $z = 3xy; z = -15$

33. $\sqrt{89} \approx 9.43; (2.5, 4)$ **35.** $\sqrt{65} \approx 8.06; (1.5, -1)$

37.

(0, 4)
(−4, 0) (4, 0)
(0, −4)

39.

(17, 0)
(1, −4)

41. $(x - 2)^2 + (y + 2)^2 = 9$ **43.** $\dfrac{y^2}{4} - \dfrac{x^2}{5} = 1$ **45.** $(-18, 0)$

47. $\left(\pm\dfrac{\sqrt{6}}{2}, -\dfrac{1}{2}\right), (\pm\sqrt{3}, 1)$ **49.** geometric; Each term is 3 times the previous term. **51.** geometric; Each term is $\dfrac{1}{10}$ the previous term. **53.** $9, 6, 1, -6, -15$ **55.** $1, 5, 14, 30, 55$

57. $a_n = 7 - 6n; a_1 = 1; a_n = a_{n-1} - 6$ **59.** $a_n = 243\left(\dfrac{1}{3}\right)^{n-1};$ $a_1 = 243; a_n = \dfrac{1}{3}a_{n-1}$ **61.** 50 **63.** 16 **65.** 720 **67.** 70

69. 21 **71.** $8x^3 + 60x^2 + 150x + 125$ **73.** $81x^4 - 108x^3 + 54x^2 - 12x + 1$ **75.** $x^6 - 12x^4 + 48x^2 - 64$ **77.** 0.2

79. $\dfrac{1}{32}$ **81.** $\dfrac{5}{16}$ **83.** $\dfrac{5}{32}$

85.
$$C(x) = \begin{cases} 11.75, & \text{if } 0 < x \le 0.5 \\ 14.00, & \text{if } 0.5 < x \le 1 \\ 15.75, & \text{if } 1 < x \le 2 \\ 18.50, & \text{if } 2 < x \le 3 \\ 21.25, & \text{if } 3 < x \le 4 \\ 24.00, & \text{if } 4 < x \le 5 \\ 26.25, & \text{if } 5 < x \le 6 \\ 28.00, & \text{if } 6 < x \le 7 \\ 30.25, & \text{if } 7 < x \le 8 \\ 31.00, & \text{if } 8 < x \le 9 \\ 32.75, & \text{if } 9 < x \le 10 \end{cases}$$

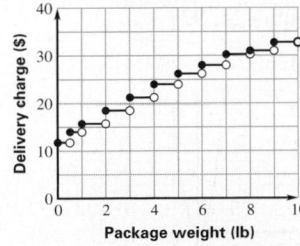

87. $a_n = 0.8a_{n-1} + 1000;$ It approaches a limit of 5000 fish. **89.** $\dfrac{2}{5}$

CHAPTER 13

SKILL REVIEW (p. 768) 1. 12 **2.** 5 **3.** $3\sqrt{2}$ **4.** $4\sqrt{6}$

5. $3\sqrt{2}$ **6.** $10\sqrt{2}$ **7.** $\sqrt{2}$ **8.** $\dfrac{2\sqrt{3}}{3}$ **9.** $\dfrac{\sqrt{3}}{2}$ **10.** -1 **11.** $-\dfrac{5}{2}, \dfrac{5}{2}$

12. 14 **13.** -10

13.1 PRACTICE (pp. 772–774) 5. $\sin\theta = \dfrac{3}{5}; \cos\theta = \dfrac{4}{5};$ $\tan\theta = \dfrac{3}{4}; \csc\theta = \dfrac{5}{3}; \sec\theta = \dfrac{5}{4}; \cot\theta = \dfrac{4}{3}$ **7.** $\sin\theta = \dfrac{\sqrt{5}}{3};$ $\cos\theta = \dfrac{2}{3}; \tan\theta = \dfrac{\sqrt{5}}{2}; \csc\theta = \dfrac{3\sqrt{5}}{5}; \sec\theta = \dfrac{3}{2}; \cot\theta = \dfrac{2\sqrt{5}}{5}$

9. $B = 15°; a \approx 19.3; b \approx 5.18$ **11.** $B = 28°; a \approx 56.4; c \approx 63.9$

13. $A = 75°; a \approx 157; c \approx 162$ **15.** $\sin\theta = \dfrac{\sqrt{5}}{5}; \cos\theta = \dfrac{2\sqrt{5}}{5};$ $\tan\theta = \dfrac{1}{2}; \csc\theta = \sqrt{5}; \sec\theta = \dfrac{\sqrt{5}}{2}; \cot\theta = 2$

17. $\sin\theta = \dfrac{2\sqrt{14}}{9}; \cos\theta = \dfrac{5}{9}; \tan\theta = \dfrac{2\sqrt{14}}{5}; \csc\theta = \dfrac{9\sqrt{14}}{28};$ $\sec\theta = \dfrac{9}{5}; \cot\theta = \dfrac{5\sqrt{14}}{28}$ **19.** $\sin\theta = \dfrac{9}{25}; \cos\theta = \dfrac{4\sqrt{34}}{25};$ $\tan\theta = \dfrac{9\sqrt{34}}{136}; \csc\theta = \dfrac{25}{9}; \sec\theta = \dfrac{25\sqrt{34}}{136}; \cot\theta = \dfrac{4\sqrt{34}}{9}$

21. 12 cm, 5 cm, 13 cm; $\sin\theta = \dfrac{5}{13}; \cos\theta = \dfrac{12}{13}; \tan\theta = \dfrac{5}{12};$ $\csc\theta = \dfrac{13}{5}; \sec\theta = \dfrac{13}{12}; \cot\theta = \dfrac{12}{5}$

23. $\dfrac{\sqrt{22}}{2}; \dfrac{\sqrt{22}}{2}$ **25.** 0.2419 **27.** 1.6643 **29.** 1.0154

31. 9.5668 **33.** $A = 66°; b \approx 3.56; c \approx 8.76$ **35.** $B = 71°;$ $a \approx 1.38; c \approx 4.23$ **37.** $B = 61°; a \approx 11.6; c \approx 24.0$

39. $A = 25°; a \approx 5.07; b \approx 10.9$ **41.** $96\sqrt{3}$ units^2, or about 166 units^2 **43.** about 400 ft **45.** about 4250 ft

47. about 425 m; about 432 m **49.** about 12,350 ft

13.1 MIXED REVIEW (p. 775) 55. 157.5 mi **57.** $\$3666$

59. parabola **61.** circle **63.** $\dfrac{16,016}{50,625}$, or about 0.316

13.2 PRACTICE (pp. 780–782) 5–11. Sample angles are given.

5.

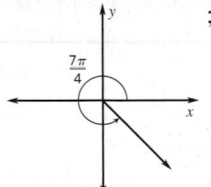

60°; **7.**

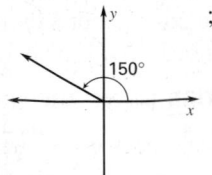

$\dfrac{7\pi}{4}$;

$420°, -300°$ $\dfrac{15\pi}{4}, -\dfrac{\pi}{4}$

9. $-\dfrac{3\pi}{2}$; **11.** 150°;

$\dfrac{\pi}{2}, -\dfrac{7\pi}{2}$ $510°, -210°$

13. $\dfrac{\pi}{6}$ **15.** $\dfrac{13\pi}{9}$ **17.** $315°$ **19.** $15°$ **21.** $\dfrac{11\pi}{9}$ in.; $\dfrac{22\pi}{9}$ in.^{2}

23. $\frac{17\pi}{18}$ cm; $\frac{17\pi}{18}$ cm^2 **25.** C **27.** A

29.
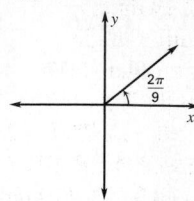
35.

9.
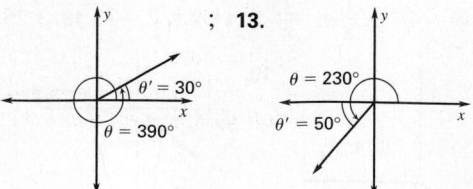
; 13.

30°   50°

37–43. Sample angles are given. **37.** 570°; −150°
39. 60°; −300° **41.** $\frac{\pi}{4}$; $-\frac{7\pi}{4}$ **43.** $\frac{4\pi}{3}$; $-\frac{2\pi}{3}$ **45.** $\frac{5\pi}{4}$ **47.** $\frac{\pi}{4}$
49. $\frac{65\pi}{36}$ **51.** $-\frac{29\pi}{18}$ **53.** −810° **55.** −75° **57.** −675°
59. 288° **61.** $\frac{\pi}{6}$ ft; $\frac{\pi}{4}$ ft^2 **63.** 6π in.; 36π in.^{2} **65.** $\frac{175\pi}{12}$ mm;
$\frac{875\pi}{8}$ mm^2 **67.** $\frac{40\pi}{9}$ cm; $\frac{320\pi}{9}$ cm^2 **69.** $\frac{1}{2}$ **71.** $\sqrt{3}$
73. 1.3764 **75.** 0.6428 **77.** 540°; 3π **79.** 1260°; 7π
81. about 1820° or $\frac{91\pi}{9}$ radians **83.** about 528 in.^{2}
85. 2π **87.** $\frac{5}{3}$ in.

13.2 MIXED REVIEW (p. 783) **93.** $5\sqrt{11}$ **95.** 16 **97.** $\frac{\sqrt{7}}{4}$
99. $\frac{2\sqrt{14}}{7}$ **101.** $\frac{4}{3}$ **103.** $\frac{144}{35}$ **105.** $\frac{100}{37}$ **107.** $y^2 = 20x$
109. $y^2 = 24x$ **111.** $x^2 = -17.6y$

QUIZ 1 (p. 783) **1.** $\sin \theta = \frac{8}{17}$; $\cos \theta = \frac{15}{17}$; $\tan \theta = \frac{8}{15}$;
$\csc \theta = \frac{17}{8}$; $\sec \theta = \frac{17}{15}$; $\cot \theta = \frac{15}{8}$ **2.** $\sin \theta = \frac{3\sqrt{58}}{58}$;
$\cos \theta = \frac{7\sqrt{58}}{58}$; $\tan \theta = \frac{3}{7}$; $\csc \theta = \frac{\sqrt{58}}{3}$; $\sec \theta = \frac{\sqrt{58}}{7}$;
$\cot \theta = \frac{7}{3}$ **3.** $\sin \theta = \frac{6\sqrt{61}}{61}$; $\cos \theta = \frac{5\sqrt{61}}{61}$; $\tan \theta = \frac{6}{5}$;
$\csc \theta = \frac{\sqrt{61}}{6}$; $\sec \theta = \frac{\sqrt{61}}{5}$; $\cot \theta = \frac{5}{6}$ **4.** $A = 40°$; $b \approx 21.5$
$c \approx 28.0$ **5.** $B = 57°$; $a \approx 6.54$; $b \approx 10.1$ **6.** $B = 80°$;
$b \approx 17.0$; $c \approx 17.3$ **7.** $A = 19°$; $a \approx 0.749$; $b \approx 2.17$
8–11. Sample answers are given. **8.** 385°; −335°
9. $\frac{4\pi}{3}$; $-\frac{8\pi}{3}$ **10.** $\frac{\pi}{4}$; $-\frac{7\pi}{4}$ **11.** 280°; −80° **12.** 2π m; 6π m^2
13. $\frac{5\pi}{3}$ ft; $\frac{5\pi}{3}$ ft^2 **14.** $\frac{8\pi}{9}$ cm; $\frac{32\pi}{9}$ cm^2 **15.** $\frac{242\pi}{9}$ in.;
$\frac{2662\pi}{9}$ in.^{2} **16.** $\frac{25\pi}{12}$ ft; $\frac{125\pi}{24}$ ft^2 **17.** $\frac{32\pi}{3}$ mm; 64π mm^2
18. The 6 in. slice has an area of 18.85 in.^{2} and costs about
$.80/in.^{2}, while the 7 in. slice has an area of about
19.24 in.^{2} and costs about $.09/in.^{2}. The 6 in. slice has
a lower unit price, so it is a better deal.

13.3 PRACTICE (pp. 788–790)
5. $\sin \theta = -\frac{5\sqrt{41}}{41}$; $\cos \theta = -\frac{4\sqrt{41}}{41}$; $\tan \theta = \frac{5}{4}$;
$\csc \theta = -\frac{\sqrt{41}}{5}$; $\sec \theta = -\frac{\sqrt{41}}{4}$; $\cot \theta = \frac{4}{5}$

15. $\sqrt{3}$ **17.** $\sqrt{2}$ **19.** $-\frac{1}{2}$ **21.** $-\frac{\sqrt{3}}{3}$ **23.** $\sin \theta = \frac{5}{13}$;
$\cos \theta = -\frac{12}{13}$; $\tan \theta = -\frac{5}{12}$; $\csc \theta = \frac{13}{5}$; $\sec \theta = -\frac{13}{12}$;
$\cot \theta = -\frac{12}{5}$ **25.** $\sin \theta = \frac{14\sqrt{277}}{277}$; $\cos \theta = \frac{-9\sqrt{277}}{277}$;
$\tan \theta = -\frac{14}{9}$; $\csc \theta = \frac{\sqrt{277}}{14}$; $\sec \theta = -\frac{\sqrt{277}}{9}$; $\cot \theta = -\frac{9}{14}$
27. $\sin \theta = \frac{\sqrt{2}}{2}$; $\cos \theta = -\frac{\sqrt{2}}{2}$; $\tan \theta = -1$; $\csc \theta = \sqrt{2}$;
$\sec \theta = -\sqrt{2}$; $\cot \theta = -1$ **29.** $\sin \theta = -\frac{3\sqrt{13}}{13}$;
$\cos \theta = \frac{2\sqrt{13}}{13}$; $\tan \theta = -\frac{3}{2}$; $\csc \theta = -\frac{\sqrt{13}}{3}$; $\sec \theta = \frac{\sqrt{13}}{2}$;
$\cot \theta = -\frac{2}{3}$ **31.** $\sin \theta = -\frac{\sqrt{3}}{2}$; $\cos \theta = \frac{1}{2}$; $\tan \theta = -\sqrt{3}$;
$\csc \theta = -\frac{2\sqrt{3}}{3}$; $\sec \theta = 2$; $\cot \theta = -\frac{\sqrt{3}}{3}$ **33.** $\sin \theta = \frac{\sqrt{7}}{4}$;
$\cos \theta = -\frac{3}{4}$; $\tan \theta = -\frac{\sqrt{7}}{3}$; $\csc \theta = \frac{4\sqrt{7}}{7}$; $\sec \theta = -\frac{4}{3}$;
$\cot \theta = -\frac{3\sqrt{7}}{7}$ **35.** $\sin 270° = -1$; $\cos 270° = 0$; $\tan 270°$
is undefined; $\csc 270° = -1$; $\sec 270°$ is undefined;
$\cot 270° = 0$.

39.
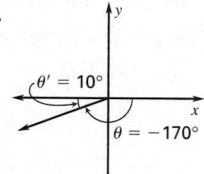
; 41.

10°   80°

43.
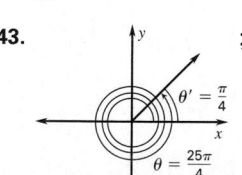
; $\frac{\pi}{4}$ **45.** $\frac{\sqrt{2}}{2}$ **47.** $\frac{2\sqrt{3}}{3}$ **49.** 2
51. $-\frac{\sqrt{2}}{2}$ **53.** $-\sqrt{3}$ **55.** $-\frac{1}{2}$
57. $-\frac{1}{2}$ **59.** $-\frac{2\sqrt{3}}{3}$ **61.** −1.3673
63. −0.1736 **65.** 1.3764

67. −0.8090 **69.** about 16.5 ft/sec **71.** about 7.4 ft
73. about 22,800 mi **75.** about (−24, 93)

13.3 MIXED REVIEW (p. 790)
81.
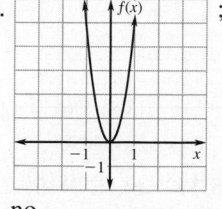
; 83. **;**

yes   no

85. 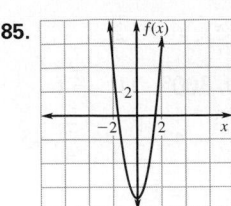 ; no **87.** $\frac{1}{52}$ **89.** $\frac{4}{13}$

91. $A = 70°$; $a \approx 20.7$; $b \approx 7.52$

93. $B = 40°$; $a \approx 2.30$; $b \approx 1.93$

95. $B = 7°$; $b \approx 6.14$; $c \approx 50.4$

13.4 PRACTICE (pp. 795–797)
5. $\frac{\pi}{3}$, or 60° **7.** $\frac{\pi}{6}$, or 30°
9. 1.32; 75.6° **11.** 1.22; 70.1° **13.** 200° **15.** 295°
17. about 42.3° **19.** $\frac{\pi}{3}$; 60° **21.** 0; 0° **23.** $-\frac{\pi}{2}$; −90°
25. $\frac{5\pi}{6}$; 150° **27** 48.2° **29.** 120° **31.** 18.4° **33.** 1.33; 76.1°
35. 0.848; 48.6° **37.** 2.21; 127° **39.** 1.15; 66.0°
41. 1.43; 81.9° **43.** 0.988; 56.6° **45.** 247° **47.** 127°
49. 224° **51.** 222° **53.** about 44.4° **55.** about 70.2°
57. $\theta = \tan^{-1}(2.127t)$ **59.** about 71.6° **61.** $y = 1.6x + 3$

13.4 MIXED REVIEW (p. 798)
65. 18 **66.** $\frac{21}{4}$ **67.** −3
68. −4 **69.** −3, 3 **70.** no solution **71.** $\frac{1}{5}$ **72.** $\frac{1}{3}$ **73.** $\frac{1}{2}$
74. $\frac{1}{3}$ **75.** $\frac{11}{30}$ **76.** $\frac{7}{30}$ **77.** 0.4540 **78.** 0.3827 **79.** 0.3907
80. 1.0642 **81.** 0.2126 **82.** −1.5890

QUIZ 2 (p. 798)
1. $\sin\theta = -\frac{16\sqrt{337}}{337}$; $\cos\theta = -\frac{9\sqrt{337}}{337}$;
$\tan\theta = \frac{16}{9}$; $\csc\theta = -\frac{\sqrt{337}}{16}$; $\sec\theta = -\frac{\sqrt{337}}{9}$; $\cot\theta = \frac{9}{16}$

2. $\sin\theta = -\frac{2\sqrt{53}}{53}$; $\cos\theta = \frac{7\sqrt{53}}{53}$; $\tan\theta = -\frac{2}{7}$;
$\csc\theta = -\frac{\sqrt{53}}{2}$; $\sec\theta = \frac{\sqrt{53}}{7}$; $\cot\theta = -\frac{7}{2}$ **3.** $\sin\theta = \frac{5\sqrt{26}}{26}$;
$\cos\theta = -\frac{\sqrt{26}}{26}$; $\tan\theta = -5$; $\csc\theta = \frac{\sqrt{26}}{5}$; $\sec\theta = -\sqrt{26}$;
$\cot\theta = -\frac{1}{5}$ **4.** $\sin\theta = -\frac{11\sqrt{157}}{157}$; $\cos\theta = \frac{6\sqrt{157}}{157}$;
$\tan\theta = -\frac{11}{6}$; $\csc\theta = -\frac{\sqrt{157}}{11}$; $\sec\theta = \frac{\sqrt{157}}{6}$; $\cot\theta = -\frac{6}{11}$
5. $\sin\theta = \frac{2\sqrt{5}}{5}$; $\cos\theta = \frac{\sqrt{5}}{5}$; $\tan\theta = 2$; $\csc\theta = \frac{\sqrt{5}}{2}$;
$\sec\theta = \sqrt{5}$; $\cot\theta = \frac{1}{2}$ **6.** $\sin\theta = \frac{\sqrt{17}}{17}$; $\cos\theta = -\frac{4\sqrt{17}}{17}$;
$\tan\theta = -\frac{1}{4}$; $\csc\theta = \sqrt{17}$; $\sec\theta = -\frac{\sqrt{17}}{4}$; $\cot\theta = -4$

7. $\sin\theta = -\frac{5\sqrt{106}}{106}$; $\cos\theta = \frac{9\sqrt{106}}{106}$; $\tan\theta = -\frac{5}{9}$;
$\csc\theta = -\frac{\sqrt{106}}{5}$; $\sec\theta = \frac{\sqrt{106}}{9}$; $\cot\theta = -\frac{9}{5}$
8. $\sin\theta = -\frac{8\sqrt{113}}{113}$; $\cos\theta = -\frac{7\sqrt{113}}{113}$; $\tan\theta = \frac{8}{7}$;
$\csc\theta = -\frac{\sqrt{113}}{8}$; $\sec\theta = -\frac{\sqrt{113}}{7}$; $\cot\theta = \frac{7}{8}$ **9.** $-\frac{\sqrt{2}}{2}$
10. $-\sqrt{3}$ **11.** $\frac{1}{2}$ **12.** $\sqrt{3}$ **13.** $-\frac{\sqrt{3}}{2}$ **14.** $-\frac{\sqrt{3}}{2}$ **15.** $-\frac{\sqrt{3}}{3}$
16. $-\frac{1}{2}$ **17.** 1.16; 66.5° **18.** −0.644; −36.9° **19.** 0.318; 18.2°
20. 0.232; 13.3° **21.** −1.33; −76.0° **22.** 2.50; 143°
23. 0.100; 5.74° **24.** 1.47; 84.3° **25.** 166° **36.** 282°
27. 262° **28.** 206° **29.** 253° **30.** 103° **31.** about 47 ft

13.5 PRACTICE (pp. 803–806)
5. no triangle **7.** two triangles
9. $A \approx 35.8°$; $B \approx 49.2°$; $a = 14.7$ **11.** 2.19 units^2
13. 125 units^2 **15.** about $62,400 **17.** no triangle
19. two triangles **21.** one triangle **23.** no triangle
25. $C = 75°$; $a \approx 24.9$; $b \approx 30.5$ **27.** $A \approx 84.7°$; $C \approx 35.3°$;
$a \approx 34.5$ **29.** no triangle **31.** $A \approx 62.3°$; $B \approx 22.7°$; $b \approx 3.48$
33. $A \approx 111.6°$; $B \approx 52.4°$; $a \approx 108$, or $A \approx 36.4°$; $B \approx 127.6°$;
$a \approx 68.9$ **35.** $A \approx 15.4°$; $C \approx 129.6°$ $c \approx 34.9$ **37.** 119 units^2
39. 17.3 units^2 **41.** 162 units^2 **43.** 9.83 units^2
45. 67.1 units^2 **47.** 76.1 units^2 **49.** 9.06 units^2
51. 85.7 units^2 **53.** *Sample answer:* Let the side lengths
be 10 and 15. The equation is $A = 75\sin x$. **55.** 90°
57. about 22.5 mi **61.** 31.8°, or 8.2° **63.** about 155.4 ft
65. 21 bags **67.** about 0.57 gal, so buy a single gallon can

13.5 MIXED REVIEW (p. 806)
71. $23\sqrt{3}$ **73.** $8\sqrt{7}$
75. $28\sqrt{2}$ **77.** 0.3090 **79.** −0.2225 **81.** 0.5736 **83.** 0.9962

13.6 PRACTICE (pp. 810–812)
5. $b \approx 43.0$; $A \approx 107.4°$;
$C \approx 52.7°$ **7.** $A \approx 82.2°$; $B \approx 25.8°$; $C \approx 72.0°$
9. 510 units^2 **11.** 1470 units^2 **13.** about 63.7 ft
15. $c \approx 4.60$; $A \approx 35.2°$; $B \approx 112.8°$ **17.** $c \approx 12.9$; $A \approx 48.6°$;
$B \approx 91.4°$ **19.** $c \approx 16.3$; $A \approx 37.7°$; $B \approx 47.3°$ **21.** $A \approx 22.3°$;
$B \approx 49.5°$; $C \approx 108.2°$ **23.** $a \approx 29.1$; $B \approx 63.4°$; $C \approx 56.6°$
25. $c \approx 10.4$; $A \approx 75°$; $B \approx 75°$ **27.** $b \approx 6.40$; $A \approx 150.9°$;
$C \approx 14.1°$ **29.** $A \approx 47.0°$; $B \approx 27.8°$; $C \approx 105.1°$
31. $A = 70°$; $a \approx 32.4$; $c \approx 17.3$ **33.** $a \approx 27.5$; $A \approx 56.5°$;
$B \approx 19.5°$ **35.** $A \approx 64.3°$; $B \approx 73.2°$; $C \approx 42.5°$
37. $c \approx 11.7$; $A \approx 20.0°$; $B \approx 70.0°$ **39.** 14.0 units^2
41. 150 units^2 **43.** 2210 units^2 **45.** 3.87 units^2
47. 27.7 units^2 **51.** about 74.4 ft **53.** about 7800 mi^2

13.6 MIXED REVIEW (p. 812)
59. $\frac{y^2}{9} - \frac{x^2}{112} = 1$
61. $y^2 - \frac{x^2}{19} = 1$ **63.** 0.137 **65.** 0.160 **67.** 0.0130

13.7 PRACTICE (pp. 816–818)
5. 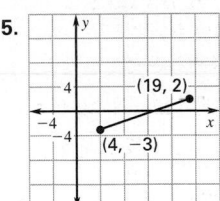 **7.** $y = \frac{3}{7}x - 2$; $0 \le x \le 35$
9. $y = (\tan 72.1°)x + 3$, or
$y = 3.10x + 3$; $0 \le x \le 35.3$

11. 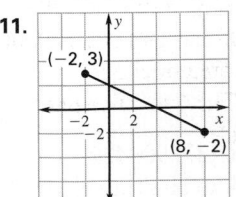 **13.**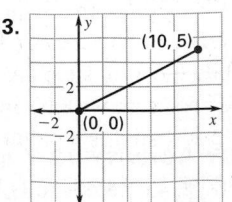

15. 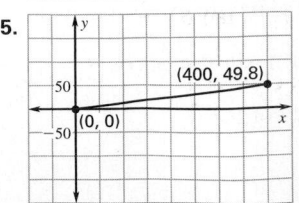 **17.** $y = 2x - 5$; $1 \le x \le 6$
19. $y = x$; $0 \le x \le 100$
21. $x = (20.0\cos 71.6°)t$, or
$x = 6.31t$;
$y = (20.0\sin 71.6°)t$, or
$y = 19.0t$; $0 \le t \le 3$

23. $x = (13.0 \cos 80.0°)t + 3$, or $x = 2.26t + 3$; $y = (13.0 \sin 80.0°)t + 2$, or $y = 12.8t + 2$; $0 \le t \le 5$ **25.** $x = (10 \cos 143.13°)t + 2.0$; $y = (10 \sin 143.13°)t$ **27.** about 3774 sec, or about 63 min **29.** $x = 260t$; $y = 10,000 - 30t$ **31.** about 333 sec, or 5 min 33 sec **33.** $x = (17.9 \cos 14.3°)t$, or $x = 17.3t$; $y = -4.9t^2 + (17.9 \sin 14.3°)t + 1.71$, or $y = -4.9t^2 + 4.42t + 1.71$ **35.** about 20.7 m **37.** about 1.49 sec **39.** $x = (v \cos 43°)t$, or $x = 0.731vt$; $y = -16t^2 + (v \sin 43°)t + 6$, or $y = -16t^2 + 0.682vt + 6$

13.7 MIXED REVIEW (p. 819)

45.
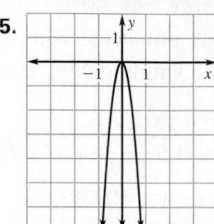

47.
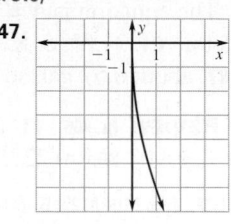

49.
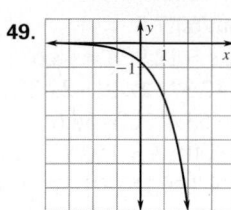

51. 6930 **53.** $-\dfrac{1}{9}$

55. 0.3413 **57.** 0.0013

QUIZ 3 (p. 819) **1.** $A \approx 58.5°$; $C \approx 51.5°$; $a \approx 27.2$ **2.** $A = 70°$; $b \approx 2.77$; $c \approx 15.7$ **3.** $C = 30°$; $a \approx 20.5$; $c \approx 16.0$ **4.** no triangle **5.** $A \approx 106.1°$; $B \approx 43.1°$; $C \approx 30.8°$ **6.** $a = 35.4$; $B = 23.9°$; $C = 49.1°$ **7.** 179 units^2 **8.** 499 units^2 **9.** 57.0 units^2 **10.** 16.3 units^2 **11.** 1950 units^2 **12.** 334 units^2

13.
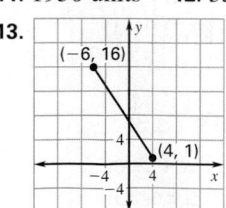

14.
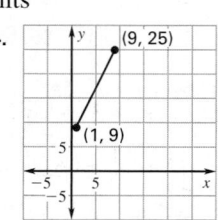

15.
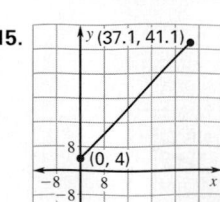

16. $y = -\dfrac{1}{5}x - \dfrac{27}{5}$; $-22 \le x \le 3$
17. $y = 0.700x$; $0 \le x \le 246$
18. about 23.0 ft

TECHNOLOGY ACTIVITY 13.7 (p. 820) **1.** 390; 423; 443; 443; 423; 390 **2.** 45°; the results look to be symmetric around the value $\theta = 45°$, with a maximum at that angle.

CHAPTER REVIEW (pp. 822–824) **1.** $\sin \theta = \dfrac{3}{5}$; $\cos \theta = \dfrac{4}{5}$; $\tan \theta = \dfrac{3}{4}$; $\csc \theta = \dfrac{5}{3}$; $\sec \theta = \dfrac{5}{4}$; $\cot \theta = \dfrac{4}{3}$

3. $\sin \theta = \dfrac{\sqrt{2}}{2}$; $\cos \theta = \dfrac{\sqrt{2}}{2}$; $\tan \theta = 1$; $\csc \theta = \sqrt{2}$; $\sec \theta = \sqrt{2}$; $\cot \theta = 1$ **5.** $\dfrac{\pi}{6}$ **7.** $-\dfrac{\pi}{12}$ **9.** 300° **11.** $\dfrac{5\pi}{2}$ ft, $\dfrac{25\pi}{4}$ ft^2 **13.** $\dfrac{56\pi}{3}$ cm, $\dfrac{448\pi}{3}$ cm^2 **15.** $\dfrac{\sqrt{3}}{2}$ **17.** $\dfrac{1}{2}$ **19.** $\dfrac{\pi}{4}$, 45°
21. $\dfrac{\pi}{2}$, 90° **23.** $\dfrac{2\pi}{3}$, 120° **25.** $A = 29.3°$; $C = 132.7°$; $c = 28.5$ or $A = 150.7°$; $C = 11.3°$; $c = 7.60$ **27.** 63.1 units^2 **29.** 98.3 units^2 **31.** $C = 107°$, $A = 24°$, $B = 49°$ **33.** 9.9 units^2 **35.** 46.4 units^2 **39.** $y = -2x - 1$; $-3 \le x \le 13$

CHAPTER 14

SKILL REVIEW (p. 830)

1.
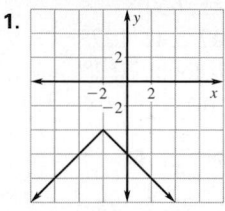

2.
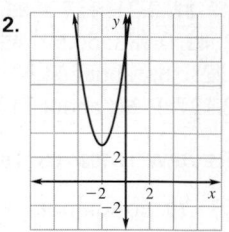

3.
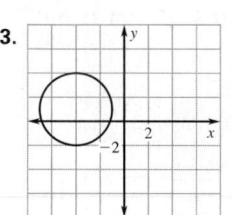

4. -8, 1 **5.** $\pm\dfrac{5}{3}$ **6.** $\dfrac{1}{6} \pm \dfrac{\sqrt{61}}{6}$ **7.** $\dfrac{\sqrt{3}}{2}$ **8.** $\dfrac{\sqrt{3}}{3}$ **9.** $\dfrac{\sqrt{2}}{2}$ **10.** 0

11. $\dfrac{\pi}{4}$, 45° **12.** $\dfrac{\pi}{6}$, 30° **13.** $\dfrac{\pi}{2}$, 90° **14.** $-\dfrac{\pi}{3}$, $-60°$

14.1 PRACTICE (pp. 835–837) **5.** amplitude: 3, period: 2 **7.** amplitude: $\dfrac{2}{3}$, period: 6 **9.** amplitude: 1, period: 4π

11.
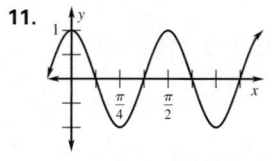

13.
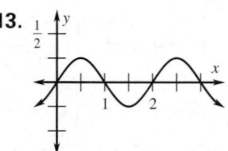

15.
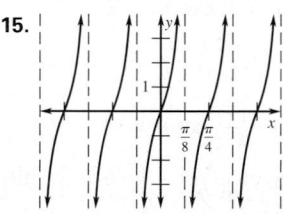

17. B **19.** D **21.** A
23. amplitude: 1, period: 6π
25. amplitude: 4, period: π
27. amplitude: 1, period: π
29. amplitude: 5, period: 4π
31. amplitude: $\dfrac{1}{3}$, period: $\dfrac{1}{2}$

33.
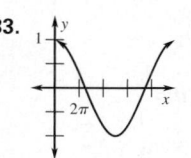

35.
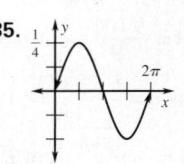

37.
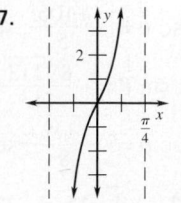

39. 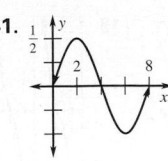 **41.** 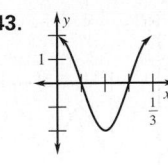 **43.**

45. $y = 10 \sin \dfrac{\pi x}{2}$ **47.** $y = \dfrac{1}{2} \sin \dfrac{2}{3}x$ **49.** $y = 3 \sin 4\pi x$

53. amplitude: $\dfrac{1}{2}$ ft, period: $\dfrac{\pi}{3}$ sec **55.** 8.7 ft, 8.9 ft, 9.2 ft; $h_t - h_{t-1}$ increases as t increases.

14.1 MIXED REVIEW (p. 837)

61. 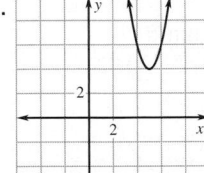 **63.**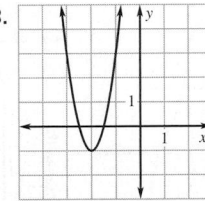

67. $\dfrac{15}{58}$ **69.** $\dfrac{7}{58}$

71. 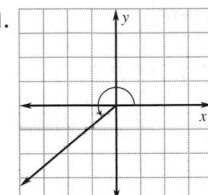 ; 40° **73.** 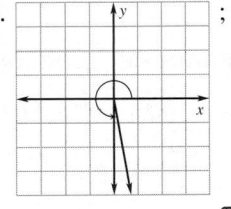 ; 80°

75. 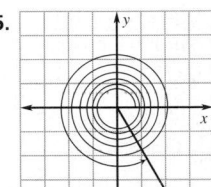 ; $\dfrac{\pi}{3}$ **77.** 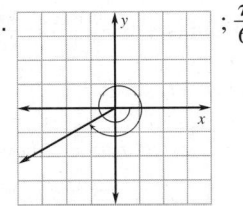 ; $\dfrac{\pi}{6}$

79. 46.2 years

TECHNOLOGY ACTIVITY 14.1 (p. 838) **1.** amplitude: $\dfrac{1}{3}$, 3, 9; period: 2π **3.** amplitude: $\dfrac{1}{2}$, 1, 2; period: 2π

5. amplitude: 1; period: 2π, π, $\dfrac{\pi}{2}$

7. amplitude: 1; period: 4π, 2π, π

14.2 PRACTICE (pp. 844–846) **1.** translation **3.** shifted right π units **5.** horizontal shift **7.** horizontal shift **9.** reflection, vertical shift

11. 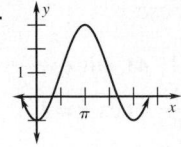 **13.**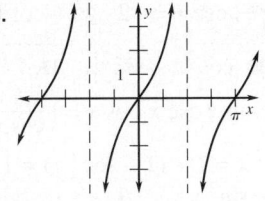

15. 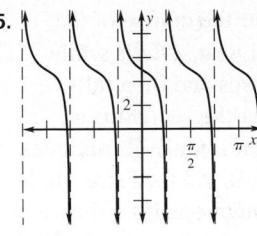 **17.** shift up 2 **19.** shift down 2
21. reflect in x-axis and shift left π **23.** reflect in x-axis, shift right $\dfrac{\pi}{4}$, shift up 5
25. shift left $\dfrac{3\pi}{4}$, shift up 3
27. B **29.** A **31.** D

33. 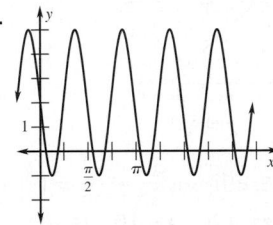 **35.**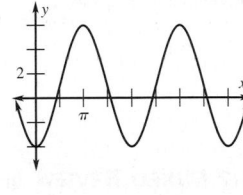

37. 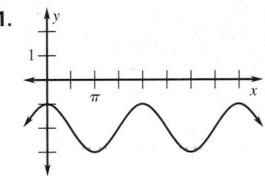 **39.**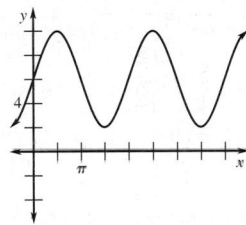

41. 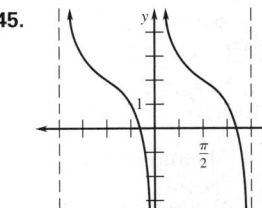 **43.**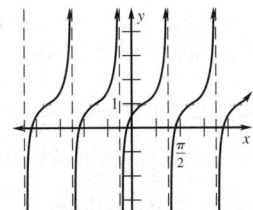

45. **49.**

51. $y = 3 \cos (x + \pi) + 3$ **53.** $y = -\dfrac{1}{3} \sin 6x - 1$

55. $y = -4 \tan \dfrac{\pi}{2}\left(x - \dfrac{1}{2}\right) + 6$

57. 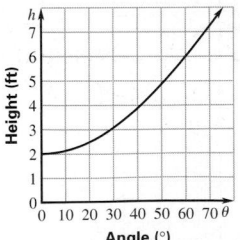 ; 4.3 ft

59. 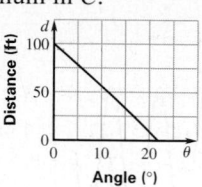 ; Over the course of the first year, R falls while C rises and then falls. Over the second year, R rises while C continues to fall and then rise. Both populations have the same period, 2 years, with the peak in R occurring 6 months before the peak in C, and the minimum in R 6 months before the minimum in C.

61. $d = -250 \tan \theta + 100$, where $0 \le \theta \le 21.8°$;

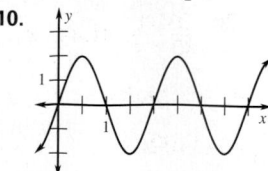

14.2 MIXED REVIEW (p. 847) 65. ellipse, $\dfrac{x^2}{25} + \dfrac{y^2}{36} = 1$

67. circle, $x^2 + y^2 = 25$ **69.** 8 **71.** 120 **73.** 10 **75.** 7

77. $\sin \theta = \dfrac{4}{5}$, $\cos \theta = \dfrac{3}{5}$, $\tan \theta = \dfrac{4}{3}$, $\sec \theta = \dfrac{5}{3}$,

$\csc \theta = \dfrac{5}{4}$, $\cot \theta = \dfrac{3}{4}$ **79.** $\sin \theta = \dfrac{3}{10}$, $\cos \theta = \dfrac{\sqrt{91}}{10}$,

$\tan \theta = \dfrac{3\sqrt{91}}{91}$, $\sec \theta = \dfrac{10\sqrt{91}}{91}$, $\csc \theta = \dfrac{10}{3}$, $\cot \theta = \dfrac{\sqrt{91}}{3}$

81. $\sin \theta = \dfrac{2\sqrt{6}}{5}$, $\cos \theta = \dfrac{1}{5}$, $\tan \theta = 2\sqrt{6}$, $\sec \theta = 5$,

$\csc \theta = \dfrac{5\sqrt{6}}{12}$, $\cot \theta = \dfrac{\sqrt{6}}{12}$ **83.** 40,320

QUIZ 1 (p. 847) 1. amplitude: $\dfrac{5}{2}$, period: $\dfrac{2\pi}{7}$ **2.** amplitude: 1,

period: π **3.** amplitude: 1, period: 4 **4.** amplitude: $\dfrac{1}{4}$,

period: 1 **5.** amplitude: 3, period: 2 **6.** amplitude: 4,

period: $\dfrac{4}{3}$ **7.** amplitude: $\dfrac{7}{3}$, period: $\dfrac{\pi}{2}$ **8.** amplitude: $\dfrac{1}{3}$,

period: 2π **9.** amplitude: 6, period: 16π

10. 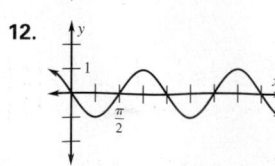 **11.**

12. 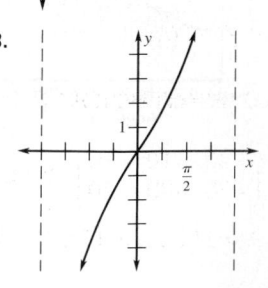 **13.**

14. 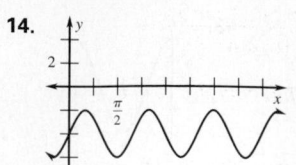 **15.**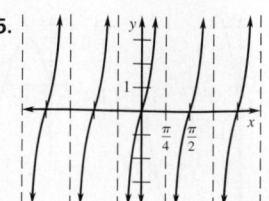

16. 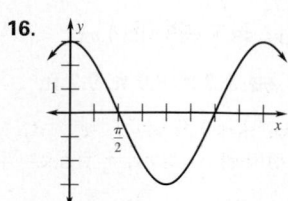 **17.**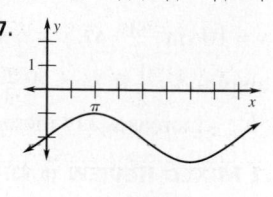

18. 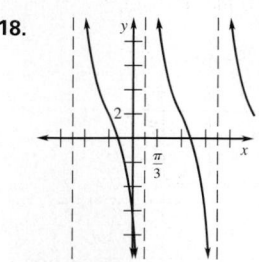 **19.** $d = 120 \tan \theta$
$0° \le \theta \le 65.2°$; 30.3°;

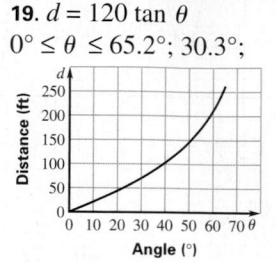

14.3 PRACTICE (pp. 852–854) 5. $\sin \theta = \dfrac{4}{5}$, $\tan \theta = -\dfrac{4}{3}$,

$\sec \theta = -\dfrac{5}{3}$, $\csc \theta = \dfrac{5}{4}$, $\cot \theta = -\dfrac{3}{4}$ **7.** $\sin \theta = -\dfrac{\sqrt{7}}{4}$, $\cos \theta = \dfrac{3}{4}$,

$\tan \theta = -\dfrac{\sqrt{7}}{3}$, $\csc \theta = -\dfrac{4\sqrt{7}}{7}$, $\cot \theta = -\dfrac{3\sqrt{7}}{7}$ **9.** $\tan x$ **11.** 1

13. $\cot x \tan (-x) = \dfrac{\cos x}{\sin x} \cdot \dfrac{\sin (-x)}{\cos (-x)} = \dfrac{\cos x}{\sin x} \cdot \dfrac{-\sin x}{\cos x} = -1$

15. ellipse **17.** $\sin \theta = \dfrac{3\sqrt{73}}{73}$, $\cos \theta = \dfrac{8\sqrt{73}}{73}$, $\sec \theta = \dfrac{\sqrt{73}}{8}$,

$\csc \theta = \dfrac{\sqrt{73}}{3}$, $\cot \theta = \dfrac{8}{3}$ **19.** $\cos \theta = -\dfrac{4}{5}$, $\tan \theta = -\dfrac{3}{4}$,

$\sec \theta = -\dfrac{5}{4}$, $\csc \theta = \dfrac{5}{3}$, $\cot \theta = -\dfrac{4}{3}$ **21.** $\sin \theta = \dfrac{\sqrt{23}}{12}$,

$\tan \theta = -\dfrac{\sqrt{23}}{11}$, $\sec \theta = -\dfrac{12}{11}$, $\csc \theta = \dfrac{12\sqrt{23}}{23}$,

$\cot \theta = -\dfrac{11\sqrt{23}}{23}$ **23.** $\sin \theta = -\dfrac{\sqrt{91}}{10}$, $\cos \theta = -\dfrac{3}{10}$,

$\tan \theta = \dfrac{\sqrt{91}}{3}$, $\csc \theta = -\dfrac{10\sqrt{91}}{91}$, $\cot \theta = \dfrac{3\sqrt{91}}{91}$

25. $\sin \theta = -\dfrac{\sqrt{3}}{2}$, $\cos \theta = \dfrac{1}{2}$, $\tan \theta = -\sqrt{3}$, $\csc \theta = -\dfrac{2\sqrt{3}}{3}$,

$\cot \theta = -\dfrac{\sqrt{3}}{3}$ **27.** $\sin \theta = -\dfrac{1}{2}$, $\cos \theta = \dfrac{\sqrt{3}}{2}$, $\tan \theta = -\dfrac{\sqrt{3}}{3}$,

$\sec \theta = \dfrac{2\sqrt{3}}{3}$, $\csc \theta = -2$ **29.** $-\cot x$ **31.** $\csc x$

33. $\cos x$ **35.** $\cos^2 x - \sin^2 x$ **37.** 1 **39.** -1 **41.** $\sin x$

43. -1 **45.** $\tan x \csc x \cos x = \left(\dfrac{\sin x}{\cos x}\right)\left(\dfrac{1}{\sin x}\right) \cos x = 1$

47. $2 - \sec^2 x = 1 + (1 - \sec^2 x) = 1 - \tan^2 x$

49. $\dfrac{\cos^2 x + \sin^2 x}{1 + \tan^2 x} = \dfrac{1}{\sec^2 x} = \cos^2 x$

51. $\dfrac{\sin \left(\dfrac{\pi}{2} - x\right) - 1}{1 - \cos (-x)} = \dfrac{\cos x - 1}{1 - \cos x} = -1$

53. $\dfrac{\cos(-x)}{1+\sin(-x)} = \dfrac{\cos x}{1-\sin x} = \dfrac{\cos x\,(1+\sin x)}{1-\sin^2 x} =$

$\dfrac{\cos x\,(1+\sin x)}{\cos^2 x} = \sec x + \tan x$ **55.** $1 = \sec^2 t - \tan^2 t =$

$\dfrac{x^2}{5} - \dfrac{y^2}{1}$, hyperbola **57.** $1 = \sin^2 \pi t + \cos^2 \pi t = \dfrac{y^2}{64} + \dfrac{x^2}{64}$,

circle **59.** $1 = \sin^2 \dfrac{t}{2} + \cos^2 \dfrac{t}{2} = \dfrac{y^2}{16} + \dfrac{x^2}{1}$, ellipse

61. $s = \dfrac{h \sin(90° - \theta)}{\sin \theta} = \dfrac{h \cos \theta}{\sin \theta} = h \cot \theta$

63. Actual wheel is 18 ft wide, model is 1 ft wide. Actual wheel rotates once every 15 sec, model once every 8 sec.

14.3 MIXED REVIEW (p. 854) **69.** $-9, 4$ **71.** $-\dfrac{3}{2}, 5$

73. $-\dfrac{1}{3}, \dfrac{1}{3}$ **75.** $60°, \dfrac{\pi}{3}$ **77.** $30°, \dfrac{\pi}{6}$ **79.** $120°, \dfrac{2\pi}{3}$

81. 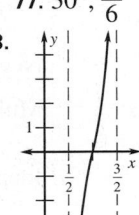 **83.** 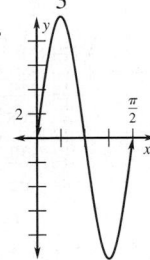 **85.**

14.4 PRACTICE (pp. 859–860) **5.** $\dfrac{\pi}{6}, \dfrac{5\pi}{6}, \dfrac{7\pi}{6}, \dfrac{11\pi}{6}$ **7.** $\dfrac{\pi}{6}, \dfrac{11\pi}{6}$

9. $0.45 + 2n\pi, 2.69 + 2n\pi$ **11.** $\dfrac{7\pi}{6} + 2n\pi, \dfrac{11\pi}{6} + 2n\pi$

13. yes **15.** yes **17.** yes **19.** $\dfrac{\pi}{3} + 2n\pi, \dfrac{5\pi}{3} + 2n\pi$

21. $\dfrac{\pi}{6} + 2n\pi, \dfrac{5\pi}{6} + 2n\pi$ **23.** $\dfrac{\pi}{4} + \dfrac{n\pi}{2}$ **25.** $\dfrac{\pi}{2} + n\pi$

27. $\dfrac{\pi}{2} + 2n\pi, \dfrac{7\pi}{6} + 2n\pi, \dfrac{11\pi}{6} + 2n\pi$

29. $\dfrac{\pi}{2} + 2n\pi, \dfrac{11\pi}{6} + 2n\pi$ **31.** $\dfrac{\pi}{3} + 2n\pi, \dfrac{5\pi}{3} + 2n\pi$

33. $0.93, 5.36$ **35.** $\dfrac{\pi}{3}, \dfrac{2\pi}{3}, \dfrac{4\pi}{3}, \dfrac{5\pi}{3}$ **37.** $\dfrac{\pi}{6}, \dfrac{5\pi}{6}, \dfrac{3\pi}{2}$

39. $\dfrac{\pi}{4}, \dfrac{7\pi}{4}$ **41.** $\dfrac{\pi}{4}, \dfrac{3\pi}{4}, \dfrac{5\pi}{4}, \dfrac{7\pi}{4}$ **43.** $1.33, 4.47$ **45.** $4.13, 5.30$

47. $\dfrac{7\pi}{6}, \dfrac{11\pi}{6}$ **49.** $0, \pi$ **51.** $\dfrac{\pi}{6}, \dfrac{2\pi}{3}, \dfrac{7\pi}{6}, \dfrac{5\pi}{3}$

53. $\dfrac{\pi}{4}, \dfrac{3\pi}{4}, \dfrac{5\pi}{4}, \dfrac{7\pi}{4}$ **55.** $\dfrac{\pi}{3}, \dfrac{5\pi}{3}$ **57.** highs: 6:12 A.M. and 6:36 P.M., lows: 12:00 A.M. and 12:24 P.M., the water depth never goes below 7 ft. **59.** June, July, August; no

14.4 MIXED REVIEW (p. 861) **65.** $\dfrac{33}{36}$ **67.** $\dfrac{33}{36}$

69. 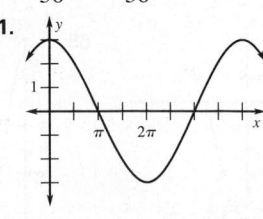 **71.**

73. 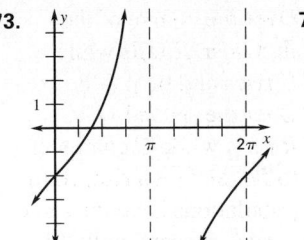 **77.** 36 ft

14.5 PRACTICE (pp. 865–867) **5.** $y = \cos \pi x - 2$

7. $y = 3 \sin \dfrac{x}{2} + 7$ **9.** $h = -20 \cos\left(\dfrac{2\pi}{15}t\right) + 25$

11. $y = 5 \sin 2x$ **13.** $y = -4 \cos \pi x$ **15.** $y = 2 \cos \dfrac{\pi x}{2} - 4$

17. $y = 8 \sin \dfrac{x}{2}$ **19.** $y = -\cos 3x + 3$ **21.** $y = -5 \sin \dfrac{\pi x}{2} + 2$

23. $y = -6 \cos 6x + 5$ **25.** $y = 4 \cos \dfrac{x}{3} - 4$

27. $y = -2 \sin 6x - 4$ **31.** $h = 6.5 \cos 60\pi t + 4.5$

33. $h = -2.5 \cos \pi t + 6.5$

35. $T = 776.4 \cdot \sin\left(0.45t + 1.49\right) + 727.7$

14.5 MIXED REVIEW (p. 867) **41.** $\dfrac{1}{36}$ **43.** $\dfrac{1}{4}$ **45.** $-\dfrac{\sqrt{2}}{2}$

47. $-\dfrac{1}{2}$ **49.** $-\dfrac{\sqrt{3}}{3}$ **51.** 9.92 **53.** 22.19 **55.** 31.53

QUIZ 2 (p. 868) **1.** $\csc x$ **2.** $2 \cos^2 x$ **3.** $\sin x \cos x$

4. $\dfrac{\pi}{6} + \pi n, \dfrac{5\pi}{6} + \pi n$ **5.** $5.94 + 2\pi n, 3.48 + 2\pi n$

6. $\dfrac{2\pi}{3} + \pi n, \dfrac{5\pi}{6} + \pi n$ **7.** $y = -5 \sin 2x$ **8.** $y = \cos \dfrac{x}{3} + 2$

9. $y = -2 \cos x + 4$ **10.** $T = 25.0 \sin(0.50t - 1.76) + 47.3$

14.6 PRACTICE (pp. 872–874) **5.** $\dfrac{\sqrt{6} - \sqrt{2}}{4}$ **7.** $-\dfrac{\sqrt{2} + \sqrt{6}}{4}$

9. $-2 - \sqrt{3}$ **11.** none **13.** $\dfrac{\pi}{3}, \dfrac{4\pi}{3}$ **15.** 0 **17.** $-\dfrac{\sqrt{3}}{2}$

19. 1 **21.** $-\dfrac{\sqrt{2}}{2}$ **23.** $-2 + \sqrt{3}$ **25.** $\dfrac{\sqrt{2} - \sqrt{6}}{4}$ **27.** $-2 - \sqrt{3}$

29. $-\dfrac{36 + \sqrt{627}}{70}$ **31.** $\dfrac{\sqrt{627} + 36}{4\sqrt{19} - 9\sqrt{33}}$ **33.** $-\dfrac{9\sqrt{33} + 4\sqrt{19}}{70}$

35. $\dfrac{4\sqrt{11} - 15}{30}$ **37.** $\dfrac{4\sqrt{11} - 15}{3\sqrt{11} + 20}$ **39.** $\dfrac{20 - 3\sqrt{11}}{30}$ **41.** $\tan x$

43. $-\sin x$ **45.** $-\cos x$ **47.** $-\sin x$ **49.** $\dfrac{3\pi}{2}$ **51.** $0, \pi$

53. $0, \dfrac{\pi}{3}, \dfrac{5\pi}{3}$ **55.** $36.9°$ **57.** $P = \dfrac{1}{40} \cos 1100t$

59. $0.26 + \dfrac{n\pi}{10}$

14.6 MIXED REVIEW (p. 874) **65.** $\begin{bmatrix} 3 & 3 & 3 \\ -1 & -1 & -1 \end{bmatrix}$ **67.** $\begin{bmatrix} -15 \\ 13 \end{bmatrix}$

69. $\begin{bmatrix} 30 & 10 & -10 \\ -70 & -20 & 30 \end{bmatrix}$ **71.** $C = 134°, a = 65.8, c = 153$

73. $A = 111°, B = 17°, C = 52°$ **75.** $\dfrac{2\pi}{3}, \dfrac{5\pi}{3}$ **77.** $\dfrac{3\pi}{4}, \dfrac{7\pi}{4}$

14.7 PRACTICE (pp. 879–881) **5.** $-\sqrt{\dfrac{29 - 5\sqrt{29}}{58}}$ **7.** $\dfrac{20}{29}$ **9.** $\dfrac{20}{21}$

11. $2 \cos x - 2 \cos^2 x$ **13.** $\dfrac{2 \tan x}{1 - \tan^4 x}$ **15.** $-2 \cos^2 x$

17. $2 - \sqrt{3}$ **19.** $1 - \sqrt{2}$ **21.** $-\left(2 + \sqrt{3}\right)$

23. $-\left(\dfrac{\sqrt{2 + \sqrt{3}}}{2}\right)$ **25.** $\dfrac{\sqrt{2 - \sqrt{3}}}{2}$

27. $\sin \dfrac{u}{2} = \dfrac{\sqrt{6}}{6}$, $\cos \dfrac{u}{2} = -\dfrac{\sqrt{30}}{6}$, $\tan \dfrac{u}{2} = -\dfrac{\sqrt{5}}{5}$

29. $\sin \dfrac{u}{2} = \dfrac{\sqrt{5}}{5}$, $\cos \dfrac{u}{2} = -\dfrac{2\sqrt{5}}{5}$, $\tan \dfrac{u}{2} = -\dfrac{1}{2}$

31. $\sin 2x = -\dfrac{4}{5}$, $\cos 2x = \dfrac{3}{5}$, $\tan 2x = -\dfrac{4}{3}$

33. $\sin 2x = -\dfrac{24}{25}$, $\cos 2x = \dfrac{7}{25}$, $\tan 2x = -\dfrac{24}{7}$ **35.** $2 \cos x$

37. $1 - 5 \sin^2 x$ **39.** $\dfrac{1}{1 + \cos x}$ **41.** $2 \sin x \cos x$

43. $(\sin x + \cos x)^2 = \sin^2 x + \cos^2 x + 2 \sin x \cos x = 1 + \sin 2x$ **45.** $\cos \theta + 2 \sin^2 \dfrac{\theta}{2} = \cos \theta + 2\left(\dfrac{1 - \cos \theta}{2}\right) = \cos \theta + 1 - \cos \theta = 1$ **47.** $\cos 3x = \cos (2x + x) = \cos 2x \cos x - \sin 2x \sin x = \cos x (\cos^2 x - \sin^2 x) - \sin x (2 \sin x \cos x) = \cos^3 x - 3 \sin^2 x \cos x$

49. $\cos^2 2x - \sin^2 2x = \cos 4x$ **51.** no solution

53. $0, \dfrac{\pi}{4}, \dfrac{3\pi}{4}, \pi, \dfrac{5\pi}{4}, \dfrac{7\pi}{4}$ **55.** $0, \pi$ **57.** $0.21, 1.38, 3.36, 4.50$

59. $0, \pi$ **61.** $n\pi, \dfrac{2\pi}{3} + 2n\pi, \dfrac{4\pi}{3} + 2n\pi$ **63.** $\pi + 2n\pi$, $\dfrac{\pi}{3} + 4n\pi, \dfrac{5\pi}{3} + 4n\pi$ **65.** $\dfrac{3\pi}{2} + 2n\pi, \dfrac{7\pi}{6} + 2n\pi, \dfrac{11\pi}{6} + 2n\pi$

67. $\tan \dfrac{u}{2} = \dfrac{1 - \cos u}{\sin u} = \dfrac{(1 - \cos u)(1 + \cos u)}{\sin u (1 + \cos u)} = \dfrac{1 - \cos^2 u}{\sin u (1 + \cos u)} = \dfrac{\sin^2 u}{\sin u (1 + \cos u)} = \dfrac{\sin u}{1 + \cos u}$

69. $y_{\max} = \dfrac{1}{64} v^2 \sin^2 \theta$ **71.** $A = 324 \sin \dfrac{\theta}{2} \cos \dfrac{\theta}{2}$

73. $n = \dfrac{\sqrt{3}}{2} + \dfrac{1}{2} \cot \dfrac{\theta}{2}$; $77°$

14.7 MIXED REVIEW (p. 882) **79.** $f(x) - g(x) = -2x + 1$, all real numbers **81.** $f(x) \div g(x) = \dfrac{4x + 1}{6x}$, all real numbers except $x = 0$ **83.** $g(f(x)) = 24x + 6$, all real numbers **85.** 0.137 **87.** 0.1601 **89.** 0.013 **91.** $-\sin x$ **93.** $-\cos x$ **95.** $\dfrac{\tan x + 1}{1 - \tan x}$

QUIZ 3 (p. 882) **1.** $\dfrac{\sqrt{2 + \sqrt{3}}}{2}$ **2.** $\dfrac{\sqrt{6} - \sqrt{2}}{4}$ **3.** $-2 + \sqrt{3}$

4. $-\dfrac{\sqrt{6} + \sqrt{2}}{4}$ **5.** $-\dfrac{\sqrt{6} + \sqrt{2}}{4}$ **6.** $-2 + \sqrt{3}$ **7.** $\dfrac{\sqrt{18 + 12\sqrt{2}}}{6}$

8. $\dfrac{\sqrt{18 + 12\sqrt{2}}}{6}$ **9.** $\dfrac{\sqrt{3 + 2\sqrt{2}}}{\sqrt{3 - 2\sqrt{2}}}$ **10.** $-\dfrac{4\sqrt{2}}{9}$ **11.** $\dfrac{7}{9}$ **12.** $-\dfrac{4\sqrt{2}}{7}$

13. $-\sin x$ **14.** $-\cos x$ **15.** $\dfrac{\tan x + 1}{1 - \tan x}$ **16.** $\sin x$ **17.** 1

18. $\dfrac{\tan x}{1 + \tan x}$ **19.** $\dfrac{\pi}{18} + \dfrac{2n\pi}{3}, \dfrac{5\pi}{18} + \dfrac{2n\pi}{3}$ **20.** $n\pi$

21. $n\pi; \dfrac{2\pi}{3} + 2n\pi; \dfrac{4\pi}{3} + 2n\pi$ **22.** $\dfrac{3\pi}{8} + \dfrac{n\pi}{2}$

23. 77 ft

CHAPTER 14 REVIEW (pp. 884–886)

1. 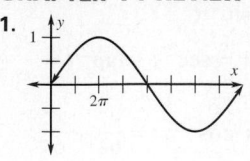 **3.**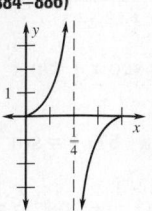

5. 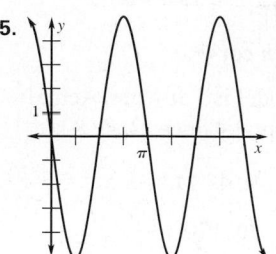 **7.** 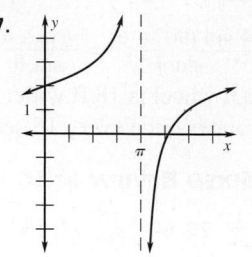 **9.** 1

11. $\sin^2 (-x) = \sin^2 x$ Negative angle identity

$= \dfrac{\sin^2 x}{\cos^2 x} \cos^2 x$ Multiply by $\dfrac{\cos^2 x}{\cos^2 x}$.

$= \dfrac{\tan^2 x}{\sec^2 x}$ Identities

$= \dfrac{\tan^2 x}{1 + \tan^2 x}$ Pythagorean identity

13. $\dfrac{\pi}{4} + \dfrac{n\pi}{2}, n\pi$ **15.** $\dfrac{\pi}{2} + 2n\pi$ **17.** $\dfrac{\pi}{6} + 2n\pi, \dfrac{5\pi}{6} + 2n\pi$

19. $y = 2 \sin x$ **21.** $y = \cos 2x$ **23.** $-\dfrac{\sqrt{6} + \sqrt{2}}{4}$ **25.** $-2 - \sqrt{3}$

27. $-2 + \sqrt{3}$ **29.** $-\dfrac{\sqrt{2 - \sqrt{2}}}{2}$ **31.** 0

CUMULATIVE PRACTICE (pp. 890–891) **1.** $y = -2x + 7$

3. $x = 4$ **5.** $(10, 4, -4)$ **7.** $\begin{bmatrix} 11 & -8 \\ -14 & 9 \end{bmatrix}$ **9.** $\begin{bmatrix} -\dfrac{3}{2} & 1 \\ -18 & 8 \end{bmatrix}$

11. $2x^3 - 5x^2 - 13x + 4$ **13.** $\dfrac{x}{4x^2 - 19x - 30}$

15. $\dfrac{4x^2 + 27x + 7}{x^2 - 49}$ **17.** $\dfrac{1}{5}$ **19.** -1 **21.** -4 **23.** 7 **25.** 0

27. $5.39, (-2.5, 1)$ **29.** $9.90, (3.5, 0.5)$ **31.** $\dfrac{1}{2}, 2^{4 - n}$

33. $14, 5n - 11$ **35.** 40 **37.** $\dfrac{3}{2}$ **39.** 90 **41.** 8 **43.** 35

45. 28.3 in.; 84.82 in.^{2} **47.** $\dfrac{\sqrt{3}}{3}$ **49.** 1 **51.** $\dfrac{1}{2}$ **53.** $\dfrac{\pi}{6}, 30°$

55. $\dfrac{3\pi}{4}, 135°$ **57.** $B = 31°, C = 84°, c = 7.68$

59. $A = 92°, B = 64°, C = 24°$ **61.** 336.7

63. 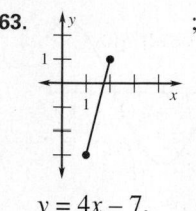 ; **65.**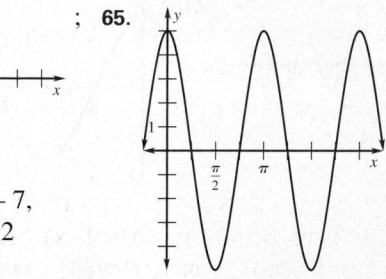

$y = 4x - 7$,
$1 \le x \le 2$

67.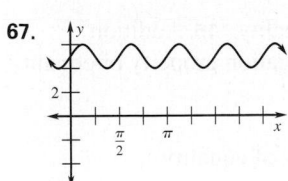

69. $\tan^3 x$ **71.** $-\csc x$

73. $\frac{\pi}{2} + n\pi$ **75.** $-\frac{\sqrt{2} + \sqrt{6}}{4}$

77. $-2 - \sqrt{3}$ **79.** $-\frac{\sqrt{2} + \sqrt{6}}{4}$

81. mean: 72.4; median: 73; modes: 76, 74; range: 12; standard deviation: 3.7; **83.** 953 ft

Heights of Girls (in.)

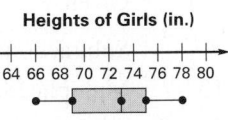

SKILLS REVIEW HANDBOOK

OPERATIONS WITH SIGNED NUMBERS (p. 905) **1.** −2 **3.** 0
5. −1 **7.** 6 **9.** −10 **11.** −21 **13.** 6 **15.** −4 **17.** 9 **19.** −5
21. −3 **23.** 15 **25.** 24 **27.** −24 **29.** 30 **31.** 25 **33.** −5
35. 8 **37.** −4 **39.** 3 **41.** −20 **43.** −2 **45.** −3 **47.** 29 **49.** −7
51. 135 **53.** −35 **55.** −3 **57.** 7 **59.** −7 **61.** −9 **63.** 132

CONVERTING DECIMALS, FRACTIONS, AND PERCENTS
(p. 906) **1.** 20% **3.** 55% **5.** 87% **7.** 40% **9.** 60% **11.** 0.5
13. 0.02 **15.** 0.4 **17.** 0.36 **19.** 1.5

CALCULATING PERCENTS (p. 907) **1.** 3 **3.** 0.3 **5.** 30
7. 0.54 **9.** 12 **11.** 0.00375 **13.** 0.025 **15.** 0.084 **17.** 14
19. 0.005 **21.** 50% **23.** 100% **25.** 35% **27.** about 22%
29. about 2.4% **31.** 20% **33.** 0.2% **35.** 0.44%

LEAST COMMON DENOMINATOR (p. 909) **1.** $2 \times 2 \times 2$
3. $2 \times 2 \times 2 \times 2 \times 2 \times 2$ **5.** prime **7.** $2 \times 2 \times 3$
9. 2×11 **11.** prime **13.** prime **15.** 5×5 **17.** 1, 28
19. 2, 60 **21.** 20, 40 **23.** 6, 72 **25.** 12, 144 **27.** 1, 6
29. 6, 18 **31.** 48 **33.** 26 **35.** 10 **37.** 12 **39.** 60 **41.** 12
43. 120 **45.** 12 **47.** 60 **49.** 60 **51.** $\frac{19}{24}$ **53.** $-\frac{5}{4}$ **55.** $-\frac{1}{10}$
57. $\frac{33}{80}$ **59.** $\frac{13}{12}$ **61.** $-\frac{111}{66}$ **63.** $\frac{1}{2}$ **65.** $-\frac{1}{20}$ **67.** $\frac{7}{6}$ **69.** $\frac{1}{3}$

WRITING RATIOS AND SOLVING PROPORTIONS (p. 910)
1. 4:5, $\frac{4}{5}$ **3.** 2:6, $\frac{2}{6}$ **5.** 1 to 5, 1:5 **7.** 8 to 5, 8:5
9. 3 to 1, $\frac{3}{1}$ **11.** 3 to 4, 3:4 **13.** 1 to 4 **15.** 1:4 **17.** $\frac{1}{5}$
19. 5 to 3 **21.** $\frac{3}{5}$ **23.** $\frac{4}{3}$ **25.** 1 **27.** 16 **29.** 3 **31.** 21
33. 5 **35.** 27 **37.** 18 **39.** 20 **41.** 16 **43.** 8 **45.** 6 **47.** 1

SIGNIFICANT DIGITS (p. 912) **1.** 8200 **3.** 9.50 **5.** 28.15
7. 700 **9.** 10 **11.** 0.74 **13.** 3.2 **15.** 1.0 **17.** 200 **19.** 24.7
21. 17.7 **23.** 89 **25.** 0.723 **27.** 0.06 **29.** 16,000
31. $7.50 **33.** $239.70 **35.** 13 mi/gal
37. 100 gal of milk **39.** 230 mL **41.** 730 computers/store
43. 15 mg **45.** 25.9 in. of rain

SCIENTIFIC NOTATION (p. 913) **1.** 4×10^{-1} **3.** 9×10^{-2}
5. 4×10^{0} **7.** 9.26×10^{-5} **9.** 2.11111×10^{2} **11.** 5×10^{-3}
13. 9.84×10^{4} **15.** 2.0489×10^{2} **17.** 3.7×10^{-4}
19. 5.98×10^{1} **21.** 2.30856×10^{7} **23.** 1.00×10^{-4}
25. 900 **27.** 3100 **29.** 0.290 **31.** 10,010 **33.** 7,926,000
35. 0.000384 **37.** 0.000037 **39.** 0.0049831 **41.** 395,020
43. 2640.95 **45.** 0.000455 **47.** 0.059438

PERIMETER, AREA, AND VOLUME (p. 916) **1.** about 6.28 m
3. 8 in. **5.** 13 m **7.** 12 ft **9.** 22 cm **11.** 18 cm **13.** about
69 in. **15.** 81 in.^{2} **17.** 21 cm^2 **19.** 24 in.^{2} **21.** about
0.79 in.^{2} **23.** 12 mi^2 **25.** 10 in.^{2} **27.** 88 ft^2 **29.** about
63 mm^2 **31.** 201 in.^{2} **33.** 288 cm^2 **35.** 1000 cm^3
37. 12 yd^3 **39.** 5 ft^3 **41.** about 127 in.^{3} **43.** 38.4 m^3

TRIANGLE RELATIONSHIPS (p. 918) **1.** 45 **3.** 76 **5.** 165
7. 60 **9.** yes **11.** no **13.** no **15.** no **17.** no **19.** yes **21.** yes
23. yes **25.** about 5.7 mm **27.** 2.5 m **29.** about 3.6 m
31. 8 cm **33.** about 7.1 in. **35.** yes **37.** no **39.** yes **41.** yes
43. no **45.** yes

SYMMETRY (p. 920) **1.** line symmetry: 4 lines of symmetry;
rotational symmetry: 90° or 180° in either direction
3. line symmetry: 6 lines of symmetry; rotational
symmetry: 60°, 120°, or 180° in either direction
5. line symmetry: 5 lines of symmetry; rotational
symmetry: 72° or 144° in either direction **7.** no line or
rotational symmetry **9.** (−3, 2) **11.** (4, 1) **13.** (4, 6)

TRANSFORMATIONS (p. 922) **1.** (−3, −6) **3.** $\left(\frac{9}{2}, -9\right)$
5. (6, 3) **7.** (3, 6) **9.** (0, −1)

11. 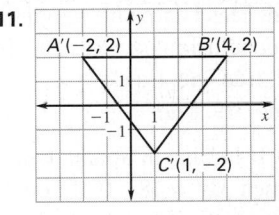 **13.**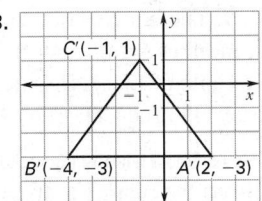

15. 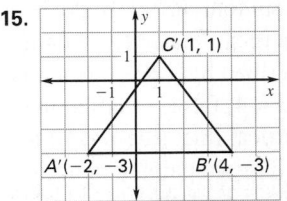 **17.**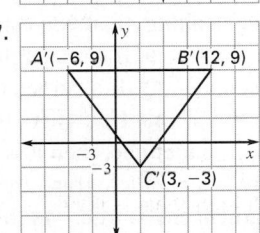

19. 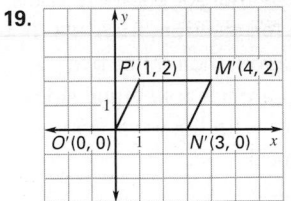 **21.**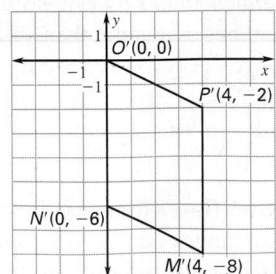

23.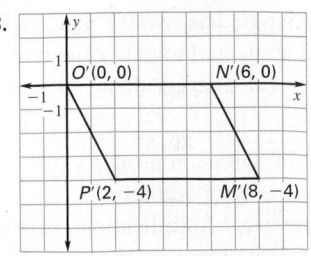

27.

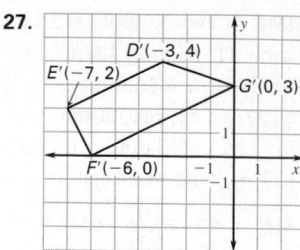

29.

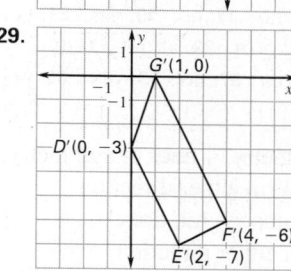

SIMILAR FIGURES (p. 923)   **1.** 2.5   **3.** 1   **5.** 70   **7.** 3.75

LOGICAL ARGUMENT (p. 925)   **1.** The conclusion is invalid. This does not follow the chain rule.   **3.** The conclusion is valid. This is not an example of the *Or* rule.
5. The conclusion is valid. This is an example of the chain rule.   **7.** The conclusion is invalid. This is not an example of an indirect argument.   **9.** The conclusion is valid. This is an example of the AND rule.   **11.** true   **13.** true
17. true   **19.** true   **21.** true   **23.** true   **25.** true

IF-THEN STATEMENTS (p. 926)   **1.** If it rains in Spain, then it falls on the plain.   **3.** If $x = 4$, then $3x^2 = 48$.   **5.** If you finish cleaning, then you can go out tonight.   **7.** If $x = 3$, then $y = 16$.   **9.** If a rectangle has four equal sides, then it is a square.   **11.** If a curve is described by $y = x^2$, then it is a parabola.   **13.** If $x^2 = 16$, then $x = 4$; false.   **15.** If a line's slope is undefined, then it is a vertical line; true.   **17.** If a figure is a parallelogram, then it has two pairs of opposite congruent sides; true.   **19.** If you are cold, then you are in Minnesota in January; false.   **21.** If Margot got more votes than her opponent, then she won the election; true.   **23.** If a convex polygon is a regular pentagon, then it has five equal sides; true.   **25.** False; a square has four equal sides and four 90° angles.   **27.** False; $x^2 = 25$ for $x = 5, -5$.
29. true   **31.** true   **33.** true   **35.** true

COUNTEREXAMPLES (p. 928)   **1.** False; any parallelogram with angles that are not right angles is not a rectangle.
3. False; the last digit of the number 16 is 6, but 16 is not divisible by 3.   **5.** False; no triangle has two 90° angles because there must be a third angle and together the three must total 180°.   **7.** False; cats can also be black.   **9.** true
11. False; if $a = 1$, then $3a - 4 = -1 < 0$.   **13.** true   **15.** true

JUSTIFY REASONING (p. 929)   **1.** Division property of equality   **3.** Multiplication property of equality
5. Addition property of equality   **7.** Multiplication property of equality   **9.** Definition of raising to a power (2)
11. Subtraction property of equality

13. Multiplication property of equality   **15.** Addition property of equality   **17.** Multiplication property of equality
19. Distributive property
21. $9x = 27$ — Given
$x = 3$ — Division property of equality
23. $\frac{x}{2} + 5 = 0$ — Given
$\frac{x}{2} = -5$ — Subtraction property of equality
$x = -10$ — Multiplication property of equality
25. $\frac{5x}{2} - 2 = -5$ — Given
$5x - 4 = -10$ — Multiplication property of equality
$5x = -6$ — Addition property of equality
$x = -\frac{6}{5}$ — Division property of equality
27. $\frac{3x}{4} = 6$ — Given
$3x = 24$ — Multiplication property of equality
$x = 8$ — Division property of equality

TRANSLATING PHRASES INTO ALGEBRAIC EXPRESSIONS (p. 930)   **1.** $x + 8$ **3.** $x - 49$ **5.** $7x$ **7.** $\frac{3}{4}x$
9. $0.90x$ **11.** $x - 4$ **13.** $\frac{x + 3}{2}$ **15.** $3b$ **17.** $67.39 - x$ **19.** $2.5x$

ADDITIONAL PROBLEM SOLVING STRATEGIES (p. 932)
1. 10   **3.** from 40 to 60 people   **5.** 128 ft/sec   **7.** 3, 6, 9, 11, 12, 14, 17, 19, 22, 27   **9.** 10   **11.** 35   **13.** 204

POINTS IN THE COORDINATE PLANE (p. 933)
1–15 odd:

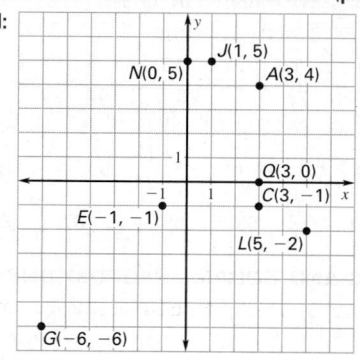

17. (0, 4), y-axis
19. (−5, 5), Quadrant II
21. (2, −5), Quadrant IV
23. (−5, −5), Quadrant III
25. (3, −3), Quadrant IV

27. (−3, 0), x-axis   **29.** (−5, 2), Quadrant II
31. (5, 5), Quadrant I   **33.** (−8, −4), Quadrant III
35. (7, −4), Quadrant IV   **37.** (4, −7), Quadrant IV

BAR, CIRCLE, AND LINE GRAPHS (p. 935)
1. about 1.2 ft   **3.** about 120   **5.** about 20%
7. Students with Each Major   **9.** Visitors to the Zoo

OPPOSITES (p. 936)   **1.** −3   **3.** −150   **5.** −4.3   **7.** $-\frac{3}{5}$
9. $-2a - b$ **11.** $-a + b + c$ **13.** $-2 - x$ **15.** $1 - 4x$

17. $-x^2 - 2x + 4$ **19.** $-2x - 3y$ **21.** $-3x + y - 11z$
23. $36x - 54y$ **25.** $x - 7y$ **27.** $-a + 3b$

MULTIPLYING BINOMIALS (p. 937)
1. $x^2 + 2x + 1$ **3.** $4x^2 + 9x + 2$ **5.** $-2x^2 - 5x + 3$ **7.** $4x^2 - 25$ **9.** $5x^2 - 7x - 6$ **11.** $2y^2 + 3y - 9$ **13.** $ac + ad + bc + bd$ **15.** $-4x^2 + 1$ **17.** $x^2 - y^2$ **19.** $3x^2 - x - 10$ **21.** $-12x^2 + 4x + 96$

FACTORING (p. 938)
1. $(x + 3)(x + 2)$ **3.** $(x + 4)(x + 5)$ **5.** $(x + 3)(x + 3)$ **7.** $(x + 3)(x - 8)$ **9.** $(x + 2)(x + 1)$ **11.** $(x + 3)(x - 2)$ **13.** $(x + 7)(x + 7)$ **15.** $(x - 10)(x + 2)$ **17.** $(x - 9)(x - 9)$ **19.** $(x - 5)(x - 3)$ **21.** $(x - 16)(x - 5)$ **23.** $(x - 4)(x + 1)$ **25.** $(x - 5)(x - 4)$ **27.** $(x + 5)(x + 5)$ **29.** $(x + 4)(x + 2)$

LEAST COMMON DENOMINATOR (p. 939)
1. $2x$ **3.** $90k^2$ **5.** $6xy$ **7.** $3z^2$ **9.** $(b - 1)(b + 1)^2$ **11.** $2(n + 2)$ **13.** $6(2 + 3x)$ **15.** $10(3h - 4)$ **17.** $12 - 20e$ **19.** $c^2(c - 1)(c - 4)$ **21.** $36x^2$ **23.** $3x^2 + 2x$

EXTRA PRACTICE

CHAPTER 1 (p. 940)

1.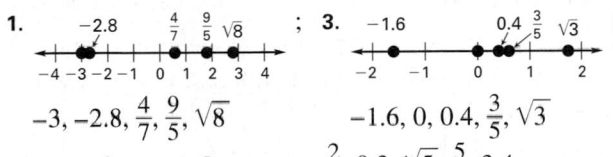
$-3, -2.8, \frac{4}{7}, \frac{9}{5}, \sqrt{8}$ $-1.6, 0, 0.4, \frac{3}{5}, \sqrt{3}$

5. $-\frac{2}{5}, 0.3, \sqrt{5}, \frac{5}{2}, 3.4$

7. commutative property of multiplication **9.** inverse property of addition **11.** commutative property of addition **13.** 9 **15.** -36 **17.** 12 **19.** $12x^2 - 13x$ **21.** $-9x^2 + 2x$ **23.** $5x + 4$ **25.** 7 **27.** -9 **29.** -2.3 **31.** $y = \dfrac{-3x + 12}{4}$ **33.** $y = \dfrac{7x + 9}{6}$ **35.** $y = \dfrac{2}{25}x + \dfrac{3}{10}$ **37.** C = Total cost (dollars), 15 = Cost of first pound (dollars), 3 = Cost per pound of each additional pound (dollars per pound), 6 = Number of additional pounds (pounds) **39.** $C = 33$; it will cost $33 to send a 7 pound package.

41. $x > 7$;

43. $x > 2$;

45. $2 \leq x \leq 10$;

47. $x < 3$ or $x \geq 8$;

49. $x \leq \dfrac{23}{3}$ or $x > 12$;

51. $28, -22$ **53.** $10.2, 4.4$ **55.** $\dfrac{62}{7}, -\dfrac{22}{7}$ **57.** 2

59. $x < -7$ or $x > 1$;

61. $-3 < x < 1$;

63. $2 < y < 3$;

65. $x \leq -\dfrac{17}{3}$ or $x \geq 5$;

67. $y < -1$ or $y > 4$;

CHAPTER 2 (p. 941)

1. 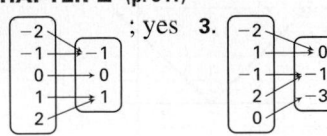 ; yes **3.** 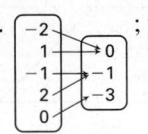 ; yes **5.** 5 **7.** -46
9. -36
11. parallel
13. perpendicular

15. parallel **17.** 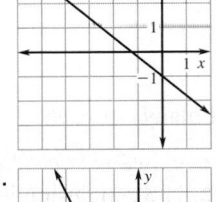 **19.**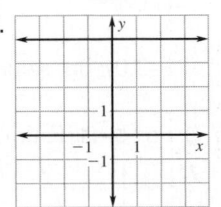

21. 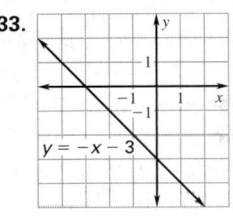 **23.** undefined; none **25.** $2; -5$
27. $2; 10$ **29.** $\dfrac{1}{3}; \dfrac{8}{3}$

31. 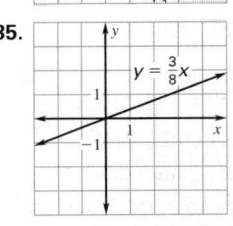 **33.**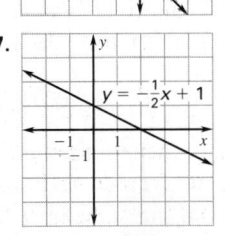

35. 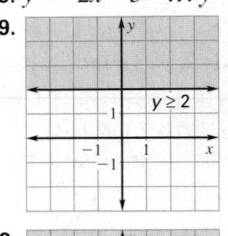 **37.**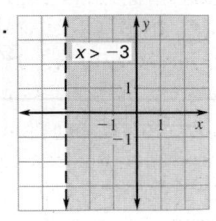

39. $y = 2$ **41.** $y = 2x - 5$ **43.** $y = -\dfrac{5}{2}x + \dfrac{7}{2}$
45. $y = -2x - 3$ **47.** $y = 6$

49. 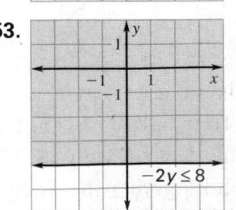 **51.**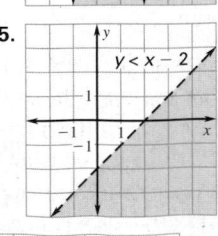

53. 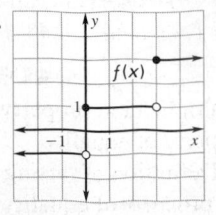 **55.**

61. -4 **63.** 9 **65.** 2 **67.**

69.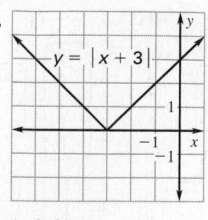

$(0, 5)$; up; narrower

71.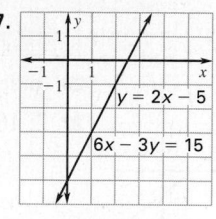

$(-3, 0)$; up; same

CHAPTER 3 (p. 943) **1.** no **3.** no **5–11.** Estimates may vary.

5.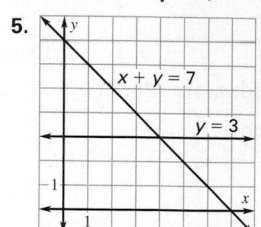

1; $(4, 3)$

7.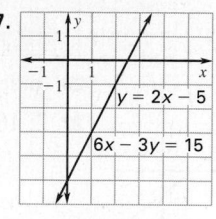

infinitely many

9.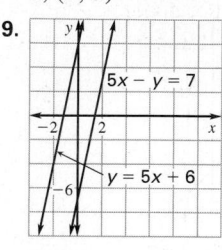

11.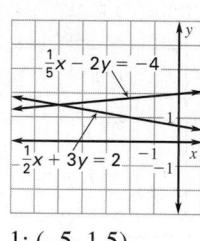

1; $(-5, 1.5)$

13. $\left(7, \dfrac{17}{2}\right)$ **15.** $(-3, -2)$ **17.** $(2, 0)$ **19.** $(-8, -9)$

21.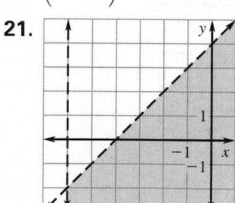

23.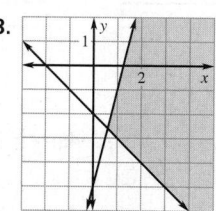

25.

27.

29. -25; 48 **31.** -27; 25

33.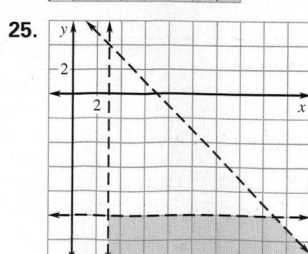

39. $f(x, y) = -\dfrac{1}{3}x - \dfrac{1}{3}y + 3$; 3

41. $f(x, y) = -x + \dfrac{5}{2}y - 5$; 4

43. $f(x, y) = \dfrac{1}{7}x - \dfrac{4}{7}y - \dfrac{31}{7}$; -4

45. $(0, -2, 5)$ **47.** $(-3, 4, 2)$

49. $\left(\dfrac{1}{2}, 3, 7\right)$

CHAPTER 4 (p. 944)

1. $\begin{bmatrix} 4 & 2 \\ -4 & 4 \end{bmatrix}$ **3.** $\begin{bmatrix} -1 & -1 & 7 \\ 1 & 0 & -4 \end{bmatrix}$ **5.** $\begin{bmatrix} 3\frac{2}{3} & \frac{1}{5} \\ 5 & -\frac{1}{3} \end{bmatrix}$ **7.** $\begin{bmatrix} 5 & -6 \\ 17 & 27 \end{bmatrix}$

9. $\begin{bmatrix} 2.6 & 3.8 & 4.9 \\ 2.3 & 3.4 & 4.2 \end{bmatrix}$ **11.** $[4.4]$ **13.** $\begin{bmatrix} 10.83 & -23.2 \\ 66.62 & 23.31 \end{bmatrix}$

15. $\begin{bmatrix} -14 & 33 & 57 \\ -66 & -3 & -36 \\ -74 & 23 & -12 \end{bmatrix}$

17.

	Total
Machine 1	$40.05
Machine 2	$50.85
Machine 3	$44.45

19. 29

21. -51 **23.** 799 **25.** $(2, -3)$ **27.** $(-6, -4)$ **29.** $(5, -1, -2)$

31. $\begin{bmatrix} 2 & -1 \\ -\frac{7}{3} & \frac{4}{3} \end{bmatrix}$ **33.** $\begin{bmatrix} -\frac{1}{6} & \frac{1}{2} \\ \frac{1}{12} & \frac{1}{4} \end{bmatrix}$ **35.** $\begin{bmatrix} \frac{1}{2} & \frac{1}{8} \\ \frac{1}{4} & -\frac{1}{16} \end{bmatrix}$ **37.** $\begin{bmatrix} 3 & 7 \\ 4 & 9 \end{bmatrix}$

39. $(5, 1)$ **41.** $(-1, -1)$ **43.** $(0, -2)$ **45.** $\left(-\dfrac{7}{5}, 5\right)$

47. $(3, -2, 1)$

CHAPTER 5 (p. 945)

1.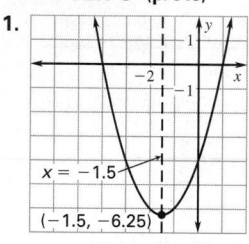

3.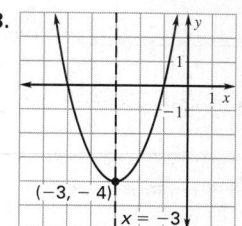

5.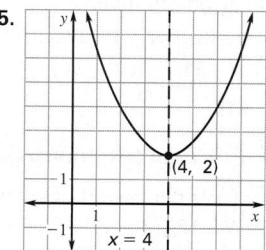

7.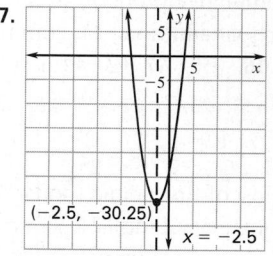

9. 0 mi/h **11.** $(m - 4)(m - 5)$ **13.** $(3x - 2)(2x + 3)$

15. $(2u + 5)(2u - 7)$ **17.** $(x - 5)^2$ **19.** $2(2x - 5)(x + 2)$

21. cannot be factored **23.** $-\dfrac{1}{2}, 7$ **25.** $\dfrac{2}{5}$ **27.** $-\dfrac{4}{3}, \dfrac{1}{2}$

29. $-\dfrac{8}{3}, \dfrac{5}{4}$ **31.** $y = x(x - 5)$; $0, 5$ **33.** $y = 6(x + 2)(x - 2)$; $2, -2$

35. $y = (5x - 3)(x - 2)$; $\dfrac{3}{5}, 2$ **37.** $y = 7(x + 3)(x - 3)$; $3, -3$

39. $5\sqrt{5}$ **41.** $9\sqrt{3}$ **43.** $\dfrac{9\sqrt{5}}{25}$ **45.** $\dfrac{4}{5}$ **47.** $4\sqrt{10}, -4\sqrt{10}$

49. $\sqrt{5} - 2, -\sqrt{5} - 2$ **51.** $5, -5$ **53.** $7, 1$ **55.** $i\sqrt{10}, -i\sqrt{10}$

57. $5i, -5i$ **59.** $6i, -6i$ **61.** $-1 + 2i\sqrt{5}, -1 - 2i\sqrt{5}$

63. $-4 - 3i$ **65.** 0 **67.** $-4 - 6i$ **69.** $11 - 11i$ **71.** $\dfrac{15}{26} - \dfrac{3}{26}i$

73. $-i$ **75.** $2 + 2i, 2 - 2i$ **77.** $0.866, -3.47$ **79.** $-\dfrac{2}{3}, 2$

81. $\dfrac{4}{5}, -2$ **83.** $\dfrac{3}{4}, -1$ **85.** $-\dfrac{3}{2} + \dfrac{\sqrt{41}}{2}, -\dfrac{3}{2} - \dfrac{\sqrt{41}}{2}$

87. $\dfrac{3}{7} + \dfrac{\sqrt{61}}{7}i, \dfrac{3}{7} - \dfrac{\sqrt{61}}{7}i$ **89.** 1; 2; real

91. -191; 2; imaginary **93.** -40; 2; imaginary

99.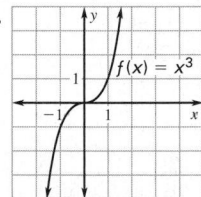

101. $y = (x-1)^2 + 1$

103. $y = \frac{1}{9}(x-2)^2 + 1$

105. $y = 2(x+3)^2 - 5$

107. $y = (x-2)(x-6)$

109. $y = 2x(x-4)$

111. $y = \frac{3}{4}(x-1)(x-2)$

113. $y = -\frac{1}{6}(x-5)(x+2)$

CHAPTER 6 (p. 947) **1.** 625; product of powers **3.** 512; power of a power **5.** $\frac{16}{25}$; power of a quotient **7.** $\frac{1}{512}$; *Sample answer:* zero exponent, negative exponent **9.** $\frac{1}{46,656}$; *Sample answer:* product of powers, power of a quotient **11.** 6; zero exponent, quotient of powers **13.** $1,048,576x^8$; power of a product, power of a power **15.** x^3; quotient of powers **17.** $\frac{1}{36x^6y^8}$; power of a product, power of a power, negative exponent **19.** $-\frac{1}{2187x^{63}y^{21}}$; power of a product, power of a power, negative exponent **21.** $\frac{1}{64x^{12}y^{16}}$; power of a product, power of a power, negative exponent **23.** $\frac{3x^8}{y^5}$; product of powers, quotient of powers, negative exponent **25.** 19 **27.** -4

29.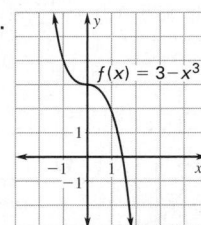

31.

33.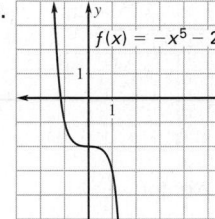

35. $5x^2 + 10x + 7$

37. $5x^3 - 10x^2 + 18$

39. $15x^3 + 9x^2 + 29x - 16$

41. $x^2 + 2x - 35$

43. $-3x^3 - 16x^2 + 17x + 30$

45. $12x^4 - 24x^3 + 42x$

47. $8x^3 + 96x^2 + 384x + 512$

49. $x^3 + 3x^2y + 3xy^2 + y^3$

51. $2(x+5)(x^2-5x+25)$ **53.** $(x+1)(x+3)^2$ **55.** $3(x-2)(x^2+2x+4)$ **57.** $(2x^2-5)(x+9)$ **59.** $(\sqrt{3}+3)$ inches by $(\sqrt{3}-1)$ inches by $\sqrt{3}$ inches **61.** $x^2 - 6x + 3$ **63.** $3x^3 - 29x^2 + 129x - 540 + \frac{2176}{x+4}$ **65.** $4x^3 + 3x^2 + 8x + 15 + \frac{35}{x-2}$ **67.** $-3, -2$ **69.** 2 **71.** -5 **73.** 1, 2, 3 **75.** $-2, 4$ **77.** $-1, 1, \sqrt{5}, -\sqrt{5}$ **79.** $x^3 + 5x^2 + 8x + 4$ **81.** $x^3 - 3x^2 + x - 3$ **83.** $x^3 - 4x^2 + 6x - 4$ **85.** $x^4 + x^3 - 6x^2 - 14x - 12$ **87.** $x^4 - 4x^3 + 41x^2 - 144x + 180$ **89.** $x^6 + 36x^4 - 625x^2 - 22,500$

91.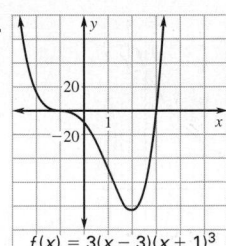

$f(x) = 3(x-3)(x+1)^3$

93.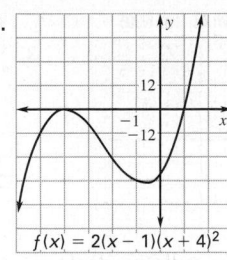

$f(x) = 2(x-1)(x+4)^2$

99. $y = \frac{1}{2x^2} + \frac{3}{2x}$ **101.** $y = x^3 - 3x^2 + 2x + 3$

CHAPTER 7 (p. 949) **1.** 3 **3.** $\frac{1}{4}$ **5.** -125 **7.** $\frac{1}{9}$ **9.** 2 **11.** 2 **13.** 5 **15.** 2 **17.** $5^{1/2}$ **19.** $7\sqrt[6]{7}$ **21.** $x^{7/10}$ **23.** $3xy^2\sqrt{x}$ **25.** $\frac{\sqrt[6]{x^5}}{4x^5}$ **27.** $\frac{2x^2y^4}{3}$ **29.** $2x^2 - 4x - 4$; all real numbers **31.** $2x^2 - 4x - 4$; all real numbers **33.** $2x^2 - 8x + 10$; all real numbers **35.** $2x^2 - 18$; all real numbers **37.** $3x^{5/6}$; nonnegative reals **39.** $3x^{5/6}$; nonnegative reals **41.** $3x^{1/6}$; nonnegative reals **43.** $3^{4/3}x^{1/9}$; nonnegative reals **45.** $f^{-1}(x) = \frac{x-1}{3}$ **47.** $f^{-1}(x) = -x - 4$ **49.** $f^{-1}(x) = \frac{x-3}{2}$ **51.** $f^{-1}(x) = 2x + 8$ **53.** $f^{-1}(x) = -3x + 15$ **55.** $f^{-1}(x) = \sqrt[4]{x + \frac{1}{8}}$ **57.** $r = \frac{\sqrt{\pi A}}{\pi}$

59.

$y = \frac{1}{4}\sqrt{x}$

$x \geq 0$; $y \geq 0$

61.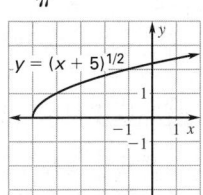

$y = (x+5)^{1/2}$

$x \geq -5$; $y \geq 0$

63.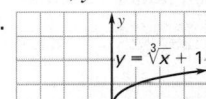

$y = \sqrt[3]{x} + 1$

all reals; all reals

65.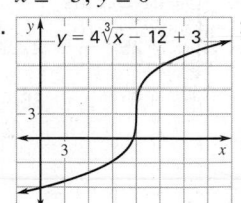

$y = 4\sqrt[3]{x-12} + 3$

all reals; all reals

67.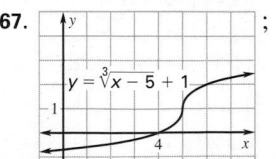

$y = \sqrt[3]{x-5} + 1$

all reals; all reals

69.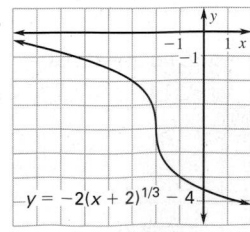

$y = -2(x+2)^{1/3} - 4$

all reals; all reals

71. 43,046,721 **73.** no solution **75.** -8 **77.** no solution **79.** 10 **81.** $\frac{101}{13}$ **83.** 58.2; 57.5; 58; 21; 5.25 **85.** 25.6; 21.3; 18.6; 46.7; 15.0

1.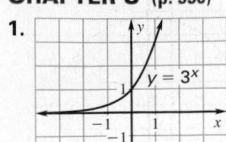

all reals; positive reals

3.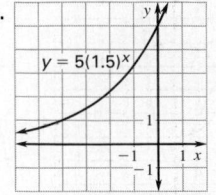

all reals; positive reals

5.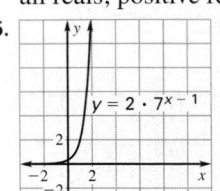

all reals; positive reals

7.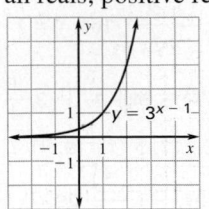

all reals; positive reals

9.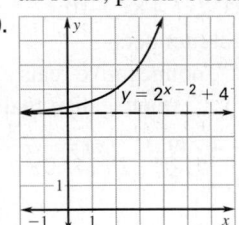

all reals; $y > 4$

11.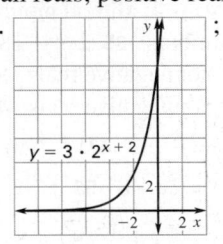

all reals; positive reals

13.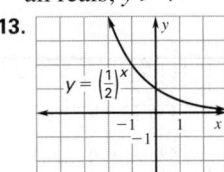

all reals; positive reals

15.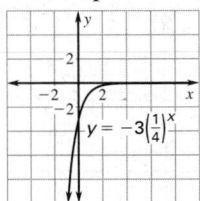

all reals; negative reals

21. e^7 **23.** $16e^{6x}$ **25.** $\dfrac{10}{e^{2x}}$ **27.** e^{6x-1} **29.** $4e^{4x-1}$ **31.** $4e^{4x}$

33.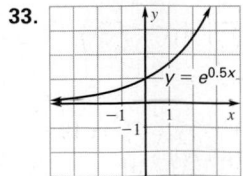

all reals; positive reals

35.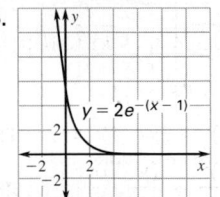

all reals; positive reals

37.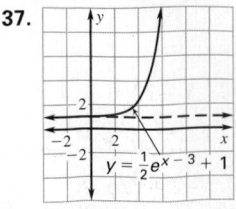

all reals; $y > 1$

39.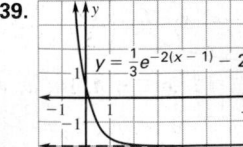

all reals; $y > -2$

41. about 8.96 lb per square inch **43.** 2 **45.** $-\dfrac{1}{2}$ **47.** 3

49. 3 **51.** $y = \left(\dfrac{1}{3}\right)^x$ **53.** $y = \dfrac{1}{3}e^x$ **55.** $y = e^x + 3$

57.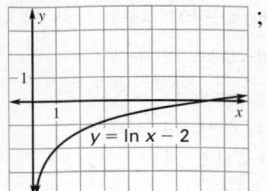

positive reals; all reals

63.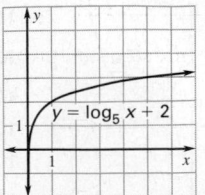

positive reals; all reals

65. 3 **67.** 3 **69.** -5 **71.** 6 **73.** $\log 3 + 4\log x$

75. $\ln 15 + \ln x$ **77.** $\log 3 + \dfrac{1}{2}\log x$

79. $2\log x + 3\log y + 4\log z$ **81.** $\ln x^4 y^6 z^3$ **83.** $\ln\left(\dfrac{27}{x}\right)^{1/4}$

85. $\log_5 5^3 10^{-1}$ **87.** 1.90 **89.** 0.778 **91.** $-163{,}000$ **93.** 5

95. $y = 0.5(2)^x$ **97.** $y = 0.25(5)^x$ **99.** $y = 0.286(1.14)^x$

101. $y = -2(4)^x$ **103.** $y = x^3$ **105.** $y = 2x^{1/2}$ **107.** $y = 3x^3$

109. $y = 0.5x^2$ **111.** 2.43 **113.** 0.196 **115.** 1.2 **117.** 0.724

119.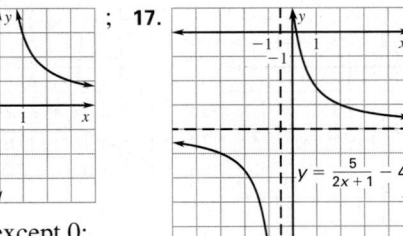

$y = 0, y = 1; \left(0, \dfrac{1}{4}\right);$

$(0.549, 0.5)$

121.

$y = 0, y = 2; (0, 1); (0, 1)$

1. $y = \dfrac{18}{x}$; 4.5 **3.** $y = -\dfrac{4}{x}$; -1

5. $y = -\dfrac{3}{x}$; $-\dfrac{3}{4}$ **7.** $y = \dfrac{1}{16x}$; $\dfrac{1}{64}$ **9.** $z = xy$; 28

11. $z = -\dfrac{xy}{30}$; $-\dfrac{14}{15}$ **13.** $z = \dfrac{64xy}{3}$; $\dfrac{1792}{3}$

15.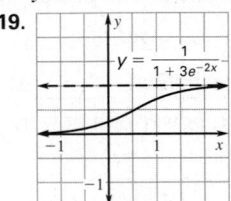

all reals except 0;
all reals except 0

17.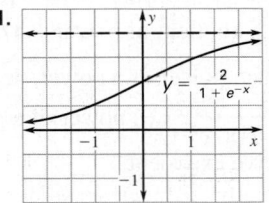

all reals except $-\dfrac{1}{2}$;
all reals except -4

19.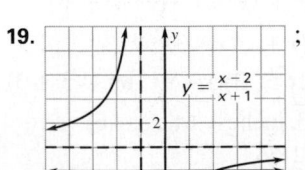

all reals except -1;
all reals except 1

21.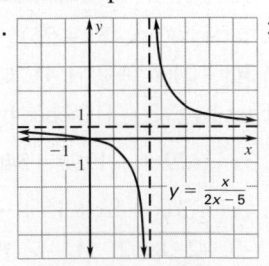

all reals except $\dfrac{5}{2}$;

all reals except $\dfrac{1}{2}$

23. $C = \dfrac{4.50n + 710}{n}$ **25.** The average cost decreases as the number of calendars printed increases.

27.
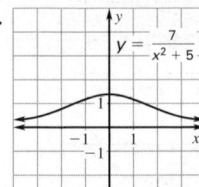

29.
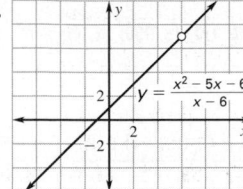

31.
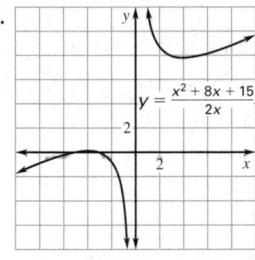

33.
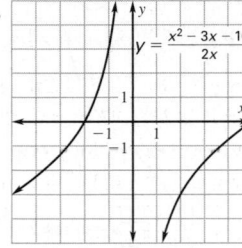

35. $2x^4$ **37.** $\dfrac{5x^4}{2x + 4}$ **39.** $\dfrac{x - 3}{x + 3}$ **41.** $\dfrac{x(x^2 - 2x + 4)(2x - 3)}{x - 2}$

43. $\dfrac{12}{5x}$ **45.** $\dfrac{26}{15x}$ **47.** $\dfrac{7x + 11}{(x + 2)(x - 2)}$ **49.** $\dfrac{-3x - 2}{(x + 3)(x + 5)}$

51. $\dfrac{-4x + 4}{2x + 1}$ **53.** $\dfrac{11}{2x^2}$ **55.** $\dfrac{9x + 13}{4x}$ **57.** $\dfrac{24x}{(x + 7)(5 - 18x)}$

59. 2 **61.** $\dfrac{12}{29}$ **63.** $-\dfrac{5}{3}$ **65.** $\dfrac{1}{3}$ **67.** $-\dfrac{3}{4}, 0$ **69.** $\dfrac{7}{2}$

CHAPTER 10 (p. 953)

1. $10; (3, 4)$ **3.** $5.83; \left(-\dfrac{3}{2}, -\dfrac{7}{2}\right)$ **5.** $5; (3, 4)$ **7.** $3.12; \left(-4, \dfrac{7}{2}\right)$

9.
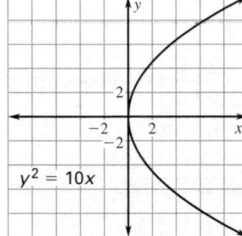
;

11.
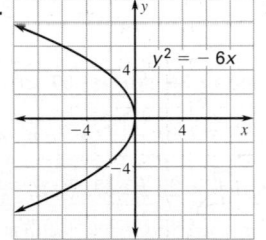
;

$\left(\dfrac{5}{2}, 0\right); x = -\dfrac{5}{2}$

$\left(-\dfrac{3}{2}, 0\right); x = \dfrac{3}{2}$

13.
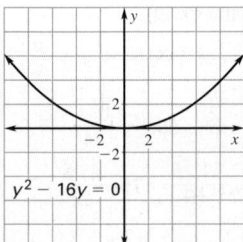
;

15.
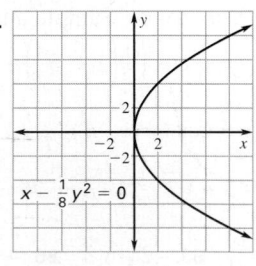
;

$(0, 4); y = -4$

$(2, 0); y = -2$

17. $y^2 = 12x$ **19.** $y^2 = 2x$ **21.** $x^2 = -24y$ **23.** $x^2 = -3y$

25.
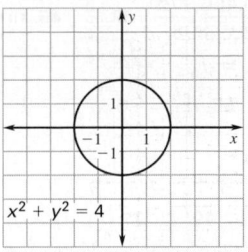

31.
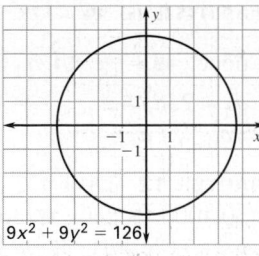

33. $x^2 + y^2 = 16$ **35.** $x^2 + y^2 = 13$ **37.** $x^2 + y^2 = 36$
39. $x^2 + y^2 = 29$ **41.** $x^2 + y^2 \le 100$

43.
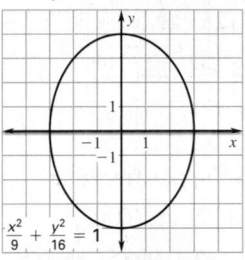

49.
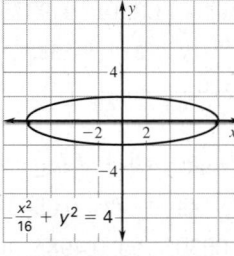

$(0, 4), (0, -4);$
$(-3, 0), (3, 0);$
$\left(0, \sqrt{7}\right), \left(0, -\sqrt{7}\right)$

$(-8, 0), (8, 0);$
$(0, 2), (0, -2);$
$\left(-2\sqrt{15}, 0\right), \left(2\sqrt{15}, 0\right)$

51. $\dfrac{x^2}{16} + \dfrac{y^2}{64} = 1$ **53.** $\dfrac{x^2}{49} + \dfrac{y^2}{4} = 1$

55. $\dfrac{x^2}{256} + \dfrac{y^2}{100} = 1$ **57.** $\dfrac{x^2}{4} + \dfrac{y^2}{400} = 1$

59.
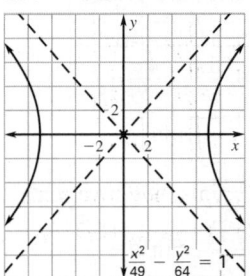

63.
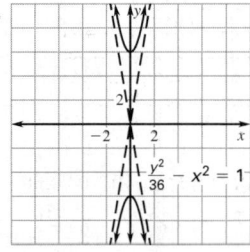

$\left(-\sqrt{113}, 0\right), \left(\sqrt{113}, 0\right);$
$y = \dfrac{8}{7}x, y = -\dfrac{8}{7}x$

$\left(0, \sqrt{37}\right), \left(0, -\sqrt{37}\right);$
$y = 6x, y = -6x$

67. $(x - 3)^2 + (y - 4)^2 = 25$ **69.** $(x - 2)^2 + (y + 5)^2 = 49$

71. $\dfrac{(x - 3)^2}{25} + \dfrac{(y - 3)^2}{9} = 1$ **73.** $\dfrac{(x - 2)^2}{9} - \dfrac{(y - 6)^2}{7} = 1$

75. parabola **77.** hyperbola **79.** $(2, 4), (-4, -2)$ **81.** none

83. $(3, 0), (5, 4)$ **85.** $\left(\dfrac{14}{5}, -\dfrac{2}{5}\right), (-2, 2)$

CHAPTER 11 (p. 955) **1.** $14; a_n = 3n - 1$ **3.** $-13;$
$a_n = -4n + 7$ **5.** $-256; a_n = -(-4)^{n - 1}$ **7.** $\dfrac{1}{1024}; a_n = \dfrac{1}{4^n}$

9. 72 **11.** 55 **13.** 440 **15.** $\dfrac{169}{20}$ **17.** $a_n = -2 + 3n; 28$

19. $a_n = 18 - 10n; -82$ **21.** $a_n = \dfrac{11}{4} - \dfrac{1}{2}n; -\dfrac{9}{4}$

23. $a_n = 2 - 2n; -18$ **25.** $a_n = -9 + 4n; 31$ **27.** the 21st row

29. $a_n = -\left(\dfrac{1}{2}\right)^{n - 1}; -\dfrac{1}{128}$ **31.** $a_n = \left(-\dfrac{1}{10}\right)^{n - 2}; \dfrac{1}{1,000,000}$

33. $a_n = -\dfrac{1}{2}(6)^n; -839{,}808$ **35.** $a_n = 750\left(\dfrac{1}{5}\right)^n; \dfrac{6}{3125}$

37. $61,035,156$ **39.** -728 **41.** $\dfrac{60,466,175}{839,808}$ **43.** $\dfrac{3}{2}$ **45.** none

47. none **49.** $-\dfrac{1}{18}$ **51.** $a_1 = 2,\ a_n = a_{n-1} + 4$

53. $a_1 = 2,\ a_n = a_{n-1} + 5(3)^{n-2}$ **55.** $a_1 = -6,\ a_2 = -9,$
$a_n = a_{n-1} \cdot a_{n-2}$

CHAPTER 12 (p. 956) **1.** 2 **3.** 12 **5.** 12 **7.** 6 **9.** 120
11. $50,400$ **13.** 840 **15.** 15 **17.** 1 **19.** 1 **21.** 1140
23. $x^7 + 7x^6y + 21x^5y^2 + 35x^4y^3 + 35x^3y^4 + 21x^2y^5 +$
$7xy^6 + y^7$ **25.** $x^{12} + 12x^{10}y + 60x^8y^2 + 160x^6y^3 +$
$240x^4y^4 + 192x^2y^5 + 64y^6$ **27.** $243x^{10} - 2025x^8 +$
$6750x^6 - 11{,}250x^4 + 9375x^2 - 3125$ **29.** $x^9 + 3x^6y^3 +$
$3x^3y^6 + y^9$ **31.** $\dfrac{1}{13}$ **33.** $\dfrac{1}{2}$ **35.** $\dfrac{3}{13}$ **37.** $\dfrac{113}{200}$ **39.** $\dfrac{87}{200}$

41. $\dfrac{127}{200}$ **43.** $\dfrac{1}{8}$ **45.** $\dfrac{1}{2}$ **47.** $\dfrac{3}{8}$ **49.** 0.5; no **51.** 43%; yes

53. 4%; no **55.** 1 **57.** $\dfrac{1}{4}$ **59.** 0.8 **61.** $\dfrac{1}{16}$ **63.** $\dfrac{8}{75}$ **65.** $\dfrac{4}{45}$

67. $\dfrac{8}{75}$ **69.** $\dfrac{2}{15}$ **71.** 0.0543 **73.** 0.117 **75.** 0.00217

77. 0.00305 **79.** 0.4985 **81.** 0.84 **83.** 0.9985 **85.** 0.5

CHAPTER 13 (p. 957) **1.** $\sin\theta = \dfrac{\sqrt{2}}{2}$; $\cos\theta = \dfrac{\sqrt{2}}{2}$, $\tan\theta = 1$;

$\sec\theta = \sqrt{2}$; $\csc\theta = \sqrt{2}$; $\cot\theta = 1$ **3.** $\sin\theta = \dfrac{2\sqrt{14}}{9}$;

$\cos\theta = \dfrac{5}{9}$, $\tan\theta = \dfrac{2\sqrt{14}}{5}$; $\sec\theta = \dfrac{9}{5}$; $\csc\theta = \dfrac{9\sqrt{14}}{28}$;

$\cot\theta = \dfrac{5\sqrt{14}}{28}$ **5–15.** Sample answers are given.

5. $395°$; $-325°$ **7.** $485°$; $-235°$ **9.** $315°$; $-405°$

11. $225°$; $-135°$ **13.** $\dfrac{8\pi}{3}$; $-\dfrac{4\pi}{3}$ **15.** $\dfrac{6\pi}{5}$; $-\dfrac{4\pi}{5}$

17. $\dfrac{4\pi}{3}$ in.; $\dfrac{8\pi}{3}$ in.^{2} **19.** $\dfrac{21\pi}{2}$ cm; $\dfrac{147\pi}{2}$ cm^2

21. $\dfrac{\pi}{5}$ cm; $\dfrac{9\pi}{10}$ cm^2 **23.** $\sin\theta = \dfrac{5\sqrt{41}}{41}$; $\cos\theta = \dfrac{4\sqrt{41}}{41}$;

$\tan\theta = \dfrac{5}{4}$; $\sec\theta = \dfrac{\sqrt{41}}{4}$; $\csc\theta = \dfrac{\sqrt{41}}{5}$; $\cot\theta = \dfrac{4}{5}$

25. $\sin\theta = -\dfrac{3\sqrt{10}}{10}$; $\cos\theta = -\dfrac{\sqrt{10}}{10}$; $\tan\theta = 3$;

$\sec\theta = -\sqrt{10}$; $\csc\theta = -\dfrac{\sqrt{10}}{3}$; $\cot\theta = \dfrac{1}{3}$

27. $\sin\theta = \dfrac{\sqrt{5}}{5}$; $\cos\theta = \dfrac{2\sqrt{5}}{5}$; $\tan\theta = \dfrac{1}{2}$; $\sec\theta = \dfrac{\sqrt{5}}{2}$;

$\csc\theta = \sqrt{5}$; $\cot\theta = 2$ **29.** $\sin\theta = -\dfrac{2\sqrt{67}}{67}$; $\cos\theta = \dfrac{3\sqrt{469}}{67}$;

$\tan\theta = -\dfrac{2\sqrt{7}}{21}$; $\sec\theta = \dfrac{\sqrt{469}}{21}$; $\csc\theta = -\dfrac{\sqrt{67}}{2}$;

$\cot\theta = -\dfrac{3\sqrt{7}}{2}$ **31.** $\sin\theta = -\dfrac{5\sqrt{34}}{34}$; $\cos\theta = \dfrac{3\sqrt{34}}{34}$;

$\tan\theta = -\dfrac{5}{3}$; $\sec\theta = \dfrac{\sqrt{34}}{3}$; $\csc\theta = -\dfrac{\sqrt{34}}{5}$; $\cot\theta = -\dfrac{3}{5}$

33. $\sin\theta = \dfrac{2\sqrt{5}}{5}$; $\cos\theta = -\dfrac{\sqrt{5}}{5}$; $\tan\theta = -2$; $\sec\theta = -\sqrt{5}$;

$\csc\theta = \dfrac{\sqrt{5}}{2}$; $\cot\theta = -\dfrac{1}{2}$ **35.** $-\dfrac{1}{2}$ **37.** $\dfrac{\sqrt{2}}{2}$ **39.** $\dfrac{\sqrt{2}}{2}$

41. $-\dfrac{\sqrt{3}}{2}$ **43.** $-45°$; $-\dfrac{\pi}{4}$ **45.** $-30°$; $-\dfrac{\pi}{6}$ **47.** $30°$; $\dfrac{\pi}{6}$

49. $60°$; $\dfrac{\pi}{3}$ **51.** $41.8°$; $30°$ **53.** $B \approx 93°$; $b \approx 7.61$; $c \approx 5.48$

55. $B \approx 65°$; $a \approx 6$; $c \approx 5.07$ **57.** about 34.4 **59.** about 4140

61. about 1720 **63.** about 63.6 **65.** about 283

67. $y = \dfrac{x-7}{2}$; $-7 \le x \le 5369$ **69.** $y = x$; $0 \le x \le 500$

CHAPTER 14 (p. 959) **1.** 6; 4π **3.** $\dfrac{1}{7}$; 2 **5.** $1, 1$ **7.** $\dfrac{2}{5}$; 8π

9. 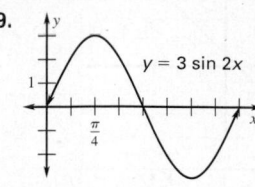 **11.**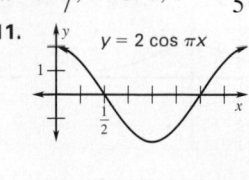

13. 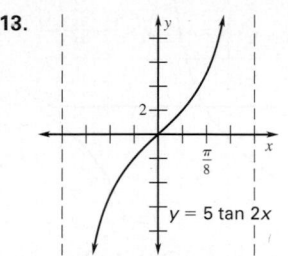 **15.**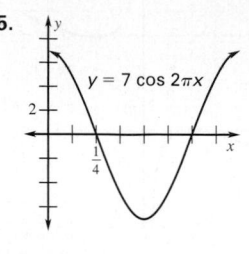

17. Shift the graph of $y = \cos x$ up 3 units. **19.** Shift the
graph of $y = \cos x$ up 4 units and reflect the graph in the
line $y = 4$. **21.** Shift the graph of $y = \cos x$ right π units.

23. Shift the graph of $y = \cos x$ right $\dfrac{\pi}{2}$ units.

27. 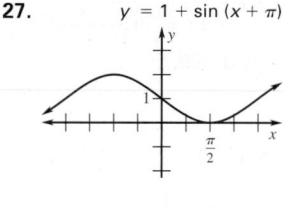 **29.**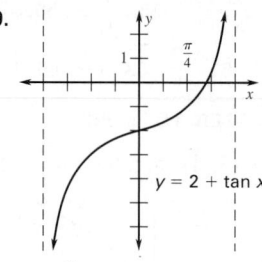

33. $\sec x$ **35.** $\sin^2 x$ **37.** $\cos x$ **39.** $\dfrac{2}{\sin x}$ **41.** $-\cos x \sin x$

43. $\dfrac{7\pi}{6} + 2n\pi,\ \dfrac{11\pi}{6} + 2n\pi$ **45.** $\dfrac{\pi}{3} + 2n\pi,\ \dfrac{2\pi}{3} + 2n\pi,\ \dfrac{4\pi}{3} +$

$2n\pi,\ \dfrac{5\pi}{3} + 2n\pi$ **47.** $2n\pi,\ \dfrac{2\pi}{3} + 2n\pi,\ \pi + 2n\pi,\ \dfrac{4\pi}{3} + 2n\pi$

49. $\dfrac{\pi}{4} + 2n\pi,\ \dfrac{7\pi}{4} + 2n\pi,\ \dfrac{3\pi}{4} + 2n\pi,\ \dfrac{5\pi}{4} + 2n\pi$

51. $0.615, 3.76$ **53.** $\dfrac{3\pi}{2}$ **55.** $\dfrac{\pi}{3},\ \dfrac{5\pi}{3}$ **57.** $0, 0.464, \pi, 3.61$

59. $0,\ \pi$ **61–65.** Sample answers are given.

61. $y = \dfrac{1}{2}\cos\left(\dfrac{1}{2}\left(x + \pi\right)\right) + \dfrac{3}{2}$ **63.** $y = 4\cos\left(3\left(x + \dfrac{\pi}{3}\right)\right) - 4$

65. $y = \cos\left(\pi(x - 1)\right) + 22$ **67.** $-\dfrac{\sqrt{2}}{2}$ **69.** $\dfrac{-\sqrt{6} - \sqrt{2}}{4}$

71. $-2 + \sqrt{3}$ **73.** $\dfrac{\sqrt{3}}{3}$ **75.** $\dfrac{11}{21}$ **77.** $\dfrac{11\sqrt{5}}{40}$ **79.** $\dfrac{4\sqrt{5}}{21}$

81. $\dfrac{19}{21}$ **83.** $-2 - \sqrt{3}$ **85.** $-\dfrac{\sqrt{2 - \sqrt{2}}}{2}$ **87.** $\dfrac{\sqrt{2 - \sqrt{2}}}{2}$

89. $-2 - \sqrt{3}$ **91.** $\dfrac{\sqrt{2 + \sqrt{2}}}{2}$ **93.** $-\dfrac{\sqrt{2 - \sqrt{3}}}{2}$

95. $\sin 2x = \dfrac{9\sqrt{19}}{50}$; $\cos 2x = \dfrac{31}{50}$; $\tan 2x = \dfrac{9\sqrt{19}}{31}$

97. $\sin 2x = \dfrac{24}{25}$; $\cos 2x = \dfrac{7}{25}$; $\tan 2x = \dfrac{24}{7}$

MATHEMATICS REFERENCE SHEET

Area

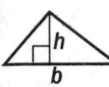 Triangle $\quad A = \frac{1}{2}bh$

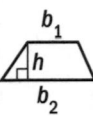 Rectangle $\quad A = lw$

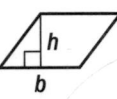 Trapezoid $\quad A = \frac{1}{2}h(b_1 + b_2)$

 Parallelogram $\quad A = bh$

Circle $\quad A = \pi r^2$

Key

b = base $\qquad\qquad d$ = diameter
h = height $\qquad\qquad r$ = radius
l = length $\qquad\qquad A$ = area
w = width $\qquad\qquad C$ = circumference
ℓ = slant height $\qquad V$ = volume
$S.\,A.$ = surface area

Use 3.14 or $\frac{22}{7}$ for π.

Circumference

$$C = \pi d = 2\pi r$$

		Volume	Total Surface Area
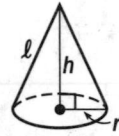	Right Circular Cone	$V = \frac{1}{3}\pi r^2 h$	$S.A. = \frac{1}{2}(2\pi r)\ell + \pi r^2 = \pi r\ell + \pi r^2$
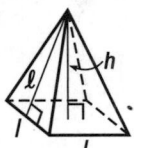	Square Pyramid	$V = \frac{1}{3}l^2 h$	$S.A. = 4\left(\frac{1}{2}l\ell\right) + l^2 = 2l\ell + l^2$
	Sphere	$V = \frac{4}{3}\pi r^3$	$S.A. = 4\pi r^2$
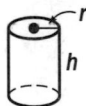	Right Circular Cylinder	$V = \pi r^2 h$	$S.A. = 2\pi rh + 2\pi r^2$
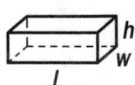	Rectangular Solid	$V = lwh$	$S.A. = 2(lw) + 2(hw) + 2(lh)$

In the following formulas, n represents the number of sides:

In a polygon, the sum of the measures of the interior angles is equal to $180(n - 2)$.

In a regular polygon, the measure of an interior angle is equal to $\dfrac{180(n - 2)}{n}$.